PENGUIN CLASSICS

THE BIBLE

DAVID NORTON was born in 1946 and educated at Rickmansworth Grammar School and Peterhouse, Cambridge, where he read English. Interest in the use of the Bible in D. H. Lawrence led him to work on literary ideas of the Bible, then to editing the King James Bible. His award-winning first book, *A History of the Bible as Literature* (2 vols., 1993; revised and condensed as *A History of the English Bible as Literature*, 2000), was followed by *The New Cambridge Paragraph Bible* (2005) and *A Textual History of the King James Bible* (2005). Married with three sons, he is Professor of English at Victoria University of Wellington, New Zealand.

THE BIBLE

King James Version
with The Apocrypha

*Edited with an Introduction
and Notes by David Norton*

PENGUIN BOOKS

PENGUIN CLASSICS

Published by the Penguin Group
Penguin Books Ltd, 80 Strand, London WC2R 0RL, England
Penguin Group (USA) Inc., 375 Hudson Street, New York,
New York 10014, USA
Penguin Group (Canada), 90 Eglinton Avenue East, Suite 700,
Toronto, Ontario, Canada M4P 2Y3
(a division of Pearson Penguin Canada Inc.)
Penguin Ireland, 25 St Stephen's Green, Dublin 2, Ireland
(a division of Penguin Books Ltd)
Penguin Group (Australia), 250 Camberwell Road, Camberwell,
Victoria 3124, Australia
(a division of Pearson Australia Group Pty Ltd)
Penguin Books India Pvt Ltd, 11 Community Centre, Panchsheel
Park, New Delhi – 110 017, India
Penguin Group (NZ), cnr Airborne and Rosedale Roads, Albany,
Auckland 1310, New Zealand
(a division of Pearson New Zealand Ltd)
Penguin Books (South Africa) (Pty) Ltd, 24 Sturdee Avenue,
Rosebank, Johannesburg 2196, South Africa

Penguin Books Ltd, Registered Offices: 80 Strand,
London WC2R 0RL, England

www.penguin.com

First published by Cambridge University Press 2005
This edition with new Introduction and Notes first published in
Penguin Classics 2006
006

Rights in the Authorised (King James) Version of the Bible
are vested in the Crown. *The New Cambridge Paragraph Bible with
the Apocrypha: King James Version*, as edited by David Norton,
copyright © Cambridge University Press, 2005
Introduction and Notes copyright © David Norton, 2006
All rights reserved

The moral right of the editor has been asserted

Printed in England by Clays Ltd, St Ives plc

ISBN-13: 978-0-141-44151-1

www.greenpenguin.co.uk

CONTENTS

CONTENTS

INTRODUCTION

In its beginnings the Bible enshrined the beliefs, law and memory of the people who took their name from Israel, the later name of Jacob, one of a line of patriarchs whose ancestry could be traced back to the original parents of mankind, Adam and Eve. Jacob was grandson of Abraham, the 'father of many nations' (Gen. 17:5), to whom God promised that his seed would be multiplied 'as the stars of the heaven, and as the sand which is upon the sea-shore' (Gen. 22:17). As the Israelites multiplied and – often perforce – spread throughout the world, they took their Bible with them. It grew to be a collection of twenty-four books (sometimes counted as twenty-two) that defined the Jewish heritage.[1] Living always in relation – but not always obedience – to their demanding God whose name they dared not say, they became twelve tribes; they lived in Egypt following Joseph's success there, then fled from it because of persecution by the pharaoh as God brought plagues on the Egyptians, finally bringing death on every firstborn son, before parting the Red Sea for Moses and the Israelites to escape safely. Forty years in the wilderness followed, during which God gave Moses the Ten Commandments, and promised the people a land flowing with milk and honey (Canaan, later, Israel). There they settled, and this is the land they have fought for ever since, sometimes winning, as in the conquest under Joshua's leadership, sometimes losing, most notably when Jerusalem, the capital and site of the Temple that Solomon had built, was captured in 597 BCE, the disaster that led to exile in Babylon.

The long period from the creation to the conquest of the promised land established what it meant to be the chosen people of God. Its story is told in the books from Genesis to Joshua, books replete with narratives and law that have such a hold on the imagination that they have become part of the general heritage of the Judaeo-Christian world. Later Jewish history, in the books from Judges to Nehemiah, tells of the development of a kingdom, its rise under David and Solomon, then its division, decline and destruction; finally there is the return of a remnant of the people to Jerusalem, and the establishment of a new religious nation. From this period of decline and reconstruction comes a substantial body of often poetic books of prophecy, Isaiah to Malachi, that further developed the people's understanding of its relationship with God. Central to these is an intensely critical awareness of how the Israelites have fallen away from their religious and moral duty, so there is a mixture of dire condemnation of the present, warnings of future catastrophe as a consequence, but also promise of a restored relationship with God if they repent. Above all there is the promise of a Messiah. Job, Psalms and other poetic and wisdom writings also became part of the Jewish Bible, further expressing and exploring this heritage and religious understanding.

A tiny new sect – the followers of Jesus, a descendant of Abraham and Jacob by way of the greatest of the kings, David – inherited the Jewish Bible and added a new religious understanding and heritage to it, the collection of books and letters that became known as the New Testament. Through faith, missionary zeal and persecution on the one hand, and conquest on the other, this sect, the Christians, also fulfilled the promise to Abraham, becoming many nations. Their Bible, focusing intensely on the proclamation of Jesus, the son of God, the Messiah who was crucified and rose again from the dead, went with them. It gave religious, legal, moral and literary shape to nations across the world until the two Testaments of the Christian Bible reigned in the consciousness of more people than any other book. It became the classic of classics.

Yet it is unlike most classics in that it is a collection of writings. The word 'bible' was originally Greek, *ta biblia*, with a plural sense, 'the little books' – something that is useful to keep in mind both when thinking about the nature of the Bible and when reading it. It is the work of many authors and compilers living over a period of roughly a millennium. The book might be thought of as an anthology but is really closer to being a library. Containing most of what survives of ancient Hebrew writings and the key texts of early Christian writings, it is a varied collection of small to medium-sized books (from less than 300 words in English to more than 40,000) united by one thing: a belief that everything in it is sacred, the word of God to man.

Just what this word of God consists of and how it is organised depends on one's particular belief or on the particular Bible one picks up. For Judaism, the Bible or Tanakh is what Christians call the Old Testament. It is divided into three parts, the Law or Torah (Genesis to Deuteronomy), the Prophets or Nevi'im (divided into the Former Prophets, Joshua to 2 Kings (excluding Ruth), and the Latter Prophets, Isaiah to Ezekiel (excluding Lamentations) and the Twelve Minor Prophets), and the Writings or Kethuvim (beginning with Psalms and ending with Chronicles). All these books were originally written in Hebrew, with just a few chapters in Aramaic. They are still read in Hebrew from scrolls in synagogues.

Christianity has the same books but in different arrangements. The Writings and the Latter Prophets change places, removing the tripartite sense of the collection, and the order of some books is significantly altered. There are also differences within Christianity. Roman Catholicism and Eastern Orthodoxy add to the Old Testament a number of books not found in the Hebrew collection. Protestantism keeps to the Hebrew books but has a separate section of additional books, the Apocrypha; here they are not so much part of Scripture as a supplement to it. Ambivalence towards the Apocrypha led in the early nineteenth century to its omission from most Protestant Bibles.

Then there is Christianity's special part of the Bible, the New Testament, with the same books in the same order in almost all churches. These books record the early history of Christianity, especially the life and teachings of Jesus, then the acts of his apostles; they include the key doctrinal letters of the apostles, especially Paul, and end with a prophetic vision, Revelation.

One of the characteristics of the Bible as a library is that it contains multiple accounts of the same events. Rather than giving a single account of the life and teachings of Jesus (as the Syrian Church did by using a synopsis of the Gospels), it includes four Gospels. The life of David is told in both Samuel and Chronicles. There can be multiple accounts within single books, beginning with the two accounts of the creation of man in Genesis. Sometimes two accounts are mixed together to become a single narrative with contradictory details in them, as in the story of the flood, also in Genesis. So, even when one reads the Bible in a single form without being aware that it has multiple versions, one gets a sense that its contents are protean. Moreover, the Bible seems quite unaware of these variations: it says things happened this way, it says they happened that way; it gives Jesus' sayings one way, it gives them another way. This is very unusual. We are familiar with historians speculating as to what happened and giving several alternatives, but not with books that give alternatives as if they are all true. In general terms, it is an effect that belongs to a library: there one can in turn pick up several authors' accounts of, say, one person's life. This aspect of the Bible can produce a sense that its truth – whether religious, historical, mythical or fictional – lies on the other side of its words or particular details. It is often as if one finds the Bible not *in* its words, but *through* or *behind* them.

The Bible is the world's most translated book. It exists in more languages than any other book, and sometimes, as in English, it has hundreds of forms within one language. However much its words are revered, in practice we accept that the meaning and content do survive translation. The Bible itself gives us grounds for accepting this position. The New Testament is written in Greek. It usually quotes the Old Testament not from the Hebrew but from the Greek translation that had become current from the third century BCE, the Septuagint, and Jesus' words are given in Greek, not the Aramaic he actually spoke. Aramaic is preserved in a few instances, as when he says to Jairus' daughter, who seemed to be dead but was sleeping, ' "Talitha cumi", which is, being interpreted, "Damsel, I say unto thee, arise" ' (Mark 5:41). Again it is as if the true text lies behind the actual words given.

How, then, can we think of any of the thousands of different bibles as *the* Bible? The translators of the King James Bible give this answer in their preface:

the very meanest translation of the Bible in English set forth by men of our profession . . . containeth the word of God, nay, is the word of God: as the King's speech which he uttered in Parliament, being translated into French, Dutch, Italian and Latin, is still the King's speech, though it be not interpreted by every translator with the like grace, nor peradventure so fitly for phrase, nor so expressly for sense, everywhere . . . No cause therefore why the word translated should be denied to be the word, or forbidden to be current, notwithstanding that some imperfections and blemishes may be noted in the setting forth of it.'[2]

In short, as a translation contains the word of God, so it is the word of God. This is indeed part of how we think of it: one translation can be as good as another as long as we are convinced it is a faithful translation rather than a rewriting.

But we usually want to go further than this, and settle on a single version as the Bible. In part this is because of our sense that, as God-given scripture, it is sacred down to the finest detail of the text. Perhaps the oldest expression of this idea is Moses' injunction to the children of Israel, 'Ye shall not add unto the word which I command you, neither shall you diminish aught from it, that ye may keep the commandments of the LORD your God which I command you' (Deut. 4:2). The first-century CE Jewish historian Josephus put it this way: 'we have given practical proof of our reverence for our own Scriptures. For, although such long ages have now passed, no one has ventured either to add, or to remove, or to alter a syllable; and it is an instinct with every Jew . . . to regard them as the decrees of God, to abide by them, and, if need be, cheerfully to die for them'.[3] The Jews still regard the Hebrew scriptures in this way.

To varying degrees, Christians have inherited this attitude, constantly inclining to grant to a single version a similar sacredness. For the Eastern Church this version was the Greek Septuagint coupled with the Greek New Testament. For the Roman Catholic Church it was St Jerome's standard Latin translation begun in 382 CE, the Vulgate. For English-speaking Protestantism it was – for many, it remains – a Bible translated from the traditional Hebrew, known as the Masoretic text, and from the Greek Received Text of the New Testament originally published in 1550: the King James Bible or Authorised Version of 1611.

There are particular reasons for reading the King James Bible. Some are to do with its intrinsic qualities, others with its place in history. It is the culmination of nearly a century of translation work that began with William Tyndale (?1494–1536). Because translation was forbidden in Roman Catholic England, he worked in sometimes horrific conditions of exile and captivity in what is now Belgium, translating the New Testament (1525 and 1526; revised 1534) and the Pentateuch (Genesis to Deuteronomy, 1530). By the time of his martyrdom for heresy in 1536, he had taken his work to the end of Chronicles. His aim was to bring the Bible to the ploughboy. Ordinary English folk were to know more of the word of God than ignorant priests did. Using straightforward, sometimes even slangy, English, he translated from the Hebrew and Greek rather than the Latin revered by the Roman Catholics. His work, especially in the Old Testament, has a sometimes remarkable freshness and clarity, and remains highly readable.

Tyndale was a pioneer of genius, one of the very great figures of both English religion and English literature. The English Bible owes more to him than any other single person. Miles Coverdale (1488–1568) revised and finished his work, publishing the first complete printed Bible in English in 1535. Both Tyndale and Coverdale worked as private translators (and there were others, now too little remembered, who did likewise), but official translation soon followed as the English Reformation under Henry VIII gained strength and the ban on translation disappeared. Under the auspices of Archbishop Thomas Cranmer and with further work from Coverdale, the Church of England's first official Bible, the Great Bible of 1539–40, was created. Then came the return to Roman Catholicism under Mary. Some Protestant exiles in Geneva further revised the text and added substantial notes. Respected for its scholarship, appreciated for the strongly Protestant understanding of the notes, for the clear print and its relative cheapness, the Geneva Bible was the most popular English Bible between 1560 and the middle of the next century. It was reprinted around 200 times.

With the return of Protestantism under Elizabeth I, the Church of England made a second official revision, the Bishops' Bible of 1568, but, less scholarly and less affordable, it proved no rival for the Geneva. The Roman Catholics in exile in France also produced a translation (New Testament, 1582; Old Testament, 1609, 1610). It too depended largely on the foundations Tyndale had created. Like the Geneva Bible, it had copious notes, this time giving the Roman Catholic understanding.

The King James Bible built on these predecessors. It was initiated at a 1604 conference at Hampton Court called by the new king, James I, in an effort to produce religious harmony in his kingdoms. A leader of the Puritans moved 'his Majesty that there might be a new translation of the Bible because those which were allowed in the reigns of Henry VIII and Edward VI were corrupt and not answerable to the truth of the original'. In short, there were mistakes in the Great Bible. Psalm 105:28, for instance, should not read, 'they were not obedient' but 'they were not disobedient' (the King James Bible reads, 'they rebelled not').[4] He evidently did not mention that this was a Geneva Bible reading, but the intention seems clear: let the Church adopt the Bible favoured by the Puritans. If he had wished to crush the suggestion, James might have responded that the Church had already revised the Great Bible and that the sense was correct in the Bishops' Bible. Perhaps a few more corrections to that were all that was needed. Certainly he was aware of the unstated desire to have the Geneva Bible, for he let fly against it: it was the worst of translations because of the anti-monarchist tendency of some of the notes. Perhaps to the Puritans' dismay, he took the suggestion for a new translation literally. The idea probably appealed to the scholar in him, and he may have had more than one kingly motive for liking it: it would keep the religious leaders busy – indeed, it might even get them working together – and it might become a monument to his reign. There should be a new translation that the whole Church would use, and, following his objection to Geneva, it should have no annotations.

Everything but the provision of money for the work was done on a grand scale. Forty-seven men – future archbishops and lifelong country parsons, king's professors and men without college positions, high Church men and Puritans, but united across party and position by their devotion and learning – were appointed to six companies. Two companies at Westminster were assigned Genesis to 2 Kings, and the Epistles; two at Oxford, the Prophets (Isaiah to Malachi), and the Gospels, Acts and Revelation; and two at Cambridge, 1 Chronicles to the Song of Solomon, and the Apocrypha. Under the king's supervision, detailed instructions were drawn up (James seems to have had little further direct involvement other than intervening to hurry the work to completion). In spite of the Puritans, it was to be a light revision of the Church's official Bible, the Bishops' Bible: this was to be 'as little altered as the truth of the original will permit'. Older English Bibles could be used 'where they agree better with the text than the Bishops' Bible'. This gave the translators both a base text and the freedom to draw on the collective labours of their predecessors in their pursuit of truth to the original Greek and Hebrew. They were to keep traditional forms of names and 'old ecclesiastical words' such as 'Church' (this to avoid the tendentiousness of words like 'Congregation'), to follow traditional understanding in cases of ambiguity, and to avoid tinkering with the division into chapters and verses.[5]

Some detailed matters of practice were laid down. Each member of a company was individually to work over the piece of scripture in hand, and then the company would collectively agree on the revisions. As books were finished they were to be sent to the other companies for comment, and advice could be sought from outside. The clergy were to be invited to submit suggestions. A general meeting was envisaged once the companies had finished their work. One translator later noted some further practices. Where a word in the original had two possible and suitable meanings, one meaning was put in the text, the other in the margin, and similarly where there was a variant reading in the original. Difficult Hebrew and Greek expressions were placed in the margin, so the text contained an equivalent to the meaning while the margin gave a literal translation. Words which were necessary for English expression but had no equivalent in the originals were set in a different typeface (this is the origin of the italics found in most editions of the King James Bible); chapter summaries were added, and new page headings, also summarising the content, were supplied.

As might be expected, these rules and notes do not cover everything the translators had to do, nor were they perfectly adhered to. Most importantly, what had been envisaged as a light revision became, to good effect, a thorough revision: all the scholarship of the time was employed to get the best possible understanding of the texts in the original languages, and the work of their English predecessors was scrupulously examined and discriminatingly used. Yet not everything was perfectly done. Names were inconsistently treated, the marking of added words was erratic, not all the textual variants were noted, and the paragraphing was never finished (there is one paragraph division in the Psalms and six in the Apocrypha; paragraphing ceases entirely after Acts 20). The translators did not always follow the specified ways of working. Some of the companies appear to have subdivided their work, and there was much less consultation than anticipated (in part because of James's intervention to cut short the time the translators were spending on the first part of the work). Nor did the general meeting finish things. This was left to two of the translators, Miles Smith and Thomas Bilson, who oversaw the final revisions as the work went through the press.

Sometime in 1611 the King's Printer, Robert Barker, issued what we now call the King James Bible or Authorised Version. There is no record of exactly when, nor of its being officially authorised. Designed as a Church Bible, it was a large and heavy folio printed in imposing but rather antiquated black-letter type (a stiff contrast with the modern roman type of most Geneva Bibles). Following a fine title-page (an engraving that must have suffered a printing-house accident, for it disappeared from use), there is a fulsome dedication to the king that remains a standard part of most British editions. Then comes Miles Smith's 'The Translators to the Reader'; this valuable but long and elaborately written statement of the history of – and justification for – translation, and of the translators' intentions, is usually omitted (as are the Calendar, the Tables of Lessons, the thirty-four pages of ornately engraved genealogies beginning with God and ending with Jesus, and the map and gazetteer of the Holy Land). The Bible text itself is in two-column form, with each verse beginning as a separate line. New paragraphs are marked with a paraph (¶). As well as the headers and chapter summaries, there are marginal notes giving alternative translations, literal renderings of the original and cross-references; occasional miscellaneous information is also given, such as equivalent values for money and weights.

The translators described their work in this way:

> Truly, good Christian reader, we never thought from the begin-
> ning that we should need to make a new translation, nor yet to
> make of a bad one a good one . . . but to make a good one better,
> or out of many good ones one principal good one, not justly to

be excepted against, that hath been our endeavour, that our mark. To that purpose there were many chosen that were greater in other men's eyes than in their own, and that sought the truth rather than their own praise.

They saw themselves as revisers. Their idea of what would make the good work of their predecessors better is contained in the word 'truth'. They say this of 'truth' and the Bible: 'But now what piety without truth? what truth, what saving truth, without the word of God? what word of God, whereof we may be sure, without the Scripture?' They exhort readers to search and study the Scriptures, having in mind particularly Jesus' words, 'Search the scriptures, for in them ye think ye have eternal life, and they are they which testify of me' (John 5:39). '[H]appy is the man that delighteth in the Scripture,' they declare, 'and thrice happy that meditateth in it day and night'.[6] As the essence of truth, as God's direct communication to man, the Bible is to be studied and meditated on. The translators envisage their work as being true to the truth in such a way that no man can say, 'this is not correctly translated'. Accuracy was vital, and achieved by studying the original texts with erudition, intensity and subtlety. One of the translators, John Bois, made notes on some of their discussions that show all these qualities being exercised. We might imagine that the translators spent most time discussing their English, but these notes show above all a painstaking attention to the precise, nuanced meaning of the original.[7]

In the first place, then, the King James Bible is a highly scholarly translation. William Blake as he was beginning to learn Hebrew wrote to a correspondent, 'I read Greek as fluently as an Oxford scholar, & the [New] Testament is my chief master: astonishing indeed is the English translation, it is almost word for word, & if the Hebrew Bible is as well translated . . . we need not doubt of its having been translated as well as written by the Holy Ghost'.[8] Modern readers who can read this Bible in the light of the originals can share this astonishment. More than many recent versions, it trusts the original texts, believing that their way of saying things can speak with clarity, without much resort to paraphrase.

Its language is, of course, antiquated, and this presents the reader with both challenges and rewards. The challenges are the old grammatical forms (these only take a little getting used to), a number of unfamiliar words and the changed sense of some words. The rewards are a language that is usually highly meaningful (there are places where, like the originals, it can be obscure) and also highly pleasing. The King James Bible offers the reader both the meaning of the Bible and a religious or aesthetic experience of language that no modern translation can match. For instance, after Adam and Eve have eaten fruit from the tree of the knowledge of good and evil, the King James Bible has Adam give this simple reply to God: 'And the man said, "The woman whom thou gavest to be with me, she gave me of the tree, and I did eat"' (Gen. 3:12). The meaning is clear except perhaps for 'she gave me of the tree', but in context it is obvious that he is saying she gave him fruit from the tree. The language is simple, almost entirely monosyllabic English, without a trace of pretence to grandeur. Only the archaic form, 'thou gavest', marks it out as biblical English. It is when one listens to it that its power becomes obvious. Two words stand out, 'she' and 'did'. 'The woman ... she gave' places the stress on her in a way that 'the woman ... gave' could not. Then 'I did eat' rather than 'I ate' gives a strong sense of Adam's guilt, as if he was saying, 'yes I did, I ate from the tree'. As well as these ringing words, stressing both accusation and confession, there is a rhythm to the verse. The last ten words make a pentameter. Milton recognised this, and 'she gave me of the tree, and I did eat' became a line of *Paradise Lost* (1667).

Modern versions usually stay close to the King James in this verse. Here is the New International Version: 'The man said, "The woman you put here with me – she gave me some fruit from the tree, and I ate it." ' It is still powerful, but not as powerful. There are no uncertainties of meaning, nor any archaism, but the rhythm has almost vanished, and there are several touches, all of them associated with a move from literal translation towards paraphrase, which make it less effective. The dash before 'she gave me' underlines the effect of having the subject stated twice (as it is in the Hebrew), but it goes along with changes that make Adam close to vindictive in his attitude to Eve. 'The woman you put here with me' is a bitter statement, as if Eve were inflicted on him. The sense of Eve as a gift is lost – 'The woman whom thou *gavest* to be with me'; lost too is the parallel between Eve being given and Eve giving – 'she gave' (the Hebrew uses the same verb in both places). The change at the end of the verse, 'and I ate it', comes about not just because modern translators are uncomfortable with using 'did', but because the New International Version, paraphrasing for clarity, has added 'some fruit' (not in the Hebrew), and so must finish with 'it' (again not in the Hebrew). The reader should not make too much of a single example of this sort. By itself it does not prove the King James great, and it certainly does not prove that the New International Version is bad. The Bible is a massive book, and there are places where the King James is not so easily admired.

I have kept the Hebrew in sight in discussing this example because most readers of the Bible would agree that fidelity to the meaning of the originals is essential, and that felicity of language is less important. Every detail in the King James rendering of the verse comes from the Hebrew. The excellence of the writing comes from the excellence of the Hebrew. Yet the language of the King James does matter for its own sake. Beauty and truth are not always close companions, but they can never be entirely divorced. '[W]orship the LORD in the beauty of holiness,' cries the Psalmist (Psalms 29:2, 96:9). If beauty is lacking, some of the holiness is lost.

In the English-speaking world the King James Bible is the supremely beautiful Bible, and has long been praised as such. The most eloquent example of this praise comes from a convert to Catholicism, Father William Faber, in the middle of the nineteenth century. Though he opposes Protestantism, he makes the most important points about the place of the King James Bible in the English consciousness:

> who will say that the uncommon beauty and marvellous English of the Protestant Bible is not one of the great strongholds of heresy in this country? It lives on in the ear like a music that never can be forgotten, like the sound of church bells which the convert hardly knows how he can forego. Its felicities seem often to be things rather than mere words. It is part of the national mind and the anchor of the national seriousness. Nay, it is worshipped with a positive idolatry, in extenuation of whose grotesque fanaticism its intrinsic beauty pleads availingly with the man of letters and the scholar. The memory of the dead passes into it. The potent traditions of childhood are stereotyped in its verses. The power of all the griefs and trials of a man is hidden beneath its words. It is the representative of his best moments, and all that there has been about him of soft, and gentle, and pure, and penitent, and good, speaks to him forever out of his English Bible. It is his sacred thing which doubt never dimmed and controversy never soiled. It has been to him all along as the silent, but O how intelligible voice, of his guardian angel; and in the length and breadth of the land there is not a Protestant, with one spark of religiousness about him, whose spiritual biography is not in his Saxon Bible.[9]

Experienced throughout life by generations of English-speakers, it is at the heart of English-speaking religion and culture, shaping emotional history, law, language and literature. Whether or not one is a Christian, one cannot know what it means to be part of an English-speaking heritage without knowledge of the King James Bible.

READING THE BIBLE FOR THE FIRST TIME

Readers encountering the Bible for the first time may find it helpful to remember that, in spite of its physical appearance as a single book, it is a library. Pick up a book, and one usually begins at the beginning intending to read it all, but this is not how one uses a library: there one chooses what to pick off the shelves. Some books appeal, some do not; one puts these latter back on the shelves, finds something more congenial, and so goes on reading. In short, first-time readers of the Bible may be defeated if they try to read it consecutively from beginning to end.

The reader opening this book as an unknown classic may find that narrative is its most appealing aspect. Though one can begin with either Testament, there is some value to starting with the Old Testament: not only does it give the essential framework of belief and heritage on which the New Testament is built, but, save for the gospel story, it contains the Bible's most famous and powerful narratives.

From Genesis to Exodus 20 there is the story of the creation of the world and humanity which leads by way of Noah and the flood to the histories of the founding fathers of Israel, the captivity in Egypt and the escape under Moses' leadership into the wilderness where the fundamental Jewish law is established. Here are some of the world's great stories, many of them still alive in our collective consciousness even if we think we know nothing of the Bible. Numbers 9–14 covers some essential parts of the time in the wilderness, then Joshua 1–11 tells the story of the fight for the promised land.

Judges, featuring the story of Samson but replete with other sometimes horrifying stories, and Ruth lead into the period of the kings, notably Saul, David and Solomon in the two books of Samuel and 1 Kings 1–3 and 10–11. David is the towering character here, and his story is told in unblinking detail as he moves from the young hero who slays Goliath to the morally corrupt king who sets up the death of Uriah so that he can have Uriah's wife Bathsheba. But, taken as a whole, he is a hero, the more so for being the chief creator of Hebrew poetry.

Among the many other narrative books, Jonah, in which the rebellious prophet is swallowed by a great fish or whale, is not to be missed. In the Apocrypha, there are Tobit, Judith and what is one of the world's earliest detective stories, Bel and the Dragon.

There is much besides narrative. Old Testament poetry reaches its pinnacle in the Song of Solomon, a series of love poems often read in allegorical ways, for instance by Christians as expressing God and the Church's mutual love. Nevertheless, the heart of the Bible's religious poetry is the Psalms, a collection of 150 poems that have consoled and inspired through the ages. Among them are some of the most moving expressions of belief, such as Psalm 23, 'The Lord is my shepherd'.

Job and Ecclesiastes are essential philosophical books. Written almost entirely as poetic dialogues, Job explores the problem of suffering and God's justice as Job is afflicted with torments. Ecclesiastes reflects on the state of the world, asking the perennial question, 'What profit hath a man of all his labour which he taketh under the sun?' (1:3) when all is 'vanity of vanities'.

Often difficult, the prophetic books are best approached through Isaiah, bearing in mind Matthew Arnold's judgement that 'by virtue of the original it is a monument of the Hebrew genius at its best, and by virtue of the translation it is a monument of the English language at its best'.[10]

The essential story and teaching of the New Testament is in the Gospels. Jesus' life emerges as a complex whole from the four tellings, and none can be dispensed with. However, Matthew, more often than the others, gives the incidents and the teaching in their best-known form, and John is theologically essential. Next in theological importance are the epistles of Paul, which are best begun in the order they appear, with Romans and 1 Corinthians. Acts, narrating what happened to Jesus' followers after his death, provides an important context for these epistles, and also narrates stories that are essential to the Christian heritage, such as the martyrdom of Stephen and the conversion of Saul (thereafter Paul) on the road to Damascus.

THE TEXT

The text of this Penguin Bible, giving both Testaments and the Apocrypha, is that of *The New Cambridge Paragraph Bible* (2005), with some corrections. It gives the closest possible realisation of the text decided on by the King James translators in a format that is as readable as possible.

Other texts of the King James Bible misrepresent to some extent the work of the translators. Even the first edition of 1611 had its unavoidable share of printing errors. Subsequent editions corrected these and also revised some readings, often because, in the editor's judgement, his reading was what the translators should have adopted, either for accuracy to the original or for the sake of English expression. This gradual process effectively came to an end with an Oxford Bible published in 1769. Most modern editions give this revised yet antiquated Oxford text with almost no changes.

The *New Cambridge Paragraph Bible* text is based on a collation of all the variations between the first edition and the modern text. In each case the translators' preferred reading was established and adopted. This work involved comparison of printed editions of the King James Bible, examination of the history of the readings in earlier English Bibles and of the Hebrew and Greek texts. Some of the most enlightening evidence came from a source never before used in preparing a text of the King James Bible: manuscript work and notes from the translators themselves. The most important of these is a Bishops' Bible of 1602 (in the Bodleian Library, Oxford), in which the Old Testament is intensively annotated by the translators: it is very close to being their final manuscript.

Few of the variations in the King James text have theological significance. One of these illustrates both how the translators worked and what happened to their text. At Hosea 6:5 God declares, according to current editions of the King James Bible, 'Therefore have I hewed them by the prophets; I have slain them by the words of my mouth'. Earlier English Bibles had had 'cut down' instead of 'hewed', both good literal translations of the Hebrew. The first edition of the King James is different by one letter, 'shewed' instead of 'hewed'. Rather than God appearing, by way of the prophets, to be a killer, in this reading he reveals things to the people; he warns them, and the words of truth are so terrible to the backsliders that, metaphorically rather than literally, they are struck dead. 'Hewed' appeared in the second edition, and the assumption has been that 'shewed' was a misprint. It was not. The translators struck through 'cut down' in the Bishops' Bible and substituted 'shewed them by'. They had decided to bring out the gentler sense of the text, probably influenced by the Geneva Bible's explanatory note: 'I have still laboured by my prophets, and as it were, framed you to bring you to amendment, but all was in vain: for my word was not meat to feed them, but a sword to slay them'. What may have decided the translators was the reading in the ancient Aramaic translation-paraphrase of the prophets, Targum Jonathan, 'I warned them' (a copy of this was in Oxford at the time the Oxford translators were working on Hosea). This, then, gives a sense of the translators' scholarly work and of how it could be lost by later editors who did not understand what they had done. The *New Cambridge Paragraph Bible* text restores such readings, placing the reader closer to the King James translators than ever before.

Hosea 6:5 now reads, 'Therefore have I shown them'. 'Shown' instead of 'showed' is an example of the other major aspect of the *New Cambridge Paragraph Bible* text: its spelling, punctuation and presentation are modernised. 'Spake' becomes 'spoke', 'musick' 'music', 'bason' 'basin', 'digged' 'dug', and so on. The punctuation is revised towards that found in the original 1611 edition (seventeenth-century punctuation is closer to modern punctuation than that of the eighteenth century), speech marks have been added, and the imperfect and incomplete paragraphing has been fully revised. These changes have been made because the spelling and punctuation, like the readings, are as they were settled in the Oxford edition of 1769: they belong neither to the time of the translators nor to the present, so have no special authority, and are often an obstacle to clear understanding of the text.

There are strict limits to the revisions: what the translators wrote is never rewritten. Consequently, old linguistic forms such as 'thou shalt' remain because they are an essential part of the character of the translators' language. To change them is to begin to rewrite and so to make another version. Original words that had been obscured by changes of spelling or the substitution of similar but different words are restored. Though sometimes challenging, this act of faithfulness to the translators' text may help the reader to a better understanding. For instance, the original spelling of 'instead' as two words is restored. In the King James Bible, 'stead' is often used by itself to mean 'place'; 'in stead' usually means 'in the place of' rather than 'as an alternative to', which is our normal sense of 'instead'. When God tells Moses, in the words of most King James Bibles, that Aaron 'shall be to thee instead of a mouth, and thou shalt be to him instead of God' (Exod. 4:16), it does not mean that Moses has no mouth and, alarmingly, Aaron no God other than his own brother. The old spelling, 'in stead of God' makes it clear that Moses is in the place of God for Aaron, relaying to him the divine words.

Traditional presentation of the text in two columns of separate numbered verses was originally dictated by the economics of manuscripts and printing and by the utility of a quick reference system. Except for the avoidance of very long lines on large pages, it does nothing for the reader. Rather, it is a great barrier to insight and pleasure.[11] It militates against what William Tyndale wanted his readers to perceive, 'the process, order and meaning' of the text.[12] The text given here retains verse numbering unobtrusively, so that it can be used as a reference text, but is presented in our familiar reading forms of paragraphed prose and lineated poetry. In this way, the words of this classic of classics can speak with the greatest possible clarity.[13]

NOTES

1. In its Protestant form, the Old Testament has thirty-nine books. The Hebrew Bible counts the two-part books (Samuel, Kings, Chronicles and Ezra–Nehemiah) and the Twelve Minor Prophets (Hosea to Malachi) as one each, giving twenty-four. Judges and Ruth, and Jeremiah and Lamentations could be counted as single books, giving twenty-two. This had a certain magic to it, for this is the number of letters in the Hebrew alphabet (and also of founding fathers from Adam to Jacob). Moreover five of these letters have alternative forms, and five of the books could be reckoned as two each. The attraction of twenty-two is clear as a reflection of divine inspiration: just as God created the letters of the alphabet, so he created the Scriptures and conformed this creation to the number of letters.

2. *The New Cambridge Paragraph Bible*, ed. David Norton (Cambridge University Press, 2005), p. xxviii.

3. *Against Apion*, 1:42; *Josephus*, trans. H. St J. Thackeray, 8 vols. (Heinemann and Putnam's, 1926), vol. 1, pp. 179–81.

4. William Barlow, *The Sum and Substance of the Conference ... at Hampton Court* (1604), p. 45.

5. For the complete rules and other evidence about the making of the King James Bible, see David Norton, *A Textual History of the King James Bible* (Cambridge University Press, 2005), pp. 7–28.

6. *The New Cambridge Paragraph Bible*, ed. Norton, pp. xxxi, xix–xx, xxi.

7. See Ward S. Allen, *Translating for King James* (Vanderbilt University Press, 1969).

8. Letter to James Blake, 30 January 1803, *The Complete Writings of William Blake*, ed. Geoffrey Keynes (Oxford University Press, 1966), pp. 821–2.

9. F. W. Faber, 'An essay on the interest and characteristics of the Lives of the Saints', in *The Life of S. Francis of Assisi* (1853), pp. 116–17.

10. Matthew Arnold, *A Bible Reading for Schools* (1872), in *The Complete Prose Works of Matthew Arnold*, ed. R. H. Super, 11 vols. (University of Michigan Press, 1960–77), vol. 7, p. 58.

11. This text does not include the marginal annotations.

12. 'W. T. to the Reader', *Tyndale's Old Testament*, ed. David Daniell (Yale University Press, 1992), p. 4.

13. Norton, *Textual History*, chapters 8 and 9, gives a full account of the revisions to the text.

FURTHER READING

Only a very few of the innumerable books about the Bible can be noted here. Readers should choose according to what they want to know and according to the kind of denominational or scholarly viewpoint likely to be most congenial.

Bible dictionaries, companions or encyclopaedias are a ready source of information. Most are excellent, including those now found only second-hand. *The Oxford Companion to the Bible* is as good as any. For help in understanding a particular passage or book, Bible commentaries or annotated Bibles are invaluable. It can be enlightening to use more than one because theological understanding and scholarly opinions vary. *Eerdmans Commentary on the Bible* is very useful, and like several of the others includes the apocryphal books.

The best way of finding words or phrases in the Bible is a searchable electronic text. *Logos Bible Software* offers an ever-expanding range of reliable biblical texts and supplementary works, and can be used to correlate the English, including the Apocrypha, with the original languages. Similar though more limited resources can be found on the internet at sites such as www.blueletterbible.org. Concordances, that is, alphabetical listings of words with a brief indication of the context, remain useful. The best is *Strong's Exhaustive Concordance*, available in many editions; it ties the words to their Hebrew and Greek originals, and includes Hebrew and Greek dictionaries. It is rare to find a concordance that gives the Apocrypha. None of these resources will exactly match the *New Cambridge Paragraph Bible* text, particularly because of its revised spelling, but a little ingenuity, such as looking for 'bason' rather than 'basin', will usually solve the problem.

The following is a very brief selection of books about the history of the Bible, the English Bible and the King James Bible.

Alter, Robert, and Frank Kermode, *The Literary Guide to the Bible* (Collins, 1987).

The Cambridge History of the Bible, 3 vols. (Cambridge University Press, 1963–70).

Daniell, David, *The Bible in English: Its History and Influence* (Yale University Press, 2003).

de Hamel, Christopher, *The Book: A History of the Bible* (Phaidon, 2001).

Hammond, Gerald, *The Making of the English Bible* (Carcanet, 1982).

Miller, Stephen M., and Robert V. Huber, *The Bible: A History* (Lion Hudson, 2003).

Nicolson, Adam, *Power and Glory: Jacobean England and the Making of the*

King James Bible (HarperCollins, 2003). The American edition published as *God's Secretaries: The Making of the King James Bible*.

Norton, David, *A History of the English Bible as Literature* (Cambridge University Press, 2000).

——, *A Textual History of the King James Bible* (Cambridge University Press, 2005).

Paine, Gustavus S., *The Men Behind the King James Version* (Baker, 1977). Originally published as *The Learned Men* (1959).

Rogerson, John (ed.), *The Oxford Illustrated History of the Bible* (Oxford University Press, 2001).

THE
HOLY BIBLE

CONTAINING THE

OLD AND NEW TESTAMENT

AND THE BOOKS CALLED APOCRYPHA

TRANSLATED OUT OF THE ORIGINAL TONGUES
AND WITH THE FORMER TRANSLATIONS
DILIGENTLY COMPARED AND REVISED
BY HIS MAJESTY'S SPECIAL COMMANDMENT

Appointed to be read in Churches

CUM PRIVILEGIO

TO THE MOST HIGH AND MIGHTY

Prince, JAMES, by the grace of GOD,
King of Great Britain, France and Ireland,
Defender of the Faith, etc.

THE TRANSLATORS OF THE BIBLE
wish grace, mercy, and peace, through JESUS
CHRIST our LORD

Great and manifold were the blessings, most dread Sovereign, which Almighty GOD, the Father of all mercies, bestowed upon us the people of England, when first he sent your Majesty's royal person to rule and reign over us. For whereas it was the expectation of many, who wished not well unto our Sion, that upon the setting of that bright occidental star, Queen Elizabeth of most happy memory, some thick and palpable clouds of darkness would so have overshadowed this land, that men should have been in doubt which way they were to walk, and that it should hardly be known, who was to direct the unsettled state: the appearance of your Majesty, as of the sun in his strength, instantly dispelled those supposed and surmised mists, and gave unto all that were well affected exceeding cause of comfort; especially when we beheld the government established in your Highness, and your hopeful seed, by an undoubted title, and this also accompanied with peace and tranquillity at home and abroad.

But amongst all our joys, there was none that more filled our hearts, than the blessed continuance of the preaching of GOD's sacred word amongst us, which is that inestimable treasure, which excelleth all the riches of the earth, because the fruit thereof extendeth itself, not only to the time spent in this transitory world, but directeth and disposeth men unto that eternal happiness which is above in heaven.

Then, not to suffer this to fall to the ground, but rather to take it up, and to continue it in that state, wherein the famous predecessor of your Highness did leave it: nay, to go forward with the confidence and resolution of a man in maintaining the truth of CHRIST, and propagating it far and near, is that which have so bound and firmly knit the hearts of all your Majesty's loyal and religious people unto you, that your very name is precious among them, their eye doth behold you with comfort, and they bless you in their hearts, as that sanctified person, who, under GOD, is the immediate author of their true happiness. And this their contentment doth not diminish or decay, but every day increaseth and taketh strength, when they observe that the zeal of your Majesty towards the house of GOD doth not slack or go backward, but is more and more kindled, manifesting itself abroad in the farthest parts of Christendom, by writing in defence of the Truth (which hath given such a blow unto that man of sin, as will not be healed), and every day at home, by religious and learned discourse, by frequenting the house of GOD, by hearing the word preached, by cherishing the teachers thereof, by caring for the Church as a most tender and loving nursing father.

There are infinite arguments of this right Christian and religious affection in your Majesty: but none is more forcible to declare it to others than the vehement and perpetuated desire of accomplishing and publishing of this work, which now with all humility we present unto your Majesty, For when your Highness had once out of deep judgement apprehended how convenient it was, that out of the original sacred tongues, together with comparing of the labours, both in our own and other foreign languages, of many worthy men who went before us, there should be one more exact translation of the Holy Scriptures into the English tongue; your Majesty did never desist to urge and to excite those to whom it was commended, that the work might be hastened, and that the business might be expedited in so decent a manner, as a matter of such importance might justly require.

And now at last, by the mercy of GOD, and the continuance of our labours, it being brought unto such a conclusion, as that we have great hope that the Church of England shall reap good fruit thereby; we hold it our duty to offer it to your Majesty, not only as to our King and Sovereign, but as to the principal mover and author of the work: humbly craving of your most sacred Majesty, that since things of this quality have ever been subject to the censures of ill-meaning and discontented persons, it may receive approbation and patronage from so learned and judicious a prince as your Highness is, whose allowance and acceptance of our labours shall more honour and encourage us, than all the calumniations and hard interpretations of other men shall dismay us. So that if, on the one side, we shall be traduced by Popish persons at home or abroad, who therefore will malign us, because we are poor instruments to make GOD's holy Truth to be yet more and more known unto the people, whom they desire still to keep in ignorance and darkness; or if, on the other side, we shall be maligned by self-conceited brethren, who run their own ways, and give liking unto nothing but what is framed by themselves, and hammered on their anvil; we may rest secure, supported within by the truth and innocence of a good conscience, having walked the ways of simplicity and integrity, as before the Lord; and sustained without by the powerful protection of your Majesty's grace and favour, which will ever give countenance to honest and Christian endeavours against bitter censures and uncharitable imputations.

The LORD of heaven and earth bless your Majesty with many and happy days, that, as his heavenly hand hath enriched your Highness with many singular and extraordinary graces, so you may be the wonder of the world in this latter age for happiness and true felicity, to the honour of that great GOD, and the good of his Church, through JESUS CHRIST our Lord and only Saviour.

THE NAMES AND ORDER
of all the Books of the
Old and New Testament
and the Books called Apocrypha

THE BOOKS OF THE NEW TESTAMENT

THE OLD TESTAMENT

THE FIRST BOOK OF MOSES,
CALLED
GENESIS

1 In the beginning God created the heaven and the earth. ²And the earth was without form, and void, and darkness was upon the face of the deep. And the Spirit of God moved upon the face of the waters. ³And God said, 'Let there be light': and there was light. ⁴And God saw the light, that it was good: and God divided the light from the darkness. ⁵And God called the light Day, and the darkness he called Night. And the evening and the morning were the first day.

⁶And God said, 'Let there be a firmament in the midst of the waters, and let it divide the waters from the waters'. ⁷And God made the firmament, and divided the waters which were under the firmament from the waters which were above the firmament: and it was so. ⁸And God called the firmament Heaven. And the evening and the morning were the second day.

⁹And God said, 'Let the waters under the heaven be gathered together unto one place, and let the dry land appear': and it was so. ¹⁰And God called the dry land Earth, and the gathering together of the waters called he Seas: and God saw that it was good. ¹¹And God said, 'Let the earth bring forth grass, the herb yielding seed, and the fruit tree yielding fruit after his kind, whose seed is in itself, upon the earth': and it was so. ¹²And the earth brought forth grass, and herb yielding seed after his kind, and the tree yielding fruit, whose seed was in itself, after his kind: and God saw that it was good. ¹³And the evening and the morning were the third day.

¹⁴And God said, 'Let there be lights in the firmament of the heaven to divide the day from the night: and let them be for signs and for seasons, and for days and years. ¹⁵And let them be for lights in the firmament of the heaven to give light upon the earth': and it was so. ¹⁶And God made two great lights: the greater light to rule the day, and the lesser light to rule the night: he made the stars also. ¹⁷And God set them in the firmament of the heaven to give light upon the earth, ¹⁸and to rule over the day and over the night, and to divide the light from the darkness: and God saw that it was good. ¹⁹And the evening and the morning were the fourth day.

²⁰And God said, 'Let the waters bring forth abundantly the moving creature that hath life, and fowl that may fly above the earth in the open firmament of heaven'. ²¹And God created great whales, and every living creature that moveth, which the waters brought forth abundantly, after their kind, and every winged fowl after his kind: and God saw that it was good. ²²And God blessed them, saying, 'Be fruitful, and multiply, and fill the waters in the seas, and let fowl multiply in the earth'. ²³And the evening and the morning were the fifth day.

²⁴And God said, 'Let the earth bring forth the living creature after his

kind, cattle, and creeping thing, and beast of the earth after his kind': and it was so. ²⁵And God made the beast of the earth after his kind, and cattle after their kind, and everything that creepeth upon the earth after his kind: and God saw that it was good.

²⁶And God said, 'Let us make man in our image, after our likeness: and let them have dominion over the fish of the sea, and over the fowl of the air, and over the cattle, and over all the earth, and over every creeping thing that creepeth upon the earth'. ²⁷So God created man in his own image, in the image of God created he him; male and female created he them. ²⁸And God blessed them, and God said unto them, 'Be fruitful, and multiply, and replenish the earth, and subdue it, and have dominion over the fish of the sea, and over the fowl of the air, and over every living thing that moveth upon the earth'.

²⁹And God said, 'Behold, I have given you every herb bearing seed, which is upon the face of all the earth, and every tree, in the which is the fruit of a tree yielding seed; to you it shall be for meat: ³⁰and to every beast of the earth, and to every fowl of the air, and to everything that creepeth upon the earth, wherein there is life, I have given every green herb for meat': and it was so. ³¹And God saw everything that he had made, and behold, it was very good. And the evening and the morning were the sixth day.

2 Thus the heavens and the earth were finished, and all the host of them. ²And on the seventh day God ended his work which he had made: and he rested on the seventh day from all his work which he had made. ³And God blessed the seventh day, and sanctified it: because that in it he had rested from all his work which God created and made.

⁴These are the generations of the heavens and of the earth when they were created, in the day that the LORD God made the earth and the heavens, ⁵and every plant of the field before it was in the earth, and every herb of the field before it grew: for the LORD God had not caused it to rain upon the earth, and there was not a man to till the ground. ⁶But there went up a mist from the earth, and watered the whole face of the ground. ⁷And the LORD God formed man of the dust of the ground, and breathed into his nostrils the breath of life; and man became a living soul.

⁸And the LORD God planted a garden eastward in Eden; and there he put the man whom he had formed. ⁹And out of the ground made the LORD God to grow every tree that is pleasant to the sight, and good for food; the tree of life also in the midst of the garden, and the tree of knowledge of good and evil. ¹⁰And a river went out of Eden to water the garden, and from thence it was parted, and became into four heads. ¹¹The name of the first is Pison: that is it which compasseth the whole land of Havilah, where there is gold. ¹²And the gold of that land is good: there is bdellium and the onyx stone. ¹³And the name of the second river is Gihon: the same is it that compasseth the whole land of Ethiopia. ¹⁴And the name of the third river is Hiddekel: that is it which goeth toward the east of Assyria. And the fourth river is Euphrates. ¹⁵And the LORD God took the man, and put him into the

garden of Eden to dress it and to keep it. [16]And the LORD God commanded the man, saying, 'Of every tree of the garden thou mayest freely eat. [17]But of the tree of the knowledge of good and evil, thou shalt not eat of it: for in the day that thou eatest thereof thou shalt surely die.'

[18]And the LORD God said, 'It is not good that the man should be alone: I will make him a help meet for him'. [19]And out of the ground the LORD God formed every beast of the field, and every fowl of the air, and brought them unto Adam to see what he would call them: and whatsoever Adam called every living creature, that was the name thereof. [20]And Adam gave names to all cattle, and to the fowl of the air, and to every beast of the field; but for Adam there was not found a help meet for him. [21]And the LORD God caused a deep sleep to fall upon Adam, and he slept; and he took one of his ribs, and closed up the flesh in stead thereof. [22]And the rib which the LORD God had taken from man, made he a woman, and brought her unto the man. [23]And Adam said, 'This is now bone of my bones, and flesh of my flesh: she shall be called Woman, because she was taken out of Man'. [24]Therefore shall a man leave his father and his mother, and shall cleave unto his wife: and they shall be one flesh. [25]And they were both naked, the man and his wife, and were not ashamed.

3 Now the serpent was more subtle than any beast of the field which the LORD God had made. And he said unto the woman, 'Yea, hath God said, "Ye shall not eat of every tree of the garden"?' [2]And the woman said unto the serpent, 'We may eat of the fruit of the trees of the garden: [3]but of the fruit of the tree which is in the midst of the garden, God hath said, "Ye shall not eat of it, neither shall ye touch it, lest ye die"'. [4]And the serpent said unto the woman, 'Ye shall not surely die. [5]For God doth know that in the day ye eat thereof, then your eyes shall be opened, and ye shall be as gods, knowing good and evil.' [6]And when the woman saw that the tree was good for food, and that it was pleasant to the eyes, and a tree to be desired to make one wise, she took of the fruit thereof, and did eat, and gave also unto her husband with her, and he did eat. [7]And the eyes of them both were opened, and they knew that they were naked; and they sewed fig leaves together, and made themselves aprons.

[8]And they heard the voice of the LORD God walking in the garden in the cool of the day: and Adam and his wife hid themselves from the presence of the LORD God amongst the trees of the garden. [9]And the LORD God called unto Adam, and said unto him, 'Where art thou?' [10]And he said, 'I heard thy voice in the garden, and I was afraid, because I was naked, and I hid myself'. [11]And he said, 'Who told thee that thou wast naked? Hast thou eaten of the tree, whereof I commanded thee that thou shouldst not eat?' [12]And the man said, 'The woman whom thou gavest to be with me, she gave me of the tree, and I did eat'. [13]And the LORD God said unto the woman, 'What is this that thou hast done?' And the woman said, 'The serpent beguiled me, and I did eat'. [14]And the LORD God said unto the serpent, 'Because thou hast done this, thou art

cursed above all cattle, and above every beast of the field: upon thy belly shalt thou go, and dust shalt thou eat all the days of thy life. ¹⁵And I will put enmity between thee and the woman, and between thy seed and her seed: it shall bruise thy head, and thou shalt bruise his heel.' ¹⁶Unto the woman he said, 'I will greatly multiply thy sorrow and thy conception. In sorrow thou shalt bring forth children: and thy desire shall be to thy husband, and he shall rule over thee.' ¹⁷And unto Adam he said, 'Because thou hast hearkened unto the voice of thy wife, and hast eaten of the tree, of which I commanded thee, saying, "Thou shalt not eat of it": cursed is the ground for thy sake: in sorrow shalt thou eat of it all the days of thy life. ¹⁸Thorns also and thistles shall it bring forth to thee; and thou shalt eat the herb of the field. ¹⁹In the sweat of thy face shalt thou eat bread, till thou return unto the ground: for out of it wast thou taken, for dust thou art, and unto dust shalt thou return.' ²⁰And Adam called his wife's name Eve, because she was the mother of all living. ²¹Unto Adam also and to his wife did the LORD God make coats of skins, and clothed them.

²²And the LORD God said, 'Behold, the man is become as one of us, to know good and evil. And now, lest he put forth his hand, and take also of the tree of life, and eat, and live for ever': ²³therefore the LORD God sent him forth from the garden of Eden, to till the ground from whence he was taken. ²⁴So he drove out the man; and he placed at the east of the garden of Eden Cherubims, and a flaming sword which turned every way, to keep the way of the tree of life.

4 And Adam knew Eve his wife, and she conceived, and bore Cain, and said, 'I have gotten a man from the LORD'. ²And she again bore his brother Abel. And Abel was a keeper of sheep, but Cain was a tiller of the ground. ³And in process of time it came to pass, that Cain brought of the fruit of the ground an offering unto the LORD. ⁴And Abel, he also brought of the firstlings of his flock and of the fat thereof. And the LORD had respect unto Abel and to his offering. ⁵But unto Cain and to his offering he had not respect. And Cain was very wroth, and his countenance fell. ⁶And the LORD said unto Cain, 'Why art thou wroth? and why is thy countenance fallen? ⁷If thou doest well, shalt thou not be accepted? and if thou doest not well, sin lieth at the door. And unto thee shall be his desire, and thou shalt rule over him.' ⁸And Cain talked with Abel his brother: and it came to pass, when they were in the field, that Cain rose up against Abel his brother, and slew him. ⁹And the LORD said unto Cain, 'Where is Abel thy brother?' And he said, 'I know not: am I my brother's keeper?' ¹⁰And he said, 'What hast thou done? the voice of thy brother's blood crieth unto me from the ground. ¹¹And now art thou cursed from the earth, which hath opened her mouth to receive thy brother's blood from thy hand. ¹²When thou tillest the ground, it shall not henceforth yield unto thee her strength: a fugitive and a vagabond shalt thou be in the earth.' ¹³And Cain said unto the LORD, 'My punishment is greater than I can bear. ¹⁴Behold, thou hast driven me out this day from the face of the earth, and from thy face shall I be hid, and I shall be a fugitive and a vagabond in the earth: and it shall come to pass, that every one that findeth me shall slay me.' [15]And the LORD said unto him, 'Therefore whosoever slayeth Cain, vengeance shall be taken on him sevenfold'. And the LORD set a mark upon Cain, lest any finding him should kill him.

[16]And Cain went out from the presence of the LORD, and dwelt in the land of Nod, on the east of Eden. [17]And Cain knew his wife, and she conceived, and bore Enoch: and he built a city, and called the name of the city, after the name of his son, Enoch. [18]And unto Enoch was born Irad: and Irad begot Mehujael, and Mehujael begot Methusael, and Methusael begot Lamech.

[19]And Lamech took unto him two wives: the name of the one was Adah, and the name of the other Zillah. [20]And Adah bore Jabal: he was the father of such as dwell in tents, and of such as have cattle. [21]And his brother's name was Jubal: he was the father of all such as handle the harp and organ. [22]And Zillah, she also bore Tubal-cain, an instructor of every artificer in brass and iron: and the sister of Tubal-cain was Naamah. [23]And Lamech said unto his wives, Adah and Zillah, 'Hear my voice, ye wives of Lamech, hearken unto my speech: for I have slain a man to my wounding, and a young man to my hurt. [24]If Cain shall be avenged sevenfold, truly Lamech seventy and sevenfold.'

[25]And Adam knew his wife again, and she bore a son, and called his name Seth: 'For God', said she, 'hath appointed me another seed in stead of Abel, whom Cain slew'. [26]And to Seth, to him also there was born a son, and he called his name Enos: then began men to call upon the name of the LORD.

5 This is the book of the generations of Adam. In the day that God created man, in the likeness of God made he him. [2]Male and female created he them, and blessed them, and called their name Adam, in the day when they were created.

[3]And Adam lived a hundred and thirty years, and begot a son in his own likeness, after his image; and called his name Seth. [4]And the days of Adam after he had begotten Seth were eight hundred years: and he begot sons and daughters. [5]And all the days that Adam lived were nine hundred and thirty years: and he died.

[6]And Seth lived a hundred and five years, and begot Enos. [7]And Seth lived after he begot Enos eight hundred and seven years, and begot sons and daughters. [8]And all the days of Seth were nine hundred and twelve years: and he died.

[9]And Enos lived ninety years, and begot Cainan. [10]And Enos lived after he begot Cainan eight hundred and fifteen years, and begot sons and daughters. [11]And all the days of Enos were nine hundred and five years: and he died.

[12]And Cainan lived seventy years, and begot Mahalaleel. [13]And Cainan lived after he begot Mahalaleel eight hundred and forty years, and begot sons and daughters. [14]And all the days of Cainan were nine hundred and ten years: and he died.

[15]And Mahalaleel lived sixty and five years, and begot Jared. [16]And Mahalaleel lived after he begot Jared eight hundred and thirty years,

and begot sons and daughters. ¹⁷And all the days of Mahalaleel were eight hundred ninety and five years: and he died.

¹⁸And Jared lived a hundred sixty and two years, and he begot Enoch. ¹⁹And Jared lived after he begot Enoch eight hundred years, and begot sons and daughters. ²⁰And all the days of Jared were nine hundred sixty and two years: and he died.

²¹And Enoch lived sixty and five years, and begot Methuselah. ²²And Enoch walked with God after he begot Methuselah three hundred years, and begot sons and daughters. ²³And all the days of Enoch were three hundred sixty and five years. ²⁴And Enoch walked with God: and he was not; for God took him.

²⁵And Methuselah lived a hundred eighty and seven years, and begot Lamech. ²⁶And Methuselah lived after he begot Lamech seven hundred eighty and two years, and begot sons and daughters. ²⁷And all the days of Methuselah were nine hundred sixty and nine years: and he died.

²⁸And Lamech lived a hundred eighty and two years, and begot a son: ²⁹and he called his name Noah, saying, 'This same shall comfort us concerning our work and toil of our hands, because of the ground which the LORD hath cursed'. ³⁰And Lamech lived after he begot Noah five hundred ninety and five years, and begot sons and daughters. ³¹And all the days of Lamech were seven hundred seventy and seven years: and he died. ³²And Noah was five hundred years old: and Noah begot Shem, Ham, and Japheth.

6 And it came to pass, when men began to multiply on the face of the earth, and daughters were born unto them, ²that the sons of God saw the daughters of men that they were fair, and they took them wives of all which they chose. ³And the LORD said, 'My spirit shall not always strive with man, for that he also is flesh: yet his days shall be a hundred and twenty years'. ⁴There were giants in the earth in those days; and also after that, when the sons of God came in unto the daughters of men, and they bore children to them, the same became mighty men which were of old, men of renown.

⁵And GOD saw that the wickedness of man was great in the earth, and that every imagination of the thoughts of his heart was only evil continually. ⁶And it repented the LORD that he had made man on the earth, and it grieved him at his heart. ⁷And the LORD said, 'I will destroy man whom I have created from the face of the earth; both man, and beast, and the creeping thing, and the fowls of the air: for it repenteth me that I have made them'. ⁸But Noah found grace in the eyes of the LORD.

⁹These are the generations of Noah: Noah was a just man and perfect in his generations, and Noah walked with God. ¹⁰And Noah begot three sons, Shem, Ham, and Japheth. ¹¹The earth also was corrupt before God, and the earth was filled with violence. ¹²And God looked upon the earth, and behold, it was corrupt: for all flesh had corrupted his way upon the earth. ¹³And God said unto Noah, 'The end of all flesh is come before me; for the earth is filled with violence through them; and behold, I will destroy them with the earth. ¹⁴Make thee an ark of gopher

wood: rooms shalt thou make in the ark, and shalt pitch it within and without with pitch. ¹⁵And this is the fashion which thou shalt make it of: the length of the ark shall be three hundred cubits, the breadth of it fifty cubits, and the height of it thirty cubits. ¹⁶A window shalt thou make to the ark, and in a cubit shalt thou finish it above; and the door of the ark shalt thou set in the side thereof; with lower, second, and third storeys shalt thou make it. ¹⁷And behold, I, even I, do bring a flood of waters upon the earth, to destroy all flesh, wherein is the breath of life, from under heaven, and everything that is in the earth shall die. ¹⁸But with thee will I establish my covenant: and thou shalt come into the ark, thou, and thy sons, and thy wife, and thy sons' wives with thee. ¹⁹And of every living thing of all flesh, two of every sort shalt thou bring into the ark, to keep them alive with thee: they shall be male and female. ²⁰Of fowls after their kind, and of cattle after their kind, of every creeping thing of the earth after his kind, two of every sort shall come unto thee, to keep them alive. ²¹And take thou unto thee of all food that is eaten, and thou shalt gather it to thee; and it shall be for food for thee, and for them.' ²²Thus did Noah; according to all that God commanded him, so did he.

7 And the LORD said unto Noah, 'Come thou and all thy house into the ark: for thee have I seen righteous before me in this generation. ²Of every clean beast thou shalt take to thee by sevens, the male and his female: and of beasts that are not clean by two, the male and his female. ³Of fowls also of the air by sevens, the male and the female; to keep seed alive upon the face of all the earth. ⁴For yet seven days, and I will cause it to rain upon the earth forty days and forty nights: and every living substance that I have made will I destroy from off the face of the earth.' ⁵And Noah did according unto all that the LORD commanded him. ⁶And Noah was six hundred years old when the flood of waters was upon the earth.

⁷And Noah went in, and his sons, and his wife, and his sons' wives with him, into the ark, because of the waters of the flood. ⁸Of clean beasts, and of beasts that are not clean, and of fowls, and of everything that creepeth upon the earth, ⁹there went in two and two unto Noah into the ark, the male and the female, as God had commanded Noah. ¹⁰And it came to pass after seven days, that the waters of the flood were upon the earth.

¹¹In the six hundredth year of Noah's life, in the second month, the seventeenth day of the month, the same day were all the fountains of the great deep broken up, and the windows of heaven were opened. ¹²And the rain was upon the earth forty days and forty nights. ¹³In the selfsame day entered Noah, and Shem, and Ham, and Japheth, the sons of Noah, and Noah's wife, and the three wives of his sons with them, into the ark, ¹⁴they, and every beast after his kind, and all the cattle after their kind, and every creeping thing that creepeth upon the earth after his kind, and every fowl after his kind, every bird of every sort. ¹⁵And they went in unto Noah into the ark, two and two of all flesh, wherein is the breath of life. ¹⁶And they that went in, went in

male and female of all flesh, as God had commanded him: and the LORD shut him in. ¹⁷And the flood was forty days upon the earth, and the waters increased, and bore up the ark, and it was lifted up above the earth. ¹⁸And the waters prevailed, and were increased greatly upon the earth; and the ark went upon the face of the waters. ¹⁹And the waters prevailed exceedingly upon the earth, and all the high hills, that were under the whole heaven, were covered. ²⁰Fifteen cubits upward did the waters prevail; and the mountains were covered. ²¹And all flesh died that moved upon the earth, both of fowl, and of cattle, and of beast, and of every creeping thing that creepeth upon the earth, and every man: ²²all in whose nostrils was the breath of life, of all that was in the dry land, died. ²³And every living substance was destroyed which was upon the face of the ground, both man, and cattle, and the creeping things, and the fowl of the heaven; and they were destroyed from the earth: and Noah only remained alive, and they that were with him in the ark. ²⁴And the waters prevailed upon the earth a hundred and fifty days.

8 And God remembered Noah, and every living thing, and all the cattle that was with him in the ark: and God made a wind to pass over the earth, and the waters assuaged. ²The fountains also of the deep and the windows of heaven were stopped, and the rain from heaven was restrained. ³And the waters returned from off the earth continually: and after the end of the hundred and fifty days the waters were abated. ⁴And the ark rested in the seventh month, on the seventeenth day of the month, upon the mountains of Ararat. ⁵And the waters decreased continually until the tenth month: in the tenth month, on the first day of the month, were the tops of the mountains seen.

⁶And it came to pass at the end of forty days, that Noah opened the window of the ark which he had made. ⁷And he sent forth a raven, which went forth to and fro, until the waters were dried up from off the earth. ⁸Also he sent forth a dove from him, to see if the waters were abated from off the face of the ground. ⁹But the dove found no rest for the sole of her foot, and she returned unto him into the ark, for the waters were on the face of the whole earth. Then he put forth his hand, and took her, and pulled her in unto him into the ark. ¹⁰And he stayed yet other seven days; and again he sent forth the dove out of the ark. ¹¹And the dove came in to him in the evening, and lo, in her mouth was an olive leaf plucked off: so Noah knew that the waters were abated from off the earth. ¹²And he stayed yet other seven days, and sent forth the dove, which returned not again unto him any more.

¹³And it came to pass in the six hundredth and first year, in the first month, the first day of the month, the waters were dried up from off the earth: and Noah removed the covering of the ark, and looked, and behold, the face of the ground was dry. ¹⁴And in the second month, on the seven and twentieth day of the month, was the earth dried.

¹⁵And God spoke unto Noah, saying, ¹⁶'Go forth of the ark, thou, and thy wife, and thy sons, and thy sons' wives with thee. ¹⁷Bring forth with

thee every living thing that is with thee, of all flesh, both of fowl, and of cattle, and of every creeping thing that creepeth upon the earth, that they may breed abundantly in the earth, and be fruitful, and multiply upon the earth.' ¹⁸And Noah went forth, and his sons, and his wife, and his sons' wives with him: ¹⁹every beast, every creeping thing, and every fowl, and whatsoever creepeth upon the earth, after their kinds, went forth out of the ark.

²⁰And Noah built an altar unto the LORD, and took of every clean beast, and of every clean fowl, and offered burnt offerings on the altar. ²¹And the LORD smelled a sweet savour, and the LORD said in his heart, 'I will not again curse the ground any more for man's sake; for the imagination of man's heart is evil from his youth; neither will I again smite any more everything living, as I have done. ²²While the earth remaineth, seed-time and harvest, and cold and heat, and summer and winter, and day and night shall not cease.'

9 And God blessed Noah and his sons, and said unto them, 'Be fruitful, and multiply, and replenish the earth. ²And the fear of you and the dread of you shall be upon every beast of the earth, and upon every fowl of the air, upon all that moveth upon the earth, and upon all the fishes of the sea; into your hand are they delivered. ³Every moving thing that liveth shall be meat for you; even as the green herb have I given you all things. ⁴But flesh with the life thereof, which is the blood thereof, shall you not eat. ⁵And surely your blood of your lives will I require: at the hand of every beast will I require it, and at the hand of man; at the hand of every man's brother will I require the life of man. ⁶Whoso sheddeth man's blood, by man shall his blood be shed: for in the image of God made he man. ⁷And you, be ye fruitful, and multiply, bring forth abundantly in the earth, and multiply therein.'

⁸And God spoke unto Noah, and to his sons with him, saying, ⁹'And I, behold, I establish my covenant with you, and with your seed after you; ¹⁰and with every living creature that is with you, of the fowl, of the cattle, and of every beast of the earth with you, from all that go out of the ark, to every beast of the earth. ¹¹And I will establish my covenant with you; neither shall all flesh be cut off any more by the waters of a flood, neither shall there any more be a flood to destroy the earth.' ¹²And God said, 'This is the token of the covenant which I make between me and you and every living creature that is with you, for perpetual generations. ¹³I do set my bow in the cloud, and it shall be for a token of a covenant between me and the earth. ¹⁴And it shall come to pass, when I bring a cloud over the earth, that the bow shall be seen in the cloud. ¹⁵And I will remember my covenant, which is between me and you and every living creature of all flesh: and the waters shall no more become a flood to destroy all flesh. ¹⁶And the bow shall be in the cloud; and I will look upon it, that I may remember the everlasting covenant between God and every living creature of all flesh that is upon the earth.' ¹⁷And God said unto Noah, 'This is the token of the covenant, which I have established between me and all flesh that is upon the earth'.

¹⁸And the sons of Noah, that went forth of the ark, were Shem, and Ham, and Japheth: and Ham is the father of Canaan. ¹⁹These are the three sons of Noah: and of them was the whole earth overspread.

²⁰And Noah began to be a husbandman, and he planted a vineyard. ²¹And he drank of the wine, and was drunken, and he was uncovered within his tent. ²²And Ham, the father of Canaan, saw the nakedness of his father, and told his two brethren without. ²³And Shem and Japheth took a garment, and laid it upon both their shoulders, and went backward, and covered the nakedness of their father; and their faces were backward, and they saw not their father's nakedness. ²⁴And Noah awoke from his wine, and knew what his younger son had done unto him. ²⁵And he said, 'Cursed be Canaan: a servant of servants shall he be unto his brethren'. ²⁶And he said, 'Blessed be the LORD God of Shem, and Canaan shall be his servant. ²⁷God shall enlarge Japheth, and he shall dwell in the tents of Shem, and Canaan shall be his servant.'

²⁸And Noah lived after the flood three hundred and fifty years. ²⁹And all the days of Noah were nine hundred and fifty years: and he died.

10 Now these are the generations of the sons of Noah, Shem, Ham, and Japheth: and unto them were sons born after the flood. ²The sons of Japheth: Gomer, and Magog, and Madai, and Javan, and Tubal, and Meshech, and Tiras. ³And the sons of Gomer: Ashkenaz, and Riphath, and Togarmah. ⁴And the sons of Javan: Elishah, and Tarshish, Kittim, and Dodanim. ⁵By these were the isles of the Gentiles divided in their lands, every one after his tongue, after their families, in their nations.

⁶And the sons of Ham: Cush, and Mizraim, and Phut, and Canaan. ⁷And the sons of Cush: Seba, and Havilah, and Sabtah, and Raamah, and Sabtecha: and the sons of Raamah: Sheba, and Dedan. ⁸And Cush begot Nimrod: he began to be a mighty one in the earth. ⁹He was a mighty hunter before the LORD: wherefore it is said, 'Even as Nimrod the mighty hunter before the LORD'. ¹⁰And the beginning of his kingdom was Babel, and Erech, and Accad, and Calneh, in the land of Shinar. ¹¹Out of that land went forth Asshur, and built Nineveh, and the city Rehoboth, and Calah, ¹²and Resen between Nineveh and Calah: the same is a great city. ¹³And Mizraim begot Ludim, and Anamim, and Lehabim, and Naphtuhim, ¹⁴and Pathrusim, and Casluhim (out of whom came Philistim), and Caphtorim.

¹⁵And Canaan begot Sidon his firstborn, and Heth, ¹⁶and the Jebusite, and the Amorite, and the Girgashite, ¹⁷and the Hivite, and the Arkite, and the Sinite, ¹⁸and the Arvadite, and the Zemarite, and the Hamathite: and afterward were the families of the Canaanites spread abroad. ¹⁹And the border of the Canaanites was from Sidon, as thou comest to Gerar, unto Gaza; as thou goest unto Sodom, and Gomorrah, and Admah, and Zeboim, even unto Lasha. ²⁰These are the sons of Ham, after their families, after their tongues, in their countries, and in their nations.

²¹Unto Shem also, the father of all the children of Eber, the brother

of Japheth the elder, even to him were children born. ²²The children of Shem: Elam, and Asshur, and Arphaxad, and Lud, and Aram. ²³And the children of Aram: Uz, and Hul, and Gether, and Mash. ²⁴And Arphaxad begot Salah, and Salah begot Eber. ²⁵And unto Eber were born two sons: the name of one was Peleg, for in his days was the earth divided; and his brother's name was Joktan. ²⁶And Joktan begot Almodad, and Sheleph, and Hazarmaveth, and Jerah, ²⁷and Hadoram, and Uzal, and Diklah, ²⁸and Obal, and Abimael, and Sheba, ²⁹and Ophir, and Havilah, and Jobab: all these were the sons of Joktan. ³⁰And their dwelling was from Mesha, as thou goest unto Sephar, a mount of the east. ³¹These are the sons of Shem, after their families, after their tongues, in their lands, after their nations.

³²These are the families of the sons of Noah, after their generations, in their nations: and by these were the nations divided in the earth after the flood.

11 And the whole earth was of one language, and of one speech. ²And it came to pass, as they journeyed from the east, that they found a plain in the land of Shinar, and they dwelt there. ³And they said one to another, 'Go to, let us make brick, and burn them thoroughly'. And they had brick for stone, and slime had they for mortar. ⁴And they said, 'Go to, let us build us a city and a tower, whose top may reach unto heaven, and let us make us a name, lest we be scattered abroad upon the face of the whole earth'. ⁵And the LORD came down to see the city and the tower, which the children of men built. ⁶And the LORD said, 'Behold, the people is one, and they have all one language: and this they begin to do: and now nothing will be restrained from them, which they have imagined to do. ⁷Go to, let us go down, and there confound their language, that they may not understand one another's speech.' ⁸So the LORD scattered them abroad from thence upon the face of all the earth: and they left off to build the city. ⁹Therefore is the name of it called Babel, because the LORD did there confound the language of all the earth: and from thence did the LORD scatter them abroad upon the face of all the earth.

¹⁰These are the generations of Shem: Shem was a hundred years old, and begot Arphaxad two years after the flood. ¹¹And Shem lived after he begot Arphaxad five hundred years, and begot sons and daughters. ¹²And Arphaxad lived five and thirty years, and begot Salah. ¹³And Arphaxad lived after he begot Salah four hundred and three years, and begot sons and daughters. ¹⁴And Salah lived thirty years, and begot Eber. ¹⁵And Salah lived after he begot Eber four hundred and three years, and begot sons and daughters. ¹⁶And Eber lived four and thirty years, and begot Peleg. ¹⁷And Eber lived after he begot Peleg four hundred and thirty years, and begot sons and daughters. ¹⁸And Peleg lived thirty years, and begot Reu. ¹⁹And Peleg lived after he begot Reu two hundred and nine years, and begot sons and daughters. ²⁰And Reu lived two and thirty years, and begot Serug. ²¹And Reu lived after he begot Serug two hundred and seven years, and begot sons and daughters. ²²And Serug lived thirty years, and begot Nahor. ²³And Serug lived

after he begot Nahor two hundred years, and begot sons and daughters. ²⁴And Nahor lived nine and twenty years, and begot Terah. ²⁵And Nahor lived after he begot Terah a hundred and nineteen years, and begot sons and daughters. ²⁶And Terah lived seventy years, and begot Abram, Nahor, and Haran.

²⁷Now these are the generations of Terah: Terah begot Abram, Nahor, and Haran; and Haran begot Lot. ²⁸And Haran died before his father Terah in the land of his nativity, in Ur of the Chaldees. ²⁹And Abram and Nahor took them wives: the name of Abram's wife was Sarai, and the name of Nahor's wife, Milcah, the daughter of Haran, the father of Milcah, and the father of Iscah. ³⁰But Sarai was barren; she had no child. ³¹And Terah took Abram his son, and Lot the son of Haran his son's son, and Sarai his daughter-in-law, his son Abram's wife, and they went forth with them from Ur of the Chaldees, to go into the land of Canaan; and they came unto Haran, and dwelt there. ³²And the days of Terah were two hundred and five years: and Terah died in Haran.

12 Now the LORD had said unto Abram, 'Get thee out of thy country, and from thy kindred, and from thy father's house, unto a land that I will show thee: ²and I will make of thee a great nation, and I will bless thee, and make thy name great; and thou shalt be a blessing: ³and I will bless them that bless thee, and curse him that curseth thee: and in thee shall all families of the earth be blessed'. ⁴So Abram departed, as the LORD had spoken unto him, and Lot went with him: and Abram was seventy and five years old when he departed out of Haran. ⁵And Abram took Sarai his wife, and Lot his brother's son, and all their substance that they had gathered, and the souls that they had gotten in Haran, and they went forth to go into the land of Canaan; and into the land of Canaan they came.

⁶And Abram passed through the land unto the place of Sichem, unto the plain of Moreh. And the Canaanite was then in the land. ⁷And the LORD appeared unto Abram, and said, 'Unto thy seed will I give this land': and there built he an altar unto the LORD, who appeared unto him. ⁸And he removed from thence unto a mountain on the east of Beth-el, and pitched his tent, having Beth-el on the west, and Hai on the east: and there he built an altar unto the LORD, and called upon the name of the LORD. ⁹And Abram journeyed, going on still toward the south.

¹⁰And there was a famine in the land: and Abram went down into Egypt to sojourn there: for the famine was grievous in the land. ¹¹And it came to pass, when he was come near to enter into Egypt, that he said unto Sarai his wife, 'Behold now, I know that thou art a fair woman to look upon. ¹²Therefore it shall come to pass, when the Egyptians shall see thee, that they shall say, "This is his wife": and they will kill me, but they will save thee alive. ¹³Say, I pray thee, thou art my sister, that it may be well with me for thy sake; and my soul shall live because of thee.' ¹⁴And it came to pass, that, when Abram was come into Egypt, the Egyptians beheld the woman that she was very fair. ¹⁵The princes also of Pharaoh saw her, and commended her before Pharaoh: and the

woman was taken into Pharaoh's house. ¹⁶And he entreated Abram well for her sake: and he had sheep, and oxen, and he-asses, and menservants, and maidservants, and she-asses, and camels. ¹⁷And the LORD plagued Pharaoh and his house with great plagues because of Sarai Abram's wife. ¹⁸And Pharaoh called Abram, and said, 'What is this that thou hast done unto me? why didst thou not tell me that she was thy wife? ¹⁹Why saidst thou, "She is my sister"? so I might have taken her to me to wife: now therefore behold thy wife, take her, and go thy way.' ²⁰And Pharaoh commanded his men concerning him: and they sent him away, and his wife, and all that he had.

13 And Abram went up out of Egypt, he, and his wife, and all that he had, and Lot with him, into the south. ²And Abram was very rich in cattle, in silver, and in gold. ³And he went on his journeys from the south even to Beth-el, unto the place where his tent had been at the beginning, between Beth-el and Hai; ⁴unto the place of the altar, which he had made there at the first: and there Abram called on the name of the LORD.

⁵And Lot also, which went with Abram, had flocks, and herds, and tents. ⁶And the land was not able to bear them, that they might dwell together: for their substance was great, so that they could not dwell together. ⁷And there was a strife between the herdsmen of Abram's cattle and the herdsmen of Lot's cattle: and the Canaanite and the Perizzite dwelt then in the land. ⁸And Abram said unto Lot, 'Let there be no strife, I pray thee, between me and thee, and between my herdsmen and thy herdsmen: for we be brethren. ⁹Is not the whole land before thee? Separate thyself, I pray thee, from me: if thou wilt take the left hand, then I will go to the right; or if thou depart to the right hand, then I will go to the left.' ¹⁰And Lot lifted up his eyes, and beheld all the plain of Jordan, that it was well watered everywhere, before the LORD destroyed Sodom and Gomorrah, even as the garden of the LORD, like the land of Egypt, as thou comest unto Zoar. ¹¹Then Lot chose him all the plain of Jordan; and Lot journeyed east: and they separated themselves the one from the other. ¹²Abram dwelt in the land of Canaan, and Lot dwelt in the cities of the plain, and pitched his tent toward Sodom. ¹³But the men of Sodom were wicked, and sinners before the LORD exceedingly.

¹⁴And the LORD said unto Abram, after that Lot was separated from him, 'Lift up now thy eyes, and look from the place where thou art, northward, and southward, and eastward, and westward: ¹⁵for all the land which thou seest, to thee will I give it, and to thy seed for ever. ¹⁶And I will make thy seed as the dust of the earth: so that if a man can number the dust of the earth, then shall thy seed also be numbered. ¹⁷Arise, walk through the land in the length of it and in the breadth of it: for I will give it unto thee.' ¹⁸Then Abram removed his tent, and came and dwelt in the plain of Mamre, which is in Hebron, and built there an altar unto the LORD.

14 And it came to pass in the days of Amraphel king of Shinar, Arioch king of Ellasar, Chedorlaomer king of Elam, and Tidal king of nations; [2]that these made war with Bera king of Sodom, and with Birsha king of Gomorrah, Shinab king of Admah, and Shemeber king of Zeboiim, and the king of Bela, which is Zoar. [3]All these were joined together in the vale of Siddim, which is the salt sea. [4]Twelve years they served Chedorlaomer, and in the thirteenth year they rebelled. [5]And in the fourteenth year came Chedorlaomer, and the kings that were with him, and smote the Rephaims in Ashteroth Karnaim, and the Zuzims in Ham, and the Emims in Shaveh Kiriathaim, [6]and the Horites in their mount Seir, unto El-paran, which is by the wilderness. [7]And they returned, and came to En-mishpat, which is Kadesh, and smote all the country of the Amalekites, and also the Amorites, that dwelt in Hazezon-tamar. [8]And there went out the king of Sodom, and the king of Gomorrah, and the king of Admah, and the king of Zeboiim, and the king of Bela (the same is Zoar), and they joined battle with them in the vale of Siddim; [9]with Chedorlaomer the king of Elam, and with Tidal king of nations, and Amraphel king of Shinar, and Arioch king of Ellasar; four kings with five. [10]And the vale of Siddim was full of slime-pits; and the kings of Sodom and Gomorrah fled, and fell there; and they that remained fled to the mountain. [11]And they took all the goods of Sodom and Gomorrah, and all their victuals, and went their way. [12]And they took Lot, Abram's brother's son, who dwelt in Sodom, and his goods, and departed.

[13]And there came one that had escaped, and told Abram the Hebrew; for he dwelt in the plain of Mamre the Amorite, brother of Eshcol, and brother of Aner: and these were confederate with Abram. [14]And when Abram heard that his brother was taken captive, he armed his trained servants, born in his own house, three hundred and eighteen, and pursued them unto Dan. [15]And he divided himself against them, he and his servants, by night, and smote them, and pursued them unto Hobah, which is on the left hand of Damascus. [16]And he brought back all the goods, and also brought again his brother Lot, and his goods, and the women also, and the people.

[17]And the king of Sodom went out to meet him (after his return from the slaughter of Chedorlaomer, and of the kings that were with him), at the valley of Shaveh, which is the king's dale. [18]And Melchizedek king of Salem brought forth bread and wine: and he was the priest of the most high God. [19]And he blessed him, and said, 'Blessed be Abram of the most high God, possessor of heaven and earth, [20]and blessed be the most high God, which hath delivered thy enemies into thy hand'. And he gave him tithes of all. [21]And the king of Sodom said unto Abram, 'Give me the persons, and take the goods to thyself'. [22]And Abram said to the king of Sodom, 'I have lifted up my hand unto the LORD, the most high God, the possessor of heaven and earth, [23]that I will not take from a thread even to a shoe-latchet, and that I will not take anything that is thine, lest thou shouldst say, "I have made Abram rich": [24]save only that which the young men have eaten, and the portion of the men which went with me, Aner, Eshcol, and Mamre; let them take their portion'.

15 After these things the word of the LORD came unto Abram in a vision, saying, 'Fear not, Abram: I am thy shield, and thy exceeding great reward'. ²And Abram said, 'LORD GOD, what wilt thou give me, seeing I go childless, and the steward of my house is this Eliezer of Damascus?' ³And Abram said, 'Behold, to me thou hast given no seed: and lo, one born in my house is my heir'. ⁴And behold, the word of the LORD came unto him, saying, 'This shall not be thy heir: but he that shall come forth out of thy own bowels shall be thy heir'. ⁵And he brought him forth abroad, and said, 'Look now towards heaven, and tell the stars, if thou be able to number them'. And he said unto him, 'So shall thy seed be'. ⁶And he believed in the LORD; and he counted it to him for righteousness. ⁷And he said unto him, 'I am the LORD that brought thee out of Ur of the Chaldees, to give thee this land to inherit it'. ⁸And he said, 'LORD GOD, whereby shall I know that I shall inherit it?' ⁹And he said unto him, 'Take me a heifer of three years old, and a she-goat of three years old, and a ram of three years old, and a turtle dove, and a young pigeon'. ¹⁰And he took unto him all these, and divided them in the midst, and laid each piece one against another: but the birds divided he not. ¹¹And when the fowls came down upon the carcases, Abram drove them away. ¹²And when the sun was going down, a deep sleep fell upon Abram: and lo, a horror of great darkness fell upon him. ¹³And he said unto Abram, 'Know of a surety that thy seed shall be a stranger in a land that is not theirs, and shall serve them, and they shall afflict them four hundred years. ¹⁴And also that nation, whom they shall serve, will I judge: and afterward shall they come out with great substance. ¹⁵And thou shalt go to thy fathers in peace; thou shalt be buried in a good old age. ¹⁶But in the fourth generation they shall come hither again: for the iniquity of the Amorites is not yet full.' ¹⁷And it came to pass, that, when the sun went down, and it was dark, behold a smoking furnace, and a burning lamp that passed between those pieces. ¹⁸In that same day the LORD made a covenant with Abram, saying, 'Unto thy seed have I given this land, from the river of Egypt unto the great river, the river Euphrates: ¹⁹the Kenites, and the Kenizzites, and the Kadmonites, ²⁰and the Hittites, and the Perizzites, and the Rephaims, ²¹and the Amorites, and the Canaanites, and the Girgashites, and the Jebusites'.

16 Now Sarai Abram's wife bore him no children: and she had a handmaid, an Egyptian, whose name was Hagar. ²And Sarai said unto Abram, 'Behold now, the LORD hath restrained me from bearing: I pray thee, go in unto my maid: it may be that I may obtain children by her'. And Abram hearkened to the voice of Sarai. ³And Sarai Abram's wife took Hagar her maid the Egyptian, after Abram had dwelt ten years in the land of Canaan, and gave her to her husband Abram to be his wife. ⁴And he went in unto Hagar, and she conceived: and when she saw that she had conceived, her mistress was despised in her eyes. ⁵And Sarai said unto Abram, 'My wrong be upon thee: I have given my maid into thy bosom, and when she saw that she had conceived, I was despised in her eyes: the LORD judge between me and thee'. ⁶And Abram said unto Sarai, 'Behold, thy maid is in thy hand; do to her as it pleaseth thee'. And when Sarai dealt hardly with her, she fled from her face.

⁷And the angel of the Lᴏʀᴅ found her by a fountain of water in the wilderness, by the fountain in the way to Shur. ⁸And he said, 'Hagar, Sarai's maid, whence camest thou? and whither wilt thou go?' And she said, 'I flee from the face of my mistress Sarai'. ⁹And the angel of the Lᴏʀᴅ said unto her, 'Return to thy mistress, and submit thyself under her hands'. ¹⁰And the angel of the Lᴏʀᴅ said unto her, 'I will multiply thy seed exceedingly, that it shall not be numbered for multitude'. ¹¹And the angel of the Lᴏʀᴅ said unto her, 'Behold, thou art with child, and shalt bear a son, and shalt call his name Ishmael; because the Lᴏʀᴅ hath heard thy affliction. ¹²And he will be a wild man; his hand will be against every man, and every man's hand against him; and he shall dwell in the presence of all his brethren.' ¹³And she called the name of the Lᴏʀᴅ that spoke unto her, 'Thou God seest me': for she said, 'Have I also here looked after him that seeth me?' ¹⁴Wherefore the well was called Beer-lahai-roi; behold, it is between Kadesh and Bered. ¹⁵And Hagar bore Abram a son: and Abram called his son's name, which Hagar bore, Ishmael. ¹⁶And Abram was fourscore and six years old, when Hagar bore Ishmael to Abram.

17 And when Abram was ninety years old and nine, the Lᴏʀᴅ appeared to Abram, and said unto him, 'I am the Almighty God, walk before me, and be thou perfect. ²And I will make my covenant between me and thee, and will multiply thee exceedingly.' ³And Abram fell on his face, and God talked with him, saying, ⁴'As for me, behold, my covenant is with thee, and thou shalt be a father of many nations. ⁵Neither shall thy name any more be called Abram, but thy name shall be Abraham: for a father of many nations have I made thee. ⁶And I will make thee exceeding fruitful, and I will make nations of thee, and kings shall come out of thee. ⁷And I will establish my covenant between me and thee and thy seed after thee in their generations for an everlasting covenant, to be a God unto thee, and to thy seed after thee. ⁸And I will give unto thee, and to thy seed after thee, the land wherein thou art a stranger, all the land of Canaan, for an everlasting possession, and I will be their God.'

⁹And God said unto Abraham, 'Thou shalt keep my covenant therefore, thou, and thy seed after thee in their generations. ¹⁰This is my covenant, which ye shall keep, between me and you and thy seed after thee: every man-child among you shall be circumcised. ¹¹And ye shall circumcise the flesh of your foreskin; and it shall be a token of the covenant betwixt me and you. ¹²And he that is eight days old shall be circumcised among you, every man-child in your generations, he that is born in the house, or bought with money of any stranger, which is not of thy seed. ¹³He that is born in thy house, and he that is bought with thy money, must needs be circumcised: and my covenant shall be in your flesh for an everlasting covenant. ¹⁴And the uncircumcised man-child whose flesh of his foreskin is not circumcised, that soul shall be cut off from his people: he hath broken my covenant.'

¹⁵And God said unto Abraham, 'As for Sarai thy wife, thou shalt not call her name Sarai, but Sarah shall her name be. ¹⁶And I will bless her, and give thee a son also of her: yea, I will bless her, and she shall be a mother of nations; kings of people shall be of her.' ¹⁷Then Abraham fell upon his face, and laughed, and said in his heart, 'Shall a child be born unto him that is a hundred years old? and shall Sarah, that is ninety years old, bear?' ¹⁸And Abraham said unto God, 'O that Ishmael might live before thee'. ¹⁹And God said, 'Sarah thy wife shall bear thee a son indeed, and thou shalt call his name Isaac: and I will establish my covenant with him for an everlasting covenant, and with his seed after him. ²⁰And as for Ishmael, I have heard thee: behold, I have blessed him, and will make him fruitful, and will multiply him exceedingly: twelve princes shall he beget, and I will make him a great nation. ²¹But my covenant will I establish with Isaac, which Sarah shall bear unto thee at this set time in the next year.' ²²And he left off talking with him, and God went up from Abraham.

²³And Abraham took Ishmael his son, and all that were born in his house, and all that were bought with his money, every male among the men of Abraham's house, and circumcised the flesh of their foreskin in the selfsame day, as God had said unto him. ²⁴And Abraham was ninety years old and nine, when he was circumcised in the flesh of his foreskin. ²⁵And Ishmael his son was thirteen years old, when he was circumcised in the flesh of his foreskin. ²⁶In the selfsame day was Abraham circumcised, and Ishmael his son. ²⁷And all the men of his house, born in the house, and bought with money of the stranger, were circumcised with him.

18 And the Lord appeared unto him in the plains of Mamre: and he sat in the tent door in the heat of the day. ²And he lifted up his eyes and looked, and lo, three men stood by him: and when he saw them, he ran to meet them from the tent door, and bowed himself toward the ground, ³and said, 'My Lord, if now I have found favour in thy sight, pass not away, I pray thee, from thy servant: ⁴let a little water, I pray you, be fetched, and wash your feet, and rest yourselves under the tree: ⁵and I will fetch a morsel of bread, and comfort ye your hearts; after that you shall pass on: for therefore are you come to your servant'. And they said, 'So do, as thou hast said'. ⁶And Abraham hastened into the tent unto Sarah, and said, 'Make ready quickly three measures of fine meal, knead it, and make cakes upon the hearth'. ⁷And Abraham ran unto the herd, and fetched a calf tender and good, and gave it unto a young man; and he hasted to dress it. ⁸And he took butter, and milk, and the calf which he had dressed, and set it before them; and he stood by them under the tree, and they did eat.

⁹And they said unto him, 'Where is Sarah thy wife?' And he said, 'Behold, in the tent'. ¹⁰And he said, 'I will certainly return unto thee according to the time of life; and lo, Sarah thy wife shall have a son'. And Sarah heard it in the tent door, which was behind him. ¹¹Now Abraham and Sarah were old and well stricken in age: and it ceased to be with Sarah after the manner of women. ¹²Therefore Sarah laughed

within herself, saying, 'After I am waxed old shall I have pleasure, my lord being old also?' ¹³And the Lᴏʀᴅ said unto Abraham, 'Wherefore did Sarah laugh, saying, "Shall I of a surety bear a child, which am old?" ¹⁴Is anything too hard for the Lᴏʀᴅ? At the time appointed I will return unto thee, according to the time of life, and Sarah shall have a son.' ¹⁵Then Sarah denied, saying, 'I laughed not'; for she was afraid. And he said, 'Nay, but thou didst laugh'.

¹⁶And the men rose up from thence, and looked toward Sodom: and Abraham went with them to bring them on the way. ¹⁷And the Lᴏʀᴅ said, 'Shall I hide from Abraham that thing which I do; ¹⁸seeing that Abraham shall surely become a great and mighty nation, and all the nations of the earth shall be blessed in him? ¹⁹For I know him, that he will command his children and his household after him, and they shall keep the way of the Lᴏʀᴅ, to do justice and judgement, that the Lᴏʀᴅ may bring upon Abraham that which he hath spoken of him.' ²⁰And the Lᴏʀᴅ said, 'Because the cry of Sodom and Gomorrah is great, and because their sin is very grievous: ²¹I will go down now, and see whether they have done altogether according to the cry of it, which is come unto me: and if not, I will know'. ²²And the men turned their faces from thence, and went toward Sodom: but Abraham stood yet before the Lᴏʀᴅ.

²³And Abraham drew near, and said, 'Wilt thou also destroy the righteous with the wicked? ²⁴Peradventure there be fifty righteous within the city: wilt thou also destroy and not spare the place for the fifty righteous that are therein? ²⁵That be far from thee to do after this manner, to slay the righteous with the wicked: and that the righteous should be as the wicked, that be far from thee: shall not the Judge of all the earth do right?' ²⁶And the Lᴏʀᴅ said, 'If I find in Sodom fifty righteous within the city, then I will spare all the place for their sakes'. ²⁷And Abraham answered and said, 'Behold now, I have taken upon me to speak unto the Lᴏʀᴅ, which am but dust and ashes. ²⁸Peradventure there shall lack five of the fifty righteous: wilt thou destroy all the city for lack of five?' And he said, 'If I find there forty and five, I will not destroy it'. ²⁹And he spoke unto him yet again, and said, 'Peradventure there shall be forty found there'. And he said, 'I will not do it for forty's sake'. ³⁰And he said unto him, 'O let not the Lᴏʀᴅ be angry, and I will speak: peradventure there shall thirty be found there'. And he said, 'I will not do it, if I find thirty there'. ³¹And he said, 'Behold now, I have taken upon me to speak unto the Lᴏʀᴅ: peradventure there shall be twenty found there'. And he said, 'I will not destroy it for twenty's sake'. ³²And he said, 'O let not the Lᴏʀᴅ be angry, and I will speak yet but this once: peradventure ten shall be found there'. And he said, 'I will not destroy it for ten's sake'. ³³And the Lᴏʀᴅ went his way, as soon as he had left communing with Abraham: and Abraham returned unto his place.

19 And there came two angels to Sodom at even, and Lot sat in the gate of Sodom: and Lot seeing them rose up to meet them, and he bowed himself with his face toward the ground. ²And he said,

'Behold now, my lords, turn in, I pray you, into your servant's house, and tarry all night, and wash your feet, and ye shall rise up early, and go on your ways'. And they said, 'Nay: but we will abide in the street all night'. ³And he pressed upon them greatly, and they turned in unto him, and entered into his house: and he made them a feast, and did bake unleavened bread, and they did eat.

⁴But before they lay down, the men of the city, even the men of Sodom, compassed the house round, both old and young, all the people from every quarter. ⁵And they called unto Lot, and said unto him, 'Where are the men which came in to thee this night? bring them out unto us, that we may know them'. ⁶And Lot went out at the door unto them, and shut the door after him, ⁷and said, 'I pray you, brethren, do not so wickedly. ⁸Behold now, I have two daughters which have not known man; let me, I pray you, bring them out unto you, and do ye to them as is good in your eyes: only unto these men do nothing: for therefore came they under the shadow of my roof.' ⁹And they said, 'Stand back'. And they said again, 'This one fellow came in to sojourn, and he will needs be a judge: now will we deal worse with thee, than with them'. And they pressed sore upon the man, even Lot, and came near to break the door. ¹⁰But the men put forth their hand, and pulled Lot into the house to them, and shut to the door. ¹¹And they smote the men that were at the door of the house with blindness, both small and great: so that they wearied themselves to find the door.

¹²And the men said unto Lot, 'Hast thou here any besides? son-in-law, and thy sons, and thy daughters, and whatsoever thou hast in the city, bring them out of this place. ¹³For we will destroy this place, because the cry of them is waxed great before the face of the LORD: and the LORD hath sent us to destroy it.' ¹⁴And Lot went out, and spoke unto his sons-in-law, which married his daughters, and said, 'Up, get you out of this place: for the LORD will destroy this city'. But he seemed as one that mocked unto his sons-in-law.

¹⁵And when the morning arose, then the angels hastened Lot, saying, 'Arise, take thy wife, and thy two daughters, which are here, lest thou be consumed in the iniquity of the city'. ¹⁶And while he lingered, the men laid hold upon his hand, and upon the hand of his wife, and upon the hand of his two daughters, the LORD being merciful unto him: and they brought him forth, and set him without the city.

¹⁷And it came to pass, when they had brought them forth abroad, that he said, 'Escape for thy life, look not behind thee, neither stay thou in all the plain: escape to the mountain, lest thou be consumed'. ¹⁸And Lot said unto them, 'O, not so, my Lord. ¹⁹Behold now, thy servant hath found grace in thy sight, and thou hast magnified thy mercy, which thou hast shown unto me in saving my life; and I cannot escape to the mountain, lest some evil take me, and I die. ²⁰Behold now, this city is near to flee unto, and it is a little one: O, let me escape thither (is it not a little one?), and my soul shall live.' ²¹And he said unto him, 'See, I have accepted thee concerning this thing, that I will not overthrow this city, for the which thou hast spoken. ²²Haste thee, escape thither: for I can-

not do anything till thou be come thither.' Therefore the name of the city was called Zoar. ²³The sun was risen upon the earth when Lot entered into Zoar. ²⁴Then the LORD rained upon Sodom and upon Gomorrah brimstone and fire from the LORD out of heaven. ²⁵And he overthrew those cities, and all the plain, and all the inhabitants of the cities, and that which grew upon the ground.

²⁶But his wife looked back from behind him, and she became a pillar of salt. ²⁷And Abraham got up early in the morning to the place where he stood before the LORD. ²⁸And he looked toward Sodom and Gomorrah, and toward all the land of the plain, and beheld, and lo, the smoke of the country went up as the smoke of a furnace.

²⁹And it came to pass, when God destroyed the cities of the plain, that God remembered Abraham, and sent Lot out of the midst of the overthrow, when he overthrew the cities in the which Lot dwelt.

³⁰And Lot went up out of Zoar, and dwelt in the mountain, and his two daughters with him: for he feared to dwell in Zoar: and he dwelt in a cave, he and his two daughters. ³¹And the firstborn said unto the younger, 'Our father is old, and there is not a man in the earth to come in unto us after the manner of all the earth. ³²Come, let us make our father drink wine, and we will lie with him, that we may preserve seed of our father.' ³³And they made their father drink wine that night, and the firstborn went in, and lay with her father: and he perceived not when she lay down, nor when she arose. ³⁴And it came to pass on the morrow, that the firstborn said unto the younger, 'Behold, I lay yesternight with my father: let us make him drink wine this night also, and go thou in, and lie with him, that we may preserve seed of our father'. ³⁵And they made their father drink wine that night also, and the younger arose, and lay with him: and he perceived not when she lay down, nor when she arose. ³⁶Thus were both the daughters of Lot with child by their father. ³⁷And the firstborn bore a son, and called his name Moab: the same is the father of the Moabites unto this day. ³⁸And the younger, she also bore a son, and called his name Ben-ammi: the same is the father of the children of Ammon unto this day.

20 And Abraham journeyed from thence toward the south country, and dwelt between Kadesh and Shur, and sojourned in Gerar. ²And Abraham said of Sarah his wife, 'She is my sister': and Abimelech king of Gerar sent, and took Sarah. ³But God came to Abimelech in a dream by night, and said to him, 'Behold, thou art but a dead man, for the woman which thou hast taken: for she is a man's wife'. ⁴But Abimelech had not come near her: and he said, 'Lord, wilt thou slay also a righteous nation? ⁵Said he not unto me, "She is my sister"? and she, even she herself said, "He is my brother": in the integrity of my heart and innocence of my hands have I done this.' ⁶And God said unto him in a dream, 'Yea, I know that thou didst this in the integrity of thy heart: for I also withheld thee from sinning against me: therefore suffered I thee not to touch her. ⁷Now therefore restore the man his wife: for he is a prophet, and he shall pray for thee, and thou shalt live: and if thou restore her not, know thou that thou shalt surely die, thou, and all that are thine.' ⁸Therefore Abimelech rose early in the morning, and called all his servants, and told all these things in their ears: and the men were sore afraid. ⁹Then Abimelech called Abraham, and said unto him, 'What hast thou done unto us? and what have I offended thee, that thou hast brought on me and on my kingdom a great sin? thou hast done deeds unto me that ought not to be done'. ¹⁰And Abimelech said unto Abraham, 'What sawest thou, that thou hast done this thing?' ¹¹And Abraham said, 'Because I thought, surely the fear of God is not in this place: and they will slay me for my wife's sake. ¹²And yet indeed she is my sister: she is the daughter of my father, but not the daughter of my mother; and she became my wife. ¹³And it came to pass when God caused me to wander from my father's house, that I said unto her, "This is thy kindness which thou shalt show unto me; at every place whither we shall come, say of me, 'He is my brother'".' ¹⁴And Abimelech took sheep, and oxen, and menservants, and womenservants, and gave them unto Abraham, and restored him Sarah his wife. ¹⁵And Abimelech said, 'Behold, my land is before thee: dwell where it pleaseth thee'. ¹⁶And unto Sarah he said, 'Behold, I have given thy brother a thousand pieces of silver: behold, he is to thee a covering of the eyes, unto all that are with thee, and with all others': thus she was reproved.

¹⁷So Abraham prayed unto God: and God healed Abimelech, and his wife, and his maidservants, and they bore children. ¹⁸For the LORD had fast closed up all the wombs of the house of Abimelech, because of Sarah Abraham's wife.

21 And the LORD visited Sarah as he had said, and the LORD did unto Sarah as he had spoken. ²For Sarah conceived, and bore Abraham a son in his old age, at the set time of which God had spoken to him. ³And Abraham called the name of his son that was born unto him, whom Sarah bore to him, Isaac. ⁴And Abraham circumcised his son Isaac, being eight days old, as God had commanded him. ⁵And Abraham was a hundred years old, when his son Isaac was born unto him.

⁶And Sarah said, 'God hath made me to laugh, so that all that hear will laugh with me'. ⁷And she said, 'Who would have said unto Abraham, that Sarah should have given children suck? for I have borne him a son in his old age'. ⁸And the child grew, and was weaned: and Abraham made a great feast the same day that Isaac was weaned.

⁹And Sarah saw the son of Hagar the Egyptian, which she had borne unto Abraham, mocking. ¹⁰Wherefore she said unto Abraham, 'Cast out this bondwoman and her son: for the son of this bondwoman shall not be heir with my son, even with Isaac'. ¹¹And the thing was very grievous in Abraham's sight because of his son. ¹²And God said unto Abraham, 'Let it not be grievous in thy sight because of the lad, and because of thy bondwoman. In all that Sarah hath said unto thee, hearken unto her voice: for in Isaac shall thy seed be called. ¹³And also of the son of the bondwoman will I make a nation, because he is thy seed.'

¹⁴And Abraham rose up early in the morning, and took bread, and a bottle of water, and gave it unto Hagar, putting it on her shoulder, and the child, and sent her away: and she departed, and wandered in the wilderness of Beer-sheba. ¹⁵And the water was spent in the bottle, and she cast the child under one of the shrubs. ¹⁶And she went, and sat her down over against him a good way off, as it were a bowshot: for she said, 'Let me not see the death of the child'. And she sat over against him, and lifted up her voice, and wept. ¹⁷And God heard the voice of the lad; and the angel of God called to Hagar out of heaven, and said unto her, 'What aileth thee, Hagar? fear not: for God hath heard the voice of the lad where he is. ¹⁸Arise, lift up the lad, and hold him in thy hand: for I will make him a great nation.' ¹⁹And God opened her eyes, and she saw a well of water; and she went, and filled the bottle with water, and gave the lad drink. ²⁰And God was with the lad, and he grew, and dwelt in the wilderness, and became an archer. ²¹And he dwelt in the wilderness of Paran: and his mother took him a wife out of the land of Egypt.

²²And it came to pass at that time, that Abimelech and Phichol the chief captain of his host spoke unto Abraham, saying, 'God is with thee in all that thou doest. ²³Now therefore swear unto me here by God that thou wilt not deal falsely with me, nor with my son, nor with my son's son: but according to the kindness that I have done unto thee, thou shalt do unto me, and to the land wherein thou hast sojourned.' ²⁴And Abraham said, 'I will swear'. ²⁵And Abraham reproved Abimelech because of a well of water, which Abimelech's servants had violently taken away. ²⁶And Abimelech said, 'I wot not who hath done this thing: neither didst thou tell me, neither yet heard I of it, but today'. ²⁷And Abraham took sheep and oxen, and gave them unto Abimelech: and both of them made a covenant. ²⁸And Abraham set seven ewe lambs of the flock by themselves. ²⁹And Abimelech said unto Abraham, 'What mean these seven ewe lambs which thou hast set by themselves?' ³⁰And he said, 'For these seven ewe lambs shalt thou take of my hand, that they may be a witness unto me, that I have dug this well'. ³¹Wherefore he called that place Beer-sheba: because there they swore both of them. ³²Thus they made a covenant at Beer-sheba: then Abimelech rose up, and Phichol the chief captain of his host, and they returned into the land of the Philistines.

³³And Abraham planted a grove in Beer-sheba, and called there on the name of the LORD, the everlasting God. ³⁴And Abraham sojourned in the Philistines' land many days.

22 And it came to pass after these things, that God did tempt Abraham, and said unto him, 'Abraham'. And he said, 'Behold, here I am'. ²And he said, 'Take now thy son, thy only son Isaac, whom thou lovest, and get thee into the land of Moriah: and offer him there for a burnt offering upon one of the mountains which I will tell thee of'.

³And Abraham rose up early in the morning, and saddled his ass, and took two of his young men with him, and Isaac his son, and cleft the wood for the burnt offering, and rose up, and went unto the place

of which God had told him. ⁴Then on the third day Abraham lifted up his eyes, and saw the place afar off. ⁵And Abraham said unto his young men, 'Abide you here with the ass, and I and the lad will go yonder and worship, and come again to you'. ⁶And Abraham took the wood of the burnt offering, and laid it upon Isaac his son; and he took the fire in his hand, and a knife; and they went both of them together. ⁷And Isaac spoke unto Abraham his father, and said, 'My father': and he said, 'Here am I, my son'. And he said, 'Behold the fire and wood: but where is the lamb for a burnt offering?' ⁸And Abraham said, 'My son, God will provide himself a lamb for a burnt offering': so they went both of them together. ⁹And they came to the place which God had told him of, and Abraham built an altar there, and laid the wood in order, and bound Isaac his son, and laid him on the altar upon the wood. ¹⁰And Abraham stretched forth his hand, and took the knife to slay his son. ¹¹And the angel of the LORD called unto him out of heaven, and said, 'Abraham, Abraham'. And he said, 'Here am I'. ¹²And he said, 'Lay not thy hand upon the lad, neither do thou anything unto him: for now I know that thou fearest God, seeing thou hast not withheld thy son, thy only son from me'. ¹³And Abraham lifted up his eyes, and looked, and behold, behind him a ram caught in a thicket by his horns: and Abraham went and took the ram, and offered him up for a burnt offering in the stead of his son. ¹⁴And Abraham called the name of that place Jehovah-jireh, as it is said to this day, 'In the mount of the LORD it shall be seen'.

¹⁵And the angel of the LORD called unto Abraham out of heaven the second time, ¹⁶and said, 'By myself have I sworn,' saith the LORD, 'for because thou hast done this thing, and hast not withheld thy son, thine only son, ¹⁷that in blessing I will bless thee, and in multiplying I will multiply thy seed as the stars of the heaven, and as the sand which is upon the sea-shore, and thy seed shall possess the gate of his enemies. ¹⁸And in thy seed shall all the nations of the earth be blessed, because thou hast obeyed my voice.' ¹⁹So Abraham returned unto his young men, and they rose up and went together to Beer-sheba, and Abraham dwelt at Beer-sheba.

²⁰And it came to pass after these things, that it was told Abraham, saying, 'Behold Milcah, she hath also borne children unto thy brother Nahor, ²¹Huz his firstborn, and Buz his brother, and Kemuel the father of Aram, ²²and Chesed, and Hazo, and Pildash, and Jidlaph, and Bethuel'. ²³And Bethuel begot Rebekah: these eight Milcah did bear to Nahor, Abraham's brother. ²⁴And his concubine, whose name was Reumah, she bore also Tebah, and Gaham, and Thahash, and Maachah.

23 And Sarah was a hundred and seven and twenty years old: these were the years of the life of Sarah. ²And Sarah died in Kirjath-arba; the same is Hebron in the land of Canaan: and Abraham came to mourn for Sarah, and to weep for her.

³And Abraham stood up from before his dead, and spoke unto the sons of Heth, saying, ⁴'I am a stranger and a sojourner with you: give me a possession of a burying-place with you, that I may bury my dead out of my sight'. ⁵And the children of Heth answered Abraham, saying

unto him, ⁶'Hear us, my lord, thou art a mighty prince amongst us: in the choice of our sepulchres bury thy dead: none of us shall withhold from thee his sepulchre, but that thou mayest bury thy dead'. ⁷And Abraham stood up, and bowed himself to the people of the land, even to the children of Heth. ⁸And he communed with them, saying, 'If it be your mind that I should bury my dead out of my sight, hear me, and entreat for me to Ephron the son of Zohar, ⁹that he may give me the cave of Machpelah, which he hath, which is in the end of his field; for as much money as it is worth he shall give it me for a possession of a burying-place amongst you'. ¹⁰And Ephron dwelt amongst the children of Heth. And Ephron the Hittite answered Abraham in the audience of the children of Heth, even of all that went in at the gates of his city, saying, ¹¹'Nay, my lord, hear me: the field give I thee, and the cave that is therein, I give it thee; in the presence of the sons of my people give I it thee: bury thy dead'. ¹²And Abraham bowed down himself before the people of the land. ¹³And he spoke unto Ephron in the audience of the people of the land, saying, 'But if thou wilt give it, I pray thee, hear me: I will give thee money for the field: take it of me, and I will bury my dead there'. ¹⁴And Ephron answered Abraham, saying unto him, ¹⁵'My lord, hearken unto me: the land is worth four hundred shekels of silver: what is that betwixt me and thee? bury therefore thy dead'. ¹⁶And Abraham hearkened unto Ephron, and Abraham weighed to Ephron the silver, which he had named in the audience of the sons of Heth, four hundred shekels of silver, current money with the merchant.

¹⁷And the field of Ephron, which was in Machpelah, which was before Mamre, the field, and the cave which was therein, and all the trees that were in the field, that were in all the borders round about, were made sure ¹⁸unto Abraham for a possession in the presence of the children of Heth, before all that went in at the gates of his city. ¹⁹And after this, Abraham buried Sarah his wife in the cave of the field of Machpelah before Mamre: the same is Hebron in the land of Canaan. ²⁰And the field, and the cave that is therein, were made sure unto Abraham for a possession of a burying-place by the sons of Heth.

24 And Abraham was old, and well stricken in age: and the LORD had blessed Abraham in all things. ²And Abraham said unto his eldest servant of his house, that ruled over all that he had, 'Put, I pray thee, thy hand under my thigh: ³and I will make thee swear by the LORD, the God of heaven, and the God of the earth, that thou shalt not take a wife unto my son of the daughters of the Canaanites amongst whom I dwell: ⁴but thou shalt go unto my country, and to my kindred, and take a wife unto my son Isaac'. ⁵And the servant said unto him, 'Peradventure the woman will not be willing to follow me unto this land: must I needs bring thy son again unto the land from whence thou camest?' ⁶And Abraham said unto him, 'Beware thou that thou bring not my son thither again. ⁷The LORD God of heaven, which took me from my father's house, and from the land of my kindred, and which spoke unto me, and that swore unto me, saying, "Unto thy seed will I give this land", he shall send his angel before thee, and thou shalt take a wife unto my son from thence. ⁸And if the woman will not be willing to follow thee, then thou shalt be clear from this my oath: only bring not my son thither again.' ⁹And the servant put his hand under the thigh of Abraham his master, and swore to him concerning that matter.

¹⁰And the servant took ten camels of the camels of his master, and departed; for all the goods of his master were in his hand: and he arose, and went to Mesopotamia, unto the city of Nahor. ¹¹And he made his camels to kneel down without the city by a well of water at the time of the evening, even the time that women go out to draw water. ¹²And he said, 'O LORD God of my master Abraham, I pray thee, send me good speed this day, and show kindness unto my master Abraham. ¹³Behold, I stand here by the well of water; and the daughters of the men of the city come out to draw water: ¹⁴and let it come to pass, that the damsel to whom I shall say, "Let down thy pitcher, I pray thee, that I may drink"; and she shall say, "Drink, and I will give thy camels drink also": let the same be she that thou hast appointed for thy servant Isaac: and thereby shall I know that thou hast shown kindness unto my master.' ¹⁵And it came to pass, before he had done speaking, that behold, Rebekah came out, who was born to Bethuel, son of Milcah, the wife of Nahor, Abraham's brother, with her pitcher upon her shoulder. ¹⁶And the damsel was very fair to look upon, a virgin, neither had any man known her; and she went down to the well, and filled her pitcher, and came up. ¹⁷And the servant ran to meet her, and said, 'Let me, I pray thee, drink a little water of thy pitcher'. ¹⁸And she said, 'Drink, my lord': and she hasted, and let down her pitcher upon her hand, and gave him drink. ¹⁹And when she had done giving him drink, she said, 'I will draw water for thy camels also, until they have done drinking'. ²⁰And she hasted, and emptied her pitcher into the trough, and ran again unto the well to draw water, and drew for all his camels. ²¹And the man wondering at her held his peace, to wit whether the LORD had made his journey prosperous or not.

²²And it came to pass, as the camels had done drinking, that the man took a golden earring of half a shekel weight, and two bracelets for her hands of ten shekels weight of gold, ²³and said, 'Whose daughter art thou? tell me, I pray thee: is there room in thy father's house for us to lodge in?' ²⁴And she said unto him, 'I am the daughter of Bethuel the son of Milcah, which she bore unto Nahor'. ²⁵She said moreover unto him, 'We have both straw and provender enough, and room to lodge in'. ²⁶And the man bowed down his head, and worshipped the LORD. ²⁷And he said, 'Blessed be the LORD God of my master Abraham, who hath not left destitute my master of his mercy and his truth: I being in the way, the LORD led me to the house of my master's brethren'.

²⁸And the damsel ran, and told them of her mother's house these things. ²⁹And Rebekah had a brother, and his name was Laban: and Laban ran out unto the man, unto the well. ³⁰And it came to pass when he saw the earring and bracelets upon his sister's hands, and when he heard the words of Rebekah his sister, saying, 'Thus spoke the man unto me', that he came unto the man; and behold, he stood by the

camels at the well. ³¹And he said, 'Come in, thou blessed of the LORD, wherefore standest thou without? for I have prepared the house, and room for the camels'.

³²And the man came into the house: and he ungirded his camels, and gave straw and provender for the camels, and water to wash his feet, and the men's feet that were with him. ³³And there was set meat before him to eat: but he said, 'I will not eat, until I have told my errand'. And he said, 'Speak on'. ³⁴And he said, 'I am Abraham's servant. ³⁵And the LORD hath blessed my master greatly, and he is become great: and he hath given him flocks, and herds, and silver, and gold, and menservants, and maidservants, and camels, and asses. ³⁶And Sarah my master's wife bore a son to my master when she was old: and unto him hath he given all that he hath. ³⁷And my master made me swear, saying, "Thou shalt not take a wife to my son of the daughters of the Canaanites, in whose land I dwell: ³⁸but thou shalt go unto my father's house, and to my kindred, and take a wife unto my son". ³⁹And I said unto my master, "Peradventure the woman will not follow me". ⁴⁰And he said unto me, "The LORD, before whom I walk, will send his angel with thee, and prosper thy way: and thou shalt take a wife for my son of my kindred, and of my father's house. ⁴¹Then shalt thou be clear from this my oath, when thou comest to my kindred, and if they give not thee one, thou shalt be clear from my oath." ⁴²And I came this day unto the well, and said, "O LORD God of my master Abraham, if now thou do prosper my way which I go: ⁴³behold, I stand by the well of water; and it shall come to pass, that when the virgin cometh forth to draw water, and I say to her, 'Give me, I pray thee, a little water of thy pitcher to drink'; ⁴⁴and she say to me, 'Both drink thou, and I will also draw for thy camels': let the same be the woman whom the LORD hath appointed out for my master's son". ⁴⁵And before I had done speaking in my heart, behold, Rebekah came forth with her pitcher on her shoulder; and she went down unto the well, and drew water: and I said unto her, "Let me drink, I pray thee". ⁴⁶And she made haste, and let down her pitcher from her shoulder, and said, "Drink, and I will give thy camels drink also": so I drank, and she made the camels drink also. ⁴⁷And I asked her, and said, "Whose daughter art thou?" And she said, "The daughter of Bethuel, Nahor's son, whom Milcah bore unto him": and I put the earring upon her face, and the bracelets upon her hands. ⁴⁸And I bowed down my head, and worshipped the LORD, and blessed the LORD God of my master Abraham, which had led me in the right way to take my master's brother's daughter unto his son. ⁴⁹And now if you will deal kindly and truly with my master, tell me: and if not, tell me; that I may turn to the right hand, or to the left.'

⁵⁰Then Laban and Bethuel answered and said, 'The thing proceedeth from the LORD: we cannot speak unto thee bad or good. ⁵¹Behold, Rebekah is before thee, take her, and go, and let her be thy master's son's wife, as the LORD hath spoken.' ⁵²And it came to pass, that, when Abraham's servant heard their words, he worshipped the LORD, bowing himself to the earth. ⁵³And the servant brought forth jewels of silver,

and jewels of gold, and raiment, and gave them to Rebekah: he gave also to her brother and to her mother precious things. ⁵⁴And they did eat and drink, he and the men that were with him, and tarried all night; and they rose up in the morning, and he said, 'Send me away unto my master'. ⁵⁵And her brother and her mother said, 'Let the damsel abide with us a few days, at the least ten; after that she shall go'. ⁵⁶And he said unto them, 'Hinder me not, seeing the LORD hath prospered my way: send me away that I may go to my master'. ⁵⁷And they said, 'We will call the damsel, and inquire at her mouth'. ⁵⁸And they called Rebekah, and said unto her, 'Wilt thou go with this man?' And she said, 'I will go'. ⁵⁹And they sent away Rebekah their sister, and her nurse, and Abraham's servant, and his men. ⁶⁰And they blessed Rebekah, and said unto her, 'Thou art our sister, be thou the mother of thousands of millions, and let thy seed possess the gate of those which hate them'.

⁶¹And Rebekah arose, and her damsels, and they rode upon the camels, and followed the man: and the servant took Rebekah, and went his way.

⁶²And Isaac came from the way of the well Lahai-roi, for he dwelt in the south country. ⁶³And Isaac went out to meditate in the field at the eventide: and he lifted up his eyes, and saw, and behold, the camels were coming. ⁶⁴And Rebekah lifted up her eyes, and when she saw Isaac, she lighted off the camel. ⁶⁵For she had said unto the servant, 'What man is this that walketh in the field to meet us?' And the servant had said, 'It is my master': therefore she took a veil, and covered herself. ⁶⁶And the servant told Isaac all things that he had done. ⁶⁷And Isaac brought her into his mother Sarah's tent, and took Rebekah, and she became his wife, and he loved her: and Isaac was comforted after his mother's death.

25 Then again Abraham took a wife, and her name was Keturah. ²And she bore him Zimran, and Jokshan, and Medan, and Midian, and Ishbak, and Shuah. ³And Jokshan begot Sheba, and Dedan. And the sons of Dedan were Asshurim, and Letushim, and Leummim. ⁴And the sons of Midian, Ephah, and Epher, and Hanoch, and Abida, and Eldaah: all these were the children of Keturah. ⁵And Abraham gave all that he had unto Isaac. ⁶But unto the sons of the concubines which Abraham had, Abraham gave gifts, and sent them away from Isaac his son, while he yet lived, eastward, unto the east country. ⁷And these are the days of the years of Abraham's life which he lived, a hundred threescore and fifteen years. ⁸Then Abraham gave up the ghost, and died in a good old age, an old man, and full of years, and was gathered to his people. ⁹And his sons Isaac and Ishmael buried him in the cave of Machpelah, in the field of Ephron the son of Zohar the Hittite, which is before Mamre; ¹⁰the field which Abraham purchased of the sons of Heth: there was Abraham buried, and Sarah his wife. ¹¹And it came to pass after the death of Abraham, that God blessed his son Isaac, and Isaac dwelt by the well Lahai-roi.

¹²Now these are the generations of Ishmael, Abraham's son, whom

Hagar the Egyptian, Sarah's handmaid, bore unto Abraham: [13]and these are the names of the sons of Ishmael, by their names, according to their generations: the firstborn of Ishmael, Nebajoth, and Kedar, and Adbeel, and Mibsam, [14]and Mishma, and Dumah, and Massa, [15]Hadar, and Tema, Jetur, Naphish, and Kedemah. [16]These are the sons of Ishmael, and these are their names, by their towns, and by their castles; twelve princes according to their nations. [17]And these are the years of the life of Ishmael, a hundred and thirty and seven years: and he gave up the ghost and died, and was gathered unto his people. [18]And they dwelt from Havilah unto Shur, that is before Egypt, as thou goest towards Assyria: and he died in the presence of all his brethren.

[19]And these are the generations of Isaac, Abraham's son: Abraham begot Isaac. [20]And Isaac was forty years old when he took Rebekah to wife, the daughter of Bethuel the Syrian of Padan-aram, the sister to Laban the Syrian. [21]And Isaac entreated the LORD for his wife, because she was barren: and the LORD was entreated of him, and Rebekah his wife conceived. [22]And the children struggled together within her; and she said, 'If it be so, why am I thus?' And she went to inquire of the LORD. [23]And the LORD said unto her, 'Two nations are in thy womb, and two manner of people shall be separated from thy bowels: and the one people shall be stronger than the other people: and the elder shall serve the younger'.

[24]And when her days to be delivered were fulfilled, behold, there were twins in her womb. [25]And the first came out red, all over like a hairy garment: and they called his name Esau. [26]And after that came his brother out, and his hand took hold on Esau's heel; and his name was called Jacob: and Isaac was threescore years old when she bore them. [27]And the boys grew: and Esau was a cunning hunter, a man of the field; and Jacob was a plain man, dwelling in tents. [28]And Isaac loved Esau, because he did eat of his venison: but Rebekah loved Jacob.

[29]And Jacob seethed pottage: and Esau came from the field, and he was faint. [30]And Esau said to Jacob, 'Feed me, I pray thee, with that same red pottage: for I am faint': therefore was his name called Edom. [31]And Jacob said, 'Sell me this day thy birthright'. [32]And Esau said, 'Behold, I am at the point to die: and what profit shall this birthright do to me?' [33]And Jacob said, 'Swear to me this day'; and he swore unto him: and he sold his birthright unto Jacob. [34]Then Jacob gave Esau bread and pottage of lentils; and he did eat and drink, and rose up, and went his way: thus Esau despised his birthright.

26

And there was a famine in the land, besides the first famine that was in the days of Abraham. And Isaac went unto Abimelech king of the Philistines, unto Gerar. [2]And the LORD appeared unto him, and said, 'Go not down into Egypt; dwell in the land which I shall tell thee of. [3]Sojourn in this land, and I will be with thee, and will bless thee: for unto thee, and unto thy seed, I will give all these countries, and I will perform the oath which I swore unto Abraham thy father. [4]And I will make thy seed to multiply as the stars of heaven, and will give unto thy seed all these countries; and in thy seed shall all the nations of the earth be blessed: [5]because that Abraham obeyed my voice, and kept my charge, my commandments, my statutes, and my laws.'

[6]And Isaac dwelt in Gerar. [7]And the men of the place asked him of his wife; and he said, 'She is my sister': for he feared to say, 'She is my wife'; 'lest', said he, 'the men of the place should kill me for Rebekah'; because she was fair to look upon. [8]And it came to pass, when he had been there a long time, that Abimelech king of the Philistines looked out at a window, and saw, and behold, Isaac was sporting with Rebekah his wife. [9]And Abimelech called Isaac, and said, 'Behold, of a surety she is thy wife: and how saidst thou, "She is my sister"?' And Isaac said unto him, 'Because I said, "Lest I die for her"'. [10]And Abimelech said, 'What is this thou hast done unto us? one of the people might lightly have lain with thy wife, and thou shouldst have brought guiltiness upon us'. [11]And Abimelech charged all his people, saying, 'He that toucheth this man or his wife shall surely be put to death'.

[12]Then Isaac sowed in that land, and received in the same year a hundredfold: and the LORD blessed him. [13]And the man waxed great, and went forward, and grew until he became very great: [14]for he had possession of flocks, and possession of herds, and great store of servants, and the Philistines envied him. [15]For all the wells which his father's servants had dug in the days of Abraham his father, the Philistines had stopped them, and filled them with earth. [16]And Abimelech said unto Isaac, 'Go from us: for thou art much mightier than we'.

[17]And Isaac departed thence, and pitched his tent in the valley of Gerar, and dwelt there. [18]And Isaac dug again the wells of water, which they had dug in the days of Abraham his father: for the Philistines had stopped them after the death of Abraham, and he called their names after the names by which his father had called them. [19]And Isaac's servants dug in the valley, and found there a well of springing water. [20]And the herdsmen of Gerar did strive with Isaac's herdsmen, saying, 'The water is ours': and he called the name of the well Esek, because they strove with him. [21]And they dug another well, and strove for that also: and he called the name of it Sitnah. [22]And he removed from thence, and dug another well, and for that they strove not: and he called the name of it Rehoboth: and he said, 'For now the LORD hath made room for us, and we shall be fruitful in the land'.

[23]And he went up from thence to Beer-sheba. [24]And the LORD appeared unto him the same night, and said, 'I am the God of Abraham thy father: fear not, for I am with thee, and will bless thee, and multiply thy seed for my servant Abraham's sake'. [25]And he built an altar there, and called upon the name of the LORD, and pitched his tent there: and there Isaac's servants dug a well.

[26]Then Abimelech went to him from Gerar, and Ahuzzath one of his friends, and Phichol the chief captain of his army. [27]And Isaac said unto them, 'Wherefore come ye to me, seeing ye hate me, and have sent me away from you?' [28]And they said, 'We saw certainly that the LORD was with thee: and we said, "Let there be now an oath betwixt us, even

betwixt us and thee, and let us make a covenant with thee"; ²⁹that thou wilt do us no hurt, as we have not touched thee, and as we have done unto thee nothing but good, and have sent thee away in peace: thou art now the blessed of the LORD'. ³⁰And he made them a feast, and they did eat and drink. ³¹And they rose up betimes in the morning, and swore one to another: and Isaac sent them away, and they departed from him in peace. ³²And it came to pass the same day, that Isaac's servants came, and told him concerning the well which they had dug, and said unto him, 'We have found water'. ³³And he called it Shebah: therefore the name of the city is Beer-sheba unto this day.

³⁴And Esau was forty years old when he took to wife Judith the daughter of Beeri the Hittite, and Bashemath the daughter of Elon the Hittite: ³⁵which were a grief of mind unto Isaac and to Rebekah.

27 And it came to pass that when Isaac was old, and his eyes were dim, so that he could not see, he called Esau his eldest son, and said unto him, 'My son'. And he said unto him, 'Behold, here am I'. ²And he said, 'Behold now, I am old, I know not the day of my death. ³Now therefore take, I pray thee, thy weapons, thy quiver and thy bow, and go out to the field, and take me some venison; ⁴and make me savoury meat, such as I love, and bring it to me, that I may eat, that my soul may bless thee before I die.'

⁵And Rebekah heard when Isaac spoke to Esau his son. And Esau went to the field to hunt for venison, and to bring it. ⁶And Rebekah spoke unto Jacob her son, saying, 'Behold, I heard thy father speak unto Esau thy brother, saying, ⁷"Bring me venison, and make me savoury meat, that I may eat, and bless thee before the LORD before my death". ⁸Now therefore, my son, obey my voice according to that which I command thee. ⁹Go now to the flock, and fetch me from thence two good kids of the goats, and I will make them savoury meat for thy father, such as he loveth. ¹⁰And thou shalt bring it to thy father, that he may eat, and that he may bless thee before his death.' ¹¹And Jacob said to Rebekah his mother, 'Behold, Esau my brother is a hairy man, and I am a smooth man. ¹²My father peradventure will feel me, and I shall seem to him as a deceiver, and I shall bring a curse upon me, and not a blessing.' ¹³And his mother said unto him, 'Upon me be thy curse, my son: only obey my voice, and go fetch me them'. ¹⁴And he went, and fetched, and brought them to his mother, and his mother made savoury meat, such as his father loved. ¹⁵And Rebekah took goodly raiment of her eldest son Esau, which were with her in the house, and put them upon Jacob her younger son: ¹⁶and she put the skins of the kids of the goats upon his hands, and upon the smooth of his neck. ¹⁷And she gave the savoury meat and the bread, which she had prepared, into the hand of her son Jacob.

¹⁸And he came unto his father, and said, 'My father': and he said, 'Here am I: who art thou, my son?' ¹⁹And Jacob said unto his father, 'I am Esau thy firstborn; I have done according as thou badest me: arise, I pray thee, sit and eat of my venison, that thy soul may bless me'. ²⁰And Isaac said unto his son, 'How is it that thou hast found it so quickly, my

son?' And he said, 'Because the LORD thy God brought it to me'. ²¹And Isaac said unto Jacob, 'Come near, I pray thee, that I may feel thee, my son, whether thou be my very son Esau or not'. ²²And Jacob went near unto Isaac his father: and he felt him, and said, 'The voice is Jacob's voice, but the hands are the hands of Esau'. ²³And he discerned him not, because his hands were hairy, as his brother Esau's hands: so he blessed him. ²⁴And he said, 'Art thou my very son Esau?' And he said, 'I am'. ²⁵And he said, 'Bring it near to me, and I will eat of my son's venison, that my soul may bless thee'. And he brought it near to him, and he did eat: and he brought him wine, and he drank. ²⁶And his father Isaac said unto him, 'Come near now, and kiss me, my son'. ²⁷And he came near, and kissed him: and he smelled the smell of his raiment, and blessed him, and said, 'See, the smell of my son is as the smell of a field which the LORD hath blessed: ²⁸therefore God give thee of the dew of heaven, and the fatness of the earth, and plenty of corn and wine. ²⁹Let people serve thee, and nations bow down to thee: be lord over thy brethren, and let thy mother's sons bow down to thee: cursed be every one that curseth thee, and blessed be he that blesseth thee.'

³⁰And it came to pass, as soon as Isaac had made an end of blessing Jacob, and Jacob was yet scarce gone out from the presence of Isaac his father, that Esau his brother came in from his hunting. ³¹And he also had made savoury meat, and brought it unto his father, and said unto his father, 'Let my father arise, and eat of his son's venison, that thy soul may bless me'. ³²And Isaac his father said unto him, 'Who art thou?' And he said, 'I am thy son, thy firstborn Esau'. ³³And Isaac trembled very exceedingly, and said, 'Who? where is he that hath taken venison, and brought it me, and I have eaten of all before thou camest, and have blessed him? yea, and he shall be blessed'. ³⁴And when Esau heard the words of his father, he cried with a great and exceeding bitter cry, and said unto his father, 'Bless me, even me also, O my father'. ³⁵And he said, 'Thy brother came with subtlety, and hath taken away thy blessing'. ³⁶And he said, 'Is not he rightly named Jacob? for he hath supplanted me these two times: he took away my birthright, and behold, now he hath taken away my blessing'. And he said, 'Hast thou not reserved a blessing for me?' ³⁷And Isaac answered and said unto Esau, 'Behold, I have made him thy lord, and all his brethren have I given to him for servants; and with corn and wine have I sustained him: and what shall I do now unto thee, my son?' ³⁸And Esau said unto his father, 'Hast thou but one blessing, my father? bless me, even me also, O my father'. And Esau lifted up his voice, and wept. ³⁹And Isaac his father answered and said unto him, 'Behold, thy dwelling shall be the fatness of the earth, and of the dew of heaven from above. ⁴⁰And by thy sword shalt thou live, and shalt serve thy brother: and it shall come to pass when thou shalt have the dominion, that thou shalt break his yoke from off thy neck.'

⁴¹And Esau hated Jacob because of the blessing wherewith his father blessed him: and Esau said in his heart, 'The days of mourning for my father are at hand; then will I slay my brother Jacob'. ⁴²And these words

of Esau her elder son were told to Rebekah: and she sent and called Jacob her younger son, and said unto him, 'Behold, thy brother Esau, as touching thee, doth comfort himself, purposing to kill thee. ⁴³Now therefore, my son, obey my voice: and arise, flee thou to Laban my brother to Haran. ⁴⁴And tarry with him a few days, until thy brother's fury turn away; ⁴⁵until thy brother's anger turn away from thee, and he forget that which thou hast done to him: then I will send, and fetch thee from thence: why should I be deprived also of you both in one day?'

⁴⁶And Rebekah said to Isaac, 'I am weary of my life because of the daughters of Heth: if Jacob take a wife of the daughters of Heth, such as these which are of the daughters of the land, what good shall my life do me?'

28 And Isaac called Jacob, and blessed him, and charged him, and said unto him, 'Thou shalt not take a wife of the daughters of Canaan. ²Arise, go to Padan-aram, to the house of Bethuel thy mother's father, and take thee a wife from thence of the daughters of Laban thy mother's brother. ³And God Almighty bless thee, and make thee fruitful, and multiply thee, that thou mayest be a multitude of people; ⁴and give thee the blessing of Abraham, to thee, and to thy seed with thee, that thou mayest inherit the land wherein thou art a stranger, which God gave unto Abraham.' ⁵And Isaac sent away Jacob: and he went to Padan-aram unto Laban, son of Bethuel the Syrian, the brother of Rebekah, Jacob's and Esau's mother.

⁶When Esau saw that Isaac had blessed Jacob, and sent him away to Padan-aram, to take him a wife from thence; and that as he blessed him he gave him a charge, saying, 'Thou shalt not take a wife of the daughters of Canaan'; ⁷and that Jacob obeyed his father and his mother, and was gone to Padan-aram; ⁸and Esau seeing that the daughters of Canaan pleased not Isaac his father; ⁹then went Esau unto Ishmael, and took unto the wives which he had Mahalath the daughter of Ishmael Abraham's son, the sister of Nebajoth, to be his wife.

¹⁰And Jacob went out from Beer-sheba, and went toward Haran. ¹¹And he lighted upon a certain place, and tarried there all night, because the sun was set; and he took of the stones of that place, and put them for his pillows, and lay down in that place to sleep. ¹²And he dreamed, and behold, a ladder set up on the earth, and the top of it reached to heaven: and behold, the angels of God ascending and descending on it. ¹³And behold, the LORD stood above it, and said, 'I am the LORD God of Abraham thy father, and the God of Isaac: the land whereon thou liest, to thee will I give it, and to thy seed. ¹⁴And thy seed shall be as the dust of the earth, and thou shalt spread abroad to the west, and to the east, and to the north, and to the south: and in thee and in thy seed shall all the families of the earth be blessed. ¹⁵And behold, I am with thee, and will keep thee in all places whither thou goest, and will bring thee again into this land: for I will not leave thee, until I have done that which I have spoken to thee of.' ¹⁶And Jacob awoke out of his sleep, and he said, 'Surely the LORD is in this place, and I knew it not'. ¹⁷And he was

afraid, and said, 'How dreadful is this place? this is no other but the house of God, and this is the gate of heaven'. ¹⁸And Jacob rose up early in the morning, and took the stone that he had put for his pillows, and set it up for a pillar, and poured oil upon the top of it. ¹⁹And he called the name of that place Beth-el: but the name of that city was called Luz at the first. ²⁰And Jacob vowed a vow, saying, 'If God will be with me, and will keep me in this way that I go, and will give me bread to eat, and raiment to put on, ²¹so that I come again to my father's house in peace: then shall the LORD be my God. ²²And this stone, which I have set for a pillar, shall be God's house: and of all that thou shalt give me I will surely give the tenth unto thee.'

29 Then Jacob went on his journey, and came into the land of the people of the east. ²And he looked, and behold, a well in the field, and lo, there were three flocks of sheep lying by it: for out of that well they watered the flocks: and a great stone was upon the well's mouth. ³And thither were all the flocks gathered: and they rolled the stone from the well's mouth, and watered the sheep, and put the stone again upon the well's mouth in his place. ⁴And Jacob said unto them, 'My brethren, whence be ye?' And they said, 'Of Haran are we'. ⁵And he said unto them, 'Know ye Laban the son of Nahor?' And they said, 'We know him'. ⁶And he said unto them, 'Is he well?' And they said, 'He is well: and behold, Rachel his daughter cometh with the sheep'. ⁷And he said, 'Lo, it is yet high day, neither is it time that the cattle should be gathered together: water ye the sheep, and go and feed them'. ⁸And they said, 'We cannot, until all the flocks be gathered together, and till they roll the stone from the well's mouth: then we water the sheep'.

⁹And while he yet spoke with them, Rachel came with her father's sheep: for she kept them. ¹⁰And it came to pass, when Jacob saw Rachel the daughter of Laban his mother's brother, and the sheep of Laban his mother's brother, that Jacob went near, and rolled the stone from the well's mouth, and watered the flock of Laban his mother's brother. ¹¹And Jacob kissed Rachel, and lifted up his voice, and wept. ¹²And Jacob told Rachel that he was her father's brother, and that he was Rebekah's son: and she ran and told her father. ¹³And it came to pass, when Laban heard the tidings of Jacob his sister's son, that he ran to meet him, and embraced him, and kissed him, and brought him to his house. And he told Laban all these things. ¹⁴And Laban said to him, 'Surely thou art my bone and my flesh'. And he abode with him the space of a month.

¹⁵And Laban said unto Jacob, 'Because thou art my brother, shouldst thou therefore serve me for nought? tell me, what shall thy wages be?' ¹⁶And Laban had two daughters: the name of the elder was Leah, and the name of the younger was Rachel. ¹⁷Leah was tender-eyed: but Rachel was beautiful and well-favoured. ¹⁸And Jacob loved Rachel, and said, 'I will serve thee seven years for Rachel thy younger daughter'. ¹⁹And Laban said, 'It is better that I give her to thee, than that I should give her to another man: abide with me'. ²⁰And Jacob served seven years for Rachel: and they seemed unto him but a few days, for the love he had to her.

²¹And Jacob said unto Laban, 'Give me my wife, for my days are fulfilled, that I may go in unto her'. ²²And Laban gathered together all the men of the place, and made a feast. ²³And it came to pass in the evening, that he took Leah his daughter, and brought her to him, and he went in unto her. ²⁴And Laban gave unto his daughter Leah Zilpah his maid for a handmaid. ²⁵And it came to pass, that in the morning, behold, it was Leah: and he said to Laban, 'What is this thou hast done unto me? did not I serve with thee for Rachel? wherefore then hast thou beguiled me?' ²⁶And Laban said, 'It must not be so done in our country, to give the younger before the firstborn. ²⁷Fulfil her week, and we will give thee this also for the service which thou shalt serve with me yet seven other years.' ²⁸And Jacob did so, and fulfilled her week: and he gave him Rachel his daughter to wife also. ²⁹And Laban gave to Rachel his daughter Bilhah his handmaid to be her maid. ³⁰And he went in also unto Rachel, and he loved also Rachel more than Leah, and served with him yet seven other years.

³¹And when the LORD saw that Leah was hated, he opened her womb: but Rachel was barren. ³²And Leah conceived, and bore a son, and she called his name Reuben: for she said, 'Surely the LORD hath looked upon my affliction; now therefore my husband will love me'. ³³And she conceived again, and bore a son, and said, 'Because the LORD hath heard that I was hated, he hath therefore given me this son also': and she called his name Simeon. ³⁴And she conceived again, and bore a son, and said, 'Now this time will my husband be joined unto me, because I have borne him three sons': therefore was his name called Levi. ³⁵And she conceived again, and bore a son: and she said, 'Now will I praise the LORD': therefore she called his name Judah; and left bearing.

30

And when Rachel saw that she bore Jacob no children, Rachel envied her sister, and said unto Jacob, 'Give me children, or else I die'. ²And Jacob's anger was kindled against Rachel, and he said, 'Am I in God's stead, who hath withheld from thee the fruit of the womb?' ³And she said, 'Behold my maid Bilhah: go in unto her, and she shall bear upon my knees, that I may also have children by her'. ⁴And she gave him Bilhah her handmaid to wife: and Jacob went in unto her. ⁵And Bilhah conceived, and bore Jacob a son. ⁶And Rachel said, 'God hath judged me, and hath also heard my voice, and hath given me a son': therefore called she his name Dan. ⁷And Bilhah Rachel's maid conceived again, and bore Jacob a second son. ⁸And Rachel said, 'With great wrestlings have I wrestled with my sister, and I have prevailed': and she called his name Naphtali.

⁹When Leah saw that she had left bearing, she took Zilpah her maid, and gave her Jacob to wife. ¹⁰And Zilpah Leah's maid bore Jacob a son. ¹¹And Leah said, 'A troop cometh': and she called his name Gad. ¹²And Zilpah Leah's maid bore Jacob a second son. ¹³And Leah said, 'Happy am I, for the daughters will call me blessed': and she called his name Asher.

¹⁴And Reuben went in the days of wheat harvest, and found mandrakes in the field, and brought them unto his mother Leah. Then

Rachel said to Leah, 'Give me, I pray thee, of thy son's mandrakes'. ¹⁵And she said unto her, 'Is it a small matter that thou hast taken my husband? and wouldst thou take away my son's mandrakes also?' And Rachel said, 'Therefore he shall lie with thee tonight for thy son's mandrakes'. ¹⁶And Jacob came out of the field in the evening, and Leah went out to meet him, and said, 'Thou must come in unto me: for surely I have hired thee with my son's mandrakes'. And he lay with her that night. ¹⁷And God hearkened unto Leah, and she conceived, and bore Jacob the fifth son. ¹⁸And Leah said, 'God hath given me my hire, because I have given my maiden to my husband': and she called his name Issachar. ¹⁹And Leah conceived again, and bore Jacob the sixth son. ²⁰And Leah said, 'God hath endowed me with a good dowry: now will my husband dwell with me, because I have borne him six sons': and she called his name Zebulun. ²¹And afterwards she bore a daughter, and called her name Dinah.

²²And God remembered Rachel, and God hearkened to her, and opened her womb. ²³And she conceived, and bore a son, and said, 'God hath taken away my reproach': ²⁴and she called his name Joseph, and said, 'The LORD shall add to me another son'.

²⁵And it came to pass, when Rachel had borne Joseph, that Jacob said unto Laban, 'Send me away, that I may go unto my own place, and to my country. ²⁶Give me my wives and my children, for whom I have served thee, and let me go: for thou knowest my service which I have done thee.' ²⁷And Laban said unto him, 'I pray thee, if I have found favour in thy eyes, tarry: for I have learned by experience that the LORD hath blessed me for thy sake'. ²⁸And he said, 'Appoint me thy wages, and I will give it'. ²⁹And he said unto him, 'Thou knowest how I have served thee, and how thy cattle was with me. ³⁰For it was little which thou hadst before I came, and it is now increased unto a multitude; and the LORD hath blessed thee since my coming: and now when shall I provide for my own house also?' ³¹And he said, 'What shall I give thee?' And Jacob said, 'Thou shalt not give me anything: if thou wilt do this thing for me, I will again feed and keep thy flock. ³²I will pass through all thy flock today, removing from thence all the speckled and spotted cattle, and all the brown cattle among the sheep, and the spotted and speckled among the goats: and of such shall be my hire. ³³So shall my righteousness answer for me in time to come, when it shall come for my hire before thy face: every one that is not speckled and spotted amongst the goats, and brown amongst the sheep, that shall be counted stolen with me.' ³⁴And Laban said, 'Behold, I would it might be according to thy word'. ³⁵And he removed that day the he-goats that were ring-streaked and spotted, and all the she-goats that were speckled and spotted, and every one that had some white in it, and all the brown amongst the sheep, and gave them into the hand of his sons. ³⁶And he set three days' journey betwixt himself and Jacob: and Jacob fed the rest of Laban's flocks.

³⁷And Jacob took him rods of green poplar, and of the hazel and chestnut tree, and peeled white streaks in them, and made the white

appear which was in the rods. [38]And he set the rods which he had peeled before the flocks in the gutters in the watering-trough when the flocks came to drink, that they should conceive when they came to drink. [39]And the flocks conceived before the rods, and brought forth cattle ring-streaked, speckled, and spotted. [40]And Jacob did separate the lambs, and set the faces of the flocks toward the ring-streaked, and all the brown in the flock of Laban; and he put his own flocks by themselves, and put them not unto Laban's cattle. [41]And it came to pass, whensoever the stronger cattle did conceive, that Jacob laid the rods before the eyes of the cattle in the gutters, that they might conceive among the rods. [42]But when the cattle were feeble, he put them not in: so the feebler were Laban's, and the stronger Jacob's. [43]And the man increased exceedingly, and had much cattle, and maidservants, and menservants, and camels, and asses.

31 And he heard the words of Laban's sons, saying, 'Jacob hath taken away all that was our father's; and of that which was of our father's hath he gotten all this glory'. [2]And Jacob beheld the countenance of Laban, and behold, it was not toward him as before. [3]And the LORD said unto Jacob, 'Return unto the land of thy fathers, and to thy kindred; and I will be with thee'. [4]And Jacob sent and called Rachel and Leah to the field unto his flock, [5]and said unto them, 'I see your father's countenance, that it is not toward me as before; but the God of my father hath been with me. [6]And ye know that with all my power I have served your father. [7]And your father hath deceived me, and changed my wages ten times: but God suffered him not to hurt me. [8]If he said thus, "The speckled shall be thy wages", then all the cattle bore speckled: and if he said thus, "The ring-streaked shall be thy hire", then bore all the cattle ring-streaked. [9]Thus God hath taken away the cattle of your father, and given them to me. [10]And it came to pass at the time that the cattle conceived, that I lifted up my eyes, and saw in a dream, and behold, the rams which leapt upon the cattle were ring-streaked, speckled, and grisled. [11]And the angel of God spoke unto me in a dream, saying, "Jacob": and I said, "Here am I". [12]And he said, "Lift up now thy eyes, and see, all the rams which leap upon the cattle are ring-streaked, speckled, and grisled: for I have seen all that Laban doeth unto thee. [13]I am the God of Beth-el, where thou anointedst the pillar, and where thou vowedst a vow unto me: now arise, get thee out from this land, and return unto the land of thy kindred."' [14]And Rachel and Leah answered and said unto him, 'Is there yet any portion or inheritance for us in our father's house? [15]Are we not counted of him strangers? for he hath sold us, and hath quite devoured also our money. [16]For all the riches which God hath taken from our father, that is ours, and our children's: now then, whatsoever God hath said unto thee, do.'

[17]Then Jacob rose up, and set his sons and his wives upon camels. [18]And he carried away all his cattle, and all his goods which he had gotten, the cattle of his getting, which he had gotten in Padan-aram, for to go to Isaac his father in the land of Canaan. [19]And Laban went to shear his sheep: and Rachel had stolen the images that were

her father's. ²⁰And Jacob stole away unawares to Laban the Syrian, in that he told him not that he fled. ²¹So he fled with all that he had; and he rose up, and passed over the river, and set his face toward the mount Gilead.

²²And it was told Laban on the third day that Jacob was fled. ²³And he took his brethren with him, and pursued after him seven days' journey, and they overtook him in the mount Gilead. ²⁴And God came to Laban the Syrian in a dream by night, and said unto him, 'Take heed that thou speak not to Jacob either good or bad'. ²⁵Then Laban overtook Jacob. Now Jacob had pitched his tent in the mount: and Laban with his brethren pitched in the mount of Gilead. ²⁶And Laban said to Jacob, 'What hast thou done, that thou hast stolen away unawares to me, and carried away my daughters, as captives taken with the sword? ²⁷Wherefore didst thou fly away secretly, and steal away from me, and didst not tell me, that I might have sent thee away with mirth, and with songs, with tabret, and with harp? ²⁸and hast not suffered me to kiss my sons and my daughters? thou hast now done foolishly in so doing. ²⁹It is in the power of my hand to do you hurt: but the God of your father spoke unto me yesternight, saying, "Take thou heed that thou speak not to Jacob either good or bad". ³⁰And now, though thou wouldst needs be gone, because thou sore longedst after thy father's house, yet wherefore hast thou stolen my gods?' ³¹And Jacob answered and said to Laban, 'Because I was afraid: for I said, peradventure thou wouldst take by force thy daughters from me. ³²With whomsoever thou findest thy gods, let him not live: before our brethren discern thou what is thine with me, and take it to thee.' For Jacob knew not that Rachel had stolen them. ³³And Laban went into Jacob's tent, and into Leah's tent, and into the two maidservants' tents: but he found them not. Then went he out of Leah's tent, and entered into Rachel's tent. ³⁴Now Rachel had taken the images, and put them in the camel's furniture, and sat upon them. And Laban searched all the tent, but found them not. ³⁵And she said to her father, 'Let it not displease my lord that I cannot rise up before thee; for the custom of women is upon me'. And he searched, but found not the images.

³⁶And Jacob was wroth, and chided with Laban: and Jacob answered and said to Laban, 'What is my trespass? what is my sin, that thou hast so hotly pursued after me? ³⁷Whereas thou hast searched all my stuff, what hast thou found of all thy household stuff? set it here before my brethren and thy brethren, that they may judge betwixt us both. ³⁸This twenty years have I been with thee: thy ewes and thy she-goats have not cast their young, and the rams of thy flock have I not eaten. ³⁹That which was torn of beasts I brought not unto thee; I bore the loss of it; of my hand didst thou require it, whether stolen by day, or stolen by night. ⁴⁰Thus I was: in the day the drought consumed me, and the frost by night, and my sleep departed from my eyes. ⁴¹Thus have I been twenty years in thy house: I served thee fourteen years for thy two daughters, and six years for thy cattle; and thou hast changed my wages ten times. ⁴²Except the God of my father, the God of Abraham,

and the fear of Isaac, had been with me, surely thou hadst sent me away now empty. God hath seen my affliction and the labour of my hands, and rebuked thee yesternight.'

[43]And Laban answered and said unto Jacob, 'These daughters are my daughters, and these children are my children, and these cattle are my cattle, and all that thou seest is mine: and what can I do this day unto these my daughters, or unto their children which they have borne? [44]Now therefore come thou, let us make a covenant, I and thou: and let it be for a witness between me and thee.' [45]And Jacob took a stone, and set it up for a pillar. [46]And Jacob said unto his brethren, 'Gather stones', and they took stones, and made a heap, and they did eat there upon the heap. [47]And Laban called it Jegar-sahadutha: but Jacob called it Galeed. [48]And Laban said, 'This heap is a witness between me and thee this day'. Therefore was the name of it called Galeed, [49]and Mizpah: for he said, 'The LORD watch between me and thee, when we are absent one from another. [50]If thou shalt afflict my daughters, or if thou shalt take other wives besides my daughters, no man is with us; see, God is witness betwixt me and thee.' [51]And Laban said to Jacob, 'Behold this heap, and behold this pillar, which I have cast betwixt me and thee. [52]This heap be witness, and this pillar be witness, that I will not pass over this heap to thee, and that thou shalt not pass over this heap and this pillar unto me, for harm. [53]The God of Abraham, and the God of Nahor, the God of their father, judge betwixt us.' And Jacob swore by the fear of his father Isaac. [54]Then Jacob offered sacrifice upon the mount, and called his brethren to eat bread: and they did eat bread, and tarried all night in the mount. [55]And early in the morning Laban rose up, and kissed his sons and his daughters, and blessed them: and Laban departed, and returned unto his place.

32 And Jacob went on his way, and the angels of God met him. [2]And when Jacob saw them, he said, 'This is God's host': and he called the name of that place Mahanaim. [3]And Jacob sent messengers before him to Esau his brother unto the land of Seir, the country of Edom. [4]And he commanded them, saying, 'Thus shall ye speak unto my lord Esau, "Thy servant Jacob saith thus, 'I have sojourned with Laban, and stayed there until now: [5]and I have oxen, and asses, flocks, and menservants, and womenservants: and I have sent to tell my lord, that I may find grace in thy sight'"'.

[6]And the messengers returned to Jacob, saying, 'We came to thy brother Esau, and also he cometh to meet thee, and four hundred men with him'. [7]Then Jacob was greatly afraid and distressed: and he divided the people that was with him, and the flocks, and herds, and the camels, into two bands, [8]and said, 'If Esau come to the one company, and smite it, then the other company which is left shall escape'.

[9]And Jacob said, 'O God of my father Abraham, and God of my father Isaac, the LORD which saidst unto me, "Return unto thy country, and to thy kindred, and I will deal well with thee": [10]I am not worthy of the least of all the mercies, and of all the truth, which thou hast shown unto thy servant: for with my staff I passed over this Jordan, and now I

am become two bands. ¹¹Deliver me, I pray thee, from the hand of my brother, from the hand of Esau: for I fear him, lest he will come and smite me, and the mother with the children. ¹²And thou saidst, "I will surely do thee good, and make thy seed as the sand of the sea, which cannot be numbered for multitude".'

¹³And he lodged there that same night, and took of that which came to his hand a present for Esau his brother: ¹⁴two hundred she-goats, and twenty he-goats, two hundred ewes, and twenty rams, ¹⁵thirty milch camels with their colts, forty kine, and ten bulls, twenty she-asses, and ten foals. ¹⁶And he delivered them into the hand of his servants, every drove by themselves; and said unto his servants, 'Pass over before me, and put a space betwixt drove and drove'. ¹⁷And he commanded the foremost, saying, 'When Esau my brother meeteth thee, and asketh thee, saying, "Whose art thou? and whither goest thou? and whose are these before thee?" ¹⁸then thou shalt say, "They be thy servant Jacob's: it is a present sent unto my lord Esau: and behold also, he is behind us"'. ¹⁹And so commanded he the second, and the third, and all that followed the droves, saying, 'On this manner shall you speak unto Esau, when you find him. ²⁰And say ye moreover, "Behold, thy servant Jacob is behind us".' For he said, 'I will appease him with the present that goeth before me, and afterward I will see his face; peradventure he will accept of me'. ²¹So went the present over before him: and himself lodged that night in the company. ²²And he rose up that night, and took his two wives, and his two womenservants, and his eleven sons, and passed over the ford Jabbok. ²³And he took them, and sent them over the brook, and sent over that he had.

²⁴And Jacob was left alone: and there wrestled a man with him until the breaking of the day. ²⁵And when he saw that he prevailed not against him, he touched the hollow of his thigh: and the hollow of Jacob's thigh was out of joint, as he wrestled with him. ²⁶And he said, 'Let me go, for the day breaketh'. And he said, 'I will not let thee go, except thou bless me'. ²⁷And he said unto him, 'What is thy name?' And he said, 'Jacob'. ²⁸And he said, 'Thy name shall be called no more Jacob, but Israel: for as a prince hast thou power with God and with men, and hast prevailed'. ²⁹And Jacob asked him, and said, 'Tell me, I pray thee, thy name'. And he said, 'Wherefore is it that thou dost ask after my name?' And he blessed him there. ³⁰And Jacob called the name of the place Peniel: 'For I have seen God face to face, and my life is preserved'. ³¹And as he passed over Penuel the sun rose upon him, and he halted upon his thigh. ³²Therefore the children of Israel eat not of the sinew which shrank, which is upon the hollow of the thigh, unto this day: because he touched the hollow of Jacob's thigh in the sinew that shrank.

33 And Jacob lifted up his eyes, and looked, and behold, Esau came, and with him four hundred men. And he divided the children unto Leah, and unto Rachel, and unto the two handmaids. ²And he put the handmaids and their children foremost, and Leah and her children after, and Rachel and Joseph hindmost. ³And he passed over before them, and bowed himself to the ground seven times, until he came near to his brother. ⁴And Esau ran to meet him, and embraced him, and fell on his neck, and kissed him, and they wept. ⁵And he lifted up his eyes, and saw the women and the children, and said, 'Who are those with thee?' And he said, 'The children which God hath graciously given thy servant'. ⁶Then the handmaidens came near, they and their children, and they bowed themselves. ⁷And Leah also with her children came near, and bowed themselves: and after came Joseph near and Rachel, and they bowed themselves. ⁸And he said, 'What meanest thou by all this drove which I met?' And he said, 'These are to find grace in the sight of my lord'. ⁹And Esau said, 'I have enough: my brother, keep that thou hast unto thyself'. ¹⁰And Jacob said, 'Nay, I pray thee, if now I have found grace in thy sight, then receive my present at my hand: for therefore I have seen thy face, as though I had seen the face of God, and thou wast pleased with me. ¹¹Take, I pray thee, my blessing that is brought to thee; because God hath dealt graciously with me, and because I have enough.' And he urged him, and he took it. ¹²And he said, 'Let us take our journey, and let us go, and I will go before thee'. ¹³And he said unto him, 'My lord knoweth that the children are tender, and the flocks and herds with young are with me: and if men should overdrive them one day, all the flock will die. ¹⁴Let my lord, I pray thee, pass over before his servant, and I will lead on softly, according as the cattle that goeth before me and the children be able to endure, until I come unto my lord unto Seir.' ¹⁵And Esau said, 'Let me now leave with thee some of the folk that are with me'. And he said, 'What needeth it? let me find grace in the sight of my lord'.

¹⁶So Esau returned that day on his way unto Seir. ¹⁷And Jacob journeyed to Succoth, and built him a house, and made booths for his cattle: therefore the name of the place is called Succoth.

¹⁸And Jacob came to Shalem, a city of Shechem, which is in the land of Canaan, when he came from Padan-aram, and pitched his tent before the city. ¹⁹And he bought a parcel of a field, where he had spread his tent, at the hand of the children of Hamor, Shechem's father, for a hundred pieces of money. ²⁰And he erected there an altar, and called it El-elohe-Israel.

34 And Dinah the daughter of Leah, which she bore unto Jacob, went out to see the daughters of the land. ²And when Shechem the son of Hamor the Hivite, prince of the country, saw her, he took her, and lay with her, and defiled her. ³And his soul cleaved unto Dinah the daughter of Jacob, and he loved the damsel, and spoke kindly unto the damsel. ⁴And Shechem spoke unto his father Hamor, saying, 'Get me this damsel to wife'. ⁵And Jacob heard that he had defiled Dinah his daughter: now his sons were with his cattle in the field: and Jacob held his peace until they were come.

⁶And Hamor the father of Shechem went out unto Jacob to commune with him. ⁷And the sons of Jacob came out of the field when they heard it, and the men were grieved: and they were very wroth, because he had wrought folly in Israel in lying with Jacob's daughter; which

thing ought not to be done. ⁸And Hamor communed with them, saying, 'The soul of my son Shechem longeth for your daughter: I pray you give her him to wife. ⁹And make ye marriages with us, and give your daughters unto us, and take our daughters unto you. ¹⁰And ye shall dwell with us, and the land shall be before you: dwell and trade you therein, and get you possessions therein.' ¹¹And Shechem said unto her father and unto her brethren, 'Let me find grace in your eyes, and what ye shall say unto me I will give. ¹²Ask me never so much dowry and gift, and I will give according as ye shall say unto me: but give me the damsel to wife.' ¹³And the sons of Jacob answered Shechem and Hamor his father deceitfully, and said, because he had defiled Dinah their sister. ¹⁴And they said unto them, 'We cannot do this thing, to give our sister to one that is uncircumcised: for that were a reproach unto us. ¹⁵But in this will we consent unto you: if ye will be as we be, that every male of you be circumcised: ¹⁶then will we give our daughters unto you, and we will take your daughters to us, and we will dwell with you, and we will become one people. ¹⁷But if ye will not hearken unto us, to be circumcised, then will we take our daughter, and we will be gone.' ¹⁸And their words pleased Hamor, and Shechem Hamor's son. ¹⁹And the young man deferred not to do the thing, because he had delight in Jacob's daughter: and he was more honourable than all the house of his father.

²⁰And Hamor and Shechem his son came unto the gate of their city, and communed with the men of their city, saying, ²¹'These men are peaceable with us, therefore let them dwell in the land, and trade therein: for the land, behold, it is large enough for them: let us take their daughters to us for wives, and let us give them our daughters. ²²Only herein will the men consent unto us for to dwell with us, to be one people, if every male among us be circumcised, as they are circumcised. ²³Shall not their cattle and their substance and every beast of theirs be ours? only let us consent unto them, and they will dwell with us.' ²⁴And unto Hamor and unto Shechem his son hearkened all that went out of the gate of his city; and every male was circumcised, all that went out of the gate of his city.

²⁵And it came to pass on the third day, when they were sore, that two of the sons of Jacob, Simeon and Levi, Dinah's brethren, took each man his sword, and came upon the city boldly, and slew all the males. ²⁶And they slew Hamor and Shechem his son with the edge of the sword, and took Dinah out of Shechem's house, and went out. ²⁷The sons of Jacob came upon the slain, and spoiled the city, because they had defiled their sister. ²⁸They took their sheep, and their oxen, and their asses, and that which was in the city, and that which was in the field. ²⁹And all their wealth, and all their little ones, and their wives took they captive, and spoiled even all that was in the house. ³⁰And Jacob said to Simeon and Levi, 'Ye have troubled me to make me to stink among the inhabitants of the land, amongst the Canaanites and the Perizzites: and I being few in number, they shall gather themselves together against me, and slay me; and I shall be destroyed, I and my house'. ³¹And they said, 'Should he deal with our sister as with a harlot?'

35 And God said unto Jacob, 'Arise, go up to Beth-el, and dwell there: and make there an altar unto God, that appeared unto thee when thou fleddest from the face of Esau thy brother'. ²Then Jacob said unto his household, and to all that were with him, 'Put away the strange gods that are among you, and be clean, and change your garments, ³and let us arise, and go up to Beth-el, and I will make there an altar unto God, who answered me in the day of my distress, and was with me in the way which I went'. ⁴And they gave unto Jacob all the strange gods which were in their hand, and all their earrings which were in their ears, and Jacob hid them under the oak which was by Shechem. ⁵And they journeyed: and the terror of God was upon the cities that were round about them, and they did not pursue after the sons of Jacob.

⁶So Jacob came to Luz, which is in the land of Canaan, that is, Beth-el, he and all the people that were with him. ⁷And he built there an altar, and called the place El-beth-el: because there God appeared unto him, when he fled from the face of his brother. ⁸But Deborah Rebekah's nurse died, and she was buried beneath Beth-el under an oak: and the name of it was called Allon-bachuth.

⁹And God appeared unto Jacob again, when he came out of Padan-aram, and blessed him. ¹⁰And God said unto him, 'Thy name is Jacob: thy name shall not be called any more Jacob, but Israel shall be thy name': and he called his name Israel. ¹¹And God said unto him, 'I am God Almighty: be fruitful and multiply: a nation and a company of nations shall be of thee, and kings shall come out of thy loins. ¹²And the land which I gave Abraham and Isaac, to thee I will give it, and to thy seed after thee will I give the land.' ¹³And God went up from him in the place where he talked with him. ¹⁴And Jacob set up a pillar in the place where he talked with him, even a pillar of stone: and he poured a drink offering thereon, and he poured oil thereon. ¹⁵And Jacob called the name of the place where God spoke with him, Beth-el.

¹⁶And they journeyed from Beth-el; and there was but a little way to come to Ephrath: and Rachel travailed, and she had hard labour. ¹⁷And it came to pass, when she was in hard labour, that the midwife said unto her, 'Fear not: thou shalt have this son also'. ¹⁸And it came to pass, as her soul was in departing (for she died), that she called his name Ben-oni: but his father called him Benjamin. ¹⁹And Rachel died, and was buried in the way to Ephrath, which is Beth-lehem. ²⁰And Jacob set a pillar upon her grave: that is the pillar of Rachel's grave unto this day.

²¹And Israel journeyed, and spread his tent beyond the tower of Edar. ²²And it came to pass, when Israel dwelt in that land, that Reuben went and lay with Bilhah his father's concubine: and Israel heard it. Now the sons of Jacob were twelve. ²³The sons of Leah: Reuben, Jacob's firstborn, and Simeon, and Levi, and Judah, and Issachar, and Zebulun. ²⁴The sons of Rachel: Joseph, and Benjamin. ²⁵And the sons of Bilhah, Rachel's handmaid: Dan, and Naphtali. ²⁶And the sons of Zilpah, Leah's handmaid: Gad, and Asher. These are the sons of Jacob, which were born to him in Padan-aram.

²⁷And Jacob came unto Isaac his father unto Mamre, unto the city of Arbah, which is Hebron, where Abraham and Isaac sojourned. ²⁸And the days of Isaac were a hundred and fourscore years. ²⁹And Isaac gave up the ghost, and died, and was gathered unto his people, being old and full of days: and his sons Esau and Jacob buried him.

36 Now these are the generations of Esau, who is Edom. ²Esau took his wives of the daughters of Canaan: Adah the daughter of Elon the Hittite, and Aholibamah the daughter of Anah the daughter of Zibeon the Hivite; ³and Bashemath Ishmael's daughter, sister of Nebajoth. ⁴And Adah bore to Esau Eliphaz; and Bashemath bore Reuel. ⁵And Aholibamah bore Jeush, and Jaalam, and Korah: these are the sons of Esau, which were born unto him in the land of Canaan. ⁶And Esau took his wives, and his sons, and his daughters, and all the persons of his house, and his cattle, and all his beasts, and all his substance, which he had got in the land of Canaan; and went into the country from the face of his brother Jacob. ⁷For their riches were more than that they might dwell together: and the land wherein they were strangers could not bear them because of their cattle. ⁸Thus dwelt Esau in mount Seir: Esau is Edom.

⁹And these are the generations of Esau the father of the Edomites in mount Seir. ¹⁰These are the names of Esau's sons: Eliphaz the son of Adah the wife of Esau, Reuel the son of Bashemath the wife of Esau. ¹¹And the sons of Eliphaz were Teman, Omar, Zepho, and Gatam, and Kenaz. ¹²And Timna was concubine to Eliphaz Esau's son, and she bore to Eliphaz Amalek: these were the sons of Adah Esau's wife. ¹³And these are the sons of Reuel: Nahath, and Zerah, Shammah, and Mizzah: these were the sons of Bashemath Esau's wife.

¹⁴And these were the sons of Aholibamah, the daughter of Anah, daughter of Zibeon, Esau's wife: and she bore to Esau Jeush, and Jaalam, and Korah.

¹⁵These were dukes of the sons of Esau: the sons of Eliphaz the firstborn son of Esau, duke Teman, duke Omar, duke Zepho, duke Kenaz, ¹⁶duke Korah, duke Gatam, and duke Amalek: these are the dukes that came of Eliphaz in the land of Edom: these were the sons of Adah.

¹⁷And these are the sons of Reuel Esau's son: duke Nahath, duke Zerah, duke Shammah, duke Mizzah: these are the dukes that came of Reuel in the land of Edom: these are the sons of Bashemath Esau's wife.

¹⁸And these are the sons of Aholibamah Esau's wife: duke Jeush, duke Jaalam, duke Korah: these were the dukes that came of Aholibamah the daughter of Anah, Esau's wife. ¹⁹These are the sons of Esau, who is Edom, and these are their dukes.

²⁰These are the sons of Seir the Horite, who inhabited the land: Lotan, and Shobal, and Zibeon, and Anah, ²¹and Dishon, and Ezer, and Dishan: these are the dukes of the Horites, the children of Seir in the land of Edom. ²²And the children of Lotan were Hori and Hemam; and Lotan's sister was Timna. ²³And the children of Shobal were these: Alvan, and Manahath, and Ebal, Shepho, and Onam. ²⁴And these are the

children of Zibeon: both Aiah, and Anah: this was that Anah that found the mules in the wilderness, as he fed the asses of Zibeon his father. ²⁵And the children of Anah were these: Dishon, and Aholibamah the daughter of Anah. ²⁶And these are the children of Dishon: Hemdan, and Eshban, and Ithran, and Cheran. ²⁷The children of Ezer are these: Bilhan, and Zaavan, and Akan. ²⁸The children of Dishan are these: Uz, and Aran. ²⁹These are the dukes that came of the Horites: duke Lotan, duke Shobal, duke Zibeon, duke Anah, ³⁰duke Dishon, duke Ezer, duke Dishan: these are the dukes that came of Hori, among their dukes in the land of Seir.

³¹And these are the kings that reigned in the land of Edom, before there reigned any king over the children of Israel. ³²And Bela the son of Beor reigned in Edom: and the name of his city was Dinhabah. ³³And Bela died, and Jobab the son of Zerah of Bozrah reigned in his stead. ³⁴And Jobab died, and Husham of the land of Temani reigned in his stead. ³⁵And Husham died, and Hadad the son of Bedad, who smote Midian in the field of Moab, reigned in his stead: and the name of his city was Avith. ³⁶And Hadad died, and Samlah of Masrekah reigned in his stead. ³⁷And Samlah died, and Saul of Rehoboth by the river reigned in his stead. ³⁸And Saul died, and Baal-hanan the son of Achbor reigned in his stead. ³⁹And Baal-hanan the son of Achbor died, and Hadar reigned in his stead: and the name of his city was Pau; and his wife's name was Mehetabel, the daughter of Matred, the daughter of Mezahab.

⁴⁰And these are the names of the dukes that came of Esau, according to their families, after their places, by their names: duke Timnah, duke Alvah, duke Jetheth, ⁴¹duke Aholibamah, duke Elah, duke Pinon, ⁴²duke Kenaz, duke Teman, duke Mibzar, ⁴³duke Magdiel, duke Iram. These be the dukes of Edom, according to their habitations in the land of their possession: he is Esau the father of the Edomites.

37

And Jacob dwelt in the land wherein his father was a stranger, in the land of Canaan. ²These are the generations of Jacob. Joseph, being seventeen years old, was feeding the flock with his brethren, and the lad was with the sons of Bilhah, and with the sons of Zilpah, his father's wives: and Joseph brought unto his father their evil report. ³Now Israel loved Joseph more than all his children, because he was the son of his old age: and he made him a coat of many colours. ⁴And when his brethren saw that their father loved him more than all his brethren, they hated him, and could not speak peaceably unto him.

⁵And Joseph dreamed a dream, and he told it his brethren, and they hated him yet the more. ⁶And he said unto them, 'Hear, I pray you, this dream which I have dreamed. ⁷For behold, we were binding sheaves in the field, and lo, my sheaf arose, and also stood upright; and behold, your sheaves stood round about, and made obeisance to my sheaf.' ⁸And his brethren said to him, 'Shalt thou indeed reign over us? or shalt thou indeed have dominion over us?' And they hated him yet the more for his dreams, and for his words.

⁹And he dreamed yet another dream, and told it his brethren, and said, 'Behold, I have dreamed a dream more: and behold, the sun and the moon and the eleven stars made obeisance to me'. ¹⁰And he told it to his father, and to his brethren: and his father rebuked him, and said unto him, 'What is this dream that thou hast dreamed? Shall I and thy mother and thy brethren indeed come to bow down ourselves to thee to the earth?' ¹¹And his brethren envied him: but his father observed the saying.

¹²And his brethren went to feed their father's flock in Shechem. ¹³And Israel said unto Joseph, 'Do not thy brethren feed the flock in Shechem? Come, and I will send thee unto them.' And he said to him, 'Here am I'. ¹⁴And he said to him, 'Go, I pray thee, see whether it be well with thy brethren, and well with the flocks, and bring me word again'. So he sent him out of the vale of Hebron, and he came to Shechem.

¹⁵And a certain man found him, and behold, he was wandering in the field: and the man asked him, saying, 'What seekest thou?' ¹⁶And he said, 'I seek my brethren: tell me, I pray thee, where they feed their flocks'. ¹⁷And the man said, 'They are departed hence: for I heard them say, "Let us go to Dothan"'. And Joseph went after his brethren, and found them in Dothan. ¹⁸And when they saw him afar off, even before he came near unto them, they conspired against him to slay him. ¹⁹And they said one to another, 'Behold, this dreamer cometh. ²⁰Come now therefore, and let us slay him, and cast him into some pit, and we will say, "Some evil beast hath devoured him": and we shall see what will become of his dreams.' ²¹And Reuben heard it, and he delivered him out of their hands, and said, 'Let us not kill him'. ²²And Reuben said unto them, 'Shed no blood, but cast him into this pit that is in the wilderness, and lay no hand upon him'; that he might rid him out of their hands, to deliver him to his father again.

²³And it came to pass, when Joseph was come unto his brethren, that they stripped Joseph out of his coat, his coat of many colours that was on him. ²⁴And they took him, and cast him into a pit: and the pit was empty, there was no water in it. ²⁵And they sat down to eat bread: and they lifted up their eyes and looked, and behold, a company of Ishmeelites came from Gilead, with their camels bearing spicery and balm and myrrh, going to carry it down to Egypt. ²⁶And Judah said unto his brethren, 'What profit is it if we slay our brother, and conceal his blood? ²⁷Come, and let us sell him to the Ishmeelites, and let not our hand be upon him: for he is our brother and our flesh.' And his brethren were content. ²⁸Then there passed by Midianites merchantmen, and they drew and lifted up Joseph out of the pit, and sold Joseph to the Ishmeelites for twenty pieces of silver: and they brought Joseph into Egypt.

²⁹And Reuben returned unto the pit, and behold, Joseph was not in the pit: and he rent his clothes. ³⁰And he returned unto his brethren, and said, 'The child is not, and I, whither shall I go?' ³¹And they took Joseph's coat, and killed a kid of the goats, and dipped the coat in the blood. ³²And they sent the coat of many colours, and they brought it to

their father, and said, 'This have we found: know now whether it be thy son's coat or no'. ³³And he knew it, and said, 'It is my son's coat: an evil beast hath devoured him; Joseph is without doubt rent in pieces'. ³⁴And Jacob rent his clothes, and put sackcloth upon his loins, and mourned for his son many days. ³⁵And all his sons and all his daughters rose up to comfort him: but he refused to be comforted: and he said, 'For I will go down into the grave unto my son mourning'. Thus his father wept for him. ³⁶And the Midianites sold him into Egypt unto Potiphar, an officer of Pharaoh's, and captain of the guard.

38 And it came to pass at that time, that Judah went down from his brethren, and turned in to a certain Adullamite, whose name was Hirah. ²And Judah saw there a daughter of a certain Canaanite, whose name was Shuah; and he took her, and went in unto her. ³And she conceived, and bore a son, and he called his name Er. ⁴And she conceived again, and bore a son, and she called his name Onan. ⁵And she yet again conceived, and bore a son, and called his name Shelah: and he was at Chezib, when she bore him. ⁶And Judah took a wife for Er his firstborn, whose name was Tamar. ⁷And Er, Judah's firstborn, was wicked in the sight of the LORD, and the LORD slew him. ⁸And Judah said unto Onan, 'Go in unto thy brother's wife, and marry her, and raise up seed to thy brother'. ⁹And Onan knew that the seed should not be his; and it came to pass, when he went in unto his brother's wife, that he spilt it on the ground, lest that he should give seed to his brother. ¹⁰And the thing which he did displeased the LORD: wherefore he slew him also. ¹¹Then said Judah to Tamar his daughter-in-law, 'Remain a widow at thy father's house, till Shelah my son be grown': for he said, 'Lest peradventure he die also, as his brethren did'. And Tamar went and dwelt in her father's house.

¹²And in process of time the daughter of Shuah Judah's wife died; and Judah was comforted, and went up unto his sheep-shearers to Timnath, he and his friend Hirah the Adullamite. ¹³And it was told Tamar, saying, 'Behold thy father-in-law goeth up to Timnath to shear his sheep'. ¹⁴And she put her widow's garments off from her, and covered her with a veil, and wrapped herself, and sat in an open place, which is by the way to Timnath: for she saw that Shelah was grown, and she was not given unto him to wife. ¹⁵When Judah saw her, he thought her to be a harlot: because she had covered her face. ¹⁶And he turned unto her by the way, and said, 'Go to, I pray thee, let me come in unto thee' (for he knew not that she was his daughter-in-law). And she said, 'What wilt thou give me, that thou mayest come in unto me?' ¹⁷And he said, 'I will send thee a kid from the flock'. And she said, 'Wilt thou give me a pledge, till thou send it?' ¹⁸And he said, 'What pledge shall I give thee?' And she said, 'Thy signet, and thy bracelets, and thy staff that is in thy hand'. And he gave it her, and came in unto her, and she conceived by him. ¹⁹And she arose, and went away, and laid by her veil from her, and put on the garments of her widowhood. ²⁰And Judah sent the kid by the hand of his friend the Adullamite, to receive his pledge from the woman's hand: but he found her not. ²¹Then he asked the men

of that place, saying, 'Where is the harlot, that was openly by the wayside?' And they said, 'There was no harlot in this place'. ²²And he returned to Judah, and said, 'I cannot find her; and also the men of the place said, that there was no harlot in this place'. ²³And Judah said, 'Let her take it to her, lest we be shamed: behold, I sent this kid, and thou hast not found her'.

²⁴And it came to pass about three months after, that it was told Judah, saying, 'Tamar thy daughter-in-law hath played the harlot, and also behold, she is with child by whoredom'. And Judah said, 'Bring her forth, and let her be burnt'. ²⁵When she was brought forth, she sent to her father-in-law, saying, 'By the man whose these are, am I with child': and she said, 'Discern, I pray thee, whose are these, the signet, and bracelets, and staff'. ²⁶And Judah acknowledged them, and said, 'She hath been more righteous than I: because that I gave her not to Shelah my son'. And he knew her again no more.

²⁷And it came to pass in the time of her travail, that, behold, twins were in her womb. ²⁸And it came to pass, when she travailed, that the one put out his hand, and the midwife took and bound upon his hand a scarlet thread, saying, 'This came out first'. ²⁹And it came to pass, as he drew back his hand, that, behold, his brother came out: and she said, 'How hast thou broken forth? this breach be upon thee': therefore his name was called Pharez. ³⁰And afterward came out his brother, that had the scarlet thread upon his hand, and his name was called Zerah.

39 And Joseph was brought down to Egypt, and Potiphar, an officer of Pharaoh, captain of the guard, an Egyptian, bought him of the hand of the Ishmeelites, which had brought him down thither. ²And the LORD was with Joseph, and he was a prosperous man, and he was in the house of his master the Egyptian. ³And his master saw that the LORD was with him, and that the LORD made all that he did to prosper in his hand. ⁴And Joseph found grace in his sight, and he served him; and he made him overseer over his house, and all that he had he put into his hand. ⁵And it came to pass from the time that he had made him overseer in his house, and over all that he had, that the LORD blessed the Egyptian's house for Joseph's sake: and the blessing of the LORD was upon all that he had in the house, and in the field. ⁶And he left all that he had in Joseph's hand: and he knew not aught he had, save the bread which he did eat. And Joseph was a goodly person, and well-favoured.

⁷And it came to pass after these things, that his master's wife cast her eyes upon Joseph, and she said, 'Lie with me'. ⁸But he refused, and said unto his master's wife, 'Behold, my master wotteth not what is with me in the house, and he hath committed all that he hath to my hand. ⁹There is none greater in this house than I; neither hath he kept back anything from me but thee, because thou art his wife: how then can I do this great wickedness, and sin against God?' ¹⁰And it came to pass, as she spoke to Joseph day by day, that he hearkened not unto her, to lie by her, or to be with her. ¹¹And it came to pass about this time, that Joseph went into the house to do his business, and there was none

of the men of the house there within. ¹²And she caught him by his garment, saying, 'Lie with me': and he left his garment in her hand, and fled, and got him out. ¹³And it came to pass, when she saw that he had left his garment in her hand, and was fled forth, ¹⁴that she called unto the men of her house, and spoke unto them, saying, 'See, he hath brought in a Hebrew unto us to mock us; he came in unto me to lie with me, and I cried with a loud voice. ¹⁵And it came to pass, when he heard that I lifted up my voice and cried, that he left his garment with me, and fled, and got him out.' ¹⁶And she laid up his garment by her, until her lord came home. ¹⁷And she spoke unto him according to these words, saying, 'The Hebrew servant, which thou hast brought unto us, came in unto me to mock me. ¹⁸And it came to pass, as I lifted up my voice and cried, that he left his garment with me, and fled out.' ¹⁹And it came to pass, when his master heard the words of his wife, which she spoke unto him, saying, 'After this manner did thy servant to me', that his wrath was kindled. ²⁰And Joseph's master took him, and put him into the prison, a place where the king's prisoners were bound: and he was there in the prison.

²¹But the LORD was with Joseph, and showed him mercy, and gave him favour in the sight of the keeper of the prison. ²²And the keeper of the prison committed to Joseph's hand all the prisoners that were in the prison, and whatsoever they did there, he was the doer of it. ²³The keeper of the prison looked not to anything that was under his hand: because the LORD was with him, and that which he did, the LORD made it to prosper.

40 And it came to pass after these things, that the butler of the king of Egypt and his baker had offended their lord the king of Egypt. ²And Pharaoh was wroth against two of his officers, against the chief of the butlers, and against the chief of the bakers. ³And he put them in ward in the house of the captain of the guard, into the prison, the place where Joseph was bound. ⁴And the captain of the guard charged Joseph with them, and he served them, and they continued a season in ward.

⁵And they dreamed a dream both of them, each man his dream in one night, each man according to the interpretation of his dream, the butler and the baker of the king of Egypt, which were bound in the prison. ⁶And Joseph came in unto them in the morning, and looked upon them, and, behold, they were sad. ⁷And he asked Pharaoh's officers that were with him in the ward of his lord's house, saying, 'Wherefore look ye so sadly today?' ⁸And they said unto him, 'We have dreamed a dream, and there is no interpreter of it'. And Joseph said unto them, 'Do not interpretations belong to God? tell me them, I pray you'. ⁹And the chief butler told his dream to Joseph, and said to him, 'In my dream, behold, a vine was before me; ¹⁰and in the vine were three branches, and it was as though it budded, and her blossoms shot forth; and the clusters thereof brought forth ripe grapes. ¹¹And Pharaoh's cup was in my hand, and I took the grapes, and pressed them into Pharaoh's cup, and I gave the cup into Pharaoh's hand.' ¹²And Joseph

said unto him, 'This is the interpretation of it: the three branches are three days: [13]yet within three days shall Pharaoh lift up thy head, and restore thee unto thy place, and thou shalt deliver Pharaoh's cup into his hand, after the former manner when thou wast his butler. [14]But think on me when it shall be well with thee, and show kindness, I pray thee, unto me, and make mention of me unto Pharaoh, and bring me out of this house. [15]For indeed I was stolen away out of the land of the Hebrews: and here also have I done nothing that they should put me into the dungeon.'

[16]When the chief baker saw that the interpretation was good, he said unto Joseph, 'I also was in my dream, and behold, I had three white baskets on my head. [17]And in the uppermost basket there was of all manner of bakemeats for Pharaoh, and the birds did eat them out of the basket upon my head.' [18]And Joseph answered and said, 'This is the interpretation thereof: the three baskets are three days: [19]yet within three days shall Pharaoh lift up thy head from off thee, and shall hang thee on a tree, and the birds shall eat thy flesh from off thee'.

[20]And it came to pass the third day, which was Pharaoh's birthday, that he made a feast unto all his servants: and he lifted up the head of the chief butler and of the chief baker among his servants. [21]And he restored the chief butler unto his butlership again, and he gave the cup into Pharaoh's hand. [22]But he hanged the chief baker, as Joseph had interpreted to them. [23]Yet did not the chief butler remember Joseph, but forgot him.

41 And it came to pass at the end of two full years, that Pharaoh dreamed: and behold, he stood by the river. [2]And behold, there came up out of the river seven well-favoured kine and fat-fleshed, and they fed in a meadow. [3]And behold, seven other kine came up after them out of the river, ill-favoured and lean-fleshed, and stood by the other kine upon the brink of the river. [4]And the ill-favoured and lean-fleshed kine did eat up the seven well-favoured and fat kine. So Pharaoh awoke. [5]And he slept and dreamed the second time: and behold, seven ears of corn came up upon one stalk, rank and good. [6]And behold, seven thin ears and blasted with the east wind sprang up after them. [7]And the seven thin ears devoured the seven rank and full ears. And Pharaoh awoke, and behold, it was a dream. [8]And it came to pass in the morning that his spirit was troubled, and he sent and called for all the magicians of Egypt, and all the wise men thereof: and Pharaoh told them his dream; but there was none that could interpret them unto Pharaoh.

[9]Then spoke the chief butler unto Pharaoh, saying, 'I do remember my faults this day. [10]Pharaoh was wroth with his servants, and put me in ward in the captain of the guard's house, both me and the chief baker. [11]And we dreamed a dream in one night, I and he: we dreamed each man according to the interpretation of his dream. [12]And there was there with us a young man, a Hebrew, servant to the captain of the guard; and we told him, and he interpreted to us our dreams, to each man according to his dream he did interpret. [13]And it came to pass, as

he interpreted to us, so it was; me he restored unto my office, and him he hanged.'

[14]Then Pharaoh sent and called Joseph, and they brought him hastily out of the dungeon: and he shaved himself, and changed his raiment, and came in unto Pharaoh. [15]And Pharaoh said unto Joseph, 'I have dreamed a dream, and there is none that can interpret it: and I have heard say of thee, that thou canst understand a dream to interpret it'. [16]And Joseph answered Pharaoh, saying, 'It is not in me: God shall give Pharaoh an answer of peace'. [17]And Pharaoh said unto Joseph, 'In my dream, behold, I stood upon the bank of the river. [18]And behold, there came up out of the river seven kine, fat-fleshed and well-favoured, and they fed in a meadow. [19]And behold, seven other kine came up after them, poor and very ill-favoured and lean-fleshed, such as I never saw in all the land of Egypt for badness. [20]And the lean and the ill-favoured kine did eat up the first seven fat kine. [21]And when they had eaten them up, it could not be known that they had eaten them, but they were still ill-favoured, as at the beginning. So I awoke. [22]And I saw in my dream, and behold, seven ears came up in one stalk, full and good. [23]And behold, seven ears, withered, thin, and blasted with the east wind, sprang up after them. [24]And the thin ears devoured the seven good ears: and I told this unto the magicians, but there was none that could declare it to me.'

[25]And Joseph said unto Pharaoh, 'The dream of Pharaoh is one: God hath shown Pharaoh what he is about to do. [26]The seven good kine are seven years; and the seven good ears are seven years: the dream is one. [27]And the seven thin and ill-favoured kine that came up after them are seven years; and the seven empty ears blasted with the east wind shall be seven years of famine. [28]This is the thing which I have spoken unto Pharaoh: what God is about to do he showeth unto Pharaoh. [29]Behold, there come seven years of great plenty throughout all the land of Egypt. [30]And there shall arise after them seven years of famine, and all the plenty shall be forgotten in the land of Egypt: and the famine shall consume the land. [31]And the plenty shall not be known in the land by reason of that famine following: for it shall be very grievous. [32]And for that the dream was doubled unto Pharaoh twice, it is because the thing is established by God: and God will shortly bring it to pass. [33]Now therefore let Pharaoh look out a man discreet and wise, and set him over the land of Egypt. [34]Let Pharaoh do this, and let him appoint officers over the land, and take up the fifth part of the land of Egypt in the seven plenteous years. [35]And let them gather all the food of those good years that come, and lay up corn under the hand of Pharaoh, and let them keep food in the cities. [36]And that food shall be for store to the land against the seven years of famine, which shall be in the land of Egypt, that the land perish not through the famine.'

[37]And the thing was good in the eyes of Pharaoh, and in the eyes of all his servants. [38]And Pharaoh said unto his servants, 'Can we find such a one as this is, a man in whom the Spirit of God is?' [39]And Pharaoh said unto Joseph, 'Forasmuch as God hath shown thee all this, there is none

so discreet and wise as thou art: ⁴⁰thou shalt be over my house, and according unto thy word shall all my people be ruled: only in the throne will I be greater than thou'. ⁴¹And Pharaoh said unto Joseph, 'See, I have set thee over all the land of Egypt'. ⁴²And Pharaoh took off his ring from his hand, and put it upon Joseph's hand, and arrayed him in vestures of fine linen, and put a gold chain about his neck. ⁴³And he made him to ride in the second chariot which he had; and they cried before him, 'Bow the knee': and he made him ruler over all the land of Egypt. ⁴⁴And Pharaoh said unto Joseph, 'I am Pharaoh, and without thee shall no man lift up his hand or foot in all the land of Egypt'. ⁴⁵And Pharaoh called Joseph's name Zaphnath-paaneah, and he gave him to wife Asenath the daughter of Poti-pherah priest of On. And Joseph went out over all the land of Egypt.

⁴⁶And Joseph was thirty years old when he stood before Pharaoh king of Egypt. And Joseph went out from the presence of Pharaoh, and went throughout all the land of Egypt. ⁴⁷And in the seven plenteous years the earth brought forth by handfuls. ⁴⁸And he gathered up all the food of the seven years, which were in the land of Egypt, and laid up the food in the cities: the food of the field which was round about every city, laid he up in the same. ⁴⁹And Joseph gathered corn as the sand of the sea, very much, until he left numbering: for it was without number.

⁵⁰And unto Joseph were born two sons before the years of famine came, which Asenath the daughter of Poti-pherah priest of On bore unto him. ⁵¹And Joseph called the name of the firstborn Manasseh: 'For God', said he, 'hath made me forget all my toil, and all my father's house'. ⁵²And the name of the second called he Ephraim: 'For God hath caused me to be fruitful in the land of my affliction'.

⁵³And the seven years of plenteousness, that was in the land of Egypt, were ended. ⁵⁴And the seven years of dearth began to come, according as Joseph had said, and the dearth was in all lands; but in all the land of Egypt there was bread. ⁵⁵And when all the land of Egypt was famished, the people cried to Pharaoh for bread: and Pharaoh said unto all the Egyptians, 'Go unto Joseph: what he saith to you, do'. ⁵⁶And the famine was over all the face of the earth; and Joseph opened all the storehouses, and sold unto the Egyptians; and the famine waxed sore in the land of Egypt. ⁵⁷And all countries came into Egypt to Joseph for to buy corn, because that the famine was so sore in all lands.

42 Now when Jacob saw that there was corn in Egypt, Jacob said unto his sons, 'Why do ye look one upon another?' ²And he said, 'Behold, I have heard that there is corn in Egypt: get you down thither, and buy for us from thence, that we may live, and not die'. ³And Joseph's ten brethren went down to buy corn in Egypt. ⁴But Benjamin, Joseph's brother, Jacob sent not with his brethren: for he said, 'Lest peradventure mischief befall him'.

⁵And the sons of Israel came to buy corn among those that came: for the famine was in the land of Canaan. ⁶And Joseph was the governor over the land, and he it was that sold to all the people of the land: and Joseph's brethren came, and bowed down themselves before him with

their faces to the earth. ⁷And Joseph saw his brethren, and he knew them, but made himself strange unto them, and spoke roughly unto them; and he said unto them, 'Whence come ye?' And they said, 'From the land of Canaan to buy food'. ⁸And Joseph knew his brethren, but they knew not him. ⁹And Joseph remembered the dreams which he dreamed of them, and said unto them, 'Ye are spies: to see the nakedness of the land you are come'. ¹⁰And they said unto him, 'Nay, my lord, but to buy food are thy servants come. ¹¹We are all one man's sons; we are true men, thy servants are no spies.' ¹²And he said unto them, 'Nay, but to see the nakedness of the land you are come'. ¹³And they said, 'Thy servants are twelve brethren, the sons of one man in the land of Canaan; and behold, the youngest is this day with our father, and one is not'. ¹⁴And Joseph said unto them, 'That is it that I spoke unto you, saying, "Ye are spies". ¹⁵Hereby ye shall be proved: by the life of Pharaoh ye shall not go forth hence, except your youngest brother come hither. ¹⁶Send one of you, and let him fetch your brother, and ye shall be kept in prison, that your words may be proved, whether there be any truth in you: or else by the life of Pharaoh surely ye are spies.' ¹⁷And he put them all together into ward three days. ¹⁸And Joseph said unto them the third day, 'This do, and live: for I fear God: ¹⁹if ye be true men, let one of your brethren be bound in the house of your prison: go ye, carry corn for the famine of your houses: ²⁰but bring your youngest brother unto me; so shall your words be verified, and ye shall not die'. And they did so.

²¹And they said one to another, 'We are verily guilty concerning our brother, in that we saw the anguish of his soul, when he besought us, and we would not hear: therefore is this distress come upon us'. ²²And Reuben answered them, saying, 'Spoke I not unto you, saying, "Do not sin against the child"; and ye would not hear? therefore behold, also his blood is required'. ²³And they knew not that Joseph understood them: for he spoke unto them by an interpreter. ²⁴And he turned himself about from them, and wept, and returned to them again, and communed with them, and took from them Simeon, and bound him before their eyes.

²⁵Then Joseph commanded to fill their sacks with corn, and to restore every man's money into his sack, and to give them provision for the way: and thus did he unto them. ²⁶And they loaded their asses with the corn, and departed thence. ²⁷And as one of them opened his sack to give his ass provender in the inn, he espied his money: for behold, it was in his sack's mouth. ²⁸And he said unto his brethren, 'My money is restored, and lo, it is even in my sack': and their heart failed them, and they were afraid, saying one to another, 'What is this that God hath done unto us?'

²⁹And they came unto Jacob their father unto the land of Canaan, and told him all that befell unto them, saying, ³⁰'The man who is the lord of the land, spoke roughly to us, and took us for spies of the country. ³¹And we said unto him, "We are true men; we are no spies. ³²We be twelve brethren, sons of our father: one is not, and the youngest is this

day with our father in the land of Canaan."³³And the man, the lord of the country, said unto us, "Hereby shall I know that ye are true men: leave one of your brethren here with me, and take food for the famine of your households, and be gone. ³⁴And bring your youngest brother unto me: then shall I know that you are no spies, but that you are true men: so will I deliver you your brother, and ye shall traffic in the land."'

³⁵And it came to pass as they emptied their sacks, that behold, every man's bundle of money was in his sack: and when both they and their father saw the bundles of money, they were afraid. ³⁶And Jacob their father said unto them, 'Me have ye bereaved of my children: Joseph is not, and Simeon is not, and ye will take Benjamin away: all these things are against me'. ³⁷And Reuben spoke unto his father, saying, 'Slay my two sons, if I bring him not to thee: deliver him into my hand, and I will bring him to thee again'. ³⁸And he said, 'My son shall not go down with you; for his brother is dead, and he is left alone: if mischief befall him by the way in the which ye go, then shall ye bring down my grey hairs with sorrow to the grave'.

43 And the famine was sore in the land. ²And it came to pass, when they had eaten up the corn which they had brought out of Egypt, their father said unto them, 'Go again, buy us a little food'. ³And Judah spoke unto him, saying, 'The man did solemnly protest unto us, saying, "Ye shall not see my face, except your brother be with you". ⁴If thou wilt send our brother with us, we will go down and buy thee food. ⁵But if thou wilt not send him, we will not go down: for the man said unto us, "Ye shall not see my face, except your brother be with you".' ⁶And Israel said, 'Wherefore dealt ye so ill with me, as to tell the man whether ye had yet a brother?' ⁷And they said, 'The man asked us straitly of our state, and of our kindred, saying, 'Is your father yet alive? have ye another brother?" and we told him according to the tenor of these words: could we certainly know that he would say, "Bring your brother down"?' ⁸And Judah said unto Israel his father, 'Send the lad with me, and we will arise and go, that we may live, and not die, both we, and thou, and also our little ones. ⁹I will be surety for him; of my hand shalt thou require him: if I bring him not unto thee, and set him before thee, then let me bear the blame for ever. ¹⁰For except we had lingered, surely now we had returned this second time.' ¹¹And their father Israel said unto them, 'If it must be so now, do this: take of the best fruits in the land in your vessels, and carry down the man a present, a little balm, and a little honey, spices, and myrrh, nuts, and almonds. ¹²And take double money in your hand, and the money that was brought again in the mouth of your sacks, carry it again in your hand; peradventure it was an oversight. ¹³Take also your brother, and arise, go again unto the man. ¹⁴And God Almighty give you mercy before the man, that he may send away your other brother, and Benjamin. If I be bereaved of my children, I am bereaved.'

¹⁵And the men took that present, and they took double money in their hand, and Benjamin; and rose up, and went down to Egypt, and stood before Joseph. ¹⁶And when Joseph saw Benjamin with them, he

said to the ruler of his house, 'Bring these men home, and slay, and make ready: for these men shall dine with me at noon'. ¹⁷And the man did as Joseph bade: and the man brought the men into Joseph's house. ¹⁸And the men were afraid, because they were brought into Joseph's house, and they said, 'Because of the money that was returned in our sacks at the first time are we brought in, that he may seek occasion against us, and fall upon us, and take us for bondmen, and our asses'. ¹⁹And they came near to the steward of Joseph's house, and they communed with him at the door of the house, ²⁰and said, 'O sir, we came indeed down at the first time to buy food: ²¹and it came to pass when we came to the inn, that we opened our sacks, and behold, every man's money was in the mouth of his sack, our money in full weight: and we have brought it again in our hand. ²²And other money have we brought down in our hands to buy food: we cannot tell who put our money in our sacks.' ²³And he said, 'Peace be to you, fear not: your God, and the God of your father, hath given you treasure in your sacks: I had your money'. And he brought Simeon out unto them. ²⁴And the man brought the men into Joseph's house, and gave them water, and they washed their feet; and he gave their asses provender. ²⁵And they made ready the present against Joseph came at noon: for they heard that they should eat bread there.

²⁶And when Joseph came home, they brought him the present which was in their hand into the house, and bowed themselves to him to the earth. ²⁷And he asked them of their welfare, and said, 'Is your father well, the old man of whom ye spoke? Is he yet alive?' ²⁸And they answered, 'Thy servant our father is in good health, he is yet alive'. And they bowed down their heads, and made obeisance. ²⁹And he lifted up his eyes, and saw his brother Benjamin, his mother's son, and said, 'Is this your younger brother, of whom ye spoke unto me?' And he said, 'God be gracious unto thee, my son'. ³⁰And Joseph made haste: for his bowels did yearn upon his brother: and he sought where to weep, and he entered into his chamber, and wept there. ³¹And he washed his face, and went out, and refrained himself, and said, 'Set on bread'. ³²And they set on for him by himself, and for them by themselves, and for the Egyptians, which did eat with him, by themselves: because the Egyptians might not eat bread with the Hebrews: for that is an abomination unto the Egyptians. ³³And they sat before him, the firstborn according to his birthright, and the youngest according to his youth: and the men marvelled one at another. ³⁴And he took and sent messes unto them from before him: but Benjamin's mess was five times so much as any of theirs. And they drank, and were merry with him.

44 And he commanded the steward of his house, saying, 'Fill the men's sacks with food, as much as they can carry, and put every man's money in his sack's mouth. ²And put my cup, the silver cup, in the sack's mouth of the youngest, and his corn money.' And he did according to the word that Joseph had spoken. ³As soon as the morning was light, the men were sent away, they and their asses. ⁴And when they were gone out of the city, and not yet far off, Joseph said unto his steward, 'Up, follow after the men; and when thou dost overtake them, say unto them, "Wherefore have ye rewarded evil for good? ⁵Is not this it in which my lord drinketh, and whereby indeed he divineth? ye have done evil in so doing."'

⁶And he overtook them, and he spoke unto them these same words. ⁷And they said unto him, 'Wherefore saith my lord these words? God forbid that thy servants should do according to this thing. ⁸Behold, the money, which we found in our sacks' mouths, we brought again unto thee out of the land of Canaan: how then should we steal out of thy lord's house silver or gold? ⁹With whomsoever of thy servants it be found, both let him die, and we also will be my lord's bondmen.' ¹⁰And he said, 'Now also let it be according unto your words: he with whom it is found shall be my servant; and ye shall be blameless'. ¹¹Then they speedily took down every man his sack to the ground, and opened every man his sack. ¹²And he searched, and began at the eldest, and left at the youngest: and the cup was found in Benjamin's sack. ¹³Then they rent their clothes, and loaded every man his ass, and returned to the city.

¹⁴And Judah and his brethren came to Joseph's house; for he was yet there: and they fell before him on the ground. ¹⁵And Joseph said unto them, 'What deed is this that ye have done? wot ye not that such a man as I can certainly divine?' ¹⁶And Judah said, 'What shall we say unto my lord? what shall we speak? or how shall we clear ourselves? God hath found out the iniquity of thy servants: behold, we are my lord's servants, both we, and he also with whom the cup is found.' ¹⁷And he said, 'God forbid that I should do so: but the man in whose hand the cup is found, he shall be my servant; and as for you, get you up in peace unto your father'.

¹⁸Then Judah came near unto him, and said, 'O my lord, let thy servant, I pray thee, speak a word in my lord's ears, and let not thy anger burn against thy servant: for thou art even as Pharaoh. ¹⁹My lord asked his servants, saying, "Have ye a father, or a brother?" ²⁰And we said unto my lord, "We have a father, an old man, and a child of his old age, a little one; and his brother is dead, and he alone is left of his mother, and his father loveth him". ²¹And thou saidst unto thy servants, "Bring him down unto me, that I may set my eyes upon him". ²²And we said unto my lord, "The lad cannot leave his father: for if he should leave his father, his father would die". ²³And thou saidst unto thy servants, "Except your youngest brother come down with you, you shall see my face no more". ²⁴And it came to pass when we came up unto thy servant my father, we told him the words of my lord. ²⁵And our father said, "Go again, and buy us a little food". ²⁶And we said, "We cannot go down: if our youngest brother be with us, then will we go down: for we may not see the man's face, except our youngest brother be with us". ²⁷And thy servant my father said unto us, "Ye know that my wife bore me two sons. ²⁸And the one went out from me, and I said, 'Surely he is torn in pieces'; and I saw him not since. ²⁹And if ye take this also from me, and mischief befall him, ye shall bring down my grey hairs with sorrow to

the grave. [30]Now therefore when I come to thy servant my father, and the lad be not with us; seeing that his life is bound up in the lad's life; [31]it shall come to pass, when he seeth that the lad is not with us, that he will die: and thy servants shall bring down the grey hairs of thy servant our father with sorrow to the grave." [32]For thy servant became surety for the lad unto my father, saying, "If I bring him not unto thee, then I shall bear the blame to my father for ever". [33]Now therefore, I pray thee, let thy servant abide in stead of the lad a bondman to my lord, and let the lad go up with his brethren. [34]For how shall I go up to my father, and the lad be not with me? lest peradventure I see the evil that shall come on my father.'

45 Then Joseph could not refrain himself before all them that stood by him: and he cried, 'Cause every man to go out from me'. And there stood no man with him, while Joseph made himself known unto his brethren. [2]And he wept aloud: and the Egyptians and the house of Pharaoh heard. [3]And Joseph said unto his brethren, 'I am Joseph; doth my father yet live?' And his brethren could not answer him: for they were troubled at his presence. [4]And Joseph said unto his brethren, 'Come near to me, I pray you'. And they came near. And he said, 'I am Joseph your brother, whom ye sold into Egypt. [5]Now therefore be not grieved, nor angry with yourselves, that ye sold me hither: for God did send me before you to preserve life. [6]For these two years hath the famine been in the land: and yet there are five years, in the which there shall neither be earing nor harvest. [7]And God sent me before you to preserve you a posterity in the earth, and to save your lives by a great deliverance. [8]So now it was not you that sent me hither, but God: and he hath made me a father to Pharaoh, and lord of all his house, and a ruler throughout all the land of Egypt. [9]Haste you, and go up to my father, and say unto him, "Thus saith thy son Joseph, 'God hath made me lord of all Egypt: come down unto me, tarry not. [10]And thou shalt dwell in the land of Goshen, and thou shalt be near unto me, thou, and thy children, and thy children's children, and thy flocks, and thy herds, and all that thou hast. [11]And there will I nourish thee; for yet there are five years of famine; lest thou, and thy household, and all that thou hast, come to poverty.'" [12]And behold, your eyes see, and the eyes of my brother Benjamin, that it is my mouth that speaketh unto you. [13]And you shall tell my father of all my glory in Egypt, and of all that you have seen, and ye shall haste and bring down my father hither.' [14]And he fell upon his brother Benjamin's neck, and wept: and Benjamin wept upon his neck. [15]Moreover he kissed all his brethren, and wept upon them: and after that his brethren talked with him.

[16]And the fame thereof was heard in Pharaoh's house, saying, 'Joseph's brethren are come': and it pleased Pharaoh well, and his servants. [17]And Pharaoh said unto Joseph, 'Say unto thy brethren, "This do ye, load your beasts, and go, get you unto the land of Canaan. [18]And take your father and your households, and come unto me: and I will give you the good of the land of Egypt, and ye shall eat the fat of the land. [19]Now thou art

commanded, this do ye; take you wagons out of the land of Egypt for your little ones, and for your wives, and bring your father, and come. ²⁰Also regard not your stuff: for the good of all the land of Egypt is yours."' ²¹And the children of Israel did so: and Joseph gave them wagons, according to the commandment of Pharaoh, and gave them provision for the way. ²²To all of them he gave each man changes of raiment; but to Benjamin he gave three hundred pieces of silver, and five changes of raiment. ²³And to his father he sent after this manner: ten asses laden with the good things of Egypt, and ten she-asses laden with corn and bread and meat for his father by the way. ²⁴So he sent his brethren away, and they departed: and he said unto them, 'See that ye fall not out by the way'.

²⁵And they went up out of Egypt, and came into the land of Canaan unto Jacob their father, ²⁶and told him, saying, 'Joseph is yet alive, and he is governor over all the land of Egypt'. And Jacob's heart fainted, for he believed them not. ²⁷And they told him all the words of Joseph, which he had said unto them: and when he saw the wagons which Joseph had sent to carry him, the spirit of Jacob their father revived. ²⁸And Israel said, 'It is enough; Joseph my son is yet alive: I will go and see him before I die'.

46 And Israel took his journey with all that he had, and came to Beer-sheba, and offered sacrifices unto the God of his father Isaac. ²And God spoke unto Israel in the visions of the night, and said, 'Jacob, Jacob'. And he said, 'Here am I'. ³And he said, 'I am God, the God of thy father, fear not to go down into Egypt: for I will there make of thee a great nation. ⁴I will go down with thee into Egypt; and I will also surely bring thee up again: and Joseph shall put his hand upon thy eyes.' ⁵And Jacob rose up from Beer-sheba: and the sons of Israel carried Jacob their father, and their little ones, and their wives, in the wagons which Pharaoh had sent to carry him. ⁶And they took their cattle, and their goods, which they had gotten in the land of Canaan, and came into Egypt, Jacob, and all his seed with him: ⁷his sons, and his sons' sons with him, his daughters, and his sons' daughters, and all his seed brought he with him into Egypt.

⁸And these are the names of the children of Israel, which came into Egypt, Jacob and his sons: Reuben, Jacob's firstborn. ⁹And the sons of Reuben: Hanoch, and Phallu, and Hezron, and Carmi.

¹⁰And the sons of Simeon: Jemuel, and Jamin, and Ohad, and Jachin, and Zohar, and Shaul the son of a Canaanitish woman.

¹¹And the sons of Levi: Gershon, Kohath, and Merari.

¹²And the sons of Judah: Er, and Onan, and Shelah, and Pharez, and Zerah: but Er and Onan died in the land of Canaan. And the sons of Pharez were Hezron and Hamul.

¹³And the sons of Issachar: Tola, and Phuvah, and Job, and Shimron.

¹⁴And the sons of Zebulun: Sered, and Elon, and Jahleel. ¹⁵These be the sons of Leah, which she bore unto Jacob in Padan-aram, with his daughter Dinah: all the souls of his sons and his daughters were thirty and three.

¹⁶And the sons of Gad: Ziphion, and Haggi, Shuni, and Ezbon, Eri, and Arodi, and Areli.

¹⁷And the sons of Asher: Jimnah, and Ishuah, and Ishui, and Beriah, and Serah their sister: and the sons of Beriah: Heber, and Malchiel. ¹⁸These are the sons of Zilpah, whom Laban gave to Leah his daughter, and these she bore unto Jacob, even sixteen souls.

¹⁹The sons of Rachel Jacob's wife: Joseph, and Benjamin.

²⁰And unto Joseph in the land of Egypt were born Manasseh and Ephraim, which Asenath the daughter of Poti-pherah priest of On bore unto him.

²¹And the sons of Benjamin were Belah, and Becher, and Ashbel, Gera, and Naaman, Ehi, and Rosh, Muppim, and Huppim, and Ard. ²²These are the sons of Rachel, which were born to Jacob: all the souls were fourteen.

²³And the sons of Dan: Hushim.

²⁴And the sons of Naphtali: Jahzeel, and Guni, and Jezer, and Shillem. ²⁵These are the sons of Bilhah, which Laban gave unto Rachel his daughter, and she bore these unto Jacob: all the souls were seven.

²⁶All the souls that came with Jacob into Egypt, which came out of his loins, besides Jacob's sons' wives, all the souls were threescore and six. ²⁷And the sons of Joseph, which were born him in Egypt, were two souls: all the souls of the house of Jacob, which came into Egypt, were threescore and ten.

²⁸And he sent Judah before him unto Joseph, to direct his face unto Goshen, and they came into the land of Goshen. ²⁹And Joseph made ready his chariot, and went up to meet Israel his father, to Goshen, and presented himself unto him: and he fell on his neck, and wept on his neck a good while. ³⁰And Israel said unto Joseph, 'Now let me die, since I have seen thy face, because thou art yet alive'. ³¹And Joseph said unto his brethren, and unto his father's house, 'I will go up, and show Pharaoh, and say unto him, "My brethren, and my father's house, which were in the land of Canaan, are come unto me. ³²And the men are shepherds, for their trade hath been to feed cattle; and they have brought their flocks, and their herds, and all that they have." ³³And it shall come to pass, when Pharaoh shall call you, and shall say, "What is your occupation?" ³⁴that ye shall say, "Thy servants' trade hath been about cattle from our youth even until now, both we, and also our fathers": that ye may dwell in the land of Goshen; for every shepherd is an abomination unto the Egyptians.'

47 Then Joseph came and told Pharaoh, and said, 'My father and my brethren, and their flocks, and their herds, and all that they have, are come out of the land of Canaan: and behold, they are in the land of Goshen'. ²And he took some of his brethren, even five men, and presented them unto Pharaoh. ³And Pharaoh said unto his brethren, 'What is your occupation?' And they said unto Pharaoh, 'Thy servants are shepherds, both we, and also our fathers'. ⁴They said moreover unto Pharaoh, 'For to sojourn in the land are we come: for thy servants have no pasture for their flocks, for the famine is sore in the land of Canaan:

now therefore, we pray thee, let thy servants dwell in the land of Goshen'. ⁵And Pharaoh spoke unto Joseph, saying, 'Thy father and thy brethren are come unto thee. ⁶The land of Egypt is before thee: in the best of the land make thy father and brethren to dwell, in the land of Goshen let them dwell: and if thou knowest any men of activity amongst them, then make them rulers over my cattle.' ⁷And Joseph brought in Jacob his father, and set him before Pharaoh: and Jacob blessed Pharaoh. ⁸And Pharaoh said unto Jacob, 'How old art thou?' ⁹And Jacob said unto Pharaoh, 'The days of the years of my pilgrimage are a hundred and thirty years: few and evil have the days of the years of my life been, and have not attained unto the days of the years of the life of my fathers in the days of their pilgrimage'. ¹⁰And Jacob blessed Pharaoh, and went out from before Pharaoh.

¹¹And Joseph placed his father and his brethren, and gave them a possession in the land of Egypt, in the best of the land, in the land of Rameses, as Pharaoh had commanded. ¹²And Joseph nourished his father, and his brethren, and all his father's household, with bread, according to their families.

¹³And there was no bread in all the land: for the famine was very sore, so that the land of Egypt and all the land of Canaan fainted by reason of the famine. ¹⁴And Joseph gathered up all the money that was found in the land of Egypt, and in the land of Canaan, for the corn which they bought: and Joseph brought the money into Pharaoh's house. ¹⁵And when money failed in the land of Egypt, and in the land of Canaan, all the Egyptians came unto Joseph, and said, 'Give us bread: for why should we die in thy presence? for the money faileth'. ¹⁶And Joseph said, 'Give your cattle: and I will give you for your cattle, if money fail'. ¹⁷And they brought their cattle unto Joseph: and Joseph gave them bread in exchange for horses, and for the flocks, and for the cattle of the herds, and for the asses, and he fed them with bread for all their cattle for that year. ¹⁸When that year was ended, they came unto him the second year, and said unto him, 'We will not hide it from my lord, how that our money is spent; my lord also had our herds of cattle: there is not aught left in the sight of my lord, but our bodies, and our lands. ¹⁹Wherefore shall we die before thy eyes, both we and our land? buy us and our land for bread, and we and our land will be servants unto Pharaoh: and give us seed, that we may live, and not die, that the land be not desolate.' ²⁰And Joseph bought all the land of Egypt for Pharaoh: for the Egyptians sold every man his field, because the famine prevailed over them: so the land became Pharaoh's. ²¹And as for the people, he removed them to cities from one end of the borders of Egypt even to the other end thereof. ²²Only the land of the priests bought he not: for the priests had a portion assigned them of Pharaoh, and did eat their portion which Pharaoh gave them: wherefore they sold not their lands. ²³Then Joseph said unto the people, 'Behold, I have bought you this day and your land for Pharaoh: lo, here is seed for you, and ye shall sow the land. ²⁴And it shall come to pass in the increase, that you shall give the fifth part unto Pharaoh, and four parts shall be your own, for

seed of the field, and for your food, and for them of your households, and for food for your little ones.' ²⁵And they said, 'Thou hast saved our lives: let us find grace in the sight of my lord, and we will be Pharaoh's servants'. ²⁶And Joseph made it a law over the land of Egypt unto this day, that Pharaoh should have the fifth part; except the land of the priests only, which became not Pharaoh's.

²⁷And Israel dwelt in the land of Egypt, in the country of Goshen, and they had possessions therein, and grew, and multiplied exceedingly. ²⁸And Jacob lived in the land of Egypt seventeen years: so the whole age of Jacob was a hundred forty and seven years. ²⁹And the time drew nigh that Israel must die, and he called his son Joseph, and said unto him, 'If now I have found grace in thy sight, put, I pray thee, thy hand under my thigh, and deal kindly and truly with me; bury me not, I pray thee, in Egypt. ³⁰But I will lie with my fathers, and thou shalt carry me out of Egypt, and bury me in their burying-place.' And he said, 'I will do as thou hast said'. ³¹And he said, 'Swear unto me'. And he swore unto him. And Israel bowed himself upon the bed's head.

48 And it came to pass after these things, that one told Joseph, 'Behold, thy father is sick': and he took with him his two sons, Manasseh and Ephraim. ²And one told Jacob, and said, 'Behold, thy son Joseph cometh unto thee': and Israel strengthened himself, and sat upon the bed. ³And Jacob said unto Joseph, 'God Almighty appeared unto me at Luz in the land of Canaan, and blessed me, ⁴and said unto me, "Behold, I will make thee fruitful, and multiply thee, and I will make of thee a multitude of people, and will give this land to thy seed after thee for an everlasting possession". ⁵And now thy two sons, Ephraim and Manasseh, which were born unto thee in the land of Egypt before I came unto thee into Egypt, are mine: as Reuben and Simeon, they shall be mine. ⁶And thy issue, which thou begettest after them, shall be thine, and shall be called after the name of their brethren in their inheritance. ⁷And as for me, when I came from Padan, Rachel died by me in the land of Canaan in the way, when yet there was but a little way to come unto Ephrath: and I buried her there in the way of Ephrath; the same is Beth-lehem.'

⁸And Israel beheld Joseph's sons, and said, 'Who are these?' ⁹And Joseph said unto his father, 'They are my sons, whom God hath given me in this place'. And he said, 'Bring them, I pray thee, unto me, and I will bless them'. ¹⁰Now the eyes of Israel were dim for age, so that he could not see. And he brought them near unto him, and he kissed them, and embraced them. ¹¹And Israel said unto Joseph, 'I had not thought to see thy face: and lo, God hath shown me also thy seed'. ¹²And Joseph brought them out from between his knees, and he bowed himself with his face to the earth. ¹³And Joseph took them both, Ephraim in his right hand toward Israel's left hand, and Manasseh in his left hand towards Israel's right hand, and brought them near unto him. ¹⁴And Israel stretched out his right hand, and laid it upon Ephraim's head, who was the younger, and his left hand upon Manasseh's head, guiding his hands wittingly: for Manasseh was the firstborn.

¹⁵And he blessed Joseph, and said, 'God, before whom my fathers Abraham and Isaac did walk, the God which fed me all my life long unto this day, ¹⁶the Angel which redeemed me from all evil, bless the lads, and let my name be named on them, and the name of my fathers Abraham and Isaac, and let them grow into a multitude in the midst of the earth'. ¹⁷And when Joseph saw that his father laid his right hand upon the head of Ephraim, it displeased him: and he held up his father's hand, to remove it from Ephraim's head unto Manasseh's head. ¹⁸And Joseph said unto his father, 'Not so, my father: for this is the firstborn; put thy right hand upon his head'. ¹⁹And his father refused, and said, 'I know it, my son, I know it: he also shall become a people, and he also shall be great: but truly his younger brother shall be greater than he, and his seed shall become a multitude of nations'. ²⁰And he blessed them that day, saying, 'In thee shall Israel bless, saying, "God make thee as Ephraim and as Manasseh"': and he set Ephraim before Manasseh. ²¹And Israel said unto Joseph, 'Behold, I die: but God shall be with you, and bring you again unto the land of your fathers. ²²Moreover I have given to thee one portion above thy brethren, which I took out of the hand of the Amorite with my sword and with my bow.'

49 And Jacob called unto his sons, and said, 'Gather yourselves together, that I may tell you that which shall befall you in the last days.

² 'Gather yourselves together, and hear, ye sons of Jacob,
   and hearken unto Israel your father.

³ 'Reuben, thou art my firstborn,
   my might, and the beginning of my strength,
   the excellence of dignity, and the excellence of power:
⁴ unstable as water, thou shalt not excel,
   because thou wentest up to thy father's bed:
   then defiledst thou it. He went up to my couch.

⁵ 'Simeon and Levi are brethren,
   instruments of cruelty are in their habitations.
⁶ O my soul, come not thou into their secret:
   unto their assembly, my honour, be not thou united:
   for in their anger they slew a man,
   and in their self-will they dug down a wall.
⁷ Cursed be their anger, for it was fierce;
   and their wrath, for it was cruel:
   I will divide them in Jacob,
   and scatter them in Israel.

⁸ 'Judah, thou art he whom thy brethren shall praise:
   thy hand shall be in the neck of thy enemies,
   thy father's children shall bow down before thee.

⁹ Judah is a lion's whelp:
  from the prey, my son, thou art gone up:
  he stooped down, he couched as a lion,
  and as an old lion: who shall rouse him up?
¹⁰ The sceptre shall not depart from Judah,
  nor a lawgiver from between his feet, until Shiloh come:
  and unto him shall the gathering of the people be:
¹¹ binding his foal unto the vine,
  and his ass's colt unto the choice vine;
  he washed his garments in wine,
  and his clothes in the blood of grapes.
¹² His eyes shall be red with wine,
  and his teeth white with milk.

¹³ 'Zebulun shall dwell at the haven of the sea,
  and he shall be for a haven of ships:
  and his border shall be unto Zidon.

¹⁴ 'Issachar is a strong ass
  couching down between two burdens.
¹⁵ And he saw that rest was good,
  and the land that it was pleasant:
  and bowed his shoulder to bear,
  and became a servant unto tribute.

¹⁶ 'Dan shall judge his people,
  as one of the tribes of Israel.
¹⁷ Dan shall be a serpent by the way,
  an adder in the path,
  that biteth the horse-heels,
  so that his rider shall fall backward.
¹⁸ I have waited for thy salvation, O Lord.

¹⁹ 'Gad, a troop shall overcome him:
  but he shall overcome at the last.

²⁰ 'Out of Asher his bread shall be fat,
  and he shall yield royal dainties.

²¹ 'Naphtali is a hind let loose:
  he giveth goodly words.

²² 'Joseph is a fruitful bough,
  even a fruitful bough by a well,
  whose branches run over the wall.
²³ The archers have sorely grieved him,
  and shot at him, and hated him.
²⁴ But his bow abode in strength,

and the arms of his hands were made strong
by the hands of the mighty God of Jacob
(from thence is the shepherd, the stone of Israel),
25 even by the God of thy father, who shall help thee,
and by the Almighty, who shall bless thee
with blessings of heaven above,
blessings of the deep that lieth under,
blessings of the breasts, and of the womb.
26 The blessings of thy father have prevailed
above the blessings of my progenitors:
unto the utmost bound of the everlasting hills,
they shall be on the head of Joseph,
and on the crown of the head of him that was separate from his
     brethren.

27 'Benjamin shall raven as a wolf:
in the morning he shall devour the prey,
and at night he shall divide the spoil.'

28All these are the twelve tribes of Israel, and this is it that their father
spoke unto them, and blessed them: every one according to his blessing
he blessed them. 29And he charged them, and said unto them, 'I am to
be gathered unto my people: bury me with my fathers in the cave that
is in the field of Ephron the Hittite, 30in the cave that is in the field of
Machpelah, which is before Mamre, in the land of Canaan, which
Abraham bought with the field of Ephron the Hittite for a possession of
a burying-place. 31There they buried Abraham and Sarah his wife, there
they buried Isaac and Rebekah his wife, and there I buried Leah. 32The
purchase of the field and of the cave that is therein was from the children of Heth.' 33And when Jacob had made an end of commanding his
sons, he gathered up his feet into the bed, and yielded up the ghost,
and was gathered unto his people.

50 And Joseph fell upon his father's face, and wept upon him, and
kissed him. 2And Joseph commanded his servants the physicians
to embalm his father: and the physicians embalmed Israel. 3And forty
days were fulfilled for him (for so are fulfilled the days of those which
are embalmed), and the Egyptians mourned for him threescore and ten
days.

4And when the days of his mourning were past, Joseph spoke unto
the house of Pharaoh, saying, 'If now I have found grace in your eyes,
speak, I pray you, in the ears of Pharaoh, saying, 5"My father made
me swear, saying, 'Lo, I die: in my grave which I have dug for me in
the land of Canaan, there shalt thou bury me'. Now therefore let me
go up, I pray thee, and bury my father, and I will come again."' 6And
Pharaoh said, 'Go up, and bury thy father, according as he made thee
swear'.

7And Joseph went up to bury his father: and with him went up all the
servants of Pharaoh, the elders of his house, and all the elders of the

land of Egypt, [8]and all the house of Joseph, and his brethren, and his father's house: only their little ones, and their flocks, and their herds, they left in the land of Goshen. [9]And there went up with him both chariots and horsemen: and it was a very great company. [10]And they came to the threshing-floor of Atad, which is beyond Jordan, and there they mourned with a great and very sore lamentation: and he made a mourning for his father seven days. [11]And when the inhabitants of the land, the Canaanites, saw the mourning in the floor of Atad, they said, 'This is a grievous mourning to the Egyptians': wherefore the name of it was called Abel-mizraim, which is beyond Jordan. [12]And his sons did unto him according as he commanded them. [13]For his sons carried him into the land of Canaan, and buried him in the cave of the field of Machpelah, which Abraham bought with the field for a possession of a burying-place of Ephron the Hittite, before Mamre.

[14]And Joseph returned into Egypt, he, and his brethren, and all that went up with him to bury his father, after he had buried his father.

[15]And when Joseph's brethren saw that their father was dead, they said, 'Joseph will peradventure hate us, and will certainly requite us all the evil which we did unto him'. [16]And they sent a messenger unto Joseph, saying, 'Thy father did command before he died, saying, [17]"So shall ye say unto Joseph, 'Forgive, I pray thee now, the trespass of thy brethren, and their sin: for they did unto thee evil'": and now, we pray thee, forgive the trespass of the servants of the God of thy father'. And Joseph wept when they spoke unto him. [18]And his brethren also went and fell down before his face, and they said, 'Behold, we be thy servants'. [19]And Joseph said unto them, 'Fear not: for am I in the place of God? [20]But as for you, ye thought evil against me, but God meant it unto good, to bring to pass, as it is this day, to save much people alive. [21]Now therefore fear ye not: I will nourish you, and your little ones.' And he comforted them, and spoke kindly unto them.

[22]And Joseph dwelt in Egypt, he, and his father's house: and Joseph lived a hundred and ten years. [23]And Joseph saw Ephraim's children of the third generation: the children also of Machir the son of Manasseh were brought up upon Joseph's knees. [24]And Joseph said unto his brethren, 'I die: and God will surely visit you, and bring you out of this land unto the land which he swore to Abraham, to Isaac, and to Jacob'. [25]And Joseph took an oath of the children of Israel, saying, 'God will surely visit you, and ye shall carry up my bones from hence'. [26]So Joseph died, being a hundred and ten years old: and they embalmed him, and he was put in a coffin in Egypt.

THE SECOND BOOK OF MOSES,

CALLED

EXODUS

1 Now these are the names of the children of Israel, which came into Egypt; every man and his household came with Jacob. ²Reuben, Simeon, Levi, and Judah, ³Issachar, Zebulun, and Benjamin, ⁴Dan, and Naphtali, Gad, and Asher. ⁵And all the souls that came out of the loins of Jacob were seventy souls: for Joseph was in Egypt already. ⁶And Joseph died, and all his brethren, and all that generation.

⁷And the children of Israel were fruitful, and increased abundantly, and multiplied, and waxed exceeding mighty, and the land was filled with them. ⁸Now there arose up a new king over Egypt, which knew not Joseph. ⁹And he said unto his people, 'Behold, the people of the children of Israel are more and mightier than we. ¹⁰Come on, let us deal wisely with them, lest they multiply, and it come to pass that, when there falleth out any war, they join also unto our enemies, and fight against us, and so get them up out of the land.' ¹¹Therefore they did set over them taskmasters to afflict them with their burdens. And they built for Pharaoh treasure-cities, Pithom and Raamses. ¹²But the more they afflicted them, the more they multiplied and grew. And they were grieved because of the children of Israel. ¹³And the Egyptians made the children of Israel to serve with rigour. ¹⁴And they made their lives bitter with hard bondage, in mortar, and in brick, and in all manner of service in the field: all their service, wherein they made them serve, was with rigour.

¹⁵And the king of Egypt spoke to the Hebrew midwives, of which the name of the one was Shiphrah, and the name of the other Puah: ¹⁶and he said, 'When ye do the office of a midwife to the Hebrew women, and see them upon the stools, if it be a son, then ye shall kill him: but if it be a daughter, then she shall live'. ¹⁷But the midwives feared God, and did not as the king of Egypt commanded them, but saved the men-children alive. ¹⁸And the king of Egypt called for the midwives, and said unto them, 'Why have ye done this thing, and have saved the men-children alive?' ¹⁹And the midwives said unto Pharaoh, 'Because the Hebrew women are not as the Egyptian women: for they are lively, and are delivered ere the midwives come in unto them'. ²⁰Therefore God dealt well with the midwives: and the people multiplied, and waxed very mighty. ²¹And it came to pass, because the midwives feared God, that he made them houses. ²²And Pharaoh charged all his people, saying, 'Every son that is born ye shall cast into the river, and every daughter ye shall save alive'.

2 And there went a man of the house of Levi, and took to wife a daughter of Levi. ²And the woman conceived, and bore a son: and when she saw him that he was a goodly child, she hid him three

67

months. ³And when she could not longer hide him, she took for him an ark of bulrushes, and daubed it with slime and with pitch, and put the child therein, and she laid it in the flags by the river's brink. ⁴And his sister stood afar off, to wit what would be done to him.

⁵And the daughter of Pharaoh came down to wash herself at the river, and her maidens walked along by the river's side: and when she saw the ark among the flags, she sent her maid to fetch it. ⁶And when she had opened it, she saw the child: and behold, the babe wept. And she had compassion on him, and said, 'This is one of the Hebrews' children'. ⁷Then said his sister to Pharaoh's daughter, 'Shall I go and call to thee a nurse of the Hebrew women, that she may nurse the child for thee?' ⁸And Pharaoh's daughter said to her, 'Go'. And the maid went and called the child's mother. ⁹And Pharaoh's daughter said unto her, 'Take this child away, and nurse it for me, and I will give thee thy wages'. And the woman took the child, and nursed it. ¹⁰And the child grew, and she brought him unto Pharaoh's daughter, and he became her son. And she called his name Moses: and she said, 'Because I drew him out of the water'.

¹¹And it came to pass in those days, when Moses was grown, that he went out unto his brethren, and looked on their burdens, and he spied an Egyptian smiting a Hebrew, one of his brethren. ¹²And he looked this way and that way, and when he saw that there was no man, he slew the Egyptian, and hid him in the sand. ¹³And when he went out the second day, behold, two men of the Hebrews strove together: and he said to him that did the wrong, 'Wherefore smitest thou thy fellow?' ¹⁴And he said, 'Who made thee a prince and a judge over us? intendest thou to kill me, as thou killedst the Egyptian?' And Moses feared, and said, 'Surely this thing is known'.

¹⁵Now when Pharaoh heard this thing, he sought to slay Moses. But Moses fled from the face of Pharaoh, and dwelt in the land of Midian: and he sat down by a well. ¹⁶Now the priest of Midian had seven daughters, and they came and drew water, and filled the troughs to water their father's flock. ¹⁷And the shepherds came and drove them away: but Moses stood up and helped them, and watered their flock. ¹⁸And when they came to Reuel their father, he said, 'How is it that you are come so soon today?' ¹⁹And they said, 'An Egyptian delivered us out of the hand of the shepherds, and also drew water enough for us, and watered the flock'. ²⁰And he said unto his daughters, 'And where is he? why is it that ye have left the man? Call him, that he may eat bread.' ²¹And Moses was content to dwell with the man, and he gave Moses Zipporah his daughter. ²²And she bore him a son, and he called his name Gershom: for he said, 'I have been a stranger in a strange land'.

²³And it came to pass in process of time, that the king of Egypt died, and the children of Israel sighed by reason of the bondage, and they cried, and their cry came up unto God by reason of the bondage. ²⁴And God heard their groaning, and God remembered his covenant with Abraham, with Isaac, and with Jacob. ²⁵And God looked upon the children of Israel, and God had respect unto them.

3 Now Moses kept the flock of Jethro his father-in-law, the priest of Midian: and he led the flock to the backside of the desert, and came to the mountain of God, even to Horeb. ²And the angel of the LORD appeared unto him in a flame of fire out of the midst of a bush, and he looked, and behold, the bush burnt with fire, and the bush was not consumed. ³And Moses said, 'I will now turn aside, and see this great sight, why the bush is not burnt'. ⁴And when the LORD saw that he turned aside to see, God called unto him out of the midst of the bush, and said, 'Moses, Moses'. And he said, 'Here am I'. ⁵And he said, 'Draw not nigh hither: put off thy shoes from off thy feet, for the place whereon thou standest is holy ground'. ⁶Moreover he said, 'I am the God of thy father, the God of Abraham, the God of Isaac, and the God of Jacob'. And Moses hid his face: for he was afraid to look upon God.

⁷And the LORD said, 'I have surely seen the affliction of my people which are in Egypt, and have heard their cry by reason of their taskmasters: for I know their sorrows; ⁸and I am come down to deliver them out of the hand of the Egyptians, and to bring them up out of that land unto a good land and a large, unto a land flowing with milk and honey, unto the place of the Canaanites, and the Hittites, and the Amorites, and the Perizzites, and the Hivites, and the Jebusites. ⁹Now therefore behold, the cry of the children of Israel is come unto me: and I have also seen the oppression wherewith the Egyptians oppress them. ¹⁰Come now therefore, and I will send thee unto Pharaoh, that thou mayest bring forth my people the children of Israel out of Egypt.'

¹¹And Moses said unto God, 'Who am I, that I should go unto Pharaoh, and that I should bring forth the children of Israel out of Egypt?' ¹²And he said, 'Certainly I will be with thee, and this shall be a token unto thee, that I have sent thee: when thou hast brought forth the people out of Egypt, ye shall serve God upon this mountain'. ¹³And Moses said unto God, 'Behold, when I come unto the children of Israel, and shall say unto them, "The God of your fathers hath sent me unto you"; and they shall say to me, "What is his name?" what shall I say unto them?' ¹⁴And God said unto Moses, 'I AM THAT I AM': and he said, 'Thus shalt thou say unto the children of Israel, "I AM hath sent me unto you"'. ¹⁵And God said moreover unto Moses, 'Thus shalt thou say unto the children of Israel, "The LORD God of your fathers, the God of Abraham, the God of Isaac, and the God of Jacob, hath sent me unto you: this is my name for ever, and this is my memorial unto all generations". ¹⁶Go, and gather the elders of Israel together, and say unto them, "The LORD God of your fathers, the God of Abraham, of Isaac, and of Jacob, appeared unto me, saying, 'I have surely visited you, and seen that which is done to you in Egypt'". ¹⁷And I have said, "I will bring you up out of the affliction of Egypt unto the land of the Canaanites, and the Hittites, and the Amorites, and the Perizzites, and the Hivites, and the Jebusites, unto a land flowing with milk and honey". ¹⁸And they shall hearken to thy voice: and thou shalt come, thou and the elders of

Israel, unto the king of Egypt, and you shall say unto him, "The LORD God of the Hebrews hath met with us: and now let us go, we beseech thee, three days' journey into the wilderness, that we may sacrifice to the LORD our God". ¹⁹And I am sure that the king of Egypt will not let you go, no, not by a mighty hand. ²⁰And I will stretch out my hand, and smite Egypt with all my wonders which I will do in the midst thereof: and after that he will let you go. ²¹And I will give this people favour in the sight of the Egyptians: and it shall come to pass, that, when ye go, ye shall not go empty: ²²but every woman shall borrow of her neighbour, and of her that sojourneth in her house, jewels of silver, and jewels of gold, and raiment: and ye shall put them upon your sons, and upon your daughters, and ye shall spoil the Egyptians.'

4 And Moses answered and said, 'But behold, they will not believe me, nor hearken unto my voice: for they will say, "The LORD hath not appeared unto thee"'. ²And the LORD said unto him, 'What is that in thy hand?' And he said, 'A rod'. ³And he said, 'Cast it on the ground'. And he cast it on the ground, and it became a serpent: and Moses fled from before it. ⁴And the LORD said unto Moses, 'Put forth thy hand, and take it by the tail'. And he put forth his hand, and caught it, and it became a rod in his hand: ⁵'That they may believe that the LORD God of their fathers, the God of Abraham, the God of Isaac, and the God of Jacob, hath appeared unto thee'.

⁶And the LORD said furthermore unto him, 'Put now thy hand into thy bosom'. And he put his hand into his bosom: and when he took it out, behold, his hand was leprous as snow. ⁷And he said, 'Put thy hand into thy bosom again'. And he put his hand into his bosom again, and plucked it out of his bosom, and behold, it was turned again as his other flesh. ⁸'And it shall come to pass, if they will not believe thee, neither hearken to the voice of the first sign, that they will believe the voice of the latter sign. ⁹And it shall come to pass, if they will not believe also these two signs, neither hearken unto thy voice, that thou shalt take of the water of the river, and pour it upon the dry land: and the water which thou takest out of the river shall become blood upon the dry land.'

¹⁰And Moses said unto the LORD, 'O my Lord, I am not eloquent, neither heretofore, nor since thou hast spoken unto thy servant: but I am slow of speech, and of a slow tongue'. ¹¹And the LORD said unto him, 'Who hath made man's mouth? or who maketh the dumb, or deaf, or the seeing, or the blind? have not I the LORD? ¹²Now therefore go, and I will be with thy mouth, and teach thee what thou shalt say.' ¹³And he said, 'O my Lord, send, I pray thee, by the hand of him whom thou wilt send'. ¹⁴And the anger of the LORD was kindled against Moses, and he said, 'Is not Aaron the Levite thy brother? I know that he can speak well. And also behold, he cometh forth to meet thee: and when he seeth thee, he will be glad in his heart. ¹⁵And thou shalt speak unto him, and put words in his mouth: and I will be with thy mouth, and with his mouth, and will teach you what ye shall do. ¹⁶And he shall be thy spokesman unto the people: and he shall be, even he shall be to thee in

stead of a mouth, and thou shalt be to him in stead of God. ¹⁷And thou shalt take this rod in thy hand, wherewith thou shalt do signs.'

¹⁸And Moses went and returned to Jethro his father-in-law, and said unto him, 'Let me go, I pray thee, and return unto my brethren which are in Egypt, and see whether they be yet alive'. And Jethro said to Moses, 'Go in peace'. ¹⁹And the LORD said unto Moses in Midian, 'Go, return into Egypt: for all the men are dead which sought thy life'. ²⁰And Moses took his wife and his sons, and set them upon an ass, and he returned to the land of Egypt. And Moses took the rod of God in his hand. ²¹And the LORD said unto Moses, 'When thou goest to return into Egypt, see that thou do all those wonders before Pharaoh, which I have put in thy hand: but I will harden his heart, that he shall not let the people go. ²²And thou shalt say unto Pharaoh, "Thus saith the LORD, Israel is my son, even my firstborn. ²³And I say unto thee, let my son go, that he may serve me: and if thou refuse to let him go, behold, I will slay thy son, even thy firstborn."'

²⁴And it came to pass by the way in the inn, that the LORD met him, and sought to kill him. ²⁵Then Zipporah took a sharp stone, and cut off the foreskin of her son, and cast it at his feet, and said, 'Surely a bloody husband art thou to me'. ²⁶So he let him go: then she said, 'A bloody husband thou art, because of the circumcision'.

²⁷And the LORD said to Aaron, 'Go into the wilderness to meet Moses'. And he went, and met him in the mount of God, and kissed him. ²⁸And Moses told Aaron all the words of the LORD who had sent him, and all the signs which he had commanded him.

²⁹And Moses and Aaron went and gathered together all the elders of the children of Israel. ³⁰And Aaron spoke all the words which the LORD had spoken unto Moses, and did the signs in the sight of the people. ³¹And the people believed: and when they heard that the LORD had visited the children of Israel, and that he had looked upon their affliction, then they bowed their heads and worshipped.

5 And afterward Moses and Aaron went in, and told Pharaoh, 'Thus saith the LORD God of Israel, "Let my people go, that they may hold a feast unto me in the wilderness"'. ²And Pharaoh said, 'Who is the LORD, that I should obey his voice to let Israel go? I know not the LORD, neither will I let Israel go.' ³And they said, 'The God of the Hebrews hath met with us: let us go, we pray thee, three days' journey into the desert, and sacrifice unto the LORD our God, lest he fall upon us with pestilence, or with the sword'. ⁴And the king of Egypt said unto them, 'Wherefore do ye, Moses and Aaron, let the people from their works? get you unto your burdens'. ⁵And Pharaoh said, 'Behold, the people of the land now are many, and you make them rest from their burdens'.

⁶And Pharaoh commanded the same day the taskmasters of the people, and their officers, saying, ⁷'Ye shall no more give the people straw to make brick, as heretofore: let them go and gather straw for themselves. ⁸And the tale of the bricks, which they did make heretofore, you shall lay upon them: you shall not diminish aught thereof: for they be idle; therefore they cry, saying, "Let us go and sacrifice to our God". ⁹Let

there more work be laid upon the men, that they may labour therein; and let them not regard vain words.'

¹⁰And the taskmasters of the people went out, and their officers, and they spoke to the people, saying, 'Thus saith Pharaoh, "I will not give you straw. ¹¹Go ye, get you straw where you can find it: yet not aught of your work shall be diminished."' ¹²So the people were scattered abroad throughout all the land of Egypt to gather stubble instead of straw. ¹³And the taskmasters hasted them, saying, 'Fulfil your works, your daily tasks, as when there was straw'. ¹⁴And the officers of the children of Israel, which Pharaoh's taskmasters had set over them, were beaten, and demanded, 'Wherefore have ye not fulfilled your task in making brick both yesterday and today, as heretofore?'

¹⁵Then the officers of the children of Israel came and cried unto Pharaoh, saying, 'Wherefore dealest thou thus with thy servants? ¹⁶There is no straw given unto thy servants, and they say to us, "Make brick": and behold, thy servants are beaten; but the fault is in thy own people.' ¹⁷But he said, 'Ye are idle, ye are idle: therefore ye say, "Let us go and do sacrifice to the LORD". ¹⁸Go therefore now, and work: for there shall no straw be given you, yet shall ye deliver the tale of bricks.' ¹⁹And the officers of the children of Israel did see that they were in evil case, after it was said, 'Ye shall not minish aught from your bricks of your daily task'.

²⁰And they met Moses and Aaron, who stood in the way, as they came forth from Pharaoh. ²¹And they said unto them, 'The LORD look upon you, and judge; because you have made our savour to be abhorred in the eyes of Pharaoh, and in the eyes of his servants, to put a sword in their hand to slay us'. ²²And Moses returned unto the LORD, and said, 'Lord, wherefore hast thou so evil entreated this people? why is it that thou hast sent me? ²³For since I came to Pharaoh to speak in thy name, he hath done evil to this people, neither hast thou delivered thy people at all.'

6 Then the LORD said unto Moses, 'Now shalt thou see what I will do to Pharaoh: for with a strong hand shall he let them go, and with a strong hand shall he drive them out of his land'.

²And God spoke unto Moses, and said unto him, 'I am the LORD. ³And I appeared unto Abraham, unto Isaac, and unto Jacob, by the name of God Almighty, but by my name JEHOVAH was I not known to them. ⁴And I have also established my covenant with them, to give them the land of Canaan, the land of their pilgrimage, wherein they were strangers. ⁵And I have also heard the groaning of the children of Israel, whom the Egyptians keep in bondage; and I have remembered my covenant. ⁶Wherefore say unto the children of Israel, "I am the LORD, and I will bring you out from under the burdens of the Egyptians, and I will rid you out of their bondage, and I will redeem you with a stretched out arm, and with great judgements. ⁷And I will take you to me for a people, and I will be to you a God: and ye shall know that I am the LORD your God, which bringeth you out from under the burdens of the Egyptians. ⁸And I will bring you in unto the land,

concerning the which I did swear to give it to Abraham, to Isaac, and to Jacob, and I will give it you for a heritage: I am the LORD."' ⁹And Moses spoke so unto the children of Israel: but they hearkened not unto Moses for anguish of spirit, and for cruel bondage.

¹⁰And the LORD spoke unto Moses, saying, ¹¹'Go in, speak unto Pharaoh king of Egypt, that he let the children of Israel go out of his land'. ¹²And Moses spoke before the LORD, saying, 'Behold, the children of Israel have not hearkened unto me: how then shall Pharaoh hear me, who am of uncircumcised lips?' ¹³And the LORD spoke unto Moses and unto Aaron, and gave them a charge unto the children of Israel, and unto Pharaoh king of Egypt, to bring the children of Israel out of the land of Egypt.

¹⁴These be the heads of their fathers' houses: the sons of Reuben the firstborn of Israel, Hanoch, and Pallu, Hezron, and Carmi: these be the families of Reuben. ¹⁵And the sons of Simeon: Jemuel, and Jamin, and Ohad, and Jachin, and Zohar, and Shaul the son of a Canaanitish woman: these are the families of Simeon.

¹⁶And these are the names of the sons of Levi according to their generations: Gershon, and Kohath, and Merari: and the years of the life of Levi were a hundred thirty and seven years. ¹⁷The sons of Gershon: Libni, and Shimi, according to their families. ¹⁸And the sons of Kohath: Amram, and Izhar, and Hebron, and Uzziel. And the years of the life of Kohath were a hundred thirty and three years. ¹⁹And the sons of Merari: Mahali and Mushi: these are the families of Levi according to their generations. ²⁰And Amram took him Jochebed his father's sister to wife, and she bore him Aaron and Moses: and the years of the life of Amram were a hundred and thirty and seven years. ²¹And the sons of Izhar: Korah, and Nepheg, and Zichri. ²²And the sons of Uzziel: Mishael, and Elzaphan, and Zithri. ²³And Aaron took him Elisheba, daughter of Amminadab, sister of Naashon, to wife, and she bore him Nadab, and Abihu, Eleazar, and Ithamar. ²⁴And the sons of Korah: Assir, and Elkanah, and Abiasaph: these are the families of the Korhites. ²⁵And Eleazar Aaron's son took him one of the daughters of Putiel to wife, and she bore him Phinehas: these are the heads of the fathers of the Levites according to their families. ²⁶These are that Aaron and Moses, to whom the LORD said, 'Bring out the children of Israel from the land of Egypt according to their armies'. ²⁷These are they which spoke to Pharaoh king of Egypt, to bring out the children of Israel from Egypt: these are that Moses and Aaron.

²⁸And it came to pass on the day when the LORD spoke unto Moses in the land of Egypt, ²⁹that the LORD spoke unto Moses, saying, 'I am the LORD: speak thou unto Pharaoh king of Egypt all that I say unto thee'. ³⁰And Moses said before the LORD, 'Behold, I am of uncircumcised lips, and how shall Pharaoh hearken unto me?'

7 And the LORD said unto Moses, 'See, I have made thee a god to Pharaoh: and Aaron thy brother shall be thy prophet. ²Thou shalt speak all that I command thee: and Aaron thy brother shall speak unto Pharaoh, that he send the children of Israel out of his land. ³And I will

harden Pharaoh's heart, and multiply my signs and my wonders in the land of Egypt. ⁴But Pharaoh shall not hearken unto you, that I may lay my hand upon Egypt, and bring forth my armies, and my people the children of Israel, out of the land of Egypt by great judgements. ⁵And the Egyptians shall know that I am the LORD, when I stretch forth my hand upon Egypt, and bring out the children of Israel from among them.' ⁶And Moses and Aaron did as the LORD commanded them, so did they. ⁷And Moses was fourscore years old, and Aaron fourscore and three years old, when they spoke unto Pharaoh.

⁸And the LORD spoke unto Moses and unto Aaron, saying, ⁹'When Pharaoh shall speak unto you, saying, "Show a miracle for you": then thou shalt say unto Aaron, "Take thy rod, and cast it before Pharaoh, and it shall become a serpent"'.

¹⁰And Moses and Aaron went in unto Pharaoh, and they did so as the LORD had commanded: and Aaron cast down his rod before Pharaoh, and before his servants, and it became a serpent. ¹¹Then Pharaoh also called the wise men and the sorcerers; now the magicians of Egypt, they also did in like manner with their enchantments. ¹²For they cast down every man his rod, and they became serpents: but Aaron's rod swallowed up their rods. ¹³And he hardened Pharaoh's heart, that he hearkened not unto them, as the LORD had said.

¹⁴And the LORD said unto Moses, 'Pharaoh's heart is hardened, he refuseth to let the people go. ¹⁵Get thee unto Pharaoh in the morning, lo, he goeth out unto the water, and thou shalt stand by the river's brink against he come: and the rod which was turned to a serpent shalt thou take in thy hand. ¹⁶And thou shalt say unto him, "The LORD God of the Hebrews hath sent me unto thee, saying, 'Let my people go, that they may serve me in the wilderness: and behold, hitherto thou wouldst not hear'. ¹⁷Thus saith the LORD, 'In this thou shalt know that I am the LORD: behold, I will smite with the rod that is in my hand upon the waters which are in the river, and they shall be turned to blood. ¹⁸And the fish that is in the river shall die, and the river shall stink, and the Egyptians shall loathe to drink of the water of the river.'"'

¹⁹And the LORD spoke unto Moses, 'Say unto Aaron, "Take thy rod, and stretch out thy hand upon the waters of Egypt, upon their streams, upon their rivers, and upon their ponds, and upon all their pools of water, that they may become blood, and that there may be blood throughout all the land of Egypt, both in vessels of wood, and in vessels of stone"'. ²⁰And Moses and Aaron did so, as the LORD commanded: and he lifted up the rod, and smote the waters that were in the river, in the sight of Pharaoh, and in the sight of his servants: and all the waters that were in the river were turned to blood. ²¹And the fish that was in the river died: and the river stank, and the Egyptians could not drink of the water of the river; and there was blood throughout all the land of Egypt. ²²And the magicians of Egypt did so with their enchantments: and Pharaoh's heart was hardened, neither did he hearken unto them; as the LORD had said. ²³And Pharaoh turned and went into his house,

neither did he set his heart to this also. ²⁴And all the Egyptians dug round about the river for water to drink: for they could not drink of the water of the river. ²⁵And seven days were fulfilled after that the LORD had smitten the river.

8 And the LORD spoke unto Moses, 'Go unto Pharaoh, and say unto him, "Thus saith the LORD, 'Let my people go, that they may serve me. ²And if thou refuse to let them go, behold, I will smite all thy borders with frogs. ³And the river shall bring forth frogs abundantly, which shall go up and come into thy house, and into thy bedchamber, and upon thy bed, and into the house of thy servants, and upon thy people, and into thy ovens, and into thy kneading-troughs: ⁴and the frogs shall come up both on thee, and upon thy people, and upon all thy servants.'"'

⁵And the LORD spoke unto Moses, 'Say unto Aaron, "Stretch forth thy hand with thy rod over the streams, over the rivers, and over the ponds, and cause frogs to come up upon the land of Egypt"'. ⁶And Aaron stretched out his hand over the waters of Egypt,and the frogs came up, and covered the land of Egypt. ⁷And the magicians did so with their enchantments, and brought up frogs upon the land of Egypt.

⁸Then Pharaoh called for Moses and Aaron, and said, 'Entreat the LORD, that he may take away the frogs from me, and from my people: and I will let the people go, that they may do sacrifice unto the LORD'. ⁹And Moses said unto Pharaoh, 'Glory over me: when shall I entreat for thee, and for thy servants, and for thy people, to destroy the frogs from thee and thy houses, that they may remain in the river only?' ¹⁰And he said, 'Tomorrow'. And he said, 'Be it according to thy word: that thou mayest know that there is none like unto the LORD our God. ¹¹And the frogs shall depart from thee, and from thy houses, and from thy servants, and from thy people; they shall remain in the river only.' ¹²And Moses and Aaron went out from Pharaoh: and Moses cried unto the LORD because of the frogs which he had brought against Pharaoh. ¹³And the LORD did according to the word of Moses: and the frogs died out of the houses, out of the villages, and out of the fields. ¹⁴And they gathered them together upon heaps, and the land stank. ¹⁵But when Pharaoh saw that there was respite, he hardened his heart, and hearkened not unto them, as the LORD had said.

¹⁶And the LORD said unto Moses, 'Say unto Aaron, "Stretch out thy rod, and smite the dust of the land, that it may become lice throughout all the land of Egypt"'. ¹⁷And they did so: for Aaron stretched out his hand with his rod, and smote the dust of the earth, and it became lice in man, and in beast: all the dust of the land became lice throughout all the land of Egypt. ¹⁸And the magicians did so with their enchantments to bring forth lice, but they could not: so there were lice upon man, and upon beast. ¹⁹Then the magicians said unto Pharaoh, 'This is the finger of God'. And Pharaoh's heart was hardened, and he hearkened not unto them, as the LORD had said.

²⁰And the LORD said unto Moses, 'Rise up early in the morning, and stand before Pharaoh: lo, he cometh forth to the water, and say unto

him, "Thus saith the LORD, 'Let my people go, that they may serve me. ²¹Else, if thou wilt not let my people go, behold, I will send swarms of flies upon thee, and upon thy servants, and upon thy people, and into thy houses: and the houses of the Egyptians shall be full of swarms of flies, and also the ground whereon they are. ²²And I will sever in that day the land of Goshen, in which my people dwell, that no swarms of flies shall be there, to the end thou mayest know that I am the LORD in the midst of the earth. ²³And I will put a division between my people and thy people: tomorrow shall this sign be.'"' ²⁴And the LORD did so: and there came a grievous swarm of flies into the house of Pharaoh, and into his servants' houses, and into all the land of Egypt: the land was corrupted by reason of the swarm of flies.

²⁵And Pharaoh called for Moses and for Aaron, and said, 'Go ye, sacrifice to your God in the land'. ²⁶And Moses said, 'It is not meet so to do; for we shall sacrifice the abomination of the Egyptians to the LORD our God: lo, shall we sacrifice the abomination of the Egyptians before their eyes, and will they not stone us? ²⁷We will go three days' journey into the wilderness, and sacrifice to the LORD our God, as he shall command us.' ²⁸And Pharaoh said, 'I will let you go, that ye may sacrifice to the LORD your God in the wilderness; only you shall not go very far away: entreat for me'. ²⁹And Moses said, 'Behold, I go out from thee, and I will entreat the LORD that the swarms of flies may depart from Pharaoh, from his servants, and from his people, tomorrow: but let not Pharaoh deal deceitfully any more in not letting the people go to sacrifice to the LORD'.

³⁰And Moses went out from Pharaoh, and entreated the LORD. ³¹And the LORD did according to the word of Moses: and he removed the swarms of flies from Pharaoh, from his servants, and from his people: there remained not one. ³²And Pharaoh hardened his heart at this time also, neither would he let the people go.

9 Then the LORD said unto Moses, 'Go in unto Pharaoh, and tell him, "Thus saith the LORD God of the Hebrews, 'Let my people go, that they may serve me. ²For if thou refuse to let them go, and wilt hold them still, ³behold, the hand of the LORD is upon thy cattle which is in the field, upon the horses, upon the asses, upon the camels, upon the oxen, and upon the sheep: there shall be a very grievous murrain. ⁴And the LORD shall sever between the cattle of Israel and the cattle of Egypt, and there shall nothing die of all that is the children's of Israel.'"' ⁵And the LORD appointed a set time, saying, 'Tomorrow the LORD shall do this thing in the land'. ⁶And the LORD did that thing on the morrow, and all the cattle of Egypt died, but of the cattle of the children of Israel died not one. ⁷And Pharaoh sent, and behold, there was not one of the cattle of the Israelites dead. And the heart of Pharaoh was hardened, and he did not let the people go.

⁸And the LORD said unto Moses and unto Aaron, 'Take to you handfuls of ashes of the furnace, and let Moses sprinkle it towards the heaven in the sight of Pharaoh. ⁹And it shall become small dust in all the land of Egypt, and shall be a boil breaking forth with blains upon

man, and upon beast, throughout all the land of Egypt.' ¹⁰And they took ashes of the furnace, and stood before Pharaoh, and Moses sprinkled it up toward heaven: and it became a boil breaking forth with blains upon man, and upon beast. ¹¹And the magicians could not stand before Moses because of the boils: for the boil was upon the magicians, and upon all the Egyptians. ¹²And the LORD hardened the heart of Pharaoh, and he hearkened not unto them, as the LORD had spoken unto Moses.

¹³And the LORD said unto Moses, 'Rise up early in the morning, and stand before Pharaoh, and say unto him, "Thus saith the LORD God of the Hebrews, 'Let my people go, that they may serve me. ¹⁴For I will at this time send all my plagues upon thy heart, and upon thy servants, and upon thy people: that thou mayest know that there is none like me in all the earth. ¹⁵For now I will stretch out my hand, that I may smite thee and thy people with pestilence, and thou shalt be cut off from the earth. ¹⁶And in very deed for this cause have I raised thee up, for to show in thee my power, and that my name may be declared throughout all the earth. ¹⁷As yet exaltest thou thyself against my people, that thou wilt not let them go? ¹⁸Behold, tomorrow about this time I will cause it to rain a very grievous hail, such as hath not been in Egypt since the foundation thereof even until now. ¹⁹Send therefore now, and gather thy cattle, and all that thou hast in the field: for upon every man and beast which shall be found in the field, and shall not be brought home, the hail shall come down upon them, and they shall die.'"' ²⁰He that feared the word of the LORD amongst the servants of Pharaoh made his servants and his cattle flee into the houses. ²¹And he that regarded not the word of the LORD left his servants and his cattle in the field.

²²And the LORD said unto Moses, 'Stretch forth thy hand toward heaven, that there may be hail in all the land of Egypt, upon man, and upon beast, and upon every herb of the field, throughout the land of Egypt'. ²³And Moses stretched forth his rod toward heaven, and the LORD sent thunder and hail, and the fire ran along upon the ground, and the LORD rained hail upon the land of Egypt. ²⁴So there was hail, and fire mingled with the hail, very grievous, such as there was none like it in all the land of Egypt since it became a nation. ²⁵And the hail smote throughout all the land of Egypt all that was in the field, both man and beast; and the hail smote every herb of the field, and broke every tree of the field. ²⁶Only in the land of Goshen, where the children of Israel were, was there no hail.

²⁷And Pharaoh sent, and called for Moses and Aaron, and said unto them, 'I have sinned this time: the LORD is righteous, and I and my people are wicked. ²⁸Entreat the LORD (for it is enough) that there be no more mighty thunderings and hail, and I will let you go, and ye shall stay no longer.' ²⁹And Moses said unto him, 'As soon as I am gone out of the city, I will spread abroad my hands unto the LORD, and the thunder shall cease, neither shall there be any more hail: that thou mayest know how that the earth is the LORD's. ³⁰But as for thee and thy servants, I know that ye will not yet fear the LORD God.' ³¹And the flax and

the barley was smitten: for the barley was in the ear, and the flax was bolled. ³²But the wheat and the rye were not smitten: for they were not grown up. ³³And Moses went out of the city from Pharaoh, and spread abroad his hands unto the LORD: and the thunders and hail ceased, and the rain was not poured upon the earth. ³⁴And when Pharaoh saw that the rain and the hail and the thunders were ceased, he sinned yet more, and hardened his heart, he and his servants. ³⁵And the heart of Pharaoh was hardened, neither would he let the children of Israel go, as the LORD had spoken by Moses.

10 And the LORD said unto Moses, 'Go in unto Pharaoh: for I have hardened his heart, and the heart of his servants, that I might show these my signs before him: ²and that thou mayest tell in the ears of thy son, and of thy son's son, what things I have wrought in Egypt, and my signs which I have done amongst them, that ye may know how that I am the LORD'. ³And Moses and Aaron came in unto Pharaoh, and said unto him, 'Thus saith the LORD God of the Hebrews, "How long wilt thou refuse to humble thyself before me? Let my people go, that they may serve me. ⁴Else, if thou refuse to let my people go, behold, tomorrow will I bring the locusts into thy coast. ⁵And they shall cover the face of the earth, that one cannot be able to see the earth, and they shall eat the residue of that which is escaped, which remaineth unto you from the hail, and shall eat every tree which groweth for you out of the field. ⁶And they shall fill thy houses, and the houses of all thy servants, and the houses of all the Egyptians, which neither thy fathers, nor thy fathers' fathers have seen, since the day that they were upon the earth unto this day."' And he turned himself, and went out from Pharaoh. ⁷And Pharaoh's servants said unto him, 'How long shall this man be a snare unto us? Let the men go, that they may serve the LORD their God: knowest thou not yet that Egypt is destroyed?' ⁸And Moses and Aaron were brought again unto Pharaoh: and he said unto them, 'Go, serve the LORD your God: but who are they that shall go?' ⁹And Moses said, 'We will go with our young and with our old, with our sons and with our daughters, with our flocks and with our herds will we go: for we must hold a feast unto the LORD'. ¹⁰And he said unto them, 'Let the LORD be so with you, as I will let you go, and your little ones. Look to it, for evil is before you. ¹¹Not so: go now ye that are men, and serve the LORD, for that you did desire.' And they were driven out from Pharaoh's presence.

¹²And the LORD said unto Moses, 'Stretch out thy hand over the land of Egypt for the locusts, that they may come up upon the land of Egypt, and eat every herb of the land, even all that the hail hath left'. ¹³And Moses stretched forth his rod over the land of Egypt, and the LORD brought an east wind upon the land all that day, and all that night; and when it was morning, the east wind brought the locusts. ¹⁴And the locusts went up over all the land of Egypt, and rested in all the coasts of Egypt: very grievous were they: before them there were no such locusts as they, neither after them shall be such. ¹⁵For they covered the face of the whole earth, so that the land was darkened, and they did eat every

herb of the land, and all the fruit of the trees which the hail had left, and there remained not any green thing in the trees, or in the herbs of the field, through all the land of Egypt. ¹⁶Then Pharaoh called for Moses and Aaron in haste: and he said, 'I have sinned against the LORD your God, and against you. ¹⁷Now therefore forgive, I pray thee, my sin only this once, and entreat the LORD your God, that he may take away from me this death only.' ¹⁸And he went out from Pharaoh, and entreated the LORD. ¹⁹And the LORD turned a mighty strong west wind, which took away the locusts, and cast them into the Red Sea: there remained not one locust in all the coasts of Egypt. ²⁰But the LORD hardened Pharaoh's heart, so that he would not let the children of Israel go.

²¹And the LORD said unto Moses, 'Stretch out thy hand toward heaven, that there may be darkness over the land of Egypt, even darkness which may be felt'. ²²And Moses stretched forth his hand toward heaven: and there was a thick darkness in all the land of Egypt three days. ²³They saw not one another, neither rose any from his place for three days: but all the children of Israel had light in their dwellings.

²⁴And Pharaoh called unto Moses, and said, 'Go ye, serve the LORD: only let your flocks and your herds be stayed: let your little ones also go with you'. ²⁵And Moses said, 'Thou must give us also sacrifices and burnt offerings, that we may sacrifice unto the LORD our God. ²⁶Our cattle also shall go with us: there shall not a hoof be left behind: for thereof must we take to serve the LORD our God: and we know not with what we must serve the LORD, until we come thither.'

²⁷But the LORD hardened Pharaoh's heart, and he would not let them go. ²⁸And Pharaoh said unto him, 'Get thee from me, take heed to thyself, see my face no more: for in that day thou seest my face thou shalt die'. ²⁹And Moses said, 'Thou hast spoken well, I will see thy face again no more'.

11 And the LORD said unto Moses, 'Yet will I bring one plague more upon Pharaoh, and upon Egypt; afterwards he will let you go hence: when he shall let you go, he shall surely thrust you out hence altogether. ²Speak now in the ears of the people, and let every man borrow of his neighbour, and every woman of her neighbour, jewels of silver, and jewels of gold.' ³And the LORD gave the people favour in the sight of the Egyptians. Moreover, the man Moses was very great in the land of Egypt, in the sight of Pharaoh's servants, and in the sight of the people.

⁴And Moses said, 'Thus saith the LORD, "About midnight will I go out into the midst of Egypt. ⁵And all the firstborn in the land of Egypt shall die, from the firstborn of Pharaoh that sitteth upon his throne, even unto the firstborn of the maidservant that is behind the mill, and all the firstborn of beasts. ⁶And there shall be a great cry throughout all the land of Egypt, such as there was none like it, nor shall be like it any more." ⁷But against any of the children of Israel shall not a dog move his tongue, against man or beast: that ye may know how that the LORD doth put a difference between the Egyptians and Israel. ⁸And all these

thy servants shall come down unto me, and bow down themselves unto me, saying, "Get thee out, and all the people that follow thee": and after that I will go out.' And he went out from Pharaoh in a great anger.

⁹And the LORD said unto Moses, 'Pharaoh shall not hearken unto you, that my wonders may be multiplied in the land of Egypt'. ¹⁰And Moses and Aaron did all these wonders before Pharaoh: and the LORD hardened Pharaoh's heart, so that he would not let the children of Israel go out of his land.

12 And the LORD spoke unto Moses and Aaron in the land of Egypt, saying, ²'This month shall be unto you the beginning of months: it shall be the first month of the year to you.

³'Speak ye unto all the congregation of Israel, saying, "In the tenth day of this month they shall take to them every man a lamb, according to the house of their fathers, a lamb for a house. ⁴And if the household be too little for the lamb, let him and his neighbour next unto his house take it according to the number of the souls: every man according to his eating shall make your count for the lamb. ⁵Your lamb shall be without blemish, a male of the first year: ye shall take it out from the sheep, or from the goats. ⁶And ye shall keep it up until the fourteenth day of the same month: and the whole assembly of the congregation of Israel shall kill it in the evening. ⁷And they shall take of the blood, and strike it on the two side-posts and on the upper door-post of the houses wherein they shall eat it. ⁸And they shall eat the flesh in that night, roast with fire, and unleavened bread, and with bitter herbs they shall eat it. ⁹Eat not of it raw, nor seethed at all with water, but roast with fire: his head with his legs, and with the purtenance thereof. ¹⁰And ye shall let nothing of it remain until the morning: and that which remaineth of it until the morning ye shall burn with fire.

¹¹'"And thus shall ye eat it: with your loins girded, your shoes on your feet, and your staff in your hand; and ye shall eat it in haste: it is the LORD's passover. ¹²For I will pass through the land of Egypt this night, and will smite all the firstborn in the land of Egypt, both man and beast, and against all the gods of Egypt I will execute judgement: I am the LORD. ¹³And the blood shall be to you for a token upon the houses where you are: and when I see the blood, I will pass over you, and the plague shall not be upon you to destroy you, when I smite the land of Egypt. ¹⁴And this day shall be unto you for a memorial: and you shall keep it a feast to the LORD throughout your generations: you shall keep it a feast by an ordinance for ever. ¹⁵Seven days shall ye eat unleavened bread, even the first day ye shall put away leaven out of your houses: for whosoever eateth leavened bread from the first day until the seventh day, that soul shall be cut off from Israel. ¹⁶And in the first day there shall be a holy convocation, and in the seventh day there shall be a holy convocation to you: no manner of work shall be done in them, save that which every man must eat, that only may be done of you. ¹⁷And ye shall observe the feast of unleavened bread: for in this selfsame day have I brought your armies out of the land of Egypt: therefore shall ye observe this day in your generations by an ordinance for ever.

[18]"'In the first month, on the fourteenth day of the month at even, ye shall eat unleavened bread, until the one and twentieth day of the month at even. [19]Seven days shall there be no leaven found in your houses: for whosoever eateth that which is leavened, even that soul shall be cut off from the congregation of Israel, whether he be a stranger, or born in the land. [20]Ye shall eat nothing leavened: in all your habitations shall ye eat unleavened bread."'

[21]Then Moses called for all the elders of Israel, and said unto them, 'Draw out and take you a lamb according to your families, and kill the passover. [22]And ye shall take a bunch of hyssop, and dip it in the blood that is in the basin, and strike the lintel and the two side-posts with the blood that is in the basin: and none of you shall go out at the door of his house until the morning. [23]For the LORD will pass through to smite the Egyptians; and when he seeth the blood upon the lintel, and on the two side-posts, the LORD will pass over the door, and will not suffer the destroyer to come in unto your houses to smite you. [24]And ye shall observe this thing for an ordinance to thee and to thy sons for ever. [25]And it shall come to pass, when ye be come to the land which the LORD will give you, according as he hath promised, that ye shall keep this service. [26]And it shall come to pass, when your children shall say unto you, "What mean you by this service?" [27]that ye shall say, "It is the sacrifice of the LORD's passover, who passed over the houses of the children of Israel in Egypt, when he smote the Egyptians, and delivered our houses".' And the people bowed the head and worshipped. [28]And the children of Israel went away, and did as the LORD had commanded Moses and Aaron, so did they.

[29]And it came to pass, that at midnight the LORD smote all the firstborn in the land of Egypt, from the firstborn of Pharaoh that sat on his throne unto the firstborn of the captive that was in the dungeon, and all the firstborn of cattle. [30]And Pharaoh rose up in the night, he, and all his servants, and all the Egyptians; and there was a great cry in Egypt: for there was not a house where there was not one dead.

[31]And he called for Moses and Aaron by night, and said, 'Rise up, and get you forth from amongst my people, both you and the children of Israel: and go, serve the LORD, as ye have said. [32]Also take your flocks and your herds, as ye have said, and be gone, and bless me also.' [33]And the Egyptians were urgent upon the people, that they might send them out of the land in haste: for they said, 'We be all dead men'. [34]And the people took their dough before it was leavened, their kneading-troughs being bound up in their clothes upon their shoulders. [35]And the children of Israel did according to the word of Moses: and they borrowed of the Egyptians jewels of silver, and jewels of gold, and raiment. [36]And the LORD gave the people favour in the sight of the Egyptians, so that they lent unto them such things as they required. And they spoiled the Egyptians.

[37]And the children of Israel journeyed from Rameses to Succoth, about six hundred thousand on foot that were men, besides children. [38]And a mixed multitude went up also with them, and flocks, and

herds, even very much cattle. ³⁹And they baked unleavened cakes of the dough which they brought forth out of Egypt, for it was not leavened: because they were thrust out of Egypt, and could not tarry, neither had they prepared for themselves any victual.

⁴⁰Now the sojourning of the children of Israel, who dwelt in Egypt, was four hundred and thirty years. ⁴¹And it came to pass at the end of the four hundred and thirty years, even the selfsame day it came to pass, that all the hosts of the LORD went out from the land of Egypt. ⁴²It is a night to be much observed unto the LORD for bringing them out from the land of Egypt: this is that night of the LORD to be observed of all the children of Israel in their generations.

⁴³And the LORD said unto Moses and Aaron, 'This is the ordinance of the passover: there shall no stranger eat thereof. ⁴⁴But every man's servant that is bought for money, when thou hast circumcised him, then shall he eat thereof. ⁴⁵A foreigner and a hired servant shall not eat thereof. ⁴⁶In one house shall it be eaten; thou shalt not carry forth aught of the flesh abroad out of the house, neither shall ye break a bone thereof. ⁴⁷All the congregation of Israel shall keep it. ⁴⁸And when a stranger shall sojourn with thee, and will keep the passover to the LORD, let all his males be circumcised, and then let him come near and keep it: and he shall be as one that is born in the land: for no uncircumcised person shall eat thereof. ⁴⁹One law shall be to him that is home-born, and unto the stranger that sojourneth among you.'

⁵⁰Thus did all the children of Israel: as the LORD commanded Moses and Aaron, so did they. ⁵¹And it came to pass the selfsame day, that the LORD did bring the children of Israel out of the land of Egypt by their armies.

13 And the LORD spoke unto Moses, saying, ²'Sanctify unto me all the firstborn, whatsoever openeth the womb among the children of Israel, both of man and of beast: it is mine'.

³And Moses said unto the people, 'Remember this day, in which ye came out from Egypt, out of the house of bondage: for by strength of hand the LORD brought you out from this place: there shall no leavened bread be eaten. ⁴This day came ye out in the month Abib.

⁵'And it shall be when the LORD shall bring thee into the land of the Canaanites, and the Hittites, and the Amorites, and the Hivites, and the Jebusites, which he swore unto thy fathers to give thee, a land flowing with milk and honey, that thou shalt keep this service in this month. ⁶Seven days thou shalt eat unleavened bread, and in the seventh day shall be a feast to the LORD. ⁷Unleavened bread shall be eaten seven days: and there shall no leavened bread be seen with thee, neither shall there be leaven seen with thee in all thy quarters.

⁸'And thou shalt show thy son in that day, saying, "This is done because of that which the LORD did unto me when I came forth out of Egypt". ⁹And it shall be for a sign unto thee upon thy hand, and for a memorial between thine eyes, that the LORD's law may be in thy mouth: for with a strong hand hath the LORD brought thee out of Egypt. ¹⁰Thou shalt therefore keep this ordinance in his season from year to year.

¹¹"And it shall be when the LORD shall bring thee into the land of the Canaanites, as he swore unto thee and to thy fathers, and shall give it thee, ¹²that thou shalt set apart unto the LORD all that openeth the matrix, and every firstling that cometh of a beast which thou hast, the males shall be the LORD's. ¹³And every firstling of an ass thou shalt redeem with a lamb; and if thou wilt not redeem it, then thou shalt break his neck: and all the firstborn of man amongst thy children shalt thou redeem.

¹⁴And it shall be when thy son asketh thee in time to come, saying, "What is this?" that thou shalt say unto him, "By strength of hand the LORD brought us out from Egypt, from the house of bondage. ¹⁵And it came to pass, when Pharaoh would hardly let us go, that the LORD slew all the firstborn in the land of Egypt, both the firstborn of man, and the firstborn of beast: therefore I sacrifice to the LORD all that openeth the matrix, being males; but all the firstborn of my children I redeem. ¹⁶And it shall be for a token upon thy hand, and for frontlets between thy eyes: for by strength of hand the LORD brought us forth out of Egypt."'

¹⁷And it came to pass, when Pharaoh had let the people go, that God led them not through the way of the land of the Philistines, although that was near: for God said, 'Lest peradventure the people repent when they see war, and they return to Egypt': ¹⁸but God led the people about, through the way of the wilderness of the Red Sea: and the children of Israel went up harnessed out of the land of Egypt. ¹⁹And Moses took the bones of Joseph with him: for he had straitly sworn the children of Israel, saying, 'God will surely visit you, and ye shall carry up my bones away hence with you'.

²⁰And they took their journey from Succoth, and encamped in Etham, in the edge of the wilderness. ²¹And the LORD went before them by day in a pillar of a cloud, to lead them the way, and by night in a pillar of fire, to give them light to go by day and night. ²²He took not away the pillar of the cloud by day, nor the pillar of fire by night, from before the people.

14 And the LORD spoke unto Moses, saying, ²'Speak unto the children of Israel, that they turn and encamp before Pi-hahiroth, between Migdol and the sea, over against Baal-zephon: before it shall ye encamp by the sea. ³For Pharaoh will say of the children of Israel, "They are entangled in the land, the wilderness hath shut them in". ⁴And I will harden Pharaoh's heart, that he shall follow after them, and I will be honoured upon Pharaoh, and upon all his host, that the Egyptians may know that I am the LORD.' And they did so.

⁵And it was told the king of Egypt that the people fled: and the heart of Pharaoh and of his servants was turned against the people, and they said, 'Why have we done this, that we have let Israel go from serving us?' ⁶And he made ready his chariot, and took his people with him. ⁷And he took six hundred chosen chariots, and all the chariots of Egypt, and captains over every one of them. ⁸And the LORD hardened the heart of Pharaoh king of Egypt, and he pursued after the children

of Israel: and the children of Israel went out with a high hand. ⁹But the Egyptians pursued after them, all the horses and chariots of Pharaoh, and his horsemen, and his army, and overtook them encamping by the sea, beside Pi-hahiroth, before Baal-zephon.

¹⁰And when Pharaoh drew nigh, the children of Israel lifted up their eyes, and, behold, the Egyptians marched after them, and they were sore afraid: and the children of Israel cried out unto the LORD. ¹¹And they said unto Moses, 'Because there were no graves in Egypt, hast thou taken us away to die in the wilderness? Wherefore hast thou dealt thus with us, to carry us forth out of Egypt? ¹²Is not this the word that we did tell thee in Egypt, saying, "Let us alone, that we may serve the Egyptians?" For it had been better for us to serve the Egyptians, than that we should die in the wilderness.' ¹³And Moses said unto the people, 'Fear ye not, stand still, and see the salvation of the LORD, which he will show to you today: for the Egyptians whom ye have seen today, ye shall see them again no more for ever. ¹⁴The LORD shall fight for you, and ye shall hold your peace.'

¹⁵And the LORD said unto Moses, 'Wherefore criest thou unto me? Speak unto the children of Israel, that they go forward. ¹⁶But lift thou up thy rod, and stretch out thy hand over the sea, and divide it: and the children of Israel shall go on dry ground through the midst of the sea. ¹⁷And I, behold, I will harden the hearts of the Egyptians, and they shall follow them: and I will get me honour upon Pharaoh, and upon all his host, upon his chariots, and upon his horsemen. ¹⁸And the Egyptians shall know that I am the LORD, when I have gotten me honour upon Pharaoh, upon his chariots, and upon his horsemen.'

¹⁹And the angel of God, which went before the camp of Israel, removed and went behind them; and the pillar of the cloud went from before their face, and stood behind them. ²⁰And it came between the camp of the Egyptians and the camp of Israel, and it was a cloud and darkness to them, but it gave light by night to these: so that the one came not near the other all the night. ²¹And Moses stretched out his hand over the sea, and the LORD caused the sea to go back by a strong east wind all that night, and made the sea dry land, and the waters were divided. ²²And the children of Israel went into the midst of the sea upon the dry ground, and the waters were a wall unto them on their right hand, and on their left.

²³And the Egyptians pursued, and went in after them to the midst of the sea, even all Pharaoh's horses, his chariots, and his horsemen. ²⁴And it came to pass, that in the morning watch the LORD looked unto the host of the Egyptians through the pillar of fire and of the cloud, and troubled the host of the Egyptians, ²⁵and took off their chariot wheels, that they drove them heavily: so that the Egyptians said, 'Let us flee from the face of Israel: for the LORD fighteth for them against the Egyptians'.

²⁶And the LORD said unto Moses, 'Stretch out thy hand over the sea, that the waters may come again upon the Egyptians, upon their chariots, and upon their horsemen'. ²⁷And Moses stretched forth his hand

over the sea, and the sea returned to his strength when the morning appeared; and the Egyptians fled against it; and the LORD overthrew the Egyptians in the midst of the sea. ²⁸And the waters returned, and covered the chariots, and the horsemen, and all the host of Pharaoh that came into the sea after them: there remained not so much as one of them. ²⁹But the children of Israel walked upon dry land in the midst of the sea, and the waters were a wall unto them on their right hand, and on their left. ³⁰Thus the LORD saved Israel that day out of the hand of the Egyptians: and Israel saw the Egyptians dead upon the sea-shore. ³¹And Israel saw that great work which the LORD did upon the Egyptians: and the people feared the LORD, and believed the LORD, and his servant Moses.

15 Then sang Moses and the children of Israel this song unto the LORD, and spoke, saying,

'I will sing unto the LORD, for he hath triumphed gloriously:
the horse and his rider hath he thrown into the sea.
² The LORD is my strength and song, and he is become my salvation:
he is my God, and I will prepare him a habitation;
my father's God, and I will exalt him.
³ The LORD is a man of war:
the LORD is his name.
⁴ Pharaoh's chariots and his host hath he cast into the sea:
his chosen captains also are drowned in the Red Sea.
⁵ The depths have covered them:
they sank into the bottom as a stone.
⁶ Thy right hand, O LORD, is become glorious in power:
thy right hand, O LORD, hath dashed in pieces the enemy.
⁷ And in the greatness of thy excellence thou hast overthrown
them that rose up against thee:
thou sentest forth thy wrath, which consumed them as stubble.
⁸ And with the blast of thy nostrils the waters were gathered
together,
the floods stood upright as a heap,
and the depths were congealed in the heart of the sea.
⁹ The enemy said, "I will pursue, I will overtake, I will divide the
spoil:
my lust shall be satisfied upon them:
I will draw my sword, my hand shall destroy them".
¹⁰ Thou didst blow with thy wind, the sea covered them:
they sank as lead in the mighty waters.
¹¹ Who is like unto thee, O LORD, amongst the gods?
who is like thee, glorious in holiness, fearful in praises, doing
wonders?
¹² Thou stretchedst out thy right hand,
the earth swallowed them.
¹³ Thou in thy mercy hast led forth the people which thou hast
redeemed:

thou hast guided them in thy strength unto thy holy habitation.
¹⁴ The people shall hear, and be afraid:
sorrow shall take hold on the inhabitants of Palestina.
¹⁵ Then the dukes of Edom shall be amazed:
the mighty men of Moab trembling shall take hold upon them:
all the inhabitants of Canaan shall melt away.
¹⁶ Fear and dread shall fall upon them,
by the greatness of thy arm they shall be as still as a stone,
till thy people pass over, O LORD,
till the people pass over, which thou hast purchased.
¹⁷ Thou shalt bring them in, and plant them in the mountain of
thy inheritance,
in the place, O LORD, which thou hast made for thee to dwell in,
in the Sanctuary, O LORD, which thy hands have established.
¹⁸ The LORD shall reign for ever and ever.

¹⁹'For the horse of Pharaoh went in with his chariots and with his horsemen into the sea, and the LORD brought again the waters of the sea upon them: but the children of Israel went on dry land in the midst of the sea.'

²⁰And Miriam the prophetess, the sister of Aaron, took a timbrel in her hand, and all the women went out after her with timbrels and with dances. ²¹And Miriam answered them,

'Sing ye to the LORD, for he hath triumphed gloriously:
the horse and his rider hath he thrown into the sea'.

²²So Moses brought Israel from the Red Sea, and they went out into the wilderness of Shur: and they went three days in the wilderness, and found no water. ²³And when they came to Marah, they could not drink of the waters of Marah, for they were bitter: therefore the name of it was called Marah. ²⁴And the people murmured against Moses, saying, 'What shall we drink?' ²⁵And he cried unto the LORD: and the LORD showed him a tree, which when he had cast into the waters, the waters were made sweet: there he made a statute and an ordinance, and there he proved them, ²⁶and said, 'If thou wilt diligently hearken to the voice of the LORD thy God, and wilt do that which is right in his sight, and wilt give ear to his commandments, and keep all his statutes, I will put none of these diseases upon thee, which I have brought upon the Egyptians: for I am the LORD that healeth thee'.

²⁷And they came to Elim, where were twelve wells of water, and threescore and ten palm trees, and they encamped there by the waters.

16 And they took their journey from Elim, and all the congregation of the children of Israel came unto the wilderness of Sin, which is between Elim and Sinai, on the fifteenth day of the second month after their departing out of the land of Egypt. ²And the whole congregation of the children of Israel murmured against Moses and Aaron in the wilderness. ³And the children of Israel said unto them, 'Would to God we had died by the hand of the LORD in the land of Egypt, when we sat by the flesh-pots, and when we did eat bread to the full: for ye have brought us forth into this wilderness, to kill this whole assembly with hunger'.

⁴Then said the LORD unto Moses, 'Behold, I will rain bread from heaven for you: and the people shall go out and gather a certain rate every day, that I may prove them, whether they will walk in my law, or no. ⁵And it shall come to pass, that on the sixth day they shall prepare that which they bring in, and it shall be twice as much as they gather daily.' ⁶And Moses and Aaron said unto all the children of Israel, 'At even, then ye shall know that the LORD hath brought you out from the land of Egypt. ⁷And in the morning, then ye shall see the glory of the LORD, for that he heareth your murmurings against the LORD: and what are we, that ye murmur against us?' ⁸And Moses said, 'This shall be, when the LORD shall give you in the evening flesh to eat, and in the morning bread to the full: for that the LORD heareth your murmurings which ye murmur against him; and what are we? your murmurings are not against us, but against the LORD'.

⁹And Moses spoke unto Aaron, 'Say unto all the congregation of the children of Israel, "Come near before the LORD: for he hath heard your murmurings"'. ¹⁰And it came to pass, as Aaron spoke unto the whole congregation of the children of Israel, that they looked toward the wilderness, and behold, the glory of the LORD appeared in the cloud.

¹¹And the LORD spoke unto Moses, saying, ¹²'I have heard the murmurings of the children of Israel: speak unto them, saying, "At even ye shall eat flesh, and in the morning ye shall be filled with bread: and ye shall know that I am the LORD your God"'. ¹³And it came to pass, that at even the quails came up, and covered the camp: and in the morning the dew lay round about the host. ¹⁴And when the dew that lay was gone up, behold, upon the face of the wilderness there lay a small round thing, as small as the hoar frost on the ground. ¹⁵And when the children of Israel saw it, they said one to another, 'It is manna': for they wist not what it was. And Moses said unto them, 'This is the bread which the LORD hath given you to eat. ¹⁶This is the thing which the LORD hath commanded, gather of it every man according to his eating, an omer for every man, according to the number of your persons; take ye every man for them which are in his tents.' ¹⁷And the children of Israel did so, and gathered some more, some less. ¹⁸And when they did mete it with an omer, he that gathered much had nothing over, and he that gathered little had no lack: they gathered every man according to his eating. ¹⁹And Moses said, 'Let no man leave of it till the morning'. ²⁰Notwithstanding they hearkened not unto Moses; but some of them left of it until the morning, and it bred worms, and stank: and Moses was wroth with them. ²¹And they gathered it every morning, every man according to his eating: and when the sun waxed hot, it melted.

²²And it came to pass, that on the sixth day they gathered twice as much bread, two omers for one man: and all the rulers of the congregation came and told Moses. ²³And he said unto them, 'This is that which the LORD hath said, "Tomorrow is the rest of the holy sabbath

unto the LORD: bake that which you will bake today, and seethe that ye will seethe, and that which remaineth over lay up for you to be kept until the morning"'. [24]And they laid it up till the morning, as Moses bade: and it did not stink, neither was there any worm therein. [25]And Moses said, 'Eat that today, for today is a sabbath unto the LORD: today ye shall not find it in the field. [26]Six days ye shall gather it, but on the seventh day, which is the sabbath, in it there shall be none.'

[27]And it came to pass, that there went out some of the people on the seventh day for to gather, and they found none. [28]And the LORD said unto Moses, 'How long refuse ye to keep my commandments and my laws? [29]See, for that the LORD hath given you the sabbath, therefore he giveth you on the sixth day the bread of two days: abide ye every man in his place, let no man go out of his place on the seventh day.' [30]So the people rested on the seventh day. [31]And the house of Israel called the name thereof manna: and it was like coriander seed, white: and the taste of it was like wafers made with honey.

[32]And Moses said, 'This is the thing which the LORD commandeth, "Fill an omer of it to be kept for your generations: that they may see the bread wherewith I have fed you in the wilderness, when I brought you forth from the land of Egypt"'. [33]And Moses said unto Aaron, 'Take a pot, and put an omer full of manna therein, and lay it up before the LORD, to be kept for your generations'. [34]As the LORD commanded Moses, so Aaron laid it up before the Testimony, to be kept. [35]And the children of Israel did eat manna forty years, until they came to a land inhabited: they did eat manna, until they came unto the borders of the land of Canaan. [36]Now an omer is the tenth part of an ephah.

17 And all the congregation of the children of Israel journeyed from the wilderness of Sin after their journeys, according to the commandment of the LORD, and pitched in Rephidim: and there was no water for the people to drink. [2]Wherefore the people did chide with Moses, and said, 'Give us water that we may drink'. And Moses said unto them, 'Why chide you with me? Wherefore do ye tempt the LORD?' [3]And the people thirsted there for water, and the people murmured against Moses, and said, 'Wherefore is this that thou hast brought us up out of Egypt, to kill us and our children and our cattle with thirst?' [4]And Moses cried unto the LORD, saying, 'What shall I do unto this people? they be almost ready to stone me'. [5]And the LORD said unto Moses, 'Go on before the people, and take with thee of the elders of Israel; and thy rod, wherewith thou smotest the river, take in thy hand, and go. [6]Behold, I will stand before thee there upon the rock in Horeb, and thou shalt smite the rock, and there shall come water out of it, that the people may drink.' And Moses did so in the sight of the elders of Israel. [7]And he called the name of the place Massah, and Meribah, because of the chiding of the children of Israel, and because they tempted the LORD, saying, 'Is the LORD amongst us, or not?'

[8]Then came Amalek, and fought with Israel in Rephidim. [9]And Moses said unto Joshua, 'Choose us out men, and go out, fight with Amalek: tomorrow I will stand on the top of the hill with the rod of God in my

hand'. ¹⁰So Joshua did as Moses had said to him, and fought with Amalek: and Moses, Aaron, and Hur went up to the top of the hill. ¹¹And it came to pass when Moses held up his hand, that Israel prevailed: and when he let down his hand, Amalek prevailed. ¹²But Moses' hands were heavy; and they took a stone, and put it under him, and he sat thereon: and Aaron and Hur stayed up his hands, the one on the one side, and the other on the other side, and his hands were steady until the going down of the sun. ¹³And Joshua discomfited Amalek and his people with the edge of the sword. ¹⁴And the Lᴏʀᴅ said unto Moses, 'Write this for a memorial in a book, and rehearse it in the ears of Joshua: for I will utterly put out the remembrance of Amalek from under heaven'. ¹⁵And Moses built an altar, and called the name of it Jehovah-nissi: ¹⁶for he said, 'Because the Lᴏʀᴅ hath sworn that the Lᴏʀᴅ will have war with Amalek from generation to generation'.

18 When Jethro, the priest of Midian, Moses' father-in-law, heard of all that God had done for Moses, and for Israel his people, and that the Lᴏʀᴅ had brought Israel out of Egypt: ²then Jethro, Moses' father-in-law, took Zipporah, Moses' wife, after he had sent her back, ³and her two sons, of which the name of the one was Gershom: for he said, 'I have been an alien in a strange land': ⁴and the name of the other was Eliezer: 'For the God of my father,' said he, 'was my help, and delivered me from the sword of Pharaoh'. ⁵And Jethro, Moses' father-in-law, came with his sons and his wife unto Moses into the wilderness, where he encamped at the mount of God. ⁶And he said unto Moses, 'I thy father-in-law Jethro am come unto thee, and thy wife, and her two sons with her'. ⁷And Moses went out to meet his father-in-law, and did obeisance, and kissed him; and they asked each other of their welfare, and they came into the tent. ⁸And Moses told his father-in-law all that the Lᴏʀᴅ had done unto Pharaoh and to the Egyptians for Israel's sake, and all the travail that had come upon them by the way, and how the Lᴏʀᴅ delivered them. ⁹And Jethro rejoiced for all the goodness which the Lᴏʀᴅ had done to Israel, whom he had delivered out of the hand of the Egyptians. ¹⁰And Jethro said, 'Blessed be the Lᴏʀᴅ, who hath delivered you out of the hand of the Egyptians, and out of the hand of Pharaoh, who hath delivered the people from under the hand of the Egyptians. ¹¹Now I know that the Lᴏʀᴅ is greater than all gods: for in the thing wherein they dealt proudly he was above them.' ¹²And Jethro, Moses' father-in-law, took a burnt offering and sacrifices for God: and Aaron came, and all the elders of Israel, to eat bread with Moses' father-in-law before God.

¹³And it came to pass on the morrow, that Moses sat to judge the people: and the people stood by Moses from the morning unto the evening. ¹⁴And when Moses' father-in-law saw all that he did to the people, he said, 'What is this thing that thou doest to the people? Why sittest thou thyself alone, and all the people stand by thee from morning unto even?' ¹⁵And Moses said unto his father-in-law, 'Because the people come unto me to inquire of God. ¹⁶When they have a matter, they come unto me, and I judge between one and another, and I do

make them know the statutes of God, and his laws.' [17]And Moses' father-in-law said unto him, 'The thing that thou doest is not good. [18]Thou wilt surely wear away, both thou, and this people that is with thee: for this thing is too heavy for thee: thou art not able to perform it thyself alone. [19]Hearken now unto my voice, I will give thee counsel, and God shall be with thee: be thou for the people to God-ward, that thou mayest bring the causes unto God: [20]and thou shalt teach them ordinances and laws, and shalt show them the way wherein they must walk, and the work that they must do. [21]Moreover thou shalt provide out of all the people able men, such as fear God, men of truth, hating covetousness, and place such over them, to be rulers of thousands, and rulers of hundreds, rulers of fifties, and rulers of tens. [22]And let them judge the people at all seasons: and it shall be that every great matter they shall bring unto thee, but every small matter they shall judge: so shall it be easier for thyself, and they shall bear the burden with thee. [23]If thou shalt do this thing, and God command thee so, then thou shalt be able to endure, and all this people shall also go to their place in peace.' [24]So Moses hearkened to the voice of his father-in-law, and did all that he had said. [25]And Moses chose able men out of all Israel, and made them heads over the people, rulers of thousands, rulers of hundreds, rulers of fifties, and rulers of tens. [26]And they judged the people at all seasons: the hard causes they brought unto Moses, but every small matter they judged themselves.

[27]And Moses let his father-in-law depart, and he went his way into his own land.

19 In the third month, when the children of Israel were gone forth out of the land of Egypt, the same day came they into the wilderness of Sinai. [2]For they were departed from Rephidim, and were come to the desert of Sinai, and had pitched in the wilderness; and there Israel camped before the mount. [3]And Moses went up unto God: and the LORD called unto him out of the mountain, saying, 'Thus shalt thou say to the house of Jacob, and tell the children of Israel: [4]"Ye have seen what I did unto the Egyptians, and how I bore you on eagles' wings, and brought you unto myself. [5]Now therefore, if ye will obey my voice indeed, and keep my covenant, then ye shall be a peculiar treasure unto me above all people: for all the earth is mine. [6]And ye shall be unto me a kingdom of priests, and a holy nation." These are the words which thou shalt speak unto the children of Israel.'

[7]And Moses came and called for the elders of the people, and laid before their faces all these words which the LORD commanded him. [8]And all the people answered together, and said, 'All that the LORD hath spoken we will do'. And Moses returned the words of the people unto the LORD. [9]And the LORD said unto Moses, 'Lo, I come unto thee in a thick cloud, that the people may hear when I speak with thee, and believe thee for ever'. And Moses told the words of the people unto the LORD.

[10]And the LORD said unto Moses, 'Go unto the people, and sanctify them today and tomorrow, and let them wash their clothes. [11]And be

ready against the third day: for the third day the LORD will come down in the sight of all the people upon mount Sinai. ¹²And thou shalt set bounds unto the people round about, saying, "Take heed to yourselves, that ye go not up into the mount, or touch the border of it: whosoever toucheth the mount shall be surely put to death. ¹³There shall not a hand touch it, but he shall surely be stoned, or shot through, whether it be beast or man, it shall not live: when the trumpet soundeth long, they shall come up to the mount."'

¹⁴And Moses went down from the mount unto the people, and sanctified the people; and they washed their clothes. ¹⁵And he said unto the people, 'Be ready against the third day: come not at your wives'.

¹⁶And it came to pass on the third day in the morning, that there were thunders and lightnings, and a thick cloud upon the mount, and the voice of the trumpet exceeding loud, so that all the people that was in the camp trembled. ¹⁷And Moses brought forth the people out of the camp to meet with God, and they stood at the nether part of the mount. ¹⁸And mount Sinai was altogether on a smoke, because the LORD descended upon it in fire: and the smoke thereof ascended as the smoke of a furnace, and the whole mount quaked greatly. ¹⁹And when the voice of the trumpet sounded long, and waxed louder and louder, Moses spoke, and God answered him by a voice. ²⁰And the LORD came down upon mount Sinai, on the top of the mount: and the LORD called Moses up to the top of the mount; and Moses went up. ²¹And the LORD said unto Moses, 'Go down, charge the people, lest they break through unto the LORD to gaze, and many of them perish. ²²And let the priests also, which come near to the LORD, sanctify themselves, lest the LORD break forth upon them.' ²³And Moses said unto the LORD, 'The people cannot come up to mount Sinai: for thou chargedst us, saying, "Set bounds about the mount, and sanctify it"'. ²⁴And the LORD said unto him, 'Away, get thee down, and thou shalt come up, thou, and Aaron with thee: but let not the priests and the people break through to come up unto the LORD, lest he break forth upon them'. ²⁵So Moses went down unto the people, and spoke unto them.

20 And God spoke all these words, saying, ²'I am the LORD thy God, which have brought thee out of the land of Egypt, out of the house of bondage.

³'Thou shalt have no other gods before me.

⁴'Thou shalt not make unto thee any graven image, or any likeness of anything that is in heaven above, or that is in the earth beneath, or that is in the water under the earth. ⁵Thou shalt not bow down thyself to them, nor serve them: for I the LORD thy God am a jealous God, visiting the iniquity of the fathers upon the children unto the third and fourth generation of them that hate me; ⁶and showing mercy unto thousands of them that love me, and keep my commandments.

⁷'Thou shalt not take the name of the LORD thy God in vain: for the LORD will not hold him guiltless that taketh his name in vain.

⁸'Remember the sabbath day, to keep it holy. ⁹Six days shalt thou labour, and do all thy work: ¹⁰but the seventh day is the sabbath of the

LORD thy God: in it thou shalt not do any work, thou, nor thy son, nor thy daughter, thy manservant, nor thy maidservant, nor thy cattle, nor thy stranger that is within thy gates: [11]for in six days the LORD made heaven and earth, the sea, and all that in them is, and rested the seventh day: wherefore the LORD blessed the sabbath day, and hallowed it.

[12]'Honour thy father and thy mother: that thy days may be long upon the land which the LORD thy God giveth thee.

[13]'Thou shalt not kill.

[14]'Thou shalt not commit adultery.

[15]'Thou shalt not steal.

[16]'Thou shalt not bear false witness against thy neighbour.

[17]'Thou shalt not covet thy neighbour's house, thou shalt not covet thy neighbour's wife, nor his manservant, nor his maidservant, nor his ox, nor his ass, nor anything that is thy neighbour's.'

[18]And all the people saw the thunderings, and the lightnings, and the noise of the trumpet, and the mountain smoking: and when the people saw it, they removed, and stood afar off. [19]And they said unto Moses, 'Speak thou with us, and we will hear: but let not God speak with us, lest we die'. [20]And Moses said unto the people, 'Fear not: for God is come to prove you, and that his fear may be before your faces, that ye sin not'. [21]And the people stood afar off, and Moses drew near unto the thick darkness where God was.

[22]And the LORD said unto Moses, 'Thus thou shalt say unto the children of Israel, "Ye have seen that I have talked with you from heaven. [23]Ye shall not make with me gods of silver, neither shall ye make unto you gods of gold. [24]An altar of earth thou shalt make unto me, and shalt sacrifice thereon thy burnt offerings, and thy peace offerings, thy sheep, and thy oxen: in all places where I record my name I will come unto thee, and I will bless thee. [25]And if thou wilt make me an altar of stone, thou shalt not build it of hewn stone: for if thou lift up thy tool upon it, thou hast polluted it. [26]Neither shalt thou go up by steps unto my altar, that thy nakedness be not discovered thereon."

21 'Now these are the judgements which thou shalt set before them.

[2]'If thou buy a Hebrew servant, six years he shall serve, and in the seventh he shall go out free for nothing. [3]If he came in by himself, he shall go out by himself: if he were married, then his wife shall go out with him. [4]If his master have given him a wife, and she have borne him sons or daughters; the wife and her children shall be her master's, and he shall go out by himself. [5]And if the servant shall plainly say, "I love my master, my wife, and my children, I will not go out free": [6]then his master shall bring him unto the judges; he shall also bring him to the door, or unto the door-post; and his master shall bore his ear through with an awl, and he shall serve him for ever.

[7]'And if a man sell his daughter to be a maidservant, she shall not go out as the menservants do. [8]If she please not her master, who hath betrothed her to himself, then shall he let her be redeemed: to sell her unto a strange nation he shall have no power, seeing he hath dealt

deceitfully with her. ⁹And if he have betrothed her unto his son, he shall deal with her after the manner of daughters. ¹⁰If he take him another wife, her food, her raiment, and her duty of marriage, shall he not diminish. ¹¹And if he do not these three unto her, then shall she go out free without money.

¹²'He that smiteth a man, so that he die, shall be surely put to death. ¹³And if a man lie not in wait, but God deliver him into his hand, then I will appoint thee a place whither he shall flee. ¹⁴But if a man come presumptuously upon his neighbour, to slay him with guile, thou shalt take him from my altar, that he may die.

¹⁵'And he that smiteth his father, or his mother, shall be surely put to death.

¹⁶'And he that stealeth a man, and selleth him, or if he be found in his hand, he shall surely be put to death.

¹⁷'And he that curseth his father, or his mother, shall surely be put to death.

¹⁸'And if men strive together, and one smite another with a stone, or with his fist, and he die not, but keepeth his bed: ¹⁹if he rise again, and walk abroad upon his staff, then shall he that smote him be quit: only he shall pay for the loss of his time, and shall cause him to be thoroughly healed.

²⁰'And if a man smite his servant, or his maid, with a rod, and he die under his hand, he shall be surely punished. ²¹Notwithstanding, if he continue a day or two, he shall not be punished, for he is his money.

²²'If men strive, and hurt a woman with child, so that her fruit depart from her, and yet no mischief follow, he shall be surely punished, according as the woman's husband will lay upon him, and he shall pay as the judges determine. ²³And if any mischief follow, then thou shalt give life for life, ²⁴eye for eye, tooth for tooth, hand for hand, foot for foot, ²⁵burning for burning, wound for wound, stripe for stripe.

²⁶'And if a man smite the eye of his servant, or the eye of his maid, that it perish, he shall let him go free for his eye's sake. ²⁷And if he smite out his manservant's tooth, or his maidservant's tooth, he shall let him go free for his tooth's sake.

²⁸'If an ox gore a man or a woman, that they die, then the ox shall be surely stoned, and his flesh shall not be eaten: but the owner of the ox shall be quit. ²⁹But if the ox were wont to push with his horn in time past, and it hath been testified to his owner, and he hath not kept him in, but that he hath killed a man or a woman; the ox shall be stoned, and his owner also shall be put to death. ³⁰If there be laid on him a sum of money, then he shall give for the ransom of his life whatsoever is laid upon him. ³¹Whether he have gored a son, or have gored a daughter, according to this judgement shall it be done unto him. ³²If the ox shall push a manservant or a maidservant, he shall give unto their master thirty shekels, and the ox shall be stoned.

³³'And if a man shall open a pit, or if a man shall dig a pit, and not cover it, and an ox or an ass fall therein: ³⁴the owner of the pit shall

make it good, and give money unto the owner of them, and the dead beast shall be his.

³⁵'And if one man's ox hurt another's, that he die, then they shall sell the live ox, and divide the money of it, and the dead ox also they shall divide. ³⁶Or if it be known that the ox hath used to push in time past, and his owner hath not kept him in, he shall surely pay ox for ox, and the dead shall be his own.

22 'If a man shall steal an ox, or a sheep, and kill it, or sell it; he shall restore five oxen for an ox, and four sheep for a sheep. ²'If a thief be found breaking up, and be smitten that he die, there shall no blood be shed for him. ³If the sun be risen upon him, there shall be blood shed for him: for he should make full restitution: if he have nothing, then he shall be sold for his theft. ⁴If the theft be certainly found in his hand alive, whether it be ox, or ass, or sheep, he shall restore double.

⁵'If a man shall cause a field or vineyard to be eaten, and shall put in his beast, and shall feed in another man's field: of the best of his own field, and of the best of his own vineyard, shall he make restitution.

⁶'If fire break out, and catch in thorns, so that the stacks of corn, or the standing corn, or the field, be consumed therewith; he that kindled the fire shall surely make restitution.

⁷'If a man shall deliver unto his neighbour money or stuff to keep, and it be stolen out of the man's house; if the thief be found, let him pay double. ⁸If the thief be not found, then the master of the house shall be brought unto the judges, to see whether he have put his hand unto his neighbour's goods. ⁹For all manner of trespass, whether it be for ox, for ass, for sheep, for raiment, or for any manner of lost thing, which another challengeth to be his, the cause of both parties shall come before the judges, and whom the judges shall condemn, he shall pay double unto his neighbour.

¹⁰'If a man deliver unto his neighbour an ass, or an ox, or a sheep, or any beast, to keep, and it die, or be hurt, or driven away, no man seeing it, ¹¹then shall an oath of the Lᴏʀᴅ be between them both, that he hath not put his hand unto his neighbour's goods: and the owner of it shall accept thereof, and he shall not make it good. ¹²And if it be stolen from him, he shall make restitution unto the owner thereof. ¹³If it be torn in pieces, then let him bring it for witness, and he shall not make good that which was torn.

¹⁴'And if a man borrow aught of his neighbour, and it be hurt, or die, the owner thereof being not with it, he shall surely make it good. ¹⁵But if the owner thereof be with it, he shall not make it good: if it be a hired thing, it came for his hire.

¹⁶'And if a man entice a maid that is not betrothed, and lie with her, he shall surely endow her to be his wife. ¹⁷If her father utterly refuse to give her unto him, he shall pay money according to the dowry of virgins.

¹⁸'Thou shalt not suffer a witch to live.

¹⁹'Whosoever lieth with a beast shall surely be put to death.

²⁰'He that sacrificeth unto any god, save unto the Lord only, he shall be utterly destroyed.

²¹'Thou shalt neither vex a stranger, nor oppress him: for ye were strangers in the land of Egypt.

²²'Ye shall not afflict any widow, or fatherless child. ²³If thou afflict them in any wise, and they cry at all unto me, I will surely hear their cry; ²⁴and my wrath shall wax hot, and I will kill you with the sword: and your wives shall be widows, and your children fatherless.

²⁵'If thou lend money to any of my people that is poor by thee, thou shalt not be to him as an usurer, neither shalt thou lay upon him usury. ²⁶If thou at all take thy neighbour's raiment to pledge, thou shalt deliver it unto him by that the sun goeth down: ²⁷for that is his covering only, it is his raiment for his skin: wherein shall he sleep? and it shall come to pass, when he crieth unto me, that I will hear: for I am gracious.

²⁸'Thou shalt not revile the gods, nor curse the ruler of thy people.

²⁹'Thou shalt not delay to offer the first of thy ripe fruits, and of thy liquors: the firstborn of thy sons shalt thou give unto me. ³⁰Likewise shalt thou do with thy oxen, and with thy sheep: seven days it shall be with his dam, on the eighth day thou shalt give it me.

³¹'And ye shall be holy men unto me: neither shall ye eat any flesh that is torn of beasts in the field: ye shall cast it to the dogs.

23 'Thou shalt not raise a false report: put not thy hand with the wicked to be an unrighteous witness.

²'Thou shalt not follow a multitude to do evil; neither shalt thou speak in a cause to decline after many to wrest judgement.

³'Neither shalt thou countenance a poor man in his cause.

⁴'If thou meet thy enemy's ox or his ass going astray, thou shalt surely bring it back to him again. ⁵If thou see the ass of him that hateth thee lying under his burden, and wouldst forbear to help him, thou shalt surely help with him.

⁶'Thou shalt not wrest the judgement of thy poor in his cause. ⁷Keep thee far from a false matter; and the innocent and righteous slay thou not: for I will not justify the wicked.

⁸'And thou shalt take no gift: for the gift blindeth the wise, and perverteth the words of the righteous.

⁹'Also thou shalt not oppress a stranger: for ye know the heart of a stranger, seeing ye were strangers in the land of Egypt.

¹⁰'And six years thou shalt sow thy land, and shalt gather in the fruits thereof: ¹¹but the seventh year thou shalt let it rest and lie still, that the poor of thy people may eat: and what they leave the beasts of the field shall eat. In like manner thou shalt deal with thy vineyard, and with thy olive-yard. ¹²Six days thou shalt do thy work, and on the seventh day thou shalt rest: that thy ox and thy ass may rest, and the son of thy handmaid, and the stranger may be refreshed. ¹³And in all things that I have said unto you be circumspect: and make no mention of the names of other gods, neither let it be heard out of thy mouth.

¹⁴'Three times thou shalt keep a feast unto me in the year. ¹⁵Thou

shalt keep the feast of unleavened bread: thou shalt eat unleavened bread seven days, as I commanded thee, in the time appointed of the month Abib: for in it thou camest out from Egypt: and none shall appear before me empty: ¹⁶and the feast of harvest, the first-fruits of thy labours, which thou hast sown in the field: and the feast of ingathering, which is in the end of the year, when thou hast gathered in thy labours out of the field. ¹⁷Three times in the year all thy males shall appear before the LORD GOD.

¹⁸'Thou shalt not offer the blood of my sacrifice with leavened bread, neither shall the fat of my sacrifice remain until the morning. ¹⁹The first of the first-fruits of thy land thou shalt bring into the house of the LORD thy God. Thou shalt not seethe a kid in his mother's milk.

²⁰'Behold, I send an Angel before thee to keep thee in the way, and to bring thee into the place which I have prepared. ²¹Beware of him, and obey his voice, provoke him not; for he will not pardon your transgressions: for my name is in him. ²²But if thou shalt indeed obey his voice, and do all that I speak, then I will be an enemy unto thy enemies, and an adversary unto thy adversaries. ²³For my Angel shall go before thee, and bring thee in unto the Amorites, and the Hittites, and the Perizzites, and the Canaanites, the Hivites, and the Jebusites: and I will cut them off. ²⁴Thou shalt not bow down to their gods, nor serve them, nor do after their works: but thou shalt utterly overthrow them, and quite break down their images. ²⁵And ye shall serve the LORD your God, and he shall bless thy bread, and thy water: and I will take sickness away from the midst of thee.

²⁶'There shall nothing cast their young, nor be barren, in thy land: the number of thy days I will fulfil. ²⁷I will send my fear before thee, and will destroy all the people to whom thou shalt come, and I will make all thy enemies turn their backs unto thee. ²⁸And I will send hornets before thee, which shall drive out the Hivite, the Canaanite, and the Hittite, from before thee. ²⁹I will not drive them out from before thee in one year, lest the land become desolate, and the beast of the field multiply against thee. ³⁰By little and little I will drive them out from before thee, until thou be increased, and inherit the land. ³¹And I will set thy bounds from the Red Sea even unto the sea of the Philistines, and from the desert unto the river: for I will deliver the inhabitants of the land into your hand: and thou shalt drive them out before thee. ³²Thou shalt make no covenant with them, nor with their gods. ³³They shall not dwell in thy land, lest they make thee sin against me: for if thou serve their gods, it will surely be a snare unto thee.'

24 And he said unto Moses, 'Come up unto the LORD, thou, and Aaron, Nadab, and Abihu, and seventy of the elders of Israel; and worship ye afar off. ²And Moses alone shall come near the LORD: but they shall not come nigh, neither shall the people go up with him.'

³And Moses came and told the people all the words of the LORD, and all the judgements: and all the people answered with one voice, and said, 'All the words which the LORD hath said will we do'. ⁴And Moses wrote all the words of the LORD, and rose up early in the morning, and

built an altar under the hill, and twelve pillars, according to the twelve tribes of Israel. [5]And he sent young men of the children of Israel, which offered burnt offerings, and sacrificed peace offerings of oxen unto the LORD. [6]And Moses took half of the blood, and put it in basins, and half of the blood he sprinkled on the altar. [7]And he took the book of the covenant, and read in the audience of the people: and they said, 'All that the LORD hath said will we do, and be obedient'. [8]And Moses took the blood, and sprinkled it on the people, and said, 'Behold the blood of the covenant, which the LORD hath made with you concerning all these words'.

[9]Then went up Moses, and Aaron, Nadab, and Abihu, and seventy of the elders of Israel: [10]and they saw the God of Israel: and there was under his feet as it were a paved work of a sapphire stone, and as it were the body of heaven in his clearness. [11]And upon the nobles of the children of Israel he laid not his hand: also they saw God, and did eat and drink.

[12]And the LORD said unto Moses, 'Come up to me into the mount, and be there, and I will give thee tablets of stone, and a law, and commandments which I have written, that thou mayest teach them'. [13]And Moses rose up, and his minister Joshua: and Moses went up into the mount of God. [14]And he said unto the elders, 'Tarry ye here for us, until we come again unto you: and behold, Aaron and Hur are with you: if any man have any matters to do, let him come unto them'. [15]And Moses went up into the mount, and a cloud covered the mount. [16]And the glory of the LORD abode upon mount Sinai, and the cloud covered it six days: and the seventh day he called unto Moses out of the midst of the cloud. [17]And the sight of the glory of the LORD was like devouring fire on the top of the mount in the eyes of the children of Israel. [18]And Moses went into the midst of the cloud, and got him up into the mount: and Moses was in the mount forty days and forty nights.

25 And the LORD spoke unto Moses, saying, [2]'Speak unto the children of Israel, that they bring me an offering: of every man that giveth it willingly with his heart ye shall take my offering. [3]And this is the offering which ye shall take of them: gold, and silver, and brass, [4]and blue, and purple, and scarlet, and fine linen, and goats' hair, [5]and rams' skins dyed red, and badgers' skins, and shittim wood, [6]oil for the light, spices for anointing oil, and for sweet incense, [7]onyx stones, and stones to be set in the ephod, and in the breastplate. [8]And let them make me a sanctuary, that I may dwell amongst them. [9]According to all that I show thee, after the pattern of the tabernacle, and the pattern of all the instruments thereof, even so shall ye make it.

[10]'And they shall make an ark of shittim wood: two cubits and a half shall be the length thereof, and a cubit and a half the breadth thereof, and a cubit and a half the height thereof. [11]And thou shalt overlay it with pure gold, within and without shalt thou overlay it, and shalt make upon it a crown of gold round about. [12]And thou shalt cast four rings of gold for it, and put them in the four corners thereof, and two rings shall be in the one side of it, and two rings in the other side

of it. [13]And thou shalt make staves of shittim wood, and overlay them with gold. [14]And thou shalt put the staves into the rings by the sides of the ark, that the ark may be borne with them. [15]The staves shall be in the rings of the ark: they shall not be taken from it. [16]And thou shalt put into the ark the testimony which I shall give thee. [17]And thou shalt make a mercy-seat of pure gold: two cubits and a half shall be the length thereof, and a cubit and a half the breadth thereof. [18]And thou shalt make two cherubims of gold: of beaten work shalt thou make them, in the two ends of the mercy-seat. [19]And make one cherub on the one end, and the other cherub on the other end: even of the mercy-seat shall ye make the cherubims on the two ends thereof. [20]And the cherubims shall stretch forth their wings on high, covering the mercy-seat with their wings, and their faces shall look one to another; toward the mercy-seat shall the faces of the cherubims be. [21]And thou shalt put the mercy-seat above upon the ark, and in the ark thou shalt put the testimony that I shall give thee. [22]And there I will meet with thee, and I will commune with thee from above the mercy-seat, from between the two cherubims which are upon the ark of the testimony, of all things which I will give thee in commandment unto the children of Israel.

[23]'Thou shalt also make a table of shittim wood: two cubits shall be the length thereof, and a cubit the breadth thereof, and a cubit and a half the height thereof. [24]And thou shalt overlay it with pure gold, and make thereto a crown of gold round about. [25]And thou shalt make unto it a border of a handbreadth round about, and thou shalt make a golden crown to the border thereof round about. [26]And thou shalt make for it four rings of gold, and put the rings in the four corners that are on the four feet thereof. [27]Over against the border shall the rings be for places of the staves to bear the table. [28]And thou shalt make the staves of shittim wood, and overlay them with gold, that the table may be borne with them. [29]And thou shalt make the dishes thereof, and spoons thereof, and covers thereof, and bowls thereof, to cover withal: of pure gold shalt thou make them. [30]And thou shalt set upon the table show-bread before me always.

[31]'And thou shalt make a candlestick of pure gold: of beaten work shall the candlestick be made: his shaft, and his branches, his bowls, his knops, and his flowers, shall be of the same. [32]And six branches shall come out of the sides of it: three branches of the candlestick out of the one side, and three branches of the candlestick out of the other side: [33]three bowls made like unto almonds, with a knop and a flower in one branch; and three bowls made like almonds in the other branch, with a knop and a flower: so in the six branches that come out of the candlestick. [34]And in the candlestick shall be four bowls made like unto almonds, with their knops and their flowers. [35]And there shall be a knop under two branches of the same, and a knop under two branches of the same, and a knop under two branches of the same, according to the six branches that proceed out of the candlestick. [36]Their knops and their branches shall be of the same: all it shall be one beaten work of

pure gold. ³⁷And thou shalt make the seven lamps thereof: and they shall light the lamps thereof, that they may give light over against it. ³⁸And the tongs thereof, and the snuff-dishes thereof, shall be of pure gold. ³⁹Of a talent of pure gold shall he make it, with all these vessels. ⁴⁰And look that thou make them after their pattern, which was shown thee in the mount.

26 ¹Moreover thou shalt make the tabernacle with ten curtains of fine twined linen, and blue, and purple, and scarlet: with cherubims of cunning work shalt thou make them. ²The length of one curtain shall be eight and twenty cubits, and the breadth of one curtain four cubits: and every one of the curtains shall have one measure. ³The five curtains shall be coupled together one to another; and other five curtains shall be coupled one to another. ⁴And thou shalt make loops of blue upon the edge of the one curtain from the selvedge in the coupling, and likewise shalt thou make in the outermost edge of another curtain, in the coupling of the second. ⁵Fifty loops shalt thou make in the one curtain, and fifty loops shalt thou make in the edge of the curtain that is in the coupling of the second, that the loops may take hold one of another. ⁶And thou shalt make fifty taches of gold, and couple the curtains together with the taches: and it shall be one tabernacle.

⁷And thou shalt make curtains of goats' hair to be a covering upon the tabernacle: eleven curtains shalt thou make. ⁸The length of one curtain shall be thirty cubits, and the breadth of one curtain four cubits: and the eleven shall be all of one measure. ⁹And thou shalt couple five curtains by themselves, and six curtains by themselves, and shalt double the sixth curtain in the forefront of the tabernacle. ¹⁰And thou shalt make fifty loops on the edge of the one curtain that is outmost in the coupling, and fifty loops in the edge of the curtain which coupleth the second. ¹¹And thou shalt make fifty taches of brass, and put the taches into the loops, and couple the tent together, that it may be one. ¹²And the remnant that remaineth of the curtains of the tent, the half curtain that remaineth, shall hang over the backside of the tabernacle. ¹³And a cubit on the one side, and a cubit on the other side of that which remaineth in the length of the curtains of the tent, it shall hang over the sides of the tabernacle on this side and on that side, to cover it. ¹⁴And thou shalt make a covering for the tent of rams' skins dyed red, and a covering above of badgers' skins.

¹⁵And thou shalt make boards for the tabernacle of shittim wood standing up. ¹⁶Ten cubits shall be the length of a board, and a cubit and a half shall be the breadth of one board. ¹⁷Two tenons shall there be in one board, set in order one against another: thus shalt thou make for all the boards of the tabernacle. ¹⁸And thou shalt make the boards for the tabernacle, twenty boards on the south side southward. ¹⁹And thou shalt make forty sockets of silver under the twenty boards: two sockets under one board for his two tenons, and two sockets under another board for his two tenons. ²⁰And for the second side of the tabernacle on the north side there shall be twenty boards, ²¹and their forty sockets of

silver: two sockets under one board, and two sockets under another board. ²²And for the sides of the tabernacle westward thou shalt make six boards. ²³And two boards shalt thou make for the corners of the tabernacle in the two sides. ²⁴And they shall be coupled together beneath, and they shall be coupled together above the head of it unto one ring: thus shall it be for them both; they shall be for the two corners. ²⁵And they shall be eight boards, and their sockets of silver, sixteen sockets: two sockets under one board, and two sockets under another board.

²⁶‘And thou shalt make bars of shittim wood: five for the boards of the one side of the tabernacle, ²⁷and five bars for the boards of the other side of the tabernacle, and five bars for the boards of the side of the tabernacle, for the two sides westward. ²⁸And the middle bar in the midst of the boards shall reach from end to end. ²⁹And thou shalt overlay the boards with gold, and make their rings of gold for places for the bars: and thou shalt overlay the bars with gold. ³⁰And thou shalt rear up the tabernacle according to the fashion thereof which was shown thee in the mount.

³¹‘And thou shalt make a veil of blue, and purple, and scarlet, and fine twined linen of cunning work: with cherubims shall it be made. ³²And thou shalt hang it upon four pillars of shittim wood overlaid with gold: their hooks shall be of gold, upon the four sockets of silver. ³³And thou shalt hang up the veil under the taches, that thou mayest bring in thither within the veil the ark of the testimony: and the veil shall divide unto you between the holy place and the most holy. ³⁴And thou shalt put the mercy-seat upon the ark of the testimony in the most holy place. ³⁵And thou shalt set the table without the veil, and the candlestick over against the table on the side of the tabernacle toward the south: and thou shalt put the table on the north side. ³⁶And thou shalt make a hanging for the door of the tent, of blue, and purple, and scarlet, and fine twined linen, wrought with needlework. ³⁷And thou shalt make for the hanging five pillars of shittim wood, and overlay them with gold, and their hooks shall be of gold: and thou shalt cast five sockets of brass for them.

27 ‘And thou shalt make an altar of shittim wood, five cubits long, and five cubits broad: the altar shall be four-square, and the height thereof shall be three cubits. ²And thou shalt make the horns of it upon the four corners thereof: his horns shall be of the same: and thou shalt overlay it with brass. ³And thou shalt make his pans to receive his ashes, and his shovels, and his basins, and his fleshhooks, and his fire-pans: all the vessels thereof thou shalt make of brass. ⁴And thou shalt make for it a grate of network of brass; and upon the net shalt thou make four brazen rings in the four corners thereof. ⁵And thou shalt put it under the compass of the altar beneath, that the net may be even to the midst of the altar. ⁶And thou shalt make staves for the altar, staves of shittim wood, and overlay them with brass. ⁷And the staves shall be put into the rings, and the staves shall be upon the two sides of the altar, to bear it. ⁸Hollow with boards shalt thou make it: as it was shown thee in the mount, so shall they make it.

⁹'And thou shalt make the court of the tabernacle: for the south side southward there shall be hangings for the court of fine twined linen of a hundred cubits long for one side. ¹⁰And the twenty pillars thereof and their twenty sockets shall be of brass; the hooks of the pillars and their fillets shall be of silver. ¹¹And likewise for the north side in length there shall be hangings of a hundred cubits long, and his twenty pillars and their twenty sockets of brass; the hooks of the pillars and their fillets of silver. ¹²And for the breadth of the court on the west side shall be hangings of fifty cubits: their pillars ten, and their sockets ten. ¹³And the breadth of the court on the east side eastward shall be fifty cubits. ¹⁴The hangings of one side of the gate shall be fifteen cubits: their pillars three, and their sockets three. ¹⁵And on the other side shall be hangings fifteen cubits: their pillars three, and their sockets three.

¹⁶'And for the gate of the court shall be a hanging of twenty cubits, of blue, and purple, and scarlet, and fine twined linen, wrought with needlework: and their pillars shall be four, and their sockets four. ¹⁷All the pillars round about the court shall be filleted with silver: their hooks shall be of silver, and their sockets of brass.

¹⁸'The length of the court shall be a hundred cubits, and the breadth fifty everywhere, and the height five cubits of fine twined linen, and their sockets of brass. ¹⁹All the vessels of the tabernacle in all the service thereof, and all the pins thereof, and all the pins of the court, shall be of brass.

²⁰'And thou shalt command the children of Israel, that they bring thee pure oil olive beaten for the light, to cause the lamp to burn always. ²¹In the tabernacle of the congregation without the veil, which is before the testimony, Aaron and his sons shall order it from evening to morning before the LORD: it shall be a statute for ever unto their generations on the behalf of the children of Israel.

28

'And take thou unto thee Aaron thy brother, and his sons with him, from among the children of Israel, that he may minister unto me in the priest's office, even Aaron, Nadab and Abihu, Eleazar and Ithamar, Aaron's sons. ²And thou shalt make holy garments for Aaron thy brother for glory and for beauty. ³And thou shalt speak unto all that are wise-hearted, whom I have filled with the spirit of wisdom, that they may make Aaron's garments to consecrate him, that he may minister unto me in the priest's office. ⁴And these are the garments which they shall make: a breastplate, and an ephod, and a robe, and a broidered coat, a mitre, and a girdle: and they shall make holy garments for Aaron thy brother, and his sons, that he may minister unto me in the priest's office. ⁵And they shall take gold, and blue, and purple, and scarlet, and fine linen.

⁶'And they shall make the ephod of gold, of blue, and of purple, of scarlet, and fine twined linen, with cunning work. ⁷It shall have the two shoulder-pieces thereof joined at the two edges thereof; and so it shall be joined together. ⁸And the curious girdle of the ephod, which is upon it, shall be of the same, according to the work thereof, even of gold, of blue, and purple, and scarlet, and fine twined linen. ⁹And thou

shalt take two onyx stones, and grave on them the names of the children of Israel: [10]six of their names on one stone, and the other six names of the rest on the other stone, according to their birth. [11]With the work of an engraver in stone, like the engravings of a signet, shalt thou engrave the two stones with the names of the children of Israel; thou shalt make them to be set in ouches of gold. [12]And thou shalt put the two stones upon the shoulders of the ephod for stones of memorial unto the children of Israel. And Aaron shall bear their names before the LORD upon his two shoulders for a memorial.

[13]'And thou shalt make ouches of gold; [14]and two chains of pure gold at the ends; of wreathen work shalt thou make them, and fasten the wreathen chains to the ouches.

[15]'And thou shalt make the breastplate of judgement with cunning work; after the work of the ephod thou shalt make it: of gold, of blue, and of purple, and of scarlet, and of fine twined linen, shalt thou make it. [16]Four-square it shall be being doubled; a span shall be the length thereof, and a span shall be the breadth thereof. [17]And thou shalt set in it settings of stones, even four rows of stones: the first row shall be a sardius, a topaz, and a carbuncle: this shall be the first row. [18]And the second row shall be an emerald, a sapphire, and a diamond. [19]And the third row a ligure, an agate, and an amethyst. [20]And the fourth row a beryl, and an onyx, and a jasper: they shall be set in gold in their enclosings. [21]And the stones shall be with the names of the children of Israel, twelve, according to their names, like the engravings of a signet: every one with his name shall they be according to the twelve tribes.

[22]'And thou shalt make upon the breastplate chains at the ends of wreathen work of pure gold. [23]And thou shalt make upon the breastplate two rings of gold, and shalt put the two rings on the two ends of the breastplate. [24]And thou shalt put the two wreathen chains of gold in the two rings which are on the ends of the breastplate. [25]And the other two ends of the two wreathen chains thou shalt fasten in the two ouches, and put them on the shoulder-pieces of the ephod before it.

[26]'And thou shalt make two rings of gold, and thou shalt put them upon the two ends of the breastplate in the border thereof, which is in the side of the ephod inward. [27]And two other rings of gold thou shalt make, and shalt put them on the two sides of the ephod underneath, towards the forepart thereof, over against the other coupling thereof, above the curious girdle of the ephod. [28]And they shall bind the breastplate by the rings thereof unto the rings of the ephod with a lace of blue, that it may be above the curious girdle of the ephod, and that the breastplate be not loosed from the ephod. [29]And Aaron shall bear the names of the children of Israel in the breastplate of judgement upon his heart, when he goeth in unto the holy place, for a memorial before the LORD continually.

[30]'And thou shalt put in the breastplate of judgement the Urim and the Thummim, and they shall be upon Aaron's heart, when he goeth in

before the LORD: and Aaron shall bear the judgement of the children of Israel upon his heart before the LORD continually.

[31]'And thou shalt make the robe of the ephod all of blue. [32]And there shall be a hole in the top of it, in the midst thereof: it shall have a binding of woven work round about the hole of it, as it were the hole of a habergeon, that it be not rent.

[33]'And beneath upon the hem of it thou shalt make pomegranates of blue, and of purple, and of scarlet, round about the hem thereof, and bells of gold between them round about: [34]a golden bell and a pomegranate, a golden bell and a pomegranate, upon the hem of the robe round about. [35]And it shall be upon Aaron to minister: and his sound shall be heard when he goeth in unto the holy place before the LORD, and when he cometh out, that he die not.

[36]'And thou shalt make a plate of pure gold, and grave upon it, like the engravings of a signet, HOLINESS TO THE LORD. [37]And thou shalt put it on a blue lace, that it may be upon the mitre; upon the forefront of the mitre it shall be. [38]And it shall be upon Aaron's forehead, that Aaron may bear the iniquity of the holy things, which the children of Israel shall hallow in all their holy gifts: and it shall be always upon his forehead, that they may be accepted before the LORD.

[39]'And thou shalt embroider the coat of fine linen, and thou shalt make the mitre of fine linen, and thou shalt make the girdle of needlework.

[40]'And for Aaron's sons thou shalt make coats, and thou shalt make for them girdles, and bonnets shalt thou make for them, for glory and for beauty. [41]And thou shalt put them upon Aaron thy brother, and his sons with him; and shalt anoint them, and consecrate them, and sanctify them, that they may minister unto me in the priest's office. [42]And thou shalt make them linen breeches to cover their nakedness; from the loins even unto the thighs they shall reach. [43]And they shall be upon Aaron, and upon his sons, when they come in unto the tabernacle of the congregation, or when they come near unto the altar to minister in the holy place, that they bear not iniquity, and die: it shall be a statute for ever unto him and his seed after him.

29 'And this is the thing that thou shalt do unto them to hallow them, to minister unto me in the priest's office: take one young bullock, and two rams without blemish, [2]and unleavened bread, and cakes unleavened tempered with oil, and wafers unleavened anointed with oil: of wheaten flour shalt thou make them. [3]And thou shalt put them into one basket, and bring them in the basket, with the bullock and the two rams. [4]And Aaron and his sons thou shalt bring unto the door of the tabernacle of the congregation, and shalt wash them with water. [5]And thou shalt take the garments, and put upon Aaron the coat, and the robe of the ephod, and the ephod, and the breastplate, and gird him with the curious girdle of the ephod. [6]And thou shalt put the mitre upon his head, and put the holy crown upon the mitre. [7]Then shalt thou take the anointing oil, and pour it upon his head, and anoint him. [8]And thou shalt bring his sons, and put coats upon them. [9]And

thou shalt gird them with girdles, Aaron and his sons, and put the bonnets on them: and the priest's office shall be theirs for a perpetual statute: and thou shalt consecrate Aaron and his sons. ¹⁰And thou shalt cause a bullock to be brought before the tabernacle of the congregation: and Aaron and his sons shall put their hands upon the head of the bullock. ¹¹And thou shalt kill the bullock before the LORD, by the door of the tabernacle of the congregation. ¹²And thou shalt take of the blood of the bullock, and put it upon the horns of the altar with thy finger, and pour all the blood beside the bottom of the altar. ¹³And thou shalt take all the fat that covereth the inwards, and the caul that is above the liver, and the two kidneys, and the fat that is upon them, and burn them upon the altar. ¹⁴But the flesh of the bullock, and his skin, and his dung, shalt thou burn with fire without the camp: it is a sin offering.

¹⁵'Thou shalt also take one ram, and Aaron and his sons shall put their hands upon the head of the ram. ¹⁶And thou shalt slay the ram, and thou shalt take his blood, and sprinkle it around about upon the altar. ¹⁷And thou shalt cut the ram in pieces, and wash the inwards of him, and his legs, and put them unto his pieces, and unto his head. ¹⁸And thou shalt burn the whole ram upon the altar: it is a burnt offering unto the LORD: it is a sweet savour, an offering made by fire unto the LORD.

¹⁹'And thou shalt take the other ram: and Aaron and his sons shall put their hands upon the head of the ram. ²⁰Then shalt thou kill the ram, and take of his blood, and put it upon the tip of the right ear of Aaron, and upon the tip of the right ear of his sons, and upon the thumb of their right hand, and upon the great toe of their right foot, and sprinkle the blood upon the altar round about. ²¹And thou shalt take of the blood that is upon the altar, and of the anointing oil, and sprinkle it upon Aaron, and upon his garments, and upon his sons, and upon the garments of his sons with him: and he shall be hallowed, and his garments, and his sons, and his sons' garments with him. ²²Also thou shalt take of the ram the fat and the rump, and the fat that covereth the inwards, and the caul above the liver, and the two kidneys, and the fat that is upon them, and the right shoulder; for it is a ram of consecration: ²³and one loaf of bread, and one cake of oiled bread, and one wafer out of the basket of the unleavened bread that is before the LORD. ²⁴And thou shalt put all in the hands of Aaron, and in the hands of his sons, and shalt wave them for a wave offering before the LORD. ²⁵And thou shalt receive them of their hands, and burn them upon the altar for a burnt offering, for a sweet savour before the LORD: it is an offering made by fire unto the LORD. ²⁶And thou shalt take the breast of the ram of Aaron's consecrations, and wave it for a wave offering before the LORD: and it shall be thy part. ²⁷And thou shalt sanctify the breast of the wave offering, and the shoulder of the heave offering, which is waved, and which is heaved up, of the ram of the consecration, even of that which is for Aaron, and of that which is for his sons. ²⁸And it shall be Aaron's and his sons' by a statute for ever from the children of Israel:

for it is a heave offering: and it shall be a heave offering from the children of Israel of the sacrifice of their peace offerings, even their heave offering unto the LORD.

[29] 'And the holy garments of Aaron shall be his sons' after him, to be anointed therein, and to be consecrated in them. [30]And that son that is priest in his stead shall put them on seven days, when he cometh into the tabernacle of the congregation to minister in the holy place.

[31] 'And thou shalt take the ram of the consecration, and seethe his flesh in the holy place. [32]And Aaron and his sons shall eat the flesh of the ram, and the bread that is in the basket, by the door of the tabernacle of the congregation. [33]And they shall eat those things wherewith the atonement was made, to consecrate and to sanctify them: but a stranger shall not eat thereof, because they are holy. [34]And if aught of the flesh of the consecrations, or of the bread, remain unto the morning, then thou shalt burn the remainder with fire: it shall not be eaten, because it is holy.

[35] 'And thus shalt thou do unto Aaron, and to his sons, according to all things which I have commanded thee: seven days shalt thou consecrate them. [36]And thou shalt offer every day a bullock for a sin offering for atonement: and thou shalt cleanse the altar, when thou hast made an atonement for it, and thou shalt anoint it, to sanctify it. [37]Seven days thou shalt make an atonement for the altar, and sanctify it: and it shall be an altar most holy: whatsoever toucheth the altar shall be holy.

[38] 'Now this is that which thou shalt offer upon the altar: two lambs of the first year day by day continually. [39]The one lamb thou shalt offer in the morning; and the other lamb thou shalt offer at even: [40]and with the one lamb a tenth deal of flour mingled with the fourth part of a hin of beaten oil; and the fourth part of a hin of wine for a drink offering. [41]And the other lamb thou shalt offer at even, and shalt do thereto according to the meat offering of the morning, and according to the drink offering thereof, for a sweet savour, an offering made by fire unto the LORD. [42]This shall be a continual burnt offering throughout your generations at the door of the tabernacle of the congregation before the LORD: where I will meet you, to speak there unto thee. [43]And there I will meet with the children of Israel, and the tabernacle shall be sanctified by my glory. [44]And I will sanctify the tabernacle of the congregation, and the altar: I will sanctify also both Aaron and his sons, to minister to me in the priest's office. [45]And I will dwell amongst the children of Israel, and will be their God. [46]And they shall know that I am the LORD their God, that brought them forth out of the land of Egypt, that I may dwell amongst them: I am the LORD their God.

30

'And thou shalt make an altar to burn incense upon: of shittim wood shalt thou make it. [2]A cubit shall be the length thereof, and a cubit the breadth thereof; four-square shall it be: and two cubits shall be the height thereof: the horns thereof shall be of the same. [3]And thou shalt overlay it with pure gold, the top thereof, and the sides thereof round about, and the horns thereof; and thou shalt make unto it a crown of gold round about. [4]And two golden rings shalt thou make to it under the crown of it, by the two corners thereof, upon the two sides of it shalt thou make it: and they shall be for places for the staves to bear it withal. ⁵And thou shalt make the staves of shittim wood, and overlay them with gold. ⁶And thou shalt put it before the veil that is by the ark of the testimony, before the mercy-seat that is over the testimony, where I will meet with thee. ⁷And Aaron shall burn thereon sweet incense every morning: when he dresseth the lamps, he shall burn incense upon it. ⁸And when Aaron lighteth the lamps at even, he shall burn incense upon it, a perpetual incense before the LORD throughout your generations. ⁹Ye shall offer no strange incense thereon, nor burnt sacrifice, nor meat offering, neither shall ye pour drink offering thereon. ¹⁰And Aaron shall make an atonement upon the horns of it once in a year with the blood of the sin offering of atonements: once in the year shall he make atonement upon it throughout your generations: it is most holy unto the LORD.'

¹¹And the LORD spoke unto Moses, saying, ¹²'When thou takest the sum of the children of Israel after their number, then shall they give every man a ransom for his soul unto the LORD, when thou numberest them, that there be no plague amongst them, when thou numberest them. ¹³This they shall give, every one that passeth among them that are numbered, half a shekel after the shekel of the sanctuary (a shekel is twenty gerahs): a half shekel shall be the offering of the LORD. ¹⁴Every one that passeth among them that are numbered, from twenty years old and above, shall give an offering unto the LORD. ¹⁵The rich shall not give more, and the poor shall not give less than half a shekel, when they give an offering unto the LORD, to make an atonement for your souls. ¹⁶And thou shalt take the atonement money of the children of Israel, and shalt appoint it for the service of the tabernacle of the congregation, that it may be a memorial unto the children of Israel before the LORD, to make an atonement for your souls.'

¹⁷And the LORD spoke unto Moses, saying, ¹⁸'Thou shalt also make a laver of brass, and his foot also of brass, to wash withal, and thou shalt put it between the tabernacle of the congregation and the altar, and thou shalt put water therein. ¹⁹For Aaron and his sons shall wash their hands and their feet thereat. ²⁰When they go into the tabernacle of the congregation, they shall wash with water, that they die not; or when they come near to the altar to minister, to burn offering made by fire unto the LORD: ²¹so they shall wash their hands and their feet, that they die not: and it shall be a statute for ever to them, even to him and to his seed throughout their generations.'

²²Moreover the LORD spoke unto Moses, saying, ²³'Take thou also unto thee principal spices, of pure myrrh five hundred shekels, and of sweet cinnamon half so much, even two hundred and fifty shekels, and of sweet calamus two hundred and fifty shekels, ²⁴and of cassia five hundred shekels, after the shekel of the sanctuary, and of oil olive a hin. ²⁵And thou shalt make it an oil of holy ointment, an ointment compound after the art of the apothecary: it shall be a holy anointing oil. ²⁶And thou shalt anoint the tabernacle of the congregation there-

with, and the ark of the testimony, ²⁷and the table and all his vessels, and the candlestick and his vessels, and the altar of incense, ²⁸and the altar of burnt offering with all his vessels, and the laver and his foot. ²⁹And thou shalt sanctify them, that they may be most holy: whatsoever toucheth them shall be holy. ³⁰And thou shalt anoint Aaron and his sons, and consecrate them, that they may minister unto me in the priest's office. ³¹And thou shalt speak unto the children of Israel, saying, "This shall be a holy anointing oil unto me throughout your generations. ³²Upon man's flesh shall it not be poured, neither shall ye make any other like it, after the composition of it: it is holy, and it shall be holy unto you. ³³Whosoever compoundeth any like it, or whosoever putteth any of it upon a stranger, shall even be cut off from his people."'

³⁴And the LORD said unto Moses, 'Take unto thee sweet spices, stacte, and onycha, and galbanum: these sweet spices with pure frankincense, of each shall there be a like weight. ³⁵And thou shalt make it a perfume, a confection after the art of the apothecary, tempered together, pure and holy. ³⁶And thou shalt beat some of it very small, and put of it before the testimony in the tabernacle of the congregation, where I will meet with thee: it shall be unto you most holy. ³⁷And as for the perfume which thou shalt make, you shall not make to yourselves according to the composition thereof: it shall be unto thee holy for the LORD. ³⁸Whosoever shall make like unto that, to smell thereto, shall even be cut off from his people.'

31 And the LORD spoke unto Moses, saying, ²'See, I have called by name Bezaleel the son of Uri, the son of Hur, of the tribe of Judah: ³and I have filled him with the Spirit of God, in wisdom, and in understanding, and in knowledge, and in all manner of workmanship, ⁴to devise cunning works, to work in gold, and in silver, and in brass, ⁵and in cutting of stones, to set them, and in carving of timber, to work in all manner of workmanship. ⁶And I, behold, I have given with him Aholiab, the son of Ahisamach, of the tribe of Dan: and in the hearts of all that are wise-hearted I have put wisdom, that they may make all that I have commanded thee: ⁷the tabernacle of the congregation, and the ark of the testimony, and the mercy-seat that is thereupon, and all the furniture of the tabernacle, ⁸and the table and his furniture, and the pure candlestick with all his furniture, and the altar of incense, ⁹and the altar of burnt offering with all his furniture, and the laver and his foot, ¹⁰and the cloths of service, and the holy garments for Aaron the priest, and the garments of his sons, to minister in the priest's office, ¹¹and the anointing oil, and sweet incense for the holy place: according to all that I have commanded thee shall they do.'

¹²And the LORD spoke unto Moses, saying, ¹³'Speak thou also unto the children of Israel, saying, "Verily my sabbaths ye shall keep: for it is a sign between me and you throughout your generations, that ye may know that I am the LORD that doth sanctify you. ¹⁴Ye shall keep the sabbath therefore: for it is holy unto you: every one that defileth it shall surely be put to death: for whosoever doeth any work therein, that soul

shall be cut off from amongst his people. [15]Six days may work be done, but in the seventh is the sabbath of rest, holy to the LORD: whosoever doeth any work in the sabbath day, he shall surely be put to death. [16]Wherefore the children of Israel shall keep the sabbath, to observe the sabbath throughout their generations, for a perpetual covenant. [17]It is a sign between me and the children of Israel for ever: for in six days the LORD made heaven and earth, and on the seventh day he rested, and was refreshed."'

[18]And he gave unto Moses, when he had made an end of communing with him upon mount Sinai, two tablets of testimony, tablets of stone, written with the finger of God.

32 And when the people saw that Moses delayed to come down out of the mount, the people gathered themselves together unto Aaron, and said unto him, 'Up, make us gods which shall go before us: for as for this Moses, the man that brought us up out of the land of Egypt, we wot not what is become of him'. [2]And Aaron said unto them, 'Break off the golden earrings, which are in the ears of your wives, of your sons, and of your daughters, and bring them unto me'. [3]And all the people broke off the golden earrings which were in their ears, and brought them unto Aaron. [4]And he received them at their hand, and fashioned it with a graving tool, after he had made it a molten calf: and they said, 'These be thy gods, O Israel, which brought thee up out of the land of Egypt'. [5]And when Aaron saw it, he built an altar before it; and Aaron made proclamation, and said, 'Tomorrow is a feast to the LORD'. [6]And they rose up early on the morrow, and offered burnt offerings, and brought peace offerings; and the people sat down to eat and to drink, and rose up to play.

[7]And the LORD said unto Moses, 'Go, get thee down: for thy people, which thou broughtest out of the land of Egypt, have corrupted themselves. [8]They have turned aside quickly out of the way which I commanded them: they have made them a molten calf, and have worshipped it, and have sacrificed thereunto, and said, "These be thy gods, O Israel, which have brought thee up out of the land of Egypt".' [9]And the LORD said unto Moses, 'I have seen this people, and behold, it is a stiff-necked people. [10]Now therefore let me alone, that my wrath may wax hot against them, and that I may consume them: and I will make of thee a great nation.' [11]And Moses besought the LORD his God, and said, 'LORD, why doth thy wrath wax hot against thy people, which thou hast brought forth out of the land of Egypt with great power, and with a mighty hand? [12]Wherefore should the Egyptians speak, and say, "For mischief did he bring them out, to slay them in the mountains, and to consume them from the face of the earth"? Turn from thy fierce wrath, and repent of this evil against thy people. [13]Remember Abraham, Isaac, and Israel, thy servants, to whom thou sworest by thy own self, and saidst unto them, "I will multiply your seed as the stars of heaven, and all this land that I have spoken of will I give unto your seed, and they shall inherit it for ever".' [14]And the LORD repented of the evil which he thought to do unto his people.

¹⁵And Moses turned, and went down from the mount, and the two tablets of the testimony were in his hand: the tablets were written on both their sides; on the one side and on the other were they written. ¹⁶And the tablets were the work of God, and the writing was the writing of God, graven upon the tablets. ¹⁷And when Joshua heard the noise of the people as they shouted, he said unto Moses, 'There is a noise of war in the camp'. ¹⁸And he said, 'It is not the voice of them that shout for mastery, neither is it the voice of them that cry for being overcome: but the noise of them that sing do I hear'.

¹⁹And it came to pass, as soon as he came nigh unto the camp, that he saw the calf, and the dancing: and Moses' anger waxed hot, and he cast the tablets out of his hands, and broke them beneath the mount. ²⁰And he took the calf which they had made, and burnt it in the fire, and ground it to powder, and strewed it upon the water, and made the children of Israel drink of it. ²¹And Moses said unto Aaron, 'What did this people unto thee, that thou hast brought so great a sin upon them?' ²²And Aaron said, 'Let not the anger of my lord wax hot: thou knowest the people, that they are set on mischief. ²³For they said unto me, "Make us gods, which shall go before us: for as for this Moses, the man that brought us up out of the land of Egypt, we wot not what is become of him". ²⁴And I said unto them, "Whosoever hath any gold, let them break it off". So they gave it me: then I cast it into the fire, and there came out this calf.'

²⁵And when Moses saw that the people were naked (for Aaron had made them naked unto their shame amongst their enemies), ²⁶then Moses stood in the gate of the camp, and said, 'Who is on the Lord's side? let him come unto me'. And all the sons of Levi gathered themselves together unto him. ²⁷And he said unto them, 'Thus saith the Lord God of Israel, "Put every man his sword by his side, and go in and out from gate to gate throughout the camp, and slay every man his brother, and every man his companion, and every man his neighbour"'. ²⁸And the children of Levi did according to the word of Moses: and there fell of the people that day about three thousand men. ²⁹For Moses had said, 'Consecrate yourselves today to the Lord, even every man upon his son, and upon his brother; that he may bestow upon you a blessing this day'.

³⁰And it came to pass on the morrow, that Moses said unto the people, 'Ye have sinned a great sin: and now I will go up unto the Lord; peradventure I shall make an atonement for your sin'. ³¹And Moses returned unto the Lord, and said, 'Oh, this people have sinned a great sin, and have made them gods of gold. ³²Yet now, if thou wilt forgive their sin—; and if not, blot me, I pray thee, out of thy book which thou hast written.' ³³And the Lord said unto Moses, 'Whosoever hath sinned against me, him will I blot out of my book. ³⁴Therefore now go, lead the people unto the place of which I have spoken unto thee: behold, my Angel shall go before thee; nevertheless in the day when I visit I will visit their sin upon them.' ³⁵And the Lord plagued the people, because they made the calf, which Aaron made.

33

And the LORD said unto Moses, 'Depart, and go up hence, thou and the people which thou hast brought up out of the land of Egypt, unto the land which I swore unto Abraham, to Isaac, and to Jacob, saying, "Unto thy seed will I give it". ²And I will send an angel before thee, and I will drive out the Canaanite, the Amorite, and the Hittite, and the Perizzite, the Hivite, and the Jebusite: ³unto a land flowing with milk and honey: for I will not go up in the midst of thee: for thou art a stiff-necked people: lest I consume thee in the way.'

⁴And when the people heard these evil tidings, they mourned: and no man did put on him his ornaments. ⁵For the LORD had said unto Moses, 'Say unto the children of Israel, "Ye are a stiff-necked people: I will come up into the midst of thee in a moment, and consume thee: therefore now put off thy ornaments from thee, that I may know what to do unto thee"'. ⁶And the children of Israel stripped themselves of their ornaments by the mount Horeb.

⁷And Moses took the tabernacle, and pitched it without the camp, afar off from the camp, and called it the Tabernacle of the Congregation. And it came to pass, that every one which sought the LORD went out unto the tabernacle of the congregation, which was without the camp. ⁸And it came to pass, when Moses went out unto the tabernacle, that all the people rose up, and stood every man at his tent door, and looked after Moses, until he was gone into the tabernacle. ⁹And it came to pass, as Moses entered into the tabernacle, the cloudy pillar descended, and stood at the door of the tabernacle, and the LORD talked with Moses. ¹⁰And all the people saw the cloudy pillar stand at the tabernacle door: and all the people rose up and worshipped, every man in his tent door. ¹¹And the LORD spoke unto Moses face to face, as a man speaketh unto his friend. And he turned again into the camp, but his servant Joshua, the son of Nun, a young man, departed not out of the tabernacle.

¹²And Moses said unto the LORD, 'See, thou sayest unto me, "Bring up this people", and thou hast not let me know whom thou wilt send with me. Yet thou hast said, "I know thee by name, and thou hast also found grace in my sight". ¹³Now therefore, I pray thee, if I have found grace in thy sight, show me now thy way, that I may know thee, that I may find grace in thy sight: and consider that this nation is thy people.' ¹⁴And he said, 'My presence shall go with thee, and I will give thee rest'. ¹⁵And he said unto him, 'If thy presence go not with me, carry us not up hence. ¹⁶For wherein shall it be known here that I and thy people have found grace in thy sight? is it not in that thou goest with us? So shall we be separated, I and thy people, from all the people that are upon the face of the earth.' ¹⁷And the LORD said unto Moses, 'I will do this thing also that thou hast spoken: for thou hast found grace in my sight, and I know thee by name'. ¹⁸And he said, 'I beseech thee, show me thy glory'. ¹⁹And he said, 'I will make all my goodness pass before thee, and I will proclaim the name of the LORD before thee; and will be gracious to whom I will be gracious, and will show mercy on whom I will show mercy'. ²⁰And he said, 'Thou canst not see my face: for there shall no

man see me, and live'. ²¹And the LORD said, 'Behold, there is a place by me, and thou shalt stand upon a rock. ²²And it shall come to pass, while my glory passeth by, that I will put thee in a cleft of the rock, and will cover thee with my hand while I pass by. ²³And I will take away my hand, and thou shalt see my back parts: but my face shall not be seen.'

34 And the LORD said unto Moses, 'Hew thee two tablets of stone like unto the first: and I will write upon these tablets the words that were in the first tablets, which thou brokest. ²And be ready in the morning, and come up in the morning unto mount Sinai, and present thyself there to me in the top of the mount.' ³And no man shall come up with thee, neither let any man be seen throughout all the mount; neither let the flocks nor herds feed before that mount.

⁴And he hewed two tablets of stone like unto the first; and Moses rose up early in the morning, and went up unto mount Sinai, as the LORD had commanded him, and took in his hand the two tablets of stone. ⁵And the LORD descended in the cloud, and stood with him there, and proclaimed the name of the LORD. ⁶And the LORD passed by before him, and proclaimed, 'The LORD, the LORD God, merciful and gracious, long-suffering, and abundant in goodness and truth, ⁷keeping mercy for thousands, forgiving iniquity and transgression and sin, and that will by no means clear the guilty, visiting the iniquity of the fathers upon the children, and upon the children's children, unto the third and to the fourth generation'. ⁸And Moses made haste, and bowed his head toward the earth, and worshipped. ⁹And he said, 'If now I have found grace in thy sight, O Lord, let my Lord, I pray thee, go amongst us (for it is a stiff-necked people), and pardon our iniquity and our sin, and take us for thy inheritance'.

¹⁰And he said, 'Behold, I make a covenant: before all thy people I will do marvels, such as have not been done in all the earth, nor in any nation: and all the people amongst which thou art shall see the work of the LORD: for it is a terrible thing that I will do with thee. ¹¹Observe thou that which I command thee this day: behold, I drive out before thee the Amorite, and the Canaanite, and the Hittite, and the Perizzite, and the Hivite, and the Jebusite. ¹²Take heed to thyself, lest thou make a covenant with the inhabitants of the land whither thou goest, lest it be for a snare in the midst of thee: ¹³but ye shall destroy their altars, break their images, and cut down their groves: ¹⁴for thou shalt worship no other god: for the LORD, whose name is Jealous, is a jealous God: ¹⁵lest thou make a covenant with the inhabitants of the land, and they go a-whoring after their gods, and do sacrifice unto their gods, and one call thee, and thou eat of his sacrifice, ¹⁶and thou take of their daughters unto thy sons, and their daughters go a-whoring after their gods, and make thy sons go a-whoring after their gods.

¹⁷'Thou shalt make thee no molten gods.

¹⁸'The feast of unleavened bread shalt thou keep. Seven days thou shalt eat unleavened bread, as I commanded thee, in the time of the month Abib: for in the month Abib thou camest out from Egypt.

¹⁹'All that openeth the matrix is mine: and every firstling amongst

thy cattle, whether ox or sheep, that is male. ²⁰But the firstling of an ass thou shalt redeem with a lamb: and if thou redeem him not, then shalt thou break his neck. All the firstborn of thy sons thou shalt redeem. And none shall appear before me empty.

²¹'Six days thou shalt work, but on the seventh day thou shalt rest: in earing time and in harvest thou shalt rest.

²²'And thou shalt observe the feast of weeks, of the first-fruits of wheat harvest, and the feast of ingathering at the year's end.

²³'Thrice in the year shall all your men-children appear before the Lord God, the God of Israel. ²⁴For I will cast out the nations before thee, and enlarge thy borders: neither shall any man desire thy land, when thou shalt go up to appear before the Lord thy God thrice in the year.

²⁵'Thou shalt not offer the blood of my sacrifice with leaven, neither shall the sacrifice of the feast of passover be left unto the morning.

²⁶'The first of the first-fruits of thy land thou shalt bring unto the house of the Lord thy God. Thou shalt not seethe a kid in his mother's milk.'

²⁷'And the Lord said unto Moses, 'Write thou these words: for after the tenor of these words I have made a covenant with thee and with Israel'. ²⁸And he was there with the Lord forty days and forty nights: he did neither eat bread, nor drink water. And he wrote upon the tablets the words of the covenant, the ten commandments.

²⁹And it came to pass, when Moses came down from mount Sinai with the two tablets of testimony in Moses' hand, when he came down from the mount, that Moses wist not that the skin of his face shone while he talked with him. ³⁰And when Aaron and all the children of Israel saw Moses, behold, the skin of his face shone, and they were afraid to come nigh him. ³¹And Moses called unto them, and Aaron and all the rulers of the congregation returned unto him, and Moses talked with them. ³²And afterward all the children of Israel came nigh: and he gave them in commandment all that the Lord had spoken with him in mount Sinai. ³³And till Moses had done speaking with them, he put a veil on his face. ³⁴But when Moses went in before the Lord to speak with him, he took the veil off, until he came out. And he came out, and spoke unto the children of Israel that which he was commanded. ³⁵And the children of Israel saw the face of Moses, that the skin of Moses' face shone: and Moses put the veil upon his face again, until he went in to speak with him.

35 And Moses gathered all the congregation of the children of Israel together, and said unto them, 'These are the words which the Lord hath commanded, that ye should do them. ²"Six days shall work be done, but on the seventh day there shall be to you a holy day, a sabbath of rest to the Lord: whosoever doeth work therein shall be put to death. ³Ye shall kindle no fire throughout your habitations upon the sabbath day."'

⁴And Moses spoke unto all the congregation of the children of Israel, saying, 'This is the thing which the Lord commanded, saying, ⁵"Take ye from amongst you an offering unto the Lord: whosoever is of a willing

heart, let him bring it, an offering of the LORD; gold, and silver, and brass, [6]and blue, and purple, and scarlet, and fine linen, and goats' hair, [7]and rams' skins dyed red, and badgers' skins, and shittim wood, [8]and oil for the light, and spices for anointing oil, and for the sweet incense, [9]and onyx stones, and stones to be set for the ephod, and for the breastplate. [10]And every wise-hearted among you shall come, and make all that the LORD hath commanded: [11]the tabernacle, his tent, and his covering, his taches, and his boards, his bars, his pillars, and his sockets, [12]the ark, and the staves thereof, with the mercy-seat, and the veil of the covering, [13]the table, and his staves, and all his vessels, and the showbread, [14]the candlestick also for the light, and his furniture, and his lamps, with the oil for the light, [15]and the incense altar, and his staves, and the anointing oil, and the sweet incense, and the hanging for the door at the entering in of the tabernacle, [16]the altar of burnt offering, with his brazen grate, his staves, and all his vessels, the laver and his foot, [17]the hangings of the court, his pillars, and their sockets, and the hanging for the door of the court, [18]the pins of the tabernacle, and the pins of the court, and their cords, [19]the cloths of service, to do service in the holy place, the holy garments for Aaron the priest, and the garments of his sons, to minister in the priest's office."'

[20]And all the congregation of the children of Israel departed from the presence of Moses. [21]And they came, every one whose heart stirred him up, and every one whom his spirit made willing, and they brought the LORD's offering to the work of the tabernacle of the congregation, and for all his service, and for the holy garments. [22]And they came, both men and women, as many as were willing-hearted, and brought bracelets, and earrings, and rings, and tablets, all jewels of gold: and every man that offered offered an offering of gold unto the LORD. [23]And every man, with whom was found blue, and purple, and scarlet, and fine linen, and goats' hair, and red skins of rams, and badgers' skins, brought them. [24]Every one that did offer an offering of silver and brass brought the LORD's offering: and every man, with whom was found shittim wood for any work of the service, brought it. [25]And all the women that were wise-hearted did spin with their hands, and brought that which they had spun, both of blue, and of purple, and of scarlet, and of fine linen. [26]And all the women whose heart stirred them up in wisdom spun goats' hair. [27]And the rulers brought onyx stones, and stones to be set, for the ephod, and for the breastplate; [28]and spice, and oil for the light, and for the anointing oil, and for the sweet incense. [29]The children of Israel brought a willing offering unto the LORD, every man and woman, whose heart made them willing to bring for all manner of work, which the LORD had commanded to be made by the hands of Moses.

[30]And Moses said unto the children of Israel, 'See, the LORD hath called by name Bezaleel the son of Uri, the son of Hur, of the tribe of Judah. [31]And he hath filled him with the Spirit of God, in wisdom, in understanding, and in knowledge, and in all manner of workmanship; [32]and to devise curious works, to work in gold, and in silver, and in

brass, ³³and in the cutting of stones, to set them, and in carving of wood, to make any manner of cunning work. ³⁴And he hath put in his heart that he may teach, both he, and Aholiab, the son of Ahisamach, of the tribe of Dan. ³⁵Them hath he filled with wisdom of heart, to work all manner of work, of the engraver, and of the cunning workman, and of the embroiderer, in blue, and in purple, in scarlet, and in fine linen, and of the weaver, even of them that do any work, and of those that devise cunning work.'

36 Then wrought Bezaleel and Aholiab, and every wise-hearted man, in whom the LORD put wisdom and understanding to know how to work all manner of work for the service of the sanctuary, according to all that the LORD had commanded. ²And Moses called Bezaleel and Aholiab, and every wise-hearted man, in whose heart the LORD had put wisdom, even every one whose heart stirred him up to come unto the work to do it. ³And they received of Moses all the offering, which the children of Israel had brought for the work of the service of the sanctuary, to make it withal. And they brought yet unto him free offerings every morning. ⁴And all the wise men, that wrought all the work of the sanctuary, came every man from his work which they made.

⁵And they spoke unto Moses, saying, 'The people bring much more than enough for the service of the work, which the LORD commanded to make'. ⁶And Moses gave commandment, and they caused it to be proclaimed throughout the camp, saying, 'Let neither man nor woman make any more work for the offering of the sanctuary'. So the people were restrained from bringing. ⁷For the stuff they had was sufficient for all the work to make it, and too much.

⁸And every wise-hearted man among them that wrought the work of the tabernacle made ten curtains of fine twined linen, and blue, and purple, and scarlet: with cherubims of cunning work made he them. ⁹The length of one curtain was twenty and eight cubits, and the breadth of one curtain four cubits: the curtains were all of one size. ¹⁰And he coupled the five curtains one unto another: and the other five curtains he coupled one unto another. ¹¹And he made loops of blue on the edge of one curtain from the selvedge in the coupling: likewise he made in the outermost side of another curtain, in the coupling of the second. ¹²Fifty loops made he in one curtain, and fifty loops made he in the edge of the curtain which was in the coupling of the second: the loops held one curtain to another. ¹³And he made fifty taches of gold, and coupled the curtains one unto another with the taches. So it became one tabernacle.

¹⁴And he made curtains of goats' hair for the tent over the tabernacle: eleven curtains he made them. ¹⁵The length of one curtain was thirty cubits, and four cubits was the breadth of one curtain: the eleven curtains were of one size. ¹⁶And he coupled five curtains by themselves, and six curtains by themselves. ¹⁷And he made fifty loops upon the outermost edge of the curtain in the coupling, and fifty loops made he upon the edge of the curtain which coupleth the second. ¹⁸And he

made fifty taches of brass to couple the tent together, that it might be one. ¹⁹And he made a covering for the tent of rams' skins dyed red, and a covering of badgers' skins above that.

²⁰And he made boards for the tabernacle of shittim wood, standing up. ²¹The length of a board was ten cubits, and the breadth of a board one cubit and a half. ²²One board had two tenons, equally distant one from another: thus did he make for all the boards of the tabernacle. ²³And he made boards for the tabernacle: twenty boards for the south side southward. ²⁴And forty sockets of silver he made under the twenty boards: two sockets under one board for his two tenons, and two sockets under another board for his two tenons. ²⁵And for the other side of the tabernacle, which is toward the north corner, he made twenty boards, ²⁶and their forty sockets of silver: two sockets under one board, and two sockets under another board. ²⁷And for the sides of the tabernacle westward he made six boards. ²⁸And two boards made he for the corners of the tabernacle in the two sides. ²⁹And they were coupled beneath, and coupled together at the head thereof, to one ring: thus he did to both of them in both the corners. ³⁰And there were eight boards, and their sockets were sixteen sockets of silver: under every board two sockets.

³¹And he made bars of shittim wood: five for the boards of the one side of the tabernacle, ³²and five bars for the boards of the other side of the tabernacle, and five bars for the boards of the tabernacle for the sides westward. ³³And he made the middle bar to shoot through the boards from the one end to the other. ³⁴And he overlaid the boards with gold, and made their rings of gold to be places for the bars, and overlaid the bars with gold.

³⁵And he made a veil of blue, and purple, and scarlet, and fine twined linen: with cherubims made he it of cunning work. ³⁶And he made thereunto four pillars of shittim wood, and overlaid them with gold: their hooks were of gold; and he cast for them four sockets of silver.

³⁷And he made a hanging for the tabernacle door of blue, and purple, and scarlet, and fine twined linen, of needlework, ³⁸and the five pillars of it with their hooks: and he overlaid their chapiters and their fillets with gold: but their five sockets were of brass.

37 And Bezaleel made the ark of shittim wood: two cubits and a half was the length of it, and a cubit and a half the breadth of it, and a cubit and a half the height of it. ²And he overlaid it with pure gold within and without, and made a crown of gold to it round about. ³And he cast for it four rings of gold, to be set by the four corners of it: even two rings upon the one side of it, and two rings upon the other side of it. ⁴And he made staves of shittim wood, and overlaid them with gold. ⁵And he put the staves into the rings by the sides of the ark, to bear the ark.

⁶And he made the mercy-seat of pure gold: two cubits and a half was the length thereof, and one cubit and a half the breadth thereof. ⁷And he made two cherubims of gold, beaten out of one piece made he them, on the two ends of the mercy-seat: ⁸one cherub on the end on this side,

and another cherub on the other end on that side: out of the mercy-seat made he the cherubims on the two ends thereof. ⁹And the cherubims spread out their wings on high, and covered with their wings over the mercy-seat, with their faces one to another: even to the mercy-seat-ward were the faces of the cherubims.

¹⁰And he made the table of shittim wood: two cubits was the length thereof, and a cubit the breadth thereof, and a cubit and a half the height thereof. ¹¹And he overlaid it with pure gold, and made thereunto a crown of gold round about. ¹²Also he made thereunto a border of a handbreadth round about; and made a crown of gold for the border thereof round about. ¹³And he cast for it four rings of gold, and put the rings upon the four corners that were in the four feet thereof. ¹⁴Over against the border were the rings, the places for the staves to bear the table. ¹⁵And he made the staves of shittim wood, and overlaid them with gold, to bear the table. ¹⁶And he made the vessels which were upon the table, his dishes, and his spoons, and his bowls, and his covers to cover withal, of pure gold.

¹⁷And he made the candlestick of pure gold: of beaten work made he the candlestick; his shaft, and his branch, his bowls, his knops, and his flowers, were of the same: ¹⁸and six branches going out of the sides thereof: three branches of the candlestick out of the one side thereof, and three branches of the candlestick out of the other side thereof. ¹⁹Three bowls made after the fashion of almonds in one branch, a knop and a flower; and three bowls made like almonds in another branch, a knop and a flower: so throughout the six branches going out of the candlestick. ²⁰And in the candlestick were four bowls made like almonds, his knops, and his flowers: ²¹and a knop under two branches of the same, and a knop under two branches of the same, and a knop under two branches of the same, according to the six branches going out of it. ²²Their knops and their branches were of the same: all of it was one beaten work of pure gold. ²³And he made his seven lamps, and his snuffers, and his snuff-dishes, of pure gold. ²⁴Of a talent of pure gold made he it, and all the vessels thereof.

²⁵And he made the incense altar of shittim wood: the length of it was a cubit, and the breadth of it a cubit: it was four-square; and two cubits was the height of it; the horns thereof were of the same. ²⁶And he overlaid it with pure gold, both the top of it, and the sides thereof round about, and the horns of it: also he made unto it a crown of gold round about. ²⁷And he made two rings of gold for it under the crown thereof, by the two corners of it, upon the two sides thereof, to be places for the staves to bear it withal. ²⁸And he made the staves of shittim wood, and overlaid them with gold.

²⁹And he made the holy anointing oil, and the pure incense of sweet spices, according to the work of the apothecary.

38 And he made the altar of burnt offering of shittim wood: five cubits was the length thereof, and five cubits the breadth thereof: it was four-square, and three cubits the height thereof. ²And he made the horns thereof on the four corners of it; the horns thereof were of the same: and he overlaid it with brass. ³And he made all the vessels of the altar, the pots, and the shovels, and the basins, and the fleshhooks, and the fire-pans: all the vessels thereof made he of brass. ⁴And he made for the altar a brazen grate of network under the compass thereof beneath unto the midst of it. ⁵And he cast four rings for the four ends of the grate of brass, to be places for the staves. ⁶And he made the staves of shittim wood, and overlaid them with brass. ⁷And he put the staves into the rings on the sides of the altar, to bear it withal; he made the altar hollow with boards.

⁸And he made the laver of brass, and the foot of it of brass, of the looking-glasses of the women assembling, which assembled at the door of the tabernacle of the congregation.

⁹And he made the court: on the south side southward the hangings of the court were of fine twined linen, a hundred cubits. ¹⁰Their pillars were twenty, and their brazen sockets twenty; the hooks of the pillars and their fillets were of silver. ¹¹And for the north side the hangings were a hundred cubits, their pillars were twenty, and their sockets of brass twenty: the hooks of the pillars and their fillets of silver. ¹²And for the west side were hangings of fifty cubits, their pillars ten, and their sockets ten: the hooks of the pillars and their fillets of silver. ¹³And for the east side eastward fifty cubits. ¹⁴The hangings of the one side of the gate were fifteen cubits, their pillars three, and their sockets three. ¹⁵And for the other side of the court gate, on this hand and that hand, were hangings of fifteen cubits, their pillars three, and their sockets three. ¹⁶All the hangings of the court round about were of fine twined linen. ¹⁷And the sockets for the pillars were of brass, the hooks of the pillars and their fillets of silver, and the overlaying of their chapiters of silver, and all the pillars of the court were filleted with silver. ¹⁸And the hanging for the gate of the court was needlework, of blue, and purple, and scarlet, and fine twined linen: and twenty cubits was the length, and the height in the breadth was five cubits, answerable to the hangings of the court. ¹⁹And their pillars were four, and their sockets of brass four, their hooks of silver, and the overlaying of their chapiters and their fillets of silver. ²⁰And all the pins of the tabernacle, and of the court round about, were of brass.

²¹This is the sum of the tabernacle, even of the tabernacle of testimony, as it was counted, according to the commandment of Moses, for the service of the Levites, by the hand of Ithamar, son to Aaron the priest. ²²And Bezaleel the son of Uri, the son of Hur, of the tribe of Judah, made all that the LORD commanded Moses. ²³And with him was Aholiab, son of Ahisamach, of the tribe of Dan, an engraver, and a cunning workman, and an embroiderer in blue, and in purple, and in scarlet, and fine linen.

²⁴All the gold that was occupied for the work in all the work of the holy place, even the gold of the offering, was twenty and nine talents, and seven hundred and thirty shekels, after the shekel of the sanctuary. ²⁵And the silver of them that were numbered of the congregation was a hundred talents, and a thousand seven hundred and threescore

and fifteen shekels, after the shekel of the sanctuary: ²⁶a bekah for every man, that is, half a shekel, after the shekel of the sanctuary, for every one that went to be numbered, from twenty years old and upward, for six hundred thousand and three thousand and five hundred and fifty men. ²⁷And of the hundred talents of silver were cast the sockets of the sanctuary, and the sockets of the veil: a hundred sockets of the hundred talents, a talent for a socket. ²⁸And of the thousand seven hundred seventy and five shekels he made hooks for the pillars, and overlaid their chapiters, and filleted them. ²⁹And the brass of the offering was seventy talents, and two thousand and four hundred shekels. ³⁰And therewith he made the sockets to the door of the tabernacle of the congregation, and the brazen altar, and the brazen grate for it, and all the vessels of the altar, ³¹and the sockets of the court round about, and the sockets of the court gate, and all the pins of the tabernacle, and all the pins of the court round about.

39 And of the blue, and purple, and scarlet, they made clothes of service, to do service in the holy place, and made the holy garments for Aaron, as the LORD commanded Moses. ²And he made the ephod of gold, blue, and purple, and scarlet, and fine twined linen. ³And they did beat the gold into thin plates, and cut it into wires, to work it in the blue, and in the purple, and in the scarlet, and in the fine linen, with cunning work. ⁴They made shoulder-pieces for it, to couple it together; by the two edges was it coupled together. ⁵And the curious girdle of his ephod, that was upon it, was of the same, according to the work thereof: of gold, blue, and purple, and scarlet, and fine twined linen, as the LORD commanded Moses.

⁶And they wrought onyx stones enclosed in ouches of gold, graven, as signets are graven, with the names of the children of Israel. ⁷And he put them on the shoulders of the ephod, that they should be stones for a memorial to the children of Israel, as the LORD commanded Moses.

⁸And he made the breastplate of cunning work, like the work of the ephod, of gold, blue, and purple, and scarlet, and fine twined linen. ⁹It was four-square; they made the breastplate double: a span was the length thereof, and a span the breadth thereof, being doubled. ¹⁰And they set in it four rows of stones: the first row was a sardius, a topaz, and a carbuncle: this was the first row. ¹¹And the second row, an emerald, a sapphire, and a diamond. ¹²And the third row, a ligure, an agate, and an amethyst. ¹³And the fourth row, a beryl, an onyx, and a jasper: they were enclosed in ouches of gold in their enclosings. ¹⁴And the stones were according to the names of the children of Israel, twelve, according to their names, like the engravings of a signet, every one with his name, according to the twelve tribes. ¹⁵And they made upon the breastplate chains at the ends, of wreathen work of pure gold. ¹⁶And they made two ouches of gold, and two gold rings: and put the two rings in the two ends of the breastplate. ¹⁷And they put the two wreathen chains of gold in the two rings on the ends of the breastplate. ¹⁸And the two ends of the two wreathen chains they fastened in the two

ouches, and put them on the shoulder-pieces of the ephod, before it. ¹⁹And they made two rings of gold, and put them on the two ends of the breastplate, upon the border of it, which was on the side of the ephod inward. ²⁰And they made two other golden rings, and put them on the two sides of the ephod underneath, toward the forepart of it, over against the other coupling thereof, above the curious girdle of the ephod. ²¹And they did bind the breastplate by his rings unto the rings of the ephod with a lace of blue, that it might be above the curious girdle of the ephod, and that the breastplate might not be loosed from the ephod, as the LORD commanded Moses.

²²And he made the robe of the ephod of woven work, all of blue. ²³And there was a hole in the midst of the robe, as the hole of a habergeon, with a band round about the hole, that it should not rend. ²⁴And they made upon the hems of the robe pomegranates of blue, and purple, and scarlet, and twined linen. ²⁵And they made bells of pure gold, and put the bells between the pomegranates upon the hem of the robe, round about between the pomegranates; ²⁶a bell and a pomegranate, a bell and a pomegranate, round about the hem of the robe to minister in, as the LORD commanded Moses.

²⁷And they made coats of fine linen of woven work for Aaron, and for his sons, ²⁸and a mitre of fine linen, and goodly bonnets of fine linen, and linen breeches of fine twined linen, ²⁹and a girdle of fine twined linen, and blue, and purple, and scarlet, of needlework, as the LORD commanded Moses.

³⁰And they made the plate of the holy crown of pure gold, and wrote upon it a writing, like to the engravings of a signet, 'HOLINESS TO THE LORD'. ³¹And they tied unto it a lace of blue, to fasten it on high upon the mitre, as the LORD commanded Moses.

³²Thus was all the work of the tabernacle of the tent of the congregation finished: and the children of Israel did according to all that the LORD commanded Moses, so did they.

³³And they brought the tabernacle unto Moses, the tent, and all his furniture, his taches, his boards, his bars, and his pillars, and his sockets, ³⁴and the covering of rams' skins dyed red, and the covering of badgers' skins, and the veil of the covering, ³⁵the ark of the testimony, and the staves thereof, and the mercy-seat, ³⁶the table, and all the vessels thereof, and the showbread, ³⁷the pure candlestick, with the lamps thereof, even with the lamps to be set in order, and all the vessels thereof, and the oil for light, ³⁸and the golden altar, and the anointing oil, and the sweet incense, and the hanging for the tabernacle door, ³⁹the brazen altar, and his grate of brass, his staves, and all his vessels, the laver and his foot, ⁴⁰the hangings of the court, his pillars, and his sockets, and the hanging for the court gate, his cords, and his pins, and all the vessels of the service of the tabernacle, for the tent of the congregation, ⁴¹the cloths of service to do service in the holy place, and the holy garments for Aaron the priest, and his sons' garments, to minister in the priest's office. ⁴²According to all that the LORD commanded Moses, so the children of Israel made all the work. ⁴³And Moses did look upon all the

work, and behold, they had done it as the LORD had commanded, even so had they done it: and Moses blessed them.

40 And the LORD spoke unto Moses, saying, [2]'On the first day of the first month shalt thou set up the tabernacle of the tent of the congregation. [3]And thou shalt put therein the ark of the testimony, and cover the ark with the veil. [4]And thou shalt bring in the table, and set in order the things that are to be set in order upon it, and thou shalt bring in the candlestick, and light the lamps thereof. [5]And thou shalt set the altar of gold for the incense before the ark of the testimony, and put the hanging of the door to the tabernacle. [6]And thou shalt set the altar of the burnt offering before the door of the tabernacle of the tent of the congregation. [7]And thou shalt set the laver between the tent of the congregation and the altar, and shalt put water therein. [8]And thou shalt set up the court round about, and hang up the hanging at the court gate. [9]And thou shalt take the anointing oil, and anoint the tabernacle, and all that is therein, and shalt hallow it, and all the vessels thereof: and it shall be holy. [10]And thou shalt anoint the altar of the burnt offering, and all his vessels, and sanctify the altar: and it shall be an altar most holy. [11]And thou shalt anoint the laver and his foot, and sanctify it. [12]And thou shalt bring Aaron and his sons unto the door of the tabernacle of the congregation, and wash them with water. [13]And thou shalt put upon Aaron the holy garments, and anoint him, and sanctify him, that he may minister unto me in the priest's office. [14]And thou shalt bring his sons, and clothe them with coats. [15]And thou shalt anoint them, as thou didst anoint their father, that they may minister unto me in the priest's office: for their anointing shall surely be an everlasting priesthood throughout their generations.' [16]Thus did Moses: according to all that the LORD commanded him, so did he.

[17]And it came to pass in the first month in the second year, on the first day of the month, that the tabernacle was reared up. [18]And Moses reared up the tabernacle, and fastened his sockets, and set up the boards thereof, and put in the bars thereof, and reared up his pillars. [19]And he spread abroad the tent over the tabernacle, and put the covering of the tent above upon it, as the LORD commanded Moses.

[20]And he took and put the testimony into the ark, and set the staves on the ark, and put the mercy-seat above upon the ark. [21]And he brought the ark into the tabernacle, and set up the veil of the covering, and covered the ark of the testimony, as the LORD commanded Moses.

[22]And he put the table in the tent of the congregation, upon the side of the tabernacle northward, without the veil. [23]And he set the bread in order upon it before the LORD, as the LORD had commanded Moses.

[24]And he put the candlestick in the tent of the congregation, over against the table, on the side of the tabernacle southward. [25]And he lighted the lamps before the LORD, as the LORD commanded Moses.

[26]And he put the golden altar in the tent of the congregation before the veil. [27]And he burnt sweet incense thereon, as the LORD commanded Moses.

[28]And he set up the hanging at the door of the tabernacle. [29]And he

put the altar of burnt offering by the door of the tabernacle of the tent of the congregation, and offered upon it the burnt offering and the meat offering, as the LORD commanded Moses.

[30]And he set the laver between the tent of the congregation and the altar, and put water there, to wash withal. [31]And Moses and Aaron and his sons washed their hands and their feet thereat. [32]When they went into the tent of the congregation, and when they came near unto the altar, they washed, as the LORD commanded Moses. [33]And he reared up the court round about the tabernacle and the altar, and set up the hanging of the court gate. So Moses finished the work.

[34]Then a cloud covered the tent of the congregation, and the glory of the LORD filled the tabernacle. [35]And Moses was not able to enter into the tent of the congregation, because the cloud abode thereon, and the glory of the LORD filled the tabernacle. [36]And when the cloud was taken up from over the tabernacle, the children of Israel went onward in all their journeys: [37]but if the cloud were not taken up, then they journeyed not till the day that it was taken up. [38]For the cloud of the LORD was upon the tabernacle by day, and fire was on it by night, in the sight of all the house of Israel, throughout all their journeys.

THE THIRD BOOK OF MOSES,
CALLED
LEVITICUS

1 And the Lord called unto Moses, and spoke unto him out of the tabernacle of the congregation, saying, ²"Speak unto the children of Israel, and say unto them, "If any man of you bring an offering unto the Lord, ye shall bring your offering of the cattle, even of the herd, and of the flock.

³"If his offering be a burnt sacrifice of the herd, let him offer a male without blemish: he shall offer it of his own voluntary will at the door of the tabernacle of the congregation before the Lord. ⁴And he shall put his hand upon the head of the burnt offering; and it shall be accepted for him to make atonement for him. ⁵And he shall kill the bullock before the Lord: and the priests, Aaron's sons, shall bring the blood, and sprinkle the blood round about upon the altar that is by the door of the tabernacle of the congregation. ⁶And he shall flay the burnt offering, and cut it into his pieces. ⁷And the sons of Aaron the priest shall put fire upon the altar, and lay the wood in order upon the fire. ⁸And the priests, Aaron's sons, shall lay the parts, the head, and the fat, in order upon the wood that is in the fire which is upon the altar. ⁹But the inwards and his legs shall he wash in water: and the priest shall burn all on the altar, to be a burnt sacrifice, an offering made by fire, of a sweet savour unto the Lord.

¹⁰"And if his offering be of the flocks, namely, of the sheep, or of the goats, for a burnt sacrifice, he shall bring it a male without blemish. ¹¹And he shall kill it on the side of the altar northward before the Lord: and the priests, Aaron's sons, shall sprinkle his blood round about upon the altar. ¹²And he shall cut it into his pieces, with his head and his fat: and the priest shall lay them in order on the wood that is on the fire which is upon the altar: ¹³but he shall wash the inwards and the legs with water: and the priest shall bring it all, and burn it upon the altar: it is a burnt sacrifice, an offering made by fire, of a sweet savour unto the Lord.

¹⁴"And if the burnt sacrifice for his offering to the Lord be of fowls, then he shall bring his offering of turtle doves, or of young pigeons. ¹⁵And the priest shall bring it unto the altar, and wring off his head, and burn it on the altar; and the blood thereof shall be wrung out at the side of the altar. ¹⁶And he shall pluck away his crop with his feathers, and cast it beside the altar on the east part, by the place of the ashes. ¹⁷And he shall cleave it with the wings thereof, but shall not divide it asunder: and the priest shall burn it upon the altar, upon the wood that is upon the fire: it is a burnt sacrifice, an offering made by fire of a sweet savour unto the Lord.

2 "And when any will offer a meat offering unto the Lord, his offering shall be of fine flour; and he shall pour oil upon it, and put frankincense thereon. ²And he shall bring it to Aaron's sons the priests: and he shall take thereout his handful of the flour thereof, and of the oil thereof, with all the frankincense thereof; and the priest shall burn the memorial of it upon the altar, to be an offering made by fire of a sweet savour unto the LORD. ³And the remnant of the meat offering shall be Aaron's and his sons': it is a thing most holy of the offerings of the LORD made by fire.

⁴"And if thou bring an oblation of a meat offering baked in the oven, it shall be an unleavened cake of fine flour mingled with oil, or unleavened wafers anointed with oil.

⁵"And if thy oblation be a meat offering baked in a pan, it shall be of fine flour unleavened, mingled with oil. ⁶Thou shalt part it in pieces, and pour oil thereon: it is a meat offering.

⁷"And if thy oblation be a meat offering baked in the frying-pan, it shall be made of fine flour with oil. ⁸And thou shalt bring the meat offering that is made of these things unto the LORD: and when it is presented unto the priest, he shall bring it unto the altar. ⁹And the priest shall take from the meat offering a memorial thereof, and shall burn it upon the altar: it is an offering made by fire of a sweet savour unto the LORD. ¹⁰And that which is left of the meat offering shall be Aaron's and his sons': it is a thing most holy of the offerings of the LORD made by fire. ¹¹No meat offering, which ye shall bring unto the LORD, shall be made with leaven: for ye shall burn no leaven, nor any honey, in any offering of the LORD made by fire.

¹²"As for the oblation of the first-fruits, ye shall offer them unto the LORD: but they shall not be burnt on the altar for a sweet savour. ¹³And every oblation of thy meat offering shalt thou season with salt; neither shalt thou suffer the salt of the covenant of thy God to be lacking from thy meat offering: with all thy offerings thou shalt offer salt. ¹⁴And if thou offer a meat offering of thy first-fruits unto the LORD, thou shalt offer for the meat offering of thy first-fruits green ears of corn dried by the fire, even corn beaten out of full ears. ¹⁵And thou shalt put oil upon it, and lay frankincense thereon: it is a meat offering. ¹⁶And the priest shall burn the memorial of it, part of the beaten corn thereof, and part of the oil thereof, with all the frankincense thereof: it is an offering made by fire unto the LORD.

3 ¹"And if his oblation be a sacrifice of peace offering, if he offer it of the herd, whether it be a male or female, he shall offer it without blemish before the LORD. ²And he shall lay his hand upon the head of his offering, and kill it at the door of the tabernacle of the congregation: and Aaron's sons the priests shall sprinkle the blood upon the altar round about. ³And he shall offer of the sacrifice of the peace offering an offering made by fire unto the LORD: the fat that covereth the inwards, and all the fat that is upon the inwards, ⁴and the two kidneys, and the fat that is on them, which is by the flanks, and the caul above the liver, with the kidneys, it shall he take away. ⁵And Aaron's sons shall burn it on the altar upon the burnt sacrifice, which is upon the wood that is on the fire: it is an offering made by fire, of a sweet savour unto the LORD.

⁶'"And if his offering for a sacrifice of peace offering unto the LORD be of the flock, male or female, he shall offer it without blemish. ⁷If he offer a lamb for his offering, then shall he offer it before the LORD. ⁸And he shall lay his hand upon the head of his offering, and kill it before the tabernacle of the congregation: and Aaron's sons shall sprinkle the blood thereof round about upon the altar. ⁹And he shall offer of the sacrifice of the peace offering an offering made by fire unto the LORD: the fat thereof, and the whole rump, it shall he take off hard by the backbone; and the fat that covereth the inwards, and all the fat that is upon the inwards, ¹⁰and the two kidneys, and the fat that is upon them, which is by the flanks, and the caul above the liver, with the kidneys, it shall he take away. ¹¹And the priest shall burn it upon the altar: it is the food of the offering made by fire unto the LORD.

¹²'"And if his offering be a goat, then he shall offer it before the LORD. ¹³And he shall lay his hand upon the head of it, and kill it before the tabernacle of the congregation: and the sons of Aaron shall sprinkle the blood thereof upon the altar round about. ¹⁴And he shall offer thereof his offering, even an offering made by fire unto the LORD: the fat that covereth the inwards, and all the fat that is upon the inwards, ¹⁵and the two kidneys, and the fat that is upon them, which is by the flanks, and the caul above the liver, with the kidneys, it shall he take away. ¹⁶And the priest shall burn them upon the altar: it is the food of the offering made by fire for a sweet savour: all the fat is the LORD's. ¹⁷It shall be a perpetual statute for your generations throughout all your dwellings, that ye eat neither fat nor blood."'

4 And the LORD spoke unto Moses, saying, ²'Speak unto the children of Israel, saying, "If a soul shall sin through ignorance against any of the commandments of the LORD concerning things which ought not to be done, and shall do against any of them: ³if the priest that is anointed do sin according to the sin of the people, then let him bring for his sin, which he hath sinned, a young bullock without blemish unto the LORD for a sin offering. ⁴And he shall bring the bullock unto the door of the tabernacle of the congregation before the LORD, and shall lay his hand upon the bullock's head, and kill the bullock before the LORD. ⁵And the priest that is anointed shall take of the bullock's blood, and bring it to the tabernacle of the congregation. ⁶And the priest shall dip his finger in the blood, and sprinkle of the blood seven times before the LORD, before the veil of the sanctuary. ⁷And the priest shall put some of the blood upon the horns of the altar of sweet incense before the LORD, which is in the tabernacle of the congregation; and shall pour all the blood of the bullock at the bottom of the altar of the burnt offering, which is at the door of the tabernacle of the congregation. ⁸And he shall take off from it all the fat of the bullock for the sin offering: the fat that covereth the inwards, and all the fat that is upon the inwards, ⁹and the two kidneys, and the fat that is upon them, which is by the flanks, and the caul above the liver, with the kidneys, it shall he take away, ¹⁰as it was taken off from the bullock of the sacrifice of peace offerings: and the priest shall burn them upon the altar of the burnt offering. [11]And the skin of the bullock, and all his flesh, with his head, and with his legs, and his inwards, and his dung, [12]even the whole bullock shall he carry forth without the camp unto a clean place, where the ashes are poured out, and burn him on the wood with fire: where the ashes are poured out shall he be burnt.

[13]"And if the whole congregation of Israel sin through ignorance, and the thing be hid from the eyes of the assembly, and they have done somewhat against any of the commandments of the LORD concerning things which should not be done, and are guilty: [14]when the sin, which they have sinned against it, is known, then the congregation shall offer a young bullock for the sin, and bring him before the tabernacle of the congregation. [15]And the elders of the congregation shall lay their hands upon the head of the bullock before the LORD: and the bullock shall be killed before the LORD. [16]And the priest that is anointed shall bring of the bullock's blood to the tabernacle of the congregation. [17]And the priest shall dip his finger in some of the blood, and sprinkle it seven times before the LORD, even before the veil. [18]And he shall put some of the blood upon the horns of the altar which is before the LORD, that is in the tabernacle of the congregation, and shall pour out all the blood at the bottom of the altar of the burnt offering, which is at the door of the tabernacle of the congregation. [19]And he shall take all his fat from him, and burn it upon the altar. [20]And he shall do with the bullock as he did with the bullock for a sin offering, so shall he do with this: and the priest shall make an atonement for them, and it shall be forgiven them. [21]And he shall carry forth the bullock without the camp, and burn him as he burnt the first bullock: it is a sin offering for the congregation.

[22]"When a ruler hath sinned, and done somewhat through ignorance against any of the commandments of the LORD his God concerning things which should not be done, and is guilty; [23]or if his sin, wherein he hath sinned, come to his knowledge: he shall bring his offering, a kid of the goats, a male without blemish. [24]And he shall lay his hand upon the head of the goat, and kill it in the place where they kill the burnt offering before the LORD: it is a sin offering. [25]And the priest shall take of the blood of the sin offering with his finger, and put it upon the horns of the altar of burnt offering, and shall pour out his blood at the bottom of the altar of burnt offering. [26]And he shall burn all his fat upon the altar, as the fat of the sacrifice of peace offerings: and the priest shall make an atonement for him as concerning his sin, and it shall be forgiven him.

[27]"And if any one of the common people sin through ignorance, while he doeth somewhat against any of the commandments of the LORD concerning things which ought not to be done, and be guilty; [28]or if his sin, which he hath sinned, come to his knowledge: then he shall bring his offering, a kid of the goats, a female without blemish, for his sin which he hath sinned. [29]And he shall lay his hand upon the head of the sin offering, and slay the sin offering in the place of the burnt offering. [30]And the priest shall take of the blood thereof with his finger, and

put it upon the horns of the altar of burnt offering, and shall pour out all the blood thereof at the bottom of the altar. ³¹And he shall take away all the fat thereof, as the fat is taken away from off the sacrifice of peace offerings; and the priest shall burn it upon the altar for a sweet savour unto the LORD; and the priest shall make an atonement for him, and it shall be forgiven him. ³²And if he bring a lamb for a sin offering, he shall bring it a female without blemish. ³³And he shall lay his hand upon the head of the sin offering, and slay it for a sin offering in the place where they kill the burnt offering. ³⁴And the priest shall take of the blood of the sin offering with his finger, and put it upon the horns of the altar of burnt offering, and shall pour out all the blood thereof at the bottom of the altar. ³⁵And he shall take away all the fat thereof, as the fat of the lamb is taken away from the sacrifice of the peace offerings; and the priest shall burn them upon the altar, according to the offerings made by fire unto the LORD: and the priest shall make an atonement for his sin that he hath committed, and it shall be forgiven him.

5 ¹'"And if a soul sin, and hear the voice of swearing, and is a witness, whether he hath seen or known of it, if he do not utter it, then he shall bear his iniquity. ²Or if a soul touch any unclean thing, whether it be a carcase of an unclean beast, or a carcase of unclean cattle, or the carcase of unclean creeping things, and if it be hidden from him, he also shall be unclean, and guilty. ³Or if he touch the uncleanness of man, whatsoever uncleanness it be that a man shall be defiled withal, and it be hid from him, when he knoweth of it, then he shall be guilty. ⁴Or if a soul swear, pronouncing with his lips to do evil, or to do good, whatsoever it be that a man shall pronounce with an oath, and it be hid from him, when he knoweth of it, then he shall be guilty in one of these. ⁵And it shall be, when he shall be guilty in one of these things, that he shall confess that he hath sinned in that thing: ⁶and he shall bring his trespass offering unto the LORD for his sin which he hath sinned, a female from the flock, a lamb or a kid of the goats, for a sin offering; and the priest shall make an atonement for him concerning his sin. ⁷And if he be not able to bring a lamb, then he shall bring for his trespass which he hath committed, two turtle doves, or two young pigeons, unto the LORD: one for a sin offering, and the other for a burnt offering. ⁸And he shall bring them unto the priest, who shall offer that which is for the sin offering first, and wring off his head from his neck, but shall not divide it asunder. ⁹And he shall sprinkle of the blood of the sin offering upon the side of the altar, and the rest of the blood shall be wrung out at the bottom of the altar: it is a sin offering. ¹⁰And he shall offer the second for a burnt offering, according to the manner: and the priest shall make an atonement for him for his sin which he had sinned, and it shall be forgiven him.

¹¹'"But if he be not able to bring two turtle doves, or two young pigeons, then he that sinned shall bring for his offering the tenth part of an ephah of fine flour for a sin offering; he shall put no oil upon it, neither shall he put any frankincense thereon: for it is a sin offer-

ing. ¹²Then shall he bring it to the priest, and the priest shall take his handful of it, even a memorial thereof, and burn it on the altar, according to the offerings made by fire unto the LORD: it is a sin offering. ¹³And the priest shall make an atonement for him as touching his sin that he hath sinned in one of these, and it shall be forgiven him: and the remnant shall be the priest's, as a meat offering."'

¹⁴And the LORD spoke unto Moses, saying, ¹⁵'If a soul commit a trespass, and sin through ignorance, in the holy things of the LORD; then he shall bring for his trespass unto the LORD a ram without blemish out of the flocks, with thy estimation by shekels of silver, after the shekel of the sanctuary, for a trespass offering: ¹⁶and he shall make amends for the harm that he hath done in the holy thing, and shall add the fifth part thereto, and give it unto the priest: and the priest shall make an atonement for him with the ram of the trespass offering, and it shall be forgiven him.

¹⁷'And if a soul sin, and commit any of these things which are forbidden to be done by the commandments of the LORD, though he wist it not, yet is he guilty, and shall bear his iniquity. ¹⁸And he shall bring a ram without blemish out of the flock, with thy estimation, for a trespass offering, unto the priest: and the priest shall make an atonement for him concerning his ignorance wherein he erred and wist it not, and it shall be forgiven him. ¹⁹It is a trespass offering: he hath certainly trespassed against the LORD.'

6 And the LORD spoke unto Moses, saying, ²'If a soul sin, and commit a trespass against the LORD, and lie unto his neighbour in that which was delivered him to keep, or in fellowship, or in a thing taken away by violence, or hath deceived his neighbour; ³or have found that which was lost, and lieth concerning it, and sweareth falsely; in any of all these that a man doeth, sinning therein: ⁴then it shall be, because he hath sinned, and is guilty, that he shall restore that which he took violently away, or the thing which he hath deceitfully gotten, or that which was delivered him to keep, or the lost thing which he found, ⁵or all that about which he hath sworn falsely; he shall even restore it in the principal, and shall add the fifth part more thereto, and give it unto him to whom it appertaineth, in the day of his trespass offering. ⁶And he shall bring his trespass offering unto the LORD, a ram without blemish out of the flock, with thy estimation, for a trespass offering, unto the priest. ⁷And the priest shall make an atonement for him before the LORD: and it shall be forgiven him for any thing of all that he hath done in trespassing therein.'

⁸And the LORD spoke unto Moses, saying, ⁹'Command Aaron and his sons, saying, "This is the law of the burnt offering: it is the burnt offering, because of the burning upon the altar all night unto the morning, and the fire of the altar shall be burning in it. ¹⁰And the priest shall put on his linen garment, and his linen breeches shall he put upon his flesh, and take up the ashes which the fire hath consumed with the burnt offering on the altar, and he shall put them beside the altar. ¹¹And he shall put off his garments, and put on other garments,

and carry forth the ashes without the camp unto a clean place. ¹²And the fire upon the altar shall be burning in it; it shall not be put out: and the priest shall burn wood on it every morning, and lay the burnt offering in order upon it, and he shall burn thereon the fat of the peace offerings. ¹³The fire shall ever be burning upon the altar; it shall never go out.

¹⁴'"And this is the law of the meat offering: the sons of Aaron shall offer it before the LORD, before the altar. ¹⁵And he shall take of it his handful, of the flour of the meat offering, and of the oil thereof, and all the frankincense which is upon the meat offering, and shall burn it upon the altar for a sweet savour, even the memorial of it, unto the LORD. ¹⁶And the remainder thereof shall Aaron and his sons eat: with unleavened bread shall it be eaten in the holy place; in the court of the tabernacle of the congregation they shall eat it. ¹⁷It shall not be baked with leaven. I have given it unto them for their portion of my offerings made by fire: it is most holy, as is the sin offering, and as the trespass offering. ¹⁸All the males among the children of Aaron shall eat of it. It shall be a statute for ever in your generations concerning the offerings of the LORD made by fire: every one that toucheth them shall be holy."'

¹⁹And the LORD spoke unto Moses, saying, ²⁰'This is the offering of Aaron and of his sons, which they shall offer unto the LORD in the day when he is anointed: the tenth part of an ephah of fine flour for a meat offering perpetual, half of it in the morning, and half thereof at night. ²¹In a pan it shall be made with oil; and when it is baked, thou shalt bring it in: and the baked pieces of the meat offering shalt thou offer for a sweet savour unto the LORD. ²²And the priest of his sons that is anointed in his stead shall offer it: it is a statute for ever unto the LORD; it shall be wholly burnt. ²³For every meat offering for the priest shall be wholly burnt: it shall not be eaten.'

²⁴And the LORD spoke unto Moses, saying, ²⁵'Speak unto Aaron and to his sons, saying, "This is the law of the sin offering: in the place where the burnt offering is killed shall the sin offering be killed before the LORD: it is most holy. ²⁶The priest that offereth it for sin shall eat it: in the holy place shall it be eaten, in the court of the tabernacle of the congregation. ²⁷Whatsoever shall touch the flesh thereof shall be holy: and when there is sprinkled of the blood thereof upon any garment, thou shalt wash that whereon it was sprinkled in the holy place. ²⁸But the earthen vessel wherein it is seethed shall be broken: and if it be seethed in a brazen pot, it shall be both scoured, and rinsed in water. ²⁹All the males among the priests shall eat thereof: it is most holy. ³⁰And no sin offering, whereof any of the blood is brought into the tabernacle of the congregation to reconcile withal in the holy place, shall be eaten: it shall be burnt in the fire.

7 '"Likewise this is the law of the trespass offering: it is most holy. ²In the place where they kill the burnt offering shall they kill the trespass offering: and the blood thereof shall he sprinkle round about upon the altar. ³And he shall offer of it all the fat thereof; the rump, and the fat that covereth the inwards, ⁴and the two kidneys, and the fat

that is on them, which is by the flanks, and the caul that is above the liver, with the kidneys, it shall he take away: ⁵and the priest shall burn them upon the altar for an offering made by fire unto the LORD: it is a trespass offering. ⁶Every male among the priests shall eat thereof: it shall be eaten in the holy place: it is most holy. ⁷As the sin offering is, so is the trespass offering: there is one law for them: the priest that maketh atonement therewith shall have it. ⁸And the priest that offereth any man's burnt offering, even the priest shall have to himself the skin of the burnt offering which he hath offered. ⁹And all the meat offering that is baked in the oven, and all that is dressed in the frying-pan, and in the pan, shall be the priest's that offereth it. ¹⁰And every meat offering, mingled with oil, and dry, shall all the sons of Aaron have, one as much as another.

¹¹ "And this is the law of the sacrifice of peace offerings, which he shall offer unto the LORD. ¹²If he offer it for a thanksgiving, then he shall offer with the sacrifice of thanksgiving unleavened cakes mingled with oil, and unleavened wafers anointed with oil, and cakes mingled with oil, of fine flour, fried. ¹³Besides the cakes, he shall offer for his offering leavened bread with the sacrifice of thanksgiving of his peace offerings. ¹⁴And of it he shall offer one out of the whole oblation for a heave offering unto the LORD, and it shall be the priest's that sprinkleth the blood of the peace offerings. ¹⁵And the flesh of the sacrifice of his peace offerings for thanksgiving shall be eaten the same day that it is offered; he shall not leave any of it until the morning. ¹⁶But if the sacrifice of his offering be a vow, or a voluntary offering, it shall be eaten the same day that he offereth his sacrifice: and on the morrow also the remainder of it shall be eaten. ¹⁷But the remainder of the flesh of the sacrifice on the third day shall be burnt with fire. ¹⁸And if any of the flesh of the sacrifice of his peace offerings be eaten at all on the third day, it shall not be accepted, neither shall it be imputed unto him that offereth it: it shall be an abomination, and the soul that eateth of it shall bear his iniquity. ¹⁹And the flesh that toucheth any unclean thing shall not be eaten: it shall be burnt with fire: and as for the flesh, all that be clean shall eat thereof. ²⁰But the soul that eateth of the flesh of the sacrifice of peace offerings, that pertain unto the LORD, having his uncleanness upon him, even that soul shall be cut off from his people. ²¹Moreover the soul that shall touch any unclean thing, as the uncleanness of man, or any unclean beast, or any abominable unclean thing, and eat of the flesh of the sacrifice of peace offerings, which pertain unto the LORD, even that soul shall be cut off from his people."'

²²And the LORD spoke unto Moses, saying, ²³'Speak unto the children of Israel, saying, "Ye shall eat no manner fat, of ox, or of sheep, or of goat. ²⁴And the fat of the beast that dieth of itself, and the fat of that which is torn with beasts, may be used in any other use: but ye shall in no wise eat of it. ²⁵For whosoever eateth the fat of the beast, of which men offer an offering made by fire unto the LORD, even the soul that eateth it shall be cut off from his people. ²⁶Moreover ye shall eat no manner of blood, whether it be of fowl or of beast, in any of your

dwellings. ²⁷Whatsoever soul it be that eateth any manner of blood, even that soul shall be cut off from his people."'

²⁸And the LORD spoke unto Moses, saying, ²⁹'Speak unto the children of Israel, saying, "He that offereth the sacrifice of his peace offerings unto the LORD shall bring his oblation unto the LORD of the sacrifice of his peace offerings. ³⁰His own hands shall bring the offerings of the LORD made by fire, the fat with the breast, it shall he bring, that the breast may be waved for a wave offering before the LORD. ³¹And the priest shall burn the fat upon the altar: but the breast shall be Aaron's and his sons'. ³²And the right shoulder shall ye give unto the priest for a heave offering of the sacrifices of your peace offerings. ³³He among the sons of Aaron, that offereth the blood of the peace offerings, and the fat, shall have the right shoulder for his part. ³⁴For the wave breast and the heave shoulder have I taken of the children of Israel from off the sacrifices of their peace offerings, and have given them unto Aaron the priest and unto his sons by a statute for ever from among the children of Israel."'

³⁵This is the portion of the anointing of Aaron, and of the anointing of his sons, out of the offerings of the LORD made by fire, in the day when he presented them to minister unto the LORD in the priest's office; ³⁶which the LORD commanded to be given them of the children of Israel, in the day that he anointed them, by a statute for ever throughout their generations. ³⁷This is the law of the burnt offering, of the meat offering, and of the sin offering, and of the trespass offering, and of the consecrations, and of the sacrifice of the peace offerings; ³⁸which the LORD commanded Moses in mount Sinai, in the day that he commanded the children of Israel to offer their oblations unto the LORD, in the wilderness of Sinai.

8 And the LORD spoke unto Moses, saying, ²'Take Aaron and his sons with him, and the garments, and the anointing oil, and a bullock for the sin offering, and two rams, and a basket of unleavened bread; ³and gather thou all the congregation together unto the door of the tabernacle of the congregation'. ⁴And Moses did as the LORD commanded him; and the assembly was gathered together unto the door of the tabernacle of the congregation. ⁵And Moses said unto the congregation, 'This is the thing which the LORD commanded to be done'.

⁶And Moses brought Aaron and his sons, and washed them with water. ⁷And he put upon him the coat, and girded him with the girdle, and clothed him with the robe, and put the ephod upon him, and he girded him with the curious girdle of the ephod, and bound it unto him therewith. ⁸And he put the breastplate upon him: also he put in the breastplate the Urim and the Thummim. ⁹And he put the mitre upon his head; also upon the mitre, even upon his forefront, did he put the golden plate, the holy crown, as the LORD commanded Moses. ¹⁰And Moses took the anointing oil, and anointed the tabernacle and all that was therein, and sanctified them. ¹¹And he sprinkled thereof upon the altar seven times, and anointed the altar and all his vessels, both the laver and his foot, to sanctify them. ¹²And he poured of the anointing

oil upon Aaron's head, and anointed him, to sanctify him. [13]And Moses brought Aaron's sons, and put coats upon them, and girded them with girdles, and put bonnets upon them, as the LORD commanded Moses.

[14]And he brought the bullock for the sin offering: and Aaron and his sons laid their hands upon the head of the bullock for the sin offering. [15]And he slew it; and Moses took the blood, and put it upon the horns of the altar round about with his finger, and purified the altar, and poured the blood at the bottom of the altar, and sanctified it, to make reconciliation upon it. [16]And he took all the fat that was upon the inwards, and the caul above the liver, and the two kidneys, and their fat, and Moses burnt it upon the altar. [17]But the bullock, and his hide, his flesh, and his dung, he burnt with fire without the camp, as the LORD commanded Moses.

[18]And he brought the ram for the burnt offering: and Aaron and his sons laid their hands upon the head of the ram. [19]And he killed it; and Moses sprinkled the blood upon the altar round about. [20]And he cut the ram into pieces; and Moses burnt the head, and the pieces, and the fat. [21]And he washed the inwards and the legs in water; and Moses burnt the whole ram upon the altar: it was a burnt sacrifice for a sweet savour, and an offering made by fire unto the LORD, as the LORD commanded Moses.

[22]And he brought the other ram, the ram of consecration: and Aaron and his sons laid their hands upon the head of the ram. [23]And he slew it; and Moses took of the blood of it, and put it upon the tip of Aaron's right ear, and upon the thumb of his right hand, and upon the great toe of his right foot. [24]And he brought Aaron's sons, and Moses put of the blood upon the tip of their right ear, and upon the thumbs of their right hands, and upon the great toes of their right feet: and Moses sprinkled the blood upon the altar round about. [25]And he took the fat, and the rump, and all the fat that was upon the inwards, and the caul above the liver, and the two kidneys, and their fat, and the right shoulder: [26]and out of the basket of unleavened bread, that was before the LORD, he took one unleavened cake, and a cake of oiled bread, and one wafer, and put them on the fat, and upon the right shoulder: [27]and he put all upon Aaron's hands, and upon his sons' hands, and waved them for a wave offering before the LORD. [28]And Moses took them from off their hands, and burnt them on the altar upon the burnt offering: they were consecrations for a sweet savour: it is an offering made by fire unto the LORD. [29]And Moses took the breast, and waved it for a wave offering before the LORD: for of the ram of consecration it was Moses' part, as the LORD commanded Moses. [30]And Moses took of the anointing oil, and of the blood which was upon the altar, and sprinkled it upon Aaron, and upon his garments, and upon his sons, and upon his sons' garments with him; and sanctified Aaron, and his garments, and his sons, and his sons' garments with him.

[31]And Moses said unto Aaron and to his sons, 'Boil the flesh at the door of the tabernacle of the congregation: and there eat it with the bread that is in the basket of consecrations, as I commanded, saying,

Aaron and his sons shall eat it. ³²And that which remaineth of the flesh and of the bread shall ye burn with fire. ³³And ye shall not go out of the door of the tabernacle of the congregation in seven days, until the days of your consecration be at an end: for seven days shall he consecrate you. ³⁴As he hath done this day, so the LORD hath commanded to do, to make an atonement for you. ³⁵Therefore shall ye abide at the door of the tabernacle of the congregation day and night seven days, and keep the charge of the LORD, that ye die not: for so I am commanded.' ³⁶So Aaron and his sons did all things which the LORD commanded by the hand of Moses.

9 And it came to pass on the eighth day, that Moses called Aaron and his sons, and the elders of Israel. ²And he said unto Aaron, 'Take thee a young calf for a sin offering, and a ram for a burnt offering, without blemish, and offer them before the LORD. ³And unto the children of Israel thou shalt speak, saying, "Take ye a kid of the goats for a sin offering; and a calf and a lamb, both of the first year, without blemish, for a burnt offering; ⁴also a bullock and a ram for peace offerings, to sacrifice before the LORD; and a meat offering mingled with oil: for today the LORD will appear unto you".'

⁵And they brought that which Moses commanded before the tabernacle of the congregation: and all the congregation drew near and stood before the LORD. ⁶And Moses said, 'This is the thing which the LORD commanded that ye should do: and the glory of the LORD shall appear unto you'. ⁷And Moses said unto Aaron, 'Go unto the altar, and offer thy sin offering, and thy burnt offering, and make an atonement for thyself, and for the people: and offer the offering of the people, and make an atonement for them, as the LORD commanded'.

⁸Aaron therefore went unto the altar, and slew the calf of the sin offering, which was for himself. ⁹And the sons of Aaron brought the blood unto him: and he dipped his finger in the blood, and put it upon the horns of the altar, and poured out the blood at the bottom of the altar: ¹⁰but the fat, and the kidneys, and the caul above the liver of the sin offering, he burnt upon the altar, as the LORD commanded Moses. ¹¹And the flesh and the hide he burnt with fire without the camp. ¹²And he slew the burnt offering; and Aaron's sons presented unto him the blood, which he sprinkled round about upon the altar. ¹³And they presented the burnt offering unto him, with the pieces thereof, and the head: and he burnt them upon the altar. ¹⁴And he did wash the inwards and the legs, and burnt them upon the burnt offering on the altar.

¹⁵And he brought the people's offering, and took the goat, which was the sin offering for the people, and slew it, and offered it for sin, as the first. ¹⁶And he brought the burnt offering, and offered it according to the manner. ¹⁷And he brought the meat offering, and took a handful thereof, and burnt it upon the altar, beside the burnt sacrifice of the morning. ¹⁸He slew also the bullock and the ram for a sacrifice of peace offerings, which was for the people: and Aaron's sons presented unto him the blood, which he sprinkled upon the altar round about, ¹⁹and

the fat of the bullock and of the ram, the rump, and that which covereth the inwards, and the kidneys, and the caul above the liver: ²⁰and they put the fat upon the breasts, and he burnt the fat upon the altar: ²¹and the breasts and the right shoulder Aaron waved for a wave offering before the LORD; as Moses commanded.

²²And Aaron lifted up his hand towards the people, and blessed them, and came down from offering of the sin offering, and the burnt offering, and peace offerings. ²³And Moses and Aaron went into the tabernacle of the congregation, and came out, and blessed the people: and the glory of the LORD appeared unto all the people. ²⁴And there came a fire out from before the LORD, and consumed upon the altar the burnt offering and the fat: which when all the people saw, they shouted, and fell on their faces.

10 And Nadab and Abihu, the sons of Aaron, took either of them his censer, and put fire therein, and put incense thereon, and offered strange fire before the LORD, which he commanded them not. ²And there went out fire from the LORD, and devoured them, and they died before the LORD. ³Then Moses said unto Aaron, 'This is it that the LORD spoke, saying, "I will be sanctified in them that come nigh me, and before all the people I will be glorified"'. And Aaron held his peace. ⁴And Moses called Mishael and Elzaphan, the sons of Uzziel the uncle of Aaron, and said unto them, 'Come near, carry your brethren from before the sanctuary out of the camp'. ⁵So they went near, and carried them in their coats out of the camp, as Moses had said. ⁶And Moses said unto Aaron, and unto Eleazar and unto Ithamar, his sons, 'Uncover not your heads, neither rend your clothes, lest you die, and lest wrath come upon all the people: but let your brethren, the whole house of Israel, bewail the burning which the LORD hath kindled. ⁷And ye shall not go out from the door of the tabernacle of the congregation, lest you die: for the anointing oil of the LORD is upon you.' And they did according to the word of Moses.

⁸And the LORD spoke unto Aaron, saying, ⁹'Do not drink wine nor strong drink, thou, nor thy sons with thee, when ye go into the tabernacle of the congregation, lest ye die: it shall be a statute for ever throughout your generations: ¹⁰and that ye may put difference between holy and unholy, and between unclean and clean; ¹¹and that ye may teach the children of Israel all the statutes which the LORD hath spoken unto them by the hand of Moses'.

¹²And Moses spoke unto Aaron, and unto Eleazar and unto Ithamar, his sons that were left, 'Take the meat offering that remaineth of the offerings of the LORD made by fire, and eat it without leaven beside the altar: for it is most holy. ¹³And ye shall eat it in the holy place, because it is thy due, and thy sons' due, of the sacrifices of the LORD made by fire: for so I am commanded. ¹⁴And the wave breast and heave shoulder shall ye eat in a clean place, thou, and thy sons, and thy daughters with thee: for they be thy due, and thy sons' due, which are given out of the sacrifice of peace offerings of the children of Israel. ¹⁵The heave shoulder and the wave breast shall they bring with the offerings made by fire of

the fat, to wave it for a wave offering before the LORD; and it shall be thine, and thy sons' with thee, by a statute for ever, as the LORD hath commanded.'

¹⁶And Moses diligently sought the goat of the sin offering, and, behold, it was burnt: and he was angry with Eleazar and Ithamar, the sons of Aaron which were left alive, saying, ¹⁷'Wherefore have ye not eaten the sin offering in the holy place, seeing it is most holy, and God hath given it you to bear the iniquity of the congregation, to make atonement for them before the LORD? ¹⁸Behold, the blood of it was not brought in within the holy place: ye should indeed have eaten it in the holy place, as I commanded.' ¹⁹And Aaron said unto Moses, 'Behold, this day have they offered their sin offering and their burnt offering before the LORD; and such things have befallen me: and if I had eaten the sin offering today, should it have been accepted in the sight of the LORD?' ²⁰And when Moses heard that, he was content.

11 And the LORD spoke unto Moses and to Aaron, saying unto them, ²'Speak unto the children of Israel, saying, "These are the beasts which ye shall eat among all the beasts that are on the earth. ³Whatsoever parteth the hoof, and is cloven-footed, and cheweth the cud, among the beasts, that shall ye eat. ⁴Nevertheless these shall ye not eat of them that chew the cud, or of them that divide the hoof: as the camel, because he cheweth the cud, but divideth not the hoof, he is unclean unto you. ⁵And the coney, because he cheweth the cud, but divideth not the hoof, he is unclean unto you. ⁶And the hare, because he cheweth the cud, but divideth not the hoof, he is unclean unto you. ⁷And the swine, though he divide the hoof, and be cloven-footed, yet he cheweth not the cud: he is unclean to you. ⁸Of their flesh shall ye not eat, and their carcase shall ye not touch: they are unclean to you.

⁹'"These shall ye eat of all that are in the waters: whatsoever hath fins and scales in the waters, in the seas, and in the rivers, them shall ye eat. ¹⁰And all that have not fins nor scales in the seas, and in the rivers, of all that move in the waters, and of any living thing which is in the waters, they shall be an abomination unto you: ¹¹they shall be even an abomination unto you: ye shall not eat of their flesh, but you shall have their carcases in abomination. ¹²Whatsoever hath no fins nor scales in the waters, that shall be an abomination unto you.

¹³'"And these are they which ye shall have in abomination among the fowls; they shall not be eaten, they are an abomination: the eagle, and the ossifrage, and the osprey, ¹⁴and the vulture, and the kite after his kind; ¹⁵every raven after his kind; ¹⁶and the owl, and the night hawk, and the cuckoo, and the hawk after his kind, ¹⁷and the little owl, and the cormorant, and the great owl, ¹⁸and the swan, and the pelican, and the gier-eagle, ¹⁹and the stork, the heron after her kind, and the lapwing, and the bat. ²⁰All fowls that creep, going upon all four, shall be an abomination unto you. ²¹Yet these may ye eat of every flying creeping thing that goeth upon all four, which have legs above their feet, to leap withal upon the earth; ²²even these of them ye may eat: the locust after

his kind, and the bald locust after his kind, and the beetle after his kind, and the grasshopper after his kind. ²³But all other flying creeping things, which have four feet, shall be an abomination unto you.

²⁴"And for these ye shall be unclean: whosoever toucheth the carcase of them shall be unclean until the even. ²⁵And whosoever beareth aught of the carcase of them shall wash his clothes, and be unclean until the even. ²⁶The carcases of every beast which divideth the hoof, and is not cloven-footed, nor cheweth the cud, are unclean unto you: every one that toucheth them shall be unclean. ²⁷And whatsoever goeth upon his paws, among all manner of beasts that go on all four, those are unclean unto you: whoso toucheth their carcase shall be unclean until the even. ²⁸And he that beareth the carcase of them shall wash his clothes, and be unclean until the even: they are unclean unto you.

²⁹"These also shall be unclean unto you among the creeping things that creep upon the earth: the weasel, and the mouse, and the tortoise after his kind, ³⁰and the ferret, and the chameleon, and the lizard, and the snail, and the mole. ³¹These are unclean to you among all that creep: whosoever doth touch them, when they be dead, shall be unclean until the even. ³²And upon whatsoever any of them, when they are dead, doth fall, it shall be unclean; whether it be any vessel of wood, or raiment, or skin, or sack, whatsoever vessel it be, wherein any work is done, it must be put into water, and it shall be unclean until the even; so it shall be cleansed. ³³And every earthen vessel, whereinto any of them falleth, whatsoever is in it shall be unclean; and ye shall break it. ³⁴Of all meat which may be eaten, that on which such water cometh shall be unclean: and all drink that may be drunk in every such vessel shall be unclean. ³⁵And everything whereupon any part of their carcase falleth shall be unclean; whether it be oven, or ranges for pots, they shall be unclean unto you. ³⁶Nevertheless a fountain or pit, wherein there is plenty of water, shall be clean: but that which toucheth their carcase shall be unclean. ³⁷And if any part of their carcase fall upon any sowing seed which is to be sown, it shall be clean. ³⁸But if any water be put upon the seed, and any part of their carcase fall thereon, it shall be unclean unto you.

³⁹"And if any beast, of which ye may eat, die, he that toucheth the carcase thereof shall be unclean until the even. ⁴⁰And he that eateth of the carcase of it shall wash his clothes, and be unclean until the even: he also that beareth the carcase of it shall wash his clothes, and be unclean until the even.

⁴¹"And every creeping thing that creepeth upon the earth shall be an abomination: it shall not be eaten. ⁴²Whatsoever goeth upon the belly, and whatsoever goeth upon all four, or whatsoever hath more feet among all creeping things that creep upon the earth, them ye shall not eat, for they are an abomination. ⁴³Ye shall not make yourselves abominable with any creeping thing that creepeth, neither shall ye make yourselves unclean with them, that ye should be defiled thereby. ⁴⁴For I am the LORD your God: ye shall therefore sanctify yourselves, and ye shall be holy; for I am holy: neither shall ye defile yourselves with any manner of creeping thing that creepeth upon the earth. ⁴⁵For I am the

LORD that bringeth you up out of the land of Egypt, to be your God: ye shall therefore be holy, for I am holy. ⁴⁶This is the law of the beasts, and of the fowl, and of every living creature that moveth in the waters, and of every creature that creepeth upon the earth: ⁴⁷to make a difference between the unclean and the clean, and between the beast that may be eaten and the beast that may not be eaten."'

12 And the LORD spoke unto Moses, saying, ²'Speak unto the children of Israel, saying, "If a woman have conceived seed, and borne a man-child, then she shall be unclean seven days; according to the days of the separation for her infirmity shall she be unclean. ³And in the eighth day the flesh of his foreskin shall be circumcised. ⁴And she shall then continue in the blood of her purifying three and thirty days; she shall touch no hallowed thing, nor come into the sanctuary, until the days of her purifying be fulfilled. ⁵But if she bear a maid-child, then she shall be unclean two weeks, as in her separation: and she shall continue in the blood of her purifying threescore and six days. ⁶And when the days of her purifying are fulfilled, for a son, or for a daughter, she shall bring a lamb of the first year for a burnt offering, and a young pigeon, or a turtle dove, for a sin offering, unto the door of the tabernacle of the congregation, unto the priest: ⁷who shall offer it before the LORD, and make an atonement for her; and she shall be cleansed from the issue of her blood. This is the law for her that hath borne a male or a female. ⁸And if she be not able to bring a lamb, then she shall bring two turtles, or two young pigeons, the one for the burnt offering, and the other for a sin offering: and the priest shall make an atonement for her, and she shall be clean."'

13 And the LORD spoke unto Moses and Aaron, saying, ²'When a man shall have in the skin of his flesh a rising, a scab, or bright spot, and it be in the skin of his flesh like the plague of leprosy, then he shall be brought unto Aaron the priest, or unto one of his sons the priests. ³And the priest shall look on the plague in the skin of the flesh: and when the hair in the plague is turned white, and the plague in sight be deeper than the skin of his flesh, it is a plague of leprosy: and the priest shall look on him, and pronounce him unclean. ⁴If the bright spot be white in the skin of his flesh, and in sight be not deeper than the skin, and the hair thereof be not turned white, then the priest shall shut up him that hath the plague seven days. ⁵And the priest shall look on him the seventh day: and, behold, if the plague in his sight be at a stay, and the plague spread not in the skin, then the priest shall shut him up seven days more. ⁶And the priest shall look on him again the seventh day: and behold, if the plague be somewhat dark, and the plague spread not in the skin, the priest shall pronounce him clean: it is but a scab: and he shall wash his clothes, and be clean. ⁷But if the scab spread much abroad in the skin, after that he hath been seen of the priest for his cleansing, he shall be seen of the priest again. ⁸And if the priest see that, behold, the scab spreadeth in the skin, then the priest shall pronounce him unclean: it is a leprosy.

⁹'When the plague of leprosy is in a man, then he shall be brought

unto the priest; [10]and the priest shall see him: and behold, if the rising be white in the skin, and it have turned the hair white, and there be quick raw flesh in the rising: [11]it is an old leprosy in the skin of his flesh, and the priest shall pronounce him unclean, and shall not shut him up: for he is unclean. [12]And if a leprosy break out abroad in the skin, and the leprosy cover all the skin of him that hath the plague from his head even to his foot, wheresoever the priest looketh: [13]then the priest shall consider: and behold, if the leprosy have covered all his flesh, he shall pronounce him clean that hath the plague: it is all turned white: he is clean. [14]But when raw flesh appeareth in him, he shall be unclean. [15]And the priest shall see the raw flesh, and pronounce him to be unclean: for the raw flesh is unclean: it is a leprosy. [16]Or if the raw flesh turn again, and be changed unto white, he shall come unto the priest; [17]and the priest shall see him: and behold, if the plague be turned into white: then the priest shall pronounce him clean that hath the plague: he is clean.

[18]'The flesh also, in which, even in the skin thereof, was a boil, and is healed, [19]and in the place of the boil there be a white rising, or a bright spot, white, and somewhat reddish, and it be shown to the priest; [20]and if, when the priest seeth it, behold, it be in sight lower than the skin, and the hair thereof be turned white, the priest shall pronounce him unclean: it is a plague of leprosy broken out of the boil. [21]But if the priest look on it, and, behold, there be no white hairs therein, and if it be not lower than the skin, but be somewhat dark: then the priest shall shut him up seven days. [22]And if it spread much abroad in the skin, then the priest shall pronounce him unclean: it is a plague. [23]But if the bright spot stay in his place, and spread not, it is a burning boil; and the priest shall pronounce him clean.

[24]'Or if there be any flesh, in the skin whereof there is a hot burning, and the quick flesh that burneth have a white bright spot, somewhat reddish, or white; [25]then the priest shall look upon it: and behold, if the hair in the bright spot be turned white, and it be in sight deeper than the skin, it is a leprosy broken out of the burning: wherefore the priest shall pronounce him unclean: it is the plague of leprosy. [26]But if the priest look on it, and behold, there be no white hair in the bright spot, and it be no lower than the other skin, but be somewhat dark, then the priest shall shut him up seven days. [27]And the priest shall look upon him the seventh day: and if it be spread much abroad in the skin, then the priest shall pronounce him unclean: it is the plague of leprosy. [28]And if the bright spot stay in his place, and spread not in the skin, but it be somewhat dark; it is a rising of the burning, and the priest shall pronounce him clean: for it is an inflammation of the burning.

[29]'If a man or woman hath a plague upon the head or the beard, [30]then the priest shall see the plague: and behold, if it be in sight deeper than the skin, and there be in it a yellow thin hair; then the priest shall pronounce him unclean: it is a dry scall, even a leprosy upon the head or beard. [31]And if the priest look on the plague of the scall, and behold,

it be not in sight deeper than the skin, and that there is no black hair in it; then the priest shall shut up him that hath the plague of the scall seven days. ³²And in the seventh day the priest shall look on the plague: and behold, if the scall spread not, and there be in it no yellow hair, and the scall be not in sight deeper than the skin; ³³he shall be shaven, but the scall shall he not shave; and the priest shall shut up him that hath the scall seven days more. ³⁴And in the seventh day the priest shall look on the scall: and behold, if the scall be not spread in the skin, nor be in sight deeper than the skin, then the priest shall pronounce him clean: and he shall wash his clothes, and be clean. ³⁵But if the scall spread much in the skin after his cleansing, ³⁶then the priest shall look on him: and behold, if the scall be spread in the skin, the priest shall not seek for yellow hair: he is unclean. ³⁷But if the scall be in his sight at a stay, and that there is black hair grown up therein: the scall is healed, he is clean, and the priest shall pronounce him clean.

³⁸'If a man also or a woman have in the skin of their flesh bright spots, even white bright spots, ³⁹then the priest shall look: and behold, if the bright spots in the skin of their flesh be darkish white, it is a freckled spot that groweth in the skin: he is clean.

⁴⁰'And the man whose hair is fallen off his head, he is bald; yet is he clean. ⁴¹And he that hath his hair fallen off from the part of his head toward his face, he is forehead-bald: yet is he clean. ⁴²And if there be in the bald head, or bald forehead, a white reddish sore, it is a leprosy sprung up in his bald head, or his bald forehead. ⁴³Then the priest shall look upon it: and behold, if the rising of the sore be white reddish in his bald head, or in his bald forehead, as the leprosy appeareth in the skin of the flesh, ⁴⁴he is a leprous man, he is unclean: the priest shall pronounce him utterly unclean; his plague is in his head.

⁴⁵'And the leper in whom the plague is, his clothes shall be rent, and his head bare, and he shall put a covering upon his upper lip, and shall cry, "Unclean, unclean". ⁴⁶All the days wherein the plague shall be in him, he shall be defiled; he is unclean: he shall dwell alone; without the camp shall his habitation be.

⁴⁷'The garment also that the plague of leprosy is in, whether it be a woollen garment, or a linen garment; ⁴⁸whether it be in the warp, or woof; of linen, or of woollen; whether in a skin, or in anything made of skin; ⁴⁹and if the plague be greenish or reddish in the garment, or in the skin, either in the warp, or in the woof, or in anything of skin, it is a plague of leprosy, and shall be shown unto the priest. ⁵⁰And the priest shall look upon the plague, and shut up it that hath the plague seven days. ⁵¹And he shall look on the plague on the seventh day: if the plague be spread in the garment, either in the warp, or in the woof, or in a skin, or in any work that is made of skin, the plague is a fretting leprosy; it is unclean. ⁵²He shall therefore burn that garment, whether warp or woof, in woollen or in linen, or anything of skin, wherein the plague is: for it is a fretting leprosy; it shall be burnt in the fire. ⁵³And if the priest shall look, and, behold, the plague be not spread in the garment, either in the warp, or in the woof, or in anything of skin; ⁵⁴then

the priest shall command that they wash the thing wherein the plague is, and he shall shut it up seven days more. ⁵⁵And the priest shall look on the plague, after that it is washed: and behold, if the plague have not changed his colour, and the plague be not spread, it is unclean; thou shalt burn it in the fire; it is fretted inward, whether it be bare within or without. ⁵⁶And if the priest look, and, behold, the plague be somewhat dark after the washing of it, then he shall rend it out of the garment, or out of the skin, or out of the warp, or out of the woof. ⁵⁷And if it appear still in the garment, either in the warp, or in the woof, or in anything of skin, it is a spreading plague: thou shalt burn that wherein the plague is with fire. ⁵⁸And the garment, either warp, or woof, or whatsoever thing of skin it be, which thou shalt wash, if the plague be departed from them, then it shall be washed the second time, and shall be clean. ⁵⁹This is the law of the plague of leprosy in a garment of woollen or linen, either in the warp, or woof, or anything of skins, to pronounce it clean, or to pronounce it unclean.'

14 And the LORD spoke unto Moses, saying, ²'This shall be the law of the leper in the day of his cleansing: he shall be brought unto the priest. ³And the priest shall go forth out of the camp; and the priest shall look: and behold, if the plague of leprosy be healed in the leper, ⁴then shall the priest command to take for him that is to be cleansed two birds alive and clean, and cedar wood, and scarlet, and hyssop. ⁵And the priest shall command that one of the birds be killed in an earthen vessel over running water. ⁶As for the living bird, he shall take it, and the cedar wood, and the scarlet, and the hyssop, and shall dip them and the living bird in the blood of the bird that was killed over the running water. ⁷And he shall sprinkle upon him that is to be cleansed from the leprosy seven times, and shall pronounce him clean, and shall let the living bird loose into the open field. ⁸And he that is to be cleansed shall wash his clothes, and shave off all his hair, and wash himself in water, that he may be clean: and after that he shall come into the camp, and shall tarry abroad out of his tent seven days. ⁹But it shall be on the seventh day, that he shall shave all his hair off his head and his beard and his eyebrows, even all his hair he shall shave off: and he shall wash his clothes, also he shall wash his flesh in water, and he shall be clean. ¹⁰And on the eighth day he shall take two he-lambs without blemish, and one ewe lamb of the first year without blemish, and three tenth deals of fine flour for a meat offering, mingled with oil, and one log of oil. ¹¹And the priest that maketh him clean shall present the man that is to be made clean, and those things, before the LORD, at the door of the tabernacle of the congregation: ¹²and the priest shall take one he-lamb, and offer him for a trespass offering, and the log of oil, and wave them for a wave offering before the LORD. ¹³And he shall slay the lamb in the place where he shall kill the sin offering and the burnt offering, in the holy place: for as the sin offering is the priest's, so is the trespass offering: it is most holy. ¹⁴And the priest shall take some of the blood of the trespass offering, and the priest shall put it upon the tip of the right ear of him that is to be cleansed, and upon the thumb of his right hand, and upon the great toe of his right foot. ¹⁵And the priest shall take some of the log of oil, and pour it into the palm of his own left hand: ¹⁶and the priest shall dip his right finger in the oil that is in his left hand, and shall sprinkle of the oil with his finger seven times before the LORD. ¹⁷And of the rest of the oil that is in his hand shall the priest put upon the tip of the right ear of him that is to be cleansed, and upon the thumb of his right hand, and upon the great toe of his right foot, upon the blood of the trespass offering. ¹⁸And the remnant of the oil that is in the priest's hand he shall pour upon the head of him that is to be cleansed: and the priest shall make an atonement for him before the LORD. ¹⁹And the priest shall offer the sin offering, and make an atonement for him that is to be cleansed from his uncleanness; and afterward he shall kill the burnt offering. ²⁰And the priest shall offer the burnt offering and the meat offering upon the altar: and the priest shall make an atonement for him, and he shall be clean.

²¹ 'And if he be poor, and cannot get so much, then he shall take one lamb for a trespass offering to be waved, to make an atonement for him, and one tenth deal of fine flour mingled with oil for a meat offering, and a log of oil, ²²and two turtle doves, or two young pigeons, such as he is able to get; and the one shall be a sin offering, and the other a burnt offering. ²³And he shall bring them on the eighth day for his cleansing unto the priest, unto the door of the tabernacle of the congregation, before the LORD. ²⁴And the priest shall take the lamb of the trespass offering, and the log of oil, and the priest shall wave them for a wave offering before the LORD. ²⁵And he shall kill the lamb of the trespass offering, and the priest shall take some of the blood of the trespass offering, and put it upon the tip of the right ear of him that is to be cleansed, and upon the thumb of his right hand, and upon the great toe of his right foot. ²⁶And the priest shall pour of the oil into the palm of his own left hand. ²⁷And the priest shall sprinkle with his right finger some of the oil that is in his left hand seven times before the LORD. ²⁸And the priest shall put of the oil that is in his hand upon the tip of the right ear of him that is to be cleansed, and upon the thumb of his right hand, and upon the great toe of his right foot, upon the place of the blood of the trespass offering. ²⁹And the rest of the oil that is in the priest's hand he shall put upon the head of him that is to be cleansed, to make an atonement for him before the LORD. ³⁰And he shall offer the one of the turtle doves, or of the young pigeons, such as he can get: ³¹even such as he is able to get, the one for a sin offering, and the other for a burnt offering, with the meat offering. And the priest shall make an atonement for him that is to be cleansed before the LORD. ³²This is the law of him in whom is the plague of leprosy, whose hand is not able to get that which pertaineth to his cleansing.'

³³And the LORD spoke unto Moses and unto Aaron, saying, ³⁴'When ye be come into the land of Canaan, which I give to you for a possession, and I put the plague of leprosy in a house of the land of your possession; ³⁵and he that owneth the house shall come and tell the priest, say-

ing, "It seemeth to me there is as it were a plague in the house": [36] then the priest shall command that they empty the house, before the priest go into it to see the plague, that all that is in the house be not made unclean: and afterward the priest shall go in to see the house. [37] And he shall look on the plague, and, behold, if the plague be in the walls of the house with hollow streaks, greenish or reddish, which in sight are lower than the wall; [38] then the priest shall go out of the house to the door of the house, and shut up the house seven days. [39] And the priest shall come again the seventh day, and shall look: and behold, if the plague be spread in the walls of the house; [40] then the priest shall command that they take away the stones in which the plague is, and they shall cast them into an unclean place without the city. [41] And he shall cause the house to be scraped within round about, and they shall pour out the dust that they scrape off without the city into an unclean place. [42] And they shall take other stones, and put them in the place of those stones; and he shall take other mortar, and shall plaster the house. [43] And if the plague come again, and break out in the house, after that he hath taken away the stones, and after he hath scraped the house, and after it is plastered; [44] then the priest shall come and look, and behold, if the plague be spread in the house, it is a fretting leprosy in the house: it is unclean. [45] And he shall break down the house, the stones of it, and the timber thereof, and all the mortar of the house; and he shall carry them forth out of the city into an unclean place. [46] Moreover, he that goeth into the house all the while that it is shut up shall be unclean until the even. [47] And he that lieth in the house shall wash his clothes; and he that eateth in the house shall wash his clothes. [48] And if the priest shall come in, and look upon it, and behold, the plague hath not spread in the house, after the house was plastered: then the priest shall pronounce the house clean, because the plague is healed. [49] And he shall take to cleanse the house two birds, and cedar wood, and scarlet, and hyssop. [50] And he shall kill the one of the birds in an earthen vessel over running water. [51] And he shall take the cedar wood, and the hyssop, and the scarlet, and the living bird, and dip them in the blood of the slain bird, and in the running water, and sprinkle the house seven times. [52] And he shall cleanse the house with the blood of the bird, and with the running water, and with the living bird, and with the cedar wood, and with the hyssop, and with the scarlet. [53] But he shall let go the living bird out of the city into the open fields, and make an atonement for the house: and it shall be clean.

[54] 'This is the law for all manner plague of leprosy, and scall, [55] and for the leprosy of a garment, and of a house, [56] and for a rising, and for a scab, and for a bright spot: [57] to teach when it is unclean, and when it is clean: this is the law of leprosy.'

15 And the Lord spoke unto Moses and to Aaron, saying, [2] 'Speak unto the children of Israel, and say unto them, "When any man hath a running issue out of his flesh, because of his issue he is unclean. [3] And this shall be his uncleanness in his issue: whether his flesh run with his issue, or his flesh be stopped from his issue, it is his uncleanness. ⁴Every bed whereon he lieth that hath the issue, is unclean: and everything whereon he sitteth, shall be unclean. ⁵And whosoever toucheth his bed shall wash his clothes, and bathe himself in water, and be unclean until the even. ⁶And he that sitteth on anything whereon he sat that hath the issue shall wash his clothes, and bathe himself in water, and be unclean until the even. ⁷And he that toucheth the flesh of him that hath the issue shall wash his clothes, and bathe himself in water, and be unclean until the even. ⁸And if he that hath the issue spit upon him that is clean, then he shall wash his clothes, and bathe himself in water, and be unclean until the even. ⁹And what saddle soever he rideth upon that hath the issue shall be unclean. ¹⁰And whosoever toucheth anything that was under him shall be unclean until the even: and he that beareth any of those things shall wash his clothes, and bathe himself in water, and be unclean until the even. ¹¹And whomsoever he toucheth that hath the issue, and hath not rinsed his hands in water, he shall wash his clothes, and bathe himself in water, and be unclean until the even. ¹²And the vessel of earth, that he toucheth which hath the issue, shall be broken: and every vessel of wood shall be rinsed in water.

¹³'"And when he that hath an issue is cleansed of his issue, then he shall number to himself seven days for his cleansing, and wash his clothes, and bathe his flesh in running water, and shall be clean. ¹⁴And on the eighth day he shall take to him two turtle doves, or two young pigeons, and come before the Lord unto the door of the tabernacle of the congregation, and give them unto the priest. ¹⁵And the priest shall offer them, the one for a sin offering, and the other for a burnt offering; and the priest shall make an atonement for him before the Lord for his issue.

¹⁶'"And if any man's seed of copulation go out from him, then he shall wash all his flesh in water, and be unclean until the even. ¹⁷And every garment, and every skin, whereon is the seed of copulation, shall be washed with water, and be unclean until the even. ¹⁸The woman also with whom man shall lie with seed of copulation, they shall both bathe themselves in water, and be unclean until the even.

¹⁹'"And if a woman have an issue, and her issue in her flesh be blood, she shall be put apart seven days: and whosoever toucheth her shall be unclean until the even. ²⁰And everything that she lieth upon in her separation shall be unclean: everything also that she sitteth upon shall be unclean. ²¹And whosoever toucheth her bed shall wash his clothes, and bathe himself in water, and be unclean until the even. ²²And whosoever toucheth anything that she sat upon shall wash his clothes, and bathe himself in water, and be unclean until the even. ²³And if it be on her bed, or on anything whereon she sitteth, when he toucheth it, he shall be unclean until the even. ²⁴And if any man lie with her at all, and her flowers be upon him, he shall be unclean seven days; and all the bed whereon he lieth shall be unclean. ²⁵And if a woman have an issue of her blood many days out of the time of her separation, or if it run beyond the time of her separation, all the days of the issue of her

uncleanness shall be as the days of her separation: she shall be unclean. ²⁶Every bed whereon she lieth all the days of her issue shall be unto her as the bed of her separation: and whatsoever she sitteth upon shall be unclean, as the uncleanness of her separation. ²⁷And whosoever toucheth those things shall be unclean, and shall wash his clothes, and bathe himself in water, and be unclean until the even. ²⁸But if she be cleansed of her issue, then she shall number to herself seven days, and after that she shall be clean. ²⁹And on the eighth day she shall take unto her two turtles, or two young pigeons, and bring them unto the priest, to the door of the tabernacle of the congregation. ³⁰And the priest shall offer the one for a sin offering, and the other for a burnt offering; and the priest shall make an atonement for her before the LORD for the issue of her uncleanness.

³¹'"Thus shall ye separate the children of Israel from their uncleanness, that they die not in their uncleanness, when they defile my tabernacle that is among them. ³²This is the law of him that hath an issue, and of him whose seed goeth from him, and is defiled therewith; ³³and of her that is sick of her flowers, and of him that hath an issue, of the man, and of the woman, and of him that lieth with her which is unclean."'

16 And the LORD spoke unto Moses after the death of the two sons of Aaron, when they offered before the LORD, and died. ²And the LORD said unto Moses, 'Speak unto Aaron thy brother, that he come not at all times into the holy place within the veil before the mercy-seat, which is upon the ark, that he die not: for I will appear in the cloud upon the mercy-seat. ³Thus shall Aaron come into the holy place: with a young bullock for a sin offering, and a ram for a burnt offering. ⁴He shall put on the holy linen coat, and he shall have the linen breeches upon his flesh, and shall be girded with a linen girdle, and with the linen mitre shall he be attired. These are holy garments; therefore shall he wash his flesh in water, and so put them on. ⁵And he shall take of the congregation of the children of Israel two kids of the goats for a sin offering, and one ram for a burnt offering. ⁶And Aaron shall offer his bullock of the sin offering, which is for himself, and make an atonement for himself, and for his house. ⁷And he shall take the two goats, and present them before the LORD at the door of the tabernacle of the congregation. ⁸And Aaron shall cast lots upon the two goats: one lot for the LORD, and the other lot for the scapegoat. ⁹And Aaron shall bring the goat upon which the LORD's lot fell, and offer him for a sin offering. ¹⁰But the goat, on which the lot fell to be the scapegoat, shall be presented alive before the LORD, to make an atonement with him, and to let him go for a scapegoat into the wilderness. ¹¹And Aaron shall bring the bullock of the sin offering, which is for himself, and shall make an atonement for himself, and for his house, and shall kill the bullock of the sin offering which is for himself. ¹²And he shall take a censer full of burning coals of fire from off the altar before the LORD, and his hands full of sweet incense beaten small, and bring it within the veil. ¹³And he shall put the incense upon the fire before the LORD, that the cloud of the incense may cover the mercy-seat that is upon the testimony, that he die not. ¹⁴And he shall take of the blood of the bullock, and sprinkle it with his finger upon the mercy-seat eastward; and before the mercy-seat shall he sprinkle of the blood with his finger seven times.

¹⁵'Then shall he kill the goat of the sin offering that is for the people, and bring his blood within the veil, and do with that blood as he did with the blood of the bullock, and sprinkle it upon the mercy-seat, and before the mercy-seat. ¹⁶And he shall make an atonement for the holy place, because of the uncleanness of the children of Israel, and because of their transgressions in all their sins: and so shall he do for the tabernacle of the congregation, that remaineth among them in the midst of their uncleanness. ¹⁷And there shall be no man in the tabernacle of the congregation when he goeth in to make an atonement in the holy place, until he come out, and have made an atonement for himself, and for his household, and for all the congregation of Israel. ¹⁸And he shall go out unto the altar that is before the LORD, and make an atonement for it; and shall take of the blood of the bullock, and of the blood of the goat, and put it upon the horns of the altar round about. ¹⁹And he shall sprinkle of the blood upon it with his finger seven times, and cleanse it, and hallow it from the uncleanness of the children of Israel.

²⁰'And when he hath made an end of reconciling the holy place, and the tabernacle of the congregation, and the altar, he shall bring the live goat. ²¹And Aaron shall lay both his hands upon the head of the live goat, and confess over him all the iniquities of the children of Israel, and all their transgressions in all their sins, putting them upon the head of the goat, and shall send him away by the hand of a fit man into the wilderness. ²²And the goat shall bear upon him all their iniquities unto a land not inhabited; and he shall let go the goat in the wilderness.

²³'And Aaron shall come into the tabernacle of the congregation, and shall put off the linen garments, which he put on when he went into the holy place, and shall leave them there. ²⁴And he shall wash his flesh with water in the holy place, and put on his garments, and come forth, and offer his burnt offering, and the burnt offering of the people, and make an atonement for himself, and for the people. ²⁵And the fat of the sin offering shall he burn upon the altar. ²⁶And he that let go the goat for the scapegoat shall wash his clothes, and bathe his flesh in water, and afterward come into the camp. ²⁷And the bullock for the sin offering, and the goat for the sin offering, whose blood was brought in to make atonement in the holy place, shall one carry forth without the camp; and they shall burn in the fire their skins, and their flesh, and their dung. ²⁸And he that burneth them shall wash his clothes, and bathe his flesh in water, and afterward he shall come into the camp.

²⁹'And this shall be a statute for ever unto you: that in the seventh month, on the tenth day of the month, ye shall afflict your souls, and do no work at all, whether it be one of your own country, or a stranger that sojourneth among you: ³⁰for on that day shall the priest make an

atonement for you, to cleanse you, that ye may be clean from all your sins before the LORD. ³¹It shall be a sabbath of rest unto you, and ye shall afflict your souls, by a statute for ever. ³²And the priest, whom he shall anoint, and whom he shall consecrate to minister in the priest's office in his father's stead, shall make the atonement, and shall put on the linen clothes, even the holy garments. ³³And he shall make an atonement for the holy sanctuary, and he shall make an atonement for the tabernacle of the congregation, and for the altar: and he shall make an atonement for the priests, and for all the people of the congregation. ³⁴And this shall be an everlasting statute unto you, to make an atonement for the children of Israel for all their sins once a year.' And he did as the LORD commanded Moses.

17 And the LORD spoke unto Moses, saying, ²'Speak unto Aaron, and unto his sons, and unto all the children of Israel, and say unto them: "This is the thing which the LORD hath commanded, saying, ³What man soever there be of the house of Israel, that killeth an ox, or lamb, or goat, in the camp, or that killeth it out of the camp, ⁴and bringeth it not unto the door of the tabernacle of the congregation, to offer an offering unto the LORD before the tabernacle of the LORD, blood shall be imputed unto that man; he hath shed blood, and that man shall be cut off from among his people: ⁵to the end that the children of Israel may bring their sacrifices, which they offer in the open field, even that they may bring them unto the LORD, unto the door of the tabernacle of the congregation, unto the priest, and offer them for peace offerings unto the LORD. ⁶And the priest shall sprinkle the blood upon the altar of the LORD at the door of the tabernacle of the congregation, and burn the fat for a sweet savour unto the LORD. ⁷And they shall no more offer their sacrifices unto devils, after whom they have gone a-whoring. This shall be a statute for ever unto them throughout their generations."

⁸'And thou shalt say unto them, "Whatsoever man there be of the house of Israel, or of the strangers which sojourn among you, that offereth a burnt offering or sacrifice, ⁹and bringeth it not unto the door of the tabernacle of the congregation, to offer it unto the LORD, even that man shall be cut off from among his people.

¹⁰'"And whatsoever man there be of the house of Israel, or of the strangers that sojourn among you, that eateth any manner of blood, I will even set my face against that soul that eateth blood, and will cut him off from among his people. ¹¹For the life of the flesh is in the blood, and I have given it to you upon the altar to make an atonement for your souls: for it is the blood that maketh an atonement for the soul. ¹²Therefore I said unto the children of Israel, 'No soul of you shall eat blood, neither shall any stranger that sojourneth among you eat blood'. ¹³And whatsoever man there be of the children of Israel, or of the strangers that sojourn among you, which hunteth and catcheth any beast or fowl that may be eaten, he shall even pour out the blood thereof, and cover it with dust. ¹⁴For it is the life of all flesh, the blood of it is for the life thereof: therefore I said unto the children of Israel,

'Ye shall eat the blood of no manner of flesh: for the life of all flesh is the blood thereof': whosoever eateth it shall be cut off. ¹⁵And every soul that eateth that which died of itself, or that which was torn with beasts, whether it be one of your own country, or a stranger, he shall both wash his clothes, and bathe himself in water, and be unclean until the even: then shall he be clean. ¹⁶But if he wash them not, nor bathe his flesh, then he shall bear his iniquity.'"

18 And the LORD spoke unto Moses, saying, ²'Speak unto the children of Israel, and say unto them, "I am the LORD your God. ³After the doings of the land of Egypt, wherein ye dwelt, shall ye not do: and after the doings of the land of Canaan, whither I bring you, shall ye not do: neither shall ye walk in their ordinances. ⁴Ye shall do my judgements, and keep my ordinances, to walk therein: I am the LORD your God. ⁵Ye shall therefore keep my statutes, and my judgements: which if a man do, he shall live in them: I am the LORD.

⁶'"None of you shall approach to any that is near of kin to him, to uncover their nakedness: I am the LORD. ⁷The nakedness of thy father, or the nakedness of thy mother, shalt thou not uncover: she is thy mother; thou shalt not uncover her nakedness. ⁸The nakedness of thy father's wife shalt thou not uncover: it is thy father's nakedness. ⁹The nakedness of thy sister, the daughter of thy father, or daughter of thy mother, whether she be born at home, or born abroad, even their nakedness thou shalt not uncover. ¹⁰The nakedness of thy son's daughter, or of thy daughter's daughter, even their nakedness thou shalt not uncover: for theirs is thy own nakedness. ¹¹The nakedness of thy father's wife's daughter, begotten of thy father (she is thy sister), thou shalt not uncover her nakedness. ¹²Thou shalt not uncover the nakedness of thy father's sister: she is thy father's near kinswoman. ¹³Thou shalt not uncover the nakedness of thy mother's sister: for she is thy mother's near kinswoman. ¹⁴Thou shalt not uncover the nakedness of thy father's brother, thou shalt not approach to his wife: she is thy aunt. ¹⁵Thou shalt not uncover the nakedness of thy daughter-in-law: she is thy son's wife; thou shalt not uncover her nakedness. ¹⁶Thou shalt not uncover the nakedness of thy brother's wife: it is thy brother's nakedness. ¹⁷Thou shalt not uncover the nakedness of a woman and her daughter, neither shalt thou take her son's daughter, or her daughter's daughter, to uncover her nakedness; for they are her near kinswomen: it is wickedness. ¹⁸Neither shalt thou take a wife to her sister, to vex her, to uncover her nakedness, besides the other in her lifetime. ¹⁹Also thou shalt not approach unto a woman to uncover her nakedness, as long as she is put apart for her uncleanness.²⁰Moreover thou shalt not lie carnally with thy neighbour's wife, to defile thyself with her. ²¹And thou shalt not let any of thy seed pass through the fire to Molech, neither shalt thou profane the name of thy God: I am the LORD. ²²Thou shalt not lie with mankind, as with womankind: it is abomination. ²³Neither shalt thou lie with any beast to defile thyself therewith: neither shall any woman stand before a beast to lie down thereto: it is confusion.

²⁴'"Defile not you yourselves in any of these things: for in all these the

nations are defiled which I cast out before you:²⁵ and the land is defiled: therefore I do visit the iniquity thereof upon it, and the land itself vomiteth out her inhabitants. ²⁶Ye shall therefore keep my statutes and my judgements, and shall not commit any of these abominations; neither any of your own nation, nor any stranger that sojourneth among you ²⁷(for all these abominations have the men of the land done, which were before you, and the land is defiled): ²⁸that the land spew not you out also, when ye defile it, as it spewed out the nations that were before you. ²⁹For whosoever shall commit any of these abominations, even the souls that commit them, shall be cut off from among their people. ³⁰Therefore shall ye keep my ordinance, that ye commit not any one of these abominable customs, which were committed before you, and that ye defile not yourselves therein: I am the LORD your God."'

19 And the LORD spoke unto Moses, saying, ²'Speak unto all the congregation of the children of Israel, and say unto them, "Ye shall be holy: for I the LORD your God am holy.

³'"Ye shall fear every man his mother, and his father, and keep my sabbaths: I am the LORD your God.

⁴'"Turn ye not unto idols, nor make to yourselves molten gods: I am the LORD your God.

⁵'"And if ye offer a sacrifice of peace offerings unto the LORD, ye shall offer it at your own will. ⁶It shall be eaten the same day ye offer it, and on the morrow: and if aught remain until the third day, it shall be burnt in the fire. ⁷And if it be eaten at all on the third day, it is abominable: it shall not be accepted. ⁸Therefore every one that eateth it shall bear his iniquity, because he hath profaned the hallowed thing of the LORD: and that soul shall be cut off from among his people.

⁹'"And when ye reap the harvest of your land, thou shalt not wholly reap the corners of thy field, neither shalt thou gather the gleanings of thy harvest. ¹⁰And thou shalt not glean thy vineyard, neither shalt thou gather every grape of thy vineyard; thou shalt leave them for the poor and stranger: I am the LORD your God.

¹¹'"Ye shall not steal, neither deal falsely, neither lie one to another.

¹²'"And ye shall not swear by my name falsely, neither shalt thou profane the name of thy God: I am the LORD.

¹³'"Thou shalt not defraud thy neighbour, neither rob him: the wages of him that is hired shall not abide with thee all night until the morning.

¹⁴'"Thou shalt not curse the deaf, nor put a stumbling-block before the blind, but shalt fear thy God: I am the LORD.

¹⁵'"Ye shall do no unrighteousness in judgement: thou shalt not respect the person of the poor, nor honour the person of the mighty: but in righteousness shalt thou judge thy neighbour.

¹⁶'"Thou shalt not go up and down as a tale-bearer among thy people: neither shalt thou stand against the blood of thy neighbour: I am the LORD.

¹⁷'"Thou shalt not hate thy brother in thy heart: thou shalt in any wise rebuke thy neighbour, and not suffer sin upon him.

¹⁸ "'Thou shalt not avenge, nor bear any grudge against the children of thy people, but thou shalt love thy neighbour as thyself: I am the LORD.
¹⁹ "'Ye shall keep my statutes. Thou shalt not let thy cattle gender with a diverse kind: thou shalt not sow thy field with mingled seed: neither shall a garment mingled of linen and woollen come upon thee.
²⁰ "'And whosoever lieth carnally with a woman that is a bondmaid, betrothed to a husband, and not at all redeemed, nor freedom given her; she shall be scourged; they shall not be put to death, because she was not free. ²¹And he shall bring his trespass offering unto the LORD, unto the door of the tabernacle of the congregation, even a ram for a trespass offering. ²²And the priest shall make an atonement for him with the ram of the trespass offering before the LORD for his sin which he hath done: and the sin which he hath done shall be forgiven him.
²³ "'And when ye shall come into the land, and shall have planted all manner of trees for food, then ye shall count the fruit thereof as uncircumcised: three years shall it be as uncircumcised unto you: it shall not be eaten of. ²⁴But in the fourth year all the fruit thereof shall be holy to praise the LORD withal. ²⁵And in the fifth year shall ye eat of the fruit thereof, that it may yield unto you the increase thereof: I am the LORD your God.
²⁶ "'Ye shall not eat anything with the blood, neither shall ye use enchantment, nor observe times. ²⁷Ye shall not round the corners of your heads, neither shalt thou mar the corners of thy beard. ²⁸Ye shall not make any cuttings in your flesh for the dead, nor print any marks upon you: I am the LORD.
²⁹ "'Do not prostitute thy daughter, to cause her to be a whore, lest the land fall to whoredom, and the land become full of wickedness.
³⁰ "'Ye shall keep my sabbaths, and reverence my sanctuary: I am the LORD.
³¹ "'Regard not them that have familiar spirits, neither seek after wizards, to be defiled by them: I am the LORD your God.
³² "'Thou shalt rise up before the hoary head, and honour the face of the old man, and fear thy God: I am the LORD.
³³ "'And if a stranger sojourn with thee in your land, ye shall not vex him. ³⁴But the stranger that dwelleth with you shall be as one born amongst you, and thou shalt love him as thyself, for ye were strangers in the land of Egypt: I am the LORD your God.
³⁵ "'Ye shall do no unrighteousness in judgement, in meteyard, in weight, or in measure. ³⁶Just balances, just weights, a just ephah, and a just hin, shall ye have: I am the LORD your God, which brought you out of the land of Egypt. ³⁷Therefore shall ye observe all my statutes, and all my judgements, and do them: I am the LORD."'

20 And the LORD spoke unto Moses, saying, ²'Again, thou shalt say to the children of Israel, "Whosoever he be of the children of Israel, or of the strangers that sojourn in Israel, that giveth any of his seed unto Molech, he shall surely be put to death: the people of the land shall stone him with stones. ³And I will set my face against that man, and will cut him off from among his people: because he hath given of his seed unto Molech, to defile my sanctuary, and to profane my holy name. ⁴And if the people of the land do any ways hide their eyes from the man, when he giveth of his seed unto Molech, and kill him not: ⁵then I will set my face against that man, and against his family, and will cut him off, and all that go a-whoring after him, to commit whoredom with Molech, from among their people.

⁶'"And the soul that turneth after such as have familiar spirits, and after wizards, to go a-whoring after them, I will even set my face against that soul, and will cut him off from among his people.

⁷'"Sanctify yourselves therefore, and be ye holy: for I am the LORD your God. ⁸And ye shall keep my statutes, and do them: I am the LORD which sanctify you.

⁹'"For every one that curseth his father or his mother shall be surely put to death: he hath cursed his father or his mother; his blood shall be upon him.

¹⁰'"And the man that committeth adultery with another man's wife, even he that committeth adultery with his neighbour's wife, the adulterer and the adulteress shall surely be put to death. ¹¹And the man that lieth with his father's wife hath uncovered his father's nakedness: both of them shall be put to death; their blood shall be upon them. ¹²And if a man lie with his daughter-in-law, both of them shall surely be put to death: they have wrought confusion; their blood shall be upon them. ¹³If a man also lie with mankind, as he lieth with a woman, both of them have committed an abomination: they shall surely be put to death; their blood shall be upon them. ¹⁴And if a man take a wife and her mother, it is wickedness: they shall be burnt with fire, both he and they; that there be no wickedness among you. ¹⁵And if a man lie with a beast, he shall surely be put to death; and ye shall slay the beast. ¹⁶And if a woman approach unto any beast, and lie down thereto, thou shalt kill the woman, and the beast: they shall surely be put to death; their blood shall be upon them. ¹⁷And if a man shall take his sister, his father's daughter, or his mother's daughter, and see her nakedness, and she see his nakedness, it is a wicked thing, and they shall be cut off in the sight of their people: he hath uncovered his sister's nakedness; he shall bear his iniquity. ¹⁸And if a man shall lie with a woman having her sickness, and shall uncover her nakedness: he hath discovered her fountain, and she hath uncovered the fountain of her blood: and both of them shall be cut off from among their people. ¹⁹And thou shalt not uncover the nakedness of thy mother's sister, nor of thy father's sister: for he uncovereth his near kin: they shall bear their iniquity. ²⁰And if a man shall lie with his uncle's wife, he hath uncovered his uncle's nakedness: they shall bear their sin; they shall die childless. ²¹And if a man shall take his brother's wife, it is an unclean thing: he hath uncovered his brother's nakedness; they shall be childless.

²²'"Ye shall therefore keep all my statutes, and all my judgements, and do them: that the land, whither I bring you to dwell therein, spew you not out. ²³And ye shall not walk in the manners of the nation, which I cast out before you: for they committed all these things, and therefore

I abhorred them. ²⁴But I have said unto you, 'Ye shall inherit their land, and I will give it unto you to possess it, a land that floweth with milk and honey: I am the LORD your God, which have separated you from other people'. ²⁵Ye shall therefore put difference between clean beasts and unclean, and between unclean fowls and clean: and ye shall not make your souls abominable by beast, or by fowl, or by any manner of living thing that creepeth on the ground, which I have separated from you as unclean. ²⁶And ye shall be holy unto me: for I the LORD am holy, and have severed you from other people, that ye should be mine.

²⁷'"A man also or woman that hath a familiar spirit, or that is a wizard, shall surely be put to death: they shall stone them with stones: their blood shall be upon them."'

21 And the LORD said unto Moses, 'Speak unto the priests the sons of Aaron, and say unto them, "There shall none be defiled for the dead among his people: ²but for his kin, that is near unto him, that is, for his mother, and for his father, and for his son, and for his daughter, and for his brother, ³and for his sister a virgin, that is nigh unto him, which hath had no husband: for her may he be defiled. ⁴But he shall not defile himself, being a chief man among his people, to profane himself. ⁵They shall not make baldness upon their head, neither shall they shave off the corner of their beard, nor make any cuttings in their flesh. ⁶They shall be holy unto their God, and not profane the name of their God: for the offerings of the LORD made by fire, and the bread of their God, they do offer: therefore they shall be holy. ⁷They shall not take a wife that is a whore, or profane, neither shall they take a woman put away from her husband: for he is holy unto his God. ⁸Thou shalt sanctify him therefore, for he offereth the bread of thy God: he shall be holy unto thee: for I the LORD, which sanctify you, am holy.

⁹'"And the daughter of any priest, if she profane herself by playing the whore, she profaneth her father: she shall be burnt with fire.

¹⁰'"And he that is the high priest among his brethren, upon whose head the anointing oil was poured, and that is consecrated to put on the garments, shall not uncover his head, nor rend his clothes; ¹¹neither shall he go in to any dead body, nor defile himself for his father, or for his mother; ¹²neither shall he go out of the sanctuary, nor profane the sanctuary of his God; for the crown of the anointing oil of his God is upon him: I am the LORD. ¹³And he shall take a wife in her virginity. ¹⁴A widow, or a divorced woman, or profane, or a harlot, these shall he not take: but he shall take a virgin of his own people to wife. ¹⁵Neither shall he profane his seed among his people: for I the LORD do sanctify him."'

¹⁶And the LORD spoke unto Moses, saying, ¹⁷'Speak unto Aaron, saying, "Whosoever he be of thy seed in their generations that hath any blemish, let him not approach to offer the bread of his God. ¹⁸For whatsoever man he be that hath a blemish, he shall not approach: a blind man, or a lame, or he that hath a flat nose, or anything superfluous, ¹⁹or a man that is broken-footed, or broken-handed, ²⁰or crook-backed, or a dwarf, or that hath a blemish in his eye, or be scurvy, or scabbed, or

hath his stones broken; [21] no man that hath a blemish, of the seed of Aaron the priest shall come nigh to offer the offerings of the LORD made by fire: he hath a blemish; he shall not come nigh to offer the bread of his God. [22] He shall eat the bread of his God, both of the most holy, and of the holy. [23] Only he shall not go in unto the veil, nor come nigh unto the altar, because he hath a blemish, that he profane not my sanctuaries: for I the LORD do sanctify them."' [20] And Moses told it unto Aaron, and to his sons, and unto all the children of Israel.

22 And the LORD spoke unto Moses, saying, [2] 'Speak unto Aaron and to his sons, that they separate themselves from the holy things of the children of Israel, and that they profane not my holy name in those things which they hallow unto me: I am the LORD. [3] Say unto them, "Whosoever he be of all your seed among your generations, that goeth unto the holy things, which the children of Israel hallow unto the LORD, having his uncleanness upon him, that soul shall be cut off from my presence: I am the LORD. [4] What man soever of the seed of Aaron is a leper, or hath a running issue, he shall not eat of the holy things, until he be clean. And whoso toucheth anything that is unclean by the dead, or a man whose seed goeth from him; [5] or whosoever toucheth any creeping thing, whereby he may be made unclean, or a man of whom he may take uncleanness, whatsoever uncleanness he hath: [6] the soul which hath touched any such shall be unclean until even, and shall not eat of the holy things, unless he wash his flesh with water. [7] And when the sun is down, he shall be clean, and shall afterward eat of the holy things, because it is his food. [8] That which dieth of itself, or is torn with beasts, he shall not eat to defile himself therewith: I am the LORD. [9] They shall therefore keep my ordinance, lest they bear sin for it, and die therefore, if they profane it: I the LORD do sanctify them.

[10] '"There shall no stranger eat of the holy thing: a sojourner of the priest, or a hired servant, shall not eat of the holy thing. [11] But if the priest buy any soul with his money, he shall eat of it, and he that is born in his house: they shall eat of his meat. [12] If the priest's daughter also be married unto a stranger, she may not eat of an offering of the holy things. [13] But if the priest's daughter be a widow, or divorced, and have no child, and is returned unto her father's house, as in her youth, she shall eat of her father's meat: but there shall no stranger eat thereof.

[14] '"And if a man eat of the holy thing unwittingly, then he shall put the fifth part thereof unto it, and shall give it unto the priest with the holy thing. [15] And they shall not profane the holy things of the children of Israel, which they offer unto the LORD; [16] or suffer them to bear the iniquity of trespass, when they eat their holy things: for I the LORD do sanctify them."'

[17] And the LORD spoke unto Moses, saying, [18] 'Speak unto Aaron, and to his sons, and unto all the children of Israel, and say unto them, "Whatsoever he be of the house of Israel, or of the strangers in Israel, that will offer his oblation for all his vows, and for all his free-will offer-

ings, which they will offer unto the LORD for a burnt offering: ¹⁹ye shall offer at your own will a male without blemish, of the beeves, of the sheep, or of the goats. ²⁰But whatsoever hath a blemish, that shall ye not offer: for it shall not be acceptable for you. ²¹And whosoever offereth a sacrifice of peace offerings unto the LORD to accomplish his vow, or a free-will offering in beeves or sheep, it shall be perfect to be accepted: there shall be no blemish therein. ²²Blind, or broken, or maimed, or having a wen, or scurvy, or scabbed, ye shall not offer these unto the LORD, nor make an offering by fire of them upon the altar unto the LORD. ²³Either a bullock or a lamb that hath anything superfluous or lacking in his parts, that mayest thou offer for a free-will offering; but for a vow it shall not be accepted. ²⁴Ye shall not offer unto the LORD that which is bruised, or crushed, or broken, or cut; neither shall you make any offering thereof in your land. ²⁵Neither from a stranger's hand shall ye offer the bread of your God of any of these; because their corruption is in them, and blemishes be in them: they shall not be accepted for you.'"

²⁶And the LORD spoke unto Moses, saying, ²⁷'When a bullock, or a sheep, or a goat, is brought forth, then it shall be seven days under the dam; and from the eighth day and thenceforth it shall be accepted for an offering made by fire unto the LORD. ²⁸And whether it be cow or ewe, ye shall not kill it and her young both in one day. ²⁹And when ye will offer a sacrifice of thanksgiving unto the LORD, offer it at your own will. ³⁰On the same day it shall be eaten up; ye shall leave none of it until the morrow: I am the LORD. ³¹Therefore shall ye keep my commandments, and do them: I am the LORD. ³²Neither shall ye profane my holy name; but I will be hallowed among the children of Israel: I am the LORD which hallow you, ³³That brought you out of the land of Egypt, to be your God: I am the LORD.'

23 And the LORD spoke unto Moses, saying, ²'Speak unto the children of Israel, and say unto them, "Concerning the feasts of the LORD, which ye shall proclaim to be holy convocations, even these are my feasts. ³Six days shall work be done: but the seventh day is the sabbath of rest, a holy convocation; ye shall do no work therein: it is the sabbath of the LORD in all your dwellings.

⁴'"These are the feasts of the LORD, even holy convocations, which ye shall proclaim in their seasons. ⁵In the fourteenth day of the first month at even is the LORD's passover. ⁶And on the fifteenth day of the same month is the feast of unleavened bread unto the LORD: seven days ye must eat unleavened bread. ⁷In the first day ye shall have a holy convocation: ye shall do no servile work therein. ⁸But ye shall offer an offering made by fire unto the LORD seven days: in the seventh day is a holy convocation: ye shall do no servile work therein.'"

⁹And the LORD spoke unto Moses, saying, ¹⁰'Speak unto the children of Israel, and say unto them, "When ye be come into the land which I give unto you, and shall reap the harvest thereof, then ye shall bring a sheaf of the first-fruits of your harvest unto the priest: ¹¹and he shall wave the sheaf before the LORD, to be accepted for you: on the morrow

after the sabbath the priest shall wave it. [12]And ye shall offer that day when ye wave the sheaf a he-lamb without blemish of the first year for a burnt offering unto the LORD. [13]And the meat offering thereof shall be two tenth deals of fine flour mingled with oil, an offering made by fire unto the LORD for a sweet savour: and the drink offering thereof shall be of wine, the fourth part of a hin. [14]And ye shall eat neither bread, nor parched corn, nor green ears, until the selfsame day that ye have brought an offering unto your God: it shall be a statute for ever throughout your generations in all your dwellings.

[15]'"And ye shall count unto you from the morrow after the sabbath, from the day that ye brought the sheaf of the wave offering; seven sabbaths shall be complete: [16]even unto the morrow after the seventh sabbath shall ye number fifty days, and ye shall offer a new meat offering unto the LORD. [17]Ye shall bring out of your habitations two wave loaves of two tenth deals: they shall be of fine flour; they shall be baked with leaven; they are the first-fruits unto the LORD. [18]And ye shall offer with the bread seven lambs without blemish, of the first year, and one young bullock, and two rams: they shall be for a burnt offering unto the LORD, with their meat offering, and their drink offerings, even an offering made by fire, of sweet savour unto the LORD. [19]Then ye shall sacrifice one kid of the goats for a sin offering, and two lambs of the first year for a sacrifice of peace offerings. [20]And the priest shall wave them with the bread of the first-fruits for a wave offering before the LORD, with the two lambs: they shall be holy to the LORD for the priests. [21]And ye shall proclaim on the selfsame day, that it may be a holy convocation unto you: ye shall do no servile work therein: it shall be a statute for ever in all your dwellings throughout your generations.

[22]'"And when ye reap the harvest of your land, thou shalt not make clean riddance of the corners of the field when thou reapest, neither shalt thou gather any gleaning of thy harvest: thou shalt leave them unto the poor, and to the stranger: I am the LORD your God."'

[23]And the LORD spoke unto Moses, saying, [24]'Speak unto the children of Israel, saying, "In the seventh month, in the first day of the month, shall ye have a sabbath, a memorial of blowing of trumpets, a holy convocation. [25]Ye shall do no servile work therein: but ye shall offer an offering made by fire unto the LORD."'

[26]And the LORD spoke unto Moses, saying, [27]'Also on the tenth day of this seventh month there shall be a day of atonement: it shall be a holy convocation unto you, and ye shall afflict your souls, and offer an offering made by fire unto the LORD. [28]And ye shall do no work in that same day: for it is a day of atonement, to make an atonement for you before the LORD your God. [29]For whatsoever soul it be that shall not be afflicted in that same day, he shall be cut off from among his people. [30]And whatsoever soul it be that doeth any work in that same day, the same soul will I destroy from among his people. [31]Ye shall do no manner of work: it shall be a statute for ever throughout your generations in all your dwellings. [32]It shall be unto you a sabbath of rest, and

ye shall afflict your souls: in the ninth day of the month at even, from even unto even, shall ye celebrate your sabbath.'

[33]And the LORD spoke unto Moses, saying, [34]'Speak unto the children of Israel, saying, "The fifteenth day of this seventh month shall be the feast of tabernacles for seven days unto the LORD. [35]On the first day shall be a holy convocation: ye shall do no servile work therein. [36]Seven days ye shall offer an offering made by fire unto the LORD: on the eighth day shall be a holy convocation unto you, and ye shall offer an offering made by fire unto the LORD: it is a solemn assembly, and ye shall do no servile work therein. [37]These are the feasts of the LORD, which ye shall proclaim to be holy convocations, to offer an offering made by fire unto the LORD, a burnt offering, and a meat offering, a sacrifice, and drink offerings, everything upon his day: [38]besides the sabbaths of the LORD, and besides your gifts, and besides all your vows, and besides all your free-will offerings, which ye give unto the LORD.

[39]'"Also in the fifteenth day of the seventh month, when ye have gathered in the fruit of the land, ye shall keep a feast unto the LORD seven days: on the first day shall be a sabbath, and on the eighth day shall be a sabbath. [40]And ye shall take you on the first day the boughs of goodly trees, branches of palm trees, and the boughs of thick trees, and willows of the brook, and ye shall rejoice before the LORD your God seven days. [41]And ye shall keep it a feast unto the LORD seven days in the year: it shall be a statute for ever in your generations: ye shall celebrate it in the seventh month. [42]Ye shall dwell in booths seven days; all that are Israelites born shall dwell in booths: [43]that your generations may know that I made the children of Israel to dwell in booths, when I brought them out of the land of Egypt: I am the LORD your God."' [44]And Moses declared unto the children of Israel the feasts of the LORD.

24 And the LORD spoke unto Moses, saying, [2]'Command the children of Israel, that they bring unto thee pure oil olive beaten, for the light, to cause the lamps to burn continually. [3]Without the veil of the testimony, in the tabernacle of the congregation, shall Aaron order it from the evening unto the morning before the LORD continually: it shall be a statute for ever in your generations. [4]He shall order the lamps upon the pure candlestick before the LORD continually.

[5]'And thou shalt take fine flour, and bake twelve cakes thereof: two tenth deals shall be in one cake. [6]And thou shalt set them in two rows, six on a row, upon the pure table, before the LORD. [7]And thou shalt put pure frankincense upon each row, that it may be on the bread for a memorial, even an offering made by fire unto the LORD. [8]Every sabbath he shall set it in order before the LORD continually, being taken from the children of Israel by an everlasting covenant. [9]And it shall be Aaron's and his sons'; and they shall eat it in the holy place: for it is most holy unto him of the offerings of the LORD made by fire by a perpetual statute.'

[10]And the son of an Israelitish woman, whose father was an Egyptian, went out among the children of Israel: and this son of the Israelitish woman and a man of Israel strove together in the camp. [11]And the

Israelitish woman's son blasphemed the name of the Lord, and cursed. And they brought him unto Moses (and his mother's name was Shelomith, the daughter of Dibri, of the tribe of Dan). ¹²And they put him in ward, that the mind of the Lord might be shown them. ¹³And the Lord spoke unto Moses, saying, ¹⁴'Bring forth him that hath cursed without the camp; and let all that heard him lay their hands upon his head, and let all the congregation stone him. ¹⁵And thou shalt speak unto the children of Israel, saying, "Whosoever curseth his God shall bear his sin. ¹⁶And he that blasphemeth the name of the Lord, he shall surely be put to death, and all the congregation shall certainly stone him: as well the stranger, as he that is born in the land, when he blasphemeth the name of the Lord, shall be put to death.

¹⁷'"And he that killeth any man shall surely be put to death. ¹⁸And he that killeth a beast shall make it good; beast for beast. ¹⁹And if a man cause a blemish in his neighbour; as he hath done, so shall it be done to him: ²⁰breach for breach, eye for eye, tooth for tooth: as he hath caused a blemish in a man, so shall it be done to him again. ²¹And he that killeth a beast, he shall restore it: and he that killeth a man, he shall be put to death. ²²Ye shall have one manner of law, as well for the stranger, as for one of your own country: for I am the Lord your God."'

²³And Moses spoke to the children of Israel, that they should bring forth him that had cursed out of the camp, and stone him with stones. And the children of Israel did as the Lord commanded Moses.

25 And the Lord spoke unto Moses in mount Sinai, saying, ²'Speak unto the children of Israel, and say unto them, "When ye come into the land which I give you, then shall the land keep a sabbath unto the Lord. ³Six years thou shalt sow thy field, and six years thou shalt prune thy vineyard, and gather in the fruit thereof; ⁴but in the seventh year shall be a sabbath of rest unto the land, a sabbath for the Lord: thou shalt neither sow thy field, nor prune thy vineyard. ⁵That which groweth of its own accord of thy harvest thou shalt not reap, neither gather the grapes of thy vine undressed: for it is a year of rest unto the land. ⁶And the sabbath of the land shall be meat for you; for thee, and for thy servant, and for thy maid, and for thy hired servant, and for the stranger that sojourneth with thee, ⁷and for thy cattle, and for the beast that are in thy land, shall all the increase thereof be meat.

⁸'"And thou shalt number seven sabbaths of years unto thee, seven times seven years; and the space of the seven sabbaths of years shall be unto thee forty and nine years. ⁹Then shalt thou cause the trumpet of the jubilee to sound on the tenth day of the seventh month; in the day of atonement shall ye make the trumpet sound throughout all your land. ¹⁰And ye shall hallow the fiftieth year, and proclaim liberty throughout all the land unto all the inhabitants thereof: it shall be a jubilee unto you, and ye shall return every man unto his possession, and ye shall return every man unto his family. ¹¹A jubilee shall that fiftieth year be unto you: ye shall not sow, neither reap that which groweth of itself in it, nor gather the grapes in it of thy vine undressed. ¹²For it is the jubilee; it shall be holy unto you: ye shall eat the increase thereof

out of the field. ¹³In the year of this jubilee ye shall return every man unto his possession. ¹⁴And if thou sell aught unto thy neighbour, or buyest aught of thy neighbour's hand, ye shall not oppress one another. ¹⁵According to the number of years after the jubilee thou shalt buy of thy neighbour, and according unto the number of years of the fruits he shall sell unto thee. ¹⁶According to the multitude of years thou shalt increase the price thereof, and according to the fewness of years thou shalt diminish the price of it: for according to the number of the years of the fruits doth he sell unto thee. ¹⁷Ye shall not therefore oppress one another; but thou shalt fear thy God: for I am the LORD your God.

¹⁸'"Wherefore ye shall do my statutes, and keep my judgements, and do them; and ye shall dwell in the land in safety. ¹⁹And the land shall yield her fruit, and ye shall eat your fill, and dwell therein in safety. ²⁰And if ye shall say, 'What shall we eat the seventh year? behold, we shall not sow, nor gather in our increase': ²¹then I will command my blessing upon you in the sixth year, and it shall bring forth fruit for three years. ²²And ye shall sow the eighth year, and eat yet of old fruit until the ninth year; until her fruits come in ye shall eat of the old store.

²³'"The land shall not be sold for ever: for the land is mine, for ye are strangers and sojourners with me. ²⁴And in all the land of your possession ye shall grant a redemption for the land.

²⁵'"If thy brother be waxed poor, and hath sold away some of his possession, and if any of his kin come to redeem it, then shall he redeem that which his brother sold. ²⁶And if the man have none to redeem it, and himself be able to redeem it: ²⁷then let him count the years of the sale thereof, and restore the overplus unto the man to whom he sold it, that he may return unto his possession. ²⁸But if he be not able to restore it to him, then that which is sold shall remain in the hand of him that hath bought it until the year of jubilee: and in the jubilee it shall go out, and he shall return unto his possession.

²⁹'"And if a man sell a dwelling-house in a walled city, then he may redeem it within a whole year after it is sold; within a full year may he redeem it. ³⁰And if it be not redeemed within the space of a full year, then the house that is in the walled city shall be established for ever to him that bought it throughout his generations: it shall not go out in the jubilee. ³¹But the houses of the villages which have no walls round about them shall be counted as the fields of the country: they may be redeemed, and they shall go out in the jubilee. ³²Notwithstanding the cities of the Levites, and the houses of the cities of their possession, may the Levites redeem at any time. ³³And if a man purchase of the Levites, then the house that was sold, and the city of his possession, shall go out in the year of jubilee: for the houses of the cities of the Levites are their possession among the children of Israel. ³⁴But the field of the suburbs of their cities may not be sold, for it is their perpetual possession.

³⁵'"And if thy brother be waxed poor, and fallen in decay with thee,

then thou shalt relieve him, yea, though he be a stranger, or a sojourner, that he may live with thee. ³⁶Take thou no usury of him, or increase: but fear thy God, that thy brother may live with thee. ³⁷Thou shalt not give him thy money upon usury, nor lend him thy victuals for increase.³⁸I am the Lord your God, which brought you forth out of the land of Egypt, to give you the land of Canaan, and to be your God.

³⁹'"And if thy brother that dwelleth by thee be waxed poor, and be sold unto thee, thou shalt not compel him to serve as a bondservant: ⁴⁰but as a hired servant, and as a sojourner, he shall be with thee, and shall serve thee unto the year of jubilee: ⁴¹and then shall he depart from thee, both he and his children with him, and shall return unto his own family, and unto the possession of his fathers shall he return. ⁴²For they are my servants, which I brought forth out of the land of Egypt: they shall not be sold as bondmen. ⁴³Thou shalt not rule over him with rigour, but shalt fear thy God. ⁴⁴Both thy bondmen, and thy bondmaids, which thou shalt have, shall be of the heathen that are round about you: of them shall ye buy bondmen and bondmaids. ⁴⁵Moreover of the children of the strangers that do sojourn among you, of them shall ye buy, and of their families that are with you, which they begot in your land: and they shall be your possession. ⁴⁶And ye shall take them as an inheritance for your children after you, to inherit them for a possession; they shall be your bondmen for ever: but over your brethren the children of Israel, ye shall not rule one over another with rigour.

⁴⁷'"And if a sojourner or stranger wax rich by thee, and thy brother that dwelleth by him wax poor, and sell himself unto the stranger or sojourner by thee, or to the stock of the stranger's family: ⁴⁸after that he is sold he may be redeemed again: one of his brethren may redeem him. ⁴⁹Either his uncle, or his uncle's son, may redeem him, or any that is nigh of kin unto him of his family may redeem him; or if he be able, he may redeem himself. ⁵⁰And he shall reckon with him that bought him from the year that he was sold to him unto the year of jubilee, and the price of his sale shall be according unto the number of years, according to the time of a hired servant shall it be with him. ⁵¹If there be yet many years behind, according unto them he shall give again the price of his redemption out of the money that he was bought for. ⁵²And if there remain but few years unto the year of jubilee, then he shall count with him, and according unto his years shall he give him again the price of his redemption. ⁵³And as a yearly hired servant shall he be with him: and the other shall not rule with rigour over him in thy sight. ⁵⁴And if he be not redeemed in these years, then he shall go out in the year of jubilee, both he, and his children with him.⁵⁵For unto me the children of Israel are servants; they are my servants whom I brought forth out of the land of Egypt: I am the Lord your God.

26 '"Ye shall make you no idols nor graven image, neither rear you up a standing image, neither shall ye set up any image of stone in your land, to bow down unto it: for I am the Lord your God.

²"Ye shall keep my sabbaths, and reverence my sanctuary: I am the LORD.

³"If ye walk in my statutes, and keep my commandments, and do them; ⁴then I will give you rain in due season, and the land shall yield her increase, and the trees of the field shall yield their fruit. ⁵And your threshing shall reach unto the vintage, and the vintage shall reach unto the sowing time: and ye shall eat your bread to the full, and dwell in your land safely. ⁶And I will give peace in the land, and ye shall lie down, and none shall make you afraid: and I will rid evil beasts out of the land, neither shall the sword go through your land. ⁷And ye shall chase your enemies, and they shall fall before you by the sword. ⁸And five of you shall chase a hundred, and a hundred of you shall put ten thousand to flight: and your enemies shall fall before you by the sword. ⁹For I will have respect unto you, and make you fruitful, and multiply you, and establish my covenant with you. ¹⁰And ye shall eat old store, and bring forth the old because of the new. ¹¹And I will set my tabernacle amongst you: and my soul shall not abhor you. ¹²And I will walk among you, and will be your God, and ye shall be my people. ¹³I am the LORD your God, which brought you forth out of the land of Egypt, that ye should not be their bondmen; and I have broken the bands of your yoke, and made you go upright.

¹⁴"But if ye will not hearken unto me, and will not do all these commandments; ¹⁵and if ye shall despise my statutes, or if your soul abhor my judgements, so that ye will not do all my commandments, but that ye break my covenant: ¹⁶I also will do this unto you, I will even appoint over you terror, consumption, and the burning ague, that shall consume the eyes, and cause sorrow of heart: and ye shall sow your seed in vain, for your enemies shall eat it. ¹⁷And I will set my face against you, and ye shall be slain before your enemies: they that hate you shall reign over you; and ye shall flee when none pursueth you. ¹⁸And if ye will not yet for all this hearken unto me, then I will punish you seven times more for your sins. ¹⁹And I will break the pride of your power, and I will make your heaven as iron, and your earth as brass: ²⁰and your strength shall be spent in vain: for your land shall not yield her increase, neither shall the trees of the land yield their fruits.

²¹"And if ye walk contrary unto me, and will not hearken unto me, I will bring seven times more plagues upon you according to your sins. ²²I will also send wild beasts among you, which shall rob you of your children, and destroy your cattle, and make you few in number; and your highways shall be desolate. ²³And if ye will not be reformed by these things, but will walk contrary unto me: ²⁴then will I also walk contrary unto you, and will punish you yet seven times for your sins. ²⁵And I will bring a sword upon you, that shall avenge the quarrel of my covenant: and when ye are gathered together within your cities, I will send the pestilence among you; and ye shall be delivered into the hand of the enemy. ²⁶And when I have broken the staff of your bread, ten women shall bake your bread in one oven, and they shall deliver you your bread again by weight: and ye shall eat, and not be satisfied.

²⁷'"And if ye will not for all this hearken unto me, but walk contrary unto me, ²⁸then I will walk contrary unto you also in fury; and I, even I, will chastise you seven times for your sins. ²⁹And ye shall eat the flesh of your sons, and the flesh of your daughters shall ye eat. ³⁰And I will destroy your high places, and cut down your images, and cast your carcases upon the carcases of your idols, and my soul shall abhor you. ³¹And I will make your cities waste, and bring your sanctuaries unto desolation, and I will not smell the savour of your sweet odours. ³²And I will bring the land into desolation: and your enemies which dwell therein shall be astonished at it. ³³And I will scatter you among the heathen, and will draw out a sword after you: and your land shall be desolate, and your cities waste. ³⁴Then shall the land enjoy her sabbaths, as long as it lieth desolate, and ye be in your enemies' land; even then shall the land rest, and enjoy her sabbaths. ³⁵As long as it lieth desolate it shall rest: because it did not rest in your sabbaths, when ye dwelt upon it. ³⁶And upon them that are left alive of you I will send a faintness into their hearts in the lands of their enemies, and the sound of a shaken leaf shall chase them, and they shall flee, as fleeing from a sword: and they shall fall when none pursueth. ³⁷And they shall fall one upon another, as it were before a sword, when none pursueth: and ye shall have no power to stand before your enemies. ³⁸And ye shall perish among the heathen, and the land of your enemies shall eat you up. ³⁹And they that are left of you shall pine away in their iniquity in your enemies' lands; and also in the iniquities of their fathers shall they pine away with them. ⁴⁰If they shall confess their iniquity, and the iniquity of their fathers, with their trespass which they trespassed against me, and that also they have walked contrary unto me; ⁴¹and that I also have walked contrary unto them, and have brought them into the land of their enemies; if then their uncircumcised hearts be humbled, and they then accept of the punishment of their iniquity: ⁴²then will I remember my covenant with Jacob, and also my covenant with Isaac, and also my covenant with Abraham will I remember; and I will remember the land. ⁴³The land also shall be left of them, and shall enjoy her sabbaths, while she lieth desolate without them: and they shall accept of the punishment of their iniquity: because, even because they despised my judgements, and because their soul abhorred my statutes. ⁴⁴And yet for all that, when they be in the land of their enemies, I will not cast them away, neither will I abhor them, to destroy them utterly, and to break my covenant with them: for I am the LORD their God. ⁴⁵But I will for their sakes remember the covenant of their ancestors, whom I brought forth out of the land of Egypt in the sight of the heathen, that I might be their God: I am the LORD."' ⁴⁶These are the statutes and judgements and laws, which the LORD made between him and the children of Israel in mount Sinai by the hand of Moses.

27 And the LORD spoke unto Moses, saying, ²'Speak unto the children of Israel, and say unto them, "When a man shall make a singular vow, the persons shall be for the LORD by thy estimation. ³And thy estimation shall be of the male from twenty years old even unto sixty years old, even thy estimation shall be fifty shekels of silver, after the shekel of the sanctuary. ⁴And if it be a female, then thy estimation shall be thirty shekels. ⁵And if it be from five years old even unto twenty years old, then thy estimation shall be of the male twenty shekels, and for the female ten shekels. ⁶And if it be from a month old even unto five years old, then thy estimation shall be of the male five shekels of silver, and for the female thy estimation shall be three shekels of silver. ⁷And if it be from sixty years old and above, if it be a male, then thy estimation shall be fifteen shekels, and for the female ten shekels. ⁸But if he be poorer than thy estimation, then he shall present himself before the priest, and the priest shall value him: according to his ability that vowed shall the priest value him.

⁹'"And if it be a beast, whereof men bring an offering unto the LORD, all that any man giveth of such unto the LORD shall be holy. ¹⁰He shall not alter it, nor change it, a good for a bad, or a bad for a good: and if he shall at all change beast for beast, then it and the exchange thereof shall be holy. ¹¹And if it be any unclean beast, of which they do not offer a sacrifice unto the LORD, then he shall present the beast before the priest: ¹²and the priest shall value it, whether it be good or bad: as thou valuest it, who art the priest, so shall it be. ¹³But if he will at all redeem it, then he shall add a fifth part thereof unto thy estimation.

¹⁴'"And when a man shall sanctify his house to be holy unto the LORD, then the priest shall estimate it, whether it be good or bad: as the priest shall estimate it, so shall it stand. ¹⁵And if he that sanctified it will redeem his house, then he shall add the fifth part of the money of thy estimation unto it, and it shall be his.

¹⁶'"And if a man shall sanctify unto the LORD some part of a field of his possession, then thy estimation shall be according to the seed thereof: a homer of barley seed shall be valued at fifty shekels of silver. ¹⁷If he sanctify his field from the year of jubilee, according to thy estimation it shall stand. ¹⁸But if he sanctify his field after the jubilee, then the priest shall reckon unto him the money according to the years that remain, even unto the year of the jubile, and it shall be abated from thy estimation. ¹⁹And if he that sanctified the field will in any wise redeem it, then he shall add the fifth part of the money of thy estimation unto it, and it shall be assured to him. ²⁰And if he will not redeem the field, or if he have sold the field to another man, it shall not be redeemed any more. ²¹But the field, when it goeth out in the jubilee, shall be holy unto the LORD, as a field devoted: the possession thereof shall be the priest's. ²²And if a man sanctify unto the LORD a field which he hath bought, which is not of the fields of his possession: ²³then the priest shall reckon unto him the worth of thy estimation, even unto the year of the jubilee: and he shall give thy estimation in that day, as a holy thing unto the LORD. ²⁴In the year of the jubilee the field shall return unto him of whom it was bought, even to him to whom the possession of the land did belong. ²⁵And all thy estimations

shall be according to the shekel of the sanctuary: twenty gerahs shall be the shekel.

²⁶'"Only the firstling of the beasts, which should be the LORD's firstling, no man shall sanctify it, whether it be ox, or sheep: it is the LORD's. ²⁷And if it be of an unclean beast, then he shall redeem it according to thy estimation, and shall add a fifth part of it thereto: or if it be not redeemed, then it shall be sold according to thy estimation. ²⁸Notwithstanding no devoted thing, that a man shall devote unto the LORD of all that he hath, both of man and beast, and of the field of his possession, shall be sold or redeemed: every devoted thing is most holy unto the LORD. ²⁹None devoted, which shall be devoted of men, shall be redeemed; but shall surely be put to death.

³⁰'"And all the tithe of the land, whether of the seed of the land, or of the fruit of the tree, is the LORD's: it is holy unto the LORD. ³¹And if a man will at all redeem aught of his tithes, he shall add thereto the fifth part thereof. ³²And concerning the tithe of the herd, or of the flock, even of whatsoever passeth under the rod, the tenth shall be holy unto the LORD. ³³He shall not search whether it be good or bad, neither shall he change it: and if he change it at all, then both it and the change thereof shall be holy; it shall not be redeemed."'

³⁴These are the commandments, which the LORD commanded Moses for the children of Israel in mount Sinai.

THE FOURTH BOOK OF MOSES,
CALLED
NUMBERS

1 And the Lord spoke unto Moses in the wilderness of Sinai, in the tabernacle of the congregation, on the first day of the second month, in the second year after they were come out of the land of Egypt, saying, ²'Take ye the sum of all the congregation of the children of Israel, after their families, by the house of their fathers, with the number of their names, every male by their poll: ³from twenty years old and upward, all that are able to go forth to war in Israel: thou and Aaron shall number them by their armies. ⁴And with you there shall be a man of every tribe: every one head of the house of his fathers.

⁵'And these are the names of the men that shall stand with you: of the tribe of Reuben: Elizur the son of Shedeur. ⁶Of Simeon: Shelumiel the son of Zurishaddai. ⁷Of Judah: Nahshon the son of Amminadab. ⁸Of Issachar: Nethaneel the son of Zuar. ⁹Of Zebulun: Eliab the son of Helon. ¹⁰Of the children of Joseph: of Ephraim: Elishama the son of Ammihud: of Manasseh: Gamaliel the son of Pedahzur. ¹¹Of Benjamin: Abidan the son of Gideoni. ¹²Of Dan: Ahiezer the son of Ammishaddai. ¹³Of Asher: Pagiel the son of Ocran. ¹⁴Of Gad: Eliasaph the son of Deuel. ¹⁵Of Naphtali: Ahira the son of Enan.' ¹⁶These were the renowned of the congregation, princes of the tribes of their fathers, heads of thousands in Israel.

¹⁷And Moses and Aaron took these men which are expressed by their names. ¹⁸And they assembled all the congregation together on the first day of the second month, and they declared their pedigrees after their families, by the house of their fathers, according to the number of the names, from twenty years old and upward, by their poll. ¹⁹As the LORD commanded Moses, so he numbered them in the wilderness of Sinai.

²⁰And the children of Reuben, Israel's eldest son, by their generations, after their families, by the house of their fathers, according to the number of the names, by their poll, every male from twenty years old and upward, all that were able to go forth to war: ²¹those that were numbered of them, even of the tribe of Reuben, were forty and six thousand and five hundred.

²²Of the children of Simeon, by their generations, after their families, by the house of their fathers, those that were numbered of them, according to the number of the names, by their polls, every male from twenty years old and upward, all that were able to go forth to war: ²³those that were numbered of them, even of the tribe of Simeon, were fifty and nine thousand and three hundred.

²⁴Of the children of Gad, by their generations, after their families, by the house of their fathers, according to the number of the names, from twenty years old and upward, all that were able to go forth to war:

²⁵those that were numbered of them, even of the tribe of Gad, were forty and five thousand six hundred and fifty.

²⁶Of the children of Judah, by their generations, after their families, by the house of their fathers, according to the number of the names, from twenty years old and upward, all that were able to go forth to war: ²⁷those that were numbered of them, even of the tribe of Judah, were threescore and fourteen thousand and six hundred.

²⁸Of the children of Issachar, by their generations, after their families, by the house of their fathers, according to the number of the names, from twenty years old and upward, all that were able to go forth to war: ²⁹those that were numbered of them, even of the tribe of Issachar, were fifty and four thousand and four hundred.

³⁰Of the children of Zebulun, by their generations, after their families, by the house of their fathers, according to the number of the names, from twenty years old and upward, all that were able to go forth to war: ³¹those that were numbered of them, even of the tribe of Zebulun, were fifty and seven thousand and four hundred.

³²Of the children of Joseph: namely, of the children of Ephraim, by their generations, after their families, by the house of their fathers, according to the number of the names, from twenty years old and upward, all that were able to go forth to war: ³³those that were numbered of them, even of the tribe of Ephraim, were forty thousand and five hundred.

³⁴Of the children of Manasseh, by their generations, after their families, by the house of their fathers, according to the number of the names, from twenty years old and upward, all that were able to go forth to war: ³⁵those that were numbered of them, even of the tribe of Manasseh, were thirty and two thousand and two hundred.

³⁶Of the children of Benjamin, by their generations, after their families, by the house of their fathers, according to the number of the names, from twenty years old and upward, all that were able to go forth to war: ³⁷those that were numbered of them, even of the tribe of Benjamin, were thirty and five thousand and four hundred.

³⁸Of the children of Dan, by their generations, after their families, by the house of their fathers, according to the number of the names, from twenty years old and upward, all that were able to go forth to war: ³⁹those that were numbered of them, even of the tribe of Dan, were threescore and two thousand and seven hundred.

⁴⁰Of the children of Asher, by their generations, after their families, by the house of their fathers, according to the number of the names, from twenty years old and upward, all that were able to go forth to war: ⁴¹those that were numbered of them, even of the tribe of Asher, were forty and one thousand and five hundred.

⁴²Of the children of Naphtali, throughout their generations, after their families, by the house of their fathers, according to the number of the names, from twenty years old and upward, all that were able to go forth to war: ⁴³those that were numbered of them, even of the tribe of Naphtali, were fifty and three thousand and four hundred.

⁴⁴These are those that were numbered, which Moses and Aaron numbered, and the princes of Israel, being twelve men: each one was for the house of his fathers. ⁴⁵So were all those that were numbered of the children of Israel, by the house of their fathers, from twenty years old and upward, all that were able to go forth to war in Israel: ⁴⁶even all they that were numbered were six hundred thousand and three thousand and five hundred and fifty.

⁴⁷But the Levites after the tribe of their fathers were not numbered among them. ⁴⁸For the Lᴏʀᴅ had spoken unto Moses, saying, ⁴⁹'Only thou shalt not number the tribe of Levi, neither take the sum of them among the children of Israel. ⁵⁰But thou shalt appoint the Levites over the tabernacle of testimony, and over all the vessels thereof, and over all things that belong to it: they shall bear the tabernacle, and all the vessels thereof; and they shall minister unto it, and shall encamp round about the tabernacle. ⁵¹And when the tabernacle setteth forward, the Levites shall take it down: and when the tabernacle is to be pitched, the Levites shall set it up: and the stranger that cometh nigh shall be put to death. ⁵²And the children of Israel shall pitch their tents, every man by his own camp, and every man by his own standard, throughout their hosts. ⁵³But the Levites shall pitch round about the tabernacle of testimony, that there be no wrath upon the congregation of the children of Israel: and the Levites shall keep the charge of the tabernacle of testimony.' ⁵⁴And the children of Israel did according to all that the Lᴏʀᴅ commanded Moses, so did they.

2 And the Lᴏʀᴅ spoke unto Moses and unto Aaron, saying, ²'Every man of the children of Israel shall pitch by his own standard, with the ensign of their father's house: far off about the tabernacle of the congregation shall they pitch. ³And on the east side toward the rising of the sun shall they of the standard of the camp of Judah pitch throughout their armies: and Nahshon the son of Amminadab shall be captain of the children of Judah.' ⁴And his host, and those that were numbered of them, were threescore and fourteen thousand and six hundred. ⁵'And those that do pitch next unto him shall be the tribe of Issachar: and Nethaneel the son of Zuar shall be captain of the children of Issachar.' ⁶And his host, and those that were numbered thereof, were fifty and four thousand and four hundred. ⁷'Then the tribe of Zebulun: and Eliab the son of Helon shall be captain of the children of Zebulun.' ⁸And his host, and those that were numbered thereof, were fifty and seven thousand and four hundred. ⁹All that were numbered in the camp of Judah were a hundred thousand and fourscore thousand and six thousand and four hundred, throughout their armies. 'These shall first set forth.

¹⁰'On the south side shall be the standard of the camp of Reuben according to their armies: and the captain of the children of Reuben shall be Elizur the son of Shedeur.' ¹¹And his host, and those that were numbered thereof, were forty and six thousand and five hundred. ¹²'And those which pitch by him shall be the tribe of Simeon: and the captain of the children of Simeon shall be Shelumiel the son of

Zurishaddai.' ¹³And his host, and those that were numbered of them, were fifty and nine thousand and three hundred. ¹⁴'Then the tribe of Gad: and the captain of the sons of Gad shall be Eliasaph the son of Reuel.' ¹⁵And his host, and those that were numbered of them, were forty and five thousand and six hundred and fifty. ¹⁶All that were numbered in the camp of Reuben were a hundred thousand and fifty and one thousand and four hundred and fifty, throughout their armies. 'And they shall set forth in the second rank.

¹⁷'Then the tabernacle of the congregation shall set forward with the camp of the Levites in the midst of the camp: as they encamp, so shall they set forward, every man in his place by their standards.

¹⁸'On the west side shall be the standard of the camp of Ephraim according to their armies: and the captain of the sons of Ephraim shall be Elishama the son of Ammihud.' ¹⁹And his host, and those that were numbered of them, were forty thousand and five hundred. ²⁰'And by him shall be the tribe of Manasseh: and the captain of the children of Manasseh shall be Gamaliel the son of Pedahzur.' ²¹And his host, and those that were numbered of them, were thirty and two thousand and two hundred. ²²'Then the tribe of Benjamin: and the captain of the sons of Benjamin shall be Abidan the son of Gideoni.' ²³And his host, and those that were numbered of them, were thirty and five thousand and four hundred. ²⁴All that were numbered of the camp of Ephraim were a hundred thousand and eight thousand and a hundred, throughout their armies. 'And they shall go forward in the third rank.

²⁵'The standard of the camp of Dan shall be on the north side by their armies: and the captain of the children of Dan shall be Ahiezer the son of Ammishaddai.' ²⁶And his host, and those that were numbered of them, were threescore and two thousand and seven hundred. ²⁷'And those that encamp by him shall be the tribe of Asher: and the captain of the children of Asher shall be Pagiel the son of Ocran.' ²⁸And his host, and those that were numbered of them, were forty and one thousand and five hundred.

²⁹'Then the tribe of Naphtali: and the captain of the children of Naphtali shall be Ahira the son of Enan.' ³⁰And his host, and those that were numbered of them, were fifty and three thousand and four hundred. ³¹All they that were numbered in the camp of Dan were a hundred thousand and fifty and seven thousand and six hundred. 'They shall go hindmost with their standards.'

³²These are those which were numbered of the children of Israel by the house of their fathers: all those that were numbered of the camps throughout their hosts were six hundred thousand and three thousand and five hundred and fifty. ³³But the Levites were not numbered among the children of Israel, as the LORD commanded Moses. ³⁴And the children of Israel did according to all that the LORD commanded Moses: so they pitched by their standards, and so they set forward, every one after their families, according to the house of their fathers.

3 These also are the generations of Aaron and Moses in the day that the LORD spoke with Moses in mount Sinai. ²And these are the names of the sons of Aaron: Nadab the firstborn, and Abihu, Eleazar, and Ithamar. ³These are the names of the sons of Aaron, the priests which were anointed, whom he consecrated to minister in the priest's office. ⁴And Nadab and Abihu died before the LORD, when they offered strange fire before the LORD in the wilderness of Sinai, and they had no children: and Eleazar and Ithamar ministered in the priest's office in the sight of Aaron their father.

⁵And the LORD spoke unto Moses, saying, ⁶'Bring the tribe of Levi near, and present them before Aaron the priest, that they may minister unto him. ⁷And they shall keep his charge, and the charge of the whole congregation before the tabernacle of the congregation, to do the service of the tabernacle. ⁸And they shall keep all the instruments of the tabernacle of the congregation, and the charge of the children of Israel, to do the service of the tabernacle. ⁹And thou shalt give the Levites unto Aaron and to his sons: they are wholly given unto him out of the children of Israel. ¹⁰And thou shalt appoint Aaron and his sons, and they shall wait on their priest's office: and the stranger that cometh nigh shall be put to death.'

¹¹And the LORD spoke unto Moses, saying, ¹²'And I, behold, I have taken the Levites from among the children of Israel in stead of all the firstborn that openeth the matrix among the children of Israel: therefore the Levites shall be mine, ¹³because all the firstborn are mine; for on the day that I smote all the firstborn in the land of Egypt I hallowed unto me all the firstborn in Israel, both man and beast: mine they shall be: I am the LORD'.

¹⁴And the LORD spoke unto Moses in the wilderness of Sinai, saying, ¹⁵'Number the children of Levi after the house of their fathers, by their families: every male from a month old and upward shalt thou number them'. ¹⁶And Moses numbered them according to the word of the LORD, as he was commanded. ¹⁷And these were the sons of Levi by their names: Gershon, and Kohath, and Merari. ¹⁸And these are the names of the sons of Gershon by their families: Libni, and Shimei. ¹⁹And the sons of Kohath by their families: Amram, and Izehar, Hebron, and Uzziel. ²⁰And the sons of Merari by their families: Mahli, and Mushi. These are the families of the Levites according to the house of their fathers.

²¹Of Gershon was the family of the Libnites, and the family of the Shimites: these are the families of the Gershonites. ²²Those that were numbered of them, according to the number of all the males, from a month old and upward, even those that were numbered of them were seven thousand and five hundred. ²³'The families of the Gershonites shall pitch behind the tabernacle westward. ²⁴And the chief of the house of the father of the Gershonites shall be Eliasaph the son of Lael. ²⁵And the charge of the sons of Gershon in the tabernacle of the congregation shall be the tabernacle, and the tent, the covering thereof, and the hanging for the door of the tabernacle of the congregation, ²⁶and the hangings of the court, and the curtain for the door of the court, which is by the tabernacle, and by the altar round about, and the cords of it for all the service thereof.'

²⁷And of Kohath was the family of the Amramites, and the family of the Izeharites, and the family of the Hebronites, and the family of the Uzzielites: these are the families of the Kohathites. ²⁸In the number of all the males, from a month old and upward, were eight thousand and six hundred, keeping the charge of the sanctuary. ²⁹'The families of the sons of Kohath shall pitch on the side of the tabernacle southward. ³⁰And the chief of the house of the father of the families of the Kohathites shall be Elizaphan the son of Uzziel. ³¹And their charge shall be the ark, and the table, and the candlestick, and the altars, and the vessels of the sanctuary wherewith they minister, and the hanging, and all the service ³²And Eleazar the son of Aaron the priest shall be chief over the chief of the Levites, and have the oversight of them that keep the charge of the sanctuary.'

³³Of Merari was the family of the Mahlites, and the family of the Mushites: these are the families of Merari. ³⁴And those that were numbered of them, according to the number of all the males, from a month old and upward, were six thousand and two hundred. ³⁵And the chief of the house of the father of the families of Merari was Zuriel the son of Abihail. 'These shall pitch on the side of the tabernacle northwards. ³⁶And under the custody and charge of the sons of Merari shall be the boards of the tabernacle, and the bars thereof, and the pillars thereof, and the sockets thereof, and all the vessels thereof, and all that serveth thereto, ³⁷and the pillars of the court round about, and their sockets, and their pins, and their cords.

³⁸'But those that encamp before the tabernacle toward the east, even before the tabernacle of the congregation eastward, shall be Moses, and Aaron and his sons, keeping the charge of the sanctuary for the charge of the children of Israel; and the stranger that cometh nigh shall be put to death.'

³⁹All that were numbered of the Levites, which Moses and Aaron numbered at the commandment of the LORD, throughout their families, all the males from a month old and upward, were twenty and two thousand.

⁴⁰And the LORD said unto Moses, 'Number all the firstborn of the males of the children of Israel from a month old and upward, and take the number of their names. ⁴¹And thou shalt take the Levites for me (I am the LORD) in stead of all the firstborn among the children of Israel; and the cattle of the Levites in stead of all the firstlings among the cattle of the children of Israel.' ⁴²And Moses numbered, as the LORD commanded him, all the firstborn among the children of Israel. ⁴³And all the firstborn males by the number of names, from a month old and upward, of those that were numbered of them, were twenty and two thousand two hundred and threescore and thirteen.

⁴⁴And the LORD spoke unto Moses, saying, ⁴⁵'Take the Levites in stead of all the firstborn among the children of Israel, and the cattle of the Levites in stead of their cattle; and the Levites shall be mine: I am the LORD. ⁴⁶And for those that are to be redeemed of the two hundred and threescore and thirteen of the firstborn of the children of Israel, which

are more than the Levites; [47]thou shalt even take five shekels apiece by the poll, after the shekel of the sanctuary shalt thou take them (the shekel is twenty gerahs). [48]And thou shalt give the money, wherewith the odd number of them is to be redeemed, unto Aaron and to his sons.' [49]And Moses took the redemption money of them that were over and above them that were redeemed by the Levites: [50]of the firstborn of the children of Israel took he the money; a thousand three hundred and threescore and five shekels, after the shekel of the sanctuary: [51]and Moses gave the money of them that were redeemed unto Aaron and to his sons, according to the word of the LORD, as the LORD commanded Moses.

4 And the LORD spoke unto Moses and unto Aaron, saying, [2]'Take the sum of the sons of Kohath from among the sons of Levi, after their families, by the house of their fathers, [3]from thirty years old and upward even until fifty years old, all that enter into the host, to do the work in the tabernacle of the congregation. [4]This shall be the service of the sons of Kohath in the tabernacle of the congregation, about the most holy things.

[5]'And when the camp setteth forward, Aaron shall come, and his sons, and they shall take down the covering veil, and cover the ark of testimony with it: [6]and shall put thereon the covering of badgers' skins, and shall spread over it a cloth wholly of blue, and shall put in the staves thereof. [7]And upon the table of showbread they shall spread a cloth of blue, and put thereon the dishes, and the spoons, and the bowls, and covers to cover withal: and the continual bread shall be thereon. [8]And they shall spread upon them a cloth of scarlet, and cover the same with a covering of badgers' skins, and shall put in the staves thereof. [9]And they shall take a cloth of blue, and cover the candlestick of the light, and his lamps, and his tongs, and his snuff-dishes, and all the oil vessels thereof, wherewith they minister unto it. [10]And they shall put it and all the vessels thereof within a covering of badgers' skins, and shall put it upon a bar. [11]And upon the golden altar they shall spread a cloth of blue, and cover it with a covering of badgers' skins, and shall put to the staves thereof. [12]And they shall take all the instruments of ministry, wherewith they minister in the sanctuary, and put them in a cloth of blue, and cover them with a covering of badgers' skins, and shall put them on a bar. [13]And they shall take away the ashes from the altar, and spread a purple cloth thereon: [14]and they shall put upon it all the vessels thereof, wherewith they minister about it, even the censers, the fleshhooks, and the shovels, and the basins, all the vessels of the altar; and they shall spread upon it a covering of badgers' skins, and put to the staves of it. [15]And when Aaron and his sons have made an end of covering the sanctuary, and all the vessels of the sanctuary, as the camp is to set forward; after that, the sons of Kohath shall come to bear it: but they shall not touch any holy thing, lest they die. These things are the burden of the sons of Kohath in the tabernacle of the congregation.

[16]'And to the office of Eleazar the son of Aaron the priest pertaineth the oil for the light, and the sweet incense, and the daily meat offering,

and the anointing oil, and the oversight of all the tabernacle, and of all that therein is, in the sanctuary, and in the vessels thereof.'

[17]And the LORD spoke unto Moses and unto Aaron, saying, [18]'Cut ye not off the tribe of the families of the Kohathites from among the Levites: [19]but thus do unto them, that they may live, and not die, when they approach unto the most holy things. Aaron and his sons shall go in, and appoint them every one to his service and to his burden: [20]but they shall not go in to see when the holy things are covered, lest they die.'

[21]And the LORD spoke unto Moses, saying, [22]'Take also the sum of the sons of Gershon, throughout the houses of their fathers, by their families: [23]from thirty years old and upward until fifty years old shalt thou number them: all that enter in to perform the service, to do the work in the tabernacle of the congregation. [24]This is the service of the families of the Gershonites, to serve, and for burdens. [25]And they shall bear the curtains of the tabernacle, and the tabernacle of the congregation, his covering, and the covering of the badgers' skins that is above upon it, and the hanging for the door of the tabernacle of the congregation, [26]and the hangings of the court, and the hanging for the door of the gate of the court, which is by the tabernacle and by the altar round about, and their cords, and all the instruments of their service, and all that is made for them: so shall they serve. [27]At the appointment of Aaron and his sons shall be all the service of the sons of the Gershonites, in all their burdens, and in all their service: and ye shall appoint unto them in charge all their burdens. [28]This is the service of the families of the sons of Gershon in the tabernacle of the congregation: and their charge shall be under the hand of Ithamar the son of Aaron the priest.

[29]'As for the sons of Merari, thou shalt number them after their families, by the house of their fathers: [30]from thirty years old and upward even unto fifty years old shalt thou number them, every one that entereth into the service, to do the work of the tabernacle of the congregation. [31]And this is the charge of their burden, according to all their service in the tabernacle of the congregation: the boards of the tabernacle, and the bars thereof, and the pillars thereof, and sockets thereof, [32]and the pillars of the court round about, and their sockets, and their pins, and their cords, with all their instruments, and with all their service: and by name ye shall reckon the instruments of the charge of their burden. [33]This is the service of the families of the sons of Merari, according to all their service in the tabernacle of the congregation, under the hand of Ithamar the son of Aaron the priest.'

[34]And Moses and Aaron and the chief of the congregation numbered the sons of the Kohathites after their families, and after the house of their fathers, [35]from thirty years old and upward even unto fifty years old, every one that entereth into the service, for the work in the tabernacle of the congregation. [36]And those that were numbered of them by their families were two thousand seven hundred and fifty. [37]These were they that were numbered of the families of the Kohathites, all that

might do service in the tabernacle of the congregation, which Moses and Aaron did number according to the commandment of the LORD by the hand of Moses. ³⁸And those that were numbered of the sons of Gershon, throughout their families, and by the house of their fathers, ³⁹from thirty years old and upward even unto fifty years old, every one that entereth into the service, for the work in the tabernacle of the congregation, ⁴⁰even those that were numbered of them, throughout their families, by the houses of their fathers, were two thousand and six hundred and thirty. ⁴¹These are they that were numbered of the families of the sons of Gershon, of all that might do service in the tabernacle of the congregation, whom Moses and Aaron did number according to the commandment of the LORD.

⁴²And those that were numbered of the families of the sons of Merari, throughout their families, by the house of their fathers, ⁴³from thirty years old and upward even unto fifty years old, every one that entereth into the service, for the work in the tabernacle of the congregation, ⁴⁴even those that were numbered of them after their families, were three thousand and two hundred. ⁴⁵These be those that were numbered of the families of the sons of Merari, whom Moses and Aaron numbered according to the word of the LORD by the hand of Moses.

⁴⁶All those that were numbered of the Levites, whom Moses and Aaron and the chief of Israel numbered, after their families, and after the house of their fathers, ⁴⁷from thirty years old and upward even unto fifty years old, every one that came to do the service of the ministry, and the service of the burden in the tabernacle of the congregation, ⁴⁸even those that were numbered of them, were eight thousand and five hundred and fourscore. ⁴⁹According to the commandment of the LORD they were numbered by the hand of Moses, every one according to his service, and according to his burden: thus were they numbered of him, as the LORD commanded Moses.

5 And the LORD spoke unto Moses, saying, ²'Command the children of Israel, that they put out of the camp every leper, and every one that hath an issue, and whosoever is defiled by the dead: ³both male and female shall ye put out, without the camp shall ye put them, that they defile not their camps, in the midst whereof I dwell'. ⁴And the children of Israel did so, and put them out without the camp: as the LORD spoke unto Moses, so did the children of Israel.

⁵And the LORD spoke unto Moses, saying, ⁶'Speak unto the children of Israel, "When a man or woman shall commit any sin that men commit, to do a trespass against the LORD, and that person be guilty; ⁷then they shall confess their sin which they have done: and he shall recompense his trespass with the principal thereof, and add unto it the fifth part thereof, and give it unto him against whom he hath trespassed. ⁸But if the man have no kinsman to recompense the trespass unto, let the trespass be recompensed unto the LORD, even to the priest; besides the ram of the atonement, whereby an atonement shall be made for him. ⁹And every offering of all the holy things of the children of Israel, which they bring unto the priest, shall be his. ¹⁰And every

man's hallowed things shall be his: whatsoever any man giveth the priest, it shall be his."'

¹¹And the LORD spoke unto Moses, saying, ¹²'Speak unto the children of Israel, and say unto them, "If any man's wife go aside, and commit a trespass against him, ¹³and a man lie with her carnally, and it be hid from the eyes of her husband, and be kept close, and she be defiled, and there be no witness against her, neither she be taken with the manner; ¹⁴and the spirit of jealousy come upon him, and he be jealous of his wife, and she be defiled: or if the spirit of jealousy come upon him, and he be jealous of his wife, and she be not defiled: ¹⁵then shall the man bring his wife unto the priest, and he shall bring her offering for her, the tenth part of an ephah of barley meal; he shall pour no oil upon it, nor put frankincense thereon; for it is an offering of jealousy, an offering of memorial, bringing iniquity to remembrance. ¹⁶And the priest shall bring her near, and set her before the LORD. ¹⁷And the priest shall take holy water in an earthen vessel; and of the dust that is in the floor of the tabernacle the priest shall take, and put it into the water: ¹⁸and the priest shall set the woman before the LORD, and uncover the woman's head, and put the offering of memorial in her hands, which is the jealousy offering: and the priest shall have in his hand the bitter water that causeth the curse. ¹⁹And the priest shall charge her by an oath, and say unto the woman, 'If no man have lain with thee, and if thou hast not gone aside to uncleanness with another in stead of thy husband, be thou free from this bitter water that causeth the curse. ²⁰But if thou hast gone aside to another in stead of thy husband, and if thou be defiled, and some man hath lain with thee besides thy husband:' ²¹then the priest shall charge the woman with an oath of cursing, and the priest shall say unto the woman, 'The LORD make thee a curse and an oath among thy people, when the LORD doth make thy thigh to rot, and thy belly to swell. ²²And this water that causeth the curse shall go into thy bowels, to make thy belly to swell, and thy thigh to rot:' and the woman shall say, 'Amen, amen'. ²³And the priest shall write these curses in a book, and he shall blot them out with the bitter water: ²⁴and he shall cause the woman to drink the bitter water that causeth the curse: and the water that causeth the curse shall enter into her, and become bitter. ²⁵Then the priest shall take the jealousy offering out of the woman's hand, and shall wave the offering before the LORD, and offer it upon the altar. ²⁶And the priest shall take a handful of the offering, even the memorial thereof, and burn it upon the altar, and afterward shall cause the woman to drink the water. ²⁷And when he hath made her to drink the water, then it shall come to pass, that, if she be defiled, and have done trespass against her husband, that the water that causeth the curse shall enter into her, and become bitter, and her belly shall swell, and her thigh shall rot: and the woman shall be a curse among her people. ²⁸And if the woman be not defiled, but be clean, then she shall be free, and shall conceive seed.

²⁹'"This is the law of jealousies, when a wife goeth aside to another in stead of her husband, and is defiled; ³⁰or when the spirit of jealousy

cometh upon him, and he be jealous over his wife, and shall set the woman before the LORD, and the priest shall execute upon her all this law. ³¹Then shall the man be guiltless from iniquity, and this woman shall bear her iniquity."'

6 And the LORD spoke unto Moses, saying, ²'Speak unto the children of Israel, and say unto them, "When either man or woman shall separate themselves to vow a vow of a Nazarite, to separate themselves unto the LORD: ³he shall separate himself from wine and strong drink, and shall drink no vinegar of wine, or vinegar of strong drink, neither shall he drink any liquor of grapes, nor eat moist grapes, or dried. ⁴All the days of his separation shall he eat nothing that is made of the vine tree, from the kernels even to the husk. ⁵All the days of the vow of his separation there shall no razor come upon his head: until the days be fulfilled, in the which he separateth himself unto the LORD, he shall be holy, and shall let the locks of the hair of his head grow. ⁶All the days that he separateth himself unto the LORD he shall come at no dead body. ⁷He shall not make himself unclean for his father, or for his mother, for his brother, or for his sister, when they die: because the consecration of his God is upon his head. ⁸All the days of his separation he is holy unto the LORD. ⁹And if any man die very suddenly by him, and he hath defiled the head of his consecration, then he shall shave his head in the day of his cleansing, on the seventh day shall he shave it. ¹⁰And on the eighth day he shall bring two turtles, or two young pigeons, to the priest, to the door of the tabernacle of the congregation: ¹¹and the priest shall offer the one for a sin offering, and the other for a burnt offering, and make an atonement for him, for that he sinned by the dead, and shall hallow his head that same day. ¹²And he shall consecrate unto the LORD the days of his separation, and shall bring a lamb of the first year for a trespass offering: but the days that were before shall be lost, because his separation was defiled.

¹³'"And this is the law of the Nazarite: when the days of his separation are fulfilled, he shall be brought unto the door of the tabernacle of the congregation. ¹⁴And he shall offer his offering unto the LORD, one he-lamb of the first year without blemish for a burnt offering, and one ewe lamb of the first year without blemish for a sin offering, and one lamb without blemish for peace offerings, ¹⁵and a basket of unleavened bread, cakes of fine flour mingled with oil, and wafers of unleavened bread anointed with oil, and their meat offering, and their drink offerings. ¹⁶And the priest shall bring them before the LORD, and shall offer his sin offering, and his burnt offering. ¹⁷And he shall offer the ram for a sacrifice of peace offerings unto the LORD, with the basket of unleavened bread: the priest shall offer also his meat offering, and his drink offering. ¹⁸And the Nazarite shall shave the head of his separation at the door of the tabernacle of the congregation, and shall take the hair of the head of his separation, and put it in the fire which is under the sacrifice of the peace offerings. ¹⁹And the priest shall take the seethed shoulder of the ram, and one unleavened cake out of the basket, and one unleavened wafer, and shall put them upon the hands of the

Nazarite, after the hair of his separation is shaven. ²⁰And the priest shall wave them for a wave offering before the LORD: this is holy for the priest, with the wave breast and heave shoulder: and after that the Nazarite may drink wine. ²¹This is the law of the Nazarite who hath vowed, and of his offering unto the LORD for his separation, besides that that his hand shall get: according to the vow which he vowed, so he must do after the law of his separation."'

²²And the LORD spoke unto Moses, saying, ²³'Speak unto Aaron and unto his sons, saying, "On this wise ye shall bless the children of Israel, saying unto them, ²⁴"The LORD bless thee, and keep thee: ²⁵the LORD make his face shine upon thee, and be gracious unto thee: ²⁶the LORD lift up his countenance upon thee, and give thee peace'". ²⁷And they shall put my name upon the children of Israel; and I will bless them.'

7 And it came to pass on the day that Moses had fully set up the tabernacle, and had anointed it, and sanctified it, and all the instruments thereof, both the altar and all the vessels thereof, and had anointed them, and sanctified them; ²that the princes of Israel, heads of the house of their fathers, who were the princes of the tribes, and were over them that were numbered, offered: ³and they brought their offering before the LORD, six covered wagons, and twelve oxen: a wagon for two of the princes, and for each one an ox: and they brought them before the tabernacle. ⁴And the LORD spoke unto Moses, saying, ⁵'Take it of them, that they may be to do the service of the tabernacle of the congregation; and thou shalt give them unto the Levites, to every man according to his service'. ⁶And Moses took the wagons and the oxen, and gave them unto the Levites. ⁷Two wagons and four oxen he gave unto the sons of Gershon, according to their service. ⁸And four wagons and eight oxen he gave unto the sons of Merari, according unto their service, under the hand of Ithamar the son of Aaron the priest. ⁹But unto the sons of Kohath he gave none: because the service of the sanctuary belonging unto them was that they should bear upon their shoulders.

¹⁰And the princes offered for dedicating of the altar in the day that it was anointed, even the princes offered their offering before the altar. ¹¹And the LORD said unto Moses, 'They shall offer their offering, each prince on his day, for the dedicating of the altar'.

¹²And he that offered his offering the first day was Nahshon the son of Amminadab, of the tribe of Judah. ¹³And his offering was one silver charger, the weight thereof was a hundred and thirty shekels, one silver bowl of seventy shekels, after the shekel of the sanctuary; both of them were full of fine flour mingled with oil for a meat offering: ¹⁴one spoon of ten shekels of gold, full of incense: ¹⁵one young bullock, one ram, one lamb of the first year, for a burnt offering, ¹⁶one kid of the goats for a sin offering: ¹⁷and for a sacrifice of peace offerings, two oxen, five rams, five he-goats, five lambs of the first year: this was the offering of Nahshon the son of Amminadab.

¹⁸On the second day Nethaneel the son of Zuar, prince of Issachar, did offer. ¹⁹He offered for his offering one silver charger, the weight

whereof was a hundred and thirty shekels, one silver bowl of seventy shekels, after the shekel of the sanctuary, both of them full of fine flour mingled with oil for a meat offering: [20] one spoon of gold of ten shekels, full of incense: [21] one young bullock, one ram, one lamb of the first year, for a burnt offering: [22] one kid of the goats for a sin offering: [23] and for a sacrifice of peace offerings, two oxen, five rams, five he-goats, five lambs of the first year: this was the offering of Nethaneel the son of Zuar.

[24] On the third day Eliab the son of Helon, prince of the children of Zebulun, did offer. [25] His offering was one silver charger, the weight whereof was a hundred and thirty shekels, one silver bowl of seventy shekels, after the shekel of the sanctuary, both of them full of fine flour mingled with oil for a meat offering: [26] one golden spoon of ten shekels, full of incense: [27] one young bullock, one ram, one lamb of the first year, for a burnt offering: [28] one kid of the goats for a sin offering: [29] and for a sacrifice of peace offerings, two oxen, five rams, five he-goats, five lambs of the first year: this was the offering of Eliab the son of Helon.

[30] On the fourth day Elizur the son of Shedeur, prince of the children of Reuben, did offer. [31] His offering was one silver charger of a hundred and thirty shekels, one silver bowl of seventy shekels, after the shekel of the sanctuary, both of them full of fine flour mingled with oil for a meat offering: [32] one golden spoon of ten shekels, full of incense: [33] one young bullock, one ram, one lamb of the first year, for a burnt offering: [34] one kid of the goats for a sin offering: [35] and for a sacrifice of peace offerings, two oxen, five rams, five he-goats, five lambs of the first year: this was the offering of Elizur the son of Shedeur.

[36] On the fifth day Shelumiel the son of Zurishaddai, prince of the children of Simeon, did offer. [37] His offering was one silver charger, the weight whereof was a hundred and thirty shekels, one silver bowl of seventy shekels, after the shekel of the sanctuary, both of them full of fine flour mingled with oil for a meat offering: [38] one golden spoon of ten shekels, full of incense: [39] one young bullock, one ram, one lamb of the first year, for a burnt offering: [40] one kid of the goats for a sin offering: [41] and for a sacrifice of peace offerings, two oxen, five rams, five he-goats, five lambs of the first year: this was the offering of Shelumiel the son of Zurishaddai.

[42] On the sixth day Eliasaph the son of Deuel, prince of the children of Gad, offered. [43] His offering was one silver charger of the weight of a hundred and thirty shekels, a silver bowl of seventy shekels, after the shekel of the sanctuary, both of them full of fine flour mingled with oil for a meat offering: [44] one golden spoon of ten shekels, full of incense: [45] one young bullock, one ram, one lamb of the first year, for a burnt offering: [46] one kid of the goats for a sin offering: [47] and for a sacrifice of peace offerings, two oxen, five rams, five he-goats, five lambs of the first year: this was the offering of Eliasaph the son of Deuel.

[48] On the seventh day Elishama the son of Ammihud, prince of the children of Ephraim, offered. [49] His offering was one silver charger, the

weight whereof was a hundred and thirty shekels, one silver bowl of seventy shekels, after the shekel of the sanctuary, both of them full of fine flour mingled with oil for a meat offering: [50] one golden spoon of ten shekels, full of incense: [51] one young bullock, one ram, one lamb of the first year, for a burnt offering: [52] One kid of the goats for a sin offering: [53] and for a sacrifice of peace offerings, two oxen, five rams, five he-goats, five lambs of the first year: this was the offering of Elishama the son of Ammihud.

[54] On the eighth day offered Gamaliel the son of Pedahzur, prince of the children of Manasseh. [55] His offering was one silver charger of a hundred and thirty shekels, one silver bowl of seventy shekels, after the shekel of the sanctuary, both of them full of fine flour mingled with oil for a meat offering: [56] one golden spoon of ten shekels, full of incense: [57] one young bullock, one ram, one lamb of the first year, for a burnt offering: [58] one kid of the goats for a sin offering: [59] and for a sacrifice of peace offerings, two oxen, five rams, five he-goats, five lambs of the first year: this was the offering of Gamaliel the son of Pedahzur.

[60] On the ninth day Abidan the son of Gideoni, prince of the children of Benjamin, offered. [61] His offering was one silver charger, the weight whereof was a hundred and thirty shekels, a silver bowl of seventy shekels, after the shekel of the sanctuary, both of them full of fine flour mingled with oil for a meat offering: [62] one golden spoon of ten shekels, full of incense: [63] one young bullock, one ram, one lamb of the first year, for a burnt offering: [64] one kid of the goats for a sin offering: [65] and for a sacrifice of peace offerings, two oxen, five rams, five he-goats, five lambs of the first year: this was the offering of Abidan the son of Gideoni.

[66] On the tenth day Ahiezer the son of Ammishaddai, prince of the children of Dan, offered. [67] His offering was one silver charger, the weight whereof was a hundred and thirty shekels, one silver bowl of seventy shekels, after the shekel of the sanctuary, both of them full of fine flour mingled with oil for a meat offering: [68] one golden spoon of ten shekels, full of incense: [69] one young bullock, one ram, one lamb of the first year, for a burnt offering: [70] one kid of the goats for a sin offering: [71] and for a sacrifice of peace offerings, two oxen, five rams, five he-goats, five lambs of the first year: this was the offering of Ahiezer the son of Ammishaddai.

[72] On the eleventh day Pagiel the son of Ocran, prince of the children of Asher, offered. [73] His offering was one silver charger, the weight whereof was a hundred and thirty shekels, one silver bowl of seventy shekels, after the shekel of the sanctuary, both of them full of fine flour mingled with oil for a meat offering: [74] one golden spoon of ten shekels, full of incense: [75] one young bullock, one ram, one lamb of the first year, for a burnt offering: [76] one kid of the goats for a sin offering: [77] and for a sacrifice of peace offerings, two oxen, five rams, five he-goats, five lambs of the first year: this was the offering of Pagiel the son of Ocran.

[78] On the twelfth day Ahira the son of Enan, prince of the children of

Naphtali, offered. [79]His offering was one silver charger, the weight whereof was a hundred and thirty shekels, one silver bowl of seventy shekels, after the shekel of the sanctuary, both of them full of fine flour mingled with oil for a meat offering: [80]one golden spoon of ten shekels, full of incense: [81]one young bullock, one ram, one lamb of the first year, for a burnt offering: [82]one kid of the goats for a sin offering: [83]and for a sacrifice of peace offerings, two oxen, five rams, five he-goats, five lambs of the first year: this was the offering of Ahira the son of Enan.

[84]This was the dedication of the altar, in the day when it was anointed, by the princes of Israel: twelve chargers of silver, twelve silver bowls, twelve spoons of gold: [85]each charger of silver weighing a hundred and thirty shekels, each bowl seventy: all the silver vessels weighed two thousand and four hundred shekels, after the shekel of the sanctuary. [86]The golden spoons were twelve, full of incense, weighing ten shekels apiece, after the shekel of the sanctuary: all the gold of the spoons was a hundred and twenty shekels. [87]All the oxen for the burnt offering were twelve bullocks, the rams twelve, the lambs of the first year twelve, with their meat offering: and the kids of the goats for sin offering twelve. [88]And all the oxen for the sacrifice of the peace offerings were twenty and four bullocks, the rams sixty, the he-goats sixty, the lambs of the first year sixty. This was the dedication of the altar, after that it was anointed.

[89]And when Moses was gone into the tabernacle of the congregation to speak with him, then he heard the voice of one speaking unto him from off the mercy-seat that was upon the ark of testimony, from between the two cherubims: and he spoke unto him.

8 And the LORD spoke unto Moses, saying, [2]'Speak unto Aaron, and say unto him, "When thou lightest the lamps, the seven lamps shall give light over against the candlestick"'. [3]And Aaron did so; he lighted the lamps thereof over against the candlestick, as the LORD commanded Moses. [4]And this work of the candlestick was of beaten gold, unto the shaft thereof, unto the flowers thereof, was beaten work: according unto the pattern which the LORD had shown Moses, so he made the candlestick.

[5]And the LORD spoke unto Moses, saying, [6]'Take the Levites from among the children of Israel, and cleanse them. [7]And thus shalt thou do unto them, to cleanse them: sprinkle water of purifying upon them, and let them shave all their flesh, and let them wash their clothes, and so make themselves clean. [8]Then let them take a young bullock with his meat offering, even fine flour mingled with oil, and another young bullock shalt thou take for a sin offering. [9]And thou shalt bring the Levites before the tabernacle of the congregation; and thou shalt gather the whole assembly of the children of Israel together: [10]and thou shalt bring the Levites before the LORD: and the children of Israel shall put their hands upon the Levites. [11]And Aaron shall offer the Levites before the LORD for an offering of the children of Israel, that they may execute the service of the LORD. [12]And the Levites shall lay their hands

upon the heads of the bullocks: and thou shalt offer the one for a sin offering, and the other for a burnt offering unto the LORD, to make an atonement for the Levites. ¹³And thou shalt set the Levites before Aaron, and before his sons, and offer them for an offering unto the LORD. ¹⁴Thus shalt thou separate the Levites from among the children of Israel: and the Levites shall be mine. ¹⁵And after that shall the Levites go in to do the service of the tabernacle of the congregation: and thou shalt cleanse them, and offer them for an offering. ¹⁶For they are wholly given unto me from among the children of Israel: in stead of such as open every womb, even in stead of the firstborn of all the children of Israel, have I taken them unto me. ¹⁷For all the firstborn of the children of Israel are mine, both man and beast: on the day that I smote every firstborn in the land of Egypt I sanctified them for myself. ¹⁸And I have taken the Levites for all the firstborn of the children of Israel. ¹⁹And I have given the Levites as a gift to Aaron and to his sons from among the children of Israel, to do the service of the children of Israel in the tabernacle of the congregation, and to make an atonement for the children of Israel: that there be no plague among the children of Israel, when the children of Israel come nigh unto the sanctuary.' ²⁰And Moses, and Aaron, and all the congregation of the children of Israel, did to the Levites according unto all that the LORD commanded Moses concerning the Levites, so did the children of Israel unto them. ²¹And the Levites were purified, and they washed their clothes; and Aaron offered them as an offering before the LORD; and Aaron made an atonement for them to cleanse them. ²²And after that went the Levites in to do their service in the tabernacle of the congregation before Aaron, and before his sons: as the LORD had commanded Moses concerning the Levites, so did they unto them.

²³And the LORD spoke unto Moses, saying, ²⁴'This is it that belongeth unto the Levites: from twenty and five years old and upward they shall go in to wait upon the service of the tabernacle of the congregation: ²⁵and from the age of fifty years they shall cease waiting upon the service thereof, and shall serve no more: ²⁶but shall minister with their brethren in the tabernacle of the congregation, to keep the charge, and shall do no service. Thus shalt thou do unto the Levites touching their charge.'

9 And the LORD spoke unto Moses in the wilderness of Sinai, in the first month of the second year after they were come out of the land of Egypt, saying, ²'Let the children of Israel also keep the passover at his appointed season. ³In the fourteenth day of this month at even, ye shall keep it in his appointed season: according to all the rites of it, and according to all the ceremonies thereof, shall ye keep it.' ⁴And Moses spoke unto the children of Israel, that they should keep the passover. ⁵And they kept the passover on the fourteenth day of the first month at even in the wilderness of Sinai: according to all that the LORD commanded Moses, so did the children of Israel.

⁶And there were certain men, who were defiled by the dead body of a man, that they could not keep the passover on that day: and they came

before Moses and before Aaron on that day. ⁷And those men said unto him, 'We are defiled by the dead body of a man: wherefore are we kept back, that we may not offer an offering of the LORD in his appointed season among the children of Israel?' ⁸And Moses said unto them, 'Stand still, and I will hear what the LORD will command concerning you'.

⁹And the LORD spoke unto Moses, saying, ¹⁰'Speak unto the children of Israel, saying, "If any man of you or of your posterity shall be unclean by reason of a dead body, or be in a journey afar off, yet he shall keep the passover unto the LORD. ¹¹The fourteenth day of the second month at even they shall keep it, and eat it with unleavened bread and bitter herbs. ¹²They shall leave none of it unto the morning, nor break any bone of it: according to all the ordinances of the passover they shall keep it. ¹³But the man that is clean, and is not in a journey, and forbeareth to keep the passover, even the same soul shall be cut off from among his people, because he brought not the offering of the LORD in his appointed season: that man shall bear his sin. ¹⁴And if a stranger shall sojourn among you, and will keep the passover unto the LORD; according to the ordinance of the passover, and according to the manner thereof, so shall he do: ye shall have one ordinance, both for the stranger, and for him that was born in the land."'

¹⁵And on the day that the tabernacle was reared up the cloud covered the tabernacle, namely, the tent of the testimony: and at even there was upon the tabernacle as it were the appearance of fire, until the morning. ¹⁶So it was always: the cloud covered it by day, and the appearance of fire by night. ¹⁷And when the cloud was taken up from the tabernacle, then after that the children of Israel journeyed: and in the place where the cloud abode, there the children of Israel pitched their tents. ¹⁸At the commandment of the LORD the children of Israel journeyed, and at the commandment of the LORD they pitched: as long as the cloud abode upon the tabernacle they rested in the tents. ¹⁹And when the cloud tarried long upon the tabernacle many days, then the children of Israel kept the charge of the LORD, and journeyed not. ²⁰And so it was, when the cloud was a few days upon the tabernacle; according to the commandment of the LORD they abode in their tents, and according to the commandment of the LORD they journeyed. ²¹And so it was, when the cloud abode from even unto the morning, and that the cloud was taken up in the morning, then they journeyed: whether it was by day or by night that the cloud was taken up, they journeyed. ²²Or whether it were two days, or a month, or a year, that the cloud tarried upon the tabernacle, remaining thereon, the children of Israel abode in their tents, and journeyed not: but when it was taken up, they journeyed. ²³At the commandment of the LORD they rested in the tents, and at the commandment of the LORD they journeyed: they kept the charge of the LORD, at the commandment of the LORD by the hand of Moses.

10 And the LORD spoke unto Moses, saying, ²'Make thee two trumpets of silver: of a whole piece shalt thou make them, that thou mayest use them for the calling of the assembly, and for the journeying of the camps. ³And when they shall blow with them, all the assembly shall assemble themselves to thee at the door of the tabernacle of the congregation. ⁴And if they blow but with one trumpet, then the princes, which are heads of the thousands of Israel, shall gather themselves unto thee. ⁵When ye blow an alarm, then the camps that lie on the east parts shall go forward. ⁶When you blow an alarm the second time, then the camps that lie on the south side shall take their journey: they shall blow an alarm for their journeys. ⁷But when the congregation is to be gathered together, you shall blow, but you shall not sound an alarm. ⁸And the sons of Aaron, the priests, shall blow with the trumpets; and they shall be to you for an ordinance for ever throughout your generations. ⁹And if ye go to war in your land against the enemy that oppresseth you, then ye shall blow an alarm with the trumpets; and ye shall be remembered before the LORD your God, and ye shall be saved from your enemies. ¹⁰Also in the day of your gladness, and in your solemn days, and in the beginnings of your months, ye shall blow with the trumpets over your burnt offerings, and over the sacrifices of your peace offerings, that they may be to you for a memorial before your God: I am the LORD your God.'

¹¹And it came to pass on the twentieth day of the second month, in the second year, that the cloud was taken up from off the tabernacle of the testimony. ¹²And the children of Israel took their journeys out of the wilderness of Sinai; and the cloud rested in the wilderness of Paran. ¹³And they first took their journey according to the commandment of the LORD by the hand of Moses.

¹⁴In the first place went the standard of the camp of the children of Judah according to their armies: and over his host was Nahshon the son of Amminadab. ¹⁵And over the host of the tribe of the children of Issachar was Nethaneel the son of Zuar. ¹⁶And over the host of the tribe of the children of Zebulun was Eliab the son of Helon. ¹⁷And the tabernacle was taken down; and the sons of Gershon and the sons of Merari set forward, bearing the tabernacle.

¹⁸And the standard of the camp of Reuben set forward according to their armies: and over his host was Elizur the son of Shedeur. ¹⁹And over the host of the tribe of the children of Simeon was Shelumiel the son of Zurishaddai. ²⁰And over the host of the tribe of the children of Gad was Eliasaph the son of Deuel. ²¹And the Kohathites set forward, bearing the sanctuary, and the others did set up the tabernacle against they came.

²²And the standard of the camp of the children of Ephraim set forward according to their armies: and over his host was Elishama the son of Ammihud. ²³And over the host of the tribe of the children of Manasseh was Gamaliel the son of Pedahzur. ²⁴And over the host of the tribe of the children of Benjamin was Abidan the son of Gideoni.

²⁵And the standard of the camp of the children of Dan set forward, which was the rearward of all the camps throughout their hosts: and over his host was Ahiezer the son of Ammishaddai. ²⁶And over the host of the tribe of the children of Asher was Pagiel the son of Ocran. ²⁷And

over the host of the tribe of the children of Naphtali was Ahira the son of Enan. [28]Thus were the journeyings of the children of Israel according to their armies, when they set forward.

[29]And Moses said unto Hobab, the son of Raguel the Midianite, Moses' father-in-law, 'We are journeying unto the place of which the LORD said, "I will give it you": come thou with us, and we will do thee good: for the LORD hath spoken good concerning Israel'. [30]And he said unto him, 'I will not go, but I will depart to mine own land, and to my kindred'. [31]And he said, 'Leave us not, I pray thee, forasmuch as thou knowest how we are to encamp in the wilderness, and thou mayest be to us instead of eyes. [32]And it shall be, if thou go with us, yea, it shall be, that what goodness the LORD shall do unto us, the same will we do unto thee.'

[33]And they departed from the mount of the LORD three days' journey: and the ark of the covenant of the LORD went before them in the three days' journey, to search out a resting place for them. [34]And the cloud of the LORD was upon them by day, when they went out of the camp. [35]And it came to pass, when the ark set forward, that Moses said, 'Rise up, LORD, and let thy enemies be scattered; and let them that hate thee flee before thee'. [36]And when it rested, he said, 'Return, O LORD, unto the many thousands of Israel'.

11 And when the people complained, it displeased the LORD: and the LORD heard it; and his anger was kindled; and the fire of the LORD burnt among them, and consumed them that were in the outermost parts of the camp. [2]And the people cried unto Moses; and when Moses prayed unto the LORD, the fire was quenched. [3]And he called the name of the place Taberah: because the fire of the LORD burnt among them.

[4]And the mixed multitude that was among them fell a-lusting, and the children of Israel also wept again, and said, 'Who shall give us flesh to eat? [5]We remember the fish which we did eat in Egypt freely; the cucumbers, and the melons, and the leeks, and the onions, and the garlick. [6]But now our soul is dried away: there is nothing at all, besides this manna, before our eyes.' [7]And the manna was as coriander seed, and the colour thereof as the colour of bdellium. [8]And the people went about, and gathered it, and ground it in mills, or beat it in a mortar, and baked it in pans, and made cakes of it: and the taste of it was as the taste of fresh oil. [9]And when the dew fell upon the camp in the night, the manna fell upon it.

[10]Then Moses heard the people weep throughout their families, every man in the door of his tent: and the anger of the LORD was kindled greatly; Moses also was displeased. [11]And Moses said unto the LORD, 'Wherefore hast thou afflicted thy servant? and wherefore have I not found favour in thy sight, that thou layest the burden of all this people upon me? [12]Have I conceived all this people? have I begotten them, that thou shouldst say unto me, "Carry them in thy bosom, as a nursing father beareth the sucking child, unto the land which thou sworest unto their fathers?" [13]Whence should I have flesh to give unto

all this people? for they weep unto me, saying, "Give us flesh, that we may eat". ¹⁴I am not able to bear all this people alone, because it is too heavy for me. ¹⁵And if thou deal thus with me, kill me, I pray thee, out of hand, if I have found favour in thy sight, and let me not see my wretchedness.'

¹⁶And the LORD said unto Moses, 'Gather unto me seventy men of the elders of Israel, whom thou knowest to be the elders of the people, and officers over them; and bring them unto the tabernacle of the congregation, that they may stand there with thee. ¹⁷And I will come down and talk with thee there: and I will take of the spirit which is upon thee, and will put it upon them; and they shall bear the burden of the people with thee, that thou bear it not thyself alone. ¹⁸And say thou unto the people, "Sanctify yourselves against tomorrow, and ye shall eat flesh: for you have wept in the ears of the LORD, saying, 'Who shall give us flesh to eat? for it was well with us in Egypt': therefore the LORD will give you flesh, and ye shall eat. ¹⁹Ye shall not eat one day, nor two days, nor five days, neither ten days, nor twenty days: ²⁰but even a whole month, until it come out at your nostrils, and it be loathsome unto you, because that ye have despised the LORD which is among you, and have wept before him, saying, 'Why came we forth out of Egypt?'"' ²¹And Moses said, 'The people amongst whom I am, are six hundred thousand footmen; and thou hast said, "I will give them flesh, that they may eat a whole month". ²²Shall the flocks and the herds be slain for them, to suffice them? or shall all the fish of the sea be gathered together for them, to suffice them?' ²³And the LORD said unto Moses, 'Is the LORD's hand waxed short? thou shalt see now whether my word shall come to pass unto thee or not'.

²⁴And Moses went out, and told the people the words of the LORD, and gathered the seventy men of the elders of the people, and set them round about the tabernacle. ²⁵And the LORD came down in a cloud, and spoke unto him, and took of the spirit that was upon him, and gave it unto the seventy elders: and it came to pass that when the spirit rested upon them, they prophesied, and did not cease. ²⁶But there remained two of the men in the camp, the name of the one was Eldad, and the name of the other Medad: and the spirit rested upon them; and they were of them that were written, but went not out unto the tabernacle: and they prophesied in camp. ²⁷And there ran a young man, and told Moses, and said, 'Eldad and Medad do prophesy in the camp'. ²⁸And Joshua the son of Nun, the servant of Moses, one of his young men, answered and said, 'My lord Moses, forbid them'. ²⁹And Moses said unto him, 'Enviest thou for my sake? Would God that all the LORD's people were prophets, and that the LORD would put his spirit upon them.' ³⁰And Moses got him into the camp, he and the elders of Israel.

³¹And there went forth a wind from the LORD, and brought quails from the sea, and let them fall by the camp, as it were a day's journey on this side, and as it were a day's journey on the other side, round about the camp, and as it were two cubits high upon the face of the earth. ³²And the people stood up all that day, and all that night, and all

the next day, and they gathered the quails: he that gathered least gathered ten homers: and they spread them all abroad for themselves round about the camp. ³³And while the flesh was yet between their teeth, ere it was chewed, the wrath of the L ORD was kindled against the people, and the L ORD smote the people with a very great plague. ³⁴And he called the name of that place Kibroth-hattaavah: because there they buried the people that lusted. ³⁵And the people journeyed from Kibroth-hattaavah unto Hazeroth; and abode at Hazeroth.

12 And Miriam and Aaron spoke against Moses because of the Ethiopian woman whom he had married: for he had married an Ethiopian woman. ²And they said, 'Hath the L ORD indeed spoken only by Moses? Hath he not spoken also by us?' And the L ORD heard it. ³(Now the man Moses was very meek, above all the men which were upon the face of the earth.) ⁴And the L ORD spoke suddenly unto Moses, and unto Aaron, and unto Miriam, 'Come out ye three unto the tabernacle of the congregation'. And they three came out. ⁵And the L ORD came down in the pillar of the cloud, and stood in the door of the tabernacle, and called Aaron and Miriam: and they both came forth. ⁶And he said, 'Hear now my words: if there be a prophet among you, I the L ORD will make myself known unto him in a vision, and will speak unto him in a dream. ⁷My servant Moses is not so, who is faithful in all my house. ⁸With him will I speak mouth to mouth, even apparently, and not in dark speeches, and the similitude of the L ORD shall he behold: wherefore then were ye not afraid to speak against my servant Moses?' ⁹And the anger of the L ORD was kindled against them; and he departed. ¹⁰And the cloud departed from off the tabernacle; and behold, Miriam became leprous, white as snow: and Aaron looked upon Miriam, and behold, she was leprous. ¹¹And Aaron said unto Moses, 'Alas, my lord, I beseech thee, lay not the sin upon us, wherein we have done foolishly, and wherein we have sinned. ¹²Let her not be as one dead, of whom the flesh is half consumed when he cometh out of his mother's womb.' ¹³And Moses cried unto the L ORD, saying, 'Heal her now, O God, I beseech thee'. ¹⁴And the L ORD said unto Moses, 'If her father had but spat in her face, should she not be ashamed seven days? let her be shut out from the camp seven days, and after that let her be received in again'. ¹⁵And Miriam was shut out from the camp seven days: and the people journeyed not till Miriam was brought in again. ¹⁶And afterward the people removed from Hazeroth, and pitched in the wilderness of Paran.

13 And the L ORD spoke unto Moses, saying, ²'Send thou men, that they may search the land of Canaan, which I give unto the children of Israel: of every tribe of their fathers shall ye send a man, every one a ruler among them'. ³And Moses by the commandment of the L ORD sent them from the wilderness of Paran: all those men were heads of the children of Israel. ⁴And these were their names. Of the tribe of Reuben, Shammua the son of Zaccur. ⁵Of the tribe of Simeon, Shaphat the son of Hori. ⁶Of the tribe of Judah, Caleb the son of Jephunneh. ⁷Of the tribe of Issachar, Igal the son of Joseph. ⁸Of the tribe

of Ephraim, Oshea the son of Nun. ⁹Of the tribe of Benjamin, Palti the son of Raphu. ¹⁰Of the tribe of Zebulun, Gaddiel the son of Sodi. ¹¹Of the tribe of Joseph, namely of the tribe of Manasseh, Gaddi the son of Susi. ¹²Of the tribe of Dan, Ammiel the son of Gemalli. ¹³Of the tribe of Asher, Sethur the son of Michael. ¹⁴Of the tribe of Naphtali, Nahbi the son of Vophsi. ¹⁵Of the tribe of Gad, Geuel the son of Machi. ¹⁶These are the names of the men which Moses sent to spy out the land. And Moses called Oshea the son of Nun Jehoshua.

¹⁷And Moses sent them to spy out the land of Canaan, and said unto them, 'Get you up this way southward, and go up into the mountain: ¹⁸and see the land, what it is; and the people that dwelleth therein, whether they be strong or weak, few or many; ¹⁹and what the land is that they dwell in, whether it be good or bad; and what cities they be that they dwell in, whether in tents, or in strongholds; ²⁰and what the land is, whether it be fat or lean, whether there be wood therein, or not. And be ye of good courage, and bring of the fruit of the land.' Now the time was the time of the first-ripe grapes.

²¹So they went up, and searched the land from the wilderness of Zin unto Rehob, as men come to Hamath. ²²And they ascended by the south, and came unto Hebron: where Ahiman, Sheshai, and Talmai, the children of Anak, were (now Hebron was built seven years before Zoan in Egypt). ²³And they came unto the brook of Eshcol, and cut down from thence a branch with one cluster of grapes, and they bore it between two upon a staff; and they brought of the pomegranates, and of the figs. ²⁴The place was called the brook Eshcol, because of the cluster of grapes which the children of Israel cut down from thence. ²⁵And they returned from searching of the land after forty days.

²⁶And they went and came to Moses, and to Aaron, and to all the congregation of the children of Israel, unto the wilderness of Paran, to Kadesh; and brought back word unto them, and unto all the congregation, and showed them the fruit of the land. ²⁷And they told him, and said, 'We came unto the land whither thou sentest us, and surely it floweth with milk and honey; and this is the fruit of it. ²⁸Nevertheless the people be strong that dwell in the land, and the cities are walled, and very great: and moreover we saw the children of Anak there. ²⁹The Amalekites dwell in the land of the south: and the Hittites, and the Jebusites, and the Amorites, dwell in the mountains: and the Canaanites dwell by the sea, and by the coast of Jordan.' ³⁰And Caleb stilled the people before Moses, and said, 'Let us go up at once, and possess it; for we are well able to overcome it'. ³¹But the men that went up with him said, 'We be not able to go up against the people, for they are stronger than we'. ³²And they brought up an evil report of the land which they had searched unto the children of Israel, saying, 'The land, through which we have gone to search it, is a land that eateth up the inhabitants thereof, and all the people that we saw in it are men of a great stature. ³³And there we saw the giants, the sons of Anak, which come of the giants: and we were in our own sight as grasshoppers, and so we were in their sight.'

14 And all the congregation lifted up their voice and cried; and the people wept that night. ²And all the children of Israel murmured against Moses and against Aaron: and the whole congregation said unto them, 'Would God that we had died in the land of Egypt, or would God we had died in this wilderness. ³And wherefore hath the LORD brought us unto this land, to fall by the sword, that our wives and our children should be a prey? were it not better for us to return into Egypt?' ⁴And they said one to another, 'Let us make a captain, and let us return into Egypt'. ⁵Then Moses and Aaron fell on their faces before all the assembly of the congregation of the children of Israel.

⁶And Joshua the son of Nun, and Caleb the son of Jephunneh, which were of them that searched the land, rent their clothes. ⁷And they spoke unto all the company of the children of Israel, saying, 'The land which we passed through to search it, is an exceeding good land. ⁸If the LORD delight in us, then he will bring us into this land, and give it us, a land which floweth with milk and honey. ⁹Only rebel not ye against the LORD, neither fear ye the people of the land, for they are bread for us: their defence is departed from them, and the LORD is with us: fear them not.' ¹⁰But all the congregation bade stone them with stones. And the glory of the LORD appeared in the tabernacle of the congregation before all the children of Israel.

¹¹And the LORD said unto Moses, 'How long will this people provoke me? and how long will it be ere they believe me, for all the signs which I have shown among them? ¹²I will smite them with the pestilence, and disinherit them, and will make of thee a greater nation and mightier than they.'

¹³And Moses said unto the LORD, 'Then the Egyptians shall hear it (for thou broughtest up this people in thy might from among them), ¹⁴and they will tell it to the inhabitants of this land: for they have heard that thou LORD art among this people, that thou LORD art seen face to face, and that thy cloud standeth over them, and that thou goest before them, by day time in a pillar of a cloud, and in a pillar of fire by night. ¹⁵Now if thou shalt kill all this people as one man, then the nations which have heard the fame of thee will speak, saying, ¹⁶"Because the LORD was not able to bring this people into the land which he swore unto them, therefore he hath slain them in the wilderness". ¹⁷And now, I beseech thee, let the power of my LORD be great, according as thou hast spoken, saying, ¹⁸"The LORD is long-suffering, and of great mercy, forgiving iniquity and transgression, and by no means clearing the guilty, visiting the iniquity of the fathers upon the children unto the third and fourth generation". ¹⁹Pardon, I beseech thee, the iniquity of this people, according unto the greatness of thy mercy, and as thou hast forgiven this people, from Egypt even until now.'

²⁰And the LORD said, 'I have pardoned according to thy word. ²¹But as truly as I live, all the earth shall be filled with the glory of the LORD. ²²Because all those men which have seen my glory, and my miracles which I did in Egypt and in the wilderness, and have tempted me

now these ten times, and have not hearkened to my voice, [23]surely they shall not see the land which I swore unto their fathers, neither shall any of them that provoked me see it. [24]But my servant Caleb, because he had another spirit with him, and hath followed me fully, him will I bring into the land whereinto he went; and his seed shall possess it.' [25](Now the Amalekites and the Canaanites dwelt in the valley.) 'Tomorrow turn you, and get you into the wilderness by the way of the Red Sea.'

[26]And the LORD spoke unto Moses and unto Aaron, saying, [27]'How long shall I bear with this evil congregation, which murmur against me? I have heard the murmurings of the children of Israel, which they murmur against me. [28]Say unto them, "As truly as I live," saith the LORD, "as ye have spoken in my ears, so will I do to you: [29]your carcases shall fall in this wilderness; and all that were numbered of you, according to your whole number from twenty year old and upward, which have murmured against me, [30]doubtless ye shall not come into the land, concerning which I swore to make you dwell therein, save Caleb the son of Jephunneh, and Joshua the son of Nun. [31]But your little ones, which ye said should be a prey, them will I bring in, and they shall know the land which ye have despised. [32]But as for you, your carcases, they shall fall in this wilderness. [33]And your children shall wander in the wilderness forty years, and bear your whoredoms, until your carcases be wasted in the wilderness. [34]After the number of the days in which ye searched the land, even forty days, each day for a year, shall ye bear your iniquities, even forty years, and ye shall know my breach of promise. [35]I the LORD have said, I will surely do it unto all this evil congregation, that are gathered together against me: in this wilderness they shall be consumed, and there they shall die."' [36]And the men which Moses sent to search the land, who returned, and made all the congregation to murmur against him, by bringing up a slander upon the land, [37]even those men that did bring up the evil report upon the land, died by the plague before the LORD. [38]But Joshua the son of Nun, and Caleb the son of Jephunneh, which were of the men that went to search the land, lived still. [39]And Moses told these sayings unto all the children of Israel: and the people mourned greatly.

[40]And they rose up early in the morning, and got them up into the top of the mountain, saying, 'Lo, we be here, and will go up unto the place which the LORD hath promised: for we have sinned'. [41]And Moses said, 'Wherefore now do you transgress the commandment of the LORD? but it shall not prosper. [42]Go not up, for the LORD is not among you, that ye be not smitten before your enemies. [43]For the Amalekites and the Canaanites are there before you, and ye shall fall by the sword: because ye are turned away from the LORD, therefore the LORD will not be with you.' [44]But they presumed to go up unto the hill-top: nevertheless the ark of the covenant of the LORD, and Moses, departed not out of the camp. [45]Then the Amalekites came down, and the Canaanites which dwelt in that hill, and smote them, and discomfited them, even unto Hormah.

15 And the LORD spoke unto Moses, saying, ²'Speak unto the children of Israel, and say unto them, "When ye be come into the land of your habitations, which I give unto you, ³and will make an offering by fire unto the LORD, a burnt offering, or a sacrifice in performing a vow, or in a free-will offering, or in your solemn feasts, to make a sweet savour unto the LORD, of the herd, or of the flock: ⁴then shall he that offereth his offering unto the LORD bring a meat offering of a tenth deal of flour mingled with the fourth part of a hin of oil. ⁵And the fourth part of a hin of wine for a drink offering shalt thou prepare with the burnt offering or sacrifice, for one lamb. ⁶Or for a ram, thou shalt prepare for a meat offering two tenth deals of flour mingled with the third part of a hin of oil. ⁷And for a drink offering thou shalt offer the third part of a hin of wine, for a sweet savour unto the LORD. ⁸And when thou preparest a bullock for a burnt offering, or for a sacrifice in performing a vow, or peace offerings unto the LORD: ⁹then shall he bring with a bullock a meat offering of three tenth deals of flour, mingled with half a hin of oil. ¹⁰And thou shalt bring for a drink offering half a hin of wine, for an offering made by fire, of a sweet savour unto the LORD. ¹¹Thus shall it be done for one bullock, or for one ram, or for a lamb, or a kid. ¹²According to the number that ye shall prepare, so shall ye do to every one according to their number. ¹³All that are born of the country shall do these things after this manner, in offering an offering made by fire, of a sweet savour unto the LORD. ¹⁴And if a stranger sojourn with you, or whosoever be among you in your generations, and will offer an offering made by fire, of a sweet savour unto the LORD: as ye do, so he shall do. ¹⁵One ordinance shall be both for you of the congregation, and also for the stranger that sojourneth with you, an ordinance for ever in your generations: as ye are, so shall the stranger be before the LORD. ¹⁶One law and one manner shall be for you, and for the stranger that sojourneth with you."'

¹⁷And the LORD spoke unto Moses, saying, ¹⁸'Speak unto the children of Israel, and say unto them, "When ye come into the land whither I bring you, ¹⁹then it shall be that when ye eat of the bread of the land, ye shall offer up a heave offering unto the LORD. ²⁰Ye shall offer up a cake of the first of your dough for a heave offering: as ye do the heave offering of the threshing-floor, so shall ye heave it. ²¹Of the first of your dough ye shall give unto the LORD a heave offering in your generations.

²²'"And if ye have erred, and not observed all these commandments which the LORD hath spoken unto Moses, ²³even all that the LORD hath commanded you by the hand of Moses, from the day that the LORD commanded Moses, and henceforward among your generations: ²⁴then it shall be, if aught be committed by ignorance without the knowledge of the congregation, that all the congregation shall offer one young bullock for a burnt offering, for a sweet savour unto the LORD, with his meat offering, and his drink offering, according to the manner, and one kid of the goats for a sin offering. ²⁵And the priest shall make an atonement for all the congregation of the children of Israel, and it shall be forgiven them, for it is ignorance: and they shall bring their offer-

ing, a sacrifice made by fire unto the LORD, and their sin offering before the LORD, for their ignorance. ²⁶And it shall be forgiven all the congregation of the children of Israel, and the stranger that sojourneth among them, seeing all the people were in ignorance.

²⁷'"And if any soul sin through ignorance, then he shall bring a she-goat of the first year for a sin offering. ²⁸And the priest shall make an atonement for the soul that sinneth ignorantly, when he sinneth by ignorance before the LORD, to make an atonement for him; and it shall be forgiven him. ²⁹You shall have one law for him that sinneth through ignorance, both for him that is born amongst the children of Israel, and for the stranger that sojourneth among them.

³⁰'"But the soul that doeth aught presumptuously, whether he be born in the land, or a stranger, the same reproacheth the LORD: and that soul shall be cut off from among his people. ³¹Because he hath despised the word of the LORD, and hath broken his commandment, that soul shall utterly be cut off: his iniquity shall be upon him."'

³²And while the children of Israel were in the wilderness, they found a man that gathered sticks upon the sabbath day. ³³And they that found him gathering sticks brought him unto Moses and Aaron, and unto all the congregation. ³⁴And they put him in ward, because it was not declared what should be done to him. ³⁵And the LORD said unto Moses, 'The man shall be surely put to death: all the congregation shall stone him with stones without the camp'. ³⁶And all the congregation brought him without the camp, and stoned him with stones, and he died, as the LORD commanded Moses.

³⁷And the LORD spoke unto Moses, saying, ³⁸'Speak unto the children of Israel, and bid them that they make them fringes in the borders of their garments throughout their generations, and that they put upon the fringe of the borders a ribbon of blue. ³⁹And it shall be unto you for a fringe, that ye may look upon it, and remember all the commandments of the LORD, and do them; and that ye seek not after your own heart and your own eyes, after which ye use to go a-whoring: ⁴⁰that ye may remember, and do all my commandments, and be holy unto your God. ⁴¹I am the LORD your God, which brought you out of the land of Egypt, to be your God: I am the LORD your God.'

16 Now Korah, the son of Izhar, the son of Kohath, the son of Levi, and Dathan and Abiram, the sons of Eliab, and On, the son of Peleth, sons of Reuben, took men. ²And they rose up before Moses, with certain of the children of Israel, two hundred and fifty princes of the assembly, famous in the congregation, men of renown. ³And they gathered themselves together against Moses and against Aaron, and said unto them, 'Ye take too much upon you, seeing all the congregation are holy, every one of them, and the LORD is among them: wherefore then lift you up yourselves above the congregation of the LORD?' ⁴And when Moses heard it, he fell upon his face. ⁵And he spoke unto Korah and unto all his company, saying, 'Even tomorrow the LORD will show who are his, and who is holy; and will cause him to come near unto him: even him whom he hath chosen will he cause to come near unto him. ⁶This do: take you censers, Korah, and all his company; ⁷and put fire therein, and put incense in them before the Lord tomorrow: and it shall be that the man whom the Lord doth choose, he shall be holy: ye take too much upon you, ye sons of Levi.' ⁸And Moses said unto Korah, 'Hear, I pray you, ye sons of Levi. ⁹Seemeth it but a small thing unto you, that the God of Israel hath separated you from the congregation of Israel, to bring you near to himself to do the service of the tabernacle of the Lord, and to stand before the congregation to minister unto them? ¹⁰And he hath brought thee near to him, and all thy brethren the sons of Levi with thee: and seek ye the priesthood also? ¹¹For which cause both thou and all thy company are gathered together against the Lord: and what is Aaron, that ye murmur against him?'

¹²And Moses sent to call Dathan and Abiram, the sons of Eliab: which said, 'We will not come up. ¹³Is it a small thing that thou hast brought us up out of a land that floweth with milk and honey, to kill us in the wilderness, except thou make thyself altogether a prince over us? ¹⁴Moreover thou hast not brought us into a land that floweth with milk and honey, or given us inheritance of fields and vineyards: wilt thou put out the eyes of these men? we will not come up.' ¹⁵And Moses was very wroth, and said unto the Lord, 'Respect not thou their offering: I have not taken one ass from them, neither have I hurt one of them'. ¹⁶And Moses said unto Korah, 'Be thou and all thy company before the Lord, thou, and they, and Aaron, tomorrow. ¹⁷And take every man his censer, and put incense in them, and bring ye before the Lord every man his censer, two hundred and fifty censers; thou also, and Aaron, each of you his censer.' ¹⁸And they took every man his censer, and put fire in them, and laid incense thereon, and stood in the door of the tabernacle of the congregation with Moses and Aaron. ¹⁹And Korah gathered all the congregation against them unto the door of the tabernacle of the congregation: and the glory of the Lord appeared unto all the congregation.

²⁰And the Lord spoke unto Moses and unto Aaron, saying, ²¹'Separate yourselves from among this congregation, that I may consume them in a moment'. ²²And they fell upon their faces, and said, 'O God, the God of the spirits of all flesh, shall one man sin, and wilt thou be wroth with all the congregation?' ²³And the Lord spoke unto Moses, saying, ²⁴'Speak unto the congregation, saying, "Get you up from about the tabernacle of Korah, Dathan, and Abiram"'. ²⁵And Moses rose up and went unto Dathan and Abiram; and the elders of Israel followed him. ²⁶And he spoke unto the congregation, saying, 'Depart, I pray you, from the tents of these wicked men, and touch nothing of theirs, lest ye be consumed in all their sins'. ²⁷So they got up from the tabernacle of Korah, Dathan, and Abiram, on every side: and Dathan and Abiram came out, and stood in the door of their tents, and their wives, and their sons, and their little children. ²⁸And Moses said, 'Hereby ye shall know that the Lord hath sent me to do all these works: for I have not done them of my own mind. ²⁹If these men die the common death of all men, or if they be visited after the visitation of all men, then the

LORD hath not sent me: [30]but if the LORD make a new thing, and the earth open her mouth, and swallow them up, with all that appertain unto them, and they go down quick into the pit: then ye shall understand that these men have provoked the LORD.'

[31]And it came to pass, as he had made an end of speaking all these words, that the ground cleft asunder that was under them: [32]and the earth opened her mouth, and swallowed them up, and their houses, and all the men that appertained unto Korah, and all their goods. [33]They, and all that appertained to them, went down alive into the pit, and the earth closed upon them: and they perished from among the congregation. [34]And all Israel that were round about them fled at the cry of them: for they said, 'Lest the earth swallow us up also'. [35]And there came out a fire from the LORD, and consumed the two hundred and fifty men that offered incense.

[36]And the LORD spoke unto Moses, saying, [37]'Speak unto Eleazar the son of Aaron the priest, that he take up the censers out of the burning, and scatter thou the fire yonder, for they are hallowed. [38]The censers of these sinners against their own souls, let them make them broad plates for a covering of the altar: for they offered them before the LORD, therefore they are hallowed: and they shall be a sign unto the children of Israel.' [39]And Eleazar the priest took the brazen censers, wherewith they that were burnt had offered, and they were made broad plates for a covering of the altar: [40]to be a memorial unto the children of Israel, that no stranger, which is not of the seed of Aaron, come near to offer incense before the LORD; that he be not as Korah, and as his company, as the LORD said to him by the hand of Moses.

[41]But on the morrow all the congregation of the children of Israel murmured against Moses and against Aaron, saying, 'Ye have killed the people of the LORD'. [42]And it came to pass, when the congregation was gathered against Moses and against Aaron, that they looked toward the tabernacle of the congregation: and, behold, the cloud covered it, and the glory of the LORD appeared. [43]And Moses and Aaron came before the tabernacle of the congregation. [44]And the LORD spoke unto Moses, saying, [45]'Get you up from among this congregation, that I may consume them as in a moment'. And they fell upon their faces. [46]And Moses said unto Aaron, 'Take a censer, and put fire therein from off the altar, and put on incense, and go quickly unto the congregation, and make an atonement for them: for there is wrath gone out from the LORD; the plague is begun'. [47]And Aaron took as Moses commanded, and ran into the midst of the congregation; and behold, the plague was begun among the people: and he put on incense, and made an atonement for the people. [48]And he stood between the dead and the living; and the plague was stayed. [49]Now they that died in the plague were fourteen thousand and seven hundred, besides them that died about the matter of Korah. [50]And Aaron returned unto Moses unto the door of the tabernacle of the congregation: and the plague was stayed.

17 And the LORD spoke unto Moses, saying, [2]'Speak unto the children of Israel, and take of every one of them a rod according to the house of their fathers, of all their princes according to the house of their fathers twelve rods: write thou every man's name upon his rod. ³And thou shalt write Aaron's name upon the rod of Levi: for one rod shall be for the head of the house of their fathers. ⁴And thou shalt lay them up in the tabernacle of the congregation before the testimony, where I will meet with you. ⁵And it shall come to pass, that the man's rod, whom I shall choose, shall blossom: and I will make to cease from me the murmurings of the children of Israel, whereby they murmur against you.'

⁶And Moses spoke unto the children of Israel, and every one of their princes gave him a rod apiece, for each prince one, according to their fathers' houses, even twelve rods: and the rod of Aaron was among their rods. ⁷And Moses laid up the rods before the LORD in the tabernacle of witness. ⁸And it came to pass that on the morrow Moses went into the tabernacle of witness, and behold, the rod of Aaron for the house of Levi was budded, and brought forth buds, and bloomed blossoms, and yielded almonds. ⁹And Moses brought out all the rods from before the LORD unto all the children of Israel: and they looked, and took every man his rod.

¹⁰And the LORD said unto Moses, 'Bring Aaron's rod again before the testimony, to be kept for a token against the rebels, and thou shalt quite take away their murmurings from me, that they die not'. ¹¹And Moses did so: as the LORD commanded him, so did he. ¹²And the children of Israel spoke unto Moses, saying, 'Behold, we die, we perish, we all perish. ¹³Whosoever cometh anything near unto the tabernacle of the LORD shall die: shall we be consumed with dying?'

18 And the LORD said unto Aaron, 'Thou and thy sons and thy father's house with thee shall bear the iniquity of the sanctuary: and thou and thy sons with thee shall bear the iniquity of your priesthood. ²And thy brethren also of the tribe of Levi, the tribe of thy father, bring thou with thee, that they may be joined unto thee, and minister unto thee: but thou and thy sons with thee shall minister before the tabernacle of witness. ³And they shall keep thy charge, and the charge of all the tabernacle: only they shall not come nigh the vessels of the sanctuary and the altar, that neither they, nor you also, die. ⁴And they shall be joined unto thee, and keep the charge of the tabernacle of the congregation, for all the service of the tabernacle: and a stranger shall not come nigh unto you. ⁵And ye shall keep the charge of the sanctuary, and the charge of the altar: that there be no wrath any more upon the children of Israel. ⁶And I, behold, I have taken your brethren the Levites from among the children of Israel: to you they are given as a gift for the LORD, to do the service of the tabernacle of the congregation. ⁷Therefore thou and thy sons with thee shall keep your priest's office for everything of the altar, and within the veil; and ye shall serve: I have given your priest's office unto you as a service of gift: and the stranger that cometh nigh shall be put to death.'

⁸And the LORD spoke unto Aaron, 'Behold, I also have given thee the charge of my heave offerings of all the hallowed things of the children

of Israel; unto thee have I given them by reason of the anointing, and to thy sons, by an ordinance for ever. ⁹This shall be thine of the most holy things, reserved from the fire: every oblation of theirs, every meat offering of theirs, and every sin offering of theirs, and every trespass offering of theirs, which they shall render unto me, shall be most holy for thee and for thy sons. ¹⁰In the most holy place shalt thou eat it; every male shall eat it: it shall be holy unto thee. ¹¹And this is thine: the heave offering of their gift, with all the wave offerings of the children of Israel: I have given them unto thee, and to thy sons and to thy daughters with thee, by a statute for ever: every one that is clean in thy house shall eat of it. ¹²All the best of the oil, and all the best of the wine, and of the wheat, the first-fruits of them which they shall offer unto the LORD, them have I given thee. ¹³And whatsoever is first ripe in the land, which they shall bring unto the LORD, shall be thine; every one that is clean in thy house shall eat of it. ¹⁴Everything devoted in Israel shall be thine. ¹⁵Everything that openeth the matrix in all flesh, which they bring unto the LORD, whether it be of men or beasts, shall be thine: nevertheless the firstborn of man shalt thou surely redeem, and the firstling of unclean beasts shalt thou redeem. ¹⁶And those that are to be redeemed from a month old shalt thou redeem, according to thy estimation, for the money of five shekels, after the shekel of the sanctuary, which is twenty gerahs. ¹⁷But the firstling of a cow, or the firstling of a sheep, or the firstling of a goat, thou shalt not redeem; they are holy: thou shalt sprinkle their blood upon the altar, and shalt burn their fat for an offering made by fire, for a sweet savour unto the LORD. ¹⁸And the flesh of them shall be thine, as the wave breast and as the right shoulder are thine. ¹⁹All the heave offerings of the holy things, which the children of Israel offer unto the LORD, have I given thee, and thy sons and thy daughters with thee, by a statute for ever: it is a covenant of salt for ever before the LORD unto thee and to thy seed with thee.'

²⁰And the LORD spoke unto Aaron, 'Thou shalt have no inheritance in their land, neither shalt thou have any part among them: I am thy part and thy inheritance among the children of Israel. ²¹And behold, I have given the children of Levi all the tenth in Israel for an inheritance, for their service which they serve, even the service of the tabernacle of the congregation. ²²Neither must the children of Israel henceforth come nigh the tabernacle of the congregation, lest they bear sin, and die. ²³But the Levites shall do the service of the tabernacle of the congregation, and they shall bear their iniquity: it shall be a statute for ever throughout your generations, that among the children of Israel they have no inheritance. ²⁴But the tithes of the children of Israel which they offer as a heave offering unto the LORD, I have given to the Levites to inherit: therefore I have said unto them, among the children of Israel they shall have no inheritance.'

²⁵And the LORD spoke unto Moses, saying, ²⁶'Thus speak unto the Levites, and say unto them, "When ye take of the children of Israel the tithes which I have given you from them for your inheritance, then ye shall offer up a heave offering of it for the LORD, even a tenth part of

the tithe. ²⁷And this your heave offering shall be reckoned unto you, as though it were the corn of the threshing-floor, and as the fulness of the wine-press. ²⁸Thus you also shall offer a heave offering unto the LORD of all your tithes which ye receive of the children of Israel; and ye shall give thereof the LORD's heave offering to Aaron the priest. ²⁹Out of all your gifts ye shall offer every heave offering of the LORD, of all the best thereof, even the hallowed part thereof out of it. ³⁰Therefore thou shalt say unto them, when ye have heaved the best thereof from it, then it shall be counted unto the Levites as the increase of the threshing-floor, and as the increase of the wine-press. ³¹And ye shall eat it in every place, ye and your households: for it is your reward for your service in the tabernacle of the congregation. ³²And ye shall bear no sin by reason of it, when ye have heaved from it the best of it: neither shall ye pollute the holy things of the children of Israel, lest ye die."'

19 And the LORD spoke unto Moses and unto Aaron, saying, ²'This is the ordinance of the law which the LORD hath commanded, saying, "Speak unto the children of Israel, that they bring thee a red heifer without spot, wherein is no blemish, and upon which never came yoke. ³And ye shall give her unto Eleazar the priest, that he may bring her forth without the camp, and one shall slay her before his face. ⁴And Eleazar the priest shall take of her blood with his finger, and sprinkle of her blood directly before the tabernacle of the congregation seven times. ⁵And one shall burn the heifer in his sight: her skin, and her flesh, and her blood, with her dung, shall he burn. ⁶And the priest shall take cedar wood, and hyssop, and scarlet, and cast it into the midst of the burning of the heifer. ⁷Then the priest shall wash his clothes, and he shall bathe his flesh in water, and afterward he shall come into the camp, and the priest shall be unclean until the even. ⁸And he that burneth her shall wash his clothes in water, and bathe his flesh in water, and shall be unclean until the even. ⁹And a man that is clean shall gather up the ashes of the heifer, and lay them up without the camp in a clean place, and it shall be kept for the congregation of the children of Israel for a water of separation: it is a purification for sin. ¹⁰And he that gathereth the ashes of the heifer shall wash his clothes, and be unclean until the even: and it shall be unto the children of Israel, and unto the stranger that sojourneth among them, for a statute for ever.

¹¹'"He that toucheth the dead body of any man shall be unclean seven days. ¹²He shall purify himself with it on the third day, and on the seventh day he shall be clean: but if he purify not himself the third day, then the seventh day he shall not be clean. ¹³Whosoever toucheth the dead body of any man that is dead, and purifieth not himself, defileth the tabernacle of the LORD, and that soul shall be cut off from Israel, because the water of separation was not sprinkled upon him: he shall be unclean, his uncleanness is yet upon him. ¹⁴This is the law, when a man dieth in a tent: all that come into the tent, and all that is in the tent, shall be unclean seven days. ¹⁵And every open vessel which hath no covering bound upon it, is unclean. ¹⁶And whosoever toucheth one

that is slain with a sword in the open fields, or a dead body, or a bone of a man, or a grave, shall be unclean seven days. [17]And for an unclean person they shall take of the ashes of the burnt heifer of purification for sin, and running water shall be put thereto in a vessel: [18]and a clean person shall take hyssop, and dip it in the water, and sprinkle it upon the tent, and upon all the vessels, and upon the persons that were there, and upon him that touched a bone, or one slain, or one dead, or a grave. [19]And the clean person shall sprinkle upon the unclean on the third day, and on the seventh day: and on the seventh day he shall purify himself, and wash his clothes, and bathe himself in water, and shall be clean at even. [20]But the man that shall be unclean, and shall not purify himself, that soul shall be cut off from among the congregation, because he hath defiled the sanctuary of the LORD: the water of separation hath not been sprinkled upon him; he is unclean. [21]And it shall be a perpetual statute unto them, that he that sprinkleth the water of separation shall wash his clothes; and he that toucheth the water of separation shall be unclean until even. [22]And whatsoever the unclean person toucheth shall be unclean; and the soul that toucheth it shall be unclean until even."'

20 Then came the children of Israel, even the whole congregation, into the desert of Zin in the first month: and the people abode in Kadesh; and Miriam died there, and was buried there. [2]And there was no water for the congregation: and they gathered themselves together against Moses and against Aaron. [3]And the people chided with Moses, and spoke, saying, 'Would God that we had died when our brethren died before the LORD. [4]And why have ye brought up the congregation of the LORD into this wilderness, that we and our cattle should die there? [5]And wherefore have ye made us to come up out of Egypt, to bring us in unto this evil place? it is no place of seed, or of figs, or vines, or of pomegranates, neither is there any water to drink.' [6]And Moses and Aaron went from the presence of the assembly unto the door of the tabernacle of the congregation, and they fell upon their faces: and the glory of the LORD appeared unto them.

[7]And the LORD spoke unto Moses, saying, [8]'Take the rod, and gather thou the assembly together, thou, and Aaron thy brother, and speak ye unto the rock before their eyes, and it shall give forth his water, and thou shalt bring forth to them water out of the rock: so thou shalt give the congregation and their beasts drink'. [9]And Moses took the rod from before the LORD, as he commanded him. [10]And Moses and Aaron gathered the congregation together before the rock, and he said unto them, 'Hear now, ye rebels; must we fetch you water out of this rock?' [11]And Moses lifted up his hand, and with his rod he smote the rock twice: and the water came out abundantly, and the congregation drank, and their beasts also.

[12]And the LORD spoke unto Moses and Aaron, 'Because ye believed me not, to sanctify me in the eyes of the children of Israel, therefore ye shall not bring this congregation into the land which I have given them'. [13]This is the water of Meribah, because the children of Israel strove with the LORD; and he was sanctified in them.

¹⁴And Moses sent messengers from Kadesh unto the king of Edom: 'Thus saith thy brother Israel, "Thou knowest all the travail that hath befallen us: ¹⁵how our fathers went down into Egypt, and we have dwelt in Egypt a long time: and the Egyptians vexed us, and our fathers. ¹⁶And when we cried unto the LORD, he heard our voice, and sent an angel, and hath brought us forth out of Egypt: and behold, we are in Kadesh, a city in the outermost of thy border. ¹⁷Let us pass, I pray thee, through thy country: we will not pass through the fields, or through the vineyards, neither will we drink of the water of the wells: we will go by the king's highway, we will not turn to the right hand nor to the left, until we have passed thy borders."' ¹⁸And Edom said unto him, 'Thou shalt not pass by me, lest I come out against thee with the sword'. ¹⁹And the children of Israel said unto him, 'We will go by the highway: and if I and my cattle drink of thy water, then I will pay for it: I will only, without doing anything else, go through on my feet'. ²⁰And he said, 'Thou shalt not go through'. And Edom came out against him with much people, and with a strong hand. ²¹Thus Edom refused to give Israel passage through his border: wherefore Israel turned away from him.

²²And the children of Israel, even the whole congregation, journeyed from Kadesh, and came unto mount Hor. ²³And the LORD spoke unto Moses and Aaron in mount Hor, by the coast of the land of Edom, saying, ²⁴'Aaron shall be gathered unto his people: for he shall not enter into the land which I have given unto the children of Israel, because ye rebelled against my word at the water of Meribah. ²⁵Take Aaron and Eleazar his son, and bring them up unto mount Hor: ²⁶and strip Aaron of his garments, and put them upon Eleazar his son: and Aaron shall be gathered unto his people, and shall die there.' ²⁷And Moses did as the LORD commanded: and they went up into mount Hor in the sight of all the congregation. ²⁸And Moses stripped Aaron of his garments, and put them upon Eleazar his son; and Aaron died there in the top of the mount: and Moses and Eleazar came down from the mount. ²⁹And when all the congregation saw that Aaron was dead, they mourned for Aaron thirty days, even all the house of Israel.

21 And when king Arad the Canaanite, which dwelt in the south, heard tell that Israel came by the way of the spies, then he fought against Israel, and took some of them prisoners. ²And Israel vowed a vow unto the LORD, and said, 'If thou wilt indeed deliver this people into my hand, then I will utterly destroy their cities'. ³And the LORD hearkened to the voice of Israel, and delivered up the Canaanites: and they utterly destroyed them and their cities, and he called the name of the place Hormah.

⁴And they journeyed from mount Hor by the way of the Red Sea, to compass the land of Edom: and the soul of the people was much discouraged because of the way. ⁵And the people spoke against God, and against Moses, 'Wherefore have ye brought us up out of Egypt to die in the wilderness? for there is no bread, neither is there any water; and our soul loatheth this light bread'. ⁶And the LORD sent fiery serpents among the people, and they bit the people, and much people of Israel

died. [7]Therefore the people came to Moses, and said, 'We have sinned, for we have spoken against the LORD, and against thee: pray unto the LORD, that he take away the serpents from us'. And Moses prayed for the people. [8]And the LORD said unto Moses, 'Make thee a fiery serpent, and set it upon a pole: and it shall come to pass, that every one that is bitten, when he looketh upon it, shall live'. [9]And Moses made a serpent of brass, and put it upon a pole, and it came to pass, that if a serpent had bitten any man, when he beheld the serpent of brass, he lived.

[10]And the children of Israel set forward, and pitched in Oboth. [11]And they journeyed from Oboth, and pitched at Ije-abarim, in the wilderness which is before Moab, toward the sunrising. [12]From thence they removed, and pitched in the valley of Zared. [13]From thence they removed, and pitched on the other side of Arnon, which is in the wilderness that cometh out of the coasts of the Amorites: for Arnon is the border of Moab, between Moab and the Amorites. [14]Wherefore it is said in the book of the wars of the LORD, 'What he did in the Red Sea, and in the brooks of Arnon, [15]and at the stream of the brooks that goeth down to the dwelling of Ar, and lieth upon the border of Moab'. [16]And from thence they went to Beer: that is the well whereof the LORD spoke unto Moses, 'Gather the people together, and I will give them water'.

[17]Then Israel sang this song,

'Spring up, O well, sing ye unto it:
[18]   the princes dug the well,
   the nobles of the people dug it,
      by the direction of the lawgiver, with their staves'.

And from the wilderness they went to Mattanah: [19]and from Mattanah to Nahaliel: and from Nahaliel to Bamoth: [20]and from Bamoth in the valley, that is in the country of Moab, to the top of Pisgah, which looketh toward Jeshimon.

[21]And Israel sent messengers unto Sihon king of the Amorites, saying, [22]'Let me pass through thy land: we will not turn into the fields, or into the vineyards; we will not drink of the waters of the well: but we will go along by the king's highway, until we be past thy borders'. [23]And Sihon would not suffer Israel to pass through his border: but Sihon gathered all his people together, and went out against Israel into the wilderness: and he came to Jahaz, and fought against Israel. [24]And Israel smote him with the edge of the sword, and possessed his land from Arnon unto Jabbok, even unto the children of Ammon: for the border of the children of Ammon was strong. [25]And Israel took all these cities: and Israel dwelt in all the cities of the Amorites, in Heshbon, and in all the villages thereof. [26]For Heshbon was the city of Sihon the king of the Amorites, who had fought against the former king of Moab, and taken all his land out of his hand, even unto Arnon. [27]Wherefore they that speak in proverbs say,

'Come into Heshbon:
let the city of Sihon be built and prepared.
[28] For there is a fire gone out of Heshbon,
a flame from the city of Sihon:
it hath consumed Ar of Moab,
and the lords of the high places of Arnon.
[29] Woe to thee, Moab,
thou art undone, O people of Chemosh:
he hath given his sons that escaped, and his daughters,
into captivity unto Sihon king of the Amorites.
[30] We have shot at them;
Heshbon is perished even unto Dibon,
and we have laid them waste even unto Nophah,
which reacheth unto Medeba.'

[31]Thus Israel dwelt in the land of the Amorites. [32]And Moses sent to spy out Jaazer, and they took the villages thereof, and drove out the Amorites that were there.

[33]And they turned and went up by the way of Bashan: and Og the king of Bashan went out against them, he, and all his people, to the battle at Edrei. [34]And the LORD said unto Moses, 'Fear him not: for I have delivered him into thy hand, and all his people, and his land; and thou shalt do to him as thou didst unto Sihon king of the Amorites, which dwelt at Heshbon'. [35]So they smote him, and his sons, and all his people, until there was none left him alive: and they possessed his land.

22 And the children of Israel set forward, and pitched in the plains of Moab on this side Jordan by Jericho. [2]And Balak the son of Zippor saw all that Israel had done to the Amorites. [3]And Moab was sore afraid of the people, because they were many: and Moab was distressed because of the children of Israel. [4]And Moab said unto the elders of Midian, 'Now shall this company lick up all that are round about us, as the ox licketh up the grass of the field'. And Balak the son of Zippor was king of the Moabites at that time. [5]He sent messengers therefore unto Balaam the son of Beor to Pethor, which is by the river of the land of the children of his people, to call him, saying, 'Behold, there is a people come out from Egypt: behold, they cover the face of the earth, and they abide over against me. [6]Come now therefore, I pray thee, curse me this people; for they are too mighty for me: peradventure I shall prevail, that we may smite them, and that I may drive them out of the land: for I wot that he whom thou blessest is blessed, and he whom thou cursest is cursed.' [7]And the elders of Moab and the elders of Midian departed with the rewards of divination in their hand; and they came unto Balaam, and spoke unto him the words of Balak. [8]And he said unto them, 'Lodge here this night, and I will bring you word again, as the LORD shall speak unto me': and the princes of Moab abode with Balaam. [9]And God came unto Balaam, and said, 'What men are these with thee?' [10]And Balaam said unto God, 'Balak the son of Zippor, king

of Moab, hath sent unto me, saying, [11]"Behold, there is a people come out of Egypt, which covereth the face of the earth: come now, curse me them; peradventure I shall be able to overcome them, and drive them out"'. [12]And God said unto Balaam, 'Thou shalt not go with them, thou shalt not curse the people: for they are blessed'. [13]And Balaam rose up in the morning, and said unto the princes of Balak, 'Get you into your land: for the LORD refuseth to give me leave to go with you'. [14]And the princes of Moab rose up, and they went unto Balak, and said, 'Balaam refuseth to come with us'.

[15]And Balak sent yet again princes, more, and more honourable than they. [16]And they came to Balaam, and said to him, 'Thus saith Balak the son of Zippor, "Let nothing, I pray thee, hinder thee from coming unto me: [17]for I will promote thee unto very great honour, and I will do whatsoever thou sayest unto me: come therefore, I pray thee, curse me this people"'. [18]And Balaam answered and said unto the servants of Balak, 'If Balak would give me his house full of silver and gold, I cannot go beyond the word of the LORD my God, to do less or more. [19]Now therefore, I pray you, tarry ye also here this night, that I may know what the LORD will say unto me more.' [20]And God came unto Balaam at night, and said unto him, 'If the men come to call thee, rise up, and go with them; but yet the word which I shall say unto thee, that shalt thou do'. [21]And Balaam rose up in the morning, and saddled his ass, and went with the princes of Moab.

[22]And God's anger was kindled because he went: and the angel of the LORD stood in the way for an adversary against him. Now he was riding upon his ass, and his two servants were with him. [23]And the ass saw the angel of the LORD standing in the way, and his sword drawn in his hand: and the ass turned aside out of the way, and went into the field: and Balaam smote the ass, to turn her into the way. [24]But the angel of the LORD stood in a path of the vineyards, a wall being on this side, and a wall on that side. [25]And when the ass saw the angel of the LORD, she thrust herself unto the wall, and crushed Balaam's foot against the wall: and he smote her again. [26]And the angel of the LORD went farther, and stood in a narrow place, where was no way to turn either to the right hand or to the left. [27]And when the ass saw the angel of the LORD, she fell down under Balaam: and Balaam's anger was kindled, and he smote the ass with a staff. [28]And the LORD opened the mouth of the ass, and she said unto Balaam, 'What have I done unto thee, that thou hast smitten me these three times?' [29]And Balaam said unto the ass, 'Because thou hast mocked me: I would there were a sword in my hand, for now would I kill thee'. [30]And the ass said unto Balaam, 'Am not I thy ass, upon which thou hast ridden ever since I was thine unto this day? was I ever wont to do so unto thee?' And he said, 'Nay'. [31]Then the LORD opened the eyes of Balaam, and he saw the angel of the LORD standing in the way, and his sword drawn in his hand: and he bowed down his head, and fell flat on his face. [32]And the angel of the LORD said unto him, 'Wherefore hast thou smitten thy ass these three times? Behold, I went out to withstand thee, because thy way is perverse before

me. ³³And the ass saw me, and turned from me these three times: unless she had turned from me, surely now also I had slain thee, and saved her alive.' ³⁴And Balaam said unto the angel of the Lord, 'I have sinned: for I knew not that thou stoodest in the way against me: now therefore, if it displease thee, I will get me back again'. ³⁵And the angel of the Lord said unto Balaam, 'Go with the men: but only the word that I shall speak unto thee, that thou shalt speak'. So Balaam went with the princes of Balak.

³⁶And when Balak heard that Balaam was come, he went out to meet him unto a city of Moab, which is in the border of Arnon, which is in the utmost coast. ³⁷And Balak said unto Balaam, 'Did I not earnestly send unto thee to call thee? wherefore camest thou not unto me? Am I not able indeed to promote thee to honour?' ³⁸And Balaam said unto Balak, 'Lo, I am come unto thee: have I now any power at all to say anything? the word that God putteth in my mouth, that shall I speak'. ³⁹And Balaam went with Balak, and they came unto Kirjathhuzoth. ⁴⁰And Balak offered oxen and sheep, and sent to Balaam, and to the princes that were with him. ⁴¹And it came to pass on the morrow, that Balak took Balaam, and brought him up into the high places of Baal, that thence he might see the utmost part of the people.

23 And Balaam said unto Balak, 'Build me here seven altars, and prepare me here seven oxen and seven rams'. ²And Balak did as Balaam had spoken; and Balak and Balaam offered on every altar a bullock and a ram. ³And Balaam said unto Balak, 'Stand by thy burnt offering, and I will go: peradventure the Lord will come to meet me: and whatsoever he showeth me I will tell thee'. And he went to a high place. ⁴And God met Balaam, and he said unto him, 'I have prepared seven altars, and I have offered upon every altar a bullock and a ram'. ⁵And the Lord put a word in Balaam's mouth, and said, 'Return unto Balak, and thus thou shalt speak'. ⁶And he returned unto him, and lo, he stood by his burnt sacrifice, he, and all the princes of Moab. ⁷And he took up his parable, and said,

> 'Balak the king of Moab hath brought me from Aram,
> out of the mountains of the east,
> saying, "Come, curse me Jacob, and come, defy Israel".
> ⁸ How shall I curse, whom God hath not cursed?
> or how shall I defy, whom the Lord hath not defied?
> ⁹ For from the top of the rocks I see him,
> and from the hills I behold him:
> lo, the people shall dwell alone,
> and shall not be reckoned among the nations.
> ¹⁰ Who can count the dust of Jacob,
> and the number of the fourth part of Israel?
> Let me die the death of the righteous,
> and let my last end be like his.'

¹¹And Balak said unto Balaam, 'What hast thou done unto me? I took

thee to curse my enemies, and behold, thou hast blessed them alto-gether.' ¹²And he answered and said, 'Must I not take heed to speak that which the LORD hath put in my mouth?' ¹³And Balak said unto him, 'Come, I pray thee, with me unto another place, from whence thou mayest see them: thou shalt see but the outmost part of them, and shalt not see them all: and curse me them from thence'.

¹⁴And he brought him into the field of Zophim, to the top of Pisgah, and built seven altars, and offered a bullock and a ram on every altar. ¹⁵And he said unto Balak, 'Stand here by thy burnt offering, while I meet the LORD yonder'. ¹⁶And the LORD met Balaam, and put a word in his mouth, and said, 'Go again unto Balak, and say thus'. ¹⁷And when he came to him, behold, he stood by his burnt offering, and the princes of Moab with him. And Balak said unto him, 'What hath the LORD spoken?' ¹⁸And he took up his parable, and said,

'Rise up, Balak, and hear;
hearken unto me, thou son of Zippor:
¹⁹ God is not a man, that he should lie,
neither the son of man, that he should repent:
hath he said, and shall he not do it?
or hath he spoken, and shall he not make it good?
²⁰ Behold, I have received commandment to bless:
and he hath blessed, and I cannot reverse it.
²¹ He hath not beheld iniquity in Jacob,
neither hath he seen perverseness in Israel:
the LORD his God is with him,
and the shout of a king is among them.
²² God brought them out of Egypt;
he hath as it were the strength of an unicorn.
²³ Surely there is no enchantment against Jacob,
neither is there any divination against Israel:
according to this time it shall be said of Jacob and of Israel,
"What hath God wrought!"
²⁴ Behold, the people shall rise up as a great lion,
and lift up himself as a young lion:
he shall not lie down until he eat of the prey,
and drink the blood of the slain.'

²⁵And Balak said unto Balaam, 'Neither curse them at all, nor bless them at all'. ²⁶But Balaam answered and said unto Balak, 'Told not I thee, saying, "All that the LORD speaketh, that I must do?"'

²⁷And Balak said unto Balaam, 'Come, I pray thee, I will bring thee unto another place; peradventure it will please God that thou mayest curse me them from thence'. ²⁸And Balak brought Balaam unto the top of Peor, that looketh toward Jeshimon. ²⁹And Balaam said unto Balak, 'Build me here seven altars, and prepare me here seven bullocks and seven rams'. ³⁰And Balak did as Balaam had said, and offered a bullock and a ram on every altar.

24 And when Balaam saw that it pleased the LORD to bless Israel, he went not, as at other times, to seek for enchantments, but he set his face toward the wilderness. ²And Balaam lifted up his eyes, and he saw Israel abiding in his tents according to their tribes: and the Spirit of God came upon him. ³And he took up his parable, and said,

'Balaam the son of Beor hath said,
and the man whose eyes are open hath said:
⁴ he hath said, which heard the words of God,
which saw the vision of the Almighty,
falling into a trance, but having his eyes open:
⁵ "How goodly are thy tents,
O Jacob, and thy tabernacles, O Israel!
⁶ As the valleys are they spread forth,
as gardens by the river's side,
as the trees of lign-aloes which the LORD hath planted,
and as cedar trees beside the waters.
⁷ He shall pour the water out of his buckets,
and his seed shall be in many waters,
and his king shall be higher than Agag,
and his kingdom shall be exalted.
⁸ God brought him forth out of Egypt;
he hath as it were the strength of an unicorn:
he shall eat up the nations his enemies,
and shall break their bones,
and pierce them through with his arrows.
⁹ He couched, he lay down as a lion, and as a great lion:
who shall stir him up?
Blessed is he that blesseth thee,
and cursed is he that curseth thee."'

¹⁰And Balak's anger was kindled against Balaam, and he smote his hands together: and Balak said unto Balaam, 'I called thee to curse my enemies, and behold, thou hast altogether blessed them these three times. ¹¹Therefore now flee thou to thy place: I thought to promote thee unto great honour, but lo, the LORD hath kept thee back from honour.' ¹²And Balaam said unto Balak, 'Spoke I not also to thy messengers which thou sentest unto me, saying, ¹³"If Balak would give me his house full of silver and gold, I cannot go beyond the commandment of the LORD, to do either good or bad of my own mind; but what the LORD saith, that will I speak"? ¹⁴And now behold, I go unto my people: come therefore, and I will advertise thee what this people shall do to thy people in the latter days.'

¹⁵And he took up his parable, and said,

'Balaam the son of Beor hath said,
and the man whose eyes are open hath said:
¹⁶ He hath said, which heard the words of God,

and knew the knowledge of the most High,
which saw the vision of the Almighty,
falling into a trance, but having his eyes open:
¹⁷ "I shall see him, but not now:
I shall behold him, but not nigh:
there shall come a Star out of Jacob,
and a Sceptre shall rise out of Israel,
and shall smite the corners of Moab,
and destroy all the children of Sheth.
¹⁸ And Edom shall be a possession,
Seir also shall be a possession for his enemies,
and Israel shall do valiantly.
¹⁹ Out of Jacob shall come he that shall have dominion,
and shall destroy him that remaineth of the city."'

²⁰And when he looked on Amalek, he took up his parable, and said,

'Amalek was the first of the nations,
but his latter end shall be that he perish for ever'.

²¹And he looked on the Kenites, and took up his parable, and said,

'Strong is thy dwelling-place,
and thou puttest thy nest in a rock:
²² nevertheless the Kenite shall be wasted,
until Asshur shall carry thee away captive'.

²³And he took up his parable, and said,

'Alas! who shall live when God doeth this?
²⁴ And ships shall come from the coast of Chittim,
and shall afflict Asshur, and shall afflict Eber,
and he also shall perish for ever.'

²⁵And Balaam rose up, and went and returned to his place: and Balak also went his way.

25 And Israel abode in Shittim, and the people began to commit whoredom with the daughters of Moab. ²And they called the people unto the sacrifices of their gods: and the people did eat, and bowed down to their gods. ³And Israel joined himself unto Baal-peor: and the anger of the LORD was kindled against Israel. ⁴And the LORD said unto Moses, 'Take all the heads of the people, and hang them up before the LORD against the sun, that the fierce anger of the LORD may be turned away from Israel'. ⁵And Moses said unto the judges of Israel, 'Slay ye every one his men that were joined unto Baal-peor'.

⁶And behold, one of the children of Israel came and brought unto his brethren a Midianitish woman in the sight of Moses, and in the sight of all the congregation of the children of Israel, who were weeping before

the door of the tabernacle of the congregation. ⁷And when Phinehas the son of Eleazar, the son of Aaron the priest, saw it, he rose up from amongst the congregation, and took a javelin in his hand. ⁸And he went after the man of Israel into the tent, and thrust both of them through, the man of Israel, and the woman through her belly. So the plague was stayed from the children of Israel. ⁹And those that died in the plague were twenty and four thousand.

¹⁰And the Lord spoke unto Moses, saying, ¹¹'Phinehas, the son of Eleazar, the son of Aaron the priest, hath turned my wrath away from the children of Israel, while he was zealous for my sake among them, that I consumed not the children of Israel in my jealousy. ¹²Wherefore say, "Behold, I give unto him my covenant of peace. ¹³And he shall have it, and his seed after him, even the covenant of an everlasting priest-hood, because he was zealous for his God, and made an atonement for the children of Israel."' ¹⁴Now the name of the Israelite that was slain, even that was slain with the Midianitish woman, was Zimri, the son of Salu, a prince of a chief house among the Simeonites. ¹⁵And the name of the Midianitish woman that was slain was Cozbi, the daughter of Zur; he was head over a people, and of a chief house in Midian.

¹⁶And the Lord spoke unto Moses, saying, ¹⁷'Vex the Midianites, and smite them: ¹⁸for they vex you with their wiles, wherewith they have beguiled you in the matter of Peor, and in the matter of Cozbi, the daughter of a prince of Midian, their sister, which was slain in the day of the plague for Peor's sake'.

26 And it came to pass after the plague, that the Lord spoke unto Moses and unto Eleazar the son of Aaron the priest, saying, ²'Take the sum of all the congregation of the children of Israel, from twenty years old and upward, throughout their fathers' house, all that are able to go to war in Israel'. ³And Moses and Eleazar the priest spoke with them in the plains of Moab by Jordan near Jericho, saying, ⁴'Take the sum of the people, from twenty years old and upward', as the Lord commanded Moses and the children of Israel, which went forth out of the land of Egypt.

⁵Reuben, the eldest son of Israel: the children of Reuben, Hanoch, of whom cometh the family of the Hanochites: of Pallu, the family of the Palluites: ⁶of Hezron, the family of the Hezronites: of Carmi, the family of the Carmites. ⁷These are the families of the Reubenites: and they that were numbered of them were forty and three thousand and seven hundred and thirty. ⁸And the sons of Pallu, Eliab. ⁹And the sons of Eliab, Nemuel, and Dathan, and Abiram. This is that Dathan and Abiram, which were famous in the congregation, who strove against Moses and against Aaron in the company of Korah, when they strove against the Lord: ¹⁰and the earth opened her mouth, and swallowed them up together with Korah, when that company died, what time the fire devoured two hundred and fifty men: and they became a sign. ¹¹Notwithstanding the children of Korah died not.

¹²The sons of Simeon after their families: of Nemuel, the family of the Nemuelites: of Jamin, the family of the Jaminites: of Jachin, the

family of the Jachinites: [13]of Zerah, the family of the Zarhites: of Shaul, the family of the Shaulites. [14]These are the families of the Simeonites, twenty and two thousand and two hundred.

[15]The children of Gad after their families: of Zephon, the family of the Zephonites: of Haggi, the family of the Haggites: of Shuni, the family of the Shunites: [16]of Ozni, the family of the Oznites: of Eri, the family of the Erites: [17]of Arod, the family of the Arodites: of Areli, the family of the Arelites. [18]These are the families of the children of Gad according to those that were numbered of them, forty thousand and five hundred.

[19]The sons of Judah were Er and Onan: and Er and Onan died in the land of Canaan. [20]And the sons of Judah after their families were: of Shelah, the family of the Shelanites: of Pharez, the family of the Pharzites: of Zerah, the family of the Zarhites. [21]And the sons of Pharez were: of Hezron, the family of the Hezronites: of Hamul, the family of the Hamulites. [22]These are the families of Judah according to those that were numbered of them, threescore and sixteen thousand and five hundred.

[23]Of the sons of Issachar after their families: of Tola, the family of the Tolaites: of Pua, the family of the Punites: [24]of Jashub, the family of the Jashubites: of Shimron, the family of the Shimronites. [25]These are the families of Issachar according to those that were numbered of them, threescore and four thousand and three hundred.

[26]Of the sons of Zebulun after their families: of Sered, the family of the Sardites: of Elon, the family of the Elonites: of Jahleel, the family of the Jahleelites. [27]These are the families of the Zebulunites according to those that were numbered of them, threescore thousand and five hundred.

[28]The sons of Joseph after their families were Manasseh and Ephraim. [29]Of the sons of Manasseh: of Machir, the family of the Machirites: and Machir begot Gilead: of Gilead come the family of the Gileadites. [30]These are the sons of Gilead: of Jeezer, the family of the Jeezerites: of Helek, the family of the Helekites: [31]and of Asriel, the family of the Asrielites: and of Shechem, the family of the Shechemites: [32]and of Shemida, the family of the Shemidaites: and of Hepher, the family of the Hepherites.

[33]And Zelophehad the son of Hepher had no sons, but daughters: and the names of the daughters of Zelophehad were Mahlah, and Noah, Hoglah, Milcah, and Tirzah. [34]These are the families of Manasseh, and those that were numbered of them, fifty and two thousand and seven hundred.

[35]These are the sons of Ephraim after their families: of Shuthelah, the family of the Shuthalhites: of Becher, the family of the Bachrites: of Tahan, the family of the Tahanites. [36]And these are the sons of Shuthelah: of Eran, the family of the Eranites. [37]These are the families of the sons of Ephraim according to those that were numbered of them, thirty and two thousand and five hundred. These are the sons of Joseph after their families.

³⁸The sons of Benjamin after their families: of Bela, the family of the Belaites: of Ashbel, the family of the Ashbelites: of Ahiram, the family of the Ahiramites: ³⁹of Shupham, the family of the Shuphamites: of Hupham, the family of the Huphamites. ⁴⁰And the sons of Bela were Ard and Naaman: of Ard, the family of the Ardites: and of Naaman, the family of the Naamites. ⁴¹These are the sons of Benjamin after their families: and they that were numbered of them were forty and five thousand and six hundred.

⁴²These are the sons of Dan after their families: of Shuham, the family of the Shuhamites. These are the families of Dan after their families. ⁴³All the families of the Shuhamites, according to those that were numbered of them, were threescore and four thousand and four hundred.

⁴⁴Of the children of Asher after their families: of Jimnah, the family of the Jimnites: of Jesui, the family of the Jesuites: of Beriah, the family of the Beriites. ⁴⁵Of the sons of Beriah: of Heber, the family of the Heberites: of Malchiel, the family of the Malchielites. ⁴⁶And the name of the daughter of Asher was Sarah. ⁴⁷These are the families of the sons of Asher according to those that were numbered of them; who were fifty and three thousand and four hundred.

⁴⁸Of the sons of Naphtali after their families: of Jahzeel, the family of the Jahzeelites: of Guni, the family of the Gunites: ⁴⁹of Jezer, the family of the Jezerites: of Shillem, the family of the Shillemites. ⁵⁰These are the families of Naphtali according to their families: and they that were numbered of them were forty and five thousand and four hundred.

⁵¹These were the numbered of the children of Israel, six hundred thousand and a thousand seven hundred and thirty.

⁵²And the Lord spoke unto Moses, saying, ⁵³'Unto these the land shall be divided for an inheritance according to the number of names. ⁵⁴To many thou shalt give the more inheritance, and to few thou shalt give the less inheritance: to every one shall his inheritance be given according to those that were numbered of him. ⁵⁵Notwithstanding the land shall be divided by lot: according to the names of the tribes of their fathers they shall inherit. ⁵⁶According to the lot shall the possession thereof be divided between many and few.'

⁵⁷And these are they that were numbered of the Levites after their families: of Gershon, the family of the Gershonites: of Kohath, the family of the Kohathites: of Merari, the family of the Merarites. ⁵⁸These are the families of the Levites: the family of the Libnites, the family of the Hebronites, the family of the Mahlites, the family of the Mushites, the family of the Korahites. And Kohath begot Amram. ⁵⁹And the name of Amram's wife was Jochebed, the daughter of Levi, whom her mother bore to Levi in Egypt: and she bore unto Amram Aaron and Moses, and Miriam their sister. ⁶⁰And unto Aaron was born Nadab and Abihu, Eleazar and Ithamar. ⁶¹And Nadab and Abihu died, when they offered strange fire before the Lord. ⁶²And those that were numbered of them were twenty and three thousand, all males from a month old and upward: for they were not numbered among the children of Israel,

because there was no inheritance given them among the children of Israel.

⁶³These are they that were numbered by Moses and Eleazar the priest, who numbered the children of Israel in the plains of Moab by Jordan near Jericho. ⁶⁴But among these there was not a man of them whom Moses and Aaron the priest numbered, when they numbered the children of Israel in the wilderness of Sinai. ⁶⁵For the LORD had said of them, 'They shall surely die in the wilderness'. And there was not left a man of them, save Caleb the son of Jephunneh, and Joshua the son of Nun.

27 Then came the daughters of Zelophehad, the son of Hepher, the son of Gilead, the son of Machir, the son of Manasseh, of the families of Manasseh the son of Joseph: and these are the names of his daughters: Mahlah, Noah, and Hoglah, and Milcah, and Tirzah. ²And they stood before Moses, and before Eleazar the priest, and before the princes and all the congregation, by the door of the tabernacle of the congregation, saying, ³'Our father died in the wilderness, and he was not in the company of them that gathered themselves together against the LORD in the company of Korah; but died in his own sin, and had no sons. ⁴Why should the name of our father be done away from among his family, because he hath no son? Give unto us therefore a possession among the brethren of our father.' ⁵And Moses brought their cause before the LORD.

⁶And the LORD spoke unto Moses, saying, ⁷'The daughters of Zelophehad speak right: thou shalt surely give them a possession of an inheritance among their father's brethren, and thou shalt cause the inheritance of their father to pass unto them. ⁸And thou shalt speak unto the children of Israel, saying, "If a man die, and have no son, then ye shall cause his inheritance to pass unto his daughter. ⁹And if he have no daughter, then ye shall give his inheritance unto his brethren. ¹⁰And if he have no brethren, then ye shall give his inheritance unto his father's brethren. ¹¹And if his father have no brethren, then ye shall give his inheritance unto his kinsman that is next to him of his family, and he shall possess it: and it shall be unto the children of Israel a statute of judgement, as the LORD commanded Moses."'

¹²And the LORD said unto Moses, 'Get thee up into this mount Abarim, and see the land which I have given unto the children of Israel. ¹³And when thou hast seen it, thou also shalt be gathered unto thy people, as Aaron thy brother was gathered. ¹⁴For ye rebelled against my commandment in the desert of Zin, in the strife of the congregation, to sanctify me at the water before their eyes: that is the water of Meribah in Kadesh in the wilderness of Zin.'

¹⁵And Moses spoke unto the LORD, saying, ¹⁶'Let the LORD, the God of the spirits of all flesh, set a man over the congregation, ¹⁷which may go out before them, and which may go in before them, and which may lead them out, and which may bring them in, that the congregation of the LORD be not as sheep which have no shepherd'.

¹⁸And the LORD said unto Moses, 'Take thee Joshua the son of Nun, a

man in whom is the spirit, and lay thy hand upon him. ¹⁹And set him before Eleazar the priest, and before all the congregation: and give him a charge in their sight. ²⁰And thou shalt put some of thy honour upon him, that all the congregation of the children of Israel may be obedient. ²¹And he shall stand before Eleazar the priest, who shall ask counsel for him after the judgement of Urim before the Lord: at his word shall they go out, and at his word they shall come in, both he, and all the children of Israel with him, even all the congregation.' ²²And Moses did as the Lord commanded him: and he took Joshua, and set him before Eleazar the priest, and before all the congregation. ²³And he laid his hands upon him, and gave him a charge, as the Lord commanded by the hand of Moses.

28 And the Lord spoke unto Moses, saying, ²'Command the children of Israel, and say unto them, "My offering, and my bread for my sacrifices made by fire, for a sweet savour unto me, shall ye observe to offer unto me in their due season". ³And thou shalt say unto them, "This is the offering made by fire which ye shall offer unto the Lord: two lambs of the first year without spot day by day, for a continual burnt offering. ⁴The one lamb shalt thou offer in the morning, and the other lamb shalt thou offer at even; ⁵and a tenth part of an ephah of flour for a meat offering, mingled with the fourth part of a hin of beaten oil. ⁶It is a continual burnt offering, which was ordained in mount Sinai for a sweet savour, a sacrifice made by fire unto the Lord. ⁷And the drink offering thereof shall be the fourth part of a hin for the one lamb: in the holy place shalt thou cause the strong wine to be poured unto the Lord for a drink offering. ⁸And the other lamb shalt thou offer at even: as the meat offering of the morning, and as the drink offering thereof, thou shalt offer it, a sacrifice made by fire, of a sweet savour unto the Lord.

⁹'"And on the sabbath day two lambs of the first year without spot, and two tenth deals of flour for a meat offering, mingled with oil, and the drink offering thereof. ¹⁰This is the burnt offering of every sabbath, besides the continual burnt offering, and his drink offering.

¹¹'"And in the beginnings of your months ye shall offer a burnt offering unto the Lord: two young bullocks, and one ram, seven lambs of the first year without spot, ¹²and three tenth deals of flour for a meat offering, mingled with oil, for one bullock, and two tenth deals of flour for a meat offering, mingled with oil, for one ram; ¹³and a several tenth deal of flour mingled with oil for a meat offering unto one lamb; for a burnt offering of a sweet savour, a sacrifice made by fire unto the Lord. ¹⁴And their drink offerings shall be half a hin of wine unto a bullock, and the third part of a hin unto a ram, and a fourth part of a hin unto a lamb: this is the burnt offering of every month throughout the months of the year. ¹⁵And one kid of the goats for a sin offering unto the Lord shall be offered, besides the continual burnt offering, and his drink offering.

¹⁶'"And in the fourteenth day of the first month is the passover of the Lord. ¹⁷And in the fifteenth day of this month is the feast: seven days

shall unleavened bread be eaten. [18]In the first day shall be a holy convocation; ye shall do no manner of servile work therein. [19]But ye shall offer a sacrifice made by fire for a burnt offering unto the LORD, two young bullocks, and one ram, and seven lambs of the first year: they shall be unto you without blemish. [20]And their meat offering shall be of flour mingled with oil: three tenth deals shall ye offer for a bullock, and two tenth deals for a ram. [21]A several tenth deal shalt thou offer for every lamb, throughout the seven lambs: [22]and one goat for a sin offering, to make an atonement for you. [23]Ye shall offer these besides the burnt offering in the morning, which is for a continual burnt offering. [24]After this manner ye shall offer daily, throughout the seven days, the meat of the sacrifice made by fire, of a sweet savour unto the LORD: it shall be offered besides the continual burnt offering, and his drink offering. [25]And on the seventh day ye shall have a holy convocation; ye shall do no servile work.

[26]'Also in the day of the first-fruits, when ye bring a new meat offering unto the LORD, after your weeks be out, ye shall have a holy convocation; ye shall do no servile work. [27]But ye shall offer the burnt offering for a sweet savour unto the LORD, two young bullocks, one ram, seven lambs of the first year. [28]And their meat offering of flour mingled with oil, three tenth deals unto one bullock, two tenth deals unto one ram, [29]a several tenth deal unto one lamb, throughout the seven lambs, [30]and one kid of the goats, to make an atonement for you. [31]Ye shall offer them besides the continual burnt offering, and his meat offering (they shall be unto you without blemish), and their drink offerings.

29 '"And in the seventh month, on the first day of the month, ye shall have a holy convocation; ye shall do no servile work: it is a day of blowing the trumpets unto you. [2]And ye shall offer a burnt offering for a sweet savour unto the LORD, one young bullock, one ram, and seven lambs of the first year without blemish. [3]And their meat offering shall be of flour mingled with oil, three tenth deals for a bullock, and two tenth deals for a ram, [4]and one tenth deal for one lamb, throughout the seven lambs: [5]and one kid of the goats for a sin offering, to make an atonement for you: [6]besides the burnt offering of the month, and his meat offering, and the daily burnt offering, and his meat offering, and their drink offerings, according unto their manner, for a sweet savour, a sacrifice made by fire unto the LORD.

[7]'And ye shall have on the tenth day of this seventh month a holy convocation; and ye shall afflict your souls: ye shall not do any work therein. [8]But ye shall offer a burnt offering unto the LORD for a sweet savour, one young bullock, one ram, and seven lambs of the first year; they shall be unto you without blemish. [9]And their meat offering shall be of flour mingled with oil, three tenth deals to a bullock, and two tenth deals to one ram, [10]a several tenth deal for one lamb, throughout the seven lambs: [11]one kid of the goats for a sin offering, besides the sin offering of atonement, and the continual burnt offering, and the meat offering of it, and their drink offerings.

[12]"And on the fifteenth day of the seventh month ye shall have a holy convocation; ye shall do no servile work, and ye shall keep a feast unto the LORD seven days. [13]And ye shall offer a burnt offering, a sacrifice made by fire, of a sweet savour unto the LORD, thirteen young bullocks, two rams, and fourteen lambs of the first year: they shall be without blemish. [14]And their meat offering shall be of flour mingled with oil, three tenth deals unto every bullock of the thirteen bullocks, two tenth deals to each ram of the two rams, [15]and a several tenth deal to each lamb of the fourteen lambs: [16]and one kid of the goats for a sin offering; besides the continual burnt offering, his meat offering, and his drink offering.

[17]"And on the second day ye shall offer twelve young bullocks, two rams, fourteen lambs of the first year without spot. [18]And their meat offering and their drink offerings for the bullocks, for the rams, and for the lambs, shall be according to their number, after the manner: [19]and one kid of the goats for a sin offering; besides the continual burnt offering, and the meat offering thereof, and their drink offerings.

[20]"And on the third day eleven bullocks, two rams, fourteen lambs of the first year without blemish. [21]And their meat offering and their drink offerings for the bullocks, for the rams, and for the lambs, shall be according to their number, after the manner: [22]and one goat for a sin offering; besides the continual burnt offering, and his meat offering, and his drink offering.

[23]"And on the fourth day ten bullocks, two rams, and fourteen lambs of the first year without blemish. [24]Their meat offering and their drink offerings for the bullocks, for the rams, and for the lambs, shall be according to their number, after the manner: [25]and one kid of the goats for a sin offering; besides the continual burnt offering, his meat offering, and his drink offering.

[26]"And on the fifth day nine bullocks, two rams, and fourteen lambs of the first year without spot. [27]And their meat offering and their drink offerings for the bullocks, for the rams, and for the lambs, shall be according to their number, after the manner: [28]and one goat for a sin offering; besides the continual burnt offering, and his meat offering, and his drink offering.

[29]"And on the sixth day eight bullocks, two rams, and fourteen lambs of the first year without blemish. [30]And their meat offering and their drink offerings for the bullocks, for the rams, and for the lambs, shall be according to their number, after the manner: [31]and one goat for a sin offering; besides the continual burnt offering, his meat offering, and his drink offering.

[32]"And on the seventh day seven bullocks, two rams, and fourteen lambs of the first year without blemish. [33]And their meat offering and their drink offerings for the bullocks, for the rams, and for the lambs, shall be according to their number, after the manner: [34]and one goat for a sin offering; besides the continual burnt offering, his meat offering, and his drink offering.

³⁵'"On the eighth day ye shall have a solemn assembly: ye shall do no servile work therein: ³⁶but ye shall offer a burnt offering, a sacrifice made by fire, of a sweet savour unto the LORD: one bullock, one ram, seven lambs of the first year without blemish: ³⁷their meat offering and their drink offerings for the bullock, for the ram, and for the lambs, shall be according to their number, after the manner: ³⁸and one goat for a sin offering; besides the continual burnt offering, and his meat offering, and his drink offering. ³⁹These things ye shall do unto the LORD in your set feasts, besides your vows, and your free-will offerings, for your burnt offerings, and for your meat offerings, and for your drink offerings, and for your peace offerings."' ⁴⁰And Moses told the children of Israel according to all that the LORD commanded Moses.

30
And Moses spoke unto the heads of the tribes concerning the children of Israel, saying, 'This is the thing which the LORD hath commanded. ²"If a man vow a vow unto the LORD, or swear an oath to bind his soul with a bond: he shall not break his word, he shall do according to all that proceedeth out of his mouth. ³If a woman also vow a vow unto the LORD, and bind herself by a bond, being in her father's house in her youth; ⁴and her father hear her vow, and her bond wherewith she hath bound her soul, and her father shall hold his peace at her: then all her vows shall stand, and every bond wherewith she hath bound her soul shall stand. ⁵But if her father disallow her in the day that he heareth; not any of her vows, or of her bonds wherewith she hath bound her soul, shall stand: and the LORD shall forgive her, because her father disallowed her. ⁶And if she had at all a husband, when she vowed, or uttered aught out of her lips, wherewith she bound her soul, ⁷and her husband heard it, and held his peace at her in the day that he heard it: then her vows shall stand, and her bonds wherewith she bound her soul shall stand. ⁸But if her husband disallow her on the day that he heard it, then he shall make her vow which she vowed, and that which she uttered with her lips, wherewith she bound her soul, of no effect, and the LORD shall forgive her. ⁹But every vow of a widow, and of her that is divorced, wherewith they have bound their souls, shall stand against her. ¹⁰And if she vowed in her husband's house, or bound her soul by a bond with an oath; ¹¹and her husband heard it, and held his peace at her, and disallowed her not: then all her vows shall stand, and every bond wherewith she bound her soul shall stand. ¹²But if her husband hath utterly made them void on the day he heard them, then whatsoever proceeded out of her lips concerning her vows, or concerning the bond of her soul, shall not stand: her husband hath made them void, and the LORD shall forgive her. ¹³Every vow, and every binding oath to afflict the soul, her husband may establish it, or her husband may make it void. ¹⁴But if her husband altogether hold his peace at her from day to day, then he establisheth all her vows, or all her bonds, which are upon her: he confirmeth them, because he held his peace at her in the day that he heard them. ¹⁵But if he shall any ways make them void after that he hath heard them, then he shall bear her iniquity."' ¹⁶These are the statutes which the LORD commanded Moses,

between a man and his wife, between the father and his daughter, being yet in her youth in her father's house.

31 And the LORD spoke unto Moses, saying, [2]'Avenge the children of Israel of the Midianites: afterward shalt thou be gathered unto thy people'. [3]And Moses spoke unto the people, saying, 'Arm some of yourselves unto the war, and let them go against the Midianites, and avenge the LORD of Midian. [4]Of every tribe a thousand, throughout all the tribes of Israel, shall ye send to the war.' [5]So there were delivered out of the thousands of Israel, a thousand of every tribe, twelve thousand armed for war. [6]And Moses sent them to the war, a thousand of every tribe, them and Phinehas the son of Eleazar the priest, to the war, with the holy instruments, and the trumpets to blow in his hand. [7]And they warred against the Midianites, as the LORD commanded Moses, and they slew all the males. [8]And they slew the kings of Midian, besides the rest of them that were slain; namely, Evi, and Rekem, and Zur, and Hur, and Reba, five kings of Midian: Balaam also the son of Beor they slew with the sword. [9]And the children of Israel took all the women of Midian captives, and their little ones, and took the spoil of all their cattle, and all their flocks, and all their goods. [10]And they burnt all their cities wherein they dwelt, and all their goodly castles with fire. [11]And they took all the spoil, and all the prey, both of men and of beasts. [12]And they brought the captives, and the prey, and the spoil, unto Moses, and Eleazar the priest, and unto the congregation of the children of Israel, unto the camp at the plains of Moab, which are by Jordan near Jericho.

[13]And Moses, and Eleazar the priest, and all the princes of the congregation, went forth to meet them without the camp. [14]And Moses was wroth with the officers of the host, with the captains over thousands, and captains over hundreds, which came from the battle. [15]And Moses said unto them, 'Have ye saved all the women alive? [16]Behold, these caused the children of Israel, through the counsel of Balaam, to commit trespass against the LORD in the matter of Peor, and there was a plague among the congregation of the LORD. [17]Now therefore kill every male among the little ones, and kill every woman that hath known man by lying with him. [18]But all the women children that have not known a man by lying with him, keep alive for yourselves. [19]And do ye abide without the camp seven days: whosoever hath killed any person, and whosoever hath touched any slain, purify both yourselves and your captives on the third day, and on the seventh day. [20]And purify all your raiment, and all that is made of skins, and all work of goats' hair, and all things made of wood.'

[21]And Eleazar the priest said unto the men of war which went to the battle, 'This is the ordinance of the law which the LORD commanded Moses. [22]Only the gold, and the silver, the brass, the iron, the tin, and the lead, [23]everything that may abide the fire, ye shall make it go through the fire, and it shall be clean: nevertheless it shall be purified with the water of separation: and all that abideth not the fire ye shall make go through the water. [24]And ye shall wash your clothes on the seventh day, and ye shall be clean, and afterward ye shall come into the camp.'

^{25}And the LORD spoke unto Moses, saying, ^{26}'Take the sum of the prey that was taken, both of man and of beast, thou, and Eleazar the priest, and the chief fathers of the congregation: ^{27}and divide the prey into two parts, between them that took the war upon them, who went out to battle, and between all the congregation. ^{28}And levy a tribute unto the LORD of the men of war which went out to battle: one soul of five hundred, both of the persons, and of the beeves, and of the asses, and of the sheep. ^{29}Take it of their half, and give it unto Eleazar the priest, for a heave offering of the LORD. ^{30}And of the children of Israel's half, thou shalt take one portion of fifty, of the persons, of the beeves, of the asses, and of the flocks, of all manner of beasts, and give them unto the Levites, which keep the charge of the tabernacle of the LORD.' ^{31}And Moses and Eleazar the priest did as the LORD commanded Moses. ^{32}And the booty, being the rest of the prey which the men of war had caught, was six hundred thousand and seventy thousand and five thousand sheep, ^{33}and threescore and twelve thousand beeves, ^{34}and threescore and one thousand asses, ^{35}and thirty and two thousand persons in all, of women that had not known man by lying with him. ^{36}And the half, which was the portion of them that went out to war, was in number three hundred thousand and seven and thirty thousand and five hundred sheep. ^{37}And the LORD's tribute of the sheep was six hundred and threescore and fifteen. ^{38}And the beeves were thirty and six thousand, of which the LORD's tribute was threescore and twelve. ^{39}And the asses were thirty thousand and five hundred, of which the LORD's tribute was threescore and one. ^{40}And the persons were sixteen thousand, of which the LORD's tribute was thirty and two persons. ^{41}And Moses gave the tribute which was the LORD's heave offering, unto Eleazar the priest, as the LORD commanded Moses. ^{42}And of the children of Israel's half, which Moses divided from the men that warred ^{43}(now the half that pertained unto the congregation was three hundred thousand and thirty thousand and seven thousand and five hundred sheep, ^{44}and thirty and six thousand beeves, ^{45}and thirty thousand asses and five hundred, ^{46}and sixteen thousand persons), ^{47}even of the children of Israel's half, Moses took one portion of fifty, both of man and of beast, and gave them unto the Levites, which kept the charge of the tabernacle of the LORD, as the LORD commanded Moses.

^{48}And the officers which were over thousands of the host, the captains of thousands, and captains of hundreds, came near unto Moses. ^{49}And they said unto Moses, 'Thy servants have taken the sum of the men of war which are under our charge, and there lacketh not one man of us. ^{50}We have therefore brought an oblation for the LORD, what every man hath gotten, of jewels of gold, chains, and bracelets, rings, ear-rings, and tablets, to make an atonement for our souls before the LORD.' ^{51}And Moses and Eleazar the priest took the gold of them, even all wrought jewels. ^{52}And all the gold of the offering that they offered up to the LORD, of the captains of thousands, and of the captains of hundreds, was sixteen thousand seven hundred and fifty shekels. ^{53}(For the men of war had taken spoil, every man for himself.) ^{54}And Moses and Eleazar the priest took the gold of the captains of thousands and of hundreds, and brought it into the tabernacle of the congregation, for a memorial for the children of Israel before the LORD.

32 Now the children of Reuben and the children of Gad had a very great multitude of cattle: and when they saw the land of Jazer, and the land of Gilead, that behold, the place was a place for cattle; ²the children of Gad and the children of Reuben came and spoke unto Moses, and to Eleazar the priest, and unto the princes of the congregation, saying, ³'Ataroth, and Dibon, and Jazer, and Nimrah, and Heshbon, and Elealeh, and Shebam, and Nebo, and Beon, ⁴even the country which the LORD smote before the congregation of Israel, is a land for cattle, and thy servants have cattle. ⁵Wherefore,' said they, 'if we have found grace in thy sight, let this land be given unto thy servants for a possession, and bring us not over Jordan.'

⁶And Moses said unto the children of Gad and to the children of Reuben, 'Shall your brethren go to war, and shall ye sit here? ⁷And wherefore discourage ye the heart of the children of Israel from going over into the land which the LORD hath given them? ⁸Thus did your fathers, when I sent them from Kadesh-barnea to see the land. ⁹For when they went up unto the valley of Eshcol, and saw the land, they discouraged the heart of the children of Israel, that they should not go into the land which the LORD had given them. ¹⁰And the LORD's anger was kindled the same time, and he swore, saying, ¹¹"Surely none of the men that came up out of Egypt, from twenty years old and upward, shall see the land which I swore unto Abraham, unto Isaac, and unto Jacob, because they have not wholly followed me: ¹²save Caleb the son of Jephunneh the Kenezite, and Joshua the son of Nun: for they have wholly followed the LORD". ¹³And the LORD's anger was kindled against Israel, and he made them wander in the wilderness forty years, until all the generation that had done evil in the sight of the LORD was consumed. ¹⁴And behold, ye are risen up in your fathers' stead, an increase of sinful men, to augment yet the fierce anger of the LORD toward Israel. ¹⁵For if ye turn away from after him, he will yet again leave them in the wilderness; and ye shall destroy all this people.'

¹⁶And they came near unto him, and said, 'We will build sheepfolds here for our cattle, and cities for our little ones. ¹⁷But we ourselves will go ready armed before the children of Israel, until we have brought them unto their place: and our little ones shall dwell in the fenced cities because of the inhabitants of the land. ¹⁸We will not return unto our houses, until the children of Israel have inherited every man his inheritance: ¹⁹for we will not inherit with them on yonder side Jordan, or forward, because our inheritance is fallen to us on this side Jordan eastward.'

²⁰And Moses said unto them, 'If ye will do this thing, if ye will go armed before the LORD to war, ²¹and will go all of you armed over Jordan before the LORD, until he hath driven out his enemies from before him, ²²and the land be subdued before the LORD: then afterward ye shall return, and be guiltless before the LORD, and before Israel; and

this land shall be your possession before the LORD. ²³But if ye will not do so, behold, ye have sinned against the LORD: and be sure your sin will find you out. ²⁴Build ye cities for your little ones, and folds for your sheep; and do that which hath proceeded out of your mouth.' ²⁵And the children of Gad and the children of Reuben spoke unto Moses, saying, 'Thy servants will do as my lord commandeth. ²⁶Our little ones, our wives, our flocks, and all our cattle, shall be there in the cities of Gilead. ²⁷But thy servants will pass over, every man armed for war, before the LORD to battle, as my lord saith.' ²⁸So concerning them Moses commanded Eleazar the priest, and Joshua the son of Nun, and the chief fathers of the tribes of the children of Israel: ²⁹and Moses said unto them, 'If the children of Gad and the children of Reuben will pass with you over Jordan, every man armed to battle before the LORD, and the land shall be subdued before you, then ye shall give them the land of Gilead for a possession: ³⁰but if they will not pass over with you armed, they shall have possessions among you in the land of Canaan'. ³¹And the children of Gad and the children of Reuben answered, saying, 'As the LORD hath said unto thy servants, so will we do. ³²We will pass over armed before the LORD into the land of Canaan, that the possession of our inheritance on this side Jordan may be ours.' ³³And Moses gave unto them, even to the children of Gad, and to the children of Reuben, and unto half the tribe of Manasseh the son of Joseph, the kingdom of Sihon king of the Amorites, and the kingdom of Og king of Bashan, the land with the cities thereof, in the coasts, even the cities of the country round about.

³⁴And the children of Gad built Dibon, and Ataroth, and Aroer, ³⁵and Atroth, Shophan, and Jaazer, and Jogbehah, ³⁶and Beth-nimrah, and Beth-haran, fenced cities: and folds for sheep. ³⁷And the children of Reuben built Heshbon, and Elealeh, and Kirjathaim, ³⁸and Nebo, and Baal-meon (their names being changed), and Shibmah: and gave other names unto the cities which they built. ³⁹And the children of Machir the son of Manasseh went to Gilead, and took it, and dispossessed the Amorite which was in it. ⁴⁰And Moses gave Gilead unto Machir the son of Manasseh, and he dwelt therein. ⁴¹And Jair the son of Manasseh went and took the small towns thereof, and called them Havoth-jair. ⁴²And Nobah went and took Kenath, and the villages thereof, and called it Nobah, after his own name.

33 These are the journeys of the children of Israel, which went forth out of the land of Egypt with their armies under the hand of Moses and Aaron. ²And Moses wrote their goings out according to their journeys by the commandment of the LORD: and these are their journeys according to their goings out. ³And they departed from Rameses in the first month, on the fifteenth day of the first month; on the morrow after the passover the children of Israel went out with a high hand in the sight of all the Egyptians. ⁴For the Egyptians buried all their firstborn, which the LORD had smitten among them: upon their gods also the LORD executed judgments. ⁵And the children of Israel removed from Rameses, and pitched in Succoth. ⁶And they departed from Succoth, and pitched in Etham, which is in the edge of the wilderness. ⁷And they removed from Etham, and turned again unto Pi-hahiroth, which is before Baal-zephon: and they pitched before Migdol. ⁸And they departed from before Pi-hahiroth, and passed through the midst of the sea into the wilderness, and went three days' journey in the wilderness of Etham, and pitched in Marah. ⁹And they removed from Marah, and came unto Elim: and in Elim were twelve fountains of water, and threescore and ten palm trees; and they pitched there. ¹⁰And they removed from Elim, and encamped by the Red Sea. ¹¹And they removed from the Red Sea, and encamped in the wilderness of Sin. ¹²And they took their journey out of the wilderness of Sin, and encamped in Dophkah. ¹³And they departed from Dophkah, and encamped in Alush. ¹⁴And they removed from Alush, and encamped at Rephidim, where was no water for the people to drink. ¹⁵And they departed from Rephidim, and pitched in the wilderness of Sinai. ¹⁶And they removed from the desert of Sinai, and pitched at Kibroth-hattaavah. ¹⁷And they departed from Kibroth-hattaavah, and encamped at Hazeroth. ¹⁸And they departed from Hazeroth, and pitched in Rithmah. ¹⁹And they departed from Rithmah, and pitched at Rimmon-parez. ²⁰And they departed from Rimmon-parez, and pitched in Libnah. ²¹And they removed from Libnah, and pitched at Rissah. ²²And they journeyed from Rissah, and pitched in Kehelathah. ²³And they went from Kehelathah, and pitched in mount Shapher. ²⁴And they removed from mount Shapher, and encamped in Haradah. ²⁵And they removed from Haradah, and pitched in Makheloth. ²⁶And they removed from Makheloth, and encamped at Tahath. ²⁷And they departed from Tahath, and pitched at Tarah. ²⁸And they removed from Tarah, and pitched in Mithcah. ²⁹And they went from Mithcah, and pitched in Hashmonah. ³⁰And they departed from Hashmonah, and encamped at Moseroth. ³¹And they departed from Moseroth, and pitched in Bene-jaakan. ³²And they removed from Bene-jaakan, and encamped at Hor-hagidgad. ³³And they went from Hor-hagidgad, and pitched in Jotbathah. ³⁴And they removed from Jotbathah, and encamped at Ebronah. ³⁵And they departed from Ebronah, and encamped at Ezion-geber. ³⁶And they removed from Ezion-geber, and pitched in the wilderness of Zin, which is Kadesh. ³⁷And they removed from Kadesh, and pitched in mount Hor, in the edge of the land of Edom. ³⁸And Aaron the priest went up into mount Hor at the commandment of the LORD, and died there, in the fortieth year after the children of Israel were come out of the land of Egypt, in the first day of the fifth month. ³⁹And Aaron was a hundred and twenty and three years old when he died in mount Hor. ⁴⁰And king Arad the Canaanite, which dwelt in the south in the land of Canaan, heard of the coming of the children of Israel. ⁴¹And they departed from mount Hor, and pitched in Zalmonah. ⁴²And they departed from Zalmonah, and pitched in Punon. ⁴³And they departed from Punon, and pitched in Oboth. ⁴⁴And they departed from Oboth, and pitched in Ije-abarim, in the border of Moab. ⁴⁵And they departed from Iim, and pitched in Dibon-gad. ⁴⁶And they removed from Dibon-gad, and encamped in Almon-diblathaim. ⁴⁷And they removed from Almon-diblathaim, and pitched in the mountains of Abarim, before Nebo. ⁴⁸And they departed from the mountains of Abarim, and pitched in the plains of Moab by Jordan near Jericho. ⁴⁹And they pitched by Jordan, from Beth-jesimoth even unto Abel-shittim in the plains of Moab.

⁵⁰And the Lord spoke unto Moses in the plains of Moab by Jordan near Jericho, saying, ⁵¹'Speak unto the children of Israel, and say unto them, "When ye are passed over Jordan into the land of Canaan; ⁵²then ye shall drive out all the inhabitants of the land from before you, and destroy all their pictures, and destroy all their molten images, and quite pluck down all their high places. ⁵³And ye shall dispossess the inhabitants of the land, and dwell therein: for I have given you the land to possess it. ⁵⁴And ye shall divide the land by lot for an inheritance among your families: and to the more ye shall give the more inheritance, and to the fewer ye shall give the less inheritance: every man's inheritance shall be in the place where his lot falleth; according to the tribes of your fathers ye shall inherit. ⁵⁵But if ye will not drive out the inhabitants of the land from before you, then it shall come to pass, that those which ye let remain of them shall be pricks in your eyes, and thorns in your sides, and shall vex you in the land wherein ye dwell. ⁵⁶Moreover it shall come to pass, that I shall do unto you, as I thought to do unto them."'

34 And the Lord spoke unto Moses, saying, ²'Command the children of Israel, and say unto them, "When ye come into the land of Canaan (this is the land that shall fall unto you for an inheritance, even the land of Canaan with the coasts thereof), ³then your south quarter shall be from the wilderness of Zin along by the coast of Edom, and your south border shall be the utmost coast of the salt sea eastward. ⁴And your border shall turn from the south to the ascent of Akrabbim, and pass on to Zin: and the going forth thereof shall be from the south to Kadesh-barnea, and shall go on to Hazar-addar, and pass on to Azmon. ⁵And the border shall fetch a compass from Azmon unto the river of Egypt, and the goings out of it shall be at the sea. ⁶And as for the western border, you shall even have the great sea for a border: this shall be your west border. ⁷And this shall be your north border: from the great sea you shall point out for you mount Hor. ⁸From mount Hor ye shall point out your border unto the entrance of Hamath; and the goings forth of the border shall be to Zedad. ⁹And the border shall go on to Ziphron, and the goings out of it shall be at Hazar-enan: this shall be your north border. ¹⁰And ye shall point out your east border from Hazar-enan to Shepham. ¹¹And the coast shall go down from Shepham to Riblah, on the east side of Ain; and the border shall descend, and shall reach unto the side of the sea of Chinnereth eastward. ¹²And the border shall go down to Jordan, and the goings out of it shall be at the salt sea: this shall be your land with the coasts thereof round about."'

¹³And Moses commanded the children of Israel, saying, 'This is the land which ye shall inherit by lot, which the Lord commanded to give

unto the nine tribes, and to the half tribe: ¹⁴for the tribe of the children of Reuben according to the house of their fathers, and the tribe of the children of Gad according to the house of their fathers, have received their inheritance; and half the tribe of Manasseh have received their inheritance: ¹⁵the two tribes and the half tribe have received their inheritance on this side Jordan near Jericho eastward, toward the sun-rising.'

¹⁶And the LORD spoke unto Moses, saying, ¹⁷'These are the names of the men which shall divide the land unto you: Eleazar the priest, and Joshua the son of Nun. ¹⁸And ye shall take one prince of every tribe, to divide the land by inheritance. ¹⁹And the names of the men are these: of the tribe of Judah, Caleb the son of Jephunneh. ²⁰And of the tribe of the children of Simeon, Shemuel the son of Ammihud. ²¹Of the tribe of Benjamin, Elidad the son of Chislon. ²²And the prince of the tribe of the children of Dan, Bukki the son of Jogli. ²³The prince of the children of Joseph, for the tribe of the children of Manasseh, Hanniel the son of Ephod. ²⁴And the prince of the tribe of the children of Ephraim, Kemuel the son of Shiphtan. ²⁵And the prince of the tribe of the children of Zebulun, Elizaphan the son of Parnach. ²⁶And the prince of the tribe of the children of Issachar, Paltiel the son of Azzan. ²⁷And the prince of the tribe of the children of Asher, Ahihud the son of Shelomi. ²⁸And the prince of the tribe of the children of Naphtali, Pedahel the son of Ammihud.' ²⁹These are they whom the LORD commanded to divide the inheritance unto the children of Israel in the land of Canaan.

35 And the LORD spoke unto Moses in the plains of Moab by Jordan near Jericho, saying, ²'Command the children of Israel, that they give unto the Levites of the inheritance of their possession, cities to dwell in; and ye shall give also unto the Levites suburbs for the cities round about them. ³And the cities shall they have to dwell in; and the suburbs of them shall be for their cattle, and for their goods, and for all their beasts. ⁴And the suburbs of the cities, which ye shall give unto the Levites, shall reach from the wall of the city and outward a thousand cubits round about. ⁵And ye shall measure from without the city on the east side two thousand cubits, and on the south side two thousand cubits, and on the west side two thousand cubits, and on the north side two thousand cubits; and the city shall be in the midst: this shall be to them the suburbs of the cities. ⁶And among the cities which ye shall give unto the Levites there shall be six cities for refuge, which ye shall appoint for the man-slayer, that he may flee thither: and to them ye shall add forty and two cities. ⁷So all the cities which ye shall give to the Levites shall be forty and eight cities: them shall ye give with their sub-urbs. ⁸And the cities which ye shall give shall be of the possession of the children of Israel: from them that have many ye shall give many; but from them that have few ye shall give few: every one shall give of his cities unto the Levites according to his inheritance which he inheriteth.'

⁹And the LORD spoke unto Moses, saying, ¹⁰'Speak unto the children of Israel, and say unto them, "When ye be come over Jordan into the

land of Canaan: ¹¹then ye shall appoint you cities to be cities of refuge for you; that the slayer may flee thither which killeth any person at unawares. ¹²And they shall be unto you cities for refuge from the avenger, that the man-slayer die not, until he stand before the congregation in judgement. ¹³And of these cities which ye shall give, six cities shall ye have for refuge. ¹⁴Ye shall give three cities on this side Jordan, and three cities shall ye give in the land of Canaan, which shall be cities of refuge. ¹⁵These six cities shall be a refuge, both for the children of Israel, and for the stranger, and for the sojourner among them: that every one that killeth any person unawares may flee thither. ¹⁶And if he smite him with an instrument of iron, so that he die, he is a murderer: the murderer shall surely be put to death. ¹⁷And if he smite him with throwing a stone, wherewith he may die, and he die, he is a murderer: the murderer shall surely be put to death. ¹⁸Or if he smite him with a hand weapon of wood, wherewith he may die, and he die, he is a murderer: the murderer shall surely be put to death. ¹⁹The revenger of blood himself shall slay the murderer: when he meeteth him, he shall slay him. ²⁰But if he thrust him of hatred, or hurl at him by laying of wait, that he die, ²¹or in enmity smite him with his hand, that he die: he that smote him shall surely be put to death, for he is a murderer: the revenger of blood shall slay the murderer, when he meeteth him. ²²But if he thrust him suddenly without enmity, or have cast upon him anything without laying of wait, ²³or with any stone wherewith a man may die, seeing him not, and cast it upon him, that he die, and was not his enemy, neither sought his harm: ²⁴then the congregation shall judge between the slayer and the revenger of blood according to these judgements. ²⁵And the congregation shall deliver the slayer out of the hand of the revenger of blood, and the congregation shall restore him to the city of his refuge, whither he was fled: and he shall abide in it unto the death of the high priest, which was anointed with the holy oil. ²⁶But if the slayer shall at any time come without the border of the city of his refuge, whither he was fled: ²⁷and the revenger of blood find him without the borders of the city of his refuge, and the revenger of blood kill the slayer; he shall not be guilty of blood: ²⁸because he should have remained in the city of his refuge until the death of the high priest: but after the death of the high priest the slayer shall return into the land of his possession. ²⁹So these things shall be for a statute of judgement unto you throughout your generations in all your dwellings.

³⁰'"Whoso killeth any person, the murderer shall be put to death by the mouth of witnesses: but one witness shall not testify against any person to cause him to die. ³¹Moreover ye shall take no satisfaction for the life of a murderer, which is guilty of death, but he shall be surely put to death. ³²And ye shall take no satisfaction for him that is fled to the city of his refuge, that he should come again to dwell in the land, until the death of the priest. ³³So ye shall not pollute the land wherein ye are: for blood, it defileth the land: and the land cannot be cleansed of the blood that is shed therein, but by the blood of him that

shed it. ³⁴Defile not therefore the land which ye shall inhabit, wherein I dwell: for I the LORD dwell among the children of Israel."'

36 And the chief fathers of the families of the children of Gilead, the son of Machir, the son of Manasseh, of the families of the sons of Joseph, came near, and spoke before Moses, and before the princes, the chief fathers of the children of Israel. ²And they said, 'The LORD commanded my lord to give the land for an inheritance by lot to the children of Israel: and my lord was commanded by the LORD to give the inheritance of Zelophehad our brother unto his daughters. ³And if they be married to any of the sons of the other tribes of the children of Israel, then shall their inheritance be taken from the inheritance of our fathers, and shall be put to the inheritance of the tribe whereinto they are received: so shall it be taken from the lot of our inheritance. ⁴And when the jubilee of the children of Israel shall be, then shall their inheritance be put unto the inheritance of the tribe whereunto they are received: so shall their inheritance be taken away from the inheritance of the tribe of our fathers.' ⁵And Moses commanded the children of Israel according to the word of the LORD, saying, 'The tribe of the sons of Joseph hath said well. ⁶This is the thing which the LORD doth command concerning the daughters of Zelophehad, saying, "Let them marry to whom they think best; only to the family of the tribe of their father shall they marry. ⁷So shall not the inheritance of the children of Israel remove from tribe to tribe: for every one of the children of Israel shall keep himself to the inheritance of the tribe of his fathers. ⁸And every daughter, that possesseth an inheritance in any tribe of the children of Israel, shall be wife unto one of the family of the tribe of her father, that the children of Israel may enjoy every man the inheritance of his fathers. ⁹Neither shall the inheritance remove from one tribe to another tribe; but every one of the tribes of the children of Israel shall keep himself to his own inheritance."' ¹⁰Even as the LORD commanded Moses, so did the daughters of Zelophehad. ¹¹For Mahlah, Tirzah, and Hoglah, and Milcah, and Noah, the daughters of Zelophehad, were married unto their father's brothers' sons. ¹²And they were married into the families of the sons of Manasseh the son of Joseph, and their inheritance remained in the tribe of the family of their father. ¹³These are the commandments and the judgements, which the LORD commanded by the hand of Moses unto the children of Israel in the plains of Moab by Jordan near Jericho.

THE FIFTH BOOK OF MOSES,
CALLED
DEUTERONOMY

1 These be the words which Moses spoke unto all Israel on this side Jordan in the wilderness, in the plain over against the Red Sea, between Paran, and Tophel, and Laban, and Hazeroth, and Dizahab. ²(There are eleven days' journey from Horeb by the way of mount Seir unto Kadesh-barnea.) ³And it came to pass in the fortieth year, in the eleventh month, on the first day of the month, that Moses spoke unto the children of Israel, according unto all that the LORD had given him in commandment unto them; ⁴after he had slain Sihon the king of the Amorites, which dwelt in Heshbon, and Og the king of Bashan, which dwelt at Astaroth in Edrei: ⁵on this side Jordan, in the land of Moab, began Moses to declare this law, saying, ⁶"The Lord our God spoke unto us in Horeb, saying, "Ye have dwelt long enough in this mount: ⁷turn you, and take your journey, and go to the mount of the Amorites, and unto all the places nigh thereunto, in the plain, in the hills, and in the vale, and in the south, and by the seaside, to the land of the Canaanites, and unto Lebanon, unto the great river, the river Euphrates. ⁸Behold, I have set the land before you: go in and possess the land which the LORD swore unto your fathers, Abraham, Isaac, and Jacob, to give unto them and to their seed after them."

⁹'And I spoke unto you at that time, saying, "I am not able to bear you myself alone: ¹⁰the LORD your God hath multiplied you, and behold, you are this day as the stars of heaven for multitude. ¹¹(The LORD God of your fathers make you a thousand times so many more as ye are, and bless you, as he hath promised you.) ¹²How can I myself alone bear your cumbrance, and your burden, and your strife? ¹³Take ye wise men, and understanding, and known among your tribes, and I will make them rulers over you." ¹⁴And ye answered me, and said, "The thing which thou hast spoken is good for us to do". ¹⁵So I took the chief of your tribes, wise men, and known, and made them heads over you, captains over thousands, and captains over hundreds, and captains over fifties, and captains over tens, and officers among your tribes. ¹⁶And I charged your judges at that time, saying, "Hear the causes between your brethren, and judge righteously between every man and his brother, and the stranger that is with him. ¹⁷Ye shall not respect persons in judgement, but you shall hear the small as well as the great; you shall not be afraid of the face of man, for the judgement is God's: and the cause that is too hard for you, bring it unto me, and I will hear it." ¹⁸And I commanded you at that time all the things which ye should do.

¹⁹'And when we departed from Horeb, we went through all that great and terrible wilderness, which you saw by the way of the mountain of the Amorites, as the LORD our God commanded us; and we came to Kadesh-barnea. ²⁰And I said unto you, "Ye are come unto the mountain

of the Amorites, which the LORD our God doth give unto us. [21]Behold, the LORD thy God hath set the land before thee: go up and possess it, as the LORD God of thy fathers hath said unto thee; fear not, neither be discouraged." [22]And ye came near unto me every one of you, and said, "We will send men before us, and they shall search us out the land, and bring us word again by what way we must go up, and into what cities we shall come". [23]And the saying pleased me well: and I took twelve men of you, one of a tribe. [24]And they turned and went up into the mountain, and came unto the valley of Eshcol, and searched it out. [25]And they took of the fruit of the land in their hands, and brought it down unto us, and brought us word again, and said, "It is a good land which the LORD our God doth give us". [26]Notwithstanding ye would not go up, but rebelled against the commandment of the LORD your God. [27]And ye murmured in your tents, and said, "Because the LORD hated us, he hath brought us forth out of the land of Egypt, to deliver us into the hand of the Amorites, to destroy us. [28]Whither shall we go up? our brethren have discouraged our heart, saying, 'The people is greater and taller than we, the cities are great and walled up to heaven, and moreover we have seen the sons of the Anakims there'." [29]Then I said unto you, "Dread not, neither be afraid of them. [30]The LORD your God which goeth before you, he shall fight for you, according to all that he did for you in Egypt before your eyes; [31]and in the wilderness, where thou hast seen how that the LORD thy God bore thee, as a man doth bear his son, in all the way that ye went, until ye came into this place." [32]Yet in this thing ye did not believe the LORD your God, [33]who went in the way before you, to search you out a place to pitch your tents in, in fire by night, to show you by what way ye should go, and in a cloud by day. [34]And the LORD heard the voice of your words, and was wroth, and swore, saying, [35]"Surely there shall not one of these men of this evil generation see that good land, which I swore to give unto your fathers, [36]save Caleb the son of Jephunneh; he shall see it, and to him will I give the land that he hath trodden upon, and to his children, because he hath wholly followed the LORD". [37]Also the LORD was angry with me for your sakes, saying, "Thou also shalt not go in thither. [38]But Joshua the son of Nun, which standeth before thee, he shall go in thither. Encourage him: for he shall cause Israel to inherit it. [39]Moreover your little ones, which ye said should be a prey, and your children, which in that day had no knowledge between good and evil, they shall go in thither, and unto them will I give it, and they shall possess it. [40]But as for you, turn ye, and take your journey into the wilderness by the way of the Red Sea." [41]Then ye answered and said unto me, "We have sinned against the LORD, we will go up and fight, according to all that the LORD our God commanded us". And when ye had girded on every man his weapons of war, ye were ready to go up into the hill. [42]And the LORD said unto me, "Say unto them, 'Go not up, neither fight, for I am not among you: lest ye be smitten before your enemies'". [43]So I spoke unto you, and you would not hear, but rebelled against the commandment of the LORD, and went presumptuously up into the hill. [44]And the

Amorites which dwelt in that mountain, came out against you, and chased you, as bees do, and destroyed you in Seir, even unto Hormah. ⁴⁵And ye returned and wept before the LORD; but the LORD would not hearken to your voice, nor give ear unto you. ⁴⁶So ye abode in Kadesh many days, according unto the days that ye abode there.

2 ¹Then we turned, and took our journey into the wilderness by the way of the Red Sea, as the LORD spoke unto me: and we compassed mount Seir many days. ²And the LORD spoke unto me, saying, ³"Ye have compassed this mountain long enough: turn you northward. ⁴And command thou the people, saying, 'Ye are to pass through the coast of your brethren the children of Esau, which dwell in Seir, and they shall be afraid of you: take ye good heed unto yourselves therefore. ⁵Meddle not with them, for I will not give you of their land, no, not so much as a foot-breadth, because I have given mount Seir unto Esau for a possession. ⁶Ye shall buy meat of them for money, that ye may eat, and ye shall also buy water of them for money, that ye may drink.'" ⁷For the LORD thy God hath blessed thee in all the works of thy hand: he knoweth thy walking through this great wilderness: these forty years the LORD thy God hath been with thee; thou hast lacked nothing. ⁸And when we passed by from our brethren the children of Esau, which dwelt in Seir, through the way of the plain from Elath, and from Ezion-geber, we turned and passed by the way of the wilderness of Moab. ⁹And the LORD said unto me, "Distress not the Moabites, neither contend with them in battle: for I will not give thee of their land for a possession, because I have given Ar unto the children of Lot for a possession".' ¹⁰The Emims dwelt therein in times past, a people great, and many, and tall, as the Anakims; ¹¹which also were accounted giants, as the Anakims; but the Moabites called them Emims. ¹²The Horims also dwelt in Seir beforetime, but the children of Esau succeeded them, when they had destroyed them from before them, and dwelt in their stead, as Israel did unto the land of his possession, which the LORD gave unto them. ¹³'"Now rise up," said I, "and get you over the brook Zered". And we went over the brook Zered. ¹⁴And the space in which we came from Kadesh-barnea, until we were come over the brook Zered, was thirty and eight years; until all the generation of the men of war were wasted out from among the host, as the LORD swore unto them. ¹⁵For indeed the hand of the LORD was against them, to destroy them from among the host, until they were consumed.

¹⁶'So it came to pass, when all the men of war were consumed and dead from among the people, ¹⁷that the LORD spoke unto me, saying, ¹⁸"Thou art to pass over through Ar, the coast of Moab, this day. ¹⁹And when thou comest nigh over against the children of Ammon, distress them not, nor meddle with them: for I will not give thee of the land of the children of Ammon any possession, because I have given it unto the children of Lot for a possession." ²⁰(That also was accounted a land of giants: giants dwelt therein in old time; and the Ammonites call them Zamzummims; ²¹a people great, and many, and tall, as the Anakims; but the LORD destroyed them before them, and they succeeded them,

and dwelt in their stead: ²²as he did to the children of Esau, which dwelt in Seir, when he destroyed the Horims from before them; and they succeeded them, and dwelt in their stead even unto this day: ²³and the Avims which dwelt in Hazerim, even unto Azzah, the Caphtorims, which came forth out of Caphtor, destroyed them, and dwelt in their stead.) ²⁴Rise ye up, take your journey, and pass over the river Arnon: behold, I have given into thy hand Sihon the Amorite, king of Heshbon, and his land: begin to possess it, and contend with him in battle. ²⁵This day will I begin to put the dread of thee and the fear of thee upon the nations that are under the whole heaven, who shall hear report of thee, and shall tremble, and be in anguish because of thee."

²⁶'And I sent messengers out of the wilderness of Kedemoth unto Sihon king of Heshbon with words of peace, saying, ²⁷"Let me pass through thy land: I will go along by the highway, I will neither turn unto the right hand nor to the left. ²⁸Thou shalt sell me meat for money, that I may eat, and give me water for money, that I may drink: only I will pass through on my feet ²⁹(as the children of Esau which dwell in Seir, and the Moabites which dwell in Ar, did unto me), until I shall pass over Jordan into the land which the LORD our God giveth us." ³⁰But Sihon king of Heshbon would not let us pass by him: for the LORD thy God hardened his spirit, and made his heart obstinate, that he might deliver him into thy hand, as appeareth this day. ³¹And the LORD said unto me, "Behold, I have begun to give Sihon and his land before thee: begin to possess, that thou mayest inherit his land". ³²Then Sihon came out against us, he and all his people, to fight at Jahaz. ³³And the LORD our God delivered him before us, and we smote him, and his sons, and all his people. ³⁴And we took all his cities at that time, and utterly destroyed the men, and the women, and the little ones, of every city, we left none to remain: ³⁵only the cattle we took for a prey unto ourselves, and the spoil of the cities which we took. ³⁶From Aroer, which is by the brink of the river of Arnon, and from the city that is by the river, even unto Gilead, there was not one city too strong for us: the LORD our God delivered all unto us: ³⁷Only unto the land of the children of Ammon thou camest not, nor unto any place of the river Jabbok, nor unto the cities in the mountains, nor unto whatsoever the LORD our God forbad us.

3 'Then we turned, and went up the way to Bashan: and Og the king of Bashan came out against us, he and all his people, to battle at Edrei. ²And the LORD said unto me, "Fear him not: for I will deliver him, and all his people, and his land, into thy hand; and thou shalt do unto him as thou didst unto Sihon king of the Amorites, which dwelt at Heshbon". ³So the LORD our God delivered into our hands Og also, the king of Bashan, and all his people: and we smote him until none was left to him remaining. ⁴And we took all his cities at that time, there was not a city which we took not from them, threescore cities, all the region of Argob, the kingdom of Og in Bashan. ⁵All these cities were fenced with high walls, gates, and bars; besides unwalled towns a great many. ⁶And we utterly destroyed them, as we did unto Sihon king of

Heshbon, utterly destroying the men, women, and children, of every city. ⁷But all the cattle, and the spoil of the cities, we took for a prey to ourselves. ⁸And we took at that time out of the hand of the two kings of the Amorites the land that was on this side Jordan, from the river of Arnon unto mount Hermon ⁹(which Hermon the Sidonians call Sirion; and the Amorites call it Shenir); ¹⁰all the cities of the plain, and all Gilead, and all Bashan, unto Salchah and Edrei, cities of the kingdom of Og in Bashan. ¹¹For only Og king of Bashan remained of the remnant of giants; behold, his bedstead was a bedstead of iron; is it not in Rabbath of the children of Ammon? Nine cubits was the length thereof, and four cubits the breadth of it, after the cubit of a man. ¹²And this land, which we possessed at that time, from Aroer which is by the river Arnon, and half mount Gilead, and the cities thereof, gave I unto the Reubenites and to the Gadites. ¹³And the rest of Gilead, and all Bashan, being the kingdom of Og, gave I unto the half tribe of Manasseh: all the region of Argob, with all Bashan, which was called the land of giants. ¹⁴Jair the son of Manasseh took all the country of Argob unto the coasts of Geshuri and Maachathi; and called them after his own name, Bashan-havoth-jair, unto this day. ¹⁵And I gave Gilead unto Machir. ¹⁶And unto the Reubenites and unto the Gadites I gave from Gilead even unto the river Arnon half the valley, and the border even unto the river Jabbok, which is the border of the children of Ammon; ¹⁷the plain also, and Jordan, and the coast thereof, from Chinnereth even unto the sea of the plain, even the salt sea, under Ashdoth-pisgah eastward.

¹⁸'And I commanded you at that time, saying, "The LORD your God hath given you this land to possess it: ye shall pass over armed before your brethren the children of Israel, all that are meet for the war. ¹⁹But your wives, and your little ones, and your cattle (for I know that ye have much cattle) shall abide in your cities which I have given you; ²⁰until the LORD have given rest unto your brethren, as well as unto you, and until they also possess the land which the LORD your God hath given them beyond Jordan: and then shall ye return every man unto his possession, which I have given you."

²¹'And I commanded Joshua at that time, saying, "Thy eyes have seen all that the LORD your God hath done unto these two kings: so shall the LORD do unto all the kingdoms whither thou passest. ²²Ye shall not fear them: for the LORD your God, he shall fight for you." ²³And I besought the LORD at that time, saying, ²⁴"O Lord GOD, thou hast begun to show thy servant thy greatness, and thy mighty hand: for what God is there in heaven or in earth, that can do according to thy works, and according to thy might? ²⁵I pray thee, let me go over, and see the good land that is beyond Jordan, that goodly mountain, and Lebanon." ²⁶But the LORD was wroth with me for your sakes, and would not hear me: and the LORD said unto me, "Let it suffice thee; speak no more unto me of this matter. ²⁷Get thee up into the top of Pisgah, and lift up thy eyes westward, and northward, and southward, and eastward, and behold it with thy eyes: for thou shalt not go over this Jordan. ²⁸But charge

Joshua, and encourage him, and strengthen him: for he shall go over before this people, and he shall cause them to inherit the land which thou shalt see." ²⁹So we abode in the valley over against Beth-peor.

4 'Now therefore hearken, O Israel, unto the statutes and unto the judgements which I teach you, for to do them, that ye may live, and go in and possess the land which the LORD God of your fathers giveth you. ²Ye shall not add unto the word which I command you, neither shall you diminish aught from it, that ye may keep the commandments of the LORD your God which I command you. ³Your eyes have seen what the LORD did because of Baal-peor: for all the men that followed Baal-peor, the LORD thy God hath destroyed them from among you. ⁴But ye that did cleave unto the LORD your God are alive every one of you this day. ⁵Behold, I have taught you statutes and judgements, even as the LORD my God commanded me, that ye should do so in the land whither ye go to possess it. ⁶Keep therefore and do them; for this is your wisdom and your understanding in the sight of the nations, which shall hear all these statutes, and say, "Surely this great nation is a wise and understanding people". ⁷For what nation is there so great, who hath God so nigh unto them, as the LORD our God is in all things that we call upon him for? ⁸And what nation is there so great, that hath statutes and judgements so righteous as all this law, which I set before you this day? ⁹Only take heed to thyself, and keep thy soul diligently, lest thou forget the things which thy eyes have seen, and lest they depart from thy heart all the days of thy life: but teach them thy sons, and thy sons' sons: ¹⁰specially the day that thou stoodest before the LORD thy God in Horeb, when the LORD said unto me, "Gather me the people together, and I will make them hear my words, that they may learn to fear me all the days that they shall live upon the earth, and that they may teach their children". ¹¹And ye came near and stood under the mountain, and the mountain burnt with fire unto the midst of heaven, with darkness, clouds, and thick darkness. ¹²And the LORD spoke unto you out of the midst of the fire: ye heard the voice of the words, but saw no similitude; only ye heard a voice. ¹³And he declared unto you his covenant, which he commanded you to perform, even ten commandments; and he wrote them upon two tablets of stone.

¹⁴'And the LORD commanded me at that time to teach you statutes and judgements, that ye might do them in the land whither ye go over to possess it. ¹⁵Take ye therefore good heed unto yourselves (for ye saw no manner of similitude on the day that the LORD spoke unto you in Horeb out of the midst of the fire), ¹⁶lest ye corrupt yourselves, and make you a graven image, the similitude of any figure, the likeness of male or female, ¹⁷the likeness of any beast that is on the earth, the likeness of any winged fowl that flieth in the air, ¹⁸the likeness of anything that creepeth on the ground, the likeness of any fish that is in the waters beneath the earth: ¹⁹and lest thou lift up thine eyes unto heaven, and when thou seest the sun, and the moon, and the stars, even all the host of heaven, shouldst be driven to worship them, and serve them, which the LORD thy God hath divided unto all nations under the whole

heaven. ²⁰But the LORD hath taken you, and brought you forth out of the iron furnace, even out of Egypt, to be unto him a people of inheritance, as ye are this day. ²¹Furthermore the LORD was angry with me for your sakes, and swore that I should not go over Jordan, and that I should not go in unto that good land, which the LORD thy God giveth thee for an inheritance: ²²but I must die in this land, I must not go over Jordan: but ye shall go over, and possess that good land. ²³Take heed unto yourselves, lest ye forget the covenant of the LORD your God, which he made with you, and make you a graven image, or the likeness of anything, which the LORD thy God hath forbidden thee. ²⁴For the LORD thy God is a consuming fire, even a jealous God.

²⁵'When thou shalt beget children, and children's children, and shalt have remained long in the land, and shall corrupt yourselves, and make a graven image, or the likeness of anything, and shall do evil in the sight of the LORD thy God, to provoke him to anger: ²⁶I call heaven and earth to witness against you this day, that ye shall soon utterly perish from off the land whereunto you go over Jordan to possess it: ye shall not prolong your days upon it, but shall utterly be destroyed. ²⁷And the LORD shall scatter you among the nations, and ye shall be left few in number among the heathen, whither the LORD shall lead you. ²⁸And there ye shall serve gods, the work of men's hands, wood and stone, which neither see, nor hear, nor eat, nor smell. ²⁹But if from thence thou shalt seek the LORD thy God, thou shalt find him, if thou seek him with all thy heart and with all thy soul. ³⁰When thou art in tribulation, and all these things are come upon thee, even in the latter days, if thou turn to the LORD thy God, and shalt be obedient unto his voice ³¹(for the LORD thy God is a merciful God), he will not forsake thee, neither destroy thee, nor forget the covenant of thy fathers which he swore unto them. ³²For ask now of the days that are past, which were before thee, since the day that God created man upon the earth, and ask from the one side of heaven unto the other, whether there hath been any such thing as this great thing is, or hath been heard like it? ³³Did ever people hear the voice of God speaking out of the midst of the fire, as thou hast heard, and live? ³⁴Or hath God essayed to go and take him a nation from the midst of another nation, by temptations, by signs, and by wonders, and by war, and by a mighty hand, and by a stretched out arm, and by great terrors, according to all that the LORD your God did for you in Egypt before your eyes? ³⁵Unto thee it was shown, that thou mightest know that the LORD he is God; there is none else besides him. ³⁶Out of heaven he made thee to hear his voice, that he might instruct thee: and upon earth he showed thee his great fire, and thou heardest his words out of the midst of the fire. ³⁷And because he loved thy fathers, therefore he chose their seed after them, and brought thee out in his sight with his mighty power out of Egypt: ³⁸to drive out nations from before thee greater and mightier than thou art, to bring thee in, to give thee their land for an inheritance, as it is this day. ³⁹Know therefore this day, and consider it in thy heart, that the LORD he is God in heaven above, and upon the earth beneath: there is

none else. ⁴⁰Thou shalt keep therefore his statutes, and his commandments, which I command thee this day, that it may go well with thee, and with thy children after thee, and that thou mayest prolong thy days upon the earth, which the LORD thy God giveth thee, for ever.'

⁴¹Then Moses severed three cities on this side Jordan toward the sunrising: ⁴²that the slayer might flee thither, which should kill his neighbour unawares, and hated him not in times past, and that fleeing unto one of these cities he might live: ⁴³namely, Bezer in the wilderness, in the plain country of the Reubenites; and Ramoth in Gilead of the Gadites; and Golan in Bashan of the Manassites.

⁴⁴And this is the law which Moses set before the children of Israel: ⁴⁵these are the testimonies, and the statutes, and the judgements, which Moses spoke unto the children of Israel, after they came forth out of Egypt, ⁴⁶on this side Jordan, in the valley over against Beth-peor, in the land of Sihon king of the Amorites, who dwelt at Heshbon, whom Moses and the children of Israel smote, after they were come forth out of Egypt. ⁴⁷And they possessed his land, and the land of Og king of Bashan, two kings of the Amorites, which were on this side Jordan toward the sunrising, ⁴⁸from Aroer, which is by the bank of the river Arnon, even unto mount Sion, which is Hermon, ⁴⁹and all the plain of this side Jordan eastward, even unto the sea of the plain under the springs of Pisgah.

5 And Moses called all Israel, and said unto them, 'Hear, O Israel, the statutes and judgements which I speak in your ears this day, that ye may learn them, and keep, and do them. ²The LORD our God made a covenant with us in Horeb. ³The LORD made not this covenant with our fathers, but with us, even us, who are all of us here alive this day. ⁴The LORD talked with you face to face in the mount out of the midst of the fire ⁵(I stood between the LORD and you at that time, to show you the word of the LORD: for ye were afraid by reason of the fire, and went not up into the mount), saying, ⁶'I am the LORD thy God, which brought thee out of the land of Egypt, from the house of bondage.

⁷'"Thou shalt have no other gods before me.

⁸'"Thou shalt not make thee any graven image, or any likeness of anything that is in heaven above, or that is in the earth beneath, or that is in the waters beneath the earth. ⁹Thou shalt not bow down thyself unto them, nor serve them: for I the LORD thy God am a jealous God, visiting the iniquity of the fathers upon the children unto the third and fourth generation of them that hate me, ¹⁰and showing mercy unto thousands of them that love me and keep my commandments.

¹¹'"Thou shalt not take the name of the LORD thy God in vain: for the LORD will not hold him guiltless that taketh his name in vain.

¹²'"Keep the sabbath day to sanctify it, as the LORD thy God hath commanded thee. ¹³Six days thou shalt labour, and do all thy work: ¹⁴but the seventh day is the sabbath of the LORD thy God: in it thou shalt not do any work, thou, nor thy son, nor thy daughter, nor thy manservant, nor thy maidservant, nor thy ox, nor thy ass, nor any of thy cattle, nor thy stranger that is within thy gates, that thy manservant and thy

maidservant may rest as well as thou. ¹⁵And remember that thou wast a servant in the land of Egypt, and that the LORD thy God brought thee out thence through a mighty hand and by a stretched out arm: therefore the LORD thy God commanded thee to keep the sabbath day.

¹⁶'"Honour thy father and thy mother, as the LORD thy God hath commanded thee, that thy days may be prolonged, and that it may go well with thee, in the land which the LORD thy God giveth thee.

¹⁷'"Thou shalt not kill.

¹⁸'"Neither shalt thou commit adultery.

¹⁹'"Neither shalt thou steal.

²⁰'"Neither shalt thou bear false witness against thy neighbour.

²¹'"Neither shalt thou desire thy neighbour's wife, neither shalt thou covet thy neighbour's house, his field, or his manservant, or his maidservant, his ox, or his ass, or anything that is thy neighbour's."

²²'These words the LORD spoke unto all your assembly in the mount out of the midst of the fire, of the cloud, and of the thick darkness, with a great voice: and he added no more. And he wrote them in two tablets of stone, and delivered them unto me. ²³And it came to pass when ye heard the voice out of the midst of the darkness (for the mountain did burn with fire), that ye came near unto me, even all the heads of your tribes, and your elders. ²⁴And ye said, "Behold, the LORD our God hath shown us his glory and his greatness, and we have heard his voice out of the midst of the fire: we have seen this day that God doth talk with man, and he liveth. ²⁵Now therefore why should we die? for this great fire will consume us: if we hear the voice of the LORD our God any more, then we shall die. ²⁶For who is there of all flesh that hath heard the voice of the living God speaking out of the midst of the fire, as we have, and lived? ²⁷Go thou near, and hear all that the LORD our God shall say: and speak thou unto us all that the LORD our God shall speak unto thee, and we will hear it, and do it." ²⁸And the LORD heard the voice of your words, when ye spoke unto me; and the LORD said unto me, "I have heard the voice of the words of this people, which they have spoken unto thee: they have well said all that they have spoken. ²⁹O that there were such a heart in them, that they would fear me, and keep my commandments always, that it might be well with them, and with their children for ever. ³⁰Go say to them, 'Get you into your tents again'. ³¹But as for thee, stand thou here by me, and I will speak unto thee all the commandments, and the statutes, and the judgements, which thou shalt teach them, that they may do them in the land which I give them to possess it." ³²Ye shall observe to do therefore as the LORD your God hath commanded you: you shall not turn aside to the right hand or to the left. ³³You shall walk in all the ways which the LORD your God hath commanded you, that ye may live, and that it may be well with you, and that ye may prolong your days in the land which ye shall possess.

6 'Now these are the commandments, the statutes, and the judgements, which the LORD your God commanded to teach you, that ye might do them in the land whither ye go to possess it: ²that thou

mightest fear the Lord thy God, to keep all his statutes and his commandments, which I command thee, thou, and thy son, and thy son's son, all the days of thy life; and that thy days may be prolonged. ³Hear therefore, O Israel, and observe to do it; that it may be well with thee, and that ye may increase mightily, as the Lord God of thy fathers hath promised thee, in the land that floweth with milk and honey.

⁴'Hear, O Israel: the Lord our God is one Lord. ⁵And thou shalt love the Lord thy God with all thy heart, and with all thy soul, and with all thy might. ⁶And these words which I command thee this day, shall be in thy heart. ⁷And thou shalt teach them diligently unto thy children, and shalt talk of them when thou sittest in thy house, and when thou walkest by the way, and when thou liest down, and when thou risest up. ⁸And thou shalt bind them for a sign upon thy hand, and they shall be as frontlets between thy eyes. ⁹And thou shalt write them upon the posts of thy house, and on thy gates.

¹⁰'And it shall be, when the Lord thy God shall have brought thee into the land which he swore unto thy fathers, to Abraham, to Isaac, and to Jacob, to give thee great and goodly cities, which thou buildedst not, ¹¹and houses full of all good things, which thou filledst not, and wells dug, which thou duggedst not, vineyards and olive trees, which thou plantedst not; when thou shalt have eaten and be full; ¹²then beware lest thou forget the Lord, which brought thee forth out of the land of Egypt, from the house of bondage. ¹³Thou shalt fear the Lord thy God, and serve him, and shalt swear by his name. ¹⁴Ye shall not go after other gods, of the gods of the people which are round about you ¹⁵(for the Lord thy God is a jealous God among you), lest the anger of the Lord thy God be kindled against thee, and destroy thee from off the face of the earth.

¹⁶'Ye shall not tempt the Lord your God, as ye tempted him in Massah. ¹⁷You shall diligently keep the commandments of the Lord your God, and his testimonies, and his statutes, which he hath commanded thee. ¹⁸And thou shalt do that which is right and good in the sight of the Lord: that it may be well with thee, and that thou mayest go in and possess the good land which the Lord swore unto thy fathers, ¹⁹to cast out all thy enemies from before thee, as the Lord hath spoken. ²⁰And when thy son asketh thee in time to come, saying, "What mean the testimonies, and the statutes, and the judgements, which the Lord our God hath commanded you?" ²¹Then thou shalt say unto thy son, "We were Pharaoh's bondmen in Egypt, and the Lord brought us out of Egypt with a mighty hand. ²²And the Lord showed signs and wonders, great and sore, upon Egypt, upon Pharaoh, and upon all his household, before our eyes: ²³and he brought us out from thence, that he might bring us in, to give us the land which he swore unto our fathers. ²⁴And the Lord commanded us to do all these statutes, to fear the Lord our God, for our good always, that he might preserve us alive, as it is at this day. ²⁵And it shall be our righteousness, if we observe to do all these commandments before the Lord our God, as he hath commanded us."

7 'When the Lord thy God shall bring thee into the land whither thou goest to possess it, and hath cast out many nations before thee, the Hittites, and the Girgashites, and the Amorites, and the Canaanites, and the Perizzites, and the Hivites, and the Jebusites, seven nations greater and mightier than thou: ²and when the Lord thy God shall deliver them before thee, thou shalt smite them, and utterly destroy them; thou shalt make no covenant with them, nor show mercy unto them. ³Neither shalt thou make marriages with them: thy daughter thou shalt not give unto his son, nor his daughter shalt thou take unto thy son. ⁴For they will turn away thy son from following me, that they may serve other gods: so will the anger of the Lord be kindled against you, and destroy thee suddenly. ⁵But thus shall ye deal with them: ye shall destroy their altars, and break down their images, and cut down their groves, and burn their graven images with fire. ⁶For thou art a holy people unto the Lord thy God: the Lord thy God hath chosen thee to be a special people unto himself, above all people that are upon the face of the earth. ⁷The Lord did not set his love upon you, nor choose you, because ye were more in number than any people (for ye were the fewest of all people): ⁸but because the Lord loved you, and because he would keep the oath which he had sworn unto your fathers, hath the Lord brought you out with a mighty hand, and redeemed you out of the house of bondmen, from the hand of Pharaoh king of Egypt. ⁹Know therefore that the Lord thy God, he is God, the faithful God, which keepeth covenant and mercy with them that love him and keep his commandments to a thousand generations; ¹⁰and repayeth them that hate him to their face, to destroy them: he will not be slack to him that hateth him, he will repay him to his face. ¹¹Thou shalt therefore keep the commandments, and the statutes, and the judgements, which I command thee this day, to do them.

¹²'Wherefore it shall come to pass, if ye hearken to these judgements, and keep, and do them, that the Lord thy God shall keep unto thee the covenant and the mercy which he swore unto thy fathers. ¹³And he will love thee, and bless thee, and multiply thee: he will also bless the fruit of thy womb, and the fruit of thy land, thy corn, and thy wine, and thy oil, the increase of thy kine, and the flocks of thy sheep, in the land which he swore unto thy fathers to give thee. ¹⁴Thou shalt be blessed above all people: there shall not be male or female barren among you, or among your cattle. ¹⁵And the Lord will take away from thee all sickness, and will put none of the evil diseases of Egypt, which thou knowest, upon thee: but will lay them upon all them that hate thee. ¹⁶And thou shalt consume all the people which the Lord thy God shall deliver thee: thy eye shall have no pity upon them, neither shalt thou serve their gods; for that will be a snare unto thee. ¹⁷If thou shalt say in thy heart, "These nations are more than I, how can I dispossess them?" ¹⁸thou shalt not be afraid of them: but shalt well remember what the Lord thy God did unto Pharaoh, and unto all Egypt, ¹⁹the great temptations which thy eyes saw, and the signs, and the wonders, and the mighty hand, and the stretched out arm, whereby the Lord thy God

brought thee out: so shall the LORD thy God do unto all the people of whom thou art afraid. [20]Moreover the LORD thy God will send the hornet among them, until they that are left, and hide themselves from thee, be destroyed. [21]Thou shalt not be affrighted at them: for the LORD thy God is among you, a mighty God and terrible. [22]And the LORD thy God will put out those nations before thee by little and little: thou mayest not consume them at once, lest the beasts of the field increase upon thee. [23]But the LORD thy God shall deliver them unto thee, and shall destroy them with a mighty destruction, until they be destroyed. [24]And he shall deliver their kings into thy hand, and thou shalt destroy their name from under heaven: there shall no man be able to stand before thee, until thou have destroyed them. [25]The graven images of their gods shall ye burn with fire: thou shalt not desire the silver or gold that is on them, nor take it unto thee, lest thou be snared therein: for it is an abomination to the LORD thy God. [26]Neither shalt thou bring an abomination into thy house, lest thou be a cursed thing like it: but thou shalt utterly detest it, and thou shalt utterly abhor it, for it is a cursed thing.

8 [1]All the commandments which I command thee this day shall ye observe to do, that ye may live, and multiply, and go in and possess the land which the LORD swore unto your fathers. [2]And thou shalt remember all the way which the LORD thy God led thee these forty years in the wilderness, to humble thee, and to prove thee, to know what was in thy heart, whether thou wouldst keep his commandments, or no. [3]And he humbled thee, and suffered thee to hunger, and fed thee with manna, which thou knewest not, neither did thy fathers know: that he might make thee know that man doth not live by bread only, but by every word that proceedeth out of the mouth of the LORD doth man live. [4]Thy raiment waxed not old upon thee, neither did thy foot swell, these forty years. [5]Thou shalt also consider in thy heart, that, as a man chasteneth his son, so the LORD thy God chasteneth thee. [6]Therefore thou shalt keep the commandments of the LORD thy God, to walk in his ways, and to fear him. [7]For the LORD thy God bringeth thee into a good land, a land of brooks of water, of fountains and depths that spring out of valleys and hills, [8]a land of wheat, and barley, and vines, and fig trees, and pomegranates, a land of oil olive, and honey, [9]a land wherein thou shalt eat bread without scarceness, thou shalt not lack anything in it: a land whose stones are iron, and out of whose hills thou mayest dig brass. [10]When thou hast eaten and art full, then thou shalt bless the LORD thy God for the good land which he hath given thee. [11]Beware that thou forget not the LORD thy God, in not keeping his commandments, and his judgements, and his statutes, which I command thee this day: [12]lest when thou hast eaten and art full, and hast built goodly houses, and dwelt therein; [13]and when thy herds and thy flocks multiply, and thy silver and thy gold is multiplied, and all that thou hast is multiplied: [14]then thy heart be lifted up, and thou forget the LORD thy God (which brought thee forth out of the land of Egypt, from the house of bondage, [15]who led thee through that great and terrible wilderness, wherein were fiery serpents, and scorpions, and drought, where there was no water, who brought thee forth water out of the rock of flint, ¹⁶who fed thee in the wilderness with manna, which thy fathers knew not, that he might humble thee, and that he might prove thee, to do thee good at thy latter end): ¹⁷and thou say in thy heart, "My power and the might of my hand hath gotten me this wealth". ¹⁸But thou shalt remember the LORD thy God: for it is he that giveth thee power to get wealth, that he may establish his covenant which he swore unto thy fathers, as it is this day. ¹⁹And it shall be, if thou do at all forget the LORD thy God, and walk after other gods, and serve them, and worship them, I testify against you this day that ye shall surely perish. ²⁰As the nations which the LORD destroyeth before your face, so shall ye perish; because ye would not be obedient unto the voice of the LORD your God.

9 ¹'Hear, O Israel: thou art to pass over Jordan this day, to go in to possess nations greater and mightier than thyself, cities great and fenced up to heaven, ²a people great and tall, the children of the Anakims, whom thou knowest, and of whom thou hast heard say, "Who can stand before the children of Anak?" ³Understand therefore this day, that the LORD thy God is he which goeth over before thee, as a consuming fire: he shall destroy them, and he shall bring them down before thy face: so shalt thou drive them out, and destroy them quickly, as the LORD hath said unto thee. ⁴Speak not thou in thy heart, after that the LORD thy God hath cast them out from before thee, saying, "For my righteousness the LORD hath brought me in to possess this land": but for the wickedness of these nations the LORD doth drive them out from before thee. ⁵Not for thy righteousness, or for the uprightness of thy heart, dost thou go to possess their land: but for the wickedness of these nations the LORD thy God doth drive them out from before thee, and that he may perform the word which the LORD swore unto thy fathers, Abraham, Isaac, and Jacob. ⁶Understand therefore, that the LORD thy God giveth thee not this good land to possess it for thy righteousness; for thou art a stiff-necked people.

⁷'Remember, and forget not, how thou provokedst the LORD thy God to wrath in the wilderness: from the day that thou didst depart out of the land of Egypt, until ye came unto this place, ye have been rebellious against the LORD. ⁸Also in Horeb ye provoked the LORD to wrath, so that the LORD was angry with you to have destroyed you. ⁹When I was gone up into the mount to receive the tablets of stone, even the tablets of the covenant which the LORD made with you, then I abode in the mount forty days and forty nights, I neither did eat bread nor drink water: ¹⁰and the LORD delivered unto me two tablets of stone written with the finger of God; and on them was written according to all the words which the LORD spoke with you in the mount out of the midst of fire, in the day of the assembly. ¹¹And it came to pass at the end of forty days and forty nights, that the LORD gave me the two tablets of stone, even the tablets of the covenant. ¹²And the LORD said unto me, "Arise, get thee down quickly from hence; for thy people which thou hast brought

forth out of Egypt have corrupted themselves: they are quickly turned aside out of the way which I commanded them; they have made them a molten image". [13]Furthermore the LORD spoke unto me, saying, "I have seen this people, and behold, it is a stiff-necked people. [14]Let me alone, that I may destroy them, and blot out their name from under heaven: and I will make of thee a nation mightier and greater than they." [15]So I turned and came down from the mount, and the mount burnt with fire: and the two tablets of the covenant were in my two hands. [16]And I looked, and behold, ye had sinned against the LORD your God, and had made you a molten calf: ye had turned aside quickly out of the way which the LORD had commanded you. [17]And I took the two tablets, and cast them out of my two hands, and broke them before your eyes. [18]And I fell down before the LORD, as at the first, forty days and forty nights: I did neither eat bread, nor drink water, because of all your sins which ye sinned, in doing wickedly in the sight of the LORD, to provoke him to anger [19](for I was afraid of the anger and hot displeasure, wherewith the LORD was wroth against you to destroy you). But the LORD hearkened unto me at that time also. [20]And the LORD was very angry with Aaron, to have destroyed him: and I prayed for Aaron also the same time. [21]And I took your sin, the calf which ye had made, and burnt it with fire, and stamped it, and ground it very small, even until it was as small as dust: and I cast the dust thereof into the brook that descended out of the mount. [22]And at Taberah, and at Massah, and at Kibroth-hattaavah, ye provoked the LORD to wrath. [23]Likewise when the LORD sent you from Kadesh-barnea, saying, "Go up and possess the land which I have given you", then you rebelled against the commandment of the LORD your God, and ye believed him not, nor hearkened to his voice. [24]You have been rebellious against the LORD from the day that I knew you. [25]Thus I fell down before the LORD forty days and forty nights, as I fell down at the first, because the LORD had said he would destroy you. [26]I prayed therefore unto the LORD, and said, "O LORD GOD, destroy not thy people and thy inheritance, which thou hast redeemed through thy greatness, which thou hast brought forth out of Egypt with a mighty hand. [27]Remember thy servants, Abraham, Isaac, and Jacob; look not unto the stubbornness of this people, nor to their wickedness, nor to their sin: [28]lest the land whence thou broughtest us out say, 'Because the LORD was not able to bring them into the land which he promised them, and because he hated them, he hath brought them out to slay them in the wilderness'. [29]Yet they are thy people and thy inheritance, which thou broughtest out by thy mighty power and by thy stretched out arm."

10 [1]'At that time the LORD said unto me, "Hew thee two tablets of stone like unto the first, and come up unto me into the mount, and make thee an ark of wood. [2]And I will write on the tablets the words that were in the first tablets which thou brokest, and thou shalt put them in the ark." [3]And I made an ark of shittim wood, and hewed two tablets of stone like unto the first, and went up into the mount, having the two tablets in my hand. [4]And he wrote on the tablets, according to the first writing, the ten commandments, which the LORD spoke unto you in the mount out of the midst of the fire in the day of the assembly: and the LORD gave them unto me. ⁵And I turned myself and came down from the mount, and put the tablets in the ark which I had made; and there they be, as the LORD commanded me.'

⁶And the children of Israel took their journey from Beeroth of the children of Jaakan to Mosera; there Aaron died, and there he was buried, and Eleazar his son ministered in the priest's office in his stead. ⁷From thence they journeyed unto Gudgodah, and from Gudgodah to Jotbath, a land of rivers of waters.

⁸At that time the LORD separated the tribe of Levi, to bear the ark of the covenant of the LORD, to stand before the LORD to minister unto him, and to bless in his name, unto this day. ⁹Wherefore Levi hath no part nor inheritance with his brethren: the LORD is his inheritance, according as the LORD thy God promised him. ¹⁰And I stayed in the mount, according to the first time, forty days and forty nights; and the LORD hearkened unto me at that time also, and the LORD would not destroy thee. ¹¹And the LORD said unto me, "Arise, take thy journey before the people, that they may go in and possess the land, which I swore unto their fathers to give unto them".

¹²'And now, Israel, what doth the LORD thy God require of thee, but to fear the LORD thy God, to walk in all his ways, and to love him, and to serve the LORD thy God with all thy heart and with all thy soul, ¹³to keep the commandments of the LORD, and his statutes, which I command thee this day for thy good? ¹⁴Behold, the heaven and the heaven of heavens is the LORD's thy God, the earth also, with all that therein is. ¹⁵Only the LORD had a delight in thy fathers to love them, and he chose their seed after them, even you, above all people, as it is this day. ¹⁶Circumcise therefore the foreskin of your heart, and be no more stiff-necked. ¹⁷For the LORD your God is God of gods, and Lord of lords, a great God, a mighty, and a terrible, which regardeth not persons, nor taketh reward. ¹⁸He doth execute the judgement of the fatherless and widow, and loveth the stranger, in giving him food and raiment. ¹⁹Love ye therefore the stranger: for ye were strangers in the land of Egypt. ²⁰Thou shalt fear the LORD thy God; him shalt thou serve, and to him shalt thou cleave, and swear by his name. ²¹He is thy praise, and he is thy God, that hath done for thee these great and terrible things, which thy eyes have seen. ²²Thy fathers went down into Egypt with threescore and ten persons: and now the LORD thy God hath made thee as the stars of heaven for multitude.

11 'Therefore thou shalt love the LORD thy God, and keep his charge, and his statutes, and his judgements, and his commandments always. ²And know you this day: for I speak not with your children which have not known, and which have not seen the chastisement of the LORD your God, his greatness, his mighty hand, and his stretched out arm, ³and his miracles, and his acts, which he did in the midst of Egypt unto Pharaoh the king of Egypt, and unto all his land; ⁴and what he did unto the army of Egypt, unto their horses, and to their chariots;

how he made the water of the Red Sea to overflow them as they pursued after you, and how the LORD hath destroyed them unto this day; [5]and what he did unto you in the wilderness, until ye came into this place; [6]and what he did unto Dathan and Abiram, the sons of Eliab, the son of Reuben: how the earth opened her mouth, and swallowed them up, and their households, and their tents, and all the substance that was in their possession, in the midst of all Israel: [7]but your eyes have seen all the great acts of the LORD which he did. [8]Therefore shall ye keep all the commandments which I command you this day, that ye may be strong, and go in and possess the land, whither ye go to possess it; [9]and that ye may prolong your days in the land, which the LORD swore unto your fathers to give unto them and to their seed, a land that floweth with milk and honey.

[10]'For the land, whither thou goest in to possess it, is not as the land of Egypt from whence ye came out, where thou sowedst thy seed, and wateredst it with thy foot, as a garden of herbs: [11]but the land whither ye go to possess it, is a land of hills and valleys, and drinketh water of the rain of heaven: [12]a land which the LORD thy God careth for: the eyes of the LORD thy God are always upon it, from the beginning of the year even unto the end of the year.

[13]'And it shall come to pass, if you shall hearken diligently unto my commandments which I command you this day, to love the LORD your God, and to serve him with all your heart and with all your soul, [14]that I will give you the rain of your land in his due season, the first rain and the latter rain, that thou mayest gather in thy corn, and thy wine, and thy oil. [15]And I will send grass in thy fields for thy cattle, that thou mayest eat and be full. [16]Take heed to yourselves, that your heart be not deceived, and ye turn aside, and serve other gods, and worship them; [17]and then the LORD's wrath be kindled against you, and he shut up the heaven, that there be no rain, and that the land yield not her fruit; and lest ye perish quickly from off the good land which the LORD giveth you.

[18]'Therefore shall ye lay up these my words in your heart and in your soul, and bind them for a sign upon your hand, that they may be as frontlets between your eyes. [19]And ye shall teach them your children, speaking of them when thou sittest in thy house, and when thou walkest by the way, when thou liest down, and when thou risest up. [20]And thou shalt write them upon the door-posts of thy house, and upon thy gates: [21]that your days may be multiplied, and the days of your children, in the land which the LORD swore unto your fathers to give them, as the days of heaven upon the earth.

[22]'For if ye shall diligently keep all these commandments which I command you, to do them, to love the LORD your God, to walk in all his ways, and to cleave unto him: [23]then will the LORD drive out all these nations from before you, and ye shall possess greater nations and mightier than yourselves. [24]Every place whereon the soles of your feet shall tread shall be yours: from the wilderness and Lebanon, from the river, the river Euphrates, even unto the outermost sea shall your

coast be. ²⁵There shall no man be able to stand before you: for the LORD your God shall lay the fear of you and the dread of you upon all the land that ye shall tread upon, as he hath said unto you.

²⁶'Behold, I set before you this day a blessing and a curse: ²⁷a blessing, if ye obey the commandments of the LORD your God, which I command you this day: ²⁸and a curse, if ye will not obey the commandments of the LORD your God, but turn aside out of the way which I command you this day, to go after other gods, which ye have not known. ²⁹And it shall come to pass, when the LORD thy God hath brought thee in unto the land whither thou goest to possess it, that thou shalt put the blessing upon mount Gerizim, and the curse upon mount Ebal. ³⁰Are they not on the other side Jordan, by the way where the sun goeth down, in the land of the Canaanites, which dwell in the champaign over against Gilgal, beside the plains of Moreh? ³¹For ye shall pass over Jordan to go in to possess the land which the LORD your God giveth you, and ye shall possess it, and dwell therein. ³²And ye shall observe to do all the statutes and judgements which I set before you this day.

12 'These are the statutes and judgements, which ye shall observe to do in the land which the LORD God of thy fathers giveth thee to possess it, all the days that ye live upon the earth. ²Ye shall utterly destroy all the places, wherein the nations which ye shall possess served their gods, upon the high mountains, and upon the hills, and under every green tree. ³And you shall overthrow their altars, and break their pillars, and burn their groves with fire, and you shall hew down the graven images of their gods, and destroy the names of them out of that place. ⁴Ye shall not do so unto the LORD your God.

⁵But unto the place which the LORD your God shall choose out of all your tribes to put his name there, even unto his habitation shall ye seek, and thither thou shalt come: ⁶and thither ye shall bring your burnt offerings, and your sacrifices, and your tithes, and heave offerings of your hand, and your vows, and your free-will offerings, and the firstlings of your herds and of your flocks. ⁷And there ye shall eat before the LORD your God, and ye shall rejoice in all that you put your hand unto, ye and your households, wherein the LORD thy God hath blessed thee. ⁸Ye shall not do after all the things that we do here this day, every man whatsoever is right in his own eyes. ⁹For ye are not as yet come to the rest and to the inheritance, which the LORD your God giveth you. ¹⁰But when ye go over Jordan, and dwell in the land which the LORD your God giveth you to inherit, and when he giveth you rest from all your enemies round about, so that ye dwell in safety: ¹¹then there shall be a place which the LORD your God shall choose to cause his name to dwell there; thither shall ye bring all that I command you: your burnt offerings, and your sacrifices, your tithes, and the heave offering of your hand, and all your choice vows which ye vow unto the LORD. ¹²And ye shall rejoice before the LORD your God, ye, and your sons, and your daughters, and your menservants, and your maidservants, and the Levite that is within your gates, forasmuch as he hath no part nor inheritance with you. ¹³Take heed to thyself that thou offer not thy

burnt offerings in every place that thou seest: [14]but in the place which the Lord shall choose in one of thy tribes, there thou shalt offer thy burnt offerings, and there thou shalt do all that I command thee. [15]Notwithstanding thou mayest kill and eat flesh in all thy gates, whatsoever thy soul lusteth after, according to the blessing of the Lord thy God which he hath given thee: the unclean and the clean may eat thereof, as of the roebuck, and as of the hart. [16]Only ye shall not eat the blood: ye shall pour it upon the earth as water.

[17]'Thou mayest not eat within thy gates the tithe of thy corn, or of thy wine, or of thy oil, or the firstlings of thy herds, or of thy flock, nor any of thy vows which thou vowest, nor thy free-will offerings, or heave offering of thy hand: [18]But thou must eat them before the Lord thy God in the place which the Lord thy God shall choose, thou, and thy son, and thy daughter, and thy manservant, and thy maidservant, and the Levite that is within thy gates: and thou shalt rejoice before the Lord thy God in all that thou puttest thy hands unto. [19]Take heed to thyself that thou forsake not the Levite as long as thou livest upon the earth.

[20]'When the Lord thy God shall enlarge thy border, as he hath promised thee, and thou shalt say, "I will eat flesh", because thy soul longeth to eat flesh, thou mayest eat flesh, whatsoever thy soul lusteth after. [21]If the place which the Lord thy God hath chosen to put his name there be too far from thee, then thou shalt kill of thy herd and of thy flock, which the Lord hath given thee, as I have commanded thee, and thou shalt eat in thy gates whatsoever thy soul lusteth after. [22]Even as the roebuck and the hart is eaten, so thou shalt eat them: the unclean and the clean shall eat of them alike. [23]Only be sure that thou eat not the blood: for the blood is the life, and thou mayest not eat the life with the flesh. [24]Thou shalt not eat it; thou shalt pour it upon the earth as water. [25]Thou shalt not eat it, that it may go well with thee, and with thy children after thee, when thou shalt do that which is right in the sight of the Lord. [26]Only thy holy things which thou hast, and thy vows, thou shalt take, and go unto the place which the Lord shall choose. [27]And thou shalt offer thy burnt offerings, the flesh and the blood, upon the altar of the Lord thy God: and the blood of thy sacrifices shall be poured out upon the altar of the Lord thy God, and thou shalt eat the flesh. [28]Observe and hear all these words which I command thee, that it may go well with thee, and with thy children after thee for ever, when thou doest that which is good and right in the sight of the Lord thy God.

[29]'When the Lord thy God shall cut off the nations from before thee, whither thou goest to possess them, and thou succeedest them, and dwellest in their land: [30]take heed to thyself that thou be not snared by following them, after that they be destroyed from before thee, and that thou inquire not after their gods, saying, "How did these nations serve their gods? even so will I do likewise". [31]Thou shalt not do so unto the Lord thy God: for every abomination to the Lord which he hateth, have they done unto their gods: for even their sons and their daughters they have burnt in the fire to their gods. [32]What thing soever I command

you, observe to do it: thou shalt not add thereto, nor diminish from it.

13

¹If there arise among you a prophet, or a dreamer of dreams, and giveth thee a sign or a wonder, ²and the sign or the wonder come to pass, whereof he spoke unto thee, saying, "Let us go after other gods, which thou hast not known, and let us serve them": ³thou shalt not hearken unto the words of that prophet, or that dreamer of dreams: for the LORD your God proveth you, to know whether you love the LORD your God with all your heart and with all your soul. ⁴Ye shall walk after the LORD your God, and fear him, and keep his commandments, and obey his voice, and you shall serve him, and cleave unto him. ⁵And that prophet or that dreamer of dreams shall be put to death because he hath spoken to turn you away from the LORD your God, which brought you out of the land of Egypt, and redeemed you out of the house of bondage, to thrust thee out of the way which the LORD thy God commanded thee to walk in. So shalt thou put the evil away from the midst of thee.

⁶'If thy brother, the son of thy mother, or thy son, or thy daughter, or the wife of thy bosom, or thy friend, which is as thy own soul, entice thee secretly, saying, "Let us go and serve other gods, which thou hast not known, thou, nor thy fathers": ⁷namely, of the gods of the people which are round about you, nigh unto thee, or far off from thee, from the one end of the earth even unto the other end of the earth: ⁸thou shalt not consent unto him, nor hearken unto him, neither shall thy eye pity him, neither shalt thou spare, neither shalt thou conceal him: ⁹but thou shalt surely kill him: thy hand shall be first upon him to put him to death, and afterwards the hand of all the people. ¹⁰And thou shalt stone him with stones, that he die: because he hath sought to thrust thee away from the LORD thy God, which brought thee out of the land of Egypt, from the house of bondage. ¹¹And all Israel shall hear, and fear, and shall do no more any such wickedness as this is among you.

¹²'If thou shalt hear say in one of thy cities, which the LORD thy God hath given thee to dwell there, saying, ¹³"Certain men, the children of Belial, are gone out from among you, and have withdrawn the inhabitants of their city, saying, 'Let us go and serve other gods, which ye have not known'": ¹⁴then shalt thou inquire, and make search, and ask diligently: and behold, if it be truth, and the thing certain, that such abomination is wrought among you: ¹⁵thou shalt surely smite the inhabitants of that city with the edge of the sword, destroying it utterly, and all that is therein, and the cattle thereof, with the edge of the sword. ¹⁶And thou shalt gather all the spoil of it into the midst of the street thereof, and shalt burn with fire the city, and all the spoil thereof every whit, for the LORD thy God: and it shall be a heap for ever; it shall not be built again. ¹⁷And there shall cleave nought of the cursed thing to thy hand, that the LORD may turn from the fierceness of his anger, and show thee mercy, and have compassion upon thee, and multiply thee, as he hath sworn unto thy fathers; ¹⁸when thou shalt hearken to the voice of the LORD thy God, to keep all his command-

ments which I command thee this day, to do that which is right in the eyes of the LORD thy God.

14 ¹'Ye are the children of the LORD your God: ye shall not cut yourselves, nor make any baldness between your eyes for the dead. ²For thou art a holy people unto the LORD thy God, and the LORD hath chosen thee to be a peculiar people unto himself, above all the nations that are upon the earth.

³'Thou shalt not eat any abominable thing. ⁴These are the beasts which ye shall eat: the ox, the sheep, and the goat, ⁵the hart, and the roebuck, and the fallow deer, and the wild goat, and the pygarg, and the wild ox, and the chamois. ⁶And every beast that parteth the hoof, and cleaveth the cleft into two claws, and cheweth the cud amongst the beasts: that ye shall eat. ⁷Nevertheless these ye shall not eat of them that chew the cud, or of them that divide the cloven hoof, as the camel, and the hare, and the coney: for they chew the cud, but divide not the hoof; therefore they are unclean unto you. ⁸And the swine, because it divideth the hoof, yet cheweth not the cud, it is unclean unto you: ye shall not eat of their flesh, nor touch their dead carcase.

⁹'These ye shall eat of all that are in the waters: all that have fins and scales shall ye eat: ¹⁰and whatsoever hath not fins and scales ye may not eat: it is unclean unto you.

¹¹'Of all clean birds ye shall eat. ¹²But these are they of which ye shall not eat: the eagle, and the ossifrage, and the osprey, ¹³and the glede, and the kite, and the vulture after his kind, ¹⁴and every raven after his kind, ¹⁵and the owl, and the night hawk, and the cuckoo, and the hawk after his kind, ¹⁶the little owl, and the great owl, and the swan, ¹⁷and the pelican, and the gier-eagle, and the cormorant, ¹⁸and the stork, and the heron after her kind, and the lapwing, and the bat. ¹⁹And every creeping thing that flieth is unclean unto you: they shall not be eaten. ²⁰But of all clean fowls ye may eat.

²¹'Ye shall not eat of anything that dieth of itself: thou shalt give it unto the stranger that is in thy gates, that he may eat it, or thou mayest sell it unto an alien: for thou art a holy people unto the LORD thy God. Thou shalt not seethe a kid in his mother's milk.

²²'Thou shalt truly tithe all the increase of thy seed, that the field bringeth forth year by year. ²³And thou shalt eat before the LORD thy God, in the place which he shall choose to place his name there, the tithe of thy corn, of thy wine, and of thy oil, and the firstlings of thy herds and of thy flocks: that thou mayest learn to fear the LORD thy God always. ²⁴And if the way be too long for thee, so that thou art not able to carry it, or if the place be too far from thee, which the LORD thy God shall choose to set his name there, when the LORD thy God hath blessed thee: ²⁵then shalt thou turn it into money, and bind up the money in thy hand, and shalt go unto the place which the LORD thy God shall choose. ²⁶And thou shalt bestow that money for whatsoever thy soul lusteth after, for oxen, or for sheep, or for wine, or for strong drink, or for whatsoever thy soul desireth: and thou shalt eat there before the LORD thy God, and thou shalt rejoice, thou, and thy house-

hold. ²⁷And the Levite that is within thy gates; thou shalt not forsake him: for he hath no part nor inheritance with thee.

²⁸'At the end of three years thou shalt bring forth all the tithe of thy increase the same year, and shalt lay it up within thy gates. ²⁹And the Levite, because he hath no part nor inheritance with thee, and the stranger, and the fatherless, and the widow, which are within thy gates, shall come, and shall eat and be satisfied, that the Lord thy God may bless thee in all the work of thy hand which thou doest.

15 ¹'At the end of every seven years thou shalt make a release. ²And this is the manner of the release: every creditor that lendeth aught unto his neighbour shall release it: he shall not exact it of his neighbour, or of his brother, because it is called the Lord's release. ³Of a foreigner thou mayest exact it again: but that which is thine with thy brother thy hand shall release; ⁴save when there shall be no poor among you: for the Lord shall greatly bless thee in the land which the Lord thy God giveth thee for an inheritance to possess it: ⁵only if thou carefully hearken unto the voice of the Lord thy God, to observe to do all these commandments which I command thee this day. ⁶For the Lord thy God blesseth thee, as he promised thee: and thou shalt lend unto many nations, but thou shalt not borrow; and thou shalt reign over many nations, but they shall not reign over thee.

⁷'If there be among you a poor man of one of thy brethren within any of thy gates in thy land which the Lord thy God giveth thee, thou shalt not harden thy heart, nor shut thy hand from thy poor brother: ⁸but thou shalt open thy hand wide unto him, and shalt surely lend him sufficient for his need, in that which he wanteth. ⁹Beware that there be not a thought in thy wicked heart, saying, "The seventh year, the year of release, is at hand", and thy eye be evil against thy poor brother, and thou givest him nought, and he cry unto the Lord against thee, and it be sin unto thee. ¹⁰Thou shalt surely give him, and thy heart shall not be grieved when thou givest unto him: because that for this thing the Lord thy God shall bless thee in all thy works, and in all that thou puttest thy hand unto. ¹¹For the poor shall never cease out of the land: therefore I command thee, saying, "Thou shalt open thy hand wide unto thy brother, to thy poor, and to thy needy in the land".

¹²'And if thy brother, a Hebrew man, or a Hebrew woman, be sold unto thee, and serve thee six years, then in the seventh year thou shalt let him go free from thee. ¹³And when thou sendest him out free from thee, thou shalt not let him go away empty: ¹⁴thou shalt furnish him liberally out of thy flock, and out of thy floor, and out of thy wine-press: of that wherewith the Lord thy God hath blessed thee thou shalt give unto him. ¹⁵And thou shalt remember that thou wast a bondman in the land of Egypt, and the Lord thy God redeemed thee: therefore I command thee this thing today. ¹⁶And it shall be, if he say unto thee, "I will not go away from thee", because he loveth thee and thy house, because he is well with thee; ¹⁷Then thou shalt take an awl, and thrust it through his ear unto the door, and he shall be thy servant for ever. And also unto thy maidservant thou shalt do likewise. ¹⁸It shall not seem

hard unto thee, when thou sendest him away free from thee: for he hath been worth a double hired servant to thee, in serving thee six years: and the LORD thy God shall bless thee in all that thou doest.

[19] 'All the firstling males that come of thy herd and of thy flock thou shalt sanctify unto the LORD thy God: thou shalt do no work with the firstling of thy bullock, nor shear the firstling of thy sheep. [20]Thou shalt eat it before the LORD thy God year by year in the place which the LORD shall choose, thou and thy household. [21]And if there be any blemish therein, as if it be lame, or blind, or have any ill blemish, thou shalt not sacrifice it unto the LORD thy God. [22]Thou shalt eat it within thy gates: the unclean and the clean person shall eat it alike, as the roebuck, and as the hart. [23]Only thou shalt not eat the blood thereof: thou shalt pour it upon the ground as water.

16 'Observe the month of Abib, and keep the passover unto the LORD thy God: for in the month of Abib the LORD thy God brought thee forth out of Egypt by night. [2]Thou shalt therefore sacrifice the passover unto the LORD thy God, of the flock and the herd, in the place which the LORD shall choose to place his name there. [3]Thou shalt eat no leavened bread with it: seven days shalt thou eat unleavened bread therewith, even the bread of affliction; for thou camest forth out of the land of Egypt in haste: that thou mayest remember the day when thou camest forth out of the land of Egypt all the days of thy life. [4]And there shall be no leavened bread seen with thee in all thy coasts seven days, neither shall there anything of the flesh, which thou sacrificedst the first day at even, remain all night until the morning. [5]Thou mayest not sacrifice the passover within any of the gates which the LORD thy God giveth thee: [6]but at the place which the LORD thy God shall choose to place his name in, there thou shalt sacrifice the passover at even, at the going down of the sun, at the season that thou camest forth out of Egypt. [7]And thou shalt roast and eat it in the place which the LORD thy God shall choose, and thou shalt turn in the morning, and go unto thy tents. [8]Six days thou shalt eat unleavened bread, and on the seventh day shall be a solemn assembly to the LORD thy God: thou shalt do no work therein.

[9] 'Seven weeks shalt thou number unto thee: begin to number the seven weeks from such time as thou beginnest to put the sickle to the corn. [10]And thou shalt keep the feast of weeks unto the LORD thy God with a tribute of a free-will offering of thy hand, which thou shalt give unto the LORD thy God, according as the LORD thy God hath blessed thee. [11]And thou shalt rejoice before the LORD thy God, thou, and thy son, and thy daughter, and thy manservant, and thy maidservant, and the Levite that is within thy gates, and the stranger, and the fatherless, and the widow, that are among you, in the place which the LORD thy God hath chosen to place his name there. [12]And thou shalt remember that thou wast a bondman in Egypt: and thou shalt observe and do these statutes.

[13] 'Thou shalt observe the feast of tabernacles seven days, after that thou hast gathered in thy corn and thy wine. [14]And thou shalt rejoice in

thy feast, thou, and thy son, and thy daughter, and thy manservant, and thy maidservant, and the Levite, the stranger, and the fatherless, and the widow, that are within thy gates. [15]Seven days shalt thou keep a solemn feast unto the LORD thy God in the place which the LORD shall choose: because the LORD thy God shall bless thee in all thy increase, and in all the works of thy hands, therefore thou shalt surely rejoice.

[16]'Three times in a year shall all thy males appear before the LORD thy God in the place which he shall choose: in the feast of unleavened bread, and in the feast of weeks, and in the feast of tabernacles: and they shall not appear before the LORD empty. [17]Every man shall give as he is able, according to the blessing of the LORD thy God which he hath given thee.

[18]'Judges and officers shalt thou make thee in all thy gates, which the LORD thy God giveth thee, throughout thy tribes: and they shall judge the people with just judgement. [19]Thou shalt not wrest judgement, thou shalt not respect persons, neither take a gift: for a gift doth blind the eyes of the wise, and pervert the words of the righteous. [20]That which is altogether just shalt thou follow, that thou mayest live, and inherit the land which the LORD thy God giveth thee.

[21]'Thou shalt not plant thee a grove of any trees near unto the altar of the LORD thy God, which thou shalt make thee. [22]Neither shalt thou set thee up any image, which the LORD thy God hateth.

17 'Thou shalt not sacrifice unto the LORD thy God any bullock, or sheep, wherein is blemish, or any evilfavouredness: for that is an abomination unto the LORD thy God.

[2]'If there be found among you within any of thy gates which the LORD thy God giveth thee, man or woman, that hath wrought wickedness in the sight of the LORD thy God, in transgressing his covenant, [3]and hath gone and served other gods, and worshipped them, either the sun, or moon, or any of the host of heaven, which I have not commanded, [4]and it be told thee, and thou hast heard of it, and inquired diligently, and behold, it be true, and the thing certain, that such abomination is wrought in Israel: [5]then shalt thou bring forth that man or that woman, which have committed that wicked thing, unto thy gates, even that man or that woman, and shalt stone them with stones till they die. [6]At the mouth of two witnesses, or three witnesses, shall he that is worthy of death be put to death: but at the mouth of one witness he shall not be put to death. [7]The hands of the witnesses shall be first upon him to put him to death, and afterward the hands of all the people. So thou shalt put the evil away from among you.

[8]'If there arise a matter too hard for thee in judgement, between blood and blood, between plea and plea, and between stroke and stroke, being matters of controversy within thy gates: then shalt thou arise, and get thee up into the place which the LORD thy God shall choose; [9]and thou shalt come unto the priests the Levites, and unto the judge that shall be in those days, and inquire; and they shall show thee the sentence of judgement. [10]And thou shalt do according to the sentence, which they of that place which the LORD shall choose shall show thee,

and thou shalt observe to do according to all that they inform thee; [11]according to the sentence of the law which they shall teach thee, and according to the judgement which they shall tell thee, thou shalt do: thou shalt not decline from the sentence which they shall show thee, to the right hand, nor to the left. [12]And the man that will do presumptuously, and will not hearken unto the priest that standeth to minister there before the LORD thy God, or unto the judge, even that man shall die: and thou shalt put away the evil from Israel. [13]And all the people shall hear, and fear, and do no more presumptuously.

[14]'When thou art come unto the land which the LORD thy God giveth thee, and shalt possess it, and shalt dwell therein, and shalt say, "I will set a king over me, like as all the nations that are about me": [15]thou shalt in any wise set him king over thee, whom the LORD thy God shall choose: one from among thy brethren shalt thou set king over thee: thou mayest not set a stranger over thee, which is not thy brother. [16]But he shall not multiply horses to himself, nor cause the people to return to Egypt, to the end that he should multiply horses: forasmuch as the LORD hath said unto you, "Ye shall henceforth return no more that way". [17]Neither shall he multiply wives to himself, that his heart turn not away: neither shall he greatly multiply to himself silver and gold. [18]And it shall be, when he sitteth upon the throne of his kingdom, that he shall write him a copy of this law in a book out of that which is before the priests the Levites. [19]And it shall be with him, and he shall read therein all the days of his life, that he may learn to fear the LORD his God, to keep all the words of this law and these statutes, to do them: [20]that his heart be not lifted up above his brethren, and that he turn not aside from the commandment, to the right hand, or to the left: to the end that he may prolong his days in his kingdom, he, and his children, in the midst of Israel.

18 'The priests the Levites, and all the tribe of Levi, shall have no part nor inheritance with Israel: they shall eat the offerings of the LORD made by fire, and his inheritance. [2]Therefore shall they have no inheritance among their brethren: the LORD is their inheritance, as he hath said unto them.

[3]'And this shall be the priests' due from the people, from them that offer a sacrifice, whether it be ox or sheep: and they shall give unto the priest the shoulder, and the two cheeks, and the maw. [4]The first-fruit also of thy corn, of thy wine, and of thy oil, and the first of the fleece of thy sheep, shalt thou give him. [5]For the LORD thy God hath chosen him out of all thy tribes, to stand to minister in the name of the LORD, him and his sons for ever.

[6]'And if a Levite come from any of thy gates out of all Israel, where he sojourned, and come with all the desire of his mind unto the place which the LORD shall choose; [7]then he shall minister in the name of the LORD his God, as all his brethren the Levites do, which stand there before the LORD. [8]They shall have like portions to eat, besides that which cometh of the sale of his patrimony.

[9]'When thou art come into the land which the LORD thy God giveth

thee, thou shalt not learn to do after the abominations of those nations. [10]There shall not be found among you anyone that maketh his son or his daughter to pass through the fire, or that useth divination, or an observer of times, or an enchanter, or a witch, [11]or a charmer, or a consulter with familiar spirits, or a wizard, or a necromancer. [12]For all that do these things are an abomination unto the LORD: and because of these abominations the LORD thy God doth drive them out from before thee. [13]Thou shalt be perfect with the LORD thy God. [14]For these nations, which thou shalt possess, hearkened unto observers of times, and unto diviners: but as for thee, the LORD thy God hath not suffered thee so to do.

[15]'The LORD thy God will raise up unto thee a Prophet from the midst of thee, of thy brethren, like unto me; unto him ye shall hearken; [16]according to all that thou desiredst of the LORD thy God in Horeb in the day of the assembly, saying, "Let me not hear again the voice of the LORD my God, neither let me see this great fire any more, that I die not". [17]And the LORD said unto me, "They have well spoken that which they have spoken. [18]I will raise them up a Prophet from among their brethren, like unto thee, and will put my words in his mouth, and he shall speak unto them all that I shall command him. [19]And it shall come to pass, that whosoever will not hearken unto my words which he shall speak in my name, I will require it of him. [20]But the prophet which shall presume to speak a word in my name, which I have not commanded him to speak, or that shall speak in the name of other gods, even that prophet shall die." [21]And if thou say in thy heart, "How shall we know the word which the LORD hath not spoken?" [22]when a prophet speaketh in the name of the LORD, if the thing follow not, nor come to pass, that is the thing which the LORD hath not spoken, but the prophet hath spoken it presumptuously: thou shalt not be afraid of him.

19 'When the LORD thy God hath cut off the nations, whose land the LORD thy God giveth thee, and thou succeedest them, and dwellest in their cities, and in their houses: [2]thou shalt separate three cities for thee in the midst of thy land, which the LORD thy God giveth thee to possess it. [3]Thou shalt prepare thee a way, and divide the coasts of thy land, which the LORD thy God giveth thee to inherit, into three parts, that every slayer may flee thither.

[4]'And this is the case of the slayer which shall flee thither, that he may live: whoso killeth his neighbour ignorantly, whom he hated not in time past, [5]as when a man goeth into the wood with his neighbour to hew wood, and his hand fetcheth a stroke with the axe to cut down the tree, and the head slippeth from the helve, and lighteth upon his neighbour, that he die; he shall flee unto one of those cities, and live: [6]lest the avenger of the blood pursue the slayer, while his heart is hot, and overtake him, because the way is long, and slay him; whereas he was not worthy of death, inasmuch as he hated him not in time past. [7]Wherefore I command thee, saying, "Thou shalt separate three cities for thee". [8]And if the LORD thy God enlarge thy coast, as he hath sworn

unto thy fathers, and give thee all the land which he promised to give unto thy fathers ⁹(if thou shalt keep all these commandments to do them, which I command thee this day, to love the LORD thy God, and to walk ever in his ways): then shalt thou add three cities more for thee, besides these three: ¹⁰that innocent blood be not shed in thy land, which the LORD thy God giveth thee for an inheritance, and so blood be upon thee.

¹¹'But if any man hate his neighbour, and lie in wait for him, and rise up against him, and smite him mortally that he die, and fleeth into one of these cities: ¹²then the elders of his city shall send and fetch him thence, and deliver him into the hand of the avenger of blood, that he may die. ¹³Thy eye shall not pity him, but thou shalt put away the guilt of innocent blood from Israel, that it may go well with thee.

¹⁴'Thou shalt not remove thy neighbour's landmark, which they of old time have set in thy inheritance, which thou shalt inherit in the land that the LORD thy God giveth thee to possess it.

¹⁵'One witness shall not rise up against a man for any iniquity, or for any sin, in any sin that he sinneth: at the mouth of two witnesses, or at the mouth of three witnesses, shall the matter be established.

¹⁶'If a false witness rise up against any man to testify against him that which is wrong: ¹⁷then both the men, between whom the controversy is, shall stand before the LORD, before the priests and the judges, which shall be in those days. ¹⁸And the judges shall make diligent inquisition: and behold, if the witness be a false witness, and hath testified falsely against his brother: ¹⁹then shall ye do unto him, as he had thought to have done unto his brother: so shalt thou put the evil away from among you. ²⁰And those which remain shall hear, and fear, and shall henceforth commit no more any such evil among you. ²¹And thy eye shall not pity, but life shall go for life, eye for eye, tooth for tooth, hand for hand, foot for foot.

20 'When thou goest out to battle against thy enemies, and seest horses, and chariots, and a people more than thou, be not afraid of them: for the LORD thy God is with thee, which brought thee up out of the land of Egypt. ²And it shall be, when ye are come nigh unto the battle, that the priest shall approach and speak unto the people, ³and shall say unto them, "Hear, O Israel, you approach this day unto battle against your enemies: let not your hearts faint, fear not, and do not tremble, neither be ye terrified because of them; ⁴for the LORD your God is he that goeth with you, to fight for you against your enemies, to save you".

⁵'And the officers shall speak unto the people, saying, "What man is there that hath built a new house, and hath not dedicated it? let him go and return to his house, lest he die in the battle, and another man dedicate it. ⁶And what man is he that hath planted a vineyard, and hath not yet eaten of it? let him also go and return unto his house, lest he die in the battle, and another man eat of it. ⁷And what man is there that hath betrothed a wife, and hath not taken her? let him go and return unto his house, lest he die in battle, and another man take her." ⁸And

the officers shall speak further unto the people, and they shall say, "What man is there that is fearful and faint-hearted? let him go and return unto his house, lest his brethren's heart faint as well as his heart". ⁹And it shall be, when the officers have made an end of speaking unto the people, that they shall make captains of the armies to lead the people.

¹⁰'When thou comest nigh unto a city to fight against it, then proclaim peace unto it. ¹¹And it shall be, if it make thee answer of peace, and open unto thee, then it shall be, that all the people that is found therein shall be tributaries unto thee, and they shall serve thee. ¹²And if it will make no peace with thee, but will make war against thee, then thou shalt besiege it. ¹³And when the LORD thy God hath delivered it into thy hands, thou shalt smite every male thereof with the edge of the sword. ¹⁴But the women, and the little ones, and the cattle, and all that is in the city, even all the spoil thereof, shalt thou take unto thyself, and thou shalt eat the spoil of thy enemies, which the LORD thy God hath given thee. ¹⁵Thus shalt thou do unto all the cities which are very far off from thee, which are not of the cities of these nations. ¹⁶But of the cities of these people, which the LORD thy God doth give thee for an inheritance, thou shalt save alive nothing that breatheth: ¹⁷but thou shalt utterly destroy them, namely, the Hittites, and the Amorites, the Canaanites, and the Perizzites, the Hivites, and the Jebusites; as the LORD thy God hath commanded thee: ¹⁸that they teach you not to do after all their abominations, which they have done unto their gods; so should ye sin against the LORD your God.

¹⁹'When thou shalt besiege a city a long time, in making war against it to take it, thou shalt not destroy the trees thereof by forcing an axe against them: for thou mayest eat of them, and thou shalt not cut them down (for the tree of the field is man's life) to employ them in the siege. ²⁰Only the trees which thou knowest that they be not trees for meat, thou shalt destroy and cut them down, and thou shalt build bulwarks against the city that maketh war with thee, until it be subdued.

21 'If one be found slain in the land which the LORD thy God giveth thee to possess it, lying in the field, and it be not known who hath slain him: ²then thy elders and thy judges shall come forth, and they shall measure unto the cities which are round about him that is slain. ³And it shall be, that the city which is next unto the slain man, even the elders of that city shall take a heifer, which hath not been wrought with, and which hath not drawn in the yoke. ⁴And the elders of that city shall bring down the heifer unto a rough valley, which is neither eared nor sown, and shall strike off the heifer's neck there in the valley. ⁵And the priests the sons of Levi shall come near; for them the LORD thy God hath chosen to minister unto him, and to bless in the name of the LORD: and by their word shall every controversy and every stroke be tried. ⁶And all the elders of that city that are next unto the slain man, shall wash their hands over the heifer that is beheaded in the valley. ⁷And they shall answer and say, "Our hands have not shed this blood, neither have our eyes seen it. ⁸Be merciful, O LORD, unto thy people Israel, whom thou hast redeemed, and lay not innocent blood unto thy people of Israel's charge." And the blood shall be forgiven them. ⁹So shalt thou put away the guilt of innocent blood from among you, when thou shalt do that which is right in the sight of the LORD.

¹⁰'When thou goest forth to war against thy enemies, and the LORD thy God hath delivered them into thy hands, and thou hast taken them captive, ¹¹and seest among the captives a beautiful woman, and hast a desire unto her, that thou wouldst have her to thy wife: ¹²then thou shalt bring her home to thy house, and she shall shave her head, and pare her nails. ¹³And she shall put the raiment of her captivity from off her, and shall remain in thy house, and bewail her father and her mother a full month: and after that thou shalt go in unto her, and be her husband, and she shall be thy wife. ¹⁴And it shall be, if thou have no delight in her, then thou shalt let her go whither she will; but thou shalt not sell her at all for money, thou shalt not make merchandise of her, because thou hast humbled her.

¹⁵'If a man have two wives, one beloved, and another hated, and they have borne him children, both the beloved and the hated; and if the firstborn son be hers that was hated: ¹⁶then it shall be, when he maketh his sons to inherit that which he hath, that he may not make the son of the beloved firstborn before the son of the hated, which is indeed the firstborn: ¹⁷but he shall acknowledge the son of the hated for the first-born, by giving him a double portion of all that he hath: for he is the beginning of his strength; the right of the firstborn is his.

¹⁸'If a man have a stubborn and rebellious son, which will not obey the voice of his father, or the voice of his mother, and that, when they have chastened him, will not hearken unto them: ¹⁹then shall his father and his mother lay hold on him, and bring him out unto the elders of his city, and unto the gate of his place: ²⁰and they shall say unto the elders of his city, "This our son is stubborn and rebellious, he will not obey our voice: he is a glutton, and a drunkard". ²¹And all the men of his city shall stone him with stones, that he die: so shalt thou put evil away from among you; and all Israel shall hear, and fear.

²²'And if a man have committed a sin worthy of death, and he be to be put to death, and thou hang him on a tree: ²³his body shall not remain all night upon the tree, but thou shalt in any wise bury him that day (for he that is hanged is accursed of God), that thy land be not defiled, which the LORD thy God giveth thee for an inheritance.

22

'Thou shalt not see thy brother's ox or his sheep go astray, and hide thyself from them: thou shalt in any case bring them again unto thy brother. ²And if thy brother be not nigh unto thee, or if thou know him not, then thou shalt bring it unto thy own house, and it shall be with thee until thy brother seek after it, and thou shalt restore it to him again. ³In like manner shalt thou do with his ass, and so shalt thou do with his raiment: and with all lost thing of thy brother's which he hath lost, and thou hast found, shalt thou do likewise: thou mayest not hide thyself.

⁴'Thou shalt not see thy brother's ass or his ox fall down by the way,

and hide thyself from them: thou shalt surely help him to lift them up again.

⁵'The woman shall not wear that which pertaineth unto a man, neither shall a man put on a woman's garment: for all that do so are abomination unto the LORD thy God.

⁶'If a bird's nest chance to be before thee in the way in any tree, or on the ground, whether they be young ones, or eggs, and the dam sitting upon the young, or upon the eggs, thou shalt not take the dam with the young: ⁷but thou shalt in any wise let the dam go, and take the young to thee; that it may be well with thee, and that thou mayest prolong thy days.

⁸'When thou buildest a new house, then thou shalt make a battlement for thy roof, that thou bring not blood upon thy house, if any man fall from thence.

⁹'Thou shalt not sow thy vineyard with divers seeds: lest the fruit of thy seed which thou hast sown, and the fruit of thy vineyard be defiled.

¹⁰'Thou shalt not plough with an ox and an ass together.

¹¹'Thou shalt not wear a garment of diverse sorts, as of woollen and linen together.

¹²'Thou shalt make thee fringes upon the four quarters of thy vesture, wherewith thou coverest thyself.

¹³'If any man take a wife, and go in unto her, and hate her, ¹⁴and give occasions of speech against her, and bring up an evil name upon her, and say, "I took this woman, and when I came to her, I found her not a maid": ¹⁵then shall the father of the damsel, and her mother take and bring forth the tokens of the damsel's virginity unto the elders of the city in the gate. ¹⁶And the damsel's father shall say unto the elders, "I gave my daughter unto this man to wife, and he hateth her: ¹⁷and lo, he hath given occasions of speech against her, saying, 'I found not thy daughter a maid': and yet these are the tokens of my daughter's virginity". And they shall spread the cloth before the elders of the city. ¹⁸And the elders of that city shall take that man and chastise him. ¹⁹And they shall amerce him in a hundred shekels of silver, and give them unto the father of the damsel, because he hath brought up an evil name upon a virgin of Israel: and she shall be his wife; he may not put her away all his days. ²⁰But if this thing be true, and the tokens of virginity be not found for the damsel: ²¹then they shall bring out the damsel to the door of her father's house, and the men of her city shall stone her with stones that she die, because she hath wrought folly in Israel, to play the whore in her father's house: so shalt thou put evil away from among you.

²²'If a man be found lying with a woman married to a husband, then they shall both of them die, both the man that lay with the woman, and the woman: so shalt thou put away evil from Israel.

²³'If a damsel that is a virgin be betrothed unto a husband, and a man find her in the city, and lie with her: ²⁴then ye shall bring them both out unto the gate of that city, and ye shall stone them with stones that they die; the damsel, because she cried not, being in the city; and

the man, because he hath humbled his neighbour's wife: so thou shalt put away evil from among you.

²⁵ 'But if a man find a betrothed damsel in the field, and the man force her, and lie with her: then the man only that lay with her shall die. ²⁶But unto the damsel thou shalt do nothing; there is in the damsel no sin worthy of death: for as when a man riseth against his neighbour, and slayeth him, even so is this matter: ²⁷for he found her in the field, and the betrothed damsel cried, and there was none to save her.

²⁸ 'If a man find a damsel that is a virgin, which is not betrothed, and lay hold on her, and lie with her, and they be found: ²⁹then the man that lay with her shall give unto the damsel's father fifty shekels of silver, and she shall be his wife, because he hath humbled her: he may not put her away all his days.

³⁰ 'A man shall not take his father's wife, nor discover his father's skirt.

23 'He that is wounded in the stones, or hath his privy member cut off, shall not enter into the congregation of the LORD. ²A bastard shall not enter into the congregation of the LORD: even to his tenth generation shall he not enter into the congregation of the LORD. ³An Ammonite or Moabite shall not enter into the congregation of the LORD; even to their tenth generation shall they not enter into the congregation of the LORD for ever, ⁴because they met you not with bread and with water in the way, when ye came forth out of Egypt; and because they hired against thee Balaam the son of Beor of Pethor of Mesopotamia, to curse thee. ⁵Nevertheless the LORD thy God would not hearken unto Balaam: but the LORD thy God turned the curse into a blessing unto thee, because the LORD thy God loved thee. ⁶Thou shalt not seek their peace nor their prosperity all thy days for ever.

⁷ 'Thou shalt not abhor an Edomite, for he is thy brother: thou shalt not abhor an Egyptian, because thou wast a stranger in his land. ⁸The children that are begotten of them shall enter into the congregation of the LORD in their third generation.

⁹ 'When the host goeth forth against thy enemies, then keep thee from every wicked thing.

¹⁰ 'If there be among you any man that is not clean by reason of uncleanness that chanceth him by night, then shall he go abroad out of the camp, he shall not come within the camp: ¹¹but it shall be when evening cometh on, he shall wash himself with water: and when the sun is down, he shall come into the camp again.

¹² 'Thou shalt have a place also without the camp, whither thou shalt go forth abroad. ¹³And thou shalt have a paddle upon thy weapon; and it shall be when thou wilt ease thyself abroad, thou shalt dig therewith, and shalt turn back and cover that which cometh from thee: ¹⁴for the LORD thy God walketh in the midst of thy camp, to deliver thee, and to give up thy enemies before thee: therefore shall thy camp be holy, that he see no unclean thing in thee, and turn away from thee.

¹⁵ 'Thou shalt not deliver unto his master the servant which is escaped from his master unto thee. ¹⁶He shall dwell with thee, even among you, in that place which he shall choose in one of thy gates where it liketh

him best: thou shalt not oppress him.

[17] 'There shall be no whore of the daughters of Israel, nor a sodomite of the sons of Israel. [18]Thou shalt not bring the hire of a whore, or the price of a dog into the house of the LORD thy God for any vow: for even both these are abomination unto the LORD thy God.

[19] 'Thou shalt not lend upon usury to thy brother; usury of money, usury of victuals, usury of anything that is lent upon usury. [20]Unto a stranger thou mayest lend upon usury; but unto thy brother thou shalt not lend upon usury: that the LORD thy God may bless thee in all that thou settest thy hand to in the land whither thou goest to possess it.

[21] 'When thou shalt vow a vow unto the LORD thy God, thou shalt not slack to pay it: for the LORD thy God will surely require it of thee; and it would be sin in thee. [22]But if thou shalt forbear to vow, it shall be no sin in thee. [23]That which is gone out of thy lips thou shalt keep and perform; even a free-will offering according as thou hast vowed unto the LORD thy God, which thou hast promised with thy mouth.

[24] 'When thou comest into thy neighbour's vineyard, then thou mayest eat grapes thy fill at thy own pleasure, but thou shalt not put any in thy vessel. [25]When thou comest into the standing corn of thy neighbour, then thou mayest pluck the ears with thy hand; but thou shalt not move a sickle unto thy neighbour's standing corn.

24

'When a man hath taken a wife, and married her, and it come to pass that she find no favour in his eyes, because he hath found some uncleanness in her: then let him write her a bill of divorcement, and give it in her hand, and send her out of his house. [2]And when she is departed out of his house, she may go and be another man's wife. [3]And if the latter husband hate her, and write her a bill of divorcement, and giveth it in her hand, and sendeth her out of his house; or if the latter husband die, which took her to be his wife, [4]her former husband, which sent her away, may not take her again to be his wife, after that she is defiled: for that is abomination before the LORD, and thou shalt not cause the land to sin, which the LORD thy God giveth thee for an inheritance.

[5] 'When a man hath taken a new wife, he shall not go out to war, neither shall he be charged with any business: but he shall be free at home one year, and shall cheer up his wife which he hath taken.

[6] 'No man shall take the nether or the upper millstone to pledge: for he taketh a man's life to pledge.

[7] 'If a man be found stealing any of his brethren of the children of Israel, and maketh merchandise of him, or selleth him: then that thief shall die, and thou shalt put evil away from among you.

[8] 'Take heed in the plague of leprosy, that thou observe diligently, and do according to all that the priests the Levites shall teach you: as I commanded them, so ye shall observe to do. [9]Remember what the LORD thy God did unto Miriam by the way, after that ye were come forth out of Egypt.

[10] 'When thou dost lend thy brother anything, thou shalt not go into his house to fetch his pledge. [11]Thou shalt stand abroad, and the man to

whom thou dost lend shall bring out the pledge abroad unto thee. [12]And if the man be poor, thou shalt not sleep with his pledge: [13]in any case thou shalt deliver him the pledge again when the sun goeth down, that he may sleep in his own raiment, and bless thee: and it shall be righteousness unto thee before the LORD thy God.

[14]'Thou shalt not oppress a hired servant that is poor and needy, whether he be of thy brethren, or of thy strangers that are in thy land within thy gates. [15]At his day thou shalt give him his hire, neither shall the sun go down upon it, for he is poor, and setteth his heart upon it, lest he cry against thee unto the LORD, and it be sin unto thee.

[16]'The fathers shall not be put to death for the children, neither shall the children be put to death for the fathers: every man shall be put to death for his own sin.

[17]'Thou shalt not pervert the judgement of the stranger, nor of the fatherless, nor take a widow's raiment to pledge. [18]But thou shalt remember that thou wast a bondman in Egypt, and the LORD thy God redeemed thee thence: therefore I command thee to do this thing.

[19]'When thou cuttest down thy harvest in thy field, and hast forgotten a sheaf in the field, thou shalt not go again to fetch it: it shall be for the stranger, for the fatherless, and for the widow: that the LORD thy God may bless thee in all the work of thy hands. [20]When thou beatest thy olive tree, thou shalt not go over the boughs again: it shall be for the stranger, for the fatherless, and for the widow. [21]When thou gatherest the grapes of thy vineyard, thou shalt not glean it afterward: it shall be for the stranger, for the fatherless, and for the widow. [22]And thou shalt remember that thou wast a bondman in the land of Egypt: therefore I command thee to do this thing.

25 'If there be a controversy between men, and they come unto judgement, that the judges may judge them, then they shall justify the righteous, and condemn the wicked. [2]And it shall be, if the wicked man be worthy to be beaten, that the judge shall cause him to lie down, and to be beaten before his face, according to his fault, by a certain number. [3]Forty stripes he may give him, and not exceed: lest, if he should exceed, and beat him above these with many stripes, then thy brother should seem vile unto thee.

[4]'Thou shalt not muzzle the ox when he treadeth out the corn.

[5]'If brethren dwell together, and one of them die, and have no child, the wife of the dead shall not marry without unto a stranger: her husband's brother shall go in unto her, and take her to him to wife, and perform the duty of a husband's brother unto her. [6]And it shall be, that the firstborn which she beareth shall succeed in the name of his brother which is dead, that his name be not put out of Israel. [7]And if the man like not to take his brother's wife, then let his brother's wife go up to the gate unto the elders, and say, "My husband's brother refuseth to raise up unto his brother a name in Israel: he will not perform the duty of my husband's brother". [8]Then the elders of his city shall call him, and speak unto him: and if he stand to it, and say, "I like not to take her": [9]then shall his brother's wife come unto him in the

presence of the elders, and loose his shoe from off his foot, and spit in his face, and shall answer and say, "So shall it be done unto that man that will not build up his brother's house". [10]And his name shall be called in Israel, the house of him that hath his shoe loosed.

[11]'When men strive together one with another, and the wife of the one draweth near for to deliver her husband out of the hand of him that smiteth him, and putteth forth her hand, and taketh him by the secrets: [12]then thou shalt cut off her hand, thy eye shall not pity her.

[13]'Thou shalt not have in thy bag diverse weights, a great and a small. [14]Thou shalt not have in thy house diverse measures, a great and a small. [15]But thou shalt have a perfect and just weight, a perfect and just measure shalt thou have: that thy days may be lengthened in the land which the LORD thy God giveth thee. [16]For all that do such things, and all that do unrighteously, are an abomination unto the LORD thy God.

[17]'Remember what Amalek did unto thee by the way, when ye were come forth out of Egypt: [18]how he met thee by the way, and smote the hindmost of thee, even all that were feeble behind thee, when thou wast faint and weary; and he feared not God. [19]Therefore it shall be, when the LORD thy God hath given thee rest from all thy enemies round about, in the land which the LORD thy God giveth thee for an inheritance to possess it, that thou shalt blot out the remembrance of Amalek from under heaven: thou shalt not forget it.

26 'And it shall be, when thou art come in unto the land which the LORD giveth thee for an inheritance, and possessest it, and dwellest therein: [2]that thou shalt take of the first of all the fruit of the earth, which thou shalt bring of thy land that the LORD thy God giveth thee, and shalt put it in a basket, and shalt go unto the place which the LORD thy God shall choose to place his name there. [3]And thou shalt go unto the priest that shall be in those days, and say unto him, "I profess this day unto the LORD thy God, that I am come unto the country which the LORD swore unto our fathers for to give us". [4]And the priest shall take the basket out of thy hand, and set it down before the altar of the LORD thy God. [5]And thou shalt speak and say before the LORD thy God, "A Syrian ready to perish was my father, and he went down into Egypt, and sojourned there with a few, and became there a nation, great, mighty, and populous. [6]And the Egyptians evil entreated us, and afflicted us, and laid upon us hard bondage. [7]And when we cried unto the LORD God of our fathers, the LORD heard our voice, and looked on our affliction, and our labour, and our oppression. [8]And the LORD brought us forth out of Egypt with a mighty hand, and with an out-stretched arm, and with great terribleness, and with signs, and with wonders. [9]And he hath brought us into this place, and hath given us this land, even a land that floweth with milk and honey. [10]And now behold, I have brought the first-fruits of the land, which thou, O LORD, hast given me." And thou shalt set it before the LORD thy God, and wor-ship before the LORD thy God. [11]And thou shalt rejoice in every good thing which the LORD thy God hath given unto thee, and unto thy

house, thou, and the Levite, and the stranger that is among you.

¹²'When thou hast made an end of tithing all the tithes of thy increase the third year, which is the year of tithing, and hast given it unto the Levite, the stranger, the fatherless, and the widow, that they may eat within thy gates, and be filled: ¹³then thou shalt say before the LORD thy God, "I have brought away the hallowed things out of my house, and also have given them unto the Levite, and unto the stranger, to the fatherless, and to the widow, according to all thy commandments which thou hast commanded me: I have not transgressed thy commandments, neither have I forgotten them. ¹⁴I have not eaten thereof in my mourning, neither have I taken away aught thereof for any unclean use, nor given aught thereof for the dead: but I have hearkened to the voice of the LORD my God, and have done according to all that thou hast commanded me. ¹⁵Look down from thy holy habitation, from heaven, and bless thy people Israel, and the land which thou hast given us, as thou sworest unto our fathers, a land that floweth with milk and honey."

¹⁶'This day the LORD thy God hath commanded thee to do these statutes and judgements: thou shalt therefore keep and do them with all thy heart, and with all thy soul. ¹⁷Thou hast avowed the LORD this day to be thy God, and to walk in his ways, and to keep his statutes, and his commandments, and his judgements, and to hearken unto his voice. ¹⁸And the LORD hath avowed thee this day to be his peculiar people, as he hath promised thee, and that thou shouldst keep all his commandments; ¹⁹and to make thee high above all nations which he hath made, in praise, and in name, and in honour; and that thou mayest be a holy people unto the LORD thy God, as he hath spoken.'

27 And Moses with the elders of Israel commanded the people, saying, 'Keep all the commandments which I command you this day. ²And it shall be, on the day when you shall pass over Jordan unto the land which the LORD thy God giveth thee, that thou shalt set thee up great stones, and plaster them with plaster. ³And thou shalt write upon them all the words of this law, when thou art passed over, that thou mayest go in unto the land which the LORD thy God giveth thee, a land that floweth with milk and honey, as the LORD God of thy fathers hath promised thee. ⁴Therefore it shall be when ye be gone over Jordan, that ye shall set up these stones, which I command you this day, in mount Ebal, and thou shalt plaster them with plaster. ⁵And there shalt thou build an altar unto the LORD thy God, an altar of stones: thou shalt not lift up any iron tool upon them. ⁶Thou shalt build the altar of the LORD thy God of whole stones: and thou shalt offer burnt offerings thereon unto the LORD thy God. ⁷And thou shalt offer peace offerings, and shalt eat there, and rejoice before the LORD thy God. ⁸And thou shalt write upon the stones all the words of this law very plainly.'

⁹And Moses and the priests the Levites spoke unto all Israel, saying, 'Take heed, and hearken, O Israel, this day thou art become the people of the LORD thy God. ¹⁰Thou shalt therefore obey the voice of the LORD thy God, and do his commandments and his statutes, which I com-

mand thee this day.'

[11]And Moses charged the people the same day, saying, [12]'These shall stand upon mount Gerizim to bless the people, when ye are come over Jordan: Simeon, and Levi, and Judah, and Issachar, and Joseph, and Benjamin. [13]And these shall stand upon mount Ebal to curse: Reuben, Gad, and Asher, and Zebulun, Dan, and Naphtali.

[14]'And the Levites shall speak, and say unto all the men of Israel with a loud voice, [15]"Cursed be the man that maketh any graven or molten image, an abomination unto the LORD, the work of the hands of the craftsman, and putteth it in a secret place". And all the people shall answer and say, "Amen".

[16]'"Cursed be he that setteth light by his father or his mother." And all the people shall say, "Amen".

[17]'"Cursed be he that removeth his neighbour's landmark." And all the people shall say, "Amen".

[18]'"Cursed be he that maketh the blind to wander out of the way." And all the people shall say, "Amen".

[19]'"Cursed be he that perverteth the judgement of the stranger, fatherless, and widow." And all the people shall say, "Amen".

[20]'"Cursed be he that lieth with his father's wife, because he uncovereth his father's skirt." And all the people shall say, "Amen".

[21]'"Cursed be he that lieth with any manner of beast." And all the people shall say, "Amen".

[22]'"Cursed be he that lieth with his sister, the daughter of his father, or the daughter of his mother." And all the people shall say, "Amen".

[23]'"Cursed be he that lieth with his mother-in-law." And all the people shall say, "Amen".

[24]'"Cursed be he that smiteth his neighbour secretly." And all the people shall say, "Amen".

[25]'"Cursed be he that taketh reward to slay an innocent person." And all the people shall say, "Amen".

[26]'"Cursed be he that confirmeth not all the words of this law to do them." And all the people shall say, "Amen".

28 'And it shall come to pass, if thou shalt hearken diligently unto the voice of the LORD thy God, to observe and to do all his commandments which I command thee this day, that the LORD thy God will set thee on high above all nations of the earth. [2]And all these blessings shall come on thee, and overtake thee, if thou shalt hearken unto the voice of the LORD thy God.

[3]'Blessed shalt thou be in the city, and blessed shalt thou be in the field.

[4]'Blessed shall be the fruit of thy body, and the fruit of thy ground, and the fruit of thy cattle, the increase of thy kine, and the flocks of thy sheep.

[5]'Blessed shall be thy basket and thy store.

[6]'Blessed shalt thou be when thou comest in, and blessed shalt thou be when thou goest out.

[7]'The LORD shall cause thy enemies that rise up against thee to be

smitten before thy face: they shall come out against thee one way, and flee before thee seven ways.

⁸'The LORD shall command the blessing upon thee in thy store-houses, and in all that thou settest thy hand unto, and he shall bless thee in the land which the LORD thy God giveth thee.

⁹'The LORD shall establish thee a holy people unto himself, as he hath sworn unto thee, if thou shalt keep the commandments of the LORD thy God, and walk in his ways. ¹⁰And all people of the earth shall see that thou art called by the name of the LORD, and they shall be afraid of thee. ¹¹And the LORD shall make thee plenteous in goods, in the fruit of thy body, and in the fruit of thy cattle, and in the fruit of thy ground, in the land which the LORD swore unto thy fathers to give thee. ¹²The LORD shall open unto thee his good treasure, the heaven to give the rain unto thy land in his season, and to bless all the work of thy hand: and thou shalt lend unto many nations, and thou shalt not borrow. ¹³And the LORD shall make thee the head, and not the tail, and thou shalt be above only, and thou shalt not be beneath; if that thou hearken unto the commandments of the LORD thy God, which I com-mand thee this day, to observe and to do them: ¹⁴and thou shalt not go aside from any of the words which I command thee this day, to the right hand, or to the left, to go after other gods to serve them.

¹⁵'But it shall come to pass, if thou wilt not hearken unto the voice of the LORD thy God, to observe to do all his commandments and his statutes which I command thee this day, that all these curses shall come upon thee, and overtake thee.

¹⁶'Cursed shalt thou be in the city, and cursed shalt thou be in the field.

¹⁷'Cursed shall be thy basket and thy store.

¹⁸'Cursed shall be the fruit of thy body, and the fruit of thy land, the increase of thy kine, and the flocks of thy sheep.

¹⁹'Cursed shalt thou be when thou comest in, and cursed shalt thou be when thou goest out.

²⁰'The LORD shall send upon thee cursing, vexation, and rebuke, in all that thou settest thy hand unto for to do, until thou be destroyed, and until thou perish quickly, because of the wickedness of thy doings, whereby thou hast forsaken me. ²¹The LORD shall make the pestilence cleave unto thee, until he have consumed thee from off the land, whither thou goest to possess it. ²²The LORD shall smite thee with a con-sumption, and with a fever, and with an inflammation, and with an extreme burning, and with the sword, and with blasting, and with mildew; and they shall pursue thee until thou perish. ²³And the heaven that is over thy head shall be brass, and the earth that is under thee shall be iron. ²⁴The LORD shall make the rain of thy land powder and dust: from heaven shall it come down upon thee, until thou be destroyed. ²⁵The LORD shall cause thee to be smitten before thy ene-mies: thou shalt go out one way against them, and flee seven ways before them: and shalt be removed into all the kingdoms of the earth. ²⁶And thy carcase shall be meat unto all fowls of the air, and unto the

beasts of the earth, and no man shall fray them away. [27]The LORD will smite thee with the botch of Egypt, and with the haemorrhoids, and with the scab, and with the itch, whereof thou canst not be healed. [28]The LORD shall smite thee with madness, and blindness, and astonishment of heart. [29]And thou shalt grope at noondays, as the blind gropeth in darkness, and thou shalt not prosper in thy ways: and thou shalt be only oppressed and spoiled evermore, and no man shall save thee. [30]Thou shalt betroth a wife, and another man shall lie with her: thou shalt build a house, and thou shalt not dwell therein: thou shalt plant a vineyard, and shalt not gather the grapes thereof. [31]Thy ox shall be slain before thy eyes, and thou shalt not eat thereof: thy ass shall be violently taken away from before thy face, and shall not be restored to thee: thy sheep shall be given unto thy enemies, and thou shalt have none to rescue them. [32]Thy sons and thy daughters shall be given unto another people, and thy eyes shall look, and fail with longing for them all the day long: and there shall be no might in thy hand. [33]The fruit of thy land, and all thy labours, shall a nation which thou knowest not eat up: and thou shalt be only oppressed and crushed always: [34]so that thou shalt be mad for the sight of thy eyes which thou shalt see. [35]The LORD shall smite thee in the knees, and in the legs, with a sore botch that cannot be healed, from the sole of thy foot unto the top of thy head. [36]The LORD shall bring thee, and thy king which thou shalt set over thee, unto a nation which neither thou nor thy fathers have known, and there shalt thou serve other gods, wood and stone. [37]And thou shalt become an astonishment, a proverb, and a byword, among all nations whither the LORD shall lead thee. [38]Thou shalt carry much seed out into the field, and shalt gather but little in: for the locust shall consume it. [39]Thou shalt plant vineyards and dress them, but shalt neither drink of the wine, nor gather the grapes: for the worms shall eat them. [40]Thou shalt have olive trees throughout all thy coasts, but thou shalt not anoint thyself with the oil: for thy olive shall cast his fruit. [41]Thou shalt beget sons and daughters, but thou shalt not enjoy them: for they shall go into captivity. [42]All thy trees and fruit of thy land shall the locusts consume. [43]The stranger that is within thee shall get up above thee very high: and thou shalt come down very low. [44]He shall lend to thee, and thou shalt not lend to him: he shall be the head, and thou shalt be the tail. [45]Moreover all these curses shall come upon thee, and shall pursue thee, and overtake thee, till thou be destroyed: because thou hearkenedst not unto the voice of the LORD thy God, to keep his commandments and his statutes which he commanded thee. [46]And they shall be upon thee for a sign and for a wonder, and upon thy seed for ever: [47]because thou servedst not the LORD thy God with joyfulness, and with gladness of heart, for the abundance of all things. [48]Therefore shalt thou serve thy enemies which the LORD shall send against thee, in hunger, and in thirst, and in nakedness, and in want of all things: and he shall put a yoke of iron upon thy neck, until he have destroyed thee. [49]The LORD shall bring a nation against thee from far, from the end of the earth, as swift as the eagle flieth, a nation whose tongue thou shalt not understand; ⁵⁰a nation of fierce countenance, which shall not regard the person of the old, nor show favour to the young: ⁵¹and he shall eat the fruit of thy cattle, and the fruit of thy land, until thou be destroyed: which also shall not leave thee either corn, wine, or oil, or the increase of thy kine, or flocks of thy sheep, until he have destroyed thee. ⁵²And he shall besiege thee in all thy gates, until thy high and fenced walls come down wherein thou trustedst, throughout all thy land: and he shall besiege thee in all thy gates throughout all thy land, which the LORD thy God hath given thee. ⁵³And thou shalt eat the fruit of thy own body, the flesh of thy sons and of thy daughters, which the LORD thy God hath given thee, in the siege, and in the straitness wherewith thy enemies shall distress thee: ⁵⁴so that the man that is tender among you, and very delicate, his eye shall be evil toward his brother, and toward the wife of his bosom, and towards the remnant of his children which he shall leave: ⁵⁵so that he will not give to any of them of the flesh of his children whom he shall eat: because he hath nothing left him in the siege, and in the straitness wherewith thy enemies shall distress thee in all thy gates. ⁵⁶The tender and delicate woman among you, which would not adventure to set the sole of her foot upon the ground for delicateness and tenderness, her eye shall be evil towards the husband of her bosom, and towards her son, and towards her daughter, ⁵⁷and towards her young one that cometh out from between her feet, and towards her children which she shall bear: for she shall eat them for want of all things secretly in the siege and straitness, wherewith thy enemy shall distress thee in thy gates.

⁵⁸'If thou wilt not observe to do all the words of this law that are written in this book, that thou mayest fear this glorious and fearful name, THE LORD THY GOD: ⁵⁹then the LORD will make thy plagues wonderful, and the plagues of thy seed, even great plagues, and of long continuance, and sore sicknesses, and of long continuance. ⁶⁰Moreover he will bring upon thee all the diseases of Egypt, which thou wast afraid of, and they shall cleave unto thee. ⁶¹Also every sickness, and every plague which is not written in the book of this law, them will the LORD bring upon thee, until thou be destroyed. ⁶²And ye shall be left few in number, whereas ye were as the stars of heaven for multitude: because thou wouldst not obey the voice of the LORD thy God. ⁶³And it shall come to pass, that as the LORD rejoiced over you to do you good, and to multiply you; so the LORD will rejoice over you to destroy you, and to bring you to nought; and ye shall be plucked from off the land whither thou goest to possess it. ⁶⁴And the LORD shall scatter thee among all people, from the one end of the earth even unto the other: and there thou shalt serve other gods, which neither thou nor thy fathers have known, even wood and stone. ⁶⁵And among these nations shalt thou find no ease, neither shall the sole of thy foot have rest: but the LORD shall give thee there a trembling heart, and failing of eyes, and sorrow of mind. ⁶⁶And thy life shall hang in doubt before thee, and thou shalt fear day and night, and shalt have no assurance of thy life. ⁶⁷In the morning thou shalt say, "Would God it were even": and at even thou shalt say, "Would

God it were morning", for the fear of thy heart wherewith thou shalt fear, and for the sight of thine eyes which thou shalt see. ⁶⁸And the LORD shall bring thee into Egypt again with ships, by the way whereof I spoke unto thee, "Thou shalt see it no more again": and there ye shall be sold unto your enemies for bondmen and bondwomen, and no man shall buy you.'

29 These are the words of the covenant, which the LORD commanded Moses to make with the children of Israel in the land of Moab, besides the covenant which he made with them in Horeb.

²And Moses called unto all Israel, and said unto them, 'Ye have seen all that the LORD did before your eyes in the land of Egypt unto Pharaoh, and unto all his servants, and unto all his land; ³the great temptations which thine eyes have seen, the signs, and those great miracles: ⁴yet the LORD hath not given you a heart to perceive, and eyes to see, and ears to hear, unto this day. ⁵And I have led you forty years in the wilderness: your clothes are not waxed old upon you, and thy shoe is not waxed old upon thy foot. ⁶Ye have not eaten bread, neither have you drunk wine or strong drink: that ye might know that I am the LORD your God. ⁷And when ye came unto this place, Sihon the king of Heshbon, and Og the king of Bashan, came out against us unto battle, and we smote them. ⁸And we took their land, and gave it for an inheritance unto the Reubenites, and to the Gadites, and to the half tribe of Manasseh. ⁹Keep therefore the words of this covenant, and do them, that ye may prosper in all that ye do.

¹⁰'Ye stand this day all of you before the LORD your God: your captains of your tribes, your elders, and your officers, with all the men of Israel, ¹¹your little ones, your wives, and thy stranger that is in thy camp, from the hewer of thy wood unto the drawer of thy water: ¹²that thou shouldst enter into covenant with the LORD thy God, and into his oath, which the LORD thy God maketh with thee this day: ¹³that he may establish thee today for a people unto himself, and that he may be unto thee a God, as he hath said unto thee, and as he hath sworn unto thy fathers, to Abraham, to Isaac, and to Jacob. ¹⁴Neither with you only do I make this covenant and this oath: ¹⁵but with him that standeth here with us this day before the LORD our God, and also with him that is not here with us this day ¹⁶(for ye know how we have dwelt in the land of Egypt, and how we came through the nations which ye passed by; ¹⁷and ye have seen their abominations, and their idols, wood and stone, silver and gold, which were among them): ¹⁸lest there should be among you man or woman, or family, or tribe, whose heart turneth away this day from the LORD our God, to go and serve the gods of these nations: lest there should be among you a root that beareth gall and wormwood; ¹⁹and it come to pass, when he heareth the words of this curse, that he bless himself in his heart, saying, "I shall have peace, though I walk in the imagination of my heart, to add drunkenness to thirst": ²⁰the LORD will not spare him, but then the anger of the LORD and his jealousy shall smoke against that man, and all the curses that are written in this book shall lie upon him, and the LORD shall blot out his name from

under heaven. [21]And the LORD shall separate him unto evil out of all the tribes of Israel, according to all the curses of the covenant that are written in this book of the law: [22]so that the generation to come of your children that shall rise up after you, and the stranger that shall come from a far land, shall say, when they see the plagues of that land, and the sicknesses which the LORD hath laid upon it; [23]and that the whole land thereof is brimstone, and salt, and burning, that it is not sown, nor beareth, nor any grass groweth therein, like the overthrow of Sodom and Gomorrah, Admah, and Zeboim, which the LORD overthrew in his anger, and in his wrath: [24]even all nations shall say, "Wherefore hath the LORD done thus unto this land? what meaneth the heat of this great anger?" [25]Then men shall say, "Because they have forsaken the covenant of the LORD God of their fathers, which he made with them when he brought them forth out of the land of Egypt. [26]For they went and served other gods, and worshipped them, gods whom they knew not, and whom he had not given unto them. [27]And the anger of the LORD was kindled against this land, to bring upon it all the curses that are written in this book. [28]And the LORD rooted them out of their land in anger, and in wrath, and in great indignation, and cast them into another land, as it is this day." [29]The secret things belong unto the LORD our God: but those things which are revealed belong unto us and to our children for ever, that we may do all the words of this law.

30 [1]And it shall come to pass, when all these things are come upon thee, the blessing and the curse, which I have set before thee, and thou shalt call them to mind among all the nations whither the LORD thy God hath driven thee, [2]and shalt return unto the LORD thy God, and shalt obey his voice according to all that I command thee this day, thou and thy children, with all thy heart, and with all thy soul: [3]that then the LORD thy God will turn thy captivity, and have compassion upon thee, and will return and gather thee from all the nations, whither the LORD thy God hath scattered thee. [4]If any of thine be driven out unto the utmost parts of heaven, from thence will the LORD thy God gather thee, and from thence will he fetch thee. [5]And the LORD thy God will bring thee into the land which thy fathers possessed, and thou shalt possess it: and he will do thee good, and multiply thee above thy fathers. [6]And the LORD thy God will circumcise thy heart, and the heart of thy seed, to love the LORD thy God with all thy heart, and with all thy soul, that thou mayest live. [7]And the LORD thy God will put all these curses upon thy enemies, and on them that hate thee, which persecuted thee. [8]And thou shalt return and obey the voice of the LORD, and do all his commandments which I command thee this day. [9]And the LORD thy God will make thee plenteous in every work of thy hand, in the fruit of thy body, and in the fruit of thy cattle, and in the fruit of thy land, for good: for the LORD will again rejoice over thee for good, as he rejoiced over thy fathers: [10]if thou shalt hearken unto the voice of the LORD thy God to keep his commandments and his statutes which are written in this book of the law, and if thou turn unto the LORD thy

God with all thy heart, and with all thy soul. ¹¹'For this commandment which I command thee this day, it is not hidden from thee, neither is it far off. ¹²It is not in heaven, that thou shouldst say, "Who shall go up for us to heaven, and bring it unto us, that we may hear it, and do it?" ¹³Neither is it beyond the sea, that thou shouldst say, "Who shall go over the sea for us, and bring it unto us, that we may hear it, and do it?" ¹⁴But the word is very nigh unto thee, in thy mouth, and in thy heart, that thou mayest do it.

¹⁵'See, I have set before thee this day life and good, and death and evil: ¹⁶in that I command thee this day to love the Lord thy God, to walk in his ways, and to keep his commandments and his statutes, and his judgements, that thou mayest live and multiply: and the Lord thy God shall bless thee in the land whither thou goest to possess it. ¹⁷But if thy heart turn away, so that thou wilt not hear, but shalt be drawn away, and worship other gods, and serve them: ¹⁸I denounce unto you this day, that ye shall surely perish, and that ye shall not prolong your days upon the land, whither thou passest over Jordan to go to possess it. ¹⁹I call heaven and earth to record this day against you, that I have set before you life and death, blessing and cursing: therefore choose life, that both thou and thy seed may live: ²⁰that thou mayest love the Lord thy God, and that thou mayest obey his voice, and that thou mayest cleave unto him: for he is thy life, and the length of thy days, that thou mayest dwell in the land which the Lord swore unto thy fathers, to Abraham, to Isaac, and to Jacob, to give them.'

31 And Moses went and spoke these words unto all Israel. ²And he said unto them, 'I am a hundred and twenty years old this day; I can no more go out and come in: also the Lord hath said unto me, "Thou shalt not go over this Jordan". ³The Lord thy God, he will go over before thee, and he will destroy these nations from before thee, and thou shalt possess them: and Joshua, he shall go over before thee, as the Lord hath said. ⁴And the Lord shall do unto them as he did to Sihon and to Og, kings of the Amorites, and unto the land of them, whom he destroyed. ⁵And the Lord shall give them up before your face, that ye may do unto them according unto all the commandments which I have commanded you. ⁶Be strong and of a good courage, fear not, nor be afraid of them: for the Lord thy God, he it is that doth go with thee; he will not fail thee, nor forsake thee.'

⁷And Moses called unto Joshua, and said unto him in the sight of all Israel, 'Be strong and of a good courage: for thou must go with this people unto the land which the Lord hath sworn unto their fathers to give them; and thou shalt cause them to inherit it. ⁸And the Lord, he it is that doth go before thee; he will be with thee, he will not fail thee, neither forsake thee: fear not, neither be dismayed.'

⁹And Moses wrote this law, and delivered it unto the priests the sons of Levi, which bore the ark of the covenant of the Lord, and unto all the elders of Israel. ¹⁰And Moses commanded them, saying, 'At the end of every seven years, in the solemnity of the year of release, in the feast of tabernacles, ¹¹when all Israel is come to appear before the Lord thy

God in the place which he shall choose, thou shalt read this law before all Israel in their hearing. [12]Gather the people together, men, and women, and children, and thy stranger that is within thy gates, that they may hear, and that they may learn, and fear the LORD your God, and observe to do all the words of this law: [13]and that their children, which have not known anything, may hear, and learn to fear the LORD your God, as long as ye live in the land whither ye go over Jordan to possess it.'

[14]And the LORD said unto Moses, 'Behold, thy days approach that thou must die: call Joshua, and present yourselves in the tabernacle of the congregation, that I may give him a charge'. And Moses and Joshua went, and presented themselves in the tabernacle of the congregation. [15]And the LORD appeared in the tabernacle in a pillar of a cloud: and the pillar of the cloud stood over the door of the tabernacle.

[16]And the LORD said unto Moses, 'Behold, thou shalt sleep with thy fathers; and this people will rise up, and go a-whoring after the gods of the strangers of the land, whither they go to be amongst them, and will forsake me, and break my covenant which I have made with them. [17]Then my anger shall be kindled against them in that day, and I will forsake them, and I will hide my face from them, and they shall be devoured, and many evils and troubles shall befall them, so that they will say in that day, "Are not these evils come upon us, because our God is not amongst us?" [18]And I will surely hide my face in that day for all the evils which they shall have wrought, in that they are turned unto other gods. [19]Now therefore write ye this song for you, and teach it the children of Israel: put it in their mouths, that this song may be a witness for me against the children of Israel. [20]For when I shall have brought them into the land which I swore unto their fathers, that floweth with milk and honey; and they shall have eaten and filled themselves, and waxed fat; then will they turn unto other gods, and serve them, and provoke me, and break my covenant. [21]And it shall come to pass, when many evils and troubles are befallen them, that this song shall testify against them as a witness; for it shall not be forgotten out of the mouths of their seed: for I know their imagination which they go about, even now, before I have brought them into the land which I swore.'

[22]Moses therefore wrote this song the same day, and taught it the children of Israel. [23]And he gave Joshua the son of Nun a charge, and said, 'Be strong and of a good courage: for thou shalt bring the children of Israel into the land which I swore unto them: and I will be with thee'.

[24]And it came to pass, when Moses had made an end of writing the words of this law in a book, until they were finished, [25]that Moses commanded the Levites, which bore the ark of the covenant of the LORD, saying, [26]'Take this book of the law, and put it in the side of the ark of the covenant of the LORD your God, that it may be there for a witness against thee. [27]For I know thy rebellion, and thy stiff neck: behold, while I am yet alive with you this day, ye have been rebellious against the LORD; and how much more after my death?

[28]'Gather unto me all the elders of your tribes, and your officers, that

I may speak these words in their ears, and call heaven and earth to record against them. [29]For I know that after my death ye will utterly corrupt yourselves, and turn aside from the way which I have commanded you: and evil will befall you in the latter days, because ye will do evil in the sight of the Lord, to provoke him to anger through the work of your hands.'

[30]And Moses spoke in the ears of all the congregation of Israel the words of this song, until they were ended.

32

'Give ear, O ye heavens, and I will speak;
and hear, O earth, the words of my mouth.
[2] My doctrine shall drop as the rain:
my speech shall distil as the dew,
as the small rain upon the tender herb,
and as the showers upon the grass:
[3] because I will publish the name of the Lord:
ascribe ye greatness unto our God.
[4] He is the Rock, his work is perfect:
for all his ways are judgement:
a God of truth and without iniquity, just and right is he.
[5] They have corrupted themselves,
their spot is not the spot of his children:
they are a perverse and crooked generation.
[6] Do ye thus requite the Lord, O foolish people and unwise?
Is not he thy father that hath bought thee?
Hath he not made thee, and established thee?

[7] 'Remember the days of old,
consider the years of many generations:
ask thy father, and he will show thee;
thy elders, and they will tell thee.
[8] When the most High divided to the nations their inheritance,
when he separated the sons of Adam,
he set the bounds of the people according to the number of the
children of Israel.
[9] For the Lord's portion is his people:
Jacob is the lot of his inheritance.
[10] He found him in a desert land,
and in the waste howling wilderness:
he led him about, he instructed him,
he kept him as the apple of his eye.
[11] As an eagle stirreth up her nest,
fluttereth over her young,
spreadeth abroad her wings,
taketh them, beareth them on her wings:
[12] so the Lord alone did lead him,
and there was no strange god with him.
[13] He made him ride on the high places of the earth,

that he might eat the increase of the fields;
and he made him to suck honey out of the rock,
and oil out of the flinty rock;
¹⁴ butter of kine, and milk of sheep,
with fat of lambs, and rams of the breed of Bashan,
and goats, with the fat of kidneys of wheat;
and thou didst drink the pure blood of the grape.

¹⁵ But Jeshurun waxed fat, and kicked:
thou art waxed fat, thou art grown thick,
thou art covered with fatness:
then he forsook God which made him,
and lightly esteemed the Rock of his salvation.
¹⁶ They provoked him to jealousy with strange gods,
with abominations provoked they him to anger.
¹⁷ They sacrificed unto devils, not to God:
to gods whom they knew not, to new gods that came newly up,
whom your fathers feared not.
¹⁸ Of the Rock that begot thee thou art unmindful,
and hast forgotten God that formed thee.
¹⁹ And when the Lord saw it, he abhorred them,
because of the provoking of his sons, and of his daughters.
²⁰ And he said, "I will hide my face from them,
I will see what their end shall be:
for they are a very froward generation,
children in whom is no faith.
²¹ They have moved me to jealousy with that which is not God,
they have provoked me to anger with their vanities:
and I will move them to jealousy with those which are not a
people,
I will provoke them to anger with a foolish nation.
²² For a fire is kindled in my anger,
and shall burn unto the lowest hell,
and shall consume the earth with her increase,
and set on fire the foundations of the mountains.
²³ I will heap mischiefs upon them;
I will spend my arrows upon them.
²⁴ They shall be burnt with hunger,
and devoured with burning heat, and with bitter destruction:
I will also send the teeth of beasts upon them,
with the poison of serpents of the dust.
²⁵ The sword without, and terror within
shall destroy both the young man and the virgin,
the suckling also with the man of grey hairs.
²⁶ I said, I would scatter them into corners,
I would make the remembrance of them to cease from among
men:
²⁷ were it not that I feared the wrath of the enemy,

lest their adversaries should behave themselves strangely,
and lest they should say, 'Our hand is high,
and the LORD hath not done all this'.

²⁸ For they are a nation void of counsel,
neither is there any understanding in them.

²⁹ O that they were wise, that they understood this,
that they would consider their latter end!"

³⁰ How should one chase a thousand,
and two put ten thousand to flight,
except their Rock had sold them,
and the LORD had shut them up?

³¹ For their rock is not as our Rock,
even our enemies themselves being judges.

³² For their vine is of the vine of Sodom,
and of the fields of Gomorrah:
their grapes are grapes of gall,
their clusters are bitter.

³³ Their wine is the poison of dragons,
and the cruel venom of asps.

³⁴ Is not this laid up in store with me,
and sealed up among my treasures?

³⁵ To me belongeth vengeance, and recompense;
their foot shall slide in due time:
for the day of their calamity is at hand,
and the things that shall come upon them make haste.

³⁶ For the LORD shall judge his people,
and repent himself for his servants,
when he seeth that their power is gone,
and there is none shut up, or left.

³⁷ And he shall say, "Where are their gods,
their rock in whom they trusted,

³⁸ which did eat the fat of their sacrifices,
and drank the wine of their drink offerings?
let them rise up and help you,
and be your protection.

³⁹ See now that I, even I, am he,
and there is no god with me:
I kill, and I make alive;
I wound, and I heal:
neither is there any that can deliver out of my hand.

⁴⁰ For I lift up my hand to heaven,
and say, I live for ever.

⁴¹ If I whet my glittering sword,
and my hand take hold on judgement,
I will render vengeance to my enemies,
and will reward them that hate me.

⁴² I will make my arrows drunk with blood
(and my sword shall devour flesh),

and that with the blood of the slain and of the captives,
from the beginning of revenges upon the enemy."
43 Rejoice, O ye nations, with his people:
for he will avenge the blood of his servants,
and will render vengeance to his adversaries,
and will be merciful unto his land, and to his people.'

44And Moses came and spoke all the words of this song in the ears of the people, he, and Hoshea the son of Nun. 45And Moses made an end of speaking all these words to all Israel. 46And he said unto them, 'Set your hearts unto all the words which I testify among you this day, which ye shall command your children to observe to do, all the words of this law. 47For it is not a vain thing for you: because it is your life, and through this thing ye shall prolong your days, in the land whither ye go over Jordan to possess it.'

48And the LORD spoke unto Moses that selfsame day, saying, 49'Get thee up into this mountain Abarim, unto mount Nebo, which is in the land of Moab, that is over against Jericho, and behold the land of Canaan, which I give unto the children of Israel for a possession: 50and die in the mount whither thou goest up, and be gathered unto thy people, as Aaron thy brother died in mount Hor, and was gathered unto his people: 51because ye trespassed against me among the children of Israel at the waters of Meribah-kadesh, in the wilderness of Zin; because ye sanctified me not in the midst of the children of Israel. 52Yet thou shalt see the land before thee; but thou shalt not go thither unto the land which I give the children of Israel.'

33 And this is the blessing, wherewith Moses the man of God blessed the children of Israel before his death. 2And he said,

'The LORD came from Sinai,
and rose up from Seir unto them,
he shone forth from mount Paran,
and he came with ten thousands of saints:
from his right hand went a fiery law for them.
3 Yea, he loved the people;
all his saints are in thy hand:
and they sat down at thy feet;
every one shall receive of thy words.
4 Moses commanded us a law,
even the inheritance of the congregation of Jacob.
5 And he was king in Jeshurun,
when the heads of the people
and the tribes of Israel were gathered together.

6 'Let Reuben live, and not die,
and let not his men be few.'

7And this is the blessing of Judah: and he said,

'Hear, LORD, the voice of Judah,

and bring him unto his people:
let his hands be sufficient for him,
and be thou a help to him from his enemies'.

8 And of Levi he said,

'Let thy Thummim and thy Urim be with thy holy one,
whom thou didst prove at Massah,
and with whom thou didst strive at the waters of Meribah;
9 who said unto his father and to his mother,
"I have not seen him";
neither did he acknowledge his brethren,
nor knew his own children:
for they have observed thy word,
and kept thy covenant.
10 They shall teach Jacob thy judgements,
and Israel thy law:
they shall put incense before thee,
and whole burnt sacrifice upon thy altar.
11 Bless, LORD, his substance,
and accept the work of his hands:
smite through the loins of them that rise against him,
and of them that hate him,
that they rise not again.'

12 And of Benjamin he said,

'The beloved of the LORD shall dwell in safety by him,
and the LORD shall cover him all the day long,
and he shall dwell between his shoulders'.

13 And of Joseph he said,

'Blessed of the LORD be his land,
for the precious things of heaven,
for the dew, and for the deep that coucheth beneath,
14 and for the precious fruits brought forth by the sun,
and for the precious things put forth by the moon,
15 and for the chief things of the ancient mountains,
and for the precious things of the lasting hills,
16 and for the precious things of the earth
and fulness thereof,
and for the good will of him that dwelt in the bush:
let the blessing come upon the head of Joseph,
and upon the top of the head of him that was separated from his
brethren.
17 His glory is like the firstling of his bullock,
and his horns are like the horns of unicorns:

with them he shall push the people together to the ends of the
earth:
and they are the ten thousands of Ephraim,
and they are the thousands of Manasseh.'

[18]And of Zebulun he said,

'Rejoice, Zebulun, in thy going out;
and, Issachar, in thy tents.
[19] They shall call the people unto the mountain,
there they shall offer sacrifices of righteousness:
for they shall suck of the abundance of the seas,
and of treasures hid in the sand.'

[20]And of Gad he said,

'Blessed be he that enlargeth Gad:
he dwelleth as a lion,
and teareth the arm with the crown of the head.
[21] And he provided the first part for himself,
because there, in a portion of the lawgiver, was he seated;
and he came with the heads of the people,
he executed the justice of the LORD,
and his judgements with Israel.'

[22]And of Dan he said,

'Dan is a lion's whelp:
he shall leap from Bashan'.

[23]And of Naphtali he said,

'O Naphtali, satisfied with favour,
and full with the blessing of the LORD:
possess thou the west and the south'.

[24]And of Asher he said,

'Let Asher be blessed with children;
let him be acceptable to his brethren,
and let him dip his foot in oil.
[25] Thy shoes shall be iron and brass,
and as thy days, so shall thy strength be.

[26] 'There is none like unto the God of Jeshurun,
who rideth upon the heaven in thy help,
and in his excellence on the sky.
[27] The eternal God is thy refuge,

and underneath are the everlasting arms:
and he shall thrust out the enemy from before thee,
and shall say, "Destroy them".
²⁸ Israel then shall dwell in safety alone:
the fountain of Jacob shall be upon a land of corn and wine,
also his heavens shall drop down dew.
²⁹ Happy art thou, O Israel:
who is like unto thee, O people!
saved by the LORD, the shield of thy help,
and who is the sword of thy excellence:
and thy enemies shall be found liars unto thee,
and thou shalt tread upon their high places.'

34 And Moses went up from the plains of Moab unto the mountain of Nebo, to the top of Pisgah, that is over against Jericho. And the LORD showed him all the land of Gilead, unto Dan, ²and all Naphtali, and the land of Ephraim, and Manasseh, and all the land of Judah, unto the utmost sea, ³and the south, and the plain of the valley of Jericho, the city of palm trees, unto Zoar. ⁴And the LORD said unto him, 'This is the land which I swore unto Abraham, unto Isaac, and unto Jacob, saying, "I will give it unto thy seed": I have caused thee to see it with thy eyes, but thou shalt not go over thither'.

⁵So Moses the servant of the LORD died there in the land of Moab, according to the word of the LORD. ⁶And he buried him in a valley in the land of Moab, over against Beth-peor: but no man knoweth of his sepulchre unto this day.

⁷And Moses was a hundred and twenty years old when he died: his eye was not dim, nor his natural force abated.

⁸And the children of Israel wept for Moses in the plains of Moab thirty days: so the days of weeping and mourning for Moses were ended.

⁹And Joshua the son of Nun was full of the spirit of wisdom: for Moses had laid his hands upon him: and the children of Israel hearkened unto him, and did as the LORD commanded Moses.

¹⁰And there arose not a prophet since in Israel like unto Moses, whom the LORD knew face to face, ¹¹in all the signs and the wonders which the LORD sent him to do in the land of Egypt to Pharaoh, and to all his servants, and to all his land, ¹²and in all that mighty hand, and in all the great terror which Moses showed in the sight of all Israel.

THE BOOK OF
JOSHUA

1 Now after the death of Moses the servant of the Lord it came to pass, that the Lord spoke unto Joshua the son of Nun, Moses' minister, saying, ²'Moses my servant is dead: now therefore arise, go over this Jordan, thou, and all this people, unto the land which I do give to them, even to the children of Israel. ³Every place that the sole of your foot shall tread upon, that have I given unto you, as I said unto Moses. ⁴From the wilderness and this Lebanon even unto the great river, the river Euphrates, all the land of the Hittites, and unto the great sea toward the going down of the sun, shall be your coast. ⁵There shall not any man be able to stand before thee all the days of thy life: as I was with Moses, so I will be with thee: I will not fail thee, nor forsake thee. ⁶Be strong and of a good courage: for unto this people shalt thou divide for an inheritance the land which I swore unto their fathers to give them. ⁷Only be thou strong and very courageous, that thou mayest observe to do according to all the law, which Moses my servant commanded thee: turn not from it to the right hand or to the left, that thou mayest prosper whithersoever thou goest. ⁸This book of the law shall not depart out of thy mouth, but thou shalt meditate therein day and night, that thou mayest observe to do according to all that is written therein: for then thou shalt make thy way prosperous, and then thou shalt have good success. ⁹Have not I commanded thee? Be strong and of a good courage, be not afraid, neither be thou dismayed: for the Lord thy God is with thee whithersoever thou goest.'

¹⁰Then Joshua commanded the officers of the people, saying, ¹¹'Pass through the host, and command the people, saying, "Prepare you victuals: for within three days ye shall pass over this Jordan, to go in to possess the land which the Lord your God giveth you to possess it"'.

¹²And to the Reubenites, and to the Gadites, and to half the tribe of Manasseh, spoke Joshua, saying, ¹³'Remember the word which Moses the servant of the Lord commanded you, saying, "The Lord your God hath given you rest, and hath given you this land". ¹⁴Your wives, your little ones, and your cattle shall remain in the land which Moses gave you on this side Jordan; but ye shall pass before your brethren armed, all the mighty men of valour, and help them; ¹⁵until the Lord have given your brethren rest, as he hath given you, and they also have possessed the land which the Lord your God giveth them: then ye shall return unto the land of your possession, and enjoy it, which Moses the Lord's servant gave you on this side Jordan toward the sunrising.'

¹⁶And they answered Joshua, saying, 'All that thou commandest us we will do, and whithersoever thou sendest us, we will go. ¹⁷According as we hearkened unto Moses in all things, so will we hearken unto thee: only the Lord thy God be with thee, as he was with Moses. ¹⁸Whosoever he be that doth rebel against thy commandment, and will not hearken

unto thy words in all that thou commandest him, he shall be put to death: only be strong and of a good courage.'

2 And Joshua the son of Nun sent out of Shittim two men to spy secretly, saying, 'Go view the land, even Jericho'. And they went, and came into a harlot's house, named Rahab, and lodged there. ²And it was told the king of Jericho, saying, 'Behold, there came men in hither tonight of the children of Israel to search out the country'. ³And the king of Jericho sent unto Rahab, saying, 'Bring forth the men that are come to thee, which are entered into thy house: for they be come to search out all the country'. ⁴And the woman took the two men, and hid them, and said thus: 'There came men unto me, but I wist not whence they were: ⁵and it came to pass about the time of shutting of the gate, when it was dark, that the men went out: whither the men went I wot not: pursue after them quickly; for ye shall overtake them'. ⁶But she had brought them up to the roof of the house, and hid them with the stalks of flax, which she had laid in order upon the roof. ⁷And the men pursued after them the way to Jordan unto the fords: and as soon as they which pursued after them were gone out, they shut the gate.

⁸And before they were laid down, she came up unto them upon the roof. ⁹And she said unto the men, 'I know that the LORD hath given you the land, and that your terror is fallen upon us, and that all the inhabitants of the land faint because of you. ¹⁰For we have heard how the LORD dried up the water of the Red Sea for you, when ye came out of Egypt; and what ye did unto the two kings of the Amorites that were on the other side Jordan, Sihon and Og, whom ye utterly destroyed. ¹¹And as soon as we had heard these things, our hearts did melt, neither did there remain any more courage in any man, because of you: for the LORD your God, he is God in heaven above, and in earth beneath. ¹²Now therefore, I pray you, swear unto me by the LORD, since I have shown you kindness, that ye will also show kindness unto my father's house, and give me a true token: ¹³and that ye will save alive my father, and my mother, and my brethren, and my sisters, and all that they have, and deliver our lives from death.' ¹⁴And the men answered her, 'Our life for yours, if ye utter not this our business. And it shall be when the LORD hath given us the land, that we will deal kindly and truly with thee.'

¹⁵Then she let them down by a cord through the window: for her house was upon the town wall, and she dwelt upon the wall. ¹⁶And she said unto them, 'Get you to the mountain, lest the pursuers meet you; and hide yourselves there three days, until the pursuers be returned: and afterward may ye go your way'. ¹⁷And the men said unto her, 'We will be blameless of this thy oath which thou hast made us swear. ¹⁸Behold, when we come into the land, thou shalt bind this line of scarlet thread in the window which thou didst let us down by: and thou shalt bring thy father, and thy mother, and thy brethren, and all thy father's household home unto thee. ¹⁹And it shall be, that whosoever shall go out of the doors of thy house into the street, his blood shall be upon his head, and we will be guiltless: and whosoever shall be with thee in the house, his blood shall be on our head, if any hand be upon

him. ²⁰And if thou utter this our business, then we will be quit of thy oath which thou hast made us to swear.' ²¹And she said, 'According unto your words, so be it'. And she sent them away, and they departed: and she bound the scarlet line in the window. ²²And they went, and came unto the mountain, and abode there three days, until the pursuers were returned: and the pursuers sought them throughout all the way, but found them not.

²³So the two men returned, and descended from the mountain, and passed over, and came to Joshua the son of Nun, and told him all things that befell them. ²⁴And they said unto Joshua, 'Truly the LORD hath delivered into our hands all the land; for even all the inhabitants of the country do faint because of us'.

3 And Joshua rose early in the morning; and they removed from Shittim, and came to Jordan, he and all the children of Israel, and lodged there before they passed over. ²And it came to pass after three days, that the officers went through the host; ³and they commanded the people, saying, 'When ye see the ark of the covenant of the LORD your God, and the priests the Levites bearing it, then ye shall remove from your place, and go after it.' ⁴Yet there shall be a space between you and it, about two thousand cubits by measure: come not near unto it, that ye may know the way by which ye must go: for ye have not passed this way heretofore.' ⁵And Joshua said unto the people, 'Sanctify yourselves: for tomorrow the LORD will do wonders among you'. ⁶And Joshua spoke unto the priests, saying, 'Take up the ark of the covenant, and pass over before the people'. And they took up the ark of the covenant, and went before the people.

⁷And the LORD said unto Joshua, 'This day will I begin to magnify thee in the sight of all Israel, that they may know that as I was with Moses, so I will be with thee. ⁸And thou shalt command the priests that bear the ark of the covenant, saying, "When ye are come to the brink of the water of Jordan, ye shall stand still in Jordan".'

⁹And Joshua said unto the children of Israel, 'Come hither, and hear the words of the LORD your God'. ¹⁰And Joshua said, 'Hereby ye shall know that the living God is among you, and that he will without fail drive out from before you the Canaanites, and the Hittites, and the Hivites, and the Perizzites, and the Girgashites, and the Amorites, and the Jebusites. ¹¹Behold, the ark of the covenant, even the Lord of all the earth, passeth over before you into Jordan. ¹²Now therefore take ye twelve men out of the tribes of Israel, out of every tribe a man. ¹³And it shall come to pass, as soon as the soles of the feet of the priests that bear the ark of the LORD, the Lord of all the earth, shall rest in the waters of Jordan, that the waters of Jordan shall be cut off from the waters that come down from above; and they shall stand upon a heap.'

¹⁴And it came to pass when the people removed from their tents, to pass over Jordan, and the priests bearing the ark of the covenant before the people; ¹⁵and as they that bore the ark were come unto Jordan, and the feet of the priests that bore the ark were dipped in the brim of the water (for Jordan overfloweth all his banks at the time of harvest),

¹⁶that the waters which came down from above stood and rose up upon a heap very far from the city Adam, that is beside Zaretan: and those that came down toward the sea of the plain, even the salt sea, failed, and were cut off: and the people passed over right against Jericho. ¹⁷And the priests that bore the ark of the covenant of the LORD stood firm on dry ground in the midst of Jordan, and all the Israelites passed over on dry ground, until all the people were passed clean over Jordan.

4 And it came to pass when all the people were clean passed over Jordan, that the LORD spoke unto Joshua, saying, ²'Take you twelve men out of the people, out of every tribe a man, ³and command you them, saying, "Take you hence out of the midst of Jordan, out of the place where the priests' feet stood firm, twelve stones, and ye shall carry them over with you, and leave them in the lodging-place, where you shall lodge this night"'. ⁴Then Joshua called the twelve men, whom he had prepared of the children of Israel, out of every tribe a man: ⁵and Joshua said unto them, 'Pass over before the ark of the LORD your God into the midst of Jordan, and take ye up every man of you a stone upon his shoulder, according unto the number of the tribes of the children of Israel: ⁶that this may be a sign among you, that when your children ask their fathers in time to come, saying, "What mean you by these stones?" ⁷then ye shall answer them, that the waters of Jordan were cut off before the ark of the covenant of the LORD; when it passed over Jordan, the waters of Jordan were cut off: and these stones shall be for a memorial unto the children of Israel for ever'. ⁸And the children of Israel did so as Joshua commanded, and took up twelve stones out of the midst of Jordan, as the LORD spoke unto Joshua, according to the number of the tribes of the children of Israel, and carried them over with them unto the place where they lodged, and laid them down there. ⁹And Joshua set up twelve stones in the midst of Jordan, in the place where the feet of the priests which bore the ark of the covenant stood: and they are there unto this day.

¹⁰For the priests which bore the ark stood in the midst of Jordan, until everything was finished that the LORD commanded Joshua to speak unto the people, according to all that Moses commanded Joshua: and the people hasted and passed over. ¹¹And it came to pass, when all the people were clean passed over, that the ark of the LORD passed over, and the priests, in the presence of the people. ¹²And the children of Reuben, and the children of Gad, and half the tribe of Manasseh, passed over armed before the children of Israel, as Moses spoke unto them: ¹³about forty thousand prepared for war passed over before the LORD unto battle, to the plains of Jericho. ¹⁴On that day the LORD magnified Joshua in the sight of all Israel; and they feared him, as they feared Moses, all the days of his life.

¹⁵And the LORD spoke unto Joshua, saying, ¹⁶'Command the priests that bear the ark of the testimony, that they come up out of Jordan'. ¹⁷Joshua therefore commanded the priests, saying, 'Come ye up out of Jordan'. ¹⁸And it came to pass, when the priests that bore the ark of the covenant of the LORD were come up out of the midst of Jordan, and the

soles of the priests' feet were lifted up unto the dry land, that the waters of Jordan returned unto their place, and flowed over all his banks, as they did before. ¹⁹And the people came up out of Jordan on the tenth day of the first month, and encamped in Gilgal, in the east border of Jericho. ²⁰And those twelve stones, which they took out of Jordan, did Joshua pitch in Gilgal. ²¹And he spoke unto the children of Israel, saying, 'When your children shall ask their fathers in time to come, saying, "What mean these stones?" ²²then ye shall let your children know, saying, "Israel came over this Jordan on dry land". ²³For the LORD your God dried up the waters of Jordan from before you, until ye were passed over, as the LORD your God did to the Red Sea, which he dried up from before us, until we were gone over: ²⁴that all the people of the earth might know the hand of the LORD, that it is mighty: that ye might fear the LORD your God for ever.'

5 And it came to pass, when all the kings of the Amorites, which were on the side of Jordan westward, and all the kings of the Canaanites, which were by the sea, heard that the LORD had dried up the waters of Jordan from before the children of Israel, until we were passed over, that their heart melted, neither was there spirit in them any more, because of the children of Israel.

²At that time the LORD said unto Joshua, 'Make thee sharp knives, and circumcise again the children of Israel the second time'. ³And Joshua made him sharp knives, and circumcised the children of Israel at the hill of the foreskins. ⁴And this is the cause why Joshua did circumcise: all the people that came out of Egypt, that were males, even all the men of war, died in the wilderness by the way, after they came out of Egypt. ⁵Now all the people that came out were circumcised: but all the people that were born in the wilderness by the way as they came forth out of Egypt, them they had not circumcised. ⁶For the children of Israel walked forty years in the wilderness, till all the people that were men of war, which came out of Egypt, were consumed, because they obeyed not the voice of the LORD: unto whom the LORD swore that he would not show them the land, which the LORD swore unto their fathers that he would give us, a land that floweth with milk and honey. ⁷And their children, whom he raised up in their stead, them Joshua circumcised: for they were uncircumcised, because they had not circumcised them by the way. ⁸And it came to pass, when they had done circumcising all the people, that they abode in their places in the camp, till they were whole. ⁹And the LORD said unto Joshua, 'This day have I rolled away the reproach of Egypt from off you'. Wherefore the name of the place is called Gilgal unto this day.

¹⁰And the children of Israel encamped in Gilgal, and kept the passover on the fourteenth day of the month at even in the plains of Jericho. ¹¹And they did eat of the old corn of the land on the morrow after the passover, unleavened cakes, and parched corn in the selfsame day. ¹²And the manna ceased on the morrow after they had eaten of the old corn of the land; neither had the children of Israel manna any more, but they did eat of the fruit of the land of Canaan that year.

¹³And it came to pass when Joshua was by Jericho, that he lifted up his eyes and looked, and behold, there stood a man over against him with his sword drawn in his hand: and Joshua went unto him, and said unto him, 'Art thou for us, or for our adversaries?' ¹⁴And he said, 'Nay, but as captain of the host of the LORD am I now come'. And Joshua fell on his face to the earth, and did worship, and said unto him, 'What saith my lord unto his servant?' ¹⁵And the captain of the LORD's host said unto Joshua, 'Loose thy shoe from off thy foot, for the place whereon thou standest is holy'. And Joshua did so.

6 Now Jericho was straitly shut up because of the children of Israel: none went out, and none came in. ²And the LORD said unto Joshua, 'See, I have given into thy hand Jericho, and the king thereof, and the mighty men of valour. ³And ye shall compass the city, all ye men of war, and go round about the city once. Thus shalt thou do six days. ⁴And seven priests shall bear before the ark seven trumpets of rams' horns: and the seventh day ye shall compass the city seven times, and the priests shall blow with the trumpets. ⁵And it shall come to pass that when they make a long blast with the ram's horn, and when ye hear the sound of the trumpet, all the people shall shout with a great shout: and the wall of the city shall fall down flat, and the people shall ascend up every man straight before him.'

⁶And Joshua the son of Nun called the priests, and said unto them, 'Take up the ark of the covenant, and let seven priests bear seven trumpets of rams' horns before the ark of the LORD'. ⁷And he said unto the people, 'Pass on, and compass the city, and let him that is armed pass on before the ark of the LORD'.

⁸And it came to pass, when Joshua had spoken unto the people, that the seven priests bearing the seven trumpets of rams' horns passed on before the LORD, and blew with the trumpets: and the ark of the covenant of the LORD followed them. ⁹And the armed men went before the priests that blew with the trumpets, and the rearward came after the ark, the priests going on, and blowing with the trumpets. ¹⁰And Joshua had commanded the people, saying, 'Ye shall not shout, nor make any noise with your voice, neither shall any word proceed out of your mouth, until the day I bid you shout; then shall ye shout'. ¹¹So the ark of the LORD compassed the city, going about it once: and they came into the camp, and lodged in the camp.

¹²And Joshua rose early in the morning, and the priests took up the ark of the LORD. ¹³And seven priests bearing seven trumpets of rams' horns before the ark of the LORD went on continually, and blew with the trumpets: and the armed men went before them, but the rearward came after the ark of the LORD, the priests going on, and blowing with the trumpets. ¹⁴And the second day they compassed the city once, and returned into the camp: so they did six days. ¹⁵And it came to pass on the seventh day, that they rose early about the dawning of the day, and compassed the city after the same manner seven times: only on that day they compassed the city seven times. ¹⁶And it came to pass at the seventh time, when the priests blew with the trumpets, Joshua said

unto the people, 'Shout, for the Lord hath given you the city. ¹⁷And the city shall be accursed, even it, and all that are therein, to the Lord: only Rahab the harlot shall live, she and all that are with her in the house, because she hid the messengers that we sent. ¹⁸And you, in any wise keep yourselves from the accursed thing, lest ye make yourselves accursed, when ye take of the accursed thing, and make the camp of Israel a curse, and trouble it. ¹⁹But all the silver, and gold, and vessels of brass and iron, are consecrated unto the Lord: they shall come into the treasury of the Lord.' ²⁰So the people shouted when the priests blew with the trumpets: and it came to pass when the people heard the sound of the trumpet, and the people shouted with a great shout, that the wall fell down flat, so that the people went up into the city, every man straight before him, and they took the city. ²¹And they utterly destroyed all that was in the city, both man and woman, young and old, and ox, and sheep, and ass, with the edge of the sword. ²²But Joshua had said unto the two men that had spied out the country, 'Go into the harlot's house, and bring out thence the woman, and all that she hath, as ye swore unto her'. ²³And the young men that were spies went in, and brought out Rahab, and her father, and her mother, and her brethren, and all that she had; and they brought out all her kindred, and left them without the camp of Israel. ²⁴And they burnt the city with fire, and all that was therein: only the silver, and the gold, and the vessels of brass and of iron, they put into the treasury of the house of the Lord. ²⁵And Joshua saved Rahab the harlot alive, and her father's household, and all that she had; and she dwelleth in Israel even unto this day, because she hid the messengers, which Joshua sent to spy out Jericho.

²⁶And Joshua adjured them at that time, saying, 'Cursed be the man before the Lord, that riseth up and buildeth this city Jericho: he shall lay the foundation thereof in his firstborn, and in his youngest son shall he set up the gates of it'. ²⁷So the Lord was with Joshua; and his fame was noised throughout all the country.

7 But the children of Israel committed a trespass in the accursed thing: for Achan, the son of Carmi, the son of Zabdi, the son of Zerah, of the tribe of Judah, took of the accursed thing: and the anger of the Lord was kindled against the children of Israel. ²And Joshua sent men from Jericho to Ai, which is beside Beth-aven, on the east side of Beth-el, and spoke unto them, saying, 'Go up and view the country'. And the men went up and viewed Ai. ³And they returned to Joshua, and said unto him, 'Let not all the people go up; but let about two or three thousand men go up and smite Ai; and make not all the people to labour thither, for they are but few'. ⁴So there went up thither of the people about three thousand men: and they fled before the men of Ai. ⁵And the men of Ai smote of them about thirty and six men: for they chased them from before the gate even unto Shebarim, and smote them in the going down: wherefore the hearts of the people melted, and became as water.

⁶And Joshua rent his clothes, and fell to the earth upon his face before the ark of the Lord until the eventide, he and the elders of Israel, and

put dust upon their heads. [7]And Joshua said, 'Alas, O Lord GOD, wherefore hast thou at all brought this people over Jordan, to deliver us into the hand of the Amorites, to destroy us? Would to God we had been content, and dwelt on the other side Jordan. [8]O Lord! what shall I say, when Israel turneth their backs before their enemies? [9]For the Canaanites and all the inhabitants of the land shall hear of it, and shall environ us round, and cut off our name from the earth: and what wilt thou do unto thy great name?'

[10]And the LORD said unto Joshua, 'Get thee up; wherefore liest thou thus upon thy face? [11]Israel hath sinned, and they have also transgressed my covenant which I commanded them: for they have even taken of the accursed thing, and have also stolen, and dissembled also, and they have put it even amongst their own stuff. [12]Therefore the children of Israel could not stand before their enemies, but turned their backs before their enemies, because they were accursed: neither will I be with you any more, except ye destroy the accursed from amongst you. [13]Up, sanctify the people, and say, "Sanctify yourselves against tomorrow: for thus saith the LORD God of Israel, 'There is an accursed thing in the midst of thee, O Israel: thou canst not stand before thy enemies, until ye take away the accursed thing from among you'. [14]In the morning therefore ye shall be brought according to your tribes: and it shall be, that the tribe which the LORD taketh shall come according to the families thereof, and the family which the LORD shall take shall come by households; and the households which the LORD shall take shall come man by man. [15]And it shall be, that he that is taken with the accursed thing shall be burnt with fire, he and all that he hath: because he hath transgressed the covenant of the LORD, and because he hath wrought folly in Israel."'

[16]So Joshua rose up early in the morning, and brought Israel by their tribes; and the tribe of Judah was taken. [17]And he brought the family of Judah; and he took the family of the Zarhites, and he brought the family of the Zarhites man by man; and Zabdi was taken. [18]And he brought his household man by man; and Achan, the son of Carmi, the son of Zabdi, the son of Zerah, of the tribe of Judah, was taken. [19]And Joshua said unto Achan, 'My son, give, I pray thee, glory to the LORD God of Israel, and make confession unto him, and tell me now what thou hast done, hide it not from me'. [20]And Achan answered Joshua, and said, 'Indeed I have sinned against the LORD God of Israel, and thus and thus have I done. [21]When I saw among the spoils a goodly Babylonish garment, and two hundred shekels of silver, and a wedge of gold of fifty shekels weight, then I coveted them, and took them; and behold, they are hid in the earth in the midst of my tent, and the silver under it.'

[22]So Joshua sent messengers, and they ran unto the tent; and behold, it was hid in his tent, and the silver under it. [23]And they took them out of the midst of the tent, and brought them unto Joshua, and unto all the children of Israel, and laid them out before the LORD. [24]And Joshua and all Israel with him took Achan the son of Zerah, and the silver, and the garment, and the wedge of gold, and his sons, and his daughters, and his oxen, and his asses, and his sheep, and his tent, and all that he

had: and they brought them unto the valley of Achor. ²⁵And Joshua said, 'Why hast thou troubled us? the LORD shall trouble thee this day'. And all Israel stoned him with stones, and burnt them with fire, after they had stoned them with stones. ²⁶And they raised over him a great heap of stones unto this day. So the LORD turned from the fierceness of his anger. Wherefore the name of the place was called, the valley of Achor, unto this day.

8 And the LORD said unto Joshua, 'Fear not, neither be thou dismayed: take all the people of war with thee, and arise, go up to Ai: see, I have given into thy hand the king of Ai, and his people, and his city, and his land. ²And thou shalt do to Ai and her king as thou didst unto Jericho and her king: only the spoil thereof, and the cattle thereof, shall ye take for a prey unto yourselves: lay thee an ambush for the city behind it.'

³So Joshua arose, and all the people of war, to go up against Ai: and Joshua chose out thirty thousand mighty men of valour, and sent them away by night. ⁴And he commanded them, saying, 'Behold, ye shall lie in wait against the city, even behind the city: go not very far from the city, but be ye all ready: ⁵and I, and all the people that are with me, will approach unto the city: and it shall come to pass, when they come out against us, as at the first, that we will flee before them ⁶(for they will come out after us), till we have drawn them from the city; for they will say, "They flee before us, as at the first": therefore we will flee before them. ⁷Then ye shall rise up from the ambush, and seize upon the city: for the LORD your God will deliver it into your hand. ⁸And it shall be when ye have taken the city, that ye shall set the city on fire: according to the commandment of the LORD shall ye do. See, I have commanded you.'

⁹Joshua therefore sent them forth: and they went to lie in ambush, and abode between Beth-el and Ai, on the west side of Ai: but Joshua lodged that night among the people. ¹⁰And Joshua rose up early in the morning, and numbered the people, and went up, he and the elders of Israel, before the people to Ai. ¹¹And all the people, even the people of war that were with him, went up, and drew nigh, and came before the city, and pitched on the north side of Ai: now there was a valley between them and Ai. ¹²And he took about five thousand men, and set them to lie in ambush between Beth-el and Ai, on the west side of the city. ¹³And when they had set the people, even all the host that was on the north of the city, and their liers in wait on the west of the city, Joshua went that night into the midst of the valley.

¹⁴And it came to pass, when the king of Ai saw it, that they hasted and rose up early, and the men of the city went out against Israel to battle, he and all his people, at a time appointed, before the plain; but he wist not that there were liers in ambush against him behind the city. ¹⁵And Joshua and all Israel made as if they were beaten before them, and fled by the way of the wilderness. ¹⁶And all the people that were in Ai were called together to pursue after them: and they pursued after Joshua, and were drawn away from the city. ¹⁷And there was not a man left in Ai

or Beth-el, that went not out after Israel: and they left the city open, and pursued after Israel. ¹⁸And the LORD said unto Joshua, 'Stretch out the spear that is in thy hand toward Ai; for I will give it into thy hand'. And Joshua stretched out the spear that he had in his hand toward the city. ¹⁹And the ambush arose quickly out of their place, and they ran as soon as he had stretched out his hand: and they entered into the city, and took it, and hasted and set the city on fire. ²⁰And when the men of Ai looked behind them, they saw, and behold, the smoke of the city ascended up to heaven, and they had no power to flee this way or that way: and the people that fled to the wilderness turned back upon the pursuers. ²¹And when Joshua and all Israel saw that the ambush had taken the city, and that the smoke of the city ascended, then they turned again, and slew the men of Ai. ²²And the others issued out of the city against them; so they were in the midst of Israel, some on this side, and some on that side: and they smote them, so that they let none of them remain or escape. ²³And the king of Ai they took alive, and brought him to Joshua. ²⁴And it came to pass when Israel had made an end of slaying all the inhabitants of Ai in the field, in the wilderness wherein they chased them, and when they were all fallen on the edge of the sword, until they were consumed, that all the Israelites returned unto Ai, and smote it with the edge of the sword. ²⁵And so it was that all that fell that day, both of men and women, were twelve thousand, even all the men of Ai. ²⁶For Joshua drew not his hand back wherewith he stretched out the spear, until he had utterly destroyed all the inhabitants of Ai. ²⁷Only the cattle and the spoil of that city Israel took for a prey unto themselves, according unto the word of the LORD which he commanded Joshua. ²⁸And Joshua burnt Ai, and made it a heap for ever, even a desolation unto this day. ²⁹And the king of Ai he hanged on a tree until eventide: and as soon as the sun was down, Joshua commanded that they should take his carcase down from the tree, and cast it at the entering of the gate of the city, and raise thereon a great heap of stones that remaineth unto this day.

³⁰Then Joshua built an altar unto the LORD God of Israel in mount Ebal, ³¹as Moses the servant of the LORD commanded the children of Israel, as it is written in the book of the law of Moses, an altar of whole stones, over which no man hath lifted up any iron: and they offered thereon burnt offerings unto the LORD, and sacrificed peace offerings.

³²And he wrote there upon the stones a copy of the law of Moses, which he wrote in the presence of the children of Israel. ³³And all Israel, and their elders, and officers, and their judges, stood on this side the ark and on that side before the priests the Levites, which bore the ark of the covenant of the LORD, as well the stranger, as he that was born among them; half of them over against mount Gerizim, and half of them over against mount Ebal, as Moses the servant of the LORD had commanded before, that they should bless the people of Israel. ³⁴And afterward he read all the words of the law, the blessings and cursings, according to all that is written in the book of the law. ³⁵There was not a word of all that Moses commanded, which Joshua read not before all

the congregation of Israel, with the women, and the little ones, and the strangers that were conversant among them.

9 And it came to pass when all the kings which were on this side Jordan in the hills, and in the valleys, and in all the coasts of the great sea over against Lebanon, the Hittite, and the Amorite, the Canaanite, the Perizzite, the Hivite, and the Jebusite, heard thereof: ²that they gathered themselves together to fight with Joshua and with Israel, with one accord.

³And when the inhabitants of Gibeon heard what Joshua had done unto Jericho and to Ai, ⁴they did work wilily, and went and made as if they had been ambassadors, and took old sacks upon their asses, and wine bottles, old, and rent, and bound up, ⁵and old shoes and clouted upon their feet, and old garments upon them; and all the bread of their provision was dry and mouldy. ⁶And they went to Joshua unto the camp at Gilgal, and said unto him, and to the men of Israel, 'We be come from a far country: now therefore make ye a league with us'. ⁷And the men of Israel said unto the Hivites, 'Peradventure ye dwell among us; and how shall we make a league with you?' ⁸And they said unto Joshua, 'We are thy servants'. And Joshua said unto them, 'Who are ye? and from whence come ye?' ⁹And they said unto him, 'From a very far country thy servants are come because of the name of the LORD thy God: for we have heard the fame of him, and all that he did in Egypt, ¹⁰and all that he did to the two kings of the Amorites, that were beyond Jordan, to Sihon king of Heshbon, and to Og king of Bashan, which was at Ashtaroth. ¹¹Wherefore our elders and all the inhabitants of our country spoke to us, saying, "Take victuals with you for the journey, and go to meet them, and say unto them, 'We are your servants: therefore now make ye a league with us'". ¹²This our bread we took hot for our provision out of our houses on the day we came forth to go unto you; but now behold, it is dry, and it is mouldy. ¹³And these bottles of wine which we filled, were new, and behold, they be rent: and these our garments and our shoes are become old by reason of the very long journey.' ¹⁴And the men took of their victuals, and asked not counsel at the mouth of the LORD. ¹⁵And Joshua made peace with them, and made a league with them, to let them live: and the princes of the congregation swore unto them.

¹⁶And it came to pass at the end of three days after they had made a league with them, that they heard that they were their neighbours, and that they dwelt among them. ¹⁷And the children of Israel journeyed, and came unto their cities on the third day. Now their cities were Gibeon, and Chephirah, and Beeroth, and Kirjath-jearim. ¹⁸And the children of Israel smote them not, because the princes of the congregation had sworn unto them by the LORD God of Israel. And all the congregation murmured against the princes. ¹⁹But all the princes said unto all the congregation, 'We have sworn unto them by the LORD God of Israel: now therefore we may not touch them. ²⁰This we will do to them; we will even let them live, lest wrath be upon us, because of the oath which we swore unto them.' ²¹And the princes said unto them, 'Let

them live; but let them be hewers of wood and drawers of water unto all the congregation'; as the princes had promised them.

²²And Joshua called for them, and he spoke unto them, saying, 'Wherefore have ye beguiled us, saying, "We are very far from you"; when ye dwell among us? ²³Now therefore ye are cursed, and there shall none of you be freed from being bondmen, and hewers of wood and drawers of water for the house of my God.' ²⁴And they answered Joshua, and said, 'Because it was certainly told thy servants, how that the LORD thy God commanded his servant Moses to give you all the land, and to destroy all the inhabitants of the land from before you, therefore we were sore afraid of our lives because of you, and have done this thing. ²⁵And now, behold, we are in thy hand: as it seemeth good and right unto thee to do unto us, do.' ²⁶And so did he unto them, and delivered them out of the hand of the children of Israel, that they slew them not. ²⁷And Joshua made them that day hewers of wood and drawers of water for the congregation, and for the altar of the LORD, even unto this day, in the place which he should choose.

10 Now it came to pass, when Adoni-zedek king of Jerusalem had heard how Joshua had taken Ai, and had utterly destroyed it (as he had done to Jericho and her king, so he had done to Ai and her king), and how the inhabitants of Gibeon had made peace with Israel, and were among them, ²that they feared greatly, because Gibeon was a great city, as one of the royal cities, and because it was greater than Ai, and all the men thereof were mighty. ³Wherefore Adoni-zedek king of Jerusalem sent unto Hoham king of Hebron, and unto Piram king of Jarmuth, and unto Japhia king of Lachish, and unto Debir king of Eglon, saying, ⁴'Come up unto me, and help me, that we may smite Gibeon: for it hath made peace with Joshua and with the children of Israel'. ⁵Therefore the five kings of the Amorites, the king of Jerusalem, the king of Hebron, the king of Jarmuth, the king of Lachish, the king of Eglon, gathered themselves together, and went up, they and all their hosts, and encamped before Gibeon, and made war against it.

⁶And the men of Gibeon sent unto Joshua to the camp to Gilgal, saying, 'Slack not thy hand from thy servants; come up to us quickly, and save us, and help us: for all the kings of the Amorites that dwell in the mountains are gathered together against us'. ⁷So Joshua ascended from Gilgal, he, and all the people of war with him, and all the mighty men of valour.

⁸And the LORD said unto Joshua, 'Fear them not: for I have delivered them into thy hand; there shall not a man of them stand before thee'. ⁹Joshua therefore came unto them suddenly, and went up from Gilgal all night. ¹⁰And the LORD discomfited them before Israel, and slew them with a great slaughter at Gibeon, and chased them along the way that goeth up to Beth-horon, and smote them to Azekah, and unto Makkedah. ¹¹And it came to pass, as they fled from before Israel, and were in the going down to Beth-horon, that the LORD cast down great stones from heaven upon them unto Azekah, and they died: they were more which died with hailstones than they whom the children of Israel slew with the sword.

¹²Then spoke Joshua to the LORD in the day when the LORD delivered up the Amorites before the children of Israel, and he said in the sight of Israel, 'Sun, stand thou still upon Gibeon, and thou, Moon, in the valley of Aijalon'. ¹³And the sun stood still, and the moon stayed, until the people had avenged themselves upon their enemies. Is not this written in the book of Jasher? 'So the sun stood still in the midst of heaven, and hasted not to go down about a whole day'. ¹⁴And there was no day like that before it or after it, that the LORD hearkened unto the voice of a man: for the LORD fought for Israel.

¹⁵And Joshua returned, and all Israel with him, unto the camp to Gilgal. ¹⁶But these five kings fled, and hid themselves in a cave at Makkedah. ¹⁷And it was told Joshua, saying, 'The five kings are found hid in a cave at Makkedah'. ¹⁸And Joshua said, 'Roll great stones upon the mouth of the cave, and set men by it for to keep them. ¹⁹And stay you not, but pursue after your enemies, and smite the hindmost of them; suffer them not to enter into their cities: for the LORD your God hath delivered them into your hand.' ²⁰And it came to pass when Joshua and the children of Israel had made an end of slaying them with a very great slaughter, till they were consumed, that the rest which remained of them entered into fenced cities. ²¹And all the people returned to the camp to Joshua at Makkedah in peace: none moved his tongue against any of the children of Israel. ²²Then said Joshua, 'Open the mouth of the cave, and bring out those five kings unto me out of the cave'. ²³And they did so, and brought forth those five kings unto him out of the cave, the king of Jerusalem, the king of Hebron, the king of Jarmuth, the king of Lachish, and the king of Eglon. ²⁴And it came to pass when they brought out those kings unto Joshua, that Joshua called for all the men of Israel, and said unto the captains of the men of war which went with him, 'Come near, put your feet upon the necks of these kings'. And they came near, and put their feet upon the necks of them. ²⁵And Joshua said unto them, 'Fear not, nor be dismayed, be strong and of good courage: for thus shall the LORD do to all your enemies against whom ye fight'. ²⁶And afterward Joshua smote them, and slew them, and hanged them on five trees: and they were hanging upon the trees until the evening. ²⁷And it came to pass at the time of the going down of the sun, that Joshua commanded, and they took them down off the trees, and cast them into the cave wherein they had been hid, and laid great stones in the cave's mouth, which remain until this very day.

²⁸And that day Joshua took Makkedah, and smote it with the edge of the sword, and the king thereof he utterly destroyed, them, and all the souls that were therein; he let none remain: and he did to the king of Makkedah as he did unto the king of Jericho.

²⁹Then Joshua passed from Makkedah, and all Israel with him, unto Libnah, and fought against Libnah. ³⁰And the LORD delivered it also, and the king thereof, into the hand of Israel; and he smote it with the edge of the sword, and all the souls that were therein; he let none remain in it, but did unto the king thereof as he did unto the king of Jericho.

³¹And Joshua passed from Libnah, and all Israel with him, unto

Lachish, and encamped against it, and fought against it. ³²And the LORD delivered Lachish into the hand of Israel, which took it on the second day, and smote it with the edge of the sword, and all the souls that were therein, according to all that he had done to Libnah.

³³Then Horam king of Gezer came up to help Lachish, and Joshua smote him and his people, until he had left him none remaining.

³⁴And from Lachish Joshua passed unto Eglon, and all Israel with him, and they encamped against it, and fought against it. ³⁵And they took it on that day, and smote it with the edge of the sword, and all the souls that were therein he utterly destroyed that day, according to all that he had done to Lachish.

³⁶And Joshua went up from Eglon, and all Israel with him, unto Hebron, and they fought against it. ³⁷And they took it, and smote it with the edge of the sword, and the king thereof, and all the cities thereof, and all the souls that were therein; he left none remaining, according to all that he had done to Eglon: but destroyed it utterly, and all the souls that were therein.

³⁸And Joshua returned, and all Israel with him, to Debir, and fought against it. ³⁹And he took it, and the king thereof, and all the cities thereof, and they smote them with the edge of the sword, and utterly destroyed all the souls that were therein; he left none remaining: as he had done to Hebron, so he did to Debir, and to the king thereof, as he had done also to Libnah, and to her king.

⁴⁰So Joshua smote all the country of the hills, and of the south, and of the vale, and of the springs, and all their kings: he left none remaining, but utterly destroyed all that breathed, as the LORD God of Israel commanded. ⁴¹And Joshua smote them from Kadesh-barnea even unto Gaza, and all the country of Goshen, even unto Gibeon. ⁴²And all these kings and their land did Joshua take at one time, because the LORD God of Israel fought for Israel. ⁴³And Joshua returned, and all Israel with him, unto the camp to Gilgal.

11 And it came to pass, when Jabin king of Hazor had heard those things, that he sent to Jobab king of Madon, and to the king of Shimron, and to the king of Achshaph, ²and to the kings that were on the north of the mountains, and of the plains south of Chinneroth, and in the valley, and in the borders of Dor on the west, ³and to the Canaanite on the east and on the west, and to the Amorite, and the Hittite, and the Perizzite, and the Jebusite in the mountains, and to the Hivite under Hermon in the land of Mizpeh. ⁴And they went out, they and all their hosts with them, much people, even as the sand that is upon the sea-shore in multitude, with horses and chariots very many. ⁵And when all these kings were met together, they came and pitched together at the waters of Merom, to fight against Israel.

⁶And the LORD said unto Joshua, 'Be not afraid because of them: for tomorrow about this time will I deliver them up all slain before Israel: thou shalt hock their horses, and burn their chariots with fire'. ⁷So Joshua came, and all the people of war with him, against them by the waters of Merom suddenly; and they fell upon them. ⁸And the LORD

delivered them into the hand of Israel, who smote them, and chased them unto great Zidon, and unto Misrephoth-maim, and unto the valley of Mizpeh eastward; and they smote them, until they left them none remaining. ⁹And Joshua did unto them as the LORD bade him: he hocked their horses, and burnt their chariots with fire.

¹⁰And Joshua at that time turned back, and took Hazor, and smote the king thereof with the sword: for Hazor beforetime was the head of all those kingdoms. ¹¹And they smote all the souls that were therein with the edge of the sword, utterly destroying them: there was not any left to breathe: and he burnt Hazor with fire. ¹²And all the cities of those kings, and all the kings of them, did Joshua take, and smote them with the edge of the sword, and he utterly destroyed them, as Moses the servant of the LORD commanded. ¹³But as for the cities that stood still in their strength, Israel burnt none of them, save Hazor only; that did Joshua burn. ¹⁴And all the spoil of these cities, and the cattle, the children of Israel took for a prey unto themselves; but every man they smote with the edge of the sword, until they had destroyed them, neither left they any to breathe.

¹⁵As the LORD commanded Moses his servant, so did Moses command Joshua, and so did Joshua: he left nothing undone of all that the LORD commanded Moses. ¹⁶So Joshua took all that land, the hills, and all the south country, and all the land of Goshen, and the valley, and the plain, and the mountain of Israel, and the valley of the same: ¹⁷even from the mount Halak, that goeth up to Seir, unto Baal-gad in the valley of Lebanon under mount Hermon: and all their kings he took, and smote them, and slew them. ¹⁸Joshua made war a long time with all those kings. ¹⁹There was not a city that made peace with the children of Israel, save the Hivites the inhabitants of Gibeon: all others they took in battle. ²⁰For it was of the LORD to harden their hearts, that they should come against Israel in battle, that he might destroy them utterly, and that they might have no favour, but that he might destroy them, as the LORD commanded Moses.

²¹And at that time came Joshua, and cut off the Anakims from the mountains, from Hebron, from Debir, from Anab, and from all the mountains of Judah, and from all the mountains of Israel: Joshua destroyed them utterly with their cities. ²²There was none of the Anakims left in the land of the children of Israel: only in Gaza, in Gath, and in Ashdod, there remained. ²³So Joshua took the whole land, according to all that the LORD said unto Moses; and Joshua gave it for an inheritance unto Israel according to their divisions by their tribes. And the land rested from war.

12 Now these are the kings of the land, which the children of Israel smote, and possessed their land on the other side Jordan toward the rising of the sun, from the river Arnon unto mount Hermon, and all the plain on the east: ²Sihon king of the Amorites who dwelt in Heshbon, and ruled from Aroer, which is upon the bank of the river of Arnon, and from the middle of the river, and from half Gilead, even unto the river Jabbok, which is the border of the children of Ammon;

³and from the plain to the sea of Chinneroth on the east, and unto the sea of the plain, even the salt sea on the east, the way to Beth-jeshimoth; and from the south, under Ashdoth-pisgah: ⁴and the coast of Og king of Bashan, which was of the remnant of the giants, that dwelt at Ashtaroth and at Edrei, ⁵and reigned in mount Hermon, and in Salcah, and in all Bashan, unto the border of the Geshurites and the Maachathites, and half Gilead, the border of Sihon king of Heshbon. ⁶Them did Moses the servant of the LORD and the children of Israel smite: and Moses the servant of the LORD gave it for a possession unto the Reubenites, and Gadites, and the half tribe of Manasseh.

⁷And these are the kings of the country which Joshua and the children of Israel smote on this side Jordan on the west, from Baal-gad in the valley of Lebanon even unto the mount Halak, that goeth up to Seir, which Joshua gave unto the tribes of Israel for a possession according to their divisions; ⁸in the mountains, and in the valleys, and in the plains, and in the springs, and in the wilderness, and in the south country; the Hittites, the Amorites, and the Canaanites, the Perizzites, the Hivites, and the Jebusites: ⁹the king of Jericho, one; the king of Ai, which is beside Beth-el, one; ¹⁰the king of Jerusalem, one; the king of Hebron, one; ¹¹the king of Jarmuth, one; the king of Lachish, one; ¹²the king of Eglon, one; the king of Gezer, one; ¹³the king of Debir, one; the king of Geder, one; ¹⁴the king of Hormah, one; the king of Arad, one; ¹⁵the king of Libnah, one; the king of Adullam, one; ¹⁶the king of Makkedah, one; the king of Beth-el, one; ¹⁷the king of Tappuah, one; the king of Hepher, one; ¹⁸the king of Aphek, one; the king of Lasharon, one; ¹⁹the king of Madon, one; the king of Hazor, one; ²⁰the king of Shimron-meron, one; the king of Achshaph, one; ²¹the king of Taanach, one; the king of Megiddo, one; ²²the king of Kedesh, one; the king of Jokneam of Carmel, one; ²³the king of Dor in the coast of Dor, one; the king of the nations of Gilgal, one; ²⁴the king of Tirzah, one: all the kings thirty and one.

13 Now Joshua was old and stricken in years, and the LORD said unto him, 'Thou art old and stricken in years, and there remaineth yet very much land to be possessed. ²This is the land that yet remaineth: all the borders of the Philistines, and all Geshuri, ³from Sihor, which is before Egypt, even unto the borders of Ekron northward, which is counted to the Canaanite: five lords of the Philistines; the Gazathites, and the Ashdothites, the Eshkalonites, the Gittites, and the Ekronites; also the Avites: ⁴from the south, all the land of the Canaanites, and Mearah that is beside the Sidonians, unto Aphek, to the borders of the Amorites: ⁵and the land of the Giblites, and all Lebanon, toward the sunrising, from Baal-gad under mount Hermon unto the entering into Hamath. ⁶All the inhabitants of the hill-country from Lebanon unto Misrephoth-maim, and all the Sidonians, them will I drive out from before the children of Israel: only divide thou it by lot unto the Israelites for an inheritance, as I have commanded thee. ⁷Now therefore divide this land for an inheritance unto the nine tribes, and the half tribe of Manasseh;' ⁸with whom the Reubenites and the

Gadites have received their inheritance, which Moses gave them, beyond Jordan eastward, even as Moses the servant of the LORD gave them: ⁹from Aroer, that is upon the bank of the river Arnon, and the city that is in the midst of the river, and all the plain of Medeba unto Dibon: ¹⁰and all the cities of Sihon king of the Amorites, which reigned in Heshbon, unto the border of the children of Ammon: ¹¹and Gilead, and the border of the Geshurites and Maachathites, and all mount Hermon, and all Bashan unto Salcah: ¹²all the kingdom of Og in Bashan, which reigned in Ashtaroth and in Edrei, who remained of the remnant of the giants: for these did Moses smite, and cast them out. ¹³Nevertheless the children of Israel expelled not the Geshurites, nor the Maachathites: but the Geshurites and the Maachathites dwell among the Israelites until this day. ¹⁴Only unto the tribe of Levi he gave no inheritance: the sacrifices of the LORD God of Israel made by fire are their inheritance, as he said unto them.

¹⁵And Moses gave unto the tribe of the children of Reuben inheritance according to their families. ¹⁶And their coast was from Aroer that is on the bank of the river Arnon, and the city that is in the midst of the river, and all the plain by Medeba; ¹⁷Heshbon, and all her cities that are in the plain: Dibon, and Bamoth-baal, and Beth-baal-meon, ¹⁸And Jahazah, and Kedemoth, and Mephaath, ¹⁹And Kirjathaim, and Sibmah, and Zareth-shahar in the mount of the valley, ²⁰and Beth-peor, and Ashdoth-pisgah, and Beth-jeshimoth, ²¹and all the cities of the plain, and all the kingdom of Sihon king of the Amorites, which reigned in Heshbon, whom Moses smote with the princes of Midian, Evi, and Rekem, and Zur, and Hur, and Reba, which were dukes of Sihon, dwelling in the country.

²²Balaam also the son of Beor, the soothsayer, did the children of Israel slay with the sword among them that were slain by them. ²³And the border of the children of Reuben was Jordan, and the border thereof. This was the inheritance of the children of Reuben after their families, the cities and villages thereof.

²⁴And Moses gave inheritance unto the tribe of Gad, even unto the children of Gad according to their families. ²⁵And their coast was Jazer, and all the cities of Gilead, and half the land of the children of Ammon, unto Aroer that is before Rabbah; ²⁶and from Heshbon unto Ramath-mizpeh, and Betonim; and from Mahanaim unto the border of Debir; ²⁷and in the valley, Beth-aram, and Beth-nimrah, and Succoth, and Zaphon, the rest of the kingdom of Sihon king of Heshbon, Jordan and his border, even unto the edge of the sea of Chinnereth on the other side Jordan eastward. ²⁸This is the inheritance of the children of Gad after their families, the cities, and their villages.

²⁹And Moses gave inheritance unto the half tribe of Manasseh: and this was the possession of the half tribe of Manasseh by their families. ³⁰And their coast was from Mahanaim, all Bashan, all the kingdom of Og king of Bashan, and all the towns of Jair, which are in Bashan, three-score cities: ³¹and half Gilead, and Ashtaroth, and Edrei, cities of the kingdom of Og in Bashan, were pertaining unto the children of Machir

the son of Manasseh, even to the one half of the children of Machir by their families. ³²These are the countries which Moses did distribute for inheritance in the plains of Moab, on the other side Jordan, by Jericho, eastward. ³³But unto the tribe of Levi Moses gave not any inheritance: the LORD God of Israel was their inheritance, as he said unto them.

14 And these are the countries which the children of Israel inherited in the land of Canaan, which Eleazar the priest, and Joshua the son of Nun, and the heads of the fathers of the tribes of the children of Israel distributed for inheritance to them. ²By lot was their inheritance, as the LORD commanded by the hand of Moses, for the nine tribes, and for the half tribe. ³For Moses had given the inheritance of two tribes and a half tribe on the other side Jordan: but unto the Levites he gave no inheritance among them. ⁴For the children of Joseph were two tribes, Manasseh and Ephraim: therefore they gave no part unto the Levites in the land, save cities to dwell in, with their suburbs for their cattle and for their substance. ⁵As the LORD commanded Moses, so the children of Israel did, and they divided the land.

⁶Then the children of Judah came unto Joshua in Gilgal: and Caleb the son of Jephunneh the Kenezite said unto him, 'Thou knowest the thing that the LORD said unto Moses the man of God concerning me and thee in Kadesh-barnea. ⁷Forty years old was I when Moses the servant of the LORD sent me from Kadesh-barnea to espy out the land, and I brought him word again as it was in my heart. ⁸Nevertheless my brethren that went up with me made the heart of the people melt: but I wholly followed the LORD my God. ⁹And Moses swore on that day, saying, "Surely the land whereon thy feet have trodden shall be thy inheritance, and thy children's for ever, because thou hast wholly followed the LORD my God". ¹⁰And now, behold, the LORD hath kept me alive, as he said, these forty and five years, even since the LORD spoke this word unto Moses, while the children of Israel wandered in the wilderness: and now lo, I am this day fourscore and five years old. ¹¹As yet I am as strong this day as I was in the day that Moses sent me: as my strength was then, even so is my strength now, for war, both to go out, and to come in. ¹²Now therefore give me this mountain, whereof the LORD spoke in that day; for thou heardest in that day how the Anakims were there, and that the cities were great and fenced: if so be the LORD will be with me, then I shall be able to drive them out, as the LORD said.' ¹³And Joshua blessed him, and gave unto Caleb the son of Jephunneh Hebron for an inheritance. ¹⁴Hebron therefore became the inheritance of Caleb the son of Jephunneh the Kenezite unto this day, because that he wholly followed the LORD God of Israel. ¹⁵And the name of Hebron before was Kirjath-arba; which Arba was a great man among the Anakims. And the land had rest from war.

15 This then was the lot of the tribe of the children of Judah by their families; even to the border of Edom the wilderness of Zin southward was the uttermost part of the south coast. ²And their south border was from the shore of the salt sea, from the bay that looketh southward. ³And it went out to the south side to Maaleh-acrabbim, and passed along to Zin, and ascended up on the south side unto Kadesh-barnea, and passed along to Hezron, and went up to Adar, and fetched a compass to Karkaa. ⁴From thence it passed toward Azmon, and went out unto the river of Egypt; and the goings out of that coast were at the sea: this shall be your south coast. ⁵And the east border was the salt sea, even unto the end of Jordan. And their border in the north quarter was from the bay of the sea at the uttermost part of Jordan. ⁶And the border went up to Beth-hogla, and passed along by the north of Beth-arabah; and the border went up to the stone of Bohan the son of Reuben. ⁷And the border went up toward Debir from the valley of Achor, and so northward, looking toward Gilgal, that is before the going up to Adummim, which is on the south side of the river: and the border passed towards the waters of En-shemesh, and the goings out thereof were at En-rogel. ⁸And the border went up by the valley of the son of Hinnom unto the south side of the Jebusite; the same is Jerusalem: and the border went up to the top of the mountain that lieth before the valley of Hinnom westward, which is at the end of the valley of the giants northward. ⁹And the border was drawn from the top of the hill unto the fountain of the water of Nephtoah, and went out to the cities of mount Ephron; and the border was drawn to Baalah, which is Kirjath-jearim. ¹⁰And the border compassed from Baalah westward unto mount Seir, and passed along unto the side of mount Jearim, which is Chesalon, on the north side, and went down to Beth-shemesh, and passed on to Timnah. ¹¹And the border went out unto the side of Ekron northward: and the border was drawn to Shicron, and passed along to mount Baalah, and went out unto Jabneel; and the goings out of the border were at the sea. ¹²And the west border was to the great sea, and the coast thereof. This is the coast of the children of Judah round about according to their families.

¹³And unto Caleb the son of Jephunneh he gave a part among the children of Judah, according to the commandment of the LORD to Joshua, even the city of Arba the father of Anak, which city is Hebron. ¹⁴And Caleb drove thence the three sons of Anak, Sheshai, and Ahiman, and Talmai, the children of Anak. ¹⁵And he went up thence to the inhabitants of Debir: and the name of Debir before was Kirjath-sepher.

¹⁶And Caleb said, 'He that smiteth Kirjath-sepher, and taketh it, to him will I give Achsah my daughter to wife'. ¹⁷And Othniel the son of Kenaz, the brother of Caleb, took it: and he gave him Achsah his daughter to wife. ¹⁸And it came to pass as she came unto him, that she moved him to ask of her father a field: and she lighted off her ass; and Caleb said unto her, 'What wouldst thou?' ¹⁹Who answered, 'Give me a blessing; for thou hast given me a south land; give me also springs of water'. And he gave her the upper springs, and the nether springs.

²⁰This is the inheritance of the tribe of the children of Judah according to their families. ²¹And the uttermost cities of the tribe of the children of Judah toward the coast of Edom southward were Kabzeel, and Eder, and Jagur, ²²and Kinah, and Dimonah, and Adadah, ²³and Kedesh, and Hazor, and Ithnan, ²⁴Ziph, and Telem, and Bealoth, ²⁵and Hazor,

Hadattah, and Kerioth, and Hezron, which is Hazor, ²⁶Amam, and Shema, and Moladah, ²⁷and Hazar-gaddah, and Heshmon, and Beth-palet, ²⁸and Hazar-shual, and Beer-sheba, and Bizjothjah, ²⁹Baalah, and Iim, and Azem, ³⁰and Eltolad, and Chesil, and Hormah, ³¹and Ziklag, and Madmannah, and Sansannah, ³²and Lebaoth, and Shilhim, and Ain, and Rimmon: all the cities are twenty and nine, with their villages.

³³And in the valley, Eshtaol, and Zoreah, and Ashnah, ³⁴and Zanoah, and En-gannim, Tappuah, and Enam, ³⁵Jarmuth, and Adullam, Socoh, and Azekah, ³⁶and Sharaim, and Adithaim, and Gederah, and Gederothaim: fourteen cities with their villages. ³⁷Zenan, and Hadashah, and Migdal-gad, ³⁸and Dilean, and Mizpeh, and Joktheel, ³⁹Lachish, and Bozkath, and Eglon, ⁴⁰and Cabbon, and Lahmam, and Kithlish, ⁴¹and Gederoth, Beth-dagon, and Naamah, and Makkedah: sixteen cities with their villages. ⁴²Libnah, and Ether, and Ashan, ⁴³and Jiphtah, and Ashnah, and Nezib, ⁴⁴and Keilah, and Achzib, and Mareshah: nine cities with their villages. ⁴⁵Ekron, with her towns and her villages. ⁴⁶From Ekron even unto the sea, all that lay near Ashdod, with their villages. ⁴⁷Ashdod with her towns and her villages, Gaza with her towns and her villages, unto the river of Egypt, and the great sea, and the border thereof.

⁴⁸And in the mountains, Shamir, and Jattir, and Socoh, ⁴⁹and Dannah, and Kirjath-sannah, which is Debir, ⁵⁰and Anab, and Ashtemoh, and Anim, ⁵¹and Goshen, and Holon, and Giloh: eleven cities with their villages. ⁵²Arab, and Dumah, and Eshean, ⁵³and Janum, and Beth-tappuah, and Aphekah, ⁵⁴and Humtah, and Kirjath-arba, which is Hebron, and Zior: nine cities with their villages. ⁵⁵Maon, Carmel, and Ziph, and Juttah, ⁵⁶and Jezreel, and Jokdeam, and Zanoah, ⁵⁷Cain, Gibeah, and Timnah: ten cities with their villages. ⁵⁸Halhul, Beth-zur, and Gedor, ⁵⁹and Maarath, and Beth-anoth, and Eltekon: six cities with their villages. ⁶⁰Kirjath-baal, which is Kirjath-jearim, and Rabbah: two cities with their villages.

⁶¹In the wilderness, Beth-arabah, Middin, and Secacah, ⁶²and Nibshan, and the city of Salt, and En-gedi: six cities with their villages.

⁶³As for the Jebusites the inhabitants of Jerusalem, the children of Judah could not drive them out: but the Jebusites dwell with the children of Judah at Jerusalem unto this day.

16 And the lot of the children of Joseph fell from Jordan by Jericho, unto the water of Jericho on the east, to the wilderness that goeth up from Jericho throughout mount Beth-el, ²and goeth out from Beth-el to Luz, and passeth along unto the borders of Archi to Ataroth, ³and goeth down westward to the coast of Japhleti, unto the coast of Beth-horon the nether, and to Gezer: and the goings out thereof are at the sea. ⁴So the children of Joseph, Manasseh and Ephraim, took their inheritance.

⁵And the border of the children of Ephraim according to their families was thus: even the border of their inheritance on the east side was Ataroth-addar, unto Beth-horon the upper; ⁶and the border went out toward the sea to Michmethah on the north side; and the border went

about eastward unto Taanath-shiloh, and passed by it on the east to Janohah; ⁷and it went down from Janohah to Ataroth, and to Naarath, and came to Jericho, and went out at Jordan. ⁸The border went out from Tappuah westward unto the river Kanah; and the goings out thereof were at the sea. This is the inheritance of the tribe of the children of Ephraim by their families. ⁹And the separate cities for the children of Ephraim were among the inheritance of the children of Manasseh, all the cities with their villages. ¹⁰And they drove not out the Canaanites that dwelt in Gezer: but the Canaanites dwell among the Ephraimites unto this day, and serve under tribute.

17 There was also a lot for the tribe of Manasseh (for he was the firstborn of Joseph); to wit, for Machir the firstborn of Manasseh, the father of Gilead: because he was a man of war, therefore he had Gilead and Bashan. ²There was also a lot for the rest of the children of Manasseh by their families; for the children of Abiezer, and for the children of Helek, and for the children of Asriel, and for the children of Shechem, and for the children of Hepher, and for the children of Shemida: these were the male children of Manasseh the son of Joseph by their families.

³But Zelophehad, the son of Hepher, the son of Gilead, the son of Machir, the son of Manasseh, had no sons, but daughters: and these are the names of his daughters, Mahlah, and Noah, Hoglah, Milcah, and Tirzah. ⁴And they came near before Eleazar the priest, and before Joshua the son of Nun, and before the princes, saying, 'The LORD commanded Moses to give us an inheritance among our brethren'. Therefore according to the commandment of the LORD he gave them an inheritance among the brethren of their father. ⁵And there fell ten portions to Manasseh, besides the land of Gilead and Bashan, which were on the other side Jordan; ⁶because the daughters of Manasseh had an inheritance among his sons: and the rest of Manasseh's sons had the land of Gilead.

⁷And the coast of Manasseh was from Asher to Michmethah, that lieth before Shechem; and the border went along on the right hand unto the inhabitants of En-tappuah. ⁸Now Manasseh had the land of Tappuah: but Tappuah on the border of Manasseh belonged to the children of Ephraim. ⁹And the coast descended unto the river Kanah, southward of the river: these cities of Ephraim are among the cities of Manasseh: the coast of Manasseh also was on the north side of the river, and the outgoings of it were at the sea. ¹⁰Southward it was Ephraim's, and northward it was Manasseh's, and the sea is his border; and they met together in Asher on the north, and in Issachar on the east. ¹¹And Manasseh had in Issachar and in Asher Beth-shean and her towns, and Ibleam and her towns, and the inhabitants of Dor and her towns, and the inhabitants of En-dor and her towns, and the inhabitants of Taanach and her towns, and the inhabitants of Megiddo and her towns, even three countries. ¹²Yet the children of Manasseh could not drive out the inhabitants of those cities; but the Canaanites would dwell in that land. ¹³Yet it came to pass, when the children of Israel were waxed

strong, that they put the Canaanites to tribute; but did not utterly drive them out.

¹⁴And the children of Joseph spoke unto Joshua, saying, 'Why hast thou given me but one lot and one portion to inherit, seeing I am a great people, forasmuch as the LORD hath blessed me hitherto?' ¹⁵And Joshua answered them, 'If thou be a great people, then get thee up to the wood country, and cut down for thyself there in the land of the Perizzites and of the giants, if mount Ephraim be too narrow for thee'. ¹⁶And the children of Joseph said, 'The hill is not enough for us: and all the Canaanites that dwell in the land of the valley have chariots of iron, both they who are of Beth-shean and her towns, and they who are of the valley of Jezreel'. ¹⁷And Joshua spoke unto the house of Joseph, even to Ephraim and to Manasseh, saying, 'Thou art a great people, and hast great power: thou shalt not have one lot only. ¹⁸But the mountain shall be thine, for it is a wood, and thou shalt cut it down: and the out-goings of it shall be thine: for thou shalt drive out the Canaanites, though they have iron chariots, and though they be strong.'

18 And the whole congregation of the children of Israel assembled together at Shiloh, and set up the tabernacle of the congregation there. And the land was subdued before them. ²And there remained among the children of Israel seven tribes, which had not yet received their inheritance. ³And Joshua said unto the children of Israel, 'How long are you slack to go to possess the land, which the LORD God of your fathers hath given you? ⁴Give out from among you three men for each tribe: and I will send them, and they shall rise, and go through the land, and describe it according to the inheritance of them; and they shall come again to me. ⁵And they shall divide it into seven parts: Judah shall abide in their coast on the south, and the house of Joseph shall abide in their coasts on the north. ⁶Ye shall therefore describe the land into seven parts, and bring the description hither to me, that I may cast lots for you here before the LORD our God. ⁷But the Levites have no part among you, for the priesthood of the LORD is their inheri-tance: and Gad, and Reuben, and half the tribe of Manasseh, have received their inheritance beyond Jordan on the east, which Moses the servant of the LORD gave them.'

⁸And the men arose, and went away: and Joshua charged them that went to describe the land, saying, 'Go and walk through the land, and describe it, and come again to me, that I may here cast lots for you before the LORD in Shiloh'. ⁹And the men went and passed through the land, and described it by cities into seven parts in a book, and came again to Joshua to the host at Shiloh. ¹⁰And Joshua cast lots for them in Shiloh before the LORD: and there Joshua divided the land unto the children of Israel according to their divisions.

¹¹And the lot of the tribe of the children of Benjamin came up accord-ing to their families: and the coast of their lot came forth between the children of Judah and the children of Joseph. ¹²And their border on the north side was from Jordan; and the border went up to the side of Jericho on the north side, and went up through the mountains west-

ward; and the goings out thereof were at the wilderness of Beth-aven. ¹³And the border went over from thence toward Luz, to the side of Luz, which is Beth-el, southward; and the border descended to Ataroth-adar, near the hill that lieth on the south side of the nether Beth-horon. ¹⁴And the border was drawn thence, and compassed the corner of the sea southward, from the hill that lieth before Beth-horon southward; and the goings out thereof were at Kirjath-baal, which is Kirjath-jearim, a city of the children of Judah: this was the west quarter. ¹⁵And the south quarter was from the end of Kirjath-jearim, and the border went out on the west, and went out to the well of waters of Nephtoah. ¹⁶And the border came down to the end of the mountain that lieth before the valley of the son of Hinnom, and which is in the valley of the giants on the north, and descended to the valley of Hinnom, to the side of Jebusi on the south, and descended to En-rogel, ¹⁷and was drawn from the north, and went forth to En-shemesh, and went forth toward Geliloth, which is over against the going up of Adummim, and descended to the stone of Bohan the son of Reuben, ¹⁸and passed along toward the side over against Arabah northward, and went down unto Arabah. ¹⁹And the border passed along to the side of Beth-hoglah north-ward: and the outgoings of the border were at the north bay of the salt sea at the south end of Jordan: this was the south coast. ²⁰And Jordan was the border of it on the east side. This was the inheritance of the children of Benjamin, by the coasts thereof round about, according to their families.

²¹Now the cities of the tribe of the children of Benjamin according to their families were Jericho, and Beth-hoglah, and the valley of Keziz, ²²and Beth-arabah, and Zemaraim, and Beth-el, ²³and Avim, and Parah, and Ophrah, ²⁴and Chephar-haammonai, and Ophni, and Gaba: twelve cities with their villages. ²⁵Gibeon, and Ramah, and Beeroth, ²⁶and Mizpeh, and Chephirah, and Mozah, ²⁷and Rekem, and Irpeel, and Taralah, ²⁸and Zelah, Eleph, and Jebusi, which is Jerusalem, Gibeath, and Kirjath: fourteen cities with their villages. This is the inheritance of the children of Benjamin according to their families.

19 And the second lot came forth to Simeon, even for the tribe of the children of Simeon according to their families: and their inheritance was within the inheritance of the children of Judah. ²And they had in their inheritance Beer-sheba, or Sheba, and Moladah, ³and Hazar-shual, and Balah, and Azem, ⁴and Eltolad, and Bethul, and Hormah, ⁵and Ziklag, and Beth-marcaboth, and Hazar-susah, ⁶and Beth-lebaoth, and Sharuhen: thirteen cities and their villages. ⁷Ain, Remmon, and Ether, and Ashan: four cities and their villages, ⁸and all the villages that were round about these cities to Baalath-beer, Ramath of the south. This is the inheritance of the tribe of the children of Simeon according to their families. ⁹Out of the portion of the children of Judah was the inheritance of the children of Simeon: for the part of the children of Judah was too much for them: therefore the children of Simeon had their inheritance within the inheritance of them.

¹⁰And the third lot came up for the children of Zebulun according to

their families: and the border of their inheritance was unto Sarid. ¹¹And their border went up toward the sea, and Maralah, and reached to Dabbasheth, and reached to the river that is before Jokneam, ¹²and turned from Sarid eastward toward the sunrising unto the border of Chisloth-tabor, and then goeth out to Daberath, and goeth up to Japhia, ¹³and from thence passeth on along on the east to Gittah-hepher, to Ittah-kazin, and goeth out to Remmon-methoar to Neah. ¹⁴And the border compasseth it on the north side to Hannathon: and the outgoings thereof are in the valley of Jiphthah-el. ¹⁵And Kattath, and Nahallal, and Shimron, and Idalah, and Beth-lehem: twelve cities with their villages. ¹⁶This is the inheritance of the children of Zebulun according to their families, these cities with their villages.

¹⁷And the fourth lot came out to Issachar, for the children of Issachar according to their families. ¹⁸And their border was toward Jezreel, and Chesulloth, and Shunem, ¹⁹and Hapharaim, and Shion, and Anaharath, ²⁰and Rabbith, and Kishion, and Abez, ²¹and Remeth, and En-gannim, and En-haddah, and Beth-pazzez. ²²And the coast reached to Tabor, and Shahazimah, and Beth-shemesh; and the outgoings of their border were at Jordan: sixteen cities with their villages. ²³This is the inheritance of the tribe of the children of Issachar according to their families, the cities and their villages.

²⁴And the fifth lot came out for the tribe of the children of Asher according to their families. ²⁵And their border was Helkath, and Hali, and Beten, and Achshaph, ²⁶and Alammelech, and Amad, and Misheal; and reacheth to Carmel westward, and to Shihor-libnath, ²⁷and turneth toward the sunrising to Beth-dagon, and reacheth to Zebulun, and to the valley of Jiphthah-el toward the north side of Beth-emek, and Neiel, and goeth out to Cabul on the left hand, ²⁸and Hebron, and Rehob, and Hammon, and Kanah, even unto great Zidon; ²⁹and then the coast turneth to Ramah, and to the strong city Tyre; and the coast turneth to Hosah; and the outgoings thereof are at the sea from the coast to Achzib. ³⁰Ummah also, and Aphek, and Rehob: twenty and two cities with their villages. ³¹This is the inheritance of the tribe of the children of Asher according to their families, these cities with their villages.

³²The sixth lot came out to the children of Naphtali, even for the children of Naphtali according to their families. ³³And their coast was from Heleph, from Allon to Zaanannim, and Adami, Nekeb, and Jabneel, unto Lakum; and the outgoings thereof were at Jordan. ³⁴And then the coast turneth westward to Aznoth-tabor, and goeth out from thence to Hukkok, and reacheth to Zebulun on the south side, and reacheth to Asher on the west side, and to Judah upon Jordan toward the sunrising. ³⁵And the fenced cities are Ziddim, Zer, and Hammath, Rakkath, and Chinnereth, ³⁶and Adamah, and Ramah, and Hazor, ³⁷and Kedesh, and Edrei, and En-hazor, ³⁸and Iron, and Migdal-el, Horem, and Bethanath, and Beth-shemesh: nineteen cities with their villages. ³⁹This is the inheritance of the tribe of the children of Naphtali according to their families, the cities and their villages.

⁴⁰And the seventh lot came out for the tribe of the children of Dan

according to their families. ⁴¹And the coast of their inheritance was Zorah, and Eshtaol, and Ir-shemesh, ⁴²and Shaalabbin, and Aijalon, and Jethlah, ⁴³and Elon, and Thimnathah, and Ekron, ⁴⁴and Eltekeh, and Gibbethon, and Baalath, ⁴⁵and Jehud, and Bene-berak, and Gath-rimmon, ⁴⁶and Me-jarkon, and Rakkon, with the border before Japho. ⁴⁷And the coast of the children of Dan went out too little for them: therefore the children of Dan went up to fight against Leshem, and took it, and smote it with the edge of the sword, and possessed it, and dwelt therein, and called Leshem, Dan, after the name of Dan their father. ⁴⁸This is the inheritance of the tribe of the children of Dan according to their families, these cities with their villages.

⁴⁹When they had made an end of dividing the land for inheritance by their coasts, the children of Israel gave an inheritance to Joshua the son of Nun among them: ⁵⁰according to the word of the LORD they gave him the city which he asked, even Timnath-serah in mount Ephraim: and he built the city, and dwelt therein.

⁵¹These are the inheritances, which Eleazar the priest, and Joshua the son of Nun, and the heads of the fathers of the tribes of the children of Israel, divided for an inheritance by lot in Shiloh before the LORD, at the door of the tabernacle of the congregation. So they made an end of dividing the country.

20 The LORD also spoke unto Joshua, saying, ²'Speak to the children of Israel, saying, "Appoint out for you cities of refuge, whereof I spoke unto you by the hand of Moses: ³that the slayer that killeth any person unawares and unwittingly may flee thither: and they shall be your refuge from the avenger of blood. ⁴And when he that doth flee unto one of those cities shall stand at the entering of the gate of the city, and shall declare his cause in the ears of the elders of that city, they shall take him into the city unto them, and give him a place, that he may dwell among them. ⁵And if the avenger of blood pursue after him, then they shall not deliver the slayer up into his hand: because he smote his neighbour unwittingly, and hated him not beforetime. ⁶And he shall dwell in that city, until he stand before the congregation for judgement, and until the death of the high priest that shall be in those days: then shall the slayer return, and come unto his own city, and unto his own house, unto the city from whence he fled."'

⁷And they appointed Kedesh in Galilee in mount Naphtali, and Shechem in mount Ephraim, and Kirjath-arba, which is Hebron, in the mountain of Judah. ⁸And on the other side Jordan by Jericho eastward, they assigned Bezer in the wilderness upon the plain out of the tribe of Reuben, and Ramoth in Gilead out of the tribe of Gad, and Golan in Bashan out of the tribe of Manasseh. ⁹These were the cities appointed for all the children of Israel, and for the stranger that sojourneth among them, that whosoever killeth any person at unawares might flee thither, and not die by the hand of the avenger of blood, until he stood before the congregation.

21 Then came near the heads of the fathers of the Levites unto Eleazar the priest, and unto Joshua the son of Nun, and unto the

heads of the fathers of the tribes of the children of Israel. ²And they spoke unto them at Shiloh in the land of Canaan, saying, 'The LORD commanded by the hand of Moses to give us cities to dwell in, with the suburbs thereof for our cattle'. ³And the children of Israel gave unto the Levites out of their inheritance, at the commandment of the LORD, these cities and their suburbs. ⁴And the lot came out for the families of the Kohathites: and the children of Aaron the priest, which were of the Levites, had by lot out of the tribe of Judah, and out of the tribe of Simeon, and out of the tribe of Benjamin, thirteen cities. ⁵And the rest of the children of Kohath had by lot out of the families of the tribe of Ephraim, and out of the tribe of Dan, and out of the half tribe of Manasseh, ten cities. ⁶And the children of Gershon had by lot out of the families of the tribe of Issachar, and out of the tribe of Asher, and out of the tribe of Naphtali, and out of the half tribe of Manasseh in Bashan, thirteen cities. ⁷The children of Merari by their families had out of the tribe of Reuben, and out of the tribe of Gad, and out of the tribe of Zebulun, twelve cities. ⁸And the children of Israel gave by lot unto the Levites these cities with their suburbs, as the LORD commanded by the hand of Moses.

⁹And they gave out of the tribe of the children of Judah, and out of the tribe of the children of Simeon, these cities which are here mentioned by name, ¹⁰which the children of Aaron, being of the families of the Kohathites, who were of the children of Levi, had: for theirs was the first lot. ¹¹And they gave them the city of Arba the father of Anak, which city is Hebron, in the hill-country of Judah, with the suburbs thereof round about it. ¹²But the fields of the city, and the villages thereof, gave they to Caleb the son of Jephunneh for his possession.

¹³Thus they gave to the children of Aaron the priest Hebron with her suburbs, to be a city of refuge for the slayer; and Libnah with her suburbs, ¹⁴and Jattir with her suburbs, and Eshtemoa with her suburbs, ¹⁵and Holon with her suburbs, and Debir with her suburbs, ¹⁶and Ain with her suburbs, and Juttah with her suburbs, and Beth-shemesh with her suburbs: nine cities out of those two tribes. ¹⁷And out of the tribe of Benjamin, Gibeon with her suburbs, Geba with her suburbs, ¹⁸Anathoth with her suburbs, and Almon with her suburbs; four cities. ¹⁹All the cities of the children of Aaron, the priests, were thirteen cities with their suburbs:

²⁰And the families of the children of Kohath, the Levites which remained of the children of Kohath, even they had the cities of their lot out of the tribe of Ephraim. ²¹For they gave them Shechem with her suburbs in mount Ephraim, to be a city of refuge for the slayer; and Gezer with her suburbs, ²²and Kibzaim with her suburbs, and Beth-horon with her suburbs: four cities. ²³And out of the tribe of Dan, Eltekeh with her suburbs, Gibbethon with her suburbs, ²⁴Aijalon with her suburbs, Gath-rimmon with her suburbs: four cities. ²⁵And out of the half tribe of Manasseh, Tanach with her suburbs, and Gath-rimmon with her suburbs: two cities. ²⁶All the cities were ten with their suburbs for the families of the children of Kohath that remained.

²⁷And unto the children of Gershon, of the families of the Levites, out of the other half tribe of Manasseh they gave Golan in Bashan with her suburbs, to be a city of refuge for the slayer; and Beesh-terah with her suburbs: two cities. ²⁸And out of the tribe of Issachar, Kishon with her suburbs, Dabareh with her suburbs, ²⁹Jarmuth with her suburbs, En-gannim with her suburbs: four cities. ³⁰And out of the tribe of Asher, Mishal with her suburbs, Abdon with her suburbs, ³¹Helkath with her suburbs, and Rehob with her suburbs: four cities. ³²And out of the tribe of Naphtali, Kedesh in Galilee with her suburbs, to be a city of refuge for the slayer; and Hammoth-dor with her suburbs, and Kartan with her suburbs: three cities. ³³All the cities of the Gershonites according to their families were thirteen cities with their suburbs.

³⁴And unto the families of the children of Merari, the rest of the Levites, out of the tribe of Zebulun, Jokneam with her suburbs, and Kartah with her suburbs, ³⁵Dimnah with her suburbs, Nahalal with her suburbs: four cities. ³⁶And out of the tribe of Reuben, Bezer with her suburbs, and Jahazah with her suburbs, ³⁷Kedemoth with her suburbs, and Mephaath with her suburbs: four cities. ³⁸And out of the tribe of Gad, Ramoth in Gilead with her suburbs, to be a city of refuge for the slayer; and Mahanaim with her suburbs, ³⁹Heshbon with her suburbs, Jazer with her suburbs: four cities in all. ⁴⁰So all the cities for the children of Merari by their families, which were remaining of the families of the Levites, were by their lot twelve cities.

⁴¹All the cities of the Levites within the possession of the children of Israel were forty and eight cities with their suburbs. ⁴²These cities were every one with their suburbs round about them: thus were all these cities.

⁴³And the LORD gave unto Israel all the land which he swore to give unto their fathers: and they possessed it, and dwelt therein. ⁴⁴And the LORD gave them rest round about, according to all that he swore unto their fathers: and there stood not a man of all their enemies before them: the LORD delivered all their enemies into their hand. ⁴⁵There failed not aught of any good thing which the LORD had spoken unto the house of Israel: all came to pass.

22 Then Joshua called the Reubenites, and the Gadites, and the half tribe of Manasseh, ²and said unto them, 'Ye have kept all that Moses the servant of the LORD commanded you, and have obeyed my voice in all that I commanded you. ³Ye have not left your brethren these many days unto this day, but have kept the charge of the commandment of the LORD your God. ⁴And now the LORD your God hath given rest unto your brethren, as he promised them: therefore now return ye, and get ye unto your tents, and unto the land of your possession, which Moses the servant of the LORD gave you on the other side Jordan. ⁵But take diligent heed to do the commandment and the law, which Moses the servant of the LORD charged you, to love the LORD your God, and to walk in all his ways, and to keep his commandments, and to cleave unto him, and to serve him with all your heart and with all your soul.' ⁶So Joshua blessed them, and sent them away: and they went unto their tents. [7]Now to the one half of the tribe of Manasseh Moses had given possession in Bashan: but unto the other half thereof gave Joshua among their brethren on this side Jordan westward. And when Joshua sent them away also unto their tents, then he blessed them, [8]and he spoke unto them, saying, 'Return with much riches unto your tents, and with very much cattle, with silver, and with gold, and with brass, and with iron, and with very much raiment: divide the spoil of your enemies with your brethren'.

[9]And the children of Reuben and the children of Gad and the half tribe of Manasseh returned, and departed from the children of Israel out of Shiloh, which is in the land of Canaan, to go unto the country of Gilead, to the land of their possession, whereof they were possessed, according to the word of the LORD by the hand of Moses. [10]And when they came unto the borders of Jordan, that are in the land of Canaan, the children of Reuben and the children of Gad and the half tribe of Manasseh built there an altar by Jordan, a great altar to see to.

[11]And the children of Israel heard say, 'Behold, the children of Reuben and the children of Gad and the half tribe of Manasseh have built an altar over against the land of Canaan, in the borders of Jordan, at the passage of the children of Israel'.

[12]And when the children of Israel heard of it, the whole congregation of the children of Israel gathered themselves together at Shiloh, to go up to war against them. [13]And the children of Israel sent unto the children of Reuben, and to the children of Gad, and to the half tribe of Manasseh, into the land of Gilead, Phinehas the son of Eleazar the priest, [14]and with him ten princes, of each chief house a prince throughout all the tribes of Israel; and each one was a head of the house of their fathers among the thousands of Israel.

[15]And they came unto the children of Reuben, and to the children of Gad, and to the half tribe of Manasseh, unto the land of Gilead, and they spoke with them, saying, [16]'Thus saith the whole congregation of the LORD, "What trespass is this that ye have committed against the God of Israel, to turn away this day from following the LORD, in that ye have built you an altar, that ye might rebel this day against the LORD? [17]Is the iniquity of Peor too little for us, from which we are not cleansed until this day, although there was a plague in the congregation of the LORD, [18]but that ye must turn away this day from following the LORD? and it will be, seeing ye rebel today against the LORD, that tomorrow he will be wroth with the whole congregation of Israel. [19]Notwithstanding, if the land of your possession be unclean, then pass ye over unto the land of the possession of the LORD, wherein the LORD's tabernacle dwelleth, and take possession among us: but rebel not against the LORD, nor rebel against us, in building you an altar besides the altar of the LORD our God. [20]Did not Achan the son of Zerah commit a trespass in the accursed thing, and wrath fell on all the congregation of Israel? and that man perished not alone in his iniquity."'

[21]Then the children of Reuben and the children of Gad and the half tribe of Manasseh answered, and said unto the heads of the thousands

of Israel, ²²'The LORD God of gods, the LORD God of gods, he knoweth, and Israel he shall know, if it be in rebellion, or if in transgression against the LORD (save us not this day), ²³that we have built us an altar to turn from following the LORD, or if to offer thereon burnt offering or meat offering, or if to offer peace offerings thereon, let the LORD himself require it; ²⁴and if we have not rather done it for fear of this thing, saying, in time to come your children might speak unto our children, saying, "What have you to do with the LORD God of Israel? ²⁵for the LORD hath made Jordan a border between us and you, ye children of Reuben and children of Gad; ye have no part in the LORD": so shall your children make our children cease from fearing the LORD. ²⁶Therefore we said, "Let us now prepare to build us an altar, not for burnt offering, nor for sacrifice: ²⁷but that it may be a witness between us, and you, and our generations after us, that we might do the service of the LORD before him with our burnt offerings, and with our sacrifices, and with our peace offerings; that your children may not say to our children in time to come, 'Ye have no part in the LORD'." ²⁸Therefore said we, that it shall be, when they should so say to us or to our generations in time to come, that we may say again, "Behold the pattern of the altar of the LORD, which our fathers made, not for burnt offerings, nor for sacrifices; but it is a witness between us and you". ²⁹God forbid that we should rebel against the LORD, and turn this day from following the LORD, to build an altar for burnt offerings, for meat offerings, or for sacrifices, besides the altar of the LORD our God that is before his tabernacle.'

³⁰And when Phinehas the priest, and the princes of the congregation and heads of the thousands of Israel which were with him, heard the words that the children of Reuben and the children of Gad and the children of Manasseh spoke, it pleased them. ³¹And Phinehas the son of Eleazar the priest said unto the children of Reuben, and to the children of Gad, and to the children of Manasseh, 'This day we perceive that the LORD is among us, because ye have not committed this trespass against the LORD: now ye have delivered the children of Israel out of the hand of the LORD'.

³²And Phinehas the son of Eleazar the priest, and the princes, returned from the children of Reuben, and from the children of Gad, out of the land of Gilead, unto the land of Canaan, to the children of Israel, and brought them word again. ³³And the thing pleased the children of Israel; and the children of Israel blessed God, and did not intend to go up against them in battle, to destroy the land wherein the children of Reuben and Gad dwelt. ³⁴And the children of Reuben and the children of Gad called the altar Ed: 'for it shall be a witness between us that the LORD is God'.

23 And it came to pass a long time after that the LORD had given rest unto Israel from all their enemies round about, that Joshua waxed old and stricken in age. ²And Joshua called for all Israel, and for their elders, and for their heads, and for their judges, and for their officers, and said unto them, 'I am old and stricken in age. ³And ye have seen all that the LORD your God hath done unto all these nations because of you; for the LORD your God is he that hath fought for you. [4]Behold, I have divided unto you by lot these nations that remain, to be an inheritance for your tribes, from Jordan, with all the nations that I have cut off, even unto the great sea westward. [5]And the LORD your God, he shall expel them from before you, and drive them from out of your sight; and ye shall possess their land, as the LORD your God hath promised unto you. [6]Be ye therefore very courageous to keep and to do all that is written in the book of the law of Moses, that ye turn not aside therefrom to the right hand or to the left; [7]that ye come not among these nations, these that remain amongst you; neither make mention of the name of their gods, nor cause to swear by them, neither serve them, nor bow yourselves unto them. [8]But cleave unto the LORD your God, as ye have done unto this day. [9]For the LORD hath driven out from before you great nations and strong: but as for you, no man hath been able to stand before you unto this day. [10]One man of you shall chase a thousand: for the LORD your God, he it is that fighteth for you, as he hath promised you. [11]Take good heed therefore unto yourselves, that ye love the LORD your God. [12]Else if ye do in any wise go back, and cleave unto the remnant of these nations, even these that remain among you, and shall make marriages with them, and go in unto them, and they to you: [13]know for a certainty that the LORD your God will no more drive out any of these nations from before you; but they shall be snares and traps unto you, and scourges in your sides, and thorns in your eyes, until ye perish from off this good land which the LORD your God hath given you. [14]And behold, this day I am going the way of all the earth: and ye know in all your hearts and in all your souls, that not one thing hath failed of all the good things which the LORD your God spoke concerning you; all are come to pass unto you, and not one thing hath failed thereof. [15]Therefore it shall come to pass, that as all good things are come upon you, which the LORD your God promised you: so shall the LORD bring upon you all evil things, until he have destroyed you from off this good land which the LORD your God hath given you. [16]When ye have transgressed the covenant of the LORD your God, which he commanded you, and have gone and served other gods, and bowed yourselves to them: then shall the anger of the LORD be kindled against you, and ye shall perish quickly from off the good land which he hath given unto you.'

24 And Joshua gathered all the tribes of Israel to Shechem, and called for the elders of Israel, and for their heads, and for their judges, and for their officers; and they presented themselves before God. [2]And Joshua said unto all the people, 'Thus saith the LORD God of Israel, "Your fathers dwelt on the other side of the flood in old time, even Terah, the father of Abraham, and the father of Nachor: and they served other gods. [3]And I took your father Abraham from the other side of the flood, and led him throughout all the land of Canaan, and multiplied his seed, and gave him Isaac. [4]And I gave unto Isaac Jacob and Esau: and I gave unto Esau mount Seir, to possess it; but Jacob and his children went down into Egypt. [5]I sent Moses also and Aaron, and I plagued Egypt, according to that which I did amongst them: and afterward I brought you out. [6]And I brought your fathers out of Egypt: and you came unto the sea; and the Egyptians pursued after your fathers with chariots and horsemen unto the Red Sea. [7]And when they cried unto the LORD, he put darkness between you and the Egyptians, and brought the sea upon them, and covered them; and your eyes have seen what I have done in Egypt: and ye dwelt in the wilderness a long season. [8]And I brought you into the land of the Amorites, which dwelt on the other side Jordan; and they fought with you: and I gave them into your hand, that ye might possess their land; and I destroyed them from before you. [9]Then Balak the son of Zippor, king of Moab, arose and warred against Israel, and sent and called Balaam the son of Beor to curse you: [10]but I would not hearken unto Balaam; therefore he blessed you still: so I delivered you out of his hand. [11]And you went over Jordan, and came unto Jericho: and the men of Jericho fought against you, the Amorites, and the Perizzites, and the Canaanites, and the Hittites, and the Girgashites, the Hivites, and the Jebusites; and I delivered them into your hand. [12]And I sent the hornet before you, which drove them out from before you, even the two kings of the Amorites: but not with thy sword, nor with thy bow. [13]And I have given you a land for which ye did not labour, and cities which ye built not, and ye dwell in them; of the vineyards and olive-yards which ye planted not do ye eat."

[14]'Now therefore fear the LORD, and serve him in sincerity and in truth: and put away the gods which your fathers served on the other side of the flood, and in Egypt; and serve ye the LORD. [15]And if it seem evil unto you to serve the LORD, choose you this day whom you will serve, whether the gods which your fathers served that were on the other side of the flood, or the gods of the Amorites, in whose land ye dwell: but as for me and my house, we will serve the LORD.'

[16]And the people answered and said, 'God forbid that we should forsake the LORD, to serve other gods. [17]For the LORD our God, he it is that brought us up and our fathers out of the land of Egypt, from the house of bondage, and which did those great signs in our sight, and preserved us in all the way wherein we went, and among all the people through whom we passed. [18]And the LORD drove out from before us all the people, even the Amorites which dwelt in the land: therefore will we also serve the LORD, for he is our God.' [19]And Joshua said unto the people, 'Ye cannot serve the LORD: for he is a holy God: he is a jealous God, he will not forgive your transgressions nor your sins. [20]If ye forsake the LORD, and serve strange gods, then he will turn and do you hurt, and consume you, after that he hath done you good.' [21]And the people said unto Joshua, 'Nay, but we will serve the LORD'. [22]And Joshua said unto the people, 'Ye are witnesses against yourselves that ye have chosen you the LORD, to serve him'. And they said, 'We are witnesses'. [23]'Now therefore put away', said he, 'the strange gods which are among you, and incline your heart unto the LORD God of Israel.' [24]And the people said unto Joshua, 'The LORD our God will we serve, and his voice will we obey'. [25]So

Joshua made a covenant with the people that day, and set them a statute and an ordinance in Shechem.

²⁶And Joshua wrote these words in the book of the law of God, and took a great stone, and set it up there under an oak, that was by the sanctuary of the LORD. ²⁷And Joshua said unto all the people, 'Behold, this stone shall be a witness unto us; for it hath heard all the words of the LORD which he spoke unto us: it shall be therefore a witness unto you, lest ye deny your God'. ²⁸So Joshua let the people depart, every man unto his inheritance.

²⁹And it came to pass after these things, that Joshua the son of Nun, the servant of the LORD, died, being a hundred and ten years old. ³⁰And they buried him in the border of his inheritance in Timnath-serah, which is in mount Ephraim, on the north side of the hill of Gaash. ³¹And Israel served the LORD all the days of Joshua, and all the days of the elders that overlived Joshua, and which had known all the works of the LORD, that he had done for Israel.

³²And the bones of Joseph, which the children of Israel brought up out of Egypt, buried they in Shechem, in a parcel of ground which Jacob bought of the sons of Hamor the father of Shechem for a hundred pieces of silver: and it became the inheritance of the children of Joseph. ³³And Eleazar the son of Aaron died, and they buried him in a hill that pertained to Phinehas his son, which was given him in mount Ephraim.

THE BOOK OF
JUDGES

1 Now after the death of Joshua it came to pass, that the children of Israel asked the LORD, saying, 'Who shall go up for us against the Canaanites first, to fight against them?' ²And the LORD said, 'Judah shall go up: behold, I have delivered the land into his hand'. ³And Judah said unto Simeon his brother, 'Come up with me into my lot, that we may fight against the Canaanites, and I likewise will go with thee into thy lot'. So Simeon went with him. ⁴And Judah went up, and the LORD delivered the Canaanites and the Perizzites into their hand: and they slew of them in Bezek ten thousand men. ⁵And they found Adoni-bezek in Bezek: and they fought against him, and they slew the Canaanites and the Perizzites. ⁶But Adoni-bezek fled; and they pursued after him, and caught him, and cut off his thumbs and his great toes. ⁷And Adoni-bezek said, 'Threescore and ten kings, having their thumbs and their great toes cut off, gathered their meat under my table: as I have done, so God hath requited me'. And they brought him to Jerusalem, and there he died. ⁸(Now the children of Judah had fought against Jerusalem, and had taken it, and smitten it with the edge of the sword, and set the city on fire.)

⁹And afterward the children of Judah went down to fight against the Canaanites, that dwelt in the mountain, and in the south, and in the valley. ¹⁰And Judah went against the Canaanites that dwelt in Hebron (now the name of Hebron before was Kirjath-arba): and they slew Sheshai, and Ahiman, and Talmai. ¹¹And from thence he went against the inhabitants of Debir (and the name of Debir before was Kirjath-sepher): ¹²and Caleb said, 'He that smiteth Kirjath-sepher, and taketh it, to him will I give Achsah my daughter to wife'. ¹³And Othniel the son of Kenaz, Caleb's younger brother, took it: and he gave him Achsah his daughter to wife. ¹⁴And it came to pass when she came to him, that she moved him to ask of her father a field: and she lighted from off her ass, and Caleb said unto her, 'What wilt thou?' ¹⁵And she said unto him, 'Give me a blessing: for thou hast given me a south land; give me also springs of water'. And Caleb gave her the upper springs and the nether springs.

¹⁶And the children of the Kenite, Moses' father-in-law, went up out of the city of palm trees with the children of Judah into the wilderness of Judah, which lieth in the south of Arad; and they went and dwelt among the people. ¹⁷And Judah went with Simeon his brother, and they slew the Canaanites that inhabited Zephath, and utterly destroyed it (and the name of the city was called Hormah). ¹⁸Also Judah took Gaza with the coast thereof, and Askelon with the coast thereof, and Ekron with the coast thereof. ¹⁹And the LORD was with Judah, and he drove out the inhabitants of the mountain; but could not drive out the inhabitants of the valley, because they had chariots of iron. ²⁰And they gave

Hebron unto Caleb, as Moses said: and he expelled thence the three sons of Anak. ²¹And the children of Benjamin did not drive out the Jebusites that inhabited Jerusalem: but the Jebusites dwell with the children of Benjamin in Jerusalem unto this day.

²²And the house of Joseph, they also went up against Beth-el: and the LORD was with them. ²³And the house of Joseph sent to descry Beth-el (now the name of the city before was Luz). ²⁴And the spies saw a man come forth out of the city, and they said unto him, 'Show us, we pray thee, the entrance into the city, and we will show thee mercy'. ²⁵And when he showed them the entrance into the city, they smote the city with the edge of the sword: but they let go the man and all his family. ²⁶And the man went into the land of the Hittites, and built a city, and called the name thereof Luz: which is the name thereof unto this day.

²⁷Neither did Manasseh drive out the inhabitants of Beth-shean and her towns, nor Taanach and her towns, nor the inhabitants of Dor and her towns, nor the inhabitants of Ibleam and her towns, nor the inhabitants of Megiddo and her towns: but the Canaanites would dwell in that land. ²⁸And it came to pass, when Israel was strong, that they put the Canaanites to tribute, and did not utterly drive them out.

²⁹Neither did Ephraim drive out the Canaanites that dwelt in Gezer: but the Canaanites dwelt in Gezer among them.

³⁰Neither did Zebulun drive out the inhabitants of Kitron, nor the inhabitants of Nahalol: but the Canaanites dwelt among them, and became tributaries.

³¹Neither did Asher drive out the inhabitants of Accho, nor the inhabitants of Zidon, nor of Ahlab, nor Achzib, nor Helbah, nor Aphik, nor of Rehob: ³²but the Asherites dwelt among the Canaanites, the inhabitants of the land: for they did not drive them out.

³³Neither did Naphtali drive out the inhabitants of Beth-shemesh, nor the inhabitants of Beth-anath, but he dwelt among the Canaanites, the inhabitants of the land: nevertheless the inhabitants of Beth-shemesh and of Beth-anath became tributaries unto them.

³⁴And the Amorites forced the children of Dan into the mountain: for they would not suffer them to come down to the valley: ³⁵but the Amorites would dwell in mount Heres in Aijalon, and in Shaalbim: yet the hand of the house of Joseph prevailed, so that they became tributaries. ³⁶And the coast of the Amorites was from the going up to Akrabbim, from the rock, and upward.

2 And an angel of the LORD came up from Gilgal to Bochim, and said, 'I made you to go up out of Egypt, and have brought you unto the land which I swore unto your fathers; and I said, "I will never break my covenant with you. ²And ye shall make no league with the inhabitants of this land; you shall throw down their altars": but ye have not obeyed my voice: why have ye done this? ³Wherefore I also said, "I will not drive them out from before you; but they shall be as thorns in your sides, and their gods shall be a snare unto you".' ⁴And it came to pass when the angel of the LORD spoke these words unto all the children of Israel, that

the people lifted up their voice, and wept. ⁵And they called the name of that place Bochim: and they sacrificed there unto the LORD.

⁶And when Joshua had let the people go, the children of Israel went every man unto his inheritance to possess the land. ⁷And the people served the LORD all the days of Joshua, and all the days of the elders that outlived Joshua, who had seen all the great works of the LORD, that he did for Israel. ⁸And Joshua the son of Nun, the servant of the LORD, died, being a hundred and ten years old. ⁹And they buried him in the border of his inheritance in Timnath-heres, in the mount of Ephraim, on the north side of the hill Gaash. ¹⁰And also all that generation were gathered unto their fathers: and there arose another generation after them, which knew not the LORD, nor yet the works which he had done for Israel.

¹¹And the children of Israel did evil in the sight of the LORD, and served Baalim: ¹²and they forsook the LORD God of their fathers, which brought them out of the land of Egypt, and followed other gods, of the gods of the people that were round about them, and bowed themselves unto them, and provoked the LORD to anger. ¹³And they forsook the LORD, and served Baal and Ashtaroth.

¹⁴And the anger of the LORD was hot against Israel, and he delivered them into the hands of spoilers that spoiled them, and he sold them into the hands of their enemies round about, so that they could not any longer stand before their enemies. ¹⁵Whithersoever they went out, the hand of the LORD was against them for evil, as the LORD had said, and as the LORD had sworn unto them: and they were greatly distressed.

¹⁶Nevertheless the LORD raised up judges, which delivered them out of the hand of those that spoiled them. ¹⁷And yet they would not hearken unto their judges, but they went a-whoring after other gods, and bowed themselves unto them: they turned quickly out of the way which their fathers walked in, obeying the commandments of the LORD; but they did not so. ¹⁸And when the LORD raised them up judges, then the LORD was with the judge, and delivered them out of the hand of their enemies all the days of the judge: for it repented the LORD because of their groanings by reason of them that oppressed them and vexed them. ¹⁹And it came to pass, when the judge was dead, that they returned, and corrupted themselves more than their fathers, in following other gods to serve them, and to bow down unto them: they ceased not from their own doings, nor from their stubborn way.

²⁰And the anger of the LORD was hot against Israel, and he said, 'Because that this people hath transgressed my covenant which I commanded their fathers, and have not hearkened unto my voice: ²¹I also will not henceforth drive out any from before them of the nations which Joshua left when he died: ²²that through them I may prove Israel, whether they will keep the way of the LORD to walk therein, as their fathers did keep it, or not'. ²³Therefore the LORD left those nations, without driving them out hastily, neither delivered he them into the hand of Joshua.

3 Now these are the nations which the LORD left, to prove Israel by them (even as many of Israel as had not known all the wars of Canaan; ²only that the generations of the children of Israel might know, to teach them war, at the least such as before knew nothing thereof): ³namely, five lords of the Philistines, and all the Canaanites, and the Sidonians, and the Hivites that dwelt in mount Lebanon, from mount Baal-hermon unto the entering in of Hamath. ⁴And they were to prove Israel by them, to know whether they would hearken unto the commandments of the LORD, which he commanded their fathers by the hand of Moses.

⁵And the children of Israel dwelt among the Canaanites, Hittites, and Amorites, and Perizzites, and Hivites, and Jebusites: ⁶and they took their daughters to be their wives, and gave their daughters to their sons, and served their gods. ⁷And the children of Israel did evil in the sight of the LORD, and forgot the LORD their God, and served Baalim and the groves.

⁸Therefore the anger of the LORD was hot against Israel, and he sold them into the hand of Chushan-rishathaim king of Mesopotamia: and the children of Israel served Chushan-rishathaim eight years. ⁹And when the children of Israel cried unto the LORD, the LORD raised up a deliverer to the children of Israel, who delivered them, even Othniel the son of Kenaz, Caleb's younger brother. ¹⁰And the Spirit of the LORD came upon him, and he judged Israel, and went out to war: and the LORD delivered Chushan-rishathaim king of Mesopotamia into his hand; and his hand prevailed against Chushan-rishathaim. ¹¹And the land had rest forty years. And Othniel the son of Kenaz died.

¹²And the children of Israel did evil again in the sight of the LORD: and the LORD strengthened Eglon the king of Moab against Israel, because they had done evil in the sight of the LORD. ¹³And he gathered unto him the children of Ammon and Amalek, and went and smote Israel, and possessed the city of palm trees. ¹⁴So the children of Israel served Eglon the king of Moab eighteen years.

¹⁵But when the children of Israel cried unto the LORD, the LORD raised them up a deliverer, Ehud the son of Gera, a Benjamite, a man left-handed: and by him the children of Israel sent a present unto Eglon the king of Moab. ¹⁶But Ehud made him a dagger which had two edges, of a cubit length, and he did gird it under his raiment upon his right thigh. ¹⁷And he brought the present unto Eglon king of Moab: and Eglon was a very fat man. ¹⁸And when he had made an end to offer the present, he sent away the people that bore the present. ¹⁹But he himself turned again from the quarries that were by Gilgal, and said, 'I have a secret errand unto thee, O king': who said, 'Keep silence'. And all that stood by him went out from him. ²⁰And Ehud came unto him; and he was sitting in a summer parlour, which he had for himself alone. And Ehud said, 'I have a message from God unto thee'. And he arose out of his seat. ²¹And Ehud put forth his left hand, and took the dagger from his right thigh, and thrust it into his belly. ²²And the haft also went in after the blade; and the fat closed upon the blade, so that he could not draw

the dagger out of his belly; and the dirt came out. ²³Then Ehud went forth through the porch, and shut the doors of the parlour upon him, and locked them.

²⁴When he was gone out, his servants came; and when they saw that, behold, the doors of the parlour were locked, they said, 'Surely he covereth his feet in his summer chamber'. ²⁵And they tarried till they were ashamed: and behold, he opened not the doors of the parlour; therefore they took a key, and opened them: and behold, their lord was fallen down dead on the earth.

²⁶And Ehud escaped while they tarried, and passed beyond the quarries, and escaped unto Seirath. ²⁷And it came to pass when he was come, that he blew a trumpet in the mountain of Ephraim, and the children of Israel went down with him from the mount, and he before them. ²⁸And he said unto them, 'Follow after me: for the LORD hath delivered your enemies the Moabites into your hand'. And they went down after him, and took the fords of Jordan toward Moab, and suffered not a man to pass over. ²⁹And they slew of Moab at that time about ten thousand men, all lusty, and all men of valour; and there escaped not a man. ³⁰So Moab was subdued that day under the hand of Israel. And the land had rest fourscore years.

³¹And after him was Shamgar the son of Anath, which slew of the Philistines six hundred men with an ox-goad: and he also delivered Israel.

4 And the children of Israel again did evil in the sight of the LORD, when Ehud was dead. ²And the LORD sold them into the hand of Jabin king of Canaan, that reigned in Hazor, the captain of whose host was Sisera, which dwelt in Harosheth of the Gentiles. ³And the children of Israel cried unto the LORD: for he had nine hundred chariots of iron: and twenty years he mightily oppressed the children of Israel.

⁴And Deborah, a prophetess, the wife of Lapidoth, she judged Israel at that time.⁵And she dwelt under the palm tree of Deborah between Ramah and Beth-el in mount Ephraim: and the children of Israel came up to her for judgement. ⁶And she sent and called Barak the son of Abinoam out of Kedesh-naphtali, and said unto him, 'Hath not the LORD God of Israel commanded, saying, "Go and draw toward mount Tabor, and take with thee ten thousand men of the children of Naphtali and of the children of Zebulun? ⁷And I will draw unto thee to the river Kishon Sisera, the captain of Jabin's army, with his chariots and his multitude; and I will deliver him into thy hand."' ⁸And Barak said unto her, 'If thou wilt go with me, then I will go: but if thou wilt not go with me, then I will not go'. ⁹And she said, 'I will surely go with thee, notwithstanding the journey that thou takest shall not be for thy honour: for the LORD shall sell Sisera into the hand of a woman'. And Deborah arose, and went with Barak to Kedesh.

¹⁰And Barak called Zebulun and Naphtali to Kedesh, and he went up with ten thousand men at his feet: and Deborah went up with him. ¹¹Now Heber the Kenite, which was of the children of Hobab the father-in-law of Moses, had severed himself from the Kenites, and pitched his

tent unto the plain of Zaanaim, which is by Kedesh. ¹²And they showed Sisera that Barak the son of Abinoam was gone up to mount Tabor. ¹³And Sisera gathered together all his chariots, even nine hundred chariots of iron, and all the people that were with him, from Harosheth of the Gentiles unto the river of Kishon. ¹⁴And Deborah said unto Barak, 'Up, for this is the day in which the Lord hath delivered Sisera into thy hand: is not the Lord gone out before thee?' So Barak went down from mount Tabor, and ten thousand men after him. ¹⁵And the Lord discomfited Sisera, and all his chariots, and all his host with the edge of the sword before Barak: so that Sisera lighted down off his chariot, and fled away on his feet. ¹⁶But Barak pursued after the chariots, and after the host, unto Harosheth of the Gentiles: and all the host of Sisera fell upon the edge of the sword; and there was not a man left.

¹⁷Howbeit Sisera fled away on his feet to the tent of Jael the wife of Heber the Kenite: for there was peace between Jabin the king of Hazor and the house of Heber the Kenite. ¹⁸And Jael went out to meet Sisera, and said unto him, 'Turn in, my lord, turn in to me, fear not'. And when he had turned in unto her into the tent, she covered him with a mantle. ¹⁹And he said unto her, 'Give me, I pray thee, a little water to drink, for I am thirsty'. And she opened a bottle of milk, and gave him drink, and covered him. ²⁰Again he said unto her, 'Stand in the door of the tent, and it shall be, when any man doth come and inquire of thee, and say, "Is there any man here?" that thou shalt say, "No"'. ²¹Then Jael Heber's wife took a nail of the tent, and took a hammer in her hand, and went softly unto him, and smote the nail into his temples, and fastened it into the ground: for he was fast asleep and weary. So he died. ²²And behold, as Barak pursued Sisera, Jael came out to meet him, and said unto him, 'Come, and I will show thee the man whom thou seekest'. And when he came into her tent, behold, Sisera lay dead, and the nail was in his temples. ²³So God subdued on that day Jabin the king of Canaan before the children of Israel. ²⁴And the hand of the children of Israel prospered, and prevailed against Jabin the king of Canaan, until they had destroyed Jabin king of Canaan.

5 Then sang Deborah and Barak the son of Abinoam on that day, saying,

² 'Praise ye the Lord for the avenging of Israel,
  when the people willingly offered themselves.
³ Hear, O ye kings, give ear, O ye princes:
  I, even I, will sing unto the Lord,
  I will sing praise to the Lord God of Israel.
⁴ Lord, when thou wentest out of Seir,
  when thou marchedst out of the field of Edom,
  the earth trembled, and the heavens dropped,
  the clouds also dropped water.
⁵ The mountains melted from before the Lord,
  even that Sinai from before the Lord God of Israel.
⁶ In the days of Shamgar the son of Anath,

in the days of Jael,
the highways were unoccupied,
and the travellers walked through byways.
⁷ The inhabitants of the villages ceased,
they ceased in Israel,
until that I Deborah arose,
that I arose a mother in Israel.
⁸ They chose new gods;
then was war in the gates:
was there a shield or spear seen among forty thousand in Israel?
⁹ My heart is toward the governors of Israel,
that offered themselves willingly among the people.
Bless ye the LORD.
¹⁰ Speak, ye that ride on white asses,
ye that sit in judgement, and walk by the way.
¹¹ they that are delivered from the noise of archers in the places of
drawing water,
there shall they rehearse the righteous acts of the LORD,
even the righteous acts towards the inhabitants of his villages in
Israel:
then shall the people of the LORD go down to the gates.
¹² Awake, awake, Deborah: awake, awake, utter a song:
arise, Barak, and lead thy captivity captive,
thou son of Abinoam.
¹³ Then he made him that remaineth have dominion over the
nobles among the people:
the LORD made me have dominion over the mighty.
¹⁴ Out of Ephraim was there a root of them against Amalek;
after thee, Benjamin, among thy people;
out of Machir came down governors,
and out of Zebulun they that handle the pen of the writer.
¹⁵ And the princes of Issachar were with Deborah:
even Issachar, and also Barak:
he was sent on foot into the valley.
For the divisions of Reuben there were great thoughts of heart.
¹⁶ Why abodest thou among the sheepfolds,
to hear the bleatings of the flocks?
For the divisions of Reuben there were great searchings of heart.
¹⁷ Gilead abode beyond Jordan:
and why did Dan remain in ships?
Asher continued on the sea-shore,
and abode in his breaches.
¹⁸ Zebulun and Naphtali were a people that jeoparded their lives
unto the death in the high places of the field.
¹⁹ The kings came and fought,
then fought the kings of Canaan in Taanach by the waters of
Megiddo;
they took no gain of money.

²⁰ They fought from heaven,
    the stars in their courses fought against Sisera.
²¹ The river of Kishon swept them away,
    that ancient river, the river Kishon:
  O my soul, thou hast trodden down strength.
²² Then were the horse-hoofs broken by the means of the prancings,
    the prancings of their mighty ones.
²³ "Curse ye Meroz," said the angel of the LORD,
    "curse ye bitterly the inhabitants thereof:
  because they came not to the help of the LORD,
    to the help of the LORD against the mighty".
²⁴ Blessed above women shall Jael the wife of Heber the Kenite be,
    blessed shall she be above women in the tent.
²⁵ He asked water, and she gave him milk,
    she brought forth butter in a lordly dish.
²⁶ She put her hand to the nail,
    and her right hand to the workmen's hammer:
  and with the hammer she smote Sisera,
  she smote off his head,
  when she had pierced and stricken through his temples.
²⁷ At her feet he bowed, he fell, he lay down:
    at her feet he bowed, he fell:
  where he bowed, there he fell down dead.
²⁸ The mother of Sisera looked out at a window,
    and cried through the lattice,
  "Why is his chariot so long in coming?
  Why tarry the wheels of his chariots?"
²⁹ Her wise ladies answered her, yea, she returned answer to
    herself,
³⁰ "Have they not sped?
  have they not divided the prey;
  to every man a damsel or two;
  to Sisera a prey of divers colours,
  a prey of divers colours of needlework,
  of divers colours of needlework on both sides,
  meet for the necks of them that take the spoil?"
³¹ So let all thy enemies perish, O LORD:
  but let them that love him be as the sun when he goeth forth in
    his might.'

And the land had rest forty years.

6 And the children of Israel did evil in the sight of the LORD: and the LORD delivered them into the hand of Midian seven years. ²And the hand of Midian prevailed against Israel: and because of the Midianites the children of Israel made them the dens which are in the mountains, and caves, and strongholds. ³And so it was when Israel had sown, that the Midianites came up, and the Amalekites, and the children of the east, even they came up against them, ⁴and they encamped against them, and destroyed the increase of the earth, till thou come unto Gaza, and left no sustenance for Israel, neither sheep, nor ox, nor ass. ⁵For they came up with their cattle and their tents, and they came as grasshoppers for multitude, for both they and their camels were without number: and they entered into the land to destroy it. ⁶And Israel was greatly impoverished because of the Midianites; and the children of Israel cried unto the LORD.

⁷And it came to pass, when the children of Israel cried unto the LORD because of the Midianites, ⁸that the LORD sent a prophet unto the children of Israel, which said unto them, 'Thus saith the LORD God of Israel, "I brought you up from Egypt, and brought you forth out of the house of bondage, ⁹and I delivered you out of the hand of the Egyptians, and out of the hand of all that oppressed you, and drove them out from before you, and gave you their land; ¹⁰and I said unto you, 'I am the LORD your God, fear not the gods of the Amorites, in whose land ye dwell': but ye have not obeyed my voice"'.

¹¹And there came an angel of the LORD, and sat under an oak which was in Ophrah, that pertained unto Joash the Abi-ezrite: and his son Gideon threshed wheat by the wine-press, to hide it from the Midianites. ¹²And the angel of the LORD appeared unto him, and said unto him, 'The LORD is with thee, thou mighty man of valour'. ¹³And Gideon said unto him, 'O my Lord, if the LORD be with us, why then is all this befallen us? and where be all his miracles which our fathers told us of, saying, "Did not the LORD bring us up from Egypt?" but now the LORD hath forsaken us, and delivered us into the hands of the Midianites'. ¹⁴And the LORD looked upon him, and said, 'Go in this thy might, and thou shalt save Israel from the hand of the Midianites: have not I sent thee?' ¹⁵And he said unto him, 'O my Lord, wherewith shall I save Israel? behold, my family is poor in Manasseh, and I am the least in my father's house'. ¹⁶And the LORD said unto him, 'Surely I will be with thee, and thou shalt smite the Midianites as one man'. ¹⁷And he said unto him, 'If now I have found grace in thy sight, then show me a sign that thou talkest with me. ¹⁸Depart not hence, I pray thee, until I come unto thee, and bring forth my present, and set it before thee.' And he said, 'I will tarry until thou come again'.

¹⁹And Gideon went in, and made ready a kid, and unleavened cakes of an ephah of flour: the flesh he put in a basket, and he put the broth in a pot, and brought it out unto him under the oak, and presented it. ²⁰And the angel of God said unto him, 'Take the flesh and the unleavened cakes, and lay them upon this rock, and pour out the broth'. And he did so. ²¹Then the angel of the LORD put forth the end of the staff that was in his hand, and touched the flesh and the unleavened cakes; and there rose up fire out of the rock, and consumed the flesh and the unleavened cakes. Then the angel of the LORD departed out of his sight. ²²And when Gideon perceived that he was an angel of the LORD, Gideon said, 'Alas, O Lord GOD: for because I have seen an angel of the LORD face to face'. ²³And the LORD said unto him, 'Peace be unto thee, fear not, thou shalt not die'. ²⁴Then Gideon built an altar there unto the LORD,

and called it Jehovah-shalom: unto this day it is yet in Ophrah of the Abi-ezrites.

²⁵And it came to pass the same night, that the LORD said unto him, 'Take thy father's young bullock, even the second bullock of seven years old, and throw down the altar of Baal that thy father hath, and cut down the grove that is by it: ²⁶and build an altar unto the LORD thy God upon the top of this rock, in the ordered place, and take the second bullock, and offer a burnt sacrifice with the wood of the grove which thou shalt cut down'. ²⁷Then Gideon took ten men of his servants, and did as the LORD had said unto him: and so it was, because he feared his father's household, and the men of the city, that he could not do it by day, that he did it by night.

²⁸And when the men of the city arose early in the morning, behold, the altar of Baal was cast down, and the grove was cut down that was by it, and the second bullock was offered upon the altar that was built. ²⁹And they said one to another, 'Who hath done this thing?' And when they inquired and asked, they said, 'Gideon the son of Joash hath done this thing'. ³⁰Then the men of the city said unto Joash, 'Bring out thy son, that he may die: because he hath cast down the altar of Baal, and because he hath cut down the grove that was by it'. ³¹And Joash said unto all that stood against him, 'Will ye plead for Baal? will ye save him? He that will plead for him, let him be put to death whilst it is yet morning: if he be a god, let him plead for himself, because one hath cast down his altar.' ³²Therefore on that day he called him Jerubbaal, saying, 'Let Baal plead against him, because he hath thrown down his altar'.

³³Then all the Midianites and the Amalekites and the children of the east were gathered together, and went over, and pitched in the valley of Jezreel. ³⁴But the Spirit of the LORD came upon Gideon, and he blew a trumpet; and Abi-ezer was gathered after him. ³⁵And he sent messengers throughout all Manasseh, who also was gathered after him, and he sent messengers unto Asher, and unto Zebulun, and unto Naphtali, and they came up to meet them.

³⁶And Gideon said unto God, 'If thou wilt save Israel by my hand, as thou hast said, ³⁷behold, I will put a fleece of wool in the floor: and if the dew be on the fleece only, and it be dry upon all the earth beside, then shall I know that thou wilt save Israel by my hand, as thou hast said'. ³⁸And it was so: for he rose up early on the morrow, and thrust the fleece together, and wrung the dew out of the fleece, a bowl full of water. ³⁹And Gideon said unto God, 'Let not thy anger be hot against me, and I will speak but this once: let me prove, I pray thee, but this once with the fleece. Let it now be dry only upon the fleece, and upon all the ground let there be dew.' ⁴⁰And God did so that night: for it was dry upon the fleece only, and there was dew on all the ground.

7 Then Jerubbaal, who is Gideon, and all the people that were with him, rose up early, and pitched beside the well of Harod: so that the host of the Midianites were on the north side of them, by the hill of Moreh, in the valley. ²And the LORD said unto Gideon, 'The people that

are with thee are too many for me to give the Midianites into their hands, lest Israel vaunt themselves against me, saying, "My own hand hath saved me". ³Now therefore go to, proclaim in the ears of the people, saying, "Whosoever is fearful and afraid, let him return and depart early from mount Gilead".' And there returned of the people twenty and two thousand; and there remained ten thousand. ⁴And the LORD said unto Gideon, 'The people are yet too many: bring them down unto the water, and I will try them for thee there: and it shall be, that of whom I say unto thee, "This shall go with thee", the same shall go with thee; and of whomsoever I say unto thee, "This shall not go with thee", the same shall not go'. ⁵So he brought down the people unto the water: and the LORD said unto Gideon, 'Every one that lappeth of the water with his tongue, as a dog lappeth, him shalt thou set by himself, likewise every one that boweth down upon his knees to drink'. ⁶And the number of them that lapped, putting their hand to their mouth, were three hundred men: but all the rest of the people bowed down upon their knees to drink water. ⁷And the LORD said unto Gideon, 'By the three hundred men that lapped will I save you, and deliver the Midianites into thy hand: and let all the other people go every man unto his place'. ⁸So the people took victuals in their hand, and their trumpets: and he sent all the rest of Israel every man unto his tent, and retained those three hundred men: and the host of Midian was beneath him in the valley.

⁹And it came to pass the same night, that the LORD said unto him, 'Arise, get thee down unto the host, for I have delivered it into thy hand. ¹⁰But if thou fear to go down, go thou with Phurah thy servant down to the host. ¹¹And thou shalt hear what they say, and afterward shall thy hands be strengthened to go down unto the host.' Then went he down with Phurah his servant unto the outside of the armed men that were in the host. ¹²And the Midianites and the Amalekites and all the children of the east lay along in the valley like grasshoppers for multitude, and their camels were without number, as the sand by the seaside for multitude. ¹³And when Gideon was come, behold, there was a man that told a dream unto his fellow, and said, 'Behold, I dreamed a dream, and lo, a cake of barley bread tumbled into the host of Midian, and came unto a tent, and smote it that it fell, and overturned it, that the tent lay along'. ¹⁴And his fellow answered and said, 'This is nothing else save the sword of Gideon the son of Joash, a man of Israel: for into his hand hath God delivered Midian, and all the host'.

¹⁵And it was so, when Gideon heard the telling of the dream, and the interpretation thereof, that he worshipped, and returned into the host of Israel, and said, 'Arise, for the LORD hath delivered into your hand the host of Midian'. ¹⁶And he divided the three hundred men into three companies, and he put a trumpet in every man's hand, with empty pitchers, and lamps within the pitchers. ¹⁷And he said unto them, 'Look on me, and do likewise: and behold, when I come to the outside of the camp, it shall be that, as I do, so shall ye do. ¹⁸When I blow with a trumpet, I and all that are with me, then blow ye the trumpets also

on every side of all the camp, and say, "The sword of the LORD, and of Gideon".'

¹⁹So Gideon, and the hundred men that were with him, came unto the outside of the camp in the beginning of the middle watch; and they had but newly set the watch: and they blew the trumpets, and broke the pitchers that were in their hands. ²⁰And the three companies blew the trumpets, and broke the pitchers, and held the lamps in their left hands, and the trumpets in their right hands to blow withal: and they cried, 'The sword of the LORD, and of Gideon'. ²¹And they stood every man in his place round about the camp: and all the host ran, and cried, and fled. ²²And the three hundred blew the trumpets, and the LORD set every man's sword against his fellow, even throughout all the host: and the host fled to Beth-shittah in Zererath, and to the border of Abel-meholah, unto Tabbath. ²³And the men of Israel gathered themselves together out of Naphtali, and out of Asher, and out of all Manasseh, and pursued after the Midianites.

²⁴And Gideon sent messengers throughout all mount Ephraim, saying, 'Come down against the Midianites, and take before them the waters unto Beth-barah and Jordan'. Then all the men of Ephraim gathered themselves together, and took the waters unto Beth-barah and Jordan. ²⁵And they took two princes of the Midianites, Oreb and Zeeb; and they slew Oreb upon the rock Oreb, and Zeeb they slew at the winepress of Zeeb, and pursued Midian, and brought the heads of Oreb and Zeeb to Gideon on the other side Jordan.

8 And the men of Ephraim said unto him, 'Why hast thou served us thus, that thou calledst us not, when thou wentest to fight with the Midianites?' And they did chide with him sharply. ²And he said unto them, 'What have I done now in comparison of you? Is not the gleaning of the grapes of Ephraim better than the vintage of Abi-ezer? ³God hath delivered into your hands the princes of Midian, Oreb and Zeeb: and what was I able to do in comparison of you?' Then their anger was abated toward him, when he had said that.

⁴And Gideon came to Jordan, and passed over, he, and the three hundred men that were with him, faint, yet pursuing them. ⁵And he said unto the men of Succoth, 'Give, I pray you, loaves of bread unto the people that follow me, for they be faint, and I am pursuing after Zebah and Zalmunna, kings of Midian'. ⁶And the princes of Succoth said, 'Are the hands of Zebah and Zalmunna now in thy hand, that we should give bread unto thy army?' ⁷And Gideon said, 'Therefore when the LORD hath delivered Zebah and Zalmunna into my hand, then I will tear your flesh with the thorns of the wilderness and with briers'.

⁸And he went up thence to Penuel, and spoke unto them likewise: and the men of Penuel answered him as the men of Succoth had answered him. ⁹And he spoke also unto the men of Penuel, saying, 'When I come again in peace, I will break down this tower'.

¹⁰Now Zebah and Zalmunna were in Karkor, and their hosts with them, about fifteen thousand men, all that were left of all the hosts of the children of the east: for there fell a hundred and twenty thousand

men that drew sword. ¹¹And Gideon went up by the way of them that dwelt in tents on the east of Nobah and Jogbehah, and smote the host: for the host was secure. ¹²And when Zebah and Zalmunna fled, he pursued after them, and took the two kings of Midian, Zebah and Zalmunna, and discomfited all the host.

¹³And Gideon the son of Joash returned from battle before the sun was up, ¹⁴and caught a young man of the men of Succoth, and inquired of him: and he described unto him the princes of Succoth, and the elders thereof, even threescore and seventeen men. ¹⁵And he came unto the men of Succoth, and said, 'Behold Zebah and Zalmunna, with whom ye did upbraid me, saying, "Are the hands of Zebah and Zalmunna now in thy hand, that we should give bread unto thy men that are weary?"' ¹⁶And he took the elders of the city, and thorns of the wilderness and briers, and with them he taught the men of Succoth. ¹⁷And he beat down the tower of Penuel, and slew the men of the city.

¹⁸Then said he unto Zebah and Zalmunna, 'What manner of men were they whom ye slew at Tabor?' And they answered, 'As thou art, so were they; each one resembled the children of a king'. ¹⁹And he said, 'They were my brethren, even the sons of my mother: as the LORD liveth, if ye had saved them alive, I would not slay you'. ²⁰And he said unto Jether his firstborn, 'Up, and slay them'. But the youth drew not his sword: for he feared, because he was yet a youth. ²¹Then Zebah and Zalmunna said, 'Rise thou, and fall upon us: for as the man is, so is his strength'. And Gideon arose, and slew Zebah and Zalmunna, and took away the ornaments that were on their camels' necks.

²²Then the men of Israel said unto Gideon, 'Rule thou over us, both thou, and thy son, and thy son's son also: for thou hast delivered us from the hand of Midian'. ²³And Gideon said unto them, 'I will not rule over you, neither shall my son rule over you: the LORD shall rule over you'.

²⁴And Gideon said unto them, 'I would desire a request of you, that you would give me every man the earrings of his prey' (for they had golden earrings, because they were Ishmaelites). ²⁵And they answered, 'We will willingly give them'. And they spread a garment, and did cast therein every man the earrings of his prey. ²⁶And the weight of the golden earrings that he requested was a thousand and seven hundred shekels of gold, besides ornaments, and collars, and purple raiment that was on the kings of Midian, and besides the chains that were about their camels' necks. ²⁷And Gideon made an ephod thereof, and put it in his city, even in Ophrah: and all Israel went thither a-whoring after it: which thing became a snare unto Gideon, and to his house.

²⁸Thus was Midian subdued before the children of Israel, so that they lifted up their heads no more. And the country was in quietness forty years in the days of Gideon.

²⁹And Jerubbaal the son of Joash went and dwelt in his own house. ³⁰And Gideon had threescore and ten sons of his body begotten: for he had many wives. ³¹And his concubine that was in Shechem, she also bore him a son, whose name he called Abimelech.

³²And Gideon the son of Joash died in a good old age, and was buried in the sepulchre of Joash his father, in Ophrah of the Abi-ezrites. ³³And it came to pass, as soon as Gideon was dead, that the children of Israel turned again, and went a-whoring after Baalim, and made Baal-berith their god. ³⁴And the children of Israel remembered not the LORD their God, who had delivered them out of the hands of all their enemies on every side: ³⁵neither showed they kindness to the house of Jerubbaal, namely Gideon, according to all the goodness which he had shown unto Israel.

9 And Abimelech the son of Jerubbaal went to Shechem unto his mother's brethren, and communed with them, and with all the family of the house of his mother's father, saying, ²'Speak, I pray you, in the ears of all the men of Shechem, "Whether is better for you, either that all the sons of Jerubbaal, which are threescore and ten persons, reign over you, or that one reign over you? Remember also that I am your bone and your flesh."' ³And his mother's brethren spoke of him in the ears of all the men of Shechem all these words, and their hearts inclined to follow Abimelech: for they said, 'He is our brother'. ⁴And they gave him threescore and ten pieces of silver out of the house of Baal-berith, wherewith Abimelech hired vain and light persons, which followed him. ⁵And he went unto his father's house at Ophrah, and slew his brethren the sons of Jerubbaal, being threescore and ten persons, upon one stone: notwithstanding yet Jotham the youngest son of Jerubbaal was left; for he hid himself. ⁶And all the men of Shechem gathered together, and all the house of Millo, and went, and made Abimelech king, by the plain of the pillar that was in Shechem.

⁷And when they told it to Jotham, he went and stood in the top of mount Gerizim, and lifted up his voice, and cried, and said unto them, 'Hearken unto me, you men of Shechem, that God may hearken unto you. ⁸The trees went forth on a time to anoint a king over them; and they said unto the olive tree, "Reign thou over us". ⁹But the olive tree said unto them, "Should I leave my fatness, wherewith by me they honour God and man, and go to be promoted over the trees?" ¹⁰And the trees said to the fig tree, "Come thou, and reign over us". ¹¹But the fig tree said unto them, "Should I forsake my sweetness, and my good fruit, and go to be promoted over the trees?" ¹²Then said the trees unto the vine, "Come thou, and reign over us". ¹³And the vine said unto them, "Should I leave my wine, which cheereth God and man, and go to be promoted over the trees?" ¹⁴Then said all the trees unto the bramble, "Come thou, and reign over us". ¹⁵And the bramble said unto the trees, "If in truth ye anoint me king over you, then come and put your trust in my shadow: and if not, let fire come out of the bramble, and devour the cedars of Lebanon". ¹⁶Now therefore, if ye have done truly and sincerely, in that ye have made Abimelech king, and if ye have dealt well with Jerubbaal and his house, and have done unto him according to the deserving of his hands ¹⁷(for my father fought for you, and adventured his life far, and delivered you out of the hand of Midian: ¹⁸and ye are risen up against my father's house this day, and have slain his sons,

threescore and ten persons, upon one stone, and have made Abimelech, the son of his maidservant, king over the men of Shechem, because he is your brother): ¹⁹if ye then have dealt truly and sincerely with Jerubbaal and with his house this day, then rejoice ye in Abimelech, and let him also rejoice in you: ²⁰but if not, let fire come out from Abimelech, and devour the men of Shechem, and the house of Millo; and let fire come out from the men of Shechem, and from the house of Millo, and devour Abimelech.' ²¹And Jotham ran away, and fled, and went to Beer, and dwelt there, for fear of Abimelech his brother.

²²When Abimelech had reigned three years over Israel, ²³then God sent an evil spirit between Abimelech and the men of Shechem: and the men of Shechem dealt treacherously with Abimelech: ²⁴that the cruelty done to the threescore and ten sons of Jerubbaal might come, and their blood be laid upon Abimelech their brother, which slew them, and upon the men of Shechem, which aided him in the killing of his brethren. ²⁵And the men of Shechem set liers in wait for him in the top of the mountains, and they robbed all that came along that way by them: and it was told Abimelech.

²⁶And Gaal the son of Ebed came with his brethren, and went over to Shechem: and the men of Shechem put their confidence in him. ²⁷And they went out into the fields, and gathered their vineyards, and trod the grapes, and made merry, and went into the house of their god, and did eat and drink, and cursed Abimelech. ²⁸And Gaal the son of Ebed said, 'Who is Abimelech, and who is Shechem, that we should serve him? Is not he the son of Jerubbaal? and Zebul his officer? serve the men of Hamor the father of Shechem: for why should we serve him? ²⁹And would to God this people were under my hand; then would I remove Abimelech.' And he said to Abimelech, 'Increase thy army, and come out'.

³⁰And when Zebul the ruler of the city heard the words of Gaal the son of Ebed, his anger was kindled. ³¹And he sent messengers unto Abimelech privily, saying, 'Behold, Gaal the son of Ebed and his brethren be come to Shechem, and behold, they fortify the city against thee. ³²Now therefore up by night, thou and the people that is with thee, and lie in wait in the field. ³³And it shall be, that in the morning, as soon as the sun is up, thou shalt rise early, and set upon the city: and behold, when he and the people that is with him come out against thee, then mayest thou do to them as thou shalt find occasion.'

³⁴And Abimelech rose up, and all the people that were with him, by night, and they laid wait against Shechem in four companies. ³⁵And Gaal the son of Ebed went out, and stood in the entering of the gate of the city: and Abimelech rose up, and the people that were with him, from lying in wait. ³⁶And when Gaal saw the people, he said to Zebul, 'Behold, there come people down from the top of the mountains'. And Zebul said unto him, 'Thou seest the shadow of the mountains as if they were men'. ³⁷And Gaal spoke again and said, 'See there come people down by the middle of the land, and another company come

along by the plain of Meonenim'. ³⁸Then said Zebul unto him, 'Where is now thy mouth, wherewith thou saidst, "Who is Abimelech, that we should serve him?" Is not this the people that thou hast despised? Go out, I pray now, and fight with them.' ³⁹And Gaal went out before the men of Shechem, and fought with Abimelech. ⁴⁰And Abimelech chased him, and he fled before him, and many were overthrown and wounded, even unto the entering of the gate. ⁴¹And Abimelech dwelt at Arumah: and Zebul thrust out Gaal and his brethren, that they should not dwell in Shechem. ⁴²And it came to pass on the morrow, that the people went out into the field, and they told Abimelech. ⁴³And he took the people, and divided them into three companies, and laid wait in the field, and looked, and behold, the people were come forth out of the city; and he rose up against them, and smote them. ⁴⁴And Abimelech, and the company that was with him, rushed forward, and stood in the entering of the gate of the city: and the two other companies ran upon all the people that were in the fields, and slew them. ⁴⁵And Abimelech fought against the city all that day; and he took the city, and slew the people that was therein, and beat down the city, and sowed it with salt.

⁴⁶And when all the men of the tower of Shechem heard that, they entered into a hold of the house of the god Berith. ⁴⁷And it was told Abimelech, that all the men of the tower of Shechem were gathered together. ⁴⁸And Abimelech got him up to mount Zalmon, he and all the people that were with him; and Abimelech took an axe in his hand, and cut down a bough from the trees, and took it, and laid it on his shoulder, and said unto the people that were with him, 'What ye have seen me do, make haste, and do as I have done'. ⁴⁹And all the people likewise cut down every man his bough, and followed Abimelech, and put them to the hold, and set the hold on fire upon them: so that all the men of the tower of Shechem died also, about a thousand men and women.

⁵⁰Then went Abimelech to Thebez, and encamped against Thebez, and took it. ⁵¹But there was a strong tower within the city, and thither fled all the men and women, and all they of the city, and shut it to them, and got them up to the top of the tower. ⁵²And Abimelech came unto the tower, and fought against it, and went hard unto the door of the tower to burn it with fire. ⁵³And a certain woman cast a piece of a millstone upon Abimelech's head, and all to broke his skull. ⁵⁴Then he called hastily unto the young man his armour-bearer, and said unto him, 'Draw thy sword, and slay me, that men say not of me, "A woman slew him"'. And his young man thrust him through, and he died. ⁵⁵And when the men of Israel saw that Abimelech was dead, they departed every man unto his place.

⁵⁶Thus God rendered the wickedness of Abimelech, which he did unto his father, in slaying his seventy brethren: ⁵⁷and all the evil of the men of Shechem did God render upon their heads: and upon them came the curse of Jotham the son of Jerubbaal.

10 And after Abimelech there arose to defend Israel Tola the son of Puah, the son of Dodo, a man of Issachar; and he dwelt in

Shamir in mount Ephraim. ²And he judged Israel twenty and three years, and died, and was buried in Shamir.

³And after him arose Jair, a Gileadite, and judged Israel twenty and two years. ⁴And he had thirty sons that rode on thirty ass-colts, and they had thirty cities, which are called Havoth-jair unto this day, which are in the land of Gilead. ⁵And Jair died, and was buried in Camon.

⁶And the children of Israel did evil again in the sight of the Lord, and served Baalim, and Ashtaroth, and the gods of Syria, and the gods of Zidon, and the gods of Moab, and the gods of the children of Ammon, and the gods of the Philistines, and forsook the Lord, and served not him. ⁷And the anger of the Lord was hot against Israel, and he sold them into the hands of the Philistines, and into the hands of the children of Ammon. ⁸And that year they vexed and oppressed the children of Israel: eighteen years, all the children of Israel that were on the other side Jordan in the land of the Amorites, which is in Gilead. ⁹Moreover the children of Ammon passed over Jordan to fight also against Judah, and against Benjamin, and against the house of Ephraim; so that Israel was sore distressed.

¹⁰And the children of Israel cried unto the Lord, saying, 'We have sinned against thee, both because we have forsaken our God, and also served Baalim'. ¹¹And the Lord said unto the children of Israel, 'Did not I deliver you from the Egyptians, and from the Amorites, from the children of Ammon, and from the Philistines? ¹²The Zidonians also, and the Amalekites, and the Maonites, did oppress you, and ye cried to me, and I delivered you out of their hand. ¹³Yet ye have forsaken me, and served other gods: wherefore I will deliver you no more. ¹⁴Go and cry unto the gods which ye have chosen, let them deliver you in the time of your tribulation.'

¹⁵And the children of Israel said unto the Lord, 'We have sinned: do thou unto us whatsoever seemeth good unto thee; deliver us only, we pray thee, this day'. ¹⁶And they put away the strange gods from among them, and served the Lord: and his soul was grieved for the misery of Israel. ¹⁷Then the children of Ammon were gathered together, and encamped in Gilead. And the children of Israel assembled themselves together, and encamped in Mizpeh. ¹⁸And the people and princes of Gilead said one to another, 'What man is he that will begin to fight against the children of Ammon? he shall be head over all the inhabitants of Gilead'.

11 Now Jephthah the Gileadite was a mighty man of valour, and he was the son of a harlot: and Gilead begot Jephthah. ²And Gilead's wife bore him sons; and his wife's sons grew up, and they thrust out Jephthah, and said unto him, 'Thou shalt not inherit in our father's house, for thou art the son of a strange woman'. ³Then Jephthah fled from his brethren, and dwelt in the land of Tob: and there were gathered vain men to Jephthah, and went out with him.

⁴And it came to pass in process of time, that the children of Ammon made war against Israel. ⁵And it was so, that when the children of Ammon made war against Israel, the elders of Gilead went to fetch

Jephthah out of the land of Tob: [6]and they said unto Jephthah, 'Come, and be our captain, that we may fight with the children of Ammon'. [7]And Jephthah said unto the elders of Gilead, 'Did not ye hate me, and expel me out of my father's house? And why are ye come unto me now when ye are in distress?' [8]And the elders of Gilead said unto Jephthah, 'Therefore we turn again to thee now, that thou mayest go with us, and fight against the children of Ammon, and be our head over all the inhabitants of Gilead'. [9]And Jephthah said unto the elders of Gilead, 'If ye bring me home again to fight against the children of Ammon, and the LORD deliver them before me, shall I be your head?' [10]And the elders of Gilead said unto Jephthah, 'The LORD be witness between us, if we do not so according to thy words'. [11]Then Jephthah went with the elders of Gilead, and the people made him head and captain over them: and Jephthah uttered all his words before the LORD in Mizpeh.

[12]And Jephthah sent messengers unto the king of the children of Ammon, saying, 'What hast thou to do with me, that thou art come against me to fight in my land?' [13]And the king of the children of Ammon answered unto the messengers of Jephthah, 'Because Israel took away my land, when they came up out of Egypt, from Arnon even unto Jabbok, and unto Jordan: now therefore restore those lands again peaceably'. [14]And Jephthah sent messengers again unto the king of the children of Ammon: [15]and said unto him, 'Thus saith Jephthah, "Israel took not away the land of Moab, nor the land of the children of Ammon: [16]but when Israel came up from Egypt, and walked through the wilderness unto the Red Sea, and came to Kadesh; [17]then Israel sent messengers unto the king of Edom, saying, 'Let me, I pray thee, pass through thy land'. But the king of Edom would not hearken thereto. And in like manner they sent unto the king of Moab: but he would not consent: and Israel abode in Kadesh. [18]Then they went along through the wilderness, and compassed the land of Edom, and the land of Moab, and came by the east side of the land of Moab, and pitched on the other side of Arnon, but came not within the border of Moab: for Arnon was the border of Moab. [19]And Israel sent messengers unto Sihon king of the Amorites, the king of Heshbon, and Israel said unto him, 'Let us pass, we pray thee, through thy land unto my place'. [20]But Sihon trusted not Israel to pass through his coast: but Sihon gathered all his people together, and pitched in Jahaz, and fought against Israel. [21]And the LORD God of Israel delivered Sihon and all his people into the hand of Israel, and they smote them: so Israel possessed all the land of the Amorites, the inhabitants of that country. [22]And they possessed all the coasts of the Amorites, from Arnon even unto Jabbok, and from the wilderness even unto Jordan. [23]So now the LORD God of Israel hath dispossessed the Amorites from before his people Israel, and shouldst thou possess it? [24]Wilt not thou possess that which Chemosh thy god giveth thee to possess? So whomsoever the LORD our God shall drive out from before us, them will we possess. [25]And now art thou anything better than Balak the son of Zippor, king of Moab? Did he ever strive against Israel, or did he ever fight against them, [26]while Israel dwelt in

Heshbon and her towns, and in Aroer and her towns, and in all the cities that be along by the coasts of Arnon, three hundred years? Why therefore did ye not recover them within that time? [27]Wherefore I have not sinned against thee, but thou doest me wrong to war against me: the LORD the Judge be judge this day between the children of Israel and the children of Ammon."' [28]Howbeit the king of the children of Ammon hearkened not unto the words of Jephthah which he sent him.

[29]Then the Spirit of the LORD came upon Jephthah, and he passed over Gilead, and Manasseh, and passed over Mizpeh of Gilead, and from Mizpeh of Gilead he passed over unto the children of Ammon. [30]And Jephthah vowed a vow unto the LORD, and said, 'If thou shalt without fail deliver the children of Ammon into my hands, [31]then it shall be, that whatsoever cometh forth of the doors of my house to meet me, when I return in peace from the children of Ammon, shall surely be the LORD's, and I will offer it up for a burnt offering'.

[32]So Jephthah passed over unto the children of Ammon to fight against them, and the LORD delivered them into his hands. [33]And he smote them from Aroer, even till thou come to Minnith, even twenty cities, and unto the plain of the vineyards, with a very great slaughter. Thus the children of Ammon were subdued before the children of Israel.

[34]And Jephthah came to Mizpeh unto his house, and behold, his daughter came out to meet him with timbrels and with dances, and she was his only child: besides her he had neither son nor daughter. [35]And it came to pass, when he saw her, that he rent his clothes, and said, 'Alas, my daughter, thou hast brought me very low, and thou art one of them that trouble me: for I have opened my mouth unto the LORD, and I cannot go back'. [36]And she said unto him, 'My father, if thou hast opened thy mouth unto the LORD, do to me according to that which hath proceeded out of thy mouth; forasmuch as the LORD hath taken vengeance for thee of thy enemies, even of the children of Ammon'. [37]And she said unto her father, 'Let this thing be done for me: let me alone two months, that I may go up and down upon the mountains, and bewail my virginity, I and my fellows'. [38]And he said, 'Go'. And he sent her away for two months: and she went with her companions, and bewailed her virginity upon the mountains. [39]And it came to pass at the end of two months that she returned unto her father, who did with her according to his vow which he had vowed: and she knew no man. And it was a custom in Israel, [40]that the daughters of Israel went yearly to lament the daughter of Jephthah the Gileadite four days in a year.

12 And the men of Ephraim gathered themselves together, and went northward, and said unto Jephthah, 'Wherefore passedst thou over to fight against the children of Ammon, and didst not call us to go with thee? We will burn thy house upon thee with fire.' [2]And Jephthah said unto them, 'I and my people were at great strife with the children of Ammon; and when I called you, ye delivered me not out of their hands. ³And when I saw that ye delivered me not, I put my life in my hands, and passed over against the children of Ammon, and the LORD delivered them into my hand: wherefore then are ye come up unto me this day, to fight against me?' ⁴Then Jephthah gathered together all the men of Gilead, and fought with Ephraim: and the men of Gilead smote Ephraim, because they said, 'Ye Gileadites are fugitives of Ephraim among the Ephraimites, and among the Manassites'. ⁵And the Gileadites took the passages of Jordan before the Ephraimites: and it was so, that when those Ephraimites which were escaped said, 'Let me go over', that the men of Gilead said unto him, 'Art thou an Ephraimite?' If he said, 'Nay': ⁶then said they unto him, 'Say now "Shibboleth"': and he said "Sibboleth": for he could not frame to pronounce it right. Then they took him, and slew him at the passages of Jordan: and there fell at that time of the Ephraimites forty and two thousand. ⁷And Jephthah judged Israel six years. Then died Jephthah the Gileadite, and was buried in one of the cities of Gilead.

⁸And after him Ibzan of Beth-lehem judged Israel. ⁹And he had thirty sons, and thirty daughters, whom he sent abroad, and took in thirty daughters from abroad for his sons. And he judged Israel seven years. ¹⁰Then died Ibzan, and was buried at Beth-lehem.

¹¹And after him Elon, a Zebulonite, judged Israel; and he judged Israel ten years. ¹²And Elon the Zebulonite died, and was buried in Aijalon in the country of Zebulun.

¹³And after him Abdon the son of Hillel, a Pirathonite, judged Israel. ¹⁴And he had forty sons and thirty nephews, that rode on threescore and ten ass-colts: and he judged Israel eight years. ¹⁵And Abdon the son of Hillel the Pirathonite died, and was buried in Pirathon in the land of Ephraim, in the mount of the Amalekites.

13 And the children of Israel did evil again in the sight of the LORD, and the LORD delivered them into the hand of the Philistines forty years.

²And there was a certain man of Zorah, of the family of the Danites, whose name was Manoah; and his wife was barren, and bore not. ³And the angel of the LORD appeared unto the woman, and said unto her, 'Behold now, thou art barren, and bearest not: but thou shalt conceive, and bear a son. ⁴Now therefore beware, I pray thee, and drink not wine nor strong drink, and eat not any unclean thing. ⁵For lo, thou shalt conceive, and bear a son; and no razor shall come on his head: for the child shall be a Nazarite unto God from the womb: and he shall begin to deliver Israel out of the hand of the Philistines.'

⁶Then the woman came and told her husband, saying, 'A man of God came unto me, and his countenance was like the countenance of an angel of God, very terrible: but I asked him not whence he was, neither told he me his name: ⁷but he said unto me, "Behold, thou shalt conceive, and bear a son; and now drink no wine nor strong drink, neither eat any unclean thing: for the child shall be a Nazarite to God from the womb to the day of his death"'.

⁸Then Manoah entreated the LORD, and said, 'O my Lord, let the man

of God which thou didst send come again unto us, and teach us what we shall do unto the child that shall be born'. ⁹And God hearkened to the voice of Manoah; and the angel of God came again unto the woman as she sat in the field: but Manoah her husband was not with her. ¹⁰And the woman made haste, and ran, and showed her husband, and said unto him, 'Behold, the man hath appeared unto me, that came unto me the other day'. ¹¹And Manoah arose, and went after his wife, and came to the man, and said unto him, 'Art thou the man that spokest unto the woman?' And he said, 'I am'. ¹²And Manoah said, 'Now let thy words come to pass. How shall we order the child, and how shall we do unto him?' ¹³And the angel of the LORD said unto Manoah, 'Of all that I said unto the woman let her beware. ¹⁴She may not eat of anything that cometh of the vine, neither let her drink wine or strong drink, nor eat any unclean thing: all that I commanded her let her observe.'

¹⁵And Manoah said unto the angel of the LORD, 'I pray thee, let us detain thee, until we shall have made ready a kid for thee'. ¹⁶And the angel of the LORD said unto Manoah, 'Though thou detain me, I will not eat of thy bread: and if thou wilt offer a burnt offering, thou must offer it unto the LORD'. For Manoah knew not that he was an angel of the LORD. ¹⁷And Manoah said unto the angel of the LORD, 'What is thy name, that when thy sayings come to pass we may do thee honour?' ¹⁸And the angel of the LORD said unto him, 'Why askest thou thus after my name, seeing it is secret?' ¹⁹So Manoah took a kid with a meat offering, and offered it upon a rock unto the LORD: and the angel did wondrously, and Manoah and his wife looked on. ²⁰For it came to pass, when the flame went up toward heaven from off the altar, that the angel of the LORD ascended in the flame of the altar. And Manoah and his wife looked on it, and fell on their faces to the ground. ²¹(But the angel of the LORD did no more appear to Manoah and to his wife): then Manoah knew that he was an angel of the LORD. ²²And Manoah said unto his wife, 'We shall surely die, because we have seen God'. ²³But his wife said unto him, 'If the LORD were pleased to kill us, he would not have received a burnt offering and a meat offering at our hands, neither would he have shown us all these things, nor would as at this time have told us such things as these'.

²⁴And the woman bore a son, and called his name Samson: and the child grew, and the LORD blessed him. ²⁵And the Spirit of the LORD began to move him at times in the camp of Dan between Zorah and Eshtaol.

14 And Samson went down to Timnath, and saw a woman in Timnath of the daughters of the Philistines. ²And he came up, and told his father and his mother, and said, 'I have seen a woman in Timnath of the daughters of the Philistines: now therefore get her for me to wife'. ³Then his father and his mother said unto him, 'Is there never a woman among the daughters of thy brethren, or among all my people, that thou goest to take a wife of the uncircumcised Philistines?' And Samson said unto his father, 'Get her for me; for she pleaseth me well'. ⁴But his father and his mother knew not that it was of the LORD, that he sought an occasion against the Philistines: for at that time the Philistines had dominion over Israel.

⁵Then went Samson down, and his father and his mother, to Timnath, and came to the vineyards of Timnath: and behold, a young lion roared against him. ⁶And the Spirit of the LORD came mightily upon him, and he rent him as he would have rent a kid, and he had nothing in his hand: but he told not his father or his mother what he had done. ⁷And he went down, and talked with the woman, and she pleased Samson well.

⁸And after a time he returned to take her, and he turned aside to see the carcase of the lion: and behold, there was a swarm of bees and honey in the carcase of the lion. ⁹And he took thereof in his hands, and went on eating, and came to his father and mother, and he gave them, and they did eat: but he told not them that he had taken the honey out of the carcase of the lion.

¹⁰So his father went down unto the woman, and Samson made there a feast: for so used the young men to do. ¹¹And it came to pass when they saw him, that they brought thirty companions to be with him. ¹²And Samson said unto them, 'I will now put forth a riddle unto you: if you can certainly declare it me within the seven days of the feast, and find it out, then I will give you thirty sheets and thirty change of garments: ¹³but if ye cannot declare it me, then shall ye give me thirty sheets and thirty change of garments'. And they said unto him, 'Put forth thy riddle, that we may hear it'. ¹⁴And he said unto them, 'Out of the eater came forth meat, and out of the strong came forth sweetness'. And they could not in three days expound the riddle. ¹⁵And it came to pass on the seventh day, that they said unto Samson's wife, 'Entice thy husband, that he may declare unto us the riddle, lest we burn thee and thy father's house with fire: have ye called us to take that we have? is it not so?' ¹⁶And Samson's wife wept before him, and said, 'Thou dost but hate me, and lovest me not: thou hast put forth a riddle unto the children of my people, and hast not told it me'. And he said unto her, 'Behold, I have not told it my father nor my mother, and shall I tell it thee?' ¹⁷And she wept before him the seven days, while the feast lasted: and it came to pass on the seventh day, that he told her, because she lay sore upon him: and she told the riddle to the children of her people. ¹⁸And the men of the city said unto him on the seventh day before the sun went down, 'What is sweeter than honey? and what is stronger than a lion?' And he said unto them, 'If ye had not ploughed with my heifer, ye had not found out my riddle'.

¹⁹And the Spirit of the LORD came upon him, and he went down to Ashkelon, and slew thirty men of them, and took their spoil, and gave change of garments unto them which expounded the riddle. And his anger was kindled, and he went up to his father's house. ²⁰But Samson's wife was given to his companion, whom he had used as his friend.

15 But it came to pass within a while after, in the time of wheat harvest, that Samson visited his wife with a kid; and he said, 'I will go in to my wife into the chamber'. But her father would not suffer him to go in. ²And her father said, 'I verily thought that thou hadst utterly hated her; therefore I gave her to thy companion: is not her younger sister fairer than she? take her, I pray thee, in stead of her'.

³And Samson said concerning them, 'Now shall I be more blameless than the Philistines, though I do them a displeasure'. ⁴And Samson went and caught three hundred foxes, and took fire-brands, and turned tail to tail, and put a fire-brand in the midst between two tails. ⁵And when he had set the brands on fire, he let them go into the standing corn of the Philistines, and burnt up both the shocks, and also the standing corn, with the vineyards and olives.

⁶Then the Philistines said, 'Who hath done this?' And they answered, 'Samson, the son-in-law of the Timnite, because he had taken his wife, and given her to his companion'. And the Philistines came up, and burnt her and her father with fire.

⁷And Samson said unto them, 'Though ye have done this, yet will I be avenged of you, and after that I will cease'. ⁸And he smote them hip and thigh with a great slaughter: and he went down and dwelt in the top of the rock Etam.

⁹Then the Philistines went up, and pitched in Judah, and spread themselves in Lehi. ¹⁰And the men of Judah said, 'Why are ye come up against us?' And they answered, 'To bind Samson are we come up, to do to him as he hath done to us'. ¹¹Then three thousand men of Judah went to the top of the rock Etam, and said to Samson, 'Knowest thou not that the Philistines are rulers over us? What is this that thou hast done unto us?' And he said unto them, 'As they did unto me, so have I done unto them'. ¹²And they said unto him, 'We are come down to bind thee, that we may deliver thee into the hand of the Philistines'. And Samson said unto them, 'Swear unto me, that ye will not fall upon me yourselves'. ¹³And they spoke unto him, saying, 'No: but we will bind thee fast, and deliver thee into their hand: but surely we will not kill thee'. And they bound him with two new cords, and brought him up from the rock.

¹⁴And when he came unto Lehi, the Philistines shouted against him: and the Spirit of the LORD came mightily upon him, and the cords that were upon his arms became as flax that was burnt with fire, and his bands loosed from off his hands. ¹⁵And he found a new jawbone of an ass, and put forth his hand, and took it, and slew a thousand men therewith. ¹⁶And Samson said, 'With the jawbone of an ass, heaps upon heaps, with the jaw of an ass have I slain a thousand men'. ¹⁷And it came to pass when he had made an end of speaking, that he cast away the jawbone out of his hand, and called that place Ramath-lehi.

¹⁸And he was sore athirst, and called on the LORD, and said, 'Thou hast given this great deliverance into the hand of thy servant: and now shall I die for thirst, and fall into the hand of the uncircumcised?' ¹⁹But God cleft a hollow place that was in the jaw, and there came water thereout; and when he had drunk, his spirit came again, and he revived: wherefore he called the name thereof En-hakkore, which is in Lehi unto this day. ²⁰And he judged Israel in the days of the Philistines twenty years.

16 Then went Samson to Gaza, and saw there a harlot, and went in unto her. ²And it was told the Gazites, saying, 'Samson is come hither'. And they compassed him in, and laid wait for him all night in the gate of the city, and were quiet all the night, saying, 'In the morning, when it is day, we shall kill him'. ³And Samson lay till midnight, and arose at midnight, and took the doors of the gate of the city, and the two posts, and went away with them, bar and all, and put them upon his shoulders, and carried them up to the top of a hill that is before Hebron.

⁴And it came to pass afterward, that he loved a woman in the valley of Sorek, whose name was Delilah. ⁵And the lords of the Philistines came up unto her, and said unto her, 'Entice him, and see wherein his great strength lieth, and by what means we may prevail against him, that we may bind him to afflict him: and we will give thee every one of us eleven hundred pieces of silver'.

⁶And Delilah said to Samson, 'Tell me, I pray thee, wherein thy great strength lieth, and wherewith thou mightest be bound to afflict thee'. ⁷And Samson said unto her, 'If they bind me with seven green withs that were never dried, then shall I be weak, and be as another man'. ⁸Then the lords of the Philistines brought up to her seven green withs which had not been dried, and she bound him with them. ⁹Now there were men lying in wait, abiding with her in the chamber. And she said unto him, 'The Philistines be upon thee, Samson'. And he broke the withs, as a thread of tow is broken when it toucheth the fire. So his strength was not known. ¹⁰And Delilah said unto Samson, 'Behold, thou hast mocked me, and told me lies: now tell me, I pray thee, wherewith thou mightest be bound'. ¹¹And he said unto her, 'If they bind me fast with new ropes that never were occupied, then shall I be weak, and be as another man'. ¹²Delilah therefore took new ropes, and bound him therewith, and said unto him, 'The Philistines be upon thee, Samson'. And there were liers in wait abiding in the chamber. And he broke them from off his arms like a thread. ¹³And Delilah said unto Samson, 'Hitherto thou hast mocked me, and told me lies: tell me wherewith thou mightest be bound'. And he said unto her, 'If thou weavest the seven locks of my head with the web'. ¹⁴And she fastened it with the pin, and said unto him, 'The Philistines be upon thee, Samson'. And he awoke out of his sleep, and went away with the pin of the beam, and with the web.

¹⁵And she said unto him, 'How canst thou say, "I love thee", when thy heart is not with me? Thou hast mocked me these three times, and hast not told me wherein thy great strength lieth.' ¹⁶And it came to pass, when she pressed him daily with her words, and urged him, so that his soul was vexed unto death, ¹⁷that he told her all his heart, and said unto her, 'There hath not come a razor upon my head: for I have been a Nazarite unto God from my mother's womb: if I be shaven, then my strength will go from me, and I shall become weak, and be like any other man'. ¹⁸And when Delilah saw that he had told her all his heart, she sent and called for the lords of the Philistines, saying, 'Come up this once, for he hath shown me all his heart'. Then the lords of the

Philistines came up unto her, and brought money in their hand. ¹⁹And she made him sleep upon her knees; and she called for a man, and she caused him to shave off the seven locks of his head; and she began to afflict him, and his strength went from him. ²⁰And she said, 'The Philistines be upon thee, Samson'. And he awoke out of his sleep, and said, 'I will go out as at other times before, and shake myself'. And he wist not that the LORD was departed from him.

²¹But the Philistines took him, and put out his eyes, and brought him down to Gaza, and bound him with fetters of brass; and he did grind in the prison-house. ²²Howbeit the hair of his head began to grow again after he was shaven.

²³Then the lords of the Philistines gathered them together for to offer a great sacrifice unto Dagon their god, and to rejoice: for they said, 'Our god hath delivered Samson our enemy into our hand'. ²⁴And when the people saw him, they praised their god: for they said, 'Our god hath delivered into our hands our enemy, and the destroyer of our country, which slew many of us'. ²⁵And it came to pass, when their hearts were merry, that they said, 'Call for Samson, that he may make us sport'. And they called for Samson out of the prison-house, and he made them sport, and they set him between the pillars. ²⁶And Samson said unto the lad that held him by the hand, 'Suffer me that I may feel the pillars whereupon the house standeth, that I may lean upon them'. ²⁷Now the house was full of men and women, and all the lords of the Philistines were there; and there were upon the roof about three thousand men and women, that beheld while Samson made sport. ²⁸And Samson called unto the LORD, and said, 'O Lord GOD, remember me, I pray thee, and strengthen me, I pray thee, only this once, O God, that I may be at once avenged of the Philistines for my two eyes'. ²⁹And Samson took hold of the two middle pillars upon which the house stood, and on which it was borne up, of the one with his right hand, and of the other with his left. ³⁰And Samson said, 'Let me die with the Philistines'. And he bowed himself with all his might: and the house fell upon the lords, and upon all the people that were therein. So the dead which he slew at his death were more than they which he slew in his life. ³¹Then his brethren and all the house of his father came down, and took him, and brought him up, and buried him between Zorah and Eshtaol in the burying-place of Manoah his father. And he judged Israel twenty years.

17 And there was a man of mount Ephraim, whose name was Micah. ²And he said unto his mother, 'The eleven hundred shekels of silver that were taken from thee, about which thou cursedst, and spokest of also in my ears, behold, the silver is with me; I took it'. And his mother said, 'Blessed be thou of the LORD, my son'. ³And when he had restored the eleven hundred shekels of silver to his mother, his mother said, 'I had wholly dedicated the silver unto the LORD from my hand for my son, to make a graven image and a molten image: now therefore I will restore it unto thee'. ⁴Yet he restored the money unto his mother; and his mother took two hundred shekels of silver, and gave them to the founder, who made thereof a graven image and a molten image: and they were in the house of Micah. ⁵And the man Micah had a house of gods, and made an ephod, and teraphim, and consecrated one of his sons, who became his priest. ⁶In those days there was no king in Israel, but every man did that which was right in his own eyes.

⁷And there was a young man out of Beth-lehem-judah of the family of Judah, who was a Levite, and he sojourned there. ⁸And the man departed out of the city from Beth-lehem-judah to sojourn where he could find a place: and he came to mount Ephraim to the house of Micah, as he journeyed. ⁹And Micah said unto him, 'Whence comest thou?' And he said unto him, 'I am a Levite of Beth-lehem-judah, and I go to sojourn where I may find a place'. ¹⁰And Micah said unto him, 'Dwell with me, and be unto me a father and a priest, and I will give thee ten shekels of silver by the year, and a suit of apparel, and thy victuals'. So the Levite went in. ¹¹And the Levite was content to dwell with the man; and the young man was unto him as one of his sons. ¹²And Micah consecrated the Levite; and the young man became his priest, and was in the house of Micah. ¹³Then said Micah, 'Now know I that the LORD will do me good, seeing I have a Levite to my priest'.

18 In those days there was no king in Israel: and in those days the tribe of the Danites sought them an inheritance to dwell in: for unto that day all their inheritance had not fallen unto them among the tribes of Israel. ²And the children of Dan sent of their family five men from their coasts, men of valour, from Zorah, and from Eshtaol, to spy out the land, and to search it; and they said unto them, 'Go, search the land': who when they came to mount Ephraim, to the house of Micah, they lodged there. ³When they were by the house of Micah, they knew the voice of the young man the Levite: and they turned in thither, and said unto him, 'Who brought thee hither? And what makest thou in this place? and what hast thou here?' ⁴And he said unto them, 'Thus and thus dealeth Micah with me, and hath hired me, and I am his priest'. ⁵And they said unto him, 'Ask counsel, we pray thee, of God, that we may know whether our way which we go shall be prosperous'. ⁶And the priest said unto them, 'Go in peace: before the LORD is your way wherein ye go'.

⁷Then the five men departed, and came to Laish, and saw the people that were therein, how they dwelt careless, after the manner of the Zidonians, quiet and secure; and there was no magistrate in the land that might put them to shame in anything; and they were far from the Zidonians, and had no business with any man. ⁸And they came unto their brethren to Zorah and Eshtaol: and their brethren said unto them, 'What say ye?' ⁹And they said, 'Arise, that we may go up against them: for we have seen the land, and behold, it is very good: and are ye still? Be not slothful to go, and to enter to possess the land. ¹⁰When ye go, ye shall come unto a people secure, and to a large land: for God hath given it into your hands: a place where there is no want of anything that is in the earth.'

¹¹And there went from thence of the family of the Danites, out of

Zorah and out of Eshtaol, six hundred men appointed with weapons of war. [12]And they went up, and pitched in Kirjath-jearim, in Judah: wherefore they called that place Mahaneh-dan unto this day: behold, it is behind Kirjath-jearim. [13]And they passed thence unto mount Ephraim, and came unto the house of Micah.

[14]Then answered the five men that went to spy out the country of Laish, and said unto their brethren, 'Do ye know that there is in these houses an ephod, and teraphim, and a graven image, and a molten image? Now therefore consider what ye have to do.' [15]And they turned thitherward, and came to the house of the young man the Levite, even unto the house of Micah, and saluted him. [16]And the six hundred men appointed with their weapons of war, which were of the children of Dan, stood by the entering of the gate. [17]And the five men that went to spy out the land went up, and came in thither, and took the graven image, and the ephod, and the teraphim, and the molten image: and the priest stood in the entering of the gate with the six hundred men that were appointed with weapons of war. [18]And these went into Micah's house, and fetched the carved image, the ephod, and the teraphim, and the molten image. Then said the priest unto them, 'What do ye?' [19]And they said unto him, 'Hold thy peace, lay thy hand upon thy mouth, and go with us, and be to us a father and a priest: is it better for thee to be a priest unto the house of one man, or that thou be a priest unto a tribe and a family in Israel?' [20]And the priest's heart was glad, and he took the ephod, and the teraphim, and the graven image, and went in the midst of the people. [21]So they turned and departed, and put the little ones and the cattle and the carriage before them.

[22]And when they were a good way from the house of Micah, the men that were in the houses near to Micah's house were gathered together, and overtook the children of Dan. [23]And they cried unto the children of Dan. And they turned their faces, and said unto Micah, 'What aileth thee, that thou comest with such a company?' [24]And he said, 'Ye have taken away my gods which I made, and the priest, and ye are gone away: and what have I more? and what is this that ye say unto me, "What aileth thee?"' [25]And the children of Dan said unto him, 'Let not thy voice be heard among us, lest angry fellows run upon thee, and thou lose thy life, with the lives of thy household'. [26]And the children of Dan went their way: and when Micah saw that they were too strong for him, he turned and went back unto his house. [27]And they took the things which Micah had made, and the priest which he had, and came unto Laish, unto a people that were at quiet and secure, and they smote them with the edge of the sword, and burnt the city with fire. [28]And there was no deliverer, because it was far from Zidon, and they had no business with any man; and it was in the valley that lieth by Beth-rehob. And they built a city, and dwelt therein. [29]And they called the name of the city Dan, after the name of Dan their father, who was born unto Israel: howbeit the name of the city was Laish at the first.

[30]And the children of Dan set up the graven image: and Jonathan, the son of Gershom, the son of Manasseh, he and his sons were priests

to the tribe of Dan until the day of the captivity of the land. ³¹And they set them up Micah's graven image, which he made, all the time that the house of God was in Shiloh.

19 And it came to pass in those days, when there was no king in Israel, that there was a certain Levite sojourning on the side of mount Ephraim, who took to him a concubine out of Beth-lehem-judah. ²And his concubine played the whore against him, and went away from him unto her father's house to Beth-lehem-judah, and was there four whole months. ³And her husband arose, and went after her to speak friendly unto her, and to bring her again, having his servant with him, and a couple of asses: and she brought him into her father's house, and when the father of the damsel saw him, he rejoiced to meet him. ⁴And his father-in-law, the damsel's father, retained him, and he abode with him three days: so they did eat and drink, and lodged there. ⁵And it came to pass on the fourth day, when they arose early in the morning, that he rose up to depart: and the damsel's father said unto his son-in-law, 'Comfort thy heart with a morsel of bread, and afterward go your way'. ⁶And they sat down, and did eat and drink both of them together: for the damsel's father had said unto the man, 'Be content, I pray thee, and tarry all night, and let thy heart be merry'. ⁷And when the man rose up to depart, his father-in-law urged him: therefore he lodged there again. ⁸And he arose early in the morning on the fifth day to depart, and the damsel's father said, 'Comfort thy heart, I pray thee'. And they tarried until afternoon, and they did eat both of them. ⁹And when the man rose up to depart, he and his concubine, and his servant, his father-in-law, the damsel's father, said unto him, 'Behold, now the day draweth towards evening, I pray you tarry all night: behold, the day groweth to an end, lodge here, that thy heart may be merry; and tomorrow get you early on your way, that thou mayest go home'. ¹⁰But the man would not tarry that night, but he rose up and departed, and came over against Jebus, which is Jerusalem; and there were with him two asses saddled, his concubine also was with him. ¹¹And when they were by Jebus, the day was far spent, and the servant said unto his master, 'Come, I pray thee, and let us turn in into this city of the Jebusites, and lodge in it'. ¹²And his master said unto him, 'We will not turn aside hither into the city of a stranger, that is not of the children of Israel; we will pass over to Gibeah'. ¹³And he said unto his servant, 'Come, and let us draw near to one of these places to lodge all night, in Gibeah, or in Ramah'. ¹⁴And they passed on and went their way, and the sun went down upon them when they were by Gibeah, which belongeth to Benjamin. ¹⁵And they turned aside thither, to go in and to lodge in Gibeah: and when he went in, he sat him down in a street of the city: for there was no man that took them into his house to lodging.

¹⁶And behold, there came an old man from his work out of the field at even, which was also of mount Ephraim; and he sojourned in Gibeah, but the men of the place were Benjamites. ¹⁷And when he had lifted up his eyes, he saw a wayfaring man in the street of the city: and the old

man said, 'Whither goest thou? and whence comest thou?' ¹⁸And he said unto him, 'We are passing from Beth-lehem-judah toward the side of mount Ephraim; from thence am I: and I went to Beth-lehem-judah, but I am now going to the house of the Lᴏʀᴅ; and there is no man that receiveth me to house. ¹⁹Yet there is both straw and provender for our asses, and there is bread and wine also for me, and for thy handmaid, and for the young man which is with thy servants: there is no want of anything. ²⁰And the old man said, 'Peace be with thee; howsoever let all thy wants lie upon me; only lodge not in the street'. ²¹So he brought him into his house, and gave provender unto the asses: and they washed their feet, and did eat and drink.

²²Now as they were making their hearts merry, behold, the men of the city, certain sons of Belial, beset the house round about, and beat at the door, and spoke to the master of the house, the old man, saying, 'Bring forth the man that came into thy house, that we may know him'. ²³And the man, the master of the house, went out unto them, and said unto them, 'Nay, my brethren, nay, I pray you, do not so wickedly; seeing that this man is come into my house, do not this folly. ²⁴Behold, here is my daughter a maiden, and his concubine, them I will bring out now, and humble ye them, and do with them what seemeth good unto you: but unto this man do not so vile a thing.' ²⁵But the men would not hearken to him: so the man took his concubine, and brought her forth unto them, and they knew her, and abused her all the night until the morning: and when the day began to spring, they let her go. ²⁶Then came the woman in the dawning of the day, and fell down at the door of the man's house where her lord was, till it was light. ²⁷And her lord rose up in the morning, and opened the doors of the house, and went out to go his way: and behold, the woman his concubine was fallen down at the door of the house, and her hands were upon the threshold. ²⁸And he said unto her, 'Up, and let us be going'. But none answered. Then the man took her up upon an ass, and the man rose up, and got him unto his place.

²⁹And when he was come into his house, he took a knife, and laid hold on his concubine, and divided her, together with her bones, into twelve pieces, and sent her into all the coasts of Israel. ³⁰And it was so, that all that saw it said, 'There was no such deed done nor seen from the day that the children of Israel came up out of the land of Egypt unto this day: consider of it, take advice, and speak your minds'.

20 Then all the children of Israel went out, and the congregation was gathered together as one man, from Dan even to Beer-sheba, with the land of Gilead, unto the Lᴏʀᴅ in Mizpeh. ²And the chief of all the people, even of all the tribes of Israel, presented themselves in the assembly of the people of God, four hundred thousand footmen that drew sword. ³(Now the children of Benjamin heard that the children of Israel were gone up to Mizpeh.) Then said the children of Israel, 'Tell us, how was this wickedness?' ⁴And the Levite, the husband of the woman that was slain, answered and said, 'I came into Gibeah that belongeth to Benjamin, I and my concubine, to lodge. ⁵And the men of Gibeah rose against me, and beset the house round about upon me by night, and thought to have slain me: and my concubine have they forced, that she is dead. ⁶And I took my concubine, and cut her in pieces, and sent her throughout all the country of the inheritance of Israel: for they have committed lewdness and folly in Israel. ⁷Behold, ye are all children of Israel; give here your advice and counsel.'

⁸And all the people arose as one man, saying, 'We will not any of us go to his tent, neither will we any of us turn into his house. ⁹But now this shall be the thing which we will do to Gibeah, we will go up by lot against it: ¹⁰and we will take ten men of a hundred throughout all the tribes of Israel, and a hundred of a thousand, and a thousand out of ten thousand, to fetch victual for the people, that they may do, when they come to Gibeah of Benjamin, according to all the folly that they have wrought in Israel.' ¹¹So all the men of Israel were gathered against the city, knit together as one man.

¹²And the tribes of Israel sent men through all the tribe of Benjamin, saying, 'What wickedness is this that is done among you? ¹³Now therefore deliver us the men, the children of Belial, which are in Gibeah, that we may put them to death, and put away evil from Israel.' But the children of Benjamin would not hearken to the voice of their brethren the children of Israel. ¹⁴But the children of Benjamin gathered themselves together out of the cities unto Gibeah, to go out to battle against the children of Israel. ¹⁵And the children of Benjamin were numbered at that time out of the cities twenty and six thousand men that drew sword, besides the inhabitants of Gibeah, which were numbered seven hundred chosen men. ¹⁶Among all this people there were seven hundred chosen men left-handed; every one could sling stones at a hairbreadth, and not miss. ¹⁷And the men of Israel, besides Benjamin, were numbered four hundred thousand men that drew sword: all these were men of war.

¹⁸And the children of Israel arose, and went up to the house of God, and asked counsel of God, and said, 'Which of us shall go up first to the battle against the children of Benjamin?' And the LORD said, 'Judah shall go up first'. ¹⁹And the children of Israel rose up in the morning, and encamped against Gibeah. ²⁰And the men of Israel went out to battle against Benjamin, and the men of Israel put themselves in array to fight against them at Gibeah. ²¹And the children of Benjamin came forth out of Gibeah, and destroyed down to the ground of the Israelites that day twenty and two thousand men. ²²And the people the men of Israel encouraged themselves, and set their battle again in array in the place where they put themselves in array the first day. ²³(And the children of Israel went up and wept before the LORD until even, and asked counsel of the LORD, saying, 'Shall I go up again to battle against the children of Benjamin my brother?' And the LORD said, 'Go up against him'.) ²⁴And the children of Israel came near against the children of Benjamin the second day. ²⁵And Benjamin went forth against them out of Gibeah the second day, and destroyed down to the ground of the children of Israel again eighteen thousand men; all these drew the sword.

²⁶Then all the children of Israel, and all the people went up, and came unto the house of God, and wept, and sat there before the LORD, and fasted that day until even, and offered burnt offerings and peace offerings before the LORD. ²⁷And the children of Israel inquired of the LORD (for the ark of the covenant of God was there in those days, ²⁸and Phinehas, the son of Eleazar, the son of Aaron, stood before it in those days), saying, 'Shall I yet again go out to battle against the children of Benjamin my brother, or shall I cease?' And the LORD said, 'Go up; for tomorrow I will deliver them into thy hand'. ²⁹And Israel set liers in wait round about Gibeah. ³⁰And the children of Israel went up against the children of Benjamin on the third day, and put themselves in array against Gibeah, as at other times. ³¹And the children of Benjamin went out against the people, and were drawn away from the city; and they began to smite of the people, and kill, as at other times, in the highways, of which one goeth up to the house of God, and the other to Gibeah in the field, about thirty men of Israel. ³²And the children of Benjamin said, 'They are smitten down before us, as at the first'. But the children of Israel said, 'Let us flee, and draw them from the city unto the highways'. ³³And all the men of Israel rose up out of their place, and put themselves in array at Baal-tamar: and the liers in wait of Israel came forth out of their places, even out of the meadows of Gibeah. ³⁴And there came against Gibeah ten thousand chosen men out of all Israel, and the battle was sore: but they knew not that evil was near them. ³⁵And the LORD smote Benjamin before Israel: and the children of Israel destroyed of the Benjamites that day twenty and five thousand and a hundred men: all these drew the sword.

³⁶So the children of Benjamin saw that they were smitten: for the men of Israel gave place to the Benjamites, because they trusted unto the liers in wait which they had set beside Gibeah. ³⁷And the liers in wait hasted, and rushed upon Gibeah; and the liers in wait drew themselves along, and smote all the city with the edge of the sword. ³⁸Now there was an appointed sign between the men of Israel and the liers in wait, that they should make a great flame with smoke rise up out of the city. ³⁹And when the men of Israel retired in the battle, Benjamin began to smite and kill of the men of Israel about thirty persons: for they said, 'Surely they are smitten down before us, as in the first battle'. ⁴⁰But when the flame began to arise up out of the city with a pillar of smoke, the Benjamites looked behind them, and behold, the flame of the city ascended up to heaven. ⁴¹And when the men of Israel turned again, the men of Benjamin were amazed: for they saw that evil was come upon them. ⁴²Therefore they turned their backs before the men of Israel unto the way of the wilderness, but the battle overtook them; and them which came out of the cities they destroyed in the midst of them. ⁴³Thus they enclosed the Benjamites round about, and chased them, and trod them down with ease over against Gibeah toward the sunrising. ⁴⁴And there fell of Benjamin eighteen thousand men; all these were men of valour. ⁴⁵And they turned and fled toward the wilderness unto the rock of Rimmon: and they gleaned of them in the highways five

thousand men; and pursued hard after them unto Gidom, and slew two thousand men of them. ⁴⁶So that all which fell that day of Benjamin were twenty and five thousand men that drew the sword; all these were men of valour. ⁴⁷But six hundred men turned and fled to the wilderness unto the rock Rimmon, and abode in the rock Rimmon four months. ⁴⁸And the men of Israel turned again upon the children of Benjamin, and smote them with the edge of the sword, as well the men of every city, as the beast, and all that came to hand: also they set on fire all the cities that they came to.

21 Now the men of Israel had sworn in Mizpeh, saying, 'There shall not any of us give his daughter unto Benjamin to wife'. ²And the people came to the house of God, and abode there till even before God, and lifted up their voices, and wept sore: ³and said, 'O LORD God of Israel, why is this come to pass in Israel, that there should be today one tribe lacking in Israel?' ⁴And it came to pass on the morrow, that the people rose early, and built there an altar, and offered burnt offerings and peace offerings. ⁵And the children of Israel said, 'Who is there among all the tribes of Israel that came not up with the congregation unto the LORD?' For they had made a great oath concerning him that came not up to the LORD to Mizpeh, saying, 'He shall surely be put to death'. ⁶And the children of Israel repented them for Benjamin their brother, and said, 'There is one tribe cut off from Israel this day. ⁷How shall we do for wives for them that remain, seeing we have sworn by the LORD that we will not give them of our daughters to wives?'

⁸And they said, 'What one is there of the tribes of Israel that came not up to Mizpeh to the LORD?' And behold, there came none to the camp from Jabesh-gilead to the assembly. ⁹For the people were numbered, and behold, there were none of the inhabitants of Jabesh-gilead there. ¹⁰And the congregation sent thither twelve thousand men of the valiantest, and commanded them, saying, 'Go and smite the inhabitants of Jabesh-gilead with the edge of the sword, with the women and the children. ¹¹And this is the thing that ye shall do, ye shall utterly destroy every male, and every woman that hath lain by man.' ¹²And they found among the inhabitants of Jabesh-gilead four hundred young virgins that had known no man by lying with any male: and they brought them unto the camp to Shiloh, which is in the land of Canaan. ¹³And the whole congregation sent some to speak to the children of Benjamin that were in the rock Rimmon, and to call peaceably unto them. ¹⁴And Benjamin came again at that time, and they gave them wives which they had saved alive of the women of Jabesh-gilead: and yet so they sufficed them not. ¹⁵And the people repented them for Benjamin, because that the LORD had made a breach in the tribes of Israel.

¹⁶Then the elders of the congregation said, 'How shall we do for wives for them that remain, seeing the women are destroyed out of Benjamin?' ¹⁷And they said, 'There must be an inheritance for them that be escaped of Benjamin, that a tribe be not destroyed out of Israel. ¹⁸Howbeit we may not give them wives of our daughters: for the children

of Israel have sworn, saying, "Cursed be he that giveth a wife to Benjamin".' [19]Then they said, 'Behold, there is a feast of the Lord in Shiloh yearly in a place which is on the north side of Beth-el, on the east side of the highway that goeth up from Beth-el to Shechem, and on the south of Lebanon'. [20]Therefore they commanded the children of Benjamin, saying, 'Go and lie in wait in the vineyards. [21]And see, and behold, if the daughters of Shiloh come out to dance in dances, then come ye out of the vineyards, and catch you every man his wife of the daughters of Shiloh, and go to the land of Benjamin. [22]And it shall be, when their fathers or their brethren come unto us to complain, that we will say unto them, "Be favourable unto them for our sakes: because we reserved not to each man his wife in the war: for ye did not give unto them at this time, that you should be guilty".' [23]And the children of Benjamin did so, and took them wives, according to their number, of them that danced, whom they caught: and they went and returned unto their inheritance, and repaired the cities, and dwelt in them. [24]And the children of Israel departed thence at that time, every man to his tribe and to his family, and they went out from thence every man to his inheritance.

[25]In those days there was no king in Israel: every man did that which was right in his own eyes.

THE BOOK OF
RUTH

1 Now it came to pass in the days when the judges ruled, that there was a famine in the land. And a certain man of Beth-lehem-judah went to sojourn in the country of Moab, he, and his wife, and his two sons. ²And the name of the man was Elimelech, and the name of his wife Naomi, and the name of his two sons Mahlon and Chilion, Ephrathites of Beth-lehem-judah. And they came into the country of Moab, and continued there. ³And Elimelech Naomi's husband died; and she was left, and her two sons. ⁴And they took them wives of the women of Moab: the name of the one was Orpah, and the name of the other Ruth: and they dwelt there about ten years. ⁵And Mahlon and Chilion died also both of them, and the woman was left of her two sons and her husband.

⁶Then she arose with her daughters-in-law, that she might return from the country of Moab: for she had heard in the country of Moab how that the LORD had visited his people in giving them bread. ⁷Wherefore she went forth out of the place where she was, and her two daughters-in-law with her: and they went on the way to return unto the land of Judah. ⁸And Naomi said unto her two daughters-in-law, 'Go, return each to her mother's house: the LORD deal kindly with you, as ye have dealt with the dead, and with me. ⁹The LORD grant you that you may find rest, each of you in the house of her husband.' Then she kissed them; and they lifted up their voice, and wept. ¹⁰And they said unto her, 'Surely we will return with thee unto thy people'. ¹¹And Naomi said, 'Turn again, my daughters: why will you go with me? Are there yet any more sons in my womb, that they may be your husbands? ¹²Turn again, my daughters, go your way, for I am too old to have a husband. If I should say, I have hope, if I should have a husband also tonight, and should also bear sons: ¹³would ye tarry for them till they were grown? would ye stay for them from having husbands? nay, my daughters: for it grieveth me much for your sakes that the hand of the LORD is gone out against me.' ¹⁴And they lifted up their voice, and wept again: and Orpah kissed her mother-in-law, but Ruth cleaved unto her. ¹⁵And she said, 'Behold, thy sister-in-law is gone back unto her people, and unto her gods: return thou after thy sister-in-law'. ¹⁶And Ruth said, 'Entreat me not to leave thee, or to return from following after thee: for whither thou goest, I will go; and where thou lodgest, I will lodge: thy people shall be my people, and thy God my God: ¹⁷where thou diest, will I die, and there will I be buried: the LORD do so to me, and more also, if aught but death part thee and me'. ¹⁸When she saw that she was steadfastly minded to go with her, then she left speaking unto her.

¹⁹So they two went until they came to Beth-lehem. And it came to pass, when they were come to Beth-lehem, that all the city was moved about them, and they said,' Is this Naomi?' ²⁰And she said unto them,

'Call me not Naomi, call me Mara: for the Almighty hath dealt very bitterly with me. ²¹I went out full, and the LORD hath brought me home again empty: why then call ye me Naomi, seeing the LORD hath testified against me, and the Almighty hath afflicted me?' ²²So Naomi returned, and Ruth the Moabitess, her daughter-in-law, with her, which returned out of the country of Moab: and they came to Beth-lehem in the beginning of barley harvest.

2 And Naomi had a kinsman of her husband's, a mighty man of wealth, of the family of Elimelech, and his name was Boaz. ²And Ruth the Moabitess said unto Naomi, 'Let me now go to the field, and glean ears of corn after him in whose sight I shall find grace'. And she said unto her, 'Go, my daughter'. ³And she went, and came, and gleaned in the field after the reapers: and her hap was to light on a part of the field belonging unto Boaz, who was of the kindred of Elimelech.

⁴And behold, Boaz came from Beth-lehem, and said unto the reapers, 'The LORD be with you'. And they answered him, 'The LORD bless thee'. ⁵Then said Boaz unto his servant that was set over the reapers, 'Whose damsel is this?' ⁶And the servant that was set over the reapers answered and said, 'It is the Moabitish damsel that came back with Naomi out of the country of Moab: ⁷and she said, "I pray you, let me glean and gather after the reapers amongst the sheaves": so she came, and hath continued even from the morning until now, that she tarried a little in the house'. ⁸Then said Boaz unto Ruth, 'Hearest thou not, my daughter? Go not to glean in another field, neither go from hence, but abide here fast by my maidens. ⁹Let thy eyes be on the field that they do reap, and go thou after them: have I not charged the young men that they shall not touch thee? and when thou art athirst, go unto the vessels, and drink of that which the young men have drawn.' ¹⁰Then she fell on her face, and bowed herself to the ground, and said unto him, 'Why have I found grace in thy eyes, that thou shouldst take knowledge of me, seeing I am a stranger?' ¹¹And Boaz answered and said unto her, 'It hath fully been shown me, all that thou hast done unto thy mother-in-law since the death of thy husband: and how thou hast left thy father and thy mother, and the land of thy nativity, and art come unto a people which thou knewest not heretofore. ¹²The LORD recompense thy work, and a full reward be given thee of the LORD God of Israel, under whose wings thou art come to trust.' ¹³Then she said, 'Let me find favour in thy sight, my lord, for that thou hast comforted me, and for that thou hast spoken friendly unto thy handmaid, though I be not like unto one of thy handmaidens'. ¹⁴And Boaz said unto her, 'At meal-time come thou hither, and eat of the bread, and dip thy morsel in the vinegar'. And she sat beside the reapers: and he reached her parched corn, and she did eat, and was sufficed, and left. ¹⁵And when she was risen up to glean, Boaz commanded his young men, saying, 'Let her glean even among the sheaves, and reproach her not. ¹⁶And let fall also some of the handfuls of purpose for her, and leave them that she may glean them, and rebuke her not.' ¹⁷So she gleaned in the field until even, and beat out that she had gleaned: and it was about an ephah of barley.

¹⁸And she took it up, and went into the city: and her mother-in-law saw what she had gleaned: and she brought forth, and gave to her that she had reserved after she was sufficed. ¹⁹And her mother-in-law said unto her, 'Where hast thou gleaned today? and where wroughtest thou? blessed be he that did take knowledge of thee'. And she showed her mother-in-law with whom she had wrought, and said, 'The man's name with whom I wrought to day is Boaz'. ²⁰And Naomi said unto her daughter-in-law, 'Blessed be he of the LORD, who hath not left off his kindness to the living and to the dead'. And Naomi said unto her, 'The man is near of kin unto us, one of our next kinsmen'. ²¹And Ruth the Moabitess said, 'He said unto me also, "Thou shalt keep fast by my young men, until they have ended all my harvest"'. ²²And Naomi said unto Ruth her daughter-in-law, 'It is good, my daughter, that thou go out with his maidens, that they meet thee not in any other field'. ²³So she kept fast by the maidens of Boaz to glean unto the end of barley harvest and of wheat harvest; and dwelt with her mother-in-law.

3 Then Naomi her mother-in-law said unto her, 'My daughter, shall I not seek rest for thee, that it may be well with thee? ²And now is not Boaz of our kindred, with whose maidens thou wast? Behold, he winnoweth barley tonight in the threshing-floor. ³Wash thyself therefore, and anoint thee, and put thy raiment upon thee, and get thee down to the floor: but make not thyself known unto the man, until he shall have done eating and drinking. ⁴And it shall be, when he lieth down, that thou shalt mark the place where he shall lie, and thou shalt go in, and uncover his feet, and lay thee down, and he will tell thee what thou shalt do.' ⁵And she said unto her, 'All that thou sayest unto me I will do'.

⁶And she went down unto the floor, and did according to all that her mother-in-law bade her. ⁷And when Boaz had eaten and drunk, and his heart was merry, he went to lie down at the end of the heap of corn: and she came softly, and uncovered his feet, and laid her down.

⁸And it came to pass at midnight, that the man was afraid, and turned himself: and behold, a woman lay at his feet. ⁹And he said, 'Who art thou?' And she answered, 'I am Ruth thy handmaid: spread therefore thy skirt over thy handmaid, for thou art a near kinsman'. ¹⁰And he said, 'Blessed be thou of the LORD, my daughter: for thou hast shown more kindness in the latter end than at the beginning, inasmuch as thou followedst not young men, whether poor or rich. ¹¹And now, my daughter, fear not, I will do to thee all that thou requirest: for all the city of my people doth know that thou art a virtuous woman. ¹²And now it is true that I am thy near kinsman: howbeit there is a kinsman nearer than I. ¹³Tarry this night, and it shall be in the morning, that if he will perform unto thee the part of a kinsman, well, let him do the kinsman's part: but if he will not do the part of a kinsman to thee, then will I do the part of a kinsman to thee, as the LORD liveth: lie down until the morning.'

¹⁴And she lay at his feet until the morning: and she rose up before one could know another. And he said, 'Let it not be known that a woman came into the floor'. ¹⁵Also he said, 'Bring the veil that thou

hast upon thee, and hold it'. And when she held it, he measured six measures of barley, and laid it on her: and he went into the city. ¹⁶And when she came to her mother-in-law, she said, 'Who art thou, my daughter?' And she told her all that the man had done to her. ¹⁷And she said, 'These six measures of barley gave he me, for he said to me, "Go not empty unto thy mother-in-law"'. ¹⁸Then said she, 'Sit still, my daughter, until thou know how the matter will fall: for the man will not be in rest, until he have finished the thing this day'.

4 Then went Boaz up to the gate, and sat him down there: and behold, the kinsman of whom Boaz spoke came by; unto whom he said, 'Ho, such a one: turn aside, sit down here'. And he turned aside, and sat down. ²And he took ten men of the elders of the city, and said, 'Sit ye down here'. And they sat down. ³And he said unto the kinsman, 'Naomi, that is come again out of the country of Moab, selleth a parcel of land, which was our brother Elimelech's. ⁴And I thought to advertise thee, saying, "Buy it before the inhabitants, and before the elders of my people". If thou wilt redeem it, redeem it, but if thou wilt not redeem it, then tell me, that I may know: for there is none to redeem it besides thee, and I am after thee'. And he said, 'I will redeem it'. ⁵Then said Boaz, 'What day thou buyest the field of the hand of Naomi, thou must buy it also of Ruth the Moabitess, the wife of the dead, to raise up the name of the dead upon his inheritance'.

⁶And the kinsman said, 'I cannot redeem it for myself, lest I mar my own inheritance: redeem thou my right to thyself, for I cannot redeem it'. ⁷Now this was the manner in former time in Israel concerning redeeming and concerning changing, for to confirm all things: a man plucked off his shoe, and gave it to his neighbour: and this was a testimony in Israel. ⁸Therefore the kinsman said unto Boaz, 'Buy it for thee'. So he drew off his shoe.

⁹And Boaz said unto the elders, and unto all the people, 'Ye are witnesses this day, that I have bought all that was Elimelech's, and all that was Chilion's and Mahlon's, of the hand of Naomi. ¹⁰Moreover Ruth the Moabitess, the wife of Mahlon, have I purchased to be my wife, to raise up the name of the dead upon his inheritance, that the name of the dead be not cut off from among his brethren, and from the gate of his place: ye are witnesses this day.' ¹¹And all the people that were in the gate, and the elders said, 'We are witnesses. The LORD make the woman that is come into thy house like Rachel and like Leah, which two did build the house of Israel: and do thou worthily in Ephratah, and be famous in Beth-lehem. ¹²And let thy house be like the house of Pharez, whom Tamar bore unto Judah, of the seed which the LORD shall give thee of this young woman.'

¹³So Boaz took Ruth, and she was his wife: and when he went in unto her, the LORD gave her conception, and she bore a son. ¹⁴And the women said unto Naomi, 'Blessed be the LORD, which hath not left thee this day without a kinsman, that his name may be famous in Israel. ¹⁵And he shall be unto thee a restorer of thy life, and a nourisher of thy old age: for thy daughter-in-law, which loveth thee, which is better to thee than

seven sons, hath borne him.' [16]And Naomi took the child, and laid it in her bosom, and became nurse unto it. [17]And the women her neighbours gave it a name, saying, 'There is a son born to Naomi', and they called his name Obed: he is the father of Jesse, the father of David.

[18]Now these are the generations of Pharez: Pharez begot Hezron, [19]and Hezron begot Ram, and Ram begot Amminadab, [20]and Amminadab begot Nahshon, and Nahshon begot Salmon, [21]and Salmon begot Boaz, and Boaz begot Obed, [22]and Obed begot Jesse, and Jesse begot David.

begot = father of

Ruth became an

THE FIRST BOOK OF
SAMUEL
OTHERWISE CALLED
THE FIRST BOOK OF THE KINGS

1 Now there was a certain man of Ramathaim-zophim, of mount Ephraim, and his name was Elkanah, the son of Jeroham, the son of Elihu, the son of Tohu, the son of Zuph, an Ephrathite: ²and he had two wives; the name of the one was Hannah, and the name of the other Peninnah: and Peninnah had children, but Hannah had no children. ³And this man went up out of his city yearly to worship and to sacrifice unto the LORD of hosts in Shiloh. And the two sons of Eli, Hophni and Phinehas, the priests of the LORD, were there.

⁴And when the time was that Elkanah offered, he gave to Peninnah his wife, and to all her sons and her daughters, portions. ⁵But unto Hannah he gave a worthy portion; for he loved Hannah, but the LORD had shut up her womb. ⁶And her adversary also provoked her sore, for to make her fret, because the LORD had shut up her womb. ⁷And as he did so year by year, when she went up to the house of the LORD, so she provoked her; therefore she wept, and did not eat. ⁸Then said Elkanah her husband to her, 'Hannah, why weepest thou? and why eatest thou not? and why is thy heart grieved? Am not I better to thee than ten sons?'

⁹So Hannah rose up after they had eaten in Shiloh, and after they had drunk (now Eli the priest sat upon a seat by a post of the temple of the LORD). ¹⁰And she was in bitterness of soul, and prayed unto the LORD, and wept sore. ¹¹And she vowed a vow, and said, 'O LORD of hosts, if thou wilt indeed look on the affliction of thy handmaid, and remember me, and not forget thy handmaid, but wilt give unto thy handmaid a man-child, then I will give him unto the LORD all the days of his life, and there shall no razor come upon his head'. ¹²And it came to pass, as she continued praying before the LORD, that Eli marked her mouth. ¹³Now Hannah, she spoke in her heart, only her lips moved, but her voice was not heard: therefore Eli thought she had been drunken. ¹⁴And Eli said unto her, 'How long wilt thou be drunken? put away thy wine from thee'. ¹⁵And Hannah answered and said, 'No, my lord, I am a woman of a sorrowful spirit: I have drunk neither wine nor strong drink, but have poured out my soul before the LORD. ¹⁶Count not thy handmaid for a daughter of Belial: for out of the abundance of my complaint and grief have I spoken hitherto.' ¹⁷Then Eli answered and said, 'Go in peace: and the God of Israel grant thee thy petition that thou hast asked of him'. ¹⁸And she said, 'Let thy handmaid find grace in thy sight'. So the woman went her way, and did eat, and her countenance was no more sad.

¹⁹And they rose up in the morning early, and worshipped before the LORD, and returned, and came to their house to Ramah: and Elkanah

knew Hannah his wife, and the Lord remembered her. ²⁰Wherefore it came to pass, when the time was come about after Hannah had conceived, that she bore a son, and called his name Samuel, saying, 'Because I have asked him of the Lord'. ²¹And the man Elkanah, and all his house, went up to offer unto the Lord the yearly sacrifice, and his vow. ²²But Hannah went not up; for she said unto her husband, 'I will not go up until the child be weaned, and then I will bring him, that he may appear before the Lord, and there abide for ever'. ²³And Elkanah her husband said unto her, 'Do what seemeth thee good, tarry until thou have weaned him, only the Lord establish his word'. So the woman abode, and gave her son suck until she weaned him.

²⁴And when she had weaned him, she took him up with her, with three bullocks, and one ephah of flour, and a bottle of wine, and brought him unto the house of the Lord in Shiloh: and the child was young. ²⁵And they slew a bullock, and brought the child to Eli. ²⁶And she said, 'O my lord, as thy soul liveth, my lord, I am the woman that stood by thee here, praying unto the Lord. ²⁷For this child I prayed, and the Lord hath given me my petition which I asked of him: ²⁸therefore also I have lent him to the Lord; as long as he liveth he shall be lent to the Lord.' And he worshipped the Lord there.

2 And Hannah prayed, and said,

> 'My heart rejoiceth in the Lord,
>   my horn is exalted in the Lord:
>   my mouth is enlarged over my enemies:
>   because I rejoice in thy salvation.
> ² There is none holy as the Lord:
>   for there is none besides thee:
>   neither is there any rock like our God.
> ³ Talk no more so exceeding proudly,
>   let not arrogance come out of your mouth:
>   for the Lord is a God of knowledge,
>   and by him actions are weighed.
> ⁴ The bows of the mighty men are broken,
>   and they that stumbled are girt with strength.
> ⁵ They that were full have hired out themselves for bread;
>   and they that were hungry ceased:
>   so that the barren hath borne seven,
>   and she that hath many children is waxed feeble.
> ⁶ The Lord killeth, and maketh alive:
>   he bringeth down to the grave, and bringeth up.
> ⁷ The Lord maketh poor, and maketh rich:
>   he bringeth low, and lifteth up.
> ⁸ He raiseth up the poor out of the dust,
>   and lifteth up the beggar from the dunghill,
>   to set them among princes,
>   and to make them inherit the throne of glory:

for the pillars of the earth are the LORD's,
and he hath set the world upon them.
⁹ He will keep the feet of his saints,
and the wicked shall be silent in darkness;
for by strength shall no man prevail.
¹⁰ The adversaries of the LORD shall be broken to pieces;
out of heaven shall he thunder upon them:
the LORD shall judge the ends of the earth,
and he shall give strength unto his king,
and exalt the horn of his anointed.'

¹¹And Elkanah went to Ramah to his house. And the child did minister unto the LORD before Eli the priest.

¹²Now the sons of Eli were sons of Belial, they knew not the LORD. ¹³And the priests' custom with the people was, that when any man offered sacrifice, the priest's servant came, while the flesh was in seething, with a fleshhook of three teeth in his hand, ¹⁴and he struck it into the pan, or kettle, or cauldron, or pot: all that the fleshhook brought up the priest took for himself. So they did in Shiloh unto all the Israelites that came thither. ¹⁵Also before they burnt the fat, the priest's servant came, and said to the man that sacrificed, 'Give flesh to roast for the priest, for he will not have seethed flesh of thee, but raw'. ¹⁶And if any man said unto him, 'Let them not fail to burn the fat presently, and then take as much as thy soul desireth': then he would answer him, 'Nay, but thou shalt give it me now: and if not, I will take it by force'. ¹⁷Wherefore the sin of the young men was very great before the LORD: for men abhorred the offering of the LORD.

¹⁸But Samuel ministered before the LORD, being a child, girded with a linen ephod. ¹⁹Moreover his mother made him a little coat, and brought it to him from year to year, when she came up with her husband to offer the yearly sacrifice.

²⁰And Eli blessed Elkanah and his wife, and said, 'The LORD give thee seed of this woman for the loan which is lent to the LORD'. And they went unto their own home. ²¹And the LORD visited Hannah, so that she conceived, and bore three sons and two daughters. And the child Samuel grew before the LORD.

²²Now Eli was very old, and heard all that his sons did unto all Israel, and how they lay with the women that assembled at the door of the tabernacle of the congregation. ²³And he said unto them, 'Why do ye such things? for I hear of your evil dealings by all this people. ²⁴Nay, my sons: for it is no good report that I hear; ye make the LORD's people to transgress. ²⁵If one man sin against another, the judge shall judge him: but if a man sin against the LORD, who shall entreat for him?' Notwithstanding they hearkened not unto the voice of their father, because the LORD would slay them. ²⁶(And the child Samuel grew on, and was in favour both with the LORD, and also with men.)

²⁷And there came a man of God unto Eli, and said unto him, 'Thus saith the LORD, "Did I plainly appear unto the house of thy father, when

they were in Egypt in Pharaoh's house? ²⁸And did I choose him out of all the tribes of Israel to be my priest, to offer upon my altar, to burn incense, to wear an ephod before me? and did I give unto the house of thy father all the offerings made by fire of the children of Israel? ²⁹Wherefore kick ye at my sacrifice and at my offering, which I have commanded in my habitation, and honourest thy sons above me, to make yourselves fat with the chiefest of all the offerings of Israel my people?" ³⁰Wherefore the Lᴏʀᴅ God of Israel saith, "I said indeed that thy house, and the house of thy father, should walk before me for ever": but now the Lᴏʀᴅ saith, "Be it far from me; for them that honour me I will honour, and they that despise me shall be lightly esteemed. ³¹Behold, the days come, that I will cut off thy arm, and the arm of thy father's house, that there shall not be an old man in thy house. ³²And thou shalt see an enemy in my habitation, in all the wealth which God shall give Israel: and there shall not be an old man in thy house for ever. ³³And the man of thine, whom I shall not cut off from my altar, shall be to consume thy eyes, and to grieve thy heart: and all the increase of thy house shall die in the flower of their age. ³⁴And this shall be a sign unto thee, that shall come upon thy two sons, on Hophni and Phinehas: in one day they shall die both of them. ³⁵And I will raise me up a faithful priest, that shall do according to that which is in my heart and in my mind, and I will build him a sure house, and he shall walk before my anointed for ever. ³⁶And it shall come to pass, that every one that is left in thy house shall come and crouch to him for a piece of silver and a morsel of bread, and shall say, 'Put me, I pray thee, into one of the priests' offices, that I may eat a piece of bread'."'

3 And the child Samuel ministered unto the Lᴏʀᴅ before Eli. And the word of the Lᴏʀᴅ was precious in those days; there was no open vision. ²And it came to pass at that time, when Eli was laid down in his place, and his eyes began to wax dim, that he could not see; ³and ere the lamp of God went out in the temple of the Lᴏʀᴅ, where the ark of God was, and Samuel was laid down to sleep, ⁴that the Lᴏʀᴅ called Samuel, and he answered, 'Here am I'. ⁵And he ran unto Eli, and said, 'Here am I, for thou calledst me'. And he said, 'I called not, lie down again'. And he went and lay down. ⁶And the Lᴏʀᴅ called yet again, 'Samuel'. And Samuel arose and went to Eli, and said, 'Here am I, for thou didst call me'. And he answered, 'I called not, my son; lie down again'. ⁷Now Samuel did not yet know the Lᴏʀᴅ, neither was the word of the Lᴏʀᴅ yet revealed unto him. ⁸And the Lᴏʀᴅ called Samuel again the third time. And he arose and went to Eli, and said, 'Here am I, for thou didst call me'. And Eli perceived that the Lᴏʀᴅ had called the child. ⁹Therefore Eli said unto Samuel, 'Go, lie down, and it shall be, if he call thee, that thou shalt say, "Speak, Lᴏʀᴅ, for thy servant heareth"'. So Samuel went and lay down in his place. ¹⁰And the Lᴏʀᴅ came, and stood, and called as at other times, 'Samuel, Samuel'. Then Samuel answered, 'Speak, for thy servant heareth'.

¹¹And the Lᴏʀᴅ said to Samuel, 'Behold, I will do a thing in Israel, at which both the ears of every one that heareth it shall tingle. ¹²In that

day I will perform against Eli all things which I have spoken concerning his house: when I begin, I will also make an end. [13]For I have told him that I will judge his house for ever for the iniquity which he knoweth: because his sons made themselves vile, and he restrained them not. [14]And therefore I have sworn unto the house of Eli, that the iniquity of Eli's house shall not be purged with sacrifice nor offering for ever.'

[15]And Samuel lay until the morning, and opened the doors of the house of the LORD. And Samuel feared to show Eli the vision. [16]Then Eli called Samuel, and said, 'Samuel, my son'. And he answered, 'Here am I'. [17]And he said, 'What is the thing that the LORD hath said unto thee? I pray thee hide it not from me: God do so to thee, and more also, if thou hide anything from me of all the things that he said unto thee.' [18]And Samuel told him every whit, and hid nothing from him. And he said, 'It is the LORD: let him do what seemeth him good'.

[19]And Samuel grew, and the LORD was with him, and did let none of his words fall to the ground. [20]And all Israel from Dan even to Beersheba knew that Samuel was established to be a prophet of the LORD. [21]And the LORD appeared again in Shiloh: for the LORD revealed himself to Samuel in Shiloh by the word of the LORD.

4 And the word of Samuel came to all Israel. Now Israel went out against the Philistines to battle, and pitched beside Eben-ezer: and the Philistines pitched in Aphek. [2]And the Philistines put themselves in array against Israel: and when they joined battle, Israel was smitten before the Philistines: and they slew of the army in the field about four thousand men. [3]And when the people were come into the camp, the elders of Israel said, 'Wherefore hath the LORD smitten us today before the Philistines? Let us fetch the ark of the covenant of the LORD out of Shiloh unto us, that when it cometh among us, it may save us out of the hand of our enemies.' [4]So the people sent to Shiloh, that they might bring from thence the ark of the covenant of the LORD of hosts, which dwelleth between the cherubims: and the two sons of Eli, Hophni and Phinehas, were there with the ark of the covenant of God. [5]And when the ark of the covenant of the LORD came into the camp, all Israel shouted with a great shout, so that the earth rang again. [6]And when the Philistines heard the noise of the shout, they said, 'What meaneth the noise of this great shout in the camp of the Hebrews?' And they understood that the ark of the LORD was come into the camp. [7]And the Philistines were afraid, for they said, 'God is come into the camp'. And they said, 'Woe unto us: for there hath not been such a thing heretofore. [8]Woe unto us: who shall deliver us out of the hand of these mighty Gods? these are the Gods that smote the Egyptians with all the plagues in the wilderness. [9]Be strong, and quit yourselves like men, O ye Philistines, that ye be not servants unto the Hebrews, as they have been to you: quit yourselves like men, and fight.' [10]And the Philistines fought, and Israel was smitten, and they fled every man into his tent: and there was a very great slaughter, for there fell of Israel thirty thousand footmen. [11]And the ark of God was taken, and the two sons of Eli, Hophni and Phinehas, were slain.

¹²And there ran a man of Benjamin out of the army, and came to Shiloh the same day with his clothes rent, and with earth upon his head. ¹³And when he came, lo, Eli sat upon a seat by the wayside watching: for his heart trembled for the ark of God. And when the man came into the city, and told it, all the city cried out. ¹⁴And when Eli heard the noise of the crying, he said, 'What meaneth the noise of this tumult?' And the man came in hastily, and told Eli. ¹⁵Now Eli was ninety and eight years old, and his eyes were dim, that he could not see. ¹⁶And the man said unto Eli, 'I am he that came out of the army, and I fled today out of the army'. And he said, 'What is there done, my son?' ¹⁷And the messenger answered and said, 'Israel is fled before the Philistines, and there hath been also a great slaughter among the people, and thy two sons also, Hophni and Phinehas, are dead, and the ark of God is taken'. ¹⁸And it came to pass, when he made mention of the ark of God, that he fell from off the seat backward by the side of the gate, and his neck broke, and he died: for he was an old man, and heavy. And he had judged Israel forty years.

¹⁹And his daughter-in-law, Phinehas' wife, was with child, near to be delivered: and when she heard the tidings that the ark of God was taken, and that her father-in-law and her husband were dead, she bowed herself and travailed; for her pains came upon her. ²⁰And about the time of her death the women that stood by her said unto her, 'Fear not, for thou hast borne a son'. But she answered not, neither did she regard it. ²¹And she named the child Ichabod, saying, 'The glory is departed from Israel': because the ark of God was taken, and because of her father-in-law and her husband. ²²And she said, 'The glory is departed from Israel: for the ark of God is taken'.

5 And the Philistines took the ark of God, and brought it from Ebenezer unto Ashdod. ²When the Philistines took the ark of God, they brought it into the house of Dagon, and set it by Dagon. ³And when they of Ashdod arose early on the morrow, behold, Dagon was fallen upon his face to the earth before the ark of the LORD. And they took Dagon, and set him in his place again. ⁴And when they arose early on the morrow morning, behold, Dagon was fallen upon his face to the ground before the ark of the LORD: and the head of Dagon and both the palms of his hands were cut off upon the threshold; only the stump of Dagon was left to him. ⁵Therefore neither the priests of Dagon, nor any that come into Dagon's house, tread on the threshold of Dagon in Ashdod unto this day.

⁶But the hand of the LORD was heavy upon them of Ashdod, and he destroyed them, and smote them with haemorrhoids, even Ashdod and the coasts thereof. ⁷And when the men of Ashdod saw that it was so, they said, 'The ark of the God of Israel shall not abide with us: for his hand is sore upon us, and upon Dagon our god'. ⁸They sent therefore and gathered all the lords of the Philistines unto them, and said, 'What shall we do with the ark of the God of Israel?' And they answered, 'Let the ark of the God of Israel be carried about unto Gath'. And they carried the ark of the God of Israel about thither. ⁹And it was so, that after

they had carried it about, the hand of the LORD was against the city with a very great destruction: and he smote the men of the city, both small and great, and they had haemorrhoids in their secret parts. ¹⁰Therefore they sent the ark of God to Ekron. And it came to pass, as the ark of God came to Ekron, that the Ekronites cried out, saying, 'They have brought about the ark of the God of Israel to us, to slay us and our people'. ¹¹So they sent and gathered together all the lords of the Philistines, and said, 'Send away the ark of the God of Israel, and let it go again to his own place, that it slay us not, and our people': for there was a deadly destruction throughout all the city: the hand of God was very heavy there. ¹²And the men that died not were smitten with the haemorrhoids: and the cry of the city went up to heaven.

6 And the ark of the LORD was in the country of the Philistines seven months. ²And the Philistines called for the priests and the diviners, saying, 'What shall we do to the ark of the LORD? Tell us wherewith we shall send it to his place.' ³And they said, 'If ye send away the ark of the God of Israel, send it not empty: but in any wise return him a trespass offering: then ye shall be healed, and it shall be known to you why his hand is not removed from you'. ⁴Then said they, 'What shall be the trespass offering which we shall return to him?' They answered, 'Five golden haemorrhoids, and five golden mice, according to the number of the lords of the Philistines: for one plague was on you all, and on your lords. ⁵Wherefore ye shall make images of your haemorrhoids, and images of your mice that mar the land; and ye shall give glory unto the God of Israel: peradventure he will lighten his hand from off you, and from off your gods, and from off your land. ⁶Wherefore then do ye harden your hearts, as the Egyptians and Pharaoh hardened their hearts? when he had wrought wonderfully among them, did they not let the people go, and they departed? ⁷Now therefore make a new cart, and take two milch-kine, on which there hath come no yoke, and tie the kine to the cart, and bring the calves home from them. ⁸And take the ark of the LORD, and lay it upon the cart, and put the jewels of gold, which ye return him for a trespass offering, in a coffer by the side thereof, and send it away, that it may go. ⁹And see, if it goeth up by the way of his own coast to Beth-shemesh, then he hath done us this great evil: but if not, then we shall know that it is not his hand that smote us; it was a chance that happened to us.'

¹⁰And the men did so: and took two milch-kine, and tied them to the cart, and shut up their calves at home. ¹¹And they laid the ark of the LORD upon the cart, and the coffer with the mice of gold and the images of their haemorrhoids. ¹²And the kine took the straight way to the way of Beth-shemesh, and went along the highway, lowing as they went, and turned not aside to the right hand or to the left; and the lords of the Philistines went after them unto the border of Beth-shemesh. ¹³And they of Beth-shemesh were reaping their wheat harvest in the valley: and they lifted up their eyes, and saw the ark, and rejoiced to see it. ¹⁴And the cart came into the field of Joshua, a Beth-shemite, and stood there, where there was a great stone: and they cleft

the wood of the cart, and offered the kine, a burnt offering unto the LORD. ¹⁵And the Levites took down the ark of the LORD, and the coffer that was with it, wherein the jewels of gold were, and put them on the great stone: and the men of Beth-shemesh offered burnt offerings and sacrificed sacrifices the same day unto the LORD. ¹⁶And when the five lords of the Philistines had seen it, they returned to Ekron the same day.

¹⁷And these are the golden haemorrhoids which the Philistines returned for a trespass offering unto the LORD; for Ashdod one, for Gaza one, for Askelon one, for Gath one, for Ekron one; ¹⁸and the golden mice, according to the number of all the cities of the Philistines belonging to the five lords, both of fenced cities, and of country villages, even unto the great stone of Abel, whereon they set down the ark of the LORD: which stone remaineth unto this day in the field of Joshua, the Beth-shemite.

¹⁹And he smote the men of Beth-shemesh, because they had looked into the ark of the LORD, even he smote of the people fifty thousand and threescore and ten men: and the people lamented, because the LORD had smitten many of the people with a great slaughter. ²⁰And the men of Beth-shemesh said, 'Who is able to stand before this holy LORD God? and to whom shall he go up from us?'

²¹And they sent messengers to the inhabitants of Kirjath-jearim, saying, 'The Philistines have brought again the ark of the LORD; come ye down, and fetch it up to you'.

7 And the men of Kirjath-jearim came, and fetched up the ark of the LORD, and brought it into the house of Abinadab in the hill, and sanctified Eleazar his son to keep the ark of the LORD. ²And it came to pass, while the ark abode in Kirjath-jearim, that the time was long: for it was twenty years: and all the house of Israel lamented after the LORD. ³And Samuel spoke unto all the house of Israel, saying, 'If ye do return unto the LORD with all your hearts, then put away the strange gods and Ashtaroth from among you, and prepare your hearts unto the LORD, and serve him only: and he will deliver you out of the hand of the Philistines'. ⁴Then the children of Israel did put away Baalim and Ashtaroth, and served the LORD only.

⁵And Samuel said, 'Gather all Israel to Mizpeh, and I will pray for you unto the LORD'. ⁶And they gathered together to Mizpeh, and drew water, and poured it out before the LORD, and fasted on that day, and said there, 'We have sinned against the LORD'. And Samuel judged the children of Israel in Mizpeh.

⁷And when the Philistines heard that the children of Israel were gathered together to Mizpeh, the lords of the Philistines went up against Israel: and when the children of Israel heard it, they were afraid of the Philistines. ⁸And the children of Israel said to Samuel, 'Cease not to cry unto the LORD our God for us, that he will save us out of the hand of the Philistines'. ⁹And Samuel took a sucking lamb, and offered it for a burnt offering wholly unto the LORD; and Samuel cried unto the LORD for Israel, and the LORD heard him. ¹⁰And as Samuel was offering up the

burnt offering, the Philistines drew near to battle against Israel: but the LORD <u>thundered</u> with a great thunder on that day upon the Philistines, and discomfited them, and they were smitten before Israel. ¹¹And the men of Israel went out of Mizpeh, and pursued the Philistines, and smote them, until they came under Beth-car. ¹²Then Samuel took a stone, and set it between Mizpeh and Shen, and called the name of it Eben-ezer, saying, 'Hitherto hath the LORD helped us'.

¹³So the Philistines were subdued, and they came no more into the coast of Israel: and the hand of the LORD was against the Philistines all the days of Samuel. ¹⁴And the cities which the Philistines had taken from Israel were restored to Israel, from Ekron even unto Gath; and the coasts thereof did Israel deliver out of the hands of the Philistines. And there was peace between Israel and the Amorites.

¹⁵And Samuel judged Israel all the days of his life. ¹⁶And he went from year to year in circuit to Beth-el, and Gilgal, and Mizpeh, and judged Israel in all those places. ¹⁷And his return was to Ramah: for there was his house: and there he judged Israel, and there he built an altar unto the LORD.

8 And it came to pass, when Samuel was old, that he made his sons judges over Israel. ²Now the name of his firstborn was Joel, and the name of his second, Abiah: they were judges in Beer-sheba. ³And his sons walked not in his ways, but turned aside after lucre, and took bribes, and perverted judgement. ⁴Then all the elders of Israel gathered themselves together, and came to Samuel unto Ramah, ⁵and said unto him, 'Behold, thou art old, and thy sons walk not in thy ways: now make us a king to judge us like all the nations'.

⁶But the thing displeased Samuel, when they said, 'Give us a king to judge us'. And Samuel prayed unto the LORD. ⁷And the LORD said unto Samuel, 'Hearken unto the voice of the people in all that they say unto thee: for they have not rejected thee, but they have rejected me, that I should not reign over them. ⁸According to all the works which they have done since the day that I brought them up out of Egypt even unto this day, wherewith they have forsaken me, and served other gods, so do they also unto thee. ⁹Now therefore hearken unto their voice: howbeit yet protest solemnly unto them, and show them the manner of the king that shall reign over them.'

¹⁰And Samuel told all the words of the LORD unto the people that asked of him a king. ¹¹And he said, 'This will be the manner of the king that shall reign over you: he will take your sons, and appoint them for himself, for his chariots, and to be his horsemen; and some shall run before his chariots. ¹²And he will appoint him captains over thousands, and captains over fifties; and will set them to ear his ground, and to reap his harvest, and to make his instruments of war, and instruments of his chariots. ¹³And he will take your daughters to be confectionaries, and to be cooks, and to be bakers. ¹⁴And he will take your fields, and your vineyards, and your olive-yards, even the best of them, and give them to his servants. ¹⁵And he will take the tenth of your seed, and of your vineyards, and give to his officers, and to his servants. ¹⁶And he

will take your menservants, and your maidservants, and your goodliest young men, and your asses, and put them to his work. ¹⁷He will take the tenth of your sheep: and ye shall be his servants. ¹⁸And ye shall cry out in that day because of your king which ye shall have chosen you; and the LORD will not hear you in that day.'

¹⁹Nevertheless the people refused to obey the voice of Samuel; and they said, 'Nay, but we will have a king over us: ²⁰that we also may be like all the nations, and that our king may judge us, and go out before us, and fight our battles'. ²¹And Samuel heard all the words of the people, and he rehearsed them in the ears of the LORD. ²²And the LORD said to Samuel, 'Hearken unto their voice, and make them a king'. And Samuel said unto the men of Israel, 'Go ye every man unto his city'.

9 Now there was a man of Benjamin, whose name was Kish, the son of Abiel, the son of Zeror, the son of Bechorath, the son of Aphiah, a Benjamite, a mighty man of power. ²And he had a son, whose name was Saul, a choice young man, and a goodly: and there was not among the children of Israel a goodlier person than he: from his shoulders and upward he was higher than any of the people. ³And the asses of Kish, Saul's father, were lost. And Kish said to Saul his son, 'Take now one of the servants with thee, and arise, go seek the asses'. ⁴And he passed through mount Ephraim, and passed through the land of Shalisha, but they found them not: then they passed through the land of Shalim, and there they were not: and he passed through the land of the Benjamites, but they found them not. ⁵And when they were come to the land of Zuph, Saul said to his servant that was with him, 'Come, and let us return, lest my father leave caring for the asses, and take thought for us'. ⁶And he said unto him, 'Behold now, there is in this city a man of God, and he is an honourable man; all that he saith cometh surely to pass: now let us go thither; peradventure he can show us our way that we should go'. ⁷Then said Saul to his servant, 'But behold, if we go, what shall we bring the man? for the bread is spent in our vessels, and there is not a present to bring to the man of God: what have we?' ⁸And the servant answered Saul again, and said, 'Behold, I have here at hand the fourth part of a shekel of silver: that will I give to the man of God, to tell us our way'. ⁹(Beforetime in Israel, when a man went to inquire of God, thus he spoke, 'Come, and let us go to the seer': for he that is now called a Prophet was beforetime called a Seer.) ¹⁰Then said Saul to his servant, 'Well said; come, let us go'. So they went unto the city where the man of God was.

¹¹And as they went up the hill to the city, they found young maidens going out to draw water, and said unto them, 'Is the seer here?' ¹²And they answered them, and said, 'He is: behold, he is before you: make haste now, for he came today to the city; for there is a sacrifice of the people today in the high place. ¹³As soon as ye be come into the city, ye shall straightway find him, before he go up to the high place to eat: for the people will not eat until he come, because he doth bless the sacrifice; and afterwards they eat that be bidden. Now therefore get you up; for about this time ye shall find him.' ¹⁴And they went up into the city:

and when they were come into the city, behold, Samuel came out against them, for to go up to the high place.

¹⁵Now the LORD had told Samuel in his ear a day before Saul came, saying, ¹⁶'Tomorrow about this time I will send thee a man out of the land of Benjamin, and thou shalt anoint him to be captain over my people Israel, that he may save my people out of the hand of the Philistines: for I have looked upon my people, because their cry is come unto me'. ¹⁷And when Samuel saw Saul, the LORD said unto him, 'Behold the man whom I spoke to thee of: this same shall reign over my people'. ¹⁸Then Saul drew near to Samuel in the gate, and said, 'Tell me, I pray thee, where the seer's house is'. ¹⁹And Samuel answered Saul, and said, 'I am the seer: go up before me unto the high place, for ye shall eat with me today, and tomorrow I will let thee go, and will tell thee all that is in thy heart. ²⁰And as for thy asses that were lost three days ago, set not thy mind on them, for they are found. And on whom is all the desire of Israel? Is it not on thee, and on all thy father's house?' ²¹And Saul answered and said, 'Am not I a Benjamite, of the smallest of the tribes of Israel? and my family the least of all the families of the tribe of Benjamin? Wherefore then speakest thou so to me?' ²²And Samuel took Saul and his servant, and brought them into the parlour, and made them sit in the chiefest place among them that were bidden, which were about thirty persons. ²³And Samuel said unto the cook, 'Bring the portion which I gave thee, of which I said unto thee, "Set it by thee"'. ²⁴And the cook took up the shoulder, and that which was upon it, and set it before Saul. And Samuel said, 'Behold that which is left, set it before thee, and eat: for unto this time hath it been kept for thee, since I said I have invited the people'. So Saul did eat with Samuel that day.

²⁵And when they were come down from the high place into the city, Samuel communed with Saul upon the top of the house. ²⁶And they arose early: and it came to pass about the spring of the day, that Samuel called Saul to the top of the house, saying, 'Up, that I may send thee away'. And Saul arose, and they went out both of them, he and Samuel, abroad. ²⁷And as they were going down to the end of the city, Samuel said to Saul, 'Bid the servant pass on before us' (and he passed on), 'but stand thou still a while, that I may show thee the word of God'.

10 Then Samuel took a vial of oil, and poured it upon his head, and kissed him, and said, 'Is it not because the LORD hath anointed thee to be captain over his inheritance? ²When thou art departed from me today, then thou shalt find two men by Rachel's sepulchre in the border of Benjamin at Zelzah: and they will say unto thee, "The asses which thou wentest to seek are found: and lo, thy father hath left the care of the asses, and soroweth for you, saying, 'What shall I do for my son?'" ³Then shalt thou go on forward from thence, and thou shalt come to the plain of Tabor, and there shall meet thee three men going up to God to Beth-el, one carrying three kids, and another carrying three loaves of bread, and another carrying a bottle of wine. ⁴And they will salute thee, and give thee two loaves of bread; which thou shalt receive of their hands. ⁵After that thou shalt come to the hill of God, where is the garrison of the Philistines: and it shall come to pass when thou art come thither to the city, that thou shalt meet a company of prophets coming down from the high place with a psaltery, and a tabret, and a pipe, and a harp before them; and they shall prophesy. ⁶And the Spirit of the LORD will come upon thee, and thou shalt prophesy with them, and shalt be turned into another man. ⁷And let it be when these signs are come unto thee, that thou do as occasion serve thee, for God is with thee. ⁸And thou shalt go down before me to Gilgal; and behold, I will come down unto thee, to offer burnt offerings, and to sacrifice sacrifices of peace offerings: seven days shalt thou tarry, till I come to thee, and show thee what thou shalt do.'

⁹And it was so that when he had turned his back to go from Samuel, God gave him another heart: and all those signs came to pass that day. ¹⁰And when they came thither to the hill, behold, a company of the prophets met him, and the Spirit of God came upon him, and he prophesied among them. ¹¹And it came to pass, when all that knew him beforetime saw that, behold, he prophesied among the prophets, then the people said one to another, 'What is this that is come unto the son of Kish? Is Saul also among the prophets?' ¹²And one of the same place answered and said, 'But who is their father?' Therefore it became a proverb, 'Is Saul also among the prophets?' ¹³And when he had made an end of prophesying, he came to the high place.

¹⁴And Saul's uncle said unto him and to his servant, 'Whither went ye?' And he said, 'To seek the asses: and when we saw that they were nowhere, we came to Samuel'. ¹⁵And Saul's uncle said, 'Tell me, I pray thee, what Samuel said unto you'. ¹⁶And Saul said unto his uncle, 'He told us plainly that the asses were found'. But of the matter of the kingdom, whereof Samuel spoke, he told him not.

¹⁷And Samuel called the people together unto the LORD to Mizpeh; ¹⁸and said unto the children of Israel, 'Thus saith the LORD God of Israel, "I brought up Israel out of Egypt, and delivered you out of the hand of the Egyptians, and out of the hand of all kingdoms, and of them that oppressed you". ¹⁹And ye have this day rejected your God, who himself saved you out of all your adversities and your tribulations: and ye have said unto him, "Nay, but set a king over us". Now therefore present yourselves before the LORD by your tribes, and by your thousands.' ²⁰And when Samuel had caused all the tribes of Israel to come near, the tribe of Benjamin was taken. ²¹When he had caused the tribe of Benjamin to come near by their families, the family of Matri was taken, and Saul the son of Kish was taken: and when they sought him, he could not be found. ²²Therefore they inquired of the LORD further, if the man should yet come thither. And the LORD answered, 'Behold, he hath hid himself among the stuff'. ²³And they ran and fetched him thence: and when he stood among the people, he was higher than any of the people from the shoulders and upward. ²⁴And Samuel said to all the people, 'See ye him whom the LORD hath chosen, that there is none like him among all the people?' And all the people shouted, and said, 'God save the king'. ²⁵Then Samuel told the people the manner of the kingdom, and wrote

it in a book, and laid it up before the LORD. And Samuel sent all the people away, every man to his house.

²⁶And Saul also went home to Gibeah; and there went with him a band of men, whose hearts God had touched. ²⁷But the children of Belial said, 'How shall this man save us?' And they despised him, and brought him no presents. But he held his peace.

11 Then Nahash the Ammonite came up, and encamped against Jabesh-gilead: and all the men of Jabesh said unto Nahash, 'Make a covenant with us, and we will serve thee'. ²And Nahash the Ammonite answered them, 'On this condition will I make a covenant with you, that I may thrust out all your right eyes, and lay it for a reproach upon all Israel'. ³And the elders of Jabesh said unto him, 'Give us seven days' respite, that we may send messengers unto all the coasts of Israel: and then, if there be no man to save us, we will come out to thee'.

⁴Then came the messengers to Gibeah of Saul, and told the tidings in the ears of the people: and all the people lifted up their voices, and wept. ⁵And behold, Saul came after the herd out of the field; and Saul said, 'What aileth the people that they weep?' And they told him the tidings of the men of Jabesh. ⁶And the Spirit of God came upon Saul when he heard those tidings, and his anger was kindled greatly. ⁷And he took a yoke of oxen, and hewed them in pieces, and sent them throughout all the coasts of Israel by the hands of messengers, saying, 'Whosoever cometh not forth after Saul and after Samuel, so shall it be done unto his oxen'. And the fear of the LORD fell on the people, and they came out with one consent. ⁸And when he numbered them in Bezek, the children of Israel were three hundred thousand, and the men of Judah thirty thousand. ⁹And they said unto the messengers that came, 'Thus shall ye say unto the men of Jabesh-gilead, "Tomorrow, by that time the sun be hot, ye shall have help"'. And the messengers came and showed it to the men of Jabesh, and they were glad. ¹⁰Therefore the men of Jabesh said, 'Tomorrow we will come out unto you, and ye shall do with us all that seemeth good unto you'. ¹¹And it was so on the morrow, that Saul put the people in three companies; and they came into the midst of the host in the morning watch, and slew the Ammonites until the heat of the day: and it came to pass, that they which remained were scattered, so that two of them were not left together.

¹²And the people said unto Samuel, 'Who is he that said, "Shall Saul reign over us?" bring the men, that we may put them to death'. ¹³And Saul said, 'There shall not a man be put to death this day: for today the LORD hath wrought salvation in Israel'. ¹⁴Then said Samuel to the people, 'Come, and let us go to Gilgal, and renew the kingdom there'. ¹⁵And all the people went to Gilgal, and there they made Saul king before the LORD in Gilgal: and there they sacrificed sacrifices of peace offerings before the LORD: and there Saul and all the men of Israel rejoiced greatly.

12 And Samuel said unto all Israel, 'Behold, I have hearkened unto your voice in all that ye said unto me, and have made a king over you. ²And now, behold, the king walketh before you: and I am old and grey-headed, and behold, my sons are with you: and I have walked before you from my childhood unto this day. ³Behold, here I am: witness against me before the LORD, and before his anointed: whose ox have I taken? or whose ass have I taken? or whom have I defrauded? whom have I oppressed? or of whose hand have I received any bribe to blind my eyes therewith? and I will restore it you.' ⁴And they said, 'Thou hast not defrauded us, nor oppressed us, neither hast thou taken aught of any man's hand'. ⁵And he said unto them, 'The LORD is witness against you, and his anointed is witness this day, that ye have not found aught in my hand'. And they answered, 'He is witness'.

⁶And Samuel said unto the people, 'It is the LORD that advanced Moses and Aaron, and that brought your fathers up out of the land of Egypt. ⁷Now therefore stand still, that I may reason with you before the LORD of all the righteous acts of the LORD, which he did to you and to your fathers. ⁸When Jacob was come into Egypt, and your fathers cried unto the LORD, then the LORD sent Moses and Aaron, which brought forth your fathers out of Egypt, and made them dwell in this place. ⁹And when they forgot the LORD their God, he sold them into the hand of Sisera, captain of the host of Hazor, and into the hand of the Philistines, and into the hand of the king of Moab, and they fought against them. ¹⁰And they cried unto the LORD, and said, "We have sinned, because we have forsaken the LORD, and have served Baalim and Ashtaroth: but now deliver us out of the hand of our enemies, and we will serve thee". ¹¹And the LORD sent Jerubbaal, and Bedan, and Jephthah, and Samuel, and delivered you out of the hand of your enemies on every side, and ye dwelt safe. ¹²And when ye saw that Nahash the king of the children of Ammon came against you, ye said unto me, "Nay, but a king shall reign over us", when the LORD your God was your king. ¹³Now therefore behold the king whom ye have chosen, and whom ye have desired: and behold, the LORD hath set a king over you. ¹⁴If ye will fear the LORD, and serve him, and obey his voice, and not rebel against the commandment of the LORD, then shall both ye and also the king that reigneth over you continue following the LORD your God. ¹⁵But if ye will not obey the voice of the LORD, but rebel against the commandment of the LORD, then shall the hand of the LORD be against you, as it was against your fathers.

¹⁶'Now therefore stand and see this great thing, which the LORD will do before your eyes. ¹⁷Is it not wheat harvest today? I will call unto the LORD, and he shall send thunder and rain, that ye may perceive and see that your wickedness is great, which ye have done in the sight of the LORD, in asking you a king.' ¹⁸So Samuel called unto the LORD, and the LORD sent thunder and rain that day: and all the people greatly feared the LORD and Samuel. ¹⁹And all the people said unto Samuel, 'Pray for thy servants unto the LORD thy God, that we die not: for we have added unto all our sins this evil, to ask us a king'.

²⁰And Samuel said unto the people, 'Fear not (ye have done all this wickedness: yet turn not aside from following the LORD, but serve the

LORD with all your heart; [21] and turn ye not aside, for then should ye go after vain things, which cannot profit nor deliver, for they are vain): [22] for the LORD will not forsake his people for his great name's sake: because it hath pleased the LORD to make you his people. [23] Moreover, as for me, God forbid that I should sin against the LORD in ceasing to pray for you: but I will teach you the good and the right way. [24] Only fear the LORD, and serve him in truth with all your heart: for consider how great things he hath done for you. [25] But if ye shall still do wickedly, ye shall be consumed, both ye and your king.'

13 Saul reigned one year; and when he had reigned two years over Israel, [2] Saul chose him three thousand men of Israel: whereof two thousand were with Saul in Michmash and in mount Beth-el, and a thousand were with Jonathan in Gibeah of Benjamin: and the rest of the people he sent every man to his tent. [3] And Jonathan smote the garrison of the Philistines that was in Geba, and the Philistines heard of it. And Saul blew the trumpet throughout all the land, saying, 'Let the Hebrews hear'. [4] And all Israel heard say that Saul had smitten a garrison of the Philistines, and that Israel also was had in abomination with the Philistines. And the people were called together after Saul to Gilgal.

[5] And the Philistines gathered themselves together to fight with Israel, thirty thousand chariots, and six thousand horsemen, and people as the sand which is on the sea-shore in multitude: and they came up, and pitched in Michmash, eastward from Beth-aven. [6] When the men of Israel saw that they were in a strait (for the people were distressed), then the people did hide themselves in caves, and in thickets, and in rocks, and in high places, and in pits. [7] And some of the Hebrews went over Jordan to the land of Gad and Gilead. As for Saul, he was yet in Gilgal, and all the people followed him trembling.

[8] And he tarried seven days, according to the set time that Samuel had appointed: but Samuel came not to Gilgal; and the people were scattered from him. [9] And Saul said, 'Bring hither a burnt offering to me, and peace offerings'. And he offered the burnt offering. [10] And it came to pass that as soon as he had made an end of offering the burnt offering, behold, Samuel came; and Saul went out to meet him, that he might salute him. [11] And Samuel said, 'What hast thou done?' And Saul said, 'Because I saw that the people were scattered from me, and that thou camest not within the days appointed, and that the Philistines gathered themselves together at Michmash: [12] therefore said I, "The Philistines will come down now upon me to Gilgal, and I have not made supplication unto the LORD": I forced myself therefore, and offered a burnt offering'. [13] And Samuel said to Saul, 'Thou hast done foolishly: thou hast not kept the commandment of the LORD thy God, which he commanded thee: for now would the LORD have established thy kingdom upon Israel for ever. [14] But now thy kingdom shall not continue: the LORD hath sought him a man after his own heart, and the LORD hath commanded him to be captain over his people, because thou hast not kept that which the LORD commanded thee.'

¹⁵And Samuel arose, and got him up from Gilgal unto Gibeah of Benjamin. And Saul numbered the people that were present with him, about six hundred men. ¹⁶And Saul, and Jonathan his son, and the people that were present with them, abode in Gibeah of Benjamin: but the Philistines encamped in Michmash.

¹⁷And the spoilers came out of the camp of the Philistines in three companies: one company turned unto the way that leadeth to Ophrah, unto the land of Shual: ¹⁸and another company turned the way to Bethhoron: and another company turned to the way of the border that looketh to the valley of Zeboim toward the wilderness.

¹⁹Now there was no smith found throughout all the land of Israel: for the Philistines said, 'Lest the Hebrews make them swords or spears'. ²⁰But all the Israelites went down to the Philistines, to sharpen every man his share, and his coulter, and his axe, and his mattock. ²¹Yet they had a file for the mattocks, and for the coulters, and for the forks, and for the axes, and to sharpen the goads. ²²So it came to pass in the day of battle, that there was neither sword nor spear found in the hand of any of the people that were with Saul and Jonathan: but with Saul and with Jonathan his son was there found. ²³And the garrison of the Philistines went out to the passage of Michmash.

14 Now it came to pass upon a day, that Jonathan the son of Saul said unto the young man that bore his armour, 'Come, and let us go over to the Philistines' garrison, that is on the other side'. But he told not his father. ²And Saul tarried in the uttermost part of Gibeah under a pomegranate tree which is in Migron: and the people that were with him were about six hundred men; ³and Ahiah, the son of Ahitub, Ichabod's brother, the son of Phinehas, the son of Eli, the LORD's priest in Shiloh, wearing an ephod. And the people knew not that Jonathan was gone.

⁴And between the passages, by which Jonathan sought to go over unto the Philistines' garrison, there was a sharp rock on the one side, and a sharp rock on the other side: and the name of the one was Bozez, and the name of the other Seneh. ⁵The forefront of the one was situated northward over against Michmash, and the other southward over against Gibeah. ⁶And Jonathan said to the young man that bore his armour, 'Come, and let us go over unto the garrison of these uncircumcised: it may be that the LORD will work for us: for there is no restraint to the LORD to save by many or by few'. ⁷And his armour-bearer said unto him, 'Do all that is in thy heart: turn thee, behold, I am with thee according to thy heart'. ⁸Then said Jonathan, 'Behold, we will pass over unto these men, and we will discover ourselves unto them. ⁹If they say thus unto us, "Tarry until we come to you": then we will stand still in our place, and will not go up unto them. ¹⁰But if they say thus, "Come up unto us": then we will go up: for the LORD hath delivered them into our hand: and this shall be a sign unto us.' ¹¹And both of them discovered themselves unto the garrison of the Philistines: and the Philistines said, 'Behold, the Hebrews come forth out of the holes where they had hid themselves'. ¹²And the men of the garrison answered Jonathan and

his armour-bearer, and said, 'Come up to us, and we will show you a thing'. And Jonathan said unto his armour-bearer, 'Come up after me: for the LORD hath delivered them into the hand of Israel'. [13]And Jonathan climbed up upon his hands and upon his feet, and his armour-bearer after him: and they fell before Jonathan; and his armour-bearer slew after him. [14]And that first slaughter, which Jonathan and his armour-bearer made, was about twenty men, within as it were a half acre of land, which a yoke of oxen might plough. [15]And there was trembling in the host, in the field, and among all the people: the garrison, and the spoilers, they also trembled, and the earth quaked: so it was a very great trembling.

[16]And the watchmen of Saul in Gibeah of Benjamin looked: and behold, the multitude melted away, and they went on beating down one another. [17]Then said Saul unto the people that were with him, 'Number now, and see who is gone from us'. And when they had numbered, behold, Jonathan and his armour-bearer were not there. [18]And Saul said unto Ahiah, 'Bring hither the ark of God' (for the ark of God was at that time with the children of Israel). [19]And it came to pass, while Saul talked unto the priest, that the noise that was in the host of the Philistines went on and increased: and Saul said unto the priest, 'Withdraw thy hand'. [20]And Saul and all the people that were with him assembled themselves, and they came to the battle: and behold, every man's sword was against his fellow, and there was a very great discomfiture. [21]Moreover, the Hebrews that were with the Philistines before that time, which went up with them into the camp from the country round about, even they also turned to be with the Israelites that were with Saul and Jonathan. [22]Likewise all the men of Israel which had hid themselves in mount Ephraim, when they heard that the Philistines fled, even they also followed hard after them in the battle. [23]So the LORD saved Israel that day: and the battle passed over unto Beth-aven.

[24]And the men of Israel were distressed that day: for Saul had adjured the people, saying, 'Cursed be the man that eateth any food until evening, that I may be avenged on my enemies'. So none of the people tasted any food. [25]And all they of the land came to a wood, and there was honey upon the ground. [26]And when the people were come into the wood, behold, the honey dropped; but no man put his hand to his mouth: for the people feared the oath. [27]But Jonathan heard not when his father charged the people with the oath: wherefore he put forth the end of the rod that was in his hand, and dipped it in a honeycomb, and put his hand to his mouth; and his eyes were enlightened. [28]Then answered one of the people, and said, 'Thy father straitly charged the people with an oath, saying, "Cursed be the man that eateth any food this day"'. And the people were faint. [29]Then said Jonathan, 'My father hath troubled the land: see, I pray you, how my eyes have been enlightened, because I tasted a little of this honey. [30]How much more, if haply the people had eaten freely today of the spoil of their enemies which they found? for had there not been now a much greater slaughter

among the Philistines?' ³¹And they smote the Philistines that day from Michmash to Aijalon: and the people were very faint. ³²And the people flew upon the spoil, and took sheep, and oxen, and calves, and slew them on the ground: and the people did eat them with the blood. ³³Then they told Saul, saying, 'Behold, the people sin against the LORD, in that they eat with the blood'. And he said, 'Ye have transgressed: roll a great stone unto me this day'. ³⁴And Saul said, 'Disperse yourselves among the people, and say unto them, "Bring me hither every man his ox, and every man his sheep, and slay them here, and eat, and sin not against the LORD in eating with the blood"'. And all the people brought every man his ox with him that night, and slew them there. ³⁵And Saul built an altar unto the LORD: the same was the first altar that he built unto the LORD.

³⁶And Saul said, 'Let us go down after the Philistines by night, and spoil them until the morning light, and let us not leave a man of them'. And they said, 'Do whatsoever seemeth good unto thee'. Then said the priest, 'Let us draw near hither unto God'. ³⁷And Saul asked counsel of God, 'Shall I go down after the Philistines? Wilt thou deliver them into the hand of Israel?' But he answered him not that day. ³⁸And Saul said, 'Draw ye near hither, all the chief of the people: and know and see wherein this sin hath been this day. ³⁹For, as the LORD liveth, which saveth Israel, though it be in Jonathan my son, he shall surely die.' But there was not a man among all the people that answered him. ⁴⁰Then said he unto all Israel, 'Be ye on one side, and I and Jonathan my son will be on the other side'. And the people said unto Saul, 'Do what seemeth good unto thee'. ⁴¹Therefore Saul said unto the LORD God of Israel, 'Give a perfect lot'. And Saul and Jonathan were taken: but the people escaped. ⁴²And Saul said, 'Cast lots between me and Jonathan my son'. And Jonathan was taken. ⁴³Then Saul said to Jonathan, 'Tell me what thou hast done'. And Jonathan told him, and said, 'I did but taste a little honey with the end of the rod that was in my hand, and lo, I must die'. ⁴⁴And Saul answered, 'God do so and more also: for thou shalt surely die, Jonathan'. ⁴⁵And the people said unto Saul, 'Shall Jonathan die, who hath wrought this great salvation in Israel? God forbid: as the LORD liveth, there shall not one hair of his head fall to the ground: for he hath wrought with God this day.' So the people rescued Jonathan, that he died not. ⁴⁶Then Saul went up from following the Philistines: and the Philistines went to their own place.

⁴⁷So Saul took the kingdom over Israel, and fought against all his enemies on every side, against Moab, and against the children of Ammon, and against Edom, and against the kings of Zobah, and against the Philistines: and whithersoever he turned himself, he vexed them. ⁴⁸And he gathered a host, and smote the Amalekites, and delivered Israel out of the hands of them that spoiled them.

⁴⁹Now the sons of Saul were Jonathan, and Ishui, and Melchi-shua: and the names of his two daughters were these: the name of the first-born Merab, and the name of the younger Michal: ⁵⁰and the name of Saul's wife was Ahinoam, the daughter of Ahimaaz: and the name of

the captain of his host was Abner, the son of Ner, Saul's uncle. ⁵¹And Kish was the father of Saul; and Ner the father of Abner was the son of Abiel. ⁵²And there was sore war against the Philistines all the days of Saul: and when Saul saw any strong man, or any valiant man, he took him unto him.

15 Samuel also said unto Saul, 'The Lord sent me to anoint thee to be king over his people, over Israel: now therefore hearken thou unto the voice of the words of the Lord. ²Thus saith the Lord of hosts, "I remember that which Amalek did to Israel, how he laid wait for him in the way, when he came up from Egypt. ³Now go and smite Amalek, and utterly destroy all that they have, and spare them not; but slay both man and woman, infant and suckling, ox and sheep, camel and ass."'

⁴And Saul gathered the people together, and numbered them in Telaim, two hundred thousand footmen, and ten thousand men of Judah. ⁵And Saul came to a city of Amalek, and laid wait in the valley. ⁶And Saul said unto the Kenites, 'Go, depart, get you down from among the Amalekites, lest I destroy you with them: for ye showed kindness to all the children of Israel, when they came up out of Egypt'. So the Kenites departed from among the Amalekites. ⁷And Saul smote the Amalekites from Havilah until thou comest to Shur, that is over against Egypt. ⁸And he took Agag the king of the Amalekites alive, and utterly destroyed all the people with the edge of the sword. ⁹But Saul and the people spared Agag, and the best of the sheep, and of the oxen, and of the fatlings, and the lambs, and all that was good, and would not utterly destroy them: but everything that was vile and refuse, that they destroyed utterly.

¹⁰Then came the word of the Lord unto Samuel, saying, ¹¹'It repenteth me that I have set up Saul to be king: for he is turned back from following me, and hath not performed my commandments'. And it grieved Samuel; and he cried unto the Lord all night. ¹²And when Samuel rose early to meet Saul in the morning, it was told Samuel, saying, 'Saul came to Carmel, and behold, he set him up a place, and is gone about, and passed on, and gone down to Gilgal'. ¹³And Samuel came to Saul, and Saul said unto him, 'Blessed be thou of the Lord: I have performed the commandment of the Lord'. ¹⁴And Samuel said, 'What meaneth then this bleating of the sheep in my ears, and the lowing of the oxen which I hear?' ¹⁵And Saul said, 'They have brought them from the Amalekites: for the people spared the best of the sheep and of the oxen, to sacrifice unto the Lord thy God; and the rest we have utterly destroyed'. ¹⁶Then Samuel said unto Saul, 'Stay, and I will tell thee what the Lord hath said to me this night'. And he said unto him, 'Say on'. ¹⁷And Samuel said, 'When thou wast little in thy own sight, wast thou not made the head of the tribes of Israel, and the Lord anointed thee king over Israel? ¹⁸And the Lord sent thee on a journey, and said, "Go and utterly destroy the sinners the Amalekites, and fight against them until they be consumed". ¹⁹Wherefore then didst thou not obey the voice of the Lord, but didst fly upon the spoil, and didst evil in the sight of the Lord?' ²⁰And Saul said unto Samuel, 'Yea, I have obeyed the

voice of the LORD, and have gone the way which the LORD sent me, and have brought Agag the king of Amalek, and have utterly destroyed the Amalekites. ²¹But the people took of the spoil, sheep and oxen, the chief of the things which should have been utterly destroyed, to sacrifice unto the LORD thy God in Gilgal.' ²²And Samuel said, 'Hath the LORD as great delight in burnt offerings and sacrifices, as in obeying the voice of the LORD? Behold, to obey is better than sacrifice, and to hearken than the fat of rams. ²³For rebellion is as the sin of witchcraft, and stubbornness is as iniquity and idolatry: because thou hast rejected the word of the LORD, he hath also rejected thee from being king.'

²⁴And Saul said unto Samuel, 'I have sinned: for I have transgressed the commandment of the LORD, and thy words: because I feared the people, and obeyed their voice. ²⁵Now therefore, I pray thee, pardon my sin, and turn again with me, that I may worship the LORD.' ²⁶And Samuel said unto Saul, 'I will not return with thee: for thou hast rejected the word of the LORD, and the LORD hath rejected thee from being king over Israel'. ²⁷And as Samuel turned about to go away, he laid hold upon the skirt of his mantle, and it rent. ²⁸And Samuel said unto him, 'The LORD hath rent the kingdom of Israel from thee this day, and hath given it to a neighbour of thine, that is better than thou. ²⁹And also the Strength of Israel will not lie nor repent: for he is not a man, that he should repent.' ³⁰Then he said, 'I have sinned: yet honour me now, I pray thee, before the elders of my people, and before Israel, and turn again with me, that I may worship the LORD thy God'. ³¹So Samuel turned again after Saul; and Saul worshipped the LORD.

³²Then said Samuel, 'Bring you hither to me Agag the king of the Amalekites'. And Agag came unto him delicately. And Agag said, 'Surely the bitterness of death is past'. ³³And Samuel said, 'As thy sword hath made women childless, so shall thy mother be childless among women'. And Samuel hewed Agag in pieces before the LORD in Gilgal.

³⁴Then Samuel went to Ramah, and Saul went up to his house to Gibeah of Saul. ³⁵And Samuel came no more to see Saul until the day of his death: nevertheless Samuel mourned for Saul: and the LORD repented that he had made Saul king over Israel.

16 And the LORD said unto Samuel, 'How long wilt thou mourn for Saul, seeing I have rejected him from reigning over Israel? Fill thy horn with oil, and go, I will send thee to Jesse the Beth-lehemite: for I have provided me a king among his sons.' ²And Samuel said, 'How can I go? if Saul hear it, he will kill me'. And the LORD said, 'Take a heifer with thee, and say, "I am come to sacrifice to the LORD". ³And call Jesse to the sacrifice, and I will show thee what thou shalt do: and thou shalt anoint unto me him whom I name unto thee.' ⁴And Samuel did that which the LORD spoke, and came to Beth-lehem. And the elders of the town trembled at his coming, and said, 'Comest thou peaceably?' ⁵And he said, 'Peaceably: I am come to sacrifice unto the LORD: sanctify yourselves, and come with me to the sacrifice'. And he sanctified Jesse and his sons, and called them to the sacrifice.

⁶And it came to pass when they were come, that he looked on Eliab,

and said, 'Surely the LORD's anointed is before him'. [7]But the LORD said unto Samuel, 'Look not on his countenance, or on the height of his stature, because I have refused him: for the LORD seeth not as man seeth; for man looketh on the outward appearance, but the LORD looketh on the heart'. [8]Then Jesse called Abinadab, and made him pass before Samuel. And he said, 'Neither hath the LORD chosen this'. [9]Then Jesse made Shammah to pass by. And he said, 'Neither hath the LORD chosen this'. [10]Again, Jesse made seven of his sons to pass before Samuel. And Samuel said unto Jesse, 'The LORD hath not chosen these'. [11]And Samuel said unto Jesse, 'Are here all thy children?' And he said, 'There remaineth yet the youngest, and behold, he keepeth the sheep'. And Samuel said unto Jesse, 'Send and fetch him: for we will not sit down till he come hither'. [12]And he sent, and brought him in. Now he was ruddy, and withal of a beautiful countenance, and goodly to look to. And the LORD said, 'Arise, anoint him: for this is he'. [13]Then Samuel took the horn of oil, and anointed him in the midst of his brethren: and the Spirit of the LORD came upon David from that day forward. So Samuel rose up, and went to Ramah.

[14]But the Spirit of the LORD departed from Saul, and an evil spirit from the LORD troubled him. [15]And Saul's servants said unto him, 'Behold now, an evil spirit from God troubleth thee. [16]Let our lord now command thy servants, which are before thee, to seek out a man, who is a cunning player on a harp: and it shall come to pass, when the evil spirit from God is upon thee, that he shall play with his hand, and thou shalt be well.' [17]And Saul said unto his servants, 'Provide me now a man that can play well, and bring him to me'. [18]Then answered one of the servants, and said, 'Behold, I have seen a son of Jesse the Beth-lehemite, that is cunning in playing, and a mighty valiant man, and a man of war, and prudent in matters, and a comely person, and the LORD is with him'. aka David

[19]Wherefore Saul sent messengers unto Jesse, and said, 'Send me David thy son, which is with the sheep'. [20]And Jesse took an ass laden with bread, and a bottle of wine, and a kid, and sent them by David his son unto Saul. [21]And David came to Saul, and stood before him: and he loved him greatly, and he became his armour-bearer. [22]And Saul sent to Jesse, saying, 'Let David, I pray thee, stand before me: for he hath found favour in my sight'. [23]And it came to pass, when the evil spirit from God was upon Saul, that David took a harp, and played with his hand: so Saul was refreshed, and was well, and the evil spirit departed from him.

17 Now the Philistines gathered together their armies to battle, and were gathered together at Shochoh, which belongeth to Judah, and pitched between Shochoh and Azekah, in Ephes-dammim. [2]And Saul and the men of Israel were gathered together, and pitched by the valley of Elah, and set the battle in array against the Philistines. [3]And the Philistines stood on a mountain on the one side, and Israel stood on a mountain on the other side: and there was a valley between them. youngest, weakest

[4]And there went out a champion out of the camp of the Philistines, named Goliath, of Gath, whose height was six cubits and a span. [5]And

he had a helmet of brass upon his head, and he was armed with a coat of mail: and the weight of the coat was five thousand shekels of brass. ⁶And he had greaves of brass upon his legs, and a target of brass between his shoulders. ⁷And the staff of his spear was like a weaver's beam, and his spear's head weighed six hundred shekels of iron: and one bearing a shield went before him. ⁸And he stood and cried unto the armies of Israel, and said unto them, 'Why are ye come out to set your battle in array? am not I a Philistine, and you servants to Saul? choose you a man for you, and let him come down to me. ⁹If he be able to fight with me, and to kill me, then will we be your servants: but if I prevail against him, and kill him, then shall ye be our servants, and serve us.' ¹⁰And the Philistine said, 'I defy the armies of Israel this day; give me a man, that we may fight together'. ¹¹When Saul and all Israel heard those words of the Philistine, they were dismayed, and greatly afraid.

¹²Now David was the son of that Ephrathite of Beth-lehem-judah, whose name was Jesse; and he had eight sons: and the man went among men for an old man in the days of Saul. ¹³And the three eldest sons of Jesse went and followed Saul to the battle: and the names of his three sons that went to the battle were Eliab the firstborn, and next unto him Abinadab, and the third Shammah. ¹⁴And David was the youngest: and the three eldest followed Saul. ¹⁵But David went and returned from Saul to feed his father's sheep at Beth-lehem. ¹⁶And the Philistine drew near morning and evening, and presented himself forty days. ¹⁷And Jesse said unto David his son, 'Take now for thy brethren an ephah of this parched corn, and these ten loaves, and run to the camp to thy brethren. ¹⁸And carry these ten cheeses unto the captain of their thousand, and look how thy brethren fare, and take their pledge.' ¹⁹Now Saul, and they, and all the men of Israel were in the valley of Elah, fighting with the Philistines.

²⁰And David rose up early in the morning, and left the sheep with a keeper, and took, and went, as Jesse had commanded him; and he came to the trench, as the host was going forth to the fight, and shouted for the battle. ²¹For Israel and the Philistines had put the battle in array, army against army. ²²And David left his carriage in the hand of the keeper of the carriage, and ran into the army, and came and saluted his brethren. ²³And as he talked with them, behold, there came up the champion, the Philistine of Gath, Goliath by name, out of the armies of the Philistines, and spoke according to the same words: and David heard them. ²⁴And all the men of Israel, when they saw the man, fled from him, and were sore afraid. ²⁵And the men of Israel said, 'Have ye seen this man that is come up? Surely to defy Israel is he come up: and it shall be that the man who killeth him, the king will enrich him with great riches, and will give him his daughter, and make his father's house free in Israel.' ²⁶And David spoke to the men that stood by him, saying, 'What shall be done to the man that killeth this Philistine, and taketh away the reproach from Israel? for who is this uncircumcised Philistine, that he should defy the armies of the living God?' ²⁷And the

people answered him after this manner, saying, 'So shall it be done to the man that killeth him'.

²⁸And Eliab his eldest brother heard when he spoke unto the men, and Eliab's anger was kindled against David, and he said, 'Why camest thou down hither? and with whom hast thou left those few sheep in the wilderness? I know thy pride, and the naughtiness of thy heart; for thou art come down that thou mightest see the battle.' ²⁹And David said, 'What have I now done? Is there not a cause?'

³⁰And he turned from him towards another, and spoke after the same manner: and the people answered him again after the former manner. ³¹And when the words were heard which David spoke, they rehearsed them before Saul: and he sent for him.

³²And David said to Saul, 'Let no man's heart fail because of him: thy servant will go and fight with this Philistine'. ³³And Saul said to David, 'Thou art not able to go against this Philistine to fight with him: for thou art but a youth, and he a man of war from his youth'. ³⁴And David said unto Saul, 'Thy servant kept his father's sheep, and there came a lion, and a bear, and took a lamb out of the flock: ³⁵and I went out after him, and smote him, and delivered it out of his mouth: and when he arose against me, I caught him by his beard, and smote him, and slew him. ³⁶Thy servant slew both the lion and the bear: and this uncircumcised Philistine shall be as one of them, seeing he hath defied the armies of the living God.' ³⁷David said moreover, 'The LORD that delivered me out of the paw of the lion, and out of the paw of the bear, he will deliver me out of the hand of this Philistine'. And Saul said unto David, 'Go, and the LORD be with thee'.

³⁸And Saul armed David with his armour, and he put a helmet of brass upon his head; also he armed him with a coat of mail. ³⁹And David girded his sword upon his armour, and he essayed to go, for he had not proved it: and David said unto Saul, 'I cannot go with these: for I have not proved them'. And David put them off him. ⁴⁰And he took his staff in his hand, and chose him five smooth stones out of the brook, and put them in a shepherd's bag which he had, even in a scrip; and his sling was in his hand: and he drew near to the Philistine. ⁴¹And the Philistine came on and drew near unto David, and the man that bore the shield went before him. ⁴²And when the Philistine looked about, and saw David, he disdained him: for he was but a youth, and ruddy, and of a fair countenance. ⁴³And the Philistine said unto David, 'Am I a dog, that thou comest to me with staves?' And the Philistine cursed David by his gods. ⁴⁴And the Philistine said to David, 'Come to me, and I will give thy flesh unto the fowls of the air, and to the beasts of the field'. ⁴⁵Then said David to the Philistine, 'Thou comest to me with a sword, and with a spear, and with a shield: but I come to thee in the name of the LORD of hosts, the God of the armies of Israel, whom thou hast defied. ⁴⁶This day will the LORD deliver thee into my hand, and I will smite thee, and take thy head from thee; and I will give the carcases of the host of the Philistines this day unto the fowls of the air, and to the wild beasts of the earth, that all the earth may know that there

is a God in Israel. ⁴⁷And all this assembly shall know that the LORD saveth not with sword and spear: for the battle is the LORD's, and he will give you into our hands.'

⁴⁸And it came to pass, when the Philistine arose, and came and drew nigh to meet David, that David hasted, and ran toward the army to meet the Philistine. ⁴⁹And David put his hand in his bag, and took thence a stone, and slung it, and smote the Philistine in his forehead, that the stone sank into his forehead, and he fell upon his face to the earth. ⁵⁰So David prevailed over the Philistine with a sling and with a stone, and smote the Philistine, and slew him; but there was no sword in the hand of David. ⁵¹Therefore David ran, and stood upon the Philistine, and took his sword, and drew it out of the sheath thereof, and slew him, and cut off his head therewith. And when the Philistines saw their champion was dead, they fled. ⁵²And the men of Israel and of Judah arose, and shouted, and pursued the Philistines, until thou come to the valley, and to the gates of Ekron. And the wounded of the Philistines fell down by the way to Shaaraim, even unto Gath, and unto Ekron. ⁵³And the children of Israel returned from chasing after the Philistines, and they spoiled their tents. ⁵⁴And David took the head of the Philistine, and brought it to Jerusalem; but he put his armour in his tent.

⁵⁵And when Saul saw David go forth against the Philistine, he said unto Abner, the captain of the host, 'Abner, whose son is this youth?' And Abner said, 'As thy soul liveth, O king, I cannot tell'. ⁵⁶And the king said, 'Inquire thou whose son the stripling is'. ⁵⁷And as David returned from the slaughter of the Philistine, Abner took him, and brought him before Saul with the head of the Philistine in his hand. ⁵⁸And Saul said to him, 'Whose son art thou, thou young man?' And David answered, 'I am the son of thy servant Jesse the Beth-lehemite'.

18 And it came to pass, when he had made an end of speaking unto Saul, that the soul of Jonathan was knit with the soul of David, and Jonathan loved him as his own soul. ²And Saul took him that day, and would let him go no more home to his father's house. ³Then Jonathan and David made a covenant, because he loved him as his own soul. ⁴And Jonathan stripped himself of the robe that was upon him, and gave it to David, and his garments, even to his sword, and to his bow, and to his girdle.

⁵And David went out whithersoever Saul sent him, and behaved himself wisely: and Saul set him over the men of war, and he was accepted in the sight of all the people, and also in the sight of Saul's servants. ⁶And it came to pass as they came, when David was returned from the slaughter of the Philistine, that the women came out of all cities of Israel, singing and dancing, to meet king Saul, with tabrets, with joy, and with instruments of music. ⁷And the women answered one another as they played, and said, 'Saul hath slain his thousands, and David his ten thousands'. ⁸And Saul was very wroth, and the saying displeased him; and he said, 'They have ascribed unto David ten thousands, and to me they have ascribed but thousands: and what can he

have more but the kingdom?' ⁹And Saul eyed David from that day and forward.

¹⁰And it came to pass on the morrow, that the evil spirit from God came upon Saul, and he prophesied in the midst of the house: and David played with his hand, as at other times: and there was a javelin in Saul's hand. ¹¹And Saul cast the javelin; for he said, 'I will smite David even to the wall with it'. And David avoided out of his presence twice.

¹²And Saul was afraid of David, because the LORD was with him, and was departed from Saul. ¹³Therefore Saul removed him from him, and made him his captain over a thousand; and he went out and came in before the people. ¹⁴And David behaved himself wisely in all his ways; and the LORD was with him. ¹⁵Wherefore when Saul saw that he behaved himself very wisely, he was afraid of him. ¹⁶But all Israel and Judah loved David, because he went out and came in before them.

¹⁷And Saul said to David, 'Behold my elder daughter Merab, her will I give thee to wife: only be thou valiant for me, and fight the LORD's battles'. For Saul said, 'Let not my hand be upon him, but let the hand of the Philistines be upon him'. ¹⁸And David said unto Saul, 'Who am I? and what is my life, or my father's family in Israel, that I should be son-in-law to the king?' ¹⁹But it came to pass at the time when Merab Saul's daughter should have been given to David, that she was given unto Adriel the Meholathite to wife. ²⁰And Michal Saul's daughter loved David: and they told Saul, and the thing pleased him. ²¹And Saul said, 'I will give him her, that she may be a snare to him, and that the hand of the Philistines may be against him'. Wherefore Saul said to David, 'Thou shalt this day be my son-in-law in the one of the twain'.

²²And Saul commanded his servants, saying, 'Commune with David secretly, and say, "Behold, the king hath delight in thee, and all his servants love thee: now therefore be the king's son-in-law"'. ²³And Saul's servants spoke those words in the ears of David. And David said, 'Seemeth it to you a light thing to be a king's son-in-law, seeing that I am a poor man, and lightly esteemed?' ²⁴And the servants of Saul told him, saying, 'On this manner spoke David'. ²⁵And Saul said, 'Thus shall ye say to David, "The king desireth not any dowry, but a hundred foreskins of the Philistines, to be avenged of the king's enemies"'. But Saul thought to make David fall by the hand of the Philistines. ²⁶And when his servants told David these words, it pleased David well to be the king's son-in-law: and the days were not expired. ²⁷Wherefore David arose, he and his men, and slew of the Philistines two hundred men; and David brought their foreskins, and they gave them in full tale to the king, that he might be the king's son-in-law. And Saul gave him Michal his daughter to wife.

²⁸And Saul saw and knew that the LORD was with David, and that Michal Saul's daughter loved him. ²⁹And Saul was yet the more afraid of David; and Saul became David's enemy continually.

³⁰Then the princes of the Philistines went forth: and it came to pass, after they went forth, that David behaved himself more wisely than all the servants of Saul; so that his name was much set by.

19

And Saul spoke to Jonathan his son, and to all his servants, that they should kill David. [2]But Jonathan Saul's son delighted much in David: and Jonathan told David, saying, 'Saul my father seeketh to kill thee: now therefore, I pray thee, take heed to thyself until the morning, and abide in a secret place, and hide thyself: [3]and I will go out and stand beside my father in the field where thou art, and I will commune with my father of thee; and what I see, that I will tell thee'.

[4]And Jonathan spoke good of David unto Saul his father, and said unto him, 'Let not the king sin against his servant, against David: because he hath not sinned against thee, and because his works have been to thee-ward very good. [5]For he did put his life in his hand, and slew the Philistine, and the LORD wrought a great salvation for all Israel: thou sawest it, and didst rejoice: wherefore then wilt thou sin against innocent blood, to slay David without a cause?' [6]And Saul hearkened unto the voice of Jonathan: and Saul swore, 'As the LORD liveth, he shall not be slain'. [7]And Jonathan called David, and Jonathan showed him all those things. And Jonathan brought David to Saul, and he was in his presence, as in times past.

[8]And there was war again: and David went out, and fought with the Philistines, and slew them with a great slaughter; and they fled from him. [9]And the evil spirit from the LORD was upon Saul, as he sat in his house with his javelin in his hand: and David played with his hand. [10]And Saul sought to smite David even to the wall with the javelin: but he slipped away out of Saul's presence, and he smote the javelin into the wall: and David fled, and escaped that night. [11]Saul also sent messengers unto David's house, to watch him, and to slay him in the morning: and Michal David's wife told him, saying, 'If thou save not thy life tonight, tomorrow thou shalt be slain'.

[12]So Michal let David down through a window: and he went and fled, and escaped. [13]And Michal took an image, and laid it in the bed, and put a pillow of goats' hair for his bolster, and covered it with a cloth. [14]And when Saul sent messengers to take David, she said, 'He is sick'. [15]And Saul sent the messengers again to see David, saying, 'Bring him up to me in the bed, that I may slay him'. [16]And when the messengers were come in, behold, there was an image in the bed, with a pillow of goats' hair for his bolster. [17]And Saul said unto Michal, 'Why hast thou deceived me so, and sent away my enemy, that he is escaped?' And Michal answered Saul, 'He said unto me, "Let me go; why should I kill thee?"'

[18]So David fled, and escaped, and came to Samuel to Ramah, and told him all that Saul had done to him. And he and Samuel went and dwelt in Naioth. [19]And it was told Saul, saying, 'Behold, David is at Naioth in Ramah'. [20]And Saul sent messengers to take David: and when they saw the company of the prophets prophesying, and Samuel standing as appointed over them, the Spirit of God was upon the messengers of Saul, and they also prophesied. [21]And when it was told Saul, he sent other messengers, and they prophesied likewise. And Saul sent messengers again the third time, and they prophesied also. [22]Then went he

also to Ramah, and came to a great well that is in Sechu: and he asked and said, 'Where are Samuel and David?' And one said, 'Behold, they be at Naioth in Ramah'. ²³And he went thither to Naioth in Ramah: and the Spirit of God was upon him also, and he went on, and prophesied, until he came to Naioth in Ramah. ²⁴And he stripped off his clothes also, and prophesied before Samuel in like manner, and lay down naked all that day and all that night. Wherefore they say, 'Is Saul also among the prophets?'

20 And David fled from Naioth in Ramah, and came and said before Jonathan, 'What have I done? what is my iniquity? and what is my sin before thy father, that he seeketh my life?' ²And he said unto him, 'God forbid, thou shalt not die: behold, my father will do nothing either great or small, but that he will show it me: and why should my father hide this thing from me? it is not so'. ³And David swore moreover, and said, 'Thy father certainly knoweth that I have found grace in thy eyes, and he saith, "Let not Jonathan know this, lest he be grieved": but truly, as the LORD liveth, and as thy soul liveth, there is but a step between me and death'. ⁴Then said Jonathan unto David, 'Whatsoever thy soul desireth, I will even do it for thee'. ⁵And David said unto Jonathan, 'Behold, tomorrow is the new moon, and I should not fail to sit with the king at meat: but let me go, that I may hide myself in the fields unto the third day at even. ⁶If thy father at all miss me, then say, "David earnestly asked leave of me that he might run to Beth-lehem his city: for there is a yearly sacrifice there for all the family". ⁷If he say thus, "It is well", thy servant shall have peace: but if he be very wroth, then be sure that evil is determined by him. ⁸Therefore thou shalt deal kindly with thy servant, for thou hast brought thy servant into a covenant of the LORD with thee: notwithstanding, if there be in me iniquity, slay me thyself: for why shouldst thou bring me to thy father?' ⁹And Jonathan said, 'Far be it from thee: for if I knew certainly that evil were determined by my father to come upon thee, then would not I tell it thee?' ¹⁰Then said David to Jonathan, 'Who shall tell me? or what if thy father answer thee roughly?'

¹¹And Jonathan said unto David, 'Come, and let us go out into the field'. And they went out both of them into the field. ¹²And Jonathan said unto David, 'O LORD God of Israel, when I have sounded my father about tomorrow any time, or the third day, and behold, if there be good toward David, and I then send not unto thee, and show it thee; ¹³the LORD do so and much more to Jonathan: but if it please my father to do thee evil, then I will show it thee, and send thee away, that thou mayest go in peace, and the LORD be with thee, as he hath been with my father. ¹⁴And thou shalt not only while yet I live show me the kindness of the LORD, that I die not: ¹⁵but also thou shalt not cut off thy kindness from my house for ever: no, not when the LORD hath cut off the enemies of David every one from the face of the earth.' ¹⁶So Jonathan made a covenant with the house of David, saying, 'Let the LORD even require it at the hand of David's enemies'. ¹⁷And Jonathan caused David to swear again, because he loved him: for he loved him as he loved his own soul.

¹⁸Then Jonathan said to David, 'Tomorrow is the new moon: and thou shalt be missed, because thy seat will be empty. ¹⁹And when thou hast stayed three days, then thou shalt go down quickly, and come to the place where thou didst hide thyself when the business was in hand, and shalt remain by the stone Ezel. ²⁰And I will shoot three arrows on the side thereof, as though I shot at a mark. ²¹And behold, I will send a lad, saying, "Go, find out the arrows". If I expressly say unto the lad, "Behold, the arrows are on this side of thee, take them": then come thou, for there is peace to thee, and no hurt, as the LORD liveth. ²²But if I say thus unto the young man, "Behold, the arrows are beyond thee": go thy way, for the LORD hath sent thee away. ²³And as touching the matter which thou and I have spoken of, behold, the LORD be between thee and me for ever.'

²⁴So David hid himself in the field: and when the new moon was come, the king sat him down to eat meat. ²⁵And the king sat upon his seat, as at other times, even upon a seat by the wall: and Jonathan arose, and Abner sat by Saul's side, and David's place was empty. ²⁶Nevertheless Saul spoke not anything that day: for he thought, something hath befallen him, he is not clean; surely he is not clean. ²⁷And it came to pass on the morrow, which was the second day of the month, that David's place was empty: and Saul said unto Jonathan his son, 'Wherefore cometh not the son of Jesse to meat, neither yesterday, nor today?' ²⁸And Jonathan answered Saul, 'David earnestly asked leave of me to go to Beth-lehem. ²⁹And he said, "Let me go, I pray thee; for our family hath a sacrifice in the city, and my brother, he hath commanded me to be there: and now, if I have found favour in thy eyes, let me get away, I pray thee, and see my brethren". Therefore he cometh not unto the king's table.' ³⁰Then Saul's anger was kindled against Jonathan, and he said unto him, 'Thou son of the perverse rebellious woman, do not I know that thou hast chosen the son of Jesse to thy own confusion, and unto the confusion of thy mother's nakedness? ³¹For as long as the son of Jesse liveth upon the ground, thou shalt not be established, nor thy kingdom. Wherefore now send and fetch him unto me, for he shall surely die.' ³²And Jonathan answered Saul his father, and said unto him, 'Wherefore shall he be slain? what hath he done?' ³³And Saul cast a javelin at him to smite him, whereby Jonathan knew that it was determined of his father to slay David. ³⁴So Jonathan arose from the table in fierce anger, and did eat no meat the second day of the month: for he was grieved for David, because his father had done him shame.

³⁵And it came to pass in the morning, that Jonathan went out into the field at the time appointed with David, and a little lad with him. ³⁶And he said unto his lad, 'Run, find out now the arrows which I shoot'. And as the lad ran, he shot an arrow beyond him. ³⁷And when the lad was come to the place of the arrow which Jonathan had shot, Jonathan cried after the lad, and said, 'Is not the arrow beyond thee?' ³⁸And Jonathan cried after the lad, 'Make speed, haste, stay not'. And Jonathan's lad gathered up the arrows, and came to his master. ³⁹But the lad knew not anything: only Jonathan and David knew the matter.

⁴⁰And Jonathan gave his artillery unto his lad, and said unto him, 'Go, carry them to the city'. ⁴¹And as soon as the lad was gone, David arose out of a place toward the south, and fell on his face to the ground, and bowed himself three times: and they kissed one another, and wept one with another, until David exceeded. ⁴²And Jonathan said to David, 'Go in peace, forasmuch as we have sworn both of us in the name of the LORD, saying, "The LORD be between me and thee, and between my seed and thy seed for ever"'. And he arose and departed: and Jonathan went into the city.

21 Then came David to Nob to Ahimelech the priest: and Ahimelech was afraid at the meeting of David, and said unto him, 'Why art thou alone, and no man with thee?' ²And David said unto Ahimelech the priest, 'The king hath commanded me a business, and hath said unto me, "Let no man know anything of the business whereabout I send thee, and what I have commanded thee: and I have appointed my servants to such and such a place". ³Now therefore what is under thy hand? give me five loaves of bread in my hand, or what there is present.' ⁴And the priest answered David, and said, 'There is no common bread under my hand, but there is hallowed bread: if the young men have kept themselves at least from women'. ⁵And David answered the priest, and said unto him, 'Of a truth women have been kept from us about these three days, since I came out, and the vessels of the young men are holy, and the bread is in a manner common, yea, though it were sanctified this day in the vessel'. ⁶So the priest gave him hallowed bread: for there was no bread there but the showbread, that was taken from before the LORD, to put hot bread in the day when it was taken away. ⁷Now a certain man of the servants of Saul was there that day, detained before the LORD, and his name was Doeg, an Edomite, the chiefest of the herdsmen that belonged to Saul.

⁸And David said unto Ahimelech, 'And is there not here under thy hand spear or sword? for I have neither brought my sword nor my weapons with me, because the king's business required haste'. ⁹And the priest said, 'The sword of Goliath the Philistine, whom thou slewest in the valley of Elah, behold, it is here wrapped in a cloth behind the ephod: if thou wilt take that, take it: for there is no other save that here'. And David said, 'There is none like that; give it me'.

¹⁰And David arose, and fled that day for fear of Saul, and went to Achish the king of Gath. ¹¹And the servants of Achish said unto him, 'Is not this David the king of the land? Did they not sing one to another of him in dances, saying, "Saul hath slain his thousands, and David his ten thousands"?' ¹²And David laid up these words in his heart, and was sore afraid of Achish the king of Gath. ¹³And he changed his behaviour before them, and feigned himself mad in their hands, and scrabbled on the doors of the gate, and let his spittle fall down upon his beard. ¹⁴Then said Achish unto his servants, 'Lo, you see the man is mad: wherefore then have ye brought him to me? ¹⁵Have I need of madmen, that ye have brought this fellow to play the madman in my presence? Shall this fellow come into my house?'

22 David therefore departed thence, and escaped to the cave Adullam: and when his brethren and all his father's house heard it, they went down thither to him. ²And every one that was in distress, and every one that was in debt, and every one that was discontented, gathered themselves unto him, and he became a captain over them: and there were with him about four hundred men.

³And David went thence to Mizpeh of Moab: and he said unto the king of Moab, 'Let my father and my mother, I pray thee, come forth, and be with you, till I know what God will do for me'. ⁴And he brought them before the king of Moab: and they dwelt with him all the while that David was in the hold.

⁵And the prophet Gad said unto David, 'Abide not in the hold; depart, and get thee into the land of Judah'. Then David departed, and came into the forest of Hareth.

⁶When Saul heard that David was discovered, and the men that were with him (now Saul abode in Gibeah under a tree in Ramah, having his spear in his hand, and all his servants were standing about him): ⁷then Saul said unto his servants that stood about him, 'Hear now, ye Benjamites; will the son of Jesse give every one of you fields and vineyards, and make you all captains of thousands, and captains of hundreds; ⁸that all of you have conspired against me, and there is none that showeth me that my son hath made a league with the son of Jesse, and there is none of you that is sorry for me, or showeth unto me that my son hath stirred up my servant against me, to lie in wait, as at this day?'

⁹Then answered Doeg the Edomite, which was set over the servants of Saul, and said, 'I saw the son of Jesse coming to Nob, to Ahimelech the son of Ahitub. ¹⁰And he inquired of the LORD for him, and gave him victuals, and gave him the sword of Goliath the Philistine.' ¹¹Then the king sent to call Ahimelech the priest, the son of Ahitub, and all his father's house, the priests that were in Nob: and they came all of them to the king. ¹²And Saul said, 'Hear now, thou son of Ahitub'. And he answered, 'Here I am, my lord'. ¹³And Saul said unto him, 'Why have ye conspired against me, thou and the son of Jesse, in that thou hast given him bread, and a sword, and hast inquired of God for him, that he should rise against me, to lie in wait, as at this day?' ¹⁴Then Ahimelech answered the king, and said, 'And who is so faithful among all thy servants as David, which is the king's son-in-law, and goeth at thy bidding, and is honourable in thy house? ¹⁵Did I then begin to inquire of God for him? be it far from me: let not the king impute anything unto his servant, nor to all the house of my father: for thy servant knew nothing of all this, less or more.' ¹⁶And the king said, 'Thou shalt surely die, Ahimelech, thou, and all thy father's house'.

¹⁷And the king said unto the footmen that stood about him, 'Turn and slay the priests of the LORD, because their hand also is with David, and because they knew when he fled, and did not show it to me'. But the servants of the king would not put forth their hand to fall upon the priests of the LORD. ¹⁸And the king said to Doeg, 'Turn thou, and fall

upon the priests'. And Doeg the Edomite turned, and he fell upon the priests, and slew on that day fourscore and five persons that did wear a linen ephod. ¹⁹And Nob the city of the priests smote he with the edge of the sword, both men and women, children and sucklings, and oxen, and asses, and sheep, with the edge of the sword.

²⁰And one of the sons of Ahimelech the son of Ahitub, named Abiathar, escaped, and fled after David. ²¹And Abiathar showed David that Saul had slain the Lord's priests. ²²And David said unto Abiathar, 'I knew it that day, when Doeg the Edomite was there, that he would surely tell Saul: I have occasioned the death of all the persons of thy father's house. ²³Abide thou with me, fear not: for he that seeketh my life seeketh thy life: but with me thou shalt be in safeguard.'

23 Then they told David, saying, 'Behold, the Philistines fight against Keilah, and they rob the threshing-floors'. ²Therefore David inquired of the Lord, saying, 'Shall I go and smite these Philistines?' And the Lord said unto David, 'Go, and smite the Philistines, and save Keilah'. ³And David's men said unto him, 'Behold, we be afraid here in Judah: how much more then if we come to Keilah against the armies of the Philistines?' ⁴Then David inquired of the Lord yet again. And the Lord answered him and said, 'Arise, go down to Keilah: for I will deliver the Philistines into thy hand'. ⁵So David and his men went to Keilah, and fought with the Philistines, and brought away their cattle, and smote them with a great slaughter. So David saved the inhabitants of Keilah.

⁶And it came to pass, when Abiathar the son of Ahimelech fled to David to Keilah, that he came down with an ephod in his hand. ⁷And it was told Saul that David was come to Keilah. And Saul said, 'God hath delivered him into my hand: for he is shut in, by entering into a town that hath gates and bars'. ⁸And Saul called all the people together to war, to go down to Keilah, to besiege David and his men.

⁹And David knew that Saul secretly practised mischief against him, and he said to Abiathar the priest, 'Bring hither the ephod'. ¹⁰Then said David, 'O Lord God of Israel, thy servant hath certainly heard that Saul seeketh to come to Keilah, to destroy the city for my sake. ¹¹Will the men of Keilah deliver me up into his hand? will Saul come down, as thy servant hath heard, O Lord God of Israel? I beseech thee, tell thy servant.' And the Lord said, 'He will come down'. ¹²Then said David, 'Will the men of Keilah deliver me and my men into the hand of Saul?' And the Lord said, 'They will deliver thee up'.

¹³Then David and his men, which were about six hundred, arose and departed out of Keilah, and went whithersoever they could go. And it was told Saul that David was escaped from Keilah; and he forbore to go forth. ¹⁴And David abode in the wilderness in strongholds, and remained in a mountain in the wilderness of Ziph. And Saul sought him every day, but God delivered him not into his hand. ¹⁵And David saw that Saul was come out to seek his life: and David was in the wilderness of Ziph in a wood.

¹⁶And Jonathan Saul's son arose, and went to David into the wood,

and strengthened his hand in God. [17]And he said unto him, 'Fear not: for the hand of Saul my father shall not find thee, and thou shalt be king over Israel, and I shall be next unto thee; and that also Saul my father knoweth'. [18]And they two made a covenant before the LORD: and David abode in the wood, and Jonathan went to his house.

[19]Then came up the Ziphites to Saul to Gibeah, saying, 'Doth not David hide himself with us in strongholds in the wood, in the hill of Hachilah, which is on the south of Jeshimon? [20]Now therefore, O king, come down according to all the desire of thy soul to come down, and our part shall be to deliver him into the king's hand.' [21]And Saul said, 'Blessed be ye of the LORD, for ye have compassion on me. [22]Go, I pray you, prepare yet, and know and see his place where his haunt is, and who hath seen him there: for it is told me that he dealeth very subtly. [23]See therefore, and take knowledge of all the lurking-places where he hideth himself, and come ye again to me with the certainty, and I will go with you: and it shall come to pass, if he be in the land, that I will search him out throughout all the thousands of Judah.' [24]And they arose, and went to Ziph before Saul: but David and his men were in the wilderness of Maon, in the plain on the south of Jeshimon. [25]Saul also and his men went to seek him. And they told David: wherefore he came down into a rock, and abode in the wilderness of Maon. And when Saul heard that, he pursued after David in the wilderness of Maon. [26]And Saul went on this side of the mountain, and David and his men on that side of the mountain: and David made haste to get away for fear of Saul: for Saul and his men compassed David and his men round about to take them.

[27]But there came a messenger unto Saul, saying, 'Haste thee, and come: for the Philistines have invaded the land'. [28]Wherefore Saul returned from pursuing after David, and went against the Philistines: therefore they called that place Sela-hammahlekoth.

[29]And David went up from thence, and dwelt in strongholds at En-gedi.

24 And it came to pass, when Saul was returned from following the Philistines, that it was told him, saying, 'Behold, David is in the wilderness of En-gedi'. [2]Then Saul took three thousand chosen men out of all Israel, and went to seek David and his men upon the rocks of the wild goats. [3]And he came to the sheepcotes by the way, where was a cave; and Saul went in to cover his feet: and David and his men remained in the sides of the cave. [4]And the men of David said unto him, 'Behold the day of which the LORD said unto thee, "Behold, I will deliver thy enemy into thy hand, that thou mayest do to him as it shall seem good unto thee"'. Then David arose, and cut off the skirt of Saul's robe privily. [5]And it came to pass afterward, that David's heart smote him, because he had cut off Saul's skirt. [6]And he said unto his men, 'The LORD forbid that I should do this thing unto my master, the LORD's anointed, to stretch forth my hand against him, seeing he is the anointed of the LORD'. [7]So David stayed his servants with these words and suffered them not to rise against Saul. But Saul rose up out of the cave, and went on his way. [8]David also arose afterward, and went out of the cave, and cried after Saul, saying, 'My lord the king'. And when Saul looked behind him, David stooped with his face to the earth, and bowed himself.

[9]And David said to Saul, 'Wherefore hearest thou men's words, saying, "Behold, David seeketh thy hurt"? [10]Behold, this day thy eyes have seen how that the LORD had delivered thee today into my hand in the cave: and some bade me kill thee: but my eye spared thee; and I said, I will not put forth my hand against my lord, for he is the LORD's anointed. [11]Moreover, my father, see, yea, see the skirt of thy robe in my hand: for in that I cut off the skirt of thy robe, and killed thee not, know thou and see that there is neither evil nor transgression in my hand, and I have not sinned against thee; yet thou huntest my soul to take it. [12]The LORD judge between me and thee, and the LORD avenge me of thee: but my hand shall not be upon thee. [13]As saith the proverb of the ancients, "Wickedness proceedeth from the wicked": but my hand shall not be upon thee. [14]After whom is the king of Israel come out? after whom dost thou pursue? After a dead dog, after a flea. [15]The LORD therefore be judge, and judge between me and thee, and see, and plead my cause, and deliver me out of thy hand.'

[16]And it came to pass, when David had made an end of speaking these words unto Saul, that Saul said, 'Is this thy voice, my son David?' And Saul lifted up his voice, and wept. [17]And he said to David, 'Thou art more righteous than I: for thou hast rewarded me good, whereas I have rewarded thee evil. [18]And thou hast shown this day how that thou hast dealt well with me: forasmuch as when the LORD had delivered me into thy hand, thou killedst me not. [19]For if a man find his enemy, will he let him go well away? wherefore the LORD reward thee good for that thou hast done unto me this day. [20]And now behold, I know well that thou shalt surely be king, and that the kingdom of Israel shall be established in thy hand. [21]Swear now therefore unto me by the LORD, that thou wilt not cut off my seed after me, and that thou wilt not destroy my name out of my father's house.' [22]And David swore unto Saul. And Saul went home: but David and his men got them up unto the hold.

25 And Samuel died; and all the Israelites were gathered together, and lamented him, and buried him in his house at Ramah. And David arose, and went down to the wilderness of Paran.

[2]And there was a man in Maon, whose possessions were in Carmel, and the man was very great, and he had three thousand sheep, and a thousand goats: and he was shearing his sheep in Carmel. [3]Now the name of the man was Nabal, and the name of his wife Abigail: and she was a woman of good understanding, and of a beautiful countenance: but the man was churlish and evil in his doings; and he was of the house of Caleb.

[4]And David heard in the wilderness that Nabal did shear his sheep. [5]And David sent out ten young men, and David said unto the young men, 'Get you up to Carmel, and go to Nabal, and greet him in my name: [6]and thus shall ye say to him that liveth in prosperity, "Peace be both to thee, and peace be to thy house, and peace be unto all that thou

hast. ⁷And now I have heard that thou hast shearers: now thy shepherds which were with us, we hurt them not, neither was there aught missing unto them, all the while they were in Carmel. ⁸Ask thy young men, and they will show thee. Wherefore let the young men find favour in thy eyes (for we come in a good day): give, I pray thee, whatsoever cometh to thy hand unto thy servants, and to thy son David."' ⁹And when David's young men came, they spoke to Nabal according to all those words in the name of David, and ceased. ¹⁰And Nabal answered David's servants, and said, 'Who is David? and who is the son of Jesse? There be many servants nowadays that break away every man from his master. ¹¹Shall I then take my bread, and my water, and my flesh that I have killed for my shearers, and give it unto men, whom I know not whence they be?' ¹²So David's young men turned their way, and went again, and came and told him all those sayings. ¹³And David said unto his men, 'Gird you on every man his sword'. And they girded on every man his sword, and David also girded on his sword: and there went up after David about four hundred men; and two hundred abode by the stuff.

¹⁴But one of the young men told Abigail, Nabal's wife, saying, 'Behold, David sent messengers out of the wilderness to salute our master: and he railed on them. ¹⁵But the men were very good unto us, and we were not hurt, neither missed we anything, as long as we were conversant with them, when we were in the fields. ¹⁶They were a wall unto us both by night and day, all the while we were with them keeping sheep. ¹⁷Now therefore know and consider what thou wilt do: for evil is determined against our master, and against all his household: for he is such a son of Belial, that a man cannot speak to him.'

¹⁸Then Abigail made haste, and took two hundred loaves, and two bottles of wine, and five sheep ready dressed, and five measures of parched corn, and a hundred clusters of raisins, and two hundred cakes of figs, and laid them on asses. ¹⁹And she said unto her servants, 'Go on before me; behold, I come after you'. But she told not her husband Nabal. ²⁰And it was so, as she rode on the ass, that she came down by the covert of the hill, and behold, David and his men came down against her; and she met them. ²¹(Now David had said, 'Surely in vain have I kept all that this fellow hath in the wilderness, so that nothing was missed of all that pertained unto him: and he hath requited me evil for good. ²²So and more also do God unto the enemies of David, if I leave of all that pertain to him by the morning light any that pisseth against the wall.') ²³And when Abigail saw David, she hasted, and lighted off the ass, and fell before David on her face, and bowed herself to the ground, ²⁴and fell at his feet, and said, 'Upon me, my lord, upon me let this iniquity be: and let thy handmaid, I pray thee, speak in thy audience, and hear the words of thy handmaid. ²⁵Let not my lord, I pray thee, regard this man of Belial, even Nabal: for as his name is, so is he: Nabal is his name, and folly is with him: but I thy handmaid saw not the young men of my lord, whom thou didst send. ²⁶Now therefore, my lord, as the LORD liveth, and as thy soul liveth, seeing the LORD hath withheld thee from

coming to shed blood, and from avenging thyself with thy own hand, now let thy enemies, and they that seek evil to my lord, be as Nabal. ²⁷And now this blessing which thy handmaid hath brought unto my lord, let it even be given unto the young men that follow my lord. ²⁸I pray thee, forgive the trespass of thy handmaid: for the LORD will certainly make my lord a sure house, because my lord fighteth the battles of the LORD, and evil hath not been found in thee all thy days. ²⁹Yet a man is risen to pursue thee, and to seek thy soul: but the soul of my lord shall be bound in the bundle of life with the LORD thy God; and the souls of thy enemies, them shall he sling out, as out of the middle of a sling. ³⁰And it shall come to pass when the LORD shall have done to my lord according to all the good that he hath spoken concerning thee, and shall have appointed thee ruler over Israel; ³¹that this shall be no grief unto thee, nor offence of heart unto my lord, either that thou hast shed blood causeless, or that my lord hath avenged himself: but when the LORD shall have dealt well with my lord, then remember thy handmaid.'

³²And David said to Abigail, 'Blessed be the LORD God of Israel, which sent thee this day to meet me. ³³And blessed be thy advice, and blessed be thou, which hast kept me this day from coming to shed blood, and from avenging myself with my own hand. ³⁴For in very deed, as the LORD God of Israel liveth, which hath kept me back from hurting thee, except thou hadst hasted and come to meet me, surely there had not been left unto Nabal by the morning light any that pisseth against the wall.' ³⁵So David received of her hand that which she had brought him, and said unto her, 'Go up in peace to thy house; see, I have hearkened to thy voice, and have accepted thy person'.

³⁶And Abigail came to Nabal, and behold, he held a feast in his house, like the feast of a king; and Nabal's heart was merry within him, for he was very drunken: wherefore she told him nothing, less or more, until the morning light. ³⁷But it came to pass in the morning, when the wine was gone out of Nabal, and his wife had told him these things, that his heart died within him, and he became as a stone. ³⁸And it came to pass about ten days after, that the LORD smote Nabal, that he died.

³⁹And when David heard that Nabal was dead, he said, 'Blessed be the LORD, that hath pleaded the cause of my reproach from the hand of Nabal, and hath kept his servant from evil: for the LORD hath returned the wickedness of Nabal upon his own head'. And David sent and communed with Abigail, to take her to him to wife. ⁴⁰And when the servants of David were come to Abigail to Carmel, they spoke unto her, saying, 'David sent us unto thee, to take thee to him to wife'. ⁴¹And she arose, and bowed herself on her face to the earth, and said, 'Behold, let thy handmaid be a servant to wash the feet of the servants of my lord'. ⁴²And Abigail hasted, and arose, and rode upon an ass, with five damsels of hers that went after her; and she went after the messengers of David, and became his wife. ⁴³David also took Ahinoam of Jezreel; and they were also both of them his wives.

⁴⁴But Saul had given Michal his daughter, David's wife, to Phalti the son of Laish, which was of Gallim.

26 And the Ziphites came unto Saul to Gibeah, saying, 'Doth not David hide himself in the hill of Hachilah, which is before Jeshimon?' ²Then Saul arose, and went down to the wilderness of Ziph, having three thousand chosen men of Israel with him, to seek David in the wilderness of Ziph. ³And Saul pitched in the hill of Hachilah, which is before Jeshimon by the way. But David abode in the wilderness, and he saw that Saul came after him into the wilderness. ⁴David therefore sent out spies, and understood that Saul was come in very deed.

⁵And David arose, and came to the place where Saul had pitched: and David beheld the place where Saul lay, and Abner the son of Ner, the captain of his host: and Saul lay in the trench, and the people pitched round about him. ⁶Then answered David and said to Ahimelech the Hittite, and to Abishai the son of Zeruiah, brother to Joab, saying, 'Who will go down with me to Saul to the camp?' And Abishai said, 'I will go down with thee'. ⁷So David and Abishai came to the people by night: and behold, Saul lay sleeping within the trench, and his spear stuck in the ground at his bolster: but Abner and the people lay round about him. ⁸Then said Abishai to David, 'God hath delivered thy enemy into thy hand this day: now therefore let me smite him, I pray thee, with the spear even to the earth at once, and I will not smite him the second time'. ⁹And David said to Abishai, 'Destroy him not: for who can stretch forth his hand against the LORD's anointed, and be guiltless?' ¹⁰David said furthermore, 'As the LORD liveth, the LORD shall smite him, or his day shall come to die, or he shall descend into battle, and perish. ¹¹The LORD forbid that I should stretch forth my hand against the LORD's anointed: but, I pray thee, take thou now the spear that is at his bolster, and the cruse of water, and let us go.' ¹²So David took the spear and the cruse of water from Saul's bolster, and they got them away, and no man saw it, nor knew it, neither awoke: for they were all asleep; because a deep sleep from the LORD was fallen upon them.

¹³Then David went over to the other side, and stood on the top of a hill afar off; a great space being between them: ¹⁴and David cried to the people, and to Abner the son of Ner, saying, 'Answerest thou not, Abner?' Then Abner answered and said, 'Who art thou that criest to the king?' ¹⁵And David said to Abner, 'Art not thou a valiant man? and who is like to thee in Israel? Wherefore then hast thou not kept thy lord the king? for there came one of the people in to destroy the king thy lord. ¹⁶This thing is not good that thou hast done. As the LORD liveth, ye are worthy to die, because ye have not kept your master, the LORD's anointed. And now see where the king's spear is, and the cruse of water that was at his bolster.'

¹⁷And Saul knew David's voice, and said, 'Is this thy voice, my son David?' And David said, 'It is my voice, my lord, O king'. ¹⁸And he said, 'Wherefore doth my lord thus pursue after his servant? for what have I done? or what evil is in my hand? ¹⁹Now therefore, I pray thee, let my lord the king hear the words of his servant. If the LORD have stirred thee up against me, let him accept an offering: but if they be the children of men, cursed be they before the LORD: for they have driven me out this

day from abiding in the inheritance of the L ORD, saying, "Go serve other gods." ²⁰Now therefore, let not my blood fall to the earth before the face of the L ORD: for the king of Israel is come out to seek a flea, as when one doth hunt a partridge in the mountains.'

²¹Then said Saul, 'I have sinned: return, my son David, for I will no more do thee harm, because my soul was precious in thy eyes this day: behold, I have played the fool, and have erred exceedingly'. ²²And David answered and said, 'Behold the king's spear, and let one of the young men come over and fetch it. ²³The L ORD render to every man his right-eousness and his faithfulness: for the L ORD delivered thee into my hand today, but I would not stretch forth my hand against the L ORD's anointed. ²⁴And behold, as thy life was much set by this day in my eyes, so let my life be much set by in the eyes of the L ORD, and let him deliver me out of all tribulation.' ²⁵Then Saul said to David, 'Blessed be thou, my son David: thou shalt both do great things, and also shalt still pre-vail'. So David went on his way, and Saul returned to his place.

27 And David said in his heart, 'I shall now perish one day by the hand of Saul: there is nothing better for me than that I should speedily escape into the land of the Philistines; and Saul shall despair of me, to seek me any more in any coast of Israel: so shall I escape out of his hand'. ²And David arose, and he passed over with the six hundred men that were with him unto Achish, the son of Maoch, king of Gath. ³And David dwelt with Achish at Gath, he and his men, every man with his household, even David with his two wives, Ahinoam the Jezreelitess, and Abigail the Carmelitess, Nabal's wife. ⁴And it was told Saul that David was fled to Gath, and he sought no more again for him.

⁵And David said unto Achish, 'If I have now found grace in thy eyes, let them give me a place in some town in the country, that I may dwell there: for why should thy servant dwell in the royal city with thee?' ⁶Then Achish gave him Ziklag that day: wherefore Ziklag pertaineth unto the kings of Judah unto this day. ⁷And the time that David dwelt in the country of the Philistines was a full year and four months.

⁸And David and his men went up and invaded the Geshurites, and the Gezrites, and the Amalekites: for those nations were of old the inhabi-tants of the land, as thou goest to Shur, even unto the land of Egypt. ⁹And David smote the land, and left neither man nor woman alive, and took away the sheep, and the oxen, and the asses, and the camels, and the apparel, and returned, and came to Achish. ¹⁰And Achish said, 'Whither have ye made a road today?' And David said, 'Against the south of Judah, and against the south of the Jerahmeelites, and against the south of the Kenites'. ¹¹And David saved neither man nor woman alive, to bring tidings to Gath, saying, 'Lest they should tell on us, say-ing, "So did David, and so will be his manner all the while he dwelleth in the country of the Philistines"'. ¹²And Achish believed David, saying, 'He hath made his people Israel utterly to abhor him, therefore he shall be my servant for ever'.

28 And it came to pass in those days, that the Philistines gathered their armies together for warfare, to fight with Israel. And

Achish said unto David, 'Know thou assuredly, that thou shalt go out with me to battle, thou and thy men'. ²And David said to Achish, 'Surely thou shalt know what thy servant can do'. And Achish said to David, 'Therefore will I make thee keeper of my head for ever'.

³Now Samuel was dead, and all Israel had lamented him, and buried him in Ramah, even in his own city. And Saul had put away those that had familiar spirits, and the wizards, out of the land. ⁴And the Philistines gathered themselves together, and came and pitched in Shunem: and Saul gathered all Israel together, and they pitched in Gilboa. ⁵And when Saul saw the host of the Philistines, he was afraid, and his heart greatly trembled. ⁶And when Saul inquired of the LORD, the LORD answered him not, neither by dreams, nor by Urim, nor by prophets.

⁷Then said Saul unto his servants, 'Seek me a woman that hath a familiar spirit, that I may go to her, and inquire of her'. And his servant said to him, 'Behold, there is a woman that hath a familiar spirit at Endor'. ⁸And Saul disguised himself, and put on other raiment, and he went, and two men with him, and they came to the woman by night: and he said, 'I pray thee, divine unto me by the familiar spirit, and bring me him up, whom I shall name unto thee'. ⁹And the woman said unto him, 'Behold, thou knowest what Saul hath done, how he hath cut off those that have familiar spirits, and the wizards, out of the land: wherefore then layest thou a snare for my life, to cause me to die?' ¹⁰And Saul swore to her by the LORD, saying, 'As the LORD liveth, there shall no punishment happen to thee for this thing'. ¹¹Then said the woman, 'Whom shall I bring up unto thee?' And he said, 'Bring me up Samuel'. ¹²And when the woman saw Samuel, she cried with a loud voice: and the woman spoke to Saul, saying, 'Why hast thou deceived me? for thou art Saul'. ¹³And the king said unto her, 'Be not afraid: for what sawest thou?' And the woman said unto Saul, 'I saw gods ascending out of the earth'. ¹⁴And he said unto her, 'What form is he of?' And she said, 'An old man cometh up, and he is covered with a mantle'. And Saul perceived that it was Samuel, and he stooped with his face to the ground, and bowed himself.

¹⁵And Samuel said to Saul, 'Why hast thou disquieted me, to bring me up?' And Saul answered, 'I am sore distressed; for the Philistines make war against me, and God is departed from me, and answereth me no more, neither by prophets, nor by dreams: therefore I have called thee, that thou mayest make known unto me what I shall do'. ¹⁶Then said Samuel, 'Wherefore then dost thou ask of me, seeing the LORD is departed from thee, and is become thy enemy? ¹⁷And the LORD hath done to him, as he spoke by me: for the LORD hath rent the kingdom out of thy hand, and given it to thy neighbour, even to David: ¹⁸because thou obeyedst not the voice of the LORD, nor executedst his fierce wrath upon Amalek, therefore hath the LORD done this thing unto thee this day. ¹⁹Moreover the LORD will also deliver Israel with thee into the hand of the Philistines: and tomorrow shalt thou and thy sons be with me: the LORD also shall deliver the host of Israel into the hand of the

Philistines.' [20]Then Saul fell straightway all along on the earth, and was sore afraid, because of the words of Samuel, and there was no strength in him: for he had eaten no bread all the day, nor all the night.

[21]And the woman came unto Saul, and saw that he was sore troubled, and said unto him, 'Behold, thy handmaid hath obeyed thy voice, and I have put my life in my hand, and have hearkened unto thy words which thou spokest unto me. [22]Now therefore, I pray thee, hearken thou also unto the voice of thy handmaid, and let me set a morsel of bread before thee; and eat, that thou mayest have strength, when thou goest on thy way.' [23]But he refused, and said, 'I will not eat'. But his servants, together with the woman, compelled him, and he hearkened unto their voice. So he arose from the earth, and sat upon the bed. [24]And the woman had a fat calf in the house, and she hasted, and killed it, and took flour, and kneaded it, and did bake unleavened bread thereof. [25]And she brought it before Saul, and before his servants, and they did eat. Then they rose up, and went away that night.

29 Now the Philistines gathered together all their armies to Aphek: and the Israelites pitched by a fountain which is in Jezreel. [2]And the lords of the Philistines passed on by hundreds, and by thousands: but David and his men passed on in the rearward with Achish. [3]Then said the princes of the Philistines, 'What do these Hebrews here?' And Achish said unto the princes of the Philistines, 'Is not this David, the servant of Saul the king of Israel, which hath been with me these days, or these years, and I have found no fault in him since he fell unto me unto this day?' [4]And the princes of the Philistines were wroth with him; and the princes of the Philistines said unto him, 'Make this fellow return, that he may go again to his place which thou hast appointed him, and let him not go down with us to battle, lest in the battle he be an adversary to us: for wherewith should he reconcile himself unto his master? should it not be with the heads of these men? [5]Is not this David, of whom they sang one to another in dances, saying, "Saul slew his thousands, and David his ten thousands"?'

[6]Then Achish called David, and said unto him, 'Surely, as the LORD liveth, thou hast been upright, and thy going out and thy coming in with me in the host is good in my sight: for I have not found evil in thee since the day of thy coming unto me unto this day: nevertheless the lords favour thee not. [7]Wherefore now return, and go in peace, that thou displease not the lords of the Philistines.' [8]And David said unto Achish, 'But what have I done? and what hast thou found in thy servant so long as I have been with thee unto this day, that I may not go fight against the enemies of my lord the king?' [9]And Achish answered and said to David, 'I know that thou art good in my sight, as an angel of God: notwithstanding the princes of the Philistines have said, "He shall not go up with us to the battle". [10]Wherefore now rise up early in the morning with thy master's servants that are come with thee: and as soon as ye be up early in the morning, and have light, depart.' [11]So David and his men rose up early to depart in the morning, to return into the land of the Philistines. And the Philistines went up to Jezreel.

30 And it came to pass, when David and his men were come to Ziklag on the third day, that the Amalekites had invaded the south and Ziklag, and smitten Ziklag, and burnt it with fire; ²and had taken the women captives, that were therein: they slew not any, either great or small, but carried them away, and went on their way. ³So David and his men came to the city, and behold, it was burnt with fire, and their wives, and their sons, and their daughters were taken captives. ⁴Then David and the people that were with him lifted up their voice and wept, until they had no more power to weep. ⁵And David's two wives were taken captives, Ahinoam the Jezreelitess, and Abigail the wife of Nabal the Carmelite. ⁶And David was greatly distressed: for the people spoke of stoning him, because the soul of all the people was grieved, every man for his sons and for his daughters: but David encouraged himself in the LORD his God. ⁷And David said to Abiathar the priest, Ahimelech's son, 'I pray thee, bring me hither the ephod'. And Abiathar brought thither the ephod to David. ⁸And David inquired at the LORD, saying, 'Shall I pursue after this troop? shall I overtake them?' And he answered him, 'Pursue: for thou shalt surely overtake them, and without fail recover all'. ⁹So David went, he and the six hundred men that were with him, and came to the brook Besor, where those that were left behind stayed. ¹⁰But David pursued, he and four hundred men (for two hundred abode behind, which were so faint that they could not go over the brook Besor).

¹¹And they found an Egyptian in the field, and brought him to David, and gave him bread, and he did eat, and they made him drink water. ¹²And they gave him a piece of a cake of figs, and two clusters of raisins: and when he had eaten, his spirit came again to him: for he had eaten no bread, nor drunk any water, three days and three nights. ¹³And David said unto him, 'To whom belongest thou? and whence art thou?' And he said, 'I am a young man of Egypt, servant to an Amalekite; and my master left me, because three days agone I fell sick. ¹⁴We made an invasion upon the south of the Cherethites, and upon the coast which belongeth to Judah, and upon the south of Caleb, and we burnt Ziklag with fire.' ¹⁵And David said to him, 'Canst thou bring me down to this company?' And he said, 'Swear unto me by God, that thou wilt neither kill me, nor deliver me into the hands of my master, and I will bring thee down to this company'.

¹⁶And when he had brought him down, behold, they were spread abroad upon all the earth, eating and drinking, and dancing, because of all the great spoil that they had taken out of the land of the Philistines, and out of the land of Judah. ¹⁷And David smote them from the twilight even unto the evening of the next day: and there escaped not a man of them, save four hundred young men, which rode upon camels, and fled. ¹⁸And David recovered all that the Amalekites had carried away: and David rescued his two wives. ¹⁹And there was nothing lacking to them, neither small nor great, neither sons nor daughters, neither spoil, nor anything that they had taken to them: David recovered all. ²⁰And David took all the flocks and the herds,

which they drove before those other cattle, and said, 'This is David's spoil'.

²¹And David came to the two hundred men which were so faint that they could not follow David, whom they had made also to abide at the brook Besor: and they went forth to meet David, and to meet the people that were with him: and when David came near to the people, he saluted them. ²²Then answered all the wicked men, and men of Belial, of those that went with David, and said, 'Because they went not with us, we will not give them aught of the spoil that we have recovered, save to every man his wife and his children, that they may lead them away, and depart'. ²³Then said David, 'Ye shall not do so, my brethren, with that which the LORD hath given us, who hath preserved us, and delivered the company that came against us into our hand. ²⁴For who will hearken unto you in this matter? But as his part is that goeth down to the battle, so shall his part be that tarrieth by the stuff: they shall part alike.' ²⁵And it was so from that day forward, that he made it a statute and an ordinance for Israel unto this day.

²⁶And when David came to Ziklag, he sent of the spoil unto the elders of Judah, even to his friends, saying, 'Behold a present for you of the spoil of the enemies of the LORD'; ²⁷to them which were in Beth-el, and to them which were in south Ramoth, and to them which were in Jattir, ²⁸and to them which were in Aroer, and to them which were in Siphmoth, and to them which were in Eshtemoa, ²⁹and to them which were in Rachal, and to them which were in the cities of the Jerahmeelites, and to them which were in the cities of the Kenites, ³⁰and to them which were in Hormah, and to them which were in Chorashan, and to them which were in Athach, ³¹and to them which were in Hebron, and to all the places where David himself and his men were wont to haunt.

31 Now the Philistines fought against Israel: and the men of Israel fled from before the Philistines, and fell down slain in mount Gilboa. ²And the Philistines followed hard upon Saul and upon his sons; and the Philistines slew Jonathan, and Abinadab, and Malchishua, Saul's sons. ³And the battle went sore against Saul, and the archers hit him, and he was sore wounded of the archers. ⁴Then said Saul unto his armour-bearer, 'Draw thy sword, and thrust me through therewith, lest these uncircumcised come and thrust me through, and abuse me'. But his armour-bearer would not, for he was sore afraid. Therefore Saul took a sword, and fell upon it. ⁵And when his armour-bearer saw that Saul was dead, he fell likewise upon his sword, and died with him. ⁶So Saul died, and his three sons, and his armour-bearer, and all his men, that same day together.

⁷And when the men of Israel that were on the other side of the valley, and they that were on the other side Jordan, saw that the men of Israel fled, and that Saul and his sons were dead, they forsook the cities, and fled; and the Philistines came and dwelt in them. ⁸And it came to pass on the morrow when the Philistines came to strip the slain, that they found Saul and his three sons fallen in mount Gilboa. ⁹And they cut off

his head, and stripped off his armour, and sent into the land of the Philistines round about to publish it in the house of their idols, and among the people. ¹⁰And they put his armour in the house of Ashtaroth: and they fastened his body to the wall of Beth-shan.

¹¹And when the inhabitants of Jabesh-gilead heard of that which the Philistines had done to Saul: ¹²all the valiant men arose, and went all night, and took the body of Saul and the bodies of his sons from the wall of Beth-shan, and came to Jabesh, and burnt them there. ¹³And they took their bones, and buried them under a tree at Jabesh, and fasted seven days.

THE SECOND BOOK OF
SAMUEL
OTHERWISE CALLED
THE SECOND BOOK OF THE KINGS

1 Now it came to pass after the death of Saul, when David was returned from the slaughter of the Amalekites, and David had abode two days in Ziklag, ²it came even to pass on the third day, that behold, a man came out of the camp from Saul with his clothes rent, and earth upon his head: and so it was when he came to David, that he fell to the earth, and did obeisance. ³And David said unto him, 'From whence comest thou?' And he said unto him, 'Out of the camp of Israel am I escaped'. ⁴And David said unto him, 'How went the matter? I pray thee, tell me'. And he answered, 'That the people are fled from the battle, and many of the people also are fallen and dead; and Saul and Jonathan his son are dead also'. ⁵And David said unto the young man that told him, 'How knowest thou that Saul and Jonathan his son be dead?' ⁶And the young man that told him said, 'As I happened by chance upon mount Gilboa, behold, Saul leaned upon his spear: and lo, the chariots and horsemen followed hard after him. ⁷And when he looked behind him, he saw me, and called unto me. And I answered, "Here am I". ⁸And he said unto me, "Who art thou?" And I answered him, "I am an Amalekite". ⁹He said unto me again, "Stand, I pray thee, upon me, and slay me: for anguish is come upon me, because my life is yet whole in me". ¹⁰So I stood upon him, and slew him, because I was sure that he could not live after that he was fallen: and I took the crown that was upon his head, and the bracelet that was on his arm, and have brought them hither unto my lord." ¹¹Then David took hold on his clothes, and rent them, and likewise all the men that were with him. ¹²And they mourned and wept, and fasted until even, for Saul and for Jonathan his son, and for the people of the Lord, and for the house of Israel, because they were fallen by the sword.

¹³And David said unto the young man that told him, 'Whence art thou?' And he answered, 'I am the son of a stranger, an Amalekite'. ¹⁴And David said unto him, 'How wast thou not afraid to stretch forth thy hand to destroy the Lord's anointed?' ¹⁵And David called one of the young men, and said, 'Go near, and fall upon him'. And he smote him that he died. ¹⁶And David said unto him, 'Thy blood be upon thy head: for thy mouth hath testified against thee, saying, "I have slain the Lord's anointed"'.

¹⁷And David lamented with this lamentation over Saul and over Jonathan his son ¹⁸(also he bade them teach the children of Judah the use of the bow: behold, it is written in the book of Jasher):

¹⁹ 'The beauty of Israel is slain upon thy high places:
  how are the mighty fallen!

²⁰ Tell it not in Gath, publish it not in the streets of Askelon:
lest the daughters of the Philistines rejoice,
lest the daughters of the uncircumcised triumph.
²¹ Ye mountains of Gilboa, let there be no dew,
neither let there be rain upon you, nor fields of offerings:
for there the shield of the mighty is vilely cast away,
the shield of Saul, as though he had not been anointed with oil.
²² From the blood of the slain, from the fat of the mighty,
the bow of Jonathan turned not back,
and the sword of Saul returned not empty.
²³ Saul and Jonathan were lovely and pleasant in their lives,
and in their death they were not divided:
they were swifter than eagles, they were stronger than lions.
²⁴ Ye daughters of Israel, weep over Saul,
who clothed you in scarlet, with other delights,
who put on ornaments of gold upon your apparel.
²⁵ How are the mighty fallen in the midst of the battle!
O Jonathan, thou wast slain in thy high places.
²⁶ I am distressed for thee, my brother Jonathan:
very pleasant hast thou been unto me:
thy love to me was wonderful, passing the love of women.
²⁷ How are the mighty fallen,
and the weapons of war perished!'

2 And it came to pass after this, that David inquired of the LORD, saying, 'Shall I go up into any of the cities of Judah?' And the LORD said unto him, 'Go up'. And David said, 'Whither shall I go up?' And he said, 'Unto Hebron'. ²So David went up thither, and his two wives also, Ahinoam the Jezreelitess, and Abigail Nabal's wife the Carmelite. ³And his men that were with him did David bring up, every man with his household: and they dwelt in the cities of Hebron. ⁴And the men of Judah came, and there they anointed David king over the house of Judah. And they told David, saying, that the men of Jabesh-gilead were they that buried Saul.

⁵And David sent messengers unto the men of Jabesh-gilead, and said unto them, 'Blessed be ye of the LORD, that ye have shown this kindness unto your lord, even unto Saul, and have buried him. ⁶And now the LORD show kindness and truth unto you: and I also will requite you this kindness, because ye have done this thing. ⁷Therefore now let your hands be strengthened, and be ye valiant: for your master Saul is dead, and also the house of Judah have anointed me king over them.'

⁸But Abner the son of Ner, captain of Saul's host, took Ish-bosheth the son of Saul, and brought him over to Mahanaim. ⁹And he made him king over Gilead, and over the Ashurites, and over Jezreel, and over Ephraim, and over Benjamin, and over all Israel. ¹⁰Ish-bosheth Saul's son was forty years old when he began to reign over Israel, and reigned two years. But the house of Judah followed David. ¹¹And the time that David was king in Hebron over the house of Judah was seven years and six months.

¹²And Abner the son of Ner, and the servants of Ish-bosheth the son of Saul, went out from Mahanaim to Gibeon. ¹³And Joab the son of Zeruiah, and the servants of David went out, and met together by the pool of Gibeon: and they sat down, the one on the one side of the pool, and the other on the other side of the pool. ¹⁴And Abner said to Joab, 'Let the young men now arise, and play before us'. And Joab said, 'Let them arise'. ¹⁵Then there arose and went over by number twelve of Benjamin, which pertained to Ish-bosheth the son of Saul, and twelve of the servants of David. ¹⁶And they caught every one his fellow by the head, and thrust his sword in his fellow's side, so they fell down together: wherefore that place was called Helkath-hazzurim, which is in Gibeon. ¹⁷And there was a very sore battle that day: and Abner was beaten, and the men of Israel, before the servants of David.

¹⁸And there were three sons of Zeruiah there, Joab, and Abishai, and Asahel: and Asahel was as light of foot as a wild roe. ¹⁹And Asahel pursued after Abner, and in going he turned not to the right hand nor to the left from following Abner. ²⁰Then Abner looked behind him, and said, 'Art thou Asahel?' And he answered, 'I am'. ²¹And Abner said to him, 'Turn thee aside to thy right hand or to thy left, and lay thee hold on one of the young men, and take thee his armour'. But Asahel would not turn aside from following of him. ²²And Abner said again to Asahel, 'Turn thee aside from following me: wherefore should I smite thee to the ground? how then should I hold up my face to Joab thy brother?' ²³Howbeit he refused to turn aside: wherefore Abner with the hinder end of the spear smote him under the fifth rib, that the spear came out behind him; and he fell down there, and died in the same place: and it came to pass, that as many as came to the place where Asahel fell down and died stood still. ²⁴Joab also and Abishai pursued after Abner: and the sun went down when they were come to the hill of Ammah, that lieth before Giah by the way of the wilderness of Gibeon.

²⁵And the children of Benjamin gathered themselves together after Abner, and became one troop, and stood on the top of a hill. ²⁶Then Abner called to Joab, and said, 'Shall the sword devour for ever? Knowest thou not that it will be bitterness in the latter end? How long shall it be then, ere thou bid the people return from following their brethren?' ²⁷And Joab said, 'As God liveth, unless thou hadst spoken, surely then in the morning the people had gone up every one from following his brother'. ²⁸So Joab blew a trumpet, and all the people stood still, and pursued after Israel no more, neither fought they any more. ²⁹And Abner and his men walked all that night through the plain, and passed over Jordan, and went through all Bithron, and they came to Mahanaim. ³⁰And Joab returned from following Abner: and when he had gathered all the people together, there lacked of David's servants nineteen men and Asahel. ³¹But the servants of David had smitten of Benjamin and of Abner's men, so that three hundred and threescore men died.

³²And they took up Asahel, and buried him in the sepulchre of his father which was in Beth-lehem. And Joab and his men went all night, and they came to Hebron at break of day.

3 Now there was long war between the house of Saul and the house of David: but David waxed stronger and stronger, and the house of Saul waxed weaker and weaker.

²And unto David were sons born in Hebron: and his firstborn was Amnon, of Ahinoam the Jezreelitess; ³and his second, Chileab, of Abigail the wife of Nabal the Carmelite; and the third, Absalom the son of Maachah the daughter of Talmai king of Geshur; ⁴and the fourth, Adonijah the son of Haggith; and the fifth, Shephatiah the son of Abital; ⁵and the sixth, Ithream, by Eglah David's wife. These were born to David in Hebron.

⁶And it came to pass, while there was war between the house of Saul and the house of David, that Abner made himself strong for the house of Saul. ⁷And Saul had a concubine, whose name was Rizpah, the daughter of Aiah: and Ish-bosheth said to Abner, 'Wherefore hast thou gone in unto my father's concubine?' ⁸Then was Abner very wroth for the words of Ish-bosheth, and said, 'Am I a dog's head, which against Judah do show kindness this day unto the house of Saul thy father, to his brethren, and to his friends, and have not delivered thee into the hand of David, that thou chargest me today with a fault concerning this woman? ⁹So do God to Abner, and more also, except, as the LORD hath sworn to David, even so I do to him: ¹⁰to translate the kingdom from the house of Saul, and to set up the throne of David over Israel and over Judah, from Dan even to Beer-sheba.' ¹¹And he could not answer Abner a word again, because he feared him.

¹²And Abner sent messengers to David on his behalf, saying, 'Whose is the land?' saying also, 'Make thy league with me, and behold, my hand shall be with thee, to bring about all Israel unto thee'. ¹³And he said, 'Well, I will make a league with thee: but one thing I require of thee, that is, thou shalt not see my face, except thou first bring Michal Saul's daughter, when thou comest to see my face'. ¹⁴And David sent messengers to Ish-bosheth Saul's son, saying, 'Deliver me my wife Michal, which I espoused to me for a hundred foreskins of the Philistines'. ¹⁵And Ish-bosheth sent, and took her from her husband, even from Phaltiel the son of Laish. ¹⁶And her husband went with her along weeping behind her to Bahurim. Then said Abner unto him, 'Go, return'. And he returned.

¹⁷And Abner had communication with the elders of Israel, saying, 'Ye sought for David in times past to be king over you. ¹⁸Now then do it: for the LORD hath spoken of David, saying, "By the hand of my servant David I will save my people Israel out of the hand of the Philistines, and out of the hand of all their enemies".' ¹⁹And Abner also spoke in the ears of Benjamin: and Abner went also to speak in the ears of David in Hebron all that seemed good to Israel, and that seemed good to the whole house of Benjamin. ²⁰So Abner came to David to Hebron, and twenty men with him. And David made Abner and the men that were with him a feast. ²¹And Abner said unto David, 'I will arise and go, and will gather all Israel unto my lord the king, that they may make a league with thee, and that thou mayest reign over all that thy heart desireth'. And David sent Abner away; and he went in peace.

²²And behold, the servants of David and Joab came from pursuing a troop, and brought in a great spoil with them (but Abner was not with David in Hebron, for he had sent him away, and he was gone in peace). ²³When Joab and all the host that was with him were come, they told Joab, saying, 'Abner the son of Ner came to the king, and he hath sent him away, and he is gone in peace'. ²⁴Then Joab came to the king, and said, 'What hast thou done? behold, Abner came unto thee; why is it that thou hast sent him away, and he is quite gone? ²⁵Thou knowest Abner the son of Ner, that he came to deceive thee, and to know thy going out and thy coming in, and to know all that thou doest.' ²⁶And when Joab was come out from David, he sent messengers after Abner, which brought him again from the well of Sirah; but David knew it not. ²⁷And when Abner was returned to Hebron, Joab took him aside in the gate to speak with him quietly, and smote him there under the fifth rib, that he died, for the blood of Asahel his brother.

²⁸And afterward when David heard it, he said, 'I and my kingdom are guiltless before the Lord for ever from the blood of Abner the son of Ner: ²⁹let it rest on the head of Joab, and on all his father's house; and let there not fail from the house of Joab one that hath an issue, or that is a leper, or that leaneth on a staff, or that falleth on the sword, or that lacketh bread'. ³⁰So Joab, and Abishai his brother slew Abner, because he had slain their brother Asahel at Gibeon in the battle.

³¹And David said to Joab, and to all the people that were with him, 'Rend your clothes, and gird you with sackcloth, and mourn before Abner'. And king David himself followed the bier. ³²And they buried Abner in Hebron: and the king lifted up his voice, and wept at the grave of Abner; and all the people wept. ³³And the king lamented over Abner, and said, 'Died Abner as a fool dieth? ³⁴Thy hands were not bound, nor thy feet put into fetters: as a man falleth before wicked men, so fellest thou.' And all the people wept again over him. ³⁵And when all the people came to cause David to eat meat while it was yet day, David swore, saying, 'So do God to me, and more also, if I taste bread, or aught else, till the sun be down'. ³⁶And all the people took notice of it, and it pleased them: as whatsoever the king did pleased all the people. ³⁷For all the people and all Israel understood that day that it was not of the king to slay Abner the son of Ner. ³⁸And the king said unto his servants, 'Know ye not that there is a prince and a great man fallen this day in Israel? ³⁹And I am this day weak, though anointed king; and these men the sons of Zeruiah be too hard for me: the Lord shall reward the doer of evil according to his wickedness.'

4 And when Saul's son heard that Abner was dead in Hebron, his hands were feeble, and all the Israelites were troubled. ²And Saul's son had two men that were captains of bands: the name of the one was Baanah, and the name of the other Rechab, the sons of Rimmon a Beerothite, of the children of Benjamin (for Beeroth also was reckoned to Benjamin: ³and the Beerothites fled to Gittaim, and were sojourners there until this day). ⁴And Jonathan, Saul's son, had a son that was lame of his feet, and was five years old when the tidings came of Saul and

Jonathan out of Jezreel, and his nurse took him up, and fled: and it came to pass, as she made haste to flee, that he fell, and became lame. And his name was Mephibosheth. ⁵And the sons of Rimmon the Beerothite, Rechab and Baanah, went, and came about the heat of the day to the house of Ish-bosheth, who lay on a bed at noon. ⁶And they came thither into the midst of the house, as though they would have fetched wheat, and they smote him under the fifth rib: and Rechab and Baanah his brother escaped. ⁷For when they came into the house, he lay on his bed in his bedchamber, and they smote him, and slew him, and beheaded him, and took his head, and got them away through the plain all night. ⁸And they brought the head of Ish-bosheth unto David to Hebron, and said to the king, 'Behold the head of Ish-bosheth the son of Saul thy enemy, which sought thy life; and the LORD hath avenged my lord the king this day of Saul, and of his seed'.

⁹And David answered Rechab and Baanah his brother, the sons of Rimmon the Beerothite, and said unto them, 'As the LORD liveth, who hath redeemed my soul out of all adversity, ¹⁰when one told me, saying, "Behold, Saul is dead", thinking to have brought good tidings, I took hold of him, and slew him in Ziklag, who thought that I would have given him a reward for his tidings: ¹¹how much more, when wicked men have slain a righteous person in his own house upon his bed? Shall I not therefore now require his blood of your hand, and take you away from the earth?' ¹²And David commanded his young men, and they slew them, and cut off their hands and their feet, and hanged them up over the pool in Hebron. But they took the head of Ish-bosheth, and buried it in the sepulchre of Abner in Hebron.

5 Then came all the tribes of Israel to David unto Hebron, and spoke, saying, 'Behold, we are thy bone and thy flesh. ²Also in time past, when Saul was king over us, thou wast he that leddest out and brought-est in Israel: and the LORD said to thee, "Thou shalt feed my people Israel, and thou shalt be a captain over Israel".' ³So all the elders of Israel came to the king to Hebron; and king David made a league with them in Hebron before the LORD: and they anointed David king over Israel.

⁴David was thirty years old when he began to reign, and he reigned forty years. ⁵In Hebron he reigned over Judah seven years and six months: and in Jerusalem he reigned thirty and three years over all Israel and Judah.

⁶And the king and his men went to Jerusalem unto the Jebusites, the inhabitants of the land: which spoke unto David, saying, 'Except thou take away the blind and the lame, thou shalt not come in hither': thinking, David cannot come in hither. ⁷Nevertheless, David took the stronghold of Zion: the same is the city of David. ⁸And David said on that day, 'Whosoever getteth up to the gutter, and smiteth the Jebusites, and the lame and the blind, that are hated of David's soul, he shall be chief and captain'. Wherefore they said, 'The blind and the lame shall not come into the house'. ⁹So David dwelt in the fort, and called it the city of David. And David built round about, from Millo and

inward. ¹⁰And David went on, and grew great, and the LORD God of hosts was with him.

¹¹And Hiram king of Tyre sent messengers to David, and cedar trees, and carpenters, and masons: and they built David a house. ¹²And David perceived that the LORD had established him king over Israel, and that he had exalted his kingdom for his people Israel's sake.

¹³And David took him more concubines and wives out of Jerusalem, after he was come from Hebron: and there were yet sons and daughters born to David. ¹⁴And these be the names of those that were born unto him in Jerusalem; Shammua, and Shobab, and Nathan, and Solomon, ¹⁵Ibhar also, and Elishua, and Nepheg, and Japhia, ¹⁶and Elishama, and Eliada, and Eliphalet.

¹⁷But when the Philistines heard that they had anointed David king over Israel, all the Philistines came up to seek David; and David heard of it, and went down to the hold. ¹⁸The Philistines also came and spread themselves in the valley of Rephaim. ¹⁹And David inquired of the LORD, saying, 'Shall I go up to the Philistines? wilt thou deliver them into my hand?' And the LORD said unto David, 'Go up: for I will doubtless deliver the Philistines into thy hand'. ²⁰And David came to Baal-perazim, and David smote them there, and said, 'The LORD hath broken forth upon my enemies before me, as the breach of waters'. Therefore he called the name of that place Baal-perazim. ²¹And there they left their images, and David and his men burnt them.

²²And the Philistines came up yet again, and spread themselves in the valley of Rephaim. ²³And when David inquired of the LORD, he said, 'Thou shalt not go up: but fetch a compass behind them, and come upon them over against the mulberry trees. ²⁴And let it be, when thou hearest the sound of a going in the tops of the mulberry trees, that then thou shalt bestir thyself: for then shall the LORD go out before thee, to smite the host of the Philistines.' ²⁵And David did so, as the LORD had commanded him; and smote the Philistines from Geba until thou come to Gazer.

6 Again, David gathered together all the chosen men of Israel, thirty thousand. ²And David arose, and went with all the people that were with him from Baale of Judah, to bring up from thence the ark of God, whose name is called by the name of the LORD of hosts that dwelleth between the cherubims. ³And they set the ark of God upon a new cart, and brought it out of the house of Abinadab that was in Gibeah: and Uzzah and Ahio, the sons of Abinadab, drove the new cart. ⁴And they brought it out of the house of Abinadab which was at Gibeah, accompanying the ark of God; and Ahio went before the ark. ⁵And David and all the house of Israel played before the LORD on all manner of instruments made of fir wood, even on harps, and on psalteries, and on timbrels, and on cornets, and on cymbals.

⁶And when they came to Nachon's threshing-floor, Uzzah put forth his hand to the ark of God, and took hold of it, for the oxen shook it. ⁷And the anger of the LORD was kindled against Uzzah, and God smote him there for his error; and there he died by the ark of God. ⁸And David

was displeased, because the LORD had made a breach upon Uzzah: and he called the name of the place Perez-uzzah to this day. ⁹And David was afraid of the LORD that day, and said, 'How shall the ark of the LORD come to me?' ¹⁰So David would not remove the ark of the LORD unto him into the city of David: but David carried it aside into the house of Obed-edom the Gittite. ¹¹And the ark of the LORD continued in the house of Obed-edom the Gittite three months: and the LORD blessed Obed-edom, and all his household.

¹²And it was told king David, saying, 'The LORD hath blessed the house of Obed-edom, and all that pertaineth unto him, because of the ark of God'. So David went and brought up the ark of God from the house of Obed-edom into the city of David with gladness. ¹³And it was so, that when they that bore the ark of the LORD had gone six paces, he sacrificed oxen and fatlings. ¹⁴And David danced before the LORD with all his might; and David was girded with a linen ephod. ¹⁵So David and all the house of Israel brought up the ark of the LORD with shouting, and with the sound of the trumpet. ¹⁶And as the ark of the LORD came into the city of David, Michal Saul's daughter looked through a window, and saw king David leaping and dancing before the LORD, and she despised him in her heart.

¹⁷And they brought in the ark of the LORD, and set it in his place, in the midst of the tabernacle that David had pitched for it: and David offered burnt offerings and peace offerings before the LORD. ¹⁸And as soon as David had made an end of offering burnt offerings and peace offerings, he blessed the people in the name of the LORD of hosts. ¹⁹And he dealt among all the people, even among the whole multitude of Israel, as well to the women as men, to every one a cake of bread, and a good piece of flesh, and a flagon of wine. So all the people departed every one to his house.

²⁰Then David returned to bless his household. And Michal the daughter of Saul came out to meet David, and said, 'How glorious was the king of Israel today, who uncovered himself today in the eyes of the handmaids of his servants, as one of the vain fellows shamelessly uncovereth himself!' ²¹And David said unto Michal, 'It was before the LORD, which chose me before thy father, and before all his house, to appoint me ruler over the people of the LORD, over Israel: therefore will I play before the LORD. ²²And I will yet be more vile than thus, and will be base in my own sight: and of the maidservants which thou hast spoken of, of them shall I be had in honour.' ²³Therefore Michal the daughter of Saul had no child unto the day of her death.

7 And it came to pass, when the king sat in his house, and the LORD had given him rest round about from all his enemies; ²that the king said unto Nathan the prophet, 'See now, I dwell in a house of cedar, but the ark of God dwelleth within curtains'. ³And Nathan said to the king, 'Go, do all that is in thy heart: for the LORD is with thee'.

⁴And it came to pass that night, that the word of the LORD came unto Nathan, saying, ⁵'Go and tell my servant David, "Thus saith the LORD, 'Shalt thou build me a house for me to dwell in? ⁶Whereas I have not

dwelt in any house since the time that I brought up the children of Israel out of Egypt, even to this day, but have walked in a tent and in a tabernacle. ⁷In all the places wherein I have walked with all the children of Israel spoke I a word with any of the tribes of Israel, whom I commanded to feed my people Israel, saying, "Why build ye not me a house of cedar?"'" ⁸Now therefore so shalt thou say unto my servant David, "Thus saith the LORD of hosts, 'I took thee from the sheepcote, from following the sheep, to be ruler over my people, over Israel. ⁹And I was with thee whithersoever thou wentest, and have cut off all thy enemies out of thy sight, and have made thee a great name, like unto the name of the great men that are in the earth. ¹⁰(Moreover I will appoint a place for my people Israel, and will plant them, that they may dwell in a place of their own, and move no more; neither shall the children of wickedness afflict them any more, as beforetime, ¹¹and as since the time that I commanded judges to be over my people Israel, and have caused thee to rest from all thy enemies.)'" Also the LORD telleth thee that he will make thee a house.

¹²'"And when thy days be fulfilled, and thou shalt sleep with thy fathers, I will set up thy seed after thee, which shall proceed out of thy bowels, and I will establish his kingdom. ¹³He shall build a house for my name, and I will establish the throne of his kingdom for ever. ¹⁴I will be his father, and he shall be my son. If he commit iniquity, I will chasten him with the rod of men, and with the stripes of the children of men. ¹⁵But my mercy shall not depart away from him, as I took it from Saul, whom I put away before thee. ¹⁶And thy house and thy kingdom shall be established for ever before thee: thy throne shall be established for ever."' ¹⁷According to all these words, and according to all this vision, so did Nathan speak unto David.

¹⁸Then went king David in, and sat before the LORD, and he said, 'Who am I, O Lord GOD? and what is my house, that thou hast brought me hitherto? ¹⁹And this was yet a small thing in thy sight, O Lord GOD; but thou hast spoken also of thy servant's house for a great while to come. And is this the manner of man, O Lord GOD? ²⁰And what can David say more unto thee? for thou, Lord GOD, knowest thy servant. ²¹For thy word's sake, and according to thy own heart, hast thou done all these great things, to make thy servant know them. ²²Wherefore thou art great, O LORD God: for there is none like thee, neither is there any God besides thee, according to all that we have heard with our ears. ²³And what one nation in the earth is like thy people, even like Israel, whom God went to redeem for a people to himself, and to make him a name, and to do for you great things and terrible, for thy land, before thy people which thou redeemedst to thee from Egypt, from the nations and their gods? ²⁴For thou hast confirmed to thyself thy people Israel to be a people unto thee for ever: and thou, LORD, art become their God. ²⁵And now, O LORD God, the word that thou hast spoken concerning thy servant, and concerning his house, establish it for ever, and do as thou hast said. ²⁶And let thy name be magnified for ever, saying, "The LORD of hosts is the God over Israel": and let the house of thy servant David be

established before thee. ²⁷For thou, O LORD of hosts, God of Israel, hast revealed to thy servant, saying, "I will build thee a house": therefore hath thy servant found in his heart to pray this prayer unto thee. ²⁸And now, O Lord GOD (thou art that God, and thy words be true, and thou hast promised this goodness unto thy servant): ²⁹therefore now let it please thee to bless the house of thy servant, that it may continue for ever before thee: for thou, O Lord GOD, hast spoken it: and with thy blessing let the house of thy servant be blessed for ever.'

8 And after this it came to pass, that David smote the Philistines, and subdued them: and David took Metheg-ammah out of the hand of the Philistines. ²And he smote Moab, and measured them with a line, casting them down to the ground: even with two lines measured he to put to death, and with one full line to keep alive. And so the Moabites became David's servants, and brought gifts.

³David smote also Hadadezer, the son of Rehob, king of Zobah, as he went to recover his border at the river Euphrates. ⁴And David took from him a thousand chariots, and seven hundred horsemen, and twenty thousand footmen: and David hocked all the chariot-horses, but reserved of them for a hundred chariots. ⁵And when the Syrians of Damascus came to succour Hadadezer king of Zobah, David slew of the Syrians two and twenty thousand men. ⁶Then David put garrisons in Syria of Damascus: and the Syrians became servants to David, and brought gifts. And the LORD preserved David whithersoever he went. ⁷And David took the shields of gold that were on the servants of Hadadezer, and brought them to Jerusalem. ⁸And from Betah, and from Berothai, cities of Hadadezer, king David took exceeding much brass.

⁹When Toi king of Hamath heard that David had smitten all the host of Hadadezer, ¹⁰then Toi sent Joram his son unto king David, to salute him, and to bless him, because he had fought against Hadadezer, and smitten him: for Hadadezer had wars with Toi. And Joram brought with him vessels of silver, and vessels of gold, and vessels of brass; ¹¹which also king David did dedicate unto the LORD, with the silver and gold that he had dedicated of all nations which he subdued: ¹²of Syria, and of Moab, and of the children of Ammon, and of the Philistines, and of Amalek, and of the spoil of Hadadezer, son of Rehob, king of Zobah. ¹³And David got him a name when he returned from smiting of the Syrians in the valley of salt, being eighteen thousand men.

¹⁴And he put garrisons in Edom; throughout all Edom put he garrisons, and all they of Edom became David's servants. And the LORD preserved David whithersoever he went.

¹⁵And David reigned over all Israel, and David executed judgement and justice unto all his people. ¹⁶And Joab the son of Zeruiah was over the host, and Jehoshaphat the son of Ahilud was recorder, ¹⁷and Zadok the son of Ahitub, and Ahimelech the son of Abiathar, were the priests, and Seraiah was the scribe. ¹⁸And Benaiah the son of Jehoiada was over both the Cherethites and the Pelethites, and David's sons were chief rulers.

9 And David said, 'Is there yet any that is left of the house of Saul, that I may show him kindness for Jonathan's sake?' ²And there was

of the house of Saul a servant whose name was Ziba. And when they had called him unto David, the king said unto him, 'Art thou Ziba?' And he said, 'Thy servant is he'. ³And the king said, 'Is there not yet any of the house of Saul, that I may show the kindness of God unto him?' And Ziba said unto the king, 'Jonathan hath yet a son, which is lame on his feet'. ⁴And the king said unto him, 'Where is he?' And Ziba said unto the king, 'Behold, he is in the house of Machir, the son of Ammiel, in Lo-debar'.

⁵Then king David sent, and fetched him out of the house of Machir, the son of Ammiel, from Lo-debar. ⁶Now when Mephibosheth, the son of Jonathan the son of Saul, was come unto David, he fell on his face, and did reverence. And David said, 'Mephibosheth!' And he answered, 'Behold thy servant'.

⁷And David said unto him, 'Fear not, for I will surely show thee kindness for Jonathan thy father's sake, and will restore thee all the land of Saul thy father, and thou shalt eat bread at my table continually'. ⁸And he bowed himself, and said, 'What is thy servant, that thou shouldst look upon such a dead dog as I am?'

⁹Then the king called to Ziba, Saul's servant, and said unto him, 'I have given unto thy master's son all that pertained to Saul and to all his house. ¹⁰Thou therefore, and thy sons, and thy servants, shall till the land for him, and thou shalt bring in the fruits, that thy master's son may have food to eat: but Mephibosheth thy master's son shall eat bread always at my table.' Now Ziba had fifteen sons and twenty servants. ¹¹Then said Ziba unto the king, 'According to all that my lord the king hath commanded his servant, so shall thy servant do'. 'As for Mephibosheth,' said the king, 'he shall eat at my table, as one of the king's sons.' ¹²And Mephibosheth had a young son, whose name was Micha. And all that dwelt in the house of Ziba were servants unto Mephibosheth. ¹³So Mephibosheth dwelt in Jerusalem: for he did eat continually at the king's table; and was lame on both his feet.

10 And it came to pass after this, that the king of the children of Ammon died, and Hanun his son reigned in his stead. ²Then said David, 'I will show kindness unto Hanun the son of Nahash, as his father showed kindness unto me'. And David sent to comfort him by the hand of his servants for his father. And David's servants came into the land of the children of Ammon. ³And the princes of the children of Ammon said unto Hanun their lord, 'Thinkest thou that David doth honour thy father, that he hath sent comforters unto thee? Hath not David rather sent his servants unto thee, to search the city, and to spy it out, and to overthrow it?' ⁴Wherefore Hanun took David's servants, and shaved off the one half of their beards, and cut off their garments in the middle, even to their buttocks, and sent them away. ⁵When they told it unto David, he sent to meet them, because the men were greatly ashamed: and the king said, 'Tarry at Jericho until your beards be grown, and then return'.

⁶And when the children of Ammon saw that they stank before David, the children of Ammon sent and hired the Syrians of Beth-rehob, and

the Syrians of Zoba, twenty thousand footmen, and of king Maachah a thousand men, and of Ish-tob twelve thousand men. [7]And when David heard of it, he sent Joab, and all the host of the mighty men. [8]And the children of Ammon came out, and put the battle in array at the entering in of the gate: and the Syrians of Zoba and of Rehob, and Ish-tob, and Maachah, were by themselves in the field. [9]When Joab saw that the front of the battle was against him, before and behind, he chose of all the choice men of Israel, and put them in array against the Syrians. [10]And the rest of the people he delivered into the hand of Abishai his brother, that he might put them in array against the children of Ammon. [11]And he said, 'If the Syrians be too strong for me, then thou shalt help me: but if the children of Ammon be too strong for thee, then I will come and help thee. [12]Be of good courage, and let us play the men for our people, and for the cities of our God: and the LORD do that which seemeth him good.' [13]And Joab drew nigh, and the people that were with him, unto the battle against the Syrians: and they fled before him. [14]And when the children of Ammon saw that the Syrians were fled, then fled they also before Abishai, and entered into the city. So Joab returned from the children of Ammon, and came to Jerusalem.

[15]And when the Syrians saw that they were smitten before Israel, they gathered themselves together. [16]And Hadarezer sent, and brought out the Syrians that were beyond the river, and they came to Helam; and Shobach the captain of the host of Hadarezer went before them. [17]And when it was told David, he gathered all Israel together, and passed over Jordan, and came to Helam. And the Syrians set themselves in array against David, and fought with him. [18]And the Syrians fled before Israel; and David slew the men of seven hundred chariots of the Syrians, and forty thousand horsemen, and smote Shobach the captain of their host, who died there. [19]And when all the kings that were servants to Hadarezer saw that they were smitten before Israel, they made peace with Israel, and served them. So the Syrians feared to help the children of Ammon any more.

11 And it came to pass, that after the year was expired, at the time when kings go forth to battle, that David sent Joab, and his servants with him, and all Israel; and they destroyed the children of Ammon, and besieged Rabbah. But David tarried still at Jerusalem.

[2]And it came to pass in an evening-tide, that David arose from off his bed, and walked upon the roof of the king's house: and from the roof he saw a woman washing herself; and the woman was very beautiful to look upon. [3]And David sent and inquired after the woman. And one said, 'Is not this Bath-sheba, the daughter of Eliam, the wife of Uriah the Hittite?' [4]And David sent messengers, and took her, and she came in unto him, and he lay with her (for she was purified from her uncleanness), and she returned unto her house. [5]And the woman conceived, and sent and told David, and said, 'I am with child'.

[6]And David sent to Joab, saying, 'Send me Uriah the Hittite'. And Joab sent Uriah to David. [7]And when Uriah was come unto him, David demanded of him how Joab did, and how the people did, and how the

war prospered. [8]And David said to Uriah, 'Go down to thy house, and wash thy feet'. And Uriah departed out of the king's house, and there followed him a mess of meat from the king. [9]But Uriah slept at the door of the king's house with all the servants of his lord, and went not down to his house. [10]And when they had told David, saying, 'Uriah went not down unto his house', David said unto Uriah, 'Camest thou not from thy journey? why then didst thou not go down unto thy house?' [11]And Uriah said unto David, 'The ark, and Israel, and Judah, abide in tents, and my lord Joab, and the servants of my lord are encamped in the open fields; shall I then go into my house, to eat and to drink, and to lie with my wife? As thou livest, and as thy soul liveth, I will not do this thing.' [12]And David said to Uriah, 'Tarry here today also, and tomorrow I will let thee depart'. So Uriah abode in Jerusalem that day, and the morrow. [13]And when David had called him, he did eat and drink before him, and he made him drunk: and at even he went out to lie on his bed with the servants of his lord, but went not down to his house.

[14]And it came to pass in the morning, that David wrote a letter to Joab, and sent it by the hand of Uriah. [15]And he wrote in the letter, saying, 'Set ye Uriah in the forefront of the hottest battle, and retire ye from him, that he may be smitten, and die'. [16]And it came to pass, when Joab observed the city, that he assigned Uriah unto a place where he knew that valiant men were. [17]And the men of the city went out, and fought with Joab: and there fell some of the people of the servants of David, and Uriah the Hittite died also.

[18]Then Joab sent and told David all the things concerning the war: [19]and charged the messenger, saying, 'When thou hast made an end of telling the matters of the war unto the king, [20]and if so be that the king's wrath arise, and he say unto thee, "Wherefore approached ye so nigh unto the city when ye did fight? Knew ye not that they would shoot from the wall? [21]Who smote Abimelech the son of Jerubbesheth? Did not a woman cast a piece of a millstone upon him from the wall, that he died in Thebez? why went ye nigh the wall?" Then say thou, "Thy servant Uriah the Hittite is dead also".'

[22]So the messenger went, and came and showed David all that Joab had sent him for. [23]And the messenger said unto David, 'Surely the men prevailed against us, and came out unto us into the field, and we were upon them even unto the entering of the gate. [24]And the shooters shot from off the wall upon thy servants, and some of the king's servants be dead, and thy servant Uriah the Hittite is dead also.' [25]Then David said unto the messenger, 'Thus shalt thou say unto Joab, "Let not this thing displease thee, for the sword devoureth one as well as another: make thy battle more strong against the city, and overthrow it": and encourage thou him'.

[26]And when the wife of Uriah heard that Uriah her husband was dead, she mourned for her husband. [27]And when the mourning was past, David sent and fetched her to his house, and she became his wife, and bore him a son: but the thing that David had done displeased the LORD.

prophet i speak

12 And the LORD sent Nathan unto David. And he came unto him, and said unto him, 'There were two men in one city; the one rich, and the other poor. ²The rich man had exceeding many flocks and herds. ³But the poor man had nothing, save one little ewe lamb, which he had bought and nourished up: and it grew up together with him, and with his children; it did eat of his own meat, and drank of his own cup, and lay in his bosom, and was unto him as a daughter. ⁴And there came a traveller unto the rich man, and he spared to take of his own flock and of his own herd, to dress for the wayfaring man that was come unto him, but took the poor man's lamb, and dressed it for the man that was come to him.' ⁵And David's anger was greatly kindled against the man, and he said to Nathan, 'As the LORD liveth, the man that hath done this thing shall surely die. ⁶And he shall restore the lamb fourfold, because he did this thing, and because he had no pity.'

⁷And Nathan said to David, 'Thou art the man. Thus saith the LORD God of Israel, "I anointed thee king over Israel, and I delivered thee out of the hand of Saul, ⁸and I gave thee thy master's house, and thy master's wives into thy bosom, and gave thee the house of Israel and of Judah; and if that had been too little, I would moreover have given unto thee such and such things. ⁹Wherefore hast thou despised the commandment of the LORD, to do evil in his sight? thou hast killed Uriah the Hittite with the sword, and hast taken his wife to be thy wife, and hast slain him with the sword of the children of Ammon. ¹⁰Now therefore the sword shall never depart from thy house, because thou hast despised me, and hast taken the wife of Uriah the Hittite to be thy wife." ¹¹Thus saith the LORD, "Behold, I will raise up evil against thee out of thy own house, and I will take thy wives before thy eyes, and give them unto thy neighbour, and he shall lie with thy wives in the sight of this sun. ¹²For thou didst it secretly: but I will do this thing before all Israel, and before the sun."' ¹³And David said unto Nathan, 'I have sinned against the LORD'. And Nathan said unto David, 'The LORD also hath put away thy sin; thou shalt not die. ¹⁴Howbeit, because by this deed thou hast given great occasion to the enemies of the LORD to blaspheme, the child also that is born unto thee shall surely die.'

¹⁵And Nathan departed unto his house. And the LORD struck the child that Uriah's wife bore unto David, and it was very sick. ¹⁶David therefore besought God for the child; and David fasted, and went in, and lay all night upon the earth. ¹⁷And the elders of his house arose, and went to him, to raise him up from the earth: but he would not, neither did he eat bread with them. ¹⁸And it came to pass on the seventh day, that the child died. And the servants of David feared to tell him that the child was dead: for they said, 'Behold, while the child was yet alive, we spoke unto him, and he would not hearken unto our voice: how will he then vex himself, if we tell him that the child is dead?' ¹⁹But when David saw that his servants whispered, David perceived that the child was dead: therefore David said unto his servants, 'Is the child dead?' And they said, 'He is dead'. ²⁰Then David arose from the earth and washed, and anointed himself, and changed his apparel, and came into

for Karma Crime for David

Confession

Punishment

the house of the LORD, and worshipped: then he came to his own house, and when he required, they set bread before him, and he did eat. ²¹Then said his servants unto him, 'What thing is this that thou hast done? thou didst fast and weep for the child, while it was alive, but when the child was dead, thou didst rise and eat bread'. ²²And he said, 'While the child was yet alive, I fasted and wept: for I said, "Who can tell whether GOD will be gracious to me, that the child may live?" ²³But now he is dead, wherefore should I fast? Can I bring him back again? I shall go to him, but he shall not return to me.'

²⁴And David comforted Bath-sheba his wife, and went in unto her, and lay with her: and she bore a son, and he called his name Solomon: and the LORD loved him. ²⁵And he sent by the hand of Nathan the prophet, and he called his name Jedidiah, because of the LORD.

²⁶And Joab fought against Rabbah of the children of Ammon, and took the royal city. ²⁷And Joab sent messengers to David, and said, 'I have fought against Rabbah, and have taken the city of waters. ²⁸Now therefore gather the rest of the people together, and encamp against the city, and take it: lest I take the city, and it be called after my name.' ²⁹And David gathered all the people together, and went to Rabbah, and fought against it, and took it. ³⁰And he took their king's crown from off his head, the weight whereof was a talent of gold with the precious stones: and it was set on David's head. And he brought forth the spoil of the city in great abundance. ³¹And he brought forth the people that were therein, and put them under saws, and under harrows of iron, and under axes of iron, and made them pass through the brick-kiln: and thus did he unto all the cities of the children of Ammon. So David and all the people returned unto Jerusalem.

13 And it came to pass after this, that Absalom the son of David had a fair sister, whose name was Tamar: and Amnon the son of David loved her. ²And Amnon was so vexed, that he fell sick for his sister Tamar: for she was a virgin, and Amnon thought it hard for him to do anything to her. ³But Amnon had a friend, whose name was Jonadab, the son of Shimeah David's brother: and Jonadab was a very subtle man. ⁴And he said unto him, 'Why art thou, being the king's son, lean from day to day? Wilt thou not tell me?' And Amnon said unto him, 'I love Tamar, my brother Absalom's sister'. ⁵And Jonadab said unto him, 'Lay thee down on thy bed, and make thyself sick: and when thy father cometh to see thee, say unto him, "I pray thee, let my sister Tamar come, and give me meat, and dress the meat in my sight, that I may see it, and eat it at her hand"'.

⁶So Amnon lay down, and made himself sick: and when the king was come to see him, Amnon said unto the king, 'I pray thee, let Tamar my sister come, and make me a couple of cakes in my sight, that I may eat at her hand'. ⁷Then David sent home to Tamar, saying, 'Go now to thy brother Amnon's house, and dress him meat'. ⁸So Tamar went to her brother Amnon's house; and he was laid down. And she took flour, and kneaded it, and made cakes in his sight, and did bake the cakes.

⁹And she took a pan, and poured them out before him, but he

refused to eat. And Amnon said, 'Have out all men from me'. And they went out every man from him. ¹⁰And Amnon said unto Tamar, 'Bring the meat into the chamber, that I may eat of thy hand'. And Tamar took the cakes which she had made, and brought them into the chamber to Amnon her brother. ¹¹And when she had brought them unto him to eat, he took hold of her, and said unto her, 'Come lie with me, my sister'. ¹²And she answered him, 'Nay, my brother, do not force me: for no such thing ought to be done in Israel; do not thou this folly. ¹³And I, whither shall I cause my shame to go? and as for thee, thou shalt be as one of the fools in Israel. Now therefore, I pray thee, speak unto the king, for he will not withhold me from thee.' ¹⁴Howbeit he would not hearken unto her voice: but, being stronger than she, forced her, and lay with her.

¹⁵Then Amnon hated her exceedingly, so that the hatred wherewith he hated her was greater than the love wherewith he had loved her. And Amnon said unto her, 'Arise, be gone'. ¹⁶And she said unto him, 'There is no cause: this evil in sending me away is greater than the other that thou didst unto me'. But he would not hearken unto her. ¹⁷Then he called his servant that ministered unto him, and said, 'Put now this woman out from me, and bolt the door after her'. ¹⁸And she had a garment of divers colours upon her: for with such robes were the king's daughters that were virgins apparelled. Then his servant brought her out, and bolted the door after her. ¹⁹And Tamar put ashes on her head, and rent her garment of divers colours that was on her, and laid her hand on her head, and went on, crying. ²⁰And Absalom her brother said unto her, 'Hath Amnon thy brother been with thee? But hold now thy peace, my sister: he is thy brother, regard not this thing.' So Tamar remained desolate in her brother Absalom's house.

²¹But when king David heard of all these things, he was very wroth. ²²And Absalom spoke unto his brother Amnon neither good nor bad: for Absalom hated Amnon, because he had forced his sister Tamar.

²³And it came to pass after two full years, that Absalom had sheep-shearers in Baal-hazor, which is beside Ephraim: and Absalom invited all the king's sons. ²⁴And Absalom came to the king, and said, 'Behold now, thy servant hath sheep-shearers; let the king, I beseech thee, and his servants go with thy servant'. ²⁵And the king said to Absalom, 'Nay, my son, let us not all now go, lest we be chargeable unto thee'. And he pressed him: howbeit he would not go, but blessed him. ²⁶Then said Absalom, 'If not, I pray thee, let my brother Amnon go with us'. And the king said unto him, 'Why should he go with thee?' ²⁷But Absalom pressed him, that he let Amnon and all the king's sons go with him.

²⁸Now Absalom had commanded his servants, saying, 'Mark ye now when Amnon's heart is merry with wine, and when I say unto you, "Smite Amnon", then kill him, fear not: have not I commanded you? be courageous, and be valiant'. ²⁹And the servants of Absalom did unto Amnon as Absalom had commanded. Then all the king's sons arose, and every man got him up upon his mule, and fled.

³⁰And it came to pass, while they were in the way, that tidings came to

David, saying, 'Absalom hath slain all the king's sons, and there is not one of them left'. ³¹Then the king arose, and tore his garments, and lay on the earth; and all his servants stood by with their clothes rent. ³²And Jonadab, the son of Shimeah David's brother, answered and said, 'Let not my lord suppose that they have slain all the young men the king's sons; for Amnon only is dead: for by the appointment of Absalom this hath been determined from the day that he forced his sister Tamar. ³³Now therefore let not my lord the king take the thing to his heart, to think that all the king's sons are dead: for Amnon only is dead.' ³⁴But Absalom fled. And the young man that kept the watch lifted up his eyes, and looked, and behold, there came much people by the way of the hill side behind him. ³⁵And Jonadab said unto the king, 'Behold, the king's sons come: as thy servant said, so it is'. ³⁶And it came to pass, as soon as he had made an end of speaking, that behold, the king's sons came, and lifted up their voice and wept: and the king also and all his servants wept very sore.

³⁷But Absalom fled, and went to Talmai the son of Ammihud, king of Geshur. And David mourned for his son every day. ³⁸So Absalom fled, and went to Geshur, and was there three years. ³⁹And the soul of king David longed to go forth unto Absalom: for he was comforted concerning Amnon, seeing he was dead.

14 Now Joab the son of Zeruiah perceived that the king's heart was toward Absalom. ²And Joab sent to Tekoah, and fetched thence a wise woman, and said unto her, 'I pray thee, feign thyself to be a mourner, and put on now mourning apparel, and anoint not thyself with oil, but be as a woman that had a long time mourned for the dead: ³and come to the king, and speak on this manner unto him'. So Joab put the words in her mouth.

⁴And when the woman of Tekoah spoke to the king, she fell on her face to the ground, and did obeisance, and said, 'Help, O king'. ⁵And the king said unto her, 'What aileth thee?' And she answered, 'I am indeed a widow woman, and my husband is dead. ⁶And thy handmaid had two sons, and they two strove together in the field, and there was none to part them, but the one smote the other, and slew him. ⁷And behold, the whole family is risen against thy handmaid, and they said, "Deliver him that smote his brother, that we may kill him, for the life of his brother whom he slew; and we will destroy the heir also": and so they shall quench my coal which is left, and shall not leave to my husband neither name nor remainder upon the earth.' ⁸And the king said unto the woman, 'Go to thy house, and I will give charge concerning thee'. ⁹And the woman of Tekoah said unto the king, 'My lord, O king, the iniquity be on me, and on my father's house: and the king and his throne be guiltless'. ¹⁰And the king said, 'Whosoever saith aught unto thee, bring him to me, and he shall not touch thee any more'. ¹¹Then said she, 'I pray thee, let the king remember the LORD thy God, that thou wouldst not suffer the revengers of blood to destroy any more, lest they destroy my son'. And he said, 'As the LORD liveth, there shall not one hair of thy son fall to the earth'. ¹²Then the woman said, 'Let thy

handmaid, I pray thee, speak one word unto my lord the king'. And he said, 'Say on'. [13]And the woman said, 'Wherefore then hast thou thought such a thing against the people of God? For the king doth speak this thing as one which is faulty, in that the king doth not fetch home again his banished. [14]For we must needs die, and are as water spilt on the ground, which cannot be gathered up again: neither doth God respect any person, yet doth he devise means, that his banished be not expelled from him. [15]Now therefore that I am come to speak of this thing unto my lord the king, it is because the people have made me afraid: and thy handmaid said, "I will now speak unto the king; it may be that the king will perform the request of his handmaid. [16]For the king will hear, to deliver his handmaid out of the hand of the man that would destroy me and my son together out of the inheritance of God." [17]Then thy handmaid said, "The word of my lord the king shall now be comfortable: for as an angel of God, so is my lord the king to discern good and bad: therefore the LORD thy God will be with thee".' [18]Then the king answered and said unto the woman, 'Hide not from me, I pray thee, the thing that I shall ask thee'. And the woman said, 'Let my lord the king now speak'. [19]And the king said, 'Is not the hand of Joab with thee in all this?' And the woman answered and said, 'As thy soul liveth, my lord the king, none can turn to the right hand or to the left from aught that my lord the king hath spoken: for thy servant Joab, he bade me, and he put all these words in the mouth of thy handmaid: [20]to fetch about this form of speech hath thy servant Joab done this thing: and my lord is wise, according to the wisdom of an angel of God, to know all things that are in the earth'.

[21]And the king said unto Joab, 'Behold now, I have done this thing: go therefore, bring the young man Absalom again'. [22]And Joab fell to the ground on his face, and bowed himself, and thanked the king: and Joab said, 'Today thy servant knoweth that I have found grace in thy sight, my lord, O king, in that the king hath fulfilled the request of his servant'. [23]So Joab arose and went to Geshur, and brought Absalom to Jerusalem. [24]And the king said, 'Let him turn to his own house, and let him not see my face'. So Absalom returned to his own house, and saw not the king's face.

[25]But in all Israel there was none to be so much praised as Absalom for his beauty: from the sole of his foot even to the crown of his head there was no blemish in him. [26]And when he polled his head (for it was at every year's end that he polled it: because the hair was heavy on him, therefore he polled it), he weighed the hair of his head at two hundred shekels after the king's weight. [27]And unto Absalom there were born three sons, and one daughter, whose name was Tamar: she was a woman of a fair countenance.

[28]So Absalom dwelt two full years in Jerusalem, and saw not the king's face. [29]Therefore Absalom sent for Joab, to have sent him to the king, but he would not come to him: and when he sent again the second time, he would not come. [30]Therefore he said unto his servants, 'See, Joab's field is near mine, and he hath barley there: go and set it on fire'.

And Absalom's servants set the field on fire. ³¹Then Joab arose, and came to Absalom unto his house, and said unto him, 'Wherefore have thy servants set my field on fire?' ³²And Absalom answered Joab, 'Behold, I sent unto thee, saying, "Come hither, that I may send thee to the king, to say, 'Wherefore am I come from Geshur? It had been good for me to have been there still: now therefore let me see the king's face: and if there be any iniquity in me, let him kill me'."' ³³So Joab came to the king, and told him: and when he had called for Absalom, he came to the king, and bowed himself on his face to the ground before the king, and the king kissed Absalom.

15 And it came to pass after this, that Absalom prepared him chariots and horses, and fifty men to run before him. ²And Absalom rose up early, and stood beside the way of the gate: and it was so, that when any man that had a controversy came to the king for judgement, then Absalom called unto him, and said, 'Of what city art thou?' And he said, 'Thy servant is of one of the tribes of Israel'. ³And Absalom said unto him, 'See, thy matters are good and right, but there is no man deputed of the king to hear thee'. ⁴Absalom said moreover, 'O that I were made judge in the land, that every man which hath any suit or cause might come unto me, and I would do him justice!' ⁵And it was so, that when any man came nigh to him to do him obeisance, he put forth his hand, and took him, and kissed him. ⁶And on this manner did Absalom to all Israel that came to the king for judgement: so Absalom stole the hearts of the men of Israel.

⁷And it came to pass after forty years, that Absalom said unto the king, 'I pray thee, let me go and pay my vow, which I have vowed unto the LORD in Hebron. ⁸For thy servant vowed a vow while I abode at Geshur in Syria, saying, "If the LORD shall bring me again indeed to Jerusalem, then I will serve the LORD".' ⁹And the king said unto him, 'Go in peace'. So he arose, and went to Hebron.

¹⁰But Absalom sent spies throughout all the tribes of Israel, saying, 'As soon as ye hear the sound of the trumpet, then ye shall say, "Absalom reigneth in Hebron"'. ¹¹And with Absalom went two hundred men out of Jerusalem, that were called; and they went in their simplicity, and they knew not anything. ¹²And Absalom sent for Ahithophel the Gilonite, David's counsellor, from his city, even from Giloh, while he offered sacrifices. And the conspiracy was strong, for the people increased continually with Absalom.

¹³And there came a messenger to David, saying, 'The hearts of the men of Israel are after Absalom'. ¹⁴And David said unto all his servants that were with him at Jerusalem, 'Arise, and let us flee; for we shall not else escape from Absalom: make speed to depart, lest he overtake us suddenly, and bring evil upon us, and smite the city with the edge of the sword'. ¹⁵And the king's servants said unto the king, 'Behold, thy servants are ready to do whatsoever my lord the king shall appoint'. ¹⁶And the king went forth, and all his household after him. And the king left ten women, which were concubines, to keep the house. ¹⁷And the king went forth, and all the people after him, and tarried in a place that was

far off. ¹⁸And all his servants passed on beside him: and all the Cherethites, and all the Pelethites, and all the Gittites, six hundred men which came after him from Gath, passed on before the king.

¹⁹Then said the king to Ittai the Gittite, 'Wherefore goest thou also with us? Return to thy place, and abide with the king: for thou art a stranger, and also an exile. ²⁰Whereas thou camest but yesterday, should I this day make thee go up and down with us? Seeing I go whither I may, return thou, and take back thy brethren: mercy and truth be with thee.' ²¹And Ittai answered the king, and said, 'As the LORD liveth, and as my lord the king liveth, surely in what place my lord the king shall be, whether in death or life, even there also will thy servant be'. ²²And David said to Ittai, 'Go and pass over'. And Ittai the Gittite passed over, and all his men, and all the little ones that were with him. ²³And all the country wept with a loud voice, and all the people passed over: the king also himself passed over the brook Kidron, and all the people passed over, toward the way of the wilderness.

²⁴And lo, Zadok also, and all the Levites were with him, bearing the ark of the covenant of God: and they set down the ark of God; and Abiathar went up, until all the people had done passing out of the city. ²⁵And the king said unto Zadok, 'Carry back the ark of God into the city: if I shall find favour in the eyes of the LORD, he will bring me again, and show me both it, and his habitation. ²⁶But if he thus say, "I have no delight in thee": behold, here am I, let him do to me as seemeth good unto him.' ²⁷The king said also unto Zadok the priest, 'Art not thou a seer? Return into the city in peace, and your two sons with you, Ahimaaz thy son, and Jonathan the son of Abiathar. ²⁸See, I will tarry in the plain of the wilderness, until there come word from you to certify me.' ²⁹Zadok therefore and Abiathar carried the ark of God again to Jerusalem: and they tarried there.

³⁰And David went up by the ascent of mount Olivet, and wept as he went up, and had his head covered, and he went barefoot: and all the people that was with him covered every man his head, and they went up, weeping as they went up.

³¹And one told David, saying, 'Ahithophel is among the conspirators with Absalom'. And David said, 'O LORD, I pray thee, turn the counsel of Ahithophel into foolishness'.

³²And it came to pass, that when David was come to the top of the mount, where he worshipped God, behold, Hushai the Archite came to meet him with his coat rent, and earth upon his head: ³³unto whom David said, 'If thou passest on with me, then thou shalt be a burden unto me. ³⁴But if thou return to the city, and say unto Absalom, "I will be thy servant, O king: as I have been thy father's servant hitherto, so will I now also be thy servant": then mayest thou for me defeat the counsel of Ahithophel. ³⁵And hast thou not there with thee Zadok and Abiathar the priests? therefore it shall be, that what thing soever thou shalt hear out of the king's house, thou shalt tell it to Zadok and Abiathar the priests. ³⁶Behold, they have there with them their two sons: Ahimaaz Zadok's son, and Jonathan Abiathar's son: and by them

ye shall send unto me everything that ye can hear.' ³⁷So Hushai David's friend came into the city, and Absalom came into Jerusalem.

16 And when David was a little past the top of the hill, behold, Ziba the servant of Mephibosheth met him with a couple of asses saddled, and upon them two hundred loaves of bread, and a hundred bunches of raisins, and a hundred of summer fruits, and a bottle of wine. ²And the king said unto Ziba, 'What meanest thou by these?' And Ziba said, 'The asses be for the king's household to ride on, and the bread and summer fruit for the young men to eat, and the wine, that such as be faint in the wilderness may drink'. ³And the king said, 'And where is thy master's son?' And Ziba said unto the king, 'Behold, he abideth at Jerusalem: for he said, "Today shall the house of Israel restore me the kingdom of my father"'. ⁴Then said the king to Ziba, 'Behold, thine are all that pertained unto Mephibosheth'. And Ziba said, 'I humbly beseech thee that I may find grace in thy sight, my lord, O king'.

⁵And when king David came to Bahurim, behold, thence came out a man of the family of the house of Saul, whose name was Shimei, the son of Gera: he came forth, and cursed still as he came. ⁶And he cast stones at David, and at all the servants of king David: and all the people and all the mighty men were on his right hand and on his left. ⁷And thus said Shimei when he cursed, 'Come out, come out thou bloody man, and thou man of Belial: ⁸the LORD hath returned upon thee all the blood of the house of Saul, in whose stead thou hast reigned, and the LORD hath delivered the kingdom into the hand of Absalom thy son: and behold, thou art taken to thy mischief, because thou art a bloody man'.

⁹Then said Abishai the son of Zeruiah unto the king, 'Why should this dead dog curse my lord the king? let me go over, I pray thee, and take off his head'. ¹⁰And the king said, 'What have I to do with you, ye sons of Zeruiah? So let him curse, because the LORD hath said unto him, "Curse David". Who shall then say, "Wherefore hast thou done so?"' ¹¹And David said to Abishai, and to all his servants, 'Behold, my son which came forth of my bowels, seeketh my life: how much more now may this Benjamite do it? let him alone, and let him curse: for the LORD hath bidden him. ¹²It may be that the LORD will look on my affliction, and that the LORD will requite good for his cursing this day.' ¹³And as David and his men went by the way, Shimei went along on the hill's side over against him, and cursed as he went, and threw stones at him, and cast dust. ¹⁴And the king, and all the people that were with him, came weary, and refreshed themselves there.

¹⁵And Absalom and all the people the men of Israel, came to Jerusalem, and Ahithophel with him. ¹⁶And it came to pass when Hushai the Archite, David's friend, was come unto Absalom, that Hushai said unto Absalom, 'God save the king, God save the king'. ¹⁷And Absalom said to Hushai, 'Is this thy kindness to thy friend? Why wentest thou not with thy friend?' ¹⁸And Hushai said unto Absalom, 'Nay, but whom the LORD and this people, and all the men of Israel choose,

his will I be, and with him will I abide. ¹⁹And again, whom should I serve? should I not serve in the presence of his son? as I have served in thy father's presence, so will I be in thy presence.'

²⁰Then said Absalom to Ahithophel, 'Give counsel among you what we shall do'. ²¹And Ahithophel said unto Absalom, 'Go in unto thy father's concubines, which he hath left to keep the house, and all Israel shall hear that thou art abhorred of thy father: then shall the hands of all that are with thee be strong'. ²²So they spread Absalom a tent upon the top of the house, and Absalom went in unto his father's concubines in the sight of all Israel. ²³And the counsel of Ahithophel which he counselled in those days, was as if a man had inquired at the oracle of God: so was all the counsel of Ahithophel both with David and with Absalom.

17 Moreover Ahithophel said unto Absalom, 'Let me now choose out twelve thousand men, and I will arise and pursue after David this night. ²And I will come upon him while he is weary and weakhanded, and will make him afraid: and all the people that are with him shall flee, and I will smite the king only. ³And I will bring back all the people unto thee: the man whom thou seekest is as if all returned: so all the people shall be in peace.' ⁴And the saying pleased Absalom well, and all the elders of Israel. ⁵Then said Absalom, 'Call now Hushai the Archite also, and let us hear likewise what he saith'. ⁶And when Hushai was come to Absalom, Absalom spoke unto him, saying, 'Ahithophel hath spoken after this manner: shall we do after his saying? if not; speak thou'. ⁷And Hushai said unto Absalom, 'The counsel that Ahithophel hath given is not good at this time. ⁸For,' said Hushai, 'thou knowest thy father and his men, that they be mighty men, and they be chafed in their minds, as a bear robbed of her whelps in the field: and thy father is a man of war, and will not lodge with the people. ⁹Behold, he is hid now in some pit, or in some other place: and it will come to pass when some of them be overthrown at the first, that whosoever heareth it will say, "There is a slaughter among the people that follow Absalom". ¹⁰And he also that is valiant, whose heart is as the heart of a lion, shall utterly melt: for all Israel knoweth that thy father is a mighty man, and they which be with him are valiant men. ¹¹Therefore I counsel that all Israel be generally gathered unto thee, from Dan even to Beer-sheba, as the sand that is by the sea for multitude, and that thou go to battle in thy own person. ¹²So shall we come upon him in some place where he shall be found, and we will light upon him as the dew falleth on the ground: and of him and of all the men that are with him there shall not be left so much as one. ¹³Moreover, if he be gotten into a city, then shall all Israel bring ropes to that city, and we will draw it into the river, until there be not one small stone found there.' ¹⁴And Absalom and all the men of Israel said, 'The counsel of Hushai the Archite is better than the counsel of Ahithophel'. For the LORD had appointed to defeat the good counsel of Ahithophel, to the intent that the LORD might bring evil upon Absalom.

¹⁵Then said Hushai unto Zadok and to Abiathar the priests, 'Thus and

thus did Ahithophel counsel Absalom and the elders of Israel, and thus and thus have I counselled. ¹⁶Now therefore send quickly, and tell David, saying, "Lodge not this night in the plains of the wilderness, but speedily pass over, lest the king be swallowed up, and all the people that are with him".' ¹⁷Now Jonathan and Ahimaaz stayed by En-rogel (for they might not be seen to come into the city): and a wench went and told them; and they went and told king David. ¹⁸Nevertheless a lad saw them, and told Absalom: but they went both of them away quickly, and came to a man's house in Bahurim, which had a well in his court, whither they went down. ¹⁹And the woman took and spread a covering over the well's mouth, and spread ground corn thereon; and the thing was not known. ²⁰And when Absalom's servants came to the woman to the house, they said, 'Where is Ahimaaz and Jonathan?' And the woman said unto them, 'They be gone over the brook of water'. And when they had sought and could not find them, they returned to Jerusalem. ²¹And it came to pass after they were departed, that they came up out of the well, and went and told king David, and said unto David, 'Arise, and pass quickly over the water: for thus hath Ahithophel counselled against you'. ²²Then David arose, and all the people that were with him, and they passed over Jordan: by the morning light there lacked not one of them that was not gone over Jordan.

²³And when Ahithophel saw that his counsel was not followed, he saddled his ass, and arose, and got him home to his house, to his city, and put his household in order, and hanged himself, and died, and was buried in the sepulchre of his father.

²⁴Then David came to Mahanaim. And Absalom passed over Jordan, he and all the men of Israel with him. ²⁵And Absalom made Amasa captain of the host in stead of Joab: which Amasa was a man's son whose name was Ithra an Israelite, that went in to Abigail the daughter of Nahash, sister to Zeruiah Joab's mother. ²⁶So Israel and Absalom pitched in the land of Gilead.

²⁷And it came to pass when David was come to Mahanaim, that Shobi the son of Nahash of Rabbah of the children of Ammon, and Machir the son of Ammiel of Lo-debar, and Barzillai the Gileadite of Rogelim, ²⁸brought beds, and basins, and earthen vessels, and wheat, and barley, and flour, and parched corn, and beans, and lentils, and parched pulse, ²⁹and honey, and butter, and sheep, and cheese of kine for David, and for the people that were with him, to eat: for they said, 'The people is hungry, and weary, and thirsty, in the wilderness'.

18 And David numbered the people that were with him, and set captains of thousands and captains of hundreds over them. ²And David sent forth a third part of the people under the hand of Joab, and a third part under the hand of Abishai the son of Zeruiah, Joab's brother, and a third part under the hand of Ittai the Gittite. And the king said unto the people, 'I will surely go forth with you myself also'. ³But the people answered, 'Thou shalt not go forth: for if we flee away, they will not care for us, neither if half of us die will they care for us: but now thou art worth ten thousand of us: therefore now it is better that thou succour us out of the city'. ⁴And the king said unto them, 'What seemeth you best I will do'. And the king stood by the gate side, and all the people came out by hundreds and by thousands. ⁵And the king commanded Joab and Abishai and Ittai, saying, 'Deal gently for my sake with the young man, even with Absalom'. And all the people heard when the king gave all the captains charge concerning Absalom.

⁶So the people went out into the field against Israel: and the battle was in the wood of Ephraim, ⁷where the people of Israel were slain before the servants of David, and there was there a great slaughter that day of twenty thousand men. ⁸For the battle was there scattered over the face of all the country: and the wood devoured more people that day than the sword devoured.

⁹And Absalom met the servants of David. And Absalom rode upon a mule, and the mule went under the thick boughs of a great oak, and his head caught hold of the oak, and he was taken up between the heaven and the earth; and the mule that was under him went away. ¹⁰And a certain man saw it, and told Joab, and said, 'Behold, I saw Absalom hanged in an oak'. ¹¹And Joab said unto the man that told him, 'And behold, thou sawest him, and why didst thou not smite him there to the ground? and I would have given thee ten shekels of silver, and a girdle'. ¹²And the man said unto Joab, 'Though I should receive a thousand shekels of silver in my hand, yet would I not put forth my hand against the king's son: for in our hearing the king charged thee and Abishai and Ittai, saying, "Beware that none touch the young man Absalom". ¹³Otherwise I should have wrought falsehood against my own life: for there is no matter hid from the king, and thou thyself wouldst have set thyself against me.' ¹⁴Then said Joab, 'I may not tarry thus with thee'. And he took three darts in his hand, and thrust them through the heart of Absalom, while he was yet alive in the midst of the oak. ¹⁵And ten young men that bore Joab's armour compassed about and smote Absalom, and slew him. ¹⁶And Joab blew the trumpet, and the people returned from pursuing after Israel: for Joab held back the people. ¹⁷And they took Absalom, and cast him into a great pit in the wood, and laid a very great heap of stones upon him: and all Israel fled every one to his tent.

¹⁸Now Absalom in his lifetime had taken and reared up for himself a pillar, which is in the king's dale: for he said, 'I have no son to keep my name in remembrance': and he called the pillar after his own name: and it is called unto this day, Absalom's place.

¹⁹Then said Ahimaaz the son of Zadok, 'Let me now run, and bear the king tidings, how that the LORD hath avenged him of his enemies'. ²⁰And Joab said unto him, 'Thou shalt not bear tidings this day, but thou shalt bear tidings another day: but this day thou shalt bear no tidings, because the king's son is dead'. ²¹Then said Joab to Cushi, 'Go tell the king what thou hast seen'. And Cushi bowed himself unto Joab, and ran. ²²Then said Ahimaaz the son of Zadok yet again to Joab, 'But howsoever, let me, I pray thee, also run after Cushi'. And Joab said, 'Wherefore wilt thou run, my son, seeing that thou hast no tidings

ready?' ²³'But howsoever,' said he, 'let me run'. And he said unto him, 'Run'. Then Ahimaaz ran by the way of the plain, and overran Cushi.

²⁴And David sat between the two gates: and the watchman went up to the roof over the gate unto the wall, and lifted up his eyes, and looked, and behold, a man running alone. ²⁵And the watchman cried, and told the king. And the king said, 'If he be alone, there is tidings in his mouth'. And he came apace, and drew near. ²⁶And the watchman saw another man running: and the watchman called unto the porter, and said, 'Behold another man running alone'. And the king said, 'He also bringeth tidings'. ²⁷And the watchman said, 'Me thinketh the running of the foremost is like the running of Ahimaaz the son of Zadok'. And the king said, 'He is a good man, and cometh with good tidings'. ²⁸And Ahimaaz called, and said unto the king, 'All is well'. And he fell down to the earth upon his face before the king, and said, 'Blessed be the LORD thy God, which hath delivered up the men that lifted up their hand against my lord the king'. ²⁹And the king said, 'Is the young man Absalom safe?' And Ahimaaz answered, 'When Joab sent the king's servant, and me thy servant, I saw a great tumult, but I knew not what it was'. ³⁰And the king said unto him, 'Turn aside, and stand here'. And he turned aside, and stood still. ³¹And behold, Cushi came; and Cushi said, 'Tidings, my lord the king: for the LORD hath avenged thee this day of all them that rose up against thee'. ³²And the king said unto Cushi, 'Is the young man Absalom safe?' And Cushi answered, 'The enemies of my lord the king, and all that rise against thee to do thee hurt, be as that young man is'.

³³And the king was much moved, and went up to the chamber over the gate, and wept: and as he went, thus he said, 'O my son Absalom, my son, my son Absalom: would God I had died for thee, O Absalom, my son, my son'.

19 And it was told Joab, 'Behold, the king weepeth and mourneth for Absalom'. ²And the victory that day was turned into mourning unto all the people: for the people heard say that day how the king was grieved for his son. ³And the people got them by stealth that day into the city, as people being ashamed steal away when they flee in battle. ⁴But the king covered his face, and the king cried with a loud voice, 'O my son Absalom, O Absalom, my son, my son'. ⁵And Joab came into the house to the king, and said, 'Thou hast shamed this day the faces of all thy servants, which this day have saved thy life, and the lives of thy sons and of thy daughters, and the lives of thy wives, and the lives of thy concubines, ⁶in that thou lovest thy enemies, and hatest thy friends. For thou hast declared this day, that thou regardest neither princes nor servants: for this day I perceive, that if Absalom had lived, and all we had died this day, then it had pleased thee well. ⁷Now therefore arise, go forth, and speak comfortably unto thy servants: for I swear by the LORD, if thou go not forth, there will not tarry one with thee this night, and that will be worse unto thee than all the evil that befell thee from thy youth until now.' ⁸Then the king arose, and sat in the gate. And they told unto all the people, saying, 'Behold, the king doth sit in the gate'. And all the people came before the king: for Israel had fled every man to his tent.

⁹And all the people were at strife throughout all the tribes of Israel, saying, 'The king saved us out of the hand of our enemies, and he delivered us out of the hand of the Philistines; and now he is fled out of the land for Absalom. ¹⁰And Absalom, whom we anointed over us, is dead in battle. Now therefore why speak ye not a word of bringing the king back?'

¹¹And king David sent to Zadok and to Abiathar the priests, saying, 'Speak unto the elders of Judah, saying, "Why are ye the last to bring the king back to his house?"' (seeing the speech of all Israel is come to the king, even to his house). ¹²'"Ye are my brethren, ye are my bones and my flesh: wherefore then are ye the last to bring back the king?" ¹³And say ye to Amasa, "Art thou not of my bone, and of my flesh? God do so to me, and more also, if thou be not captain of the host before me continually in the room of Joab."' ¹⁴And he bowed the heart of all the men of Judah, even as the heart of one man, so that they sent this word unto the king, 'Return thou, and all thy servants'. ¹⁵So the king returned, and came to Jordan. And Judah came to Gilgal, to go to meet the king, to conduct the king over Jordan.

¹⁶And Shimei the son of Gera, a Benjamite, which was of Bahurim, hasted and came down with the men of Judah to meet king David. ¹⁷And there were a thousand men of Benjamin with him, and Ziba the servant of the house of Saul, and his fifteen sons and his twenty servants with him; and they went over Jordan before the king. ¹⁸And there went over a ferry-boat to carry over the king's household, and to do what he thought good. And Shimei the son of Gera fell down before the king as he was come over Jordan; ¹⁹and said unto the king, 'Let not my lord impute iniquity unto me, neither do thou remember that which thy servant did perversely the day that my lord the king went out of Jerusalem, that the king should take it to his heart. ²⁰For thy servant doth know that I have sinned: therefore behold, I am come the first this day of all the house of Joseph to go down to meet my lord the king.' ²¹But Abishai the son of Zeruiah answered and said, 'Shall not Shimei be put to death for this, because he cursed the LORD's anointed?' ²²And David said, 'What have I to do with you, ye sons of Zeruiah, that ye should this day be adversaries unto me? shall there any man be put to death this day in Israel? for do not I know that I am this day king over Israel?' ²³Therefore the king said unto Shimei, 'Thou shalt not die'. And the king swore unto him.

²⁴And Mephibosheth the son of Saul came down to meet the king, and had neither dressed his feet, nor trimmed his beard, nor washed his clothes, from the day the king departed until the day he came again in peace. ²⁵And it came to pass when he was come to Jerusalem to meet the king, that the king said unto him, 'Wherefore wentest not thou with me, Mephibosheth?' ²⁶And he answered, 'My lord, O king, my servant deceived me: for thy servant said, "I will saddle me an ass, that I may ride thereon, and go to the king"; because thy servant is lame. ²⁷And he

hath slandered thy servant unto my lord the king; but my lord the king is as an angel of God: do therefore what is good in thy eyes. [28]For all of my father's house were but dead men before my lord the king: yet didst thou set thy servant among them that did eat at thy own table. What right therefore have I yet to cry any more unto the king?' [29]And the king said unto him, 'Why speakest thou any more of thy matters? I have said, "Thou and Ziba divide the land".' [30]And Mephibosheth said unto the king, 'Yea, let him take all, forasmuch as my lord the king is come again in peace unto his own house'.

[31]And Barzillai the Gileadite came down from Rogelim, and went over Jordan with the king, to conduct him over Jordan. [32]Now Barzillai was a very aged man, even fourscore years old: and he had provided the king of sustenance while he lay at Mahanaim: for he was a very great man. [33]And the king said unto Barzillai, 'Come thou over with me, and I will feed thee with me in Jerusalem'. [34]And Barzillai said unto the king, 'How long have I to live, that I should go up with the king unto Jerusalem? [35]I am this day fourscore years old: and can I discern between good and evil? Can thy servant taste what I eat or what I drink? can I hear any more the voice of singing men and singing women? wherefore then should thy servant be yet a burden unto my lord the king? [36]Thy servant will go a little way over Jordan with the king: and why should the king recompense it me with such a reward? [37]Let thy servant, I pray thee, turn back again, that I may die in my own city, and be buried by the grave of my father and of my mother. But behold thy servant Chimham, let him go over with my lord the king, and do to him what shall seem good unto thee.' [38]And the king answered, 'Chimham shall go over with me, and I will do to him that which shall seem good unto thee: and whatsoever thou shalt require of me, that will I do for thee'. [39]And all the people went over Jordan. And when the king was come over, the king kissed Barzillai, and blessed him; and he returned unto his own place. [40]Then the king went on to Gilgal, and Chimham went on with him: and all the people of Judah conducted the king, and also half the people of Israel.

[41]And behold, all the men of Israel came to the king, and said unto the king, 'Why have our brethren the men of Judah stolen thee away, and have brought the king, and his household, and all David's men with him, over Jordan?' [42]And all the men of Judah answered the men of Israel, 'Because the king is near of kin to us: wherefore then be ye angry for this matter? Have we eaten at all of the king's cost? or hath he given us any gift?' [43]And the men of Israel answered the men of Judah, and said, 'We have ten parts in the king, and we have also more right in David than ye: why then did ye despise us, that our advice should not be first had in bringing back our king?' And the words of the men of Judah were fiercer than the words of the men of Israel.

20 And there happened to be there a man of Belial, whose name was Sheba, the son of Bichri, a Benjamite: and he blew a trumpet, and said, 'We have no part in David, neither have we inheritance in the son of Jesse: every man to his tents, O Israel'. [2]So every man of Israel went up from after David, and followed Sheba the son of Bichri: but the men of Judah cleaved unto their king, from Jordan even to Jerusalem.

³And David came to his house at Jerusalem; and the king took the ten women his concubines, whom he had left to keep the house, and put them in ward, and fed them, but went not in unto them. So they were shut up unto the day of their death, living in widowhood.

⁴Then said the king to Amasa, 'Assemble me the men of Judah within three days, and be thou here present'. ⁵So Amasa went to assemble the men of Judah: but he tarried longer than the set time which he had appointed him. ⁶And David said to Abishai, 'Now shall Sheba the son of Bichri do us more harm than did Absalom: take thou thy lord's servants, and pursue after him, lest he get him fenced cities, and escape us'. ⁷And there went out after him Joab's men, and the Cherethites, and the Pelethites, and all the mighty men: and they went out of Jerusalem, to pursue after Sheba the son of Bichri. ⁸When they were at the great stone which is in Gibeon, Amasa went before them. And Joab's garment that he had put on was girded unto him, and upon it a girdle with a sword fastened upon his loins in the sheath thereof; and as he went forth it fell out. ⁹And Joab said to Amasa, 'Art thou in health, my brother?' And Joab took Amasa by the beard with the right hand to kiss him. ¹⁰But Amasa took no heed to the sword that was in Joab's hand: so he smote him therewith in the fifth rib, and shed out his bowels to the ground, and struck him not again; and he died. So Joab and Abishai his brother pursued after Sheba the son of Bichri. ¹¹And one of Joab's men stood by him, and said, 'He that favoureth Joab, and he that is for David, let him go after Joab'. ¹²And Amasa wallowed in blood in the midst of the highway. And when the man saw that all the people stood still, he removed Amasa out of the highway into the field, and cast a cloth upon him, when he saw that every one that came by him stood still. ¹³When he was removed out of the highway, all the people went on after Joab, to pursue after Sheba the son of Bichri.

¹⁴And he went through all the tribes of Israel unto Abel, and to Beth-maachah, and all the Berites: and they were gathered together, and went also after him. ¹⁵And they came and besieged him in Abel of Beth-maachah, and they cast up a bank against the city, and it stood in the trench: and all the people that were with Joab battered the wall, to throw it down.

¹⁶Then cried a wise woman out of the city, 'Hear, hear; say, I pray you, unto Joab, "Come near hither, that I may speak with thee"'. ¹⁷And when he was come near unto her, the woman said, 'Art thou Joab?' And he answered, 'I am he'. Then she said unto him, 'Hear the words of thy handmaid'. And he answered, 'I do hear'. ¹⁸Then she spoke, saying, 'They were wont to speak in old time, saying, "They shall surely ask counsel at Abel": and so they ended the matter. ¹⁹I am one of them that are peaceable and faithful in Israel: thou seekest to destroy a city and a mother in Israel: why wilt thou swallow up the inheritance of the LORD?' ²⁰And Joab answered and said, 'Far be it, far be it from me, that I should swallow up or destroy. ²¹The matter is not so: but a man of

mount Ephraim, Sheba the son of Bichri by name, hath lifted up his hand against the king, even against David: deliver him only and I will depart from the city'. And the woman said unto Joab, 'Behold, his head shall be thrown to thee over the wall'. ²²Then the woman went unto all the people in her wisdom, and they cut off the head of Sheba the son of Bichri, and cast it out to Joab. And he blew a trumpet, and they retired from the city, every man to his tent. And Joab returned to Jerusalem unto the king.

²³Now Joab was over all the host of Israel, and Benaiah the son of Jehoiada was over the Cherethites and over the Pelethites. ²⁴And Adoram was over the tribute, and Jehoshaphat the son of Ahilud was recorder. ²⁵And Sheva was scribe, and Zadok and Abiathar were the priests. ²⁶And Ira also the Jairite was a chief ruler about David.

21 Then there was a famine in the days of David three years, year after year, and David inquired of the LORD. And the LORD answered, 'It is for Saul, and for his bloody house, because he slew the Gibeonites'. ²And the king called the Gibeonites, and said unto them (now the Gibeonites were not of the children of Israel, but of the remnant of the Amorites, and the children of Israel had sworn unto them: and Saul sought to slay them in his zeal to the children of Israel and Judah); ³wherefore David said unto the Gibeonites, 'What shall I do for you? and wherewith shall I make the atonement, that ye may bless the inheritance of the LORD?' ⁴And the Gibeonites said unto him, 'We will have no silver nor gold of Saul, nor of his house, neither for us shalt thou kill any man in Israel'. And he said, 'What you shall say, that will I do for you'. ⁵And they answered the king, 'The man that consumed us, and that devised against us that we should be destroyed from remaining in any of the coasts of Israel, ⁶let seven men of his sons be delivered unto us, and we will hang them up unto the LORD in Gibeah of Saul, whom the LORD did choose'. And the king said, 'I will give them'. ⁷But the king spared Mephibosheth, the son of Jonathan the son of Saul, because of the LORD's oath that was between them, between David and Jonathan the son of Saul. ⁸But the king took the two sons of Rizpah the daughter of Aiah, whom she bore unto Saul, Armoni and Mephibosheth, and the five sons of Michal the daughter of Saul, whom she brought up for Adriel the son of Barzillai the Meholathite. ⁹And he delivered them into the hands of the Gibeonites, and they hanged them in the hill before the LORD: and they fell all seven together, and were put to death in the days of harvest, in the first days, in the beginning of barley harvest.

¹⁰And Rizpah the daughter of Aiah took sackcloth, and spread it for her upon the rock, from the beginning of harvest until water dropped upon them out of heaven, and suffered neither the birds of the air to rest on them by day, nor the beasts of the field by night. ¹¹And it was told David what Rizpah the daughter of Aiah, the concubine of Saul, had done.

¹²And David went and took the bones of Saul and the bones of Jonathan his son from the men of Jabesh-gilead, which had stolen

them from the street of Beth-shan, where the Philistines had hanged them, when the Philistines had slain Saul in Gilboa: ¹³And he brought up from thence the bones of Saul and the bones of Jonathan his son; and they gathered the bones of them that were hanged. ¹⁴And the bones of Saul and Jonathan his son buried they in the country of Benjamin in Zelah, in the sepulchre of Kish his father: and they performed all that the king commanded. And after that God was entreated for the land.

¹⁵Moreover the Philistines had yet war again with Israel; and David went down, and his servants with him, and fought against the Philistines, and David waxed faint. ¹⁶And Ishbi-benob, which was of the sons of the giant, the weight of whose spear weighed three hundred shekels of brass in weight, he being girded with a new sword, thought to have slain David. ¹⁷But Abishai the son of Zeruiah succoured him, and smote the Philistine, and killed him. Then the men of David swore unto him, saying, Thou shalt go no more out with us to battle, that thou quench not the light of Israel. ¹⁸And it came to pass after this, that there was again a battle with the Philistines at Gob: then Sibbechai the Hushathite slew Saph, which was of the sons of the giant. ¹⁹And there was again a battle in Gob with the Philistines, where Elhanan the son of Jaare-oregim, a Beth-lehemite, slew the brother of Goliath the Gittite, the staff of whose spear was like a weaver's beam. ²⁰And there was yet a battle in Gath, where was a man of great stature, that had on every hand six fingers, and on every foot six toes, four and twenty in number; and he also was born to the giant. ²¹And when he defied Israel, Jonathan the son of Shimea the brother of David slew him. ²²These four were born to the giant in Gath, and fell by the hand of David, and by the hand of his servants.

22 And David spoke unto the LORD the words of this song in the day that the LORD had delivered him out of the hand of all his enemies, and out of the hand of Saul: ²and he said,

'The LORD is my rock, and my fortress, and my deliverer:
³ the God of my rock; in him will I trust:
    he is my shield, and the horn of my salvation,
    my high tower, and my refuge, my saviour;
    thou savest me from violence.
⁴ I will call on the LORD, who is worthy to be praised:
    so shall I be saved from my enemies.

⁵ 'When the waves of death compassed me,
    the floods of ungodly men made me afraid.
⁶ The sorrows of hell compassed me about:
    the snares of death prevented me.
⁷ In my distress I called upon the LORD, and cried to my God,
    and he did hear my voice out of his temple,
    and my cry did enter into his ears.

⁸ 'Then the earth shook and trembled,
the foundations of heaven moved and shook, because he was
wroth.
⁹ There went up a smoke out of his nostrils,
and fire out of his mouth devoured: coals were kindled by it.
¹⁰ He bowed the heavens also, and came down:
and darkness was under his feet.
¹¹ And he rode upon a cherub, and did fly:
and he was seen upon the wings of the wind.
¹² And he made darkness pavilions round about him,
dark waters, and thick clouds of the skies.
¹³ Through the brightness before him were coals of fire kindled.
¹⁴ The LORD thundered from heaven:
and the most High uttered his voice.
¹⁵ And he sent out arrows, and scattered them;
lightning, and discomfited them.
¹⁶ And the channels of the sea appeared,
the foundations of the world were discovered,
at the rebuking of the LORD,
at the blast of the breath of his nostrils.

¹⁷ 'He sent from above, he took me:
he drew me out of many waters.
¹⁸ He delivered me from my strong enemy, and from them that
hated me:
for they were too strong for me.
¹⁹ They prevented me in the day of my calamity:
but the LORD was my stay.
²⁰ He brought me forth also into a large place:
he delivered me, because he delighted in me.

²¹ 'The LORD rewarded me according to my righteousness:
according to the cleanness of my hands hath he
recompensed me.
²² For I have kept the ways of the LORD,
and have not wickedly departed from my God.
²³ For all his judgements were before me:
and as for his statutes, I did not depart from them.
²⁴ I was also upright before him:
and have kept myself from my iniquity.
²⁵ Therefore the LORD hath recompensed me according to my
righteousness:
according to my cleanness in his eyesight.

²⁶ 'With the merciful thou wilt show thyself merciful,
and with the upright man thou wilt show thyself upright.
²⁷ With the pure thou wilt show thyself pure:
and with the froward thou wilt show thyself unsavoury.

²⁸ And the afflicted people thou wilt save:
  but thy eyes are upon the haughty, that thou mayest bring them
      down.
²⁹ For thou art my lamp, O LORD:
  and the LORD will lighten my darkness.
³⁰ For by thee I have run through a troop:
  by my God have I leapt over a wall.

³¹ 'As for God, his way is perfect,
  the word of the LORD is tried:
  he is a buckler to all them that trust in him.
³² For who is God, save the LORD?
  and who is a rock, save our God?
³³ God is my strength and power:
  and he maketh my way perfect.
³⁴ He maketh my feet like hinds' feet:
  and setteth me upon my high places.
³⁵ He teacheth my hands to war:
  so that a bow of steel is broken by my arms.
³⁶ Thou hast also given me the shield of thy salvation:
  and thy gentleness hath made me great.
³⁷ Thou hast enlarged my steps under me:
  so that my feet did not slip.

³⁸ 'I have pursued my enemies, and destroyed them:
  and turned not again until I had consumed them.
³⁹ And I have consumed them, and wounded them, that they could
      not arise:
  yea, they are fallen under my feet.
⁴⁰ For thou hast girded me with strength to battle:
  them that rose up against me hast thou subdued under me.
⁴¹ Thou hast also given me the necks of my enemies,
  that I might destroy them that hate me.
⁴² They looked, but there was none to save:
  even unto the LORD, but he answered them not.
⁴³ Then did I beat them as small as the dust of the earth:
  I did stamp them as the mire of the street,
  and did spread them abroad.

⁴⁴ 'Thou also hast delivered me from the strivings of my
      people,
  thou hast kept me to be head of the heathen:
  a people which I knew not shall serve me.
⁴⁵ Strangers shall submit themselves unto me:
  as soon as they hear, they shall be obedient unto me.
⁴⁶ Strangers shall fade away:
  and they shall be afraid out of their close places.

⁴⁷ 'The Lᴏʀᴅ liveth, and blessed be my rock:
and exalted be the God of the rock of my salvation.
⁴⁸ It is God that avengeth me,
and that bringeth down the people under me:
⁴⁹ and that bringeth me forth from my enemies:
thou also hast lifted me up on high above them that rose up
against me:
thou hast delivered me from the violent man.
⁵⁰ Therefore I will give thanks unto thee, O Lᴏʀᴅ, among the
heathen:
and I will sing praises unto thy name.
⁵¹ He is the tower of salvation for his king:
and showeth mercy to his anointed,
unto David, and to his seed for evermore.'

23 Now these be the last words of David.

David the son of Jesse said,
and the man who was raised up on high,
the anointed of the God of Jacob,
and the sweet psalmist of Israel, said,
² 'The Spirit of the Lᴏʀᴅ spoke by me,
and his word was in my tongue.
³ The God of Israel said,
the Rock of Israel spoke to me,
"He that ruleth over men must be just,
ruling in the fear of God.
⁴ And he shall be as the light of the morning,
when the sun riseth,
even a morning without clouds;
as the tender grass springing out of the earth
by clear shining after rain."
⁵ Although my house be not so with God:
yet he hath made with me an everlasting covenant,
ordered in all things, and sure:
for this is all my salvation, and all my desire,
although he make it not to grow.

⁶ 'But the sons of Belial shall be all of them as thorns thrust away,
because they cannot be taken with hands:
⁷ but the man that shall touch them must be fenced with iron
and the staff of a spear,
and they shall be utterly burnt with fire in the same place.'

⁸These be the names of the mighty men whom David had: the
Tachmonite that sat in the seat, chief among the captains; the same
was Adino the Eznite: he lifted up his spear against eight hundred,
whom he slew at one time. ⁹And after him was Eleazar the son of Dodo

the Ahohite, one of the three mighty men with David, when they defied the Philistines that were there gathered together to battle, and the men of Israel were gone away: ¹⁰he arose, and smote the Philistines until his hand was weary, and his hand cleaved unto the sword: and the LORD wrought a great victory that day; and the people returned after him only to spoil. ¹¹And after him was Shammah the son of Agee the Hararite. And the Philistines were gathered together into a troop, where was a piece of ground full of lentils: and the people fled from the Philistines. ¹²But he stood in the midst of the ground, and defended it, and slew the Philistines: and the LORD wrought a great victory.

¹³And three of the thirty chief went down, and came to David in the harvest time unto the cave of Adullam: and the troop of the Philistines pitched in the valley of Rephaim. ¹⁴And David was then in a hold, and the garrison of the Philistines was then in Beth-lehem. ¹⁵And David longed, and said, 'O that one would give me drink of the water of the well of Beth-lehem, which is by the gate'. ¹⁶And the three mighty men broke through the host of the Philistines, and drew water out of the well of Beth-lehem, that was by the gate, and took it, and brought it to David: nevertheless he would not drink thereof, but poured it out unto the LORD. ¹⁷And he said, 'Be it far from me, O LORD, that I should do this: is not this the blood of the men that went in jeopardy of their lives?' therefore he would not drink it. These things did these three mighty men.

¹⁸And Abishai, the brother of Joab, the son of Zeruiah, was chief among three. And he lifted up his spear against three hundred, and slew them, and had the name among three. ¹⁹Was he not most honourable of three? therefore he was their captain: howbeit he attained not unto the first three. ²⁰And Benaiah the son of Jehoiada, the son of a valiant man, of Kabzeel, who had done many acts, he slew two lion-like men of Moab: he went down also and slew a lion in the midst of a pit in time of snow. ²¹And he slew an Egyptian, a goodly man: and the Egyptian had a spear in his hand; but he went down to him with a staff, and plucked the spear out of the Egyptian's hand, and slew him with his own spear. ²²These things did Benaiah the son of Jehoiada, and had the name among three mighty men. ²³He was more honourable than the thirty, but he attained not to the first three. And David set him over his guard.

²⁴Asahel the brother of Joab was one of the thirty: Elhanan the son of Dodo of Beth-lehem, ²⁵Shammah the Harodite, Elika the Harodite, ²⁶Helez the Paltite, Ira the son of Ikkesh the Tekoite, ²⁷Abiezer the Anethothite, Mebunnai the Hushathite, ²⁸Zalmon the Ahohite, Maharai the Netophathite, ²⁹Heleb the son of Baanah, a Netophathite, Ittai the son of Ribai out of Gibeah of the children of Benjamin, ³⁰Benaiah the Pirathonite, Hiddai of the brooks of Gaash, ³¹Abi-albon the Arbathite, Azmaveth the Barhumite, ³²Elihaba the Shaalbonite, of the sons of Jashen, Jonathan, ³³Shammah the Hararite, Ahiam the son of Sharar the Hararite, ³⁴Eliphelet the son of Ahasbai, the son of the Maachathite, Eliam the son of Ahithophel the Gilonite, ³⁵Hezrai the

Carmelite, Paarai the Arbite, [36]Igal the son of Nathan of Zobah, Bani the Gadite, [37]Zelek the Ammonite, Naharai the Beerothite, armour-bearer to Joab the son of Zeruiah, [38]Ira an Ithrite, Gareb an Ithrite, [39]Uriah the Hittite: thirty and seven in all.

24 And again the anger of the Lord was kindled against Israel, and he moved David against them to say, 'Go, number Israel and Judah'. [2]For the king said to Joab the captain of the host, which was with him, 'Go now through all the tribes of Israel, from Dan even to Beer-sheba, and number ye the people, that I may know the number of the people'. [3]And Joab said unto the king, 'Now the Lord thy God add unto the people, how many soever they be, a hundredfold, and that the eyes of my lord the king may see it: but why doth my lord the king delight in this thing?' [4]Notwithstanding the king's word prevailed against Joab, and against the captains of the host. And Joab and the captains of the host went out from the presence of the king, to number the people of Israel.

[5]And they passed over Jordan, and pitched in Aroer, on the right side of the city that lieth in the midst of the river of Gad, and toward Jazer: [6]then they came to Gilead, and to the land of Tahtim-hodshi; and they came to Dan-jaan, and about to Zidon, [7]and came to the stronghold of Tyre, and to all the cities of the Hivites, and of the Canaanites: and they went out to the south of Judah, even to Beer-sheba. [8]So when they had gone through all the land, they came to Jerusalem at the end of nine months and twenty days. [9]And Joab gave up the sum of the number of the people unto the king: and there were in Israel eight hundred thousand valiant men that drew the sword; and the men of Judah were five hundred thousand men.

[10]And David's heart smote him after that he had numbered the people. And David said unto the Lord, 'I have sinned greatly in that I have done: and now, I beseech thee, O Lord, take away the iniquity of thy servant, for I have done very foolishly'. [11]For when David was up in the morning, the word of the Lord came unto the prophet Gad, David's seer, saying, [12]'Go and say unto David, "Thus saith the Lord, 'I offer thee three things; choose thee one of them, that I may do it unto thee'"'. [13]So Gad came to David, and told him, and said unto him, 'Shall seven years of famine come unto thee in thy land? or wilt thou flee three months before thy enemies, while they pursue thee? or that there be three days' pestilence in thy land? Now advise, and see what answer I shall return to him that sent me.' [14]And David said unto Gad, 'I am in a great strait: let us fall now into the hand of the Lord (for his mercies are great), and let me not fall into the hand of man'.

[15]So the Lord sent a pestilence upon Israel from the morning even to the time appointed: and there died of the people from Dan even to Beer-sheba seventy thousand men. [16]And when the angel stretched out his hand upon Jerusalem to destroy it, the Lord repented him of the evil, and said to the angel that destroyed the people, 'It is enough: stay now thy hand'. And the angel of the Lord was by the threshing-place of Araunah the Jebusite. [17]And David spoke unto the Lord when he saw the angel that smote the people, and said, 'Lo, I have sinned, and I have

done wickedly: but these sheep, what have they done? Let thy hand, I pray thee, be against me, and against my father's house.'

¹⁸And Gad came that day to David, and said unto him, 'Go up, rear an altar unto the LORD in the threshing-floor of Araunah the Jebusite'. ¹⁹And David, according to the saying of Gad, went up as the LORD commanded. ²⁰And Araunah looked, and saw the king and his servants coming on toward him: and Araunah went out, and bowed himself before the king on his face upon the ground. ²¹And Araunah said, 'Wherefore is my lord the king come to his servant?' And David said, 'To buy the threshing-floor of thee, to build an altar unto the LORD, that the plague may be stayed from the people'. ²²And Araunah said unto David, 'Let my lord the king take and offer up what seemeth good unto him: behold, here be oxen for burnt sacrifice, and threshing instruments and other instruments of the oxen for wood'. ²³All these things did Araunah, as a king, give unto the king. And Araunah said unto the king, 'The LORD thy God accept thee'. ²⁴And the king said unto Araunah, 'Nay, but I will surely buy it of thee at a price: neither will I offer burnt offerings unto the LORD my God of that which doth cost me nothing'. So David bought the threshing-floor and the oxen for fifty shekels of silver. ²⁵And David built there an altar unto the LORD, and offered burnt offerings and peace offerings. So the LORD was entreated for the land, and the plague was stayed from Israel.

THE FIRST BOOK OF THE
KINGS
COMMONLY CALLED
THE THIRD BOOK OF THE KINGS

1 Now king David was old and stricken in years, and they covered him with clothes, but he got no heat. ²Wherefore his servants said unto him, 'Let there be sought for my lord the king a young virgin: and let her stand before the king, and let her cherish him, and let her lie in thy bosom, that my lord the king may get heat'. ³So they sought for a fair damsel throughout all the coasts of Israel, and found Abishag a Shunammite, and brought her to the king. ⁴And the damsel was very fair, and cherished the king, and ministered to him: but the king knew her not.

⁵Then Adonijah the son of Haggith exalted himself, saying, 'I will be king': and he prepared him chariots and horsemen, and fifty men to run before him. ⁶And his father had not displeased him at any time in saying, 'Why hast thou done so?' And he also was a very goodly man; and his mother bore him after Absalom. ⁷And he conferred with Joab the son of Zeruiah, and with Abiathar the priest: and they following Adonijah helped him. ⁸But Zadok the priest, and Benaiah the son of Jehoiada, and Nathan the prophet, and Shimei, and Rei, and the mighty men which belonged to David, were not with Adonijah. ⁹And Adonijah slew sheep and oxen and fat cattle by the stone of Zoheleth, which is by En-rogel, and called all his brethren the king's sons, and all the men of Judah the king's servants. ¹⁰But Nathan the prophet, and Benaiah, and the mighty men, and Solomon his brother he called not.

¹¹Wherefore Nathan spoke unto Bath-sheba the mother of Solomon, saying, 'Hast thou not heard that Adonijah the son of Haggith doth reign, and David our lord knoweth it not? ¹²Now therefore come, let me, I pray thee, give thee counsel, that thou mayest save thy own life, and the life of thy son Solomon. ¹³Go and get thee in unto king David, and say unto him, "Didst not thou, my lord, O king, swear unto thy handmaid, saying, 'Assuredly Solomon thy son shall reign after me, and he shall sit upon my throne'? why then doth Adonijah reign?" ¹⁴Behold, while thou yet talkest there with the king, I also will come in after thee, and confirm thy words.'

¹⁵And Bath-sheba went in unto the king into the chamber: and the king was very old, and Abishag the Shunammite ministered unto the king. ¹⁶And Bath-sheba bowed, and did obeisance unto the king. And the king said, 'What wouldst thou?' ¹⁷And she said unto him, 'My lord, thou sworest by the LORD thy God unto thy handmaid, saying, "Assuredly Solomon thy son shall reign after me, and he shall sit upon my throne". ¹⁸And now, behold, Adonijah reigneth; and now, my lord the king, thou knowest it not. ¹⁹And he hath slain oxen and fat cattle

and sheep in abundance, and hath called all the sons of the king, and Abiathar the priest, and Joab the captain of the host: but Solomon thy servant hath he not called. ²⁰And thou, my lord, O king, the eyes of all Israel are upon thee, that thou shouldst tell them who shall sit on the throne of my lord the king after him. ²¹Otherwise it shall come to pass, when my lord the king shall sleep with his fathers, that I and my son Solomon shall be counted offenders.'

²²And lo, while she yet talked with the king, Nathan the prophet also came in. ²³And they told the king, saying, 'Behold Nathan the prophet'. And when he was come in before the king, he bowed himself before the king with his face to the ground. ²⁴And Nathan said, 'My lord, O king, hast thou said, "Adonijah shall reign after me, and he shall sit upon my throne?" ²⁵For he is gone down this day, and hath slain oxen and fat cattle and sheep in abundance, and hath called all the king's sons, and the captains of the host, and Abiathar the priest: and behold, they eat and drink before him, and say, "God save king Adonijah". ²⁶But me, even me thy servant, and Zadok the priest, and Benaiah the son of Jehoiada, and thy servant Solomon, hath he not called. ²⁷Is this thing done by my lord the king, and thou hast not shown it unto thy servant, who should sit on the throne of my lord the king after him?'

²⁸Then king David answered and said, 'Call me Bath-sheba'. And she came into the king's presence, and stood before the king. ²⁹And the king swore, and said, 'As the LORD liveth, that hath redeemed my soul out of all distress, ³⁰even as I swore unto thee by the LORD God of Israel, saying, "Assuredly Solomon thy son shall reign after me, and he shall sit upon my throne in my stead"; even so will I certainly do this day'. ³¹Then Bath-sheba bowed with her face to the earth, and did reverence to the king, and said, 'Let my lord king David live for ever'.

³²And king David said, 'Call me Zadok the priest, and Nathan the prophet, and Benaiah the son of Jehoiada'. And they came before the king. ³³The king also said unto them, 'Take with you the servants of your lord, and cause Solomon my son to ride upon my own mule, and bring him down to Gihon. ³⁴And let Zadok the priest and Nathan the prophet anoint him there king over Israel: and blow ye with the trumpet, and say, "God save king Solomon". ³⁵Then ye shall come up after him, that he may come and sit upon my throne; for he shall be king in my stead: and I have appointed him to be ruler over Israel and over Judah.' ³⁶And Benaiah the son of Jehoiada answered the king, and said, 'Amen: the LORD God of my lord the king say so too. ³⁷As the LORD hath been with my lord the king, even so be he with Solomon, and make his throne greater than the throne of my lord king David.' ³⁸So Zadok the priest, and Nathan the prophet, and Benaiah the son of Jehoiada, and the Cherethites, and the Pelethites, went down, and caused Solomon to ride upon king David's mule, and brought him to Gihon. ³⁹And Zadok the priest took a horn of oil out of the tabernacle, and anointed Solomon. And they blew the trumpet, and all the people said, 'God save king Solomon'. ⁴⁰And all the people came up after him, and the people piped with pipes, and rejoiced with great joy, so that the earth rent with the sound of them.

⁴¹And Adonijah and all the guests that were with him heard it as they had made an end of eating. And when Joab heard the sound of the trumpet, he said, 'Wherefore is this noise of the city being in an uproar?' ⁴²And while he yet spoke, behold, Jonathan the son of Abiathar the priest came: and Adonijah said unto him, 'Come in, for thou art a valiant man, and bringest good tidings'. ⁴³And Jonathan answered and said to Adonijah, 'Verily our lord king David hath made Solomon king. ⁴⁴And the king hath sent with him Zadok the priest, and Nathan the prophet, and Benaiah the son of Jehoiada, and the Cherethites, and the Pelethites, and they have caused him to ride upon the king's mule. ⁴⁵And Zadok the priest and Nathan the prophet have anointed him king in Gihon: and they are come up from thence rejoicing, so that the city rang again. This is the noise that ye have heard. ⁴⁶And also Solomon sitteth on the throne of the kingdom. ⁴⁷And moreover the king's servants came to bless our lord king David, saying, "God make the name of Solomon better than thy name, and make his throne greater than thy throne". And the king bowed himself upon the bed. ⁴⁸And also thus said the king, "Blessed be the LORD God of Israel, which hath given one to sit on my throne this day, my eyes even seeing it".' ⁴⁹And all the guests that were with Adonijah were afraid, and rose up, and went every man his way.

⁵⁰And Adonijah feared because of Solomon, and arose, and went, and caught hold on the horns of the altar. ⁵¹And it was told Solomon, saying, 'Behold, Adonijah feareth king Solomon: for lo, he hath caught hold on the horns of the altar, saying, "Let king Solomon swear unto me today that he will not slay his servant with the sword"'. ⁵²And Solomon said, 'If he will show himself a worthy man, there shall not a hair of him fall to the earth: but if wickedness shall be found in him, he shall die'. ⁵³So king Solomon sent, and they brought him down from the altar. And he came and bowed himself to king Solomon: and Solomon said unto him, 'Go to thy house'.

2 Now the days of David drew nigh that he should die, and he charged Solomon his son, saying, ²'I go the way of all the earth: be thou strong therefore, and show thyself a man. ³And keep the charge of the LORD thy God, to walk in his ways, to keep his statutes, and his commandments, and his judgements, and his testimonies, as it is written in the law of Moses, that thou mayest prosper in all that thou doest, and whithersoever thou turnest thyself: ⁴that the LORD may continue his word which he spoke concerning me, saying, "If thy children take heed to their way, to walk before me in truth with all their heart and with all their soul, there shall not fail thee" (said he) "a man on the throne of Israel". ⁵Moreover thou knowest also what Joab the son of Zeruiah did to me, and what he did to the two captains of the hosts of Israel, unto Abner the son of Ner, and unto Amasa the son of Jether, whom he slew, and shed the blood of war in peace, and put the blood of war upon his girdle that was about his loins, and in his shoes that were on his feet. ⁶Do therefore according to thy wisdom, and let not his hoar head go down to the grave in peace. ⁷But show kindness unto the sons

of Barzillai the Gileadite, and let them be of those that eat at thy table: for so they came to me when I fled because of Absalom thy brother. ⁸And behold, thou hast with thee Shimei the son of Gera, a Benjamite of Bahurim, which cursed me with a grievous curse in the day when I went to Mahanaim: but he came down to meet me at Jordan, and I swore to him by the LORD, saying, "I will not put thee to death with the sword". ⁹Now therefore hold him not guiltless: for thou art a wise man, and knowest what thou oughtest to do unto him, but his hoar head bring thou down to the grave with blood.'

¹⁰So David slept with his fathers, and was buried in the city of David. ¹¹And the days that David reigned over Israel were forty years: seven years reigned he in Hebron, and thirty and three years reigned he in Jerusalem.

¹²Then sat Solomon upon the throne of David his father, and his kingdom was established greatly.

¹³And Adonijah the son of Haggith came to Bath-sheba the mother of Solomon. And she said, 'Comest thou peaceably?' And he said, 'Peaceably'. ¹⁴He said moreover, 'I have somewhat to say unto thee'. And she said, 'Say on'. ¹⁵And he said, 'Thou knowest that the kingdom was mine, and that all Israel set their faces on me, that I should reign: howbeit the kingdom is turned about, and is become my brother's: for it was his from the LORD. ¹⁶And now I ask one petition of thee, deny me not.' And she said unto him, 'Say on'. ¹⁷And he said, 'Speak, I pray thee, unto Solomon the king (for he will not say thee nay), that he give me Abishag the Shunammite to wife'. ¹⁸And Bath-sheba said, 'Well, I will speak for thee unto the king'.

¹⁹Bath-sheba therefore went unto king Solomon, to speak unto him for Adonijah. And the king rose up to meet her, and bowed himself unto her, and sat down on his throne, and caused a seat to be set for the king's mother, and she sat on his right hand. ²⁰Then she said, 'I desire one small petition of thee; I pray thee, say me not nay'. And the king said unto her, 'Ask on, my mother, for I will not say thee nay'. ²¹And she said, 'Let Abishag the Shunammite be given to Adonijah thy brother to wife'. ²²And king Solomon answered and said unto his mother, 'And why dost thou ask Abishag the Shunammite for Adonijah? Ask for him the kingdom also; for he is my elder brother; even for him, and for Abiathar the priest, and for Joab the son of Zeruiah.' ²³Then king Solomon swore by the LORD, saying, 'God do so to me, and more also, if Adonijah have not spoken this word against his own life. ²⁴Now therefore, as the LORD liveth, which hath established me, and set me on the throne of David my father, and who hath made me a house as he promised, Adonijah shall be put to death this day.' ²⁵And king Solomon sent by the hand of Benaiah the son of Jehoiada, and he fell upon him that he died.

²⁶And unto Abiathar the priest said the king, 'Get thee to Anathoth, unto thy own fields, for thou art worthy of death: but I will not at this time put thee to death, because thou borest the ark of the Lord GOD before David my father, and because thou hast been afflicted in all

wherein my father was afflicted'. ²⁷So Solomon thrust out Abiathar from being priest unto the LORD: that he might fulfil the word of the LORD, which he spoke concerning the house of Eli in Shiloh.

²⁸Then tidings came to Joab (for Joab had turned after Adonijah, though he turned not after Absalom), and Joab fled unto the tabernacle of the LORD, and caught hold on the horns of the altar. ²⁹And it was told king Solomon that Joab was fled unto the tabernacle of the LORD, and behold, he is by the altar. Then Solomon sent Benaiah the son of Jehoiada, saying, 'Go, fall upon him'. ³⁰And Benaiah came to the tabernacle of the LORD, and said unto him, 'Thus saith the king, "Come forth"'. And he said, 'Nay, but I will die here'. And Benaiah brought the king word again, saying, 'Thus said Joab, and thus he answered me'. ³¹And the king said unto him, 'Do as he hath said, and fall upon him, and bury him, that thou mayest take away the innocent blood, which Joab shed, from me, and from the house of my father. ³²And the LORD shall return his blood upon his own head, who fell upon two men more righteous and better than he, and slew them with the sword, my father David not knowing thereof, to wit, Abner the son of Ner, captain of the host of Israel, and Amasa the son of Jether, captain of the host of Judah. ³³Their blood shall therefore return upon the head of Joab, and upon the head of his seed for ever: but upon David, and upon his seed, and upon his house, and upon his throne, shall there be peace for ever from the LORD.' ³⁴So Benaiah the son of Jehoiada went up, and fell upon him, and slew him: and he was buried in his own house in the wilderness. ³⁵And the king put Benaiah the son of Jehoiada in his room over the host: and Zadok the priest did the king put in the room of Abiathar.

³⁶And the king sent and called for Shimei, and said unto him, 'Build thee a house in Jerusalem, and dwell there, and go not forth thence any whither. ³⁷For it shall be, that on the day thou goest out, and passest over the brook Kidron, thou shalt know for certain that thou shalt surely die: thy blood shall be upon thy own head.' ³⁸And Shimei said unto the king, 'The saying is good: as my lord the king hath said, so will thy servant do'. And Shimei dwelt in Jerusalem many days. ³⁹And it came to pass at the end of three years, that two of the servants of Shimei ran away unto Achish son of Maachah king of Gath. And they told Shimei, saying, 'Behold, thy servants be in Gath'. ⁴⁰And Shimei arose, and saddled his ass, and went to Gath to Achish to seek his servants: and Shimei went, and brought his servants from Gath. ⁴¹And it was told Solomon that Shimei had gone from Jerusalem to Gath, and was come again. ⁴²And the king sent and called for Shimei, and said unto him, 'Did I not make thee to swear by the LORD, and protested unto thee, saying, "Know for a certain that on the day thou goest out, and walkest abroad any whither, that thou shalt surely die?" And thou saidst unto me, "The word that I have heard is good". ⁴³Why then hast thou not kept the oath of the LORD, and the commandment that I have charged thee with?" ⁴⁴The king said moreover to Shimei, 'Thou knowest all the wickedness which thy heart is privy to, that thou didst to David my father: therefore the LORD shall return thy wickedness upon thy

own head. ⁴⁵And king Solomon shall be blessed, and the throne of David shall be established before the LORD for ever.' ⁴⁶So the king commanded Benaiah the son of Jehoiada, which went out, and fell upon him, that he died. And the kingdom was established in the hand of Solomon.

3 And Solomon made affinity with Pharaoh king of Egypt, and took Pharaoh's daughter, and brought her into the city of David, until he had made an end of building his own house, and the house of the LORD, and the wall of Jerusalem round about. ²Only the people sacrificed in high places, because there was no house built unto the name of the LORD until those days. ³And Solomon loved the LORD, walking in the statutes of David his father: only he sacrificed and burnt incense in high places. ⁴And the king went to Gibeon to sacrifice there; for that was the great high place: a thousand burnt offerings did Solomon offer up on that altar.

⁵In Gibeon the LORD appeared to Solomon in a dream by night: and God said, 'Ask what I shall give thee'. ⁶And Solomon said, 'Thou hast shown unto thy servant David my father great mercy, according as he walked before thee in truth, and in righteousness, and in uprightness of heart with thee, and thou hast kept for him this great kindness, that thou hast given him a son to sit on his throne, as it is this day. ⁷And now, O LORD my God, thou hast made thy servant king in stead of David my father: and I am but a little child: I know not how to go out or come in. ⁸And thy servant is in the midst of thy people which thou hast chosen, a great people, that cannot be numbered nor counted for multitude. ⁹Give therefore thy servant an understanding heart to judge thy people, that I may discern between good and bad: for who is able to judge this thy so great a people?' ¹⁰And the speech pleased the Lord, that Solomon had asked this thing. ¹¹And God said unto him, 'Because thou hast asked this thing, and hast not asked for thyself long life, neither hast asked riches for thyself, nor hast asked the life of thy enemies, but hast asked for thyself understanding to discern judgement; ¹²behold, I have done according to thy word: lo, I have given thee a wise and an understanding heart, so that there was none like thee before thee, neither after thee shall any arise like unto thee. ¹³And I have also given thee that which thou hast not asked, both riches, and honour: so that there shall not be any among the kings like unto thee all thy days. ¹⁴And if thou wilt walk in my ways, to keep my statutes and my commandments, as thy father David did walk, then I will lengthen thy days.' ¹⁵And Solomon awoke, and behold, it was a dream. And he came to Jerusalem, and stood before the ark of the covenant of the LORD, and offered up burnt offerings, and offered peace offerings, and made a feast to all his servants.

¹⁶Then came there two women that were harlots, unto the king, and stood before him. ¹⁷And the one woman said, 'O my lord, I and this woman dwell in one house, and I was delivered of a child with her in the house. ¹⁸And it came to pass the third day after that I was delivered, that this woman was delivered also: and we were together; there was

no stranger with us in the house, save we two in the house. ¹⁹And this woman's child died in the night: because she overlaid it. ²⁰And she arose at midnight, and took my son from beside me, while thy handmaid slept, and laid it in her bosom, and laid her dead child in my bosom. ²¹And when I rose in the morning to give my child suck, behold, it was dead: but when I had considered it in the morning, behold, it was not my son, which I did bear.' ²²And the other woman said, 'Nay, but the living is my son, and the dead is thy son'. And this said, 'No, but the dead is thy son, and the living is my son'. Thus they spoke before the king. ²³Then said the king, 'The one saith, "This is my son that liveth, and thy son is the dead": and the other saith, "Nay: but thy son is the dead, and my son is the living"'. ²⁴And the king said, 'Bring me a sword'. And they brought a sword before the king. ²⁵And the king said, 'Divide the living child in two, and give half to the one, and half to the other'. ²⁶Then spoke the woman whose the living child was unto the king, for her bowels yearned upon her son, and she said, 'O my lord, give her the living child, and in no wise slay it'. But the other said, 'Let it be neither mine nor thine, but divide it'. ²⁷Then the king answered and said, 'Give her the living child, and in no wise slay it: she is the mother thereof'. ²⁸And all Israel heard of the judgement which the king had judged, and they feared the king: for they saw that the wisdom of God was in him, to do judgement.

4 So king Solomon was king over all Israel. ²And these were the princes which he had, Azariah the son of Zadok the priest, ³Elihoreph and Ahiah, the sons of Shisha, scribes: Jehoshaphat the son of Ahilud, the recorder. ⁴And Benaiah the son of Jehoiada was over the host: and Zadok and Abiathar were the priests: ⁵and Azariah the son of Nathan was over the officers: and Zabud the son of Nathan was principal officer, and the king's friend. ⁶And Ahishar was over the household: and Adoniram the son of Abda was over the tribute.

⁷And Solomon had twelve officers over all Israel, which provided victuals for the king and his household: each man his month in a year made provision. ⁸And these are their names: the son of Hur in mount Ephraim, ⁹the son of Dekar in Makaz, and in Shaalbim, and Beth-shemesh, and Elon-beth-hanan. ¹⁰The son of Hesed, in Aruboth; to him pertained Sochoh, and all the land of Hepher: ¹¹the son of Abinadab in all the region of Dor, which had Taphath the daughter of Solomon to wife: ¹²Baana the son of Ahilud; to him pertained Taanach and Megiddo, and all Beth-shean, which is by Zartanah beneath Jezreel, from Beth-shean to Abel-meholah, even unto the place that is beyond Jokmeam: ¹³the son of Geber in Ramoth-gilead; to him pertained the towns of Jair the son of Manasseh, which are in Gilead; to him also pertained the region of Argob, which is in Bashan, threescore great cities with walls and brazen bars. ¹⁴Ahinadab the son of Iddo had Mahanaim. ¹⁵Ahimaaz was in Naphtali; he also took Basmath the daughter of Solomon to wife. ¹⁶Baanah the son of Hushai was in Asher and in Aloth: ¹⁷Jehoshaphat the son of Paruah, in Issachar: ¹⁸Shimei the son of Elah, in Benjamin: ¹⁹Geber the son of Uri was in the country of Gilead, in the

country of Sihon king of the Amorites, and of Og king of Bashan; and he was the only officer which was in the land.

²⁰Judah and Israel were many, as the sand which is by the sea in multitude, eating and drinking, and making merry. ²¹And Solomon reigned over all kingdoms from the river unto the land of the Philistines, and unto the border of Egypt: they brought presents, and served Solomon all the days of his life.

²²And Solomon's provision for one day was thirty measures of fine flour, and threescore measures of meal, ²³ten fat oxen, and twenty oxen out of the pastures, and a hundred sheep, besides harts, and roebucks, and fallow deer, and fatted fowl. ²⁴For he had dominion over all the region on this side the river, from Tiphsah even to Azzah, over all the kings on this side the river: and he had peace on all sides round about him. ²⁵And Judah and Israel dwelt safely, every man under his vine and under his fig tree, from Dan even to Beer-sheba, all the days of Solomon.

²⁶And Solomon had forty thousand stalls of horses for his chariots, and twelve thousand horsemen. ²⁷And those officers provided victual for king Solomon, and for all that came unto king Solomon's table, every man in his month: they lacked nothing. ²⁸Barley also and straw for the horses and dromedaries brought they unto the place where the officers were, every man according to his charge.

²⁹And God gave Solomon wisdom and understanding exceeding much, and largeness of heart, even as the sand that is on the sea-shore. ³⁰And Solomon's wisdom excelled the wisdom of all the children of the east country, and all the wisdom of Egypt. ³¹For he was wiser than all men; than Ethan the Ezrahite, and Heman, and Chalcol, and Darda, the sons of Mahol: and his fame was in all nations round about. ³²And he spoke three thousand proverbs: and his songs were a thousand and five. ³³And he spoke of trees, from the cedar tree that is in Lebanon even unto the hyssop that springeth out of the wall: he spoke also of beasts, and of fowl, and of creeping things, and of fishes. ³⁴And there came of all people to hear the wisdom of Solomon, from all kings of the earth, which had heard of his wisdom.

5 And Hiram king of Tyre sent his servants unto Solomon (for he had heard that they had anointed him king in the room of his father): for Hiram was ever a lover of David. ²And Solomon sent to Hiram, saying, ³'Thou knowest how that David my father could not build a house unto the name of the LORD his God for the wars which were about him on every side, until the LORD put them under the soles of his feet. ⁴But now the LORD my God hath given me rest on every side, so that there is neither adversary nor evil occurrent. ⁵And behold, I purpose to build a house unto the name of the LORD my God, as the LORD spoke unto David my father, saying, "Thy son, whom I will set upon thy throne in thy room, he shall build a house unto my name". ⁶Now therefore command thou that they hew me cedar trees out of Lebanon; and my servants shall be with thy servants: and unto thee will I give hire for thy servants according to all that thou shalt appoint: for thou knowest that there is not among us any that can skill to hew timber like unto the Sidonians.'

⁷And it came to pass when Hiram heard the words of Solomon, that he rejoiced greatly, and said, 'Blessed be the LORD this day, which hath given unto David a wise son over this great people'. ⁸And Hiram sent to Solomon, saying, 'I have considered the things which thou sentest to me for: and I will do all thy desire concerning timber of cedar, and concerning timber of fir. ⁹My servants shall bring them down from Lebanon unto the sea: and I will convey them by sea in floats unto the place that thou shalt appoint me, and will cause them to be discharged there, and thou shalt receive them: and thou shalt accomplish my desire, in giving food for my household.' ¹⁰So Hiram gave Solomon cedar trees and fir trees according to all his desire. ¹¹And Solomon gave Hiram twenty thousand measures of wheat for food to his household, and twenty measures of pure oil: thus gave Solomon to Hiram year by year. ¹²And the LORD gave Solomon wisdom, as he promised him: and there was peace between Hiram and Solomon; and they two made a league together.

¹³And king Solomon raised a levy out of all Israel, and the levy was thirty thousand men. ¹⁴And he sent them to Lebanon, ten thousand a month by courses: a month they were in Lebanon, and two months at home: and Adoniram was over the levy. ¹⁵And Solomon had threescore and ten thousand that bore burdens, and fourscore thousand hewers in the mountains; ¹⁶besides the chief of Solomon's officers which were over the work, three thousand and three hundred, which ruled over the people that wrought in the work. ¹⁷And the king commanded, and they brought great stones, costly stones, and hewn stones, to lay the foundation of the house. ¹⁸And Solomon's builders and Hiram's builders did hew them, and the stone-squarers: so they prepared timber and stones to build the house.

6 And it came to pass in the four hundred and fourscore year after the children of Israel were come out of the land of Egypt, in the fourth year of Solomon's reign over Israel, in the month Zif, which is the second month, that he began to build the house of the LORD. ²And the house which king Solomon built for the LORD, the length thereof was threescore cubits, and the breadth thereof twenty cubits, and the height thereof thirty cubits. ³And the porch before the temple of the house, twenty cubits was the length thereof, according to the breadth of the house, and ten cubits was the breadth thereof before the house. ⁴And for the house he made windows of narrow lights.

⁵And against the wall of the house he built chambers round about, against the walls of the house round about, both of the temple and of the oracle: and he made chambers round about. ⁶The nethermost chamber was five cubits broad, and the middle was six cubits broad, and the third was seven cubits broad: for without in the wall of the house he made narrowed rests round about, that the beams should not be fastened in the walls of the house. ⁷And the house when it was in building, was built of stone made ready before it was brought thither:

so that there was neither hammer nor axe nor any tool of iron heard in the house, while it was in building. ⁸The door for the middle chamber was in the right side of the house: and they went up with winding stairs into the middle chamber, and out of the middle into the third. ⁹So he built the house, and finished it; and covered the house with beams and boards of cedar. ¹⁰And then he built chambers against all the house, five cubits high: and they rested on the house with timber of cedar.

¹¹And the word of the LORD came to Solomon, saying, ¹²'Concerning this house which thou art in building, if thou wilt walk in my statutes, and execute my judgements, and keep all my commandments to walk in them: then will I perform my word with thee, which I spoke unto David thy father. ¹³And I will dwell among the children of Israel, and will not forsake my people Israel.'

¹⁴So Solomon built the house, and finished it. ¹⁵And he built the walls of the house within with boards of cedar, both the floor of the house, and the walls of the ceiling: and he covered them on the inside with wood, and covered the floor of the house with planks of fir. ¹⁶And he built twenty cubits on the sides of the house, both the floor and the walls with boards of cedar: he even built them for it within, even for the oracle, even for the most holy place. ¹⁷And the house, that is, the temple before it, was forty cubits long. ¹⁸And the cedar of the house within was carved with knops and open flowers: all was cedar, there was no stone seen. ¹⁹And the oracle he prepared in the house within, to set there the ark of the covenant of the LORD. ²⁰And the oracle in the forepart was twenty cubits in length, and twenty cubits in breadth, and twenty cubits in the height thereof: and he overlaid it with pure gold, and so covered the altar which was of cedar. ²¹So Solomon overlaid the house within with pure gold: and he made a partition by the chains of gold before the oracle, and he overlaid it with gold. ²²And the whole house he overlaid with gold until he had finished all the house: also the whole altar that was by the oracle he overlaid with gold.

²³And within the oracle he made two cherubims of olive tree, each ten cubits high. ²⁴And five cubits was the one wing of the cherub, and five cubits the other wing of the cherub: from the outermost part of the one wing unto the outermost part of the other were ten cubits. ²⁵And the other cherub was ten cubits: both the cherubims were of one measure and one size. ²⁶The height of the one cherub was ten cubits, and so was it of the other cherub. ²⁷And he set the cherubims within the inner house: and they stretched forth the wings of the cherubims, so that the wing of the one touched the one wall, and the wing of the other cherub touched the other wall: and their wings touched one another in the midst of the house. ²⁸And he overlaid the cherubims with gold. ²⁹And he carved all the walls of the house round about with carved figures of cherubims and palm trees and open flowers, within and without. ³⁰And the floor of the house he overlaid with gold, within and without.

³¹And for the entering of the oracle he made doors of olive tree: the lintel and side-posts were a fifth part of the wall. ³²The two doors also

were of olive tree, and he carved upon them carvings of cherubims and palm trees and open flowers, and overlaid them with gold, and spread gold upon the cherubims, and upon the palm trees. ³³So also made he for the door of the temple posts of olive tree, a fourth part of the wall. ³⁴And the two doors were of fir tree: the two leaves of the one door were folding, and the two leaves of the other door were folding. ³⁵And he carved thereon cherubims and palm trees and open flowers: and covered them with gold fitted upon the carved work.

³⁶And he built the inner court with three rows of hewn stone, and a row of cedar beams.

³⁷In the fourth year was the foundation of the house of the LORD laid, in the month Zif. ³⁸And in the eleventh year, in the month Bul, which is the eighth month, was the house finished throughout all the parts thereof, and according to all the fashion of it. So was he seven years in building it.

7 But Solomon was building his own house thirteen years, and he finished all his house. ²He built also the house of the forest of Lebanon; the length thereof was a hundred cubits, and the breadth thereof fifty cubits, and the height thereof thirty cubits, upon four rows of cedar pillars, with cedar beams upon the pillars. ³And it was covered with cedar above upon the beams, that lay on forty-five pillars, fifteen in a row. ⁴And there were windows in three rows, and light was against light in three ranks. ⁵And all the doors and posts were square, with the windows: and light was against light in three ranks.

⁶And he made a porch of pillars, the length thereof was fifty cubits, and the breadth thereof thirty cubits: and the porch was before them: and the other pillars and the thick beam were before them.

⁷Then he made a porch for the throne where he might judge, even the porch of judgement: and it was covered with cedar from one side of the floor to the other.

⁸And his house where he dwelt had another court within the porch, which was of the like work. Solomon made also a house for Pharaoh's daughter, whom he had taken to wife, like unto this porch. ⁹All these were of costly stones, according to the measures of hewn stones, sawn with saws, within and without, even from the foundation unto the coping, and so on the outside toward the great court. ¹⁰And the foundation was of costly stones, even great stones, stones of ten cubits, and stones of eight cubits. ¹¹And above were costly stones, after the measures of hewn stones, and cedars. ¹²And the great court round about was with three rows of hewn stones, and a row of cedar beams, both for the inner court of the house of the LORD, and for the porch of the house.

¹³And king Solomon sent and fetched Hiram out of Tyre. ¹⁴He was a widow's son of the tribe of Naphtali, and his father was a man of Tyre, a worker in brass: and he was filled with wisdom, and understanding, and cunning to work all works in brass. And he came to king Solomon, and wrought all his work. ¹⁵For he cast two pillars of brass, of eighteen cubits high apiece: and a line of twelve cubits did compass either of them about. ¹⁶And he made two chapiters of molten brass, to set upon

the tops of the pillars: the height of the one chapiter was five cubits, and the height of the other chapiter was five cubits: [17] and nets of checker work, and wreaths of chain work, for the chapiters which were upon the top of the pillars: seven for the one chapiter, and seven for the other chapiter. [18] And he made the pillars, and two rows round about upon the one network, to cover the chapiters that were upon the top, with pomegranates: and so did he for the other chapiter. [19] And the chapiters that were upon the top of the pillars were of lily-work in the porch, four cubits. [20] And the chapiters upon the two pillars had pomegranates also above, over against the belly which was by the network: and the pomegranates were two hundred in rows round about upon the other chapiter. [21] And he set up the pillars in the porch of the temple: and he set up the right pillar, and called the name thereof Jachin: and he set up the left pillar, and called the name thereof Boaz. [22] And upon the top of the pillars was lily-work: so was the work of the pillars finished.

[23] And he made a molten sea, ten cubits from the one brim to the other: it was round all about, and his height was five cubits: and a line of thirty cubits did compass it round about. [24] And under the brim of it round about there were knops compassing it, ten in a cubit, compassing the sea round about: the knops were cast in two rows, when it was cast. [25] It stood upon twelve oxen, three looking toward the north, and three looking toward the west, and three looking toward the south, and three looking toward the east: and the sea was set above upon them, and all their hinder parts were inward. [26] And it was a handbreadth thick, and the brim thereof was wrought like the brim of a cup, with flowers of lilies: it contained two thousand baths.

[27] And he made ten bases of brass; four cubits was the length of one base, and four cubits the breadth thereof, and three cubits the height of it. [28] And the work of the bases was on this manner: they had borders, and the borders were between the ledges: [29] and on the borders that were between the ledges were lions, oxen, and cherubims: and upon the ledges there was a base above: and beneath the lions and oxen were certain additions made of thin work. [30] And every base had four brazen wheels, and plates of brass: and the four corners thereof had undersetters: under the laver were undersetters molten, at the side of every addition. [31] And the mouth of it within the chapiter and above was a cubit: but the mouth thereof was round after the work of the base, a cubit and a half: and also upon the mouth of it were gravings with their borders, four-square, not round. [32] And under the borders were four wheels: and the axletrees of the wheels were joined to the base, and the height of a wheel was a cubit and half a cubit. [33] And the work of the wheels was like the work of a chariot wheel: their axletrees, and their naves, and their felloes, and their spokes were all molten. [34] And there were four undersetters to the four corners of one base: and the undersetters were of the very base itself. [35] And in the top of the base was there a round compass of half a cubit high: and on the top of the base the ledges thereof and the borders thereof were of the same. [36] For

on the plates of the ledges thereof, and on the borders thereof, he graved cherubims, lions, and palm trees, according to the proportion of every one, and additions round about. ³⁷After this manner he made the ten bases: all of them had one casting, one measure, and one size.

³⁸Then made he ten lavers of brass: one laver contained forty baths: and every laver was four cubits: and upon every one of the ten bases one laver. ³⁹And he put five bases on the right side of the house, and five on the left side of the house: and he set the sea on the right side of the house eastward over against the south.

⁴⁰And Hiram made the lavers, and the shovels, and the basins. So Hiram made an end of doing all the work that he made king Solomon for the house of the LORD: ⁴¹the two pillars, and the two bowls of the chapiters that were on the top of the two pillars; and the two networks, to cover the two bowls of the chapiters which were upon the top of the pillars; ⁴²and four hundred pomegranates for the two networks, even two rows of pomegranates for one network, to cover the two bowls of the chapiters that were upon the pillars; ⁴³and the ten bases, and ten lavers on the bases; ⁴⁴and one sea, and twelve oxen under the sea; ⁴⁵and the pots, and the shovels, and the basins: and all these vessels which Hiram made to king Solomon for the house of the LORD, were of bright brass. ⁴⁶In the plain of Jordan did the king cast them, in the clay ground between Succoth and Zarthan. ⁴⁷And Solomon left all the vessels unweighed, because they were exceeding many: neither was the weight of the brass found out. ⁴⁸And Solomon made all the vessels that pertained unto the house of the LORD: the altar of gold, and the table of gold, whereupon the showbread was, ⁴⁹and the candlesticks of pure gold, five on the right side, and five on the left, before the oracle, with the flowers, and the lamps, and the tongs of gold, ⁵⁰and the bowls, and the snuffers, and the basins, and the spoons, and the censers of pure gold; and the hinges of gold, both for the doors of the inner house, the most holy place, and for the doors of the house, to wit, of the temple. ⁵¹So was ended all the work that king Solomon made for the house of the LORD. And Solomon brought in the things which David his father had dedicated, even the silver, and the gold, and the vessels did he put among the treasures of the house of the LORD.

8 Then Solomon assembled the elders of Israel, and all the heads of the tribes, the chief of the fathers of the children of Israel, unto king Solomon in Jerusalem, that they might bring up the ark of the covenant of the LORD out of the city of David, which is Zion. ²And all the men of Israel assembled themselves unto king Solomon at the feast in the month Ethanim, which is the seventh month. ³And all the elders of Israel came, and the priests took up the ark. ⁴And they brought up the ark of the LORD, and the tabernacle of the congregation, and all the holy vessels that were in the tabernacle, even those did the priests and the Levites bring up. ⁵And king Solomon, and all the congregation of Israel, that were assembled unto him, were with him before the ark, sacrificing sheep and oxen, that could not be told nor numbered for multitude. ⁶And the priests brought in the ark of the covenant of the

LORD unto his place, into the oracle of the house to the most holy place, even under the wings of the cherubims. ⁷For the cherubims spread forth their two wings over the place of the ark, and the cherubims covered the ark and the staves thereof above. ⁸And they drew out the staves, that the ends of the staves were seen out in the holy place before the oracle, and they were not seen without: and there they are unto this day. ⁹There was nothing in the ark save the two tablets of stone, which Moses put there at Horeb, when the LORD made a covenant with the children of Israel, when they came out of the land of Egypt. ¹⁰And it came to pass, when the priests were come out of the holy place, that the cloud filled the house of the LORD, ¹¹so that the priests could not stand to minister because of the cloud: for the glory of the LORD had filled the house of the LORD.

¹²Then spoke Solomon, 'The LORD said that he would dwell in the thick darkness. ¹³I have surely built thee a house to dwell in, a settled place for thee to abide in for ever.' ¹⁴And the king turned his face about, and blessed all the congregation of Israel (and all the congregation of Israel stood): ¹⁵and he said, 'Blessed be the LORD God of Israel, which spoke with his mouth unto David my father, and hath with his hand fulfilled it, saying, ¹⁶"Since the day that I brought forth my people Israel out of Egypt, I chose no city out of all the tribes of Israel to build a house that my name might be therein; but I chose David to be over my people Israel". ¹⁷And it was in the heart of David my father to build a house for the name of the LORD God of Israel. ¹⁸And the LORD said unto David my father, "Whereas it was in thy heart to build a house unto my name, thou didst well that it was in thy heart. ¹⁹Nevertheless thou shalt not build the house, but thy son that shall come forth out of thy loins, he shall build the house unto my name." ²⁰And the LORD hath performed his word that he spoke, and I am risen up in the room of David my father, and sit on the throne of Israel, as the LORD promised, and have built a house for the name of the LORD God of Israel. ²¹And I have set there a place for the ark, wherein is the covenant of the LORD, which he made with our fathers, when he brought them out of the land of Egypt.'

²²And Solomon stood before the altar of the LORD in the presence of all the congregation of Israel, and spread forth his hands toward heaven: ²³and he said, 'LORD God of Israel, there is no God like thee, in heaven above, or on earth beneath, who keepest covenant and mercy with thy servants that walk before thee with all their heart: ²⁴who hast kept with thy servant David my father that thou promisedst him: thou spokest also with thy mouth, and hast fulfilled it with thy hand, as it is this day. ²⁵Therefore now, LORD God of Israel, keep with thy servant David my father that thou promisedst him, saying, "There shall not fail thee a man in my sight to sit on the throne of Israel; so that thy children take heed to their way, that they walk before me as thou hast walked before me". ²⁶And now, O God of Israel, let thy word, I pray thee, be verified, which thou spokest unto thy servant David my father. ²⁷But will God indeed dwell on the earth? Behold, the heaven and heaven of heav-

ens cannot contain thee: how much less this house that I have built? 28Yet have thou respect unto the prayer of thy servant, and to his supplication, O LORD my God, to hearken unto the cry and to the prayer, which thy servant prayeth before thee today: 29that thy eyes may be open toward this house night and day, even toward the place of which thou hast said, "My name shall be there": that thou mayest hearken unto the prayer which thy servant shall make towards this place. 30And hearken thou to the supplication of thy servant, and of thy people Israel, when they shall pray towards this place: and hear thou in heaven thy dwelling place: and when thou hearest, forgive.

31'If any man trespass against his neighbour, and an oath be laid upon him to cause him to swear, and the oath come before thy altar in this house: 32then hear thou in heaven, and do, and judge thy servants, condemning the wicked to bring his way upon his head, and justifying the righteous to give him according to his righteousness.

33'When thy people Israel be smitten down before the enemy, because they have sinned against thee, and shall turn again to thee, and confess thy name, and pray, and make supplication unto thee in this house: 34then hear thou in heaven, and forgive the sin of thy people Israel, and bring them again unto the land which thou gavest unto their fathers.

35'When heaven is shut up, and there is no rain, because they have sinned against thee: if they pray towards this place, and confess thy name, and turn from their sin, when thou afflictest them: 36then hear thou in heaven, and forgive the sin of thy servants, and of thy people Israel, that thou teach them the good way wherein they should walk, and give rain upon thy land which thou hast given to thy people for an inheritance.

37'If there be in the land famine, if there be pestilence, blasting, mildew, locust, or if there be caterpillar: if their enemy besiege them in the land of their cities, whatsoever plague, whatsoever sickness there be; 38what prayer and supplication soever be made by any man, or by all thy people Israel, which shall know every man the plague of his own heart, and spread forth his hands towards this house: 39then hear thou in heaven thy dwelling place, and forgive, and do, and give to every man according to his ways, whose heart thou knowest (for thou, even thou only, knowest the hearts of all the children of men), 40that they may fear thee all the days that they live in the land which thou gavest unto our fathers.

41'Moreover concerning a stranger that is not of thy people Israel, but cometh out of a far country for thy name's sake 42(for they shall hear of thy great name, and of thy strong hand, and of thy stretched out arm); when he shall come and pray towards this house: 43hear thou in heaven thy dwelling place, and do according to all that the stranger calleth to thee for: that all people of the earth may know thy name, to fear thee, as do thy people Israel, and that they may know that this house, which I have built, is called by thy name.

44'If thy people go out to battle against their enemy, whithersoever thou shalt send them, and shall pray unto the LORD toward the city which thou hast chosen, and toward the house that I have built for thy name: ⁴⁵then hear thou in heaven their prayer and their supplication, and maintain their cause. ⁴⁶If they sin against thee (for there is no man that sinneth not), and thou be angry with them, and deliver them to the enemy, so that they carry them away captives unto the land of the enemy, far or near; ⁴⁷yet if they shall bethink themselves in the land whither they were carried captives, and repent, and make supplication unto thee in the land of them that carried them captives, saying, "We have sinned, and have done perversely, we have committed wickedness"; ⁴⁸and so return unto thee with all their heart, and with all their soul, in the land of their enemies, which led them away captive, and pray unto thee toward their land, which thou gavest unto their fathers, the city which thou hast chosen, and the house which I have built for thy name: ⁴⁹then hear thou their prayer and their supplication in heaven thy dwelling place, and maintain their cause, ⁵⁰and forgive thy people that have sinned against thee, and all their transgressions wherein they have transgressed against thee, and give them compassion before them who carried them captive, that they may have compassion on them: ⁵¹for they be thy people, and thy inheritance, which thou broughtest forth out of Egypt, from the midst of the furnace of iron: ⁵²that thy eyes may be open unto the supplication of thy servant, and unto the supplication of thy people Israel, to hearken unto them in all that they call for unto thee. ⁵³For thou didst separate them from among all the people of the earth, to be thy inheritance, as thou spokest by the hand of Moses thy servant, when thou broughtest our fathers out of Egypt, O Lord God.'

⁵⁴And it was so, that when Solomon had made an end of praying all this prayer and supplication unto the LORD, he arose from before the altar of the LORD, from kneeling on his knees with his hands spread up to heaven. ⁵⁵And he stood, and blessed all the congregation of Israel with a loud voice, saying, ⁵⁶'Blessed be the LORD, that hath given rest unto his people Israel, according to all that he promised: there hath not failed one word of all his good promise, which he promised by the hand of Moses his servant. ⁵⁷The LORD our God be with us, as he was with our fathers: let him not leave us, nor forsake us: ⁵⁸that he may incline our hearts unto him, to walk in all his ways, and to keep his commandments, and his statutes, and his judgements, which he commanded our fathers. ⁵⁹And let these my words wherewith I have made supplication before the LORD, be nigh unto the LORD our God day and night, that he maintain the cause of his servant, and the cause of his people Israel at all times, as the matter shall require: ⁶⁰that all the people of the earth may know that the LORD is God, and that there is none else. ⁶¹Let your heart therefore be perfect with the LORD our God, to walk in his statutes, and to keep his commandments, as at this day.'

⁶²And the king, and all Israel with him, offered sacrifice before the LORD. ⁶³And Solomon offered a sacrifice of peace offerings, which he offered unto the LORD, two and twenty thousand oxen, and a hundred and twenty thousand sheep. So the king and all the children of Israel

dedicated the house of the LORD. ⁶⁴The same day did the king hallow the middle of the court that was before the house of the LORD: for there he offered burnt offerings, and meat offerings, and the fat of the peace offerings: because the brazen altar that was before the LORD was too little to receive the burnt offerings, and meat offerings, and the fat of the peace offerings.

⁶⁵And at that time Solomon held a feast, and all Israel with him, a great congregation, from the entering in of Hamath unto the river of Egypt, before the LORD our God, seven days and seven days, even fourteen days. ⁶⁶On the eighth day he sent the people away: and they blessed the king, and went unto their tents joyful and glad of heart for all the goodness that the LORD had done for David his servant, and for Israel his people.

9 And it came to pass, when Solomon had finished the building of the house of the LORD, and the king's house, and all Solomon's desire which he was pleased to do, ²that the LORD appeared to Solomon the second time, as he had appeared unto him at Gibeon. ³And the LORD said unto him, 'I have heard thy prayer and thy supplication that thou hast made before me: I have hallowed this house which thou hast built, to put my name there for ever, and my eyes and my heart shall be there perpetually. ⁴And if thou wilt walk before me, as David thy father walked, in integrity of heart, and in uprightness, to do according to all that I have commanded thee, and wilt keep my statutes and my judgements: ⁵then I will establish the throne of thy kingdom upon Israel for ever, as I promised to David thy father, saying, "There shall not fail thee a man upon the throne of Israel". ⁶But if you shall at all turn from following me, you or your children, and will not keep my commandments and my statutes which I have set before you, but go and serve other gods, and worship them: ⁷then will I cut off Israel out of the land which I have given them; and this house, which I have hallowed for my name, will I cast out of my sight, and Israel shall be a proverb and a byword among all people: ⁸and at this house which is high, every one that passeth by it shall be astonished, and shall hiss, and they shall say, "Why hath the LORD done thus unto this land, and to this house?" ⁹And they shall answer, "Because they forsook the LORD their God, who brought forth their fathers out of the land of Egypt, and have taken hold upon other gods, and have worshipped them, and served them: therefore hath the LORD brought upon them all this evil".'

¹⁰And it came to pass at the end of twenty years, when Solomon had built the two houses, the house of the LORD, and the king's house ¹¹(now Hiram the king of Tyre had furnished Solomon with cedar trees and fir trees, and with gold according to all his desire), that then Solomon gave Hiram twenty cities in the land of Galilee. ¹²And Hiram came out from Tyre to see the cities which Solomon had given him, and they pleased him not. ¹³And he said, 'What cities are these which thou hast given me, my brother?' And he called them the land of Cabul unto this day. ¹⁴And Hiram sent to the king sixscore talents of gold.

¹⁵And this is the reason of the levy which king Solomon raised, for to

build the house of the LORD, and his own house, and Millo, and the wall of Jerusalem, and Hazor, and Megiddo, and Gezer. ¹⁶For Pharaoh king of Egypt had gone up, and taken Gezer, and burnt it with fire, and slain the Canaanites that dwelt in the city, and given it for a present unto his daughter, Solomon's wife. ¹⁷And Solomon built Gezer, and Beth-horon the nether, ¹⁸and Baalath, and Tadmor in the wilderness, in the land, ¹⁹and all the cities of store that Solomon had, and cities for his chariots, and cities for his horsemen, and that which Solomon desired to build in Jerusalem, and in Lebanon, and in all the land of his dominion. ²⁰And all the people that were left of the Amorites, Hittites, Perizzites, Hivites, and Jebusites, which were not of the children of Israel, ²¹their children that were left after them in the land, whom the children of Israel also were not able utterly to destroy, upon those did Solomon levy a tribute of bondservice unto this day. ²²But of the children of Israel did Solomon make no bondmen: but they were men of war, and his servants, and his princes, and his captains, and rulers of his chariots, and his horsemen. ²³These were the chief of the officers that were over Solomon's work, five hundred and fifty, which bore rule over the people that wrought in the work.

²⁴But Pharaoh's daughter came up out of the city of David unto her house which Solomon had built for her: then did he build Millo.

²⁵And three times in a year did Solomon offer burnt offerings and peace offerings upon the altar which he built unto the LORD, and he burnt incense upon the altar that was before the LORD. So he finished the house.

²⁶And king Solomon made a navy of ships in Ezion-geber, which is beside Eloth, on the shore of the Red Sea, in the land of Edom. ²⁷And Hiram sent in the navy his servants, shipmen that had knowledge of the sea, with the servants of Solomon. ²⁸And they came to Ophir, and fetched from thence gold, four hundred and twenty talents, and brought it to king Solomon.

10 And when the queen of Sheba heard of the fame of Solomon concerning the name of the LORD, she came to prove him with hard questions. ²And she came to Jerusalem with a very great train, with camels that bore spices, and very much gold, and precious stones: and when she was come to Solomon, she communed with him of all that was in her heart. ³And Solomon told her all her questions: there was not anything hid from the king, which he told her not. ⁴And when the queen of Sheba had seen all Solomon's wisdom, and the house that he had built, ⁵and the meat of his table, and the sitting of his servants, and the attendance of his ministers, and their apparel, and his cupbearers, and his ascent by which he went up unto the house of the LORD: there was no more spirit in her. ⁶And she said to the king, 'It was a true report that I heard in my own land of thy acts and of thy wisdom. ⁷Howbeit I believed not the words, until I came, and my eyes had seen it: and behold, the half was not told me: thy wisdom and prosperity exceedeth the fame which I heard. ⁸Happy are thy men, happy are these thy servants, which stand continually before thee, and that hear thy wisdom. ⁹Blessed be the LORD thy God which delighted in thee, to set thee on the throne of Israel: because the LORD loved Israel for ever, therefore made he thee king, to do judgement and justice.' ¹⁰And she gave the king a hundred and twenty talents of gold, and of spices very great store, and precious stones: there came no more such abundance of spices as these which the queen of Sheba gave to king Solomon. ¹¹And the navy also of Hiram that brought gold from Ophir, brought in from Ophir great plenty of almug trees, and precious stones. ¹²And the king made of the almug trees pillars for the house of the LORD, and for the king's house, harps also and psalteries for singers: there came no such almug trees, nor were seen unto this day. ¹³And king Solomon gave unto the queen of Sheba all her desire, whatsoever she asked, besides that which Solomon gave her of his royal bounty. So she turned and went to her own country, she and her servants.

¹⁴Now the weight of gold that came to Solomon in one year was six hundred threescore and six talents of gold, ¹⁵besides that he had of the merchantmen, and of the traffic of the spice-merchants, and of all the kings of Arabia, and of the governors of the country.

¹⁶And king Solomon made two hundred targets of beaten gold: six hundred shekels of gold went to one target. ¹⁷And he made three hundred shields of beaten gold; three pound of gold went to one shield: and the king put them in the house of the forest of Lebanon.

¹⁸Moreover the king made a great throne of ivory, and overlaid it with the best gold. ¹⁹The throne had six steps, and the top of the throne was round behind: and there were stays on either side on the place of the seat, and two lions stood beside the stays. ²⁰And twelve lions stood there on the one side and on the other upon the six steps: there was not the like made in any kingdom.

²¹And all king Solomon's drinking vessels were of gold, and all the vessels of the house of the forest of Lebanon were of pure gold; none were of silver: it was nothing accounted of in the days of Solomon. ²²For the king had at sea a navy of Tarshish with the navy of Hiram: once in three years came the navy of Tarshish, bringing gold, and silver, ivory, and apes, and peacocks. ²³So king Solomon exceeded all the kings of the earth for riches and for wisdom.

²⁴And all the earth sought to Solomon, to hear his wisdom, which God had put in his heart. ²⁵And they brought every man his present, vessels of silver, and vessels of gold, and garments, and armour, and spices, horses, and mules, a rate year by year.

²⁶And Solomon gathered together chariots and horsemen: and he had a thousand and four hundred chariots, and twelve thousand horsemen, whom he bestowed in the cities for chariots, and with the king at Jerusalem. ²⁷And the king made silver to be in Jerusalem as stones, and cedars made he to be as the sycamore trees that are in the vale, for abundance.

²⁸And Solomon had horses brought out of Egypt, and linen yarn: the king's merchants received the linen yarn at a price. ²⁹And a chariot came up and went out of Egypt for six hundred shekels of silver, and a

11 But king Solomon loved many strange women (together with the daughter of Pharaoh), women of the Moabites, Ammonites, Edomites, Zidonians, and Hittites: ²of the nations concerning which the LORD said unto the children of Israel, 'Ye shall not go in to them, neither shall they come in unto you: for surely they will turn away your heart after their gods': Solomon cleaved unto these in love. ³And he had seven hundred wives, princesses, and three hundred concubines: and his wives turned away his heart. ⁴For it came to pass, when Solomon was old, that his wives turned away his heart after other gods: and his heart was not perfect with the LORD his God, as was the heart of David his father. ⁵For Solomon went after Ashtoreth the goddess of the Zidonians, and after Milcom the abomination of the Ammonites. ⁶And Solomon did evil in the sight of the LORD, and went not fully after the LORD, as did David his father. ⁷Then did Solomon build a high place for Chemosh, the abomination of Moab, in the hill that is before Jerusalem, and for Molech, the abomination of the children of Ammon. ⁸And likewise did he for all his strange wives, which burnt incense and sacrificed unto their gods.

⁹And the LORD was angry with Solomon, because his heart was turned from the LORD God of Israel, which had appeared unto him twice, ¹⁰and had commanded him concerning this thing, that he should not go after other gods: but he kept not that which the LORD commanded. ¹¹Wherefore the LORD said unto Solomon, 'Forasmuch as this is done of thee, and thou hast not kept my covenant and my statutes which I have commanded thee, I will surely rend the kingdom from thee, and will give it to thy servant. ¹²Notwithstanding in thy days I will not do it for David thy father's sake: but I will rend it out of the hand of thy son. ¹³Howbeit I will not rend away all the kingdom: but will give one tribe to thy son for David my servant's sake, and for Jerusalem's sake which I have chosen.'

¹⁴And the LORD stirred up an adversary unto Solomon, Hadad the Edomite: he was of the king's seed in Edom. ¹⁵For it came to pass when David was in Edom, and Joab the captain of the host was gone up to bury the slain, after he had smitten every male in Edom ¹⁶(for six months did Joab remain there with all Israel, until he had cut off every male in Edom), ¹⁷that Hadad fled, he and certain Edomites of his father's servants with him, to go into Egypt: Hadad being yet a little child. ¹⁸And they arose out of Midian, and came to Paran, and they took men with them out of Paran, and they came to Egypt, unto Pharaoh king of Egypt, which gave him a house, and appointed him victuals, and gave him land. ¹⁹And Hadad found great favour in the sight of Pharaoh, so that he gave him to wife the sister of his own wife, the sister of Tahpenes the queen. ²⁰And the sister of Tahpenes bore him Genubath his son, whom Tahpenes weaned in Pharaoh's house: and Genubath was in Pharaoh's household among the sons of Pharaoh. ²¹And when Hadad heard in Egypt that David slept with his fathers, and

that Joab the captain of the host was dead, Hadad said to Pharaoh, 'Let me depart, that I may go to my own country'. ²²Then Pharaoh said unto him, 'But what hast thou lacked with me, that, behold, thou seekest to go to thy own country?' And he answered, 'Nothing: howbeit let me go in any wise'.

²³And God stirred him up another adversary, Rezon the son of Eliadah, which fled from his lord Hadadezer king of Zobah: ²⁴and he gathered men unto him, and became captain over a band, when David slew them of Zobah: and they went to Damascus, and dwelt therein, and reigned in Damascus. ²⁵And he was an adversary to Israel all the days of Solomon, besides the mischief that Hadad did: and he abhorred Israel, and reigned over Syria.

²⁶And Jeroboam the son of Nebat, an Ephrathite of Zereda, Solomon's servant, whose mother's name was Zeruah, a widow woman, even he lifted up his hand against the king. ²⁷And this was the cause that he lifted up his hand against the king: Solomon built Millo, and repaired the breaches of the city of David his father. ²⁸And the man Jeroboam was a mighty man of valour: and Solomon seeing the young man that he was industrious, he made him ruler over all the charge of the house of Joseph. ²⁹And it came to pass at that time when Jeroboam went out of Jerusalem, that the prophet Ahijah the Shilonite found him in the way: and he had clad himself with a new garment; and they two were alone in the field: ³⁰and Ahijah caught the new garment that was on him, and rent it in twelve pieces. ³¹And he said to Jeroboam, 'Take thee ten pieces: for thus saith the LORD, the God of Israel, "Behold, I will rend the kingdom out of the hand of Solomon, and will give ten tribes to thee ³²(but he shall have one tribe for my servant David's sake, and for Jerusalem's sake, the city which I have chosen out of all the tribes of Israel): ³³because that they have forsaken me, and have worshipped Ashtoreth the goddess of the Zidonians, Chemosh the god of the Moabites, and Milcom the god of the children of Ammon, and have not walked in my ways, to do that which is right in my eyes, and to keep my statutes and my judgements, as did David his father. ³⁴Howbeit I will not take the whole kingdom out of his hand: but I will make him prince all the days of his life for David my servant's sake, whom I chose, because he kept my commandments and my statutes: ³⁵but I will take the kingdom out of his son's hand, and will give it unto thee, even ten tribes. ³⁶And unto his son will I give one tribe, that David my servant may have a light always before me in Jerusalem, the city which I have chosen me to put my name there. ³⁷And I will take thee, and thou shalt reign according to all that thy soul desireth, and shalt be king over Israel. ³⁸And it shall be, if thou wilt hearken unto all that I command thee, and wilt walk in my ways, and do that is right in my sight, to keep my statutes and my commandments, as David my servant did; that I will be with thee, and build thee a sure house, as I built for David, and will give Israel unto thee. ³⁹And I will for this afflict the seed of David, but not for ever."' ⁴⁰Solomon sought therefore to kill Jeroboam. And Jeroboam arose, and fled into Egypt, unto Shishak king of Egypt, and was in Egypt until the death of Solomon.

⁴¹And the rest of the acts of Solomon, and all that he did, and his wisdom, are they not written in the book of the acts of Solomon? ⁴²And the time that Solomon reigned in Jerusalem over all Israel was forty years. ⁴³And Solomon slept with his fathers, and was buried in the city of David his father: and Rehoboam his son reigned in his stead.

12 And Rehoboam went to Shechem: for all Israel were come to Shechem to make him king. ²And it came to pass when Jeroboam the son of Nebat, who was yet in Egypt, heard of it (for he was fled from the presence of king Solomon, and Jeroboam dwelt in Egypt), ³that they sent and called him. And Jeroboam and all the congregation of Israel came, and spoke unto Rehoboam, saying, ⁴'Thy father made our yoke grievous: now therefore make thou the grievous service of thy father, and his heavy yoke which he put upon us, lighter, and we will serve thee'. ⁵And he said unto them, 'Depart yet for three days, then come again to me'. And the people departed.

⁶And king Rehoboam consulted with the old men that stood before Solomon his father while he yet lived, and said, 'How do you advise that I may answer this people?' ⁷And they spoke unto him, saying, 'If thou wilt be a servant unto this people this day, and wilt serve them, and answer them, and speak good words to them, then they will be thy servants for ever'. ⁸But he forsook the counsel of the old men, which they had given him, and consulted with the young men that were grown up with him, and which stood before him. ⁹And he said unto them, 'What counsel give ye that we may answer this people, who have spoken to me, saying, "Make the yoke which thy father did put upon us lighter"?' ¹⁰And the young men that were grown up with him spoke unto him, saying, 'Thus shalt thou speak unto this people that spoke unto thee, saying, "Thy father made our yoke heavy, but make thou it lighter unto us"; thus shalt thou say unto them, "My little finger shall be thicker than my father's loins. ¹¹And now whereas my father did load you with a heavy yoke, I will add to your yoke: my father hath chastised you with whips, but I will chastise you with scorpions."'

¹²So Jeroboam and all the people came to Rehoboam the third day, as the king had appointed, saying, 'Come to me again the third day'. ¹³And the king answered the people roughly, and forsook the old men's counsel that they gave him: ¹⁴and spoke to them after the counsel of the young men, saying, 'My father made your yoke heavy, and I will add to your yoke: my father also chastised you with whips, but I will chastise you with scorpions'. ¹⁵Wherefore the king hearkened not unto the people: for the cause was from the LORD, that he might perform his saying, which the LORD spoke by Ahijah the Shilonite unto Jeroboam the son of Nebat.

¹⁶So when all Israel saw that the king hearkened not unto them, the people answered the king, saying, 'What portion have we in David? neither have we inheritance in the son of Jesse: to your tents, O Israel: now see to thy own house, David'. So Israel departed unto their tents. ¹⁷But as for the children of Israel which dwelt in the cities of Judah, Rehoboam reigned over them. ¹⁸Then king Rehoboam sent Adoram,

who was over the tribute, and all Israel stoned him with stones that he died. Therefore king Rehoboam made speed to get him up to his chariot, to flee to Jerusalem. ¹⁹So Israel rebelled against the house of David unto this day. ²⁰And it came to pass when all Israel heard that Jeroboam was come again, that they sent and called him unto the congregation, and made him king over all Israel: there was none that followed the house of David, but the tribe of Judah only.

²¹And when Rehoboam was come to Jerusalem, he assembled all the house of Judah, with the tribe of Benjamin, a hundred and fourscore thousand chosen men which were warriors, to fight against the house of Israel, to bring the kingdom again to Rehoboam the son of Solomon. ²²But the word of God came unto Shemaiah the man of God, saying, ²³'Speak unto Rehoboam, the son of Solomon, king of Judah, and unto all the house of Judah and Benjamin, and to the remnant of the people, saying, ²⁴"Thus saith the LORD, 'Ye shall not go up, nor fight against your brethren the children of Israel: return every man to his house, for this thing is from me'"'. They hearkened therefore to the word of the LORD, and returned to depart, according to the word of the LORD.

²⁵Then Jeroboam built Shechem in mount Ephraim, and dwelt therein; and went out from thence, and built Penuel. ²⁶And Jeroboam said in his heart, 'Now shall the kingdom return to the house of David: ²⁷if this people go up to do sacrifice in the house of the LORD at Jerusalem, then shall the heart of this people turn again unto their lord, even unto Rehoboam king of Judah, and they shall kill me, and go again to Rehoboam king of Judah'. ²⁸Whereupon the king took counsel, and made two calves of gold, and said unto them, 'It is too much for you to go up to Jerusalem: behold thy gods, O Israel, which brought thee up out of the land of Egypt'. ²⁹And he set the one in Beth-el, and the other put he in Dan. ³⁰And this thing became a sin: for the people went to worship before the one, even unto Dan. ³¹And he made a house of high places, and made priests of the lowest of the people, which were not of the sons of Levi. ³²And Jeroboam ordained a feast in the eighth month, on the fifteenth day of the month, like unto the feast that is in Judah, and he offered upon the altar (so did he in Beth-el), sacrificing unto the calves that he had made: and he placed in Beth-el the priests of the high places which he had made. ³³So he offered upon the altar which he had made in Beth-el the fifteenth day of the eighth month, even in the month which he had devised of his own heart: and ordained a feast unto the children of Israel, and he offered upon the altar, and burnt incense.

13 And behold, there came a man of God out of Judah by the word of the LORD unto Beth-el: and Jeroboam stood by the altar to burn incense. ²And he cried against the altar in the word of the LORD, and said, 'O altar, altar, thus saith the LORD, "Behold, a child shall be born unto the house of David, Josiah by name, and upon thee shall he offer the priests of the high places that burn incense upon thee, and men's bones shall be burnt upon thee"'. ³And he gave a sign the same day, saying, 'This is the sign which the LORD hath spoken, "Behold, the altar shall be rent, and the ashes that are upon it shall be poured out"'. ⁴And it came to pass, when king Jeroboam heard the saying of the man of God, which had cried against the altar in Beth-el, that he put forth his hand from the altar, saying, 'Lay hold on him'. And his hand which he put forth against him, dried up, so that he could not pull it in again to him. ⁵The altar also was rent, and the ashes poured out from the altar, according to the sign which the man of God had given by the word of the LORD. ⁶And the king answered and said unto the man of God, 'Entreat now the face of the LORD thy God, and pray for me, that my hand may be restored me again'. And the man of God besought the LORD, and the king's hand was restored again, and became as it was before. ⁷And the king said unto the man of God, 'Come home with me, and refresh thyself, and I will give thee a reward'. ⁸And the man of God said unto the king, 'If thou wilt give me half thy house, I will not go in with thee, neither will I eat bread nor drink water in this place: ⁹for so was it charged me by the word of the LORD, saying, "Eat no bread, nor drink water, nor turn again by the same way that thou camest"'. ¹⁰So he went another way, and returned not by the way that he came to Beth-el.

¹¹Now there dwelt an old prophet in Beth-el, and his son came and told him all the works that the man of God had done that day in Beth-el: the words which he had spoken unto the king, them they told also to their father. ¹²And their father said unto them, 'What way went he?' For his sons had seen what way the man of God went, which came from Judah. ¹³And he said unto his sons, 'Saddle me the ass'. So they saddled him the ass, and he rode thereon, ¹⁴and went after the man of God, and found him sitting under an oak: and he said unto him, 'Art thou the man of God that camest from Judah?' And he said, 'I am'. ¹⁵Then he said unto him, 'Come home with me, and eat bread'. ¹⁶And he said, 'I may not return with thee, nor go in with thee: neither will I eat bread nor drink water with thee in this place. ¹⁷For it was said to me by the word of the LORD, "Thou shalt eat no bread nor drink water there, nor turn again to go by the way that thou camest".' ¹⁸He said unto him, 'I am a prophet also as thou art, and an angel spoke unto me by the word of the LORD, saying, "Bring him back with thee into thy house, that he may eat bread and drink water"'. But he lied unto him. ¹⁹So he went back with him, and did eat bread in his house, and drank water.

²⁰And it came to pass as they sat at the table, that the word of the LORD came unto the prophet that brought him back: ²¹and he cried unto the man of God that came from Judah, saying, 'Thus saith the LORD, "Forasmuch as thou hast disobeyed the mouth of the LORD, and hast not kept the commandment which the LORD thy God commanded thee, ²²but camest back, and hast eaten bread and drunk water in the place, of the which the LORD did say to thee, 'Eat no bread, and drink no water'; thy carcase shall not come unto the sepulchre of thy fathers"'.

²³And it came to pass after he had eaten bread, and after he had drunk, that he saddled for him the ass, to wit, for the prophet whom he had brought back. ²⁴And when he was gone, a lion met him by the way,

and slew him: and his carcase was cast in the way, and the ass stood by it, the lion also stood by the carcase. ²⁵And behold, men passed by, and saw the carcase cast in the way, and the lion standing by the carcase: and they came and told it in the city where the old prophet dwelt. ²⁶And when the prophet that brought him back from the way heard thereof, he said, 'It is the man of God, who was disobedient unto the word of the LORD: therefore the LORD hath delivered him unto the lion, which hath torn him, and slain him, according to the word of the LORD, which he spoke unto him'. ²⁷And he spoke to his sons, saying, 'Saddle me the ass'. And they saddled him. ²⁸And he went and found his carcase cast in the way, and the ass and the lion standing by the carcase: the lion had not eaten the carcase, nor torn the ass. ²⁹And the prophet took up the carcase of the man of God, and laid it upon the ass, and brought it back: and the old prophet came to the city, to mourn and to bury him. ³⁰And he laid his carcase in his own grave, and they mourned over him, saying, 'Alas, my brother'. ³¹And it came to pass after he had buried him, that he spoke to his sons, saying, 'When I am dead, then bury me in the sepulchre wherein the man of God is buried; lay my bones beside his bones. ³²For the saying which he cried by the word of the LORD against the altar in Beth-el, and against all the houses of the high places which are in the cities of Samaria, shall surely come to pass.'

³³After this thing Jeroboam returned not from his evil way, but made again of the lowest of the people priests of the high places: whosoever would, he consecrated him, and he became one of the priests of the high places. ³⁴And this thing became sin unto the house of Jeroboam, even to cut it off, and to destroy it from off the face of the earth.

14 At that time Abijah the son of Jeroboam fell sick. ²And Jeroboam said to his wife, 'Arise, I pray thee, and disguise thyself, that thou be not known to be the wife of Jeroboam: and get thee to Shiloh: behold, there is Ahijah the prophet, which told me that I should be king over this people. ³And take with thee ten loaves, and cracknels, and a cruse of honey, and go to him: he shall tell thee what shall become of the child.' ⁴And Jeroboam's wife did so, and arose, and went to Shiloh, and came to the house of Ahijah. But Ahijah could not see, for his eyes were set by reason of his age.

⁵And the LORD said unto Ahijah, 'Behold, the wife of Jeroboam cometh to ask a thing of thee for her son, for he is sick: thus and thus shalt thou say unto her: for it shall be when she cometh in, that she shall feign herself to be another woman'. ⁶And it was so, when Ahijah heard the sound of her feet, as she came in at the door, that he said, 'Come in, thou wife of Jeroboam; why feignest thou thyself to be another? for I am sent to thee with heavy tidings. ⁷Go, tell Jeroboam, "Thus saith the LORD God of Israel, 'Forasmuch as I exalted thee from among the people, and made thee prince over my people Israel, ⁸and rent the kingdom away from the house of David, and gave it thee: and yet thou hast not been as my servant David, who kept my commandments, and who followed me with all his heart, to do that only which was right in my eyes, ⁹but hast done evil above all that were before thee: for thou hast

gone and made thee other gods, and molten images, to provoke me to anger, and hast cast me behind thy back: [10]therefore behold, I will bring evil upon the house of Jeroboam, and will cut off from Jeroboam him that pisseth against the wall, and him that is shut up and left in Israel, and will take away the remnant of the house of Jeroboam, as a man taketh away dung, till it be all gone. [11]Him that dieth of Jeroboam in the city shall the dogs eat; and him that dieth in the field shall the fowls of the air eat': for the LORD hath spoken it." [12]Arise thou therefore, get thee to thine own house: and when thy feet enter into the city, the child shall die. [13]And all Israel shall mourn for him, and bury him: for he only of Jeroboam shall come to the grave, because in him there is found some good thing toward the LORD God of Israel in the house of Jeroboam.

[14]'Moreover the LORD shall raise him up a king over Israel, who shall cut off the house of Jeroboam that day: but what? even now. [15]For the LORD shall smite Israel, as a reed is shaken in the water, and he shall root up Israel out of this good land, which he gave to their fathers, and shall scatter them beyond the river, because they have made their groves, provoking the LORD to anger. [16]And he shall give Israel up because of the sins of Jeroboam, who did sin, and who made Israel to sin.'

[17]And Jeroboam's wife arose, and departed, and came to Tirzah: and when she came to the threshold of the door, the child died. [18]And they buried him, and all Israel mourned for him, according to the word of the LORD, which he spoke by the hand of his servant Ahijah the prophet.

[19]And the rest of the acts of Jeroboam, how he warred, and how he reigned, behold, they are written in the book of the chronicles of the kings of Israel. [20]And the days which Jeroboam reigned were two and twenty years: and he slept with his fathers, and Nadab his son reigned in his stead.

[21]And Rehoboam the son of Solomon reigned in Judah. Rehoboam was forty and one years old when he began to reign, and he reigned seventeen years in Jerusalem, the city which the LORD did choose out of all the tribes of Israel, to put his name there. And his mother's name was Naamah an Ammonitess. [22]And Judah did evil in the sight of the LORD, and they provoked him to jealousy with their sins which they had committed, above all that their fathers had done. [23]For they also built them high places, and images, and groves, on every high hill, and under every green tree. [24]And there were also sodomites in the land: and they did according to all the abominations of the nations which the LORD cast out before the children of Israel.

[25]And it came to pass in the fifth year of king Rehoboam, that Shishak king of Egypt came up against Jerusalem: [26]and he took away the treasures of the house of the LORD, and the treasures of the king's house; he even took away all: and he took away all the shields of gold which Solomon had made. [27]And king Rehoboam made in their stead brazen shields, and committed them unto the hands of the chief of the guard,

which kept the door of the king's house. ²⁸And it was so, when the king went into the house of the Lord, that the guard bore them, and brought them back into the guard chamber.

²⁹Now the rest of the acts of Rehoboam, and all that he did, are they not written in the book of the chronicles of the kings of Judah? ³⁰And there was war between Rehoboam and Jeroboam all their days. ³¹And Rehoboam slept with his fathers, and was buried with his fathers in the city of David. And his mother's name was Naamah an Ammonitess. And Abijam his son reigned in his stead.

15

Now in the eighteenth year of king Jeroboam the son of Nebat reigned Abijam over Judah. ²Three years reigned he in Jerusalem. And his mother's name was Maachah, the daughter of Abishalom. ³And he walked in all the sins of his father, which he had done before him: and his heart was not perfect with the Lord his God, as the heart of David his father. ⁴Nevertheless for David's sake did the Lord his God give him a lamp in Jerusalem, to set up his son after him, and to establish Jerusalem: ⁵because David did that which was right in the eyes of the Lord, and turned not aside from anything that he commanded him all the days of his life, save only in the matter of Uriah the Hittite. ⁶And there was war between Rehoboam and Jeroboam all the days of his life.

⁷Now the rest of the acts of Abijam, and all that he did, are they not written in the book of the chronicles of the kings of Judah? And there was war between Abijam and Jeroboam. ⁸And Abijam slept with his fathers, and they buried him in the city of David: and Asa his son reigned in his stead.

⁹And in the twentieth year of Jeroboam king of Israel reigned Asa over Judah. ¹⁰And forty and one years reigned he in Jerusalem. And his mother's name was Maachah, the daughter of Abishalom. ¹¹And Asa did that which was right in the eyes of the Lord, as did David his father. ¹²And he took away the sodomites out of the land, and removed all the idols that his fathers had made. ¹³And also Maachah his mother, even her he removed from being queen, because she had made an idol in a grove; and Asa destroyed her idol, and burnt it by the brook Kidron. ¹⁴But the high places were not removed: nevertheless Asa's heart was perfect with the Lord all his days. ¹⁵And he brought in the things which his father had dedicated, and the things which himself had dedicated, into the house of the Lord, silver, and gold, and vessels.

¹⁶And there was war between Asa and Baasha king of Israel all their days. ¹⁷And Baasha king of Israel went up against Judah, and built Ramah, that he might not suffer any to go out or come in to Asa king of Judah. ¹⁸Then Asa took all the silver and the gold that were left in the treasures of the house of the Lord, and the treasures of the king's house, and delivered them into the hand of his servants: and king Asa sent them to Ben-hadad, the son of Tabrimon, the son of Hezion, king of Syria, that dwelt at Damascus, saying, ¹⁹'There is a league between me and thee, and between my father and thy father: behold, I have sent unto thee a present of silver and gold; come and break thy

league with Baasha king of Israel, that he may depart from me'. ²⁰So Ben-hadad hearkened unto king Asa, and sent the captains of the hosts which he had against the cities of Israel, and smote Ijon, and Dan, and Abel-beth-maachah, and all Chinneroth, with all the land of Naphtali. ²¹And it came to pass, when Baasha heard thereof, that he left off building of Ramah, and dwelt in Tirzah. ²²Then king Asa made a proclamation throughout all Judah; none was exempted: and they took away the stones of Ramah, and the timber thereof wherewith Baasha had built, and king Asa built with them Geba of Benjamin, and Mizpah.

²³The rest of all the acts of Asa, and all his might, and all that he did, and the cities which he built, are they not written in the book of the chronicles of the kings of Judah? Nevertheless in the time of his old age he was diseased in his feet. ²⁴And Asa slept with his fathers, and was buried with his fathers in the city of David his father: and Jehoshaphat his son reigned in his stead.

²⁵And Nadab the son of Jeroboam began to reign over Israel in the second year of Asa king of Judah, and reigned over Israel two years. ²⁶And he did evil in the sight of the LORD, and walked in the way of his father, and in his sin wherewith he made Israel to sin.

²⁷And Baasha the son of Ahijah, of the house of Issachar, conspired against him; and Baasha smote him at Gibbethon, which belongeth to the Philistines; for Nadab and all Israel laid siege to Gibbethon. ²⁸Even in the third year of Asa king of Judah did Baasha slay him, and reigned in his stead. ²⁹And it came to pass, when he reigned, that he smote all the house of Jeroboam; he left not to Jeroboam any that breathed, until he had destroyed him, according unto the saying of the LORD, which he spoke by his servant Ahijah the Shilonite: ³⁰because of the sins of Jeroboam which he sinned, and which he made Israel sin, by his provocation wherewith he provoked the LORD God of Israel to anger.

³¹Now the rest of the acts of Nadab, and all that he did, are they not written in the book of the chronicles of the kings of Israel?

³²And there was war between Asa and Baasha king of Israel all their days. ³³In the third year of Asa king of Judah began Baasha the son of Ahijah to reign over all Israel in Tirzah, twenty and four years. ³⁴And he did evil in the sight of the LORD, and walked in the way of Jeroboam, and in his sin wherewith he made Israel to sin.

16 Then the word of the LORD came to Jehu the son of Hanani against Baasha, saying, ²'Forasmuch as I exalted thee out of the dust, and made thee prince over my people Israel, and thou hast walked in the way of Jeroboam, and hast made my people Israel to sin, to provoke me to anger with their sins; ³behold, I will take away the posterity of Baasha, and the posterity of his house: and will make thy house like the house of Jeroboam the son of Nebat. ⁴Him that dieth of Baasha in the city shall the dogs eat: and him that dieth of his in the fields shall the fowls of the air eat.'

⁵Now the rest of the acts of Baasha, and what he did, and his might, are they not written in the book of the chronicles of the kings of Israel?

⁶So Baasha slept with his fathers, and was buried in Tirzah: and Elah his son reigned in his stead.

⁷And also by the hand of the prophet Jehu the son of Hanani came the word of the LORD against Baasha, and against his house, even for all the evil that he did in the sight of the LORD, in provoking him to anger with the work of his hands, in being like the house of Jeroboam; and because he killed him.

⁸In the twenty and sixth year of Asa king of Judah began Elah the son of Baasha to reign over Israel in Tirzah, two years. ⁹And his servant Zimri, captain of half his chariots, conspired against him as he was in Tirzah drinking himself drunk in the house of Arza steward of his house in Tirzah. ¹⁰And Zimri went in and smote him, and killed him, in the twenty and seventh year of Asa king of Judah, and reigned in his stead.

¹¹And it came to pass when he began to reign, as soon as he sat on his throne, that he slew all the house of Baasha: he left him not one that pisseth against a wall, neither of his kinsfolks, nor of his friends. ¹²Thus did Zimri destroy all the house of Baasha, according to the word of the LORD, which he spoke against Baasha by Jehu the prophet, ¹³for all the sins of Baasha, and the sins of Elah his son, by which they sinned, and by which they made Israel to sin, in provoking the LORD God of Israel to anger with their vanities.

¹⁴Now the rest of the acts of Elah, and all that he did, are they not written in the book of the chronicles of the kings of Israel?

¹⁵In the twenty and seventh year of Asa king of Judah did Zimri reign seven days in Tirzah. And the people were encamped against Gibbethon, which belonged to the Philistines. ¹⁶And the people that were encamped heard say, 'Zimri hath conspired, and hath also slain the king': wherefore all Israel made Omri, the captain of the host, king over Israel that day in the camp. ¹⁷And Omri went up from Gibbethon, and all Israel with him, and they besieged Tirzah. ¹⁸And it came to pass when Zimri saw that the city was taken, that he went into the palace of the king's house, and burnt the king's house over him with fire, and died, ¹⁹for his sins which he sinned in doing evil in the sight of the LORD, in walking in the way of Jeroboam, and in his sin which he did, to make Israel sin.

²⁰Now the rest of the acts of Zimri, and his treason that he wrought, are they not written in the book of the chronicles of the kings of Israel?

²¹Then were the people of Israel divided into two parts: half of the people followed Tibni the son of Ginath, to make him king: and half followed Omri. ²²But the people that followed Omri prevailed against the people that followed Tibni the son of Ginath: so Tibni died, and Omri reigned.

²³In the thirty and first year of Asa king of Judah began Omri to reign over Israel twelve years: six years reigned he in Tirzah. ²⁴And he bought the hill Samaria of Shemer for two talents of silver, and built on the hill, and called the name of the city which he built, after the name of Shemer, owner of the hill, Samaria.

²⁵But Omri wrought evil in the eyes of the LORD, and did worse than all that were before him. ²⁶For he walked in all the way of Jeroboam the son of Nebat, and in his sin wherewith he made Israel to sin, to provoke the LORD God of Israel to anger with their vanities.

²⁷Now the rest of the acts of Omri which he did, and his might that he showed, are they not written in the book of the chronicles of the kings of Israel? ²⁸So Omri slept with his fathers, and was buried in Samaria: and Ahab his son reigned in his stead.

²⁹And in the thirty and eighth year of Asa king of Judah began Ahab the son of Omri to reign over Israel: and Ahab the son of Omri reigned over Israel in Samaria twenty and two years. ³⁰And Ahab the son of Omri did evil in the sight of the LORD above all that were before him. ³¹And it came to pass, as if it had been a light thing for him to walk in the sins of Jeroboam the son of Nebat, that he took to wife Jezebel the daughter of Ethbaal king of the Zidonians, and went and served Baal, and worshipped him. ³²And he reared up an altar for Baal in the house of Baal, which he had built in Samaria. ³³And Ahab made a grove; and Ahab did more to provoke the LORD God of Israel to anger than all the kings of Israel that were before him.

³⁴In his days did Hiel the Beth-elite build Jericho: he laid the foundation thereof in Abiram his firstborn, and set up the gates thereof in his youngest son Segub, according to the word of the LORD, which he spoke by Joshua the son of Nun.

17 And Elijah the Tishbite, who was of the inhabitants of Gilead, said unto Ahab, 'As the LORD God of Israel liveth, before whom I stand, there shall not be dew nor rain these years, but according to my word'. ²And the word of the LORD came unto him, saying, ³'Get thee hence, and turn thee eastward, and hide thyself by the brook Cherith, that is before Jordan. ⁴And it shall be, that thou shalt drink of the brook, and I have commanded the ravens to feed thee there.' ⁵So he went and did according unto the word of the LORD: for he went and dwelt by the brook Cherith, that is before Jordan. ⁶And the ravens brought him bread and flesh in the morning, and bread and flesh in the evening; and he drank of the brook. ⁷And it came to pass after a while, that the brook dried up, because there had been no rain in the land.

⁸And the word of the LORD came unto him, saying, ⁹'Arise, get thee to Zarephath, which belongeth to Zidon, and dwell there: behold, I have commanded a widow woman there to sustain thee'. ¹⁰So he arose and went to Zarephath. And when he came to the gate of the city, behold, the widow woman was there gathering of sticks: and he called to her, and said, 'Fetch me, I pray thee, a little water in a vessel, that I may drink'. ¹¹And as she was going to fetch it, he called to her, and said, 'Bring me, I pray thee, a morsel of bread in thy hand'. ¹²And she said, 'As the LORD thy God liveth, I have not a cake, but a handful of meal in a barrel, and a little oil in a cruse: and behold, I am gathering two sticks, that I may go in and dress it for me and my son, that we may eat it, and die'. ¹³And Elijah said unto her, 'Fear not, go and do as thou hast said: but make me thereof a little cake first, and bring it unto me, and after make for thee

and for thy son. ¹⁴For thus saith the LORD God of Israel, "The barrel of meal shall not waste, neither shall the cruse of oil fail, until the day that the LORD sendeth rain upon the earth".' ¹⁵And she went and did according to the saying of Elijah: and she, and he, and her house, did eat many days. ¹⁶And the barrel of meal wasted not, neither did the cruse of oil fail, according to the word of the LORD, which he spoke by Elijah.

¹⁷And it came to pass after these things, that the son of the woman, the mistress of the house, fell sick; and his sickness was so sore, that there was no breath left in him. ¹⁸And she said unto Elijah, 'What have I to do with thee? O thou man of God! Art thou come unto me to call my sin to remembrance, and to slay my son?' ¹⁹And he said unto her, 'Give me thy son'. And he took him out of her bosom, and carried him up into a loft, where he abode, and laid him upon his own bed. ²⁰And he cried unto the LORD, and said, 'O LORD my God, hast thou also brought evil upon the widow with whom I sojourn, by slaying her son?' ²¹And he stretched himself upon the child three times, and cried unto the LORD, and said, 'O LORD my God, I pray thee, let this child's soul come into him again'. ²²And the LORD heard the voice of Elijah, and the soul of the child came into him again, and he revived. ²³And Elijah took the child, and brought him down out of the chamber into the house, and delivered him unto his mother: and Elijah said, 'See, thy son liveth'. ²⁴And the woman said to Elijah, 'Now by this I know that thou art a man of God, and that the word of the LORD in thy mouth is truth'.

18 And it came to pass after many days, that the word of the LORD came to Elijah in the third year, saying, 'Go show thyself unto Ahab, and I will send rain upon the earth'. ²And Elijah went to show himself unto Ahab. And there was a sore famine in Samaria. ³And Ahab called Obadiah, which was the governor of his house. (Now Obadiah feared the LORD greatly: ⁴for it was so, when Jezebel cut off the prophets of the LORD, that Obadiah took a hundred prophets, and hid them by fifty in a cave, and fed them with bread and water.) ⁵And Ahab said unto Obadiah, 'Go into the land, unto all fountains of water, and unto all brooks: peradventure we may find grass to save the horses and mules alive, that we lose not all the beasts'. ⁶So they divided the land between them to pass throughout it: Ahab went one way by himself, and Obadiah went another way by himself.

⁷And as Obadiah was in the way, behold, Elijah met him: and he knew him, and fell on his face, and said, 'Art thou that my lord Elijah?' ⁸And he answered him, 'I am: go, tell thy lord, "Behold, Elijah is here"'. ⁹And he said, 'What have I sinned, that thou wouldst deliver thy servant into the hand of Ahab, to slay me? ¹⁰As the LORD thy God liveth, there is no nation or kingdom, whither my lord hath not sent to seek thee: and when they said, "He is not there", he took an oath of the kingdom and nation, that they found thee not. ¹¹And now thou sayest, "Go, tell thy lord, 'Behold, Elijah is here'". ¹²And it shall come to pass, as soon as I am gone from thee, that the Spirit of the LORD shall carry thee whither I know not; and so when I come and tell Ahab, and he cannot find thee, he shall slay me: but I thy servant fear the LORD from my youth. ¹³Was it

not told my lord what I did when Jezebel slew the prophets of the LORD, how I hid a hundred men of the LORD's prophets by fifty in a cave, and fed them with bread and water? ¹⁴And now thou sayest, "Go, tell thy lord, 'Behold, Elijah is here'": and he shall slay me.' ¹⁵And Elijah said, 'As the LORD of hosts liveth, before whom I stand, I will surely show myself unto him today'. ¹⁶So Obadiah went to meet Ahab, and told him: and Ahab went to meet Elijah.

¹⁷And it came to pass, when Ahab saw Elijah, that Ahab said unto him, 'Art thou he that troubleth Israel?' ¹⁸And he answered, 'I have not troubled Israel, but thou, and thy father's house, in that ye have forsaken the commandments of the LORD, and thou hast followed Baalim. ¹⁹Now therefore send, and gather to me all Israel unto mount Carmel, and the prophets of Baal four hundred and fifty, and the prophets of the groves four hundred, which eat at Jezebel's table.' ²⁰So Ahab sent unto all the children of Israel, and gathered the prophets together unto mount Carmel.

²¹And Elijah came unto all the people, and said, 'How long halt ye between two opinions? If the LORD be God, follow him: but if Baal, then follow him.' And the people answered him not a word. ²²Then said Elijah unto the people, 'I, even I only remain a prophet of the LORD: but Baal's prophets are four hundred and fifty men. ²³Let them therefore give us two bullocks, and let them choose one bullock for themselves, and cut it in pieces, and lay it on wood, and put no fire under: and I will dress the other bullock, and lay it on wood, and put no fire under. ²⁴And call ye on the name of your gods, and I will call on the name of the LORD: and the God that answereth by fire, let him be God.' And all the people answered and said, 'It is well spoken'.

²⁵And Elijah said unto the prophets of Baal, 'Choose you one bullock for yourselves, and dress it first, for ye are many: and call on the name of your gods, but put no fire under'. ²⁶And they took the bullock which was given them, and they dressed it, and called on the name of Baal from morning even until noon, saying, 'O Baal, hear us'. But there was no voice, nor any that answered. And they leapt upon the altar which was made. ²⁷And it came to pass at noon, that Elijah mocked them, and said, 'Cry aloud: for he is a god; either he is talking, or he is pursuing, or he is in a journey, or peradventure he sleepeth, and must be awaked'. ²⁸And they cried loud, and cut themselves after their manner with knives and lancets, till the blood gushed out upon them. ²⁹And it came to pass, when midday was past, and they prophesied until the time of the offering of the evening sacrifice, that there was neither voice, nor any to answer, nor any that regarded.

³⁰And Elijah said unto all the people, 'Come near unto me'. And all the people came near unto him. And he repaired the altar of the LORD that was broken down. ³¹And Elijah took twelve stones, according to the number of the tribes of the sons of Jacob, unto whom the word of the LORD came, saying, 'Israel shall be thy name'. ³²And with the stones he built an altar in the name of the LORD, and he made a trench about the altar, as great as would contain two measures of seed. ³³And he put the wood in order, and cut the bullock in pieces, and laid him on the wood,

and said, 'Fill four barrels with water, and pour it on the burnt sacrifice, and on the wood'. ³⁴And he said, 'Do it the second time'. And they did it the second time. And he said, 'Do it the third time'. And they did it the third time. ³⁵And the water ran round about the altar, and he filled the trench also with water.

³⁶And it came to pass at the time of the offering of the evening sacrifice, that Elijah the prophet came near, and said, 'LORD God of Abraham, Isaac, and of Israel, let it be known this day that thou art God in Israel, and that I am thy servant, and that I have done all these things at thy word. ³⁷Hear me, O LORD, hear me, that this people may know that thou art the LORD God, and that thou hast turned their heart back again.' ³⁸Then the fire of the LORD fell, and consumed the burnt sacrifice, and the wood, and the stones, and the dust, and licked up the water that was in the trench. ³⁹And when all the people saw it, they fell on their faces: and they said, 'The LORD, he is the God, the LORD, he is the God'. ⁴⁰And Elijah said unto them, 'Take the prophets of Baal, let not one of them escape'. And they took them: and Elijah brought them down to the brook Kishon, and slew them there.

⁴¹And Elijah said unto Ahab, 'Get thee up, eat and drink, for there is a sound of abundance of rain'. ⁴²So Ahab went up to eat and to drink. And Elijah went up to the top of Carmel; and he cast himself down upon the earth, and put his face between his knees, ⁴³and said to his servant, 'Go up now, look toward the sea'. And he went up, and looked, and said, 'There is nothing'. And he said, 'Go again seven times'. ⁴⁴And it came to pass at the seventh time, that he said, 'Behold, there ariseth a little cloud out of the sea, like a man's hand'. And he said, 'Go up, say unto Ahab, "Prepare thy chariot, and get thee down, that the rain stop thee not"'. ⁴⁵And it came to pass in the mean while, that the heaven was black with clouds and wind, and there was a great rain. And Ahab rode, and went to Jezreel. ⁴⁶And the hand of the LORD was on Elijah; and he girded up his loins, and ran before Ahab to the entrance of Jezreel.

19 And Ahab told Jezebel all that Elijah had done, and withal how he had slain all the prophets with the sword. ²Then Jezebel sent a messenger unto Elijah, saying, 'So let the gods do to me, and more also, if I make not thy life as the life of one of them by tomorrow about this time'. ³And when he saw that, he arose, and went for his life, and came to Beer-sheba, which belongeth to Judah, and left his servant there.

⁴But he himself went a day's journey into the wilderness, and came and sat down under a juniper tree: and he requested for himself that he might die, and said, 'It is enough; now, O LORD, take away my life: for I am not better than my fathers'. ⁵And as he lay and slept under a juniper tree, behold then, an angel touched him, and said unto him, 'Arise and eat'. ⁶And he looked, and behold, there was a cake baked on the coals, and a cruse of water at his head. And he did eat and drink, and laid him down again. ⁷And the angel of the LORD came again the second time, and touched him, and said, 'Arise and eat, because the journey is too great for thee'. ⁸And he arose, and did eat and drink, and went in the strength of that meat forty days and forty nights unto Horeb the mount of God.

⁹And he came thither unto a cave, and lodged there, and behold, the word of the Lord came to him, and he said unto him, 'What doest thou here, Elijah?' ¹⁰And he said, 'I have been very jealous for the Lord God of hosts: for the children of Israel have forsaken thy covenant, thrown down thy altars, and slain thy prophets with the sword: and I, even I only am left, and they seek my life, to take it away'. ¹¹And he said, 'Go forth, and stand upon the mount before the Lord'. And behold, the Lord passed by, and a great and strong wind rent the mountains, and broke in pieces the rocks before the Lord; but the Lord was not in the wind: and after the wind an earthquake, but the Lord was not in the earthquake: ¹²and after the earthquake a fire, but the Lord was not in the fire: and after the fire, a still small voice. ¹³And it was so, when Elijah heard it, that he wrapped his face in his mantle, and went out, and stood in the entering in of the cave. And behold, there came a voice unto him, and said, 'What doest thou here, Elijah?' ¹⁴And he said, 'I have been very jealous for the Lord God of hosts, because the children of Israel have forsaken thy covenant, thrown down thy altars, and slain thy prophets with the sword, and I, even I only am left; and they seek my life, to take it away'. ¹⁵And the Lord said unto him, 'Go, return on thy way to the wilderness of Damascus: and when thou comest, anoint Hazael to be king over Syria. ¹⁶And Jehu the son of Nimshi shalt thou anoint to be king over Israel: and Elisha the son of Shaphat of Abel-meholah shalt thou anoint to be prophet in thy room. ¹⁷And it shall come to pass, that him that escapeth the sword of Hazael shall Jehu slay: and him that escapeth from the sword of Jehu shall Elisha slay. ¹⁸Yet I have left me seven thousand in Israel, all the knees which have not bowed unto Baal, and every mouth which hath not kissed him.'

¹⁹So he departed thence, and found Elisha the son of Shaphat, who was ploughing with twelve yoke of oxen before him, and he with the twelfth: and Elijah passed by him, and cast his mantle upon him. ²⁰And he left the oxen, and ran after Elijah, and said, 'Let me, I pray thee, kiss my father and my mother, and then I will follow thee'. And he said unto him, 'Go back again: for what have I done to thee?' ²¹And he returned back from him, and took a yoke of oxen, and slew them, and boiled their flesh with the instruments of the oxen, and gave unto the people, and they did eat. Then he arose, and went after Elijah, and ministered unto him.

20 And Ben-hadad the king of Syria gathered all his host together: and there were thirty and two kings with him, and horses, and chariots: and he went up and besieged Samaria, and warred against it. ²And he sent messengers to Ahab king of Israel into the city, and said unto him, 'Thus saith Ben-hadad, ³"Thy silver and thy gold is mine; thy wives also and thy children, even the goodliest, are mine"'. ⁴And the king of Israel answered and said, 'My lord, O king, according to thy saying, I am thine, and all that I have'. ⁵And the messengers came again, and said, 'Thus speaketh Ben-hadad, saying, "Although I have sent unto thee, saying, 'Thou shalt deliver me thy silver, and thy gold, and thy wives, and thy children': ⁶yet I will send my servants unto thee tomorrow about this time, and they shall search thy house, and the houses of thy servants; and it shall be, that whatsoever is pleasant in thy eyes, they shall put it in their hand, and take it away"'. ⁷Then the king of Israel called all the elders of the land, and said, 'Mark, I pray you, and see how this man seeketh mischief: for he sent unto me for my wives, and for my children, and for my silver, and for my gold, and I denied him not'. ⁸And all the elders and all the people said unto him, 'Hearken not unto him, nor consent'. ⁹Wherefore he said unto the messengers of Ben-hadad, 'Tell my lord the king, "All that thou didst send for to thy servant at the first I will do: but this thing I may not do"'. And the messengers departed, and brought him word again. ¹⁰And Ben-hadad sent unto him, and said, 'The gods do so unto me, and more also, if the dust of Samaria shall suffice for handfuls for all the people that follow me'. ¹¹And the king of Israel answered and said, 'Tell him, "Let not him that girdeth on his harness boast himself as he that putteth it off"'. ¹²And it came to pass, when Ben-hadad heard this message, as he was drinking, he and the kings in the pavilions, that he said unto his servants, 'Set yourselves in array'. And they set themselves in array against the city.

¹³And behold, there came a prophet unto Ahab king of Israel, saying, 'Thus saith the LORD, "Hast thou seen all this great multitude? behold, I will deliver it into thy hand this day, and thou shalt know that I am the LORD"'. ¹⁴And Ahab said, 'By whom?' And he said, 'Thus saith the LORD, "Even by the young men of the princes of the provinces"'. Then he said, 'Who shall order the battle?' And he answered, 'Thou'. ¹⁵Then he numbered the young men of the princes of the provinces, and they were two hundred and thirty-two: and after them he numbered all the people, even all the children of Israel, being seven thousand. ¹⁶And they went out at noon. But Ben-hadad was drinking himself drunk in the pavilions, he and the kings, the thirty and two kings that helped him. ¹⁷And the young men of the princes of the provinces went out first; and Ben-hadad sent out, and they told him, saying, 'There are men come out of Samaria'. ¹⁸And he said, 'Whether they be come out for peace, take them alive; or whether they be come out for war, take them alive'. ¹⁹So these young men of the princes of the provinces came out of the city, and the army which followed them. ²⁰And they slew every one his man: and the Syrians fled, and Israel pursued them: and Ben-hadad the king of Syria escaped on a horse with the horsemen. ²¹And the king of Israel went out, and smote the horses and chariots, and slew the Syrians with a great slaughter.

²²And the prophet came to the king of Israel, and said unto him, 'Go, strengthen thyself, and mark and see what thou doest: for at the return of the year the king of Syria will come up against thee'.

²³And the servants of the king of Syria said unto him, 'Their gods are gods of the hills, therefore they were stronger than we: but let us fight against them in the plain, and surely we shall be stronger than they. ²⁴And do this thing, take the kings away, every man out of his place, and put captains in their rooms. ²⁵And number thee an army, like the army that thou hast lost, horse for horse, and chariot for chariot: and we will

fight against them in the plain, and surely we shall be stronger than they.' And he hearkened unto their voice, and did so.

²⁶And it came to pass at the return of the year, that Ben-hadad numbered the Syrians, and went up to Aphek, to fight against Israel. ²⁷And the children of Israel were numbered, and were all present, and went against them: and the children of Israel pitched before them like two little flocks of kids: but the Syrians filled the country.

²⁸And there came a man of God, and spoke unto the king of Israel, and said, 'Thus saith the LORD, "Because the Syrians have said, 'The LORD is God of the hills, but he is not God of the valleys', therefore will I deliver all this great multitude into thy hand, and ye shall know that I am the LORD"'. ²⁹And they pitched one over against the other seven days. And so it was, that in the seventh day the battle was joined: and the children of Israel slew of the Syrians a hundred thousand footmen in one day. ³⁰But the rest fled to Aphek, into the city, and there a wall fell upon twenty and seven thousand of the men that were left. And Ben-hadad fled, and came into the city, into an inner chamber.

³¹And his servants said unto him, 'Behold now, we have heard that the kings of the house of Israel are merciful kings: let us, I pray thee, put sackcloth on our loins, and ropes upon our heads, and go out to the king of Israel: peradventure he will save thy life'. ³²So they girded sackcloth on their loins, and put ropes on their heads, and came to the king of Israel, and said, 'Thy servant Ben-hadad saith, "I pray thee, let me live"'. And he said, 'Is he yet alive? he is my brother'. ³³Now the men did diligently observe whether anything would come from him, and did hastily catch it: and they said, 'Thy brother Ben-hadad'. Then he said, 'Go ye, bring him'. Then Ben-hadad came forth to him: and he caused him to come up into the chariot. ³⁴And Ben-hadad said unto him, 'The cities, which my father took from thy father, I will restore, and thou shalt make streets for thee in Damascus, as my father made in Samaria'. Then said Ahab, 'I will send thee away with this covenant'. So he made a covenant with him, and sent him away.

³⁵And a certain man of the sons of the prophets said unto his neighbour in the word of the LORD, 'Smite me, I pray thee'. And the man refused to smite him. ³⁶Then said he unto him, 'Because thou hast not obeyed the voice of the LORD, behold, as soon as thou art departed from me, a lion shall slay thee'. And as soon as he was departed from him, a lion found him, and slew him. ³⁷Then he found another man, and said, 'Smite me, I pray thee'. And the man smote him, so that in smiting he wounded him. ³⁸So the prophet departed, and waited for the king by the way, and disguised himself with ashes upon his face. ³⁹And as the king passed by, he cried unto the king: and he said, 'Thy servant went out into the midst of the battle, and behold, a man turned aside, and brought a man unto me, and said, "Keep this man: if by any means he be missing, then shall thy life be for his life, or else thou shalt pay a talent of silver". ⁴⁰And as thy servant was busy here and there, he was gone.' And the king of Israel said unto him, 'So shall thy judgement be; thyself hast decided it'. ⁴¹And he hasted, and took the ashes away from his face,

and the king of Israel discerned him that he was of the prophets. ⁴²And he said unto him, 'Thus saith the LORD, "Because thou hast let go out of thy hand a man whom I appointed to utter destruction, therefore thy life shall go for his life, and thy people for his people"'. ⁴³And the king of Israel went to his house heavy and displeased, and came to Samaria.

21 And it came to pass after these things, that Naboth the Jezreelite had a vineyard, which was in Jezreel, hard by the palace of Ahab king of Samaria. ²And Ahab spoke unto Naboth, saying, 'Give me thy vineyard, that I may have it for a garden of herbs, because it is near unto my house: and I will give thee for it a better vineyard than it; or, if it seem good to thee, I will give thee the worth of it in money'. ³And Naboth said to Ahab, 'The LORD forbid it me, that I should give the inheritance of my fathers unto thee'. ⁴And Ahab came into his house heavy and displeased because of the word which Naboth the Jezreelite had spoken to him: for he had said, 'I will not give thee the inheritance of my fathers'. And he laid him down upon his bed, and turned away his face, and would eat no bread.

⁵But Jezebel his wife came to him, and said unto him, 'Why is thy spirit so sad, that thou eatest no bread?' ⁶And he said unto her, 'Because I spoke unto Naboth the Jezreelite, and said unto him, "Give me thy vineyard for money; or else, if it please thee, I will give thee another vineyard for it": and he answered, "I will not give thee my vineyard"'. ⁷And Jezebel his wife said unto him, 'Dost thou now govern the kingdom of Israel? Arise, and eat bread, and let thy heart be merry: I will give thee the vineyard of Naboth the Jezreelite.' ⁸So she wrote letters in Ahab's name, and sealed them with his seal, and sent the letters unto the elders and to the nobles that were in his city, dwelling with Naboth. ⁹And she wrote in the letters, saying, 'Proclaim a fast, and set Naboth on high among the people: ¹⁰and set two men, sons of Belial, before him, to bear witness against him, saying, "Thou didst blaspheme God and the king". And then carry him out, and stone him, that he may die.' ¹¹And the men of his city, even the elders and the nobles who were the inhabitants in his city, did as Jezebel had sent unto them, and as it was written in the letters which she had sent unto them. ¹²They proclaimed a fast, and set Naboth on high among the people. ¹³And there came in two men, children of Belial, and sat before him: and the men of Belial witnessed against him, even against Naboth, in the presence of the people, saying, 'Naboth did blaspheme God and the king'. Then they carried him forth out of the city, and stoned him with stones, that he died. ¹⁴Then they sent to Jezebel, saying, 'Naboth is stoned, and is dead'.

¹⁵And it came to pass, when Jezebel heard that Naboth was stoned and was dead, that Jezebel said to Ahab, 'Arise, take possession of the vineyard of Naboth the Jezreelite, which he refused to give thee for money: for Naboth is not alive, but dead'. ¹⁶And it came to pass when Ahab heard that Naboth was dead, that Ahab rose up to go down to the vineyard of Naboth the Jezreelite, to take possession of it.

¹⁷And the word of the LORD came to Elijah the Tishbite, saying, ¹⁸'Arise, go down to meet Ahab king of Israel, which is in Samaria:

behold, he is in the vineyard of Naboth, whither he is gone down to possess it. ¹⁹And thou shalt speak unto him, saying, "Thus saith the LORD, 'Hast thou killed, and also taken possession?'" And thou shalt speak unto him, saying, "Thus saith the LORD, 'In the place where dogs licked the blood of Naboth shall dogs lick thy blood, even thine'".' ²⁰And Ahab said to Elijah, 'Hast thou found me, O my enemy?' And he answered, 'I have found thee: because thou hast sold thyself to work evil in the sight of the LORD. ²¹Behold, I will bring evil upon thee, and will take away thy posterity, and will cut off from Ahab him that pisseth against the wall, and him that is shut up and left in Israel, ²²and will make thy house like the house of Jeroboam the son of Nebat, and like the house of Baasha the son of Ahijah, for the provocation wherewith thou hast provoked me to anger, and made Israel to sin.' ²³And of Jezebel also spoke the LORD, saying, 'The dogs shall eat Jezebel by the wall of Jezreel. ²⁴Him that dieth of Ahab in the city the dogs shall eat: and him that dieth in the field shall the fowls of the air eat.'

²⁵But there was none like unto Ahab, which did sell himself to work wickedness in the sight of the LORD, whom Jezebel his wife stirred up. ²⁶And he did very abominably in following idols, according to all things as did the Amorites, whom the LORD cast out before the children of Israel.

²⁷And it came to pass when Ahab heard those words, that he rent his clothes, and put sackcloth upon his flesh, and fasted, and lay in sackcloth, and went softly. ²⁸And the word of the LORD came to Elijah the Tishbite, saying, ²⁹'Seest thou how Ahab humbleth himself before me? because he humbleth himself before me, I will not bring the evil in his days: but in his son's days will I bring the evil upon his house'.

22 And they continued three years without war between Syria and Israel. ²And it came to pass on the third year, that Jehoshaphat the king of Judah came down to the king of Israel. ³And the king of Israel said unto his servants, 'Know ye that Ramoth in Gilead is ours, and we be still, and take it not out of the hand of the king of Syria?' ⁴And he said unto Jehoshaphat, 'Wilt thou go with me to battle to Ramoth-gilead?' And Jehoshaphat said to the king of Israel, 'I am as thou art, my people as thy people, my horses as thy horses'. ⁵And Jehoshaphat said unto the king of Israel, 'Inquire, I pray thee, at the word of the LORD today'. ⁶Then the king of Israel gathered the prophets together, about four hundred men, and said unto them, 'Shall I go against Ramoth-gilead to battle, or shall I forbear?' And they said, 'Go up, for the Lord shall deliver it into the hand of the king'. ⁷And Jehoshaphat said, 'Is there not here a prophet of the LORD besides, that we might inquire of him?' ⁸And the king of Israel said unto Jehoshaphat, 'There is yet one man, Micaiah the son of Imlah, by whom we may inquire of the LORD: but I hate him, for he doth not prophesy good concerning me, but evil'. And Jehoshaphat said, 'Let not the king say so'. ⁹Then the king of Israel called an officer, and said, 'Hasten hither Micaiah the son of Imlah'. ¹⁰And the king of Israel and Jehoshaphat the king of Judah sat each on his throne, having put on their robes, in a void place in the entrance of the gate of Samaria, and

all the prophets prophesied before them. ¹¹And Zedekiah the son of Chenaanah made him horns of iron: and he said, 'Thus saith the LORD, "With these shalt thou push the Syrians, until thou have consumed them"'. ¹²And all the prophets prophesied so, saying, 'Go up to Ramoth-gilead, and prosper: for the LORD shall deliver it into the king's hand'.

¹³And the messenger that was gone to call Micaiah spoke unto him, saying, 'Behold now, the words of the prophets declare good unto the king with one mouth: let thy word, I pray thee, be like the word of one of them, and speak that which is good'. ¹⁴And Micaiah said, 'As the LORD liveth, what the LORD saith unto me, that will I speak'.

¹⁵So he came to the king. And the king said unto him, 'Micaiah, shall we go against Ramoth-gilead to battle, or shall we forbear?' And he answered him, 'Go, and prosper: for the LORD shall deliver it into the hand of the king'. ¹⁶And the king said unto him, 'How many times shall I adjure thee that thou tell me nothing but that which is true in the name of the LORD?' ¹⁷And he said, 'I saw all Israel scattered upon the hills, as sheep that have not a shepherd. And the LORD said, "These have no master: let them return every man to his house in peace".' ¹⁸And the king of Israel said unto Jehoshaphat, 'Did I not tell thee that he would prophesy no good concerning me, but evil?' ¹⁹And he said, 'Hear thou therefore the word of the LORD: I saw the LORD sitting on his throne, and all the host of heaven standing by him on his right hand and on his left. ²⁰And the LORD said, "Who shall persuade Ahab, that he may go up and fall at Ramoth-gilead?" And one said on this manner, and another said on that manner. ²¹And there came forth a spirit, and stood before the LORD, and said, "I will persuade him". ²²And the LORD said unto him, "Wherewith?" And he said, "I will go forth, and I will be a lying spirit in the mouth of all his prophets". And he said, "Thou shalt persuade him, and prevail also: go forth, and do so". ²³Now therefore behold, the LORD hath put a lying spirit in the mouth of all these thy prophets, and the LORD hath spoken evil concerning thee.' ²⁴But Zedekiah the son of Chenaanah went near, and smote Micaiah on the cheek, and said, 'Which way went the Spirit of the LORD from me to speak unto thee?' ²⁵And Micaiah said, 'Behold, thou shalt see in that day, when thou shalt go into an inner chamber to hide thyself'. ²⁶And the king of Israel said, 'Take Micaiah, and carry him back unto Amon the governor of the city, and to Joash the king's son: ²⁷and say, "Thus saith the king, 'Put this fellow in the prison, and feed him with bread of affliction and with water of affliction, until I come in peace'"'. ²⁸And Micaiah said, 'If thou return at all in peace, the LORD hath not spoken by me'. And he said, 'Hearken, O people, every one of you'.

²⁹So the king of Israel and Jehoshaphat the king of Judah went up to Ramoth-gilead. ³⁰And the king of Israel said unto Jehoshaphat, 'I will disguise myself, and enter into the battle; but put thou on thy robes'. And the king of Israel disguised himself, and went into the battle. ³¹But the king of Syria commanded his thirty and two captains that had rule over his chariots, saying, 'Fight neither with small nor great, save only with the king of Israel'. ³²And it came to pass, when the captains of the

chariots saw Jehoshaphat, that they said, 'Surely it is the king of Israel'. And they turned aside to fight against him: and Jehoshaphat cried out. ³³And it came to pass, when the captains of the chariots perceived that it was not the king of Israel, that they turned back from pursuing him. ³⁴And a certain man drew a bow at a venture, and smote the king of Israel between the joints of the harness: wherefore he said unto the driver of his chariot, 'Turn thy hand, and carry me out of the host, for I am wounded'. ³⁵And the battle increased that day: and the king was stayed up in his chariot against the Syrians, and died at even: and the blood ran out of the wound into the midst of the chariot. ³⁶And there went a proclamation throughout the host about the going down of the sun, saying, 'Every man to his city, and every man to his own country'.

³⁷So the king died, and was brought to Samaria; and they buried the king in Samaria. ³⁸And one washed the chariot in the pool of Samaria, and the dogs licked up his blood, and they washed his armour, according unto the word of the LORD which he spoke.

³⁹Now the rest of the acts of Ahab, and all that he did, and the ivory house which he made, and all the cities that he built, are they not written in the book of the chronicles of the kings of Israel? ⁴⁰So Ahab slept with his fathers, and Ahaziah his son reigned in his stead.

⁴¹And Jehoshaphat the son of Asa began to reign over Judah in the fourth year of Ahab king of Israel. ⁴²Jehoshaphat was thirty and five years old when he began to reign, and he reigned twenty and five years in Jerusalem. And his mother's name was Azubah the daughter of Shilhi. ⁴³And he walked in all the ways of Asa his father; he turned not aside from it, doing that which was right in the eyes of the LORD: nevertheless the high places were not taken away: for the people offered and burnt incense yet in the high places. ⁴⁴And Jehoshaphat made peace with the king of Israel.

⁴⁵Now the rest of the acts of Jehoshaphat, and his might that he showed, and how he warred, are they not written in the book of the chronicles of the kings of Judah? ⁴⁶And the remnant of the sodomites, which remained in the days of his father Asa, he took out of the land.

⁴⁷There was then no king in Edom: a deputy was king. ⁴⁸Jehoshaphat made ships of Tarshish to go to Ophir for gold: but they went not, for the ships were broken at Ezion-geber. ⁴⁹Then said Ahaziah the son of Ahab unto Jehoshaphat, 'Let my servants go with thy servants in the ships'. But Jehoshaphat would not.

⁵⁰And Jehoshaphat slept with his fathers, and was buried with his fathers in the city of David his father: and Jehoram his son reigned in his stead.

⁵¹Ahaziah the son of Ahab began to reign over Israel in Samaria the seventeenth year of Jehoshaphat king of Judah, and reigned two years over Israel. ⁵²And he did evil in the sight of the LORD, and walked in the way of his father, and in the way of his mother, and in the way of Jeroboam the son of Nebat, who made Israel to sin: ⁵³for he served Baal, and worshipped him, and provoked to anger the LORD God of Israel, according unto all that his father had done.

THE SECOND BOOK OF THE
KINGS
COMMONLY CALLED
THE FOURTH BOOK OF THE KINGS

1 Then Moab rebelled against Israel after the death of Ahab. ²And Ahaziah fell down through a lattice in his upper chamber that was in Samaria, and was sick: and he sent messengers, and said unto them, 'Go, inquire of Baal-zebub the god of Ekron whether I shall recover of this disease'. ³But the angel of the LORD said to Elijah the Tishbite, 'Arise, go up to meet the messengers of the king of Samaria, and say unto them, "Is it not because there is not a God in Israel, that ye go to inquire of Baal-zebub the god of Ekron? ⁴Now therefore thus saith the LORD, 'Thou shalt not come down from that bed on which thou art gone up, but shalt surely die'." ' And Elijah departed.

⁵And when the messengers turned back unto him, he said unto them, 'Why are ye now turned back?' ⁶And they said unto him, 'There came a man up to meet us, and said unto us, "Go, turn again unto the king that sent you, and say unto him, 'Thus saith the LORD, "Is it not because there is not a God in Israel, that thou sendest to inquire of Baal-zebub the god of Ekron? therefore thou shalt not come down from that bed on which thou art gone up, but shalt surely die" ' ". ⁷And he said unto them, 'What manner of man was he which came up to meet you, and told you these words?' ⁸And they answered him, 'He was a hairy man, and girt with a girdle of leather about his loins'. And he said, 'It is Elijah the Tishbite'.

⁹Then the king sent unto him a captain of fifty with his fifty. And he went up to him: and behold, he sat on the top of a hill. And he spoke unto him, 'Thou man of God, the king hath said, "Come down" '. ¹⁰And Elijah answered and said to the captain of fifty, 'If I be a man of God, then let fire come down from heaven, and consume thee and thy fifty'. And there came down fire from heaven, and consumed him and his fifty.

¹¹Again also he sent unto him another captain of fifty with his fifty. And he answered and said unto him, 'O man of God, thus hath the king said, "Come down quickly" '. ¹²And Elijah answered and said unto them, 'If I be a man of God, let fire come down from heaven, and consume thee and thy fifty'. And the fire of God came down from heaven, and consumed him and his fifty.

¹³And he sent again a captain of the third fifty with his fifty. And the third captain of fifty went up, and came and fell on his knees before Elijah, and besought him, and said unto him, 'O man of God, I pray thee, let my life, and the life of these fifty thy servants, be precious in thy sight. ¹⁴Behold, there came fire down from heaven, and burnt up the two captains of the former fifties with their fifties: therefore let my

life now be precious in thy sight.' ¹⁵And the angel of the LORD said unto Elijah, 'Go down with him: be not afraid of him'. And he arose, and went down with him unto the king. ¹⁶And he said unto him, 'Thus saith the LORD, "Forasmuch as thou hast sent messengers to inquire of Baal-zebub the god of Ekron (is it not because there is no God in Israel to inquire of his word?), therefore thou shalt not come down off that bed on which thou art gone up, but shalt surely die"'.

¹⁷So he died according to the word of the LORD which Elijah had spoken. And Jehoram reigned in his stead, in the second year of Jehoram the son of Jehoshaphat king of Judah, because he had no son.

¹⁸Now the rest of the acts of Ahaziah which he did, are they not written in the book of the chronicles of the kings of Israel?

2 And it came to pass when the LORD would take up Elijah into heaven by a whirlwind, that Elijah went with Elisha from Gilgal. ²And Elijah said unto Elisha, 'Tarry here, I pray thee: for the LORD hath sent me to Beth-el'. And Elisha said unto him, 'As the LORD liveth, and as thy soul liveth, I will not leave thee'. So they went down to Beth-el. ³And the sons of the prophets that were at Beth-el came forth to Elisha, and said unto him, 'Knowest thou that the LORD will take away thy master from thy head today?' And he said, 'Yea, I know it; hold you your peace'. ⁴And Elijah said unto him, 'Elisha, tarry here, I pray thee: for the LORD hath sent me to Jericho'. And he said, 'As the LORD liveth, and as thy soul liveth, I will not leave thee'. So they came to Jericho. ⁵And the sons of the prophets that were at Jericho came to Elisha, and said unto him, 'Knowest thou that the LORD will take away thy master from thy head today?' And he answered, 'Yea, I know it; hold you your peace'. ⁶And Elijah said unto him, 'Tarry, I pray thee, here: for the LORD hath sent me to Jordan'. And he said, 'As the LORD liveth, and as thy soul liveth, I will not leave thee'. And they two went on. ⁷And fifty men of the sons of the prophets went, and stood to view afar off: and they two stood by Jordan. ⁸And Elijah took his mantle, and wrapped it together, and smote the waters, and they were divided hither and thither, so that they two went over on dry ground.

⁹And it came to pass, when they were gone over, that Elijah said unto Elisha, 'Ask what I shall do for thee, before I be taken away from thee'. And Elisha said, 'I pray thee, let a double portion of thy spirit be upon me'. ¹⁰And he said, 'Thou hast asked a hard thing: nevertheless, if thou see me when I am taken from thee, it shall be so unto thee: but if not, it shall not be so'. ¹¹And it came to pass as they still went on, and talked, that behold, there appeared a chariot of fire, and horses of fire, and parted them both asunder; and Elijah went up by a whirlwind into heaven.

¹²And Elisha saw it, and he cried, 'My father, my father, the chariot of Israel, and the horsemen thereof'. And he saw him no more: and he took hold of his own clothes, and rent them in two pieces. ¹³He took up also the mantle of Elijah that fell from him, and went back, and stood by the bank of Jordan. ¹⁴And he took the mantle of Elijah that fell from him, and smote the waters, and said, 'Where is the LORD God of Elijah?'

And when he also had smitten the waters, they parted hither and thither: and Elisha went over. ¹⁵And when the sons of the prophets which were to view at Jericho saw him, they said, 'The spirit of Elijah doth rest on Elisha'. And they came to meet him, and bowed themselves to the ground before him.

¹⁶And they said unto him, 'Behold now, there be with thy servants fifty strong men; let them go, we pray thee, and seek thy master: lest peradventure the Spirit of the LORD hath taken him up, and cast him upon some mountain, or into some valley'. And he said, 'Ye shall not send'. ¹⁷And when they urged him till he was ashamed, he said, 'Send'. They sent therefore fifty men, and they sought three days, but found him not. ¹⁸And when they came again to him (for he tarried at Jericho), he said unto them, 'Did I not say unto you, "Go not?"'

¹⁹And the men of the city said unto Elisha, 'Behold, I pray thee, the situation of this city is pleasant, as my lord seeth: but the water is naught, and the ground barren'. ²⁰And he said, 'Bring me a new cruse, and put salt therein'. And they brought it to him. ²¹And he went forth unto the spring of the waters, and cast the salt in there, and said, 'Thus saith the LORD, "I have healed these waters; there shall not be from thence any more death or barren land"'. ²²So the waters were healed unto this day, according to the saying of Elisha which he spoke.

²³And he went up from thence unto Beth-el: and as he was going up by the way, there came forth little children out of the city, and mocked him, and said unto him, 'Go up, thou bald-head, go up, thou bald-head'. ²⁴And he turned back, and looked on them, and cursed them in the name of the LORD. And there came forth two she bears out of the wood, and tore forty and two children of them. ²⁵And he went from thence to mount Carmel, and from thence he returned to Samaria.

3 Now Jehoram the son of Ahab began to reign over Israel in Samaria the eighteenth year of Jehoshaphat king of Judah, and reigned twelve years. ²And he wrought evil in the sight of the LORD, but not like his father, and like his mother: for he put away the image of Baal that his father had made. ³Nevertheless he cleaved unto the sins of Jeroboam the son of Nebat, which made Israel to sin; he departed not therefrom.

⁴And Mesha king of Moab was a sheepmaster, and rendered unto the king of Israel a hundred thousand lambs, and a hundred thousand rams, with the wool. ⁵But it came to pass when Ahab was dead, that the king of Moab rebelled against the king of Israel.

⁶And king Jehoram went out of Samaria the same time, and numbered all Israel. ⁷And he went and sent to Jehoshaphat the king of Judah, saying, 'The king of Moab hath rebelled against me: wilt thou go with me against Moab to battle?' And he said, 'I will go up: I am as thou art, my people as thy people, and my horses as thy horses'. ⁸And he said, 'Which way shall we go up?' And he answered, 'The way through the wilderness of Edom'.

⁹So the king of Israel went, and the king of Judah, and the king of Edom: and they fetched a compass of seven days' journey: and there

was no water for the host, and for the cattle that followed them. ¹⁰And the king of Israel said, 'Alas, that the LORD hath called these three kings together, to deliver them into the hand of Moab'. ¹¹But Jehoshaphat said, 'Is there not here a prophet of the LORD, that we may inquire of the LORD by him?' And one of the king of Israel's servants answered and said, 'Here is Elisha the son of Shaphat, which poured water on the hands of Elijah'. ¹²And Jehoshaphat said, 'The word of the LORD is with him'. So the king of Israel and Jehoshaphat and the king of Edom went down to him. ¹³And Elisha said unto the king of Israel, 'What have I to do with thee? Get thee to the prophets of thy father, and to the prophets of thy mother.' And the king of Israel said unto him, 'Nay: for the LORD hath called these three kings together, to deliver them into the hand of Moab'. ¹⁴And Elisha said, 'As the LORD of hosts liveth, before whom I stand, surely were it not that I regard the presence of Jehoshaphat the king of Judah, I would not look toward thee, nor see thee. ¹⁵But now bring me a minstrel.' And it came to pass when the minstrel played, that the hand of the LORD came upon him. ¹⁶And he said, 'Thus saith the LORD, "Make this valley full of ditches". ¹⁷For thus saith the LORD, "Ye shall not see wind, neither shall ye see rain, yet that valley shall be filled with water, that ye may drink, both ye, and your cattle, and your beasts". ¹⁸And this is but a light thing in the sight of the LORD: he will deliver the Moabites also into your hand. ¹⁹And ye shall smite every fenced city, and every choice city, and shall fell every good tree, and stop all wells of water, and mar every good piece of land with stones.' ²⁰And it came to pass in the morning when the meat offering was offered, that behold, there came water by the way of Edom, and the country was filled with water.

²¹And when all the Moabites heard that the kings were come up to fight against them, they gathered all that were able to put on armour, and upward, and stood in the border. ²²And they rose up early in the morning, and the sun shone upon the water, and the Moabites saw the water on the other side as red as blood. ²³And they said, 'This is blood: the kings are surely slain, and they have smitten one another: now therefore, Moab, to the spoil'. ²⁴And when they came to the camp of Israel, the Israelites rose up and smote the Moabites, so that they fled before them: but they went forward smiting the Moabites, even in their country. ²⁵And they beat down the cities, and on every good piece of land cast every man his stone, and filled it; and they stopped all the wells of water, and felled all the good trees: only in Kir-haraseth left they the stones thereof; howbeit the slingers went about it, and smote it.

²⁶And when the king of Moab saw that the battle was too sore for him, he took with him seven hundred men that drew swords, to break through even unto the king of Edom: but they could not. ²⁷Then he took his eldest son that should have reigned in his stead, and offered him for a burnt offering upon the wall. And there was great indignation against Israel, and they departed from him, and returned to their own land.

4 Now there cried a certain woman of the wives of the sons of the prophets unto Elisha, saying, 'Thy servant my husband is dead, and thou knowest that thy servant did fear the LORD: and the creditor is come to take unto him my two sons to be bondmen'. ²And Elisha said unto her, 'What shall I do for thee? Tell me, what hast thou in the house?' And she said, 'Thy handmaid hath not anything in the house, save a pot of oil'. ³Then he said, 'Go, borrow thee vessels abroad of all thy neighbours, even empty vessels; borrow not a few. ⁴And when thou art come in, thou shalt shut the door upon thee and upon thy sons, and shalt pour out into all those vessels, and thou shalt set aside that which is full.' ⁵So she went from him, and shut the door upon her and upon her sons: who brought the vessels to her, and she poured out. ⁶And it came to pass, when the vessels were full, that she said unto her son, 'Bring me yet a vessel'. And he said unto her, 'There is not a vessel more'. And the oil stayed. ⁷Then she came and told the man of God. And he said, 'Go, sell the oil, and pay thy debt, and live thou and thy children of the rest'.

⁸And it fell on a day, that Elisha passed to Shunem, where was a great woman; and she constrained him to eat bread. And so it was, that as oft as he passed by, he turned in thither to eat bread. ⁹And she said unto her husband, 'Behold now, I perceive that this is a holy man of God, which passeth by us continually. ¹⁰Let us make a little chamber, I pray thee, on the wall, and let us set for him there a bed, and a table, and a stool, and a candlestick: and it shall be, when he cometh to us, that he shall turn in thither.'

¹¹And it fell on a day, that he came thither, and he turned into the chamber, and lay there. ¹²And he said to Gehazi his servant, 'Call this Shunammite'. And when he had called her, she stood before him. ¹³And he said unto him, 'Say now unto her, "Behold, thou hast been careful for us with all this care; what is to be done for thee? Wouldst thou be spoken for to the king, or to the captain of the host?"' And she answered, 'I dwell among my own people'. ¹⁴And he said, 'What then is to be done for her?' And Gehazi answered, 'Verily she hath no child, and her husband is old'. ¹⁵And he said, 'Call her'. And when he had called her, she stood in the door. ¹⁶And he said, 'About this season, according to the time of life, thou shalt embrace a son'. And she said, 'Nay, my lord, thou man of God, do not lie unto thy handmaid'. ¹⁷And the woman conceived, and bore a son at that season that Elisha had said unto her, according to the time of life.

¹⁸And when the child was grown, it fell on a day that he went out to his father to the reapers. ¹⁹And he said unto his father, 'My head, my head'. And he said to a lad, 'Carry him to his mother'. ²⁰And when he had taken him, and brought him to his mother, he sat on her knees till noon, and then died. ²¹And she went up, and laid him on the bed of the man of God, and shut the door upon him, and went out. ²²And she called unto her husband, and said, 'Send me, I pray thee, one of the young men, and one of the asses, that I may run to the man of God, and come again'. ²³And he said, 'Wherefore wilt thou go to him today? it is

neither new moon, nor sabbath'. And she said, 'It shall be well'. ²⁴Then she saddled an ass, and said to her servant, 'Drive, and go forward: slack not thy riding for me, except I bid thee'. ²⁵So she went and came unto the man of God to mount Carmel. And it came to pass when the man of God saw her afar off, that he said to Gehazi his servant, 'Behold, yonder is that Shunammite: ²⁶run now, I pray thee, to meet her, and say unto her, "Is it well with thee? is it well with thy husband? is it well with the child?"' And she answered, 'It is well'. ²⁷And when she came to the man of God to the hill, she caught him by the feet: but Gehazi came near to thrust her away. And the man of God said, 'Let her alone, for her soul is vexed within her: and the LORD hath hid it from me, and hath not told me'. ²⁸Then she said, 'Did I desire a son of my lord? did I not say, "Do not deceive me?"' ²⁹Then he said to Gehazi, 'Gird up thy loins, and take my staff in thy hand, and go thy way: if thou meet any man, salute him not: and if any salute thee, answer him not again: and lay my staff upon the face of the child'. ³⁰And the mother of the child said, 'As the LORD liveth, and as thy soul liveth, I will not leave thee'. And he arose, and followed her.

³¹And Gehazi passed on before them, and laid the staff upon the face of the child, but there was neither voice, nor hearing. Wherefore he went again to meet him, and told him, saying, 'The child is not awaked'. ³²And when Elisha was come into the house, behold, the child was dead, and laid upon his bed. ³³He went in therefore, and shut the door upon them twain, and prayed unto the LORD. ³⁴And he went up, and lay upon the child, and put his mouth upon his mouth, and his eyes upon his eyes, and his hands upon his hands: and he stretched himself upon the child, and the flesh of the child waxed warm. ³⁵Then he returned, and walked in the house to and fro; and went up, and stretched himself upon him: and the child sneezed seven times, and the child opened his eyes. ³⁶And he called Gehazi, and said, 'Call this Shunammite'. So he called her. And when she was come in unto him, he said, 'Take up thy son'. ³⁷Then she went in, and fell at his feet, and bowed herself to the ground, and took up her son, and went out.

³⁸And Elisha came again to Gilgal, and there was a dearth in the land, and the sons of the prophets were sitting before him: and he said unto his servant, 'Set on the great pot, and seethe pottage for the sons of the prophets'. ³⁹And one went out into the field to gather herbs, and found a wild vine, and gathered thereof wild gourds his lap full, and came and shredded them into the pot of pottage: for they knew them not. ⁴⁰So they poured out for the men to eat. And it came to pass, as they were eating of the pottage, that they cried out, and said, 'O thou man of God, there is death in the pot'. And they could not eat thereof. ⁴¹But he said, 'Then bring meal'. And he cast it into the pot: and he said, 'Pour out for the people, that they may eat'. And there was no harm in the pot.

⁴²And there came a man from Baal-shalisha, and brought the man of God bread of the first-fruits, twenty loaves of barley, and full ears of corn in the husk thereof. And he said, 'Give unto the people, that they

may eat'. ⁴³And his servitor said, 'What, should I set this before a hundred men?' He said again, 'Give the people, that they may eat: for thus saith the LORD, "They shall eat, and shall leave thereof"'. ⁴⁴So he set it before them, and they did eat, and left thereof, according to the word of the LORD.

5 Now Naaman, captain of the host of the king of Syria, was a great man with his master, and honourable, because by him the LORD had given deliverance unto Syria: he was also a mighty man in valour, but he was a leper. ²And the Syrians had gone out by companies, and had brought away captive out of the land of Israel a little maid; and she waited on Naaman's wife. ³And she said unto her mistress, 'Would God my lord were with the prophet that is in Samaria, for he would recover him of his leprosy'. ⁴And one went in, and told his lord, saying, 'Thus and thus said the maid that is of the land of Israel'. ⁵And the king of Syria said, 'Go to, go, and I will send a letter unto the king of Israel'. And he departed, and took with him ten talents of silver, and six thousand pieces of gold, and ten changes of raiment. ⁶And he brought the letter to the king of Israel, saying, 'Now when this letter is come unto thee, behold, I have therewith sent Naaman my servant to thee, that thou mayest recover him of his leprosy'. ⁷And it came to pass when the king of Israel had read the letter, that he rent his clothes, and said, 'Am I God, to kill and to make alive, that this man doth send unto me to recover a man of his leprosy? Wherefore consider, I pray you, and see how he seeketh a quarrel against me.'

⁸And it was so, when Elisha the man of God had heard that the king of Israel had rent his clothes, that he sent to the king, saying, 'Wherefore hast thou rent thy clothes? Let him come now to me, and he shall know that there is a prophet in Israel.' ⁹So Naaman came with his horses and with his chariot, and stood at the door of the house of Elisha. ¹⁰And Elisha sent a messenger unto him, saying, 'Go and wash in Jordan seven times, and thy flesh shall come again to thee, and thou shalt be clean'. ¹¹But Naaman was wroth, and went away, and said, 'Behold, I thought, he will surely come out to me, and stand, and call on the name of the LORD his God, and strike his hand over the place, and recover the leper. ¹²Are not Abana and Pharpar, rivers of Damascus, better than all the waters of Israel? May I not wash in them, and be clean?' So he turned and went away in a rage. ¹³And his servants came near and spoke unto him, and said, 'My father, if the prophet had bid thee do some great thing, wouldst thou not have done it? How much rather then, when he saith to thee, "Wash, and be clean"?' ¹⁴Then went he down, and dipped himself seven times in Jordan, according to the saying of the man of God: and his flesh came again like unto the flesh of a little child, and he was clean.

¹⁵And he returned to the man of God, he and all his company, and came, and stood before him: and he said, 'Behold, now I know that there is no God in all the earth, but in Israel: now therefore, I pray thee, take a blessing of thy servant'. ¹⁶But he said, 'As the LORD liveth, before whom I stand, I will receive none'. And he urged him to take it, but he

refused. ¹⁷And Naaman said, 'Shall there not then, I pray thee, be given to thy servant two mules' burden of earth? for thy servant will henceforth offer neither burnt offering nor sacrifice unto other gods, but unto the LORD. ¹⁸In this thing the LORD pardon thy servant, that when my master goeth into the house of Rimmon to worship there, and he leaneth on my hand, and I bow myself in the house of Rimmon: when I bow down myself in the house of Rimmon, the LORD pardon thy servant in this thing.' ¹⁹And he said unto him, 'Go in peace'. So he departed from him a little way.

²⁰But Gehazi, the servant of Elisha the man of God, said, 'Behold, my master hath spared Naaman this Syrian, in not receiving at his hands that which he brought: but as the LORD liveth, I will run after him, and take somewhat of him'. ²¹So Gehazi followed after Naaman. And when Naaman saw him running after him, he lighted down from the chariot to meet him, and said, 'Is all well?' ²²And he said, 'All is well. My master hath sent me, saying, "Behold, even now there be come to me from mount Ephraim two young men of the sons of the prophets: give them, I pray thee, a talent of silver, and two changes of garments".' ²³And Naaman said, 'Be content, take two talents'. And he urged him, and bound two talents of silver in two bags, with two changes of garments, and laid them upon two of his servants, and they bore them before him. ²⁴And when he came to the tower, he took them from their hand, and bestowed them in the house: and he let the men go, and they departed. ²⁵But he went in, and stood before his master. And Elisha said unto him, 'Whence comest thou, Gehazi?' And he said, 'Thy servant went no whither'. ²⁶And he said unto him, 'Went not my heart with thee, when the man turned again from his chariot to meet thee? Is it a time to receive money, and to receive garments, and olive-yards, and vineyards, and sheep, and oxen, and menservants, and maidservants? ²⁷The leprosy therefore of Naaman shall cleave unto thee, and unto thy seed for ever.' And he went out from his presence a leper as white as snow.

6 And the sons of the prophets said unto Elisha, 'Behold now, the place where we dwell with thee is too strait for us. ²Let us go, we pray thee, unto Jordan, and take thence every man a beam, and let us make us a place there where we may dwell.' And he answered, 'Go ye'. ³And one said, 'Be content, I pray thee, and go with thy servants'. And he answered, 'I will go'. ⁴So he went with them. And when they came to Jordan, they cut down wood. ⁵But as one was felling a beam, the axehead fell into the water: and he cried, and said, 'Alas, master', for it was borrowed. ⁶And the man of God said, 'Where fell it?' And he showed him the place. And he cut down a stick, and cast it in thither, and the iron did swim. ⁷Therefore said he, 'Take it up to thee'. And he put out his hand, and took it.

⁸Then the king of Syria warred against Israel, and took counsel with his servants, saying, 'In such and such a place shall be my camp'. ⁹And the man of God sent unto the king of Israel, saying, 'Beware that thou pass not such a place; for thither the Syrians are come down'. ¹⁰And the

king of Israel sent to the place which the man of God told him and warned him of, and saved himself there, not once nor twice. ¹¹Therefore the heart of the king of Syria was sore troubled for this thing, and he called his servants, and said unto them, 'Will ye not show me which of us is for the king of Israel?' ¹²And one of his servants said, 'None, my lord, O king: but Elisha, the prophet that is in Israel, telleth the king of Israel the words that thou speakest in thy bedchamber.' ¹³And he said, 'Go and spy where he is, that I may send and fetch him'. And it was told him, saying, 'Behold, he is in Dothan'. ¹⁴Therefore sent he thither horses, and chariots, and a great host: and they came by night, and compassed the city about.

¹⁵And when the servant of the man of God was risen early and gone forth, behold, a host compassed the city both with horses and chariots. And his servant said unto him, 'Alas, my master, how shall we do?' ¹⁶And he answered, 'Fear not: for they that be with us are more than they that be with them'. ¹⁷And Elisha prayed, and said, 'LORD, I pray thee, open his eyes, that he may see'. And the LORD opened the eyes of the young man, and he saw: and behold, the mountain was full of horses and chariots of fire round about Elisha. ¹⁸And when they came down to him, Elisha prayed unto the LORD, and said, 'Smite this people, I pray thee, with blindness'. And he smote them with blindness according to the word of Elisha. ¹⁹And Elisha said unto them, 'This is not the way, neither is this the city: follow me, and I will bring you to the man whom ye seek'. But he led them to Samaria.

²⁰And it came to pass when they were come into Samaria, that Elisha said, 'LORD, open the eyes of these men, that they may see'. And the LORD opened their eyes, and they saw, and behold, they were in the midst of Samaria. ²¹And the king of Israel said unto Elisha, when he saw them, 'My father, shall I smite them? shall I smite them?' ²²And he answered, 'Thou shalt not smite them: wouldst thou smite those whom thou hast taken captive with thy sword and with thy bow? set bread and water before them, that they may eat and drink, and go to their master'. ²³And he prepared great provision for them: and when they had eaten and drunk, he sent them away, and they went to their master. So the bands of Syria came no more into the land of Israel.

²⁴And it came to pass after this, that Ben-hadad king of Syria gathered all his host, and went up, and besieged Samaria. ²⁵And there was a great famine in Samaria: and behold, they besieged it, until an ass's head was sold for fourscore pieces of silver, and the fourth part of a kab of dove's dung for five pieces of silver. ²⁶And as the king of Israel was passing by upon the wall, there cried a woman unto him, saying, 'Help, my lord, O king'. ²⁷And he said, 'If the LORD do not help thee, whence shall I help thee? out of the barn-floor, or out of the wine-press?' ²⁸And the king said unto her, 'What aileth thee?' And she answered, 'This woman said unto me, "Give thy son, that we may eat him today, and we will eat my son tomorrow". ²⁹So we boiled my son, and did eat him: and I said unto her on the next day, "Give thy son, that we may eat him": and she hath hid her son.' ³⁰And it came to pass, when the king heard the words of

the woman, that he rent his clothes; and he passed by upon the wall, and the people looked, and behold, he had sackcloth within upon his flesh. ³¹Then he said, 'God do so and more also to me, if the head of Elisha the son of Shaphat shall stand on him this day'. ³²But Elisha sat in his house, and the elders sat with him; and the king sent a man from before him: but ere the messenger came to him, he said to the elders, 'See ye how this son of a murderer hath sent to take away my head? Look, when the messenger cometh, shut the door, and hold him fast at the door: is not the sound of his master's feet behind him?' ³³And while he yet talked with them, behold, the messenger came down unto him: and he said, 'Behold, this evil is of the Lord; what should I wait for the Lord any longer?'

7 Then Elisha said, 'Hear ye the word of the Lord; thus saith the Lord, "Tomorrow about this time shall a measure of fine flour be sold for a shekel, and two measures of barley for a shekel, in the gate of Samaria"'. ²Then a lord on whose hand the king leaned answered the man of God, and said, 'Behold, if the Lord would make windows in heaven, might this thing be?' And he said, 'Behold, thou shalt see it with thy eyes, but shalt not eat thereof'.

³And there were four leprous men at the entering in of the gate: and they said one to another, 'Why sit we here until we die? ⁴If we say, we will enter into the city, then the famine is in the city, and we shall die there: and if we sit still here, we die also. Now therefore come, and let us fall unto the host of the Syrians: if they save us alive, we shall live; and if they kill us, we shall but die.' ⁵And they rose up in the twilight, to go unto the camp of the Syrians: and when they were come to the uttermost part of the camp of Syria, behold, there was no man there. ⁶For the Lord had made the host of the Syrians to hear a noise of chariots, and a noise of horses, even the noise of a great host: and they said one to another, 'Lo, the king of Israel hath hired against us the kings of the Hittites, and the kings of the Egyptians, to come upon us'. ⁷Wherefore they arose and fled in the twilight, and left their tents, and their horses, and their asses, even the camp as it was, and fled for their life. ⁸And when these lepers came to the uttermost part of the camp, they went into one tent, and did eat and drink, and carried thence silver, and gold, and raiment, and went and hid it; and came again, and entered into another tent, and carried thence also, and went and hid it. ⁹Then they said one to another, 'We do not well: this day is a day of good tidings, and we hold our peace: if we tarry till the morning light, some mischief will come upon us: now therefore come, that we may go and tell the king's household'. ¹⁰So they came and called unto the porter of the city: and they told them, saying, 'We came to the camp of the Syrians, and behold, there was no man there, neither voice of man, but horses tied, and asses tied, and the tents as they were'. ¹¹And he called the porters, and they told it to the king's house within.

¹²And the king arose in the night, and said unto his servants, 'I will now show you what the Syrians have done to us. They know that we be hungry; therefore are they gone out of the camp to hide themselves

in the field, saying, "When they come out of the city, we shall catch them alive, and get into the city".' [13]And one of his servants answered and said, 'Let some take, I pray thee, five of the horses that remain, which are left in the city (behold, they are as all the multitude of Israel that are left in it: behold, I say, they are even as all the multitude of the Israelites that are consumed), and let us send and see'. [14]They took therefore two chariot-horses, and the king sent after the host of the Syrians, saying, 'Go and see'. [15]And they went after them unto Jordan: and lo, all the way was full of garments and vessels, which the Syrians had cast away in their haste. And the messengers returned, and told the king. [16]And the people went out, and spoiled the tents of the Syrians. So a measure of fine flour was sold for a shekel, and two measures of barley for a shekel, according to the word of the LORD.

[17]And the king appointed the lord on whose hand he leaned to have the charge of the gate: and the people trod upon him in the gate, and he died, as the man of God had said, who spoke when the king came down to him. [18]And it came to pass as the man of God had spoken to the king, saying, 'Two measures of barley for a shekel, and a measure of fine flour for a shekel, shall be tomorrow about this time in the gate of Samaria': [19]and that lord answered the man of God, and said, 'Now behold, if the LORD should make windows in heaven, might such a thing be?' And he said, 'Behold, thou shalt see it with thy eyes, but shalt not eat thereof'. [20]And so it fell out unto him: for the people trod upon him in the gate, and he died.

8 Then spoke Elisha unto the woman, whose son he had restored to life, saying, 'Arise, and go thou and thy household, and sojourn wheresoever thou canst sojourn: for the LORD hath called for a famine, and it shall also come upon the land seven years'. [2]And the woman arose, and did after the saying of the man of God: and she went with her household, and sojourned in the land of the Philistines seven years. [3]And it came to pass at the seven years' end, that the woman returned out of the land of the Philistines: and she went forth to cry unto the king for her house and for her land. [4]And the king talked with Gehazi the servant of the man of God, saying, 'Tell me, I pray thee, all the great things that Elisha hath done'. [5]And it came to pass, as he was telling the king how he had restored a dead body to life, that behold, the woman whose son he had restored to life, cried to the king for her house and for her land. And Gehazi said, 'My lord, O king, this is the woman, and this is her son, whom Elisha restored to life'. [6]And when the king asked the woman, she told him. So the king appointed unto her a certain officer, saying, 'Restore all that was hers, and all the fruits of the field since the day that she left the land, even until now'.

[7]And Elisha came to Damascus; and Ben-hadad the king of Syria was sick; and it was told him, saying, 'The man of God is come hither'. [8]And the king said unto Hazael, 'Take a present in thy hand, and go meet the man of God, and inquire of the LORD by him, saying, "Shall I recover of this disease?"' [9]So Hazael went to meet him, and took a present with

him, even of every good thing of Damascus, forty camels' burden, and came and stood before him, and said, 'Thy son Ben-hadad king of Syria hath sent me to thee, saying, "Shall I recover of this disease?"' ¹⁰And Elisha said unto him, 'Go, say unto him, "Thou mayest certainly recover": howbeit the LORD hath shown me that he shall surely die'. ¹¹And he settled his countenance steadfastly, until he was ashamed: and the man of God wept. ¹²And Hazael said, 'Why weepeth my lord?' And he answered, 'Because I know the evil that thou wilt do unto the children of Israel: their strongholds wilt thou set on fire, and their young men wilt thou slay with the sword, and wilt dash their children, and rip up their women with child'. ¹³And Hazael said, 'But what, is thy servant a dog, that he should do this great thing?' And Elisha answered, 'The LORD hath shown me that thou shalt be king over Syria'. ¹⁴So he departed from Elisha, and came to his master, who said to him, 'What said Elisha to thee?' And he answered, 'He told me that thou shouldst surely recover'. ¹⁵And it came to pass on the morrow, that he took a thick cloth, and dipped it in water, and spread it on his face, so that he died: and Hazael reigned in his stead.

¹⁶And in the fifth year of Joram the son of Ahab king of Israel, Jehoshaphat being then king of Judah, Jehoram the son of Jehoshaphat king of Judah began to reign. ¹⁷Thirty and two years old was he when he began to reign, and he reigned eight years in Jerusalem. ¹⁸And he walked in the way of the kings of Israel, as did the house of Ahab: for the daughter of Ahab was his wife: and he did evil in the sight of the LORD. ¹⁹Yet the LORD would not destroy Judah for David his servant's sake, as he promised to give to him always a light, and to his children.

²⁰In his days Edom revolted from under the hand of Judah, and made a king over themselves. ²¹So Joram went over to Zair, and all the chariots with him: and he rose by night, and smote the Edomites which compassed him about: and the captains of the chariots, and the people fled into their tents. ²²Yet Edom revolted from under the hand of Judah unto this day. Then Libnah revolted at the same time.

²³And the rest of the acts of Joram, and all that he did, are they not written in the book of the chronicles of the kings of Judah? ²⁴And Joram slept with his fathers, and was buried with his fathers in the city of David: and Ahaziah his son reigned in his stead.

²⁵In the twelfth year of Joram the son of Ahab king of Israel did Ahaziah the son of Jehoram king of Judah begin to reign. ²⁶Two and twenty years old was Ahaziah when he began to reign, and he reigned one year in Jerusalem. And his mother's name was Athaliah, the daughter of Omri king of Israel. ²⁷And he walked in the way of the house of Ahab, and did evil in the sight of the LORD, as did the house of Ahab: for he was the son-in-law of the house of Ahab.

²⁸And he went with Joram the son of Ahab to the war against Hazael king of Syria in Ramoth-gilead; and the Syrians wounded Joram. ²⁹And king Joram went back to be healed in Jezreel of the wounds which the Syrians had given him at Ramah, when he fought against Hazael king

letter cometh to you, seeing your master's sons are with you, and there are with you chariots and horses, a fenced city also, and armour: ³look even out the best and meetest of your master's sons, and set him on his father's throne, and fight for your master's house'. ⁴But they were exceedingly afraid, and said, 'Behold, two kings stood not before him: how then shall we stand?' ⁵And he that was over the house, and he that was over the city, the elders also, and the bringers up of the children, sent to Jehu, saying, 'We are thy servants, and will do all that thou shalt bid us; we will not make any king: do thou that which is good in thy eyes'.

⁶Then he wrote a letter the second time to them, saying, 'If ye be mine, and if ye will hearken unto my voice, take ye the heads of the men your master's sons, and come to me to Jezreel by tomorrow this time'. Now the king's sons, being seventy persons, were with the great men of the city, which brought them up. ⁷And it came to pass, when the letter came to them, that they took the king's sons, and slew seventy persons, and put their heads in baskets, and sent him them to Jezreel.

⁸And there came a messenger, and told him, saying, 'They have brought the heads of the king's sons'. And he said, 'Lay ye them in two heaps at the entering in of the gate until the morning'. ⁹And it came to pass in the morning, that he went out, and stood, and said to all the people, 'Ye be righteous: behold, I conspired against my master, and slew him: but who slew all these? ¹⁰Know now that there shall fall unto the earth nothing of the word of the LORD, which the LORD spoke concerning the house of Ahab: for the LORD hath done that which he spoke by his servant Elijah.' ¹¹So Jehu slew all that remained of the house of Ahab in Jezreel, and all his great men, and his kinsfolks, and his priests, until he left him none remaining.

¹²And he arose and departed, and came to Samaria. And as he was at the shearing-house in the way, ¹³Jehu met with the brethren of Ahaziah king of Judah, and said, 'Who are ye?' And they answered, 'We are the brethren of Ahaziah, and we go down to salute the children of the king and the children of the queen'. ¹⁴And he said, 'Take them alive'. And they took them alive, and slew them at the pit of the shearing-house, even two and forty men; neither left he any of them.

¹⁵And when he was departed thence, he lighted on Jehonadab the son of Rechab coming to meet him: and he saluted him, and said to him, 'Is thy heart right, as my heart is with thy heart?' And Jehonadab answered, 'It is'. 'If it be, give me thy hand'. And he gave him his hand, and he took him up to him into the chariot. ¹⁶And he said, 'Come with me, and see my zeal for the LORD'. So they made him ride in his chariot. ¹⁷And when he came to Samaria, he slew all that remained unto Ahab in Samaria, till he had destroyed him, according to the saying of the LORD, which he spoke to Elijah.

¹⁸And Jehu gathered all the people together, and said unto them, 'Ahab served Baal a little, but Jehu shall serve him much. ¹⁹Now therefore call unto me all the prophets of Baal, all his servants, and all his priests; let none be wanting: for I have a great sacrifice to do to Baal; whosoever

shall be wanting, he shall not live.' But Jehu did it in subtlety, to the intent that he might destroy the worshippers of Baal. ²⁰And Jehu said, 'Proclaim a solemn assembly for Baal'. And they proclaimed it. ²¹And Jehu sent through all Israel, and all the worshippers of Baal came, so that there was not a man left that came not. And they came into the house of Baal; and the house of Baal was full from one end to another. ²²And he said unto him that was over the vestry, 'Bring forth vestments for all the worshippers of Baal'. And he brought them forth vestments. ²³And Jehu went, and Jehonadab the son of Rechab, into the house of Baal, and said unto the worshippers of Baal, 'Search, and look that there be here with you none of the servants of the LORD, but the worshippers of Baal only'. ²⁴And when they went in to offer sacrifices and burnt offerings, Jehu appointed fourscore men without, and said, 'If any of the men whom I have brought into your hands escape, he that letteth him go, his life shall be for the life of him'. ²⁵And it came to pass, as soon as he had made an end of offering the burnt offering, that Jehu said to the guard and to the captains, 'Go in, and slay them, let none come forth'. And they smote them with the edge of the sword, and the guard and the captains cast them out, and went to the city of the house of Baal. ²⁶And they brought forth the images out of the house of Baal, and burnt them. ²⁷And they broke down the image of Baal, and broke down the house of Baal, and made it a draught-house unto this day. ²⁸Thus Jehu destroyed Baal out of Israel.

²⁹Howbeit, from the sins of Jeroboam the son of Nebat, who made Israel to sin, Jehu departed not from after them, to wit, the golden calves that were in Beth-el, and that were in Dan. ³⁰And the LORD said unto Jehu, 'Because thou hast done well in executing that which is right in my eyes, and hast done unto the house of Ahab according to all that was in my heart, thy children of the fourth generation shall sit on the throne of Israel'. ³¹But Jehu took no heed to walk in the law of the LORD God of Israel with all his heart: for he departed not from the sins of Jeroboam, which made Israel to sin.

³²In those days the LORD began to cut Israel short: and Hazael smote them in all the coasts of Israel: ³³from Jordan eastward, all the land of Gilead, the Gadites, and the Reubenites, and the Manassites, from Aroer, which is by the river Arnon, even Gilead and Bashan.

³⁴Now the rest of the acts of Jehu, and all that he did, and all his might, are they not written in the book of the chronicles of the kings of Israel? ³⁵And Jehu slept with his fathers, and they buried him in Samaria. And Jehoahaz his son reigned in his stead. ³⁶And the time that Jehu reigned over Israel in Samaria was twenty and eight years.

11 And when Athaliah the mother of Ahaziah saw that her son was dead, she arose and destroyed all the seed royal. ²But Jehosheba, the daughter of king Joram, sister of Ahaziah, took Joash the son of Ahaziah, and stole him from among the king's sons which were slain; and they hid him, even him and his nurse, in the bedchamber from Athaliah, so that he was not slain. ³And he was with her hid in the house of the LORD six years. And Athaliah did reign over the land.

⁴And the seventh year Jehoiada sent and fetched the rulers over hundreds, with the captains and the guard, and brought them to him into the house of the LORD, and made a covenant with them, and took an oath of them in the house of the LORD, and showed them the king's son. ⁵And he commanded them, saying, 'This is the thing that ye shall do: a third part of you that enter in on the sabbath shall even be keepers of the watch of the king's house: ⁶and a third part shall be at the gate of Sur, and a third part at the gate behind the guard: so shall ye keep the watch of the house, that it be not broken down. ⁷And two parts of all you that go forth on the sabbath, even they shall keep the watch of the house of the LORD about the king. ⁸And ye shall compass the king round about, every man with his weapons in his hand: and he that cometh within the ranges, let him be slain: and be ye with the king as he goeth out and as he cometh in.' ⁹And the captains over the hundreds did according to all things that Jehoiada the priest commanded: and they took every man his men that were to come in on the sabbath, with them that should go out on the sabbath, and came to Jehoiada the priest. ¹⁰And to the captains over hundreds did the priest give king David's spears and shields, that were in the temple. ¹¹And the guard stood, every man with his weapons in his hand, round about the king, from the right corner of the temple to the left corner of the temple, along by the altar and the temple. ¹²And he brought forth the king's son, and put the crown upon him, and gave him the testimony; and they made him king, and anointed him; and they clapped their hands, and said, 'God save the king'.

¹³And when Athaliah heard the noise of the guard and of the people, she came to the people into the temple of the LORD. ¹⁴And when she looked, behold, the king stood by a pillar, as the manner was, and the princes and the trumpeters by the king, and all the people of the land rejoiced, and blew with trumpets: and Athaliah rent her clothes, and cried, 'Treason, Treason'. ¹⁵But Jehoiada the priest commanded the captains of the hundreds, the officers of the host, and said unto them, 'Have her forth without the ranges: and him that followeth her kill with the sword'. For the priest had said, 'Let her not be slain in the house of the LORD'. ¹⁶And they laid hands on her; and she went by the way by the which the horses came into the king's house: and there was she slain.

¹⁷And Jehoiada made a covenant between the LORD and the king and the people, that they should be the LORD's people; between the king also and the people. ¹⁸And all the people of the land went into the house of Baal, and broke it down; his altars and his images broke they in pieces thoroughly, and slew Mattan the priest of Baal before the altars. And the priest appointed officers over the house of the LORD. ¹⁹And he took the rulers over hundreds, and the captains, and the guard, and all the people of the land, and they brought down the king from the house of the LORD, and came by the way of the gate of the guard to the king's house. And he sat on the throne of the kings. ²⁰And all the people of the land rejoiced, and the city was in quiet: and they

slew Athaliah with the sword beside the king's house. ²¹Seven years old was Jehoash when he began to reign.

12 In the seventh year of Jehu Jehoash began to reign, and forty years reigned he in Jerusalem. And his mother's name was Zibiah of Beer-sheba. ²And Jehoash did that which was right in the sight of the LORD all his days wherein Jehoiada the priest instructed him. ³But the high places were not taken away: the people still sacrificed and burnt incense in the high places.

⁴And Jehoash said to the priests, 'All the money of the dedicated things that is brought into the house of the LORD, even the money of every one that passeth the account, the money that every man is set at, and all the money that cometh into any man's heart to bring into the house of the LORD, ⁵let the priests take it to them, every man of his acquaintance, and let them repair the breaches of the house, wheresoever any breach shall be found'. ⁶But it was so that in the three and twentieth year of king Jehoash the priests had not repaired the breaches of the house. ⁷Then king Jehoash called for Jehoiada the priest, and the other priests, and said unto them, 'Why repair ye not the breaches of the house? now therefore receive no more money of your acquaintance, but deliver it for the breaches of the house'. ⁸And the priests consented to receive no more money of the people, neither to repair the breaches of the house. ⁹But Jehoiada the priest took a chest, and bored a hole in the lid of it, and set it beside the altar, on the right side as one cometh into the house of the LORD: and the priests that kept the door put therein all the money that was brought into the house of the LORD. ¹⁰And it was so, when they saw that there was much money in the chest, that the king's scribe and the high priest came up, and they put up in bags, and told the money that was found in the house of the LORD. ¹¹And they gave the money, being told, into the hands of them that did the work, that had the oversight of the house of the LORD: and they laid it out to the carpenters and builders, that wrought upon the house of the LORD, ¹²and to masons, and hewers of stone, and to buy timber and hewn stone to repair the breaches of the house of the LORD, and for all that was laid out for the house to repair it. ¹³Howbeit there were not made for the house of the LORD bowls of silver, snuffers, basins, trumpets, any vessels of gold, or vessels of silver, of the money that was brought into the house of the LORD: ¹⁴but they gave that to the workmen, and repaired therewith the house of the LORD. ¹⁵Moreover they reckoned not with the men, into whose hand they delivered the money to be bestowed on workmen: for they dealt faithfully. ¹⁶The trespass money and sin money was not brought into the house of the LORD: it was the priests'.

¹⁷Then Hazael king of Syria went up, and fought against Gath, and took it: and Hazael set his face to go up to Jerusalem. ¹⁸And Jehoash king of Judah took all the hallowed things that Jehoshaphat, and Jehoram, and Ahaziah, his fathers, kings of Judah, had dedicated, and his own hallowed things, and all the gold that was found in the treasures of the house of the LORD, and in the king's house, and sent it to Hazael king of Syria: and he went away from Jerusalem.

¹⁹And the rest of the acts of Jehoash, and all that he did, are they not written in the book of the chronicles of the kings of Judah? ²⁰And his servants arose, and made a conspiracy, and slew Jehoash in the house of Millo, which goeth down to Silla. ²¹For Jozachar the son of Shimeath, and Jehozabad the son of Shomer, his servants, smote him, and he died; and they buried him with his fathers in the city of David, and Amaziah his son reigned in his stead.

13 In the three and twentieth year of Joash the son of Ahaziah king of Judah Jehoahaz the son of Jehu began to reign over Israel in Samaria, and reigned seventeen years. ²And he did that which was evil in the sight of the LORD, and followed the sins of Jeroboam the son of Nebat, which made Israel to sin; he departed not therefrom.

³And the anger of the LORD was kindled against Israel, and he delivered them into the hand of Hazael king of Syria, and into the hand of Ben-hadad the son of Hazael, all their days. ⁴And Jehoahaz besought the LORD, and the LORD hearkened unto him: for he saw the oppression of Israel, because the king of Syria oppressed them. ⁵(And the LORD gave Israel a saviour, so that they went out from under the hand of the Syrians: and the children of Israel dwelt in their tents, as beforetime. ⁶Nevertheless they departed not from the sins of the house of Jeroboam, who made Israel sin, but walked therein: and there remained the grove also in Samaria.) ⁷Neither did he leave of the people to Jehoahaz but fifty horsemen, and ten chariots, and ten thousand footmen: for the king of Syria had destroyed them, and had made them like the dust by threshing.

⁸Now the rest of the acts of Jehoahaz, and all that he did, and his might, are they not written in the book of the chronicles of the kings of Israel? ⁹And Jehoahaz slept with his fathers, and they buried him in Samaria, and Joash his son reigned in his stead.

¹⁰In the thirty and seventh year of Joash king of Judah began Jehoash the son of Jehoahaz to reign over Israel in Samaria, and reigned sixteen years. ¹¹And he did that which was evil in the sight of the LORD; he departed not from all the sins of Jeroboam the son of Nebat, who made Israel sin: but he walked therein.

¹²And the rest of the acts of Joash, and all that he did, and his might wherewith he fought against Amaziah king of Judah, are they not written in the book of the chronicles of the kings of Israel? ¹³And Joash slept with his fathers, and Jeroboam sat upon his throne: and Joash was buried in Samaria with the kings of Israel.

¹⁴Now Elisha was fallen sick of his sickness whereof he died. And Joash the king of Israel came down unto him, and wept over his face, and said, 'O my father, my father, the chariot of Israel, and the horsemen thereof'. ¹⁵And Elisha said unto him, 'Take bow and arrows'. And he took unto him bow and arrows. ¹⁶And he said to the king of Israel, 'Put thy hand upon the bow'. And he put his hand upon it: and Elisha put his hands upon the king's hands. ¹⁷And he said, 'Open the window eastward'. And he opened it. Then Elisha said, 'Shoot'. And he shot. And he said, 'The arrow of the LORD's deliverance, and the arrow of deliverance

from Syria: for thou shalt smite the Syrians in Aphek, till thou have consumed them'. ¹⁸And he said, 'Take the arrows'. And he took them. And he said unto the king of Israel, 'Smite upon the ground'. And he smote thrice, and stayed. ¹⁹And the man of God was wroth with him, and said, 'Thou shouldst have smitten five or six times, then hadst thou smitten Syria till thou hadst consumed it: whereas now thou shalt smite Syria but thrice'.

²⁰And Elisha died, and they buried him. And the bands of the Moabites invaded the land at the coming in of the year. ²¹And it came to pass as they were burying a man, that behold, they spied a band of men, and they cast the man into the sepulchre of Elisha: and when the man was let down, and touched the bones of Elisha, he revived, and stood up on his feet.

²²But Hazael king of Syria oppressed Israel all the days of Jehoahaz. ²³And the Lord was gracious unto them, and had compassion on them, and had respect unto them, because of his covenant with Abraham, Isaac, and Jacob, and would not destroy them, neither cast he them from his presence as yet. ²⁴So Hazael the king of Syria died, and Ben-hadad his son reigned in his stead. ²⁵And Jehoash the son of Jehoahaz took again out of the hand of Ben-hadad the son of Hazael the cities which he had taken out of the hand of Jehoahaz his father by war. Three times did Joash beat him, and recovered the cities of Israel.

14 In the second year of Joash son of Jehoahaz king of Israel reigned Amaziah the son of Joash king of Judah. ²He was twenty and five years old when he began to reign, and reigned twenty and nine years in Jerusalem. And his mother's name was Jehoaddan of Jerusalem. ³And he did that which was right in the sight of the Lord, yet not like David his father: he did according to all things as Joash his father did. ⁴Howbeit the high places were not taken away: as yet the people did sacrifice and burnt incense on the high places.

⁵And it came to pass, as soon as the kingdom was confirmed in his hand, that he slew his servants which had slain the king his father. ⁶But the children of the murderers he slew not, according unto that which is written in the book of the law of Moses, wherein the Lord commanded, saying, 'The fathers shall not be put to death for the children, nor the children be put to death for the fathers: but every man shall be put to death for his own sin'. ⁷He slew of Edom in the valley of salt ten thousand, and took Selah by war, and called the name of it Joktheel unto this day.

⁸Then Amaziah sent messengers to Jehoash, the son of Jehoahaz son of Jehu, king of Israel, saying, 'Come, let us look one another in the face'. ⁹And Jehoash the king of Israel sent to Amaziah king of Judah, saying, 'The thistle that was in Lebanon sent to the cedar that was in Lebanon, saying, "Give thy daughter to my son to wife". And there passed by a wild beast that was in Lebanon, and trod down the thistle. ¹⁰Thou hast indeed smitten Edom, and thy heart hath lifted thee up: glory of this, and tarry at home: for why shouldst thou meddle to thy hurt, that thou shouldst fall, even thou, and Judah with thee?' ¹¹But

Amaziah would not hear. Therefore Jehoash king of Israel went up; and he and Amaziah king of Judah looked one another in the face at Beth-shemesh, which belongeth to Judah. ¹²And Judah was put to the worse before Israel, and they fled every man to their tents. ¹³And Jehoash king of Israel took Amaziah king of Judah, the son of Jehoash the son of Ahaziah, at Beth-shemesh, and came to Jerusalem, and broke down the wall of Jerusalem from the gate of Ephraim unto the corner gate, four hundred cubits. ¹⁴And he took all the gold and silver, and all the vessels that were found in the house of the LORD, and in the treasures of the king's house, and hostages, and returned to Samaria.

¹⁵Now the rest of the acts of Jehoash which he did, and his might, and how he fought with Amaziah king of Judah, are they not written in the book of the chronicles of the kings of Israel? ¹⁶And Jehoash slept with his fathers, and was buried in Samaria with the kings of Israel, and Jeroboam his son reigned in his stead.

¹⁷And Amaziah the son of Joash king of Judah lived after the death of Jehoash son of Jehoahaz king of Israel fifteen years. ¹⁸And the rest of the acts of Amaziah, are they not written in the book of the chronicles of the kings of Judah? ¹⁹Now they made a conspiracy against him in Jerusalem: and he fled to Lachish, but they sent after him to Lachish, and slew him there. ²⁰And they brought him on horses, and he was buried at Jerusalem with his fathers in the city of David.

²¹And all the people of Judah took Azariah, which was sixteen years old, and made him king instead of his father Amaziah. ²²He built Elath, and restored it to Judah, after that the king slept with his fathers.

²³In the fifteenth year of Amaziah the son of Joash king of Judah Jeroboam the son of Joash king of Israel began to reign in Samaria, and reigned forty and one years. ²⁴And he did that which was evil in the sight of the LORD: he departed not from all the sins of Jeroboam the son of Nebat, who made Israel to sin. ²⁵He restored the coast of Israel from the entering of Hamath unto the sea of the plain, according to the word of the LORD God of Israel, which he spoke by the hand of his servant Jonah, the son of Amittai, the prophet, which was of Gath-hepher. ²⁶For the LORD saw the affliction of Israel, that it was very bitter: for there was not any shut up, nor any left, nor any helper for Israel. ²⁷And the LORD said not that he would blot out the name of Israel from under heaven: but he saved them by the hand of Jeroboam the son of Joash.

²⁸Now the rest of the acts of Jeroboam, and all that he did, and his might, how he warred, and how he recovered Damascus, and Hamath, which belonged to Judah, for Israel, are they not written in the book of the chronicles of the kings of Israel? ²⁹And Jeroboam slept with his fathers, even with the kings of Israel, and Zachariah his son reigned in his stead.

15 In the twenty and seventh year of Jeroboam king of Israel began Azariah son of Amaziah king of Judah to reign. ²Sixteen years old was he when he began to reign, and he reigned two and fifty years in Jerusalem. And his mother's name was Jecholiah of Jerusalem. ³And he did that which was right in the sight of the LORD, according to all that his father Amaziah had done; ⁴save that the high places were not removed: the people sacrificed and burnt incense still on the high places.

⁵And the LORD smote the king, so that he was a leper unto the day of his death, and dwelt in a several house. And Jotham the king's son was over the house, judging the people of the land.

⁶And the rest of the acts of Azariah, and all that he did, are they not written in the book of the chronicles of the kings of Judah? ⁷So Azariah slept with his fathers, and they buried him with his fathers in the city of David, and Jotham his son reigned in his stead.

⁸In the thirty and eighth year of Azariah king of Judah did Zachariah the son of Jeroboam reign over Israel in Samaria six months. ⁹And he did that which was evil in the sight of the LORD, as his fathers had done: he departed not from the sins of Jeroboam the son of Nebat, who made Israel to sin. ¹⁰And Shallum the son of Jabesh conspired against him, and smote him before the people, and slew him, and reigned in his stead.

¹¹And the rest of the acts of Zachariah, behold, they are written in the book of the chronicles of the kings of Israel.

¹²This was the word of the LORD which he spoke unto Jehu, saying, 'Thy sons shall sit on the throne of Israel unto the fourth generation'. And so it came to pass.

¹³Shallum the son of Jabesh began to reign in the nine and thirtieth year of Uzziah king of Judah; and he reigned a full month in Samaria. ¹⁴For Menahem the son of Gadi went up from Tirzah, and came to Samaria, and smote Shallum the son of Jabesh in Samaria, and slew him, and reigned in his stead.

¹⁵And the rest of the acts of Shallum, and the conspiracy which he made, behold, they are written in the book of the chronicles of the kings of Israel.

¹⁶Then Menahem smote Tiphsah, and all that were therein, and the coasts thereof from Tirzah: because they opened not to him, therefore he smote it, and all the women therein that were with child he ripped up. ¹⁷In the nine and thirtieth year of Azariah king of Judah began Menahem the son of Gadi to reign over Israel, and reigned ten years in Samaria. ¹⁸And he did that which was evil in the sight of the LORD: he departed not all his days from the sins of Jeroboam the son of Nebat, who made Israel to sin. ¹⁹And Pul the king of Assyria came against the land: and Menahem gave Pul a thousand talents of silver, that his hand might be with him to confirm the kingdom in his hand. ²⁰And Menahem exacted the money of Israel, even of all the mighty men of wealth, of each man fifty shekels of silver, to give to the king of Assyria. So the king of Assyria turned back, and stayed not there in the land.

²¹And the rest of the acts of Menahem, and all that he did, are they not written in the book of the chronicles of the kings of Israel? ²²And Menahem slept with his fathers, and Pekahiah his son reigned in his stead.

²³ In the fiftieth year of Azariah king of Judah Pekahiah the son of Menahem began to reign over Israel in Samaria, and reigned two years. ²⁴ And he did that which was evil in the sight of the LORD: he departed not from the sins of Jeroboam the son of Nebat, who made Israel to sin. ²⁵ But Pekah the son of Remaliah, a captain of his, conspired against him, and smote him in Samaria, in the palace of the king's house, with Argob and Arieh, and with him fifty men of the Gileadites: and he killed him, and reigned in his room.

²⁶ And the rest of the acts of Pekahiah, and all that he did, behold, they are written in the book of the chronicles of the kings of Israel.

²⁷ In the two and fiftieth year of Azariah king of Judah Pekah the son of Remaliah began to reign over Israel in Samaria, and reigned twenty years. ²⁸ And he did that which was evil in the sight of the LORD: he departed not from the sins of Jeroboam the son of Nebat, who made Israel to sin. ²⁹ In the days of Pekah king of Israel came Tiglath-pileser king of Assyria, and took Ijon, and Abel-beth-maachah, and Janoah, and Kedesh, and Hazor, and Gilead, and Galilee, all the land of Naphtali, and carried them captive to Assyria. ³⁰ And Hoshea the son of Elah made a conspiracy against Pekah the son of Remaliah, and smote him, and slew him, and reigned in his stead, in the twentieth year of Jotham the son of Uzziah.

³¹ And the rest of the acts of Pekah, and all that he did, behold, they are written in the book of the chronicles of the kings of Israel.

³² In the second year of Pekah the son of Remaliah king of Israel began Jotham the son of Uzziah king of Judah to reign. ³³ Five and twenty years old was he when he began to reign, and he reigned sixteen years in Jerusalem. And his mother's name was Jerusha, the daughter of Zadok. ³⁴ And he did that which was right in the sight of the LORD: he did according to all that his father Uzziah had done.

³⁵ Howbeit the high places were not removed: the people sacrificed and burnt incense still in the high places. He built the higher gate of the house of the LORD.

³⁶ Now the rest of the acts of Jotham, and all that he did, are they not written in the book of the chronicles of the kings of Judah? ³⁷ (In those days the LORD began to send against Judah Rezin the king of Syria, and Pekah the son of Remaliah.) ³⁸ And Jotham slept with his fathers, and was buried with his fathers in the city of David his father: and Ahaz his son reigned in his stead.

16 In the seventeenth year of Pekah the son of Remaliah Ahaz the son of Jotham king of Judah began to reign. ² Twenty years old was Ahaz when he began to reign, and reigned sixteen years in Jerusalem, and did not that which was right in the sight of the LORD his God, like David his father. ³ But he walked in the way of the kings of Israel, yea, and made his son to pass through the fire, according to the abominations of the heathen, whom the LORD cast out from before the children of Israel. ⁴ And he sacrificed and burnt incense in the high places, and on the hills, and under every green tree.

⁵ Then Rezin king of Syria and Pekah son of Remaliah king of Israel

came up to Jerusalem to war: and they besieged Ahaz, but could not overcome him. [6]At that time Rezin king of Syria recovered Elath to Syria, and drove the Jews from Elath: and the Syrians came to Elath, and dwelt there unto this day. [7]So Ahaz sent messengers to Tiglath-pileser king of Assyria, saying, 'I am thy servant and thy son: come up, and save me out of the hand of the king of Syria, and out of the hand of the king of Israel, which rise up against me'. [8]And Ahaz took the silver and gold that was found in the house of the LORD, and in the treasures of the king's house, and sent it for a present to the king of Assyria. [9]And the king of Assyria hearkened unto him: for the king of Assyria went up against Damascus, and took it, and carried the people of it captive to Kir, and slew Rezin.

[10]And king Ahaz went to Damascus to meet Tiglath-pileser king of Assyria, and saw an altar that was at Damascus: and king Ahaz sent to Urijah the priest the fashion of the altar, and the pattern of it, according to all the workmanship thereof. [11]And Urijah the priest built an altar according to all that king Ahaz had sent from Damascus: so Urijah the priest made it against king Ahaz came from Damascus. [12]And when the king was come from Damascus, the king saw the altar: and the king approached to the altar, and offered thereon. [13]And he burnt his burnt offering and his meat offering, and poured his drink offering, and sprinkled the blood of his peace offerings, upon the altar. [14]And he brought also the brazen altar which was before the LORD, from the forefront of the house, from between the altar and the house of the LORD, and put it on the north side of the altar. [15]And king Ahaz commanded Urijah the priest, saying, 'Upon the great altar burn the morning burnt offering, and the evening meat offering, and the king's burnt sacrifice, and his meat offering, with the burnt offering of all the people of the land, and their meat offering, and their drink offerings; and sprinkle upon it all the blood of the burnt offering, and all the blood of the sacrifice: and the brazen altar shall be for me to inquire by'. [16]Thus did Urijah the priest, according to all that king Ahaz commanded.

[17]And king Ahaz cut off the borders of the bases, and removed the laver from off them, and took down the sea from off the brazen oxen that were under it, and put it upon a pavement of stones. [18]And the covert for the sabbath that they had built in the house, and the king's entry without, turned he from the house of the LORD for the king of Assyria.

[19]Now the rest of the acts of Ahaz which he did, are they not written in the book of the chronicles of the kings of Judah? [20]And Ahaz slept with his fathers, and was buried with his fathers in the city of David, and Hezekiah his son reigned in his stead.

17 In the twelfth year of Ahaz king of Judah began Hoshea the son of Elah to reign in Samaria over Israel nine years. [2]And he did that which was evil in the sight of the LORD, but not as the kings of Israel that were before him. [3]Against him came up Shalmaneser king of Assyria, and Hoshea became his servant, and gave him presents. [4]And the king of Assyria found conspiracy in Hoshea: for he had sent messengers to So king of Egypt, and brought no present to the king of Assyria, as he had done year by year: therefore the king of Assyria shut him up, and bound him in prison. ⁵Then the king of Assyria came up throughout all the land, and went up to Samaria, and besieged it three years. ⁶In the ninth year of Hoshea the king of Assyria took Samaria, and carried Israel away into Assyria, and placed them in Halah and in Habor by the river of Gozan, and in the cities of the Medes.

⁷For so it was, that the children of Israel had sinned against the LORD their God, which had brought them up out of the land of Egypt, from under the hand of Pharaoh king of Egypt, and had feared other gods, ⁸and walked in the statutes of the heathen, whom the LORD cast out from before the children of Israel, and of the kings of Israel, which they had made. ⁹And the children of Israel did secretly those things that were not right against the LORD their God, and they built them high places in all their cities, from the tower of the watchmen to the fenced city. ¹⁰And they set them up images and groves in every high hill, and under every green tree. ¹¹And there they burnt incense in all the high places, as did the heathen whom the LORD carried away before them, and wrought wicked things to provoke the LORD to anger: ¹²for they served idols, whereof the LORD had said unto them, 'Ye shall not do this thing'. ¹³Yet the LORD testified against Israel, and against Judah, by all the prophets, and by all the seers, saying, 'Turn ye from your evil ways, and keep my commandments and my statutes, according to all the law which I commanded your fathers, and which I sent to you by my servants the prophets'. ¹⁴Notwithstanding they would not hear, but hardened their necks, like to the neck of their fathers, that did not believe in the LORD their God. ¹⁵And they rejected his statutes, and his covenant that he made with their fathers, and his testimonies which he testified against them; and they followed vanity, and became vain, and went after the heathen that were round about them, concerning whom the LORD had charged them, that they should not do like them. ¹⁶And they left all the commandments of the LORD their God, and made them molten images, even two calves, and made a grove, and worshipped all the host of heaven, and served Baal. ¹⁷And they caused their sons and their daughters to pass through the fire, and used divination and enchantments, and sold themselves to do evil in the sight of the LORD, to provoke him to anger. ¹⁸Therefore the LORD was very angry with Israel, and removed them out of his sight: there was none left but the tribe of Judah only. ¹⁹Also Judah kept not the commandments of the LORD their God, but walked in the statutes of Israel which they made. ²⁰And the LORD rejected all the seed of Israel, and afflicted them, and delivered them into the hand of spoilers, until he had cast them out of his sight. ²¹For he rent Israel from the house of David, and they made Jeroboam the son of Nebat king: and Jeroboam drove Israel from following the LORD, and made them sin a great sin. ²²For the children of Israel walked in all the sins of Jeroboam which he did, they departed not from them: ²³until the LORD removed Israel out of his sight, as he

had said by all his servants the prophets. So was Israel carried away out of their own land to Assyria unto this day.

²⁴And the king of Assyria brought men from Babylon, and from Cuthah, and from Ava, and from Hamath, and from Sepharvaim, and placed them in the cities of Samaria instead of the children of Israel: and they possessed Samaria, and dwelt in the cities thereof. ²⁵And so it was at the beginning of their dwelling there, that they feared not the LORD: therefore the LORD sent lions among them, which slew some of them. ²⁶Wherefore they spoke to the king of Assyria, saying, 'The nations which thou hast removed, and placed in the cities of Samaria, know not the manner of the God of the land: therefore he hath sent lions among them, and behold, they slay them, because they know not the manner of the God of the land'. ²⁷Then the king of Assyria commanded, saying, 'Carry thither one of the priests whom ye brought from thence, and let them go and dwell there, and let him teach them the manner of the God of the land'. ²⁸Then one of the priests whom they had carried away from Samaria came and dwelt in Beth-el, and taught them how they should fear the LORD.

²⁹Howbeit every nation made gods of their own, and put them in the houses of the high places which the Samaritans had made, every nation in their cities wherein they dwelt. ³⁰And the men of Babylon made Succoth-benoth, and the men of Cuth made Nergal, and the men of Hamath made Ashima, ³¹and the Avites made Nibhaz and Tartak, and the Sepharvites burnt their children in fire to Adrammelech and Anammelech, the gods of Sepharvaim. ³²So they feared the LORD, and made unto themselves of the lowest of them priests of the high places, which sacrificed for them in the houses of the high places. ³³They feared the LORD, and served their own gods, after the manner of the nations whom they carried away from thence. ³⁴Unto this day they do after the former manners: they fear not the LORD, neither do they after their statutes, or after their ordinances, or after the law and commandment which the LORD commanded the children of Jacob, whom he named Israel; ³⁵with whom the LORD had made a covenant, and charged them, saying, 'Ye shall not fear other gods, nor bow yourselves to them, nor serve them, nor sacrifice to them: ³⁶but the LORD, who brought you up out of the land of Egypt with great power and a stretched out arm, him shall ye fear, and him shall ye worship, and to him shall ye do sacrifice. ³⁷And the statutes, and the ordinances, and the law, and the commandment, which he wrote for you, ye shall observe to do for evermore, and ye shall not fear other gods. ³⁸And the covenant that I have made with you ye shall not forget, neither shall ye fear other gods. ³⁹But the LORD your God ye shall fear, and he shall deliver you out of the hand of all your enemies.' ⁴⁰Howbeit they did not hearken, but they did after their former manner. ⁴¹So these nations feared the LORD, and served their graven images, both their children, and their children's children: as did their fathers, so do they unto this day.

18 Now it came to pass in the third year of Hoshea son of Elah king of Israel, that Hezekiah the son of Ahaz king of Judah began to

reign. ²Twenty and five years old was he when he began to reign, and he reigned twenty and nine years in Jerusalem. His mother's name also was Abi, the daughter of Zachariah. ³And he did that which was right in the sight of the LORD, according to all that David his father did.

⁴He removed the high places, and broke the images, and cut down the groves, and broke in pieces the brazen serpent that Moses had made: for unto those days the children of Israel did burn incense to it: and he called it Nehushtan. ⁵He trusted in the LORD God of Israel, so that after him was none like him among all the kings of Judah, nor any that were before him. ⁶For he cleaved to the LORD, and departed not from following him, but kept his commandments, which the LORD commanded Moses. ⁷And the LORD was with him, and he prospered whithersoever he went forth: and he rebelled against the king of Assyria, and served him not. ⁸He smote the Philistines, even unto Gaza, and the borders thereof, from the tower of the watchmen to the fenced cities.

⁹And it came to pass in the fourth year of king Hezekiah (which was the seventh year of Hoshea son of Elah king of Israel), that Shalmaneser king of Assyria came up against Samaria, and besieged it. ¹⁰And at the end of three years they took it: even in the sixth year of Hezekiah (that is the ninth year of Hoshea king of Israel) Samaria was taken. ¹¹And the king of Assyria did carry away Israel unto Assyria, and put them in Halah and in Habor by the river of Gozan, and in the cities of the Medes: ¹²because they obeyed not the voice of the LORD their God, but transgressed his covenant, and all that Moses the servant of the LORD commanded, and would not hear them, nor do them.

¹³Now in the fourteenth year of king Hezekiah did Sennacherib king of Assyria come up against all the fenced cities of Judah, and took them. ¹⁴And Hezekiah king of Judah sent to the king of Assyria to Lachish, saying, 'I have offended; return from me: that which thou puttest on me will I bear'. And the king of Assyria appointed unto Hezekiah king of Judah three hundred talents of silver and thirty talents of gold. ¹⁵And Hezekiah gave him all the silver that was found in the house of the LORD, and in the treasures of the king's house. ¹⁶At that time did Hezekiah cut off the gold from the doors of the temple of the LORD, and from the pillars which Hezekiah king of Judah had overlaid, and gave it to the king of Assyria. ¹⁷And the king of Assyria sent Tartan and Rabsaris and Rab-shakeh from Lachish to king Hezekiah with a great host against Jerusalem. And they went up and came to Jerusalem. And when they were come up, they came and stood by the conduit of the upper pool, which is in the highway of the fuller's field. ¹⁸And when they had called to the king, there came out to them Eliakim the son of Hilkiah, which was over the household, and Shebna the scribe, and Joah the son of Asaph the recorder. ¹⁹And Rab-shakeh said unto them, 'Speak ye now to Hezekiah, "Thus saith the great king, the king of Assyria, 'What confidence is this wherein thou trustest?' ²⁰Thou sayest (but they are but vain words), 'I have counsel and strength for the war'. Now on whom dost thou trust, that thou rebellest against me? ²¹Now behold, thou trustest upon the staff of this bruised reed, even upon

Egypt, on which if a man lean, it will go into his hand, and pierce it: so is Pharaoh king of Egypt unto all that trust on him. ²²But if ye say unto me, 'We trust in the LORD our God': is not that he, whose high places and whose altars Hezekiah hath taken away, and hath said to Judah and Jerusalem, 'Ye shall worship before this altar in Jerusalem?' ²³Now therefore, I pray thee, give pledges to my lord the king of Assyria, and I will deliver thee two thousand horses, if thou be able on thy part to set riders upon them. ²⁴How then wilt thou turn away the face of one captain of the least of my master's servants, and put thy trust on Egypt for chariots and for horsemen? ²⁵Am I now come up without the LORD against this place to destroy it? The LORD said to me, 'Go up against this land, and destroy it'."' ²⁶Then said Eliakim the son of Hilkiah, and Shebna, and Joah, unto Rab-shakeh, 'Speak, I pray thee, to thy servants in the Syrian language, for we understand it, and talk not with us in the Jews' language in the ears of the people that are on the wall'. ²⁷But Rab-shakeh said unto them, 'Hath my master sent me to thy master, and to thee, to speak these words? hath he not sent me to the men which sit on the wall, that they may eat their own dung, and drink their own piss with you?' ²⁸Then Rab-shakeh stood and cried with a loud voice in the Jews' language, and spoke, saying, 'Hear the word of the great king, the king of Assyria. ²⁹Thus saith the king, "Let not Hezekiah deceive you, for he shall not be able to deliver you out of his hand: ³⁰neither let Hezekiah make you trust in the LORD, saying, 'The LORD will surely deliver us, and this city shall not be delivered into the hand of the king of Assyria'". ³¹Hearken not to Hezekiah: for thus saith the king of Assyria, "Make an agreement with me by a present, and come out to me, and then eat ye every man of his own vine, and every one of his fig tree, and drink ye every one the waters of his cistern: ³²until I come and take you away to a land like your own land, a land of corn and wine, a land of bread and vineyards, a land of oil olive and of honey, that ye may live, and not die: and hearken not unto Hezekiah, when he persuadeth you, saying, 'The LORD will deliver us'. ³³Hath any of the gods of the nations delivered at all his land out of the hand of the king of Assyria? ³⁴Where are the gods of Hamath, and of Arpad? where are the gods of Sepharvaim, Hena, and Ivah? have they delivered Samaria out of my hand? ³⁵Who are they among all the gods of the countries, that have delivered their country out of my hand, that the LORD should deliver Jerusalem out of my hand?"' ³⁶But the people held their peace, and answered him not a word: for the king's commandment was, saying, 'Answer him not'. ³⁷Then came Eliakim the son of Hilkiah, which was over the household, and Shebna the scribe, and Joah the son of Asaph the recorder, to Hezekiah with their clothes rent, and told him the words of Rab-shakeh.

19 And it came to pass, when king Hezekiah heard it, that he rent his clothes, and covered himself with sackcloth, and went into the house of the LORD. ²And he sent Eliakim, which was over the household, and Shebna the scribe, and the elders of the priests, covered with sackcloth, to Isaiah the prophet the son of Amoz. ³And they said unto him, 'Thus saith Hezekiah, "This day is a day of trouble, and of rebuke, and blasphemy: for the children are come to the birth, and there is not strength to bring forth. ⁴It may be the LORD thy God will hear all the words of Rab-shakeh, whom the king of Assyria his master hath sent to reproach the living God, and will reprove the words which the LORD thy God hath heard: wherefore lift up thy prayer for the remnant that are left."' ⁵So the servants of king Hezekiah came to Isaiah. ⁶And Isaiah said unto them, 'Thus shall ye say to your master, "Thus saith the LORD, 'Be not afraid of the words which thou hast heard, with which the servants of the king of Assyria have blasphemed me. ⁷Behold, I will send a blast upon him, and he shall hear a rumour, and shall return to his own land; and I will cause him to fall by the sword in his own land.'"'

⁸So Rab-shakeh returned, and found the king of Assyria warring against Libnah: for he had heard that he was departed from Lachish. ⁹And when he heard say of Tirhakah king of Ethiopia, 'Behold, he is come out to fight against thee': he sent messengers again unto Hezekiah, saying, ¹⁰'Thus shall ye speak to Hezekiah king of Judah, saying, "Let not thy God in whom thou trustest deceive thee, saying, Jerusalem shall not be delivered into the hand of the king of Assyria. ¹¹Behold, thou hast heard what the kings of Assyria have done to all lands, by destroying them utterly: and shalt thou be delivered? ¹²Have the gods of the nations delivered them which my fathers have destroyed? As Gozan, and Haran, and Rezeph, and the children of Eden which were in Thelasar? ¹³Where is the king of Hamath, and the king of Arpad, and the king of the city of Sepharvaim, of Hena, and Ivah?"'

¹⁴And Hezekiah received the letter of the hand of the messengers, and read it: and Hezekiah went up into the house of the LORD, and spread it before the LORD. ¹⁵And Hezekiah prayed before the LORD, and said, 'O LORD God of Israel, which dwellest between the cherubims, thou art the God, even thou alone, of all the kingdoms of the earth; thou hast made heaven and earth. ¹⁶LORD, bow down thy ear, and hear: open, LORD, thy eyes, and see: and hear the words of Sennacherib, which hath sent him to reproach the living God. ¹⁷Of a truth, LORD, the kings of Assyria have destroyed the nations and their lands, ¹⁸and have cast their gods into the fire: for they were no gods, but the work of men's hands, wood and stone: therefore they have destroyed them. ¹⁹Now therefore, O LORD our God, I beseech thee, save thou us out of his hand, that all the kingdoms of the earth may know that thou art the LORD God, even thou only.'

²⁰Then Isaiah the son of Amoz sent to Hezekiah, saying, 'Thus saith the LORD God of Israel, "That which thou hast prayed to me against Sennacherib king of Assyria I have heard". ²¹This is the word that the LORD hath spoken concerning him:

'"The virgin the daughter of Zion hath despised thee,
    and laughed thee to scorn,
    the daughter of Jerusalem hath shaken her head at thee.
²² Whom hast thou reproached and blasphemed?
    and against whom hast thou exalted thy voice,

him. 'Thus saith Hezekiah, 'This
and lifted up thy eyes on high?
even against the Holy One of Israel.

²³ By thy messengers thou hast reproached the Lord,
and hast said, 'With the multitude of my chariots
I am come up to the height of the mountains,
to the sides of Lebanon,
and will cut down the tall cedar trees thereof,
and the choice fir trees thereof:
and I will enter into the lodgings of his borders,
and into the forest of his Carmel.

²⁴ I have dug and drunk strange waters,
and with the sole of my feet have I dried up
all the rivers of besieged places.'

²⁵ Hast thou not heard long ago how I have done it,
and of ancient times that I have formed it?
now have I brought it to pass,
that thou shouldst be to lay waste
fenced cities into ruinous heaps.

²⁶ Therefore their inhabitants were of small power,
they were dismayed and confounded,
they were as the grass of the field,
and as the green herb,
as the grass on the housetops,
and as corn blasted before it be grown up.

²⁷ But I know thy abode,
and thy going out, and thy coming in,
and thy rage against me.

²⁸ Because thy rage against me
and thy tumult is come up into my ears,
therefore I will put my hook in thy nose,
and my bridle in thy lips,
and I will turn thee back
by the way by which thou camest.

²⁹ "And this shall be a sign unto thee, ye shall eat this year such things as grow of themselves, and in the second year that which springeth of the same, and in the third year sow ye, and reap, and plant vineyards, and eat the fruits thereof. ³⁰And the remnant that is escaped of the house of Judah shall yet again take root downward, and bear fruit upward. ³¹For out of Jerusalem shall go forth a remnant, and they that escape out of mount Zion: the zeal of the LORD of hosts shall do this." ³²Therefore thus saith the LORD concerning the king of Assyria, "He shall not come into this city, nor shoot an arrow there, nor come before it with shield, nor cast a bank against it. ³³By the way that he came, by the same shall he return, and shall not come into this city," saith the LORD. ³⁴"For I will defend this city, to save it, for my own sake, and for my servant David's sake.'"

³⁵And it came to pass that night, that the angel of the LORD went out,

and smote in the camp of the Assyrians a hundred fourscore and five thousand: and when they arose early in the morning, behold, they were all dead corpses. ³⁶So Sennacherib king of Assyria departed, and went and returned, and dwelt at Nineveh. ³⁷And it came to pass as he was worshipping in the house of Nisroch his god, that Adrammelech and Sharezer his sons smote him with the sword: and they escaped into the land of Armenia. And Esar-haddon his son reigned in his stead.

20 In those days was Hezekiah sick unto death. And the prophet Isaiah the son of Amoz came to him, and said unto him, 'Thus saith the LORD, "Set thy house in order: for thou shalt die, and not live"'. ²Then he turned his face to the wall, and prayed unto the LORD, saying, ³'I beseech thee, O LORD, remember now how I have walked before thee in truth and with a perfect heart, and have done that which is good in thy sight'. And Hezekiah wept sore. ⁴And it came to pass afore Isaiah was gone out into the middle court, that the word of the LORD came to him, saying, ⁵'Turn again, and tell Hezekiah the captain of my people, "Thus saith the LORD, the God of David thy father, 'I have heard thy prayer, I have seen thy tears: behold, I will heal thee: on the third day thou shalt go up unto the house of the LORD. ⁶And I will add unto thy days fifteen years, and I will deliver thee and this city out of the hand of the king of Assyria, and I will defend this city for my own sake, and for my servant David's sake.'"'

⁷And Isaiah said, 'Take a lump of figs'. And they took and laid it on the boil, and he recovered.

⁸And Hezekiah said unto Isaiah, 'What shall be the sign that the LORD will heal me, and that I shall go up into the house of the LORD the third day?' ⁹And Isaiah said, 'This sign shalt thou have of the LORD, that the LORD will do the thing that he hath spoken: shall the shadow go forward ten degrees, or go back ten degrees?' ¹⁰And Hezekiah answered, 'It is a light thing for the shadow to go down ten degrees: nay, but let the shadow return backward ten degrees'. ¹¹And Isaiah the prophet cried unto the LORD, and he brought the shadow ten degrees backward, by which it had gone down in the dial of Ahaz.

¹²At that time Berodach-baladan, the son of Baladan, king of Babylon, sent letters and a present unto Hezekiah: for he had heard that Hezekiah had been sick. ¹³And Hezekiah hearkened unto them, and showed them the house of his precious things, the silver, and the gold, and the spices, and the precious ointment, and all the house of his armour, and all that was found in his treasures: there was nothing in his house, nor in all his dominion, that Hezekiah showed them not.

¹⁴Then came Isaiah the prophet unto king Hezekiah, and said unto him, 'What said these men? and from whence came they unto thee?' And Hezekiah said, 'They are come from a far country, even from Babylon'. ¹⁵And he said, 'What have they seen in thy house?' And Hezekiah answered, 'All the things that are in my house have they seen: there is nothing among my treasures that I have not shown them'. ¹⁶And Isaiah said unto Hezekiah, 'Hear the word of the LORD. ¹⁷"Behold, the days come, that all that is in thy house, and that which thy fathers

have laid up in store unto this day, shall be carried unto Babylon: nothing shall be left," saith the LORD. [18]"And of thy sons that shall issue from thee, which thou shalt beget, shall they take away, and they shall be eunuchs in the palace of the king of Babylon."' [19]Then said Hezekiah unto Isaiah, 'Good is the word of the LORD which thou hast spoken'. And he said, 'Is it not good, if peace and truth be in my days?'

[20]And the rest of the acts of Hezekiah, and all his might, and how he made a pool and a conduit, and brought water into the city, are they not written in the book of the chronicles of the kings of Judah? [21]And Hezekiah slept with his fathers: and Manasseh his son reigned in his stead.

21 Manasseh was twelve years old when he began to reign, and reigned fifty and five years in Jerusalem. And his mother's name was Hephzi-bah. [2]And he did that which was evil in the sight of the LORD, after the abominations of the heathen, whom the LORD cast out before the children of Israel. [3]For he built up again the high places which Hezekiah his father had destroyed, and he reared up altars for Baal, and made a grove, as did Ahab king of Israel, and worshipped all the host of heaven, and served them. [4]And he built altars in the house of the LORD, of which the LORD said, 'In Jerusalem will I put my name'. [5]And he built altars for all the host of heaven in the two courts of the house of the LORD. [6]And he made his son pass through the fire, and observed times, and used enchantments, and dealt with familiar spirits and wizards: he wrought much wickedness in the sight of the LORD, to provoke him to anger. [7]And he set a graven image of the grove that he had made in the house, of which the LORD said to David, and to Solomon his son, 'In this house, and in Jerusalem, which I have chosen out of all tribes of Israel, will I put my name for ever: [8]neither will I make the feet of Israel move any more out of the land which I gave their fathers: only if they will observe to do according to all that I have commanded them, and according to all the law that my servant Moses commanded them'. [9]But they hearkened not: and Manasseh seduced them to do more evil than did the nations whom the LORD destroyed before the children of Israel.

[10]And the LORD spoke by his servants the prophets, saying, [11]'Because Manasseh king of Judah hath done these abominations, and hath done wickedly above all that the Amorites did, which were before him, and hath made Judah also to sin with his idols: [12]therefore thus saith the LORD God of Israel, "Behold, I am bringing such evil upon Jerusalem and Judah, that whosoever heareth of it, both his ears shall tingle. [13]And I will stretch over Jerusalem the line of Samaria, and the plummet of the house of Ahab: and I will wipe Jerusalem as a man wipeth a dish, wiping it, and turning it upside down. [14]And I will forsake the remnant of my inheritance, and deliver them into the hand of their enemies, and they shall become a prey and a spoil to all their enemies, [15]because they have done that which was evil in my sight, and have provoked me to anger since the day their fathers came forth out of Egypt, even unto this day."' [16]Moreover Manasseh shed innocent blood very

much, till he had filled Jerusalem from one end to another; besides his sin wherewith he made Judah to sin, in doing that which was evil in the sight of the LORD.

[17] Now the rest of the acts of Manasseh, and all that he did, and his sin that he sinned, are they not written in the book of the chronicles of the kings of Judah? [18] And Manasseh slept with his fathers, and was buried in the garden of his own house, in the garden of Uzza: and Amon his son reigned in his stead.

[19] Amon was twenty and two years old when he began to reign, and he reigned two years in Jerusalem. And his mother's name was Meshullemeth, the daughter of Haruz of Jotbah. [20] And he did that which was evil in the sight of the LORD, as his father Manasseh did. [21] And he walked in all the ways that his father walked in, and served the idols that his father served, and worshipped them: [22] and he forsook the LORD God of his fathers, and walked not in the way of the LORD.

[23] And the servants of Amon conspired against him, and slew the king in his own house. [24] And the people of the land slew all them that had conspired against king Amon, and the people of the land made Josiah his son king in his stead.

[25] Now the rest of the acts of Amon which he did, are they not written in the book of the chronicles of the kings of Judah? [26] And he was buried in his sepulchre in the garden of Uzza, and Josiah his son reigned in his stead.

22 Josiah was eight years old when he began to reign, and he reigned thirty and one years in Jerusalem. And his mother's name was Jedidah, the daughter of Adaiah of Boscath. [2] And he did that which was right in the sight of the LORD, and walked in all the ways of David his father, and turned not aside to the right hand or to the left.

[3] And it came to pass in the eighteenth year of king Josiah, that the king sent Shaphan the son of Azaliah, the son of Meshullam the scribe, to the house of the LORD, saying, [4] 'Go up to Hilkiah the high priest, that he may sum the silver which is brought into the house of the LORD, which the keepers of the door have gathered of the people. [5] And let them deliver it into the hand of the doers of the work, that have the oversight of the house of the LORD: and let them give it to the doers of the work which is in the house of the LORD, to repair the breaches of the house, [6] unto carpenters, and builders, and masons, and to buy timber and hewn stone to repair the house.' [7] Howbeit there was no reckoning made with them of the money that was delivered into their hand, because they dealt faithfully.

[8] And Hilkiah the high priest said unto Shaphan the scribe, 'I have found the book of the law in the house of the LORD'. And Hilkiah gave the book to Shaphan, and he read it. [9] And Shaphan the scribe came to the king, and brought the king word again, and said, 'Thy servants have gathered the money that was found in the house, and have delivered it into the hand of them that do the work, that have the oversight of the house of the LORD'. [10] And Shaphan the scribe showed the king, saying, 'Hilkiah the priest hath delivered me a book'. And Shaphan read it

before the king. [11]And it came to pass when the king had heard the words of the book of the law, that he rent his clothes. [12]And the king commanded Hilkiah the priest, and Ahikam the son of Shaphan, and Achbor the son of Michaiah, and Shaphan the scribe, and Asaiah a servant of the king, saying, [13]'Go ye, inquire of the LORD for me, and for the people, and for all Judah, concerning the words of this book that is found: for great is the wrath of the LORD that is kindled against us, because our fathers have not hearkened unto the words of this book, to do according unto all that which is written concerning us'.

[14]So Hilkiah the priest, and Ahikam, and Achbor, and Shaphan, and Asaiah, went unto Huldah the prophetess, the wife of Shallum the son of Tikvah, the son of Harhas, keeper of the wardrobe (now she dwelt in Jerusalem in the college), and they communed with her. [15]And she said unto them, 'Thus saith the LORD God of Israel, "Tell the man that sent you to me, [16]'Thus saith the LORD, "Behold, I will bring evil upon this place, and upon the inhabitants thereof, even all the words of the book which the king of Judah hath read. [17]Because they have forsaken me, and have burnt incense unto other gods, that they might provoke me to anger with all the works of their hands: therefore my wrath shall be kindled against this place, and shall not be quenched."' [18]But to the king of Judah which sent you to inquire of the LORD, thus shall ye say to him, 'Thus saith the LORD God of Israel, as touching the words which thou hast heard: [19]"Because thy heart was tender, and thou hast humbled thyself before the LORD, when thou heardest what I spoke against this place, and against the inhabitants thereof, that they should become a desolation and a curse, and hast rent thy clothes, and wept before me; I also have heard thee," saith the LORD. [20]"Behold therefore, I will gather thee unto thy fathers, and thou shalt be gathered into thy grave in peace, and thy eyes shall not see all the evil which I will bring upon this place."'"' And they brought the king word again.

23 And the king sent, and they gathered unto him all the elders of Judah and of Jerusalem. [2]And the king went up into the house of the LORD, and all the men of Judah and all the inhabitants of Jerusalem with him, and the priests, and the prophets, and all the people, both small and great: and he read in their ears all the words of the book of the covenant which was found in the house of the LORD.

[3]And the king stood by a pillar, and made a covenant before the LORD, to walk after the LORD, and to keep his commandments and his testimonies and his statutes with all their heart and all their soul, to perform the words of this covenant that were written in this book. And all the people stood to the covenant.

[4]And the king commanded Hilkiah the high priest, and the priests of the second order, and the keepers of the door, to bring forth out of the temple of the LORD all the vessels that were made for Baal, and for the grove, and for all the host of heaven: and he burnt them without Jerusalem in the fields of Kidron, and carried the ashes of them unto Beth-el. [5]And he put down the idolatrous priests whom the kings of Judah had ordained to burn incense in the high places in the cities of

Judah, and in the places round about Jerusalem; them also that burnt incense unto Baal, to the sun, and to the moon, and to the planets, and to all the host of heaven. ⁶And he brought out the grove from the house of the LORD, without Jerusalem, unto the brook Kidron, and burnt it at the brook Kidron, and stamped it small to powder, and cast the powder thereof upon the graves of the children of the people. ⁷And he broke down the houses of the sodomites that were by the house of the LORD, where the women wove hangings for the grove. ⁸And he brought all the priests out of the cities of Judah, and defiled the high places where the priests had burnt incense, from Geba to Beer-sheba, and broke down the high places of the gates that were in the entering in of the gate of Joshua the governor of the city, which were on a man's left hand at the gate of the city. ⁹Nevertheless the priests of the high places came not up to the altar of the LORD in Jerusalem, but they did eat of the unleavened bread among their brethren. ¹⁰And he defiled Topheth, which is in the valley of the children of Hinnom, that no man might make his son or his daughter to pass through the fire to Molech. ¹¹And he took away the horses that the kings of Judah had given to the sun, at the entering in of the house of the LORD, by the chamber of Nathan-melech the chamberlain, which was in the suburbs, and burnt the chariots of the sun with fire. ¹²And the altars that were on the top of the upper chamber of Ahaz, which the kings of Judah had made, and the altars which Manasseh had made in the two courts of the house of the LORD, did the king beat down, and broke them down from thence, and cast the dust of them into the brook Kidron. ¹³And the high places that were before Jerusalem, which were on the right hand of the mount of corruption, which Solomon the king of Israel had built for Ashtoreth the abomination of the Zidonians, and for Chemosh the abomination of the Moabites, and for Milcom the abomination of the children of Ammon, did the king defile. ¹⁴And he broke in pieces the images, and cut down the groves, and filled their places with the bones of men.

¹⁵Moreover the altar that was at Beth-el, and the high place which Jeroboam the son of Nebat, who made Israel to sin, had made, both that altar and the high place he broke down, and burnt the high place, and stamped it small to powder, and burnt the grove. ¹⁶And as Josiah turned himself, he spied the sepulchres that were there in the mount, and sent, and took the bones out of the sepulchres, and burnt them upon the altar, and polluted it, according to the word of the LORD which the man of God proclaimed, who proclaimed these words. ¹⁷Then he said, 'What title is that that I see?' And the men of the city told him, 'It is the sepulchre of the man of God, which came from Judah, and proclaimed these things that thou hast done against the altar of Beth-el'. ¹⁸And he said, 'Let him alone: let no man move his bones'. So they let his bones alone, with the bones of the prophet that came out of Samaria. ¹⁹And all the houses also of the high places that were in the cities of Samaria, which the kings of Israel had made to provoke the LORD to anger, Josiah took away, and did to them according to all the acts that he had done in Beth-el. ²⁰And he slew all the priests of the high places that were there

upon the altars, and burnt men's bones upon them, and returned to Jerusalem.

[21] And the king commanded all the people, saying, 'Keep the passover unto the Lord your God, as it is written in this book of the covenant'. [22] Surely there was not held such a passover from the days of the judges that judged Israel, nor in all the days of the kings of Israel, nor of the kings of Judah: [23] but in the eighteenth year of king Josiah, wherein this passover was held to the Lord in Jerusalem.

[24] Moreover the workers with familiar spirits, and the wizards, and the images, and the idols, and all the abominations that were spied in the land of Judah and in Jerusalem, did Josiah put away, that he might perform the words of the law, which were written in the book that Hilkiah the priest found in the house of the Lord. [25] And like unto him was there no king before him, that turned to the Lord with all his heart, and with all his soul, and with all his might, according to all the law of Moses; neither after him arose there any like him.

[26] Notwithstanding the Lord turned not from the fierceness of his great wrath, wherewith his anger was kindled against Judah, because of all the provocations that Manasseh had provoked him withal. [27] And the Lord said, 'I will remove Judah also out of my sight, as I have removed Israel, and will cast off this city Jerusalem which I have chosen, and the house of which I said, "My name shall be there"'.

[28] Now the rest of the acts of Josiah, and all that he did, are they not written in the book of the chronicles of the kings of Judah?

[29] In his days Pharaoh-nechoh king of Egypt went up against the king of Assyria to the river Euphrates: and king Josiah went against him, and he slew him at Megiddo, when he had seen him. [30] And his servants carried him in a chariot dead from Megiddo, and brought him to Jerusalem, and buried him in his own sepulchre. And the people of the land took Jehoahaz the son of Josiah, and anointed him, and made him king in his father's stead.

[31] Jehoahaz was twenty and three years old when he began to reign, and he reigned three months in Jerusalem. And his mother's name was Hamutal, the daughter of Jeremiah of Libnah. [32] And he did that which was evil in the sight of the Lord, according to all that his fathers had done. [33] And Pharaoh-nechoh put him in bands at Riblah in the land of Hamath, that he might not reign in Jerusalem, and put the land to a tribute of a hundred talents of silver, and a talent of gold. [34] And Pharaoh-nechoh made Eliakim the son of Josiah king in the room of Josiah his father, and turned his name to Jehoiakim, and took Jehoahaz away: and he came to Egypt, and died there. [35] And Jehoiakim gave the silver and the gold to Pharaoh, but he taxed the land to give the money according to the commandment of Pharaoh: he exacted the silver and the gold of the people of the land, of every one according to his taxation, to give it unto Pharaoh-nechoh.

[36] Jehoiakim was twenty and five years old when he began to reign, and he reigned eleven years in Jerusalem. And his mother's name was Zebudah, the daughter of Pedaiah of Rumah. [37] And he did that which

was evil in the sight of the LORD, according to all that his fathers had done.

24 In his days Nebuchadnezzar king of Babylon came up, and Jehoiakim became his servant three years: then he turned and rebelled against him. ²And the LORD sent against him bands of the Chaldees, and bands of the Syrians, and bands of the Moabites, and bands of the children of Ammon, and sent them against Judah to destroy it, according to the word of the LORD, which he spoke by his servants the prophets. ³Surely at the commandment of the LORD came this upon Judah, to remove them out of his sight, for the sins of Manasseh, according to all that he did; ⁴and also for the innocent blood that he shed: for he filled Jerusalem with innocent blood; which the LORD would not pardon.

⁵Now the rest of the acts of Jehoiakim, and all that he did, are they not written in the book of the chronicles of the kings of Judah? ⁶So Jehoiakim slept with his fathers: and Jehoiachin his son reigned in his stead. ⁷And the king of Egypt came not again any more out of his land: for the king of Babylon had taken from the river of Egypt unto the river Euphrates all that pertained to the king of Egypt.

⁸Jehoiachin was eighteen years old when he began to reign, and he reigned in Jerusalem three months. And his mother's name was Nehushta, the daughter of Elnathan of Jerusalem. ⁹And he did that which was evil in the sight of the LORD, according to all that his father had done.

¹⁰At that time the servants of Nebuchadnezzar king of Babylon came up against Jerusalem, and the city was besieged. ¹¹And Nebuchadnezzar king of Babylon came against the city, and his servants did besiege it. ¹²And Jehoiachin the king of Judah went out to the king of Babylon, he, and his mother, and his servants, and his princes, and his officers: and the king of Babylon took him in the eighth year of his reign. ¹³And he carried out thence all the treasures of the house of the LORD, and the treasure of the king's house, and cut in pieces all the vessels of gold which Solomon king of Israel had made in the temple of the LORD, as the LORD had said. ¹⁴And he carried away all Jerusalem, and all the princes, and all the mighty men of valour, even ten thousand captives, and all the craftsmen and smiths: none remained, save the poorest sort of the people of the land. ¹⁵And he carried away Jehoiachin to Babylon, and the king's mother, and the king's wives, and his officers, and the mighty of the land, those carried he into captivity from Jerusalem to Babylon. ¹⁶And all the men of might, even seven thousand, and craftsmen and smiths a thousand, all that were strong and apt for war, even them the king of Babylon brought captive to Babylon.

¹⁷And the king of Babylon made Mattaniah his father's brother king in his stead, and changed his name to Zedekiah. ¹⁸Zedekiah was twenty and one years old when he began to reign, and he reigned eleven years in Jerusalem. And his mother's name was Hamutal, the daughter of Jeremiah of Libnah. ¹⁹And he did that which was evil in the sight of the LORD, according to all that Jehoiakim had done. ²⁰For through the

anger of the LORD it came to pass in Jerusalem and Judah, until he had cast them out from his presence, that Zedekiah rebelled against the king of Babylon.

25 And it came to pass in the ninth year of his reign, in the tenth month, in the tenth day of the month, that Nebuchadnezzar king of Babylon came, he, and all his host, against Jerusalem, and pitched against it, and they built forts against it round about. ²And the city was besieged unto the eleventh year of king Zedekiah. ³And on the ninth day of the fourth month the famine prevailed in the city, and there was no bread for the people of the land.

⁴And the city was broken up, and all the men of war fled by night by the way of the gate between two walls, which is by the king's garden (now the Chaldees were against the city round about), and the king went the way toward the plain. ⁵And the army of the Chaldees pursued after the king, and overtook him in the plains of Jericho: and all his army were scattered from him. ⁶So they took the king, and brought him up to the king of Babylon to Riblah, and they gave judgement upon him. ⁷And they slew the sons of Zedekiah before his eyes, and put out the eyes of Zedekiah, and bound him with fetters of brass, and carried him to Babylon.

⁸And in the fifth month, on the seventh day of the month (which is the nineteenth year of king Nebuchadnezzar king of Babylon), came Nebuzar-adan, captain of the guard, a servant of the king of Babylon, unto Jerusalem: ⁹and he burnt the house of the LORD, and the king's house, and all the houses of Jerusalem, and every great man's house burnt he with fire. ¹⁰And all the army of the Chaldees that were with the captain of the guard, broke down the walls of Jerusalem round about. ¹¹Now the rest of the people that were left in the city, and the fugitives that fell away to the king of Babylon, with the remnant of the multitude, did Nebuzar-adan the captain of the guard carry away. ¹²But the captain of the guard left of the poor of the land to be vine-dressers and husbandmen.

¹³And the pillars of brass that were in the house of the LORD, and the bases, and the brazen sea that was in the house of the LORD, did the Chaldees break in pieces, and carried the brass of them to Babylon. ¹⁴And the pots, and the shovels, and the snuffers, and the spoons, and all the vessels of brass wherewith they ministered, took they away. ¹⁵And the fire-pans, and the bowls, and such things as were of gold, in gold, and of silver, in silver, the captain of the guard took away. ¹⁶The two pillars, one sea, and the bases which Solomon had made for the house of the LORD; the brass of all these vessels was without weight. ¹⁷The height of the one pillar was eighteen cubits, and the chapiter upon it was brass: and the height of the chapiter three cubits; and the wreathen work, and pomegranates upon the chapiter round about, all of brass: and like unto these had the second pillar with wreathen work.

¹⁸And the captain of the guard took Seraiah the chief priest, and Zephaniah the second priest, and the three keepers of the door. ¹⁹And out of the city he took an officer that was set over the men of war, and

five men of them that were in the king's presence, which were found in the city, and the principal scribe of the host, which mustered the people of the land, and threescore men of the people of the land that were found in the city. ²⁰And Nebuzar-adan captain of the guard took these, and brought them to the king of Babylon to Riblah. ²¹And the king of Babylon smote them, and slew them at Riblah in the land of Hamath. So Judah was carried away out of their land.

²²And as for the people that remained in the land of Judah, whom Nebuchadnezzar king of Babylon had left, even over them he made Gedaliah the son of Ahikam, the son of Shaphan, ruler. ²³And when all the captains of the armies, they and their men, heard that the king of Babylon had made Gedaliah governor, there came to Gedaliah to Mizpah, even Ishmael the son of Nethaniah, and Johanan the son of Careah, and Seraiah the son of Tanhumeth the Netophathite, and Jaazaniah the son of a Maachathite, they and their men. ²⁴And Gedaliah swore to them, and to their men, and said unto them, 'Fear not to be the servants of the Chaldees: dwell in the land, and serve the king of Babylon; and it shall be well with you'. ²⁵But it came to pass in the seventh month, that Ishmael the son of Nethaniah, the son of Elishama, of the seed royal, came, and ten men with him, and smote Gedaliah, that he died, and the Jews and the Chaldees that were with him at Mizpah. ²⁶And all the people both small and great, and the captains of the armies arose, and came to Egypt: for they were afraid of the Chaldees.

²⁷And it came to pass in the seven and thirtieth year of the captivity of Jehoiachin king of Judah, in the twelfth month, on the seven and twentieth day of the month, that Evil-merodach king of Babylon in the year that he began to reign did lift up the head of Jehoiachin king of Judah out of prison. ²⁸And he spoke kindly to him, and set his throne above the throne of the kings that were with him in Babylon, ²⁹and changed his prison garments: and he did eat bread continually before him all the days of his life. ³⁰And his allowance was a continual allowance given him of the king, a daily rate for every day, all the days of his life.

THE FIRST BOOK OF THE
CHRONICLES

1 Adam, Sheth, Enosh, ²Kenan, Mahalaleel, Jered, ³Henoch, Methuselah, Lamech, ⁴Noah, Shem, Ham, and Japheth.

⁵The sons of Japheth: Gomer, and Magog, and Madai, and Javan, and Tubal, and Meshech, and Tiras. ⁶And the sons of Gomer: Ashchenaz, and Riphath, and Togarmah. ⁷And the sons of Javan: Elishah, and Tarshish, Kittim, and Dodanim.

⁸The sons of Ham: Cush, and Mizraim, Put, and Canaan. ⁹And the sons of Cush: Seba, and Havilah, and Sabta, and Raamah, and Sabtecha. And the sons of Raamah: Sheba, and Dedan. ¹⁰And Cush begot Nimrod: he began to be mighty upon the earth. ¹¹And Mizraim begot Ludim, and Anamim, and Lehabim, and Naphtuhim, ¹²and Pathrusim, and Casluhim (of whom came the Philistines), and Caphthorim. ¹³And Canaan begot Zidon his firstborn, and Heth, ¹⁴the Jebusite also, and the Amorite, and the Girgashite, ¹⁵and the Hivite, and the Arkite, and the Sinite, ¹⁶and the Arvadite, and the Zemarite, and the Hamathite.

¹⁷The sons of Shem: Elam, and Asshur, and Arphaxad, and Lud, and Aram, and Uz, and Hul, and Gether, and Meshech. ¹⁸And Arphaxad begot Shelah, and Shelah begot Eber. ¹⁹And unto Eber were born two sons: the name of the one was Peleg (because in his days the earth was divided), and his brother's name was Joktan. ²⁰And Joktan begot Almodad, and Sheleph, and Hazarmaveth, and Jerah, ²¹Hadoram also, and Uzal, and Diklah, ²²and Ebal, and Abimael, and Sheba, ²³and Ophir, and Havilah, and Jobab. All these were the sons of Joktan.

²⁴Shem, Arphaxad, Shelah, ²⁵Eber, Peleg, Reu, ²⁶Serug, Nahor, Terah, ²⁷Abram; the same is Abraham. ²⁸The sons of Abraham: Isaac, and Ishmael.

²⁹These are their generations: the firstborn of Ishmael, Nebaioth, then Kedar, and Adbeel, and Mibsam, ³⁰Mishma, and Dumah, Massa, Hadad, and Tema, ³¹Jetur, Naphish, and Kedemah. These are the sons of Ishmael.

³²Now the sons of Keturah, Abraham's concubine: she bore Zimran, and Jokshan, and Medan, and Midian, and Ishbak, and Shuah. And the sons of Jokshan: Sheba, and Dedan. ³³And the sons of Midian: Ephah, and Epher, and Henoch, and Abida, and Eldaah. All these are the sons of Keturah. ³⁴And Abraham begot Isaac. The sons of Isaac: Esau and Israel.

³⁵The sons of Esau: Eliphaz, Reuel, and Jeush, and Jaalam, and Korah. ³⁶The sons of Eliphaz: Teman, and Omar, Zephi, and Gatam, Kenaz, and Timna, and Amalek. ³⁷The sons of Reuel: Nahath, Zerah, Shammah, and Mizzah. ³⁸And the sons of Seir: Lotan, and Shobal, and Zibeon, and Anah, and Dishon, and Ezer, and Dishan. ³⁹And the sons of Lotan: Hori, and Homam: and Timna was Lotan's sister. ⁴⁰The sons of Shobal: Alian, and Manahath, and Ebal, Shephi, and Onam. And the sons of Zibeon:

Aiah, and Anah. ⁴¹The sons of Anah: Dishon. And the sons of Dishon: Amram, and Eshban, and Ithran, and Cheran. ⁴²The sons of Ezer: Bilhan, and Zavan, and Jakan. The sons of Dishan: Uz, and Aran.

⁴³Now these are the kings that reigned in the land of Edom before any king reigned over the children of Israel. Bela the son of Beor; and the name of his city was Dinhabah. ⁴⁴And when Bela was dead, Jobab the son of Zerah of Bozrah reigned in his stead. ⁴⁵And when Jobab was dead, Husham of the land of the Temanites reigned in his stead. ⁴⁶And when Husham was dead, Hadad the son of Bedad (which smote Midian in the field of Moab), reigned in his stead: and the name of his city was Avith. ⁴⁷And when Hadad was dead, Samlah of Masrekah reigned in his stead. ⁴⁸And when Samlah was dead, Shaul of Rehoboth by the river reigned in his stead. ⁴⁹And when Shaul was dead, Baal-hanan the son of Achbor reigned in his stead. ⁵⁰And when Baal-hanan was dead, Hadad reigned in his stead: and the name of his city was Pai: and his wife's name was Mehetabel, the daughter of Matred, the daughter of Mezahab.

⁵¹Hadad died also. And the dukes of Edom were: duke Timnah, duke Aliah, duke Jetheth, ⁵²duke Aholibamah, duke Elah, duke Pinon, ⁵³duke Kenaz, duke Teman, duke Mibzar, ⁵⁴duke Magdiel, duke Iram. These are the dukes of Edom.

2 These are the sons of Israel: Reuben, Simeon, Levi, and Judah, Issachar, and Zebulun, ²Dan, Joseph, and Benjamin, Naphtali, Gad, and Asher.

³The sons of Judah: Er, and Onan, and Shelah. Which three were born unto him of the daughter of Shua the Canaanitess. And Er, the first-born of Judah, was evil in the sight of the LORD, and he slew him. ⁴And Tamar his daughter-in-law bore him Pharez and Zerah. All the sons of Judah were five. ⁵The sons of Pharez: Hezron, and Hamul. ⁶And the sons of Zerah: Zimri, and Ethan, and Heman, and Calcol, and Dara. Five of them in all. ⁷And the sons of Carmi: Achar, the troubler of Israel, who transgressed in the thing accursed. ⁸And the sons of Ethan: Azariah. ⁹The sons also of Hezron, that were born unto him: Jerahmeel, and Ram, and Chelubai. ¹⁰And Ram begot Amminadab, and Amminadab begot Nahshon, prince of the children of Judah. ¹¹And Nahshon begot Salma, and Salma begot Boaz. ¹²And Boaz begot Obed, and Obed begot Jesse.

¹³And Jesse begot his firstborn Eliab, and Abinadab the second, and Shimma the third, ¹⁴Nethaneel the fourth, Raddai the fifth, ¹⁵Ozem the sixth, David the seventh: ¹⁶whose sisters were Zeruiah, and Abigail. And the sons of Zeruiah: Abishai, and Joab, and Asahel, three. ¹⁷And Abigail bore Amasa. And the father of Amasa was Jether the Ishmeelite.

¹⁸And Caleb the son of Hezron begot children of Azubah his wife, and of Jerioth: her sons are these: Jesher, Shobab, and Ardon. ¹⁹And when Azubah was dead, Caleb took unto him Ephrath, which bore him Hur. ²⁰And Hur begot Uri, and Uri begot Bezaleel.

²¹And afterward Hezron went in to the daughter of Machir the father of Gilead, whom he married when he was threescore years old; and she bore him Segub. ²²And Segub begot Jair, who had three and twenty

cities in the land of Gilead. ²³And he took Geshur, and Aram, with the towns of Jair, from them, with Kenath, and the towns thereof, even threescore cities. All these belonged to the sons of Machir the father of Gilead. ²⁴And after that Hezron was dead in Caleb-ephratah, then Abiah Hezron's wife bore him Ashur the father of Tekoa.

²⁵And the sons of Jerahmeel the firstborn of Hezron were Ram the firstborn, and Bunah, and Oren, and Ozem, and Ahijah. ²⁶Jerahmeel had also another wife, whose name was Atarah; she was the mother of Onam. ²⁷And the sons of Ram the firstborn of Jerahmeel were Maaz, and Jamin, and Eker. ²⁸And the sons of Onam were Shammai, and Jada. And the sons of Shammai: Nadab, and Abishur. ²⁹And the name of the wife of Abishur was Abihail, and she bore him Ahban, and Molid. ³⁰And the sons of Nadab: Seled, and Appaim. But Seled died without children. ³¹And the sons of Appaim, Ishi. And the sons of Ishi, Sheshan. And the children of Sheshan, Ahlai. ³²And the sons of Jada the brother of Shammai, Jether, and Jonathan: and Jether died without children. ³³And the sons of Jonathan, Peleth, and Zaza. These were the sons of Jerahmeel.

³⁴Now Sheshan had no sons, but daughters. And Sheshan had a servant, an Egyptian, whose name was Jarha. ³⁵And Sheshan gave his daughter to Jarha his servant to wife, and she bore him Attai. ³⁶And Attai begot Nathan, and Nathan begot Zabad, ³⁷and Zabad begot Ephlal, and Ephlal begot Obed, ³⁸and Obed begot Jehu, and Jehu begot Azariah, ³⁹and Azariah begot Helez, and Helez begot Eleasah, ⁴⁰and Eleasah begot Sisamai, and Sisamai begot Shallum, ⁴¹and Shallum begot Jekamiah, and Jekamiah begot Elishama.

⁴²Now the sons of Caleb the brother of Jerahmeel were, Mesha his firstborn, which was the father of Ziph: and the sons of Mareshah the father of Hebron. ⁴³And the sons of Hebron: Korah, and Tappuah, and Rekem, and Shema. ⁴⁴And Shema begot Raham, the father of Jorkoam: and Rekem begot Shammai. ⁴⁵And the son of Shammai was Maon: and Maon was the father of Beth-zur. ⁴⁶And Ephah Caleb's concubine bore Haran, and Moza, and Gazez: and Haran begot Gazez. ⁴⁷And the sons of Jahdai: Regem, and Jotham, and Geshan, and Pelet, and Ephah, and Shaaph. ⁴⁸Maachah, Caleb's concubine, bore Sheber, and Tirhanah. ⁴⁹She bore also Shaaph the father of Madmannah, Sheva the father of Machbenah, and the father of Gibea: and the daughter of Caleb was Achsah.

⁵⁰These were the sons of Caleb the son of Hur, the firstborn of Ephratah: Shobal the father of Kirjath-jearim, ⁵¹Salma the father of Beth-lehem, Hareph the father of Beth-gader. ⁵²And Shobal the father of Kirjath-jearim had sons, Haroeh, and half of the Manahethites. ⁵³And the families of Kirjath-jearim, the Ithrites, and the Puhites, and the Shumathites, and the Mishraites: of them came the Zareathites, and the Eshtaulites. ⁵⁴The sons of Salma: Beth-lehem, and the Netophathites, Ataroth, the house of Joab, and half of the Manahethites, the Zorites. ⁵⁵And the families of the scribes which dwelt at Jabez: the Tirathites, the Shimeathites, and Suchathites. These are the Kenites that came of Hamath, the father of the house of Rechab.

3 Now these were the sons of David, which were born unto him in Hebron: the firstborn Amnon, of Ahinoam the Jezreelitess: the second Daniel, of Abigail the Carmelitess: ²the third, Absalom the son of Maachah the daughter of Talmai king of Geshur: the fourth, Adonijah the son of Haggith: ³the fifth, Shephatiah of Abital: the sixth, Ithream by Eglah his wife. ⁴These six were born unto him in Hebron, and there he reigned seven years and six months: and in Jerusalem he reigned thirty and three years. ⁵And these were born unto him in Jerusalem. Shimea, and Shobab, and Nathan, and Solomon, four, of Bath-shua the daughter of Ammiel. ⁶Ibhar also, and Elishama, and Eliphelet, ⁷and Nogah, and Nepheg, and Japhia, ⁸and Elishama, and Eliada, and Eliphelet, nine. ⁹These were all the sons of David, besides the sons of the concubines, and Tamar their sister.

¹⁰And Solomon's son was Rehoboam: Abiah his son: Asa his son: Jehoshaphat his son: ¹¹Joram his son: Ahaziah his son: Joash his son: ¹²Amaziah his son: Azariah his son: Jotham his son: ¹³Ahaz his son: Hezekiah his son: Manasseh his son: ¹⁴Amon his son: Josiah his son. ¹⁵And the sons of Josiah were: the firstborn Johanan, the second Jehoiakim, the third Zedekiah, the fourth Shallum. ¹⁶And the sons of Jehoiakim: Jeconiah his son, Zedekiah his son.

¹⁷And the sons of Jeconiah, Assir, Salathiel his son, ¹⁸Malchiram also, and Pedaiah, and Shenazar, Jecamiah, Hoshama, and Nedabiah. ¹⁹And the sons of Pedaiah were: Zerubbabel, and Shimei: and the son of Zerubbabel, Meshullam, and Hananiah, and Shelomith their sister. ²⁰And Hashubah, and Ohel, and Berechiah, and Hasadiah, Jushab-hesed, five. ²¹And the sons of Hananiah, Pelatiah, and Jesaiah: the sons of Rephaiah, the sons of Arnan, the sons of Obadiah, the sons of Shechaniah. ²²And the sons of Shechaniah, Shemaiah: and the sons of Shemaiah, Hattush, and Igeal, and Bariah, and Neariah, and Shaphat, six. ²³And the sons of Neariah: Elioenai, and Hezekiah, and Azrikam, three. ²⁴And the sons of Elioenai were: Hodaiah, and Eliashib, and Pelaiah, and Akkub, and Johanan, and Dalaiah, and Anani, seven.

4 The sons of Judah: Pharez, Hezron, and Carmi, and Hur, and Shobal. ²And Reaiah the son of Shobal begot Jahath, and Jahath begot Ahumai, and Lahad. These are the families of the Zorathites. ³And these were of the father of Etam: Jezreel, and Ishma, and Idbash: and the name of their sister was Hazelelponi: ⁴and Penuel the father of Gedor, and Ezer the father of Hushah. These are the sons of Hur, the firstborn of Ephratah, the father of Beth-lehem.

⁵And Ashur the father of Tekoa had two wives, Helah and Naarah. ⁶And Naarah bore him Ahuzam, and Hepher, and Temeni, and Haahashtari. These were the sons of Naarah. ⁷And the sons of Helah were Zereth, and Zohar, and Ethnan. ⁸And Coz begot Anub, and Zobebah, and the families of Aharhel the son of Harum.

⁹And Jabez was more honourable than his brethren: and his mother called his name Jabez, saying, 'Because I bore him with sorrow'. ¹⁰And Jabez called on the God of Israel, saying, 'O that thou wouldst bless me indeed, and enlarge my coast, and that thy hand might be with me,

and that thou wouldst keep me from evil, that it may not grieve me'. And God granted him that which he requested.

[11]And Chelub the brother of Shuah begot Mehir, which was the father of Eshton. [12]And Eshton begot Beth-rapha, and Paseah, and Tehinnah the father of Ir-nahash. These are the men of Rechah. [13]And the sons of Kenaz: Othniel, and Seraiah: and the sons of Othniel, Hathath. [14]And Meonothai begot Ophrah: and Seraiah begot Joab, the father of the valley of Charashim, for they were craftsmen. [15]And the sons of Caleb the son of Jephunneh: Iru, Elah, and Naam: and the sons of Elah, even Kenaz. [16]And the sons of Jehaleleel: Ziph, and Ziphah, Tiria, and Asareel. [17]And the sons of Ezra were: Jether, and Mered, and Epher, and Jalon: and she bore Miriam, and Shammai, and Ishbah the father of Eshtemoa. [18]And his wife Jehudijah bore Jered the father of Gedor, and Heber the father of Socho, and Jekuthiel the father of Zanoah. And these are the sons of Bithiah the daughter of Pharaoh, which Mered took. [19]And the sons of his wife Hodijah the sister of Naham, the father of Keilah the Garmite, and Eshtemoa the Maachathite. [20]And the sons of Shimon were: Amnon, and Rinnah, Ben-hanan, and Tilon. And the sons of Ishi were: Zoheth, and Ben-zoheth.

[21]The sons of Shelah the son of Judah were: Er the father of Lecah, and Laadah the father of Mareshah, and the families of the house of them that wrought fine linen, of the house of Ashbea, [22]and Jokim, and the men of Chozeba, and Joash, and Saraph, who had the dominion in Moab, and Jashubi-lehem. And these are ancient things. [23]These were the potters, and those that dwelt amongst plants and hedges. There they dwelt with the king for his work.

[24]The sons of Simeon were: Nemuel, and Jamin, Jarib, Zerah, and Shaul: [25]Shallum his son, Mibsam his son, Mishma his son. [26]And the sons of Mishma: Hamuel his son, Zacchur his son, Shimei his son. [27]And Shimei had sixteen sons and six daughters, but his brethren had not many children, neither did all their family multiply like to the children of Judah. [28]And they dwelt at Beer-sheba, and Moladah, and Hazar-shual, [29]and at Bilhah, and at Ezem, and at Tolad, [30]and at Bethuel, and at Hormah, and at Ziklag, [31]and at Beth-marcaboth, and Hazar-susim, and at Beth-birei, and at Shaaraim. These were their cities unto the reign of David. [32]And their villages were: Etam, and Ain, Rimmon, and Tochen, and Ashan, five cities: [33]and all their villages that were round about the same cities, unto Baal. These were their habitations, and their genealogy.

[34]And Meshobab, and Jamlech, and Joshah the son of Amaziah, [35]and Joel, and Jehu the son of Josibiah, the son of Seraiah, the son of Asiel, [36]and Elioenai, and Jaakobah, and Jeshohaiah, and Asaiah, and Adiel, and Jesimiel, and Benaiah, [37]and Ziza the son of Shiphi, the son of Allon, the son of Jedaiah, the son of Shimri, the son of Shemaiah. [38]These mentioned by their names were princes in their families, and the house of their fathers increased greatly.

[39]And they went to the entrance of Gedor, even unto the east side of the valley, to seek pasture for their flocks. [40]And they found fat pasture

and good, and the land was wide, and quiet, and peaceable: for they of Ham had dwelt there of old. ⁴¹And these written by name came in the days of Hezekiah king of Judah, and smote their tents, and the habitations that were found there, and destroyed them utterly unto this day, and dwelt in their rooms: because there was pasture there for their flocks. ⁴²And some of them, even of the sons of Simeon, five hundred men, went to mount Seir, having for their captains Pelatiah, and Neariah, and Rephaiah, and Uzziel, the sons of Ishi. ⁴³And they smote the rest of the Amalekites that were escaped, and dwelt there unto this day.

5 Now the sons of Reuben the firstborn of Israel (for he was the firstborn, but, forasmuch as he defiled his father's bed, his birthright was given unto the sons of Joseph the son of Israel: and the genealogy is not to be reckoned after the birthright. ²For Judah prevailed above his brethren, and of him came the chief ruler, but the birthright was Joseph's); ³the sons, I say, of Reuben the firstborn of Israel were: Hanoch, and Pallu, Hezron, and Carmi. ⁴The sons of Joel: Shemaiah his son, Gog his son, Shimei his son, ⁵Micah his son, Reaiah his son, Baal his son, ⁶Beerah his son, whom Tilgath-pilneser king of Assyria carried away captive: he was prince of the Reubenites. ⁷And his brethren by their families, when the genealogy of their generations was reckoned, were the chief, Jeiel, and Zechariah, ⁸and Bela the son of Azaz, the son of Shema, the son of Joel, who dwelt in Aroer, even unto Nebo and Baal-meon: ⁹and eastward he inhabited unto the entering in of the wilderness from the river Euphrates: because their cattle were multiplied in the land of Gilead. ¹⁰And in the days of Saul they made war with the Hagarites, who fell by their hand: and they dwelt in their tents throughout all the east land of Gilead.

¹¹And the children of Gad dwelt over against them, in the land of Bashan unto Salchah: ¹²Joel the chief, and Shapham the next, and Jaanai, and Shaphat in Bashan. ¹³And their brethren of the house of their fathers were: Michael, and Meshullam, and Sheba, and Jorai, and Jachan, and Zia, and Heber, seven. ¹⁴These are the children of Abihail the son of Huri, the son of Jaroah, the son of Gilead, the son of Michael, the son of Jeshishai, the son of Jahdo, the son of Buz: ¹⁵Ahi the son of Abdiel, the son of Guni, chief of the house of their fathers. ¹⁶And they dwelt in Gilead in Bashan, and in her towns, and in all the suburbs of Sharon, upon their borders. ¹⁷All these were reckoned by genealogies in the days of Jotham king of Judah, and in the days of Jeroboam king of Israel.

¹⁸The sons of Reuben, and the Gadites, and half the tribe of Manasseh, of valiant men, men able to bear buckler and sword, and to shoot with bow, and skilful in war, were four and forty thousand seven hundred and threescore, that went out to the war. ¹⁹And they made war with the Hagarites, with Jetur, and Nephish, and Nodab. ²⁰And they were helped against them, and the Hagarites were delivered into their hand, and all that were with them, for they cried to God in the battle, and he was entreated of them, because they put their trust in him. ²¹And they took

away their cattle: of their camels fifty thousand, and of sheep two hundred and fifty thousand, and of asses two thousand, and of men a hundred thousand. ²²For there fell down many slain, because the war was of God. And they dwelt in their steads until the captivity.

²³And the children of the half tribe of Manasseh dwelt in the land: they increased from Bashan unto Baal-hermon and Senir, and unto mount Hermon. ²⁴And these were the heads of the house of their fathers, even Epher, and Ishi, and Eliel, and Azriel, and Jeremiah, and Hodaviah, and Jahdiel, mighty men of valour, famous men, and heads of the house of their fathers.

²⁵And they transgressed against the God of their fathers, and went a-whoring after the gods of the people of the land, whom God destroyed before them. ²⁶And the God of Israel stirred up the spirit of Pul king of Assyria, and the spirit of Tilgath-pilneser king of Assyria, and he carried them away, even the Reubenites, and the Gadites, and the half tribe of Manasseh, and brought them unto Halah, and Habor, and Hara, and to the river Gozan, unto this day.

6 The sons of Levi: Gershon, Kohath, and Merari. ²And the sons of Kohath: Amram, Izhar, and Hebron, and Uzziel. ³And the children of Amram: Aaron, and Moses, and Miriam. The sons also of Aaron: Nadab, and Abihu, Eleazar, and Ithamar.

⁴Eleazar begot Phinehas, Phinehas begot Abishua, ⁵and Abishua begot Bukki, and Bukki begot Uzzi ⁶and Uzzi begot Zerahiah, and Zerahiah begot Meraioth, ⁷Meraioth begot Amariah, and Amariah begot Ahitub, ⁸and Ahitub begot Zadok, and Zadok begot Ahimaaz, ⁹and Ahimaaz begot Azariah, and Azariah begot Johanan, ¹⁰and Johanan begot Azariah (he it is that executed the priest's office in the temple that Solomon built in Jerusalem), ¹¹and Azariah begot Amariah, and Amariah begot Ahitub, ¹²and Ahitub begot Zadok, and Zadok begot Shallum, ¹³and Shallum begot Hilkiah, and Hilkiah begot Azariah, ¹⁴and Azariah begot Seraiah, and Seraiah begot Jehozadak, ¹⁵and Jehozadak went into captivity, when the Lord carried away Judah and Jerusalem by the hand of Nebuchadnezzar.

¹⁶The sons of Levi: Gershom, Kohath, and Merari. ¹⁷And these be the names of the sons of Gershom: Libni, and Shimei. ¹⁸And the sons of Kohath were: Amram, and Izhar, and Hebron, and Uzziel. ¹⁹The sons of Merari: Mahli, and Mushi. And these are the families of the Levites according to their fathers. ²⁰Of Gershom: Libni his son, Jahath his son, Zimmah his son, ²¹Joah his son, Iddo his son, Zerah his son, Jeaterai his son. ²²The sons of Kohath: Amminadab his son, Korah his son, Assir his son, ²³Elkanah his son, and Ebiasaph his son, and Assir his son, ²⁴Tahath his son, Uriel his son, Uzziah his son, and Shaul his son. ²⁵And the sons of Elkanah: Amasai, and Ahimoth. ²⁶As for Elkanah: the sons of Elkanah, Zophai his son, and Nahath his son, ²⁷Eliab his son, Jeroham his son, Elkanah his son. ²⁸And the sons of Samuel: the firstborn Vashni, and Abiah. ²⁹The sons of Merari: Mahli, Libni his son, Shimei his son, Uzzah his son, ³⁰Shimea his son, Haggiah his son, Asaiah his son.

³¹And these are they whom David set over the service of song in the

house of the Lord, after that the ark had rest. ³²And they ministered before the dwelling place of the tabernacle of the congregation with singing, until Solomon had built the house of the Lord in Jerusalem: and then they waited on their office according to their order. ³³And these are they that waited with their children. Of the sons of the Kohathites: Heman a singer, the son of Joel, the son of Shemuel, ³⁴the son of Elkanah, the son of Jeroham, the son of Eliel, the son of Toah, ³⁵the son of Zuph, the son of Elkanah, the son of Mahath, the son of Amasai, ³⁶the son of Elkanah, the son of Joel, the son of Azariah, the son of Zephaniah, ³⁷the son of Tahath, the son of Assir, the son of Ebiasaph, the son of Korah, ³⁸the son of Izhar, the son of Kohath, the son of Levi, the son of Israel. ³⁹And his brother Asaph, who stood on his right hand, even Asaph the son of Berechiah, the son of Shimea, ⁴⁰the son of Michael, the son of Baaseiah, the son of Malchiah, ⁴¹the son of Ethni, the son of Zerah, the son of Adaiah, ⁴²the son of Ethan, the son of Zimmah, the son of Shimei, ⁴³the son of Jahath, the son of Gershom, the son of Levi. ⁴⁴And their brethren the sons of Merari stood on the left hand: Ethan the son of Kishi, the son of Abdi, the son of Malluch, ⁴⁵the son of Hashabiah, the son of Amaziah, the son of Hilkiah, ⁴⁶the son of Amzi, the son of Bani, the son of Shamer, ⁴⁷the son of Mahli, the son of Mushi, the son of Merari, the son of Levi. ⁴⁸Their brethren also the Levites were appointed unto all manner of service of the tabernacle of the house of God.

⁴⁹But Aaron and his sons offered upon the altar of the burnt offering, and on the altar of incense, and were appointed for all the work of the place most holy, and to make an atonement for Israel, according to all that Moses the servant of God had commanded. ⁵⁰And these are the sons of Aaron: Eleazar his son, Phinehas his son, Abishua his son, ⁵¹Bukki his son, Uzzi his son, Zerahiah his son, ⁵²Meraioth his son, Amariah his son, Ahitub his son, ⁵³Zadok his son, Ahimaaz his son.

⁵⁴Now these are their dwelling places throughout their castles in their coasts, of the sons of Aaron: of the families of the Kohathites: for theirs was the lot. ⁵⁵And they gave them Hebron in the land of Judah, and the suburbs thereof round about it. ⁵⁶But the fields of the city, and the villages thereof, they gave to Caleb the son of Jephunneh. ⁵⁷And to the sons of Aaron they gave the cities of Judah, namely, Hebron, the city of refuge, and Libnah with her suburbs, and Jattir, and Eshtemoa, with their suburbs, ⁵⁸and Hilen with her suburbs, Debir with her suburbs, ⁵⁹and Ashan with her suburbs, and Beth-shemesh with her suburbs: ⁶⁰and out of the tribe of Benjamin, Geba with her suburbs, and Alemeth with her suburbs, Anathoth with her suburbs. All their cities throughout their families were thirteen cities.

⁶¹And unto the sons of Kohath, which were left of the family of that tribe, were cities given out of the half tribe, namely, out of the half tribe of Manasseh, by lot, ten cities. ⁶²And to the sons of Gershom throughout their families out of the tribe of Issachar, and out of the tribe of Asher, and out of the tribe of Naphtali, and out of the tribe of Manasseh in Bashan, thirteen cities. ⁶³Unto the sons of Merari were

given by lot, throughout their families, out of the tribe of Reuben, and out of the tribe of Gad, and out of the tribe of Zebulun, twelve cities. ⁶⁴And the children of Israel gave to the Levites these cities with their suburbs. ⁶⁵And they gave by lot out of the tribe of the children of Judah, and out of the tribe of the children of Simeon, and out of the tribe of the children of Benjamin, these cities, which are called by their names. ⁶⁶And the residue of the families of the sons of Kohath had cities of their coasts out of the tribe of Ephraim. ⁶⁷And they gave unto them of the cities of refuge, Shechem in mount Ephraim with her suburbs; they gave also Gezer with her suburbs, ⁶⁸and Jokmeam with her suburbs, and Beth-horon with her suburbs, ⁶⁹and Aijalon with her suburbs, and Gath-rimmon with her suburbs. ⁷⁰And out of the half tribe of Manasseh, Aner with her suburbs, and Bileam with her suburbs, for the family of the remnant of the sons of Kohath.

⁷¹Unto the sons of Gershom were given out of the family of the half tribe of Manasseh, Golan in Bashan with her suburbs, and Ashtaroth with her suburbs. ⁷²And out of the tribe of Issachar; Kedesh with her suburbs, Daberath with her suburbs, ⁷³and Ramoth with her suburbs, and Anem with her suburbs. ⁷⁴And out of the tribe of Asher, Mashal with her suburbs, and Abdon with her suburbs, ⁷⁵and Hukok with her suburbs, and Rehob with her suburbs. ⁷⁶And out of the tribe of Naphtali, Kedesh in Galilee with her suburbs, and Hammon with her suburbs, and Kirjathaim with her suburbs.

⁷⁷Unto the rest of the children of Merari were given out of the tribe of Zebulun, Rimmon with her suburbs, Tabor with her suburbs. ⁷⁸And on the other side Jordan by Jericho, on the east side of Jordan, were given them out of the tribe of Reuben, Bezer in the wilderness with her suburbs, and Jahzah with her suburbs, ⁷⁹Kedemoth also with her suburbs, and Mephaath with her suburbs. ⁸⁰And out of the tribe of Gad, Ramoth in Gilead with her suburbs, and Mahanaim with her suburbs, ⁸¹and Heshbon with her suburbs, and Jazer with her suburbs.

7 Now the sons of Issachar were, Tola, and Puah, Jashub, and Shimron, four. ²And the sons of Tola: Uzzi, and Rephaiah, and Jeriel, and Jahmai, and Jibsam, and Shemuel, heads of their fathers' house, to wit, of Tola: they were valiant men of might in their generations, whose number was in the days of David two and twenty thousand and six hundred. ³And the sons of Uzzi: Izrahiah: and the sons of Izrahiah: Michael, and Obadiah, and Joel, Ishiah, five: all of them chief men. ⁴And with them, by their generations, after the house of their fathers, were bands of soldiers for war, six and thirty thousand men: for they had many wives and sons. ⁵And their brethren among all the families of Issachar were men of might, reckoned in all by their genealogies fourscore and seven thousand.

⁶The sons of Benjamin: Bela, and Becher, and Jediael, three. ⁷And the sons of Bela: Ezbon, and Uzzi, and Uzziel, and Jerimoth, and Iri, five, heads of the house of their fathers, mighty men of valour, and were reckoned by their genealogies twenty and two thousand and thirty and four. ⁸And the sons of Becher: Zemira, and Joash, and Eliezer, and

Elioenai, and Omri, and Jeremoth, and Abiah, and Anathoth, and Alameth. All these are the sons of Becher. ⁹And the number of them, after their genealogy by their generations, heads of the house of their fathers, mighty men of valour, was twenty thousand and two hundred. ¹⁰The sons also of Jediael: Bilhan: and the sons of Bilhan: Jeush, and Benjamin, and Ehud, and Chenaanah, and Zethan, and Tarshish, and Ahishahar. ¹¹All these the sons of Jediael, by the heads of their fathers, mighty men of valour, were seventeen thousand and two hundred soldiers, fit to go out for war and battle. ¹²Shuppim also, and Huppim, the children of Ir, and Hushim, the sons of Aher.

¹³The sons of Naphtali: Jahziel, and Guni, and Jezer, and Shallum, the sons of Bilhah.

¹⁴The sons of Manasseh: Ashriel, whom she bore (but his concubine the Aramitess bore Machir the father of Gilead: ¹⁵and Machir took to wife the sister of Huppim and Shuppim, whose sister's name was Maachah); and the name of the second was Zelophehad: and Zelophehad had daughters. ¹⁶And Maachah the wife of Machir bore a son, and she called his name Peresh, and the name of his brother was Sheresh, and his sons were Ulam and Rakem. ¹⁷And the sons of Ulam: Bedan. These were the sons of Gilead, the son of Machir, the son of Manasseh. ¹⁸And his sister Hammoleketh bore Ishod, and Abiezer, and Mahalah. ¹⁹And the sons of Shemida were: Ahian, and Shechem, and Likhi, and Aniam.

²⁰And the sons of Ephraim: Shuthelah, and Bered his son, and Tahath his son, and Eladah his son, and Tahath his son, ²¹and Zabad his son, and Shuthelah his son, and Ezer, and Elead, whom the men of Gath that were born in that land slew, because they came down to take away their cattle. ²²And Ephraim their father mourned many days, and his brethren came to comfort him. ²³And when he went in to his wife, she conceived, and bore a son, and he called his name Beriah, because it went evil with his house. ²⁴(And his daughter was Sherah, who built Beth-horon the nether, and the upper, and Uzzen-sherah.) ²⁵And Rephah was his son, also Resheph, and Telah his son, and Tahan his son, ²⁶Laadan his son, Ammihud his son, Elishama his son, ²⁷Non his son, Jehoshua his son.

²⁸And their possessions and habitations were, Beth-el and the towns thereof, and eastward Naaran, and westward Gezer, with the towns thereof, Shechem also and the towns thereof, unto Gaza and the towns thereof: ²⁹and by the borders of the children of Manasseh, Beth-shean and her towns, Taanach and her towns, Megiddo and her towns, Dor and her towns. In these dwelt the children of Joseph the son of Israel.

³⁰The sons of Asher: Imnah, and Isuah, and Ishuai, and Beriah, and Serah their sister. ³¹And the sons of Beriah: Heber, and Malchiel, who is the father of Birzavith. ³²And Heber begot Japhlet, and Shomer, and Hotham, and Shua their sister. ³³And the sons of Japhlet: Pasach, and Bimhal, and Ashvath. These are the children of Japhlet. ³⁴And the sons of Shamer: Ahi, and Rohgah, Jehubbah, and Aram. ³⁵And the son of his brother Helem: Zophah, and Imna, and Shelesh, and Amal. ³⁶The sons

of Zophah: Suah, and Harnepher, and Shual, and Beri, and Imrah, ³⁷Bezer, and Hod, and Shamma, and Shilshah, and Ithran, and Beera. ³⁸And the sons of Jether: Jephunneh, and Pispah, and Ara. ³⁹And the sons of Ulla: Arah, and Haniel, and Rezia. ⁴⁰All these were the children of Asher, heads of their fathers' house, choice and mighty men of valour, chief of the princes. And the number throughout the genealogy of them that were apt to the war and to battle was twenty and six thousand men.

8 Now Benjamin begot Bela his firstborn, Ashbel the second, and Aharah the third, ²Nohah the fourth, and Rapha the fifth. ³And the sons of Bela were: Addar, and Gera, and Abihud, ⁴and Abishua, and Naaman, and Ahoah, ⁵and Gera, and Shephuphan, and Huram. ⁶And these are the sons of Ehud: these are the heads of the fathers of the inhabitants of Geba, and they removed them to Manahath: ⁷and Naaman, and Ahiah, and Gera, he removed them, and begot Uzza, and Ahihud. ⁸And Shaharaim begot children in the country of Moab, after he had sent them away; Hushim and Baara were his wives. ⁹And he begot of Hodesh his wife, Jobab, and Zibia, and Mesha, and Malcham, ¹⁰and Jeuz, and Shachia, and Mirma. These were his sons, heads of the fathers. ¹¹And of Hushim he begot Abitub, and Elpaal. ¹²The sons of Elpaal: Eber, and Misham, and Shamed, who built Ono, and Lod, with the towns thereof. ¹³Beriah also, and Shema, who were heads of the fathers of the inhabitants of Aijalon, who drove away the inhabitants of Gath. ¹⁴And Ahio, Shashak, and Jeremoth, ¹⁵and Zebadiah, and Arad, and Ader, ¹⁶and Michael, and Ispah, and Joha, the sons of Beriah, ¹⁷and Zebadiah, and Meshullam, and Hezeki, and Heber, ¹⁸Ishmerai also, and Jezliah, and Jobab, the sons of Elpaal. ¹⁹And Jakim, and Zichri, and Zabdi, ²⁰and Elienai, and Zilthai, and Eliel, ²¹and Adaiah, and Beraiah, and Shimrath, the sons of Shimhi, ²²and Ishpan, and Heber, and Eliel, ²³and Abdon, and Zichri, and Hanan, ²⁴and Hananiah, and Elam, and Antothijah, ²⁵and Iphedeiah, and Penuel, the sons of Shashak, ²⁶and Shamsherai, and Shehariah, and Athaliah, ²⁷and Jaresiah, and Eliah, and Zichri, the sons of Jeroham. ²⁸These were heads of the fathers, by their generations, chief men. These dwelt in Jerusalem.

²⁹And at Gibeon dwelt the father of Gibeon, whose wife's name was Maachah: ³⁰and his firstborn son Abdon, and Zur, and Kish, and Baal, and Nadab, ³¹and Gedor, and Ahio, and Zacher. ³²And Mikloth begot Shimeah. And these also dwelt with their brethren in Jerusalem, over against them.

³³And Ner begot Kish, and Kish begot Saul, and Saul begot Jonathan, and Malchi-shua, and Abinadab, and Esh-baal. ³⁴And the son of Jonathan was Merib-baal; and Merib-baal begot Micah. ³⁵And the sons of Micah were Pithon, and Melech, and Tarea, and Ahaz. ³⁶And Ahaz begot Jehoadah, and Jehoadah begot Alemeth, and Azmaveth, and Zimri, and Zimri begot Moza, ³⁷and Moza begot Binea: Rapha was his son, Eleasah his son, Azel his son: ³⁸and Azel had six sons, whose names are these, Azrikam, Bocheru, and Ishmael, and Sheariah, and Obadiah, and Hanan. All these were the sons of Azel. ³⁹And the sons of Eshek his

brother were Ulam his firstborn, Jehush the second, and Eliphelet the third. ⁴⁰And the sons of Ulam were mighty men of valour, archers, and had many sons, and sons' sons, a hundred and fifty. All these are of the sons of Benjamin.

9 So all Israel were reckoned by genealogies, and behold, they were written in the book of the kings of Israel and Judah, who were carried away to Babylon for their transgression.

²Now the first inhabitants that dwelt in their possessions in their cities were the Israelites, the priests, Levites, and the Nethinims. ³And in Jerusalem dwelt of the children of Judah, and of the children of Benjamin, and of the children of Ephraim, and Manasseh. ⁴Uthai the son of Ammihud, the son of Omri, the son of Imri, the son of Bani, of the children of Pharez the son of Judah. ⁵And of the Shilonites: Asaiah the firstborn, and his sons. ⁶And of the sons of Zerah: Jeuel, and their brethren, six hundred and ninety. ⁷And of the sons of Benjamin: Sallu the son of Meshullam, the son of Hodaviah, the son of Hasenuah, ⁸and Ibneiah the son of Jeroham, and Elah the son of Uzzi, the son of Michri, and Meshullam the son of Shephathiah, the son of Reuel, the son of Ibnijah, ⁹and their brethren, according to their generations, nine hundred and fifty and six. All these men were chief of the fathers in the house of their fathers.

¹⁰And of the priests: Jedaiah, and Jehoiarib, and Jachin, ¹¹and Azariah the son of Hilkiah, the son of Meshullam, the son of Zadok, the son of Meraioth, the son of Ahitub, the ruler of the house of God. ¹²And Adaiah the son of Jeroham, the son of Pashur, the son of Malchiah, and Maasai the son of Adiel, the son of Jahzerah, the son of Meshullam, the son of Meshillemith, the son of Immer. ¹³And their brethren, heads of the house of their fathers, a thousand and seven hundred and threescore, very able men for the work of the service of the house of God.

¹⁴And of the Levites: Shemaiah the son of Hasshub, the son of Azrikam, the son of Hashabiah, of the sons of Merari. ¹⁵And Bakbakkar, Heresh, and Galal, and Mattaniah the son of Micha, the son of Zichri, the son of Asaph. ¹⁶And Obadiah the son of Shemaiah, the son of Galal, the son of Jeduthun, and Berechiah the son of Asa, the son of Elkanah, that dwelt in the villages of the Netophathites. ¹⁷And the porters were, Shallum, and Akkub, and Talmon, and Ahiman, and their brethren: Shallum was the chief; ¹⁸who hitherto waited in the king's gate eastward: they were porters in the companies of the children of Levi. ¹⁹And Shallum the son of Kore, the son of Ebiasaph, the son of Korah, and his brethren (of the house of his father) the Korahites, were over the work of the service, keepers of the gates of the tabernacle: and their fathers being over the host of the LORD, were keepers of the entry. ²⁰And Phinehas the son of Eleazar was the ruler over them in time past, and the LORD was with him. ²¹And Zechariah the son of Meshelemiah was porter of the door of the tabernacle of the congregation. ²²All these which were chosen to be porters in the gates were two hundred and twelve. These were reckoned by their genealogy in their villages, whom David and Samuel the seer did ordain in their set office. ²³So they and

their children had the oversight of the gates of the house of the LORD, namely, the house of the tabernacle, by wards. ²⁴In four quarters were the porters, toward the east, west, north, and south. ²⁵And their brethren, which were in their villages, were to come after seven days from time to time with them. ²⁶For these Levites, the four chief porters, were in their set office, and were over the chambers and treasuries of the house of God.

²⁷And they lodged round about the house of God, because the charge was upon them, and the opening thereof every morning pertained to them. ²⁸And certain of them had the charge of the ministering vessels, that they should bring them in and out by tale. ²⁹Some of them also were appointed to oversee the vessels, and all the instruments of the sanctuary, and the fine flour, and the wine, and the oil, and the frankincense, and the spices. ³⁰And some of the sons of the priests made the ointment of the spices. ³¹And Mattithiah, one of the Levites, who was the firstborn of Shallum the Korahite, had the set office over the things that were made in the pans. ³²And others of their brethren of the sons of the Kohathites, were over the showbread, to prepare it every sabbath. ³³And these are the singers, chief of the fathers of the Levites, who remaining in the chambers were free: for they were employed in that work day and night. ³⁴These chief fathers of the Levites were chief throughout their generations; these dwelt at Jerusalem.

³⁵And in Gibeon dwelt the father of Gibeon, Jeiel, whose wife's name was Maachah: ³⁶and his firstborn son Abdon, then Zur, and Kish, and Baal, and Ner, and Nadab, ³⁷and Gedor, and Ahio, and Zechariah, and Mikloth. ³⁸And Mikloth begot Shimeam. And they also dwelt with their brethren at Jerusalem, over against their brethren. ³⁹And Ner begot Kish, and Kish begot Saul, and Saul begot Jonathan, and Malchi-shua, and Abinadab, and Esh-baal. ⁴⁰And the son of Jonathan was Merib-baal: and Merib-baal begot Micah. ⁴¹And the sons of Micah were Pithon, and Melech, and Tahrea, and Ahaz. ⁴²And Ahaz begot Jarah, and Jarah begot Alemeth, and Azmaveth, and Zimri: and Zimri begot Moza, ⁴³and Moza begot Binea: and Rephaiah his son, Eleasah his son, Azel his son. ⁴⁴And Azel had six sons, whose names are these: Azrikam, Bocheru, and Ishmael, and Sheariah, and Obadiah, and Hanan. These were the sons of Azel.

10 Now the Philistines fought against Israel, and the men of Israel fled from before the Philistines, and fell down slain in mount Gilboa. ²And the Philistines followed hard after Saul, and after his sons, and the Philistines slew Jonathan, and Abinadab, and Malchi-shua, the sons of Saul. ³And the battle went sore against Saul, and the archers hit him, and he was wounded of the archers. ⁴Then said Saul to his armour-bearer, 'Draw thy sword, and thrust me through therewith, lest these uncircumcised come and abuse me'. But his armour-bearer would not, for he was sore afraid. So Saul took a sword, and fell upon it. ⁵And when his armour-bearer saw that Saul was dead, he fell likewise on the sword, and died. ⁶So Saul died, and his three sons, and all his house died together. ⁷And when all the men of Israel that were in the valley saw that they fled, and that Saul and his sons were dead: then they forsook their cities, and fled, and the Philistines came and dwelt in them.

⁸And it came to pass on the morrow, when the Philistines came to strip the slain, that they found Saul and his sons fallen in mount Gilboa. ⁹And when they had stripped him, they took his head, and his armour, and sent into the land of the Philistines round about, to carry tidings unto their idols, and to the people. ¹⁰And they put his armour in the house of their gods, and fastened his head in the temple of Dagon.

¹¹And when all Jabesh-gilead heard all that the Philistines had done to Saul, ¹²they arose, all the valiant men, and took away the body of Saul, and the bodies of his sons, and brought them to Jabesh, and buried their bones under the oak in Jabesh, and fasted seven days.

¹³So Saul died for his transgression which he committed against the LORD, even against the word of the LORD which he kept not, and also for asking counsel of one that had a familiar spirit, to inquire of it: ¹⁴and inquired not of the LORD: therefore he slew him, and turned the kingdom unto David the son of Jesse.

11 Then all Israel gathered themselves to David unto Hebron, saying, 'Behold, we are thy bone and thy flesh. ²And moreover in time past, even when Saul was king, thou wast he that leddest out and broughtest in Israel: and the LORD thy God said unto thee, "Thou shalt feed my people Israel, and thou shalt be ruler over my people Israel".' ³Therefore came all the elders of Israel to the king to Hebron: and David made a covenant with them in Hebron before the LORD, and they anointed David king over Israel, according to the word of the LORD by Samuel.

⁴And David and all Israel went to Jerusalem, which is Jebus, where the Jebusites were the inhabitants of the land. ⁵And the inhabitants of Jebus said to David, 'Thou shalt not come hither'. Nevertheless David took the castle of Zion, which is the city of David. ⁶And David said, 'Whosoever smiteth the Jebusites first shall be chief and captain'. So Joab the son of Zeruiah went first up, and was chief. ⁷And David dwelt in the castle: therefore they called it the city of David. ⁸And he built the city round about, even from Millo round about: and Joab repaired the rest of the city. ⁹So David waxed greater and greater: for the LORD of hosts was with him.

¹⁰These also are the chief of the mighty men whom David had, who strengthened themselves with him in his kingdom, and with all Israel, to make him king according to the word of the LORD concerning Israel. ¹¹And this is the number of the mighty men whom David had: Jashobeam, a Hachmonite, the chief of the captains: he lifted up his spear against three hundred slain by him at one time. ¹²And after him was Eleazar the son of Dodo, the Ahohite, who was one of the three mighties. ¹³He was with David at Pas-dammim; and there the Philistines were gathered together to battle, where was a parcel of ground full of barley, and the people fled from before the Philistines. ¹⁴And they set themselves in the midst of that parcel, and delivered

it, and slew the Philistines, and the LORD saved them by a great deliverance.

¹⁵Now three of the thirty captains went down to the rock of David, into the cave of Adullam, and the host of the Philistines encamped in the valley of Rephaim. ¹⁶And David was then in the hold, and the Philistines' garrison was then at Beth-lehem. ¹⁷And David longed, and said, 'O that one would give me drink of the water of the well of Beth-lehem, that is at the gate'. ¹⁸And the three broke through the host of the Philistines, and drew water out of the well of Beth-lehem, that was by the gate, and took it, and brought it to David: but David would not drink of it, but poured it out to the LORD, ¹⁹and said, 'My God forbid it me, that I should do this thing. Shall I drink the blood of these men that have put their lives in jeopardy? for with the jeopardy of their lives they brought it.' Therefore he would not drink it. These things did these three mightiest.

²⁰And Abishai the brother of Joab, he was chief of the three. For lifting up his spear against three hundred, he slew them, and had a name among the three. ²¹Of the three, he was more honourable than the two, for he was their captain: howbeit he attained not to the first three. ²²Benaiah the son of Jehoiada, the son of a valiant man of Kabzeel, who had done many acts: he slew two lion-like men of Moab, also he went down and slew a lion in a pit in a snowy day. ²³And he slew an Egyptian, a man of great stature, five cubits high, and in the Egyptian's hand was a spear like a weaver's beam: and he went down to him with a staff, and plucked the spear out of the Egyptian's hand, and slew him with his own spear. ²⁴These things did Benaiah the son of Jehoiada, and had the name among the three mighties. ²⁵Behold, he was honourable among the thirty, but attained not to the first three: and David set him over his guard.

²⁶Also the valiant men of the armies were Asahel the brother of Joab, Elhanan the son of Dodo of Beth-lehem, ²⁷Shammoth the Harorite, Helez the Pelonite, ²⁸Ira the son of Ikkesh the Tekoite, Abi-ezer the Antothite, ²⁹Sibbecai the Hushathite, Ilai the Ahohite, ³⁰Maharai the Netophathite, Heled the son of Baanah the Netophathite, ³¹Ithai the son of Ribai of Gibeah, that pertained to the children of Benjamin, Benaiah the Pirathonite, ³²Hurai of the brooks of Gaash, Abiel the Arbathite, ³³Azmaveth the Baharumite, Elihaba the Shaalbonite, ³⁴the sons of Hashem the Gizonite, Jonathan the son of Shageh the Hararite, ³⁵Ahiam the son of Sacar the Hararite, Eliphal the son of Ur, ³⁶Hepher the Mecherathite, Ahijah the Pelonite, ³⁷Hezro the Carmelite, Naarai the son of Ezbai, ³⁸Joel the brother of Nathan, Mibhar the son of Haggeri, ³⁹Zelek the Ammonite, Naharai the Berothite, the armour-bearer of Joab the son of Zeruiah, ⁴⁰Ira the Ithrite, Gareb the Ithrite, ⁴¹Uriah the Hittite, Zabad the son of Ahlai, ⁴²Adina the son of Shiza the Reubenite, a captain of the Reubenites, and thirty with him, ⁴³Hanan the son of Maachah, and Joshaphat the Mithnite, ⁴⁴Uzzia the Ashterathite, Shama and Jeiel the sons of Hothan the Aroerite, ⁴⁵Jediael the son of Shimri, and Joha his brother, the Tizite, ⁴⁶Eliel the Mahavite,

and Jeribai, and Joshaviah, the sons of Elnaam, and Ithmah the Moabite, [47]Eliel, and Obed, and Jasiel the Mesobaite.

12 Now these are they that came to David to Ziklag, while he yet kept himself close because of Saul the son of Kish: and they were among the mighty men, helpers of the war. [2]They were armed with bows, and could use both the right hand and the left in hurling stones and shooting arrows out of a bow, even of Saul's brethren of Benjamin. [3]The chief was Ahiezer, then Joash, the sons of Shemaah the Gibeathite, and Jeziel, and Pelet, the sons of Azmaveth, and Berachah, and Jehu the Antothite, [4]and Ismaiah the Gibeonite, a mighty man among the thirty, and over the thirty, and Jeremiah, and Jahaziel, and Johanan, and Jozabad the Gederathite, [5]Eleuzai, and Jerimoth, and Bealiah, and Shemariah, and Shephatiah the Haruphite, [6]Elkanah, and Jesiah, and Azareel, and Joezer, and Jashobeam, the Korhites, [7]and Joelah, and Zebadiah, the sons of Jeroham of Gedor. [8]And of the Gadites there separated themselves unto David into the hold to the wilderness, men of might, and men of war fit for the battle, that could handle shield and buckler, whose faces were like the faces of lions, and were as swift as the roes upon the mountains: [9]Ezer the first, Obadiah the second, Eliab the third, [10]Mishmannah the fourth, Jeremiah the fifth, [11]Attai the sixth, Eliel the seventh, [12]Johanan the eighth, Elzabad the ninth, [13]Jeremiah the tenth, Machbanai the eleventh. [14]These were of the sons of Gad, captains of the host: one of the least was over a hundred, and the greatest over a thousand. [15]These are they that went over Jordan in the first month, when it had overflowed all his banks, and they put to flight all them of the valleys, both toward the east, and toward the west. [16]And there came of the children of Benjamin and Judah to the hold unto David. [17]And David went out to meet them, and answered and said unto them, 'If ye be come peaceably unto me to help me, my heart shall be knit unto you: but if ye be come to betray me to my enemies, seeing there is no wrong in my hands, the God of our fathers look thereon, and rebuke it' . [18]Then the spirit came upon Amasai, who was chief of the captains, and he said, 'Thine are we, David, and on thy side, thou son of Jesse: peace, peace be unto thee, and peace be to thy helpers; for thy God helpeth thee'. Then David received them, and made them captains of the band. [19]And there fell some of Manasseh to David, when he came with the Philistines against Saul to battle, but they helped them not. For the lords of the Philistines upon advisement sent him away, saying, 'He will fall to his master Saul to the jeopardy of our heads'. [20]As he went to Ziklag, there fell to him of Manasseh, Adnah, and Jozabad, and Jediael, and Michael, and Jozabad, and Elihu, and Zilthai, captains of the thousands that were of Manasseh. [21]And they helped David against the band of the rovers: for they were all mighty men of valour, and were captains in the host. [22]For at that time day by day there came to David to help him, until it was a great host, like the host of God.

[23]And these are the numbers of the bands that were ready armed to the war, and came to David to Hebron, to turn the kingdom of Saul to

him, according to the word of the LORD. [24]The children of Judah that bore shield and spear were six thousand and eight hundred, ready armed to the war. [25]Of the children of Simeon, mighty men of valour for the war, seven thousand and one hundred. [26]Of the children of Levi four thousand and six hundred. [27]And Jehoiada was the leader of the Aaronites, and with him were three thousand and seven hundred. [28]And Zadok, a young man mighty of valour, and of his father's house twenty and two captains. [29]And of the children of Benjamin, the kindred of Saul, three thousand: for hitherto the greatest part of them had kept the ward of the house of Saul. [30]And of the children of Ephraim twenty thousand and eight hundred, mighty men of valour, famous throughout the house of their fathers. [31]And of the half tribe of Manasseh eighteen thousand, which were expressed by name, to come and make David king. [32]And of the children of Issachar, which were men that had understanding of the times, to know what Israel ought to do: the heads of them were two hundred; and all their brethren were at their commandment. [33]Of Zebulun, such as went forth to battle, expert in war, with all instruments of war, fifty thousand which could keep rank: they were not of double heart. [34]And of Naphtali a thousand captains, and with them with shield and spear thirty and seven thousand. [35]And of the Danites expert in war twenty and eight thousand and six hundred. [36]And of Asher, such as went forth to battle, expert in war, forty thousand. [37]And on the other side of Jordan, of the Reubenites, and the Gadites, and of the half tribe of Manasseh, with all manner of instruments of war for the battle, a hundred and twenty thousand. [38]All these men of war, that could keep rank, came with a perfect heart to Hebron, to make David king over all Israel: and all the rest also of Israel were of one heart to make David king. [39]And there they were with David three days, eating and drinking: for their brethren had prepared for them. [40]Moreover they that were nigh them, even unto Issachar and Zebulun and Naphtali, brought bread on asses, and on camels, and on mules, and on oxen, and meat, meal, cakes of figs, and bunches of raisins, and wine, and oil, and oxen, and sheep abundantly: for there was joy in Israel.

13 And David consulted with the captains of thousands and hundreds, and with every leader. [2]And David said unto all the congregation of Israel, 'If it seem good unto you, and that it be of the LORD our God, let us send abroad unto our brethren everywhere, that are left in all the land of Israel, and with them also to the priests and Levites which are in their cities and suburbs, that they may gather themselves unto us. [3]And let us bring again the ark of our God to us: for we inquired not at it in the days of Saul.' [4]And all the congregation said that they would do so: for the thing was right in the eyes of all the people. [5]So David gathered all Israel together, from Shihor of Egypt even unto the entering of Hamath, to bring the ark of God from Kirjath-jearim. [6]And David went up, and all Israel, to Baalah, that is, to Kirjath-jearim, which belonged to Judah, to bring up thence the ark of God the LORD, that dwelleth between the cherubims, whose name is called on it. [7]And they carried the ark of God in a new cart out of the house of Abinadab: and Uzza and Ahio drove the cart. [8]And David and all Israel played before God with all their might, and with singing, and with harps, and with psalteries, and with timbrels, and with cymbals, and with trumpets.

[9]And when they came unto the threshing-floor of Chidon, Uzza put forth his hand to hold the ark, for the oxen stumbled. [10]And the anger of the LORD was kindled against Uzza, and he smote him, because he put his hand to the ark: and there he died before God. [11]And David was displeased, because the LORD had made a breach upon Uzza: wherefore that place is called Perez-uzza to this day. [12]And David was afraid of God that day, saying, 'How shall I bring the ark of God home to me?' [13]So David brought not the ark home to himself to the city of David, but carried it aside into the house of Obed-edom the Gittite. [14]And the ark of God remained with the family of Obed-edom in his house three months. And the LORD blessed the house of Obed-edom, and all that he had.

14 Now Hiram king of Tyre sent messengers to David, and timber of cedars, with masons and carpenters, to build him a house. [2]And David perceived that the LORD had confirmed him king over Israel, for his kingdom was lifted up on high, because of his people Israel.

[3]And David took more wives at Jerusalem: and David begot more sons and daughters. [4]Now these are the names of his children which he had in Jerusalem: Shammua, and Shobab, Nathan, and Solomon, [5]and Ibhar, and Elishua, and Elpalet, [6]and Nogah, and Nepheg, and Japhia, [7]and Elishama, and Beeliada, and Eliphalet.

[8]And when the Philistines heard that David was anointed king over all Israel, all the Philistines went up to seek David. And David heard of it, and went out against them. [9]And the Philistines came and spread themselves in the valley of Rephaim. [10]And David inquired of God, saying, 'Shall I go up against the Philistines? and wilt thou deliver them into my hand?' And the LORD said unto him, 'Go up, for I will deliver them into thy hand'. [11]So they came up to Baal-perazim, and David smote them there. Then David said, 'God hath broken in upon my enemies by my hand like the breaking forth of waters': therefore they called the name of that place Baal-perazim. [12]And when they had left their gods there, David gave a commandment, and they were burnt with fire. [13]And the Philistines yet again spread themselves abroad in the valley. [14]Therefore David inquired again of God, and God said unto him, 'Go not up after them, turn away from them, and come upon them over against the mulberry trees. [15]And it shall be, when thou shalt hear a sound of going in the tops of the mulberry trees, that then thou shalt go out to battle: for God is gone forth before thee to smite the host of the Philistines.' [16]David therefore did as God commanded him: and they smote the host of the Philistines from Gibeon even to Gazer. [17]And the fame of David went out into all lands, and the LORD brought the fear of him upon all nations.

15 And David made him houses in the city of David, and prepared a place for the ark of God, and pitched for it a tent. [2]Then David said, 'None ought to carry the ark of God but the Levites: for them hath the LORD chosen to carry the ark of God, and to minister unto him for ever'. ³And David gathered all Israel together to Jerusalem, to bring up the ark of the LORD unto his place, which he had prepared for it. ⁴And David assembled the children of Aaron, and the Levites. ⁵Of the sons of Kohath: Uriel the chief, and his brethren a hundred and twenty. ⁶Of the sons of Merari: Asaiah the chief, and his brethren two hundred and twenty. ⁷Of the sons of Gershom: Joel the chief, and his brethren a hundred and thirty. ⁸Of the sons of Elizaphan: Shemaiah the chief, and his brethren two hundred. ⁹Of the sons of Hebron: Eliel the chief, and his brethren fourscore. ¹⁰Of the sons of Uzziel: Amminadab the chief, and his brethren a hundred and twelve.

¹¹And David called for Zadok and Abiathar the priests, and for the Levites, for Uriel, Asaiah, and Joel, Shemaiah, and Eliel, and Amminadab, ¹²and said unto them, 'Ye are the chief of the fathers of the Levites: sanctify yourselves, both ye and your brethren, that you may bring up the ark of the LORD God of Israel unto the place that I have prepared for it. ¹³For because ye did it not at the first, the LORD our God made a breach upon us, for that we sought him not after the due order.' ¹⁴So the priests and the Levites sanctified themselves to bring up the ark of the LORD God of Israel. ¹⁵And the children of the Levites bore the ark of God upon their shoulders with the staves thereon, as Moses commanded according to the word of the LORD. ¹⁶And David spoke to the chief of the Levites to appoint their brethren to be the singers with instruments of music, psalteries and harps and cymbals, sounding, by lifting up the voice with joy. ¹⁷So the Levites appointed Heman the son of Joel; and of his brethren, Asaph the son of Berechiah; and of the sons of Merari their brethren, Ethan the son of Kushaiah. ¹⁸And with them their brethren of the second degree, Zechariah, Ben, and Jaaziel, and Shemiramoth, and Jehiel, and Unni, Eliab, and Benaiah, and Maaseiah, and Mattithiah, and Elipheleh, and Mikneiah, and Obed-edom, and Jeiel, the porters. ¹⁹So the singers, Heman, Asaph, and Ethan, were appointed to sound with cymbals of brass. ²⁰And Zechariah, and Aziel, and Shemiramoth, and Jehiel, and Unni, and Eliab, and Maaseiah, and Benaiah, with psalteries on Alamoth. ²¹And Mattithiah, and Elipheleh, and Mikneiah, and Obed-edom, and Jeiel, and Azaziah, with harps on the Sheminith to excel. ²²And Chenaniah chief of the Levites was for song: he instructed about the song, because he was skilful. ²³And Berechiah and Elkanah were doorkeepers for the ark. ²⁴And Shebaniah, and Jehoshaphat, and Nethaneel, and Amasai, and Zechariah, and Benaiah, and Eliezer, the priests, did blow with the trumpets before the ark of God: and Obed-edom and Jehiah were doorkeepers for the ark.

²⁵So David, and the elders of Israel, and the captains over thousands, went to bring up the ark of the covenant of the LORD out of the house of Obed-edom with joy. ²⁶And it came to pass, when God helped the Levites that bore the ark of the covenant of the LORD, that they offered seven bullocks and seven rams. ²⁷And David was clothed with a robe of fine

linen, and all the Levites that bore the ark, and the singers, and Chenaniah the master of the song with the singers. David also had upon him an ephod of linen. ²⁸Thus all Israel brought up the ark of the covenant of the LORD with shouting, and with sound of the cornet, and with trumpets, and with cymbals, making a noise with psalteries and harps.

²⁹And it came to pass as the ark of the covenant of the LORD came to the city of David, that Michal the daughter of Saul looking out at a window saw king David dancing and playing: and she despised him in her heart.

16

So they brought the ark of God, and set it in the midst of the tent that David had pitched for it: and they offered burnt sacrifices and peace offerings before God. ²And when David had made an end of offering the burnt offerings and the peace offerings, he blessed the people in the name of the LORD. ³And he dealt to every one of Israel, both man and woman, to every one a loaf of bread, and a good piece of flesh, and a flagon of wine.

⁴And he appointed certain of the Levites to minister before the ark of the LORD, and to record, and to thank and praise the LORD God of Israel: ⁵Asaph the chief, and next to him Zechariah, Jeiel, and Shemiramoth, and Jehiel, and Mattithiah, and Eliab, and Benaiah, and Obed-edom: and Jeiel with psalteries and with harps; but Asaph made a sound with cymbals; ⁶Benaiah also and Jahaziel the priests with trumpets continually before the ark of the covenant of God.

⁷Then on that day David delivered first this psalm to thank the LORD into the hand of Asaph and his brethren.

⁸ Give thanks unto the LORD, call upon his name,
   make known his deeds among the people.
⁹ Sing unto him, sing psalms unto him,
   talk you of all his wondrous works.
¹⁰ Glory ye in his holy name,
   let the heart of them rejoice that seek the LORD.
¹¹ Seek the LORD and his strength,
   seek his face continually.
¹² Remember his marvellous works that he hath done,
   his wonders, and the judgements of his mouth,
¹³ O ye seed of Israel his servant,
   ye children of Jacob, his chosen ones.

¹⁴ He is the LORD our God,
   his judgements are in all the earth.
¹⁵ Be ye mindful always of his covenant:
   the word which he commanded to a thousand generations:
¹⁶ even of the covenant which he made with Abraham,
   and of his oath unto Isaac:
¹⁷ and hath confirmed the same to Jacob for a law,
   and to Israel for an everlasting covenant,

¹⁸ saying, 'Unto thee will I give the land of Canaan,
the lot of your inheritance'.

¹⁹ When ye were but few,
even a few, and strangers in it:

²⁰ and when they went from nation to nation,
and from one kingdom to another people:

²¹ he suffered no man to do them wrong:
yea, he reproved kings for their sakes,

²² saying, 'Touch not my anointed,
and do my prophets no harm'.

²³ Sing unto the LORD, all the earth:
show forth from day to day his salvation.

²⁴ Declare his glory among the heathen:
his marvellous works among all nations.

²⁵ For great is the LORD, and greatly to be praised:
he also is to be feared above all gods.

²⁶ For all the gods of the people are idols:
but the LORD made the heavens.

²⁷ Glory and honour are in his presence:
strength and gladness are in his place.

²⁸ Give unto the LORD, ye kindreds of the people,
give unto the LORD glory and strength.

²⁹ Give unto the LORD the glory due unto his name:
bring an offering, and come before him,
worship the LORD in the beauty of holiness.

³⁰ Fear before him, all the earth:
the world also shall be stable, that it be not moved.

³¹ Let the heavens be glad, and let the earth rejoice:
and let men say among the nations, 'The LORD reigneth'.

³² Let the sea roar, and the fulness thereof:
let the fields rejoice, and all that is therein.

³³ Then shall the trees of the wood sing out at the presence of the
LORD,
because he cometh to judge the earth.

³⁴ O give thanks unto the LORD, for he is good:
for his mercy endureth for ever.

³⁵ And say ye, 'Save us, O God of our salvation,
and gather us together,
and deliver us from the heathen,
that we may give thanks to thy holy name,
and glory in thy praise'.

³⁶ Blessed be the LORD God of Israel for ever and ever.

And all the people said, 'Amen', and praised the LORD.

³⁷So he left there before the ark of the covenant of the LORD Asaph and his brethren, to minister before the ark continually, as every day's work required: ³⁸and Obed-edom with their brethren, threescore and eight: Obed-edom also the son of Jeduthun and Hosah to be porters: ³⁹and Zadok the priest, and his brethren the priests, before the tabernacle of the LORD in the high place that was at Gibeon, ⁴⁰to offer burnt offerings unto the LORD upon the altar of the burnt offering continually morning and evening, and to do according to all that is written in the law of the LORD, which he commanded Israel: ⁴¹and with them Heman and Jeduthun, and the rest that were chosen, who were expressed by name, to give thanks to the LORD, because his mercy endureth for ever. ⁴²And with them Heman and Jeduthun, with trumpets and cymbals for those that should make a sound, and with musical instruments of God. And the sons of Jeduthun were porters. ⁴³And all the people departed every man to his house, and David returned to bless his house.

17 Now it came to pass, as David sat in his house, that David said to Nathan the prophet, 'Lo, I dwell in a house of cedars, but the ark of the covenant of the LORD remaineth under curtains'. ²Then Nathan said unto David, 'Do all that is in thy heart, for God is with thee'.

³And it came to pass the same night, that the word of God came to Nathan, saying, ⁴'Go and tell David my servant, "Thus saith the LORD, 'Thou shalt not build me a house to dwell in: ⁵for I have not dwelt in a house since the day that I brought up Israel unto this day, but have gone from tent to tent, and from one tabernacle to another. ⁶Wheresoever I have walked with all Israel, spoke I a word to any of the judges of Israel, whom I commanded to feed my people, saying, "Why have ye not built me a house of cedars?"'" ⁷Now therefore thus shalt thou say unto my servant David, "Thus saith the LORD of hosts, 'I took thee from the sheepcote, even from following the sheep, that thou shouldst be ruler over my people Israel: ⁸and I have been with thee whithersoever thou hast walked, and have cut off all thy enemies from before thee, and have made thee a name like the name of the great men that are in the earth. ⁹Also I will ordain a place for my people Israel, and will plant them, and they shall dwell in their place, and shall be moved no more: neither shall the children of wickedness waste them any more, as at the beginning, ¹⁰and since the time that I commanded judges to be over my people Israel. Moreover I will subdue all thy enemies. Furthermore I tell thee, that the LORD will build thee a house.

¹¹"'And it shall come to pass, when thy days be expired that thou must go to be with thy fathers, that I will raise up thy seed after thee, which shall be of thy sons, and I will establish his kingdom. ¹²He shall build me a house, and I will establish his throne for ever. ¹³I will be his father, and he shall be my son, and I will not take my mercy away from him, as I took it from him that was before thee. ¹⁴But I will settle him in my house and in my kingdom for ever, and his throne shall be established for evermore.'"' ¹⁵According to all these words, and according to all this vision, so did Nathan speak unto David.

¹⁶And David the king came and sat before the LORD, and said, 'Who am I, O LORD God, and what is my house, that thou hast brought me hitherto? ¹⁷And yet this was a small thing in thy eyes, O God: for thou hast also spoken of thy servant's house for a great while to come, and hast regarded me according to the estate of a man of high degree, O LORD God. ¹⁸What can David speak more to thee for the honour of thy servant? for thou knowest thy servant. ¹⁹O LORD, for thy servant's sake, and according to thy own heart, hast thou done all this greatness in making known all these great things. ²⁰O LORD, there is none like thee, neither is there any God besides thee, according to all that we have heard with our ears. ²¹And what one nation in the earth is like thy people Israel, whom God went to redeem to be his own people, to make thee a name of greatness and terribleness, by driving out nations from before thy people, whom thou hast redeemed out of Egypt? ²²For thy people Israel didst thou make thy own people for ever, and thou, LORD, becamest their God. ²³Therefore now, LORD, let the thing that thou hast spoken concerning thy servant and concerning his house be established for ever, and do as thou hast said. ²⁴Let it even be established, that thy name may be magnified for ever, saying, "The LORD of hosts is the God of Israel, even a God to Israel": and let the house of David thy servant be established before thee. ²⁵For thou, O my God, hast told thy servant that thou wilt build him a house: therefore thy servant hath found in his heart to pray before thee. ²⁶And now, LORD (thou art God, and hast promised this goodness unto thy servant), ²⁷now therefore let it please thee to bless the house of thy servant, that it may be before thee for ever: for thou blessest, O LORD, and it shall be blessed for ever.'

18 Now after this it came to pass, that David smote the Philistines and subdued them, and took Gath and her towns out of the hand of the Philistines. ²And he smote Moab, and the Moabites became David's servants, and brought gifts.

³And David smote Hadarezer king of Zobah unto Hamath, as he went to establish his dominion by the river Euphrates. ⁴And David took from him a thousand chariots, and seven thousand horsemen, and twenty thousand footmen: David also hocked all the chariot-horses, but reserved of them a hundred chariots. ⁵And when the Syrians of Damascus came to help Hadarezer king of Zobah, David slew of the Syrians two and twenty thousand men. ⁶Then David put garrisons in Syria-damascus, and the Syrians became David's servants, and brought gifts. Thus the LORD preserved David whithersoever he went. ⁷And David took the shields of gold that were on the servants of Hadarezer, and brought them to Jerusalem. ⁸Likewise from Tibhath, and from Chun, cities of Hadarezer, brought David very much brass, wherewith Solomon made the brazen sea, and the pillars, and the vessels of brass.

⁹Now when Tou king of Hamath heard how David had smitten all the host of Hadarezer king of Zobah: ¹⁰he sent Hadoram his son to king David, to inquire of his welfare, and to congratulate him, because he had fought against Hadarezer, and smitten him (for Hadarezer had war with Tou), and with him all manner of vessels of gold and silver and

brass. [11]Them also king David dedicated unto the LORD, with the silver and the gold that he brought from all these nations: from Edom, and from Moab, and from the children of Ammon, and from the Philistines, and from Amalek. [12]Moreover Abishai the son of Zeruiah slew of the Edomites in the valley of salt eighteen thousand. [13]And he put garrisons in Edom; and all the Edomites became David's servants. Thus the LORD preserved David whithersoever he went.

[14]So David reigned over all Israel, and executed judgement and justice among all his people. [15]And Joab the son of Zeruiah was over the host, and Jehoshaphat the son of Ahilud, recorder. [16]And Zadok the son of Ahitub, and Abimelech the son of Abiathar, were the priests, and Shavsha was scribe. [17]And Benaiah the son of Jehoiada was over the Cherethites and the Pelethites: and the sons of David were chief about the king.

19 Now it came to pass after this, that Nahash the king of the children of Ammon died, and his son reigned in his stead. [2]And David said, 'I will show kindness unto Hanun the son of Nahash, because his father showed kindness to me'. And David sent messengers to comfort him concerning his father. So the servants of David came into the land of the children of Ammon to Hanun, to comfort him. [3]But the princes of the children of Ammon said to Hanun, 'Thinkest thou that David doth honour thy father, that he hath sent comforters unto thee? Are not his servants come unto thee for to search, and to overthrow, and to spy out the land?' [4]Wherefore Hanun took David's servants, and shaved them, and cut off their garments in the midst hard by their buttocks, and sent them away. [5]Then there went certain, and told David how the men were served. And he sent to meet them: for the men were greatly ashamed. And the king said, 'Tarry at Jericho until your beards be grown, and then return'.

[6]And when the children of Ammon saw that they had made themselves odious to David, Hanun and the children of Ammon sent a thousand talents of silver to hire them chariots and horsemen out of Mesopotamia, and out of Syria-maachah, and out of Zobah. [7]So they hired thirty and two thousand chariots, and the king of Maachah and his people, who came and pitched before Medeba. And the children of Ammon gathered themselves together from their cities, and came to battle. [8]And when David heard of it, he sent Joab, and all the host of the mighty men. [9]And the children of Ammon came out, and put the battle in array before the gate of the city, and the kings that were come were by themselves in the field. [10]Now when Joab saw that the battle was set against him before and behind, he chose out of all the choice of Israel, and put them in array against the Syrians. [11]And the rest of the people he delivered unto the hand of Abishai his brother, and they set themselves in array against the children of Ammon. [12]And he said, 'If the Syrians be too strong for me, then thou shalt help me: but if the children of Ammon be too strong for thee, then I will help thee. [13]Be of good courage, and let us behave ourselves valiantly for our people, and for the cities of our God: and let the LORD do that which is good in his sight.'

¹⁴So Joab and the people that were with him drew nigh before the Syrians unto the battle; and they fled before him. ¹⁵And when the children of Ammon saw that the Syrians were fled, they likewise fled before Abishai his brother, and entered into the city. Then Joab came to Jerusalem.

¹⁶And when the Syrians saw that they were put to the worse before Israel, they sent messengers, and drew forth the Syrians that were beyond the river: and Shophach the captain of the host of Hadarezer went before them. ¹⁷And it was told David, and he gathered all Israel, and passed over Jordan, and came upon them, and set the battle in array against them. So when David had put the battle in array against the Syrians, they fought with him. ¹⁸But the Syrians fled before Israel, and David slew of the Syrians seven thousand men which fought in chariots, and forty thousand footmen, and killed Shophach the captain of the host. ¹⁹And when the servants of Hadarezer saw that they were put to the worse before Israel, they made peace with David, and became his servants: neither would the Syrians help the children of Ammon any more.

20 And it came to pass, that after the year was expired, at the time that kings go out to battle, Joab led forth the power of the army, and wasted the country of the children of Ammon, and came and besieged Rabbah. But David tarried at Jerusalem. And Joab smote Rabbah, and destroyed it. ²And David took the crown of their king from off his head, and found it to weigh a talent of gold, and there were precious stones in it; and it was set upon David's head; and he brought also exceeding much spoil out of the city. ³And he brought out the people that were in it, and cut them with saws, and with harrows of iron, and with axes. Even so dealt David with all the cities of the children of Ammon. And David and all the people returned to Jerusalem.

⁴And it came to pass after this, that there arose war at Gezer with the Philistines, at which time Sibbechai the Hushathite slew Sippai, that was of the children of the giant: and they were subdued. ⁵And there was war again with the Philistines, and Elhanan the son of Jair slew Lahmi the brother of Goliath the Gittite, whose spear-staff was like a weaver's beam. ⁶And yet again there was war at Gath, where was a man of great stature, whose fingers and toes were four and twenty, six on each hand, and six on each foot. And he also was the son of the giant. ⁷But when he defied Israel, Jonathan the son of Shimea David's brother slew him. ⁸These were born unto the giant in Gath, and they fell by the hand of David, and by the hand of his servants.

21 And Satan stood up against Israel, and provoked David to number Israel. ²And David said to Joab and to the rulers of the people, 'Go, number Israel from Beer-sheba even to Dan: and bring the number of them to me, that I may know it'. ³And Joab answered, 'The LORD make his people a hundred times so many more as they be: but, my lord the king, are they not all my lord's servants? why then doth my lord require this thing? why will he be a cause of trespass to Israel?' ⁴Nevertheless the king's word prevailed against Joab: wherefore Joab departed, and went throughout all Israel, and came to Jerusalem.

⁵And Joab gave the sum of the number of the people unto David. And all they of Israel were a thousand thousand and a hundred thousand men that drew sword: and Judah was four hundred threescore and ten thousand men that drew sword. ⁶But Levi and Benjamin counted he not among them: for the king's word was abominable to Joab. ⁷And God was displeased with this thing; therefore he smote Israel. ⁸And David said unto God, 'I have sinned greatly, because I have done this thing: but now, I beseech thee, do away the iniquity of thy servant, for I have done very foolishly'.

⁹And the LORD spoke unto Gad, David's seer, saying, ¹⁰'Go and tell David, saying, "Thus saith the LORD, 'I offer thee three things: choose thee one of them, that I may do it unto thee'"'. ¹¹So Gad came to David, and said unto him, 'Thus saith the LORD, "Choose thee ¹²either three years' famine, or three months to be destroyed before thy foes, while that the sword of thy enemies overtaketh thee, or else three days the sword of the LORD, even the pestilence in the land, and the angel of the LORD destroying throughout all the coasts of Israel". Now therefore advise thyself what word I shall bring again to him that sent me.' ¹³And David said unto Gad, 'I am in a great strait. Let me fall now into the hand of the LORD (for very great are his mercies), but let me not fall into the hand of man.'

¹⁴So the LORD sent pestilence upon Israel: and there fell of Israel seventy thousand men. ¹⁵And God sent an angel unto Jerusalem to destroy it: and as he was destroying, the LORD beheld, and he repented him of the evil, and said to the angel that destroyed, 'It is enough, stay now thy hand'. And the angel of the LORD stood by the threshing-floor of Ornan the Jebusite. ¹⁶And David lifted up his eyes, and saw the angel of the LORD stand between the earth and the heaven, having a drawn sword in his hand stretched out over Jerusalem. Then David and the elders of Israel, who were clothed in sackcloth, fell upon their faces. ¹⁷And David said unto God, 'Is it not I that commanded the people to be numbered? even I it is that have sinned and done evil indeed; but as for these sheep, what have they done? Let thy hand, I pray thee, O LORD my God, be on me, and on my father's house, but not on thy people, that they should be plagued.'

¹⁸Then the angel of the LORD commanded Gad to say to David, that David should go up and set up an altar unto the LORD in the threshing-floor of Ornan the Jebusite. ¹⁹And David went up at the saying of Gad, which he spoke in the name of the LORD. ²⁰And Ornan turned back, and saw the angel; and his four sons with him hid themselves. Now Ornan was threshing wheat. ²¹And as David came to Ornan, Ornan looked and saw David, and went out of the threshing-floor, and bowed himself to David with his face to the ground. ²²Then David said to Ornan, 'Grant me the place of this threshing-floor, that I may build an altar therein unto the LORD: thou shalt grant it me for the full price, that the plague may be stayed from the people'. ²³And Ornan said unto David, 'Take it to thee, and let my lord the king do that which is good in his eyes: lo, I give thee the oxen also for burnt offerings, and the threshing instru-

ments for wood, and the wheat for the meat offering, I give it all'. ²⁴And king David said to Ornan, 'Nay, but I will verily buy it for the full price: for I will not take that which is thine for the LORD, nor offer burnt offerings without cost'. ²⁵So David gave to Ornan for the place six hundred shekels of gold by weight. ²⁶And David built there an altar unto the LORD, and offered burnt offerings and peace offerings, and called upon the LORD; and he answered him from heaven by fire upon the altar of burnt offering. ²⁷And the LORD commanded the angel, and he put up his sword again into the sheath thereof.

²⁸At that time when David saw that the LORD had answered him in the threshing-floor of Ornan the Jebusite, then he sacrificed there. ²⁹For the tabernacle of the LORD which Moses made in the wilderness, and the altar of the burnt offering were at that season in the high place at Gibeon. ³⁰But David could not go before it to inquire of God: for he was afraid because of the sword of the angel of the LORD.

22 Then David said, 'This is the house of the LORD God, and this is the altar of the burnt offering for Israel'. ²And David commanded to gather together the strangers that were in the land of Israel: and he set masons to hew wrought stones to build the house of God. ³And David prepared iron in abundance for the nails for the doors of the gates, and for the joinings, and brass in abundance without weight; ⁴also cedar trees in abundance: for the Zidonians and they of Tyre brought much cedar wood to David. ⁵And David said, 'Solomon my son is young and tender, and the house that is to be built for the LORD must be exceeding magnifical, of fame and of glory throughout all countries: I will therefore now make preparation for it'. So David prepared abundantly before his death.

⁶Then he called for Solomon his son, and charged him to build a house for the LORD God of Israel. ⁷And David said to Solomon, 'My son, as for me, it was in my mind to build a house unto the name of the LORD my God. ⁸But the word of the LORD came to me, saying, "Thou hast shed blood abundantly, and hast made great wars: thou shalt not build a house unto my name, because thou hast shed much blood upon the earth in my sight. ⁹Behold, a son shall be born to thee, who shall be a man of rest, and I will give him rest from all his enemies round about: for his name shall be Solomon, and I will give peace and quietness unto Israel in his days. ¹⁰He shall build a house for my name, and he shall be my son, and I will be his father, and I will establish the throne of his kingdom over Israel for ever." ¹¹Now my son, the LORD be with thee, and prosper thou, and build the house of the LORD thy God, as he hath said of thee. ¹²Only the LORD give thee wisdom and understanding, and give thee charge concerning Israel, that thou mayest keep the law of the LORD thy God. ¹³Then shalt thou prosper, if thou takest heed to fulfil the statutes and judgements which the LORD charged Moses with concerning Israel: be strong, and of good courage, dread not, nor be dismayed. ¹⁴Now behold, in my trouble I have prepared for the house of the LORD a hundred thousand talents of gold, and a thousand thousand talents of silver, and of brass and iron without weight (for it is in abundance):

timber also and stone have I prepared, and thou mayest add thereto. ¹⁵Moreover there are workmen with thee in abundance, hewers and workers of stone and timber, and all manner of cunning men for every manner of work. ¹⁶Of the gold, the silver, and the brass, and the iron, there is no number. Arise therefore, and be doing, and the LORD be with thee.'

¹⁷David also commanded all the princes of Israel to help Solomon his son, saying, ¹⁸'Is not the LORD your God with you? and hath he not given you rest on every side? for he hath given the inhabitants of the land into my hand, and the land is subdued before the LORD, and before his people. ¹⁹Now set your heart and your soul to seek the LORD your God: arise therefore, and build ye the sanctuary of the LORD God, to bring the ark of the covenant of the LORD, and the holy vessels of God, into the house that is to be built to the name of the LORD.'

23

So when David was old and full of days, he made Solomon his son king over Israel.

²And he gathered together all the princes of Israel, with the priests and the Levites. ³Now the Levites were numbered from the age of thirty years and upward: and their number by their polls, man by man, was thirty and eight thousand. ⁴Of which, twenty and four thousand were to set forward the work of the house of the LORD; and six thousand were officers and judges. ⁵Moreover four thousand were porters, and four thousand praised the LORD with the instruments which I made, said David, to praise therewith. ⁶And David divided them into courses among the sons of Levi, namely, Gershon, Kohath, and Merari.

⁷Of the Gershonites were Laadan, and Shimei. ⁸The sons of Laadan: the chief was Jehiel, and Zetham, and Joel, three. ⁹The sons of Shimei: Shelomith, and Haziel, and Haran, three. These were the chief of the fathers of Laadan. ¹⁰And the sons of Shimei were: Jahath, Zina, and Jeush, and Beriah. These four were the sons of Shimei. ¹¹And Jahath was the chief, and Zizah the second: but Jeush and Beriah had not many sons: therefore they were in one reckoning, according to their father's house.

¹²The sons of Kohath: Amram, Izhar, Hebron, and Uzziel, four. ¹³The sons of Amram: Aaron and Moses: and Aaron was separated, that he should sanctify the most holy things, he and his sons for ever, to burn incense before the LORD, to minister unto him, and to bless in his name for ever. ¹⁴Now concerning Moses the man of God, his sons were named of the tribe of Levi. ¹⁵The sons of Moses were: Gershom, and Eliezer. ¹⁶Of the sons of Gershom Shebuel was the chief. ¹⁷And the sons of Eliezer were: Rehabiah the chief. And Eliezer had no other sons: but the sons of Rehabiah were very many. ¹⁸Of the sons of Izhar: Shelomith the chief. ¹⁹Of the sons of Hebron: Jeriah the first, Amariah the second, Jahaziel the third, and Jekameam the fourth. ²⁰Of the sons of Uzziel: Michah the first and Jesiah the second.

²¹The sons of Merari: Mahli, and Mushi. The sons of Mahli: Eleazar, and Kish. ²²And Eleazar died, and had no sons, but daughters: and their brethren the sons of Kish took them. ²³The sons of Mushi: Mahli, and Eder, and Jeremoth, three.

²⁴These were the sons of Levi after the house of their fathers; even the chief of the fathers, as they were counted by number of names by their polls, that did the work for the service of the house of the LORD, from the age of twenty years and upward. ²⁵For David said, 'The LORD God of Israel hath given rest unto his people, that they may dwell in Jerusalem for ever. ²⁶And also unto the Levites: they shall no more carry the tabernacle, nor any vessels of it for the service thereof.' ²⁷For by the last words of David the Levites were numbered from twenty years old and above: ²⁸because their office was to wait on the sons of Aaron for the service of the house of the LORD, in the courts, and in the chambers, and in the purifying of all holy things, and the work of the service of the house of God: ²⁹both for the showbread, and for the fine flour for meat offering, and for the unleavened cakes, and for that which is baked in the pan, and for that which is fried, and for all manner of measure and size; ³⁰and to stand every morning to thank and praise the LORD, and likewise at even; ³¹and to offer all burnt sacrifices unto the LORD in the sabbaths, in the new moons, and on the set feasts, by number, according to the order commanded unto them continually before the LORD: ³²and that they should keep the charge of the tabernacle of the congregation, and the charge of the holy place, and the charge of the sons of Aaron their brethren, in the service of the house of the LORD.

24 Now these are the divisions of the sons of Aaron. The sons of Aaron: Nadab, and Abihu, Eleazar, and Ithamar. ²But Nadab and Abihu died before their father, and had no children: therefore Eleazar and Ithamar executed the priest's office. ³And David distributed them, both Zadok of the sons of Eleazar, and Ahimelech of the sons of Ithamar, according to their offices in their service. ⁴And there were more chief men found of the sons of Eleazar than of the sons of Ithamar: and thus were they divided. Among the sons of Eleazar there were sixteen chief men of the house of their fathers, and eight among the sons of Ithamar according to the house of their fathers. ⁵Thus were they divided by lot, one sort with another; for the governors of the sanctuary, and governors of the house of God, were of the sons of Eleazar, and of the sons of Ithamar. ⁶And Shemaiah the son of Nethaneel the scribe, one of the Levites, wrote them before the king, and the princes, and Zadok the priest, and Ahimelech the son of Abiathar, and before the chief of the fathers of the priests and Levites: one principal household being taken for Eleazar, and one taken for Ithamar. ⁷Now the first lot came forth to Jehoiarib, the second to Jedaiah, ⁸the third to Harim, the fourth to Seorim, ⁹the fifth to Malchijah, the sixth to Mijamin, ¹⁰the seventh to Hakkoz, the eighth to Abijah, ¹¹the ninth to Jeshua, the tenth to Shechaniah, ¹²the eleventh to Eliashib, the twelfth to Jakim, ¹³the thirteenth to Huppah, the fourteenth to Jeshebeab, ¹⁴the fifteenth to Bilgah, the sixteenth to Immer, ¹⁵the seventeenth to Hezir, the eighteenth to Aphses, ¹⁶the nineteenth to Pethahiah, the twentieth to Jehezekel, ¹⁷the one and twentieth to Jachin, the two and twentieth to Gamul, ¹⁸the three and twentieth to Delaiah, the four and twentieth to Maaziah. ¹⁹These were the orderings of them in their service to come into the house of the LORD, according to their manner, under Aaron their father, as the LORD God of Israel had commanded him.

²⁰And the rest of the sons of Levi were these: of the sons of Amram, Shubael: of the sons of Shubael, Jehdeiah. ²¹Concerning Rehabiah: of the sons of Rehabiah, the first was Isshiah. ²²Of the Izharites, Shelomoth: of the sons of Shelomoth, Jahath. ²³And the sons of Hebron, Jeriah the first, Amariah the second, Jahaziel the third, Jekameam the fourth. ²⁴Of the sons of Uzziel, Michah: of the sons of Michah, Shamir. ²⁵The brother of Michah was Isshiah: of the sons of Isshiah, Zechariah. ²⁶The sons of Merari were Mahli and Mushi: the sons of Jaaziah, Beno. ²⁷The sons of Merari by Jaaziah: Beno, and Shoham, and Zaccur, and Ibri. ²⁸Of Mahli came Eleazar, who had no sons. ²⁹Concerning Kish: the son of Kish was Jerahmeel. ³⁰The sons also of Mushi: Mahli, and Eder, and Jerimoth. These were the sons of the Levites after the house of their fathers. ³¹These likewise cast lots over against their brethren the sons of Aaron in the presence of David the king, and Zadok, and Ahimelech, and the chief of the fathers of the priests and Levites, even the principal fathers over against their younger brethren.

25 Moreover David and the captains of the host separated to the service of the sons of Asaph, and of Heman, and of Jeduthun, who should prophesy with harps, with psalteries, and with cymbals: and the number of the workmen according to their service was: ²of the sons of Asaph: Zaccur, and Joseph, and Nethaniah, and Asarelah, the sons of Asaph under the hands of Asaph, which prophesied according to the order of the king. ³Of Jeduthun: the sons of Jeduthun, Gedaliah, and Zeri, and Jeshaiah, Hashabiah, and Mattithiah, six, under the hands of their father Jeduthun, who prophesied with a harp, to give thanks and to praise the LORD. ⁴Of Heman: the sons of Heman, Bukkiah, Mattaniah, Uzziel, Shebuel, and Jerimoth, Hananiah, Hanani, Eliathah, Giddalti, and Romamti-ezer, Joshbekashah, Mallothi, Hothir, and Mahazioth: ⁵all these were the sons of Heman the king's seer in the words of God, to lift up the horn. And God gave to Heman fourteen sons and three daughters. ⁶All these were under the hands of their father for song in the house of the LORD with cymbals, psalteries, and harps, for the service of the house of God, according to the king's order to Asaph, Jeduthun, and Heman. ⁷So the number of them, with their brethren that were instructed in the songs of the LORD, even all that were cunning, was two hundred fourscore and eight.

⁸And they cast lots ward against ward, as well the small as the great, the teacher as the scholar. ⁹Now the first lot came forth for Asaph to Joseph: the second to Gedaliah, who with his brethren and sons were twelve: ¹⁰the third to Zaccur, he, his sons, and his brethren, were twelve: ¹¹the fourth to Izri, he, his sons, and his brethren, were twelve: ¹²the fifth to Nethaniah, he, his sons, and his brethren, were twelve: ¹³the sixth to Bukkiah, he, his sons, and his brethren, were twelve: ¹⁴the seventh to Jesharelah, he, his sons, and his brethren, were twelve: ¹⁵the eighth to Jeshaiah, he, his sons, and his brethren, were twelve: ¹⁶the

ninth to Mattaniah, he, his sons, and his brethren, were twelve: [17] the tenth to Shimei, he, his sons, and his brethren, were twelve: [18] the eleventh to Azareel, he, his sons, and his brethren, were twelve: [19] the twelfth to Hashabiah, he, his sons, and his brethren, were twelve: [20] the thirteenth to Shubael, he, his sons, and his brethren, were twelve: [21] the fourteenth to Mattithiah, he, his sons, and his brethren, were twelve: [22] the fifteenth to Jeremoth, he, his sons, and his brethren, were twelve: [23] the sixteenth to Hananiah, he, his sons, and his brethren, were twelve: [24] the seventeenth to Joshbekashah, he, his sons, and his brethren, were twelve: [25] the eighteenth to Hanani, he, his sons, and his brethren, were twelve: [26] the nineteenth to Mallothi, he, his sons, and his brethren, were twelve: [27] the twentieth to Eliathah, he, his sons, and his brethren, were twelve: [28] the one and twentieth to Hothir, he, his sons, and his brethren, were twelve: [29] the two and twentieth to Giddalti, he, his sons, and his brethren, were twelve: [30] the three and twentieth to Mahazioth, he, his sons, and his brethren, were twelve: [31] the four and twentieth to Romamti-ezer, he, his sons, and his brethren, were twelve.

26

Concerning the divisions of the porters: of the Korhites was Meshelemiah the son of Kore, of the sons of Asaph. [2] And the sons of Meshelemiah were Zechariah the firstborn, Jediael the second, Zebadiah the third, Jathniel the fourth, [3] Elam the fifth, Jehohanan the sixth, Elioenai the seventh. [4] Moreover the sons of Obed-edom were Shemaiah the firstborn, Jehozabad the second, Joah the third, and Sacar the fourth, and Nethaneel the fifth, [5] Ammiel the sixth, Issachar the seventh, Peulthai the eighth: for God blessed him. [6] Also unto Shemaiah his son were sons born, that ruled throughout the house of their father: for they were mighty men of valour. [7] The sons of Shemaiah: Othni, and Rephael, and Obed, Elzabad, whose brethren were strong men, Elihu, and Semachiah. [8] All these of the sons of Obed-edom: they and their sons and their brethren, able men for strength for the service, were threescore and two of Obed-edom. [9] And Meshelemiah had sons and brethren, strong men, eighteen. [10] Also Hosah, of the children of Merari, had sons: Simri the chief (for though he was not the firstborn, yet his father made him the chief), [11] Hilkiah the second, Tebaliah the third, Zechariah the fourth: all the sons and brethren of Hosah were thirteen. [12] Among these were the divisions of the porters, even among the chief men, having wards one against another, to minister in the house of the LORD.

[13] And they cast lots, as well the small as the great, according to the house of their fathers, for every gate. [14] And the lot eastward fell to Shelemiah. Then for Zechariah his son, a wise counsellor, they cast lots, and his lot came out northward. [15] To Obed-edom southward, and to his sons the house of Asuppim. [16] To Shuppim and Hosah the lot came forth westward, with the gate Shallecheth, by the causeway of the going up, ward against ward. [17] Eastward were six Levites, northward four a day, southward four a day, and toward Asuppim two and two. [18] And Parbar westward, four at the causeway, and two at Parbar. [19] These are the divi-

sions of the porters among the sons of Kore, and among the sons of Merari.

²⁰And of the Levites, Ahijah was over the treasures of the house of God, and over the treasures of the dedicated things. ²¹As concerning the sons of Laadan; the sons of the Gershonite Laadan, chief fathers, even of Laadan the Gershonite, were Jehieli. ²²The sons of Jehieli, Zetham, and Joel his brother, which were over the treasures of the house of the LORD. ²³Of the Amramites, and the Izharites, the Hebronites, and the Uzzielites: ²⁴and Shebuel the son of Gershom, the son of Moses, was ruler of the treasures. ²⁵And his brethren by Eliezer: Rehabiah his son, and Jeshaiah his son, and Joram his son, and Zichri his son, and Shelomith his son. ²⁶Which Shelomith and his brethren were over all the treasures of the dedicated things, which David the king, and the chief fathers, the captains over thousands and hundreds, and the captains of the host had dedicated. ²⁷Out of the spoils won in battles did they dedicate to maintain the house of the LORD. ²⁸And all that Samuel the seer, and Saul the son of Kish, and Abner the son of Ner, and Joab the son of Zeruiah, had dedicated and whosoever had dedicated anything, it was under the hand of Shelomith, and of his brethren.

²⁹Of the Izharites, Chenaniah and his sons were for the outward business over Israel, for officers and judges. ³⁰And of the Hebronites, Hashabiah and his brethren, men of valour, a thousand and seven hundred, were officers among them of Israel on this side Jordan westward in all business of the LORD, and in the service of the king. ³¹Among the Hebronites was Jerijah the chief, even among the Hebronites, according to the generations of his fathers. In the fortieth year of the reign of David they were sought for, and there were found among them mighty men of valour at Jazer of Gilead. ³²And his brethren, men of valour, were two thousand and seven hundred chief fathers, whom king David made rulers over the Reubenites, the Gadites, and the half tribe of Manasseh, for every matter pertaining to God, and affairs of the king.

27 Now the children of Israel after their number, to wit, the chief fathers and captains of thousands and hundreds, and their officers that served the king in any matter of the courses, which came in and went out month by month throughout all the months of the year, of every course were twenty and four thousand. ²Over the first course for the first month was Jashobeam the son of Zabdiel: and in his course were twenty and four thousand. ³Of the children of Perez was the chief of all the captains of the host for the first month. ⁴And over the course of the second month was Dodai an Ahohite, and of his course was Mikloth also the ruler: in his course likewise were twenty and four thousand. ⁵The third captain of the host for the third month was Benaiah the son of Jehoiada, a chief priest: and in his course were twenty and four thousand. ⁶This is that Benaiah, who was mighty among the thirty, and above the thirty: and in his course was Ammizabad his son. ⁷The fourth captain for the fourth month was Asahel the brother of Joab, and Zebadiah his son after him: and in his course were twenty and four thousand. ⁸The fifth captain for the fifth month was Shamhuth the Izrahite: and in his course were twenty and four thousand. ⁹The sixth captain for the sixth month was Ira the son of Ikkesh the Tekoite: and in his course were twenty and four thousand. ¹⁰The seventh captain for the seventh month was Helez the Pelonite, of the children of Ephraim: and in his course were twenty and four thousand. ¹¹The eighth captain for the eighth month was Sibbecai the Hushathite, of the Zarhites: and in his course were twenty and four thousand. ¹²The ninth captain for the ninth month was Abi-ezer the Anetothite, of the Benjamites: and in his course were twenty and four thousand. ¹³The tenth captain for the tenth month was Maharai the Netophathite, of the Zarhites: and in his course were twenty and four thousand. ¹⁴The eleventh captain for the eleventh month was Benaiah the Pirathonite, of the children of Ephraim: and in his course were twenty and four thousand. ¹⁵The twelfth captain for the twelfth month was Heldai the Netophathite, of Othniel: and in his course were twenty and four thousand.

¹⁶Furthermore over the tribes of Israel: the ruler of the Reubenites was Eliezer the son of Zichri: of the Simeonites, Shephatiah the son of Maachah: ¹⁷of the Levites, Hashabiah the son of Kemuel: of the Aaronites, Zadok: ¹⁸of Judah, Elihu, one of the brethren of David: of Issachar, Omri the son of Michael: ¹⁹of Zebulun, Ishmaiah the son of Obadiah: of Naphtali, Jerimoth the son of Azriel: ²⁰of the children of Ephraim, Hoshea the son of Azaziah: of the half tribe of Manasseh, Joel the son of Pedaiah: ²¹of the half tribe of Manasseh in Gilead, Iddo the son of Zechariah: of Benjamin, Jaasiel the son of Abner: ²²of Dan, Azareel the son of Jeroham. These were the princes of the tribes of Israel.

²³But David took not the number of them from twenty years old and under: because the LORD had said he would increase Israel like to the stars of the heavens. ²⁴Joab the son of Zeruiah began to number, but he finished not, because there fell wrath for it against Israel; neither was the number put in the account of the chronicles of king David.

²⁵And over the king's treasures was Azmaveth the son of Adiel: and over the storehouses in the fields, in the cities, and in the villages, and in the castles, was Jehonathan the son of Uzziah: ²⁶and over them that did the work of the field for tillage of the ground was Ezri the son of Chelub: ²⁷and over the vineyards was Shimei the Ramathite: over the increase of the vineyards for the wine-cellars was Zabdi the Shiphmite: ²⁸and over the olive trees and the sycamore trees that were in the low plains was Baal-hanan the Gederite: and over the cellars of oil was Joash: ²⁹and over the herds that fed in Sharon was Shitrai the Sharonite: and over the herds that were in the valleys was Shaphat the son of Adlai: ³⁰over the camels also was Obil the Ishmaelite: and over the asses was Jehdeiah the Meronothite: ³¹and over the flocks was Jaziz the Hagerite. All these were the rulers of the substance which was king David's. ³²Also Jonathan David's uncle was a counsellor, a wise man, and a scribe: and Jehiel the son of Hachmoni was with the king's sons: ³³and Ahithophel was the king's counsellor: and Hushai the Archite was

the king's companion: ³⁴and after Ahithophel was Jehoiada the son of Benaiah, and Abiathar: and the general of the king's army was Joab.

28 And David assembled all the princes of Israel, the princes of the tribes, and the captains of the companies that ministered to the king by course, and the captains over the thousands, and captains over the hundreds, and the stewards over all the substance and possession of the king, and of his sons, with the officers, and with the mighty men, and with all the valiant men, unto Jerusalem. ²Then David the king stood up upon his feet, and said, 'Hear me, my brethren, and my people: as for me, I had in my heart to build a house of rest for the ark of the covenant of the LORD, and for the footstool of our God, and had made ready for the building: ³but God said unto me, "Thou shalt not build a house for my name, because thou hast been a man of war, and hast shed blood". ⁴Howbeit the LORD God of Israel chose me before all the house of my father to be king over Israel for ever: for he hath chosen Judah to be the ruler; and of the house of Judah, the house of my father; and among the sons of my father he liked me to make me king over all Israel: ⁵and of all my sons (for the LORD hath given me many sons), he hath chosen Solomon my son to sit upon the throne of the kingdom of the LORD over Israel. ⁶And he said unto me, "Solomon thy son, he shall build my house and my courts: for I have chosen him to be my son, and I will be his father. ⁷Moreover I will establish his kingdom for ever, if he be constant to do my commandments and my judgements, as at this day." ⁸Now therefore in the sight of all Israel, the congregation of the LORD, and in the audience of our God, keep and seek for all the commandments of the LORD your God, that ye may possess this good land, and leave it for an inheritance for your children after you for ever.

⁹'And thou, Solomon my son, know thou the God of thy father, and serve him with a perfect heart and with a willing mind: for the LORD searcheth all hearts, and understandeth all the imaginations of the thoughts: if thou seek him, he will be found of thee; but if thou forsake him, he will cast thee off for ever. ¹⁰Take heed now, for the LORD hath chosen thee to build a house for the sanctuary: be strong, and do it.'

¹¹Then David gave to Solomon his son the pattern of the porch, and of the houses thereof, and of the treasuries thereof, and of the upper chambers thereof, and of the inner parlours thereof, and of the place of the mercy-seat, ¹²and the pattern of all that he had by the spirit, of the courts of the house of the LORD, and of all the chambers round about, of the treasuries of the house of God, and of the treasuries of the dedicated things: ¹³also for the courses of the priests and the Levites, and for all the work of the service of the house of the LORD, and for all the vessels of service in the house of the LORD. ¹⁴He gave of gold by weight for things of gold, for all instruments of all manner of service; silver also for all instruments of silver by weight, for all instruments of every kind of service: ¹⁵even the weight for the candlesticks of gold, and for their lamps of gold, by weight for every candlestick, and for the lamps thereof: and for the candlesticks of silver by weight, both for the

candlestick, and also for the lamps thereof, according to the use of every candlestick. ¹⁶And by weight he gave gold for the tables of show-bread, for every table, and likewise silver for the tables of silver: ¹⁷also pure gold for the fleshhooks, and the bowls, and the cups: and for the golden basins he gave gold by weight for every basin; and likewise silver by weight for every basin of silver: ¹⁸and for the altar of incense refined gold by weight; and gold for the pattern of the chariot of the cherubims, that spread out their wings, and covered the ark of the covenant of the Lord. ¹⁹'All this,' said David, 'the Lord made me understand in writing by his hand upon me, even all the works of this pattern.' ²⁰And David said to Solomon his son, 'Be strong and of good courage, and do it: fear not, nor be dismayed, for the Lord God, even my God, will be with thee; he will not fail thee, nor forsake thee, until thou hast finished all the work for the service of the house of the Lord. ²¹And behold, the courses of the priests and the Levites, even they shall be with thee for all the service of the house of God: and there shall be with thee for all manner of workmanship every willing skilful man, for any manner of service: also the princes and all the people will be wholly at thy commandment.'

29 Furthermore David the king said unto all the congregation, 'Solomon my son, whom alone God hath chosen, is yet young and tender, and the work is great: for the palace is not for man, but for the Lord God. ²Now I have prepared with all my might for the house of my God the gold for things to be made of gold, the silver for things of silver, and the brass for things of brass, the iron for things of iron, and wood for things of wood, onyx stones, and stones to be set, glistering stones, and of divers colours, and all manner of precious stones, and marble stones in abundance. ³Moreover, because I have set my affection to the house of my God, I have of my own proper good, of gold and silver, which I have given to the house of my God, over and above all that I have prepared for the holy house: ⁴even three thousand talents of gold, of the gold of Ophir, and seven thousand talents of refined silver, to overlay the walls of the houses withal: ⁵the gold for things of gold, and the silver for things of silver, and for all manner of work to be made by the hands of artificers. And who then is willing to consecrate his service this day unto the Lord?'

⁶Then the chief of the fathers and princes of the tribes of Israel, and the captains of thousands and of hundreds, with the rulers over the king's work, offered willingly, ⁷and gave for the service of the house of God of gold five thousand talents and ten thousand drams, and of silver ten thousand talents, and of brass eighteen thousand talents, and one hundred thousand talents of iron. ⁸And they with whom precious stones were found gave them to the treasure of the house of the Lord, by the hand of Jehiel the Gershonite. ⁹Then the people rejoiced, for that they offered willingly, because with perfect heart they offered willingly to the Lord: and David the king also rejoiced with great joy.

¹⁰Wherefore David blessed the Lord before all the congregation: and David said, 'Blessed be thou, Lord God of Israel our father, for ever and

ever. ¹¹Thine, O LORD, is the greatness, and the power, and the glory, and the victory, and the majesty: for all that is in the heaven and in the earth is thine: thine is the kingdom, O LORD, and thou art exalted as head above all. ¹²Both riches and honour come of thee, and thou reignest over all; and in thy hand is power and might, and in thy hand it is to make great, and to give strength unto all. ¹³Now therefore, our God, we thank thee, and praise thy glorious name. ¹⁴But who am I, and what is my people, that we should be able to offer so willingly after this sort? for all things come of thee, and of thy own have we given thee. ¹⁵For we are strangers before thee, and sojourners, as were all our fathers: our days on the earth are as a shadow, and there is no abiding. ¹⁶O LORD our God, all this store that we have prepared to build thee a house for thy holy name cometh of thy hand, and is all thy own. ¹⁷I know also, my God, that thou triest the heart, and hast pleasure in uprightness. As for me, in the uprightness of my heart I have willingly offered all these things: and now have I seen with joy thy people, which are present here, to offer willingly unto thee. ¹⁸O LORD God of Abraham, Isaac, and of Israel, our fathers, keep this for ever in the imagination of the thoughts of the heart of thy people, and prepare their heart unto thee: ¹⁹and give unto Solomon my son a perfect heart to keep thy commandments, thy testimonies, and thy statutes, and to do all these things, and to build the palace, for the which I have made provision.'

²⁰And David said to all the congregation, 'Now bless the LORD your God'. And all the congregation blessed the LORD God of their fathers, and bowed down their heads, and worshipped the LORD, and the king. ²¹And they sacrificed sacrifices unto the LORD, and offered burnt offerings unto the LORD on the morrow after that day, even a thousand bullocks, a thousand rams, and a thousand lambs, with their drink offerings, and sacrifices in abundance for all Israel: ²²and did eat and drink before the LORD on that day with great gladness. And they made Solomon the son of David king the second time, and anointed him unto the LORD to be the chief governor, and Zadok to be priest. ²³Then Solomon sat on the throne of the LORD as king instead of David his father, and prospered, and all Israel obeyed him. ²⁴And all the princes, and the mighty men, and all the sons likewise of king David, submitted themselves unto Solomon the king. ²⁵And the LORD magnified Solomon exceedingly in the sight of all Israel, and bestowed upon him such royal majesty as had not been on any king before him in Israel.

²⁶Thus David the son of Jesse reigned over all Israel. ²⁷And the time that he reigned over Israel was forty years. Seven years reigned he in Hebron, and thirty and three years reigned he in Jerusalem. ²⁸And he died in a good old age, full of days, riches, and honour: and Solomon his son reigned in his stead. ²⁹Now the acts of David the king, first and last, behold, they are written in the book of Samuel the seer, and in the book of Nathan the prophet, and in the book of Gad the seer, ³⁰with all his reign and his might, and the times that went over him, and over Israel, and over all the kingdoms of the countries.

THE SECOND BOOK OF THE
CHRONICLES

1 And Solomon the son of David was strengthened in his kingdom, and the LORD his God was with him, and magnified him exceedingly. ²Then Solomon spoke unto all Israel, to the captains of thousands and of hundreds, and to the judges, and to every governor in all Israel, the chief of the fathers. ³So Solomon, and all the congregation with him, went to the high place that was at Gibeon, for there was the tabernacle of the congregation of God, which Moses the servant of the LORD had made in the wilderness. ⁴But the ark of God had David brought up from Kirjath-jearim to the place which David had prepared for it: for he had pitched a tent for it at Jerusalem. ⁵Moreover the brazen altar that Bezaleel the son of Uri, the son of Hur, had made, he put before the tabernacle of the LORD: and Solomon and the congregation sought unto it. ⁶And Solomon went up thither to the brazen altar before the LORD, which was at the tabernacle of the congregation, and offered a thousand burnt offerings upon it.

⁷In that night did God appear unto Solomon, and said unto him, 'Ask what I shall give thee'. ⁸And Solomon said unto God, 'Thou hast shown great mercy unto David my father, and hast made me to reign in his stead. ⁹Now, O LORD God, let thy promise unto David my father be established: for thou hast made me king over a people like the dust of the earth in multitude. ¹⁰Give me now wisdom and knowledge, that I may go out and come in before this people. For who can judge this thy people, that is so great?' ¹¹And God said to Solomon, 'Because this was in thy heart, and thou hast not asked riches, wealth, or honour, nor the life of thy enemies, neither yet hast asked long life; but hast asked wisdom and knowledge for thyself, that thou mayest judge my people, over whom I have made thee king: ¹²wisdom and knowledge is granted unto thee, and I will give thee riches, and wealth, and honour, such as none of the kings have had that have been before thee, neither shall there any after thee have the like'.

¹³Then Solomon came from his journey to the high place that was at Gibeon to Jerusalem, from before the tabernacle of the congregation, and reigned over Israel. ¹⁴And Solomon gathered chariots and horsemen: and he had a thousand and four hundred chariots, and twelve thousand horsemen, which he placed in the chariot-cities, and with the king at Jerusalem. ¹⁵And the king made silver and gold at Jerusalem as plenteous as stones, and cedar trees made he as the sycamore trees that are in the vale for abundance. ¹⁶And Solomon had horses brought out of Egypt, and linen yarn: the king's merchants received the linen yarn at a price. ¹⁷And they fetched up, and brought forth out of Egypt a chariot for six hundred shekels of silver, and a horse for a hundred and fifty: and so brought they out horses for all the kings of the Hittites, and for the kings of Syria, by their means.

2 And Solomon determined to build a house for the name of the LORD, and a house for his kingdom. [2]And Solomon told out threescore and ten thousand men to bear burdens, and fourscore thousand to hew in the mountain, and three thousand and six hundred to oversee them.

[3]And Solomon sent to Huram the king of Tyre, saying, 'As thou didst deal with David my father, and didst send him cedars to build him a house to dwell therein, even so deal with me. [4]Behold, I build a house to the name of the LORD my God, to dedicate it to him, and to burn before him sweet incense, and for the continual showbread, and for the burnt offerings morning and evening, on the sabbaths, and on the new moons, and on the solemn feasts of the LORD our God. This is an ordinance for ever to Israel. [5]And the house which I build is great: for great is our God above all gods. [6]But who is able to build him a house, seeing the heaven and heaven of heavens cannot contain him? who am I then, that I should build him a house, save only to burn sacrifice before him? [7]Send me now therefore a man cunning to work in gold, and in silver, and in brass, and in iron, and in purple, and crimson, and blue, and that can skill to grave with the cunning men that are with me in Judah and in Jerusalem, whom David my father did provide. [8]Send me also cedar trees, fir trees, and algum trees, out of Lebanon (for I know that thy servants can skill to cut timber in Lebanon): and behold, my servants shall be with thy servants, [9]even to prepare me timber in abundance: for the house which I am about to build shall be wonderful great. [10]And behold, I will give to thy servants, the hewers that cut timber, twenty thousand measures of beaten wheat, and twenty thousand measures of barley, and twenty thousand baths of wine, and twenty thousand baths of oil.'

[11]Then Huram the king of Tyre answered in writing, which he sent to Solomon, 'Because the LORD hath loved his people, he hath made thee king over them'. [12]Huram said moreover, 'Blessed be the LORD God of Israel that made heaven and earth, who hath given to David the king a wise son, endued with prudence and understanding, that might build a house for the LORD, and a house for his kingdom. [13]And now I have sent a cunning man, endued with understanding, of Huram my father's, [14]the son of a woman of the daughters of Dan, and his father was a man of Tyre, skilful to work in gold, and in silver, in brass, in iron, in stone, and in timber, in purple, in blue, and in fine linen, and in crimson; also to grave any manner of graving, and to find out every device which shall be put to him, with thy cunning men, and with the cunning men of my lord David thy father. [15]Now therefore the wheat, and the barley, the oil, and the wine, which my lord hath spoken of, let him send unto his servants: [16]and we will cut wood out of Lebanon, as much as thou shalt need, and we will bring it to thee in floats by sea to Joppa, and thou shalt carry it up to Jerusalem.'

[17]And Solomon numbered all the strangers that were in the land of Israel, after the numbering wherewith David his father had numbered them: and they were found a hundred and fifty thousand and three

thousand and six hundred. [18]And he set threescore and ten thousand of them to be bearers of burdens, and fourscore thousand to be hewers in the mountain, and three thousand and six hundred overseers to set the people a-work.

3 Then Solomon began to build the house of the LORD at Jerusalem in mount Moriah, where the LORD appeared unto David his father, in the place that David had prepared in the threshing-floor of Ornan the Jebusite. [2]And he began to build in the second day of the second month, in the fourth year of his reign.

[3]Now these are the things wherein Solomon was instructed for the building of the house of God. The length by cubits after the first measure was threescore cubits, and the breadth twenty cubits. [4]And the porch that was in the front of the house, the length of it was according to the breadth of the house, twenty cubits, and the height was a hundred and twenty: and he overlaid it within with pure gold. [5]And the greater house he ceiled with fir tree, which he overlaid with fine gold, and set thereon palm trees and chains. [6]And he garnished the house with precious stones for beauty, and the gold was gold of Parvaim. [7]He overlaid also the house, the beams, the posts, and the walls thereof, and the doors thereof with gold, and graved cherubims on the walls. [8]And he made the most holy house, the length whereof was according to the breadth of the house, twenty cubits, and the breadth thereof twenty cubits: and he overlaid it with fine gold, amounting to six hundred talents. [9]And the weight of the nails was fifty shekels of gold. And he overlaid the upper chambers with gold.

[10]And in the most holy place he made two cherubims of image work, and overlaid them with gold. [11]And the wings of the cherubims were twenty cubits long: one wing of the one cherub was five cubits, reaching to the wall of the house: and the other wing was likewise five cubits, reaching to the wing of the other cherub. [12]And one wing of the other cherub was five cubits, reaching to the wall of the house: and the other wing was five cubits also, joining to the wing of the other cherub. [13]The wings of these cherubims spread themselves forth twenty cubits: and they stood on their feet, and their faces were inward.

[14]And he made the veil of blue, and purple, and crimson, and fine linen, and wrought cherubims thereon. [15]Also he made before the house two pillars of thirty and five cubits high, and the chapiter that was on the top of each of them was five cubits. [16]And he made chains, as in the oracle, and put them on the heads of the pillars, and made a hundred pomegranates, and put them on the chains. [17]And he reared up the pillars before the temple, one on the right hand, and the other on the left, and called the name of that on the right hand Jachin, and the name of that on the left Boaz.

4 Moreover he made an altar of brass, twenty cubits the length thereof, and twenty cubits the breadth thereof, and ten cubits the height thereof.

[2]Also he made a molten sea of ten cubits from brim to brim, round in compass, and five cubits the height thereof, and a line of thirty cubits

did compass it round about. ³And under it was the similitude of oxen, which did compass it round about: ten in a cubit, compassing the sea round about. Two rows of oxen were cast, when it was cast. ⁴It stood upon twelve oxen, three looking toward the north, and three looking toward the west, and three looking toward the south, and three looking toward the east: and the sea was set above upon them, and all their hinder parts were inward. ⁵And the thickness of it was a handbreadth, and the brim of it like the work of the brim of a cup, with flowers of lilies: and it received and held three thousand baths.

⁶He made also ten lavers, and put five on the right hand, and five on the left, to wash in them: such things as they offered for the burnt offering they washed in them, but the sea was for the priests to wash in. ⁷And he made ten candlesticks of gold according to their form, and set them in the temple, five on the right hand, and five on the left. ⁸He made also ten tables, and placed them in the temple, five on the right side, and five on the left. And he made a hundred basins of gold. ⁹Furthermore he made the court of the priests, and the great court, and doors for the court, and overlaid the doors of them with brass. ¹⁰And he set the sea on the right side of the east end, over against the south.

¹¹And Huram made the pots, and the shovels, and the basins. And Huram finished the work that he was to make for king Solomon for the house of God: ¹²to wit, the two pillars, and the pommels, and the chapiters which were on the top of the two pillars, and the two wreaths to cover the two pommels of the chapiters which were on the top of the pillars; ¹³and four hundred pomegranates on the two wreaths: two rows of pomegranates on each wreath, to cover the two pommels of the chapiters which were upon the pillars. ¹⁴He made also bases, and lavers made he upon the bases; ¹⁵one sea, and twelve oxen under it. ¹⁶The pots also, and the shovels, and the fleshhooks, and all their instruments, did Huram his father make to king Solomon for the house of the LORD of bright brass. ¹⁷In the plain of Jordan did the king cast them, in the clay ground between Succoth and Zeredathah. ¹⁸Thus Solomon made all these vessels in great abundance: for the weight of the brass could not be found out.

¹⁹And Solomon made all the vessels that were for the house of God, the golden altar also, and the tables whereon the showbread was set; ²⁰moreover the candlesticks with their lamps, that they should burn after the manner before the oracle, of pure gold; ²¹and the flowers, and the lamps, and the tongs, made he of gold, and that perfect gold; ²²and the snuffers, and the basins, and the spoons, and the censers, of pure gold. And the entry of the house, the inner doors thereof for the most holy place, and the doors of the house of the temple, were of gold.

5 Thus all the work that Solomon made for the house of the LORD was finished: and Solomon brought in all the things that David his father had dedicated; and the silver, and the gold, and all the instruments, put he among the treasures of the house of God.

²Then Solomon assembled the elders of Israel, and all the heads of the

tribes, the chief of the fathers of the children of Israel, unto Jerusalem, to bring up the ark of the covenant of the LORD out of the city of David, which is Zion. ³Wherefore all the men of Israel assembled themselves unto the king in the feast which was in the seventh month. ⁴And all the elders of Israel came, and the Levites took up the ark. ⁵And they brought up the ark, and the tabernacle of the congregation, and all the holy vessels that were in the tabernacle, these did the priests and the Levites bring up. ⁶Also king Solomon and all the congregation of Israel that were assembled unto him before the ark, sacrificed sheep and oxen, which could not be told nor numbered for multitude. ⁷And the priests brought in the ark of the covenant of the LORD unto his place, to the oracle of the house, into the most holy place, even under the wings of the cherubims: ⁸for the cherubims spread forth their wings over the place of the ark, and the cherubims covered the ark and the staves thereof, above. ⁹And they drew out the staves of the ark, that the ends of the staves were seen from the ark before the oracle; but they were not seen without. And there it is unto this day. ¹⁰There was nothing in the ark save the two tablets which Moses put therein at Horeb, when the LORD made a covenant with the children of Israel, when they came out of Egypt.

¹¹And it came to pass when the priests were come out of the holy place (for all the priests that were present were sanctified, and did not then wait by course: ¹²also the Levites which were the singers, all of them of Asaph, of Heman, of Jeduthun, with their sons and their brethren, being arrayed in white linen, having cymbals and psalteries and harps, stood at the east end of the altar, and with them a hundred and twenty priests sounding with trumpets): ¹³it came even to pass, as the trumpeters and singers were as one, to make one sound to be heard in praising and thanking the LORD; and when they lifted up their voice with the trumpets and cymbals and instruments of music, and praised the LORD, saying, 'For he is good, for his mercy endureth for ever': that then the house was filled with a cloud, even the house of the LORD; ¹⁴so that the priests could not stand to minister by reason of the cloud: for the glory of the LORD had filled the house of God.

6 Then said Solomon, 'The LORD hath said that he would dwell in the thick darkness. ²But I have built a house of habitation for thee, and a place for thy dwelling for ever.' ³And the king turned his face, and blessed the whole congregation of Israel: and all the congregation of Israel stood. ⁴And he said, 'Blessed be the LORD God of Israel, who hath with his hands fulfilled that which he spoke with his mouth to my father David, saying, ⁵"Since the day that I brought forth my people out of the land of Egypt, I chose no city among all the tribes of Israel to build a house in, that my name might be there, neither chose I any man to be a ruler over my people Israel: ⁶but I have chosen Jerusalem, that my name might be there, and have chosen David to be over my people Israel". ⁷Now it was in the heart of David my father to build a house for the name of the LORD God of Israel. ⁸But the LORD said to David my father, "Forasmuch as it was in thy heart to build a house for my name, thou didst well in that it was in thy heart. ⁹Notwithstanding thou shalt not build the house, but thy son which shall come forth out of thy loins, he shall build the house for my name." ¹⁰The LORD therefore hath performed his word that he hath spoken: for I am risen up in the room of David my father, and am set on the throne of Israel, as the LORD promised, and have built the house for the name of the LORD God of Israel. ¹¹And in it have I put the ark, wherein is the covenant of the LORD, that he made with the children of Israel.'

¹²And he stood before the altar of the LORD in the presence of all the congregation of Israel, and spread forth his hands ¹³(for Solomon had made a brazen scaffold of five cubits long, and five cubits broad, and three cubits high, and had set it in the midst of the court: and upon it he stood, and kneeled down upon his knees before all the congregation of Israel, and spread forth his hands towards heaven): ¹⁴and said, 'O LORD God of Israel, there is no God like thee in the heaven, nor in the earth; which keepest covenant, and showest mercy unto thy servants, that walk before thee with all their hearts: ¹⁵thou which hast kept with thy servant David my father that which thou hast promised him; and spokest with thy mouth, and hast fulfilled it with thy hand, as it is this day. ¹⁶Now therefore, O LORD God of Israel, keep with thy servant David my father that which thou hast promised him, saying, "There shall not fail thee a man in my sight to sit upon the throne of Israel; yet so, that thy children take heed to their way to walk in my law, as thou hast walked before me". ¹⁷Now then, O LORD God of Israel, let thy word be verified, which thou hast spoken unto thy servant David. ¹⁸(But will God in very deed dwell with men on the earth? behold, heaven and the heaven of heavens cannot contain thee: how much less this house which I have built?) ¹⁹Have respect therefore to the prayer of thy servant, and to his supplication, O LORD my God, to hearken unto the cry and the prayer which thy servant prayeth before thee: ²⁰that thy eyes may be open upon this house day and night, upon the place whereof thou hast said that thou wouldst put thy name there, to hearken unto the prayer which thy servant prayeth towards this place. ²¹Hearken therefore unto the supplications of thy servant, and of thy people Israel, which they shall make towards this place: hear thou from thy dwelling place, even from heaven; and when thou hearest, forgive.

²²'If a man sin against his neighbour, and an oath be laid upon him to make him swear, and the oath come before thy altar in this house: ²³then hear thou from heaven, and do, and judge thy servants by requiting the wicked, by recompensing his way upon his own head, and by justifying the righteous, by giving him according to his righteousness.

²⁴'And if thy people Israel be put to the worse before the enemy, because they have sinned against thee, and shall return and confess thy name, and pray and make supplication before thee in this house: ²⁵then hear thou from the heavens, and forgive the sin of thy people Israel, and bring them again unto the land which thou gavest to them and to their fathers.

²⁶'When the heaven is shut up, and there is no rain, because they have sinned against thee: yet if they pray towards this place, and confess thy name, and turn from their sin, when thou dost afflict them: ²⁷then hear thou from heaven, and forgive the sin of thy servants, and of thy people Israel, when thou hast taught them the good way, wherein they should walk, and send rain upon the land, which thou hast given unto thy people for an inheritance.

²⁸'If there be dearth in the land, if there be pestilence, if there be blasting, or mildew, locusts, or caterpillars; if their enemies besiege them in the cities of their land; whatsoever sore or whatsoever sickness there be: ²⁹then what prayer or what supplication soever shall be made of any man, or of all thy people Israel, when every one shall know his own sore and his own grief, and shall spread forth his hands in this house: ³⁰then hear thou from heaven thy dwelling place, and forgive, and render unto every man according unto all his ways, whose heart thou knowest (for thou only knowest the hearts of the children of men): ³¹that they may fear thee, to walk in thy ways so long as they live in the land which thou gavest unto our fathers.

³²'Moreover concerning the stranger which is not of thy people Israel, but is come from a far country for thy great name's sake, and thy mighty hand, and thy stretched out arm: if they come and pray in this house: ³³then hear thou from the heavens, even from thy dwelling place, and do according to all that the stranger calleth to thee for; that all people of the earth may know thy name, and fear thee, as doth thy people Israel, and may know that this house which I have built is called by thy name.

³⁴'If thy people go out to war against their enemies by the way that thou shalt send them, and they pray unto thee toward this city which thou hast chosen, and the house which I have built for thy name: ³⁵then hear thou from the heavens their prayer and their supplication, and maintain their cause. ³⁶If they sin against thee (for there is no man which sinneth not), and thou be angry with them, and deliver them over before their enemies, and they carry them away captives unto a land far off or near: ³⁷yet if they bethink themselves in the land whither they are carried captive, and turn and pray unto thee in the land of their captivity, saying, "We have sinned, we have done amiss, and have dealt wickedly": ³⁸if they return to thee with all their heart and with all their soul in the land of their captivity, whither they have carried them captives, and pray toward their land which thou gavest unto their fathers, and toward the city which thou hast chosen, and toward the house which I have built for thy name: ³⁹then hear thou from the heavens, even from thy dwelling place, their prayer and their supplications, and maintain their cause, and forgive thy people which have sinned against thee.

⁴⁰'Now, my God, let, I beseech thee, thy eyes be open, and let thy ears be attentive unto the prayer that is made in this place. ⁴¹Now therefore arise, O Lᴏʀᴅ God, into thy resting place, thou, and the ark of thy strength: let thy priests, O Lᴏʀᴅ God, be clothed with salvation, and let

thy saints rejoice in goodness. [42]O Lord God, turn not away the face of thy anointed: remember the mercies of David thy servant.'

7 Now when Solomon had made an end of praying, the fire came down from heaven, and consumed the burnt offering and the sacrifices, and the glory of the Lord filled the house. [2]And the priests could not enter into the house of the Lord, because the glory of the Lord had filled the Lord's house. [3]And when all the children of Israel saw how the fire came down, and the glory of the Lord upon the house, they bowed themselves with their faces to the ground upon the pavement, and worshipped, and praised the Lord, saying, 'For he is good, for his mercy endureth for ever'.

[4]Then the king and all the people offered sacrifices before the Lord. [5]And king Solomon offered a sacrifice of twenty and two thousand oxen, and a hundred and twenty thousand sheep. So the king and all the people dedicated the house of God. [6]And the priests waited on their offices: the Levites also with instruments of music of the Lord, which David the king had made to praise the Lord, because his mercy endureth for ever, when David praised by their ministry; and the priests sounded trumpets before them, and all Israel stood. [7]Moreover Solomon hallowed the middle of the court that was before the house of the Lord: for there he offered burnt offerings, and the fat of the peace offerings, because the brazen altar which Solomon had made was not able to receive the burnt offerings, and the meat offerings, and the fat.

[8]Also at the same time Solomon kept the feast seven days, and all Israel with him, a very great congregation, from the entering in of Hamath unto the river of Egypt. [9]And in the eighth day they made a solemn assembly: for they kept the dedication of the altar seven days, and the feast seven days. [10]And on the three and twentieth day of the seventh month he sent the people away into their tents, glad and merry in heart for the goodness that the Lord had shown unto David, and to Solomon, and to Israel his people.

[11]Thus Solomon finished the house of the Lord, and the king's house: and all that came into Solomon's heart to make in the house of the Lord, and in his own house, he prosperously effected.

[12]And the Lord appeared to Solomon by night, and said unto him, 'I have heard thy prayer, and have chosen this place to myself for a house of sacrifice. [13]If I shut up heaven that there be no rain, or if I command the locusts to devour the land, or if I send pestilence among my people; [14]if my people, which are called by my name, shall humble themselves, and pray, and seek my face, and turn from their wicked ways: then will I hear from heaven, and will forgive their sin, and will heal their land. [15]Now my eyes shall be open, and my ears attentive unto the prayer that is made in this place. [16]For now have I chosen and sanctified this house, that my name may be there for ever: and my eyes and my heart shall be there perpetually. [17]And as for thee, if thou wilt walk before me, as David thy father walked, and do according to all that I have commanded thee, and shalt observe my statutes and my judgements: [18]then will I establish the throne of thy kingdom, according as I have

covenanted with David thy father, saying, "There shall not fail thee a man to be ruler in Israel". ¹⁹But if ye turn away and forsake my statutes and my commandments which I have set before you, and shall go and serve other gods, and worship them: ²⁰then will I pluck them up by the roots out of my land which I have given them, and this house, which I have sanctified for my name, will I cast out of my sight, and will make it to be a proverb and a byword among all nations. ²¹And this house which is high, shall be an astonishment to every one that passeth by it: so that he shall say, "Why hath the LORD done thus unto this land, and unto this house?" ²²And it shall be answered, "Because they forsook the LORD God of their fathers, which brought them forth out of the land of Egypt, and laid hold on other gods, and worshipped them, and served them: therefore hath he brought all this evil upon them".'

8 And it came to pass at the end of twenty years, wherein Solomon had built the house of the LORD, and his own house, ²that the cities which Huram had restored to Solomon, Solomon built them, and caused the children of Israel to dwell there. ³And Solomon went to Hamath-zobah, and prevailed against it. ⁴And he built Tadmor in the wilderness, and all the store-cities, which he built in Hamath. ⁵Also he built Beth-horon the upper, and Beth-horon the nether, fenced cities, with walls, gates, and bars; ⁶and Baalath, and all the store-cities that Solomon had, and all the chariot-cities, and the cities of the horsemen, and all that Solomon desired to build in Jerusalem, and in Lebanon, and throughout all the land of his dominion.

⁷As for all the people that were left of the Hittites, and the Amorites, and the Perizzites, and the Hivites, and the Jebusites, which were not of Israel, ⁸but of their children, who were left after them in the land, whom the children of Israel consumed not, them did Solomon make to pay tribute until this day. ⁹But of the children of Israel did Solomon make no servants for his work: but they were men of war, and chief of his captains, and captains of his chariots and horsemen. ¹⁰And these were the chief of king Solomon's officers, even two hundred and fifty, that bore rule over the people.

¹¹And Solomon brought up the daughter of Pharaoh out of the city of David unto the house that he had built for her: for he said, 'My wife shall not dwell in the house of David king of Israel, because the places are holy, whereunto the ark of the LORD hath come'.

¹²Then Solomon offered burnt offerings unto the LORD on the altar of the LORD, which he had built before the porch, ¹³even after a certain rate every day, offering according to the commandment of Moses, on the sabbaths, and on the new moons, and on the solemn feasts three times in the year, even in the feast of unleavened bread, and in the feast of weeks, and in the feast of tabernacles.

¹⁴And he appointed, according to the order of David his father, the courses of the priests to their service, and the Levites to their charges, to praise and minister before the priests, as the duty of every day required: the porters also by their courses at every gate: for so had David the man of God commanded. ¹⁵And they departed not from the

commandment of the king unto the priests and Levites concerning any matter, or concerning the treasures. ¹⁶Now all the work of Solomon was prepared unto the day of the foundation of the house of the LORD, and until it was finished. So the house of the LORD was perfected.

¹⁷Then went Solomon to Ezion-geber, and to Eloth, at the seaside in the land of Edom. ¹⁸And Huram sent him by the hands of his servants ships, and servants that had knowledge of the sea; and they went with the servants of Solomon to Ophir, and took thence four hundred and fifty talents of gold, and brought them to king Solomon.

9 And when the queen of Sheba heard of the fame of Solomon, she came to prove Solomon with hard questions at Jerusalem, with a very great company, and camels that bore spices, and gold in abundance, and precious stones: and when she was come to Solomon, she communed with him of all that was in her heart. ²And Solomon told her all her questions: and there was nothing hid from Solomon which he told her not. ³And when the queen of Sheba had seen the wisdom of Solomon, and the house that he had built, ⁴and the meat of his table, and the sitting of his servants, and the attendance of his ministers, and their apparel, his cup-bearers also, and their apparel; and his ascent by which he went up into the house of the LORD; there was no more spirit in her. ⁵And she said to the king, 'It was a true report which I heard in my own land of thy acts, and of thy wisdom: ⁶howbeit I believed not their words, until I came, and my eyes had seen it: and behold, the one half of the greatness of thy wisdom was not told me: for thou exceedest the fame that I heard. ⁷Happy are thy men, and happy are these thy servants, which stand continually before thee, and hear thy wisdom. ⁸Blessed be the LORD thy God, which delighted in thee to set thee on his throne, to be king for the LORD thy God: because thy God loved Israel, to establish them for ever, therefore made he thee king over them, to do judgement and justice.' ⁹And she gave the king a hundred and twenty talents of gold, and of spices great abundance, and precious stones: neither was there any such spice as the queen of Sheba gave king Solomon. ¹⁰And the servants also of Huram, and the servants of Solomon, which brought gold from Ophir, brought algum trees and precious stones. ¹¹And the king made of the algum trees terraces to the house of the LORD, and to the king's palace, and harps and psalteries for singers: and there were none such seen before in the land of Judah. ¹²And king Solomon gave to the queen of Sheba all her desire, whatsoever she asked, besides that which she had brought unto the king. So she turned, and went away to her own land, she and her servants.

¹³Now the weight of gold that came to Solomon in one year was six hundred and threescore and six talents of gold; ¹⁴besides that which chapmen and merchants brought. And all the kings of Arabia and governors of the country brought gold and silver to Solomon.

¹⁵And king Solomon made two hundred targets of beaten gold: six hundred shekels of beaten gold went to one target. ¹⁶And three hundred shields made he of beaten gold: three hundred shekels of gold went to one shield. And the king put them in the house of the forest of

Lebanon. ¹⁷Moreover the king made a great throne of ivory, and over-laid it with pure gold. ¹⁸And there were six steps to the throne, with a footstool of gold, which were fastened to the throne, and stays on each side of the sitting-place, and two lions standing by the stays: ¹⁹and twelve lions stood there on the one side and on the other upon the six steps. There was not the like made in any kingdom.

²⁰And all the drinking vessels of king Solomon were of gold, and all the vessels of the house of the forest of Lebanon were of pure gold: none were of silver; it was not anything accounted of in the days of Solomon. ²¹For the king's ships went to Tarshish with the servants of Huram: every three years once came the ships of Tarshish bringing gold, and silver, ivory, and apes, and peacocks. ²²And king Solomon passed all the kings of the earth in riches and wisdom.

²³And all the kings of the earth sought the presence of Solomon, to hear his wisdom, that God had put in his heart. ²⁴And they brought every man his present, vessels of silver, and vessels of gold, and rai-ment, harness, and spices, horses, and mules, a rate year by year.

²⁵And Solomon had four thousand stalls for horses and chariots, and twelve thousand horsemen, whom he bestowed in the chariot-cities, and with the king at Jerusalem.

²⁶And he reigned over all the kings from the river even unto the land of the Philistines, and to the border of Egypt. ²⁷And the king made silver in Jerusalem as stones, and cedar trees made he as the sycamore trees that are in the low plains in abundance. ²⁸And they brought unto Solomon horses out of Egypt, and out of all lands.

²⁹Now the rest of the acts of Solomon, first and last, are they not writ-ten in the book of Nathan the prophet, and in the prophecy of Ahijah the Shilonite, and in the visions of Iddo the seer against Jeroboam the son of Nebat? ³⁰And Solomon reigned in Jerusalem over all Israel forty years. ³¹And Solomon slept with his fathers, and he was buried in the city of David his father, and Rehoboam his son reigned in his stead.

10 And Rehoboam went to Shechem: for to Shechem were all Israel come to make him king. ²And it came to pass when Jeroboam the son of Nebat, who was in Egypt, whither he had fled from the presence of Solomon the king, heard it, that Jeroboam returned out of Egypt. ³And they sent and called him. So Jeroboam and all Israel came and spoke to Rehoboam, saying, ⁴'Thy father made our yoke grievous: now therefore ease thou somewhat the grievous servitude of thy father, and his heavy yoke that he put upon us, and we will serve thee'. ⁵And he said unto them, 'Come again unto me after three days'. And the people departed.

⁶And king Rehoboam took counsel with the old men that had stood before Solomon his father while he yet lived, saying, 'What counsel give ye me to return answer to this people?' ⁷And they spoke unto him, saying, 'If thou be kind to this people, and please them, and speak good words to them, they will be thy servants for ever'. ⁸But he forsook the counsel which the old men gave him, and took counsel with the young men that were brought up with him, that stood before him. ⁹And he

said unto them, 'What advice give ye that we may return answer to this people, which have spoken to me, saying, "Ease somewhat the yoke that thy father did put upon us"?' ¹⁰And the young men that were brought up with him spoke unto him, saying, 'Thus shalt thou answer the people that spoke unto thee, saying, "Thy father made our yoke heavy, but make thou it somewhat lighter for us": thus shalt thou say unto them, "My little finger shall be thicker than my father's loins. ¹¹For whereas my father put a heavy yoke upon you, I will put more to your yoke: my father chastised you with whips, but I will chastise you with scorpions."' ¹²So Jeroboam and all the people came to Rehoboam on the third day, as the king bade, saying, 'Come again to me on the third day'. ¹³And the king answered them roughly; and king Rehoboam forsook the counsel of the old men, ¹⁴and answered them after the advice of the young men, saying, 'My father made your yoke heavy, but I will add thereto: my father chastised you with whips, but I will chastise you with scorpions'. ¹⁵So the king hearkened not unto the people, for the cause was of God, that the LORD might perform his word, which he spoke by the hand of Ahijah the Shilonite to Jeroboam the son of Nebat.

¹⁶And when all Israel saw that the king would not hearken unto them, the people answered the king, saying, 'What portion have we in David? and we have no inheritance in the son of Jesse: every man to your tents, O Israel: and now, David, see to thy own house'. So all Israel went to their tents. ¹⁷But as for the children of Israel that dwelt in the cities of Judah, Rehoboam reigned over them. ¹⁸Then king Rehoboam sent Hadoram that was over the tribute, and the children of Israel stoned him with stones, that he died. But king Rehoboam made speed to get him up to his chariot, to flee to Jerusalem. ¹⁹And Israel rebelled against the house of David unto this day.

11 And when Rehoboam was come to Jerusalem, he gathered of the house of Judah and Benjamin a hundred and fourscore thousand chosen men, which were warriors, to fight against Israel, that he might bring the kingdom again to Rehoboam. ²But the word of the LORD came to Shemaiah the man of God, saying, ³'Speak unto Rehoboam the son of Solomon, king of Judah, and to all Israel in Judah and Benjamin, saying, ⁴"Thus saith the LORD, 'Ye shall not go up, nor fight against your brethren: return every man to his house, for this thing is done of me'"'. And they obeyed the words of the LORD, and returned from going against Jeroboam.

⁵And Rehoboam dwelt in Jerusalem, and built cities for defence in Judah. ⁶He built even Beth-lehem, and Etam, and Tekoa, ⁷and Beth-zur, and Shoco, and Adullam, ⁸and Gath, and Mareshah, and Ziph, ⁹and Adoraim, and Lachish, and Azekah, ¹⁰and Zorah, and Aijalon, and Hebron, which are in Judah and in Benjamin fenced cities. ¹¹And he fortified the strongholds, and put captains in them, and store of victual, and of oil and wine. ¹²And in every several city he put shields and spears, and made them exceeding strong, having Judah and Benjamin on his side.

¹³And the priests and the Levites that were in all Israel resorted to him out of all their coasts. ¹⁴For the Levites left their suburbs and their possession, and came to Judah and Jerusalem: for Jeroboam and his sons had cast them off from executing the priest's office unto the LORD. ¹⁵And he ordained him priests for the high places, and for the devils, and for the calves which he had made. ¹⁶And after them out of all the tribes of Israel such as set their hearts to seek the LORD God of Israel came to Jerusalem, to sacrifice unto the LORD God of their fathers. ¹⁷So they strengthened the kingdom of Judah, and made Rehoboam the son of Solomon strong, three years: for three years they walked in the way of David and Solomon.

¹⁸And Rehoboam took him Mahalath the daughter of Jerimoth the son of David to wife, and Abihail the daughter of Eliab the son of Jesse: ¹⁹which bore him children, Jeush, and Shamariah, and Zaham. ²⁰And after her he took Maachah the daughter of Absalom, which bore him Abijah, and Attai, and Ziza, and Shelomith. ²¹And Rehoboam loved Maachah the daughter of Absalom above all his wives and his concubines (for he took eighteen wives, and threescore concubines, and begot twenty and eight sons, and threescore daughters). ²²And Rehoboam made Abijah the son of Maachah the chief, to be ruler among his brethren: for he thought to make him king. ²³And he dealt wisely, and dispersed of all his children throughout all the countries of Judah and Benjamin, unto every fenced city: and he gave them victual in abundance. And he desired many wives.

12 And it came to pass when Rehoboam had established the kingdom, and had strengthened himself, he forsook the law of the LORD, and all Israel with him. ²And it came to pass, that in the fifth year of king Rehoboam Shishak king of Egypt came up against Jerusalem, because they had transgressed against the LORD, ³with twelve hundred chariots, and threescore thousand horsemen: and the people were without number that came with him out of Egypt: the Lubims, the Sukkiims, and the Ethiopians. ⁴And he took the fenced cities which pertained to Judah, and came to Jerusalem.

⁵Then came Shemaiah the prophet to Rehoboam, and to the princes of Judah that were gathered together to Jerusalem because of Shishak, and said unto them, 'Thus saith the LORD, "Ye have forsaken me, and therefore have I also left you in the hand of Shishak"'. ⁶Whereupon the princes of Israel and the king humbled themselves; and they said, 'The LORD is righteous'. ⁷And when the LORD saw that they humbled themselves, the word of the LORD came to Shemaiah, saying, 'They have humbled themselves, therefore I will not destroy them, but I will grant them some deliverance, and my wrath shall not be poured out upon Jerusalem by the hand of Shishak. ⁸Nevertheless they shall be his servants, that they may know my service, and the service of the kingdoms of the countries.' ⁹So Shishak king of Egypt came up against Jerusalem, and took away the treasures of the house of the LORD, and the treasures of the king's house; he took all: he carried away also the shields of gold which Solomon had made. ¹⁰Instead of which king Rehoboam made

shields of brass, and committed them to the hands of the chief of the guard, that kept the entrance of the king's house. ¹¹And when the king entered into the house of the LORD, the guard came and fetched them, and brought them again into the guard chamber. ¹²And when he humbled himself, the wrath of the LORD turned from him, that he would not destroy him altogether: and also in Judah things went well.

¹³So king Rehoboam strengthened himself in Jerusalem, and reigned: for Rehoboam was one and forty years old when he began to reign, and he reigned seventeen years in Jerusalem, the city which the LORD had chosen out of all the tribes of Israel, to put his name there. And his mother's name was Naamah an Ammonitess. ¹⁴And he did evil, because he prepared not his heart to seek the LORD. ¹⁵Now the acts of Rehoboam, first and last, are they not written in the book of Shemaiah the prophet, and of Iddo the seer concerning genealogies? And there were wars between Rehoboam and Jeroboam continually. ¹⁶And Rehoboam slept with his fathers, and was buried in the city of David, and Abijah his son reigned in his stead.

13 Now in the eighteenth year of king Jeroboam began Abijah to reign over Judah. ²He reigned three years in Jerusalem. His mother's name also was Michaiah the daughter of Uriel of Gibeah. And there was war between Abijah and Jeroboam. ³And Abijah set the battle in array with an army of valiant men of war, even four hundred thousand chosen men: Jeroboam also set the battle in array against him with eight hundred thousand chosen men, being mighty men of valour.

⁴And Abijah stood up upon mount Zemaraim, which is in mount Ephraim, and said, 'Hear me, thou Jeroboam, and all Israel: ⁵ought you not to know that the LORD God of Israel gave the kingdom over Israel to David for ever, even to him and to his sons by a covenant of salt? ⁶Yet Jeroboam the son of Nebat, the servant of Solomon the son of David, is risen up, and hath rebelled against his lord. ⁷And there are gathered unto him vain men, the children of Belial, and have strengthened themselves against Rehoboam the son of Solomon, when Rehoboam was young and tender-hearted, and could not withstand them. ⁸And now ye think to withstand the kingdom of the LORD in the hand of the sons of David, and ye be a great multitude, and there are with you golden calves, which Jeroboam made you for gods. ⁹Have ye not cast out the priests of the LORD, the sons of Aaron, and the Levites, and have made you priests after the manner of the nations of other lands? so that whosoever cometh to consecrate himself with a young bullock and seven rams, the same may be a priest of them that are no gods. ¹⁰But as for us, the LORD is our God, and we have not forsaken him, and the priests which minister unto the LORD, are the sons of Aaron, and the Levites wait upon their business. ¹¹And they burn unto the LORD every morning and every evening burnt sacrifices and sweet incense: the showbread also set they in order upon the pure table, and the candlestick of gold with the lamps thereof, to burn every evening: for we keep the charge of the LORD our God, but ye have forsaken him. ¹²And behold,

God himself is with us for our captain, and his priests with sounding trumpets to cry alarm against you. O children of Israel, fight ye not against the LORD God of your fathers, for ye shall not prosper.'

[13]But Jeroboam caused an ambushment to come about behind them: so they were before Judah, and the ambushment was behind them. [14]And when Judah looked back, behold, the battle was before and behind: and they cried unto the LORD, and the priests sounded with the trumpets. [15]Then the men of Judah gave a shout: and as the men of Judah shouted, it came to pass that God smote Jeroboam and all Israel before Abijah and Judah. [16]And the children of Israel fled before Judah: and God delivered them into their hand. [17]And Abijah and his people slew them with a great slaughter: so there fell down slain of Israel five hundred thousand chosen men. [18]Thus the children of Israel were brought under at that time, and the children of Judah prevailed, because they relied upon the LORD God of their fathers. [19]And Abijah pursued after Jeroboam, and took cities from him, Beth-el with the towns thereof, and Jeshanah with the towns thereof, and Ephraim with the towns thereof. [20]Neither did Jeroboam recover strength again in the days of Abijah: and the LORD struck him, and he died.

[21]But Abijah waxed mighty, and married fourteen wives, and begot twenty and two sons, and sixteen daughters. [22]And the rest of the acts of Abijah, and his ways, and his sayings, are written in the story of the prophet Iddo.

14 So Abijah slept with his fathers, and they buried him in the city of David, and Asa his son reigned in his stead. In his days the land was quiet ten years. [2]And Asa did that which was good and right in the eyes of the LORD his God. [3]For he took away the altars of the strange gods, and the high places, and broke down the images, and cut down the groves: [4]and commanded Judah to seek the LORD God of their fathers, and to do the law and the commandment. [5]Also he took away out of all the cities of Judah the high places and the images: and the kingdom was quiet before him.

[6]And he built fenced cities in Judah: for the land had rest, and he had no war in those years; because the LORD had given him rest. [7]Therefore he said unto Judah, 'Let us build these cities, and make about them walls and towers, gates, and bars, while the land is yet before us: because we have sought the LORD our God, we have sought him, and he hath given us rest on every side'. So they built and prospered. [8]And Asa had an army of men that bore targets and spears, out of Judah three hundred thousand, and out of Benjamin, that bore shields and drew bows, two hundred and fourscore thousand: all these were mighty men of valour.

[9]And there came out against them Zerah the Ethiopian with a host of a thousand thousand, and three hundred chariots, and came unto Mareshah. [10]Then Asa went out against him, and they set the battle in array in the valley of Zephathah at Mareshah. [11]And Asa cried unto the LORD his God, and said, 'LORD, it is nothing with thee to help, whether with many, or with them that have no power. Help us, O LORD our God,

for we rest on thee, and in thy name we go against this multitude. O Lord, thou art our God, let not man prevail against thee.' ¹²So the Lord smote the Ethiopians before Asa, and before Judah, and the Ethiopians fled. ¹³And Asa and the people that were with him pursued them unto Gerar: and the Ethiopians were overthrown, that they could not recover themselves, for they were destroyed before the Lord, and before his host, and they carried away very much spoil. ¹⁴And they smote all the cities round about Gerar, for the fear of the Lord came upon them: and they spoiled all the cities, for there was exceeding much spoil in them. ¹⁵They smote also the tents of cattle, and carried away sheep and camels in abundance, and returned to Jerusalem.

15 And the Spirit of God came upon Azariah the son of Oded. ²And he went out to meet Asa, and said unto him, 'Hear ye me, Asa, and all Judah and Benjamin, the Lord is with you, while ye be with him: and if ye seek him, he will be found of you: but if ye forsake him, he will forsake you. ³Now for a long season Israel hath been without the true God, and without a teaching priest, and without law. ⁴But when they in their trouble did turn unto the Lord God of Israel, and sought him, he was found of them. ⁵And in those times there was no peace to him that went out, nor to him that came in, but great vexations were upon all the inhabitants of the countries. ⁶And nation was destroyed of nation, and city of city: for God did vex them with all adversity. ⁷Be ye strong therefore, and let not your hands be weak: for your work shall be rewarded.'

⁸And when Asa heard these words, and the prophecy of Oded the prophet, he took courage, and put away the abominable idols out of all the land of Judah and Benjamin, and out of the cities which he had taken from mount Ephraim, and renewed the altar of the Lord, that was before the porch of the Lord. ⁹And he gathered all Judah and Benjamin, and the strangers with them out of Ephraim and Manasseh, and out of Simeon: for they fell to him out of Israel in abundance, when they saw that the Lord his God was with him. ¹⁰So they gathered themselves together at Jerusalem in the third month, in the fifteenth year of the reign of Asa. ¹¹And they offered unto the Lord the same time, of the spoil which they had brought, seven hundred oxen and seven thousand sheep. ¹²And they entered into a covenant to seek the Lord God of their fathers with all their heart and with all their soul: ¹³that whosoever would not seek the Lord God of Israel should be put to death, whether small or great, whether man or woman. ¹⁴And they swore unto the Lord with a loud voice, and with shouting, and with trumpets, and with cornets. ¹⁵And all Judah rejoiced at the oath: for they had sworn with all their heart, and sought him with their whole desire, and he was found of them: and the Lord gave them rest round about.

¹⁶And also concerning Maachah the mother of Asa the king, he removed her from being queen, because she had made an idol in a grove: and Asa cut down her idol, and stamped it, and burnt it at the brook Kidron. ¹⁷But the high places were not taken away out of Israel: nevertheless the heart of Asa was perfect all his days.

¹⁸And he brought into the house of God the things that his father had dedicated, and that he himself had dedicated, silver, and gold, and vessels. ¹⁹And there was no more war unto the five and thirtieth year of the reign of Asa.

16 In the six and thirtieth year of the reign of Asa Baasha king of Israel came up against Judah, and built Ramah, to the intent that he might let none go out or come in to Asa king of Judah. ²Then Asa brought out silver and gold out of the treasures of the house of the LORD and of the king's house, and sent to Ben-hadad king of Syria that dwelt at Damascus, saying, ³'There is a league between me and thee, as there was between my father and thy father: behold, I have sent thee silver and gold; go, break thy league with Baasha king of Israel, that he may depart from me'. ⁴And Ben-hadad hearkened unto king Asa, and sent the captains of his armies against the cities of Israel, and they smote Ijon, and Dan, and Abel-maim, and all the store-cities of Naphtali. ⁵And it came to pass, when Baasha heard it, that he left off building of Ramah, and let his work cease. ⁶Then Asa the king took all Judah, and they carried away the stones of Ramah, and the timber thereof, wherewith Baasha was a-building; and he built therewith Geba and Mizpah.

⁷And at that time Hanani the seer came to Asa king of Judah, and said unto him, 'Because thou hast relied on the king of Syria, and not relied on the LORD thy God, therefore is the host of the king of Syria escaped out of thy hand. ⁸Were not the Ethiopians and the Lubims a huge host, with very many chariots and horsemen? Yet because thou didst rely on the LORD, he delivered them into thy hand. ⁹For the eyes of the LORD run to and fro throughout the whole earth, to show himself strong in the behalf of them whose heart is perfect towards him. Herein thou hast done foolishly: therefore from henceforth thou shalt have wars.' ¹⁰Then Asa was wroth with the seer, and put him in a prison-house; for he was in a rage with him because of this thing. And Asa oppressed some of the people the same time.

¹¹And behold, the acts of Asa, first and last, lo, they are written in the book of the kings of Judah and Israel. ¹²And Asa in the thirty and ninth year of his reign was diseased in his feet, until his disease was exceeding great: yet in his disease he sought not to the LORD, but to the physicians.

¹³And Asa slept with his fathers, and died in the one and fortieth year of his reign. ¹⁴And they buried him in his own sepulchres which he had made for himself in the city of David, and laid him in the bed which was filled with sweet odours and divers kinds of spices prepared by the apothecaries' art: and they made a very great burning for him.

17 And Jehoshaphat his son reigned in his stead, and strengthened himself against Israel. ²And he placed forces in all the fenced cities of Judah, and set garrisons in the land of Judah, and in the cities of Ephraim, which Asa his father had taken. ³And the LORD was with Jehoshaphat, because he walked in the first ways of his father David, and sought not unto Baalim; ⁴but sought to the LORD God of his father, and walked in his commandments, and not after the doings of Israel. [5]Therefore the LORD established the kingdom in his hand, and all Judah brought to Jehoshaphat presents, and he had riches and honour in abundance. [6]And his heart was lifted up in the ways of the LORD: moreover he took away the high places and groves out of Judah.

[7]Also in the third year of his reign he sent to his princes, even to Ben-hail, and to Obadiah, and to Zechariah, and to Nethaneel, and to Michaiah, to teach in the cities of Judah. [8]And with them he sent Levites, even Shemaiah, and Nethaniah, and Zebadiah, and Asahel, and Shemiramoth, and Jehonathan, and Adonijah, and Tobijah, and Tob-adonijah, Levites; and with them Elishama and Jehoram, priests. [9]And they taught in Judah, and had the book of the law of the LORD with them, and went about throughout all the cities of Judah, and taught the people.

[10]And the fear of the LORD fell upon all the kingdoms of the lands that were round about Judah, so that they made no war against Jehoshaphat. [11]Also some of the Philistines brought Jehoshaphat presents, and tribute silver; and the Arabians brought him flocks, seven thousand and seven hundred rams, and seven thousand and seven hundred he-goats.

[12]And Jehoshaphat waxed great exceedingly; and he built in Judah castles, and cities of store. [13]And he had much business in the cities of Judah: and the men of war, mighty men of valour, were in Jerusalem. [14]And these are the numbers of them according to the house of their fathers: of Judah, the captains of thousands; Adnah the chief, and with him mighty men of valour three hundred thousand. [15]And next to him was Jehohanan the captain, and with him two hundred and fourscore thousand. [16]And next him was Amasiah the son of Zichri, who willingly offered himself unto the LORD; and with him two hundred thousand mighty men of valour. [17]And of Benjamin; Eliada a mighty man of valour, and with him armed men with bow and shield two hundred thousand. [18]And next him was Jehozabad, and with him a hundred and fourscore thousand ready prepared for the war. [19]These waited on the king, besides those whom the king put in the fenced cities throughout all Judah.

18 Now Jehoshaphat had riches and honour in abundance, and joined affinity with Ahab. [2]And after certain years he went down to Ahab to Samaria: and Ahab killed sheep and oxen for him in abundance, and for the people that he had with him, and persuaded him to go up with him to Ramoth-gilead. [3]And Ahab king of Israel said unto Jehoshaphat king of Judah, 'Wilt thou go with me to Ramoth-gilead?' And he answered him, 'I am as thou art, and my people as thy people, and we will be with thee in the war'.

[4]And Jehoshaphat said unto the king of Israel, 'Inquire, I pray thee, at the word of the LORD today'. [5]Therefore the king of Israel gathered together of prophets four hundred men, and said unto them, 'Shall we go to Ramoth-gilead to battle, or shall I forbear?' And they said, 'Go up, for God will deliver it into the king's hand'. [6]But Jehoshaphat said, 'Is

there not here a prophet of the LORD besides, that we might inquire of him?' ⁷And the king of Israel said unto Jehoshaphat, 'There is yet one man, by whom we may inquire of the LORD: but I hate him, for he never prophesied good unto me, but always evil: the same is Micaiah the son of Imla'. And Jehoshaphat said, 'Let not the king say so'. ⁸And the king of Israel called for one of his officers, and said, 'Fetch quickly Micaiah the son of Imla'.

⁹And the king of Israel and Jehoshaphat king of Judah sat either of them on his throne, clothed in their robes, and they sat in a void place at the entering in of the gate of Samaria, and all the prophets prophesied before them. ¹⁰And Zedekiah the son of Chenaanah had made him horns of iron, and said, 'Thus saith the LORD, "With these thou shalt push Syria until they be consumed"'. ¹¹And all the prophets prophesied so, saying, 'Go up to Ramoth-gilead, and prosper: for the LORD shall deliver it into the hand of the king'.

¹²And the messenger that went to call Micaiah spoke to him, saying, 'Behold, the words of the prophets declare good to the king with one assent: let thy word therefore, I pray thee, be like one of theirs, and speak thou good'. ¹³And Micaiah said, 'As the LORD liveth, even what my God saith, that will I speak'. ¹⁴And when he was come to the king, the king said unto him, 'Micaiah, shall we go to Ramoth-gilead to battle, or shall I forbear?' And he said, 'Go ye up, and prosper, and they shall be delivered into your hand'. ¹⁵And the king said to him, 'How many times shall I adjure thee that thou say nothing but the truth to me in the name of the LORD?' ¹⁶Then he said, 'I did see all Israel scattered upon the mountains, as sheep that have no shepherd: and the LORD said, "These have no master, let them return therefore every man to his house in peace"'. ¹⁷(And the king of Israel said to Jehoshaphat, 'Did I not tell thee that he would not prophesy good unto me, but evil?') ¹⁸Again he said, 'Therefore hear the word of the LORD: I saw the LORD sitting upon his throne, and all the host of heaven standing on his right hand and on his left. ¹⁹And the LORD said, "Who shall entice Ahab king of Israel, that he may go up and fall at Ramoth-gilead?" And one spoke saying after this manner, and another saying after that manner. ²⁰Then there came out a spirit, and stood before the LORD, and said, "I will entice him". And the LORD said unto him, "Wherewith?" ²¹And he said, "I will go out, and be a lying spirit in the mouth of all his prophets". And the LORD said, "Thou shalt entice him, and thou shalt also prevail: go out, and do even so". ²²Now therefore behold, the LORD hath put a lying spirit in the mouth of these thy prophets, and the LORD hath spoken evil against thee.'

²³Then Zedekiah the son of Chenaanah came near, and smote Micaiah upon the cheek, and said, 'Which way went the Spirit of the LORD from me to speak unto thee?' ²⁴And Micaiah said, 'Behold, thou shalt see on that day when thou shalt go into an inner chamber to hide thyself'. ²⁵Then the king of Israel said, 'Take ye Micaiah, and carry him back to Amon the governor of the city, and to Joash the king's son. ²⁶And say, "Thus saith the king, 'Put this fellow in the prison, and feed him with

bread of affliction and with water of affliction, until I return in peace'".' ²⁷And Micaiah said, 'If thou certainly return in peace, then hath not the LORD spoken by me'. And he said, 'Hearken, all ye people'.

²⁸So the king of Israel and Jehoshaphat the king of Judah went up to Ramoth-gilead. ²⁹And the king of Israel said unto Jehoshaphat, 'I will disguise myself, and will go to the battle, but put thou on thy robes'. So the king of Israel disguised himself, and they went to the battle. ³⁰Now the king of Syria had commanded the captains of the chariots that were with him, saying, 'Fight ye not with small or great, save only with the king of Israel'. ³¹And it came to pass when the captains of the chariots saw Jehoshaphat, that they said, 'It is the king of Israel'. Therefore they compassed about him to fight. But Jehoshaphat cried out, and the LORD helped him; and God moved them to depart from him. ³²For it came to pass that, when the captains of the chariots perceived that it was not the king of Israel, they turned back again from pursuing him. ³³And a certain man drew a bow at a venture, and smote the king of Israel between the joints of the harness: therefore he said to his chariot-man, 'Turn thy hand, that thou mayest carry me out of the host, for I am wounded'. ³⁴And the battle increased that day: howbeit the king of Israel stayed himself up in his chariot against the Syrians until the even: and about the time of the sun going down he died.

19 And Jehoshaphat the king of Judah returned to his house in peace to Jerusalem. ²And Jehu the son of Hanani the seer went out to meet him, and said to king Jehoshaphat, 'Shouldst thou help the ungodly, and love them that hate the LORD? Therefore is wrath upon thee from before the LORD. ³Nevertheless there are good things found in thee, in that thou hast taken away the groves out of the land, and hast prepared thy heart to seek God.' ⁴And Jehoshaphat dwelt at Jerusalem: and he went out again through the people from Beer-sheba to mount Ephraim, and brought them back unto the LORD God of their fathers.

⁵And he set judges in the land throughout all the fenced cities of Judah, city by city, ⁶and said to the judges, 'Take heed what ye do: for ye judge not for man, but for the LORD, who is with you in the judgement. ⁷Wherefore now let the fear of the LORD be upon you; take heed and do it: for there is no iniquity with the LORD our God, nor respect of persons, nor taking of gifts.'

⁸Moreover in Jerusalem did Jehoshaphat set of the Levites, and of the priests, and of the chief of the fathers of Israel, for the judgement of the LORD, and for controversies, when they returned to Jerusalem. ⁹And he charged them, saying, 'Thus shall ye do in the fear of the LORD faithfully, and with a perfect heart. ¹⁰And what cause soever shall come to you of your brethren that dwell in their cities, between blood and blood, between law and commandment, statutes and judgements, ye shall even warn them that they trespass not against the LORD, and so wrath come upon you, and upon your brethren: this do, and ye shall not trespass. ¹¹And behold, Amariah the chief priest is over you in all matters of the LORD and Zebadiah the son of Ishmael, the ruler of the

ॉ

house of Judah, for all the king's matters: also the Levites shall be officers before you. Deal courageously, and the LORD shall be with the good.'

20 It came to pass after this also, that the children of Moab, and the children of Ammon, and with them others besides the Ammonites, came against Jehoshaphat to battle. ²Then there came some that told Jehoshaphat, saying, 'There cometh a great multitude against thee from beyond the sea on this side Syria, and behold, they be in Hazazon-tamar, which is En-gedi'. ³And Jehoshaphat feared, and set himself to seek the LORD, and proclaimed a fast throughout all Judah. ⁴And Judah gathered themselves together, to ask help of the LORD: even out of all the cities of Judah they came to seek the LORD.

⁵And Jehoshaphat stood in the congregation of Judah and Jerusalem, in the house of the LORD before the new court, ⁶and said, 'O LORD God of our fathers, art not thou God in heaven? and rulest not thou over all the kingdoms of the heathen? and in thy hand is there not power and might, so that none is able to withstand thee? ⁷Art not thou our God, who didst drive out the inhabitants of this land before thy people Israel, and gavest it to the seed of Abraham thy friend for ever? ⁸And they dwelt therein, and have built thee a sanctuary therein for thy name, saying, ⁹"If, when evil cometh upon us, as the sword, judgement, or pestilence, or famine, we stand before this house, and in thy presence (for thy name is in this house), and cry unto thee in our affliction, then thou wilt hear and help". ¹⁰And now behold, the children of Ammon and Moab and mount Seir, whom thou wouldst not let Israel invade, when they came out of the land of Egypt, but they turned from them, and destroyed them not: ¹¹behold, I say, how they reward us, to come to cast us out of thy possession, which thou hast given us to inherit. ¹²O our God, wilt thou not judge them? for we have no might against this great company that cometh against us, neither know we what to do: but our eyes are upon thee.' ¹³And all Judah stood before the LORD, with their little ones, their wives, and their children.

¹⁴Then upon Jahaziel the son of Zechariah, the son of Benaiah, the son of Jeiel, the son of Mattaniah, a Levite of the sons of Asaph, came the Spirit of the LORD in the midst of the congregation: ¹⁵and he said, 'Hearken ye, all Judah, and ye inhabitants of Jerusalem, and thou king Jehoshaphat, thus saith the LORD unto you, "Be not afraid nor dismayed by reason of this great multitude; for the battle is not yours, but God's. ¹⁶Tomorrow go ye down against them: behold, they come up by the cliff of Ziz, and ye shall find them at the end of the brook, before the wilderness of Jeruel. ¹⁷Ye shall not need to fight in this battle: set yourselves, stand ye still, and see the salvation of the LORD with you, O Judah and Jerusalem: fear not, nor be dismayed; tomorrow go out against them, for the LORD will be with you."' ¹⁸And Jehoshaphat bowed his head with his face to the ground: and all Judah and the inhabitants of Jerusalem fell before the LORD, worshipping the LORD. ¹⁹And the Levites, of the children of the Kohathites, and of the children of

the Korhites, stood up to praise the Lord God of Israel with a loud voice on high.

²⁰And they rose early in the morning, and went forth into the wilderness of Tekoa: and as they went forth, Jehoshaphat stood and said, 'Hear me, O Judah, and ye inhabitants of Jerusalem; believe in the Lord your God, so shall you be established; believe his prophets, so shall ye prosper'. ²¹And when he had consulted with the people, he appointed singers unto the Lord, and that should praise the beauty of holiness, as they went out before the army; and to say, 'Praise the Lord, for his mercy endureth for ever'.

²²And when they began to sing and to praise, the Lord set ambushments against the children of Ammon, Moab, and mount Seir, which were come against Judah, and they were smitten. ²³For the children of Ammon and Moab stood up against the inhabitants of mount Seir, utterly to slay and destroy them: and when they had made an end of the inhabitants of Seir, every one helped to destroy another. ²⁴And when Judah came toward the watch-tower in the wilderness, they looked unto the multitude, and behold, they were dead bodies fallen to the earth, and none escaped. ²⁵And when Jehoshaphat and his people came to take away the spoil of them, they found among them in abundance both riches with the dead bodies, and precious jewels (which they stripped off for themselves), more than they could carry away: and they were three days in gathering of the spoil, it was so much.

²⁶And on the fourth day they assembled themselves in the valley of Berachah; for there they blessed the Lord: therefore the name of the same place was called the valley of Berachah unto this day. ²⁷Then they returned, every man of Judah and Jerusalem, and Jehoshaphat in the forefront of them, to go again to Jerusalem with joy: for the Lord had made them to rejoice over their enemies. ²⁸And they came to Jerusalem with psalteries and harps and trumpets unto the house of the Lord. ²⁹And the fear of God was on all the kingdoms of those countries, when they had heard that the Lord fought against the enemies of Israel. ³⁰So the realm of Jehoshaphat was quiet: for his God gave him rest round about.

³¹And Jehoshaphat reigned over Judah: he was thirty and five years old when he began to reign, and he reigned twenty and five years in Jerusalem. And his mother's name was Azubah the daughter of Shilhi. ³²And he walked in the way of Asa his father, and departed not from it, doing that which was right in the sight of the Lord. ³³Howbeit the high places were not taken away: for as yet the people had not prepared their hearts unto the God of their fathers.

³⁴Now the rest of the acts of Jehoshaphat, first and last, behold, they are written in the book of Jehu the son of Hanani, who is mentioned in the book of the kings of Israel.

³⁵And after this did Jehoshaphat king of Judah join himself with Ahaziah king of Israel, who did very wickedly: ³⁶and he joined himself with him to make ships to go to Tarshish: and they made the ships in Ezion-geber. ³⁷Then Eliezer the son of Dodavah of Mareshah prophesied

against Jehoshaphat, saying, 'Because thou hast joined thyself with Ahaziah, the Lord hath broken thy works'. And the ships were broken, that they were not able to go to Tarshish.

21 Now Jehoshaphat slept with his fathers, and was buried with his fathers in the city of David. And Jehoram his son reigned in his stead. ²And he had brethren the sons of Jehoshaphat, Azariah, and Jehiel, and Zechariah, and Azariah, and Michael, and Shephatiah: all these were the sons of Jehoshaphat king of Israel. ³And their father gave them great gifts of silver and of gold, and of precious things, with fenced cities in Judah: but the kingdom gave he to Jehoram, because he was the firstborn. ⁴Now when Jehoram was risen up to the kingdom of his father, he strengthened himself, and slew all his brethren with the sword, and divers also of the princes of Israel.

⁵Jehoram was thirty and two years old when he began to reign, and he reigned eight years in Jerusalem. ⁶And he walked in the way of the kings of Israel, like as did the house of Ahab: for he had the daughter of Ahab to wife: and he wrought that which was evil in the eyes of the Lord. ⁷Howbeit the Lord would not destroy the house of David, because of the covenant that he had made with David, and as he promised, to give a light to him and to his sons for ever.

⁸In his days the Edomites revolted from under the dominion of Judah, and made themselves a king. ⁹Then Jehoram went forth with his princes, and all his chariots with him: and he rose up by night, and smote the Edomites which compassed him in, and the captains of the chariots. ¹⁰So the Edomites revolted from under the hand of Judah unto this day. The same time also did Libnah revolt from under his hand, because he had forsaken the Lord God of his fathers. ¹¹Moreover he made high places in the mountains of Judah, and caused the inhabitants of Jerusalem to commit fornication, and compelled Judah thereto.

¹²And there came a writing to him from Elijah the prophet, saying, Thus saith the Lord God of David thy father, 'Because thou hast not walked in the ways of Jehoshaphat thy father, nor in the ways of Asa king of Judah, ¹³but hast walked in the way of the kings of Israel, and hast made Judah and the inhabitants of Jerusalem to go a-whoring, like to the whoredoms of the house of Ahab, and also hast slain thy brethren of thy father's house, which were better than thyself: ¹⁴behold, with a great plague will the Lord smite thy people, and thy children, and thy wives, and all thy goods. ¹⁵And thou shalt have great sickness by disease of thy bowels, until thy bowels fall out by reason of the sickness day by day.'

¹⁶Moreover the Lord stirred up against Jehoram the spirit of the Philistines, and of the Arabians, that were near the Ethiopians. ¹⁷And they came up into Judah, and broke into it, and carried away all the substance that was found in the king's house, and his sons also, and his wives; so that there was never a son left him, save Jehoahaz, the youngest of his sons.

¹⁸And after all this the Lord smote him in his bowels with an incur-

able disease. ¹⁹And it came to pass, that in process of time, after the end of two years, his bowels fell out by reason of his sickness: so he died of sore diseases. And his people made no burning for him, like the burning of his fathers. ²⁰Thirty and two years old was he when he began to reign, and he reigned in Jerusalem eight years, and departed without being desired. Howbeit they buried him in the city of David, but not in the sepulchres of the kings.

22 And the inhabitants of Jerusalem made Ahaziah his youngest son king in his stead: for the band of men that came with the Arabians to the camp had slain all the eldest. So Ahaziah the son of Jehoram king of Judah reigned. ²Forty and two years old was Ahaziah when he began to reign, and he reigned one year in Jerusalem. His mother's name also was Athaliah the daughter of Omri. ³He also walked in the ways of the house of Ahab: for his mother was his counsellor to do wickedly. ⁴Wherefore he did evil in the sight of the LORD like the house of Ahab: for they were his counsellors, after the death of his father to his destruction.

⁵He walked also after their counsel, and went with Jehoram the son of Ahab king of Israel to war against Hazael king of Syria at Ramoth-gilead: and the Syrians smote Joram. ⁶And he returned to be healed in Jezreel because of the wounds which were given him at Ramah when he fought with Hazael king of Syria. And Azariah the son of Jehoram king of Judah went down to see Jehoram the son of Ahab at Jezreel, because he was sick. ⁷And the destruction of Ahaziah was of God by coming to Joram: for when he was come, he went out with Jehoram against Jehu the son of Nimshi, whom the LORD had anointed to cut off the house of Ahab. ⁸And it came to pass that, when Jehu was executing judgement upon the house of Ahab, and found the princes of Judah, and the sons of the brethren of Ahaziah, that ministered to Ahaziah, he slew them. ⁹And he sought Ahaziah: and they caught him (for he was hid in Samaria), and brought him to Jehu: and when they had slain him, they buried him: 'Because,' said they, 'he is the son of Jehoshaphat, who sought the LORD with all his heart'. So the house of Ahaziah had no power to keep still the kingdom.

¹⁰But when Athaliah the mother of Ahaziah saw that her son was dead, she arose and destroyed all the seed royal of the house of Judah. ¹¹But Jehoshabeath, the daughter of the king, took Joash the son of Ahaziah, and stole him from among the king's sons that were slain, and put him and his nurse in a bedchamber. So Jehoshabeath, the daughter of king Jehoram, the wife of Jehoiada the priest (for she was the sister of Ahaziah), hid him from Athaliah, so that she slew him not. ¹²And he was with them hid in the house of God six years: and Athaliah reigned over the land.

23 And in the seventh year Jehoiada strengthened himself, and took the captains of hundreds, Azariah the son of Jeroham, and Ishmael the son of Jehohanan, and Azariah the son of Obed, and Maaseiah the son of Adaiah, and Elishaphat the son of Zichri, into covenant with him. ²And they went about in Judah, and gathered the

Levites out of all the cities of Judah, and the chief of the fathers of Israel, and they came to Jerusalem. ³And all the congregation made a covenant with the king in the house of God. And he said unto them, 'Behold, the king's son shall reign, as the LORD hath said of the sons of David. ⁴This is the thing that ye shall do: a third part of you entering on the sabbath, of the priests and of the Levites, shall be porters of the doors. ⁵And a third part shall be at the king's house; and a third part at the gate of the foundation: and all the people shall be in the courts of the house of the LORD. ⁶But let none come into the house of the LORD, save the priests, and they that minister of the Levites; they shall go in, for they are holy: but all the people shall keep the watch of the LORD. ⁷And the Levites shall compass the king round about, every man with his weapons in his hand; and whosoever else cometh into the house, he shall be put to death: but be you with the king when he cometh in, and when he goeth out.' ⁸So the Levites and all Judah did according to all things that Jehoiada the priest had commanded, and took every man his men that were to come in on the sabbath, with them that were to go out on the sabbath: for Jehoiada the priest dismissed not the courses. ⁹Moreover Jehoiada the priest delivered to the captains of hundreds spears, and bucklers, and shields, that had been king David's, which were in the house of God. ¹⁰And he set all the people, every man having his weapon in his hand, from the right side of the temple to the left side of the temple, along by the altar and the temple, by the king round about. ¹¹Then they brought out the king's son, and put upon him the crown, and gave him the testimony, and made him king. And Jehoiada and his sons anointed him, and said, 'God save the king'.

¹²Now when Athaliah heard the noise of the people running and praising the king, she came to the people into the house of the LORD. ¹³And she looked, and, behold, the king stood at his pillar at the entering in, and the princes and the trumpets by the king: and all the people of the land rejoiced, and sounded with trumpets, also the singers with instruments of music, and such as taught to sing praise. Then Athaliah rent her clothes, and said, 'Treason, Treason'. ¹⁴Then Jehoiada the priest brought out the captains of hundreds that were set over the host, and said unto them, 'Have her forth of the ranges: and whoso followeth her, let him be slain with the sword'. For the priest said, 'Slay her not in the house of the LORD'. ¹⁵So they laid hands on her; and when she was come to the entering of the horse gate by the king's house, they slew her there.

¹⁶And Jehoiada made a covenant between him, and between all the people, and between the king, that they should be the LORD's people. ¹⁷Then all the people went to the house of Baal, and broke it down, and broke his altars and his images in pieces, and slew Mattan the priest of Baal before the altars. ¹⁸Also Jehoiada appointed the offices of the house of the LORD by the hand of the priests the Levites, whom David had distributed in the house of the LORD, to offer the burnt offerings of the LORD, as it is written in the law of Moses, with rejoicing and with singing, as it was ordained by David. ¹⁹And he set the porters at the

gates of the house of the Lord, that none which was unclean in any-thing should enter in. ²⁰And he took the captains of hundreds, and the nobles, and the governors of the people, and all the people of the land, and brought down the king from the house of the Lord: and they came through the high gate into the king's house, and set the king upon the throne of the kingdom. ²¹And all the people of the land rejoiced: and the city was quiet, after that they had slain Athaliah with the sword.

24 Joash was seven years old when he began to reign, and he reigned forty years in Jerusalem. His mother's name also was Zibiah of Beer-sheba. ²And Joash did that which was right in the sight of the Lord all the days of Jehoiada the priest. ³And Jehoiada took for him two wives, and he begot sons and daughters.

⁴And it came to pass after this that Joash was minded to repair the house of the Lord. ⁵And he gathered together the priests and the Levites, and said to them, 'Go out unto the cities of Judah, and gather of all Israel money to repair the house of your God from year to year, and see that ye haste the matter'. Howbeit the Levites hastened it not. ⁶And the king called for Jehoiada the chief, and said unto him, 'Why hast thou not required of the Levites to bring in out of Judah and out of Jerusalem the collection, according to the commandment of Moses the servant of the Lord, and of the congregation of Israel, for the taberna-cle of witness?' ⁷For the sons of Athaliah, that wicked woman, had bro-ken up the house of God; and also all the dedicated things of the house of the Lord did they bestow upon Baalim. ⁸And at the king's command-ment they made a chest, and set it without, at the gate of the house of the Lord. ⁹And they made a proclamation through Judah and Jerusalem, to bring in to the Lord the collection that Moses the servant of God laid upon Israel in the wilderness. ¹⁰And all the princes and all the people rejoiced, and brought in, and cast into the chest, until they had made an end. ¹¹Now it came to pass that at what time the chest was brought unto the king's office by the hand of the Levites, and when they saw that there was much money, the king's scribe and the high priest's officer came and emptied the chest, and took it, and carried it to his place again. Thus they did day by day, and gathered money in abundance. ¹²And the king and Jehoiada gave it to such as did the work of the service of the house of the Lord, and hired masons and carpen-ters to repair the house of the Lord, and also such as wrought iron and brass to mend the house of the Lord. ¹³So the workmen wrought, and the work was perfected by them: and they set the house of God in his state, and strengthened it. ¹⁴And when they had finished it, they brought the rest of the money before the king and Jehoiada, whereof were made vessels for the house of the Lord, even vessels to minister, and to offer withal, and spoons, and vessels of gold and silver. And they offered burnt offerings in the house of the Lord continually all the days of Jehoiada.

¹⁵But Jehoiada waxed old, and was full of days when he died: a hun-dred and thirty years old was he when he died. ¹⁶And they buried him in the city of David among the kings, because he had done good in Israel,

both towards God, and towards his house. ¹⁷Now after the death of Jehoiada came the princes of Judah, and made obeisance to the king. Then the king hearkened unto them. ¹⁸And they left the house of the LORD God of their fathers, and served groves and idols: and wrath came upon Judah and Jerusalem for this their trespass. ¹⁹Yet he sent prophets to them to bring them again unto the LORD, and they testified against them: but they would not give ear. ²⁰And the Spirit of God came upon Zechariah the son of Jehoiada the priest, which stood above the people, and said unto them, 'Thus saith God, "Why transgress ye the commandments of the LORD, that ye cannot prosper? because ye have forsaken the LORD, he hath also forsaken you"'. ²¹And they conspired against him, and stoned him with stones at the commandment of the king in the court of the house of the LORD. ²²Thus Joash the king remembered not the kindness which Jehoiada his father had done to him, but slew his son. And when he died, he said, 'The LORD look upon it, and require it'.

²³And it came to pass at the end of the year, that the host of Syria came up against him: and they came to Judah and Jerusalem, and destroyed all the princes of the people from among the people, and sent all the spoil of them unto the king of Damascus. ²⁴For the army of the Syrians came with a small company of men, and the LORD delivered a very great host into their hand, because they had forsaken the LORD God of their fathers. So they executed judgement against Joash. ²⁵And when they were departed from him (for they left him in great diseases), his own servants conspired against him for the blood of the sons of Jehoiada the priest, and slew him on his bed, and he died: and they buried him in the city of David, but they buried him not in the sepulchres of the kings. ²⁶And these are they that conspired against him: Zabad the son of Shimeath an Ammonitess, and Jehozabad the son of Shimrith a Moabitess.

²⁷Now concerning his sons, and the greatness of the burdens laid upon him, and the repairing of the house of God, behold, they are written in the story of the book of the kings. And Amaziah his son reigned in his stead.

25 Amaziah was twenty and five years old when he began to reign, and he reigned twenty and nine years in Jerusalem. And his mother's name was Jehoaddan of Jerusalem. ²And he did that which was right in the sight of the LORD, but not with a perfect heart.

³Now it came to pass, when the kingdom was established to him, that he slew his servants that had killed the king his father. ⁴But he slew not their children, but did as it is written in the law in the book of Moses, where the LORD commanded, saying, 'The fathers shall not die for the children, neither shall the children die for the fathers, but every man shall die for his own sin'.

⁵Moreover Amaziah gathered Judah together, and made them captains over thousands, and captains over hundreds, according to the houses of their fathers, throughout all Judah and Benjamin: and he numbered them from twenty years old and above, and found them

three hundred thousand choice men, able to go forth to war, that could handle spear and shield. ⁶He hired also a hundred thousand mighty men of valour out of Israel for a hundred talents of silver. ⁷But there came a man of God to him, saying, 'O king, let not the army of Israel go with thee: for the LORD is not with Israel, to wit, with all the children of Ephraim. ⁸But if thou wilt go, do it, be strong for the battle: God shall make thee fall before the enemy: for God hath power to help, and to cast down.' ⁹And Amaziah said to the man of God, 'But what shall we do for the hundred talents which I have given to the army of Israel?' And the man of God answered, 'The LORD is able to give thee much more than this'. ¹⁰Then Amaziah separated them, to wit, the army that was come to him out of Ephraim, to go home again. Wherefore their anger was greatly kindled against Judah, and they returned home in great anger.

¹¹And Amaziah strengthened himself, and led forth his people, and went to the valley of salt, and smote of the children of Seir ten thousand. ¹²And other ten thousand left alive did the children of Judah carry away captive, and brought them unto the top of the rock, and cast them down from the top of the rock, that they all were broken in pieces. ¹³But the soldiers of the army which Amaziah sent back, that they should not go with him to battle, fell upon the cities of Judah, from Samaria even unto Beth-horon, and smote three thousand of them, and took much spoil.

¹⁴Now it came to pass, after that Amaziah was come from the slaughter of the Edomites, that he brought the gods of the children of Seir, and set them up to be his gods, and bowed down himself before them, and burnt incense unto them. ¹⁵Wherefore the anger of the LORD was kindled against Amaziah, and he sent unto him a prophet, which said unto him, 'Why hast thou sought after the gods of the people, which could not deliver their own people out of thy hand?' ¹⁶And it came to pass as he talked with him, that the king said unto him, 'Art thou made of the king's counsel? forbear; why shouldst thou be smitten?' Then the prophet forbore, and said, 'I know that God hath determined to destroy thee, because thou hast done this, and hast not hearkened unto my counsel'.

¹⁷Then Amaziah king of Judah took advice, and sent to Joash, the son of Jehoahaz, the son of Jehu, king of Israel, saying, 'Come, let us see one another in the face'. ¹⁸And Joash king of Israel sent to Amaziah king of Judah, saying, 'The thistle that was in Lebanon sent to the cedar that was in Lebanon, saying, "Give thy daughter to my son to wife": and there passed by a wild beast that was in Lebanon, and trod down the thistle. ¹⁹Thou sayest, lo, thou hast smitten the Edomites; and thy heart lifteth thee up to boast. Abide now at home; why shouldst thou meddle to thy hurt, that thou shouldst fall, even thou, and Judah with thee?' ²⁰But Amaziah would not hear: for it came of God, that he might deliver them into the hand of their enemies, because they sought after the gods of Edom. ²¹So Joash the king of Israel went up, and they saw one another in the face, both he and Amaziah king of Judah, at Beth-

shemesh, which belongeth to Judah. ²²And Judah was put to the worse before Israel, and they fled every man to his tent. ²³And Joash the king of Israel took Amaziah king of Judah, the son of Joash, the son of Jehoahaz, at Beth-shemesh, and brought him to Jerusalem, and broke down the wall of Jerusalem from the gate of Ephraim to the corner gate, four hundred cubits. ²⁴And he took all the gold and the silver, and all the vessels that were found in the house of God with Obed-edom, and the treasures of the king's house, the hostages also, and returned to Samaria.

²⁵And Amaziah the son of Joash king of Judah lived after the death of Joash son of Jehoahaz king of Israel fifteen years. ²⁶Now the rest of the acts of Amaziah, first and last, behold, are they not written in the book of the kings of Judah and Israel?

²⁷Now after the time that Amaziah did turn away from following the LORD they made a conspiracy against him in Jerusalem, and he fled to Lachish: but they sent to Lachish after him, and slew him there. ²⁸And they brought him upon horses, and buried him with his fathers in the city of Judah.

26 Then all the people of Judah took Uzziah, who was sixteen years old, and made him king in the room of his father Amaziah. ²He built Eloth, and restored it to Judah, after that the king slept with his fathers. ³Sixteen years old was Uzziah when he began to reign, and he reigned fifty and two years in Jerusalem. His mother's name also was Jecoliah of Jerusalem. ⁴And he did that which was right in the sight of the LORD, according to all that his father Amaziah did. ⁵And he sought God in the days of Zechariah, who had understanding in the visions of God: and as long as he sought the LORD, God made him to prosper. ⁶And he went forth and warred against the Philistines, and broke down the wall of Gath, and the wall of Jabneh, and the wall of Ashdod, and built cities about Ashdod, and among the Philistines. ⁷And God helped him against the Philistines, and against the Arabians that dwelt in Gur-baal, and the Mehunims. ⁸And the Ammonites gave gifts to Uzziah, and his name spread abroad even to the entering in of Egypt: for he strengthened himself exceedingly. ⁹Moreover Uzziah built towers in Jerusalem at the corner gate, and at the valley gate, and at the turning of the wall, and fortified them. ¹⁰Also he built towers in the desert, and dug many wells: for he had much cattle, both in the low country, and in the plains: husbandmen also, and vine-dressers in the mountains, and in Carmel: for he loved husbandry. ¹¹Moreover Uzziah had a host of fighting men, that went out to war by bands, according to the number of their account by the hand of Jeiel the scribe and Maaseiah the ruler, under the hand of Hananiah, one of the king's captains. ¹²The whole number of the chief of the fathers of the mighty men of valour were two thousand and six hundred. ¹³And under their hand was an army, three hundred thousand and seven thousand and five hundred, that made war with mighty power, to help the king against the enemy. ¹⁴And Uzziah prepared for them throughout all the host shields, and spears, and helmets, and habergeons, and bows, and slings to cast stones. ¹⁵And

he made in Jerusalem engines invented by cunning men, to be on the towers and upon the bulwarks, to shoot arrows and great stones withal. And his name spread far abroad, for he was marvellously helped, till he was strong.

¹⁶But when he was strong, his heart was lifted up to his destruction: for he transgressed against the LORD his God, and went into the temple of the LORD to burn incense upon the altar of incense. ¹⁷And Azariah the priest went in after him, and with him fourscore priests of the LORD, that were valiant men. ¹⁸And they withstood Uzziah the king, and said unto him, 'It pertaineth not unto thee, Uzziah, to burn incense unto the LORD, but to the priests the sons of Aaron, that are consecrated to burn incense. Go out of the sanctuary; for thou hast trespassed; neither shall it be for thy honour from the LORD God.' ¹⁹Then Uzziah was wroth, and had a censer in his hand to burn incense: and while he was wroth with the priests, the leprosy even rose up in his forehead before the priests in the house of the LORD, from beside the incense altar. ²⁰And Azariah the chief priest, and all the priests, looked upon him, and behold, he was leprous in his forehead, and they thrust him out from thence, yea, himself hasted also to go out, because the LORD had smitten him. ²¹And Uzziah the king was a leper unto the day of his death, and dwelt in a several house, being a leper, for he was cut off from the house of the LORD: and Jotham his son was over the king's house, judging the people of the land.

²²Now the rest of the acts of Uzziah, first and last, did Isaiah the prophet, the son of Amoz, write. ²³So Uzziah slept with his fathers, and they buried him with his fathers in the field of the burial which belonged to the kings: for they said, 'He is a leper': and Jotham his son reigned in his stead.

27 Jotham was twenty and five years old when he began to reign, and he reigned sixteen years in Jerusalem. His mother's name also was Jerushah, the daughter of Zadok. ²And he did that which was right in the sight of the LORD, according to all that his father Uzziah did: howbeit he entered not into the temple of the LORD. And the people did yet corruptly. ³He built the high gate of the house of the LORD, and on the wall of Ophel he built much. ⁴Moreover he built cities in the mountains of Judah, and in the forests he built castles and towers.

⁵He fought also with the king of the Ammonites, and prevailed against them. And the children of Ammon gave him the same year a hundred talents of silver, and ten thousand measures of wheat, and ten thousand of barley. So much did the children of Ammon pay unto him, both the second year, and the third. ⁶So Jotham became mighty, because he prepared his ways before the LORD his God.

⁷Now the rest of the acts of Jotham, and all his wars, and his ways, lo, they are written in the book of the kings of Israel and Judah. ⁸He was five and twenty years old when he began to reign, and reigned sixteen years in Jerusalem.

⁹And Jotham slept with his fathers, and they buried him in the city of David: and Ahaz his son reigned in his stead.

28 Ahaz was twenty years old when he began to reign, and he reigned sixteen years in Jerusalem: but he did not that which was right in the sight of the LORD, like David his father: ²for he walked in the ways of the kings of Israel, and made also molten images for Baalim. ³Moreover he burnt incense in the valley of the son of Hinnom, and burnt his children in the fire, after the abominations of the heathen whom the LORD had cast out before the children of Israel. ⁴He sacrificed also and burnt incense in the high places, and on the hills, and under every green tree. ⁵Wherefore the LORD his God delivered him into the hand of the king of Syria; and they smote him, and carried away a great multitude of them captives, and brought them to Damascus. And he was also delivered into the hand of the king of Israel, who smote him with a great slaughter.

⁶For Pekah the son of Remaliah slew in Judah a hundred and twenty thousand in one day, which were all valiant men; because they had forsaken the LORD God of their fathers. ⁷And Zichri, a mighty man of Ephraim, slew Maaseiah the king's son, and Azrikam the governor of the house, and Elkanah that was next to the king. ⁸And the children of Israel carried away captive of their brethren two hundred thousand, women, sons, and daughters, and took also away much spoil from them, and brought the spoil to Samaria. ⁹But a prophet of the LORD was there, whose name was Oded: and he went out before the host that came to Samaria, and said unto them, 'Behold, because the LORD God of your fathers was wroth with Judah, he hath delivered them into your hand, and ye have slain them in a rage that reacheth up unto heaven. ¹⁰And now ye purpose to keep under the children of Judah and Jerusalem for bondmen and bondwomen unto you: but are there not with you, even with you, sins against the LORD your God? ¹¹Now hear me therefore, and deliver the captives again, which ye have taken captive of your brethren: for the fierce wrath of God is upon you.' ¹²Then certain of the heads of the children of Ephraim, Azariah the son of Johanan, Berechiah the son of Meshillemoth, and Jehizkiah the son of Shallum, and Amasa the son of Hadlai, stood up against them that came from the war, ¹³and said unto them, 'Ye shall not bring in the captives hither: for whereas we have offended against the LORD already, ye intend to add more to our sins and to our trespass: for our trespass is great, and there is fierce wrath against Israel'. ¹⁴So the armed men left the captives and the spoil before the princes and all the congregation. ¹⁵And the men which were expressed by name rose up, and took the captives, and with the spoil clothed all that were naked among them, and arrayed them, and shod them, and gave them to eat and to drink, and anointed them, and carried all the feeble of them upon asses, and brought them to Jericho, the city of palm trees, to their brethren: then they returned to Samaria.

¹⁶At that time did king Ahaz send unto the kings of Assyria to help him. ¹⁷For again the Edomites had come and smitten Judah, and carried away captives. ¹⁸The Philistines also had invaded the cities of the low country, and of the south of Judah, and had taken Beth-shemesh, and

Aijalon, and Gederoth, and Shocho with the villages thereof, and Timnah with the villages thereof, Gimzo also and the villages thereof: and they dwelt there. [19]For the LORD brought Judah low because of Ahaz king of Israel; for he made Judah naked, and transgressed sore against the LORD. [20]And Tilgath-pilneser king of Assyria came unto him, and distressed him, but strengthened him not. [21]For Ahaz took away a portion out of the house of the LORD, and out of the house of the king, and of the princes, and gave it unto the king of Assyria: but he helped him not.

[22]And in the time of this distress did he trespass yet more against the LORD: this is that king Ahaz. [23]For he sacrificed unto the gods of Damascus, which smote him: and he said, 'Because the gods of the kings of Syria help them, therefore will I sacrifice to them, that they may help me'. But they were the ruin of him, and of all Israel. [24]And Ahaz gathered together the vessels of the house of God, and cut in pieces the vessels of the house of God, and shut up the doors of the house of the LORD, and he made him altars in every corner of Jerusalem. [25]And in every several city of Judah he made high places to burn incense unto other gods, and provoked to anger the LORD God of his fathers.

[26]Now the rest of his acts and of all his ways, first and last, behold, they are written in the book of the kings of Judah and Israel. [27]And Ahaz slept with his fathers, and they buried him in the city, even in Jerusalem: but they brought him not into the sepulchres of the kings of Israel: and Hezekiah his son reigned in his stead.

29 Hezekiah began to reign when he was five and twenty years old, and he reigned nine and twenty years in Jerusalem. And his mother's name was Abijah, the daughter of Zechariah. [2]And he did that which was right in the sight of the LORD, according to all that David his father had done.

[3]He in the first year of his reign, in the first month, opened the doors of the house of the LORD, and repaired them. [4]And he brought in the priests and the Levites, and gathered them together into the east street, [5]and said unto them, 'Hear me, ye Levites, sanctify now yourselves, and sanctify the house of the LORD God of your fathers, and carry forth the filthiness out of the holy place. [6]For our fathers have trespassed, and done that which was evil in the eyes of the LORD our God, and have forsaken him, and have turned away their faces from the habitation of the LORD, and turned their backs. [7]Also they have shut up the doors of the porch, and put out the lamps, and have not burnt incense nor offered burnt offerings in the holy place unto the God of Israel. [8]Wherefore the wrath of the LORD was upon Judah and Jerusalem, and he hath delivered them to trouble, to astonishment, and to hissing, as ye see with your eyes. [9]For lo, our fathers have fallen by the sword, and our sons and our daughters and our wives are in captivity for this. [10]Now it is in my heart to make a covenant with the LORD God of Israel, that his fierce wrath may turn away from us. [11]My sons, be not now negligent: for the LORD hath chosen you to stand before him, to serve him, and that you should minister unto him, and burn incense.'

¹²Then the Levites arose, Mahath the son of Amasai, and Joel the son of Azariah, of the sons of the Kohathites: and of the sons of Merari, Kish the son of Abdi, and Azariah the son of Jehalelel: and of the Gershonites, Joah the son of Zimmah, and Eden the son of Joah: ¹³and of the sons of Elizaphan, Shimri, and Jeiel: and of the sons of Asaph, Zechariah, and Mattaniah: ¹⁴and of the sons of Heman, Jehiel, and Shimei: and of the sons of Jeduthun, Shemaiah, and Uzziel. ¹⁵And they gathered their brethren, and sanctified themselves, and came according to the commandment of the king, by the words of the LORD, to cleanse the house of the LORD. ¹⁶And the priests went into the inner part of the house of the LORD, to cleanse it, and brought out all the uncleanness that they found in the temple of the LORD into the court of the house of the LORD. And the Levites took it, to carry it out abroad into the brook Kidron. ¹⁷Now they began on the first day of the first month to sanctify, and on the eighth day of the month came they to the porch of the LORD. So they sanctified the house of the LORD in eight days, and in the sixteenth day of the first month they made an end. ¹⁸Then they went in to Hezekiah the king, and said, 'We have cleansed all the house of the LORD, and the altar of burnt offering, with all the vessels thereof, and the showbread table, with all the vessels thereof. ¹⁹Moreover all the vessels, which king Ahaz in his reign did cast away in his transgression, have we prepared and sanctified, and behold, they are before the altar of the LORD.'

²⁰Then Hezekiah the king rose early, and gathered the rulers of the city, and went up to the house of the LORD. ²¹And they brought seven bullocks, and seven rams, and seven lambs, and seven he-goats, for a sin offering for the kingdom, and for the sanctuary, and for Judah. And he commanded the priests the sons of Aaron to offer them on the altar of the LORD. ²²So they killed the bullocks, and the priests received the blood, and sprinkled it on the altar: likewise, when they had killed the rams, they sprinkled the blood upon the altar: they killed also the lambs, and they sprinkled the blood upon the altar. ²³And they brought forth the he-goats for the sin offering before the king and the congregation, and laid their hands upon them: ²⁴and the priests killed them, and they made reconciliation with their blood upon the altar, to make an atonement for all Israel: for the king commanded that the burnt offering and the sin offering should be made for all Israel. ²⁵And he set the Levites in the house of the LORD with cymbals, with psalteries, and with harps, according to the commandment of David, and of Gad the king's seer, and Nathan the prophet: for so was the commandment of the LORD by his prophets. ²⁶And the Levites stood with the instruments of David, and the priests with the trumpets. ²⁷And Hezekiah commanded to offer the burnt offering upon the altar. And when the burnt offering began, the song of the LORD began also with the trumpets, and with the instruments ordained by David king of Israel. ²⁸And all the congregation worshipped, and the singers sang, and the trumpeters sounded: and all this continued until the burnt offering was finished. ²⁹And when they had made an end of offering, the king and all that

were present with him bowed themselves, and worshipped. ³⁰Moreover Hezekiah the king and the princes commanded the Levites to sing praise unto the LORD with the words of David, and of Asaph the seer. And they sang praises with gladness, and they bowed their heads and worshipped. ³¹Then Hezekiah answered and said, 'Now ye have consecrated yourselves unto the LORD, come near and bring sacrifices and thanks offerings into the house of the LORD'. And the congregation brought in sacrifices and thanks offerings, and as many as were of a free heart, burnt offerings. ³²And the number of the burnt offerings which the congregation brought, was threescore and ten bullocks, a hundred rams, and two hundred lambs: all these were for a burnt offering to the LORD. ³³And the consecrated things were six hundred oxen and three thousand sheep. ³⁴But the priests were too few, so that they could not flay all the burnt offerings: wherefore their brethren the Levites did help them, till the work was ended, and until the other priests had sanctified themselves: for the Levites were more upright in heart to sanctify themselves than the priests. ³⁵And also the burnt offerings were in abundance, with the fat of the peace offerings, and the drink offerings for every burnt offering. So the service of the house of the LORD was set in order. ³⁶And Hezekiah rejoiced, and all the people, that God had prepared the people: for the thing was done suddenly.

30 And Hezekiah sent to all Israel and Judah, and wrote letters also to Ephraim and Manasseh, that they should come to the house of the LORD at Jerusalem, to keep the passover unto the LORD God of Israel. ²For the king had taken counsel, and his princes, and all the congregation in Jerusalem, to keep the passover in the second month. ³For they could not keep it at that time, because the priests had not sanctified themselves sufficiently, neither had the people gathered themselves together to Jerusalem. ⁴And the thing pleased the king and all the congregation. ⁵So they established a decree to make proclamation throughout all Israel, from Beer-sheba even to Dan, that they should come to keep the passover unto the LORD God of Israel at Jerusalem: for they had not done it of a long time in such sort, as it was written. ⁶So the posts went with the letters from the king and his princes throughout all Israel and Judah, and according to the commandment of the king, saying, 'Ye children of Israel, turn again unto the LORD God of Abraham, Isaac, and Israel, and he will return to the remnant of you, that are escaped out of the hand of the kings of Assyria. ⁷And be not ye like your fathers, and like your brethren, which trespassed against the LORD God of their fathers, who therefore gave them up to desolation, as ye see. ⁸Now be ye not stiff-necked, as your fathers were, but yield yourselves unto the LORD, and enter into his sanctuary, which he hath sanctified for ever: and serve the LORD your God, that the fierceness of his wrath may turn away from you. ⁹For if ye turn again unto the LORD, your brethren and your children shall find compassion before them that lead them captive, so that they shall come again into this land: for the LORD your God is gracious and merciful, and will not turn away his face from you, if ye return unto him.' ¹⁰So the posts passed from city to city through the country of Ephraim and Manasseh even unto Zebulun: but they laughed them to scorn, and mocked them. [11]Nevertheless divers of Asher and Manasseh and of Zebulun humbled themselves, and came to Jerusalem. [12]Also in Judah the hand of God was to give them one heart to do the commandment of the king and of the princes, by the word of the LORD.

[13]And there assembled at Jerusalem much people to keep the feast of unleavened bread in the second month, a very great congregation. [14]And they arose and took away the altars that were in Jerusalem, and all the altars for incense took they away, and cast them into the brook Kidron. [15]Then they killed the passover on the fourteenth day of the second month: and the priests and the Levites were ashamed, and sanctified themselves, and brought in the burnt offerings into the house of the LORD. [16]And they stood in their place after their manner, according to the law of Moses the man of God: the priests sprinkled the blood, which they received of the hand of the Levites. [17]For there were many in the congregation that were not sanctified: therefore the Levites had the charge of the killing of the passovers for every one that was not clean, to sanctify them unto the LORD. [18]For a multitude of the people, even many of Ephraim and Manasseh, Issachar and Zebulun, had not cleansed themselves: yet did they eat the passover otherwise than it was written. But Hezekiah prayed for them, saying, 'The good LORD pardon every one [19]that prepareth his heart to seek God, the LORD God of his fathers, though he be not cleansed according to the purification of the sanctuary'. [20]And the LORD hearkened to Hezekiah, and healed the people.

[21]And the children of Israel that were present at Jerusalem kept the feast of unleavened bread seven days with great gladness: and the Levites and the priests praised the LORD day by day, singing with loud instruments unto the LORD. [22]And Hezekiah spoke comfortably unto all the Levites that taught the good knowledge of the LORD: and they did eat throughout the feast seven days, offering peace offerings, and making confession to the LORD God of their fathers. [23]And the whole assembly took counsel to keep other seven days: and they kept other seven days with gladness. [24]For Hezekiah king of Judah did give to the congregation a thousand bullocks and seven thousand sheep; and the princes gave to the congregation a thousand bullocks and ten thousand sheep: and a great number of priests sanctified themselves. [25]And all the congregation of Judah, with the priests and the Levites, and all the congregation that came out of Israel, and the strangers that came out of the land of Israel, and that dwelt in Judah, rejoiced. [26]So there was great joy in Jerusalem: for since the time of Solomon the son of David king of Israel there was not the like in Jerusalem.

[27]Then the priests the Levites arose and blessed the people: and their voice was heard, and their prayer came up to his holy dwelling place, even unto heaven.

31 Now when all this was finished, all Israel that were present went out to the cities of Judah, and broke the images in pieces, and

cut down the groves, and threw down the high places and the altars out of all Judah and Benjamin, in Ephraim also and Manasseh, until they had utterly destroyed them all. Then all the children of Israel returned every man to his possession into their own cities.

²And Hezekiah appointed the courses of the priests and the Levites after their courses, every man according to his service, the priests and Levites for burnt offerings and for peace offerings, to minister, and to give thanks, and to praise in the gates of the tents of the LORD. ³He appointed also the king's portion of his substance for the burnt offerings, to wit, for the morning and evening burnt offerings, and the burnt offerings for the sabbaths, and for the new moons, and for the set feasts, as it is written in the law of the LORD. ⁴Moreover he commanded the people that dwelt in Jerusalem to give the portion of the priests and the Levites, that they might be encouraged in the law of the LORD.

⁵And as soon as the commandment came abroad, the children of Israel brought in abundance the first-fruits of corn, wine, and oil, and honey, and of all the increase of the field; and the tithe of all things brought they in abundantly. ⁶And concerning the children of Israel and Judah, that dwelt in the cities of Judah, they also brought in the tithes of oxen and sheep, and the tithe of holy things which were consecrated unto the LORD their God, and laid them by heaps. ⁷In the third month they began to lay the foundation of the heaps, and finished them in the seventh month. ⁸And when Hezekiah and the princes came and saw the heaps, they blessed the LORD, and his people Israel. ⁹Then Hezekiah questioned with the priests and the Levites concerning the heaps. ¹⁰And Azariah the chief priest of the house of Zadok answered him, and said, 'Since the people began to bring the offerings into the house of the LORD, we have had enough to eat, and have left plenty: for the LORD hath blessed his people; and that which is left is this great store'.

¹¹Then Hezekiah commanded to prepare chambers in the house of the LORD, and they prepared them, ¹²and brought in the offerings and the tithes and the dedicated things faithfully: over which Cononiah the Levite was ruler, and Shimei his brother was the next. ¹³And Jehiel, and Azaziah, and Nahath, and Asahel, and Jerimoth, and Jozabad, and Eliel, and Ismachiah, and Mahath, and Benaiah were overseers under the hand of Cononiah and Shimei his brother, at the commandment of Hezekiah the king, and Azariah the ruler of the house of God. ¹⁴And Kore the son of Imnah the Levite, the porter toward the east, was over the free-will offerings of God, to distribute the oblations of the LORD, and the most holy things. ¹⁵And next him were Eden, and Miniamin, and Jeshua, and Shemaiah, Amariah, and Shechaniah, in the cities of the priests, in their set office, to give to their brethren by courses, as well to the great as to the small: ¹⁶besides their genealogy of males, from three years old and upward, even unto every one that entereth into the house of the LORD, his daily portion for their service in their charges according to their courses: ¹⁷both to the genealogy of the priests by the house of their fathers, and the Levites from twenty years

old and upward, in their charges by their courses: ¹⁸and to the genealogy of all their little ones, their wives, and their sons, and their daughters, through all the congregation: for in their set office they sanctified themselves in holiness: ¹⁹also of the sons of Aaron the priests, which were in the fields of the suburbs of their cities, in every several city, the men that were expressed by name, to give portions to all the males among the priests, and to all that were reckoned by genealogies among the Levites.

²⁰And thus did Hezekiah throughout all Judah, and wrought that which was good and right and truth before the LORD his God. ²¹And in every work that he began in the service of the house of God, and in the law, and in the commandments, to seek his God, he did it with all his heart, and prospered.

32 After these things, and the establishment thereof, Sennacherib king of Assyria came, and entered into Judah, and encamped against the fenced cities, and thought to win them for himself. ²And when Hezekiah saw that Sennacherib was come, and that he was purposed to fight against Jerusalem, ³he took counsel with his princes and his mighty men to stop the waters of the fountains which were without the city: and they did help him. ⁴So there was gathered much people together, who stopped all the fountains, and the brook that ran through the midst of the land, saying, 'Why should the kings of Assyria come, and find much water?' ⁵Also he strengthened himself, and built up all the wall that was broken, and raised it up to the towers, and another wall without, and prepared Millo in the city of David, and made darts and shields in abundance. ⁶And he set captains of war over the people, and gathered them together to him in the street of the gate of the city, and spoke comfortably to them, saying, ⁷'Be strong and courageous, be not afraid nor dismayed for the king of Assyria, nor for all the multitude that is with him: for there be more with us than with him. ⁸With him is an arm of flesh, but with us is the LORD our God to help us, and to fight our battles.' And the people rested themselves upon the words of Hezekiah king of Judah.

⁹After this did Sennacherib king of Assyria send his servants to Jerusalem (but he himself laid siege against Lachish, and all his power with him) unto Hezekiah king of Judah, and unto all Judah that were at Jerusalem, saying, ¹⁰'Thus saith Sennacherib king of Assyria, "Whereon do ye trust, that ye abide in the siege in Jerusalem? ¹¹Doth not Hezekiah persuade you to give over yourselves to die by famine and by thirst, saying, 'The LORD our God shall deliver us out of the hand of the king of Assyria'? ¹²Hath not the same Hezekiah taken away his high places and his altars, and commanded Judah and Jerusalem, saying, 'Ye shall worship before one altar, and burn incense upon it'? ¹³Know ye not what I and my fathers have done unto all the people of other lands? were the gods of the nations of those lands any ways able to deliver their lands out of my hand? ¹⁴Who was there among all the gods of those nations that my fathers utterly destroyed, that could deliver his people out of my hand, that your God should be able to deliver you out of my hand?

[15]Now therefore let not Hezekiah deceive you, nor persuade you on this manner, neither yet believe him: for no god of any nation or kingdom was able to deliver his people out of my hand, and out of the hand of my fathers: how much less shall your God deliver you out of my hand?"' [16]And his servants spoke yet more against the LORD God, and against his servant Hezekiah. [17]He wrote also letters to rail on the LORD God of Israel, and to speak against him, saying, 'As the gods of the nations of other lands have not delivered their people out of my hand, so shall not the God of Hezekiah deliver his people out of my hand'. [18]Then they cried with a loud voice in the Jews' speech unto the people of Jerusalem that were on the wall, to affright them, and to trouble them, that they might take the city. [19]And they spoke against the God of Jerusalem, as against the gods of the people of the earth, which were the work of the hands of man. [20]For this cause Hezekiah the king, and the prophet Isaiah the son of Amoz, prayed and cried to heaven.

[21]And the LORD sent an angel, which cut off all the mighty men of valour, and the leaders and captains in the camp of the king of Assyria. So he returned with shame of face to his own land. And when he was come into the house of his god, they that came forth of his own bowels slew him there with the sword. [22]Thus the LORD saved Hezekiah and the inhabitants of Jerusalem from the hand of Sennacherib the king of Assyria, and from the hand of all others, and guided them on every side. [23]And many brought gifts unto the LORD to Jerusalem, and presents to Hezekiah king of Judah: so that he was magnified in the sight of all nations from thenceforth.

[24]In those days Hezekiah was sick to the death, and prayed unto the LORD: and he spoke unto him, and he gave him a sign. [25]But Hezekiah rendered not again according to the benefit done unto him; for his heart was lifted up: therefore there was wrath upon him, and upon Judah and Jerusalem. [26]Notwithstanding Hezekiah humbled himself for the pride of his heart, both he and the inhabitants of Jerusalem, so that the wrath of the LORD came not upon them in the days of Hezekiah.

[27]And Hezekiah had exceeding much riches and honour: and he made himself treasuries for silver, and for gold, and for precious stones, and for spices, and for shields, and for all manner of pleasant jewels; [28]storehouses also for the increase of corn, and wine, and oil; and stalls for all manner of beasts, and cotes for flocks. [29]Moreover he provided him cities, and possessions of flocks and herds in abundance: for God had given him substance very much. [30]This same Hezekiah also stopped the upper watercourse of Gihon, and brought it straight down to the west side of the city of David. And Hezekiah prospered in all his works. [31]Howbeit in the business of the ambassadors of the princes of Babylon, who sent unto him to inquire of the wonder that was done in the land, God left him, to try him, that he might know all that was in his heart.

[32]Now the rest of the acts of Hezekiah, and his goodness, behold, they are written in the vision of Isaiah the prophet, the son of Amoz, and in

the book of the kings of Judah and Israel. ³³And Hezekiah slept with his fathers, and they buried him in the chiefest of the sepulchres of the sons of David: and all Judah and the inhabitants of Jerusalem did him honour at his death. And Manasseh his son reigned in his stead.

33 Manasseh was twelve years old when he began to reign, and he reigned fifty and five years in Jerusalem: ²but did that which was evil in the sight of the LORD, like unto the abominations of the heathen, whom the LORD had cast out before the children of Israel. ³For he built again the high places which Hezekiah his father had broken down, and he reared up altars for Baalim, and made groves, and worshipped all the host of heaven, and served them. ⁴Also he built altars in the house of the LORD, whereof the LORD had said, 'In Jerusalem shall my name be for ever'. ⁵And he built altars for all the host of heaven in the two courts of the house of the LORD. ⁶And he caused his children to pass through the fire in the valley of the son of Hinnom: also he observed times, and used enchantments, and used witchcraft, and dealt with a familiar spirit, and with wizards: he wrought much evil in the sight of the LORD, to provoke him to anger. ⁷And he set a carved image, the idol which he had made, in the house of God, of which God had said to David and to Solomon his son, 'In this house, and in Jerusalem, which I have chosen before all the tribes of Israel, will I put my name for ever. ⁸Neither will I any more remove the foot of Israel from out of the land which I have appointed for your fathers; so that they will take heed to do all that I have commanded them, according to the whole law and the statutes and the ordinances by the hand of Moses.' ⁹So Manasseh made Judah and the inhabitants of Jerusalem to err, and to do worse than the heathen, whom the LORD had destroyed before the children of Israel.

¹⁰And the LORD spoke to Manasseh, and to his people: but they would not hearken. ¹¹Wherefore the LORD brought upon them the captains of the host of the king of Assyria, which took Manasseh among the thorns, and bound him with fetters, and carried him to Babylon. ¹²And when he was in affliction, he besought the LORD his God, and humbled himself greatly before the God of his fathers, ¹³and prayed unto him: and he was entreated of him, and heard his supplication, and brought him again to Jerusalem into his kingdom. Then Manasseh knew that the LORD he was God.

¹⁴Now after this he built a wall without the city of David, on the west side of Gihon, in the valley, even to the entering in at the fish gate, and compassed about Ophel, and raised it up a very great height, and put captains of war in all the fenced cities of Judah. ¹⁵And he took away the strange gods, and the idol out of the house of the LORD, and all the altars that he had built in the mount of the house of the LORD, and in Jerusalem, and cast them out of the city. ¹⁶And he repaired the altar of the LORD, and sacrificed thereon peace offerings and thanks offerings, and commanded Judah to serve the LORD God of Israel. ¹⁷Nevertheless the people did sacrifice still in the high places, yet unto the LORD their God only.

¹⁸Now the rest of the acts of Manasseh, and his prayer unto his God, and the words of the seers that spoke to him in the name of the LORD God of Israel, behold, they are written in the book of the kings of Israel. ¹⁹His prayer also, and how God was entreated of him, and all his sin, and his trespass, and the places wherein he built high places, and set up groves and graven images before he was humbled: behold, they are written among the sayings of the seers.

²⁰So Manasseh slept with his fathers, and they buried him in his own house: and Amon his son reigned in his stead.

²¹Amon was two and twenty years old when he began to reign, and reigned two years in Jerusalem. ²²But he did that which was evil in the sight of the LORD, as did Manasseh his father: for Amon sacrificed unto all the carved images which Manasseh his father had made, and served them; ²³and humbled not himself before the LORD, as Manasseh his father had humbled himself: but Amon trespassed more and more. ²⁴And his servants conspired against him, and slew him in his own house.

²⁵But the people of the land slew all them that had conspired against king Amon, and the people of the land made Josiah his son king in his stead.

34 Josiah was eight years old when he began to reign, and he reigned in Jerusalem one and thirty years. ²And he did that which was right in the sight of the LORD, and walked in the ways of David his father, and declined neither to the right hand, nor to the left.

³For in the eighth year of his reign, while he was yet young, he began to seek after the God of David his father: and in the twelfth year he began to purge Judah and Jerusalem from the high places, and the groves, and the carved images, and the molten images. ⁴And they broke down the altars of Baalim in his presence; and the images, that were on high above them, he cut down; and the groves, and the carved images, and the molten images, he broke in pieces, and made dust of them, and strewed it upon the graves of them that had sacrificed unto them. ⁵And he burnt the bones of the priests upon their altars, and cleansed Judah and Jerusalem. ⁶And so did he in the cities of Manasseh, and Ephraim, and Simeon, even unto Naphtali, with their mattocks, round about. ⁷And when he had broken down the altars and the groves, and had beaten the graven images into powder, and cut down all the idols throughout all the land of Israel, he returned to Jerusalem.

⁸Now in the eighteenth year of his reign, when he had purged the land, and the house, he sent Shaphan the son of Azaliah, and Maaseiah the governor of the city, and Joah the son of Joahaz the recorder, to repair the house of the LORD his God. ⁹And when they came to Hilkiah the high priest, they delivered the money that was brought into the house of God, which the Levites that kept the doors had gathered of the hand of Manasseh and Ephraim, and of all the remnant of Israel, and of all Judah and Benjamin, and they returned to Jerusalem. ¹⁰And they put it in the hand of the workmen that had the oversight of the house of the LORD, and they gave it to the workmen that wrought in the house of

the LORD, to repair and mend the house. ¹¹Even to the artificers and builders gave they it, to buy hewn stone, and timber for couplings, and to floor the houses which the kings of Judah had destroyed. ¹²And the men did the work faithfully: and the overseers of them were Jahath and Obadiah, the Levites, of the sons of Merari, and Zechariah and Meshullam, of the sons of the Kohathites, to set it forward; and others of the Levites, all that could skill of instruments of music. ¹³Also they were over the bearers of burdens, and were overseers of all that wrought the work in any manner of service: and of the Levites there were scribes, and officers, and porters.

¹⁴And when they brought out the money that was brought into the house of the LORD, Hilkiah the priest found a book of the law of the LORD given by Moses. ¹⁵And Hilkiah answered and said to Shaphan the scribe, 'I have found the book of the law in the house of the LORD'. And Hilkiah delivered the book to Shaphan: ¹⁶and Shaphan carried the book to the king, and brought the king word back again, saying, 'All that was committed to thy servants, they do it. ¹⁷And they have gathered together the money that was found in the house of the LORD, and have delivered it into the hand of the overseers, and to the hand of the workmen.' ¹⁸Then Shaphan the scribe told the king, saying, 'Hilkiah the priest hath given me a book'. And Shaphan read it before the king. ¹⁹And it came to pass when the king had heard the words of the law, that he rent his clothes. ²⁰And the king commanded Hilkiah, and Ahikam the son of Shaphan, and Abdon the son of Micah, and Shaphan the scribe, and Asaiah a servant of the king, saying, ²¹'Go, inquire of the LORD for me, and for them that are left in Israel and in Judah, concerning the words of the book that is found: for great is the wrath of the LORD that is poured out upon us, because our fathers have not kept the word of the LORD, to do after all that is written in this book'.

²²And Hilkiah, and they that the king had appointed, went to Huldah the prophetess, the wife of Shallum the son of Tikvath, the son of Hasrah, keeper of the wardrobe (now she dwelt in Jerusalem in the college), and they spoke to her to that effect. ²³And she answered them, 'Thus saith the LORD God of Israel, "Tell ye the man that sent you to me, ²⁴"Thus saith the LORD, "Behold, I will bring evil upon this place, and upon the inhabitants thereof, even all the curses that are written in the book which they have read before the king of Judah: ²⁵because they have forsaken me, and have burnt incense unto other gods, that they might provoke me to anger with all the works of their hands; therefore my wrath shall be poured out upon this place, and shall not be quenched"'. ²⁶And as for the king of Judah, who sent you to inquire of the LORD, so shall ye say unto him, 'Thus saith the LORD God of Israel concerning the words which thou hast heard: ²⁷"Because thy heart was tender, and thou didst humble thyself before God, when thou heardest his words against this place, and against the inhabitants thereof, and humbledst thyself before me, and didst rend thy clothes, and weep before me, I have even heard thee also," saith the LORD. ²⁸"Behold, I will gather thee to thy fathers, and thou shalt be gathered to thy grave in

peace, neither shall thy eyes see all the evil that I will bring upon this place, and upon the inhabitants of the same."'" So they brought the king word again.

²⁹Then the king sent and gathered together all the elders of Judah and Jerusalem. ³⁰And the king went up into the house of the LORD, and all the men of Judah, and the inhabitants of Jerusalem, and the priests, and the Levites, and all the people, great and small: and he read in their ears all the words of the book of the covenant that was found in the house of the LORD. ³¹And the king stood in his place, and made a covenant before the LORD, to walk after the LORD, and to keep his commandments, and his testimonies, and his statutes, with all his heart, and with all his soul, to perform the words of the covenant which are written in this book. ³²And he caused all that were present in Jerusalem and Benjamin to stand to it. And the inhabitants of Jerusalem did according to the covenant of God, the God of their fathers. ³³And Josiah took away all the abominations out of all the countries that pertained to the children of Israel, and made all that were present in Israel to serve, even to serve the LORD their God. And all his days they departed not from following the LORD, the God of their fathers.

35 Moreover Josiah kept a passover unto the LORD in Jerusalem: and they killed the passover on the fourteenth day of the first month. ²And he set the priests in their charges, and encouraged them to the service of the house of the LORD, ³and said unto the Levites that taught all Israel, which were holy unto the LORD, 'Put the holy ark in the house which Solomon the son of David king of Israel did build; it shall not be a burden upon your shoulders: serve now the LORD your God, and his people Israel. ⁴And prepare yourselves by the houses of your fathers, after your courses, according to the writing of David king of Israel, and according to the writing of Solomon his son. ⁵And stand in the holy place according to the divisions of the families of the fathers of your brethren the people, and after the division of the families of the Levites. ⁶So kill the passover, and sanctify yourselves, and prepare your brethren, that they may do according to the word of the LORD by the hand of Moses.'

⁷And Josiah gave to the people, of the flock, lambs and kids, all for the passover offerings, for all that were present, to the number of thirty thousand, and three thousand bullocks: these were of the king's substance. ⁸And his princes gave willingly unto the people, to the priests, and to the Levites: Hilkiah and Zechariah and Jehiel, rulers of the house of God, gave unto the priests for the passover offerings two thousand and six hundred small cattle, and three hundred oxen. ⁹Conaniah also, and Shemaiah and Nethaneel, his brethren, and Hashabiah and Jeiel and Jozabad, chief of the Levites, gave unto the Levites for passover offerings five thousand small cattle, and five hundred oxen.

¹⁰So the service was prepared, and the priests stood in their place, and the Levites in their courses, according to the king's commandment. ¹¹And they killed the passover, and the priests sprinkled the blood from their hands, and the Levites flayed them. ¹²And they removed the burnt

offerings, that they might give according to the divisions of the families of the people, to offer unto the LORD, as it is written in the book of Moses: and so did they with the oxen. ¹³And they roasted the passover with fire according to the ordinance: but the other holy offerings seethed they in pots, and in cauldrons, and in pans, and divided them speedily among all the people. ¹⁴And afterward they made ready for themselves, and for the priests: because the priests the sons of Aaron were busied in offering of burnt offerings and the fat until night; therefore the Levites prepared for themselves, and for the priests the sons of Aaron. ¹⁵And the singers the sons of Asaph were in their place, according to the commandment of David, and Asaph, and Heman, and Jeduthun the king's seer; and the porters waited at every gate: they might not depart from their service; for their brethren the Levites prepared for them. ¹⁶So all the service of the LORD was prepared the same day, to keep the passover, and to offer burnt offerings upon the altar of the LORD, according to the commandment of king Josiah. ¹⁷And the children of Israel that were present kept the passover at that time, and the feast of unleavened bread seven days. ¹⁸And there was no passover like to that kept in Israel from the days of Samuel the prophet; neither did all the kings of Israel keep such a passover as Josiah kept, and the priests, and the Levites, and all Judah and Israel that were present, and the inhabitants of Jerusalem. ¹⁹In the eighteenth year of the reign of Josiah was this passover kept.

²⁰After all this, when Josiah had prepared the temple, Necho king of Egypt came up to fight against Carchemish by Euphrates: and Josiah went out against him. ²¹But he sent ambassadors to him, saying, 'What have I to do with thee, thou king of Judah? I come not against thee this day, but against the house wherewith I have war: for God commanded me to make haste: forbear thee from meddling with God, who is with me, that he destroy thee not.' ²²Nevertheless Josiah would not turn his face from him, but disguised himself that he might fight with him, and hearkened not unto the words of Necho from the mouth of God, and came to fight in the valley of Megiddo. ²³And the archers shot at king Josiah: and the king said to his servants, 'Have me away, for I am sore wounded'. ²⁴His servants therefore took him out of that chariot, and put him in the second chariot that he had: and they brought him to Jerusalem, and he died, and was buried in one of the sepulchres of his fathers. And all Judah and Jerusalem mourned for Josiah.

²⁵And Jeremiah lamented for Josiah: and all the singing men and the singing women spoke of Josiah in their lamentations to this day, and made them an ordinance in Israel; and behold, they are written in the lamentations.

²⁶Now the rest of the acts of Josiah, and his goodness, according to that which was written in the law of the LORD, ²⁷and his deeds, first and last, behold, they are written in the book of the kings of Israel and Judah.

36 Then the people of the land took Jehoahaz the son of Josiah, and made him king in his father's stead in Jerusalem. ²Jehoahaz was twenty and three years old when he began to reign, and he reigned three months in Jerusalem. ³And the king of Egypt put him down at Jerusalem, and condemned the land in a hundred talents of silver and a talent of gold. ⁴And the king of Egypt made Eliakim his brother king over Judah and Jerusalem, and turned his name to Jehoiakim. And Necho took Jehoahaz his brother, and carried him to Egypt.

⁵Jehoiakim was twenty and five years old when he began to reign, and he reigned eleven years in Jerusalem: and he did that which was evil in the sight of the LORD his God. ⁶Against him came up Nebuchadnezzar king of Babylon, and bound him in fetters, to carry him to Babylon. ⁷Nebuchadnezzar also carried of the vessels of the house of the LORD to Babylon, and put them in his temple at Babylon.

⁸Now the rest of the acts of Jehoiakim, and his abominations which he did, and that which was found in him, behold, they are written in the book of the kings of Israel and Judah: and Jehoiachin his son reigned in his stead.

⁹Jehoiachin was eight years old when he began to reign, and he reigned three months and ten days in Jerusalem: and he did that which was evil in the sight of the LORD. ¹⁰And when the year was expired, king Nebuchadnezzar sent, and brought him to Babylon, with the goodly vessels of the house of the LORD, and made Zedekiah his brother king over Judah and Jerusalem.

¹¹Zedekiah was one and twenty years old when he began to reign, and reigned eleven years in Jerusalem. ¹²And he did that which was evil in the sight of the LORD his God, and humbled not himself before Jeremiah the prophet speaking from the mouth of the LORD. ¹³And he also rebelled against king Nebuchadnezzar, who had made him swear by God: but he stiffened his neck, and hardened his heart from turning unto the LORD God of Israel.

¹⁴Moreover all the chief of the priests, and the people transgressed very much after all the abominations of the heathen, and polluted the house of the LORD which he had hallowed in Jerusalem. ¹⁵And the LORD God of their fathers sent to them by his messengers, rising up betimes, and sending: because he had compassion on his people, and on his dwelling place: ¹⁶but they mocked the messengers of God, and despised his words, and misused his prophets, until the wrath of the LORD arose against his people, till there was no remedy. ¹⁷Therefore he brought upon them the king of the Chaldees, who slew their young men with the sword in the house of their sanctuary, and had no compassion upon young man or maiden, old man, or him that stooped for age: he gave them all into his hand. ¹⁸And all the vessels of the house of God, great and small, and the treasures of the house of the LORD, and the treasures of the king, and of his princes: all these he brought to Babylon. ¹⁹And they burnt the house of God, and broke down the wall of Jerusalem, and burnt all the palaces thereof with fire, and destroyed all the goodly vessels thereof. ²⁰And them that had escaped from the sword carried he away to Babylon: where they were servants to him and his sons until the reign of the kingdom of Persia: ²¹to fulfil the word of the

LORD by the mouth of Jeremiah, until the land had enjoyed her sab-baths: for as long as she lay desolate she kept sabbath, to fulfil three-score and ten years.

²²Now in the first year of Cyrus king of Persia, that the word of the LORD spoken by the mouth of Jeremiah might be accomplished, the LORD stirred up the spirit of Cyrus king of Persia, that he made a procla-mation throughout all his kingdom, and put it also in writing, saying,

²³Thus saith Cyrus king of Persia, 'All the kingdoms of the earth hath the Lord God of heaven given me, and he hath charged me to build him a house in Jerusalem, which is in Judah. Who is there among you of all his people? The Lord his God be with him, and let him go up.'

EZRA

1 Now in the first year of Cyrus king of Persia, that the word of the Lord by the mouth of Jeremiah might be fulfilled, the Lord stirred up the spirit of Cyrus king of Persia, that he made a proclamation throughout all his kingdom, and put it also in writing, saying,

²Thus saith Cyrus king of Persia, 'The Lord God of heaven hath given me all the kingdoms of the earth, and he hath charged me to build him a house at Jerusalem, which is in Judah. ³Who is there among you of all his people? his God be with him, and let him go up to Jerusalem, which is in Judah, and build the house of the Lord God of Israel (he is the God) which is in Jerusalem. ⁴And whosoever remaineth in any place where he sojourneth, let the men of his place help him with silver, and with gold, and with goods, and with beasts, besides the free-will offering for the house of God that is in Jerusalem.'

⁵Then rose up the chief of the fathers of Judah and Benjamin, and the priests, and the Levites, with all them whose spirit God had raised, to go up to build the house of the Lord which is in Jerusalem. ⁶And all they that were about them strengthened their hands with vessels of silver, with gold, with goods, and with beasts, and with precious things, besides all that was willingly offered.

⁷Also Cyrus the king brought forth the vessels of the house of the Lord, which Nebuchadnezzar had brought forth out of Jerusalem, and had put them in the house of his gods: ⁸even those did Cyrus king of Persia bring forth by the hand of Mithredath the treasurer, and numbered them unto Sheshbazzar, the prince of Judah. ⁹And this is the number of them: thirty chargers of gold, a thousand chargers of silver, nine and twenty knives, ¹⁰thirty basins of gold, silver basins of a second sort four hundred and ten, and other vessels a thousand. ¹¹All the vessels of gold and of silver were five thousand and four hundred. All these did Sheshbazzar bring up with them of the captivity that were brought up from Babylon unto Jerusalem.

2 Now these are the children of the province that went up out of the captivity, of those which had been carried away, whom Nebuchadnezzar the king of Babylon had carried away unto Babylon, and came again unto Jerusalem and Judah, every one unto his city; ²which came with Zerubbabel: Jeshua, Nehemiah, Seraiah, Reelaiah, Mordecai, Bilshan, Mispar, Bigvai, Rehum, Baanah. The number of the men of the people of Israel. ³The children of Parosh, two thousand a hundred seventy and two. ⁴The children of Shephatiah, three hundred seventy and two. ⁵The children of Arah, seven hundred seventy and five. ⁶The children of Pahath-moab, of the children of Jeshua and Joab, two thousand eight hundred and twelve. ⁷The children of Elam, a thousand two hundred fifty and four. ⁸The children of Zattu, nine hundred forty and five. ⁹The children of Zaccai, seven hundred and threescore. ¹⁰The children of Bani, six hundred forty and two. ¹¹The children of Bebai, six hundred twenty and three. ¹²The children of Azgad, a thousand two hundred twenty and two. ¹³The children of Adonikam, six hundred sixty and six. ¹⁴The children of Bigvai, two thousand fifty and six. ¹⁵The children of Adin, four hundred fifty and four. ¹⁶The children of Ater of Hezekiah, ninety and eight. ¹⁷The children of Bezai, three hundred twenty and three. ¹⁸The children of Jorah, a hundred and twelve. ¹⁹The children of Hashum, two hundred twenty and three. ²⁰The children of Gibbar, ninety and five. ²¹The children of Beth-lehem, a hundred twenty and three. ²²The men of Netophah, fifty and six. ²³The men of Anathoth, a hundred twenty and eight. ²⁴The children of Azmaveth, forty and two. ²⁵The children of Kirjath-arim, Chephirah, and Beeroth, seven hundred and forty and three. ²⁶The children of Ramah and Gaba, six hundred twenty and one. ²⁷The men of Michmas, a hundred twenty and two. ²⁸The men of Beth-el and Ai, two hundred twenty and three. ²⁹The children of Nebo, fifty and two. ³⁰The children of Magbish, a hundred fifty and six. ³¹The children of the other Elam, a thousand two hundred fifty and four. ³²The children of Harim, three hundred and twenty. ³³The children of Lod, Hadid, and Ono, seven hundred twenty and five. ³⁴The children of Jericho, three hundred forty and five. ³⁵The children of Senaah, three thousand and six hundred and thirty.

³⁶The priests. The children of Jedaiah, of the house of Jeshua, nine hundred seventy and three. ³⁷The children of Immer, a thousand fifty and two. ³⁸The children of Pashur, a thousand two hundred forty and seven. ³⁹The children of Harim, a thousand and seventeen.

⁴⁰The Levites. The children of Jeshua and Kadmiel, of the children of Hodaviah, seventy and four.

⁴¹The singers. The children of Asaph, a hundred twenty and eight.

⁴²The children of the porters. The children of Shallum, the children of Ater, the children of Talmon, the children of Akkub, the children of Hatita, the children of Shobai, in all a hundred thirty and nine.

⁴³The Nethinims. The children of Ziha, the children of Hasupha, the children of Tabbaoth, ⁴⁴the children of Keros, the children of Siaha, the children of Padon, ⁴⁵the children of Lebanah, the children of Hagabah, the children of Akkub, ⁴⁶the children of Hagab, the children of Shalmai, the children of Hanan, ⁴⁷the children of Giddel, the children of Gahar, the children of Reaiah, ⁴⁸the children of Rezin, the children of Nekoda, the children of Gazzam, ⁴⁹the children of Uzza, the children of Paseah, the children of Besai, ⁵⁰the children of Asnah, the children of Mehunim, the children of Nephusim, ⁵¹the children of Bakbuk, the children of Hakupha, the children of Harhur, ⁵²the children of Bazluth, the children of Mehida, the children of Harsha, ⁵³the children of Barkos, the children of Sisera, the children of Thamah, ⁵⁴the children of Neziah, the children of Hatipha.

⁵⁵The children of Solomon's servants. The children of Sotai, the children of Sophereth, the children of Peruda, ⁵⁶the children of Jaalah, the children of Darkon, the children of Giddel, ⁵⁷the children of

Shephatiah, the children of Hattil, the children of Pochereth of Zebaim, the children of Ami. ⁵⁸All the Nethinims, and the children of Solomon's servants, were three hundred ninety and two.

⁵⁹And these were they which went up from Tel-melah, Tel-harsa, Cherub, Addan, and Immer: but they could not show their fathers' house, and their seed, whether they were of Israel. ⁶⁰The children of Delaiah, the children of Tobiah, the children of Nekoda, six hundred fifty and two.

⁶¹And of the children of the priests. The children of Habaiah, the children of Koz, the children of Barzillai (which took a wife of the daughters of Barzillai the Gileadite, and was called after their name). ⁶²These sought their register among those that were reckoned by genealogy, but they were not found: therefore were they, as polluted, put from the priesthood. ⁶³And the Tirshatha said unto them, that they should not eat of the most holy things, till there stood up a priest with Urim and with Thummim.

⁶⁴The whole congregation together was forty and two thousand three hundred and threescore, ⁶⁵besides their servants and their maids, of whom there were seven thousand three hundred thirty and seven: and there were among them two hundred singing men and singing women. ⁶⁶Their horses were seven hundred thirty and six: their mules, two hundred forty and five: ⁶⁷their camels, four hundred thirty and five: their asses, six thousand seven hundred and twenty.

⁶⁸And some of the chief of the fathers, when they came to the house of the LORD which is at Jerusalem, offered freely for the house of God to set it up in his place: ⁶⁹they gave after their ability unto the treasure of the work threescore and one thousand drams of gold, and five thousand pound of silver, and one hundred priests' garments. ⁷⁰So the priests, and the Levites, and some of the people, and the singers, and the porters, and the Nethinims, dwelt in their cities, and all Israel in their cities.

3 And when the seventh month was come, and the children of Israel were in the cities, the people gathered themselves together as one man to Jerusalem. ²Then stood up Jeshua the son of Jozadak, and his brethren the priests, and Zerubbabel the son of Shealtiel, and his brethren, and built the altar of the God of Israel, to offer burnt offerings thereon, as it is written in the law of Moses the man of God. ³And they set the altar upon his bases (for fear was upon them because of the people of those countries), and they offered burnt offerings thereon unto the LORD, even burnt offerings morning and evening. ⁴They kept also the feast of tabernacles, as it is written, and offered the daily burnt offerings by number, according to the custom, as the duty of every day required; ⁵and afterward offered the continual burnt offering, both of the new moons, and of all the set feasts of the LORD that were consecrated, and of every one that willingly offered a free-will offering unto the LORD. ⁶From the first day of the seventh month began they to offer burnt offerings unto the LORD. But the foundation of the temple of the LORD was not yet laid. ⁷They gave money also unto the masons, and to

the carpenters; and meat, and drink, and oil, unto them of Zidon, and to them of Tyre, to bring cedar trees from Lebanon to the sea of Joppa, according to the grant that they had of Cyrus king of Persia.

[8]Now in the second year of their coming unto the house of God at Jerusalem, in the second month, began Zerubbabel the son of Shealtiel, and Jeshua the son of Jozadak, and the remnant of their brethren the priests and the Levites, and all they that were come out of the captivity unto Jerusalem; and appointed the Levites, from twenty years old and upward, to set forward the work of the house of the LORD. [9]Then stood Jeshua with his sons and his brethren, Kadmiel and his sons, the sons of Judah, together, to set forward the workmen in the house of God: the sons of Henadad, with their sons and their brethren the Levites. [10]And when the builders laid the foundation of the temple of the LORD, they set the priests in their apparel with trumpets, and the Levites the sons of Asaph with cymbals, to praise the LORD, after the ordinance of David king of Israel. [11]And they sang together by course in praising and giving thanks unto the LORD, 'Because he is good, for his mercy endureth for ever towards Israel'. And all the people shouted with a great shout, when they praised the LORD, because the foundation of the house of the LORD was laid. [12]But many of the priests and Levites and chief of the fathers, who were ancient men, that had seen the first house, when the foundation of this house was laid before their eyes, wept with a loud voice, and many shouted aloud for joy: [13]so that the people could not discern the noise of the shout of joy from the noise of the weeping of the people: for the people shouted with a loud shout, and the noise was heard afar off.

4 Now when the adversaries of Judah and Benjamin heard that the children of the captivity built the temple unto the LORD God of Israel: [2]then they came to Zerubbabel, and to the chief of the fathers, and said unto them, 'Let us build with you, for we seek your God, as ye do, and we do sacrifice unto him since the days of Esar-haddon king of Assur, which brought us up hither'. [3]But Zerubbabel, and Jeshua, and the rest of the chief of the fathers of Israel, said unto them, 'You have nothing to do with us to build a house unto our God; but we ourselves together will build unto the LORD God of Israel, as king Cyrus the king of Persia hath commanded us'. [4]Then the people of the land weakened the hands of the people of Judah, and troubled them in building, [5]and hired counsellors against them, to frustrate their purpose, all the days of Cyrus king of Persia, even until the reign of Darius king of Persia. [6]And in the reign of Ahasuerus, in the beginning of his reign, wrote they unto him an accusation against the inhabitants of Judah and Jerusalem.

[7]And in the days of Artaxerxes wrote Bishlam, Mithredath, Tabeel, and the rest of their companions, unto Artaxerxes king of Persia; and the writing of the letter was written in the Syrian tongue, and interpreted in the Syrian tongue. [8]Rehum the chancellor and Shimshai the scribe wrote a letter against Jerusalem to Artaxerxes the king in this sort: [9]then wrote Rehum the chancellor, and Shimshai the scribe, and the

rest of their companions; the Dinaites, the Apharsathchites, the Tarpelites, the Apharsites, the Archevites, the Babylonians, the Susanchites, the Dehavites, and the Elamites, [10]and the rest of the nations whom the great and noble Asnappar brought over, and set in the cities of Samaria, and the rest that are on this side the river, and at such a time.

[11]This is the copy of the letter that they sent unto him, even unto Artaxerxes the king:

> Thy servants the men on this side the river, and at such a time. [12]Be it known unto the king, that the Jews which came up from thee to us are come unto Jerusalem, building the rebellious and the bad city, and have set up the walls thereof, and joined the foundations. [13]Be it known now unto the king, that if this city be built, and the walls set up again, then will they not pay toll, tribute, and custom, and so thou shalt endamage the revenue of the kings. [14]Now because we have maintenance from the king's palace, and it was not meet for us to see the king's dishonour, therefore have we sent and certified the king, [15]that search may be made in the book of the records of thy fathers: so shalt thou find in the book of the records, and know that this city is a rebellious city, and hurtful unto kings and provinces, and that they have moved sedition within the same of old time: for which cause was this city destroyed. [16]We certify the king that if this city be built again, and the walls thereof set up, by this means thou shalt have no portion on this side the river.

[17]Then sent the king an answer unto Rehum the chancellor, and to Shimshai the scribe, and to the rest of their companions that dwell in Samaria, and unto the rest beyond the river,

> Peace, and at such a time. [18]The letter which ye sent unto us hath been plainly read before me. [19]And I commanded, and search hath been made, and it is found that this city of old time hath made insurrection against kings, and that rebellion and sedition have been made therein. [20]There have been mighty kings also over Jerusalem, which have ruled over all countries beyond the river, and toll, tribute, and custom, was paid unto them. [21]Give ye now commandment to cause these men to cease, and that this city be not built, until another commandment shall be given from me. [22]Take heed now that ye fail not to do this: why should damage grow to the hurt of the kings?

[23]Now when the copy of king Artaxerxes' letter was read before Rehum and Shimshai the scribe, and their companions, they went up in haste to Jerusalem unto the Jews, and made them to cease by force and power. [24]Then ceased the work of the house of the God which is at Jerusalem. So it ceased unto the second year of the reign of Darius king of Persia.

5 Then the prophets, Haggai the prophet, and Zechariah the son of Iddo, prophesied unto the Jews that were in Judah and Jerusalem in the name of the God of Israel, even unto them. [2]Then rose up

Zerubbabel the son of Shealtiel, and Jeshua the son of Jozadak, and began to build the house of God which is at Jerusalem: and with them were the prophets of God helping them.

³At the same time came to them Tatnai, governor on this side the river, and Shethar-boznai, and their companions, and said thus unto them, 'Who hath commanded you to build this house, and to make up this wall?' ⁴Then said we unto them after this manner, 'What are the names of the men that make this building?' ⁵But the eye of their God was upon the elders of the Jews, that they could not cause them to cease, till the matter came to Darius: and then they returned answer by letter concerning this matter.

⁶The copy of the letter that Tatnai, governor on this side the river, and Shethar-boznai, and his companions the Apharsachites, which were on this side the river, sent unto Darius the king: ⁷they sent a letter unto him, wherein was written thus:

Unto Darius the king, all peace. ⁸Be it known unto the king, that we went into the province of Judea, to the house of the great God, which is built with great stones, and timber is laid in the walls, and this work goeth fast on, and prospereth in their hands. ⁹Then asked we those elders, and said unto them thus, 'Who commanded you to build this house, and to make up these walls?' ¹⁰We asked their names also, to certify thee, that we might write the names of the men that were the chief of them. ¹¹And thus they returned us answer, saying, 'We are the servants of the God of heaven and earth, and build the house that was built these many years ago, which a great king of Israel built and set up. ¹²But after that our fathers had provoked the God of heaven unto wrath, he gave them into the hand of Nebuchadnezzar the king of Babylon, the Chaldean, who destroyed this house, and carried the people away into Babylon. ¹³But in the first year of Cyrus the king of Babylon the same king Cyrus made a decree to build this house of God. ¹⁴And the vessels also of gold and silver of the house of God, which Nebuchadnezzar took out of the temple that was in Jerusalem, and brought them into the temple of Babylon, those did Cyrus the king take out of the temple of Babylon, and they were delivered unto one, whose name was Sheshbazzar, whom he had made governor; ¹⁵and said unto him, "Take these vessels, go, carry them into the temple that is in Jerusalem, and let the house of God be built in his place". ¹⁶Then came the same Sheshbazzar, and laid the foundation of the house of God which is in Jerusalem. And since that time even until now hath it been in building, and yet it is not finished.' ¹⁷Now therefore, if it seem good to the king, let there be search made in the king's treasure-house, which is there at Babylon, whether it be so that a decree was made of Cyrus the king to build this house of God at Jerusalem, and let the king send his pleasure to us concerning this matter.

6 Then Darius the king made a decree, and search was made in the house of the rolls, where the treasures were laid up in Babylon. ²And there was found at Achmetha, in the palace that is in the province of the Medes, a roll, and therein was a record thus written:

³In the first year of Cyrus the king the same Cyrus the king made a decree concerning the house of God at Jerusalem: 'Let the house be built, the place where they offered sacrifices, and let the foundations thereof be strongly laid, the height thereof threescore cubits, and the breadth thereof threescore cubits: ⁴with three rows of great stones, and a row of new timber: and let the expenses be given out of the king's house. ⁵And also let the golden and silver vessels of the house of God, which Nebuchadnezzar took forth out of the temple which is at Jerusalem, and brought unto Babylon, be restored, and brought again unto the temple which is at Jerusalem, every one to his place, and place them in the house of God.'

⁶Now therefore, Tatnai, governor beyond the river, Shethar-boznai, and your companions the Apharsachites, which are beyond the river, be ye far from thence: ⁷let the work of this house of God alone, let the governor of the Jews and the elders of the Jews build this house of God in his place. ⁸Moreover I make a decree what ye shall do to the elders of these Jews for the building of this house of God: that of the king's goods, even of the tribute beyond the river, forthwith expenses be given unto these men, that they be not hindered. ⁹And that which they have need of, both young bullocks, and rams, and lambs, for the burnt offerings of the God of heaven, wheat, salt, wine, and oil, according to the appointment of the priests which are at Jerusalem, let it be given them day by day without fail: ¹⁰that they may offer sacrifices of sweet savours unto the God of heaven, and pray for the life of the king, and of his sons. ¹¹Also I have made a decree, that whosoever shall alter this word, let timber be pulled down from his house, and being set up, let him be hanged thereon, and let his house be made a dunghill for this. ¹²And the God that hath caused his name to dwell there destroy all kings and people that shall put to their hand to alter and to destroy this house of God which is at Jerusalem. I Darius have made a decree, let it be done with speed.

¹³Then Tatnai, governor on this side the river, Shethar-boznai, and their companions, according to that which Darius the king had sent, so they did speedily. ¹⁴And the elders of the Jews built, and they prospered through the prophesying of Haggai the prophet and Zechariah the son of Iddo. And they built, and finished it, according to the commandment of the God of Israel, and according to the commandment of Cyrus, and Darius, and Artaxerxes king of Persia. ¹⁵And this house was finished on the third day of the month Adar, which was in the sixth year of the reign of Darius the king.

¹⁶And the children of Israel, the priests, and the Levites, and the rest of the children of the captivity, kept the dedication of this house of God with joy, ¹⁷and offered at the dedication of this house of God a hundred bullocks, two hundred rams, four hundred lambs; and for a sin offering for all Israel, twelve he-goats, according to the number of the tribes of Israel. ¹⁸And they set the priests in their divisions, and the Levites in their courses, for the service of God, which is at Jerusalem, as it is written in the book of Moses.

¹⁹And the children of the captivity kept the passover upon the fourteenth day of the first month. ²⁰For the priests and the Levites were purified together, all of them were pure, and killed the passover for all the children of the captivity, and for their brethren the priests, and for themselves. ²¹And the children of Israel, which were come again out of captivity, and all such as had separated themselves unto them from the filthiness of the heathen of the land, to seek the LORD God of Israel, did eat, ²²and kept the feast of unleavened bread seven days with joy: for the LORD had made them joyful, and turned the heart of the king of Assyria unto them, to strengthen their hands in the work of the house of God, the God of Israel.

7 Now after these things, in the reign of Artaxerxes king of Persia, Ezra the son of Seraiah, the son of Azariah, the son of Hilkiah, ²the son of Shallum, the son of Zadok, the son of Ahitub, ³the son of Amariah, the son of Azariah, the son of Meraioth, ⁴the son of Zerahiah, the son of Uzzi, the son of Bukki, ⁵the son of Abishua, the son of Phinehas, the son of Eleazar, the son of Aaron the chief priest: ⁶this Ezra went up from Babylon, and he was a ready scribe in the law of Moses, which the LORD God of Israel had given: and the king granted him all his request, according to the hand of the LORD his God upon him. ⁷And there went up some of the children of Israel, and of the priests, and the Levites, and the singers, and the porters, and the Nethinims, unto Jerusalem, in the seventh year of Artaxerxes the king. ⁸And he came to Jerusalem in the fifth month, which was in the seventh year of the king. ⁹For upon the first day of the first month began he to go up from Babylon, and on the first day of the fifth month came he to Jerusalem, according to the good hand of his God upon him. ¹⁰For Ezra had prepared his heart to seek the law of the LORD, and to do it, and to teach in Israel statutes and judgements.

¹¹Now this is the copy of the letter that the king Artaxerxes gave unto Ezra the priest, the scribe, even a scribe of the words of the commandments of the LORD, and of his statutes to Israel.

¹²Artaxerxes, king of kings, unto Ezra the priest, a scribe of the law of the God of heaven, perfect peace, and at such a time. ¹³I make a decree, that all they of the people of Israel, and of his priests and Levites in my realm, which are minded of their own free will to go up to Jerusalem, go with thee. ¹⁴Forasmuch as thou art sent of the king, and of his seven counsellors, to inquire concerning Judah and Jerusalem, according to the law of thy God which is in thy hand; ¹⁵and to carry the silver and

gold, which the king and his counsellors have freely offered unto the God of Israel, whose habitation is in Jerusalem, [16]and all the silver and gold that thou canst find in all the province of Babylon, with the free-will offering of the people, and of the priests, offering willingly for the house of their God which is in Jerusalem: [17]that thou mayest buy speedily with this money bullocks, rams, lambs, with their meat offerings and their drink offerings, and offer them upon the altar of the house of your God which is in Jerusalem. [18]And whatsoever shall seem good to thee, and to thy brethren, to do with the rest of the silver and gold, that do after the will of your God. [19]The vessels also that are given thee for the service of the house of thy God, those deliver thou before the God of Jerusalem. [20]And whatsoever more shall be needful for the house of thy God, which thou shalt have occasion to bestow, bestow it out of the king's treasure-house. [21]And I, even I Artaxerxes the king, do make a decree to all the treasurers which are beyond the river, that whatsoever Ezra the priest, the scribe of the law of the God of heaven, shall require of you, it be done speedily, [22]unto a hundred talents of silver, and to a hundred measures of wheat, and to a hundred baths of wine, and to a hundred baths of oil, and salt, without prescribing how much. [23]Whatsoever is commanded by the God of heaven, let it be diligently done for the house of the God of heaven: for why should there be wrath against the realm of the king and his sons? [24]Also we certify you, that touching any of the priests and Levites, singers, porters, Nethinims, or ministers of this house of God, it shall not be lawful to impose toll, tribute, or custom, upon them. [25]And thou, Ezra, after the wisdom of thy God, that is in thy hand, set magistrates and judges, which may judge all the people that are beyond the river, all such as know the laws of thy God; and teach ye them that know them not. [26]And whosoever will not do the law of thy God, and the law of the king, let judgement be executed speedily upon him, whether it be unto death, or to banishment, or to confiscation of goods, or to imprisonment.

[27]Blessed be the LORD God of our fathers, which hath put such a thing as this in the king's heart, to beautify the house of the LORD which is in Jerusalem: [28]and hath extended mercy unto me before the king, and his counsellors, and before all the king's mighty princes. And I was strengthened as the hand of the LORD my God was upon me, and I gathered together out of Israel chief men to go up with me.

8 These are now the chief of their fathers, and this is the genealogy of them that went up with me from Babylon, in the reign of Artaxerxes the king. [2]Of the sons of Phinehas, Gershom: of the sons of Ithamar, Daniel: of the sons of David, Hattush. [3]Of the sons of Shechaniah, of the sons of Pharosh, Zechariah, and with him were reckoned by genealogy of the males a hundred and fifty. [4]Of the sons of Pahath-moab, Elihoenai the son of Zerahiah, and with him two hun-

dred males. ⁵Of the sons of Shechaniah, the son of Jahaziel, and with him three hundred males. ⁶Of the sons also of Adin, Ebed the son of Jonathan, and with him fifty males. ⁷And of the sons of Elam, Jeshaiah the son of Athaliah, and with him seventy males. ⁸And of the sons of Shephatiah, Zebadiah the son of Michael, and with him fourscore males. ⁹Of the sons of Joab, Obadiah the son of Jehiel, and with him two hundred and eighteen males. ¹⁰And of the sons of Shelomith, the son of Josiphiah, and with him a hundred and threescore males. ¹¹And of the sons of Bebai, Zechariah the son of Bebai, and with him twenty and eight males. ¹²And of the sons of Azgad, Johanan the son of Hakkatan, and with him a hundred and ten males. ¹³And of the last sons of Adonikam, whose names are these, Eliphelet, Jeiel, and Shemaiah, and with them threescore males. ¹⁴Of the sons also of Bigvai, Uthai, and Zabbud, and with them seventy males.

¹⁵And I gathered them together to the river that runneth to Ahava, and there abode we in tents three days: and I viewed the people, and the priests, and found there none of the sons of Levi. ¹⁶Then sent I for Eliezer, for Ariel, for Shemaiah, and for Elnathan, and for Jarib, and for Elnathan, and for Nathan, and for Zechariah, and for Meshullam, chief men; also for Joiarib, and for Elnathan, men of understanding. ¹⁷And I sent them with commandment unto Iddo the chief at the place Casiphia, and I told them what they should say unto Iddo, and to his brethren the Nethinims, at the place Casiphia, that they should bring unto us ministers for the house of our God. ¹⁸And by the good hand of our God upon us they brought us a man of understanding, of the sons of Mahli, the son of Levi, the son of Israel; and Sherebiah, with his sons and his brethren, eighteen; ¹⁹and Hashabiah, and with him Jeshaiah of the sons of Merari, his brethren and their sons, twenty; ²⁰also of the Nethinims, whom David and the princes had appointed for the service of the Levites, two hundred and twenty Nethinims: all of them were expressed by name.

²¹Then I proclaimed a fast there, at the river Ahava, that we might afflict ourselves before our God, to seek of him a right way for us, and for our little ones, and for all our substance. ²²For I was ashamed to require of the king a band of soldiers and horsemen to help us against the enemy in the way: because we had spoken unto the king, saying, 'The hand of our God is upon all them for good that seek him, but his power and his wrath is against all them that forsake him'. ²³So we fasted and besought our God for this, and he was entreated of us.

²⁴Then I separated twelve of the chief of the priests, Sherebiah, Hashabiah, and ten of their brethren with them, ²⁵and weighed unto them the silver, and the gold, and the vessels, even the offering of the house of our God, which the king, and his counsellors, and his lords, and all Israel there present, had offered: ²⁶I even weighed unto their hand six hundred and fifty talents of silver, and silver vessels a hundred talents, and of gold a hundred talents; ²⁷also twenty basins of gold, of a thousand drams, and two vessels of fine copper, precious as gold. ²⁸And I said unto them, 'Ye are holy unto the LORD, the vessels are

holy also, and the silver and the gold are a free-will offering unto the LORD God of your fathers. ²⁹Watch ye, and keep them, until ye weigh them before the chief of the priests and the Levites, and chief of the fathers of Israel, at Jerusalem, in the chambers of the house of the LORD.' ³⁰So took the priests and the Levites the weight of the silver, and the gold, and the vessels, to bring them to Jerusalem unto the house of our God.

³¹Then we departed from the river of Ahava on the twelfth day of the first month, to go unto Jerusalem; and the hand of our God was upon us, and he delivered us from the hand of the enemy, and of such as lay in wait by the way. ³²And we came to Jerusalem, and abode there three days.

³³Now on the fourth day was the silver and the gold and the vessels weighed in the house of our God by the hand of Meremoth the son of Uriah the priest; and with him was Eleazar the son of Phinehas; and with them was Jozabad the son of Jeshua, and Noadiah the son of Binnui, Levites; ³⁴by number and by weight of every one: and all the weight was written at that time. ³⁵Also the children of those that had been carried away which were come out of the captivity, offered burnt offerings unto the God of Israel, twelve bullocks for all Israel, ninety and six rams, seventy and seven lambs, twelve he-goats for a sin offering: all this was a burnt offering unto the LORD.

³⁶And they delivered the king's commissions unto the king's lieutenants, and to the governors on this side the river, and they furthered the people, and the house of God.

9 Now when these things were done, the princes came to me, saying, 'The people of Israel, and the priests, and the Levites, have not separated themselves from the people of the lands, doing according to their abominations, even of the Canaanites, the Hittites, the Perizzites, the Jebusites, the Ammonites, the Moabites, the Egyptians, and the Amorites. ²For they have taken of their daughters for themselves, and for their sons: so that the holy seed have mingled themselves with the people of those lands: yea, the hand of the princes and rulers hath been chief in this trespass.' ³And when I heard this thing, I rent my garment and my mantle, and plucked off the hair of my head and of my beard, and sat down astonished. ⁴Then were assembled unto me every one that trembled at the words of the God of Israel, because of the transgression of those that had been carried away, and I sat astonished until the evening sacrifice.

⁵And at the evening sacrifice I arose up from my heaviness, and having rent my garment and my mantle, I fell upon my knees, and spread out my hands unto the LORD my God, ⁶and said, 'O my God, I am ashamed and blush to lift up my face to thee, my God: for our iniquities are increased over our head, and our trespass is grown up unto the heavens. ⁷Since the days of our fathers have we been in a great trespass unto this day, and for our iniquities have we, our kings, and our priests, been delivered into the hand of the kings of the lands, to the sword, to captivity, and to a spoil, and to confusion of face, as it is this day. ⁸And

now for a little space grace hath been shown from the LORD our God, to leave us a remnant to escape, and to give us a nail in his holy place, that our God may lighten our eyes, and give us a little reviving in our bondage. ⁹For we were bondmen, yet our God hath not forsaken us in our bondage, but hath extended mercy unto us in the sight of the kings of Persia, to give us a reviving to set up the house of our God, and to repair the desolations thereof, and to give us a wall in Judah and in Jerusalem. ¹⁰And now, O our God, what shall we say after this? for we have forsaken thy commandments, ¹¹which thou hast commanded by thy servants the prophets, saying, "The land unto which ye go to possess it, is an unclean land with the filthiness of the people of the lands, with their abominations, which have filled it from one end to another with their uncleanness. ¹²Now therefore give not your daughters unto their sons, neither take their daughters unto your sons, nor seek their peace or their wealth for ever: that ye may be strong, and eat the good of the land, and leave it for an inheritance to your children for ever." ¹³And after all that is come upon us for our evil deeds, and for our great trespass, seeing that thou our God hast punished us less than our iniquities deserve, and hast given us such deliverance as this; ¹⁴should we again break thy commandments, and join in affinity with the people of these abominations? wouldst not thou be angry with us till thou hadst consumed us, so that there should be no remnant nor escaping? ¹⁵O LORD God of Israel, thou art righteous, for we remain yet escaped, as it is this day: behold, we are before thee in our trespasses: for we cannot stand before thee because of this.'

10 Now when Ezra had prayed, and when he had confessed, weeping and casting himself down before the house of God, there assembled unto him out of Israel a very great congregation of men and women and children: for the people wept very sore. ²And Shechaniah the son of Jehiel, one of the sons of Elam, answered and said unto Ezra, 'We have trespassed against our God, and have taken strange wives of the people of the land: yet now there is hope in Israel concerning this thing. ³Now therefore let us make a covenant with our God to put away all the wives, and such as are born of them, according to the counsel of my lord, and of those that tremble at the commandment of our God, and let it be done according to the law. ⁴Arise, for this matter belongeth unto thee: we also will be with thee: be of good courage, and do it.' ⁵Then arose Ezra, and made the chief priests, the Levites, and all Israel, to swear that they should do according to this word. And they swore.

⁶Then Ezra rose up from before the house of God, and went into the chamber of Johanan the son of Eliashib: and when he came thither, he did eat no bread, nor drink water: for he mourned because of the transgression of them that had been carried away. ⁷And they made proclamation throughout Judah and Jerusalem unto all the children of the captivity, that they should gather themselves together unto Jerusalem; ⁸and that whosoever would not come within three days, according to the counsel of the princes and the elders, all his substance should be

forfeited, and himself separated from the congregation of those that had been carried away. ⁹Then all the men of Judah and Benjamin gathered themselves together unto Jerusalem within three days. It was the ninth month, on the twentieth day of the month, and all the people sat in the street of the house of God, trembling because of this matter, and for the great rain. ¹⁰And Ezra the priest stood up, and said unto them, 'Ye have transgressed, and have taken strange wives, to increase the trespass of Israel. ¹¹Now therefore make confession unto the LORD God of your fathers, and do his pleasure: and separate yourselves from the people of the land, and from the strange wives.' ¹²Then all the congregation answered and said with a loud voice, 'As thou hast said, so must we do. ¹³But the people are many, and it is a time of much rain, and we are not able to stand without, neither is this a work of one day or two: for we are many that have transgressed in this thing. ¹⁴Let now our rulers of all the congregation stand, and let all them which have taken strange wives in our cities come at appointed times, and with them the elders of every city, and the judges thereof, until the fierce wrath of our God for this matter be turned from us.'

¹⁵Only Jonathan the son of Asahel and Jahaziah the son of Tikvah were employed about this matter: and Meshullam and Shabbethai the Levite helped them. ¹⁶And the children of the captivity did so. And Ezra the priest, with certain chief of the fathers, after the house of their fathers, and all of them by their names, were separated, and sat down in the first day of the tenth month to examine the matter. ¹⁷And they made an end with all the men that had taken strange wives by the first day of the first month.

¹⁸And among the sons of the priests there were found that had taken strange wives: namely, of the sons of Jeshua the son of Jozadak, and his brethren, Maaseiah, and Eliezer, and Jarib, and Gedaliah. ¹⁹And they gave their hands that they would put away their wives: and being guilty, they offered a ram of the flock for their trespass. ²⁰And of the sons of Immer, Hanani, and Zebadiah. ²¹And of the sons of Harim, Maaseiah, and Elijah, and Shemaiah, and Jehiel, and Uzziah. ²²And of the sons of Pashur, Elioenai, Maaseiah, Ishmael, Nethaneel, Jozabad, and Elasah. ²³Also of the Levites, Jozabad, and Shimei, and Kelaiah (the same is Kelita), Pethahiah, Judah, and Eliezer. ²⁴Of the singers also, Eliashib: and of the porters, Shallum, and Telem, and Uri. ²⁵Moreover of Israel: of the sons of Parosh, Ramiah, and Jezziah, and Malchiah, and Miamin, and Eleazar, and Malchijah, and Benaiah. ²⁶And of the sons of Elam, Mattaniah, Zechariah, and Jehiel, and Abdi, and Jeremoth, and Eliah. ²⁷And of the sons of Zattu, Elioenai, Eliashib, Mattaniah, and Jeremoth, and Zabad, and Aziza. ²⁸Of the sons also of Bebai, Jehohanan, Hananiah, Zabbai, and Athlai. ²⁹And of the sons of Bani, Meshullam, Malluch, and Adaiah, Jashub, and Sheal, and Ramoth. ³⁰And of the sons of Pahath-moab, Adna, and Chelal, Benaiah, Maaseiah, Mattaniah, Bezaleel, and Binnui, and Manasseh. ³¹And of the sons of Harim, Eliezer, Ishijah, Malchiah, Shemaiah, Shimeon, ³²Benjamin, Malluch,

and Shemariah. ³³Of the sons of Hashum, Mattenai, Mattathah, Zabad, Eliphelet, Jeremai, Manasseh, and Shimei. ³⁴Of the sons of Bani, Maadai, Amram, and Uel, ³⁵Benaiah, Bedeiah, Chelluh, ³⁶Vaniah, Meremoth, Eliashib, ³⁷Mattaniah, Mattenai, and Jaasau, ³⁸and Bani, and Binnui, Shimei, ³⁹and Shelemiah, and Nathan, and Adaiah, ⁴⁰Machnadebai, Shashai, Sharai, ⁴¹Azareel, and Shelemiah, Shemariah, ⁴²Shallum, Amariah, and Joseph. ⁴³Of the sons of Nebo, Jeiel, Mattithiah, Zabad, Zebina, Jadau, and Joel, Benaiah. ⁴⁴All these had taken strange wives: and some of them had wives by whom they had children.

THE BOOK OF
NEHEMIAH

1 The words of Nehemiah the son of Hachaliah. And it came to pass in the month Chisleu, in the twentieth year, as I was in Shushan the palace, ²that Hanani, one of my brethren, came, he and certain men of Judah, and I asked them concerning the Jews that had escaped, which were left of the captivity, and concerning Jerusalem. ³And they said unto me, 'The remnant that are left of the captivity there in the province are in great affliction and reproach: the wall of Jerusalem also is broken down, and the gates thereof are burnt with fire'.

⁴And it came to pass when I heard these words, that I sat down and wept, and mourned certain days, and fasted, and prayed before the God of heaven, ⁵and said, 'I beseech thee, O LORD God of heaven, the great and terrible God, that keepeth covenant and mercy for them that love him and observe his commandments: ⁶let thy ear now be attentive, and thy eyes open, that thou mayest hear the prayer of thy servant, which I pray before thee now, day and night, for the children of Israel thy servants, and confess the sins of the children of Israel, which we have sinned against thee: both I and my father's house have sinned. ⁷We have dealt very corruptly against thee, and have not kept the commandments, nor the statutes, nor the judgements, which thou commandedst thy servant Moses. ⁸Remember, I beseech thee, the word that thou commandedst thy servant Moses, saying, "If ye transgress, I will scatter you abroad among the nations: ⁹but if ye turn unto me, and keep my commandments, and do them: though there were of you cast out unto the uttermost part of the heaven, yet will I gather them from thence, and will bring them unto the place that I have chosen to set my name there". ¹⁰Now these are thy servants and thy people, whom thou hast redeemed by thy great power, and by thy strong hand. ¹¹O Lord, I beseech thee, let now thy ear be attentive to the prayer of thy servant, and to the prayer of thy servants, who desire to fear thy name: and prosper, I pray thee, thy servant this day, and grant him mercy in the sight of this man.' For I was the king's cup-bearer.

2 And it came to pass in the month Nisan, in the twentieth year of Artaxerxes the king, that wine was before him: and I took up the wine, and gave it unto the king. Now I had not been beforetime sad in his presence. ²Wherefore the king said unto me, 'Why is thy countenance sad, seeing thou art not sick? this is nothing else but sorrow of heart'. Then I was very sore afraid, ³and said unto the king, 'Let the king live for ever: why should not my countenance be sad, when the city, the place of my fathers' sepulchres, lieth waste, and the gates thereof are consumed with fire?' ⁴Then the king said unto me, 'For what dost thou make request?' So I prayed to the God of heaven. ⁵And I said unto the king, 'If it please the king, and if thy servant have found favour in thy sight, that thou wouldst send me unto Judah, unto the city of my fathers' sepulchres, that I may build it'. ⁶And the king said unto me (the queen also sitting by him), 'For how long shall thy journey be? and when wilt thou return?' So it pleased the king to send me, and I set him a time. ⁷Moreover I said unto the king, 'If it please the king, let letters be given me to the governors beyond the river, that they may convey me over till I come into Judah; ⁸and a letter unto Asaph the keeper of the king's forest, that he may give me timber to make beams for the gates of the palace which appertained to the house, and for the wall of the city, and for the house that I shall enter into'. And the king granted me, according to the good hand of my God upon me.

⁹Then I came to the governors beyond the river, and gave them the king's letters. Now the king had sent captains of the army and horsemen with me. ¹⁰When Sanballat the Horonite, and Tobiah the servant, the Ammonite, heard of it, it grieved them exceedingly that there was come a man to seek the welfare of the children of Israel. ¹¹So I came to Jerusalem, and was there three days.

¹²And I arose in the night, I and some few men with me; neither told I any man what God had put in my heart to do at Jerusalem: neither was there any beast with me, save the beast that I rode upon. ¹³And I went out by night by the gate of the valley, even before the dragon well, and to the dung port, and viewed the walls of Jerusalem, which were broken down, and the gates thereof were consumed with fire. ¹⁴Then I went on to the gate of the fountain, and to the king's pool: but there was no place for the beast that was under me to pass. ¹⁵Then went I up in the night by the brook, and viewed the wall, and turned back, and entered by the gate of the valley, and so returned. ¹⁶And the rulers knew not whither I went, or what I did; neither had I as yet told it to the Jews, nor to the priests, nor to the nobles, nor to the rulers, nor to the rest that did the work.

¹⁷Then said I unto them, 'Ye see the distress that we are in, how Jerusalem lieth waste, and the gates thereof are burnt with fire: come, and let us build up the wall of Jerusalem, that we be no more a reproach'. ¹⁸Then I told them of the hand of my God which was good upon me; as also the king's words that he had spoken unto me. And they said, 'Let us rise up and build'. So they strengthened their hands for this good work.

¹⁹But when Sanballat the Horonite, and Tobiah the servant, the Ammonite, and Geshem the Arabian heard it, they laughed us to scorn, and despised us, and said, 'What is this thing that ye do? will ye rebel against the king?' ²⁰Then answered I them, and said unto them, 'The God of heaven, he will prosper us, therefore we his servants will arise and build: but you have no portion, nor right, nor memorial, in Jerusalem'.

3 Then Eliashib the high priest rose up with his brethren the priests, and they built the sheep gate; they sanctified it, and set up the doors of it; even unto the tower of Meah they sanctified it, unto the tower of Hananeel. ²And next unto him built the men of Jericho. And next to them built Zaccur the son of Imri. ³But the fish gate did the sons of Hassenaah build, who also laid the beams thereof, and set up the doors thereof, the locks thereof, and the bars thereof. ⁴And next unto them repaired Meremoth the son of Urijah, the son of Koz. And next unto them repaired Meshullam the son of Berechiah, the son of Meshezabeel. And next unto them repaired Zadok the son of Baana. ⁵And next unto them the Tekoites repaired; but their nobles put not their necks to the work of their Lord. ⁶Moreover the old gate repaired Jehoiada the son of Paseah, and Meshullam the son of Besodeiah; they laid the beams thereof, and set up the doors thereof, and the locks thereof, and the bars thereof. ⁷And next unto them repaired Melatiah the Gibeonite, and Jadon the Meronothite, the men of Gibeon, and of Mizpah, unto the throne of the governor on this side the river. ⁸Next unto him repaired Uzziel the son of Harhaiah, of the goldsmiths. Next unto him also repaired Hananiah the son of one of the apothecaries, and they fortified Jerusalem unto the broad wall. ⁹And next unto them repaired Rephaiah the son of Hur, the ruler of the half part of Jerusalem. ¹⁰And next unto them repaired Jedaiah the son of Harumaph, even over against his house. And next unto him repaired Hattush the son of Hashabniah. ¹¹Malchijah the son of Harim, and Hashub the son of Pahath-moab, repaired the other piece, and the tower of the furnaces. ¹²And next unto him repaired Shallum the son of Hallohesh, the ruler of the half part of Jerusalem, he and his daughters. ¹³The valley gate repaired Hanun, and the inhabitants of Zanoah; they built it, and set up the doors thereof, the locks thereof, and the bars thereof, and a thousand cubits on the wall unto the dung gate. ¹⁴But the dung gate repaired Malchiah the son of Rechab, the ruler of part of Beth-haccerem: he built it, and set up the doors thereof, the locks thereof, and the bars thereof. ¹⁵But the gate of the fountain repaired Shallun the son of Col-hozeh, the ruler of part of Mizpah: he built it, and covered it, and set up the doors thereof, the locks thereof, and the bars thereof, and the wall of the pool of Siloah by the king's garden, and unto the stairs that go down from the city of David. ¹⁶After him repaired Nehemiah the son of Azbuk, the ruler of the half part of Beth-zur, unto the place over against the sepulchres of David, and to the pool that was made, and unto the house of the mighty. ¹⁷After him repaired the Levites, Rehum the son of Bani. Next unto him repaired Hashabiah, the ruler of the half part of Keilah in his part. ¹⁸After him repaired their brethren, Bavai the son of Henadad, the ruler of the half part of Keilah. ¹⁹And next to him repaired Ezer the son of Jeshua, the ruler of Mizpah, another piece over against the going up to the armoury at the turning of the wall. ²⁰After him Baruch the son of Zabbai earnestly repaired the other piece, from the turning of the wall unto the door of the house of Eliashib the high priest. ²¹After him repaired Meremoth the son of Urijah the son of Koz another piece, from the door of the house of Eliashib even to the end of the house of Eliashib. ²²And after him repaired the priests, the men of the plain. ²³After him repaired Benjamin and Hashub over against their house. After him repaired Azariah the son of Maaseiah the son of Ananiah by his house. ²⁴After him repaired Binnui the son of Henadad another piece, from the house of Azariah unto the turning of the wall, even unto the corner. ²⁵Palal the son of Uzai, over against the turning of the wall, and the tower which lieth out from the king's high house, that was by the court of the prison. After him Pedaiah the son of Parosh. ²⁶Moreover the Nethinims dwelt in Ophel, unto the place over against the water gate toward the east, and the tower that lieth out. ²⁷After them the Tekoites repaired another piece, over against the great tower that lieth out, even unto the wall of Ophel. ²⁸From above the horse gate repaired the priests, every one over against his house. ²⁹After them repaired Zadok the son of Immer over against his house. After him repaired also Shemaiah the son of Shechaniah, the keeper of the east gate. ³⁰After him repaired Hananiah the son of Shelemiah, and Hanun the sixth son of Zalaph, another piece. After him repaired Meshullam the son of Berechiah over against his chamber. ³¹After him repaired Malchiah the goldsmith's son unto the place of the Nethinims, and of the merchants, over against the gate Miphkad, and to the going up of the corner. ³²And between the going up of the corner unto the sheep gate repaired the goldsmiths and the merchants.

4 But it came to pass, that when Sanballat heard that we built the wall, he was wroth, and took great indignation, and mocked the Jews. ²And he spoke before his brethren and the army of Samaria, and said, 'What do these feeble Jews? will they fortify themselves? will they sacrifice? will they make an end in a day? will they revive the stones out of the heaps of the rubbish which are burnt?' ³Now Tobiah the Ammonite was by him, and he said, 'Even that which they build, if a fox go up, he shall even break down their stone wall'. ⁴'Hear, O our God, for we are despised: and turn their reproach upon their own head, and give them for a prey in the land of captivity. ⁵And cover not their iniquity, and let not their sin be blotted out from before thee: for they have provoked thee to anger before the builders.' ⁶So built we the wall, and all the wall was joined together unto the half thereof: for the people had a mind to work.

⁷But it came to pass that when Sanballat, and Tobiah, and the Arabians, and the Ammonites, and the Ashdodites, heard that the walls of Jerusalem were made up, and that the breaches began to be stopped, then they were very wroth, ⁸and conspired all of them together to come and to fight against Jerusalem, and to hinder it. ⁹Nevertheless we made our prayer unto our God, and set a watch against them day and night, because of them. ¹⁰And Judah said, 'The strength of the bearers of burdens is decayed, and there is much rubbish, so that we are not able to build the wall'. ¹¹And our adversaries said, 'They shall not know, neither see, till we come in the midst among them, and slay them, and cause the work to cease'. ¹²And it came to pass, that when the Jews which dwelt by them came, they said unto us ten times, 'From all places whence ye shall return unto us they will be upon you'.

¹³Therefore set I in the lower places behind the wall, and on the

higher places, I even set the people after their families with their swords, their spears, and their bows. [14]And I looked, and rose up, and said unto the nobles, and to the rulers, and to the rest of the people, 'Be not ye afraid of them: remember the Lord, which is great and terrible, and fight for your brethren, your sons, and your daughters, your wives, and your houses'. [15]And it came to pass when our enemies heard that it was known unto us, and God had brought their counsel to nought, that we returned all of us to the wall, every one unto his work. [16]And it came to pass from that time forth, that the half of my servants wrought in the work, and the other half of them held both the spears, the shields, and the bows, and the habergeons; and the rulers were behind all the house of Judah. [17]They which built on the wall, and they that bore burdens, with those that loaded, every one with one of his hands wrought in the work, and with the other hand held a weapon. [18]For the builders, every one had his sword girded by his side, and so built. And he that sounded the trumpet was by me.

[19]And I said unto the nobles, and to the rulers, and to the rest of the people, 'The work is great and large, and we are separated upon the wall, one far from another. [20]In what place therefore ye hear the sound of the trumpet, resort ye thither unto us: our God shall fight for us.' [21]So we laboured in the work: and half of them held the spears from the rising of the morning till the stars appeared. [22]Likewise at the same time said I unto the people, 'Let every one with his servant lodge within Jerusalem, that in the night they may be a guard to us, and labour on the day'. [23]So neither I, nor my brethren, nor my servants, nor the men of the guard which followed me, none of us put off our clothes, saving that every one put them off for washing.

5 And there was a great cry of the people and of their wives against their brethren the Jews. [2]For there were that said, 'We, our sons, and our daughters are many: therefore we take up corn for them, that we may eat, and live'. [3]Some also there were that said, 'We have mortgaged our lands, vineyards, and houses, that we might buy corn, because of the dearth'. [4]There were also that said, 'We have borrowed money for the king's tribute, and that upon our lands and vineyards. [5]Yet now our flesh is as the flesh of our brethren, our children as their children: and lo, we bring into bondage our sons and our daughters to be servants, and some of our daughters are brought unto bondage already: neither is it in our power to redeem them: for other men have our lands and vineyards.'

[6]And I was very angry when I heard their cry and these words. [7]Then I consulted with myself, and I rebuked the nobles, and the rulers, and said unto them, 'You exact usury, every one of his brother'. And I set a great assembly against them. [8]And I said unto them, 'We after our ability have redeemed our brethren the Jews, which were sold unto the heathen; and will you even sell your brethren? or shall they be sold unto us?' Then held they their peace, and found nothing to answer. [9]Also I said, 'It is not good that ye do: ought ye not to walk in the fear of our God because of the reproach of the heathen our enemies? [10]I like-

wise, and my brethren, and my servants, might exact of them money and corn: I pray you, let us leave off this usury. ¹¹Restore, I pray you, to them, even this day, their lands, their vineyards, their olive-yards, and their houses, also the hundredth part of the money, and of the corn, the wine, and the oil, that ye exact of them.' ¹²Then said they, 'We will restore them, and will require nothing of them; so will we do as thou sayest'. Then I called the priests, and took an oath of them, that they should do according to this promise. ¹³Also I shook my lap, and said, 'So God shake out every man from his house, and from his labour, that performeth not this promise, even thus be he shaken out, and emptied'. And all the congregation said, 'Amen', and praised the LORD. And the people did according to this promise.

¹⁴Moreover from the time that I was appointed to be their governor in the land of Judah, from the twentieth year even unto the two and thirtieth year of Artaxerxes the king, that is, twelve years, I and my brethren have not eaten the bread of the governor. ¹⁵But the former governors that had been before me were chargeable unto the people, and had taken of them bread and wine, besides forty shekels of silver; yea, even their servants bore rule over the people: but so did not I, because of the fear of God. ¹⁶Yea also I continued in the work of this wall, neither bought we any land: and all my servants were gathered thither unto the work. ¹⁷Moreover there were at my table a hundred and fifty of the Jews and rulers, besides those that came unto us from among the heathen that are about us. ¹⁸Now that which was prepared for me daily was one ox and six choice sheep; also fowls were prepared for me, and once in ten days store of all sorts of wine: yet for all this required not I the bread of the governor, because the bondage was heavy upon this people. ¹⁹Think upon me, my God, for good, according to all that I have done for this people.

6 Now it came to pass when Sanballat, and Tobiah, and Geshem the Arabian, and the rest of our enemies, heard that I had built the wall, and that there was no breach left therein (though at that time I had not set up the doors upon the gates), ²that Sanballat and Geshem sent unto me, saying, 'Come, let us meet together in some one of the villages in the plain of Ono'. But they thought to do me mischief. ³And I sent messengers unto them, saying, 'I am doing a great work, so that I cannot come down: why should the work cease, whilst I leave it, and come down to you?' ⁴Yet they sent unto me four times after this sort; and I answered them after the same manner. ⁵Then sent Sanballat his servant unto me in like manner the fifth time with an open letter in his hand: ⁶wherein was written, 'It is reported among the heathen, and Gashmu saith it, that thou and the Jews think to rebel: for which cause thou buildest the wall, that thou mayest be their king, according to these words. ⁷And thou hast also appointed prophets to preach of thee at Jerusalem, saying, "There is a king in Judah". And now shall it be reported to the king according to these words. Come now therefore, and let us take counsel together.' ⁸Then I sent unto him, saying, 'There are no such things done as thou sayest, but thou feignest them out of

thy own heart'. ⁹For they all made us afraid, saying, 'Their hands shall be weakened from the work that it be not done'. Now therefore, O God, strengthen my hands.

¹⁰Afterward I came unto the house of Shemaiah the son of Delaiah the son of Mehetabeel, who was shut up; and he said, 'Let us meet together in the house of God, within the temple, and let us shut the doors of the temple: for they will come to slay thee; yea, in the night will they come to slay thee'. ¹¹And I said, 'Should such a man as I flee? and who is there, that, being as I am, would go into the temple to save his life? I will not go in.' ¹²And lo, I perceived that God had not sent him, but that he pronounced this prophecy against me: for Tobiah and Sanballat had hired him. ¹³Therefore was he hired, that I should be afraid, and do so, and sin, and that they might have matter for an evil report, that they might reproach me. ¹⁴My God, think thou upon Tobiah and Sanballat according to these their works, and on the prophetess Noadiah, and the rest of the prophets, that would have put me in fear.

¹⁵So the wall was finished in the twenty and fifth day of the month Elul, in fifty and two days. ¹⁶And it came to pass that when all our enemies heard thereof, and all the heathen that were about us saw these things, they were much cast down in their own eyes: for they perceived that this work was wrought of our God.

¹⁷Moreover in those days the nobles of Judah sent many letters unto Tobiah, and the letters of Tobiah came unto them. ¹⁸For there were many in Judah sworn unto him, because he was the son-in-law of Shechaniah the son of Arah, and his son Johanan had taken the daughter of Meshullam the son of Berechiah. ¹⁹Also they reported his good deeds before me, and uttered my words to him. And Tobiah sent letters to put me in fear.

7 Now it came to pass, when the wall was built, and I had set up the doors, and the porters and the singers and the Levites were appointed, ²that I gave my brother Hanani, and Hananiah the ruler of the palace, charge over Jerusalem: for he was a faithful man, and feared God above many. ³And I said unto them, 'Let not the gates of Jerusalem be opened until the sun be hot; and while they stand by, let them shut the doors, and bar them. And appoint watches of the inhabitants of Jerusalem, every one in his watch, and every one to be over against his house.' ⁴Now the city was large and great, but the people were few therein, and the houses were not built.

⁵And my God put into my heart to gather together the nobles, and the rulers, and the people, that they might be reckoned by genealogy. And I found a register of the genealogy of them which came up at the first, and found written therein:

⁶These are the children of the province, that went up out of the captivity, of those that had been carried away, whom Nebuchadnezzar the king of Babylon had carried away, and came again to Jerusalem and to Judah, every one unto his city; ⁷who came with Zerubbabel, Jeshua, Nehemiah, Azariah, Raamiah, Nahamani, Mordecai, Bilshan, Mispereth, Bigvai,

Nehum, Baanah. The number, I say, of the men of the people of Israel was this. [8]The children of Parosh, two thousand a hundred seventy and two. [9]The children of Shephatiah, three hundred seventy and two. [10]The children of Arah, six hundred fifty and two. [11]The children of Pahath-moab, of the children of Jeshua and Joab, two thousand and eight hundred and eighteen. [12]The children of Elam, a thousand two hundred fifty and four. [13]The children of Zattu, eight hundred forty and five. [14]The children of Zaccai, seven hundred and threescore. [15]The children of Binnui, six hundred forty and eight. [16]The children of Bebai, six hundred twenty and eight. [17]The children of Azgad, two thousand three hundred twenty and two. [18]The children of Adonikam, six hundred threescore and seven. [19]The children of Bigvai, two thousand threescore and seven. [20]The children of Adin, six hundred fifty and five. [21]The children of Ater of Hezekiah, ninety and eight. [22]The children of Hashum, three hundred twenty and eight. [23]The children of Bezai, three hundred twenty and four. [24]The children of Hariph, a hundred and twelve. [25]The children of Gibeon, ninety and five. [26]The men of Beth-lehem and Netophah, a hundred fourscore and eight. [27]The men of Anathoth, a hundred twenty and eight. [28]The men of Beth-azmaveth, forty and two. [29]The men of Kirjath-jearim, Chephirah, and Beeroth, seven hundred forty and three. [30]The men of Ramah and Gaba, six hundred twenty and one. [31]The men of Michmas, a hundred and twenty and two. [32]The men of Beth-el and Ai, a hundred twenty and three. [33]The men of the other Nebo, fifty and two. [34]The children of the other Elam, a thousand two hundred fifty and four. [35]The children of Harim, three hundred and twenty. [36]The children of Jericho, three hundred forty and five. [37]The children of Lod, Hadid, and Ono, seven hundred twenty and one. [38]The children of Senaah, three thousand nine hundred and thirty.

[39]The priests. The children of Jedaiah, of the house of Jeshua, nine hundred seventy and three. [40]The children of Immer, a thousand fifty and two. [41]The children of Pashur, a thousand two hundred forty and seven. [42]The children of Harim, a thousand and seventeen.

[43]The Levites. The children of Jeshua, of Kadmiel, and of the children of Hodevah, seventy and four.

[44]The singers. The children of Asaph, a hundred forty and eight.

[45]The porters. The children of Shallum, the children of Ater, the children of Talmon, the children of Akkub, the children of Hatita, the children of Shobai, a hundred thirty and eight.

[46]The Nethinims. The children of Ziha, the children of Hashupha, the children of Tabbaoth, [47]the children of Keros, the children of Sia, the children of Padon, [48]the children of Lebana, the children of Hagaba, the children of Shalmai, [49]the

children of Hanan, the children of Giddel, the children of Gahar, [50]the children of Reaiah, the children of Rezin, the children of Nekoda, [51]the children of Gazzam, the children of Uzza, the children of Phaseah, [52]the children of Besai, the children of Meunim, the children of Nephishesim, [53]the children of Bakbuk, the children of Hakupha, the children of Harhur, [54]the children of Bazlith, the children of Mehida, the children of Harsha, [55]the children of Barkos, the children of Sisera, the children of Tamah, [56]the children of Neziah, the children of Hatipha.

[57]The children of Solomon's servants. The children of Sotai, the children of Sophereth, the children of Perida, [58]the children of Jaala, the children of Darkon, the children of Giddel, [59]the children of Shephatiah, the children of Hattil, the children of Pochereth of Zebaim, the children of Amon. [60]All the Nethinims, and the children of Solomon's servants, were three hundred ninety and two. [61]And these were they which went up also from Tel-melah, Tel-haresha, Cherub, Addon, and Immer: but they could not show their fathers' house, nor their seed, whether they were of Israel. [62]The children of Delaiah, the children of Tobiah, the children of Nekoda, six hundred forty and two.

[63]And of the priests. The children of Habaiah, the children of Koz, the children of Barzillai, which took one of the daughters of Barzillai the Gileadite to wife, and was called after their name. [64]These sought their register among those that were reckoned by genealogy, but it was not found: therefore were they, as polluted, put from the priesthood. [65]And the Tirshatha said unto them, that they should not eat of the most holy things, till there stood up a priest with Urim and Thummim.

[66]The whole congregation together was forty and two thousand three hundred and threescore, [67]besides their manservants and their maidservants, of whom there were seven thousand three hundred thirty and seven: and they had two hundred forty and five singing men and singing women. [68]Their horses, seven hundred thirty and six: their mules, two hundred forty and five: [69]their camels, four hundred thirty and five: six thousand seven hundred and twenty asses.

[70]And some of the chief of the fathers gave unto the work. The Tirshatha gave to the treasure a thousand drams of gold, fifty basins, five hundred and thirty priests' garments. [71]And some of the chief of the fathers gave to the treasure of the work twenty thousand drams of gold, and two thousand and two hundred pound of silver. [72]And that which the rest of the people gave was twenty thousand drams of gold, and two thousand pound of silver, and threescore and seven priests' garments. [73]So the priests, and the Levites, and the porters, and the singers,

and some of the people, and the Nethinims, and all Israel, dwelt in their cities.

And when the seventh month came, the children of Israel were in their cities.

8 And all the people gathered themselves together as one man into the street that was before the water gate, and they spoke unto Ezra the scribe to bring the book of the law of Moses, which the LORD had commanded to Israel. ²And Ezra the priest brought the law before the congregation both of men and women, and all that could hear with understanding, upon the first day of the seventh month. ³And he read therein before the street that was before the water gate from the morning until midday, before the men and the women, and those that could understand: and the ears of all the people were attentive unto the book of the law. ⁴And Ezra the scribe stood upon a pulpit of wood, which they had made for the purpose, and beside him stood Mattithiah, and Shema, and Anaiah, and Urijah, and Hilkiah, and Maaseiah, on his right hand; and on his left hand, Pedaiah, and Mishael, and Malchiah, and Hashum, and Hashbadana, Zechariah, and Meshullam. ⁵And Ezra opened the book in the sight of all the people (for he was above all the people), and when he opened it, all the people stood up: ⁶and Ezra blessed the LORD, the great God. And all the people answered, 'Amen, Amen', with lifting up their hands: and they bowed their heads, and worshipped the LORD with their faces to the ground. ⁷Also Jeshua, and Bani, and Sherebiah, Jamin, Akkub, Shabbethai, Hodijah, Maaseiah, Kelita, Azariah, Jozabad, Hanan, Pelaiah, and the Levites, caused the people to understand the law: and the people stood in their place. ⁸So they read in the book in the law of God distinctly, and gave the sense, and caused them to understand the reading.

⁹And Nehemiah, which is the Tirshatha, and Ezra the priest the scribe, and the Levites that taught the people, said unto all the people, 'This day is holy unto the LORD your God, mourn not, nor weep'. For all the people wept, when they heard the words of the law. ¹⁰Then he said unto them, 'Go your way, eat the fat, and drink the sweet, and send portions unto them for whom nothing is prepared: for this day is holy unto our Lord: neither be ye sorry, for the joy of the LORD is your strength'. ¹¹So the Levites stilled all the people, saying, 'Hold your peace, for the day is holy, neither be ye grieved'. ¹²And all the people went their way to eat, and to drink, and to send portions, and to make great mirth, because they had understood the words that were declared unto them.

¹³And on the second day were gathered together the chief of the fathers of all the people, the priests, and the Levites, unto Ezra the scribe, even to understand the words of the law. ¹⁴And they found written in the law which the LORD had commanded by Moses, that the children of Israel should dwell in booths in the feast of the seventh month: ¹⁵and that they should publish and proclaim in all their cities, and in Jerusalem, saying, 'Go forth unto the mount, and fetch olive branches, and pine branches, and myrtle branches, and palm branches, and

branches of thick trees, to make booths, as it is written'. ¹⁶So the people went forth, and brought them, and made themselves booths, every one upon the roof of his house, and in their courts, and in the courts of the house of God, and in the street of the water gate, and in the street of the gate of Ephraim. ¹⁷And all the congregation of them that were come again out of the captivity made booths, and sat under the booths: for since the days of Jeshua the son of Nun unto that day had not the children of Israel done so. And there was very great gladness. ¹⁸Also day by day from the first day unto the last day, he read in the book of the law of God. And they kept the feast seven days, and on the eighth day was a solemn assembly, according unto the manner.

9 Now in the twenty and fourth day of this month the children of Israel were assembled with fasting, and with sackclothes, and earth upon them. ²And the seed of Israel separated themselves from all strangers, and stood and confessed their sins, and the iniquities of their fathers. ³And they stood up in their place, and read in the book of the law of the LORD their God one fourth part of the day; and another fourth part they confessed, and worshipped the LORD their God.

⁴Then stood up upon the stairs of the Levites, Jeshua, and Bani, Kadmiel, Shebaniah, Bunni, Sherebiah, Bani, and Chenani, and cried with a loud voice unto the LORD their God. ⁵Then the Levites, Jeshua, and Kadmiel, Bani, Hashabniah, Sherebiah, Hodijah, Shebaniah, and Pethahiah, said, 'Stand up and bless the LORD your God for ever and ever, and blessed be thy glorious name, which is exalted above all blessing and praise. ⁶Thou, even thou, art LORD alone, thou hast made heaven, the heaven of heavens, with all their host, the earth, and all things that are therein, the seas, and all that is therein, and thou preservest them all, and the host of heaven worshippeth thee. ⁷Thou art the LORD the God, who didst choose Abram, and broughtest him forth out of Ur of the Chaldees, and gavest him the name of Abraham; ⁸and foundest his heart faithful before thee, and madest a covenant with him to give the land of the Canaanites, the Hittites, the Amorites, and the Perizzites, and the Jebusites, and the Girgashites, to give it, I say, to his seed, and hast performed thy words, for thou art righteous: ⁹and didst see the affliction of our fathers in Egypt, and heardest their cry by the Red Sea, ¹⁰and showedst signs and wonders upon Pharaoh, and on all his servants, and on all the people of his land: for thou knewest that they dealt proudly against them. So didst thou get thee a name, as it is this day. ¹¹And thou didst divide the sea before them, so that they went through the midst of the sea on the dry land, and their persecutors thou threwest into the deeps, as a stone into the mighty waters. ¹²Moreover thou leddest them in the day by a cloudy pillar, and in the night by a pillar of fire, to give them light in the way wherein they should go. ¹³Thou camest down also upon mount Sinai, and spokest with them from heaven, and gavest them right judgements, and true laws, good statutes and commandments: ¹⁴and madest known unto them thy holy sabbath, and commandedst them precepts, statutes, and laws, by the hand of Moses thy servant: ¹⁵and gavest them bread from

heaven for their hunger, and broughtest forth water for them out of the rock for their thirst, and promisedst them that they should go in to possess the land which thou hadst sworn to give them. ¹⁶But they and our fathers dealt proudly, and hardened their necks, and hearkened not to thy commandments: ¹⁷and refused to obey, neither were mindful of the wonders that thou didst among them; but hardened their necks, and in their rebellion appointed a captain to return to their bondage; but thou art a God ready to pardon, gracious and merciful, slow to anger, and of great kindness, and forsookest them not. ¹⁸Yea, when they had made them a molten calf, and said, "This is thy God that brought thee up out of Egypt", and had wrought great provocations: ¹⁹yet thou in thy manifold mercies forsookest them not in the wilderness: the pillar of the cloud departed not from them by day, to lead them in the way, neither the pillar of fire by night, to show them light, and the way wherein they should go. ²⁰Thou gavest also thy good spirit to instruct them, and withheldest not thy manna from their mouth, and gavest them water for their thirst. ²¹Yea, forty years didst thou sustain them in the wilderness, so that they lacked nothing; their clothes waxed not old, and their feet swelled not. ²²Moreover thou gavest them kingdoms and nations, and didst divide them into corners: so they possessed the land of Sihon, and the land of the king of Heshbon, and the land of Og king of Bashan. ²³Their children also multipliedst thou as the stars of heaven, and broughtest them into the land, concerning which thou hadst promised to their fathers, that they should go in to possess it. ²⁴So the children went in and possessed the land, and thou subduedst before them the inhabitants of the land, the Canaanites, and gavest them into their hands, with their kings, and the people of the land, that they might do with them as they would. ²⁵And they took strong cities, and a fat land, and possessed houses full of all goods, wells dug, vineyards, and olive-yards, and fruit trees in abundance: so they did eat, and were filled, and became fat, and delighted themselves in thy great goodness. ²⁶Nevertheless they were disobedient, and rebelled against thee, and cast thy law behind their backs, and slew thy prophets which testified against them to turn them to thee, and they wrought great provocations. ²⁷Therefore thou deliveredst them into the hand of their enemies, who vexed them, and in the time of their trouble, when they cried unto thee, thou heardest them from heaven: and according to thy manifold mercies thou gavest them saviours, who saved them out of the hand of their enemies. ²⁸But after they had rest, they did evil again before thee: therefore leftest thou them in the hand of their enemies, so that they had the dominion over them: yet when they returned, and cried unto thee, thou heardest them from heaven, and many times didst thou deliver them according to thy mercies; ²⁹and testifiedst against them, that thou mightest bring them again unto thy law: yet they dealt proudly, and hearkened not unto thy commandments, but sinned against thy judgements (which if a man do, he shall live in them), and withdrew the shoulder, and hardened their neck, and would not hear. ³⁰Yet many years didst thou forbear them, and testifiedst against them by thy spirit in thy prophets: yet would they not give ear: therefore gavest thou them into the hand of the people of the lands. ³¹Nevertheless for thy great mercies' sake thou didst not utterly consume them, nor forsake them; for thou art a gracious and merciful God. ³²Now therefore, our God, the great, the mighty, and the terrible God, who keepest covenant and mercy: let not all the trouble seem little before thee, that hath come upon us, on our kings, on our princes, and on our priests, and on our prophets, and on our fathers, and on all thy people, since the time of the kings of Assyria unto this day. ³³Howbeit, thou art just in all that is brought upon us, for thou hast done right, but we have done wickedly: ³⁴neither have our kings, our princes, our priests, nor our fathers kept thy law, nor hearkened unto thy commandments and thy testimonies, wherewith thou didst testify against them. ³⁵For they have not served thee in their kingdom, and in thy great goodness that thou gavest them, and in the large and fat land which thou gavest before them, neither turned they from their wicked works. ³⁶Behold, we are servants this day, and for the land that thou gavest unto our fathers to eat the fruit thereof and the good thereof, behold, we are servants in it. ³⁷And it yieldeth much increase unto the kings whom thou hast set over us because of our sins: also they have dominion over our bodies, and over our cattle, at their pleasure, and we are in great distress. ³⁸And because of all this we make a sure covenant, and write it, and our princes, Levites, and priests, seal unto it.'

10 Now those that sealed were, Nehemiah, the Tirshatha, the son of Hachaliah, and Zidkijah, ²Seraiah, Azariah, Jeremiah, ³Pashur, Amariah, Malchiah, ⁴Hattush, Shebaniah, Malluch, ⁵Harim, Meremoth, Obadiah, ⁶Daniel, Ginnethon, Baruch, ⁷Meshullam, Abijah, Mijamin, ⁸Maaziah, Bilgai, Shemaiah: these were the priests. ⁹And the Levites: both Jeshua the son of Azaniah, Binnui of the sons of Henadad, Kadmiel; ¹⁰and their brethren, Shebaniah, Hodijah, Kelita, Pelaiah, Hanan, ¹¹Micha, Rehob, Hashabiah, ¹²Zaccur, Sherebiah, Shebaniah, ¹³Hodijah, Bani, Beninu. ¹⁴The chief of the people. Parosh, Pahath-moab, Elam, Zatthu, Bani, ¹⁵Bunni, Azgad, Bebai, ¹⁶Adonijah, Bigvai, Adin, ¹⁷Ater, Hizkijah, Azzur, ¹⁸Hodijah, Hashum, Bezai, ¹⁹Hariph, Anathoth, Nebai, ²⁰Magpiash, Meshullam, Hezir, ²¹Meshezabeel, Zadok, Jaddua, ²²Pelatiah, Hanan, Anaiah, ²³Hoshea, Hananiah, Hashub, ²⁴Hallohesh, Pileha, Shobek, ²⁵Rehum, Hashabnah, Maaseiah, ²⁶and Ahijah, Hanan, Anan, ²⁷Malluch, Harim, Baanah.

²⁸And the rest of the people, the priests, the Levites, the porters, the singers, the Nethinims, and all they that had separated themselves from the people of the lands unto the law of God, their wives, their sons, and their daughters, every one having knowledge, and having understanding. ²⁹They cleaved to their brethren, their nobles, and entered into a curse, and into an oath, to walk in God's law, which was given by Moses the servant of God, and to observe and do all the commandments of the LORD our Lord, and his judgements and his statutes: ³⁰and that we would not give our daughters unto the people of the land,

nor take their daughters for our sons. [31]And if the people of the land bring ware or any victuals on the sabbath day to sell, that we would not buy it of them on the sabbath, or on the holy day, and that we would leave the seventh year, and the exaction of every debt. [32]Also we made ordinances for us, to charge ourselves yearly with the third part of a shekel for the service of the house of our God, [33]for the showbread, and for the continual meat offering, and for the continual burnt offering, of the sabbaths, of the new moons, for the set feasts, and for the holy things, and for the sin offerings to make an atonement for Israel, and for all the work of the house of our God. [34]And we cast the lots among the priests, the Levites, and the people, for the wood offering, to bring it into the house of our God, after the houses of our fathers, at times appointed year by year, to burn upon the altar of the LORD our God, as it is written in the law: [35]and to bring the first-fruits of our ground, and the first-fruits of all fruit of all trees, year by year, unto the house of the LORD. [36]Also the firstborn of our sons, and of our cattle, as it is written in the law, and the firstlings of our herds and of our flocks, to bring to the house of our God, unto the priests that minister in the house of our God: [37]and that we should bring the first-fruits of our dough, and our offerings, and the fruit of all manner of trees, of wine and of oil, unto the priests, to the chambers of the house of our God, and the tithes of our ground unto the Levites, that the same Levites might have the tithes in all the cities of our tillage. [38]And the priest the son of Aaron shall be with the Levites, when the Levites take tithes, and the Levites shall bring up the tithe of the tithes unto the house of our God, to the chambers, into the treasure-house. [39]For the children of Israel and the children of Levi shall bring the offering of the corn, of the new wine, and the oil, unto the chambers, where are the vessels of the sanctuary, and the priests that minister, and the porters, and the singers: and we will not forsake the house of our God.

11 And the rulers of the people dwelt at Jerusalem: the rest of the people also cast lots, to bring one of ten to dwell in Jerusalem the holy city, and nine parts to dwell in other cities. [2]And the people blessed all the men, that willingly offered themselves to dwell at Jerusalem.

[3]Now these are the chief of the province that dwelt in Jerusalem: but in the cities of Judah dwelt every one in his possession in their cities, to wit, Israel, the priests, and the Levites, and the Nethinims, and the children of Solomon's servants. [4]And at Jerusalem dwelt certain of the children of Judah, and of the children of Benjamin. Of the children of Judah: Athaiah the son of Uzziah, the son of Zechariah, the son of Amariah, the son of Shephatiah, the son of Mahalaleel, of the children of Perez; [5]and Maaseiah the son of Baruch, the son of Col-hozeh, the son of Hazaiah, the son of Adaiah, the son of Joiarib, the son of Zechariah, the son of Shiloni. [6]All the sons of Perez that dwelt at Jerusalem were four hundred threescore and eight valiant men. [7]And these are the sons of Benjamin: Sallu the son of Meshullam, the son of Joed, the son of Pedaiah, the son of Kolaiah, the son of Maaseiah, the

son of Ithiel, the son of Jesaiah. ⁸And after him Gabbai, Sallai, nine hundred twenty and eight. ⁹And Joel the son of Zichri was their overseer: and Judah the son of Senuah was second over the city. ¹⁰Of the priests: Jedaiah the son of Joiarib, Jachin. ¹¹Seraiah the son of Hilkiah, the son of Meshullam, the son of Zadok, the son of Meraioth, the son of Ahitub, was the ruler of the house of God. ¹²And their brethren that did the work of the house were eight hundred twenty and two: and Adaiah the son of Jeroham, the son of Pelaliah, the son of Amzi, the son of Zechariah, the son of Pashur, the son of Malchiah, ¹³and his brethren, chief of the fathers, two hundred forty and two: and Amashai the son of Azareel, the son of Ahasai, the son of Meshillemoth, the son of Immer, ¹⁴and their brethren, mighty men of valour, a hundred twenty and eight; and their overseer was Zabdiel, the son of one of the great men. ¹⁵Also of the Levites: Shemaiah the son of Hashub, the son of Azrikam, the son of Hashabiah, the son of Bunni. ¹⁶And Shabbethai and Jozabad, of the chief of the Levites, had the oversight of the outward business of the house of God. ¹⁷And Mattaniah the son of Micha, the son of Zabdi, the son of Asaph, was the principal to begin the thanksgiving in prayer: and Bakbukiah the second among his brethren, and Abda the son of Shammua, the son of Galal, the son of Jeduthun. ¹⁸All the Levites in the holy city were two hundred fourscore and four. ¹⁹Moreover the porters, Akkub, Talmon, and their brethren that kept the gates, were a hundred seventy and two.

²⁰And the residue of Israel, of the priests, and the Levites, were in all the cities of Judah, every one in his inheritance. ²¹But the Nethinims dwelt in Ophel: and Ziha and Gispa were over the Nethinims. ²²The overseer also of the Levites at Jerusalem was Uzzi the son of Bani, the son of Hashabiah, the son of Mattaniah, the son of Micha. Of the sons of Asaph, the singers were over the business of the house of God. ²³For it was the king's commandment concerning them, that a certain portion should be for the singers, due for every day. ²⁴And Pethahiah the son of Meshezabeel, of the children of Zerah the son of Judah, was at the king's hand in all matters concerning the people. ²⁵And for the villages, with their fields, some of the children of Judah dwelt at Kirjath-arba, and in the villages thereof, and at Dibon, and in the villages thereof, and at Jekabzeel, and in the villages thereof, ²⁶and at Jeshua, and at Moladah, and at Beth-phelet, ²⁷and at Hazar-shual, and at Beer-sheba, and in the villages thereof, ²⁸and at Ziklag, and at Mekonah, and in the villages thereof, ²⁹and at En-rimmon, and at Zareah, and at Jarmuth, ³⁰Zanoah, Adullam, and in their villages, at Lachish, and the fields thereof, at Azekah, and in the villages thereof. And they dwelt from Beer-sheba unto the valley of Hinnom. ³¹The children also of Benjamin from Geba dwelt at Michmash, and Aija, and Beth-el, and in their villages, ³²and at Anathoth, Nob, Ananiah, ³³Hazor, Ramah, Gittaim, ³⁴Hadid, Zeboim, Neballat, ³⁵Lod, and Ono, the valley of craftsmen. ³⁶And of the Levites were divisions in Judah, and in Benjamin.

12 Now these are the priests and the Levites that went up with Zerubbabel the son of Shealtiel, and Jeshua: Seraiah, Jeremiah,

Ezra, ²Amariah, Malluch, Hattush, ³Shechaniah, Rehum, Meremoth, ⁴Iddo, Ginnetho, Abijah, ⁵Miamin, Maadiah, Bilgah, ⁶Shemaiah, and Joiarib, Jedaiah, ⁷Sallu, Amok, Hilkiah, Jedaiah. These were the chief of the priests and of their brethren in the days of Jeshua. ⁸Moreover the Levites: Jeshua, Binnui, Kadmiel, Sherebiah, Judah, and Mattaniah, which was over the thanksgiving, he and his brethren. ⁹Also Bakbukiah and Unni, their brethren, were over against them in the watches.

¹⁰And Jeshua begot Joiakim, Joiakim also begot Eliashib, and Eliashib begot Joiada, ¹¹and Joiada begot Jonathan, and Jonathan begot Jaddua. ¹²And in the days of Joiakim were priests, the chief of the fathers: of Seraiah, Meraiah; of Jeremiah, Hananiah; ¹³of Ezra, Meshullam; of Amariah, Jehohanan; ¹⁴of Melicu, Jonathan; of Shebaniah, Joseph; ¹⁵of Harim, Adna; of Meraioth, Helkai; ¹⁶of Iddo, Zechariah; of Ginnethon, Meshullam; ¹⁷of Abijah, Zichri; of Miniamin, of Moadiah, Piltai; ¹⁸of Bilgah, Shammua; of Shemaiah, Jehonathan; ¹⁹and of Joiarib, Mattenai; of Jedaiah, Uzzi; ²⁰of Sallai, Kallai; of Amok, Eber; ²¹of Hilkiah, Hashabiah; of Jedaiah, Nethaneel.

²²The Levites in the days of Eliashib, Joiada, and Johanan, and Jaddua, were recorded chief of the fathers: also the priests, to the reign of Darius the Persian. ²³The sons of Levi, the chief of the fathers, were written in the book of the chronicles, even until the days of Johanan the son of Eliashib. ²⁴And the chief of the Levites: Hashabiah, Sherebiah, and Jeshua the son of Kadmiel, with their brethren over against them, to praise and to give thanks, according to the commandment of David the man of God, ward over against ward. ²⁵Mattaniah, and Bakbukiah, Obadiah, Meshullam, Talmon, Akkub, were porters keeping the ward at the thresholds of the gates. ²⁶These were in the days of Joiakim the son of Jeshua, the son of Jozadak, and in the days of Nehemiah the governor, and of Ezra the priest, the scribe.

²⁷And at the dedication of the wall of Jerusalem they sought the Levites out of all their places, to bring them to Jerusalem, to keep the dedication with gladness, both with thanksgivings, and with singing, with cymbals, psalteries, and with harps. ²⁸And the sons of the singers gathered themselves together, both out of the plain country round about Jerusalem, and from the villages of Netophathi; ²⁹also from the house of Gilgal, and out of the fields of Geba and Azmaveth: for the singers had built them villages round about Jerusalem. ³⁰And the priests and the Levites purified themselves, and purified the people, and the gates, and the wall.

³¹Then I brought up the princes of Judah upon the wall, and appointed two great companies of them that gave thanks, whereof one went on the right hand upon the wall toward the dung gate: ³²and after them went Hoshaiah, and half of the princes of Judah, ³³and Azariah, Ezra, and Meshullam, ³⁴Judah, and Benjamin, and Shemaiah, and Jeremiah, ³⁵and certain of the priests' sons with trumpets: namely, Zechariah the son of Jonathan, the son of Shemaiah, the son of Mattaniah, the son of Michaiah, the son of Zaccur, the son of Asaph: ³⁶and his brethren, Shemaiah, and Azareel, Milalai, Gilalai, Maai,

Nethaneel, and Judah, Hanani, with the musical instruments of David the man of God, and Ezra the scribe before them. [37]And at the fountain gate, which was over against them, they went up by the stairs of the city of David, at the going up of the wall, above the house of David, even unto the water gate eastward. [38]And the other company of them that gave thanks went over against them, and I after them, and the half of the people upon the wall, from beyond the tower of the furnaces even unto the broad wall; [39]and from above the gate of Ephraim, and above the old gate, and above the fish gate, and the tower of Hananeel, and the tower of Meah, even unto the sheep gate: and they stood still in the prison gate. [40]So stood the two companies of them that gave thanks in the house of God, and I, and the half of the rulers with me: [41]and the priests: Eliakim, Maaseiah, Miniamin, Michaiah, Elioenai, Zechariah, and Hananiah, with trumpets; [42]and Maaseiah, and Shemaiah, and Eleazar, and Uzzi, and Jehohanan, and Malchijah, and Elam, and Ezer. And the singers sang loud, with Jezrahiah their overseer. [43]Also that day they offered great sacrifices, and rejoiced: for God had made them rejoice with great joy: the wives also and the children rejoiced: so that the joy of Jerusalem was heard even afar off.

[44]And at that time were some appointed over the chambers for the treasures, for the offerings, for the first-fruits, and for the tithes, to gather into them out of the fields of the cities the portions of the law for the priests and Levites: for Judah rejoiced for the priests and for the Levites that waited. [45]And both the singers and the porters kept the ward of their God, and the ward of the purification, according to the commandment of David, and of Solomon his son. [46]For in the days of David and Asaph of old there were chief of the singers, and songs of praise and thanksgiving unto God. [47]And all Israel in the days of Zerubbabel, and in the days of Nehemiah, gave the portions of the singers and the porters, every day his portion: and they sanctified holy things unto the Levites, and the Levites sanctified them unto the children of Aaron.

13 On that day they read in the book of Moses in the audience of the people, and therein was found written, that the Ammonite and the Moabite should not come into the congregation of God for ever, [2]because they met not the children of Israel with bread and with water, but hired Balaam against them, that he should curse them: howbeit our God turned the curse into a blessing. [3]Now it came to pass when they had heard the law, that they separated from Israel all the mixed multitude.

[4]And before this Eliashib the priest, having the oversight of the chamber of the house of our God, was allied unto Tobiah: [5]and he had prepared for him a great chamber, where aforetime they laid the meat offerings, the frankincense, and the vessels, and the tithes of the corn, the new wine, and the oil, which was commanded to be given to the Levites, and the singers, and the porters, and the offerings of the priests. [6]But in all this time was not I at Jerusalem: for in the two and thirtieth year of Artaxerxes king of Babylon came I unto the king, and

after certain days obtained I leave of the king: ⁷and I came to Jerusalem, and understood of the evil that Eliashib did for Tobiah, in preparing him a chamber in the courts of the house of God. ⁸And it grieved me sore: therefore I cast forth all the household stuff of Tobiah out of the chamber. ⁹Then I commanded, and they cleansed the chambers, and thither brought I again the vessels of the house of God, with the meat offering and the frankincense.

¹⁰And I perceived that the portions of the Levites had not been given them: for the Levites and the singers, that did the work, were fled every one to his field. ¹¹Then contended I with the rulers, and said, 'Why is the house of God forsaken?' And I gathered them together, and set them in their place. ¹²Then brought all Judah the tithe of the corn and the new wine and the oil unto the treasuries. ¹³And I made treasurers over the treasuries, Shelemiah the priest, and Zadok the scribe, and of the Levites, Pedaiah: and next to them was Hanan the son of Zaccur, the son of Mattaniah: for they were counted faithful, and their office was to distribute unto their brethren. ¹⁴Remember me, O my God, concerning this, and wipe not out my good deeds that I have done for the house of my God, and for the offices thereof.

¹⁵In those days saw I in Judah some treading wine-presses on the sabbath, and bringing in sheaves, and loading asses, as also wine, grapes, and figs, and all manner of burdens, which they brought into Jerusalem on the sabbath day: and I testified against them in the day wherein they sold victuals. ¹⁶There dwelt men of Tyre also therein, which brought fish, and all manner of ware, and sold on the sabbath unto the children of Judah, and in Jerusalem. ¹⁷Then I contended with the nobles of Judah, and said unto them, 'What evil thing is this that ye do, and profane the sabbath day? ¹⁸Did not your fathers thus, and did not our God bring all this evil upon us, and upon this city? yet ye bring more wrath upon Israel by profaning the sabbath.' ¹⁹And it came to pass, that when the gates of Jerusalem began to be dark before the sabbath, I commanded that the gates should be shut, and charged that they should not be opened till after the sabbath: and some of my servants set I at the gates, that there should no burden be brought in on the sabbath day. ²⁰So the merchants and sellers of all kind of ware lodged without Jerusalem once or twice. ²¹Then I testified against them, and said unto them, 'Why lodge ye about the wall? if ye do so again, I will lay hands on you'. From that time forth came they no more on the sabbath. ²²And I commanded the Levites that they should cleanse themselves, and that they should come and keep the gates, to sanctify the sabbath day. Remember me, O my God, concerning this also, and spare me according to the greatness of thy mercy.

²³In those days also saw I Jews that had married wives of Ashdod, of Ammon, and of Moab: ²⁴and their children spoke half in the speech of Ashdod, and could not speak in the Jews' language, but according to the language of each people. ²⁵And I contended with them, and cursed them, and smote certain of them, and plucked off their hair, and made them swear by God, saying, 'Ye shall not give your daughters unto their

sons, nor take their daughters unto your sons, or for yourselves. [26]Did not Solomon king of Israel sin by these things? yet among many nations was there no king like him, who was beloved of his God, and God made him king over all Israel: nevertheless even him did outlandish women cause to sin. [27]Shall we then hearken unto you to do all this great evil, to transgress against our God in marrying strange wives?' [28]And one of the sons of Joiada, the son of Eliashib the high priest, was son-in-law to Sanballat the Horonite: therefore I chased him from me. [29]Remember them, O my God, because they have defiled the priesthood, and the covenant of the priesthood, and of the Levites. [30]Thus cleansed I them from all strangers, and appointed the wards of the priests and the Levites, every one in his business: [31]and for the wood offering, at times appointed, and for the first-fruits. Remember me, O my God, for good.

THE BOOK OF
ESTHER

1 Now it came to pass in the days of Ahasuerus (this is Ahasuerus which reigned from India even unto Ethiopia, over a hundred and seven and twenty provinces), ²that in those days, when the king Ahasuerus sat on the throne of his kingdom, which was in Shushan the palace, ³in the third year of his reign, he made a feast unto all his princes and his servants, the power of Persia and Media, the nobles and princes of the provinces being before him: ⁴when he showed the riches of his glorious kingdom and the honour of his excellent majesty many days, even a hundred and fourscore days. ⁵And when these days were expired, the king made a feast unto all the people that were present in Shushan the palace, both unto great and small, seven days, in the court of the garden of the king's palace, ⁶where were white, green, and blue hangings, fastened with cords of fine linen and purple to silver rings and pillars of marble: the beds were of gold and silver, upon a pavement of red, and blue, and white, and black marble. ⁷And they gave them drink in vessels of gold (the vessels being diverse one from another), and royal wine in abundance, according to the state of the king. ⁸And the drinking was according to the law, none did compel: for the king had appointed to all the officers of his house, that they should do according to every man's pleasure. ⁹Also Vashti the queen made a feast for the women in the royal house which belonged to king Ahasuerus.

¹⁰On the seventh day, when the heart of the king was merry with wine, he commanded Mehuman, Biztha, Harbona, Bigtha, and Abagtha, Zethar, and Carcas, the seven chamberlains that served in the presence of Ahasuerus the king, ¹¹to bring Vashti the queen before the king with the crown royal, to show the people and the princes her beauty: for she was fair to look on. ¹²But the queen Vashti refused to come at the king's commandment by his chamberlains: therefore was the king very wroth, and his anger burnt in him.

¹³Then the king said to the wise men, which knew the times (for so was the king's manner towards all that knew law and judgement: ¹⁴and the next unto him was Carshena, Shethar, Admatha, Tarshish, Meres, Marsena, and Memucan, the seven princes of Persia and Media, which saw the king's face, and which sat the first in the kingdom), ¹⁵'What shall we do unto the queen Vashti according to law, because she hath not performed the commandment of the king Ahasuerus by the chamberlains?' ¹⁶And Memucan answered before the king and the princes, 'Vashti the queen hath not done wrong to the king only, but also to all the princes, and to all the people that are in all the provinces of the king Ahasuerus. ¹⁷For this deed of the queen shall come abroad unto all women, so that they shall despise their husbands in their eyes, when it shall be reported, "The king Ahasuerus commanded Vashti the queen

to be brought in before him, but she came not". [18]Likewise shall the ladies of Persia and Media say this day unto all the king's princes, which have heard of the deed of the queen. Thus shall there arise too much contempt and wrath. [19]If it please the king, let there go a royal commandment from him, and let it be written among the laws of the Persians and the Medes, that it be not altered, that Vashti come no more before king Ahasuerus; and let the king give her royal estate unto another that is better than she. [20]And when the king's decree which he shall make shall be published throughout all his empire (for it is great), all the wives shall give to their husbands honour, both to great and small.' [21]And the saying pleased the king and the princes, and the king did according to the word of Memucan: [22]for he sent letters into all the king's provinces, into every province according to the writing thereof, and to every people after their language, that every man should bear rule in his own house, and that it should be published according to the language of every people.

2 After these things, when the wrath of king Ahasuerus was appeased, he remembered Vashti, and what she had done, and what was decreed against her. [2]Then said the king's servants that ministered unto him, 'Let there be fair young virgins sought for the king: [3]and let the king appoint officers in all the provinces of his kingdom, that they may gather together all the fair young virgins unto Shushan the palace, to the house of the women, unto the custody of Hege the king's chamberlain, keeper of the women, and let their things for purification be given them: [4]and let the maiden which pleaseth the king be queen instead of Vashti'. And the thing pleased the king, and he did so.

[5]Now in Shushan the palace there was a certain Jew, whose name was Mordecai, the son of Jair, the son of Shimei, the son of Kish, a Benjamite, [6]who had been carried away from Jerusalem with the captivity which had been carried away with Jeconiah king of Judah, whom Nebuchadnezzar the king of Babylon had carried away. [7]And he brought up Hadassah, that is, Esther, his uncle's daughter, for she had neither father nor mother, and the maid was fair and beautiful, whom Mordecai, when her father and mother were dead, took for his own daughter.

[8]So it came to pass, when the king's commandment and his decree was heard, and when many maidens were gathered together unto Shushan the palace, to the custody of Hegai, that Esther was brought also unto the king's house, to the custody of Hegai, keeper of the women. [9]And the maiden pleased him, and she obtained kindness of him, and he speedily gave her her things for purification, with such things as belonged to her, and seven maidens, which were meet to be given her, out of the king's house: and he preferred her and her maids unto the best place of the house of the women. [10]Esther had not shown her people nor her kindred: for Mordecai had charged her that she should not show it. [11]And Mordecai walked every day before the court of the women's house, to know how Esther did, and what should become of her.

¹²Now when every maid's turn was come to go in to king Ahasuerus, after that she had been twelve months, according to the manner of the women (for so were the days of their purifications accomplished, to wit, six months with oil of myrrh, and six months with sweet odours, and with other things for the purifying of the women), ¹³then thus came every maiden unto the king; whatsoever she desired was given her to go with her out of the house of the women unto the king's house. ¹⁴In the evening she went, and on the morrow she returned into the second house of the women, to the custody of Shaashgaz, the king's chamberlain, which kept the concubines: she came in unto the king no more, except the king delighted in her, and that she were called by name.

¹⁵Now when the turn of Esther, the daughter of Abihail the uncle of Mordecai, who had taken her for his daughter, was come to go in unto the king, she required nothing but what Hegai the king's chamberlain, the keeper of the women, appointed. And Esther obtained favour in the sight of all them that looked upon her. ¹⁶So Esther was taken unto king Ahasuerus into his house royal in the tenth month, which is the month Tebeth, in the seventh year of his reign. ¹⁷And the king loved Esther above all the women, and she obtained grace and favour in his sight more than all the virgins; so that he set the royal crown upon her head, and made her queen in stead of Vashti. ¹⁸Then the king made a great feast unto all his princes and his servants, even Esther's feast, and he made a release to the provinces, and gave gifts, according to the state of the king. ¹⁹And when the virgins were gathered together the second time, then Mordecai sat in the king's gate. ²⁰Esther had not yet shown her kindred nor her people, as Mordecai had charged her: for Esther did the commandment of Mordecai, like as when she was brought up with him.

²¹In those days, while Mordecai sat in the king's gate, two of the king's chamberlains, Bigthan and Teresh, of those which kept the door, were wroth, and sought to lay hand on the king Ahasuerus. ²²And the thing was known to Mordecai, who told it unto Esther the queen, and Esther certified the king thereof in Mordecai's name. ²³And when inquisition was made of the matter, it was found out; therefore they were both hanged on a tree: and it was written in the book of the chronicles before the king.

3 After these things did king Ahasuerus promote Haman the son of Hammedatha the Agagite, and advanced him, and set his seat above all the princes that were with him. ²And all the king's servants, that were in the king's gate, bowed, and reverenced Haman, for the king had so commanded concerning him. But Mordecai bowed not, nor did him reverence. ³Then the king's servants, which were in the king's gate, said unto Mordecai, 'Why transgressest thou the king's commandment?' ⁴Now it came to pass, when they spoke daily unto him, and he hearkened not unto them, that they told Haman, to see whether Mordecai's matters would stand: for he had told them that he was a Jew. ⁵And when Haman saw that Mordecai bowed not, nor did him rev-

erence, then was Haman full of wrath. ⁶And he thought scorn to lay hands on Mordecai alone, for they had shown him the people of Mordecai: wherefore Haman sought to destroy all the Jews that were throughout the whole kingdom of Ahasuerus, even the people of Mordecai.

⁷In the first month, that is, the month Nisan, in the twelfth year of king Ahasuerus, they cast Pur, that is, the lot, before Haman from day to day, and from month to month, to the twelfth month, that is, the month Adar.

⁸And Haman said unto king Ahasuerus, 'There is a certain people scattered abroad and dispersed among the people in all the provinces of thy kingdom; and their laws are diverse from all people, neither keep they the king's laws: therefore it is not for the king's profit to suffer them. ⁹If it please the king, let it be written that they may be destroyed: and I will pay ten thousand talents of silver to the hands of those that have the charge of the business, to bring it into the king's treasuries.' ¹⁰And the king took his ring from his hand, and gave it unto Haman the son of Hammedatha the Agagite, the Jews' enemy. ¹¹And the king said unto Haman, 'The silver is given to thee, the people also, to do with them as it seemeth good to thee'. ¹²Then were the king's scribes called on the thirteenth day of the first month, and there was written according to all that Haman had commanded unto the king's lieutenants, and to the governors that were over every province, and to the rulers of every people of every province according to the writing thereof, and to every people after their language; in the name of king Ahasuerus was it written, and sealed with the king's ring. ¹³And the letters were sent by posts into all the king's provinces, to destroy, to kill, and to cause to perish all Jews, both young and old, little children and women, in one day, even upon the thirteenth day of the twelfth month, which is the month Adar, and to take the spoil of them for a prey. ¹⁴The copy of the writing for a commandment to be given in every province was published unto all people, that they should be ready against that day. ¹⁵The posts went out, being hastened by the king's commandment, and the decree was given in Shushan the palace. And the king and Haman sat down to drink; but the city Shushan was perplexed.

4 When Mordecai perceived all that was done, Mordecai rent his clothes, and put on sackcloth with ashes, and went out into the midst of the city, and cried with a loud and a bitter cry; ²and came even before the king's gate: for none might enter into the king's gate clothed with sackcloth. ³And in every province, whithersoever the king's commandment and his decree came, there was great mourning among the Jews, and fasting, and weeping, and wailing; and many lay in sackcloth and ashes.

⁴So Esther's maids and her chamberlains came and told it her. Then was the queen exceedingly grieved; and she sent raiment to clothe Mordecai, and to take away his sackcloth from him: but he received it not. ⁵Then called Esther for Hatach, one of the king's chamberlains, whom he had appointed to attend upon her, and gave him a command-

ment to Mordecai, to know what it was, and why it was. ⁶So Hatach went forth to Mordecai unto the street of the city, which was before the king's gate. ⁷And Mordecai told him of all that had happened unto him, and of the sum of the money that Haman had promised to pay to the king's treasuries for the Jews, to destroy them. ⁸Also he gave him the copy of the writing of the decree that was given at Shushan to destroy them, to show it unto Esther, and to declare it unto her, and to charge her that she should go in unto the king, to make supplication unto him, and to make request before him for her people. ⁹And Hatach came and told Esther the words of Mordecai.

¹⁰Again Esther spoke unto Hatach, and gave him commandment unto Mordecai; ¹¹'All the king's servants, and the people of the king's provinces do know, that whosoever, whether man or woman, shall come unto the king into the inner court, who is not called, there is one law of his to put him to death, except such to whom the king shall hold out the golden sceptre, that he may live: but I have not been called to come in unto the king these thirty days'. ¹²And they told to Mordecai Esther's words. ¹³Then Mordecai commanded to answer Esther, 'Think not with thyself that thou shalt escape in the king's house, more than all the Jews. ¹⁴For if thou altogether holdest thy peace at this time, then shall there enlargement and deliverance arise to the Jews from another place, but thou and thy father's house shall be destroyed: and who knoweth whether thou art come to the kingdom for such a time as this?'

¹⁵Then Esther bade them return Mordecai this answer, ¹⁶'Go, gather together all the Jews that are present in Shushan, and fast ye for me, and neither eat nor drink three days, night or day: I also and my maidens will fast likewise, and so will I go in unto the king, which is not according to the law: and if I perish, I perish'. ¹⁷So Mordecai went his way, and did according to all that Esther had commanded him.

5 Now it came to pass on the third day, that Esther put on her royal apparel, and stood in the inner court of the king's house, over against the king's house: and the king sat upon his royal throne in the royal house, over against the gate of the house. ²And it was so, when the king saw Esther the queen standing in the court, that she obtained favour in his sight: and the king held out to Esther the golden sceptre that was in his hand. So Esther drew near, and touched the top of the sceptre. ³Then said the king unto her, 'What wilt thou, queen Esther? and what is thy request? it shall be even given thee to the half of the kingdom'. ⁴And Esther answered, 'If it seem good unto the king, let the king and Haman come this day unto the banquet that I have prepared for him'. ⁵Then the king said, 'Cause Haman to make haste, that he may do as Esther hath said'. So the king and Haman came to the banquet that Esther had prepared.

⁶And the king said unto Esther at the banquet of wine, 'What is thy petition? and it shall be granted thee: and what is thy request? even to the half of the kingdom it shall be performed'. ⁷Then answered Esther, and said, 'My petition and my request is, ⁸if I have found favour in the

sight of the king, and if it please the king to grant my petition, and to perform my request, let the king and Haman come to the banquet that I shall prepare for them, and I will do tomorrow as the king hath said'.

⁹Then went Haman forth that day joyful and with a glad heart: but when Haman saw Mordecai in the king's gate, that he stood not up, nor moved for him, he was full of indignation against Mordecai. ¹⁰Nevertheless Haman refrained himself: and when he came home, he sent and called for his friends, and Zeresh his wife. ¹¹And Haman told them of the glory of his riches, and the multitude of his children, and all the things wherein the king had promoted him, and how he had advanced him above the princes and servants of the king. ¹²Haman said moreover, 'Yea, Esther the queen did let no man come in with the king unto the banquet that she had prepared but myself; and tomorrow am I invited unto her also with the king. ¹³Yet all this availeth me nothing, so long as I see Mordecai the Jew sitting at the king's gate.'

¹⁴Then said Zeresh his wife and all his friends unto him, 'Let a gallows be made of fifty cubits high, and tomorrow speak thou unto the king that Mordecai may be hanged thereon: then go thou in merrily with the king unto the banquet'. And the thing pleased Haman, and he caused the gallows to be made.

6 On that night could not the king sleep, and he commanded to bring the book of records of the chronicles: and they were read before the king. ²And it was found written, that Mordecai had told of Bigthana and Teresh, two of the king's chamberlains, the keepers of the door, who sought to lay hand on the king Ahasuerus. ³And the king said, 'What honour and dignity hath been done to Mordecai for this?' Then said the king's servants that ministered unto him, 'There is nothing done for him'.

⁴And the king said, 'Who is in the court?' Now Haman was come into the outward court of the king's house, to speak unto the king to hang Mordecai on the gallows that he had prepared for him. ⁵And the king's servants said unto him, 'Behold, Haman standeth in the court'. And the king said, 'Let him come in'. ⁶So Haman came in. And the king said unto him, 'What shall be done unto the man whom the king delighteth to honour?' Now Haman thought in his heart, 'To whom would the king delight to do honour more than to myself?' ⁷And Haman answered the king, 'For the man whom the king delighteth to honour, ⁸let the royal apparel be brought which the king useth to wear, and the horse that the king rideth upon, and the crown royal which is set upon his head: ⁹and let this apparel and horse be delivered to the hand of one of the king's most noble princes, that they may array the man withal whom the king delighteth to honour, and bring him on horseback through the street of the city, and proclaim before him, "Thus shall it be done to the man whom the king delighteth to honour"'. ¹⁰Then the king said to Haman, 'Make haste, and take the apparel and the horse, as thou hast said, and do even so to Mordecai the Jew, that sitteth at the king's gate: let nothing fail of all that thou hast spoken'. ¹¹Then took Haman the apparel and the horse, and arrayed Mordecai, and brought

him on horseback through the street of the city, and proclaimed before him, 'Thus shall it be done unto the man whom the king delighteth to honour'.

[12]And Mordecai came again to the king's gate. But Haman hasted to his house mourning, and having his head covered. [13]And Haman told Zeresh his wife and all his friends everything that had befallen him. Then said his wise men and Zeresh his wife unto him, 'If Mordecai be of the seed of the Jews, before whom thou hast begun to fall, thou shalt not prevail against him, but shalt surely fall before him'. [14]And while they were yet talking with him, came the king's chamberlains, and hasted to bring Haman unto the banquet that Esther had prepared.

7 So the king and Haman came to banquet with Esther the queen. [2]And the king said again unto Esther on the second day at the banquet of wine, 'What is thy petition, queen Esther, and it shall be granted thee? and what is thy request? and it shall be performed, even to the half of the kingdom'. [3]Then Esther the queen answered and said, 'If I have found favour in thy sight, O king, and if it please the king, let my life be given me at my petition, and my people at my request. [4]For we are sold, I and my people, to be destroyed, to be slain, and to perish. But if we had been sold for bondmen and bondwomen, I had held my tongue, although the enemy could not countervail the king's damage.'

[5]Then the king Ahasuerus answered and said unto Esther the queen, 'Who is he, and where is he, that durst presume in his heart to do so?' [6]And Esther said, 'The adversary and enemy is this wicked Haman'. Then Haman was afraid before the king and the queen.

[7]And the king arising from the banquet of wine in his wrath went into the palace garden: and Haman stood up to make request for his life to Esther the queen: for he saw that there was evil determined against him by the king. [8]Then the king returned out of the palace garden into the place of the banquet of wine, and Haman was fallen upon the bed whereon Esther was. Then said the king, 'Will he force the queen also before me in the house?' As the word went out of the king's mouth, they covered Haman's face. [9]And Harbonah, one of the chamberlains, said before the king, 'Behold also the gallows fifty cubits high, which Haman had made for Mordecai, who had spoken good for the king, standeth in the house of Haman'. Then the king said, 'Hang him thereon'. [10]So they hanged Haman on the gallows that he had prepared for Mordecai. Then was the king's wrath pacified.

8 On that day did the king Ahasuerus give the house of Haman the Jews' enemy unto Esther the queen. And Mordecai came before the king; for Esther had told what he was unto her. [2]And the king took off his ring, which he had taken from Haman, and gave it unto Mordecai. And Esther set Mordecai over the house of Haman.

[3]And Esther spoke yet again before the king, and fell down at his feet, and besought him with tears to put away the mischief of Haman the Agagite, and his device that he had devised against the Jews. [4]Then the king held out the golden sceptre toward Esther. So Esther arose, and stood before the king, [5]and said, 'If it please the king, and if I have

found favour in his sight, and the thing seem right before the king, and I be pleasing in his eyes, let it be written to reverse the letters devised by Haman the son of Hammedatha the Agagite, which he wrote to destroy the Jews which are in all the king's provinces. ⁶For how can I endure to see the evil that shall come unto my people? or how can I endure to see the destruction of my kindred?'

⁷Then the king Ahasuerus said unto Esther the queen and to Mordecai the Jew, 'Behold, I have given Esther the house of Haman, and him they have hanged upon the gallows, because he laid his hand upon the Jews. ⁸Write ye also for the Jews, as it liketh you, in the king's name, and seal it with the king's ring: for the writing which is written in the king's name, and sealed with the king's ring, may no man reverse.' ⁹Then were the king's scribes called at that time in the third month, that is, the month Sivan, on the three and twentieth day thereof, and it was written according to all that Mordecai commanded unto the Jews, and to the lieutenants, and the deputies and rulers of the provinces which are from India unto Ethiopia, a hundred twenty and seven provinces, unto every province according to the writing thereof, and unto every people after their language, and to the Jews according to their writing, and according to their language. ¹⁰And he wrote in the king Ahasuerus' name, and sealed it with the king's ring, and sent letters by posts on horseback, and riders on mules, camels, and young dromedaries: ¹¹wherein the king granted the Jews which were in every city to gather themselves together, and to stand for their life, to destroy, to slay, and to cause to perish all the power of the people and province that would assault them, both little ones and women, and to take the spoil of them for a prey, ¹²upon one day in all the provinces of king Ahasuerus, namely, upon the thirteenth day of the twelfth month, which is the month Adar. ¹³The copy of the writing for a commandment to be given in every province was published unto all people, and that the Jews should be ready against that day to avenge themselves on their enemies. ¹⁴So the posts that rode upon mules and camels went out, being hastened and pressed on by the king's commandment. And the decree was given at Shushan the palace.

¹⁵And Mordecai went out from the presence of the king in royal apparel of blue and white, and with a great crown of gold, and with a garment of fine linen and purple: and the city of Shushan rejoiced and was glad. ¹⁶The Jews had light, and gladness, and joy, and honour. ¹⁷And in every province, and in every city, whithersoever the king's commandment and his decree came, the Jews had joy and gladness, a feast and a good day. And many of the people of the land became Jews; for the fear of the Jews fell upon them.

9 Now in the twelfth month, that is, the month Adar, on the thirteenth day of the same, when the king's commandment and his decree drew near to be put in execution, in the day that the enemies of the Jews hoped to have power over them (though it was turned to the contrary, that the Jews had rule over them that hated them), ²the Jews gathered themselves together in their cities throughout all the

provinces of the king Ahasuerus, to lay hand on such as sought their hurt, and no man could withstand them: for the fear of them fell upon all people. ³And all the rulers of the provinces, and the lieutenants, and the deputies, and officers of the king, helped the Jews: because the fear of Mordecai fell upon them. ⁴For Mordecai was great in the king's house, and his fame went out throughout all the provinces: for this man Mordecai waxed greater and greater. ⁵Thus the Jews smote all their enemies with the stroke of the sword, and slaughter, and destruction, and did what they would unto those that hated them. ⁶And in Shushan the palace the Jews slew and destroyed five hundred men: ⁷and Parshandatha, and Dalphon, and Aspatha, ⁸and Poratha, and Adalia, and Aridatha, ⁹and Parmashta, and Arisai, and Aridai, and Vajezatha, ¹⁰the ten sons of Haman the son of Hammedatha, the enemy of the Jews, slew they; but on the spoil laid they not their hand.

¹¹On that day the number of those that were slain in Shushan the palace was brought before the king. ¹²And the king said unto Esther the queen, 'The Jews have slain and destroyed five hundred men in Shushan the palace, and the ten sons of Haman; what have they done in the rest of the king's provinces? now what is thy petition? and it shall be granted thee: or what is thy request further? and it shall be done'. ¹³Then said Esther, 'If it please the king, let it be granted to the Jews which are in Shushan to do tomorrow also according unto this day's decree, and let Haman's ten sons be hanged upon the gallows'. ¹⁴And the king commanded it so to be done: and the decree was given at Shushan, and they hanged Haman's ten sons. ¹⁵For the Jews that were in Shushan gathered themselves together on the fourteenth day also of the month Adar, and slew three hundred men at Shushan; but on the prey they laid not their hand.

¹⁶But the other Jews that were in the king's provinces gathered themselves together, and stood for their lives, and had rest from their enemies, and slew of their foes seventy and five thousand, but they laid not their hands on the prey. ¹⁷On the thirteenth day of the month Adar, and on the fourteenth day of the same rested they, and made it a day of feasting and gladness. ¹⁸But the Jews that were at Shushan assembled together on the thirteenth day thereof, and on the fourteenth thereof; and on the fifteenth day of the same they rested, and made it a day of feasting and gladness. ¹⁹Therefore the Jews of the villages, that dwelt in the unwalled towns, made the fourteenth day of the month Adar a day of gladness and feasting, and a good day, and of sending portions one to another.

²⁰And Mordecai wrote these things, and sent letters unto all the Jews that were in all the provinces of the king Ahasuerus, both nigh and far, ²¹to establish this among them, that they should keep the fourteenth day of the month Adar, and the fifteenth day of the same, yearly, ²²as the days wherein the Jews rested from their enemies, and the month which was turned unto them from sorrow to joy, and from mourning into a good day: that they should make them days of feasting and joy, and of sending portions one to another, and gifts to the poor. ²³And the

Jews undertook to do as they had begun, and as Mordecai had written unto them: ²⁴because Haman the son of Hammedatha the Agagite, the enemy of all the Jews, had devised against the Jews to destroy them, and had cast Pur, that is, the lot, to consume them, and to destroy them. ²⁵But when Esther came before the king, he commanded by letters that his wicked device, which he devised against the Jews, should return upon his own head, and that he and his sons should be hanged on the gallows. ²⁶Wherefore they called these days Purim after the name of Pur. Therefore for all the words of this letter, and of that which they had seen concerning this matter, and which had come unto them, ²⁷the Jews ordained, and took upon them, and upon their seed, and upon all such as joined themselves unto them, so as it should not fail, that they would keep these two days according to their writing, and according to their appointed time every year; ²⁸and that these days should be remembered and kept throughout every generation, every family, every province, and every city; and that these days of Purim should not fail from among the Jews, nor the memorial of them perish from their seed. ²⁹Then Esther the queen, the daughter of Abihail, and Mordecai the Jew, wrote with all authority, to confirm this second letter of Purim. ³⁰And he sent the letters unto all the Jews, to the hundred twenty and seven provinces of the kingdom of Ahasuerus, with words of peace and truth, ³¹to confirm these days of Purim in their times appointed, according as Mordecai the Jew and Esther the queen had enjoined them, and as they had decreed for themselves and for their seed, the matters of the fastings and their cry. ³²And the decree of Esther confirmed these matters of Purim; and it was written in the book.

10 And the king Ahasuerus laid a tribute upon the land, and upon the isles of the sea. ²And all the acts of his power and of his might, and the declaration of the greatness of Mordecai, whereunto the king advanced him, are they not written in the book of the chronicles of the kings of Media and Persia? ³For Mordecai the Jew was next unto king Ahasuerus, and great among the Jews, and accepted of the multitude of his brethren, seeking the wealth of his people, and speaking peace to all his seed.

THE BOOK OF
JOB

1 There was a man in the land of Uz, whose name was Job, and that man was perfect and upright, and one that feared God, and eschewed evil. ²And there were born unto him seven sons and three daughters. ³His substance also was seven thousand sheep, and three thousand camels, and five hundred yoke of oxen, and five hundred she-asses, and a very great household; so that this man was the greatest of all the men of the east.

⁴And his sons went and feasted in their houses, every one his day, and sent and called for their three sisters to eat and to drink with them. ⁵And it was so, when the days of their feasting were gone about, that Job sent and sanctified them, and rose up early in the morning, and offered burnt offerings according to the number of them all: for Job said, 'It may be that my sons have sinned, and cursed God in their hearts'. Thus did Job continually.

⁶Now there was a day when the sons of God came to present themselves before the LORD, and Satan came also among them. ⁷And the LORD said unto Satan, 'Whence comest thou?' Then Satan answered the LORD, and said, 'From going to and fro in the earth, and from walking up and down in it'. ⁸And the LORD said unto Satan, 'Hast thou considered my servant Job, that there is none like him in the earth, a perfect and an upright man, one that feareth God, and escheweth evil?' ⁹Then Satan answered the LORD, and said, 'Doth Job fear God for nought? ¹⁰Hast not thou made a hedge about him, and about his house, and about all that he hath on every side? thou hast blessed the work of his hands, and his substance is increased in the land. ¹¹But put forth thy hand now, and touch all that he hath, and he will curse thee to thy face.' ¹²And the LORD said unto Satan, 'Behold, all that he hath is in thy power, only upon himself put not forth thy hand'. So Satan went forth from the presence of the LORD.

¹³And there was a day when his sons and his daughters were eating and drinking wine in their eldest brother's house: ¹⁴and there came a messenger unto Job, and said, 'The oxen were ploughing, and the asses feeding beside them, ¹⁵and the Sabeans fell upon them, and took them away: yea, they have slain the servants with the edge of the sword, and I only am escaped alone to tell thee'. ¹⁶While he was yet speaking, there came also another, and said, 'The fire of God is fallen from heaven, and hath burnt up the sheep, and the servants, and consumed them, and I only am escaped alone to tell thee'. ¹⁷While he was yet speaking, there came also another, and said, 'The Chaldeans made out three bands, and fell upon the camels, and have carried them away, yea, and slain the servants with the edge of the sword, and I only am escaped alone to tell thee'. ¹⁸While he was yet speaking, there came also another, and said, 'Thy sons and thy daughters were eating and drinking wine in

their eldest brother's house. [19]And behold, there came a great wind from the wilderness, and smote the four corners of the house, and it fell upon the young men, and they are dead, and I only am escaped alone to tell thee.' [20]Then Job arose, and rent his mantle, and shaved his head, and fell down upon the ground, and worshipped, [21]and said,

> 'Naked came I out of my mother's womb,
> and naked shall I return thither:
> the Lord gave, and the Lord hath taken away;
> blessed be the name of the Lord'.

[22]In all this Job sinned not, nor charged God foolishly.

2 Again there was a day when the sons of God came to present themselves before the LORD, and Satan came also among them to present himself before the LORD. [2]And the LORD said unto Satan, 'From whence comest thou?' And Satan answered the LORD, and said, 'From going to and fro in the earth, and from walking up and down in it'. [3]And the LORD said unto Satan, 'Hast thou considered my servant Job, that there is none like him in the earth, a perfect and an upright man, one that feareth God, and escheweth evil? and still he holdeth fast his integrity, although thou movedst me against him, to destroy him without cause'. [4]And Satan answered the LORD, and said, 'Skin for skin, yea, all that a man hath will he give for his life. [5]But put forth thy hand now, and touch his bone and his flesh, and he will curse thee to thy face.' [6]And the LORD said unto Satan, 'Behold, he is in thy hand, but save his life'.

[7]So went Satan forth from the presence of the LORD, and smote Job with sore boils from the sole of his foot unto his crown. [8]And he took him a potsherd to scrape himself withal; and he sat down among the ashes. [9]Then said his wife unto him, 'Dost thou still retain thy integrity? Curse God, and die.' [10]But he said unto her, 'Thou speakest as one of the foolish women speaketh. What? shall we receive good at the hand of God, and shall we not receive evil?' In all this did not Job sin with his lips.

[11]Now when Job's three friends heard of all this evil that was come upon him, they came every one from his own place, Eliphaz the Temanite, and Bildad the Shuhite, and Zophar the Naamathite: for they had made an appointment together to come to mourn with him and to comfort him. [12]And when they lifted up their eyes afar off, and knew him not, they lifted up their voice, and wept; and they rent every one his mantle, and sprinkled dust upon their heads toward heaven. [13]So they sat down with him upon the ground seven days and seven nights, and none spoke a word unto him: for they saw that his grief was very great.

3 After this opened Job his mouth, and cursed his day. [2]And Job spoke, and said,

> [3] 'Let the day perish wherein I was born,
> and the night in which it was said,
> "There is a man-child conceived".
> [4] Let that day be darkness,

let not God regard it from above,
    neither let the light shine upon it.
⁵ Let darkness and the shadow of death stain it,
    let a cloud dwell upon it,
    let the blackness of the day terrify it.
⁶ As for that night, let darkness seize upon it,
    let it not be joined unto the days of the year,
    let it not come into the number of the months.
⁷ Lo, let that night be solitary,
    let no joyful voice come therein.
⁸ Let them curse it that curse the day,
    who are ready to raise up their mourning.
⁹ Let the stars of the twilight thereof be dark,
    let it look for light, but have none,
    neither let it see the dawning of the day:
¹⁰ because it shut not up the doors of my mother's womb,
    nor hid sorrow from my eyes.

¹¹ 'Why died I not from the womb?
    why did I not give up the ghost when I came out of the belly?
¹² Why did the knees prevent me?
    or why the breasts that I should suck?
¹³ For now should I have lain still and been quiet,
    I should have slept:
    then had I been at rest,
¹⁴ with kings and counsellors of the earth,
    which built desolate places for themselves,
¹⁵ or with princes that had gold,
    who filled their houses with silver:
¹⁶ or as a hidden untimely birth I had not been;
    as infants which never saw light.
¹⁷ There the wicked cease from troubling:
    and there the weary be at rest.
¹⁸ There the prisoners rest together,
    they hear not the voice of the oppressor.
¹⁹ The small and great are there,
    and the servant is free from his master.

²⁰ 'Wherefore is light given to him that is in misery,
    and life unto the bitter in soul?
²¹ which long for death, but it cometh not,
    and dig for it more than for hid treasures;
²² which rejoice exceedingly, and are glad,
    when they can find the grave?
²³ Why is light given to a man whose way is hid,
    and whom God hath hedged in?
²⁴ For my sighing cometh before I eat,
    and my roarings are poured out like the waters.

Conventional wisdom and skeptical wisdom [handwritten annotation]

²⁵ For the thing which I greatly feared is come upon me,
and that which I was afraid of is come unto me.
²⁶ I was not in safety, neither had I rest,
neither was I quiet: yet trouble came.'

4 Then Eliphaz the Temanite answered and said,

Job, you people can't take your own advice? [handwritten annotation]

² 'If we essay to commune with thee, wilt thou be grieved?
But who can withhold himself from speaking?
³ Behold, thou hast instructed many,
and thou hast strengthened the weak hands.
⁴ Thy words have upheld him that was falling,
and thou hast strengthened the feeble knees.
⁵ But now it is come upon thee, and thou faintest;
it toucheth thee, and thou art troubled.
⁶ Is not this thy fear, thy confidence,
the uprightness of thy ways and thy hope?
⁷ Remember, I pray thee, who ever perished, being innocent?
or where were the righteous cut off?
⁸ Even as I have seen, they that plough iniquity,
and sow wickedness, reap the same.
⁹ By the blast of God they perish,
and by the breath of his nostrils are they consumed.

dramatic irony / we know why Job is being punished [handwritten annotation]

¹⁰ The roaring of the lion, and the voice of the fierce lion,
and the teeth of the young lions are broken.
¹¹ The old lion perisheth for lack of prey,
and the stout lion's whelps are scattered abroad.
¹² 'Now a thing was secretly brought to me,
and my ear received a little thereof.
¹³ In thoughts from the visions of the night,
when deep sleep falleth on men,
¹⁴ fear came upon me, and trembling,
which made all my bones to shake.
¹⁵ Then a spirit passed before my face:
the hair of my flesh stood up.
¹⁶ It stood still, but I could not discern the form thereof:
an image was before my eyes, there was silence,
and I heard a voice, saying,
¹⁷ "Shall mortal man be more just than God?
shall a man be more pure than his maker?
¹⁸ Behold, he put no trust in his servants;
and his angels he charged with folly:
¹⁹ how much less on them that dwell in houses of clay,
whose foundation is in the dust,
which are crushed before the moth?
²⁰ They are destroyed from morning to evening:
they perish for ever without any regarding it.

²¹ Doth not their excellence which is in them go away?
   they die, even without wisdom."

5 'Call now, if there be any that will answer thee;
   and to which of the saints wilt thou turn?
² For wrath killeth the foolish man,
   and envy slayeth the silly one.
³ I have seen the foolish taking root:
   but suddenly I cursed his habitation.
⁴ His children are far from safety,
   and they are crushed in the gate,
   neither is there any to deliver them.
⁵ Whose harvest the hungry eateth up,
   and taketh it even out of the thorns,
   and the robber swalloweth up their substance.
⁶ Although affliction cometh not forth of the dust,
   neither doth trouble spring out of the ground:
⁷ yet man is born unto trouble,
   as the sparks fly upward.

⁸ 'I would seek unto God,
   and unto God would I commit my cause:
⁹ which doeth great things and unsearchable:
   marvellous things without number:
¹⁰ who giveth rain upon the earth,
   and sendeth waters upon the fields:
¹¹ to set up on high those that be low;
   that those which mourn may be exalted to safety.
¹² He disappointeth the devices of the crafty,
   so that their hands cannot perform their enterprise.
¹³ He taketh the wise in their own craftiness:
   and the counsel of the froward is carried headlong.
¹⁴ They meet with darkness in the daytime,
   and grope in the noonday as in the night.
¹⁵ But he saveth the poor from the sword,
   from their mouth, and from the hand of the mighty.
¹⁶ So the poor hath hope,
   and iniquity stoppeth her mouth.

¹⁷ 'Behold, happy is the man whom God correcteth:
   therefore despise not thou the chastening of the Almighty:
¹⁸ for he maketh sore, and bindeth up:
   he woundeth, and his hands make whole.
¹⁹ He shall deliver thee in six troubles,
   yea, in seven there shall no evil touch thee.
²⁰ In famine he shall redeem thee from death:
   and in war from the power of the sword.
²¹ Thou shalt be hid from the scourge of the tongue:

neither shalt thou be afraid of destruction when it cometh.
²² At destruction and famine thou shalt laugh:
   neither shalt thou be afraid of the beasts of the earth.
²³ For thou shalt be in league with the stones of the field:
   and the beasts of the field shall be at peace with thee.
²⁴ And thou shalt know that thy tabernacle shall be in peace,
   and thou shalt visit thy habitation, and shalt not sin.
²⁵ Thou shalt know also that thy seed shall be great,
   and thy offspring as the grass of the earth.
²⁶ Thou shalt come to thy grave in a full age,
   like as a shock of corn cometh in in his season.
²⁷ Lo this, we have searched it, so it is;
   hear it, and know thou it for thy good.'

6

But Job answered and said,

² 'O that my grief were thoroughly weighed,
   and my calamity laid in the balances together!
³ For now it would be heavier than the sand of the sea:
   therefore my words are swallowed up.
⁴ For the arrows of the Almighty are within me,
   the poison whereof drinketh up my spirit:
   the terrors of God do set themselves in array against me.
⁵ Doth the wild ass bray when he hath grass?
   or loweth the ox over his fodder?
⁶ Can that which is unsavoury be eaten without salt?
   or is there any taste in the white of an egg?
⁷ The things that my soul refused to touch
   are as my sorrowful meat.

⁸ 'O that I might have my request!
   and that God would grant me the thing that I long for!
⁹ Even that it would please God to destroy me,
   that he would let loose his hand, and cut me off!
¹⁰ Then should I yet have comfort,
   yea, I would harden myself in sorrow: let him not spare,
   for I have not concealed the words of the Holy One.
¹¹ What is my strength, that I should hope?
   and what is my end, that I should prolong my life?
¹² Is my strength the strength of stones?
   or is my flesh of brass?
¹³ Is not my help in me?
   and is wisdom driven quite from me?

¹⁴ 'To him that is afflicted pity should be shown from his friend;
   but he forsaketh the fear of the Almighty.
¹⁵ My brethren have dealt deceitfully as a brook,
   and as the stream of brooks they pass away,

¹⁶ which are blackish by reason of the ice,
   and wherein the snow is hid:
¹⁷ what time they wax warm, they vanish:
   when it is hot, they are consumed out of their place.
¹⁸ The paths of their way are turned aside;
   they go to nothing, and perish.
¹⁹ The troops of Tema looked,
   the companies of Sheba waited for them.
²⁰ They were confounded because they had hoped;
   they came thither, and were ashamed.
²¹ For now ye are nothing;
   ye see my casting down, and are afraid.
²² Did I say, "Bring unto me"?
   or, "Give a reward for me of your substance"?
²³ or, "Deliver me from the enemy's hand"?
   or, "Redeem me from the hand of the mighty"?
²⁴ Teach me, and I will hold my tongue:
   and cause me to understand wherein I have erred.
²⁵ How forcible are right words!
   but what doth your arguing reprove?
²⁶ Do ye imagine to reprove words,
   and the speeches of one that is desperate, which are as wind?
²⁷ Yea, ye overwhelm the fatherless,
   and you dig a pit for your friend.
²⁸ Now therefore be content, look upon me,
   for it is evident unto you if I lie.
²⁹ Return, I pray you, let it not be iniquity;
   yea, return again: my righteousness is in it.
³⁰ Is there iniquity in my tongue?
   cannot my taste discern perverse things?

7 'Is there not an appointed time to man upon earth?
   are not his days also like the days of a hireling?
² As a servant earnestly desireth the shadow,
   and as a hireling looketh for the reward of his work:
³ so am I made to possess months of vanity,
   and wearisome nights are appointed to me.
⁴ When I lie down, I say, "When shall I arise, and the night be gone?"
   and I am full of tossings to and fro unto the dawning of the day.
⁵ My flesh is clothed with worms and clods of dust,
   my skin is broken, and become loathsome.
⁶ My days are swifter than a weaver's shuttle,
   and are spent without hope.
⁷ O remember that my life is wind:
   my eye shall no more see good.
⁸ The eye of him that hath seen me shall see me no more:
   thy eyes are upon me, and I am not.
⁹ As the cloud is consumed and vanisheth away:

so he that goeth down to the grave shall come up no more.
¹⁰ He shall return no more to his house,
neither shall his place know him any more.

¹¹ 'Therefore I will not refrain my mouth,
I will speak in the anguish of my spirit,
I will complain in the bitterness of my soul.
¹² Am I a sea, or a whale, that thou settest a watch over me?
¹³ When I say, "My bed shall comfort me,
my couch shall ease my complaint":
¹⁴ then thou scarest me with dreams,
and terrifiest me through visions:
¹⁵ so that my soul chooseth strangling,
and death rather than my life.
¹⁶ I loathe it; I would not live always:
let me alone, for my days are vanity.
¹⁷ What is man, that thou shouldst magnify him?
and that thou shouldst set thy heart upon him?
¹⁸ and that thou shouldst visit him every morning,
and try him every moment?
¹⁹ How long wilt thou not depart from me,
nor let me alone till I swallow down my spittle?
²⁰ I have sinned, what shall I do unto thee,
O thou preserver of men?
why hast thou set me as a mark against thee,
so that I am a burden to myself?
²¹ And why dost thou not pardon my transgression,
and take away my iniquity?
for now shall I sleep in the dust,
and thou shalt seek me in the morning,
but I shall not be.'

8 Then answered Bildad the Shuhite, and said,

² 'How long wilt thou speak these things?
and how long shall the words of thy mouth be like a strong
wind?
³ Doth God pervert judgement?
or doth the Almighty pervert justice?
⁴ If thy children have sinned against him,
and he have cast them away for their transgression:
⁵ if thou wouldst seek unto God betimes,
and make thy supplication to the Almighty:
⁶ if thou wert pure and upright,
surely now he would awake for thee,
and make the habitation of thy righteousness prosperous.
⁷ Though thy beginning was small,
yet thy latter end should greatly increase.

⁸ 'For inquire, I pray thee, of the former age,
   and prepare thyself to the search of their fathers.
⁹ (For we are but of yesterday, and know nothing,
   because our days upon earth are a shadow.)
¹⁰ Shall not they teach thee, and tell thee,
   and utter words out of their heart?
¹¹ Can the rush grow up without mire?
   can the flag grow without water?
¹² Whilst it is yet in his greenness, and not cut down,
   it withereth before any other herb.
¹³ So are the paths of all that forget God,
   and the hypocrite's hope shall perish:
¹⁴ whose hope shall be cut off,
   and whose trust shall be a spider's web.
¹⁵ He shall lean upon his house, but it shall not stand:
   he shall hold it fast, but it shall not endure.
¹⁶ He is green before the sun,
   and his branch shooteth forth in his garden.
¹⁷ His roots are wrapped about the heap,
   and seeth the place of stones.
¹⁸ If he destroy him from his place,
   then it shall deny him,
   saying, "I have not seen thee".
¹⁹ Behold, this is the joy of his way,
   and out of the earth shall others grow.
²⁰ Behold, God will not cast away a perfect man,
   neither will he help the evil doers:
²¹ till he fill thy mouth with laughing,
   and thy lips with rejoicing.
²² They that hate thee shall be clothed with shame,
   and the dwelling place of the wicked shall come to nought.'

9 Then Job answered and said,

² 'I know it is so of a truth:
   but how should man be just with God?
³ If he will contend with him,
   he cannot answer him one of a thousand.
⁴ He is wise in heart, and mighty in strength:
   who hath hardened himself against him, and hath prospered?
⁵ which removeth the mountains, and they know not:
   which overturneth them in his anger:
⁶ which shaketh the earth out of her place,
   and the pillars thereof tremble:
⁷ which commandeth the sun, and it riseth not:
   and sealeth up the stars:
⁸ which alone spreadeth out the heavens,
   and treadeth upon the waves of the sea:

⁹ which maketh Arcturus, Orion, and Pleiades,
 and the chambers of the south:
¹⁰ which doeth great things past finding out,
 yea, and wonders without number.

¹¹ 'Lo, he goeth by me, and I see him not:
 he passeth on also, but I perceive him not.
¹² Behold, he taketh away, who can hinder him?
 who will say unto him, "What doest thou?"
¹³ If God will not withdraw his anger,
 the proud helpers do stoop under him.
¹⁴ How much less shall I answer him,
 and choose out my words to reason with him?
¹⁵ whom, though I were righteous, yet would I not answer,
 but I would make supplication to my judge.

¹⁶ 'If I had called, and he had answered me,
 yet would I not believe that he had hearkened unto my voice:
¹⁷ for he breaketh me with a tempest,
 and multiplieth my wounds without cause.
¹⁸ He will not suffer me to take my breath,
 but filleth me with bitterness.
¹⁹ If I speak of strength, lo, he is strong:
 and if of judgement, who shall set me a time to plead?
²⁰ If I justify myself, my own mouth shall condemn me:
 if I say, "I am perfect", it shall also prove me perverse.
²¹ Though I were perfect, yet would I not know my soul:
 I would despise my life.
²² This is one thing, therefore I said it;
 he destroyeth the perfect and the wicked.
²³ If the scourge slay suddenly,
 he will laugh at the trial of the innocent.
²⁴ The earth is given into the hand of the wicked:
 he covereth the faces of the judges thereof;
 if not, where, and who is he?
²⁵ Now my days are swifter than a post:
 they flee away, they see no good.
²⁶ They are passed away as the swift ships:
 as the eagle that hasteth to the prey.

²⁷ 'If I say, "I will forget my complaint,
 I will leave off my heaviness, and comfort myself":
²⁸ I am afraid of all my sorrows,
 I know that thou wilt not hold me innocent.
²⁹ If I be wicked, why then labour I in vain?
³⁰ If I wash myself with snow water,
 and make my hands never so clean:
³¹ yet shalt thou plunge me in the ditch,
 and my own clothes shall abhor me.

³² For he is not a man, as I am, that I should answer him,
and we should come together in judgement.
³³ Neither is there any daysman betwixt us,
that might lay his hand upon us both.
³⁴ Let him take his rod away from me,
and let not his fear terrify me:
³⁵ then would I speak, and not fear him;
but it is not so with me.

10

'My soul is weary of my life,
I will leave my complaint upon myself;
I will speak in the bitterness of my soul.
² I will say unto God, "Do not condemn me;
show me wherefore thou contendest with me.
³ Is it good unto thee that thou shouldst oppress,
that thou shouldst despise the work of thy hands,
and shine upon the counsel of the wicked?
⁴ Hast thou eyes of flesh?
or seest thou as man seeth?
⁵ Are thy days as the days of man?
are thy years as man's days,
⁶ that thou inquirest after my iniquity,
and searchest after my sin?
⁷ Thou knowest that I am not wicked,
and there is none that can deliver out of thy hand.

⁸ '"Thy hands have made me
and fashioned me together round about;
yet thou dost destroy me.
⁹ Remember, I beseech thee, that thou hast made me as the clay,
and wilt thou bring me into dust again?
¹⁰ Hast thou not poured me out as milk,
and curdled me like cheese?
¹¹ Thou hast clothed me with skin and flesh,
and hast fenced me with bones and sinews.
¹² Thou hast granted me life and favour,
and thy visitation hath preserved my spirit.

¹³ '"And these things hast thou hid in thy heart:
I know that this is with thee.
¹⁴ If I sin, then thou markest me,
and thou wilt not acquit me from my iniquity.
¹⁵ If I be wicked, woe unto me;
and if I be righteous, yet will I not lift up my head:
I am full of confusion,
therefore see thou my affliction; ¹⁶for it increaseth.
Thou huntest me as a fierce lion:
and again thou showest thyself marvellous upon me.

¹⁷ Thou renewest thy witnesses against me,
and increasest thy indignation upon me;
changes and war are against me.
¹⁸ '"Wherefore then hast thou brought me forth out of the womb?
O that I had given up the ghost, and no eye had seen me!
¹⁹ I should have been as though I had not been,
I should have been carried from the womb to the grave.
²⁰ Are not my days few?
cease then, and let me alone,
that I may take comfort a little,
²¹ before I go whence I shall not return,
even to the land of darkness and the shadow of death,
²² a land of darkness, as darkness itself;
and of the shadow of death, without any order,
and where the light is as darkness."'

11 Then answered Zophar the Naamathite, and said,

² 'Should not the multitude of words be answered?
and should a man full of talk be justified?
³ Should thy lies make men hold their peace?
and when thou mockest, shall no man make thee ashamed?
⁴ For thou hast said, "My doctrine is pure,
and I am clean in thy eyes".
⁵ But O that God would speak,
and open his lips against thee,
⁶ and that he would show thee the secrets of wisdom,
that they are double to that which is:
know therefore that God exacteth of thee less than thy iniquity
deserveth.

⁷ 'Canst thou by searching find out God?
canst thou find out the Almighty unto perfection?
⁸ It is as high as heaven, what canst thou do?
deeper than hell, what canst thou know?
⁹ The measure thereof is longer than the earth,
and broader than the sea.
¹⁰ If he cut off, and shut up, or gather together,
then who can hinder him?
¹¹ For he knoweth vain men:
he seeth wickedness also, will he not then consider it?
¹² For vain man would be wise,
though man be born like a wild ass's colt.

¹³ 'If thou prepare thy heart,
and stretch out thy hands toward him:
¹⁴ if iniquity be in thy hand, put it far away,

and let not wickedness dwell in thy tabernacles.
¹⁵ For then shalt thou lift up thy face without spot,
yea, thou shalt be steadfast, and shalt not fear:
¹⁶ because thou shalt forget thy misery,
and remember it as waters that pass away:
¹⁷ and thy age shall be clearer than the noonday;
thou shalt shine forth, thou shalt be as the morning.
¹⁸ And thou shalt be secure, because there is hope,
yea, thou shalt dig about thee,
and thou shalt take thy rest in safety.
¹⁹ Also thou shalt lie down, and none shall make thee afraid;
yea, many shall make suit unto thee.
²⁰ But the eyes of the wicked shall fail,
and they shall not escape,
and their hope shall be as the giving up of the ghost.'

12

And Job answered and said,

² 'No doubt but ye are the people,
and wisdom shall die with you.
³ But I have understanding as well as you,
I am not inferior to you:
yea, who knoweth not such things as these?
⁴ I am as one mocked of his neighbour,
who calleth upon God, and he answereth him:
the just upright man is laughed to scorn.
⁵ He that is ready to slip with his feet
is as a lamp despised in the thought of him that is at ease.
⁶ The tabernacles of robbers prosper,
and they that provoke God are secure,
into whose hand God bringeth abundantly.

⁷ 'But ask now the beasts, and they shall teach thee;
and the fowls of the air, and they shall tell thee.
⁸ Or speak to the earth, and it shall teach thee:
and the fishes of the sea shall declare unto thee.
⁹ Who knoweth not in all these
that the hand of the LORD hath wrought this?
¹⁰ in whose hand is the soul of every living thing,
and the breath of all mankind.

¹¹ 'Doth not the ear try words?
and the mouth taste his meat?
¹² With the ancient is wisdom,
and in length of days understanding.
¹³ With him is wisdom and strength,
he hath counsel and understanding.
¹⁴ Behold, he breaketh down, and it cannot be built again:

he shutteth up a man, and there can be no opening.
¹⁵ Behold, he withholdeth the waters, and they dry up:
also he sendeth them out, and they overturn the earth.
¹⁶ With him is strength and wisdom:
the deceived and the deceiver are his.
¹⁷ He leadeth counsellors away spoiled,
and maketh the judges fools.
¹⁸ He looseth the bond of kings,
and girdeth their loins with a girdle.
¹⁹ He leadeth princes away spoiled,
and overthroweth the mighty.
²⁰ He removeth away the speech of the trusty,
and taketh away the understanding of the aged.
²¹ He poureth contempt upon princes,
and weakeneth the strength of the mighty.
²² He discovereth deep things out of darkness,
and bringeth out to light the shadow of death.
²³ He increaseth the nations, and destroyeth them:
he enlargeth the nations, and straiteneth them again.
²⁴ He taketh away the heart of the chief of the people of the earth,
and causeth them to wander in a wilderness where there is no
way.
²⁵ They grope in the dark without light,
and he maketh them to stagger like a drunken man.

13 ¹Lo, my eye hath seen all this,
my ear hath heard and understood it.
² What ye know, the same do I know also:
I am not inferior unto you.
³ Surely I would speak to the Almighty,
and I desire to reason with God.
⁴ But ye are forgers of lies,
ye are all physicians of no value.
⁵ O that you would altogether hold your peace,
and it should be your wisdom.

⁶ 'Hear now my reasoning,
and hearken to the pleadings of my lips.
⁷ Will you speak wickedly for God?
and talk deceitfully for him?
⁸ Will ye accept his person?
will ye contend for God?
⁹ Is it good that he should search you out?
or as one man mocketh another, do ye so mock him?
¹⁰ He will surely reprove you,
if ye do secretly accept persons.
¹¹ Shall not his excellence make you afraid?
and his dread fall upon you?

¹² Your remembrances are like unto ashes,
your bodies to bodies of clay.

¹³ 'Hold your peace, let me alone that I may speak,
and let come on me what will.
¹⁴ Wherefore do I take my flesh in my teeth,
and put my life in my hand?
¹⁵ Though he slay me, yet will I trust in him:
but I will maintain my own ways before him.
¹⁶ He also shall be my salvation:
for a hypocrite shall not come before him.

¹⁷ 'Hear diligently my speech,
and my declaration with your ears.
¹⁸ Behold now, I have ordered my cause,
I know that I shall be justified.
¹⁹ Who is he that will plead with me?
for now if I hold my tongue, I shall give up the ghost.
²⁰ Only do not two things unto me:
then will I not hide myself from thee.
²¹ Withdraw thy hand far from me:
and let not thy dread make me afraid.
²² Then call thou, and I will answer:
or let me speak, and answer thou me.
²³ How many are my iniquities and sins?
make me to know my transgression and my sin.
²⁴ Wherefore hidest thou thy face,
and holdest me for thy enemy?
²⁵ Wilt thou break a leaf driven to and fro?
and wilt thou pursue the dry stubble?
²⁶ For thou writest bitter things against me,
and makest me to possess the iniquities of my youth.
²⁷ Thou puttest my feet also in the stocks,
and lookest narrowly unto all my paths;
thou settest a print upon the heels of my feet.
²⁸ And he, as a rotten thing, consumeth,
as a garment that is moth-eaten.

14 'Man that is born of a woman is of few days,
and full of trouble.
² He cometh forth like a flower, and is cut down:
he fleeth also as a shadow, and continueth not.
³ And dost thou open thy eyes upon such a one,
and bringest me into judgment with thee?
⁴ Who can bring a clean thing out of an unclean? not one.
⁵ Seeing his days are determined,
the number of his months are with thee,
thou hast appointed his bounds that he cannot pass.

⁶ Turn from him, that he may rest,
  till he shall accomplish, as a hireling, his day.
⁷ For there is hope of a tree, if it be cut down,
  that it will sprout again,
  and that the tender branch thereof will not cease.
⁸ Though the root thereof wax old in the earth,
  and the stock thereof die in the ground:
⁹ yet through the scent of water it will bud,
  and bring forth boughs like a plant.
¹⁰ But man dieth, and wasteth away:
  yea, man giveth up the ghost, and where is he?
¹¹ As the waters fail from the sea,
  and the flood decayeth and drieth up:
¹² so man lieth down, and riseth not:
  till the heavens be no more, they shall not awake,
  nor be raised out of their sleep.

¹³ 'O that thou wouldst hide me in the grave,
  that thou wouldst keep me secret, until thy wrath be past,
  that thou wouldst appoint me a set time, and remember me!
¹⁴ If a man die, shall he live again?
  All the days of my appointed time will I wait, till my change come.
¹⁵ Thou shalt call, and I will answer thee:
  thou wilt have a desire to the work of thy hands.
¹⁶ For now thou numberest my steps:
  dost thou not watch over my sin?
¹⁷ My transgression is sealed up in a bag,
  and thou sewest up my iniquity.
¹⁸ And surely the mountain falling cometh to nought,
  and the rock is removed out of his place.
¹⁹ The waters wear the stones,
  thou washest away the things which grow out of the dust of the
    earth,
  and thou destroyest the hope of man.
²⁰ Thou prevailest for ever against him, and he passeth:
  thou changest his countenance, and sendest him away.
²¹ His sons come to honour, and he knoweth it not;
  and they are brought low, but he perceiveth it not of them.
²² But his flesh upon him shall have pain,
  and his soul within him shall mourn.'

15 Then answered Eliphaz the Temanite, and said,

² 'Should a wise man utter vain knowledge,
  and fill his belly with the east wind?
³ Should he reason with unprofitable talk?
  or with speeches wherewith he can do no good?
⁴ Yea, thou castest off fear,

and restrainest prayer before God.

⁵ For thy mouth uttereth thy iniquity,
and thou choosest the tongue of the crafty.

⁶ Thy own mouth condemneth thee, and not I:
yea, thy own lips testify against thee.

⁷ 'Art thou the first man that was born?
or wast thou made before the hills?

⁸ Hast thou heard the secret of God?
and dost thou restrain wisdom to thyself?

⁹ What knowest thou that we know not?
what understandest thou, which is not in us?

¹⁰ With us are both the grey-headed and very aged men,
much elder than thy father.

¹¹ Are the consolations of God small with thee?
is there any secret thing with thee?

¹² Why doth thy heart carry thee away?
and what do thy eyes wink at,

¹³ that thou turnest thy spirit against God,
and lettest such words go out of thy mouth?

¹⁴ 'What is man, that he should be clean?
and he which is born of a woman, that he should be
righteous?

¹⁵ Behold, he putteth no trust in his saints,
yea, the heavens are not clean in his sight.

¹⁶ How much more abominable and filthy is man,
which drinketh iniquity like water?

¹⁷ 'I will show thee, hear me;
and that which I have seen I will declare;

¹⁸ which wise men have told from their fathers,
and have not hid it:

¹⁹ unto whom alone the earth was given,
and no stranger passed among them.

²⁰ The wicked man travaileth with pain all his days,
and the number of years is hidden to the oppressor.

²¹ A dreadful sound is in his ears;
in prosperity the destroyer shall come upon him.

²² He believeth not that he shall return out of darkness,
and he is waited for of the sword.

²³ He wandereth abroad for bread, saying, "Where is it?"
he knoweth that the day of darkness is ready at his hand.

²⁴ Trouble and anguish shall make him afraid;
they shall prevail against him, as a king ready to the battle.

²⁵ For he stretcheth out his hand against God,
and strengtheneth himself against the Almighty.

²⁶ He runneth upon him, even on his neck,

upon the thick bosses of his bucklers:
²⁷ because he covereth his face with his fatness,
and maketh collops of fat on his flanks.
²⁸ And he dwelleth in desolate cities,
and in houses which no man inhabiteth,
which are ready to become heaps.
²⁹ He shall not be rich, neither shall his substance continue,
neither shall he prolong the perfection thereof upon the earth.
³⁰ He shall not depart out of darkness,
the flame shall dry up his branches,
and by the breath of his mouth shall he go away.

³¹ 'Let not him that is deceived trust in vanity:
for vanity shall be his recompense.
³² It shall be accomplished before his time,
and his branch shall not be green.
³³ He shall shake off his unripe grape as the vine,
and shall cast off his flower as the olive.
³⁴ For the congregation of hypocrites shall be desolate,
and fire shall consume the tabernacles of bribery.
³⁵ They conceive mischief, and bring forth vanity,
and their belly prepareth deceit.'

16

Then Job answered and said,

² 'I have heard many such things:
miserable comforters are ye all.
³ Shall vain words have an end?
or what emboldeneth thee that thou answerest?
⁴ I also could speak as ye do:
if your soul were in my soul's stead,
I could heap up words against you,
and shake my head at you.
⁵ But I would strengthen you with my mouth,
and the moving of my lips should assuage your grief.
⁶ Though I speak, my grief is not assuaged:
and though I forbear, what am I eased?
⁷ But now he hath made me weary:
thou hast made desolate all my company.
⁸ And thou hast filled me with wrinkles,
which is a witness against me:
and my leanness rising up in me beareth witness to my face.

⁹ 'He teareth me in his wrath, who hateth me:
he gnasheth upon me with his teeth;
my enemy sharpeneth his eyes upon me.
¹⁰ They have gaped upon me with their mouth,
they have smitten me upon the cheek reproachfully,

they have gathered themselves together against me.

11 God hath delivered me to the ungodly,
and turned me over into the hands of the wicked.
12 I was at ease, but he hath broken me asunder:
he hath also taken me by my neck, and shaken me to pieces,
and set me up for his mark.
13 His archers compass me round about,
he cleaveth my reins asunder, and doth not spare;
he poureth out my gall upon the ground.
14 He breaketh me with breach upon breach,
he runneth upon me like a giant.

15 'I have sewed sackcloth upon my skin,
and defiled my horn in the dust.
16 My face is foul with weeping,
and on my eyelids is the shadow of death;
17 not for any injustice in my hands:
also my prayer is pure.

18 'O earth, cover not thou my blood,
and let my cry have no place.
19 Also now, behold, my witness is in heaven,
and my record is on high.
20 My friends scorn me:
but my eye poureth out tears unto God.
21 O that one might plead for a man with God,
as a man pleadeth for his neighbour!
22 When a few years are come,
then I shall go the way whence I shall not return.

17 'My breath is corrupt, my days are extinct,
the graves are ready for me.
2 Are there not mockers with me?
and doth not my eye continue in their provocation?
3 Lay down now, put me in a surety with thee;
who is he that will strike hands with me?
4 For thou hast hid their heart from understanding:
therefore shalt thou not exalt them.
5 He that speaketh flattery to his friends,
even the eyes of his children shall fail.
6 He hath made me also a byword of the people,
and aforetime I was as a tabret.
7 My eye also is dim by reason of sorrow,
and all my members are as a shadow.
8 Upright men shall be astonished at this,
and the innocent shall stir up himself against the hypocrite.
9 The righteous also shall hold on his way,
and he that hath clean hands shall be stronger and stronger.

¹⁰ But as for you all, do you return, and come now,
   for I cannot find one wise man among you.

¹¹ 'My days are past, my purposes are broken off,
   even the thoughts of my heart.
¹² They change the night into day:
   the light is short because of darkness.
¹³ If I wait, the grave is my house:
   I have made my bed in the darkness.
¹⁴ I have said to corruption, "Thou art my father":
   to the worm, "Thou art my mother, and my sister".
¹⁵ And where is now my hope?
   as for my hope, who shall see it?
¹⁶ They shall go down to the bars of the pit,
   when our rest together is in the dust.'

18 Then answered Bildad the Shuhite, and said,

² 'How long will it be ere you make an end of words?
   Mark, and afterward we will speak.
³ Wherefore are we counted as beasts,
   and reputed vile in your sight?
⁴ He teareth himself in his anger:
   shall the earth be forsaken for thee?
   and shall the rock be removed out of his place?
⁵ Yea, the light of the wicked shall be put out,
   and the spark of his fire shall not shine.
⁶ The light shall be dark in his tabernacle,
   and his candle shall be put out with him.
⁷ The steps of his strength shall be straitened,
   and his own counsel shall cast him down.
⁸ For he is cast into a net by his own feet,
   and he walketh upon a snare.

⁹ 'The gin shall take him by the heel,
   and the robber shall prevail against him.
¹⁰ The snare is laid for him in the ground,
   and a trap for him in the way.
¹¹ Terrors shall make him afraid on every side,
   and shall drive him to his feet.
¹² His strength shall be hunger-bitten,
   and destruction shall be ready at his side.
¹³ It shall devour the strength of his skin:
   even the firstborn of death shall devour his strength.
¹⁴ His confidence shall be rooted out of his tabernacle,
   and it shall bring him to the king of terrors.
¹⁵ It shall dwell in his tabernacle, because it is none of his:
   brimstone shall be scattered upon his habitation.

¹⁶ His roots shall be dried up beneath,
and above shall his branch be cut off.
¹⁷ His remembrance shall perish from the earth,
and he shall have no name in the street.
¹⁸ He shall be driven from light into darkness,
and chased out of the world.
¹⁹ He shall neither have son nor nephew among his people,
nor any remaining in his dwellings.

²⁰ 'They that come after him shall be astonished at his day,
as they that went before were affrighted.
²¹ Surely such are the dwellings of the wicked,
and this is the place of him that knoweth not God.'

19

Then Job answered and said,

² 'How long will ye vex my soul,
and break me in pieces with words?
³ These ten times have ye reproached me:
you are not ashamed that you make yourselves strange to
me.
⁴ And be it indeed that I have erred,
my error remaineth with myself.
⁵ If indeed ye will magnify yourselves against me,
and plead against me my reproach:
⁶ know now that God hath overthrown me,
and hath compassed me with his net.

⁷ 'Behold, I cry out of wrong, but I am not heard:
I cry aloud, but there is no judgement.
⁸ He hath fenced up my way that I cannot pass,
and he hath set darkness in my paths.
⁹ He hath stripped me of my glory,
and taken the crown from my head.
¹⁰ He hath destroyed me on every side, and I am gone:
and my hope hath he removed like a tree.
¹¹ He hath also kindled his wrath against me,
and he counteth me unto him as one of his enemies.
¹² His troops come together, and raise up their way against me,
and encamp round about my tabernacle.
¹³ He hath put my brethren far from me,
and my acquaintance are verily estranged from me.
¹⁴ My kinsfolk have failed,
and my familiar friends have forgotten me.
¹⁵ They that dwell in my house, and my maids
count me for a stranger:
I am an alien in their sight.
¹⁶ I called my servant, and he gave me no answer;

I entreated him with my mouth.

¹⁷ My breath is strange to my wife,
though I entreated for the children's sake of my own body.

¹⁸ Yea, young children despised me;
I arose, and they spoke against me.

¹⁹ All my inward friends abhorred me:
and they whom I loved are turned against me.

²⁰ My bone cleaveth to my skin and to my flesh,
and I am escaped with the skin of my teeth.

²¹ 'Have pity upon me, have pity upon me, O ye my friends,
for the hand of God hath touched me.

²² Why do ye persecute me as God,
and are not satisfied with my flesh?

²³ O that my words were now written,
O that they were printed in a book!

²⁴ that they were graven with an iron pen and lead
in the rock for ever.

²⁵ For I know that my redeemer liveth,
and that he shall stand at the latter day upon the earth:

²⁶ and though after my skin worms destroy this body,
yet in my flesh shall I see God:

²⁷ whom I shall see for myself,
and my eyes shall behold, and not another,
though my reins be consumed within me.

²⁸ 'But ye should say, "Why persecute we him?"
seeing the root of the matter is found in me.

²⁹ Be ye afraid of the sword:
for wrath bringeth the punishments of the sword,
that ye may know there is a judgement.'

20 Then answered Zophar the Naamathite, and said,

² 'Therefore do my thoughts cause me to answer,
and for this I make haste.

³ I have heard the check of my reproach,
and the spirit of my understanding causeth me to answer.

⁴ Knowest thou not this of old,
since man was placed upon earth,

⁵ that the triumphing of the wicked is short,
and the joy of the hypocrite but for a moment?

⁶ Though his excellence mount up to the heavens,
and his head reach unto the clouds:

⁷ yet he shall perish for ever like his own dung:
they which have seen him shall say, "Where is he?"

⁸ He shall fly away as a dream, and shall not be found:
yea, he shall be chased away as a vision of the night.

⁹ The eye also which saw him shall see him no more;
   neither shall his place any more behold him.
¹⁰ His children shall seek to please the poor,
   and his hands shall restore their goods.
¹¹ His bones are full of the sin of his youth,
   which shall lie down with him in the dust.
¹² Though wickedness be sweet in his mouth,
   though he hide it under his tongue;
¹³ though he spare it, and forsake it not,
   but keep it still within his mouth:
¹⁴ yet his meat in his bowels is turned,
   it is the gall of asps within him.
¹⁵ He hath swallowed down riches,
   and he shall vomit them up again:
   God shall cast them out of his belly.
¹⁶ He shall suck the poison of asps:
   the viper's tongue shall slay him.
¹⁷ He shall not see the rivers, the floods,
   the brooks of honey and butter.
¹⁸ That which he laboured for shall he restore,
   and shall not swallow it down:
   according to his substance shall the restitution be,
   and he shall not rejoice therein.
¹⁹ Because he hath oppressed and hath forsaken the poor;
   because he hath violently taken away a house which he built not:
²⁰ surely he shall not feel quietness in his belly,
   he shall not save of that which he desired.
²¹ There shall none of his meat be left;
   therefore shall no man look for his goods.
²² In the fulness of his sufficiency he shall be in straits:
   every hand of the wicked shall come upon him.
²³ When he is about to fill his belly,
   God shall cast the fury of his wrath upon him,
   and shall rain it upon him while he is eating.
²⁴ He shall flee from the iron weapon,
   and the bow of steel shall strike him through.
²⁵ It is drawn, and cometh out of the body;
   yea, the glittering sword cometh out of his gall:
   terrors are upon him.
²⁶ All darkness shall be hid in his secret places:
   a fire not blown shall consume him;
   it shall go ill with him that is left in his tabernacle.
²⁷ The heaven shall reveal his iniquity;
   and the earth shall rise up against him.
²⁸ The increase of his house shall depart,
   and his goods shall flow away in the day of his wrath.
²⁹ This is the portion of a wicked man from God,
   and the heritage appointed unto him by God.'

21 But Job answered and said,

² 'Hear diligently my speech,
    and let this be your consolations.
³ Suffer me that I may speak,
    and after that I have spoken, mock on.
⁴ As for me, is my complaint to man?
    and if it were so, why should not my spirit be troubled?
⁵ Mark me, and be astonished,
    and lay your hand upon your mouth.
⁶ Even when I remember, I am afraid,
    and trembling taketh hold on my flesh.

⁷ 'Wherefore do the wicked live, become old,
    yea, are mighty in power?
⁸ Their seed is established in their sight with them,
    and their offspring before their eyes.
⁹ Their houses are safe from fear,
    neither is the rod of God upon them.
¹⁰ Their bull gendereth, and faileth not,
    their cow calveth, and casteth not her calf.
¹¹ They send forth their little ones like a flock,
    and their children dance.
¹² They take the timbrel and harp,
    and rejoice at the sound of the organ.
¹³ They spend their days in wealth,
    and in a moment go down to the grave.
¹⁴ Therefore they say unto God, "Depart from us:
    for we desire not the knowledge of thy ways.
¹⁵ What is the Almighty, that we should serve him?
    and what profit should we have, if we pray unto him?"
¹⁶ Lo, their good is not in their hand:
    the counsel of the wicked is far from me.

¹⁷ 'How oft is the candle of the wicked put out!
    and how oft cometh their destruction upon them!
    God distributeth sorrows in his anger.
¹⁸ They are as stubble before the wind,
    and as chaff that the storm carrieth away.
¹⁹ God layeth up his iniquity for his children:
    he rewardeth him, and he shall know it.
²⁰ His eyes shall see his destruction,
    and he shall drink of the wrath of the Almighty.
²¹ For what pleasure hath he in his house after him,
    when the number of his months is cut off in the midst?

²² 'Shall any teach God knowledge?
    seeing he judgeth those that are high.

²³ One dieth in his full strength,
  being wholly at ease and quiet.
²⁴ His breasts are full of milk,
  and his bones are moistened with marrow.
²⁵ And another dieth in the bitterness of his soul,
  and never eateth with pleasure.
²⁶ They shall lie down alike in the dust,
  and the worms shall cover them.

²⁷ 'Behold, I know your thoughts,
  and the devices which ye wrongfully imagine against me.
²⁸ For ye say, "Where is the house of the prince?
  and where are the dwelling places of the wicked?"
²⁹ Have ye not asked them that go by the way?
  and do ye not know their tokens?
³⁰ that the wicked is reserved to the day of destruction;
  they shall be brought forth to the day of wrath.
³¹ Who shall declare his way to his face?
  and who shall repay him what he hath done?
³² Yet shall he be brought to the grave,
  and shall remain in the tomb.
³³ The clods of the valley shall be sweet unto him,
  and every man shall draw after him,
  as there are innumerable before him.
³⁴ How then comfort ye me in vain,
  seeing in your answers there remaineth falsehood?'

22

Then Eliphaz the Temanite answered and said,

² 'Can a man be profitable unto God,
  as he that is wise may be profitable unto himself?
³ Is it any pleasure to the Almighty, that thou art righteous?
  or is it gain to him, that thou makest thy ways perfect?
⁴ Will he reprove thee for fear of thee?
  will he enter with thee into judgement?

⁵ 'Is not thy wickedness great?
  and thy iniquities infinite?
⁶ For thou hast taken a pledge from thy brother for nought,
  and stripped the naked of their clothing.
⁷ Thou hast not given water to the weary to drink,
  and thou hast withheld bread from the hungry.
⁸ But as for the mighty man, he had the earth,
  and the honourable man dwelt in it.
⁹ Thou hast sent widows away empty,
  and the arms of the fatherless have been broken.
¹⁰ Therefore snares are round about thee,
  and sudden fear troubleth thee,

¹¹ or darkness, that thou canst not see;
and abundance of waters cover thee.

¹² 'Is not God in the height of heaven?
and behold the height of the stars, how high they are.
¹³ And thou sayest, "How doth God know?
can he judge through the dark cloud?
¹⁴ Thick clouds are a covering to him that he seeth not,
and he walketh in the circuit of heaven."

¹⁵ 'Hast thou marked the old way which wicked men have trodden?
¹⁶ which were cut down out of time,
whose foundation was overflowed with a flood:
¹⁷ which said unto God, "Depart from us":
and what can the Almighty do for them?
¹⁸ Yet he filled their houses with good things:
but the counsel of the wicked is far from me.
¹⁹ The righteous see it, and are glad,
and the innocent laugh them to scorn.
²⁰ Whereas our substance is not cut down,
but the remnant of them the fire consumeth.

²¹ 'Acquaint now thyself with him, and be at peace:
Thereby good shall come unto thee.
²² Receive, I pray thee, the law from his mouth,
and lay up his words in thy heart.
²³ If thou return to the Almighty, thou shalt be built up,
thou shalt put away iniquity far from thy tabernacles.
²⁴ Then shalt thou lay up gold as dust,
and the gold of Ophir as the stones of the brooks.
²⁵ Yea, the Almighty shall be thy defence,
and thou shalt have plenty of silver.
²⁶ For then shalt thou have thy delight in the Almighty,
and shalt lift up thy face unto God.
²⁷ Thou shalt make thy prayer unto him, and he shall hear thee,
and thou shalt pay thy vows.
²⁸ Thou shalt also decree a thing,
and it shall be established unto thee:
and the light shall shine upon thy ways.
²⁹ When men are cast down,
then thou shalt say, "There is lifting up":
and he shall save the humble person.
³⁰ He shall deliver the island of the innocent:
and it is delivered by the pureness of thy hands.'

23 Then Job answered and said,

² 'Even today is my complaint bitter:

my stroke is heavier than my groaning.
3 O that I knew where I might find him!
  that I might come even to his seat!
4 I would order my cause before him,
  and fill my mouth with arguments.
5 I would know the words which he would answer me,
  and understand what he would say unto me.
6 Will he plead against me with his great power?
  No, but he would put strength in me.
7 There the righteous might dispute with him;
  so should I be delivered for ever from my judge.
8 Behold, I go forward, but he is not there,
  and backward, but I cannot perceive him:
9 on the left hand where he doth work, but I cannot behold him:
  he hideth himself on the right hand, that I cannot see him.
10 But he knoweth the way that I take:
  when he hath tried me, I shall come forth as gold.
11 My foot hath held his steps,
  his way have I kept, and not declined.
12 Neither have I gone back from the commandment of his lips,
  I have esteemed the words of his mouth more than my necessary
    food.
13 But he is in one mind, and who can turn him?
  and what his soul desireth, even that he doeth.
14 For he performeth the thing that is appointed for me:
  and many such things are with him.
15 Therefore am I troubled at his presence:
  when I consider, I am afraid of him.
16 For God maketh my heart soft,
  and the Almighty troubleth me:
17 because I was not cut off before the darkness,
  neither hath he covered the darkness from my face.

24 'Why, seeing times are not hidden from the Almighty,
  do they that know him not see his days?
2 Some remove the landmarks;
  they violently take away flocks, and feed thereof.
3 They drive away the ass of the fatherless,
  they take the widow's ox for a pledge.
4 They turn the needy out of the way:
  the poor of the earth hide themselves together.
5 Behold, as wild asses in the desert, go they forth to their work,
    rising betimes for a prey:
  the wilderness yieldeth food for them and for their children.
6 They reap every one his corn in the field:
  and they gather the vintage of the wicked.
7 They cause the naked to lodge without clothing,
  that they have no covering in the cold.

⁸ They are wet with the showers of the mountains,
  and embrace the rock for want of a shelter.
⁹ They pluck the fatherless from the breast,
  and take a pledge of the poor.
¹⁰ They cause him to go naked without clothing,
  and they take away the sheaf from the hungry,
¹¹ Which make oil within their walls,
  and tread their wine-presses, and suffer thirst.
¹² Men groan from out of the city,
  and the soul of the wounded crieth out:
  yet God layeth not folly to them.
¹³ They are of those that rebel against the light,
  they know not the ways thereof, nor abide in the paths thereof.
¹⁴ The murderer rising with the light killeth the poor and needy,
  and in the night is as a thief.
¹⁵ The eye also of the adulterer waiteth for the twilight,
  saying, "No eye shall see me": and disguiseth his face.
¹⁶ In the dark they dig through houses,
  which they had marked for themselves in the daytime:
  they know not the light.
¹⁷ For the morning is to them even as the shadow of death:
  if one know them, they are in the terrors of the shadow of death.
¹⁸ He is swift as the waters; their portion is cursed in the earth:
  he beholdeth not the way of the vineyards.
¹⁹ Drought and heat consume the snow waters:
  so doth the grave those which have sinned.
²⁰ The womb shall forget him,
  the worm shall feed sweetly on him,
  he shall be no more remembered,
  and wickedness shall be broken as a tree.
²¹ He evil entreateth the barren that beareth not:
  and doeth not good to the widow.
²² He draweth also the mighty with his power:
  he riseth up, and no man is sure of life.
²³ Though it be given him to be in safety, whereon he resteth;
  yet his eyes are upon their ways.
²⁴ They are exalted for a little while,
  but are gone and brought low,
  they are taken out of the way as all others,
  and cut off as the tops of the ears of corn.
²⁵ And if it be not so now, who will make me a liar,
  and make my speech nothing worth?'

25

Then answered Bildad the Shuhite, and said,

² 'Dominion and fear are with him,
  he maketh peace in his high places.
³ Is there any number of his armies?

and upon whom doth not his light arise?
⁴ How then can man be justified with God?
 or how can he be clean that is born of a woman?
⁵ Behold even to the moon, and it shineth not,
 yea, the stars are not pure in his sight.
⁶ How much less man, that is a worm?
 and the son of man, which is a worm?'

26
But Job answered and said,

² 'How hast thou helped him that is without power?
 how savest thou the arm that hath no strength?
³ How hast thou counselled him that hath no wisdom?
 and how hast thou plentifully declared the thing as it is?
⁴ To whom hast thou uttered words?
 and whose spirit came from thee?

⁵ 'Dead things are formed from under the waters,
 and the inhabitants thereof.
⁶ Hell is naked before him,
 and destruction hath no covering.
⁷ He stretcheth out the north over the empty place,
 and hangeth the earth upon nothing.
⁸ He bindeth up the waters in his thick clouds;
 and the cloud is not rent under them.
⁹ He holdeth back the face of his throne,
 and spreadeth his cloud upon it.
¹⁰ He hath compassed the waters with bounds,
 until the day and night come to an end.
¹¹ The pillars of heaven tremble
 and are astonished at his reproof.
¹² He divideth the sea with his power,
 and by his understanding he smiteth through the proud.
¹³ By his spirit he hath garnished the heavens;
 his hand hath formed the crooked serpent.
¹⁴ Lo, these are parts of his ways:
 but how little a portion is heard of him?
 but the thunder of his power who can understand?'

27
Moreover Job continued his parable, and said,

² 'As God liveth, who hath taken away my judgement,
 and the Almighty, who hath vexed my soul;
³ all the while my breath is in me,
 and the Spirit of God is in my nostrils;
⁴ my lips shall not speak wickedness,
 nor my tongue utter deceit.
⁵ God forbid that I should justify you:

till I die I will not remove my integrity from me.
⁶ My righteousness I hold fast, and will not let it go:
my heart shall not reproach me so long as I live.

⁷ 'Let my enemy be as the wicked,
and he that riseth up against me as the unrighteous.
⁸ For what is the hope of the hypocrite, though he hath gained,
when God taketh away his soul?
⁹ Will God hear his cry when trouble cometh upon him?
¹⁰ Will he delight himself in the Almighty?
will he always call upon God?
¹¹ I will teach you by the hand of God:
that which is with the Almighty will I not conceal.
¹² Behold, all ye yourselves have seen it;
why then are ye thus altogether vain?
¹³ This is the portion of a wicked man with God,
and the heritage of oppressors which they shall receive of the
Almighty.
¹⁴ If his children be multiplied, it is for the sword:
and his offspring shall not be satisfied with bread.
¹⁵ Those that remain of him shall be buried in death:
and his widows shall not weep.
¹⁶ Though he heap up silver as the dust,
and prepare raiment as the clay:
¹⁷ he may prepare it, but the just shall put it on,
and the innocent shall divide the silver.
¹⁸ He buildeth his house as a moth,
and as a booth that the keeper maketh.
¹⁹ The rich man shall lie down, but he shall not be gathered:
he openeth his eyes, and he is not:
²⁰ terrors take hold on him as waters,
a tempest stealeth him away in the night.
²¹ The east wind carrieth him away, and he departeth:
and as a storm hurleth him out of his place.
²² For God shall cast upon him, and not spare:
he would fain flee out of his hand.
²³ Men shall clap their hands at him,
and shall hiss him out of his place.

28 'Surely there is a vein for the silver,
and a place for gold where they fine it.
² Iron is taken out of the earth,
and brass is molten out of the stone.
³ He setteth an end to darkness,
and searcheth out all perfection:
the stones of darkness, and the shadow of death.
⁴ The flood breaketh out from the inhabitant;
even the waters forgotten of the foot:

they are dried up, they are gone away from men.

⁵ As for the earth, out of it cometh bread:
   and under it, is turned up as it were fire.
⁶ The stones of it are the place of sapphires:
   and it hath dust of gold.
⁷ There is a path which no fowl knoweth,
   and which the vulture's eye hath not seen:
⁸ the lion's whelps have not trodden it,
   nor the fierce lion passed by it.
⁹ He putteth forth his hand upon the rock;
   he overturneth the mountains by the roots.
¹⁰ He cutteth out rivers among the rocks,
   and his eye seeth every precious thing.
¹¹ He bindeth the floods from overflowing,
   and the thing that is hid bringeth he forth to light.

¹² 'But where shall wisdom be found?
   and where is the place of understanding?
¹³ Man knoweth not the price thereof;
   neither is it found in the land of the living.
¹⁴ The depth saith, "It is not in me":
   and the sea saith, "It is not with me".
¹⁵ It cannot be gotten for gold,
   neither shall silver be weighed for the price thereof.
¹⁶ It cannot be valued with the gold of Ophir,
   with the precious onyx, or the sapphire.
¹⁷ The gold and the crystal cannot equal it:
   and the exchange of it shall not be for jewels of fine gold.
¹⁸ No mention shall be made of coral, or of pearls:
   for the price of wisdom is above rubies.
¹⁹ The topaz of Ethiopia shall not equal it,
   neither shall it be valued with pure gold.
²⁰ Whence then cometh wisdom?
   and where is the place of understanding?
²¹ Seeing it is hid from the eyes of all living,
   and kept close from the fowls of the air.
²² Destruction and death say,
   "We have heard the fame thereof with our ears".
²³ God understandeth the way thereof,
   and he knoweth the place thereof.
²⁴ For he looketh to the ends of the earth,
   and seeth under the whole heaven:
²⁵ to make the weight for the winds,
   and he weigheth the waters by measure.
²⁶ When he made a decree for the rain,
   and a way for the lightning of the thunder:
²⁷ then did he see it, and declare it,
   he prepared it, yea, and searched it out.

²⁸ And unto man he said,
"Behold, the fear of the Lord, that is wisdom,
and to depart from evil is understanding".'

29

Moreover Job continued his parable, and said,

² 'O that I were as in months past,
as in the days when God preserved me:
³ when his candle shone upon my head,
and when by his light I walked through darkness:
⁴ as I was in the days of my youth,
when the secret of God was upon my tabernacle:
⁵ when the Almighty was yet with me,
when my children were about me:
⁶ when I washed my steps with butter,
and the rock poured me out rivers of oil:
⁷ when I went out to the gate through the city,
when I prepared my seat in the street.
⁸ The young men saw me, and hid themselves:
and the aged arose, and stood up.
⁹ The princes refrained talking,
and laid their hand on their mouth.
¹⁰ The nobles held their peace,
and their tongue cleaved to the roof of their mouth.
¹¹ When the ear heard me, then it blessed me,
and when the eye saw me, it gave witness to me:
¹² because I delivered the poor that cried, and the fatherless,
and him that had none to help him.
¹³ The blessing of him that was ready to perish came upon me:
and I caused the widow's heart to sing for joy.
¹⁴ I put on righteousness, and it clothed me:
my judgement was as a robe and a diadem.
¹⁵ I was eyes to the blind,
and feet was I to the lame.
¹⁶ I was a father to the poor:
and the cause which I knew not I searched out.
¹⁷ And I broke the jaws of the wicked,
and plucked the spoil out of his teeth.
¹⁸ Then I said, "I shall die in my nest,
and I shall multiply my days as the sand".
¹⁹ My root was spread out by the waters,
and the dew lay all night upon my branch.
²⁰ My glory was fresh in me,
and my bow was renewed in my hand.
²¹ Unto me men gave ear, and waited,
and kept silence at my counsel.
²² After my words they spoke not again,
and my speech dropped upon them,

²³ and they waited for me as for the rain,
   and they opened their mouth wide as for the latter rain.
²⁴ If I laughed on them, they believed it not,
   and the light of my countenance they cast not down.
²⁵ I chose out their way, and sat chief,
   and dwelt as a king in the army,
   as one that comforteth the mourners.

30 ¹But now they that are younger than I have me in derision,
   whose fathers I would have disdained to have set with the dogs of
   my flock.
² Yea, whereto might the strength of their hands profit me,
   in whom old age was perished?
³ For want and famine they were solitary:
   flying into the wilderness in former time desolate and waste:
⁴ who cut up mallows by the bushes,
   and juniper roots for their meat.
⁵ They were driven forth from among men
   (they cried after them as after a thief),
⁶ to dwell in the clefts of the valleys,
   in caves of the earth, and in the rocks.
⁷ Among the bushes they brayed:
   under the nettles they were gathered together.
⁸ They were children of fools, yea, children of base men:
   they were viler than the earth.

⁹ 'And now am I their song,
   yea, I am their byword.
¹⁰ They abhor me, they flee far from me,
   and spare not to spit in my face.
¹¹ Because he hath loosed my cord, and afflicted me,
   they have also let loose the bridle before me.
¹² Upon my right hand rise the youth,
   they push away my feet,
   and they raise up against me the ways of their destruction.
¹³ They mar my path,
   they set forward my calamity,
   they have no helper.
¹⁴ They came upon me as a wide breaking in of waters:
   in the desolation they rolled themselves upon me.

¹⁵ 'Terrors are turned upon me:
   they pursue my soul as the wind:
   and my welfare passeth away as a cloud.
¹⁶ And now my soul is poured out upon me:
   the days of affliction have taken hold upon me.
¹⁷ My bones are pierced in me in the night season:
   and my sinews take no rest.

¹⁸ By the great force of my disease is my garment changed:
  it bindeth me about as the collar of my coat.
¹⁹ He hath cast me into the mire,
  and I am become like dust and ashes.

²⁰ 'I cry unto thee, and thou dost not hear me:
  I stand up, and thou regardest me not.
²¹ Thou art become cruel to me:
  with thy strong hand thou opposest thyself against me.
²² Thou liftest me up to the wind:
  thou causest me to ride upon it, and dissolvest my substance.
²³ For I know that thou wilt bring me to death,
  and to the house appointed for all living.
²⁴ Howbeit he will not stretch out his hand to the grave,
  though they cry in his destruction.

²⁵ 'Did not I weep for him that was in trouble?
  was not my soul grieved for the poor?
²⁶ When I looked for good, then evil came unto me:
  and when I waited for light, there came darkness.
²⁷ My bowels boiled, and rested not:
  the days of affliction prevented me.
²⁸ I went mourning without the sun:
  I stood up, and I cried in the congregation.
²⁹ I am a brother to dragons,
  and a companion to owls.
³⁰ My skin is black upon me,
  and my bones are burnt with heat.
³¹ My harp also is turned to mourning,
  and my organ into the voice of them that weep.

31 'I made a covenant with my eyes;
  why then should I think upon a maid?
² For what portion of God is there from above?
  and what inheritance of the Almighty from on high?
³ Is not destruction to the wicked?
  and a strange punishment to the workers of iniquity?
⁴ Doth not he see my ways,
  and count all my steps?
⁵ If I have walked with vanity,
  or if my foot hath hasted to deceit;
⁶ let me be weighed in an even balance,
  that God may know my integrity.
⁷ If my step hath turned out of the way,
  and my heart walked after my eyes,
  and if any blot hath cleaved to my hands:
⁸ then let me sow, and let another eat,
  yea, let my offspring be rooted out.

⁹ If my heart have been deceived by a woman,
  or if I have laid wait at my neighbour's door:
¹⁰ then let my wife grind unto another,
  and let others bow down upon her.
¹¹ For this is a heinous crime,
  yea, it is an iniquity to be punished by the judges.
¹² For it is a fire that consumeth to destruction,
  and would root out all my increase.

¹³ 'If I did despise the cause of my manservant or of my
    maidservant,
  when they contended with me:
¹⁴ what then shall I do when God riseth up?
  and when he visiteth, what shall I answer him?
¹⁵ Did not he that made me in the womb make him?
  and did not one fashion us in the womb?

¹⁶ 'If I have withheld the poor from their desire,
  or have caused the eyes of the widow to fail;
¹⁷ or have eaten my morsel myself alone,
  and the fatherless hath not eaten thereof
¹⁸ (for from my youth he was brought up with me, as with a father,
  and I have guided her from my mother's womb);
¹⁹ if I have seen any perish for want of clothing,
  or any poor without covering;
²⁰ if his loins have not blessed me,
  and if he were not warmed with the fleece of my sheep;
²¹ if I have lifted up my hand against the fatherless,
  when I saw my help in the gate:
²² then let my arm fall from my shoulder-blade,
  and my arm be broken from the bone.
²³ For destruction from God was a terror to me,
  and by reason of his highness I could not endure.

²⁴ 'If I have made gold my hope,
  or have said to the fine gold, "Thou art my confidence";
²⁵ if I rejoiced because my wealth was great,
  and because my hand had gotten much;
²⁶ if I beheld the sun when it shone,
  or the moon walking in brightness;
²⁷ and my heart hath been secretly enticed,
  or my mouth hath kissed my hand:
²⁸ this also were an iniquity to be punished by the judge:
  for I should have denied the God that is above.

²⁹ 'If I rejoiced at the destruction of him that hated me,
  or lifted up myself when evil found him:
³⁰ neither have I suffered my mouth to sin

by wishing a curse to his soul.
³¹ If the men of my tabernacle said not,
"O that we had of his flesh! we cannot be satisfied".
³² The stranger did not lodge in the street:
but I opened my doors to the traveller.
³³ If I covered my transgressions as Adam,
by hiding my iniquity in my bosom:
³⁴ did I fear a great multitude,
or did the contempt of families terrify me,
that I kept silence, and went not out of the door?

³⁵ 'O that one would hear me!
behold, my desire is, that the Almighty would answer me,
and that my adversary had written a book.
³⁶ Surely I would take it upon my shoulder,
and bind it as a crown to me.
³⁷ I would declare unto him the number of my steps,
as a prince would I go near unto him.
³⁸ If my land cry against me,
or that the furrows likewise thereof complain;
³⁹ if I have eaten the fruits thereof without money,
or have caused the owners thereof to lose their life:
⁴⁰ Let thistles grow instead of wheat,
and cockle instead of barley.'

The words of Job are ended.

32 So these three men ceased to answer Job, because he was right-eous in his own eyes. ²Then was kindled the wrath of Elihu the son of Barachel the Buzite, of the kindred of Ram: against Job was his wrath kindled, because he justified himself rather than God. ³Also against his three friends was his wrath kindled, because they had found no answer, and yet had condemned Job. ⁴Now Elihu had waited till Job had spoken, because they were elder than he. ⁵When Elihu saw that there was no answer in the mouth of these three men, then his wrath was kindled. ⁶And Elihu the son of Barachel the Buzite answered and said,

'I am young, and ye are very old,
wherefore I was afraid, and durst not show you my opinion.
⁷ I said, "Days should speak,
and multitude of years should teach wisdom".
⁸ But there is a spirit in man:
and the inspiration of the Almighty giveth them
understanding.
⁹ Great men are not always wise:
neither do the aged understand judgement.
¹⁰ Therefore I said, "Hearken to me:
I also will show my opinion".
¹¹ Behold, I waited for your words;

I gave ear to your reasons, whilst you searched out what to say.

¹² Yea, I attended unto you,
and behold, there was none of you that convinced Job,
or that answered his words:

¹³ lest ye should say, "We have found out wisdom:
God thrusteth him down, not man".

¹⁴ Now he hath not directed his words against me:
neither will I answer him with your speeches.

¹⁵ They were amazed, they answered no more,
they left off speaking.

¹⁶ When I had waited (for they spoke not,
but stood still, and answered no more),

¹⁷ I said, "I will answer also my part,
I also will show my opinion".

¹⁸ For I am full of matter,
the spirit within me constraineth me.

¹⁹ Behold, my belly is as wine which hath no vent,
it is ready to burst like new bottles.

²⁰ I will speak, that I may be refreshed:
I will open my lips and answer.

²¹ Let me not, I pray you, accept any man's person,
neither let me give flattering titles unto man.

²² For I know not to give flattering titles:
in so doing my maker would soon take me away.

33

¹ 'Wherefore, Job, I pray thee, hear my speeches,
and hearken to all my words.

² Behold, now I have opened my mouth,
my tongue hath spoken in my mouth.

³ My words shall be of the uprightness of my heart:
and my lips shall utter knowledge clearly.

⁴ The Spirit of God hath made me,
and the breath of the Almighty hath given me life.

⁵ If thou canst answer me,
set thy words in order before me, stand up.

⁶ Behold, I am according to thy wish in God's stead:
I also am formed out of the clay.

⁷ Behold, my terror shall not make thee afraid,
neither shall my hand be heavy upon thee.

⁸ 'Surely thou hast spoken in my hearing,
and I have heard the voice of thy words, saying,

⁹ "I am clean without transgression, I am innocent;
neither is there iniquity in me.

¹⁰ Behold, he findeth occasions against me,
he counteth me for his enemy,

¹¹ he putteth my feet in the stocks,
he marketh all my paths."

¹² 'Behold, in this thou art not just:
   I will answer thee, that God is greater than man.
¹³ Why dost thou strive against him?
   for he giveth not account of any of his matters.
¹⁴ For God speaketh once, yea twice,
   yet man perceiveth it not.
¹⁵ In a dream, in a vision of the night,
   when deep sleep falleth upon men, in slumberings upon the bed:
¹⁶ then he openeth the ears of men,
   and sealeth their instruction,
¹⁷ that he may withdraw man from his purpose,
   and hide pride from man.
¹⁸ He keepeth back his soul from the pit,
   and his life from perishing by the sword.
¹⁹ He is chastened also with pain upon his bed,
   and the multitude of his bones with strong pain:
²⁰ so that his life abhorreth bread,
   and his soul dainty meat.
²¹ His flesh is consumed away, that it cannot be seen;
   and his bones that were not seen stick out.
²² His soul draweth near unto the grave,
   and his life to the destroyers.

²³ 'If there be a messenger with him, an interpreter,
   one among a thousand, to show unto man his uprightness:
²⁴ then he is gracious unto him, and saith,
   "Deliver him from going down to the pit: I have found a ransom".
²⁵ His flesh shall be fresher than a child's:
   he shall return to the days of his youth.
²⁶ He shall pray unto God,
   and he will be favourable unto him,
   and he shall see his face with joy:
   for he will render unto man his righteousness.
²⁷ He looketh upon men, and if any say, "I have sinned,
   and perverted that which was right, and it profited me not":
²⁸ he will deliver his soul from going into the pit,
   and his life shall see the light.
²⁹ Lo, all these things worketh God oftentimes with man,
³⁰ to bring back his soul from the pit,
   to be enlightened with the light of the living.

³¹ 'Mark well, O Job, hearken unto me:
   hold thy peace, and I will speak.
³² If thou hast anything to say, answer me:
   speak, for I desire to justify thee.
³³ If not, hearken unto me:
   hold thy peace, and I shall teach thee wisdom.'

34

Furthermore Elihu answered and said,

² 'Hear my words, O ye wise men,
   and give ear unto me, ye that have knowledge.
³ For the ear trieth words, as the mouth tasteth meat.
⁴ Let us choose to us judgement:
   let us know among ourselves what is good.
⁵ For Job hath said, "I am righteous:
   and God hath taken away my judgement.
⁶ Should I lie against my right?
   my wound is incurable without transgression."
⁷ What man is like Job,
   who drinketh up scorning like water?
⁸ which goeth in company with the workers of iniquity,
   and walketh with wicked men.
⁹ For he hath said, "It profiteth a man nothing
   that he should delight himself with God".
¹⁰ Therefore hearken unto me, ye men of understanding:
   far be it from God, that he should do wickedness,
   and from the Almighty, that he should commit iniquity.
¹¹ For the work of a man shall he render unto him,
   and cause every man to find according to his ways.
¹² Yea, surely God will not do wickedly,
   neither will the Almighty pervert judgement.
¹³ Who hath given him a charge over the earth?
   or who hath disposed the whole world?
¹⁴ If he set his heart upon man,
   if he gather unto himself his spirit and his breath;
¹⁵ all flesh shall perish together,
   and man shall turn again unto dust.
¹⁶ If now thou hast understanding, hear this:
   hearken to the voice of my words.
¹⁷ Shall even he that hateth right govern?
   and wilt thou condemn him that is most just?
¹⁸ Is it fit to say to a king, "Thou art wicked"?
   and to princes, "Ye are ungodly"?
¹⁹ How much less to him that accepteth not the persons of princes,
   nor regardeth the rich more than the poor?
   for they all are the work of his hands.
²⁰ In a moment shall they die,
   and the people shall be troubled at midnight, and pass away:
   and the mighty shall be taken away without hand.
²¹ For his eyes are upon the ways of man,
   and he seeth all his goings.
²² There is no darkness, nor shadow of death,
   where the workers of iniquity may hide themselves.
²³ For he will not lay upon man more than right;
   that he should enter into judgement with God.

²⁴ He shall break in pieces mighty men without number,
and set others in their stead.
²⁵ Therefore he knoweth their works,
and he overturneth them in the night, so that they are
destroyed.
²⁶ He striketh them as wicked men in the open sight of others:
²⁷ because they turned back from him,
and would not consider any of his ways:
²⁸ so that they cause the cry of the poor to come unto him,
and he heareth the cry of the afflicted.
²⁹ When he giveth quietness, who then can make trouble?
and when he hideth his face, who then can behold him?
whether it be done against a nation, or against a man only:
³⁰ that the hypocrite reign not, lest the people be ensnared.
³¹ Surely it is meet to be said unto God,
"I have borne chastisement, I will not offend any more.
³² That which I see not teach thou me:
if I have done iniquity, I will do no more."
³³ Should it be according to thy mind?
he will recompense it, whether thou refuse, or whether thou
choose, and not I:
therefore speak what thou knowest.
³⁴ Let men of understanding tell me,
and let a wise man hearken unto me.
³⁵ Job hath spoken without knowledge,
and his words were without wisdom.
³⁶ My desire is that Job may be tried unto the end
because of his answers for wicked men.
³⁷ For he addeth rebellion unto his sin,
he clappeth his hands amongst us,
and multiplieth his words against God.'

35

Elihu spoke moreover, and said,

² 'Thinkest thou this to be right, that thou saidst,
"My righteousness is more than God's"?
³ For thou saidst, "What advantage will it be unto thee?"
and, "What profit shall I have, if I be cleansed from my sin?"
⁴ I will answer thee, and thy companions with thee.
⁵ Look unto the heavens, and see,
and behold the clouds which are higher than thou.
⁶ If thou sinnest, what doest thou against him?
or if thy transgressions be multiplied, what doest thou unto him?
⁷ If thou be righteous, what givest thou him?
or what receiveth he of thy hand?
⁸ Thy wickedness may hurt a man as thou art,
and thy righteousness may profit the son of man.

9 'By reason of the multitude of oppressions they make the
oppressed to cry:
they cry out by reason of the arm of the mighty.
10 But none saith, "Where is God my maker,
who giveth songs in the night;
11 who teacheth us more than the beasts of the earth,
and maketh us wiser than the fowls of heaven?"
12 There they cry, but none giveth answer,
because of the pride of evil men.
13 Surely God will not hear vanity,
neither will the Almighty regard it.

14 'Although thou sayest thou shalt not see him,
yet judgement is before him; therefore trust thou in him.
15 But now, because it is not so, he hath visited in his anger;
yet he knoweth it not in great extremity:
16 Therefore doth Job open his mouth in vain:
he multiplieth words without knowledge.'

36 Elihu also proceeded, and said,

2 'Suffer me a little, and I will show thee that I have yet to speak
on God's behalf.
3 I will fetch my knowledge from afar,
and will ascribe righteousness to my Maker.
4 For truly my words shall not be false:
he that is perfect in knowledge is with thee.

5 'Behold, God is mighty, and despiseth not any:
he is mighty in strength and wisdom.
6 He preserveth not the life of the wicked:
but giveth right to the poor.
7 He withdraweth not his eyes from the righteous:
but with kings are they on the throne;
yea, he doth establish them for ever, and they are exalted.
8 And if they be bound in fetters,
and be held in cords of affliction:
9 then he showeth them their work,
and their transgressions that they have exceeded.
10 He openeth also their ear to discipline,
and commandeth that they return from iniquity.
11 If they obey and serve him,
they shall spend their days in prosperity, and their years in
pleasures.
12 But if they obey not,
they shall perish by the sword,
and they shall die without knowledge.
13 But the hypocrites in heart heap up wrath:

they cry not when he bindeth them.

¹⁴ They die in youth,
and their life is among the unclean.

¹⁵ He delivereth the poor in his affliction,
and openeth their ears in oppression.

¹⁶ 'Even so would he have removed thee out of the strait
into a broad place, where there is no straitness,
and that which should be set on thy table should be full of
fatness.

¹⁷ But thou hast fulfilled the judgement of the wicked:
judgement and justice take hold on thee.

¹⁸ Because there is wrath, beware lest he take thee away with his
stroke:
then a great ransom cannot deliver thee.

¹⁹ Will he esteem thy riches?
no, not gold, nor all the forces of strength.

²⁰ Desire not the night,
when people are cut off in their place.

²¹ Take heed, regard not iniquity:
for this hast thou chosen rather than affliction.

²² 'Behold, God exalteth by his power:
who teacheth like him?

²³ Who hath enjoined him his way?
or who can say, "Thou hast wrought iniquity"?

²⁴ Remember that thou magnify his work, which men behold.

²⁵ Every man may see it, man may behold it afar off.

²⁶ Behold, God is great, and we know him not,
neither can the number of his years be searched out.

²⁷ For he maketh small the drops of water:
they pour down rain according to the vapour thereof:

²⁸ which the clouds do drop and distil upon man abundantly.

²⁹ Also can any understand the spreadings of the clouds,
or the noise of his tabernacle?

³⁰ Behold, he spreadeth his light upon it,
and covereth the bottom of the sea.

³¹ For by them judgeth he the people;
he giveth meat in abundance.

³² With clouds he covereth the light,
and commandeth it not to shine by the cloud that cometh
betwixt.

³³ The noise thereof showeth concerning it,
the cattle also concerning the vapour.

37

'At this also my heart trembleth,
and is moved out of his place.

² Hear attentively the noise of his voice,

and the sound that goeth out of his mouth.
3 He directeth it under the whole heaven,
  and his lightning unto the ends of the earth.
4 After it a voice roareth:
  he thundereth with the voice of his excellence,
  and he will not stay them when his voice is heard.
5 God thundereth marvellously with his voice:
  great things doeth he, which we cannot comprehend.
6 For he saith to the snow, "Be thou on the earth";
  likewise to the small rain, and to the great rain of his
    strength.
7 He sealeth up the hand of every man;
  that all men may know his work.
8 Then the beasts go into dens,
  and remain in their places.
9 Out of the south cometh the whirlwind:
  and cold out of the north.
10 By the breath of God frost is given:
  and the breadth of the waters is straitened.
11 Also by watering he wearieth the thick cloud:
  he scattereth his bright cloud.
12 And it is turned round about by his counsels:
  that they may do whatsoever he commandeth them
  upon the face of the world in the earth.
13 He causeth it to come, whether for correction,
  or for his land, or for mercy.

14 'Hearken unto this, O Job:
  stand still, and consider the wondrous works of God.
15 Dost thou know when God disposed them,
  and caused the light of his cloud to shine?
16 Dost thou know the balancings of the clouds,
  the wondrous works of him which is perfect in knowledge?
17 how thy garments are warm,
  when he quieteth the earth by the south wind?
18 Hast thou with him spread out the sky, which is strong,
  and as a molten looking-glass?

19 'Teach us what we shall say unto him;
  for we cannot order our speech by reason of darkness.
20 Shall it be told him that I speak?
  if a man speak, surely he shall be swallowed up.
21 And now men see not the bright light which is in the
    clouds:
  but the wind passeth, and cleanseth them.
22 Fair weather cometh out of the north:
  with God is terrible majesty.
23 Touching the Almighty, we cannot find him out:

he is excellent in power, and in judgement, and in plenty of
justice:
he will not afflict.
²⁴ Men do therefore fear him:
he respecteth not any that are wise of heart.'

38 Then the LORD answered Job out of the whirlwind, and said,

² 'Who is this that darkeneth counsel
by words without knowledge?
³ Gird up now thy loins like a man;
for I will demand of thee, and answer thou me.
⁴ 'Where wast thou when I laid the foundations of the earth?
declare, if thou hast understanding.
⁵ Who hath laid the measures thereof, if thou knowest?
or who hath stretched the line upon it?
⁶ Whereupon are the foundations thereof fastened?
or who laid the corner-stone thereof,
⁷ when the morning stars sang together,
and all the sons of God shouted for joy?
⁸ Or who shut up the sea with doors, when it broke forth,
as if it had issued out of the womb?
⁹ when I made the cloud the garment thereof,
and thick darkness a swaddling-band for it,
¹⁰ and broke up for it my decreed place,
and set bars and doors,
¹¹ and said, "Hitherto shalt thou come, but no farther:
and here shall thy proud waves be stayed?"

¹² 'Hast thou commanded the morning since thy days,
and caused the day-spring to know his place,
¹³ that it might take hold of the ends of the earth,
that the wicked might be shaken out of it?
¹⁴ It is turned as clay to the seal, and they stand as a garment.
¹⁵ And from the wicked their light is withheld,
and the high arm shall be broken.
¹⁶ Hast thou entered into the springs of the sea?
or hast thou walked in the search of the depth?
¹⁷ Have the gates of death been opened unto thee?
or hast thou seen the doors of the shadow of death?
¹⁸ Hast thou perceived the breadth of the earth?
Declare if thou knowest it all.

¹⁹ 'Where is the way where light dwelleth?
and as for darkness, where is the place thereof,
²⁰ that thou shouldst take it to the bound thereof,
and that thou shouldst know the paths to the house thereof?

²¹ Knowest thou it, because thou wast then born?
  or because the number of thy days is great?
²² Hast thou entered into the treasures of the snow?
  or hast thou seen the treasures of the hail,
²³ which I have reserved against the time of trouble,
  against the day of battle and war?
²⁴ By what way is the light parted,
  which scattereth the east wind upon the earth?
²⁵ Who hath divided a watercourse for the overflowing of waters,
  or a way for the lightning of thunder,
²⁶ to cause it to rain on the earth, where no man is:
  on the wilderness, wherein there is no man,
²⁷ to satisfy the desolate and waste ground,
  and to cause the bud of the tender herb to spring forth?
²⁸ Hath the rain a father?
  or who hath begotten the drops of dew?
²⁹ Out of whose womb came the ice?
  and the hoary frost of heaven, who hath gendered it?
³⁰ The waters are hid as with a stone,
  and the face of the deep is frozen.

³¹ 'Canst thou bind the sweet influences of Pleiades,
  or loose the bands of Orion?
³² Canst thou bring forth Mazzaroth in his season,
  or canst thou guide Arcturus with his sons?
³³ Knowest thou the ordinances of heaven?
  canst thou set the dominion thereof in the earth?
³⁴ Canst thou lift up thy voice to the clouds,
  that abundance of waters may cover thee?
³⁵ Canst thou send lightnings, that they may go,
  and say unto thee, "Here we are"?
³⁶ Who hath put wisdom in the inward parts?
  or who hath given understanding to the heart?
³⁷ Who can number the clouds in wisdom?
  or who can stay the bottles of heaven,
³⁸ when the dust groweth into hardness,
  and the clods cleave fast together?
³⁹ Wilt thou hunt the prey for the lion?
  or fill the appetite of the young lions,
⁴⁰ when they couch in their dens,
  and abide in the covert to lie in wait?
⁴¹ Who provideth for the raven his food?
  when his young ones cry unto God, they wander for lack of
    meat.

39 'Knowest thou the time when the wild goats of the rock bring
    forth?
  or canst thou mark when the hinds do calve?

² Canst thou number the months that they fulfil?
  or knowest thou the time when they bring forth?
³ They bow themselves, they bring forth their young ones,
  they cast out their sorrows.
⁴ Their young ones are in good liking, they grow up with corn:
  they go forth, and return not unto them.

⁵ 'Who hath sent out the wild ass free?
  or who hath loosed the bands of the wild ass,
⁶ whose house I have made the wilderness,
  and the barren land his dwellings?
⁷ He scorneth the multitude of the city,
  neither regardeth he the crying of the driver.
⁸ The range of the mountains is his pasture,
  and he searcheth after every green thing.

⁹ 'Will the unicorn be willing to serve thee,
  or abide by thy crib?
¹⁰ Canst thou bind the unicorn with his band in the furrow?
  or will he harrow the valleys after thee?
¹¹ Wilt thou trust him, because his strength is great?
  or wilt thou leave thy labour to him?
¹² Wilt thou believe him that he will bring home thy seed,
  and gather it into thy barn?

¹³ 'Gavest thou the goodly wings unto the peacocks?
  or wings and feathers unto the ostrich?
¹⁴ which leaveth her eggs in the earth,
  and warmeth them in dust,
¹⁵ and forgetteth that the foot may crush them,
  or that the wild beast may break them.
¹⁶ She is hardened against her young ones, as though they were not
    hers:
  her labour is in vain without fear.
¹⁷ Because God hath deprived her of wisdom,
  neither hath he imparted to her understanding.
¹⁸ What time she lifteth up herself on high,
  she scorneth the horse and his rider.

¹⁹ 'Hast thou given the horse strength?
  hast thou clothed his neck with thunder?
²⁰ Canst thou make him afraid as a grasshopper?
  the glory of his nostrils is terrible.
²¹ He paweth in the valley, and rejoiceth in his strength:
  he goeth on to meet the armed men.
²² He mocketh at fear, and is not affrighted:
  neither turneth he back from the sword.
²³ The quiver rattleth against him,

the glittering spear and the shield.

²⁴ He swalloweth the ground with fierceness and rage:
and neither believeth he that it is the sound of the trumpet.

²⁵ He saith among the trumpets, "Ha, ha":
and he smelleth the battle afar off,
the thunder of the captains, and the shouting.

²⁶ 'Doth the hawk fly by thy wisdom,
and stretch her wings toward the south?

²⁷ Doth the eagle mount up at thy command,
and make her nest on high?

²⁸ She dwelleth and abideth on the rock,
upon the crag of the rock, and the strong place.

²⁹ From thence she seeketh the prey,
and her eyes behold afar off.

³⁰ Her young ones also suck up blood:
and where the slain are, there is she.'

40

Moreover the LORD answered Job, and said,

² 'Shall he that contendeth with the Almighty instruct him?
he that reproveth God, let him answer it'.

³Then Job answered the LORD, and said,

⁴ 'Behold, I am vile, what shall I answer thee?
I will lay my hand upon my mouth.

⁵ Once have I spoken, but I will not answer:
yea, twice, but I will proceed no further.'

⁶Then answered the LORD unto Job out of the whirlwind, and said,

⁷ 'Gird up thy loins now like a man:
I will demand of thee, and declare thou unto me.

⁸ Wilt thou also disannul my judgement?
wilt thou condemn me, that thou mayest be righteous?

⁹ Hast thou an arm like God?
or canst thou thunder with a voice like him?

¹⁰ Deck thyself now with majesty and excellence,
and array thyself with glory and beauty.

¹¹ Cast abroad the rage of thy wrath:
and behold every one that is proud, and abase him.

¹² Look on every one that is proud, and bring him low:
and tread down the wicked in their place.

¹³ Hide them in the dust together,
and bind their faces in secret.

¹⁴ Then will I also confess unto thee
that thy own right hand can save thee.

¹⁵ 'Behold now behemoth, which I made with thee,
he eateth grass as an ox.
¹⁶ Lo now, his strength is in his loins,
and his force is in the navel of his belly.
¹⁷ He moveth his tail like a cedar:
the sinews of his stones are wrapped together.
¹⁸ His bones are as strong pieces of brass:
his bones are like bars of iron.
¹⁹ He is the chief of the ways of God:
he that made him can make his sword to approach unto him.
²⁰ Surely the mountains bring him forth food,
where all the beasts of the field play.
²¹ He lieth under the shady trees,
in the covert of the reed, and fens.
²² The shady trees cover him with their shadow:
the willows of the brook compass him about.
²³ Behold, he drinketh up a river, and hasteth not:
he trusteth that he can draw up Jordan into his mouth.
²⁴ He taketh it with his eyes:
his nose pierceth through snares.

41 'Canst thou draw out leviathan with a hook?
or his tongue with a cord which thou lettest down?
² Canst thou put a hook into his nose?
or bore his jaw through with a thorn?
³ Will he make many supplications unto thee?
will he speak soft words unto thee?
⁴ Will he make a covenant with thee?
wilt thou take him for a servant for ever?
⁵ Wilt thou play with him as with a bird?
wilt thou bind him for thy maidens?
⁶ Shall the companions make a banquet of him?
shall they part him among the merchants?
⁷ Canst thou fill his skin with barbed irons?
or his head with fish-spears?
⁸ Lay thy hand upon him,
remember the battle, do no more.
⁹ Behold, the hope of him is in vain:
shall not one be cast down even at the sight of him?
¹⁰ None is so fierce that dare stir him up:
who then is able to stand before me?
¹¹ Who hath prevented me, that I should repay him?
whatsoever is under the whole heaven is mine.

¹² 'I will not conceal his parts, nor his power,
nor his comely proportion.
¹³ Who can discover the face of his garment?
or who can come to him with his double bridle?

¹⁴ Who can open the doors of his face?
his teeth are terrible round about.

¹⁵ His scales are his pride,
shut up together as with a close seal.

¹⁶ One is so near to another, that no air can come between them.

¹⁷ They are joined one to another,
they stick together, that they cannot be sundered.

¹⁸ By his neesings a light doth shine,
and his eyes are like the eyelids of the morning.

¹⁹ Out of his mouth go burning lamps,
and sparks of fire leap out.

²⁰ Out of his nostrils goeth smoke,
as out of a seething pot or cauldron.

²¹ His breath kindleth coals,
and a flame goeth out of his mouth.

²² In his neck remaineth strength,
and sorrow is turned into joy before him.

²³ The flakes of his flesh are joined together:
they are firm in themselves, they cannot be moved.

²⁴ His heart is as firm as a stone,
yea, as hard as a piece of the nether millstone.

²⁵ 'When he raiseth up himself, the mighty are afraid:
by reason of breakings they purify themselves.

²⁶ The sword of him that layeth at him cannot hold:
the spear, the dart, nor the habergeon.

²⁷ He esteemeth iron as straw,
and brass as rotten wood.

²⁸ The arrow cannot make him flee:
sling-stones are turned with him into stubble.

²⁹ Darts are counted as stubble:
he laugheth at the shaking of a spear.

³⁰ 'Sharp stones are under him:
he spreadeth sharp pointed things upon the mire.

³¹ He maketh the deep to boil like a pot:
he maketh the sea like a pot of ointment.

³² He maketh a path to shine after him;
one would think the deep to be hoary.

³³ Upon earth there is not his like,
who is made without fear.

³⁴ He beholdeth all high things:
he is a king over all the children of pride.'

42 Then Job answered the LORD, and said,

² 'I know that thou canst do everything,
and that no thought can be withheld from thee.

³ Who is he that hideth counsel without knowledge?
therefore have I uttered that I understood not,
things too wonderful for me, which I knew not.
⁴ Hear, I beseech thee, and I will speak:
I will demand of thee, and declare thou unto me.
⁵ I have heard of thee by the hearing of the ear:
but now my eye seeth thee.
⁶ Wherefore I abhor myself,
and repent in dust and ashes.'

⁷And it was so, that after the LORD had spoken these words unto Job, the LORD said to Eliphaz the Temanite, 'My wrath is kindled against thee, and against thy two friends: for ye have not spoken of me the thing that is right, as my servant Job hath. ⁸Therefore take unto you now seven bullocks and seven rams, and go to my servant Job, and offer up for yourselves a burnt offering, and my servant Job shall pray for you, for him will I accept: lest I deal with you after your folly, in that ye have not spoken of me the thing which is right, like my servant Job.' ⁹So Eliphaz the Temanite and Bildad the Shuhite and Zophar the Naamathite went, and did according as the LORD commanded them: the LORD also accepted Job.

¹⁰And the LORD turned the captivity of Job, when he prayed for his friends: also the LORD gave Job twice as much as he had before. ¹¹Then came there unto him all his brethren, and all his sisters, and all they that had been of his acquaintance before, and did eat bread with him in his house: and they bemoaned him, and comforted him over all the evil that the LORD had brought upon him: every man also gave him a piece of money, and every one an earring of gold. ¹²So the LORD blessed the latter end of Job more than his beginning: for he had fourteen thousand sheep, and six thousand camels, and a thousand yoke of oxen, and a thousand she-asses. ¹³He had also seven sons and three daughters. ¹⁴And he called the name of the first, Jemima, and the name of the second, Kezia, and the name of the third, Keren-happuch. ¹⁵And in all the land were no women found so fair as the daughters of Job: and their father gave them inheritance among their brethren.

¹⁶After this lived Job a hundred and forty years, and saw his sons, and his sons' sons, even four generations. ¹⁷So Job died, being old and full of days.

THE BOOK OF
PSALMS

PSALM 1

¹ Blessed is the man that walketh not in the counsel of the
   ungodly,
 nor standeth in the way of sinners,
 nor sitteth in the seat of the scornful.
² But his delight is in the law of the LORD,
 and in his law doth he meditate day and night.
³ And he shall be like a tree planted by the rivers of water,
 that bringeth forth his fruit in his season;
 his leaf also shall not wither,
 and whatsoever he doeth shall prosper.

⁴ The ungodly are not so:
 but are like the chaff which the wind driveth away.
⁵ Therefore the ungodly shall not stand in the judgement,
 nor sinners in the congregation of the righteous.

⁶ For the LORD knoweth the way of the righteous:
 but the way of the ungodly shall perish.

PSALM 2

¹ Why do the heathen rage,
 and the people imagine a vain thing?
² The kings of the earth set themselves,
 and the rulers take counsel together,
 against the LORD, and against his anointed, saying,
³ 'Let us break their bands asunder,
 and cast away their cords from us'.
⁴ He that sitteth in the heavens shall laugh:
 the LORD shall have them in derision.
⁵ Then shall he speak unto them in his wrath,
 and vex them in his sore displeasure.
⁶ 'Yet have I set my king upon my holy hill of Zion'.

⁷ I will declare the decree: the LORD hath said unto me,
 'Thou art my Son, this day have I begotten thee.
⁸ Ask of me, and I shall give thee the heathen for thy inheritance,
 and the uttermost parts of the earth for thy possession.
⁹ Thou shalt break them with a rod of iron,
 thou shalt dash them in pieces like a potter's vessel.'

¹⁰ Be wise now therefore, O ye kings:
    be instructed, ye judges of the earth.
¹¹ Serve the LORD with fear, and rejoice with trembling.
¹² Kiss the Son, lest he be angry,
    and ye perish from the way, when his wrath is kindled but a
       little.
    Blessed are all they that put their trust in him.

PSALM 3

A psalm of David when he fled from Absalom his son.

¹ LORD, how are they increased that trouble me?
    many are they that rise up against me.
² Many there be which say of my soul,
    'There is no help for him in God'. Selah.
³ But thou, O LORD, art a shield for me;
    my glory, and the lifter up of my head.
⁴ I cried unto the LORD with my voice,
    and he heard me out of his holy hill. Selah.
⁵ I laid me down and slept;
    I awoke, for the LORD sustained me.
⁶ I will not be afraid of ten thousands of people,
    that have set themselves against me round about.
⁷ Arise, O LORD, save me, O my God:
    for thou hast smitten all my enemies upon the cheek-bone;
    thou hast broken the teeth of the ungodly.
⁸ Salvation belongeth unto the LORD:
    thy blessing is upon thy people. Selah.

PSALM 4

To the chief musician on neginoth.
A psalm of David.

¹ Hear me when I call, O God of my righteousness:
    thou hast enlarged me when I was in distress;
    have mercy upon me, and hear my prayer.
² O ye sons of men, how long will ye turn my glory into shame?
    how long will ye love vanity, and seek after leasing? Selah.
³ But know that the LORD hath set apart him that is godly for
      himself:
    the LORD will hear when I call unto him.
⁴ Stand in awe, and sin not:
    commune with your own heart upon your bed, and be still.
      Selah.
⁵ Offer the sacrifices of righteousness,
    and put your trust in the LORD.

⁶ There be many that say, 'Who will show us any good?'
LORD, lift thou up the light of thy countenance upon us.
⁷ Thou hast put gladness in my heart,
more than in the time that their corn and their wine
increased.
⁸ I will both lay me down in peace, and sleep:
for thou LORD only makest me dwell in safety.

PSALM 5

To the chief musician upon nehiloth.
A psalm of David.

¹ Give ear to my words, O LORD,
consider my meditation.
² Hearken unto the voice of my cry, my King, and my God:
for unto thee will I pray.
³ My voice shalt thou hear in the morning, O LORD;
in the morning will I direct my prayer unto thee, and will
look up.
⁴ For thou art not a God that hath pleasure in wickedness:
neither shall evil dwell with thee.
⁵ The foolish shall not stand in thy sight:
thou hatest all workers of iniquity.
⁶ Thou shalt destroy them that speak leasing:
the LORD will abhor the bloody and deceitful man.
⁷ But as for me, I will come into thy house in the multitude of thy
mercy:
and in thy fear will I worship toward thy holy temple.
⁸ Lead me, O LORD, in thy righteousness because of my
enemies;
make thy way straight before my face.
⁹ For there is no faithfulness in their mouth,
their inward part is very wickedness:
their throat is an open sepulchre,
they flatter with their tongue.
¹⁰ Destroy thou them, O God,
let them fall by their own counsels:
cast them out in the multitude of their transgressions,
for they have rebelled against thee.
¹¹ But let all those that put their trust in thee rejoice:
let them ever shout for joy, because thou defendest them:
let them also that love thy name be joyful in thee.
¹² For thou, LORD, wilt bless the righteous:
with favour wilt thou compass him as with a shield.

PSALM 6

To the chief musician on neginoth upon sheminith.
A psalm of David.

¹ O LORD, rebuke me not in thy anger,
  neither chasten me in thy hot displeasure.
² Have mercy upon me, O LORD, for I am weak:
  O LORD, heal me, for my bones are vexed.
³ My soul is also sore vexed:
  but thou, O LORD, how long?
⁴ Return, O LORD, deliver my soul:
  O save me for thy mercy's sake.
⁵ For in death there is no remembrance of thee:
  in the grave who shall give thee thanks?
⁶ I am weary with my groaning,
  all the night make I my bed to swim:
  I water my couch with my tears.
⁷ My eye is consumed because of grief;
  it waxeth old because of all my enemies.

⁸ Depart from me, all ye workers of iniquity;
  for the LORD hath heard the voice of my weeping.
⁹ The LORD hath heard my supplication;
  the LORD will receive my prayer.
¹⁰ Let all my enemies be ashamed and sore vexed:
  let them return and be ashamed suddenly.

PSALM 7

Shiggaion of David, which he sang unto the LORD concerning the words
of Cush the Benjamite.

¹ O LORD my God, in thee do I put my trust:
  save me from all them that persecute me, and deliver me:
² lest he tear my soul like a lion,
  rending it in pieces, while there is none to deliver.
³ O LORD my God, if I have done this;
  if there be iniquity in my hands;
⁴ if I have rewarded evil unto him that was at peace with me
  (yea, I have delivered him that without cause is my enemy):
⁵ let the enemy persecute my soul, and take it;
  yea, let him tread down my life upon the earth,
  and lay my honour in the dust. Selah.

⁶ Arise, O LORD, in thy anger,
  lift up thyself because of the rage of my enemies:
  and awake for me to the judgement that thou hast
    commanded.

7 So shall the congregation of the people compass thee about:
  for their sakes therefore return thou on high.

8 The LORD shall judge the people:
  judge me, O LORD, according to my righteousness,
  and according to my integrity that is in me.

9 O let the wickedness of the wicked come to an end,
  but establish the just:
  for the righteous God trieth the hearts and reins.

10 My defence is of God,
   which saveth the upright in heart.

11 God judgeth the righteous,
   and God is angry with the wicked every day.

12 If he turn not, he will whet his sword;
   he hath bent his bow, and made it ready.

13 He hath also prepared for him the instruments of death;
   he ordaineth his arrows against the persecutors.

14 Behold, he travaileth with iniquity,
   and hath conceived mischief, and brought forth falsehood.

15 He made a pit, and dug it,
   and is fallen into the ditch which he made.

16 His mischief shall return upon his own head,
   and his violent dealing shall come down upon his own pate.

17 I will praise the LORD according to his righteousness:
   and will sing praise to the name of the LORD most high.

PSALM 8

To the chief musician upon gittith.
A psalm of David.

1 O LORD our Lord, how excellent is thy name in all the earth!
  who hast set thy glory above the heavens.

2 Out of the mouth of babes and sucklings
  hast thou ordained strength because of thy enemies,
  that thou mightest still the enemy and the avenger.

3 When I consider thy heavens, the work of thy fingers,
  the moon and the stars, which thou hast ordained;

4 what is man, that thou art mindful of him?
  and the son of man, that thou visitest him?

5 For thou hast made him a little lower than the angels,
  and hast crowned him with glory and honour.

6 Thou madest him to have dominion over the works of thy
     hands;
  thou hast put all things under his feet:

681

7 all sheep and oxen, yea, and the beasts of the field;
8 the fowl of the air, and the fish of the sea,
and whatsoever passeth through the paths of the seas.

9 O Lord our Lord, how excellent is thy name in all the earth!

PSALM 9

To the chief musician upon Muth Labben.
A psalm of David.

1 I will praise thee, O Lord, with my whole heart:
I will show forth all thy marvellous works.
2 I will be glad and rejoice in thee:
I will sing praise to thy name, O thou most High.

3 When my enemies are turned back,
they shall fall and perish at thy presence.
4 For thou hast maintained my right and my cause:
thou sattest in the throne judging right.
5 Thou hast rebuked the heathen,
thou hast destroyed the wicked,
thou hast put out their name for ever and ever.
6 O thou enemy, destructions are come to a perpetual end:
and thou hast destroyed cities;
their memorial is perished with them.

7 But the Lord shall endure for ever:
he hath prepared his throne for judgement.
8 And he shall judge the world in righteousness,
he shall minister judgement to the people in uprightness.
9 The Lord also will be a refuge for the oppressed,
a refuge in times of trouble.
10 And they that know thy name will put their trust in thee:
for thou, Lord, hast not forsaken them that seek thee.

11 Sing praises to the Lord, which dwelleth in Zion:
declare among the people his doings.
12 When he maketh inquisition for blood, he remembereth
them:
he forgetteth not the cry of the humble.
13 Have mercy upon me, O Lord,
consider my trouble which I suffer of them that hate me,
thou that liftest me up from the gates of death:
14 that I may show forth all thy praise in the gates of the daughter
of Zion:
I will rejoice in thy salvation.

¹⁵ The heathen are sunk down in the pit that they made:
　　in the net which they hid is their own foot taken.
¹⁶ The Lord is known by the judgement which he executeth:
　　the wicked is snared in the work of his own hands.
　　Higgaion. Selah.
¹⁷ The wicked shall be turned into hell,
　　and all the nations that forget God.
¹⁸ For the needy shall not always be forgotten:
　　the expectation of the poor shall not perish for ever.

¹⁹ Arise, O Lord; let not man prevail:
　　let the heathen be judged in thy sight.
²⁰ Put them in fear, O Lord:
　　that the nations may know themselves to be but men. Selah.

PSALM 10

¹ Why standest thou afar off, O Lord?
　　why hidest thou thyself in times of trouble?
² The wicked in his pride doth persecute the poor:
　　let them be taken in the devices that they have imagined.
³ For the wicked boasteth of his heart's desire,
　　and blesseth the covetous, whom the Lord abhorreth.
⁴ The wicked, through the pride of his countenance, will not seek
　　　after God:
　　God is not in all his thoughts.
⁵ His ways are always grievous,
　　thy judgements are far above out of his sight:
　　as for all his enemies, he puffeth at them.
⁶ He hath said in his heart, 'I shall not be moved:
　　for I shall never be in adversity'.
⁷ His mouth is full of cursing and deceit and fraud:
　　under his tongue is mischief and vanity.
⁸ He sitteth in the lurking-places of the villages:
　　in the secret places doth he murder the innocent:
　　his eyes are privily set against the poor.
⁹ He lieth in wait secretly as a lion in his den,
　　he lieth in wait to catch the poor:
　　he doth catch the poor, when he draweth him into his net.
¹⁰ He croucheth, and humbleth himself,
　　that the poor may fall by his strong ones.
¹¹ He hath said in his heart, 'God hath forgotten:
　　he hideth his face, he will never see it'.

¹² Arise, O Lord; O God, lift up thy hand:
　　forget not the humble.
¹³ Wherefore doth the wicked contemn God?

he hath said in his heart, 'Thou wilt not require it'.
¹⁴ Thou hast seen it,
for thou beholdest mischief and spite, to requite it with thy hand:
the poor committeth himself unto thee,
thou art the helper of the fatherless.
¹⁵ Break thou the arm of the wicked and the evil man:
seek out his wickedness till thou find none.
¹⁶ The LORD is King for ever and ever:
the heathen are perished out of his land.
¹⁷ LORD, thou hast heard the desire of the humble:
thou wilt prepare their heart,
thou wilt cause thy ear to hear,
¹⁸ to judge the fatherless and the oppressed,
that the man of the earth may no more oppress.

PSALM 11

To the chief musician.
A psalm of David.

¹ In the LORD put I my trust:
how say ye to my soul,
'Fly as a bird to your mountain'?
² For lo, the wicked bend their bow,
they make ready their arrow upon the string,
that they may privily shoot at the upright in heart.
³ If the foundations be destroyed,
what can the righteous do?

⁴ The LORD is in his holy temple,
the LORD's throne is in heaven:
his eyes behold,
his eyelids try the children of men.
⁵ The LORD trieth the righteous:
but the wicked and him that loveth violence his soul hateth.
⁶ Upon the wicked he shall rain snares,
fire and brimstone, and a horrible tempest:
this shall be the portion of their cup.
⁷ For the righteous LORD loveth righteousness:
his countenance doth behold the upright.

PSALM 12

To the chief musician upon sheminith.
A psalm of David.

¹ Help, LORD, for the godly man ceaseth;
for the faithful fail from among the children of men.

² They speak vanity every one with his neighbour:
  with flattering lips and with a double heart do they speak.
³ The LORD shall cut off all flattering lips,
  and the tongue that speaketh proud things:
⁴ Who have said, 'With our tongue will we prevail,
  our lips are our own: who is lord over us?'
⁵ 'For the oppression of the poor, for the sighing of the needy,
  now will I arise,' saith the LORD,
  'I will set him in safety from him that puffeth at him.'
⁶ The words of the LORD are pure words:
  as silver tried in a furnace of earth, purified seven times.
⁷ Thou shalt keep them, O LORD,
  thou shalt preserve them from this generation for ever.
⁸ The wicked walk on every side,
  when the vilest men are exalted.

PSALM 13

To the chief musician.
A psalm of David.

¹ How long wilt thou forget me, O LORD? for ever?
  how long wilt thou hide thy face from me?
² How long shall I take counsel in my soul,
  having sorrow in my heart daily?
  how long shall my enemy be exalted over me?
³ Consider and hear me, O LORD my God:
  lighten my eyes, lest I sleep the sleep of death;
⁴ lest my enemy say, 'I have prevailed against him':
  and those that trouble me rejoice when I am moved.
⁵ But I have trusted in thy mercy;
  my heart shall rejoice in thy salvation.
⁶ I will sing unto the LORD,
  because he hath dealt bountifully with me.

PSALM 14

To the chief musician.
A psalm of David.

¹ The fool hath said in his heart, 'There is no God'.
  They are corrupt, they have done abominable works,
  there is none that doeth good.
² The LORD looked down from heaven upon the children of men,
  to see if there were any that did understand and seek God.
³ They are all gone aside, they are all together become filthy:
  there is none that doeth good, no, not one.

⁴ Have all the workers of iniquity no knowledge?
who eat up my people as they eat bread, and call not upon the
LORD.
⁵ There were they in great fear:
for God is in the generation of the righteous.
⁶ You have shamed the counsel of the poor,
because the LORD is his refuge.

⁷ O that the salvation of Israel were come out of Zion!
when the LORD bringeth back the captivity of his people,
Jacob shall rejoice, and Israel shall be glad.

PSALM 15
A psalm of David.

¹ LORD, who shall abide in thy tabernacle?
who shall dwell in thy holy hill?
² He that walketh uprightly,
and worketh righteousness,
and speaketh the truth in his heart.
³ He that backbiteth not with his tongue,
nor doeth evil to his neighbour,
nor taketh up a reproach against his neighbour.
⁴ In whose eyes a vile person is contemned;
but he honoureth them that fear the LORD.
He that sweareth to his own hurt, and changeth not.
⁵ He that putteth not out his money to usury,
nor taketh reward against the innocent.
He that doeth these things shall never be moved.

PSALM 16
Michtam of David.

¹ Preserve me, O God:
for in thee do I put my trust.
² O my soul thou hast said unto the LORD,
'Thou art my Lord': my goodness extendeth not to thee:
³ but to the saints that are in the earth,
and to the excellent, in whom is all my delight.
⁴ Their sorrows shall be multiplied that hasten after another god:
their drink offerings of blood will I not offer,
nor take up their names into my lips.
⁵ The LORD is the portion of my inheritance and of my cup:
thou maintainest my lot.
⁶ The lines are fallen unto me in pleasant places;
yea, I have a goodly heritage.

⁷ I will bless the LORD, who hath given me counsel:
    my reins also instruct me in the night seasons.
⁸ I have set the LORD always before me:
    because he is at my right hand, I shall not be moved.
⁹ Therefore my heart is glad, and my glory rejoiceth:
    my flesh also shall rest in hope.
¹⁰ For thou wilt not leave my soul in hell;
    neither wilt thou suffer thy Holy One to see corruption.
¹¹ Thou wilt show me the path of life:
    in thy presence is fulness of joy;
    at thy right hand there are pleasures for evermore.

PSALM 17

A prayer of David.

¹ Hear the right, O LORD, attend unto my cry,
    give ear unto my prayer, that goeth not out of feigned lips.
² Let my sentence come forth from thy presence:
    let thy eyes behold the things that are equal.
³ Thou hast proved my heart, thou hast visited me in the night,
    thou hast tried me, and shalt find nothing:
    I am purposed that my mouth shall not transgress.
⁴ Concerning the works of men, by the word of thy lips
    I have kept me from the paths of the destroyer.
⁵ Hold up my goings in thy paths, that my footsteps slip not.

⁶ I have called upon thee, for thou wilt hear me, O God:
    incline thine ear unto me, and hear my speech.
⁷ Show thy marvellous loving-kindness,
    O thou that savest by thy right hand
    them which put their trust in thee
    from those that rise up against them.
⁸ Keep me as the apple of the eye:
    hide me under the shadow of thy wings,
⁹ from the wicked that oppress me,
    from my deadly enemies, who compass me about.
¹⁰ They are enclosed in their own fat:
    with their mouth they speak proudly.
¹¹ They have now compassed us in our steps:
    they have set their eyes bowing down to the earth:
¹² like as a lion that is greedy of his prey,
    and as it were a young lion lurking in secret places.

¹³ Arise, O LORD, disappoint him, cast him down:
    deliver my soul from the wicked, which is thy sword:
¹⁴ from men which are thy hand, O LORD,
    from men of the world, which have their portion in this life,

and whose belly thou fillest with thy hid treasure:
they are full of children,
and leave the rest of their substance to their babes.

¹⁵ As for me, I will behold thy face in righteousness:
I shall be satisfied, when I awake, with thy likeness.

PSALM 18

To the chief musician.

A psalm of David, the servant of the Lord, who spoke unto the Lord the words of this song in the day that the Lord delivered him from the hand of all his enemies, and from the hand of Saul: and he said,

¹ I will love thee, O LORD, my strength.
² The LORD is my rock, and my fortress, and my deliverer:
my God, my strength, in whom I will trust,
my buckler, and the horn of my salvation, and my high tower.
³ I will call upon the LORD, who is worthy to be praised:
so shall I be saved from my enemies.

⁴ The sorrows of death compassed me,
and the floods of ungodly men made me afraid.
⁵ The sorrows of hell compassed me about:
the snares of death prevented me.
⁶ In my distress I called upon the LORD, and cried unto my God:
he heard my voice out of his temple,
and my cry came before him, even into his ears.

⁷ Then the earth shook and trembled;
the foundations also of the hills moved and were shaken,
because he was wroth.
⁸ There went up a smoke out of his nostrils,
and fire out of his mouth devoured:
coals were kindled by it.
⁹ He bowed the heavens also, and came down:
and darkness was under his feet.
¹⁰ And he rode upon a cherub, and did fly:
yea, he did fly upon the wings of the wind.
¹¹ He made darkness his secret place:
his pavilion round about him were dark waters
and thick clouds of the skies.
¹² At the brightness that was before him his thick clouds passed,
hail stones and coals of fire.
¹³ The LORD also thundered in the heavens,
and the Highest gave his voice;
hail stones and coals of fire.

¹⁴ Yea, he sent out his arrows, and scattered them;
    and he shot out lightnings, and discomfited them.
¹⁵ Then the channels of waters were seen,
    and the foundations of the world were discovered:
    at thy rebuke, O LORD,
    at the blast of the breath of thy nostrils.

¹⁶ He sent from above, he took me,
    he drew me out of many waters.
¹⁷ He delivered me from my strong enemy,
    and from them which hated me:
    for they were too strong for me.
¹⁸ They prevented me in the day of my calamity:
    but the LORD was my stay.
¹⁹ He brought me forth also into a large place:
    he delivered me, because he delighted in me.

²⁰ The LORD rewarded me according to my righteousness,
    according to the cleanness of my hands hath he
        recompensed me.
²¹ For I have kept the ways of the LORD,
    and have not wickedly departed from my God.
²² For all his judgements were before me,
    and I did not put away his statutes from me.
²³ I was also upright before him:
    and I kept myself from my iniquity.
²⁴ Therefore hath the LORD recompensed me according to my
        righteousness,
    according to the cleanness of my hands in his eyesight.

²⁵ With the merciful thou wilt show thyself merciful,
    with an upright man thou wilt show thyself upright.
²⁶ With the pure thou wilt show thyself pure,
    and with the froward thou wilt show thyself froward.
²⁷ For thou wilt save the afflicted people:
    but wilt bring down high looks.
²⁸ For thou wilt light my candle:
    the LORD my God will enlighten my darkness.
²⁹ For by thee I have run through a troop;
    and by my God have I leapt over a wall.

³⁰ As for God, his way is perfect:
    the word of the LORD is tried:
    he is a buckler to all those that trust in him.
³¹ For who is God save the LORD?
    or who is a rock save our God?
³² It is God that girdeth me with strength,
    and maketh my way perfect.

³³ He maketh my feet like hinds' feet,
and setteth me upon my high places.
³⁴ He teacheth my hands to war,
so that a bow of steel is broken by my arms.
³⁵ Thou hast also given me the shield of thy salvation:
and thy right hand hath held me up,
and thy gentleness hath made me great.
³⁶ Thou hast enlarged my steps under me,
that my feet did not slip.

³⁷ I have pursued my enemies, and overtaken them:
neither did I turn again till they were consumed.
³⁸ I have wounded them that they were not able to rise:
they are fallen under my feet.
³⁹ For thou hast girded me with strength unto the battle:
thou hast subdued under me those that rose up against
me.
⁴⁰ Thou hast also given me the necks of my enemies:
that I might destroy them that hate me.
⁴¹ They cried, but there was none to save them:
even unto the LORD, but he answered them not.
⁴² Then did I beat them small as the dust before the wind:
I did cast them out as the dirt in the streets.

⁴³ Thou hast delivered me from the strivings of the people,
and thou hast made me the head of the heathen:
a people whom I have not known shall serve me.
⁴⁴ As soon as they hear of me, they shall obey me:
the strangers shall submit themselves unto me.
⁴⁵ The strangers shall fade away,
and be afraid out of their close places.

⁴⁶ The LORD liveth, and blessed be my rock:
and let the God of my salvation be exalted.
⁴⁷ It is God that avengeth me,
and subdueth the people under me.
⁴⁸ He delivereth me from my enemies:
yea, thou liftest me up above those that rise up against
me:
thou hast delivered me from the violent man.
⁴⁹ Therefore will I give thanks unto thee, O LORD, among the
heathen,
and sing praises unto thy name.
⁵⁰ Great deliverance giveth he to his king:
and showeth mercy to his anointed,
to David, and to his seed for evermore.

PSALM 19

To the chief musician.
A psalm of David.

¹ The heavens declare the glory of God:
  and the firmament showeth his handiwork.
² Day unto day uttereth speech,
  and night unto night showeth knowledge.
³ There is no speech nor language,
  where their voice is not heard.
⁴ Their line is gone out through all the earth,
  and their words to the end of the world.
  In them hath he set a tabernacle for the sun,
⁵ which is as a bridegroom coming out of his chamber,
  and rejoiceth as a strong man to run a race.
⁶ His going forth is from the end of the heaven,
  and his circuit unto the ends of it:
  and there is nothing hid from the heat thereof.

⁷ The law of the LORD is perfect, converting the soul:
  the testimony of the LORD is sure, making wise the simple.
⁸ The statutes of the LORD are right, rejoicing the heart:
  the commandment of the LORD is pure, enlightening the eyes.
⁹ The fear of the LORD is clean, enduring for ever:
  the judgements of the LORD are true and righteous altogether.
¹⁰ More to be desired are they than gold, yea, than much fine gold:
  sweeter also than honey and the honeycomb.
¹¹ Moreover by them is thy servant warned:
  and in keeping of them there is great reward.
¹² Who can understand his errors?
  cleanse thou me from secret faults.
¹³ Keep back thy servant also from presumptuous sins,
  let them not have dominion over me: then shall I be upright,
  and I shall be innocent from the great transgression.

¹⁴ Let the words of my mouth, and the meditation of my heart,
  be acceptable in thy sight, O LORD,
  my strength, and my redeemer.

PSALM 20

To the chief musician.
A psalm of David.

¹ The LORD hear thee in the day of trouble,
  the name of the God of Jacob defend thee;
² send thee help from the sanctuary,
  and strengthen thee out of Zion;

³ remember all thy offerings,
and accept thy burnt sacrifice. Selah.
⁴ Grant thee according to thy own heart,
and fulfil all thy counsel.
⁵ We will rejoice in thy salvation,
and in the name of our God we will set up our banners:
the LORD fulfil all thy petitions.

⁶ Now know I that the LORD saveth his anointed:
he will hear him from his holy heaven,
with the saving strength of his right hand.
⁷ Some trust in chariots, and some in horses:
but we will remember the name of the LORD our God.
⁸ They are brought down and fallen:
but we are risen, and stand upright.
⁹ Save, LORD: let the king hear us when we call.

PSALM 21

To the chief musician.
A psalm of David.

¹ The king shall joy in thy strength, O LORD:
and in thy salvation how greatly shall he rejoice?
² Thou hast given him his heart's desire,
and hast not withheld the request of his lips. Selah.
³ For thou preventest him with the blessings of goodness:
thou settest a crown of pure gold on his head.
⁴ He asked life of thee, and thou gavest it him,
even length of days for ever and ever.
⁵ His glory is great in thy salvation:
honour and majesty hast thou laid upon him.
⁶ For thou hast made him most blessed for ever:
thou hast made him exceeding glad with thy countenance.
⁷ For the king trusteth in the LORD,
and through the mercy of the most High he shall not be
moved.

⁸ Thy hand shall find out all thy enemies:
thy right hand shall find out those that hate thee.
⁹ Thou shalt make them as a fiery oven in the time of thy anger:
the LORD shall swallow them up in his wrath,
and the fire shall devour them.
¹⁰ Their fruit shalt thou destroy from the earth,
and their seed from among the children of men.
¹¹ For they intended evil against thee:
they imagined a mischievous device,
which they are not able to perform.

¹² Therefore shalt thou make them turn their back,
  when thou shalt make ready thy arrows upon thy strings against
    the face of them.

¹³ Be thou exalted, LORD, in thy own strength:
  so will we sing and praise thy power.

PSALM 22
To the chief musician upon Aijeleth Shahar.
A psalm of David.

¹ My God, my God, why hast thou forsaken me?
  why art thou so far from helping me,
    and from the words of my roaring?
² O my God, I cry in the daytime, but thou hearest not;
  and in the night season, and am not silent.
³ But thou art holy, O thou that inhabitest the praises of Israel.
⁴ Our fathers trusted in thee:
  they trusted, and thou didst deliver them.
⁵ They cried unto thee, and were delivered:
  they trusted in thee, and were not confounded.
⁶ But I am a worm, and no man;
  a reproach of men, and despised of the people.
⁷ All they that see me laugh me to scorn:
  they shoot out the lip, they shake the head, saying,
⁸ 'He trusted on the LORD that he would deliver him:
  let him deliver him, seeing he delighted in him'.

⁹ But thou art he that took me out of the womb:
  thou didst make me hope when I was upon my mother's breasts.
¹⁰ I was cast upon thee from the womb:
  thou art my God from my mother's belly.
¹¹ Be not far from me, for trouble is near;
  for there is none to help.
¹² Many bulls have compassed me:
  strong bulls of Bashan have beset me round.
¹³ They gaped upon me with their mouths,
  as a ravening and a roaring lion.
¹⁴ I am poured out like water,
  and all my bones are out of joint:
  my heart is like wax,
  it is melted in the midst of my bowels.
¹⁵ My strength is dried up like a potsherd;
  and my tongue cleaveth to my jaws;
  and thou hast brought me into the dust of death.
¹⁶ For dogs have compassed me:
  the assembly of the wicked have enclosed me:

they pierced my hands and my feet.
[17] I may tell all my bones:
they look and stare upon me.
[18] They part my garments among them,
and cast lots upon my vesture.

[19] But be not thou far from me, O LORD:
O my strength, haste thee to help me.
[20] Deliver my soul from the sword:
my darling from the power of the dog.
[21] Save me from the lion's mouth:
for thou hast heard me from the horns of the unicorns.

[22] I will declare thy name unto my brethren:
in the midst of the congregation will I praise thee.
[23] Ye that fear the LORD, praise him;
all ye the seed of Jacob, glorify him,
and fear him, all ye the seed of Israel.
[24] For he hath not despised nor abhorred the affliction of the
afflicted;
neither hath he hid his face from him,
but when he cried unto him, he heard.
[25] My praise shall be of thee in the great congregation:
I will pay my vows before them that fear him.
[26] The meek shall eat and be satisfied:
they shall praise the LORD that seek him:
your heart shall live for ever.
[27] All the ends of the world shall remember and turn unto the LORD:
and all the kindreds of the nations shall worship before thee.
[28] For the kingdom is the LORD's:
and he is the governor among the nations.
[29] All they that be fat upon earth shall eat and worship:
all they that go down to the dust shall bow before him,
and none can keep alive his own soul.
[30] A seed shall serve him;
it shall be accounted to the Lord for a generation.
[31] They shall come, and shall declare his righteousness
unto a people that shall be born,
that he hath done this.

PSALM 23
A psalm of David.

The LORD is my shepherd; I shall not want.
[2] He maketh me to lie down in green pastures:
he leadeth me beside the still waters.
[3] He restoreth my soul:

he leadeth me in the paths of righteousness for his name's sake.
⁴ Yea, though I walk through the valley of the shadow of death,
I will fear no evil: for thou art with me;
thy rod and thy staff they comfort me.
⁵ Thou preparest a table before me in the presence of my enemies:
thou anointest my head with oil, my cup runneth over.
⁶ Surely goodness and mercy shall follow me all the days of my life:
and I will dwell in the house of the LORD for ever.

PSALM 24
A psalm of David.

¹ The earth is the LORD's, and the fulness thereof;
the world, and they that dwell therein.
² For he hath founded it upon the seas,
and established it upon the floods.
³ Who shall ascend into the hill of the LORD?
and who shall stand in his holy place?
⁴ He that hath clean hands, and a pure heart;
who hath not lifted up his soul unto vanity, nor sworn deceitfully.
⁵ He shall receive the blessing from the LORD,
and righteousness from the God of his salvation.
⁶ This is the generation of them that seek him,
that seek thy face, O Jacob. Selah.

⁷ Lift up your heads, O ye gates,
and be ye lifted up, ye everlasting doors;
and the King of glory shall come in.
⁸ Who is this King of glory?
The LORD strong and mighty,
the LORD mighty in battle.
⁹ Lift up your heads, O ye gates,
even lift them up, ye everlasting doors;
and the King of glory shall come in.
¹⁰ Who is this King of glory?
The LORD of hosts, he is the King of glory. Selah.

PSALM 25
A psalm of David.

¹ Unto thee, O LORD, do I lift up my soul.
² O my God, I trust in thee, let me not be ashamed:
let not my enemies triumph over me.
³ Yea, let none that wait on thee be ashamed:
let them be ashamed which transgress without cause.
⁴ Show me thy ways, O LORD: teach me thy paths.

⁵ Lead me in thy truth, and teach me:
  for thou art the God of my salvation;
  on thee do I wait all the day.
⁶ Remember, O LORD, thy tender mercies and thy loving-kindnesses:
  for they have been ever of old.
⁷ Remember not the sins of my youth, nor my transgressions:
  according to thy mercy remember thou me
  for thy goodness' sake, O LORD.

⁸ Good and upright is the LORD:
  therefore will he teach sinners in the way.
⁹ The meek will he guide in judgement:
  and the meek will he teach his way.
¹⁰ All the paths of the LORD are mercy and truth
  unto such as keep his covenant and his testimonies.
¹¹ For thy name's sake, O LORD, pardon my iniquity:
  for it is great.
¹² What man is he that feareth the LORD?
  him shall he teach in the way that he shall choose.
¹³ His soul shall dwell at ease:
  and his seed shall inherit the earth.
¹⁴ The secret of the LORD is with them that fear him:
  and he will show them his covenant.
¹⁵ My eyes are ever towards the LORD:
  for he shall pluck my feet out of the net.

¹⁶ Turn thee unto me, and have mercy upon me:
  for I am desolate and afflicted.
¹⁷ The troubles of my heart are enlarged:
  O bring thou me out of my distresses.
¹⁸ Look upon my affliction and my pain,
  and forgive all my sins.
¹⁹ Consider my enemies: for they are many,
  and they hate me with cruel hatred.
²⁰ O keep my soul, and deliver me:
  let me not be ashamed, for I put my trust in thee.
²¹ Let integrity and uprightness preserve me:
  for I wait on thee.

²² Redeem Israel, O God, out of all his troubles.

PSALM 26
A psalm of David.

¹ Judge me, O LORD, for I have walked in my integrity:
  I have trusted also in the LORD: therefore I shall not slide.
² Examine me, O LORD, and prove me;

try my reins and my heart.
3 For thy loving-kindness is before my eyes:
  and I have walked in thy truth.

4 I have not sat with vain persons,
  neither will I go in with dissemblers.
5 I have hated the congregation of evil-doers:
  and will not sit with the wicked.
6 I will wash my hands in innocence:
  so will I compass thy altar, O LORD:
7 that I may publish with the voice of thanksgiving,
  and tell of all thy wondrous works.
8 LORD, I have loved the habitation of thy house,
  and the place where thy honour dwelleth.
9 Gather not my soul with sinners,
  nor my life with bloody men:
10 in whose hands is mischief:
  and their right hand is full of bribes.
11 But as for me, I will walk in my integrity:
  redeem me, and be merciful unto me.
12 My foot standeth in an even place:
  in the congregations will I bless the LORD.

PSALM 27

A psalm of David.

1 The LORD is my light and my salvation, whom shall I fear?
  the LORD is the strength of my life, of whom shall I be afraid?
2 When the wicked, even my enemies and my foes, came upon me
    to eat up my flesh,
  they stumbled and fell.
3 Though a host should encamp against me, my heart shall not
    fear:
  though war should rise against me, in this will I be confident.
4 One thing have I desired of the LORD, that will I seek after:
  that I may dwell in the house of the LORD all the days of my
    life,
  to behold the beauty of the LORD, and to inquire in his
    temple.
5 For in the time of trouble he shall hide me in his pavilion:
  in the secret of his tabernacle shall he hide me;
  he shall set me up upon a rock.
6 And now shall my head be lifted up above my enemies round
    about me:
  therefore will I offer in his tabernacle sacrifices of joy,
  I will sing, yea, I will sing praises unto the LORD.

⁷ Hear, O Lᴏʀᴅ, when I cry with my voice:
have mercy also upon me, and answer me.
⁸ When thou saidst, 'Seek ye my face',
my heart said unto thee, 'Thy face, Lᴏʀᴅ, will I seek'.
⁹ Hide not thy face far from me,
put not thy servant away in anger: thou hast been my help;
leave me not, neither forsake me, O God of my salvation.
¹⁰ When my father and my mother forsake me,
then the Lᴏʀᴅ will take me up.
¹¹ Teach me thy way, O Lᴏʀᴅ,
and lead me in a plain path, because of my enemies.
¹² Deliver me not over unto the will of my enemies:
for false witnesses are risen up against me,
and such as breathe out cruelty.
¹³ I had fainted, unless I had believed to see the goodness of the
Lᴏʀᴅ in the land of the living.

¹⁴ Wait on the Lᴏʀᴅ:
be of good courage, and he shall strengthen thy heart:
wait, I say, on the Lᴏʀᴅ.

PSALM 28
A psalm of David.

¹ Unto thee will I cry, O Lᴏʀᴅ, my rock,
be not silent to me:
lest, if thou be silent to me,
I become like them that go down into the pit.
² Hear the voice of my supplications, when I cry unto thee:
when I lift up my hands toward thy holy oracle.
³ Draw me not away with the wicked, and with the workers of
iniquity:
which speak peace to their neighbours, but mischief is in their
hearts.
⁴ Give them according to their deeds,
and according to the wickedness of their endeavours:
give them after the work of their hands,
render to them their desert.
⁵ Because they regard not the works of the Lᴏʀᴅ,
nor the operation of his hands,
he shall destroy them, and not build them up.

⁶ Blessed be the Lᴏʀᴅ,
because he hath heard the voice of my supplications.
⁷ The Lᴏʀᴅ is my strength and my shield,
my heart trusted in him, and I am helped:
therefore my heart greatly rejoiceth,

and with my song will I praise him.
⁸ The LORD is their strength,
and he is the saving strength of his anointed.
⁹ Save thy people, and bless thy inheritance:
feed them also, and lift them up for ever.

PSALM 29
A psalm of David.

¹ Give unto the LORD, O ye mighty,
give unto the LORD glory and strength.
² Give unto the LORD the glory due unto his name;
worship the LORD in the beauty of holiness.

³ The voice of the LORD is upon the waters:
the God of glory thundereth, the LORD is upon many waters.
⁴ The voice of the LORD is powerful;
the voice of the LORD is full of majesty.
⁵ The voice of the LORD breaketh the cedars:
yea, the LORD breaketh the cedars of Lebanon.
⁶ He maketh them also to skip like a calf;
Lebanon and Sirion like a young unicorn.
⁷ The voice of the LORD divideth the flames of fire.
⁸ The voice of the LORD shaketh the wilderness:
the LORD shaketh the wilderness of Kadesh.
⁹ The voice of the LORD maketh the hinds to calve,
and discovereth the forests:
and in his temple doth every one speak of his glory.

¹⁰ The LORD sitteth upon the flood:
yea, the LORD sitteth King for ever.
¹¹ The LORD will give strength unto his people;
the LORD will bless his people with peace.

PSALM 30
A psalm and song at the dedication of the house of David.

¹ I will extol thee, O LORD, for thou hast lifted me up,
and hast not made my foes to rejoice over me.
² O LORD my God, I cried unto thee,
and thou hast healed me.
³ O LORD, thou hast brought up my soul from the grave:
thou hast kept me alive, that I should not go down to the pit.

⁴ Sing unto the LORD, O ye saints of his,
and give thanks at the remembrance of his holiness.

⁵ For his anger endureth but a moment; in his favour is life:
  weeping may endure for a night, but joy cometh in the morning.

⁶ And in my prosperity I said, 'I shall never be moved'.
⁷ LORD, by thy favour thou hast made my mountain to stand
    strong:
  thou didst hide thy face, and I was troubled.
⁸ I cried to thee, O LORD:
  and unto the LORD I made supplication.
⁹ What profit is there in my blood, when I go down to the pit?
  Shall the dust praise thee? shall it declare thy truth?
¹⁰ Hear, O LORD, and have mercy upon me:
  LORD, be thou my helper.

¹¹ Thou hast turned for me my mourning into dancing:
  thou hast put off my sackcloth, and girded me with gladness:
¹² to the end that my glory may sing praise to thee,
  and not be silent. O LORD my God, I will give thanks unto thee for
    ever.

PSALM 31

To the chief musician.
A psalm of David.

¹ In thee, O LORD, do I put my trust, let me never be ashamed:
  deliver me in thy righteousness.
² Bow down thy ear to me, deliver me speedily:
  be thou my strong rock, for a house of defence to save me.
³ For thou art my rock and my fortress:
  therefore for thy name's sake lead me, and guide me.
⁴ Pull me out of the net that they have laid privily for me:
  for thou art my strength.
⁵ Into thy hand I commit my spirit:
  thou hast redeemed me, O LORD God of truth.
⁶ I have hated them that regard lying vanities:
  but I trust in the LORD.
⁷ I will be glad and rejoice in thy mercy:
  for thou hast considered my trouble;
  thou hast known my soul in adversities;
⁸ and hast not shut me up into the hand of the enemy:
  thou hast set my feet in a large room.

⁹ Have mercy upon me, O LORD, for I am in trouble:
  my eye is consumed with grief, yea, my soul and my belly.
¹⁰ For my life is spent with grief, and my years with sighing:
  my strength faileth because of my iniquity,
  and my bones are consumed.

¹¹ I was a reproach among all my enemies,
   but especially among my neighbours, and a fear to my
      acquaintance:
   they that did see me without fled from me.
¹² I am forgotten as a dead man out of mind:
   I am like a broken vessel.
¹³ For I have heard the slander of many, fear was on every
      side:
   while they took counsel together against me,
   they devised to take away my life.

¹⁴ But I trusted in thee, O LORD:
   I said, 'Thou art my God'.
¹⁵ My times are in thy hand:
   deliver me from the hand of my enemies,
   and from them that persecute me.
¹⁶ Make thy face to shine upon thy servant:
   save me for thy mercy's sake.
¹⁷ Let me not be ashamed, O LORD, for I have called upon
      thee:
   let the wicked be ashamed, and let them be silent in the
      grave.
¹⁸ Let the lying lips be put to silence:
   which speak grievous things proudly and contemptuously
      against the righteous.

¹⁹ O how great is thy goodness,
   which thou hast laid up for them that fear thee:
   which thou hast wrought for them that trust in thee before the
      sons of men!
²⁰ Thou shalt hide them in the secret of thy presence from the
      pride of man:
   thou shalt keep them secretly in a pavilion from the strife of
      tongues.
²¹ Blessed be the LORD:
   for he hath shown me his marvellous kindness in a strong
      city.
²² For I said in my haste, 'I am cut off from before thy eyes':
   nevertheless thou heardest the voice of my supplications when I
      cried unto thee.

²³ O love the LORD, all ye his saints:
   for the LORD preserveth the faithful,
   and plentifully rewardeth the proud doer.
²⁴ Be of good courage, and he shall strengthen your heart:
   all ye that hope in the LORD.

PSALM 32

A psalm of David, maschil.

[1] Blessed is he whose transgression is forgiven,
   whose sin is covered.
[2] Blessed is the man unto whom the LORD imputeth not iniquity,
   and in whose spirit there is no guile.

[3] When I kept silence,
   my bones waxed old through my roaring all the day long.
[4] For day and night thy hand was heavy upon me:
   my moisture is turned into the drought of summer. Selah.

[5] I acknowledged my sin unto thee,
   and my iniquity have I not hid.
   I said, 'I will confess my transgressions unto the LORD';
   and thou forgavest the iniquity of my sin. Selah.

[6] For this shall every one that is godly pray unto thee in a time
      when thou mayest be found:
   surely in the floods of great waters, they shall not come nigh
      unto him.
[7] Thou art my hiding-place,
   thou shalt preserve me from trouble:
   thou shalt compass me about with songs of deliverance. Selah.

[8] I will instruct thee and teach thee in the way which thou shalt
      go:
   I will guide thee with my eye.
[9] Be ye not as the horse, or as the mule,
   which have no understanding:
   whose mouth must be held in with bit and bridle,
   lest they come near unto thee.

[10] Many sorrows shall be to the wicked:
   but he that trusteth in the LORD, mercy shall compass him
      about.
[11] Be glad in the LORD, and rejoice, ye righteous:
   and shout for joy, all ye that are upright in heart.

PSALM 33

[1] Rejoice in the LORD, O ye righteous:
   for praise is comely for the upright.
[2] Praise the LORD with harp:
   sing unto him with the psaltery and an instrument of ten
      strings.

³ Sing unto him a new song:
  play skilfully with a loud noise.
⁴ For the word of the LORD is right:
  and all his works are done in truth.
⁵ He loveth righteousness and judgement:
  the earth is full of the goodness of the LORD.

⁶ By the word of the LORD were the heavens made:
  and all the host of them by the breath of his mouth.
⁷ He gathereth the waters of the sea together as a heap:
  he layeth up the depth in storehouses.
⁸ Let all the earth fear the LORD:
  let all the inhabitants of the world stand in awe of him.
⁹ For he spoke, and it was done:
  he commanded, and it stood fast.

¹⁰ The LORD bringeth the counsel of the heathen to nought:
  he maketh the devices of the people of no effect.
¹¹ The counsel of the LORD standeth for ever,
  the thoughts of his heart to all generations.
¹² Blessed is the nation whose God is the LORD:
  and the people whom he hath chosen for his own
    inheritance.
¹³ The LORD looketh from heaven:
  he beholdeth all the sons of men.
¹⁴ From the place of his habitation,
  he looketh upon all the inhabitants of the earth.
¹⁵ He fashioneth their hearts alike:
  he considereth all their works.

¹⁶ There is no king saved by the multitude of a host:
  a mighty man is not delivered by much strength.
¹⁷ A horse is a vain thing for safety:
  neither shall he deliver any by his great strength.
¹⁸ Behold, the eye of the LORD is upon them that fear him:
  upon them that hope in his mercy:
¹⁹ to deliver their soul from death,
  and to keep them alive in famine.
²⁰ Our soul waiteth for the LORD:
  he is our help and our shield.
²¹ For our heart shall rejoice in him:
  because we have trusted in his holy name.

²² Let thy mercy, O LORD, be upon us:
  according as we hope in thee.

PSALM 34

A psalm of David, when he changed his behaviour before Abimelech:
who drove him away, and he departed.

¹ I will bless the LORD at all times:
his praise shall continually be in my mouth.
² My soul shall make her boast in the LORD:
the humble shall hear thereof, and be glad.
³ O magnify the LORD with me,
and let us exalt his name together.

⁴ I sought the LORD, and he heard me,
and delivered me from all my fears.
⁵ They looked unto him, and were lightened:
and their faces were not ashamed.
⁶ This poor man cried, and the LORD heard him,
and saved him out of all his troubles.
⁷ The angel of the LORD encampeth round about them that fear
him,
and delivereth them.
⁸ O taste and see that the LORD is good:
blessed is the man that trusteth in him.
⁹ O fear the LORD, ye his saints:
for there is no want to them that fear him.
¹⁰ The young lions do lack, and suffer hunger:
but they that seek the LORD shall not want any good thing.

¹¹ Come, ye children, hearken unto me:
I will teach you the fear of the LORD.
¹² What man is he that desireth life,
and loveth many days, that he may see good?
¹³ Keep thy tongue from evil,
and thy lips from speaking guile.
¹⁴ Depart from evil, and do good:
seek peace, and pursue it.
¹⁵ The eyes of the LORD are upon the righteous,
and his ears are open unto their cry.
¹⁶ The face of the LORD is against them that do evil,
to cut off the remembrance of them from the earth.
¹⁷ The righteous cry, and the LORD heareth,
and delivereth them out of all their troubles.
¹⁸ The LORD is nigh unto them that are of a broken heart:
and saveth such as be of a contrite spirit.
¹⁹ Many are the afflictions of the righteous:
but the LORD delivereth him out of them all.
²⁰ He keepeth all his bones:
not one of them is broken.
²¹ Evil shall slay the wicked:

and they that hate the righteous shall be desolate.
²² The Lord redeemeth the soul of his servants:
and none of them that trust in him shall be desolate.

PSALM 35
A psalm of David.

¹ Plead my cause, O Lord, with them that strive with me:
fight against them that fight against me.
² Take hold of shield and buckler,
and stand up for my help.
³ Draw out also the spear, and stop the way against them that
persecute me:
say unto my soul, 'I am thy salvation'.

⁴ Let them be confounded and put to shame that seek after my soul:
let them be turned back and brought to confusion that devise
my hurt.
⁵ Let them be as chaff before the wind:
and let the angel of the Lord chase them.
⁶ Let their way be dark and slippery:
and let the angel of the Lord persecute them.
⁷ For without cause have they hid for me their net in a pit,
which without cause they have dug for my soul.
⁸ Let destruction come upon him at unawares,
and let his net that he hath hid catch himself:
into that very destruction let him fall.

⁹ And my soul shall be joyful in the Lord:
it shall rejoice in his salvation.
¹⁰ All my bones shall say, 'Lord, who is like unto thee,
which deliverest the poor from him that is too strong for him,
yea, the poor and the needy from him that spoileth him?'

¹¹ False witnesses did rise up;
they laid to my charge things that I knew not.
¹² They rewarded me evil for good,
to the spoiling of my soul.
¹³ But as for me, when they were sick, my clothing was sackcloth:
I humbled my soul with fasting, and my prayer returned into my
own bosom.
¹⁴ I behaved myself as though he had been my friend or brother:
I bowed down heavily, as one that mourneth for his mother.
¹⁵ But in my adversity they rejoiced, and gathered themselves
together:
yea, the abjects gathered themselves together against me, and I
knew it not;

they did tear me, and ceased not:
¹⁶ with hypocritical mockers in feasts,
they gnashed upon me with their teeth.

¹⁷ Lord, how long wilt thou look on?
rescue my soul from their destructions,
my darling from the lions.
¹⁸ I will give thee thanks in the great congregation:
I will praise thee among much people.

¹⁹ Let not them that are my enemies wrongfully rejoice over
me:
neither let them wink with the eye that hate me without a
cause.
²⁰ For they speak not peace:
but they devise deceitful matters against them that are quiet in
the land.
²¹ Yea, they opened their mouth wide against me,
and said, 'Aha, aha, our eye hath seen it'.
²² This thou hast seen, O LORD: keep not silence:
O Lord, be not far from me.
²³ Stir up thyself, and awake to my judgement,
even unto my cause, my God and my Lord.
²⁴ Judge me, O LORD my God, according to thy righteousness,
and let them not rejoice over me.
²⁵ Let them not say in their hearts, 'Ah, so would we have it':
let them not say, 'We have swallowed him up'.
²⁶ Let them be ashamed and brought to confusion together that
rejoice at my hurt:
let them be clothed with shame and dishonour that magnify
themselves against me.

²⁷ Let them shout for joy, and be glad, that favour my righteous
cause:
yea, let them say continually, 'Let the LORD be magnified,
which hath pleasure in the prosperity of his servant'.
²⁸ And my tongue shall speak of thy righteousness,
and of thy praise all the day long.

PSALM 36

To the chief musician.
A psalm of David the servant of the Lord.

¹ The transgression of the wicked saith within my heart,
that there is no fear of God before his eyes.
² For he flattereth himself in his own eyes,
until his iniquity be found to be hateful.

³ The words of his mouth are iniquity and deceit:
he hath left off to be wise, and to do good.
⁴ He deviseth mischief upon his bed;
he setteth himself in a way that is not good; he abhorreth not
   evil.

⁵ Thy mercy, O Lord, is in the heavens;
and thy faithfulness reacheth unto the clouds.
⁶ Thy righteousness is like the great mountains;
thy judgements are a great deep:
O Lord, thou preservest man and beast.
⁷ How excellent is thy loving-kindness, O God!
therefore the children of men put their trust under the shadow
   of thy wings.
⁸ They shall be abundantly satisfied with the fatness of thy
   house:
and thou shalt make them drink of the river of thy pleasures.
⁹ For with thee is the fountain of life:
in thy light shall we see light.
¹⁰ O continue thy loving-kindness unto them that know thee;
and thy righteousness to the upright in heart.

¹¹ Let not the foot of pride come against me,
and let not the hand of the wicked remove me.
¹² There are the workers of iniquity fallen:
they are cast down, and shall not be able to rise.

PSALM 37
A psalm of David.

¹ Fret not thyself because of evil-doers,
neither be thou envious against the workers of iniquity.
² For they shall soon be cut down like the grass,
and wither as the green herb.
³ Trust in the Lord, and do good;
so shalt thou dwell in the land, and verily thou shalt be fed.
⁴ Delight thyself also in the Lord;
and he shall give thee the desires of thy heart.
⁵ Commit thy way unto the Lord;
trust also in him, and he shall bring it to pass.
⁶ And he shall bring forth thy righteousness as the light,
and thy judgement as the noonday.
⁷ Rest in the Lord, and wait patiently for him:
fret not thyself because of him who prospereth in his way,
because of the man who bringeth wicked devices to pass.
⁸ Cease from anger, and forsake wrath:
fret not thyself in any wise to do evil.

⁹ For evil-doers shall be cut off:
but those that wait upon the Lord, they shall inherit the earth.
¹⁰ For yet a little while, and the wicked shall not be:
yea, thou shalt diligently consider his place, and it shall not be.
¹¹ But the meek shall inherit the earth:
and shall delight themselves in the abundance of peace.
¹² The wicked plotteth against the just,
and gnasheth upon him with his teeth.
¹³ The Lord shall laugh at him:
for he seeth that his day is coming.
¹⁴ The wicked have drawn out the sword, and have bent their
bow,
to cast down the poor and needy, and to slay such as be of
upright conversation.
¹⁵ Their sword shall enter into their own heart,
and their bows shall be broken.
¹⁶ A little that a righteous man hath is better than the riches of
many wicked.
¹⁷ For the arms of the wicked shall be broken:
but the Lord upholdeth the righteous.
¹⁸ The Lord knoweth the days of the upright:
and their inheritance shall be for ever.
¹⁹ They shall not be ashamed in the evil time:
and in the days of famine they shall be satisfied.
²⁰ But the wicked shall perish,
and the enemies of the Lord shall be as the fat of lambs:
they shall consume;
into smoke shall they consume away.
²¹ The wicked borroweth, and payeth not again:
but the righteous showeth mercy, and giveth.
²² For such as be blessed of him shall inherit the earth:
and they that be cursed of him shall be cut off.
²³ The steps of a good man are ordered by the Lord:
and he delighteth in his way.
²⁴ Though he fall, he shall not be utterly cast down:
for the Lord upholdeth him with his hand.
²⁵ I have been young, and now am old;
yet have I not seen the righteous forsaken, nor his seed begging
bread.
²⁶ He is ever merciful, and lendeth:
and his seed is blessed.
²⁷ Depart from evil, and do good;
and dwell for evermore.
²⁸ For the Lord loveth judgement, and forsaketh not his saints;
they are preserved for ever:
but the seed of the wicked shall be cut off.
²⁹ The righteous shall inherit the land,
and dwell therein for ever.

³⁰ The mouth of the righteous speaketh wisdom,
and his tongue talketh of judgement.
³¹ The law of his God is in his heart:
none of his steps shall slide.
³² The wicked watcheth the righteous,
and seeketh to slay him.
³³ The LORD will not leave him in his hand,
nor condemn him when he is judged.
³⁴ Wait on the LORD, and keep his way,
and he shall exalt thee to inherit the land:
when the wicked are cut off, thou shalt see it.
³⁵ I have seen the wicked in great power,
and spreading himself like a green bay tree.
³⁶ Yet he passed away, and lo, he was not:
yea, I sought him, but he could not be found.
³⁷ Mark the perfect man, and behold the upright:
for the end of that man is peace.
³⁸ But the transgressors shall be destroyed together:
the end of the wicked shall be cut off.
³⁹ But the salvation of the righteous is of the LORD:
he is their strength in the time of trouble.
⁴⁰ And the LORD shall help them, and deliver them:
he shall deliver them from the wicked, and save them,
because they trust in him.

PSALM 38

A psalm of David, to bring to remembrance.

¹ O LORD, rebuke me not in thy wrath:
neither chasten me in thy hot displeasure.
² For thy arrows stick fast in me,
and thy hand presseth me sore.
³ There is no soundness in my flesh because of thy anger:
neither is there any rest in my bones because of my sin.
⁴ For my iniquities are gone over my head:
as a heavy burden they are too heavy for me.
⁵ My wounds stink and are corrupt
because of my foolishness.
⁶ I am troubled, I am bowed down greatly;
I go mourning all the day long.
⁷ For my loins are filled with a loathsome disease:
and there is no soundness in my flesh.
⁸ I am feeble and sore broken:
I have roared by reason of the disquietness of my heart.

⁹ Lord, all my desire is before thee:
and my groaning is not hid from thee.

¹⁰ My heart panteth, my strength faileth me:
   as for the light of my eyes, it also is gone from me.
¹¹ My lovers and my friends stand aloof from my sore:
   and my kinsmen stand afar off.
¹² They also that seek after my life lay snares for me:
   and they that seek my hurt speak mischievous things,
   and imagine deceits all the day long.

¹³ But I, as a deaf man, heard not;
   and I was as a dumb man that openeth not his mouth.
¹⁴ Thus I was as a man that heareth not,
   and in whose mouth are no reproofs.
¹⁵ For in thee, O LORD, do I hope:
   thou wilt hear, O Lord my God.
¹⁶ For I said, 'Hear me, lest otherwise they should rejoice over
      me':
   when my foot slippeth, they magnify themselves against me.
¹⁷ For I am ready to halt,
   and my sorrow is continually before me.
¹⁸ For I will declare my iniquity;
   I will be sorry for my sin.
¹⁹ But my enemies are lively, and they are strong:
   and they that hate me wrongfully are multiplied.
²⁰ They also that render evil for good are my adversaries:
   because I follow the thing that good is.

²¹ Forsake me not, O LORD:
   O my God, be not far from me.
²² Make haste to help me, O Lord my salvation.

PSALM 39

To the chief musician, even to Jeduthun.
A psalm of David.

¹ I said, 'I will take heed to my ways,
   that I sin not with my tongue:
   I will keep my mouth with a bridle,
   while the wicked is before me'.
² I was dumb with silence,
   I held my peace, even from good;
   and my sorrow was stirred.
³ My heart was hot within me,
   while I was musing the fire burnt:
   then spoke I with my tongue,
⁴ 'LORD, make me to know my end,
   and the measure of my days, what it is:
   that I may know how frail I am.

⁵ Behold, thou hast made my days as a handbreadth,
   and my age is as nothing before thee:
   verily every man at his best state is altogether vanity. Selah.
⁶ Surely every man walketh in a vain show:
   surely they are disquieted in vain:
   he heapeth up riches,
   and knoweth not who shall gather them.'

⁷ And now, Lord, what wait I for?
   my hope is in thee.
⁸ Deliver me from all my transgressions:
   make me not the reproach of the foolish.
⁹ I was dumb, I opened not my mouth;
   because thou didst it.
¹⁰ Remove thy stroke away from me:
   I am consumed by the blow of thy hand.
¹¹ When thou with rebukes dost correct man for iniquity,
   thou makest his beauty to consume away like a moth:
   surely every man is vanity. Selah.

¹² Hear my prayer, O LORD, and give ear unto my cry,
   hold not thy peace at my tears:
   for I am a stranger with thee,
   and a sojourner, as all my fathers were.
¹³ O spare me, that I may recover strength:
   before I go hence, and be no more.

PSALM 40

To the chief musician.
A psalm of David.

¹ I waited patiently for the LORD,
   and he inclined unto me, and heard my cry.
² He brought me up also out of a horrible pit, out of the miry
      clay,
   and set my feet upon a rock, and established my goings.
³ And he hath put a new song in my mouth, even praise unto our
      God:
   many shall see it, and fear, and shall trust in the LORD.
⁴ Blessed is that man that maketh the LORD his trust,
   and respecteth not the proud, nor such as turn aside to
      lies.
⁵ Many, O LORD my God, are thy wonderful works which thou hast
      done,
   and thy thoughts which are to us-ward:
   they cannot be reckoned up in order unto thee:
   if I would declare and speak of them,

they are more than can be numbered.
⁶ Sacrifice and offering thou didst not desire,
my ears hast thou opened:
burnt offering and sin offering hast thou not required.

⁷ Then said I, 'Lo, I come':
in the volume of the book it is written of me:
⁸ I delight to do thy will, O my God:
yea, thy law is within my heart.
⁹ I have preached righteousness in the great congregation:
lo, I have not refrained my lips, O LORD, thou knowest.
¹⁰ I have not hid thy righteousness within my heart;
I have declared thy faithfulness and thy salvation:
I have not concealed thy loving-kindness and thy truth from the
great congregation.

¹¹ Withhold not thou thy tender mercies from me, O LORD:
let thy loving-kindness and thy truth continually preserve me.
¹² For innumerable evils have compassed me about:
my iniquities have taken hold upon me,
so that I am not able to look up:
they are more than the hairs of my head,
therefore my heart faileth me.
¹³ Be pleased, O LORD, to deliver me:
O LORD, make haste to help me.
¹⁴ Let them be ashamed and confounded together that seek after
my soul to destroy it:
let them be driven backward and put to shame that wish me evil.
¹⁵ Let them be desolate for a reward of their shame that say unto
me, 'Aha, aha!'
¹⁶ Let all those that seek thee rejoice and be glad in thee:
let such as love thy salvation say continually, 'The LORD be
magnified'.
¹⁷ But I am poor and needy,
yet the Lord thinketh upon me:
thou art my help and my deliverer,
make no tarrying, O my God.

PSALM 41
To the chief musician.
A psalm of David.

¹ Blessed is he that considereth the poor:
the LORD will deliver him in time of trouble.
² The LORD will preserve him, and keep him alive,
and he shall be blessed upon the earth:
and thou wilt not deliver him unto the will of his enemies.

³ The LORD will strengthen him upon the bed of languishing:
   thou wilt make all his bed in his sickness.

⁴ I said, 'LORD, be merciful unto me,
   heal my soul, for I have sinned against thee'.
⁵ My enemies speak evil of me,
   'When shall he die, and his name perish?'
⁶ And if he come to see me, he speaketh vanity:
   his heart gathereth iniquity to itself;
   when he goeth abroad, he telleth it.
⁷ All that hate me whisper together against me:
   against me do they devise my hurt.
⁸ 'An evil disease,' say they, 'cleaveth fast unto him:
   and now that he lieth he shall rise up no more.'
⁹ Yea, my own familiar friend in whom I trusted, which did eat of
      my bread,
   hath lifted up his heel against me.

¹⁰ But thou, O LORD, be merciful unto me,
   and raise me up, that I may requite them.
¹¹ By this I know that thou favourest me:
   because my enemy doth not triumph over me.
¹² And as for me, thou upholdest me in my integrity,
   and settest me before thy face for ever.

¹³ Blessed be the LORD God of Israel,
   from everlasting, and to everlasting. Amen, and Amen.

PSALM 42

To the chief musician, maschil, for the sons of Korah.

¹ As the hart panteth after the water brooks,
   so panteth my soul after thee, O God.
² My soul thirsteth for God, for the living God:
   when shall I come and appear before God?
³ My tears have been my meat day and night;
   while they continually say unto me, 'Where is thy God?'
⁴ When I remember these things, I pour out my soul in me:
   for I had gone with the multitude,
   I went with them to the house of God,
   with the voice of joy and praise,
   with a multitude that kept holy day.

⁵ Why art thou cast down, O my soul?
   and why art thou disquieted in me?
   hope thou in God,
   for I shall yet praise him for the help of his countenance.

⁶ O my God, my soul is cast down within me:
therefore will I remember thee from the land of Jordan,
and of the Hermonites, from the hill Mizar.
⁷ Deep calleth unto deep at the noise of thy water-spouts:
all thy waves and thy billows are gone over me.
⁸ Yet the LORD will command his loving-kindness in the
daytime,
and in the night his song shall be with me,
and my prayer unto the God of my life.
⁹ I will say unto God, 'My rock, why hast thou forgotten me?'
why go I mourning because of the oppression of the enemy?
¹⁰ As with a sword in my bones, my enemies reproach me;
while they say daily unto me, 'Where is thy God?'

¹¹ Why art thou cast down, O my soul?
and why art thou disquieted within me?
hope thou in God, for I shall yet praise him,
who is the health of my countenance, and my God.

PSALM 43

¹ Judge me, O God, and plead my cause against an ungodly
nation:
O deliver me from the deceitful and unjust man.
² For thou art the God of my strength: why dost thou cast me
off?
why go I mourning because of the oppression of the enemy?
³ O send out thy light and thy truth: let them lead me,
let them bring me unto thy holy hill, and to thy tabernacles.
⁴ Then will I go unto the altar of God, unto God my exceeding
joy:
yea, upon the harp will I praise thee, O God my God.

⁵ Why art thou cast down, O my soul?
and why art thou disquieted within me?
hope in God, for I shall yet praise him,
who is the health of my countenance, and my God.

PSALM 44

To the chief musician for the sons of Korah, maschil.

¹ We have heard with our ears, O God, our fathers have told us,
what work thou didst in their days, in the times of old.
² How thou didst drive out the heathen with thy hand, and
plantedst them;
how thou didst afflict the people, and cast them out.

³ For they got not the land in possession by their own sword,
  neither did their own arm save them:
  but thy right hand, and thy arm, and the light of thy
    countenance,
  because thou hadst a favour unto them.

⁴ Thou art my King, O God:
  command deliverances for Jacob.
⁵ Through thee will we push down our enemies:
  through thy name will we tread them under that rise up
    against us.
⁶ For I will not trust in my bow, neither shall my sword save
    me.
⁷ But thou hast saved us from our enemies,
  and hast put them to shame that hated us.
⁸ In God we boast all the day long,
  and praise thy name for ever. Selah.

⁹ But thou hast cast off, and put us to shame;
  and goest not forth with our armies.
¹⁰ Thou makest us to turn back from the enemy:
  and they which hate us spoil for themselves.
¹¹ Thou hast given us like sheep appointed for meat:
  and hast scattered us among the heathen.
¹² Thou sellest thy people for nought,
  and dost not increase thy wealth by their price.
¹³ Thou makest us a reproach to our neighbours,
  a scorn and a derision to them that are round about us.
¹⁴ Thou makest us a byword among the heathen:
  a shaking of the head among the people.
¹⁵ My confusion is continually before me,
  and the shame of my face hath covered me,
¹⁶ for the voice of him that reproacheth and blasphemeth;
  by reason of the enemy and avenger.

¹⁷ All this is come upon us; yet have we not forgotten thee,
  neither have we dealt falsely in thy covenant.
¹⁸ Our heart is not turned back,
  neither have our steps declined from thy way,
¹⁹ though thou hast sore broken us in the place of dragons,
  and covered us with the shadow of death.
²⁰ If we have forgotten the name of our God,
  or stretched out our hands to a strange god:
²¹ shall not God search this out?
  for he knoweth the secrets of the heart.
²² Yea, for thy sake are we killed all the day long:
  we are counted as sheep for the slaughter.

²³ Awake, why sleepest thou, O Lord?
arise, cast us not off for ever.
²⁴ Wherefore hidest thou thy face,
and forgettest our affliction and our oppression?
²⁵ For our soul is bowed down to the dust:
our belly cleaveth unto the earth.
²⁶ Arise for our help,
and redeem us for thy mercy's sake.

PSALM 45

To the chief musician upon Shoshannim, for the sons of Korah, maschil:
a song of loves.

¹ My heart is inditing a good matter:
I speak of the things which I have made touching the king:
my tongue is the pen of a ready writer.

² Thou art fairer than the children of men:
grace is poured into thy lips:
therefore God hath blessed thee for ever.
³ Gird thy sword upon thy thigh, O most mighty,
with thy glory and thy majesty.
⁴ And in thy majesty ride prosperously because of truth and
meekness and righteousness:
and thy right hand shall teach thee terrible things.
⁵ Thy arrows are sharp in the heart of the king's enemies;
whereby the people fall under thee.
⁶ Thy throne, O God, is for ever and ever:
the sceptre of thy kingdom is a right sceptre.
⁷ Thou lovest righteousness, and hatest wickedness:
therefore God, thy God, hath anointed thee with the oil of
gladness above thy fellows.
⁸ All thy garments smell of myrrh, and aloes, and cassia,
out of the ivory palaces, whereby they have made thee glad.
⁹ Kings' daughters were among thy honourable women:
upon thy right hand did stand the queen in gold of Ophir.

¹⁰ Hearken, O daughter, and consider, and incline thy ear;
forget also thy own people, and thy father's house;
¹¹ so shall the king greatly desire thy beauty:
for he is thy Lord, and worship thou him.
¹² And the daughter of Tyre shall be there with a gift;
even the rich among the people shall entreat thy favour.
¹³ The king's daughter is all glorious within:
her clothing is of wrought gold.
¹⁴ She shall be brought unto the king in raiment of
needlework:

the virgins her companions that follow her shall be brought unto
thee.

[15] With gladness and rejoicing shall they be brought:
they shall enter into the king's palace.

[16] In stead of thy fathers shall be thy children,
whom thou mayest make princes in all the earth.

[17] I will make thy name to be remembered in all generations:
therefore shall the people praise thee for ever and ever.

PSALM 46

To the chief musician for the sons of Korah.
A song upon Alamoth.

[1] God is our refuge and strength:
a very present help in trouble.

[2] Therefore will not we fear, though the earth be removed:
and though the mountains be carried into the midst of the sea;

[3] though the waters thereof roar and be troubled,
though the mountains shake with the swelling thereof. Selah.

[4] There is a river, the streams whereof shall make glad the city of
God:
the holy place of the tabernacles of the most High.

[5] God is in the midst of her; she shall not be moved:
God shall help her, and that right early.

[6] The heathen raged, the kingdoms were moved:
he uttered his voice, the earth melted.

[7] The LORD of hosts is with us;
the God of Jacob is our refuge. Selah.

[8] Come, behold the works of the LORD,
what desolations he hath made in the earth.

[9] He maketh wars to cease unto the end of the earth:
he breaketh the bow, and cutteth the spear in sunder,
he burneth the chariot in the fire.

[10] Be still, and know that I am God:
I will be exalted among the heathen,
I will be exalted in the earth.

[11] The LORD of hosts is with us;
the God of Jacob is our refuge. Selah.

PSALM 47

To the chief musician.
A psalm for the sons of Korah.

[1] O clap your hands, all ye people:
shout unto God with the voice of triumph.

² For the Lord most high is terrible;
he is a great King over all the earth.
³ He shall subdue the people under us,
and the nations under our feet.
⁴ He shall choose our inheritance for us,
the excellence of Jacob whom he loved. Selah.

⁵ God is gone up with a shout,
the Lord with the sound of a trumpet.
⁶ Sing praises to God, sing praises:
sing praises unto our King, sing praises.
⁷ For God is the King of all the earth:
sing ye praises with understanding.
⁸ God reigneth over the heathen:
God sitteth upon the throne of his holiness.
⁹ The princes of the people are gathered together,
even the people of the God of Abraham:
for the shields of the earth belong unto God:
he is greatly exalted.

PSALM 48

A song and psalm for the sons of Korah.

¹ Great is the Lord, and greatly to be praised in the city of our God,
in the mountain of his holiness.
² Beautiful for situation, the joy of the whole earth is mount Zion,
on the sides of the north, the city of the great King.
³ God is known in her palaces for a refuge.
⁴ For lo, the kings were assembled: they passed by together.
⁵ They saw it, and so they marvelled;
they were troubled, and hasted away.
⁶ Fear took hold upon them there,
and pain, as of a woman in travail.
⁷ Thou breakest the ships of Tarshish with an east wind.
⁸ As we have heard, so have we seen
in the city of the Lord of hosts, in the city of our God:
God will establish it for ever. Selah.

⁹ We have thought of thy loving-kindness, O God, in the midst of
thy temple.
¹⁰ According to thy name, O God, so is thy praise unto the ends of
the earth:
thy right hand is full of righteousness.
¹¹ Let mount Zion rejoice, let the daughters of Judah be glad,
because of thy judgements.
¹² Walk about Zion, and go round about her:
tell the towers thereof.

¹³ Mark ye well her bulwarks, consider her palaces;
   that ye may tell it to the generation following.
¹⁴ For this God is our God for ever and ever:
   he will be our guide even unto death.

PSALM 49

To the chief musician.
A psalm for the sons of Korah.

¹ Hear this, all ye people,
   give ear, all ye inhabitants of the world:
² Both low and high,
   rich and poor, together.
³ My mouth shall speak of wisdom:
   and the meditation of my heart shall be of understanding.
⁴ I will incline my ear to a parable:
   I will open my dark saying upon the harp.

⁵ Wherefore should I fear in the days of evil,
   when the iniquity of my heels shall compass me about?
⁶ They that trust in their wealth,
   and boast themselves in the multitude of their riches:
⁷ none of them can by any means redeem his brother,
   nor give to God a ransom for him
⁸ (for the redemption of their soul is precious,
   and it ceaseth for ever):
⁹ that he should still live for ever,
   and not see corruption.
¹⁰ For he seeth that wise men die,
   likewise the fool and the brutish person perish,
   and leave their wealth to others.
¹¹ Their inward thought is, that their houses shall continue for ever,
   and their dwelling places to all generations;
   they call their lands after their own names.
¹² Nevertheless man being in honour abideth not:
   he is like the beasts that perish.
¹³ This their way is their folly:
   yet their posterity approve their sayings. Selah.

¹⁴ Like sheep they are laid in the grave, death shall feed on them;
   and the upright shall have dominion over them in the morning;
   and their beauty shall consume in the grave from their dwelling.
¹⁵ But God will redeem my soul from the power of the grave:
   for he shall receive me. Selah.
¹⁶ Be not thou afraid when one is made rich,
   when the glory of his house is increased;
¹⁷ for when he dieth he shall carry nothing away:

his glory shall not descend after him.
¹⁸ Though whilst he lived he blessed his soul:
and men will praise thee, when thou doest well to thyself.
¹⁹ He shall go to the generation of his fathers;
they shall never see light.

²⁰ Man that is in honour, and understandeth not,
is like the beasts that perish.

PSALM 50
A psalm of Asaph.

¹ The mighty God, even the LORD, hath spoken,
and called the earth from the rising of the sun unto the going
down thereof.
² Out of Zion, the perfection of beauty, God hath shone.
³ Our God shall come, and shall not keep silence:
a fire shall devour before him,
and it shall be very tempestuous round about him.
⁴ He shall call to the heavens from above, and to the earth,
that he may judge his people.
⁵ Gather my saints together unto me:
those that have made a covenant with me by sacrifice.
⁶ And the heavens shall declare his righteousness:
for God is judge himself. Selah.
⁷ Hear, O my people, and I will speak,
O Israel, and I will testify against thee:
I am God, even thy God.
⁸ I will not reprove thee for thy sacrifices,
or thy burnt offerings, to have been continually before me.
⁹ I will take no bullock out of thy house,
nor he-goats out of thy folds.
¹⁰ For every beast of the forest is mine,
and the cattle upon a thousand hills.
¹¹ I know all the fowls of the mountains:
and the wild beasts of the field are mine.
¹² If I were hungry, I would not tell thee:
for the world is mine, and the fulness thereof.
¹³ Will I eat the flesh of bulls,
or drink the blood of goats?
¹⁴ Offer unto God thanksgiving,
and pay thy vows unto the most High.
¹⁵ And call upon me in the day of trouble:
I will deliver thee, and thou shalt glorify me.

¹⁶ But unto the wicked God saith,
'What hast thou to do to declare my statutes,

or that thou shouldst take my covenant in thy mouth?
¹⁷ seeing thou hatest instruction,
and castest my words behind thee.
¹⁸ When thou sawest a thief, then thou consentedst with him,
and hast been partaker with adulterers.
¹⁹ Thou givest thy mouth to evil,
and thy tongue frameth deceit.
²⁰ Thou sittest and speakest against thy brother;
thou slanderest thy own mother's son.
²¹ These things hast thou done, and I kept silence:
thou thoughtest that I was altogether such a one as thyself:
but I will reprove thee, and set them in order before thy eyes.
²² Now consider this, ye that forget God,
lest I tear you in pieces, and there be none to deliver.
²³ Whoso offereth praise glorifieth me:
and to him that ordereth his conversation aright will I show the
salvation of God.'

PSALM 51

To the chief musician.
A psalm of David, when Nathan the prophet came unto him, after he
had gone in to Bath-sheba.

¹ Have mercy upon me, O God, according to thy loving-kindness:
according unto the multitude of thy tender mercies blot out my
transgressions.
² Wash me thoroughly from my iniquity,
and cleanse me from my sin.
³ For I acknowledge my transgressions:
and my sin is ever before me.

⁴ Against thee, thee only, have I sinned,
and done this evil in thy sight:
that thou mightest be justified when thou speakest,
and be clear when thou judgest.
⁵ Behold, I was shaped in iniquity:
and in sin did my mother conceive me.
⁶ Behold, thou desirest truth in the inward parts:
and in the hidden part thou shalt make me to know
wisdom.

⁷ Purge me with hyssop, and I shall be clean:
wash me, and I shall be whiter than snow.
⁸ Make me to hear joy and gladness:
that the bones which thou hast broken may rejoice.
⁹ Hide thy face from my sins,
and blot out all my iniquities.

¹⁰ Create in me a clean heart, O God;
and renew a right spirit within me.
¹¹ Cast me not away from thy presence;
and take not thy holy spirit from me.
¹² Restore unto me the joy of thy salvation:
and uphold me with thy free spirit.
¹³ Then will I teach transgressors thy ways,
and sinners shall be converted unto thee.

¹⁴ Deliver me from blood-guiltiness, O God, thou God of my salvation:
and my tongue shall sing aloud of thy righteousness.
¹⁵ O Lord, open thou my lips,
and my mouth shall show forth thy praise.
¹⁶ For thou desirest not sacrifice: else would I give it:
thou delightest not in burnt offering.
¹⁷ The sacrifices of God are a broken spirit:
a broken and a contrite heart, O God, thou wilt not despise.

¹⁸ Do good in thy good pleasure unto Zion:
build thou the walls of Jerusalem.
¹⁹ Then shalt thou be pleased with the sacrifices of righteousness,
with burnt offering and whole burnt offering:
then shall they offer bullocks upon thy altar.

PSALM 52

To the chief musician, maschil.
A psalm of David, when Doeg the Edomite came and told Saul, and said
unto him, 'David is come to the house of Ahimelech'.

¹ Why boastest thou thyself in mischief, O mighty man?
the goodness of God endureth continually.

² Thy tongue deviseth mischiefs:
like a sharp razor, working deceitfully.
³ Thou lovest evil more than good;
and lying rather than to speak righteousness. Selah.
⁴ Thou lovest all devouring words, O thou deceitful tongue.
⁵ God shall likewise destroy thee for ever,
he shall take thee away, and pluck thee out of thy dwelling place,
and root thee out of the land of the living. Selah.

⁶ The righteous also shall see, and fear,
and shall laugh at him:
⁷ 'Lo, this is the man that made not God his strength:
but trusted in the abundance of his riches,
and strengthened himself in his wickedness'.

⁸ But I am like a green olive tree in the house of God:
I trust in the mercy of God for ever and ever.
⁹ I will praise thee for ever, because thou hast done it:
and I will wait on thy name, for it is good before thy saints.

PSALM 53

To the chief musician upon Mahalath, maschil.
A psalm of David.

¹ The fool hath said in his heart, 'There is no God'.
Corrupt are they, and have done abominable iniquity:
there is none that doeth good.
² God looked down from heaven upon the children of men,
to see if there were any that did understand, that did seek God.
³ Every one of them is gone back: they are altogether become filthy:
there is none that doeth good, no, not one.
⁴ Have the workers of iniquity no knowledge?
who eat up my people as they eat bread:
they have not called upon God.
⁵ There were they in great fear, where no fear was:
for God hath scattered the bones of him that encampeth against
thee:
thou hast put them to shame, because God hath despised them.

⁶ O that the salvation of Israel were come out of Zion!
When God bringeth back the captivity of his people,
Jacob shall rejoice, and Israel shall be glad.

PSALM 54

To the chief musician on neginoth, maschil.
A psalm of David, when the Ziphims came and said to Saul, 'Doth not
David hide himself with us?'

¹ Save me, O God, by thy name,
and judge me by thy strength.
² Hear my prayer, O God;
give ear to the words of my mouth.
³ For strangers are risen up against me,
and oppressors seek after my soul:
they have not set God before them. Selah.

⁴ Behold, God is my helper:
the Lord is with them that uphold my soul.
⁵ He shall reward evil unto my enemies:
cut them off in thy truth.

⁶ I will freely sacrifice unto thee:
   I will praise thy name, O Lord: for it is good.
⁷ For he hath delivered me out of all trouble:
   and my eye hath seen his desire upon my enemies.

PSALM 55

To the chief musician on neginoth, maschil.
A psalm of David.

¹ Give ear to my prayer, O God:
   and hide not thyself from my supplication.
² Attend unto me, and hear me:
   I mourn in my complaint, and make a noise;
³ because of the voice of the enemy, because of the oppression of
      the wicked:
   for they cast iniquity upon me, and in wrath they hate me.
⁴ My heart is sore pained within me:
   and the terrors of death are fallen upon me.
⁵ Fearfulness and trembling are come upon me,
   and horror hath overwhelmed me.
⁶ And I said, 'O that I had wings like a dove;
   for then would I fly away, and be at rest'.
⁷ Lo, then would I wander far off, and remain in the wilderness.
      Selah.
⁸ I would hasten my escape from the windy storm and tempest.

⁹ Destroy, O Lord, and divide their tongues:
   for I have seen violence and strife in the city.
¹⁰ Day and night they go about it upon the walls thereof:
   mischief also and sorrow are in the midst of it.
¹¹ Wickedness is in the midst thereof:
   deceit and guile depart not from her streets.
¹² For it was not an enemy that reproached me;
   then I could have borne it:
   neither was it he that hated me that did magnify himself against
      me;
   then I would have hid myself from him:
¹³ but it was thou, a man my equal, my guide, and my
      acquaintance.
¹⁴ We took sweet counsel together,
   and walked unto the house of God in company.

¹⁵ Let death seize upon them,
   and let them go down quick into hell:
   for wickedness is in their dwellings, and among them.
¹⁶ As for me, I will call upon God: and the Lord shall save me.

¹⁷ Evening, and morning, and at noon, will I pray, and cry aloud:

and he shall hear my voice.

¹⁸ He hath delivered my soul in peace from the battle that was against me:

for there were many with me.

¹⁹ God shall hear, and afflict them, even he that abideth of old. Selah.

Because they have no changes, therefore they fear not God.

²⁰ He hath put forth his hands against such as be at peace with him:

he hath broken his covenant.

²¹ The words of his mouth were smoother than butter, but war was in his heart:

his words were softer than oil, yet were they drawn swords.

²² Cast thy burden upon the LORD, and he shall sustain thee:

he shall never suffer the righteous to be moved.

²³ But thou, O God, shalt bring them down into the pit of destruction:

bloody and deceitful men shall not live out half their days,

but I will trust in thee.

PSALM 56

To the chief musician upon Jonath Elem Rechokim,
michtam of David, when the Philistines took him in Gath.

¹ Be merciful unto me, O God, for man would swallow me up:

he fighting daily oppresseth me.

² My enemies would daily swallow me up:

for they be many that fight against me, O thou most High.

³ What time I am afraid, I will trust in thee.

⁴ In God I will praise his word, in God I have put my trust,

I will not fear what flesh can do unto me.

⁵ Every day they wrest my words:

all their thoughts are against me for evil.

⁶ They gather themselves together;

they hide themselves,

they mark my steps when they wait for my soul.

⁷ Shall they escape by iniquity?

in thy anger cast down the people, O God.

⁸ Thou tellest my wanderings:

put thou my tears into thy bottle: are they not in thy book?

⁹ When I cry unto thee, then shall my enemies turn back:

this I know, for God is for me.

¹⁰ In God will I praise his word:
in the LORD will I praise his word.
¹¹ In God have I put my trust:
I will not be afraid what man can do unto me.

¹² Thy vows are upon me, O God:
I will render praises unto thee.
¹³ For thou hast delivered my soul from death:
wilt not thou deliver my feet from falling,
that I may walk before God in the light of the living?

PSALM 57

To the chief musician, Al-taschith,
michtam of David, when he fled from Saul in the cave.

¹ Be merciful unto me, O God, be merciful unto me,
for my soul trusteth in thee:
yea, in the shadow of thy wings will I make my refuge,
until these calamities be overpast.
² I will cry unto God most high:
unto God that performeth all things for me.
³ He shall send from heaven, and save me
from the reproach of him that would swallow me up. Selah.
God shall send forth his mercy and his truth.

⁴ My soul is among lions,
and I lie even among them that are set on fire:
even the sons of men,
whose teeth are spears and arrows,
and their tongue a sharp sword.
⁵ Be thou exalted, O God, above the heavens:
let thy glory be above all the earth.
⁶ They have prepared a net for my steps,
my soul is bowed down: they have dug a pit before me,
into the midst whereof they are fallen themselves. Selah.

⁷ My heart is fixed, O God, my heart is fixed:
I will sing and give praise.
⁸ Awake up, my glory,
awake, psaltery and harp:
I myself will awake early.
⁹ I will praise thee, O Lord, among the people:
I will sing unto thee among the nations.
¹⁰ For thy mercy is great unto the heavens,
and thy truth unto the clouds.
¹¹ Be thou exalted, O God, above the heavens:
let thy glory be above all the earth.

PSALM 58

To the chief musician, Al-taschith,
michtam of David.

¹ Do ye indeed speak righteousness, O congregation?
  do ye judge uprightly, O ye sons of men?
² Yea, in heart you work wickedness;
  you weigh the violence of your hands in the earth.
³ The wicked are estranged from the womb:
  they go astray as soon as they be born, speaking lies.
⁴ Their poison is like the poison of a serpent:
  they are like the deaf adder that stoppeth her ear:
⁵ which will not hearken to the voice of charmers,
  charming never so wisely.

⁶ Break their teeth, O God, in their mouth:
  break out the great teeth of the young lions, O LORD.
⁷ Let them melt away as waters which run continually:
  when he bendeth his bow to shoot his arrows, let them be as cut
    in pieces.
⁸ As a snail which melteth, let every one of them pass away:
  like the untimely birth of a woman, that they may not see the sun.
⁹ Before your pots can feel the thorns,
  he shall take them away as with a whirlwind, both living, and in
    his wrath.

¹⁰ The righteous shall rejoice when he seeth the vengeance:
   he shall wash his feet in the blood of the wicked.
¹¹ So that a man shall say,
   'Verily there is a reward for the righteous:
   verily he is a God that judgeth in the earth'.

PSALM 59

To the chief musician, Al-taschith,
michtam of David, when Saul sent, and they watched the house to kill
him.

¹ Deliver me from my enemies, O my God:
  defend me from them that rise up against me.
² Deliver me from the workers of iniquity,
  and save me from bloody men.

³ For lo, they lie in wait for my soul:
  the mighty are gathered against me;
  not for my transgression, nor for my sin, O LORD.
⁴ They run and prepare themselves without my fault:
  awake to help me, and behold.

⁵ Thou therefore, O LORD God of hosts, the God of Israel, awake to
   visit all the heathen:
be not merciful to any wicked transgressors. Selah.
⁶ They return at evening:
   they make a noise like a dog, and go round about the city.
⁷ Behold, they belch out with their mouth:
   swords are in their lips:
   'For who,' say they, 'doth hear?'
⁸ But thou, O LORD, shalt laugh at them;
   thou shalt have all the heathen in derision.
⁹ Because of his strength will I wait upon thee:
   for God is my defence.
¹⁰ The God of my mercy shall prevent me:
   God shall let me see my desire upon my enemies.
¹¹ Slay them not, lest my people forget:
   scatter them by thy power;
   and bring them down, O Lord our shield.
¹² For the sin of their mouth and the words of their lips let them
   even be taken in their pride:
   and for cursing and lying which they speak.
¹³ Consume them in wrath, consume them, that they may not be:
   and let them know that God ruleth in Jacob unto the ends of the
   earth. Selah.
¹⁴ And at evening let them return,
   and let them make a noise like a dog, and go round about the
   city.
¹⁵ Let them wander up and down for meat,
   and grudge if they be not satisfied.

¹⁶ But I will sing of thy power;
   yea, I will sing aloud of thy mercy in the morning:
   for thou hast been my defence and refuge in the day of my
   trouble.
¹⁷ Unto thee, O my strength, will I sing:
   for God is my defence, and the God of my mercy.

PSALM 60

To the chief musician upon Shushan Eduth,
michtam of David, to teach.
When he strove with Aram-naharaim and with Aram-zobah,
when Joab returned, and smote of Edom in the valley of salt
twelve thousand.

¹ O God, thou hast cast us off, thou hast scattered us, thou hast
   been displeased;
   O turn thyself to us again.

² Thou hast made the earth to tremble; thou hast broken it:
  heal the breaches thereof, for it shaketh.
³ Thou hast shown thy people hard things:
  thou hast made us to drink the wine of astonishment.
⁴ Thou hast given a banner to them that fear thee,
  that it may be displayed because of the truth. Selah.
⁵ That thy beloved may be delivered;
  save with thy right hand, and hear me.

⁶ God hath spoken in his holiness, 'I will rejoice:
  I will divide Shechem, and mete out the valley of Succoth.
⁷ Gilead is mine, and Manasseh is mine;
  Ephraim also is the strength of my head; Judah is my lawgiver.
⁸ Moab is my wash-pot; over Edom will I cast out my shoe:
  Philistia, triumph thou because of me.'

⁹ Who will bring me into the strong city?
  who will lead me into Edom?
¹⁰ Wilt not thou, O God, which hadst cast us off?
  and thou, O God, which didst not go out with our armies?
¹¹ Give us help from trouble:
  for vain is the help of man.
¹² Through God we shall do valiantly:
  for he it is that shall tread down our enemies.

PSALM 61

To the chief musician upon neginah.
A psalm of David.

¹ Hear my cry, O God, attend unto my prayer.

² From the end of the earth will I cry unto thee, when my heart is
    overwhelmed:
  lead me to the rock that is higher than I.
³ For thou hast been a shelter for me,
  and a strong tower from the enemy.
⁴ I will abide in thy tabernacle for ever:
  I will trust in the covert of thy wings. Selah.
⁵ For thou, O God, hast heard my vows:
  thou hast given me the heritage of those that fear thy name.
⁶ Thou wilt prolong the king's life:
  and his years as many generations.
⁷ He shall abide before God for ever:
  O prepare mercy and truth which may preserve him.

⁸ So will I sing praise unto thy name for ever,
  that I may daily perform my vows.

PSALM 62

To the chief musician to Jeduthun.
A psalm of David.

¹ Truly my soul waiteth upon God:
  from him cometh my salvation.
² He only is my rock and my salvation:
  he is my defence, I shall not be greatly moved.

³ How long will ye imagine mischief against a man?
  ye shall be slain all of you:
  as a bowing wall shall ye be, and as a tottering fence.
⁴ They only consult to cast him down from his excellence,
  they delight in lies:
  they bless with their mouth, but they curse inwardly. Selah.

⁵ My soul, wait thou only upon God:
  for my expectation is from him.
⁶ He only is my rock and my salvation:
  he is my defence; I shall not be moved.
⁷ In God is my salvation and my glory:
  the rock of my strength, and my refuge, is in God.
⁸ Trust in him at all times;
  ye people, pour out your heart before him:
  God is a refuge for us. Selah.

⁹ Surely men of low degree are vanity,
  and men of high degree are a lie:
  to be laid in the balance, they are altogether lighter than vanity.
¹⁰ Trust not in oppression,
  become not vain in robbery:
  if riches increase, set not your heart upon them.

¹¹ God hath spoken once;
  twice have I heard this,
  that power belongeth unto God.
¹² Also unto thee, O Lord, belongeth mercy:
  for thou renderest to every man according to his work.

PSALM 63

A psalm of David,
when he was in the wilderness of Judah.

¹ O God, thou art my God, early will I seek thee:
  my soul thirsteth for thee,
  my flesh longeth for thee in a dry and thirsty land, where no
    water is:

² to see thy power and thy glory,
   so as I have seen thee in the sanctuary.
³ Because thy loving-kindness is better than life,
   my lips shall praise thee.
⁴ Thus will I bless thee while I live:
   I will lift up my hands in thy name.
⁵ My soul shall be satisfied as with marrow and fatness:
   and my mouth shall praise thee with joyful lips:
⁶ when I remember thee upon my bed,
   and meditate on thee in the night watches.
⁷ Because thou hast been my help,
   therefore in the shadow of thy wings will I rejoice.
⁸ My soul followeth hard after thee:
   thy right hand upholdeth me.
⁹ But those that seek my soul to destroy it, shall go into the lower
      parts of the earth.
¹⁰ They shall fall by the sword:
   they shall be a portion for foxes.
¹¹ But the king shall rejoice in God;
   every one that sweareth by him shall glory:
   but the mouth of them that speak lies shall be stopped.

PSALM 64
To the chief musician.
A psalm of David.

¹ Hear my voice, O God, in my prayer:
   preserve my life from fear of the enemy.
² Hide me from the secret counsel of the wicked:
   from the insurrection of the workers of iniquity:
³ who whet their tongue like a sword,
   and bend their bows to shoot their arrows, even bitter words:
⁴ that they may shoot in secret at the perfect:
   suddenly do they shoot at him, and fear not.
⁵ They encourage themselves in an evil matter:
   they commune of laying snares privily;
   they say, 'Who shall see them?'
⁶ They search out iniquities, they accomplish a diligent search:
   both the inward thought of every one of them, and the heart, is
      deep.

⁷ But God shall shoot at them:
   with an arrow, suddenly shall they be wounded.
⁸ So they shall make their own tongue to fall upon themselves:
   all that see them shall flee away.
⁹ And all men shall fear, and shall declare the work of God;
   for they shall wisely consider of his doing.

¹⁰ The righteous shall be glad in the LORD, and shall trust in
    him;
  and all the upright in heart shall glory.

PSALM 65

To the chief musician.
A psalm and song of David.

¹ Praise waiteth for thee, O God, in Zion:
  and unto thee shall the vow be performed.
² O thou that hearest prayer,
  unto thee shall all flesh come.
³ Iniquities prevail against me:
  as for our transgressions, thou shalt purge them away.
⁴ Blessed is the man whom thou choosest,
  and causest to approach unto thee, that he may dwell in thy
    courts:
  we shall be satisfied with the goodness of thy house, even of thy
    holy temple.
⁵ By terrible things in righteousness wilt thou answer us, O God of
    our salvation:
  who art the confidence of all the ends of the earth,
  and of them that are afar off upon the sea.
⁶ Which by his strength setteth fast the mountains;
  being girded with power.
⁷ Which stilleth the noise of the seas;
  the noise of their waves, and the tumult of the people.
⁸ They also that dwell in the uttermost parts are afraid at thy
    tokens:
  thou makest the outgoings of the morning and evening to
    rejoice.

⁹ Thou visitest the earth, and waterest it:
  thou greatly enrichest it with the river of God which is full of water:
  thou preparest them corn, when thou hast so provided for it.
¹⁰ Thou waterest the ridges thereof abundantly:
  thou settlest the furrows thereof:
  thou makest it soft with showers, thou blessest the springing
    thereof.
¹¹ Thou crownest the year with thy goodness;
  and thy paths drop fatness.
¹² They drop upon the pastures of the wilderness;
  and the little hills rejoice on every side.
¹³ The pastures are clothed with flocks;
  the valleys also are covered over with corn;
  they shout for joy, they also sing.

PSALM 66

To the chief musician.
A song or psalm.

¹ Make a joyful noise unto God, all ye lands.
² Sing forth the honour of his name:
  make his praise glorious.
³ Say unto God, 'How terrible art thou in thy works!
  through the greatness of thy power shall thy enemies submit
    themselves unto thee.
⁴ All the earth shall worship thee, and shall sing unto thee;
  they shall sing to thy name.' Selah.

⁵ Come and see the works of God:
  he is terrible in his doing toward the children of men.
⁶ He turned the sea into dry land:
  they went through the flood on foot:
  there did we rejoice in him.
⁷ He ruleth by his power for ever, his eyes behold the
    nations:
  let not the rebellious exalt themselves. Selah.

⁸ O bless our God, ye people,
  and make the voice of his praise to be heard.
⁹ Which holdeth our soul in life,
  and suffereth not our feet to be moved.
¹⁰ For thou, O God, hast proved us:
  thou hast tried us, as silver is tried.
¹¹ Thou broughtest us into the net;
  thou laidst affliction upon our loins.
¹² Thou hast caused men to ride over our heads;
  we went through fire and through water:
  but thou broughtest us out into a wealthy place.

¹³ I will go into thy house with burnt offerings:
  I will pay thee my vows,
¹⁴ which my lips have uttered,
  and my mouth hath spoken, when I was in trouble.
¹⁵ I will offer unto thee burnt sacrifices of fatlings, with the
    incense of rams:
  I will offer bullocks with goats. Selah.

¹⁶ Come and hear, all ye that fear God,
  and I will declare what he hath done for my soul.
¹⁷ I cried unto him with my mouth,
  and he was extolled with my tongue.
¹⁸ If I regard iniquity in my heart,
  the Lord will not hear me.

¹⁹ But verily God hath heard me;
    he hath attended to the voice of my prayer.

²⁰ Blessed be God,
    which hath not turned away my prayer, nor his mercy from
       me.

PSALM 67
To the chief musician on neginoth.
A psalm or song.

¹ God be merciful unto us, and bless us;
    and cause his face to shine upon us. Selah.
² That thy way may be known upon earth,
    thy saving health among all nations.

³ Let the people praise thee, O God;
    let all the people praise thee.
⁴ O let the nations be glad and sing for joy:
    for thou shalt judge the people righteously,
    and govern the nations upon earth. Selah.
⁵ Let the people praise thee, O God;
    let all the people praise thee.

⁶ Then shall the earth yield her increase;
    and God, even our own God, shall bless us.
⁷ God shall bless us;
    and all the ends of the earth shall fear him.

PSALM 68
To the chief musician.
A psalm or song of David.

¹ Let God arise, let his enemies be scattered:
    let them also that hate him flee before him.
² As smoke is driven away, so drive them away:
    as wax melteth before the fire, so let the wicked perish at the
      presence of God.
³ But let the righteous be glad:
    let them rejoice before God, yea, let them exceedingly rejoice.

⁴ Sing unto God, sing praises to his name:
    extol him that rideth upon the heavens by his name JAH,
    and rejoice before him.

⁵ A father of the fatherless, and a judge of the widows,
   is God in his holy habitation.
⁶ God setteth the solitary in families:
   he bringeth out those which are bound with chains,
   but the rebellious dwell in a dry land.

⁷ O God, when thou wentest forth before thy people,
   when thou didst march through the wilderness; Selah:
⁸ the earth shook, the heavens also dropped at the presence of
      God:
   even Sinai itself was moved at the presence of God, the God of
      Israel.
⁹ Thou, O God, didst send a plentiful rain,
   whereby thou didst confirm thine inheritance, when it was
      weary.
¹⁰ Thy congregation hath dwelt therein:
   thou, O God, hast prepared of thy goodness for the poor.

¹¹ The Lord gave the word:
   great was the company of those that published it.
¹² Kings of armies did flee apace:
   and she that tarried at home divided the spoil.
¹³ Though ye have lain among the pots,
   yet shall ye be as the wings of a dove, covered with silver,
   and her feathers with yellow gold.
¹⁴ When the Almighty scattered kings in it,
   it was white as snow in Salmon.

¹⁵ The hill of God is as the hill of Bashan,
   a high hill as the hill of Bashan.
¹⁶ Why leap ye, ye high hills?
   this is the hill which God desireth to dwell in;
   yea, the LORD will dwell in it for ever.
¹⁷ The chariots of God are twenty thousand, even thousands of
      angels:
   the Lord is among them as in Sinai, in the holy place.
¹⁸ Thou hast ascended on high, thou hast led captivity captive:
   thou hast received gifts for men;
   yea, for the rebellious also, that the LORD God might dwell
      among them.

¹⁹ Blessed be the Lord, who daily loadeth us with benefits,
   even the God of our salvation. Selah.
²⁰ He that is our God is the God of salvation;
   and unto GOD the Lord belong the issues from death.
²¹ But God shall wound the head of his enemies,
   and the hairy scalp of such a one as goeth on still in his
      trespasses.

²² The Lord said, 'I will bring again from Bashan,
   I will bring my people again from the depths of the sea:
²³ that thy foot may be dipped in the blood of thy enemies,
   and the tongue of thy dogs in the same'.

²⁴ They have seen thy goings, O God,
   even the goings of my God, my King, in the sanctuary.
²⁵ The singers went before, the players on instruments followed after;
   amongst them were the damsels playing with timbrels.
²⁶ Bless ye God in the congregations,
   even the Lord, from the fountain of Israel.
²⁷ There is little Benjamin with their ruler,
   the princes of Judah and their council,
   the princes of Zebulun, and the princes of Naphtali.
²⁸ Thy God hath commanded thy strength:
   strengthen, O God, that which thou hast wrought for us.
²⁹ Because of thy temple at Jerusalem shall kings bring presents
   unto thee.
³⁰ Rebuke the company of spearmen,
   the multitude of the bulls, with the calves of the people,
   till every one submit himself with pieces of silver:
   scatter thou the people that delight in war.
³¹ Princes shall come out of Egypt,
   Ethiopia shall soon stretch out her hands unto God.

³² Sing unto God, ye kingdoms of the earth:
   O sing praises unto the Lord; Selah:
³³ to him that rideth upon the heavens of heavens, which were of old;
   lo, he doth send out his voice, and that a mighty voice.
³⁴ Ascribe ye strength unto God:
   his excellence is over Israel,
   and his strength is in the clouds.

³⁵ O God, thou art terrible out of thy holy places:
   the God of Israel is he that giveth strength and power unto his
      people.
   Blessed be God.

PSALM 69

To the chief musician upon Shoshannim.
A psalm of David.

¹ Save me, O God, for the waters are come in unto my soul.
² I sink in deep mire, where there is no standing:
   I am come into deep waters, where the floods overflow me.
³ I am weary of my crying: my throat is dried:
   my eyes fail while I wait for my God.

⁴ They that hate me without a cause are more than the hairs of my
    head:
they that would destroy me, being my enemies wrongfully, are
    mighty:
then I restored that which I took not away.

⁵ O God, thou knowest my foolishness;
and my sins are not hid from thee.
⁶ Let not them that wait on thee, O Lord GOD of hosts, be ashamed
    for my sake:
let not those that seek thee be confounded for my sake, O God of
    Israel.
⁷ Because for thy sake I have borne reproach:
shame hath covered my face.
⁸ I am become a stranger unto my brethren,
and an alien unto my mother's children.
⁹ For the zeal of thy house hath eaten me up;
and the reproaches of them that reproached thee are fallen
    upon me.
¹⁰ When I wept, and chastened my soul with fasting,
that was to my reproach.
¹¹ I made sackcloth also my garment:
and I became a proverb to them.
¹² They that sit in the gate speak against me;
and I was the song of the drunkards.

¹³ But as for me, my prayer is unto thee, O LORD, in an acceptable
    time:
O God, in the multitude of thy mercy hear me,
in the truth of thy salvation.
¹⁴ Deliver me out of the mire, and let me not sink:
let me be delivered from them that hate me, and out of the deep
    waters.
¹⁵ Let not the water-flood overflow me,
neither let the deep swallow me up,
and let not the pit shut her mouth upon me.
¹⁶ Hear me, O LORD, for thy loving-kindness is good:
turn unto me according to the multitude of thy tender mercies.
¹⁷ And hide not thy face from thy servant,
for I am in trouble: hear me speedily.
¹⁸ Draw nigh unto my soul, and redeem it:
deliver me because of my enemies.

¹⁹ Thou hast known my reproach, and my shame, and my
    dishonour:
my adversaries are all before thee.
²⁰ Reproach hath broken my heart, and I am full of heaviness:
and I looked for some to take pity, but there was none;

and for comforters, but I found none.
²¹ They gave me also gall for my meat,
and in my thirst they gave me vinegar to drink.
²² Let their table become a snare before them:
and that which should have been for their welfare, let it become
a trap.
²³ Let their eyes be darkened, that they see not;
and make their loins continually to shake.
²⁴ Pour out thy indignation upon them,
and let thy wrathful anger take hold of them.
²⁵ Let their habitation be desolate,
and let none dwell in their tents.
²⁶ For they persecute him whom thou hast smitten,
and they talk to the grief of those whom thou hast wounded.
²⁷ Add iniquity unto their iniquity:
and let them not come into thy righteousness.
²⁸ Let them be blotted out of the book of the living,
and not be written with the righteous.

²⁹ But I am poor and sorrowful:
let thy salvation, O God, set me up on high.
³⁰ I will praise the name of God with a song,
and will magnify him with thanksgiving.
³¹ This also shall please the LORD better than an ox or bullock that
hath horns and hoofs.
³² The humble shall see this, and be glad:
and your heart shall live that seek God.
³³ For the LORD heareth the poor,
and despiseth not his prisoners.

³⁴ Let the heaven and earth praise him,
the seas, and everything that moveth therein.
³⁵ For God will save Zion, and will build the cities of Judah,
that they may dwell there, and have it in possession.
³⁶ The seed also of his servants shall inherit it:
and they that love his name shall dwell therein.

PSALM 70

To the chief musician.
A psalm of David, to bring to remembrance.

¹ Make haste, O God, to deliver me,
make haste to help me, O LORD.
² Let them be ashamed and confounded that seek after my
soul:
let them be turned backward, and put to confusion, that desire
my hurt.

³ Let them be turned back for a reward of their shame that say,
  'Aha, aha'.
⁴ Let all those that seek thee rejoice and be glad in thee:
  and let such as love thy salvation say continually, 'Let God be
  magnified'.

⁵ But I am poor and needy:
  make haste unto me, O God:
  thou art my help and my deliverer;
  O LORD, make no tarrying.

PSALM 71

¹ In thee, O LORD, do I put my trust:
  let me never be put to confusion.
² Deliver me in thy righteousness, and cause me to escape:
  incline thy ear unto me, and save me.
³ Be thou my strong habitation, whereunto I may continually
    resort:
  thou hast given commandment to save me, for thou art my rock
    and my fortress.
⁴ Deliver me, O my God, out of the hand of the wicked,
  out of the hand of the unrighteous and cruel man.

⁵ For thou art my hope, O Lord GOD:
  thou art my trust from my youth.
⁶ By thee have I been held up from the womb:
  thou art he that took me out of my mother's bowels:
  my praise shall be continually of thee.
⁷ I am as a wonder unto many,
  but thou art my strong refuge.
⁸ Let my mouth be filled with thy praise and with thy honour all
    the day.
⁹ Cast me not off in the time of old age;
  forsake me not when my strength faileth.
¹⁰ For my enemies speak against me:
  and they that lay wait for my soul take counsel together,
¹¹ saying, 'God hath forsaken him:
  persecute and take him, for there is none to deliver him'.
¹² O God, be not far from me:
  my God, make haste for my help.
¹³ Let them be confounded and consumed that are adversaries to
    my soul:
  let them be covered with reproach and dishonour that seek my
    hurt.
¹⁴ But I will hope continually,
  and will yet praise thee more and more.

¹⁵ My mouth shall show forth thy righteousness and thy salvation all the day:
for I know not the numbers thereof.
¹⁶ I will go in the strength of the Lord GOD:
I will make mention of thy righteousness, even of thine only.

¹⁷ O God, thou hast taught me from my youth:
and hitherto have I declared thy wondrous works.
¹⁸ Now also when I am old and grey-headed, O God, forsake me not:
until I have shown thy strength unto this generation,
and thy power to every one that is to come.
¹⁹ Thy righteousness also, O God, is very high, who hast done great things:
O God, who is like unto thee?
²⁰ Thou, which hast shown me great and sore troubles, shalt quicken me again,
and shalt bring me up again from the depths of the earth.
²¹ Thou shalt increase my greatness,
and comfort me on every side.
²² I will also praise thee with the psaltery, even thy truth, O my God:
unto thee will I sing with the harp, O thou Holy One of Israel.
²³ My lips shall greatly rejoice when I sing unto thee:
and my soul, which thou hast redeemed.
²⁴ My tongue also shall talk of thy righteousness all the day long:
for they are confounded, for they are brought unto shame, that seek my hurt.

PSALM 72

A psalm for Solomon.

¹ Give the king thy judgements, O God,
and thy righteousness unto the king's son.
² He shall judge thy people with righteousness,
and thy poor with judgement.
³ The mountains shall bring peace to the people,
and the little hills, by righteousness.
⁴ He shall judge the poor of the people,
he shall save the children of the needy,
and shall break in pieces the oppressor.
⁵ They shall fear thee as long as the sun and moon endure,
throughout all generations.
⁶ He shall come down like rain upon the mown grass:
as showers that water the earth.
⁷ In his days shall the righteous flourish:

and abundance of peace so long as the moon endureth.
⁸ He shall have dominion also from sea to sea,
  and from the river unto the ends of the earth.
⁹ They that dwell in the wilderness shall bow before him:
  and his enemies shall lick the dust.
¹⁰ The kings of Tarshish and of the isles shall bring presents:
  the kings of Sheba and Seba shall offer gifts.
¹¹ Yea, all kings shall fall down before him:
  all nations shall serve him.
¹² For he shall deliver the needy when he crieth:
  the poor also, and him that hath no helper.
¹³ He shall spare the poor and needy,
  and shall save the souls of the needy.
¹⁴ He shall redeem their soul from deceit and violence:
  and precious shall their blood be in his sight.
¹⁵ And he shall live, and to him shall be given of the gold of
    Sheba:
  prayer also shall be made for him continually,
  and daily shall he be praised.
¹⁶ There shall be a handful of corn in the earth upon the top
    of the mountains;
  the fruit thereof shall shake like Lebanon,
  and they of the city shall flourish like grass of the earth.
¹⁷ His name shall endure for ever:
  his name shall be continued as long as the sun:
  and men shall be blessed in him:
  all nations shall call him blessed.

¹⁸ Blessed be the LORD God,
  the God of Israel, who only doeth wondrous things.
¹⁹ And blessed be his glorious name for ever:
  and let the whole earth be filled with his glory.
  Amen, and Amen.

²⁰The prayers of David the son of Jesse are ended.

PSALM 73
A psalm of Asaph.

¹ Truly God is good to Israel,
  even to such as are of a clean heart.
² But as for me, my feet were almost gone,
  my steps had well nigh slipped.
³ For I was envious at the foolish,
  when I saw the prosperity of the wicked.
⁴ For there are no bands in their death:
  but their strength is firm.

⁵ They are not in trouble as other men:
  neither are they plagued like other men.
⁶ Therefore pride compasseth them about as a chain:
  violence covereth them as a garment.
⁷ Their eyes stand out with fatness:
  they have more than heart could wish.
⁸ They are corrupt, and speak wickedly concerning
    oppression:
  they speak loftily.
⁹ They set their mouth against the heavens,
  and their tongue walketh through the earth.
¹⁰ Therefore his people return hither:
  and waters of a full cup are wrung out to them.
¹¹ And they say, 'How doth God know?
  and is there knowledge in the most High?'
¹² Behold, these are the ungodly, who prosper in the world;
  they increase in riches.

¹³ Verily I have cleansed my heart in vain,
  and washed my hands in innocence.
¹⁴ For all the day long have I been plagued,
  and chastened every morning.
¹⁵ If I say, I will speak thus:
  behold, I should offend against the generation of thy
    children.
¹⁶ When I thought to know this,
  it was too painful for me,
¹⁷ until I went into the sanctuary of God;
  then understood I their end.
¹⁸ Surely thou didst set them in slippery places:
  thou castedst them down into destruction.
¹⁹ How are they brought into desolation as in a moment!
  they are utterly consumed with terrors.
²⁰ As a dream when one awaketh;
  so, O Lord, when thou awakest, thou shalt despise their image.

²¹ Thus my heart was grieved,
  and I was pricked in my reins.
²² So foolish was I, and ignorant:
  I was as a beast before thee.
²³ Nevertheless I am continually with thee:
  thou hast held me by my right hand.
²⁴ Thou shalt guide me with thy counsel,
  and afterward receive me to glory.
²⁵ Whom have I in heaven but thee?
  and there is none upon earth that I desire besides thee.
²⁶ My flesh and my heart faileth:
  but God is the strength of my heart, and my portion for ever.

²⁷ For lo, they that are far from thee shall perish:
thou hast destroyed all them that go a-whoring from thee.
²⁸ But it is good for me to draw near to God:
I have put my trust in the Lord God,
that I may declare all thy works.

PSALM 74
Maschil of Asaph.

¹ O God, why hast thou cast us off for ever?
why doth thy anger smoke against the sheep of thy pasture?
² Remember thy congregation which thou hast purchased of old:
the rod of thy inheritance which thou hast redeemed,
this mount Zion, wherein thou hast dwelt.
³ Lift up thy feet unto the perpetual desolations:
even all that the enemy hath done wickedly in the sanctuary.

⁴ Thy enemies roar in the midst of thy congregations:
they set up their ensigns for signs.
⁵ A man was famous according as he had lifted up axes upon the
thick trees.
⁶ But now they break down the carved work thereof at once with
axes and hammers.
⁷ They have cast fire into thy sanctuary,
they have defiled by casting down the dwelling place of thy
name to the ground.
⁸ They said in their hearts, 'Let us destroy them together':
they have burnt up all the synagogues of God in the land.

⁹ We see not our signs: there is no more any prophet,
neither is there among us any that knoweth how long.
¹⁰ O God, how long shall the adversary reproach?
shall the enemy blaspheme thy name for ever?
¹¹ Why withdrawest thou thy hand, even thy right hand?
pluck it out of thy bosom.

¹² For God is my King of old,
working salvation in the midst of the earth.
¹³ Thou didst divide the sea by thy strength:
thou brokest the heads of the dragons in the waters.
¹⁴ Thou brokest the heads of leviathan in pieces,
and gavest him to be meat to the people inhabiting the
wilderness.
¹⁵ Thou didst cleave the fountain and the flood:
thou driedst up mighty rivers.
¹⁶ The day is thine, the night also is thine:
thou hast prepared the light and the sun.

¹⁷ Thou hast set all the borders of the earth:
  thou hast made summer and winter.

¹⁸ Remember this, that the enemy hath reproached, O LORD,
  and that the foolish people have blasphemed thy name.
¹⁹ O deliver not the soul of thy turtle dove unto the multitude of
    the wicked:
  forget not the congregation of thy poor for ever.
²⁰ Have respect unto the covenant:
  for the dark places of the earth are full of the habitations of
    cruelty.
²¹ O let not the oppressed return ashamed:
  let the poor and needy praise thy name.

²² Arise, O God, plead thy own cause:
  remember how the foolish man reproacheth thee daily.
²³ Forget not the voice of thy enemies:
  the tumult of those that rise up against thee increaseth
    continually.

PSALM 75

To the chief musician, Al-taschith.
A psalm or song of Asaph.

¹ Unto thee, O God, do we give thanks, unto thee do we give thanks:
  for that thy name is near, thy wondrous works declare.
² When I shall receive the congregation I will judge uprightly.
³ The earth and all the inhabitants thereof are dissolved:
  I bear up the pillars of it. Selah.

⁴ I said unto the fools, 'Deal not foolishly':
  and to the wicked, 'Lift not up the horn.
⁵ Lift not up your horn on high:
  speak not with a stiff neck.'
⁶ For promotion cometh neither from the east,
  nor from the west, nor from the south.
⁷ But God is the judge:
  he putteth down one, and setteth up another.
⁸ For in the hand of the LORD there is a cup, and the wine is red:
  it is full of mixture, and he poureth out of the same:
  but the dregs thereof, all the wicked of the earth shall wring
    them out, and drink them.

⁹ But I will declare for ever;
  I will sing praises to the God of Jacob.
¹⁰ All the horns of the wicked also will I cut off;
  but the horns of the righteous shall be exalted.

PSALM 76

To the chief musician on neginoth.
A psalm or song of Asaph.

¹ In Judah is God known:
  his name is great in Israel.
² In Salem also is his tabernacle,
  and his dwelling place in Zion.
³ There broke he the arrows of the bow,
  the shield, and the sword, and the battle. Selah.

⁴ Thou art more glorious and excellent than the mountains of prey.
⁵ The stout-hearted are spoiled, they have slept their sleep:
  and none of the men of might have found their hands.
⁶ At thy rebuke, O God of Jacob, both the chariot and horse are
    cast into a dead sleep.
⁷ Thou, even thou, art to be feared:
  and who may stand in thy sight when once thou art angry?
⁸ Thou didst cause judgement to be heard from heaven:
  the earth feared, and was still,
⁹ when God arose to judgement,
  to save all the meek of the earth. Selah.

¹⁰ Surely the wrath of man shall praise thee:
  the remainder of wrath shalt thou restrain.
¹¹ Vow, and pay unto the LORD your God:
  let all that be round about him bring presents unto him that
    ought to be feared.
¹² He shall cut off the spirit of princes:
  he is terrible to the kings of the earth.

PSALM 77

To the chief musician, to Jeduthun.
A psalm of Asaph.

¹ I cried unto God with my voice:
  even unto God with my voice, and he gave ear unto me.
² In the day of my trouble I sought the Lord:
  my sore ran in the night, and ceased not:
  my soul refused to be comforted.
³ I remembered God, and was troubled:
  I complained, and my spirit was overwhelmed. Selah.

⁴ Thou holdest my eyes waking:
  I am so troubled that I cannot speak.
⁵ I have considered the days of old,
  the years of ancient times.

⁶ I call to remembrance my song in the night:
  I commune with my own heart, and my spirit made diligent
    search.

⁷ Will the Lord cast off for ever?
  and will he be favourable no more?
⁸ Is his mercy clean gone for ever?
  doth his promise fail for evermore?
⁹ Hath God forgotten to be gracious?
  hath he in anger shut up his tender mercies? Selah.

¹⁰ And I said, 'This is my infirmity:
  but I will remember the years of the right hand of the most
    High'.
¹¹ I will remember the works of the Lord:
  surely I will remember thy wonders of old.
¹² I will meditate also of all thy work,
  and talk of thy doings.
¹³ Thy way, O God, is in the sanctuary:
  who is so great a God as our God?
¹⁴ Thou art the God that doest wonders:
  thou hast declared thy strength among the people.
¹⁵ Thou hast with thy arm redeemed thy people,
  the sons of Jacob and Joseph. Selah.

¹⁶ The waters saw thee, O God, the waters saw thee:
  they were afraid; the depths also were troubled.
¹⁷ The clouds poured out water, the skies sent out a sound:
  thy arrows also went abroad.
¹⁸ The voice of thy thunder was in the heaven:
  the lightnings lightened the world,
  the earth trembled and shook.
¹⁹ Thy way is in the sea, and thy path in the great waters,
  and thy footsteps are not known.
²⁰ Thou leddest thy people like a flock
  by the hand of Moses and Aaron.

PSALM 78
Maschil of Asaph.

¹ Give ear, O my people, to my law:
  incline your ears to the words of my mouth.
² I will open my mouth in a parable:
  I will utter dark sayings of old:
³ which we have heard and known,
  and our fathers have told us.
⁴ We will not hide them from their children,

showing to the generation to come the praises of the
  LORD,
and his strength, and his wonderful works that he hath
  done.

⁵ For he established a testimony in Jacob,
  and appointed a law in Israel,
  which he commanded our fathers,
  that they should make them known to their children:
⁶ that the generation to come might know them,
  even the children which should be born:
  who should arise and declare them to their children:
⁷ that they might set their hope in God,
  and not forget the works of God,
  but keep his commandments:
⁸ and might not be as their fathers,
  a stubborn and rebellious generation,
  a generation that set not their heart aright,
  and whose spirit was not steadfast with God.

⁹ The children of Ephraim, being armed, and carrying bows,
  turned back in the day of battle.
¹⁰ They kept not the covenant of God,
  and refused to walk in his law:
¹¹ and forgot his works,
  and his wonders that he had shown them.

¹² Marvellous things did he in the sight of their fathers,
  in the land of Egypt, in the field of Zoan.
¹³ He divided the sea, and caused them to pass through:
  and he made the waters to stand as a heap.
¹⁴ In the daytime also he led them with a cloud,
  and all the night with a light of fire.
¹⁵ He cleft the rocks in the wilderness,
  and gave them drink as out of the great depths.
¹⁶ He brought streams also out of the rock,
  and caused waters to run down like rivers.

¹⁷ And they sinned yet more against him
  by provoking the most High in the wilderness.
¹⁸ And they tempted God in their heart
  by asking meat for their lust.
¹⁹ Yea, they spoke against God:
  they said, 'Can God furnish a table in the wilderness?
²⁰ Behold, he smote the rock,
  that the waters gushed out, and the streams overflowed;
  can he give bread also? can he provide flesh for his people?'

21 Therefore the LORD heard this, and was wroth:
so a fire was kindled against Jacob,
and anger also came up against Israel;
22 because they believed not in God,
and trusted not in his salvation:
23 though he had commanded the clouds from above,
and opened the doors of heaven,
24 and had rained down manna upon them to eat,
and had given them of the corn of heaven.
25 Man did eat angels' food:
he sent them meat to the full.
26 He caused an east wind to blow in the heaven:
and by his power he brought in the south wind.
27 He rained flesh also upon them as dust,
and feathered fowls like as the sand of the sea.
28 And he let it fall in the midst of their camp,
round about their habitations.
29 So they did eat, and were well filled:
for he gave them their own desire.
30 They were not estranged from their lust.
But while their meat was yet in their mouths,
31 the wrath of God came upon them, and slew the fattest of
them,
and smote down the chosen men of Israel.

32 For all this they sinned still,
and believed not for his wondrous works.
33 Therefore their days did he consume in vanity,
and their years in trouble.
34 When he slew them, then they sought him:
and they returned and inquired early after God.
35 And they remembered that God was their rock,
and the high God their redeemer.
36 Nevertheless they did flatter him with their mouth,
and they lied unto him with their tongues.
37 For their heart was not right with him,
neither were they steadfast in his covenant.
38 But he, being full of compassion,
forgave their iniquity, and destroyed them not:
yea, many a time turned he his anger away,
and did not stir up all his wrath.
39 For he remembered that they were but flesh;
a wind that passeth away, and cometh not again.

40 How oft did they provoke him in the wilderness,
and grieve him in the desert!
41 Yea, they turned back and tempted God,
and limited the Holy One of Israel.

⁴² They remembered not his hand,
   nor the day when he delivered them from the enemy:
⁴³ how he had wrought his signs in Egypt,
   and his wonders in the field of Zoan:
⁴⁴ and had turned their rivers into blood:
   and their floods, that they could not drink.
⁴⁵ He sent divers sorts of flies among them, which devoured
      them:
   and frogs which destroyed them.
⁴⁶ He gave also their increase unto the caterpillar,
   and their labour unto the locust.
⁴⁷ He destroyed their vines with hail,
   and their sycamore trees with frost.
⁴⁸ He gave up their cattle also to the hail,
   and their flocks to hot thunderbolts.
⁴⁹ He cast upon them the fierceness of his anger,
   wrath, and indignation, and trouble,
   by sending evil angels among them.
⁵⁰ He made a way to his anger,
   he spared not their soul from death,
   but gave their life over to the pestilence;
⁵¹ And smote all the firstborn in Egypt:
   the chief of their strength in the tabernacles of Ham:
⁵² but made his own people to go forth like sheep,
   and guided them in the wilderness like a flock.
⁵³ And he led them on safely, so that they feared not:
   but the sea overwhelmed their enemies.
⁵⁴ And he brought them to the border of his sanctuary,
   even to this mountain which his right hand had
      purchased.
⁵⁵ He cast out the heathen also before them,
   and divided them an inheritance by line,
   and made the tribes of Israel to dwell in their tents.

⁵⁶ Yet they tempted and provoked the most high God,
   and kept not his testimonies:
⁵⁷ but turned back, and dealt unfaithfully like their fathers:
   they were turned aside like a deceitful bow.
⁵⁸ For they provoked him to anger with their high places,
   and moved him to jealousy with their graven images.
⁵⁹ When God heard this, he was wroth,
   and greatly abhorred Israel:
⁶⁰ so that he forsook the tabernacle of Shiloh,
   the tent which he placed among men,
⁶¹ and delivered his strength into captivity,
   and his glory into the enemy's hand.
⁶² He gave his people over also unto the sword:
   and was wroth with his inheritance.

⁶³ The fire consumed their young men:
and their maidens were not given to marriage.
⁶⁴ Their priests fell by the sword:
and their widows made no lamentation.

⁶⁵ Then the Lord awoke as one out of sleep,
and like a mighty man that shouteth by reason of wine.
⁶⁶ And he smote his enemies in the hinder parts:
he put them to a perpetual reproach.
⁶⁷ Moreover he refused the tabernacle of Joseph,
and chose not the tribe of Ephraim:
⁶⁸ but chose the tribe of Judah,
the mount Zion which he loved.
⁶⁹ And he built his sanctuary like high palaces,
like the earth which he hath established for ever.
⁷⁰ He chose David also his servant,
and took him from the sheepfolds:
⁷¹ from following the ewes great with young, he brought him to
feed Jacob his people,
and Israel his inheritance.
⁷² So he fed them according to the integrity of his heart:
and guided them by the skilfulness of his hands.

PSALM 79
A psalm of Asaph.

¹ O God, the heathen are come into thy inheritance,
thy holy temple have they defiled:
they have laid Jerusalem on heaps.
² The dead bodies of thy servants have they given to be meat unto
the fowls of the heaven,
the flesh of thy saints unto the beasts of the earth.
³ Their blood have they shed like water round about Jerusalem:
and there was none to bury them.
⁴ We are become a reproach to our neighbours,
a scorn and derision to them that are round about us.

⁵ How long, LORD, wilt thou be angry, for ever?
shall thy jealousy burn like fire?
⁶ Pour out thy wrath upon the heathen that have not known thee,
and upon the kingdoms that have not called upon thy name.
⁷ For they have devoured Jacob,
and laid waste his dwelling place.
⁸ O remember not against us former iniquities:
let thy tender mercies speedily prevent us:
for we are brought very low.
⁹ Help us, O God of our salvation, for the glory of thy name:

and deliver us, and purge away our sins for thy name's sake.
¹⁰ Wherefore should the heathen say, 'Where is their God?'
    let him be known among the heathen in our sight
    by the revenging of the blood of thy servants which is shed.

¹¹ Let the sighing of the prisoner come before thee,
    according to the greatness of thy power:
    preserve thou those that are appointed to die.
¹² And render unto our neighbours sevenfold into their bosom
    their reproach wherewith they have reproached thee, O Lord.
¹³ So we thy people and sheep of thy pasture will give thee thanks
      for ever:
    we will show forth thy praise to all generations.

PSALM 80

To the chief musician upon Shoshannim Eduth.
A psalm of Asaph.

¹ Give ear, O Shepherd of Israel,
    thou that leadest Joseph like a flock;
    thou that dwellest between the cherubims, shine forth.
² Before Ephraim and Benjamin and Manasseh stir up thy strength,
    and come and save us.

³ Turn us again, O God,
    and cause thy face to shine,
    and we shall be saved.

⁴ O Lord God of hosts,
    how long wilt thou be angry against the prayer of thy
      people?
⁵ Thou feedest them with the bread of tears:
    and givest them tears to drink in great measure.
⁶ Thou makest us a strife unto our neighbours:
    and our enemies laugh among themselves.

⁷ Turn us again, O God of hosts,
    and cause thy face to shine;
    and we shall be saved.

⁸ Thou hast brought a vine out of Egypt:
    thou hast cast out the heathen, and planted it.
⁹ Thou preparedst room before it,
    and didst cause it to take deep root,
    and it filled the land.
¹⁰ The hills were covered with the shadow of it,
    and the boughs thereof were like the goodly cedars.

¹¹ She sent out her boughs unto the sea,
  and her branches unto the river.
¹² Why hast thou then broken down her hedges,
  so that all they which pass by the way do pluck her?
¹³ The boar out of the wood doth waste it,
  and the wild beast of the field doth devour it.

¹⁴ Return, we beseech thee, O God of hosts:
  look down from heaven, and behold, and visit this vine:
¹⁵ and the vineyard which thy right hand hath planted,
  and the branch that thou madest strong for thyself.
¹⁶ It is burnt with fire, it is cut down:
  they perish at the rebuke of thy countenance.
¹⁷ Let thy hand be upon the man of thy right hand,
  upon the son of man whom thou madest strong for
    thyself.
¹⁸ So will not we go back from thee:
  quicken us, and we will call upon thy name.

¹⁹ Turn us again, O LORD God of hosts,
  cause thy face to shine,
  and we shall be saved.

PSALM 81
To the chief musician upon gittith.
A psalm of Asaph.

¹ Sing aloud unto God our strength:
  make a joyful noise unto the God of Jacob.
² Take a psalm, and bring hither the timbrel,
  the pleasant harp with the psaltery.
³ Blow up the trumpet in the new moon,
  in the time appointed on our solemn feast day.
⁴ For this was a statute for Israel,
  and a law of the God of Jacob.
⁵ This he ordained in Joseph for a testimony, when he went out
    through the land of Egypt:
  where I heard a language that I understood not.

⁶ 'I removed his shoulder from the burden:
  his hands were delivered from the pots.
⁷ Thou calledst in trouble, and I delivered thee;
  I answered thee in the secret place of thunder:
  I proved thee at the waters of Meribah. Selah.
⁸ Hear, O my people, and I will testify unto thee:
  O Israel, if thou wilt hearken unto me:
⁹ there shall no strange god be in thee:

neither shalt thou worship any strange god.
¹⁰ I am the LORD thy God, which brought thee out of the land of
   Egypt:
   open thy mouth wide, and I will fill it.

¹¹ 'But my people would not hearken to my voice:
   and Israel would none of me.
¹² So I gave them up unto their own hearts' lust:
   and they walked in their own counsels.

¹³ 'O that my people had hearkened unto me,
   and Israel had walked in my ways!
¹⁴ I should soon have subdued their enemies,
   and turned my hand against their adversaries.'
¹⁵ The haters of the LORD should have submitted themselves unto
   him:
   but their time should have endured for ever.
¹⁶ He should have fed them also with the finest of the
   wheat:
   and with honey out of the rock should I have satisfied
   thee.

PSALM 82

A psalm of Asaph.

¹ God standeth in the congregation of the mighty:
   he judgeth among the gods.

² 'How long will ye judge unjustly,
   and accept the persons of the wicked? Selah.
³ Defend the poor and fatherless:
   do justice to the afflicted and needy.
⁴ Deliver the poor and needy:
   rid them out of the hand of the wicked.
⁵ They know not, neither will they understand;
   they walk on in darkness:
   all the foundations of the earth are out of course.
⁶ I have said, "Ye are gods:
   and all of you are children of the most High.
⁷ But ye shall die like men,
   and fall like one of the princes."'

⁸ Arise, O God, judge the earth:
   for thou shalt inherit all nations.

PSALM 83

A song or psalm of Asaph.

[1] Keep not thou silence, O God:
  hold not thy peace, and be not still, O God.
[2] For lo, thy enemies make a tumult:
  and they that hate thee have lifted up the head.

[3] They have taken crafty counsel against thy people,
  and consulted against thy hidden ones.
[4] They have said, 'Come, and let us cut them off from being a
    nation:
  that the name of Israel may be no more in remembrance'.
[5] For they have consulted together with one consent:
  they are confederate against thee:
[6] the tabernacles of Edom, and the Ishmaelites;
  of Moab, and the Hagarenes;
[7] Gebal, and Ammon, and Amalek;
  the Philistines with the inhabitants of Tyre;
[8] Assur also is joined with them:
  they have helped the children of Lot. Selah.

[9] Do unto them as unto the Midianites:
  as to Sisera, as to Jabin, at the brook of Kison:
[10] which perished at En-dor:
  they became as dung for the earth.
[11] Make their nobles like Oreb, and like Zeeb:
  yea, all their princes as Zebah, and as Zalmunna:
[12] who said, 'Let us take to ourselves the houses of God in
    possession'.
[13] O my God, make them like a wheel:
  as the stubble before the wind.
[14] As the fire burneth a wood,
  and as the flame setteth the mountains on fire:
[15] so persecute them with thy tempest,
  and make them afraid with thy storm.
[16] Fill their faces with shame:
  that they may seek thy name, O LORD.
[17] Let them be confounded and troubled for ever:
  yea, let them be put to shame, and perish:
[18] that men may know that thou, whose name alone is JEHOVAH,
  art the most high over all the earth.

PSALM 84

To the chief musician upon gittith.
A psalm for the sons of Korah.

[1] How amiable are thy tabernacles,
   O LORD of hosts!

[2] My soul longeth, yea, even fainteth for the courts of the LORD:
   my heart and my flesh crieth out for the living God.
[3] Yea, the sparrow hath found a house,
   and the swallow a nest for herself, where she may lay her
      young,
   even thy altars, O LORD of hosts, my King, and my God.
[4] Blessed are they that dwell in thy house:
   they will be still praising thee. Selah.
[5] Blessed is the man whose strength is in thee;
   in whose heart are the ways of them:
[6] who passing through the valley of Baca make it a well:
   the rain also filleth the pools.
[7] They go from strength to strength:
   every one of them in Zion appeareth before God.

[8] O LORD God of hosts, hear my prayer:
   give ear, O God of Jacob. Selah.
[9] Behold, O God our shield,
   and look upon the face of thy anointed.
[10] For a day in thy courts is better than a thousand:
   I had rather be a doorkeeper in the house of my God,
   than to dwell in the tents of wickedness.
[11] For the LORD God is a sun and shield:
   the LORD will give grace and glory:
   no good thing will he withhold from them that walk uprightly.

[12] O LORD of hosts:
   blessed is the man that trusteth in thee.

PSALM 85

To the chief musician.
A psalm for the sons of Korah.

[1] LORD, thou hast been favourable unto thy land:
   thou hast brought back the captivity of Jacob.
[2] Thou hast forgiven the iniquity of thy people,
   thou hast covered all their sin. Selah.
[3] Thou hast taken away all thy wrath:
   thou hast turned thyself from the fierceness of thy anger.

⁴ Turn us, O God of our salvation,
and cause thy anger towards us to cease.
⁵ Wilt thou be angry with us for ever?
wilt thou draw out thy anger to all generations?
⁶ Wilt thou not revive us again:
that thy people may rejoice in thee?
⁷ Show us thy mercy, O LORD,
and grant us thy salvation.

⁸ I will hear what God the LORD will speak:
for he will speak peace unto his people, and to his saints:
but let them not turn again to folly.
⁹ Surely his salvation is nigh them that fear him;
that glory may dwell in our land.
¹⁰ Mercy and truth are met together:
righteousness and peace have kissed each other.
¹¹ Truth shall spring out of the earth:
and righteousness shall look down from heaven.
¹² Yea, the LORD shall give that which is good:
and our land shall yield her increase.
¹³ Righteousness shall go before him:
and shall set us in the way of his steps.

PSALM 86

A prayer of David.

¹ Bow down thy ear, O LORD, hear me:
for I am poor and needy.
² Preserve my soul, for I am holy:
O thou my God, save thy servant that trusteth in thee.
³ Be merciful unto me, O Lord:
for I cry unto thee daily.
⁴ Rejoice the soul of thy servant:
for unto thee, O Lord, do I lift up my soul.
⁵ For thou, Lord, art good, and ready to forgive:
and plenteous in mercy unto all them that call upon
thee.
⁶ Give ear, O LORD, unto my prayer:
and attend to the voice of my supplications.
⁷ In the day of my trouble I will call upon thee:
for thou wilt answer me.

⁸ Among the gods there is none like unto thee, O Lord:
neither are there any works like unto thy works.
⁹ All nations whom thou hast made shall come and worship
before thee, O Lord:
and shall glorify thy name.

¹⁰ For thou art great, and doest wondrous things:
   thou art God alone.

¹¹ Teach me thy way, O LORD, I will walk in thy truth:
   unite my heart to fear thy name.
¹² I will praise thee, O Lord my God, with all my heart:
   and I will glorify thy name for evermore.
¹³ For great is thy mercy toward me:
   and thou hast delivered my soul from the lowest hell.
¹⁴ O God, the proud are risen against me,
   and the assemblies of violent men have sought after my
      soul:
   and have not set thee before them.
¹⁵ But thou, O Lord, art a God full of compassion, and gracious:
   long-suffering, and plenteous in mercy and truth.
¹⁶ O turn unto me, and have mercy upon me,
   give thy strength unto thy servant,
   and save the son of thy handmaid.
¹⁷ Show me a token for good,
   that they which hate me may see it, and be ashamed:
   because thou, LORD, hast helped me, and comforted me.

PSALM 87

A psalm or song for the sons of Korah.

¹ His foundation is in the holy mountains.
² The LORD loveth the gates of Zion
   more than all the dwellings of Jacob.
³ Glorious things are spoken of thee, O city of God. Selah.

⁴ I will make mention of Rahab and Babylon to them that know
      me:
   behold Philistia, and Tyre, with Ethiopia:
   this man was born there.
⁵ And of Zion it shall be said,
   'This and that man was born in her':
   and the highest himself shall establish her.
⁶ The LORD shall count, when he writeth up the people,
   that this man was born there. Selah.
⁷ As well the singers as the players on instruments shall be
      there:
   all my springs are in thee.

PSALM 88

A song or psalm for the sons of Korah,
to the chief musician upon Mahalath Leannoth.
Maschil of Heman the Ezrahite.

[1] O LORD God of my salvation,
I have cried day and night before thee.
[2] Let my prayer come before thee:
incline thy ear unto my cry.

[3] For my soul is full of troubles:
and my life draweth nigh unto the grave.
[4] I am counted with them that go down into the pit:
I am as a man that hath no strength:
[5] free among the dead, like the slain that lie in the grave, whom
thou rememberest no more:
and they are cut off from thy hand.
[6] Thou hast laid me in the lowest pit,
in darkness, in the deeps.
[7] Thy wrath lieth hard upon me,
and thou hast afflicted me with all thy waves. Selah.
[8] Thou hast put away my acquaintance far from me:
thou hast made me an abomination unto them:
I am shut up, and I cannot come forth.
[9] My eye mourneth by reason of affliction,
LORD, I have called daily upon thee:
I have stretched out my hands unto thee.

[10] Wilt thou show wonders to the dead?
shall the dead arise and praise thee? Selah.
[11] Shall thy loving-kindness be declared in the grave?
or thy faithfulness in destruction?
[12] Shall thy wonders be known in the dark?
and thy righteousness in the land of forgetfulness?

[13] But unto thee have I cried, O LORD,
and in the morning shall my prayer prevent thee.

[14] LORD, why castest thou off my soul?
why hidest thou thy face from me?
[15] I am afflicted and ready to die from my youth up:
while I suffer thy terrors I am distracted.
[16] Thy fierce wrath goeth over me:
thy terrors have cut me off.
[17] They came round about me daily like water:
they compassed me about together.
[18] Lover and friend hast thou put far from me,
and my acquaintance into darkness.

PSALM 89

Maschil of Ethan the Ezrahite.

¹ I will sing of the mercies of the LORD for ever:
  with my mouth will I make known thy faithfulness to all
    generations.
² For I have said, 'Mercy shall be built up for ever:
  thy faithfulness shalt thou establish in the very heavens'.

³ 'I have made a covenant with my chosen,
  I have sworn unto David my servant,
⁴ "Thy seed will I establish for ever,
  and build up thy throne to all generations".' Selah.

⁵ And the heavens shall praise thy wonders, O LORD:
  thy faithfulness also in the congregation of the saints.
⁶ For who in the heaven can be compared unto the LORD?
  who among the sons of the mighty can be likened unto the
    LORD?
⁷ God is greatly to be feared in the assembly of the saints:
  and to be had in reverence of all them that are about him.
⁸ O LORD God of hosts, who is a strong LORD like unto thee?
  or to thy faithfulness round about thee?
⁹ Thou rulest the raging of the sea:
  when the waves thereof arise, thou stillest them.
¹⁰ Thou hast broken Rahab in pieces, as one that is slain:
  thou hast scattered thy enemies with thy strong arm.
¹¹ The heavens are thine, the earth also is thine:
  as for the world and the fulness thereof, thou hast founded them.
¹² The north and the south, thou hast created them:
  Tabor and Hermon shall rejoice in thy name.
¹³ Thou hast a mighty arm:
  strong is thy hand, and high is thy right hand.
¹⁴ Justice and judgement are the habitation of thy throne:
  mercy and truth shall go before thy face.

¹⁵ Blessed is the people that know the joyful sound:
  they shall walk, O LORD, in the light of thy countenance.
¹⁶ In thy name shall they rejoice all the day:
  and in thy righteousness shall they be exalted.
¹⁷ For thou art the glory of their strength:
  and in thy favour our horn shall be exalted.
¹⁸ For the LORD is our defence:
  and the Holy One of Israel is our king.

¹⁹ Then thou spokest in vision to thy holy one,
  and saidst, 'I have laid help upon one that is mighty:
  I have exalted one chosen out of the people.

²⁰ I have found David my servant:
  with my holy oil have I anointed him:
²¹ with whom my hand shall be established:
  my arm also shall strengthen him.
²² The enemy shall not exact upon him:
  nor the son of wickedness afflict him.
²³ And I will beat down his foes before his face,
  and plague them that hate him.
²⁴ But my faithfulness and my mercy shall be with him:
  and in my name shall his horn be exalted.
²⁵ I will set his hand also in the sea,
  and his right hand in the rivers.
²⁶ He shall cry unto me, "Thou art my father:
  my God, and the rock of my salvation".
²⁷ Also I will make him my firstborn,
  higher than the kings of the earth.
²⁸ My mercy will I keep for him for evermore,
  and my covenant shall stand fast with him.
²⁹ His seed also will I make to endure for ever,
  and his throne as the days of heaven.

³⁰ 'If his children forsake my law, and walk not in my judgements:
³¹ if they break my statutes, and keep not my commandments:
³² then will I visit their transgression with the rod, and their
  iniquity with stripes.
³³ Nevertheless my loving-kindness will I not utterly take from him,
  nor suffer my faithfulness to fail.
³⁴ My covenant will I not break,
  nor alter the thing that is gone out of my lips.
³⁵ Once have I sworn by my holiness
  that I will not lie unto David.
³⁶ His seed shall endure for ever,
  and his throne as the sun before me.
³⁷ It shall be established for ever as the moon,
  and as a faithful witness in heaven.' Selah.

³⁸ But thou hast cast off and abhorred:
  thou hast been wroth with thy anointed.
³⁹ Thou hast made void the covenant of thy servant:
  thou hast profaned his crown by casting it to the ground.
⁴⁰ Thou hast broken down all his hedges:
  thou hast brought his strongholds to ruin.
⁴¹ All that pass by the way spoil him:
  he is a reproach to his neighbours.
⁴² Thou hast set up the right hand of his adversaries:
  thou hast made all his enemies to rejoice.
⁴³ Thou hast also turned the edge of his sword,
  and hast not made him to stand in the battle.

⁴⁴ Thou hast made his glory to cease,
and cast his throne down to the ground.
⁴⁵ The days of his youth hast thou shortened:
thou hast covered him with shame. Selah.

⁴⁶ How long, LORD, wilt thou hide thyself, for ever?
shall thy wrath burn like fire?
⁴⁷ Remember how short my time is:
wherefore hast thou made all men in vain?
⁴⁸ What man is he that liveth, and shall not see death?
shall he deliver his soul from the hand of the grave? Selah.
⁴⁹ Lord, where are thy former loving-kindnesses,
which thou sworest unto David in thy truth?
⁵⁰ Remember, Lord, the reproach of thy servants:
how I do bear in my bosom the reproach of all the mighty
people;
⁵¹ wherewith thy enemies have reproached, O LORD:
wherewith they have reproached the footsteps of thy anointed.

⁵² Blessed be the LORD for evermore.
Amen, and Amen.

PSALM 90

A prayer of Moses the man of God.

¹ LORD, thou hast been our dwelling place in all generations.
² Before the mountains were brought forth,
or ever thou hadst formed the earth and the world:
even from everlasting to everlasting, thou art God.

³ Thou turnest man to destruction:
and sayest, 'Return, ye children of men'.
⁴ For a thousand years in thy sight are but as yesterday when it is
past,
and as a watch in the night.
⁵ Thou carriest them away as with a flood, they are as a sleep:
in the morning they are like grass which groweth up.
⁶ In the morning it flourisheth, and groweth up:
in the evening it is cut down, and withereth.

⁷ For we are consumed by thy anger,
and by thy wrath are we troubled.
⁸ Thou hast set our iniquities before thee,
our secret sins in the light of thy countenance.
⁹ For all our days are passed away in thy wrath:
we spend our years as a tale that is told.
¹⁰ The days of our years are threescore years and ten,

and if by reason of strength they be fourscore years, yet is their
    strength labour and sorrow:
for it is soon cut off, and we fly away.

[11] Who knoweth the power of thy anger?
    even according to thy fear, so is thy wrath.

[12] So teach us to number our days,
    that we may apply our hearts unto wisdom.

[13] Return, O Lord, how long?
    and let it repent thee concerning thy servants.

[14] O satisfy us early with thy mercy:
    that we may rejoice and be glad all our days.

[15] Make us glad according to the days wherein thou hast afflicted
    us,
and the years wherein we have seen evil.

[16] Let thy work appear unto thy servants,
    and thy glory unto their children.

[17] And let the beauty of the Lord our God be upon us,
    and establish thou the work of our hands upon us:
yea, the work of our hands establish thou it.

PSALM 91

[1] He that dwelleth in the secret place of the most High
    shall abide under the shadow of the Almighty.

[2] I will say of the Lord, 'He is my refuge and my fortress:
    my God, in him will I trust'.

[3] Surely he shall deliver thee from the snare of the fowler,
    and from the noisome pestilence.

[4] He shall cover thee with his feathers,
    and under his wings shalt thou trust:
his truth shall be thy shield and buckler.

[5] Thou shalt not be afraid for the terror by night:
    nor for the arrow that flieth by day:

[6] nor for the pestilence that walketh in darkness:
    nor for the destruction that wasteth at noonday.

[7] A thousand shall fall at thy side,
    and ten thousand at thy right hand:
but it shall not come nigh thee.

[8] Only with thy eyes shalt thou behold
    and see the reward of the wicked.

[9] Because thou hast made the Lord, which is my refuge,
    even the most High, thy habitation:

[10] there shall no evil befall thee,
    neither shall any plague come nigh thy dwelling.

¹¹ For he shall give his angels charge over thee,
 to keep thee in all thy ways.
¹² They shall bear thee up in their hands,
 lest thou dash thy foot against a stone.
¹³ Thou shalt tread upon the lion and adder:
 the young lion and the dragon shalt thou trample under feet.

¹⁴ 'Because he hath set his love upon me, therefore will I deliver him:
 I will set him on high, because he hath known my name.
¹⁵ He shall call upon me, and I will answer him:
 I will be with him in trouble,
 I will deliver him, and honour him.
¹⁶ With long life will I satisfy him,
 and show him my salvation.'

PSALM 92

A psalm or song for the sabbath day.

¹ It is a good thing to give thanks unto the LORD,
 and to sing praises unto thy name, O most High:
² to show forth thy loving-kindness in the morning,
 and thy faithfulness every night,
³ upon an instrument of ten strings, and upon the psaltery:
 upon the harp with a solemn sound.
⁴ For thou, LORD, hast made me glad through thy work:
 I will triumph in the works of thy hands.
⁵ O LORD, how great are thy works!
 and thy thoughts are very deep.
⁶ A brutish man knoweth not:
 neither doth a fool understand this.
⁷ When the wicked spring as the grass,
 and when all the workers of iniquity do flourish:
 it is that they shall be destroyed for ever.

⁸ But thou, LORD, art most high for evermore.
⁹ For lo, thy enemies, O LORD, for lo, thy enemies shall perish:
 all the workers of iniquity shall be scattered.
¹⁰ But my horn shalt thou exalt like the horn of an unicorn:
 I shall be anointed with fresh oil.
¹¹ My eye also shall see my desire on my enemies,
 and my ears shall hear my desire of the wicked that rise up
  against me.
¹² The righteous shall flourish like the palm tree:
 he shall grow like a cedar in Lebanon.
¹³ Those that be planted in the house of the LORD
 shall flourish in the courts of our God.
¹⁴ They shall still bring forth fruit in old age:

they shall be fat and flourishing:
¹⁵ to show that the LORD is upright:
    he is my rock, and there is no unrighteousness in him.

PSALM 93

¹ The LORD reigneth, he is clothed with majesty,
    the LORD is clothed with strength, wherewith he hath girded
       himself:
    the world also is established, that it cannot be moved.
² Thy throne is established of old:
    thou art from everlasting.

³ The floods have lifted up, O LORD, the floods have lifted up their
      voice:
    the floods lift up their waves.
⁴ The LORD on high is mightier than the noise of many waters,
    yea, than the mighty waves of the sea.

⁵ Thy testimonies are very sure:
    holiness becometh thy house, O LORD, for ever.

PSALM 94

¹ O LORD God, to whom vengeance belongeth:
    O God, to whom vengeance belongeth, show thyself.
² Lift up thyself, thou judge of the earth:
    render a reward to the proud.

³ LORD, how long shall the wicked,
    how long shall the wicked triumph?
⁴ How long shall they utter and speak hard things?
    and all the workers of iniquity boast themselves?
⁵ They break in pieces thy people, O LORD,
    and afflict thy heritage.
⁶ They slay the widow and the stranger:
    and murder the fatherless.
⁷ Yet they say, 'The LORD shall not see,
    neither shall the God of Jacob regard it'.

⁸ Understand, ye brutish among the people:
    and ye fools, when will ye be wise?
⁹ He that planted the ear, shall he not hear?
    he that formed the eye, shall he not see?
¹⁰ He that chastiseth the heathen, shall not he correct?
    he that teacheth man knowledge, shall not he know?

¹¹ The LORD knoweth the thoughts of man,
   that they are vanity.
¹² Blessed is the man whom thou chastenest, O LORD,
   and teachest him out of thy law:
¹³ that thou mayest give him rest from the days of adversity,
   until the pit be dug for the wicked.
¹⁴ For the LORD will not cast off his people,
   neither will he forsake his inheritance.
¹⁵ But judgement shall return unto righteousness:
   and all the upright in heart shall follow it.

¹⁶ Who will rise up for me against the evil-doers?
   or who will stand up for me against the workers of iniquity?
¹⁷ Unless the LORD had been my help,
   my soul had almost dwelt in silence.
¹⁸ When I said, 'My foot slippeth':
   thy mercy, O LORD, held me up.
¹⁹ In the multitude of my thoughts within me
   thy comforts delight my soul.
²⁰ Shall the throne of iniquity have fellowship with thee,
   which frameth mischief by a law?

²¹ They gather themselves together against the soul of the
      righteous,
   and condemn the innocent blood.
²² But the LORD is my defence:
   and my God is the rock of my refuge.
²³ And he shall bring upon them their own iniquity,
   and shall cut them off in their own wickedness:
   yea, the LORD our God shall cut them off.

PSALM 95

¹ O come, let us sing unto the LORD:
   let us make a joyful noise to the rock of our salvation.
² Let us come before his presence with thanksgiving,
   and make a joyful noise unto him with psalms.

³ For the LORD is a great God,
   and a great King above all gods.
⁴ In his hand are the deep places of the earth:
   the strength of the hills is his also.
⁵ The sea is his, and he made it:
   and his hands formed the dry land.

⁶ O come, let us worship and bow down:
   let us kneel before the LORD our maker.

⁷ For he is our God,
  and we are the people of his pasture,
  and the sheep of his hand.

Today if ye will hear his voice,
⁸ 'Harden not your heart, as in the provocation,
  and as in the day of temptation in the wilderness:
⁹ when your fathers tempted me,
  proved me, and saw my work.
¹⁰ Forty years long was I grieved with this generation,
  and said, "It is a people that do err in their heart,
  and they have not known my ways":
¹¹ unto whom I swore in my wrath
  that they should not enter into my rest.'

PSALM 96

¹ O sing unto the LORD a new song:
  sing unto the LORD, all the earth.
² Sing unto the LORD, bless his name:
  show forth his salvation from day to day.
³ Declare his glory among the heathen:
  his wonders among all people.
⁴ For the LORD is great, and greatly to be praised:
  he is to be feared above all gods.
⁵ For all the gods of the nations are idols:
  but the LORD made the heavens.
⁶ Honour and majesty are before him:
  strength and beauty are in his sanctuary.
⁷ Give unto the LORD, O ye kindreds of the people,
  give unto the LORD glory and strength.

⁸ Give unto the LORD the glory due unto his name:
  bring an offering, and come into his courts.
⁹ O worship the LORD in the beauty of holiness:
  fear before him all the earth.
¹⁰ Say among the heathen that the LORD reigneth:
  the world also shall be established that it shall not be moved:
  he shall judge the people righteously.

¹¹ Let the heavens rejoice, and let the earth be glad:
  let the sea roar, and the fulness thereof.
¹² Let the field be joyful, and all that is therein:
  then shall all the trees of the wood rejoice ¹³before the LORD,
  for he cometh, for he cometh to judge the earth:
  he shall judge the world with righteousness,
  and the people with his truth.

PSALM 97

1 The LORD reigneth, let the earth rejoice:
  let the multitude of isles be glad thereof.
2 Clouds and darkness are round about him:
  righteousness and judgement are the habitation of his throne.
3 A fire goeth before him,
  and burneth up his enemies round about.
4 His lightnings enlightened the world:
  the earth saw, and trembled.
5 The hills melted like wax at the presence of the LORD,
  at the presence of the Lord of the whole earth.
6 The heavens declare his righteousness,
  and all the people see his glory.
7 Confounded be all they that serve graven images,
  that boast themselves of idols:
  worship him, all ye gods.

8 Zion heard, and was glad, and the daughters of Judah rejoiced
  because of thy judgements, O LORD.
9 For thou, LORD, art high above all the earth:
  thou art exalted far above all gods.

10 Ye that love the LORD, hate evil:
  he preserveth the souls of his saints:
  he delivereth them out of the hand of the wicked.
11 Light is sown for the righteous,
  and gladness for the upright in heart.
12 Rejoice in the LORD, ye righteous:
  and give thanks at the remembrance of his holiness.

PSALM 98

A psalm.

1 O sing unto the LORD a new song, for he hath done marvellous
    things:
  his right hand, and his holy arm hath gotten him the victory.
2 The LORD hath made known his salvation:
  his righteousness hath he openly shown in the sight of the heathen.
3 He hath remembered his mercy and his truth toward the house
    of Israel:
  all the ends of the earth have seen the salvation of our God.

4 Make a joyful noise unto the LORD, all the earth:
  make a loud noise, and rejoice, and sing praise.
5 Sing unto the LORD with the harp:
  with the harp, and the voice of a psalm.

⁶ With trumpets and sound of cornet
  make a joyful noise before the Lord, the King.
⁷ Let the sea roar, and the fulness thereof:
  the world, and they that dwell therein.
⁸ Let the floods clap their hands:
  let the hills be joyful together ⁹before the Lord,
  for he cometh to judge the earth:
  with righteousness shall he judge the world,
  and the people with equity.

PSALM 99

¹ The Lord reigneth, let the people tremble:
  he sitteth between the cherubims, let the earth be moved.
² The Lord is great in Zion:
  and he is high above all people.
³ Let them praise thy great and terrible name:
  for it is holy.

⁴ The king's strength also loveth judgement;
  thou dost establish equity:
  thou executest judgement and righteousness in Jacob.
⁵ Exalt ye the Lord our God, and worship at his footstool:
  for he is holy.

⁶ Moses and Aaron among his priests,
  and Samuel among them that call upon his name:
  they called upon the Lord, and he answered them.
⁷ He spoke unto them in the cloudy pillar:
  they kept his testimonies,
  and the ordinance that he gave them.
⁸ Thou answeredst them, O Lord our God:
  thou wast a God that forgavest them,
  though thou tookest vengeance of their inventions.

⁹ Exalt the Lord our God,
  and worship at his holy hill:
  for the Lord our God is holy.

PSALM 100
A psalm of praise.

¹ Make a joyful noise unto the Lord, all ye lands.
² Serve the Lord with gladness:
  come before his presence with singing.
³ Know ye that the Lord, he is God:

it is he that hath made us, and not we ourselves:
we are his people, and the sheep of his pasture.
⁴ Enter into his gates with thanksgiving,
and into his courts with praise:
be thankful unto him, and bless his name.
⁵ For the LORD is good, his mercy is everlasting:
and his truth endureth to all generations.

PSALM 101
A psalm of David.

¹ I will sing of mercy and judgement:
unto thee, O LORD, will I sing.
² I will behave myself wisely in a perfect way,
O when wilt thou come unto me?
I will walk within my house with a perfect heart.
³ I will set no wicked thing before my eyes:
I hate the work of them that turn aside, it shall not cleave to me.
⁴ A froward heart shall depart from me:
I will not know a wicked person.
⁵ Whoso privily slandereth his neighbour, him will I cut off:
him that hath a high look and a proud heart will not I suffer.

⁶ My eyes shall be upon the faithful of the land, that they may
dwell with me:
he that walketh in a perfect way, he shall serve me.
⁷ He that worketh deceit shall not dwell within my house:
he that telleth lies shall not tarry in my sight.
⁸ I will early destroy all the wicked of the land:
that I may cut off all wicked-doers from the city of the LORD.

PSALM 102
A prayer of the afflicted when he is overwhelmed, and poureth out his
complaint before the Lord.

¹ Hear my prayer, O LORD,
and let my cry come unto thee.
² Hide not thy face from me in the day when I am in trouble,
incline thy ear unto me:
in the day when I call, answer me speedily.
³ For my days are consumed like smoke,
and my bones are burnt as a hearth.
⁴ My heart is smitten, and withered like grass:
so that I forget to eat my bread.
⁵ By reason of the voice of my groaning,
my bones cleave to my skin.

⁶ I am like a pelican of the wilderness:
  I am like an owl of the desert.
⁷ I watch, and am as a sparrow alone upon the house top.

⁸ My enemies reproach me all the day:
  and they that are mad against me are sworn against me.
⁹ For I have eaten ashes like bread,
  and mingled my drink with weeping,
¹⁰ because of thy indignation and thy wrath:
  for thou hast lifted me up, and cast me down.
¹¹ My days are like a shadow that declineth:
  and I am withered like grass.

¹² But thou, O LORD, shalt endure for ever:
  and thy remembrance unto all generations.
¹³ Thou shalt arise, and have mercy upon Zion:
  for the time to favour her, yea, the set time is come.
¹⁴ For thy servants take pleasure in her stones,
  and favour the dust thereof.
¹⁵ So the heathen shall fear the name of the LORD,
  and all the kings of the earth thy glory.
¹⁶ When the LORD shall build up Zion,
  he shall appear in his glory.
¹⁷ He will regard the prayer of the destitute,
  and not despise their prayer.

¹⁸ This shall be written for the generation to come:
  and the people which shall be created shall praise the
    LORD.
¹⁹ For he hath looked down from the height of his sanctuary:
  from heaven did the LORD behold the earth:
²⁰ to hear the groaning of the prisoner:
  to loose those that are appointed to death:
²¹ to declare the name of the LORD in Zion,
  and his praise in Jerusalem:
²² when the people are gathered together,
  and the kingdoms to serve the LORD.

²³ He weakened my strength in the way:
  he shortened my days.
²⁴ I said, 'O my God, take me not away in the midst of my days:
  thy years are throughout all generations'.
²⁵ Of old hast thou laid the foundation of the earth:
  and the heavens are the work of thy hands.
²⁶ They shall perish, but thou shalt endure:
  yea, all of them shall wax old like a garment:
  as a vesture shalt thou change them, and they shall be changed.
²⁷ But thou art the same,

and thy years shall have no end.
²⁸ The children of thy servants shall continue,
and their seed shall be established before thee.

PSALM 103

A psalm of David.

¹ Bless the LORD, O my soul:
and all that is within me, bless his holy name.
² Bless the LORD, O my soul,
and forget not all his benefits:
³ who forgiveth all thy iniquities:
who healeth all thy diseases:
⁴ who redeemeth thy life from destruction:
who crowneth thee with loving-kindness and tender mercies:
⁵ who satisfieth thy mouth with good things
so that thy youth is renewed like the eagle's.

⁶ The LORD executeth righteousness,
and judgement for all that are oppressed.
⁷ He made known his ways unto Moses,
his acts unto the children of Israel.
⁸ The LORD is merciful and gracious,
slow to anger, and plenteous in mercy.
⁹ He will not always chide:
neither will he keep his anger for ever.
¹⁰ He hath not dealt with us after our sins,
nor rewarded us according to our iniquities.
¹¹ For as the heaven is high above the earth,
so great is his mercy toward them that fear him.
¹² As far as the east is from the west,
so far hath he removed our transgressions from us.
¹³ Like as a father pitieth his children,
so the LORD pitieth them that fear him.
¹⁴ For he knoweth our frame:
he remembereth that we are dust.

¹⁵ As for man, his days are as grass:
as a flower of the field, so he flourisheth.
¹⁶ For the wind passeth over it, and it is gone;
and the place thereof shall know it no more.
¹⁷ But the mercy of the LORD is from everlasting to everlasting upon
them that fear him,
and his righteousness unto children's children:
¹⁸ to such as keep his covenant,
and to those that remember his commandments to do them.

¹⁹ The Lord hath prepared his throne in the heavens:
and his kingdom ruleth over all.
²⁰ Bless the Lord, ye his angels,
that excel in strength, that do his commandments,
hearkening unto the voice of his word.
²¹ Bless ye the Lord, all ye his hosts:
ye ministers of his that do his pleasure.
²² Bless the Lord, all his works in all places of his dominion:
bless the Lord, O my soul.

PSALM 104

¹ Bless the Lord, O my soul.

O Lord my God, thou art very great:
thou art clothed with honour and majesty.
² Who coverest thyself with light as with a garment:
who stretchest out the heavens like a curtain:
³ who layeth the beams of his chambers in the waters:
who maketh the clouds his chariot:
who walketh upon the wings of the wind:
⁴ who maketh his angels spirits:
his ministers a flaming fire:
⁵ who laid the foundations of the earth,
that it should not be removed for ever.

⁶ Thou coveredst it with the deep as with a garment:
the waters stood above the mountains.
⁷ At thy rebuke they fled:
at the voice of thy thunder they hasted away.
⁸ They go up by the mountains:
they go down by the valleys unto the place which thou hast
founded for them.
⁹ Thou hast set a bound that they may not pass over:
that they turn not again to cover the earth.

¹⁰ He sendeth the springs into the valleys,
which run among the hills.
¹¹ They give drink to every beast of the field:
the wild asses quench their thirst.
¹² By them shall the fowls of the heaven have their habitation,
which sing among the branches.
¹³ He watereth the hills from his chambers:
the earth is satisfied with the fruit of thy works.
¹⁴ He causeth the grass to grow for the cattle,
and herb for the service of man:
that he may bring forth food out of the earth:

¹⁵ and wine that maketh glad the heart of man,
and oil to make his face to shine,
and bread which strengtheneth man's heart.

¹⁶ The trees of the LORD are full of sap:
the cedars of Lebanon, which he hath planted;
¹⁷ where the birds make their nests:
as for the stork, the fir trees are her house.
¹⁸ The high hills are a refuge for the wild goats:
and the rocks for the conies.
¹⁹ He appointed the moon for seasons:
the sun knoweth his going down.
²⁰ Thou makest darkness, and it is night:
wherein all the beasts of the forest do creep forth.
²¹ The young lions roar after their prey,
and seek their meat from God.
²² The sun ariseth, they gather themselves together,
and lay them down in their dens.
²³ Man goeth forth unto his work:
and to his labour until the evening.

²⁴ O LORD, how manifold are thy works!
in wisdom hast thou made them all:
the earth is full of thy riches.
²⁵ So is this great and wide sea, wherein are things creeping
innumerable,
both small and great beasts.
²⁶ There go the ships:
there is that leviathan, whom thou hast made to play
therein.
²⁷ These wait all upon thee:
that thou mayest give them their meat in due season.
²⁸ That thou givest them they gather:
thou openest thy hand, they are filled with good.
²⁹ Thou hidest thy face, they are troubled:
thou takest away their breath, they die,
and return to their dust.
³⁰ Thou sendest forth thy spirit, they are created:
and thou renewest the face of the earth.

³¹ The glory of the LORD shall endure for ever:
the LORD shall rejoice in his works.
³² He looketh on the earth, and it trembleth:
he toucheth the hills, and they smoke.
³³ I will sing unto the LORD as long as I live:
I will sing praise to my God while I have my being.
³⁴ My meditation of him shall be sweet:
I will be glad in the LORD.

³⁵ Let the sinners be consumed out of the earth,
and let the wicked be no more.

Bless thou the LORD, O my soul.
Praise ye the LORD.

PSALM 105

¹ O give thanks unto the LORD, call upon his name:
make known his deeds among the people.
² Sing unto him, sing psalms unto him:
talk ye of all his wondrous works.
³ Glory ye in his holy name:
let the heart of them rejoice that seek the LORD.
⁴ Seek the LORD, and his strength:
seek his face evermore.
⁵ Remember his marvellous works that he hath done:
his wonders, and the judgements of his mouth,
⁶ O ye seed of Abraham his servant,
ye children of Jacob his chosen.

⁷ He is the LORD our God:
his judgements are in all the earth.
⁸ He hath remembered his covenant for ever,
the word which he commanded to a thousand generations.
⁹ Which covenant he made with Abraham,
and his oath unto Isaac:
¹⁰ and confirmed the same unto Jacob for a law,
and to Israel for an everlasting covenant:
¹¹ saying, 'Unto thee will I give the land of Canaan,
the lot of your inheritance'.

¹² When they were but a few men in number:
yea, very few, and strangers in it:
¹³ when they went from one nation to another,
from one kingdom to another people:
¹⁴ he suffered no man to do them wrong:
yea, he reproved kings for their sakes:
¹⁵ saying, 'Touch not my anointed,
and do my prophets no harm'.
¹⁶ Moreover he called for a famine upon the land:
he broke the whole staff of bread.
¹⁷ He sent a man before them,
even Joseph, who was sold for a servant:
¹⁸ whose feet they hurt with fetters:
he was laid in iron:
¹⁹ until the time that his word came:

the word of the LORD tried him.
20 The king sent and loosed him:
even the ruler of the people, and let him go free.
21 He made him lord of his house,
and ruler of all his substance:
22 to bind his princes at his pleasure:
and teach his senators wisdom.
23 Israel also came into Egypt:
and Jacob sojourned in the land of Ham.
24 And he increased his people greatly:
and made them stronger than their enemies.
25 He turned their heart to hate his people,
to deal subtly with his servants.

26 He sent Moses his servant:
and Aaron whom he had chosen.
27 They showed his signs among them,
and wonders in the land of Ham.
28 He sent darkness, and made it dark:
and they rebelled not against his word.
29 He turned their waters into blood,
and slew their fish.
30 The land brought forth frogs in abundance,
in the chambers of their kings.
31 He spoke, and there came divers sorts of flies,
and lice in all their coasts.
32 He gave them hail for rain,
and flaming fire in their land.
33 He smote their vines also and their fig trees:
and broke the trees of their coasts.
34 He spoke, and the locusts came,
and caterpillars, and that without number,
35 and did eat up all the herbs in their land,
and devoured the fruit of their ground.
36 He smote also all the firstborn in their land,
the chief of all their strength.

37 He brought them forth also with silver and gold:
and there was not one feeble person among their tribes.
38 Egypt was glad when they departed:
for the fear of them fell upon them.
39 He spread a cloud for a covering:
and fire to give light in the night.
40 The people asked, and he brought quails,
and satisfied them with the bread of heaven.
41 He opened the rock, and the waters gushed out:
they ran in the dry places like a river.
42 For he remembered his holy promise,

and Abraham his servant.
⁴³ And he brought forth his people with joy,
and his chosen with gladness:
⁴⁴ and gave them the lands of the heathen:
and they inherited the labour of the people:
⁴⁵ that they might observe his statutes, and keep his laws.

Praise ye the LORD.

PSALM 106

¹ Praise ye the LORD.

O give thanks unto the LORD,
for he is good: for his mercy endureth for ever.
² Who can utter the mighty acts of the LORD?
who can show forth all his praise?
³ Blessed are they that keep judgement,
and he that doeth righteousness at all times.

⁴ Remember me, O LORD, with the favour that thou bearest unto
thy people:
O visit me with thy salvation:
⁵ that I may see the good of thy chosen,
that I may rejoice in the gladness of thy nation,
that I may glory with thy inheritance.

⁶ We have sinned with our fathers,
we have committed iniquity, we have done wickedly.
⁷ Our fathers understood not thy wonders in Egypt,
they remembered not the multitude of thy mercies:
but provoked him at the sea, even at the Red Sea.
⁸ Nevertheless he saved them for his name's sake,
that he might make his mighty power to be known.
⁹ He rebuked the Red Sea also, and it was dried up:
so he led them through the depths, as through the
wilderness.
¹⁰ And he saved them from the hand of him that hated them,
and redeemed them from the hand of the enemy.
¹¹ And the waters covered their enemies:
there was not one of them left.
¹² Then believed they his words:
they sang his praise.
¹³ They soon forgot his works:
they waited not for his counsel:
¹⁴ but lusted exceedingly in the wilderness,
and tempted God in the desert.

¹⁵ And he gave them their request:
  but sent leanness into their soul.
¹⁶ They envied Moses also in the camp,
  and Aaron the saint of the LORD.
¹⁷ The earth opened and swallowed up Dathan,
  and covered the company of Abiram.
¹⁸ And a fire was kindled in their company:
  the flame burnt up the wicked.

¹⁹ They made a calf in Horeb,
  and worshipped the molten image.
²⁰ Thus they changed their glory
  into the similitude of an ox that eateth grass.
²¹ They forgot God their saviour,
  which had done great things in Egypt:
²² wondrous works in the land of Ham,
  and terrible things by the Red Sea.
²³ Therefore he said that he would destroy them,
  had not Moses his chosen stood before him in the breach,
  to turn away his wrath, lest he should destroy them.

²⁴ Yea, they despised the pleasant land,
  they believed not his word:
²⁵ but murmured in their tents,
  and hearkened not unto the voice of the LORD.
²⁶ Therefore he lifted up his hand against them,
  to overthrow them in the wilderness:
²⁷ to overthrow their seed also among the nations,
  and to scatter them in the lands.

²⁸ They joined themselves also unto Baal-peor,
  and ate the sacrifices of the dead.
²⁹ Thus they provoked him to anger with their inventions:
  and the plague broke in upon them.
³⁰ Then stood up Phinehas, and executed judgement:
  and so the plague was stayed.
³¹ And that was counted unto him for righteousness:
  unto all generations for evermore.

³² They angered him also at the waters of strife,
  so that it went ill with Moses for their sakes:
³³ because they provoked his spirit,
  so that he spoke unadvisedly with his lips.
³⁴ They did not destroy the nations,
  concerning whom the LORD commanded them:
³⁵ but were mingled among the heathen,
  and learned their works.

³⁶ And they served their idols:
  which were a snare unto them.
³⁷ Yea, they sacrificed their sons and their daughters unto devils,
³⁸ and shed innocent blood, even the blood of their sons and of
    their daughters,
  whom they sacrificed unto the idols of Canaan:
  and the land was polluted with blood.
³⁹ Thus were they defiled with their own works,
  and went a-whoring with their own inventions.

⁴⁰ Therefore was the wrath of the LORD kindled against his
    people,
  insomuch that he abhorred his own inheritance.
⁴¹ And he gave them into the hand of the heathen:
  and they that hated them ruled over them.
⁴² Their enemies also oppressed them,
  and they were brought into subjection under their hand.
⁴³ Many times did he deliver them:
  but they provoked him with their counsel,
  and were brought low for their iniquity.
⁴⁴ Nevertheless he regarded their affliction,
  when he heard their cry.
⁴⁵ And he remembered for them his covenant,
  and repented according to the multitude of his mercies.
⁴⁶ He made them also to be pitied of all those that carried them
    captives.

⁴⁷ Save us, O LORD our God,
  and gather us from among the heathen,
  to give thanks unto thy holy name,
  and to triumph in thy praise.

⁴⁸ Blessed be the LORD God of Israel from everlasting to everlasting:
  and let all the people say, 'Amen'.

  Praise ye the LORD.

PSALM 107

¹ O give thanks unto the LORD, for he is good:
  for his mercy endureth for ever.
² Let the redeemed of the LORD say so,
  whom he hath redeemed from the hand of the enemy:
³ and gathered them out of the lands,
  from the east, and from the west,
  from the north, and from the south.

⁴ They wandered in the wilderness in a solitary way:
   they found no city to dwell in.
⁵ Hungry and thirsty,
   their soul fainted in them.
⁶ Then they cried unto the LORD in their trouble,
   and he delivered them out of their distresses.
⁷ And he led them forth by the right way,
   that they might go to a city of habitation.

⁸ O that men would praise the LORD for his goodness,
   and for his wonderful works to the children of men!
⁹ For he satisfieth the longing soul,
   and filleth the hungry soul with goodness.

¹⁰ Such as sit in darkness and in the shadow of death,
   being bound in affliction and iron:
¹¹ because they rebelled against the words of God,
   and contemned the counsel of the most High:
¹² therefore he brought down their heart with labour:
   they fell down, and there was none to help.
¹³ Then they cried unto the LORD in their trouble,
   and he saved them out of their distresses.
¹⁴ He brought them out of darkness and the shadow of
      death,
   and broke their bands in sunder.

¹⁵ O that men would praise the LORD for his goodness,
   and for his wonderful works to the children of men!
¹⁶ For he hath broken the gates of brass,
   and cut the bars of iron in sunder.

¹⁷ Fools because of their transgression, and because of their
      iniquities, are afflicted.
¹⁸ Their soul abhorreth all manner of meat:
   and they draw near unto the gates of death.
¹⁹ Then they cry unto the LORD in their trouble:
   he saveth them out of their distresses.
²⁰ He sent his word, and healed them,
   and delivered them from their destructions.

²¹ O that men would praise the LORD for his goodness,
   and for his wonderful works to the children of men!
²² And let them sacrifice the sacrifices of thanksgiving,
   and declare his works with rejoicing.

²³ They that go down to the sea in ships,
   that do business in great waters:
²⁴ these see the works of the LORD,

and his wonders in the deep.

²⁵ For he commandeth, and raiseth the stormy wind,
  which lifteth up the waves thereof.

²⁶ They mount up to the heaven,
  they go down again to the depths:
  their soul is melted because of trouble.

²⁷ They reel to and fro, and stagger like a drunken man,
  and are at their wits' end.

²⁸ Then they cry unto the LORD in their trouble,
  and he bringeth them out of their distresses.

²⁹ He maketh the storm a calm,
  so that the waves thereof are still.

³⁰ Then are they glad because they be quiet:
  so he bringeth them unto their desired haven.

³¹ O that men would praise the LORD for his goodness,
  and for his wonderful works to the children of men!

³² Let them exalt him also in the congregation of the people,
  and praise him in the assembly of the elders.

³³ He turneth rivers into a wilderness,
  and the water-springs into dry ground:

³⁴ a fruitful land into barrenness,
  for the wickedness of them that dwell therein.

³⁵ He turneth the wilderness into a standing water,
  and dry ground into water-springs.

³⁶ And there he maketh the hungry to dwell,
  that they may prepare a city for habitation,

³⁷ and sow the fields, and plant vineyards,
  which may yield fruits of increase.

³⁸ He blesseth them also, so that they are multiplied greatly:
  and suffereth not their cattle to decrease.

³⁹ Again, they are minished and brought low
  through oppression, affliction, and sorrow.

⁴⁰ He poureth contempt upon princes,
  and causeth them to wander in the wilderness, where there is no
      way.

⁴¹ Yet setteth he the poor on high from affliction,
  and maketh him families like a flock.

⁴² The righteous shall see it, and rejoice:
  and all iniquity shall stop her mouth.

⁴³ Whoso is wise, and will observe those things,
  even they shall understand the loving-kindness of the
      LORD.

PSALM 108

A song or psalm of David.

¹ O God, my heart is fixed:
  I will sing and give praise, even with my glory.

² Awake, psaltery and harp:
  I myself will awake early.
³ I will praise thee, O LORD, among the people:
  and I will sing praises unto thee among the nations.
⁴ For thy mercy is great above the heavens:
  and thy truth reacheth unto the clouds.
⁵ Be thou exalted, O God, above the heavens:
  and thy glory above all the earth:
⁶ that thy beloved may be delivered:
  save with thy right hand, and answer me.

⁷ God hath spoken in his holiness,
  'I will rejoice, I will divide Shechem,
  and mete out the valley of Succoth.
⁸ Gilead is mine, Manasseh is mine,
  Ephraim also is the strength of my head:
  Judah is my lawgiver.
⁹ Moab is my wash-pot, over Edom will I cast out my shoe:
  over Philistia will I triumph.'

¹⁰ Who will bring me into the strong city?
  who will lead me into Edom?
¹¹ Wilt not thou, O God, who hast cast us off?
  and wilt not thou, O God, go forth with our hosts?
¹² Give us help from trouble:
  for vain is the help of man.
¹³ Through God we shall do valiantly:
  for he it is that shall tread down our enemies.

PSALM 109

To the chief musician.
A psalm of David.

¹ Hold not thy peace, O God of my praise.
² For the mouth of the wicked and the mouth of the deceitful are
    opened against me:
  they have spoken against me with a lying tongue.
³ They compassed me about also with words of hatred:
  and fought against me without a cause.
⁴ For my love, they are my adversaries:

but I give myself unto prayer.
⁵ And they have rewarded me evil for good,
  and hatred for my love.

⁶ Set thou a wicked man over him:
  and let Satan stand at his right hand.
⁷ When he shall be judged, let him be condemned:
  and let his prayer become sin.
⁸ Let his days be few:
  and let another take his office.
⁹ Let his children be fatherless,
  and his wife a widow.
¹⁰ Let his children be continually vagabonds, and beg:
  let them seek their bread also out of their desolate places.
¹¹ Let the extortioner catch all that he hath:
  and let the strangers spoil his labour.
¹² Let there be none to extend mercy unto him:
  neither let there be any to favour his fatherless children.
¹³ Let his posterity be cut off:
  and in the generation following let their name be blotted out.
¹⁴ Let the iniquity of his fathers be remembered with the LORD:
  and let not the sin of his mother be blotted out.
¹⁵ Let them be before the LORD continually,
  that he may cut off the memory of them from the earth.
¹⁶ Because that he remembered not to show mercy,
  but persecuted the poor and needy man,
  that he might even slay the broken in heart.
¹⁷ As he loved cursing, so let it come unto him:
  as he delighted not in blessing, so let it be far from him.
¹⁸ As he clothed himself with cursing like as with his garment,
  so let it come into his bowels like water,
  and like oil into his bones.
¹⁹ Let it be unto him as the garment which covereth him,
  and for a girdle wherewith he is girded continually.
²⁰ Let this be the reward of my adversaries from the LORD,
  and of them that speak evil against my soul.

²¹ But do thou for me, O GOD the Lord, for thy name's sake:
  because thy mercy is good:
  deliver thou me.
²² For I am poor and needy,
  and my heart is wounded within me.
²³ I am gone like the shadow when it declineth:
  I am tossed up and down as the locust.
²⁴ My knees are weak through fasting:
  and my flesh faileth of fatness.
²⁵ I became also a reproach unto them:
  when they looked upon me they shook their heads.

²⁶ Help me, O LORD my God:
   O save me according to thy mercy:
²⁷ that they may know that this is thy hand:
   that thou, LORD, hast done it.
²⁸ Let them curse, but bless thou:
   when they arise, let them be ashamed,
   but let thy servant rejoice.
²⁹ Let my adversaries be clothed with shame,
   and let them cover themselves with their own confusion, as with
      a mantle.

³⁰ I will greatly praise the LORD with my mouth:
   yea, I will praise him among the multitude.
³¹ For he shall stand at the right hand of the poor,
   to save him from those that condemn his soul.

PSALM 110

A psalm of David.

¹ The LORD said unto my Lord, 'Sit thou at my right hand,
   until I make thy enemies thy footstool'.
² The LORD shall send the rod of thy strength out of Zion:
   rule thou in the midst of thy enemies.
³ Thy people shall be willing in the day of thy power,
   in the beauties of holiness from the womb of the morning:
   thou hast the dew of thy youth.
⁴ The LORD hath sworn, and will not repent,
   'Thou art a priest for ever after the order of Melchizedek'.
⁵ The Lord at thy right hand shall strike through kings in the day
      of his wrath.
⁶ He shall judge among the heathen,
   he shall fill the places with the dead bodies:
   he shall wound the heads over many countries.
⁷ He shall drink of the brook in the way:
   therefore shall he lift up the head.

PSALM 111

¹ Praise ye the LORD.

   I will praise the LORD with my whole heart,
   in the assembly of the upright, and in the congregation.
² The works of the LORD are great,
   sought out of all them that have pleasure therein.
³ His work is honourable and glorious:
   and his righteousness endureth for ever.

⁴ He hath made his wonderful works to be remembered:
  the LORD is gracious and full of compassion.
⁵ He hath given meat unto them that fear him:
  he will ever be mindful of his covenant.
⁶ He hath shown his people the power of his works,
  that he may give them the heritage of the heathen.
⁷ The works of his hands are verity and judgement:
  all his commandments are sure.
⁸ They stand fast for ever and ever,
  and are done in truth and uprightness.
⁹ He sent redemption unto his people,
  he hath commanded his covenant for ever:
  holy and reverend is his name.
¹⁰ The fear of the LORD is the beginning of wisdom:
  a good understanding have all they that do his commandments:
  his praise endureth for ever.

PSALM 112

¹ Praise ye the LORD.

  Blessed is the man that feareth the LORD,
  that delighteth greatly in his commandments.
² His seed shall be mighty upon earth:
  the generation of the upright shall be blessed.
³ Wealth and riches shall be in his house:
  and his righteousness endureth for ever.
⁴ Unto the upright there ariseth light in the darkness:
  he is gracious, and full of compassion, and righteous.
⁵ A good man showeth favour, and lendeth:
  he will guide his affairs with discretion.
⁶ Surely he shall not be moved for ever:
  the righteous shall be in everlasting remembrance.
⁷ He shall not be afraid of evil tidings:
  his heart is fixed, trusting in the LORD.
⁸ His heart is established, he shall not be afraid,
  until he see his desire upon his enemies.
⁹ He hath dispersed, he hath given to the poor:
  his righteousness endureth for ever;
  his horn shall be exalted with honour.
¹⁰ The wicked shall see it, and be grieved;
  he shall gnash with his teeth, and melt away:
  the desire of the wicked shall perish.

PSALM 113

¹ Praise ye the LORD.

Praise, O ye servants of the LORD,
  praise the name of the LORD.
² Blessed be the name of the LORD
  from this time forth and for evermore.
³ From the rising of the sun unto the going down of the same
  the LORD's name is to be praised.

⁴ The LORD is high above all nations,
  and his glory above the heavens.
⁵ Who is like unto the LORD our God,
  who dwelleth on high:
⁶ who humbleth himself to behold the things that are in heaven,
    and in the earth!
⁷ He raiseth up the poor out of the dust,
  and lifteth the needy out of the dunghill:
⁸ that he may set him with princes,
  even with the princes of his people.
⁹ He maketh the barren woman to keep house,
  to be a joyful mother of children.

Praise ye the LORD.

PSALM 114

¹ When Israel went out of Egypt,
  the house of Jacob from a people of strange language:
² Judah was his sanctuary,
  and Israel his dominion.

³ The sea saw it, and fled:
  Jordan was driven back.
⁴ The mountains skipped like rams,
  and the little hills like lambs.

⁵ What ailed thee, O thou sea, that thou fleddest?
  thou Jordan, that thou wast driven back?
⁶ Ye mountains, that ye skipped like rams:
  and ye little hills like lambs?

⁷ Tremble, thou earth, at the presence of the Lord,
  at the presence of the God of Jacob:
⁸ which turned the rock into a standing water,
  the flint into a fountain of waters.

PSALM 115

¹ Not unto us, O Lord, not unto us, but unto thy name give
   glory:
   for thy mercy, and for thy truth's sake.
² Wherefore should the heathen say, 'Where is now their God?'
³ But our God is in the heavens:
   he hath done whatsoever he pleased.

⁴ Their idols are silver and gold:
   the work of men's hands.
⁵ They have mouths, but they speak not:
   eyes have they, but they see not.
⁶ They have ears, but they hear not:
   noses have they, but they smell not.
⁷ They have hands, but they handle not:
   feet have they, but they walk not:
   neither speak they through their throat.
⁸ They that make them are like unto them:
   so is every one that trusteth in them.

⁹ O Israel, trust thou in the Lord:
   he is their help and their shield.
¹⁰ O house of Aaron, trust in the Lord:
   he is their help and their shield.
¹¹ Ye that fear the Lord, trust in the Lord:
   he is their help and their shield.

¹² The Lord hath been mindful of us:
   he will bless us, he will bless the house of Israel:
   he will bless the house of Aaron.
¹³ He will bless them that fear the Lord,
   both small and great.
¹⁴ The Lord shall increase you more and more,
   you and your children.
¹⁵ You are blessed of the Lord
   which made heaven and earth.
¹⁶ The heaven, even the heavens are the Lord's:
   but the earth hath he given to the children of men.
¹⁷ The dead praise not the Lord,
   neither any that go down into silence.
¹⁸ But we will bless the Lord from this time forth and for evermore.

Praise the Lord.

PSALM 116

¹ I love the LORD,
  because he hath heard my voice and my supplications.
² Because he hath inclined his ear unto me,
  therefore will I call upon him as long as I live.

³ The sorrows of death compassed me,
  and the pains of hell got hold upon me:
  I found trouble and sorrow.
⁴ Then called I upon the name of the LORD:
  'O LORD, I beseech thee, deliver my soul'.
⁵ Gracious is the LORD, and righteous:
  yea, our God is merciful.
⁶ The LORD preserveth the simple:
  I was brought low, and he helped me.
⁷ Return unto thy rest, O my soul:
  for the LORD hath dealt bountifully with thee.
⁸ For thou hast delivered my soul from death,
  my eyes from tears, and my feet from falling.
⁹ I will walk before the LORD
  in the land of the living.

¹⁰ I believed, therefore have I spoken:
  I was greatly afflicted.
¹¹ I said in my haste, 'All men are liars'.
¹² What shall I render unto the LORD
  for all his benefits towards me?
¹³ I will take the cup of salvation,
  and call upon the name of the LORD.
¹⁴ I will pay my vows unto the LORD
  now in the presence of all his people.
¹⁵ Precious in the sight of the LORD
  is the death of his saints.
¹⁶ O LORD, truly I am thy servant,
  I am thy servant, and the son of thy handmaid:
  thou hast loosed my bonds.
¹⁷ I will offer to thee the sacrifice of thanksgiving,
  and will call upon the name of the LORD.
¹⁸ I will pay my vows unto the LORD
  now in the presence of all his people:
¹⁹ in the courts of the LORD's house,
  in the midst of thee, O Jerusalem.

Praise ye the LORD.

PSALM 117

¹ O praise the LORD, all ye nations:
  praise him, all ye people.
² For his merciful kindness is great toward us:
  and the truth of the LORD endureth for ever.

Praise ye the LORD.

PSALM 118

¹ O give thanks unto the LORD, for he is good:
  because his mercy endureth for ever.
² Let Israel now say,
  that his mercy endureth for ever.
³ Let the house of Aaron now say,
  that his mercy endureth for ever.
⁴ Let them now that fear the LORD say,
  that his mercy endureth for ever.

⁵ I called upon the LORD in distress:
  the LORD answered me, and set me in a large place.
⁶ The LORD is on my side, I will not fear:
  what can man do unto me?
⁷ The LORD taketh my part with them that help me:
  therefore shall I see my desire upon them that hate me.
⁸ It is better to trust in the LORD
  than to put confidence in man.
⁹ It is better to trust in the LORD
  than to put confidence in princes.

¹⁰ All nations compassed me about:
  but in the name of the LORD will I destroy them.
¹¹ They compassed me about, yea, they compassed me
    about:
  but in the name of the LORD I will destroy them.
¹² They compassed me about like bees,
  they are quenched as the fire of thorns:
  for in the name of the LORD I will destroy them.
¹³ Thou hast thrust sore at me that I might fall:
  but the LORD helped me.
¹⁴ The LORD is my strength and song,
  and is become my salvation.

¹⁵ The voice of rejoicing and salvation is in the tabernacles of the
    righteous:
  the right hand of the LORD doeth valiantly.

¹⁶ The right hand of the LORD is exalted:
  the right hand of the LORD doeth valiantly.
¹⁷ I shall not die, but live,
  and declare the works of the LORD.
¹⁸ The LORD hath chastened me sore:
  but he hath not given me over unto death.
¹⁹ Open to me the gates of righteousness:
  I will go into them, and I will praise the LORD:
²⁰ this gate of the LORD,
  into which the righteous shall enter.
²¹ I will praise thee, for thou hast heard me,
  and art become my salvation.
²² The stone which the builders refused
  is become the head stone of the corner.
²³ This is the LORD's doing:
  it is marvellous in our eyes.
²⁴ This is the day which the LORD hath made:
  we will rejoice and be glad in it.

²⁵ Save now, I beseech thee, O LORD:
  O LORD, I beseech thee, send now prosperity.
²⁶ Blessed be he that cometh in the name of the LORD:
  we have blessed you out of the house of the LORD.
²⁷ God is the LORD, which hath shown us light,
  bind the sacrifice with cords, even unto the horns of the altar.
²⁸ Thou art my God, and I will praise thee:
  thou art my God, I will exalt thee.

²⁹ O give thanks unto the LORD,
  for he is good:
  for his mercy endureth for ever.

PSALM 119

Aleph

¹ Blessed are the undefiled in the way,
  who walk in the law of the LORD.
² Blessed are they that keep his testimonies,
  and that seek him with the whole heart.
³ They also do no iniquity:
  they walk in his ways.
⁴ Thou hast commanded us to keep thy precepts diligently.
⁵ O that my ways were directed to keep thy statutes!
⁶ Then shall I not be ashamed,
  when I have respect unto all thy commandments.

⁷ I will praise thee with uprightness of heart,
  when I shall have learned thy righteous judgements.
⁸ I will keep thy statutes:
  O forsake me not utterly.

Beth

⁹ Wherewithal shall a young man cleanse his way?
  by taking heed thereto according to thy word.
¹⁰ With my whole heart have I sought thee:
  O let me not wander from thy commandments.
¹¹ Thy word have I hid in my heart,
  that I might not sin against thee.
¹² Blessed art thou, O LORD:
  teach me thy statutes.
¹³ With my lips have I declared all the judgements of thy
    mouth.
¹⁴ I have rejoiced in the way of thy testimonies,
  as much as in all riches.
¹⁵ I will meditate in thy precepts,
  and have respect unto thy ways.
¹⁶ I will delight myself in thy statutes:
  I will not forget thy word.

Gimel

¹⁷ Deal bountifully with thy servant,
  that I may live, and keep thy word.
¹⁸ Open thou my eyes,
  that I may behold wondrous things out of thy law.
¹⁹ I am a stranger in the earth:
  hide not thy commandments from me.
²⁰ My soul breaketh for the longing
  that it hath unto thy judgements at all times.
²¹ Thou hast rebuked the proud that are cursed,
  which do err from thy commandments.
²² Remove from me reproach and contempt:
  for I have kept thy testimonies.
²³ Princes also did sit and speak against me:
  but thy servant did meditate in thy statutes.
²⁴ Thy testimonies also are my delight
  and my counsellors.

Daleth

²⁵ My soul cleaveth unto the dust:
  quicken thou me according to thy word.
²⁶ I have declared my ways, and thou heardest me:
  teach me thy statutes.
²⁷ Make me to understand the way of thy precepts:
  so shall I talk of thy wondrous works.

²⁸ My soul melteth for heaviness:
strengthen thou me according unto thy word.
²⁹ Remove from me the way of lying:
and grant me thy law graciously.
³⁰ I have chosen the way of truth:
thy judgements have I laid before me.
³¹ I have stuck unto thy testimonies:
O Lord, put me not to shame.
³² I will run the way of thy commandments,
when thou shalt enlarge my heart.

He

³³ Teach me, O Lord, the way of thy statutes:
and I shall keep it unto the end.
³⁴ Give me understanding, and I shall keep thy law:
yea, I shall observe it with my whole heart.
³⁵ Make me to go in the path of thy commandments:
for therein do I delight.
³⁶ Incline my heart unto thy testimonies,
and not to covetousness.
³⁷ Turn away my eyes from beholding vanity:
and quicken thou me in thy way.
³⁸ Establish thy word unto thy servant,
who is devoted to thy fear.
³⁹ Turn away my reproach which I fear:
for thy judgements are good.
⁴⁰ Behold, I have longed after thy precepts:
quicken me in thy righteousness.

Waw

⁴¹ Let thy mercies come also unto me, O Lord,
even thy salvation, according to thy word.
⁴² So shall I have wherewith to answer him that reproacheth me:
for I trust in thy word.
⁴³ And take not the word of truth utterly out of my mouth:
for I have hoped in thy judgements.
⁴⁴ So shall I keep thy law continually
for ever and ever.
⁴⁵ And I will walk at liberty:
for I seek thy precepts.
⁴⁶ I will speak of thy testimonies also before kings, and will not be
ashamed.
⁴⁷ And I will delight myself in thy commandments, which I have
loved.
⁴⁸ My hands also will I lift up unto thy commandments, which I
have loved:
and I will meditate in thy statutes.

Zayin

⁴⁹ Remember the word unto thy servant,
upon which thou hast caused me to hope.
⁵⁰ This is my comfort in my affliction:
for thy word hath quickened me.
⁵¹ The proud have had me greatly in derision:
yet have I not declined from thy law.
⁵² I remembered thy judgements of old, O LORD:
and have comforted myself.
⁵³ Horror hath taken hold upon me because of the wicked that
forsake thy law.
⁵⁴ Thy statutes have been my songs in the house of my
pilgrimage.
⁵⁵ I have remembered thy name, O LORD, in the night, and have
kept thy law.
⁵⁶ This I had,
because I kept thy precepts.

Heth

⁵⁷ Thou art my portion, O LORD:
I have said that I would keep thy words.
⁵⁸ I entreated thy favour with my whole heart:
be merciful unto me according to thy word.
⁵⁹ I thought on my ways,
and turned my feet unto thy testimonies.
⁶⁰ I made haste, and delayed not to keep thy commandments.
⁶¹ The bands of the wicked have robbed me:
but I have not forgotten thy law.
⁶² At midnight I will rise to give thanks unto thee
because of thy righteous judgements.
⁶³ I am a companion of all them that fear thee,
and of them that keep thy precepts.
⁶⁴ The earth, O LORD, is full of thy mercy:
teach me thy statutes.

Teth

⁶⁵ Thou hast dealt well with thy servant, O LORD,
according unto thy word.
⁶⁶ Teach me good judgement and knowledge:
for I have believed thy commandments.
⁶⁷ Before I was afflicted I went astray:
but now have I kept thy word.
⁶⁸ Thou art good, and doest good:
teach me thy statutes.
⁶⁹ The proud have forged a lie against me:
but I will keep thy precepts with my whole heart.
⁷⁰ Their heart is as fat as grease:

but I delight in thy law.
71 It is good for me that I have been afflicted:
that I might learn thy statutes.
72 The law of thy mouth is better unto me
than thousands of gold and silver.

Yodh

73 Thy hands have made me and fashioned me:
give me understanding, that I may learn thy commandments.
74 They that fear thee will be glad when they see me:
because I have hoped in thy word.
75 I know, O LORD, that thy judgements are right,
and that thou in faithfulness hast afflicted me.
76 Let, I pray thee, thy merciful kindness be for my comfort,
according to thy word unto thy servant.
77 Let thy tender mercies come unto me, that I may live:
for thy law is my delight.
78 Let the proud be ashamed, for they dealt perversely with me
without a cause:
but I will meditate in thy precepts.
79 Let those that fear thee turn unto me,
and those that have known thy testimonies.
80 Let my heart be sound in thy statutes;
that I be not ashamed.

Kaph

81 My soul fainteth for thy salvation:
but I hope in thy word.
82 My eyes fail for thy word,
saying, 'When wilt thou comfort me?'
83 For I am become like a bottle in the smoke:
yet do I not forget thy statutes.
84 How many are the days of thy servant?
when wilt thou execute judgement on them that persecute
me?
85 The proud have dug pits for me,
which are not after thy law.
86 All thy commandments are faithful:
they persecute me wrongfully; help thou me.
87 They had almost consumed me upon earth:
but I forsook not thy precepts.
88 Quicken me after thy loving-kindness:
so shall I keep the testimony of thy mouth.

Lamedh

89 For ever, O LORD, thy word is settled in heaven.
90 Thy faithfulness is unto all generations:
thou hast established the earth, and it abideth.

⁹¹ They continue this day according to thy ordinances:
for all are thy servants.
⁹² Unless thy law had been my delights,
I should then have perished in my affliction.
⁹³ I will never forget thy precepts:
for with them thou hast quickened me.
⁹⁴ I am thine, save me:
for I have sought thy precepts.
⁹⁵ The wicked have waited for me to destroy me:
but I will consider thy testimonies.
⁹⁶ I have seen an end of all perfection:
but thy commandment is exceeding broad.

Mem

⁹⁷ O how love I thy law!
it is my meditation all the day.
⁹⁸ Thou through thy commandments hast made me wiser than my
enemies:
for they are ever with me.
⁹⁹ I have more understanding than all my teachers:
for thy testimonies are my meditation.
¹⁰⁰ I understand more than the ancients,
because I keep thy precepts.
¹⁰¹ I have refrained my feet from every evil way,
that I may keep thy word.
¹⁰² I have not departed from thy judgements:
for thou hast taught me.
¹⁰³ How sweet are thy words unto my taste!
yea, sweeter than honey to my mouth!
¹⁰⁴ Through thy precepts I get understanding:
therefore I hate every false way.

Nun

¹⁰⁵ Thy word is a lamp unto my feet,
and a light unto my path.
¹⁰⁶ I have sworn, and I will perform it,
that I will keep thy righteous judgements.
¹⁰⁷ I am afflicted very much:
quicken me, O LORD, according unto thy word.
¹⁰⁸ Accept, I beseech thee, the free-will offerings of my mouth,
O LORD,
and teach me thy judgements.
¹⁰⁹ My soul is continually in my hand:
yet do I not forget thy law.
¹¹⁰ The wicked have laid a snare for me:
yet I erred not from thy precepts.
¹¹¹ Thy testimonies have I taken as a heritage for ever:
for they are the rejoicing of my heart.

¹¹² I have inclined my heart to perform thy statutes always, even
    unto the end.

Samech

¹¹³ I hate vain thoughts:
    but thy law do I love.
¹¹⁴ Thou art my hiding-place and my shield:
    I hope in thy word.
¹¹⁵ Depart from me, ye evil-doers:
    for I will keep the commandments of my God.
¹¹⁶ Uphold me according unto thy word, that I may live:
    and let me not be ashamed of my hope.
¹¹⁷ Hold thou me up, and I shall be safe:
    and I will have respect unto thy statutes continually.
¹¹⁸ Thou hast trodden down all them that err from thy statutes:
    for their deceit is falsehood.
¹¹⁹ Thou puttest away all the wicked of the earth like dross:
    therefore I love thy testimonies.
¹²⁰ My flesh trembleth for fear of thee:
    and I am afraid of thy judgements.

Ayin

¹²¹ I have done judgement and justice:
    leave me not to my oppressors.
¹²² Be surety for thy servant for good:
    let not the proud oppress me.
¹²³ My eyes fail for thy salvation,
    and for the word of thy righteousness.
¹²⁴ Deal with thy servant according unto thy mercy,
    and teach me thy statutes.
¹²⁵ I am thy servant, give me understanding,
    that I may know thy testimonies.
¹²⁶ It is time for thee, LORD, to work:
    for they have made void thy law.
¹²⁷ Therefore I love thy commandments
    above gold, yea, above fine gold.
¹²⁸ Therefore I esteem all thy precepts concerning all things to be
    right:
    and I hate every false way.

Pe

¹²⁹ Thy testimonies are wonderful:
    therefore doth my soul keep them.
¹³⁰ The entrance of thy words giveth light:
    it giveth understanding unto the simple.
¹³¹ I opened my mouth, and panted:
    for I longed for thy commandments.

¹³² Look thou upon me, and be merciful unto me,
   as thou usest to do unto those that love thy name.
¹³³ Order my steps in thy word:
   and let not any iniquity have dominion over me.
¹³⁴ Deliver me from the oppression of man:
   so will I keep thy precepts.
¹³⁵ Make thy face to shine upon thy servant:
   and teach me thy statutes.
¹³⁶ Rivers of waters run down my eyes,
   because they keep not thy law.

Tsade

¹³⁷ Righteous art thou, O LORD,
   and upright are thy judgements.
¹³⁸ Thy testimonies that thou hast commanded are righteous
   and very faithful.
¹³⁹ My zeal hath consumed me,
   because my enemies have forgotten thy words.
¹⁴⁰ Thy word is very pure:
   therefore thy servant loveth it.
¹⁴¹ I am small and despised:
   yet do not I forget thy precepts.
¹⁴² Thy righteousness is an everlasting righteousness,
   and thy law is the truth.
¹⁴³ Trouble and anguish have taken hold on me:
   yet thy commandments are my delights.
¹⁴⁴ The righteousness of thy testimonies is everlasting:
   give me understanding, and I shall live.

Qoph

¹⁴⁵ I cried with my whole heart:
   'Hear me, O LORD, I will keep thy statutes'.
¹⁴⁶ I cried unto thee, 'Save me,
   and I shall keep thy testimonies'.
¹⁴⁷ I prevented the dawning of the morning, and cried:
   I hoped in thy word.
¹⁴⁸ My eyes prevent the night watches,
   that I might meditate in thy word.
¹⁴⁹ Hear my voice according unto thy loving-kindness:
   O LORD, quicken me according to thy judgement.
¹⁵⁰ They draw nigh that follow after mischief:
   they are far from thy law.
¹⁵¹ Thou art near, O LORD:
   and all thy commandments are truth.
¹⁵² Concerning thy testimonies, I have known of old
   that thou hast founded them for ever.

Resh

¹⁵³ Consider my affliction, and deliver me:
  for I do not forget thy law.
¹⁵⁴ Plead my cause, and deliver me:
  quicken me according to thy word.
¹⁵⁵ Salvation is far from the wicked:
  for they seek not thy statutes.
¹⁵⁶ Great are thy tender mercies, O LORD:
  quicken me according to thy judgements.
¹⁵⁷ Many are my persecutors and my enemies:
  yet do I not decline from thy testimonies.
¹⁵⁸ I beheld the transgressors, and was grieved;
  because they kept not thy word.
¹⁵⁹ Consider how I love thy precepts:
  quicken me, O LORD, according to thy loving-kindness.
¹⁶⁰ Thy word is true from the beginning:
  and every one of thy righteous judgements endureth for ever.

Shin

¹⁶¹ Princes have persecuted me without a cause:
  but my heart standeth in awe of thy word.
¹⁶² I rejoice at thy word,
  as one that findeth great spoil.
¹⁶³ I hate and abhor lying:
  but thy law do I love.
¹⁶⁴ Seven times a day do I praise thee
  because of thy righteous judgements.
¹⁶⁵ Great peace have they which love thy law:
  and nothing shall offend them.
¹⁶⁶ LORD, I have hoped for thy salvation,
  and done thy commandments.
¹⁶⁷ My soul hath kept thy testimonies:
  and I love them exceedingly.
¹⁶⁸ I have kept thy precepts and thy testimonies:
  for all my ways are before thee.

Taw

¹⁶⁹ Let my cry come near before thee, O LORD:
  give me understanding according to thy word.
¹⁷⁰ Let my supplication come before thee:
  deliver me according to thy word.
¹⁷¹ My lips shall utter praise,
  when thou hast taught me thy statutes.
¹⁷² My tongue shall speak of thy word:
  for all thy commandments are righteousness.
¹⁷³ Let thy hand help me:
  for I have chosen thy precepts.

¹⁷⁴ I have longed for thy salvation, O L<small>ORD</small>:
and thy law is my delight.
¹⁷⁵ Let my soul live, and it shall praise thee:
and let thy judgements help me.
¹⁷⁶ I have gone astray like a lost sheep, seek thy servant:
for I do not forget thy commandments.

PSALM 120

A song of degrees.

¹ In my distress I cried unto the L<small>ORD</small>,
and he heard me.
² 'Deliver my soul, O L<small>ORD</small>, from lying lips,
and from a deceitful tongue.'
³ What shall be given unto thee?
or what shall be done unto thee, thou false tongue?
⁴ Sharp arrows of the mighty,
with coals of juniper.

⁵ Woe is me, that I sojourn in Mesech,
that I dwell in the tents of Kedar.
⁶ My soul hath long dwelt with him that hateth peace.
⁷ I am for peace:
but when I speak, they are for war.

PSALM 121

A song of degrees.

¹ I will lift up my eyes unto the hills,
from whence cometh my help.
² My help cometh from the L<small>ORD</small>,
which made heaven and earth.
³ He will not suffer thy foot to be moved:
he that keepeth thee will not slumber.
⁴ Behold, he that keepeth Israel
shall neither slumber nor sleep.

⁵ The L<small>ORD</small> is thy keeper:
the L<small>ORD</small> is thy shade upon thy right hand.
⁶ The sun shall not smite thee by day,
nor the moon by night.
⁷ The L<small>ORD</small> shall preserve thee from all evil:
he shall preserve thy soul.
⁸ The L<small>ORD</small> shall preserve thy going out and thy coming in
from this time forth, and even for evermore.

PSALM 122
A song of degrees of David.

[1] I was glad when they said unto me,
  'Let us go into the house of the LORD'.
[2] Our feet shall stand within thy gates, O Jerusalem.
[3] Jerusalem is built as a city that is compact together:
[4] whither the tribes go up, the tribes of the LORD, unto the
    testimony of Israel,
  to give thanks unto the name of the LORD.
[5] For there are set thrones of judgement,
  the thrones of the house of David.

[6] Pray for the peace of Jerusalem:
  they shall prosper that love thee.
[7] Peace be within thy walls,
  and prosperity within thy palaces.
[8] For my brethren and companions' sakes,
  I will now say, 'Peace be within thee'.
[9] Because of the house of the LORD our God
  I will seek thy good.

PSALM 123
A song of degrees.

[1] Unto thee lift I up my eyes,
  O thou that dwellest in the heavens.
[2] Behold, as the eyes of servants look unto the hand of their
    masters,
  and as the eyes of a maiden unto the hand of her mistress:
  so our eyes wait upon the LORD our God,
  until that he have mercy upon us.

[3] Have mercy upon us, O LORD, have mercy upon us:
  for we are exceedingly filled with contempt.
[4] Our soul is exceedingly filled with the scorning of those that are
    at ease,
  and with the contempt of the proud.

PSALM 124
A song of degrees of David.

[1] 'If it had not been the LORD who was on our side,'
  now may Israel say:
[2] 'if it had not been the LORD who was on our side,
  when men rose up against us:

³ then they had swallowed us up quick,
   when their wrath was kindled against us.
⁴ Then the waters had overwhelmed us,
   the stream had gone over our soul.
⁵ Then the proud waters had gone over our soul.'

⁶ Blessed be the LORD,
   who hath not given us as a prey to their teeth.
⁷ Our soul is escaped as a bird out of the snare of the fowlers:
   the snare is broken, and we are escaped.
⁸ Our help is in the name of the LORD,
   who made heaven and earth.

PSALM 125
A song of degrees.

¹ They that trust in the LORD shall be as mount Zion,
   which cannot be removed, but abideth for ever.
² As the mountains are round about Jerusalem,
   so the LORD is round about his people
   from henceforth even for ever.
³ For the rod of the wicked shall not rest upon the lot of the
      righteous,
   lest the righteous put forth their hands unto iniquity.
⁴ Do good, O LORD, unto those that be good,
   and to them that are upright in their hearts.
⁵ As for such as turn aside unto their crooked ways,
   the LORD shall lead them forth with the workers of iniquity:
   but peace shall be upon Israel.

PSALM 126
A song of degrees.

¹ When the LORD turned again the captivity of Zion,
   we were like them that dream.
² Then was our mouth filled with laughter,
   and our tongue with singing,
   then said they among the heathen,
   'The LORD hath done great things for them'.
³ The LORD hath done great things for us:
   whereof we are glad.

⁴ Turn again our captivity, O LORD,
   as the streams in the south.
⁵ They that sow in tears shall reap in joy.

⁶ He that goeth forth and weepeth, bearing precious seed,
   shall doubtless come again with rejoicing,
   bringing his sheaves with him.

PSALM 127

A song of degrees for Solomon.

¹ Except the LORD build the house, they labour in vain that build
      it:
   except the LORD keep the city, the watchman waketh but in vain.
² It is vain for you to rise up early, to sit up late, to eat the bread of
      sorrows:
   for so he giveth his beloved sleep.

³ Lo, children are a heritage of the LORD:
   and the fruit of the womb is his reward.
⁴ As arrows are in the hand of a mighty man:
   so are children of the youth.
⁵ Happy is the man that hath his quiver full of them,
   they shall not be ashamed:
   but they shall speak with the enemies in the gate.

PSALM 128

A song of degrees.

¹ Blessed is every one that feareth the LORD:
   that walketh in his ways.
² For thou shalt eat the labour of thy hands:
   happy shalt thou be, and it shall be well with thee.
³ Thy wife shall be as a fruitful vine by the sides of thy house,
   thy children like olive plants round about thy table.
⁴ Behold, that thus shall the man be blessed
   that feareth the LORD.
⁵ The LORD shall bless thee out of Zion:
   and thou shalt see the good of Jerusalem all the days of thy life.
⁶ Yea, thou shalt see thy children's children,
   and peace upon Israel.

PSALM 129

A song of degrees.

¹ 'Many a time have they afflicted me from my youth,'
   may Israel now say:
² 'many a time have they afflicted me from my youth:
   yet they have not prevailed against me.

³ The ploughers ploughed upon my back:
  they made long their furrows.'
⁴ The LORD is righteous:
  he hath cut asunder the cords of the wicked.

⁵ Let them all be confounded and turned back that hate Zion.
⁶ Let them be as the grass upon the house-tops,
  which withereth afore it groweth up:
⁷ wherewith the mower filleth not his hand:
  nor he that bindeth sheaves his bosom.
⁸ Neither do they which go by say,
  'The blessing of the LORD be upon you:
  we bless you in the name of the LORD'.

PSALM 130
A song of degrees.

¹ Out of the depths have I cried unto thee, O LORD.
² Lord, hear my voice:
  let thy ears be attentive to the voice of my supplications.
³ If thou, LORD, shouldst mark iniquities,
  O Lord, who shall stand?
⁴ But there is forgiveness with thee,
  that thou mayest be feared.

⁵ I wait for the LORD, my soul doth wait,
  and in his word do I hope.
⁶ My soul waiteth for the Lord more than they that watch for the
    morning:
  I say, more than they that watch for the morning.

⁷ Let Israel hope in the LORD:
  for with the LORD there is mercy,
  and with him is plenteous redemption.
⁸ And he shall redeem Israel from all his iniquities.

PSALM 131
A song of degrees of David.

¹ LORD, my heart is not haughty, nor my eyes lofty:
  neither do I exercise myself in great matters, or in things too
    high for me.
² Surely I have behaved and quieted myself, as a child that is
    weaned of his mother:
  my soul is even as a weaned child.
³ Let Israel hope in the LORD from henceforth and for ever.

PSALM 132
A song of degrees.

¹ LORD, remember David, and all his afflictions:
² how he swore unto the LORD, and vowed unto the mighty God of
   Jacob.
³ 'Surely I will not come into the tabernacle of my house,
   nor go up into my bed.
⁴ I will not give sleep to my eyes,
   or slumber to my eyelids,
⁵ until I find out a place for the LORD,
   a habitation for the mighty God of Jacob.'

⁶ Lo, we heard of it at Ephratah:
   we found it in the fields of the wood.
⁷ We will go into his tabernacles:
   we will worship at his footstool.
⁸ Arise, O LORD, into thy rest:
   thou, and the ark of thy strength.
⁹ Let thy priests be clothed with righteousness:
   and let thy saints shout for joy.
¹⁰ For thy servant David's sake
   turn not away the face of thy anointed.

¹¹ The LORD hath sworn in truth unto David, he will not turn from it:
   'Of the fruit of thy body will I set upon thy throne.
¹² If thy children will keep my covenant and my testimony that I
      shall teach them,
   their children also shall sit upon thy throne for evermore.'
¹³ For the LORD hath chosen Zion:
   he hath desired it for his habitation.
¹⁴ 'This is my rest for ever:
   here will I dwell, for I have desired it.
¹⁵ I will abundantly bless her provision:
   I will satisfy her poor with bread.
¹⁶ I will also clothe her priests with salvation:
   and her saints shall shout aloud for joy.
¹⁷ There will I make the horn of David to bud:
   I have ordained a lamp for my anointed.
¹⁸ His enemies will I clothe with shame:
   but upon himself shall his crown flourish.'

PSALM 133
A song of degrees of David.

¹ Behold how good and how pleasant it is
   for brethren to dwell together in unity.

² It is like the precious ointment upon the head,
  that ran down upon the beard, even Aaron's beard:
  that went down to the skirts of his garments;
³ as the dew of Hermon, and as the dew that descended upon the
  mountains of Zion,
  for there the LORD commanded the blessing,
  even life for evermore.

PSALM 134
A song of degrees.

¹ Behold, bless ye the LORD, all ye servants of the LORD,
  which by night stand in the house of the LORD.
² Lift up your hands in the sanctuary,
  and bless the LORD.
³ The LORD that made heaven and earth
  bless thee out of Zion.

PSALM 135

¹ Praise ye the LORD, praise ye the name of the LORD:
  praise him, O ye servants of the LORD.
² Ye that stand in the house of the LORD,
  in the courts of the house of our God,
³ praise the LORD, for the LORD is good:
  sing praises unto his name, for it is pleasant.
⁴ For the LORD hath chosen Jacob unto himself,
  and Israel for his peculiar treasure.
⁵ For I know that the LORD is great,
  and that our Lord is above all gods.
⁶ Whatsoever the LORD pleased,
  that did he in heaven, and in earth,
  in the seas, and all deep places.
⁷ He causeth the vapours to ascend from the ends of the earth,
  he maketh lightnings for the rain:
  he bringeth the wind out of his treasuries.
⁸ Who smote the firstborn of Egypt,
  both of man and beast.
⁹ Who sent tokens and wonders into the midst of thee, O Egypt,
  upon Pharaoh, and upon all his servants.
¹⁰ Who smote great nations, and slew mighty kings:
¹¹ Sihon king of the Amorites, and Og king of Bashan,
  and all the kingdoms of Canaan,
¹² and gave their land for a heritage,
  a heritage unto Israel his people.
¹³ Thy name, O LORD, endureth for ever:

and thy memorial, O LORD, throughout all generations.

¹⁴ For the LORD will judge his people,
and he will repent himself concerning his servants.

¹⁵ The idols of the heathen are silver and gold,
the work of men's hands.

¹⁶ They have mouths, but they speak not:
eyes have they, but they see not;

¹⁷ They have ears, but they hear not:
neither is there any breath in their mouths.

¹⁸ They that make them are like unto them:
so is every one that trusteth in them.

¹⁹ Bless the LORD, O house of Israel:
bless the LORD, O house of Aaron.

²⁰ Bless the LORD, O house of Levi:
ye that fear the LORD, bless the LORD.

²¹ Blessed be the LORD out of Zion,
which dwelleth at Jerusalem.

Praise ye the LORD.

PSALM 136

¹ O give thanks unto the LORD, for he is good:
for his mercy endureth for ever.

² O give thanks unto the God of gods:
for his mercy endureth for ever.

³ O give thanks to the Lord of lords:
for his mercy endureth for ever.

⁴ To him who alone doeth great wonders:
for his mercy endureth for ever.

⁵ To him that by wisdom made the heavens:
for his mercy endureth for ever.

⁶ To him that stretched out the earth above the waters:
for his mercy endureth for ever.

⁷ To him that made great lights:
for his mercy endureth for ever.

⁸ The sun to rule by day:
for his mercy endureth for ever.

⁹ The moon and stars to rule by night:
for his mercy endureth for ever.

¹⁰ To him that smote Egypt in their firstborn:
for his mercy endureth for ever.

¹¹ And brought out Israel from among them:
for his mercy endureth for ever.

¹² With a strong hand, and with a stretched out arm:

for his mercy endureth for ever.

¹³ To him which divided the Red Sea into parts:
for his mercy endureth for ever.
¹⁴ And made Israel to pass through the midst of it:
for his mercy endureth for ever.
¹⁵ But overthrew Pharaoh and his host in the Red Sea:
for his mercy endureth for ever.
¹⁶ To him which led his people through the wilderness:
for his mercy endureth for ever.
¹⁷ To him which smote great kings:
for his mercy endureth for ever.
¹⁸ And slew famous kings:
for his mercy endureth for ever.
¹⁹ Sihon king of the Amorites:
for his mercy endureth for ever.
²⁰ And Og the king of Bashan:
for his mercy endureth for ever.
²¹ And gave their land for a heritage:
for his mercy endureth for ever.
²² Even a heritage unto Israel his servant:
for his mercy endureth for ever.
²³ Who remembered us in our low estate:
for his mercy endureth for ever.
²⁴ And hath redeemed us from our enemies:
for his mercy endureth for ever.
²⁵ Who giveth food to all flesh:
for his mercy endureth for ever.
²⁶ O give thanks unto the God of heaven:
for his mercy endureth for ever.

PSALM 137

¹ By the rivers of Babylon, there we sat down,
yea, we wept, when we remembered Zion.
² We hanged our harps upon the willows in the midst thereof.
³ For there they that carried us away captive required of us a
song,
and they that wasted us required of us mirth:
saying, 'Sing us one of the songs of Zion'.

⁴ How shall we sing the LORD's song in a strange land?
⁵ If I forget thee, O Jerusalem,
let my right hand forget her cunning.
⁶ If I do not remember thee, let my tongue cleave to the roof of my
mouth;
if I prefer not Jerusalem above my chief joy.

⁷ Remember, O LORD, the children of Edom in the day of
 Jerusalem;
 who said, 'Rase it, rase it: even to the foundation thereof'.
⁸ O daughter of Babylon, who art to be destroyed:
 happy shall he be that rewardeth thee as thou hast served us.
⁹ Happy shall he be that taketh and dasheth thy little ones against
 the stones.

PSALM 138
A psalm of David.

¹ I will praise thee with my whole heart:
 before the gods will I sing praise unto thee.
² I will worship towards thy holy temple, and praise thy name
 for thy loving-kindness and for thy truth:
 for thou hast magnified thy word above all thy name.
³ In the day when I cried thou answeredst me,
 and strengthenedst me with strength in my soul.

⁴ All the kings of the earth shall praise thee, O LORD,
 when they hear the words of thy mouth.
⁵ Yea, they shall sing in the ways of the LORD:
 for great is the glory of the LORD.
⁶ Though the LORD be high, yet hath he respect unto the lowly:
 but the proud he knoweth afar off.

⁷ Though I walk in the midst of trouble, thou wilt revive me:
 thou shalt stretch forth thy hand against the wrath of my
 enemies,
 and thy right hand shall save me.
⁸ The LORD will perfect that which concerneth me:
 thy mercy, O LORD, endureth for ever:
 forsake not the works of thy own hands.

PSALM 139
To the chief musician.
A psalm of David.

¹ O LORD, thou hast searched me, and known me.
² Thou knowest my down-sitting and my uprising:
 thou understandest my thought afar off.
³ Thou compassest my path and my lying down,
 and art acquainted with all my ways.
⁴ For there is not a word in my tongue,
 but lo, O LORD, thou knowest it altogether.
⁵ Thou hast beset me behind and before,

and laid thy hand upon me.
⁶ Such knowledge is too wonderful for me:
  it is high, I cannot attain unto it.

⁷ Whither shall I go from thy spirit?
  or whither shall I fly from thy presence?
⁸ If I ascend up into heaven, thou art there:
  if I make my bed in hell, behold, thou art there.
⁹ If I take the wings of the morning,
  and dwell in the uttermost parts of the sea:
¹⁰ even there shall thy hand lead me,
  and thy right hand shall hold me.
¹¹ If I say, 'Surely the darkness shall cover me:
  even the night shall be light about me'.
¹² Yea, the darkness hideth not from thee, but the night shineth as
      the day:
  the darkness and the light are both alike to thee.

¹³ For thou hast possessed my reins:
  thou hast covered me in my mother's womb.
¹⁴ I will praise thee, for I am fearfully and wonderfully made:
  marvellous are thy works:
  and that my soul knoweth right well.
¹⁵ My substance was not hid from thee, when I was made in
      secret,
  and curiously wrought in the lowest parts of the earth.
¹⁶ Thy eyes did see my substance yet being unperfect,
  and in thy book all my members were written,
  which in continuance were fashioned,
  when as yet there was none of them.
¹⁷ How precious also are thy thoughts unto me, O God:
  how great is the sum of them!
¹⁸ If I should count them, they are more in number than the sand:
  when I awake, I am still with thee.

¹⁹ Surely thou wilt slay the wicked, O God:
  depart from me therefore, ye bloody men.
²⁰ For they speak against thee wickedly,
  and thy enemies take thy name in vain.
²¹ Do not I hate them, O LORD, that hate thee?
  and am not I grieved with those that rise up against thee?
²² I hate them with perfect hatred:
  I count them my enemies.

²³ Search me, O God, and know my heart:
  try me, and know my thoughts:
²⁴ and see if there be any wicked way in me,
  and lead me in the way everlasting.

PSALM 140

To the chief musician.
A psalm of David.

¹ Deliver me, O L ord, from the evil man:
  preserve me from the violent man;
² which imagine mischiefs in their heart:
  continually are they gathered together for war.
³ They have sharpened their tongues like a serpent:
  adder's poison is under their lips. Selah.
⁴ Keep me, O L ord, from the hands of the wicked,
  preserve me from the violent man:
  who have purposed to overthrow my goings.
⁵ The proud have hid a snare for me, and cords,
  they have spread a net by the wayside:
  they have set gins for me. Selah.

⁶ I said unto the L ord, 'Thou art my God:
  hear the voice of my supplications, O L ord.
⁷ O G od the Lord, the strength of my salvation:
  thou hast covered my head in the day of battle.
⁸ Grant not, O L ord, the desires of the wicked:
  further not his wicked device: lest they exalt themselves.
    Selah.

⁹ 'As for the head of those that compass me about,
  let the mischief of their own lips cover them.
¹⁰ Let burning coals fall upon them,
  let them be cast into the fire:
  into deep pits, that they rise not up again.
¹¹ Let not an evil speaker be established in the earth:
  evil shall hunt the violent man to overthrow him.'

¹² I know that the L ord will maintain the cause of the
    afflicted,
  and the right of the poor.
¹³ Surely the righteous shall give thanks unto thy name:
  the upright shall dwell in thy presence.

PSALM 141

A psalm of David.

¹ L ord, I cry unto thee, make haste unto me:
  give ear unto my voice, when I cry unto thee.
² Let my prayer be set forth before thee as incense:
  and the lifting up of my hands as the evening sacrifice.

³ Set a watch, O Lord, before my mouth:
keep the door of my lips.
⁴ Incline not my heart to any evil thing,
to practise wicked works with men that work iniquity:
and let me not eat of their dainties.

⁵ Let the righteous smite me, it shall be a kindness:
and let him reprove me, it shall be an excellent oil, which shall
not break my head:
for yet my prayer also shall be in their calamities.

⁶ When their judges are overthrown in stony places,
they shall hear my words, for they are sweet.
⁷ Our bones are scattered at the grave's mouth,
as when one cutteth and cleaveth wood upon the earth.

⁸ But my eyes are unto thee, O God the Lord:
in thee is my trust, leave not my soul destitute.
⁹ Keep me from the snare which they have laid for me,
and the gins of the workers of iniquity.
¹⁰ Let the wicked fall into their own nets,
whilst that I withal escape.

PSALM 142
Maschil of David.
A prayer when he was in the cave.

¹ I cried unto the Lord with my voice:
with my voice unto the Lord did I make my supplication.
² I poured out my complaint before him:
I showed before him my trouble.

³ When my spirit was overwhelmed within me, then thou knewest
my path.
In the way wherein I walked have they privily laid a snare for
me.
⁴ I looked on my right hand, and beheld,
but there was no man that would know me, refuge failed me:
no man cared for my soul.
⁵ I cried unto thee, O Lord, I said,
'Thou art my refuge and my portion in the land of the living.
⁶ Attend unto my cry, for I am brought very low,
deliver me from my persecutors: for they are stronger than I.
⁷ Bring my soul out of prison, that I may praise thy name:
the righteous shall compass me about:
for thou shalt deal bountifully with me.'

PSALM 143
A psalm of David.

¹ Hear my prayer, O Lord, give ear to my supplications:
　in thy faithfulness answer me, and in thy righteousness.
² And enter not into judgement with thy servant:
　for in thy sight shall no man living be justified.
³ For the enemy hath persecuted my soul,
　he hath smitten my life down to the ground:
　he hath made me to dwell in darkness, as those that have been
　　long dead.
⁴ Therefore is my spirit overwhelmed within me:
　my heart within me is desolate.
⁵ I remember the days of old, I meditate on all thy works:
　I muse on the work of thy hands.
⁶ I stretch forth my hands unto thee:
　my soul thirsteth after thee, as a thirsty land. Selah.

⁷ Hear me speedily, O Lord, my spirit faileth, hide not thy face
　　from me:
　lest I be like unto them that go down into the pit.
⁸ Cause me to hear thy loving-kindness in the morning, for in thee
　　do I trust:
　cause me to know the way wherein I should walk:
　for I lift up my soul unto thee.
⁹ Deliver me, O Lord, from my enemies:
　I fly unto thee to hide me.
¹⁰ Teach me to do thy will, for thou art my God, thy spirit is good:
　lead me into the land of uprightness.
¹¹ Quicken me, O Lord, for thy name's sake:
　for thy righteousness' sake bring my soul out of trouble.
¹² And of thy mercy cut off my enemies, and destroy all them that
　　afflict my soul:
　for I am thy servant.

PSALM 144
A psalm of David.

¹ Blessed be the Lord my strength,
　which teacheth my hands to war, and my fingers to fight:
² My goodness, and my fortress,
　my high tower, and my deliverer,
　my shield, and he in whom I trust:
　who subdueth my people under me.

³ Lord, what is man, that thou takest knowledge of him?
　or the son of man, that thou makest account of him?

⁴ Man is like to vanity:
his days are as a shadow that passeth away.

⁵ Bow thy heavens, O LORD, and come down:
touch the mountains, and they shall smoke.
⁶ Cast forth lightning, and scatter them:
shoot out thy arrows, and destroy them.
⁷ Send thy hand from above,
rid me, and deliver me out of great waters,
from the hand of strange children;
⁸ whose mouth speaketh vanity:
and their right hand is a right hand of falsehood.

⁹ I will sing a new song unto thee, O God:
upon a psaltery and an instrument of ten strings will I sing
praises unto thee.
¹⁰ It is he that giveth salvation unto kings:
who delivereth David his servant from the hurtful sword.

¹¹ Rid me, and deliver me from the hand of strange children, whose
mouth speaketh vanity:
and their right hand is a right hand of falsehood:
¹² that our sons may be as plants grown up in their youth:
that our daughters may be as corner-stones,
polished after the similitude of a palace:
¹³ that our garners may be full, affording all manner of
store:
that our sheep may bring forth thousands and ten thousands in
our streets:
¹⁴ that our oxen may be strong to labour,
that there be no breaking in, nor going out;
that there be no complaining in our streets.
¹⁵ Happy is that people, that is in such a case:
yea, happy is that people, whose God is the LORD.

PSALM 145
David's psalm of praise.

¹ I will extol thee, my God, O king:
and I will bless thy name for ever and ever.
² Every day will I bless thee:
and I will praise thy name for ever and ever.

³ Great is the LORD, and greatly to be praised:
and his greatness is unsearchable.
⁴ One generation shall praise thy works to another,
and shall declare thy mighty acts.

⁵ I will speak of the glorious honour of thy majesty,
and of thy wondrous works.
⁶ And men shall speak of the might of thy terrible acts:
and I will declare thy greatness.
⁷ They shall abundantly utter the memory of thy great goodness,
and shall sing of thy righteousness.

⁸ The LORD is gracious, and full of compassion:
slow to anger, and of great mercy.
⁹ The LORD is good to all:
and his tender mercies are over all his works.

¹⁰ All thy works shall praise thee, O LORD:
and thy saints shall bless thee.
¹¹ They shall speak of the glory of thy kingdom,
and talk of thy power;
¹² to make known to the sons of men his mighty acts,
and the glorious majesty of his kingdom.
¹³ Thy kingdom is an everlasting kingdom,
and thy dominion endureth throughout all generations.

¹⁴ The LORD upholdeth all that fall,
and raiseth up all those that be bowed down.
¹⁵ The eyes of all wait upon thee:
and thou givest them their meat in due season.
¹⁶ Thou openest thy hand,
and satisfiest the desire of every living thing.

¹⁷ The LORD is righteous in all his ways,
and holy in all his works.
¹⁸ The LORD is nigh unto all them that call upon him,
to all that call upon him in truth.
¹⁹ He will fulfil the desire of them that fear him:
he also will hear their cry, and will save them.
²⁰ The LORD preserveth all them that love him:
but all the wicked will he destroy.

²¹ My mouth shall speak the praise of the LORD:
and let all flesh bless his holy name for ever and ever.

PSALM 146

¹ Praise ye the LORD.
Praise the LORD, O my soul.
² While I live will I praise the LORD:
I will sing praises unto my God while I have any being.

³ Put not your trust in princes,
nor in the son of man, in whom there is no help.
⁴ His breath goeth forth, he returneth to his earth:
in that very day his thoughts perish.

⁵ Happy is he that hath the God of Jacob for his help,
whose hope is in the LORD his God:
⁶ which made heaven, and earth, the sea, and all that therein
is:
which keepeth truth for ever:
⁷ which executeth judgement for the oppressed,
which giveth food to the hungry.
The LORD looseth the prisoners:
⁸ the LORD openeth the eyes of the blind,
the LORD raiseth them that are bowed down:
the LORD loveth the righteous:
⁹ the LORD preserveth the strangers,
he relieveth the fatherless and widow:
but the way of the wicked he turneth upside down.
¹⁰ The LORD shall reign for ever,
even thy God, O Zion, unto all generations.

Praise ye the LORD.

PSALM 147

¹ Praise ye the LORD:
for it is good to sing praises unto our God:
for it is pleasant, and praise is comely.

² The LORD doth build up Jerusalem:
he gathereth together the outcasts of Israel.
³ He healeth the broken in heart,
and bindeth up their wounds.
⁴ He telleth the number of the stars:
he calleth them all by their names.
⁵ Great is our Lord, and of great power:
his understanding is infinite.
⁶ The LORD lifteth up the meek:
he casteth the wicked down to the ground.

⁷ Sing unto the LORD with thanksgiving:
sing praise upon the harp unto our God:
⁸ who covereth the heaven with clouds,
who prepareth rain for the earth:
who maketh grass to grow upon the mountains.
⁹ He giveth to the beast his food,

and to the young ravens which cry.

¹⁰ He delighteth not in the strength of the horse:
he taketh not pleasure in the legs of a man.

¹¹ The LORD taketh pleasure in them that fear him,
in those that hope in his mercy.

¹² Praise the LORD, O Jerusalem:
praise thy God, O Zion.

¹³ For he hath strengthened the bars of thy gates:
he hath blessed thy children within thee.

¹⁴ He maketh peace in thy borders,
and filleth thee with the finest of the wheat.

¹⁵ He sendeth forth his commandment upon earth:
his word runneth very swiftly.

¹⁶ He giveth snow like wool:
he scattereth the hoar frost like ashes.

¹⁷ He casteth forth his ice like morsels:
who can stand before his cold?

¹⁸ He sendeth out his word, and melteth them:
he causeth his wind to blow, and the waters flow.

¹⁹ He showeth his word unto Jacob,
his statutes and his judgements unto Israel.

²⁰ He hath not dealt so with any nation:
and as for his judgements, they have not known them.

Praise ye the LORD.

PSALM 148

¹ Praise ye the LORD.

Praise ye the LORD from the heavens:
praise him in the heights.

² Praise ye him, all his angels:
praise ye him, all his hosts.

³ Praise ye him, sun and moon:
praise him, all ye stars of light.

⁴ Praise him, ye heavens of heavens,
and ye waters that be above the heavens.

⁵ Let them praise the name of the LORD:
for he commanded, and they were created.

⁶ He hath also established them for ever and ever:
he hath made a decree which shall not pass.

⁷ Praise the LORD from the earth,
ye dragons, and all deeps:

⁸ fire, and hail, snow, and vapour:

stormy wind fulfilling his word:
⁹ mountains, and all hills:
  fruitful trees, and all cedars:
¹⁰ beasts, and all cattle:
   creeping things, and flying fowl:
¹¹ kings of the earth, and all people:
   princes, and all judges of the earth:
¹² both young men, and maidens:
   old men, and children.
¹³ Let them praise the name of the LORD,
   for his name alone is excellent:
   his glory is above the earth and heaven.
¹⁴ He also exalteth the horn of his people,
   the praise of all his saints;
   even of the children of Israel,
   a people near unto him.

Praise ye the LORD.

PSALM 149

¹ Praise ye the LORD.
  Sing unto the LORD a new song,
  and his praise in the congregation of saints.
² Let Israel rejoice in him that made him:
  let the children of Zion be joyful in their King.
³ Let them praise his name in the dance:
  let them sing praises unto him with the timbrel and harp.
⁴ For the LORD taketh pleasure in his people:
  he will beautify the meek with salvation.

⁵ Let the saints be joyful in glory:
  let them sing aloud upon their beds.
⁶ Let the high praises of God be in their mouth,
  and a two-edged sword in their hand:
⁷ to execute vengeance upon the heathen,
  and punishments upon the people;
⁸ to bind their kings with chains,
  and their nobles with fetters of iron;
⁹ to execute upon them the judgement written:
  this honour have all his saints.

Praise ye the LORD.

PSALM 150

[1] Praise ye the LORD.

Praise God in his sanctuary:
praise him in the firmament of his power.
[2] Praise him for his mighty acts:
praise him according to his excellent greatness.
[3] Praise him with the sound of the trumpet:
praise him with the psaltery and harp.
[4] Praise him with the timbrel and dance:
praise him with stringed instruments and organs.
[5] Praise him upon the loud cymbals:
praise him upon the high sounding cymbals.
[6] Let everything that hath breath praise the LORD.

Praise ye the LORD.

THE PROVERBS

1 The proverbs of Solomon the son of David, king of Israel,
² to know wisdom and instruction,
to perceive the words of understanding,
³ to receive the instruction of wisdom,
justice, and judgement, and equity,
⁴ to give subtlety to the simple,
to the young man knowledge and discretion.
⁵ A wise man will hear, and will increase learning:
and a man of understanding shall attain unto wise counsels:
⁶ to understand a proverb, and the interpretation;
the words of the wise, and their dark sayings.

⁷ The fear of the LORD is the beginning of knowledge:
but fools despise wisdom and instruction.
⁸ My son, hear the instruction of thy father,
and forsake not the law of thy mother:
⁹ for they shall be an ornament of grace unto thy head,
and chains about thy neck.

¹⁰ My son, if sinners entice thee, consent thou not.
¹¹ If they say, 'Come with us, let us lay wait for blood,
let us lurk privily for the innocent without cause:
¹² let us swallow them up alive as the grave,
and whole, as those that go down into the pit:
¹³ we shall find all precious substance,
we shall fill our houses with spoil:
¹⁴ cast in thy lot among us,
let us all have one purse':
¹⁵ my son, walk not thou in the way with them;
refrain thy foot from their path:
¹⁶ for their feet run to evil,
and make haste to shed blood.
¹⁷ Surely in vain the net is spread in the sight of any bird.
¹⁸ And they lay wait for their own blood,
they lurk privily for their own lives.
¹⁹ So are the ways of every one that is greedy of gain:
which taketh away the life of the owners thereof.

²⁰ Wisdom crieth without,
she uttereth her voice in the streets:
²¹ she crieth in the chief place of concourse,
in the openings of the gates:
in the city she uttereth her words, saying,
²² 'How long, ye simple ones, will ye love simplicity?

and the scorners delight in their scorning,
and fools hate knowledge?
²³ Turn you at my reproof:
behold, I will pour out my spirit unto you,
I will make known my words unto you.

²⁴ 'Because I have called, and ye refused,
I have stretched out my hand, and no man regarded:
²⁵ but ye have set at nought all my counsel,
and would none of my reproof:
²⁶ I also will laugh at your calamity,
I will mock when your fear cometh.
²⁷ When your fear cometh as desolation,
and your destruction cometh as a whirlwind;
when distress and anguish cometh upon you:
²⁸ then shall they call upon me, but I will not answer;
they shall seek me early, but they shall not find me:
²⁹ for that they hated knowledge,
and did not choose the fear of the LORD.
³⁰ They would none of my counsel:
they despised all my reproof.
³¹ Therefore shall they eat of the fruit of their own way,
and be filled with their own devices.
³² For the turning away of the simple shall slay them,
and the prosperity of fools shall destroy them.
³³ But whoso hearkeneth unto me shall dwell safely,
and shall be quiet from fear of evil.'

2 My son, if thou wilt receive my words,
and hide my commandments with thee;
² so that thou incline thy ear unto wisdom,
and apply thy heart to understanding:
³ yea, if thou criest after knowledge,
and liftest up thy voice for understanding;
⁴ if thou seekest her as silver,
and searchest for her as for hid treasures:
⁵ then shalt thou understand the fear of the LORD,
and find the knowledge of God.
⁶ For the LORD giveth wisdom:
out of his mouth cometh knowledge and understanding.
⁷ He layeth up sound wisdom for the righteous:
he is a buckler to them that walk uprightly.
⁸ He keepeth the paths of judgement,
and preserveth the way of his saints.
⁹ Then shalt thou understand righteousness, and judgement, and
equity;
yea, every good path.

¹⁰ When wisdom entereth into thy heart,
  and knowledge is pleasant unto thy soul;
¹¹ discretion shall preserve thee,
  understanding shall keep thee:
¹² to deliver thee from the way of the evil man,
  from the man that speaketh froward things;
¹³ who leave the paths of uprightness,
  to walk in the ways of darkness;
¹⁴ who rejoice to do evil,
  and delight in the frowardness of the wicked;
¹⁵ whose ways are crooked,
  and they froward in their paths:
¹⁶ to deliver thee from the strange woman,
  even from the stranger which flattereth with her words:
¹⁷ which forsaketh the guide of her youth,
  and forgetteth the covenant of her God.
¹⁸ For her house inclineth unto death,
  and her paths unto the dead.
¹⁹ None that go unto her return again,
  neither take they hold of the paths of life.
²⁰ That thou mayest walk in the way of good men,
  and keep the paths of the righteous.
²¹ For the upright shall dwell in the land,
  and the perfect shall remain in it.
²² But the wicked shall be cut off from the earth,
  and the transgressors shall be rooted out of it.

3 My son, forget not my law;
  but let thy heart keep my commandments:
² for length of days, and long life, and peace
  shall they add to thee.
³ Let not mercy and truth forsake thee:
  bind them about thy neck,
  write them upon the tablet of thy heart:
⁴ so shalt thou find favour and good understanding
  in the sight of God and man.

⁵ Trust in the LORD with all thy heart;
  and lean not unto thy own understanding.
⁶ In all thy ways acknowledge him,
  and he shall direct thy paths.

⁷ Be not wise in thy own eyes:
  fear the LORD, and depart from evil.
⁸ It shall be health to thy navel,
  and marrow to thy bones.
⁹ Honour the LORD with thy substance,
  and with the first-fruits of all thy increase:

¹⁰ so shall thy barns be filled with plenty,
and thy presses shall burst out with new wine.

¹¹ My son, despise not the chastening of the LORD:
neither be weary of his correction:
¹² for whom the LORD loveth he correcteth,
even as a father the son in whom he delighteth.

¹³ Happy is the man that findeth wisdom,
and the man that getteth understanding.
¹⁴ For the merchandise of it is better than the merchandise of
silver,
and the gain thereof than fine gold.
¹⁵ She is more precious than rubies:
and all the things thou canst desire are not to be compared unto
her.
¹⁶ Length of days is in her right hand:
and in her left hand riches and honour.
¹⁷ Her ways are ways of pleasantness,
and all her paths are peace.
¹⁸ She is a tree of life to them that lay hold upon her:
and happy is every one that retaineth her.

¹⁹ The LORD by wisdom hath founded the earth;
by understanding hath he established the heavens.
²⁰ By his knowledge the depths are broken up,
and the clouds drop down the dew.

²¹ My son, let not them depart from thy eyes:
keep sound wisdom and discretion:
²² so shall they be life unto thy soul,
and grace to thy neck.
²³ Then shalt thou walk in thy way safely,
and thy foot shall not stumble.
²⁴ When thou liest down, thou shalt not be afraid:
yea, thou shalt lie down, and thy sleep shall be sweet.
²⁵ Be not afraid of sudden fear,
neither of the desolation of the wicked, when it cometh.
²⁶ For the LORD shall be thy confidence,
and shall keep thy foot from being taken.

²⁷ Withhold not good from them to whom it is due,
when it is in the power of thy hand to do it.
²⁸ Say not unto thy neighbour,
'Go, and come again, and tomorrow I will give',
when thou hast it by thee.
²⁹ Devise not evil against thy neighbour,
seeing he dwelleth securely by thee.

³⁰ Strive not with a man without cause,
    if he have done thee no harm.

³¹ Envy thou not the oppressor,
    and choose none of his ways.

³² For the froward is abomination to the LORD:
    but his secret is with the righteous.

³³ The curse of the LORD is in the house of the wicked:
    but he blesseth the habitation of the just.

³⁴ Surely he scorneth the scorners:
    but he giveth grace unto the lowly.

³⁵ The wise shall inherit glory:
    but shame shall be the promotion of fools.

4

Hear, ye children, the instruction of a father,
    and attend to know understanding.

² For I give you good doctrine:
    forsake you not my law.

³ For I was my father's son,
    tender and only beloved in the sight of my mother.

⁴ He taught me also, and said unto me,
    'Let thy heart retain my words:
    keep my commandments, and live.

⁵ Get wisdom, get understanding:
    forget it not, neither decline from the words of my mouth.

⁶ Forsake her not, and she shall preserve thee:
    love her, and she shall keep thee.

⁷ Wisdom is the principal thing, therefore get wisdom:
    and with all thy getting get understanding.

⁸ Exalt her, and she shall promote thee:
    she shall bring thee to honour, when thou dost embrace
      her.

⁹ She shall give to thy head an ornament of grace:
    a crown of glory shall she deliver to thee.

¹⁰ Hear, O my son, and receive my sayings:
    and the years of thy life shall be many.

¹¹ I have taught thee in the way of wisdom:
    I have led thee in right paths.

¹² When thou goest, thy steps shall not be straitened,
    and when thou runnest, thou shalt not stumble.

¹³ Take fast hold of instruction, let her not go:
    keep her, for she is thy life.

¹⁴ 'Enter not into the path of the wicked,
    and go not in the way of evil men.

¹⁵ Avoid it, pass not by it,
    turn from it, and pass away.

¹⁶ For they sleep not, except they have done mischief:
   and their sleep is taken away, unless they cause some to fall.
¹⁷ For they eat the bread of wickedness,
   and drink the wine of violence.
¹⁸ But the path of the just is as the shining light
   that shineth more and more unto the perfect day.
¹⁹ The way of the wicked is as darkness:
   they know not at what they stumble.

²⁰ 'My son, attend to my words,
   incline thy ear unto my sayings.
²¹ Let them not depart from thy eyes:
   keep them in the midst of thy heart.
²² For they are life unto those that find them,
   and health to all their flesh.

²³ 'Keep thy heart with all diligence:
   for out of it are the issues of life.
²⁴ Put away from thee a froward mouth,
   and perverse lips put far from thee.
²⁵ Let thy eyes look right on,
   and let thy eyelids look straight before thee.
²⁶ Ponder the path of thy feet,
   and let all thy ways be established.
²⁷ Turn not to the right hand nor to the left:
   remove thy foot from evil.

5 'My son, attend unto my wisdom,
   and bow thy ear to my understanding:
² that thou mayest regard discretion,
   and that thy lips may keep knowledge.

³ 'For the lips of a strange woman drop as a honeycomb,
   and her mouth is smoother than oil:
⁴ but her end is bitter as wormwood,
   sharp as a two-edged sword.
⁵ Her feet go down to death:
   her steps take hold on hell.
⁶ Lest thou shouldst ponder the path of life,
   her ways are movable, that thou canst not know them.
⁷ Hear me now therefore, O ye children,
   and depart not from the words of my mouth.
⁸ Remove thy way far from her,
   and come not nigh the door of her house:
⁹ lest thou give thy honour unto others,
   and thy years unto the cruel:
¹⁰ lest strangers be filled with thy wealth,
   and thy labours be in the house of a stranger,

¹¹ and thou mourn at the last,
when thy flesh and thy body are consumed,
¹² and say, "How have I hated instruction,
and my heart despised reproof!
¹³ and have not obeyed the voice of my teachers,
nor inclined my ear to them that instructed me!
¹⁴ I was almost in all evil
in the midst of the congregation and assembly."

¹⁵ 'Drink waters out of thy own cistern,
and running waters out of thy own well.
¹⁶ Let thy fountains be dispersed abroad,
and rivers of waters in the streets.
¹⁷ Let them be only thy own,
and not strangers' with thee.
¹⁸ Let thy fountain be blessed:
and rejoice with the wife of thy youth.
¹⁹ Let her be as the loving hind and pleasant roe,
let her breasts satisfy thee at all times,
and be thou ravished always with her love.
²⁰ And why wilt thou, my son, be ravished with a strange woman,
and embrace the bosom of a stranger?
²¹ For the ways of man are before the eyes of the LORD,
and he pondereth all his goings.

²² 'His own iniquities shall take the wicked himself,
and he shall be held with the cords of his sins.
²³ He shall die without instruction,
and in the greatness of his folly he shall go astray.

6 'My son, if thou be surety for thy friend,
if thou hast stricken thy hand with a stranger,
² thou art snared with the words of thy mouth,
thou art taken with the words of thy mouth.
³ Do this now, my son, and deliver thyself,
when thou art come into the hand of thy friend:
go, humble thyself, and make sure thy friend.
⁴ Give not sleep to thy eyes,
nor slumber to thy eyelids.
⁵ Deliver thyself as a roe from the hand of the hunter,
and as a bird from the hand of the fowler.

⁶ 'Go to the ant, thou sluggard,
consider her ways, and be wise:
⁷ which having no guide, overseer, or ruler,
⁸ provideth her meat in the summer,
and gathereth her food in the harvest.

⁹ How long wilt thou sleep, O sluggard?
   when wilt thou arise out of thy sleep?
¹⁰ Yet a little sleep, a little slumber,
   a little folding of the hands to sleep:
¹¹ so shall thy poverty come as one that travelleth,
   and thy want as an armed man.

¹² 'A naughty person, a wicked man,
   walketh with a froward mouth.
¹³ He winketh with his eyes,
   he speaketh with his feet,
   he teacheth with his fingers.
¹⁴ Frowardness is in his heart,
   he deviseth mischief continually,
   he soweth discord.
¹⁵ Therefore shall his calamity come suddenly;
   suddenly shall he be broken without remedy.

¹⁶ 'These six things doth the LORD hate:
   yea, seven are an abomination unto him:
¹⁷ a proud look, a lying tongue,
   and hands that shed innocent blood,
¹⁸ a heart that deviseth wicked imaginations,
   feet that be swift in running to mischief,
¹⁹ a false witness that speaketh lies,
   and him that soweth discord among brethren.

²⁰ 'My son, keep thy father's commandment,
   and forsake not the law of thy mother.
²¹ Bind them continually upon thy heart,
   and tie them about thy neck.
²² When thou goest, it shall lead thee;
   when thou sleepest, it shall keep thee;
   and when thou awakest, it shall talk with thee.
²³ For the commandment is a lamp, and the law is light:
   and reproofs of instruction are the way of life:
²⁴ to keep thee from the evil woman,
   from the flattery of the tongue of a strange woman.
²⁵ Lust not after her beauty in thy heart;
   neither let her take thee with her eyelids.
²⁶ For by means of a whorish woman a man is brought to a piece of
      bread:
   and the adulteress will hunt for the precious life.
²⁷ Can a man take fire in his bosom,
   and his clothes not be burnt?
²⁸ Can one go upon hot coals,
   and his feet not be burnt?
²⁹ So he that goeth in to his neighbour's wife;

whosoever toucheth her shall not be innocent.

³⁰ Men do not despise a thief,
    if he steal to satisfy his soul when he is hungry:
³¹ but if he be found, he shall restore sevenfold,
    he shall give all the substance of his house.
³² But whoso committeth adultery with a woman lacketh
      understanding:
    he that doeth it destroyeth his own soul.
³³ A wound and dishonour shall he get,
    and his reproach shall not be wiped away.
³⁴ For jealousy is the rage of a man:
    therefore he will not spare in the day of vengeance.
³⁵ He will not regard any ransom;
    neither will he rest content, though thou givest many gifts.

7

'My son, keep my words,
    and lay up my commandments with thee.
² Keep my commandments, and live:
    and my law as the apple of thy eye.
³ Bind them upon thy fingers,
    write them upon the tablet of thy heart.
⁴ Say unto wisdom, "Thou art my sister",
    and call understanding thy kinswoman,
⁵ that they may keep thee from the strange woman,
    from the stranger which flattereth with her words.

⁶ 'For at the window of my house
    I looked through my casement,
⁷ and beheld among the simple ones,
    I discerned among the youths, a young man void of understanding,
⁸ passing through the street near her corner,
    and he went the way to her house,
⁹ in the twilight, in the evening,
    in the black and dark night:
¹⁰ and behold, there met him a woman
    with the attire of a harlot, and subtle of heart.
¹¹ (She is loud and stubborn,
    her feet abide not in her house:
¹² now is she without, now in the streets,
    and lieth in wait at every corner.)
¹³ So she caught him, and kissed him,
    and with an impudent face said unto him,
¹⁴ "I have peace offerings with me:
    this day have I paid my vows.
¹⁵ Therefore came I forth to meet thee,
    diligently to seek thy face, and I have found thee.
¹⁶ I have decked my bed with coverings of tapestry,
    with carved works, with fine linen of Egypt.

¹⁷ I have perfumed my bed with myrrh,
  aloes, and cinnamon.
¹⁸ Come, let us take our fill of love until the morning:
  let us solace ourselves with loves.
¹⁹ For the goodman is not at home,
  he is gone a long journey:
²⁰ he hath taken a bag of money with him,
  and will come home at the day appointed."
²¹ With much fair speech she caused him to yield,
  with the flattering of her lips she forced him.
²² He goeth after her straightway,
  as an ox goeth to the slaughter,
  or as a fool to the correction of the stocks,
²³ till a dart strike through his liver,
  as a bird hasteth to the snare,
  and knoweth not that it is for his life.

²⁴ 'Hearken unto me now therefore, O ye children,
  and attend to the words of my mouth.
²⁵ Let not thy heart decline to her ways,
  go not astray in her paths.
²⁶ For she hath cast down many wounded:
  yea, many strong men have been slain by her.
²⁷ Her house is the way to hell,
  going down to the chambers of death.'

8 Doth not wisdom cry?
  and understanding put forth her voice?
² She standeth in the top of high places,
  by the way in the places of the paths.
³ She crieth at the gates, at the entry of the city,
  at the coming in at the doors.
⁴ 'Unto you, O men, I call,
  and my voice is to the sons of man.
⁵ O ye simple, understand wisdom:
  and ye fools, be ye of an understanding heart.
⁶ Hear, for I will speak of excellent things:
  and the opening of my lips shall be right things.
⁷ For my mouth shall speak truth,
  and wickedness is an abomination to my lips.
⁸ All the words of my mouth are in righteousness,
  there is nothing froward or perverse in them.
⁹ They are all plain to him that understandeth,
  and right to them that find knowledge.
¹⁰ Receive my instruction, and not silver:
  and knowledge rather than choice gold.
¹¹ For wisdom is better than rubies:
  and all the things that may be desired are not to be compared to it.

¹² 'I wisdom dwell with prudence,
    and find out knowledge of witty inventions.
¹³ The fear of the LORD is to hate evil:
    pride, and arrogance, and the evil way, and the froward mouth,
        do I hate.
¹⁴ Counsel is mine, and sound wisdom:
    I am understanding, I have strength.
¹⁵ By me kings reign,
    and princes decree justice.
¹⁶ By me princes rule, and nobles,
    even all the judges of the earth.
¹⁷ I love them that love me,
    and those that seek me early shall find me.
¹⁸ Riches and honour are with me,
    yea, durable riches and righteousness.
¹⁹ My fruit is better than gold, yea, than fine gold,
    and my revenue than choice silver.
²⁰ I lead in the way of righteousness,
    in the midst of the paths of judgement,
²¹ that I may cause those that love me to inherit substance:
    and I will fill their treasures.

²² 'The LORD possessed me in the beginning of his way,
    before his works of old.
²³ I was set up from everlasting,
    from the beginning, or ever the earth was.
²⁴ When there were no depths, I was brought forth:
    when there were no fountains abounding with water.
²⁵ Before the mountains were settled,
    before the hills was I brought forth:
²⁶ while as yet he had not made the earth, nor the fields,
    nor the highest part of the dust of the world.
²⁷ When he prepared the heavens, I was there:
    when he set a compass upon the face of the depth:
²⁸ when he established the clouds above:
    when he strengthened the fountains of the deep:
²⁹ when he gave to the sea his decree,
    that the waters should not pass his commandment:
    when he appointed the foundations of the earth:
³⁰ then I was by him, as one brought up with him:
    and I was daily his delight, rejoicing always before him:
³¹ rejoicing in the habitable part of his earth;
    and my delights were with the sons of men.

³² 'Now therefore hearken unto me, O ye children:
    for blessed are they that keep my ways.
³³ Hear instruction, and be wise,
    and refuse it not.

³⁴ Blessed is the man that heareth me,
  watching daily at my gates,
  waiting at the posts of my doors.
³⁵ For whoso findeth me findeth life,
  and shall obtain favour of the Lord.
³⁶ But he that sinneth against me wrongeth his own soul:
  all they that hate me love death.'

9 Wisdom hath built her house,
  she hath hewn out her seven pillars:
² she hath killed her beasts;
  she hath mingled her wine:
  she hath also furnished her table.
³ She hath sent forth her maidens:
  she crieth upon the highest places of the city,
⁴ 'Whoso is simple, let him turn in hither':
  as for him that wanteth understanding, she saith to him,
⁵ 'Come, eat of my bread,
  and drink of the wine which I have mingled.
⁶ Forsake the foolish, and live;
  and go in the way of understanding.'

⁷ He that reproveth a scorner getteth to himself shame:
  and he that rebuketh a wicked man getteth himself a blot.
⁸ Reprove not a scorner, lest he hate thee:
  rebuke a wise man, and he will love thee.
⁹ Give instruction to a wise man, and he will be yet wiser:
  teach a just man, and he will increase in learning.

¹⁰ The fear of the Lord is the beginning of wisdom:
  and the knowledge of the holy is understanding.
¹¹ For by me thy days shall be multiplied,
  and the years of thy life shall be increased.
¹² If thou be wise, thou shalt be wise for thyself:
  but if thou scornest, thou alone shalt bear it.

¹³ A foolish woman is clamorous:
  she is simple, and knoweth nothing.
¹⁴ For she sitteth at the door of her house on a seat,
  in the high places of the city,
¹⁵ to call passengers who go right on their ways:
¹⁶ 'Whoso is simple, let him turn in hither':
  and as for him that wanteth understanding, she saith to him,
¹⁷ 'Stolen waters are sweet,
  and bread eaten in secret is pleasant'.
¹⁸ But he knoweth not that the dead are there;
  and that her guests are in the depths of hell.

10

The proverbs of Solomon.

A wise son maketh a glad father:
but a foolish son is the heaviness of his mother.

2 Treasures of wickedness profit nothing:
but righteousness delivereth from death.

3 The LORD will not suffer the soul of the righteous to famish:
but he casteth away the substance of the wicked.

4 He becometh poor that dealeth with a slack hand:
but the hand of the diligent maketh rich.

5 He that gathereth in summer is a wise son:
but he that sleepeth in harvest is a son that causeth shame.

6 Blessings are upon the head of the just:
but violence covereth the mouth of the wicked.

7 The memory of the just is blessed:
but the name of the wicked shall rot.

8 The wise in heart will receive commandments:
but a prating fool shall fall.

9 He that walketh uprightly walketh surely:
but he that perverteth his ways shall be known.

10 He that winketh with the eye causeth sorrow:
but a prating fool shall fall.

11 The mouth of a righteous man is a well of life:
but violence covereth the mouth of the wicked.

12 Hatred stirreth up strifes:
but love covereth all sins.

13 In the lips of him that hath understanding wisdom is found:
but a rod is for the back of him that is void of understanding.

14 Wise men lay up knowledge:
but the mouth of the foolish is near destruction.

15 The rich man's wealth is his strong city:
the destruction of the poor is their poverty.

16 The labour of the righteous tendeth to life:
the fruit of the wicked to sin.

17 He is in the way of life that keepeth instruction:
but he that refuseth reproof erreth.

18 He that hideth hatred with lying lips,
and he that uttereth a slander, is a fool.

19 In the multitude of words there wanteth not sin:
but he that refraineth his lips is wise.

20 The tongue of the just is as choice silver:
the heart of the wicked is little worth.

²¹ The lips of the righteous feed many:
  but fools die for want of wisdom.

²² The blessing of the Lᴏʀᴅ, it maketh rich,
  and he addeth no sorrow with it.

²³ It is as a sport to a fool to do mischief:
  but a man of understanding hath wisdom.

²⁴ The fear of the wicked, it shall come upon him:
  but the desire of the righteous shall be granted.

²⁵ As the whirlwind passeth, so is the wicked no more:
  but the righteous is an everlasting foundation.

²⁶ As vinegar to the teeth, and as smoke to the eyes,
  so is the sluggard to them that send him.

²⁷ The fear of the Lᴏʀᴅ prolongeth days:
  but the years of the wicked shall be shortened.

²⁸ The hope of the righteous shall be gladness:
  but the expectation of the wicked shall perish.

²⁹ The way of the Lᴏʀᴅ is strength to the upright:
  but destruction shall be to the workers of iniquity.

³⁰ The righteous shall never be removed:
  but the wicked shall not inhabit the earth.

³¹ The mouth of the just bringeth forth wisdom:
  but the froward tongue shall be cut out.

³² The lips of the righteous know what is acceptable:
  but the mouth of the wicked speaketh frowardness.

11 A false balance is abomination to the Lᴏʀᴅ:
  but a just weight is his delight.

² When pride cometh, then cometh shame:
  but with the lowly is wisdom.

³ The integrity of the upright shall guide them:
  but the perverseness of transgressors shall destroy them.

⁴ Riches profit not in the day of wrath:
  but righteousness delivereth from death.

⁵ The righteousness of the perfect shall direct his way:
  but the wicked shall fall by his own wickedness.

⁶ The righteousness of the upright shall deliver them:
  but transgressors shall be taken in their own naughtiness.

⁷ When a wicked man dieth, his expectation shall perish:
  and the hope of unjust men perisheth.

⁸ The righteous is delivered out of trouble,
  and the wicked cometh in his stead.

⁹ A hypocrite with his mouth destroyeth his neighbour:
  but through knowledge shall the just be delivered.

¹⁰ When it goeth well with the righteous, the city rejoiceth:
  and when the wicked perish, there is shouting.

¹¹ By the blessing of the upright the city is exalted:
  but it is overthrown by the mouth of the wicked.

¹² He that is void of wisdom despiseth his neighbour:
  but a man of understanding holdeth his peace.

¹³ A tale-bearer revealeth secrets:
  but he that is of a faithful spirit concealeth the matter.

¹⁴ Where no counsel is, the people fall:
  but in the multitude of counsellors there is safety.

¹⁵ He that is surety for a stranger shall smart for it:
  and he that hateth suretyship is sure.

¹⁶ A gracious woman retaineth honour:
  and strong men retain riches.

¹⁷ The merciful man doeth good to his own soul:
  but he that is cruel troubleth his own flesh.

¹⁸ The wicked worketh a deceitful work:
  but to him that soweth righteousness shall be a sure reward.

¹⁹ As righteousness tendeth to life:
  so he that pursueth evil pursueth it to his own death.

²⁰ They that are of a froward heart are abomination to the Lord:
  but such as are upright in their way are his delight.

²¹ Though hand join in hand, the wicked shall not be unpunished:
  but the seed of the righteous shall be delivered.

²² As a jewel of gold in a swine's snout,
  so is a fair woman which is without discretion.

²³ The desire of the righteous is only good:
  but the expectation of the wicked is wrath.

²⁴ There is that scattereth, and yet increaseth;
  and there is that withholdeth more than is meet, but it
    tendeth to poverty.

²⁵ The liberal soul shall be made fat:
  and he that watereth shall be watered also himself.

²⁶ He that withholdeth corn, the people shall curse him:
  but blessing shall be upon the head of him that selleth it.

²⁷ He that diligently seeketh good procureth favour:
  but he that seeketh mischief, it shall come unto him.

²⁸ He that trusteth in his riches shall fall:
  but the righteous shall flourish as a branch.

²⁹ He that troubleth his own house shall inherit the wind:
    and the fool shall be servant to the wise of heart.

³⁰ The fruit of the righteous is a tree of life:
    and he that winneth souls is wise.

³¹ Behold, the righteous shall be recompensed in the earth:
    much more the wicked and the sinner.

12 Whoso loveth instruction loveth knowledge:
    but he that hateth reproof is brutish.

² A good man obtaineth favour of the Lord:
    but a man of wicked devices will he condemn.

³ A man shall not be established by wickedness:
    but the root of the righteous shall not be moved.

⁴ A virtuous woman is a crown to her husband:
    but she that maketh ashamed is as rottenness in his bones.

⁵ The thoughts of the righteous are right:
    but the counsels of the wicked are deceit.

⁶ The words of the wicked are to lie in wait for blood:
    but the mouth of the upright shall deliver them.

⁷ The wicked are overthrown, and are not:
    but the house of the righteous shall stand.

⁸ A man shall be commended according to his wisdom:
    but he that is of a perverse heart shall be despised.

⁹ He that is despised, and hath a servant,
    is better than he that honoureth himself, and lacketh bread.

¹⁰ A righteous man regardeth the life of his beast:
    but the tender mercies of the wicked are cruel.

¹¹ He that tilleth his land shall be satisfied with bread:
    but he that followeth vain persons is void of understanding.

¹² The wicked desireth the net of evil men:
    but the root of the righteous yieldeth fruit.

¹³ The wicked is snared by the transgression of his lips:
    but the just shall come out of trouble.

¹⁴ A man shall be satisfied with good by the fruit of his mouth:
    and the recompense of a man's hands shall be rendered unto
      him.

¹⁵ The way of a fool is right in his own eyes:
    but he that hearkeneth unto counsel is wise.

¹⁶ A fool's wrath is presently known:
    but a prudent man covereth shame.

¹⁷ He that speaketh truth showeth forth righteousness:
    but a false witness deceit.

¹⁸ There is that speaketh like the piercings of a sword:
  but the tongue of the wise is health.

¹⁹ The lip of truth shall be established for ever:
  but a lying tongue is but for a moment.

²⁰ Deceit is in the heart of them that imagine evil:
  but to the counsellors of peace is joy.

²¹ There shall no evil happen to the just:
  but the wicked shall be filled with mischief.

²² Lying lips are abomination to the LORD:
  but they that deal truly are his delight.

²³ A prudent man concealeth knowledge:
  but the heart of fools proclaimeth foolishness.

²⁴ The hand of the diligent shall bear rule:
  but the slothful shall be under tribute.

²⁵ Heaviness in the heart of man maketh it stoop:
  but a good word maketh it glad.

²⁶ The righteous is more excellent than his neighbour:
  but the way of the wicked seduceth them.

²⁷ The slothful man roasteth not that which he took in hunting:
  but the substance of a diligent man is precious.

²⁸ In the way of righteousness is life,
  and in the pathway thereof there is no death.

13 A wise son heareth his father's instruction:
  but a scorner heareth not rebuke.

² A man shall eat good by the fruit of his mouth:
  but the soul of the transgressors shall eat violence.

³ He that keepeth his mouth keepeth his life:
  but he that openeth wide his lips shall have destruction.

⁴ The soul of the sluggard desireth, and hath nothing:
  but the soul of the diligent shall be made fat.

⁵ A righteous man hateth lying:
  but a wicked man is loathsome, and cometh to shame.

⁶ Righteousness keepeth him that is upright in the way:
  but wickedness overthroweth the sinner.

⁷ There is that maketh himself rich, yet hath nothing:
  there is that maketh himself poor, yet hath great riches.

⁸ The ransom of a man's life are his riches:
  but the poor heareth not rebuke.

⁹ The light of the righteous rejoiceth:
  but the lamp of the wicked shall be put out.

¹⁰ Only by pride cometh contention:
    but with the well advised is wisdom.

¹¹ Wealth gotten by vanity shall be diminished:
    but he that gathereth by labour shall increase.

¹² Hope deferred maketh the heart sick:
    but when the desire cometh, it is a tree of life.

¹³ Whoso despiseth the word shall be destroyed:
    but he that feareth the commandment shall be rewarded.

¹⁴ The law of the wise is a fountain of life,
    to depart from the snares of death.

¹⁵ Good understanding giveth favour:
    but the way of transgressors is hard.

¹⁶ Every prudent man dealeth with knowledge:
    but a fool layeth open his folly.

¹⁷ A wicked messenger falleth into mischief:
    but a faithful ambassador is health.

¹⁸ Poverty and shame shall be to him that refuseth instruction:
    but he that regardeth reproof shall be honoured.

¹⁹ The desire accomplished is sweet to the soul:
    but it is abomination to fools to depart from evil.

²⁰ He that walketh with wise men shall be wise:
    but a companion of fools shall be destroyed.

²¹ Evil pursueth sinners:
    but to the righteous good shall be repaid.

²² A good man leaveth an inheritance to his children's children:
    and the wealth of the sinner is laid up for the just.

²³ Much food is in the tillage of the poor:
    but there is that is destroyed for want of judgement.

²⁴ He that spareth his rod hateth his son:
    but he that loveth him chasteneth him betimes.

²⁵ The righteous eateth to the satisfying of his soul:
    but the belly of the wicked shall want.

14 Every wise woman buildeth her house:
    but the foolish plucketh it down with her hands.

² He that walketh in his uprightness feareth the LORD:
    but he that is perverse in his ways despiseth him.

³ In the mouth of the foolish is a rod of pride:
    but the lips of the wise shall preserve them.

⁴ Where no oxen are, the crib is clean:
    but much increase is by the strength of the ox.

⁵ A faithful witness will not lie:
  but a false witness will utter lies.

⁶ A scorner seeketh wisdom, and findeth it not:
  but knowledge is easy unto him that understandeth.

⁷ Go from the presence of a foolish man,
  when thou perceivest not in him the lips of knowledge.

⁸ The wisdom of the prudent is to understand his way:
  but the folly of fools is deceit.

⁹ Fools make a mock at sin:
  but among the righteous there is favour.

¹⁰ The heart knoweth his own bitterness;
  and a stranger doth not intermeddle with his joy.

¹¹ The house of the wicked shall be overthrown:
  but the tabernacle of the upright shall flourish.

¹² There is a way which seemeth right unto a man,
  but the end thereof are the ways of death.

¹³ Even in laughter the heart is sorrowful;
  and the end of that mirth is heaviness.

¹⁴ The backslider in heart shall be filled with his own ways:
  and a good man shall be satisfied from himself.

¹⁵ The simple believeth every word:
  but the prudent man looketh well to his going.

¹⁶ A wise man feareth, and departeth from evil:
  but the fool rageth, and is confident.

¹⁷ He that is soon angry dealeth foolishly:
  and a man of wicked devices is hated.

¹⁸ The simple inherit folly:
  but the prudent are crowned with knowledge.

¹⁹ The evil bow before the good:
  and the wicked at the gates of the righteous.

²⁰ The poor is hated even of his own neighbour:
  but the rich hath many friends.

²¹ He that despiseth his neighbour sinneth:
  but he that hath mercy on the poor, happy is he.

²² Do they not err that devise evil?
  but mercy and truth shall be to them that devise good.

²³ In all labour there is profit:
  but the talk of the lips tendeth only to penury.

²⁴ The crown of the wise is their riches:
  but the foolishness of fools is folly.

²⁵ A true witness delivereth souls:
  but a deceitful witness speaketh lies.

²⁶ In the fear of the LORD is strong confidence:
    and his children shall have a place of refuge.

²⁷ The fear of the LORD is a fountain of life,
    to depart from the snares of death.

²⁸ In the multitude of people is the king's honour:
    but in the want of people is the destruction of the prince.

²⁹ He that is slow to wrath is of great understanding:
    but he that is hasty of spirit exalteth folly.

³⁰ A sound heart is the life of the flesh:
    but envy the rottenness of the bones.

³¹ He that oppresseth the poor reproacheth his Maker:
    but he that honoureth him hath mercy on the poor.

³² The wicked is driven away in his wickedness:
    but the righteous hath hope in his death.

³³ Wisdom resteth in the heart of him that hath understanding:
    but that which is in the midst of fools is made known.

³⁴ Righteousness exalteth a nation:
    but sin is a reproach to any people.

³⁵ The king's favour is toward a wise servant:
    but his wrath is against him that causeth shame.

15 A soft answer turneth away wrath:
    but grievous words stir up anger.

² The tongue of the wise useth knowledge aright:
    but the mouth of fools poureth out foolishness.

³ The eyes of the LORD are in every place,
    beholding the evil and the good.

⁴ A wholesome tongue is a tree of life:
    but perverseness therein is a breach in the spirit.

⁵ A fool despiseth his father's instruction:
    but he that regardeth reproof is prudent.

⁶ In the house of the righteous is much treasure:
    but in the revenues of the wicked is trouble.

⁷ The lips of the wise disperse knowledge:
    but the heart of the foolish doeth not so.

⁸ The sacrifice of the wicked is an abomination to the LORD:
    but the prayer of the upright is his delight.

⁹ The way of the wicked is an abomination unto the LORD:
    but he loveth him that followeth after righteousness.

¹⁰ Correction is grievous unto him that forsaketh the way:
    and he that hateth reproof shall die.

¹¹ Hell and destruction are before the LORD:
    how much more then the hearts of the children of men?

¹² A scorner loveth not one that reproveth him:
    neither will he go unto the wise.

¹³ A merry heart maketh a cheerful countenance:
    but by sorrow of the heart the spirit is broken.

¹⁴ The heart of him that hath understanding seeketh knowledge:
    but the mouth of fools feedeth on foolishness.

¹⁵ All the days of the afflicted are evil:
    but he that is of a merry heart hath a continual feast.

¹⁶ Better is little with the fear of the LORD
    than great treasure and trouble therewith.

¹⁷ Better is a dinner of herbs where love is,
    than a stalled ox and hatred therewith.

¹⁸ A wrathful man stirreth up strife:
    but he that is slow to anger appeaseth strife.

¹⁹ The way of the slothful man is as a hedge of thorns:
    but the way of the righteous is made plain.

²⁰ A wise son maketh a glad father:
    but a foolish man despiseth his mother.

²¹ Folly is joy to him that is destitute of wisdom:
    but a man of understanding walketh uprightly.

²² Without counsel purposes are disappointed:
    but in the multitude of counsellors they are established.

²³ A man hath joy by the answer of his mouth:
    and a word spoken in due season, how good is it!

²⁴ The way of life is above to the wise,
    that he may depart from hell beneath.

²⁵ The LORD will destroy the house of the proud:
    but he will establish the border of the widow.

²⁶ The thoughts of the wicked are an abomination to the LORD:
    but the words of the pure are pleasant words.

²⁷ He that is greedy of gain troubleth his own house:
    but he that hateth gifts shall live.

²⁸ The heart of the righteous studieth to answer:
    but the mouth of the wicked poureth out evil things.

²⁹ The LORD is far from the wicked:
    but he heareth the prayer of the righteous.

³⁰ The light of the eyes rejoiceth the heart:
    and a good report maketh the bones fat.

³¹ The ear that heareth the reproof of life
    abideth among the wise.

³² He that refuseth instruction despiseth his own soul:
    but he that heareth reproof getteth understanding.

³³ The fear of the LORD is the instruction of wisdom:
    and before honour is humility.

16 The preparations of the heart in man,
    and the answer of the tongue, is from the LORD.

² All the ways of a man are clean in his own eyes:
    but the LORD weigheth the spirits.

³ Commit thy works unto the LORD,
    and thy thoughts shall be established.

⁴ The LORD hath made all things for himself:
    yea, even the wicked for the day of evil.

⁵ Every one that is proud in heart is an abomination to the LORD:
    though hand join in hand, he shall not be unpunished.

⁶ By mercy and truth iniquity is purged:
    and by the fear of the LORD men depart from evil.

⁷ When a man's ways please the LORD,
    he maketh even his enemies to be at peace with him.

⁸ Better is a little with righteousness
    than great revenues without right.

⁹ A man's heart deviseth his way:
    but the LORD directeth his steps.

¹⁰ A divine sentence is in the lips of the king:
    his mouth transgresseth not in judgement.

¹¹ A just weight and balance are the LORD's:
    all the weights of the bag are his work.

¹² It is an abomination to kings to commit wickedness:
    for the throne is established by righteousness.

¹³ Righteous lips are the delight of kings:
    and they love him that speaketh right.

¹⁴ The wrath of a king is as messengers of death:
    but a wise man will pacify it.

¹⁵ In the light of the king's countenance is life,
    and his favour is as a cloud of the latter rain.

¹⁶ How much better is it to get wisdom than gold!
    and to get understanding rather to be chosen than silver!

¹⁷ The highway of the upright is to depart from evil:
    he that keepeth his way preserveth his soul.

¹⁸ Pride goeth before destruction,
    and a haughty spirit before a fall.

¹⁹ Better it is to be of a humble spirit with the lowly,
than to divide the spoil with the proud.

²⁰ He that handleth a matter wisely shall find good:
and whoso trusteth in the LORD, happy is he.

²¹ The wise in heart shall be called prudent:
and the sweetness of the lips increaseth learning.

²² Understanding is a well-spring of life unto him that hath it:
but the instruction of fools is folly.

²³ The heart of the wise teacheth his mouth,
and addeth learning to his lips.

²⁴ Pleasant words are as a honeycomb,
sweet to the soul, and health to the bones.

²⁵ There is a way that seemeth right unto a man,
but the end thereof are the ways of death.

²⁶ He that laboureth laboureth for himself;
for his mouth craveth it of him.

²⁷ An ungodly man diggeth up evil:
and in his lips there is as a burning fire.

²⁸ A froward man soweth strife:
and a whisperer separateth chief friends.

²⁹ A violent man enticeth his neighbour,
and leadeth him into the way that is not good.

³⁰ He shutteth his eyes to devise froward things:
moving his lips he bringeth evil to pass.

³¹ The hoary head is a crown of glory,
if it be found in the way of righteousness.

³² He that is slow to anger is better than the mighty:
and he that ruleth his spirit than he that taketh a city.

³³ The lot is cast into the lap:
but the whole disposing thereof is of the LORD.

17 Better is a dry morsel, and quietness therewith,
than a house full of sacrifices with strife.

² A wise servant shall have rule over a son that causeth shame,
and shall have part of the inheritance among the brethren.

³ The fining-pot is for silver, and the furnace for gold:
but the LORD trieth the hearts.

⁴ A wicked-doer giveth heed to false lips:
and a liar giveth ear to a naughty tongue.

⁵ Whoso mocketh the poor reproacheth his Maker:
and he that is glad at calamities shall not be unpunished.

⁶ Children's children are the crown of old men:
  and the glory of children are their fathers.

⁷ Excellent speech becometh not a fool:
  much less do lying lips a prince.

⁸ A gift is as a precious stone in the eyes of him that hath it:
  whithersoever it turneth, it prospereth.

⁹ He that covereth a transgression seeketh love;
  but he that repeateth a matter separateth very friends.

¹⁰ A reproof entereth more into a wise man
  than a hundred stripes into a fool.

¹¹ An evil man seeketh only rebellion:
  therefore a cruel messenger shall be sent against him.

¹² Let a bear robbed of her whelps meet a man,
  rather than a fool in his folly.

¹³ Whoso rewardeth evil for good,
  evil shall not depart from his house.

¹⁴ The beginning of strife is as when one letteth out water:
  therefore leave off contention, before it be meddled with.

¹⁵ He that justifieth the wicked, and he that condemneth the just,
  even they both are abomination to the LORD.

¹⁶ Wherefore is there a price in the hand of a fool to get wisdom,
  seeing he hath no heart to it?

¹⁷ A friend loveth at all times,
  and a brother is born for adversity.

¹⁸ A man void of understanding striketh hands,
  and becometh surety in the presence of his friend.

¹⁹ He loveth transgression that loveth strife:
  and he that exalteth his gate seeketh destruction.

²⁰ He that hath a froward heart findeth no good,
  and he that hath a perverse tongue falleth into mischief.

²¹ He that begetteth a fool doeth it to his sorrow:
  and the father of a fool hath no joy.

²² A merry heart doeth good like a medicine:
  but a broken spirit drieth the bones.

²³ A wicked man taketh a gift out of the bosom
  to pervert the ways of judgement.

²⁴ Wisdom is before him that hath understanding:
  but the eyes of a fool are in the ends of the earth.

²⁵ A foolish son is a grief to his father,
  and bitterness to her that bore him.

²⁶ Also to punish the just is not good,
  nor to strike princes for equity.

²⁷ He that hath knowledge spareth his words:
    and a man of understanding is of an excellent spirit.

²⁸ Even a fool, when he holdeth his peace, is counted wise:
    and he that shutteth his lips is esteemed a man of
        understanding.

18 Through desire a man, having separated himself,
    seeketh and intermeddleth with all wisdom.

² A fool hath no delight in understanding,
    but that his heart may discover itself.

³ When the wicked cometh, then cometh also contempt,
    and with ignominy reproach.

⁴ The words of a man's mouth are as deep waters,
    and the well-spring of wisdom as a flowing brook.

⁵ It is not good to accept the person of the wicked,
    to overthrow the righteous in judgement.

⁶ A fool's lips enter into contention,
    and his mouth calleth for strokes.

⁷ A fool's mouth is his destruction,
    and his lips are the snare of his soul.

⁸ The words of a tale-bearer are as wounds,
    and they go down into the innermost parts of the belly.

⁹ He also that is slothful in his work
    is brother to him that is a great waster.

¹⁰ The name of the LORD is a strong tower:
    the righteous runneth into it, and is safe.

¹¹ The rich man's wealth is his strong city,
    and as a high wall in his own conceit.

¹² Before destruction the heart of man is haughty,
    and before honour is humility.

¹³ He that answereth a matter before he heareth it,
    it is folly and shame unto him.

¹⁴ The spirit of a man will sustain his infirmity:
    but a wounded spirit who can bear?

¹⁵ The heart of the prudent getteth knowledge;
    and the ear of the wise seeketh knowledge.

¹⁶ A man's gift maketh room for him,
    and bringeth him before great men.

¹⁷ He that is first in his own cause seemeth just;
    but his neighbour cometh and searcheth him.

¹⁸ The lot causeth contentions to cease,
    and parteth between the mighty.

¹⁹ A brother offended is harder to be won than a strong city:
    and their contentions are like the bars of a castle.

²⁰ A man's belly shall be satisfied with the fruit of his mouth;
    and with the increase of his lips shall he be filled.

²¹ Death and life are in the power of the tongue:
    and they that love it shall eat the fruit thereof.

²² Whoso findeth a wife findeth a good thing,
    and obtaineth favour of the LORD.

²³ The poor useth entreaties,
    but the rich answereth roughly.

²⁴ A man that hath friends must show himself friendly:
    and there is a friend that sticketh closer than a brother.

19 Better is the poor that walketh in his integrity,
    than he that is perverse in his lips, and is a fool.

² Also, that the soul be without knowledge, it is not good;
    and he that hasteth with his feet sinneth.

³ The foolishness of man perverteth his way:
    and his heart fretteth against the LORD.

⁴ Wealth maketh many friends:
    but the poor is separated from his neighbour.

⁵ A false witness shall not be unpunished,
    and he that speaketh lies shall not escape.

⁶ Many will entreat the favour of the prince:
    and every man is a friend to him that giveth gifts.

⁷ All the brethren of the poor do hate him:
    how much more do his friends go far from him?
  he pursueth them with words,
    yet they are wanting to him.

⁸ He that getteth wisdom loveth his own soul:
    he that keepeth understanding shall find good.

⁹ A false witness shall not be unpunished,
    and he that speaketh lies shall perish.

¹⁰ Delight is not seemly for a fool:
    much less for a servant to have rule over princes.

¹¹ The discretion of a man deferreth his anger:
    and it is his glory to pass over a transgression.

¹² The king's wrath is as the roaring of a lion:
    but his favour is as dew upon the grass.

¹³ A foolish son is the calamity of his father:
    and the contentions of a wife are a continual dropping.

¹⁴ House and riches are the inheritance of fathers:
  and a prudent wife is from the LORD.

¹⁵ Slothfulness casteth into a deep sleep:
  and an idle soul shall suffer hunger.

¹⁶ He that keepeth the commandment keepeth his own soul:
  but he that despiseth his ways shall die.

¹⁷ He that hath pity upon the poor lendeth unto the LORD,
  and that which he hath given will he pay him again.

¹⁸ Chasten thy son while there is hope,
  and let not thy soul spare for his crying.

¹⁹ A man of great wrath shall suffer punishment:
  for if thou deliver him, yet thou must do it again.

²⁰ Hear counsel, and receive instruction,
  that thou mayest be wise in thy latter end.

²¹ There are many devices in a man's heart:
  nevertheless the counsel of the LORD, that shall stand.

²² The desire of a man is his kindness:
  and a poor man is better than a liar.

²³ The fear of the LORD tendeth to life, and he that hath it shall
    abide satisfied:
  he shall not be visited with evil.

²⁴ A slothful man hideth his hand in his bosom,
  and will not so much as bring it to his mouth again.

²⁵ Smite a scorner, and the simple will beware:
  and reprove one that hath understanding, and he will
    understand knowledge.

²⁶ He that wasteth his father, and chaseth away his mother,
  is a son that causeth shame, and bringeth reproach.

²⁷ Cease, my son, to hear the instruction
  that causeth to err from the words of knowledge.

²⁸ An ungodly witness scorneth judgement:
  and the mouth of the wicked devoureth iniquity.

²⁹ Judgements are prepared for scorners,
  and stripes for the back of fools.

20 Wine is a mocker, strong drink is raging:
  and whosoever is deceived thereby is not wise.

² The fear of a king is as the roaring of a lion:
  whoso provoketh him to anger sinneth against his own soul.

³ It is an honour for a man to cease from strife:
  but every fool will be meddling.

⁴ The sluggard will not plough by reason of the cold;
    therefore shall he beg in harvest, and have nothing.

⁵ Counsel in the heart of man is like deep water:
    but a man of understanding will draw it out.

⁶ Most men will proclaim every one his own goodness:
    but a faithful man who can find?

⁷ The just man walketh in his integrity:
    his children are blessed after him.

⁸ A king that sitteth in the throne of judgement
    scattereth away all evil with his eyes.

⁹ Who can say, 'I have made my heart clean,
    I am pure from my sin?'

¹⁰ Divers weights, and divers measures,
    both of them are alike abomination to the LORD.

¹¹ Even a child is known by his doings,
    whether his work be pure, and whether it be right.

¹² The hearing ear, and the seeing eye,
    the LORD hath made even both of them.

¹³ Love not sleep, lest thou come to poverty:
    open thy eyes, and thou shalt be satisfied with bread.

¹⁴ 'It is naught, it is naught,' saith the buyer:
    but when he is gone his way, then he boasteth.

¹⁵ There is gold, and a multitude of rubies:
    but the lips of knowledge are a precious jewel.

¹⁶ Take his garment that is surety for a stranger:
    and take a pledge of him for a strange woman.

¹⁷ Bread of deceit is sweet to a man:
    but afterwards his mouth shall be filled with gravel.

¹⁸ Every purpose is established by counsel:
    and with good advice make war.

¹⁹ He that goeth about as a tale-bearer revealeth secrets:
    therefore meddle not with him that flattereth with his lips.

²⁰ Whoso curseth his father or his mother,
    his lamp shall be put out in obscure darkness.

²¹ An inheritance may be gotten hastily at the beginning:
    but the end thereof shall not be blessed.

²² Say not thou, 'I will recompense evil':
    but wait on the LORD, and he shall save thee.

²³ Divers weights are an abomination unto the LORD:
    and a false balance is not good.

²⁴ Man's goings are of the LORD;
    how can a man then understand his own way?

²⁵ It is a snare to the man who devoureth that which is holy,
and after vows to make inquiry.

²⁶ A wise king scattereth the wicked,
and bringeth the wheel over them.

²⁷ The spirit of man is the candle of the LORD,
searching all the inward parts of the belly.

²⁸ Mercy and truth preserve the king:
and his throne is upheld by mercy.

²⁹ The glory of young men is their strength:
and the beauty of old men is the grey head.

³⁰ The blueness of a wound cleanseth away evil:
so do stripes the inward parts of the belly.

21 The king's heart is in the hand of the LORD, as the rivers of
water:
he turneth it whithersoever he will.

² Every way of a man is right in his own eyes:
but the LORD pondereth the hearts.

³ To do justice and judgement
is more acceptable to the LORD than sacrifice.

⁴ A high look, and a proud heart,
and the ploughing of the wicked, is sin.

⁵ The thoughts of the diligent tend only to plenteousness:
but of every one that is hasty only to want.

⁶ The getting of treasures by a lying tongue
is a vanity tossed to and fro of them that seek death.

⁷ The robbery of the wicked shall destroy them;
because they refuse to do judgement.

⁸ The way of man is froward and strange:
but as for the pure, his work is right.

⁹ It is better to dwell in a corner of the house-top,
than with a brawling woman in a wide house.

¹⁰ The soul of the wicked desireth evil:
his neighbour findeth no favour in his eyes.

¹¹ When the scorner is punished, the simple is made wise:
and when the wise is instructed, he receiveth knowledge.

¹² The righteous man wisely considereth the house of the wicked:
but God overthroweth the wicked for their wickedness.

¹³ Whoso stoppeth his ears at the cry of the poor,
he also shall cry himself, but shall not be heard.

¹⁴ A gift in secret pacifieth anger:
and a reward in the bosom strong wrath.

¹⁵ It is joy to the just to do judgement:
  but destruction shall be to the workers of iniquity.

¹⁶ The man that wandereth out of the way of understanding
  shall remain in the congregation of the dead.

¹⁷ He that loveth pleasure shall be a poor man:
  he that loveth wine and oil shall not be rich.

¹⁸ The wicked shall be a ransom for the righteous,
  and the transgressor for the upright.

¹⁹ It is better to dwell in the wilderness,
  than with a contentious and an angry woman.

²⁰ There is treasure to be desired and oil in the dwelling of the
    wise:
  but a foolish man spendeth it up.

²¹ He that followeth after righteousness and mercy
  findeth life, righteousness, and honour.

²² A wise man scaleth the city of the mighty,
  and casteth down the strength of the confidence thereof.

²³ Whoso keepeth his mouth and his tongue
  keepeth his soul from troubles.

²⁴ Proud and haughty scorner is his name,
  who dealeth in proud wrath.

²⁵ The desire of the slothful killeth him:
  for his hands refuse to labour.

²⁶ He coveteth greedily all the day long:
  but the righteous giveth and spareth not.

²⁷ The sacrifice of the wicked is abomination:
  how much more, when he bringeth it with a wicked mind?

²⁸ A false witness shall perish:
  but the man that heareth speaketh constantly.

²⁹ A wicked man hardeneth his face:
  but as for the upright, he directeth his way.

³⁰ There is no wisdom nor understanding
  nor counsel against the LORD.

³¹ The horse is prepared against the day of battle:
  but safety is of the LORD.

22

A good name is rather to be chosen than great riches,
  and loving favour rather than silver and gold.

² The rich and poor meet together:
  the LORD is the maker of them all.

³ A prudent man foreseeth the evil, and hideth himself:
  but the simple pass on, and are punished.

⁴ By humility and the fear of the LORD
    are riches, and honour, and life.

⁵ Thorns and snares are in the way of the froward:
    he that doth keep his soul shall be far from them.

⁶ Train up a child in the way he should go:
    and when he is old, he will not depart from it.

⁷ The rich ruleth over the poor,
    and the borrower is servant to the lender.

⁸ He that soweth iniquity shall reap vanity:
    and the rod of his anger shall fail.

⁹ He that hath a bountiful eye shall be blessed:
    for he giveth of his bread to the poor.

¹⁰ Cast out the scorner, and contention shall go out;
    yea, strife and reproach shall cease.

¹¹ He that loveth pureness of heart,
    for the grace of his lips the king shall be his friend.

¹² The eyes of the LORD preserve knowledge,
    and he overthroweth the words of the transgressor.

¹³ The slothful man saith, 'There is a lion without,
    I shall be slain in the streets'.

¹⁴ The mouth of strange women is a deep pit:
    he that is abhorred of the LORD shall fall therein.

¹⁵ Foolishness is bound in the heart of a child:
    but the rod of correction shall drive it far from him.

¹⁶ He that oppresseth the poor to increase his riches,
    and he that giveth to the rich, shall surely come to want.

¹⁷ Bow down thy ear, and hear the words of the wise,
    and apply thy heart unto my knowledge.

¹⁸ For it is a pleasant thing if thou keep them within thee;
    they shall withal be fitted in thy lips.

¹⁹ That thy trust may be in the LORD,
    I have made known to thee this day, even to thee.

²⁰ Have not I written to thee excellent things
    in counsels and knowledge,

²¹ that I might make thee know the certainty of the words of
    truth;
    that thou mightest answer the words of truth to them that send
    unto thee?

²² Rob not the poor, because he is poor,
    neither oppress the afflicted in the gate:

²³ for the LORD will plead their cause,
    and spoil the soul of those that spoiled them.

²⁴ Make no friendship with an angry man:
  and with a furious man thou shalt not go;
²⁵ lest thou learn his ways,
  and get a snare to thy soul.
²⁶ Be not thou one of them that strike hands,
  or of them that are sureties for debts.
²⁷ If thou hast nothing to pay,
  why should he take away thy bed from under thee?
²⁸ Remove not the ancient landmark,
  which thy fathers have set.
²⁹ Seest thou a man diligent in his business?
  he shall stand before kings,
  he shall not stand before mean men.

23 When thou sittest to eat with a ruler,
  consider diligently what is before thee:
² and put a knife to thy throat,
  if thou be a man given to appetite.
³ Be not desirous of his dainties:
  for they are deceitful meat.
⁴ Labour not to be rich:
  cease from thy own wisdom.
⁵ Wilt thou set thine eyes upon that which is not?
  for riches certainly make themselves wings,
  they fly away as an eagle toward heaven.
⁶ Eat thou not the bread of him that hath an evil eye,
  neither desire thou his dainty meats:
⁷ for as he thinketh in his heart, so is he:
  'Eat and drink,' saith he to thee,
  but his heart is not with thee.
⁸ The morsel which thou hast eaten shalt thou vomit up,
  and lose thy sweet words.
⁹ Speak not in the ears of a fool:
  for he will despise the wisdom of thy words.
¹⁰ Remove not the old landmark;
  and enter not into the fields of the fatherless:
¹¹ for their redeemer is mighty;
  he shall plead their cause with thee.
¹² Apply thine heart unto instruction,
  and thine ears to the words of knowledge.
¹³ Withhold not correction from the child:
  for if thou beatest him with the rod, he shall not die.
¹⁴ Thou shalt beat him with the rod,
  and shalt deliver his soul from hell.

¹⁵ My son, if thine heart be wise,
  my heart shall rejoice, even mine.
¹⁶ Yea, my reins shall rejoice,

when thy lips speak right things.

¹⁷ Let not thy heart envy sinners:
  but be thou in the fear of the LORD all the day long.
¹⁸ For surely there is an end,
  and thy expectation shall not be cut off.
¹⁹ Hear thou, my son, and be wise,
  and guide thy heart in the way.
²⁰ Be not amongst wine-bibbers;
  amongst riotous eaters of flesh:
²¹ For the drunkard and the glutton shall come to poverty:
  and drowsiness shall clothe a man with rags.

²² Hearken unto thy father that begot thee,
  and despise not thy mother when she is old.
²³ Buy the truth, and sell it not;
  also wisdom and instruction and understanding.
²⁴ The father of the righteous shall greatly rejoice:
  he that begetteth a wise child shall have joy of him.
²⁵ Thy father and thy mother shall be glad,
  and she that bore thee shall rejoice.
²⁶ My son, give me thy heart,
  and let thy eyes observe my ways.
²⁷ For a whore is a deep ditch;
  and a strange woman is a narrow pit.
²⁸ She also lieth in wait as for a prey,
  and increaseth the transgressors among men.

²⁹ Who hath woe? who hath sorrow?
  who hath contentions? who hath babbling?
  who hath wounds without cause? who hath redness of eyes?
³⁰ they that tarry long at the wine,
  they that go to seek mixed wine.
³¹ Look not thou upon the wine when it is red,
  when it giveth his colour in the cup,
  when it moveth itself aright.
³² At the last it biteth like a serpent,
  and stingeth like an adder.
³³ Thy eyes shall behold strange women,
  and thy heart shall utter perverse things.
³⁴ Yea, thou shalt be as he that lieth down in the midst of the sea,
  or as he that lieth upon the top of a mast.
³⁵ 'They have stricken me,' shalt thou say, 'and I was not sick:
  they have beaten me, and I felt it not:
  when shall I awake? I will seek it yet again.'

24 Be not thou envious against evil men,
  neither desire to be with them.
² For their heart studieth destruction,

and their lips talk of mischief.

³ Through wisdom is a house built,
  and by understanding it is established:
⁴ and by knowledge shall the chambers be filled
  with all precious and pleasant riches.
⁵ A wise man is strong,
  yea, a man of knowledge increaseth strength.
⁶ For by wise counsel thou shalt make thy war:
  and in multitude of counsellors there is safety.
⁷ Wisdom is too high for a fool:
  he openeth not his mouth in the gate.
⁸ He that deviseth to do evil
  shall be called a mischievous person.
⁹ The thought of foolishness is sin:
  and the scorner is an abomination to men.
¹⁰ If thou faint in the day of adversity,
  thy strength is small.
¹¹ If thou forbear to deliver them that are drawn unto death,
  and those that are ready to be slain:
¹² if thou sayest, 'Behold, we knew it not': doth not he that
      pondereth the heart consider it?
  and he that keepeth thy soul, doth not he know it?
  and shall not he render to every man according to his works?
¹³ My son, eat thou honey, because it is good,
  and the honeycomb, which is sweet to thy taste.
¹⁴ So shall the knowledge of wisdom be unto thy soul:
  when thou hast found it, then there shall be a reward,
  and thy expectation shall not be cut off.
¹⁵ Lay not wait, O wicked man, against the dwelling of the
      righteous:
  spoil not his resting place:
¹⁶ for a just man falleth seven times, and riseth up again:
  but the wicked shall fall into mischief.
¹⁷ Rejoice not when thy enemy falleth,
  and let not thy heart be glad when he stumbleth:
¹⁸ lest the LORD see it, and it displease him,
  and he turn away his wrath from him.
¹⁹ Fret not thyself because of evil men,
  neither be thou envious at the wicked;
²⁰ for there shall be no reward to the evil man:
  the candle of the wicked shall be put out.
²¹ My son, fear thou the LORD and the king:
  and meddle not with them that are given to change:
²² for their calamity shall rise suddenly,
  and who knoweth the ruin of them both?

²³ These things also belong to the wise.

It is not good to have respect of persons in judgement.

²⁴ He that saith unto the wicked, 'Thou art righteous',
him shall the people curse, nations shall abhor him:
²⁵ but to them that rebuke him shall be delight,
and a good blessing shall come upon them.
²⁶ Every man shall kiss his lips
that giveth a right answer.
²⁷ Prepare thy work without, and make it fit for thyself in the
field;
and afterwards build thy house.
²⁸ Be not a witness against thy neighbour without cause:
and deceive not with thy lips.
²⁹ Say not, 'I will do so to him as he hath done to me:
I will render to the man according to his work'.

³⁰ I went by the field of the slothful,
and by the vineyard of the man void of understanding:
³¹ and lo, it was all grown over with thorns,
and nettles had covered the face thereof,
and the stone wall thereof was broken down.
³² Then I saw, and considered it well:
I looked upon it, and received instruction.
³³ Yet a little sleep, a little slumber,
a little folding of the hands to sleep:
³⁴ so shall thy poverty come as one that travelleth,
and thy want as an armed man.

25 These are also proverbs of Solomon, which the men of Hezekiah
king of Judah copied out.

² It is the glory of God to conceal a thing:
but the honour of kings is to search out a matter.

³ The heaven for height, and the earth for depth,
and the heart of kings is unsearchable.

⁴ Take away the dross from the silver,
and there shall come forth a vessel for the finer.

⁵ Take away the wicked from before the king,
and his throne shall be established in righteousness.

⁶ Put not forth thyself in the presence of the king,
and stand not in the place of great men:
⁷ for better it is that it be said unto thee, 'Come up hither';
than that thou shouldst be put lower in the presence of the
prince whom thy eyes have seen.

⁸ Go not forth hastily to strive,
lest thou know not what to do in the end thereof,
when thy neighbour hath put thee to shame.

⁹ Debate thy cause with thy neighbour himself;
and discover not a secret to another:
¹⁰ lest he that heareth it put thee to shame,
and thy infamy turn not away.

¹¹ A word fitly spoken
is like apples of gold in pictures of silver.

¹² As an earring of gold, and an ornament of fine gold,
so is a wise reprover upon an obedient ear.

¹³ As the cold of snow in the time of harvest,
so is a faithful messenger to them that send him:
for he refresheth the soul of his masters.

¹⁴ Whoso boasteth himself of a false gift
is like clouds and wind without rain.

¹⁵ By long forbearing is a prince persuaded,
and a soft tongue breaketh the bone.

¹⁶ Hast thou found honey? eat so much as is sufficient for thee,
lest thou be filled therewith, and vomit it.

¹⁷ Withdraw thy foot from thy neighbour's house:
lest he be weary of thee, and so hate thee.

¹⁸ A man that beareth false witness against his neighbour
is a maul, and a sword, and a sharp arrow.

¹⁹ Confidence in an unfaithful man in time of trouble
is like a broken tooth, and a foot out of joint.

²⁰ As he that taketh away a garment in cold weather,
and as vinegar upon nitre,
so is he that singeth songs to a heavy heart.

²¹ If thy enemy be hungry, give him bread to eat:
and if he be thirsty, give him water to drink:
²² for thou shalt heap coals of fire upon his head,
and the LORD shall reward thee.

²³ The north wind driveth away rain:
so doth an angry countenance a backbiting tongue.

²⁴ It is better to dwell in a corner of the house-top,
than with a brawling woman and in a wide house.

²⁵ As cold waters to a thirsty soul,
so is good news from a far country.

²⁶ A righteous man falling down before the wicked
is as a troubled fountain, and a corrupt spring.

²⁷ It is not good to eat much honey:
so for men to search their own glory is not glory.

²⁸ He that hath no rule over his own spirit
is like a city that is broken down, and without walls.

26 As snow in summer, and as rain in harvest,
so honour is not seemly for a fool.

2 As the bird by wandering, as the swallow by flying,
so the curse causeless shall not come.

3 A whip for the horse, a bridle for the ass,
and a rod for the fool's back.

4 Answer not a fool according to his folly,
lest thou also be like unto him.

5 Answer a fool according to his folly,
lest he be wise in his own conceit.

6 He that sendeth a message by the hand of a fool
cutteth off the feet, and drinketh damage.

7 The legs of the lame are not equal:
so is a parable in the mouth of fools.

8 As he that bindeth a stone in a sling,
so is he that giveth honour to a fool.

9 As a thorn goeth up into the hand of a drunkard,
so is a parable in the mouth of fools.

10 The great God that formed all things
both rewardeth the fool, and rewardeth transgressors.

11 As a dog returneth to his vomit,
so a fool returneth to his folly.

12 Seest thou a man wise in his own conceit?
there is more hope of a fool than of him.

13 The slothful man saith, 'There is a lion in the way,
a lion is in the streets.'

14 As the door turneth upon his hinges,
so doth the slothful upon his bed.

15 The slothful hideth his hand in his bosom;
it grieveth him to bring it again to his mouth.

16 The sluggard is wiser in his own conceit
than seven men that can render a reason.

17 He that passeth by, and meddleth with strife belonging not to him,
is like one that taketh a dog by the ears.

18 As a madman who casteth fire-brands, arrows, and death,
19 so is the man that deceiveth his neighbour,
and saith, 'Am not I in sport?'

20 Where no wood is, there the fire goeth out:
so where there is no tale-bearer, the strife ceaseth.

21 As coals are to burning coals, and wood to fire;
so is a contentious man to kindle strife.

²² The words of a tale-bearer are as wounds,
  and they go down into the innermost parts of the belly.

²³ Burning lips and a wicked heart
  are like a potsherd covered with silver dross.

²⁴ He that hateth dissembleth with his lips,
  and layeth up deceit within him.

²⁵ When he speaketh fair, believe him not:
  for there are seven abominations in his heart.

²⁶ Whose hatred is covered by deceit,
  his wickedness shall be shown before the whole congregation.

²⁷ Whoso diggeth a pit shall fall therein:
  and he that rolleth a stone, it will return upon him.

²⁸ A lying tongue hateth those that are afflicted by it,
  and a flattering mouth worketh ruin.

27 Boast not thyself of tomorrow:
  for thou knowest not what a day may bring forth.

² Let another man praise thee, and not thy own mouth;
  a stranger, and not thy own lips.

³ A stone is heavy, and the sand weighty:
  but a fool's wrath is heavier than them both.

⁴ Wrath is cruel, and anger is outrageous:
  but who is able to stand before envy?

⁵ Open rebuke is better than secret love.

⁶ Faithful are the wounds of a friend:
  but the kisses of an enemy are deceitful.

⁷ The full soul loatheth a honeycomb:
  but to the hungry soul every bitter thing is sweet.

⁸ As a bird that wandereth from her nest,
  so is a man that wandereth from his place.

⁹ Ointment and perfume rejoice the heart:
  so doth the sweetness of a man's friend by hearty counsel.

¹⁰ Thy own friend, and thy father's friend, forsake not;
  neither go into thy brother's house in the day of thy calamity:
  for better is a neighbour that is near than a brother far off.

¹¹ My son, be wise, and make my heart glad,
  that I may answer him that reproacheth me.

¹² A prudent man foreseeth the evil, and hideth himself:
  but the simple pass on, and are punished.

¹³ Take his garment that is surety for a stranger,
  and take a pledge of him for a strange woman.

¹⁴ He that blesseth his friend with a loud voice, rising early in the
morning,
it shall be counted a curse to him.

¹⁵ A continual dropping in a very rainy day
and a contentious woman are alike.

¹⁶ Whosoever hideth her hideth the wind,
and the ointment of his right hand, which bewrayeth itself.

¹⁷ Iron sharpeneth iron:
so a man sharpeneth the countenance of his friend.

¹⁸ Whoso keepeth the fig tree shall eat the fruit thereof:
so he that waiteth on his master shall be honoured.

¹⁹ As in water face answereth to face, so the heart of man to man.

²⁰ Hell and destruction are never full:
so the eyes of man are never satisfied.

²¹ As the fining-pot for silver, and the furnace for gold:
so is a man to his praise.

²² Though thou shouldst bray a fool in a mortar among wheat
with a pestle,
yet will not his foolishness depart from him.

²³ Be thou diligent to know the state of thy flocks,
and look well to thy herds.

²⁴ For riches are not for ever:
and doth the crown endure to every generation?

²⁵ The hay appeareth, and the tender grass showeth itself,
and herbs of the mountains are gathered.

²⁶ The lambs are for thy clothing,
and the goats are the price of thy field.

²⁷ And thou shalt have goats' milk enough for thy food,
for the food of thy household,
and for the maintenance for thy maidens.

28

The wicked flee when no man pursueth:
but the righteous are bold as a lion.

² For the transgression of a land many are the princes thereof:
but by a man of understanding and knowledge the state thereof
shall be prolonged.

³ A poor man that oppresseth the poor
is like a sweeping rain which leaveth no food.

⁴ They that forsake the law praise the wicked:
but such as keep the law contend with them.

⁵ Evil men understand not judgement:
but they that seek the LORD understand all things.

⁶ Better is the poor that walketh in his uprightness,
than he that is perverse in his ways, though he be rich.

⁷ Whoso keepeth the law is a wise son:
but he that is a companion of riotous men shameth his father.

⁸ He that by usury and unjust gain increaseth his substance,
he shall gather it for him that will pity the poor.

⁹ He that turneth away his ear from hearing the law,
even his prayer shall be abomination.

¹⁰ Whoso causeth the righteous to go astray in an evil way,
he shall fall himself into his own pit:
but the upright shall have good things in possession.

¹¹ The rich man is wise in his own conceit:
but the poor that hath understanding searcheth him out.

¹² When righteous men do rejoice, there is great glory:
but when the wicked rise, a man is hidden.

¹³ He that covereth his sins shall not prosper:
but whoso confesseth and forsaketh them shall have mercy.

¹⁴ Happy is the man that feareth always:
but he that hardeneth his heart shall fall into mischief.

¹⁵ As a roaring lion, and a ranging bear:
so is a wicked ruler over the poor people.

¹⁶ The prince that wanteth understanding is also a great
oppressor:
but he that hateth covetousness shall prolong his days.

¹⁷ A man that doeth violence to the blood of any person
shall fly to the pit, let no man stay him.

¹⁸ Whoso walketh uprightly shall be saved:
but he that is perverse in his ways shall fall at once.

¹⁹ He that tilleth his land shall have plenty of bread:
but he that followeth after vain persons shall have poverty
enough.

²⁰ A faithful man shall abound with blessings:
but he that maketh haste to be rich shall not be innocent.

²¹ To have respect of persons is not good:
for for a piece of bread that man will transgress.

²² He that hasteth to be rich hath an evil eye,
and considereth not that poverty shall come upon him.

²³ He that rebuketh a man afterwards shall find more favour
than he that flattereth with the tongue.

²⁴ Whoso robbeth his father or his mother,
and saith, 'It is no transgression',
the same is the companion of a destroyer.

²⁵ He that is of a proud heart stirreth up strife:
  but he that putteth his trust in the LORD shall be made fat.

²⁶ He that trusteth in his own heart is a fool:
  but whoso walketh wisely, he shall be delivered.

²⁷ He that giveth unto the poor shall not lack:
  but he that hideth his eyes shall have many a curse.

²⁸ When the wicked rise, men hide themselves:
  but when they perish, the righteous increase.

29 He, that being often reproved hardeneth his neck,
  shall suddenly be destroyed, and that without remedy.

² When the righteous are in authority, the people rejoice:
  but when the wicked beareth rule, the people mourn.

³ Whoso loveth wisdom rejoiceth his father:
  but he that keepeth company with harlots spendeth his
    substance.

⁴ The king by judgement establisheth the land:
  but he that receiveth gifts overthroweth it.

⁵ A man that flattereth his neighbour
  spreadeth a net for his feet.

⁶ In the transgression of an evil man there is a snare:
  but the righteous doth sing and rejoice.

⁷ The righteous considereth the cause of the poor:
  but the wicked regardeth not to know it.

⁸ Scornful men bring a city into a snare:
  but wise men turn away wrath.

⁹ If a wise man contendeth with a foolish man,
  whether he rage or laugh, there is no rest.

¹⁰ The bloodthirsty hate the upright:
  but the just seek his soul.

¹¹ A fool uttereth all his mind:
  but a wise man keepeth it in till afterwards.

¹² If a ruler hearken to lies,
  all his servants are wicked.

¹³ The poor and the deceitful man meet together:
  the LORD lighteneth both their eyes.

¹⁴ The king that faithfully judgeth the poor,
  his throne shall be established for ever.

¹⁵ The rod and reproof give wisdom:
  but a child left to himself bringeth his mother to shame.

¹⁶ When the wicked are multiplied, transgression increaseth:
  but the righteous shall see their fall.

¹⁷ Correct thy son, and he shall give thee rest:
yea, he shall give delight unto thy soul.

¹⁸ Where there is no vision, the people perish:
but he that keepeth the law, happy is he.

¹⁹ A servant will not be corrected by words:
for though he understand he will not answer.

²⁰ Seest thou a man that is hasty in his words?
there is more hope of a fool than of him.

²¹ He that delicately bringeth up his servant from a child
shall have him become his son at the length.

²² An angry man stirreth up strife,
and a furious man aboundeth in transgression.

²³ A man's pride shall bring him low:
but honour shall uphold the humble in spirit.

²⁴ Whoso is partner with a thief hateth his own soul:
he heareth cursing, and bewrayeth it not.

²⁵ The fear of man bringeth a snare:
but whoso putteth his trust in the LORD shall be safe.

²⁶ Many seek the ruler's favour,
but every man's judgement cometh from the LORD.

²⁷ An unjust man is an abomination to the just:
and he that is upright in the way is abomination to the wicked.

30

The words of Agur the son of Jakeh, even the prophecy: the man spoke unto Ithiel, even unto Ithiel and Ucal.

² Surely I am more brutish than any man,
and have not the understanding of a man.
³ I neither learned wisdom, nor have the knowledge of the holy.
⁴ Who hath ascended up into heaven, or descended?
who hath gathered the wind in his fists?
who hath bound the waters in a garment?
who hath established all the ends of the earth?
what is his name, and what is his son's name,
if thou canst tell?

⁵ Every word of God is pure:
he is a shield unto them that put their trust in him.
⁶ Add thou not unto his words,
lest he reprove thee, and thou be found a liar.

⁷ Two things have I required of thee;
deny me them not before I die.
⁸ Remove far from me vanity and lies:
give me neither poverty nor riches;

feed me with food convenient for me:
⁹ lest I be full, and deny thee, and say, 'Who is the LORD?'
   or lest I be poor, and steal, and take the name of my God in vain.

¹⁰ Accuse not a servant unto his master,
   lest he curse thee, and thou be found guilty.
¹¹ There is a generation that curseth their father,
   and doth not bless their mother.
¹² There is a generation that are pure in their own eyes,
   and yet is not washed from their filthiness.
¹³ There is a generation, O how lofty are their eyes!
   and their eyelids are lifted up.
¹⁴ There is a generation, whose teeth are as swords,
   and their jaw-teeth as knives,
   to devour the poor from off the earth,
   and the needy from among men.

¹⁵ The horse-leech hath two daughters, crying, 'Give, give'.
   There are three things that are never satisfied,
   yea, four things say not, 'It is enough':
¹⁶ the grave; and the barren womb;
   the earth that is not filled with water;
   and the fire that saith not, 'It is enough'.
¹⁷ The eye that mocketh at his father,
   and despiseth to obey his mother,
   the ravens of the valley shall pick it out,
   and the young eagles shall eat it.

¹⁸ There be three things which are too wonderful for me,
   yea, four which I know not:
¹⁹ the way of an eagle in the air;
   the way of a serpent upon a rock;
   the way of a ship in the midst of the sea;
   and the way of a man with a maid.
²⁰ Such is the way of an adulterous woman:
   she eateth, and wipeth her mouth,
   and saith, 'I have done no wickedness'.

²¹ For three things the earth is disquieted,
   and for four which it cannot bear:
²² for a servant when he reigneth,
   and a fool when he is filled with meat:
²³ for an odious woman when she is married,
   and a handmaid that is heir to her mistress.

²⁴ There be four things which are little upon the earth,
   but they are exceeding wise:
²⁵ the ants are a people not strong,

yet they prepare their meat in the summer;
²⁶ the conies are but a feeble folk,
   yet make they their houses in the rocks;
²⁷ the locusts have no king,
   yet go they forth all of them by bands;
²⁸ the spider taketh hold with her hands,
   and is in kings' palaces.

²⁹ There be three things which go well,
   yea, four are comely in going:
³⁰ a lion which is strongest among beasts,
   and turneth not away for any;
³¹ a greyhound; a he-goat also;
   and a king, against whom there is no rising up.

³² If thou hast done foolishly in lifting up thyself,
   or if thou hast thought evil,
   lay thy hand upon thy mouth.
³³ Surely the churning of milk bringeth forth butter,
   and the wringing of the nose bringeth forth blood:
   so the forcing of wrath bringeth forth strife.

31

The words of king Lemuel, the prophecy that his mother taught him.

² What, my son? and what, the son of my womb?
   and what, the son of my vows?
³ Give not thy strength unto women,
   nor thy ways to that which destroyeth kings.
⁴ It is not for kings, O Lemuel, it is not for kings to drink wine,
   nor for princes strong drink:
⁵ lest they drink, and forget the law,
   and pervert the judgement of any of the afflicted.
⁶ Give strong drink unto him that is ready to perish,
   and wine unto those that be of heavy hearts.
⁷ Let him drink, and forget his poverty,
   and remember his misery no more.
⁸ Open thy mouth for the dumb
   in the cause of all such as are appointed to destruction.
⁹ Open thy mouth, judge righteously,
   and plead the cause of the poor and needy.

¹⁰ Who can find a virtuous woman?
   for her price is far above rubies.
¹¹ The heart of her husband doth safely trust in her,
   so that he shall have no need of spoil.
¹² She will do him good and not evil
   all the days of her life.

¹³ She seeketh wool and flax,
and worketh willingly with her hands.
¹⁴ She is like the merchant's ships,
she bringeth her food from afar.
¹⁵ She riseth also while it is yet night,
and giveth meat to her household,
and a portion to her maidens.
¹⁶ She considereth a field, and buyeth it:
with the fruit of her hands she planteth a vineyard.
¹⁷ She girdeth her loins with strength,
and strengtheneth her arms.
¹⁸ She perceiveth that her merchandise is good:
her candle goeth not out by night.
¹⁹ She layeth her hands to the spindle,
and her hands hold the distaff.
²⁰ She stretcheth out her hand to the poor,
yea, she reacheth forth her hands to the needy.
²¹ She is not afraid of the snow for her household:
for all her household are clothed with scarlet.
²² She maketh herself coverings of tapestry;
her clothing is silk and purple.
²³ Her husband is known in the gates,
when he sitteth among the elders of the land.
²⁴ She maketh fine linen, and selleth it,
and delivereth girdles unto the merchant.
²⁵ Strength and honour are her clothing;
and she shall rejoice in time to come.
²⁶ She openeth her mouth with wisdom;
and in her tongue is the law of kindness.
²⁷ She looketh well to the ways of her household,
and eateth not the bread of idleness.
²⁸ Her children arise up, and call her blessed;
her husband also, and he praiseth her.
²⁹ Many daughters have done virtuously,
but thou excellest them all.
³⁰ Favour is deceitful, and beauty is vain:
but a woman that feareth the LORD, she shall be praised.
³¹ Give her of the fruit of her hands,
and let her own works praise her in the gates.

ECCLESIASTES

OR, THE PREACHER

1 The words of the Preacher, the son of David, king in Jerusalem.

² Vanity of vanities, saith the Preacher,
vanity of vanities, all is vanity.

³ What profit hath a man of all his labour
which he taketh under the sun?

⁴ One generation passeth away, and another generation
cometh:
but the earth abideth for ever.

⁵ The sun also ariseth, and the sun goeth down,
and hasteth to the place where he arose.

⁶ The wind goeth toward the south,
and turneth about unto the north;
it whirleth about continually,
and the wind returneth again according to his circuits.

⁷ All the rivers run into the sea, yet the sea is not full:
unto the place from whence the rivers come, thither they return
again.

⁸ All things are full of labour; man cannot utter it:
the eye is not satisfied with seeing, nor the ear filled with
hearing.

⁹ The thing that hath been, it is that which shall be:
and that which is done is that which shall be done:
and there is no new thing under the sun.

¹⁰ Is there anything whereof it may be said, 'See, this is new'?
it hath been already of old time, which was before us.

¹¹ There is no remembrance of former things;
neither shall there be any remembrance of things
that are to come with those that shall come after.

¹²I the Preacher was king over Israel in Jerusalem. ¹³And I gave my heart to seek and search out by wisdom concerning all things that are done under heaven: this sore travail hath God given to the sons of man to be exercised therewith. ¹⁴I have seen all the works that are done under the sun, and behold, all is vanity and vexation of spirit. ¹⁵That which is crooked cannot be made straight: and that which is wanting cannot be numbered. ¹⁶I communed with my own heart, saying, 'Lo, I am come to great estate, and have gotten more wisdom than all they that have been before me in Jerusalem': yea, my heart had great experience of wisdom and knowledge. ¹⁷And I gave my heart to know wisdom, and to know madness and folly: I perceived that this also is vexation of spirit. ¹⁸For in much wisdom is much grief: and he that increaseth knowledge increaseth sorrow.

2 I said in my heart, 'Go to now, I will prove thee with mirth, there-fore enjoy pleasure': and behold, this also is vanity. ²I said of laugh-ter, 'It is mad': and of mirth, 'What doeth it?' ³I sought in my heart to give myself unto wine (yet acquainting my heart with wisdom), and to lay hold on folly, till I might see what was that good for the sons of men, which they should do under the heaven all the days of their life.

⁴I made me great works, I built me houses, I planted me vineyards. ⁵I made me gardens and orchards, and I planted trees in them of all kind of fruits. ⁶I made me pools of water, to water therewith the wood that bringeth forth trees: ⁷I got me servants and maidens, and had servants born in my house; also I had great possessions of great and small cattle above all that were in Jerusalem before me: ⁸I gathered me also silver and gold, and the peculiar treasure of kings and of the provinces: I got me men singers and women singers, and the delights of the sons of men, as musical instruments, and that of all sorts. ⁹So I was great, and increased more than all that were before me in Jerusalem: also my wis-dom remained with me. ¹⁰And whatsoever my eyes desired I kept not from them; I withheld not my heart from any joy: for my heart rejoiced in all my labour; and this was my portion of all my labour. ¹¹Then I looked on all the works that my hands had wrought, and on the labour that I had laboured to do: and behold, all was vanity and vexation of spirit, and there was no profit under the sun.

¹²And I turned myself to behold wisdom, and madness, and folly: for what can the man do that cometh after the king? even that which hath been already done. ¹³Then I saw that wisdom excelleth folly, as far as light excelleth darkness. ¹⁴The wise man's eyes are in his head, but the fool walketh in darkness: and I myself perceived also that one event happeneth to them all. ¹⁵Then said I in my heart, 'As it happeneth to the fool, so it happeneth even to me, and why was I then more wise?' Then I said in my heart, that this also is vanity. ¹⁶For there is no remem-brance of the wise more than of the fool for ever; seeing that which now is, in the days to come shall be forgotten. And how dieth the wise man? as the fool. ¹⁷Therefore I hated life, because the work that is wrought under the sun is grievous unto me: for all is vanity and vexa-tion of spirit. ¹⁸Yea, I hated all my labour which I had taken under the sun: because I should leave it unto the man that shall be after me. ¹⁹And who knoweth whether he shall be a wise man or a fool? yet shall he have rule over all my labour wherein I have laboured, and wherein I have shown myself wise under the sun. This is also vanity.

²⁰Therefore I went about to cause my heart to despair of all the labour which I took under the sun. ²¹For there is a man whose labour is in wisdom, and in knowledge, and in equity: yet to a man that hath not laboured therein shall he leave it for his portion. This also is vanity and a great evil. ²²For what hath man of all his labour, and of the vexation of his heart, wherein he hath laboured under the sun? ²³For all his days are sorrows, and his travail grief; yea, his heart taketh not rest in the night. This is also vanity.

²⁴There is nothing better for a man, than that he should eat and

drink, and that he should make his soul enjoy good in his labour. This also I saw, that it was from the hand of God. [25]For who can eat, or who else can hasten hereunto, more than I? [26]For God giveth to a man that is good in his sight, wisdom, and knowledge, and joy: but to the sinner he giveth travail, to gather and to heap up, that he may give to him that is good before God. This also is vanity and vexation of spirit.

3 To everything there is a season,
  and a time to every purpose under the heaven.
  [2]A time to be born, and a time to die:
  a time to plant, and a time to pluck up that which is planted.
  [3]A time to kill, and a time to heal:
  a time to break down, and a time to build up.
  [4]A time to weep, and a time to laugh:
  a time to mourn, and a time to dance.
  [5]A time to cast away stones,
  and a time to gather stones together:
  a time to embrace, and a time to refrain from embracing.
  [6]A time to get, and a time to lose:
  a time to keep, and a time to cast away.
  [7]A time to rend, and a time to sew:
  a time to keep silence, and a time to speak.
  [8]A time to love, and a time to hate:
  a time of war, and a time of peace.

[9]What profit hath he that worketh in that wherein he laboureth? [10]I have seen the travail which God hath given to the sons of men to be exercised in it. [11]He hath made everything beautiful in his time: also he hath set the world in their heart, so that no man can find out the work that God maketh from the beginning to the end. [12]I know that there is no good in them, but for a man to rejoice, and to do good in his life. [13]And also that every man should eat and drink, and enjoy the good of all his labour: it is the gift of God. [14]I know that whatsoever God doeth, it shall be for ever: nothing can be put to it, nor anything taken from it: and God doeth it, that men should fear before him. [15]That which hath been is now: and that which is to be hath already been; and God requireth that which is past.

[16]And moreover I saw under the sun the place of judgement, that wickedness was there; and the place of righteousness, that iniquity was there. [17]I said in my heart, 'God shall judge the righteous and the wicked: for there is a time there for every purpose and for every work'.

[18]I said in my heart concerning the estate of the sons of men, that God might manifest them, and that they might see that they themselves are beasts. [19]For that which befalleth the sons of men befalleth beasts; even one thing befalleth them: as the one dieth, so dieth the other; yea, they have all one breath, so that a man hath no pre-eminence above a beast: for all is vanity. [20]All go unto one place, all are of the dust, and all turn to dust again. [21]Who knoweth the spirit of man that goeth upward, and

the spirit of the beast that goeth downward to the earth? ²²Wherefore I perceive that there is nothing better, than that a man should rejoice in his own works: for that is his portion; for who shall bring him to see what shall be after him?

4 So I returned, and considered all the oppressions that are done under the sun: and behold the tears of such as were oppressed, and they had no comforter: and on the side of their oppressors there was power, but they had no comforter. ²Wherefore I praised the dead which are already dead more than the living which are yet alive. ³Yea, better is he than both they, which hath not yet been, who hath not seen the evil work that is done under the sun.

⁴Again, I considered all travail, and every right work, that for this a man is envied of his neighbour: this is also vanity and vexation of spirit. ⁵The fool foldeth his hands together, and eateth his own flesh. ⁶Better is a handful with quietness, than both the hands full with travail and vexation of spirit.

⁷Then I returned, and I saw vanity under the sun. ⁸There is one alone, and there is not a second; yea, he hath neither child nor brother: yet is there no end of all his labour, neither is his eye satisfied with riches, neither saith he, 'For whom do I labour, and bereave my soul of good?' This is also vanity, yea, it is a sore travail. ⁹Two are better than one, because they have a good reward for their labour. ¹⁰For if they fall, the one will lift up his fellow, but woe to him that is alone when he falleth: for he hath not another to help him up. ¹¹Again, if two lie together, then they have heat: but how can one be warm alone? ¹²And if one prevail against him, two shall withstand him; and a threefold cord is not quickly broken.

¹³Better is a poor and a wise child than an old and foolish king, who will no more be admonished. ¹⁴For out of prison he cometh to reign, whereas also he that is born in his kingdom becometh poor. ¹⁵I considered all the living which walk under the sun, with the second child that shall stand up in his stead. ¹⁶There is no end of all the people, even of all that have been before them: they also that come after shall not rejoice in him. Surely this also is vanity and vexation of spirit.

5 Keep thy foot when thou goest to the house of God, and be more ready to hear, than to give the sacrifice of fools: for they consider not that they do evil. ²Be not rash with thy mouth, and let not thy heart be hasty to utter anything before God: for God is in heaven, and thou upon earth: therefore let thy words be few. ³For a dream cometh through the multitude of business, and a fool's voice is known by multitude of words. ⁴When thou vowest a vow unto God, defer not to pay it: for he hath no pleasure in fools: pay that which thou hast vowed. ⁵Better is it that thou shouldst not vow, than that thou shouldst vow and not pay. ⁶Suffer not thy mouth to cause thy flesh to sin, neither say thou before the angel, that it was an error: wherefore should God be angry at thy voice, and destroy the work of thy hands? ⁷For in the multitude of dreams and many words there are also divers vanities: but fear thou God.

⁸If thou seest the oppression of the poor, and violent perverting of judgement and justice in a province, marvel not at the matter: for he that is higher than the highest regardeth; and there be higher than they.

⁹Moreover the profit of the earth is for all: the king himself is served by the field. ¹⁰He that loveth silver shall not be satisfied with silver; nor he that loveth abundance with increase: this is also vanity. ¹¹When goods increase, they are increased that eat them: and what good is there to the owners thereof, saving the beholding of them with their eyes? ¹²The sleep of a labouring man is sweet, whether he eat little or much: but the abundance of the rich will not suffer him to sleep. ¹³There is a sore evil which I have seen under the sun, namely, riches kept for the owners thereof to their hurt. ¹⁴But those riches perish by evil travail: and he begetteth a son, and there is nothing in his hand. ¹⁵As he came forth of his mother's womb, naked shall he return to go as he came, and shall take nothing of his labour, which he may carry away in his hand. ¹⁶And this also is a sore evil, that in all points as he came, so shall he go: and what profit hath he that hath laboured for the wind? ¹⁷All his days also he eateth in darkness, and he hath much sorrow and wrath with his sickness.

¹⁸Behold that which I have seen: it is good and comely for one to eat and to drink, and to enjoy the good of all his labour that he taketh under the sun all the days of his life, which God giveth him: for it is his portion. ¹⁹Every man also to whom God hath given riches and wealth, and hath given him power to eat thereof, and to take his portion, and to rejoice in his labour; this is the gift of God. ²⁰For he shall not much remember the days of his life: because God answereth him in the joy of his heart.

6 There is an evil which I have seen under the sun, and it is common among men: ²a man to whom God hath given riches, wealth, and honour, so that he wanteth nothing for his soul of all that he desireth, yet God giveth him not power to eat thereof, but a stranger eateth it: this is vanity, and it is an evil disease.

³If a man beget a hundred children, and live many years, so that the days of his years be many, and his soul be not filled with good, and also that he have no burial; I say, that an untimely birth is better than he. ⁴For he cometh in with vanity, and departeth in darkness, and his name shall be covered with darkness. ⁵Moreover he hath not seen the sun, nor known anything: this hath more rest than the other. ⁶Yea, though he live a thousand years twice told, yet hath he seen no good: do not all go to one place?

⁷All the labour of man is for his mouth, and yet the appetite is not filled. ⁸For what hath the wise more than the fool? what hath the poor, that knoweth to walk before the living? ⁹Better is the sight of the eyes than the wandering of the desire: this is also vanity and vexation of spirit.

¹⁰That which hath been is named already, and it is known that it is man: neither may he contend with him that is mightier than he.

¹¹Seeing there be many things that increase vanity, what is man the better? ¹²For who knoweth what is good for man in this life, all the days of his vain life which he spendeth as a shadow? for who can tell a man what shall be after him under the sun?

7

A good name is better than precious ointment:
and the day of death than the day of one's birth.

² It is better to go to the house of mourning,
than to go to the house of feasting:
for that is the end of all men,
and the living will lay it to his heart.
³ Sorrow is better than laughter:
for by the sadness of the countenance the heart is made better.
⁴ The heart of the wise is in the house of mourning:
but the heart of fools is in the house of mirth.
⁵ It is better to hear the rebuke of the wise,
than for a man to hear the song of fools.
⁶ For as the crackling of thorns under a pot,
so is the laughter of the fool:
this also is vanity.
⁷ Surely oppression maketh a wise man mad:
and a gift destroyeth the heart.
⁸ Better is the end of a thing than the beginning thereof:
and the patient in spirit is better than the proud in spirit.
⁹ Be not hasty in thy spirit to be angry:
for anger resteth in the bosom of fools.
¹⁰ Say not thou, 'What is the cause that the former days were better than these?'
for thou dost not inquire wisely concerning this.

¹¹ Wisdom is good with an inheritance:
and by it there is profit to them that see the sun.
¹² For wisdom is a defence, and money is a defence:
but the excellence of knowledge is,
that wisdom giveth life to them that have it.
¹³ Consider the work of God:
for who can make that straight, which he hath made crooked?

¹⁴In the day of prosperity be joyful, but in the day of adversity consider: God also hath set the one over against the other, to the end that man should find nothing after him. ¹⁵All things have I seen in the days of my vanity: there is a just man that perisheth in his righteousness, and there is a wicked man that prolongeth his life in his wickedness. ¹⁶Be not righteous over much, neither make thyself over wise: why shouldst thou destroy thyself? ¹⁷Be not over much wicked, neither be thou foolish: why shouldst thou die before thy time? ¹⁸It is good that thou shouldst take hold of this; yea, also from this withdraw not thy hand:

for he that feareth God shall come forth of them all. ¹⁹Wisdom strengtheneth the wise more than ten mighty men which are in the city. ²⁰For there is not a just man upon earth, that doeth good, and sinneth not. ²¹Also take no heed unto all words that are spoken; lest thou hear thy servant curse thee. ²²For oftentimes also thy own heart knoweth that thou thyself likewise hast cursed others.

²³All this have I proved by wisdom: I said, 'I will be wise', but it was far from me. ²⁴That which is far off, and exceeding deep, who can find it out? ²⁵I applied my heart to know, and to search, and to seek out wisdom, and the reason of things, and to know the wickedness of folly, even of foolishness and madness. ²⁶And I find more bitter than death the woman whose heart is snares and nets, and her hands as bands: whoso pleaseth God shall escape from her, but the sinner shall be taken by her. ²⁷Behold, this have I found (saith the preacher), counting one by one, to find out the account: ²⁸which yet my soul seeketh, but I find not: one man among a thousand have I found, but a woman among all those have I not found. ²⁹Lo, this only have I found, that God hath made man upright: but they have sought out many inventions.

8 Who is as the wise man? and who knoweth the interpretation of a thing? a man's wisdom maketh his face to shine, and the boldness of his face shall be changed. ²I counsel thee to keep the king's commandment, and that in regard of the oath of God. ³Be not hasty to go out of his sight: stand not in an evil thing, for he doeth whatsoever pleaseth him. ⁴Where the word of a king is, there is power: and who may say unto him, 'What doest thou?' ⁵Whoso keepeth the commandment shall feel no evil thing: and a wise man's heart discerneth both time and judgement.

⁶Because to every purpose there is time and judgement, therefore the misery of man is great upon him. ⁷For he knoweth not that which shall be: for who can tell him when it shall be? ⁸There is no man that hath power over the spirit to retain the spirit; neither hath he power in the day of death: and there is no discharge in that war, neither shall wickedness deliver those that are given to it. ⁹All this have I seen, and applied my heart unto every work that is done under the sun: there is a time wherein one man ruleth over another to his own hurt.

¹⁰And so I saw the wicked buried, who had come and gone from the place of the holy, and they were forgotten in the city where they had so done: this is also vanity. ¹¹Because sentence against an evil work is not executed speedily, therefore the heart of the sons of men is fully set in them to do evil. ¹²Though a sinner do evil a hundred times, and his days be prolonged, yet surely I know that it shall be well with them that fear God, which fear before him. ¹³But it shall not be well with the wicked, neither shall he prolong his days, which are as a shadow; because he feareth not before God. ¹⁴There is a vanity which is done upon the earth, that there be just men, unto whom it happeneth according to the work of the wicked: again, there be wicked men, to whom it happeneth according to the work of the righteous: I said that this also is vanity. ¹⁵Then I commended mirth, because a man hath no better thing under the sun, than to eat, and to drink, and to be merry: for that shall

abide with him of his labour the days of his life, which God giveth him under the sun.

^{16}When I applied my heart to know wisdom, and to see the business that is done upon the earth (for also there is that neither day nor night seeth sleep with his eyes): ^{17}then I beheld all the work of God, that a man cannot find out the work that is done under the sun: because though a man labour to seek it out, yet he shall not find it; yea farther; though a wise man think to know it, yet shall he not be able to find it.

9 For all this I considered in my heart even to declare all this, that the righteous, and the wise, and their works, are in the hand of God: no man knoweth either love or hatred by all that is before them. ^{2}All things come alike to all: there is one event to the righteous, and to the wicked; to the good and to the clean, and to the unclean; to him that sacrificeth, and to him that sacrificeth not: as is the good, so is the sinner; and he that sweareth, as he that feareth an oath. ^{3}This is an evil among all things that are done under the sun, that there is one event unto all: yea, also the heart of the sons of men is full of evil, and madness is in their heart while they live, and after that they go to the dead.

^{4}For to him that is joined to all the living there is hope: for a living dog is better than a dead lion. ^{5}For the living know that they shall die: but the dead know not anything, neither have they any more a reward, for the memory of them is forgotten. ^{6}Also their love, and their hatred, and their envy is now perished; neither have they any more a portion for ever in anything that is done under the sun.

^{7}Go thy way, eat thy bread with joy, and drink thy wine with a merry heart; for God now accepteth thy works. ^{8}Let thy garments be always white; and let thy head lack no ointment. ^{9}Live joyfully with the wife whom thou lovest all the days of the life of thy vanity, which he hath given thee under the sun, all the days of thy vanity: for that is thy portion in this life, and in thy labour which thou takest under the sun. ^{10}Whatsoever thy hand findeth to do, do it with thy might: for there is no work, nor device, nor knowledge, nor wisdom, in the grave, whither thou goest.

^{11}I returned, and saw under the sun, that the race is not to the swift, nor the battle to the strong, neither yet bread to the wise, nor yet riches to men of understanding, nor yet favour to men of skill; but time and chance happeneth to them all. ^{12}For man also knoweth not his time: as the fishes that are taken in an evil net, and as the birds that are caught in the snare; so are the sons of men snared in an evil time, when it falleth suddenly upon them.

^{13}This wisdom have I seen also under the sun, and it seemed great unto me: ^{14}there was a little city, and few men within it; and there came a great king against it, and besieged it, and built great bulwarks against it: ^{15}now there was found in it a poor wise man, and he by his wisdom delivered the city; yet no man remembered that same poor man. ^{16}Then said I, 'Wisdom is better than strength: nevertheless the poor man's wisdom is despised, and his words are not heard'. ^{17}The words of wise men are heard in quiet more than the cry of him that ruleth among fools. [18]Wisdom is better than weapons of war: but one sinner destroyeth much good.

10

Dead flies cause the ointment of the apothecary to send forth a stinking savour:
so doth a little folly him that is in reputation for wisdom and honour.
[2] A wise man's heart is at his right hand:
but a fool's heart at his left.
[3] Yea also, when he that is a fool walketh by the way, his wisdom faileth him,
and he saith to every one that he is a fool.

[4] If the spirit of the ruler rise up against thee, leave not thy place;
for yielding pacifieth great offences.
[5] There is an evil which I have seen under the sun,
as an error which proceedeth from the ruler:
[6] Folly is set in great dignity,
and the rich sit in low place.
[7] I have seen servants upon horses,
and princes walking as servants upon the earth.

[8] He that diggeth a pit shall fall into it;
and whoso breaketh a hedge, a serpent shall bite him.
[9] Whoso removeth stones shall be hurt therewith:
and he that cleaveth wood shall be endangered thereby.
[10] If the iron be blunt, and he do not whet the edge,
then must he put to more strength:
but wisdom is profitable to direct.

[11] Surely the serpent will bite without enchantment,
and a babbler is no better.
[12] The words of a wise man's mouth are gracious:
but the lips of a fool will swallow up himself.
[13] The beginning of the words of his mouth is foolishness:
and the end of his talk is mischievous madness.
[14] A fool also is full of words:
a man cannot tell what shall be;
and what shall be after him, who can tell him?
[15] The labour of the foolish wearieth every one of them,
because he knoweth not how to go to the city.

[16] Woe to thee, O land, when thy king is a child,
and thy princes eat in the morning.
[17] Blessed art thou, O land, when thy king is the son of nobles,
and thy princes eat in due season,
for strength, and not for drunkenness.

¹⁸ By much slothfulness the building decayeth;
and through idleness of the hands the house droppeth
through.

¹⁹ A feast is made for laughter, and wine maketh merry:
but money answereth all things.

²⁰ Curse not the king, no not in thy thought;
and curse not the rich in thy bedchamber:
for a bird of the air shall carry the voice,
and that which hath wings shall tell the matter.

11 Cast thy bread upon the waters:
for thou shalt find it after many days.
² Give a portion to seven, and also to eight;
for thou knowest not what evil shall be upon the earth.
³ If the clouds be full of rain,
they empty themselves upon the earth:
and if the tree fall toward the south, or toward the north,
in the place where the tree falleth, there it shall be.
⁴ He that observeth the wind shall not sow:
and he that regardeth the clouds shall not reap.

⁵As thou knowest not what is the way of the spirit, nor how the bones
do grow in the womb of her that is with child: even so thou knowest
not the works of God who maketh all. ⁶In the morning sow thy seed,
and in the evening withhold not thy hand: for thou knowest not
whether shall prosper, either this or that, or whether they both shall be
alike good.

⁷Truly the light is sweet, and a pleasant thing is it for the eyes to
behold the sun. ⁸But if a man live many years, and rejoice in them all;
yet let him remember the days of darkness, for they shall be many. All
that cometh is vanity.

⁹Rejoice, O young man, in thy youth, and let thy heart cheer thee in
the days of thy youth, and walk in the ways of thy heart, and in the
sight of thy eyes: but know thou, that for all these things God will bring
thee into judgement. ¹⁰Therefore remove sorrow from thy heart, and
put away evil from thy flesh: for childhood and youth are vanity.

12 Remember now thy Creator in the days of thy youth, while the
evil days come not, nor the years draw nigh, when thou shalt
say, 'I have no pleasure in them': ²while the sun, or the light, or the
moon, or the stars be not darkened, nor the clouds return after the
rain: ³in the day when the keepers of the house shall tremble, and the
strong men shall bow themselves, and the grinders cease because they
are few, and those that look out of the windows be darkened, ⁴and the
doors shall be shut in the streets, when the sound of the grinding is
low, and he shall rise up at the voice of the bird, and all the daughters
of music shall be brought low. ⁵Also when they shall be afraid of that

which is high, and fears shall be in the way, and the almond tree shall flourish, and the grasshopper shall be a burden, and desire shall fail: because man goeth to his long home, and the mourners go about the streets: ⁶or ever the silver cord be loosed, or the golden bowl be broken, or the pitcher be broken at the fountain, or the wheel broken at the cistern. ⁷Then shall the dust return to the earth as it was: and the spirit shall return unto God who gave it.

⁸Vanity of vanities (saith the preacher); all is vanity.

⁹And moreover, because the preacher was wise, he still taught the people knowledge, yea, he gave good heed, and sought out, and set in order many proverbs. ¹⁰The preacher sought to find out acceptable words, and that which was written was upright, even words of truth. ¹¹The words of the wise are as goads, and as nails fastened by the masters of assemblies, which are given from one shepherd. ¹²And further, by these, my son, be admonished: of making many books there is no end, and much study is a weariness of the flesh.

¹³Let us hear the conclusion of the whole matter: fear God, and keep his commandments, for this is the whole duty of man. ¹⁴For God shall bring every work into judgement, with every secret thing, whether it be good, or whether it be evil.

THE SONG OF
SOLOMON

1 The song of songs, which is Solomon's.

2 Let him kiss me with the kisses of his mouth:
for thy love is better than wine.
3 Because of the savour of thy good ointments
thy name is as ointment poured forth,
therefore do the virgins love thee.
4 Draw me, we will run after thee:
the king hath brought me into his chambers:
we will be glad and rejoice in thee,
we will remember thy love more than wine:
the upright love thee.
5 I am black, but comely, O ye daughters of Jerusalem,
as the tents of Kedar, as the curtains of Solomon.
6 Look not upon me because I am black,
because the sun hath looked upon me:
my mother's children were angry with me,
they made me the keeper of the vineyards,
but my own vineyard have I not kept.
7 Tell me, O thou whom my soul loveth, where thou feedest,
where thou makest thy flock to rest at noon:
for why should I be as one that turneth aside by the flocks of thy
companions?

8 If thou know not, O thou fairest among women,
go thy way forth by the footsteps of the flock,
and feed thy kids beside the shepherds' tents.
9 I have compared thee, O my love,
to a company of horses in Pharaoh's chariots.
10 Thy cheeks are comely with rows of jewels,
thy neck with chains of gold.
11 We will make thee borders of gold with studs of silver.

12 While the king sitteth at his table,
my spikenard sendeth forth the smell thereof.
13 A bundle of myrrh is my well-beloved unto me;
he shall lie all night betwixt my breasts.
14 My beloved is unto me as a cluster of camphire in the vineyards
of En-gedi.
15 Behold, thou art fair, my love:
behold, thou art fair, thou hast doves' eyes.
16 Behold, thou art fair, my beloved, yea, pleasant:
also our bed is green.

877

¹⁷ The beams of our house are cedar,
and our rafters of fir.

2 I am the rose of Sharon,
and the lily of the valleys.

² As the lily among thorns,
so is my love among the daughters.

³ As the apple tree among the trees of the wood,
so is my beloved among the sons.
I sat down under his shadow with great delight,
and his fruit was sweet to my taste.
⁴ He brought me to the banqueting-house,
and his banner over me was love.
⁵ Stay me with flagons, comfort me with apples,
for I am sick of love.
⁶ His left hand is under my head,
and his right hand doth embrace me.
⁷ I charge you, O ye daughters of Jerusalem,
by the roes, and by the hinds of the field,
that ye stir not up, nor awake my love, till he please.

⁸ The voice of my beloved!
behold, he cometh leaping upon the mountains,
skipping upon the hills.
⁹ My beloved is like a roe or a young hart:
behold, he standeth behind our wall,
he looketh forth at the windows,
showing himself through the lattice.
¹⁰ My beloved spoke, and said unto me,
'Rise up, my love, my fair one, and come away.
¹¹ For, lo, the winter is past,
the rain is over and gone;
¹² The flowers appear on the earth,
the time of the singing of birds is come,
and the voice of the turtle is heard in our land.
¹³ The fig tree putteth forth her green figs,
and the vines with the tender grape give a good smell.
Arise, my love, my fair one, and come away.'

¹⁴ O my dove! that art in the clefts of the rock,
in the secret places of the stairs:
let me see thy countenance, let me hear thy voice,
for sweet is thy voice, and thy countenance is comely.
¹⁵ Take us the foxes, the little foxes, that spoil the vines:
for our vines have tender grapes.

¹⁶ My beloved is mine, and I am his:
    he feedeth among the lilies.
¹⁷ Until the day break, and the shadows flee away,
    turn, my beloved, and be thou like a roe
    or a young hart upon the mountains of Bether.

3 By night on my bed I sought him whom my soul loveth.
    I sought him, but I found him not.
² I will rise now, and go about the city in the streets,
    and in the broad ways I will seek him whom my soul loveth:
    I sought him, but I found him not.
³ The watchmen that go about the city found me:
    to whom I said, 'Saw ye him whom my soul loveth?'
⁴ It was but a little that I passed from them,
    but I found him whom my soul loveth:
    I held him, and would not let him go,
    until I had brought him into my mother's house,
    and into the chamber of her that conceived me.
⁵ I charge you, O ye daughters of Jerusalem,
    by the roes, and by the hinds of the field,
    that ye stir not up, nor awake my love, till he please.

⁶ Who is this that cometh out of the wilderness like pillars of
      smoke,
    perfumed with myrrh and frankincense,
    with all powders of the merchant?
⁷ Behold his bed, which is Solomon's:
    threescore valiant men are about it, of the valiant of Israel.
⁸ They all hold swords, being expert in war:
    every man hath his sword upon his thigh
    because of fear in the night.
⁹ King Solomon made himself a chariot of the wood of Lebanon.
¹⁰ He made the pillars thereof of silver,
    the bottom thereof of gold, the covering of it of purple,
    the midst thereof being paved with love,
    for the daughters of Jerusalem.
¹¹ Go forth, O ye daughters of Zion, and behold king Solomon
    with the crown wherewith his mother crowned him in the day of
      his espousals,
    and in the day of the gladness of his heart.

4 Behold, thou art fair, my love, behold, thou art fair;
    thou hast doves' eyes within thy locks:
    thy hair is as a flock of goats, that appear from mount Gilead.
² Thy teeth are like a flock of sheep that are even shorn,
    which came up from the washing:
    whereof every one bear twins, and none is barren among them.
³ Thy lips are like a thread of scarlet, and thy speech is comely:

thy temples are like a piece of a pomegranate within thy locks.

⁴ Thy neck is like the tower of David built for an armoury,
whereon there hang a thousand bucklers,
all shields of mighty men.

⁵ Thy two breasts are like two young roes that are twins,
which feed among the lilies.

⁶ Until the day break, and the shadows flee away,
I will get me to the mountains of myrrh,
and to the hill of frankincense.

⁷ Thou art all fair, my love,
there is no spot in thee.

⁸ Come with me from Lebanon, my spouse, with me from
Lebanon:
look from the top of Amana, from the top of Shenir and
Hermon,
from the lions' dens, from the mountains of the leopards.

⁹ Thou hast ravished my heart, my sister, my spouse;
thou hast ravished my heart with one of thy eyes,
with one chain of thy neck.

¹⁰ How fair is thy love, my sister, my spouse!
how much better is thy love than wine!
and the smell of thy ointments than all spices!

¹¹ Thy lips, O my spouse! drop as the honeycomb:
honey and milk are under thy tongue,
and the smell of thy garments is like the smell of Lebanon.

¹² A garden enclosed is my sister, my spouse:
a spring shut up, a fountain sealed.

¹³ Thy plants are an orchard of pomegranates,
with pleasant fruits, camphire, with spikenard,

¹⁴ spikenard and saffron,
calamus and cinnamon,
with all trees of frankincense,
myrrh and aloes, with all the chief spices.

¹⁵ A fountain of gardens,
a well of living waters, and streams from Lebanon.

¹⁶ Awake, O north wind, and come, thou south;
blow upon my garden, that the spices thereof may flow out.
Let my beloved come into his garden,
and eat his pleasant fruits.

5 I am come into my garden, my sister, my spouse:
I have gathered my myrrh with my spice,
I have eaten my honeycomb with my honey,
I have drunk my wine with my milk:
eat, O friends, drink, yea, drink abundantly, O beloved.

2 I sleep, but my heart waketh:
  it is the voice of my beloved that knocketh, saying,
  'Open to me, my sister, my love, my dove, my undefiled:
  for my head is filled with dew,
  and my locks with the drops of the night.'
3 I have put off my coat, how shall I put it on?
  I have washed my feet, how shall I defile them?
4 My beloved put in his hand by the hole of the door,
  and my bowels were moved for him.
5 I rose up to open to my beloved,
  and my hands dropped with myrrh,
  and my fingers with sweet-smelling myrrh,
  upon the handles of the lock.
6 I opened to my beloved,
  but my beloved had withdrawn himself, and was gone:
  my soul failed when he spoke:
  I sought him, but I could not find him:
  I called him, but he gave me no answer.
7 The watchmen that went about the city found me,
  they smote me, they wounded me,
  the keepers of the walls took away my veil from me.
8 I charge you, O daughters of Jerusalem, if ye find my beloved,
  that ye tell him, that I am sick of love.

9 What is thy beloved more than another beloved,
  O thou fairest among women?
  what is thy beloved more than another beloved,
  that thou dost so charge us?

10 My beloved is white and ruddy,
   the chiefest among ten thousand.
11 His head is as the most fine gold,
   his locks are bushy, and black as a raven.
12 His eyes are as the eyes of doves by the rivers of water,
   washed with milk, and fitly set.
13 His cheeks are as a bed of spices, as sweet flowers:
   his lips like lilies, dropping sweet-smelling myrrh.
14 His hands are as gold rings set with the beryl:
   his belly is as bright ivory overlaid with sapphires.
15 His legs are as pillars of marble, set upon sockets of fine gold:
   his countenance is as Lebanon, excellent as the cedars.
16 His mouth is most sweet, yea, he is altogether lovely.
   This is my beloved, and this is my friend,
   O daughters of Jerusalem.

6 Whither is thy beloved gone, O thou fairest among women?
  whither is thy beloved turned aside?
  that we may seek him with thee.

² My beloved is gone down into his garden, to the beds of spices,
  to feed in the gardens, and to gather lilies.
³ I am my beloved's, and my beloved is mine:
  he feedeth among the lilies.

⁴ Thou art beautiful, O my love, as Tirzah,
  comely as Jerusalem,
  terrible as an army with banners.
⁵ Turn away thy eyes from me, for they have overcome me:
  thy hair is as a flock of goats that appear from Gilead.
⁶ Thy teeth are as a flock of sheep which go up from the washing,
  whereof every one beareth twins,
  and there is not one barren among them.
⁷ As a piece of a pomegranate are thy temples within thy locks.
⁸ There are threescore queens, and fourscore concubines,
  and virgins without number.
⁹ My dove, my undefiled is but one;
  she is the only one of her mother,
  she is the choice one of her that bore her.
  The daughters saw her, and blessed her;
  yea, the queens and the concubines, and they praised her.

¹⁰ Who is she that looketh forth as the morning,
  fair as the moon, clear as the sun,
  and terrible as an army with banners?

¹¹ I went down into the garden of nuts
  to see the fruits of the valley,
  and to see whether the vine flourished,
  and the pomegranates budded.
¹² Or ever I was aware, my soul made me like the chariots of
      Ammi-nadib.

¹³ Return, return, O Shulamite;
  return, return, that we may look upon thee.
  What will ye see in the Shulamite?
  As it were the company of two armies.

7 How beautiful are thy feet with shoes, O prince's daughter!
  the joints of thy thighs are like jewels,
  the work of the hands of a cunning workman.
² Thy navel is like a round goblet, which wanteth not liquor:
  thy belly is like a heap of wheat set about with lilies.
³ Thy two breasts are like two young roes that are twins.
⁴ Thy neck is as a tower of ivory:
  thy eyes like the fish-pools in Heshbon, by the gate of Bath-rabbim:
  thy nose is as the tower of Lebanon which looketh toward
      Damascus.

⁵ Thy head upon thee is like Carmel,
  and the hair of thy head like purple;
  the king is held in the galleries.
⁶ How fair and how pleasant art thou, O love, for delights!
⁷ This thy stature is like to a palm tree,
  and thy breasts to clusters of grapes.
⁸ I said, 'I will go up to the palm tree,
  I will take hold of the boughs thereof':
  now also thy breasts shall be as clusters of the vine,
  and the smell of thy nose like apples;
⁹ and the roof of thy mouth like the best wine for my beloved,
  that goeth down sweetly,
  causing the lips of those that are asleep to speak.

¹⁰ I am my beloved's, and his desire is towards me.
¹¹ Come, my beloved, let us go forth into the field:
  let us lodge in the villages.
¹² Let us get up early to the vineyards,
  let us see if the vine flourish,
  whether the tender grape appear,
  and the pomegranates bud forth:
  there will I give thee my loves.
¹³ The mandrakes give a smell,
  and at our gates are all manner of pleasant fruits, new and old,
  which I have laid up for thee, O my beloved.

8 O that thou wert as my brother,
  that sucked the breasts of my mother!
  when I should find thee without, I would kiss thee,
  yet I should not be despised.
² I would lead thee, and bring thee into my mother's house, who
    would instruct me:
  I would cause thee to drink of spiced wine, of the juice of my
    pomegranate.
³ His left hand should be under my head,
  and his right hand should embrace me.
⁴ I charge you, O daughters of Jerusalem, that ye stir not up,
  nor awake my love, until he please.

⁵ Who is this that cometh up from the wilderness, leaning upon
    her beloved?
  I raised thee up under the apple tree:
  there thy mother brought thee forth,
  there she brought thee forth that bore thee.

⁶ Set me as a seal upon thy heart,
  as a seal upon thy arm:
  for love is strong as death,

jealousy is cruel as the grave:
the coals thereof are coals of fire,
which hath a most vehement flame.
7 Many waters cannot quench love,
neither can the floods drown it:
if a man would give all the substance of his house for love,
it would utterly be contemned.

8 We have a little sister, and she hath no breasts:
what shall we do for our sister in the day when she shall be
spoken for?
9 If she be a wall, we will build upon her a palace of silver:
and if she be a door, we will enclose her with boards of cedar.

10 I am a wall, and my breasts like towers:
then was I in his eyes as one that found favour.
11 Solomon had a vineyard at Baal-hamon,
he let out the vineyard unto keepers:
every one for the fruit thereof was to bring a thousand pieces of
silver.
12 My vineyard, which is mine, is before me:
thou, O Solomon, must have a thousand,
and those that keep the fruit thereof two hundred.

13 Thou that dwellest in the gardens,
the companions hearken to thy voice:
cause me to hear it.

14 Make haste, my beloved,
and be thou like to a roe or to a young hart
upon the mountains of spices.

THE BOOK OF THE PROPHET
ISAIAH

1 The vision of Isaiah the son of Amoz, which he saw concerning Judah and Jerusalem in the days of Uzziah, Jotham, Ahaz, and Hezekiah, kings of Judah.

² Hear, O heavens, and give ear, O earth:
  for the LORD hath spoken,
  'I have nourished and brought up children,
  and they have rebelled against me.
³ The ox knoweth his owner, and the ass his master's crib:
  but Israel doth not know, my people doth not consider.'
⁴ Ah sinful nation, a people laden with iniquity,
  a seed of evil-doers, children that are corrupters:
  they have forsaken the LORD,
  they have provoked the Holy One of Israel unto anger,
  they are gone away backward.
⁵ Why should ye be stricken any more?
  ye will revolt more and more:
  the whole head is sick, and the whole heart faint.
⁶ From the sole of the foot even unto the head
  there is no soundness in it;
  but wounds, and bruises, and putrifying sores:
  they have not been closed,
  neither bound up, neither mollified with ointment.
⁷ Your country is desolate, your cities are burnt with fire:
  your land, strangers devour it in your presence,
  and it is desolate, as overthrown by strangers.
⁸ And the daughter of Zion is left as a cottage in a vineyard,
  as a lodge in a garden of cucumbers,
  as a besieged city.
⁹ Except the LORD of hosts had left unto us a very small remnant,
  we should have been as Sodom,
  and we should have been like unto Gomorrah.

¹⁰ Hear the word of the LORD, ye rulers of Sodom,
  give ear unto the law of our God, ye people of Gomorrah.
¹¹ 'To what purpose is the multitude of your sacrifices unto me?'
    saith the LORD:
  'I am full of the burnt offerings of rams, and the fat of fed beasts,
  and I delight not in the blood of bullocks, or of lambs, or of he-
    goats.
¹² When ye come to appear before me,
  who hath required this at your hand, to tread my courts?

¹³ Bring no more vain oblations,
incense is an abomination unto me:
the new moons and sabbaths, the calling of assemblies, I cannot
away with;
it is iniquity, even the solemn meeting.
¹⁴ Your new moons and your appointed feasts my soul hateth:
they are a trouble unto me, I am weary to bear them.
¹⁵ And when ye spread forth your hands, I will hide my eyes from
you:
yea, when ye make many prayers, I will not hear:
your hands are full of blood.

¹⁶ 'Wash ye, make you clean,
put away the evil of your doings from before my eyes,
cease to do evil, ¹⁷learn to do well,
seek judgement, relieve the oppressed,
judge the fatherless, plead for the widow.

¹⁸ 'Come now, and let us reason together,' saith the LORD:
'though your sins be as scarlet, they shall be as white as snow;
though they be red like crimson, they shall be as wool.
¹⁹ If ye be willing and obedient,
ye shall eat the good of the land.
²⁰ But if ye refuse and rebel,
ye shall be devoured with the sword':
for the mouth of the LORD hath spoken it.

²¹ How is the faithful city become a harlot?
it was full of judgement, righteousness lodged in it;
but now murderers.
²² Thy silver is become dross, thy wine mixed with water.
²³ Thy princes are rebellious, and companions of thieves:
every one loveth gifts, and followeth after rewards:
they judge not the fatherless,
neither doth the cause of the widow come unto them.

²⁴ Therefore saith the Lord,
the LORD of hosts, the mighty One of Israel,
'Ah, I will ease me of my adversaries, and avenge me of my
enemies.
²⁵ And I will turn my hand upon thee,
and purely purge away thy dross, and take away all thy tin.
²⁶ And I will restore thy judges as at the first,
and thy counsellors as at the beginning:
afterward thou shalt be called the city of righteousness, the
faithful city.'
²⁷ Zion shall be redeemed with judgement,
and her converts with righteousness.

²⁸ And the destruction of the transgressors and of the sinners shall
    be together:
  and they that forsake the LORD shall be consumed.
²⁹ For they shall be ashamed of the oaks which ye have desired
  and ye shall be confounded for the gardens that ye have chosen.
³⁰ For ye shall be as an oak whose leaf fadeth,
  and as a garden that hath no water.
³¹ And the strong shall be as tow, and the maker of it as a spark,
  and they shall both burn together, and none shall quench them.

2 The word that Isaiah the son of Amoz saw concerning Judah and
  Jerusalem.

² And it shall come to pass in the last days,
  that the mountain of the LORD's house shall be established
  in the top of the mountains,
  and shall be exalted above the hills;
  and all nations shall flow unto it.
³ And many people shall go and say,
  'Come ye, and let us go up to the mountain of the LORD,
  to the house of the God of Jacob,
  and he will teach us of his ways,
  and we will walk in his paths':
  for out of Zion shall go forth the law,
  and the word of the LORD from Jerusalem.
⁴ And he shall judge among the nations,
  and shall rebuke many people:
  and they shall beat their swords into ploughshares,
  and their spears into pruning-hooks:
  nation shall not lift up sword against nation,
  neither shall they learn war any more.
⁵ O house of Jacob, come ye,
  and let us walk in the light of the LORD.

⁶ Therefore thou hast forsaken thy people the house of Jacob,
  because they be replenished from the east,
  and are soothsayers like the Philistines,
  and they please themselves in the children of strangers.
⁷ Their land also is full of silver and gold,
  neither is there any end of their treasures:
  their land is also full of horses,
  neither is there any end of their chariots.
⁸ Their land also is full of idols:
  they worship the work of their own hands,
  that which their own fingers have made:
⁹ And the mean man boweth down,
  and the great man humbleth himself:
  therefore forgive them not.

¹⁰ Enter into the rock, and hide thee in the dust,
   for fear of the LORD, and for the glory of his majesty.
¹¹ The lofty looks of man shall be humbled,
   and the haughtiness of men shall be bowed down:
   and the LORD alone shall be exalted in that day.
¹² For the day of the LORD of hosts shall be upon every one that is
      proud and lofty,
   and upon every one that is lifted up,
   and he shall be brought low:
¹³ and upon all the cedars of Lebanon, that are high and lifted up,
   and upon all the oaks of Bashan,
¹⁴ and upon all the high mountains,
   and upon all the hills that are lifted up,
¹⁵ and upon every high tower,
   and upon every fenced wall,
¹⁶ and upon all the ships of Tarshish,
   and upon all pleasant pictures.
¹⁷ And the loftiness of man shall be bowed down,
   and the haughtiness of men shall be made low:
   and the LORD alone shall be exalted in that day.
¹⁸ And the idols he shall utterly abolish.
¹⁹ And they shall go into the holes of the rocks,
   and into the caves of the earth,
   for fear of the LORD, and for the glory of his majesty,
   when he ariseth to shake terribly the earth.
²⁰ In that day a man shall cast his idols of silver,
   and his idols of gold,
   which they made each one for himself to worship,
   to the moles and to the bats:
²¹ to go into the clefts of the rocks,
   and into the tops of the ragged rocks,
   for fear of the LORD, and for the glory of his majesty,
   when he ariseth to shake terribly the earth.
²² Cease ye from man, whose breath is in his nostrils:
   for wherein is he to be accounted of?

3 For behold, the Lord, the LORD of hosts,
   doth take away from Jerusalem and from Judah the stay and the
      staff,
   the whole stay of bread, and the whole stay of water,
² the mighty man, and the man of war,
   the judge, and the prophet, and the prudent, and the ancient,
³ the captain of fifty, and the honourable man,
   and the counsellor, and the cunning artificer, and the eloquent
      orator.
⁴ And I will give children to be their princes,
   and babes shall rule over them.
⁵ And the people shall be oppressed,

every one by another, and every one by his neighbour:
the child shall behave himself proudly against the ancient,
and the base against the honourable.

⁶ When a man shall take hold of his brother of the house of his
father, saying,
'Thou hast clothing, be thou our ruler,
and let this ruin be under thy hand':

⁷ in that day shall he swear, saying, 'I will not be a healer:
for in my house is neither bread nor clothing:
make me not a ruler of the people'.

⁸ For Jerusalem is ruined, and Judah is fallen:
because their tongue and their doings are against the LORD,
to provoke the eyes of his glory.

⁹ The show of their countenance doth witness against them,
and they declare their sin as Sodom, they hide it not.
Woe unto their soul, for they have rewarded evil unto themselves.

¹⁰ Say ye to the righteous, that it shall be well with him:
for they shall eat the fruit of their doings.

¹¹ Woe unto the wicked, it shall be ill with him:
for the reward of his hands shall be given him.

¹² As for my people, children are their oppressors,
and women rule over them.
O my people, they which lead thee cause thee to err,
and destroy the way of thy paths.

¹³ The LORD standeth up to plead,
and standeth to judge the people.

¹⁴ The LORD will enter into judgement
with the ancients of his people, and the princes thereof:
for ye have eaten up the vineyard;
the spoil of the poor is in your houses.

¹⁵ 'What mean ye that ye beat my people to pieces,
and grind the faces of the poor?' saith the Lord GOD of hosts.

¹⁶ Moreover the LORD saith,
'Because the daughters of Zion are haughty,
and walk with stretched forth necks and wanton eyes,
walking and mincing as they go,
and making a tinkling with their feet:

¹⁷ therefore the Lord will smite with a scab
the crown of the head of the daughters of Zion,
and the LORD will discover their secret parts'.

¹⁸ In that day the Lord will take away
the bravery of their tinkling ornaments about their feet,
and their cauls, and their round tires like the moon,

¹⁹ the chains, and the bracelets, and the mufflers,

²⁰ the bonnets, and the ornaments of the legs,

and the headbands, and the tablets, and the earrings,
²¹ the rings, and nose-jewels,
²² the changeable suits of apparel,
and the mantles, and the wimples, and the crisping-pins,
²³ the glasses, and the fine linen,
and the hoods, and the veils.
²⁴ And it shall come to pass, that in stead of sweet smell there shall
be stink,
and in stead of a girdle a rent;
and in stead of well set hair baldness;
and in stead of a stomacher a girding of sackcloth;
and burning in stead of beauty.
²⁵ Thy men shall fall by the sword,
and thy mighty in the war.
²⁶ And her gates shall lament and mourn;
and she being desolate shall sit upon the ground.

4 And in that day seven women shall take hold of one man, saying,
'We will eat our own bread, and wear our own apparel: only let us
be called by thy name, to take away our reproach'. ²In that day shall the
branch of the LORD be beautiful and glorious, and the fruit of the earth
shall be excellent and comely for them that are escaped of Israel. ³And it
shall come to pass, that he that is left in Zion, and he that remaineth in
Jerusalem, shall be called holy, even every one that is written among the
living in Jerusalem, ⁴when the Lord shall have washed away the filth of
the daughters of Zion, and shall have purged the blood of Jerusalem from
the midst thereof by the spirit of judgement, and by the spirit of burning. ⁵And the LORD will create upon every dwelling place of mount Zion,
and upon her assemblies, a cloud and smoke by day, and the shining of
a flaming fire by night: for upon all the glory shall be a defence. ⁶And
there shall be a tabernacle for a shadow in the daytime from the heat,
and for a place of refuge, and for a covert from storm and from rain.

5 Now will I sing to my well-beloved a song of my beloved touching
his vineyard.

My well-beloved hath a vineyard in a very fruitful hill.
² And he fenced it, and gathered out the stones thereof,
and planted it with the choicest vine,
and built a tower in the midst of it,
and also made a wine-press therein:
and he looked that it should bring forth grapes,
and it brought forth wild grapes.
³ And now, O inhabitants of Jerusalem, and men of Judah,
judge, I pray you, betwixt me and my vineyard.
⁴ What could have been done more to my vineyard,
that I have not done in it?
wherefore, when I looked that it should bring forth grapes,
brought it forth wild grapes?

⁵ And now go to; I will tell you what I will do to my vineyard:
  I will take away the hedge thereof,
  and it shall be eaten up;
  and break down the wall thereof,
  and it shall be trodden down.
⁶ And I will lay it waste:
  it shall not be pruned, nor dug,
  but there shall come up briers and thorns:
  I will also command the clouds that they rain no rain upon it.
⁷ For the vineyard of the LORD of hosts is the house of Israel,
  and the men of Judah his pleasant plant:
  and he looked for judgement, but behold oppression;
  for righteousness, but behold a cry.

⁸ Woe unto them that join house to house,
  that lay field to field, till there be no place,
  that they may be placed alone in the midst of the earth.
⁹ In my ears said the LORD of hosts,
  'Of a truth many houses shall be desolate,
  even great and fair, without inhabitant.
¹⁰ Yea, ten acres of vineyard shall yield one bath,
  and the seed of a homer shall yield an ephah.'

¹¹ Woe unto them that rise up early in the morning,
  that they may follow strong drink,
  that continue until night, till wine inflame them.
¹² And the harp, and the viol, the tabret, and pipe, and wine, are in
      their feasts:
  but they regard not the work of the LORD,
  neither consider the operation of his hands.

¹³ Therefore my people are gone into captivity,
  because they have no knowledge:
  and their honourable men are famished,
  and their multitude dried up with thirst.
¹⁴ Therefore hell hath enlarged herself,
  and opened her mouth without measure:
  and their glory, and their multitude, and their pomp,
  and he that rejoiceth, shall descend into it.
¹⁵ And the mean man shall be brought down,
  and the mighty man shall be humbled,
  and the eyes of the lofty shall be humbled.
¹⁶ But the LORD of hosts shall be exalted in judgement,
  and God that is holy shall be sanctified in righteousness.
¹⁷ Then shall the lambs feed after their manner,
  and the waste places of the fat ones shall strangers eat.
¹⁸ Woe unto them that draw iniquity with cords of vanity,
  and sin as it were with a cart rope:

¹⁹ that say, 'Let him make speed, and hasten his work,
that we may see it:
and let the counsel of the Holy One of Israel draw nigh and
come,
that we may know it'.

²⁰ Woe unto them that call evil good, and good evil,
that put darkness for light, and light for darkness,
that put bitter for sweet, and sweet for bitter.
²¹ Woe unto them that are wise in their own eyes,
and prudent in their own sight.
²² Woe unto them that are mighty to drink wine,
and men of strength to mingle strong drink:
²³ which justify the wicked for reward,
and take away the righteousness of the righteous from him.
²⁴ Therefore as the fire devoureth the stubble,
and the flame consumeth the chaff,
so their root shall be as rottenness,
and their blossom shall go up as dust:
because they have cast away the law of the LORD of hosts,
and despised the word of the Holy One of Israel.
²⁵ Therefore is the anger of the LORD kindled against his people,
and he hath stretched forth his hand against them,
and hath smitten them:
and the hills did tremble,
and their carcases were torn in the midst of the streets.
For all this his anger is not turned away,
but his hand is stretched out still.

²⁶ And he will lift up an ensign to the nations from far,
and will hiss unto them from the end of the earth:
and behold, they shall come with speed swiftly.
²⁷ None shall be weary nor stumble amongst them:
none shall slumber nor sleep,
neither shall the girdle of their loins be loosed,
nor the latchet of their shoes be broken:
²⁸ whose arrows are sharp, and all their bows bent,
their horses' hoofs shall be counted like flint,
and their wheels like a whirlwind:
²⁹ their roaring shall be like a lion,
they shall roar like young lions:
yea, they shall roar, and lay hold of the prey,
and shall carry it away safe, and none shall deliver it.
³⁰ And in that day they shall roar against them like the roaring of
the sea:
and if one look unto the land, behold darkness and sorrow,
and the light is darkened in the heavens thereof.

6 In the year that king Uzziah died I saw also the Lord sitting upon a throne, high and lifted up, and his train filled the temple. ²Above it stood the seraphims: each one had six wings; with twain he covered his face, and with twain he covered his feet, and with twain he did fly.

³And one cried unto another, and said,

> 'Holy, holy, holy, is the LORD of hosts,
> the whole earth is full of his glory'.

⁴And the posts of the door moved at the voice of him that cried, and the house was filled with smoke.

⁵Then said I, 'Woe is me; for I am undone, because I am a man of unclean lips, and I dwell in the midst of a people of unclean lips: for my eyes have seen the King, the LORD of hosts'. ⁶Then flew one of the seraphims unto me, having a live coal in his hand, which he had taken with the tongs from off the altar: ⁷and he laid it upon my mouth, and said, 'Lo, this hath touched thy lips, and thy iniquity is taken away, and thy sin purged'. ⁸Also I heard the voice of the Lord, saying, 'Whom shall I send, and who will go for us?' Then I said, 'Here am I, send me'.

⁹And he said, 'Go, and tell this people,

> '"Hear ye indeed, but understand not:
> and see ye indeed, but perceive not".

¹⁰ Make the heart of this people fat,
> and make their ears heavy, and shut their eyes:
> lest they see with their eyes, and hear with their ears,
> and understand with their heart, and convert, and be healed.'

¹¹Then said I, 'Lord, how long?' And he answered,

> 'Until the cities be wasted without inhabitant,
> and the houses without man,
> and the land be utterly desolate,
¹² and the LORD have removed men far away,
> and there be a great forsaking in the midst of the land.
¹³ But yet in it shall be a tenth,
> and it shall return, and shall be eaten:
> as a teil tree, and as an oak,
> whose substance is in them, when they cast their leaves:
> so the holy seed shall be the substance thereof.'

7 And it came to pass in the days of Ahaz the son of Jotham, the son of Uzziah, king of Judah, that Rezin the king of Syria, and Pekah the son of Remaliah, king of Israel, went up towards Jerusalem to war against it, but could not prevail against it. ²And it was told the house of David, saying, 'Syria is confederate with Ephraim': and his heart was moved, and the heart of his people, as the trees of the wood are moved with the wind. ³Then said the LORD unto Isaiah, 'Go forth now to meet

Ahaz, thou, and Shear-jashub thy son, at the end of the conduit of the upper pool in the highway of the fuller's field. ⁴And say unto him, "Take heed and be quiet: fear not, neither be faint-hearted for the two tails of these smoking fire-brands, for the fierce anger of Rezin with Syria, and of the son of Remaliah. ⁵Because Syria, Ephraim, and the son of Remaliah, have taken evil counsel against thee, saying, ⁶'Let us go up against Judah, and vex it, and let us make a breach therein for us, and set a king in the midst of it, even the son of Tabeal'."' ⁷Thus saith the Lord GOD, 'It shall not stand, neither shall it come to pass. ⁸For the head of Syria is Damascus, and the head of Damascus is Rezin; and within threescore and five years shall Ephraim be broken, that it be not a people. ⁹And the head of Ephraim is Samaria, and the head of Samaria is Remaliah's son: if ye will not believe, surely ye shall not be established.'

¹⁰Moreover the LORD spoke again unto Ahaz, saying, ¹¹'Ask thee a sign of the LORD thy God; ask it either in the depth, or in the height above'. ¹²But Ahaz said, 'I will not ask, neither will I tempt the LORD'. ¹³And he said, 'Hear ye now, O house of David; is it a small thing for you to weary men, but will ye weary my God also? ¹⁴Therefore the Lord himself shall give you a sign: behold, a virgin shall conceive and bear a son, and shall call his name Immanuel. ¹⁵Butter and honey shall he eat, that he may know to refuse the evil, and choose the good. ¹⁶For before the child shall know to refuse the evil and choose the good, the land that thou abhorrest shall be forsaken of both her kings.

¹⁷'The LORD shall bring upon thee, and upon thy people, and upon thy father's house, days that have not come, from the day that Ephraim departed from Judah; even the king of Assyria. ¹⁸And it shall come to pass in that day, that the LORD shall hiss for the fly that is in the uttermost part of the rivers of Egypt, and for the bee that is in the land of Assyria. ¹⁹And they shall come, and shall rest all of them in the desolate valleys, and in the holes of the rocks, and upon all thorns, and upon all bushes. ²⁰In the same day shall the Lord shave with a razor that is hired, namely, by them beyond the river, by the king of Assyria, the head, and the hair of the feet: and it shall also consume the beard. ²¹And it shall come to pass in that day, that a man shall nourish a young cow, and two sheep. ²²And it shall come to pass, for the abundance of milk that they shall give he shall eat butter: for butter and honey shall every one eat that is left in the land. ²³And it shall come to pass in that day, that every place shall be, where there were a thousand vines at a thousand silverlings, it shall even be for briers and thorns. ²⁴With arrows and with bows shall men come thither; because all the land shall become briers and thorns. ²⁵And on all hills that shall be dug with the mattock, there shall not come thither the fear of briers and thorns: but it shall be for the sending forth of oxen, and for the treading of lesser cattle.'

8 Moreover the LORD said unto me, 'Take thee a great roll, and write in it with a man's pen concerning Maher-shalal-hash-baz'. ²And I took unto me faithful witnesses to record, Uriah the priest, and Zechariah the son of Jeberechiah. ³And I went unto the prophetess, and she conceived, and bore a son. Then said the LORD to me, 'Call his name

Maher-shalal-hash-baz. ⁴For before the child shall have knowledge to cry, "My father, and my mother", the riches of Damascus and the spoil of Samaria shall be taken away before the king of Assyria.'

⁵The LORD spoke also unto me again, saying, ⁶'Forsomuch as this people refuseth the waters of Shiloah that go softly, and rejoice in Rezin and Remaliah's son: ⁷now therefore behold, the Lord bringeth up upon them the waters of the river, strong and many, even the king of Assyria, and all his glory: and he shall come up over all his channels, and go over all his banks. ⁸And he shall pass through Judah, he shall overflow and go over, he shall reach even to the neck; and the stretching out of his wings shall fill the breadth of thy land, O Immanuel.

⁹'Associate yourselves, O ye people, and ye shall be broken in pieces; and give ear, all ye of far countries: gird yourselves, and ye shall be broken in pieces; gird yourselves, and ye shall be broken in pieces. ¹⁰Take counsel together, and it shall come to nought: speak the word, and it shall not stand; for God is with us.'

¹¹For the LORD spoke thus to me with a strong hand, and instructed me that I should not walk in the way of this people, saying, ¹²'Say ye not, "A confederacy", to all them to whom this people shall say, "A confederacy"; neither fear ye their fear, nor be afraid. ¹³Sanctify the LORD of hosts himself, and let him be your fear, and let him be your dread. ¹⁴And he shall be for a sanctuary; but for a stone of stumbling and for a rock of offence to both the houses of Israel, for a gin and for a snare to the inhabitants of Jerusalem. ¹⁵And many among them shall stumble and fall, and be broken, and be snared, and be taken.' ¹⁶Bind up the testimony, seal the law among my disciples. ¹⁷And I will wait upon the LORD, that hideth his face from the house of Jacob, and I will look for him. ¹⁸Behold, I and the children whom the LORD hath given me are for signs and for wonders in Israel from the LORD of hosts, which dwelleth in mount Zion.

¹⁹And when they shall say unto you, 'Seek unto them that have familiar spirits, and unto wizards that peep and that mutter': should not a people seek unto their God? for the living to the dead? ²⁰to the law and to the testimony: if they speak not according to this word, it is because there is no light in them. ²¹And they shall pass through it, hardly bestead and hungry: and it shall come to pass, that when they shall be hungry, they shall fret themselves, and curse their king and their God, and look upward. ²²And they shall look unto the earth: and behold trouble and darkness, dimness of anguish; and they shall be driven to darkness.

9 ¹Nevertheless the dimness shall not be such as was in her vexation, when at the first he lightly afflicted the land of Zebulun and the land of Naphtali, and afterward did more grievously afflict her by the way of the sea, beyond Jordan, in Galilee of the nations.

² The people that walked in darkness have seen a great light
  they that dwell in the land of the shadow of death,
  upon them hath the light shone.
³ Thou hast multiplied the nation, and not increased the joy:

they joy before thee according to the joy in harvest,
and as men rejoice when they divide the spoil.
⁴ For thou hast broken the yoke of his burden, and the staff of his
shoulder,
the rod of his oppressor, as in the day of Midian.
⁵ For every battle of the warrior is with confused noise, and
garments rolled in blood;
but this shall be with burning and fuel of fire.
⁶ For unto us a child is born, unto us a son is given,
and the government shall be upon his shoulder:
and his name shall be called Wonderful, Counsellor,
The mighty God,
The everlasting Father,
The Prince of peace.
⁷ Of the increase of his government and peace there shall be no end,
upon the throne of David and upon his kingdom,
to order it, and to establish it with judgement and with justice,
from henceforth even for ever:
the zeal of the LORD of hosts will perform this.

⁸ The Lord sent a word into Jacob,
and it hath lighted upon Israel.
⁹ And all the people shall know,
even Ephraim and the inhabitant of Samaria,
that say in the pride and stoutness of heart,
¹⁰ 'The bricks are fallen down, but we will build with hewn stones:
the sycamores are cut down, but we will change them into
cedars'.
¹¹ Therefore the LORD shall set up the adversaries of Rezin against
him,
and join his enemies together;
¹² the Syrians before, and the Philistines behind,
and they shall devour Israel with open mouth:
for all this his anger is not turned away,
but his hand is stretched out still.

¹³ For the people turneth not unto him that smiteth them,
neither do they seek the LORD of hosts.
¹⁴ Therefore the LORD will cut off from Israel head and tail,
branch and rush, in one day.
¹⁵ The ancient and honourable, he is the head:
and the prophet that teacheth lies, he is the tail.
¹⁶ For the leaders of this people cause them to err,
and they that are led of them are destroyed.
¹⁷ Therefore the Lord shall have no joy in their young men,
neither shall have mercy on their fatherless and widows:
for every one is a hypocrite and an evil-doer,
and every mouth speaketh folly:

for all this his anger is not turned away,
but his hand is stretched out still.

¹⁸ For wickedness burneth as the fire:
it shall devour the briers and thorns,
and shall kindle in the thickets of the forest,
and they shall mount up like the lifting up of smoke.
¹⁹ Through the wrath of the LORD of hosts is the land darkened,
and the people shall be as the fuel of the fire:
no man shall spare his brother.
²⁰ And he shall snatch on the right hand, and be hungry,
and he shall eat on the left hand, and they shall not be satisfied:
they shall eat every man the flesh of his own arm:
²¹ Manasseh, Ephraim; and Ephraim, Manasseh:
and they together shall be against Judah:
for all this his anger is not turned away,
but his hand is stretched out still.

10 Woe unto them that decree unrighteous decrees,
and that write grievousness which they have prescribed:
² to turn aside the needy from judgement,
and to take away the right from the poor of my people,
that widows may be their prey,
and that they may rob the fatherless.
³ And what will ye do in the day of visitation,
and in the desolation which shall come from far?
to whom will ye flee for help?
and where will ye leave your glory?
⁴ Without me they shall bow down under the prisoners,
and they shall fall under the slain:
for all this his anger is not turned away,
but his hand is stretched out still.

⁵ O Assyrian, the rod of my anger,
and the staff in their hand is my indignation.
⁶ I will send him against a hypocritical nation,
and against the people of my wrath will I give him a charge
to take the spoil, and to take the prey,
and to tread them down like the mire of the streets.
⁷ Howbeit he meaneth not so,
neither doth his heart think so,
but it is in his heart to destroy
and cut off nations not a few.
⁸ For he saith, 'Are not my princes altogether kings?
⁹ Is not Calno as Carchemish?
is not Hamath as Arpad?
is not Samaria as Damascus?
¹⁰ As my hand hath found the kingdoms of the idols,

and whose graven images did excel them of Jerusalem and of
Samaria:
11 shall I not, as I have done unto Samaria and her idols,
so do to Jerusalem and her idols?'

12 Wherefore it shall come to pass,
that when the Lord hath performed his whole work upon mount
Zion and on Jerusalem,
I will punish the fruit of the stout heart of the king of Assyria,
and the glory of his high looks.
13 For he saith, 'By the strength of my hand I have done it,
and by my wisdom; for I am prudent:
and I have removed the bounds of the people,
and have robbed their treasures,
and I have put down the inhabitants like a valiant man.
14 And my hand hath found as a nest the riches of the people:
and as one gathereth eggs that are left,
have I gathered all the earth,
and there was none that moved the wing,
or opened the mouth, or peeped.'
15 Shall the axe boast itself against him that heweth therewith?
or shall the saw magnify itself against him that shaketh it?
as if the rod should shake itself against them that lift it up,
or as if the staff should lift up itself, as if it were no wood.
16 Therefore shall the Lord, the Lord of hosts,
send among his fat ones leanness,
and under his glory he shall kindle a burning
like the burning of a fire.
17 And the light of Israel shall be for a fire,
and his Holy One for a flame:
and it shall burn and devour his thorns and his briers in one day:
18 and shall consume the glory of his forest,
and of his fruitful field, both soul and body:
and they shall be as when a standard-bearer fainteth.
19 And the rest of the trees of his forest shall be few,
that a child may write them.

20 And it shall come to pass in that day, that the remnant of Israel,
and such as are escaped of the house of Jacob,
shall no more again stay upon him that smote them:
but shall stay upon the LORD, the Holy One of Israel, in truth.
21 The remnant shall return, even the remnant of Jacob,
unto the mighty God.
22 For though thy people Israel be as the sand of the sea,
yet a remnant of them shall return:
the consumption decreed shall overflow with righteousness.
23 For the Lord GOD of hosts shall make a consumption,
even determined in the midst of all the land.

²⁴ Therefore thus saith the Lord GOD of hosts,
'O my people that dwellest in Zion, be not afraid of the
Assyrian:
he shall smite thee with a rod,
and shall lift up his staff against thee,
after the manner of Egypt.
²⁵ For yet a very little while, and the indignation shall cease,
and my anger in their destruction.'
²⁶ And the LORD of hosts shall stir up a scourge for him
according to the slaughter of Midian at the rock Oreb:
and as his rod was upon the sea,
so shall he lift it up after the manner of Egypt.
²⁷ And it shall come to pass in that day,
that his burden shall be taken away from off thy shoulder,
and his yoke from off thy neck,
and the yoke shall be destroyed because of the anointing.

²⁸ He is come to Aiath, he is passed to Migron:
at Michmash he hath laid up his carriages.
²⁹ They are gone over the passage:
they have taken up their lodging at Geba,
Ramah is afraid, Gibeah of Saul is fled.
³⁰ Lift up thy voice, O daughter of Gallim:
cause it to be heard unto Laish, O poor Anathoth.
³¹ Madmenah is removed,
the inhabitants of Gebim gather themselves to flee.
³² As yet shall he remain at Nob that day:
he shall shake his hand against the mount of the daughter of
Zion,
the hill of Jerusalem.
³³ Behold, the Lord, the LORD of hosts, shall lop the bough with
terror:
and the high ones of stature shall be hewn down,
and the haughty shall be humbled.
³⁴ And he shall cut down the thickets of the forests with iron,
and Lebanon shall fall by a mighty one.

11 And there shall come forth a rod out of the stem of Jesse,
and a branch shall grow out of his roots.
² And the Spirit of the LORD shall rest upon him,
the spirit of wisdom and understanding,
the spirit of counsel and might,
the spirit of knowledge and of the fear of the LORD:
³ and shall make him of quick understanding in the fear of the
LORD:
and he shall not judge after the sight of his eyes,
neither reprove after the hearing of his ears.
⁴ But with righteousness shall he judge the poor,

and reprove with equity for the meek of the earth:
and he shall smite the earth with the rod of his mouth,
and with the breath of his lips shall he slay the wicked.

⁵ And righteousness shall be the girdle of his loins,
and faithfulness the girdle of his reins.

⁶ The wolf also shall dwell with the lamb,
and the leopard shall lie down with the kid:
and the calf and the young lion and the fatling together,
and a little child shall lead them.

⁷ And the cow and the bear shall feed,
their young ones shall lie down together:
and the lion shall eat straw like the ox.

⁸ And the sucking child shall play on the hole of the asp,
and the weaned child shall put his hand on the cockatrice's den.

⁹ They shall not hurt nor destroy in all my holy mountain:
for the earth shall be full of the knowledge of the LORD,
as the waters cover the sea.

¹⁰ And in that day there shall be a root of Jesse,
which shall stand for an ensign of the people;
to it shall the Gentiles seek,
and his rest shall be glorious.

¹¹ And it shall come to pass in that day,
that the Lord shall set his hand again
the second time to recover the remnant of his people which shall
     be left,
from Assyria, and from Egypt, and from Pathros,
and from Cush, and from Elam, and from Shinar,
and from Hamath, and from the islands of the sea.

¹² And he shall set up an ensign for the nations,
and shall assemble the outcasts of Israel,
and gather together the dispersed of Judah
from the four corners of the earth.

¹³ The envy also of Ephraim shall depart,
and the adversaries of Judah shall be cut off:
Ephraim shall not envy Judah,
and Judah shall not vex Ephraim.

¹⁴ But they shall fly upon the shoulders of the Philistines toward
     the west,
they shall spoil them of the east together:
they shall lay their hand upon Edom and Moab,
and the children of Ammon shall obey them.

¹⁵ And the LORD shall utterly destroy the tongue of the Egyptian
     sea,
and with his mighty wind shall he shake his hand over the river,
and shall smite it in the seven streams,
and make men go over dry-shod.

¹⁶ And there shall be a highway for the remnant of his people,

which shall be left from Assyria;
like as it was to Israel in the day that he came up out of the land
    of Egypt.

12 And in that day thou shalt say,
    'O LORD, I will praise thee:
though thou wast angry with me,
thy anger is turned away, and thou comfortedst me.
² Behold, God is my salvation:
I will trust, and not be afraid:
for the LORD JEHOVAH is my strength and my song,
he also is become my salvation.'
³ Therefore with joy shall ye draw water
out of the wells of salvation.
⁴ And in that day shall ye say,
'Praise the LORD, call upon his name,
declare his doings among the people,
make mention that his name is exalted.
⁵ Sing unto the LORD,
for he hath done excellent things:
this is known in all the earth.
⁶ Cry out and shout, thou inhabitant of Zion:
for great is the Holy One of Israel in the midst of thee.'

13 The burden of Babylon, which Isaiah the son of Amoz did see.

² Lift ye up a banner upon the high mountain,
exalt the voice unto them, shake the hand,
that they may go into the gates of the nobles.
³ I have commanded my sanctified ones:
I have also called my mighty ones for my anger,
even them that rejoice in my highness.
⁴ The noise of a multitude in the mountains, like as of a great
    people:
a tumultuous noise of the kingdoms of nations gathered
    together:
the LORD of hosts mustereth the host of the battle.
⁵ They come from a far country, from the end of heaven,
even the LORD and the weapons of his indignation,
to destroy the whole land.

⁶ Howl ye; for the day of the LORD is at hand;
it shall come as a destruction from the Almighty.
⁷ Therefore shall all hands be faint,
and every man's heart shall melt.
⁸ And they shall be afraid:
pangs and sorrows shall take hold of them,
they shall be in pain as a woman that travaileth:

they shall be amazed one at another,
their faces shall be as flames.

⁹ Behold, the day of the LORD cometh,
cruel both with wrath and fierce anger,
to lay the land desolate:
and he shall destroy the sinners thereof out of it.

¹⁰ For the stars of heaven and the constellations thereof shall not
give their light:
the sun shall be darkened in his going forth,
and the moon shall not cause her light to shine.

¹¹ And I will punish the world for their evil,
and the wicked for their iniquity;
and I will cause the arrogance of the proud to cease,
and will lay low the haughtiness of the terrible.

¹² I will make a man more precious than fine gold;
even a man than the golden wedge of Ophir.

¹³ Therefore I will shake the heavens,
and the earth shall remove out of her place,
in the wrath of the LORD of hosts,
and in the day of his fierce anger.

¹⁴ And it shall be as the chased roe,
and as a sheep that no man taketh up:
they shall every man turn to his own people,
and flee every one into his own land.

¹⁵ Every one that is found shall be thrust through:
and every one that is joined unto them shall fall by the sword.

¹⁶ Their children also shall be dashed to pieces before their eyes,
their houses shall be spoiled, and their wives ravished.

¹⁷ Behold, I will stir up the Medes against them,
which shall not regard silver,
and as for gold, they shall not delight in it.

¹⁸ Their bows also shall dash the young men to pieces,
and they shall have no pity on the fruit of the womb;
their eye shall not spare children.

¹⁹ And Babylon, the glory of kingdoms,
the beauty of the Chaldees' excellence,
shall be as when God overthrew Sodom and Gomorrah.

²⁰ It shall never be inhabited,
neither shall it be dwelt in from generation to generation:
neither shall the Arabian pitch tent there,
neither shall the shepherds make their fold there.

²¹ But wild beasts of the desert shall lie there,
and their houses shall be full of doleful creatures,
and owls shall dwell there,
and satyrs shall dance there.

²² And the wild beasts of the islands shall cry in their desolate
houses,

and dragons in their pleasant palaces:
and her time is near to come,
and her days shall not be prolonged.

14 For the LORD will have mercy on Jacob, and will yet choose Israel, and set them in their own land: and the strangers shall be joined with them, and they shall cleave to the house of Jacob. ²And the people shall take them, and bring them to their place: and the house of Israel shall possess them in the land of the LORD for servants and handmaids: and they shall take them captives, whose captives they were, and they shall rule over their oppressors. ³And it shall come to pass in the day that the LORD shall give thee rest from thy sorrow, and from thy fear, and from the hard bondage wherein thou wast made to serve, ⁴that thou shalt take up this proverb against the king of Babylon, and say,

'How hath the oppressor ceased? the golden city ceased?
⁵ The LORD hath broken the staff of the wicked,
and the sceptre of the rulers.
⁶ He who smote the people in wrath with a continual stroke,
he that ruled the nations in anger,
is persecuted, and none hindereth.
⁷ The whole earth is at rest, and is quiet:
they break forth into singing.
⁸ Yea, the fir trees rejoice at thee,
and the cedars of Lebanon, saying,
"Since thou art laid down, no feller is come up against us".
⁹ Hell from beneath is moved for thee to meet thee at thy coming:
it stirreth up the dead for thee, even all the chief ones of the
earth;
it hath raised up from their thrones all the kings of the nations.
¹⁰ All they shall speak and say unto thee,
"Art thou also become weak as we?
art thou become like unto us?"
¹¹ Thy pomp is brought down to the grave,
and the noise of thy viols:
the worm is spread under thee,
and the worms cover thee.
¹² How art thou fallen from heaven,
O Lucifer, son of the morning?
how art thou cut down to the ground,
which didst weaken the nations?
¹³ For thou hast said in thy heart,
"I will ascend into heaven,
I will exalt my throne above the stars of God:
I will sit also upon the mount of the congregation,
in the sides of the north.
¹⁴ I will ascend above the heights of the clouds,
I will be like the most High."

¹⁵ Yet thou shalt be brought down to hell,
  to the sides of the pit.
¹⁶ They that see thee shall narrowly look upon thee,
  and consider thee, saying,
  "Is this the man that made the earth to tremble,
  that did shake kingdoms?
¹⁷ that made the world as a wilderness,
  and destroyed the cities thereof;
  that opened not the house of his prisoners?"
¹⁸ All the kings of the nations,
  even all of them, lie in glory,
  every one in his own house.
¹⁹ But thou art cast out of thy grave like an abominable branch
  and as the raiment of those that are slain, thrust through with a
    sword,
  that go down to the stones of the pit, as a carcase trodden under
    feet.
²⁰ Thou shalt not be joined with them in burial,
  because thou hast destroyed thy land, and slain thy people:
  the seed of evil-doers shall never be renowned.
²¹ Prepare slaughter for his children for the iniquity of their
    fathers,
  that they do not rise nor possess the land,
  nor fill the face of the world with cities.'

²²'For I will rise up against them,' saith the Lord of hosts, 'and cut off
from Babylon the name, and remnant, and son, and nephew,' saith the
Lord. ²³'I will also make it a possession for the bittern, and pools of
water: and I will sweep it with the besom of destruction,' saith the Lord
of hosts.

²⁴ The Lord of hosts hath sworn, saying,
  'Surely as I have thought, so shall it come to pass;
  and as I have purposed, so shall it stand:
²⁵ that I will break the Assyrian in my land,
  and upon my mountains tread him under foot:
  then shall his yoke depart from off them,
  and his burden depart from off their shoulders.
²⁶ This is the purpose that is purposed upon the whole earth:
  and this is the hand that is stretched out upon all the nations.
²⁷ For the Lord of hosts hath purposed,
  and who shall disannul it?
  and his hand is stretched out,
  and who shall turn it back?'

²⁸In the year that king Ahaz died was this burden.

²⁹ Rejoice not thou, whole Palestina,
because the rod of him that smote thee is broken:
for out of the serpent's root shall come forth a cockatrice,
and his fruit shall be a fiery flying serpent.
³⁰ And the firstborn of the poor shall feed,
and the needy shall lie down in safety:
and I will kill thy root with famine,
and he shall slay thy remnant.
³¹ Howl, O gate, cry, O city,
thou, whole Palestina, art dissolved,
for there shall come from the north a smoke,
and none shall be alone in his appointed times.
³² What shall one then answer the messengers of the nation?
that the LORD hath founded Zion,
and the poor of his people shall trust in it.

15

The burden of Moab.

Because in the night Ar of Moab is laid waste, and brought to
silence;
because in the night Kir of Moab is laid waste, and brought to
silence:
² he is gone up to Bajith, and to Dibon, the high places, to weep:
Moab shall howl over Nebo, and over Medeba,
on all their heads shall be baldness, and every beard cut off.
³ In their streets they shall gird themselves with sackcloth:
on the tops of their houses, and in their streets,
every one shall howl, weeping abundantly.
⁴ And Heshbon shall cry, and Elealeh:
their voice shall be heard even unto Jahaz:
therefore the armed soldiers of Moab shall cry out;
his life shall be grievous unto him.
⁵ My heart shall cry out for Moab,
his fugitives shall flee unto Zoar, a heifer of three years old:
for by the mounting up of Luhith with weeping shall they go it up:
for in the way of Horonaim they shall raise up a cry of destruction.
⁶ For the waters of Nimrim shall be desolate:
for the hay is withered away,
the grass faileth,
there is no green thing.
⁷ Therefore the abundance they have gotten,
and that which they have laid up,
shall they carry away to the brook of the willows.
⁸ For the cry is gone round about the borders of Moab:
the howling thereof unto Eglaim,
and the howling thereof unto Beer-elim.
⁹ For the waters of Dimon shall be full of blood:
for I will bring more upon Dimon,

lions upon him that escapeth of Moab,
and upon the remnant of the land.

16 Send ye the lamb to the ruler of the land
from Sela to the wilderness,
unto the mount of the daughter of Zion.
² For it shall be that, as a wandering bird cast out of the nest,
so the daughters of Moab shall be at the fords of Arnon.
³ Take counsel, execute judgement,
make thy shadow as the night in the midst of the noonday,
hide the outcasts, bewray not him that wandereth.
⁴ Let my outcasts dwell with thee, Moab,
be thou a covert to them from the face of the spoiler:
for the extortioner is at an end, the spoiler ceaseth,
the oppressors are consumed out of the land.
⁵ And in mercy shall the throne be established:
and he shall sit upon it in truth in the tabernacle of David,
judging, and seeking judgement, and hasting righteousness.

⁶ We have heard of the pride of Moab (he is very proud):
even of his haughtiness, and his pride, and his wrath:
but his lies shall not be so.
⁷ Therefore shall Moab howl for Moab,
every one shall howl:
for the foundations of Kir-hareseth shall ye mourn;
surely they are stricken.
⁸ For the fields of Heshbon languish, and the vine of Sibmah:
the lords of the heathen have broken down the principal plants
thereof,
they are come even unto Jazer,
they wandered through the wilderness:
her branches are stretched out,
they are gone over the sea.
⁹ Therefore I will bewail with the weeping of Jazer the vine of
Sibmah:
I will water thee with my tears, O Heshbon, and Elealeh:
for the shouting for thy summer fruits and for thy harvest is fallen.
¹⁰ And gladness is taken away, and joy out of the plentiful field,
and in the vineyards there shall be no singing,
neither shall there be shouting:
the treaders shall tread out no wine in their presses;
I have made their vintage-shouting to cease.
¹¹ Wherefore my bowels shall sound like a harp for Moab,
and my inward parts for Kir-haresh.
¹² And it shall come to pass,
when it is seen that Moab is weary on the high place,
that he shall come to his sanctuary to pray:
but he shall not prevail.

¹³This is the word that the Lord hath spoken concerning Moab since that time. ¹⁴But now the Lord hath spoken, saying, 'Within three years, as the years of a hireling, and the glory of Moab shall be contemned, with all that great multitude; and the remnant shall be very small and feeble'.

17 The burden of Damascus.

'Behold, Damascus is taken away from being a city,
and it shall be a ruinous heap.
² The cities of Aroer are forsaken:
they shall be for flocks, which shall lie down,
and none shall make them afraid.
³ The fortress also shall cease from Ephraim,
and the kingdom from Damascus, and the remnant of Syria:
they shall be as the glory of the children of Israel,' saith the Lord
of hosts.

⁴ 'And in that day it shall come to pass,
that the glory of Jacob shall be made thin,
and the fatness of his flesh shall wax lean.
⁵ And it shall be as when the harvestman gathereth the corn,
and reapeth the ears with his arm;
and it shall be as he that gathereth ears in the valley of Rephaim.
⁶ Yet gleaning grapes shall be left in it, as the shaking of an olive
tree,
two or three berries in the top of the uppermost bough,
four or five in the outmost fruitful branches thereof,' saith the
Lord God of Israel.

⁷ At that day shall a man look to his Maker,
and his eyes shall have respect to the Holy One of Israel.
⁸ And he shall not look to the altars, the work of his hands,
neither shall respect that which his fingers have made,
either the groves or the images.

⁹ In that day shall his strong cities be as a forsaken bough,
and an uppermost branch, which they left because of the
children of Israel:
and there shall be desolation.
¹⁰ Because thou hast forgotten the God of thy salvation,
and hast not been mindful of the rock of thy strength,
therefore shalt thou plant pleasant plants,
and shalt set it with strange slips.
¹¹ In the day shalt thou make thy plant to grow,
and in the morning shalt thou make thy seed to flourish:
but the harvest shall be a heap in the day of grief
and of desperate sorrow.

¹² Woe to the multitude of many people,
    which make a noise like the noise of the seas;
    and to the rushing of nations,
    that make a rushing like the rushing of mighty waters.
¹³ The nations shall rush like the rushing of many waters:
    but God shall rebuke them, and they shall flee far off,
    and shall be chased as the chaff of the mountains before the wind,
    and like a rolling thing before the whirlwind.
¹⁴ And behold at evening-tide trouble,
    and before the morning he is not:
    this is the portion of them that spoil us,
    and the lot of them that rob us.

18

Woe to the land shadowing with wings,
    which is beyond the rivers of Ethiopia:
² that sendeth ambassadors by the sea,
    even in vessels of bulrushes upon the waters, saying,
    'Go, ye swift messengers, to a nation scattered and peeled,
    to a people terrible from their beginning hitherto,
    a nation meted out and trodden down;
    whose land the rivers have spoiled.
³ All ye inhabitants of the world, and dwellers on the earth,
    see ye, when he lifteth up an ensign on the mountains;
    and when he bloweth a trumpet, hear ye.'
⁴ For so the LORD said unto me,
    'I will take my rest, and I will consider in my dwelling place
    like a clear heat upon herbs,
    and like a cloud of dew in the heat of harvest'.
⁵ For afore the harvest, when the bud is perfect,
    and the sour grape is ripening in the flower,
    he shall both cut off the sprigs with pruning-hooks,
    and take away and cut down the branches.
⁶ They shall be left together unto the fowls of the mountains,
    and to the beasts of the earth:
    and the fowls shall summer upon them,
    and all the beasts of the earth shall winter upon them.

⁷ In that time shall the present be brought unto the LORD of hosts
    of a people scattered and peeled,
    and from a people terrible from their beginning hitherto;
    a nation meted out and trodden under foot,
    whose land the rivers have spoiled,
    to the place of the name of the LORD of hosts, the mount Zion.

19

The burden of Egypt.

Behold, the LORD rideth upon a swift cloud,
    and shall come into Egypt,

and the idols of Egypt shall be moved at his presence,
and the heart of Egypt shall melt in the midst of it.
² 'And I will set the Egyptians against the Egyptians:
and they shall fight every one against his brother,
and every one against his neighbour;
city against city, and kingdom against kingdom.
³ And the spirit of Egypt shall fail in the midst thereof;
and I will destroy the counsel thereof:
and they shall seek to the idols, and to the charmers,
and to them that have familiar spirits, and to the wizards.
⁴ And the Egyptians will I give over into the hand of a cruel lord;
and a fierce king shall rule over them,'
saith the Lord, the LORD of hosts.
⁵ And the waters shall fail from the sea,
and the river shall be wasted and dried up.
⁶ And they shall turn the rivers far away,
and the brooks of defence shall be emptied and dried up:
the reeds and flags shall wither.
⁷ The paper-reeds by the brooks, by the mouth of the brooks,
and everything sown by the brooks shall wither,
be driven away, and be no more.
⁸ The fishers also shall mourn,
and all they that cast angle into the brooks shall lament,
and they that spread nets upon the waters shall languish.
⁹ Moreover they that work in fine flax,
and they that weave networks shall be confounded.
¹⁰ And they shall be broken in the purposes thereof,
all that make sluices and ponds for fish.

¹¹ Surely the princes of Zoan are fools,
the counsel of the wise counsellors of Pharaoh is become brutish:
how say ye unto Pharaoh,
'I am the son of the wise, the son of ancient kings'?
¹² Where are they? where are thy wise men?
and let them tell thee now, and let them know
what the LORD of hosts hath purposed upon Egypt.
¹³ The princes of Zoan are become fools,
the princes of Noph are deceived;
they have also seduced Egypt, even they that are the stay of the
tribes thereof.
¹⁴ The LORD hath mingled a perverse spirit in the midst thereof:
and they have caused Egypt to err in every work thereof,
as a drunken man staggereth in his vomit.
¹⁵ Neither shall there be any work for Egypt,
which the head or tail, branch or rush may do.

¹⁶ In that day shall Egypt be like unto women: and it shall be afraid and
fear because of the shaking of the hand of the LORD of hosts, which he

shaketh over it. [17]And the land of Judah shall be a terror unto Egypt, every one that maketh mention thereof shall be afraid in himself, because of the counsel of the LORD of hosts, which he hath determined against it.

[18]In that day shall five cities in the land of Egypt speak the language of Canaan, and swear to the LORD of hosts: one shall be called, The city of destruction. [19]In that day shall there be an altar to the LORD in the midst of the land of Egypt, and a pillar at the border thereof to the LORD. [20]And it shall be for a sign and for a witness unto the LORD of hosts in the land of Egypt: for they shall cry unto the LORD because of the oppressors, and he shall send them a saviour, and a great one, and he shall deliver them. [21]And the LORD shall be known to Egypt, and the Egyptians shall know the LORD in that day, and shall do sacrifice and oblation, yea, they shall vow a vow unto the LORD, and perform it. [22]And the LORD shall smite Egypt: he shall smite and heal it: and they shall return even to the LORD, and he shall be entreated of them, and shall heal them.

[23]In that day shall there be a highway out of Egypt to Assyria, and the Assyrian shall come into Egypt, and the Egyptian into Assyria, and the Egyptians shall serve with the Assyrians. [24]In that day shall Israel be the third with Egypt and with Assyria, even a blessing in the midst of the land: [25]whom the LORD of hosts shall bless, saying, 'Blessed be Egypt my people, and Assyria the work of my hands, and Israel my inheritance'.

20 In the year that Tartan came unto Ashdod (when Sargon the king of Assyria sent him), and fought against Ashdod, and took it: [2]at the same time spoke the LORD by Isaiah the son of Amoz, saying, 'Go and loose the sackcloth from off thy loins, and put off thy shoe from thy foot'. And he did so, walking naked and barefoot. [3]And the LORD said, 'Like as my servant Isaiah hath walked naked and barefoot three years for a sign and wonder upon Egypt and upon Ethiopia: [4]so shall the king of Assyria lead away the Egyptians prisoners, and the Ethiopians captives, young and old, naked and barefoot, even with their buttocks uncovered, to the shame of Egypt. [5]And they shall be afraid and ashamed of Ethiopia their expectation, and of Egypt their glory. [6]And the inhabitant of this isle shall say in that day, "Behold, such is our expectation, whither we flee for help to be delivered from the king of Assyria: and how shall we escape?"'

21 The burden of the desert of the sea.

As whirlwinds in the south pass through;
so it cometh from the desert, from a terrible land.
[2] A grievous vision is declared unto me;
the treacherous dealer dealeth treacherously,
and the spoiler spoileth.
Go up, O Elam: besiege, O Media:
all the sighing thereof have I made to cease.
[3] Therefore are my loins filled with pain:

pangs have taken hold upon me,
as the pangs of a woman that travaileth:
I was bowed down at the hearing of it,
I was dismayed at the seeing of it.

4 My heart panted, fearfulness affrighted me:
the night of my pleasure hath he turned into fear unto me.

5 Prepare the table, watch in the watch-tower, eat, drink:
arise, ye princes, and anoint the shield.

6 For thus hath the Lord said unto me,
'Go, set a watchman,
let him declare what he seeth'.

7 And he saw a chariot with a couple of horsemen,
a chariot of asses, and a chariot of camels;
and he hearkened diligently with much heed.

8 And he cried, 'A lion:
my lord, I stand continually upon the watch-tower in the
daytime,
and I am set in my ward whole nights.

9 And behold, here cometh a chariot of men, with a couple of
horsemen.'
And he answered and said,
'Babylon is fallen, is fallen,
and all the graven images of her gods
he hath broken unto the ground'.

10 O my threshing, and the corn of my floor:
that which I have heard of the LORD of hosts, the God of Israel,
have I declared unto you.

11 The burden of Dumah.

He calleth to me out of Seir,
'Watchman, what of the night?
Watchman, what of the night?'

12 The watchman said, 'The morning cometh, and also the night:
if ye will inquire, inquire ye: return, come'.

13 The burden upon Arabia.

In the forest in Arabia shall ye lodge,
O ye travelling companies of Dedanim.

14 The inhabitants of the land of Tema brought water to him that
was thirsty,
they prevented with their bread him that fled.

15 For they fled from the swords,
from the drawn sword, and from the bent bow,
and from the grievousness of war.

16 For thus hath the Lord said unto me,
'Within a year, according to the years of a hireling,

and all the glory of Kedar shall fail.
¹⁷ And the residue of the number of archers,
the mighty men of the children of Kedar shall be diminished':
for the Lord God of Israel hath spoken it.

22

The burden of the valley of vision.

What aileth thee now,
that thou art wholly gone up to the house-tops?
² Thou that art full of stirs,
a tumultuous city, a joyous city:
thy slain men are not slain with the sword,
nor dead in battle.
³ All thy rulers are fled together,
they are bound by the archers:
all that are found in thee are bound together,
which have fled from far.
⁴ Therefore said I, 'Look away from me,
I will weep bitterly, labour not to comfort me,
because of the spoiling of the daughter of my people'.
⁵ For it is a day of trouble, and of treading down,
and of perplexity by the Lord God of hosts in the valley of vision,
breaking down the walls,
and of crying to the mountains.
⁶ And Elam bore the quiver with chariots of men and horsemen,
and Kir uncovered the shield.
⁷ And it shall come to pass, that thy choicest valleys shall be full of
chariots,
and the horsemen shall set themselves in array at the gate.

⁸ And he discovered the covering of Judah,
and thou didst look in that day to the armour of the house of the
forest.
⁹ Ye have seen also the breaches of the city of David, that they are
many:
and ye gathered together the waters of the lower pool.
¹⁰ And ye have numbered the houses of Jerusalem,
and the houses have ye broken down to fortify the wall.
¹¹ Ye made also a ditch between the two walls for the water of the
old pool:
but ye have not looked unto the maker thereof,
neither had respect unto him that fashioned it long ago.
¹² And in that day did the Lord God of hosts call
to weeping, and to mourning,
and to baldness, and to girding with sackcloth.
¹³ And behold joy and gladness,
slaying oxen, and killing sheep,
eating flesh, and drinking wine:

let us eat and drink, for tomorrow we shall die.

[14] And it was revealed in my ears by the LORD of hosts,
'Surely this iniquity shall not be purged from you till ye die,'
saith the Lord GOD of hosts.

[15] Thus saith the Lord GOD of hosts, 'Go, get thee unto this treasurer, even unto Shebna, which is over the house, and say,

[16] '"What hast thou here? and whom hast thou here,
that thou hast hewn thee out a sepulchre here,
as he that heweth him out a sepulchre on high,
and that graveth a habitation for himself in a rock?
[17] Behold, the LORD will carry thee away with a mighty captivity,
and will surely cover thee.
[18] He will surely violently turn and toss thee
like a ball into a large country:
there shalt thou die,
and there the chariots of thy glory shall be the shame of thy
lord's house.
[19] And I will drive thee from thy station,
and from thy state shall he pull thee down."

[20] 'And it shall come to pass in that day,
that I will call my servant Eliakim the son of Hilkiah:
[21] and I will clothe him with thy robe,
and strengthen him with thy girdle,
and I will commit thy government into his hand,
and he shall be a father to the inhabitants of Jerusalem,
and to the house of Judah.
[22] And the key of the house of David will I lay upon his shoulder:
so he shall open, and none shall shut,
and he shall shut, and none shall open.
[23] And I will fasten him as a nail in a sure place,
and he shall be for a glorious throne to his father's house.
[24] And they shall hang upon him all the glory of his father's house,
the offspring and the issue,
all vessels of small quantity,
from the vessels of cups, even to all the vessels of flagons.
[25] In that day,' saith the LORD of hosts,
'shall the nail that is fastened in the sure place be removed,
and be cut down, and fall:
and the burden that was upon it shall be cut off:
for the LORD hath spoken it.'

23 The burden of Tyre.

Howl, ye ships of Tarshish,
for it is laid waste,

so that there is no house, no entering in:
from the land of Chittim it is revealed to them.
² Be still, ye inhabitants of the isle,
thou whom the merchants of Zidon, that pass over the sea, have
   replenished.
³ And by great waters the seed of Sihor,
the harvest of the river, is her revenue,
and she is a mart of nations.
⁴ Be thou ashamed, O Zidon:
for the sea hath spoken, even the strength of the sea, saying,
'I travail not, nor bring forth children,
neither do I nourish up young men,
nor bring up virgins'.
⁵ As at the report concerning Egypt,
so shall they be sorely pained at the report of Tyre.
⁶ Pass ye over to Tarshish,
howl, ye inhabitants of the isle.
⁷ Is this your joyous city, whose antiquity is of ancient days?
her own feet shall carry her afar off to sojourn.
⁸ Who hath taken this counsel against Tyre, the crowning city,
whose merchants are princes,
whose traffickers are the honourable of the earth?
⁹ The LORD of hosts hath purposed it,
to stain the pride of all glory,
and to bring into contempt all the honourable of the earth.
¹⁰ Pass through thy land as a river, O daughter of Tarshish:
there is no more strength.
¹¹ He stretched out his hand over the sea,
he shook the kingdoms:
the LORD hath given a commandment against the merchant-city,
to destroy the strongholds thereof.
¹² And he said, 'Thou shalt no more rejoice,
O thou oppressed virgin, daughter of Zidon:
arise, pass over to Chittim,
there also shalt thou have no rest'.
¹³ Behold the land of the Chaldeans;
this people was not, till the Assyrian founded it
for them that dwell in the wilderness:
they set up the towers thereof,
they raised up the palaces thereof, and he brought it to ruin.
¹⁴ Howl, ye ships of Tarshish:
for your strength is laid waste.

¹⁵And it shall come to pass in that day, that Tyre shall be forgotten seventy years, according to the days of one king: after the end of seventy years shall Tyre sing as a harlot. ¹⁶Take a harp, go about the city, thou harlot that hast been forgotten, make sweet melody, sing many songs, that thou mayest be remembered.

¹⁷And it shall come to pass after the end of seventy years, that the LORD will visit Tyre, and she shall turn to her hire, and shall commit fornication with all the kingdoms of the world upon the face of the earth. ¹⁸And her merchandise and her hire shall be holiness to the LORD: it shall not be treasured nor laid up: for her merchandise shall be for them that dwell before the LORD, to eat sufficiently, and for durable clothing.

24 Behold, the LORD maketh the earth empty,
and maketh it waste,
and turneth it upside down,
and scattereth abroad the inhabitants thereof.
² And it shall be, as with the people, so with the priest,
as with the servant, so with his master,
as with the maid, so with her mistress,
as with the buyer, so with the seller,
as with the lender, so with the borrower,
as with the taker of usury, so with the giver of usury to him.
³ The land shall be utterly emptied, and utterly spoiled:
for the LORD hath spoken this word.
⁴ The earth mourneth and fadeth away,
the world languisheth and fadeth away,
the haughty people of the earth do languish.
⁵ The earth also is defiled under the inhabitants thereof:
because they have transgressed the laws,
changed the ordinance,
broken the everlasting covenant.
⁶ Therefore hath the curse devoured the earth,
and they that dwell therein are desolate:
therefore the inhabitants of the earth are burnt,
and few men left.
⁷ The new wine mourneth,
the vine languisheth,
all the merry-hearted do sigh.
⁸ The mirth of tabrets ceaseth,
the noise of them that rejoice endeth,
the joy of the harp ceaseth.
⁹ They shall not drink wine with a song,
strong drink shall be bitter to them that drink it.
¹⁰ The city of confusion is broken down:
every house is shut up, that no man may come in.
¹¹ There is a crying for wine in the streets,
all joy is darkened,
the mirth of the land is gone.
¹² In the city is left desolation,
and the gate is smitten with destruction.

¹³ When thus it shall be in the midst of the land among the people,
there shall be as the shaking of an olive tree,

and as the gleaning grapes when the vintage is done.

¹⁴ They shall lift up their voice,
they shall sing for the majesty of the LORD,
they shall cry aloud from the sea.

¹⁵ Wherefore glorify ye the LORD in the fires,
even the name of the LORD God of Israel in the isles of the sea.

¹⁶ From the uttermost part of the earth have we heard songs,
even glory to the righteous.
But I said, 'My leanness, my leanness, woe unto me:
the treacherous dealers have dealt treacherously,
yea, the treacherous dealers have dealt very treacherously'.

¹⁷ Fear, and the pit, and the snare, are upon thee,
O inhabitant of the earth.

¹⁸ And it shall come to pass,
that he who fleeth from the noise of the fear shall fall into the
pit;
and he that cometh up out of the midst of the pit shall be taken
in the snare:
for the windows from on high are open,
and the foundations of the earth do shake.

¹⁹ The earth is utterly broken down,
the earth is clean dissolved,
the earth is moved exceedingly.

²⁰ The earth shall reel to and fro like a drunkard,
and shall be removed like a cottage,
and the transgression thereof shall be heavy upon it,
and it shall fall, and not rise again.

²¹ And it shall come to pass in that day,
that the LORD shall punish the host of the high ones that are on
high,
and the kings of the earth upon the earth.

²² And they shall be gathered together
as prisoners are gathered in the pit,
and shall be shut up in the prison,
and after many days shall they be visited.

²³ Then the moon shall be confounded,
and the sun ashamed,
when the LORD of hosts shall reign in mount Zion,
and in Jerusalem, and before his ancients gloriously.

25

O LORD, thou art my God,
I will exalt thee, I will praise thy name;
for thou hast done wonderful things;
thy counsels of old are faithfulness and truth.

² For thou hast made of a city a heap;
of a defenced city a ruin:
a palace of strangers to be no city,

it shall never be built.
³ Therefore shall the strong people glorify thee,
    the city of the terrible nations shall fear thee.
⁴ For thou hast been a strength to the poor,
    a strength to the needy in his distress,
    a refuge from the storm, a shadow from the heat,
    when the blast of the terrible ones is as a storm against the wall.
⁵ Thou shalt bring down the noise of strangers, as the heat in a dry
        place;
    even the heat with the shadow of a cloud:
    the branch of the terrible ones shall be brought low.

⁶ And in this mountain shall the LORD of hosts make unto all
        people
    a feast of fat things, a feast of wines on the lees,
    of fat things full of marrow, of wines on the lees well refined.
⁷ And he will destroy in this mountain
    the face of the covering cast over all people,
    and the veil that is spread over all nations.
⁸ He will swallow up death in victory,
    and the Lord GOD will wipe away tears from off all faces,
    and the rebuke of his people shall he take away from off all the
        earth:
    for the LORD hath spoken it.

⁹ And it shall be said in that day,
    'Lo, this is our God,
    we have waited for him, and he will save us:
    this is the LORD,
    we have waited for him,
    we will be glad and rejoice in his salvation'.
¹⁰ For in this mountain shall the hand of the LORD rest,
    and Moab shall be trodden down under him,
    even as straw is trodden down for the dunghill.
¹¹ And he shall spread forth his hands in the midst of them,
    as he that swimmeth spreadeth forth his hands to swim:
    and he shall bring down their pride
    together with the spoils of their hands.
¹² And the fortress of the high fort of thy walls shall he bring down,
    lay low, and bring to the ground,
    even to the dust.

26 In that day shall this song be sung in the land of Judah:
    We have a strong city,
        salvation will God appoint for walls and bulwarks.
    ² Open ye the gates,

that the righteous nation which keepeth the truth may enter in.

³ Thou wilt keep him in perfect peace, whose mind is stayed on
thee:
because he trusteth in thee.

⁴ Trust ye in the LORD for ever:
for in the LORD JEHOVAH is everlasting strength.

⁵ For he bringeth down them that dwell on high,
the lofty city, he layeth it low;
he layeth it low, even to the ground,
he bringeth it even to the dust.

⁶ The foot shall tread it down,
even the feet of the poor, and the steps of the needy.

⁷ The way of the just is uprightness:
thou, most upright, dost weigh the path of the just.

⁸ Yea, in the way of thy judgements, O LORD, have we waited for
thee;
the desire of our soul is to thy name,
and to the remembrance of thee.

⁹ With my soul have I desired thee in the night,
yea, with my spirit within me will I seek thee early:
for when thy judgements are in the earth,
the inhabitants of the world will learn righteousness.

¹⁰ Let favour be shown to the wicked,
yet will he not learn righteousness:
in the land of uprightness will he deal unjustly,
and will not behold the majesty of the LORD.

¹¹ LORD, when thy hand is lifted up, they will not see:
but they shall see, and be ashamed for their envy at the people,
yea, the fire of thy enemies shall devour them.

¹² LORD, thou wilt ordain peace for us:
for thou also hast wrought all our works in us.

¹³ O LORD our God, other lords besides thee have had dominion
over us:
but by thee only will we make mention of thy name.

¹⁴ They are dead, they shall not live;
they are deceased, they shall not rise:
therefore hast thou visited and destroyed them,
and made all their memory to perish.

¹⁵ Thou hast increased the nation, O LORD,
thou hast increased the nation, thou art glorified:
thou hadst removed it far unto all the ends of the earth.

¹⁶ LORD, in trouble have they visited thee:
they poured out a prayer when thy chastening was upon them.

¹⁷ Like as a woman with child,
that draweth near the time of her delivery,
is in pain, and crieth out in her pangs;

so have we been in thy sight, O LORD.
¹⁸ We have been with child, we have been in pain,
we have as it were brought forth wind,
we have not wrought any deliverance in the earth,
neither have the inhabitants of the world fallen.
¹⁹ Thy dead men shall live,
together with my dead body shall they arise.
Awake and sing, ye that dwell in dust:
for thy dew is as the dew of herbs,
and the earth shall cast out the dead.

²⁰ Come, my people, enter thou into thy chambers,
and shut thy doors about thee:
hide thyself as it were for a little moment,
until the indignation be overpast.
²¹ For behold, the LORD cometh out of his place
to punish the inhabitants of the earth for their iniquity:
the earth also shall disclose her blood,
and shall no more cover her slain.

27 In that day the LORD with his sore and great and strong sword
shall punish leviathan the piercing serpent,
even leviathan that crooked serpent,
and he shall slay the dragon that is in the sea.

² In that day sing ye unto her,
'A vineyard of red wine.
³ I the LORD do keep it;
I will water it every moment:
lest any hurt it, I will keep it night and day.
⁴ Fury is not in me:
who would set the briers and thorns against me in battle?
I would go through them,
I would burn them together.
⁵ Or let him take hold of my strength,
that he may make peace with me,
and he shall make peace with me.'

⁶ He shall cause them that come of Jacob to take root:
Israel shall blossom and bud,
and fill the face of the world with fruit.

⁷ Hath he smitten him, as he smote those that smote him?
or is he slain according to the slaughter of them that are slain by
him?
⁸ In measure, when it shooteth forth, thou wilt debate with it:
he stayeth his rough wind in the day of the east wind.
⁹ By this therefore shall the iniquity of Jacob be purged,

and this is all the fruit to take away his sin:
when he maketh all the stones of the altar as chalk-stones that
    are beaten in sunder,
the groves and images shall not stand up.
¹⁰ Yet the defenced city shall be desolate,
and the habitation forsaken, and left like a wilderness:
there shall the calf feed, and there shall he lie down,
and consume the branches thereof.
¹¹ When the boughs thereof are withered,
they shall be broken off:
the women come, and set them on fire:
for it is a people of no understanding:
therefore he that made them will not have mercy on them,
and he that formed them will show them no favour.

¹² And it shall come to pass in that day,
that the Lord shall beat off from the channel of the river unto
    the stream of Egypt,
and ye shall be gathered one by one,
O ye children of Israel.
¹³ And it shall come to pass in that day,
that the great trumpet shall be blown,
and they shall come which were ready to perish in the land of
    Assyria,
and the outcasts in the land of Egypt,
and shall worship the Lord in the holy mount at Jerusalem.

28 Woe to the crown of pride, to the drunkards of Ephraim,
whose glorious beauty is a fading flower,
which are on the head of the fat valleys of them that are
    overcome with wine.
² Behold, the Lord hath a mighty and strong one,
which as a tempest of hail and a destroying storm,
as a flood of mighty waters overflowing,
shall cast down to the earth with the hand.
³ The crown of pride, the drunkards of Ephraim
shall be trodden under feet.
⁴ And the glorious beauty, which is on the head of the fat valley,
shall be a fading flower,
and as the hasty fruit before the summer:
which when he that looketh upon it seeth it,
while it is yet in his hand he eateth it up.

⁵ In that day shall the Lord of hosts be for a crown of glory,
and for a diadem of beauty, unto the residue of his people,
⁶ and for a spirit of judgement to him that sitteth in judgement,
and for strength to them that turn the battle to the gate.

⁷ But they also have erred through wine,
and through strong drink are out of the way:
the priest and the prophet have erred through strong drink,
they are swallowed up of wine:
they are out of the way through strong drink,
they err in vision, they stumble in judgement.
⁸ For all tables are full of vomit and filthiness,
so that there is no place clean.

⁹ Whom shall he teach knowledge?
and whom shall he make to understand doctrine?
them that are weaned from the milk,
and drawn from the breasts.
¹⁰ For precept must be upon precept, precept upon precept,
line upon line, line upon line,
here a little, and there a little.
¹¹ For with stammering lips and another tongue
will he speak to this people.
¹² To whom he said,
'This is the rest wherewith ye may cause the weary to rest,
and this is the refreshing':
yet they would not hear.
¹³ But the word of the LORD was unto them
precept upon precept, precept upon precept,
line upon line, line upon line,
here a little, and there a little:
that they might go, and fall backward,
and be broken, and snared, and taken.

¹⁴ Wherefore hear the word of the LORD,
ye scornful men, that rule this people which is in Jerusalem.
¹⁵ Because ye have said, 'We have made a covenant with death,
and with hell are we at agreement,
when the overflowing scourge shall pass through, it shall not
come unto us:
for we have made lies our refuge,
and under falsehood have we hid ourselves':
¹⁶ therefore thus saith the Lord GOD,
'Behold, I lay in Zion for a foundation a stone, a tried stone,
a precious corner-stone, a sure foundation:
he that believeth shall not make haste.
¹⁷ Judgement also will I lay to the line,
and righteousness to the plummet:
and the hail shall sweep away the refuge of lies,
and the waters shall overflow the hiding-place.'
¹⁸ And your covenant with death shall be disannulled,
and your agreement with hell shall not stand;
when the overflowing scourge shall pass through,

then ye shall be trodden down by it.

¹⁹ From the time that it goeth forth it shall take you:
for morning by morning shall it pass over, by day and by night,
and it shall be a vexation only to understand the report.

²⁰ For the bed is shorter than that a man can stretch himself on it:
and the covering narrower than that he can wrap himself in it.

²¹ For the LORD shall rise up as in mount Perazim,
he shall be wroth as in the valley of Gibeon,
that he may do his work, his strange work;
and bring to pass his act, his strange act.

²² Now therefore be ye not mockers,
lest your bands be made strong:
for I have heard from the Lord GOD of hosts
a consumption even determined upon the whole earth.

²³ Give ye ear, and hear my voice,
hearken, and hear my speech.

²⁴ Doth the ploughman plough all day to sow?
doth he open and break the clods of his ground?

²⁵ When he hath made plain the face thereof,
doth he not cast abroad the fitches, and scatter the cummin,
and cast in the principal wheat and the appointed barley and the
rye in their place?

²⁶ For his God doth instruct him to discretion, and doth teach
him.

²⁷ For the fitches are not threshed with a threshing instrument,
neither is a cartwheel turned about upon the cummin:
but the fitches are beaten out with a staff,
and the cummin with a rod.

²⁸ Bread corn is bruised;
because he will not ever be threshing it,
nor break it with the wheel of his cart,
nor bruise it with his horsemen.

²⁹ This also cometh forth from the LORD of hosts,
which is wonderful in counsel,
and excellent in working.

29 Woe to Ariel, to Ariel, the city where David dwelt:
add ye year to year; let them kill sacrifices.

² Yet I will distress Ariel,
and there shall be heaviness and sorrow:
and it shall be unto me as Ariel.

³ And I will camp against thee round about,
and will lay siege against thee with a mount,
and I will raise forts against thee.

⁴ And thou shalt be brought down,
and shalt speak out of the ground,
and thy speech shall be low out of the dust,

and thy voice shall be as of one that hath a familiar spirit, out of
  the ground,
and thy speech shall whisper out of the dust.
⁵ Moreover the multitude of thy strangers shall be like small dust,
and the multitude of the terrible ones shall be as chaff that
  passeth away:
yea, it shall be at an instant suddenly.
⁶ Thou shalt be visited of the LORD of hosts
with thunder, and with earthquake, and great noise,
with storm and tempest, and the flame of devouring fire.

⁷ And the multitude of all the nations that fight against Ariel,
even all that fight against her and her munition, and that
  distress her,
shall be as a dream of a night vision.
⁸ It shall even be as when a hungry man dreameth, and behold, he
  eateth;
but he awaketh, and his soul is empty:
or as when a thirsty man dreameth, and behold, he drinketh;
but he awaketh, and behold, he is faint, and his soul hath
  appetite:
so shall the multitude of all the nations be, that fight against
  mount Zion.

⁹ Stay yourselves, and wonder, cry ye out, and cry:
they are drunken, but not with wine,
they stagger, but not with strong drink.
¹⁰ For the LORD hath poured out upon you the spirit of deep sleep,
and hath closed your eyes:
the prophets and your rulers, the seers hath he covered.

¹¹And the vision of all is become unto you as the words of a book that is
sealed, which men deliver to one that is learned, saying, 'Read this, I
pray thee': and he saith, 'I cannot, for it is sealed'. ¹²And the book is
delivered to him that is not learned, saying, 'Read this, I pray thee': and
he saith, 'I am not learned'.
  ¹³ Wherefore the Lord said,

  'Forasmuch as this people draw near me with their mouth,
  and with their lips do honour me,
  but have removed their heart far from me,
  and their fear towards me is taught by the precept of men:
¹⁴ therefore behold, I will proceed to do a marvellous work
    amongst this people,
  even a marvellous work and a wonder:
  for the wisdom of their wise men shall perish,
  and the understanding of their prudent men shall be hid'.

¹⁵ Woe unto them that seek deep to hide their counsel from the LORD,
and their works are in the dark, and they say,
'Who seeth us? and who knoweth us?'
¹⁶ Surely your turning of things upside down shall be esteemed as
the potter's clay:
for shall the work say of him that made it,
'He made me not'?
or shall the thing framed say of him that framed it,
'He had no understanding'?

¹⁷ Is it not yet a very little while,
and Lebanon shall be turned into a fruitful field,
and the fruitful field shall be esteemed as a forest?
¹⁸ And in that day shall the deaf hear the words of the book,
and the eyes of the blind shall see out of obscurity,
and out of darkness.
¹⁹ The meek also shall increase their joy in the LORD,
and the poor among men shall rejoice in the Holy One of Israel.
²⁰ For the terrible one is brought to nought,
and the scorner is consumed,
and all that watch for iniquity are cut off:
²¹ that make a man an offender for a word,
and lay a snare for him that reproveth in the gate,
and turn aside the just for a thing of nought.

²²Therefore thus saith the LORD, who redeemed Abraham, concerning the house of Jacob,

'Jacob shall not now be ashamed,
neither shall his face now wax pale.
²³ But when he seeth his children, the work of my hands, in the
midst of him,
they shall sanctify my name,
and sanctify the Holy One of Jacob,
and shall fear the God of Israel.
²⁴ They also that erred in spirit shall come to understanding,
and they that murmured shall learn doctrine.'

30 'Woe to the rebellious children,' saith the LORD,
'that take counsel, but not of me;
and that cover with a covering, but not of my Spirit,
that they may add sin to sin:
² that walk to go down into Egypt,
and have not asked at my mouth;
to strengthen themselves in the strength of Pharaoh,
and to trust in the shadow of Egypt.
³ Therefore shall the strength of Pharaoh be your shame,
and the trust in the shadow of Egypt your confusion.

⁴ For his princes were at Zoan,
   and his ambassadors came to Hanes.
⁵ They were all ashamed of a people that could not profit them,
   nor be a help nor profit,
   but a shame, and also a reproach.'

⁶The burden of the beasts of the south:

   into the land of trouble and anguish,
   from whence come the young and old lion,
   the viper and fiery flying serpent,
   they will carry their riches upon the shoulders of young asses,
   and their treasures upon the bunches of camels,
   to a people that shall not profit them.
⁷ For the Egyptians shall help in vain, and to no purpose:
   therefore have I cried concerning this,
   'Their strength is to sit still'.

⁸ Now go, write it before them in a tablet, and note it in a book,
   that it may be for the time to come for ever and ever:
⁹ that this is a rebellious people, lying children,
   children that will not hear the law of the LORD:
¹⁰ which say to the seers, 'See not';
   and to the prophets, 'Prophesy not unto us right things,
   speak unto us smooth things,
   prophesy deceits.
¹¹ Get ye out of the way,
   turn aside out of the path,
   cause the Holy One of Israel to cease from before us.'
¹² Wherefore thus saith the Holy One of Israel,
   'Because ye despise this word,
   and trust in oppression and perverseness,
   and stay thereon:
¹³ therefore this iniquity shall be to you as a breach ready to fall,
   swelling out in a high wall,
   whose breaking cometh suddenly at an instant.
¹⁴ And he shall break it as the breaking of the potters' vessel that is
     broken in pieces,
   he shall not spare:
   so that there shall not be found in the bursting of it
   a shard to take fire from the hearth,
   or to take water withal out of the pit.'
¹⁵ For thus saith the Lord GOD, the Holy One of Israel,
   'In returning and rest shall ye be saved,
   in quietness and in confidence shall be your strength':
   and ye would not.
¹⁶ But ye said, 'No, for we will flee upon horses';
   therefore shall ye flee.

And, 'We will ride upon the swift';
therefore shall they that pursue you be swift.
¹⁷ One thousand shall flee at the rebuke of one:
at the rebuke of five shall ye flee,
till ye be left as a beacon upon the top of a mountain,
and as an ensign on a hill.

¹⁸ And therefore will the LORD wait,
that he may be gracious unto you,
and therefore will he be exalted,
that he may have mercy upon you:
for the LORD is a God of judgement.
Blessed are all they that wait for him.

¹⁹For the people shall dwell in Zion at Jerusalem: thou shalt weep no more: he will be very gracious unto thee at the voice of thy cry; when he shall hear it, he will answer thee. ²⁰And though the Lord give you the bread of adversity, and the water of affliction, yet shall not thy teachers be removed into a corner any more, but thy eyes shall see thy teachers. ²¹And thy ears shall hear a word behind thee, saying, 'This is the way, walk ye in it', when ye turn to the right hand, and when ye turn to the left. ²²Ye shall defile also the covering of thy graven images of silver, and the ornament of thy molten images of gold: thou shalt cast them away as a menstruous cloth, thou shalt say unto it, 'Get thee hence'. ²³Then shall he give the rain of thy seed, that thou shalt sow the ground withal; and bread of the increase of the earth, and it shall be fat and plenteous: in that day shall thy cattle feed in large pastures. ²⁴The oxen likewise and the young asses that ear the ground shall eat clean provender which hath been winnowed with the shovel and with the fan. ²⁵And there shall be upon every high mountain, and upon every high hill, rivers and streams of waters in the day of the great slaughter when the towers fall. ²⁶Moreover the light of the moon shall be as the light of the sun, and the light of the sun shall be sevenfold, as the light of seven days, in the day that the LORD bindeth up the breach of his people, and healeth the stroke of their wound.

²⁷ Behold, the name of the LORD cometh from far,
burning with his anger,
and the burden thereof is heavy:
his lips are full of indignation,
and his tongue as a devouring fire.
²⁸ And his breath, as an overflowing stream,
shall reach to the midst of the neck,
to sift the nations with the sieve of vanity:
and there shall be a bridle in the jaws of the people
causing them to err.
²⁹ Ye shall have a song,
as in the night when a holy solemnity is kept,

and gladness of heart,
as when one goeth with a pipe to come into the mountain of the
  LORD,
to the mighty One of Israel.
³⁰ And the LORD shall cause his glorious voice to be heard,
and shall show the lighting down of his arm,
with the indignation of his anger,
and with the flame of a devouring fire,
with scattering and tempest and hailstones.
³¹ For through the voice of the LORD shall the Assyrian be beaten
  down,
which smote with a rod.
³² And in every place where the grounded staff shall pass,
which the LORD shall lay upon him,
it shall be with tabrets and harps:
and in battles of shaking will he fight with it.
³³ For Tophet is ordained of old;
yea, for the king it is prepared,
he hath made it deep and large:
the pile thereof is fire and much wood;
the breath of the LORD, like a stream of brimstone,
doth kindle it.

31 Woe to them that go down to Egypt for help,
and stay on horses, and trust in chariots, because they are
  many;
and in horsemen, because they are very strong:
but they look not unto the Holy One of Israel,
neither seek the LORD.
² Yet he also is wise, and will bring evil,
and will not call back his words:
but will arise against the house of the evil-doers,
and against the help of them that work iniquity.
³ Now the Egyptians are men, and not God:
and their horses flesh, and not spirit.
When the LORD shall stretch out his hand,
both he that helpeth shall fall,
and he that is helped shall fall down,
and they all shall fail together.

⁴ For thus hath the LORD spoken unto me,
'Like as the lion and the young lion roaring on his prey,
when a multitude of shepherds is called forth against him,
he will not be afraid of their voice,
nor abase himself for the noise of them:
so shall the LORD of hosts come down to fight
for mount Zion, and for the hill thereof.
⁵ As birds flying, so will the LORD of hosts defend Jerusalem;

defending also he will deliver it,
and passing over he will preserve it.

⁶ 'Turn ye unto him from whom the children of Israel have deeply
revolted.
⁷ For in that day every man shall cast away
his idols of silver, and his idols of gold,
which your own hands have made unto you for a sin.

⁸ 'Then shall the Assyrian fall with the sword, not of a mighty
man;
and the sword, not of a mean man, shall devour him:
but he shall flee from the sword,
and his young men shall be discomfited.
⁹ And he shall pass over to his stronghold for fear,
and his princes shall be afraid of the ensign,'
saith the LORD, whose fire is in Zion,
and his furnace in Jerusalem.

32 Behold, a king shall reign in righteousness,
and princes shall rule in judgement.
² And a man shall be as a hiding-place from the wind,
and a covert from the tempest:
as rivers of water in a dry place,
as the shadow of a great rock in a weary land.
³ And the eyes of them that see shall not be dim,
and the ears of them that hear shall hearken.
⁴ The heart also of the rash shall understand knowledge,
and the tongue of the stammerers shall be ready to speak plainly.
⁵ The vile person shall be no more called liberal,
nor the churl said to be bountiful.
⁶ For the vile person will speak villainy,
and his heart will work iniquity,
to practise hypocrisy, and to utter error against the LORD,
to make empty the soul of the hungry,
and he will cause the drink of the thirsty to fail.
⁷ The instruments also of the churl are evil:
he deviseth wicked devices to destroy the poor with lying words,
even when the needy speaketh right.
⁸ But the liberal deviseth liberal things,
and by liberal things shall he stand.

⁹ Rise up, ye women that are at ease:
hear my voice, ye careless daughters,
give ear unto my speech.
¹⁰ Many days and years shall ye be troubled, ye careless women:
for the vintage shall fail, the gathering shall not come.
¹¹ Tremble, ye women that are at ease:

be troubled, ye careless ones:
strip ye, and make ye bare,
and gird sackcloth upon your loins.

¹² They shall lament for the teats,
for the pleasant fields, for the fruitful vine.

¹³ Upon the land of my people shall come up thorns and briers,
yea, upon all the houses of joy in the joyous city.

¹⁴ Because the palaces shall be forsaken,
the multitude of the city shall be left,
the forts and towers shall be for dens for ever,
a joy of wild asses, a pasture of flocks;

¹⁵ until the spirit be poured upon us from on high,
and the wilderness be a fruitful field,
and the fruitful field be counted for a forest.

¹⁶ Then judgement shall dwell in the wilderness,
and righteousness remain in the fruitful field.

¹⁷ And the work of righteousness shall be peace,
and the effect of righteousness quietness and assurance for
ever.

¹⁸ And my people shall dwell in a peaceable habitation,
and in sure dwellings, and in quiet resting places;

¹⁹ when it shall hail, coming down on the forest;
and the city shall be low in a low place.

²⁰ Blessed are ye that sow beside all waters,
that send forth thither the feet of the ox and the ass.

33 Woe to thee that spoilest, and thou wast not spoiled;
and dealest treacherously, and they dealt not treacherously
with thee:
when thou shalt cease to spoil, thou shalt be spoiled;
and when thou shalt make an end to deal treacherously,
they shall deal treacherously with thee.

² O Lord, be gracious unto us,
we have waited for thee:
be thou their arm every morning,
our salvation also in the time of trouble.

³ At the noise of the tumult the people fled:
at the lifting up of thyself the nations were scattered.

⁴ And your spoil shall be gathered like the gathering of the
caterpillar:
as the running to and fro of locusts shall he run upon them.

⁵ The Lord is exalted: for he dwelleth on high,
he hath filled Zion with judgement and righteousness.

⁶ And wisdom and knowledge shall be
the stability of thy times, and strength of salvation:
the fear of the Lord is his treasure.

⁷ Behold, their valiant ones shall cry without:
the ambassadors of peace shall weep bitterly.

⁸ The highways lie waste, the wayfaring man ceaseth:
he hath broken the covenant, he hath despised the cities,
he regardeth no man.
⁹ The earth mourneth and languisheth:
Lebanon is ashamed and hewn down:
Sharon is like a wilderness,
and Bashan and Carmel shake off their fruits.

¹⁰ 'Now will I rise,' saith the LORD:
'now will I be exalted, now will I lift up myself.
¹¹ Ye shall conceive chaff, ye shall bring forth stubble:
your breath as fire shall devour you.
¹² And the people shall be as the burnings of lime:
as thorns cut up shall they be burnt in the fire.'

¹³ Hear, ye that are far off, what I have done;
and, ye that are near, acknowledge my might.
¹⁴ The sinners in Zion are afraid,
fearfulness hath surprised the hypocrites:
who among us shall dwell with the devouring fire?
who amongst us shall dwell with everlasting burnings?
¹⁵ He that walketh righteously, and speaketh uprightly,
he that despiseth the gain of oppressions,
that shaketh his hands from holding of bribes,
that stoppeth his ears from hearing of blood,
and shutteth his eyes from seeing evil:
¹⁶ he shall dwell on high:
his place of defence shall be the munitions of rocks:
bread shall be given him, his waters shall be sure.

¹⁷ Thy eyes shall see the king in his beauty:
they shall behold the land that is very far off.
¹⁸ Thy heart shall meditate terror.
Where is the scribe?
where is the receiver?
where is he that counted the towers?
¹⁹ Thou shalt not see a fierce people,
a people of a deeper speech than thou canst perceive;
of a stammering tongue, that thou canst not understand.
²⁰ Look upon Zion, the city of our solemnities:
thy eyes shall see Jerusalem a quiet habitation,
a tabernacle that shall not be taken down;
not one of the stakes thereof shall ever be removed,
neither shall any of the cords thereof be broken.
²¹ But there the glorious LORD will be unto us a place of broad
rivers and streams;
wherein shall go no galley with oars,
neither shall gallant ship pass thereby.

²² For the Lord is our judge, the Lord is our lawgiver,
the Lord is our king, he will save us.
²³ Thy tacklings are loosed:
they could not well strengthen their mast,
they could not spread the sail:
then is the prey of a great spoil divided,
the lame take the prey.
²⁴ And the inhabitant shall not say, 'I am sick':
the people that dwell therein shall be forgiven their iniquity.

34 Come near, ye nations, to hear, and hearken, ye people:
let the earth hear, and all that is therein,
the world, and all things that come forth of it.
² For the indignation of the Lord is upon all nations,
and his fury upon all their armies:
he hath utterly destroyed them,
he hath delivered them to the slaughter.
³ Their slain also shall be cast out,
and their stink shall come up out of their carcases,
and the mountains shall be melted with their blood.
⁴ And all the host of heaven shall be dissolved,
and the heavens shall be rolled together as a scroll:
and all their host shall fall down,
as the leaf falleth off from the vine,
and as a falling fig from the fig tree.
⁵ For my sword shall be bathed in heaven:
behold, it shall come down upon Idumea,
and upon the people of my curse to judgement.
⁶ The sword of the Lord is filled with blood,
it is made fat with fatness,
and with the blood of lambs and goats,
with the fat of the kidneys of rams:
for the Lord hath a sacrifice in Bozrah,
and a great slaughter in the land of Idumea.
⁷ And the unicorns shall come down with them,
and the bullocks with the bulls,
and their land shall be soaked with blood,
and their dust made fat with fatness.
⁸ For it is the day of the Lord's vengeance,
and the year of recompenses for the controversy of Zion.
⁹ And the streams thereof shall be turned into pitch,
and the dust thereof into brimstone,
and the land thereof shall become burning pitch.
¹⁰ It shall not be quenched night nor day,
the smoke thereof shall go up for ever:
from generation to generation it shall lie waste,
none shall pass through it for ever and ever.

¹¹ The cormorant and the bittern shall possess it,
the owl also and the raven shall dwell in it:
and he shall stretch out upon it the line of confusion,
and the stones of emptiness.
¹² They shall call the nobles thereof to the kingdom,
but none shall be there,
and all her princes shall be nothing.
¹³ And thorns shall come up in her palaces,
nettles and brambles in the fortresses thereof:
and it shall be a habitation of dragons, and a court for owls.
¹⁴ The wild beasts of the desert shall also meet with the wild beasts
of the island,
and the satyr shall cry to his fellow;
the screech owl also shall rest there,
and find for herself a place of rest.
¹⁵ There shall the great owl make her nest,
and lay and hatch, and gather under her shadow:
there shall the vultures also be gathered, every one with her
mate.

¹⁶ Seek ye out of the book of the LORD, and read:
no one of these shall fail, none shall want her mate:
for my mouth, it hath commanded,
and his spirit, it hath gathered them.
¹⁷ And he hath cast the lot for them,
and his hand hath divided it unto them by line:
they shall possess it for ever,
from generation to generation shall they dwell therein.

35 The wilderness and the solitary place shall be glad for them:
and the desert shall rejoice, and blossom as the rose.
² It shall blossom abundantly,
and rejoice even with joy and singing:
the glory of Lebanon shall be given unto it,
the excellence of Carmel and Sharon:
they shall see the glory of the LORD,
and the excellence of our God.

³ Strengthen ye the weak hands,
and confirm the feeble knees.
⁴ Say to them that are of a fearful heart,
'Be strong, fear not:
behold, your God will come with vengeance,
even God with a recompense,
he will come and save you'.
⁵ Then the eyes of the blind shall be opened,
and the ears of the deaf shall be unstopped.
⁶ Then shall the lame man leap as a hart,

and the tongue of the dumb sing:
for in the wilderness shall waters break out,
and streams in the desert.
⁷ And the parched ground shall become a pool,
and the thirsty land springs of water:
in the habitation of dragons, where each lay,
shall be grass with reeds and rushes.
⁸ And a highway shall be there, and a way,
and it shall be called the way of holiness;
the unclean shall not pass over it, but it shall be for those:
the wayfaring men, though fools, shall not err therein.
⁹ No lion shall be there,
nor any ravenous beast shall go up thereon,
it shall not be found there:
but the redeemed shall walk there:
¹⁰ and the ransomed of the LORD shall return,
and come to Zion with songs
and everlasting joy upon their heads:
they shall obtain joy and gladness,
and sorrow and sighing shall flee away.

36 Now it came to pass in the fourteenth year of king Hezekiah, that Sennacherib king of Assyria came up against all the defenced cities of Judah, and took them. ²And the king of Assyria sent Rabshakeh from Lachish to Jerusalem unto king Hezekiah with a great army. And he stood by the conduit of the upper pool in the highway of the fuller's field. ³Then came forth unto him Eliakim, Hilkiah's son, which was over the house, and Shebna the scribe, and Joah, Asaph's son, the recorder.

⁴And Rabshakeh said unto them, 'Say ye now to Hezekiah, "Thus saith the great king, the king of Assyria, 'What confidence is this wherein thou trustest? ⁵I say, sayest thou (but they are but vain words), "I have counsel and strength for war": now on whom dost thou trust, that thou rebellest against me? ⁶Lo, thou trustest in the staff of this broken reed, on Egypt; whereon if a man lean, it will go into his hand, and pierce it: so is Pharaoh king of Egypt to all that trust in him. ⁷But if thou say to me, "We trust in the LORD our God": is it not he, whose high places and whose altars Hezekiah hath taken away, and said to Judah and to Jerusalem, "Ye shall worship before this altar"?' ⁸Now therefore give pledges, I pray thee, to my master the king of Assyria, and I will give thee two thousand horses, if thou be able on thy part to set riders upon them. ⁹How then wilt thou turn away the face of one captain of the least of my master's servants, and put thy trust on Egypt for chariots and for horsemen? ¹⁰And am I now come up without the LORD against this land to destroy it? the LORD said unto me, 'Go up against this land, and destroy it'."'

¹¹Then said Eliakim and Shebna and Joah unto Rabshakeh, 'Speak, I pray thee, unto thy servants in the Syrian language; for we understand

it: and speak not to us in the Jews' language, in the ears of the people that are on the wall'. ¹²But Rabshakeh said, 'Hath my master sent me to thy master and to thee to speak these words? Hath he not sent me to the men that sit upon the wall, that they may eat their own dung, and drink their own piss with you?'

¹³Then Rabshakeh stood, and cried with a loud voice in the Jews' language, and said, 'Hear ye the words of the great king, the king of Assyria. ¹⁴Thus saith the king, "Let not Hezekiah deceive you, for he shall not be able to deliver you. ¹⁵Neither let Hezekiah make you trust in the LORD, saying, 'The LORD will surely deliver us: this city shall not be delivered into the hand of the king of Assyria'." ¹⁶Hearken not to Hezekiah: for thus saith the king of Assyria, "Make an agreement with me by a present, and come out to me: and eat ye every one of his vine, and every one of his fig tree, and drink ye every one the waters of his own cistern; ¹⁷until I come and take you away to a land like your own land, a land of corn and wine, a land of bread and vineyards. ¹⁸Beware lest Hezekiah persuade you, saying, 'The LORD will deliver us'. Hath any of the gods of the nations delivered his land out of the hand of the king of Assyria? ¹⁹Where are the gods of Hamath and Arphad? where are the gods of Sepharvaim? and have they delivered Samaria out of my hand? ²⁰Who are they amongst all the gods of these lands, that have delivered their land out of my hand, that the LORD should deliver Jerusalem out of my hand?"' ²¹But they held their peace, and answered him not a word: for the king's commandment was, saying, 'Answer him not'.

²²Then came Eliakim, the son of Hilkiah, that was over the household, and Shebna the scribe, and Joah, the son of Asaph the recorder, to Hezekiah with their clothes rent, and told him the words of Rabshakeh.

37

And it came to pass when king Hezekiah heard it, that he rent his clothes, and covered himself with sackcloth, and went into the house of the LORD. ²And he sent Eliakim, who was over the household, and Shebna the scribe, and the elders of the priests covered with sackcloth, unto Isaiah the prophet the son of Amoz. ³And they said unto him, 'Thus saith Hezekiah, "This day is a day of trouble, and of rebuke, and of blasphemy: for the children are come to the birth, and there is not strength to bring forth. ⁴It may be the LORD thy God will hear the words of Rabshakeh, whom the king of Assyria his master hath sent to reproach the living God, and will reprove the words which the LORD thy God hath heard: wherefore lift up thy prayer for the remnant that is left."' ⁵So the servants of king Hezekiah came to Isaiah.

⁶And Isaiah said unto them, 'Thus shall ye say unto your master, "Thus saith the LORD, 'Be not afraid of the words that thou hast heard, wherewith the servants of the king of Assyria have blasphemed me. ⁷Behold, I will send a blast upon him, and he shall hear a rumour, and return to his own land, and I will cause him to fall by the sword in his own land.'"'

⁸So Rabshakeh returned and found the king of Assyria warring against Libnah: for he had heard that he was departed from Lachish.

⁹And he heard say concerning Tirhakah king of Ethiopia, 'He is come forth to make war with thee'. And when he heard it, he sent messengers to Hezekiah, saying, ¹⁰'Thus shall ye speak to Hezekiah king of Judah, saying, "Let not thy God in whom thou trustest deceive thee, saying, 'Jerusalem shall not be given into the hand of the king of Assyria'. ¹¹Behold, thou hast heard what the kings of Assyria have done to all lands by destroying them utterly, and shalt thou be delivered? ¹²Have the gods of the nations delivered them which my fathers have destroyed, as Gozan, and Haran, and Rezeph, and the children of Eden which were in Telassar? ¹³Where is the king of Hamath, and the king of Arphad, and the king of the city of Sepharvaim, Hena, and Ivah?"'

¹⁴And Hezekiah received the letter from the hand of the messengers, and read it: and Hezekiah went up unto the house of the LORD, and spread it before the LORD. ¹⁵And Hezekiah prayed unto the LORD, saying, ¹⁶'O LORD of hosts, God of Israel, that dwellest between the cherubims, thou art the God, even thou alone, of all the kingdoms of the earth: thou hast made heaven and earth. ¹⁷Incline thy ear, O LORD, and hear, open thy eyes, O LORD, and see, and hear all the words of Sennacherib, which hath sent to reproach the living God. ¹⁸Of a truth, LORD, the kings of Assyria have laid waste all the nations and their countries, ¹⁹and have cast their gods into the fire: for they were no gods, but the work of men's hands, wood and stone: therefore they have destroyed them. ²⁰Now therefore, O LORD our God, save us from his hand, that all the kingdoms of the earth may know that thou art the LORD, even thou only.'

²¹Then Isaiah the son of Amoz sent unto Hezekiah, saying, 'Thus saith the LORD God of Israel, "Whereas thou hast prayed to me against Sennacherib king of Assyria: ²²this is the word which the LORD hath spoken concerning him:

'"The virgin, the daughter of Zion,
    hath despised thee, and laughed thee to scorn,
    the daughter of Jerusalem hath shaken her head at thee.
²³ Whom hast thou reproached and blasphemed?
    and against whom hast thou exalted thy voice,
    and lifted up thy eyes on high?
    even against the Holy One of Israel.
²⁴ By thy servants hast thou reproached the Lord, and hast said,
    "By the multitude of my chariots am I come up
    to the height of the mountains,
    to the sides of Lebanon,
    and I will cut down the tall cedars thereof,
    and the choice fir trees thereof:
    and I will enter into the height of his border,
    and the forest of his Carmel.
²⁵ I have dug, and drunk water,
    and with the sole of my feet have I dried up
    all the rivers of the besieged places."

²⁶ Hast thou not heard long ago, how I have done it,
    and of ancient times, that I have formed it?
    now have I brought it to pass, that thou shouldst be to lay waste
    defenced cities into ruinous heaps.
²⁷ Therefore their inhabitants were of small power,
    they were dismayed and confounded:
    they were as the grass of the field, and as the green herb,
    as the grass on the house-tops,
    and as corn blasted before it be grown up.
²⁸ But I know thy abode, and thy going out,
    and thy coming in, and thy rage against me.
²⁹ Because thy rage against me, and thy tumult is come up into my
        ears,
    therefore will I put my hook in thy nose,
    and my bridle in thy lips,
    and I will turn thee back by the way by which thou camest.'"

³⁰ 'And this shall be a sign unto thee,
    ye shall eat this year such as groweth of itself:
    and the second year that which springeth of the same:
    and in the third year sow ye and reap,
    and plant vineyards, and eat the fruit thereof.
³¹ And the remnant that is escaped of the house of Judah
    shall again take root downward, and bear fruit upward.
³² For out of Jerusalem shall go forth a remnant,
    and they that escape out of mount Zion:
    the zeal of the LORD of hosts shall do this.

³³ 'Therefore thus saith the LORD concerning the king of Assyria,
    "He shall not come into this city,
    nor shoot an arrow there,
    nor come before it with shields,
    nor cast a bank against it.
³⁴ By the way that he came, by the same shall he return,
    and shall not come into this city," saith the LORD.
³⁵ "For I will defend this city to save it
    for my own sake, and for my servant David's sake."'

³⁶Then the angel of the LORD went forth, and smote in the camp of the Assyrians a hundred and fourscore and five thousand: and when they arose early in the morning, behold, they were all dead corpses.

³⁷So Sennacherib king of Assyria departed, and went, and returned, and dwelt at Nineveh. ³⁸And it came to pass as he was worshipping in the house of Nisroch his god, that Adrammelech and Sharezer his sons smote him with the sword; and they escaped into the land of Armenia: and Esar-haddon his son reigned in his stead.

38 In those days was Hezekiah sick unto death: and Isaiah the prophet the son of Amoz came unto him, and said unto him,

'Thus saith the LORD, "Set thy house in order: for thou shalt die, and not live"'. ²Then Hezekiah turned his face toward the wall, and prayed unto the LORD, ³and said, 'Remember now, O LORD, I beseech thee, how I have walked before thee in truth and with a perfect heart, and have done that which is good in thy sight'. And Hezekiah wept sore.

⁴Then came the word of the LORD to Isaiah, saying, ⁵'Go, and say to Hezekiah, "Thus saith the LORD, the God of David thy father, 'I have heard thy prayer, I have seen thy tears: behold, I will add unto thy days fifteen years. ⁶And I will deliver thee and this city out of the hand of the king of Assyria: and I will defend this city.' ⁷And this shall be a sign unto thee from the LORD, that the LORD will do this thing that he hath spoken. ⁸Behold, I will bring again the shadow of the degrees, which is gone down in the sundial of Ahaz, ten degrees backward."' So the sun returned ten degrees, by which degrees it was gone down.

⁹The writing of Hezekiah king of Judah, when he had been sick, and was recovered of his sickness:

¹⁰ 'I said in the cutting off of my days,
    I shall go to the gates of the grave:
    I am deprived of the residue of my years.
¹¹ I said, I shall not see the LORD,
    even the LORD in the land of the living:
    I shall behold man no more with the inhabitants of the world.
¹² My age is departed, and is removed from me as a shepherd's tent:
    I have cut off like a weaver my life:
    he will cut me off with pining sickness:
    from day even to night wilt thou make an end of me.
¹³ I reckoned till morning, that as a lion so will he break all my
       bones:
    from day even to night wilt thou make an end of me.
¹⁴ Like a crane or a swallow, so did I chatter:
    I did mourn as a dove:
    my eyes fail with looking upward:
    O LORD, I am oppressed, undertake for me.
¹⁵ What shall I say?
    he hath both spoken unto me, and himself hath done it:
    I shall go softly all my years in the bitterness of my soul.
¹⁶ O Lord, by these things men live:
    and in all these things is the life of my spirit,
    so wilt thou recover me, and make me to live.
¹⁷ Behold, for peace I had great bitterness:
    but thou hast in love to my soul delivered it from the pit of
       corruption:
    for thou hast cast all my sins behind thy back.
¹⁸ For the grave cannot praise thee,
    death cannot celebrate thee:
    they that go down into the pit cannot hope for thy truth.
¹⁹ The living, the living, he shall praise thee, as I do this day:

the father to the children shall make known thy truth.
20 The LORD was ready to save me:
therefore we will sing my songs to the stringed instruments
all the days of our life in the house of the LORD.'

21 For Isaiah had said, 'Let them take a lump of figs, and lay it for a plaster upon the boil, and he shall recover'. 22 Hezekiah also had said, 'What is the sign that I shall go up to the house of the LORD?'

39 At that time Merodach-baladan, the son of Baladan, king of Babylon, sent letters and a present to Hezekiah: for he had heard that he had been sick, and was recovered. 2 And Hezekiah was glad of them, and showed them the house of his precious things, the silver, and the gold, and the spices, and the precious ointment, and all the house of his armour, and all that was found in his treasures: there was nothing in his house, nor in all his dominion, that Hezekiah showed them not.

3 Then came Isaiah the prophet unto king Hezekiah, and said unto him, 'What said these men? and from whence came they unto thee?' And Hezekiah said, 'They are come from a far country unto me, even from Babylon'. 4 Then said he, 'What have they seen in thy house?' And Hezekiah answered, 'All that is in my house have they seen: there is nothing among my treasures that I have not shown them'. 5 Then said Isaiah to Hezekiah, 'Hear the word of the LORD of hosts: 6 "Behold, the days come, that all that is in thy house, and that which thy fathers have laid up in store until this day, shall be carried to Babylon: nothing shall be left," saith the LORD. 7 "And of thy sons that shall issue from thee, which thou shalt beget, shall they take away; and they shall be eunuchs in the palace of the king of Babylon."' 8 Then said Hezekiah to Isaiah, 'Good is the word of the LORD which thou hast spoken'. He said moreover, 'For there shall be peace and truth in my days'.

40 'Comfort ye, comfort ye my people,' saith your God.
2 'Speak ye comfortably to Jerusalem, and cry unto her,
that her warfare is accomplished,
that her iniquity is pardoned:
for she hath received of the LORD's hand double for all her sins.'

3 The voice of him that crieth in the wilderness,
'Prepare ye the way of the LORD,
make straight in the desert a highway for our God.
4 Every valley shall be exalted,
and every mountain and hill shall be made low:
and the crooked shall be made straight,
and the rough places plain.
5 And the glory of the LORD shall be revealed,
and all flesh shall see it together:
for the mouth of the LORD hath spoken it.'

⁶ The voice said, 'Cry'.
  And he said, 'What shall I cry?'
  'All flesh is grass,
  and all the goodliness thereof is as the flower of the field.
⁷ The grass withereth, the flower fadeth;
  because the Spirit of the LORD bloweth upon it:
  surely the people is grass.
⁸ The grass withereth, the flower fadeth;
  but the word of our God shall stand for ever.'

⁹ O Zion, that bringest good tidings,
  get thee up into the high mountain:
  O Jerusalem, that bringest good tidings,
  lift up thy voice with strength,
  lift it up, be not afraid:
  say unto the cities of Judah, 'Behold your God'.
¹⁰ Behold, the Lord GOD will come with strong hand,
  and his arm shall rule for him:
  behold, his reward is with him, and his work before him.
¹¹ He shall feed his flock like a shepherd:
  he shall gather the lambs with his arm,
  and carry them in his bosom,
  and shall gently lead those that are with young.

¹² Who hath measured the waters in the hollow of his hand,
  and meted out heaven with the span,
  and comprehended the dust of the earth in a measure,
  and weighed the mountains in scales,
  and the hills in a balance?
¹³ Who hath directed the Spirit of the LORD,
  or being his counsellor hath taught him?
¹⁴ With whom took he counsel,
  and who instructed him,
  and taught him in the path of judgement,
  and taught him knowledge,
  and showed to him the way of understanding?
¹⁵ Behold, the nations are as a drop of a bucket,
  and are counted as the small dust of the balance:
  behold, he taketh up the isles as a very little thing.
¹⁶ And Lebanon is not sufficient to burn,
  nor the beasts thereof sufficient for a burnt offering.
¹⁷ All nations before him are as nothing,
  and they are counted to him less than nothing, and vanity.

¹⁸ To whom then will ye liken God?
  or what likeness will ye compare unto him?
¹⁹ The workman melteth a graven image,
  and the goldsmith spreadeth it over with gold,

and casteth silver chains.

²⁰ He that is so impoverished that he hath no oblation
  chooseth a tree that will not rot;
  he seeketh unto him a cunning workman
  to prepare a graven image that shall not be moved.

²¹ Have ye not known? have ye not heard?
  hath it not been told you from the beginning?
  have ye not understood from the foundations of the earth?
²² It is he that sitteth upon the circle of the earth,
  and the inhabitants thereof are as grasshoppers;
  that stretcheth out the heavens as a curtain,
  and spreadeth them out as a tent to dwell in:
²³ that bringeth the princes to nothing;
  he maketh the judges of the earth as vanity.
²⁴ Yea, they shall not be planted,
  yea, they shall not be sown,
  yea, their stock shall not take root in the earth:
  and he shall also blow upon them, and they shall wither,
  and the whirlwind shall take them away as stubble.

²⁵ 'To whom then will ye liken me,
  or shall I be equal?' saith the Holy One.
²⁶ Lift up your eyes on high,
  and behold who hath created these things,
  that bringeth out their host by number:
  he calleth them all by names by the greatness of his might,
  for that he is strong in power; not one faileth.

²⁷ Why sayest thou, O Jacob, and speakest, O Israel,
  'My way is hid from the LORD,
  and my judgement is passed over from my God'?
²⁸ Hast thou not known? hast thou not heard,
  that the everlasting God, the LORD,
  the Creator of the ends of the earth,
  fainteth not, neither is weary?
  there is no searching of his understanding.
²⁹ He giveth power to the faint,
  and to them that have no might he increaseth strength.
³⁰ Even the youths shall faint and be weary,
  and the young men shall utterly fall.
³¹ But they that wait upon the LORD shall renew their strength:
  they shall mount up with wings as eagles,
  they shall run, and not be weary,
  and they shall walk, and not faint.

41

¹'Keep silence before me, O islands,
and let the people renew their strength:
let them come near, then let them speak:
let us come near together to judgement.
² Who raised up the righteous man from the east,
called him to his foot, gave the nations before him,
and made him rule over kings?
he gave them as the dust to his sword,
and as driven stubble to his bow.
³ He pursued them, and passed safely;
even by the way that he had not gone with his feet.
⁴ Who hath wrought and done it,
calling the generations from the beginning?
I the Lord, the first,
and with the last, I am he.
⁵ The isles saw it, and feared,
the ends of the earth were afraid, drew near, and came.
⁶ They helped every one his neighbour,
and every one said to his brother, "Be of good courage".
⁷ So the carpenter encouraged the goldsmith,
and he that smootheth with the hammer him that smote the
anvil,
saying, "It is ready for the soldering":
and he fastened it with nails, that it should not be moved.

⁸'But thou, Israel, art my servant,
Jacob whom I have chosen,
the seed of Abraham my friend.
⁹ Thou whom I have taken from the ends of the earth,
and called thee from the chief men thereof,
and said unto thee, "Thou art my servant,
I have chosen thee, and not cast thee away".
¹⁰ Fear thou not, for I am with thee:
be not dismayed, for I am thy God:
I will strengthen thee, yea, I will help thee,
yea, I will uphold thee with the right hand of my
righteousness.
¹¹ Behold, all they that were incensed against thee
shall be ashamed and confounded:
they shall be as nothing,
and they that strive with thee shall perish.
¹² Thou shalt seek them, and shalt not find them,
even them that contended with thee:
they that war against thee shall be as nothing,
and as a thing of nought.
¹³ For I the Lord thy God will hold thy right hand,
saying unto thee, "Fear not, I will help thee".
¹⁴ Fear not, thou worm Jacob, and ye men of Israel:

I will help thee,' saith the LORD,
and thy redeemer, the Holy One of Israel.
¹⁵ 'Behold, I will make thee a new sharp threshing instrument
having teeth:
thou shalt thresh the mountains, and beat them small,
and shalt make the hills as chaff.
¹⁶ Thou shalt fan them, and the wind shall carry them away,
and the whirlwind shall scatter them:
and thou shalt rejoice in the LORD,
and shalt glory in the Holy One of Israel.

¹⁷ 'When the poor and needy seek water, and there is none,
and their tongue faileth for thirst,
I the LORD will hear them,
I the God of Israel will not forsake them.
¹⁸ I will open rivers in high places,
and fountains in the midst of the valleys:
I will make the wilderness a pool of water,
and the dry land springs of water.
¹⁹ I will plant in the wilderness the cedar,
the shittah tree, and the myrtle, and the oil tree:
I will set in the desert the fir tree,
and the pine, and the box tree together:
²⁰ that they may see, and know,
and consider, and understand together,
that the hand of the LORD hath done this,
and the Holy One of Israel hath created it.

²¹ 'Produce your cause,' saith the LORD,
'bring forth your strong reasons,' saith the King of Jacob.
²² 'Let them bring them forth, and show us what shall happen:
let them show the former things what they be,
that we may consider them, and know the latter end of them;
or declare us things for to come.
²³ Show the things that are to come hereafter,
that we may know that ye are gods:
yea, do good, or do evil,
that we may be dismayed, and behold it together.
²⁴ Behold, ye are of nothing, and your work of nought:
an abomination is he that chooseth you.

²⁵ 'I have raised up one from the north, and he shall come:
from the rising of the sun shall he call upon my name:
and he shall come upon princes as upon mortar,
and as the potter treadeth clay.
²⁶ Who hath declared from the beginning, that we may know?
and beforetime, that we may say, "He is righteous"?

yea, there is none that showeth,
yea, there is none that declareth,
yea, there is none that heareth your words.

27 The first shall say to Zion, "Behold, behold them":
and I will give to Jerusalem one that bringeth good tidings.

28 For I beheld, and there was no man, even amongst them,
and there was no counsellor,
that, when I asked of them, could answer a word.

29 Behold, they are all vanity, their works are nothing:
their molten images are wind and confusion.

42

'Behold my servant whom I uphold,
my elect, in whom my soul delighteth:
I have put my spirit upon him,
he shall bring forth judgement to the Gentiles.

2 He shall not cry, nor lift up,
nor cause his voice to be heard in the street.

3 A bruised reed shall he not break,
and the smoking flax shall he not quench:
he shall bring forth judgement unto truth.

4 He shall not fail nor be discouraged,
till he have set judgement in the earth:
and the isles shall wait for his law.'

5 Thus saith God the LORD,
he that created the heavens, and stretched them out,
he that spread forth the earth and that which cometh out of it,
he that giveth breath unto the people upon it,
and spirit to them that walk therein:

6 'I the LORD have called thee in righteousness,
and will hold thy hand, and will keep thee,
and give thee for a covenant of the people,
for a light of the Gentiles:

7 to open the blind eyes,
to bring out the prisoners from the prison,
and them that sit in darkness out of the prison-house.

8 I am the LORD: that is my name:
and my glory will I not give to another,
neither my praise to graven images.

9 Behold, the former things are come to pass,
and new things do I declare:
before they spring forth I tell you of them.'

10 Sing unto the LORD a new song,
and his praise from the end of the earth,
ye that go down to the sea, and all that is therein;
the isles, and the inhabitants thereof.

¹¹ Let the wilderness and the cities thereof lift up their voice,
the villages that Kedar doth inhabit:
let the inhabitants of the rock sing,
let them shout from the top of the mountains.
¹² Let them give glory unto the LORD,
and declare his praise in the islands.
¹³ The LORD shall go forth as a mighty man,
he shall stir up jealousy like a man of war:
he shall cry, yea, roar;
he shall prevail against his enemies.

¹⁴ I have long time held my peace,
I have been still, and refrained myself:
now will I cry like a travailing woman,
I will destroy and devour at once.
¹⁵ I will make waste mountains and hills,
and dry up all their herbs,
and I will make the rivers islands,
and I will dry up the pools.
¹⁶ And I will bring the blind by a way that they knew not,
I will lead them in paths that they have not known:
I will make darkness light before them,
and crooked things straight.
These things will I do unto them, and not forsake them.

¹⁷ They shall be turned back,
they shall be greatly ashamed, that trust in graven images,
that say to the molten images, 'Ye are our gods'.
¹⁸ Hear, ye deaf, and look, ye blind, that ye may see.
¹⁹ Who is blind, but my servant?
or deaf, as my messenger that I sent?
who is blind as he that is perfect,
and blind as the LORD's servant?
²⁰ seeing many things, but thou observest not:
opening the ears, but he heareth not.
²¹ The LORD is well pleased for his righteousness' sake,
he will magnify the law, and make it honourable.
²² But this is a people robbed and spoiled,
they are all of them snared in holes,
and they are hid in prison-houses:
they are for a prey, and none delivereth;
for a spoil, and none saith, 'Restore'.
²³ Who among you will give ear to this?
who will hearken and hear for the time to come?
²⁴ Who gave Jacob for a spoil, and Israel to the robbers?
did not the LORD, he against whom we have sinned?
For they would not walk in his ways,
neither were they obedient unto his law.

²⁵ Therefore he hath poured upon him
the fury of his anger, and the strength of battle:
and it hath set him on fire round about, yet he knew not;
and it burnt him, yet he laid it not to heart.

43 But now thus saith the LORD that created thee, O Jacob,
and he that formed thee, O Israel,
'Fear not: for I have redeemed thee,
I have called thee by thy name, thou art mine.
² When thou passest through the waters, I will be with thee;
and through the rivers, they shall not overflow thee:
when thou walkest through the fire, thou shalt not be burnt;
neither shall the flame kindle upon thee.
³ For I am the LORD thy God,
the Holy One of Israel, thy Saviour:
I gave Egypt for thy ransom,
Ethiopia and Seba for thee.
⁴ Since thou wast precious in my sight,
thou hast been honourable, and I have loved thee:
therefore will I give men for thee, and people for thy life.
⁵ Fear not: for I am with thee:
I will bring thy seed from the east,
and gather thee from the west.
⁶ I will say to the north, "Give up";
and to the south, "Keep not back:
bring my sons from far,
and my daughters from the ends of the earth;
⁷ even every one that is called by my name:
for I have created him for my glory,
I have formed him, yea, I have made him."'

⁸ Bring forth the blind people that have eyes,
and the deaf that have ears.
⁹ Let all the nations be gathered together,
and let the people be assembled:
who among them can declare this,
and show us former things?
let them bring forth their witnesses, that they may be justified:
or let them hear, and say, 'It is truth'.
¹⁰ 'Ye are my witnesses,' saith the LORD,
'and my servant whom I have chosen:
that ye may know and believe me,
and understand that I am he:
before me there was no God formed,
neither shall there be after me.
¹¹ I, even I, am the LORD,
and besides me there is no saviour.
¹² I have declared, and have saved,

and I have shown, when there was no strange god among you:
therefore ye are my witnesses,' saith the Lord, 'that I am God.
[13] Yea, before the day was, I am he;
and there is none that can deliver out of my hand:
I will work, and who shall let it?'

[14] Thus saith the Lord, your redeemer, the Holy One of Israel,
'For your sake I have sent to Babylon,
and have brought down all their nobles,
and the Chaldeans, whose cry is in the ships.
[15] I am the Lord, your Holy One,
the creator of Israel, your King.'
[16] Thus saith the Lord, which maketh a way in the sea,
and a path in the mighty waters:
[17] which bringeth forth the chariot and horse,
the army and the power:
they shall lie down together, they shall not rise:
they are extinct, they are quenched as tow.

[18] 'Remember ye not the former things,
neither consider the things of old.
[19] Behold, I will do a new thing:
now it shall spring forth; shall ye not know it?
I will even make a way in the wilderness,
and rivers in the desert.
[20] The beast of the field shall honour me,
the dragons and the owls,
because I give waters in the wilderness,
and rivers in the desert,
to give drink to my people, my chosen.
[21] This people have I formed for myself,
they shall show forth my praise.

[22] 'But thou hast not called upon me, O Jacob,
but thou hast been weary of me, O Israel.
[23] Thou hast not brought me the small cattle of thy burnt offerings,
neither hast thou honoured me with thy sacrifices.
I have not caused thee to serve with an offering,
nor wearied thee with incense.
[24] Thou hast bought me no sweet cane with money,
neither hast thou filled me with the fat of thy sacrifices:
but thou hast made me to serve with thy sins,
thou hast wearied me with thy iniquities.
[25] I, even I am he that blotteth out thy transgressions for my own sake,
and will not remember thy sins.
[26] Put me in remembrance:
let us plead together:

declare thou, that thou mayest be justified.
²⁷ Thy first father hath sinned,
and thy teachers have transgressed against me.
²⁸ Therefore I have profaned the princes of the sanctuary,
and have given Jacob to the curse,
and Israel to reproaches.

44

'Yet now hear, O Jacob my servant,
and Israel, whom I have chosen.'
² Thus saith the Lord that made thee,
and formed thee from the womb, which will help thee:
'Fear not, O Jacob, my servant,
and thou, Jeshurun, whom I have chosen.
³ For I will pour water upon him that is thirsty,
and floods upon the dry ground:
I will pour my spirit upon thy seed,
and my blessing upon thy offspring:
⁴ and they shall spring up as among the grass,
as willows by the watercourses.
⁵ One shall say, "I am the Lord's";
and another shall call himself by the name of Jacob;
and another shall subscribe with his hand unto the Lord,
and surname himself by the name of Israel.'

⁶ Thus saith the Lord the King of Israel,
and his redeemer the Lord of hosts,
'I am the first, and I am the last,
and besides me there is no God.
⁷ And who, as I, shall call, and shall declare it,
and set it in order for me,
since I appointed the ancient people?
and the things that are coming, and shall come?
let them show unto them.
⁸ Fear ye not, neither be afraid:
have not I told thee from that time, and have declared it?
ye are even my witnesses.
Is there a God besides me?
yea, there is no God, I know not any.'

⁹ They that make a graven image are all of them vanity,
and their delectable things shall not profit,
and they are their own witnesses,
they see not, nor know;
that they may be ashamed.
¹⁰ Who hath formed a god,
or molten a graven image that is profitable for nothing?
¹¹ Behold, all his fellows shall be ashamed:
and the workmen, they are of men:

let them all be gathered together, let them stand up;
yet they shall fear, and they shall be ashamed together.

¹² The smith with the tongs both worketh in the coals,
and fashioneth it with hammers,
and worketh it with the strength of his arms:
yea, he is hungry, and his strength faileth:
he drinketh no water, and is faint.
¹³ The carpenter stretcheth out his rule:
he marketh it out with the line:
he fitteth it with planes,
and he marketh it out with the compass,
and maketh it after the figure of a man,
according to the beauty of a man;
that it may remain in the house.
¹⁴ He heweth him down cedars,
and taketh the cypress and the oak,
which he strengtheneth for himself among the trees of the forest:
he planteth an ash, and the rain doth nourish it.
¹⁵ Then shall it be for a man to burn:
for he will take thereof, and warm himself;
yea, he kindleth it, and baketh bread;
yea, he maketh a god, and worshippeth it:
he maketh it a graven image, and falleth down thereto.
¹⁶ He burneth part thereof in the fire:
with part thereof he eateth flesh:
he roasteth roast, and is satisfied:
yea, he warmeth himself, and saith,
'Aha, I am warm, I have seen the fire'.
¹⁷ And the residue thereof he maketh a god,
even his graven image:
he falleth down unto it, and worshippeth it,
and prayeth unto it, and saith,
'Deliver me, for thou art my god'.
¹⁸ They have not known nor understood:
for he hath shut their eyes, that they cannot see;
and their hearts, that they cannot understand.
¹⁹ And none considereth in his heart,
neither is there knowledge nor understanding to say,
'I have burnt part of it in the fire,
yea, also I have baked bread upon the coals thereof:
I have roasted flesh, and eaten it;
and shall I make the residue thereof an abomination?
shall I fall down to the stock of a tree?'
²⁰ He feedeth of ashes:
a deceived heart hath turned him aside,
that he cannot deliver his soul,
nor say, 'Is there not a lie in my right hand?'

21 'Remember these, O Jacob and Israel;
for thou art my servant:
I have formed thee: thou art my servant,
O Israel; thou shalt not be forgotten of me.

22 I have blotted out, as a thick cloud, thy transgressions,
and, as a cloud, thy sins:
return unto me, for I have redeemed thee.'

23 Sing, O ye heavens; for the LORD hath done it:
shout, ye lower parts of the earth:
break forth into singing, ye mountains,
O forest, and every tree therein:
for the LORD hath redeemed Jacob,
and glorified himself in Israel.

24 Thus saith the LORD, thy Redeemer,
and he that formed thee from the womb,
'I am the LORD that maketh all things,
that stretcheth forth the heavens alone,
that spreadeth abroad the earth by myself:

25 that frustrateth the tokens of the liars,
and maketh diviners mad,
that turneth wise men backward,
and maketh their knowledge foolish:

26 that confirmeth the word of his servant,
and performeth the counsel of his messengers,
that saith to Jerusalem, "Thou shalt be inhabited";
and to the cities of Judah, "Ye shall be built,
and I will raise up the decayed places thereof".

27 That saith to the deep, "Be dry,
and I will dry up thy rivers".

28 That saith of Cyrus, "He is my shepherd,
and shall perform all my pleasure":
even saying to Jerusalem, "Thou shalt be built",
and to the temple, "Thy foundation shall be laid".'

45 Thus saith the LORD to his anointed,
to Cyrus, whose right hand I have held,
to subdue nations before him:
and I will loose the loins of kings
to open before him the two leaved gates,
and the gates shall not be shut.

2 'I will go before thee, and make the crooked places straight,
I will break in pieces the gates of brass,
and cut in sunder the bars of iron.

3 And I will give thee the treasures of darkness,
and hidden riches of secret places,
that thou mayest know that I, the LORD,
which call thee by thy name, am the God of Israel.

⁴ For Jacob my servant's sake, and Israel my elect,
  I have even called thee by thy name:
  I have surnamed thee, though thou hast not known me.

⁵ 'I am the LORD, and there is none else,
  there is no God besides me:
  I girded thee, though thou hast not known me:
⁶ that they may know from the rising of the sun, and from the
    west,
  that there is none besides me.
  I am the LORD, and there is none else.
⁷ I form the light, and create darkness:
  I make peace, and create evil:
  I the LORD do all these things.
⁸ Drop down, ye heavens, from above,
  and let the skies pour down righteousness:
  let the earth open, and let them bring forth salvation,
  and let righteousness spring up together:
  I the LORD have created it.
⁹ Woe unto him that striveth with his Maker:
  let the potsherd strive with the potsherds of the earth:
  shall the clay say to him that fashioneth it, "What makest thou?"
  or thy work, "He hath no hands?"
¹⁰ Woe unto him that saith unto his father, "What begettest thou?"
  or to the woman, "What hast thou brought forth?"'
¹¹ Thus saith the LORD, the Holy One of Israel, and his Maker,
  'Ask me of things to come concerning my sons,
  and concerning the work of my hands command ye me.
¹² I have made the earth, and created man upon it:
  I, even my hands have stretched out the heavens,
  and all their host have I commanded.
¹³ I have raised him up in righteousness,
  and I will direct all his ways:
  he shall build my city, and he shall let go my captives,
  not for price nor reward,'
  saith the LORD of hosts.

¹⁴ Thus saith the LORD,
  'The labour of Egypt, and merchandise of Ethiopia and of the
    Sabeans, men of stature,
  shall come over unto thee, and they shall be thine,
  they shall come after thee,
  in chains they shall come over:
  and they shall fall down unto thee,
  they shall make supplication unto thee, saying,
  "Surely God is in thee,
  and there is none else,
  there is no God.

¹⁵ Verily thou art a God that hidest thyself,
  O God of Israel the Saviour."
¹⁶ They shall be ashamed, and also confounded all of them:
  they shall go to confusion together that are makers of idols.
¹⁷ But Israel shall be saved in the LORD with an everlasting
    salvation:
  ye shall not be ashamed nor confounded world without end.'

¹⁸ For thus saith the LORD that created the heavens,
  God himself that formed the earth and made it;
  he hath established it,
  he created it not in vain,
  he formed it to be inhabited:
  'I am the LORD, and there is none else.
¹⁹ I have not spoken in secret, in a dark place of the earth:
  I said not unto the seed of Jacob, "Seek ye me in vain":
  I the LORD speak righteousness,
  I declare things that are right.

²⁰ 'Assemble yourselves and come:
  draw near together, ye that are escaped of the nations:
  they have no knowledge that set up the wood of their graven
    image,
  and pray unto a god that cannot save.
²¹ Tell ye, and bring them near,
  yea, let them take counsel together,
  who hath declared this from ancient time?
  who hath told it from that time?
  Have not I the LORD?
  and there is no God else besides me,
  a just God and a Saviour,
  there is none besides me.
²² Look unto me, and be ye saved, all the ends of the earth:
  for I am God,
  and there is none else.
²³ I have sworn by myself:
  the word is gone out of my mouth in righteousness, and shall
    not return,
  that unto me every knee shall bow,
  every tongue shall swear.'

²⁴ 'Surely,' shall one say, 'in the LORD have I righteousness and
    strength:
  even to him shall men come,
  and all that are incensed against him shall be ashamed.'
²⁵ In the LORD shall all the seed of Israel be justified,
  and shall glory.

46

Bel boweth down, Nebo stoopeth,
their idols were upon the beasts, and upon the cattle:
your carriages were heavy laden,
they are a burden to the weary beast.
² They stoop, they bow down together,
they could not deliver the burden,
but themselves are gone into captivity.

³ 'Hearken unto me, O house of Jacob,
and all the remnant of the house of Israel,
which are borne by me from the belly,
which are carried from the womb.
⁴ And even to your old age I am he,
and even to hoar hairs will I carry you:
I have made, and I will bear,
even I will carry, and will deliver you.

⁵ 'To whom will ye liken me, and make me equal,
and compare me, that we may be like?
⁶ They lavish gold out of the bag,
and weigh silver in the balance,
and hire a goldsmith, and he maketh it a god:
they fall down, yea, they worship.
⁷ They bear him upon the shoulder,
they carry him, and set him in his place, and he standeth;
from his place shall he not remove:
yea, one shall cry unto him, yet can he not answer,
nor save him out of his trouble.
⁸ Remember this, and show yourselves men:
bring it again to mind, O ye transgressors.
⁹ Remember the former things of old,
for I am God, and there is none else,
I am God, and there is none like me,
¹⁰ declaring the end from the beginning,
and from ancient times the things that are not yet done,
saying, "My counsel shall stand, and I will do all my pleasure":
¹¹ calling a ravenous bird from the east,
the man that executeth my counsel from a far country:
yea, I have spoken it, I will also bring it to pass;
I have purposed it, I will also do it.

¹² 'Hearken unto me, ye stout-hearted,
that are far from righteousness:
¹³ I bring near my righteousness:
it shall not be far off, and my salvation shall not tarry;
and I will place salvation in Zion for Israel my glory.'

47

Come down, and sit in the dust:
O virgin daughter of Babylon, sit on the ground:
there is no throne, O daughter of the Chaldeans:
for thou shalt no more be called tender and delicate.
[2] Take the millstones, and grind meal:
uncover thy locks, make bare the leg,
uncover the thigh, pass over the rivers.
[3] Thy nakedness shall be uncovered,
yea, thy shame shall be seen:
I will take vengeance, and I will not meet thee as a man.
[4] As for our redeemer, the LORD of hosts is his name,
the Holy One of Israel.
[5] Sit thou silent, and get thee into darkness,
O daughter of the Chaldeans:
for thou shalt no more be called the lady of kingdoms.

[6] I was wroth with my people:
I have polluted my inheritance, and given them into thy hand:
thou didst show them no mercy;
upon the ancient hast thou very heavily laid the yoke.

[7] And thou saidst, 'I shall be a lady for ever':
so that thou didst not lay these things to thy heart,
neither didst remember the latter end of it.
[8] Therefore hear now this, thou that art given to pleasures,
that dwellest carelessly, that sayest in thy heart,
'I am, and none else besides me;
I shall not sit as a widow,
neither shall I know the loss of children':
[9] but these two things shall come to thee in a moment in one day,
the loss of children, and widowhood:
they shall come upon thee in their perfection for the multitude
of thy sorceries,
and for the great abundance of thy enchantments.

[10] For thou hast trusted in thy wickedness:
thou hast said, 'None seeth me'.
Thy wisdom and thy knowledge, it hath perverted thee,
and thou hast said in thy heart,
'I am, and none else besides me'.

[11] Therefore shall evil come upon thee,
thou shalt not know from whence it riseth:
and mischief shall fall upon thee,
thou shalt not be able to put it off:
and desolation shall come upon thee suddenly, which thou shalt
not know.

¹² Stand now with thy enchantments,
and with the multitude of thy sorceries,
wherein thou hast laboured from thy youth;
if so be thou shalt be able to profit,
if so be thou mayest prevail.
¹³ Thou art wearied in the multitude of thy counsels:
let now the astrologers, the star-gazers, the monthly
prognosticators stand up,
and save thee from these things that shall come upon thee.
¹⁴ Behold, they shall be as stubble:
the fire shall burn them,
they shall not deliver themselves from the power of the flame:
there shall not be a coal to warm at, nor fire to sit before it.
¹⁵ Thus shall they be unto thee with whom thou hast laboured,
even thy merchants, from thy youth,
they shall wander every one to his quarter:
none shall save thee.

48 Hear ye this, O house of Jacob,
which are called by the name of Israel,
and are come forth out of the waters of Judah,
which swear by the name of the LORD,
and make mention of the God of Israel,
but not in truth, nor in righteousness.
² For they call themselves of the holy city,
and stay themselves upon the God of Israel;
the LORD of hosts is his name.
³ 'I have declared the former things from the beginning:
and they went forth out of my mouth, and I showed them,
I did them suddenly, and they came to pass.
⁴ Because I knew that thou art obstinate,
and thy neck is an iron sinew, and thy brow brass:
⁵ I have even from the beginning declared it to thee;
before it came to pass I showed it thee:
lest thou shouldst say, "My idol hath done them, and my graven
image,
and my molten image, hath commanded them".
⁶ Thou hast heard, see all this, and will not ye declare it?
I have shown thee new things from this time,
even hidden things, and thou didst not know them.
⁷ They are created now, and not from the beginning,
even before the day when thou heardest them not;
lest thou shouldst say, "Behold, I knew them".
⁸ Yea, thou heardest not, yea, thou knewest not,
yea, from that time that thy ear was not opened:
for I knew that thou wouldst deal very treacherously,
and wast called a transgressor from the womb.

⁹ 'For my name's sake will I defer my anger,
and for my praise will I refrain for thee,
that I cut thee not off.
¹⁰ Behold, I have refined thee, but not with silver;
I have chosen thee in the furnace of affliction.
¹¹ For my own sake, even for my own sake, will I do it:
for how should my name be polluted?
and I will not give my glory unto another.

¹² 'Hearken unto me, O Jacob and Israel, my called;
I am he, I am the first,
I also am the last.
¹³ My hand also hath laid the foundation of the earth,
and my right hand hath spanned the heavens:
when I call unto them, they stand up together.
¹⁴ All ye assemble yourselves and hear:
which among them hath declared these things?
The LORD hath loved him:
he will do his pleasure on Babylon,
and his arm shall be on the Chaldeans.
¹⁵ I, even I have spoken, yea, I have called him:
I have brought him, and he shall make his way prosperous.'

¹⁶ Come ye near unto me, hear ye this;
I have not spoken in secret from the beginning;
from the time that it was, there am I:
and now the Lord GOD and his Spirit hath sent me.
¹⁷ Thus saith the LORD, thy Redeemer,
the Holy One of Israel,
'I am the LORD thy God which teacheth thee to profit,
which leadeth thee by the way that thou shouldst go.
¹⁸ O that thou hadst hearkened to my commandments!
then had thy peace been as a river,
and thy righteousness as the waves of the sea.
¹⁹ Thy seed also had been as the sand,
and the offspring of thy bowels like the gravel thereof:
his name should not have been cut off
nor destroyed from before me.'

²⁰ Go ye forth of Babylon: flee ye from the Chaldeans,
with a voice of singing declare ye, tell this,
utter it even to the end of the earth:
say ye, 'The LORD hath redeemed his servant Jacob'.
²¹ And they thirsted not when he led them through the deserts:
he caused the waters to flow out of the rock for them:
he cleft the rock also, and the waters gushed out.
²² 'There is no peace,' saith the LORD, 'unto the wicked.'

49

Listen, O isles, unto me,
and hearken ye people from far.
The LORD hath called me from the womb,
from the bowels of my mother hath he made mention of my
    name.
[2] And he hath made my mouth like a sharp sword;
in the shadow of his hand hath he hid me,
and made me a polished shaft;
in his quiver hath he hid me,
[3] and said unto me, 'Thou art my servant, O Israel,
in whom I will be glorified'.
[4] Then I said, 'I have laboured in vain,
I have spent my strength for nought, and in vain:
yet surely my judgement is with the LORD,
and my work with my God'.

[5] 'And now,' saith the LORD that formed me from the womb to be
    his servant,
to bring Jacob again to him,
'though Israel be not gathered, yet shall I be glorious in the eyes
    of the LORD,
and my God shall be my strength.'
[6] And he said, 'It is a light thing that thou shouldst be my servant
to raise up the tribes of Jacob,
and to restore the preserved of Israel:
I will also give thee for a light to the Gentiles,
that thou mayest be my salvation unto the end of the earth'.

[7] Thus saith the LORD,
the Redeemer of Israel, and his Holy One,
to him whom man despiseth,
to him whom the nation abhorreth,
to a servant of rulers,
'Kings shall see and arise,
princes also shall worship,
because of the LORD that is faithful,
and the Holy One of Israel,
and he shall choose thee'.

[8] Thus saith the LORD,
'In an acceptable time have I heard thee,
and in a day of salvation have I helped thee:
and I will preserve thee,
and give thee for a covenant of the people,
to establish the earth,
to cause to inherit the desolate heritages:
[9] that thou mayest say to the prisoners, "Go forth";
to them that are in darkness, "Show yourselves".

They shall feed in the ways,
and their pastures shall be in all high places.
¹⁰ They shall not hunger nor thirst,
neither shall the heat nor sun smite them:
for he that hath mercy on them shall lead them,
even by the springs of water shall he guide them.
¹¹ And I will make all my mountains a way,
and my highways shall be exalted.
¹² Behold, these shall come from far:
and lo, these from the north and from the west,
and these from the land of Sinim.'

¹³ Sing, O heaven, and be joyful, O earth,
and break forth into singing, O mountains:
for the Lᴏʀᴅ hath comforted his people,
and will have mercy upon his afflicted.
¹⁴ But Zion said, 'The Lᴏʀᴅ hath forsaken me,
and my Lord hath forgotten me'.
¹⁵ 'Can a woman forget her sucking child,
that she should not have compassion on the son of her womb?
yea, they may forget, yet will I not forget thee.
¹⁶ Behold, I have graven thee upon the palms of my hands:
thy walls are continually before me.
¹⁷ Thy children shall make haste;
thy destroyers and they that made thee waste shall go forth of thee.

¹⁸ 'Lift up thy eyes round about, and behold:
all these gather themselves together, and come to thee.
As I live,' saith the Lᴏʀᴅ,
'thou shalt surely clothe thee with them all,
as with an ornament,
and bind them on thee, as a bride doeth.
¹⁹ For thy waste and thy desolate places,
and the land of thy destruction
shall even now be too narrow by reason of the inhabitants,
and they that swallowed thee up shall be far away.
²⁰ The children which thou shalt have,
after thou hast lost the others,
shall say again in thy ears,
"The place is too strait for me:
give place to me that I may dwell".
²¹ Then shalt thou say in thy heart,
"Who hath begotten me these,
seeing I have lost my children, and am desolate,
a captive, and removing to and fro?
and who hath brought up these?
Behold, I was left alone;
these, where had they been?"'

²² Thus saith the Lord God,
  'Behold, I will lift up my hand to the Gentiles,
  and set up my standard to the people:
  and they shall bring thy sons in their arms,
  and thy daughters shall be carried upon their shoulders.
²³ And kings shall be thy nursing fathers,
  and their queens thy nursing mothers:
  they shall bow down to thee with their face toward the earth,
  and lick up the dust of thy feet,
  and thou shalt know that I am the Lord:
  for they shall not be ashamed that wait for me.'

²⁴ Shall the prey be taken from the mighty,
  or the lawful captive delivered?
²⁵ But thus saith the Lord,
  'Even the captives of the mighty shall be taken away,
  and the prey of the terrible shall be delivered:
  for I will contend with him that contendeth with thee,
  and I will save thy children.
²⁶ And I will feed them that oppress thee with their own flesh,
  and they shall be drunken with their own blood, as with sweet
    wine:
  and all flesh shall know that I the Lord am thy Saviour and thy
    Redeemer,
  the mighty One of Jacob.'

50 Thus saith the Lord,
  'Where is the bill of your mother's divorcement, whom I have
    put away?
  or which of my creditors is it to whom I have sold you?
  Behold, for your iniquities have you sold yourselves,
  and for your transgressions is your mother put away.
² Wherefore, when I came, was there no man?
  when I called, was there none to answer?
  Is my hand shortened at all, that it cannot redeem?
  or have I no power to deliver?
  Behold, at my rebuke I dry up the sea,
  I make the rivers a wilderness:
  their fish stinketh, because there is no water,
  and dieth for thirst.
³ I clothe the heavens with blackness,
  and I make sackcloth their covering.'

⁴ The Lord God hath given me the tongue of the learned,
  that I should know how to speak a word in season to him that is
    weary:
  he wakeneth morning by morning,
  he wakeneth my ear to hear as the learned.

⁵ The Lord GOD hath opened my ear,
  and I was not rebellious, neither turned away back.
⁶ I gave my back to the smiters,
  and my cheeks to them that plucked off the hair:
  I hid not my face from shame and spitting.
⁷ For the Lord GOD will help me,
  therefore shall I not be confounded:
  therefore have I set my face like a flint,
  and I know that I shall not be ashamed.
⁸ He is near that justifieth me, who will contend with me?
  let us stand together:
  who is my adversary? let him come near to me.
⁹ Behold, the Lord GOD will help me,
  who is he that shall condemn me?
  Lo, they all shall wax old as a garment:
  the moth shall eat them up.

¹⁰ Who is among you that feareth the LORD,
  that obeyeth the voice of his servant,
  that walketh in darkness and hath no light?
  let him trust in the name of the LORD,
  and stay upon his God.
¹¹ Behold, all ye that kindle a fire,
  that compass yourselves about with sparks:
  walk in the light of your fire,
  and in the sparks that ye have kindled.
  This shall ye have of my hand,
  ye shall lie down in sorrow.

51 ¹ 'Hearken to me, ye that follow after righteousness,
  ye that seek the LORD:
  look unto the rock whence ye are hewn,
  and to the hole of the pit whence ye are dug.
² Look unto Abraham your father,
  and unto Sarah that bore you:
  for I called him alone,
  and blessed him, and increased him.'
³ For the LORD shall comfort Zion:
  he will comfort all her waste places,
  and he will make her wilderness like Eden,
  and her desert like the garden of the LORD:
  joy and gladness shall be found therein,
  thanksgiving, and the voice of melody.

⁴ 'Hearken unto me, my people,
  and give ear unto me, O my nation:
  for a law shall proceed from me,
  and I will make my judgement to rest for a light of the people.

⁵ My righteousness is near:
my salvation is gone forth,
and my arms shall judge the people:
the isles shall wait upon me,
and on my arm shall they trust.
⁶ Lift up your eyes to the heavens,
and look upon the earth beneath:
for the heavens shall vanish away like smoke,
and the earth shall wax old like a garment,
and they that dwell therein shall die in like manner:
but my salvation shall be for ever,
and my righteousness shall not be abolished.

⁷ 'Hearken unto me, ye that know righteousness,
the people in whose heart is my law:
fear ye not the reproach of men,
neither be ye afraid of their revilings.
⁸ For the moth shall eat them up like a garment,
and the worm shall eat them like wool:
but my righteousness shall be for ever,
and my salvation from generation to generation.'

⁹ Awake, awake, put on strength, O arm of the LORD,
awake, as in the ancient days, in the generations of old.
Art thou not it that hath cut Rahab, and wounded the dragon?
¹⁰ Art thou not it which hath dried the sea,
the waters of the great deep,
that hath made the depths of the sea a way for the ransomed to
pass over?
¹¹ Therefore the redeemed of the LORD shall return,
and come with singing unto Zion,
and everlasting joy shall be upon their head:
they shall obtain gladness and joy,
and sorrow and mourning shall flee away.

¹² 'I, even I am he that comforteth you:
who art thou, that thou shouldst be afraid of a man that shall
die,
and of the son of man which shall be made as grass?
¹³ and forgettest the LORD thy maker
that hath stretched forth the heavens,
and laid the foundations of the earth?
and hast feared continually every day
because of the fury of the oppressor,
as if he were ready to destroy?
and where is the fury of the oppressor?
¹⁴ The captive exile hasteneth that he may be loosed,
and that he should not die in the pit,

nor that his bread should fail.

¹⁵ But I am the LORD thy God,
that divided the sea, whose waves roared: '
the LORD of hosts is his name.

¹⁶ 'And I have put my words in thy mouth,
and have covered thee in the shadow of my hand,
that I may plant the heavens, and lay the foundations of the earth,
and say unto Zion, "Thou art my people".'

¹⁷ Awake, awake, stand up, O Jerusalem,
which hast drunk at the hand of the LORD the cup of his fury;
thou hast drunken the dregs of the cup of trembling,
and wrung them out.

¹⁸ There is none to guide her among all the sons whom she hath
brought forth:
neither is there any that taketh her by the hand of all the sons
that she hath brought up.

¹⁹ These two things are come unto thee;
who shall be sorry for thee?
desolation and destruction,
and the famine and the sword:
by whom shall I comfort thee?

²⁰ Thy sons have fainted,
they lie at the head of all the streets as a wild bull in a net:
they are full of the fury of the LORD,
the rebuke of thy God.

²¹ Therefore hear now this, thou afflicted,
and drunken, but not with wine:

²² thus saith thy Lord,
the LORD and thy God that pleadeth the cause of his people,
'Behold, I have taken out of thy hand the cup of trembling
even the dregs of the cup of my fury:
thou shalt no more drink it again.

²³ But I will put it into the hand of them that afflict thee:
which have said to thy soul, "Bow down, that we may go over":
and thou hast laid thy body as the ground,
and as the street to them that went over.'

52 Awake, awake, put on thy strength, O Zion,
put on thy beautiful garments, O Jerusalem, the holy city:
for henceforth there shall no more come into thee the
uncircumcised and the unclean.

² Shake thyself from the dust:
arise, and sit down, O Jerusalem:
loose thyself from the bands of thy neck,
O captive daughter of Zion.

³ For thus saith the LORD,

'Ye have sold yourselves for nought:
and ye shall be redeemed without money'.
⁴ For thus saith the Lord God,
'My people went down aforetime into Egypt to sojourn there,
and the Assyrian oppressed them without cause.
⁵ Now therefore, what have I here,' saith the Lord,
'that my people is taken away for nought?
they that rule over them make them to howl,' saith the Lord,
'and my name continually every day is blasphemed.
⁶ Therefore my people shall know my name:
therefore they shall know in that day that I am he that doth speak:
behold, it is I.'

⁷ How beautiful upon the mountains are the feet of him that
bringeth good tidings,
that publisheth peace,
that bringeth good tidings of good,
that publisheth salvation,
that saith unto Zion, 'Thy God reigneth'?
⁸ Thy watchmen shall lift up the voice,
with the voice together shall they sing:
for they shall see eye to eye when the Lord shall bring again Zion.

⁹ Break forth into joy,
sing together, ye waste places of Jerusalem:
for the Lord hath comforted his people,
he hath redeemed Jerusalem.
¹⁰ The Lord hath made bare his holy arm in the eyes of all the
nations,
and all the ends of the earth shall see the salvation of our God.

¹¹ Depart ye, depart ye, go ye out from thence,
touch no unclean thing;
go ye out of the midst of her;
be ye clean, that bear the vessels of the Lord.
¹² For ye shall not go out with haste, nor go by flight:
for the Lord will go before you:
and the God of Israel will be your rearward.

¹³ Behold, my servant shall deal prudently,
he shall be exalted and extolled, and be very high.
¹⁴ As many were astonished at thee
(his visage was so marred more than any man,
and his form more than the sons of men):
¹⁵ so shall he sprinkle many nations;
the kings shall shut their mouths at him:
for that which had not been told them shall they see,
and that which they had not heard shall they consider.

53

Who hath believed our report?
and to whom is the arm of the LORD revealed?

² For he shall grow up before him as a tender plant,
and as a root out of a dry ground:
he hath no form nor comeliness:
and when we shall see him,
there is no beauty that we should desire him.

³ He is despised and rejected of men,
a man of sorrows, and acquainted with grief:
and we hid as it were our faces from him;
he was despised, and we esteemed him not.

⁴ Surely he hath borne our griefs,
and carried our sorrows:
yet we did esteem him stricken,
smitten of God, and afflicted.

⁵ But he was wounded for our transgressions,
he was bruised for our iniquities:
the chastisement of our peace was upon him,
and with his stripes we are healed.

⁶ All we like sheep have gone astray,
we have turned every one to his own way,
and the LORD hath laid on him the iniquity of us all.

⁷ He was oppressed, and he was afflicted,
yet he opened not his mouth:
he is brought as a lamb to the slaughter,
and as a sheep before her shearers is dumb,
so he openeth not his mouth.

⁸ He was taken from prison and from judgement:
and who shall declare his generation?
for he was cut off out of the land of the living,
for the transgression of my people was he stricken.

⁹ And he made his grave with the wicked,
and with the rich in his death,
because he had done no violence,
neither was any deceit in his mouth.

¹⁰ Yet it pleased the LORD to bruise him;
he hath put him to grief:
when thou shalt make his soul an offering for sin,
he shall see his seed, he shall prolong his days,
and the pleasure of the LORD shall prosper in his hand.

¹¹ He shall see of the travail of his soul, and shall be satisfied:
by his knowledge shall my righteous servant justify many:
for he shall bear their iniquities.

¹² Therefore will I divide him a portion with the great,
and he shall divide the spoil with the strong:
because he hath poured out his soul unto death:

and he was numbered with the transgressors,
and he bore the sin of many,
and made intercession for the transgressors.

54 'Sing, O barren, thou that didst not bear;
break forth into singing, and cry aloud thou that didst not
travail with child:
for more are the children of the desolate
than the children of the married wife,' saith the LORD.

² Enlarge the place of thy tent,
and let them stretch forth the curtains of thy habitations:
spare not, lengthen thy cords, and strengthen thy stakes.
³ For thou shalt break forth on the right hand and on the left;
and thy seed shall inherit the Gentiles,
and make the desolate cities to be inhabited.
⁴ Fear not: for thou shalt not be ashamed:
neither be thou confounded, for thou shalt not be put to shame:
for thou shalt forget the shame of thy youth,
and shalt not remember the reproach of thy widowhood any more.
⁵ For thy Maker is thy husband
(the LORD of hosts is his name),
and thy Redeemer the Holy One of Israel;
the God of the whole earth shall he be called.
⁶ For the LORD hath called thee as a woman forsaken and grieved
in spirit,
and a wife of youth, when thou wast refused, saith thy God.
⁷ 'For a small moment have I forsaken thee,
but with great mercies will I gather thee.
⁸ In a little wrath I hid my face from thee for a moment;
but with everlasting kindness will I have mercy on thee,'
saith the LORD thy Redeemer.
⁹ 'For this is as the waters of Noah unto me:
for as I have sworn that the waters of Noah should no more go
over the earth;
so have I sworn that I would not be wroth with thee, nor rebuke
thee.
¹⁰ For the mountains shall depart, and the hills be removed,
but my kindness shall not depart from thee,
neither shall the covenant of my peace be removed,'
saith the LORD that hath mercy on thee.

¹¹ 'O thou afflicted, tossed with tempest and not comforted,
behold, I will lay thy stones with fair colours,
and lay thy foundations with sapphires.
¹² And I will make thy windows of agates,
and thy gates of carbuncles,
and all thy borders of pleasant stones.
¹³ And all thy children shall be taught of the LORD,

and great shall be the peace of thy children.
¹⁴ In righteousness shalt thou be established:
thou shalt be far from oppression, for thou shalt not fear:
and from terror, for it shall not come near thee.
¹⁵ Behold, they shall surely gather together, but not by me:
whosoever shall gather together against thee shall fall for thy
sake.
¹⁶ Behold, I have created the smith that bloweth the coals in the
fire,
and that bringeth forth an instrument for his work,
and I have created the waster to destroy.
¹⁷ No weapon that is formed against thee shall prosper,
and every tongue that shall rise against thee in judgement thou
shalt condemn.
This is the heritage of the servants of the Lord,
and their righteousness is of me,' saith the Lord.

55 Ho, every one that thirsteth, come ye to the waters,
and he that hath no money: come ye, buy, and eat,
yea, come, buy wine and milk without money and without price.
² Wherefore do ye spend money for that which is not bread?
and your labour for that which satisfieth not?
hearken diligently unto me, and eat ye that which is good,
and let your soul delight itself in fatness.
³ Incline your ear, and come unto me:
hear, and your soul shall live;
and I will make an everlasting covenant with you,
even the sure mercies of David.
⁴ Behold, I have given him for a witness to the people,
a leader and commander to the people.
⁵ Behold, thou shalt call a nation that thou knowest not,
and nations that knew not thee shall run unto thee
because of the Lord thy God, and for the Holy One of Israel,
for he hath glorified thee.

⁶ Seek ye the Lord while he may be found,
call ye upon him while he is near.
⁷ Let the wicked forsake his way,
and the unrighteous man his thoughts:
and let him return unto the Lord,
and he will have mercy upon him,
and to our God, for he will abundantly pardon.

⁸ 'For my thoughts are not your thoughts,
neither are your ways my ways,' saith the Lord.
⁹ 'For as the heavens are higher than the earth,
so are my ways higher than your ways,
and my thoughts than your thoughts.

¹⁰ For as the rain cometh down, and the snow from heaven,
and returneth not thither, but watereth the earth,
and maketh it bring forth and bud,
that it may give seed to the sower, and bread to the eater:
¹¹ so shall my word be that goeth forth out of my mouth:
it shall not return unto me void,
but it shall accomplish that which I please,
and it shall prosper in the thing whereto I sent it.
¹² For ye shall go out with joy, and be led forth with peace:
the mountains and the hills shall break forth before you into
singing,
and all the trees of the field shall clap their hands.
¹³ Instead of the thorn shall come up the fir tree,
and instead of the brier shall come up the myrtle tree:
and it shall be to the LORD for a name,
for an everlasting sign that shall not be cut off.'

56

Thus saith the LORD, 'Keep ye judgement, and do justice:
for my salvation is near to come,
and my righteousness to be revealed'.
² Blessed is the man that doeth this,
and the son of man that layeth hold on it:
that keepeth the sabbath from polluting it,
and keepeth his hand from doing any evil.

³ Neither let the son of the stranger, that hath joined himself to
the LORD, speak, saying,
'The LORD hath utterly separated me from his people':
neither let the eunuch say, 'Behold, I am a dry tree'.
⁴ For thus saith the LORD unto the eunuchs that keep my sabbaths,
and choose the things that please me,
and take hold of my covenant:
⁵ 'Even unto them will I give in my house and within my walls
a place and a name better than of sons and of daughters:
I will give them an everlasting name, that shall not be cut off.
⁶ Also the sons of the stranger,
that join themselves to the LORD, to serve him,
and to love the name of the LORD, to be his servants,
every one that keepeth the sabbath from polluting it,
and taketh hold of my covenant:
⁷ even them will I bring to my holy mountain,
and make them joyful in my house of prayer:
their burnt offerings and their sacrifices shall be accepted upon
my altar:
for my house shall be called a house of prayer for all people.'
⁸ The Lord God which gathereth the outcasts of Israel saith,
'Yet will I gather others to him,
besides those that are gathered unto him'.

⁹ All ye beasts of the field, come to devour,
   yea, all ye beasts in the forest.
¹⁰ His watchmen are blind:
   they are all ignorant, they are all dumb dogs, they cannot bark:
   sleeping, lying down, loving to slumber.
¹¹ Yea, they are greedy dogs which can never have enough,
   and they are shepherds that cannot understand:
   they all look to their own way,
   every one for his gain, from his quarter.
¹² 'Come ye,' say they, 'I will fetch wine,
   and we will fill ourselves with strong drink,
   and tomorrow shall be as this day,
   and much more abundant.'

57 The righteous perisheth, and no man layeth it to heart:
   and merciful men are taken away,
   none considering that the righteous is taken away from the evil
      to come.
² He shall enter into peace:
   they shall rest in their beds,
   each one walking in his uprightness.

³ But draw near hither, ye sons of the sorceress,
   the seed of the adulterer and the whore.
⁴ Against whom do ye sport yourselves?
   against whom make ye a wide mouth, and draw out the tongue?
   are ye not children of transgression, a seed of falsehood?
⁵ inflaming yourselves with idols under every green tree,
   slaying the children in the valleys under the clefts of the rocks?
⁶ Among the smooth stones of the stream is thy portion;
   they, they are thy lot:
   even to them hast thou poured a drink offering,
   thou hast offered a meat offering.
   Should I receive comfort in these?
⁷ Upon a lofty and high mountain hast thou set thy bed:
   even thither wentest thou up to offer sacrifice.
⁸ Behind the doors also and the posts hast thou set up thy
      remembrance:
   for thou hast discovered thyself to another than me, and art
      gone up:
   thou hast enlarged thy bed, and made a covenant with them:
   thou lovedst their bed where thou sawest it.
⁹ And thou wentest to the king with ointment,
   and didst increase thy perfumes,
   and didst send thy messengers far off,
   and didst debase thyself even unto hell.
¹⁰ Thou art wearied in the greatness of thy way;
   yet saidst thou not, 'There is no hope':

thou hast found the life of thy hand;
therefore thou wast not grieved.
[11] And of whom hast thou been afraid or feared,
that thou hast lied, and hast not remembered me,
nor laid it to thy heart?
have not I held my peace even of old,
and thou fearest me not?
[12] I will declare thy righteousness;
and thy works, for they shall not profit thee.

[13] When thou criest, let thy companies deliver thee:
but the wind shall carry them all away; vanity shall take them:
but he that putteth his trust in me shall possess the land,
and shall inherit my holy mountain,
[14] and shall say, 'Cast ye up, cast ye up, prepare the way,
take up the stumblingblock out of the way of my people'.
[15] For thus saith the high and lofty One
that inhabiteth eternity, whose name is Holy,
'I dwell in the high and holy place,
with him also that is of a contrite and humble spirit,
to revive the spirit of the humble,
and to revive the heart of the contrite ones.
[16] For I will not contend for ever,
neither will I be always wroth:
for the spirit should fail before me,
and the souls which I have made.
[17] For the iniquity of his covetousness was I wroth, and smote him:
I hid me, and was wroth,
and he went on frowardly in the way of his heart.
[18] I have seen his ways, and will heal him:
I will lead him also,
and restore comforts unto him and to his mourners.
[19] I create the fruit of the lips;
peace, peace to him that is far off,
and to him that is near,' saith the LORD,
'and I will heal him.
[20] But the wicked are like the troubled sea, when it cannot rest,
whose waters cast up mire and dirt.
[21] There is no peace,' saith my God, 'to the wicked.'

58

Cry aloud, spare not,
lift up thy voice like a trumpet,
and show my people their transgression,
and the house of Jacob their sins.
[2] Yet they seek me daily,
and delight to know my ways,
as a nation that did righteousness,
and forsook not the ordinance of their God:

they ask of me the ordinances of justice:
they take delight in approaching to God.

[3] 'Wherefore have we fasted,' say they, 'and thou seest not?
wherefore have we afflicted our soul, and thou takest no
knowledge?'
Behold, in the day of your fast you find pleasure,
and exact all your labours.
[4] Behold, ye fast for strife and debate,
and to smite with the fist of wickedness:
ye shall not fast as ye do this day,
to make your voice to be heard on high.
[5] Is it such a fast that I have chosen?
a day for a man to afflict his soul?
Is it to bow down his head as a bulrush,
and to spread sackcloth and ashes under him?
wilt thou call this a fast,
and an acceptable day to the LORD?
[6] Is not this the fast that I have chosen?
to loose the bands of wickedness,
to undo the heavy burdens,
and to let the oppressed go free,
and that ye break every yoke?
[7] Is it not to deal thy bread to the hungry,
and that thou bring the poor that are cast out to thy house?
when thou seest the naked, that thou cover him,
and that thou hide not thyself from thy own flesh?

[8] Then shall thy light break forth as the morning,
and thy health shall spring forth speedily:
and thy righteousness shall go before thee,
the glory of the LORD shall be thy rearward.
[9] Then shalt thou call, and the LORD shall answer;
thou shalt cry, and he shall say, 'Here I am'.
If thou take away from the midst of thee the yoke,
the putting forth of the finger, and speaking vanity:
[10] and if thou draw out thy soul to the hungry,
and satisfy the afflicted soul:
then shall thy light rise in obscurity,
and thy darkness be as the noonday.
[11] And the LORD shall guide thee continually,
and satisfy thy soul in drought, and make fat thy bones:
and thou shalt be like a watered garden,
and like a spring of water, whose waters fail not.
[12] And they that shall be of thee shall build the old waste places:
thou shalt raise up the foundations of many generations;
and thou shalt be called, the repairer of the breach,
the restorer of paths to dwell in.

¹³ If thou turn away thy foot from the sabbath,
from doing thy pleasure on my holy day, and call the sabbath a
delight,
the holy of the LORD, honourable,
and shalt honour him, not doing thy own ways,
nor finding thy own pleasure, nor speaking thy own words:
¹⁴ then shalt thou delight thyself in the LORD,
and I will cause thee to ride upon the high places of the earth,
and feed thee with the heritage of Jacob thy father:
for the mouth of the LORD hath spoken it.

59

Behold, the LORD's hand is not shortened, that it cannot save:
neither his ear heavy, that it cannot hear.
² But your iniquities have separated between you and your God,
and your sins have hid his face from you, that he will not hear.
³ For your hands are defiled with blood,
and your fingers with iniquity,
your lips have spoken lies,
your tongue hath muttered perverseness.
⁴ None calleth for justice, nor any pleadeth for truth:
they trust in vanity, and speak lies;
they conceive mischief, and bring forth iniquity.
⁵ They hatch cockatrice's eggs, and weave the spider's web:
he that eateth of their eggs dieth,
and that which is crushed breaketh out into a viper.
⁶ Their webs shall not become garments,
neither shall they cover themselves with their works:
their works are works of iniquity,
and the act of violence is in their hands.
⁷ Their feet run to evil,
and they make haste to shed innocent blood:
their thoughts are thoughts of iniquity,
wasting and destruction are in their paths.
⁸ The way of peace they know not,
and there is no judgement in their goings:
they have made them crooked paths:
whosoever goeth therein shall not know peace.

⁹ Therefore is judgement far from us,
neither doth justice overtake us:
we wait for light, but behold obscurity,
for brightness, but we walk in darkness.
¹⁰ We grope for the wall like the blind,
and we grope as if we had no eyes:
we stumble at noonday as in the night,
we are in desolate places as dead men.
¹¹ We roar all like bears, and mourn sore like doves:

we look for judgement, but there is none;
for salvation, but it is far off from us.
¹² For our transgressions are multiplied before thee,
and our sins testify against us:
for our transgressions are with us,
and as for our iniquities, we know them:
¹³ in transgressing and lying against the LORD,
and departing away from our God,
speaking oppression and revolt,
conceiving and uttering from the heart words of falsehood.
¹⁴ And judgement is turned away backward,
and justice standeth afar off:
for truth is fallen in the street, and equity cannot enter.
¹⁵ Yea, truth faileth,
and he that departeth from evil maketh himself a prey.

And the LORD saw it, and it displeased him
that there was no judgement.
¹⁶ And he saw that there was no man,
and wondered that there was no intercessor:
therefore his arm brought salvation unto him,
and his righteousness, it sustained him.
¹⁷ For he put on righteousness as a breastplate,
and a helmet of salvation upon his head;
and he put on the garments of vengeance for clothing,
and was clad with zeal as a cloak.
¹⁸ According to their deeds accordingly he will repay,
fury to his adversaries, recompense to his enemies;
to the islands he will repay recompense.
¹⁹ So shall they fear the name of the LORD from the west,
and his glory from the rising of the sun.
When the enemy shall come in like a flood,
the Spirit of the LORD shall lift up a standard against him.
²⁰ And the Redeemer shall come to Zion,
and unto them that turn from transgression in Jacob, saith the
LORD.

²¹ 'As for me, this is my covenant with them,' saith the LORD;
'my spirit that is upon thee,
and my words which I have put in thy mouth,
shall not depart out of thy mouth,
nor out of the mouth of thy seed,
nor out of the mouth of thy seed's seed,'
saith the LORD, 'from henceforth and for ever.'

60 Arise, shine, for thy light is come,
and the glory of the LORD is risen upon thee.
² For behold, the darkness shall cover the earth,

and gross darkness the people:
but the LORD shall arise upon thee,
and his glory shall be seen upon thee.
³ And the Gentiles shall come to thy light,
and kings to the brightness of thy rising.
⁴ Lift up thy eyes round about, and see:
all they gather themselves together, they come to thee:
thy sons shall come from far,
and thy daughters shall be nursed at thy side.
⁵ Then thou shalt see, and flow together,
and thy heart shall fear, and be enlarged;
because the abundance of the sea shall be converted unto thee,
the forces of the Gentiles shall come unto thee.
⁶ The multitude of camels shall cover thee,
the dromedaries of Midian and Ephah:
all they from Sheba shall come:
they shall bring gold and incense,
and they shall show forth the praises of the LORD.
⁷ 'All the flocks of Kedar shall be gathered together unto thee,
the rams of Nebaioth shall minister unto thee:
they shall come up with acceptance on my altar,
and I will glorify the house of my glory.'
⁸ Who are these that fly as a cloud,
and as the doves to their windows?
⁹ Surely the isles shall wait for me,
and the ships of Tarshish first,
to bring thy sons from far,
their silver and their gold with them,
unto the name of the LORD thy God,
and to the Holy One of Israel,
because he hath glorified thee.

¹⁰ 'And the sons of strangers shall build up thy walls,
and their kings shall minister unto thee:
for in my wrath I smote thee,
but in my favour have I had mercy on thee.
¹¹ Therefore thy gates shall be open continually,
they shall not be shut day nor night,
that men may bring unto thee the forces of the Gentiles,
and that their kings may be brought.
¹² For the nation and kingdom that will not serve thee shall perish,
yea, those nations shall be utterly wasted.
¹³ The glory of Lebanon shall come unto thee,
the fir tree, the pine tree, and the box together,
to beautify the place of my sanctuary,
and I will make the place of my feet glorious.
¹⁴ The sons also of them that afflicted thee shall come bending

unto thee:
and all they that despised thee shall bow themselves down at the
soles of thy feet,
and they shall call thee the city of the LORD,
the Zion of the Holy One of Israel.

¹⁵ Whereas thou hast been forsaken and hated,
so that no man went through thee,
I will make thee an eternal excellence,
a joy of many generations.

¹⁶ Thou shalt also suck the milk of the Gentiles,
and shalt suck the breast of kings,
and thou shalt know that I the LORD am thy Saviour and thy
Redeemer,
the mighty One of Jacob.

¹⁷ For brass I will bring gold,
and for iron I will bring silver,
and for wood brass, and for stones iron:
I will also make thy officers peace, and thy exactors
righteousness.

¹⁸ Violence shall no more be heard in thy land,
wasting nor destruction within thy borders,
but thou shalt call thy walls Salvation, and thy gates Praise.'

¹⁹ The sun shall be no more thy light by day,
neither for brightness shall the moon give light unto thee:
but the LORD shall be unto thee an everlasting light,
and thy God thy glory.

²⁰ Thy sun shall no more go down,
neither shall thy moon withdraw itself:
for the LORD shall be thy everlasting light,
and the days of thy mourning shall be ended.

²¹ 'Thy people also shall be all righteous:
they shall inherit the land for ever,
the branch of my planting, the work of my hands,
that I may be glorified.

²² A little one shall become a thousand,
and a small one a strong nation:
I the LORD will hasten it in his time.'

61 The Spirit of the Lord GOD is upon me,
because the LORD hath anointed me to preach good tidings
unto the meek,
he hath sent me to bind up the broken-hearted,
to proclaim liberty to the captives,
and the opening of the prison to them that are bound:

² to proclaim the acceptable year of the LORD,
and the day of vengeance of our God,

to comfort all that mourn:
³ to appoint unto them that mourn in Zion,
to give unto them beauty for ashes,
the oil of joy for mourning,
the garment of praise for the spirit of heaviness,
that they might be called trees of righteousness,
the planting of the LORD, that he might be glorified.

⁵ And they shall build the old wastes,
they shall raise up the former desolations,
and they shall repair the waste cities,
the desolations of many generations.
⁵ And strangers shall stand and feed your flocks,
and the sons of the alien shall be your ploughmen and your vine-
dressers.
⁶ But ye shall be named the Priests of the LORD:
men shall call you the Ministers of our God:
ye shall eat the riches of the Gentiles,
and in their glory shall you boast yourselves.

⁷ For your shame you shall have double;
and for confusion they shall rejoice in their portion:
therefore in their land they shall possess the double:
everlasting joy shall be unto them.

⁸ 'For I the LORD love judgement,
I hate robbery for burnt offering,
and I will direct their work in truth,
and I will make an everlasting covenant with them.'

⁹ And their seed shall be known among the Gentiles,
and their offspring among the people:
all that see them shall acknowledge them,
that they are the seed which the LORD hath blessed.

¹⁰ I will greatly rejoice in the LORD,
my soul shall be joyful in my God:
for he hath clothed me with the garments of salvation,
he hath covered me with the robe of righteousness,
as a bridegroom decketh himself with ornaments,
and as a bride adorneth herself with her jewels.
¹¹ For as the earth bringeth forth her bud,
and as the garden causeth the things that are sown in it to
spring forth:
so the Lord GOD will cause righteousness and praise
to spring forth before all the nations.

62 For Zion's sake will I not hold my peace,
and for Jerusalem's sake I will not rest,
until the righteousness thereof go forth as brightness,
and the salvation thereof as a lamp that burneth;

² and the Gentiles shall see thy righteousness,
and all kings thy glory:
and thou shalt be called by a new name,
which the mouth of the LORD shall name.

³ Thou shalt also be a crown of glory in the hand of the LORD,
and a royal diadem in the hand of thy God.

⁴ Thou shalt no more be termed Forsaken;
neither shall thy land any more be termed Desolate:
but thou shalt be called Hephzi-bah,
and thy land Beulah:
for the LORD delighteth in thee,
and thy land shall be married.

⁵ For as a young man marrieth a virgin,
so shall thy sons marry thee:
and as the bridegroom rejoiceth over the bride,
so shall thy God rejoice over thee.

⁶ I have set watchmen upon thy walls, O Jerusalem,
which shall never hold their peace day nor night:
ye that make mention of the LORD, keep not silence,

⁷ and give him no rest till he establish,
and till he make Jerusalem a praise in the earth.

⁸ The LORD hath sworn by his right hand,
and by the arm of his strength,
'Surely I will no more give thy corn to be meat for thy enemies,
and the sons of the stranger shall not drink thy wine,
for the which thou hast laboured':

⁹ but they that have gathered it shall eat it, and praise the LORD,
and they that have brought it together shall drink it in the
courts of my holiness.

¹⁰ Go through, go through the gates:
prepare you the way of the people:
cast up, cast up the highway,
gather out the stones,
lift up a standard for the people.

¹¹ Behold, the LORD hath proclaimed unto the end of the world,
say ye to the daughter of Zion, 'Behold, thy salvation cometh;
behold, his reward is with him, and his work before him'.

¹² And they shall call them,
the holy people, the redeemed of the LORD:
and thou shalt be called,
Sought out, a city not forsaken.

63

'Who is this that cometh from Edom,
with dyed garments from Bozrah?
this that is glorious in his apparel,
travelling in the greatness of his strength?'
'I that speak in righteousness, mighty to save.'

² 'Wherefore art thou red in thy apparel,
and thy garments like him that treadeth in the wine-vat?'

³ 'I have trodden the wine-press alone,
and of the people there was none with me:
for I will tread them in my anger, and trample them in my fury,
and their blood shall be sprinkled upon my garments,
and I will stain all my raiment.

⁴ For the day of vengeance is in my heart,
and the year of my redeemed is come.

⁵ And I looked, and there was none to help;
and I wondered that there was none to uphold:
therefore my own arm brought salvation unto me,
and my fury, it upheld me.

⁶ And I will tread down the people in my anger,
and make them drunk in my fury,
and I will bring down their strength to the earth.'

⁷ I will mention the loving-kindnesses of the LORD,
and the praises of the LORD,
according to all that the LORD hath bestowed on us;
and the great goodness towards the house of Israel,
which he hath bestowed on them according to his mercies,
and according to the multitude of his loving-kindnesses.

⁸ For he said, 'Surely they are my people,
children that will not lie':
so he was their Saviour.

⁹ In all their affliction he was afflicted,
and the angel of his presence saved them:
in his love and in his pity he redeemed them,
and he bore them, and carried them all the days of old.

¹⁰ But they rebelled, and vexed his holy Spirit:
therefore he was turned to be their enemy,
and he fought against them.

¹¹ Then he remembered the days of old, Moses, and his people,
saying,
'Where is he that brought them up out of the sea
with the shepherd of his flock?
where is he that put his holy Spirit within him?

¹² that led them by the right hand of Moses with his glorious arm,
dividing the water before them,
to make himself an everlasting name?

¹³ that led them through the deep as a horse in the wilderness,

that they should not stumble?'

¹⁴ As a beast goeth down into the valley,
   the Spirit of the LORD caused him to rest:
   so didst thou lead thy people,
   to make thyself a glorious name.

¹⁵ Look down from heaven,
   and behold from the habitation of thy holiness and of thy glory:
   where is thy zeal and thy strength,
   the sounding of thy bowels and of thy mercies towards me?
   are they restrained?
¹⁶ Doubtless thou art our father,
   though Abraham be ignorant of us,
   and Israel acknowledge us not:
   thou, O LORD, art our father, our redeemer,
   thy name is from everlasting.

¹⁷ O Lord, why hast thou made us to err from thy ways,
   and hardened our heart from thy fear?
   Return for thy servants' sake,
   the tribes of thy inheritance.
¹⁸ The people of thy holiness have possessed it but a little while:
   our adversaries have trodden down thy sanctuary.
¹⁹ We are thine, thou never borest rule over them,
   they were not called by thy name.

64

O that thou wouldst rend the heavens,
   that thou wouldst come down,
   that the mountains might flow down at thy presence,
² as when the melting fire burneth,
   the fire causeth the waters to boil:
   to make thy name known to thy adversaries,
   that the nations may tremble at thy presence.
³ When thou didst terrible things which we looked not for,
   thou camest down,
   the mountains flowed down at thy presence.
⁴ For since the beginning of the world men have not heard, nor
      perceived by the ear,
   neither hath the eye seen, O God, besides thee,
   what he hath prepared for him that waiteth for him.
⁵ Thou meetest him that rejoiceth and worketh righteousness,
   those that remember thee in thy ways:
   behold, thou art wroth, for we have sinned:
   in those is continuance, and we shall be saved.
⁶ But we are all as an unclean thing,
   and all our righteousnesses are as filthy rags,
   and we all do fade as a leaf,
   and our iniquities, like the wind, have taken us away.

⁷ And there is none that calleth upon thy name,
  that stirreth up himself to take hold of thee:
  for thou hast hid thy face from us,
  and hast consumed us because of our iniquities.
⁸ But now, O Lord, thou art our father:
  we are the clay, and thou our potter,
  and we all are the work of thy hand.
⁹ Be not wroth very sore, O Lord,
  neither remember iniquity for ever:
  behold, see, we beseech thee, we are all thy people.
¹⁰ Thy holy cities are a wilderness,
  Zion is a wilderness, Jerusalem a desolation.
¹¹ Our holy and our beautiful house,
  where our fathers praised thee,
  is burnt up with fire,
  and all our pleasant things are laid waste.
¹² Wilt thou refrain thyself for these things, O Lord?
  wilt thou hold thy peace, and afflict us very sore?

65 'I am sought of them that asked not for me:
  I am found of them that sought me not:
  I said, "Behold me, behold me",
  unto a nation that was not called by my name.
² I have spread out my hands all the day
  unto a rebellious people,
  which walketh in a way that was not good,
  after their own thoughts:
³ a people that provoketh me to anger
  continually to my face,
  that sacrificeth in gardens,
  and burneth incense upon altars of brick:
⁴ which remain among the graves,
  and lodge in the monuments,
  which eat swine's flesh,
  and broth of abominable things is in their vessels:
⁵ which say, "Stand by thyself, come not near to me;
  for I am holier than thou".
  These are a smoke in my nose,
  a fire that burneth all the day.
⁶ Behold, it is written before me:
  I will not keep silence, but will recompense,
  even recompense into their bosom,
⁷ your iniquities, and the iniquities of your fathers together,' saith
    the Lord,
  'which have burnt incense upon the mountains,
  and blasphemed me upon the hills:
  therefore will I measure their former work into their bosom.'

⁸ Thus saith the LORD, 'As the new wine is found in the
   cluster,
   and one saith, "Destroy it not, for a blessing is in it":
   so will I do for my servants' sakes,
   that I may not destroy them all.
⁹ And I will bring forth a seed out of Jacob,
   and out of Judah an inheritor of my mountains:
   and my elect shall inherit it,
   and my servants shall dwell there.
¹⁰ And Sharon shall be a fold of flocks,
   and the valley of Achor a place for the herds to lie down in,
   for my people that have sought me.

¹¹ 'But ye are they that forsake the LORD,
   that forget my holy mountain,
   that prepare a table for that troop,
   and that furnish the drink offering unto that number.
¹² Therefore will I number you to the sword,
   and ye shall all bow down to the slaughter:
   because when I called, ye did not answer;
   when I spoke, ye did not hear,
   but did evil before my eyes,
   and did choose that wherein I delighted not.'

¹³ Therefore thus saith the Lord GOD,
   'Behold, my servants shall eat, but ye shall be hungry:
   behold, my servants shall drink, but ye shall be thirsty:
   behold, my servants shall rejoice, but ye shall be ashamed:
¹⁴ behold, my servants shall sing for joy of heart,
   but ye shall cry for sorrow of heart,
   and shall howl for vexation of spirit.
¹⁵ And ye shall leave your name for a curse unto my chosen:
   for the Lord GOD shall slay thee,
   and call his servants by another name:
¹⁶ that he who blesseth himself in the earth
   shall bless himself in the God of truth;
   and he that sweareth in the earth
   shall swear by the God of truth;
   because the former troubles are forgotten,
   and because they are hid from my eyes.

¹⁷ 'For behold, I create new heavens and a new earth:
   and the former shall not be remembered,
   nor come into mind.
¹⁸ But be you glad and rejoice for ever in that which I create:
   for behold, I create Jerusalem a rejoicing,
   and her people a joy.
¹⁹ And I will rejoice in Jerusalem,

and joy in my people:
and the voice of weeping shall be no more heard in her,
nor the voice of crying.
²⁰ There shall be no more thence an infant of days,
nor an old man that hath not filled his days:
for the child shall die a hundred years old:
but the sinner being a hundred years old shall be accursed.
²¹ And they shall build houses, and inhabit them,
and they shall plant vineyards, and eat the fruit of them.
²² They shall not build, and another inhabit:
they shall not plant, and another eat:
for as the days of a tree are the days of my people,
and my elect shall long enjoy the work of their hands.
²³ They shall not labour in vain, nor bring forth for trouble:
for they are the seed of the blessed of the LORD,
and their offspring with them.
²⁴ And it shall come to pass, that before they call, I will answer,
and whilst they are yet speaking, I will hear.
²⁵ The wolf and the lamb shall feed together,
and the lion shall eat straw like the bullock:
and dust shall be the serpent's meat.
They shall not hurt nor destroy in all my holy mountain,'
saith the LORD.

66 Thus saith the LORD,
'The heaven is my throne, and the earth is my footstool:
where is the house that ye build unto me?
and where is the place of my rest?
² For all those things hath my hand made,
and all those things have been,'
saith the LORD:
'but to this man will I look,
even to him that is poor and of a contrite spirit,
and trembleth at my word.

³ 'He that killeth an ox is as if he slew a man:
he that sacrificeth a lamb, as if he cut off a dog's neck:
he that offereth an oblation, as if he offered swine's blood:
he that burneth incense, as if he blessed an idol:
yea, they have chosen their own ways,
and their soul delighteth in their abominations.
⁴ I also will choose their delusions,
and will bring their fears upon them;
because when I called, none did answer,
when I spoke, they did not hear:
but they did evil before my eyes,
and chose that in which I delighted not.'

⁵ Hear the word of the LORD, ye that tremble at his word:
  'Your brethren that hated you,
  that cast you out for my name's sake, said,
  "Let the LORD be glorified":
  but he shall appear to your joy,
  and they shall be ashamed.
⁶ A voice of noise from the city,
  a voice from the temple,
  a voice of the LORD that rendereth recompense to his enemies.

⁷ 'Before she travailed, she brought forth:
  before her pain came, she was delivered of a man-child.
⁸ Who hath heard such a thing?
  who hath seen such things?
  Shall the earth be made to bring forth in one day?
  or shall a nation be born at once?
  for as soon as Zion travailed, she brought forth her children.
⁹ Shall I bring to the birth, and not cause to bring forth?'
  saith the LORD:
  'shall I cause to bring forth, and shut the womb?'
  saith thy God.

¹⁰ 'Rejoice ye with Jerusalem,
  and be glad with her, all ye that love her:
  rejoice for joy with her, all ye that mourn for her:
¹¹ that ye may suck,
  and be satisfied with the breasts of her consolations:
  that ye may milk out,
  and be delighted with the abundance of her glory.'
¹² For thus saith the LORD,
  'Behold, I will extend peace to her like a river,
  and the glory of the Gentiles like a flowing stream:
  then shall ye suck, ye shall be borne upon her sides,
  and be dandled upon her knees.
¹³ As one whom his mother comforteth,
  so will I comfort you:
  and ye shall be comforted in Jerusalem.
¹⁴ And when ye see this, your heart shall rejoice,
  and your bones shall flourish like a herb:
  and the hand of the LORD shall be known towards his servants,
  and his indignation towards his enemies.
¹⁵ For behold, the LORD will come with fire,
  and with his chariots like a whirlwind,
  to render his anger with fury,
  and his rebuke with flames of fire.
¹⁶ For by fire and by his sword will the LORD plead with all flesh:
  and the slain of the LORD shall be many.
¹⁷ They that sanctify themselves,

and purify themselves in the gardens behind one tree in the
    midst,
eating swine's flesh, and the abomination, and the mouse,
shall be consumed together,' saith the LORD.

[18]'For I know their works and their thoughts: it shall come that I will gather all nations and tongues, and they shall come, and see my glory. [19]And I will set a sign among them, and I will send those that escape of them unto the nations, to Tarshish, Pul and Lud, that draw the bow, to Tubal and Javan, to the isles afar off, that have not heard my fame, neither have seen my glory; and they shall declare my glory among the Gentiles. [20]And they shall bring all your brethren for an offering unto the LORD out of all nations upon horses, and in chariots, and in litters, and upon mules, and upon swift beasts, to my holy mountain Jerusalem,' saith the LORD, 'as the children of Israel bring an offering in a clean vessel into the house of the LORD. [21]And I will also take of them for priests and for Levites,' saith the LORD. [22]'For as the new heavens and the new earth, which I will make, shall remain before me,' saith the LORD, 'so shall your seed and your name remain. [23]And it shall come to pass, that from one new moon to another, and from one sabbath to another, shall all flesh come to worship before me,' saith the LORD. [24]And they shall go forth, and look upon the carcases of the men that have transgressed against me: for their worm shall not die, neither shall their fire be quenched, and they shall be an abhorring unto all flesh.'

THE BOOK OF THE PROPHET
JEREMIAH

1 The words of Jeremiah the son of Hilkiah, of the priests that were in Anathoth in the land of Benjamin: ²to whom the word of the LORD came in the days of Josiah the son of Amon king of Judah, in the thirteenth year of his reign. ³It came also in the days of Jehoiakim the son of Josiah king of Judah, unto the end of the eleventh year of Zedekiah the son of Josiah king of Judah, unto the carrying away of Jerusalem captive in the fifth month.

⁴Then the word of the LORD came unto me, saying,

⁵ 'Before I formed thee in the belly I knew thee;
and before thou camest forth out of the womb I sanctified thee,
and I ordained thee a prophet unto the nations'.

⁶Then said I, 'Ah, Lord GOD, behold, I cannot speak: for I am a child'. ⁷But the LORD said unto me, 'Say not, "I am a child": for thou shalt go to all that I shall send thee, and whatsoever I command thee thou shalt speak. ⁸Be not afraid of their faces: for I am with thee to deliver thee,' saith the LORD. ⁹Then the LORD put forth his hand, and touched my mouth, and the LORD said unto me, 'Behold, I have put my words in thy mouth. ¹⁰See, I have this day set thee over the nations and over the kingdoms, to root out, and to pull down, and to destroy, and to throw down, to build, and to plant.'

¹¹Moreover the word of the LORD came unto me, saying, 'Jeremiah, what seest thou?' And I said, 'I see a rod of an almond tree'. ¹²Then said the LORD unto me, 'Thou hast well seen: for I will hasten my word to perform it'.

¹³And the word of the LORD came unto me the second time, saying, 'What seest thou?' And I said, 'I see a seething pot'; and the face thereof was towards the north. ¹⁴Then the LORD said unto me, 'Out of the north an evil shall break forth upon all the inhabitants of the land. ¹⁵For lo, I will call all the families of the kingdoms of the north,' saith the LORD, 'and they shall come, and they shall set every one his throne at the entering of the gates of Jerusalem, and against all the walls thereof round about, and against all the cities of Judah. ¹⁶And I will utter my judgements against them touching all their wickedness, who have forsaken me, and have burnt incense unto other gods, and worshipped the works of their own hands.

¹⁷'Thou therefore gird up thy loins, and arise, and speak unto them all that I command thee: be not dismayed at their faces, lest I confound thee before them. ¹⁸For behold, I have made thee this day a defenced city, and an iron pillar, and brazen walls against the whole land, against the kings of Judah, against the princes thereof, against the priests thereof, and against the people of the land. ¹⁹And they shall

fight against thee, but they shall not prevail against thee: for I am with thee,' saith the LORD, 'to deliver thee.'

2 Moreover the word of the LORD came to me, saying,
² 'Go and cry in the ears of Jerusalem, saying, "Thus saith the LORD,

""'I remember thee, the kindness of thy youth,
the love of thy espousals,
when thou wentest after me in the wilderness,
in a land that was not sown.
³ Israel was holiness unto the LORD,
and the first-fruits of his increase:
all that devour him shall offend;
evil shall come upon them,' saith the LORD."'

⁴ Hear ye the word of the LORD,
O house of Jacob, and all the families of the house of Israel.

⁵ Thus saith the LORD,
'What iniquity have your fathers found in me,
that they are gone far from me,
and have walked after vanity, and are become vain?
⁶ Neither said they, "Where is the LORD
that brought us up out of the land of Egypt,
that led us through the wilderness,
through a land of deserts and of pits,
through a land of drought, and of the shadow of death,
through a land that no man passed through,
and where no man dwelt?"
⁷ And I brought you into a plentiful country,
to eat the fruit thereof and the goodness thereof;
but when ye entered ye defiled my land,
and made my heritage an abomination.
⁸ The priests said not, "Where is the LORD?"
and they that handle the law knew me not:
the pastors also transgressed against me,
and the prophets prophesied by Baal,
and walked after things that do not profit.

⁹ 'Wherefore I will yet plead with you,' saith the LORD,
'and with your children's children will I plead.
¹⁰ For pass over the isles of Chittim, and see;
and send unto Kedar, and consider diligently,
and see if there be such a thing.
¹¹ Hath a nation changed their gods, which are yet no gods?
but my people have changed their glory
for that which doth not profit.
¹² Be astonished, O ye heavens, at this,
and be horribly afraid,
be ye very desolate,' saith the LORD.

¹³ For my people have committed two evils:
  they have forsaken me, the fountain of living waters,
  and hewn them out cisterns,
  broken cisterns, that can hold no water.

¹⁴ 'Is Israel a servant? is he a home-born slave?
  why is he spoiled?
¹⁵ The young lions roared upon him, and yelled,
  and they made his land waste:
  his cities are burnt without inhabitant.
¹⁶ Also the children of Noph and Tahapanes have broken the crown
    of thy head.
¹⁷ Hast thou not procured this unto thyself,
  in that thou hast forsaken the LORD thy God,
  when he led thee by the way?
¹⁸ And now what hast thou to do in the way of Egypt,
  to drink the waters of Sihor?
  or what hast thou to do in the way of Assyria,
  to drink the waters of the river?
¹⁹ Thy own wickedness shall correct thee,
  and thy backslidings shall reprove thee:
  know therefore and see that it is an evil thing and bitter
  that thou hast forsaken the LORD thy God,
  and that my fear is not in thee,' saith the Lord GOD of hosts.

²⁰ 'For of old time I have broken thy yoke, and burst thy bands,
  and thou saidst, "I will not transgress",
  when upon every high hill and under every green tree
  thou wanderest, playing the harlot.
²¹ Yet I had planted thee a noble vine, wholly a right seed:
  how then art thou turned into the degenerate plant of a strange
    vine unto me?
²² For though thou wash thee with nitre,
  and take thee much soap,
  yet thy iniquity is marked before me,' saith the Lord GOD.
²³ 'How canst thou say, "I am not polluted,
  I have not gone after Baalim?"
  see thy way in the valley,
  know what thou hast done:
  thou art a swift dromedary traversing her ways;
²⁴ a wild ass used to the wilderness,
  that snuffeth up the wind at her pleasure;
  in her occasion who can turn her away?
  all they that seek her will not weary themselves,
  in her month they shall find her.
²⁵ Withhold thy foot from being unshod,
  and thy throat from thirst:
  but thou saidst, "There is no hope.

No, for I have loved strangers, and after them will I go."

²⁶ As the thief is ashamed when he is found,
so is the house of Israel ashamed,
they, their kings, their princes,
and their priests, and their prophets,

²⁷ saying to a stock, "Thou art my father",
and to a stone, "Thou hast brought me forth":
for they have turned their back unto me,
and not their face:
but in the time of their trouble they will say,
"Arise, and save us".

²⁸ But where are thy gods that thou hast made thee?
let them arise, if they can save thee in the time of thy trouble:
for according to the number of thy cities are thy gods, O Judah.

²⁹ Wherefore will ye plead with me?
ye all have transgressed against me,' saith the LORD.

³⁰ 'In vain have I smitten your children,
they received no correction:
your own sword hath devoured your prophets,
like a destroying lion.

³¹ 'O generation, see ye the word of the LORD.
Have I been a wilderness unto Israel?
a land of darkness?
wherefore say my people, "We are lords,
we will come no more unto thee?"

³² Can a maid forget her ornaments, or a bride her attire?
yet my people have forgotten me days without number.

³³ Why trimmest thou thy way to seek love?
therefore hast thou also taught the wicked ones thy ways.

³⁴ Also in thy skirts is found the blood of the souls of the poor
innocents:
I have not found it by secret search, but upon all these.

³⁵ Yet thou sayest, "Because I am innocent,
surely his anger shall turn from me".
Behold, I will plead with thee,
because thou sayest, "I have not sinned".

³⁶ Why gaddest thou about so much to change thy way?
thou also shalt be ashamed of Egypt,
as thou wast ashamed of Assyria.

³⁷ Yea, thou shalt go forth from him,
and thy hands upon thy head:
for the LORD hath rejected thy confidences,
and thou shalt not prosper in them.

3 'They say, "If a man put away his wife,
and she go from him, and become another man's,
shall he return unto her again?

shall not that land be greatly polluted?"
but thou hast played the harlot with many lovers;
yet return again to me,' saith the LORD.
² 'Lift up thy eyes unto the high places,
and see where thou hast not been lain with.
In the ways hast thou sat for them,
as the Arabian in the wilderness,
and thou hast polluted the land
with thy whoredoms and with thy wickedness.
³ Therefore the showers have been withheld,
and there hath been no latter rain,
and thou hadst a whore's forehead,
thou refusedst to be ashamed.
⁴ Wilt thou not from this time cry unto me,
"My father, thou art the guide of my youth"?
⁵ Will he reserve his anger for ever?
will he keep it to the end?
Behold, thou hast spoken and done evil things as thou couldst.'

⁶The LORD said also unto me in the days of Josiah the king, 'Hast thou seen that which backsliding Israel hath done? she is gone up upon every high mountain and under every green tree, and there hath played the harlot. ⁷And I said after she had done all these things, "Turn thou unto me". But she returned not. And her treacherous sister Judah saw it. ⁸And I saw, when for all the causes whereby backsliding Israel committed adultery I had put her away, and given her a bill of divorce: yet her treacherous sister Judah feared not, but went and played the harlot also. ⁹And it came to pass through the lightness of her whoredom, that she defiled the land, and committed adultery with stones and with stocks. ¹⁰And yet for all this her treacherous sister Judah hath not turned unto me with her whole heart, but feignedly,' saith the LORD. ¹¹And the LORD said unto me, 'The backsliding Israel hath justified herself more than treacherous Judah.

¹²'Go and proclaim these words toward the north, and say, "'Return, thou backsliding Israel,' saith the LORD, 'and I will not cause my anger to fall upon you: for I am merciful,' saith the LORD, 'and I will not keep anger for ever. ¹³Only acknowledge thy iniquity, that thou hast transgressed against the LORD thy God, and hast scattered thy ways to the strangers under every green tree, and ye have not obeyed my voice,' saith the LORD."

¹⁴'Turn, O backsliding children,' saith the LORD, 'for I am married unto you: and I will take you one of a city, and two of a family, and I will bring you to Zion. ¹⁵And I will give you pastors according to my heart, which shall feed you with knowledge and understanding. ¹⁶And it shall come to pass when ye be multiplied and increased in the land, in those days,' saith the LORD, 'they shall say no more, "The ark of the covenant of the LORD": neither shall it come to mind, neither shall they remember it, neither shall they visit it, neither shall that be done any more.

¹⁷At that time they shall call Jerusalem the throne of the LORD, and all the nations shall be gathered unto it, to the name of the LORD, to Jerusalem: neither shall they walk any more after the imagination of their evil heart. ¹⁸In those days the house of Judah shall walk with the house of Israel, and they shall come together out of the land of the north to the land that I have given for an inheritance unto your fathers. ¹⁹But I said, "How shall I put thee among the children, and give thee a pleasant land, a goodly heritage of the hosts of nations?" and I said, "Thou shalt call me, My father, and shalt not turn away from me".

²⁰'Surely as a wife treacherously departeth from her husband, so have you dealt treacherously with me, O house of Israel,' saith the LORD. ²¹A voice was heard upon the high places, weeping and supplications of the children of Israel: for they have perverted their way, and they have forgotten the LORD their God. ²²'Return, ye backsliding children, and I will heal your backslidings.' 'Behold, we come unto thee, for thou art the LORD our God. ²³Truly in vain is salvation hoped for from the hills, and from the multitude of mountains: truly in the LORD our God is the salvation of Israel. ²⁴For shame hath devoured the labour of our fathers from our youth: their flocks and their herds, their sons and their daughters. ²⁵We lie down in our shame, and our confusion covereth us: for we have sinned against the LORD our God, we and our fathers, from our youth even unto this day, and have not obeyed the voice of the LORD our God.'

4 'If thou wilt return, O Israel,' saith the LORD, 'return unto me: and if thou wilt put away thy abominations out of my sight, then shalt thou not remove. ² And thou shalt swear, "The LORD liveth", in truth, in judgement, and in righteousness, and the nations shall bless themselves in him, and in him shall they glory.'

³For thus saith the LORD to the men of Judah and Jerusalem,

'Break up your fallow ground,
and sow not among thorns.
⁴ Circumcise yourselves to the LORD,
and take away the foreskins of your heart,
ye men of Judah and inhabitants of Jerusalem,
lest my fury come forth like fire,
and burn that none can quench it,
because of the evil of your doings.
⁵ Declare ye in Judah, and publish in Jerusalem,
and say, "Blow ye the trumpet in the land":
cry, gather together, and say,
"Assemble yourselves, and let us go into the defenced cities".
⁶ Set up the standards toward Zion:
retire, stay not:

for I will bring evil from the north,
and a great destruction.

7 The lion is come up from his thicket,
and the destroyer of the Gentiles is on his way;
he is gone forth from his place to make thy land desolate,
and thy cities shall be laid waste, without an inhabitant.'

8 For this gird you with sackcloth, lament and howl:
for the fierce anger of the LORD is not turned back from us.

9 'And it shall come to pass at that day,' saith the LORD,
'that the heart of the king shall perish,
and the heart of the princes:
and the priests shall be astonished,
and the prophets shall wonder'.

10 Then said I, 'Ah, Lord GOD,
surely thou hast greatly deceived this people and Jerusalem,
saying, "Ye shall have peace",
whereas the sword reacheth unto the soul'.

11 At that time shall it be said to this people and to Jerusalem,
'A dry wind of the high places in the wilderness
toward the daughter of my people,
not to fan, nor to cleanse,

12 even a full wind from those places shall come unto me:
now also will I give sentence against them'.

13 Behold, he shall come up as clouds,
and his chariots shall be as a whirlwind:
his horses are swifter than eagles.
Woe unto us, for we are spoiled.

14 O Jerusalem, wash thy heart from wickedness,
that thou mayest be saved.
How long shall thy vain thoughts lodge within thee?

15 For a voice declareth from Dan,
and publisheth affliction from mount Ephraim.

16 Make ye mention to the nations,
behold, publish against Jerusalem,
that watchers come from a far country,
and give out their voice against the cities of Judah.

17 'As keepers of a field are they against her round about;
because she hath been rebellious against me,' saith the LORD.

18 'Thy way and thy doings have procured these things unto thee;
this is thy wickedness, because it is bitter,
because it reacheth unto thy heart.'

19 My bowels, my bowels,
I am pained at my very heart,
my heart maketh a noise in me,
I cannot hold my peace, because thou hast heard, O my soul,
the sound of the trumpet, the alarm of war.

²⁰ Destruction upon destruction is cried,
  for the whole land is spoiled:
  suddenly are my tents spoiled,
  and my curtains in a moment.
²¹ How long shall I see the standard,
  and hear the sound of the trumpet?
²² For my people is foolish, they have not known me;
  they are sottish children,
  and they have no understanding:
  they are wise to do evil,
  but to do good they have no knowledge.
²³ I beheld the earth, and lo, it was without form and void:
  and the heavens, and they had no light.
²⁴ I beheld the mountains, and lo, they trembled,
  and all the hills moved lightly.
²⁵ I beheld, and lo, there was no man,
  and all the birds of the heavens were fled.
²⁶ I beheld, and lo, the fruitful place was a wilderness,
  and all the cities thereof were broken down at the presence of
    the Lord,
  and by his fierce anger.
²⁷ For thus hath the Lord said,
  'The whole land shall be desolate;
  yet will I not make a full end.
²⁸ For this shall the earth mourn,
  and the heavens above be black:
  because I have spoken it, I have purposed it,
  and will not repent, neither will I turn back from it.'
²⁹ The whole city shall flee for the noise of the horsemen and
    bowmen,
  they shall go into thickets, and climb up upon the rocks:
  every city shall be forsaken, and not a man dwell therein.
³⁰ And when thou art spoiled, what wilt thou do?
  Though thou clothest thyself with crimson,
  though thou deckest thee with ornaments of gold,
  though thou rentest thy face with painting,
  in vain shalt thou make thyself fair,
  thy lovers will despise thee, they will seek thy life.
³¹ For I have heard a voice as of a woman in travail,
  and the anguish as of her that bringeth forth her first child,
  the voice of the daughter of Zion, that bewaileth herself,
  that spreadeth her hands, saying, 'Woe is me now,
  for my soul is wearied because of murderers'.

5 'Run ye to and fro through the streets of Jerusalem,
  and see now and know, and seek in the broad places thereof,
  if ye can find a man, if there be any that executeth judgement,
  that seeketh the truth, and I will pardon it.

² And though they say, "The LORD liveth",
  surely they swear falsely.'
³ O LORD, are not thy eyes upon the truth?
  thou hast stricken them, but they have not grieved;
  thou hast consumed them, but they have refused to receive
    correction:
  they have made their faces harder than a rock,
  they have refused to return.
⁴ Therefore I said, 'Surely these are poor, they are foolish:
  for they know not the way of the LORD,
  nor the judgement of their God.
⁵ I will get me unto the great men, and will speak unto them,
  for they have known the way of the LORD,
  and the judgement of their God.'
  But these have altogether broken the yoke, and burst the bonds.
⁶ Wherefore a lion out of the forest shall slay them,
  and a wolf of the evenings shall spoil them,
  a leopard shall watch over their cities:
  every one that goeth out thence shall be torn in pieces,
  because their transgressions are many,
  and their backslidings are increased.

⁷ 'How shall I pardon thee for this?
  thy children have forsaken me, and sworn by them that are no
    gods:
  when I had fed them to the full, they then committed adultery,
  and assembled themselves by troops in the harlots' houses.
⁸ They were as fed horses in the morning:
  every one neighed after his neighbour's wife.
⁹ Shall I not visit for these things?' saith the LORD,
  'and shall not my soul be avenged on such a nation as this?

¹⁰ 'Go ye up upon her walls, and destroy,
  but make not a full end:
  take away her battlements, for they are not the LORD's.
¹¹ For the house of Israel and the house of Judah
  have dealt very treacherously against me,' saith the LORD.
¹² They have belied the LORD, and said,
  'It is not he, neither shall evil come upon us,
  neither shall we see sword nor famine.
¹³ And the prophets shall become wind,
  and the word is not in them:
  thus shall it be done unto them.'
¹⁴ Wherefore thus saith the LORD God of hosts,
  'Because ye speak this word,
  behold, I will make my words in thy mouth fire,
  and this people wood, and it shall devour them.
¹⁵ Lo, I will bring a nation upon you from far,

O house of Israel,' saith the Lord:
'it is a mighty nation, it is an ancient nation,
a nation whose language thou knowest not,
neither understandest what they say.
¹⁶ Their quiver is as an open sepulchre,
they are all mighty men.
¹⁷ And they shall eat up thy harvest and thy bread,
which thy sons and thy daughters should eat:
they shall eat up thy flocks and thy herds:
they shall eat up thy vines and thy fig trees:
they shall impoverish thy fenced cities
wherein thou trustedst, with the sword.

¹⁸ 'Nevertheless in those days,' saith the Lord, 'I will not make a full end with you.

¹⁹ 'And it shall come to pass, when ye shall say, "Wherefore doeth the Lord our God all these things unto us?" then shalt thou answer them, "Like as ye have forsaken me, and served strange gods in your land, so shall ye serve strangers in a land that is not yours".

²⁰ 'Declare this in the house of Jacob,
and publish it in Judah, saying,
²¹ "Hear now this, O foolish people,
and without understanding,
which have eyes, and see not,
which have ears, and hear not:
²² 'Fear ye not me?' saith the Lord:
'will ye not tremble at my presence,
which have placed the sand for the bound of the sea
by a perpetual decree, that it cannot pass it:
and though the waves thereof toss themselves, yet can they not
prevail;
though they roar, yet can they not pass over it?
²³ But this people hath a revolting and a rebellious heart,
they are revolted and gone.
²⁴ Neither say they in their heart,
"Let us now fear the Lord our God,
that giveth rain, both the former and the latter in his season:
he reserveth unto us the appointed weeks of the harvest".
²⁵ Your iniquities have turned away these things,
and your sins have withheld good things from you.
²⁶ For among my people are found wicked men:
they lay wait, as he that setteth snares,
they set a trap, they catch men.
²⁷ As a cage is full of birds, so are their houses full of deceit:
therefore they are become great, and waxed rich.
²⁸ They are waxed fat, they shine:
yea, they overpass the deeds of the wicked:

they judge not the cause, the cause of the fatherless, yet they
    prosper:
and the right of the needy do they not judge.
²⁹ Shall I not visit for these things?' saith the LORD:
    'shall not my soul be avenged on such a nation as this?'"'

³⁰ A wonderful and horrible thing is committed in the land.
³¹ The prophets prophesy falsely,
    and the priests bear rule by their means,
    and my people love to have it so:
    and what will ye do in the end thereof?

6 O ye children of Benjamin, gather yourselves
    to flee out of the midst of Jerusalem,
    and blow the trumpet in Tekoa,
    and set up a sign of fire in Beth-haccerem:
    for evil appeareth out of the north, and great destruction.
² I have likened the daughter of Zion to a comely and delicate
    woman.
³ The shepherds with their flocks shall come unto her:
    they shall pitch their tents against her round about:
    they shall feed, every one in his place.
⁴ 'Prepare ye war against her:
    arise, and let us go up at noon.'
    'Woe unto us, for the day goeth away,
    for the shadows of the evening are stretched out.'
⁵ 'Arise, and let us go by night,
    and let us destroy her palaces.'

⁶ For thus hath the LORD of hosts said,
    'Hew ye down trees, and cast a mount against Jerusalem:
    this is the city to be visited,
    she is wholly oppression in the midst of her.
⁷ As a fountain casteth out her waters, so she casteth out her
    wickedness:
    violence and spoil is heard in her,
    before me continually is grief and wounds.
⁸ Be thou instructed, O Jerusalem,
    lest my soul depart from thee:
    lest I make thee desolate, a land not inhabited.'

⁹ Thus saith the LORD of hosts,
    'They shall thoroughly glean the remnant of Israel as a vine:
    turn back thy hand as a grape-gatherer into the baskets'.
¹⁰ To whom shall I speak and give warning, that they may hear?
    Behold, their ear is uncircumcised, and they cannot hearken:
    behold, the word of the LORD is unto them a reproach:
    they have no delight in it.

¹¹ Therefore I am full of the fury of the Lord:
I am weary with holding in:
'I will pour it out upon the children abroad,
and upon the assembly of young men together:
for even the husband with the wife shall be taken,
the aged with him that is full of days.
¹² And their houses shall be turned unto others,
with their fields and wives together:
for I will stretch out my hand upon the inhabitants of the land,'
saith the Lord.
¹³ 'For from the least of them even unto the greatest of them
every one is given to covetousness,
and from the prophet even unto the priest
every one dealeth falsely.
¹⁴ They have healed also the hurt of the daughter of my people
slightly,
saying, "Peace, peace", when there is no peace.
¹⁵ Were they ashamed when they had committed abomination?
nay, they were not at all ashamed, neither could they blush:
therefore they shall fall among them that fall:
at the time that I visit them they shall be cast down,' saith the
Lord.

¹⁶ Thus saith the Lord, 'Stand ye in the ways
and see, and ask for the old paths, where is the good way,
and walk therein, and ye shall find rest for your souls.
But they said, "We will not walk therein".
¹⁷ Also I set watchmen over you, saying,
"Hearken to the sound of the trumpet".
But they said, "We will not hearken".
¹⁸ Therefore hear, ye nations,
and know, O congregation, what is among them.
¹⁹ Hear, O earth: behold, I will bring evil upon this people,
even the fruit of their thoughts,
because they have not hearkened unto my words,
nor to my law, but rejected it.
²⁰ To what purpose cometh there to me incense from Sheba,
and the sweet cane from a far country?
your burnt offerings are not acceptable,
nor your sacrifices sweet unto me.'
²¹ Therefore thus saith the Lord,
'Behold, I will lay stumbling-blocks before this people,
and the fathers and the sons together shall fall upon them:
the neighbour and his friend shall perish'.

²² Thus saith the Lord,
'Behold, a people cometh from the north country,
and a great nation shall be raised from the sides of the earth.

²³ They shall lay hold on bow and spear:
  they are cruel, and have no mercy:
  their voice roareth like the sea, and they ride upon horses,
  set in array as men for war against thee, O daughter of Zion.
²⁴ We have heard the fame thereof, our hands wax feeble,
  anguish hath taken hold of us,
  and pain, as of a woman in travail.
²⁵ Go not forth into the field, nor walk by the way:
  for the sword of the enemy and fear is on every side.
²⁶ 'O daughter of my people, gird thee with sackcloth,
  and wallow thyself in ashes:
  make thee mourning, as for an only son, most bitter
    lamentation:
  for the spoiler shall suddenly come upon us.
²⁷ I have set thee for a tower and a fortress among my people,
  that thou mayest know and try their way.
²⁸ They are all grievous revolters, walking with slanders:
  they are brass and iron, they are all corrupters.
²⁹ The bellows are burnt, the lead is consumed of the fire:
  the founder melteth in vain:
  for the wicked are not plucked away.
³⁰ Reprobate silver shall men call them,
  because the LORD hath rejected them.'

7 The word that came to Jeremiah from the LORD, saying, ²'Stand in the gate of the LORD's house, and proclaim there this word, and say, "Hear the word of the LORD, all ye of Judah, that enter in at these gates to worship the LORD. ³Thus saith the LORD of hosts, the God of Israel, 'Amend your ways and your doings, and I will cause you to dwell in this place. ⁴Trust ye not in lying words, saying, "The temple of the LORD, the temple of the LORD, the temple of the LORD are these". ⁵For if ye thoroughly amend your ways and your doings, if you thoroughly execute judgement between a man and his neighbour: ⁶if ye oppress not the stranger, the fatherless, and the widow, and shed not innocent blood in this place, neither walk after other gods to your hurt: ⁷then will I cause you to dwell in this place, in the land that I gave to your fathers, for ever and ever.

⁸ '"Behold, ye trust in lying words, that cannot profit. ⁹Will ye steal, murder, and commit adultery, and swear falsely, and burn incense unto Baal, and walk after other gods whom ye know not; ¹⁰and come and stand before me in this house, which is called by my name, and say, "We are delivered to do all these abominations"? ¹¹Is this house, which is called by my name, become a den of robbers in your eyes? Behold, even I have seen it,' saith the LORD. ¹²'But go ye now unto my place which was in Shiloh, where I set my name at the first, and see what I did to it for the wickedness of my people Israel. ¹³And now, because ye have done all these works,' saith the LORD, 'and I spoke unto you, rising

up early and speaking, but ye heard not; and I called you, but ye answered not: [14]therefore will I do unto this house, which is called by my name, wherein ye trust, and unto the place which I gave to you and to your fathers, as I have done to Shiloh. [15]And I will cast you out of my sight, as I have cast out all your brethren, even the whole seed of Ephraim. [16]Therefore pray not thou for this people, neither lift up cry nor prayer for them, neither make intercession to me, for I will not hear thee.

[17]"'Seest thou not what they do in the cities of Judah and in the streets of Jerusalem? [18]The children gather wood, and the fathers kindle the fire, and the women knead their dough to make cakes to the queen of heaven, and to pour out drink offerings unto other gods, that they may provoke me to anger. [19]Do they provoke me to anger?' saith the LORD: 'do they not provoke themselves to the confusion of their own faces?' [20]Therefore thus saith the Lord GOD, 'Behold, my anger and my fury shall be poured out upon this place, upon man and upon beast, and upon the trees of the field, and upon the fruit of the ground, and it shall burn, and shall not be quenched'.

[21]"'Thus saith the LORD of hosts, the God of Israel, 'Put your burnt offerings unto your sacrifices, and eat flesh. [22]For I spoke not unto your fathers, nor commanded them in the day that I brought them out of the land of Egypt, concerning burnt offerings or sacrifices: [23]but this thing commanded I them, saying, "Obey my voice, and I will be your God, and ye shall be my people: and walk ye in all the ways that I have commanded you, that it may be well unto you". [24]But they hearkened not, nor inclined their ear, but walked in the counsels and in the imagination of their evil heart, and went backward, and not forward. [25]Since the day that your fathers came forth out of the land of Egypt unto this day I have even sent unto you all my servants the prophets, daily rising up early and sending them: [26]yet they hearkened not unto me, nor inclined their ear, but hardened their neck: they did worse than their fathers.' [27]Therefore thou shalt speak all these words unto them, but they will not hearken to thee: thou shalt also call unto them, but they will not answer thee. [28]But thou shalt say unto them, 'This is a nation that obeyeth not the voice of the LORD their God, nor receiveth correction: truth is perished, and is cut off from their mouth.

[29]"'Cut off thy hair, O Jerusalem, and cast it away, and take up a lamentation on high places, for the LORD hath rejected and forsaken the generation of his wrath. [30]For the children of Judah have done evil in my sight,' saith the LORD: 'they have set their abominations in the house which is called by my name, to pollute it. [31]And they have built the high places of Tophet which is in the valley of the son of Hinnom, to burn their sons and their daughters in the fire, which I commanded them not, neither came it into my heart.

[32]"'Therefore behold, the days come,' saith the LORD, 'that it shall no more be called Tophet, nor the valley of the son of Hinnom, but the valley of slaughter: for they shall bury in Tophet, till there be no place. [33]And the carcases of this people shall be meat for the fowls of the

heaven, and for the beasts of the earth, and none shall fray them away. ³⁴Then will I cause to cease from the cities of Judah, and from the streets of Jerusalem, the voice of mirth, and the voice of gladness, the voice of the bridegroom, and the voice of the bride: for the land shall be desolate.

8 '"At that time,' saith the LORD, 'they shall bring out the bones of the kings of Judah, and the bones of his princes, and the bones of the priests, and the bones of the prophets, and the bones of the inhabitants of Jerusalem out of their graves. ²And they shall spread them before the sun, and the moon, and all the host of heaven whom they have loved, and whom they have served, and after whom they have walked, and whom they have sought, and whom they have worshipped: they shall not be gathered, nor be buried, they shall be for dung upon the face of the earth. ³And death shall be chosen rather than life by all the residue of them that remain of this evil family, which remain in all the places whither I have driven them,' saith the LORD of hosts."

⁴ 'Moreover thou shalt say unto them,
  "Thus saith the LORD, 'Shall they fall, and not arise?
  shall he turn away, and not return?
⁵ Why then is this people of Jerusalem slidden back by a perpetual
    backsliding?
  they hold fast deceit, they refuse to return.
⁶ I hearkened and heard, but they spoke not aright:
  no man repented him of his wickedness,
  saying, "What have I done?"
  every one turned to his course,
  as the horse rusheth into the battle.
⁷ Yea, the stork in the heaven knoweth her appointed times,
  and the turtle and the crane and the swallow observe the time of
    their coming;
  but my people know not the judgement of the LORD.
⁸ How do ye say, "We are wise,
  and the law of the LORD is with us"?
  Lo, certainly in vain made he it,
  the pen of the scribes is in vain.
⁹ The wise men are ashamed, they are dismayed and taken:
  lo, they have rejected the word of the LORD,
  and what wisdom is in them?
¹⁰ Therefore will I give their wives unto others,
  and their fields to them that shall inherit them:
  for every one from the least even unto the greatest is given to
    covetousness,
  from the prophet even unto the priest, every one dealeth falsely.
¹¹ For they have healed the hurt of the daughter of my people
    slightly,
  saying, "Peace, peace", when there is no peace.
¹² Were they ashamed when they had committed abomination?

nay, they were not at all ashamed, neither could they blush:
therefore shall they fall among them that fall,
in the time of their visitation they shall be cast down,' saith the
    LORD.

¹³ 'I will surely consume them,' saith the LORD:
'there shall be no grapes on the vine, nor figs on the fig tree, and
    the leaf shall fade,
and the things that I have given them shall pass away from
    them.'"'

¹⁴ 'Why do we sit still? assemble yourselves,
and let us enter into the defenced cities, and let us be silent
    there:
for the LORD our God hath put us to silence,
and given us waters of gall to drink,
because we have sinned against the LORD.
¹⁵ We looked for peace, but no good came:
and for a time of health, and behold trouble.'
¹⁶ The snorting of his horses was heard from Dan:
the whole land trembled at the sound of the neighing of his
    strong ones,
for they are come and have devoured the land, and all that is in it,
the city, and those that dwell therein.
¹⁷ 'For behold, I will send serpents, cockatrices among you,
which will not be charmed,
and they shall bite you,' saith the LORD.

¹⁸ When I would comfort myself against sorrow, my heart is faint
    in me.
¹⁹ Behold the voice of the cry of the daughter of my people
because of them that dwell in a far country:
'Is not the LORD in Zion? is not her king in her?'
'Why have they provoked me to anger
with their graven images, and with strange vanities?'
²⁰ 'The harvest is past, the summer is ended,
and we are not saved.'
²¹ For the hurt of the daughter of my people am I hurt,
I am black: astonishment hath taken hold on me.
²² Is there no balm in Gilead? is there no physician there?
why then is not the health of the daughter of my people
    recovered?

9 O that my head were waters,
and my eyes a fountain of tears,
that I might weep day and night
for the slain of the daughter of my people.
² O that I had in the wilderness a lodging-place of wayfaring men,

that I might leave my people, and go from them:
for they be all adulterers, an assembly of treacherous men.
³ And they bend their tongue like their bow for lies:
but they are not valiant for the truth upon the earth:
'For they proceed from evil to evil, and they know not me,' saith
the LORD.
⁴ Take ye heed every one of his neighbour,
and trust ye not in any brother:
for every brother will utterly supplant,
and every neighbour will walk with slanders.
⁵ And they will deceive every one his neighbour,
and will not speak the truth:
they have taught their tongue to speak lies,
and weary themselves to commit iniquity.
⁶ 'Thy habitation is in the midst of deceit,
through deceit they refuse to know me,' saith the LORD.
⁷ Therefore thus saith the LORD of hosts,
'Behold, I will melt them, and try them:
for how shall I do for the daughter of my people?
⁸ Their tongue is as an arrow shot out,
it speaketh deceit:
one speaketh peaceably to his neighbour with his mouth,
but in heart he layeth his wait.
⁹ Shall I not visit them for these things?' saith the LORD:
'shall not my soul be avenged on such a nation as this?
¹⁰ For the mountains will I take up a weeping and wailing,
and for the habitations of the wilderness a lamentation,
because they are burnt up, so that none can pass through them,
neither can men hear the voice of the cattle,
both the fowl of the heavens and the beast are fled, they are gone.
¹¹ And I will make Jerusalem heaps, and a den of dragons,
and I will make the cities of Judah desolate, without an
inhabitant.'

¹²Who is the wise man that may understand this? and who is he to whom the mouth of the LORD hath spoken, that he may declare it; for what the land perisheth and is burnt up like a wilderness, that none passeth through? ¹³And the LORD saith, 'Because they have forsaken my law which I set before them, and have not obeyed my voice, neither walked therein; ¹⁴but have walked after the imagination of their own heart, and after Baalim, which their fathers taught them': ¹⁵therefore thus saith the LORD of hosts, the God of Israel, 'Behold, I will feed them, even this people, with wormwood, and give them water of gall to drink. ¹⁶I will scatter them also among the heathen, whom neither they nor their fathers have known: and I will send a sword after them, till I have consumed them.'

¹⁷Thus saith the LORD of hosts,

'Consider ye, and call for the mourning women, that they may
    come,
and send for cunning women, that they may come.
[18] And let them make haste, and take up a wailing for us,
    that our eyes may run down with tears,
    and our eyelids gush out with waters.
[19] For a voice of wailing is heard out of Zion,
    "How are we spoiled!
    we are greatly confounded, because we have forsaken the land,
    because our dwellings have cast us out".'
[20] Yet hear the word of the LORD, O ye women,
    and let your ear receive the word of his mouth,
    and teach your daughters wailing,
    and every one her neighbour lamentation.
[21] For death is come up into our windows,
    and is entered into our palaces,
    to cut off the children from without,
    and the young men from the streets.
[22] 'Speak, "Thus saith the LORD,
    'Even the carcases of men shall fall as dung upon the open field,
    and as the handful after the harvestman,
    and none shall gather them'".'

[23] Thus saith the LORD,
    'Let not the wise man glory in his wisdom,
    neither let the mighty man glory in his might,
    let not the rich man glory in his riches:
[24] but let him that glorieth glory in this,
    that he understandeth and knoweth me,
    that I am the LORD which exercise loving-kindness,
    judgement and righteousness in the earth:
    for in these things I delight,' saith the LORD.

[25] 'Behold, the days come,' saith the LORD, 'that I will punish all them
which are circumcised with the uncircumcised, [26] Egypt, and Judah,
and Edom, and the children of Ammon, and Moab, and all that are in
the utmost corners, that dwell in the wilderness: for all these nations
are uncircumcised, and all the house of Israel are uncircumcised in the
heart.'

10 Hear ye the word which the LORD speaketh unto you, O house of
Israel. [2] Thus saith the LORD,

    'Learn not the way of the heathen,
    and be not dismayed at the signs of heaven,
    for the heathen are dismayed at them.
[3] For the customs of the people are vain:
    for one cutteth a tree out of the forest,

the work of the hands of the workman, with the axe.

⁴ They deck it with silver and with gold,
they fasten it with nails and with hammers that it move not.

⁵ They are upright as the palm tree, but speak not:
they must needs be borne, because they cannot go.
Be not afraid of them, for they cannot do evil,
neither also is it in them to do good.'

⁶ Forasmuch as there is none like unto thee, O LORD,
thou art great, and thy name is great in might.

⁷ Who would not fear thee, O King of nations?
for to thee doth it appertain:
forasmuch as among all the wise men of the nations,
and in all their kingdoms,
there is none like unto thee.

⁸ But they are altogether brutish and foolish:
the stock is a doctrine of vanities.

⁹ Silver spread into plates is brought from Tarshish,
and gold from Uphaz,
the work of the workman, and of the hands of the founder:
blue and purple is their clothing:
they are all the work of cunning men.

¹⁰ But the LORD is the true God,
he is the living God, and an everlasting king:
at his wrath the earth shall tremble,
and the nations shall not be able to abide his indignation.

¹¹ Thus shall ye say unto them,
'The gods that have not made the heavens and the earth,
even they shall perish from the earth,
and from under these heavens'.

¹² He hath made the earth by his power,
he hath established the world by his wisdom,
and hath stretched out the heavens by his discretion.

¹³ When he uttereth his voice, there is a multitude of waters in the
heavens,
and he causeth the vapours to ascend from the ends of the earth:
he maketh lightnings with rain,
and bringeth forth the wind out of his treasures.

¹⁴ Every man is brutish in his knowledge,
every founder is confounded by the graven image:
for his molten image is falsehood, and there is no breath in
them.

¹⁵ They are vanity, and the work of errors:
in the time of their visitation they shall perish.

¹⁶ The portion of Jacob is not like them:
for he is the former of all things,
and Israel is the rod of his inheritance:
the LORD of hosts is his name.

¹⁷ Gather up thy wares out of the land,
O inhabitant of the fortress.
¹⁸ For thus saith the LORD,
'Behold, I will sling out the inhabitants of the land at this once,
and will distress them, that they may find it so'.

¹⁹ Woe is me for my hurt, my wound is grievous:
but I said, 'Truly this is a grief, and I must bear it'.
²⁰ My tabernacle is spoiled, and all my cords are broken:
my children are gone forth of me, and they are not:
there is none to stretch forth my tent any more,
and to set up my curtains.
²¹ For the pastors are become brutish,
and have not sought the LORD:
therefore they shall not prosper,
and all their flocks shall be scattered.
²² Behold, the noise of the bruit is come,
and a great commotion out of the north country,
to make the cities of Judah desolate,
and a den of dragons.

²³ O LORD, I know that the way of man is not in himself:
it is not in man that walketh to direct his steps.
²⁴ O LORD, correct me, but with judgement,
not in thy anger, lest thou bring me to nothing.
²⁵ Pour out thy fury upon the heathen that know thee not,
and upon the families that call not on thy name:
for they have eaten up Jacob,
and devoured him, and consumed him,
and have made his habitation desolate.

11 The word that came to Jeremiah from the LORD, saying, ²'Hear ye the words of this covenant, and speak unto the men of Judah, and to the inhabitants of Jerusalem; ³and say thou unto them, "Thus saith the LORD God of Israel, 'Cursed be the man that obeyeth not the words of this covenant, ⁴which I commanded your fathers in the day that I brought them forth out of the land of Egypt, from the iron furnace, saying, "Obey my voice, and do them, according to all which I command you: so shall ye be my people, and I will be your God: ⁵that I may perform the oath which I have sworn unto your fathers, to give them a land flowing with milk and honey, as it is this day"'"'. Then answered I, and said, 'So be it, O LORD'.

⁶Then the LORD said unto me, 'Proclaim all these words in the cities of Judah, and in the streets of Jerusalem, saying, "Hear ye the words of this covenant, and do them". ⁷For I earnestly protested unto your fathers in the day that I brought them up out of the land of Egypt, even unto this day, rising early and protesting, saying, "Obey my voice". ⁸Yet

they obeyed not, nor inclined their ear, but walked every one in the imagination of their evil heart: therefore I will bring upon them all the words of this covenant, which I commanded them to do; but they did them not.'

⁹And the LORD said unto me, 'A conspiracy is found among the men of Judah, and among the inhabitants of Jerusalem. ¹⁰They are turned back to the iniquities of their forefathers, which refused to hear my words: and they went after other gods to serve them: the house of Israel and the house of Judah have broken my covenant which I made with their fathers.'

¹¹Therefore thus saith the LORD, 'Behold, I will bring evil upon them which they shall not be able to escape; and though they shall cry unto me, I will not hearken unto them. ¹²Then shall the cities of Judah and inhabitants of Jerusalem go, and cry unto the gods unto whom they offer incense: but they shall not save them at all in the time of their trouble. ¹³For according to the number of thy cities were thy gods, O Judah, and according to the number of the streets of Jerusalem have ye set up altars to that shameful thing, even altars to burn incense unto Baal. ¹⁴Therefore pray not thou for this people, neither lift up a cry or prayer for them: for I will not hear them in the time that they cry unto me for their trouble.

¹⁵'What hath my beloved to do in my house, seeing she hath wrought lewdness with many, and the holy flesh is passed from thee? when thou doest evil, then thou rejoicest.' ¹⁶The LORD called thy name, 'A green olive tree, fair and of goodly fruit': with the noise of a great tumult he hath kindled fire upon it, and the branches of it are broken. ¹⁷For the LORD of hosts that planted thee, hath pronounced evil against thee, for the evil of the house of Israel and of the house of Judah, which they have done against themselves to provoke me to anger in offering incense unto Baal.

¹⁸And the LORD hath given me knowledge of it, and I know it: then thou showedst me their doings. ¹⁹But I was like a lamb or an ox that is brought to the slaughter, and I knew not that they had devised devices against me, saying, 'Let us destroy the tree with the fruit thereof, and let us cut him off from the land of the living, that his name may be no more remembered'. ²⁰But, O LORD of hosts, that judgest righteously, that triest the reins and the heart, let me see thy vengeance on them, for unto thee have I revealed my cause. ²¹Therefore thus saith the LORD of the men of Anathoth, that seek thy life, saying, 'Prophesy not in the name of the LORD, that thou die not by our hand': ²²therefore thus saith the LORD of hosts, 'Behold, I will punish them: the young men shall die by the sword, their sons and their daughters shall die by famine: ²³and there shall be no remnant of them: for I will bring evil upon the men of Anathoth, even the year of their visitation'.

12 Righteous art thou, O LORD, when I plead with thee:
yet let me talk with thee of thy judgements:
wherefore doth the way of the wicked prosper?

wherefore are all they happy that deal very treacherously?
² Thou hast planted them, yea, they have taken root:
they grow, yea, they bring forth fruit:
thou art near in their mouth, and far from their reins.
³ But thou, O Lord, knowest me:
thou hast seen me, and tried my heart towards thee:
pull them out like sheep for the slaughter,
and prepare them for the day of slaughter.
⁴ How long shall the land mourn,
and the herbs of every field wither,
for the wickedness of them that dwell therein?
the beasts are consumed, and the birds,
because they said, 'He shall not see our last end'.

⁵ If thou hast run with the footmen, and they have wearied thee,
then how canst thou contend with horses?
and if in the land of peace, wherein thou trustedst, they wearied
thee,
then how wilt thou do in the swelling of Jordan?
⁶ For even thy brethren and the house of thy father,
even they have dealt treacherously with thee,
yea, they have called a multitude after thee:
believe them not, though they speak fair words unto thee.

⁷ 'I have forsaken my house, I have left my heritage:
I have given the dearly beloved of my soul into the hand of her
enemies.
⁸ My heritage is unto me as a lion in the forest:
it crieth out against me, therefore have I hated it.
⁹ My heritage is unto me as a speckled bird,
the birds round about are against her;
come ye, assemble all the beasts of the field, come to devour.
¹⁰ Many pastors have destroyed my vineyard,
they have trodden my portion under foot,
they have made my pleasant portion a desolate wilderness.
¹¹ They have made it desolate,
and being desolate it mourneth unto me;
the whole land is made desolate,
because no man layeth it to heart.
¹² The spoilers are come upon all high places through the
wilderness:
for the sword of the Lord shall devour
from the one end of the land even to the other end of the land:
no flesh shall have peace.
¹³ They have sown wheat, but shall reap thorns:
they have put themselves to pain, but shall not profit:
and they shall be ashamed of your revenues
because of the fierce anger of the Lord.'

¹⁴Thus saith the LORD against all my evil neighbours, that touch the inheritance which I have caused my people Israel to inherit, 'Behold, I will pluck them out of their land, and pluck out the house of Judah from among them. ¹⁵And it shall come to pass after that I have plucked them out I will return, and have compassion on them, and will bring again every man to his heritage, and every man to his land. ¹⁶And it shall come to pass, if they will diligently learn the ways of my people, to swear by my name, "The LORD liveth", as they taught my people to swear by Baal: then shall they be built in the midst of my people. ¹⁷But if they will not obey, I will utterly pluck up and destroy that nation,' saith the LORD.

13 Thus saith the LORD unto me, 'Go and get thee a linen girdle, and put it upon thy loins, and put it not in water'. ²So I got a girdle according to the word of the LORD, and put it on my loins. ³And the word of the LORD came unto me the second time, saying, ⁴"Take the girdle that thou hast got, which is upon thy loins, and arise, go to Euphrates, and hide it there in a hole of the rock'. ⁵So I went, and hid it by Euphrates, as the LORD commanded me. ⁶And it came to pass after many days, that the LORD said unto me, 'Arise, go to Euphrates, and take the girdle from thence, which I commanded thee to hide there'. ⁷Then I went to Euphrates, and dug, and took the girdle from the place where I had hid it: and behold, the girdle was marred, it was profitable for nothing. ⁸Then the word of the LORD came unto me, saying, ⁹"Thus saith the LORD, "After this manner will I mar the pride of Judah, and the great pride of Jerusalem. ¹⁰This evil people which refuse to hear my words, which walk in the imagination of their heart, and walk after other gods to serve them and to worship them, shall even be as this girdle, which is good for nothing. ¹¹For as the girdle cleaveth to the loins of a man, so have I caused to cleave unto me the whole house of Israel and the whole house of Judah," saith the LORD; "that they might be unto me for a people, and for a name, and for a praise, and for a glory: but they would not hear."

¹²'Therefore thou shalt speak unto them this word, "Thus saith the LORD God of Israel, 'Every bottle shall be filled with wine: and they shall say unto thee, "Do we not certainly know that every bottle shall be filled with wine?"'" ¹³Then shalt thou say unto them, "Thus saith the LORD, 'Behold, I will fill all the inhabitants of this land, even the kings that sit upon David's throne, and the priests, and the prophets, and all the inhabitants of Jerusalem with drunkenness. ¹⁴And I will dash them one against another, even the fathers and the sons together,' saith the LORD: 'I will not pity, nor spare, nor have mercy, but destroy them.'"'

¹⁵ Hear ye and give ear, be not proud:
    for the LORD hath spoken.
¹⁶ Give glory to the LORD your God before he cause darkness,
    and before your feet stumble upon the dark mountains,
    and while ye look for light, he turn it into the shadow of death,
    and make it gross darkness.

¹⁷ But if ye will not hear it,
    my soul shall weep in secret places for your pride,
    and my eye shall weep sore, and run down with tears,
    because the LORD's flock is carried away captive.

¹⁸ 'Say unto the king and to the queen,
    "Humble yourselves, sit down,
    for your principalities shall come down,
    even the crown of your glory".

¹⁹ The cities of the south shall be shut up, and none shall open
        them:
    Judah shall be carried away captive all of it,
    it shall be wholly carried away captive.

²⁰ Lift up your eyes, and behold them that come from the north:
    where is the flock that was given thee, thy beautiful flock?

²¹ What wilt thou say when he shall punish thee?
    for thou hast taught them to be captains, and as chief over thee:
    shall not sorrows take thee, as a woman in travail?

²² 'And if thou say in thy heart, "Wherefore come these things
        upon me?"
    For the greatness of thy iniquity are thy skirts discovered,
    and thy heels made bare.

²³ Can the Ethiopian change his skin, or the leopard his spots?
    then may ye also do good, that are accustomed to do evil.

²⁴ Therefore will I scatter them as the stubble
    that passeth away by the wind of the wilderness.

²⁵ This is thy lot, the portion of thy measures from me,' saith the
    LORD,
    'because thou hast forgotten me, and trusted in falsehood.

²⁶ Therefore will I discover thy skirts upon thy face,
    that thy shame may appear.

²⁷ I have seen thy adulteries, and thy neighings,
    the lewdness of thy whoredom,
    and thy abominations on the hills in the fields.
    Woe unto thee, O Jerusalem,
    wilt thou not be made clean?
    when shall it once be?'

14 The word of the LORD that came to Jeremiah concerning the dearth.

² Judah mourneth, and the gates thereof languish,
    they are black unto the ground,
    and the cry of Jerusalem is gone up.

³ And their nobles have sent their little ones to the waters:
    they came to the pits, and found no water,
    they returned with their vessels empty:

they were ashamed and confounded,
and covered their heads.
⁴ Because the ground is chapped,
for there was no rain in the earth,
the ploughmen were ashamed,
they covered their heads.
⁵ Yea, the hind also calved in the field,
and forsook it, because there was no grass.
⁶ And the wild asses did stand in the high places,
they snuffed up the wind like dragons:
their eyes did fail, because there was no grass.

⁷ O Lord, though our iniquities testify against us,
do thou it for thy name's sake:
for our backslidings are many,
we have sinned against thee.
⁸ O the hope of Israel, the saviour thereof in time of trouble,
why shouldst thou be as a stranger in the land,
and as a wayfaring man that turneth aside to tarry for a night?
⁹ Why shouldst thou be as a man astonished,
as a mighty man that cannot save?
yet thou, O Lord, art in the midst of us,
and we are called by thy name,
leave us not.

¹⁰Thus saith the Lord unto this people, 'Thus have they loved to wander, they have not refrained their feet, therefore the Lord doth not accept them; he will now remember their iniquity, and visit their sins'.

¹¹Then said the Lord unto me, 'Pray not for this people, for their good. ¹²When they fast I will not hear their cry, and when they offer burnt offering and an oblation, I will not accept them: but I will consume them by the sword, and by the famine, and by the pestilence.' ¹³Then said I, 'Ah, Lord God, behold, the prophets say unto them, "Ye shall not see the sword, neither shall ye have famine, but I will give you assured peace in this place"'. ¹⁴Then the Lord said unto me, 'The prophets prophesy lies in my name: I sent them not, neither have I commanded them, neither spoke unto them: they prophesy unto you a false vision and divination, and a thing of nought, and the deceit of their heart. ¹⁵Therefore thus saith the Lord concerning the prophets that prophesy in my name, and I sent them not, yet they say, "Sword and famine shall not be in this land", "By sword and famine shall those prophets be consumed". ¹⁶And the people to whom they prophesy shall be cast out in the streets of Jerusalem because of the famine and the sword, and they shall have none to bury them, them, their wives, nor their sons, nor their daughters: for I will pour their wickedness upon them.

¹⁷ 'Therefore thou shalt say this word unto them,
"Let my eyes run down with tears night and day,

and let them not cease,
for the virgin daughter of my people is broken with a great
    breach,
with a very grievous blow.
18 If I go forth into the field,
then behold the slain with the sword,
and if I enter into the city,
then behold them that are sick with famine,
yea, both the prophet and the priest go about into a land that
    they know not."'

19 Hast thou utterly rejected Judah?
hath thy soul loathed Zion?
why hast thou smitten us, and there is no healing for us?
we looked for peace, and there is no good,
and for the time of healing, and behold trouble.
20 We acknowledge, O LORD, our wickedness,
and the iniquity of our fathers:
for we have sinned against thee.
21 Do not abhor us, for thy name's sake,
do not disgrace the throne of thy glory:
remember, break not thy covenant with us.
22 Are there any among the vanities of the Gentiles that can cause
    rain?
or can the heavens give showers?
art not thou he, O LORD our God?
therefore we will wait upon thee:
for thou hast made all these things.

15 Then said the LORD unto me, 'Though Moses and Samuel stood before me, yet my mind could not be toward this people: cast them out of my sight, and let them go forth. 2And it shall come to pass, if they say unto thee, "Whither shall we go forth?" then thou shalt tell them, "Thus saith the LORD, 'Such as are for death, to death; and such as are for the sword, to the sword; and such as are for the famine, to the famine; and such as are for the captivity, to the captivity'". 3And I will appoint over them four kinds,' saith the LORD, 'the sword to slay, and the dogs to tear, and the fowls of the heaven, and the beasts of the earth to devour and destroy. 4And I will cause them to be removed into all kingdoms of the earth, because of Manasseh the son of Hezekiah king of Judah, for that which he did in Jerusalem. 5For who shall have pity upon thee, O Jerusalem? or who shall bemoan thee? or who shall go aside to ask how thou doest? 6Thou hast forsaken me,' saith the LORD, 'thou art gone backward: therefore will I stretch out my hand against thee, and destroy thee; I am weary with repenting. 7And I will fan them with a fan in the gates of the land: I will bereave them of children, I will destroy my people, since they return not from their ways. 8Their widows are increased to me above the sand of the seas: I have brought upon them against the mother of the young men a spoiler at noonday: I have caused him to fall upon it suddenly, and terrors upon the city. ⁹She that hath borne seven languisheth: she hath given up the ghost: her sun is gone down while it was yet day: she hath been ashamed and confounded: and the residue of them will I deliver to the sword before their enemies,' saith the Lord.

¹⁰Woe is me, my mother, that thou hast borne me a man of strife and a man of contention to the whole earth: I have neither lent on usury, nor men have lent to me on usury, yet every one of them doth curse me. ¹¹The Lord said, 'Verily it shall be well with thy remnant, verily I will cause the enemy to entreat thee well in the time of evil and in the time of affliction. ¹²Shall iron break the northern iron and the steel? ¹³Thy substance and thy treasures will I give to the spoil without price, and that for all thy sins, even in all thy borders. ¹⁴And I will make thee to pass with thy enemies into a land which thou knowest not: for a fire is kindled in my anger, which shall burn upon you.'

¹⁵ O Lord, thou knowest:
    remember me, and visit me,
    and revenge me of my persecutors,
    take me not away in thy long-suffering:
    know that for thy sake I have suffered rebuke.
¹⁶ Thy words were found, and I did eat them,
    and thy word was unto me the joy and rejoicing of my heart:
    for I am called by thy name, O Lord God of hosts.
¹⁷ I sat not in the assembly of the mockers, nor rejoiced,
    I sat alone because of thy hand:
    for thou hast filled me with indignation.
¹⁸ Why is my pain perpetual, and my wound incurable,
    which refuseth to be healed?
    wilt thou be altogether unto me as a liar,
    and as waters that fail?

¹⁹ Therefore thus saith the Lord,
    'If thou return, then will I bring thee again,
    and thou shalt stand before me:
    and if thou take forth the precious from the vile,
    thou shalt be as my mouth:
    let them return unto thee, but return not thou unto them.
²⁰ And I will make thee unto this people a fenced brazen wall:
    and they shall fight against thee,
    but they shall not prevail against thee:
    for I am with thee to save thee and to deliver thee,' saith the Lord.
²¹ 'And I will deliver thee out of the hand of the wicked,
    and I will redeem thee out of the hand of the terrible.'

16 The word of the LORD came also unto me, saying, [2]'Thou shalt not take thee a wife, neither shalt thou have sons nor daughters in this place'. [3]For thus saith the LORD concerning the sons and concerning the daughters that are born in this place, and concerning their mothers that bore them, and concerning their fathers that begot them in this land: [4]'They shall die of grievous deaths, they shall not be lamented, neither shall they be buried: but they shall be as dung upon the face of the earth, and they shall be consumed by the sword, and by famine, and their carcases shall be meat for the fowls of heaven, and for the beasts of the earth'. [5]For thus saith the LORD, 'Enter not into the house of mourning, neither go to lament nor bemoan them: for I have taken away my peace from this people,' saith the LORD, 'even lovingkindness and mercies. [6]Both the great and the small shall die in this land: they shall not be buried, neither shall men lament for them, nor cut themselves, nor make themselves bald for them. [7]Neither shall men tear themselves for them in mourning, to comfort them for the dead, neither shall men give them the cup of consolation to drink for their father or for their mother. [8]Thou shalt not also go into the house of feasting, to sit with them to eat and to drink.' [9]For thus saith the LORD of hosts, the God of Israel, 'Behold, I will cause to cease out of this place in your eyes, and in your days, the voice of mirth, and the voice of gladness, the voice of the bridegroom, and the voice of the bride.

[10]'And it shall come to pass, when thou shalt show this people all these words, and they shall say unto thee, "Wherefore hath the LORD pronounced all this great evil against us? or what is our iniquity? or what is our sin that we have committed against the LORD our God?" [11]then shalt thou say unto them, "'Because your fathers have forsaken me,' saith the LORD, 'and have walked after other gods, and have served them, and have worshipped them, and have forsaken me, and have not kept my law: [12]and ye have done worse than your fathers (for behold, ye walk every one after the imagination of his evil heart, that they may not hearken unto me). [13]Therefore will I cast you out of this land into a land that ye know not, neither ye nor your fathers, and there shall ye serve other gods day and night, where I will not show you favour.

[14]'"Therefore, behold, the days come,' saith the LORD, 'that it shall no more be said, "The LORD liveth, that brought up the children of Israel out of the land of Egypt"; [15]but, "The LORD liveth, that brought up the children of Israel from the land of the north, and from all the lands whither he had driven them": and I will bring them again into their land that I gave unto their fathers.

[16]'"Behold, I will send for many fishers,' saith the LORD, 'and they shall fish them; and after will I send for many hunters, and they shall hunt them from every mountain, and from every hill, and out of the holes of the rocks. [17]For my eyes are upon all their ways: they are not hid from my face, neither is their iniquity hid from my eyes. [18]And first I will recompense their iniquity and their sin double, because they have defiled my land, they have filled my inheritance with the carcases of their detestable and abominable things.'"'

^{19} O LORD, my strength and my fortress,
and my refuge in the day of affliction,
the Gentiles shall come unto thee from the ends of the earth,
and shall say,
'Surely our fathers have inherited lies, vanity,
and things wherein there is no profit.
^{20} Shall a man make gods unto himself, and they are no gods?'
^{21} 'Therefore behold, I will this once cause them to know:
I will cause them to know my hand and my might,
and they shall know that my name is the LORD.'

17 The sin of Judah is written with a pen of iron, and with the point of a diamond: it is graven upon the tablet of their heart, and upon the horns of your altars; ^{2}whilst their children remember their altars and their groves by the green trees upon the high hills. ^{3}O my mountain, in the field I will give thy substance and all thy treasures to the spoil, and thy high places for sin, throughout all thy borders. ^{4}And thou, even thyself shalt discontinue from thy heritage that I gave thee, and I will cause thee to serve thy enemies in the land which thou knowest not: for ye have kindled a fire in my anger, which shall burn for ever.

^{5}Thus saith the LORD,

'Cursed be the man that trusteth in man,
and maketh flesh his arm,
and whose heart departeth from the LORD.
^{6} For he shall be like the heath in the desert,
and shall not see when good cometh,
but shall inhabit the parched places in the wilderness,
in a salt land and not inhabited.
^{7} Blessed is the man that trusteth in the LORD,
and whose hope the LORD is.
^{8} For he shall be as a tree planted by the waters,
and that spreadeth out her roots by the river,
and shall not see when heat cometh,
but her leaf shall be green,
and shall not be careful in the year of drought,
neither shall cease from yielding fruit.

^{9} 'The heart is deceitful above all things,
and desperately wicked: who can know it?
^{10} I the LORD search the heart, I try the reins,
even to give every man according to his ways,
and according to the fruit of his doings.'

^{11} As the partridge sitteth on eggs, and hatcheth them not:
so he that getteth riches and not by right,
shall leave them in the midst of his days,
and at his end shall be a fool.

¹² A glorious high throne from the beginning
is the place of our sanctuary.
¹³ O LORD, the hope of Israel,
all that forsake thee shall be ashamed,
and they that depart from me shall be written in the earth,
because they have forsaken the LORD,
the fountain of living waters.
¹⁴ Heal me, O LORD, and I shall be healed:
save me, and I shall be saved:
for thou art my praise.

¹⁵ Behold, they say unto me,
'Where is the word of the LORD? let it come now'.
¹⁶ As for me, I have not hastened from being a pastor to follow thee,
neither have I desired the woeful day, thou knowest:
that which came out of my lips was right before thee.
¹⁷ Be not a terror unto me,
thou art my hope in the day of evil.
¹⁸ Let them be confounded that persecute me,
but let not me be confounded:
let them be dismayed,
but let not me be dismayed:
bring upon them the day of evil,
and destroy them with double destruction.

¹⁹Thus said the LORD unto me, 'Go and stand in the gate of the children of the people, whereby the kings of Judah come in, and by the which they go out, and in all the gates of Jerusalem; ²⁰and say unto them, "Hear ye the word of the LORD, ye kings of Judah, and all Judah, and all the inhabitants of Jerusalem, that enter in by these gates. ²¹Thus saith the LORD, 'Take heed to yourselves, and bear no burden on the sabbath day, nor bring it in by the gates of Jerusalem; ²²neither carry forth a burden out of your houses on the sabbath day, neither do ye any work, but hallow ye the sabbath day, as I commanded your fathers. ²³But they obeyed not, neither inclined their ear, but made their neck stiff, that they might not hear, nor receive instruction. ²⁴And it shall come to pass, if ye diligently hearken unto me,' saith the LORD, 'to bring in no burden through the gates of this city on the sabbath day, but hallow the sabbath day, to do no work therein: ²⁵then shall there enter into the gates of this city kings and princes sitting upon the throne of David, riding in chariots and on horses, they and their princes, the men of Judah and the inhabitants of Jerusalem: and this city shall remain for ever. ²⁶And they shall come from the cities of Judah, and from the places about Jerusalem, and from the land of Benjamin, and from the plain, and from the mountains, and from the south, bringing burnt offerings, and sacrifices, and meat offerings, and incense, and bringing sacrifices of praise unto the house of the LORD. ²⁷But if you will not hearken unto me to hallow the sabbath

day, and not to bear a burden, even entering in at the gates of Jerusalem on the sabbath day: then will I kindle a fire in the gates thereof, and it shall devour the palaces of Jerusalem, and it shall not be quenched.'"'

18 The word which came to Jeremiah from the LORD, saying, ²'Arise, and go down to the potter's house, and there I will cause thee to hear my words'. ³Then I went down to the potter's house, and behold, he wrought a work on the wheels. ⁴And the vessel that he made of clay was marred in the hand of the potter: so he made it again another vessel, as seemed good to the potter to make it. ⁵Then the word of the LORD came to me, saying, ⁶'O house of Israel, cannot I do with you as this potter?' saith the LORD. 'Behold, as the clay is in the potter's hand, so are ye in my hand, O house of Israel. ⁷At what instant I shall speak concerning a nation, and concerning a kingdom, to pluck up, and to pull down, and to destroy it; ⁸if that nation against whom I have pronounced, turn from their evil, I will repent of the evil that I thought to do unto them. ⁹And at what instant I shall speak concerning a nation, and concerning a kingdom to build and to plant it; ¹⁰if it do evil in my sight, that it obey not my voice, then I will repent of the good, wherewith I said I would benefit them.

¹¹'Now therefore go to, speak to the men of Judah, and to the inhabitants of Jerusalem, saying, "Thus saith the LORD, 'Behold, I frame evil against you, and devise a device against you: return ye now every one from his evil way, and make your ways and your doings good. ¹²And they said, "There is no hope: but we will walk after our own devices, and we will every one do the imagination of his evil heart".' ¹³Therefore thus saith the LORD,

'"Ask ye now among the heathen, who hath heard such things:
   the virgin of Israel hath done a very horrible thing.
¹⁴ Will a man leave the snow of Lebanon which cometh from the
      rock of the field?
   or shall the cold flowing waters that come from another place be
      forsaken?
¹⁵ Because my people hath forgotten me,
   they have burnt incense to vanity,
   and they have caused them to stumble
   in their ways from the ancient paths,
   to walk in paths, in a way not cast up,
¹⁶ to make their land desolate, and a perpetual hissing:
   every one that passeth thereby
   shall be astonished, and wag his head.
¹⁷ I will scatter them as with an east wind before the enemy:
   I will show them the back, and not the face,
   in the day of their calamity.'"'

¹⁸Then said they, 'Come, and let us devise devices against Jeremiah: for the law shall not perish from the priest, nor counsel from the wise, nor

the word from the prophet. Come and let us smite him with the tongue, and let us not give heed to any of his words.'

¹⁹ Give heed to me, O LORD,
   and hearken to the voice of them that contend with me.
²⁰ Shall evil be recompensed for good?
   for they have dug a pit for my soul:
   remember that I stood before thee to speak good for them,
   and to turn away thy wrath from them.
²¹ Therefore deliver up their children to the famine,
   and pour out their blood by the force of the sword,
   and let their wives be bereaved of their children and be widows,
   and let their men be put to death,
   let their young men be slain by the sword in battle.
²² Let a cry be heard from their houses,
   when thou shalt bring a troop suddenly upon them,
   for they have dug a pit to take me,
   and hid snares for my feet.
²³ Yet, LORD, thou knowest all their counsel against me to slay me:
   forgive not their iniquity,
   neither blot out their sin from thy sight,
   but let them be overthrown before thee,
   deal thus with them in the time of thy anger.'

19 Thus saith the LORD, 'Go and get a potter's earthen bottle, and take of the ancients of the people, and of the ancients of the priests; ²and go forth unto the valley of the son of Hinnom, which is by the entry of the east gate, and proclaim there the words that I shall tell thee, ³and say, "Hear ye the word of the LORD, O kings of Judah, and inhabitants of Jerusalem; thus saith the LORD of hosts, the God of Israel, 'Behold, I will bring evil upon this place, the which whosoever heareth, his ears shall tingle. ⁴Because they have forsaken me, and have estranged this place, and have burnt incense in it unto other gods, whom neither they nor their fathers have known, nor the kings of Judah, and have filled this place with the blood of innocents; ⁵they have built also the high places of Baal, to burn their sons with fire for burnt offerings unto Baal, which I commanded not, nor spoke it, neither came it into my mind: ⁶therefore behold, the days come,' saith the LORD, 'that this place shall no more be called Tophet, nor the valley of the son of Hinnom, but the valley of slaughter. ⁷And I will make void the counsel of Judah and Jerusalem in this place, and I will cause them to fall by the sword before their enemies, and by the hands of them that seek their lives: and their carcases will I give to be meat for the fowls of the heaven, and for the beasts of the earth. ⁸And I will make this city desolate, and a hissing: every one that passeth thereby shall be astonished and hiss because of all the plagues thereof. ⁹And I will cause them to eat the flesh of their sons and the flesh of their daughters, and they shall eat every one the flesh of his friend in the siege and straitness, wherewith their enemies, and they that seek their lives, shall straiten them.'" ¹⁰Then shalt thou break the bottle in the sight of the men that go with thee, ¹¹and shalt say unto them, "Thus saith the LORD of hosts, 'Even so will I break this people and this city, as one breaketh a potter's vessel that cannot be made whole again, and they shall bury them in Tophet, till there be no place else to bury. ¹²Thus will I do unto this place,' saith the LORD, 'and to the inhabitants thereof, and even make this city as Tophet. ¹³And the houses of Jerusalem, and the houses of the kings of Judah shall be defiled as the place of Tophet, because of all the houses upon whose roofs they have burnt incense unto all the host of heaven, and have poured out drink offerings unto other gods.'"'

¹⁴Then came Jeremiah from Tophet, whither the LORD had sent him to prophesy, and he stood in the court of the LORD's house, and said to all the people, ¹⁵'Thus saith the LORD of hosts, the God of Israel, "Behold, I will bring upon this city and upon all her towns all the evil that I have pronounced against it, because they have hardened their necks, that they might not hear my words"'.

20 Now Pashur the son of Immer the priest, who was also chief governor in the house of the LORD, heard that Jeremiah prophesied these things. ²Then Pashur smote Jeremiah the prophet, and put him in the stocks that were in the high gate of Benjamin, which was by the house of the LORD. ³And it came to pass on the morrow, that Pashur brought forth Jeremiah out of the stocks. Then said Jeremiah unto him, 'The LORD hath not called thy name Pashur, but Magor-missabib. ⁴For thus saith the LORD, "Behold, I will make thee a terror to thyself, and to all thy friends, and they shall fall by the sword of their enemies, and thy eyes shall behold it: and I will give all Judah into the hand of the king of Babylon, and he shall carry them captive into Babylon, and shall slay them with the sword. ⁵Moreover I will deliver all the strength of this city, and all the labours thereof, and all the precious things thereof, and all the treasures of the kings of Judah will I give into the hand of their enemies, which shall spoil them, and take them, and carry them to Babylon. ⁶And thou, Pashur, and all that dwell in thy house shall go into captivity: and thou shalt come to Babylon, and there thou shalt die, and shalt be buried there, thou, and all thy friends, to whom thou hast prophesied lies."'

⁷ O LORD, thou hast deceived me,
and I was deceived:
thou art stronger than I,
and hast prevailed:
I am in derision daily,
every one mocketh me.
⁸ For since I spoke, I cried out,
I cried violence and spoil;
because the word of the LORD
was made a reproach unto me,

and a derision, daily.

⁹ Then I said, 'I will not make mention of him,
nor speak any more in his name'.
But his word was in my heart
as a burning fire shut up in my bones,
and I was weary with forbearing,
and I could not stay.

¹⁰ For I heard the defaming of many,
fear on every side.
'Report,' say they, 'and we will report it.'
All my familiars watched for my halting, saying,
'Peradventure he will be enticed,
and we shall prevail against him,
and we shall take our revenge on him'.

¹¹ But the LORD is with me as a mighty terrible one:
therefore my persecutors shall stumble,
and they shall not prevail:
they shall be greatly ashamed,
for they shall not prosper:
their everlasting confusion shall never be forgotten.

¹² But, O LORD of hosts, that triest the righteous,
and seest the reins and the heart,
let me see thy vengeance on them:
for unto thee have I opened my cause.

¹³ Sing unto the LORD, praise ye the LORD:
for he hath delivered the soul of the poor
from the hand of evil-doers.

¹⁴ Cursed be the day wherein I was born:
let not the day wherein my mother bore me be blessed.

¹⁵ Cursed be the man who brought tidings to my father,
saying, 'A man-child is born unto thee',
making him very glad.

¹⁶ And let that man be as the cities
which the LORD overthrew, and repented not:
and let him hear the cry in the morning,
and the shouting at noontide,

¹⁷ because he slew me not from the womb:
or that my mother might have been my grave,
and her womb to be always great with me.

¹⁸ Wherefore came I forth out of the womb
to see labour and sorrow,
that my days should be consumed with shame?

21 The word which came unto Jeremiah from the LORD, when king
Zedekiah sent unto him Pashur the son of Malchiah, and
Zephaniah the son of Maaseiah the priest, saying, ²'Inquire, I pray thee,
of the LORD for us (for Nebuchadrezzar king of Babylon maketh war

against us) if so be that the LORD will deal with us according to all his wondrous works, that he may go up from us'.

³Then said Jeremiah unto them, 'Thus shall ye say to Zedekiah: ⁴"Thus saith the LORD God of Israel, 'Behold, I will turn back the weapons of war that are in your hands, wherewith ye fight against the king of Babylon, and against the Chaldeans, which besiege you without the walls, and I will assemble them into the midst of this city. ⁵And I myself will fight against you with an outstretched hand and with a strong arm, even in anger, and in fury, and in great wrath. ⁶And I will smite the inhabitants of this city, both man and beast: they shall die of a great pestilence. ⁷And afterward,' saith the LORD, 'I will deliver Zedekiah king of Judah, and his servants, and the people, and such as are left in this city from the pestilence, from the sword, and from the famine, into the hand of Nebuchadrezzar king of Babylon, and into the hand of their enemies, and into the hand of those that seek their life: and he shall smite them with the edge of the sword; he shall not spare them, neither have pity, nor have mercy.'"

⁸And unto this people thou shalt say, "Thus saith the LORD, 'Behold, I set before you the way of life, and the way of death. ⁹He that abideth in this city shall die by the sword, and by the famine, and by the pestilence: but he that goeth out, and falleth to the Chaldeans that besiege you, he shall live, and his life shall be unto him for a prey. ¹⁰For I have set my face against this city for evil, and not for good,' saith the LORD: 'it shall be given into the hand of the king of Babylon, and he shall burn it with fire.'"

¹¹And touching the house of the king of Judah, say, "Hear ye the word of the LORD. ¹²O house of David, thus saith the LORD,

'"Execute judgement in the morning,
and deliver him that is spoiled
out of the hand of the oppressor,
lest my fury go out like fire,
and burn that none can quench it,
because of the evil of your doings.
¹³ Behold, I am against thee,
O inhabitant of the valley,
and rock of the plain,' saith the LORD,
'which say, "Who shall come down against us?
or who shall enter into our habitations?"
¹⁴ But I will punish you
according to the fruit of your doings,' saith the LORD:
'and I will kindle a fire in the forest thereof,
and it shall devour all things round about it.'"'

22 Thus saith the LORD, 'Go down to the house of the king of Judah, and speak there this word, ²and say, "Hear the word of the LORD, O king of Judah, that sittest upon the throne of David, thou, and thy servants, and thy people that enter in by these gates. ³Thus saith the

LORD, 'Execute ye judgement and righteousness, and deliver the spoiled out of the hand of the oppressor: and do no wrong, do no violence to the stranger, the fatherless, nor the widow, neither shed innocent blood in this place. ⁴For if ye do this thing indeed, then shall there enter in by the gates of this house kings sitting upon the throne of David, riding in chariots and on horses, he, and his servants, and his people. ⁵But if ye will not hear these words, I swear by myself,' saith the LORD, 'that this house shall become a desolation.' ⁶For thus saith the LORD unto the king's house of Judah, 'Thou art Gilead unto me, and the head of Lebanon: yet surely I will make thee a wilderness, and cities which are not inhabited. ⁷And I will prepare destroyers against thee, every one with his weapons: and they shall cut down thy choice cedars, and cast them into the fire. ⁸And many nations shall pass by this city, and they shall say every man to his neighbour, "Wherefore hath the LORD done thus unto this great city?" ⁹Then they shall answer, "Because they have forsaken the covenant of the LORD their God, and worshipped other gods, and served them".'"'

¹⁰Weep ye not for the dead, neither bemoan him, but weep sore for him that goeth away: for he shall return no more, nor see his native country. ¹¹For thus saith the LORD touching Shallum the son of Josiah king of Judah, which reigned in stead of Josiah his father, which went forth out of this place, 'He shall not return thither any more: ¹²but he shall die in the place whither they have led him captive, and shall see this land no more.

¹³'Woe unto him that buildeth his house by unrighteousness, and his chambers by wrong: that useth his neighbour's service without wages, and giveth him not for his work: ¹⁴that saith, "I will build me a wide house and large chambers", and cutteth him out windows; and it is ceiled with cedar, and painted with vermilion. ¹⁵Shalt thou reign, because thou closest thyself in cedar? did not thy father eat and drink, and do judgement and justice, and then it was well with him? ¹⁶He judged the cause of the poor and needy, then it was well with him: was not this to know me?' saith the LORD. ¹⁷'But thy eyes and thy heart are not but for thy covetousness, and for to shed innocent blood, and for oppression, and for violence, to do it.' ¹⁸Therefore thus saith the LORD concerning Jehoiakim the son of Josiah king of Judah,

> 'They shall not lament for him,
> saying, "Ah my brother", or, "Ah sister":
> they shall not lament for him,
> saying, "Ah lord", or, "Ah his glory".
> ¹⁹ He shall be buried with the burial of an ass,
> drawn and cast forth beyond the gates of Jerusalem.'

> ²⁰ Go up to Lebanon, and cry,
> and lift up thy voice in Bashan,
> and cry from the passages:
> for all thy lovers are destroyed.

²¹ I spoke unto thee in thy prosperity,
    but thou saidst, 'I will not hear'.
    This hath been thy manner from thy youth,
    that thou obeyedst not my voice.
²² The wind shall eat up all thy pastors,
    and thy lovers shall go into captivity:
    surely then shalt thou be ashamed
    and confounded for all thy wickedness.
²³ O inhabitant of Lebanon,
    that makest thy nest in the cedars,
    how gracious shalt thou be
    when pangs come upon thee,
    the pain as of a woman in travail!

²⁴'As I live,' saith the LORD, 'though Coniah the son of Jehoiakim king of Judah were the signet upon my right hand, yet would I pluck thee thence. ²⁵And I will give thee into the hand of them that seek thy life, and into the hand of them whose face thou fearest, even into the hand of Nebuchadrezzar king of Babylon, and into the hand of the Chaldeans. ²⁶And I will cast thee out, and thy mother that bore thee, into another country where ye were not born, and there shall ye die. ²⁷But to the land whereunto they desire to return, thither shall they not return.'

²⁸Is this man Coniah a despised broken idol? is he a vessel wherein is no pleasure? wherefore are they cast out, he and his seed, and are cast into a land which they know not? ²⁹O earth, earth, earth, hear the word of the LORD: ³⁰thus saith the LORD, 'Write ye this man childless, a man that shall not prosper in his days: for no man of his seed shall prosper, sitting upon the throne of David, and ruling any more in Judah'.

23 'Woe be unto the pastors that destroy and scatter the sheep of my pasture,' saith the LORD. ²Therefore thus saith the LORD God of Israel against the pastors that feed my people, 'Ye have scattered my flock, and driven them away, and have not visited them: behold, I will visit upon you the evil of your doings,' saith the LORD. ³'And I will gather the remnant of my flock out of all countries whither I have driven them, and will bring them again to their folds, and they shall be fruitful and increase. ⁴And I will set up shepherds over them which shall feed them, and they shall fear no more, nor be dismayed, neither shall they be lacking,' saith the LORD.

⁵'Behold, the days come,' saith the LORD, 'that I will raise unto David a righteous Branch, and a King shall reign and prosper, and shall execute judgement and justice in the earth. ⁶In his days Judah shall be saved, and Israel shall dwell safely: and this is his name whereby he shall be called, THE LORD OUR RIGHTEOUSNESS.

⁷'Therefore behold, the days come,' saith the LORD, 'that they shall no more say, "The LORD liveth, which brought up the children of Israel out of the land of Egypt": ⁸but, "The LORD liveth, which brought up and which led the seed of the house of Israel out of the north country, and

from all countries whither I had driven them"; and they shall dwell in their own land.'

⁹ My heart within me is broken
  because of the prophets,
  all my bones shake:
  I am like a drunken man,
  and like a man whom wine hath overcome,
  because of the LORD,
  and because of the words of his holiness.
¹⁰ For the land is full of adulterers,
  for because of swearing the land mourneth:
  the pleasant places of the wilderness are dried up,
  and their course is evil,
  and their force is not right.
¹¹ 'For both prophet and priest are profane,
  yea, in my house have I found their wickedness,' saith the LORD.
¹² 'Wherefore their way shall be unto them
  as slippery ways in the darkness:
  they shall be driven on, and fall therein:
  for I will bring evil upon them,
  even the year of their visitation,' saith the LORD.
¹³ 'And I have seen folly in the prophets of Samaria;
  they prophesied in Baal, and caused my people Israel to err.
¹⁴ I have seen also in the prophets of Jerusalem a horrible thing:
  they commit adultery, and walk in lies:
  they strengthen also the hands of evil-doers,
  that none doth return from his wickedness:
  they are all of them unto me as Sodom,
  and the inhabitants thereof as Gomorrah.'

¹⁵Therefore thus saith the LORD of hosts concerning the prophets, 'Behold, I will feed them with wormwood, and make them drink the water of gall: for from the prophets of Jerusalem is profaneness gone forth into all the land'. ¹⁶Thus saith the LORD of hosts, 'Hearken not unto the words of the prophets that prophesy unto you: they make you vain: they speak a vision of their own heart, and not out of the mouth of the LORD. ¹⁷They say still unto them that despise me, "The LORD hath said, 'Ye shall have peace'"; and they say unto every one that walketh after the imagination of his own heart, "No evil shall come upon you".'

¹⁸ For who hath stood in the counsel of the LORD,
  and hath perceived and heard his word?
  who hath marked his word, and heard it?
¹⁹ Behold, a whirlwind of the LORD is gone forth in fury,
  even a grievous whirlwind:
  it shall fall grievously upon the head of the wicked.
²⁰ The anger of the LORD shall not return,

until he have executed,
and till he have performed the thoughts of his heart:
in the latter days ye shall consider it perfectly.

²¹ 'I have not sent these prophets, yet they ran:
I have not spoken to them, yet they prophesied.
²² But if they had stood in my counsel,
and had caused my people to hear my words,
then they should have turned them from their evil way,
and from the evil of their doings.
²³ Am I a God at hand,' saith the LORD,
'and not a God afar off?
²⁴ Can any hide himself in secret places
that I shall not see him?' saith the LORD.
'Do not I fill heaven and earth?' saith the LORD.
²⁵ 'I have heard what the prophets said,
that prophesy lies in my name,
saying, "I have dreamed, I have dreamed".

²⁶'How long shall this be in the heart of the prophets that prophesy lies? yea, they are prophets of the deceit of their own heart; ²⁷which think to cause my people to forget my name by their dreams which they tell every man to his neighbour, as their fathers have forgotten my name for Baal. ²⁸The prophet that hath a dream, let him tell a dream; and he that hath my word, let him speak my word faithfully. What is the chaff to the wheat?' saith the LORD. ²⁹'Is not my word like as a fire?' saith the LORD; 'and like a hammer that breaketh the rock in pieces? ³⁰Therefore, behold, I am against the prophets,' saith the LORD, 'that steal my word every one from his neighbour. ³¹Behold, I am against the prophets,' saith the LORD, 'that use their tongues, and say, "He saith". ³²Behold, I am against them that prophesy false dreams,' saith the LORD, 'and do tell them, and cause my people to err by their lies, and by their lightness, yet I sent them not, nor commanded them: therefore they shall not profit this people at all,' saith the LORD.

³³'And when this people, or the prophet, or a priest shall ask thee, saying, "What is the burden of the LORD?" thou shalt then say unto them, "What burden?" I will even forsake you,' saith the LORD. ³⁴'And as for the prophet, and the priest, and the people that shall say, "The burden of the LORD", I will even punish that man and his house. ³⁵Thus shall ye say every one to his neighbour, and every one to his brother, "What hath the LORD answered? and what hath the LORD spoken?" ³⁶And the burden of the LORD shall ye mention no more: for every man's word shall be his burden: for ye have perverted the words of the living God, of the LORD of hosts our God. ³⁷Thus shalt thou say to the prophet, "What hath the LORD answered thee? and what hath the LORD spoken?" ³⁸But since ye say, "The burden of the LORD"; therefore thus saith the LORD, "Because you say this word, 'The burden of the LORD', and I have sent unto you, saying, 'Ye shall not say, "The burden of the LORD": ³⁹therefore

behold, I, even I, will utterly forget you, and I will forsake you, and the city that I gave you and your fathers, and cast you out of my presence. [40]And I will bring an everlasting reproach upon you, and a perpetual shame, which shall not be forgotten.'"'

24 The LORD showed me, and behold, two baskets of figs were set before the temple of the LORD, after that Nebuchadrezzar king of Babylon had carried away captive Jeconiah the son of Jehoiakim king of Judah, and the princes of Judah, with the carpenters and smiths from Jerusalem, and had brought them to Babylon. [2]One basket had very good figs, even like the figs that are first ripe: and the other basket had very naughty figs, which could not be eaten, they were so bad. [3]Then said the LORD unto me, 'What seest thou, Jeremiah?' And I said, 'Figs: the good figs, very good; and the evil, very evil, that cannot be eaten, they are so evil'.

[4]Again the word of the LORD came unto me, saying, [5]'Thus saith the LORD, the God of Israel, "Like these good figs, so will I acknowledge them that are carried away captive of Judah, whom I have sent out of this place into the land of the Chaldeans for their good. [6]For I will set my eyes upon them for good, and I will bring them again to this land, and I will build them, and not pull them down, and I will plant them, and not pluck them up. [7]And I will give them a heart to know me, that I am the LORD: and they shall be my people, and I will be their God: for they shall return unto me with their whole heart.

[8]"And as the evil figs, which cannot be eaten, they are so evil" (surely thus saith the LORD), "so will I give Zedekiah the king of Judah, and his princes, and the residue of Jerusalem, that remain in this land, and them that dwell in the land of Egypt: [9]and I will deliver them to be removed into all the kingdoms of the earth for their hurt, to be a reproach and a proverb, a taunt and a curse in all places whither I shall drive them. [10]And I will send the sword, the famine, and the pestilence among them, till they be consumed from off the land that I gave unto them and to their fathers."'

25 The word that came to Jeremiah concerning all the people of Judah in the fourth year of Jehoiakim the son of Josiah king of Judah, that was the first year of Nebuchadrezzar king of Babylon: [2]the which Jeremiah the prophet spoke unto all the people of Judah, and to all the inhabitants of Jerusalem, saying, [3]'From the thirteenth year of Josiah the son of Amon king of Judah, even unto this day, that is the three and twentieth year, the word of the LORD hath come unto me, and I have spoken unto you, rising early and speaking, but ye have not hearkened. [4]And the LORD hath sent unto you all his servants the prophets, rising early and sending them, but ye have not hearkened, nor inclined your ear to hear. [5]They said, "Turn ye again now every one from his evil way, and from the evil of your doings, and dwell in the land that the LORD hath given unto you and to your fathers for ever and ever. [6]And go not after other gods to serve them, and to worship them, and provoke me not to anger with the works of your hands, and I will do you no hurt." [7]"Yet ye have not hearkened unto me," saith the LORD,

"that ye might provoke me to anger with the works of your hands to your own hurt."

⁸'Therefore thus saith the LORD of hosts, "Because ye have not heard my words, ⁹behold, I will send and take all the families of the north," saith the LORD, "and Nebuchadrezzar the king of Babylon, my servant, and will bring them against this land, and against the inhabitants thereof, and against all these nations round about, and will utterly destroy them, and make them an astonishment, and a hissing, and perpetual desolations. ¹⁰Moreover I will take from them the voice of mirth, and the voice of gladness, the voice of the bridegroom, and the voice of the bride, the sound of the millstones, and the light of the candle. ¹¹And this whole land shall be a desolation, and an astonishment, and these nations shall serve the king of Babylon seventy years.

¹²'"And it shall come to pass, when seventy years are accomplished, that I will punish the king of Babylon, and that nation," saith the LORD, "for their iniquity, and the land of the Chaldeans, and will make it perpetual desolations. ¹³And I will bring upon that land all my words which I have pronounced against it, even all that is written in this book, which Jeremiah hath prophesied against all the nations. ¹⁴For many nations and great kings shall serve themselves of them also: and I will recompense them according to their deeds, and according to the works of their own hands."'

¹⁵For thus saith the LORD God of Israel unto me, 'Take the wine cup of this fury at my hand, and cause all the nations, to whom I send thee, to drink it. ¹⁶And they shall drink, and be moved, and be mad, because of the sword that I will send among them.' ¹⁷Then took I the cup at the LORD's hand, and made all the nations to drink, unto whom the LORD had sent me: ¹⁸to wit, Jerusalem, and the cities of Judah, and the kings thereof, and the princes thereof, to make them a desolation, an astonishment, a hissing, and a curse (as it is this day): ¹⁹Pharaoh king of Egypt, and his servants, and his princes, and all his people; ²⁰and all the mingled people, and all the kings of the land of Uz, and all the kings of the land of the Philistines, and Ashkelon, and Azzah, and Ekron, and the remnant of Ashdod, ²¹Edom, and Moab, and the children of Ammon, ²²and all the kings of Tyrus, and all the kings of Zidon, and the kings of the isles which are beyond the sea, ²³Dedan, and Tema, and Buz, and all that are in the utmost corners, ²⁴and all the kings of Arabia, and all the kings of the mingled people that dwell in the desert, ²⁵and all the kings of Zimri, and all the kings of Elam, and all the kings of the Medes, ²⁶and all the kings of the north, far and near, one with another, and all the kingdoms of the world, which are upon the face of the earth: and the king of Sheshach shall drink after them.

²⁷'Therefore thou shalt say unto them, "Thus saith the LORD of hosts, the God of Israel, 'Drink ye and be drunken, and spew and fall, and rise no more, because of the sword which I will send among you'". ²⁸And it shall be, if they refuse to take the cup at thy hand to drink, then shalt thou say unto them, "Thus saith the LORD of hosts, 'Ye shall certainly drink. ²⁹For lo, I begin to bring evil on the city which is called by my

name, and should ye be utterly unpunished? Ye shall not be unpunished: for I will call for a sword upon all the inhabitants of the earth,' saith the Lord of hosts." ³⁰Therefore prophesy thou against them all these words, and say unto them,

"The Lord shall roar from on high,
and utter his voice from his holy habitation,
he shall mightily roar upon his habitation,
he shall give a shout, as they that tread the grapes,
against all the inhabitants of the earth.
³¹ A noise shall come even to the ends of the earth;
for the Lord hath a controversy with the nations:
he will plead with all flesh,
he will give them that are wicked to the sword," saith the Lord.'

³²Thus saith the Lord of hosts, 'Behold, evil shall go forth from nation to nation, and a great whirlwind shall be raised up from the coasts of the earth. ³³And the slain of the Lord shall be at that day from one end of the earth even unto the other end of the earth: they shall not be lamented, neither gathered, nor buried, they shall be dung upon the ground.'

³⁴ Howl, ye shepherds, and cry,
and wallow yourselves in the ashes, ye principal of the flock:
for the days of your slaughter and of your dispersions are
accomplished,
and ye shall fall like a pleasant vessel.
³⁵ And the shepherds shall have no way to flee,
nor the principal of the flock to escape.
³⁶ A voice of the cry of the shepherds,
and a howling of the principal of the flock shall be heard:
for the Lord hath spoiled their pasture.
³⁷ And the peaceable habitations are cut down
because of the fierce anger of the Lord.
³⁸ He hath forsaken his covert, as the lion:
for their land is desolate
because of the fierceness of the oppressor,
and because of his fierce anger.

26 In the beginning of the reign of Jehoiakim the son of Josiah king of Judah came this word from the Lord, saying, ²'Thus saith the Lord, "Stand in the court of the Lord's house, and speak unto all the cities of Judah, which come to worship in the Lord's house, all the words that I command thee to speak unto them; diminish not a word: ³if so be they will hearken, and turn every man from his evil way, that I may repent me of the evil which I purpose to do unto them because of the evil of their doings. ⁴And thou shalt say unto them, 'Thus saith the Lord, "If ye will not hearken to me, to walk in my law, which I have set before you, ⁵to hearken to the words of my servants the prophets, whom I sent unto you, both rising up early, and sending them (but ye have not hearkened): ⁶then will I make this house like Shiloh, and will make this city a curse to all the nations of the earth"'."'' ⁷So the priests and the prophets and all the people heard Jeremiah speaking these words in the house of the LORD.

⁸Now it came to pass, when Jeremiah had made an end of speaking all that the LORD had commanded him to speak unto all the people, that the priests and the prophets and all the people took him, saying, 'Thou shalt surely die. ⁹Why hast thou prophesied in the name of the LORD, saying, "This house shall be like Shiloh, and this city shall be desolate without an inhabitant"?' And all the people were gathered against Jeremiah in the house of the LORD.

¹⁰When the princes of Judah heard these things, then they came up from the king's house unto the house of the LORD, and sat down in the entry of the new gate of the LORD's house. ¹¹Then spoke the priests and the prophets unto the princes and to all the people, saying, 'This man is worthy to die, for he hath prophesied against this city, as ye have heard with your ears'.

¹²Then spoke Jeremiah unto all the princes and to all the people, saying, 'The LORD sent me to prophesy against this house and against this city all the words that ye have heard. ¹³Therefore now amend your ways and your doings, and obey the voice of the LORD your God, and the LORD will repent him of the evil that he hath pronounced against you. ¹⁴As for me, behold, I am in your hand: do with me as seemeth good and meet unto you. ¹⁵But know ye for certain, that if ye put me to death, ye shall surely bring innocent blood upon yourselves, and upon this city, and upon the inhabitants thereof: for of a truth the LORD hath sent me unto you to speak all these words in your ears.'

¹⁶Then said the princes and all the people unto the priests and to the prophets, 'This man is not worthy to die: for he hath spoken to us in the name of the LORD our God'. ¹⁷Then rose up certain of the elders of the land, and spoke to all the assembly of the people, saying, ¹⁸'Micah the Morasthite prophesied in the days of Hezekiah king of Judah, and spoke to all the people of Judah, saying, "Thus saith the LORD of hosts,

'"'Zion shall be ploughed like a field,
and Jerusalem shall become heaps,
and the mountain of the house,
the high places of a forest'".

¹⁹'Did Hezekiah king of Judah and all Judah put him at all to death? did he not fear the LORD, and besought the LORD, and the LORD repented him of the evil which he had pronounced against them? Thus might we procure great evil against our souls.'

²⁰And there was also a man that prophesied in the name of the LORD, Urijah the son of Shemaiah of Kirjath-jearim, who prophesied against this city and against this land according to all the words of Jeremiah.

²¹And when Jehoiakim the king, with all his mighty men, and all the princes, heard his words, the king sought to put him to death; but when Urijah heard it, he was afraid and fled, and went into Egypt. ²²And Jehoiakim the king sent men into Egypt, namely, Elnathan the son of Achbor, and certain men with him into Egypt. ²³And they fetched forth Urijah out of Egypt, and brought him unto Jehoiakim the king, who slew him with the sword, and cast his dead body into the graves of the common people.

²⁴Nevertheless the hand of Ahikam the son of Shaphan was with Jeremiah, that they should not give him into the hand of the people to put him to death.

27 In the beginning of the reign of Jehoiakim the son of Josiah king of Judah came this word unto Jeremiah from the LORD, saying, ²'Thus saith the LORD to me, "Make thee bonds and yokes, and put them upon thy neck, ³and send them to the king of Edom, and to the king of Moab, and to the king of the Ammonites, and to the king of Tyrus, and to the king of Zidon, by the hand of the messengers which come to Jerusalem unto Zedekiah king of Judah. ⁴And command them to say unto their masters, 'Thus saith the LORD of hosts, the God of Israel, "Thus shall ye say unto your masters: ⁵'I have made the earth, the man and the beast that are upon the ground, by my great power and by my outstretched arm, and have given it unto whom it seemed meet unto me. ⁶And now have I given all these lands into the hand of Nebuchadnezzar the king of Babylon, my servant; and the beasts of the field have I given him also to serve him. ⁷And all nations shall serve him and his son, and his son's son, until the very time of his land come: and then many nations and great kings shall serve themselves of him. ⁸And it shall come to pass, that the nation and kingdom which will not serve the same Nebuchadnezzar the king of Babylon, and that will not put their neck under the yoke of the king of Babylon, that nation will I punish,' saith the LORD, 'with the sword, and with the famine, and with the pestilence, until I have consumed them by his hand. ⁹Therefore hearken not ye to your prophets, nor to your diviners, nor to your dreamers, nor to your enchanters, nor to your sorcerers, which speak unto you, saying, "Ye shall not serve the king of Babylon": ¹⁰for they prophesy a lie unto you, to remove you far from your land, and that I should drive you out, and ye should perish. ¹¹But the nations that bring their neck under the yoke of the king of Babylon, and serve him, those will I let remain still in their own land,' saith the LORD, 'and they shall till it, and dwell therein.'"'"'

¹²I spoke also to Zedekiah king of Judah according to all these words, saying, 'Bring your necks under the yoke of the king of Babylon, and serve him and his people, and live. ¹³Why will ye die, thou and thy people, by the sword, by the famine, and by the pestilence, as the LORD hath spoken against the nation that will not serve the king of Babylon? ¹⁴Therefore hearken not unto the words of the prophets that speak unto you, saying, "Ye shall not serve the king of Babylon": for they prophesy a lie unto you. ¹⁵"For I have not sent them," saith the LORD, "yet they

prophesy a lie in my name, that I might drive you out, and that ye might perish, ye, and the prophets that prophesy unto you."'

¹⁶Also I spoke to the priests and to all this people, saying, 'Thus saith the LORD, "Hearken not to the words of your prophets that prophesy unto you, saying, 'Behold, the vessels of the LORD's house shall now shortly be brought again from Babylon': for they prophesy a lie unto you". ¹⁷Hearken not unto them: serve the king of Babylon, and live: wherefore should this city be laid waste? ¹⁸But if they be prophets, and if the word of the LORD be with them, let them now make intercession to the LORD of hosts, that the vessels which are left in the house of the LORD, and in the house of the king of Judah, and at Jerusalem, go not to Babylon.

¹⁹'For thus saith the LORD of hosts concerning the pillars, and concerning the sea, and concerning the bases, and concerning the residue of the vessels that remain in this city, ²⁰which Nebuchadnezzar king of Babylon took not, when he carried away captive Jeconiah the son of Jehoiakim king of Judah from Jerusalem to Babylon, and all the nobles of Judah and Jerusalem; ²¹yea, thus saith the LORD of hosts, the God of Israel, concerning the vessels that remain in the house of the LORD, and in the house of the king of Judah and of Jerusalem, ²²"They shall be carried to Babylon, and there shall they be until the day that I visit them," saith the LORD: "then will I bring them up, and restore them to this place".'

28 And it came to pass the same year, in the beginning of the reign of Zedekiah king of Judah, in the fourth year, and in the fifth month, that Hananiah the son of Azur the prophet, which was of Gibeon, spoke unto me in the house of the LORD, in the presence of the priests and of all the people, saying, ²"Thus speaketh the LORD of hosts, the God of Israel, saying, "I have broken the yoke of the king of Babylon. ³Within two full years will I bring again into this place all the vessels of the LORD's house, that Nebuchadnezzar king of Babylon took away from this place, and carried them to Babylon. ⁴And I will bring again to this place Jeconiah the son of Jehoiakim king of Judah, with all the captives of Judah, that went into Babylon," saith the LORD, "for I will break the yoke of the king of Babylon."'

⁵Then the prophet Jeremiah said unto the prophet Hananiah in the presence of the priests, and in the presence of all the people that stood in the house of the LORD, ⁶even the prophet Jeremiah said, 'Amen: the LORD do so, the LORD perform the words which thou hast prophesied, to bring again the vessels of the LORD's house, and all that is carried away captive from Babylon into this place. ⁷Nevertheless hear thou now this word that I speak in thy ears, and in the ears of all the people. ⁸The prophets that have been before me and before thee of old prophesied both against many countries, and against great kingdoms, of war, and of evil, and of pestilence. ⁹The prophet which prophesieth of peace, when the word of the prophet shall come to pass, then shall the prophet be known, that the LORD hath truly sent him.'

¹⁰Then Hananiah the prophet took the yoke from off the prophet

Jeremiah's neck, and broke it. ¹¹And Hananiah spoke in the presence of all the people, saying, 'Thus saith the LORD, "Even so will I break the yoke of Nebuchadnezzar king of Babylon from the neck of all nations within the space of two full years"'. And the prophet Jeremiah went his way.

¹²Then the word of the LORD came unto Jeremiah the prophet, after that Hananiah the prophet had broken the yoke from off the neck of the prophet Jeremiah, saying, ¹³'Go and tell Hananiah, saying, "Thus saith the LORD, 'Thou hast broken the yokes of wood, but thou shalt make for them yokes of iron'. ¹⁴For thus saith the LORD of hosts, the God of Israel, 'I have put a yoke of iron upon the neck of all these nations, that they may serve Nebuchadnezzar king of Babylon; and they shall serve him: and I have given him the beasts of the field also'."'

¹⁵Then said the prophet Jeremiah unto Hananiah the prophet, 'Hear now, Hananiah: the LORD hath not sent thee, but thou makest this people to trust in a lie. ¹⁶Therefore thus saith the LORD, "Behold, I will cast thee from off the face of the earth: this year thou shalt die, because thou hast taught rebellion against the LORD".' ¹⁷So Hananiah the prophet died the same year in the seventh month.

29 Now these are the words of the letter that Jeremiah the prophet sent from Jerusalem unto the residue of the elders which were carried away captives, and to the priests, and to the prophets, and to all the people whom Nebuchadnezzar had carried away captive from Jerusalem to Babylon ²(after that Jeconiah the king, and the queen, and the eunuchs, the princes of Judah and Jerusalem, and the carpenters and the smiths were departed from Jerusalem), ³by the hand of Elasah the son of Shaphan, and Gemariah the son of Hilkiah, whom Zedekiah king of Judah sent unto Babylon to Nebuchadnezzar king of Babylon saying, ⁴'Thus saith the LORD of hosts the God of Israel unto all that are carried away captives, whom I have caused to be carried away from Jerusalem unto Babylon: ⁵"Build ye houses and dwell in them, and plant gardens, and eat the fruit of them. ⁶Take ye wives, and beget sons and daughters, and take wives for your sons, and give your daughters to husbands, that they may bear sons and daughters, that ye may be increased there, and not diminished. ⁷And seek the peace of the city whither I have caused you to be carried away captives, and pray unto the LORD for it: for in the peace thereof shall ye have peace."

⁸'For thus saith the LORD of hosts, the God of Israel, "Let not your prophets and your diviners, that be in the midst of you, deceive you, neither hearken to your dreams which ye cause to be dreamed. ⁹For they prophesy falsely unto you in my name: I have not sent them," saith the LORD.

¹⁰'For thus saith the LORD, "That after seventy years be accomplished at Babylon I will visit you, and perform my good word towards you, in causing you to return to this place. ¹¹For I know the thoughts that I think towards you," saith the LORD, "thoughts of peace, and not of evil, to give you an expected end. ¹²Then shall ye call upon me, and ye shall go and pray unto me, and I will hearken unto you. ¹³And ye shall seek

me, and find me, when ye shall search for me with all your heart. ¹⁴And I will be found of you," saith the LORD, "and I will turn away your captivity, and I will gather you from all the nations, and from all the places whither I have driven you," saith the LORD, "and I will bring you again into the place whence I caused you to be carried away captive.

¹⁵Because ye have said, "The LORD hath raised us up prophets in Babylon": ¹⁶know that thus saith the LORD of the king that sitteth upon the throne of David, and of all the people that dwelleth in this city, and of your brethren that are not gone forth with you into captivity; ¹⁷thus saith the LORD of hosts, "Behold, I will send upon them the sword, the famine, and the pestilence, and will make them like vile figs, that cannot be eaten, they are so evil. ¹⁸And I will persecute them with the sword, with the famine, and with the pestilence, and will deliver them to be removed to all the kingdoms of the earth, to be a curse, and an astonishment, and a hissing, and a reproach among all the nations whither I have driven them: ¹⁹because they have not hearkened to my words," saith the LORD, "which I sent unto them by my servants the prophets, rising up early and sending them, but ye would not hear," saith the LORD.

²⁰Hear ye therefore the word of the LORD, all ye of the captivity, whom I have sent from Jerusalem to Babylon. ²¹Thus saith the LORD of hosts, the God of Israel, of Ahab the son of Kolaiah, and of Zedekiah the son of Maaseiah, which prophesy a lie unto you in my name, "Behold, I will deliver them into the hand of Nebuchadrezzar king of Babylon, and he shall slay them before your eyes. ²²And of them shall be taken up a curse by all the captivity of Judah which are in Babylon, saying, 'The LORD make thee like Zedekiah and like Ahab, whom the king of Babylon roasted in the fire'; ²³because they have committed villainy in Israel, and have committed adultery with their neighbours' wives, and have spoken lying words in my name, which I have not commanded them; even I know, and am a witness," saith the LORD.

²⁴Thus shalt thou also speak to Shemaiah the Nehelamite, saying, ²⁵Thus speaketh the LORD of hosts, the God of Israel, saying, 'Because thou hast sent letters in thy name unto all the people that are at Jerusalem, and to Zephaniah the son of Maaseiah the priest, and to all the priests, saying, ²⁶"The LORD hath made thee priest in the stead of Jehoiada the priest, that ye should be officers in the house of the LORD, for every man that is mad, and maketh himself a prophet, that thou shouldst put him in prison, and in the stocks: ²⁷now therefore why hast thou not reproved Jeremiah of Anathoth, which maketh himself a prophet to you? ²⁸For therefore he sent unto us in Babylon, saying, 'This captivity is long: build ye houses, and dwell in them; and plant gardens, and eat the fruit of them'."'" ²⁹And Zephaniah the priest read this letter in the ears of Jeremiah the prophet.

³⁰Then came the word of the LORD unto Jeremiah, saying, ³¹'Send to all them of the captivity, saying, "Thus saith the LORD concerning Shemaiah the Nehelamite, 'Because that Shemaiah hath prophesied unto you, and I sent him not, and he caused you to trust in a lie':

³²therefore thus saith the LORD, 'Behold, I will punish Shemaiah the Nehelamite, and his seed: he shall not have a man to dwell among this people, neither shall he behold the good that I will do for my people,' saith the LORD, 'because he hath taught rebellion against the LORD'.'"

30

The word that came to Jeremiah from the LORD, saying, ²'Thus speaketh the LORD God of Israel, saying, "Write thee all the words that I have spoken unto thee in a book. ³For lo, the days come," saith the LORD, "that I will bring again the captivity of my people Israel and Judah," saith the LORD, "and I will cause them to return to the land that I gave to their fathers, and they shall possess it."'

⁴And these are the words that the LORD spoke concerning Israel and concerning Judah. ⁵For thus saith the LORD, 'We have heard a voice of trembling, of fear, and not of peace. ⁶Ask ye now, and see whether a man doth travail with child? wherefore do I see every man with his hands on his loins, as a woman in travail, and all faces are turned into paleness? ⁷Alas, for that day is great, so that none is like it: it is even the time of Jacob's trouble, but he shall be saved out of it. ⁸For it shall come to pass in that day,' saith the LORD of hosts, 'that I will break his yoke from off thy neck, and will burst thy bonds, and strangers shall no more serve themselves of him: ⁹but they shall serve the LORD their God, and David their king, whom I will raise up unto them.

¹⁰ 'Therefore fear thou not, O my servant Jacob,'
  saith the LORD, 'neither be dismayed, O Israel:
  for lo, I will save thee from afar,
  and thy seed from the land of their captivity,
  and Jacob shall return, and shall be in rest, and be quiet,
  and none shall make him afraid.
¹¹ For I am with thee,' saith the LORD, 'to save thee:
  though I make a full end of all nations whither I have scattered
    thee,
  yet will I not make a full end of thee:
  but I will correct thee in measure,
  and will not leave thee altogether unpunished.'
¹² For thus saith the LORD,
  'Thy bruise is incurable,
  and thy wound is grievous.
¹³ There is none to plead thy cause,
  that thou mayest be bound up:
  thou hast no healing medicines.
¹⁴ All thy lovers have forgotten thee:
  they seek thee not,
  for I have wounded thee
  with the wound of an enemy,
  with the chastisement of a cruel one,
  for the multitude of thy iniquity:
  because thy sins were increased.
¹⁵ Why criest thou for thy affliction?

thy sorrow is incurable for the multitude of thy iniquity:
because thy sins were increased,
I have done these things unto thee.

16 Therefore all they that devour thee shall be devoured,
and all thy adversaries, every one of them, shall go into captivity:
and they that spoil thee shall be a spoil,
and all that prey upon thee will I give for a prey.

17 For I will restore health unto thee,
and I will heal thee of thy wounds,' saith the LORD,
'because they called thee an outcast, saying,
"This is Zion, whom no man seeketh after".'

18 Thus saith the LORD,
'Behold, I will bring again the captivity of Jacob's tents,
and have mercy on his dwelling-places:
and the city shall be built upon her own heap,
and the palace shall remain after the manner thereof.

19 And out of them shall proceed thanksgiving
and the voice of them that make merry:
and I will multiply them,
and they shall not be few:
I will also glorify them,
and they shall not be small.

20 Their children also shall be as aforetime,
and their congregation shall be established before me,
and I will punish all that oppress them.

21 And their nobles shall be of themselves,
and their governor shall proceed from the midst of them,
and I will cause him to draw near,
and he shall approach unto me:
for who is this that engaged his heart
to approach unto me?' saith the LORD.

22 'And ye shall be my people,
and I will be your God.'

23 Behold, the whirlwind of the LORD goeth forth with fury,
a continuing whirlwind:
it shall fall with pain upon the head of the wicked.

24 The fierce anger of the LORD shall not return, until he have done it,
and until he have performed the intents of his heart:
in the latter days ye shall consider it.

31 'At the same time,' saith the LORD,
'will I be the God of all the families of Israel,
and they shall be my people.'

2 Thus saith the LORD,
'The people which were left of the sword

found grace in the wilderness,
even Israel, when I went to cause him to rest'.
³ The LORD hath appeared of old unto me, saying,
'Yea, I have loved thee with an everlasting love:
therefore with loving-kindness have I drawn thee.
⁴ Again I will build thee, and thou shalt be built,
O virgin of Israel:
thou shalt again be adorned with thy tabrets,
and shalt go forth in the dances of them that make merry.
⁵ Thou shalt yet plant vines upon the mountains of Samaria:
the planters shall plant, and shall eat them as common things.
⁶ For there shall be a day, that the watchmen upon the mount
Ephraim shall cry,
"Arise ye, and let us go up to Zion unto the LORD our God".'
⁷ For thus saith the LORD,
'Sing with gladness for Jacob,
and shout among the chief of the nations:
publish ye, praise ye, and say,
"O LORD, save thy people, the remnant of Israel".
⁸ Behold, I will bring them from the north country,
and gather them from the coasts of the earth,
and with them the blind and the lame,
the woman with child and her that travaileth with child
together:
a great company shall return thither.
⁹ They shall come with weeping,
and with supplications will I lead them:
I will cause them to walk by the rivers of waters,
in a straight way wherein they shall not stumble:
for I am a father to Israel,
and Ephraim is my firstborn.

¹⁰ 'Hear the word of the LORD, O ye nations,
and declare it in the isles afar off, and say,
"He that scattered Israel will gather him, and keep him,
as a shepherd doth his flock".
¹¹ For the LORD hath redeemed Jacob,
and ransomed him from the hand of him that was stronger
than he.
¹² Therefore they shall come and sing in the height of Zion,
and shall flow together to the goodness of the LORD,
for wheat, and for wine, and for oil,
and for the young of the flock and of the herd:
and their soul shall be as a watered garden,
and they shall not sorrow any more at all.
¹³ Then shall the virgin rejoice in the dance,
both young men and old together:
for I will turn their mourning into joy,

and will comfort them,
and make them rejoice from their sorrow.

¹⁴ And I will satiate the soul of the priests with fatness,
and my people shall be satisfied with goodness,' saith the LORD.

¹⁵ Thus saith the LORD,
'A voice was heard in Ramah,
lamentation, and bitter weeping:
Rachel weeping for her children
refused to be comforted for her children,
because they were not'.

¹⁶ Thus saith the LORD, 'Refrain thy voice from weeping,
and thy eyes from tears:
for thy work shall be rewarded,' saith the LORD,
'and they shall come again from the land of the enemy.

¹⁷ And there is hope in thy end,' saith the LORD,
'that thy children shall come again to their own border.

¹⁸ 'I have surely heard Ephraim bemoaning himself thus,
"Thou hast chastised me, and I was chastised,
as a bullock unaccustomed to the yoke:
turn thou me, and I shall be turned;
thou art the LORD my God.

¹⁹ Surely after that I was turned, I repented;
and after that I was instructed, I smote upon my thigh:
I was ashamed, yea even confounded,
because I did bear the reproach of my youth."

²⁰ Is Ephraim my dear son?
is he a pleasant child?
for since I spoke against him,
I do earnestly remember him still:
therefore my bowels are troubled for him;
I will surely have mercy upon him,' saith the LORD.

²¹ Set thee up way-marks, make thee high heaps:
set thy heart toward the highway,
even the way which thou wentest:
turn again, O virgin of Israel,
turn again to these thy cities.

²² How long wilt thou go about,
O thou backsliding daughter?
for the LORD hath created a new thing in the earth:
a woman shall compass a man.

²³Thus saith the LORD of hosts, the God of Israel, 'As yet they shall use this speech in the land of Judah and in the cities thereof, when I shall bring again their captivity, "The LORD bless thee, O habitation of justice, and mountain of holiness". ²⁴And there shall dwell in Judah itself,

and in all the cities thereof together, husbandmen, and they that go forth with flocks. ²⁵For I have satiated the weary soul, and I have replenished every sorrowful soul.' ²⁶Upon this I awoke, and beheld, and my sleep was sweet unto me.

²⁷'Behold, the days come,' saith the LORD, 'that I will sow the house of Israel and the house of Judah with the seed of man, and with the seed of beast. ²⁸And it shall come to pass, that like as I have watched over them, to pluck up and to break down, and to throw down, and to destroy, and to afflict: so will I watch over them, to build, and to plant,' saith the LORD. ²⁹'In those days they shall say no more, "The fathers have eaten a sour grape, and the children's teeth are set on edge". ³⁰But every one shall die for his own iniquity: every man that eateth the sour grape, his teeth shall be set on edge.

³¹'Behold, the days come,' saith the LORD, 'that I will make a new covenant with the house of Israel, and with the house of Judah: ³²not according to the covenant that I made with their fathers in the day that I took them by the hand to bring them out of the land of Egypt, which my covenant they broke, although I was a husband unto them,' saith the LORD: ³³'but this shall be the covenant that I will make with the house of Israel; after those days,' saith the LORD, 'I will put my law in their inward parts, and write it in their hearts, and will be their God, and they shall be my people. ³⁴And they shall teach no more every man his neighbour, and every man his brother, saying, "Know the LORD": for they shall all know me, from the least of them unto the greatest of them,' saith the LORD: 'for I will forgive their iniquity, and I will remember their sin no more.'

³⁵Thus saith the LORD, which giveth the sun for a light by day, and the ordinances of the moon and of the stars for a light by night, which divideth the sea when the waves thereof roar; the LORD of hosts is his name: ³⁶'If those ordinances depart from before me,' saith the LORD, 'then the seed of Israel also shall cease from being a nation before me for ever'. ³⁷Thus saith the LORD, 'If heaven above can be measured, and the foundations of the earth searched out beneath, I will also cast off all the seed of Israel for all that they have done,' saith the LORD.

³⁸'Behold, the days come,' saith the LORD, 'that the city shall be built to the LORD from the tower of Hananeel unto the gate of the corner. ³⁹And the measuring-line shall yet go forth over against it upon the hill Gareb, and shall compass about to Goath. ⁴⁰And the whole valley of the dead bodies, and of the ashes, and all the fields unto the brook of Kidron, unto the corner of the horse gate towards the east, shall be holy unto the LORD; it shall not be plucked up, nor thrown down any more for ever.'

32 The word that came to Jeremiah from the LORD in the tenth year of Zedekiah king of Judah, which was the eighteenth year of Nebuchadrezzar. ²For then the king of Babylon's army besieged Jerusalem: and Jeremiah the prophet was shut up in the court of the prison, which was in the king of Judah's house. ³For Zedekiah king of Judah had shut him up, saying, 'Wherefore dost thou prophesy, and say, "Thus saith the LORD, 'Behold, I will give this city into the hand of the king of Babylon, and he shall take it; ⁴and Zedekiah king of Judah shall not escape out of the hand of the Chaldeans, but shall surely be delivered into the hand of the king of Babylon, and shall speak with him mouth to mouth, and his eyes shall behold his eyes; ⁵and he shall lead Zedekiah to Babylon, and there shall he be until I visit him,' saith the LORD: 'though ye fight with the Chaldeans, ye shall not prosper'"?'

⁶And Jeremiah said, 'The word of the LORD came unto me, saying, ⁷"Behold, Hanameel the son of Shallum thy uncle shall come unto thee, saying, 'Buy thee my field that is in Anathoth: for the right of redemption is thine to buy it'"'. ⁸So Hanameel my uncle's son came to me in the court of the prison according to the word of the LORD, and said unto me, 'Buy my field, I pray thee, that is in Anathoth, which is in the country of Benjamin: for the right of inheritance is thine, and the redemption is thine; buy it for thyself'. Then I knew that this was the word of the LORD. ⁹And I bought the field of Hanameel my uncle's son, that was in Anathoth, and weighed him the money, even seventeen shekels of silver. ¹⁰And I subscribed the evidence, and sealed it, and took witnesses, and weighed him the money in the balances. ¹¹So I took the evidence of the purchase, both that which was sealed according to the law and custom, and that which was open. ¹²And I gave the evidence of the purchase unto Baruch the son of Neriah, the son of Maaseiah, in the sight of Hanameel my uncle's son, and in the presence of the witnesses that subscribed the book of the purchase, before all the Jews that sat in the court of the prison.

¹³And I charged Baruch before them, saying, ¹⁴"Thus saith the LORD of hosts, the God of Israel, "Take these evidences, this evidence of the purchase, both which is sealed, and this evidence which is open, and put them in an earthen vessel, that they may continue many days". ¹⁵For thus saith the LORD of hosts, the God of Israel, "Houses and fields and vineyards shall be possessed again in this land".'

¹⁶Now when I had delivered the evidence of the purchase unto Baruch the son of Neriah, I prayed unto the LORD, saying, ¹⁷'Ah Lord GOD, behold, thou hast made the heaven and the earth by thy great power and stretched out arm, and there is nothing too hard for thee. ¹⁸Thou showest loving-kindness unto thousands, and recompensest the iniquity of the fathers into the bosom of their children after them: the great, the mighty God, the LORD of hosts, is his name, ¹⁹great in counsel, and mighty in work (for thy eyes are open upon all the ways of the sons of men, to give every one according to his ways, and according to the fruit of his doings), ²⁰which hast set signs and wonders in the land of Egypt, even unto this day, and in Israel, and amongst other men, and hast made thee a name, as at this day, ²¹and hast brought forth thy people Israel out of the land of Egypt with signs, and with wonders, and with a strong hand, and with a stretched out arm, and with great terror, ²²and hast given them this land which thou didst swear to their fathers to give them, a land flowing with milk and honey. ²³And they came in, and possessed it; but they obeyed not thy voice, neither

walked in thy law; they have done nothing of all that thou command-edst them to do: therefore thou hast caused all this evil to come upon them. ²⁴Behold the mounts, they are come unto the city to take it; and the city is given into the hand of the Chaldeans that fight against it, because of the sword, and of the famine, and of the pestilence: and what thou hast spoken is come to pass, and behold, thou seest it. ²⁵And thou hast said unto me, O Lord GOD, "Buy thee the field for money, and take witnesses: for the city is given into the hand of the Chaldeans".'

²⁶Then came the word of the LORD unto Jeremiah, saying, ²⁷'Behold, I am the LORD, the God of all flesh: is there anything too hard for me?' ²⁸Therefore thus saith the LORD, 'Behold, I will give this city into the hand of the Chaldeans, and into the hand of Nebuchadrezzar king of Babylon, and he shall take it. ²⁹And the Chaldeans that fight against this city, shall come and set fire on this city, and burn it with the houses upon whose roofs they have offered incense unto Baal, and poured out drink offerings unto other gods, to provoke me to anger. ³⁰For the children of Israel and the children of Judah have only done evil before me from their youth: for the children of Israel have only pro-voked me to anger with the work of their hands,' saith the LORD. ³¹'For this city hath been to me as a provocation of my anger and of my fury from the day that they built it even unto this day; that I should remove it from before my face, ³²because of all the evil of the children of Israel and of the children of Judah, which they have done to provoke me to anger, they, their kings, their princes, their priests, and their prophets, and the men of Judah, and the inhabitants of Jerusalem. ³³And they have turned unto me the back, and not the face, though I taught them, rising up early and teaching them, yet they have not hearkened to receive instruction, ³⁴but they set their abominations in the house, which is called by my name, to defile it. ³⁵And they built the high places of Baal, which are in the valley of the son of Hinnom, to cause their sons and their daughters to pass through the fire unto Molech; which I commanded them not, neither came it into my mind, that they should do this abomination, to cause Judah to sin.'

³⁶And now therefore thus saith the LORD, the God of Israel, concern-ing this city, whereof ye say, 'It shall be delivered into the hand of the king of Babylon by the sword, and by the famine, and by the pestilence': ³⁷'Behold, I will gather them out of all countries, whither I have driven them in my anger, and in my fury, and in great wrath, and I will bring them again unto this place, and I will cause them to dwell safely. ³⁸And they shall be my people, and I will be their God. ³⁹And I will give them one heart, and one way, that they may fear me for ever, for the good of them, and of their children after them. ⁴⁰And I will make an everlasting covenant with them, that I will not turn away from them, to do them good, but I will put my fear in their hearts, that they shall not depart from me. ⁴¹Yea, I will rejoice over them to do them good, and I will plant them in this land assuredly with my whole heart and with my whole soul.' ⁴²For thus saith the LORD, 'Like as I have brought all this great evil upon this people, so will I bring upon them all the good that

I have promised them. ⁴³And fields shall be bought in this land, whereof ye say, "It is desolate without man or beast, it is given into the hand of the Chaldeans". ⁴⁴Men shall buy fields for money, and subscribe evidences, and seal them, and take witnesses in the land of Benjamin, and in the places about Jerusalem, and in the cities of Judah, and in the cities of the mountains, and in the cities of the valley, and in the cities of the south: for I will cause their captivity to return,' saith the LORD.

33 Moreover the word of the LORD came unto Jeremiah the second time, while he was yet shut up in the court of the prison, saying, ²"Thus saith the LORD the maker thereof, the LORD that formed it, to establish it; the LORD is his name; ³"Call unto me, and I will answer thee, and show thee great and mighty things, which thou knowest not". ⁴For thus saith the LORD the God of Israel concerning the houses of this city, and concerning the houses of the kings of Judah, which are thrown down by the mounts, and by the sword; ⁵"They come to fight with the Chaldeans, but it is to fill them with the dead bodies of men, whom I have slain in my anger and in my fury, and for all whose wickedness I have hid my face from this city. ⁶Behold, I will bring it health and cure, and I will cure them, and will reveal unto them the abundance of peace and truth. ⁷And I will cause the captivity of Judah and the captivity of Israel to return, and will build them, as at the first. ⁸And I will cleanse them from all their iniquity, whereby they have sinned against me; and I will pardon all their iniquities, whereby they have sinned, and whereby they have transgressed against me.

⁹"And it shall be to me a name of joy, a praise and an honour before all the nations of the earth, which shall hear all the good that I do unto them: and they shall fear and tremble for all the goodness and for all the prosperity that I procure unto it." ¹⁰Thus saith the LORD, "Again there shall be heard in this place (which ye say shall be desolate without man and without beast, even in the cities of Judah, and in the streets of Jerusalem that are desolate, without man, and without inhabitant, and without beast) ¹¹the voice of joy, and the voice of gladness, the voice of the bridegroom, and the voice of the bride, the voice of them that shall say, 'Praise the LORD of hosts: for the LORD is good, for his mercy endureth for ever': and of them that shall bring the sacrifice of praise into the house of the LORD; for I will cause to return the captivity of the land, as at the first," saith the LORD. ¹²Thus saith the LORD of hosts, "Again in this place, which is desolate without man and without beast, and in all the cities thereof, shall be a habitation of shepherds causing their flocks to lie down. ¹³In the cities of the mountains, in the cities of the vale, and in the cities of the south, and in the land of Benjamin, and in the places about Jerusalem, and in the cities of Judah, shall the flocks pass again under the hands of him that telleth them," saith the LORD. ¹⁴"Behold, the days come," saith the LORD, "that I will perform that good thing which I have promised unto the house of Israel and to the house of Judah.

¹⁵"In those days, and at that time, will I cause the branch of right-

eousness to grow up unto David, and he shall execute judgement and righteousness in the land. [16]In those days shall Judah be saved, and Jerusalem shall dwell safely: and this is the name wherewith she shall be called, 'The LORD our righteousness'."

[17]'For thus saith the LORD, "David shall never want a man to sit upon the throne of the house of Israel. [18]Neither shall the priests the Levites want a man before me to offer burnt offerings, and to kindle meat offerings, and to do sacrifice continually."'

[19]And the word of the LORD came unto Jeremiah, saying, [20]'Thus saith the LORD, "If you can break my covenant of the day, and my covenant of the night, and that there should not be day and night in their season: [21]then may also my covenant be broken with David my servant, that he should not have a son to reign upon his throne; and with the Levites the priests, my ministers. [22]As the host of heaven cannot be numbered, neither the sand of the sea measured: so will I multiply the seed of David my servant, and the Levites that minister unto me."'

[23]Moreover the word of the LORD came to Jeremiah, saying, [24]'Considerest thou not what this people have spoken, saying, "The two families which the LORD hath chosen, he hath even cast them off"? thus they have despised my people, that they should be no more a nation before them'. [25]Thus saith the LORD, 'If my covenant be not with day and night, and if I have not appointed the ordinances of heaven and earth: [26]then will I cast away the seed of Jacob, and David my servant, so that I will not take any of his seed to be rulers over the seed of Abraham, Isaac, and Jacob: for I will cause their captivity to return, and have mercy on them.'

34

The word which came unto Jeremiah from the LORD, when Nebuchadnezzar king of Babylon, and all his army, and all the kingdoms of the earth of his dominion, and all the people fought against Jerusalem, and against all the cities thereof, saying, [2]'Thus saith the LORD, the God of Israel, "Go and speak to Zedekiah king of Judah, and tell him, 'Thus saith the LORD, "Behold, I will give this city into the hand of the king of Babylon, and he shall burn it with fire. [3]And thou shalt not escape out of his hand, but shalt surely be taken, and delivered into his hand, and thy eyes shall behold the eyes of the king of Babylon, and he shall speak with thee mouth to mouth, and thou shalt go to Babylon."'" [4]Yet hear the word of the LORD, O Zedekiah king of Judah: thus saith the LORD of thee, "Thou shalt not die by the sword: [5]but thou shalt die in peace: and with the burnings of thy fathers the former kings which were before thee, so shall they burn odours for thee, and they will lament thee, saying, 'Ah lord'; for I have pronounced the word," saith the LORD.' [6]Then Jeremiah the prophet spoke all these words unto Zedekiah king of Judah in Jerusalem, [7]when the king of Babylon's army fought against Jerusalem, and against all the cities of Judah that were left, against Lachish, and against Azekah: for these defenced cities remained of the cities of Judah.

[8]This is the word that came unto Jeremiah from the LORD, after that

the king Zedekiah had made a covenant with all the people which were at Jerusalem, to proclaim liberty unto them, ⁹that every man should let his manservant, and every man his maidservant, being a Hebrew or a Hebrewess, go free, that none should serve himself of them, to wit, of a Jew his brother. ¹⁰Now when all the princes, and all the people, which had entered into the covenant, heard that every one should let his manservant, and every one his maidservant go free, that none should serve themselves of them any more, then they obeyed, and let them go. ¹¹But afterwards they turned, and caused the servants and the hand-maids, whom they had let go free, to return, and brought them into subjection for servants and for handmaids.

¹²Therefore the word of the LORD came to Jeremiah from the LORD, say-ing, ¹³"Thus saith the LORD, the God of Israel, "I made a covenant with your fathers in the day that I brought them forth out of the land of Egypt, out of the house of bondmen, saying, ¹⁴'At the end of seven years let ye go every man his brother a Hebrew which hath been sold unto thee: and when he hath served thee six years, thou shalt let him go free from thee': but your fathers hearkened not unto me, neither inclined their ear. ¹⁵And ye were now turned, and had done right in my sight, in proclaiming liberty every man to his neighbour; and ye had made a covenant before me in the house which is called by my name. ¹⁶But ye turned and polluted my name, and caused every man his servant, and every man his handmaid, whom ye had set at liberty at their pleasure, to return, and brought them into subjection, to be unto you for ser-vants and for handmaids." ¹⁷Therefore thus saith the LORD, "Ye have not hearkened unto me, in proclaiming liberty every one to his brother, and every man to his neighbour: behold, I proclaim a liberty for you," saith the LORD, "to the sword, to the pestilence, and to the famine, and I will make you to be removed into all the kingdoms of the earth. ¹⁸And I will give the men that have transgressed my covenant, which have not performed the words of the covenant which they had made before me, when they cut the calf in twain, and passed between the parts thereof, ¹⁹the princes of Judah, and the princes of Jerusalem, the eunuchs, and the priests, and all the people of the land, which passed between the parts of the calf: ²⁰I will even give them into the hand of their enemies, and into the hand of them that seek their life: and their dead bodies shall be for meat unto the fowls of the heaven, and to the beasts of the earth. ²¹And Zedekiah king of Judah and his princes will I give into the hand of their enemies, and into the hand of them that seek their life, and into the hand of the king of Babylon's army, which are gone up from you. ²²Behold, I will command," saith the LORD, "and cause them to return to this city; and they shall fight against it, and take it, and burn it with fire: and I will make the cities of Judah a desolation with-out an inhabitant."'

35 The word which came unto Jeremiah from the LORD in the days of Jehoiakim the son of Josiah king of Judah, saying, ²'Go unto the house of the Rechabites, and speak unto them, and bring them into the house of the LORD, into one of the chambers, and give them wine to drink'. ³Then I took Jaazaniah the son of Jeremiah, the son of Habaziniah, and his brethren, and all his sons, and the whole house of the Rechabites. ⁴And I brought them into the house of the LORD, into the chamber of the sons of Hanan, the son of Igdaliah, a man of God, which was by the chamber of the princes, which was above the chamber of Maaseiah the son of Shallum, the keeper of the door. ⁵And I set before the sons of the house of the Rechabites pots full of wine, and cups, and I said unto them, 'Drink ye wine'. ⁶But they said, 'We will drink no wine: for Jonadab the son of Rechab our father commanded us, saying, "Ye shall drink no wine, neither ye, nor your sons for ever: ⁷neither shall ye build house, nor sow seed, nor plant vineyard, nor have any: but all your days ye shall dwell in tents, that ye may live many days in the land where ye be strangers". ⁸Thus have we obeyed the voice of Jonadab the son of Rechab our father in all that he hath charged us, to drink no wine all our days, we, our wives, our sons, nor our daughters; ⁹nor to build houses for us to dwell in: neither have we vineyard, nor field, nor seed: ¹⁰but we have dwelt in tents, and have obeyed, and done according to all that Jonadab our father commanded us. ¹¹But it came to pass when Nebuchadrezzar king of Babylon came up into the land, that we said, "Come, and let us go to Jerusalem for fear of the army of the Chaldeans, and for fear of the army of the Syrians": so we dwell at Jerusalem.'

¹²Then came the word of the LORD unto Jeremiah, saying, ¹³'Thus saith the LORD of hosts, the God of Israel, "Go and tell the men of Judah and inhabitants of Jerusalem, 'Will ye not receive instruction to hearken to my words?' saith the LORD. ¹⁴The words of Jonadab the son of Rechab, that he commanded his sons not to drink wine, are performed; for unto this day they drink none, but obey their father's commandment: notwithstanding I have spoken unto you, rising early and speaking, but ye hearkened not unto me. ¹⁵I have sent also unto you all my servants the prophets, rising up early and sending them, saying, 'Return ye now every man from his evil way, and amend your doings, and go not after other gods to serve them, and ye shall dwell in the land which I have given to you and to your fathers': but ye have not inclined your ear, nor hearkened unto me. ¹⁶Because the sons of Jonadab the son of Rechab have performed the commandment of their father, which he commanded them; but this people hath not hearkened unto me: ¹⁷therefore thus saith the LORD God of hosts, the God of Israel, 'Behold, I will bring upon Judah and upon all the inhabitants of Jerusalem all the evil that I have pronounced against them: because I have spoken unto them, but they have not heard, and I have called unto them, but they have not answered'."'

¹⁸And Jeremiah said unto the house of the Rechabites, 'Thus saith the LORD of hosts, the God of Israel, "Because ye have obeyed the commandment of Jonadab your father, and kept all his precepts, and done according unto all that he hath commanded you": ¹⁹therefore thus saith the LORD of hosts, the God of Israel, "Jonadab the son of Rechab shall not want a man to stand before me for ever"'.

36 And it came to pass in the fourth year of Jehoiakim the son of Josiah king of Judah, that this word came unto Jeremiah from the LORD, saying, ²'Take thee a roll of a book, and write therein all the words that I have spoken unto thee against Israel, and against Judah, and against all the nations, from the day I spoke unto thee, from the days of Josiah, even unto this day. ³It may be that the house of Judah will hear all the evil which I purpose to do unto them; that they may return every man from his evil way, that I may forgive their iniquity and their sin.'

⁴Then Jeremiah called Baruch the son of Neriah, and Baruch wrote from the mouth of Jeremiah all the words of the LORD, which he had spoken unto him, upon a roll of a book. ⁵And Jeremiah commanded Baruch, saying, 'I am shut up, I cannot go into the house of the LORD. ⁶Therefore go thou and read in the roll, which thou hast written from my mouth, the words of the LORD in the ears of the people in the LORD's house upon the fasting day: and also thou shalt read them in the ears of all Judah that come out of their cities. ⁷It may be they will present their supplication before the LORD, and will return every one from his evil way: for great is the anger and the fury that the LORD hath pronounced against this people.' ⁸And Baruch the son of Neriah did according to all that Jeremiah the prophet commanded him, reading in the book the words of the LORD in the LORD's house.

⁹And it came to pass in the fifth year of Jehoiakim the son of Josiah king of Judah, in the ninth month, that they proclaimed a fast before the LORD to all the people in Jerusalem, and to all the people that came from the cities of Judah unto Jerusalem. ¹⁰Then read Baruch in the book the words of Jeremiah in the house of the LORD, in the chamber of Gemariah the son of Shaphan the scribe, in the higher court at the entry of the new gate of the LORD's house, in the ears of all the people.

¹¹When Michaiah the son of Gemariah, the son of Shaphan, had heard out of the book all the words of the LORD, ¹²then he went down into the king's house, into the scribe's chamber, and lo, all the princes sat there, even Elishama the scribe, and Delaiah the son of Shemaiah, and Elnathan the son of Achbor, and Gemariah the son of Shaphan, and Zedekiah the son of Hananiah, and all the princes. ¹³Then Michaiah declared unto them all the words that he had heard when Baruch read the book in the ears of the people. ¹⁴Therefore all the princes sent Jehudi the son of Nethaniah, the son of Shelemiah, the son of Cushi, unto Baruch, saying, 'Take in thy hand the roll wherein thou hast read in the ears of the people, and come'. So Baruch the son of Neriah took the roll in his hand, and came unto them. ¹⁵And they said unto him, 'Sit down now, and read it in our ears'. So Baruch read it in their ears. ¹⁶Now it came to pass when they had heard all the words, they were afraid both one and other, and said unto Baruch, 'We will surely tell the king of all these words'. ¹⁷And they asked Baruch, saying, 'Tell us now, how didst thou write all these words at his mouth?' ¹⁸Then Baruch answered them, 'He pronounced all these words unto me with his mouth, and I wrote them with ink in the book'. ¹⁹Then said the

princes unto Baruch, 'Go, hide thee, thou and Jeremiah, and let no man know where ye be'.

²⁰And they went in to the king into the court, but they laid up the roll in the chamber of Elishama the scribe, and told all the words in the ears of the king. ²¹So the king sent Jehudi to fetch the roll: and he took it out of Elishama the scribe's chamber. And Jehudi read it in the ears of the king, and in the ears of all the princes which stood beside the king. ²²Now the king sat in the winter-house in the ninth month: and there was a fire on the hearth burning before him. ²³And it came to pass that when Jehudi had read three or four leaves, he cut it with the penknife, and cast it into the fire that was on the hearth, until all the roll was consumed in the fire that was on the hearth. ²⁴Yet they were not afraid, nor rent their garments, neither the king, nor any of his servants that heard all these words. ²⁵Nevertheless Elnathan and Delaiah and Gemariah had made intercession to the king that he would not burn the roll: but he would not hear them. ²⁶But the king commanded Jerahmeel the son of Hammelech, and Seraiah the son of Azriel, and Shelemiah the son of Abdeel, to take Baruch the scribe and Jeremiah the prophet: but the LORD hid them.

²⁷Then the word of the LORD came to Jeremiah, after that the king had burnt the roll and the words which Baruch wrote at the mouth of Jeremiah, saying, ²⁸'Take thee again another roll, and write in it all the former words that were in the first roll, which Jehoiakim the king of Judah hath burnt. ²⁹And thou shalt say to Jehoiakim king of Judah, "Thus saith the LORD, 'Thou hast burnt this roll, saying, "Why hast thou written therein, saying, "The king of Babylon shall certainly come and destroy this land, and shall cause to cease from thence man and beast"?"' ³⁰Therefore thus saith the LORD of Jehoiakim king of Judah, 'He shall have none to sit upon the throne of David, and his dead body shall be cast out in the day to the heat, and in the night to the frost. ³¹And I will punish him and his seed and his servants for their iniquity; and I will bring upon them, and upon the inhabitants of Jerusalem, and upon the men of Judah all the evil that I have pronounced against them: but they hearkened not.'"'

³²Then took Jeremiah another roll, and gave it to Baruch the scribe, the son of Neriah, who wrote therein from the mouth of Jeremiah all the words of the book which Jehoiakim king of Judah had burnt in the fire: and there were added besides unto them many like words.

37 And king Zedekiah the son of Josiah reigned instead of Coniah the son of Jehoiakim, whom Nebuchadrezzar king of Babylon made king in the land of Judah. ²But neither he, nor his servants, nor the people of the land, did hearken unto the words of the LORD, which he spoke by the prophet Jeremiah. ³And Zedekiah the king sent Jehucal the son of Shelemiah and Zephaniah the son of Maaseiah the priest to the prophet Jeremiah, saying, 'Pray now unto the LORD our God for us'. ⁴Now Jeremiah came in and went out among the people: for they had not put him into prison. ⁵Then Pharaoh's army was come forth out of

Egypt: and when the Chaldeans that besieged Jerusalem heard tidings of them, they departed from Jerusalem. ⁶Then came the word of the LORD unto the prophet Jeremiah, saying, ⁷'Thus saith the LORD, the God of Israel, "Thus shall ye say to the king of Judah, that sent you unto me to inquire of me, 'Behold, Pharaoh's army which is come forth to help you, shall return to Egypt into their own land. ⁸And the Chaldeans shall come again, and fight against this city, and take it, and burn it with fire.'" ⁹Thus saith the LORD, "Deceive not yourselves, saying, 'The Chaldeans shall surely depart from us': for they shall not depart. ¹⁰For though ye had smitten the whole army of the Chaldeans that fight against you, and there remained but wounded men among them, yet should they rise up every man in his tent, and burn this city with fire."'

¹¹And it came to pass that when the army of the Chaldeans was broken up from Jerusalem for fear of Pharaoh's army, ¹²then Jeremiah went forth out of Jerusalem to go into the land of Benjamin, to separate himself thence in the midst of the people. ¹³And when he was in the gate of Benjamin, a captain of the ward was there, whose name was Irijah, the son of Shelemiah, the son of Hananiah; and he took Jeremiah the prophet, saying, 'Thou fallest away to the Chaldeans'. ¹⁴Then said Jeremiah, 'It is false, I fall not away to the Chaldeans'. But he hearkened not to him: so Irijah took Jeremiah, and brought him to the princes. ¹⁵Wherefore the princes were wroth with Jeremiah, and smote him, and put him in prison in the house of Jonathan the scribe, for they had made that the prison.

¹⁶When Jeremiah was entered into the dungeon, and into the cabins, and Jeremiah had remained there many days: ¹⁷then Zedekiah the king sent and took him out: and the king asked him secretly in his house, and said, 'Is there any word from the LORD?' And Jeremiah said, 'There is: for,' said he, 'thou shalt be delivered into the hand of the king of Babylon'. ¹⁸Moreover Jeremiah said unto king Zedekiah, 'What have I offended against thee, or against thy servants, or against this people, that ye have put me in prison? ¹⁹Where are now your prophets which prophesied unto you, saying, "The king of Babylon shall not come against you, nor against this land"? ²⁰Therefore hear now, I pray thee, O my lord the king: let my supplication, I pray thee, be accepted before thee, that thou cause me not to return to the house of Jonathan the scribe, lest I die there.' ²¹Then Zedekiah the king commanded that they should commit Jeremiah into the court of the prison, and that they should give him daily a piece of bread out of the bakers' street, until all the bread in the city were spent. Thus Jeremiah remained in the court of the prison.

38 Then Shephatiah the son of Mattan, and Gedaliah the son of Pashur, and Jucal the son of Shelemiah, and Pashur the son of Malchiah heard the words that Jeremiah had spoken unto all the people, saying, ²'Thus saith the LORD, "He that remaineth in this city shall die by the sword, by the famine, and by the pestilence, but he that goeth forth to the Chaldeans shall live: for he shall have his life for a prey, and shall live". ³Thus saith the LORD, "This city shall surely be given into the hand of the king of Babylon's army, which shall take it".' ⁴Therefore the princes said unto the king, 'We beseech thee, let this man be put to death: for thus he weakeneth the hands of the men of war that remain in this city, and the hands of all the people, in speaking such words unto them: for this man seeketh not the welfare of this people, but the hurt'. ⁵Then Zedekiah the king said, 'Behold, he is in your hand: for the king is not he that can do anything against you'. ⁶Then took they Jeremiah, and cast him into the dungeon of Malchiah the son of Hammelech, that was in the court of the prison: and they let down Jeremiah with cords. And in the dungeon there was no water, but mire: so Jeremiah sank in the mire.

⁷Now when Ebed-melech the Ethiopian, one of the eunuchs which was in the king's house, heard that they had put Jeremiah in the dungeon (the king then sitting in the gate of Benjamin), ⁸Ebed-melech went forth out of the king's house, and spoke to the king, saying, ⁹'My lord the king, these men have done evil in all that they have done to Jeremiah the prophet, whom they have cast into the dungeon; and he is like to die for hunger in the place where he is, for there is no more bread in the city'. ¹⁰Then the king commanded Ebed-melech the Ethiopian, saying, 'Take from hence thirty men with thee, and take up Jeremiah the prophet out of the dungeon before he die'. ¹¹So Ebed-melech took the men with him, and went into the house of the king under the treasury, and took thence old cast clouts and old rotten rags, and let them down by cords into the dungeon to Jeremiah. ¹²And Ebed-melech the Ethiopian said unto Jeremiah, 'Put now these old cast clouts and rotten rags under thy arm-holes under the cords'. And Jeremiah did so. ¹³So they drew up Jeremiah with cords, and took him up out of the dungeon: and Jeremiah remained in the court of the prison.

¹⁴Then Zedekiah the king sent, and took Jeremiah the prophet unto him into the third entry that is in the house of the LORD: and the king said unto Jeremiah, 'I will ask thee a thing: hide nothing from me'. ¹⁵Then Jeremiah said unto Zedekiah, 'If I declare it unto thee, wilt thou not surely put me to death? and if I give thee counsel, wilt thou not hearken unto me?' ¹⁶So the king swore secretly unto Jeremiah, saying, 'As the LORD liveth that made us this soul, I will not put thee to death, neither will I give thee into the hand of these men that seek thy life'. ¹⁷Then said Jeremiah unto Zedekiah, 'Thus saith the LORD the God of hosts, the God of Israel, "If thou wilt assuredly go forth unto the king of Babylon's princes, then thy soul shall live, and this city shall not be burnt with fire, and thou shalt live, and thy house. ¹⁸But if thou wilt not go forth to the king of Babylon's princes, then shall this city be given into the hand of the Chaldeans, and they shall burn it with fire, and thou shalt not escape out of their hand."' ¹⁹And Zedekiah the king said unto Jeremiah, 'I am afraid of the Jews that are fallen to the Chaldeans, lest they deliver me into their hand, and they mock me'. ²⁰But Jeremiah said, 'They shall not deliver thee. Obey, I beseech thee,

the voice of the LORD, which I speak unto thee: so it shall be well unto thee, and thy soul shall live. [21]But if thou refuse to go forth, this is the word that the LORD hath shown me: [22]"And behold, all the women that are left in the king of Judah's house shall be brought forth to the king of Babylon's princes, and those women shall say, 'Thy friends have set thee on, and have prevailed against thee: thy feet are sunk in the mire, and they are turned away back'. [23]So they shall bring out all thy wives and thy children to the Chaldeans, and thou shalt not escape out of their hand, but shalt be taken by the hand of the king of Babylon: and thou shalt cause this city to be burnt with fire."'

[24]Then said Zedekiah unto Jeremiah, 'Let no man know of these words, and thou shalt not die. [25]But if the princes hear that I have talked with thee, and they come unto thee, and say unto thee, "Declare unto us now what thou hast said unto the king; hide it not from us, and we will not put thee to death; also what the king said unto thee": [26]then thou shalt say unto them, "I presented my supplication before the king, that he would not cause me to return to Jonathan's house, to die there".' [27]Then came all the princes unto Jeremiah, and asked him: and he told them according to all these words that the king had commanded. So they left off speaking with him, for the matter was not perceived. [28]So Jeremiah abode in the court of the prison until the day that Jerusalem was taken: and he was there when Jerusalem was taken.

39 In the ninth year of Zedekiah king of Judah, in the tenth month, came Nebuchadrezzar king of Babylon and all his army against Jerusalem, and they besieged it. [2]And in the eleventh year of Zedekiah, in the fourth month, the ninth day of the month, the city was broken up. [3]And all the princes of the king of Babylon came in, and sat in the middle gate, even Nergal-sharezer, Samgar-nebo, Sarsechim, Rabsaris, Nergal-sharezer, Rab-mag, with all the residue of the princes of the king of Babylon.

[4]And it came to pass that when Zedekiah the king of Judah saw them and all the men of war, then they fled, and went forth out of the city by night, by the way of the king's garden, by the gate betwixt the two walls: and he went out the way of the plain. [5]But the Chaldeans' army pursued after them, and overtook Zedekiah in the plains of Jericho: and when they had taken him, they brought him up to Nebuchadrezzar king of Babylon to Riblah in the land of Hamath, where he gave judgement upon him. [6]Then the king of Babylon slew the sons of Zedekiah in Riblah before his eyes: also the king of Babylon slew all the nobles of Judah. [7]Moreover he put out Zedekiah's eyes, and bound him with chains, to carry him to Babylon.

[8]And the Chaldeans burnt the king's house, and the houses of the people, with fire, and broke down the walls of Jerusalem. [9]Then Nebuzaradan the captain of the guard carried away captive into Babylon the remnant of the people that remained in the city, and those that fell away, that fell to him, with the rest of the people that remained. [10]But Nebuzar-adan the captain of the guard left of the poor of the people,

which had nothing, in the land of Judah, and gave them vineyards and fields at the same time. ¹¹Now Nebuchadrezzar king of Babylon gave charge concerning Jeremiah to Nebuzar-adan the captain of the guard, saying, ¹²'Take him, and look well to him, and do him no harm, but do unto him even as he shall say unto thee'. ¹³So Nebuzar-adan the captain of the guard sent, and Nebushasban, Rabsaris, and Nergal-sharezer, Rab-mag, and all the king of Babylon's princes: ¹⁴even they sent, and took Jeremiah out of the court of the prison, and committed him unto Gedaliah the son of Ahikam the son of Shaphan, that he should carry him home: so he dwelt among the people.

¹⁵Now the word of the LORD came unto Jeremiah, while he was shut up in the court of the prison, saying, ¹⁶'Go and speak to Ebed-melech the Ethiopian, saying, "Thus saith the LORD of hosts the God of Israel, 'Behold, I will bring my words upon this city for evil, and not for good, and they shall be accomplished in that day before thee. ¹⁷But I will deliver thee in that day,' saith the LORD, 'and thou shalt not be given into the hand of the men of whom thou art afraid. ¹⁸For I will surely deliver thee, and thou shalt not fall by the sword, but thy life shall be for a prey unto thee, because thou hast put thy trust in me,' saith the LORD."'

40 The word which came to Jeremiah from the LORD, after that Nebuzar-adan the captain of the guard had let him go from Ramah, when he had taken him being bound in chains among all that were carried away captive of Jerusalem and Judah, which were carried away captive unto Babylon. ²And the captain of the guard took Jeremiah, and said unto him, 'The LORD thy God hath pronounced this evil upon this place. ³Now the LORD hath brought it, and done according as he hath said: because ye have sinned against the LORD, and have not obeyed his voice, therefore this thing is come upon you. ⁴And now behold, I loose thee this day from the chains which were upon thy hand. If it seem good unto thee to come with me into Babylon, come, and I will look well unto thee: but if it seem ill unto thee to come with me into Babylon, forbear: behold, all the land is before thee: whither it seemeth good and convenient for thee to go, thither go.' ⁵Now while he was not yet gone back, he said, 'Go back also to Gedaliah the son of Ahikam the son of Shaphan, whom the king of Babylon hath made governor over all the cities of Judah, and dwell with him among the people: or go wheresoever it seemeth convenient unto thee to go'. So the captain of the guard gave him victuals and a reward, and let him go. ⁶Then went Jeremiah unto Gedaliah the son of Ahikam to Mizpah, and dwelt with him among the people that were left in the land.

⁷Now when all the captains of the forces which were in the fields, even they and their men, heard that the king of Babylon had made Gedaliah the son of Ahikam governor in the land, and had committed unto him men, and women, and children, and of the poor of the land, of them that were not carried away captive to Babylon; ⁸then they came to Gedaliah to Mizpah, even Ishmael the son of Nethaniah, and

Johanan and Jonathan the sons of Kareah, and Seraiah the son of Tanhumeth, and the sons of Ephai the Netophathite, and Jezaniah the son of a Maachathite, they and their men. ⁹And Gedaliah the son of Ahikam the son of Shaphan swore unto them and to their men, saying, 'Fear not to serve the Chaldeans: dwell in the land, and serve the king of Babylon, and it shall be well with you. ¹⁰As for me, behold, I will dwell at Mizpah to serve the Chaldeans, which will come unto us: but ye, gather ye wine, and summer fruits, and oil, and put them in your vessels, and dwell in your cities that ye have taken.' ¹¹Likewise when all the Jews that were in Moab, and among the Ammonites, and in Edom, and that were in all the countries, heard that the king of Babylon had left a remnant of Judah, and that he had set over them Gedaliah the son of Ahikam the son of Shaphan, ¹²even all the Jews returned out of all places whither they were driven, and came to the land of Judah, to Gedaliah, unto Mizpah, and gathered wine and summer fruits very much.

¹³Moreover Johanan the son of Kareah, and all the captains of the forces that were in the fields, came to Gedaliah to Mizpah, ¹⁴and said unto him, 'Dost thou certainly know that Baalis the king of the Ammonites hath sent Ishmael the son of Nethaniah to slay thee?' But Gedaliah the son of Ahikam believed them not. ¹⁵Then Johanan the son of Kareah spoke to Gedaliah in Mizpah secretly, saying, 'Let me go, I pray thee, and I will slay Ishmael the son of Nethaniah, and no man shall know it. Wherefore should he slay thee, that all the Jews which are gathered unto thee should be scattered, and the remnant in Judah perish?' ¹⁶But Gedaliah the son of Ahikam said unto Johanan the son of Kareah, 'Thou shalt not do this thing: for thou speakest falsely of Ishmael'.

41 Now it came to pass in the seventh month, that Ishmael the son of Nethaniah the son of Elishama of the seed royal, and the princes of the king, even ten men with him, came unto Gedaliah the son of Ahikam to Mizpah; and there they did eat bread together in Mizpah. ²Then arose Ishmael the son of Nethaniah, and the ten men that were with him, and smote Gedaliah the son of Ahikam the son of Shaphan with the sword, and slew him, whom the king of Babylon had made governor over the land. ³Ishmael also slew all the Jews that were with him, even with Gedaliah, at Mizpah, and the Chaldeans that were found there, and the men of war. ⁴And it came to pass the second day after he had slain Gedaliah, and no man knew it, ⁵that there came certain from Shechem, from Shiloh, and from Samaria, even fourscore men, having their beards shaven, and their clothes rent, and having cut themselves, with offerings and incense in their hand, to bring them to the house of the LORD. ⁶And Ishmael the son of Nethaniah went forth from Mizpah to meet them, weeping all along as he went: and it came to pass as he met them, he said unto them, 'Come to Gedaliah the son of Ahikam'. ⁷And it was so when they came into the midst of the city, that Ishmael the son of Nethaniah slew them, and cast them into the midst of the pit, he, and the men that were with him. ⁸But ten men were found among them that said unto Ishmael, 'Slay us not: for we have treasures in the field, of wheat, and of barley, and of oil, and of honey'. So he forbore, and slew them not among their brethren. ⁹Now the pit wherein Ishmael had cast all the dead bodies of the men (whom he had slain because of Gedaliah) was it which Asa the king had made for fear of Baasha king of Israel: and Ishmael the son of Nethaniah filled it with them that were slain. ¹⁰Then Ishmael carried away captive all the residue of the people that were in Mizpah, even the king's daughters, and all the people that remained in Mizpah, whom Nebuzar-adan the captain of the guard had committed to Gedaliah the son of Ahikam: and Ishmael the son of Nethaniah carried them away captive, and departed to go over to the Ammonites.

¹¹But when Johanan the son of Kareah, and all the captains of the forces that were with him, heard of all the evil that Ishmael the son of Nethaniah had done, ¹²then they took all the men, and went to fight with Ishmael the son of Nethaniah, and found him by the great waters that are in Gibeon. ¹³Now it came to pass that when all the people which were with Ishmael saw Johanan the son of Kareah, and all the captains of the forces that were with him, then they were glad. ¹⁴So all the people that Ishmael had carried away captive from Mizpah cast about and returned, and went unto Johanan the son of Kareah. ¹⁵But Ishmael the son of Nethaniah escaped from Johanan with eight men, and went to the Ammonites. ¹⁶Then took Johanan the son of Kareah, and all the captains of the forces that were with him, all the remnant of the people whom he had recovered from Ishmael the son of Nethaniah, from Mizpah, after that he had slain Gedaliah the son of Ahikam, even mighty men of war, and the women, and the children, and the eunuchs, whom he had brought again from Gibeon: ¹⁷and they departed, and dwelt in the habitation of Chimham, which is by Beth-lehem, to go to enter into Egypt, ¹⁸because of the Chaldeans: for they were afraid of them, because Ishmael the son of Nethaniah had slain Gedaliah the son of Ahikam, whom the king of Babylon made governor in the land.

42 Then all the captains of the forces, and Johanan the son of Kareah, and Jezaniah the son of Hoshaiah, and all the people from the least even unto the greatest, came near, ²and said unto Jeremiah the prophet, 'Let, we beseech thee, our supplication be accepted before thee, and pray for us unto the LORD thy God, even for all this remnant (for we are left but a few of many, as thy eyes do behold us), ³that the LORD thy God may show us the way wherein we may walk, and the thing that we may do'. ⁴Then Jeremiah the prophet said unto them, 'I have heard you; behold, I will pray unto the LORD your God according to your words; and it shall come to pass that what-soever thing the LORD shall answer you, I will declare it unto you: I will keep nothing back from you'. ⁵Then they said to Jeremiah, 'The LORD be a true and faithful witness between us, if we do not even according to all things for the which the LORD thy God shall send thee to us. ⁶Whether it be good, or whether it be evil, we will obey the voice of the

LORD our God, to whom we send thee, that it may be well with us, when we obey the voice of the LORD our God.'

⁷And it came to pass after ten days, that the word of the LORD came unto Jeremiah. ⁸Then called he Johanan the son of Kareah, and all the captains of the forces which were with him, and all the people from the least even to the greatest, ⁹and said unto them, 'Thus saith the LORD, the God of Israel, unto whom ye sent me to present your supplication before him: ¹⁰"If ye will still abide in this land, then will I build you, and not pull you down, and I will plant you, and not pluck you up: for I repent me of the evil that I have done unto you. ¹¹Be not afraid of the king of Babylon, of whom ye are afraid: be not afraid of him," saith the LORD: "for I am with you to save you, and to deliver you from his hand. ¹²And I will show mercies unto you, that he may have mercy upon you, and cause you to return to your own land.

¹³ "But if ye say, 'We will not dwell in this land, neither obey the voice of the LORD your God, ¹⁴saying, "No, but we will go into the land of Egypt, where we shall see no war, nor hear the sound of the trumpet, nor have hunger of bread, and there will we dwell"'" ¹⁵(and now therefore hear the word of the LORD, ye remnant of Judah, "Thus saith the LORD of hosts, the God of Israel, 'If ye wholly set your faces to enter into Egypt, and go to sojourn there'"): ¹⁶"then it shall come to pass that the sword which ye feared, shall overtake you there in the land of Egypt, and the famine, whereof ye were afraid, shall follow close after you in Egypt, and there ye shall die. ¹⁷So shall it be with all the men that set their faces to go into Egypt to sojourn there, they shall die by the sword, by the famine, and by the pestilence: and none of them shall remain or escape from the evil that I will bring upon them." ¹⁸For thus saith the LORD of hosts, the God of Israel, "As my anger and my fury hath been poured forth upon the inhabitants of Jerusalem: so shall my fury be poured forth upon you, when ye shall enter into Egypt: and ye shall be an execration, and an astonishment, and a curse, and a reproach; and ye shall see this place no more."

¹⁹'The LORD hath said concerning you, O ye remnant of Judah, "Go ye not into Egypt": know certainly that I have admonished you this day. ²⁰For ye dissembled in your hearts, when ye sent me unto the LORD your God, saying, "Pray for us unto the LORD our God, and according unto all that the LORD our God shall say, so declare unto us, and we will do it". ²¹And now I have this day declared it to you, but ye have not obeyed the voice of the LORD your God, nor anything for the which he hath sent me unto you. ²²Now therefore know certainly that ye shall die by the sword, by the famine, and by the pestilence, in the place whither ye desire to go and to sojourn.'

43 And it came to pass that when Jeremiah had made an end of speaking unto all the people all the words of the LORD their God, for which the LORD their God had sent him to them, even all these words, ²then spoke Azariah the son of Hoshaiah, and Johanan the son of Kareah, and all the proud men, saying unto Jeremiah, 'Thou speakest falsely: the LORD our God hath not sent thee to say, "Go not into Egypt to sojourn there". ³But Baruch the son of Neriah setteth thee on against us, for to deliver us into the hand of the Chaldeans, that they might put us to death, and carry us away captives into Babylon.' ⁴So Johanan the son of Kareah, and all the captains of the forces, and all the people, obeyed not the voice of the LORD, to dwell in the land of Judah. ⁵But Johanan the son of Kareah, and all the captains of the forces, took all the remnant of Judah, that were returned from all nations whither they had been driven, to dwell in the land of Judah, ⁶even men, and women, and children, and the king's daughters, and every person that Nebuzar-adan the captain of the guard had left with Gedaliah the son of Ahikam the son of Shaphan, and Jeremiah the prophet, and Baruch the son of Neriah. ⁷So they came into the land of Egypt: for they obeyed not the voice of the LORD: thus came they even to Tahpanhes.

⁸Then came the word of the LORD unto Jeremiah in Tahpanhes, saying, ⁹"Take great stones in thy hand, and hide them in the clay in the brick-kiln, which is at the entry of Pharaoh's house in Tahpanhes, in the sight of the men of Judah: ¹⁰and say unto them, "Thus saith the LORD of hosts, the God of Israel, 'Behold, I will send and take Nebuchadrezzar the king of Babylon, my servant, and will set his throne upon these stones that I have hid, and he shall spread his royal pavilion over them. ¹¹And when he cometh, he shall smite the land of Egypt, and deliver such as are for death to death; and such as are for captivity to captivity; and such as are for the sword to the sword. ¹²And I will kindle a fire in the houses of the gods of Egypt, and he shall burn them, and carry them away captives: and he shall array himself with the land of Egypt, as a shepherd putteth on his garment; and he shall go forth from thence in peace. ¹³He shall break also the images of Beth-shemesh that is in the land of Egypt, and the houses of the gods of the Egyptians shall he burn with fire.'""

44 The word that came to Jeremiah concerning all the Jews which dwell in the land of Egypt, which dwell at Migdol, and at Tahpanhes, and at Noph, and in the country of Pathros, saying, ²"Thus saith the LORD of hosts, the God of Israel, "Ye have seen all the evil that I have brought upon Jerusalem, and upon all the cities of Judah: and behold, this day they are a desolation, and no man dwelleth therein, ³because of their wickedness which they have committed to provoke me to anger, in that they went to burn incense, and to serve other gods, whom they knew not, neither they, you, nor your fathers. ⁴Howbeit I sent unto you all my servants the prophets, rising early and sending them, saying, 'Oh, do not this abominable thing that I hate'. ⁵But they hearkened not, nor inclined their ear to turn from their wickedness, to burn no incense unto other gods. ⁶Wherefore my fury and my anger was poured forth, and was kindled in the cities of Judah and in the streets of Jerusalem, and they are wasted and desolate, as at this day." ⁷Therefore now thus saith the LORD, the God of hosts, the God of Israel, "Wherefore commit ye this great evil against your souls, to cut off from you man and woman, child and suckling, out of Judah, to leave you none to remain; ⁸in that ye provoke me unto wrath with the works of your hands, burning incense unto other gods in the land of Egypt, whither ye be gone to dwell, that ye might cut yourselves off, and that ye might be a curse and a reproach among all the nations of the earth? ⁹Have ye forgotten the wickedness of your fathers, and the wickedness of the kings of Judah, and the wickedness of their wives, and your own wickedness, and the wickedness of your wives, which they have committed in the land of Judah, and in the streets of Jerusalem? ¹⁰They are not humbled even unto this day, neither have they feared nor walked in my law, nor in my statutes, that I set before you and before your fathers."

¹¹'Therefore thus saith the LORD of hosts, the God of Israel, "Behold, I will set my face against you for evil, and to cut off all Judah. ¹²And I will take the remnant of Judah, that have set their faces to go into the land of Egypt to sojourn there, and they shall all be consumed and fall in the land of Egypt: they shall even be consumed by the sword and by the famine: they shall die, from the least even unto the greatest, by the sword and by the famine: and they shall be an execration, and an astonishment, and a curse, and a reproach. ¹³For I will punish them that dwell in the land of Egypt, as I have punished Jerusalem, by the sword, by the famine, and by the pestilence: ¹⁴so that none of the remnant of Judah which are gone into the land of Egypt to sojourn there, shall escape or remain, that they should return into the land of Judah to the which they have a desire to return to dwell there: for none shall return but such as shall escape."'

¹⁵Then all the men which knew that their wives had burnt incense unto other gods, and all the women that stood by, a great multitude, even all the people that dwelt in the land of Egypt, in Pathros, answered Jeremiah, saying, ¹⁶'As for the word that thou hast spoken unto us in the name of the LORD, we will not hearken unto thee. ¹⁷But we will certainly do whatsoever thing goeth forth out of our own mouth, to burn incense unto the queen of heaven, and to pour out drink offerings unto her, as we have done, we and our fathers, our kings, and our princes, in the cities of Judah, and in the streets of Jerusalem: for then had we plenty of victuals, and were well, and saw no evil. ¹⁸But since we left off to burn incense to the queen of heaven, and to pour out drink offerings unto her, we have wanted all things, and have been consumed by the sword and by the famine. ¹⁹And when we burnt incense to the queen of heaven, and poured out drink offerings unto her, did we make her cakes to worship her, and pour out drink offerings unto her, without our men?'

²⁰Then Jeremiah said unto all the people, to the men and to the women, and to all the people which had given him that answer, saying, ²¹'The incense that ye burnt in the cities of Judah, and in the streets of Jerusalem, ye and your fathers, your kings and your princes, and the people of the land, did not the LORD remember them, and came it not into his mind? ²²So that the LORD could no longer bear, because of the evil of your doings, and because of the abominations which ye have committed: therefore is your land a desolation, and an astonishment,

and a curse without an inhabitant, as at this day. ²³Because you have burnt incense, and because ye have sinned against the LORD, and have not obeyed the voice of the LORD, nor walked in his law, nor in his statutes, nor in his testimonies: therefore this evil is happened unto you, as at this day.'

²⁴Moreover Jeremiah said unto all the people, and to all the women, 'Hear the word of the LORD, all Judah that are in the land of Egypt. ²⁵Thus saith the LORD of hosts, the God of Israel, saying, "Ye and your wives have both spoken with your mouths, and fulfilled with your hand, saying, 'We will surely perform our vows that we have vowed, to burn incense to the queen of heaven, and to pour out drink offerings unto her': ye will surely accomplish your vows, and surely perform your vows." ²⁶Therefore hear ye the word of the LORD, all Judah that dwell in the land of Egypt, "Behold, I have sworn by my great name," saith the LORD, "that my name shall no more be named in the mouth of any man of Judah in all the land of Egypt, saying, 'The Lord GOD liveth'. ²⁷Behold, I will watch over them for evil, and not for good: and all the men of Judah that are in the land of Egypt shall be consumed by the sword and by the famine, until there be an end of them. ²⁸Yet a small number that escape the sword shall return out of the land of Egypt into the land of Judah: and all the remnant of Judah, that are gone into the land of Egypt to sojourn there, shall know whose words shall stand, mine, or theirs.

²⁹' "And this shall be a sign unto you," saith the LORD, "that I will punish you in this place, that ye may know that my words shall surely stand against you for evil." ³⁰Thus saith the LORD, "Behold, I will give Pharaoh-hophra king of Egypt into the hand of his enemies, and into the hand of them that seek his life, as I gave Zedekiah king of Judah into the hand of Nebuchadrezzar king of Babylon, his enemy, and that sought his life".'

45 The word that Jeremiah the prophet spoke unto Baruch the son of Neriah, when he had written these words in a book at the mouth of Jeremiah, in the fourth year of Jehoiakim the son of Josiah king of Judah, saying, ²'Thus saith the LORD the God of Israel unto thee, O Baruch, ³"Thou didst say, 'Woe is me now, for the LORD hath added grief to my sorrow, I fainted in my sighing, and I find no rest'." ⁴Thus shalt thou say unto him, "The LORD saith thus, 'Behold, that which I have built will I break down, and that which I have planted I will pluck up, even this whole land. ⁵And seekest thou great things for thyself? seek them not: for behold, I will bring evil upon all flesh,' saith the LORD: 'but thy life will I give unto thee for a prey in all places whither thou goest.'"'

46 The word of the LORD which came to Jeremiah the prophet against the Gentiles, ²against Egypt, against the army of Pharaoh-necho king of Egypt, which was by the river Euphrates in Carchemish, which Nebuchadrezzar king of Babylon smote in the fourth year of Jehoiakim the son of Josiah king of Judah.

³ 'Order ye the buckler and shield,
and draw near to battle.
⁴ Harness the horses,
and get up, ye horsemen, and stand forth with your helmets,
furbish the spears, and put on the brigandines.
⁵ Wherefore have I seen them dismayed and turned away back?
and their mighty ones are beaten down,
and are fled apace, and look not back:
for fear was round about,' saith the LORD.
⁶ 'Let not the swift flee away,
nor the mighty man escape:
they shall stumble,
and fall toward the north by the river Euphrates.

⁷ 'Who is this that cometh up as a flood,
whose waters are moved as the rivers?
⁸ Egypt riseth up like a flood,
and his waters are moved like the rivers,
and he saith, "I will go up, and will cover the earth,
I will destroy the city and the inhabitants thereof".

⁹ 'Come up, ye horses, and rage, ye chariots,
and let the mighty men come forth,
the Ethiopians and the Libyans that handle the shield,
and the Lydians, that handle and bend the bow.
¹⁰ For this is the day of the Lord GOD of hosts,
a day of vengeance, that he may avenge him of his adversaries:
and the sword shall devour,
and it shall be satiate and made drunk with their blood:
for the Lord GOD of hosts hath a sacrifice in the north country by
the river Euphrates.

¹¹ 'Go up into Gilead, and take balm,
O virgin, the daughter of Egypt:
in vain shalt thou use many medicines:
for thou shalt not be cured.
¹² The nations have heard of thy shame,
and thy cry hath filled the land:
for the mighty man hath stumbled against the mighty,
and they are fallen both together.'

¹³The word that the LORD spoke to Jeremiah the prophet, how Nebuchadrezzar king of Babylon should come and smite the land of Egypt.

¹⁴ 'Declare ye in Egypt, and publish in Migdol,
and publish in Noph and in Tahpanhes:
say ye, "Stand fast, and prepare thee;

for the sword shall devour round about thee".

¹⁵ Why are thy valiant men swept away?
   they stood not, because the LORD did drive them.
¹⁶ He made many to fall, yea, one fell upon another:
   and they said, "Arise, and let us go again to our own people,
   and to the land of our nativity, from the oppressing sword".
¹⁷ They did cry there, "Pharaoh king of Egypt is but a noise,
   he hath passed the time appointed".

¹⁸ 'As I live,' saith the King, whose name is the LORD of hosts,
   'Surely as Tabor is among the mountains,
   and as Carmel by the sea, so shall he come.
¹⁹ O thou daughter dwelling in Egypt,
   furnish thyself to go into captivity:
   for Noph shall be waste and desolate without an inhabitant.
²⁰ Egypt is like a very fair heifer, but destruction cometh:
   it cometh out of the north.
²¹ Also her hired men are in the midst of her like fatted bullocks,
   for they also are turned back, and are fled away together:
   they did not stand,
   because the day of their calamity was come upon them,
   and the time of their visitation.
²² The voice thereof shall go like a serpent,
   for they shall march with an army,
   and come against her with axes, as hewers of wood.
²³ They shall cut down her forest,' saith the LORD,
   'though it cannot be searched,
   because they are more than the grasshoppers, and are
      innumerable.
²⁴ The daughter of Egypt shall be confounded,
   she shall be delivered into the hand of the people of the north.'

²⁵ The LORD of hosts, the God of Israel, saith,
   'Behold, I will punish the multitude of No,
   and Pharaoh, and Egypt, with their gods, and their kings,
   even Pharaoh, and all them that trust in him.
²⁶ And I will deliver them into the hand of those that seek their
      lives,
   and into the hand of Nebuchadrezzar king of Babylon,
   and into the hand of his servants:
   and afterwards it shall be inhabited, as in the days of old,' saith
      the LORD.

²⁷ 'But fear not thou, O my servant Jacob,
   and be not dismayed, O Israel:
   for behold, I will save thee from afar off,
   and thy seed from the land of their captivity,
   and Jacob shall return, and be in rest and at ease,

and none shall make him afraid.
²⁸ Fear thou not, O Jacob my servant,' saith the LORD,
'for I am with thee,
for I will make a full end of all the nations whither I have driven
thee,
but I will not make a full end of thee,
but correct thee in measure,
yet will I not leave thee wholly unpunished.'

47 The word of the LORD that came to Jeremiah the prophet against
the Philistines, before that Pharaoh smote Gaza. ²Thus saith the
LORD,

'Behold, waters rise up out of the north,
and shall be an overflowing flood,
and shall overflow the land, and all that is therein,
the city, and them that dwell therein:
then the men shall cry,
and all the inhabitants of the land shall howl'.

³ At the noise of the stamping of the hoofs of his strong horses,
at the rushing of his chariots,
and at the rumbling of his wheels,
the fathers shall not look back to their children for feebleness of
hands;
⁴ because of the day that cometh to spoil all the Philistines,
and to cut off from Tyrus and Zidon every helper that
remaineth:
for the LORD will spoil the Philistines,
the remnant of the country of Caphtor.

⁵ Baldness is come upon Gaza;
Ashkelon is cut off with the remnant of their valley:
how long wilt thou cut thyself?

⁶ O thou sword of the LORD,
how long will it be ere thou be quiet?
put up thyself into thy scabbard,
rest and be still.
⁷ How can it be quiet,
seeing the LORD hath given it a charge against Ashkelon,
and against the sea-shore?
there hath he appointed it.

48 Against Moab thus saith the LORD of hosts, the God of Israel,

'Woe unto Nebo, for it is spoiled:
Kiriathaim is confounded and taken:

Misgab is confounded and dismayed.
² There shall be no more praise of Moab:
in Heshbon they have devised evil against it;
come and let us cut it off from being a nation.
Also thou shalt be cut down, O Madmen,
the sword shall pursue thee.
³ A voice of crying shall be from Horonaim,
spoiling and great destruction.
⁴ Moab is destroyed,
her little ones have caused a cry to be heard.
⁵ For in the going up of Luhith
continual weeping shall go up;
for in the going down of Horonaim
the enemies have heard a cry of destruction.
⁶ Flee, save your lives,
and be like the heath in the wilderness.

⁷ 'For because thou hast trusted in thy works and in thy treasures,
thou shalt also be taken:
and Chemosh shall go forth into captivity
with his priests and his princes together.
⁸ And the spoiler shall come upon every city,
and no city shall escape:
the valley also shall perish,
and the plain shall be destroyed,
as the LORD hath spoken.
⁹ Give wings unto Moab, that it may flee and get away:
for the cities thereof shall be desolate,
without any to dwell therein.
¹⁰ Cursed be he that doeth the work of the LORD deceitfully,
and cursed be he that keepeth back his sword from blood.

¹¹ 'Moab hath been at ease from his youth,
and he hath settled on his lees,
and hath not been emptied from vessel to vessel,
neither hath he gone into captivity:
therefore his taste remained in him,
and his scent is not changed.
¹² Therefore behold, the days come,' saith the LORD,
'that I will send unto him wanderers that shall cause him to
wander,
and shall empty his vessels, and break their bottles.
¹³ And Moab shall be ashamed of Chemosh,
as the house of Israel was ashamed of Beth-el their confidence.

¹⁴ 'How say ye, "We are mighty and strong men for the war"?
¹⁵ Moab is spoiled and gone up out of her cities,
and his chosen young men are gone down to the slaughter,'

saith the King, whose name is the LORD of hosts.

¹⁶ 'The calamity of Moab is near to come,
and his affliction hasteth fast.
¹⁷ All ye that are about him, bemoan him,
and all ye that know his name, say,
"How is the strong staff broken, and the beautiful rod!"
¹⁸ Thou daughter that dost inhabit Dibon,
come down from thy glory, and sit in thirst;
for the spoiler of Moab shall come upon thee,
and he shall destroy thy strongholds.
¹⁹ O inhabitant of Aroer, stand by the way, and espy,
ask him that fleeth, and her that escapeth,
and say, "What is done?"

²⁰ 'Moab is confounded, for it is broken down:
howl and cry,
tell ye it in Arnon, that Moab is spoiled,
²¹ and judgement is come upon the plain country,
upon Holon, and upon Jahazah, and upon Mephaath,
²² and upon Dibon, and upon Nebo, and upon Beth-diblathaim,
²³ and upon Kiriathaim, and upon Beth-gamul, and upon Beth-
meon,
²⁴ and upon Kerioth, and upon Bozrah,
and upon all the cities of the land of Moab, far or near.
²⁵ The horn of Moab is cut off, and his arm is broken,'
saith the LORD.

²⁶ 'Make ye him drunken:
for he magnified himself against the LORD:
Moab also shall wallow in his vomit,
and he also shall be in derision.
²⁷ For was not Israel a derision unto thee?
was he found among thieves?
for since thou spokest of him, thou skippedst for joy.
²⁸ O ye that dwell in Moab,
leave the cities, and dwell in the rock,
and be like the dove that maketh her nest in the sides of the
hole's mouth.

²⁹ 'We have heard the pride of Moab
(he is exceeding proud),
his loftiness, and his arrogance, and his pride,
and the haughtiness of his heart.
³⁰ I know his wrath,' saith the LORD,
'but it shall not be so, his lies shall not so effect it.
³¹ Therefore will I howl for Moab,
and I will cry out for all Moab,
my heart shall mourn for the men of Kir-heres.

³² O vine of Sibmah,
 I will weep for thee with the weeping of Jazer:
 thy plants are gone over the sea,
 they reach even to the sea of Jazer:
 the spoiler is fallen upon thy summer fruits
 and upon thy vintage.
³³ And joy and gladness is taken from the plentiful field,
 and from the land of Moab,
 and I have caused wine to fail from the wine-presses:
 none shall tread with shouting,
 their shouting shall be no shouting.

³⁴ 'From the cry of Heshbon even unto Elealeh,
 and even unto Jahaz, have they uttered their voice,
 from Zoar even unto Horonaim,
 as a heifer of three years old:
 for the waters also of Nimrim shall be desolate.
³⁵ Moreover I will cause to cease in Moab,' saith the LORD,
 'him that offereth in the high places,
 and him that burneth incense to his gods.
³⁶ Therefore my heart shall sound for Moab like pipes,
 and my heart shall sound like pipes for the men of Kir-heres:
 because the riches that he hath gotten are perished.
³⁷ For every head shall be bald, and every beard clipped:
 upon all the hands shall be cuttings,
 and upon the loins sackcloth.
³⁸ There shall be lamentation generally upon all the house-tops of
  Moab,
 and in the streets thereof:
 for I have broken Moab like a vessel wherein is no pleasure,' saith
  the LORD.
³⁹ 'They shall howl, saying, "How is it broken down!
 how hath Moab turned the back with shame!"
 so shall Moab be a derision and a dismaying to all them about
  him.'

⁴⁰ For thus saith the LORD,
 'Behold, he shall fly as an eagle,
 and shall spread his wings over Moab.
⁴¹ Kerioth is taken, and the strongholds are surprised,
 and the mighty men's hearts in Moab at that day
 shall be as the heart of a woman in her pangs.
⁴² And Moab shall be destroyed from being a people,
 because he hath magnified himself against the LORD.
⁴³ Fear, and the pit, and the snare,
 shall be upon thee, O inhabitant of Moab,' saith the LORD.
⁴⁴ 'He that fleeth from the fear shall fall into the pit,
 and he that getteth up out of the pit shall be taken in the snare:

for I will bring upon it, even upon Moab,
the year of their visitation,' saith the LORD.

45 'They that fled stood under the shadow of Heshbon because of
the force:
but a fire shall come forth out of Heshbon,
and a flame from the midst of Sihon,
and shall devour the corner of Moab,
and the crown of the head of the tumultuous ones.
46 Woe be unto thee, O Moab,
the people of Chemosh perisheth:
for thy sons are taken captives,
and thy daughters captives.
47 Yet will I bring again the captivity of Moab in the latter days,'
saith the LORD.

Thus far is the judgement of Moab.

49

Concerning the Ammonites, thus saith the LORD,

'Hath Israel no sons? hath he no heir?
why then doth their king inherit Gad,
and his people dwell in his cities?
2 Therefore behold, the days come,' saith the LORD,
'that I will cause an alarm of war to be heard in Rabbah of the
Ammonites,
and it shall be a desolate heap,
and her daughters shall be burnt with fire:
then shall Israel be heir unto them that were his heirs,' saith the
LORD.

3 'Howl, O Heshbon, for Ai is spoiled:
cry, ye daughters of Rabbah, gird ye with sackcloth:
lament, and run to and fro by the hedges:
for their king shall go into captivity,
and his priests and his princes together.
4 Wherefore gloriest thou in the valleys,
thy flowing valley, O backsliding daughter?
that trusted in her treasures, saying, "Who shall come unto me?"
5 Behold, I will bring a fear upon thee,' saith the Lord GOD of
hosts,
'from all those that be about thee,
and ye shall be driven out every man right forth,
and none shall gather up him that wandereth.
6 And afterward I will bring again the captivity of the children of
Ammon,' saith the LORD.

7 Concerning Edom, thus saith the LORD of hosts,

'Is wisdom no more in Teman?
is counsel perished from the prudent?
is their wisdom vanished?
⁸ Flee ye, turn back, dwell deep, O inhabitants of Dedan:
for I will bring the calamity of Esau upon him,
the time that I will visit him.
⁹ If grape-gatherers come to thee,
would they not leave some gleaning grapes?
If thieves by night,
they will destroy till they have enough.
¹⁰ But I have made Esau bare,
I have uncovered his secret places,
and he shall not be able to hide himself:
his seed is spoiled,
and his brethren and his neighbours,
and he is not.
¹¹ Leave thy fatherless children, I will preserve them alive:
and let thy widows trust in me.'

¹²For thus saith the LORD, 'Behold, they whose judgement was not to drink of the cup have assuredly drunken, and art thou he that shall altogether go unpunished? thou shalt not go unpunished, but thou shalt surely drink of it. ¹³For I have sworn by myself,' saith the LORD, 'that Bozrah shall become a desolation, a reproach, a waste, and a curse; and all the cities thereof shall be perpetual wastes.'

¹⁴ I have heard a rumour from the LORD,
and an ambassador is sent unto the heathen, saying,
'Gather ye together, and come against her,
and rise up to the battle.
¹⁵ For lo, I will make thee small among the heathen,
and despised among men.
¹⁶ Thy terribleness hath deceived thee,
and the pride of thy heart,
O thou that dwellest in the clefts of the rock,
that holdest the height of the hill:
though thou shouldst make thy nest as high as the eagle,
I will bring thee down from thence,' saith the LORD.

¹⁷Also Edom shall be a desolation: every one that goeth by it shall be astonished, and shall hiss at all the plagues thereof. ¹⁸As in the overthrow of Sodom and Gomorrah and the neighbour cities thereof,' saith the LORD, 'no man shall abide there, neither shall a son of man dwell in it. ¹⁹Behold, he shall come up like a lion from the swelling of Jordan against the habitation of the strong: but I will suddenly make him run away from her: and who is a chosen man, that I may appoint over her? for who is like me? and who will appoint me the time? and who is that shepherd that will stand before me?'

²⁰Therefore hear the counsel of the LORD, that he hath taken against Edom, and his purposes that he hath purposed against the inhabitants of Teman: surely the least of the flock shall draw them out: surely he shall make their habitations desolate with them. ²¹The earth is moved at the noise of their fall: at the cry the noise thereof was heard in the Red Sea. ²²Behold, he shall come up and fly as the eagle, and spread his wings over Bozrah: and at that day shall the heart of the mighty men of Edom be as the heart of a woman in her pangs.

²³Concerning Damascus.

'Hamath is confounded, and Arpad,
for they have heard evil tidings:
they are faint-hearted, there is sorrow on the sea,
it cannot be quiet.
²⁴ Damascus is waxed feeble, and turneth herself to flee,
and fear hath seized on her:
anguish and sorrows have taken her as a woman in travail.
²⁵ How is the city of praise not left, the city of my joy!
²⁶ Therefore her young men shall fall in her streets,
and all the men of war shall be cut off in that day,'
saith the LORD of hosts.
²⁷ 'And I will kindle a fire in the wall of Damascus,
and it shall consume the palaces of Ben-hadad.'

²⁸Concerning Kedar, and concerning the kingdoms of Hazor, which Nebuchadrezzar king of Babylon shall smite, thus saith the LORD:

'Arise ye, go up to Kedar,
and spoil the men of the east.
²⁹ Their tents and their flocks shall they take away:
they shall take to themselves their curtains,
and all their vessels, and their camels,
and they shall cry unto them,
"Fear is on every side".
³⁰ Flee, get you far off, dwell deep,
O ye inhabitants of Hazor,' saith the LORD:
'for Nebuchadrezzar king of Babylon hath taken counsel against you,
and hath conceived a purpose against you.
³¹ Arise, get you up unto the wealthy nation
that dwelleth without care,' saith the LORD,
'which have neither gates nor bars, which dwell alone.
³² And their camels shall be a booty,
and the multitude of their cattle a spoil:
and I will scatter into all winds them that are in the utmost corners,
and I will bring their calamity from all sides thereof,' saith the LORD.

³³ And Hazor shall be a dwelling for dragons,
   and a desolation for ever:
   there shall no man abide there,
   nor any son of man dwell in it.

³⁴The word of the LORD that came to Jeremiah the prophet against Elam in the beginning of the reign of Zedekiah king of Judah, saying, ³⁵'Thus saith the LORD of hosts,

'"Behold, I will break the bow of Elam,
   the chief of their might.
³⁶ And upon Elam will I bring the four winds
   from the four quarters of heaven,
   and will scatter them towards all those winds,
   and there shall be no nation whither the outcasts of Elam shall
      not come.
³⁷ For I will cause Elam to be dismayed before their enemies,
   and before them that seek their life:
   and I will bring evil upon them,
   even my fierce anger," saith the LORD,
   "and I will send the sword after them,
   till I have consumed them.
³⁸ And I will set my throne in Elam,
   and will destroy from thence the king and the princes," saith the
      LORD.

³⁹ ' "But it shall come to pass in the latter days,
   that I will bring again the captivity of Elam," saith the LORD.'

50 The word that the LORD spoke against Babylon and against the land of the Chaldeans by Jeremiah the prophet. ²'Declare ye among the nations, and publish, and set up a standard, publish, and conceal not: say, "Babylon is taken, Bel is confounded, Merodach is broken in pieces, her idols are confounded, her images are broken in pieces". ³For out of the north there cometh up a nation against her, which shall make her land desolate, and none shall dwell therein: they shall remove, they shall depart, both man and beast.

⁴'In those days, and in that time,' saith the LORD, 'the children of Israel shall come, they and the children of Judah together, going and weeping: they shall go, and seek the LORD their God. ⁵They shall ask the way to Zion with their faces thitherward, saying, "Come, and let us join ourselves to the LORD in a perpetual covenant that shall not be forgotten".

⁶'My people hath been lost sheep: their shepherds have caused them to go astray, they have turned them away on the mountains: they have gone from mountain to hill, they have forgotten their resting-place. ⁷All that found them have devoured them, and their adversaries said, "We offend not, because they have sinned against the LORD, the habita-

tion of justice, even the LORD, the hope of their fathers". ⁸Remove out of the midst of Babylon, and go forth out of the land of the Chaldeans, and be as the he-goats before the flocks.

⁹'For lo, I will raise and cause to come up against Babylon an assembly of great nations from the north country: and they shall set themselves in array against her; from thence she shall be taken: their arrows shall be as of a mighty expert man: none shall return in vain. ¹⁰And Chaldea shall be a spoil: all that spoil her shall be satisfied,' saith the LORD. ¹¹Because ye were glad, because ye rejoiced, O ye destroyers of my heritage, because ye are grown fat as the heifer at grass, and bellow as bulls: ¹²your mother shall be sore confounded, she that bore you shall be ashamed: behold, the hindmost of the nations shall be a wilderness, a dry land, and a desert. ¹³Because of the wrath of the LORD it shall not be inhabited, but it shall be wholly desolate: every one that goeth by Babylon shall be astonished, and hiss at all her plagues. ¹⁴Put yourselves in array against Babylon round about: all ye that bend the bow, shoot at her; spare no arrows: for she hath sinned against the LORD. ¹⁵Shout against her round about: she hath given her hand: her foundations are fallen, her walls are thrown down: for it is the vengeance of the LORD: take vengeance upon her; as she hath done, do unto her. ¹⁶Cut off the sower from Babylon, and him that handleth the sickle in the time of harvest: for fear of the oppressing sword they shall turn every one to his people, and they shall flee every one to his own land.

¹⁷'Israel is a scattered sheep, the lions have driven him away: first the king of Assyria hath devoured him, and last this Nebuchadrezzar king of Babylon hath broken his bones.' ¹⁸Therefore thus saith the LORD of hosts, the God of Israel: 'Behold, I will punish the king of Babylon and his land, as I have punished the king of Assyria. ¹⁹And I will bring Israel again to his habitation, and he shall feed on Carmel and Bashan, and his soul shall be satisfied upon mount Ephraim and Gilead. ²⁰In those days, and in that time,' saith the LORD, 'the iniquity of Israel shall be sought for, and there shall be none; and the sins of Judah, and they shall not be found: for I will pardon them whom I reserve.

²¹'Go up against the land of Merathaim, even against it, and against the inhabitants of Pekod: waste and utterly destroy after them,' saith the LORD, 'and do according to all that I have commanded thee.'

²²A sound of battle is in the land, and of great destruction. ²³How is the hammer of the whole earth cut asunder and broken! how is Babylon become a desolation among the nations! ²⁴I have laid a snare for thee, and thou art also taken, O Babylon, and thou wast not aware: thou art found, and also caught, because thou hast striven against the LORD. ²⁵The LORD hath opened his armoury, and hath brought forth the weapons of his indignation: for this is the work of the Lord GOD of hosts in the land of the Chaldeans. ²⁶Come against her from the utmost border, open her storehouses: cast her up as heaps, and destroy her utterly: let nothing of her be left. ²⁷Slay all her bullocks: let them go down to the slaughter: woe unto them, for their day is come, the time of their visitation. ²⁸The voice of them that flee and escape out of the land of

Babylon, to declare in Zion the vengeance of the LORD our God, the vengeance of his temple. ²⁹Call together the archers against Babylon: all ye that bend the bow, camp against it round about; let none thereof escape: recompense her according to her work; according to all that she hath done, do unto her: for she hath been proud against the LORD, against the Holy One of Israel.

³⁰'Therefore shall her young men fall in the streets, and all her men of war shall be cut off in that day,' saith the LORD. ³¹'Behold, I am against thee, O thou most proud,' saith the Lord GOD of hosts: 'for thy day is come, the time that I will visit thee. ³²And the most proud shall stumble and fall, and none shall raise him up: and I will kindle a fire in his cities, and it shall devour all round about him.'

³³Thus saith the LORD of hosts, 'The children of Israel and the children of Judah were oppressed together, and all that took them captives held them fast, they refused to let them go'.

³⁴Their Redeemer is strong; the LORD of hosts is his name: he shall thoroughly plead their cause, that he may give rest to the land, and disquiet the inhabitants of Babylon.

³⁵'A sword is upon the Chaldeans,' saith the LORD, 'and upon the inhabitants of Babylon, and upon her princes, and upon her wise men. ³⁶A sword is upon the liars, and they shall dote: a sword is upon her mighty men, and they shall be dismayed. ³⁷A sword is upon their horses, and upon their chariots, and upon all the mingled people that are in the midst of her, and they shall become as women: a sword is upon her treasures, and they shall be robbed. ³⁸A drought is upon her waters, and they shall be dried up: for it is the land of graven images, and they are mad upon their idols.

³⁹'Therefore the wild beasts of the desert with the wild beasts of the islands shall dwell there, and the owls shall dwell therein: and it shall be no more inhabited for ever; neither shall it be dwelt in from generation to generation. ⁴⁰As God overthrew Sodom and Gomorrah and the neighbour cities thereof,' saith the LORD: 'so shall no man abide there, neither shall any son of man dwell therein.

⁴¹'Behold, a people shall come from the north, and a great nation, and many kings shall be raised up from the coasts of the earth. ⁴²They shall hold the bow and the lance: they are cruel and will not show mercy: their voice shall roar like the sea, and they shall ride upon horses, every one put in array, like a man to the battle, against thee, O daughter of Babylon. ⁴³The king of Babylon hath heard the report of them, and his hands waxed feeble: anguish took hold of him, and pangs as of a woman in travail.

⁴⁴'Behold, he shall come up like a lion from the swelling of Jordan unto the habitation of the strong: but I will make them suddenly run away from her: and who is a chosen man that I may appoint over her? for who is like me? and who will appoint me the time? and who is that shepherd that will stand before me?'

⁴⁵Therefore hear ye the counsel of the LORD, that he hath taken against Babylon, and his purposes, that he hath purposed against the

land of the Chaldeans: surely the least of the flock shall draw them out: surely he shall make their habitation desolate with them. ⁴⁶At the noise of the taking of Babylon the earth is moved, and the cry is heard among the nations.

51

Thus saith the LORD,

'Behold, I will raise up against Babylon,
and against them that dwell in the midst of them that rise up
   against me,
a destroying wind;
² and will send unto Babylon fanners,
that shall fan her, and shall empty her land:
for in the day of trouble they shall be against her round about.
³ Against him that bendeth let the archer bend his bow,
and against him that lifteth himself up in his brigandine;
and spare ye not her young men,
destroy ye utterly all her host.
⁴ Thus the slain shall fall in the land of the Chaldeans,
and they that are thrust through in her streets.
⁵ For Israel hath not been forsaken,
nor Judah of his God, of the LORD of hosts;
though their land was filled with sin against the Holy One of
   Israel.'

⁶ Flee out of the midst of Babylon,
and deliver every man his soul:
be not cut off in her iniquity:
for this is the time of the LORD's vengeance:
he will render unto her a recompense.

⁷ Babylon hath been a golden cup in the LORD's hand,
that made all the earth drunken:
the nations have drunken of her wine,
therefore the nations are mad.
⁸ Babylon is suddenly fallen and destroyed:
howl for her, take balm for her pain,
if so be she may be healed.
⁹ We would have healed Babylon,
but she is not healed:
forsake her, and let us go every one into his own country:
for her judgement reacheth unto heaven,
and is lifted up even to the skies.
¹⁰ The LORD hath brought forth our righteousness:
come and let us declare in Zion
the work of the LORD our God.

¹¹ Make bright the arrows:
gather the shields:

the LORD hath raised up the spirit of the kings of the Medes:
for his device is against Babylon, to destroy it;
because it is the vengeance of the LORD,
the vengeance of his temple.
¹² Set up the standard upon the walls of Babylon,
make the watch strong, set up the watchmen,
prepare the ambushes:
for the LORD hath both devised and done
that which he spoke against the inhabitants of Babylon.

¹³ O thou that dwellest upon many waters,
abundant in treasures,
thy end is come,
and the measure of thy covetousness.
¹⁴ The LORD of hosts hath sworn by himself, saying,
'Surely I will fill thee with men, as with caterpillars;
and they shall lift up a shout against thee'.

¹⁵ He hath made the earth by his power,
he hath established the world by his wisdom,
and hath stretched out the heaven by his understanding.
¹⁶ When he uttereth his voice,
there is a multitude of waters in the heavens,
and he causeth the vapours to ascend from the ends of the
earth:
he maketh lightnings with rain,
and bringeth forth the wind out of his treasures.

¹⁷ Every man is brutish by his knowledge:
every founder is confounded by the graven image:
for his molten image is falsehood,
and there is no breath in them.
¹⁸ They are vanity, the work of errors:
in the time of their visitation they shall perish.
¹⁹ The portion of Jacob is not like them,
for he is the former of all things,
and Israel is the rod of his inheritance:
the LORD of hosts is his name.

²⁰ 'Thou art my battle-axe and weapons of war:
for with thee will I break in pieces the nations,
and with thee will I destroy kingdoms;
²¹ and with thee will I break in pieces the horse and his rider,
and with thee will I break in pieces the chariot and his rider;
²² with thee also will I break in pieces man and woman,
and with thee will I break in pieces old and young,
and with thee will I break in pieces the young man and the
maid;

²³ I will also break in pieces with thee the shepherd and his flock,
and with thee will I break in pieces the husbandman and his
yoke of oxen,
and with thee will I break in pieces captains and rulers.
²⁴ And I will render unto Babylon
and to all the inhabitants of Chaldea
all their evil that they have done in Zion in your sight,' saith the
LORD.

²⁵ 'Behold, I am against thee, O destroying mountain,' saith the
LORD,
'which destroyest all the earth:
and I will stretch out my hand upon thee,
and roll thee down from the rocks,
and will make thee a burnt mountain.
²⁶ And they shall not take of thee a stone for a corner,
nor a stone for foundations,
but thou shalt be desolate for ever,' saith the LORD.

²⁷ Set ye up a standard in the land,
blow the trumpet among the nations:
prepare the nations against her:
call together against her the kingdoms of Ararat, Minni, and
Ashchenaz:
appoint a captain against her:
cause her horses to come up as the rough caterpillars.
²⁸ Prepare against her the nations with the kings of the Medes,
the captains thereof, and all the rulers thereof,
and all the land of his dominion.
²⁹ And the land shall tremble and sorrow:
for every purpose of the LORD shall be performed against
Babylon,
to make the land of Babylon a desolation without an inhabitant.

³⁰ The mighty men of Babylon have forborn to fight:
they have remained in their holds:
their might hath failed,
they became as women:
they have burnt their dwelling-places:
her bars are broken.
³¹ One post shall run to meet another,
and one messenger to meet another,
to show the king of Babylon that his city is taken at one end,
³² and that the passages are stopped,
and the reeds they have burnt with fire,
and the men of war are affrighted.
³³ For thus saith the LORD of hosts, the God of Israel,
'The daughter of Babylon is like a threshing-floor;

it is time to thresh her:
yet a little while, and the time of her harvest shall come'.

³⁴ 'Nebuchadrezzar the king of Babylon hath devoured me,
he hath crushed me,
he hath made me an empty vessel,
he hath swallowed me up like a dragon,
he hath filled his belly with my delicates,
he hath cast me out.
³⁵ The violence done to me and to my flesh be upon Babylon,'
shall the inhabitant of Zion say;
'and my blood upon the inhabitants of Chaldea,'
shall Jerusalem say.

³⁶ Therefore thus saith the LORD,
'Behold, I will plead thy cause, and take vengeance for thee,
and I will dry up her sea, and make her springs dry.
³⁷ And Babylon shall become heaps,
a dwelling-place for dragons,
an astonishment, and a hissing
without an inhabitant.
³⁸ They shall roar together like lions:
they shall yell as lions' whelps.
³⁹ In their heat I will make their feasts,
and I will make them drunken,
that they may rejoice, and sleep a perpetual sleep,
and not wake,' saith the LORD.
⁴⁰ 'I will bring them down like lambs to the slaughter,
like rams with he-goats.'

⁴¹ How is Sheshach taken!
and how is the praise of the whole earth surprised!
how is Babylon become an astonishment among the nations!
⁴² The sea is come up upon Babylon:
she is covered with the multitude of the waves thereof.
⁴³ Her cities are a desolation,
a dry land and a wilderness,
a land wherein no man dwelleth,
neither doth any son of man pass thereby.

⁴⁴ 'And I will punish Bel in Babylon,
and I will bring forth out of his mouth that which he hath
swallowed up,
and the nations shall not flow together any more unto him:
yea, the wall of Babylon shall fall.
⁴⁵ My people, go ye out of the midst of her,
and deliver ye every man his soul from the fierce anger of the
LORD.

⁴⁶ And lest your heart faint,
and ye fear for the rumour that shall be heard in the land:
a rumour shall both come one year,
and after that in another year shall come a rumour,
and violence in the land, ruler against ruler.
⁴⁷ Therefore behold, the days come,
that I will do judgement upon the graven images of Babylon,
and her whole land shall be confounded,
and all her slain shall fall in the midst of her.
⁴⁸ Then the heaven and the earth, and all that is therein, shall sing
for Babylon:
for the spoilers shall come unto her from the north,' saith the
LORD.
⁴⁹ 'As Babylon hath caused the slain of Israel to fall,
so at Babylon shall fall the slain of all the earth.'

⁵⁰ Ye that have escaped the sword,
go away, stand not still:
remember the LORD afar off,
and let Jerusalem come into your mind.
⁵¹ We are confounded, because we have heard reproach,
shame hath covered our faces:
for strangers are come into the sanctuaries of the LORD's house.

⁵² 'Wherefore, behold, the days come,' saith the LORD,
'that I will do judgement upon her graven images,
and through all her land the wounded shall groan.
⁵³ Though Babylon should mount up to heaven,
and though she should fortify the height of her strength,
yet from me shall spoilers come unto her,' saith the LORD.

⁵⁴ A sound of a cry cometh from Babylon,
and great destruction from the land of the Chaldeans:
⁵⁵ because the LORD hath spoiled Babylon,
and destroyed out of her the great voice;
when her waves do roar like great waters,
a noise of their voice is uttered:
⁵⁶ because the spoiler is come upon her,
even upon Babylon,
and her mighty men are taken,
every one of their bows is broken:
for the LORD God of recompenses shall surely requite.

⁵⁷ 'And I will make drunk her princes and her wise men,
her captains and her rulers, and her mighty men:
and they shall sleep a perpetual sleep, and not wake,'
saith the King, whose name is the LORD of hosts.

⁵⁸ Thus saith the LORD of hosts,
  'The broad walls of Babylon shall be utterly broken,
  and her high gates shall be burnt with fire,
  and the people shall labour in vain,
  and the folk in the fire, and they shall be weary'.

⁵⁹The word which Jeremiah the prophet commanded Seraiah the son of Neriah, the son of Maaseiah, when he went with Zedekiah the king of Judah into Babylon in the fourth year of his reign. And this Seraiah was a quiet prince. ⁶⁰So Jeremiah wrote in a book all the evil that should come upon Babylon: even all these words that are written against Babylon. ⁶¹And Jeremiah said to Seraiah, 'When thou comest to Babylon, and shalt see, and shalt read all these words, ⁶²then shalt thou say, "O LORD, thou hast spoken against this place, to cut it off, that none shall remain in it, neither man nor beast, but that it shall be desolate for ever". ⁶³And it shall be, when thou hast made an end of reading this book, that thou shalt bind a stone to it, and cast it into the midst of Euphrates. ⁶⁴And thou shalt say, "Thus shall Babylon sink, and shall not rise from the evil that I will bring upon her: and they shall be weary".'
Thus far are the words of Jeremiah.

52 Zedekiah was one and twenty years old when he began to reign, and he reigned eleven years in Jerusalem. And his mother's name was Hamutal the daughter of Jeremiah of Libnah. ²And he did that which was evil in the eyes of the LORD, according to all that Jehoiakim had done. ³For through the anger of the LORD it came to pass in Jerusalem and Judah, till he had cast them out from his presence, that Zedekiah rebelled against the king of Babylon.

⁴And it came to pass in the ninth year of his reign, in the tenth month, in the tenth day of the month, that Nebuchadrezzar king of Babylon came, he and all his army against Jerusalem, and pitched against it, and built forts against it round about. ⁵So the city was besieged unto the eleventh year of king Zedekiah. ⁶And in the fourth month, in the ninth day of the month, the famine was sore in the city, so that there was no bread for the people of the land. ⁷Then the city was broken up, and all the men of war fled, and went forth out of the city by night by the way of the gate between the two walls which was by the king's garden (now the Chaldeans were by the city round about), and they went by the way of the plain.

⁸But the army of the Chaldeans pursued after the king, and overtook Zedekiah in the plains of Jericho, and all his army was scattered from him. ⁹Then they took the king, and carried him up unto the king of Babylon to Riblah in the land of Hamath: where he gave judgement upon him. ¹⁰And the king of Babylon slew the sons of Zedekiah before his eyes: he slew also all the princes of Judah in Riblah. ¹¹Then he put out the eyes of Zedekiah; and the king of Babylon bound him in chains, and carried him to Babylon, and put him in prison till the day of his death.

¹²Now in the fifth month, in the tenth day of the month (which was

the nineteenth year of Nebuchadrezzar king of Babylon), came Nebuzar-adan, captain of the guard, which served the king of Babylon, into Jerusalem, ¹³and burnt the house of the LORD, and the king's house; and all the houses of Jerusalem, and all the houses of the great men, burnt he with fire. ¹⁴And all the army of the Chaldeans that were with the captain of the guard, broke down all the walls of Jerusalem round about. ¹⁵Then Nebuzar-adan the captain of the guard carried away captive certain of the poor of the people, and the residue of the people that remained in the city, and those that fell away, that fell to the king of Babylon, and the rest of the multitude. ¹⁶But Nebuzar-adan the captain of the guard left certain of the poor of the land for vine-dressers and for husbandmen.

¹⁷Also the pillars of brass that were in the house of the LORD, and the bases, and the brazen sea that was in the house of the LORD, the Chaldeans broke, and carried all the brass of them to Babylon. ¹⁸The cauldrons also, and the shovels, and the snuffers, and the bowls, and the spoons, and all the vessels of brass wherewith they ministered, took they away. ¹⁹And the basins, and the fire-pans, and the bowls, and the cauldrons, and the candlesticks, and the spoons, and the cups; that which was of gold in gold, and that which was of silver in silver, took the captain of the guard away. ²⁰The two pillars, one sea, and twelve brazen bulls that were under the bases, which king Solomon had made in the house of the LORD: the brass of all these vessels was without weight. ²¹And concerning the pillars, the height of one pillar was eighteen cubits; and a fillet of twelve cubits did compass it; and the thickness thereof was four fingers: it was hollow. ²²And a chapiter of brass was upon it; and the height of one chapiter was five cubits, with network and pomegranates upon the chapiters round about, all of brass. The second pillar also and the pomegranates were like unto these. ²³And there were ninety and six pomegranates on a side; and all the pomegranates upon the network were a hundred round about.

²⁴And the captain of the guard took Seraiah the chief priest, and Zephaniah the second priest, and the three keepers of the door: ²⁵he took also out of the city a eunuch, which had the charge of the men of war, and seven men of them that were near the king's person, which were found in the city, and the principal scribe of the host, who mustered the people of the land, and threescore men of the people of the land, that were found in the midst of the city. ²⁶So Nebuzar-adan the captain of the guard took them, and brought them to the king of Babylon to Riblah. ²⁷And the king of Babylon smote them, and put them to death in Riblah in the land of Hamath. Thus Judah was carried away captive out of his own land.

²⁸This is the people whom Nebuchadrezzar carried away captive in the seventh year, three thousand Jews and three and twenty. ²⁹In the eighteenth year of Nebuchadrezzar he carried away captive from Jerusalem eight hundred thirty and two persons. ³⁰In the three and twentieth year of Nebuchadrezzar, Nebuzar-adan the captain of the

guard carried away captive of the Jews seven hundred forty and five persons: all the persons were four thousand and six hundred.

³¹And it came to pass in the seven and thirtieth year of the captivity of Jehoiachin king of Judah, in the twelfth month, in the five and twentieth day of the month, that Evil-merodach king of Babylon in the first year of his reign lifted up the head of Jehoiachin king of Judah, and brought him forth out of prison, ³²and spoke kindly unto him, and set his throne above the throne of the kings that were with him in Babylon, ³³and changed his prison garments: and he did continually eat bread before him all the days of his life. ³⁴And for his diet, there was a continual diet given him of the king of Babylon, every day a portion until the day of his death, all the days of his life.

THE LAMENTATIONS
OF JEREMIAH

1 How doth the city sit solitary that was full of people!
how is she become as a widow!
She that was great among the nations,
and princess among the provinces,
how is she become tributary!

[2] She weepeth sore in the night,
and her tears are on her cheeks:
among all her lovers she hath none to comfort her:
all her friends have dealt treacherously with her,
they are become her enemies.

[3] Judah is gone into captivity because of affliction,
and because of great servitude:
she dwelleth among the heathen,
she findeth no rest:
all her persecutors overtook her between the straits.

[4] The ways of Zion do mourn,
because none come to the solemn feasts:
all her gates are desolate:
her priests sigh:
her virgins are afflicted,
and she is in bitterness.

[5] Her adversaries are the chief,
her enemies prosper:
for the LORD hath afflicted her;
for the multitude of her transgressions,
her children are gone into captivity before the enemy.

[6] And from the daughter of Zion
all her beauty is departed:
her princes are become like harts that find no pasture,
and they are gone without strength before the pursuer.

[7] Jerusalem remembered in the days of her affliction
and of her miseries
all her pleasant things that she had in the days of old,
when her people fell into the hand of the enemy,
and none did help her:
the adversaries saw her,
and did mock at her sabbaths.

[8] Jerusalem hath grievously sinned,
therefore she is removed:
all that honoured her despise her,
because they have seen her nakedness:
yea, she sigheth, and turneth backward.

[9] Her filthiness is in her skirts,

she remembereth not her last end,
therefore she came down wonderfully:
she had no comforter.

'O LORD, behold my affliction:
for the enemy hath magnified himself.'

¹⁰ The adversary hath spread out his hand
upon all her pleasant things:
for she hath seen that the heathen
entered into her sanctuary,
whom thou didst command
that they should not enter into thy congregation.
¹¹ All her people sigh, they seek bread,
they have given their pleasant things
for meat to relieve the soul.

'See, O LORD, and consider:
for I am become vile.
¹² Is it nothing to you,
all ye that pass by?
behold and see if there be any sorrow
like unto my sorrow,
which is done unto me,
wherewith the LORD hath afflicted me
in the day of his fierce anger.
¹³ From above hath he sent fire into my bones,
and it prevaileth against them:
he hath spread a net for my feet,
he hath turned me back:
he hath made me desolate
and faint all the day.
¹⁴ The yoke of my transgressions is bound by his hand:
they are wreathed,
and come up upon my neck:
he hath made my strength to fall,
the Lord hath delivered me into their hands,
from whom I am not able to rise up.
¹⁵ The Lord hath trodden under foot
all my mighty men in the midst of me:
he hath called an assembly against me
to crush my young men.
The Lord hath trodden the virgin,
the daughter of Judah,
as in a wine-press.
¹⁶ For these things I weep,
my eye, my eye runneth down with water,
because the comforter that should relieve my soul is far from me:

my children are desolate,
   because the enemy prevailed.
¹⁷ Zion spreadeth forth her hands,
   and there is none to comfort her:
   the LORD hath commanded concerning Jacob,
   that his adversaries should be round about him:
   Jerusalem is as a menstruous woman among them.

¹⁸ 'The LORD is righteous,
   for I have rebelled against his commandment:
   hear, I pray you, all people,
   and behold my sorrow:
   my virgins and my young men are gone into captivity.
¹⁹ I called for my lovers, but they deceived me:
   my priests and my elders gave up the ghost in the city,
   while they sought their meat to relieve their souls.
²⁰ Behold, O LORD: for I am in distress:
   my bowels are troubled:
   my heart is turned within me,
   for I have grievously rebelled:
   abroad the sword bereaveth,
   at home there is as death.
²¹ They have heard that I sigh:
   there is none to comfort me:
   all my enemies have heard of my trouble,
   they are glad that thou hast done it:
   thou wilt bring the day that thou hast called,
   and they shall be like unto me.
²² Let all their wickedness come before thee:
   and do unto them, as thou hast done unto me
   for all my transgressions:
   for my sighs are many,
   and my heart is faint.'

2 How hath the Lord covered the daughter of Zion
   with a cloud in his anger,
   and cast down from heaven unto the earth
   the beauty of Israel,
   and remembered not his footstool
   in the day of his anger!
² The Lord hath swallowed up
   all the habitations of Jacob,
   and hath not pitied:
   he hath thrown down in his wrath
   the strongholds of the daughter of Judah:
   he hath brought them down to the ground:
   he hath polluted the kingdom
   and the princes thereof.

³ He hath cut off in his fierce anger
all the horn of Israel:
he hath drawn back his right hand
from before the enemy,
and he burnt against Jacob like a flaming fire,
which devoureth round about.
⁴ He hath bent his bow like an enemy:
he stood with his right hand as an adversary,
and slew all that were pleasant to the eye
in the tabernacle of the daughter of Zion:
he poured out his fury like fire.
⁵ The Lord was as an enemy:
he hath swallowed up Israel,
he hath swallowed up all her palaces:
he hath destroyed his strongholds,
and hath increased in the daughter of Judah
mourning and lamentation.
⁶ And he hath violently taken away his tabernacle,
as if it were of a garden:
he hath destroyed his places of the assembly:
the LORD hath caused the solemn feasts
and sabbaths to be forgotten in Zion,
and hath despised in the indignation of his anger
the king and the priest.
⁷ The Lord hath cast off his altar:
he hath abhorred his sanctuary:
he hath given up into the hand of the enemy
the walls of her palaces:
they have made a noise in the house of the LORD,
as in the day of a solemn feast.
⁸ The LORD hath purposed to destroy
the wall of the daughter of Zion:
he hath stretched out a line:
he hath not withdrawn his hand from destroying:
therefore he made the rampart and the wall to lament:
they languished together.
⁹ Her gates are sunk into the ground:
he hath destroyed and broken her bars:
her king and her princes are among the Gentiles:
the law is no more,
her prophets also find no vision from the LORD.
¹⁰ The elders of the daughter of Zion
sit upon the ground and keep silence:
they have cast up dust upon their heads:
they have girded themselves with sackcloth:
the virgins of Jerusalem hang down their heads to the
ground.

¹¹ My eyes do fail with tears:
  my bowels are troubled:
  my liver is poured upon the earth,
  for the destruction of the daughter of my people:
  because the children and the sucklings
  swoon in the streets of the city.
¹² They say to their mothers,
  'Where is corn and wine?'
  when they swooned as the wounded
  in the streets of the city,
  when their soul was poured out
  into their mothers' bosom.

¹³ What thing shall I take to witness for thee?
  what thing shall I liken to thee,
  O daughter of Jerusalem?
  what shall I equal to thee, that I may comfort thee,
  O virgin daughter of Zion?
  for thy breach is great like the sea:
  who can heal thee?
¹⁴ Thy prophets have seen vain and foolish things for thee,
  and they have not discovered thy iniquity,
  to turn away thy captivity:
  but have seen for thee false burdens
  and causes of banishment.
¹⁵ All that pass by clap their hands at thee:
  they hiss and wag their head at the daughter of Jerusalem,
  saying, 'Is this the city that men call the perfection of
      beauty,
  the joy of the whole earth?'
¹⁶ All thy enemies have opened their mouth against thee:
  they hiss and gnash the teeth:
  they say, 'We have swallowed her up:
  certainly this is the day that we looked for:
  we have found, we have seen it'.
¹⁷ The LORD hath done that which he had devised:
  he hath fulfilled his word
  that he had commanded in the days of old:
  he hath thrown down and hath not pitied:
  and he hath caused thy enemy to rejoice over thee,
  he hath set up the horn of thy adversaries.
¹⁸ Their heart cried unto the Lord,
  O wall of the daughter of Zion,
  let tears run down like a river day and night:
  give thyself no rest,
  let not the apple of thy eye cease.
¹⁹ Arise, cry out in the night:
  in the beginning of the watches

pour out thy heart like water
before the face of the Lord:
lift up thy hands toward him
for the life of thy young children,
that faint for hunger in the top of every street.

²⁰ 'Behold, O LORD, and consider
to whom thou hast done this.
Shall the women eat their fruit,
and children of a span long?
shall the priest and the prophet
be slain in the sanctuary of the Lord?
²¹ The young and the old lie on the ground in the streets:
my virgins and my young men are fallen by the sword:
thou hast slain them in the day of thy anger:
thou hast killed, and not pitied.
²² Thou hast called as in a solemn day
my terrors round about,
so that in the day of the LORD's anger
none escaped nor remained:
those that I have swaddled and brought up
hath my enemy consumed.'

3 I am the man that hath seen affliction
by the rod of his wrath.
² He hath led me and brought me into darkness,
but not into light.
³ Surely against me is he turned,
he turneth his hand against me all the day.
⁴ My flesh and my skin hath he made old,
he hath broken my bones.
⁵ He hath built against me,
and compassed me with gall and travail.
⁶ He hath set me in dark places,
as they that be dead of old.
⁷ He hath hedged me about, that I cannot get out:
he hath made my chain heavy.
⁸ Also when I cry and shout,
he shutteth out my prayer.
⁹ He hath enclosed my ways with hewn stone:
he hath made my paths crooked.
¹⁰ He was unto me as a bear lying in wait,
and as a lion in secret places.
¹¹ He hath turned aside my ways, and pulled me in pieces:
he hath made me desolate.
¹² He hath bent his bow,
and set me as a mark for the arrow.
¹³ He hath caused the arrows of his quiver

to enter into my reins.
¹⁴ I was a derision to all my people,
and their song all the day.
¹⁵ He hath filled me with bitterness,
he hath made me drunken with wormwood.
¹⁶ He hath also broken my teeth with gravel stones,
he hath covered me with ashes.
¹⁷ And thou hast removed my soul far off from peace:
I forgot prosperity.
¹⁸ And I said, 'My strength and my hope
is perished from the LORD':
¹⁹ remembering my affliction and my misery,
the wormwood and the gall.
²⁰ My soul hath them still in remembrance,
and is humbled in me.

²¹ This I recall to my mind,
therefore have I hope.
²² It is of the LORD's mercies that we are not consumed,
because his compassions fail not.
²³ They are new every morning:
great is thy faithfulness.
²⁴ 'The LORD is my portion,' saith my soul,
'therefore will I hope in him.'
²⁵ The LORD is good unto them that wait for him,
to the soul that seeketh him.
²⁶ It is good that a man should both hope
and quietly wait for the salvation of the LORD.
²⁷ It is good for a man that he bear the yoke in his youth.
²⁸ He sitteth alone and keepeth silence,
because he hath borne it upon him.
²⁹ He putteth his mouth in the dust,
if so be there may be hope.
³⁰ He giveth his cheek to him that smiteth him,
he is filled full with reproach.
³¹ For the Lord will not cast off for ever:
³² But though he cause grief,
yet will he have compassion
according to the multitude of his mercies.
³³ For he doth not afflict willingly,
nor grieve the children of men.
³⁴ To crush under his feet
all the prisoners of the earth,
³⁵ to turn aside the right of a man
before the face of the most High,
³⁶ to subvert a man in his cause,
the Lord approveth not.

³⁷ Who is he that saith, and it cometh to pass,
when the Lord commandeth it not?
³⁸ Out of the mouth of the most High
proceedeth not evil and good?
³⁹ Wherefore doth a living man complain,
a man for the punishment of his sins?
⁴⁰ Let us search and try our ways,
and turn again to the Lord.
⁴¹ Let us lift up our heart with our hands
unto God in the heavens.
⁴² We have transgressed and have rebelled:
thou hast not pardoned.
⁴³ Thou hast covered with anger, and persecuted us:
thou hast slain, thou hast not pitied.
⁴⁴ Thou hast covered thyself with a cloud,
that our prayer should not pass through.
⁴⁵ Thou hast made us as the offscouring
and refuse in the midst of the people.
⁴⁶ All our enemies have opened their mouths against us.
⁴⁷ Fear and a snare is come upon us,
desolation and destruction.

⁴⁸ My eye runneth down with rivers of water
for the destruction of the daughter of my people.
⁴⁹ My eye trickleth down, and ceaseth not,
without any intermission,
⁵⁰ till the Lord look down,
and behold from heaven.
⁵¹ My eye affecteth my heart
because of all the daughters of my city.
⁵² My enemies chased me sore
like a bird, without cause.
⁵³ They have cut off my life in the dungeon,
and cast a stone upon me.
⁵⁴ Waters flowed over my head,
then I said, 'I am cut off'.

⁵⁵ I called upon thy name, O Lord,
out of the low dungeon.
⁵⁶ Thou hast heard my voice:
hide not thy ear at my breathing, at my cry.
⁵⁷ Thou drewest near in the day that I called upon thee:
thou saidst, 'Fear not'.
⁵⁸ O Lord, thou hast pleaded the causes of my soul,
thou hast redeemed my life.
⁵⁹ O Lord, thou hast seen my wrong:
judge thou my cause.
⁶⁰ Thou hast seen all their vengeance

and all their imaginations against me.
⁶¹ Thou hast heard their reproach, O LORD,
and all their imaginations against me:
⁶² the lips of those that rose up against me,
and their device against me all the day.
⁶³ Behold their sitting down, and their rising up,
I am their music.

⁶⁴ Render unto them a recompense, O LORD,
according to the work of their hands.
⁶⁵ Give them sorrow of heart,
thy curse unto them.
⁶⁶ Persecute and destroy them in anger
from under the heavens of the LORD.

4 How is the gold become dim!
how is the most fine gold changed!
the stones of the sanctuary are poured out
in the top of every street.
² The precious sons of Zion,
comparable to fine gold,
how are they esteemed as earthen pitchers,
the work of the hands of the potter!

³ Even the sea-monsters draw out the breast,
they give suck to their young ones:
the daughter of my people is become cruel,
like the ostriches in the wilderness.
⁴ The tongue of the sucking child
cleaveth to the roof of his mouth for thirst:
the young children ask bread,
and no man breaketh it unto them.

⁵ They that did feed delicately are desolate in the streets:
they that were brought up in scarlet embrace dunghills.
⁶ For the punishment of the iniquity of the daughter of my people
is greater than the punishment of the sin of Sodom,
that was overthrown as in a moment,
and no hands stayed on her.

⁷ Her Nazarites were purer than snow,
they were whiter than milk,
they were more ruddy in body than rubies,
their polishing was of sapphire.
⁸ Their visage is blacker than a coal:
they are not known in the streets:
their skin cleaveth to their bones:
it is withered, it is become like a stick.

⁹ They that be slain with the sword are better
than they that be slain with hunger:
for these pine away,
stricken through for want of the fruits of the field.
¹⁰ The hands of the pitiful women have seethed their own children:
they were their meat in the destruction of the daughter of my
people.

¹¹ The LORD hath accomplished his fury,
he hath poured out his fierce anger,
and hath kindled a fire in Zion,
and it hath devoured the foundations thereof.
¹² The kings of the earth, and all the inhabitants of the
world
would not have believed that the adversary and the enemy
should have entered into the gates of Jerusalem.

¹³ For the sins of her prophets,
and the iniquities of her priests,
that have shed the blood of the just in the midst of her,
¹⁴ they have wandered as blind men in the streets,
they have polluted themselves with blood,
so that men could not touch their garments.

¹⁵ They cried unto them, 'Depart ye, it is unclean,
depart, depart, touch not',
when they fled away and wandered:
they said among the heathen, 'They shall no more sojourn there'.
¹⁶ The anger of the LORD hath divided them,
he will no more regard them:
they respected not the persons of the priests,
they favoured not the elders.

¹⁷ As for us, our eyes as yet failed for our vain help:
in our watching we have watched
for a nation that could not save us.
¹⁸ They hunt our steps that we cannot go in our streets:
our end is near, our days are fulfilled,
for our end is come.

¹⁹ Our persecutors are swifter than the eagles of the heaven:
they pursued us upon the mountains,
they laid wait for us in the wilderness.
²⁰ The breath of our nostrils,
the anointed of the LORD,
was taken in their pits,
of whom we said,
'Under his shadow we shall live among the heathen'.

²¹ Rejoice and be glad, O daughter of Edom,
    that dwellest in the land of Uz,
    the cup also shall pass through unto thee:
    thou shalt be drunken,
    and shalt make thyself naked.
²² The punishment of thy iniquity is accomplished,
    O daughter of Zion,
    he will no more carry thee away into captivity:
    he will visit thy iniquity,
    O daughter of Edom,
    he will discover thy sins.

5 Remember, O Lord, what is come upon us:
    consider and behold our reproach.
² Our inheritance is turned to strangers,
    our houses to aliens.
³ We are orphans and fatherless,
    our mothers are as widows.
⁴ We have drunken our water for money,
    our wood is sold unto us.
⁵ Our necks are under persecution:
    we labour, and have no rest.
⁶ We have given the hand to the Egyptians,
    and to the Assyrians, to be satisfied with bread.
⁷ Our fathers have sinned and are not,
    and we have borne their iniquities.
⁸ Servants have ruled over us:
    there is none that doth deliver us out of their hand.
⁹ We got our bread with the peril of our lives
    because of the sword of the wilderness.
¹⁰ Our skin was black like an oven
    because of the terrible famine.
¹¹ They ravished the women in Zion,
    and the maids in the cities of Judah.
¹² Princes are hanged up by their hand:
    the faces of elders were not honoured.
¹³ They took the young men to grind,
    and the children fell under the wood.
¹⁴ The elders have ceased from the gate,
    the young men from their music.
¹⁵ The joy of our heart is ceased,
    our dance is turned into mourning.
¹⁶ The crown is fallen from our head:
    'Woe unto us, that we have sinned!'
¹⁷ For this our heart is faint,
    for these things our eyes are dim.
¹⁸ Because of the mountain of Zion, which is desolate,
    the foxes walk upon it.

¹⁹ Thou, O LORD, remainest for ever:
thy throne from generation to generation.
²⁰ Wherefore dost thou forget us for ever,
and forsake us so long time?
²¹ Turn thou us unto thee, O LORD, and we shall be turned:
renew our days as of old.
²² But thou hast utterly rejected us:
thou art very wroth against us.

THE BOOK OF THE PROPHET
EZEKIEL

1 Now it came to pass in the thirtieth year, in the fourth month, in the fifth day of the month, as I was among the captives by the river of Chebar, that the heavens were opened, and I saw visions of God. ²In the fifth day of the month, which was the fifth year of king Jehoiachin's captivity, ³the word of the LORD came expressly unto Ezekiel the priest, the son of Buzi, in the land of the Chaldeans by the river Chebar, and the hand of the LORD was there upon him.

⁴And I looked, and behold, a whirlwind came out of the north, a great cloud, and a fire infolding itself, and a brightness was about it, and out of the midst thereof as the colour of amber, out of the midst of the fire. ⁵Also out of the midst thereof came the likeness of four living creatures. And this was their appearance: they had the likeness of a man. ⁶And every one had four faces, and every one had four wings. ⁷And their feet were straight feet, and the sole of their feet was like the sole of a calf's foot, and they sparkled like the colour of burnished brass. ⁸And they had the hands of a man under their wings on their four sides, and they four had their faces and their wings. ⁹Their wings were joined one to another, they turned not when they went: they went every one straight forward. ¹⁰As for the likeness of their faces, they four had the face of a man, and the face of a lion on the right side, and they four had the face of an ox on the left side: they four also had the face of an eagle. ¹¹Thus were their faces: and their wings were stretched upward; two wings of every one were joined one to another, and two covered their bodies. ¹²And they went every one straight forward: whither the spirit was to go, they went: and they turned not when they went. ¹³As for the likeness of the living creatures, their appearance was like burning coals of fire, and like the appearance of lamps: it went up and down among the living creatures, and the fire was bright, and out of the fire went forth lightning. ¹⁴And the living creatures ran and returned as the appearance of a flash of lightning.

¹⁵Now as I beheld the living creatures, behold one wheel upon the earth by the living creatures, with his four faces. ¹⁶The appearance of the wheels and their work was like unto the colour of a beryl: and they four had one likeness, and their appearance and their work was as it were a wheel in the middle of a wheel. ¹⁷When they went, they went upon their four sides: and they returned not when they went. ¹⁸As for their rings, they were so high that they were dreadful; and their rings were full of eyes round about them four. ¹⁹And when the living creatures went, the wheels went by them: and when the living creatures were lifted up from the earth, the wheels were lifted up. ²⁰Whithersoever the spirit was to go, they went, thither was their spirit to go, and the wheels were lifted up over against them: for the spirit of the living creature was in the wheels. ²¹When those went, these went,

and when those stood, these stood; and when those were lifted up from the earth, the wheels were lifted up over against them: for the spirit of the living creature was in the wheels. ²²And the likeness of the firmament upon the heads of the living creature was as the colour of the terrible crystal, stretched forth over their heads above. ²³And under the firmament were their wings straight, the one toward the other: every one had two, which covered on this side, and every one had two, which covered on that side, their bodies. ²⁴And when they went, I heard the noise of their wings, like the noise of great waters, as the voice of the Almighty, the voice of speech, as the noise of a host: when they stood, they let down their wings. ²⁵And there was a voice from the firmament that was over their heads, when they stood, and had let down their wings.

²⁶And above the firmament that was over their heads was the likeness of a throne, as the appearance of a sapphire stone: and upon the likeness of the throne was the likeness as the appearance of a man above upon it. ²⁷And I saw as the colour of amber, as the appearance of fire round about within it: from the appearance of his loins even upward, and from the appearance of his loins even downward, I saw as it were the appearance of fire, and it had brightness round about. ²⁸As the appearance of the bow that is in the cloud in the day of rain, so was the appearance of the brightness round about. This was the appearance of the likeness of the glory of the LORD. And when I saw it, I fell upon my face, and I heard a voice of one that spoke.

2 And he said unto me, 'Son of man, stand upon thy feet, and I will speak unto thee'. ²And the spirit entered into me when he spoke unto me, and set me upon my feet, that I heard him that spoke unto me. ³And he said unto me, 'Son of man, I send thee to the children of Israel, to a rebellious nation that hath rebelled against me: they and their fathers have transgressed against me, even unto this very day. ⁴For they are impudent children and stiff-hearted. I do send thee unto them, and thou shalt say unto them, "Thus saith the Lord GOD". ⁵And they, whether they will hear or whether they will forbear (for they are a rebellious house), yet shall know that there hath been a prophet among them.

⁶'And thou, son of man, be not afraid of them, neither be afraid of their words, though briers and thorns be with thee, and thou dost dwell among scorpions: be not afraid of their words, nor be dismayed at their looks, though they be a rebellious house. ⁷And thou shalt speak my words unto them, whether they will hear or whether they will forbear, for they are most rebellious. ⁸But thou, son of man, hear what I say unto thee; be not thou rebellious like that rebellious house: open thy mouth, and eat that I give thee.'

⁹And when I looked, behold, a hand was sent unto me, and lo, a roll of a book was therein. ¹⁰And he spread it before me, and it was written within and without: and there was written therein lamentations, and mourning, and woe.

3 Moreover he said unto me, 'Son of man, eat that thou findest: eat this roll, and go speak unto the house of Israel'. ²So I opened my

mouth, and he caused me to eat that roll. ³And he said unto me, 'Son of man, cause thy belly to eat, and fill thy bowels with this roll that I give thee'. Then did I eat it, and it was in my mouth as honey for sweetness.

⁴And he said unto me, 'Son of man, go, get thee unto the house of Israel, and speak with my words unto them. ⁵For thou art not sent to a people of a strange speech and of a hard language, but to the house of Israel; ⁶not to many people of a strange speech and of a hard language, whose words thou canst not understand. Surely, had I sent thee to them, they would have hearkened unto thee. ⁷But the house of Israel will not hearken unto thee; for they will not hearken unto me: for all the house of Israel are impudent and hard-hearted. ⁸Behold, I have made thy face strong against their faces, and thy forehead strong against their foreheads. ⁹As an adamant harder than flint have I made thy forehead: fear them not, neither be dismayed at their looks, though they be a rebellious house.'

¹⁰Moreover he said unto me, 'Son of man, all my words that I shall speak unto thee receive in thy heart, and hear with thy ears. ¹¹And go, get thee to them of the captivity, unto thy people, and speak unto them, and tell them, "Thus saith the Lord GOD", whether they will hear, or whether they will forbear.'

¹²Then the spirit took me up, and I heard behind me a voice of a great rushing, saying, 'Blessed be the glory of the LORD from his place'. ¹³I heard also the noise of the wings of the living creatures that touched one another, and the noise of the wheels over against them, and a noise of a great rushing. ¹⁴So the spirit lifted me up, and took me away, and I went in bitterness, in the heat of my spirit; but the hand of the LORD was strong upon me. ¹⁵Then I came to them of the captivity at Tel-abib, that dwelt by the river of Chebar, and I sat where they sat, and remained there astonished among them seven days.

¹⁶And it came to pass at the end of seven days, that the word of the LORD came unto me, saying, ¹⁷'Son of man, I have made thee a watchman unto the house of Israel: therefore hear the word at my mouth, and give them warning from me. ¹⁸When I say unto the wicked, "Thou shalt surely die", and thou givest him not warning, nor speakest to warn the wicked from his wicked way, to save his life; the same wicked man shall die in his iniquity: but his blood will I require at thy hand. ¹⁹Yet if thou warn the wicked, and he turn not from his wickedness, nor from his wicked way, he shall die in his iniquity; but thou hast delivered thy soul. ²⁰Again, when a righteous man doth turn from his righteousness and commit iniquity, and I lay a stumbling-block before him, he shall die: because thou hast not given him warning, he shall die in his sin, and his righteousness which he hath done shall not be remembered: but his blood will I require at thy hand. ²¹Nevertheless if thou warn the righteous man, that the righteous sin not, and he doth not sin, he shall surely live, because he is warned: also thou hast delivered thy soul.'

²²And the hand of the LORD was there upon me, and he said unto me, "Arise, go forth into the plain, and I will there talk with thee". ²³Then I arose, and went forth into the plain: and behold, the glory of the LORD

stood there as the glory which I saw by the river of Chebar, and I fell on my face. [24]Then the spirit entered into me, and set me upon my feet, and spoke with me, and said unto me, 'Go, shut thyself within thy house. [25]But thou, O son of man, behold, they shall put bands upon thee, and shall bind thee with them, and thou shalt not go out among them. [26]And I will make thy tongue cleave to the roof of thy mouth, that thou shalt be dumb, and shalt not be to them a reprover: for they are a rebellious house. [27]But when I speak with thee, I will open thy mouth, and thou shalt say unto them, "Thus saith the Lord GOD", he that heareth, let him hear, and he that forbeareth, let him forbear: for they are a rebellious house.

4 'Thou also, son of man, take thee a tile, and lay it before thee, and portray upon it the city, even Jerusalem, [2]and lay siege against it, and build a fort against it, and cast a mount against it: set the camp also against it, and set battering-rams against it round about. [3]Moreover take thou unto thee an iron pan, and set it for a wall of iron between thee and the city: and set thy face against it, and it shall be besieged, and thou shalt lay siege against it: this shall be a sign to the house of Israel. [4]Lie thou also upon thy left side, and lay the iniquity of the house of Israel upon it: according to the number of the days that thou shalt lie upon it thou shalt bear their iniquity. [5]For I have laid upon thee the years of their iniquity, according to the number of the days, three hundred and ninety days. So shalt thou bear the iniquity of the house of Israel. [6]And when thou hast accomplished them, lie again on thy right side, and thou shalt bear the iniquity of the house of Judah forty days: I have appointed thee each day for a year. [7]Therefore thou shalt set thy face toward the siege of Jerusalem, and thy arm shall be uncovered, and thou shalt prophesy against it. [8]And behold, I will lay bands upon thee, and thou shalt not turn thee from one side to another, till thou hast ended the days of thy siege.

[9]'Take thou also unto thee wheat, and barley, and beans, and lentils, and millet, and fitches, and put them in one vessel, and make thee bread thereof according to the number of the days that thou shalt lie upon thy side; three hundred and ninety days shalt thou eat thereof. [10]And thy meat which thou shalt eat shall be by weight twenty shekels a day: from time to time shalt thou eat it. [11]Thou shalt drink also water by measure, the sixth part of a hin: from time to time shalt thou drink. [12]And thou shalt eat it as barley cakes, and thou shalt bake it with dung that cometh out of man in their sight.' [13]And the LORD said, 'Even thus shall the children of Israel eat their defiled bread among the Gentiles, whither I will drive them'.

[14]Then said I, 'Ah Lord GOD, behold, my soul hath not been polluted: for from my youth up even till now have I not eaten of that which dieth of itself, or is torn in pieces, neither came there abominable flesh into my mouth'. [15]Then he said unto me, 'Lo, I have given thee cow's dung for man's dung, and thou shalt prepare thy bread therewith'.

[16]Moreover he said unto me, 'Son of man, behold, I will break the staff of bread in Jerusalem, and they shall eat bread by weight, and with

care, and they shall drink water by measure, and with astonishment: [17]that they may want bread and water, and be astonished one with another, and consume away for their iniquity.

5 'And thou, son of man, take thee a sharp knife, take thee a barber's razor, and cause it to pass upon thy head and upon thy beard: then take thee balances to weigh, and divide the hair. [2]Thou shalt burn with fire a third part in the midst of the city, when the days of the siege are fulfilled, and thou shalt take a third part, and smite about it with a knife, and a third part thou shalt scatter in the wind, and I will draw out a sword after them. [3]Thou shalt also take thereof a few in number, and bind them in thy skirts. [4]Then take of them again, and cast them into the midst of the fire, and burn them in the fire: for thereof shall a fire come forth into all the house of Israel.'

[5]Thus saith the Lord GOD, 'This is Jerusalem: I have set it in the midst of the nations and countries that are round about her. [6]And she hath changed my judgements into wickedness more than the nations, and my statutes more than the countries that are round about her: for they have refused my judgements and my statutes, they have not walked in them.'

[7]Therefore thus saith the Lord GOD, 'Because ye multiplied more than the nations that are round about you, and have not walked in my statutes, neither have kept my judgements, neither have done according to the judgements of the nations that are round about you': [8]therefore thus saith the Lord GOD, 'Behold, I, even I am against thee, and will execute judgements in the midst of thee in the sight of the nations. [9]And I will do in thee that which I have not done, and whereunto I will not do any more the like, because of all thy abominations. [10]Therefore the fathers shall eat the sons in the midst of thee, and the sons shall eat their fathers; and I will execute judgements in thee, and the whole remnant of thee will I scatter into all the winds. [11]Wherefore, as I live,' saith the Lord GOD, 'surely because thou hast defiled my sanctuary with all thy detestable things, and with all thy abominations, therefore will I also diminish thee, neither shall my eye spare, neither will I have any pity.

[12]'A third part of thee shall die with the pestilence, and with famine shall they be consumed in the midst of thee: and a third part shall fall by the sword round about thee: and I will scatter a third part into all the winds, and I will draw out a sword after them. [13]Thus shall my anger be accomplished, and I will cause my fury to rest upon them, and I will be comforted: and they shall know that I the LORD have spoken it in my zeal, when I have accomplished my fury in them. [14]Moreover I will make thee waste, and a reproach among the nations that are round about thee, in the sight of all that pass by. [15]So it shall be a reproach and a taunt, an instruction and an astonishment unto the nations that are round about thee, when I shall execute judgements in thee in anger and in fury and in furious rebukes: I the LORD have spoken it. [16]When I shall send upon them the evil arrows of famine, which shall be for their destruction, and which I will send to destroy you: and

I will increase the famine upon you, and will break your staff of bread. [17]So will I send upon you famine and evil beasts, and they shall bereave thee, and pestilence and blood shall pass through thee, and I will bring the sword upon thee: I the LORD have spoken it.'

6 And the word of the LORD came unto me, saying, [2]'Son of man, set thy face towards the mountains of Israel, and prophesy against them, [3]and say, "Ye mountains of Israel, hear the word of the Lord GOD; thus saith the Lord GOD to the mountains and to the hills, to the rivers and to the valleys, 'Behold, I, even I will bring a sword upon you, and I will destroy your high places. [4]And your altars shall be desolate, and your images shall be broken: and I will cast down your slain men before your idols. [5]And I will lay the dead carcases of the children of Israel before their idols, and I will scatter your bones round about your altars. [6]In all your dwelling-places the cities shall be laid waste, and the high places shall be desolate, that your altars may be laid waste and made desolate, and your idols may be broken and cease, and your images may be cut down, and your works may be abolished. [7]And the slain shall fall in the midst of you, and ye shall know that I am the LORD.

[8]"'Yet will I leave a remnant, that ye may have some that shall escape the sword among the nations, when ye shall be scattered through the countries. [9]And they that escape of you shall remember me among the nations whither they shall be carried captives, because I am broken with their whorish heart which hath departed from me, and with their eyes which go a-whoring after their idols: and they shall loathe themselves for the evils which they have committed in all their abominations. [10]And they shall know that I am the LORD, and that I have not said in vain that I would do this evil unto them.'

[11]"'Thus saith the Lord GOD, 'Smite with thy hand, and stamp with thy foot, and say, "Alas for all the evil abominations of the house of Israel": for they shall fall by the sword, by the famine, and by the pestilence. [12]He that is far off shall die of the pestilence, and he that is near shall fall by the sword, and he that remaineth and is besieged shall die by the famine: thus will I accomplish my fury upon them. [13]Then shall ye know that I am the LORD, when their slain men shall be among their idols round about their altars, upon every high hill in all the tops of the mountains, and under every green tree, and under every thick oak, the place where they did offer sweet savour to all their idols. [14]So will I stretch out my hand upon them, and make the land desolate, yea, more desolate than the wilderness towards Diblath, in all their habitations: and they shall know that I am the LORD.'"'

7 Moreover the word of the LORD came unto me, saying, [2]'Also, thou son of man, thus saith the Lord GOD unto the land of Israel, "An end, the end is come upon the four corners of the land. [3]Now is the end come upon thee, and I will send my anger upon thee, and will judge thee according to thy ways, and will recompense upon thee all thy abominations. [4]And my eye shall not spare thee, neither will I have pity: but I will recompense thy ways upon thee, and thy abominations shall be in the midst of thee, and ye shall know that I am the LORD." [5]Thus

saith the Lord GOD, "An evil, an only evil, behold, is come. ⁶An end is come, the end is come: it watcheth for thee, behold, it is come. ⁷The morning is come unto thee, O thou that dwellest in the land: the time is come, the day of trouble is near, and not the sounding again of the mountains. ⁸Now will I shortly pour out my fury upon thee, and accomplish my anger upon thee: and I will judge thee according to thy ways, and will recompense thee for all thy abominations. ⁹And my eye shall not spare, neither will I have pity: I will recompense thee according to thy ways and thy abominations that are in the midst of thee, and ye shall know that I am the LORD that smiteth. ¹⁰Behold the day, behold, it is come: the morning is gone forth, the rod hath blossomed, pride hath budded. ¹¹Violence is risen up into a rod of wickedness: none of them shall remain, nor of their multitude, nor of any of theirs, neither shall there be wailing for them. ¹²The time is come, the day draweth near: let not the buyer rejoice, nor the seller mourn: for wrath is upon all the multitude thereof. ¹³For the seller shall not return to that which is sold, although they were yet alive: for the vision is touching the whole multitude thereof, which shall not return; neither shall any strengthen himself in the iniquity of his life. ¹⁴They have blown the trumpet, even to make all ready, but none goeth to the battle: for my wrath is upon all the multitude thereof. ¹⁵The sword is without, and the pestilence and the famine within: he that is in the field shall die with the sword, and he that is in the city, famine and pestilence shall devour him.

¹⁶'"But they that escape of them shall escape, and shall be on the mountains like doves of the valleys, all of them mourning, every one for his iniquity. ¹⁷All hands shall be feeble, and all knees shall be weak as water. ¹⁸They shall also gird themselves with sackcloth, and horror shall cover them, and shame shall be upon all faces, and baldness upon all their heads. ¹⁹They shall cast their silver in the streets, and their gold shall be removed: their silver and their gold shall not be able to deliver them in the day of the wrath of the LORD: they shall not satisfy their souls, neither fill their bowels: because it is the stumbling-block of their iniquity.

²⁰'"As for the beauty of his ornament, he set it in majesty: but they made the images of their abominations and of their detestable things therein: therefore have I set it far from them. ²¹And I will give it into the hands of the strangers for a prey, and to the wicked of the earth for a spoil, and they shall pollute it. ²²My face will I turn also from them, and they shall pollute my secret place: for the robbers shall enter into it, and defile it.

²³'"Make a chain: for the land is full of bloody crimes, and the city is full of violence. ²⁴Wherefore I will bring the worst of the heathen, and they shall possess their houses: I will also make the pomp of the strong to cease, and their holy places shall be defiled. ²⁵Destruction cometh, and they shall seek peace, and there shall be none. ²⁶Mischief shall come upon mischief, and rumour shall be upon rumour; then shall they seek a vision of the prophet: but the law shall perish from the priest, and counsel from the ancients. ²⁷The king shall mourn, and the prince shall be clothed with desolation, and the hands of the people of

the land shall be troubled: I will do unto them after their way, and according to their deserts will I judge them, and they shall know that I am the LORD."'

8 And it came to pass in the sixth year, in the sixth month, in the fifth day of the month, as I sat in my house, and the elders of Judah sat before me, that the hand of the Lord GOD fell there upon me. ²Then I beheld, and lo, a likeness as the appearance of fire: from the appearance of his loins even downward, fire: and from his loins even upward, as the appearance of brightness, as the colour of amber. ³And he put forth the form of a hand, and took me by a lock of my head; and the spirit lifted me up between the earth and the heaven, and brought me in the visions of God to Jerusalem, to the door of the inner gate that looketh toward the north, where was the seat of the image of jealousy, which provoketh to jealousy. ⁴And behold, the glory of the God of Israel was there, according to the vision that I saw in the plain.

⁵Then said he unto me, 'Son of man, lift up thy eyes now the way towards the north'. So I lifted up my eyes the way toward the north, and behold, northward at the gate of the altar this image of jealousy in the entry. ⁶He said furthermore unto me, 'Son of man, seest thou what they do? even the great abominations that the house of Israel committeth here, that I should go far off from my sanctuary? but turn thee yet again, and thou shalt see greater abominations'.

⁷And he brought me to the door of the court; and when I looked, behold a hole in the wall. ⁸Then said he unto me, 'Son of man, dig now in the wall': and when I had dug in the wall, behold a door. ⁹And he said unto me, 'Go in, and behold the wicked abominations that they do here'. ¹⁰So I went in and saw; and behold every form of creeping things, and abominable beasts, and all the idols of the house of Israel portrayed upon the wall round about. ¹¹And there stood before them seventy men of the ancients of the house of Israel, and in the midst of them stood Jaazaniah the son of Shaphan, with every man his censer in his hand; and a thick cloud of incense went up. ¹²Then said he unto me, 'Son of man, hast thou seen what the ancients of the house of Israel do in the dark, every man in the chambers of his imagery? for they say, "The LORD seeth us not, the LORD hath forsaken the earth"'.

¹³He said also unto me, 'Turn thee yet again, and thou shalt see greater abominations that they do'. ¹⁴Then he brought me to the door of the gate of the LORD's house which was towards the north; and behold, there sat women weeping for Tammuz.

¹⁵Then said he unto me, 'Hast thou seen this, O son of man? Turn thee yet again, and thou shalt see greater abominations than these.' ¹⁶And he brought me into the inner court of the LORD's house, and behold, at the door of the temple of the LORD, between the porch and the altar, were about five and twenty men, with their backs toward the temple of the LORD, and their faces towards the east, and they worshipped the sun towards the east.

¹⁷Then he said unto me, 'Hast thou seen this, O son of man? Is it a light thing to the house of Judah that they commit the abominations

which they commit here? for they have filled the land with violence, and have returned to provoke me to anger: and lo, they put the branch to their nose. ¹⁸Therefore will I also deal in fury: my eye shall not spare, neither will I have pity: and though they cry in my ears with a loud voice, yet will I not hear them.'

9 He cried also in my ears with a loud voice, saying, 'Cause them that have charge over the city to draw near, even every man with his destroying weapon in his hand. ²And behold, six men came from the way of the higher gate, which lieth toward the north, and every man a slaughter weapon in his hand: and one man among them was clothed with linen, with a writer's inkhorn by his side: and they went in, and stood beside the brazen altar. ³And the glory of the God of Israel was gone up from the cherub whereupon he was, to the threshold of the house. And he called to the man clothed with linen, which had the writer's inkhorn by his side. ⁴And the LORD said unto him, 'Go through the midst of the city, through the midst of Jerusalem, and set a mark upon the foreheads of the men that sigh and that cry for all the abominations that be done in the midst thereof'.

⁵And to the others he said in my hearing, 'Go ye after him through the city, and smite: let not your eye spare, neither have ye pity. ⁶Slay utterly old and young, both maids, and little children, and women: but come not near any man upon whom is the mark; and begin at my sanctuary.' Then they began at the ancient men which were before the house. ⁷And he said unto them, 'Defile the house, and fill the courts with the slain: go ye forth'. And they went forth, and slew in the city.

⁸And it came to pass, while they were slaying them, and I was left, that I fell upon my face, and cried, and said, 'Ah Lord GOD, wilt thou destroy all the residue of Israel in thy pouring out of thy fury upon Jerusalem?' ⁹Then said he unto me, 'The iniquity of the house of Israel and Judah is exceeding great, and the land is full of blood, and the city full of perverseness: for they say, "The LORD hath forsaken the earth, and the LORD seeth not". ¹⁰And as for me also, my eye shall not spare, neither will I have pity, but I will recompense their way upon their head.' ¹¹And behold, the man clothed with linen, which had the inkhorn by his side, reported the matter, saying, 'I have done as thou hast commanded me'.

10 Then I looked, and behold, in the firmament that was above the head of the cherubims there appeared over them as it were a sapphire stone, as the appearance of the likeness of a throne. ²And he spoke unto the man clothed with linen, and said, 'Go in between the wheels, even under the cherub, and fill thy hand with coals of fire from between the cherubims, and scatter them over the city'. And he went in in my sight. ³Now the cherubims stood on the right side of the house, when the man went in, and the cloud filled the inner court. ⁴Then the glory of the LORD went up from the cherub, and stood over the threshold of the house, and the house was filled with the cloud, and the court was full of the brightness of the LORD's glory. ⁵And the sound of the cherubims' wings was heard even to the outer court, as the voice of the Almighty God when he speaketh. ⁶And it came to pass that when he had commanded the man clothed with linen, saying, 'Take fire from between the wheels, from between the cherubims'; then he went in, and stood beside the wheels. ⁷And one cherub stretched forth his hand from between the cherubims unto the fire that was between the cherubims, and took thereof, and put it into the hands of him that was clothed with linen, who took it, and went out.

⁸And there appeared in the cherubims the form of a man's hand under their wings.

⁹And when I looked, behold the four wheels by the cherubims, one wheel by one cherub, and another wheel by another cherub: and the appearance of the wheels was as the colour of a beryl stone. ¹⁰And as for their appearances, they four had one likeness, as if a wheel had been in the midst of a wheel. ¹¹When they went, they went upon their four sides; they turned not as they went, but to the place whither the head looked they followed it; they turned not as they went. ¹²And their whole body, and their backs, and their hands, and their wings, and the wheels, were full of eyes round about, even the wheels that they four had. ¹³As for the wheels, it was cried unto them in my hearing, 'O wheel'. ¹⁴And every one had four faces: the first face was the face of a cherub, and the second face was the face of a man, and the third the face of a lion, and the fourth the face of an eagle. ¹⁵And the cherubims were lifted up. This is the living creature that I saw by the river of Chebar. ¹⁶And when the cherubims went, the wheels went by them: and when the cherubims lifted up their wings to mount up from the earth, the same wheels also turned not from beside them. ¹⁷When they stood, these stood; and when they were lifted up, these lifted up themselves also: for the spirit of the living creature was in them.

¹⁸Then the glory of the LORD departed from off the threshold of the house, and stood over the cherubims. ¹⁹And the cherubims lifted up their wings, and mounted up from the earth in my sight: when they went out, the wheels also were beside them, and every one stood at the door of the east gate of the LORD's house, and the glory of the God of Israel was over them above.

²⁰This is the living creature that I saw under the God of Israel by the river of Chebar, and I knew that they were the cherubims. ²¹Every one had four faces apiece, and every one four wings, and the likeness of the hands of a man was under their wings. ²²And the likeness of their faces was the same faces which I saw by the river of Chebar, their appearances and themselves: they went every one straight forward.

11 Moreover the spirit lifted me up, and brought me unto the east gate of the LORD's house, which looketh eastward: and behold at the door of the gate five and twenty men; among whom I saw Jaazaniah the son of Azur, and Pelatiah the son of Benaiah, princes of the people. ²Then said he unto me, 'Son of man, these are the men that devise mischief, and give wicked counsel in this city: ³ which say, "It is not near, let us build houses: this city is the cauldron, and we be the flesh". ⁴Therefore prophesy against them, prophesy, O son of man.'

⁵And the Spirit of the LORD fell upon me, and said unto me, 'Speak,

"Thus saith the Lord, 'Thus have ye said, O house of Israel: for I know the things that come into your mind, every one of them. ⁶Ye have multiplied your slain in this city, and ye have filled the streets thereof with the slain.'" ⁷Therefore thus saith the Lord God, "Your slain whom ye have laid in the midst of it, they are the flesh, and this city is the cauldron: but I will bring you forth out of the midst of it. ⁸Ye have feared the sword, and I will bring a sword upon you," saith the Lord God. ⁹"And I will bring you out of the midst thereof, and deliver you into the hands of strangers, and will execute judgements among you. ¹⁰Ye shall fall by the sword; I will judge you in the border of Israel; and ye shall know that I am the Lord. ¹¹This city shall not be your cauldron, neither shall ye be the flesh in the midst thereof, but I will judge you in the border of Israel. ¹²And ye shall know that I am the Lord: for ye have not walked in my statutes, neither executed my judgements, but have done after the manners of the heathen that are round about you."'

¹³And it came to pass, when I prophesied, that Pelatiah the son of Benaiah died. Then fell I down upon my face, and cried with a loud voice, and said, 'Ah Lord God, wilt thou make a full end of the remnant of Israel?'

¹⁴Again the word of the Lord came unto me, saying, ¹⁵'Son of man, thy brethren, even thy brethren, the men of thy kindred, and all the house of Israel wholly, are they unto whom the inhabitants of Jerusalem have said, "Get ye far from the Lord: unto us is this land given in possession". ¹⁶Therefore say, "Thus saith the Lord God, 'Although I have cast them far off among the heathen, and although I have scattered them among the countries, yet will I be to them as a little sanctuary in the countries where they shall come'". ¹⁷Therefore say, "Thus saith the Lord God, 'I will even gather you from the people, and assemble you out of the countries where ye have been scattered, and I will give you the land of Israel'". ¹⁸And they shall come thither, and they shall take away all the detestable things thereof and all the abominations thereof from thence. ¹⁹And I will give them one heart, and I will put a new spirit within you: and I will take the stony heart out of their flesh, and will give them a heart of flesh, ²⁰that they may walk in my statutes, and keep my ordinances, and do them: and they shall be my people, and I will be their God. ²¹But as for them whose heart walketh after the heart of their detestable things and their abominations, I will recompense their way upon their own heads,' saith the Lord God.

²²Then did the cherubims lift up their wings, and the wheels beside them, and the glory of the God of Israel was over them above. ²³And the glory of the Lord went up from the midst of the city, and stood upon the mountain which is on the east side of the city.

²⁴Afterwards the spirit took me up, and brought me in a vision by the Spirit of God into Chaldea to them of the captivity. So the vision that I had seen went up from me. ²⁵Then I spoke unto them of the captivity all the things that the Lord had shown me.

12 The word of the Lord also came unto me, saying, ²'Son of man, thou dwellest in the midst of a rebellious house, which have eyes to see, and see not: they have ears to hear, and hear not: for they are a rebellious house. ³Therefore, thou son of man, prepare thee stuff for removing, and remove by day in their sight; and thou shalt remove from thy place to another place in their sight: it may be they will consider, though they be a rebellious house. ⁴Then shalt thou bring forth thy stuff by day in their sight, as stuff for removing: and thou shalt go forth at even in their sight, as they that go forth into captivity. ⁵Dig thou through the wall in their sight, and carry out thereby. ⁶In their sight shalt thou bear it upon thy shoulders, and carry it forth in the twilight: thou shalt cover thy face, that thou see not the ground: for I have set thee for a sign unto the house of Israel.'

⁷And I did so as I was commanded: I brought forth my stuff by day, as stuff for captivity, and in the even I dug through the wall with my hand; I brought it forth in the twilight, and I bore it upon my shoulder in their sight.

⁸And in the morning came the word of the LORD unto me, saying, ⁹'Son of man, hath not the house of Israel, the rebellious house, said unto thee, "What doest thou?" ¹⁰Say thou unto them, "Thus saith the Lord GOD, 'This burden concerneth the prince in Jerusalem, and all the house of Israel that are among them'". ¹¹Say, "I am your sign: like as I have done, so shall it be done unto them: they shall remove and go into captivity". ¹²And the prince that is among them shall bear upon his shoulder in the twilight, and shall go forth: they shall dig through the wall to carry out thereby: he shall cover his face, that he see not the ground with his eyes. ¹³My net also will I spread upon him, and he shall be taken in my snare, and I will bring him to Babylon to the land of the Chaldeans; yet shall he not see it, though he shall die there. ¹⁴And I will scatter toward every wind all that are about him to help him, and all his bands; and I will draw out the sword after them. ¹⁵And they shall know that I am the LORD, when I shall scatter them among the nations, and disperse them in the countries. ¹⁶But I will leave a few men of them from the sword, from the famine, and from the pestilence, that they may declare all their abominations among the heathen whither they come; and they shall know that I am the LORD.'

¹⁷Moreover the word of the LORD came to me, saying, ¹⁸'Son of man, eat thy bread with quaking, and drink thy water with trembling and with carefulness; ¹⁹and say unto the people of the land, "Thus saith the Lord GOD of the inhabitants of Jerusalem, and of the land of Israel, 'They shall eat their bread with carefulness, and drink their water with astonishment, that her land may be desolate from all that is therein, because of the violence of them that dwell therein. ²⁰And the cities that are inhabited shall be laid waste, and the land shall be desolate; and ye shall know that I am the LORD.'"'

²¹And the word of the LORD came unto me, saying, ²²'Son of man, what is that proverb that ye have in the land of Israel, saying, "The days are prolonged, and every vision faileth"? ²³Tell them therefore, "Thus saith the Lord GOD, 'I will make this proverb to cease, and they shall no more use it as a proverb in Israel'": but say unto them, "'The days are at

hand, and the effect of every vision. ²⁴For there shall be no more any vain vision nor flattering divination within the house of Israel. ²⁵For I am the LORD: I will speak, and the word that I shall speak shall come to pass: it shall be no more prolonged: for in your days, O rebellious house, will I say the word, and will perform it,' saith the Lord GOD."'

²⁶Again the word of the LORD came to me, saying, ²⁷'Son of man, behold, they of the house of Israel say, "The vision that he seeth is for many days to come, and he prophesieth of the times that are far off". ²⁸Therefore say unto them, "Thus saith the Lord GOD, 'There shall none of my words be prolonged any more, but the word which I have spoken shall be done,' saith the Lord GOD".'

13 And the word of the LORD came unto me, saying, ²'Son of man, prophesy against the prophets of Israel that prophesy, and say thou unto them that prophesy out of their own hearts, "Hear ye the word of the LORD. ³Thus saith the Lord GOD, 'Woe unto the foolish prophets, that follow their own spirit, and have seen nothing. ⁴O Israel, thy prophets are like the foxes in the deserts. ⁵Ye have not gone up into the gaps, neither made up the hedge for the house of Israel to stand in the battle in the day of the LORD. ⁶They have seen vanity and lying divination, saying, "The LORD saith", and the LORD hath not sent them: and they have made others to hope that they would confirm the word. ⁷Have ye not seen a vain vision, and have ye not spoken a lying divination, whereas ye say, "The LORD saith it", albeit I have not spoken?' ⁸Therefore thus saith the Lord GOD, 'Because ye have spoken vanity, and seen lies, therefore behold, I am against you,' saith the Lord GOD. ⁹'And my hand shall be upon the prophets that see vanity, and that divine lies: they shall not be in the assembly of my people, neither shall they be written in the writing of the house of Israel, neither shall they enter into the land of Israel; and ye shall know that I am the Lord GOD.

¹⁰'''Because, even because they have seduced my people, saying, "Peace", and there was no peace: and one built up a wall, and lo, others daubed it with untempered mortar: ¹¹say unto them which daub it with untempered mortar, that it shall fall: there shall be an overflowing shower; and ye, O great hailstones, shall fall, and a stormy wind shall rend it. ¹²Lo, when the wall is fallen, shall it not be said unto you, "Where is the daubing wherewith ye have daubed it?"' ¹³Therefore thus saith the Lord GOD, 'I will even rend it with a stormy wind in my fury: and there shall be an overflowing shower in my anger, and great hailstones in my fury to consume it. ¹⁴So will I break down the wall that ye have daubed with untempered mortar, and bring it down to the ground, so that the foundation thereof shall be discovered, and it shall fall, and ye shall be consumed in the midst thereof: and ye shall know that I am the LORD. ¹⁵Thus will I accomplish my wrath upon the wall, and upon them that have daubed it with untempered mortar, and will say unto you, "The wall is no more, neither they that daubed it": ¹⁶to wit, the prophets of Israel which prophesy concerning Jerusalem, and which see visions of peace for her, and there is no peace,' saith the Lord GOD."

¹⁷'Likewise, thou son of man, set thy face against the daughters of thy people, which prophesy out of their own heart; and prophesy thou against them, ¹⁸and say, "Thus saith the Lord GOD, 'Woe to the women that sew pillows to all arm-holes, and make kerchiefs upon the head of every stature to hunt souls: will ye hunt the souls of my people, and will ye save the souls alive that come unto you? ¹⁹And will ye pollute me among my people for handfuls of barley and for pieces of bread, to slay the souls that should not die, and to save the souls alive that should not live, by your lying to my people that hear your lies?' ²⁰Wherefore thus saith the Lord GOD, 'Behold, I am against your pillows, wherewith ye there hunt the souls to make them fly, and I will tear them from your arms, and will let the souls go, even the souls that ye hunt to make them fly. ²¹Your kerchiefs also will I tear, and deliver my people out of your hand, and they shall be no more in your hand to be hunted; and ye shall know that I am the LORD. ²²Because with lies ye have made the heart of the righteous sad whom I have not made sad; and strengthened the hands of the wicked, that he should not return from his wicked way, by promising him life: ²³therefore ye shall see no more vanity, nor divine divinations, for I will deliver my people out of your hand: and ye shall know that I am the LORD.'"'

14 Then came certain of the elders of Israel unto me, and sat before me. ²And the word of the LORD came unto me, saying, ³'Son of man, these men have set up their idols in their heart, and put the stumbling-block of their iniquity before their face: should I be inquired of at all by them? ⁴Therefore speak unto them, and say unto them, "Thus saith the Lord GOD, 'Every man of the house of Israel that setteth up his idols in his heart, and putteth the stumbling-block of his iniquity before his face, and cometh to the prophet, I the LORD will answer him that cometh according to the multitude of his idols, ⁵that I may take the house of Israel in their own heart, because they are all estranged from me through their idols.'"

⁶'Therefore say unto the house of Israel, "Thus saith the Lord GOD, 'Repent, and turn yourselves from your idols, and turn away your faces from all your abominations. ⁷For every one of the house of Israel, or of the stranger that sojourneth in Israel, which separateth himself from me, and setteth up his idols in his heart, and putteth the stumbling-block of his iniquity before his face, and cometh to a prophet to inquire of him concerning me, I the LORD will answer him by myself. ⁸And I will set my face against that man, and will make him a sign and a proverb, and I will cut him off from the midst of my people; and ye shall know that I am the LORD. ⁹And if the prophet be deceived when he hath spoken a thing, I the LORD have deceived that prophet, and I will stretch out my hand upon him, and will destroy him from the midst of my people Israel. ¹⁰And they shall bear the punishment of their iniquity: the punishment of the prophet shall be even as the punishment of him that seeketh unto him: ¹¹that the house of Israel may go no more astray from me, neither be polluted any more with all their transgressions; but that they may be my people, and I may be their God,' saith the Lord GOD."'

¹²The word of the LORD came again to me, saying, ¹³'Son of man, when the land sinneth against me by trespassing grievously, then will I stretch out my hand upon it, and will break the staff of the bread thereof, and will send famine upon it, and will cut off man and beast from it. ¹⁴Though these three men, Noah, Daniel, and Job, were in it, they should deliver but their own souls by their righteousness,' saith the Lord GOD.

¹⁵'If I cause noisome beasts to pass through the land, and they spoil it, so that it be desolate, that no man may pass through because of the beasts: ¹⁶though these three men were in it, as I live,' saith the Lord GOD, 'they shall deliver neither sons nor daughters: they only shall be delivered, but the land shall be desolate.

¹⁷'Or if I bring a sword upon that land, and say, "Sword, go through the land", so that I cut off man and beast from it: ¹⁸though these three men were in it, as I live,' saith the Lord GOD, 'they shall deliver neither sons nor daughters, but they only shall be delivered themselves.

¹⁹'Or if I send a pestilence into that land, and pour out my fury upon it in blood, to cut off from it man and beast: ²⁰though Noah, Daniel, and Job were in it, as I live,' saith the Lord GOD, 'they shall deliver neither son nor daughter: they shall but deliver their own souls by their righteousness. ²¹For thus saith the Lord GOD, 'How much more when I send my four sore judgements upon Jerusalem, the sword, and the famine, and the noisome beast, and the pestilence, to cut off from it man and beast?

²²'Yet behold, therein shall be left a remnant that shall be brought forth, both sons and daughters: behold, they shall come forth unto you, and ye shall see their way and their doings: and ye shall be comforted concerning the evil that I have brought upon Jerusalem, even concerning all that I have brought upon it. ²³And they shall comfort you, when ye see their ways and their doings: and ye shall know that I have not done without cause all that I have done in it,' saith the Lord GOD.

15 And the word of the LORD came unto me, saying, ²'Son of man, what is the vine tree more than any tree, or than a branch which is among the trees of the forest? ³Shall wood be taken thereof to do any work? or will men take a pin of it to hang any vessel thereon? ⁴Behold, it is cast into the fire for fuel: the fire devoureth both the ends of it, and the midst of it is burnt. Is it meet for any work? ⁵Behold, when it was whole, it was meet for no work: how much less shall it be meet yet for any work, when the fire hath devoured it, and it is burnt?'

⁶Therefore thus saith the Lord GOD, 'As the vine tree among the trees of the forest, which I have given to the fire for fuel, so will I give the inhabitants of Jerusalem. ⁷And I will set my face against them, they shall go out from one fire, and another fire shall devour them; and ye shall know that I am the LORD, when I set my face against them. ⁸And I will make the land desolate, because they have committed a trespass,' saith the Lord GOD.

16 Again the word of the LORD came unto me, saying, ²'Son of man, cause Jerusalem to know her abominations, ³and say, "Thus

saith the Lord GOD unto Jerusalem, 'Thy birth and thy nativity is of the land of Canaan; thy father was an Amorite, and thy mother a Hittite. ⁴And as for thy nativity, in the day thou wast born thy navel was not cut, neither wast thou washed in water to supple thee: thou wast not salted at all, nor swaddled at all. ⁵No eye pitied thee to do any of these unto thee, to have compassion upon thee, but thou wast cast out in the open field, to the loathing of thy person, in the day that thou wast born.

⁶"" 'And when I passed by thee, and saw thee polluted in thy own blood, I said unto thee when thou wast in thy blood, "Live": yea, I said unto thee when thou wast in thy blood, "Live". ⁷I have caused thee to multiply as the bud of the field, and thou hast increased and waxed great, and thou art come to excellent ornaments: thy breasts are fashioned, and thy hair is grown, whereas thou wast naked and bare. ⁸Now when I passed by thee, and looked upon thee, behold, thy time was the time of love, and I spread my skirt over thee, and covered thy nakedness: yea, I swore unto thee, and entered into a covenant with thee,' saith the Lord GOD, 'and thou becamest mine. ⁹Then washed I thee with water: yea, I thoroughly washed away thy blood from thee, and I anointed thee with oil. ¹⁰I clothed thee also with broidered work, and shod thee with badgers' skin, and I girded thee about with fine linen, and I covered thee with silk. ¹¹I decked thee also with ornaments, and I put bracelets upon thy hands, and a chain on thy neck. ¹²And I put a jewel on thy forehead, and earrings in thy ears, and a beautiful crown upon thy head. ¹³Thus wast thou decked with gold and silver; and thy raiment was of fine linen, and silk, and broidered work; thou didst eat fine flour, and honey, and oil: and thou wast exceeding beautiful, and thou didst prosper into a kingdom. ¹⁴And thy renown went forth among the heathen for thy beauty: for it was perfect through my comeliness, which I had put upon thee,' saith the Lord GOD.

¹⁵"" 'But thou didst trust in thy own beauty, and playedst the harlot because of thy renown, and pouredst out thy fornications on every one that passed by; his it was. ¹⁶And of thy garments thou didst take, and deckedst thy high places with divers colours, and playedst the harlot thereupon: the like things shall not come, neither shall it be so. ¹⁷Thou hast also taken thy fair jewels of my gold and of my silver, which I had given thee, and madest to thyself images of men, and didst commit whoredom with them, ¹⁸and tookest thy broidered garments, and coveredst them: and thou hast set my oil and my incense before them. ¹⁹My meat also which I gave thee, fine flour, and oil, and honey wherewith I fed thee, thou hast even set it before them for a sweet savour: and thus it was,' saith the Lord GOD.

²⁰"" 'Moreover thou hast taken thy sons and thy daughters, whom thou hast borne unto me, and these hast thou sacrificed unto them to be devoured: is this of thy whoredoms a small matter, ²¹that thou hast slain my children, and delivered them to cause them to pass through the fire for them? ²²And in all thy abominations and thy whoredoms thou hast not remembered the days of thy youth, when thou wast naked and bare, and wast polluted in thy blood.

²³'"'And it came to pass after all thy wickedness (woe, woe unto thee,' saith the Lord GOD), ²⁴'that thou hast also built unto thee an eminent place, and hast made thee a high place in every street. ²⁵Thou hast built thy high place at every head of the way, and hast made thy beauty to be abhorred, and hast opened thy feet to every one that passed by, and multiplied thy whoredoms. ²⁶Thou hast also committed fornication with the Egyptians thy neighbours, great of flesh, and hast increased thy whoredoms, to provoke me to anger. ²⁷Behold therefore, I have stretched out my hand over thee, and have diminished thy ordinary food, and delivered thee unto the will of them that hate thee, the daughters of the Philistines, which are ashamed of thy lewd way. ²⁸Thou hast played the whore also with the Assyrians, because thou wast insatiable: yea, thou hast played the harlot with them, and yet couldst not be satisfied. ²⁹Thou hast moreover multiplied thy fornication in the land of Canaan unto Chaldea, and yet thou wast not satisfied herewith. ³⁰How weak is thy heart,' saith the Lord GOD, 'seeing thou doest all these things, the work of an imperious whorish woman! ³¹in that thou buildest thy eminent place in the head of every way, and makest thy high place in every street, and hast not been as a harlot, in that thou scornest hire: ³²but as a wife that committeth adultery, which taketh strangers instead of her husband. ³³They give gifts to all whores, but thou givest thy gifts to all thy lovers, and hirest them, that they may come unto thee on every side for thy whoredom. ³⁴And the contrary is in thee from other women in thy whoredoms, whereas none followeth thee to commit whoredoms: and in that thou givest a reward, and no reward is given unto thee, therefore thou art contrary.

³⁵'"'Wherefore, O harlot, hear the word of the LORD.' ³⁶Thus saith the Lord GOD, 'Because thy filthiness was poured out, and thy nakedness discovered through thy whoredoms with thy lovers, and with all the idols of thy abominations, and by the blood of thy children, which thou didst give unto them, ³⁷behold therefore, I will gather all thy lovers, with whom thou hast taken pleasure, and all them that thou hast loved, with all them that thou hast hated: I will even gather them round about against thee, and will discover thy nakedness unto them, that they may see all thy nakedness. ³⁸And I will judge thee, as women that break wedlock and shed blood are judged, and I will give thee blood in fury and jealousy. ³⁹And I will also give thee into their hand, and they shall throw down thy eminent place, and shall break down thy high places: they shall strip thee also of thy clothes, and shall take thy fair jewels, and leave thee naked and bare. ⁴⁰They shall also bring up a company against thee, and they shall stone thee with stones, and thrust thee through with their swords. ⁴¹And they shall burn thy houses with fire, and execute judgements upon thee in the sight of many women: and I will cause thee to cease from playing the harlot, and thou also shalt give no hire any more. ⁴²So will I make my fury towards thee to rest, and my jealousy shall depart from thee, and I will be quiet, and will be no more angry. ⁴³Because thou hast not remembered the days of thy youth, but hast fretted me in all these things;

behold therefore, I also will recompense thy way upon thy head,' saith the Lord GOD: 'and thou shalt not commit this lewdness above all thy abominations.

⁴⁴ '"Behold, every one that useth proverbs shall use this proverb against thee, saying, "As is the mother, so is her daughter". ⁴⁵Thou art thy mother's daughter, that loatheth her husband and her children, and thou art the sister of thy sisters which loathed their husbands and their children: your mother was a Hittite, and your father an Amorite. ⁴⁶And thy elder sister is Samaria, she and her daughters that dwell at thy left hand: and thy younger sister, that dwelleth at thy right hand, is Sodom and her daughters. ⁴⁷Yet hast thou not walked after their ways, nor done after their abominations: but, as if that were a very little thing, thou wast corrupted more than they in all thy ways. ⁴⁸As I live,' saith the Lord GOD, 'Sodom thy sister hath not done, she nor her daughters, as thou hast done, thou and thy daughters. ⁴⁹Behold, this was the iniquity of thy sister Sodom; pride, fulness of bread, and abundance of idleness was in her and in her daughters, neither did she strengthen the hand of the poor and needy. ⁵⁰And they were haughty, and committed abomination before me: therefore I took them away as I saw good. ⁵¹Neither hath Samaria committed half of thy sins, but thou hast multiplied thy abominations more than they, and hast justified thy sisters in all thy abominations which thou hast done. ⁵²Thou also, which hast judged thy sisters, bear thy own shame for thy sins that thou hast committed more abominable than they: they are more righteous than thou: yea, be thou confounded also, and bear thy shame, in that thou hast justified thy sisters.

⁵³ '"When I shall bring again their captivity, the captivity of Sodom and her daughters, and the captivity of Samaria and her daughters, then will I bring again the captivity of thy captives in the midst of them; ⁵⁴that thou mayest bear thy own shame, and mayest be confounded in all that thou hast done, in that thou art a comfort unto them. ⁵⁵When thy sisters, Sodom and her daughters shall return to their former estate, and Samaria and her daughters shall return to their former estate, then thou and thy daughters shall return to your former estate. ⁵⁶For thy sister Sodom was not mentioned by thy mouth in the day of thy pride, ⁵⁷before thy wickedness was discovered, as at the time of thy reproach of the daughters of Syria, and all that are round about her, the daughters of the Philistines which despise thee round about. ⁵⁸Thou hast borne thy lewdness and thy abominations,' saith the LORD. ⁵⁹For thus saith the Lord GOD, 'I will even deal with thee as thou hast done, which hast despised the oath in breaking the covenant.

⁶⁰ '"Nevertheless I will remember my covenant with thee in the days of thy youth, and I will establish unto thee an everlasting covenant. ⁶¹Then thou shalt remember thy ways, and be ashamed, when thou shalt receive thy sisters, thy elder and thy younger: and I will give them unto thee for daughters, but not by thy covenant. ⁶²And I will establish my covenant with thee; and thou shalt know that I am the LORD: ⁶³that thou mayest remember, and be confounded, and never open thy mouth

any more: because of thy shame, when I am pacified toward thee for all that thou hast done,' saith the Lord God."'

17 And the word of the LORD came unto me, saying, ²'Son of man, put forth a riddle, and speak a parable unto the house of Israel, ³and say, "Thus saith the Lord GOD, 'A great eagle with great wings, long-winged, full of feathers, which had divers colours, came unto Lebanon, and took the highest branch of the cedar. ⁴He cropped off the top of his young twigs, and carried it into a land of traffic; he set it in a city of merchants. ⁵He took also of the seed of the land, and planted it in a fruitful field; he placed it by great waters, and set it as a willow tree. ⁶And it grew, and became a spreading vine of low stature, whose branches turned toward him, and the roots thereof were under him: so it became a vine, and brought forth branches, and shot forth sprigs.

⁷'"There was also another great eagle with great wings and many feathers: and behold, this vine did bend her roots towards him, and shot forth her branches toward him, that he might water it by the furrows of her plantation. ⁸It was planted in a good soil by great waters, that it might bring forth branches, and that it might bear fruit, that it might be a goodly vine.'"

⁹'Say thou, "Thus saith the Lord GOD, 'Shall it prosper? shall he not pull up the roots thereof, and cut off the fruit thereof, that it wither? it shall wither in all the leaves of her spring, even without great power or many people to pluck it up by the roots thereof. ¹⁰Yea behold, being planted, shall it prosper? shall it not utterly wither, when the east wind toucheth it? it shall wither in the furrows where it grew.'"'

¹¹Moreover the word of the LORD came unto me, saying, ¹²'Say now to the rebellious house, "Know ye not what these things mean?" tell them, "Behold, the king of Babylon is come to Jerusalem, and hath taken the king thereof, and the princes thereof, and led them with him to Babylon, ¹³and hath taken of the king's seed, and made a covenant with him, and hath taken an oath of him: he hath also taken the mighty of the land, ¹⁴that the kingdom might be base, that it might not lift itself up, but that by keeping of his covenant it might stand. ¹⁵But he rebelled against him in sending his ambassadors into Egypt, that they might give him horses and much people. Shall he prosper? shall he escape that doeth such things? or shall he break the covenant, and be delivered? ¹⁶As I live," saith the Lord GOD, "surely in the place where the king dwelleth that made him king, whose oath he despised, and whose covenant he broke, even with him in the midst of Babylon he shall die. ¹⁷Neither shall Pharaoh with his mighty army and great company make for him in the war by casting up mounts, and building forts, to cut off many persons. ¹⁸Seeing he despised the oath by breaking the covenant, when lo, he had given his hand, and hath done all these things, he shall not escape."

¹⁹'Therefore thus saith the Lord GOD, "As I live, surely my oath that he hath despised, and my covenant that he hath broken, even it will I recompense upon his own head. ²⁰And I will spread my net upon him, and he shall be taken in my snare, and I will bring him to Babylon, and will

plead with him there for his trespass that he hath trespassed against me. ²¹And all his fugitives with all his bands shall fall by the sword, and they that remain shall be scattered towards all winds: and ye shall know that I the Lᴏʀᴅ have spoken it."

²²'Thus saith the Lord Gᴏᴅ, "I will also take of the highest branch of the high cedar, and will set it; I will crop off from the top of his young twigs a tender one, and will plant it upon a high mountain and eminent. ²³In the mountain of the height of Israel will I plant it: and it shall bring forth boughs, and bear fruit, and be a goodly cedar: and under it shall dwell all fowl of every wing: in the shadow of the branches thereof shall they dwell. ²⁴And all the trees of the field shall know that I the Lᴏʀᴅ have brought down the high tree, have exalted the low tree, have dried up the green tree, and have made the dry tree to flourish: I the Lᴏʀᴅ have spoken and have done it."'

18 And the word of the Lᴏʀᴅ came unto me again, saying, ²'What mean ye, that ye use this proverb concerning the land of Israel, saying, "The fathers have eaten sour grapes, and the children's teeth are set on edge"? ³As I live,' saith the Lord Gᴏᴅ, 'ye shall not have occasion any more to use this proverb in Israel. ⁴Behold, all souls are mine; as the soul of the father, so also the soul of the son is mine: the soul that sinneth, it shall die.

⁵'But if a man be just, and do that which is lawful and right, ⁶and hath not eaten upon the mountains, neither hath lifted up his eyes to the idols of the house of Israel, neither hath defiled his neighbour's wife, neither hath come near to a menstruous woman, ⁷and hath not oppressed any, but hath restored to the debtor his pledge, hath spoiled none by violence, hath given his bread to the hungry, and hath covered the naked with a garment, ⁸he that hath not given forth upon usury, neither hath taken any increase, that hath withdrawn his hand from iniquity, hath executed true judgement between man and man, ⁹hath walked in my statutes, and hath kept my judgements, to deal truly, he is just, he shall surely live,' saith the Lord Gᴏᴅ.

¹⁰'If he beget a son that is a robber, a shedder of blood, and that doeth the like to any one of these things, ¹¹and that doeth not any of those duties, but even hath eaten upon the mountains, and defiled his neighbour's wife, ¹²hath oppressed the poor and needy, hath spoiled by violence, hath not restored the pledge, and hath lifted up his eyes to the idols, hath committed abomination, ¹³hath given forth upon usury, and hath taken increase: shall he then live? he shall not live: he hath done all these abominations, he shall surely die, his blood shall be upon him.

¹⁴'Now lo, if he beget a son that seeth all his father's sins which he hath done, and considereth, and doeth not such like, ¹⁵that hath not eaten upon the mountains, neither hath lifted up his eyes to the idols of the house of Israel, hath not defiled his neighbour's wife, ¹⁶neither hath oppressed any, hath not withheld the pledge, neither hath spoiled by violence, but hath given his bread to the hungry, and hath covered the naked with a garment, ¹⁷that hath taken off his hand from the

poor, that hath not received usury nor increase, hath executed my judgements, hath walked in my statutes, he shall not die for the iniquity of his father, he shall surely live. [18]As for his father, because he cruelly oppressed, spoiled his brother by violence, and did that which is not good among his people, lo, even he shall die in his iniquity.

[19]'Yet say ye, "Why? doth not the son bear the iniquity of the father?" when the son hath done that which is lawful and right, and hath kept all my statutes, and hath done them, he shall surely live. [20]The soul that sinneth, it shall die. The son shall not bear the iniquity of the father, neither shall the father bear the iniquity of the son: the righteousness of the righteous shall be upon him, and the wickedness of the wicked shall be upon him.

[21]'But if the wicked will turn from all his sins that he hath committed, and keep all my statutes, and do that which is lawful and right, he shall surely live, he shall not die. [22]All his transgressions that he hath committed, they shall not be mentioned unto him: in his righteousness that he hath done he shall live. [23]Have I any pleasure at all that the wicked should die?' saith the Lord GOD: 'and not that he should return from his ways, and live?

[24]'But when the righteous turneth away from his righteousness, and committeth iniquity, and doeth according to all the abominations that the wicked man doeth, shall he live? All his righteousness that he hath done shall not be mentioned: in his trespass that he hath trespassed, and in his sin that he hath sinned, in them shall he die.

[25]'Yet ye say, "The way of the Lord is not equal". Hear now, O house of Israel, is not my way equal? are not your ways unequal? [26]When a righteous man turneth away from his righteousness, and committeth iniquity, and dieth in them; for his iniquity that he hath done shall he die. [27]Again, when the wicked man turneth away from his wickedness that he hath committed, and doeth that which is lawful and right, he shall save his soul alive. [28]Because he considereth and turneth away from all his transgressions that he hath committed, he shall surely live, he shall not die. [29]Yet saith the house of Israel, "The way of the Lord is not equal". O house of Israel, are not my ways equal? are not your ways unequal?

[30]'Therefore I will judge you, O house of Israel, every one according to his ways,' saith the Lord GOD. 'Repent, and turn yourselves from all your transgressions: so iniquity shall not be your ruin. [31]Cast away from you all your transgressions, whereby ye have transgressed, and make you a new heart and a new spirit: for why will ye die, O house of Israel? [32]For I have no pleasure in the death of him that dieth,' saith the Lord GOD: 'wherefore turn yourselves, and live ye.

19 'Moreover take thou up a lamentation for the princes of Israel, [2]and say,

'"What is thy mother? a lioness:
she lay down among lions,
she nourished her whelps among young lions.
[3] And she brought up one of her whelps:

it became a young lion, and it learned to catch the prey,
it devoured men.
⁴ The nations also heard of him, he was taken in their pit,
and they brought him with chains unto the land of Egypt.
⁵ Now when she saw that she had waited,
and her hope was lost,
then she took another of her whelps,
and made him a young lion.
⁶ And he went up and down among the lions,
he became a young lion, and learned to catch the prey,
and devoured men.
⁷ And he knew their desolate palaces,
and he laid waste their cities,
and the land was desolate, and the fulness thereof,
by the noise of his roaring.
⁸ Then the nations set against him on every side from the provinces,
and spread their net over him:
he was taken in their pit.
⁹ And they put him in ward in chains, and brought him to the
king of Babylon:
they brought him into holds,
that his voice should no more be heard upon the mountains of
Israel.

¹⁰ '"Thy mother is like a vine in thy blood, planted by the waters:
she was fruitful and full of branches by reason of many waters,
¹¹ and she had strong rods for the sceptres of them that bore rule,
and her stature was exalted among the thick branches,
and she appeared in her height with the multitude of her
branches.
¹² But she was plucked up in fury:
she was cast down to the ground, and the east wind dried up her
fruit:
her strong rods were broken and withered,
the fire consumed them.
¹³ And now she is planted in the wilderness,
in a dry and thirsty ground.
¹⁴ And fire is gone out of a rod of her branches, which hath
devoured her fruit,
so that she hath no strong rod to be a sceptre to rule."

'This is a lamentation, and shall be for a lamentation.'

20 And it came to pass in the seventh year, in the fifth month, the tenth day of the month, that certain of the elders of Israel came to inquire of the LORD, and sat before me. ²Then came the word of the LORD unto me, saying, ³'Son of man, speak unto the elders of Israel, and say unto them, "Thus saith the Lord GOD, 'Are ye come to inquire of me? As I live,' saith the Lord GOD, 'I will not be inquired of by you'".

⁴'Wilt thou judge them, son of man, wilt thou judge them? cause them to know the abominations of their fathers: ⁵and say unto them, "Thus saith the Lord GOD, 'In the day when I chose Israel, and lifted up my hand unto the seed of the house of Jacob, and made myself known unto them in the land of Egypt, when I lifted up my hand unto them, saying, "I am the LORD your God", ⁶in the day that I lifted up my hand unto them to bring them forth of the land of Egypt into a land that I had espied for them, flowing with milk and honey, which is the glory of all lands: ⁷then said I unto them, "Cast ye away every man the abominations of his eyes, and defile not yourselves with the idols of Egypt: I am the LORD your God".'"

⁸'But they rebelled against me, and would not hearken unto me: they did not every man cast away the abominations of their eyes, neither did they forsake the idols of Egypt: then I said, "I will pour out my fury upon them, to accomplish my anger against them in the midst of the land of Egypt". ⁹But I wrought for my name's sake that it should not be polluted before the heathen, among whom they were, in whose sight I made myself known unto them, in bringing them forth out of the land of Egypt.

¹⁰'Wherefore I caused them to go forth out of the land of Egypt, and brought them into the wilderness. ¹¹And I gave them my statutes, and showed them my judgements, which if a man do, he shall even live in them. ¹²Moreover also I gave them my sabbaths, to be a sign between me and them, that they might know that I am the LORD that sanctify them. ¹³But the house of Israel rebelled against me in the wilderness: they walked not in my statutes, and they despised my judgements, which if a man do, he shall even live in them; and my sabbaths they greatly polluted: then I said I would pour out my fury upon them in the wilderness, to consume them: ¹⁴but I wrought for my name's sake, that it should not be polluted before the heathen, in whose sight I brought them out.

¹⁵'Yet also I lifted up my hand unto them in the wilderness, that I would not bring them into the land which I had given them, flowing with milk and honey, which is the glory of all lands, ¹⁶because they despised my judgements, and walked not in my statutes, but polluted my sabbaths: for their heart went after their idols. ¹⁷Nevertheless my eye spared them from destroying them, neither did I make an end of them in the wilderness. ¹⁸But I said unto their children in the wilderness, "Walk ye not in the statutes of your fathers, neither observe their judgements, nor defile yourselves with their idols. ¹⁹I am the LORD your God: walk in my statutes, and keep my judgements, and do them: ²⁰and hallow my sabbaths, and they shall be a sign between me and you, that ye may know that I am the LORD your God." ²¹Notwithstanding the children rebelled against me: they walked not in my statutes, neither kept my judgements to do them, which if a man do, he shall even live in them; they polluted my sabbaths: then I said I would pour out my fury upon them, to accomplish my anger against them in the wilderness.

²²'Nevertheless I withdrew my hand and wrought for my name's sake, that it should not be polluted in the sight of the heathen, in whose

sight I brought them forth. ²³I lifted up my hand unto them also in the wilderness, that I would scatter them among the heathen, and disperse them through the countries; ²⁴because they had not executed my judgements, but had despised my statutes, and had polluted my sabbaths, and their eyes were after their fathers' idols. ²⁵Wherefore I gave them also statutes that were not good, and judgements whereby they should not live. ²⁶And I polluted them in their own gifts, in that they caused to pass through the fire all that openeth the womb, that I might make them desolate, to the end that they might know that I am the LORD.

²⁷'Therefore, son of man, speak unto the house of Israel, and say unto them, "Thus saith the Lord GOD, 'Yet in this your fathers have blasphemed me, in that they have committed a trespass against me. ²⁸For when I had brought them into the land, for the which I lifted up my hand to give it to them, then they saw every high hill, and all the thick trees, and they offered there their sacrifices, and there they presented the provocation of their offering: there also they made their sweet savour, and poured out there their drink offerings. ²⁹Then I said unto them, "What is the high place whereunto ye go?" And the name thereof is called Bamah unto this day.'" ³⁰Wherefore say unto the house of Israel, "Thus saith the Lord GOD, 'Are ye polluted after the manner of your fathers? and commit ye whoredom after their abominations? ³¹For when ye offer your gifts, when ye make your sons to pass through the fire, ye pollute yourselves with all your idols even unto this day: and shall I be inquired of by you, O house of Israel? As I live,' saith the Lord GOD, 'I will not be inquired of by you. ³²And that which cometh into your mind shall not be at all, that ye say, "We will be as the heathen, as the families of the countries, to serve wood and stone".

³³'"'As I live,' saith the Lord GOD, 'surely with a mighty hand, and with a stretched out arm, and with fury poured out, will I rule over you. ³⁴And I will bring you out from the people, and will gather you out of the countries wherein ye are scattered, with a mighty hand, and with a stretched out arm, and with fury poured out. ³⁵And I will bring you into the wilderness of the people, and there will I plead with you face to face. ³⁶Like as I pleaded with your fathers in the wilderness of the land of Egypt, so will I plead with you,' saith the Lord GOD. ³⁷'And I will cause you to pass under the rod, and I will bring you into the bond of the covenant. ³⁸And I will purge out from among you the rebels, and them that transgress against me: I will bring them forth out of the country where they sojourn, and they shall not enter into the land of Israel: and ye shall know that I am the LORD.

³⁹'"'As for you, O house of Israel,' thus saith the Lord GOD, 'Go ye, serve ye every one his idols, and hereafter also, if ye will not hearken unto me: but pollute ye my holy name no more with your gifts, and with your idols. ⁴⁰For in my holy mountain, in the mountain of the height of Israel,' saith the Lord GOD, 'there shall all the house of Israel, all of them in the land, serve me: there will I accept them, and there will I require your offerings, and the first-fruits of your oblations, with

all your holy things. ⁴¹I will accept you with your sweet savour, when I bring you out from the people, and gather you out of the countries wherein ye have been scattered, and I will be sanctified in you before the heathen. ⁴²And ye shall know that I am the LORD, when I shall bring you into the land of Israel, into the country for the which I lifted up my hand to give it to your fathers. ⁴³And there shall ye remember your ways, and all your doings, wherein ye have been defiled, and ye shall loathe yourselves in your own sight for all your evils that ye have committed. ⁴⁴And ye shall know that I am the LORD, when I have wrought with you for my name's sake, not according to your wicked ways, nor according to your corrupt doings, O ye house of Israel,' saith the Lord GOD."'

⁴⁵Moreover the word of the LORD came unto me, saying, ⁴⁶'Son of man, set thy face toward the south, and drop thy word toward the south, and prophesy against the forest of the south field. ⁴⁷And say to the forest of the south, "Hear the word of the LORD: thus saith the Lord GOD, 'Behold, I will kindle a fire in thee, and it shall devour every green tree in thee, and every dry tree: the flaming flame shall not be quenched, and all faces from the south to the north shall be burnt therein. ⁴⁸And all flesh shall see that I the LORD have kindled it: it shall not be quenched.'"'

⁴⁹Then said I, 'Ah Lord GOD, they say of me, "Doth he not speak parables?"'

21 And the word of the LORD came unto me, saying, ²'Son of man, set thy face toward Jerusalem, and drop thy word toward the holy places, and prophesy against the land of Israel, ³and say to the land of Israel, "Thus saith the LORD, 'Behold, I am against thee, and will draw forth my sword out of his sheath, and will cut off from thee the righteous and the wicked. ⁴Seeing then that I will cut off from thee the righteous and the wicked, therefore shall my sword go forth out of his sheath against all flesh from the south to the north: ⁵that all flesh may know that I the LORD have drawn forth my sword out of his sheath: it shall not return any more. ⁶Sigh therefore, thou son of man, with the breaking of thy loins, and with bitterness sigh before their eyes. ⁷And it shall be, when they say unto thee, "Wherefore sighest thou?" that thou shalt answer, "For the tidings", because it cometh: and every heart shall melt, and all hands shall be feeble, and every spirit shall faint, and all knees shall be weak as water: behold, it cometh, and shall be brought to pass,' saith the Lord GOD."'

⁸Again the word of the LORD came unto me, saying, ⁹'Son of man, prophesy, and say, "Thus saith the LORD," say, "A sword, a sword is sharpened, and also furbished. ¹⁰It is sharpened to make a sore slaughter; it is furbished that it may glitter: should we then make mirth? It contemneth the rod of my son, as every tree. ¹¹And he hath given it to be furbished, that it may be handled: this sword is sharpened, and it is furbished, to give it into the hand of the slayer. ¹²Cry and howl, son of man, for it shall be upon my people, it shall be upon all the princes of Israel: terrors by reason of the sword shall be upon my people: smite therefore

upon thy thigh. [13]Because it is a trial, and what if the sword contemn even the rod? it shall be no more," saith the Lord God.

[14]"Thou therefore, son of man, prophesy, and smite thy hands together, and let the sword be doubled the third time, the sword of the slain: it is the sword of the great men that are slain, which entereth into their privy chambers. [15]I have set the point of the sword against all their gates, that their heart may faint, and their ruins be multiplied. Ah, it is made bright, it is wrapped up for the slaughter. [16]Go thee one way or other, either on the right hand, or on the left, whithersoever thy face is set. [17]I will also smite my hands together, and I will cause my fury to rest: I the Lord have said it.'

[18]The word of the Lord came unto me again, saying, [19]'Also, thou son of man, appoint thee two ways, that the sword of the king of Babylon may come: both twain shall come forth out of one land: and choose thou a place, choose it at the head of the way to the city. [20]Appoint a way, that the sword may come to Rabbath of the Ammonites, and to Judah in Jerusalem the defenced. [21]For the king of Babylon stood at the parting of the way, at the head of the two ways, to use divination: he made his arrows bright, he consulted with images, he looked in the liver. [22]At his right hand was the divination for Jerusalem, to appoint captains, to open the mouth in the slaughter, to lift up the voice with shouting, to appoint battering-rams against the gates, to cast a mount, and to build a fort. [23]And it shall be unto them as a false divination in their sight, to them that have sworn oaths: but he will call to remembrance the iniquity, that they may be taken.' [24]Therefore thus saith the Lord God, 'Because ye have made your iniquity to be remembered, in that your transgressions are discovered, so that in all your doings your sins do appear: because, I say, that ye are come to remembrance, ye shall be taken with the hand.

[25]'And thou, profane wicked prince of Israel, whose day is come, when iniquity shall have an end,' [26]thus saith the Lord God, 'remove the diadem, and take off the crown: this shall not be the same: exalt him that is low, and abase him that is high. [27]I will overturn, overturn, overturn, it: and it shall be no more, until he come whose right it is; and I will give it him.

[28]'And thou, son of man, prophesy and say, "Thus saith the Lord God concerning the Ammonites, and concerning their reproach: even say thou, 'The sword, the sword is drawn, for the slaughter it is furbished, to consume because of the glittering: [29]whilst they see vanity unto thee, whilst they divine a lie unto thee, to bring thee upon the necks of them that are slain, of the wicked whose day is come, when their iniquity shall have an end. [30]Shall I cause it to return into his sheath? I will judge thee in the place where thou wast created, in the land of thy nativity. [31]And I will pour out my indignation upon thee, I will blow against thee in the fire of my wrath, and deliver thee into the hand of brutish men, and skilful to destroy. [32]Thou shalt be for fuel to the fire: thy blood shall be in the midst of the land, thou shalt be no more remembered: for I the Lord have spoken it.'"'

22 Moreover the word of the LORD came unto me, saying, ²'Now, thou son of man, wilt thou judge, wilt thou judge the bloody city? yea, thou shalt show her all her abominations. ³Then say thou, "Thus saith the Lord GOD, 'The city sheddeth blood in the midst of it, that her time may come, and maketh idols against herself to defile herself. ⁴Thou art become guilty in thy blood that thou hast shed, and hast defiled thyself in thy idols which thou hast made, and thou hast caused thy days to draw near, and art come even unto thy years: therefore have I made thee a reproach unto the heathen, and a mocking to all countries. ⁵Those that be near, and those that be far from thee, shall mock thee, which art infamous and much vexed. ⁶Behold, the princes of Israel, every one were in thee to their power to shed blood. ⁷In thee have they set light by father and mother: in the midst of thee have they dealt by oppression with the stranger: in thee have they vexed the fatherless and the widow. ⁸Thou hast despised my holy things, and hast profaned my sabbaths: ⁹in thee are men that carry tales to shed blood: and in thee they eat upon the mountains: in the midst of thee they commit lewdness. ¹⁰In thee have they discovered their fathers' nakedness: in thee have they humbled her that was set apart for pollution. ¹¹And one hath committed abomination with his neighbour's wife, and another hath lewdly defiled his daughter-in-law, and another in thee hath humbled his sister, his father's daughter. ¹²In thee have they taken gifts to shed blood: thou hast taken usury and increase, and thou hast greedily gained of thy neighbours by extortion, and hast forgotten me,' saith the Lord GOD.

¹³'"Behold, therefore I have smitten my hand at thy dishonest gain which thou hast made, and at thy blood which hath been in the midst of thee. ¹⁴Can thy heart endure, or can thy hands be strong in the days that I shall deal with thee? I the LORD have spoken it, and will do it. ¹⁵And I will scatter thee among the heathen, and disperse thee in the countries, and will consume thy filthiness out of thee. ¹⁶And thou shalt take thy inheritance in thyself in the sight of the heathen, and thou shalt know that I am the LORD.'"'

¹⁷And the word of the LORD came unto me, saying, ¹⁸'Son of man, the house of Israel is to me become dross: all they are brass, and tin, and iron, and lead in the midst of the furnace: they are even the dross of silver. ¹⁹Therefore thus saith the Lord GOD, "Because ye are all become dross, behold, therefore I will gather you into the midst of Jerusalem. ²⁰As they gather silver, and brass, and iron, and lead, and tin into the midst of the furnace, to blow the fire upon it, to melt it: so will I gather you in my anger and in my fury, and I will leave you there, and melt you. ²¹Yea, I will gather you, and blow upon you in the fire of my wrath, and ye shall be melted in the midst therof. ²²As silver is melted in the midst of the furnace, so shall ye be melted in the midst thereof, and ye shall know that I the LORD have poured out my fury upon you."'

²³And the word of the LORD came unto me, saying, ²⁴'Son of man, say unto her, "Thou art the land that is not cleansed, nor rained upon in the day of indignation. ²⁵There is a conspiracy of her prophets in the

midst thereof, like a roaring lion ravening the prey: they have devoured souls: they have taken the treasure and precious things: they have made her many widows in the midst thereof. ²⁶Her priests have violated my law, and have profaned my holy things: they have put no difference between the holy and profane, neither have they shown difference between the unclean and the clean, and have hid their eyes from my sabbaths, and I am profaned among them. ²⁷Her princes in the midst thereof are like wolves ravening the prey to shed blood, and to destroy souls, to get dishonest gain. ²⁸And her prophets have daubed them with untempered mortar, seeing vanity, and divining lies unto them, saying, 'Thus saith the Lord GOD', when the LORD hath not spoken. ²⁹The people of the land have used oppression, and exercised robbery, and have vexed the poor and needy: yea, they have oppressed the stranger wrongfully. ³⁰And I sought for a man among them, that should make up the hedge, and stand in the gap before me for the land, that I should not destroy it: but I found none. ³¹Therefore have I poured out my indignation upon them, I have consumed them with the fire of my wrath: their own way have I recompensed upon their heads,' saith the Lord GOD."'

23 The word of the LORD came again unto me, saying, ²'Son of man, there were two women, the daughters of one mother. ³And they committed whoredoms in Egypt, they committed whoredoms in their youth: there were their breasts pressed, and there they bruised the teats of their virginity. ⁴And the names of them were Aholah the elder, and Aholibah her sister: and they were mine, and they bore sons and daughters. Thus were their names: Samaria is Aholah, and Jerusalem Aholibah.

⁵'And Aholah played the harlot when she was mine, and she doted on her lovers, on the Assyrians her neighbours, ⁶which were clothed with blue, captains and rulers, all of them desirable young men, horsemen riding upon horses. ⁷Thus she committed her whoredoms with them, with all them that were the chosen men of Assyria, and with all on whom she doted: with all their idols she defiled herself. ⁸Neither left she her whoredoms brought from Egypt: for in her youth they lay with her, and they bruised the breasts of her virginity, and poured their whoredom upon her. ⁹Wherefore I have delivered her into the hand of her lovers, into the hand of the Assyrians, upon whom she doted. ¹⁰These discovered her nakedness, they took her sons and her daughters, and slew her with the sword: and she became famous among women, for they had executed judgement upon her.

¹¹'And when her sister Aholibah saw this, she was more corrupt in her inordinate love than she, and in her whoredoms more than her sister in her whoredoms. ¹²She doted upon the Assyrians her neighbours, captains and rulers clothed most gorgeously, horsemen riding upon horses, all of them desirable young men. ¹³Then I saw that she was defiled, that they took both one way, ¹⁴and that she increased her whoredoms: for when she saw men portrayed upon the wall, the images of the Chaldeans portrayed with vermilion, ¹⁵girded with girdles upon their loins, exceeding in dyed attire upon their heads, all of

them princes to look to, after the manner of the Babylonians of Chaldea, the land of their nativity: ¹⁶and as soon as she saw them with her eyes, she doted upon them, and sent messengers unto them into Chaldea. ¹⁷And the Babylonians came to her into the bed of love, and they defiled her with their whoredom, and she was polluted with them, and her mind was alienated from them. ¹⁸So she discovered her whoredoms, and discovered her nakedness: then my mind was alienated from her, like as my mind was alienated from her sister. ¹⁹Yet she multiplied her whoredoms, in calling to remembrance the days of her youth, wherein she had played the harlot in the land of Egypt. ²⁰For she doted upon their paramours, whose flesh is as the flesh of asses, and whose issue is like the issue of horses. ²¹Thus thou calledst to remembrance the lewdness of thy youth, in bruising thy teats by the Egyptians for the paps of thy youth.'

²²Therefore, O Aholibah, thus saith the Lord GOD, 'Behold, I will raise up thy lovers against thee, from whom thy mind is alienated, and I will bring them against thee on every side, ²³the Babylonians, and all the Chaldeans, Pekod, and Shoa, and Koa, all the Assyrians with them, all of them desirable young men, captains and rulers, great lords and renowned, all of them riding upon horses. ²⁴And they shall come against thee with chariots, wagons, and wheels, and with an assembly of people, which shall set against thee buckler and shield and helmet round about: and I will set judgement before them, and they shall judge thee according to their judgements. ²⁵And I will set my jealousy against thee, and they shall deal furiously with thee: they shall take away thy nose and thy ears, and thy remnant shall fall by the sword: they shall take thy sons and thy daughters, and thy residue shall be devoured by the fire. ²⁶They shall also strip thee out of thy clothes, and take away thy fair jewels. ²⁷Thus will I make thy lewdness to cease from thee, and thy whoredom brought from the land of Egypt: so that thou shalt not lift up thy eyes unto them, nor remember Egypt any more.'

²⁸For thus saith the Lord GOD, 'Behold, I will deliver thee into the hand of them whom thou hatest, into the hand of them from whom thy mind is alienated. ²⁹And they shall deal with thee hatefully, and shall take away all thy labour, and shall leave thee naked and bare: and the nakedness of thy whoredoms shall be discovered, both thy lewdness and thy whoredoms. ³⁰I will do these things unto thee, because thou hast gone a-whoring after the heathen, and because thou art polluted with their idols. ³¹Thou hast walked in the way of thy sister, therefore will I give her cup into thy hand.'

³²Thus saith the Lord GOD, 'Thou shalt drink of thy sister's cup deep and large: thou shalt be laughed to scorn and had in derision; it containeth much. ³³Thou shalt be filled with drunkenness and sorrow, with the cup of astonishment and desolation, with the cup of thy sister Samaria. ³⁴Thou shalt even drink it and suck it out, and thou shalt break the shards thereof, and pluck off thy own breasts: for I have spoken it,' saith the Lord GOD.

³⁵Therefore thus saith the Lord GOD, 'Because thou hast forgotten me,

and cast me behind thy back, therefore bear thou also thy lewdness and thy whoredoms'.

³⁶The Lord said moreover unto me, 'Son of man, wilt thou judge Aholah and Aholibah? yea, declare unto them their abominations; ³⁷that they have committed adultery, and blood is in their hands, and with their idols have they committed adultery, and have also caused their sons, whom they bore unto me, to pass for them through the fire, to devour them. ³⁸Moreover this they have done unto me: they have defiled my sanctuary in the same day, and have profaned my sabbaths. ³⁹For when they had slain their children to their idols, then they came the same day into my sanctuary to profane it; and, lo, thus have they done in the midst of my house.

⁴⁰'And furthermore, that ye have sent for men to come from far, unto whom a messenger was sent; and lo, they came: for whom thou didst wash thyself, paintedst thy eyes, and deckedst thyself with ornaments, ⁴¹and sattest upon a stately bed, and a table prepared before it, whereupon thou hast set my incense and my oil. ⁴²And a voice of a multitude being at ease was with her: and with the men of the common sort were brought Sabeans from the wilderness, which put bracelets upon their hands, and beautiful crowns upon their heads.

⁴³'Then said I unto her that was old in adulteries, "Will they now commit whoredoms with her, and she with them?" ⁴⁴Yet they went in unto her, as they go in unto a woman that playeth the harlot: so went they in unto Aholah and unto Aholibah, the lewd women.

⁴⁵'And the righteous men, they shall judge them after the manner of adulteresses, and after the manner of women that shed blood; because they are adulteresses, and blood is in their hands.' ⁴⁶For thus saith the Lord God, 'I will bring up a company upon them, and will give them to be removed and spoiled. ⁴⁷And the company shall stone them with stones, and dispatch them with their swords: they shall slay their sons and their daughters, and burn up their houses with fire. ⁴⁸Thus will I cause lewdness to cease out of the land, that all women may be taught not to do after your lewdness. ⁴⁹And they shall recompense your lewdness upon you, and ye shall bear the sins of your idols: and ye shall know that I am the Lord God.'

24 Again in the ninth year, in the tenth month, in the tenth day of the month, the word of the Lord came unto me, saying, ²'Son of man, write thee the name of the day, even of this same day: the king of Babylon set himself against Jerusalem this same day. ³And utter a parable unto the rebellious house, and say unto them, "Thus saith the Lord God, 'Set on a pot, set it on, and also pour water into it. ⁴Gather the pieces thereof into it, even every good piece, the thigh, and the shoulder; fill it with the choice bones. ⁵Take the choice of the flock, and burn also the bones under it, and make it boil well, and let them seethe the bones of it therein.'

⁶'"Wherefore thus saith the Lord God, 'Woe to the bloody city, to the pot whose scum is therein, and whose scum is not gone out of it; bring it out piece by piece, let no lot fall upon it. ⁷For her blood is in the midst

of her: she set it upon the top of a rock, she poured it not upon the ground, to cover it with dust: ⁸that it might cause fury to come up to take vengeance: I have set her blood upon the top of a rock, that it should not be covered.'

⁹'"Therefore thus saith the Lord GOD, 'Woe to the bloody city, I will even make the pile for fire great. ¹⁰Heap on wood, kindle the fire, consume the flesh, and spice it well, and let the bones be burnt. ¹¹Then set it empty upon the coals thereof, that the brass of it may be hot and may burn, and that the filthiness of it may be molten in it, that the scum of it may be consumed. ¹²She hath wearied herself with lies, and her great scum went not forth out of her: her scum shall be in the fire. ¹³In thy filthiness is lewdness: because I have purged thee, and thou wast not purged, thou shalt not be purged from thy filthiness any more, till I have caused my fury to rest upon thee. ¹⁴I the LORD have spoken it: it shall come to pass, and I will do it, I will not go back, neither will I spare, neither will I repent, according to thy ways, and according to thy doings, shall they judge thee,' saith the Lord GOD."'

¹⁵Also the word of the LORD came unto me, saying, ¹⁶'Son of man, behold, I take away from thee the desire of thy eyes with a stroke: yet neither shalt thou mourn nor weep, neither shall thy tears run down. ¹⁷Forbear to cry, make no mourning for the dead, bind the tire of thy head upon thee, and put on thy shoes upon thy feet, and cover not thy lips, and eat not the bread of men.' ¹⁸So I spoke unto the people in the morning, and at even my wife died, and I did in the morning as I was commanded.

¹⁹And the people said unto me, 'Wilt thou not tell us what these things are to us, that thou doest so?' ²⁰Then I answered them, 'The word of the LORD came unto me, saying, ²¹"Speak unto the house of Israel, 'Thus saith the Lord GOD, "Behold, I will profane my sanctuary, the excellence of your strength, the desire of your eyes, and that which your soul pitieth; and your sons and your daughters whom ye have left shall fall by the sword. ²²And ye shall do as I have done: ye shall not cover your lips, nor eat the bread of men. ²³And your tires shall be upon your heads, and your shoes upon your feet: ye shall not mourn nor weep, but ye shall pine away for your iniquities, and mourn one towards another. ²⁴Thus Ezekiel is unto you a sign: according to all that he hath done shall ye do: and when this cometh, ye shall know that I am the Lord GOD."'

²⁵'"Also, thou son of man, shall it not be in the day when I take from them their strength, the joy of their glory, the desire of their eyes, and that whereupon they set their minds, their sons and their daughters, ²⁶that he that escapeth in that day shall come unto thee, to cause thee to hear it with thy ears? ²⁷In that day shall thy mouth be opened to him which is escaped, and thou shalt speak, and be no more dumb: and thou shalt be a sign unto them; and they shall know that I am the LORD."'

25 The word of the LORD came again unto me, saying, ²'Son of man, set thy face against the Ammonites, and prophesy against them,

³and say unto the Ammonites, "Hear the word of the Lord GOD; thus saith the Lord GOD, 'Because thou saidst, "Aha", against my sanctuary, when it was profaned, and against the land of Israel, when it was desolate, and against the house of Judah, when they went into captivity; ⁴behold therefore, I will deliver thee to the men of the east for a possession, and they shall set their palaces in thee, and make their dwellings in thee: they shall eat thy fruit, and they shall drink thy milk. ⁵And I will make Rabbah a stable for camels, and the Ammonites a couching-place for flocks: and ye shall know that I am the LORD.' ⁶For thus saith the Lord GOD, 'Because thou hast clapped thy hands, and stamped with the feet, and rejoiced in heart with all thy despite against the land of Israel: ⁷behold therefore, I will stretch out my hand upon thee, and will deliver thee for a spoil to the heathen, and I will cut thee off from the people, and I will cause thee to perish out of the countries: I will destroy thee, and thou shalt know that I am the LORD.'"'

⁸Thus saith the Lord GOD, 'Because that Moab and Seir do say, "Behold, the house of Judah is like unto all the heathen": ⁹therefore behold, I will open the side of Moab from the cities, from his cities which are on his frontiers, the glory of the country, Beth-jeshimoth, Baal-meon, and Kiriathaim, ¹⁰unto the men of the east with the Ammonites, and will give them in possession, that the Ammonites may not be remembered among the nations. ¹¹And I will execute judgements upon Moab; and they shall know that I am the LORD.'

¹²Thus saith the Lord GOD, 'Because that Edom hath dealt against the house of Judah by taking vengeance, and hath greatly offended, and revenged himself upon them': ¹³therefore thus saith the Lord GOD, 'I will also stretch out my hand upon Edom, and will cut off man and beast from it, and I will make it desolate from Teman, and they of Dedan shall fall by the sword. ¹⁴And I will lay my vengeance upon Edom by the hand of my people Israel: and they shall do in Edom according to my anger and according to my fury; and they shall know my vengeance,' saith the Lord GOD.

¹⁵Thus saith the Lord GOD, 'Because the Philistines have dealt by revenge, and have taken vengeance with a despiteful heart, to destroy it for the old hatred: ¹⁶therefore thus saith the Lord GOD, "Behold, I will stretch out my hand upon the Philistines, and I will cut off the Cherethims, and destroy the remnant of the sea-coast. ¹⁷And I will execute great vengeance upon them with furious rebukes; and they shall know that I am the LORD, when I shall lay my vengeance upon them."'

26 And it came to pass in the eleventh year, in the first day of the month, that the word of the LORD came unto me, saying, ²'Son of man, because that Tyrus hath said against Jerusalem, "Aha, she is broken that was the gates of the people, she is turned unto me, I shall be replenished now she is laid waste"': ³therefore thus saith the Lord GOD, 'Behold, I am against thee, O Tyrus, and will cause many nations to come up against thee, as the sea causeth his waves to come up. ⁴And they shall destroy the walls of Tyrus, and break down her towers: I will also scrape her dust from her, and make her like the top of a rock. ⁵It shall be a place for the spreading of nets in the midst of the sea: for I have spoken it,' saith the Lord GOD, 'and it shall become a spoil to the nations. ⁶And her daughters which are in the field shall be slain by the sword; and they shall know that I am the LORD.'

⁷For thus saith the Lord GOD, 'Behold, I will bring upon Tyrus Nebuchadrezzar king of Babylon, a king of kings, from the north, with horses, and with chariots, and with horsemen, and companies, and much people. ⁸He shall slay with the sword thy daughters in the field, and he shall make a fort against thee, and cast a mount against thee, and lift up the buckler against thee. ⁹And he shall set engines of war against thy walls, and with his axes he shall break down thy towers. ¹⁰By reason of the abundance of his horses their dust shall cover thee: thy walls shall shake at the noise of the horsemen, and of the wheels, and of the chariots, when he shall enter into thy gates, as men enter into a city wherein is made a breach. ¹¹With the hoofs of his horses shall he tread down all thy streets: he shall slay thy people by the sword, and thy strong garrisons shall go down to the ground. ¹²And they shall make a spoil of thy riches, and make a prey of thy merchandise: and they shall break down thy walls, and destroy thy pleasant houses: and they shall lay thy stones and thy timber and thy dust in the midst of the water. ¹³And I will cause the noise of thy songs to cease, and the sound of thy harps shall be no more heard. ¹⁴And I will make thee like the top of a rock: thou shalt be a place to spread nets upon: thou shalt be built no more: for I the LORD have spoken it,' saith the Lord GOD.

¹⁵Thus saith the Lord GOD to Tyrus, 'Shall not the isles shake at the sound of thy fall, when the wounded cry, when the slaughter is made in the midst of thee? ¹⁶Then all the princes of the sea shall come down from their thrones, and lay away their robes, and put off their broidered garments: they shall clothe themselves with trembling, they shall sit upon the ground, and shall tremble at every moment, and be astonished at thee. ¹⁷And they shall take up a lamentation for thee, and say to thee, "How art thou destroyed that wast inhabited of seafaring men, the renowned city, which wast strong in the sea, she and her inhabitants, which cause their terror to be on all that haunt it! ¹⁸Now shall the isles tremble in the day of thy fall, yea, the isles that are in the sea shall be troubled at thy departure."' ¹⁹For thus saith the Lord GOD, 'When I shall make thee a desolate city, like the cities that are not inhabited; when I shall bring up the deep upon thee, and great waters shall cover thee; ²⁰when I shall bring thee down with them that descend into the pit, with the people of old time, and shall set thee in the low parts of the earth, in places desolate of old, with them that go down to the pit, that thou be not inhabited, and I shall set glory in the land of the living: ²¹I will make thee a terror, and thou shalt be no more: though thou be sought for, yet shalt thou never be found again,' saith the Lord GOD.

27 The word of the LORD came again unto me, saying, ²'Now, thou son of man, take up a lamentation for Tyrus; ³and say unto

Tyrus, "O thou that art situated at the entry of the sea, which art a merchant of the people for many isles, thus saith the Lord GOD,

'"'O Tyrus, thou hast said, "I am of perfect beauty".

⁴ Thy borders are in the midst of the seas,
thy builders have perfected thy beauty.

⁵ They have made all thy ship boards of fir trees of Senir:
they have taken cedars from Lebanon to make masts for thee.

⁶ Of the oaks of Bashan have they made thy oars:
the company of the Ashurites have made thy benches of ivory,
brought out of the isles of Chittim.

⁷ Fine linen with broidered work from Egypt
was that which thou spreadest forth to be thy sail,
blue and purple from the isles of Elishah was that which covered thee.

⁸ '"'The inhabitants of Zidon and Arvad were thy mariners:
thy wise men, O Tyrus, that were in thee, were thy pilots.

⁹ The ancients of Gebal and the wise men thereof were in thee thy caulkers,
all the ships of the sea with their mariners were in thee to occupy thy merchandise.

¹⁰ They of Persia and of Lud and of Phut were in thy army, thy men of war:
they hanged the shield and helmet in thee:
they set forth thy comeliness.

¹¹ The men of Arvad with thy army were upon thy walls round about,
and the Gammadims were in thy towers:
they hanged their shields upon thy walls round about:
they have made thy beauty perfect.

¹²'"'Tarshish was thy merchant by reason of the multitude of all kind of riches: with silver, iron, tin, and lead, they traded in thy fairs. ¹³Javan, Tubal, and Meshech, they were thy merchants: they traded the persons of men and vessels of brass in thy market. ¹⁴They of the house of Togarmah traded in thy fairs with horses and horsemen and mules. ¹⁵The men of Dedan were thy merchants, many isles were the merchandise of thy hand: they brought thee for a present horns of ivory and ebony. ¹⁶Syria was thy merchant by reason of the multitude of the wares of thy making: they occupied in thy fairs with emeralds, purple, and broidered work, and fine linen, and coral, and agate. ¹⁷Judah, and the land of Israel, they were thy merchants: they traded in thy market wheat of Minnith, and Pannag, and honey, and oil, and balm. ¹⁸Damascus was thy merchant in the multitude of the wares of thy making, for the multitude of all riches; in the wine of Helbon, and white wool. ¹⁹Dan also and Javan going to and fro occupied in thy fairs: bright iron, cassia, and calamus, were in thy market. ²⁰Dedan was thy

merchant in precious cloths for chariots. ²¹Arabia, and all the princes of Kedar, they occupied with thee in lambs and rams and goats: in these were they thy merchants. ²²The merchants of Sheba and Raamah, they were thy merchants: they occupied in thy fairs with chief of all spices, and with all precious stones and gold. ²³Haran, and Canneh, and Eden, the merchants of Sheba, Asshur, and Chilmad, were thy merchants. ²⁴These were thy merchants in all sorts of things, in blue clothes, and broidered work, and in chests of rich apparel, bound with cords, and made of cedar, among thy merchandise. ²⁵The ships of Tarshish did sing of thee in thy market, and thou wast replenished, and made very glorious in the midst of the seas.

²⁶'"Thy rowers have brought thee into great waters: the east wind hath broken thee in the midst of the seas. ²⁷Thy riches, and thy fairs, thy merchandise, thy mariners, and thy pilots, thy caulkers, and the occupiers of thy merchandise, and all thy men of war that are in thee, and in all thy company which is in the midst of thee, shall fall into the midst of the seas in the day of thy ruin. ²⁸The suburbs shall shake at the sound of the cry of thy pilots. ²⁹And all that handle the oar, the mariners, and all the pilots of the sea, shall come down from their ships, they shall stand upon the land; ³⁰and shall cause their voice to be heard against thee, and shall cry bitterly, and shall cast up dust upon their heads, they shall wallow themselves in the ashes. ³¹And they shall make themselves utterly bald for thee, and gird them with sackcloth, and they shall weep for thee with bitterness of heart and bitter wailing. ³²And in their wailing they shall take up a lamentation for thee, and lament over thee, saying, "What city is like Tyrus, like the destroyed in the midst of the sea? ³³When thy wares went forth out of the seas, thou filledst many people, thou didst enrich the kings of the earth with the multitude of thy riches and of thy merchandise. ³⁴In the time when thou shalt be broken by the seas in the depths of the waters thy merchandise and all thy company in the midst of thee shall fall. ³⁵All the inhabitants of the isles shall be astonished at thee, and their kings shall be sore afraid, they shall be troubled in their countenance. ³⁶The merchants among the people shall hiss at thee, thou shalt be a terror, and never shalt be any more."'"

28 The word of the LORD came again unto me, saying, ²"Son of man, say unto the prince of Tyrus, "Thus saith the Lord GOD,

'"Because thy heart is lifted up,
and thou hast said, "I am a God,
I sit in the seat of God, in the midst of the seas",
yet thou art a man, and not God,
though thou set thy heart as the heart of God.
³ Behold, thou art wiser than Daniel:
there is no secret that they can hide from thee.
⁴ With thy wisdom and with thy understanding thou hast gotten
thee riches,
and hast gotten gold and silver into thy treasures.

⁵ By thy great wisdom and by thy traffic hast thou increased thy
   riches,
   and thy heart is lifted up because of thy riches.'
⁶ Therefore thus saith the Lord GOD,
   'Because thou hast set thy heart as the heart of God;
⁷ behold therefore, I will bring strangers upon thee, the terrible of
   the nations:
   and they shall draw their swords against the beauty of thy wisdom,
   and they shall defile thy brightness.
⁸ They shall bring thee down to the pit,
   and thou shalt die the deaths of them that are slain in the midst
   of the seas.
⁹ Wilt thou yet say before him that slayeth thee, "I am God"?
   but thou shalt be a man, and no God in the hand of him that
   slayeth thee.
¹⁰ Thou shalt die the deaths of the uncircumcised by the hand of
   strangers:
   for I have spoken it,' saith the Lord GOD."'

¹¹Moreover the word of the LORD came unto me, saying, ¹²'Son of man,
take up a lamentation upon the king of Tyrus, and say unto him, "Thus
saith the Lord God,

   '"Thou sealest up the sum, full of wisdom, and perfect in beauty.
¹³ Thou hast been in Eden the garden of God;
   every precious stone was thy covering,
   the sardius, topaz, and the diamond,
   the beryl, the onyx, and the jasper,
   the sapphire, the emerald, and the carbuncle, and gold:
   the workmanship of thy tabrets and of thy pipes
   was prepared in thee in the day that thou wast created.
¹⁴ Thou art the anointed cherub that covereth: and I have set thee so;
   thou wast upon the holy mountain of God;
   thou hast walked up and down in the midst of the stones of fire.
¹⁵ Thou wast perfect in thy ways from the day that thou wast created,
   till iniquity was found in thee.
¹⁶ By the multitude of thy merchandise
   they have filled the midst of thee with violence, and thou hast
      sinned:
   therefore I will cast thee as profane out of the mountain of God:
   and I will destroy thee, O covering cherub,
   from the midst of the stones of fire.
¹⁷ Thy heart was lifted up because of thy beauty,
   thou hast corrupted thy wisdom by reason of thy brightness:
   I will cast thee to the ground:
   I will lay thee before kings, that they may behold thee.
¹⁸ Thou hast defiled thy sanctuaries by the multitude of thy
      iniquities,

by the iniquity of thy traffic:
therefore will I bring forth a fire from the midst of thee,
it shall devour thee:
and I will bring thee to ashes upon the earth
in the sight of all them that behold thee.
¹⁹ All they that know thee among the people shall be astonished at
thee:
thou shalt be a terror, and never shalt thou be any more.'"'

²⁰Again the word of the LORD came unto me, saying, ²¹'Son of man, set
thy face against Zidon, and prophesy against it, ²²and say, "Thus saith
the Lord GOD,

'"'Behold, I am against thee, O Zidon,
and I will be glorified in the midst of thee:
and they shall know that I am the LORD,
when I shall have executed judgements in her,
and shall be sanctified in her.
²³ For I will send into her pestilence, and blood into her streets,
and the wounded shall be judged in the midst of her
by the sword upon her on every side,
and they shall know that I am the LORD.

²⁴'"'And there shall be no more a pricking brier unto the house of
Israel, nor any grieving thorn of all that are round about them that
despised them; and they shall know that I am the Lord GOD.' ²⁵Thus
saith the Lord GOD, 'When I shall have gathered the house of Israel
from the people among whom they are scattered, and shall be sanctified in them in the sight of the heathen, then shall they dwell in their
land that I have given to my servant Jacob. ²⁶And they shall dwell safely
therein, and shall build houses, and plant vineyards: yea, they shall
dwell with confidence when I have executed judgements upon all
those that despise them round about them; and they shall know that I
am the LORD their God.'"'

29

In the tenth year, in the tenth month, in the twelfth day of the
month, the word of the LORD came unto me, saying, ²'Son of
man, set thy face against Pharaoh king of Egypt, and prophesy against
him, and against all Egypt. ³Speak, and say, "Thus saith the Lord GOD,

'"'Behold, I am against thee, Pharaoh king of Egypt,
the great dragon that lieth in the midst of his rivers,
which hath said, "My river is my own,
and I have made it for myself".
⁴ But I will put hooks in thy jaws,
and I will cause the fish of thy rivers to stick unto thy scales,
and I will bring thee up out of the midst of thy rivers,

and all the fish of thy rivers shall stick unto thy scales.
⁵ And I will leave thee thrown into the wilderness,
thee and all the fish of thy rivers:
thou shalt fall upon the open fields,
thou shalt not be brought together, nor gathered:
I have given thee for meat to the beasts of the field
and to the fowls of the heaven.
⁶ And all the inhabitants of Egypt shall know that I am the LORD,
because they have been a staff of reed to the house of Israel.
⁷ When they took hold of thee by thy hand,
thou didst break, and rend all their shoulder:
and when they leaned upon thee,
thou brokest, and madest all their loins to be at a stand.'

⁸'"Therefore thus saith the Lord GOD, 'Behold, I will bring a sword upon thee, and cut off man and beast out of thee. ⁹And the land of Egypt shall be desolate and waste; and they shall know that I am the LORD: because he hath said, "The river is mine, and I have made it". ¹⁰Behold therefore, I am against thee, and against thy rivers, and I will make the land of Egypt utterly waste and desolate, from the tower of Syene even unto the border of Ethiopia. ¹¹No foot of man shall pass through it, nor foot of beast shall pass through it, neither shall it be inhabited forty years. ¹²And I will make the land of Egypt desolate in the midst of the countries that are desolate, and her cities among the cities that are laid waste shall be desolate forty years: and I will scatter the Egyptians among the nations, and will disperse them through the countries.'

¹³'"Yet thus saith the Lord GOD, 'At the end of forty years will I gather the Egyptians from the people whither they were scattered. ¹⁴And I will bring again the captivity of Egypt, and will cause them to return into the land of Pathros, into the land of their habitation, and they shall be there a base kingdom. ¹⁵It shall be the basest of the kingdoms, neither shall it exalt itself any more above the nations: for I will diminish them, that they shall no more rule over the nations. ¹⁶And it shall be no more the confidence of the house of Israel, which bringeth their iniquity to remembrance, when they shall look after them: but they shall know that I am the Lord GOD.'"'

¹⁷And it came to pass in the seven and twentieth year, in the first month, in the first day of the month, the word of the LORD came unto me, saying, ¹⁸'Son of man, Nebuchadrezzar king of Babylon caused his army to serve a great service against Tyrus: every head was made bald, and every shoulder was peeled: yet had he no wages, nor his army for Tyrus, for the service that he had served against it'. ¹⁹Therefore thus saith the Lord GOD, 'Behold, I will give the land of Egypt unto Nebuchadrezzar king of Babylon, and he shall take her multitude, and take her spoil, and take her prey, and it shall be the wages for his army. ²⁰I have given him the land of Egypt for his labour wherewith he served against it, because they wrought for me,' saith the Lord GOD.

²¹'In that day will I cause the horn of the house of Israel to bud forth, and I will give thee the opening of the mouth in the midst of them; and they shall know that I am the LORD.'

30

The word of the LORD came again unto me, saying, ²'Son of man, prophesy and say, "Thus saith the Lord GOD,

'"'Howl ye, woe worth the day.
³ For the day is near,
even the day of the LORD is near,
a cloudy day;
it shall be the time of the heathen.
⁴ And the sword shall come upon Egypt,
and great pain shall be in Ethiopia,
when the slain shall fall in Egypt,
and they shall take away her multitude,
and her foundations shall be broken down.
⁵ Ethiopia, and Libya, and Lydia,
and all the mingled people, and Chub,
and the men of the land that is in league,
shall fall with them by the sword.'

⁶ '"Thus saith the LORD,
'They also that uphold Egypt shall fall,
and the pride of her power shall come down:
from the tower of Syene shall they fall in it by the sword,'
saith the Lord GOD.
⁷ 'And they shall be desolate in the midst of the countries that are
desolate,
and her cities shall be in the midst of the cities that are wasted.
⁸ And they shall know that I am the LORD,
when I have set a fire in Egypt,
and when all her helpers shall be destroyed.
⁹ In that day shall messengers go forth from me
in ships to make the careless Ethiopians afraid,
and great pain shall come upon them,
as in the day of Egypt:
for lo, it cometh.'

¹⁰ '"Thus saith the Lord GOD,
'I will also make the multitude of Egypt to cease
by the hand of Nebuchadrezzar king of Babylon.
¹¹ He and his people with him, the terrible of the nations,
shall be brought to destroy the land:
and they shall draw their swords against Egypt,
and fill the land with the slain.
¹² And I will make the rivers dry,
and sell the land into the hand of the wicked,
and I will make the land waste,

and all that is therein,
by the hand of strangers:
I the LORD have spoken it.'

[13] '"Thus saith the Lord GOD,
'I will also destroy the idols,
and I will cause their images to cease out of Noph:
and there shall be no more a prince of the land of Egypt,
and I will put a fear in the land of Egypt.
[14] And I will make Pathros desolate,
and will set fire in Zoan,
and will execute judgements in No.
[15] And I will pour my fury upon Sin,
the strength of Egypt,
and I will cut off the multitude of No.
[16] And I will set fire in Egypt:
Sin shall have great pain,
and No shall be rent asunder,
and Noph shall have distresses daily.
[17] The young men of Aven and of Phibeseth shall fall by the sword:
and these cities shall go into captivity.
[18] At Tehaphnehes also the day shall be darkened
when I shall break there the yokes of Egypt:
and the pomp of her strength shall cease in her:
as for her, a cloud shall cover her,
and her daughters shall go into captivity.
[19] Thus will I execute judgements in Egypt:
and they shall know that I am the LORD.'"'

[20]And it came to pass in the eleventh year, in the first month, in the seventh day of the month, that the word of the LORD came unto me, saying, [21]'Son of man, I have broken the arm of Pharaoh king of Egypt, and lo, it shall not be bound up to be healed, to put a roller to bind it, to make it strong to hold the sword'. [22]Therefore thus saith the Lord GOD, 'Behold, I am against Pharaoh king of Egypt, and will break his arms, the strong, and that which was broken; and I will cause the sword to fall out of his hand. [23]And I will scatter the Egyptians among the nations, and will disperse them through the countries. [24]And I will strengthen the arms of the king of Babylon, and put my sword in his hand: but I will break Pharaoh's arms, and he shall groan before him with the groanings of a deadly wounded man. [25]But I will strengthen the arms of the king of Babylon, and the arms of Pharaoh shall fall down; and they shall know that I am the LORD, when I shall put my sword into the hand of the king of Babylon, and he shall stretch it out upon the land of Egypt. [26]And I will scatter the Egyptians among the nations, and disperse them among the countries; and they shall know that I am the LORD.'

31 And it came to pass in the eleventh year, in the third month, in the first day of the month, that the word of the Lord came unto me, saying, ²'Son of man, speak unto Pharaoh king of Egypt, and to his multitude,

'"Whom art thou like in thy greatness?

³ '"Behold, the Assyrian was a cedar in Lebanon with fair branches,
    and with a shadowing shroud, and of a high stature,
    and his top was among the thick boughs.
⁴ The waters made him great,
    the deep set him up on high
    with her rivers running round about his plants,
    and sent out her little rivers unto all the trees of the field.
⁵ Therefore his height was exalted above all the trees of the field,
    and his boughs were multiplied,
    and his branches became long because of the multitude of waters,
    when he shot forth.
⁶ All the fowls of heaven made their nests in his boughs,
    and under his branches did all the beasts of the field bring forth
        their young,
    and under his shadow dwelt all great nations.
⁷ Thus was he fair in his greatness,
    in the length of his branches:
    for his root was by great waters.
⁸ The cedars in the garden of God could not hide him:
    the fir trees were not like his boughs,
    and the chestnut trees were not like his branches:
    nor any tree in the garden of God was like unto him in his beauty.
⁹ I have made him fair by the multitude of his branches:
    so that all the trees of Eden, that were in the garden of God,
        envied him."

¹⁰'Therefore thus saith the Lord God, "Because thou hast lifted up thyself in height, and he hath shot up his top among the thick boughs, and his heart is lifted up in his height; ¹¹I have therefore delivered him into the hand of the mighty one of the heathen: he shall surely deal with him, I have driven him out for his wickedness. ¹²And strangers, the terrible of the nations, have cut him off, and have left him: upon the mountains and in all the valleys his branches are fallen, and his boughs are broken by all the rivers of the land, and all the people of the earth are gone down from his shadow, and have left him. ¹³Upon his ruin shall all the fowls of the heaven remain, and all the beasts of the field shall be upon his branches, ¹⁴to the end that none of all the trees by the waters exalt themselves for their height, neither shoot up their top among the thick boughs, neither their trees stand up in their height, all that drink water: for they are all delivered unto death, to the

nether parts of the earth in the midst of the children of men, with them that go down to the pit."

¹⁵Thus saith the Lord God, "In the day when he went down to the grave I caused a mourning: I covered the deep for him, and I restrained the floods thereof, and the great waters were stayed: and I caused Lebanon to mourn for him, and all the trees of the field fainted for him. ¹⁶I made the nations to shake at the sound of his fall, when I cast him down to hell with them that descend into the pit: and all the trees of Eden, the choice and best of Lebanon, all that drink water, shall be comforted in the nether parts of the earth. ¹⁷They also went down into hell with him unto them that be slain with the sword, and they that were his arm, that dwelt under his shadow in the midst of the heathen.

¹⁸‘“To whom art thou thus like in glory and in greatness among the trees of Eden? yet shalt thou be brought down with the trees of Eden unto the nether parts of the earth: thou shalt lie in the midst of the uncircumcised with them that be slain by the sword. This is Pharaoh and all his multitude," saith the Lord God.'

32 And it came to pass in the twelfth year, in the twelfth month, in the first day of the month, that the word of the Lord came unto me, saying, ²‘Son of man, take up a lamentation for Pharaoh king of Egypt, and say unto him,

> ‘“Thou art like a young lion of the nations,
> and thou art as a whale in the seas:
> and thou camest forth with thy rivers,
> and troubledst the waters with thy feet,
> and fouledst their rivers.
> ³ Thus saith the Lord God,
> ‘I will therefore spread out my net over thee with a company of
>   many people,
> and they shall bring thee up in my net.
> ⁴ Then will I leave thee upon the land,
> I will cast thee forth upon the open field,
> and will cause all the fowls of the heaven to remain upon thee,
> and I will fill the beasts of the whole earth with thee.
> ⁵ And I will lay thy flesh upon the mountains,
> and fill the valleys with thy height.
> ⁶ I will also water with thy blood
> the land wherein thou swimmest, even to the mountains,
> and the rivers shall be full of thee.
> ⁷ And when I shall put thee out, I will cover the heaven,
> and make the stars thereof dark:
> I will cover the sun with a cloud,
> and the moon shall not give her light.
> ⁸ All the bright lights of heaven will I make dark over thee,
> and set darkness upon thy land,'
> saith the Lord God.
> ⁹ ‘I will also vex the hearts of many people,

when I shall bring thy destruction among the nations,
into the countries which thou hast not known.
¹⁰ Yea, I will make many people amazed at thee,
and their kings shall be horribly afraid for thee,
when I shall brandish my sword before them,
and they shall tremble at every moment,
every man for his own life, in the day of thy fall.'

¹¹ '"For thus saith the Lord GOD,
'The sword of the king of Babylon shall come upon thee.
¹² By the swords of the mighty will I cause thy multitude to fall,
the terrible of the nations, all of them:
and they shall spoil the pomp of Egypt,
and all the multitude thereof shall be destroyed.
¹³ I will destroy also all the beasts thereof from beside the great
waters,
neither shall the foot of man trouble them any more,
nor the hoofs of beasts trouble them.
¹⁴ Then will I make their waters deep,
and cause their rivers to run like oil,'
saith the Lord GOD.
¹⁵ 'When I shall make the land of Egypt desolate,
and the country shall be destitute of that whereof it was full,
when I shall smite all them that dwell therein,
then shall they know that I am the LORD.
¹⁶ This is the lamentation wherewith they shall lament her:
the daughters of the nations shall lament her:
they shall lament for her,
even for Egypt, and for all her multitude,'
saith the Lord GOD."'

¹⁷It came to pass also in the twelfth year, in the fifteenth day of the
month, that the word of the LORD came unto me, saying, ¹⁸'Son of man,
wail for the multitude of Egypt, and cast them down, even her, and the
daughters of the famous nations, unto the nether parts of the earth,
with them that go down into the pit. ¹⁹"Whom dost thou pass in
beauty? go down, and be thou laid with the uncircumcised." ²⁰They
shall fall in the midst of them that are slain by the sword: she is delivered to the sword: draw her and all her multitudes. ²¹The strong among
the mighty shall speak to him out of the midst of hell with them that
help him: they are gone down, they lie uncircumcised, slain by the
sword.

²²'Asshur is there and all her company: his graves are about him: all
of them slain, fallen by the sword: ²³whose graves are set in the sides of
the pit, and her company is round about her grave: all of them slain,
fallen by the sword, which caused terror in the land of the living.

²⁴"There is Elam and all her multitude round about her grave, all of
them slain, fallen by the sword, which are gone down uncircumcised

into the nether parts of the earth, which caused their terror in the land of the living; yet have they borne their shame with them that go down to the pit. ²⁵They have set her a bed in the midst of the slain with all her multitudes: her graves are round about him: all of them uncircumcised, slain by the sword: though their terror was caused in the land of the living, yet have they borne their shame with them that go down to the pit: he is put in the midst of them that be slain.

²⁶'There is Meshech, Tubal, and all her multitude: her graves are round about him: all of them uncircumcised, slain by the sword, though they caused their terror in the land of the living. ²⁷And they shall not lie with the mighty that are fallen of the uncircumcised, which are gone down to hell with their weapons of war: and they have laid their swords under their heads, but their iniquities shall be upon their bones, though they were the terror of the mighty in the land of the living. ²⁸Yea, thou shalt be broken in the midst of the uncircumcised, and shalt lie with them that are slain with the sword.

²⁹'There is Edom, her kings and all her princes, which with their might are laid by them that were slain by the sword: they shall lie with the uncircumcised, and with them that go down to the pit.

³⁰'There be the princes of the north, all of them, and all the Zidonians, which are gone down with the slain; with their terror they are ashamed of their might, and they lie uncircumcised with them that be slain by the sword, and bear their shame with them that go down to the pit.

³¹'Pharaoh shall see them, and shall be comforted over all his multitude, even Pharaoh and all his army slain by the sword,' saith the Lord GOD. ³²'For I have caused my terror in the land of the living: and he shall be laid in the midst of the uncircumcised with them that are slain with the sword, even Pharaoh and all his multitude,' saith the Lord GOD.

33 Again the word of the LORD came unto me, saying, ²'Son of man, speak to the children of thy people, and say unto them, "When I bring the sword upon a land, if the people of the land take a man of their coasts, and set him for their watchman, ³if when he seeth the sword come upon the land, he blow the trumpet, and warn the people, ⁴then whosoever heareth the sound of the trumpet, and taketh not warning, if the sword come, and take him away, his blood shall be upon his own head. ⁵He heard the sound of the trumpet, and took not warning, his blood shall be upon him. But he that taketh warning shall deliver his soul. ⁶But if the watchman see the sword come, and blow not the trumpet, and the people be not warned: if the sword come, and take any person from among them, he is taken away in his iniquity: but his blood will I require at the watchman's hand."

⁷'So thou, O son of man, I have set thee a watchman unto the house of Israel: therefore thou shalt hear the word at my mouth, and warn them from me. ⁸When I say unto the wicked, "O wicked man, thou shalt surely die", if thou dost not speak to warn the wicked from his way, that wicked man shall die in his iniquity: but his blood will I require at thy hand. ⁹Nevertheless, if thou warn the wicked of his way to turn

from it: if he do not turn from his way, he shall die in his iniquity: but thou hast delivered thy soul.

¹⁰'Therefore, O thou son of man, speak unto the house of Israel, "Thus ye speak, saying, 'If our transgressions and our sins be upon us, and we pine away in them, how should we then live?'" ¹¹Say unto them, "As I live," saith the Lord GOD, "I have no pleasure in the death of the wicked, but that the wicked turn from his way and live: turn ye, turn ye from your evil ways, for why will ye die, O house of Israel?"

¹²'Therefore, thou son of man, say unto the children of thy people, "The righteousness of the righteous shall not deliver him in the day of his transgression: as for the wickedness of the wicked, he shall not fall thereby in the day that he turneth from his wickedness, neither shall the righteous be able to live for his righteousness in the day that he sinneth". ¹³When I shall say to the righteous, that he shall surely live; if he trust to his own righteousness and commit iniquity, all his righteousnesses shall not be remembered; but for his iniquity that he hath committed, he shall die for it. ¹⁴Again, when I say unto the wicked, "Thou shalt surely die", if he turn from his sin, and do that which is lawful and right; ¹⁵if the wicked restore the pledge, give again that he had robbed, walk in the statutes of life without committing iniquity, he shall surely live, he shall not die. ¹⁶None of his sins that he hath committed shall be mentioned unto him: he hath done that which is lawful and right; he shall surely live.

¹⁷'Yet the children of thy people say, "The way of the Lord is not equal": but as for them, their way is not equal. ¹⁸When the righteous turneth from his righteousness, and committeth iniquity, he shall even die thereby. ¹⁹But if the wicked turn from his wickedness, and do that which is lawful and right, he shall live thereby.

²⁰'Yet ye say, "The way of the Lord is not equal". O ye house of Israel, I will judge you every one after his ways.'

²¹And it came to pass in the twelfth year of our captivity, in the tenth month, in the fifth day of the month, that one that had escaped out of Jerusalem came unto me, saying, 'The city is smitten'. ²²Now the hand of the LORD was upon me in the evening, afore he that was escaped came, and had opened my mouth until he came to me in the morning; and my mouth was opened, and I was no more dumb.

²³Then the word of the LORD came unto me, saying, ²⁴'Son of man, they that inhabit those wastes of the land of Israel speak, saying, "Abraham was one, and he inherited the land: but we are many, the land is given us for inheritance". ²⁵Wherefore say unto them, "Thus saith the Lord GOD, 'Ye eat with the blood, and lift up your eyes toward your idols, and shed blood: and shall ye possess the land? ²⁶Ye stand upon your sword, ye work abomination, and ye defile every one his neighbour's wife: and shall ye possess the land?'" ²⁷Say thou thus unto them, "Thus saith the Lord GOD, 'As I live, surely they that are in the wastes shall fall by the sword, and him that is in the open field will I give to the beasts to be devoured, and they that be in the forts and in the caves shall die of the pestilence'". ²⁸For I will lay the land most desolate, and the pomp of her

strength shall cease: and the mountains of Israel shall be desolate, that none shall pass through. ²⁹Then shall they know that I am the LORD, when I have laid the land most desolate because of all their abominations which they have committed.

³⁰'Also, thou son of man, the children of thy people still are talking against thee by the walls and in the doors of the houses, and speak one to another, every one to his brother, saying, "Come, I pray you, and hear what is the word that cometh forth from the LORD". ³¹And they come unto thee as the people cometh, and they sit before thee as my people, and they hear thy words, but they will not do them: for with their mouth they show much love, but their heart goeth after their covetousness. ³²And lo, thou art unto them as a very lovely song of one that hath a pleasant voice, and can play well on an instrument: for they hear thy words, but they do them not. ³³And when this cometh to pass (lo, it will come), then shall they know that a prophet hath been among them.'

34 And the word of the LORD came unto me, saying, ²'Son of man, prophesy against the shepherds of Israel, prophesy and say unto them, "Thus saith the Lord GOD unto the shepherds, 'Woe be to the shepherds of Israel that do feed themselves: should not the shepherds feed the flocks? ³Ye eat the fat, and ye clothe you with the wool, ye kill them that are fed: but ye feed not the flock. ⁴The diseased have ye not strengthened, neither have ye healed that which was sick, neither have ye bound up that which was broken, neither have ye brought again that which was driven away, neither have ye sought that which was lost; but with force and with cruelty have ye ruled them. ⁵And they were scattered because there is no shepherd: and they became meat to all the beasts of the field, when they were scattered. ⁶My sheep wandered through all the mountains, and upon every high hill: yea, my flock was scattered upon all the face of the earth, and none did search or seek after them.'

⁷'"Therefore, ye shepherds, hear the word of the LORD. ⁸As I live,' saith the Lord GOD, 'surely because my flock became a prey, and my flock became meat to every beast of the field, because there was no shepherd, neither did my shepherds search for my flock, but the shepherds fed themselves, and fed not my flock': ⁹therefore, O ye shepherds, hear the word of the LORD. ¹⁰Thus saith the Lord GOD, 'Behold, I am against the shepherds, and I will require my flock at their hand, and cause them to cease from feeding the flock; neither shall the shepherds feed themselves any more: for I will deliver my flock from their mouth, that they may not be meat for them'.

¹¹'"For thus saith the Lord GOD, 'Behold, I, even I will both search my sheep, and seek them out. ¹²As a shepherd seeketh out his flock in the day that he is among his sheep that are scattered: so will I seek out my sheep, and will deliver them out of all places where they have been scattered in the cloudy and dark day. ¹³And I will bring them out from the people, and gather them from the countries, and will bring them to their own land, and feed them upon the mountains of Israel by the

rivers, and in all the inhabited places of the country. ¹⁴I will feed them in a good pasture, and upon the high mountains of Israel shall their fold be: there shall they lie in a good fold, and in a fat pasture shall they feed upon the mountains of Israel. ¹⁵I will feed my flock, and I will cause them to lie down,' saith the Lord God. ¹⁶'I will seek that which was lost, and bring again that which was driven away, and will bind up that which was broken, and will strengthen that which was sick: but I will destroy the fat and the strong, I will feed them with judgement.

¹⁷'"'And as for you, O my flock,' thus saith the Lord God, 'behold, I judge between cattle and cattle, between the rams and the he-goats. ¹⁸Seemeth it a small thing unto you to have eaten up the good pasture, but ye must tread down with your feet the residue of your pastures? and to have drunk of the deep waters, but ye must foul the residue with your feet? ¹⁹And as for my flock, they eat that which ye have trodden with your feet: and they drink that which ye have fouled with your feet.'

²⁰'"Therefore thus saith the Lord God unto them, 'Behold, I, even I will judge between the fat cattle and between the lean cattle. ²¹Because ye have thrust with side and with shoulder, and pushed all the diseased with your horns, till ye have scattered them abroad: ²²therefore will I save my flock, and they shall no more be a prey, and I will judge between cattle and cattle. ²³And I will set up one shepherd over them, and he shall feed them, even my servant David; he shall feed them, and he shall be their shepherd. ²⁴And I the Lord will be their God, and my servant David a prince among them; I the Lord have spoken it. ²⁵And I will make with them a covenant of peace, and will cause the evil beasts to cease out of the land: and they shall dwell safely in the wilderness, and sleep in the woods. ²⁶And I will make them and the places round about my hill a blessing; and I will cause the shower to come down in his season: there shall be showers of blessing. ²⁷And the tree of the field shall yield her fruit, and the earth shall yield her increase, and they shall be safe in their land, and shall know that I am the Lord, when I have broken the bands of their yoke, and delivered them out of the hand of those that served themselves of them. ²⁸And they shall no more be a prey to the heathen, neither shall the beasts of the land devour them; but they shall dwell safely, and none shall make them afraid. ²⁹And I will raise up for them a plant of renown, and they shall be no more consumed with hunger in the land, neither bear the shame of the heathen any more. ³⁰Thus shall they know that I the Lord their God am with them, and that they, even the house of Israel, are my people,' saith the Lord God. ³¹'And ye my flock, the flock of my pasture, are men, and I am your God,' saith the Lord God.'"

35 Moreover the word of the Lord came unto me, saying, ²'Son of man, set thy face against mount Seir, and prophesy against it, ³and say unto it, "Thus saith the Lord God, 'Behold, O mount Seir, I am against thee, and I will stretch out my hand against thee, and I will make thee most desolate. ⁴I will lay thy cities waste, and thou shalt be desolate, and thou shalt know that I am the Lord. ⁵Because thou hast had a perpetual hatred, and hast shed the blood of the children of Israel by the force of the sword in the time of their calamity, in the time that their iniquity had an end: ⁶therefore, as I live,' saith the Lord GOD, 'I will prepare thee unto blood, and blood shall pursue thee: since thou hast not hated blood, even blood shall pursue thee. ⁷Thus will I make mount Seir most desolate, and cut off from it him that passeth out and him that returneth. ⁸And I will fill his mountains with his slain men: in thy hills, and in thy valleys, and in all thy rivers, shall they fall that are slain with the sword. ⁹I will make thee perpetual desolations, and thy cities shall not return: and ye shall know that I am the LORD.

¹⁰'"Because thou hast said, "These two nations and these two countries shall be mine, and we will possess it", whereas the LORD was there: ¹¹therefore, as I live,' saith the Lord GOD, 'I will even do according to thy anger, and according to thy envy which thou hast used out of thy hatred against them: and I will make myself known amongst them, when I have judged thee. ¹²And thou shalt know that I am the LORD, and that I have heard all thy blasphemies which thou hast spoken against the mountains of Israel, saying, "They are laid desolate, they are given us to consume". ¹³Thus with your mouth ye have boasted against me, and have multiplied your words against me: I have heard them.' ¹⁴Thus saith the Lord GOD, 'When the whole earth rejoiceth, I will make thee desolate. ¹⁵As thou didst rejoice at the inheritance of the house of Israel, because it was desolate, so will I do unto thee: thou shalt be desolate, O mount Seir, and all Idumea, even all of it: and they shall know that I am the LORD.'"

36 ¹Also, thou son of man, prophesy unto the mountains of Israel, and say, "Ye mountains of Israel, hear the word of the LORD. ²Thus saith the Lord GOD, 'Because the enemy hath said against you, "Aha, even the ancient high places are ours in possession"'": ³therefore prophesy and say, "Thus saith the Lord GOD, 'Because they have made you desolate, and swallowed you up on every side, that ye might be a possession unto the residue of the heathen, and ye are taken up in the lips of talkers, and are an infamy of the people': ⁴therefore, ye mountains of Israel, hear the word of the Lord GOD, thus saith the Lord GOD to the mountains and to the hills, to the rivers and to the valleys, to the desolate wastes, and to the cities that are forsaken, which became a prey and derision to the residue of the heathen that are round about: ⁵therefore thus saith the Lord GOD, 'Surely in the fire of my jealousy have I spoken against the residue of the heathen, and against all Idumea, which have appointed my land into their possession with the joy of all their heart, with despiteful minds, to cast it out for a prey'". ⁶Prophesy therefore concerning the land of Israel, and say unto the mountains and to the hills, to the rivers and to the valleys, "Thus saith the Lord GOD, 'Behold, I have spoken in my jealousy and in my fury, because ye have borne the shame of the heathen': ⁷therefore thus saith the Lord GOD, 'I have lifted up my hand, surely the heathen that are about you, they shall bear their shame.

⁸'"But ye, O mountains of Israel, ye shall shoot forth your branches,

and yield your fruit to my people of Israel, for they are at hand to come. ⁹For behold, I am for you, and I will turn unto you, and ye shall be tilled and sown. ¹⁰And I will multiply men upon you, all the house of Israel, even all of it: and the cities shall be inhabited, and the wastes shall be built. ¹¹And I will multiply upon you man and beast, and they shall increase and bring fruit, and I will settle you after your old estates: and will do better unto you than at your beginnings; and ye shall know that I am the LORD. ¹²Yea, I will cause men to walk upon you, even my people Israel, and they shall possess thee, and thou shalt be their inheritance, and thou shalt no more henceforth bereave them of men.' ¹³Thus saith the Lord GOD, 'Because they say unto you, "Thou land devourest up men, and hast bereaved thy nations", ¹⁴therefore thou shalt devour men no more, neither bereave thy nations any more,' saith the Lord GOD. ¹⁵'Neither will I cause men to hear in thee the shame of the heathen any more, neither shalt thou bear the reproach of the people any more, neither shalt thou cause the nations to fall any more,' saith the Lord GOD."'

¹⁶Moreover the word of the LORD came unto me, saying, ¹⁷'Son of man, when the house of Israel dwelt in their own land, they defiled it by their own way and by their doings: their way was before me as the uncleanness of a removed woman. ¹⁸Wherefore I poured my fury upon them for the blood that they had shed upon the land, and for their idols wherewith they had polluted it. ¹⁹And I scattered them among the heathen, and they were dispersed through the countries: according to their way and according to their doings I judged them. ²⁰And when they entered unto the heathen whither they went, they profaned my holy name, when they said to them, "These are the people of the LORD, and are gone forth out of his land".

²¹'But I had pity for my holy name, which the house of Israel had profaned among the heathen, whither they went. ²²Therefore say unto the house of Israel, "Thus saith the Lord GOD, 'I do not this for your sakes, O house of Israel, but for my holy name's sake, which ye have profaned among the heathen, whither ye went. ²³And I will sanctify my great name which was profaned among the heathen, which ye have profaned in the midst of them, and the heathen shall know that I am the LORD,' saith the Lord GOD, 'when I shall be sanctified in you before their eyes. ²⁴For I will take you from among the heathen, and gather you out of all countries, and will bring you into your own land.

²⁵'"Then will I sprinkle clean water upon you, and ye shall be clean: from all your filthiness, and from all your idols will I cleanse you. ²⁶A new heart also will I give you, and a new spirit will I put within you: and I will take away the stony heart out of your flesh, and I will give you a heart of flesh. ²⁷And I will put my Spirit within you, and cause you to walk in my statutes, and ye shall keep my judgements, and do them. ²⁸And ye shall dwell in the land that I gave to your fathers, and ye shall be my people, and I will be your God. ²⁹I will also save you from all your uncleannesses: and I will call for the corn, and will increase it, and lay no famine upon you. ³⁰And I will multiply the fruit of the tree, and the

increase of the field, that ye shall receive no more reproach of famine among the heathen. [31]Then shall ye remember your own evil ways, and your doings that were not good, and shall loathe yourselves in your own sight for your iniquities and for your abominations. [32]Not for your sakes do I this,' saith the Lord GOD, 'be it known unto you: be ashamed and confounded for your own ways, O house of Israel.'

[33]'"Thus saith the Lord GOD, 'In the day that I shall have cleansed you from all your iniquities I will also cause you to dwell in the cities, and the wastes shall be built. [34]And the desolate land shall be tilled, whereas it lay desolate in the sight of all that passed by. [35]And they shall say, "This land that was desolate is become like the garden of Eden, and the waste and desolate and ruined cities are become fenced, and are inhabited". [36]Then the heathen that are left round about you shall know that I the LORD build the ruined places, and plant that that was desolate: I the LORD have spoken it, and I will do it.'

[37]'"Thus saith the Lord GOD, 'I will yet for this be inquired of by the house of Israel, to do it for them: I will increase them with men like a flock. [38]As the holy flock, as the flock of Jerusalem in her solemn feasts, so shall the waste cities be filled with flocks of men: and they shall know that I am the LORD.'"'

37 The hand of the LORD was upon me, and carried me out in the Spirit of the LORD, and set me down in the midst of the valley which was full of bones, [2]and caused me to pass by them round about: and behold, there were very many in the open valley, and lo, they were very dry. [3]And he said unto me, 'Son of man, can these bones live?' And I answered, 'O Lord GOD, thou knowest'.

[4]Again he said unto me, 'Prophesy upon these bones, and say unto them, "O ye dry bones, hear the word of the LORD. [5]Thus saith the Lord GOD unto these bones, 'Behold, I will cause breath to enter into you, and ye shall live. [6]And I will lay sinews upon you, and will bring up flesh upon you, and cover you with skin, and put breath in you, and ye shall live; and ye shall know that I am the LORD.'"'

[7]So I prophesied as I was commanded: and as I prophesied, there was a noise, and behold a shaking, and the bones came together, bone to his bone. [8]And when I beheld, lo, the sinews and the flesh came up upon them, and the skin covered them above: but there was no breath in them. [9]Then said he unto me, 'Prophesy unto the wind, prophesy, son of man, and say to the wind, "Thus saith the Lord GOD, 'Come from the four winds, O breath, and breathe upon these slain, that they may live'"'. [10]So I prophesied as he commanded me, and the breath came into them, and they lived, and stood up upon their feet, an exceeding great army.

[11]Then he said unto me, 'Son of man, these bones are the whole house of Israel: behold, they say, "Our bones are dried, and our hope is lost: we are cut off for our parts". [12]Therefore prophesy and say unto them, "Thus saith the Lord GOD, 'Behold, O my people, I will open your graves, and cause you to come up out of your graves, and bring you into the land of Israel. [13]And ye shall know that I am the LORD, when I have

opened your graves, O my people, and brought you up out of your graves, ¹⁴and shall put my Spirit in you, and ye shall live, and I shall place you in your own land: then shall ye know that I the LORD have spoken it, and performed it,' saith the LORD."'

¹⁵The word of the LORD came again unto me, saying, ¹⁶'Moreover, thou son of man, take thee one stick, and write upon it, "For Judah and for the children of Israel his companions": then take another stick, and write upon it, "For Joseph the stick of Ephraim and for all the house of Israel his companions". ¹⁷And join them one to another into one stick, and they shall become one in thy hand.

¹⁸'And when the children of thy people shall speak unto thee, saying, "Wilt thou not show us what thou meanest by these?" ¹⁹say unto them, "Thus saith the Lord GOD, 'Behold, I will take the stick of Joseph, which is in the hand of Ephraim, and the tribes of Israel his fellows, and will put them with him, even with the stick of Judah, and make them one stick, and they shall be one in my hand'".

²⁰'And the sticks whereon thou writest shall be in thy hand before their eyes. ²¹And say unto them, "Thus saith the Lord GOD, 'Behold, I will take the children of Israel from among the heathen whither they be gone, and will gather them on every side, and bring them into their own land. ²²And I will make them one nation in the land upon the mountains of Israel, and one king shall be king to them all: and they shall be no more two nations, neither shall they be divided into two kingdoms any more at all. ²³Neither shall they defile themselves any more with their idols, nor with their detestable things, nor with any of their transgressions: but I will save them out of all their dwelling-places, wherein they have sinned, and will cleanse them: so shall they be my people, and I will be their God. ²⁴And David my servant shall be king over them, and they all shall have one shepherd: they shall also walk in my judgements, and observe my statutes, and do them. ²⁵And they shall dwell in the land that I have given unto Jacob my servant, wherein your fathers have dwelt, and they shall dwell therein, even they and their children, and their children's children for ever: and my servant David shall be their prince for ever. ²⁶Moreover I will make a covenant of peace with them, it shall be an everlasting covenant with them: and I will place them and multiply them, and will set my sanctuary in the midst of them for evermore. ²⁷My tabernacle also shall be with them: yea, I will be their God, and they shall be my people. ²⁸And the heathen shall know that I the LORD do sanctify Israel, when my sanctuary shall be in the midst of them for evermore.'"'

38 And the word of the LORD came unto me, saying, ²'Son of man, set thy face against Gog, the land of Magog, the chief prince of Meshech and Tubal, and prophesy against him, ³and say, "Thus saith the Lord GOD, 'Behold, I am against thee, O Gog, the chief prince of Meshech and Tubal. ⁴And I will turn thee back, and put hooks into thy jaws, and I will bring thee forth, and all thy army, horses and horsemen, all of them clothed with all sorts of armour, even a great company with bucklers and shields, all of them handling swords: ⁵Persia,

Ethiopia, and Libya with them; all of them with shield and helmet: ⁶Gomer, and all his bands, the house of Togarmah of the north quarters, and all his bands, and many people with thee. ⁷Be thou prepared, and prepare for thyself, thou, and all thy company that are assembled unto thee, and be thou a guard unto them.

⁸ " 'After many days thou shalt be visited: in the latter years thou shalt come into the land that is brought back from the sword, and is gathered out of many people against the mountains of Israel, which have been always waste: but it is brought forth out of the nations, and they shall dwell safely all of them. ⁹Thou shalt ascend and come like a storm, thou shalt be like a cloud to cover the land, thou and all thy bands, and many people with thee.'

¹⁰ " 'Thus saith the Lord GOD, 'It shall also come to pass, that at the same time shall things come into thy mind, and thou shalt think an evil thought. ¹¹And thou shalt say, "I will go up to the land of unwalled villages; I will go to them that are at rest, that dwell safely, all of them dwelling without walls, and having neither bars nor gates"; ¹²to take a spoil, and to take a prey, to turn thy hand upon the desolate places that are now inhabited, and upon the people that are gathered out of the nations, which have gotten cattle and goods, that dwell in the midst of the land. ¹³Sheba, and Dedan, and the merchants of Tarshish, with all the young lions thereof, shall say unto thee, "Art thou come to take a spoil? hast thou gathered thy company to take a prey? to carry away silver and gold, to take away cattle and goods, to take a great spoil?" ' "

¹⁴ 'Therefore, son of man, prophesy and say unto Gog, "Thus saith the Lord GOD, 'In that day when my people of Israel dwelleth safely, shalt thou not know it? ¹⁵And thou shalt come from thy place out of the north parts, thou and many people with thee, all of them riding upon horses, a great company, and a mighty army. ¹⁶And thou shalt come up against my people of Israel, as a cloud to cover the land; it shall be in the latter days, and I will bring thee against my land, that the heathen may know me, when I shall be sanctified in thee, O Gog, before their eyes.'

¹⁷ " 'Thus saith the Lord GOD, 'Art thou he of whom I have spoken in old time by my servants the prophets of Israel, which prophesied in those days many years that I would bring thee against them? ¹⁸And it shall come to pass at the same time when Gog shall come against the land of Israel,' saith the Lord GOD, 'that my fury shall come up in my face. ¹⁹For in my jealousy and in the fire of my wrath have I spoken: surely in that day there shall be a great shaking in the land of Israel; ²⁰so that the fishes of the sea, and the fowls of the heaven, and the beasts of the field, and all creeping things that creep upon the earth, and all the men that are upon the face of the earth, shall shake at my presence, and the mountains shall be thrown down, and the steep places shall fall, and every wall shall fall to the ground. ²¹And I will call for a sword against him throughout all my mountains,' saith the Lord GOD: 'every man's sword shall be against his brother. ²²And I will plead against him with pestilence and with blood, and I will rain upon him, and upon his

bands, and upon the many people that are with him, an overflowing rain, and great hailstones, fire, and brimstone. ²³Thus will I magnify myself, and sanctify myself; and I will be known in the eyes of many nations, and they shall know that I am the LORD.'"

39 'Therefore, thou son of man, prophesy against Gog, and say, "Thus saith the Lord GOD, 'Behold, I am against thee, O Gog, the chief prince of Meshech and Tubal. ²And I will turn thee back, and leave but the sixth part of thee, and will cause thee to come up from the north parts, and will bring thee upon the mountains of Israel: ³and I will smite thy bow out of thy left hand, and will cause thy arrows to fall out of thy right hand. ⁴Thou shalt fall upon the mountains of Israel, thou and all thy bands, and the people that is with thee: I will give thee unto the ravenous birds of every sort, and to the beasts of the field to be devoured. ⁵Thou shalt fall upon the open field, for I have spoken it,' saith the Lord GOD."

⁶'And I will send a fire on Magog, and among them that dwell carelessly in the isles: and they shall know that I am the LORD. ⁷So will I make my holy name known in the midst of my people Israel, and I will not let them pollute my holy name any more: and the heathen shall know that I am the LORD, the Holy One in Israel.

⁸'Behold, it is come, and it is done,' saith the Lord GOD, 'this is the day whereof I have spoken. ⁹And they that dwell in the cities of Israel shall go forth, and shall set on fire and burn the weapons, both the shields and the bucklers, the bows and the arrows, and the handstaves and the spears, and they shall burn them with fire seven years: ¹⁰so that they shall take no wood out of the field, neither cut down any out of the forests: for they shall burn the weapons with fire, and they shall spoil those that spoiled them, and rob those that robbed them,' saith the Lord GOD.

¹¹'And it shall come to pass at that day, that I will give unto Gog a place there of graves in Israel, the valley of the passengers on the east of the sea: and it shall stop the noses of the passengers, and there shall they bury Gog and all his multitude: and they shall call it the valley of Hamon-gog. ¹²And seven months shall the house of Israel be burying of them, that they may cleanse the land. ¹³Yea, all the people of the land shall bury them, and it shall be to them a renown the day that I shall be glorified,' saith the Lord GOD.

¹⁴'And they shall sever out men of continual employment, passing through the land to bury with the passengers those that remain upon the face of the earth to cleanse it: after the end of seven months shall they search. ¹⁵And the passengers that pass through the land, when any seeth a man's bone, then shall he set up a sign by it, till the buriers have buried it in the valley of Hamon-gog. ¹⁶And also the name of the city shall be Hamonah. Thus shall they cleanse the land.

¹⁷'And, thou son of man, thus saith the Lord GOD, "Speak unto every feathered fowl, and to every beast of the field, 'Assemble yourselves, and come, gather yourselves on every side to my sacrifice that I do sacrifice for you, even a great sacrifice upon the mountains of Israel, that

ye may eat flesh and drink blood. [18]Ye shall eat the flesh of the mighty, and drink the blood of the princes of the earth, of rams, of lambs and of goats, of bullocks, all of them fatlings of Bashan. [19]And ye shall eat fat till ye be full, and drink blood till ye be drunken, of my sacrifice which I have sacrificed for you. [20]Thus ye shall be filled at my table with horses and chariots, with mighty men, and with all men of war,' saith the Lord GOD."

[21]'And I will set my glory among the heathen, and all the heathen shall see my judgement that I have executed, and my hand that I have laid upon them. [22]So the house of Israel shall know that I am the LORD their God from that day and forward.

[23]'And the heathen shall know that the house of Israel went into captivity for their iniquity: because they trespassed against me, therefore hid I my face from them, and gave them into the hand of their enemies: so fell they all by the sword. [24]According to their uncleanness and according to their transgressions have I done unto them, and hid my face from them.'

[25]Therefore thus saith the Lord GOD, 'Now will I bring again the captivity of Jacob, and have mercy upon the whole house of Israel, and will be jealous for my holy name; [26]after that they have borne their shame, and all their trespasses whereby they have trespassed against me, when they dwelt safely in their land, and none made them afraid. [27]When I have brought them again from the people, and gathered them out of their enemies' lands, and am sanctified in them in the sight of many nations; [28]then shall they know that I am the LORD their God, which caused them to be led into captivity among the heathen: but I have gathered them unto their own land, and have left none of them any more there. [29]Neither will I hide my face any more from them: for I have poured out my Spirit upon the house of Israel,' saith the Lord GOD.

40 In the five and twentieth year of our captivity, in the beginning of the year, in the tenth day of the month, in the fourteenth year after that the city was smitten, in the selfsame day the hand of the LORD was upon me, and brought me thither. [2]In the visions of God brought he me into the land of Israel, and set me upon a very high mountain, by which was as the frame of a city on the south. [3]And he brought me thither, and behold, there was a man, whose appearance was like the appearance of brass, with a line of flax in his hand, and a measuring-reed; and he stood in the gate. [4]And the man said unto me, 'Son of man, behold with thy eyes, and hear with thy ears, and set thy heart upon all that I shall show thee: for to the intent that I might show them unto thee art thou brought hither: declare all that thou seest to the house of Israel'. [5]And behold a wall on the outside of the house round about, and in the man's hand a measuring-reed of six cubits long by the cubit and a handbreadth: so he measured the breadth of the building, one reed, and the height, one reed.

[6]Then came he unto the gate which looketh toward the east, and went up the stairs thereof, and measured the threshold of the gate, which

was one reed broad, and the other threshold of the gate, which was one reed broad. ⁷And every little chamber was one reed long, and one reed broad, and between the little chambers were five cubits, and the threshold of the gate by the porch of the gate within was one reed. ⁸He measured also the porch of the gate within, one reed. ⁹Then measured he the porch of the gate, eight cubits, and the posts thereof, two cubits, and the porch of the gate was inward. ¹⁰And the little chambers of the gate eastward were three on this side, and three on that side, they three were of one measure, and the posts had one measure on this side and on that side. ¹¹And he measured the breadth of the entry of the gate, ten cubits, and the length of the gate, thirteen cubits. ¹²The space also before the little chambers was one cubit on this side, and the space was one cubit on that side, and the little chambers were six cubits on this side, and six cubits on that side. ¹³He measured then the gate from the roof of one little chamber to the roof of another: the breadth was five and twenty cubits, door against door. ¹⁴He made also posts of three-score cubits, even unto the post of the court round about the gate. ¹⁵And from the face of the gate of the entrance unto the face of the porch of the inner gate were fifty cubits. ¹⁶And there were narrow windows to the little chambers, and to their posts within the gate round about, and likewise to the arches: and windows were round about inward: and upon each post were palm trees.

¹⁷Then brought he me into the outward court, and lo, there were chambers, and a pavement made for the court round about: thirty chambers were upon the pavement. ¹⁸And the pavement by the side of the gates over against the length of the gates was the lower pavement. ¹⁹Then he measured the breadth from the forefront of the lower gate unto the forefront of the inner court without, a hundred cubits eastward and northward.

²⁰And the gate of the outward court that looked toward the north, he measured the length thereof, and the breadth thereof. ²¹And the little chambers thereof were three on this side and three on that side, and the posts thereof and the arches thereof were after the measure of the first gate: the length thereof was fifty cubits, and the breadth five and twenty cubits. ²²And their windows, and their arches, and their palm trees, were after the measure of the gate that looketh towards the east, and they went up unto it by seven steps, and the arches thereof were before them. ²³And the gate of the inner court was over against the gate toward the north, and toward the east, and he measured from gate to gate a hundred cubits.

²⁴After that he brought me toward the south, and behold a gate toward the south, and he measured the posts thereof and the arches thereof according to these measures. ²⁵And there were windows in it and in the arches thereof round about, like those windows: the length was fifty cubits, and the breadth five and twenty cubits. ²⁶And there were seven steps to go up to it, and the arches thereof were before them, and it had palm trees, one on this side, and another on that side, upon the posts thereof. ²⁷And there was a gate in the inner court toward

the south, and he measured from gate to gate toward the south a hundred cubits.

²⁸And he brought me to the inner court by the south gate, and he measured the south gate according to these measures, ²⁹and the little chambers thereof, and the posts thereof, and the arches thereof, according to these measures: and there were windows in it and in the arches thereof round about: it was fifty cubits long, and five and twenty cubits broad. ³⁰And the arches round about were five and twenty cubits long, and five cubits broad. ³¹And the arches thereof were toward the outer court, and palm trees were upon the posts thereof, and the going up to it had eight steps.

³²And he brought me into the inner court toward the east, and he measured the gate according to these measures. ³³And the little chambers thereof, and the posts thereof, and the arches thereof were according to these measures: and there were windows therein and in the arches thereof round about: it was fifty cubits long, and five and twenty cubits broad. ³⁴And the arches thereof were toward the outward court, and palm trees were upon the posts thereof, on this side, and on that side and the going up to it had eight steps.

³⁵And he brought me to the north gate, and measured it according to these measures; ³⁶the little chambers thereof, the posts thereof, and the arches thereof, and the windows to it round about: the length was fifty cubits, and the breadth five and twenty cubits. ³⁷And the posts thereof were toward the outer court, and palm trees were upon the posts thereof, on this side, and on that side, and the going up to it had eight steps. ³⁸And the chambers and the entries thereof were by the posts of the gates, where they washed the burnt offering.

³⁹And in the porch of the gate were two tables on this side, and two tables on that side, to slay thereon the burnt offering and the sin offering and the trespass offering. ⁴⁰And at the side without, as one goeth up to the entry of the north gate, were two tables, and on the other side, which was at the porch of the gate, were two tables. ⁴¹Four tables were on this side, and four tables on that side, by the side of the gate; eight tables, whereupon they slew their sacrifices. ⁴²And the four tables were of hewn stone for the burnt offering, of a cubit and a half long, and a cubit and a half broad, and one cubit high: whereupon also they laid the instruments wherewith they slew the burnt offering and the sacrifice. ⁴³And within were hooks, a hand broad, fastened round about, and upon the tables was the flesh of the offering.

⁴⁴And without the inner gate were the chambers of the singers in the inner court, which was at the side of the north gate: and their prospect was toward the south, one at the side of the east gate having the prospect toward the north. ⁴⁵And he said unto me, 'This chamber, whose prospect is toward the south, is for the priests, the keepers of the charge of the house. ⁴⁶And the chamber whose prospect is toward the north is for the priests, the keepers of the charge of the altar: these are the sons of Zadok among the sons of Levi, which come near to the LORD to minister unto him.' ⁴⁷So he measured the court, a hundred cubits

long, and a hundred cubits broad, four-square, and the altar that was before the house.

⁴⁸And he brought me to the porch of the house, and measured each post of the porch, five cubits on this side, and five cubits on that side: and the breadth of the gate was three cubits on this side, and three cubits on that side. ⁴⁹The length of the porch was twenty cubits, and the breadth eleven cubits, and he brought me by the steps whereby they went up to it, and there were pillars by the posts, one on this side, and another on that side.

41 Afterward he brought me to the temple, and measured the posts, six cubits broad on the one side, and six cubits broad on the other side, which was the breadth of the tabernacle. ²And the breadth of the door was ten cubits, and the sides of the door were five cubits on the one side, and five cubits on the other side, and he measured the length thereof, forty cubits, and the breadth, twenty cubits. ³Then went he inward, and measured the post of the door, two cubits, and the door, six cubits, and the breadth of the door, seven cubits. ⁴So he measured the length thereof, twenty cubits, and the breadth, twenty cubits, before the temple: and he said unto me, 'This is the most holy place'.

⁵After he measured the wall of the house, six cubits, and the breadth of every side-chamber, four cubits, round about the house on every side. ⁶And the side-chambers were three, one over another, and thirty in order, and they entered into the wall which was of the house for the side-chambers round about, that they might have hold, but they had not hold in the wall of the house. ⁷And there was an enlarging and a winding about still upward to the side-chambers, for the winding about of the house went still upward round about the house: therefore the breadth of the house was still upward, and so increased from the lowest chamber to the highest by the midst.

⁸I saw also the height of the house round about: the foundations of the side-chambers were a full reed of six great cubits. ⁹The thickness of the wall which was for the side-chamber without, was five cubits, and that which was left was the place of the side-chambers that were within. ¹⁰And between the chambers was the wideness of twenty cubits round about the house on every side. ¹¹And the doors of the side-chambers were toward the place that was left, one door toward the north, and another door toward the south, and the breadth of the place that was left was five cubits round about. ¹²Now the building that was before the separate place at the end toward the west was seventy cubits broad, and the wall of the building was five cubits thick round about, and the length thereof ninety cubits.

¹³So he measured the house, a hundred cubits long, and the separate place, and the building, with the walls thereof, a hundred cubits long; ¹⁴also the breadth of the face of the house, and of the separate place toward the east, a hundred cubits. ¹⁵And he measured the length of the building over against the separate place which was behind it, and the galleries thereof on the one side and on the other side, a hundred

cubits, with the inner temple, and the porches of the court; ¹⁶the door-posts, and the narrow windows, and the galleries round about on their three storeys, over against the door, ceiled with wood round about, and from the ground up to the windows, and the windows were covered; ¹⁷to that above the door, even unto the inner house, and without, and by all the wall round about within and without, by measure. ¹⁸And it was made with cherubims and palm trees, so that a palm tree was between a cherub and a cherub, and every cherub had two faces; ¹⁹so that the face of a man was toward the palm tree on the one side, and the face of a young lion toward the palm tree on the other side: it was made through all the house round about. ²⁰From the ground unto above the door were cherubims and palm trees made, and on the wall of the temple. ²¹The posts of the temple were squared, and the face of the sanctuary, the appearance of the one as the appearance of the other. ²²The altar of wood was three cubits high, and the length thereof two cubits; and the corners thereof and the length thereof and the walls thereof were of wood: and he said unto me, 'This is the table that is before the LORD'.

²³And the temple and the sanctuary had two doors. ²⁴And the doors had two leaves apiece, two turning leaves, two leaves for the one door, and two leaves for the other door. ²⁵And there were made on them, on the doors of the temple, cherubims and palm trees, like as were made upon the walls, and there were thick planks upon the face of the porch without. ²⁶And there were narrow windows and palm trees on the one side and on the other side, on the sides of the porch, and upon the side-chambers of the house, and thick planks.

42 Then he brought me forth into the outer court, the way toward the north, and he brought me into the chamber that was over against the separate place, and which was before the building toward the north. ²Before the length of a hundred cubits was the north door, and the breadth was fifty cubits. ³Over against the twenty cubits which were for the inner court, and over against the pavement which was for the outer court, was gallery against gallery in three storeys. ⁴And before the chambers was a walk of ten cubits breadth inward, a way of one cubit, and their doors toward the north. ⁵Now the upper chambers were shorter: for the galleries were higher than these, than the lower, and than the middlemost of the building. ⁶For they were in three storeys, but had not pillars as the pillars of the courts: therefore the building was straitened more than the lowest and the middlemost from the ground. ⁷And the wall that was without over against the chambers, towards the outer court on the forepart of the chambers, the length thereof was fifty cubits. ⁸For the length of the chambers that were in the outer court was fifty cubits: and lo, before the temple were a hundred cubits. ⁹And from under these chambers was the entry on the east side, as one goeth into them from the outer court. ¹⁰The chambers were in the thickness of the wall of the court toward the east, over against the separate place, and over against the building. ¹¹And the way before them was like the appearance of the chambers which were toward the north, as long as they and as broad as they, and all their goings out were both according to their fashions, and according to their doors. ¹²And according to the doors of the chambers that were toward the south was a door in the head of the way, even the way directly before the wall toward the east, as one entereth into them.

¹³Then said he unto me, 'The north chambers and the south chambers, which are before the separate place, they be holy chambers, where the priests that approach unto the LORD shall eat the most holy things: there shall they lay the most holy things, and the meat offering, and the sin offering, and the trespass offering, for the place is holy. ¹⁴When the priests enter therein, then shall they not go out of the holy place into the outer court, but there they shall lay their garments wherein they minister: for they are holy; and shall put on other garments, and shall approach to those things which are for the people.'

¹⁵Now when he had made an end of measuring the inner house, he brought me forth toward the gate whose prospect is toward the east, and measured it round about. ¹⁶He measured the east side with the measuring-reed, five hundred reeds, with the measuring-reed round about. ¹⁷He measured the north side, five hundred reeds, with the measuring-reed round about. ¹⁸He measured the south side, five hundred reeds, with the measuring-reed.

¹⁹He turned about to the west side, and measured five hundred reeds with the measuring-reed. ²⁰He measured it by the four sides: it had a wall round about, five hundred reeds long, and five hundred broad, to make a separation between the sanctuary and the profane place.

43 Afterward he brought me to the gate, even the gate that looketh toward the east. ²And behold, the glory of the God of Israel came from the way of the east: and his voice was like a noise of many waters, and the earth shone with his glory. ³And it was according to the appearance of the vision which I saw, even according to the vision that I saw when I came to destroy the city: and the visions were like the vision that I saw by the river Chebar: and I fell upon my face. ⁴And the glory of the LORD came into the house by the way of the gate whose prospect is toward the east. ⁵So the spirit took me up, and brought me into the inner court, and behold, the glory of the LORD filled the house. ⁶And I heard him speaking unto me out of the house, and the man stood by me.

⁷And he said unto me, 'Son of man, the place of my throne, and the place of the soles of my feet, where I will dwell in the midst of the children of Israel for ever, and my holy name, shall the house of Israel no more defile, neither they, nor their kings, by their whoredom, nor by the carcases of their kings in their high places. ⁸In their setting of their threshold by my thresholds, and their post by my posts, and the wall between me and them, they have even defiled my holy name by their abominations that they have committed: wherefore I have consumed them in my anger. ⁹Now let them put away their whoredom, and the carcases of their kings far from me, and I will dwell in the midst of them for ever.

[10]'Thou son of man, show the house to the house of Israel, that they may be ashamed of their iniquities, and let them measure the pattern. [11]And if they be ashamed of all that they have done, show them the form of the house, and the fashion thereof, and the goings out thereof, and the comings in thereof, and all the forms thereof, and all the ordinances thereof, and all the forms thereof, and all the laws thereof: and write it in their sight, that they may keep the whole form thereof, and all the ordinances thereof, and do them. [12]This is the law of the house; upon the top of the mountain the whole limit thereof round about shall be most holy. Behold, this is the law of the house.

[13]'And these are the measures of the altar after the cubits: the cubit is a cubit and a handbreadth; even the bottom shall be a cubit, and the breadth a cubit, and the border thereof by the edge thereof round about shall be a span, and this shall be the higher place of the altar. [14]And from the bottom upon the ground even to the lower settle shall be two cubits, and the breadth one cubit, and from the lesser settle even to the greater settle shall be four cubits, and the breadth one cubit. [15]So the altar shall be four cubits, and from the altar and upward shall be four horns. [16]And the altar shall be twelve cubits long, twelve broad, square in the four squares thereof. [17]And the settle shall be fourteen cubits long and fourteen broad in the four squares thereof, and the border about it shall be half a cubit, and the bottom thereof shall be a cubit about, and his stairs shall look toward the east.'

[18]And he said unto me, 'Son of man, thus saith the Lord GOD, "These are the ordinances of the altar in the day when they shall make it to offer burnt offerings thereon, and to sprinkle blood thereon. [19]And thou shalt give to the priests the Levites that be of the seed of Zadok, which approach unto me, to minister unto me," saith the Lord GOD, "a young bullock for a sin offering. [20]And thou shalt take of the blood thereof, and put it on the four horns of it, and on the four corners of the settle, and upon the border round about: thus shalt thou cleanse and purge it. [21]Thou shalt take the bullock also of the sin offering, and he shall burn it in the appointed place of the house, without the sanctuary. [22]And on the second day thou shalt offer a kid of the goats without blemish for a sin offering, and they shall cleanse the altar, as they did cleanse it with the bullock. [23]When thou hast made an end of cleansing it, thou shalt offer a young bullock without blemish, and a ram out of the flock without blemish. [24]And thou shalt offer them before the LORD, and the priests shall cast salt upon them, and they shall offer them up for a burnt offering unto the LORD. [25]Seven days shalt thou prepare every day a goat for a sin offering: they shall also prepare a young bullock, and a ram out of the flock, without blemish. [26]Seven days shall they purge the altar and purify it, and they shall consecrate themselves. [27]And when these days are expired, it shall be that upon the eighth day, and so forward, the priests shall make your burnt offerings upon the altar, and your peace offerings; and I will accept you," saith the Lord GOD.'

44 Then he brought me back the way of the gate of the outward sanctuary which looketh toward the east, and it was shut. ²Then said the LORD unto me, 'This gate shall be shut, it shall not be opened, and no man shall enter in by it; because the LORD the God of Israel hath entered in by it, therefore it shall be shut. ³It is for the prince; the prince, he shall sit in it to eat bread before the LORD: he shall enter by the way of the porch of that gate, and shall go out by the way of the same.'

⁴Then brought he me the way of the north gate before the house, and I looked, and behold, the glory of the LORD filled the house of the LORD, and I fell upon my face. ⁵And the LORD said unto me, 'Son of man, mark well, and behold with thy eyes, and hear with thy ears all that I say unto thee concerning all the ordinances of the house of the LORD, and all the laws thereof, and mark well the entering in of the house, with every going forth of the sanctuary. ⁶And thou shalt say to the rebellious, even to the house of Israel, "Thus saith the Lord GOD, 'O ye house of Israel, let it suffice you of all your abominations, ⁷in that ye have brought into my sanctuary strangers, uncircumcised in heart, and uncircumcised in flesh, to be in my sanctuary to pollute it, even my house, when ye offer my bread, the fat and the blood, and they have broken my covenant because of all your abominations. ⁸And ye have not kept the charge of my holy things: but ye have set keepers of my charge in my sanctuary for yourselves.'

⁹'"Thus saith the Lord GOD, 'No stranger uncircumcised in heart, nor uncircumcised in flesh, shall enter into my sanctuary, of any stranger that is among the children of Israel. ¹⁰And the Levites that are gone away far from me, when Israel went astray, which went astray away from me after their idols, they shall even bear their iniquity. ¹¹Yet they shall be ministers in my sanctuary, having charge at the gates of the house, and ministering to the house: they shall slay the burnt offering and the sacrifice for the people, and they shall stand before them to minister unto them. ¹²Because they ministered unto them before their idols, and caused the house of Israel to fall into iniquity; therefore have I lifted up my hand against them,' saith the Lord GOD, 'and they shall bear their iniquity. ¹³And they shall not come near unto me to do the office of a priest unto me, nor to come near to any of my holy things, in the most holy place: but they shall bear their shame, and their abominations which they have committed. ¹⁴But I will make them keepers of the charge of the house for all the service thereof, and for all that shall be done therein.

¹⁵'"But the priests the Levites, the sons of Zadok, that kept the charge of my sanctuary when the children of Israel went astray from me, they shall come near to me to minister unto me, and they shall stand before me to offer unto me the fat and the blood,' saith the Lord GOD. ¹⁶'They shall enter into my sanctuary, and they shall come near to my table, to minister unto me, and they shall keep my charge.

¹⁷'"And it shall come to pass that when they enter in at the gates of the inner court, they shall be clothed with linen garments, and no

wool shall come upon them, whilst they minister in the gates of the inner court and within. ¹⁸They shall have linen bonnets upon their heads, and shall have linen breeches upon their loins: they shall not gird themselves with anything that causeth sweat. ¹⁹And when they go forth into the outer court, even into the outer court to the people, they shall put off their garments wherein they ministered, and lay them in the holy chambers, and they shall put on other garments, and they shall not sanctify the people with their garments. ²⁰Neither shall they shave their heads, nor suffer their locks to grow long, they shall only poll their heads. ²¹Neither shall any priest drink wine, when they enter into the inner court. ²²Neither shall they take for their wives a widow, or her that is put away: but they shall take maidens of the seed of the house of Israel, or a widow that had a priest before. ²³And they shall teach my people the difference between the holy and profane, and cause men to discern between the unclean and the clean. ²⁴And in controversy they shall stand in judgement, and they shall judge it according to my judgements: and they shall keep my laws and my statutes in all my assemblies, and they shall hallow my sabbaths. ²⁵And they shall come at no dead person to defile themselves: but for father or for mother, or for son or for daughter, for brother or for sister that hath had no husband, they may defile themselves. ²⁶And after he is cleansed, they shall reckon unto him seven days. ²⁷And in the day that he goeth into the sanctuary, unto the inner court to minister in the sanctuary, he shall offer his sin offering,' saith the Lord GOD. ²⁸'And it shall be unto them for an inheritance: I am their inheritance: and ye shall give them no possession in Israel: I am their possession. ²⁹They shall eat the meat offering, and the sin offering, and the trespass offering, and every dedicated thing in Israel shall be theirs. ³⁰And the first of all the first-fruits of all things, and every oblation of all of every sort of your oblations shall be the priests': ye shall also give unto the priest the first of your dough, that he may cause the blessing to rest in thy house. ³¹The priests shall not eat of anything that is dead of itself, or torn, whether it be fowl or beast.

45 '"Moreover, when ye shall divide by lot the land for inheritance, ye shall offer an oblation unto the LORD, a holy portion of the land: the length shall be the length of five and twenty thousand reeds, and the breadth shall be ten thousand. This shall be holy in all the borders thereof round about. ²Of this there shall be for the sanctuary five hundred in length, with five hundred in breadth, square round about, and fifty cubits round about for the suburbs thereof. ³And of this measure shalt thou measure the length of five and twenty thousand, and the breadth of ten thousand: and in it shall be the sanctuary and the most holy place. ⁴The holy portion of the land shall be for the priests the ministers of the sanctuary, which shall come near to minister unto the LORD, and it shall be a place for their houses, and a holy place for the sanctuary. ⁵And the five and twenty thousand of length, and the ten thousand of breadth, shall also the Levites the ministers of the house have for themselves, for a possession for twenty chambers.

⁶'"And ye shall appoint the possession of the city five thousand broad, and five and twenty thousand long, over against the oblation of the holy portion: it shall be for the whole house of Israel.

⁷'"And a portion shall be for the prince on the one side and on the other side of the oblation of the holy portion, and of the possession of the city, before the oblation of the holy portion, and before the possession of the city, from the west side westward, and from the east side eastward, and the length shall be over against one of the portions from the west border unto the east border. ⁸In the land shall be his possession in Israel, and my princes shall no more oppress my people; and the rest of the land shall they give to the house of Israel according to their tribes.'

⁹'"Thus saith the Lord GOD, 'Let it suffice you, O princes of Israel: remove violence and spoil, and execute judgement and justice, take away your exactions from my people,' saith the Lord GOD. ¹⁰Ye shall have just balances, and a just ephah, and a just bath. ¹¹The ephah and the bath shall be of one measure, that the bath may contain the tenth part of a homer, and the ephah the tenth part of a homer: the measure thereof shall be after the homer. ¹²And the shekel shall be twenty gerahs: twenty shekels, five and twenty shekels, fifteen shekels, shall be your maneh.

¹³'"This is the oblation that ye shall offer, the sixth part of an ephah of a homer of wheat, and ye shall give the sixth part of an ephah of a homer of barley: ¹⁴concerning the ordinance of oil, the bath of oil, ye shall offer the tenth part of a bath out of the cor, which is a homer of ten baths, for ten baths are a homer: ¹⁵and one lamb out of the flock, out of two hundred, out of the fat pastures of Israel for a meat offering, and for a burnt offering, and for peace offerings to make reconciliation for them,' saith the Lord GOD. ¹⁶'All the people of the land shall give this oblation for the prince in Israel. ¹⁷And it shall be the prince's part to give burnt offerings, and meat offerings, and drink offerings, in the feasts, and in the new moons, and in the sabbaths, in all solemnities of the house of Israel: he shall prepare the sin offering, and the meat offering, and the burnt offering, and the peace offerings, to make reconciliation for the house of Israel.'

¹⁸'"Thus saith the Lord GOD, 'In the first month, in the first day of the month, thou shalt take a young bullock without blemish, and cleanse the sanctuary. ¹⁹And the priest shall take of the blood of the sin offering, and put it upon the posts of the house, and upon the four corners of the settle of the altar, and upon the posts of the gate of the inner court. ²⁰And so thou shalt do the seventh day of the month for every one that erreth, and for him that is simple: so shall ye reconcile the house. ²¹In the first month, in the fourteenth day of the month, ye shall have the passover a feast of seven days, unleavened bread shall be eaten. ²²And upon that day shall the prince prepare for himself and for all the people of the land a bullock for a sin offering. ²³And seven days of the feast he shall prepare a burnt offering to the LORD, seven bullocks and seven rams without blemish daily the seven days, and a kid of

the goats daily for a sin offering. ²⁴And he shall prepare a meat offering of an ephah for a bullock, and an ephah for a ram, and a hin of oil for an ephah. ²⁵In the seventh month, in the fifteenth day of the month shall he do the like in the feast of the seven days, according to the sin offering, according to the burnt offering, and according to the meat offering, and according to the oil.'

46 '"Thus saith the Lord GOD, 'The gate of the inner court that looketh toward the east shall be shut the six working days: but on the sabbath it shall be opened, and in the day of the new moon it shall be opened. ²And the prince shall enter by the way of the porch of that gate without, and shall stand by the post of the gate, and the priests shall prepare his burnt offering and his peace offerings, and he shall worship at the threshold of the gate: then he shall go forth, but the gate shall not be shut until the evening. ³Likewise the people of the land shall worship at the door of this gate before the LORD in the sabbaths and in the new moons. ⁴And the burnt offering that the prince shall offer unto the LORD in the sabbath day shall be six lambs without blemish, and a ram without blemish. ⁵And the meat offering shall be an ephah for a ram, and the meat offering for the lambs as he shall be able to give, and a hin of oil to an ephah. ⁶And in the day of the new moon it shall be a young bullock without blemish, and six lambs, and a ram: they shall be without blemish. ⁷And he shall prepare a meat offering, an ephah for a bullock, and an ephah for a ram, and for the lambs according as his hand shall attain unto, and a hin of oil to an ephah. ⁸And when the prince shall enter, he shall go in by the way of the porch of that gate, and he shall go forth by the way thereof.

⁹'"'But when the people of the land shall come before the LORD in the solemn feasts, he that entereth in by the way of the north gate to worship shall go out by the way of the south gate; and he that entereth by the way of the south gate shall go forth by the way of the north gate: he shall not return by the way of the gate whereby he came in, but shall go forth over against it. ¹⁰And the prince in the midst of them when they go in, shall go in, and when they go forth, shall go forth. ¹¹And in the feasts and in the solemnities the meat offering shall be an ephah to a bullock, and an ephah to a ram, and to the lambs as he is able to give, and a hin of oil to an ephah. ¹²Now when the prince shall prepare a voluntary burnt offering or peace offerings voluntarily unto the LORD, one shall then open him the gate that looketh toward the east, and he shall prepare his burnt offering and his peace offerings, as he did on the sabbath day: then he shall go forth, and after his going forth one shall shut the gate. ¹³Thou shalt daily prepare a burnt offering unto the LORD of a lamb of the first year without blemish: thou shalt prepare it every morning. ¹⁴And thou shalt prepare a meat offering for it every morning, the sixth part of an ephah, and the third part of a hin of oil, to temper with the fine flour; a meat offering continually by a perpetual ordinance unto the LORD. ¹⁵Thus shall they prepare the lamb, and the meat offering, and the oil, every morning for a continual burnt offering.'

¹⁶'"Thus saith the Lord GOD, 'If the prince give a gift unto any of his

sons, the inheritance thereof shall be his sons'; it shall be their possession by inheritance. [17]But if he give a gift of his inheritance to one of his servants, then it shall be his to the year of liberty: after it shall return to the prince, but his inheritance shall be his sons' for them. [18]Moreover the prince shall not take of the people's inheritance by oppression, to thrust them out of their possession: but he shall give his sons inheritance out of his own possession, that my people be not scattered every man from his possession.'"'

[19]After he brought me through the entry, which was at the side of the gate, into the holy chambers of the priests which looked toward the north: and behold, there was a place on the two sides westward. [20]Then said he unto me, 'This is the place where the priests shall boil the trespass offering and the sin offering, where they shall bake the meat offering: that they bear them not out into the outer court, to sanctify the people'.

[21]Then he brought me forth into the outer court, and caused me to pass by the four corners of the court, and behold, in every corner of the court there was a court. [22]In the four corners of the court there were courts joined of forty cubits long and thirty broad: these four corners were of one measure. [23]And there was a row of building round about in them, round about them four, and it was made with boiling places under the rows round about. [24]Then said he unto me, 'These are the places of them that boil, where the ministers of the house shall boil the sacrifice of the people'.

47 Afterward he brought me again unto the door of the house, and behold, waters issued out from under the threshold of the house eastward: for the forefront of the house stood toward the east, and the waters came down from under from the right side of the house, at the south side of the altar. [2]Then brought he me out of the way of the gate northward, and led me about the way without unto the outer gate by the way that looketh eastward, and behold, there ran out waters on the right side. [3]And when the man that had the line in his hand went forth eastward, he measured a thousand cubits, and he brought me through the waters: the waters were to the ankles. [4]Again he measured a thousand, and brought me through the waters; the waters were to the knees. Again he measured a thousand, and brought me through; the waters were to the loins. [5]Afterward he measured a thousand, and it was a river that I could not pass over: for the waters were risen, waters to swim in, a river that could not be passed over.

[6]And he said unto me, 'Son of man, hast thou seen this?' Then he brought me, and caused me to return to the brink of the river. [7]Now when I had returned, behold, at the bank of the river were very many trees on the one side and on the other. [8]Then said he unto me, 'These waters issue out toward the east country, and go down into the desert, and go into the sea: which being brought forth into the sea, the waters shall be healed. [9]And it shall come to pass that everything that liveth, which moveth, whithersoever the rivers shall come, shall live, and there shall be a very great multitude of fish, because these waters shall

come thither: for they shall be healed, and everything shall live whither the river cometh. ¹⁰And it shall come to pass that the fishers shall stand upon it from En-gedi even unto En-eglaim; they shall be a place to spread forth nets, their fish shall be according to their kinds, as the fish of the great sea, exceeding many. ¹¹But the miry places thereof and the marshes thereof shall not be healed, they shall be given to salt. ¹²And by the river upon the bank thereof, on this side and on that side, shall grow all trees for meat, whose leaf shall not fade, neither shall the fruit thereof be consumed: it shall bring forth new fruit according to his months, because their waters they issued out of the sanctuary, and the fruit thereof shall be for meat, and the leaf thereof for medicine.'

¹³Thus saith the Lord GOD, 'This shall be the border, whereby ye shall inherit the land according to the twelve tribes of Israel: Joseph shall have two portions. ¹⁴And ye shall inherit it, one as well as another: concerning the which I lifted up my hand to give it unto your fathers: and this land shall fall unto you for inheritance. ¹⁵And this shall be the border of the land toward the north side from the great sea, the way of Hethlon, as men go to Zedad: ¹⁶Hamath, Berothah, Sibraim, which is between the border of Damascus and the border of Hamath; Hazar-hatticon, which is by the coast of Hauran. ¹⁷And the border from the sea shall be Hazar-enan, the border of Damascus, and the north northward, and the border of Hamath. And this is the north side. ¹⁸And the east side ye shall measure from Hauran, and from Damascus, and from Gilead, and from the land of Israel by Jordan, from the border unto the east sea. And this is the east side. ¹⁹And the south side southward, from Tamar even to the waters of strife in Kadesh, the river to the great sea. And this is the south side southward. ²⁰The west side also shall be the great sea from the border, till a man come over against Hamath. This is the west side. ²¹So shall ye divide this land unto you according to the tribes of Israel.

²²'And it shall come to pass that ye shall divide it by lot for an inheritance unto you, and to the strangers that sojourn among you, which shall beget children among you: and they shall be unto you as born in the country among the children of Israel; they shall have inheritance with you among the tribes of Israel. ²³And it shall come to pass that in what tribe the stranger sojourneth, there shall ye give him his inheritance,' saith the Lord GOD.

48 'Now these are the names of the tribes. From the north end to the coast of the way of Hethlon, as one goeth to Hamath, Hazar-enan, the border of Damascus northward, to the coast of Hamath (for these are his sides east and west), a portion for Dan. ²And by the border of Dan, from the east side unto the west, a portion for Asher. ³And by the border of Asher, from the east side even unto the west side, a portion for Naphtali. ⁴And by the border of Naphtali, from the east side unto the west side, a portion for Manasseh. ⁵And by the border of Manasseh, from the east side unto the west side, a portion for Ephraim. ⁶And by the border of Ephraim, from the east side even unto the west side, a portion for Reuben. ⁷And by the border of Reuben, from the east side unto the west side, a portion for Judah.

⁸'And by the border of Judah, from the east side unto the west side, shall be the offering which they shall offer of five and twenty thousand reeds in breadth, and in length as one of the other parts, from the east side unto the west side, and the sanctuary shall be in the midst of it. ⁹The oblation that ye shall offer unto the LORD shall be of five and twenty thousand in length, and of ten thousand in breadth. ¹⁰And for them, even for the priests shall be this holy oblation, toward the north five and twenty thousand in length, and toward the west ten thousand in breadth, and toward the east ten thousand in breadth, and toward the south five and twenty thousand in length, and the sanctuary of the LORD shall be in the midst thereof. ¹¹It shall be for the priests that are sanctified of the sons of Zadok, which have kept my charge, which went not astray when the children of Israel went astray, as the Levites went astray. ¹²And this oblation of the land that is offered shall be unto them a thing most holy by the border of the Levites. ¹³And over against the border of the priests the Levites shall have five and twenty thousand in length, and ten thousand in breadth: all the length shall be five and twenty thousand, and the breadth ten thousand. ¹⁴And they shall not sell of it, neither exchange, nor alienate the first-fruits of the land: for it is holy unto the LORD.

¹⁵'And the five thousand that are left in the breadth over against the five and twenty thousand, shall be a profane place for the city, for dwelling, and for suburbs, and the city shall be in the midst thereof. ¹⁶And these shall be the measures thereof, the north side four thousand and five hundred, and the south side four thousand and five hundred, and on the east side four thousand and five hundred, and the west side four thousand and five hundred. ¹⁷And the suburbs of the city shall be toward the north two hundred and fifty, and toward the south two hundred and fifty, and toward the east two hundred and fifty, and toward the west two hundred and fifty. ¹⁸And the residue in length over against the oblation of the holy portion shall be ten thousand eastward, and ten thousand westward: and it shall be over against the oblation of the holy portion, and the increase thereof shall be for food unto them that serve the city. ¹⁹And they that serve the city shall serve it out of all the tribes of Israel. ²⁰All the oblation shall be five and twenty thousand by five and twenty thousand: ye shall offer the holy oblation four-square, with the possession of the city.

²¹'And the residue shall be for the prince, on the one side and on the other of the holy oblation, and of the possession of the city over against the five and twenty thousand of the oblation toward the east border, and westward over against the five and twenty thousand toward the west border, over against the portions for the prince, and it shall be the holy oblation, and the sanctuary of the house shall be in the midst thereof. ²²Moreover from the possession of the Levites, and from the possession of the city, being in the midst of that which is the prince's, between the border of Judah and the border of Benjamin, shall be for

the prince. ²³As for the rest of the tribes, from the east side unto the west side, Benjamin shall have a portion. ²⁴And by the border of Benjamin, from the east side unto the west side, Simeon shall have a portion. ²⁵And by the border of Simeon, from the east side unto the west side, Issachar a portion. ²⁶And by the border of Issachar, from the east side unto the west side, Zebulun a portion. ²⁷And by the border of Zebulun, from the east side unto the west side, Gad a portion. ²⁸And by the border of Gad, at the south side southward, the border shall be even from Tamar unto the waters of strife in Kadesh, and to the river toward the great sea. ²⁹This is the land which ye shall divide by lot unto the tribes of Israel for inheritance, and these are their portions,' saith the Lord God.

³⁰'And these are the goings out of the city, on the north side four thousand and five hundred measures. ³¹And the gates of the city shall be after the names of the tribes of Israel, three gates northward, one gate of Reuben, one gate of Judah, one gate of Levi. ³²And at the east side four thousand and five hundred: and three gates; and one gate of Joseph, one gate of Benjamin, one gate of Dan. ³³And at the south side four thousand and five hundred measures, and three gates: one gate of Simeon, one gate of Issachar, one gate of Zebulun. ³⁴At the west side four thousand and five hundred, with their three gates: one gate of Gad, one gate of Asher, one gate of Naphtali. ³⁵It was round about eighteen thousand measures: and the name of the city from that day shall be, the Lord is there.'

THE BOOK OF
DANIEL

1 In the third year of the reign of Jehoiakim king of Judah came Nebuchadnezzar king of Babylon unto Jerusalem, and besieged it. ²And the Lord gave Jehoiakim king of Judah into his hand, with part of the vessels of the house of God, which he carried into the land of Shinar to the house of his god, and he brought the vessels into the treasure-house of his god.

³And the king spoke unto Ashpenaz the master of his eunuchs, that he should bring certain of the children of Israel, and of the king's seed, and of the princes: ⁴children in whom was no blemish, but well-favoured, and skilful in all wisdom, and cunning in knowledge, and understanding science, and such as had ability in them to stand in the king's palace, and whom they might teach the learning and the tongue of the Chaldeans. ⁵And the king appointed them a daily provision of the king's meat, and of the wine which he drank: so nourishing them three years, that at the end thereof they might stand before the king. ⁶Now among these were of the children of Judah, Daniel, Hananiah, Mishael, and Azariah: ⁷unto whom the prince of the eunuchs gave names: for he gave unto Daniel the name of Belteshazzar; and to Hananiah, of Shadrach; and to Mishael, of Meshach; and to Azariah, of Abed-nego.

⁸But Daniel purposed in his heart that he would not defile himself with the portion of the king's meat, nor with the wine which he drank: therefore he requested of the prince of the eunuchs that he might not defile himself. ⁹Now God had brought Daniel into favour and tender love with the prince of the eunuchs. ¹⁰And the prince of the eunuchs said unto Daniel, 'I fear my lord the king, who hath appointed your meat and your drink: for why should he see your faces worse liking than the children which are of your sort? then shall ye make me endanger my head to the king'. ¹¹Then said Daniel to Melzar, whom the prince of the eunuchs had set over Daniel, Hananiah, Mishael, and Azariah, ¹²'Prove thy servants, I beseech thee, ten days, and let them give us pulse to eat, and water to drink. ¹³Then let our countenances be looked upon before thee, and the countenance of the children that eat of the portion of the king's meat: and as thou seest, deal with thy servants.' ¹⁴So he consented to them in this matter, and proved them ten days. ¹⁵And at the end of ten days their countenances appeared fairer and fatter in flesh than all the children which did eat the portion of the king's meat. ¹⁶Thus Melzar took away the portion of their meat, and the wine that they should drink: and gave them pulse.

¹⁷As for these four children, God gave them knowledge and skill in all learning and wisdom, and Daniel had understanding in all visions and dreams. ¹⁸Now at the end of the days that the king had said he should bring them in, then the prince of the eunuchs brought them in before

Nebuchadnezzar. ¹⁹And the king communed with them: and among them all was found none like Daniel, Hananiah, Mishael, and Azariah: therefore stood they before the king. ²⁰And in all matters of wisdom and understanding, that the king inquired of them, he found them ten times better than all the magicians and astrologers that were in all his realm. ²¹And Daniel continued even unto the first year of king Cyrus.

2 And in the second year of the reign of Nebuchadnezzar, Nebuchadnezzar dreamed dreams, wherewith his spirit was troubled, and his sleep broke from him. ²Then the king commanded to call the magicians, and the astrologers, and the sorcerers, and the Chaldeans, for to show the king his dreams. So they came and stood before the king. ³And the king said unto them, 'I have dreamed a dream, and my spirit was troubled to know the dream'. ⁴Then spoke the Chaldeans to the king in Syriac, 'O king, live for ever: tell thy servants the dream, and we will show the interpretation'. ⁵The king answered and said to the Chaldeans, 'The thing is gone from me: if ye will not make known unto me the dream, with the interpretation thereof, ye shall be cut in pieces, and your houses shall be made a dunghill. ⁶But if ye show the dream, and the interpretation thereof, ye shall receive of me gifts and rewards and great honour: therefore show me the dream, and the interpretation thereof.' ⁷They answered again and said, 'Let the king tell his servants the dream, and we will show the interpretation of it'. ⁸The king answered and said, 'I know of certainty that ye would gain the time, because ye see the thing is gone from me. ⁹But if ye will not make known unto me the dream, there is but one decree for you: for ye have prepared lying and corrupt words to speak before me, till the time be changed: therefore tell me the dream, and I shall know that ye can show me the interpretation thereof.'

¹⁰The Chaldeans answered before the king, and said, 'There is not a man upon the earth that can show the king's matter: therefore there is no king, lord, nor ruler, that asked such things at any magician, or astrologer, or Chaldean. ¹¹And it is a rare thing that the king requireth, and there is no other that can show it before the king, except the gods, whose dwelling is not with flesh.' ¹²For this cause the king was angry and very furious, and commanded to destroy all the wise men of Babylon. ¹³And the decree went forth that the wise men should be slain; and they sought Daniel and his fellows to be slain.

¹⁴Then Daniel answered with counsel and wisdom to Arioch the captain of the king's guard, which was gone forth to slay the wise men of Babylon. ¹⁵He answered and said to Arioch the king's captain, 'Why is the decree so hasty from the king?' Then Arioch made the thing known to Daniel. ¹⁶Then Daniel went in, and desired of the king that he would give him time, and that he would show the king the interpretation. ¹⁷Then Daniel went to his house, and made the thing known to Hananiah, Mishael, and Azariah, his companions: ¹⁸that they would desire mercies of the God of heaven concerning this secret, that Daniel and his fellows should not perish with the rest of the wise men of Babylon.

¹⁹Then was the secret revealed unto Daniel in a night vision. Then Daniel blessed the God of heaven. ²⁰Daniel answered and said,

'Blessed be the name of God for ever and ever:
for wisdom and might are his:
²¹ and he changeth the times and the seasons:
he removeth kings, and setteth up kings:
he giveth wisdom unto the wise,
and knowledge to them that know understanding.
²² He revealeth the deep and secret things:
he knoweth what is in the darkness,
and the light dwelleth with him.
²³ I thank thee, and praise thee,
O thou God of my fathers,
who hast given me wisdom and might,
and hast made known unto me now what we desired of thee:
for thou hast now made known unto us the king's matter.'

²⁴Therefore Daniel went in unto Arioch, whom the king had ordained to destroy the wise men of Babylon: he went and said thus unto him, 'Destroy not the wise men of Babylon: bring me in before the king, and I will show unto the king the interpretation'. ²⁵Then Arioch brought in Daniel before the king in haste, and said thus unto him, 'I have found a man of the captives of Judah, that will make known unto the king the interpretation'. ²⁶The king answered and said to Daniel, whose name was Belteshazzar, 'Art thou able to make known unto me the dream which I have seen, and the interpretation thereof?' ²⁷Daniel answered in the presence of the king, and said, 'The secret which the king hath demanded cannot the wise men, the astrologers, the magicians, the soothsayers show unto the king: ²⁸but there is a God in heaven that revealeth secrets, and maketh known to the king Nebuchadnezzar what shall be in the latter days. Thy dream, and the visions of thy head upon thy bed, are these. ²⁹As for thee, O king, thy thoughts came into thy mind upon thy bed, what should come to pass hereafter: and he that revealeth secrets maketh known to thee what shall come to pass. ³⁰But as for me, this secret is not revealed to me for any wisdom that I have more than any living, but for their sakes that shall make known the interpretation to the king, and that thou mightest know the thoughts of thy heart.

³¹'Thou, O king, sawest, and behold a great image. This great image, whose brightness was excellent, stood before thee, and the form thereof was terrible. ³²This image's head was of fine gold, his breast and his arms of silver, his belly and his thighs of brass, ³³his legs of iron, his feet part of iron and part of clay. ³⁴Thou sawest till that a stone was cut out without hands, which smote the image upon his feet that were of iron and clay, and broke them to pieces. ³⁵Then was the iron, the clay, the brass, the silver, and the gold broken to pieces together, and became like the chaff of the summer threshing-floors, and the wind carried

them away, that no place was found for them: and the stone that smote the image became a great mountain, and filled the whole earth.

[36]'This is the dream, and we will tell the interpretation thereof before the king. [37]Thou, O king, art a king of kings: for the God of heaven hath given thee a kingdom, power, and strength, and glory. [38]And whereso-ever the children of men dwell, the beasts of the field and the fowls of the heaven hath he given into thy hand, and hath made thee ruler over them all. Thou art this head of gold. [39]And after thee shall arise another kingdom inferior to thee, and another third kingdom of brass, which shall bear rule over all the earth. [40]And the fourth kingdom shall be strong as iron: forasmuch as iron breaketh in pieces and subdueth all things: and as iron that breaketh all these, shall it break in pieces and bruise. [41]And whereas thou sawest the feet and toes, part of potter's clay, and part of iron, the kingdom shall be divided; but there shall be in it of the strength of the iron, forasmuch as thou sawest the iron mixed with miry clay. [42]And as the toes of the feet were part of iron, and part of clay, so the kingdom shall be partly strong, and partly broken. [43]And whereas thou sawest iron mixed with miry clay, they shall mingle themselves with the seed of men: but they shall not cleave one to another, even as iron is not mixed with clay. [44]And in the days of these kings shall the God of heaven set up a kingdom, which shall never be destroyed: and the kingdom shall not be left to other people, but it shall break in pieces and consume all these kingdoms, and it shall stand for ever. [45]Forasmuch as thou sawest that the stone was cut out of the mountain without hands, and that it broke in pieces the iron, the brass, the clay, the silver, and the gold: the great God hath made known to the king what shall come to pass hereafter, and the dream is certain, and the interpretation thereof sure.'

[46]Then the king Nebuchadnezzar fell upon his face, and worshipped Daniel, and commanded that they should offer an oblation and sweet odours unto him. [47]The king answered unto Daniel, and said, 'Of a truth it is, that your God is a God of gods, and a Lord of kings, and a revealer of secrets, seeing thou couldst reveal this secret'. [48]Then the king made Daniel a great man, and gave him many great gifts, and made him ruler over the whole province of Babylon, and chief of the governors over all the wise men of Babylon. [49]Then Daniel requested of the king, and he set Shadrach, Meshach, and Abed-nego, over the affairs of the province of Babylon: but Daniel sat in the gate of the king.

3 Nebuchadnezzar the king made an image of gold, whose height was threescore cubits, and the breadth thereof six cubits: he set it up in the plain of Dura, in the province of Babylon. [2]Then Nebuchadnezzar the king sent to gather together the princes, the gov-ernors, and the captains, the judges, the treasurers, the counsellors, the sheriffs, and all the rulers of the provinces, to come to the dedica-tion of the image which Nebuchadnezzar the king had set up. [3]Then the princes, the governors and captains, the judges, the treasurers, the counsellors, the sheriffs, and all the rulers of the provinces were gath-ered together unto the dedication of the image that Nebuchadnezzar

the king had set up, and they stood before the image that Nebuchadnezzar had set up. ⁴Then a herald cried aloud, 'To you it is commanded, O people, nations, and languages, ⁵that at what time ye hear the sound of the cornet, flute, harp, sackbut, psaltery, dulcimer, and all kinds of music, ye fall down and worship the golden image that Nebuchadnezzar the king hath set up: ⁶and whoso falleth not down and worshippeth shall the same hour be cast into the midst of a burning fiery furnace'. ⁷Therefore at that time, when all the people heard the sound of the cornet, flute, harp, sackbut, psaltery, and all kinds of music, all the people, the nations, and the languages fell down and worshipped the golden image that Nebuchadnezzar the king had set up.

⁸Wherefore at that time certain Chaldeans came near, and accused the Jews. ⁹They spoke and said to the king Nebuchadnezzar, 'O king, live for ever. ¹⁰Thou, O king, hast made a decree, that every man that shall hear the sound of the cornet, flute, harp, sackbut, psaltery, and dulcimer, and all kinds of music, shall fall down and worship the golden image: ¹¹and whoso falleth not down and worshippeth, that he should be cast into the midst of a burning fiery furnace. ¹²There are certain Jews whom thou hast set over the affairs of the province of Babylon, Shadrach, Meshach, and Abed-nego: these men, O king, have not regarded thee: they serve not thy gods, nor worship the golden image which thou hast set up.'

¹³Then Nebuchadnezzar in his rage and fury commanded to bring Shadrach, Meshach, and Abed-nego. Then they brought these men before the king. ¹⁴Nebuchadnezzar spoke and said unto them, 'Is it true, O Shadrach, Meshach, and Abed-nego, do not ye serve my gods, nor worship the golden image which I have set up? ¹⁵Now if ye be ready that at what time ye hear the sound of the cornet, flute, harp, sackbut, psaltery, and dulcimer, and all kinds of music, ye fall down and worship the image which I have made, well: but if ye worship not, ye shall be cast the same hour into the midst of a fiery furnace, and who is that God that shall deliver you out of my hands?' ¹⁶Shadrach, Meshach, and Abed-nego answered and said to the king, 'O Nebuchadnezzar, we are not careful to answer thee in this matter. ¹⁷If it be so, our God whom we serve is able to deliver us from the burning fiery furnace, and he will deliver us out of thy hand, O king. ¹⁸But if not, be it known unto thee, O king, that we will not serve thy gods, nor worship thy golden image which thou hast set up.'

¹⁹Then was Nebuchadnezzar full of fury, and the form of his visage was changed against Shadrach, Meshach, and Abed-nego: therefore he spoke, and commanded that they should heat the furnace one seven times more than it was wont to be heated. ²⁰And he commanded the most mighty men that were in his army to bind Shadrach, Meshach, and Abed-nego, and to cast them into the burning fiery furnace. ²¹Then these men were bound in their coats, their hose, and their hats, and their other garments, and were cast into the midst of the burning fiery furnace. ²²Therefore because the king's commandment was urgent,

and the furnace exceeding hot, the flame of the fire slew those men that took up Shadrach, Meshach, and Abed-nego. ²³And these three men, Shadrach, Meshach, and Abed-nego, fell down bound into the midst of the burning fiery furnace. ²⁴Then Nebuchadnezzar the king was astonished, and rose up in haste, and spoke and said unto his counsellors, 'Did not we cast three men bound into the midst of the fire?' They answered and said unto the king, 'True, O king'. ²⁵He answered and said, 'Lo, I see four men loose, walking in the midst of the fire, and they have no hurt; and the form of the fourth is like the Son of God'.

²⁶Then Nebuchadnezzar came near to the mouth of the burning fiery furnace, and spoke and said, 'Shadrach, Meshach, and Abed-nego, ye servants of the most high God, come forth, and come hither'. Then Shadrach, Meshach, and Abed-nego came forth of the midst of the fire. ²⁷And the princes, governors, and captains, and the king's counsellors, being gathered together, saw these men, upon whose bodies the fire had no power, nor was a hair of their head singed, neither were their coats changed, nor the smell of fire had passed on them. ²⁸Then Nebuchadnezzar spoke and said, 'Blessed be the God of Shadrach, Meshach, and Abed-nego, who hath sent his angel, and delivered his servants that trusted in him, and have changed the king's word, and yielded their bodies, that they might not serve nor worship any god, except their own God. ²⁹Therefore I make a decree, that every people, nation, and language, which speak anything amiss against the God of Shadrach, Meshach, and Abed-nego, shall be cut in pieces, and their houses shall be made a dunghill, because there is no other God that can deliver after this sort.' ³⁰Then the king promoted Shadrach, Meshach, and Abed-nego, in the province of Babylon.

4 ¹'Nebuchadnezzar the king, unto all people, nations, and languages that dwell in all the earth, peace be multiplied unto you. ²I thought it good to show the signs and wonders that the high God hath wrought toward me. ³How great are his signs! and how mighty are his wonders! his kingdom is an everlasting kingdom, and his dominion is from generation to generation.

⁴'I Nebuchadnezzar was at rest in my house, and flourishing in my palace. ⁵I saw a dream which made me afraid, and the thoughts upon my bed and the visions of my head troubled me. ⁶Therefore made I a decree to bring in all the wise men of Babylon before me, that they might make known unto me the interpretation of the dream. ⁷Then came in the magicians, the astrologers, the Chaldeans, and the soothsayers: and I told the dream before them; but they did not make known unto me the interpretation thereof.

⁸'But at the last Daniel came in before me, whose name was Belteshazzar, according to the name of my god, and in whom is the spirit of the holy gods: and before him I told the dream, saying, ⁹"O Belteshazzar, master of the magicians, because I know that the spirit of the holy gods is in thee, and no secret troubleth thee, tell me the visions of my dream that I have seen, and the interpretation thereof. ¹⁰Thus were the visions of my head in my bed: I saw, and behold, a tree

in the midst of the earth, and the height thereof was great. ¹¹The tree grew, and was strong, and the height thereof reached unto heaven, and the sight thereof to the end of all the earth. ¹²The leaves thereof were fair, and the fruit thereof much, and in it was meat for all: the beasts of the field had shadow under it, and the fowls of the heaven dwelt in the boughs thereof, and all flesh was fed of it. ¹³I saw in the visions of my head upon my bed, and behold, a watcher and a holy one came down from heaven. ¹⁴He cried aloud, and said thus, 'Hew down the tree, and cut off his branches, shake off his leaves, and scatter his fruit: let the beasts get away from under it, and the fowls from his branches. ¹⁵Nevertheless leave the stump of his roots in the earth, even with a band of iron and brass, in the tender grass of the field, and let it be wet with the dew of heaven, and let his portion be with the beasts in the grass of the earth. ¹⁶Let his heart be changed from man's, and let a beast's heart be given unto him, and let seven times pass over him. ¹⁷This matter is by the decree of the watchers, and the demand by the word of the holy ones: to the intent that the living may know that the most High ruleth in the kingdom of men, and giveth it to whomsoever he will, and setteth up over it the basest of men.' ¹⁸This dream I king Nebuchadnezzar have seen. Now thou, O Belteshazzar, declare the interpretation thereof, forasmuch as all the wise men of my kingdom are not able to make known unto me the interpretation: but thou art able; for the spirit of the holy gods is in thee."'

¹⁹Then Daniel, whose name was Belteshazzar, was astonished for one hour, and his thoughts troubled him. The king spoke, and said, 'Belteshazzar, let not the dream, or the interpretation thereof, trouble thee'. Belteshazzar answered and said, 'My lord, the dream be to them that hate thee, and the interpretation thereof to thy enemies. ²⁰The tree that thou sawest, which grew, and was strong, whose height reached unto the heaven, and the sight thereof to all the earth: ²¹whose leaves were fair, and the fruit thereof much, and in it was meat for all, under which the beasts of the field dwelt, and upon whose branches the fowls of the heaven had their habitation: ²²it is thou, O king, that art grown and become strong: for thy greatness is grown, and reacheth unto heaven, and thy dominion to the end of the earth. ²³And whereas the king saw a watcher and a holy one coming down from heaven, and saying, "Hew the tree down, and destroy it, yet leave the stump of the roots thereof in the earth, even with a band of iron and brass in the tender grass of the field, and let it be wet with the dew of heaven, and let his portion be with the beasts of the field, till seven times pass over him": ²⁴this is the interpretation, O king, and this is the decree of the most High, which is come upon my lord the king: ²⁵that they shall drive thee from men, and thy dwelling shall be with the beasts of the field, and they shall make thee to eat grass as oxen, and they shall wet thee with the dew of heaven, and seven times shall pass over thee, till thou know that the most High ruleth in the kingdom of men, and giveth it to whomsoever he will. ²⁶And whereas they commanded to leave the stump of the tree roots; thy kingdom shall be sure unto thee, after that

thou shalt have known that the heavens do rule. ²⁷Wherefore, O king, let my counsel be acceptable unto thee, and break off thy sins by righteousness, and thy iniquities by showing mercy to the poor; if it may be a lengthening of thy tranquillity.'

²⁸All this came upon the king Nebuchadnezzar. ²⁹At the end of twelve months he walked in the palace of the kingdom of Babylon. ³⁰The king spoke, and said, 'Is not this great Babylon, that I have built for the house of the kingdom by the might of my power, and for the honour of my majesty?' ³¹While the word was in the king's mouth, there fell a voice from heaven, saying, 'O king Nebuchadnezzar, to thee it is spoken; the kingdom is departed from thee. ³²And they shall drive thee from men, and thy dwelling shall be with the beasts of the field: they shall make thee to eat grass as oxen, and seven times shall pass over thee, until thou know that the most High ruleth in the kingdom of men, and giveth it to whomsoever he will.' ³³The same hour was the thing fulfilled upon Nebuchadnezzar: and he was driven from men, and did eat grass as oxen, and his body was wet with the dew of heaven, till his hairs were grown like eagles' feathers, and his nails like birds' claws.

³⁴'And at the end of the days I Nebuchadnezzar lifted up my eyes unto heaven, and my understanding returned unto me, and I blessed the most High, and I praised and honoured him that liveth for ever, whose dominion is an everlasting dominion, and his kingdom is from generation to generation. ³⁵And all the inhabitants of the earth are reputed as nothing: and he doeth according to his will in the army of heaven, and among the inhabitants of the earth: and none can stay his hand, or say unto him, "What doest thou?" ³⁶At the same time my reason returned unto me; and for the glory of my kingdom, my honour and brightness returned unto me, and my counsellors and my lords sought unto me, and I was established in my kingdom, and excellent majesty was added unto me. ³⁷Now I Nebuchadnezzar praise and extol and honour the King of heaven, all whose works are truth, and his ways judgement: and those that walk in pride he is able to abase.'

5 Belshazzar the king made a great feast to a thousand of his lords, and drank wine before the thousand. ²Belshazzar, whilst he tasted the wine, commanded to bring the golden and silver vessels which his father Nebuchadnezzar had taken out of the temple which was in Jerusalem, that the king, and his princes, his wives, and his concubines might drink therein. ³Then they brought the golden vessels that were taken out of the temple of the house of God which was at Jerusalem, and the king, and his princes, his wives, and his concubines drank in them. ⁴They drank wine, and praised the gods of gold, and of silver, of brass, of iron, of wood, and of stone.

⁵In the same hour came forth fingers of a man's hand, and wrote over against the candlestick upon the plaster of the wall of the king's palace, and the king saw the part of the hand that wrote. ⁶Then the king's countenance was changed, and his thoughts troubled him, so that the joints of his loins were loosed, and his knees smote one against

another. ⁷The king cried aloud to bring in the astrologers, the Chaldeans, and the soothsayers. And the king spoke and said to the wise men of Babylon, 'Whosoever shall read this writing, and show me the interpretation thereof, shall be clothed with scarlet, and have a chain of gold about his neck, and shall be the third ruler in the kingdom'. ⁸Then came in all the king's wise men, but they could not read the writing, nor make known to the king the interpretation thereof. ⁹Then was king Belshazzar greatly troubled, and his countenance was changed in him, and his lords were astonished.

¹⁰Now the queen, by reason of the words of the king and his lords, came into the banquet-house: and the queen spoke and said, 'O king, live for ever: let not thy thoughts trouble thee, nor let thy countenance be changed. ¹¹There is a man in thy kingdom, in whom is the spirit of the holy gods, and in the days of thy father light and understanding and wisdom, like the wisdom of the gods, was found in him: whom the king Nebuchadnezzar thy father, the king, I say, thy father, made master of the magicians, astrologers, Chaldeans, and soothsayers, ¹²forasmuch as an excellent spirit, and knowledge, and understanding, interpreting of dreams, and showing of hard sentences, and dissolving of doubts were found in the same Daniel, whom the king named Belteshazzar: now let Daniel be called, and he will show the interpretation.' ¹³Then was Daniel brought in before the king. And the king spoke and said unto Daniel, 'Art thou that Daniel, which art of the children of the captivity of Judah, whom the king my father brought out of Jewry? ¹⁴I have even heard of thee, that the spirit of the gods is in thee, and that light and understanding and excellent wisdom is found in thee. ¹⁵And now the wise men, the astrologers, have been brought in before me, that they should read this writing, and make known unto me the interpretation thereof: but they could not show the interpretation of the thing. ¹⁶And I have heard of thee, that thou canst make interpretations, and dissolve doubts: now if thou canst read the writing, and make known to me the interpretation thereof, thou shalt be clothed with scarlet, and have a chain of gold about thy neck, and shalt be the third ruler in the kingdom.'

¹⁷Then Daniel answered and said before the king, 'Let thy gifts be to thyself, and give thy rewards to another; yet I will read the writing unto the king, and make known to him the interpretation. ¹⁸O thou king, the most high God gave Nebuchadnezzar thy father a kingdom, and majesty, and glory, and honour. ¹⁹And for the majesty that he gave him, all people, nations, and languages trembled and feared before him: whom he would he slew, and whom he would he kept alive, and whom he would he set up, and whom he would he put down. ²⁰But when his heart was lifted up, and his mind hardened in pride, he was deposed from his kingly throne, and they took his glory from him. ²¹And he was driven from the sons of men, and his heart was made like the beasts, and his dwelling was with the wild asses: they fed him with grass like oxen, and his body was wet with the dew of heaven, till he knew that the most high God ruled in the kingdom of men, and that he

appointeth over it whomsoever he will. [22]And thou his son, O Belshazzar, hast not humbled thy heart, though thou knewest all this: [23]but hast lifted up thyself against the Lord of heaven, and they have brought the vessels of his house before thee, and thou, and thy lords, thy wives and thy concubines have drunk wine in them, and thou hast praised the gods of silver, and gold, of brass, iron, wood and stone, which see not, nor hear, nor know: and the God in whose hand thy breath is, and whose are all thy ways, hast thou not glorified. [24]Then was the part of the hand sent from him; and this writing was written.

[25]'And this is the writing that was written, "MENE, MENE, TEKEL, UPHARSIN". [26]This is the interpretation of the thing: "MENE", God hath numbered thy kingdom, and finished it. [27]"TEKEL", thou art weighed in the balances, and art found wanting. [28]"PERES", thy kingdom is divided, and given to the Medes and Persians.' [29]Then commanded Belshazzar, and they clothed Daniel with scarlet, and put a chain of gold about his neck, and made a proclamation concerning him, that he should be the third ruler in the kingdom.

[30]In that night was Belshazzar the king of the Chaldeans slain. [31]And Darius the Median took the kingdom, being about threescore and two years old.

6 It pleased Darius to set over the kingdom a hundred and twenty princes, which should be over the whole kingdom; [2]and over these three presidents (of whom Daniel was first) that the princes might give accounts unto them, and the king should have no damage. [3]Then this Daniel was preferred above the presidents and princes, because an excellent spirit was in him, and the king thought to set him over the whole realm.

[4]Then the presidents and princes sought to find occasion against Daniel concerning the kingdom, but they could find no occasion nor fault: forasmuch as he was faithful, neither was there any error or fault found in him. [5]Then said these men, 'We shall not find any occasion against this Daniel, except we find it against him concerning the law of his God'. [6]Then these presidents and princes assembled together to the king, and said thus unto him, 'King Darius, live for ever. [7]All the presidents of the kingdom, the governors, and the princes, the counsellors, and the captains have consulted together to establish a royal statute, and to make a firm decree, that whosoever shall ask a petition of any God or man for thirty days, save of thee, O king, he shall be cast into the den of lions. [8]Now, O king, establish the decree, and sign the writing, that it be not changed, according to the law of the Medes and Persians, which altereth not.' [9]Wherefore king Darius signed the writing and the decree.

[10]Now when Daniel knew that the writing was signed, he went into his house, and his windows being open in his chamber toward Jerusalem, he kneeled upon his knees three times a day, and prayed, and gave thanks before his God, as he did aforetime. [11]Then these men assembled, and found Daniel praying and making supplication before

his God. ¹²Then they came near, and spoke before the king concerning the king's decree, 'Hast thou not signed a decree, that every man that shall ask a petition of any God or man within thirty days, save of thee, O king, shall be cast into the den of lions?' The king answered and said, 'The thing is true, according to the law of the Medes and Persians, which altereth not'. ¹³Then answered they and said before the king, 'That Daniel, which is of the children of the captivity of Judah, regardeth not thee, O king, nor the decree that thou hast signed, but maketh his petition three times a day'. ¹⁴Then the king, when he heard these words, was sore displeased with himself, and set his heart on Daniel to deliver him: and he laboured till the going down of the sun to deliver him. ¹⁵Then these men assembled unto the king, and said unto the king, 'Know, O king, that the law of the Medes and Persians is, that no decree nor statute which the king establisheth may be changed'. ¹⁶Then the king commanded, and they brought Daniel, and cast him into the den of lions. Now the king spoke and said unto Daniel, 'Thy God whom thou servest continually, he will deliver thee'. ¹⁷And a stone was brought and laid upon the mouth of the den, and the king sealed it with his own signet, and with the signet of his lords; that the purpose might not be changed concerning Daniel.

¹⁸Then the king went to his palace, and passed the night fasting: neither were instruments of music brought before him, and his sleep went from him. ¹⁹Then the king arose very early in the morning, and went in haste unto the den of lions. ²⁰And when he came to the den, he cried with a lamentable voice unto Daniel: and the king spoke and said to Daniel, 'O Daniel, servant of the living God, is thy God, whom thou servest continually, able to deliver thee from the lions?' ²¹Then said Daniel unto the king, 'O king, live for ever. ²²My God hath sent his angel, and hath shut the lions' mouths that they have not hurt me: forasmuch as before him innocence was found in me; and also before thee, O king, have I done no hurt'. ²³Then was the king exceedingly glad for him, and commanded that they should take Daniel up out of the den. So Daniel was taken up out of the den, and no manner of hurt was found upon him, because he believed in his God.

²⁴And the king commanded, and they brought those men which had accused Daniel, and they cast them into the den of lions, them, their children, and their wives: and the lions had the mastery of them, and broke all their bones in pieces or ever they came at the bottom of the den.

²⁵Then king Darius wrote unto all people, nations, and languages, that dwell in all the earth, 'Peace be multiplied unto you. ²⁶I make a decree, that in every dominion of my kingdom men tremble and fear before the God of Daniel: for he is the living God, and steadfast for ever, and his kingdom that which shall not be destroyed, and his dominion shall be even unto the end. ²⁷He delivereth and rescueth, and he worketh signs and wonders in heaven and in earth, who hath delivered Daniel from the power of the lions.' ²⁸So this Daniel prospered in the reign of Darius, and in the reign of Cyrus the Persian.

7 In the first year of Belshazzar king of Babylon Daniel had a dream and visions of his head upon his bed: then he wrote the dream, and told the sum of the matters. ²Daniel spoke and said, 'I saw in my vision by night, and behold, the four winds of the heaven strove upon the great sea. ³And four great beasts came up from the sea, diverse one from another. ⁴The first was like a lion, and had eagle's wings: I beheld till the wings thereof were plucked, and it was lifted up from the earth, and made stand upon the feet as a man, and a man's heart was given to it. ⁵And behold, another beast, a second, like to a bear, and it raised up itself on one side, and it had three ribs in the mouth of it between the teeth of it: and they said thus unto it, "Arise, devour much flesh". ⁶After this I beheld, and lo, another, like a leopard, which had upon the back of it four wings of a fowl; the beast had also four heads, and dominion was given to it. ⁷After this I saw in the night visions, and behold, a fourth beast, dreadful and terrible, and strong exceedingly; and it had great iron teeth: it devoured and broke in pieces, and stamped the residue with the feet of it: and it was diverse from all the beasts that were before it, and it had ten horns. ⁸I considered the horns, and behold, there came up among them another little horn, before whom there were three of the first horns plucked up by the roots: and behold, in this horn were eyes like the eyes of man, and a mouth speaking great things.

⁹'I beheld till the thrones were cast down, and the Ancient of days did sit, whose garment was white as snow, and the hair of his head like the pure wool: his throne was like the fiery flame, and his wheels as burning fire. ¹⁰A fiery stream issued and came forth from before him: thousand thousands ministered unto him, and ten thousand times ten thousand stood before him: the judgement was set, and the books were opened. ¹¹I beheld then because of the voice of the great words which the horn spoke: I beheld even till the beast was slain, and his body destroyed, and given to the burning flame. ¹²As concerning the rest of the beasts, they had their dominion taken away: yet their lives were prolonged for a season and time. ¹³I saw in the night visions, and behold, one like the Son of man came with the clouds of heaven, and came to the Ancient of days, and they brought him near before him. ¹⁴And there was given him dominion and glory, and a kingdom, that all people, nations, and languages, should serve him: his dominion is an everlasting dominion, which shall not pass away, and his kingdom that which shall not be destroyed.

¹⁵'I Daniel was grieved in my spirit in the midst of my body, and the visions of my head troubled me. ¹⁶I came near unto one of them that stood by, and asked him the truth of all this. So he told me, and made me know the interpretation of the things. ¹⁷"These great beasts, which are four, are four kings, which shall arise out of the earth. ¹⁸But the saints of the most High shall take the kingdom, and possess the kingdom for ever, even for ever and ever."

¹⁹'Then I would know the truth of the fourth beast, which was diverse from all the others, exceeding dreadful, whose teeth were of iron, and

his nails of brass, which devoured, broke in pieces, and stamped the residue with his feet, ²⁰and of the ten horns that were in his head, and of the other which came up, and before whom three fell, even of that horn that had eyes, and a mouth that spoke very great things, whose look was more stout than his fellows. ²¹I beheld, and the same horn made war with the saints, and prevailed against them; ²²until the Ancient of days came, and judgement was given to the saints of the most High: and the time came that the saints possessed the kingdom.

²³'Thus he said, "The fourth beast shall be the fourth kingdom upon earth, which shall be diverse from all kingdoms, and shall devour the whole earth, and shall tread it down, and break it in pieces. ²⁴And the ten horns out of this kingdom are ten kings that shall arise: and another shall rise after them, and he shall be diverse from the first, and he shall subdue three kings. ²⁵And he shall speak great words against the most High, and shall wear out the saints of the most High, and think to change times and laws: and they shall be given into his hand until a time and times and the dividing of time. ²⁶But the judgement shall sit, and they shall take away his dominion, to consume and to destroy it unto the end. ²⁷And the kingdom and dominion, and the greatness of the kingdom under the whole heaven, shall be given to the people of the saints of the most High, whose kingdom is an everlasting kingdom, and all dominions shall serve and obey him." ²⁸Hitherto is the end of the matter. As for me Daniel, my cogitations much troubled me, and my countenance changed in me: but I kept the matter in my heart.

8 ¹In the third year of the reign of king Belshazzar a vision appeared unto me, even unto me Daniel, after that which appeared unto me at the first. ²And I saw in a vision; and it came to pass, when I saw, that I was at Shushan in the palace, which is in the province of Elam; and I saw in a vision, and I was by the river of Ulai. ³Then I lifted up my eyes, and saw, and behold, there stood before the river a ram which had two horns, and the two horns were high: but one was higher than the other, and the higher came up last. ⁴I saw the ram pushing westward, and northward, and southward: so that no beasts might stand before him, neither was there any that could deliver out of his hand, but he did according to his will, and became great. ⁵And as I was considering, behold, a he-goat came from the west on the face of the whole earth, and touched not the ground: and the goat had a notable horn between his eyes. ⁶And he came to the ram that had two horns, which I had seen standing before the river, and ran unto him in the fury of his power. ⁷And I saw him come close unto the ram, and he was moved with choler against him, and smote the ram, and broke his two horns: and there was no power in the ram to stand before him, but he cast him down to the ground, and stamped upon him: and there was none that could deliver the ram out of his hand. ⁸Therefore the he-goat waxed very great, and when he was strong, the great horn was broken: and for it came up four notable ones toward the four winds of heaven. ⁹And out of one of them came forth a little horn, which waxed exceeding great, toward the south, and toward the east, and toward the pleasant land. ¹⁰And it waxed great even to the host of heaven, and it cast down some of the host and of the stars to the ground, and stamped upon them. ¹¹Yea, he magnified himself even to the prince of the host, and by him the daily sacrifice was taken away, and the place of his sanctuary was cast down. ¹²And a host was given him against the daily sacrifice by reason of transgression, and it cast down the truth to the ground, and it practised, and prospered.

¹³'Then I heard one saint speaking, and another saint said unto that certain saint which spoke, "How long shall be the vision concerning the daily sacrifice, and the transgression of desolation, to give both the sanctuary and the host to be trodden under foot?" ¹⁴And he said unto me, "Unto two thousand and three hundred days: then shall the sanctuary be cleansed".

¹⁵'And it came to pass, when I, even I Daniel had seen the vision, and sought for the meaning, then behold, there stood before me as the appearance of a man. ¹⁶And I heard a man's voice between the banks of Ulai, which called, and said, "Gabriel, make this man to understand the vision". ¹⁷So he came near where I stood: and when he came, I was afraid, and fell upon my face: but he said unto me, "Understand, O son of man: for at the time of the end shall be the vision". ¹⁸Now as he was speaking with me, I was in a deep sleep on my face toward the ground: but he touched me, and set me upright. ¹⁹And he said, "Behold, I will make thee know what shall be in the last end of the indignation: for at the time appointed the end shall be. ²⁰The ram which thou sawest having two horns are the kings of Media and Persia. ²¹And the rough goat is the king of Grecia, and the great horn that is between his eyes is the first king. ²²Now that being broken, whereas four stood up for it, four kingdoms shall stand up out of the nation, but not in his power. ²³And in the latter time of their kingdom, when the transgressors are come to the full, a king of fierce countenance, and understanding dark sentences, shall stand up. ²⁴And his power shall be mighty, but not by his own power: and he shall destroy wonderfully, and shall prosper, and practise, and shall destroy the mighty and the holy people. ²⁵And through his policy also he shall cause craft to prosper in his hand, and he shall magnify himself in his heart, and by peace shall destroy many: he shall also stand up against the Prince of princes, but he shall be broken without hand. ²⁶And the vision of the evening and the morning which was told is true: wherefore shut thou up the vision, for it shall be for many days." ²⁷And I Daniel fainted, and was sick certain days: afterward I rose up and did the king's business, and I was astonished at the vision, but none understood it.

9 'In the first year of Darius the son of Ahasuerus, of the seed of the Medes, which was made king over the realm of the Chaldeans, ²in the first year of his reign, I Daniel understood by books the number of the years, whereof the word of the LORD came to Jeremiah the prophet, that he would accomplish seventy years in the desolations of Jerusalem.

³'And I set my face unto the Lord God to seek by prayer and supplica-

tions, with fasting, and sackcloth, and ashes: ⁴and I prayed unto the LORD my God, and made my confession, and said, "O Lord, the great and dreadful God, keeping the covenant and mercy to them that love him, and to them that keep his commandments: ⁵we have sinned, and have committed iniquity, and have done wickedly, and have rebelled, even by departing from thy precepts and from thy judgements. ⁶Neither have we hearkened unto thy servants the prophets, which spoke in thy name to our kings, our princes, and our fathers, and to all the people of the land. ⁷O Lord, righteousness belongeth unto thee, but unto us confusion of faces, as at this day: to the men of Judah, and to the inhabitants of Jerusalem, and unto all Israel that are near, and that are far off, through all the countries whither thou hast driven them, because of their trespass that they have trespassed against thee. ⁸O Lord, to us belongeth confusion of face, to our kings, to our princes, and to our fathers, because we have sinned against thee. ⁹To the Lord our God belong mercies and forgivenesses, though we have rebelled against him. ¹⁰Neither have we obeyed the voice of the LORD our God, to walk in his laws, which he set before us by his servants the prophets. ¹¹Yea, all Israel have transgressed thy law, even by departing, that they might not obey thy voice; therefore the curse is poured upon us, and the oath that is written in the law of Moses the servant of God, because we have sinned against him. ¹²And he hath confirmed his words, which he spoke against us, and against our judges that judged us, by bringing upon us a great evil: for under the whole heaven hath not been done as hath been done upon Jerusalem. ¹³As it is written in the law of Moses, all this evil is come upon us: yet made we not our prayer before the LORD our God, that we might turn from our iniquities, and understand thy truth. ¹⁴Therefore hath the LORD watched upon the evil, and brought it upon us: for the LORD our God is righteous in all his works which he doeth: for we obeyed not his voice. ¹⁵And now, O Lord our God, that hast brought thy people forth out of the land of Egypt with a mighty hand, and hast gotten thee renown, as at this day; we have sinned, we have done wickedly.

¹⁶'"O Lord, according to all thy righteousness, I beseech thee, let thy anger and thy fury be turned away from thy city Jerusalem, thy holy mountain: because for our sins, and for the iniquities of our fathers, Jerusalem and thy people are become a reproach to all that are about us. ¹⁷Now therefore, O our God, hear the prayer of thy servant, and his supplications, and cause thy face to shine upon thy sanctuary that is desolate, for the Lord's sake. ¹⁸O my God, incline thy ear, and hear: open thy eyes, and behold our desolations, and the city which is called by thy name: for we do not present our supplications before thee for our righteousnesses, but for thy great mercies. ¹⁹O Lord, hear, O Lord, forgive, O Lord, hearken and do: defer not, for thy own sake, O my God: for thy city and thy people are called by thy name."

²⁰'And whilst I was speaking, and praying, and confessing my sin and the sin of my people Israel, and presenting my supplication before the LORD my God for the holy mountain of my God: ²¹yea, whilst I was

speaking in prayer, even the man Gabriel, whom I had seen in the vision at the beginning, being caused to fly swiftly, touched me about the time of the evening oblation. ²²And he informed me, and talked with me, and said, "O Daniel, I am now come forth to give thee skill and understanding. ²³At the beginning of thy supplications the commandment came forth, and I am come to show thee: for thou art greatly beloved: therefore understand the matter, and consider the vision. ²⁴Seventy weeks are determined upon thy people and upon thy holy city, to finish the transgression, and to make an end of sins, and to make reconciliation for iniquity, and to bring in everlasting righteousness, and to seal up the vision and prophecy, and to anoint the most Holy. ²⁵Know therefore and understand, that from the going forth of the commandment to restore and to build Jerusalem unto the Messiah the Prince, shall be seven weeks, and threescore and two weeks: the street shall be built again, and the wall, even in troublous times. ²⁶And after threescore and two weeks shall Messiah be cut off, but not for himself: and the people of the prince that shall come shall destroy the city and the sanctuary, and the end thereof shall be with a flood, and unto the end of the war desolations are determined. ²⁷And he shall confirm the covenant with many for one week: and in the midst of the week he shall cause the sacrifice and the oblation to cease, and for the overspreading of abominations he shall make it desolate, even until the consummation, and that determined shall be poured upon the desolate."'

10 In the third year of Cyrus king of Persia a thing was revealed unto Daniel, whose name was called Belteshazzar; and the thing was true, but the time appointed was long: and he understood the thing, and had understanding of the vision.

²'In those days I Daniel was mourning three full weeks. ³I ate no pleasant bread, neither came flesh nor wine in my mouth, neither did I anoint myself at all, till three whole weeks were fulfilled. ⁴And in the four and twentieth day of the first month, as I was by the side of the great river, which is Hiddekel; ⁵then I lifted up my eyes, and looked, and behold, a certain man clothed in linen, whose loins were girded with fine gold of Uphaz. ⁶His body also was like the beryl, and his face as the appearance of lightning, and his eyes as lamps of fire, and his arms and his feet like in colour to polished brass, and the voice of his words like the voice of a multitude. ⁷And I Daniel alone saw the vision: for the men that were with me saw not the vision: but a great quaking fell upon them, so that they fled to hide themselves. ⁸Therefore I was left alone, and saw this great vision, and there remained no strength in me: for my comeliness was turned in me into corruption, and I retained no strength. ⁹Yet heard I the voice of his words: and when I heard the voice of his words, then was I in a deep sleep on my face, and my face toward the ground.

¹⁰'And behold, a hand touched me, which set me upon my knees and upon the palms of my hands. ¹¹And he said unto me, "O Daniel, a man greatly beloved, understand the words that I speak unto thee, and

stand upright: for unto thee am I now sent". And when he had spoken this word unto me, I stood trembling. [12]Then said he unto me, "Fear not, Daniel: for from the first day that thou didst set thy heart to understand, and to chasten thyself before thy God, thy words were heard, and I am come for thy words. [13]But the prince of the kingdom of Persia withstood me one and twenty days: but lo, Michael, one of the chief princes, came to help me, and I remained there with the kings of Persia. [14]Now I am come to make thee understand what shall befall thy people in the latter days: for yet the vision is for many days."

[15]And when he had spoken such words unto me, I set my face toward the ground, and I became dumb. [16]And behold, one like the similitude of the sons of men touched my lips: then I opened my mouth, and spoke, and said unto him that stood before me, "O my Lord, by the vision my sorrows are turned upon me, and I have retained no strength. [17]For how can the servant of this my Lord talk with this my Lord? for as for me, straightway there remained no strength in me, neither is there breath left in me."

[18]Then there came again and touched me one like the appearance of a man, and he strengthened me, [19]and said, "O man greatly beloved, fear not: peace be unto thee, be strong, yea, be strong". And when he had spoken unto me, I was strengthened, and said, "Let my Lord speak: for thou hast strengthened me". [20]Then said he, "Knowest thou wherefore I come unto thee? and now will I return to fight with the prince of Persia: and when I am gone forth, lo, the prince of Grecia shall come. [21]But I will show thee that which is noted in the scripture of truth: and there is none that holdeth with me in these things, but Michael your prince."

11 [1]Also I in the first year of Darius the Mede, even I stood to confirm and to strengthen him.

[2]"And now will I show thee the truth. Behold, there shall stand up yet three kings in Persia, and the fourth shall be far richer than they all: and by his strength through his riches he shall stir up all against the realm of Grecia. [3]And a mighty king shall stand up, that shall rule with great dominion, and do according to his will. [4]And when he shall stand up, his kingdom shall be broken, and shall be divided toward the four winds of heaven; and not to his posterity, nor according to his dominion which he ruled: for his kingdom shall be plucked up, even for others besides those.

[5]"And the king of the south shall be strong, and one of his princes, and he shall be strong above him, and have dominion: his dominion shall be a great dominion. [6]And in the end of years they shall join themselves together: for the king's daughter of the south shall come to the king of the north to make an agreement, but she shall not retain the power of the arm, neither shall he stand, nor his arm: but she shall be given up, and they that brought her, and he that begot her, and he that strengthened her in these times. [7]But out of a branch of her roots shall one stand up in his estate, which shall come with an army, and shall enter into the fortress of the king of the north, and shall deal against

them, and shall prevail: [8]and shall also carry captives into Egypt their gods, with their princes, and with their precious vessels of silver and of gold, and he shall continue more years than the king of the north. [9]So the king of the south shall come into his kingdom, and shall return into his own land.

[10]"But his sons shall be stirred up, and shall assemble a multitude of great forces: and one shall certainly come and overflow and pass through: then shall he return, and be stirred up, even to his fortress. [11]And the king of the south shall be moved with choler, and shall come forth and fight with him, even with the king of the north: and he shall set forth a great multitude, but the multitude shall be given into his hand. [12]And when he hath taken away the multitude, his heart shall be lifted up: and he shall cast down many ten thousands: but he shall not be strengthened by it. [13]For the king of the north shall return, and shall set forth a multitude greater than the former, and shall certainly come after certain years with a great army and with much riches.

[14]"And in those times there shall many stand up against the king of the south: also the robbers of thy people shall exalt themselves to establish the vision, but they shall fall. [15]So the king of the north shall come, and cast up a mount, and take the most fenced cities, and the arms of the south shall not withstand, neither his chosen people, neither shall there be any strength to withstand. [16]But he that cometh against him shall do according to his own will, and none shall stand before him: and he shall stand in the glorious land, which by his hand shall be consumed. [17]He shall also set his face to enter with the strength of his whole kingdom, and upright ones with him: thus shall he do, and he shall give him the daughter of women, corrupting her: but she shall not stand on his side, neither be for him. [18]After this shall he turn his face unto the isles, and shall take many, but a prince for his own behalf shall cause the reproach offered by him to cease without his own reproach: he shall cause it to turn upon him. [19]Then he shall turn his face towards the fort of his own land: but he shall stumble and fall, and not be found.

[20]"Then shall stand up in his estate a raiser of taxes in the glory of the kingdom, but within few days he shall be destroyed, neither in anger, nor in battle. [21]And in his estate shall stand up a vile person, to whom they shall not give the honour of the kingdom: but he shall come in peaceably, and obtain the kingdom by flatteries. [22]And with the arms of a flood shall they be overflowed from before him, and shall be broken: yea, also the prince of the covenant. [23]And after the league made with him he shall work deceitfully, for he shall come up, and shall become strong with a small people. [24]He shall enter peaceably even upon the fattest places of the province, and he shall do that which his fathers have not done, nor his fathers' fathers, he shall scatter among them the prey, and spoil, and riches: yea, and he shall forecast his devices against the strongholds, even for a time. [25]And he shall stir up his power and his courage against the king of the south with a great army, and the king of the south shall be stirred up to battle with a very great and

mighty army: but he shall not stand: for they shall forecast devices against him. ²⁶Yea, they that feed of the portion of his meat shall destroy him, and his army shall overflow: and many shall fall down slain. ²⁷And both these kings' hearts shall be to do mischief, and they shall speak lies at one table: but it shall not prosper: for yet the end shall be at the time appointed. ²⁸Then shall he return into his land with great riches, and his heart shall be against the holy covenant: and he shall do exploits, and return to his own land.

²⁹'"At the time appointed he shall return, and come toward the south: but it shall not be as the former, or as the latter. ³⁰For the ships of Chittim shall come against him: therefore he shall be grieved, and return, and have indignation against the holy covenant: so shall he do, he shall even return, and have intelligence with them that forsake the holy covenant. ³¹And arms shall stand on his part, and they shall pollute the sanctuary of strength, and shall take away the daily sacrifice, and they shall place the abomination that maketh desolate. ³²And such as do wickedly against the covenant shall he corrupt by flatteries: but the people that do know their God shall be strong and do exploits. ³³And they that understand among the people shall instruct many: yet they shall fall by the sword, and by flame, by captivity, and by spoil, many days. ³⁴Now when they shall fall, they shall be helped with a little help: but many shall cleave to them with flatteries. ³⁵And some of them of understanding shall fall, to try them, and to purge, and to make them white, even to the time of the end: because it is yet for a time appointed.

³⁶'"And the king shall do according to his will, and he shall exalt himself, and magnify himself above every god, and shall speak marvellous things against the God of gods, and shall prosper till the indignation be accomplished: for that that is determined shall be done. ³⁷Neither shall he regard the God of his fathers, nor the desire of women, nor regard any god: for he shall magnify himself above all. ³⁸But in his estate shall he honour the God of forces: and a God whom his fathers knew not shall he honour with gold, and silver, and with precious stones, and pleasant things. ³⁹Thus shall he do in the most strong holds with a strange god, whom he shall acknowledge and increase with glory: and he shall cause them to rule over many, and shall divide the land for gain.

⁴⁰'"And at the time of the end shall the king of the south push at him, and the king of the north shall come against him like a whirlwind, with chariots, and with horsemen, and with many ships, and he shall enter into the countries, and shall overflow and pass over. ⁴¹He shall enter also into the glorious land, and many countries shall be overthrown: but these shall escape out of his hand, even Edom, and Moab, and the chief of the children of Ammon. ⁴²He shall stretch forth his hand also upon the countries, and the land of Egypt shall not escape. ⁴³But he shall have power over the treasures of gold and of silver, and over all the precious things of Egypt: and the Libyans and the Ethiopians shall be at his steps. ⁴⁴But tidings out of the east and out of

the north shall trouble him: therefore he shall go forth with great fury to destroy, and utterly to make away many. ⁴⁵And he shall plant the tabernacles of his palace between the seas in the glorious holy mountain; yet he shall come to his end, and none shall help him.

12 ¹"And at that time shall Michael stand up, the great prince which standeth for the children of thy people, and there shall be a time of trouble, such as never was since there was a nation even to that same time: and at that time thy people shall be delivered, every one that shall be found written in the book. ²And many of them that sleep in the dust of the earth shall awake, some to everlasting life, and some to shame and everlasting contempt. ³And they that be wise shall shine as the brightness of the firmament, and they that turn many to righteousness as the stars for ever and ever. ⁴But thou, O Daniel, shut up the words, and seal the book, even to the time of the end: many shall run to and fro, and knowledge shall be increased."

⁵"Then I Daniel looked, and behold, there stood other two, the one on this side of the bank of the river, and the other on that side of the bank of the river. ⁶And one said to the man clothed in linen, which was upon the waters of the river, "How long shall it be to the end of these wonders?" ⁷And I heard the man clothed in linen, which was upon the waters of the river, when he held up his right hand and his left hand unto heaven, and swore by him that liveth for ever that it shall be for a time, times, and a half; and when he shall have accomplished to scatter the power of the holy people, all these things shall be finished.

⁸'And I heard, but I understood not: then said I, "O my lord, what shall be the end of these things?" ⁹And he said, "Go thy way, Daniel: for the words are closed up and sealed till the time of the end. ¹⁰Many shall be purified, and made white, and tried: but the wicked shall do wickedly: and none of the wicked shall understand, but the wise shall understand. ¹¹And from the time that the daily sacrifice shall be taken away, and the abomination that maketh desolate set up, there shall be a thousand two hundred and ninety days. ¹²Blessed is he that waiteth, and cometh to the thousand three hundred and five and thirty days. ¹³But go thou thy way till the end be: for thou shalt rest, and stand in the lot at the end of the days."'

HOSEA

1 The word of the LORD that came unto Hosea, the son of Beeri, in the days of Uzziah, Jotham, Ahaz, and Hezekiah, kings of Judah, and in the days of Jeroboam the son of Joash, king of Israel.

²The beginning of the word of the LORD by Hosea. And the LORD said to Hosea, 'Go, take unto thee a wife of whoredoms, and children of whoredoms: for the land hath committed great whoredom, departing from the LORD'. ³So he went and took Gomer the daughter of Diblaim, which conceived, and bore him a son. ⁴And the LORD said unto him, 'Call his name Jezreel, for yet a little while, and I will avenge the blood of Jezreel upon the house of Jehu, and will cause to cease the kingdom of the house of Israel. ⁵And it shall come to pass at that day, that I will break the bow of Israel, in the valley of Jezreel.'

⁶And she conceived again and bore a daughter. And God said unto him, 'Call her name Lo-ruhamah: for I will no more have mercy upon the house of Israel: but I will utterly take them away. ⁷But I will have mercy upon the house of Judah, and will save them by the LORD their God, and will not save them by bow, nor by sword, nor by battle, by horses, nor by horsemen.'

⁸Now when she had weaned Lo-ruhamah, she conceived and bore a son. ⁹Then said God, 'Call his name 'Lo-ammi: for ye are not my people, and I will not be your God.

¹⁰'Yet the number of the children of Israel shall be as the sand of the sea, which cannot be measured nor numbered; and it shall come to pass, that in the place where it was said unto them, "Ye are not my people", there it shall be said unto them, "Ye are the sons of the living God". ¹¹Then shall the children of Judah and the children of Israel be gathered together, and appoint themselves one head, and they shall come up out of the land: for great shall be the day of Jezreel.

2 'Say ye unto your brethren, Ammi, and to your sisters, Ruhamah.

² 'Plead with your mother, plead:
for she is not my wife, neither am I her husband:
let her therefore put away her whoredoms out of her sight,
and her adulteries from between her breasts;
³ lest I strip her naked,
and set her as in the day that she was born,
and make her as a wilderness,
and set her like a dry land,
and slay her with thirst.
⁴ And I will not have mercy upon her children,
for they be the children of whoredoms.
⁵ For their mother hath played the harlot:
she that conceived them hath done shamefully:
for she said, "I will go after my lovers,

that give me my bread and my water,
my wool and my flax, my oil and my drink".

⁶ 'Therefore behold, I will hedge up thy way with thorns,
and make a wall, that she shall not find her paths.
⁷ And she shall follow after her lovers,
but she shall not overtake them,
and she shall seek them, but shall not find them:
then shall she say, "I will go and return to my first husband,
for then was it better with me than now".
⁸ For she did not know that I gave her corn, and wine, and oil,
and multiplied her silver and gold, which they prepared for Baal.
⁹ Therefore will I return,
and take away my corn in the time thereof,
and my wine in the season thereof,
and will recover my wool and my flax
given to cover her nakedness.
¹⁰ And now will I discover her lewdness in the sight of her lovers,
and none shall deliver her out of my hand.
¹¹ I will also cause all her mirth to cease,
her feast days, her new moons,
and her sabbaths, and all her solemn feasts.
¹² And I will destroy her vines and her fig trees,
whereof she hath said, "These are my rewards
that my lovers have given me":
and I will make them a forest,
and the beasts of the field shall eat them.
¹³ And I will visit upon her the days of Baalim,
wherein she burnt incense to them,
and she decked herself with her earrings and her jewels,
and she went after her lovers,
and forgot me,' saith the LORD.

¹⁴ 'Therefore behold, I will allure her,
and bring her into the wilderness,
and speak comfortably unto her.
¹⁵ And I will give her her vineyards from thence,
and the valley of Achor for a door of hope,
and she shall sing there, as in the days of her youth,
and as in the day when she came up out of the land of Egypt.
¹⁶ And it shall be at that day,' saith the LORD,
'that thou shalt call me Ishi;
and shalt call me no more Baali.
¹⁷ For I will take away the names of Baalim out of her mouth,
and they shall no more be remembered by their name.
¹⁸ And in that day will I make a covenant for them
with the beasts of the field and with the fowls of heaven,
and with the creeping things of the ground:

and I will break the bow and the sword
and the battle out of the earth,
and will make them to lie down safely.
¹⁹ And I will betroth thee unto me for ever;
yea, I will betroth thee unto me in righteousness,
and in judgement, and in loving-kindness, and in mercies.
²⁰ I will even betroth thee unto me in faithfulness:
and thou shalt know the LORD.

²¹ 'And it shall come to pass in that day,
I will hear,' saith the LORD,
'I will hear the heavens, and they shall hear the earth,
²² and the earth shall hear the corn, and the wine, and the oil,
and they shall hear Jezreel.
²³ And I will sow her unto me in the earth,
and I will have mercy upon her that had not obtained mercy,
and I will say to them which were not my people,
"Thou art my people",
and they shall say, "Thou art my God".

3 Then said the LORD unto me, 'Go yet, love a woman beloved of her friend, yet an adulteress, according to the love of the LORD toward the children of Israel, who look to other gods, and love flagons of wine'. ²So I bought her to me for fifteen pieces of silver, and for a homer of barley, and a half homer of barley. ³And I said unto her, 'Thou shalt abide for me many days, thou shalt not play the harlot, and thou shalt not be for another man: so will I also be for thee'. ⁴For the children of Israel shall abide many days without a king, and without a prince, and without a sacrifice, and without an image, and without an ephod, and without teraphim. ⁵Afterward shall the children of Israel return, and seek the LORD their God, and David their king, and shall fear the LORD and his goodness in the latter days.

4 Hear the word of the LORD, ye children of Israel:
for the LORD hath a controversy with the inhabitants of the land,
because there is no truth, nor mercy,
nor knowledge of God in the land.
² 'By swearing, and lying, and killing,
and stealing, and committing adultery,
they break out, and blood toucheth blood.
³ Therefore shall the land mourn,
and every one that dwelleth therein shall languish,
with the beasts of the field,
and with the fowls of heaven,
yea, the fishes of the sea also shall be taken away.
⁴ Yet let no man strive, nor reprove another:
for this people are as they that strive with the priest.
⁵ Therefore shalt thou fall in the day,

and the prophet also shall fall with thee in the night,
and I will destroy thy mother.

⁶ 'My people are destroyed for lack of knowledge:
because thou hast rejected knowledge, I will also reject thee,
that thou shalt be no priest to me:
seeing thou hast forgotten the law of thy God,
I will also forget thy children.
⁷ As they were increased, so they sinned against me:
therefore will I change their glory into shame.
⁸ They eat up the sin of my people,
and they set their heart on their iniquity.
⁹ And there shall be like people, like priest:
and I will punish them for their ways,
and reward them their doings.
¹⁰ For they shall eat, and not have enough:
they shall commit whoredom, and shall not increase,
because they have left off to take heed to the LORD.
¹¹ Whoredom and wine and new wine take away the heart.

¹² 'My people ask counsel at their stocks,
and their staff declareth unto them:
for the spirit of whoredoms hath caused them to err,
and they have gone a-whoring from under their God.
¹³ They sacrifice upon the tops of the mountains,
and burn incense upon the hills
under oaks and poplars and elms,
because the shadow thereof is good:
therefore your daughters shall commit whoredom,
and your spouses shall commit adultery.
¹⁴ I will not punish your daughters when they commit
whoredom,
nor your spouses when they commit adultery:
for themselves are separated with whores,
and they sacrifice with harlots:
therefore the people that doth not understand shall fall.

¹⁵ 'Though thou, Israel, play the harlot,
yet let not Judah offend,
and come not ye unto Gilgal,
neither go ye up to Beth-aven,
nor swear, "The LORD liveth".
¹⁶ For Israel slideth back as a backsliding heifer:
now the LORD will feed them as a lamb in a large place.
¹⁷ Ephraim is joined to idols: let him alone.
¹⁸ Their drink is sour:
they have committed whoredom continually:
her rulers with shame do love, "Give ye".

¹⁹ The wind hath bound her up in her wings,
   and they shall be ashamed because of their sacrifices.

5 'Hear ye this, O priests,
   and hearken, ye house of Israel,
   and give ye ear, O house of the king:
   for judgement is toward you,
   because ye have been a snare on Mizpah,
   and a net spread upon Tabor.
² And the revolters are profound to make slaughter,
   though I have been a rebuker of them all.
³ I know Ephraim,
   and Israel is not hid from me:
   for now, O Ephraim, thou committest whoredom,
   and Israel is defiled.
⁴ They will not frame their doings to turn unto their God:
   for the spirit of whoredoms is in the midst of them,
   and they have not known the LORD.
⁵ And the pride of Israel doth testify to his face:
   therefore shall Israel and Ephraim fall in their iniquity:
   Judah also shall fall with them.
⁶ They shall go with their flocks and with their herds to seek the
      LORD:
   but they shall not find him,
   he hath withdrawn himself from them.
⁷ They have dealt treacherously against the LORD:
   for they have begotten strange children:
   now shall a month devour them with their portions.
⁸ Blow ye the cornet in Gibeah,
   and the trumpet in Ramah:
   cry aloud at Beth-aven, "After thee, O Benjamin".
⁹ Ephraim shall be desolate in the day of rebuke:
   among the tribes of Israel have I made known that which shall
      surely be.
¹⁰ The princes of Judah were like them that remove the bound:
   therefore I will pour out my wrath upon them like water.
¹¹ Ephraim is oppressed and broken in judgement,
   because he willingly walked after the commandment.
¹² Therefore will I be unto Ephraim as a moth,
   and to the house of Judah as rottenness.
¹³ When Ephraim saw his sickness,
   and Judah saw his wound,
   then went Ephraim to the Assyrian,
   and sent to king Jareb:
   yet could he not heal you,
   nor cure you of your wound.
¹⁴ For I will be unto Ephraim as a lion,
   and as a young lion to the house of Judah:

I, even I will tear and go away:
I will take away, and none shall rescue him.

¹⁵ 'I will go and return to my place,
till they acknowledge their offence, and seek my face:
in their affliction they will seek me early.'

6 'Come, and let us return unto the LORD:
for he hath torn, and he will heal us:
he hath smitten, and he will bind us up.
² After two days will he revive us:
in the third day he will raise us up,
and we shall live in his sight.
³ Then shall we know, if we follow on to know the LORD:
his going forth is prepared as the morning;
and he shall come unto us as the rain,
as the latter and former rain unto the earth.'

⁴ 'O Ephraim, what shall I do unto thee?
O Judah, what shall I do unto thee?
for your goodness is as a morning cloud,
and as the early dew it goeth away.
⁵ Therefore have I shown them by the prophets:
I have slain them by the words of my mouth:
and thy judgements are as the light that goeth forth.
⁶ For I desired mercy, and not sacrifice;
and the knowledge of God more than burnt offerings.
⁷ But they like men have transgressed the covenant:
there have they dealt treacherously against me.
⁸ Gilead is a city of them that work iniquity,
and is polluted with blood.
⁹ And as troops of robbers wait for a man,
so the company of priests murder in the way by consent:
for they commit lewdness.
¹⁰ I have seen a horrible thing in the house of Israel:
there is the whoredom of Ephraim, Israel is defiled.
¹¹ Also, O Judah, he hath set a harvest for thee,
when I returned the captivity of my people.

7 'When I would have healed Israel,
then the iniquity of Ephraim was discovered,
and the wickedness of Samaria:
for they commit falsehood:
and the thief cometh in,
and the troop of robbers spoileth without.
² And they consider not in their hearts
that I remember all their wickedness:
now their own doings have beset them about,

they are before my face.
³ They make the king glad with their wickedness,
   and the princes with their lies.
⁴ They are all adulterers, as an oven heated by the baker:
   who ceaseth from raising after he hath kneaded the dough, until
      it be leavened.
⁵ In the day of our king the princes have made him sick with
      bottles of wine,
   he stretched out his hand with scorners.
⁶ For they have made ready their heart like an oven, whilst they lie
      in wait:
   their baker sleepeth all the night,
   in the morning it burneth as a flaming fire.
⁷ They are all hot as an oven, and have devoured their judges;
   all their kings are fallen:
   there is none among them that calleth unto me.
⁸ Ephraim, he hath mixed himself among the people,
   Ephraim is a cake not turned.
⁹ Strangers have devoured his strength,
   and he knoweth it not:
   yea, grey hairs are here and there upon him,
   yet he knoweth not.
¹⁰ And the pride of Israel testifieth to his face:
   and they do not return to the Lord their God,
   nor seek him for all this.

¹¹ 'Ephraim also is like a silly dove without heart:
   they call to Egypt, they go to Assyria.
¹² When they shall go, I will spread my net upon them,
   I will bring them down as the fowls of the heaven:
   I will chastise them, as their congregation hath heard.
¹³ Woe unto them, for they have fled from me:
   destruction unto them, because they have transgressed against
      me:
   though I have redeemed them, yet they have spoken lies
      against me.
¹⁴ And they have not cried unto me with their heart,
   when they howled upon their beds:
   they assemble themselves for corn and wine,
   and they rebel against me.
¹⁵ Though I have bound and strengthened their arms,
   yet do they imagine mischief against me.
¹⁶ They return, but not to the most High:
   they are like a deceitful bow:
   their princes shall fall by the sword for the rage of their tongue:
   this shall be their derision in the land of Egypt.

8 ‘Set the trumpet to thy mouth.
He shall come as an eagle against the house of the LORD,
because they have transgressed my covenant,
and trespassed against my law.
² Israel shall cry unto me, "My God, we know thee".
³ Israel hath cast off the thing that is good:
the enemy shall pursue him.
⁴ They have set up kings, but not by me:
they have made princes, and I knew it not:
of their silver and their gold have they made them idols,
that they may be cut off.

⁵ ‘Thy calf, O Samaria, hath cast thee off:
my anger is kindled against them:
how long will it be ere they attain to innocence?
⁶ For from Israel was it also,
the workman made it, therefore it is not God:
but the calf of Samaria shall be broken in pieces.
⁷ For they have sown the wind,
and they shall reap the whirlwind:
it hath no stalk:
the bud shall yield no meal:
if so be it yield,
the strangers shall swallow it up.
⁸ Israel is swallowed up:
now shall they be among the Gentiles as a vessel wherein is no
    pleasure.
⁹ For they are gone up to Assyria,
a wild ass alone by himself;
Ephraim hath hired lovers.
¹⁰ Yea, though they have hired among the nations,
now will I gather them,
and they shall sorrow a little
for the burden of the king of princes.
¹¹ Because Ephraim hath made many altars to sin,
altars shall be unto him to sin.
¹² I have written to him the great things of my law,
but they were counted as a strange thing.
¹³ They sacrifice flesh for the sacrifices of my offerings, and eat it;
but the LORD accepteth them not:
now will he remember their iniquity, and visit their sins:
they shall return to Egypt.
¹⁴ For Israel hath forgotten his Maker, and buildeth temples;
and Judah hath multiplied fenced cities:
but I will send a fire upon his cities,
and it shall devour the palaces thereof.’

9

Rejoice not, O Israel, for joy, as other people:
for thou hast gone a-whoring from thy God,
thou hast loved a reward upon every corn-floor.

2 The floor and the wine-press shall not feed them,
and the new wine shall fail in her.

3 They shall not dwell in the LORD's land:
but Ephraim shall return to Egypt,
and they shall eat unclean things in Assyria.

4 They shall not offer wine offerings to the LORD,
neither shall they be pleasing unto him:
their sacrifices shall be unto them as the bread of mourners:
all that eat thereof shall be polluted:
for their bread for their soul shall not come into the house of the
LORD.

5 What will ye do in the solemn day,
and in the day of the feast of the LORD?

6 For lo, they are gone because of destruction:
Egypt shall gather them up,
Memphis shall bury them:
the pleasant places for their silver, nettles shall possess them:
thorns shall be in their tabernacles.

7 The days of visitation are come,
the days of recompense are come,
Israel shall know it:
the prophet is a fool,
the spiritual man is mad,
for the multitude of thy iniquity,
and the great hatred.

8 The watchman of Ephraim was with my God:
but the prophet is a snare of a fowler in all his ways,
and hatred in the house of his God.

9 They have deeply corrupted themselves as in the days of Gibeah:
therefore he will remember their iniquity,
he will visit their sins.

10 I found Israel like grapes in the wilderness:
I saw your fathers as the first-ripe in the fig tree at her first time:
but they went to Baal-peor,
and separated themselves unto that shame,
and their abominations were according as they loved.

11 As for Ephraim, their glory shall fly away like a bird,
from the birth, and from the womb,
and from the conception.

12 Though they bring up their children, yet will I bereave them,
that there shall not be a man left:
yea, woe also to them when I depart from them.

13 Ephraim, as I saw Tyrus, is planted in a pleasant place:
but Ephraim shall bring forth his children to the murderer.

¹⁴ Give them, O LORD: what wilt thou give?
  give them a miscarrying womb and dry breasts.
¹⁵ All their wickedness is in Gilgal:
  for there I hated them:
  for the wickedness of their doings
  I will drive them out of my house,
  I will love them no more:
  all their princes are revolters.
¹⁶ Ephraim is smitten,
  their root is dried up, they shall bear no fruit:
  yea, though they bring forth,
  yet will I slay even the beloved fruit of their womb.
¹⁷ My God will cast them away,
  because they did not hearken unto him:
  and they shall be wanderers among the nations.

10 Israel is an empty vine,
  he bringeth forth fruit unto himself:
  according to the multitude of his fruit
  he hath increased the altars,
  according to the goodness of his land
  they have made goodly images.
² Their heart is divided:
  now shall they be found faulty:
  he shall break down their altars,
  he shall spoil their images.
³ For now they shall say, 'We have no king,
  because we feared not the LORD;
  what then should a king do to us?'
⁴ They have spoken words,
  swearing falsely in making a covenant:
  thus judgement springeth up as hemlock in the furrows of the
    field.
⁵ The inhabitants of Samaria shall fear
  because of the calves of Beth-aven:
  for the people thereof shall mourn over it,
  and the priests thereof that rejoiced on it,
  for the glory thereof, because it is departed from it.
⁶ It shall be also carried unto Assyria for a present to king Jareb:
  Ephraim shall receive shame,
  and Israel shall be ashamed of his own counsel.
⁷ As for Samaria, her king is cut off as the foam upon the water.
⁸ The high places also of Aven, the sin of Israel, shall be
    destroyed:
  the thorn and the thistle shall come up on their altars;
  and they shall say to the mountains, 'Cover us';
  and to the hills, 'Fall on us'.

⁹ O Israel, thou hast sinned from the days of Gibeah:
   there they stood:
   the battle in Gibeah against the children of iniquity did not
      overtake them.
¹⁰ It is in my desire that I should chastise them,
   and the people shall be gathered against them,
   when they shall bind themselves in their two furrows.
¹¹ And Ephraim is as a heifer that is taught,
   and loveth to tread out the corn,
   but I passed over upon her fair neck:
   I will make Ephraim to ride:
   Judah shall plough,
   and Jacob shall break his clods.
¹² Sow to yourselves in righteousness, reap in mercy:
   break up your fallow ground:
   for it is time to seek the LORD,
   till he come and rain righteousness upon you.
¹³ Ye have ploughed wickedness,
   ye have reaped iniquity,
   ye have eaten the fruit of lies:
   because thou didst trust in thy way,
   in the multitude of thy mighty men.
¹⁴ Therefore shall a tumult arise among thy people,
   and all thy fortresses shall be spoiled,
   as Shalman spoiled Beth-arbel in the day of battle:
   the mother was dashed in pieces upon her children.
¹⁵ So shall Beth-el do unto you
   because of your great wickedness:
   in a morning shall the king of Israel utterly be cut off.

11 'When Israel was a child, then I loved him,
   and called my son out of Egypt.
² As they called them, so they went from them:
   they sacrificed unto Baalim,
   and burnt incense to graven images.
³ I taught Ephraim also to go,
   taking them by their arms:
   but they knew not that I healed them.
⁴ I drew them with cords of a man,
   with bands of love:
   and I was to them as they that take off the yoke on their jaws,
   and I laid meat unto them.

⁵ 'He shall not return into the land of Egypt,
   but the Assyrian shall be his king,
   because they refused to return.
⁶ And the sword shall abide on his cities,

and shall consume his branches, and devour them,
because of their own counsels.
⁷ And my people are bent to backsliding from me:
though they called them to the most High,
none at all would exalt him.

⁸ 'How shall I give thee up, Ephraim?
how shall I deliver thee, Israel?
how shall I make thee as Admah?
how shall I set thee as Zeboim?
my heart is turned within me,
my repentings are kindled together.
⁹ I will not execute the fierceness of my anger,
I will not return to destroy Ephraim:
for I am God, and not man,
the Holy One in the midst of thee,
and I will not enter into the city.
¹⁰ They shall walk after the LORD:
he shall roar like a lion:
when he shall roar,
then the children shall tremble from the west.
¹¹ They shall tremble as a bird out of Egypt,
and as a dove out of the land of Assyria:
and I will place them in their houses,' saith the LORD.
¹² 'Ephraim compasseth me about with lies,
and the house of Israel with deceit:
but Judah yet ruleth with God,
and is faithful with the saints.'

12 Ephraim feedeth on wind,
and followeth after the east wind:
he daily increaseth lies and desolation,
and they do make a covenant with the Assyrians,
and oil is carried into Egypt.
² The LORD hath also a controversy with Judah,
and will punish Jacob according to his ways;
according to his doings will he recompense him.

³ He took his brother by the heel in the womb,
and by his strength he had power with God.
⁴ Yea, he had power over the angel, and prevailed:
he wept, and made supplication unto him:
he found him in Beth-el, and there he spoke with us.
⁵ Even the LORD God of hosts, the LORD is his memorial.
⁶ Therefore turn thou to thy God:
keep mercy and judgement
and wait on thy God continually.

⁷ He is a merchant,
  the balances of deceit are in his hand:
  he loveth to oppress.
⁸ And Ephraim said, 'Yet I am become rich,
  I have found me out substance:
  in all my labours they shall find no iniquity in me that were sin'.
⁹ 'And I that am the LORD thy God from the land of Egypt
  will yet make thee to dwell in tabernacles,
  as in the days of the solemn feast.
¹⁰ I have also spoken by the prophets,
  and I have multiplied visions, and used similitudes,
  by the ministry of the prophets.
¹¹ Is there iniquity in Gilead? surely they are vanity:
  they sacrifice bullocks in Gilgal,
  yea, their altars are as heaps in the furrows of the fields.'

¹² And Jacob fled into the country of Syria,
  and Israel served for a wife,
  and for a wife he kept sheep.
¹³ And by a prophet the LORD brought Israel out of Egypt,
  and by a prophet was he preserved.
¹⁴ Ephraim provoked him to anger most bitterly:
  therefore shall he leave his blood upon him,
  and his reproach shall his Lord return unto him.

13 'When Ephraim spoke trembling, he exalted himself in Israel,
  but when he offended in Baal, he died.
² And now they sin more and more,
  and have made them molten images of their silver,
  and idols according to their own understanding,
  all of it the work of the craftsmen:
  they say of them, "Let the men that sacrifice kiss the calves".
³ Therefore they shall be as the morning cloud
  and as the early dew it passeth away,
  as the chaff that is driven with a whirlwind out of the floor,
  and as the smoke out of the chimney.
⁴ Yet I am the LORD thy God from the land of Egypt,
  and thou shalt know no god but me:
  for there is no saviour besides me.
⁵ 'I did know thee in the wilderness,
  in the land of great drought.
⁶ According to their pasture, so were they filled:
  they were filled, and their heart was exalted:
  therefore have they forgotten me.
⁷ Therefore I will be unto them as a lion:
  as a leopard by the way will I observe them:
⁸ I will meet them as a bear that is bereaved of her whelps,

and will rend the caul of their heart,
and there will I devour them like a lion:
the wild beast shall tear them.

[9] 'O Israel, thou hast destroyed thyself,
but in me is thy help.
[10] I will be thy king:
where is any other that may save thee in all thy cities?
and thy judges of whom thou saidst,
"Give me a king and princes?"
[11] I gave thee a king in my anger,
and took him away in my wrath.
[12] The iniquity of Ephraim is bound up:
his sin is hid.
[13] The sorrows of a travailing woman shall come upon him:
he is an unwise son,
for he should not stay long in the place of the breaking forth of
children.
[14] I will ransom them from the power of the grave:
I will redeem them from death:
O death, I will be thy plagues,
O grave, I will be thy destruction:
repentance shall be hid from my eyes.'

[15] Though he be fruitful among his brethren,
an east wind shall come,
the wind of the LORD shall come up from the wilderness,
and his spring shall become dry,
and his fountain shall be dried up:
he shall spoil the treasure of all pleasant vessels.
[16] Samaria shall become desolate,
for she hath rebelled against her God:
they shall fall by the sword:
their infants shall be dashed in pieces,
and their women with child shall be ripped up.

14 O Israel, return unto the LORD thy God;
for thou hast fallen by thy iniquity.
[2] Take with you words, and turn to the LORD:
say unto him, 'Take away all iniquity, and receive us graciously:
so will we render the calves of our lips.
[3] Asshur shall not save us,
we will not ride upon horses,
neither will we say any more to the work of our hands,
"Ye are our gods": for in thee the fatherless findeth mercy.'

[4] 'I will heal their backsliding,
I will love them freely:

for my anger is turned away from him.
⁵ I will be as the dew unto Israel:
  he shall grow as the lily,
  and cast forth his roots as Lebanon.
⁶ His branches shall spread,
  and his beauty shall be as the olive tree,
  and his smell as Lebanon.
⁷ They that dwell under his shadow shall return:
  they shall revive as the corn, and grow as the vine:
  the scent thereof shall be as the wine of Lebanon.
⁸ Ephraim shall say, "What have I to do any more with idols?"
  I have heard him, and observed him:
  I am like a green fir tree.
  From me is thy fruit found.'

⁹ Who is wise, and he shall understand these things?
  prudent, and he shall know them?
  for the ways of the Lord are right,
  and the just shall walk in them:
  but the transgressors shall fall therein.

JOEL

1 The word of the LORD that came to Joel the son of Pethuel.

² Hear this, ye old men,
and give ear, all ye inhabitants of the land.
Hath this been in your days,
or even in the days of your fathers?
³ Tell ye your children of it,
and let your children tell their children,
and their children another generation.
⁴ That which the palmer-worm hath left hath the locust eaten;
and that which the locust hath left hath the canker-worm eaten;
and that which the canker-worm hath left hath the caterpillar
eaten.

⁵ Awake, ye drunkards, and weep,
and howl, all ye drinkers of wine,
because of the new wine,
for it is cut off from your mouth.
⁶ For a nation is come up upon my land,
strong, and without number,
whose teeth are the teeth of a lion,
and he hath the cheek-teeth of a great lion.
⁷ He hath laid my vine waste,
and barked my fig tree:
he hath made it clean bare,
and cast it away,
the branches thereof are made white.

⁸ Lament like a virgin girded with sackcloth
for the husband of her youth.
⁹ The meat offering and the drink offering
is cut off from the house of the LORD,
the priests the LORD's ministers mourn.
¹⁰ The field is wasted, the land mourneth;
for the corn is wasted:
the new wine is dried up,
the oil languisheth.

¹¹ Be ye ashamed, O ye husbandmen:
howl, O ye vine-dressers, for the wheat and for the barley;
because the harvest of the field is perished.
¹² The vine is dried up, and the fig tree languisheth,
the pomegranate tree, the palm tree also, and the apple tree,
even all the trees of the field are withered:
because joy is withered away from the sons of men.

¹³ Gird yourselves, and lament, ye priests:
   howl, ye ministers of the altar:
   come, lie all night in sackcloth,
   ye ministers of my God:
   for the meat offering and the drink offering
   is withheld from the house of your God.

¹⁴ Sanctify ye a fast, call a solemn assembly,
   gather the elders and all the inhabitants of the land
   into the house of the LORD your God,
   and cry unto the LORD,
¹⁵ 'Alas for the day:
   for the day of the LORD is at hand,
   and as a destruction from the Almighty shall it come'.
¹⁶ Is not the meat cut off before your eyes,
   yea, joy and gladness from the house of our God?
¹⁷ The seed is rotten under their clods,
   the garners are laid desolate,
   the barns are broken down,
   for the corn is withered.
¹⁸ How do the beasts groan!
   the herds of cattle are perplexed, because they have no pasture,
   yea, the flocks of sheep are made desolate.

¹⁹ O LORD, to thee will I cry:
   for the fire hath devoured the pastures of the wilderness,
   and the flame hath burnt all the trees of the field.
²⁰ The beasts of the field cry also unto thee:
   for the rivers of waters are dried up,
   and the fire hath devoured the pastures of the wilderness.

2   Blow ye the trumpet in Zion,
    and sound an alarm in my holy mountain:
    let all the inhabitants of the land tremble:
    for the day of the LORD cometh,
    for it is nigh at hand;
²   a day of darkness and of gloominess,
    a day of clouds and of thick darkness,
    as the morning spread upon the mountains:
    a great people and a strong,
    there hath not been ever the like,
    neither shall be any more after it,
    even to the years of many generations.
³   A fire devoureth before them,
    and behind them a flame burneth:
    the land is as the garden of Eden before them,
    and behind them a desolate wilderness,
    yea, and nothing shall escape them.

⁴ The appearance of them is as the appearance of horses;
    and as horsemen, so shall they run.
⁵ Like the noise of chariots on the tops of mountains shall they leap,
    like the noise of a flame of fire that devoureth the stubble,
    as a strong people set in battle array.
⁶ Before their face the people shall be much pained:
    all faces shall gather blackness.
⁷ They shall run like mighty men,
    they shall climb the wall like men of war,
    and they shall march every one on his ways,
    and they shall not break their ranks.
⁸ Neither shall one thrust another,
    they shall walk every one in his path:
    and when they fall upon the sword,
    they shall not be wounded.
⁹ They shall run to and fro in the city:
    they shall run upon the wall:
    they shall climb up upon the houses:
    they shall enter in at the windows like a thief.
¹⁰ The earth shall quake before them,
    the heavens shall tremble,
    the sun and the moon shall be dark,
    and the stars shall withdraw their shining.
¹¹ And the LORD shall utter his voice before his army,
    for his camp is very great:
    for he is strong that executeth his word:
    for the day of the LORD is great and very terrible,
    and who can abide it?

¹² 'Therefore also now,' saith the LORD,
    'turn ye even to me with all your heart, and with fasting,
    and with weeping, and with mourning.'
¹³ And rend your heart, and not your garments,
    and turn unto the LORD your God:
    for he is gracious and merciful,
    slow to anger, and of great kindness,
    and repenteth him of the evil.
¹⁴ Who knoweth if he will return and repent,
    and leave a blessing behind him,
    even a meat offering and a drink offering
    unto the LORD your God?

¹⁵ Blow the trumpet in Zion,
    sanctify a fast, call a solemn assembly.
¹⁶ Gather the people,
    sanctify the congregation,
    assemble the elders,
    gather the children,

and those that suck the breasts:
let the bridegroom go forth of his chamber,
and the bride out of her closet.

¹⁷ Let the priests, the ministers of the LORD,
weep between the porch and the altar,
and let them say, 'Spare thy people, O LORD,
and give not thy heritage to reproach,
that the heathen should rule over them':
wherefore should they say among the people,
'Where is their God?'

¹⁸ Then will the LORD be jealous for his land,
and pity his people.
¹⁹ Yea, the LORD will answer and say unto his people,
'Behold, I will send you corn, and wine, and oil,
and ye shall be satisfied therewith:
and I will no more make you a reproach among the heathen.
²⁰ But I will remove far off from you the northern army,
and will drive him into a land barren and desolate,
with his face toward the east sea,
and his hinder part towards the utmost sea,
and his stink shall come up,
and his ill savour shall come up,
because he hath done great things.'

²¹ Fear not, O land, be glad and rejoice:
for the LORD will do great things.
²² Be not afraid, ye beasts of the field:
for the pastures of the wilderness do spring,
for the tree beareth her fruit,
the fig tree and the vine do yield their strength.
²³ Be glad then, ye children of Zion,
and rejoice in the LORD your God:
for he hath given you the former rain moderately,
and he will cause to come down for you the rain,
the former rain, and the latter rain in the first month.
²⁴ And the floors shall be full of wheat,
and the vats shall overflow with wine and oil.

²⁵ 'And I will restore to you the years that the locust hath eaten,
the canker-worm, and the caterpillar, and the palmer-worm,
my great army which I sent among you.
²⁶ And ye shall eat in plenty, and be satisfied,
and praise the name of the LORD your God,
that hath dealt wondrously with you:
and my people shall never be ashamed.
²⁷ And ye shall know that I am in the midst of Israel,
and that I am the LORD your God, and none else:
and my people shall never be ashamed.

²⁸ 'And it shall come to pass afterward,
   that I will pour out my Spirit upon all flesh,
   and your sons and your daughters shall prophesy,
   your old men shall dream dreams,
   your young men shall see visions.
²⁹ And also upon the servants and upon the handmaids
   in those days will I pour out my Spirit.
³⁰ And I will show wonders in the heavens and in the earth,
   blood, and fire, and pillars of smoke.'
³¹ The sun shall be turned into darkness,
   and the moon into blood,
   before the great and the terrible day of the LORD come.
³² And it shall come to pass that whosoever shall call on the name
    of the LORD shall be delivered:
   for in mount Zion and in Jerusalem shall be deliverance,
   as the LORD hath said,
   and in the remnant whom the LORD shall call.

3

   'For behold, in those days and in that time,
   when I shall bring again the captivity of Judah and Jerusalem,
² I will also gather all nations,
   and will bring them down into the valley of Jehoshaphat,
   and will plead with them there for my people
   and for my heritage Israel,
   whom they have scattered among the nations,
   and parted my land.
³ And they have cast lots for my people,
   and have given a boy for a harlot,
   and sold a girl for wine, that they might drink.
⁴ Yea, and what have ye to do with me,
   O Tyre and Zidon, and all the coasts of Palestina?
   will ye render me a recompense?
   and if ye recompense me,
   swiftly and speedily will I return your recompense upon your
    own head;
⁵ because ye have taken my silver and my gold,
   and have carried into your temples
   my goodly pleasant things.
⁶ The children also of Judah and the children of Jerusalem
   have ye sold unto the Grecians,
   that ye might remove them far from their border.
⁷ Behold, I will raise them out of the place whither ye have sold them,
   and will return your recompense upon your own head.
⁸ And I will sell your sons and your daughters
   into the hand of the children of Judah,
   and they shall sell them to the Sabeans, to a people far off:
   for the LORD hath spoken it.

⁹ 'Proclaim ye this among the Gentiles:
"Prepare war, wake up the mighty men,
let all the men of war draw near,
let them come up.
¹⁰ Beat your ploughshares into swords,
and your pruning-hooks into spears,
let the weak say, 'I am strong'.
¹¹ Assemble yourselves, and come, all ye heathen,
and gather yourselves together round about:
thither cause thy mighty ones to come down, O LORD."
¹² Let the heathen be wakened,
and come up to the valley of Jehoshaphat:
for there will I sit to judge all the heathen round about.'

¹³ Put ye in the sickle, for the harvest is ripe:
come, get you down, for the press is full,
the vats overflow, for the wickedness is great.
¹⁴ Multitudes, multitudes in the valley of decision:
for the day of the LORD is near in the valley of decision.
¹⁵ The sun and the moon shall be darkened,
and the stars shall withdraw their shining.
¹⁶ The LORD also shall roar out of Zion,
and utter his voice from Jerusalem,
and the heavens and the earth shall shake:
but the LORD will be the hope of his people,
and the strength of the children of Israel.

¹⁷ 'So shall ye know that I am the LORD your God
dwelling in Zion, my holy mountain:
then shall Jerusalem be holy,
and there shall no strangers pass through her any more.

¹⁸ 'And it shall come to pass in that day,
that the mountains shall drop down new wine,
and the hills shall flow with milk,
and all the rivers of Judah shall flow with waters,
and a fountain shall come forth of the house of the LORD,
and shall water the valley of Shittim.
¹⁹ Egypt shall be a desolation,
and Edom shall be a desolate wilderness,
for the violence against the children of Judah,
because they have shed innocent blood in their land.
²⁰ But Judah shall dwell for ever,
and Jerusalem from generation to generation.
²¹ For I will cleanse their blood that I have not cleansed,
for the LORD dwelleth in Zion.'

AMOS

1 The words of Amos, who was among the herdsmen of Tekoa, which he saw concerning Israel in the days of Uzziah king of Judah, and in the days of Jeroboam the son of Joash king of Israel, two years before the earthquake. ²And he said,

> The LORD will roar from Zion,
> and utter his voice from Jerusalem:
> and the habitations of the shepherds shall mourn,
> and the top of Carmel shall wither.
> ³   Thus saith the LORD,
> 'For three transgressions of Damascus,
> and for four,
> I will not turn away the punishment thereof,
> because they have threshed Gilead
> with threshing instruments of iron.
> ⁴   But I will send a fire into the house of Hazael,
> which shall devour the palaces of Ben-hadad.
> ⁵   I will break also the bar of Damascus,
> and cut off the inhabitant from the plain of Aven,
> and him that holdeth the sceptre from the house of Eden:
> and the people of Syria shall go into captivity unto Kir,'
> saith the LORD.

> ⁶ Thus saith the LORD,
> 'For three transgressions of Gaza,
> and for four,
> I will not turn away the punishment thereof,
> because they carried away captive the whole captivity,
> to deliver them up to Edom.
> ⁷   But I will send a fire on the wall of Gaza,
> which shall devour the palaces thereof.
> ⁸   And I will cut off the inhabitant from Ashdod,
> and him that holdeth the sceptre from Ashkelon,
> and I will turn my hand against Ekron:
> and the remnant of the Philistines shall perish,'
> saith the Lord GOD.

> ⁹ Thus saith the LORD,
> 'For three transgressions of Tyrus,
> and for four,
> I will not turn away the punishment thereof,
> because they delivered up the whole captivity to Edom,
> and remembered not the brotherly covenant.
> ¹⁰   But I will send a fire on the wall of Tyrus,
> which shall devour the palaces thereof.'

¹¹ Thus saith the LORD,
    'For three transgressions of Edom,
    and for four,
    I will not turn away the punishment thereof,
    because he did pursue his brother with the sword,
    and did cast off all pity,
    and his anger did tear perpetually,
    and kept his wrath for ever.
¹²   But I will send a fire upon Teman,
    which shall devour the palaces of Bozrah.'

¹³ Thus saith the LORD,
    'For three transgressions of the children of Ammon,
    and for four,
    I will not turn away the punishment thereof,
    because they have ripped up the women with child of Gilead,
    that they might enlarge their border.
¹⁴   But I will kindle a fire in the wall of Rabbah,
    and it shall devour the palaces thereof,
    with shouting in the day of battle,
    with a tempest in the day of the whirlwind.
¹⁵   And their king shall go into captivity,
    he and his princes together,' saith the LORD.

2 Thus saith the LORD,
    'For three transgressions of Moab,
    and for four,
    I will not turn away the punishment thereof,
    because he burnt the bones of the king of Edom into lime.
²   But I will send a fire upon Moab,
    and it shall devour the palaces of Kerioth:
    and Moab shall die with tumult,
    with shouting, and with the sound of the trumpet:
³   and I will cut off the judge from the midst thereof,
    and will slay all the princes thereof with him,'
    saith the LORD.

⁴ Thus saith the LORD,
    'For three transgressions of Judah,
    and for four,
    I will not turn away the punishment thereof,
    because they have despised the law of the LORD,
    and have not kept his commandments,
    and their lies caused them to err,
    after the which their fathers have walked.
⁵   But I will send a fire upon Judah,
    and it shall devour the palaces of Jerusalem.'

⁶ Thus saith the Lord,
 'For three transgressions of Israel,
 and for four,
 I will not turn away the punishment thereof,
 because they sold the righteous for silver,
 and the poor for a pair of shoes:
⁷   that pant after the dust of the earth on the head of
 the poor,
 and turn aside the way of the meek:
 and a man and his father will go in unto the same maid,
 to profane my holy name.
⁸   And they lay themselves down upon clothes laid to
 pledge by every altar,
 and they drink the wine of the condemned in the house of
 their god.

⁹ 'Yet destroyed I the Amorite before them,
 whose height was like the height of the cedars,
 and he was strong as the oaks;
 yet I destroyed his fruit from above,
 and his roots from beneath.
¹⁰   Also I brought you up from the land of Egypt,
 and led you forty years through the wilderness,
 to possess the land of the Amorite.
¹¹   And I raised up of your sons for prophets,
 and of your young men for Nazarites.
 Is it not even thus, O ye children of Israel?'
 saith the Lord.
¹²   'But ye gave the Nazarites wine to drink,
 and commanded the prophets, saying, "Prophesy not".
¹³   Behold, I am pressed under you,
 as a cart is pressed that is full of sheaves.
¹⁴   Therefore the flight shall perish from the swift,
 and the strong shall not strengthen his force,
 neither shall the mighty deliver himself:
¹⁵   neither shall he stand that handleth the bow,
 and he that is swift of foot shall not deliver himself,
 neither shall he that rideth the horse deliver himself.
¹⁶   And he that is courageous among the mighty
 shall flee away naked in that day,'
 saith the Lord.

3 'Hear this word that the Lord hath spoken against you,
 O children of Israel,
 against the whole family
 which I brought up from the land of Egypt, saying,
²   "You only have I known of all the families of the
 earth:

therefore I will punish you for all your iniquities.
3   Can two walk together, except they be agreed?
4   Will a lion roar in the forest, when he hath no prey?
will a young lion cry out of his den, if he have taken nothing?
5   Can a bird fall in a snare upon the earth, where no gin
is for him?
shall one take up a snare from the earth, and have taken
nothing at all?
6   Shall a trumpet be blown in the city, and the people
not be afraid?
shall there be evil in a city, and the LORD hath not done it?
7   Surely the Lord GOD will do nothing,
but he revealeth his secret unto his servants the prophets.
8   The lion hath roared, who will not fear?
the Lord GOD hath spoken, who can but prophesy?"'

9 'Publish in the palaces at Ashdod,
    and in the palaces in the land of Egypt,
    and say, "Assemble yourselves upon the mountains of
    Samaria,
    and behold the great tumults in the midst thereof,
    and the oppressed in the midst thereof".
10   For they know not to do right,' saith the LORD,
'who store up violence and robbery in their palaces.'
11   Therefore thus saith the Lord GOD,
'An adversary there shall be even round about the land:
and he shall bring down thy strength from thee,
and thy palaces shall be spoiled'.

12 Thus saith the LORD,
    'As the shepherd taketh out of the mouth of the lion two legs,
    or a piece of an ear;
    so shall the children of Israel be taken out
    that dwell in Samaria in the corner of a bed,
    and in Damascus in a couch.

13 'Hear ye, and testify in the house of Jacob,'
    saith the Lord GOD, the God of hosts,
14   'that in the day that I shall visit the transgressions of
Israel upon him
I will also visit the altars of Beth-el,
and the horns of the altar shall be cut off,
and fall to the ground.
15   And I will smite the winter-house with the summer-
house
and the houses of ivory shall perish,
and the great houses shall have an end,'
saith the LORD.

4 'Hear this word, ye kine of Bashan,
that are in the mountain of Samaria,
    which oppress the poor, which crush the needy,
    which say to their masters, "Bring, and let us drink".
      ²   The Lord GOD hath sworn by his holiness,
    that lo, the days shall come upon you,
    that he will take you away with hooks,
    and your posterity with fish-hooks.
      ³   And ye shall go out at the breaches,
    every cow at that which is before her,
    and ye shall cast them into the palace,'
    saith the LORD.

⁴ 'Come to Beth-el, and transgress,
    at Gilgal multiply transgression;
    and bring your sacrifices every morning,
    and your tithes after three years.
      ⁵   And offer a sacrifice of thanksgiving with leaven,
    and proclaim and publish the free offerings:
    for this liketh you, O ye children of Israel,'
    saith the Lord GOD.

⁶ 'And I also have given you cleanness of teeth in all your cities,
    and want of bread in all your places:
    yet have ye not returned unto me,' saith the LORD.
      ⁷   'And also I have withheld the rain from you,
    when there were yet three months to the harvest:
    and I caused it to rain upon one city,
    and caused it not to rain upon another city:
    one piece was rained upon,
    and the piece whereupon it rained not withered.
      ⁸   So two or three cities wandered unto one city, to drink
    water;
    but they were not satisfied:
    yet have ye not returned unto me,'
    saith the LORD.

⁹ 'I have smitten you with blasting and mildew:
    when your gardens and your vineyards
    and your fig trees and your olive trees increased,
    the palmer-worm devoured them:
    yet have ye not returned unto me,'
    saith the LORD.
      ¹⁰   'I have sent among you the pestilence after the
    manner of Egypt:
    your young men have I slain with the sword,
    and have taken away your horses,

and I have made the stink of your camps to come up unto your
nostrils,
yet have ye not returned unto me,'
saith the LORD.

[11] 'I have overthrown some of you,
as God overthrew Sodom and Gomorrah,
and ye were as a fire-brand plucked out of the burning:
yet have ye not returned unto me,'
saith the LORD.
[12] 'Therefore thus will I do unto thee, O Israel:
and because I will do this unto thee,
prepare to meet thy God, O Israel.'

[13] For lo, he that formeth the mountains, and createth the wind,
and declareth unto man what is his thought,
that maketh the morning darkness,
and treadeth upon the high places of the earth:
the LORD, the God of hosts is his name.

5 Hear ye this word which I take up against you,
even a lamentation, O house of Israel.
[2] The virgin of Israel is fallen,
she shall no more rise:
she is forsaken upon her land,
there is none to raise her up.
[3] For thus saith the Lord GOD,
'The city that went out by a thousand shall leave a hundred,
and that which went forth by a hundred shall leave ten
to the house of Israel'.

[4] For thus saith the LORD unto the house of Israel,
'Seek ye me, and ye shall live.
[5] But seek not Beth-el, nor enter into Gilgal,
and pass not to Beer-sheba:
for Gilgal shall surely go into captivity,
and Beth-el shall come to nought.'

[6] Seek the LORD, and ye shall live;
lest he break out like fire in the house of Joseph, and devour
it,
and there be none to quench it in Beth-el.
[7] Ye who turn judgement to wormwood,
and leave off righteousness in the earth,
[8] seek him that maketh the seven stars and Orion,
and turneth the shadow of death into the morning,
and maketh the day dark with night:
that calleth for the waters of the sea,

and poureth them out upon the face of the earth:
the LORD is his name:

⁹ that strengtheneth the spoiled against the strong,
so that the spoiled shall come against the fortress.

¹⁰ They hate him that rebuketh in the gate,
and they abhor him that speaketh uprightly.

¹¹ Forasmuch therefore as your treading is upon the
poor,
and ye take from him burdens of wheat,
ye have built houses of hewn stone,
but ye shall not dwell in them:
ye have planted pleasant vineyards,
but ye shall not drink wine of them.

¹² For I know your manifold transgressions
and your mighty sins:
they afflict the just, they take a bribe,
and they turn aside the poor in the gate from their right.

¹³ Therefore the prudent shall keep silence in that time,
for it is an evil time.

¹⁴ Seek good and not evil, that ye may live:
and so the LORD, the God of hosts shall be with you,
as ye have spoken.

¹⁵ Hate the evil, and love the good,
and establish judgement in the gate:
it may be that the LORD God of hosts
will be gracious unto the remnant of Joseph.

¹⁶ Therefore the LORD, the God of hosts, the Lord saith thus,
'Wailing shall be in all streets,
and they shall say in all the highways, "Alas! alas!"
and they shall call the husbandman to mourning,
and such as are skilful of lamentation to wailing.

¹⁷ And in all vineyards shall be wailing:
for I will pass through thee,' saith the LORD.

¹⁸ Woe unto you that desire the day of the LORD:
to what end is it for you?
the day of the LORD is darkness, and not light.

¹⁹ As if a man did flee from a lion,
and a bear met him;
or went into the house, and leaned his hand on the wall,
and a serpent bit him.

²⁰ Shall not the day of the LORD be darkness, and not
light?
even very dark, and no brightness in it?

²¹ 'I hate, I despise your feast days,
and I will not smell in your solemn assemblies.
²² Though ye offer me burnt offerings and your meat offerings,
I will not accept them:
neither will I regard the peace offerings of your fat beasts.
²³ Take thou away from me the noise of thy songs:
for I will not hear the melody of thy viols.
²⁴ But let judgement run down as waters,
and righteousness as a mighty stream.
²⁵ Have ye offered unto me sacrifices
and offerings in the wilderness forty years,
O house of Israel?
²⁶ But ye have borne the tabernacle of your Moloch and Chiun your images,
the star of your god, which ye made to yourselves.
²⁷ Therefore will I cause you to go into captivity beyond Damascus,'
saith the LORD, whose name is the God of hosts.

6 Woe to them that are at ease in Zion,
and trust in the mountain of Samaria,
which are named chief of the nations,
to whom the house of Israel came.
² Pass ye unto Calneh, and see,
and from thence go ye to Hamath the great:
then go down to Gath of the Philistines:
be they better than these kingdoms?
or their border greater than your border?
³ Ye that put far away the evil day,
and cause the seat of violence to come near:
⁴ that lie upon beds of ivory,
and stretch themselves upon their couches,
and eat the lambs out of the flock,
and the calves out of the midst of the stall:
⁵ that chant to the sound of the viol,
and invent to themselves instruments of music, like David:
⁶ that drink wine in bowls,
and anoint themselves with the chief ointments:
but they are not grieved for the affliction of Joseph.
⁷ Therefore now shall they go captive with the first that go captive,
and the banquet of them that stretched themselves shall be removed.

⁸ The Lord GOD hath sworn by himself,
saith the LORD the God of hosts,
'I abhor the excellence of Jacob,

and hate his palaces:
therefore will I deliver up the city with all that is therein'.

⁹And it shall come to pass, if there remain ten men in one house, that they shall die. ¹⁰And a man's uncle shall take him up, and he that burneth him, to bring out the bones out of the house, and shall say unto him that is by the sides of the house, 'Is there yet any with thee?' and he shall say, 'No'. Then shall he say, 'Hold thy tongue: for we may not make mention of the name of the LORD'.

¹¹ For behold, the LORD commandeth,
and he will smite the great house with breaches,
and the little house with clefts.

¹² Shall horses run upon the rock?
will one plough there with oxen?
for ye have turned judgement into gall,
and the fruit of righteousness into hemlock:
¹³   ye which rejoice in a thing of nought,
which say, 'Have we not taken to us horns by our own
strength?'
¹⁴   'But behold, I will raise up against you a nation,
O house of Israel,'
saith the LORD the God of hosts;
'and they shall afflict you from the entering in of Hamath
unto the river of the wilderness'.

7 Thus hath the Lord GOD shown unto me: and behold, he formed grasshoppers in the beginning of the shooting up of the latter growth: and lo, it was the latter growth after the king's mowings. ²And it came to pass, that when they had made an end of eating the grass of the land, then I said, 'O Lord GOD, forgive, I beseech thee: by whom shall Jacob arise? for he is small'. ³The LORD repented for this. 'It shall not be,' saith the LORD.

⁴Thus hath the Lord GOD shown unto me: and behold, the Lord GOD called to contend by fire, and it devoured the great deep, and did eat up a part. ⁵Then said I, 'O Lord GOD, cease, I beseech thee: by whom shall Jacob arise? for he is small'. ⁶The LORD repented for this. 'This also shall not be,' saith the Lord GOD.

⁷Thus he showed me: and behold, the Lord stood upon a wall made by a plumbline, with a plumbline in his hand. ⁸And the LORD said unto me, 'Amos, what seest thou?' And I said, 'A plumbline'. Then said the Lord, 'Behold, I will set a plumbline in the midst of my people Israel: I will not again pass by them any more. ⁹And the high places of Isaac shall be desolate, and the sanctuaries of Israel shall be laid waste; and I will rise against the house of Jeroboam with the sword.'

¹⁰Then Amaziah the priest of Beth-el sent to Jeroboam king of Israel, saying, 'Amos hath conspired against thee in the midst of the house of

Israel: the land is not able to bear all his words. ¹¹For thus Amos saith, "Jeroboam shall die by the sword, and Israel shall surely be led away captive out of their own land".' ¹²Also Amaziah said unto Amos, 'O thou seer, go, flee thee away into the land of Judah, and there eat bread, and prophesy there. ¹³But prophesy not again any more at Beth-el: for it is the king's chapel, and it is the king's court.'

¹⁴Then answered Amos, and said to Amaziah, 'I was no prophet, neither was I a prophet's son, but I was a herdsman, and a gatherer of sycamore fruit. ¹⁵And the LORD took me as I followed the flock, and the LORD said unto me, "Go, prophesy unto my people Israel". ¹⁶Now therefore hear thou the word of the LORD: thou sayest, "Prophesy not against Israel, and drop not thy word against the house of Isaac". ¹⁷Therefore thus saith the LORD, "Thy wife shall be a harlot in the city, and thy sons and thy daughters shall fall by the sword, and thy land shall be divided by line: and thou shalt die in a polluted land, and Israel shall surely go into captivity forth of his land".'

8 Thus hath the Lord GOD shown unto me: and behold, a basket of summer fruit. ²And he said, 'Amos, what seest thou?' And I said, 'A basket of summer fruit'. Then said the LORD unto me,

> 'The end is come upon my people of Israel;
> I will not again pass by them any more.
> ³   And the songs of the temples shall be howlings in that day,'
> saith the Lord GOD:
> 'there shall be many dead bodies in every place,
> they shall cast them forth with silence.'

> ⁴ Hear this, O ye that swallow up the needy,
> even to make the poor of the land to fail,
> ⁵   saying, 'When will the new moon be gone, that we
> may sell corn?
> and the sabbath, that we may set forth wheat,
> making the ephah small, and the shekel great,
> and falsifying the balances by deceit?
> ⁶   that we may buy the poor for silver,
> and the needy for a pair of shoes;
> yea, and sell the refuse of the wheat?'
> ⁷   The LORD hath sworn by the excellence of Jacob,
> 'Surely I will never forget any of their works.
> ⁸   Shall not the land tremble for this,
> and every one mourn that dwelleth therein?
> and it shall rise up wholly as a flood;
> and it shall be cast out and drowned,
> as by the flood of Egypt.
> ⁹   And it shall come to pass in that day,' saith the Lord
> GOD,
> 'that I will cause the sun to go down at noon,

and I will darken the earth in the clear day.
¹⁰　　　And I will turn your feasts into mourning,
and all your songs into lamentation,
and I will bring up sackcloth upon all loins,
and baldness upon every head:
and I will make it as the mourning of an only son,
and the end thereof as a bitter day.

¹¹ 'Behold, the days come,' saith the Lord GOD,
'that I will send a famine in the land,
not a famine of bread, nor a thirst for water,
but of hearing the words of the LORD.
¹²　　　And they shall wander from sea to sea,
and from the north even to the east,
they shall run to and fro to seek the word of the LORD,
and shall not find it.
¹³　　　In that day shall the fair virgins and young men faint
for thirst.
¹⁴　　　They that swear by the sin of Samaria, and say,
"Thy god, O Dan, liveth,
and the manner of Beer-sheba liveth",
even they shall fall, and never rise up again.'

9 I saw the Lord standing upon the altar: and he said,
'Smite the lintel of the door, that the posts may shake:
and cut them in the head, all of them,
and I will slay the last of them with the sword:
he that fleeth of them shall not flee away,
and he that escapeth of them shall not be delivered.
²　　　Though they dig into hell,
thence shall my hand take them:
though they climb up to heaven,
thence will I bring them down:
³　　　And though they hide themselves in the top of
Carmel,
I will search and take them out thence,
and though they be hid from my sight in the bottom of the
sea,
thence will I command the serpent, and he shall bite them.
⁴　　　And though they go into captivity before their
enemies,
thence will I command the sword, and it shall slay them:
and I will set my eyes upon them for evil, and not for good.'

⁵ And the Lord GOD of hosts is he that toucheth the land,
and it shall melt, and all that dwell therein shall mourn,
and it shall rise up wholly like a flood,
and shall be drowned, as by the flood of Egypt.

⁶   It is he that buildeth his storeys in the heaven,
and hath founded his troop in the earth,
he that calleth for the waters of the sea,
and poureth them out upon the face of the earth:
the LORD is his name.

⁷ 'Are ye not as children of the Ethiopians unto me, O children of
Israel?'
saith the LORD.
'Have not I brought up Israel out of the land of Egypt?
and the Philistines from Caphtor,
and the Syrians from Kir?
⁸   Behold, the eyes of the Lord GOD are upon the sinful
kingdom,
and I will destroy it from off the face of the earth;
saving that I will not utterly destroy the house of Jacob,'
saith the LORD.
⁹   'For lo, I will command,
and I will sift the house of Israel among all nations,
like as corn is sifted in a sieve,
yet shall not the least grain fall upon the earth.
¹⁰   All the sinners of my people shall die by the sword,
which say, "The evil shall not overtake nor prevent us".

¹¹ 'In that day will I raise up the tabernacle of David that is fallen,
and close up the breaches thereof,
and I will raise up his ruins,
and I will build it as in the days of old:
¹²   that they may possess the remnant of Edom,
and of all the heathen, which are called by my name,'
saith the LORD that doeth this.

¹³ 'Behold, the days come,' saith the LORD,
'that the ploughman shall overtake the reaper,
and the treader of grapes him that soweth seed,
and the mountains shall drop sweet wine,
and all the hills shall melt.
¹⁴   And I will bring again the captivity of my people of
Israel:
and they shall build the waste cities, and inhabit them;
and they shall plant vineyards, and drink the wine thereof:
they shall also make gardens, and eat the fruit of them.
¹⁵   And I will plant them upon their land,
and they shall no more be pulled up
out of their land which I have given them,'
saith the LORD thy God.

OBADIAH

The vision of Obadiah. Thus saith the Lord GOD concerning Edom,

'We have heard a rumour from the LORD,
and an ambassador is sent among the heathen:
"Arise ye, and let us rise up against her in battle".
² Behold, I have made thee small among the heathen:
thou art greatly despised.

³ 'The pride of thy heart hath deceived thee,
thou that dwellest in the clefts of the rock,
whose habitation is high,
that saith in his heart, "Who shall bring me down to the
ground?"
⁴ Though thou exalt thyself as the eagle,
and though thou set thy nest among the stars,
thence will I bring thee down,' saith the LORD.
⁵ 'If thieves came to thee, if robbers by night
(how art thou cut off!),
would they not have stolen till they had enough?
if the grape-gatherers came to thee,
would they not leave some grapes?
⁶ How are the things of Esau searched out!
how are his hidden things sought up!
⁷ All the men of thy confederacy have brought thee even to the
border:
the men that were at peace with thee have deceived thee,
and prevailed against thee:
they that eat thy bread have laid a wound under thee:
there is no understanding in him.
⁸ Shall I not in that day', saith the LORD,
'even destroy the wise men out of Edom,
and understanding out of the mount of Esau?
⁹ And thy mighty men, O Teman, shall be dismayed,
to the end that every one of the mount of Esau may be cut off by
slaughter.

¹⁰ 'For thy violence against thy brother Jacob shame shall cover
thee,
and thou shalt be cut off for ever.
¹¹ In the day that thou stoodest on the other side,
in the day that the strangers carried away captive his forces,
and foreigners entered into his gates,
and cast lots upon Jerusalem, even thou wast as one of them.
¹² But thou shouldst not have looked on the day of thy brother

in the day that he became a stranger,
neither shouldst thou have rejoiced over the children of Judah
in the day of their destruction:
neither shouldst thou have spoken proudly in the day of distress.
¹³ Thou shouldst not have entered into the gate of my people
in the day of their calamity:
yea, thou shouldst not have looked on their affliction
in the day of their calamity,
nor have laid hands on their substance
in the day of their calamity.
¹⁴ Neither shouldst thou have stood in the cross-way
to cut off those of his that did escape,
neither shouldst thou have delivered up those of his that did
remain in the day of distress.
¹⁵ For the day of the LORD is near upon all the heathen:
as thou hast done, it shall be done unto thee:
thy reward shall return upon thy own head.
¹⁶ For as ye have drunk upon my holy mountain,
so shall all the heathen drink continually:
yea, they shall drink, and they shall swallow down,
and they shall be as though they had not been.

¹⁷ 'But upon mount Zion shall be deliverance,
and there shall be holiness,
and the house of Jacob shall possess their possessions.
¹⁸ And the house of Jacob shall be a fire,
and the house of Joseph a flame,
and the house of Esau for stubble,
and they shall kindle in them, and devour them,
and there shall not be any remaining of the house of Esau,
for the LORD hath spoken it.

¹⁹ 'And they of the south shall possess the mount of Esau, and they of the plain the Philistines: and they shall possess the fields of Ephraim, and the fields of Samaria, and Benjamin shall possess Gilead. ²⁰And the captivity of this host of the children of Israel shall possess that of the Canaanites even unto Zarephath, and the captivity of Jerusalem, which is in Sepharad, shall possess the cities of the south. ²¹And saviours shall come up on mount Zion to judge the mount of Esau, and the kingdom shall be the LORD's.'

JONAH

1 Now the word of the LORD came unto Jonah the son of Amittai, saying, ²'Arise, go to Nineveh, that great city, and cry against it: for their wickedness is come up before me'. ³But Jonah rose up to flee unto Tarshish from the presence of the LORD, and went down to Joppa; and he found a ship going to Tarshish: so he paid the fare thereof, and went down into it, to go with them unto Tarshish from the presence of the LORD.

⁴But the LORD sent out a great wind into the sea, and there was a mighty tempest in the sea, so that the ship was like to be broken. ⁵Then the mariners were afraid, and cried every man unto his god, and cast forth the wares that were in the ship into the sea, to lighten it of them. But Jonah was gone down into the sides of the ship, and he lay, and was fast asleep. ⁶So the shipmaster came to him, and said unto him, 'What meanest thou, O sleeper? arise, call upon thy God, if so be that God will think upon us, that we perish not'.

⁷And they said every one to his fellow, 'Come, and let us cast lots, that we may know for whose cause this evil is upon us'. So they cast lots, and the lot fell upon Jonah. ⁸Then said they unto him, 'Tell us, we pray thee, for whose cause this evil is upon us: what is thy occupation? and whence comest thou? What is thy country? and of what people art thou?' ⁹And he said unto them, 'I am a Hebrew, and I fear the LORD the God of heaven, which hath made the sea and the dry land'. ¹⁰Then were the men exceedingly afraid, and said unto him, 'Why hast thou done this?' For the men knew that he fled from the presence of the LORD, because he had told them.

¹¹Then said they unto him, 'What shall we do unto thee, that the sea may be calm unto us?' (for the sea wrought and was tempestuous). ¹²And he said unto them, 'Take me up, and cast me forth into the sea; so shall the sea be calm unto you: for I know that for my sake this great tempest is upon you'. ¹³Nevertheless the men rowed hard to bring it to the land, but they could not: for the sea wrought, and was tempestuous against them. ¹⁴Wherefore they cried unto the LORD, and said, 'We beseech thee, O LORD, we beseech thee, let us not perish for this man's life, and lay not upon us innocent blood: for thou, O LORD, hast done as it pleased thee'. ¹⁵So they took up Jonah, and cast him forth into the sea: and the sea ceased from her raging. ¹⁶Then the men feared the LORD exceedingly, and offered a sacrifice unto the LORD, and made vows.

¹⁷Now the LORD had prepared a great fish to swallow up Jonah. And Jonah was in the belly of the fish three days and three nights.

2 Then Jonah prayed unto the LORD his God out of the fish's belly, ²and said,

'I cried by reason of my affliction unto the LORD,
    and he heard me;

out of the belly of hell cried I,
and thou heardest my voice.
³ For thou hadst cast me into the deep,
in the midst of the seas,
and the floods compassed me about:
all thy billows and thy waves passed over me.
⁴ Then I said, "I am cast out of thy sight;
yet I will look again toward thy holy temple".
⁵ The waters compassed me about even to the soul:
the depth closed me round about,
the weeds were wrapped about my head.
⁶ I went down to the bottoms of the mountains:
the earth with her bars was about me for ever:
yet hast thou brought up my life from corruption,
O LORD my God.
⁷ When my soul fainted within me
I remembered the LORD,
and my prayer came in unto thee,
into thy holy temple.
⁸ They that observe lying vanities forsake their own mercy.
⁹ But I will sacrifice unto thee with the voice of thanksgiving,
I will pay that that I have vowed:
salvation is of the LORD.'

¹⁰And the LORD spoke unto the fish, and it vomited out Jonah upon the dry land.

3 And the word of the LORD came unto Jonah the second time, saying, ²'Arise, go unto Nineveh, that great city, and preach unto it the preaching that I bid thee'. ³So Jonah arose and went unto Nineveh, according to the word of the LORD. Now Nineveh was an exceeding great city of three days' journey. ⁴And Jonah began to enter into the city a day's journey, and he cried, and said, 'Yet forty days, and Nineveh shall be overthrown'.

⁵So the people of Nineveh believed God, and proclaimed a fast, and put on sackcloth, from the greatest of them even to the least of them. ⁶For word came unto the king of Nineveh, and he arose from his throne, and he laid his robe from him, and covered him with sackcloth, and sat in ashes. ⁷And he caused it to be proclaimed and published through Nineveh by the decree of the king and his nobles, saying, 'Let neither man nor beast, herd nor flock, taste anything: let them not feed, nor drink water. ⁸But let man and beast be covered with sackcloth, and cry mightily unto God: yea, let them turn every one from his evil way, and from the violence that is in their hands. ⁹Who can tell if God will turn and repent, and turn away from his fierce anger, that we perish not?'

¹⁰And God saw their works, that they turned from their evil way, and God repented of the evil that he had said that he would do unto them and he did it not.

4 But it displeased Jonah exceedingly, and he was very angry. [2]And he prayed unto the LORD, and said, 'I pray thee, O LORD, was not this my saying, when I was yet in my country? Therefore I fled before unto Tarshish: for I knew that thou art a gracious God, and merciful, slow to anger, and of great kindness, and repentest thee of the evil. [3]Therefore now, O LORD, take, I beseech thee, my life from me; for it is better for me to die than to live.'

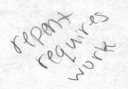

[4]Then said the LORD, 'Doest thou well to be angry?'

[5]So Jonah went out of the city, and sat on the east side of the city, and there made him a booth, and sat under it in the shadow, till he might see what would become of the city. [6]And the LORD God prepared a gourd, and made it to come up over Jonah, that it might be a shadow over his head, to deliver him from his grief. So Jonah was exceeding glad of the gourd. [7]But God prepared a worm when the morning rose the next day, and it smote the gourd that it withered. [8]And it came to pass when the sun did arise, that God prepared a vehement east wind; and the sun beat upon the head of Jonah, that he fainted, and wished in himself to die, and said, 'It is better for me to die than to live'.

[9]And God said to Jonah, 'Doest thou well to be angry for the gourd?' And he said, 'I do well to be angry, even unto death'. [10]Then said the LORD, 'Thou hast had pity on the gourd, for the which thou hast not laboured, neither madest it grow, which came up in a night, and perished in a night: [11]and should not I spare Nineveh, that great city, wherein are more than sixscore thousand persons that cannot discern between their right hand and their left hand, and also much cattle?'

MICAH

1 The word of the LORD that came to Micah the Morasthite in the days of Jotham, Ahaz, and Hezekiah, kings of Judah, which he saw concerning Samaria and Jerusalem.

² Hear, all ye people,
  hearken, O earth, and all that therein is,
  and let the Lord GOD be witness against you,
  the Lord from his holy temple.
³ For behold, the LORD cometh forth out of his place,
  and will come down, and tread upon the high places of the earth.
⁴ And the mountains shall be molten under him,
  and the valleys shall be cleft:
  as wax before the fire,
  and as the waters that are poured down a steep place.
⁵ For the transgression of Jacob is all this,
  and for the sins of the house of Israel.
  What is the transgression of Jacob?
  is it not Samaria?
  and what are the high places of Judah?
  are they not Jerusalem?
⁶ Therefore I will make Samaria as a heap of the field,
  and as plantings of a vineyard:
  and I will pour down the stones thereof into the valley,
  and I will discover the foundations thereof.
⁷ And all the graven images thereof shall be beaten to pieces,
  and all the hires thereof shall be burnt with the fire,
  and all the idols thereof will I lay desolate:
  for she gathered it of the hire of a harlot,
  and they shall return to the hire of a harlot.
⁸ Therefore I will wail and howl,
  I will go stripped and naked:
  I will make a wailing like the dragons,
  and mourning as the owls.
⁹ For her wound is incurable,
  for it is come unto Judah:
  he is come unto the gate of my people,
  even to Jerusalem.

¹⁰ Declare ye it not at Gath, weep ye not at all:
  in the house of Aphrah roll thyself in the dust.
¹¹ Pass ye away, thou inhabitant of Saphir,
  having thy shame naked:
  the inhabitant of Zaanan came not forth in the mourning of
    Beth-ezel;

he shall receive of you his standing.

¹² For the inhabitant of Maroth waited carefully for good:
but evil came down from the LORD unto the gate of Jerusalem.

¹³ O thou inhabitant of Lachish, bind the chariot to the swift beast:
she is the beginning of the sin to the daughter of Zion:
for the transgressions of Israel were found in thee.

¹⁴ Therefore shalt thou give presents to Moresheth-gath:
the houses of Achzib shall be a lie to the kings of Israel.

¹⁵ Yet will I bring an heir unto thee, O inhabitant of Mareshah:
he shall come unto Adullam, the glory of Israel.

¹⁶ Make thee bald, and poll thee for thy delicate children,
enlarge thy baldness as the eagle,
for they are gone into captivity from thee.

2 Woe to them that devise iniquity,
and work evil upon their beds:
when the morning is light, they practise it,
because it is in the power of their hand.

² And they covet fields, and take them by violence:
and houses, and take them away:
so they oppress a man and his house,
even a man and his heritage.

³ Therefore thus saith the LORD,
'Behold, against this family do I devise an evil,
from which ye shall not remove your necks,
neither shall ye go haughtily:
for this time is evil'.

⁴ In that day shall one take up a parable against you,
and lament with a doleful lamentation,
and say, 'We be utterly spoiled:
he hath changed the portion of my people:
how hath he removed it from me!
turning away he hath divided our fields'.

⁵ Therefore thou shalt have none that shall cast a cord by lot
in the congregation of the LORD.

⁶ 'Prophesy ye not', say they to them that prophesy:
they shall not prophesy to them, that they shall not take shame.

⁷ O thou that art named the house of Jacob,
is the Spirit of the LORD straitened?
are these his doings?
do not my words do good to him that walketh uprightly?

⁸ Even of late my people is risen up as an enemy:
ye pull off the robe with the garment
from them that pass by securely as men averse from war.

⁹ The women of my people have ye cast out from their pleasant
houses,

from their children have ye taken away my glory for ever.

¹⁰ Arise ye, and depart, for this is not your rest:
because it is polluted, it shall destroy you
even with a sore destruction.

¹¹ If a man walking in the spirit and falsehood do lie,
saying, 'I will prophesy unto thee of wine and of strong drink',
he shall even be the prophet of this people.

¹² I will surely assemble, O Jacob, all of thee:
I will surely gather the remnant of Israel,
I will put them together as the sheep of Bozrah,
as the flock in the midst of their fold:
they shall make great noise by reason of the multitude of men.

¹³ The breaker is come up before them:
they have broken up, and have passed through the gate,
and are gone out by it, and their king shall pass before them,
and the LORD on the head of them.

3 And I said, 'Hear, I pray you,
O heads of Jacob, and ye princes of the house of Israel:
is it not for you to know judgement?

² who hate the good, and love the evil,
who pluck off their skin from off them,
and their flesh from off their bones;

³ who also eat the flesh of my people,
and flay their skin from off them;
and they break their bones, and chop them in pieces,
as for the pot, and as flesh within the cauldron'.

⁴ Then shall they cry unto the LORD,
but he will not hear them:
he will even hide his face from them at that time,
as they have behaved themselves ill in their doings.

⁵ Thus saith the LORD concerning the prophets that make my
people err,
that bite with their teeth, and cry, 'Peace':
and he that putteth not into their mouths,
they even prepare war against him.

⁶ Therefore night shall be unto you,
that ye shall not have a vision,
and it shall be dark unto you,
that ye shall not divine,
and the sun shall go down over the prophets,
and the day shall be dark over them.

⁷ Then shall the seers be ashamed,
and the diviners confounded:
yea, they shall all cover their lips,
for there is no answer of God.

⁸ But truly I am full of power by the Spirit of the Lord,
and of judgement and of might,
to declare unto Jacob his transgression,
and to Israel his sin.
⁹ Hear this, I pray you, ye heads of the house of Jacob,
and princes of the house of Israel,
that abhor judgement, and pervert all equity.
¹⁰ They build up Zion with blood,
and Jerusalem with iniquity.
¹¹ The heads thereof judge for reward,
and the priests thereof teach for hire,
and the prophets thereof divine for money:
yet will they lean upon the Lord,
and say, 'Is not the Lord among us?
no evil can come upon us'.
¹² Therefore shall Zion for your sake be ploughed as a field,
and Jerusalem shall become heaps,
and the mountain of the house as the high places of the forest.

4

But in the last days it shall come to pass,
that the mountain of the house of the Lord
shall be established in the top of the mountains,
and it shall be exalted above the hills,
and people shall flow unto it.
² And many nations shall come, and say,
'Come, and let us go up to the mountain of the Lord,
and to the house of the God of Jacob,
and he will teach us of his ways,
and we will walk in his paths':
for the law shall go forth of Zion,
and the word of the Lord from Jerusalem.
³ And he shall judge among many people,
and rebuke strong nations afar off,
and they shall beat their swords into ploughshares,
and their spears into pruning-hooks:
nation shall not lift up a sword against nation,
neither shall they learn war any more.
⁴ But they shall sit every man under his vine and under his fig tree,
and none shall make them afraid:
for the mouth of the Lord of hosts hath spoken it.
⁵ For all people will walk every one in the name of his god,
and we will walk in the name of the Lord our God for ever and
ever.

⁶ 'In that day,' saith the Lord, 'will I assemble her that halteth,
and I will gather her that is driven out,

and her that I have afflicted.
7 And I will make her that halted a remnant,
and her that was cast far off a strong nation:
and the LORD shall reign over them in mount Zion from
henceforth,
even for ever.'

8 And thou, O tower of the flock,
the stronghold of the daughter of Zion,
unto thee shall it come,
even the first dominion,
the kingdom shall come to the daughter of Jerusalem.
9 Now why dost thou cry out aloud?
is there no king in thee? is thy counsellor perished?
for pangs have taken thee as a woman in travail.
10 Be in pain and labour to bring forth, O daughter of Zion,
like a woman in travail:
for now shalt thou go forth out of the city,
and thou shalt dwell in the field,
and thou shalt go even to Babylon:
there shalt thou be delivered:
there the LORD shall redeem thee from the hand of thy enemies.

11 Now also many nations are gathered against thee,
that say, 'Let her be defiled, and let our eye look upon Zion'.
12 But they know not the thoughts of the LORD,
neither understand they his counsel:
for he shall gather them as the sheaves into the floor.
13 Arise and thresh, O daughter of Zion:
for I will make thy horn iron,
and I will make thy hoofs brass,
and thou shalt beat in pieces many people:
and I will consecrate their gain unto the LORD,
and their substance unto the Lord of the whole earth.

5 Now gather thyself in troops, O daughter of troops:
he hath laid siege against us:
they shall smite the judge of Israel with a rod upon the cheek.
2 But thou, Beth-lehem Ephratah,
though thou be little among the thousands of Judah,
yet out of thee shall he come forth unto me that is to be ruler in
Israel:
whose goings forth have been from of old, from everlasting.
3 Therefore will he give them up,
until the time that she which travaileth hath brought forth:
then the remnant of his brethren shall return unto the children
of Israel.

⁴ And he shall stand and feed in the strength of the Lord,
  in the majesty of the name of the Lord his God,
  and they shall abide:
  for now shall he be great unto the ends of the earth.
⁵ And this man shall be the peace,
  when the Assyrian shall come into our land:
  and when he shall tread in our palaces,
  then shall we raise against him seven shepherds,
  and eight principal men.
⁶ And they shall waste the land of Assyria with the sword,
  and the land of Nimrod in the entrances thereof:
  thus shall he deliver us from the Assyrian,
  when he cometh into our land,
  and when he treadeth within our borders.
⁷ And the remnant of Jacob shall be in the midst of many people
  as a dew from the Lord,
  as the showers upon the grass that tarrieth not for man,
  nor waiteth for the sons of men.

⁸ And the remnant of Jacob shall be among the Gentiles
  in the midst of many people as a lion among the beasts of the
    forest,
  as a young lion among the flocks of sheep:
  who, if he go through,
  both treadeth down, and teareth in pieces,
  and none can deliver.
⁹ Thy hand shall be lifted up upon thy adversaries,
  and all thy enemies shall be cut off.

¹⁰ 'And it shall come to pass in that day,' saith the Lord,
  'that I will cut off thy horses out of the midst of thee,
  and I will destroy thy chariots.
¹¹ And I will cut off the cities of thy land,
  and throw down all thy strongholds.
¹² And I will cut off witchcrafts out of thy hand,
  and thou shalt have no more soothsayers:
¹³ Thy graven images also will I cut off,
  and thy standing images out of the midst of thee:
  and thou shalt no more worship the work of thy hands.
¹⁴ And I will pluck up thy groves out of the midst of thee:
  so will I destroy thy cities.
¹⁵ And I will execute vengeance in anger and fury upon the
    heathen,
  such as they have not heard.'

6 Hear ye now what the Lord saith,
  'Arise, contend thou before the mountains,
  and let the hills hear thy voice.

² Hear ye, O mountains, the LORD's controversy,
  and ye strong foundations of the earth:
  for the LORD hath a controversy with his people,
  and he will plead with Israel.
³ O my people, what have I done unto thee?
  and wherein have I wearied thee? testify against me.
⁴ For I brought thee up out of the land of Egypt,
  and redeemed thee out of the house of servants,
  and I sent before thee Moses, Aaron, and Miriam.
⁵ O my people, remember now what Balak king of Moab consulted,
  and what Balaam the son of Beor answered him from Shittim
    unto Gilgal,
  that ye may know the righteousness of the LORD.'

⁶ Wherewith shall I come before the LORD,
  and bow myself before the high God?
  shall I come before him with burnt offerings,
  with calves of a year old?
⁷ Will the LORD be pleased with thousands of rams,
  or with ten thousands of rivers of oil?
  shall I give my firstborn for my transgression,
  the fruit of my body for the sin of my soul?
⁸ He hath shown thee, O man, what is good;
  and what doth the LORD require of thee,
  but to do justly, and to love mercy,
  and to walk humbly with thy God?
⁹ The LORD's voice crieth unto the city,
  and the man of wisdom shall see thy name:
  hear ye the rod, and who hath appointed it.

¹⁰ Are there yet the treasures of wickedness in the house of the
    wicked,
  and the scant measure that is abominable?
¹¹ Shall I count them pure with the wicked balances,
  and with the bag of deceitful weights?
¹² For the rich men thereof are full of violence,
  and the inhabitants thereof have spoken lies,
  and their tongue is deceitful in their mouth.
¹³ Therefore also will I make thee sick in smiting thee,
  in making thee desolate because of thy sins.
¹⁴ Thou shalt eat, but not be satisfied,
  and thy casting down shall be in the midst of thee,
  and thou shalt take hold, but shalt not deliver:
  and that which thou deliverest will I give up to the sword.
¹⁵ Thou shalt sow, but thou shalt not reap:
  thou shalt tread the olives, but thou shalt not anoint thee with
    oil;
  and sweet wine, but shalt not drink wine.

16 For the statutes of Omri are kept,
and all the works of the house of Ahab,
and ye walk in their counsels,
that I should make thee a desolation,
and the inhabitants thereof a hissing:
therefore ye shall bear the reproach of my people.

7 Woe is me,
for I am as when they have gathered the summer fruits,
as the grape-gleanings of the vintage:
there is no cluster to eat:
my soul desired the first-ripe fruit.
2 The good man is perished out of the earth,
and there is none upright among men:
they all lie in wait for blood:
they hunt every man his brother with a net.

3 That they may do evil with both hands earnestly,
the prince asketh, and the judge asketh for a reward:
and the great man, he uttereth his mischievous desire:
so they wrap it up.
4 The best of them is as a brier:
the most upright is sharper than a thorn hedge:
the day of thy watchmen and thy visitation cometh;
now shall be their perplexity.

5 Trust ye not in a friend,
put ye not confidence in a guide:
keep the doors of thy mouth from her that lieth in thy bosom.
6 For the son dishonoureth the father,
the daughter riseth up against her mother,
the daughter-in-law against her mother-in-law;
a man's enemies are the men of his own house.
7 Therefore I will look unto the LORD:
I will wait for the God of my salvation:
my God will hear me.

8 Rejoice not against me, O my enemy:
when I fall, I shall arise;
when I sit in darkness, the LORD shall be a light unto me.
9 I will bear the indignation of the LORD,
because I have sinned against him,
until he plead my cause,
and execute judgement for me:
he will bring me forth to the light,
and I shall behold his righteousness.
10 Then she that is my enemy shall see it,
and shame shall cover her which said unto me,

'Where is the LORD thy God?' my eyes shall behold her:
now shall she be trodden down as the mire of the streets.
¹¹ In the day that thy walls are to be built,
in that day shall the decree be far removed.
¹² In that day also he shall come even to thee from Assyria,
and from the fortified cities,
and from the fortress even to the river,
and from sea to sea,
and from mountain to mountain.
¹³ Notwithstanding the land shall be desolate
because of them that dwell therein,
for the fruit of their doings.

¹⁴ Feed thy people with thy rod,
the flock of thy heritage, which dwell solitarily in the wood,
in the midst of Carmel:
let them feed in Bashan and Gilead,
as in the days of old.
¹⁵ According to the days of thy coming out of the land of Egypt
will I show unto him marvellous things.

¹⁶ The nations shall see and be confounded at all their might:
they shall lay their hand upon their mouth,
their ears shall be deaf.
¹⁷ They shall lick the dust like a serpent,
they shall move out of their holes like worms of the earth:
they shall be afraid of the LORD our God,
and shall fear because of thee.

¹⁸ Who is a God like unto thee,
that pardoneth iniquity,
and passeth by the transgression of the remnant of his heritage?
he retaineth not his anger for ever,
because he delighteth in mercy.
¹⁹ He will turn again,
he will have compassion upon us:
he will subdue our iniquities,
and thou wilt cast all their sins into the depths of the sea.
²⁰ Thou wilt perform the truth to Jacob,
and the mercy to Abraham,
which thou hast sworn unto our fathers
from the days of old.

NAHUM

1 The burden of Nineveh. The book of the vision of Nahum the Elkoshite.

² God is jealous, and the LORD revengeth:
the LORD revengeth, and is furious,
the LORD will take vengeance on his adversaries,
and he reserveth wrath for his enemies.
³ The LORD is slow to anger, and great in power,
and will not at all acquit the wicked:
the LORD hath his way in the whirlwind and in the storm,
and the clouds are the dust of his feet.
⁴ He rebuketh the sea, and maketh it dry,
and drieth up all the rivers:
Bashan languisheth, and Carmel,
and the flower of Lebanon languisheth.
⁵ The mountains quake at him, and the hills melt,
and the earth is burnt at his presence,
yea, the world and all that dwell therein.
⁶ Who can stand before his indignation?
and who can abide in the fierceness of his anger?
his fury is poured out like fire,
and the rocks are thrown down by him.
⁷ The LORD is good, a stronghold in the day of trouble,
and he knoweth them that trust in him.
⁸ But with an overrunning flood he will make an utter end of the
place thereof,
and darkness shall pursue his enemies.

⁹ What do ye imagine against the LORD?
he will make an utter end:
affliction shall not rise up the second time.
¹⁰ For while they be folded together as thorns,
and while they are drunken as drunkards,
they shall be devoured as stubble fully dry.
¹¹ There is one come out of thee, that imagineth evil against the LORD,
a wicked counsellor.

¹² Thus saith the LORD,
'Though they be quiet, and likewise many,
yet thus shall they be cut down,
when he shall pass through.
Though I have afflicted thee,
I will afflict thee no more.
¹³ For now will I break his yoke from off thee,

and will burst thy bonds in sunder.'
¹⁴ And the LORD hath given a commandment concerning thee,
that no more of thy name be sown:
'Out of the house of thy gods will I cut off the graven image and
the molten image:
I will make thy grave, for thou art vile'.
¹⁵ Behold upon the mountains
the feet of him that bringeth good tidings,
that publisheth peace.
O Judah, keep thy solemn feasts, perform thy vows:
for the wicked shall no more pass through thee,
he is utterly cut off.

2 He that dasheth in pieces is come up before thy face:
keep the munition, watch the way,
make thy loins strong, fortify thy power mightily.
² For the LORD hath turned away the excellence of Jacob,
as the excellence of Israel:
for the emptiers have emptied them out,
and marred their vine branches.
³ The shield of his mighty men is made red,
the valiant men are in scarlet:
the chariots shall be with flaming torches in the day of his
preparation,
and the fir trees shall be terribly shaken.
⁴ The chariots shall rage in the streets,
they shall jostle one against another in the broad ways:
they shall seem like torches,
they shall run like the lightnings.
⁵ He shall recount his worthies:
they shall stumble in their walk:
they shall make haste to the wall thereof,
and the defence shall be prepared.
⁶ The gates of the rivers shall be opened,
and the palace shall be dissolved.
⁷ And Huzzab shall be led away captive,
she shall be brought up,
and her maids shall lead her as with the voice of doves,
taboring upon their breasts.
⁸ But Nineveh is of old like a pool of water:
yet they shall flee away.
'Stand, stand', shall they cry:
but none shall look back.
⁹ Take ye the spoil of silver, take the spoil of gold:
for there is no end of the store and glory out of all the pleasant
furniture.
¹⁰ She is empty, and void, and waste,
and the heart melteth, and the knees smite together,

and much pain is in all loins,
and the faces of them all gather blackness.

11 Where is the dwelling of the lions,
and the feeding-place of the young lions,
where the lion, even the old lion walked,
and the lion's whelp, and none made them afraid?
12 The lion did tear in pieces enough for his whelps,
and strangled for his lionesses,
and filled his holes with prey, and his dens with raven.

13 'Behold, I am against thee,' saith the LORD of hosts,
'and I will burn her chariots in the smoke,
and the sword shall devour thy young lions:
and I will cut off thy prey from the earth,
and the voice of thy messengers shall no more be heard.'

3 Woe to the bloody city,
it is all full of lies and robbery,
the prey departeth not.
2 The noise of a whip, and the noise of the rattling of the wheels,
and of the prancing horses, and of the jumping chariots.
3 The horseman lifteth up both the bright sword and the glittering
spear,
and there is a multitude of slain, and a great number of carcases:
and there is no end of their corpses:
they stumble upon their corpses,
4 because of the multitude of the whoredoms
of the well-favoured harlot, the mistress of witchcrafts,
that selleth nations through her whoredoms,
and families through her witchcrafts.

5 'Behold, I am against thee,' saith the LORD of hosts,
'and I will discover thy skirts upon thy face,
and I will show the nations thy nakedness,
and the kingdoms thy shame.
6 And I will cast abominable filth upon thee, and make thee vile,
and will set thee as a gazing-stock.
7 And it shall come to pass, that all they that look upon thee shall
flee from thee,
and say, "Nineveh is laid waste":
who will bemoan her?
whence shall I seek comforters for thee?'

8 Art thou better than populous No,
that was situated among the rivers,
that had the waters round about it,

whose rampart was the sea,
and her wall was from the sea?
⁹ Ethiopia and Egypt were her strength, and it was infinite,
Put and Lubim were thy helpers.
¹⁰ Yet was she carried away, she went into captivity:
her young children also were dashed in pieces at the top of all
the streets:
and they cast lots for her honourable men,
and all her great men were bound in chains.
¹¹ Thou also shalt be drunken:
thou shalt be hid,
thou also shalt seek strength because of the enemy.
¹² All thy strongholds shall be like fig trees with the first-ripe figs:
if they be shaken, they shall even fall into the mouth of the eater.
¹³ Behold, thy people in the midst of thee are women:
the gates of thy land shall be set wide open unto thy enemies:
the fire shall devour thy bars.

¹⁴ Draw thee waters for the siege:
fortify thy strongholds,
go into clay, and tread the mortar:
make strong the brick-kiln.
¹⁵ There shall the fire devour thee:
the sword shall cut thee off:
it shall eat thee up like the canker-worm:
make thyself many as the canker-worm,
make thyself many as the locusts.
¹⁶ Thou hast multiplied thy merchants above the stars of heaven:
the canker-worm spoileth and flieth away.
¹⁷ The crowned are as the locusts,
and thy captains as the great grasshoppers,
which camp in the hedges in the cold day:
but when the sun ariseth they flee away,
and their place is not known where they are.

¹⁸ Thy shepherds slumber, O king of Assyria:
thy nobles shall dwell in the dust:
thy people is scattered upon the mountains,
and no man gathereth them.
¹⁹ There is no healing of thy bruise:
thy wound is grievous:
all that hear the bruit of thee shall clap the hands over thee:
for upon whom hath not thy wickedness passed continually?

HABAKKUK

1 The burden which Habakkuk the prophet did see.

² O LORD, how long shall I cry,
  and thou wilt not hear!
  even cry out unto thee of violence,
  and thou wilt not save!
³ Why dost thou show me iniquity,
  and cause me to behold grievance?
  for spoiling and violence are before me:
  and there are that raise up strife and contention.
⁴ Therefore the law is slacked,
  and judgement doth never go forth:
  for the wicked doth compass about the righteous:
  therefore wrong judgement proceedeth.

⁵ 'Behold ye among the heathen,
  and regard, and wonder marvellously:
  for I will work a work in your days,
  which ye will not believe, though it be told you.
⁶ For lo, I raise up the Chaldeans, that bitter and hasty nation,
  which shall march through the breadth of the land,
  to possess the dwelling-places that are not theirs.
⁷ They are terrible and dreadful:
  their judgement and their dignity shall proceed of themselves.
⁸ Their horses also are swifter than the leopards,
  and are more fierce than the evening wolves:
  and their horsemen shall spread themselves,
  and their horsemen shall come from far,
  they shall fly as the eagle that hasteth to eat.
⁹ They shall come all for violence:
  their faces shall sup up as the east wind,
  and they shall gather the captivity as the sand.
¹⁰ And they shall scoff at the kings,
  and the princes shall be a scorn unto them:
  they shall deride every stronghold,
  for they shall heap dust and take it.
¹¹ Then shall his mind change, and he shall pass over,
  and offend, imputing this his power unto his god.'

¹² Art thou not from everlasting,
  O LORD my God, my Holy One?
  we shall not die.
  O LORD, thou hast ordained them for judgement,
  and, O mighty God, thou hast established them for correction.

¹³ Thou art of purer eyes than to behold evil,
　and canst not look on iniquity:
　wherefore lookest thou upon them that deal treacherously,
　and holdest thy tongue when the wicked devoureth the man
　　that is more righteous than he?
¹⁴ And makest men as the fishes of the sea,
　as the creeping things, that have no ruler over them?
¹⁵ They take up all of them with the angle:
　they catch them in their net, and gather them in their drag:
　therefore they rejoice and are glad.
¹⁶ Therefore they sacrifice unto their net,
　and burn incense unto their drag:
　because by them their portion is fat,
　and their meat plenteous.
¹⁷ Shall they therefore empty their net,
　and not spare continually to slay the nations?

2 I will stand upon my watch, and set me upon the tower,
　and will watch to see what he will say unto me,
　and what I shall answer when I am reproved.
² And the Lord answered me, and said,
　'Write the vision, and make it plain upon tablets,
　that he may run that readeth it.
³ For the vision is yet for an appointed time,
　but at the end it shall speak, and not lie:
　though it tarry, wait for it,
　because it will surely come, it will not tarry.'

⁴ Behold, his soul which is lifted up is not upright in him:
　but the just shall live by his faith.
⁵ Yea also, because he transgresseth by wine, he is a proud man,
　neither keepeth at home, who enlargeth his desire as hell,
　and is as death, and cannot be satisfied,
　but gathereth unto him all nations,
　and heapeth unto him all people:
⁶ shall not all these take up a parable against him,
　and a taunting proverb against him,
　and say, 'Woe to him that increaseth that which is not his: how
　　long?
　and to him that loadeth himself with thick clay'.
⁷ Shall they not rise up suddenly that shall bite thee,
　and awake that shall vex thee,
　and thou shalt be for booties unto them?
⁸ Because thou hast spoiled many nations,
　all the remnant of the people shall spoil thee:
　because of men's blood, and for the violence of the land,
　of the city, and of all that dwell therein.

⁹ Woe to him that coveteth an evil covetousness to his house,
    that he may set his nest on high,
    that he may be delivered from the power of evil.
¹⁰ Thou hast consulted shame to thy house by cutting off many
      people,
    and hast sinned against thy soul.
¹¹ For the stone shall cry out of the wall,
    and the beam out of the timber shall answer it.

¹² Woe to him that buildeth a town with blood,
    and establisheth a city by iniquity.
¹³ Behold, is it not of the LORD of hosts that the people shall labour
    in the very fire,
    and the people shall weary themselves for very vanity?
¹⁴ For the earth shall be filled with the knowledge of the glory of
    the LORD,
    as the waters cover the sea.

¹⁵ Woe unto him that giveth his neighbour drink:
    that puttest thy bottle to him, and makest him drunken also,
    that thou mayest look on their nakedness.
¹⁶ Thou art filled with shame for glory:
    drink thou also, and let thy foreskin be uncovered:
    the cup of the LORD's right hand shall be turned unto thee,
    and shameful spewing shall be on thy glory.
¹⁷ For the violence of Lebanon shall cover thee:
    and the spoil of beasts, which made them afraid,
    because of men's blood, and for the violence of the land,
    of the city, and of all that dwell therein.

¹⁸ What profiteth the graven image that the maker thereof hath
    graven it:
    the molten image, and a teacher of lies,
    that the maker of his work trusteth therein, to make dumb idols?
¹⁹ Woe unto him that saith to the wood, 'Awake':
    to the dumb stone, 'Arise, it shall teach':
    behold, it is laid over with gold and silver,
    and there is no breath at all in the midst of it.
²⁰ But the LORD is in his holy temple:
    let all the earth keep silence before him.

3 A prayer of Habakkuk the prophet upon Shigionoth.

² O LORD, I have heard thy speech, and was afraid:
    O LORD, revive thy work in the midst of the years,
    in the midst of the years make known;
    in wrath remember mercy.

³ God came from Teman,
and the Holy One from mount Paran. Selah.
His glory covered the heavens,
and the earth was full of his praise.
⁴ And his brightness was as the light:
he had horns coming out of his hand,
and there was the hiding of his power:
⁵ before him went the pestilence,
and burning coals went forth at his feet.
⁶ He stood, and measured the earth:
he beheld, and drove asunder the nations,
and the everlasting mountains were scattered,
the perpetual hills did bow:
his ways are everlasting.
⁷ I saw the tents of Cushan in affliction:
and the curtains of the land of Midian did tremble.

⁸ Was the LORD displeased against the rivers?
was thy anger against the rivers?
was thy wrath against the sea,
that thou didst ride upon thy horses
and thy chariots of salvation?
⁹ Thy bow was made quite naked,
according to the oaths of the tribes, even thy word. Selah.
Thou didst cleave the earth with rivers.
¹⁰ The mountains saw thee, and they trembled:
the overflowing of the water passed by:
the deep uttered his voice, and lifted up his hands on high.
¹¹ The sun and moon stood still in their habitation:
at the light of thy arrows they went,
and at the shining of thy glittering spear.
¹² Thou didst march through the land in indignation,
thou didst thresh the heathen in anger.
¹³ Thou wentest forth for the salvation of thy people,
even for salvation with thy anointed,
thou woundedst the head out of the house of the wicked,
by discovering the foundation unto the neck. Selah.
¹⁴ Thou didst strike through with his staves the head of his
villages:
they came out as a whirlwind to scatter me:
their rejoicing was as to devour the poor secretly.
¹⁵ Thou didst walk through the sea with thy horses,
through the heap of great waters.
¹⁶ When I heard, my belly trembled:
my lips quivered at the voice:
rottenness entered into my bones,
and I trembled in myself,
that I might rest in the day of trouble:

when he cometh up unto the people,
he will invade them with his troops.

¹⁷ Although the fig tree shall not blossom,
neither shall fruit be in the vines:
the labour of the olive shall fail,
and the fields shall yield no meat,
the flock shall be cut off from the fold,
and there shall be no herd in the stalls:
¹⁸ yet I will rejoice in the LORD:
I will joy in the God of my salvation.
¹⁹ The LORD God is my strength,
and he will make my feet like hinds' feet,
and he will make me to walk upon my high places.

To the chief singer on my stringed instruments.

ZEPHANIAH

1 The word of the LORD which came unto Zephaniah the son of Cushi, the son of Gedaliah, the son of Amariah, the son of Hizkiah, in the days of Josiah the son of Amon, king of Judah.

² 'I will utterly consume all things from off the land,' saith the
   LORD.
³ 'I will consume man and beast:
   I will consume the fowls of the heaven, and the fishes of the sea,
   and the stumbling-blocks with the wicked,
   and I will cut off man from off the land,' saith the LORD.
⁴ 'I will also stretch out my hand upon Judah,
   and upon all the inhabitants of Jerusalem,
   and I will cut off the remnant of Baal from this place,
   and the name of the Chemarims with the priests:
⁵ and them that worship the host of heaven upon the house-tops,
   and them that worship and that swear by the LORD,
   and that swear by Malcham:
⁶ and them that are turned back from the LORD,
   and those that have not sought the LORD, nor inquired for him.'

⁷ Hold thy peace at the presence of the Lord GOD:
   for the day of the LORD is at hand:
   for the LORD hath prepared a sacrifice:
   he hath bid his guests.

⁸ 'And it shall come to pass in the day of the LORD's sacrifice,
   that I will punish the princes, and the king's children,
   and all such as are clothed with strange apparel.
⁹ In the same day also will I punish all those that leap on the
      threshold,
   which fill their masters' houses with violence and deceit.
¹⁰ And it shall come to pass in that day,' saith the LORD,
   'that there shall be the noise of a cry from the fish gate,
   and a howling from the second,
   and a great crashing from the hills.
¹¹ Howl, ye inhabitants of Maktesh,
   for all the merchant people are cut down:
   all they that bear silver are cut off.
¹² And it shall come to pass at that time, that I will search
      Jerusalem with candles,
   and punish the men that are settled on their lees,
   that say in their heart,
   "The LORD will not do good, neither will he do evil".
¹³ Therefore their goods shall become a booty,

and their houses a desolation:
they shall also build houses, but not inhabit them,
and they shall plant vineyards, but not drink the wine thereof.'

¹⁴ The great day of the LORD is near,
it is near, and hasteth greatly,
even the voice of the day of the LORD:
the mighty man shall cry there bitterly.
¹⁵ That day is a day of wrath,
a day of trouble and distress,
a day of wasteness and desolation,
a day of darkness and gloominess,
a day of clouds and thick darkness,
¹⁶ a day of the trumpet and alarm
against the fenced cities, and against the high towers.
¹⁷ And I will bring distress upon men, that they shall walk like
blind men,
because they have sinned against the LORD:
and their blood shall be poured out as dust,
and their flesh as the dung.
¹⁸ Neither their silver nor their gold shall be able to deliver them
in the day of the LORD's wrath;
but the whole land shall be devoured by the fire of his jealousy:
for he shall make even a speedy riddance of all them that dwell
in the land.

2 Gather yourselves together, yea, gather together,
O nation not desired;
² before the decree bring forth,
before the day pass as the chaff,
before the fierce anger of the LORD come upon you,
before the day of the LORD's anger come upon you.
³ Seek ye the LORD, all ye meek of the earth,
which have wrought his judgement,
seek righteousness, seek meekness:
it may be ye shall be hid in the day of the LORD's anger.

⁴ For Gaza shall be forsaken,
and Ashkelon a desolation:
they shall drive out Ashdod at the noon day,
and Ekron shall be rooted up.
⁵ Woe unto the inhabitants of the sea-coast:
the nation of the Cherethites,
the word of the LORD is against you:
O Canaan, the land of the Philistines,
I will even destroy thee, that there shall be no inhabitant.
⁶ And the sea-coast shall be dwellings and cottages for shepherds,
and folds for flocks.

7 And the coast shall be for the remnant of the house of Judah,
  they shall feed thereupon,
    in the houses of Ashkelon shall they lie down in the evening:
    for the LORD their God shall visit them, and turn away their
      captivity.

8 'I have heard the reproach of Moab,
  and the revilings of the children of Ammon,
    whereby they have reproached my people,
    and magnified themselves against their border.
9 Therefore as I live,' saith the LORD of hosts, the God of Israel,
  'surely Moab shall be as Sodom,
  and the children of Ammon as Gomorrah,
    even the breeding of nettles, and saltpits, and a perpetual
      desolation:
    the residue of my people shall spoil them,
    and the remnant of my people shall possess them.'
10 This shall they have for their pride,
  because they have reproached and magnified themselves
    against the people of the LORD of hosts.
11 The LORD will be terrible unto them:
  for he will famish all the gods of the earth,
    and men shall worship him, every one from his place,
    even all the isles of the heathen.

12 'Ye Ethiopians also, ye shall be slain by my sword.'
13 And he will stretch out his hand against the north,
  and destroy Assyria,
    and will make Nineveh a desolation,
    and dry like a wilderness.
14 And flocks shall lie down in the midst of her,
  all the beasts of the nations:
    both the cormorant and the bittern shall lodge in the upper
      lintels of it:
    their voice shall sing in the windows,
    desolation shall be in the thresholds:
    for he shall uncover the cedar work.
15 This is the rejoicing city that dwelt carelessly,
  that said in her heart, 'I am, and there is none besides me':
    how is she become a desolation, a place for beasts to lie down in!
    every one that passeth by her shall hiss, and wag his hand.

3 Woe to her that is filthy and polluted,
  to the oppressing city.
2 She obeyed not the voice:
  she received not correction:
  she trusted not in the LORD:
  she drew not near to her God.

³ Her princes within her are roaring lions;
her judges are evening wolves,
they gnaw not the bones till the morrow.
⁴ Her prophets are light and treacherous persons:
her priests have polluted the sanctuary,
they have done violence to the law.
⁵ The just LORD is in the midst thereof:
he will not do iniquity:
every morning doth he bring his judgement to light,
he faileth not:
but the unjust knoweth no shame.

⁶ 'I have cut off the nations:
their towers are desolate,
I made their streets waste, that none passeth by:
their cities are destroyed, so that there is no man,
that there is no inhabitant.
⁷ I said, "Surely thou wilt fear me:
thou wilt receive instruction":
so their dwelling should not be cut off,
howsoever I punished them:
but they rose early, and corrupted all their doings.

⁸ 'Therefore wait ye upon me,' saith the LORD,
'until the day that I rise up to the prey:
for my determination is to gather the nations,
that I may assemble the kingdoms to pour upon them my
    indignation,
even all my fierce anger:
for all the earth shall be devoured with the fire of my jealousy.
⁹ For then will I turn to the people a pure language,
that they may all call upon the name of the LORD,
to serve him with one consent.
¹⁰ From beyond the rivers of Ethiopia my suppliants,
even the daughter of my dispersed shall bring my offering.

¹¹ 'In that day shalt thou not be ashamed for all thy doings,
wherein thou hast transgressed against me:
for then I will take away out of the midst of thee them that
    rejoice in thy pride,
and thou shalt no more be haughty because of my holy
    mountain.
¹² I will also leave in the midst of thee an afflicted and poor people:
and they shall trust in the name of the LORD.
¹³ The remnant of Israel shall not do iniquity, nor speak lies:
neither shall a deceitful tongue be found in their mouth:
for they shall feed and lie down,
and none shall make them afraid.'

¹⁴ Sing, O daughter of Zion:
   shout, O Israel:
   be glad and rejoice with all the heart,
   O daughter of Jerusalem.
¹⁵ The LORD hath taken away thy judgements,
   he hath cast out thy enemy:
   the king of Israel, even the LORD, is in the midst of thee:
   thou shalt not see evil any more.
¹⁶ In that day it shall be said to Jerusalem, 'Fear thou not':
   and to Zion, 'Let not thy hands be slack'.
¹⁷ The LORD thy God in the midst of thee is mighty:
   he will save, he will rejoice over thee with joy:
   he will rest in his love, he will joy over thee with singing.

¹⁸ 'I will gather them that are sorrowful for the solemn assembly,
      who are of thee,
   to whom the reproach of it was a burden.
¹⁹ Behold, at that time I will undo all that afflict thee:
   and I will save her that halteth,
   and gather her that was driven out,
   and I will get them praise and fame
   in every land where they have been put to shame.
²⁰ At that time will I bring you again,
   even in the time that I gather you:
   for I will make you a name and a praise among all people of the
      earth,
   when I turn back your captivity before your eyes,'
   saith the LORD.

HAGGAI

1 In the second year of Darius the king, in the sixth month, in the first day of the month, came the word of the LORD by Haggai the prophet unto Zerubbabel the son of Shealtiel, governor of Judah, and to Joshua the son of Josedech, the high priest, saying, ²"Thus speaketh the LORD of hosts, saying, "This people say, 'The time is not come, the time that the LORD's house should be built'"'. ³Then came the word of the LORD by Haggai the prophet, saying, ⁴"Is it time for you, O ye, to dwell in your ceiled houses, and this house lie waste? ⁵Now therefore thus saith the LORD of hosts, "Consider your ways. ⁶Ye have sown much, and bring in little: ye eat, but ye have not enough: ye drink, but ye are not filled with drink: ye clothe you, but there is none warm: and he that earneth wages earneth wages to put it into a bag with holes."

⁷"Thus saith the LORD of hosts, "Consider your ways. ⁸Go up to the mountain, and bring wood, and build the house; and I will take pleasure in it, and I will be glorified," saith the LORD. ⁹"Ye looked for much, and lo it came to little: and when ye brought it home, I did blow upon it. Why?" saith the LORD of hosts. "Because of my house that is waste, and ye run every man unto his own house. ¹⁰Therefore the heaven over you is stayed from dew, and the earth is stayed from her fruit. ¹¹And I called for a drought upon the land, and upon the mountains, and upon the corn, and upon the new wine, and upon the oil, and upon that which the ground bringeth forth, and upon men, and upon cattle, and upon all the labour of the hands."'

¹²Then Zerubbabel the son of Shealtiel, and Joshua the son of Josedech, the high priest, with all the remnant of the people, obeyed the voice of the LORD their God, and the words of Haggai the prophet, as the LORD their God had sent him, and the people did fear before the LORD. ¹³Then spoke Haggai the LORD's messenger in the LORD's message unto the people, saying, '"I am with you," saith the LORD'. ¹⁴And the LORD stirred up the spirit of Zerubbabel the son of Shealtiel, governor of Judah, and the spirit of Joshua the son of Josedech, the high priest, and the spirit of all the remnant of the people, and they came and did work in the house of the LORD of hosts, their God, ¹⁵in the four and twentieth day of the sixth month, in the second year of Darius the king.

2 In the seventh month, in the one and twentieth day of the month, came the word of the LORD by the prophet Haggai, saying, ²"Speak now to Zerubbabel the son of Shealtiel, governor of Judah, and to Joshua the son of Josedech, the high priest, and to the residue of the people, saying, ³"Who is left among you that saw this house in her first glory? and how do ye see it now? is it not in your eyes in comparison of it as nothing? ⁴Yet now be strong, O Zerubbabel," saith the LORD, "and be strong, O Joshua, son of Josedech, the high priest, and be strong, all ye people of the land," saith the LORD, "and work: for I am with you," saith the LORD of hosts: ⁵"according to the word that I covenanted with you when ye came out of Egypt, so my spirit remaineth among you: fear ye not."

⁶'For thus saith the LORD of hosts, "Yet once, it is a little while, and I will shake the heavens, and the earth, and the sea, and the dry land. ⁷And I will shake all nations, and the desire of all nations shall come, and I will fill this house with glory," saith the LORD of hosts. ⁸"The silver is mine, and the gold is mine," saith the LORD of hosts. ⁹"The glory of this latter house shall be greater than of the former," saith the LORD of hosts: "and in this place will I give peace," saith the LORD of hosts.'

¹⁰In the four and twentieth day of the ninth month, in the second year of Darius, came the word of the LORD by Haggai the prophet, saying, ¹¹'Thus saith the LORD of hosts, "Ask now the priests concerning the law, saying, ¹²'If one bear holy flesh in the skirt of his garment, and with his skirt do touch bread, or pottage, or wine, or oil, or any meat, shall it be holy?'"' And the priests answered and said, 'No'. ¹³Then said Haggai, 'If one that is unclean by a dead body touch any of these, shall it be unclean?' And the priests answered and said, 'It shall be unclean'. ¹⁴Then answered Haggai, and said, '"So is this people, and so is this nation before me," saith the LORD, "and so is every work of their hands, and that which they offer there is unclean". ¹⁵And now, I pray you, consider from this day and upward, from before a stone was laid upon a stone in the temple of the LORD: ¹⁶since those days were, when one came to a heap of twenty measures, there were but ten: when one came to the press-vat for to draw out fifty vessels out of the press, there were but twenty. ¹⁷"I smote you with blasting and with mildew and with hail in all the labours of your hands: yet ye turned not to me," saith the LORD. ¹⁸Consider now from this day and upward, from the four and twentieth day of the ninth month, even from the day that the foundation of the LORD's temple was laid, consider it. ¹⁹Is the seed yet in the barn? yea, as yet the vine, and the fig tree, and the pomegranate, and the olive tree hath not brought forth: from this day will I bless you.'

²⁰And again the word of the LORD came unto Haggai in the four and twentieth day of the month, saying, ²¹'Speak to Zerubbabel, governor of Judah, saying, "I will shake the heavens and the earth. ²²And I will overthrow the throne of kingdoms, and I will destroy the strength of the kingdoms of the heathen, and I will overthrow the chariots, and those that ride in them, and the horses and their riders shall come down, every one by the sword of his brother. ²³In that day," saith the LORD of hosts, "will I take thee, O Zerubbabel, my servant, the son of Shealtiel," saith the LORD, "and will make thee as a signet: for I have chosen thee," saith the LORD of hosts.'

ZECHARIAH

1 In the eighth month, in the second year of Darius, came the word of the LORD unto Zechariah, the son of Berechiah, the son of Iddo the prophet, saying, ²'The LORD hath been sore displeased with your fathers. ³Therefore say thou unto them, "Thus saith the LORD of hosts, 'Turn ye unto me,' saith the LORD of hosts, 'and I will turn unto you,' saith the LORD of hosts. ⁴'Be ye not as your fathers, unto whom the former prophets have cried, saying, "Thus saith the LORD of hosts, 'Turn ye now from your evil ways, and from your evil-doings'": but they did not hear, nor hearken unto me,' saith the LORD. ⁵'Your fathers, where are they? and the prophets, do they live for ever? ⁶But my words and my statutes, which I commanded my servants the prophets, did they not take hold of your fathers? and they returned and said, "Like as the LORD of hosts thought to do unto us, according to our ways, and according to our doings, so hath he dealt with us".'"'

⁷Upon the four and twentieth day of the eleventh month, which is the month Sebat, in the second year of Darius, came the word of the LORD unto Zechariah, the son of Berechiah, the son of Iddo the prophet, saying, ⁸'I saw by night, and behold a man riding upon a red horse, and he stood among the myrtle trees that were in the bottom, and behind him were there red horses, speckled, and white'. ⁹Then said I, 'O my lord, what are these?' And the angel that talked with me said unto me, 'I will show thee what these be'. ¹⁰And the man that stood among the myrtle trees answered and said, 'These are they whom the LORD hath sent to walk to and fro through the earth'. ¹¹And they answered the angel of the LORD that stood among the myrtle trees, and said, 'We have walked to and fro through the earth, and behold, all the earth sitteth still, and is at rest'.

¹²Then the angel of the LORD answered and said, 'O LORD of hosts, how long wilt thou not have mercy on Jerusalem and on the cities of Judah, against which thou hast had indignation these threescore and ten years?' ¹³And the LORD answered the angel that talked with me with good words and comfortable words. ¹⁴So the angel that communed with me said unto me, 'Cry thou, saying, "Thus saith the LORD of hosts, 'I am jealous for Jerusalem and for Zion with a great jealousy. ¹⁵And I am very sore displeased with the heathen that are at ease: for I was but a little displeased, and they helped forward the affliction.' ¹⁶Therefore thus saith the LORD, 'I am returned to Jerusalem with mercies: my house shall be built in it,' saith the LORD of hosts, 'and a line shall be stretched forth upon Jerusalem'." ¹⁷Cry yet, saying, "Thus saith the LORD of hosts, 'My cities through prosperity shall yet be spread abroad, and the LORD shall yet comfort Zion, and shall yet choose Jerusalem'".'

¹⁸Then lifted I up my eyes, and saw, and behold, four horns. ¹⁹And I said unto the angel that talked with me, 'What be these?' And he answered me, 'These are the horns which have scattered Judah, Israel, and

Jerusalem'. ²⁰And the Lord showed me four carpenters. ²¹Then said I, 'What come these to do?' And he spoke, saying, 'These are the horns which have scattered Judah, so that no man did lift up his head: but these are come to fray them, to cast out the horns of the Gentiles, which lifted up their horn over the land of Judah to scatter it'.

2 I lifted up my eyes again, and looked, and behold, a man with a measuring-line in his hand. ²Then said I, 'Whither goest thou?' And he said unto me, 'To measure Jerusalem, to see what is the breadth thereof, and what is the length thereof'. ³And behold, the angel that talked with me went forth, and another angel went out to meet him, ⁴and said unto him, 'Run, speak to this young man, saying, "Jerusalem shall be inhabited as towns without walls for the multitude of men and cattle therein: ⁵for I," saith the Lord, "will be unto her a wall of fire round about, and will be the glory in the midst of her.

⁶'"Ho, ho, come forth, and flee from the land of the north," saith the Lord: "for I have spread you abroad as the four winds of the heaven," saith the Lord. ⁷"Deliver thyself, O Zion, that dwellest with the daughter of Babylon." ⁸For thus saith the Lord of hosts, "After the glory hath he sent me unto the nations which spoiled you: for he that toucheth you toucheth the apple of his eye". ⁹For behold, I will shake my hand upon them, and they shall be a spoil to their servants: and ye shall know that the Lord of hosts hath sent me.

¹⁰'"Sing and rejoice, O daughter of Zion: for lo, I come, and I will dwell in the midst of thee," saith the Lord. ¹¹And many nations shall be joined to the Lord in that day, and shall be my people: and I will dwell in the midst of thee, and thou shalt know that the Lord of hosts hath sent me unto thee. ¹²And the Lord shall inherit Judah his portion in the holy land, and shall choose Jerusalem again.

¹³'Be silent, O all flesh, before the Lord: for he is raised up out of his holy habitation.'

3 And he showed me Joshua the high priest standing before the angel of the Lord, and Satan standing at his right hand to resist him. ²And the Lord said unto Satan, 'The Lord rebuke thee, O Satan, even the Lord that hath chosen Jerusalem rebuke thee. Is not this a brand plucked out of the fire?' ³Now Joshua was clothed with filthy garments, and stood before the angel. ⁴And he answered and spoke unto those that stood before him, saying, 'Take away the filthy garments from him'. And unto him he said, 'Behold, I have caused thy iniquity to pass from thee, and I will clothe thee with change of raiment'. ⁵And I said, 'Let them set a fair mitre upon his head'. So they set a fair mitre upon his head, and clothed him with garments. And the angel of the Lord stood by. ⁶And the angel of the Lord protested unto Joshua, saying, ⁷'Thus saith the Lord of hosts, "If thou wilt walk in my ways, and if thou wilt keep my charge, then thou shalt also judge my house, and shalt also keep my courts, and I will give thee places to walk among these that stand by. ⁸Hear now, O Joshua the high priest, thou and thy fellows that sit before thee: for they are men wondered at: for behold, I will bring forth my servant the Branch. ⁹For behold the stone that I

have laid before Joshua: upon one stone shall be seven eyes: behold, I will engrave the graving thereof," saith the LORD of hosts, "and I will remove the iniquity of that land in one day. [10]In that day," saith the LORD of hosts, "shall ye call every man his neighbour under the vine and under the fig tree."'

4 And the angel that talked with me came again and woke me, as a man that is wakened out of his sleep, [2]and said unto me, 'What seest thou?' And I said, 'I have looked, and behold a candlestick all of gold, with a bowl upon the top of it, and his seven lamps thereon, and seven pipes to the seven lamps, which are upon the top thereof: [3]and two olive trees by it, one upon the right side of the bowl, and the other upon the left side thereof'. [4]So I answered and spoke to the angel that talked with me, saying, 'What are these, my lord?' [5]Then the angel that talked with me answered and said unto me, 'Knowest thou not what these be?' And I said, 'No, my lord'. [6]Then he answered and spoke unto me, saying, 'This is the word of the LORD unto Zerubbabel, saying, "Not by might, nor by power, but by my spirit," saith the LORD of hosts. [7]"Who art thou, O great mountain? before Zerubbabel thou shalt become a plain: and he shall bring forth the headstone thereof with shoutings, crying, 'Grace, grace unto it'."'

[8]Moreover the word of the LORD came unto me, saying, [9]'The hands of Zerubbabel have laid the foundation of this house: his hands shall also finish it, and thou shalt know that the LORD of hosts hath sent me unto you. [10]For who hath despised the day of small things? for they shall rejoice, and shall see the plummet in the hand of Zerubbabel with those seven: they are the eyes of the LORD, which run to and fro through the whole earth.'

[11]Then answered I, and said unto him, 'What are these two olive trees upon the right side of the candlestick and upon the left side thereof?' [12]And I answered again, and said unto him, 'What be these two olive branches which through the two golden pipes empty the golden oil out of themselves?' [13]And he answered me and said, 'Knowest thou not what these be?' And I said, 'No, my lord'. [14]Then said he, 'These are the two anointed ones, that stand by the Lord of the whole earth'.

5 Then I turned, and lifted up my eyes, and looked, and behold, a flying roll. [2]And he said unto me, 'What seest thou?' And I answered, 'I see a flying roll, the length thereof is twenty cubits, and the breadth thereof ten cubits'. [3]Then said he unto me, 'This is the curse that goeth forth over the face of the whole earth: for every one that stealeth shall be cut off as on this side according to it; and every one that sweareth shall be cut off as on that side according to it. [4]I will bring it forth,' saith the LORD of hosts, 'and it shall enter into the house of the thief, and into the house of him that sweareth falsely by my name: and it shall remain in the midst of his house, and shall consume it with the timber thereof and the stones thereof.'

[5]Then the angel that talked with me went forth and said unto me, 'Lift up now thy eyes, and see what is this that goeth forth'. [6]And I said, 'What is it?' And he said, 'This is an ephah that goeth forth'. He said

moreover, 'This is their resemblance through all the earth'. ⁷And behold, there was lifted up a talent of lead: and this is a woman that sitteth in the midst of the ephah. ⁸And he said, 'This is wickedness'. And he cast it into the midst of the ephah, and he cast the weight of lead upon the mouth thereof. ⁹Then lifted I up my eyes, and looked, and behold, there came out two women, and the wind was in their wings (for they had wings like the wings of a stork): and they lifted up the ephah between the earth and the heaven. ¹⁰Then said I to the angel that talked with me, 'Whither do these bear the ephah?' ¹¹And he said unto me, 'To build it a house in the land of Shinar: and it shall be established, and set there upon her own base'.

6 And I turned, and lifted up my eyes, and looked, and behold, there came four chariots out from between two mountains, and the mountains were mountains of brass. ²In the first chariot were red horses, and in the second chariot black horses; ³and in the third chariot white horses, and in the fourth chariot grisled and bay horses. ⁴Then I answered and said unto the angel that talked with me, 'What are these, my lord?' ⁵And the angel answered and said unto me, 'These are the four spirits of the heavens, which go forth from standing before the Lord of all the earth. ⁶The black horses which are therein go forth into the north country, and the white go forth after them, and the grisled go forth toward the south country.' ⁷And the bay went forth, and sought to go that they might walk to and fro through the earth: and he said, 'Get ye hence, walk to and fro through the earth'. So they walked to and fro through the earth. ⁸Then cried he upon me, and spoke unto me, saying, 'Behold, these that go toward the north country have quieted my spirit in the north country'.

⁹And the word of the LORD came unto me, saying, ¹⁰'Take of them of the captivity, even of Heldai, of Tobijah, and of Jedaiah, which are come from Babylon, and come thou the same day, and go into the house of Josiah the son of Zephaniah. ¹¹Then take silver and gold, and make crowns, and set them upon the head of Joshua the son of Josedech, the high priest. ¹²And speak unto him, saying, "Thus speaketh the LORD of hosts, saying, 'Behold the man whose name is the BRANCH, and he shall grow up out of his place, and he shall build the temple of the LORD: ¹³even he shall build the temple of the LORD, and he shall bear the glory, and shall sit and rule upon his throne, and he shall be a priest upon his throne, and the counsel of peace shall be between them both'". ¹⁴And the crowns shall be to Helem, and to Tobijah, and to Jedaiah, and to Hen the son of Zephaniah for a memorial in the temple of the LORD. ¹⁵And they that are far off shall come and build in the temple of the LORD, and ye shall know that the LORD of hosts hath sent me unto you. And this shall come to pass, if ye will diligently obey the voice of the LORD your God.'

7 And it came to pass in the fourth year of king Darius, that the word of the LORD came unto Zechariah in the fourth day of the ninth month, even in Chisleu; ²when they had sent unto the house of God Sherezer and Regem-melech, and their men to pray before the LORD, ³and to speak unto the priests which were in the house of the LORD of

hosts, and to the prophets, saying, 'Should I weep in the fifth month, separating myself, as I have done these so many years?'

⁴Then came the word of the LORD of hosts unto me, saying, ⁵'Speak unto all the people of the land, and to the priests, saying, "When ye fasted and mourned in the fifth and seventh month, even those seventy years, did ye at all fast unto me, even to me? ⁶And when ye did eat, and when ye did drink, did not ye eat for yourselves, and drink for yourselves? ⁷Should ye not hear the words which the LORD hath cried by the former prophets, when Jerusalem was inhabited and in prosperity, and the cities thereof round about her, when men inhabited the south of the plain?"'

⁸And the word of the LORD came unto Zechariah, saying, ⁹'Thus speaketh the LORD of hosts, saying, "Execute true judgement, and show mercy and compassions every man to his brother. ¹⁰And oppress not the widow, nor the fatherless, the stranger, nor the poor, and let none of you imagine evil against his brother in your heart."' ¹¹But they refused to hearken, and pulled away the shoulder, and stopped their ears, that they should not hear. ¹²Yea, they made their hearts as an adamant stone, lest they should hear the law, and the words which the LORD of hosts hath sent in his spirit by the former prophets: therefore came a great wrath from the LORD of hosts. ¹³'Therefore it is come to pass, that as he cried, and they would not hear, so they cried, and I would not hear,' saith the LORD of hosts. ¹⁴'But I scattered them with a whirlwind among all the nations whom they knew not. Thus the land was desolate after them, that no man passed through nor returned: for they laid the pleasant land desolate.'

8 Again the word of the LORD of hosts came to me, saying, ²'Thus saith the LORD of hosts, "I was jealous for Zion with great jealousy, and I was jealous for her with great fury". ³Thus saith the LORD, "I am returned unto Zion, and will dwell in the midst of Jerusalem, and Jerusalem shall be called a city of truth, and the mountain of the LORD of hosts the holy mountain". ⁴Thus saith the LORD of hosts, "There shall yet old men and old women dwell in the streets of Jerusalem, and every man with his staff in his hand for very age. ⁵And the streets of the city shall be full of boys and girls playing in the streets thereof." ⁶Thus saith the LORD of hosts, "If it be marvellous in the eyes of the remnant of this people in these days, should it also be marvellous in my eyes?" saith the LORD of hosts. ⁷Thus saith the LORD of hosts, "Behold, I will save my people from the east country, and from the west country. ⁸And I will bring them, and they shall dwell in the midst of Jerusalem: and they shall be my people, and I will be their God, in truth and in righteousness."

⁹'Thus saith the LORD of hosts, "Let your hands be strong, ye that hear in these days these words by the mouth of the prophets, which were in the day that the foundation of the house of the LORD of hosts was laid, that the temple might be built. ¹⁰For before these days there was no hire for man, nor any hire for beast, neither was there any peace to him that went out or came in because of the affliction: for I set all men every one against his neighbour. ¹¹But now I will not be unto the

residue of this people as in the former days," saith the LORD of hosts. [12] "For the seed shall be prosperous: the vine shall give her fruit, and the ground shall give her increase, and the heavens shall give their dew, and I will cause the remnant of this people to possess all these things. [13]And it shall come to pass, that as ye were a curse among the heathen, O house of Judah, and house of Israel; so will I save you, and ye shall be a blessing: fear not, but let your hands be strong." [14]For thus saith the LORD of hosts, "As I thought to punish you, when your fathers provoked me to wrath," saith the LORD of hosts, "and I repented not: [15]so again have I thought in these days to do well unto Jerusalem and to the house of Judah: fear ye not.

[16]'"These are the things that ye shall do: speak ye every man the truth to his neighbour: execute the judgement of truth and peace in your gates. [17]And let none of you imagine evil in your hearts against his neighbour, and love no false oath: for all these are things that I hate," saith the LORD.'

[18]And the word of the LORD of hosts came unto me, saying, [19]'Thus saith the LORD of hosts, "The fast of the fourth month, and the fast of the fifth, and the fast of the seventh, and the fast of the tenth shall be to the house of Judah joy and gladness, and cheerful feasts: therefore love the truth and peace".

[20]'Thus saith the LORD of hosts, "It shall yet come to pass, that there shall come people, and the inhabitants of many cities. [21]And the inhabitants of one city shall go to another, saying, 'Let us go speedily to pray before the LORD, and to seek the LORD of hosts: I will go also'." [22]Yea, many people and strong nations shall come to seek the LORD of hosts in Jerusalem, and to pray before the LORD. [23]Thus saith the LORD of hosts, "In those days it shall come to pass, that ten men shall take hold out of all languages of the nations, even shall take hold of the skirt of him that is a Jew, saying, 'We will go with you: for we have heard that God is with you'".'

9 The burden of the word of the LORD in the land of Hadrach,
and Damascus shall be the rest thereof:
when the eyes of man, as of all the tribes of Israel, shall be
toward the LORD.
[2] And Hamath also shall border thereby;
Tyrus, and Zidon, though it be very wise.
[3] And Tyrus did build herself a stronghold,
and heaped up silver as the dust,
and fine gold as the mire of the streets.
[4] Behold, the Lord will cast her out,
and he will smite her power in the sea,
and she shall be devoured with fire.
[5] Ashkelon shall see it, and fear,
Gaza also shall see it, and be very sorrowful,
and Ekron: for her expectation shall be ashamed,
and the king shall perish from Gaza,
and Ashkelon shall not be inhabited.

⁶ And a bastard shall dwell in Ashdod,
   and I will cut off the pride of the Philistines.
⁷ And I will take away his blood out of his mouth,
   and his abominations from between his teeth:
   but he that remaineth, even he shall be for our God,
   and he shall be as a governor in Judah,
   and Ekron as a Jebusite.
⁸ And I will encamp about my house because of the army,
   because of him that passeth by,
   and because of him that returneth:
   and no oppressor shall pass through them any more:
   for now have I seen with my eyes.

⁹ Rejoice greatly, O daughter of Zion;
   shout, O daughter of Jerusalem:
   behold, thy King cometh unto thee:
   he is just, and having salvation,
   lowly, and riding upon an ass,
   and upon a colt the foal of an ass.
¹⁰ And I will cut off the chariot from Ephraim,
   and the horse from Jerusalem:
   and the battle-bow shall be cut off,
   and he shall speak peace unto the heathen,
   and his dominion shall be from sea even to sea,
   and from the river even to the ends of the earth.
¹¹ As for thee also, by the blood of thy covenant
   I have sent forth thy prisoners out of the pit wherein is no
      water.

¹² Turn ye to the stronghold, ye prisoners of hope:
   even today do I declare that I will render double unto thee:
¹³ when I have bent Judah for me,
   filled the bow with Ephraim,
   and raised up thy sons, O Zion, against thy sons, O Greece,
   and made thee as the sword of a mighty man.
¹⁴ And the LORD shall be seen over them,
   and his arrow shall go forth as the lightning:
   and the Lord GOD shall blow the trumpet,
   and shall go with whirlwinds of the south.
¹⁵ The LORD of hosts shall defend them,
   and they shall devour, and subdue with sling-stones,
   and they shall drink and make a noise as through wine,
   and they shall be filled like bowls,
   and as the corners of the altar.
¹⁶ And the LORD their God shall save them in that day
   as the flock of his people,
   for they shall be as the stones of a crown
   lifted up as an ensign upon his land.

¹⁷ For how great is his goodness,
and how great is his beauty!
corn shall make the young men cheerful,
and new wine the maids.

10 Ask ye of the LORD rain in the time of the latter rain,
so the LORD shall make bright clouds, and give them showers of
rain,
to every one grass in the field.
² For the idols have spoken vanity,
and the diviners have seen a lie,
and have told false dreams;
they comfort in vain:
therefore they went their way as a flock,
they were troubled because there was no shepherd.

³ 'My anger was kindled against the shepherds,
and I punished the goats':
for the LORD of hosts hath visited his flock the house of Judah,
and hath made them as his goodly horse in the battle.
⁴ Out of him came forth the corner,
out of him the nail, out of him the battle-bow,
out of him every oppressor together.
⁵ And they shall be as mighty men,
which tread down their enemies in the mire of the streets in the
battle:
and they shall fight because the LORD is with them,
and the riders on horses shall be confounded.

⁶ 'And I will strengthen the house of Judah,
and I will save the house of Joseph,
and I will bring them again to place them,
for I have mercy upon them:
and they shall be as though I had not cast them off:
for I am the LORD their God, and will hear them.
⁷ And they of Ephraim shall be like a mighty man,
and their heart shall rejoice as through wine:
yea, their children shall see it, and be glad,
their heart shall rejoice in the LORD.
⁸ I will hiss for them, and gather them,
for I have redeemed them:
and they shall increase as they have increased.
⁹ And I will sow them among the people,
and they shall remember me in far countries,
and they shall live with their children, and turn again.
¹⁰ I will bring them again also out of the land of Egypt,
and gather them out of Assyria,

and I will bring them into the land of Gilead and Lebanon,
and place shall not be found for them.
¹¹ And he shall pass through the sea with affliction,
and shall smite the waves in the sea,
and all the deeps of the river shall dry up:
and the pride of Assyria shall be brought down,
and the sceptre of Egypt shall depart away.
¹² And I will strengthen them in the LORD,
and they shall walk up and down in his name,'
saith the LORD.

11 Open thy doors, O Lebanon,
that the fire may devour thy cedars.
² Howl, fir tree, for the cedar is fallen;
because all the mighty are spoiled:
howl, O ye oaks of Bashan,
for the forest of the vintage is come down.
³ There is a voice of the howling of the shepherds;
for their glory is spoiled:
a voice of the roaring of young lions;
for the pride of Jordan is spoiled.

⁴Thus saith the LORD my God, 'Feed the flock of the slaughter; ⁵whose possessors slay them, and hold themselves not guilty: and they that sell them say, "Blessed be the LORD; for I am rich": and their own shepherds pity them not. ⁶For I will no more pity the inhabitants of the land,' saith the LORD: 'but lo, I will deliver the men every one into his neighbour's hand, and into the hand of his king, and they shall smite the land, and out of their hand I will not deliver them.' ⁷And I will feed the flock of slaughter, even you, O poor of the flock. And I took unto me two staves; the one I called Beauty, and the other I called Bands, and I fed the flock. ⁸Three shepherds also I cut off in one month, and my soul loathed them, and their soul also abhorred me. ⁹Then said I, 'I will not feed you: that that dieth, let it die: and that that is to be cut off, let it be cut off, and let the rest eat every one the flesh of another'.

¹⁰And I took my staff, even Beauty, and cut it asunder, that I might break my covenant which I had made with all the people. ¹¹And it was broken in that day: and so the poor of the flock that waited upon me knew that it was the word of the LORD. ¹²And I said unto them, 'If ye think good, give me my price: and if not, forbear'. So they weighed for my price thirty pieces of silver. ¹³And the LORD said unto me, 'Cast it unto the potter: a goodly price that I was priced at of them'. And I took the thirty pieces of silver, and cast them to the potter in the house of the LORD. ¹⁴Then I cut asunder my other staff, even Bands, that I might break the brotherhood between Judah and Israel.

¹⁵And the LORD said unto me, 'Take unto thee yet the instruments of a foolish shepherd. ¹⁶For lo, I will raise up a shepherd in the land, which shall not visit those that be cut off, neither shall seek the young one,

nor heal that that is broken, nor feed that that standeth still: but he shall eat the flesh of the fat, and tear their claws in pieces. [17]Woe to the idol shepherd that leaveth the flock! the sword shall be upon his arm, and upon his right eye: his arm shall be clean dried up, and his right eye shall be utterly darkened.'

12 The burden of the word of the LORD for Israel, saith the LORD, which stretcheth forth the heavens, and layeth the foundation of the earth, and formeth the spirit of man within him. [2]'Behold, I will make Jerusalem a cup of trembling unto all the people round about, when they shall be in the siege both against Judah and against Jerusalem. [3]And in that day will I make Jerusalem a burdensome stone for all people: all that burden themselves with it shall be cut in pieces, though all the people of the earth be gathered together against it. [4]In that day,' saith the LORD, 'I will smite every horse with astonishment, and his rider with madness: and I will open my eyes upon the house of Judah, and will smite every horse of the people with blindness. [5]And the governors of Judah shall say in their heart, "The inhabitants of Jerusalem shall be my strength in the LORD of hosts their God".

[6]'In that day will I make the governors of Judah like a hearth of fire among the wood, and like a torch of fire in a sheaf; and they shall devour all the people round about, on the right hand and on the left: and Jerusalem shall be inhabited again in her own place, even in Jerusalem.' [7]The LORD also shall save the tents of Judah first, that the glory of the house of David and the glory of the inhabitants of Jerusalem do not magnify themselves against Judah. [8]In that day shall the LORD defend the inhabitants of Jerusalem, and he that is feeble among them at that day shall be as David; and the house of David shall be as God, as the angel of the LORD before them.

[9]'And it shall come to pass in that day, that I will seek to destroy all the nations that come against Jerusalem. [10]And I will pour upon the house of David, and upon the inhabitants of Jerusalem the spirit of grace and of supplications: and they shall look upon me whom they have pierced, and they shall mourn for him, as one mourneth for his only son, and shall be in bitterness for him, as one that is in bitterness for his firstborn. [11]In that day shall there be a great mourning in Jerusalem, as the mourning of Hadadrimmon in the valley of Megiddon. [12]And the land shall mourn, every family apart, the family of the house of David apart, and their wives apart, the family of the house of Nathan apart, and their wives apart: [13]the family of the house of Levi apart, and their wives apart: the family of Shimei apart, and their wives apart: [14]all the families that remain, every family apart, and their wives apart.

13 'In that day there shall be a fountain opened to the house of David and to the inhabitants of Jerusalem for sin and for uncleanness.

[2]'And it shall come to pass in that day,' saith the LORD of hosts, 'that I will cut off the names of the idols out of the land: and they shall no more be remembered: and also I will cause the prophets and the unclean spirit to pass out of the land. [3]And it shall come to pass that

when any shall yet prophesy, then his father and his mother that begot him shall say unto him, "Thou shalt not live: for thou speakest lies in the name of the Lord": and his father and his mother that begot him shall thrust him through when he prophesieth. ⁴And it shall come to pass in that day, that the prophets shall be ashamed every one of his vision, when he hath prophesied: neither shall they wear a rough garment to deceive: ⁵But he shall say, "I am no prophet, I am a husband-man: for man taught me to keep cattle from my youth". ⁶And one shall say unto him, "What are these wounds in thy hands?" Then he shall answer, "Those with which I was wounded in the house of my friends".

⁷'Awake, O sword, against my shepherd, and against the man that is my fellow,' saith the Lord of hosts: 'smite the shepherd, and the sheep shall be scattered: and I will turn my hand upon the little ones. ⁸And it shall come to pass, that in all the land,' saith the Lord, 'two parts therein shall be cut off and die, but the third shall be left therein. ⁹And I will bring the third part through the fire, and will refine them as silver is refined, and will try them as gold is tried: they shall call on my name, and I will hear them: I will say, "It is my people": and they shall say, "The Lord is my God".'

14 Behold, the day of the Lord cometh, and thy spoil shall be divided in the midst of thee. ²For I will gather all nations against Jerusalem to battle, and the city shall be taken, and the houses rifled, and the women ravished; and half of the city shall go forth into captivity, and the residue of the people shall not be cut off from the city. ³Then shall the Lord go forth, and fight against those nations, as when he fought in the day of battle.

⁴And his feet shall stand in that day upon the mount of Olives, which is before Jerusalem on the east, and the mount of Olives shall cleave in the midst thereof toward the east and toward the west, and there shall be a very great valley, and half of the mountain shall remove toward the north, and half of it toward the south. ⁵And ye shall flee to the valley of the mountains: for the valley of the mountains shall reach unto Azal: yea, ye shall flee like as ye fled from before the earthquake in the days of Uzziah king of Judah: and the Lord my God shall come, and all the saints with thee. ⁶And it shall come to pass in that day, that the light shall not be clear, nor dark. ⁷But it shall be one day which shall be known to the Lord, not day, nor night: but it shall come to pass that at evening time it shall be light. ⁸And it shall be in that day, that living waters shall go out from Jerusalem: half of them toward the former sea, and half of them toward the hinder sea: in summer and in winter shall it be. ⁹And the Lord shall be king over all the earth: in that day shall there be one Lord, and his name one. ¹⁰All the land shall be turned as a plain from Geba to Rimmon south of Jerusalem: and it shall be lifted up and inhabited in her place, from Benjamin's gate unto the place of the first gate, unto the corner gate, and from the tower of Hananeel unto the king's wine-presses. ¹¹And men shall dwell in it, and there shall be no more utter destruction: but Jerusalem shall be safely inhabited.

¹²And this shall be the plague wherewith the LORD will smite all the people that have fought against Jerusalem: their flesh shall consume away while they stand upon their feet, and their eyes shall consume away in their holes, and their tongue shall consume away in their mouth. ¹³And it shall come to pass in that day, that a great tumult from the LORD shall be among them, and they shall lay hold every one on the hand of his neighbour, and his hand shall rise up against the hand of his neighbour. ¹⁴And Judah also shall fight at Jerusalem; and the wealth of all the heathen round about shall be gathered together, gold and silver, and apparel in great abundance. ¹⁵And so shall be the plague of the horse, of the mule, of the camel, and of the ass, and of all the beasts that shall be in these tents, as this plague.

¹⁶And it shall come to pass, that every one that is left of all the nations which came against Jerusalem shall even go up from year to year to worship the King, the LORD of hosts, and to keep the feast of tabernacles. ¹⁷And it shall be, that whoso will not come up of all the families of the earth unto Jerusalem to worship the King, the LORD of hosts, even upon them shall be no rain. ¹⁸And if the family of Egypt go not up, and come not, that have no rain: there shall be the plague wherewith the LORD will smite the heathen that come not up to keep the feast of tabernacles. ¹⁹This shall be the punishment of Egypt, and the punishment of all nations that come not up to keep the feast of tabernacles.

²⁰In that day shall there be upon the bells of the horses, HOLINESS UNTO THE LORD, and the pots in the LORD's house shall be like the bowls before the altar. ²¹Yea, every pot in Jerusalem and in Judah shall be holiness unto the LORD of hosts, and all they that sacrifice shall come and take of them, and seethe therein: and in that day there shall be no more the Canaanite in the house of the LORD of hosts.

MALACHI

1 The burden of the word of the LORD to Israel by Malachi. ²'I have loved you,' saith the LORD. Yet ye say, 'Wherein hast thou loved us?' 'Was not Esau Jacob's brother?' saith the LORD: 'yet I loved Jacob, ³and I hated Esau, and laid his mountains and his heritage waste for the dragons of the wilderness.' ⁴Whereas Edom saith, 'We are impoverished, but we will return and build the desolate places'; thus saith the LORD of hosts, 'They shall build, but I will throw down; and they shall call them, the border of wickedness, and the people against whom the LORD hath indignation for ever'. ⁵And your eyes shall see, and ye shall say, 'The LORD will be magnified from the border of Israel'.

⁶'A son honoureth his father, and a servant his master. If then I be a father, where is my honour? and if I be a master, where is my fear? saith the LORD of hosts unto you, O priests, that despise my name. And ye say, "Wherein have we despised thy name?" ⁷Ye offer polluted bread upon my altar; and ye say, "Wherein have we polluted thee?" In that ye say, "The table of the LORD is contemptible". ⁸And if ye offer the blind for sacrifice, is it not evil? and if ye offer the lame and sick, is it not evil? offer it now unto thy governor: will he be pleased with thee, or accept thy person?' saith the LORD of hosts. ⁹'And now, I pray you, beseech God that he will be gracious unto us: this hath been by your means: will he regard your persons?' saith the LORD of hosts. ¹⁰'Who is there even among you that would shut the doors for nought? neither do ye kindle fire on my altar for nought. I have no pleasure in you,' saith the LORD of hosts, 'neither will I accept an offering at your hand. ¹¹For from the rising of the sun even unto the going down of the same my name shall be great among the Gentiles, and in every place incense shall be offered unto my name, and a pure offering: for my name shall be great among the heathen,' saith the LORD of hosts.

¹²'But ye have profaned it, in that ye say, "The table of the LORD is polluted, and the fruit thereof, even his meat, is contemptible". ¹³Ye said also, "Behold, what a weariness is it", and ye have snuffed at it,' saith the LORD of hosts, 'and ye brought that which was torn, and the lame, and the sick: thus ye brought an offering: should I accept this of your hand?' saith the LORD. ¹⁴'But cursed be the deceiver, which hath in his flock a male, and voweth and sacrificeth unto the Lord a corrupt thing: for I am a great King,' saith the LORD of hosts, 'and my name is dreadful among the heathen.

2 'And now, O ye priests, this commandment is for you. ²If ye will not hear, and if ye will not lay it to heart, to give glory unto my name,' saith the LORD of hosts, 'I will even send a curse upon you, and will curse your blessings: yea, I have cursed them already, because ye do not lay it to heart. ³Behold, I will corrupt your seed, and spread dung upon your faces, even the dung of your solemn feasts, and one shall take you away with it. ⁴And ye shall know that I have sent this commandment unto you, that my covenant might be with Levi,' saith the LORD of hosts.

⁵'My covenant was with him of life and peace, and I gave them to him for the fear wherewith he feared me, and was afraid before my name. ⁶The law of truth was in his mouth, and iniquity was not found in his lips: he walked with me in peace and equity, and did turn many away from iniquity. ⁷For the priest's lips should keep knowledge, and they should seek the law at his mouth: for he is the messenger of the LORD of hosts. ⁸But ye are departed out of the way: ye have caused many to stumble at the law: ye have corrupted the covenant of Levi,' saith the LORD of hosts. ⁹'Therefore have I also made you contemptible and base before all the people, according as ye have not kept my ways, but have been partial in the law.'

¹⁰Have we not all one father? hath not one God created us? why do we deal treacherously every man against his brother, by profaning the covenant of our fathers? ¹¹Judah hath dealt treacherously, and an abomination is committed in Israel and in Jerusalem: for Judah hath profaned the holiness of the LORD which he loved, and hath married the daughter of a strange god. ¹²The LORD will cut off the man that doeth this, the master and the scholar out of the tabernacles of Jacob, and him that offereth an offering unto the LORD of hosts. ¹³And this have ye done again, covering the altar of the LORD with tears, with weeping, and with crying out, insomuch that he regardeth not the offering any more, or receiveth it with good will at your hand.

¹⁴Yet ye say, 'Wherefore?' Because the LORD hath been witness between thee and the wife of thy youth, against whom thou hast dealt treacherously: yet is she thy companion, and the wife of thy covenant. ¹⁵And did not he make one? Yet had he the residue of the spirit. And wherefore one? that he might seek a godly seed: therefore take heed to your spirit, and let none deal treacherously against the wife of his youth. ¹⁶For the LORD the God of Israel saith that he hateth putting away: 'For one covereth violence with his garment,' saith the LORD of hosts, 'therefore take heed to your spirit, that ye deal not treacherously'.

¹⁷Ye have wearied the LORD with your words. Yet ye say, 'Wherein have we wearied him?' When ye say, 'Every one that doeth evil is good in the sight of the LORD, and he delighteth in them', or, 'Where is the God of judgement?'

3 'Behold, I will send my messenger, and he shall prepare the way before me: and the Lord whom ye seek, shall suddenly come to his temple, even the messenger of the covenant, whom ye delight in: behold, he shall come,' saith the LORD of hosts.

²But who may abide the day of his coming? and who shall stand when he appeareth? for he is like a refiner's fire, and like fullers' soap. ³And he shall sit as a refiner and purifier of silver: and he shall purify the sons of Levi, and purge them as gold and silver, that they may offer unto the LORD an offering in righteousness. ⁴Then shall the offerings of Judah and Jerusalem be pleasant unto the LORD, as in the days of old, and as in former years.

⁵'And I will come near to you to judgement, and I will be a swift witness against the sorcerers, and against the adulterers, and against false

swearers, and against those that oppress the hireling in his wages, the widow, and the fatherless, and that turn aside the stranger from his right, and fear not me,' saith the LORD of hosts. ⁶'For I am the LORD, I change not: therefore ye sons of Jacob are not consumed.

⁷'Even from the days of your fathers ye are gone away from my ordinances, and have not kept them. Return unto me, and I will return unto you,' saith the LORD of hosts. But ye said, 'Wherein shall we return?'

⁸'Will a man rob God? Yet ye have robbed me. But ye say, "Wherein have we robbed thee?" In tithes and offerings. ⁹Ye are cursed with a curse: for ye have robbed me, even this whole nation. ¹⁰Bring ye all the tithes into the storehouse, that there may be meat in my house, and prove me now herewith,' saith the LORD of hosts, 'if I will not open you the windows of heaven, and pour you out a blessing, that there shall not be room enough to receive it. ¹¹And I will rebuke the devourer for your sakes: and he shall not destroy the fruits of your ground, neither shall your vine cast her fruit before the time in the field,' saith the LORD of hosts. ¹²'And all nations shall call you blessed: for ye shall be a delightsome land,' saith the LORD of hosts.

¹³'Your words have been stout against me,' saith the LORD. 'Yet ye say, "What have we spoken so much against thee?" ¹⁴Ye have said, "It is vain to serve God: and what profit is it that we have kept his ordinance, and that we have walked mournfully before the LORD of hosts? ¹⁵And now we call the proud happy: yea, they that work wickedness are set up, yea, they that tempt God are even delivered."'

¹⁶Then they that feared the LORD spoke often one to another, and the LORD hearkened, and heard it, and a book of remembrance was written before him for them that feared the LORD, and that thought upon his name. ¹⁷'And they shall be mine,' saith the LORD of hosts, 'in that day when I make up my jewels, and I will spare them as a man spareth his own son that serveth him. ¹⁸Then shall ye return, and discern between the righteous and the wicked, between him that serveth God and him that serveth him not. ¹For behold, the day cometh, that shall burn as an oven, and all the proud, yea, and all that do wickedly, shall be stubble: and the day that cometh shall burn them up,' saith the LORD of hosts, 'that it shall leave them neither root nor branch.

²'But unto you that fear my name shall the Sun of righteousness arise with healing in his wings, and shall go forth, and grow up as calves of the stall. ³And ye shall tread down the wicked: for they shall be ashes under the soles of your feet in the day that I shall do this,' saith the LORD of hosts.

⁴'Remember ye the law of Moses my servant, which I commanded unto him in Horeb for all Israel, with the statutes and judgements.

⁵'Behold, I will send you Elijah the prophet before the coming of the great and dreadful day of the LORD. ⁶And he shall turn the heart of the fathers to the children, and the heart of the children to their fathers, lest I come and smite the earth with a curse.'

THE APOCRYPHA

THE FIRST BOOK OF
ESDRAS

1 And Josias held the feast of the passover in Jerusalem unto his Lord, and offered the passover the fourteenth day of the first month: [2] having set the priests according to their daily courses, being arrayed in long garments, in the temple of the Lord. [3] And he spoke unto the Levites, the holy ministers of Israel, that they should hallow themselves unto the Lord, to set the holy ark of the Lord in the house that king Solomon the son of David had built: [4] and said, 'Ye shall no more bear the ark upon your shoulders: now therefore serve the Lord your God, and minister unto his people Israel, and prepare you after your families and kindreds, [5] according as David the king of Israel prescribed, and according to the magnificence of Solomon his son: and standing in the temple according to the several dignity of the families of you the Levites, who minister in the presence of your brethren the children of Israel. [6] Offer the passover in order, and make ready the sacrifices for your brethren, and keep the passover according to the commandment of the Lord, which was given unto Moses.'

[7] And unto the people that was found there Josias gave thirty thousand lambs and kids, and three thousand calves: these things were given of the king's allowance, according as he promised, to the people, to the priests, and to the Levites. [8] And Helkias, Zacharias, and Syelus, the governors of the temple, gave to the priests for the passover two thousand and six hundred sheep, and three hundred calves. [9] And Jechonias, and Samaias, and Nathanael his brother, and Assabias, and Ochiel, and Joram, captains over thousands, gave to the Levites for the passover five thousand sheep, and seven hundred calves.

[10] And when these things were done, the priests and Levites, having the unleavened bread, stood in very comely order according to the kindreds, [11] and according to the several dignities of the fathers, before the people, to offer to the Lord, as it is written in the book of Moses: and thus did they in the morning. [12] And they roasted the passover with fire, as appertaineth: as for the sacrifices, they seethed them in brass pots and pans with a good savour, [13] and set them before all the people: and afterward they prepared for themselves, and for the priests their brethren, the sons of Aaron. [14] For the priests offered the fat until night: and the Levites prepared for themselves, and the priests their brethren, the sons of Aaron. [15] The holy singers also, the sons of Asaph, were in their order, according to the appointment of David, to wit, Asaph, Zacharias, and Jeduthun, who was of the king's retinue. [16] Moreover the porters were at every gate: it was not lawful for any to go from his ordinary service: for their brethren the Levites prepared for them.

[17] Thus were the things that belonged to the sacrifices of the Lord accomplished in that day, that they might hold the passover, [18] and offer sacrifices upon the altar of the Lord, according to the commandment

of king Josias. ¹⁹So the children of Israel which were present held the passover at that time, and the feast of sweet bread seven days. ²⁰And such a passover was not kept in Israel since the time of the prophet Samuel. ²¹Yea, all the kings of Israel held not such a passover as Josias, and the priests, and the Levites, and the Jews held with all Israel that were found dwelling at Jerusalem. ²²In the eighteenth year of the reign of Josias was this passover kept.

²³And the works of Josias were upright before his Lord with a heart full of godliness. ²⁴As for the things that came to pass in his time, they were written in former times, concerning those that sinned, and did wickedly against the Lord above all people and kingdoms, and how they grieved him exceedingly, so that the words of the Lord rose up against Israel.

²⁵Now after all these acts of Josias it came to pass that Pharaoh the king of Egypt came to raise war at Carchamis upon Euphrates: and Josias went out against him. ²⁶But the king of Egypt sent to him, saying, 'What have I to do with thee, O king of Judea? ²⁷I am not sent out from the Lord God against thee: for my war is upon Euphrates, and now the Lord is with me, yea, the Lord is with me hasting me forward: depart from me, and be not against the Lord.' ²⁸Howbeit Josias did not turn back his chariot from him, but undertook to fight with him, not regarding the words of the prophet Jeremy spoken by the mouth of the Lord: ²⁹but joined battle with him in the plain of Magiddo, and the princes came against king Josias. ³⁰Then said the king unto his servants, 'Carry me away out of the battle for I am very weak'. And immediately his servants took him away out of the battle. ³¹Then got he up upon his second chariot, and being brought back to Jerusalem died, and was buried in his father's sepulchre.

³²And in all Jewry they mourned for Josias, yea, Jeremy the prophet lamented for Josias, and the chief men with the women made lamentation for him unto this day: and this was given out for an ordinance to be done continually in all the nation of Israel. ³³These things are written in the book of the stories of the kings of Juda, and every one of the acts that Josias did, and his glory, and his understanding in the law of the Lord, and the things that he had done before, and the things now recited, are reported in the book of the kings of Israel and Judea.

³⁴And the people took Joachaz the son of Josias, and made him king in stead of Josias his father, when he was twenty and three years old. ³⁵And he reigned in Judea and in Jerusalem three months: and then the king of Egypt deposed him from reigning in Jerusalem. ³⁶And he set a tax upon the land of a hundred talents of silver and one talent of gold. ³⁷The king of Egypt also made king Joacim his brother king of Judea and Jerusalem. ³⁸And he bound Joacim and the nobles: but Zaraces his brother he apprehended, and brought him out of Egypt.

³⁹Five and twenty years old was Joacim when he was made king in the land of Judea and Jerusalem, and he did evil before the Lord. ⁴⁰Wherefore against him Nabuchodonosor the king of Babylon came up, and bound him with a chain of brass, and carried him unto

Babylon. ⁴¹Nabuchodonosor also took of the holy vessels of the Lord, and carried them away, and set them in his own temple at Babylon. ⁴²But those things that are recorded of him, and of his uncleanness and impiety, are written in the chronicles of the kings.

⁴³And Joacim his son reigned in his stead: he was made king being eighteen years old, ⁴⁴and reigned but three months and ten days in Jerusalem, and did evil before the Lord. ⁴⁵So after a year Nabuchodonosor sent and caused him to be brought into Babylon with the holy vessels of the Lord, ⁴⁶and made Zedechias king of Judea and Jerusalem, when he was one and twenty years old, and he reigned eleven years: ⁴⁷and he did evil also in the sight of the Lord, and cared not for the words that were spoken unto him by the prophet Jeremy from the mouth of the Lord. ⁴⁸And after that king Nabuchodonosor had made him to swear by the name of the Lord, he forswore himself, and rebelled; and hardening his neck, and his heart, he transgressed the laws of the Lord God of Israel.

⁴⁹The governors also of the people and of the priests did many things against the laws, and passed all the pollutions of all nations, and defiled the temple of the Lord which was sanctified in Jerusalem. ⁵⁰Nevertheless the God of their fathers sent by his messenger to call them back, because he spared them and his tabernacle also: ⁵¹but they had his messengers in derision; and, look, when the Lord spoke unto them, they made a sport of his prophets, ⁵²so far forth that he, being wroth with his people for their great ungodliness, commanded the kings of the Chaldees to come up against them; ⁵³who slew their young men with the sword, yea, even within the compass of their holy temple, and spared neither young man nor maid, old man nor child, among them, for he delivered all into their hands. ⁵⁴And they took all the holy vessels of the Lord, both great and small, with the vessels of the ark of God, and the king's treasures, and carried them away into Babylon.

⁵⁵As for the house of the Lord, they burnt it, broke down the walls of Jerusalem, set fire upon her towers. ⁵⁶And as for her glorious things, they never ceased till they had consumed and brought them all to nought: and the people that were not slain with the sword he carried unto Babylon: ⁵⁷who became servants to him and his children, till the Persians reigned, to fulfil the word of the Lord spoken by the mouth of Jeremy: ⁵⁸'Until the land had enjoyed her sabbaths, the whole time of her desolation shall she rest, until the full term of seventy years'.

2 In the first year of Cyrus king of the Persians, that the word of the Lord might be accomplished, that he had promised by the mouth of Jeremy: ²the Lord raised up the spirit of Cyrus the king of the Persians, and he made proclamation through all his kingdom, and also by writing, ³saying, 'Thus saith Cyrus king of the Persians: "The Lord of Israel, the most high Lord, hath made me king of the whole world, ⁴and commanded me to build him a house at Jerusalem in Jewry. ⁵If therefore there be any of you that are of his people, let the Lord, even his Lord, be with him, and let him go up to Jerusalem that is in Judea, and build the house of the Lord of Israel: for he is the Lord that dwelleth in

Jerusalem. ⁶Whosoever then dwell in the places about, let them help him (those, I say, that are his neighbours) with gold and with silver, ⁷with gifts, with horses, and with cattle, and other things, which have been set forth by vow, for the temple of the Lord at Jerusalem."'

⁸Then the chief of the families of Judea and of the tribes of Benjamin stood up: the priests also, and the Levites, and all they whose mind the Lord had moved to go up, and to build a house for the Lord at Jerusalem, ⁹and they that dwelt round about them, and helped them in all things with silver and gold, with horses and cattle, and with very many free gifts of a great number whose minds were stirred up thereto. ¹⁰King Cyrus also brought forth the holy vessels, which Nabuchodonosor had carried away from Jerusalem, and had set up in his temple of idols.

¹¹Now when Cyrus king of the Persians had brought them forth, he delivered them to Mithridates his treasurer: ¹²and by him they were delivered to Sanabassar the governor of Judea. ¹³And this was the number of them, a thousand golden cups, and a thousand of silver, censers of silver twenty nine, vials of gold thirty, and of silver two thousand four hundred and ten, and a thousand other vessels. ¹⁴So all the vessels of gold and of silver which were carried away, were five thousand four hundred threescore and nine. ¹⁵These were brought back by Sanabassar, together with them of the captivity, from Babylon to Jerusalem.

¹⁶But in the time of Artaxerxes king of the Persians, Belemus, and Mithridates, and Tabellius, and Rathumus, and Beeltethmus, and Semellius the secretary, with others that were in commission with them, dwelling in Samaria and other places, wrote unto him against them that dwelt in Judea and Jerusalem these letters following:

¹⁷To king Artaxerxes our lord, thy servants Rathumus the story-writer, and Semellius the scribe, and the rest of their council, and the judges that are in Coelosyria and Phenice. ¹⁸Be it now known to the lord the king, that the Jews that are come up from you to us, being come into Jerusalem (that rebellious and wicked city), do build the market-places, and repair the walls of it, and do lay the foundation of the temple. ¹⁹Now if this city and the walls thereof be made up again, they will not only refuse to give tribute, but also rebel against kings. ²⁰And forasmuch as the things pertaining to the temple are now in hand, we think it meet not to neglect such a matter, ²¹but to speak unto our lord the king, to the intent that, if it be thy pleasure, it may be sought out in the books of thy fathers: ²²and thou shalt find in the chronicles what is written concerning these things, and shalt understand that that city was rebellious, troubling both kings and cities: ²³and that the Jews were rebellious, and raised always wars therein, for the which cause even this city was made desolate. ²⁴Wherefore now we do declare unto thee, O lord the king, that if this city be built again, and the walls thereof set up anew, thou shalt from henceforth have no passage into Coelosyria and Phenice.

²⁵Then the king wrote back again to Rathumus the storywriter, to

Beeltethmus, to Semellius the scribe, and to the rest that were in commission, and dwellers in Samaria and Syria and Phenice, after this manner.

²⁶I have read the epistle which ye have sent unto me: therefore I commanded to make diligent search, and it hath been found that that city was from the beginning practising against kings; ²⁷and the men therein were given to rebellion and war, and that mighty kings and fierce were in Jerusalem, who reigned and exacted tributes in Coelosyria and Phenice. ²⁸Now therefore I have commanded to hinder those men from building the city, and heed to be taken that there be no more done in it, ²⁹and that those wicked workers proceed no further to the annoyance of kings.

³⁰Then king Artaxerxes' letters being read, Rathumus, and Semellius the scribe, and the rest that were in commission with them, removing in haste towards Jerusalem with a troop of horsemen and a multitude of people in battle array, began to hinder the builders; and the building of the temple in Jerusalem ceased until the second year of the reign of Darius king of the Persians.

3 Now when Darius reigned, he made a great feast unto all his subjects, and unto all his household, and unto all the princes of Media and Persia, ²and to all the governors and captains and lieutenants that were under him, from India unto Ethiopia, of a hundred twenty and seven provinces. ³And when they had eaten and drunken, and being satisfied were gone home, then Darius the king went into his bedchamber, and slept, and soon after awoke. ⁴Then three young men, that were of the guard that kept the king's body, spoke one to another: ⁵'Let every one of us speak a sentence: he that shall overcome, and whose sentence shall seem wiser than the others, unto him shall the king Darius give great gifts, and great things in token of victory: ⁶as, to be clothed in purple, to drink in gold, and to sleep upon gold, and a chariot with bridles of gold, and a head-tire of fine linen, and a chain about his neck: ⁷and he shall sit next to Darius because of his wisdom, and shall be called Darius's cousin.' ⁸And then every one wrote his sentence, sealed it, and laid it under king Darius's pillow; ⁹and said that, when the king is risen, some will give him the writings, and of whose side the king and the three princes of Persia shall judge that his sentence is the wisest, to him shall the victory be given, as was appointed.

¹⁰The first wrote, 'Wine is the strongest'. ¹¹The second wrote, 'The king is strongest'. ¹²The third wrote, 'Women are strongest: but above all things truth beareth away the victory'.

¹³Now when the king was risen up, they took their writings, and delivered them unto him, and so he read them. ¹⁴And sending forth, he called all the princes of Persia and Media, and the governors, and the captains, and the lieutenants, and the chief officers, ¹⁵and sat him down in the royal seat of judgement; and the writings were read before them. ¹⁶And he said, 'Call the young men, and they shall declare their own sentences'. So they were called, and came in. ¹⁷And he said unto

them, 'Declare unto us your mind concerning the writings'. Then began the first, who had spoken of the strength of wine; [18] and he said thus, 'O ye men, how exceeding strong is wine! it causeth all men to err that drink it: [19] it maketh the mind of the king and of the fatherless child to be all one; of the bondman and of the freeman, of the poor man and of the rich: [20] it turneth also every thought into jollity and mirth, so that a man remembereth neither sorrow nor debt: [21] and it maketh every heart rich, so that a man remembereth neither king nor governor; and it maketh to speak all things by talents: [22] and when they are in their cups, they forget their love both to friends and brethren, and a little after draw out swords: [23] but when they are from the wine, they remember not what they have done. [24] O ye men, is not wine the strongest, that enforceth to do thus?' And when he had so spoken, he held his peace.

4 Then the second, that had spoken of the strength of the king, began to say, [2] 'O ye men, do not men excel in strength, that bear rule over sea and land, and all things in them? [3] But yet the king is more mighty: for he is lord of all these things, and hath dominion over them, and whatsoever he commandeth them they do: [4] if he bid them make war the one against the other, they do it: if he send them out against the enemies, they go, and break down mountains, walls, and towers. [5] They slay and are slain, and transgress not the king's commandment: if they get the victory, they bring all to the king, as well the spoil as all things else. [6] Likewise for those that are no soldiers, and have not to do with wars, but use husbandry; when they have reaped again that which they had sown, they bring it to the king, and compel one another to pay tribute unto the king. [7] And yet he is but one man: if he command to kill, they kill; if he command to spare, they spare; [8] if he command to smite, they smite; if he command to make desolate, they make desolate; if he command to build, they build; [9] if he command to cut down, they cut down; if he command to plant, they plant. [10] So all his people and his armies obey him: furthermore he lieth down, he eateth and drinketh, and taketh his rest. [11] And these keep watch round about him, neither may anyone depart, and do his own business, neither disobey they him in anything. [12] O ye men, how should not the king be mightiest, when in such sort he is obeyed?' And he held his tongue.

[13] Then the third, who had spoken of women, and of the truth (this was Zorobabel), began to speak. [14] 'O ye men, it is not the great king, nor the multitude of men, neither is it wine, that excelleth; who is it then that ruleth them, or hath the lordship over them? are they not women? [15] Women have borne the king and all the people that bear rule by sea and land. [16] Even of them came they: and they nourished them up that planted the vineyards from whence the wine cometh. [17] These also make garments for men; these bring glory unto men, and without women cannot men be. [18] Yea, and if men have gathered together gold and silver, or any other goodly thing, do they not love a woman which is comely in favour and beauty? [19] And letting all those things go, do they not gape, and even with open mouth fix their eyes fast on her; and

have not all men more desire unto her than unto silver or gold, or any goodly thing whatsoever? ²⁰A man leaveth his own father that brought him up, and his own country, and cleaveth unto his wife. ²¹He sticks not to spend his life with his wife, and remembereth neither father, nor mother, nor country. ²²By this also you must know that women have dominion over you: do ye not labour and toil, and give and bring all to the woman? ²³Yea, a man taketh his sword, and goeth his way to rob and to steal, to sail upon the sea and upon rivers, ²⁴and looketh upon a lion, and goeth in the darkness; and when he hath stolen, spoiled and robbed, he bringeth it to his love. ²⁵Wherefore a man loveth his wife better than father or mother. ²⁶Yea, many there be that have run out of their wits for women, and become servants for their sakes. ²⁷Many also have perished, have erred, and sinned, for women.

²⁸'And now do ye not believe me? is not the king great in his power? do not all regions fear to touch him? ²⁹Yet did I see him and Apame the king's concubine, the daughter of the admirable Bartacus, sitting at the right hand of the king, ³⁰and taking the crown from the king's head, and setting it upon her own head; she also struck the king with her left hand. ³¹And yet for all this the king gaped and gazed upon her with open mouth: if she laughed upon him, he laughed also: but if she took any displeasure at him, the king was fain to flatter, that she might be reconciled to him again. ³²O ye men, how can it be but women should be strong, seeing they do thus?'

³³Then the king and the princes looked one upon another: so he began to speak of the truth.

³⁴'O ye men, are not women strong? great is the earth, high is the heaven, swift is the sun in his course, for he compasseth the heavens round about, and fetcheth his course again to his own place in one day. ³⁵Is he not great that maketh these things? therefore great is the truth, and stronger than all things. ³⁶All the earth calleth upon the truth, and the heaven blesseth it: all works shake and tremble at it, and with it is no unrighteous thing. ³⁷Wine is wicked, the king is wicked, women are wicked, all the children of men are wicked, and such are all their wicked works, and there is no truth in them. In their unrighteousness also they shall perish. ³⁸As for the truth, it endureth, and is always strong; it liveth and conquereth for evermore. ³⁹With her there is no accepting of persons or rewards, but she doeth the things that are just, and refraineth from all unjust and wicked things; and all men do well like of her works. ⁴⁰Neither in her judgement is any unrighteousness, and she is the strength, kingdom, power and majesty, of all ages. Blessed be the God of truth.'

⁴¹And with that he held his peace. And all the people then shouted, and said, 'Great is truth, and mighty above all things'. ⁴²Then said the king unto him, 'Ask what thou wilt, more than is appointed in the writing, and we will give it thee, because thou art found wisest, and thou shalt sit next me, and shalt be called my cousin'. ⁴³Then said he unto the king, 'Remember thy vow, which thou hast vowed to build Jerusalem in the day when thou camest to the kingdom, ⁴⁴and to send

away all the vessels that were taken away out of Jerusalem, which Cyrus set apart, when he vowed to destroy Babylon, and to send them again thither. [45]Thou also hast vowed to build up the temple, which the Edomites burnt when Judea was made desolate by the Chaldees. [46]And now, O lord the king, this is that which I require, and which I desire of thee, and this is the princely liberality proceeding from thyself: I desire therefore that thou make good the vow, the performance whereof with thy own mouth thou hast vowed to the King of heaven.'

[47]Then Darius the king stood up and kissed him, and wrote letters for him unto all the treasurers and lieutenants and captains and governors that they should safely convey on their way both him, and all those that go up with him to build Jerusalem. [48]He wrote letters also unto the lieutenants that were in Coelosyria and Phenice, and unto them in Libanus, that they should bring cedar wood from Libanus unto Jerusalem, and that they should build the city with him. [49]Moreover he wrote for all the Jews that went out of his realm up into Jewry, concerning their freedom, that no officer, no ruler, no lieutenant, nor treasurer, should forcibly enter into their doors, [50]and that all the country which they hold should be free without tribute, and that the Edomites should give over the villages of the Jews which then they held, [51]yea, that there should be yearly given twenty talents to the building of the temple, until the time that it were built, [52]and other ten talents yearly, to maintain the burnt offerings upon the altar every day (as they had a commandment to offer seventeen); [53]and that all they that went from Babylon to build the city should have free liberty, as well they as their posterity, and all the priests that went away.

[54]He wrote also concerning the charges, and the priests' vestments wherein they minister; [55]and likewise for the charges of the Levites, to be given them until the day that the house were finished, and Jerusalem built up. [56]And he commanded to give to all that kept the city pensions and wages. [57]He sent away also all the vessels from Babylon that Cyrus had set apart, and all that Cyrus had given in commandment, the same charged he also to be done, and sent unto Jerusalem.

[58]Now when this young man was gone forth, he lifted up his face to heaven toward Jerusalem, and praised the King of heaven, [59]and said, 'From thee cometh victory, from thee cometh wisdom, and thine is the glory, and I am thy servant. [60]Blessed art thou who hast given me wisdom: for to thee I give thanks, O Lord of our fathers.'

[61]And so he took the letters, and went out, and came unto Babylon, and told it all his brethren. [62]And they praised the God of their fathers, because he had given them freedom and liberty [63]to go up, and to build Jerusalem, and the temple which is called by his name: and they feasted with instruments of music and gladness seven days.

5 After this were the principal men of the families chosen according to their tribes, to go up with their wives and sons and daughters, with their menservants and maidservants, and their cattle. [2]And Darius sent with them a thousand horsemen, till they had brought

them back to Jerusalem safely, and with musical instruments, tabrets
and flutes: 3 and all their brethren played, and he made them go up
together with them.

4 And these are the names of the men which went up, according to
their families amongst their tribes, after their several heads. 5 The
priests, the sons of Phinees the son of Aaron: Jesus the son of Josedec,
the son of Saraias, and [a]Joacim the son of Zorobabel, the son of Salathiel
of the house of David, out of the kindred of Phares of the tribe of Juda;
6 [b]who spoke wise sentences before Darius the king of Persia in the
second year of his reign, in the month Nisan, which is the first month.

7 And these are they of Jewry that came up from the captivity, where
they dwelt as strangers, whom Nabuchodonosor the king of Babylon
had carried away unto Babylon: 8 and they returned unto Jerusalem,
and to the other parts of Jewry, every man to his own city, who came
with Zorobabel, with Jesus, Nehemias, and [c]Zacharias, and Resaias,
Enenius, Mardocheus, Beelsarus, [d]Aspharasus, [e]Reelius, Roimus, and
Baana, their guides.

9 The number of them of the nation, and their governors: sons of
[f]Phoros, two thousand a hundred seventy and two; the sons of [g]Saphat,
[h]four hundred seventy and two; 10 the sons of Ares, seven hundred fifty
and six; 11 the sons of Phaath Moab, two thousand eight hundred and
twelve; 12 the sons of Elam, a thousand two hundred fifty and four; the
sons of [i]Zathui, nine hundred forty and five; the sons of [j]Corbe, seven
hundred and five; the sons of Bani, six hundred forty and eight; 13 the
sons of Bebai, six hundred twenty and three; the sons of [k]Sadas, three
thousand two hundred twenty and two; 14 the sons of Adonikam, six
hundred sixty and seven; the sons of [l]Bagoi, two thousand sixty and six;
the sons of Adin, four hundred fifty and four; 15 the sons of [m]Aterezias,
ninety and two; the sons of Ceilan and Azetas, threescore and seven;
the sons of Azuran, four hundred thirty and two; 16 the sons of Ananias,
a hundred and one; the sons of Arom, thirty two; and the sons of [n]Bassa,
three hundred twenty and three; the sons of Azephurith, a hundred
and two; 17 the sons of Meterus, three thousand and five; the sons of
[o]Bethlomon, a hundred twenty and three.

18 They of Netophah, fifty and five; they of Anathoth, a hundred fifty
and eight; they of [p]Bethsamos, forty and two; 19 they of [q]Kiriathiarius,
twenty and five; they of Caphira and Beroth, seven hundred forty and
three; they of Pira, seven hundred; 20 they of Chadias and Ammidioi,
four hundred twenty and two; they of [r]Cirama and [s]Gabdes, six hundred
twenty and one; 21 they of [t]Macalon, a hundred twenty and two; they of
[u]Betolius, fifty and two; the sons of [v]Nephis, a hundred fifty and six;
22 the sons of [w]Calamolalus and Onus, seven hundred twenty and five;
the sons of Jerechus, two hundred forty and five; 23 the sons of [x]Annaas,
three thousand three hundred and thirty.

24 The priests: the sons of [y]Jeddu, the son of Jesus, among the sons of
Sanasib, nine hundred seventy and two; the sons of [z]Meruth, a thousand fifty and two; 25 the sons of [a]Phassaron, a thousand forty and seven;
the sons of [b]Carme, [c]a thousand and seventeen.

26 The Levites: the sons of [d]Jessue, and Cadmiel, and Banuas, and Sudias, seventy and four.

27 The holy singers: the sons of Asaph, a hundred twenty and eight.

28 The porters: the sons of [e]Salum, the sons of [f]Jatal, the sons of Talmon, the sons of [g]Dacobi, the sons of [h]Teta, the sons of [i]Sami, in all a hundred thirty and nine.

29 The servants of the temple: the sons of [j]Esau, the sons of [k]Asipha, the sons of Tabaoth, the sons of [l]Ceras, the sons of [m]Sud, the sons of [n]Phaleas, the sons of Labana, the sons of [o]Graba, 30 the sons of [p]Acua, the sons of Uta, the sons of [q]Cetab, the sons of Agaba, the sons of [r]Subai, the sons of Anan, the sons of [s]Cathua, the sons of [t]Geddur, 31 the sons of [u]Airus, the sons of [v]Daisan, the sons of [w]Noeba, the sons of Chaseba, the sons of [x]Gazera, the sons of [y]Azia, the sons of [z]Phinees, the sons of Azara, the sons of [a]Bastai, the sons of [b]Asana, the sons of [c]Meani, the sons of [d]Naphisi, the sons of [e]Acub, the sons of [f]Acipha, the sons of [g]Assur, the sons of Pharacim, the sons of [h]Basaloth, 32 the sons of [i]Meeda, the sons of Coutha, the sons of [j]Charea, the sons of [k]Charcus, the sons of [l]Aserer, the sons of [m]Thomoi, the sons of [n]Nasith, the sons of Atipha. 33 The sons of the servants of Solomon: the sons of [o]Azaphion, the sons of [p]Pharira, the sons of [q]Jeeli, the sons of [r]Lozon, the sons of [s]Isdael, the sons of [t]Sapheth, 34 the sons of [u]Hagia, the sons of [v]Phacareth, the sons of Sabie, the sons of Sarothie, the sons of Masias, the sons of Gar, the sons of Addus, the sons of Suba, the sons of Apherra, the sons of Barodis, the sons of Sabat, the sons of Allom. 35 All the ministers of the temple, and the sons of the servants of Solomon, were three hundred seventy and two.

36 These came up from Thermeleth and Thelersas, Charaathalar leading them, and Aalar; 37 neither could they show their families, nor their stock, how they were of Israel: the sons of [w]Ladan, the sons of [x]Ban, the sons of [y]Necodan, six hundred fifty and two.

38 And of the priests that usurped the office of the priesthood, and were not found: the sons of [z]Obdia, the sons of [a]Accoz, the sons of [b]Addus, who married Augia one of the daughters of Berzelus, and was named after his name. 39 And when the description of the kindred of these men was sought in the register, and was not found, they were removed from executing the office of the priesthood: 40 for unto them said [c]Nehemias and Atharias, that they should not be partakers of the holy things, till there arose up a high priest clothed with [d]doctrine and truth.

41 So of Israel, from them of twelve years old and upward, they were all in number forty thousand, besides menservants and womenservants two thousand three hundred and sixty. 42 Their menservants and handmaids were seven thousand three hundred forty and seven: the singing men and singing women, two hundred forty and five: 43 four hundred thirty and five camels, seven thousand thirty and six horses, two hundred forty and five mules, five thousand five hundred twenty and five beasts used to the yoke.

44 And certain of the chief of their families, when they came to the

temple of God that is in Jerusalem, vowed to set up the house again in his own place according to their ability, ⁴⁵ and to give into the holy treasury of the works a thousand pounds of gold, five thousand of silver, and a hundred priestly vestments.

⁴⁶And so dwelt the priests and the Levites and the people in Jerusalem, and in the country; the singers also and the porters, and all Israel in their villages.

⁴⁷But when the seventh month was at hand, and when the children of Israel were every man in his own place, they came all together with one consent into the open place of the first gate which is towards the east. ⁴⁸Then stood up Jesus the son of Josedec, and his brethren the priests, and Zorobabel the son of Salathiel, and his brethren, and made ready the altar of the God of Israel, ⁴⁹to offer burnt sacrifices upon it, according as it is expressly commanded in the book of Moses the man of God. ⁵⁰And there were gathered unto them out of the other nations of the land, and they erected the altar upon his own place, because all the nations of the land were at enmity with them, and oppressed them, and they offered sacrifices according to the time, and burnt offerings to the Lord both morning and evening. ⁵¹Also they held the feast of tabernacles, as it is commanded in the law, and offered sacrifices daily, as was meet: ⁵²and after that, the continual oblations, and the sacrifice of the sabbaths, and of the new moons, and of all holy feasts. ⁵³And all they that had made any vow to God began to offer sacrifices to God from the first day of the seventh month, although the temple of the Lord was not yet built. ⁵⁴And they gave unto the masons and carpenters money, meat, and drink with cheerfulness. ⁵⁵Unto them of Sidon also and Tyre they gave carrs that they should bring cedar trees from Libanus, which should be brought by floats to the haven of Joppe, according as it was commanded them by Cyrus king of the Persians.

⁵⁶And in the second year and second month after his coming to the temple of God at Jerusalem began Zorobabel the son of Salathiel, and Jesus the son of Josedec, and their brethren, and the priests, and the Levites, and all they that were come unto Jerusalem out of the captivity: ⁵⁷and they laid the foundation of the house of God in the first day of the second month, in the second year after they were come to Jewry and Jerusalem. ⁵⁸And they appointed the Levites from twenty years old over the works of the Lord. Then stood up Jesus, and his sons and brethren, and Cadmiel his brother, and the sons of Madiabun, with the sons of Joda the son of Eliadun, with their sons and brethren, all Levites, with one accord setters forward of the business, labouring to advance the works in the house of God. So the workmen built the temple of the Lord.

⁵⁹And the priests stood arrayed in their vestments with musical instruments and trumpets, and the Levites the sons of Asaph had cymbals, ⁶⁰singing songs of thanksgiving, and praising the Lord according as David the king of Israel had ordained. ⁶¹And they sang with loud voices songs to the praise of the Lord, because his mercy and glory is for ever in all Israel. ⁶²And all the people sounded trumpets, and shouted with a

loud voice, singing songs of thanksgiving unto the Lord for the rearing up of the house of the Lord.

⁶³Also of the priests and Levites, and of the chief of their families, the ancients who had seen the former house came to the building of this with weeping and great crying. ⁶⁴But many with trumpets and joy shouted with loud voice, ⁶⁵insomuch that the trumpets might not be heard for the weeping of the people: yet the multitude sounded marvellously, so that it was heard afar off.

⁶⁶Wherefore when the enemies of the tribe of Juda and Benjamin heard it, they came to know what that noise of trumpets should mean. ⁶⁷And they perceived that they that were of the captivity did build the temple unto the Lord God of Israel. ⁶⁸So they went to Zorobabel and Jesus, and to the chief of the families, and said unto them, 'We will build together with you. ⁶⁹For we likewise, as you, do obey your Lord, and do sacrifice unto him from the days of Asbazareth the king of the Assyrians, who brought us hither.' ⁷⁰Then Zorobabel and Jesus and the chief of the families of Israel said unto them, 'It is not for us and you to build together a house unto the Lord our God. ⁷¹We ourselves alone will build unto the Lord of Israel, according as Cyrus the king of the Persians hath commanded us.' ⁷²But the heathen of the land lying heavy upon the inhabitants of Judea, and holding them strait, hindered their building: ⁷³and by their secret plots, and popular persuasions and commotions, they hindered the finishing of the building all the time that king Cyrus lived: so they were hindered from building for the space of two years, until the reign of Darius.

6 Now in the second year of the reign of Darius, Aggeus and Zacharias the son of Addo, the prophets, prophesied unto the Jews in Jewry and Jerusalem in the name of the Lord God of Israel, which was upon them. ²Then stood up Zorobabel the son of Salathiel, and Jesus the son of Josedec, and began to build the house of the Lord at Jerusalem, the prophets of the Lord being with them, and helping them. ³At the same time came unto them Sisinnes the governor of Syria and Phenice, with Sathrabuzanes and his companions, and said unto them, ⁴'By whose appointment do you build this house and this roof, and perform all the other things? and who are the workmen that perform these things?' ⁵Nevertheless the elders of the Jews obtained favour, because the Lord had visited the captivity; ⁶and they were not hindered from building until such time as signification was given unto Darius concerning them, and an answer received.

⁷The copy of the letters which Sisinnes, governor of Syria and Phenice, and Sathrabuzanes, with their companions, rulers in Syria and Phenice, wrote and sent unto Darius,

To king Darius, greeting. ⁸Let all things be known unto our lord the king, that being come into the country of Judea, and entered into the city of Jerusalem, we found in the city of Jerusalem the ancients of the Jews that were of the captivity, ⁹building a house unto the Lord, great and new, of hewn and costly stones, and the timber already laid upon the walls. ¹⁰And those works are done with great speed, and the work goeth on prosperously in their hands, and with all glory and diligence is it made. ¹¹Then asked we these elders, saying, 'By whose commandment build you this house, and lay the foundations of these works?' ¹²Therefore to the intent that we might give knowledge unto thee by writing, we demanded of them who were the chief doers, and we required of them the names in writing of their principal men.

¹³So they gave us this answer, 'We are the servants of the Lord which made heaven and earth. ¹⁴And as for this house, it was built many years ago by a king of Israel great and strong, and was finished. ¹⁵But when our fathers provoked God unto wrath, and sinned against the Lord of Israel which is in heaven, he gave them over into the power of Nabuchodonosor king of Babylon, of the Chaldees: ¹⁶who pulled down the house, and burnt it, and carried away the people captives unto Babylon. ¹⁷But in the first year that king Cyrus reigned over the country of Babylon, Cyrus the king wrote to build up this house. ¹⁸And the holy vessels of gold and of silver, that Nabuchodonosor had carried away out of the house at Jerusalem, and had set them in his own temple, those Cyrus the king brought forth again out of the temple at Babylon, and they were delivered to Zorobabel and to Sanabassarus the ruler, ¹⁹with commandment that he should carry away the same vessels, and put them in the temple at Jerusalem, and that the temple of the Lord should be built in his place. ²⁰Then the same Sanabassarus, being come hither, laid the foundations of the house of the Lord at Jerusalem, and from that time to this being still a-building, it is not yet fully ended.'

²¹Now therefore if it seem good unto the king, let search be made among the records of king Cyrus, ²²and if it be found that the building of the house of the Lord at Jerusalem hath been done with the consent of king Cyrus, and if our lord the king be so minded, let him signify unto us thereof.

²³Then commanded king Darius to seek among the records at Babylon: and so at Ecbatana the palace, which is in the country of Media, there was found a roll wherein these things were recorded.

²⁴In the first year of the reign of Cyrus, king Cyrus commanded that the house of the Lord at Jerusalem should be built again where they do sacrifice with continual fire: ²⁵whose height shall be sixty cubits, and the breadth sixty cubits, with three rows of hewn stones, and one row of new wood of that country; and the expenses thereof to be given out of the house of king Cyrus: ²⁶and that the holy vessels of the house of the Lord, both of gold and silver, that Nabuchodonosor took out of the house at Jerusalem, and brought to Babylon, should be restored to the house at Jerusalem, and be set in the place where they were before.

²⁷And also he commanded that Sisinnes the governor of Syria and Phenice, and Sathrabuzanes, and their companions, and those which were appointed rulers in Syria and Phenice should be careful not to meddle with the place, but suffer Zorobabel, the servant of the Lord, and governor of Judea, and the elders of the Jews, to build the house of the Lord in that place. ²⁸'I have commanded also to have it built up whole again, and that they look diligently to help those that be of the captivity of the Jews, till the house of the Lord be finished: ²⁹and out of of the tribute of Coelosyria and Phenice a portion carefully to be given these men for the sacrifices of the Lord, that is, to Zorobabel the governor, for bullocks, and rams, and lambs; ³⁰and also corn, salt, wine and oil, and that continually every year without further question, according as the priests that be in Jerusalem shall signify to be daily spent: ³¹that offerings may be made to the most high God for the king and for his children, and that they may pray for their lives.' ³²And he commanded that 'Whosoever should transgress, yea, or make light of anything afore spoken or written, out of his own house should a tree be taken, and he thereon be hanged, and all his goods seized for the king. ³³The Lord therefore, whose name is there called upon, utterly destroy every king and nation, that stretcheth out his hand to hinder or endamage that house of the Lord in Jerusalem. ³⁴I Darius the king have ordained that according unto these things it be done with diligence.'

7 Then Sisinnes the governor of Coelosyria and Phenice, and Sathrabuzanes, with their companions, following the commandments of king Darius, ²did very carefully oversee the holy works, assisting the ancients of the Jews and governors of the temple. ³And so the holy works prospered, when Aggeus and Zacharias the prophets prophesied. ⁴And they finished these things by the commandment of the Lord God of Israel, and with the consent of Cyrus, Darius and Artaxerxes, kings of Persia. ⁵And thus was the holy house finished in the three and twentieth day of the month Adar, in the sixth year of Darius king of the Persians.

⁶And the children of Israel, the priests, and the Levites, and others that were of the captivity, that were added unto them, did according to the things written in the book of Moses. ⁷And to the dedication of the temple of the Lord they offered a hundred bullocks, two hundred rams, four hundred lambs; ⁸and twelve goats for the sin of all Israel, according to the number of the chief of the tribes of Israel. ⁹The priests also and the Levites stood arrayed in their vestments according to their kindreds, in the services of the Lord God of Israel, according to the book of Moses: and the porters at every gate.

¹⁰And the children of Israel that were of the captivity held the passover the fourteenth day of the first month, after that the priests and the Levites were sanctified. ¹¹They that were of the captivity were not all sanctified together: but the Levites were all sanctified together. ¹²And so they offered the passover for all them of the captivity, and for their brethren the priests, and for themselves. ¹³And the children of

Israel that came out of the captivity did eat, even all they that had separated themselves from the abominations of the people of the land, and sought the Lord. ¹⁴And they kept the feast of unleavened bread seven days, making merry before the Lord, ¹⁵for that he had turned the counsel of the king of Assyria towards them, to strengthen their hands in the works of the Lord God of Israel.

8 And after these things, when Artaxerxes the king of the Persians reigned, came Esdras the son of Saraias, the son of Ezerias, the son of Helchiah, the son of Salum, ²the son of Sadduc, the son of Achitob, the son of Amarias, the son of Ozias, the son of Memeroth, the son of Zaraias, the son of Savias, the son of Boccas, the son of Abisum, the son of Phinees, the son of Eleazar, the son of Aaron the chief priest. ³This Esdras went up from Babylon, as a scribe being very ready in the law of Moses, that was given by the God of Israel. ⁴And the king did him honour: for he found grace in his sight in all his requests.

⁵There went up with him also certain of the children of Israel, of the priests, of the Levites, of the holy singers, porters, and ministers of the temple, unto Jerusalem, ⁶in the seventh year of the reign of Artaxerxes, in the fifth month, this was the king's seventh year; for they went from Babylon in the first day of the first month, and came to Jerusalem, according to the prosperous journey which the Lord gave them. ⁷For Esdras had very great skill, so that he omitted nothing of the law and commandments of the Lord, but taught all Israel the ordinances and judgements.

⁸Now the copy of the commission, which was written from Artaxerxes the king, and came to Esdras the priest and reader of the law of the Lord, is this that followeth.

⁹King Artaxerxes unto Esdras the priest and reader of the law of the Lord sendeth greeting. ¹⁰Having determined to deal graciously, I have given order, that such of the nation of the Jews, and of the priests and Levites being within our realm, as are willing and desirous, should go with thee unto Jerusalem. ¹¹As many therefore as have a mind thereunto, let them depart with thee, as it hath seemed good both to me and my seven friends the counsellors, ¹²that they may look unto the affairs of Judea and Jerusalem, agreeably to that which is in the law of the Lord; ¹³and carry the gifts unto the Lord of Israel to Jerusalem, which I and my friends have vowed, and all the gold and silver that in the country of Babylon can be found, to the Lord in Jerusalem, ¹⁴with that also which is given of the people for the temple of the Lord their God at Jerusalem: and that silver and gold may be collected for bullocks, rams, and lambs, and things thereunto appertaining, ¹⁵to the end that they may offer sacrifices unto the Lord upon the altar of the Lord their God, which is in Jerusalem. ¹⁶And whatsoever thou and thy brethren will do with the silver and gold, that do according to the will of thy God. ¹⁷And the holy vessels of the Lord which are given thee for the use of the temple of thy

God which is in Jerusalem, thou shalt set before God in Jerusalem. [18]And whatsoever thing else thou shalt remember for the use of the temple of thy God, thou shalt give it out of the king's treasury.

[19]And I king Artaxerxes have also commanded the keepers of the treasures in Syria and Phenice, that whatsoever Esdras the priest and the reader of the law of the most high God shall send for, they should give it him with speed, [20]to the sum of a hundred talents of silver: likewise also of wheat even to a hundred cors, and a hundred pieces of wine, and other things in abundance. [21]Let all things be performed after the law of God diligently unto the most high God, that wrath come not upon the kingdom of the king and his sons. [22]I command you also, that ye require no tax, nor any other imposition of any of the priests, or Levites, or holy singers, or porters, or ministers of the temple, or of any that have doings in this temple, and that no man have authority to impose anything upon them.

[23]And thou, Esdras, according to the wisdom of God ordain judges and justices, that they may judge in all Syria and Phenice all those that know the law of thy God; and those that know it not thou shalt teach. [24]And whosoever shall transgress the law of thy God, and of the king, shall be punished diligently, whether it be by death, or other punishment, by penalty of money, or by imprisonment.

[25]Then said Esdras the scribe, 'Blessed be the only Lord God of my fathers, who hath put these things into the heart of the king, to glorify his house that is in Jerusalem: [26]and hath honoured me in the sight of the king, and his counsellors, and all his friends and nobles. [27]Therefore was I encouraged by the help of the Lord my God, and gathered together men of Israel to go up with me.

[28]'And these are the chief according to their families and several dignities, that went up with me from Babylon in the reign of king Artaxerxes: [29]of the sons of Phinees, Gerson: of the sons of Ithamar, [a]Gamael: of the sons of David, [b]Lettus [c]the son of Sechenias: [30]of the sons of Pharez, Zacharias; and with him were counted a hundred and fifty men: [31]of the sons of Pahath Moab, Eliaonias, the son of [d]Zaraias, and with him two hundred men: [32][e]of the sons of Zathoe, Sechenias the son of Jezelus, and with him three hundred men: of the sons of Adin, Obeth the son of Jonathan, and with him [f]two hundred and fifty men: [33]of the sons of Elam, Josias son of [g]Gotholias, and with him seventy men: [34]of the sons of Saphatias, [h]Zaraias son of Michael, and with him [i]threescore and ten men: [35]of the sons of Joab, [j]Abadias son of [k]Jezelus, and with him two hundred and [l]twelve men: [36][m]of the sons of Banid, Assalimoth son of Josaphias, and with him a hundred and threescore men: [37]of the sons of Babi, Zacharias son of Bebai, and with him twenty and eight men: [38]of the sons of [n]Astath, Johannes son of [o]Acatan, and with him a hundred and ten men: [39]of the sons of Adonikam, the last, and these are the names of them, Eliphalet, Jeuel, and [p]Samaias, and

with them ᵠseventy men: ⁴⁰of the sons of ʳBago, Uthi the son of Istalcurus, and with him seventy men.

⁴¹'And these I gathered together ˢto the river called Theras, where we pitched our tents three days: and then ᵗI surveyed them, ⁴²but when I had found there none of the priests and Levites, ⁴³then sent I unto Eleazar, and ᵘIduel, and ᵛMasman, ⁴⁴and Alnathan, and Mamaias, and ʷJoribus, and Nathan, Eunatan, Zacharias, and Mosollamon, principal men and learned. ⁴⁵And I bade them that they should go unto ˣSaddeus the captain, ʸwho was in the place of ᶻthe treasury: ⁴⁶and commanded them that they should speak unto ᵃDaddeus, and to ᵇhis brethren, and to the treasurers in that place, to send us such men as might execute the priests' office in the house of the Lord. ⁴⁷And by the mighty hand of our Lord they brought unto us skilful men of the sons of ᶜMoli the son of Levi, the son of Israel, ᵈAsebebia, and his sons, and his brethren, who were eighteen. ⁴⁸ᵉAnd Asebia, and Annuus, and Osaias his brother, of the sons of Channuneus, and their sons were twenty men. ⁴⁹And of the servants of the temple whom David had ordained, and the principal men for the service of the Levites, to wit, the servants of the temple, two hundred and twenty, the catalogue of whose names was shown.

⁵⁰'And there I vowed a fast unto the young men before our Lord, to desire of him a prosperous journey both for us and them that were with us, for our children, and for the cattle: ⁵¹for I was ashamed to ask the king footmen, and horsemen, and conduct for safeguard against our adversaries. ⁵²For we had said unto the king, that the power of the Lord our God should be with them that seek him, to support them in all ways. ⁵³And again we besought our Lord as touching these things, and found him favourable unto us.

⁵⁴'Then I separated twelve of the chief of the priests, Esebrias and Assanias, and ten men of their brethren with them. ⁵⁵And I weighed them the gold, and the silver, and the holy vessels of the house of our Lord, which the king, and his council, and the princes, and all Israel had given. ⁵⁶And when I had weighed it, I delivered unto them six hundred and fifty talents of silver, and silver vessels of a hundred talents, and a hundred talents of gold, ⁵⁷and twenty golden vessels, and twelve vessels of brass, even of fine brass, glittering like gold.

⁵⁸'And I said unto them, "Both you are holy unto the Lord, and the vessels are holy, and the gold and the silver is a vow unto the Lord, the Lord of our fathers. ⁵⁹Watch ye, and keep them till ye deliver them to the chief of the priests and Levites, and to the principal men of the families of Israel in Jerusalem into the chambers of the house of our God." ⁶⁰So the priests and the Levites, who had received the silver and the gold and the vessels, brought them unto Jerusalem into the temple of the Lord.

⁶¹'And from the river Theras we departed the twelfth day of the first month, and came to Jerusalem by the mighty hand of our Lord, which was with us: and from the beginning of our journey the Lord delivered us from every enemy, and so we came to Jerusalem. ⁶²And when we had been there three days, the gold and silver that was weighed was deliv-

ered in the house of our Lord on the fourth day unto Marmoth the priest the son of Iri. ⁶³And with him was Eleazar the son of Phinees, and with them were Josabad the son of Jesu and Moeth the son of Sabban, Levites: all was delivered them by number and weight. ⁶⁴And all the weight of them was written up the same hour.

⁶⁵'Moreover they that were come out of the captivity offered sacrifice unto the Lord God of Israel, even twelve bullocks for all Israel, fourscore and sixteen rams, ⁶⁶threescore and twelve lambs, goats for a peace offering, twelve, all of them a sacrifice to the Lord. ⁶⁷And they delivered the king's commandments unto the king's stewards, and to the governors of Coelosyria and Phenice, and they honoured the people and the temple of God.

⁶⁸'Now when these things were done, the rulers came unto me, and said, ⁶⁹"The nation of Israel, the princes, the priests and Levites have not put away from them the strange people of the land, nor the pollutions of the Gentiles, to wit, of the Canaanites, Hittites, Pheresites, Jebusites, and the Moabites, Egyptians, and Edomites. ⁷⁰For both they and their sons have married with their daughters, and the holy seed is mixed with the strange people of the land; and from the beginning of this matter the rulers and the great men have been partakers of this iniquity."

⁷¹'And as soon as I had heard these things, I rent my clothes, and the holy garment, and pulled off the hair from off my head and beard, and sat me down sad and very heavy. ⁷²So all they that were then moved at the word of the Lord God of Israel assembled unto me, whilst I mourned for the iniquity: but I sat still full of heaviness until the evening sacrifice. ⁷³Then rising up from the fast with my clothes and the holy garment rent, and bowing my knees, and stretching forth my hands unto the Lord, ⁷⁴I said, "O Lord, I am confounded and ashamed before thy face; ⁷⁵for our sins are multiplied above our heads, and our ignorances have reached up unto heaven. ⁷⁶For ever since the time of our fathers we have been and are in great sin, even unto this day. ⁷⁷And for our sins and our fathers' we with our brethren and our kings and our priests were given up unto the kings of the earth, to the sword, and to captivity, and for a prey with shame, unto this day. ⁷⁸And now in some measure hath mercy been shown unto us from thee, O Lord, that there should be left us a root and a name in the place of thy sanctuary; ⁷⁹and to discover unto us a light in the house of the Lord our God, and to give us food in the time of our servitude. ⁸⁰Yea, when we were in bondage, we were not forsaken of our Lord; but he made us gracious before the kings of Persia, so that they gave us food; ⁸¹yea, and honoured the temple of our Lord, and raised up the desolate Sion, that they have given us a sure abiding in Jewry and Jerusalem. ⁸²And now, O Lord, what shall we say, having these things? for we have transgressed thy commandments, which thou gavest by the hand of thy servants the prophets, saying, ⁸³'That the land, which ye enter into to possess as a heritage, is a land polluted with the pollutions of the strangers of the land, and they have filled it with their uncleanness. ⁸⁴Therefore now

shall ye not join your daughters unto their sons, neither shall ye take their daughters unto your sons. [85]Moreover you shall never seek to have peace with them, that ye may be strong, and eat the good things of the land, and that ye may leave the inheritance of the land unto your children for evermore.' [86]And all that is befallen is done unto us for our wicked works and great sins: for thou, O Lord, didst make our sins light, [87]and didst give unto us such a root: but we have turned back again to transgress thy law, and to mingle ourselves with the uncleanness of the nations of the land. [88]Mightest not thou be angry with us to destroy us, till thou hadst left us neither root, seed, nor name? [89]Lord of Israel, thou art true: for we are left a root this day. [90]Behold, now are we before thee in our iniquities, for we cannot stand any longer by reason of these things before thee."'

[91]And as Esdras in his prayer made his confession, weeping, and lying flat upon the ground before the temple, there gathered unto him from Jerusalem a very great multitude of men and women and children: for there was great weeping among the multitude. [92]Then Jechonias the son of Jeelus, one of the sons of Israel, called out and said, 'O Esdras, we have sinned against the Lord God, we have married strange women of the nations of the land, and now is all Israel aloft. [93]Let us make an oath to the Lord, that we will put away all our wives, which we have taken of the heathen, with their children, [94]like as thou hast decreed, and as many as do obey the law of the Lord. [95]Arise, and put in execution: for to thee doth this matter appertain, and we will be with thee: do valiantly.' [96]So Esdras arose, and took an oath of the chief of the priests and Levites of all Israel to do after these things; and so they swore.

9 Then Esdras rising from the court of the temple went to the chamber of Joanan the son of Eliasib, [2]and remained there, and did eat no meat nor drink water, mourning for the great iniquities of the multitude.

[3]And there was a proclamation in all Jewry and Jerusalem to all them that there were of the captivity, that they should be gathered together at Jerusalem: [4]and that whosoever met not there within two or three days, according as the elders that bore rule appointed, their cattle should be seized to the use of the temple, and himself cast out from them that were of the captivity. [5]And in three days were all they of the tribe of Juda and Benjamin gathered together at Jerusalem the twentieth day of the ninth month. [6]And all the multitude sat trembling in the broad court of the temple because of the present foul weather.

[7]So Esdras arose up, and said unto them, 'Ye have transgressed the law in marrying strange wives, thereby to increase the sins of Israel. [8]And now by confessing give glory unto the Lord God of our fathers, [9]and do his will, and separate yourselves from the heathen of the land, and from the strange women.'

[10]Then cried the whole multitude, and said with a loud voice, 'Like as thou hast spoken, so will we do. [11]But forasmuch as the people are many, and it is foul weather, so that we cannot stand without, and this is not a work of a day or two, seeing our sin in these things is spread far:

[12]therefore let the rulers of the multitude stay, and let all them of our habitations that have strange wives come at the time appointed, [13]and with them the rulers and judges of every place, till we turn away the wrath of the Lord from us for this matter.'

[14]Then Jonathan the son of Azael and Ezechias the son of Theocanus accordingly took this matter upon them: and Mosollam and Levis and Sabbatheus helped them. [15]And they that were of the captivity did according to all these things. [16]And Esdras the priest chose unto him the principal men of their families, all by name: and in the first day of the tenth month they sat together to examine the matter. [17]So their cause that held strange wives was brought to an end in the first day of the first month.

[18]And of the priests that were come together, and had strange wives, there were found: [19]of the sons of Jesus the son of Josedec, and his brethren, [a]Matthelas, and Eleazar, and [b]Joribus, and [c]Joadanus. [20]And they gave their hands to put away their wives, and to offer [d]rams to make reconcilement for their [e]errors. [21]And of the sons of Emmer, Ananias, and Zabdeus, and [f]Eanes, and [g]Sameius, and [h]Hiereel, and [i]Azarias. [22]And of the sons of [j]Phaisur, Elionas, Massias, Ismael, and Nathanael, and [k]Ocidelus, and [l]Talsas. [23]And of the Levites: Jozabad, and Semis, and [m]Colius, who was called [n]Calitas, and [o]Patheus, and Judas, and Jonas. [24]Of the holy singers: [p]Eleazurus, Bacchurus. [25]Of the porters: Sallumus, and [q]Tolbanes. [26]Of them of Israel, of the sons of [r]Phoros, [s]Hiermas, and [t]Eddias, and [u]Melchias, and Maelus, and Eleazar, and [v]Asibias, and Baanias. [27]Of the sons of Ela, Matthanias, Zacharias, and [w]Hierielus, and Hieremoth, and [x]Aedias. [28]And of the sons of [y]Zamoth, [z]Eliadas, [a]Elisimus, [b]Othonias, Jarimoth, and [c]Sabatus, and [d]Sardeus. [29]Of the sons of Bebai, Johannes, and Ananias, and [e]Josabad, and [f]Amatheis. [30]Of the sons of [g]Mani, [h]Olamus, [i]Mamuchus, [j]Jedeus, Jasubus, [k]Jasael, and Hieremoth. [31][l]And of the sons of Addi, Naathus, and Moosias, Lacunus, and Naidus, and Mathanias, and Sesthel, Balnuus, and Manasseas. [32]And of the sons of Annas, Elionas, and Aseas, and Melchias, and Sabbeus, and Simon Chosameus. [33]And of the sons of Asom, [m]Altaneus, and [n]Matthias, and [o]Bannaia, Eliphalat, and Manasses, and Semei. [34]And of the sons of Maani, Jeremias, Momdis, Omaerus, Juel, Mabdai, and Pelias, and Anos, Carabasion, and Enasibus, and Mamnitanaimus, Eliasis, Bannus, Eliali, Samis, Selemias, Nathanias. And of the sons of Ozora, Sesis, Esril, Azaelus, Samatus, Zambis, Josephus. [35]And of the sons of Ethma, Mazitias, Zabadaias, Edes, Juel, Banaias. [36]All these had taken strange wives, and they put them away with their children.

[37]And the priests and Levites, and they that were of Israel dwelt in Jerusalem, and in the country, in the first day of the seventh month: so the children of Israel were in their habitations. [38]And the whole multitude came together with one accord into the broad place of the holy porch toward the east: [39]And they spoke unto Esdras the priest and reader, that he would bring the law of Moses, that was given of the Lord God of Israel. [40]So Esdras the chief priest brought the law unto the

whole multitude from man to woman, and to all the priests, to hear the law in the first day of the seventh month. ⁴¹And he read in the broad court before the holy porch from morning unto midday, before both men and women; and all the multitude gave heed unto the law.

⁴²And Esdras the priest and reader of the law stood up upon a pulpit of wood, which was made for that purpose. ⁴³And there stood up by him Mattathias, Sammus, Ananias, Azarias, Urias, Ezecias, Balasamus, upon the right hand. ⁴⁴And upon his left hand stood Phaldaius, Misael, Melchias, Lothasubus, and Nabarias.

⁴⁵Then took Esdras the book of the law before the multitude: for he sat honourably in the first place in the sight of them all. ⁴⁶And when he opened the law, they stood all straight up. So Esdras blessed the Lord God most High, the God of hosts, Almighty. ⁴⁷And all the people answered, 'Amen'; and lifting up their hands they fell to the ground, and worshipped the Lord. ⁴⁸Also Jesus, Anus, Sarabias, Adinus, Jacubus, Sabateus, Auteas, Maianeas, and Calitas, Azarias, and Joazabdus, and Ananias, Biatas, the Levites taught the law of the Lord, making them withal to understand it.

⁴⁹Then spoke Attharates unto Esdras the chief priest and reader, and to the Levites that taught the multitude, even to all, saying, ⁵⁰'This day is holy unto the Lord' (for they all wept when they heard the law); ⁵¹'go then, and eat the fat, and drink the sweet, and send part to them that have nothing; ⁵²for this day is holy unto the Lord: and be not sorrowful; for the Lord will bring you to honour.' ⁵³So the Levites published all things to the people, saying, 'This day is holy to the Lord, be not sorrowful'. ⁵⁴Then went they their way, every one to eat and drink, and make merry, and to give part to them that had nothing, and to make great cheer, ⁵⁵because they understood the words wherein they were instructed, and for the which they had been assembled.

THE SECOND BOOK OF
ESDRAS

1 The second book of the prophet Esdras, the son of Saraias, the son of Azarias, the son of Helchias, the son of Sadamias, the son of Sadoc, the son of Achitob, ²the son of Achias, the son of Phinees, the son of Heli, the son of Amarias, the son of Aziei, the son of Marimoth, the son of Arna, the son of Ozias, the son of Borith, the son of Abisei, the son of Phinees, the son of Eleazar, ³the son of Aaron, of the tribe of Levi, which was captive in the land of the Medes, in the reign of Artaxerxes king of the Persians.

⁴And the word of the Lord came unto me, saying, ⁵'Go thy way, and show my people their sinful deeds, and their children their wickedness which they have done against me, that they may tell their children's children, ⁶because the sins of their fathers are increased in them: for they have forgotten me, and have offered unto strange gods. ⁷Am not I even he that brought them out of the land of Egypt, from the house of bondage? but they have provoked me unto wrath, and despised my counsels. ⁸Pull thou off then the hair of thy head, and cast all evil upon them, for they have not been obedient unto my law, but it is a rebellious people. ⁹How long shall I forbear them, unto whom I have done so much good? ¹⁰Many kings have I destroyed for their sakes; Pharaoh with his servants and all his power have I smitten down. ¹¹All the nations have I destroyed before them, and in the east I have scattered the people of two provinces, even of Tyrus and Sidon, and have slain all their enemies.

¹²'Speak thou therefore unto them, saying, "Thus saith the Lord, ¹³'I led you through the sea, and in the beginning gave you a large and safe passage, I gave you Moses for a leader, and Aaron for a priest. ¹⁴I gave you light in a pillar of fire, and great wonders have I done among you, yet have you forgotten me,' saith the Lord.

¹⁵'"Thus saith the Almighty Lord, 'The quails were as a token for you; I gave you tents for your safeguard: nevertheless you murmured there, ¹⁶and triumphed not in my name for the destruction of your enemies, but ever to this day do ye yet murmur. ¹⁷Where are the benefits that I have done for you? when you were hungry and thirsty in the wilderness, did you not cry unto me, ¹⁸saying, "Why hast thou brought us into this wilderness to kill us? It had been better for us to have served the Egyptians, than to die in this wilderness." ¹⁹Then had I pity upon your mournings, and gave you manna to eat; so ye did eat angels' bread. ²⁰When ye were thirsty, did I not cleave the rock, and waters flowed out to your fill? for the heat I covered you with the leaves of the trees. ²¹I divided amongst you a fruitful land, I cast out the Canaanites, the Pherezites, and the Philistines before you: what shall I yet do more for you?' saith the Lord.

²²'"Thus saith the Almighty Lord, 'When you were in the wilderness, in the river of the Amorites, being athirst, and blaspheming my name, ²³I gave you not fire for your blasphemies, but cast a tree in the water, and made the river sweet. ²⁴What shall I do unto thee, O Jacob? thou, Juda, wouldst not obey me: I will turn me to other nations, and unto those will I give my name, that they may keep my statutes. ²⁵Seeing ye have forsaken me, I will forsake you also: when ye desire me to be gracious unto you, I shall have no mercy upon you. ²⁶Whensoever you shall call upon me, I will not hear you: for ye have defiled your hands with blood, and your feet are swift to commit manslaughter. ²⁷Ye have not as it were forsaken me, but your own selves,' saith the Lord.

²⁸'"Thus saith the Almighty Lord, 'Have I not prayed you as a father his sons, as a mother her daughters, and a nurse her young babes, ²⁹that ye would be my people, and I should be your God; that ye would be my children, and I should be your father? ³⁰I gathered you together, as a hen gathereth her chickens under her wings: but now, what shall I do unto you? I will cast you out from my face. ³¹When you offer unto me, I will turn my face from you: for your solemn feast days, your new moon, and your circumcisions, have I forsaken. ³²I sent unto you my servants the prophets, whom ye have taken and slain, and torn their bodies in pieces, whose blood I will require of your hands,' saith the Lord.

³³'"Thus saith the Almighty Lord, 'Your house is desolate, I will cast you out as the wind doth stubble. ³⁴And your children shall not be fruitful: for they have despised my commandment, and done the thing that is evil before me. ³⁵Your houses will I give to a people that shall come, which not having heard of me yet shall believe me; to whom I have shown no signs, yet they shall do that I have commanded them. ³⁶They have seen no prophets, yet they shall call their sins to remembrance, and acknowledge them. ³⁷I take to witness the grace of the people to come, whose little ones rejoice in gladness: and though they have not seen me with bodily eyes, yet in spirit they believe the thing that I say. ³⁸And now, brother, behold what glory: and see the people that cometh from the east: ³⁹unto whom I will give for leaders, Abraham, Isaac, and Jacob, Oseas, Amos, and Micheas, Joel, Abdias, and Jonas, ⁴⁰Nahum, and Abacuc, Sophonias, Aggeus, Zachary, and Malachy, which is called also an angel of the Lord.'

2 '"Thus saith the Lord, 'I brought this people out of bondage, and I gave them my commandments by my servants the prophets, whom they would not hear, but despised my counsels. ²The mother that bore them saith unto them, "Go your way, ye children, for I am a widow and forsaken. ³I brought you up with gladness, but with sorrow and heaviness have I lost you: for ye have sinned before the Lord your God, and done that thing that is evil before him. ⁴But what shall I now do unto you? I am a widow and forsaken: go your way, O my children, and ask mercy of the Lord." ⁵As for me, O father, I call upon thee for a witness over the mother of these children, which would not keep my covenant, ⁶that thou bring them to confusion, and their mother to a spoil, that there may be no offspring of them. ⁷Let them be scattered abroad

among the heathen, let their names be put out of the earth: for they have despised my covenant.

⁸'"Woe be unto thee, Assur, thou that hidest the unrighteous in thee! O thou wicked people, remember what I did unto Sodom and Gomorrha; ⁹whose land lieth in clods of pitch and heaps of ashes: even so also will I do unto them that hear me not,' saith the Almighty Lord. ¹⁰Thus saith the Lord unto Esdras, 'Tell my people that I will give them the kingdom of Jerusalem, which I would have given unto Israel. ¹¹Their glory also will I take unto me, and give these the everlasting tabernacles, which I had prepared for them. ¹²They shall have the tree of life for an ointment of sweet savour; they shall neither labour, nor be weary. ¹³Go, and ye shall receive: pray for few days unto you, that they may be shortened: the kingdom is already prepared for you: watch. ¹⁴Take heaven and earth to witness; for I have broken the evil in pieces, and created the good: for I live,' saith the Lord.

¹⁵'"Mother, embrace thy children, and bring them up with gladness, make their feet as fast as a pillar: for I have chosen thee,' saith the Lord. ¹⁶'And those that be dead will I raise up again from their places, and bring them out of the graves: for I have known my name in Israel. ¹⁷Fear not, thou mother of the children: for I have chosen thee,' saith the Lord. ¹⁸'For thy help I will send my servants Esay and Jeremy, after whose counsel I have sanctified and prepared for thee twelve trees laden with diverse fruits, ¹⁹and as many fountains flowing with milk and honey, and seven mighty mountains, whereupon there grow roses and lilies, whereby I will fill thy children with joy.

²⁰'"Do right to the widow, judge for the fatherless, give to the poor, defend the orphan, clothe the naked, ²¹heal the broken and the weak, laugh not a lame man to scorn, defend the maimed, and let the blind man come into the sight of my clearness. ²²Keep the old and young within thy walls. ²³Wheresoever thou findest the dead, take them and bury them, and I will give thee the first place in my resurrection. ²⁴Abide still, O my people, and take thy rest, for thy quietness shall come. ²⁵Nourish thy children, O thou good nurse, establish their feet. ²⁶As for the servants whom I have given thee, there shall not one of them perish; for I will require them from among thy number. ²⁷Be not weary, for when the day of trouble and heaviness cometh, others shall weep and be sorrowful, but thou shalt be merry and have abundance. ²⁸The heathen shall envy thee, but they shall be able to do nothing against thee,' saith the Lord. ²⁹'My hands shall cover thee, so that thy children shall not see hell. ³⁰Be joyful, O thou mother, with thy children, for I will deliver thee,' saith the Lord. ³¹'Remember thy children that sleep, for I shall bring them out of the sides of the earth, and show mercy unto them: for I am merciful,' saith the Lord Almighty. ³²'Embrace thy children until I come and show mercy unto them: for my wells run over, and my grace shall not fail.'"'

³³I Esdras received a charge of the Lord upon the mount Oreb, that I should go unto Israel; but when I came unto them, they set me at nought, and despised the commandment of the Lord. ³⁴And therefore I

say unto you, O ye heathen, that hear and understand, 'Look for your Shepherd, he shall give you everlasting rest; for he is nigh at hand, that shall come in the end of the world. ³⁵Be ready to the reward of the kingdom, for the everlasting light shall shine upon you for evermore. ³⁶Flee the shadow of this world, receive the joyfulness of your glory: I testify my Saviour openly. ³⁷O receive the gift that is given you, and be glad, giving thanks unto him that hath called you to the heavenly kingdom. ³⁸Arise up and stand, behold the number of those that be sealed in the feast of the Lord: ³⁹which are departed from the shadow of the world, and have received glorious garments of the Lord. ⁴⁰Take thy number, O Sion, and shut up those of thine that are clothed in white, which have fulfilled the law of the Lord. ⁴¹The number of thy children whom thou longedst for, is fulfilled: beseech the power of the Lord, that thy people which have been called from the beginning, may be hallowed.'

⁴²I Esdras saw upon the mount Sion a great people, whom I could not number, and they all praised the Lord with songs. ⁴³And in the midst of them there was a young man of a high stature, taller than all the rest, and upon every one of their heads he set crowns, and was more exalted, which I marvelled at greatly. ⁴⁴So I asked the angel, and said, 'Sir, what are these?' ⁴⁵He answered and said unto me, 'These be they that have put off the mortal clothing, and put on the immortal, and have confessed the name of God: now are they crowned, and receive palms'. ⁴⁶Then said I unto the angel, 'What young person is it that crowneth them, and giveth them palms in their hands?' ⁴⁷So he answered and said unto me, 'It is the Son of God, whom they have confessed in the world'. Then began I greatly to commend them that stood so stiffly for the name of the Lord. ⁴⁸Then the angel said unto me, 'Go thy way, and tell my people what manner of things, and how great wonders of the Lord thy God thou hast seen'.

3 In the thirtieth year after the ruin of the city I was in Babylon, and lay troubled upon my bed, and my thoughts came up over my heart: ²for I saw the desolation of Sion, and the wealth of them that dwelt at Babylon. ³And my spirit was sore moved, so that I began to speak words full of fear to the most High, and said, ⁴'O Lord, who bearest rule, thou spokest at the beginning, when thou didst plant the earth, and that thyself alone, and commandedst the people, ⁵and gavest a body unto Adam without soul, which was the workmanship of thy hands, and didst breathe into him the breath of life, and he was made living before thee. ⁶And thou leddest him into paradise, which thy right hand had planted, before ever the earth came forward. ⁷And unto him thou gavest commandment to love thy way: which he transgressed, and immediately thou appointedst death in him and in his generations, of whom came nations, tribes, people, and kindreds out of number. ⁸And every people walked after their own will, and did wonderful things before thee, and despised thy commandments. ⁹And again in process of time thou broughtest the flood upon those that dwelt in the world, and destroyedst them. ¹⁰And it came to pass in every of them, that as death was to Adam, so was the flood to these. ¹¹Nevertheless one of

them thou leftest, namely, Noah with his household, of whom came all righteous men.

¹²'And it happened, that when they that dwelt upon the earth began to multiply, and had gotten them many children, and were a great people, they began again to be more ungodly than the first ¹³Now when they lived so wickedly before thee, thou didst choose thee a man from among them, whose name was Abraham. ¹⁴Him thou lovedst, and unto him only thou showedst thy will: ¹⁵and madest an everlasting covenant with him, promising him that thou wouldst never forsake his seed. ¹⁶And unto him thou gavest Isaac, and unto Isaac also thou gavest Jacob and Esau. As for Jacob, thou didst choose him to thee, and put by Esau: and so Jacob became a great multitude.

¹⁷'And it came to pass, that when thou leddest his seed out of Egypt, thou broughtest them up to the mount Sinai. ¹⁸And bowing the heavens, thou didst set fast the earth, movedst the whole world, and madest the depth to tremble, and troubledst the men of that age. ¹⁹And thy glory went through four gates, of fire, and of earthquake, and of wind, and of cold, that thou mightest give the law unto the seed of Jacob, and diligence unto the generation of Israel. ²⁰And yet tookest thou not away from them a wicked heart, that thy law might bring forth fruit in them. ²¹For the first Adam bearing a wicked heart transgressed, and was overcome; and so be all they that are born of him. ²²Thus infirmity was made permanent; and the law also in the heart of the people with the malignity of the root, so that the good departed away, and the evil abode still.

²³'So the times passed away, and the years were brought to an end: then didst thou raise thee up a servant, called David, ²⁴whom thou commandedst to build a city unto thy name, and to offer incense and oblations unto thee therein. ²⁵When this was done many years, then they that inhabited the city forsook thee, ²⁶and in all things did even as Adam and all his generations had done, for they also had a wicked heart: ²⁷and so thou gavest the city over into the hands of thy enemies.

²⁸'Are their deeds then any better that inhabit Babylon, that they should therefore have the dominion over Sion? ²⁹For when I came thither, and had seen impieties without number, then my soul saw many evil-doers in this thirtieth year, so that my heart failed me. ³⁰For I have seen how thou sufferest them sinning, and hast spared wicked-doers: and hast destroyed thy people, and hast preserved thy enemies, and hast not signified it. ³¹I do not remember how this way may be left: are they then of Babylon better than they of Sion? ³²or is there any other people that knoweth thee besides Israel? or what generation hath so believed thy covenants as Jacob? ³³And yet their reward appeareth not, and their labour hath no fruit: for I have gone here and there through the heathen, and I see that they flow in wealth, and think not upon thy commandments. ³⁴Weigh thou therefore our wickedness now in the balance, and theirs also that dwell in the world: and so shall thy name nowhere be found but in Israel. ³⁵Or when was it that they which dwell upon the earth have not sinned in thy sight? or

what people hath so kept thy commandments? ³⁶Thou shalt find that Israel by name hath kept thy precepts: but not the heathen.'

4 And the angel that was sent unto me, whose name was Uriel, gave me an answer, ²and said, 'Thy heart hath gone too far in this world, and thinkest thou to comprehend the way of the most High?' ³Then said I, 'Yea, my Lord'. And he answered me, and said, 'I am sent to show thee three ways, and to set forth three similitudes before thee. ⁴Whereof if thou canst declare me one, I will show thee also the way that thou desirest to see, and I shall show thee from whence the wicked heart cometh.' ⁵And I said, 'Tell on, my Lord'. Then said he unto me, 'Go thy way, weigh me the weight of the fire, or measure me the blast of the wind, or call me again the day that is past'. ⁶Then answered I and said, 'What man is able to do that, that thou shouldst ask such things of me?' ⁷And he said unto me, 'If I should ask thee how great dwellings are in the midst of the sea, or how many springs are in the beginning of the deep, or how many springs are above the firmament, or which are the outgoings of paradise: ⁸peradventure thou wouldst say unto me, "I never went down into the deep, nor as yet into hell, neither did I ever climb up into heaven". ⁹Nevertheless now have I asked thee but only of the fire and wind, and of the day wherethrough thou hast passed, and of things from which thou canst not be separated, and yet canst thou give me no answer of them.'

¹⁰He said moreover unto me, 'Thy own things, and such as are grown up with thee, canst thou not know. ¹¹How should thy vessel then be able to comprehend the way of the Highest, and, the world being now outwardly corrupted, to understand the corruption that is evident in my sight?' ¹²Then said I unto him, 'It were better that we were not at all, than that we should live still in wickedness, and to suffer, and not to know wherefore'. ¹³He answered me and said, 'I went into a forest into a plain, and the trees took counsel, ¹⁴and said, "Come, let us go and make war against the sea, that it may depart away before us, and that we may make us more woods". ¹⁵The floods of the sea also in like manner took counsel, and said, "Come, let us go up and subdue the woods of the plain, that there also we may make us another country". ¹⁶The thought of the wood was in vain, for the fire came and consumed it. ¹⁷The thought of the floods of the sea came likewise to nought, for the sand stood up and stopped them. ¹⁸If thou wert judge now betwixt these two, whom wouldst thou begin to justify, or whom wouldst thou condemn?'

¹⁹I answered and said, 'Verily it is a foolish thought that they both have devised, for the ground is given unto the wood, and the sea also hath his place to bear his floods'. ²⁰Then answered he me, and said, 'Thou hast given a right judgement, but why judgest thou not thyself also? ²¹For like as the ground is given unto the wood, and the sea to his floods: even so they that dwell upon the earth may understand nothing but that which is upon the earth: and he that dwelleth above the heavens may only understand the things that are above the height of the heavens.'

²²Then answered I and said, 'I beseech thee, O Lord, let me have understanding. ²³For it was not my mind to be curious of the high things, but

of such as pass by us daily, namely, wherefore Israel is given up as a reproach to the heathen, and for what cause the people whom thou hast loved is given over unto ungodly nations, and why the law of our forefathers is brought to nought, and the written covenants come to no effect, ²⁴and we pass away out of the world as grasshoppers, and our life is astonishment and fear, and we are not worthy to obtain mercy. ²⁵What will he then do unto his name whereby we are called? of these things have I asked.'

²⁶Then answered he me, and said, 'The more thou searchest, the more thou shalt marvel, for the world hasteth fast to pass away, ²⁷and cannot comprehend the things that are promised to the righteous in time to come: for this world is full of unrighteousness and infirmities. ²⁸But as concerning the things whereof thou askest me, I will tell thee; for the evil is sown, but the destruction thereof is not yet come. ²⁹If therefore that which is sown be not turned upside down, and if the place where the evil is sown pass not away, then cannot it come that is sown with good. ³⁰For the grain of evil seed hath been sown in the heart of Adam from the beginning, and how much ungodliness hath it brought up unto this time? and how much shall it yet bring forth until the time of threshing come? ³¹Ponder now by thyself, how great fruit of wickedness the grain of evil seed hath brought forth. ³²And when the ears shall be cut down, which are without number, how great a floor shall they fill?'

³³Then I answered and said, 'How and when shall these things come to pass? wherefore are our years few and evil?' ³⁴And he answered me, saying, 'Do not thou hasten above the most Highest: for thy haste is in vain to be above him, for thou hast much exceeded. ³⁵Did not the souls also of the righteous ask question of these things in their chambers, saying, "How long shall I hope on this fashion? when cometh the fruit of the floor of our reward?" ³⁶And unto these things Uriel the archangel gave them answer, and said, "Even when the number of seeds is filled in you: for he hath weighed the world in the balance. ³⁷By measure hath he measured the times, and by number hath he numbered the times; and he doth not move nor stir them, until the said measure be fulfilled."'

³⁸Then answered I and said, 'O Lord that bearest rule, even we all are full of impiety. ³⁹And for our sakes peradventure it is that the floors of the righteous are not filled, because of the sins of them that dwell upon the earth.' ⁴⁰So he answered me, and said, 'Go thy way to a woman with child, and ask of her when she hath fulfilled her nine months, if her womb may keep the birth any longer within her'. ⁴¹Then said I, 'No, Lord, that can she not'. And he said unto me, 'In the grave the chambers of souls are like the womb of a woman: ⁴²for like as a woman that travaileth maketh haste to escape the necessity of the travail: even so do these places haste to deliver those things that are committed unto them. ⁴³From the beginning look what thou desirest to see, it shall be shown thee.'

⁴⁴Then answered I and said, 'If I have found favour in thy sight, and if it be possible, and if I be meet therefore, ⁴⁵show me then whether there be more to come than is past, or more past than is to come. ⁴⁶What is

past I know, but what is for to come I know not.' ⁴⁷And he said unto me, 'Stand up upon the right side, and I shall expound the similitude unto you'. ⁴⁸So I stood and saw, and behold, a hot burning oven passed by before me: and it happened that when the flame was gone by I looked, and behold, the smoke remained still. ⁴⁹After this there passed by before me a watery cloud, and sent down much rain with a storm; and when the stormy rain was past, the drops remained still. ⁵⁰Then said he unto me, 'Consider with thyself: as the rain is more than the drops, and as the fire is greater than the smoke: but the drops and the smoke remain behind: so the quantity which is past did more exceed'.

⁵¹Then I prayed, and said, 'May I live, thinkest thou, until that time? or what shall happen in those days?' ⁵²He answered me, and said, 'As for the tokens whereof thou askest me, I may tell thee of them in part: but as touching thy life, I am not sent to show thee; for I do not know it.

5 ¹Nevertheless as concerning the tokens, behold, the days shall come that they which dwell upon earth shall be taken in a great number, and the way of truth shall be hidden, and the land shall be barren of faith. ²But iniquity shall be increased above that which now thou seest, or that thou hast heard long ago. ³And the land that thou seest now to have root, shalt thou see wasted suddenly. ⁴But if the most High grant thee to live, thou shalt see after the third trumpet that the sun shall suddenly shine again in the night, and the moon thrice in the day: ⁵and blood shall drop out of wood, and the stone shall give his voice, and the people shall be troubled: ⁶and even he shall rule whom they look not for that dwell upon the earth, and the fowls shall take their flight away together. ⁷And the Sodomitish sea shall cast out fish, and make a noise in the night, which many have not known: but they shall all hear the voice thereof. ⁸There shall be a confusion also in many places, and the fire shall be oft sent out again, and the wild beasts shall change their places, and menstruous women shall bring forth monsters: ⁹and salt waters shall be found in the sweet, and all friends shall destroy one another: then shall wit hide itself, and understanding withdraw itself into his secret chamber, ¹⁰and shall be sought of many, and yet not be found: then shall unrighteousness and incontinence be multiplied upon earth. ¹¹One land also shall ask another, and say, "Is righteousness that maketh a man righteous gone through thee?" And it shall say, "No". ¹²At the same time shall men hope, but nothing obtain: they shall labour, but their ways shall not prosper. ¹³To show thee such tokens I have leave: and if thou wilt pray again, and weep as now, and fast seven days, thou shalt hear yet greater things.'

¹⁴Then I awoke, and an extreme fearfulness went through all my body, and my mind was troubled, so that it fainted. ¹⁵So the angel that was come to talk with me held me, comforted me, and set me up upon my feet.

¹⁶And in the second night it came to pass, that Salathiel the captain of the people came unto me, saying, 'Where hast thou been? and why is thy countenance so heavy? ¹⁷Knowest thou not that Israel is committed unto thee in the land of their captivity? ¹⁸Up then, and eat bread, and

forsake us not as the shepherd that leaveth his flock in the hands of cruel wolves.' [19]Then said I unto him, 'Go thy ways from me, and come not nigh me'. And he heard what I said, and went from me.

[20]And so I fasted seven days, mourning and weeping, like as Uriel the angel commanded me. [21]And after seven days so it was, that the thoughts of my heart were very grievous unto me again. [22]And my soul recovered the spirit of understanding, and I began to talk with the most High again, [23]and said, 'O Lord that bearest rule of every wood of the earth, and of all the trees thereof, thou hast chosen thee one only vine: [24]and of all lands of the whole world thou hast chosen thee one pit: and of all the flowers thereof one lily: [25]and of all the depths of the sea thou hast filled thee one river: and of all built cities thou hast hallowed Sion unto thyself: [26]and of all the fowls that are created thou hast named thee one dove: and of all the cattle that are made thou hast provided thee one sheep: [27]and among all the multitudes of peoples thou hast gotten thee one people: and unto this people, whom thou lovedst, thou gavest a law that is approved of all. [28]And now, O Lord, why hast thou given this one people over unto many? and upon the one root hast thou prepared others, and why hast thou scattered thy only one people among many? [29]And they which did gainsay thy promises, and believed not thy covenants, have trodden them down. [30]If thou didst so much hate thy people, yet shouldst thou punish them with thy own hands.'

[31]Now when I had spoken these words, the angel that came to me the night afore was sent unto me, [32]and said unto me, 'Hear me, and I will instruct thee, hearken to the thing that I say, and I shall tell thee more'. [33]And I said, 'Speak on, my Lord'. Then said he unto me, 'Thou art sore troubled in mind for Israel's sake: lovest thou that people better than he that made them?' [34]And I said, 'No, Lord, but of very grief have I spoken: for my reins pain me every hour, while I labour to comprehend the way of the most High, and to seek out part of his judgement'. [35]And he said unto me, 'Thou canst not'. And I said, 'Wherefore, Lord? whereunto was I born then? or why was not my mother's womb then my grave, that I might not have seen the travail of Jacob, and the wearisome toil of the stock of Israel?'

[36]And he said unto me, 'Number me the things that are not yet come, gather me together the drops that are scattered abroad, make me the flowers green again that are withered, [37]open me the places that are closed, and bring me forth the winds that in them are shut up, show me the image of a voice: and then I will declare to thee the thing that thou labourest to know'. [38]And I said, 'O Lord that bearest rule, who may know these things, but he that hath not his dwelling with men? [39]As for me, I am unwise: how may I then speak of these things whereof thou askest me?' [40]Then said he unto me, 'Like as thou canst do none of these things that I have spoken of, even so canst thou not find out my judgement, or in the end the love that I have promised unto my people'.

[41]And I said, 'Behold, O Lord, yet art thou nigh unto them that be reserved till the end: and what shall they do that have been before me, or we that be now, or they that shall come after us?' [42]And he said unto

me, 'I will liken my judgement unto a ring: like as there is no slackness of the last, even so there is no swiftness of the first'. ⁴³So I answered and said, 'Couldst thou not make those that have been made, and be now, and that are for to come, at once, that thou mightest show thy judgement the sooner?' ⁴⁴Then answered he me, and said, 'The creature may not haste above the maker, neither may the world hold them at once that shall be created therein'.

⁴⁵And I said, 'As thou hast said unto thy servant, that thou, which givest life to all, hast given life at once to the creature that thou hast created, and the creature bore it: even so it might now also bear them that now be present at once'. ⁴⁶And he said unto me, 'Ask the womb of a woman, and say unto her, "If thou bringest forth children, why doest thou it not together, but one after another?" pray her therefore to bring forth ten children at once'. ⁴⁷And I said, 'She cannot: but must do it by distance of time'. ⁴⁸Then said he unto me, 'Even so have I given the womb of the earth to those that be sown in it in their times. ⁴⁹For like as a young child may not bring forth the things that belong to the aged, even so have I disposed the world which I created.'

⁵⁰And I asked, and said, 'Seeing thou hast now given me the way, I will proceed to speak before thee: for our mother of whom thou hast told me that she is young, draweth now nigh unto age'. ⁵¹He answered me, and said, 'Ask a woman that beareth children, and she shall tell thee. ⁵²Say unto her, "Wherefore are not they whom thou hast now brought forth like those that were before, but less of stature?" ⁵³And she shall answer thee, "They that be born in the strength of youth are of one fashion, and they that are born in the time of age, when the womb faileth, are otherwise". ⁵⁴Consider thou therefore also, how that ye are less of stature than those that were before you. ⁵⁵And so are they that come after you less than ye, as the creatures which now begin to be old, and have passed over the strength of youth.'

⁵⁶Then said I, 'Lord, I beseech thee, if I have found favour in thy sight, show thy servant by whom thou visitest thy creature'. ¹And he said unto me, 'In the beginning, when the earth was made, before the borders of the world stood, or ever the winds blew, ²before it thundered and lightened, or ever the foundations of paradise were laid, ³before the fair flowers were seen, or ever the movable powers were established, before the innumerable multitude of angels were gathered together, ⁴or ever the heights of the air were lifted up, before the measures of the firmament were named, or ever the chimneys in Sion were hot, ⁵and ere the present years were sought out, and or ever the inventions of them that now sin were turned, before they were sealed that have gathered faith for a treasure: ⁶then did I consider these things, and they all were made through me alone, and through no other: by me also they shall be ended, and by no other'.

⁷Then answered I and said, 'What shall be the parting asunder of the times? or when shall be the end of the first, and the beginning of it that followeth?' ⁸And he said unto me, 'From Abraham unto Isaac, when Jacob and Esau were born of him, Jacob's hand held first the heel of

Esau. [9]For Esau is the end of the world, and Jacob is the beginning of it that followeth. [10]The hand of man is betwixt the heel and the hand: other question, Esdras, ask thou not.'

[11]I answered then and said, 'O Lord that bearest rule, if I have found favour in thy sight, [12]I beseech thee, show thy servant the end of thy tokens, whereof thou showedst me part the last night'. [13]So he answered and said unto me, 'Stand up upon thy feet, and hear a mighty sounding voice. [14]And it shall be as it were a great motion, but the place where thou standest shall not be moved. [15]And therefore when it speaketh be not afraid: for the word is of the end, and the foundation of the earth is understood. [16]And why? because the speech of these things trembleth and is moved: for it knoweth that the end of these things must be changed.'

[17]And it happened that when I had heard it I stood up upon my feet, and hearkened, and behold, there was a voice that spoke, and the sound of it was like the sound of many waters. [18]And it said, 'Behold, the days come, that I will begin to draw nigh, and to visit them that dwell upon the earth, [19]and will begin to make inquisition of them, what they be that have hurt unjustly with their unrighteousness, and when the affliction of Sion shall be fulfilled. [20]And when the world that shall begin to vanish away shall be finished, then will I show these tokens, the books shall be opened before the firmament, and they shall see all together. [21]And the children of a year old shall speak with their voices, the women with child shall bring forth untimely children of three or four months old, and they shall live, and be raised up. [22]And suddenly shall the sown places appear unsown, the full storehouses shall suddenly be found empty. [23]And the trumpet shall give a sound, which when every man heareth, they shall be suddenly afraid. [24]At that time shall friends fight one against another like enemies, and the earth shall stand in fear with those that dwell therein, the springs of the fountains shall stand still, and in three hours they shall not run.

[25]'Whosoever remaineth from all these that I have told thee shall escape, and see my salvation, and the end of your world. [26]And the men that are received shall see it, who have not tasted death from their birth: and the heart of the inhabitants shall be changed, and turned into another meaning. [27]For evil shall be put out, and deceit shall be quenched. [28]As for faith, it shall flourish, corruption shall be overcome, and the truth, which hath been so long without fruit, shall be declared.'

[29]And when he talked with me, behold, I looked by little and little upon him before whom I stood. [30]And these words said he unto me, 'I am come to show thee the time of the night to come. [31]If thou wilt pray yet more, and fast seven days again, I shall tell thee greater things by day than I have heard. [32]For thy voice is heard before the most High: for the Mighty hath seen thy righteous dealing, he hath seen also thy chastity, which thou hast had ever since thy youth. [33]And therefore hath he sent me to show thee all these things, and to say unto thee, "Be of good comfort, and fear not. [34]And hasten not, with the times that are

past, to think vain things, that thou mayest not hasten from the latter times."'

³⁵And it came to pass after this that I wept again, and fasted seven days in like manner, that I might fulfil the three weeks which he told me. ³⁶And in the eighth night was my heart vexed within me again, and I began to speak before the most High. ³⁷For my spirit was greatly set on fire, and my soul was in distress. ³⁸And I said, 'O Lord, thou spokest from the beginning of the creation, even the first day, and saidst thus, "Let heaven and earth be made": and thy word was a perfect work. ³⁹And then was the spirit, and darkness and silence were on every side; the sound of man's voice was not yet formed. ⁴⁰Then commandedst thou a fair light to come forth of thy treasures, that thy work might appear.

⁴¹'Upon the second day thou madest the spirit of the firmament, and commandedst it to part asunder and to make a division betwixt the waters, that the one part might go up, and the other remain beneath.

⁴²'Upon the third day thou didst command that the waters should be gathered in the seventh part of the earth: six parts hast thou dried up, and kept them, to the intent that of these some being planted of God and tilled might serve thee. ⁴³For as soon as thy word went forth the work was made. ⁴⁴For immediately there was great and innumerable fruit, and many and divers pleasures for the taste, and flowers of unchangeable colour, and odours of wonderful smell: and this was done the third day.

⁴⁵'Upon the fourth day thou commandedst that the sun should shine, and the moon give her light, and the stars should be in order, ⁴⁶and gavest them a charge to do service unto man, that was to be made.

⁴⁷'Upon the fifth day thou saidst unto the seventh part, where the waters were gathered, that it should bring forth living creatures, fowls and fishes: and so it came to pass. ⁴⁸For the dumb water and without life brought forth living things at the commandment of God, that all people might praise thy wondrous works. ⁴⁹Then didst thou ordain two living creatures, the one thou calledst Enoch, and the other Leviathan, ⁵⁰and didst separate the one from the other: for the seventh part (namely, where the water was gathered together) might not hold them both. ⁵¹Unto Enoch thou gavest one part, which was dried up the third day, that he should dwell in the same part, wherein are a thousand hills. ⁵²But unto Leviathan thou gavest the seventh part, namely, the moist, and hast kept him to be devoured of whom thou wilt, and when.

⁵³'Upon the sixth day thou gavest commandment unto the earth, that before thee it should bring forth beasts, cattle, and creeping things: ⁵⁴and after these, Adam also, whom thou madest lord of all thy creatures: of him come we all, and the people also whom thou hast chosen.

⁵⁵'All this have I spoken before thee, O Lord, because thou madest the world for our sakes. ⁵⁶As for the other people, which also come of Adam, thou hast said that they are nothing, but be like unto spittle, and hast likened the abundance of them unto a drop that falleth from a vessel. ⁵⁷And now, O Lord, behold, these heathen, which have ever been

reputed as nothing, have begun to be lords over us, and to devour us. ⁵⁸But we thy people (whom thou hast called thy firstborn, thy only begotten, and thy fervent lover) are given into their hands. ⁵⁹If the world now be made for our sakes, why do we not possess an inheritance with the world? how long shall this endure?'

7 And when I had made an end of speaking these words, there was sent unto me the angel which had been sent unto me the nights afore. ²And he said unto me, 'Up, Esdras, and hear the words that I am come to tell thee'. ³And I said, 'Speak on, my God'. Then said he unto me, 'The sea is set in a wide place, that it might be deep and great. ⁴But put the case the entrance were narrow, and like a river, ⁵who then could go into the sea to look upon it, and to rule it? If he went not through the narrow, how could he come into the broad? ⁶There is also another thing. A city is built, and set upon a broad field, and is full of all good things. ⁷The entrance thereof is narrow, and is set in a dangerous place to fall, like as if there were a fire on the right hand, and on the left a deep water: ⁸and one only path between them both, even between the fire and the water, so small that there could but one man go there at once. ⁹If this city now were given unto a man for an inheritance, if he never shall pass the danger set before it, how shall he receive this inheritance?' ¹⁰And I said, 'It is so, Lord'.

Then said he unto me, 'Even so also is Israel's portion. ¹¹Because for their sakes I made the world: and when Adam transgressed my statutes, then was decreed that now is done. ¹²Then were the entrances of this world made narrow, full of sorrow and travail: they are but few and evil, full of perils, and very painful. ¹³For the entrances of the elder world were wide and sure, and brought immortal fruit. ¹⁴If then they that live labour not to enter these strait and vain things, they can never receive those that are laid up for them. ¹⁵Now therefore why disquietest thou thyself, seeing thou art but a corruptible man? and why art thou moved, whereas thou art but mortal? ¹⁶Why hast thou not considered in thy mind this thing that is to come, rather than that which is present?'

¹⁷Then answered I and said, 'O Lord that bearest rule, thou hast ordained in thy law, that the righteous should inherit these things, but that the ungodly should perish. ¹⁸Nevertheless the righteous shall suffer strait things, and hope for wide: for they that have done wickedly have suffered the strait things, and yet shall not see the wide.'

¹⁹And he said unto me, 'There is no judge above God, and none that hath understanding above the Highest. ²⁰For there be many that perish in this life, because they despise the law of God that is set before them. ²¹For God hath given strait commandment to such as came, what they should do to live, even as they came, and what they should observe to avoid punishment. ²²Nevertheless they were not obedient unto him, but spoke against him, and imagined vain things: ²³and deceived themselves by their wicked deeds; and said of the most High, that he is not, and knew not his ways: ²⁴but his law have they despised, and denied his covenants: in his statutes have they not been faithful, and have not per-

formed his works. ²⁵And therefore, Esdras, for the empty are empty things, and for the full are the full things.

²⁶'Behold, the time shall come, that these tokens which I have told thee shall come to pass, and the bride shall appear, and she coming forth shall be seen, that now is withdrawn from the earth. ²⁷And whosoever is delivered from the foresaid evils shall see my wonders. ²⁸For my son Jesus shall be revealed with those that be with him, and they that remain shall rejoice within four hundred years. ²⁹After these years shall my son Christ die, and all men that have life. ³⁰And the world shall be turned into the old silence seven days, like as in the former judgements: so that no man shall remain. ³¹And after seven days the world that yet awaketh not shall be raised up, and that shall die that is corrupt. ³²And the earth shall restore those that are asleep in her, and so shall the dust those that dwell in silence, and the secret places shall deliver those souls that were committed unto them. ³³And the most High shall appear upon the seat of judgement, and misery shall pass away, and the long suffering shall have an end. ³⁴But judgement only shall remain, truth shall stand, and faith shall wax strong. ³⁵And the work shall follow, and the reward shall be shown, and the good deeds shall be of force, and wicked deeds shall bear no rule.'

³⁶Then said I, 'Abraham prayed first for the Sodomites, and Moses for the fathers that sinned in the wilderness: ³⁷and Jesus after him for Israel in the time of Achan: ³⁸and Samuel and David for the destruction: and Solomon for them that should come to the sanctuary: ³⁹and Helias for those that received rain; and for the dead, that he might live: ⁴⁰and Ezechias for the people in the time of Sennacherib: and many for many. ⁴¹Even so now, seeing corruption is grown up, and wickedness increased, and the righteous have prayed for the ungodly: wherefore shall it not be so now also?'

⁴²He answered me, and said, 'This present life is not the end where much glory doth abide; therefore have they prayed for the weak. ⁴³But the day of doom shall be the end of this time, and the beginning of the immortality for to come, wherein corruption is past, ⁴⁴intemperance is at an end, infidelity is cut off, righteousness is grown, and truth is sprung up. ⁴⁵Then shall no man be able to save him that is destroyed, nor to oppress him that hath gotten the victory.'

⁴⁶I answered then and said, 'This is my first and last saying, that it had been better not to have given the earth unto Adam: or else when it was given him, to have restrained him from sinning. ⁴⁷For what profit is it for men now in this present time to live in heaviness, and after death to look for punishment? ⁴⁸O thou Adam, what hast thou done? for though it was thou that sinned, thou art not fallen alone, but we all that come of thee. ⁴⁹For what profit is it unto us, if there be promised us an immortal time, whereas we have done the works that bring death? ⁵⁰and that there is promised us an everlasting hope, whereas ourselves being most wicked are made vain? ⁵¹and that there are laid up for us dwellings of health and safety, whereas we have lived wickedly? ⁵²and that the glory of the most High is kept to defend them which have led a

wary life, whereas we have walked in the most wicked ways of all? ⁵³and that there should be shown a paradise, whose fruit endureth for ever, wherein is security and medicine, since we shall not enter into it ⁵⁴(for we have walked in unpleasant places)? ⁵⁵and that the faces of them which have used abstinence shall shine above the stars, whereas our faces shall be blacker than darkness? ⁵⁶For while we lived and committed iniquity, we considered not that we should begin to suffer for it after death.'

⁵⁷Then answered he me and said, 'This is the condition of the battle, which man that is born upon the earth shall fight, ⁵⁸that if he be overcome, he shall suffer as thou hast said: but if he get the victory, he shall receive the thing that I say. ⁵⁹For this is the life whereof Moses spoke unto the people while he lived, saying, "Choose thee life, that thou mayest live". ⁶⁰Nevertheless they believed not him, nor yet the prophets after him, no nor me which have spoken unto them, ⁶¹that there should not be such heaviness in their destruction, as shall be joy over them that are persuaded to salvation.'

⁶²I answered then, and said, 'I know, Lord, that the most High is called merciful, in that he hath mercy upon them which are not yet come into the world, ⁶³and upon those also that turn to his law, ⁶⁴and that he is patient, and long suffereth those that have sinned, as his creatures, ⁶⁵and that he is bountiful, for he is ready to give where it needeth, ⁶⁶and that he is of great mercy, for he multiplieth more and more mercies to them that are present, and that are past, and also to them which are to come. ⁶⁷For if he shall not multiply his mercies, the world would not continue with them that inherit therein. ⁶⁸And he pardoneth; for if he did not so of his goodness, that they which have committed iniquities might be eased of them, the ten thousandth part of men should not remain living. ⁶⁹And being judge, if he should not forgive them that are cured with his word, and put out the multitude of contentions, ⁷⁰there should be very few left peradventure in an innumerable multitude.'

8 And he answered me, saying, 'The most High hath made this world for many, but the world to come for few. ²I will tell thee a similitude, Esdras: as when thou askest the earth, it shall say unto thee, that it giveth much mould whereof earthen vessels are made, but little dust that gold cometh of: even so is the course of this present world. ³There be many created, but few shall be saved.' ⁴So answered I and said, 'Swallow then down, O my soul, understanding, and devour wisdom. ⁵For thou hast agreed to give ear, and art willing to prophesy: for thou hast no longer space than only to live. ⁶O Lord, if thou suffer not thy servant, that we may pray before thee, and thou give us seed unto our heart, and culture to our understanding, that there may come fruit of it, how shall each man live that is corrupt, who beareth the place of a man? ⁷For thou art alone, and we all one workmanship of thy hands, like as thou hast said. ⁸For when the body is fashioned now in the mother's womb, and thou givest it members, thy creature is preserved in fire and water, and nine months doth thy workmanship endure thy creature which is created in her. ⁹But that which keepeth and is kept shall both be preserved: and when the time cometh, the womb preserved delivereth up the things that grew in it. [10]For thou hast commanded out of the parts of the body, that is to say, out of the breasts, milk to be given, which is the fruit of the breasts, [11]that the thing which is fashioned may be nourished for a time, till thou disposest it to thy mercy. [12]Thou broughtest it up with thy righteousness, and nurturedst it in thy law, and reformedst it with thy judgement. [13]And thou shalt mortify it as thy creature, and quicken it as thy work. [14]If therefore thou shalt destroy him which with so great labour was fashioned, it is an easy thing to be ordained by thy commandment, that the thing which was made might be preserved.

[15]'Now therefore, Lord, I will speak (touching man in general, thou knowest best) but touching thy people, for whose sake I am sorry, [16]and for thy inheritance, for whose cause I mourn, and for Israel, for whom I am heavy; and for Jacob, for whose sake I am troubled: [17]therefore will I begin to pray before thee for myself and for them: for I see the falls of us that dwell in the land. [18]But I have heard the swiftness of the judge which is to come. [19]Therefore hear my voice, and understand my words, and I shall speak before thee.'

This is the beginning of the words of Esdras, before he was taken up: and I said, [20]'O Lord, thou that dwellest in everlastingness, which beholdest from above things in the heaven and in the air, [21]whose throne is inestimable, whose glory may not be comprehended, before whom the hosts of angels stand with trembling, [22]whose service is conversant in wind and fire, whose word is true, and sayings constant, whose commandment is strong, and ordinance fearful, [23]whose look drieth up the depths, and indignation maketh the mountains to melt away, which the truth witnesseth: [24]O hear the prayer of thy servant, and give ear to the petition of thy creature. [25]For while I live I will speak, and so long as I have understanding I will answer.

[26]'O look not upon the sins of thy people: but on them which serve thee in truth. [27]Regard not the wicked inventions of the heathen: but the desire of those that keep thy testimonies in afflictions. [28]Think not upon those that have walked feignedly before thee: but remember them, which according to thy will have known thy fear. [29]Let it not be thy will to destroy them which have lived like beasts: but to look upon them that have clearly taught thy law. [30]Take thou no indignation at them which are deemed worse than beasts; but love them that always put their trust in thy righteousness and glory. [31]For we and our fathers do languish of such diseases: but because of us sinners thou shalt be called merciful. [32]For if thou hast a desire to have mercy upon us, thou shalt be called merciful, to us namely, that have no works of righteousness. [33]For the just, which have many good works laid up with thee, shall out of their own deeds receive reward. [34]For what is man, that thou shouldst take displeasure at him? or what is a corruptible generation, that thou shouldst be so bitter toward it? [35]For in truth there is no man among them that be born, but he hath dealt wickedly, and among the faithful there is none which hath not done amiss. [36]For in this, O

Lord, thy righteousness and thy goodness shall be declared, if thou be merciful unto them which have not the confidence of good works.'

37Then answered he me and said, 'Some things hast thou spoken aright, and according unto thy words it shall be. 38For indeed I will not think on the disposition of them which have sinned before death, before judgement, before destruction: 39but I will rejoice over the disposition of the righteous, and I will remember also their pilgrimage, and the salvation, and the reward that they shall have. 40Like as I have spoken now, so shall it come to pass. 41For as the husbandman soweth much seed upon the ground, and planteth many trees, and yet the thing that is sown good in his season cometh not up, neither doth all that is planted take root: even so is it of them that are sown in the world, they shall not all be saved.'

42I answered then and said, 'If I have found grace, let me speak. 43Like as the husbandman's seed perisheth, if it come not up, and receive not the rain in due season, or if there come too much rain, and corrupt it: 44even so perisheth man also which is formed with thy hands, and is called thy own image, because thou art like unto him, for whose sake thou hast made all things, and likened him unto the husbandman's seed. 45Be not wroth with us, but spare thy people, and have mercy upon thy own inheritance: for thou art merciful unto thy creature.'

46Then answered he me and said, 'Things present are for the present, and things to come for such as be to come. 47For thou comest far short that thou shouldst be able to love my creature more than I: but I have ofttimes drawn nigh unto thee, and unto it, but never to the unrighteous. 48In this also thou art marvellous before the most High: 49in that thou hast humbled thyself as it becometh thee, and hast not judged thyself worthy to be much glorified among the righteous. 50For many great miseries shall be done to them that in the latter time shall dwell in the world, because they have walked in great pride. 51But understand thou for thyself, and seek out the glory for such as be like thee. 52For unto you is paradise opened, the tree of life is planted, the time to come is prepared, plenteousness is made ready, a city is built, and rest is allowed, yea, perfect goodness and wisdom. 53The root of evil is sealed up from you, weakness and the moth is hid from you, and corruption is fled into hell to be forgotten. 54Sorrows are passed, and in the end is shown the treasure of immortality.

55'And therefore ask thou no more questions concerning the multitude of them that perish. 56For when they had taken liberty, they despised the most High, thought scorn of his law, and forsook his ways. 57Moreover they have trodden down his righteous, 58and said in their heart, that there is no God; yea, and that knowing they must die. 59For as the things aforesaid shall receive you, so thirst and pain are prepared for them: for it was not his will that men should come to nought: 60but they which be created have defiled the name of him that made them, and were unthankful unto him which prepared life for them. 61And therefore is my judgement now at hand. 62These things have I not shown unto all men, but unto thee, and a few like thee.'

Then answered I and said, ⁶³'Behold, O Lord, now hast thou shown me the multitude of the wonders which thou wilt begin to do in the last times: but at what time, thou hast not shown me'.

9 He answered me then, and said, 'Measure thou the time diligently in itself: and when thou seest part of the signs past, which I have told thee before, ²then shalt thou understand, that it is the very same time, wherein the Highest will begin to visit the world which he made. ³Therefore when there shall be seen earthquakes and uproars of the people in the world: ⁴then shalt thou well understand, that the most High spoke of those things from the days that were before thee, even from the beginning. ⁵For like as all that is made in the world hath a beginning and an end, and the end is manifest: ⁶even so the times also of the Highest have plain beginnings in wonders and powerful works, and endings in effects and signs. ⁷And every one that shall be saved, and shall be able to escape by his works, and by faith, whereby ye have believed, ⁸shall be preserved from the said perils, and shall see my salvation in my land, and within my borders: for I have sanctified them for me from the beginning. ⁹Then shall they be in pitiful case, which now have abused my ways: and they that have cast them away despitefully shall dwell in torments. ¹⁰For such as in their life have received benefits, and have not known me: ¹¹and they that have loathed my law, while they had yet liberty, and when as yet place of repentance was open unto them, understood not, but despised it: ¹²the same must know it after death by pain. ¹³And therefore be thou not curious how the ungodly shall be punished, and when: but inquire how the righteous shall be saved, whose the world is, and for whom the world is created.'

¹⁴Then answered I and said, ¹⁵'I have said before, and now do speak, and will speak it also hereafter, that there be many more of them which perish, than of them which shall be saved, ¹⁶like as a wave is greater than a drop'.

¹⁷And he answered me, saying, 'Like as the field is, so is also the seed: as the flowers be, such are the colours also: such as the workman is, such also is the work: and as the husbandman is himself, so is his husbandry also: for it was the time of the world. ¹⁸And now when I prepared the world, which was not yet made, even for them to dwell in that now live, no man spoke against me. ¹⁹For then every one obeyed: but now the manners of them which are created in this world that is made are corrupted by a perpetual seed, and by a law which is unsearchable rid themselves. ²⁰So I considered the world, and behold, there was peril because of the devices that were come into it. ²¹And I saw and spared it greatly, and have kept me a grape of the cluster, and a plant of a great people. ²²Let the multitude perish then, which was born in vain, and let my grape be kept, and my plant: for with great labour have I made it perfect. ²³Nevertheless, if thou wilt cease yet seven days more (but thou shalt not fast in them), ²⁴but go into a field of flowers, where no house is built, and eat only the flowers of the field, taste no flesh, drink no wine, but eat flowers only, ²⁵and pray unto the Highest continually, then will I come and talk with thee.'

²⁶So I went my way into the field which is called Ardath, like as he commanded me, and there I sat amongst the flowers, and did eat of the herbs of the field, and the meat of the same satisfied me. ²⁷After seven days I sat upon the grass, and my heart was vexed within me, like as before. ²⁸And I opened my mouth, and began to talk before the most High, and said, ²⁹'O Lord, thou that showest thyself unto us, thou wast shown unto our fathers in the wilderness, in a place where no man treadeth, in a barren place, when they came out of Egypt. ³⁰And thou spokest, saying, "Hear me, O Israel, and mark my words, thou seed of Jacob. ³¹For behold, I sow my law in you, and it shall bring fruit in you, and ye shall be honoured in it for ever." ³²But our fathers which received the law, kept it not, and observed not thy ordinances, and though the fruit of thy law did not perish, neither could it, for it was thine: ³³yet they that received it perished, because they kept not the thing that was sown in them. ³⁴And lo, it is a custom, when the ground hath received seed, or the sea a ship, or any vessel meat or drink, that, that being perished wherein it was sown or cast into, ³⁵that thing also which was sown, or cast therein, or received, doth perish, and remaineth not with us: but with us it hath not happened so. ³⁶For we that have received the law perish by sin, and our heart also which received it. ³⁷Notwithstanding the law perisheth not, but remaineth in his force.'

³⁸And when I spoke these things in my heart, I looked back with my eyes, and upon the right side I saw a woman, and behold, she mourned and wept with a loud voice, and was much grieved in heart, and her clothes were rent, and she had ashes upon her head. ³⁹Then let I my thoughts go that I was in, and turned me unto her, ⁴⁰and said unto her, 'Wherefore weepest thou? why art thou so grieved in thy mind?' ⁴¹And she said unto me, 'Sir, let me alone, that I may bewail myself, and add unto my sorrow, for I am sore vexed in my mind, and brought very low'. ⁴²And I said unto her, 'What aileth thee? tell me'. ⁴³She said unto me, 'I thy servant have been barren, and had no child, though I had a husband thirty years. ⁴⁴And those thirty years I did nothing else day and night, and every hour, but make my prayer to the Highest. ⁴⁵After thirty years God heard me thy handmaid, looked upon my misery, considered my trouble, and gave me a son: and I was very glad of him, so was my husband also, and all my neighbours, and we gave great honour unto the Almighty. ⁴⁶And I nourished him with great travail. ⁴⁷So when he grew up and came to the time that he should have a wife, I made a feast. ¹And it so came to pass, that when my son was entered into his wedding-chamber, he fell down, and died. ²Then we all overthrew the lights, and all my neighbours rose up to comfort me: so I took my rest unto the second day at night. ³And it came to pass when they had all left off to comfort me, to the end I might be quiet: then rose I up by night, and fled, and came hither into this field, as thou seest. ⁴And I do now purpose not to return into the city, but here to stay, and neither to eat nor drink, but continually to mourn and to fast until I die.'

⁵Then left I the meditations wherein I was, and spoke to her in anger, saying, ⁶'Thou foolish woman above all others, seest thou not our mourning, and what happeneth unto us? ⁷how that Sion our mother is full of all heaviness, and much humbled, mourning very sore? ⁸And now seeing we all mourn and are sad, for we are all in heaviness, art thou grieved for one son? ⁹For ask the earth, and she shall tell thee, that it is she which ought to mourn for the fall of so many that grow upon her. ¹⁰For out of her came all at the first, and out of her shall all others come: and behold, they walk almost all into destruction, and a multitude of them is utterly rooted out. ¹¹Who then should make more mourning than she that hath lost so great a multitude, and not thou, which art sorry but for one?

¹²'But if thou sayest unto me, "My lamentation is not like the earth's, because I have lost the fruit of my womb, which I brought forth with pains, and bore with sorrows; ¹³but the earth not so: for the multitude present in it according to the course of the earth is gone, as it came": ¹⁴then say I unto thee, "Like as thou hast brought forth with labour: even so the earth also hath given her fruit, namely, man, ever since the beginning unto him that made her". ¹⁵Now therefore keep thy sorrow to thyself, and bear with a good courage that which hath befallen thee. ¹⁶For if thou shalt acknowledge the determination of God to be just, thou shalt both receive thy son in time, and shalt be commended amongst women. ¹⁷Go thy way then into the city to thy husband.'

¹⁸And she said unto me, 'That will I not do: I will not go into the city, but here will I die'.

¹⁹So I proceeded to speak further unto her, and said, ²⁰'Do not so, but be counselled by me: for how many are the adversities of Sion? Be comforted in regard of the sorrow of Jerusalem. ²¹For thou seest that our sanctuary is laid waste, our altar broken down, our temple destroyed; ²²our psaltery is laid on the ground, our song is put to silence, our rejoicing is at an end, the light of our candlestick is put out, the ark of our covenant is spoiled, our holy things are defiled, and the name that is called upon us is almost profaned: our children are put to shame, our priests are burnt, our Levites are gone into captivity, our virgins are defiled, and our wives ravished; our righteous men carried away, our little ones destroyed, our young men are brought in bondage, and our strong men are become weak; ²³and, which is the greatest of all, the seal of Sion hath now lost her honour: for she is delivered into the hands of them that hate us. ²⁴And therefore shake off thy great heaviness, and put away the multitude of sorrows, that the Mighty may be merciful unto thee again, and the Highest shall give thee rest and ease from thy labour.'

²⁵And it came to pass while I was talking with her, behold, her face upon a sudden shone exceedingly, and her countenance glistered, so that I was afraid of her, and mused what it might be. ²⁶And behold, suddenly she made a great cry very fearful: so that the earth shook at the noise of the woman. ²⁷And I looked, and behold, the woman appeared unto me no more, but there was a city built, and a large place showed

itself from the foundations: then was I afraid, and cried with a loud voice, and said, ²⁸'Where is Uriel the angel, who came unto me at the first? for he hath caused me to fall into many trances, and my end is turned into corruption, and my prayer to rebuke'.

²⁹And as I was speaking these words, behold, he came unto me, and looked upon me. ³⁰And lo, I lay as one that had been dead, and my understanding was taken from me: and he took me by the right hand, and comforted me, and set me upon my feet, and said unto me, ³¹'What aileth thee? and why art thou so disquieted? and why is thy understanding troubled, and the thoughts of thy heart?'

³²And I said, 'Because thou hast forsaken me, and yet I did according to thy words, and I went into the field, and lo, I have seen, and yet see, that I am not able to express'.

³³And he said unto me, 'Stand up manfully, and I will advise thee'.

³⁴Then said I, 'Speak on, my lord, in me, only forsake me not, lest I die frustrate of my hope. ³⁵For I have seen that I knew not, and hear that I do not know. ³⁶Or is my sense deceived, or my soul in a dream? ³⁷Now therefore I beseech thee that thou wilt show thy servant of this vision.'

³⁸He answered me then, and said, 'Hear me, and I shall inform thee, and tell thee wherefore thou art afraid: for the Highest will reveal many secret things unto thee. ³⁹He hath seen that thy way is right: for that thou sorrowest continually for thy people, and makest great lamentation for Sion. ⁴⁰This therefore is the meaning of the vision which thou lately sawest. ⁴¹Thou sawest a woman mourning, and thou begannest to comfort her: ⁴²but now seest thou the likeness of the woman no more, but there appeared unto thee a city built. ⁴³And whereas she told thee of the death of her son, this is the solution: ⁴⁴this woman, whom thou sawest, is Sion: and whereas she said unto thee (even she whom thou seest as a city built), ⁴⁵whereas, I say, she said unto thee, that she hath been thirty years barren: those are the thirty years wherein there was no offering made in her. ⁴⁶But after thirty years Solomon built the city, and offered offerings: and then bore the barren a son. ⁴⁷And whereas she told thee that she nourished him with labour: that was the dwelling in Jerusalem. ⁴⁸But whereas she said unto thee, "That my son coming into his marriage-chamber happened to have a fall, and died": this was the destruction that came to Jerusalem. ⁴⁹And behold, thou sawest her likeness, and because she mourned for her son, thou begannest to comfort her: and of these things which have chanced, these are to be opened unto thee. ⁵⁰For now the most High seeth that thou art grieved unfeignedly, and sufferest from thy whole heart for her, so hath he shown thee the brightness of her glory, and the comeliness of her beauty. ⁵¹And therefore I bade thee remain in the field where no house was built: ⁵²for I knew that the Highest would show this unto thee. ⁵³Therefore I commanded thee to go into the field, where no foundation of any building was. ⁵⁴For in the place wherein the Highest beginneth to show his city, there can no man's building be able to stand. ⁵⁵And therefore fear not, let not thy heart be affrighted, but go thy way in, and see the beauty and greatness of the building, as

much as thy eyes be able to see: ⁵⁶and then shalt thou hear as much as thy ears may comprehend. ⁵⁷For thou art blessed above many others, and art called with the Highest, and so are but few. ⁵⁸But tomorrow at night thou shalt remain here; ⁵⁹and so shall the Highest show thee visions of the high things, which the most High will do unto them that dwell upon earth in the last days.' So I slept that night and another, like as he commanded me.

11 Then saw I a dream, and behold, there came up from the sea an eagle, which had twelve feathered wings, and three heads. ²And I saw, and behold, she spread her wings over all the earth, and all the winds of the air blew on her, and were gathered together. ³And I beheld, and out of her feathers there grew other contrary feathers, and they became little feathers and small. ⁴But her heads were at rest: the head in the midst was greater than the others, yet rested it with the residue. ⁵Moreover I beheld, and lo, the eagle flew with her feathers, and reigned upon earth, and over them that dwelt therein. ⁶And I saw that all things under heaven were subject unto her, and no man spoke against her, no, not one creature upon earth.

⁷And I beheld, and lo, the eagle rose upon her talons, and spoke to her feathers, saying, ⁸'Watch not all at once: sleep every one in his own place, and watch by course: ⁹but let the heads be preserved for the last'. ¹⁰And I beheld, and lo, the voice went not out of her heads, but from the midst of her body. ¹¹And I numbered her contrary feathers, and behold, there were eight of them.

¹²And I looked, and behold, on the right side there arose one feather, and reigned over all the earth. ¹³And so it was, that when it reigned, the end of it came, and the place thereof appeared no more: so the next following stood up, and reigned, and had a great time. ¹⁴And it happened, that when it reigned, the end of it came also, like as the first, so that it appeared no more. ¹⁵Then came there a voice unto it, and said, ¹⁶'Hear, thou that hast borne rule over the earth so long: this I say unto thee, before thou beginnest to appear no more, ¹⁷there shall none after thee attain unto thy time, neither unto the half thereof'. ¹⁸Then arose the third, and reigned as the others before, and appeared no more also. ¹⁹So went it with all the residue one after another, as that every one reigned, and then appeared no more.

²⁰Then I beheld, and lo, in process of time the feathers that followed stood up upon the right side, that they might rule also; and some of them ruled, but within a while they appeared no more: ²¹for some of them were set up, but ruled not. ²²After this I looked, and behold, the twelve feathers appeared no more, nor the two little feathers: ²³and there was no more upon the eagle's body, but three heads that rested, and six little wings. ²⁴Then saw I also that two little feathers divided themselves from the six, and remained under the head that was upon the right side: for the four continued in their place. ²⁵And I beheld, and lo, the feathers that were under the wing thought to set up themselves, and to have the rule. ²⁶And I beheld, and lo, there was one set up, but shortly it appeared no more. ²⁷And the second was sooner away than

the first. ²⁸And I beheld, and lo, the two that remained thought also in themselves to reign. ²⁹And when they so thought, behold, there awoke one of the heads that were at rest, namely, it that was in the midst, for that was greater than the two other heads. ³⁰And then I saw that the two other heads were joined with it. ³¹And behold, the head was turned with them that were with it, and did eat up the two feathers under the wing that would have reigned. ³²But this head put the whole earth in fear, and bore rule in it over all those that dwelt upon the earth with much oppression; and it had the governance of the world more than all the wings that had been. ³³And after this I beheld, and lo, the head that was in the midst suddenly appeared no more, like as the wings. ³⁴But there remained the two heads, which also in like sort ruled upon the earth, and over those that dwelt therein. ³⁵And I beheld, and lo, the head upon the right side devoured it that was upon the left side.

³⁶Then I heard a voice, which said unto me, 'Look before thee, and consider the thing that thou seest'. ³⁷And I beheld, and lo, as it were a roaring lion chased out of the wood: and I saw that he sent out a man's voice unto the eagle, and said, ³⁸'Hear thou, I will talk with thee, and the Highest shall say unto thee, ³⁹"Art not thou it that remainest of the four beasts, whom I made to reign in my world, that the end of their times might come through them? ⁴⁰And the fourth came, and over-came all the beasts that were past, and had power over the world with great fearfulness, and over the whole compass of the earth with much wicked oppression; and so long time dwelt he upon the earth with deceit. ⁴¹For the earth hast thou not judged with truth. ⁴²For thou hast afflicted the meek, thou hast hurt the peaceable, thou hast loved liars, and destroyed the dwellings of them that brought forth fruit, and hast cast down the walls of such as did thee no harm. ⁴³Therefore is thy wrongful dealing come up unto the Highest, and thy pride unto the Mighty. ⁴⁴The Highest also hath looked upon the proud times, and behold, they are ended, and his abominations are fulfilled. ⁴⁵And there-fore appear no more, thou eagle, nor thy horrible wings, nor thy wicked feathers, nor thy malicious heads, nor thy hurtful claws, nor all thy vain body: ⁴⁶that all the earth may be refreshed, and may return, being delivered from thy violence, and that she may hope for the judge-ment and mercy of him that made her."'

12 And it came to pass whilst the lion spoke these words unto the eagle, I saw: ²and behold, the head that remained and the four wings appeared no more, and the two went unto it, and set themselves up to reign, and their kingdom was small, and full of uproar. ³And I saw, and behold, they appeared no more, and the whole body of the eagle was burnt, so that the earth was in great fear: then awoke I out of the trouble and trance of my mind, and from great fear, and said unto my spirit, ⁴'Lo, this hast thou done unto me, in that thou searchest out the ways of the Highest. ⁵Lo, yet am I weary in my mind, and very weak in my spirit: and little strength is there in me, for the great fear where-with I was affrighted this night. ⁶Therefore will I now beseech the Highest, that he will comfort me unto the end.' ⁷And I said, 'Lord that bearest rule, if I have found grace before thy sight, and if I am justified with thee before many others, and if my prayer indeed be come up before thy face, [8]comfort me then, and show me thy servant the interpretation and plain difference of this fearful vision, that thou mayest perfectly comfort my soul. [9]For thou hast judged me worthy to show me the last times.'

[10]And he said unto me, 'This is the interpretation of the vision. [11]The eagle whom thou sawest come up from the sea, is the kingdom which was seen in the vision of thy brother Daniel. [12]But it was not expounded unto him, therefore now I declare it unto thee. [13]Behold, the days will come, that there shall rise up a kingdom upon earth, and it shall be feared above all the kingdoms that were before it. [14]In the same shall twelve kings reign, one after another: [15]whereof the second shall begin to reign, and shall have more time than any of the twelve. [16]And this do the twelve wings signify, which thou sawest.

[17]'As for the voice which thou heardest speak, and that thou sawest not to go out from the heads, but from the midst of the body thereof, this is the interpretation: [18]that after the time of that kingdom there shall arise great strivings, and it shall stand in peril of falling: nevertheless it shall not then fall, but shall be restored again to his beginning.

[19]'And whereas thou sawest the eight small under feathers sticking to her wings, this is the interpretation: [20]that in him there shall arise eight kings, whose times shall be but small, and their years swift. [21]And two of them shall perish, the middle time approaching: four shall be kept until their end begin to approach: but two shall be kept unto the end.

[22]'And whereas thou sawest three heads resting, this is the interpretation: [23]in his last days shall the most High raise up three kingdoms, and renew many things therein, and they shall have the dominion of the earth, [24]and of those that dwell therein with much oppression, above all those that were before them: therefore are they called the heads of the eagle. [25]For these are they that shall accomplish his wickedness, and that shall finish his last end. [26]And whereas thou sawest that the great head appeared no more, it signifieth that one of them shall die upon his bed, and yet with pain. [27]For the two that remain shall be slain with the sword. [28]For the sword of the one shall devour the other: but at the last shall he fall through the sword himself.

[29]'And whereas thou sawest two feathers under the wings passing over the head that is on the right side: [30]it signifieth that these are they whom the Highest hath kept unto their end: this is the small kingdom and full of trouble, as thou sawest.

[31]'And the lion, whom thou sawest rising up out of the wood, and roaring, and speaking to the eagle, and rebuking her for her unrighteousness with all the words which thou hast heard, [32]this is the anointed which the Highest hath kept for them and for their wickedness unto the end: he shall reprove them, and shall upbraid them with their cruelty. [33]For he shall set them before him alive in judgement, and shall

rebuke them, and correct them. ³⁴For the rest of my people shall he deliver with mercy, those that have been preserved upon my borders, and he shall make them joyful until the coming of the day of judgement, whereof I have spoken unto thee from the beginning.

³⁵'This is the dream that thou sawest, and these are the interpretations. ³⁶Thou only hast been meet to know this secret of the Highest. ³⁷Therefore write all these things that thou hast seen in a book, and hide them. ³⁸And teach them to the wise of the people, whose hearts thou knowest may comprehend and keep these secrets. ³⁹But wait thou here thyself yet seven days more, that it may be shown thee whatsoever it pleaseth the Highest to declare unto thee.' And with that he went his way.

⁴⁰And it came to pass when all the people saw that the seven days were past, and I not come again into the city, they gathered them all together, from the least unto the greatest, and came unto me, and said, ⁴¹'What have we offended thee? and what evil have we done against thee, that thou forsakest us, and sittest here in this place? ⁴²For of all the prophets thou only art left us, as a cluster of the vintage, and as a candle in a dark place, and as a haven or ship preserved from the tempest. ⁴³Are not the evils which are come to us sufficient? ⁴⁴If thou shalt forsake us, how much better had it been for us, if we also had been burnt in the midst of Sion? ⁴⁵For we are not better than they that died there.' And they wept with a loud voice.

Then answered I them, and said, ⁴⁶Be of good comfort, O Israel, and be not heavy, thou house of Jacob: ⁴⁷for the Highest hath you in remembrance, and the Mighty hath not forgotten you in temptation. ⁴⁸As for me, I have not forsaken you, neither am I departed from you: but am come into this place, to pray for the desolation of Sion, and that I might seek mercy for the low estate of your sanctuary. ⁴⁹And now go your way home every man, and after these days will I come unto you.'

⁵⁰So the people went their way into the city, like as I commanded them: ⁵¹but I remained still in the field seven days, as the angel commanded me, and did eat only in those days of the flowers of the field, and had my meat of the herbs.

13 And it came to pass after seven days, I dreamed a dream by night. ²And lo, there arose a wind from the sea, that it moved all the waves thereof. ³And I beheld, and lo, that man waxed strong with the thousands of heaven: and when he turned his countenance to look, all the things trembled that were seen under him. ⁴And whensoever the voice went out of his mouth, all they burnt that heard his voice, like as the earth faileth when it feeleth the fire.

⁵And after this I beheld, and lo, there was gathered together a multitude of men, out of number, from the four winds of the heaven, to subdue the man that came out of the sea. ⁶But I beheld, and lo, he had graved himself a great mountain, and flew up upon it. ⁷But I would have seen the region or place whereout the hill was graven, and I could not. ⁸And after this I beheld, and lo, all they which were gathered together to subdue him were sore afraid, and yet durst fight. ⁹And lo,

as he saw the violence of the multitude that came, he neither lifted up his hand, nor held sword, nor any instrument of war: ¹⁰but only I saw that he sent out of his mouth as it had been a blast of fire, and out of his lips a flaming breath, and out of his tongue he cast out sparks and tempests. ¹¹And they were all mixed together; the blast of fire, the flaming breath, and the great tempest; and fell with violence upon the multitude which was prepared to fight, and burnt them up every one, so that upon a sudden of an innumerable multitude nothing was to be perceived, but only dust and smell of smoke: when I saw this I was afraid.

¹²Afterward saw I the same man come down from the mountain, and call unto him another peaceable multitude. ¹³And there came much people unto him, whereof some were glad, some were sorry, some of them were bound, and other some brought of them that were offered: then was I sick through great fear, and I awoke, and said, ¹⁴'Thou hast shown thy servant wonders from the beginning, and hast counted me worthy that thou shouldst receive my prayer: ¹⁵show me now yet the interpretation of this dream. ¹⁶For as I conceive in my understanding, woe unto them that shall be left in those days; and much more woe unto them that are not left behind. ¹⁷For they that were not left were in heaviness. ¹⁸Now understand I the things that are laid up in the latter days, which shall happen unto them, and to those that are left behind. ¹⁹Therefore are they come into great perils and many necessities, like as these dreams declare. ²⁰Yet is it easier for him that is in danger to come into these things, than to pass away as a cloud out of the world, and not to see the things that happen in the last days.'

And he answered unto me, and said, ²¹'The interpretation of the vision shall I show thee, and I will open unto thee the thing that thou hast required. ²²Whereas thou hast spoken of them that are left behind, this is the interpretation. ²³He that shall endure the peril in that time hath kept himself: they that be fallen into danger are such as have works, and faith towards the Almighty. ²⁴Know this therefore, that they which be left behind are more blessed than they that be dead.

²⁵'This is the meaning of the vision: whereas thou sawest a man coming up from the midst of the sea: ²⁶the same is he whom God the Highest hath kept a great season, which by his own self shall deliver his creature: and he shall order them that are left behind. ²⁷And whereas thou sawest that out of his mouth there came as a blast of wind, and fire, and storm; ²⁸and that he held neither sword, nor any instrument of war, but that the rushing in of him destroyed the whole multitude that came to subdue him, this is the interpretation: ²⁹behold, the days come, when the most High will begin to deliver them that are upon the earth. ³⁰And he shall come to the astonishment of them that dwell on the earth. ³¹And one shall undertake to fight against another, one city against another, one place against another, one people against another, and one realm against another. ³²And the time shall be when these things shall come to pass, and the signs shall happen which I showed thee before, and then shall my Son be declared, whom thou

sawest as a man ascending. ³³And when all the people hear his voice, every man shall in their own land leave the battle they have one against another. ³⁴And an innumerable multitude shall be gathered together, as thou sawest them, willing to come, and to overcome him by fighting. ³⁵But he shall stand upon the top of the mount Sion. ³⁶And Sion shall come and shall be shown to all men, being prepared and built, like as thou sawest the hill graven without hands. ³⁷And this my Son shall rebuke the wicked inventions of those nations, which for their wicked life are fallen into the tempest, ³⁸and shall lay before them their evil thoughts, and the torments wherewith they shall begin to be tormented, which are like unto a flame: and he shall destroy them without labour by the law which is like unto fire.

³⁹'And whereas thou sawest that he gathered another peaceable multitude unto him; ⁴⁰those are the ten tribes, which were carried away prisoners out of their own land in the time of Osea the king, whom Salmanasar the king of Assyria led away captive, and he carried them over the waters, and so came they into another land. ⁴¹But they took this counsel amongst themselves, that they would leave the multitude of the heathen, and go forth into a farther country, where never mankind dwelt, ⁴²that they might there keep their statutes, which they never kept in their own land. ⁴³And they entered into Euphrates by the narrow passages of the river. ⁴⁴For the most High then shown signs for them, and held still the flood, till they were passed over. ⁴⁵For through that country there was a great way to go, namely, of a year and a half: and the same region is called Arsareth. ⁴⁶Then dwelt they there until the latter time: and now when they shall begin to come, ⁴⁷the Highest shall stay the springs of the stream again, that they may go through: therefore sawest thou the multitude with peace.

⁴⁸'But those that be left behind of thy people are they that are found within my borders. ⁴⁹Now when he destroyeth the multitude of the nations that are gathered together, he shall defend his people that remain. ⁵⁰And then shall he show them great wonders.'

⁵¹Then said I, 'O Lord that bearest rule, show me this: wherefore have I seen the man coming up from the midst of the sea?' ⁵²And he said unto me, 'Like as thou canst neither seek out nor know the things that are in the deep of the sea: even so can no man upon earth see my Son, or those that be with him, but in the daytime. ⁵³This is the interpretation of the dream which thou sawest, and whereby thou only art here lightened. ⁵⁴For thou hast forsaken thy own way, and applied thy diligence unto my law, and sought it. ⁵⁵Thy life hast thou ordered in wisdom, and hast called understanding thy mother. ⁵⁶And therefore have I shown thee the treasures of the Highest: after other three days I will speak other things unto thee, and declare unto thee mighty and wondrous things.'

⁵⁷Then went I forth into the field, giving praise and thanks greatly unto the most High because of his wonders, which he did in time, ⁵⁸and because he governeth the same, and such things as fall in their seasons: and there I sat three days.

14 And it came to pass upon the third day, I sat under an oak, and behold, there came a voice out of a bush over against me, and said, 'Esdras, Esdras'. ²And I said, 'Here am I, Lord'. And I stood up upon my feet. ³Then said he unto me, 'In the bush I did manifestly reveal myself unto Moses, and talked with him, when my people served in Egypt. ⁴And I sent him, and led my people out of Egypt, and brought him up to the mount of Sinai, where I held him by me a long season, ⁵and told him many wondrous things, and showed him the secrets of the times, and the end, and commanded him, saying, ⁶"These words shalt thou declare, and these shalt thou hide".

⁷'And now I say unto thee, ⁸that thou lay up in thy heart the signs that I have shown, and the dreams that thou hast seen, and the interpretations which thou hast heard: ⁹for thou shalt be taken away from all, and from henceforth thou shalt remain with my Son, and with such as be like thee, until the times be ended. ¹⁰For the world hath lost his youth, and the times begin to wax old. ¹¹For the world is divided into twelve parts, and the ten parts of it are gone already, and half of a tenth part. ¹²And there remaineth that which is after the half of the tenth part. ¹³Now therefore set thy house in order, and reprove thy people, comfort such of them as be in trouble, and now renounce corruption. ¹⁴Let go from thee mortal thoughts, cast away the burdens of man, put off now the weak nature, ¹⁵and set aside the thoughts that are most heavy unto thee, and haste thee to fly from these times. ¹⁶For yet greater evils than those which thou hast seen happen shall be done hereafter. ¹⁷For look how much the world shall be weaker through age: so much the more shall evils increase upon them that dwell therein. ¹⁸For the truth is fled far away, and leasing is hard at hand: for now hasteth the vision to come, which thou hast seen.'

¹⁹Then answered I before thee, and said, ²⁰'Behold, Lord, I will go, as thou hast commanded me, and reprove the people which are present: but they that shall be born afterward, who shall admonish them? thus the world is set in darkness, and they that dwell therein are without light. ²¹For thy law is burnt, therefore no man knoweth the things that are done of thee, or the works that shall begin. ²²But if I have found grace before thee, send the Holy Ghost into me, and I shall write all that hath been done in the world since the beginning, which were written in thy law, that men may find thy path, and that they which will live in the latter days may live.'

²³And he answered me, saying, 'Go thy way, gather the people together, and say unto them, that they seek thee not for forty days. ²⁴But look thou prepare thee many box trees, and take with thee Sarea, Dabria, Selemia, Ecanus, and Asiel, these five which are ready to write swiftly. ²⁵And come hither, and I shall light a candle of understanding in thy heart, which shall not be put out, till the things be performed which thou shalt begin to write. ²⁶And when thou hast done, some things shalt thou publish, and some things shalt thou show secretly to the wise: tomorrow this hour shalt thou begin to write.'

²⁷Then went I forth, as he commanded, and gathered all the people

together, and said, ²⁸'Hear these words, O Israel. ²⁹Our fathers at the beginning were strangers in Egypt, from whence they were delivered: ³⁰and received the law of life which they kept not, which ye also have transgressed after them. ³¹Then was the land, even the land of Sion, parted among you by lot: but your fathers, and ye yourselves have done unrighteousness, and have not kept the ways which the Highest commanded you. ³²And forasmuch as he is a righteous judge, he took from you in time the thing that he had given you. ³³And now are you here, and your brethren amongst you. ³⁴Therefore if so be that you will subdue your own understanding, and reform your hearts, ye shall be kept alive, and after death ye shall obtain mercy. ³⁵For after death shall the judgement come, when we shall live again: and then shall the names of the righteous be manifest, and the works of the ungodly shall be declared. ³⁶Let no man therefore come unto me now, nor seek after me these forty days.'

³⁷So I took the five men as he commanded me, and we went into the field, and remained there. ³⁸And the next day, behold, a voice called me, saying, 'Esdras, open thy mouth, and drink that I give thee to drink'. ³⁹Then opened I my mouth, and behold, he reached me a full cup, which was full as it were with water, but the colour of it was like fire. ⁴⁰And I took it, and drank: and when I had drunk of it, my heart uttered understanding, and wisdom grew in my breast, for my spirit strengthened my memory. ⁴¹And my mouth was opened, and shut no more. ⁴²The Highest gave understanding unto the five men, and they wrote the wonderful visions of the night that were told, which they knew not: and they sat forty days, and they wrote in the day, and at night they ate bread. ⁴³As for me, I spoke in the day, and held not my tongue by night. ⁴⁴In forty days they wrote two hundred and four books.

⁴⁵And it came to pass, when the forty days were fulfilled, that the Highest spoke, saying, 'The first that thou hast written publish openly, that the worthy and unworthy may read it. ⁴⁶But keep the seventy last, that thou mayest deliver them only to such as be wise among the people: ⁴⁷for in them is the spring of understanding, the fountains of wisdom, and the stream of knowledge.' ⁴⁸And I did so.

15 'Behold, speak thou in the ears of my people the words of prophecy, which I will put in thy mouth,' saith the Lord: ²'and cause them to be written in paper: for they are faithful and true. ³Fear not the imaginations against thee, let not the incredulity of them trouble thee, that speak against thee. ⁴For all the unfaithful shall die in their unfaithfulness.

⁵'Behold,' saith the Lord, 'I will bring plagues upon the world; the sword, famine, death, and destruction. ⁶For wickedness hath exceedingly polluted the whole earth, and their hurtful works are fulfilled.' ⁷Therefore saith the Lord, ⁸'I will hold my tongue no more as touching their wickedness, which they profanely commit, neither will I suffer them in those things, in which they wickedly exercise themselves: behold, the innocent and righteous blood crieth unto me, and the souls of the just complain continually. ⁹And therefore,' saith the Lord, 'I

will surely avenge them, and receive unto me all the innocent blood from among them. ¹⁰Behold, my people is led as a flock to the slaughter: I will not suffer them now to dwell in the land of Egypt. ¹¹But I will bring them with a mighty hand and a stretched out arm, and smite Egypt with plagues as before, and will destroy all the land thereof. ¹²Egypt shall mourn, and the foundation of it shall be smitten with the plague and punishment that God shall bring upon it. ¹³They that till the ground shall mourn: for their seeds shall fail through the blasting and hail, and with a fearful constellation.

¹⁴'Woe to the world and them that dwell therein. ¹⁵For the sword and their destruction draweth nigh, and one people shall stand up to fight against another, and swords in their hands. ¹⁶For there shall be sedition among men, and invading one another; they shall not regard their kings nor princes, and the course of their actions shall stand in their power. ¹⁷A man shall desire to go into a city, and shall not be able. ¹⁸For because of their pride the cities shall be troubled, the houses shall be destroyed, and men shall be afraid. ¹⁹A man shall have no pity upon his neighbour, but shall destroy their houses with the sword, and spoil their goods, because of the lack of bread, and for great tribulation.

²⁰'Behold,' saith God, 'I will call together all the kings of the earth to reverence me, which are from the rising of the sun, from the south, from the east, and Libanus: to turn themselves one against another, and repay the things that they have done to them. ²¹Like as they do yet this day unto my chosen, so will I do also, and recompense in their bosom.'

Thus saith the Lord God, ²²'My right hand shall not spare the sinners, and my sword shall not cease over them that shed innocent blood upon earth. ²³The fire is gone forth from his wrath, and hath consumed the foundations of the earth, and the sinners, like the straw that is kindled. ²⁴Woe to them that sin, and keep not my commandments,' saith the Lord. ²⁵'I will not spare them: go your way, ye children, from the power, defile not my sanctuary: ²⁶for the Lord knoweth all them that sin against him, and therefore delivereth he them unto death and destruction. ²⁷For now are the plagues come upon the whole earth, and ye shall remain in them, for God shall not deliver you, because ye have sinned against him.

²⁸'Behold a horrible vision, and the appearance thereof from the east: ²⁹where the nations of the dragons of Arabia shall come out with many chariots, and the multitude of them shall be carried as the wind upon earth, that all they which hear them may fear and tremble. ³⁰Also the Carmanians raging in wrath shall go forth as the wild boars of the wood, and with great power shall they come, and join battle with them, and shall waste a portion of the land of the Assyrians. ³¹And then shall the dragons have the upper hand, remembering their nature; and if they shall turn themselves, conspiring together in great power to persecute them, ³²then these shall be troubled, and keep silence through their power, and shall flee. ³³And from the land of the Assyrians shall the enemy besiege them, and consume some of them, and in their host shall be fear and dread, and strife among their kings.

³⁴'Behold clouds from the east, and from the north unto the south, and they are very horrible to look upon, full of wrath and storm. ³⁵They shall smite one upon another, and they shall smite down a great multitude of stars upon the earth, even their own star; and blood shall be from the sword unto the belly, ³⁶and dung of men unto the camel's hock. ³⁷And there shall be great fearfulness and trembling upon earth: and they that see the wrath shall be afraid, and trembling shall come upon them. ³⁸And then shall there come great storms from the south, and from the north, and another part from the west. ³⁹And strong winds shall arise from the east, and shall open it; and the cloud which he raised up in wrath, and the star stirred to cause fear toward the east and west wind, shall be destroyed. ⁴⁰The great and mighty clouds shall be lifted up full of wrath, and the star, that they may make all the earth afraid, and them that dwell therein; and they shall pour out over every high and eminent place a horrible star, ⁴¹fire, and hail, and flying swords, and many waters, that all fields may be full, and all rivers, with the abundance of great waters. ⁴²And they shall break down the cities and walls, mountains and hills, trees of the wood, and grass of the meadows, and their corn. ⁴³And they shall go steadfastly unto Babylon, and make her afraid. ⁴⁴They shall come to her, and besiege her, the star and all wrath shall they pour out upon her: then shall the dust and smoke go up unto the heaven, and all they that be about her shall bewail her. ⁴⁵And they that remain under her shall do service unto them that have put her in fear.

⁴⁶'And thou, Asia, that art partaker of the hope of Babylon, and art the glory of her person: ⁴⁷woe be unto thee, thou wretch, because thou hast made thyself like unto her, and hast decked thy daughters in whoredom, that they might please and glory in thy lovers, which have always desired to commit whoredom with thee. ⁴⁸Thou hast followed her that is hated in all her works and inventions:' therefore saith God, ⁴⁹'I will send plagues upon thee: widowhood, poverty, famine, sword, and pestilence, to waste thy houses with destruction and death. ⁵⁰And the glory of thy power shall be dried up as a flower, when the heat shall arise that is sent over thee. ⁵¹Thou shalt be weakened as a poor woman with stripes, and as one chastised with wounds, so that the mighty and lovers shall not be able to receive thee. ⁵²Would I with jealousy have so proceeded against thee,' saith the Lord, ⁵³'if thou hadst not always slain my chosen, exalting the stroke of thy hands, and saying over their dead, when thou wast drunken, ⁵⁴"Set forth the beauty of thy countenance"? ⁵⁵The reward of thy whoredom shall be in thy bosom, therefore shalt thou receive recompence.

⁵⁶'Like as thou hast done unto my chosen,' saith the Lord, 'even so shall God do unto thee, and shall deliver thee into mischief. ⁵⁷Thy children shall die of hunger, and thou shalt fall through the sword: thy cities shall be broken down, and all thine shall perish with the sword in the field. ⁵⁸They that be in the mountains shall die of hunger, and eat their own flesh, and drink their own blood, for very hunger of bread, and thirst of water. ⁵⁹Thou, as unhappy, shalt come through the sea,

and receive plagues again. ⁶⁰And in the passage they shall rush on the idle city, and shall destroy some portion of thy land, and consume part of thy glory, and shall return to Babylon that was destroyed. ⁶¹And thou shalt be cast down by them as stubble, and they shall be unto thee as fire, ⁶²and shall consume thee, and thy cities, thy land and thy mountains, all thy woods and thy fruitful trees shall they burn up with fire. ⁶³Thy children shall they carry away captive, and look what thou hast, they shall spoil it, and mar the beauty of thy face.'

16 Woe be unto thee, Babylon, and Asia, woe be unto thee, Egypt, and Syria. ²Gird up yourselves with cloths of sack and hair, bewail your children, and be sorry, for your destruction is at hand. ³A sword is sent upon you, and who may turn it back? ⁴A fire is sent among you, and who may quench it? ⁵Plagues are sent unto you, and what is he that may drive them away? ⁶May any man drive away a hungry lion in the wood? or may anyone quench the fire in stubble, when it hath begun to burn? ⁷May one turn again the arrow that is shot of a strong archer?

⁸The mighty Lord sendeth the plagues, and who is he that can drive them away? ⁹A fire shall go forth from his wrath, and who is he that may quench it? ¹⁰He shall cast lightnings, and who shall not fear? he shall thunder, and who shall not be afraid? ¹¹The Lord shall threaten, and who shall not be utterly beaten to powder at his presence? ¹²The earth quaketh, and the foundations thereof, the sea ariseth up with waves from the deep, and the waves of it are troubled, and the fishes thereof also before the Lord, and before the glory of his power: ¹³for strong is his right hand that bendeth the bow, his arrows that he shooteth are sharp, and shall not miss when they begin to be shot into the ends of the world.

¹⁴Behold, the plagues are sent, and shall not return again, until they come upon the earth. ¹⁵The fire is kindled, and shall not be put out, till it consume the foundation of the earth. ¹⁶Like as an arrow which is shot of a mighty archer returneth not backward: even so the plagues that shall be sent upon earth shall not return again.

¹⁷Woe is me, woe is me, who will deliver me in those days? ¹⁸The beginning of sorrows and great mournings; the beginning of famine and great death; the beginning of wars, and the powers shall stand in fear; the beginning of evils: what shall I do when these evils shall come? ¹⁹Behold, famine and plague, tribulation and anguish, are sent as scourges for amendment. ²⁰But for all these things they shall not turn from their wickedness, nor be always mindful of the scourges. ²¹Behold, victuals shall be so good cheap upon earth, that they shall think themselves to be in good case, and even then shall evils grow upon earth, sword, famine, and great confusion. ²²For many of them that dwell upon earth shall perish of famine, and the others, that escape the hunger, shall the sword destroy. ²³And the dead shall be cast out as dung, and there shall be no man to comfort them, for the earth shall be wasted, and the cities shall be cast down. ²⁴There shall be no man left to till the earth, and to sow it. ²⁵The trees shall give fruit, and

who shall gather them? ^{26}The grapes shall ripen, and who shall tread them? for all places shall be desolate of men: ^{27}so that one man shall desire to see another, and to hear his voice. ^{28}For of a city there shall be ten left, and two of the field which shall hide themselves in the thick groves, and in the clefts of rocks. ^{29}As in an orchard of olives upon every tree there are left three or four olives; ^{30}or, when as a vineyard is gathered, there are left some clusters of them that diligently seek through the vineyard: ^{31}even so in those days there shall be three or four left by them that search their houses with the sword. ^{32}And the earth shall be laid waste, and the fields thereof shall wax old, and her ways and all her paths shall grow full of thorns, because no man shall travel therethrough. ^{33}The virgins shall mourn having no bridegrooms, the women shall mourn having no husbands, their daughters shall mourn having no helpers. ^{34}In the wars shall their bridegrooms be destroyed, and their husbands shall perish of famine.

^{35}Hear now these things, and understand them, ye servants of the Lord. ^{36}Behold the word of the Lord, receive it: believe not the gods of whom the Lord spoke. ^{37}Behold, the plagues draw nigh, and are not slack. ^{38}As when a woman with child in the ninth month bringeth forth her son, within two or three hours of her birth great pains compass her womb, which pains, when the child cometh forth, they slack not a moment: ^{39}even so shall not the plagues be slack to come upon the earth, and the world shall mourn, and sorrows shall come upon it on every side.

^{40}O my people, hear my word: make you ready to the battle, and in those evils be even as pilgrims upon the earth. ^{41}He that selleth, let him be as he that fleeth away: and he that buyeth, as one that will lose: ^{42}he that occupieth merchandise, as he that had no profit by it: and he that buildeth, as he that shall not dwell therein: ^{43}he that soweth, as if he should not reap: so also he that planteth the vineyard, as he that shall not gather the grapes: ^{44}they that marry, as they that shall get no children; and they that marry not, as the widowers. ^{45}And therefore they that labour, labour in vain: ^{46}for strangers shall reap their fruits, and spoil their goods, overthrow their houses, and take their children captives, for in captivity and famine shall they get children. ^{47}And they that occupy their merchandise with robbery, the more they deck their cities, their houses, their possessions, and their own persons: ^{48}the more will I be angry with them for their sin, saith the Lord. ^{49}Like as a whore envieth a right honest and virtuous woman: ^{50}so shall righteousness hate iniquity, when she decketh herself, and shall accuse her to her face, when he cometh that shall defend him that diligently searcheth out every sin upon earth. ^{51}And therefore be ye not like thereunto, nor to the works thereof. ^{52}For yet a little, and iniquity shall be taken away out of the earth, and righteousness shall reign among you.

^{53}Let not the sinner say that he hath not sinned: for God shall burn coals of fire upon his head, which saith before the Lord God and his glory, 'I have not sinned'. ^{54}Behold, the Lord knoweth all the works of men, their imaginations, their thoughts, and their hearts: ^{55}which spoke but the word, 'Let the earth be made', and it was made: 'Let the heaven be made', and it was created. ⁵⁶In his word were the stars made, and he knoweth the number of them. ⁵⁷He searcheth the deep, and the treasures thereof, he hath measured the sea, and what it containeth. ⁵⁸He hath shut the sea in the midst of the waters, and with his word hath he hanged the earth upon the waters. ⁵⁹He spreadeth out the heavens like a vault; upon the waters hath he founded it. ⁶⁰In the desert hath he made springs of water, and pools upon the tops of the mountains, that the floods might pour down from the high rocks to water the earth. ⁶¹He made man, and put his heart in the midst of the body, and gave him breath, life, and understanding. ⁶²Yea, and the spirit of Almighty God, which made all things, and searcheth out all hidden things in the secrets of the earth, ⁶³surely he knoweth your inventions, and what you think in your hearts, even them that sin, and would hide their sin. ⁶⁴Therefore hath the Lord exactly searched out all your works, and he will put you all to shame. ⁶⁵And when your sins are brought forth, ye shall be ashamed before men, and your own sins shall be your accusers in that day. ⁶⁶What will ye do? or how will ye hide your sins before God and his angels? ⁶⁷Behold, God himself is the judge, fear him: leave off from your sins, and forget your iniquities to meddle no more with them for ever: so shall God lead you forth, and deliver you from all trouble. ⁶⁸For behold, the burning wrath of a great multitude is kindled over you, and they shall take away certain of you, and feed you, being idle, with things offered unto idols. ⁶⁹And they that consent unto them shall be had in derision and in reproach, and trodden under foot. ⁷⁰For there shall be in every place, and in the next cities a great insurrection upon those that fear the Lord. ⁷¹They shall be like madmen, sparing none, but still spoiling and destroying those that fear the Lord. ⁷²For they shall waste and take away their goods, and cast them out of their houses. ⁷³Then shall they be known, who are my chosen; and they shall be tried as the gold in the fire.

⁷⁴'Hear, O ye my beloved,' saith the Lord: 'behold, the days of trouble are at hand, but I will deliver you from the same. ⁷⁵Be ye not afraid, neither doubt, for God is your guide, ⁷⁶and the guide of them who keep my commandments and precepts,' saith the Lord God: 'let not your sins weigh you down, and let not your iniquities lift up themselves. ⁷⁷Woe be unto them that are bound with their sins, and covered with their iniquities, like as a field is covered over with bushes, and the path thereof covered with thorns, that no man may travel through. ⁷⁸It is left undressed, and is cast into the fire to be consumed therewith.'

TOBIT

1 The book of the words of Tobit, son of Tobiel, the son of Ananiel, the son of Aduel, the son of Gabael, of the seed of Asael, of the tribe of Nephthali, ²who in the time of Enemessar king of the Assyrians was led captive out of Thisbe, which is at the right hand of that city, which is called properly Nephthali in Galilee above Aser.

³I Tobit have walked all the days of my life in the way of truth and justice, and I did many alms-deeds to my brethren, and my nation, who came with me to Nineveh, into the land of the Assyrians. ⁴And when I was in my own country, in the land of Israel, being but young, all the tribe of Nephthali my father fell from the house of Jerusalem, which was chosen out of all the tribes of Israel, that all the tribes should sacrifice there where the temple of the habitation of the most High was consecrated and built for all ages. ⁵Now all the tribes which together revolted, and the house of my father Nephthali, sacrificed unto the heifer Baal. ⁶But I alone went often to Jerusalem at the feasts, as it was ordained unto all the people of Israel by an everlasting decree, having the first-fruits and tenths of increase, with that which was first shorn, and them gave I at the altar to the priests the children of Aaron. ⁷The first tenth part of all increase I gave to the sons of Aaron, who ministered at Jerusalem: another tenth part I sold away, and went, and spent it every year at Jerusalem. ⁸And the third I gave unto them to whom it was meet, as Debora my father's mother had commanded me, because I was left an orphan by my father.

⁹Furthermore, when I was come to the age of a man, I married Anna of my own kindred, and of her I begot Tobias. ¹⁰And when we were carried away captives to Nineveh, all my brethren and those that were of my kindred did eat of the bread of the Gentiles. ¹¹But I kept myself from eating; ¹²because I remembered God with all my heart. ¹³And the most High gave me grace and favour before Enemessar, so that I was his purveyor. ¹⁴And I went into Media, and left in trust with Gabael, the brother of Gabrias, at Rages a city of Media, ten talents of silver.

¹⁵Now when Enemessar was dead, Sennacherib his son reigned in his stead, whose estate was troubled, that I could not go into Media. ¹⁶And in the time of Enemessar I gave many alms to my brethren, and gave my bread to the hungry, ¹⁷and my clothes to the naked: and if I saw any of my nation dead, or cast about the walls of Nineveh, I buried him. ¹⁸And if the king Sennacherib had slain any, when he was come, and fled from Judea, I buried them privily (for in his wrath he killed many), but the bodies were not found, when they were sought for of the king. ¹⁹And when one of the Ninevites went and complained of me to the king that I buried them, and hid myself: understanding that I was sought for to be put to death, I withdrew myself for fear. ²⁰Then all my goods were forcibly taken away, neither was there anything left me, besides my wife Anna and my son Tobias.

²¹And there passed not five and fifty days before two of his sons killed him, and they fled into the mountains of Ararath; and Sarchedonus his son reigned in his stead, who appointed over his father's accounts, and over all his affairs, Achiacharus, my brother Anael's son. ²²And Achiacharus entreating for me, I returned to Nineveh. Now Achiacharus was cup-bearer, and keeper of the signet, and steward, and overseer of the accounts: and Sarchedonus appointed him next unto him: and he was my brother's son.

2 Now when I was come home again, and my wife Anna was restored unto me, with my son Tobias, in the feast of Pentecost, which is the holy feast of the seven weeks, there was a good dinner prepared me, in the which I sat down to eat. ²And when I saw abundance of meat, I said to my son, 'Go and bring what poor man soever thou shalt find out of our brethren, who is mindful of the Lord; and lo, I tarry for thee'. ³But he came again, and said, 'Father, one of our nation is strangled, and is cast out in the market-place'. ⁴Then before I had tasted of any meat, I started up, and took him up into a room until the going down of the sun. ⁵Then I returned and washed myself, and ate my meat in heaviness, ⁶remembering that prophecy of Amos, as he said, 'Your feasts shall be turned into mourning, and all your mirth into lamentation'. ⁷Therefore I wept: and after the going down of the sun I went and made a grave, and buried him. ⁸But my neighbours mocked me, and said, 'This man is not yet afraid to be put to death for this matter, who fled away, and yet lo, he burieth the dead again'.

⁹The same night also I returned from the burial, and slept by the wall of my courtyard, being polluted, and my face was uncovered: ¹⁰and I knew not that there were sparrows in the wall, and my eyes being open, the sparrows muted warm dung into my eyes, and a whiteness came in my eyes; and I went to the physicians, but they helped me not: moreover Achiacharus did nourish me, until I went into Elymais.

¹¹And my wife Anna did take women's works to do. ¹²And when she had sent them home to the owners, they paid her wages, and gave her also besides a kid. ¹³And when it was in my house, and began to cry, I said unto her, 'From whence is this kid? is it not stolen? render it to the owners, for it is not lawful to eat anything that is stolen'. ¹⁴But she replied upon me, 'It was given for a gift more than the wages'. Howbeit I did not believe her, but bade her render it to the owners: and I was abashed at her. But she replied upon me, 'Where are thy alms and thy righteous deeds? behold, thou and all thy works are known'.

3 Then I being grieved did weep, and in my sorrow prayed, saying, ²'O Lord, thou art just, and all thy works and all thy ways are mercy and truth, and thou judgest truly and justly for ever. ³Remember me, and look on me, punish me not for my sins and ignorances, and the sins of my fathers, who have sinned before thee: ⁴for they obeyed not thy commandments, wherefore thou hast delivered us for a spoil, and unto captivity, and unto death, and for a proverb of reproach to all the nations among whom we are dispersed. ⁵And now thy judgements are many and true: deal with me according to my sins and my fathers':

because we have not kept thy commandments, neither have walked in truth before thee. ⁶Now therefore deal with me as seemeth best unto thee, and command my spirit to be taken from me, that I may be dissolved, and become earth: for it is profitable for me to die rather than to live, because I have heard false reproaches, and have much sorrow: command therefore that I may now be delivered out of this distress, and go into the everlasting place: turn not thy face away from me.'

⁷It came to pass the same day, that in Ecbatane a city of Media Sara the daughter of Raguel was also reproached by her father's maids, ⁸because that she had been married to seven husbands, whom Asmodeus the evil spirit had killed, before they had lain with her. 'Dost thou not know,' said they, 'that thou hast strangled thy husbands? thou hast had already seven husbands, neither wast thou named after any of them. ⁹Wherefore dost thou beat us for them? If they be dead, go thy ways after them, let us never see of thee either son or daughter.'

¹⁰When she heard these things, she was very sorrowful, so that she thought to have strangled herself, and she said, 'I am the only daughter of my father, and if I do this, it shall be a reproach unto him, and I shall bring his old age with sorrow unto the grave'. ¹¹Then she prayed toward the window, and said, 'Blessed art thou, O Lord my God, and thy holy and glorious name is blessed and honourable for ever: let all thy works praise thee for ever. ¹²And now, O Lord, I set my eyes and my face toward thee, ¹³and say, "Take me out of the earth, that I may hear no more the reproach". ¹⁴Thou knowest, Lord, that I am pure from all sin with man, ¹⁵and that I never polluted my name, nor the name of my father in the land of my captivity: I am the only daughter of my father, neither hath he any child to be his heir, neither any near kinsman, nor any son of his alive, to whom I may keep myself for a wife: my seven husbands are already dead, and why should I live? but if it please not thee that I should die, command some regard to be had of me, and pity taken of me, that I hear no more reproach.'

¹⁶So the prayers of them both were heard before the majesty of the great God. ¹⁷And Raphael was sent to heal them both, that is, to scale away the whiteness of Tobit's eyes, and to give Sara the daughter of Raguel for a wife to Tobias the son of Tobit, and to bind Asmodeus the evil spirit, because she belongeth to Tobias by right of inheritance. The selfsame time came Tobit home, and entered into his house, and Sara the daughter of Raguel came down from her upper chamber.

4 In that day Tobit remembered the money which he had committed to Gabael in Rages of Media, ²and said with himself, 'I have wished for death, wherefore do I not call for my son Tobias, that I may signify to him of the money before I die?' ³And when he had called him, he said, 'My son, when I am dead, bury me, and despise not thy mother, but honour her all the days of thy life, and do that which shall please her, and grieve her not. ⁴Remember, my son, that she saw many dangers for thee, when thou wast in her womb, and when she is dead, bury her by me in one grave.

⁵'My son, be mindful of the Lord our God all thy days, and let not thy

will be set to sin, or to transgress his commandments: do uprightly all thy life long, and follow not the ways of unrighteousness. ⁶For if thou deal truly, thy doings shall prosperously succeed to thee, and to all them that live justly.

⁷'Give alms of thy substance, and when thou givest alms, let not thy eye be envious, neither turn thy face from any poor, and the face of God shall not be turned away from thee. ⁸If thou hast abundance, give alms accordingly: if thou have but a little, be not afraid to give according to that little: ⁹for thou layest up a good treasure for thyself against the day of necessity. ¹⁰Because that alms doth deliver from death, and suffereth not to come into darkness. ¹¹For alms is a good gift unto all that give it, in the sight of the most High.

¹²'Beware of all whoredom, my son, and chiefly take a wife of the seed of thy fathers, and take not a strange woman to wife, which is not of thy father's tribe: for we are the children of the prophets, Noe, Abraham, Isaac, and Jacob: remember, my son, that our fathers from the beginning, even that they all married wives of their own kindred, and were blessed in their children, and their seed shall inherit the land. ¹³Now therefore, my son, love thy brethren, and despise not in thy heart thy brethren, the sons and daughters of thy people, in not taking a wife of them: for in pride is destruction and much trouble, and in lewdness is decay and great want: for lewdness is the mother of famine.

¹⁴'Let not the wages of any man, which hath wrought for thee, tarry with thee, but give him it out of hand: for if thou serve God, he will also repay thee: be circumspect, my son, in all things thou doest, and be wise in all thy conversation. ¹⁵Do that to no man which thou hatest: drink not wine to make thee drunken: neither let drunkenness go with thee in thy journey. ¹⁶Give of thy bread to the hungry, and of thy garments to them that are naked, and according to thy abundance give alms, and let not thy eye be envious, when thou givest alms. ¹⁷Pour out thy bread on the burial of the just, but give nothing to the wicked. ¹⁸Ask counsel of all that are wise, and despise not any counsel that is profitable. ¹⁹Bless the Lord thy God always, and desire of him that thy ways may be directed, and that all thy paths and counsels may prosper: for every nation hath not counsel, but the Lord himself giveth all good things, and he humbleth whom he will, as he will; now therefore, my son, remember my commandments, neither let them be put out of thy mind.

²⁰'And now I signify this to thee, that I committed ten talents to Gabael the son of Gabrias at Rages in Media. ²¹And fear not, my son, that we are made poor: for thou hast much wealth, if thou fear God, and depart from all sin, and do that which is pleasing in his sight.'

5 Tobias then answered and said, 'Father, I will do all things which thou hast commanded me. ²But how can I receive the money, seeing I know him not?' ³Then he gave him the handwriting, and said unto him, 'Seek thee a man which may go with thee whilst I yet live, and I will give him wages: and go and receive the money'.

⁴Therefore when he went to seek a man, he found Raphael that was an

angel. ⁵But he knew not; and he said unto him, 'Canst thou go with me to Rages? and knowest thou those places well?' ⁶To whom the angel said, 'I will go with thee, and I know the way well: for I have lodged with our brother Gabael'. ⁷Then Tobias said unto him, 'Tarry for me, till I tell my father'. ⁸Then he said unto him, 'Go, and tarry not'.

So he went in and said to his father, 'Behold, I have found one which will go with me'. Then he said, 'Call him unto me, that I may know of what tribe he is, and whether he be a trusty man to go with thee'. ⁹So he called him, and he came in, and they saluted one another. ¹⁰Then Tobit said unto him, 'Brother, show me of what tribe and family thou art'. ¹¹To whom he said, 'Dost thou seek for a tribe or family, or a hired man to go with thy son?' Then Tobit said unto him, 'I would know, brother, thy kindred and name'. ¹²Then he said, 'I am Azarias, the son of Ananias the great, and of thy brethren'. ¹³Then Tobit said, 'Thou art welcome, brother, be not now angry with me, because I have inquired to know thy tribe and thy family, for thou art my brother, of an honest and good stock: for I know Ananias and Jonathas, sons of that great Samaias: as we went together to Jerusalem to worship, and offered the firstborn, and the tenths of the fruits, and they were not seduced with the error of our brethren: my brother, thou art of a good stock. ¹⁴But tell me, what wages shall I give thee? wilt thou a drachm a day, and things necessary, as to my own son? ¹⁵Yea, moreover, if ye return safe, I will add something to the wages.'

¹⁶So they were well pleased. Then said he to Tobias, 'Prepare thyself for the journey, and God send you a good journey'. And when his son had prepared all things for the journey, his father said, 'Go thou with this man, and God, which dwelleth in heaven, prosper your journey, and the angel of God keep you company'. So they went forth both, and the young man's dog with them.

¹⁷But Anna his mother wept, and said to Tobit, 'Why hast thou sent away our son? is he not the staff of our hand, in going in and out before us? ¹⁸Be not greedy to add money to money: but let it be as refuse in respect of our child. ¹⁹For that which the Lord hath given us to live with, doth suffice us.' ²⁰Then said Tobit to her, 'Take no care, my sister, he shall return in safety, and thy eyes shall see him. ²¹For the good angel will keep him company, and his journey shall be prosperous, and he shall return safe.' ²²Then she made an end of weeping.

6 And as they went on their journey, they came in the evening to the river Tigris, and they lodged there. ²And when the young man went down to wash himself, a fish leapt out of the river, and would have devoured him. ³Then the angel said unto him, 'Take the fish'. And the young man laid hold of the fish, and drew it to land. ⁴To whom the angel said, 'Open the fish, and take the heart and the liver and the gall, and put them up safely'. ⁵So the young man did as the angel commanded him; and when they had roasted the fish, they did eat it: then they both went on their way, till they drew near to Ecbatane. ⁶Then the young man said to the angel, 'Brother Azarias, to what use is the heart and the liver and the gall of the fish?' ⁷And he said unto him, 'Touching

the heart and the liver, if a devil or an evil spirit trouble any, we must make a smoke thereof before the man or the woman, and the party shall be no more vexed. ⁸As for the gall, it is good to anoint a man that hath whiteness in his eyes, and he shall be healed.'

⁹And when they were come near to Rages, ¹⁰the angel said to the young man, 'Brother, today we shall lodge with Raguel, who is thy cousin; he also hath one only daughter, named Sara; I will speak for her, that she may be given thee for a wife. ¹¹For to thee doth the right of her appertain, seeing thou only art of her kindred. ¹²And the maid is fair and wise: now therefore hear me, and I will speak to her father, and when we return from Rages we will celebrate the marriage: for I know that Raguel cannot marry her to another according to the law of Moses, but he shall be guilty of death, because the right of inheritance doth rather appertain to thee than to any other.'

¹³Then the young man answered the angel, 'I have heard, brother Azarias, that this maid hath been given to seven men, who all died in the marriage-chamber. ¹⁴And now I am the only son of my father, and I am afraid, lest if I go in unto her, I die, as the others before: for a wicked spirit loveth her, which hurteth nobody, but those which come unto her: wherefore I also fear lest I die, and bring my father's and my mother's life, because of me, to the grave with sorrow: for they have no other son to bury them.'

¹⁵Then the angel said unto him, 'Dost thou not remember the precepts which thy father gave thee, that thou shouldst marry a wife of thy own kindred? wherefore hear me, O my brother, for she shall be given thee to wife, and make thou no reckoning of the evil spirit, for this same night shall she be given thee in marriage. ¹⁶And when thou shalt come into the marriage-chamber, thou shalt take the ashes of perfume, and shalt lay upon them some of the heart and liver of the fish, and shalt make a smoke with it. ¹⁷And the devil shall smell it, and flee away, and never come again any more: but when thou shalt come to her, rise up both of you, and pray to God which is merciful, who will have pity on you, and save you: fear not, for she is appointed unto thee from the beginning; and thou shalt preserve her, and she shall go with thee. Moreover I suppose that she shall bear thee children.'

Now when Tobias had heard these things, he loved her, and his heart was effectually joined to her.

7 And when they were come to Ecbatane, they came to the house of Raguel, and Sara met them: and after that they had saluted one another, she brought them into the house. ²Then said Raguel to Edna his wife, 'How like is this young man to Tobit my cousin!' ³And Raguel asked them, 'From whence are you, brethren?' To whom they said, 'We are of the sons of Nephthali, which are captives in Nineveh'. ⁴Then he said to them, 'Do ye know Tobit our kinsman?' And they said, 'We know him'. Then said he, 'Is he in good health?' ⁵And they said, 'He is both alive, and in good health': and Tobias said, 'He is my father'. ⁶Then Raguel leapt up, and kissed him, and wept, ⁷and blessed him, and said unto him, 'Thou art the son of an honest and good man'. But when he

had heard that Tobit was blind, he was sorrowful, and wept. ⁸And likewise Edna his wife and Sara his daughter wept.

Moreover they entertained them cheerfully, and after that they had killed a ram of the flock, they set store of meat on the table. Then said Tobias to Raphael, 'Brother Azarias, speak of those things of which thou didst talk in the way, and let this business be dispatched'. ⁹So he communicated the matter with Raguel, and Raguel said to Tobias, 'Eat and drink, and make merry: ¹⁰for it is meet that thou shouldst marry my daughter: nevertheless I will declare unto thee the truth. ¹¹I have given my daughter in marriage to seven men, who died that night they came in unto her: nevertheless for the present be merry.' But Tobias said, 'I will eat nothing here, till we agree and swear one to another'. ¹²Raguel said, 'Then take her from henceforth according to the manner, for thou art her cousin, and she is thine, and the merciful God give you good success in all things'.

¹³Then he called his daughter Sara, and she came to her father, and he took her by the hand, and gave her to be wife to Tobias, saying, 'Behold, take her after the law of Moses, and lead her away to thy father'. And he blessed them, ¹⁴and called Edna his wife, and took paper, and did write an instrument of covenants, and sealed it. ¹⁵Then they began to eat.

¹⁶After Raguel called his wife Edna, and said unto her, 'Sister, prepare another chamber, and bring her in thither'. ¹⁷Which when she had done as he had bidden her, she brought her thither: and she wept, and she received the tears of her daughter, and said unto her, ¹⁸'Be of good comfort, my daughter, the Lord of heaven and earth give thee joy for this thy sorrow: be of good comfort, my daughter'.

8 And when they had supped, they brought Tobias in unto her. ²And as he went, he remembered the words of Raphael, and took the ashes of the perfumes, and put the heart and the liver of the fish thereupon, and made a smoke therewith. ³The which smell when the evil spirit had smelled, he fled into the utmost parts of Egypt, and the angel bound him.

⁴And after that they were both shut in together, Tobias rose out of the bed, and said, 'Sister, arise, and let us pray that God would have pity on us'. ⁵Then began Tobias to say, 'Blessed art thou, O God of our fathers, and blessed is thy holy and glorious name for ever, let the heavens bless thee, and all thy creatures. ⁶Thou madest Adam, and gavest him Eve his wife for a helper and stay: of them came mankind: thou hast said, "It is not good that man should be alone, let us make unto him an aid like unto himself". ⁷And now, O Lord, I take not this my sister for lust, but uprightly: therefore mercifully ordain that we may become aged together.' ⁸And she said with him, 'Amen'. ⁹So they slept both that night.

And Raguel arose, and went and made a grave, ¹⁰saying, 'I fear lest he be dead'. ¹¹But when Raguel was come into his house, ¹²he said unto his wife Edna, 'Send one of the maids, and let her see whether he be alive: if he be not, that we may bury him, and no man know it'. ¹³So the maid opened the door, and went in, and found them both asleep, [14]and came forth, and told them that he was alive.

[15]Then Raguel praised God, and said, 'O God, thou art worthy to be praised with all pure and holy praise: therefore let thy saints praise thee with all thy creatures, and let all thy angels and thy elect praise thee for ever. [16]Thou art to be praised, for thou hast made me joyful, and that is not come to me which I suspected: but thou hast dealt with us according to thy great mercy. [17]Thou art to be praised, because thou hast had mercy of two that were the only begotten children of their fathers: grant them mercy, O Lord, and finish their life in health with joy and mercy.' [18]Then Raguel bade his servants to fill the grave.

[19]And he kept the wedding feast fourteen days. [20]For before the days of the marriage were finished, Raguel had said unto him by an oath, that he should not depart till the fourteen days of the marriage were expired, [21]and then he should take the half of his goods, and go in safety to his father; and should have the rest when I and my wife be dead.

9 Then Tobias called Raphael, and said unto him, [2]'Brother Azarias, take with thee a servant, and two camels, and go to Rages of Media to Gabael, and bring me the money, and bring him to the wedding. [3]For Raguel hath sworn that I shall not depart. [4]But my father counteth the days, and if I tarry long, he will be very sorry.' [5]So Raphael went out, and lodged with Gabael, and gave him the handwriting: who brought forth bags which were sealed up, and gave them to him. [6]And early in the morning they went forth both together, and came to the wedding: and Tobias blessed his wife.

10 Now Tobit his father counted every day: and when the days of the journey were expired, and they came not, [2]then Tobit said, 'Are they detained? or is Gabael dead, and there is no man to give him the money?' [3]Therefore he was very sorry. [4]Then his wife said to him, 'My son is dead, seeing he stayeth long'; and she began to bewail him, and said, [5]'Now I care for nothing, my son, since I have let thee go, the light of my eyes'. [6]To whom Tobit said, 'Hold thy peace, take no care, for he is safe'. [7]But she said, 'Hold thy peace, and deceive me not: my son is dead'. And she went out every day into the way which they went, and did eat no meat on the daytime, and ceased not whole nights to bewail her son Tobias, until the fourteen days of the wedding were expired, which Raguel had sworn that he should spend there.

Then Tobias said to Raguel, 'Let me go, for my father and my mother look no more to see me'. [8]But his father-in-law said unto him, 'Tarry with me, and I will send to thy father, and they shall declare unto him how things go with thee'. [9]But Tobias said, 'No: but let me go to my father'. [10]Then Raguel arose, and gave him Sara his wife, and half his goods, servants, and cattle, and money. [11]And he blessed them, and sent them away, saying, 'The God of heaven give you a prosperous journey, my children'. [12]And he said to his daughter, 'Honour thy father and thy mother-in-law, which are now thy parents, that I may hear good report of thee'. And he kissed her. Edna also said to Tobias, 'The Lord of heaven restore thee, my dear brother, and grant that I may see thy children of my daughter Sara before I die, that I may rejoice before the Lord: behold, I commit my daughter unto thee of special trust; wherefore do not entreat her evil'.

11 After these things Tobias went his way, praising God that he had given him a prosperous journey, and blessed Raguel and Edna his wife, and went on his way till they drew near unto Nineveh. ²Then Raphael said to Tobias, 'Thou knowest, brother, how thou didst leave thy father. ³Let us haste before thy wife, and prepare the house. ⁴And take in thy hand the gall of the fish.' So they went their way, and the dog went after them.

⁵Now Anna sat looking about towards the way for her son. ⁶And when she espied him coming, she said to his father, 'Behold, thy son cometh, and the man that went with him'.

⁷Then said Raphael, 'I know, Tobias, that thy father will open his eyes. ⁸Therefore anoint thou his eyes with the gall, and being pricked therewith, he shall rub, and the whiteness shall fall away, and he shall see thee.'

⁹Then Anna ran forth, and fell upon the neck of her son, and said unto him, 'Seeing I have seen thee, my son, from henceforth I am content to die'. And they wept both. ¹⁰Tobit also went forth toward the door, and stumbled: but his son ran unto him, ¹¹and took hold of his father: and he struck of the gall on his father's eyes, saying, 'Be of good hope, my father'. ¹²And when his eyes began to smart, he rubbed them. ¹³And the whiteness peeled away from the corners of his eyes: and when he saw his son, he fell upon his neck. ¹⁴And he wept, and said, 'Blessed art thou, O God, and blessed is thy name for ever, and blessed are all thy holy angels: ¹⁵for thou hast scourged, and hast taken pity on me: for behold, I see my son Tobias'. And his son went in rejoicing, and told his father the great things that had happened to him in Media.

¹⁶Then Tobit went out to meet his daughter-in-law at the gate of Nineveh, rejoicing, and praising God: and they which saw him go marvelled, because he had received his sight. ¹⁷But Tobit gave thanks before them, because God had mercy on him. And when he came near to Sara his daughter-in-law, he blessed her, saying, 'Thou art welcome, daughter: God be blessed, which hath brought thee unto us, and blessed be thy father and thy mother'.

And there was joy amongst all his brethren which were at Nineveh. ¹⁸And Achiacharus, and Nasbas his brother's son, came. ¹⁹And Tobias' wedding was kept seven days with great joy.

12 Then Tobit called his son Tobias, and said unto him, 'My son, see that the man have his wages, which went with thee, and thou must give him more'. ²And Tobias said unto him, 'O father, it is no harm to me to give him half of those things which I have brought: ³for he hath brought me again to thee in safety, and made whole my wife, and brought me the money, and likewise healed thee'. ⁴Then the old man said, 'It is due unto him'. ⁵So he called the angel, and he said unto him, 'Take half of all that ye have brought, and go away in safety'.

⁶Then he took them both apart, and said unto them, 'Bless God, praise him, and magnify him, and praise him for the things which he hath done unto you in the sight of all that live. It is good to praise God, and exalt his name, and honourably to show forth the works of God, therefore be not slack to praise him. ⁷It is good to keep close the secret of a king, but it is honourable to reveal the works of God. Do that which is good, and no evil shall touch you. ⁸Prayer is good with fasting and alms and righteousness. A little with righteousness is better than much with unrighteousness. It is better to give alms than to lay up gold: ⁹for alms doth deliver from death, and shall purge away all sin. Those that exercise alms and righteousness shall be filled with life: ¹⁰but they that sin are enemies to their own life. ¹¹Surely I will keep close nothing from you. For I said, it was good to keep close the secret of a king, but that it was honourable to reveal the works of God. ¹²Now therefore, when thou didst pray, and Sara thy daughter-in-law, I did bring the remembrance of your prayers before the Holy One: and when thou didst bury the dead, I was with thee likewise. ¹³And when thou didst not delay to rise up, and leave thy dinner, to go and cover the dead, thy good deed was not hid from me: but I was with thee. ¹⁴And now God hath sent me to heal thee and Sara thy daughter-in-law. ¹⁵I am Raphael, one of the seven holy angels, which present the prayers of the saints, and which go in and out before the glory of the Holy One.'

¹⁶Then they were both troubled, and fell upon their faces: for they feared. ¹⁷But he said unto them, 'Fear not, for it shall go well with you, praise God therefore. ¹⁸For not of any favour of mine, but by the will of our God I came; wherefore praise him for ever. ¹⁹All these days I did appear unto you, but I did neither eat nor drink, but you did see a vision. ²⁰Now therefore give God thanks: for I go up to him that sent me; but write all things which are done in a book.'

²¹And when they arose, they saw him no more. ²²Then they confessed the great and wonderful works of God, and how the angel of the Lord had appeared unto them.

13

Then Tobit wrote a prayer of rejoicing, and said,

'Blessed be God that liveth for ever,
and blessed be his kingdom.
² For he doth scourge, and hath mercy:
he leadeth down to hell, and bringeth up again:
neither is there any that can avoid his hand.

³ 'Confess him before the Gentiles, ye children of Israel:
for he hath scattered us among them.
⁴ There declare his greatness, and extol him before all the living:
for he is our Lord, and he is the God our Father for ever.
⁵ And he will scourge us for our iniquities, and will have mercy again,
and will gather us out of all nations, among whom he hath scattered us.

⁶ 'If you turn to him with your whole heart, and with your whole
    mind,
and deal uprightly before him,
then will he turn unto you, and will not hide his face from you.
Therefore see what he will do with you,
and confess him with your whole mouth,
and praise the Lord of might,
and extol the everlasting King.

'In the land of my captivity do I praise him,
and declare his might and majesty to a sinful nation.
O ye sinners, turn and do justice before him:
who can tell if he will accept you, and have mercy on you?
⁷ I will extol my God,
and my soul shall praise the King of heaven,
and shall rejoice in his greatness.
⁸ Let all men speak,
and let all praise him for his righteousness.

⁹ 'O Jerusalem, the holy city,
he will scourge thee for thy children's works,
and will have mercy again on the sons of the righteous.
¹⁰ Give praise to the Lord, for he is good:
and praise the everlasting King,
that his tabernacle may be built in thee again with joy:
and let him make joyful there in thee those that are captives,
and love in thee for ever those that are miserable.

¹¹ 'Many nations shall come from far to the name of the Lord God
with gifts in their hands, even gifts to the King of heaven:
all generations shall praise thee with great joy.
¹² Cursed are all they which hate thee,
and blessed shall all be which love thee for ever.
¹³ Rejoice and be glad for the children of the just:
for they shall be gathered together, and shall bless the Lord of
    the just.
¹⁴ O blessed are they which love thee,
for they shall rejoice in thy peace:
blessed are they which have been sorrowful for all thy scourges,
for they shall rejoice for thee, when they have seen all thy glory,
and shall be glad for ever.

¹⁵ 'Let my soul bless God the great King.
¹⁶ For Jerusalem shall be built up with sapphires, and emeralds,
    and precious stone:
thy walls and towers and battlements with pure gold.
¹⁷ And the streets of Jerusalem shall be paved with beryl and
    carbuncle and stones of Ophir.

[18] And all her streets shall say, "Alleluia",
and they shall praise him, saying, "Blessed be God
which hath extolled it for ever".'

14 So Tobit made an end of praising God.
[2]And he was eight and fifty years old when he lost his sight, which was restored to him after eight years: and he gave alms, and he increased in the fear of the Lord God, and praised him. [3]And when he was very aged, he called his son, and the six sons of his son, and said to him, 'My son, take thy children; for behold, I am aged, and am ready to depart out of this life. [4]Go into Media, my son, for I surely believe those things which Jonas the prophet spoke of Nineveh, that it shall be overthrown, and that for a time peace shall rather be in Media, and that our brethren shall lie scattered in the earth from that good land, and Jerusalem shall be desolate, and the house of God in it shall be burnt, and shall be desolate for a time: [5]and that again God will have mercy on them, and bring them again into the land where they shall build a temple, but not like to the first, until the time of that age be fulfilled, and afterward they shall return from all places of their captivity, and build up Jerusalem gloriously, and the house of God shall be built in it for ever with a glorious building, as the prophets have spoken thereof. [6]And all nations shall turn, and fear the Lord God truly, and shall bury their idols. [7]So shall all nations praise the Lord, and his people shall confess God, and the Lord shall exalt his people, and all those which love the Lord God in truth and justice shall rejoice, showing mercy to our brethren.

[8]'And now, my son, depart out of Nineveh, because that those things which the prophet Jonas spoke shall surely come to pass. [9]But keep thou the law and the commandments, and show thyself merciful and just, that it may go well with thee. [10]And bury me decently, and thy mother with me, but tarry no longer at Nineveh.

'Remember, my son, how Aman handled Achiacharus that brought him up, how out of light he brought him into darkness, and how he rewarded him again: yet Achiacharus was saved, but the other had his reward, for he went down into darkness. Manasses gave alms, and escaped the snares of death which they had set for him: but Aman fell into the snare, and perished. [11]Wherefore now, my son, consider what alms doeth, and how righteousness doth deliver.'

When he had said these things, he gave up the ghost in the bed, being a hundred and eight and fifty years old; and he buried him honourably. [12]And when Anna his mother was dead, he buried her with his father.

But Tobias departed with his wife and children to Ecbatane to Raguel his father-in-law, [13]where he became old with honour, and he buried his father and mother-in-law honourably, and he inherited their substance, and his father Tobit's. [14]And he died at Ecbatane in Media, being a hundred and seven and twenty years old. [15]But before he died he heard of the destruction of Nineveh, which was taken by Nabuchodonosor and Assuerus: and before his death he rejoiced over Nineveh.

JUDITH

1 In the twelfth year of the reign of Nabuchodonosor, who reigned in Nineveh, the great city; in the days of Arphaxad, which reigned over the Medes in Ecbatane, ²and built in Ecbatane walls round about of stones hewn three cubits broad and six cubits long, and made the height of the wall seventy cubits, and the breadth thereof fifty cubits: ³and set the towers thereof upon the gates of it, an hundred cubits high, and the breadth thereof in the foundation threescore cubits: ⁴and he made the gates thereof, even gates that were raised to the height of seventy cubits, and the breadth of them was forty cubits, for the going forth of his mighty armies, and for the setting in array of his footmen: ⁵even in those days king Nabuchodonosor made war with king Arphaxad in the great plain, which is the plain in the borders of Ragau. ⁶And there came unto him all they that dwelt in the hill country, and all that dwelt by Euphrates, and Tigris, and Hydaspes, and the plain of Arioch the king of the Elymeans, and very many nations of the sons of Chelod, assembled themselves to the battle.

⁷Then Nabuchodonosor king of the Assyrians sent unto all that dwelt in Persia, and to all that dwelt westward, and to those that dwelt in Cilicia, and Damascus, and Libanus, and Antilibanus, and to all that dwelt upon the sea coast, ⁸and to those amongst the nations that were of Carmel, and Galaad, and the higher Galilee, and the great plain of Esdraelon, ⁹and to all that were in Samaria and the cities thereof, and beyond Jordan unto Jerusalem, and Betane, and Chellus, and Kades, and the river of Egypt, and Taphnes, and Ramesse, and all the land of Gesem, ¹⁰until you come beyond Tanis and Memphis, and to all the inhabitants of Egypt, until you come to the borders of Ethiopia. ¹¹But all the inhabitants of the land made light of the commandment of Nabuchodonosor king of the Assyrians, neither went they with him to the battle: for they were not afraid of him: yea, he was before them as one man, and they sent away his ambassadors from them without effect, and with disgrace. ¹²Therefore Nabuchodonosor was very angry with all this country, and swore by his throne and kingdom, that he would surely be avenged upon all those coasts of Cilicia, and Damascus, and Syria, and that he would slay with the sword all the inhabitants of the land of Moab, and the children of Ammon, and all Judea, and all that were in Egypt, till you come to the borders of the two seas.

¹³Then he marched in battle array with his power against king Arphaxad in the seventeenth year, and he prevailed in his battle: for he overthrew all the power of Arphaxad, and all his horsemen, and all his chariots, ¹⁴and became lord of his cities, and came unto Ecbatane, and took the towers, and spoiled the streets thereof, and turned the beauty thereof into shame. ¹⁵He took also Arphaxad in the mountains of Ragau, and smote him through with his darts, and destroyed him utterly that day. ¹⁶So he returned afterward to Nineveh, both he and all

his company of sundry nations, being a very great multitude of men of war, and there he took his ease, and banqueted, both he and his army, an hundred and twenty days.

2 And in the eighteenth year, the two and twentieth day of the first month, there was talk in the house of Nabuchodonosor king of the Assyrians, that he should as he said avenge himself on all the earth. ²So he called unto him all his officers, and all his nobles, and communicated with them his secret counsel, and concluded the afflicting of the whole earth out of his own mouth. ³Then they decreed to destroy all flesh, that did not obey the commandment of his mouth.

⁴And when he had ended his counsel, Nabuchodonosor king of the Assyrians called Holofernes the chief captain of his army, which was next unto him, and said unto him, ⁵'Thus saith the great king, the lord of the whole earth: behold, thou shalt go forth from my presence, and take with thee men that trust in their own strength, of footmen a hundred and twenty thousand, and the number of horses with their riders twelve thousand. ⁶And thou shalt go against all the west country, because they disobeyed my commandment. ⁷And thou shalt declare unto them that they prepare for me earth and water: for I will go forth in my wrath against them, and will cover the whole face of the earth with the feet of my army, and I will give them for a spoil unto them: ⁸so that their slain shall fill their valleys and brooks, and the river shall be filled with their dead, till it overflow. ⁹And I will lead them captives to the utmost parts of all the earth. ¹⁰Thou therefore shalt go forth, and take beforehand for me all their coasts: and if they will yield themselves unto thee, thou shalt reserve them for me till the day of their punishment. ¹¹But concerning them that rebel, let not thy eye spare them: but put them to the slaughter, and spoil them wheresoever thou goest. ¹²For as I live, and by the power of my kingdom, whatsoever I have spoken, that will I do by my hand. ¹³And take thou heed that thou transgress none of the commandments of thy lord, but accomplish them fully, as I have commanded thee, and defer not to do them.'

¹⁴Then Holofernes went forth from the presence of his lord, and called all the governors and captains, and the officers of the army of Assur. ¹⁵And he mustered the chosen men for the battle, as his lord had commanded him, unto a hundred and twenty thousand, and twelve thousand archers on horseback; ¹⁶and he ranged them, as a great army is ordered for the war. ¹⁷And he took camels and asses for their carriages, a very great number, and sheep and oxen and goats without number for their provision, ¹⁸and plenty of victual for every man of the army, and very much gold and silver out of the king's house.

¹⁹Then he went forth and all his power to go before king Nabuchodonosor in the voyage, and to cover all the face of the earth westward with their chariots, and horsemen, and their chosen footmen. ²⁰A great multitude also of sundry countries came with them like locusts, and like the sand of the earth: for the multitude was without number. ²¹And they went forth of Nineveh three days' journey toward the plain of Bectileth, and pitched from Bectileth near the mountain

which is at the left hand of the upper Cilicia. ²²Then he took all his army, his footmen, and horsemen, and chariots, and went from thence into the hill country, ²³and destroyed Phud and Lud, and spoiled all the children of Rasses, and the children of Ismael, which were toward the wilderness at the south of the land of the Chellians. ²⁴Then he went over Euphrates, and went through Mesopotamia, and destroyed all the high cities that were upon the river Arbonai, till you come to the sea. ²⁵And he took the borders of Cilicia, and killed all that resisted him, and came to the borders of Japheth, which were toward the south, over against Arabia. ²⁶He compassed also all the children of Madian, and burnt up their tabernacles, and spoiled their sheepcotes. ²⁷Then he went down into the plain of Damascus in the time of wheat harvest, and burnt up all their fields, and destroyed their flocks and herds, also he spoiled their cities, and utterly wasted their countries, and smote all their young men with the edge of the sword.

²⁸Therefore the fear and dread of him fell upon all the inhabitants of the sea coasts, which were in Sidon and Tyrus, and them that dwelt in Sur and Ocina, and all that dwelt in Jemnaan; and they that dwelt in

3 Azotus and Ascalon feared him greatly. ¹So they sent ambassadors unto him to treat of peace, saying, ²'Behold, we the servants of Nabuchodonosor the great king lie before thee: use us as shall be good in thy sight. ³Behold, our houses, and all our places, and all our fields of wheat, and flocks, and herds, and all the lodges of our tents, lie before thy face: use them as it pleaseth thee. ⁴Behold, even our cities and the inhabitants thereof are thy servants: come and deal with them as seemeth good unto thee.'

⁵So the men came to Holofernes, and declared unto him after this manner. ⁶Then came he down toward the sea coast, both he and his army, and set garrisons in the high cities, and took out of them chosen men for aid. ⁷So they and all the country round about received them with garlands, with dances, and with timbrels. ⁸Yet he did cast down their frontiers, and cut down their groves: for he had decreed to destroy all the gods of the land, that all nations should worship Nabuchodonosor only, and that all tongues and tribes should call upon him as god.

⁹Also he came over against Esdraelon near unto Judea, over against the great strait of Judea. ¹⁰And he pitched between Geba and Scythopolis, and there he tarried a whole month, that he might gather together all the carriages of his army.

4 Now the children of Israel, that dwelt in Judea, heard all that Holofernes the chief captain of Nabuchodonosor king of the Assyrians had done to the nations, and after what manner he had spoiled all their temples, and brought them to nought. ²Therefore they were exceedingly afraid of him, and were troubled for Jerusalem, and for the temple of the Lord their God: ³for they were newly returned from the captivity, and all the people of Judea were lately gathered together: and the vessels, and the altar, and the house, were sanctified after the profanation. ⁴Therefore they sent into all the coasts of

Samaria, and the villages, and to Bethoron, and Belmen, and Jericho, and to Choba, and Esora, and to the valley of Salem, ⁵and possessed themselves beforehand of all the tops of the high mountains, and fortified the villages that were in them, and laid up victuals for the provision of war: for their fields were of late reaped. ⁶Also Joacim the high priest, which was in those days in Jerusalem, wrote to them that dwelt in Bethulia, and Betomestham, which is over against Esdraelon toward the open country near to Dothaim, ⁷charging them to keep the passages of the hill country: for by them there was an entrance into Judea, and it was easy to stop them that would come up, because the passage was strait, for two men at the most.

⁸And the children of Israel did as Joacim the high priest had commanded them, with the ancients of all the people of Israel, which dwelt at Jerusalem. ⁹Then every man of Israel cried to God with great fervency, and with great vehemence did they humble their souls: ¹⁰both they, and their wives, and their children, and their cattle, and every stranger and hireling, and their servants bought with money, put sackcloth upon their loins. ¹¹Thus every man and woman, and the little children, and the inhabitants of Jerusalem fell before the temple, and cast ashes upon their heads, and spread out their sackcloth before the face of the Lord: also they put sackcloth about the altar, ¹²and cried to the God of Israel all with one consent earnestly, that he would not give their children for a prey, and their wives for a spoil, and the cities of their inheritance to destruction, and the sanctuary to profanation and reproach, and for the nations to rejoice at. ¹³So God heard their prayers, and looked upon their afflictions: for the people fasted many days in all Judea and Jerusalem before the sanctuary of the Lord Almighty. ¹⁴And Joacim the high priest, and all the priests that stood before the Lord, and they which ministered unto the Lord, had their loins girt with sackcloth, and offered the daily burnt offerings, with the vows and free gifts of the people, ¹⁵and had ashes on their mitres, and cried unto the Lord with all their power, that he would look upon all the house of Israel graciously.

5 Then was it declared to Holofernes, the chief captain of the army of Assur, that the children of Israel had prepared for war, and had shut up the passages of the hill country, and had fortified all the tops of the high hills, and had laid impediments in the champaign countries: ²wherewith he was very angry, and called all the princes of Moab, and the captains of Ammon, and all the governors of the sea coast, ³and he said unto them, 'Tell me now, ye sons of Canaan, who this people is that dwelleth in the hill country, and what are the cities that they inhabit, and what is the multitude of their army, and wherein is their power and strength, and what king is set over them, or captain of their army; ⁴and why have they determined not to come and meet me, more than all the inhabitants of the west?'

⁵Then said Achior, the captain of all the sons of Ammon, 'Let my lord now hear a word from the mouth of thy servant, and I will declare unto thee the truth concerning this people, which dwelleth near thee, and

inhabiteth the hill countries: and there shall no lie come out of the mouth of thy servant. [6]This people are descended of the Chaldeans, [7]and they sojourned heretofore in Mesopotamia, because they would not follow the gods of their fathers, which were in the land of Chaldea. [8]For they left the way of their ancestors, and worshipped the God of heaven, the God whom they knew: so they cast them out from the face of their gods, and they fled into Mesopotamia, and sojourned there many days. [9]Then their God commanded them to depart from the place where they sojourned, and to go into the land of Canaan, where they dwelt, and were increased with gold and silver, and with very much cattle. [10]But when a famine covered all the land of Canaan, they went down into Egypt, and sojourned there, while they were nourished, and became there a great multitude, so that one could not number their nation. [11]Therefore the king of Egypt rose up against them, and dealt subtly with them, and brought them low with labouring in brick, and made them slaves. [12]Then they cried unto their God, and he smote all the land of Egypt with incurable plagues: so the Egyptians cast them out of their sight. [13]And God dried the Red Sea before them, [14]and brought them to mount Sinai, and Cades-Barne, and cast forth all that dwelt in the wilderness. [15]So they dwelt in the land of the Amorites, and they destroyed by their strength all them of Esebon, and passing over Jordan they possessed all the hill country. [16]And they cast forth before them the Canaanite, the Pherezite, the Jebusite, and the Sychemite, and all the Gergesites, and they dwelt in that country many days.

[17]'And whilst they sinned not before their God, they prospered, because the God that hateth iniquity was with them. [18]But when they departed from the way which he appointed them, they were destroyed in many battles very sore, and were led captives into a land that was not theirs, and the temple of their God was cast to the ground, and their cities were taken by the enemies. [19]But now are they returned to their God, and are come up from the places where they were scattered, and have possessed Jerusalem, where their sanctuary is, and are seated in the hill country, for it was desolate. [20]Now therefore, my lord and governor, if there be any error in this people, and they sin against their God, let us consider that this shall be their ruin, and let us go up, and we shall overcome them. [21]But if there be no iniquity in their nation, let my lord now pass by, lest their Lord defend them, and their God be for them, and we become a reproach before all the world.'

[22]And when Achior had finished these sayings, all the people standing round about the tent murmured, and the chief men of Holofernes, and all that dwelt by the seaside, and in Moab, spoke that he should kill him. [23]'For,' say they, 'we will not be afraid of the face of the children of Israel: for lo, it is a people that have no strength nor power for a strong battle. [24]Now therefore, lord Holofernes, we will go up, and they shall be a prey to be devoured of all thy army.'

6 And when the tumult of men that were about the council was ceased, Holofernes the chief captain of the army of Assur said unto

Achior and all the Moabites before all the company of other nations, ²'And who art thou, Achior, and the hirelings of Ephraim, that thou hast prophesied amongst us as today, and hast said, that we should not make war with the people of Israel, because their God will defend them? and who is God but Nabuchodonosor? ³He will send his power, and will destroy them from the face of the earth, and their God shall not deliver them: but we his servants will destroy them as one man, for they are not able to sustain the power of our horses. ⁴For with them we will tread them under foot, and their mountains shall be drunken with their blood, and their fields shall be filled with their dead bodies, and their footsteps shall not be able to stand before us, for they shall utterly perish, saith king Nabuchodonosor, lord of all the earth; for he said, "None of my words shall be in vain".

⁵'And thou, Achior, a hireling of Ammon, which hast spoken these words in the day of thy iniquity, shalt see my face no more from this day, until I take vengeance of this nation that came out of Egypt. ⁶And then shall the sword of my army, and the multitude of them that serve me, pass through thy sides, and thou shalt fall among their slain, when I return. ⁷Now therefore my servants shall bring thee back into the hill country, and shall set thee in one of the cities of the passages: ⁸and thou shalt not perish, till thou be destroyed with them. ⁹And if thou persuade thyself in thy mind that they shall not be taken, let not thy countenance fall: I have spoken it, and none of my words shall be in vain.'

¹⁰Then Holofernes commanded his servants that waited in his tent, to take Achior and bring him to Bethulia, and deliver him into the hands of the children of Israel. ¹¹So his servants took him, and brought him out of the camp into the plain, and they went from the midst of the plain into the hill country, and came unto the fountains that were under Bethulia. ¹²And when the men of the city saw them, they took up their weapons, and went out of the city to the top of the hill: and every man that used a sling kept them from coming up by casting of stones against them. ¹³Nevertheless having gotten privily under the hill, they bound Achior, and cast him down, and left him at the foot of the hill, and returned to their lord.

¹⁴But the Israelites descended from their city, and came unto him, and loosed him, and brought him into Bethulia, and presented him to the governors of the city, ¹⁵which were in those days Ozias the son of Micha, of the tribe of Simeon, and Chabris the son of Gothoniel, and Charmis the son of Melchiel. ¹⁶And they called together all the ancients of the city, and all their youth ran together, and their women to the assembly, and they set Achior in the midst of all their people.

Then Ozias asked him of that which was done. ¹⁷And he answered and declared unto them the words of the council of Holofernes, and all the words that he had spoken in the midst of the princes of Assur, and whatsoever Holofernes had spoken proudly against the house of Israel. ¹⁸Then the people fell down and worshipped God, and cried unto God, saying, ¹⁹'O Lord God of heaven, behold their pride, and pity the low estate of our nation, and look upon the face of those that are sanctified unto thee this day'. ²⁰Then they comforted Achior, and praised him greatly. ²¹And Ozias took him out of the assembly unto his house, and made a feast to the elders, and they called on the God of Israel all that night for help.

7 The next day Holofernes commanded all his army, and all his people which were come to take his part, that they should remove their camp against Bethulia, to take aforehand the ascents of the hill country, and to make war against the children of Israel. ²Then their strong men removed their camps in that day, and the army of the men of war was a hundred and seventy thousand footmen, and twelve thousand horsemen, besides the baggage, and other men that were afoot amongst them, a very great multitude. ³And they camped in the valley near unto Bethulia, by the fountain, and they spread themselves in breadth over Dothaim even to Belmaim, and in length from Bethulia unto Cyamon, which is over against Esdraelon.

⁴Now the children of Israel, when they saw the multitude of them, were greatly troubled, and said every one to his neighbour, 'Now will these men lick up the face of the earth; for neither the high mountains, nor the valleys, nor the hills, are able to bear their weight'. ⁵Then every man took up his weapons of war, and when they had kindled fires upon their towers, they remained and watched all that night.

⁶But in the second day Holofernes brought forth all his horsemen in the sight of the children of Israel which were in Bethulia, ⁷and viewed the passages up to the city, and came to the fountains of their waters, and took them, and set garrisons of men of war over them, and he himself removed towards his people. ⁸Then came unto him all the chief of the children of Esau, and all the governors of the people of Moab, and the captains of the sea coast, and said, ⁹'Let our lord now hear a word, that there be not an overthrow in thy army. ¹⁰For this people of the children of Israel do not trust in their spears, but in the height of the mountains wherein they dwell, because it is not easy to come up to the tops of their mountains. ¹¹Now therefore, my lord, fight not against them in battle array, and there shall not so much as one man of thy people perish. ¹²Remain in thy camp, and keep all the men of thy army, and let thy servants get into their hands the fountain of water, which issueth forth of the foot of the mountain: ¹³for all the inhabitants of Bethulia have their water thence: so shall thirst kill them, and they shall give up their city, and we and our people shall go up to the tops of the mountains that are near, and will camp upon them, to watch that none go out of the city. ¹⁴So they and their wives and their children shall be consumed with famine, and before the sword come against them, they shall be overthrown in the streets where they dwell. ¹⁵Thus shalt thou render them an evil reward: because they rebelled, and met not thy person peaceably.'

¹⁶And these words pleased Holofernes and all his servants, and he appointed to do as they had spoken. ¹⁷So the camp of the children of Ammon departed, and with them five thousand of the Assyrians, and

they pitched in the valley, and took the waters, and the fountains of the waters of the children of Israel. [18]Then the children of Esau went up with the children of Ammon, and camped in the hill country over against Dothaim: and they sent some of them toward the south, and toward the east, over against Ekrebel, which is near unto Chusi, that is upon the brook Mochmur, and the rest of the army of the Assyrians camped in the plain, and covered the face of the whole land, and their tents and carriages were pitched to a very great multitude.

[19]Then the children of Israel cried unto the Lord their God, because their heart failed, for all their enemies had compassed them round about, and there was no way to escape out from among them. [20]Thus all the company of Assur remained about them, both their footmen, chariots and horsemen, four and thirty days, so that all their vessels of water failed all the inhabitants of Bethulia. [21]And the cisterns were emptied, and they had not water to drink their fill for one day; for they gave them drink by measure. [22]Therefore their young children were out of heart, and their women and young men fainted for thirst, and fell down in the streets of the city, and by the passages of the gates, and there was no longer any strength in them.

[23]Then all the people assembled to Ozias, and to the chief of the city, both young men, and women, and children, and cried with a loud voice, and said before all the elders, [24]'God be judge between us and you: for you have done us great injury, in that you have not required peace of the children of Assur. [25]For now we have no helper: but God hath sold us into their hands, that we should be thrown down before them with thirst and great destruction. [26]Now therefore call them unto you, and deliver the whole city for a spoil to the people of Holofernes, and to all his army. [27]For it is better for us to be made a spoil unto them, than to die for thirst: for we will be his servants, that our souls may live, and not see the death of our infants before our eyes, nor our wives nor our children to die. [28]We take to witness against you the heaven and the earth, and our God and Lord of our fathers, which punisheth us according to our sins and the sins of our fathers, that he do not according as we have said this day.'

[29]Then there was great weeping with one consent in the midst of the assembly, and they cried unto the Lord God with a loud voice. [30]Then said Ozias to them, 'Brethren, be of good courage, let us yet endure five days, in the which space the Lord our God may turn his mercy toward us, for he will not forsake us utterly. [31]And if these days pass, and there come no help unto us, I will do according to your word.' [32]And he dispersed the people, every one to their own charge; and they went unto the walls and towers of their city, and sent the women and children into their houses: and they were very low brought in the city.

8 Now at that time Judith heard thereof, which was the daughter of Merari, the son of Ox, the son of Joseph, the son of Oziel, the son of Elcia, the son of Ananias, the son of Gedeon, the son of Raphaim, the son of Acitho, the son of Eliu, the son of Eliab, the son of Nathanael, the son of Samael, the son of Salasadai, the son of Israel. [2]And Manasses was her husband, of her tribe and kindred, who died in the barley harvest. ³For as he stood overseeing them that bound sheaves in the field, the heat came upon his head, and he fell on his bed, and died in the city of Bethulia: and they buried him with his fathers in the field between Dothaim and Balamo. ⁴So Judith was a widow in her house three years and four months. ⁵And she made her a tent upon the top of her house, and put on sackcloth on her loins, and wore her widow's apparel. ⁶And she fasted all the days of her widowhood, save the eves of the sabbath, and the sabbaths, and the eves of the new moons, and the new moons, and the feasts and solemn days of the house of Israel. ⁷She was also of a goodly countenance, and very beautiful to behold: and her husband Manasses had left her gold and silver, and menservants, and maidservants, and cattle, and lands; and she remained upon them. ⁸And there was none that gave her an ill word; for she feared God greatly.

⁹Now when she heard the evil words of the people against the governor, that they fainted for lack of water (for Judith had heard all the words that Ozias had spoken unto them, and that he had sworn to deliver the city unto the Assyrians after five days); ¹⁰then she sent her waiting woman that had the government of all things that she had, to call Ozias and Chabris and Charmis, the ancients of the city. ¹¹And they came unto her, and she said unto them, 'Hear me now, O ye governors of the inhabitants of Bethulia: for your words that you have spoken before the people this day are not right, touching this oath which ye made and pronounced between God and you, and have promised to deliver the city to our enemies, unless within these days the Lord turn to help you. ¹²And now who are you that have tempted God this day, and stand in stead of God amongst the children of men? ¹³And now try the Lord Almighty, but you shall never know anything. ¹⁴For you cannot find the depth of the heart of man, neither can ye perceive the things that he thinketh: then how can you search out God, that hath made all these things, and know his mind, or comprehend his purpose? Nay, my brethren, provoke not the Lord our God to anger. ¹⁵For if he will not help us within these five days, he hath power to defend us when he will, even every day, or to destroy us before our enemies. ¹⁶Do not bind the counsels of the Lord our God: for God is not as man, that he may be threatened, neither is he as the son of man, that he should be wavering. ¹⁷Therefore let us wait for salvation of him, and call upon him to help us, and he will hear our voice, if it please him. ¹⁸For there arose none in our age, neither is there any now in these days, neither tribe, nor family, nor people, nor city among us, which worship gods made with hands, as hath been aforetime. ¹⁹For the which cause our fathers were given to the sword, and for a spoil, and had a great fall before our enemies. ²⁰But we know no other god: therefore we trust that he will not despise us, nor any of our nation. ²¹For if we be taken so, all Judea shall lie waste, and our sanctuary shall be spoiled, and he will require the profanation thereof at our mouth. ²²And the slaughter of our brethren, and the captivity of the country, and the desolation of our

inheritance, will he turn upon our heads among the Gentiles, wheresoever we shall be in bondage, and we shall be an offence and a reproach
to all them that possess us. ²³For our servitude shall not be directed to
favour: but the Lord our God shall turn it to dishonour. ²⁴Now therefore, O brethren, let us show an example to our brethren, because their
hearts depend upon us, and the sanctuary, and the house, and the altar
rest upon us.

²⁵'Moreover let us give thanks to the Lord our God, which trieth us,
even as he did our fathers. ²⁶Remember what things he did to Abraham,
and how he tried Isaac, and what happened to Jacob in Mesopotamia of
Syria, when he kept the sheep of Laban his mother's brother. ²⁷For he
hath not tried us in the fire as he did them, for the examination of
their hearts, neither hath he taken vengeance on us: but the Lord doth
scourge them that come near unto him, to admonish them.'

²⁸Then said Ozias to her, 'All that thou hast spoken hast thou spoken
with a good heart, and there is none that may gainsay thy words. ²⁹For
this is not the first day wherein thy wisdom is manifested, but from the
beginning of thy days all thy people have known thy understanding,
because the disposition of thy heart is good. ³⁰But the people were very
thirsty, and compelled us to do unto them as we have spoken, and to
bring an oath upon ourselves, which we will not break. ³¹Therefore now
pray thou for us, because thou art a godly woman, and the Lord will
send us rain to fill our cisterns, and we shall faint no more.'

³²Then said Judith unto them, 'Hear me, and I will do a thing, which
shall go throughout all generations to the children of our nation. ³³You
shall stand this night in the gate, and I will go forth with my waiting
woman: and within the days that you have promised to deliver the city
to our enemies the Lord will visit Israel by my hand. ³⁴But inquire not
you of my act: for I will not declare it unto you, till the things be finished that I do.'

³⁵Then said Ozias and the princes unto her, 'Go in peace, and the
Lord God be before thee, to take vengeance on our enemies'. ³⁶So they
returned from the tent, and went to their wards.

9 Then Judith fell upon her face, and put ashes upon her head, and
uncovered the sackcloth wherewith she was clothed; and about the
time that the incense of that evening was offered in Jerusalem in the
house of the Lord, Judith cried with a loud voice, and said, ²'O Lord God
of my father Simeon, to whom thou gavest a sword to take vengeance of
the strangers, who loosened the girdle of a maid to defile her, and discovered the thigh to her shame, and polluted her virginity to her
reproach (for thou saidst it shall not be so, and yet they did so): ³wherefore thou gavest their rulers to be slain, so that they dyed their bed in
blood, being deceived, and smotest the servants with their lords, and
the lords upon their thrones: ⁴and hast given their wives for a prey, and
their daughters to be captives, and all their spoils to be divided
amongst thy dear children: which were moved with thy zeal, and
abhorred the pollution of their blood, and called upon thee for aid: O
God, O my God, hear me also a widow. ⁵For thou hast wrought not

only those things, but also the things which fell out before, and which ensued after; thou hast thought upon the things which are now, and which are to come. ⁶Yea, what things thou didst determine were ready at hand, and said, "Lo, we are here: for all thy ways are prepared, and thy judgements are in thy foreknowledge".

⁷'For behold, the Assyrians are multiplied in their power: they are exalted with horse and man: they glory in the strength of their footmen: they trust in shield, and spear, and bow, and sling, and know not that thou art the Lord that breakest the battles: the Lord is thy name. ⁸Throw down their strength in thy power, and bring down their force in thy wrath: for they have purposed to defile thy sanctuary, and to pollute the tabernacle where thy glorious name resteth, and to cast down with sword the horn of thy altar. ⁹Behold their pride, and send thy wrath upon their heads: give into my hand, which am a widow, the power that I have conceived. ¹⁰Smite by the deceit of my lips the servant with the prince, and the prince with the servant: break down their stateliness by the hand of a woman. ¹¹For thy power standeth not in multitude, nor thy might in strong men, for thou art a God of the afflicted, a helper of the oppressed, an upholder of the weak, a protector of the forlorn, a saviour of them that are without hope. ¹²I pray thee, I pray thee, O God of my father, and God of the inheritance of Israel, Lord of the heavens and earth, Creator of the waters, King of every creature: hear thou my prayer: ¹³and make my speech and deceit to be their wound and stripe, who have purposed cruel things against thy covenant, and thy hallowed house, and against the top of Sion, and against the house of the possession of thy children. ¹⁴And make every nation and tribe to acknowledge that thou art the God of all power and might, and that there is no other that protecteth the people of Israel but thou.'

10 Now after that she had ceased to cry unto the God of Israel, and had made an end of all these words, ²she rose where she had fallen down, and called her maid, and went down into the house, in the which she abode in the sabbath days, and in her feast days, ³and pulled off the sackcloth which she had on, and put off the garments of her widowhood, and washed her body all over with water, and anointed herself with precious ointment, and braided the hair of her head, and put on a tire upon it, and put on her garments of gladness, wherewith she was clad during the life of Manasses her husband. ⁴And she took sandals upon her feet, and put about her her bracelets and her chains, and her rings, and her earrings, and all her ornaments, and decked herself bravely, to allure the eyes of all men that should see her. ⁵Then she gave her maid a bottle of wine, and a cruse of oil, and filled a bag with parched corn, and lumps of figs, and with fine bread; so she folded all these things together, and laid them upon her.

⁶Thus they went forth to the gate of the city of Bethulia, and found standing there Ozias, and the ancients of the city, Chabris and Charmis. ⁷And when they saw her, that her countenance was altered, and her apparel was changed, they wondered at her beauty very

greatly, and said unto her, [8]'The God, the God of our fathers give thee favour, and accomplish thy enterprises to the glory of the children of Israel, and to the exaltation of Jerusalem'. Then they worshipped God.

[9]And she said unto them, 'Command the gates of the city to be opened unto me, that I may go forth to accomplish the things whereof you have spoken with me'. So they commanded the young men to open unto her, as she had spoken. [10]And when they had done so, Judith went out, she and her maid with her, and the men of the city looked after her, until she was gone down the mountain, and till she had passed the valley, and could see her no more.

[11]Thus they went straight forth in the valley: and the first watch of the Assyrians met her, [12]and took her, and asked her, 'Of what people art thou? and whence comest thou? and whither goest thou?' And she said, 'I am a woman of the Hebrews, and am fled from them: for they shall be given you to be consumed: [13]and I am coming before Holofernes the chief captain of your army, to declare words of truth, and I will show him a way, whereby he shall go, and win all the hill country, without losing the body or life of any one of his men'.

[14]Now when the men heard her words, and beheld her countenance, they wondered greatly at her beauty, and said unto her, [15]'Thou hast saved thy life, in that thou hast hasted to come down to the presence of our lord: now therefore come to his tent, and some of us shall conduct thee, until they have delivered thee to his hands. [16]And when thou standest before him, be not afraid in thy heart, but show unto him according to thy word, and he will entreat thee well.' [17]Then they chose out of them a hundred men to accompany her and her maid, and they brought her to the tent of Holofernes.

[18]Then was there a concourse throughout all the camp: for her coming was noised among the tents, and they came about her, as she stood without the tent of Holofernes, till they told him of her. [19]And they wondered at her beauty, and admired the children of Israel because of her, and every one said to his neighbour, 'Who would despise this people, that have among them such women? surely it is not good that one man of them be left, who being let go might deceive the whole earth'. [20]And they that lay near Holofernes went out, and all his servants, and they brought her into the tent. [21]Now Holofernes rested upon his bed under a canopy which was woven with purple, and gold, and emeralds, and precious stones. [22]So they showed him of her; and he came out before his tent with silver lamps going before him. [23]And when Judith was come before him and his servants, they all marvelled at the beauty of her countenance; and she fell down upon her face, and did reverence unto him: and his servants took her up.

11 Then said Holofernes unto her, 'Woman, be of good comfort, fear not in thy heart: for I never hurt any that was willing to serve Nabuchodonosor, the king of all the earth. [2]Now therefore, if thy people that dwelleth in the mountains had not set light by me, I would not have lifted up my spear against them: but they have done these things to themselves. [3]But now tell me wherefore thou art fled from them,

and art come unto us: for thou art come for safeguard; be of good comfort, thou shalt live this night, and hereafter: ⁴for none shall hurt thee, but entreat thee well, as they do the servants of king Nabuchodonosor my lord.'

⁵Then Judith said unto him, 'Receive the words of thy servant, and suffer thy handmaid to speak in thy presence, and I will declare no lie to my lord this night. ⁶And if thou wilt follow the words of thy handmaid, God will bring the thing perfectly to pass by thee, and my lord shall not fail of his purposes, ⁷as Nabuchodonosor king of all the earth liveth, and as his power liveth, who hath sent thee for the upholding of every living thing: for not only men shall serve him by thee, but also the beasts of the field, and the cattle, and the fowls of the air, shall live by thy power under Nabuchodonosor and all his house. ⁸For we have heard of thy wisdom and thy policies, and it is reported in all the earth, that thou only art excellent in all the kingdom, and mighty in knowledge, and wonderful in feats of war.

⁹'Now as concerning the matter, which Achior did speak in thy council, we have heard his words; for the men of Bethulia saved him, and he declared unto them all that he had spoken unto thee. ¹⁰Therefore, O lord and governor, reject not his word, but lay it up in thy heart, for it is true: for our nation shall not be punished, neither can the sword prevail against them, except they sin against their God. ¹¹And now, that my lord be not defeated and frustrate of his purpose, even death is now fallen upon them, and their sin hath overtaken them, wherewith they will provoke their God to anger, whensoever they shall do that which is not fit to be done. ¹²For their victuals fail them, and all their water is scant, and they have determined to lay hands upon their cattle, and purposed to consume all those things, that God hath forbidden them to eat by his laws, ¹³and are resolved to spend the firstfruits of the corn, and the tenths of wine and oil, which they had sanctified, and reserved for the priests that serve in Jerusalem before the face of our God, the which things it is not lawful for any of the people so much as to touch with their hands. ¹⁴For they have sent some to Jerusalem, because they also that dwell there have done the like, to bring them a licence from the senate. ¹⁵Now when they shall bring them word, they will forthwith do it, and they shall be given thee to be destroyed the same day.

¹⁶'Wherefore I thy handmaid, knowing all this, am fled from their presence, and God hath sent me to work things with thee, whereat all the earth shall be astonished, and whosoever shall hear it. ¹⁷For thy servant is religious, and serveth the God of heaven day and night: now therefore, my lord, I will remain with thee, and thy servant will go out by night into the valley, and I will pray unto God, and he will tell me when they have committed their sins. ¹⁸And I will come and show it unto thee: then thou shalt go forth with all thy army, and there shall be none of them that shall resist thee. ¹⁹And I will lead thee through the midst of Judea, until thou come before Jerusalem, and I will set thy throne in the midst thereof, and thou shalt drive them as sheep that

have no shepherd, and a dog shall not so much as open his mouth at thee: for these things were told me according to my foreknowledge, and they were declared unto me, and I am sent to tell thee.'

²⁰Then her words pleased Holofernes and all his servants; and they marvelled at her wisdom, and said, ²¹'There is not such a woman from one end of the earth to the other, both for beauty of face, and wisdom of words'. ²²Likewise Holofernes said unto her, 'God hath done well to send thee before the people, that strength might be in our hands, and destruction upon them that lightly regard my lord. ²³And now thou art both beautiful in thy countenance, and witty in thy words: surely if thou do as thou hast spoken, thy God shall be my God, and thou shalt dwell in the house of king Nabuchodonosor, and shalt be renowned through the whole earth.'

12 Then he commanded to bring her in where his plate was set, and bade that they should prepare for her of his own meats, and that she should drink of his own wine. ²And Judith said, 'I will not eat thereof, lest there be an offence: but provision shall be made for me of the things that I have brought'. ³Then Holofernes said unto her, 'If thy provision should fail, how should we give thee the like? for there be none with us of thy nation'. ⁴Then said Judith unto him, 'As thy soul liveth, my lord, thy handmaid shall not spend those things that I have, before the Lord work by my hand the things that he hath determined'.

⁵Then the servants of Holofernes brought her into the tent, and she slept till midnight, and she arose when it was towards the morning watch, ⁶and sent to Holofernes, saying, 'Let my lord now command that thy handmaid may go forth unto prayer'. ⁷Then Holofernes commanded his guard that they should not stay her: thus she abode in the camp three days, and went out in the night into the valley of Bethulia, and washed herself in a fountain of water by the camp. ⁸And when she came out, she besought the Lord God of Israel to direct her way to the raising up of the children of her people. ⁹So she came in clean, and remained in the tent, until she did eat her meat at evening. ¹⁰And in the fourth day Holofernes made a feast to his own servants only, and called none of the officers to the banquet. ¹¹Then said he to Bagoas the eunuch, who had charge over all that he had, 'Go now, and persuade this Hebrew woman which is with thee, that she come unto us, and eat and drink with us. ¹²For lo, it will be a shame for our person, if we shall let such a woman go, not having had her company: for if we draw her not unto us, she will laugh us to scorn.' ¹³Then went Bagoas from the presence of Holofernes, and came to her, and he said, 'Let not this fair damsel fear to come to my lord, and to be honoured in his presence, and drink wine, and be merry with us, and be made this day as one of the daughters of the Assyrians, which serve in the house of Nabuchodonosor'. ¹⁴Then said Judith unto him, 'Who am I now, that I should gainsay my lord? surely whatsoever pleaseth him I will do speedily, and it shall be my joy unto the day of my death'. ¹⁵So she arose, and decked herself with her apparel and all her woman's attire, and her maid went and laid soft skins on the ground for her over against

Holofernes, which she had received of Bagoas for her daily use, that she might sit and eat upon them. ¹⁶Now when Judith came in and sat down, Holofernes' heart was ravished with her, and his mind was moved, and he desired greatly her company, for he waited a time to deceive her, from the day that he had seen her. ¹⁷Then said Holofernes unto her, 'Drink now, and be merry with us'. ¹⁸So Judith said, 'I will drink now, my lord, because my life is magnified in me this day more than all the days since I was born'. ¹⁹Then she took and ate and drank before him what her maid had prepared. ²⁰And Holofernes took great delight in her, and drank much more wine than he had drunk at any time in one day since he was born.

13 Now when the evening was come, his servants made haste to depart, and Bagoas shut his tent without, and dismissed the waiters from the presence of his lord, and they went to their beds: for they were all weary, because the feast had been long. ²And Judith was left alone in the tent, and Holofernes lying along upon his bed, for he was filled with wine. ³Now Judith had commanded her maid to stand without her bedchamber, and to wait for her coming forth, as she did daily: for she said she would go forth to her prayers, and she spoke to Bagoas according to the same purpose. ⁴So all went forth, and none was left in the bedchamber, neither little nor great. Then Judith, standing by his bed, said in her heart, 'O Lord God of all power, look at this present upon the works of my hands for the exaltation of Jerusalem. ⁵For now is the time to help thy inheritance, and to execute my enterprises to the destruction of the enemies which are risen against us.'

⁶Then she came to the pillar of the bed, which was at Holofernes' head, and took down his falchion from thence, ⁷and approached to his bed, and took hold of the hair of his head, and said, 'Strengthen me, O Lord God of Israel, this day'. ⁸And she smote twice upon his neck with all her might, and she took away his head from him, ⁹and tumbled his body down from the bed, and pulled down the canopy from the pillars, and anon after she went forth, and gave Holofernes' head to her maid. ¹⁰And she put it in her bag of meat: so they twain went together according to their custom unto prayer: and when they passed the camp, they compassed the valley, and went up the mountain of Bethulia, and came to the gates thereof.

¹¹Then said Judith afar off to the watchmen at the gate, 'Open, open now the gate: God, even our God, is with us, to show his power yet in Jerusalem, and his forces against the enemy, as he hath even done this day'. ¹²Now when the men of her city heard her voice, they made haste to go down to the gate of their city, and they called the elders of the city. ¹³And then they ran all together, both small and great, for it was strange unto them that she was come: so they opened the gate, and received them, and made a fire for a light, and stood round about them. ¹⁴Then she said to them with a loud voice, 'Praise, praise God, praise God, I say, for he hath not taken away his mercy from the house of Israel, but hath destroyed our enemies by my hands this night'. ¹⁵So she took the head out of the bag, and showed it, and said unto them,

'Behold the head of Holofernes, the chief captain of the army of Assur, and behold the canopy, wherein he did lie in his drunkenness; and the Lord hath smitten him by the hand of a woman. ¹⁶As the Lord liveth, who hath kept me in my way that I went, my countenance hath deceived him to his destruction, and yet hath he not committed sin with me, to defile and shame me.'

¹⁷Then all the people were wonderfully astonished, and bowed themselves, and worshipped God, and said with one accord, 'Blessed be thou, O our God, which hast this day brought to nought the enemies of thy people'. ¹⁸Then said Ozias unto her, 'O daughter, blessed art thou of the most high God above all the women upon the earth, and blessed be the Lord God, which hath created the heavens and the earth, which hath directed thee to the cutting off of the head of the chief of our enemies. ¹⁹For this thy confidence shall not depart from the heart of men, which remember the power of God for ever. ²⁰And God turn these things to thee for a perpetual praise, to visit thee in good things, because thou hast not spared thy life for the affliction of our nation, but hast revenged our ruin, walking a straight way before our God.' And all the people said, 'So be it, so be it'.

14 Then said Judith unto them, 'Hear me now, my brethren, and take this head, and hang it upon the highest place of your walls. ²And so soon as the morning shall appear, and the sun shall come forth upon the earth, take you every one his weapons, and go forth every valiant man out of the city, and set you a captain over them, as though you would go down into the field toward the watch of the Assyrians, but go not down. ³Then they shall take their armour, and shall go into their camp, and raise up the captains of the army of Assur, and they shall run to the tent of Holofernes, but shall not find him: then fear shall fall upon them, and they shall flee before your face. ⁴So you, and all that inhabit the coast of Israel, shall pursue them, and overthrow them as they go. ⁵But before you do these things, call me Achior the Ammonite, that he may see and know him that despised the house of Israel, and that sent him to us, as it were to his death.'

⁶Then they called Achior out of the house of Ozias, and when he was come, and saw the head of Holofernes in a man's hand in the assembly of the people, he fell down on his face, and his spirit failed. ⁷But when they had recovered him, he fell at Judith's feet, and reverenced her, and said, 'Blessed art thou in all the tabernacle of Juda, and in all nations, which hearing thy name shall be astonished. ⁸Now therefore tell me all the things that thou hast done in these days.' Then Judith declared unto him in the midst of the people all that she had done, from the day that she went forth until that hour she spoke unto them. ⁹And when she had left off speaking, the people shouted with a loud voice, and made a joyful noise in their city. ¹⁰And when Achior had seen all that the God of Israel had done, he believed in God greatly, and circumcised the foreskin of his flesh, and was joined unto the house of Israel unto this day.

¹¹And as soon as the morning arose, they hanged the head of

Holofernes upon the wall, and every man took his weapons, and they went forth by bands unto the straits of the mountain. ¹²But when the Assyrians saw them, they sent to their leaders, which came to their captains and tribunes, and to every one of their rulers. ¹³So they came to Holofernes' tent, and said to him that had the charge of all his things, 'Waken now our lord: for the slaves have been bold to come down against us to battle, that they may be utterly destroyed'. ¹⁴Then went in Bagoas, and knocked at the door of the tent: for he thought that he had slept with Judith. ¹⁵But because none answered, he opened it, and went into the bedchamber, and found him cast upon the floor dead, and his head was taken from him. ¹⁶Therefore he cried with a loud voice, with weeping, and sighing, and a mighty cry, and rent his garments. ¹⁷After he went into the tent where Judith lodged, and when he found her not, he leapt out to the people, and cried, ¹⁸'These slaves have dealt treacherously, one woman of the Hebrews hath brought shame upon the house of king Nabuchodonosor: for behold, Holofernes lieth upon the ground without a head'. ¹⁹When the captains of the Assyrians' army heard these words, they rent their coats, and their minds were wonderfully troubled, and there was a cry and a very great noise throughout the camp.

15 And when they that were in the tents heard, they were astonished at the thing that was done. ²And fear and trembling fell upon them, so that there was no man that durst abide in the sight of his neighbour, but rushing out all together, they fled into every way of the plain, and of the hill country. ³They also that had camped in the mountains round about Bethulia fled away. Then the children of Israel, every one that was a warrior among them, rushed out upon them.

⁴Then sent Ozias to Betomasthem, and to Bebai, and Chobai, and Cola, and to all the coasts of Israel, such as should tell the things that were done, and that all should rush forth upon their enemies to destroy them. ⁵Now when the children of Israel heard it, they all fell upon them with one consent, and slew them unto Chobai: likewise also they that came from Jerusalem, and from all the hill country (for men had told them what things were done in the camp of their enemies), and they that were in Galaad, and in Galilee, chased them with a great slaughter, until they were past Damascus and the borders thereof. ⁶And the residue that dwelt at Bethulia, fell upon the camp of Assur, and spoiled them, and were greatly enriched. ⁷And the children of Israel that returned from the slaughter had that which remained, and the villages and the cities that were in the mountains and in the plain, got many spoils: for the multitude was very great.

⁸Then Joacim the high priest, and the ancients of the children of Israel that dwelt in Jerusalem, came to behold the good things that God had shown to Israel, and to see Judith, and to salute her. ⁹And when they came unto her, they blessed her with one accord, and said unto her, 'Thou art the exaltation of Jerusalem, thou art the great glory of Israel, thou art the great rejoicing of our nation. ¹⁰Thou hast done all these things by thy hand: thou hast done much good to Israel, and God

is pleased therewith: blessed be thou of the Almighty Lord for ever-more.' And all the people said, 'So be it'.

¹¹And the people spoiled the camp the space of thirty days: and they gave unto Judith Holofernes' tent, and all his plate, and beds, and vessels, and all his stuff: and she took it, and laid it on her mule, and made ready her carts, and laid them thereon. ¹²Then all the women of Israel ran together to see her, and blessed her, and made a dance among them for her: and she took branches in her hand, and gave also to the women that were with her. ¹³And they put a garland of olive upon her and her maid that was with her, and she went before the people in the dance, leading all the women: and all the men of Israel followed in their armour with garlands, and with songs in their mouths.

16 Then Judith began to sing this thanksgiving in all Israel, and all the people sang after her this song of praise. ²And Judith said,

'Begin unto my God with timbrels,
sing unto my Lord with cymbals:
tune unto him a new psalm:
exalt him, and call upon his name.
³ For God breaketh the battles:
for amongst the camps in the midst of the people
he hath delivered me out of the hands of them that persecuted me.

⁴ 'Assur came out of the mountains from the north,
he came with ten thousands of his army,
the multitude whereof stopped the torrents,
and their horsemen have covered the hills.
⁵ He bragged that he would burn up my borders,
and kill my young men with the sword,
and dash the sucking children against the ground,
and make my infants as a prey,
and my virgins as a spoil.

⁶ 'But the Almighty Lord hath disappointed them
by the hand of a woman.
⁷ For the mighty one did not fall by the young men,
neither did the sons of the Titans smite him,
nor high giants set upon him:
but Judith the daughter of Merari
weakened him with the beauty of her countenance.
⁸ For she put off the garment of her widowhood
for the exaltation of those that were oppressed in Israel,
and anointed her face with ointment,
and bound her hair in a tire,
and took a linen garment to deceive him.
⁹ Her sandals ravished his eyes,
her beauty took his mind prisoner,
and the falchion passed through his neck.

¹⁰ 'The Persians quaked at her boldness,
   and the Medes were daunted at her hardiness.
¹¹ Then my afflicted shouted for joy,
   and my weak ones cried aloud;
   but they were astonished:
   these lifted up their voices,
   but they were overthrown.
¹² The sons of the damsels have pierced them through,
   and wounded them as fugitives' children:
   they perished by the battle of the Lord.

¹³ 'I will sing unto the Lord a new song:
   O Lord, thou art great and glorious,
   wonderful in strength, and invincible.
¹⁴ Let all creatures serve thee:
   for thou spokest, and they were made,
   thou didst send forth thy spirit, and it created them,
   and there is none that can resist thy voice.
¹⁵ For the mountains shall be moved
   from their foundations with the waters,
   the rocks shall melt as wax at thy presence:
   yet thou art merciful to them that fear thee.
¹⁶ For all sacrifice is too little for a sweet savour unto thee,
   and all the fat is not sufficient for thy burnt offering:
   but he that feareth the Lord is great at all times.
¹⁷ Woe to the nations that rise up against my kindred:
   the Lord Almighty will take vengeance of them in the day of
      judgement,
   in putting fire and worms in their flesh,
   and they shall feel them, and weep for ever.'

¹⁸Now as soon as they entered into Jerusalem, they worshipped the Lord, and as soon as the people were purified, they offered their burnt offerings, and their free offerings, and their gifts. ¹⁹Judith also dedicated all the stuff of Holofernes, which the people had given her, and gave the canopy, which she had taken out of his bedchamber, for a gift unto the Lord. ²⁰So the people continued feasting in Jerusalem before the sanctuary for the space of three months, and Judith remained with them.

²¹After this time everyone returned to his own inheritance, and Judith went to Bethulia, and remained in her own possession, and was in her time honourable in all the country. ²²And many desired her, but none knew her all the days of her life, after that Manasses her husband was dead, and was gathered to his people. ²³But she increased more and more in honour, and waxed old in her husband's house, being a hundred and five years old, and made her maid free; so she died in Bethulia: and they buried her in the cave of her husband Manasses. ²⁴And the house of Israel lamented her seven days: and before she

died, she did distribute her goods to all them that were nearest of kindred to Manasses her husband, and to them that were the nearest of her kindred.

²⁵And there was none that made the children of Israel any more afraid in the days of Judith, nor a long time after her death.

THE REST OF THE CHAPTERS
OF THE
BOOK OF ESTHER,
WHICH ARE FOUND NEITHER IN THE
HEBREW, NOR IN THE CHALDEE

PART OF THE TENTH CHAPTER AFTER THE GREEK

Then Mardocheus said, 'God hath done these things. ⁵For I remember a dream which I saw concerning these matters, and nothing thereof hath failed. ⁶A little fountain became a river, and there was light, and the sun, and much water: this river is Esther, whom the king married, and made queen. ⁷And the two dragons are I and Aman. ⁸And the nations were those that were assembled to destroy the name of the Jews. ⁹And my nation is this Israel, which cried to God and were saved: for the Lord hath saved his people, and the Lord hath delivered us from all those evils, and God hath wrought signs and great wonders, which have not been done among the Gentiles. ¹⁰Therefore hath he made two lots, one for the people of God, and another for all the Gentiles. ¹¹And these two lots came at the hour, and time, and day of judgement before God amongst all nations. ¹²So God remembered his people, and justified his inheritance. ¹³Therefore those days shall be unto them in the month Adar, the fourteenth and fifteenth day of the same month, with an assembly, and joy, and with gladness before God, according to the generations for ever among his people.'

11 In the fourth year of the reign of Ptolemee and Cleopatra, Dositheus, who said he was a priest and Levite, and Ptolemee his son, brought this epistle of Phurim, which they said was the same, and that Lysimachus the son of Ptolemee, that was in Jerusalem, had interpreted it.

[PLACED IN THE GREEK BEFORE CHAP. 1:1 OF THE HEBREW]
²In the second year of the reign of Artaxerxes the great, in the first day of the month Nisan, Mardocheus the son of Jairus, the son of Semei, the son of Cisai, of the tribe of Benjamin, had a dream; ³who was a Jew, and dwelt in the city of Susa, a great man, being a servitor in the king's court. ⁴He was also one of the captives, which Nabuchodonosor the king of Babylon carried from Jerusalem with Jechonias king of Judea; and this was his dream. ⁵Behold a noise of a tumult, with thunder, and earthquakes, and uproar in the land: ⁶And behold, two great dragons came forth ready to fight, and their cry was great. ⁷And at their cry all nations were prepared to battle, that they might fight against the righteous people. ⁸And lo a day of darkness and obscurity, tribulation and anguish, affliction and great uproar upon the earth. ⁹And the whole righteous nation was troubled, fearing their own evils, and were ready to perish. ¹⁰Then they cried unto God, and upon their cry, as it

were from a little fountain, was made a great flood, even much water. ¹¹The light and the sun rose up, and the lowly were exalted, and devoured the glorious. ¹²Now when Mardocheus, who had seen this dream, and what God had determined to do, was awake, he bore this dream in mind, and until night by all means was desirous to know it.

12 And Mardocheus took his rest in the court with Gabatha and Tharra, the two eunuchs of the king, and keepers of the palace. ²And he heard their devices, and searched out their purposes, and learned that they were about to lay hands upon Artaxerxes the king, and so he certified the king of them. ³Then the king examined the two eunuchs, and after that they had confessed it, they were strangled. ⁴And the king made a record of these things, and Mardocheus also wrote thereof. ⁵So the king commanded Mardocheus to serve in the court, and for this he rewarded him. ⁶Howbeit Aman the son of Amadathus the Agagite, who was in great honour with the king, sought to molest Mardocheus and his people because of the two eunuchs of the king.

[PLACED IN THE GREEK AFTER CHAP. 3:13 OF THE HEBREW]

13 The copy of the letters was this.

The great king Artaxerxes writeth these things to the princes and governors that are under him from India unto Ethiopia, in a hundred and seven and twenty provinces.

²After that I became lord over many nations, and had dominion over the whole world, not lifted up with presumption of my authority, but carrying myself always with equity and mildness, I purposed to settle my subjects continually in a quiet life, and making my kingdom peaceable, and open for passage to the utmost coasts, to renew peace, which is desired of all men. ³Now when I asked my counsellors how this might be brought to pass, Aman, that excelled in wisdom among us, and was approved for his constant good will and steadfast fidelity, and had the honour of the second place in the kingdom, ⁴declared unto us, that in all nations throughout the world there was scattered a certain malicious people, that had laws contrary to all nations, and continually despised the commandments of kings, so as the uniting of our kingdoms, honourably intended by us, cannot go forward. ⁵Seeing then we understand that this people alone is continually in opposition unto all men, differing in the strange manner of their laws, and evil-affected to our state, working all the mischief they can, that our kingdom may not be firmly established: ⁶therefore have we commanded that all they that are signified in writing unto you by Aman, who is ordained over the affairs, and is next unto us, shall all, with their wives and children, be utterly destroyed by the sword of their enemies, without all mercy and pity, the fourteenth day of the twelfth month Adar of this present year: ⁷that they, who of old and now also are malicious, may in one day with violence go into the

grave, and so ever hereafter cause our affairs to be well settled, and without trouble.

[PLACED IN THE GREEK AFTER CHAP. 4:17 OF THE HEBREW]

⁸Then Mardocheus thought upon all the works of the Lord, and made his prayer unto him, ⁹saying, 'O Lord, Lord, the King Almighty: for the whole world is in thy power, and if thou hast appointed to save Israel, there is no man that can gainsay thee: ¹⁰for thou hast made heaven and earth, and all the wondrous things under the heaven. ¹¹Thou art Lord of all things, and there is no man that can resist thee, which art the Lord. ¹²Thou knowest all things, and thou knowest, Lord, that it was neither in contempt nor pride, nor for any desire of glory, that I did not bow down to proud Aman. ¹³For I could have been content with good will for the salvation of Israel to kiss the soles of his feet. ¹⁴But I did this, that I might not prefer the glory of man above the glory of God: neither will I worship any but thee, O God, neither will I do it in pride. ¹⁵And now, O Lord God and King, spare thy people: for their eyes are upon us to bring us to nought; yea, they desire to destroy the inheritance, that hath been thine from the beginning. ¹⁶Despise not the portion, which thou hast delivered out of Egypt for thy own self. ¹⁷Hear my prayer, and be merciful unto thy inheritance: turn our sorrow into joy, that we may live, O Lord, and praise thy name: and destroy not the mouths of them that praise thee, O Lord.' ¹⁸All Israel in like manner cried most earnestly unto the Lord, because their death was before their eyes.

14 Queen Esther also, being in fear of death, resorted unto the Lord, ²and laid away her glorious apparel, and put on the garments of anguish and mourning: and instead of precious ointments, she covered her head with ashes and dung, and she humbled her body greatly, and all the places of her joy she filled with her torn hair. ³And she prayed unto the Lord God of Israel, saying, 'O my Lord, thou only art our King: help me, desolate woman, which have no helper but thee: ⁴for my danger is in my hand. ⁵From my youth up I have heard in the tribe of my family, that thou, O Lord, tookest Israel from among all people, and our fathers from all their predecessors, for a perpetual inheritance, and thou hast performed whatsoever thou didst promise them. ⁶And now we have sinned before thee: therefore hast thou given us into the hands of our enemies, ⁷because we worshipped their gods: O Lord, thou art righteous. ⁸Nevertheless it satisfieth them not that we are in bitter captivity, but they have stricken hands with their idols, ⁹that they will abolish the thing that thou with thy mouth hast ordained, and destroy thy inheritance, and stop the mouth of them that praise thee, and quench the glory of thy house, and of thy altar, ¹⁰and open the mouths of the heathen to set forth the praises of the idols, and to magnify a fleshly king for ever.

¹¹'O Lord, give not thy sceptre unto them that be nothing, and let them not laugh at our fall, but turn their device upon themselves, and make him an example that hath begun this against us. ¹²Remember, O

Lord, make thyself known in time of our affliction, and give me boldness, O King of the nations, and Lord of all power. ¹³Give me eloquent
speech in my mouth before the lion: turn his heart to hate him that
fighteth against us, that there may be an end of him, and of all that are
like-minded to him: ¹⁴but deliver us with thy hand, and help me that
am desolate, and which have no other helper but thee.

¹⁵'Thou knowest all things, O Lord, thou knowest that I hate the glory
of the unrighteous, and abhor the bed of the uncircumcised, and of all
the heathen. ¹⁶Thou knowest my necessity: for I abhor the sign of my
high estate, which is upon my head in the days wherein I show myself,
and that I abhor it as a menstruous rag, and that I wear it not when I
am private by myself, ¹⁷and that thy handmaid hath not eaten at
Aman's table, and that I have not greatly esteemed the king's feast, nor
drunk the wine of the drink offerings: ¹⁸neither had thy handmaid any
joy since the day that I was brought hither to this present, but in thee,
O Lord God of Abraham. ¹⁹O thou mighty God above all, hear the voice
of the forlorn, and deliver us out of the hands of the mischievous, and
deliver me out of my fear.'

15 And upon the third day, when she had ended her prayer, she laid
away her mourning garments, and put on her glorious apparel.
²And being gloriously adorned, after she had called upon God, who is
the beholder and saviour of all things, she took two maids with her:
³and upon the one she leaned, as carrying herself daintily; ⁴and the
other followed, bearing up her train. ⁵And she was ruddy through the
perfection of her beauty, and her countenance was cheerful and very
amiable: but her heart was in anguish for fear. ⁶Then having passed
through all the doors, she stood before the king, who sat upon his royal
throne, and was clothed with all his robes of majesty, all glittering with
gold and precious stones; and he was very dreadful. ⁷Then lifting up his
countenance that shone with majesty, he looked very fiercely upon her:
and the queen fell down, and was pale, and fainted, and bowed herself
upon the head of the maid that went before her. ⁸Then God changed
the spirit of the king into mildness, who in a fear leapt from his throne,
and took her in his arms, till she came to herself again, and comforted
her with loving words, and said unto her, ⁹'Esther, what is the matter? I
am thy brother, be of good cheer: ¹⁰thou shalt not die, though our commandment be general: come near.' ¹¹And so he held up his golden sceptre, and laid it upon her neck, ¹²And embraced her, and said, 'Speak
unto me'. ¹³Then said she unto him, 'I saw thee, my lord, as an angel of
God, and my heart was troubled for fear of thy majesty. ¹⁴For wonderful
art thou, lord, and thy countenance is full of grace.' ¹⁵And as she was
speaking, she fell down for faintness. ¹⁶Then the king was troubled, and
all his servants comforted her.

[PLACED IN THE GREEK AFTER CHAP. 8:12 OF THE HEBREW]

16 The great king Artaxerxes unto the princes and governors of a
hundred and seven and twenty provinces from India unto
Ethiopia, and unto all our faithful subjects, greeting.

²Many, the more often they are honoured with the great bounty of their gracious princes, the more proud they are waxed, ³and endeavour to hurt not our subjects only, but not being able to bear abundance, do take in hand to practise also against those that do them good: ⁴and take not only thankfulness away from among men, but also lifted up with the glorious words of lewd persons that were never good, they think to escape the justice of God, that seeth all things, and hateth evil. ⁵Oftentimes also fair speech of those that are put in trust to manage their friends' affairs, hath caused many that are in authority to be partakers of innocent blood, and hath enwrapped them in remediless calamities: ⁶beguiling with the falsehood and deceit of their lewd disposition the innocence and goodness of princes. ⁷Now ye may see this, as we have declared, not so much by ancient histories, as ye may, if ye search what hath been wickedly done of late through the pestilent behaviour of them that are unworthily placed in authority. ⁸And we must take care for the time to come, that our kingdom may be quiet and peaceable for all men, ⁹both by changing our purposes, and always judging things that are evident with more equal proceeding.

¹⁰For Aman, a Macedonian, the son of Amadatha, being indeed a stranger from the Persian blood, and far distant from our goodness, and as a stranger received of us, ¹¹had so far forth obtained the favour that we show toward every nation, as that he was called our father, and was continually honoured of all men, as the next person unto the king. ¹²But he, not bearing his great dignity, went about to deprive us of our kingdom and life: ¹³having by manifold and cunning deceits sought of us the destruction as well of Mardocheus, who saved our life, and continually procured our good, as also of blameless Esther, partaker of our kingdom, with their whole nation. ¹⁴For by these means he thought, finding us destitute of friends, to have translated the kingdom of the Persians to the Macedonians.

¹⁵But we find that the Jews, whom this wicked wretch hath delivered to utter destruction, are no evil-doers, but live by most just laws: ¹⁶and that they be children of the most high and most mighty living God, who hath ordered the kingdom both unto us and to our progenitors in the most excellent manner. ¹⁷Wherefore ye shall do well not to put in execution the letters sent unto you by Aman the son of Amadatha. ¹⁸For he, that was the worker of these things, is hanged at the gates of Susa with all his family: God, who ruleth all things, speedily rendering vengeance to him according to his deserts.

¹⁹Therefore ye shall publish the copy of this letter in all places, that the Jews may freely live after their own laws. ²⁰And ye shall aid them, that even the same day, being the thirteenth day of the twelfth month Adar, they may be avenged on them,

who in the time of their affliction shall set upon them. ²¹For Almighty God hath turned to joy unto them the day, wherein the chosen people should have perished. ²²You shall therefore among your solemn feasts keep it a high day with all feasting, ²³that both now and hereafter there may be safety to us, and the well-affected Persians; but to those which do conspire against us, a memorial of destruction. ²⁴Therefore every city and country whatsoever, which shall not do according to these things, shall be destroyed without mercy with fire and sword, and shall be made not only impassable for men, but also most hateful to wild beasts and fowls for ever.

THE
WISDOM OF SOLOMON

1 Love righteousness, ye that be judges of the earth: think of the Lord with a good heart, and in simplicity of heart seek him. [2]For he will be found of them that tempt him not: and showeth himself unto such as do not distrust him. [3]For froward thoughts separate from God: and his power, when it is tried, reproveth the unwise. [4]For into a malicious soul wisdom shall not enter: nor dwell in the body that is subject unto sin. [5]For the holy spirit of discipline will fly deceit, and remove from thoughts that are without understanding: and will not abide when unrighteousness cometh in.

[6]For wisdom is a loving spirit: and will not acquit a blasphemer of his words: for God is witness of his reins, and a true beholder of his heart, and a hearer of his tongue. [7]For the Spirit of the Lord filleth the world: and that which containeth all things hath knowledge of the voice. [8]Therefore he that speaketh unrighteous things cannot be hid: neither shall vengeance, when it punisheth, pass by him. [9]For inquisition shall be made into the counsels of the ungodly: and the sound of his words shall come unto the Lord for the manifestation of his wicked deeds. [10]For the ear of jealousy heareth all things: and the noise of murmurings is not hid. [11]Therefore beware of murmuring, which is unprofitable, and refrain your tongue from backbiting: for there is no word so secret, that shall go for nought: and the mouth that belieth slayeth the soul.

[12]Seek not death in the error of your life: and pull not upon yourselves destruction with the works of your hands. [13]For God made not death: neither hath he pleasure in the destruction of the living. [14]For he created all things, that they might have their being: and the generations of the world were healthful; and there is no poison of destruction in them, nor the kingdom of death upon the earth. [15]For righteousness is immortal. [16]But ungodly men with their works and words called it to them: for when they thought to have it their friend, they consumed to nought, and made a covenant with it, because they are worthy to take part with it.

2 For the ungodly said, reasoning with themselves, but not aright, 'Our life is short and tedious, and in the death of a man there is no remedy: neither was there any man known to have returned from the grave. [2]For we are born at all adventure: and we shall be hereafter as though we had never been: for the breath in our nostrils is as smoke, and a little spark in the moving of our heart: [3]which being extinguished, our body shall be turned into ashes, and our spirit shall vanish as the soft air, [4]and our name shall be forgotten in time, and no man shall have our works in remembrance, and our life shall pass away as the trace of a cloud: and shall be dispersed as a mist that is driven away with the beams of the sun, and overcome with the heat thereof.

⁵For our time is a very shadow that passeth away: and after our end there is no returning: for it is fast sealed, so that no man cometh again.

⁶'Come on therefore, let us enjoy the good things that are present: and let us speedily use the creatures like as in youth. ⁷Let us fill ourselves with costly wine and ointments: and let no flower of the spring pass by us: ⁸let us crown ourselves with rosebuds, before they be withered. ⁹Let none of us go without his part of our voluptuousness: let us leave tokens of our joyfulness in every place: for this is our portion and our lot is this.

¹⁰'Let us oppress the poor righteous man, let us not spare the widow, nor reverence the ancient grey hairs of the aged. ¹¹Let our strength be the law of justice: for that which is feeble is found to be nothing worth. ¹²Therefore let us lie in wait for the righteous: because he is not for our turn, and he is clean contrary to our doings: he upbraideth us with our offending the law, and objecteth to our infamy the transgressings of our education. ¹³He professeth to have the knowledge of God: and he calleth himself the child of the Lord. ¹⁴He was made to reprove our thoughts. ¹⁵He is grievous unto us even to behold: for his life is not like other men's, his ways are of another fashion. ¹⁶We are esteemed of him as counterfeits: he abstaineth from our ways as from filthiness: he pronounceth the end of the just to be blessed, and maketh his boast that God is his father. ¹⁷Let us see if his words be true: and let us prove what shall happen in the end of him. ¹⁸For if the just man be the son of God, he will help him, and deliver him from the hand of his enemies. ¹⁹Let us examine him with despitefulness and torture, that we may know his meekness, and prove his patience. ²⁰Let us condemn him with a shameful death: for by his own saying he shall be respected.'

²¹Such things they did imagine, and were deceived: for their own wickedness hath blinded them. ²²As for the mysteries of God, they knew them not: neither hoped they for the wages of righteousness, nor discerned a reward for blameless souls. ²³For God created man to be immortal, and made him to be an image of his own eternity. ²⁴Nevertheless through envy of the devil came death into the world: and they that do hold of his side do find it.

3 But the souls of the righteous are in the hand of God, and there shall no torment touch them. ²In the sight of the unwise they seemed to die: and their departure is taken for misery, ³and their going from us to be utter destruction: but they are in peace. ⁴For though they be punished in the sight of men, yet is their hope full of immortality. ⁵And having been a little chastised, they shall be greatly rewarded: for God proved them, and found them worthy for himself. ⁶As gold in the furnace hath he tried them, and received them as a burnt offering. ⁷And in the time of their visitation they shall shine, and run to and fro like sparks among the stubble. ⁸They shall judge the nations, and have dominion over the people, and their Lord shall reign for ever. ⁹They that put their trust in him shall understand the truth: and such as be faithful in love shall abide with him: for grace and mercy is to his saints, and he hath care for his elect.

¹⁰But the ungodly shall be punished according to their own imaginations, which have neglected the righteous, and forsaken the Lord. ¹¹For whoso despiseth wisdom and nurture, he is miserable, and their hope is vain, their labours unfruitful, and their works unprofitable. ¹²Their wives are foolish, and their children wicked. ¹³Their offspring is cursed. Wherefore blessed is the barren that is undefiled, which hath not known the sinful bed: she shall have fruit in the visitation of souls. ¹⁴And blessed is the eunuch which with his hands hath wrought no iniquity, nor imagined wicked things against God: for unto him shall be given the special gift of faith, and an inheritance in the temple of the Lord more acceptable to his mind. ¹⁵For glorious is the fruit of good labours: and the root of wisdom shall never fall away. ¹⁶As for the children of adulterers, they shall not come to their perfection, and the seed of an unrighteous bed shall be rooted out. ¹⁷For though they live long, yet shall they be nothing regarded: and their last age shall be without honour. ¹⁸Or if they die quickly, they have no hope, neither comfort in the day of trial. ¹⁹For horrible is the end of the unrighteous generation.

4 Better it is to have no children, and to have virtue: for the memorial thereof is immortal: because it is known with God, and with men. ²When it is present, men take example at it, and when it is gone, they desire it: it weareth a crown, and triumpheth for ever, having gotten the victory, striving for undefiled rewards. ³But the multiplying brood of the ungodly shall not thrive, nor take deep rooting from bastard slips, nor lay any fast foundation. ⁴For though they flourish in branches for a time: yet standing not fast, they shall be shaken with the wind, and through the force of winds they shall be rooted out. ⁵The imperfect branches shall be broken off, their fruit unprofitable, not ripe to eat: yea, meet for nothing. ⁶For children begotten of unlawful beds are witnesses of wickedness against their parents in their trial.

⁷But though the righteous be prevented with death, yet shall he be in rest. ⁸For honourable age is not that which standeth in length of time, nor that is measured by number of years. ⁹But wisdom is the grey hair unto men, and an unspotted life is old age. ¹⁰He pleased God, and was beloved of him: so that living amongst sinners he was translated. ¹¹Yea, speedily was he taken away, lest that wickedness should alter his understanding, or deceit beguile his soul. ¹²For the bewitching of naughtiness doth obscure things that are honest: and the wandering of concupiscence doth undermine the simple mind. ¹³He, being made perfect in a short time, fulfilled a long time: ¹⁴for his soul pleased the Lord: therefore hasted he to take him away from among the wicked. ¹⁵This the people saw, and understood it not, neither laid they up this in their minds, that his grace and mercy is with his saints, and that he hath respect unto his chosen.

¹⁶Thus the righteous that is dead shall condemn the ungodly which are living, and youth that is soon perfected, the many years and old age of the unrighteous. ¹⁷For they shall see the end of the wise, and shall not understand what God in his counsel hath decreed of him, and to

what end the Lord hath set him in safety. ¹⁸They shall see him, and despise him, but God shall laugh them to scorn: and they shall hereafter be a vile carcase, and a reproach among the dead for evermore. ¹⁹For he shall rend them, and cast them down headlong, that they shall be speechless: and he shall shake them from the foundation: and they shall be utterly laid waste, and be in sorrow: and their memorial shall perish. ²⁰And when they cast up the accounts of their sins, they shall come with fear: and their own iniquities shall convince them to their face.

5 Then shall the righteous man stand in great boldness before the face of such as have afflicted him, and made no account of his labours. ²When they see it, they shall be troubled with terrible fear, and shall be amazed at the strangeness of his salvation, so far beyond all that they looked for. ³And they repenting and groaning for anguish of spirit shall say within themselves, 'This was he, whom we had sometimes in derision, and a proverb of reproach. ⁴We fools accounted his life madness, and his end to be without honour. ⁵How is he numbered among the children of God, and his lot is among the saints! ⁶Therefore have we erred from the way of truth, and the light of righteousness hath not shone unto us, and the sun of righteousness rose not upon us. ⁷We wearied ourselves in the way of wickedness and destruction: yea, we have gone through deserts, where there lay no way: but as for the way of the Lord, we have not known it.

⁸'What hath pride profited us? or what good hath riches with our vaunting brought us? ⁹All those things are passed away like a shadow, and as a post that hasted by; ¹⁰and as a ship that passeth over the waves of the water, which when it is gone by, the trace thereof cannot be found: neither the pathway of the keel in the waves; ¹¹or as when a bird hath flown through the air, there is no token of her way to be found, but the light air being beaten with the stroke of her wings, and parted with the violent noise and motion of them, is passed through, and therein afterwards no sign where she went is to be found; ¹²or like as when an arrow is shot at a mark, it parteth the air, which immediately cometh together again, so that a man cannot know where it went through: ¹³even so we in like manner, as soon as we were born, began to draw to our end, and had no sign of virtue to show: but were consumed in our own wickedness.'

¹⁴For the hope of the ungodly is like dust that is blown away with the wind, like a thin froth that is driven away with the storm: like as the smoke which is dispersed here and there with a tempest, and passeth away as the remembrance of a guest that tarrieth but a day.

¹⁵But the righteous live for evermore; their reward also is with the Lord, and the care of them is with the most High. ¹⁶Therefore shall they receive a glorious kingdom, and a beautiful crown from the Lord's hand: for with his right hand shall he cover them, and with his arm shall he protect them. ¹⁷He shall take to him his jealousy for complete armour, and make the creature his weapon for the revenge of his enemies. ¹⁸He shall put on righteousness as a breastplate, and true judge-

ment instead of a helmet. ¹⁹He shall take holiness for an invincible shield. ²⁰His severe wrath shall he sharpen for a sword, and the world shall fight with him against the unwise.

²¹Then shall the right-aiming thunderbolts go abroad, and from the clouds, as from a well-drawn bow, shall they fly to the mark. ²²And hailstones full of wrath shall be cast as out of a stone-bow, and the water of the sea shall rage against them, and the floods shall cruelly drown them. ²³Yea, a mighty wind shall stand up against them, and like a storm shall blow them away: thus iniquity shall lay waste the whole earth, and ill dealing shall overthrow the thrones of the mighty.

6 Hear therefore, O ye kings, and understand, learn, ye that be judges of the ends of the earth. ²Give ear, you that rule the people, and glory in the multitude of nations. ³For power is given you of the Lord, and sovereignty from the Highest, who shall try your works, and search out your counsels. ⁴Because, being ministers of his kingdom, you have not judged aright, nor kept the law, nor walked after the counsel of God, ⁵horribly and speedily shall he come upon you: for a sharp judgement shall be to them that be in high places. ⁶For mercy will soon pardon the meanest: but mighty men shall be mightily tormented. ⁷For he which is Lord over all shall fear no man's person, neither shall he stand in awe of any man's greatness: for he hath made the small and great, and careth for all alike. ⁸But a sore trial shall come upon the mighty. ⁹Unto you therefore, O kings, do I speak, that ye may learn wisdom, and not fall away. ¹⁰For they that keep holiness holily shall be judged holy: and they that have learned such things shall find what to answer. ¹¹Wherefore set your affection upon my words; desire them, and ye shall be instructed.

¹²Wisdom is glorious, and never fadeth away: yea, she is easily seen of them that love her, and found of such as seek her. ¹³She preventeth them that desire her, in making herself first known unto them. ¹⁴Whoso seeketh her early shall have no great travail: for he shall find her sitting at his doors. ¹⁵To think therefore upon her is perfection of wisdom: and whoso watcheth for her shall quickly be without care. ¹⁶For she goeth about seeking such as are worthy of her, showeth herself favourably unto them in the ways, and meeteth them in every thought. ¹⁷For the very true beginning of her is the desire of discipline; and the care of discipline is love; ¹⁸and love is the keeping of her laws; and the giving heed unto her laws is the assurance of incorruption; ¹⁹and incorruption maketh us near unto God: ²⁰therefore the desire of wisdom bringeth to a kingdom. ²¹If your delight be then in thrones and sceptres, O ye kings of the people, honour wisdom, that ye may reign for evermore.

²²As for wisdom, what she is, and how she came up, I will tell you, and will not hide mysteries from you: but will seek her out from the beginning of her nativity, and bring the knowledge of her into light, and will not pass over the truth. ²³Neither will I go with consuming envy: for such a man shall have no fellowship with wisdom. ²⁴But the multitude of the wise is the welfare of the world: and a wise king is the upholding

of the people. ²⁵Receive therefore instruction through my words, and it shall do you good.

7 I myself also am a mortal man, like to all, and the offspring of him that was first made of the earth, ²and in my mother's womb was fashioned to be flesh in the time of ten months, being compacted in blood, of the seed of man, and the pleasure that came with sleep. ³And when I was born, I drew in the common air, and fell upon the earth which is of like nature, and the first voice which I uttered was crying, as all others do. ⁴I was nursed in swaddling-clothes, and that with cares. ⁵For there is no king that had any other beginning of birth. ⁶For all men have one entrance into life, and the like going out.

⁷Wherefore I prayed, and understanding was given me: I called upon God, and the spirit of wisdom came to me. ⁸I preferred her before sceptres and thrones, and esteemed riches nothing in comparison of her. ⁹Neither compared I unto her any precious stone, because all gold in respect of her is as a little sand, and silver shall be counted as clay before her. ¹⁰I loved her above health and beauty, and chose to have her instead of light: for the light that cometh from her never goeth out. ¹¹All good things together came to me with her, and innumerable riches in her hands. ¹²And I rejoiced in them all, because wisdom goeth before them: and I knew not that she was the mother of them. ¹³I learned diligently, and do communicate her liberally: I do not hide her riches. ¹⁴For she is a treasure unto men that never faileth: which they that use become the friends of God, being commended for the gifts that come from learning.

¹⁵God hath granted me to speak as I would, and to conceive as is meet for the things that are given me: because it is he that leadeth unto wisdom, and directeth the wise. ¹⁶For in his hand are born we and our words: all wisdom also, and knowledge of workmanship. ¹⁷For he hath given me certain knowledge of the things that are, namely, to know how the world was made, and the operation of the elements: ¹⁸the beginning, ending and midst of the times: the alterations of the turning of the sun, and the change of seasons: ¹⁹the circuits of years, and the positions of stars: ²⁰the natures of living creatures, and the furies of wild beasts: the violence of winds, and the reasonings of men: the diversities of plants, and the virtues of roots: ²¹and all such things as are either secret or manifest, them I know.

²²For wisdom, which is the worker of all things, taught me: for in her is an understanding spirit, holy, one only, manifold, subtle, lively, clear, undefiled, plain, not subject to hurt, loving the thing that is good, quick, which cannot be letted, ready to do good, ²³kind to man, steadfast, sure, free from care, having all power, overseeing all things, and going through all understanding, pure, and most subtle spirits. ²⁴For wisdom is more moving than any motion: she passeth and goeth through all things by reason of her pureness. ²⁵For she is the breath of the power of God, and a pure influence flowing from the glory of the Almighty: therefore can no defiled thing fall into her. ²⁶For she is the brightness of the everlasting light, the unspotted mirror of the

power of God, and the image of his goodness. ²⁷And being but one, she can do all things: and remaining in herself, she maketh all things new: and in all ages entering into holy souls, she maketh them friends of God, and prophets. ²⁸For God loveth none but him that dwelleth with wisdom. ²⁹For she is more beautiful than the sun, and above all the order of stars: being compared with the light, she is found before it. ³⁰For after this cometh night: but vice shall not prevail against wisdom.

8 Wisdom reacheth from one end to another mightily: and sweetly doth she order all things. ²I loved her, and sought her out, from my youth I desired to make her my spouse, and I was a lover of her beauty. ³In that she is conversant with God, she magnifieth her nobility: yea, the Lord of all things himself loved her. ⁴For she is privy to the mysteries of the knowledge of God, and a lover of his works. ⁵If riches be a possession to be desired in this life; what is richer than wisdom that worketh all things? ⁶And if prudence work; who of all that are is a more cunning workman than she? ⁷And if a man love righteousness, her labours are virtues: for she teacheth temperance and prudence, justice and fortitude: which are such things as men can have nothing more profitable in their life. ⁸If a man desire much experience, she knoweth things of old, and conjectureth aright what is to come: she knoweth the subtleties of speeches, and can expound dark sentences: she foreseeth signs and wonders, and the events of seasons and times.

⁹Therefore I purposed to take her to me to live with me, knowing that she would be a counsellor of good things, and a comfort in cares and grief. ¹⁰For her sake I shall have estimation among the multitude, and honour with the elders, though I be young. ¹¹I shall be found of a quick conceit in judgement, and shall be admired in the sight of great men. ¹²When I hold my tongue, they shall bide my leisure, and when I speak, they shall give good ear unto me: if I talk much, they shall lay their hands upon their mouth. ¹³Moreover by the means of her I shall obtain immortality, and leave behind me an everlasting memorial to them that come after me. ¹⁴I shall set the people in order, and the nations shall be subject unto me. ¹⁵Horrible tyrants shall be afraid when they do but hear of me; I shall be found good among the multitude, and valiant in war. ¹⁶After I am come into my house, I will repose myself with her: for her conversation hath no bitterness, and to live with her hath no sorrow, but mirth and joy.

¹⁷Now when I considered these things in myself, and pondered them in my heart, how that to be allied unto wisdom is immortality, ¹⁸and great pleasure it is to have her friendship; and in the works of her hands are infinite riches, and in the exercise of conference with her, prudence: and in talking with her a good report: I went about seeking how to take her to me. ¹⁹For I was a witty child, and had a good spirit. ²⁰Yea rather, being good, I came into a body undefiled. ²¹Nevertheless, when I perceived that I could not otherwise obtain her, except God gave her me (and that was a point of wisdom also to know whose gift she was), I prayed unto the Lord, and besought him, and with my whole

9 heart I said, '‘O God of my fathers, and Lord of mercy, who hast made all things with thy word, ²and ordained man through thy wisdom, that he should have dominion over the creatures which thou hast made, ³and order the world according to equity and righteousness, and execute judgement with an upright heart: ⁴give me wisdom that sitteth by thy throne, and reject me not from among thy children: ⁵for I thy servant and son of thy handmaid am a feeble person, and of a short time, and too young for the understanding of judgement and laws. ⁶For though a man be never so perfect among the children of men, yet if thy wisdom be not with him, he shall be nothing regarded. ⁷Thou hast chosen me to be a king of thy people, and a judge of thy sons and daughters: ⁸thou hast commanded me to build a temple upon thy holy mount, and an altar in the city wherein thou dwellest, a resemblance of the holy tabernacle, which thou hast prepared from the beginning. ⁹And wisdom was with thee: which knoweth thy works, and was present when thou madest the world, and knew what was acceptable in thy sight, and right in thy commandments. ¹⁰O send her out of thy holy heavens, and from the throne of thy glory, that being present she may labour with me, that I may know what is pleasing unto thee. ¹¹For she knoweth and understandeth all things, and she shall lead me soberly in my doings, and preserve me in her power. ¹²So shall my works be acceptable, and then shall I judge thy people righteously, and be worthy to sit in my father's seat.'

¹³For what man is he that can know the counsel of God? or who can think what the will of the Lord is? ¹⁴For the thoughts of mortal men are miserable, and our devices are but uncertain. ¹⁵For the corruptible body presseth down the soul, and the earthy tabernacle weigheth down the mind that museth upon many things. ¹⁶And hardly do we guess aright at things that are upon earth, and with labour do we find the things that are before us: but the things that are in heaven who hath searched out? ¹⁷And thy counsel who hath known, except thou give wisdom, and send thy Holy Spirit from above? ¹⁸For so the ways of them which lived on the earth were reformed, and men were taught the things that are pleasing unto thee, and were saved through wisdom.

10 She preserved the first formed father of the world, that was created alone, and brought him out of his fall, ²and gave him power to rule all things. ³But when the unrighteous went away from her in his anger, he perished also in the fury wherewith he murdered his brother. ⁴For whose cause the earth being drowned with the flood, wisdom again preserved it, and directed the course of the righteous in a piece of wood of small value. ⁵Moreover, the nations in their wicked conspiracy being confounded, she found out the righteous, and preserved him blameless unto God, and kept him strong against his tender compassion towards his son.

⁶When the ungodly perished, she delivered the righteous man, who fled from the fire which fell down upon the five cities. ⁷Of whose wickedness even to this day the waste land that smoketh is a testimony,

and plants bearing fruit that never come to ripeness: and a standing pillar of salt is a monument of an unbelieving soul. ⁸For regarding not wisdom, they got not only this hurt, that they knew not the things which were good: but also left behind them to the world a memorial of their foolishness: so that in the things wherein they offended they could not so much as be hid. ⁹But wisdom delivered from pain those that attended upon her.

¹⁰When the righteous fled from his brother's wrath, she guided him in right paths, showed him the kingdom of God, and gave him knowledge of holy things, made him rich in his travails, and multiplied the fruit of his labours. ¹¹In the covetousness of such as oppressed him she stood by him, and made him rich. ¹²She defended him from his enemies, and kept him safe from those that lay in wait, and in a sore conflict she gave him the victory, that he might know that godliness is stronger than all.

¹³When the righteous was sold, she forsook him not, but delivered him from sin: she went down with him into the pit, ¹⁴and left him not in bonds, till she brought him the sceptre of the kingdom, and power against those that oppressed him: as for them that had accused him, she showed them to be liars, and gave him perpetual glory.

¹⁵She delivered the righteous people and blameless seed from the nation that oppressed them. ¹⁶She entered into the soul of the servant of the Lord, and withstood dreadful kings in wonders and signs, ¹⁷rendered to the righteous a reward of their labours, guided them in a marvellous way, and was unto them for a cover by day, and a light of stars in the night-season: ¹⁸brought them through the Red Sea, and led them through much water: ¹⁹but she drowned their enemies, and cast them up out of the bottom of the deep. ²⁰Therefore the righteous spoiled the ungodly, and praised thy holy name, O Lord, and magnified with one accord thy hand, that fought for them. ²¹For wisdom opened the mouth of the dumb, and made the tongues of them that cannot speak eloquent.

11 She prospered their works in the hand of the holy prophet. ²They went through the wilderness that was not inhabited, and pitched tents in places where there lay no way. ³They stood against their enemies, and were avenged of their adversaries. ⁴When they were thirsty, they called upon thee, and water was given them out of the flinty rock, and their thirst was quenched out of the hard stone. ⁵For by what things their enemies were punished, by the same they in their need were benefited. ⁶For instead of a fountain of a perpetual running river troubled with foul blood, ⁷for a manifest reproof of that commandment, whereby the infants were slain, thou gavest unto them abundance of water by a means which they hoped not for, ⁸declaring by that thirst then how thou hadst punished their adversaries. ⁹For when they were tried, albeit but in mercy chastised, they knew how the ungodly were judged in wrath and tormented, thirsting in another manner than the just. ¹⁰For these thou didst admonish and try as a father: but the others, as a severe king, thou didst condemn and punish. [11]Whether they were absent or present, they were vexed alike. [12]For a double grief came upon them, and a groaning for the remembrance of things past. [13]For when they heard by their own punishments the others to be benefited, they had some feeling of the Lord. [14]For whom they rejected with scorn when he was long before thrown out at the casting forth of the infants, him in the end, when they saw what came to pass, they admired.

[15]But for the foolish devices of their wickedness, wherewith being deceived they worshipped serpents void of reason, and vile beasts, thou didst send a multitude of unreasonable beasts upon them for vengeance, [16]that they might know that wherewithal a man sinneth, by the same also shall he be punished. [17]For thy Almighty hand that made the world of matter without form, wanted not means to send among them a multitude of bears, or fierce lions, [18]or unknown wild beasts, full of rage, newly created, breathing out either a fiery vapour, or filthy sents of scattered smoke, or shooting horrible sparkles out of their eyes: [19]whereof not only the harm might dispatch them at once, but also the terrible sight utterly destroy them. [20]Yea, and without these might they have fallen down with one blast, being persecuted of vengeance, and scattered abroad through the breath of thy power, but thou hast ordered all things in measure and number and weight.

[21]For thou canst show thy great strength at all times when thou wilt, and who may withstand the power of thy arm? [22]For the whole world before thee is as a little grain of the balance, yea, as a drop of the morning dew that falleth down upon the earth. [23]But thou hast mercy upon all: for thou canst do all things, and winkest at the sins of men, because they should amend. [24]For thou lovest all the things that are, and abhorrest nothing which thou hast made: for never wouldst thou have made anything, if thou hadst hated it. [25]And how could anything have endured if it had not been thy will? or been preserved, if not called by thee? [26]But thou sparest all: for they are thine, O Lord, thou lover of souls.

12 For thy incorruptible Spirit is in all things. [2]Therefore chastenest thou them by little and little that offend, and warnest them by putting them in remembrance wherein they have offended, that leaving their wickedness they may believe on thee, O Lord. [3]For it was thy will to destroy by the hands of our fathers both those old inhabitants of thy holy land, [4]whom thou hatedst for doing most odious works of witchcrafts, and wicked sacrifices; [5]and also those merciless murderers of children, and devourers of man's flesh, and the feasts of blood; [6]with their priests out of the midst of their idolatrous crew, and the parents, that killed with their own hands souls destitute of help: [7]that the land, which thou esteemedst above all other, might receive a worthy colony of God's children. [8]Nevertheless even those thou sparedst as men, and didst send wasps, forerunners of thy host, to destroy them by little and little. [9]Not that thou wast unable to bring the ungodly under the hand of the righteous in battle, or to destroy them at once with cruel beasts, or with one rough word: [10]but executing thy judgements upon them by

little and little, thou gavest them place of repentance, not being ignorant that they were a naughty generation, and that their malice was bred in them, and that their cogitation would never be changed. ¹¹For it was a cursed seed from the beginning; neither didst thou for fear of any man give them pardon for those things wherein they sinned.

¹²For who shall say, 'What hast thou done?' or who shall withstand thy judgement? or who shall accuse thee for the nations that perish whom thou hast made? or who shall come to stand against thee, to be revenged for the unrighteous men? ¹³For neither is there any God but thou that careth for all, to whom thou mightest show that thy judgement is not unright. ¹⁴Neither shall king or tyrant be able to set his face against thee for any whom thou hast punished. ¹⁵Forsomuch then as thou art righteous thyself, thou orderest all things righteously: thinking it not agreeable with thy power to condemn him that hath not deserved to be punished. ¹⁶For thy power is the beginning of righteousness, and because thou art the Lord of all, it maketh thee to be gracious unto all. ¹⁷For when men will not believe that thou art of a full power thou showest thy strength, and among them that know it thou makest their boldness manifest. ¹⁸But thou, mastering thy power, judgest with equity, and orderest us with great favour: for thou mayest use power when thou wilt.

¹⁹But by such works hast thou taught thy people that the just man should be merciful, and hast made thy children to be of a good hope that thou givest repentance for sins. ²⁰For if thou didst punish the enemies of thy children, and the condemned to death, with such deliberation, giving them time and place, whereby they might be delivered from their malice: ²¹with how great circumspection didst thou judge thy own sons, unto whose fathers thou hast sworn, and made covenants of good promises? ²²Therefore, whereas thou dost chasten us, thou scourgest our enemies a thousand times more, to the intent that, when we judge, we should carefully think of thy goodness, and when we ourselves are judged, we should look for mercy. ²³Wherefore, whereas men have lived dissolutely and unrighteously, thou hast tormented them with their own abominations. ²⁴For they went astray very far in the ways of error, and held them for gods, which even amongst the beasts of their enemies were despised, being deceived, as children of no understanding. ²⁵Therefore unto them, as to children without the use of reason, thou didst send a judgement to mock them. ²⁶But they that would not be reformed by that correction wherein he dallied with them, shall feel a judgement worthy of God. ²⁷For look, for what things they grudged when they were punished, that is, for them whom they thought to be gods; now being punished in them, when they saw it, they acknowledged him to be the true God, whom before they denied to know: and therefore came extreme damnation upon them.

13 Surely vain are all men by nature, who are ignorant of God, and could not out of the good things that are seen know him that is: neither by considering the works did they acknowledge the workmaster; ²but deemed either fire, or wind, or the swift air, or the circle of the stars, or the violent water, or the lights of heaven to be the gods which govern the world: ³with whose beauty, if they being delighted, took them to be gods: let them know how much better the Lord of them is: for the first author of beauty hath created them. ⁴But if they were astonished at their power and virtue, let them understand by them, how much mightier he is that made them. ⁵For by the greatness and beauty of the creatures proportionably the maker of them is seen. ⁶But yet for this they are the less to be blamed: for they peradventure err, seeking God, and desirous to find him. ⁷For being conversant in his works they search him diligently, and believe their sight: because the things are beautiful that are seen. ⁸Howbeit neither are they to be pardoned. ⁹For if they were able to know so much, that they could aim at the world; how did they not sooner find out the Lord thereof?

¹⁰But miserable are they, and in dead things is their hope, who called them gods which are the works of men's hands, gold and silver, to show art in, and resemblances of beasts, or a stone good for nothing, the work of an ancient hand. ¹¹Now a carpenter that felleth timber, after he hath sawn down a tree meet for the purpose, and taken off all the bark skilfully round about, and hath wrought it handsomely, and made a vessel thereof fit for the service of man's life; ¹²and after spending the refuse of his work to dress his meat, hath filled himself; ¹³and taking the very refuse among those which served to no use (being a crooked piece of wood, and full of knots), hath carved it diligently when he had nothing else to do, and formed it by the skill of his understanding, and fashioned it to the image of a man; ¹⁴or made it like some vile beast, laying it over with vermilion, and with paint colouring it red, and covering every spot therein; ¹⁵and when he had made a convenient room for it, set it in a wall, and made it fast with iron: ¹⁶for he provided for it that it might not fall, knowing that it was unable to help itself (for it is an image, and hath need of help): ¹⁷then maketh he prayer for his goods, for his wife and children, and is not ashamed to speak to that which hath no life. ¹⁸For health he calleth upon that which is weak: for life prayeth to that which is dead: for aid humbly beseecheth that which hath least means to help: and for a good journey he asketh of that which cannot set a foot forward: ¹⁹and for gaining and getting, and for good success of his hands, asketh ability to do of him that is most unable to do anything.

14 Again, one preparing himself to sail, and about to pass through the raging waves, calleth upon a piece of wood more rotten than the vessel that carrieth him. ²For verily desire of gain devised that, and the workman built it by his skill. ³But thy providence, O Father, governeth it: for thou hast made a way in the sea, and a safe path in the waves: ⁴showing that thou canst save from all danger: yea, though a man went to sea without art. ⁵Nevertheless thou wouldst not that the works of thy wisdom should be idle, and therefore do men commit their lives to a small piece of wood, and passing the rough sea in a weak vessel are saved. ⁶For in the old time also, when the proud giants perished, the hope of the world governed by thy hand escaped in a weak vessel, and left to all ages a seed of generation. ⁷For blessed is the wood whereby righteousness cometh. ⁸But that which is made with hands is cursed, as well it, as he that made it: he, because he made it, and it, because being corruptible it was called god. ⁹For the ungodly and his ungodliness are both alike hateful unto God. ¹⁰For that which is made shall be punished together with him that made it. ¹¹Therefore even upon the idols of the Gentiles shall there be a visitation: because in the creature of God they are become an abomination, and stumbling-blocks to the souls of men, and a snare to the feet of the unwise. ¹²For the devising of idols was the beginning of spiritual fornication, and the invention of them the corruption of life. ¹³For neither were they from the beginning, neither shall they be for ever. ¹⁴For by the vain glory of men they entered into the world, and therefore shall they come shortly to an end.

¹⁵For a father afflicted with untimely mourning, when he hath made an image of his child soon taken away, now honoured him as a god, which was then a dead man, and delivered to those that were under him ceremonies and sacrifices. ¹⁶Thus in process of time an ungodly custom grown strong was kept as a law, and graven images were worshipped by the commandments of kings, ¹⁷whom men could not honour in presence, because they dwelt far off, they took the counterfeit of his visage from far, and made an express image of a king whom they honoured, to the end that by this their forwardness they might flatter him that was absent, as if he were present. ¹⁸Also the singular diligence of the artificer did help to set forward the ignorant to more superstition. ¹⁹For he, peradventure willing to please one in authority, forced all his skill to make the resemblance of the best fashion. ²⁰And so the multitude, allured by the grace of the work, took him now for a god, which a little before was but honoured as a man. ²¹And this was an occasion to deceive the world: for men, serving either calamity or tyranny, did ascribe unto stones and stocks the incommunicable name.

²²Moreover this was not enough for them, that they erred in the knowledge of God; but whereas they lived in the great war of ignorance, those so great plagues called they peace. ²³For whilst they slew their children in sacrifices, or used secret ceremonies, or made revellings of strange rites; ²⁴they kept neither lives nor marriages any longer undefiled: but either one slew another traiterously, or grieved him by adultery. ²⁵So that there reigned in all men without exception blood, manslaughter, theft, and dissimulation, corruption, unfaithfulness, tumults, perjury, ²⁶disquieting of good men, forgetfulness of good turns, defiling of souls, changing of kind, disorder in marriages, adultery, and shameless uncleanness. ²⁷For the worshipping of idols not to be named is the beginning, the cause, and the end of all evil. ²⁸For either they are mad when they be merry, or prophesy lies, or live unjustly, or else lightly forswear themselves. ²⁹For insomuch as their trust is in idols which have no life, though they swear falsely, yet they look not to be hurt. ³⁰Howbeit for both causes shall they be justly punished: both because they thought

not well of God, giving heed unto idols, and also unjustly swore in deceit, despising holiness. ³¹For it is not the power of them by whom they swear: but it is the just vengeance of sinners, that punisheth always the offence of the ungodly.

15 But thou, O God, art gracious and true, long-suffering, and in mercy ordering all things. ²For if we sin, we are thine, knowing thy power: but we will not sin, knowing that we are counted thine. ³For to know thee is perfect righteousness: yea, to know thy power is the root of immortality. ⁴For neither did the mischievous invention of men deceive us, nor an image spotted with divers colours, the painters' fruitless labour; ⁵the sight whereof enticeth fools to lust after it, and so they desire the form of a dead image, that hath no breath. ⁶Both they that make them, they that desire them, and they that worship them are lovers of evil things, and are worthy to have such things to trust upon.

⁷For the potter, tempering soft earth, fashioneth every vessel with much labour for our service: yea, of the same clay he maketh both the vessels that serve for clean uses, and likewise also all such as serve to the contrary: but what is the use of either sort, the potter himself is the judge. ⁸And employing his labours lewdly, he maketh a vain god of the same clay, even he which a little before was made of earth himself, and within a little while after returneth to the same out of the which he was taken when his life which was lent him shall be demanded. ⁹Notwithstanding his care is, not that he shall have much labour, nor that his life is short: but striveth to excel goldsmiths and silversmiths, and endeavoureth to do like the workers in brass, and counteth it his glory to make counterfeit things. ¹⁰His heart is ashes, his hope is more vile than earth, and his life of less value than clay: ¹¹forasmuch as he knew not his Maker, and him that inspired into him an active soul, and breathed in a living spirit. ¹²But they counted our life a pastime, and our time here a market for gain: for, say they, we must be getting every way, though it be by evil means. ¹³For this man that of earthly matter maketh brittle vessels and graven images knoweth himself to offend above all others.

¹⁴And all the enemies of thy people that hold them in subjection are most foolish, and are more miserable than very babes. ¹⁵For they counted all the idols of the heathen to be gods: which neither have the use of eyes to see, nor noses to draw breath, nor ears to hear, nor fingers of hands to handle, and as for their feet, they are slow to go. ¹⁶For man made them, and he that borrowed his own spirit fashioned them, but no man can make a god like unto himself. ¹⁷For being mortal, he worketh a dead thing with wicked hands: for he himself is better than the things which he worshippeth: whereas he lived once, but they never.

¹⁸Yea, they worshipped those beasts also that are most hateful: for being compared together, some are worse than others. ¹⁹Neither are they beautiful, so much as to be desired in respect of beasts: but they went without the praise of God and his blessing.

16 Therefore by the like were they punished worthily, and by the multitude of beasts tormented. ²Instead of which punishment, dealing graciously with thy own people, thou preparedst for them meat of a strange taste, even quails to stir up their appetite: ³to the end that they desiring food might for the ugly sight of the beasts sent among them loathe even that which they must needs desire: but these, suffering penury for a short space, might be made partakers of a strange taste. ⁴For it was requisite that upon them exercising tyranny should come penury which they could not avoid: but to these it should only be shown how their enemies were tormented.

⁵For when the horrible fierceness of beasts came upon these, and they perished with the stings of crooked serpents, thy wrath endured not for ever: ⁶but they were troubled for a small season that they might be admonished, having a sign of salvation, to put them in remembrance of the commandment of thy law. ⁷For he that turned himself towards it was not saved by the thing that he saw, but by thee, that art the Saviour of all. ⁸And in this thou madest thy enemies confess that it is thou who deliverest from all evil: ⁹for them the bitings of grasshoppers and flies killed, neither was there found any remedy for their life: for they were worthy to be punished by such.

¹⁰But thy sons not the very teeth of venomous dragons overcame: for thy mercy was ever by them, and healed them. ¹¹For they were pricked, that they should remember thy words, and were quickly saved, that not falling into deep forgetfulness, they might be continually mindful of thy goodness. ¹²For it was neither herb, nor mollifying plaster that restored them to health: but thy word, O Lord, which healeth all things. ¹³For thou hast power of life and death: thou leadest to the gates of hell, and bringest up again. ¹⁴A man indeed killeth through his malice: and the spirit, when it is gone forth, returneth not; neither the soul received up cometh again.

¹⁵But it is not possible to escape thy hand. ¹⁶For the ungodly, that denied to know thee, were scourged by the strength of thy arm: with strange rains, hails, and showers were they persecuted, that they could not avoid, and through fire were they consumed. ¹⁷For, which is most to be wondered at, the fire had more force in the water that quencheth all things: for the world fighteth for the righteous. ¹⁸For some time the flame was mitigated, that it might not burn up the beasts that were sent against the ungodly: but themselves might see and perceive that they were persecuted with the judgement of God. ¹⁹And at another time it burneth even in the midst of water above the power of fire, that it might destroy the fruits of an unjust land.

²⁰In stead whereof thou feddest thy own people with angels' food, and didst send them from heaven bread prepared without their labour, able to content every man's delight, and agreeing to every taste. ²¹For thy sustenance declared thy sweetness unto thy children, and serving to the appetite of the eater, tempered itself to every man's liking. ²²But snow and ice endured the fire, and melted not, that they might know that fire burning in the hail, and sparkling in the rain, did destroy the fruits of the enemies. ²³But this again did even forget his own strength, that the righteous might be nourished.

²⁴For the creature that serveth thee, who art the Maker, increaseth his strength against the unrighteous for their punishment, and abateth his strength for the benefit of such as put their trust in thee. ²⁵Therefore even then was it altered into all fashions, and was obedient to thy grace that nourisheth all things, according to the desire of them that had need: ²⁶that thy children, O Lord, whom thou lovest, might know, that it is not the growing of fruits that nourisheth man: but that it is thy word, which preserveth them that put their trust in thee. ²⁷For that which was not destroyed of the fire, being warmed with a little sunbeam, soon melted away, ²⁸that it might be known that we must prevent the sun to give thee thanks, and at the day-spring pray unto thee. ²⁹For the hope of the unthankful shall melt away as the winter's hoar frost, and shall run away as unprofitable water.

17 For great are thy judgements, and cannot be expressed: therefore unnurtured souls have erred. ²For when unrighteous men thought to oppress the holy nation: they being shut up in their houses, the prisoners of darkness, and fettered with the bonds of a long night, lay there exiled from the eternal providence. ³For while they supposed to lie hid in their secret sins, they were scattered under a dark veil of forgetfulness, being horribly astonished, and troubled with strange apparitions. ⁴For neither might the corner that held them keep them from fear: but noises as of waters falling down sounded about them, and sad visions appeared unto them with heavy countenances. ⁵No power of the fire might give them light: neither could the bright flames of the stars endure to lighten that horrible night. ⁶Only there appeared unto them a fire kindled of itself, very dreadful: for being much terrified, they thought the things which they saw to be worse than the sight they saw not.

⁷As for the illusions of art magic, they were put down, and their vaunting in wisdom was reproved with disgrace. ⁸For they that promised to drive away terrors and troubles from a sick soul were sick themselves of fear worthy to be laughed at. ⁹For though no terrible thing did fear them: yet being scared with beasts that passed by, and hissing of serpents, ¹⁰they died for fear, denying that they saw the air, which could of no side be avoided. ¹¹For wickedness, condemned by her own witness, is very timorous, and being pressed with conscience, always forecasteth grievous things.

¹²For fear is nothing else but a betraying of the succours which reason offereth. ¹³And the expectation from within, being less, counteth the ignorance more than the cause which bringeth the torment. ¹⁴But they sleeping the same sleep that night, which was indeed intolerable, and which came upon them out of the bottoms of inevitable hell, ¹⁵were partly vexed with monstrous apparitions, and partly fainted, their heart failing them: for a sudden fear, and not looked for, came upon them. ¹⁶So then whosoever there fell down was straitly kept, shut up in a prison without iron bars. ¹⁷For whether he were husbandman, or shepherd, or a labourer in the field, he was overtaken, and endured that necessity, which could not be avoided: for they were all bound

with one chain of darkness. [18]Whether it were a whistling wind, or a melodious noise of birds among the spreading branches, or a pleasing fall of water running violently, [19]or a terrible sound of stones cast down, or a running that could not be seen of skipping beasts, or a roaring voice of most savage wild beasts, or a rebounding echo from the hollow mountains: these things made them to swoon for fear. [20]For the whole world shone with clear light, and none were hindered in their labour: [21]over them only was spread a heavy night, an image of that darkness which should afterwards receive them: but yet were they unto themselves more grievous than the darkness.

18 Nevertheless thy saints had a very great light, whose voice they hearing, and not seeing their shape, because they also had not suffered the same things, they counted them happy. [2]But for that they did not hurt them now, of whom they had been wronged before, they thanked them, and besought them pardon for that they had been enemies. [3]In stead whereof thou gavest them a burning pillar of fire, both to be a guide of the unknown journey, and a harmless sun to entertain them honourably. [4]For they were worthy to be deprived of light, and imprisoned in darkness, who had kept thy sons shut up, by whom the incorrupt light of the law was to be given unto the world.

[5]And when they had determined to slay the babes of the saints, one child being cast forth, and saved, to reprove them, thou tookest away the multitude of their children, and destroyedst them altogether in a mighty water. [6]Of that night were our fathers certified afore, that assuredly knowing unto what oaths they had given credence, they might afterwards be of good cheer. [7]So of thy people was accepted both the salvation of the righteous, and destruction of the enemies. [8]For wherewith thou didst punish our adversaries, by the same thou didst glorify us whom thou hadst called. [9]For the righteous children of good men did sacrifice secretly, and with one consent made a holy law, that the saints should be alike partakers of the same good and evil, the fathers now singing out the songs of praise.

[10]But on the other side there sounded an ill according cry of the enemies, and a lamentable noise was carried abroad for children that were bewailed. [11]The master and the servant were punished after one manner, and like as the king, so suffered the common person. [12]So they all together had innumerable dead with one kind of death, neither were the living sufficient to bury them: for in one moment the noblest offspring of them was destroyed. [13]For whereas they would not believe anything by reason of the enchantments; upon the destruction of the firstborn, they acknowledged this people to be the sons of God.

[14]For while all things were in quiet silence, and that night was in the midst of her swift course, [15]thy almighty word leapt down from heaven out of thy royal throne, as a fierce man of war into the midst of a land of destruction, [16]and brought thy unfeigned commandment as a sharp sword, and standing up filled all things with death; and it touched the heaven, but it stood upon the earth. [17]Then suddenly visions of horrible dreams troubled them sore, and terrors came upon them unlooked for.

¹⁸And one thrown here, another there, half dead, showed the cause of his death. ¹⁹For the dreams that troubled them did foreshow this, lest they should perish, and not know why they were afflicted.

²⁰Yea, the tasting of death touched the righteous also, and there was a destruction of the multitude in the wilderness: but the wrath endured not long. ²¹For then the blameless man made haste, and stood forth to defend them, and bringing the shield of his proper ministry, even prayer and the propitiation of incense, set himself against the wrath, and so brought the calamity to an end, declaring that he was thy servant. ²²So he overcame the destroyer, not with strength of body, nor force of arms, but with a word subdued he him that punished, alleging the oaths and covenants made with the fathers. ²³For when the dead were now fallen down by heaps one upon another, standing between, he stayed the wrath, and parted the way to the living. ²⁴For in the long garment was the whole world, and in the four rows of the stones was the glory of the fathers graven, and thy majesty upon the diadem of his head. ²⁵Unto these the destroyer gave place, and was afraid of them: for it was enough that they only tasted of the wrath.

19 As for the ungodly, wrath came upon them without mercy unto the end: for he knew before what they would do; ²how that having given them leave to depart, and sent them hastily away, they would repent and pursue them. ³For whilst they were yet mourning and making lamentation at the graves of the dead, they added another foolish device, and pursued them as fugitives, whom they had entreated to be gone. ⁴For the destiny, whereof they were worthy, drew them unto this end, and made them forget the things that had already happened, that they might fulfil the punishment which was wanting to their torments, ⁵and that thy people might pass a wonderful way: but they might find a strange death.

⁶For the whole creature in his proper kind was fashioned again anew, serving the peculiar commandments that were given unto them, that thy children might be kept without hurt: ⁷as namely, a cloud shadowing the camp, and where water stood before, dry land appeared, and out of the Red Sea a way without impediment, and out of the violent stream a green field: ⁸wherethrough all the people went that were defended with thy hand, seeing thy marvellous strange wonders. ⁹For they went at large like horses, and leapt like lambs, praising thee, O Lord, who hadst delivered them. ¹⁰For they were yet mindful of the things that were done while they sojourned in the strange land, how the ground brought forth flies instead of cattle, and how the river cast up a multitude of frogs instead of fishes. ¹¹But afterwards they saw a new generation of fowls, when being led with their appetite they asked delicate meats. ¹²For quails came up unto them from the sea for their contentment.

¹³And punishments came upon the sinners not without former signs by the force of thunders: for they suffered justly according to their own wickedness, insomuch as they used a more hard and hateful behaviour towards strangers. ¹⁴For the Sodomites did not receive those whom they

knew not when they came: but these brought friends into bondage, that had well deserved of them. ¹⁵And not only so, but peradventure some respect shall be had of those, because they used strangers not friendly: ¹⁶but these very grievously afflicted them, whom they had received with feastings, and were already made partakers of the same laws with them. ¹⁷Therefore even with blindness were these stricken, as those were at the doors of the righteous man: when, being compassed about with horrible great darkness, every one sought the passage of his own doors.

¹⁸For the elements were changed in themselves by a kind of harmony, like as in a psaltery notes change the name of the tune, and yet are always sounds; which may well be perceived by the sight of the things that have been done: ¹⁹for earthly things were turned into watery, and the things that before swam in the water now went upon the ground. ²⁰The fire had power in the water, forgetting his own virtue: and the water forgot his own quenching nature. ²¹On the other side, the flames wasted not the flesh of the corruptible living things, though they walked therein, neither melted they the icy kind of heavenly meat, that was of nature apt to melt.

²²For in all things, O Lord, thou didst magnify thy people, and glorify them, neither didst thou lightly regard them: but didst assist them in every time and place.

THE WISDOM OF JESUS THE SON OF SIRACH, OR,
ECCLESIASTICUS

A Prologue made by an uncertain Author

THIS Jesus was the son of Sirach, and grandchild to Jesus of the same name with him: this man therefore lived in the latter times, after the people had been led away captive, and called home again, and almost after all the prophets. Now his grandfather Jesus, as he himself witnesseth, was a man of great diligence and wisdom among the Hebrews, who did not only gather the grave and short sentences of wise men, that had been before him, but himself also uttered some of his own, full of much understanding and wisdom. When as therefore the first Jesus died, leaving this book almost perfected, Sirach his son receiving it after him left it to his own son Jesus, who, having gotten it into his hands, compiled it all orderly into one volume, and called it Wisdom, entitling it both by his own name, his father's name, and his grandfather's; alluring the hearer by the very name of Wisdom to have a greater love to the study of this book. It containeth therefore wise sayings, dark sentences, and parables, and certain particular ancient godly stories of men that pleased God; also his prayer and song; moreover, what benefits God had vouchsafed his people, and what plagues he had heaped upon their enemies. This Jesus did imitate Solomon, and was no less famous for wisdom and learning, both being indeed a man of great learning, and so reputed also.

The Prologue of the Wisdom of Jesus the son of Sirach

WHEREAS many and great things have been delivered unto us by the law and the prophets, and by others that have followed their steps, for the which things Israel ought to be commended for learning and wisdom, and whereof not only the readers must needs become skilful themselves, but also they that desire to learn be able to profit them which are without, both by speaking and writing: my grandfather Jesus, when he had much given himself to the reading of the law, and the prophets, and other books of our fathers, and had gotten therein good judgement, was drawn on also himself to write something pertaining to learning and wisdom, to the intent that those which are desirous to learn, and are addicted to these things, might profit much more in living according to the law. Wherefore let me entreat you to read it with favour and attention, and to pardon us, wherein we may seem to come short of some words, which we have laboured to interpret. For the same things uttered in Hebrew, and translated into another tongue, have not the same force in them: and not only these things, but the law itself, and the prophets, and the rest of the books, have no small difference, when they are spoken in their own language. For in the eight and thirtieth year coming into Egypt, when Euergetes was king, and continuing there some time, I found a book of no small learning: therefore I thought it most necessary for me to bestow some diligence and travail to interpret it: using great watchfulness and skill in that space to bring the book to an end, and set it forth for them also, which in a strange country are willing to learn, being prepared before in manners to live after the law.

1 All wisdom cometh from the Lord,
and is with him for ever.
² Who can number the sand of the sea,
and the drops of rain, and the days of eternity?
³ Who can find out the height of heaven,
and the breadth of the earth, and the deep, and wisdom?
⁴ Wisdom hath been created before all things,
and the understanding of prudence from everlasting.
⁵ The word of God most high is the fountain of wisdom,
and her ways are everlasting commandments.

⁶ To whom hath the root of wisdom been revealed?
or who hath known her wise counsels?
⁷ Unto whom hath the knowledge of wisdom been made manifest?
and who hath understood her great experience?
⁸ There is one wise and greatly to be feared,
the Lord sitting upon his throne.
⁹ He created her, and saw her, and numbered her,
and poured her out upon all his works.
¹⁰ She is with all flesh according to his gift,
and he hath given her to them that love him.

¹¹ The fear of the Lord is honour, and glory,
and gladness, and a crown of rejoicing.
¹² The fear of the Lord maketh a merry heart,
and giveth joy and gladness, and a long life.
¹³ Whoso feareth the Lord, it shall go well with him at the last,
and he shall find favour in the day of his death.
¹⁴ To fear the lord is the beginning of wisdom:
and it was created with the faithful in the womb.
¹⁵ She hath built an everlasting foundation with men,
and she shall continue with their seed.
¹⁶ To fear the Lord is fulness of wisdom,
and filleth men with her fruits.
¹⁷ She filleth all their house with things desirable,
and the garners with her increase.
¹⁸ The fear of the Lord is a crown of wisdom,
making peace and perfect health to flourish,
both which are the gifts of God:
and it enlargeth their rejoicing that love him.

19 Wisdom raineth down skill and knowledge of understanding,
  and exalteth them to honour that hold her fast.
20 The root of wisdom is to fear the Lord,
  and the branches thereof are long life.
21 The fear of the Lord driveth away sins:
  and where it is present, it turneth away wrath.

22 A furious man cannot be justified,
  for the sway of his fury shall be his destruction.
23 A patient man will bear for a time,
  and afterward joy shall spring up unto him.
24 He will hide his words for a time,
  and the lips of many shall declare his wisdom.

25 The parables of knowledge are in the treasures of wisdom:
  but godliness is an abomination to a sinner.
26 If thou desire wisdom, keep the commandments,
  and the Lord shall give her unto thee.
27 For the fear of the Lord is wisdom and instruction:
  and faith and meekness are his delight.
28 Distrust not the fear of the Lord when thou art poor:
  and come not unto him with a double heart.
29 Be not a hypocrite in the sight of men,
  and take good heed what thou speakest.
30 Exalt not thyself, lest thou fall,
  and bring dishonour upon thy soul,
  and so God discover thy secrets,
  and cast thee down in the midst of the congregation,
  because thou camest not in truth to the fear of the Lord:
  but thy heart is full of deceit.

2 My son, if thou come to serve the Lord,
  prepare thy soul for temptation.
2 Set thy heart aright, and constantly endure,
  and make not haste in time of trouble.
3 Cleave unto him, and depart not away,
  that thou mayest be increased at thy last end.
4 Whatsoever is brought upon thee take cheerfully,
  and be patient when thou art changed to a low estate.
5 For gold is tried in the fire,
  and acceptable men in the furnace of adversity.
6 Believe in him, and he will help thee,
  order thy way aright, and trust in him.

7 Ye that fear the Lord, wait for his mercy,
  and go not aside, lest ye fall.
8 Ye that fear the Lord, believe him,
  and your reward shall not fail.

⁹ Ye that fear the Lord, hope for good,
and for everlasting joy and mercy.

¹⁰ Look at the generations of old, and see,
did ever any trust in the Lord, and was confounded?
or did any abide in his fear, and was forsaken?
or whom did he ever despise, that called upon him?
¹¹ For the Lord is full of compassion and mercy,
long-suffering, and very pitiful,
and forgiveth sins, and saveth in time of affliction.

¹² Woe be to fearful hearts, and faint hands,
and the sinner that goeth two ways.
¹³ Woe unto him that is faint-hearted, for he believeth not,
therefore shall he not be defended.
¹⁴ Woe unto you that have lost patience:
and what will ye do when the Lord shall visit you?

¹⁵ They that fear the Lord will not disobey his word,
and they that love him will keep his ways.
¹⁶ They that fear the Lord will seek that which is well-pleasing unto
him,
and they that love him shall be filled with the law.
¹⁷ They that fear the Lord will prepare their hearts,
and humble their souls in his sight,
¹⁸ saying, 'We will fall into the hands of the Lord, and not into the
hands of men:
for as his majesty is, so is his mercy'.

3 Hear me your father, O children,
and do thereafter, that ye may be safe.
² For the Lord hath given the father honour over the children,
and hath confirmed the authority of the mother over the sons.
³ Whoso honoureth his father maketh an atonement for his sins:
⁴ and he that honoureth his mother is as one that layeth up
treasure.
⁵ Whoso honoureth his father shall have joy of his own children,
and when he maketh his prayer, he shall be heard.
⁶ He that honoureth his father shall have a long life,
and he that is obedient unto the Lord shall be a comfort to his
mother.
⁷ He that feareth the Lord will honour his father,
and will do service unto his parents, as to his masters.
⁸ Honour thy father and mother both in word and deed,
that a blessing may come upon thee from them.
⁹ For the blessing of the father establisheth the houses of children,
but the curse of the mother rooteth out foundations.
¹⁰ Glory not in the dishonour of thy father,

for thy father's dishonour is no glory unto thee.

¹¹ For the glory of a man is from the honour of his father,
and a mother in dishonour is a reproach to the children.

¹² My son, help thy father in his age,
and grieve him not as long as he liveth.

¹³ And if his understanding fail, have patience with him,
and despise him not when thou art in thy full strength.

¹⁴ For the relieving of thy father shall not be forgotten:
and in stead of sins it shall be added to build thee up.

¹⁵ In the day of thy affliction it shall be remembered,
thy sins also shall melt away, as the ice in the fair warm weather.

¹⁶ He that forsaketh his father is as a blasphemer,
and he that angereth his mother is cursed of God.

¹⁷ My son, go on with thy business in meekness,
so shalt thou be beloved of him that is approved.

¹⁸ The greater thou art, the more humble thyself,
and thou shalt find favour before the Lord.

¹⁹ Many are in high place, and of renown:
but mysteries are revealed unto the meek.

²⁰ For the power of the Lord is great,
and he is honoured of the lowly.

²¹ Seek not out the things that are too hard for thee,
neither search the things that are above thy strength.

²² But what is commanded thee, think thereupon with reverence,
for it is not needful for thee to see with thy eyes the things that
are in secret.

²³ Be not curious in unnecessary matters:
for more things are shown unto thee than men understand.

²⁴ For many are deceived by their own vain opinion,
and an evil suspicion hath overthrown their judgement.

²⁵ Without eyes thou shalt want light:
profess not the knowledge therefore that thou hast not.

²⁶ A stubborn heart shall fare evil at the last,
and he that loveth danger shall perish therein.

²⁷ An obstinate heart shall be laden with sorrows,
and the wicked man shall heap sin upon sin.

²⁸ In the punishment of the proud there is no remedy:
for the plant of wickedness hath taken root in him.

²⁹ The heart of the prudent will understand a parable,
and an attentive ear is the desire of a wise man.

³⁰ Water will quench a flaming fire,
and alms maketh an atonement for sins.

³¹ And he that requiteth good turns is mindful of that which may
come hereafter:
and when he falleth, he shall find a stay.

4 My son, defraud not the poor of his living,
and make not the needy eyes to wait long.
[2] Make not a hungry soul sorrowful,
neither provoke a man in his distress.
[3] Add no more trouble to a heart that is vexed,
and defer not to give to him that is in need.
[4] Reject not the supplication of the afflicted,
neither turn away thy face from a poor man.
[5] Turn not away thy eye from the needy,
and give him no occasion to curse thee:
[6] for if he curse thee in the bitterness of his soul,
his prayer shall be heard of him that made him.
[7] Get thyself the love of the congregation,
and bow thy head to a great man.
[8] Let it not grieve thee to bow down thy ear to the poor,
and give him a friendly answer with meekness.
[9] Deliver him that suffereth wrong from the hand of the
        oppressor,
and be not faint-hearted when thou sittest in judgement.
[10] Be as a father unto the fatherless,
and in stead of a husband unto their mother:
so shalt thou be as the son of the most High,
and he shall love thee more than thy mother doth.

[11] Wisdom exalteth her children,
and layeth hold of them that seek her.
[12] He that loveth her loveth life,
and they that seek to her early shall be filled with joy.
[13] He that holdeth her fast shall inherit glory,
and wheresoever she entereth, the Lord will bless.
[14] They that serve her shall minister to the Holy One,
and them that love her the Lord doth love.
[15] Whoso giveth ear unto her shall judge the nations,
and he that attendeth unto her shall dwell securely.
[16] If a man commit himself unto her, he shall inherit her,
and his generation shall hold her in possession.
[17] For at the first she will walk with him by crooked ways,
and bring fear and dread upon him,
and torment him with her discipline,
until she may trust his soul, and try him by her laws.
[18] Then will she return the straight way unto him,
and comfort him, and show him her secrets.
[19] But if he go wrong, she will forsake him,
and give him over to his own ruin.

[20] Observe the opportunity, and beware of evil,
and be not ashamed when it concerneth thy soul.
[21] For there is a shame that bringeth sin,

and there is a shame which is glory and grace.

²² Accept no person against thy soul,
and let not the reverence of any man cause thee to fall.

²³ And refrain not to speak, when there is occasion to do good,
and hide not thy wisdom in her beauty.

²⁴ For by speech wisdom shall be known,
and learning by the word of the tongue.

²⁵ In no wise speak against the truth,
but be abashed of the error of thy ignorance.

²⁶ Be not ashamed to confess thy sins,
and force not the course of the river.

²⁷ Make not thyself an underling to a foolish man,
neither accept the person of the mighty.

²⁸ Strive for the truth unto death,
and the Lord shall fight for thee.

²⁹ Be not hasty in thy tongue,
and in thy deeds slack and remiss.

³⁰ Be not as a lion in thy house,
nor frantic among thy servants.

³¹ Let not thy hand be stretched out to receive,
and shut when thou shouldst repay.

5 Set not thy heart upon thy goods:
and say not, 'I have enough for my life'.

² Follow not thy own mind and thy strength,
to walk in the ways of thy heart:

³ and say not, 'Who shall control me for my works?'
for the Lord will surely revenge thy pride.

⁴ Say not, 'I have sinned, and what harm hath happened unto me?'
for the Lord is long-suffering, he will in no wise let thee go.

⁵ Concerning propitiation,
be not without fear to add sin unto sin:

⁶ and say not, 'His mercy is great,
he will be pacified for the multitude of my sins':
for mercy and wrath come from him,
and his indignation resteth upon sinners.

⁷ Make no tarrying to turn to the Lord,
and put not off from day to day:
for suddenly shall the wrath of the Lord come forth,
and in thy security thou shalt be destroyed,
and perish in the day of vengeance.

⁸ Set not thy heart upon goods unjustly gotten:
for they shall not profit thee in the day of calamity.

⁹ Winnow not with every wind, and go not into every way:
for so doth the sinner that hath a double tongue.

¹⁰ Be steadfast in thy understanding,
and let thy word be the same.

¹¹ Be swift to hear, and let thy life be sincere,
and with patience give answer.
¹² If thou hast understanding, answer thy neighbour,
if not, lay thy hand upon thy mouth.
¹³ Honour and shame is in talk,
and the tongue of man is his fall.
¹⁴ Be not called a whisperer, and lie not in wait with thy tongue:
for a foul shame is upon the thief,
and an evil condemnation upon the double tongue.
¹⁵ Be not ignorant of anything in a great matter or a small.

6 In stead of a friend become not an enemy;
for thereby thou shalt inherit an ill name, shame, and reproach:
even so shall a sinner that hath a double tongue.
² Extol not thyself in the counsel of thy own heart,
that thy soul be not torn in pieces as a bull straying alone.
³ Thou shalt eat up thy leaves, and lose thy fruit,
and leave thyself as a dry tree.
⁴ A wicked soul shall destroy him that hath it,
and shall make him to be laughed to scorn of his enemies.
⁵ Sweet language will multiply friends:
and a fair speaking tongue will increase kind greetings.
⁶ Be in peace with many:
nevertheless have but one counsellor of a thousand.

⁷ If thou wouldst get a friend, prove him first,
and be not hasty to credit him.
⁸ For some man is a friend for his own occasion,
and will not abide in the day of thy trouble.
⁹ And there is a friend, who being turned to enmity and strife,
will discover thy reproach.
¹⁰ Again, some friend is a companion at the table,
and will not continue in the day of thy affliction.
¹¹ But in thy prosperity he will be as thyself,
and will be bold over thy servants.
¹² If thou be brought low, he will be against thee,
and will hide himself from thy face.

¹³ Separate thyself from thy enemies,
and take heed of thy friends.
¹⁴ A faithful friend is a strong defence:
and he that hath found such a one hath found a treasure.
¹⁵ Nothing doth countervail a faithful friend,
and his excellence is invaluable.
¹⁶ A faithful friend is the medicine of life,
and they that fear the Lord shall find him.
¹⁷ Whoso feareth the Lord shall direct his friendship aright,
for as he is, so shall his neighbour be also.

¹⁸ My son, gather instruction from thy youth up:
  so shalt thou find wisdom till thy old age.
¹⁹ Come unto her as one that plougheth and soweth,
  and wait for her good fruits,
  for thou shalt not toil much in labouring about her,
  but thou shalt eat of her fruits right soon.
²⁰ She is very unpleasant to the unlearned:
  he that is without understanding will not remain with her.
²¹ She will lie upon him as a mighty stone of trial,
  and he will cast her from him ere it be long.
²² For wisdom is according to her name,
  and she is not manifest unto many.

²³ Give ear, my son, receive my advice,
  and refuse not my counsel,
²⁴ and put thy feet into her fetters, and thy neck into her chain.
²⁵ Bow down thy shoulder, and bear her,
  and be not grieved with her bonds.
²⁶ Come unto her with thy whole heart,
  and keep her ways with all thy power.
²⁷ Search, and seek, and she shall be made known unto thee:
  and when thou hast got hold of her, let her not go.
²⁸ For at the last thou shalt find her rest,
  and that shall be turned to thy joy.
²⁹ Then shall her fetters be a strong defence for thee,
  and her chains a robe of glory.
³⁰ For there is a golden ornament upon her,
  and her bands are purple lace.
³¹ Thou shalt put her on as a robe of honour,
  and shalt put her about thee as a crown of joy.

³² My son, if thou wilt, thou shalt be taught:
  and if thou wilt apply thy mind, thou shalt be prudent.
³³ If thou love to hear, thou shalt receive understanding:
  and if thou bow thy ear, thou shalt be wise.
³⁴ Stand in the multitude of the elders,
  and cleave unto him that is wise.
³⁵ Be willing to hear every godly discourse,
  and let not the parables of understanding escape thee.
³⁶ And if thou seest a man of understanding, get thee betimes unto
    him,
  and let thy foot wear the steps of his door.
³⁷ Let thy mind be upon the ordinances of the Lord,
  and meditate continually in his commandments:
  he shall establish thy heart,
  and give thee wisdom at thy own desire.

7

Do no evil,
so shall no harm come unto thee.
[2] Depart from the unjust,
and iniquity shall turn away from thee.
[3] My son, sow not upon the furrows of unrighteousness,
and thou shalt not reap them sevenfold.

[4] Seek not of the Lord pre-eminence,
neither of the king the seat of honour.
[5] Justify not thyself before the Lord,
and boast not of thy wisdom before the king.
[6] Seek not to be judge, being not able to take away iniquity,
lest at any time thou fear the person of the mighty,
and lay a stumbling-block in the way of thy uprightness.

[7] Offend not against the multitude of a city,
and then thou shalt not cast thyself down among the people.

[8] Bind not one sin upon another,
for in one thou shalt not be unpunished.

[9] Say not, 'God will look upon the multitude of my oblations,
and when I offer to the most high God, he will accept it'.

[10] Be not faint-hearted when thou makest thy prayer,
and neglect not to give alms.

[11] Laugh no man to scorn in the bitterness of his soul:
for there is one which humbleth and exalteth.

[12] Devise not a lie against thy brother:
neither do the like to thy friend.
[13] Use not to make any manner of lie:
for the custom thereof is not good.

[14] Use not many words in a multitude of elders,
and make not much babbling when thou prayest.

[15] Hate not laborious work, neither husbandry,
which the most High hath ordained.

[16] Number not thyself among the multitude of sinners,
but remember that wrath will not tarry long.
[17] Humble thy soul greatly:
for the vengeance of the ungodly is fire and worms.

[18] Change not a friend for any good by no means:
neither a faithful brother for the gold of Ophir.

¹⁹ Forego not a wise and good woman:
  for her grace is above gold.
²⁰ Whereas thy servant worketh truly, entreat him not evil,
  nor the hireling that bestoweth himself wholly for thee.
²¹ Let thy soul love a good servant,
  and defraud him not of liberty.

²² Hast thou cattle? have an eye to them,
  and if they be for thy profit, keep them with thee.
²³ Hast thou children? instruct them,
  and bow down their neck from their youth.
²⁴ Hast thou daughters? have care of their body,
  and show not thyself cheerful toward them.
²⁵ Marry thy daughter, and so shalt thou have performed a weighty
    matter:
  but give her to a man of understanding.
²⁶ Hast thou a wife after thy mind? forsake her not:
  but give not thyself over to a light woman.
²⁷ Honour thy father with thy whole heart,
  and forget not the sorrows of thy mother.
²⁸ Remember that thou wast begotten of them,
  and how canst thou recompense them the things that they have
    done for thee?

²⁹ Fear the Lord with all thy soul,
  and reverence his priests.
³⁰ Love him that made thee with all thy strength,
  and forsake not his ministers.
³¹ Fear the Lord, and honour the priest:
  and give him his portion, as it is commanded thee,
  the firstfruits, and the trespass offering,
  and the gift of the shoulders, and the sacrifice of sanctification,
  and the first-fruits of the holy things.

³² And stretch thy hand unto the poor,
  that thy blessing may be perfected.
³³ A gift hath grace in the sight of every man living,
  and for the dead detain it not.
³⁴ Fail not to be with them that weep,
  and mourn with them that mourn.
³⁵ Be not slow to visit the sick:
  for that shall make thee to be beloved.
³⁶ Whatsoever thou takest in hand, remember the end,
  and thou shalt never do amiss.

8   Strive not with a mighty man,
    lest thou fall into his hands.
  ² Be not at variance with a rich man,

lest he overweigh thee:
for gold hath destroyed many,
and perverted the hearts of kings.
[3] Strive not with a man that is full of tongue,
and heap not wood upon his fire.
[4] Jest not with a rude man,
lest thy ancestors be disgraced.
[5] Reproach not a man that turneth from sin,
but remember that we are all worthy of punishment.
[6] Dishonour not a man in his old age:
for even some of us wax old.
[7] Rejoice not over thy greatest enemy being dead,
but remember that we die all.

[8] Despise not the discourse of the wise,
but acquaint thyself with their proverbs:
for of them thou shalt learn instruction,
and how to serve great men with ease.
[9] Miss not the discourse of the elders:
for they also learned of their fathers,
and of them thou shalt learn understanding,
and to give answer as need requireth.

[10] Kindle not the coals of a sinner,
lest thou be burnt with the flame of his fire.
[11] Rise not up in anger at the presence of an injurious person,
lest he lie in wait to entrap thee in thy words.

[12] Lend not unto him that is mightier than thyself;
for if thou lendest him, count it but lost.
[13] Be not surety above thy power:
for if thou be surety, take care to pay it.

[14] Go not to law with a judge,
for they will judge for him according to his honour.

[15] Travel not by the way with a bold fellow,
lest he become grievous unto thee:
for he will do according to his own will,
and thou shalt perish with him through his folly.
[16] Strive not with an angry man,
and go not with him into a solitary place:
for blood is as nothing in his sight,
and where there is no help, he will overthrow thee.
[17] Consult not with a fool,
for he cannot keep counsel.
[18] Do no secret thing before a stranger,
for thou knowest not what he will bring forth.

¹⁹ Open not thy heart to every man,
    lest he requite thee with a shrewd turn.

9 Be not jealous over the wife of thy bosom,
    and teach her not an evil lesson against thyself.
² Give not thy soul unto a woman
    to set her foot upon thy substance.
³ Meet not with a harlot,
    lest thou fall into her snares.
⁴ Use not much the company of a woman that is a singer,
    lest thou be taken with her attempts.
⁵ Gaze not on a maid,
    that thou fall not by those things that are precious in her.
⁶ Give not thy soul unto harlots,
    that thou lose not thy inheritance.
⁷ Look not round about thee in the streets of the city,
    neither wander thou in the solitary places thereof.
⁸ Turn away thy eye from a beautiful woman,
    and look not upon another's beauty:
    for many have been deceived by the beauty of a woman,
    for herewith love is kindled as a fire.
⁹ Sit not at all with another man's wife,
    nor sit down with her in thy arms,
    and spend not thy money with her at the wine,
    lest thy heart incline unto her,
    and so through thy desire thou fall into destruction.

¹⁰ Forsake not an old friend,
    for the new is not comparable to him:
    a new friend is as new wine:
    when it is old, thou shalt drink it with pleasure.

¹¹ Envy not the glory of a sinner:
    for thou knowest not what shall be his end.
¹² Delight not in the thing that the ungodly have pleasure in,
    but remember they shall not go unpunished unto their grave.

¹³ Keep thee far from the man that hath power to kill,
    so shalt thou not doubt the fear of death:
    and if thou come unto him, make no fault,
    lest he take away thy life presently:
    remember that thou goest in the midst of snares,
    and that thou walkest upon the battlements of the city.

¹⁴ As near as thou canst, guess at thy neighbour,
    and consult with the wise.
¹⁵ Let thy talk be with the wise,
    and all thy communication in the law of the most High.

¹⁶ And let just men eat and drink with thee,
and let thy glorying be in the fear of the Lord.

¹⁷ For the hand of the artificer the work shall be commended:
and the wise ruler of the people for his speech.
¹⁸ A man of an ill tongue is dangerous in his city,
and he that is rash in his talk shall be hated.

10 A wise judge will instruct his people,
and the government of a prudent man is well ordered.
² As the judge of the people is himself,
so are his officers,
and what manner of man the ruler of the city is,
such are all they that dwell therein.
³ An unwise king destroyeth his people,
but through the prudence of them which are in authority
the city shall be inhabited.
⁴ The power of the earth is in the hand of the Lord,
and in due time he will set over it one that is profitable.
⁵ In the hand of God is the prosperity of man:
and upon the person of the scribe shall he lay his honour.

⁶ Bear not hatred to thy neighbour for every wrong,
and do nothing at all by injurious practices.

⁷ Pride is hateful before God and man:
and by both doth one commit iniquity.

⁸ Because of unrighteous dealings, injuries, and riches got by
deceit,
the kingdom is translated from one people to another.

⁹ Why is earth and ashes proud?
There is not a more wicked thing than a covetous man:
for such a one setteth his own soul to sale,
because while he liveth he casteth away his bowels.
¹⁰ The physician cutteth off a long disease,
and he that is today a king tomorrow shall die.
¹¹ For when a man is dead,
he shall inherit creeping things, beasts, and worms.

¹² The beginning of pride is when one departeth from God,
and his heart is turned away from his Maker.
¹³ For pride is the beginning of sin,
and he that hath it shall pour out abomination:
and therefore the Lord brought upon them strange calamities,
and overthrew them utterly.
¹⁴ The Lord hath cast down the thrones of proud princes,

and set up the meek in their stead.

¹⁵ The Lord hath plucked up the roots of the proud nations,
and planted the lowly in their place.

¹⁶ The Lord overthrew countries of the heathen,
and destroyed them to the foundations of the earth.

¹⁷ He took some of them away, and destroyed them,
and hath made their memorial to cease from the earth.

¹⁸ Pride was not made for men,
nor furious anger for them that are born of a woman.

¹⁹ They that fear the Lord are a sure seed,
and they that love him an honourable plant:
they that regard not the law are a dishonourable seed,
they that transgress the commandments are a deceivable seed.

²⁰ Among brethren he that is chief is honourable,
so are they that fear the Lord in his eyes.

²¹ The fear of the Lord goeth before the obtaining of authority:
but roughness and pride is the losing thereof.

²² Whether he be rich, noble, or poor,
their glory is the fear of the Lord.

²³ It is not meet to despise the poor man that hath understanding,
neither is it convenient to magnify a sinful man.

²⁴ Great men, and judges, and potentates shall be honoured,
yet is there none of them greater than he that feareth the Lord.

²⁵ Unto the servant that is wise shall they that are free do service:
and he that hath knowledge will not grudge when he is
reformed.

²⁶ Be not overwise in doing thy business,
and boast not thyself in the time of thy distress.

²⁷ Better is he that laboureth, and aboundeth in all things,
than he that boasteth himself, and wanteth bread.

²⁸ My son, glorify thy soul in meekness,
and give it honour according to the dignity thereof.

²⁹ Who will justify him that sinneth against his own soul?
and who will honour him that dishonoureth his own life?

³⁰ The poor man is honoured for his skill,
and the rich man is honoured for his riches.

³¹ He that is honoured in poverty,
how much more in riches?
and he that is dishonourable in riches,
how much more in poverty?

11 Wisdom lifteth up the head of him that is of low degree,
and maketh him to sit among great men.

² Commend not a man for his beauty,
neither abhor a man for his outward appearance.

³ The bee is little among such as fly,
  but her fruit is the chief of sweet things.
⁴ Boast not of thy clothing and raiment,
  and exalt not thyself in the day of honour:
  for the works of the Lord are wonderful,
  and his works among men are hidden.
⁵ Many kings have sat down upon the ground,
  and one that was never thought of hath worn the crown.
⁶ Many mighty men have been greatly disgraced:
  and the honourable delivered into other men's hands.

⁷ Blame not before thou hast examined the truth:
  understand first, and then rebuke.
⁸ Answer not before thou hast heard the cause:
  neither interrupt men in the midst of their talk.
⁹ Strive not in a matter that concerneth thee not:
  and sit not in judgement with sinners.
¹⁰ My son, meddle not with many matters:
  for if thou meddle much, thou shalt not be innocent:
  and if thou follow after, thou shalt not obtain,
  neither shalt thou escape by flying.

¹¹ There is one that laboureth,
  and taketh pains, and maketh haste,
  and is so much the more behind.
¹² Again, there is another that is slow, and hath need of help,
  wanting ability, and full of poverty,
  yet the eye of the Lord looked upon him for good,
  and set him up from his low estate,
¹³ and lifted up his head from misery,
  so that many that saw it marvelled at him.

¹⁴ Prosperity and adversity, life and death,
  poverty and riches, come of the Lord.
¹⁵ Wisdom, knowledge, and understanding of the law, are of the
    Lord:
  love, and the way of good works, are from him.
¹⁶ Error and darkness had their beginning together with sinners:
  and evil shall wax old with them that glory therein.
¹⁷ The gift of the Lord remaineth with the godly,
  and his favour bringeth prosperity for ever.
¹⁸ There is that waxeth rich by his wariness and pinching,
  and this is the portion of his reward:
¹⁹ whereas he saith, 'I have found rest,
  and now will eat continually of my goods',
  and yet he knoweth not what time shall come upon him,
  and that he must leave those things to others, and die.

²⁰ Be steadfast in thy covenant, and be conversant therein,
   and wax old in thy work.
²¹ Marvel not at the works of sinners,
   but trust in the Lord, and abide in thy labour:
   for it is an easy thing in the sight of the Lord
   on the sudden to make a poor man rich.
²² The blessing of the Lord is in the reward of the godly,
   and suddenly he maketh his blessing to flourish.
²³ Say not, 'What profit is there of my service?
   and what good things shall I have hereafter?'
²⁴ Again, say not, 'I have enough, and possess many things,
   and what evil can come to me hereafter?'
²⁵ In the day of prosperity there is a forgetfulness of affliction:
   and in the day of affliction there is no remembrance of prosperity.
²⁶ For it is an easy thing unto the Lord in the day of death
   to reward a man according to his ways.
²⁷ The affliction of an hour maketh a man forget pleasure:
   and in his end his deeds shall be discovered.
²⁸ Judge none blessed before his death:
   for a man shall be known in his children.

²⁹ Bring not every man into thy house:
   for the deceitful man hath many trains.
³⁰ Like as a partridge taken and kept in a cage, so is the heart of the
      proud;
   and like as a spy, watcheth he for thy fall:
³¹ for he lieth in wait, and turneth good into evil,
   and in things worthy praise will lay blame upon thee.
³² Of a spark of fire a heap of coals is kindled:
   and a sinful man layeth wait for blood.
³³ Take heed of a mischievous man, for he worketh wickedness,
   lest he bring upon thee a perpetual blot.
³⁴ Receive a stranger into thy house,
   and he will disturb thee, and turn thee out of thy own.

12 When thou wilt do good, know to whom thou doest it,
   so shalt thou be thanked for thy benefits.
² Do good to the godly man, and thou shalt find a recompence,
   and if not from him, yet from the most High.
³ There can no good come to him that is always occupied in evil:
   nor to him that giveth no alms.
⁴ Give to the godly man, and help not a sinner.
⁵ Do well unto him that is lowly, but give not to the ungodly:
   hold back thy bread, and give it not unto him,
   lest he overmaster thee thereby:
   for else thou shalt receive twice as much evil
   for all the good thou shalt have done unto him.
⁶ For the most High hateth sinners,

and will repay vengeance unto the ungodly,
and keepeth them against the mighty day of their punishment.
⁷ Give unto the good, and help not the sinner.

⁸ A friend cannot be known in prosperity,
and an enemy cannot be hidden in adversity.
⁹ In the prosperity of a man enemies will be grieved:
but in his adversity even a friend will depart.
¹⁰ Never trust thy enemy:
for like as iron rusteth, so is his wickedness.
¹¹ Though he humble himself, and go crouching,
yet take good heed and beware of him,
and thou shalt be unto him as if thou hadst wiped a looking-
glass,
and thou shalt know that his rust hath not been altogether
wiped away.
¹² Set him not by thee,
lest, when he hath overthrown thee, he stand up in thy place,
neither let him sit at thy right hand,
lest he seek to take thy seat,
and thou at the last remember my words,
and be pricked therewith.
¹³ Who will pity a charmer that is bitten with a serpent,
or any such as come nigh wild beasts?
¹⁴ So one that goeth to a sinner,
and is defiled with him in his sins, who will pity?
¹⁵ For a while he will abide with thee,
but if thou begin to fall, he will not tarry.
¹⁶ An enemy speaketh sweetly with his lips,
but in his heart he imagineth how to throw thee into a pit:
he will weep with his eyes,
but if he find opportunity, he will not be satisfied with blood.
¹⁷ If adversity come upon thee,
thou shalt find him there first,
and though he pretend to help thee,
yet shall he undermine thee.
¹⁸ He will shake his head, and clap his hands,
and whisper much, and change his countenance.

13 He that toucheth pitch shall be defiled therewith,
and he that hath fellowship with a proud man shall be like
unto him.
² Burden not thyself above thy power while thou livest,
and have no fellowship with one that is mightier and richer than
thyself.
For how agree the kettle and the earthen pot together?
for if the one be smitten against the other, it shall be broken.

³ The rich man hath done wrong,
   and yet he threateneth withal:
   the poor is wronged,
   and he must entreat also.
⁴ If thou be for his profit, he will use thee:
   but if thou have nothing, he will forsake thee.
⁵ If thou have anything, he will live with thee,
   yea, he will make thee bare, and will not be sorry for it.
⁶ If he have need of thee, he will deceive thee,
   and smile upon thee, and put thee in hope,
   he will speak thee fair, and say, 'What wantest thou?'
⁷ And he will shame thee by his meats,
   until he have drawn thee dry twice or thrice,
   and at the last he will laugh thee to scorn:
   afterward when he seeth thee, he will forsake thee,
   and shake his head at thee.
⁸ Beware that thou be not deceived,
   and brought down in thy jollity.
⁹ If thou be invited of a mighty man,
   withdraw thyself, and so much the more will he invite thee.
¹⁰ Press thou not upon him, lest thou be put back,
   stand not far off, lest thou be forgotten.
¹¹ Affect not to be made equal unto him in talk,
   and believe not his many words:
   for with much communication will he tempt thee,
   and smiling upon thee will get out thy secrets:
¹² but cruelly he will lay up thy words,
   and will not spare to do thee hurt,
   and to put thee in prison.
¹³ Observe, and take good heed,
   for thou walkest in peril of thy overthrowing:
   when thou hearest these things, awake in thy sleep.

¹⁴ Love the Lord all thy life,
   and call upon him for thy salvation.

¹⁵ Every beast loveth his like,
   and every man loveth his neighbour.
¹⁶ All flesh consorteth according to kind,
   and a man will cleave to his like.
¹⁷ What fellowship hath the wolf with the lamb?
   so the sinner with the godly.
¹⁸ What agreement is there between the hyena and a dog?
   and what peace between the rich and the poor?
¹⁹ As the wild ass is the lions' prey in the wilderness:
   so the rich eat up the poor.
²⁰ As the proud hate humility:
   so doth the rich abhor the poor.

[21] A rich man beginning to fall is held up of his friends:
but a poor man being down is thrust also away by his friends.
[22] When a rich man is fallen, he hath many helpers:
he speaketh things not to be spoken, and yet men justify him:
the poor man slipped, and yet they rebuked him too:
he spoke wisely, and could have no place.
[23] When a rich man speaketh, every man holdeth his tongue,
and look, what he saith, they extol it to the clouds:
but if the poor man speak, they say, 'What fellow is this?'
and if he stumble, they will help to overthrow him.

[24] Riches are good unto him that hath no sin,
and poverty is evil in the mouth of the ungodly.
[25] The heart of a man changeth his countenance,
whether it be for good or evil:
and a merry heart maketh a cheerful countenance.
[26] A cheerful countenance is a token of a heart that is in prosperity,
and the finding out of parables is a wearisome labour of the
mind.

14 Blessed is the man that hath not slipped with his mouth,
and is not pricked with the multitude of sins.
[2] Blessed is he whose conscience hath not condemned him,
and who is not fallen from his hope in the Lord.

[3] Riches are not comely for a niggard:
and what should an envious man do with money?
[4] He that gathereth by defrauding his own soul
gathereth for others, that shall spend his goods riotously.
[5] He that is evil to himself, to whom will he be good?
he shall not take pleasure in his goods.
[6] There is none worse than he that envieth himself;
and this is a recompence of his wickedness.
[7] And if he doeth good, he doeth it unwillingly,
and at the last he will declare his wickedness.
[8] The envious man hath a wicked eye,
he turneth away his face, and despiseth men.
[9] A covetous man's eye is not satisfied with his portion,
and the iniquity of the wicked drieth up his soul.
[10] A wicked eye envieth his bread,
and he is a niggard at his table.

[11] My son, according to thy ability do good to thyself,
and give the Lord his due offering.
[12] Remember that death will not be long in coming,
and that the covenant of the grave is not shown unto thee.
[13] Do good unto thy friend before thou die,
and according to thy ability stretch out thy hand and give to him.
[14] Defraud not thyself of the good day,

and let not the part of a good desire overpass thee.

¹⁵ Shalt thou not leave thy travails unto another?
and thy labours to be divided by lot?

¹⁶ Give, and take, and sanctify thy soul,
for there is no seeking of dainties in the grave.

¹⁷ All flesh waxeth old as a garment:
for the covenant from the beginning is, thou shalt die the
death.

¹⁸ As of the green leaves on a thick tree,
some fall, and some grow;
so is the generation of flesh and blood,
one cometh to an end, and another is born.

¹⁹ Every work rotteth and consumeth away,
and the worker thereof shall go withal.

²⁰ Blessed is the man that doth meditate good things in wisdom,
and that reasoneth of holy things by his understanding.

²¹ He that considereth her ways in his heart
shall also have understanding in her secrets.

²² Go after her as one that traceth,
and lie in wait in her ways.

²³ He that prieth in at her windows
shall also hearken at her doors.

²⁴ He that doth lodge near her house
shall also fasten a pin in her walls.

²⁵ He shall pitch his tent nigh unto her,
and shall lodge in a lodging where good things are.

²⁶ He shall set his children under her shelter,
and shall lodge under her branches.

²⁷ By her he shall be covered from heat,
and in her glory shall he dwell.

15 He that feareth the Lord will do good,
and he that hath the knowledge of the law shall obtain her.

² And as a mother shall she meet him,
and receive him as a wife married of a virgin.

³ With the bread of understanding shall she feed him,
and give him the water of wisdom to drink.

⁴ He shall be stayed upon her, and shall not be moved,
and shall rely upon her, and shall not be confounded.

⁵ She shall exalt him above his neighbours,
and in the midst of the congregation shall she open his mouth.

⁶ He shall find joy and a crown of gladness,
and she shall cause him to inherit an everlasting name.

⁷ But foolish men shall not attain unto her,
and sinners shall not see her.

⁸ For she is far from pride,

and men that are liars cannot remember her.

⁹ Praise is not seemly in the mouth of a sinner,
for it was not sent him of the Lord:

¹⁰ for praise shall be uttered in wisdom,
and the Lord will prosper it.

¹¹ Say not thou, 'It is through the Lord that I fell away',
for thou oughtest not to do the things that he hateth.

¹² Say not thou, 'He hath caused me to err',
for he hath no need of the sinful man.

¹³ The Lord hateth all abomination,
and they that fear God love it not.

¹⁴ He himself made man from the beginning,
and left him in the hand of his counsel,

¹⁵ if thou wilt, to keep the commandments,
and to perform acceptable faithfulness.

¹⁶ He hath set fire and water before thee:
stretch forth thy hand unto whether thou wilt.

¹⁷ Before man is life and death,
and whether him liketh shall be given him.

¹⁸ For the wisdom of the Lord is great,
and he is mighty in power, and beholdeth all things,

¹⁹ and his eyes are upon them that fear him,
and he knoweth every work of man.

²⁰ He hath commanded no man to do wickedly,
neither hath he given any man licence to sin.

16 Desire not a multitude of unprofitable children,
neither delight in ungodly sons.

² Though they multiply, rejoice not in them,
except the fear of the Lord be with them.

³ Trust not thou in their life, neither respect their multitude:
for one that is just is better than a thousand,
and better it is to die without children, than to have them that
are ungodly.

⁴ For by one that hath understanding shall the city be replenished:
but the kindred of the wicked shall speedily become desolate.

⁵ Many such things have I seen with my eyes,
and my ear hath heard greater things than these.

⁶ In the congregation of the ungodly shall a fire be kindled,
and in a rebellious nation wrath is set on fire.

⁷ He was not pacified towards the old giants,
who fell away in the strength of their foolishness.

⁸ Neither spared he the place where Lot sojourned,
but abhorred them for their pride.

⁹ He pitied not the people of perdition,
who were taken away in their sins:

¹⁰ nor the six hundred thousand footmen,
   who were gathered together in the hardness of their hearts.
¹¹ And if there be one stiff-necked among the people,
   it is marvel if he escape unpunished:
   for mercy and wrath are with him,
   he is mighty to forgive, and to pour out displeasure.
¹² As his mercy is great, so is his correction also:
   he judgeth a man according to his works.
¹³ The sinner shall not escape with his spoils,
   and the patience of the godly shall not be frustrate.
¹⁴ Make way for every work of mercy:
   for every man shall find according to his works.
¹⁵ The Lord hardened Pharaoh, that he should not know him,
   that his powerful works might be known to the world.
¹⁶ His mercy is manifest to every creature,
   and he hath separated his light from the darkness with an
     adamant.

¹⁷ Say not thou, 'I will hide myself from the Lord:
   shall any remember me from above?
   I shall not be remembered among so many people:
   for what is my soul among such an infinite number of
     creatures?'
¹⁸ Behold, the heaven, and the heaven of heavens,
   the deep, and the earth, and all that therein is,
   shall be moved when he shall visit.
¹⁹ The mountains also and foundations of the earth shall be shaken
     with trembling,
   when the Lord looketh upon them.
²⁰ No heart can think upon these things worthily:
   and who is able to conceive his ways?
²¹ It is a tempest which no man can see:
   for the most part of his works are hid.
²² Who can declare the works of his justice?
   or who can endure them?
   for his covenant is afar off,
   and the trial of all things is in the end.
²³ He that wanteth understanding will think upon vain things:
   and a foolish man erring imagineth follies.

²⁴ My son, hearken unto me, and learn knowledge,
   and mark my words with thy heart.
²⁵ I will show forth doctrine in weight,
   and declare his knowledge exactly.
²⁶ The works of the Lord are done in judgement from the
     beginning:
   and from the time he made them he disposed the parts thereof.
²⁷ He garnished his works for ever,

and in his hand are the chief of them unto all generations:
they neither labour, nor are weary,
nor cease from their works.
²⁸ None of them hindereth another,
and they shall never disobey his word.

²⁹ After this the Lord looked upon the earth,
and filled it with his blessings.
³⁰ With all manner of living things hath he covered the face
thereof,
and they shall return into it again.

17 The Lord created man of the earth,
and turned him into it again.
² He gave them few days, and a short time,
and power also over the things therein.
³ He endued them with strength by themselves,
and made them according to his image,
⁴ and put the fear of man upon all flesh,
and gave him dominion over beasts and fowls.
⁵ They received the use of the five operations of the Lord,
and in the sixth place he imparted them understanding,
and in the seventh, speech, an interpreter of the cogitations
thereof.
⁶ Counsel, and a tongue, and eyes, ears, and a heart,
gave he them to understand.
⁷ Withal he filled them with the knowledge of understanding,
and showed them good and evil.
⁸ He set his eye upon their hearts,
that he might show them the greatness of his works.
⁹ He gave them to glory in his marvellous acts for ever,
that they might declare his works with understanding.
¹⁰ And the elect shall praise his holy name.
¹¹ Besides this he gave them knowledge,
and the law of life for a heritage.
¹² He made an everlasting covenant with them,
and showed them his judgements.
¹³ Their eyes saw the majesty of his glory,
and their ears heard his glorious voice.
¹⁴ And he said unto them, 'Beware of all unrighteousness',
and he gave every man commandment concerning his
neighbour.

¹⁵ Their ways are ever before him,
and shall not be hid from his eyes.
¹⁶ Every man from his youth is given to evil,
neither could they make to themselves fleshy hearts for stony.
¹⁷ For in the division of the nations of the whole earth
he set a ruler over every people,

but Israel is the Lord's portion:

¹⁸ whom, being his firstborn, he nourisheth with discipline,
and giving him the light of his love doth not forsake him.

¹⁹ Therefore all their works are as the sun before him,
and his eyes are continually upon their ways.

²⁰ None of their unrighteous deeds are hid from him,
but all their sins are before the Lord:

²¹ but the Lord being gracious, and knowing his workmanship,
neither left nor forsook them, but spared them.

²² The alms of a man is as a signet with him,
and he will keep the good deeds of man as the apple of the eye,
and give repentance to his sons and daughters.

²³ Afterward he will rise up and reward them,
and render their recompence upon their heads.

²⁴ But unto them that repent, he granted them return,
and comforted those that fail in patience.

²⁵ Return unto the Lord, and forsake thy sins,
make thy prayer before his face, and offend less.

²⁶ Turn again to the most High,
and turn away from iniquity:
for he will lead thee out of darkness into the light of health,
and hate thou abomination vehemently.

²⁷ Who shall praise the most High in the grave,
in stead of them which live and give thanks?

²⁸ Thanksgiving perisheth from the dead, as from one that is not:
the living and sound in heart shall praise the Lord.

²⁹ How great is the loving-kindness of the Lord our God,
and his compassion unto such as turn unto him in holiness!

³⁰ For all things cannot be in men,
because the son of man is not immortal.

³¹ What is brighter than the sun? yet the light thereof faileth:
and flesh and blood will imagine evil.

³² He vieweth the power of the height of heaven,
and all men are but earth and ashes.

18 He that liveth for ever created all things in general.
² The Lord only is righteous,
and there is no other but he,

³ who governeth the world with the palm of his hand,
and all things obey his will:
for he is the King of all,
by his power dividing holy things among them from profane.

⁴ To whom hath he given power to declare his works?
and who shall find out his noble acts?

⁵ Who shall number the strength of his majesty?
and who shall also tell out his mercies?

⁶ As for the wondrous works of the Lord,

there may nothing be taken from them,
neither may anything be put unto them,
neither can the ground of them be found out.
⁷ When a man hath done, then he beginneth,
and when he leaveth off, then he shall be doubtful.

⁸ What is man, and whereto serveth he?
What is his good, and what is his evil?
⁹ The number of a man's days at the most are a hundred years.
¹⁰ As a drop of water unto the sea,
and a gravel stone in comparison of the sand,
so are a thousand years to the days of eternity.
¹¹ Therefore is God patient with them,
and poureth forth his mercy upon them.
¹² He saw and perceived their end to be evil,
therefore he multiplied his compassion.
¹³ The mercy of man is toward his neighbour,
but the mercy of the Lord is upon all flesh:
he reproveth, and nurtureth, and teacheth,
and bringeth again, as a shepherd his flock.
¹⁴ He hath mercy on them that receive discipline,
and that diligently seek after his judgements.

¹⁵ My son, blemish not thy good deeds,
neither use uncomfortable words when thou givest anything.
¹⁶ Shall not the dew assuage the heat?
so is a word better than a gift.
¹⁷ Lo, is not a word better than a gift?
but both are with a gracious man.
¹⁸ A fool will upbraid churlishly,
and a gift of the envious consumeth the eyes.

¹⁹ Learn before thou speak,
and use physic or ever thou be sick.
²⁰ Before judgement examine thyself,
and in the day of visitation thou shalt find mercy.
²¹ Humble thyself before thou be sick,
and in the time of sins show repentance.
²² Let nothing hinder thee to pay thy vow in due time,
and defer not until death to be justified.
²³ Before thou prayest, prepare thyself,
and be not as one that tempteth the Lord.
²⁴ Think upon the wrath that shall be at the end,
and the time of vengeance when he shall turn away his face.
²⁵ When thou hast enough, remember the time of hunger:
and when thou art rich, think upon poverty and need.
²⁶ From the morning until the evening the time is changed,
and all things are soon done before the Lord.

²⁷ A wise man will fear in everything,
and in the day of sinning he will beware of offence:
but a fool will not observe time.
²⁸ Every man of understanding knoweth wisdom,
and will give praise unto him that found her.
²⁹ They that were of understanding in sayings became also wise
themselves,
and poured forth exquisite parables.
³⁰ Go not after thy lusts,
but refrain thyself from thy appetites.
³¹ If thou givest thy soul the desires that please her,
she will make thee a laughing-stock to thy enemies that malign
thee.
³² Take not pleasure in much good cheer,
neither be tied to the expense thereof.
³³ Be not made a beggar by banqueting upon borrowing,
when thou hast nothing in thy purse,
for thou shalt lie in wait for thy own life, and be talked on.

19 A labouring man that is given to drunkenness shall not be rich,
and he that contemneth small things shall fall by little and little.
² Wine and women will make men of understanding to fall away:
and he that cleaveth to harlots will become impudent.
³ Moths and worms shall have him to heritage,
and a bold man shall be taken away.
⁴ He that is hasty to give credit is light-minded,
and he that sinneth shall offend against his own soul.
⁵ Whoso taketh pleasure in wickedness shall be condemned,
but he that resisteth pleasures crowneth his life.
⁶ He that can rule his tongue shall live without strife,
and he that hateth babbling shall have less evil.
⁷ Rehearse not unto another that which is told unto thee,
and thou shalt fare never the worse.
⁸ Whether it be to friend or foe, talk not of other men's lives,
and if thou canst without offence, reveal them not.
⁹ For he heard and observed thee,
and when time cometh he will hate thee.
¹⁰ If thou hast heard a word, let it die with thee,
and be bold, it will not burst thee.
¹¹ A fool travaileth with a word,
as a woman in labour of a child.
¹² As an arrow that sticketh in a man's thigh,
so is a word within a fool's belly.

¹³ Admonish a friend, it may be he hath not done it,
and if he have done it, that he do it no more.
¹⁴ Admonish thy friend, it may be he hath not said it,

and if he have, that he speak it not again.

¹⁵ Admonish a friend: for many times it is a slander,
  and believe not every tale.

¹⁶ There is one that slippeth in his speech, but not from his heart,
  and who is he that hath not offended with his tongue?

¹⁷ Admonish thy neighbour before thou threaten him,
  and not being angry, give place to the law of the most High.

¹⁸ The fear of the Lord is the first step to be accepted of him,
  and wisdom obtaineth his love.

¹⁹ The knowledge of the commandments of the Lord is the doctrine
    of life:
  and they that do things that please him
  shall receive the fruit of the tree of immortality.

²⁰ The fear of the Lord is all wisdom,
  and in all wisdom is the performance of the law,
  and the knowledge of his omnipotency.

²¹ If a servant say to his master, 'I will not do as it pleaseth thee',
  though afterward he do it, he angereth him that nourisheth him.

²² The knowledge of wickedness is not wisdom,
  neither at any time the counsel of sinners prudence.

²³ There is a wickedness, and the same an abomination,
  and there is a fool wanting in wisdom.

²⁴ He that hath small understanding, and feareth God,
  is better than one that hath much wisdom, and transgresseth
    the law of the most High.

²⁵ There is an exquisite subtlety, and the same is unjust,
  and there is one that turneth aside to make judgement appear:
  and there is a wise man that justifieth in judgement.

²⁶ There is a wicked man that hangeth down his head sadly;
  but inwardly he is full of deceit,

²⁷ Casting down his countenance, and making as if he heard not:
  where he is not known, he will do thee a mischief before thou be
    aware.

²⁸ And if for want of power he be hindered from sinning,
  yet when he findeth opportunity he will do evil.

²⁹ A man may be known by his look,
  and one that hath understanding by his countenance,
  when thou meetest him.

³⁰ A man's attire, and excessive laughter,
  and gait, show what he is.

20 There is a reproof that is not comely:
  again, some man holdeth his tongue, and he is wise.

² It is much better to reprove, than to be angry secretly,
  and he that confesseth his fault shall be preserved from hurt.

³ How good is it, when thou art reproved, to show repentance!
  for so shalt thou escape wilful sin.

⁴ As is the lust of a eunuch to deflower a virgin,
  so is he that executeth judgement with violence.

⁵ There is one that keepeth silence, and is found wise:
  and another by much babbling becometh hateful.
⁶ Some man holdeth his tongue, because he hath not to answer,
  and some keepeth silence, knowing his time.
⁷ A wise man will hold his tongue till he see opportunity:
  but a babbler and a fool will regard no time.
⁸ He that useth many words shall be abhorred;
  and he that taketh to himself authority therein shall be hated.

⁹ There is a sinner that hath good success in evil things;
  and there is a gain that turneth to loss.
¹⁰ There is a gift that shall not profit thee;
  and there is a gift whose recompence is double.
¹¹ There is an abasement because of glory;
  and there is that lifteth up his head from a low estate.
¹² There is that buyeth much for a little,
  and repayeth it sevenfold.

¹³ A wise man by his words maketh himself beloved:
  but the graces of fools shall be poured out.
¹⁴ The gift of a fool shall do thee no good when thou hast it;
  neither yet of the envious for his necessity:
  for he looketh to receive many things for one.
¹⁵ He giveth little, and upbraideth much;
  he openeth his mouth like a crier;
  today he lendeth and tomorrow will he ask it again:
  such a one is to be hated of God and man.
¹⁶ The fool saith, 'I have no friends,
  I have no thanks for all my good deeds,
  and they that eat my bread speak evil of me'.
¹⁷ How oft, and of how many shall he be laughed to scorn!
  for he knoweth not aright what it is to have;
  and it is all one unto him as if he had it not.

¹⁸ To slip upon a pavement is better than to slip with the tongue:
  so the fall of the wicked shall come speedily.
¹⁹ An unseasonable tale will always be in the mouth of the unwise.
²⁰ A wise sentence shall be rejected when it cometh out of a fool's
    mouth:
  for he will not speak it in due season.

²¹ There is that is hindered from sinning through want:
  and when he taketh rest, he shall not be troubled.
²² There is that destroyeth his own soul through bashfulness,
  and by accepting of persons overthroweth himself.

²³ There is that for bashfulness promiseth to his friend,
and maketh him his enemy for nothing.

²⁴ A lie is a foul blot in a man,
yet it is continually in the mouth of the untaught.

²⁵ A thief is better than a man that is accustomed to lie:
but they both shall have destruction to heritage.

²⁶ The disposition of a liar is dishonourable,
and his shame is ever with him.

²⁷ A wise man shall promote himself to honour with his words:
and he that hath understanding will please great men.

²⁸ He that tilleth his land shall increase his heap:
and he that pleaseth great men shall get pardon for iniquity.

²⁹ Presents and gifts blind the eyes of the wise,
and stop up his mouth that he cannot reprove.

³⁰ Wisdom that is hid, and treasure that is hoarded up,
what profit is in them both?

³¹ Better is he that hideth his folly
than a man that hideth his wisdom.

³² Necessary patience in seeking the Lord
is better than he that leadeth his life without a guide.

21 My son, hast thou sinned? do so no more,
but ask pardon for thy former sins.

² Flee from sin as from the face of a serpent:
for if thou comest too near it, it will bite thee:
the teeth thereof are as the teeth of a lion,
slaying the souls of men.

³ All iniquity is as a two-edged sword,
the wounds whereof cannot be healed.

⁴ To terrify and do wrong will waste riches:
thus the house of proud men shall be made desolate.

⁵ A prayer out of a poor man's mouth reacheth to the ears of God,
and his judgement cometh speedily.

⁶ He that hateth to be reproved is in the way of sinners:
but he that feareth the Lord will repent from his heart.

⁷ An eloquent man is known far and near,
but a man of understanding knoweth when he slippeth.

⁸ He that buildeth his house with other men's money
is like one that gathereth himself stones for the tomb of his burial.

⁹ The congregation of the wicked is like tow wrapped together:
and the end of them is a flame of fire to destroy them.
¹⁰ The way of sinners is made plain with stones,
but at the end thereof is the pit of hell.

¹¹ He that keepeth the law of the Lord getteth the understanding
thereof:
and the perfection of the fear of the Lord is wisdom.

¹² He that is not wise will not be taught:
but there is a wisdom which multiplieth bitterness.

¹³ The knowledge of a wise man shall abound like a flood:
and his counsel is like a pure fountain of life.
¹⁴ The inner parts of a fool are like a broken vessel,
and he will hold no knowledge as long as he liveth.
¹⁵ If a skilful man hear a wise word,
he will commend it, and add unto it:
but as soon as one of no understanding heareth it,
it displeaseth him, and he casteth it behind his back.
¹⁶ The talking of a fool is like a burden in the way:
but grace shall be found in the lips of the wise.
¹⁷ They inquire at the mouth of the wise man in the congregation,
and they shall ponder his words in their heart.

¹⁸ As is a house that is destroyed, so is wisdom to a fool:
and the knowledge of the unwise is as talk without sense.
¹⁹ Doctrine unto fools is as fetters on the feet,
and like manacles on the right hand.
²⁰ A fool lifteth up his voice with laughter,
but a wise man doth scarce smile a little.
²¹ Learning is unto a wise man as an ornament of gold,
and like a bracelet upon his right arm.
²² A foolish man's foot is soon in his neighbour's house:
but a man of experience is ashamed of him.
²³ A fool will peep in at the door into the house:
but he that is well nurtured will stand without.
²⁴ It is the rudeness of a man to hearken at the door:
but a wise man will be grieved with disgrace.
²⁵ The lips of talkers will be telling such things as pertain not unto
them:
but the words of such as have understanding are weighed in the
balance.
²⁶ The heart of fools is in their mouth,
but the mouth of the wise is in their heart.

²⁷ When the ungodly curseth Satan,
he curseth his own soul.

²⁸ A whisperer defileth his own soul,
and is hated wheresoever he dwelleth.

22 A slothful man is compared to a filthy stone,
and every one will hiss him out to his disgrace.
² A slothful man is compared to the filth of a dunghill:
every man that takes it up will shake his hand.

³ An evil-nurtured son is the dishonour of his father that begot him:
and a foolish daughter is born to his loss.
⁴ A wise daughter shall bring an inheritance to her husband:
but she that liveth dishonestly is her father's heaviness.
⁵ She that is bold dishonoureth both her father and her husband,
but they both shall despise her.

⁶ A tale out of season is as music in mourning:
but stripes and correction of wisdom are never out of time.

⁷ Whoso teacheth a fool is as one that glueth a potsherd together,
and as he that waketh one from a sound sleep.
⁸ He that telleth a tale to a fool speaketh to one in a slumber:
when he hath told his tale, he will say, 'What is the matter?'

⁹ If children live honestly, and have wherewithal,
they shall cover the baseness of their parents.
¹⁰ But children, being haughty, through disdain and want of nurture
do stain the nobility of their kindred.

¹¹ Weep for the dead, for he hath lost the light:
and weep for the fool, for he wanteth understanding:
make little weeping for the dead, for he is at rest:
but the life of the fool is worse than death.
¹² Seven days do men mourn for him that is dead;
but for a fool and an ungodly man, all the days of his life.

¹³ Talk not much with a fool,
and go not to him that hath no understanding:
beware of him, lest thou have trouble,
and thou shalt never be defiled with his fooleries:
depart from him, and thou shalt find rest,
and never be disquieted with madness.
¹⁴ What is heavier than lead?
and what is the name thereof, but a fool?
¹⁵ Sand, and salt, and a mass of iron is easier to bear
than a man without understanding.
¹⁶ As timber girt and bound together in a building cannot be
loosed with shaking:
so the heart that is established by advised counsel shall fear at
no time.

¹⁷ A heart settled upon a thought of understanding
  is as a fair plastering on the wall of a gallery.
¹⁸ Pales set on a high place will never stand against the wind:
  so a fearful heart in the imagination of a fool cannot stand
    against any fear.

¹⁹ He that pricketh the eye will make tears to fall:
  and he that pricketh the heart maketh it to show her knowledge.
²⁰ Whoso casteth a stone at the birds frayeth them away,
  and he that upbraideth his friend breaketh friendship.
²¹ Though thou drewest a sword at thy friend, yet despair not:
  for there may be a returning to favour.
²² If thou hast opened thy mouth against thy friend, fear not,
  for there may be a reconciliation:
  except for upbraiding, or pride, or disclosing of secrets, or a
    treacherous wound:
  for, for these things every friend will depart.
²³ Be faithful to thy neighbour in his poverty,
  that thou mayest rejoice in his prosperity:
  abide steadfast unto him in the time of his trouble,
  that thou mayest be heir with him in his heritage:
  for a mean estate is not always to be contemned,
  nor the rich that is foolish to be had in admiration.
²⁴ As the vapour and smoke of a furnace goeth before the fire:
  so reviling before blood.
²⁵ I will not be ashamed to defend a friend:
  neither will I hide myself from him.
²⁶ And if any evil happen unto me by him,
  every one that heareth it will beware of him.

²⁷ Who shall set a watch before my mouth,
  and a seal of wisdom upon my lips,
  that I fall not suddenly by them,
  and that my tongue destroy me not?
23 O Lord, Father and Governor of all my whole life,
  leave me not to their counsels, and let me not fall by them.
² Who will set scourges over my thoughts,
  and the discipline of wisdom over my heart?
  that they spare me not for my ignorances, and it pass not by my
    sins:
³ lest my ignorances increase,
  and my sins abound to my destruction,
  and I fall before my adversaries,
  and my enemy rejoice over me, whose hope is far from thy
    mercy.
⁴ O Lord, Father and God of my life, give me not a proud look,
  but turn away from thy servants always a haughty mind.
⁵ Turn away from me vain hopes and concupiscence,

and thou shalt hold him up that is desirous always to serve thee.
⁶ Let not the greediness of the belly nor lust of the flesh take hold
of me,
and give not over me thy servant into an impudent mind.

⁷ Hear, O ye children, the discipline of the mouth:
he that keepeth it shall never be taken in his lips.
⁸ The sinner shall be left in his foolishness:
both the evil speaker and the proud shall fall thereby.
⁹ Accustom not thy mouth to swearing:
neither use thyself to the naming of the Holy One.
¹⁰ For as a servant that is continually beaten shall not be without a
blue mark:
so he that sweareth and nameth God continually shall not be
faultless.
¹¹ A man that useth much swearing shall be filled with iniquity,
and the plague shall never depart from his house:
if he shall offend, his sin shall be upon him:
and if he acknowledge not his sin, he maketh a double offence:
and if he swear in vain, he shall not be innocent,
but his house shall be full of calamities.
¹² There is a word that is clothed about with death:
God grant that it be not found in the heritage of Jacob,
for all such things shall be far from the godly,
and they shall not wallow in their sins.
¹³ Use not thy mouth to intemperate swearing,
for therein is the word of sin.
¹⁴ Remember thy father and thy mother,
when thou sittest among great men.
Be not forgetful before them, and so thou by thy custom become
a fool,
and wish that thou hadst not been born,
and curse the day of thy nativity.
¹⁵ The man that is accustomed to opprobrious words
will never be reformed all the days of his life.

¹⁶ Two sorts of men multiply sin,
and the third will bring wrath:
a hot mind is as a burning fire,
it will never be quenched till it be consumed:
a fornicator in the body of his flesh
will never cease till he hath kindled a fire.
¹⁷ All bread is sweet to a whoremonger,
he will not leave off till he die.
¹⁸ A man that breaketh wedlock, saying thus in his heart,
'Who seeth me?
I am compassed about with darkness:
the walls cover me, and nobody seeth me,

what need I to fear?
the most High will not remember my sins':

¹⁹ such a man only feareth the eyes of men,
and knoweth not that the eyes of the Lord
are ten thousand times brighter than the sun,
beholding all the ways of men,
and considering the most secret parts.

²⁰ He knew all things ere ever they were created,
so also after they were perfected he looked upon them all.

²¹ This man shall be punished in the streets of the city,
and where he suspecteth not he shall be taken.

²² Thus shall it go also with the wife that leaveth her husband,
and bringeth in an heir by another.

²³ For first, she hath disobeyed the law of the most High;
and secondly, she hath trespassed against her own husband;
and thirdly, she hath played the whore in adultery,
and brought children by another man.

²⁴ She shall be brought out into the congregation,
and inquisition shall be made of her children.

²⁵ Her children shall not take root,
and her branches shall bring forth no fruit.

²⁶ She shall leave her memory to be cursed,
and her reproach shall not be blotted out.

²⁷ And they that remain shall know that there is nothing better
than the fear of the Lord,
and that there is nothing sweeter than to take heed unto the
commandment of the Lord.

²⁸ It is great glory to follow the Lord,
and to be received of him is long life.

24

Wisdom shall praise herself,
and shall glory in the midst of her people.

² In the congregation of the most High shall she open her mouth,
and triumph before his power.

³ 'I came out of the mouth of the most High,
and covered the earth as a cloud.

⁴ I dwelt in high places,
and my throne is in a cloudy pillar.

⁵ I alone compassed the circuit of heaven,
and walked in the bottom of the deep.

⁶ In the waves of the sea, and in all the earth,
and in every people and nation, I got a possession.

⁷ With all these I sought rest:
and in whose inheritance shall I abide?

⁸ So the Creator of all things gave me a commandment,
and he that made me caused my tabernacle to rest:

and said, "Let thy dwelling be in Jacob,
and thy inheritance in Israel".

[9] He created me from the beginning before the world,
and I shall never fail.

[10] In the holy tabernacle I served before him:
and so was I established in Sion.

[11] Likewise in the beloved city he gave me rest,
and in Jerusalem was my power.

[12] And I took root in an honourable people,
even in the portion of the Lord's inheritance.

[13] 'I was exalted like a cedar in Libanus,
and as a cypress tree upon the mountains of Hermon.

[14] I was exalted like a palm tree in En-gaddi,
and as a rose plant in Jericho,
as a fair olive tree in a pleasant field,
and grew up as a plane tree by the water.

[15] I gave a sweet smell like cinnamon and aspalathus,
and I yielded a pleasant odour like the best myrrh,
as galbanum, and onyx, and sweet storax,
and as the fume of frankincense in the tabernacle.

[16] As the turpentine tree I stretched out my branches,
and my branches are the branches of honour and grace.

[17] As the vine brought I forth pleasant savour,
and my flowers are the fruit of honour and riches.

[18] 'I am the mother of fair love, and fear, and knowledge, and holy
hope:
I therefore, being eternal, am given to all my children which are
named of him.

[19] Come unto me all ye that be desirous of me,
and fill yourselves with my fruits.

[20] For my memorial is sweeter than honey,
and my inheritance than the honeycomb.

[21] They that eat me shall yet be hungry,
and they that drink me shall yet be thirsty.

[22] He that obeyeth me shall never be confounded,
and they that work by me shall not do amiss.'

[23] All these things are the book of the covenant of the most high
God,
even the law which Moses commanded
for a heritage unto the congregations of Jacob.

[24] Faint not to be strong in the Lord;
that he may confirm you, cleave unto him:
for the Lord Almighty is God alone,
and besides him there is no other Saviour.

[25] He filleth all things with his wisdom,

as Phison, and as Tigris in the time of the new fruits.

²⁶ He maketh the understanding to abound like Euphrates,
and as Jordan in the time of the harvest.

²⁷ He maketh the doctrine of knowledge appear as the light,
and as Geon in the time of vintage.

²⁸ The first man knew her not perfectly:
no more shall the last find her out.

²⁹ For her thoughts are more than the sea,
and her counsels profounder than the great deep.

³⁰ I also came out as a brook from a river,
and as a conduit into a garden.

³¹ I said, 'I will water my best garden,
and will water abundantly my garden bed':
and lo, my brook became a river,
and my river became a sea.

³² I will yet make doctrine to shine as the morning,
and will send forth her light afar off.

³³ I will yet pour out doctrine as prophecy,
and leave it to all ages for ever.

³⁴ Behold that I have not laboured for myself only,
but for all them that seek wisdom.

25

In three things I was beautified,
and stood up beautiful both before God and men:
the unity of brethren,
the love of neighbours,
a man and a wife that agree together.

² Three sorts of men my soul hateth, and I am greatly offended at
their life:
a poor man that is proud, a rich man that is a liar,
and an old adulterer that doateth.

³ If thou hast gathered nothing in thy youth,
how canst thou find anything in thy age?

⁴ O how comely a thing is judgement for grey hairs,
and for ancient men to know counsel!

⁵ O how comely is the wisdom of old men,
and understanding and counsel to men of honour!

⁶ Much experience is the crown of old men,
and the fear of God is their glory.

⁷ There be nine things which I have judged in my heart to be
happy,
and the tenth I will utter with my tongue:
a man that hath joy of his children;
and he that liveth to see the fall of his enemy:

⁸ well is he that dwelleth with a wife of understanding,

and that hath not slipped with his tongue,
and that hath not served a man more unworthy than himself.
⁹ Well is he that hath found prudence,
and he that speaketh in the ears of him that will hear:
¹⁰ O how great is he that findeth wisdom!
yet is there none above him that feareth the Lord.
¹¹ But the love of the Lord passeth all things for illumination:
he that holdeth it, whereto shall he be likened?
¹² The fear of the Lord is the beginning of his love:
and faith is the beginning of cleaving unto him.

¹³ Give me any plague, but the plague of the heart:
and any wickedness, but the wickedness of a woman:
¹⁴ and any affliction, but the affliction from them that hate me:
and any revenge, but the revenge of enemies.
¹⁵ There is no head above the head of a serpent,
and there is no wrath above the wrath of an enemy.
¹⁶ I had rather dwell with a lion and a dragon,
than to keep house with a wicked woman.
¹⁷ The wickedness of a woman changeth her face,
and darkeneth her countenance like sackcloth.
¹⁸ Her husband shall sit among his neighbours:
and when he heareth it shall sigh bitterly.

¹⁹ All wickedness is but little to the wickedness of a woman:
let the portion of a sinner fall upon her.
²⁰ As the climbing up a sandy way is to the feet of the aged,
so is a wife full of words to a quiet man.
²¹ Stumble not at the beauty of a woman,
and desire her not for pleasure.
²² A woman, if she maintain her husband,
is full of anger, impudence, and much reproach.
²³ A wicked woman abateth the courage,
maketh a heavy countenance and a wounded heart:
a woman that will not comfort her husband in distress
maketh weak hands and feeble knees.
²⁴ Of the woman came the beginning of sin,
and through her we all die.
²⁵ Give the water no passage:
neither a wicked woman liberty to gad abroad.
²⁶ If she go not as thou wouldst have her,
cut her off from thy flesh,
and give her a bill of divorce, and let her go.

26 Blessed is the man that hath a virtuous wife,
for the number of his days shall be double.
² A virtuous woman rejoiceth her husband,
and he shall fulfil the years of his life in peace.

³ A good wife is a good portion,
which shall be given in the portion of them that fear the Lord.
⁴ Whether a man be rich or poor, if he have a good heart towards
the Lord,
he shall at all times rejoice with a cheerful countenance.
⁵ There be three things that my heart feareth:
and for the fourth I was sore afraid:
the slander of a city, the gathering together of an unruly
multitude, and a false accusation:
all these are worse than death.
⁶ But a grief of heart and sorrow is a woman that is jealous over
another woman,
and a scourge of the tongue which communicateth with all.
⁷ An evil wife is a yoke shaken to and fro:
he that hath hold of her is as though he held a scorpion.
⁸ A drunken woman and a gadder-abroad causeth great anger,
and she will not cover her own shame.

⁹ The whoredom of a woman may be known in her haughty looks
and eyelids.
¹⁰ If thy daughter be shameless, keep her in straitly,
lest she abuse herself through overmuch liberty.
¹¹ Watch over an impudent eye:
and marvel not if she trespass against thee.
¹² She will open her mouth,
as a thirsty traveller when he hath found a fountain,
and drink of every water near her:
by every hedge will she sit down,
and open her quiver against every arrow.

¹³ The grace of a wife delighteth her husband,
and her discretion will fat his bones.
¹⁴ A silent and loving woman is a gift of the Lord,
and there is nothing so much worth as a mind well instructed.
¹⁵ A shamefast and faithful woman is a double grace,
and her continent mind cannot be valued.
¹⁶ As the sun when it ariseth in the high heaven:
so is the beauty of a good wife in the ordering of her house.
¹⁷ As the clear light is upon the holy candlestick:
so is the beauty of the face in ripe age.
¹⁸ As the golden pillars are upon the sockets of silver:
so are the fair feet with a constant heart.

¹⁹ My son, keep the flower of thy age sound:
and give not thy strength to strangers.
²⁰ When thou hast gotten a fruitful possession through all the
field,
sow it with thy own seed, trusting in the goodness of thy stock.

[21] So thy race which thou leavest shall be magnified,
having the confidence of their good descent.
[22] A harlot shall be accounted as spittle:
but a married woman is a tower against death to her husband.
[23] A wicked woman is given as a portion to a wicked man:
but a godly woman is given to him that feareth the Lord.
[24] A dishonest woman contemneth shame:
but an honest woman will reverence her husband.
[25] A shameless woman shall be counted as a dog:
but she that is shamefast will fear the Lord.
[26] A woman that honoureth her husband shall be judged wise of all:
but she that dishonoureth him in her pride shall be counted
ungodly of all.
[27] A loud crying woman and a scold
shall be sought out to drive away the enemies.

[28] There be two things that grieve my heart;
and the third maketh me angry:
a man of war that suffereth poverty;
and men of understanding that are not set by;
and one that returneth from righteousness to sin:
the Lord prepareth such a one for the sword.
[29] A merchant shall hardly keep himself from doing wrong:
and a huckster shall not be freed from sin.

27

Many have sinned for a small matter:
and he that seeketh for abundance will turn his eyes away.
[2] As a nail sticketh fast between the joinings of the stones:
so doth sin stick close between buying and selling.
[3] Unless a man hold himself diligently in the fear of the Lord,
his house shall soon be overthrown.

[4] As when one sifteth with a sieve, the refuse remaineth,
so the filth of man in his talk.
[5] The furnace proveth the potter's vessel:
so the trial of man is in his reasoning.
[6] The fruit declareth if the tree have been dressed:
so is the utterance of a conceit in the heart of man.
[7] Praise no man before thou hearest him speak,
for this is the trial of men.

[8] If thou followest righteousness, thou shalt obtain her,
and put her on, as a glorious long robe.
[9] The birds will resort unto their like,
so will truth return unto them that practise in her.
[10] As the lion lieth in wait for the prey:
so sin for them that work iniquity.

¹¹ The discourse of a godly man is always with wisdom:
   but a fool changeth as the moon.
¹² If thou be among the indiscreet, observe the time:
   but be continually among men of understanding.
¹³ The discourse of fools is irksome,
   and their sport is in the wantonness of sin.
¹⁴ The talk of him that sweareth much maketh the hair stand
     upright:
   and their brawls make one stop his ears.
¹⁵ The strife of the proud is bloodshedding,
   and their revilings are grievous to the ear.

¹⁶ Whoso discovereth secrets loseth his credit:
   and shall never find friend to his mind.
¹⁷ Love thy friend, and be faithful unto him:
   but if thou bewrayest his secrets, follow no more after him.
¹⁸ For as a man hath destroyed his enemy:
   so hast thou lost the love of thy neighbour.
¹⁹ As one that letteth a bird go out of his hand,
   so hast thou let thy neighbour go, and shalt not get him again.
²⁰ Follow after him no more, for he is too far off,
   he is as a roe escaped out of the snare.
²¹ As for a wound, it may be bound up,
   and after reviling there may be reconcilement:
   but he that bewrayeth secrets is without hope.

²² He that winketh with the eyes worketh evil,
   and he that knoweth him will depart from him.
²³ When thou art present he will speak sweetly,
   and will admire thy words:
   but at the last he will writhe his mouth,
   and slander thy sayings.
²⁴ I have hated many things, but nothing like him,
   for the Lord will hate him.

²⁵ Whoso casteth a stone on high casteth it on his own head,
   and a deceitful stroke shall make wounds.
²⁶ Whoso diggeth a pit shall fall therein:
   and he that setteth a trap shall be taken therein.
²⁷ He that worketh mischief, it shall fall upon him,
   and he shall not know whence it cometh.
²⁸ Mockery and reproach are from the proud:
   but vengeance as a lion shall lie in wait for them.
²⁹ They that rejoice at the fall of the righteous shall be taken in the
     snare,
   and anguish shall consume them before they die.
³⁰ Malice and wrath, even these are abominations,
   and the sinful man shall have them both.

28

He that revengeth shall find vengeance from the Lord,
and he will surely keep his sins in remembrance.

2 Forgive thy neighbour the hurt that he hath done unto thee,
so shall thy sins also be forgiven when thou prayest.

3 One man beareth hatred against another,
and doth he seek pardon from the Lord?

4 He showeth no mercy to a man, which is like himself:
and doth he ask forgiveness of his own sins?

5 If he that is but flesh nourish hatred,
who will entreat for pardon of his sins?

6 Remember thy end, and let enmity cease,
remember corruption and death, and abide in the commandments.

7 Remember the commandments, and bear no malice to thy
neighbour:
remember the covenant of the Highest, and wink at ignorance.

8 Abstain from strife, and thou shalt diminish thy sins:
for a furious man will kindle strife.

9 A sinful man disquieteth friends,
and maketh debate among them that be at peace.

10 As the matter of the fire is, so it burneth:
and as a man's strength is, so is his wrath;
and according to his riches his anger riseth;
and the stronger they are which contend, the more they will be
inflamed.

11 A hasty contention kindleth a fire,
and a hasty fighting sheddeth blood.

12 If thou blow the spark, it shall burn:
if thou spit upon it, it shall be quenched:
and both these come out of thy mouth.

13 Curse the whisperer and double-tongued:
for such have destroyed many that were at peace.

14 A backbiting tongue hath disquieted many,
and driven them from nation to nation:
strong cities hath it pulled down,
and overthrown the houses of great men.

15 A backbiting tongue hath cast out virtuous women,
and deprived them of their labours.

16 Whoso hearkeneth unto it shall never find rest,
and never dwell quietly.

17 The stroke of the whip maketh marks in the flesh,
but the stroke of the tongue breaketh the bones.

18 Many have fallen by the edge of the sword:
but not so many as have fallen by the tongue.

19 Well is he that is defended from it,
and hath not passed through the venom thereof:
who hath not drawn the yoke thereof,

nor hath been bound in her bands.

20 For the yoke thereof is a yoke of iron,
and the bands thereof are bands of brass.

21 The death thereof is an evil death,
the grave were better than it.

22 It shall not have rule over them that fear God,
neither shall they be burnt with the flame thereof.

23 Such as forsake the Lord shall fall into it,
and it shall burn in them, and not be quenched;
it shall be sent upon them as a lion,
and devour them as a leopard.

24 Look that thou hedge thy possession about with thorns,
and bind up thy silver and gold:

25 and weigh thy words in a balance,
and make a door and bar for thy mouth.

26 Beware thou slide not by it,
lest thou fall before him that lieth in wait.

29 He that is merciful will lend unto his neighbour,
and he that strengtheneth his hand keepeth the
commandments.

2 Lend to thy neighbour in time of his need,
and pay thou thy neighbour again in due season.

3 Keep thy word and deal faithfully with him,
and thou shalt always find the thing that is necessary for thee.

4 Many, when a thing was lent them, reckoned it to be found,
and put them to trouble that helped them.

5 Till he hath received, he will kiss a man's hand:
and for his neighbour's money he will speak submissively:
but when he should repay, he will prolong the time,
and return words of grief, and complain of the time.

6 If he prevail, he shall hardly receive the half,
and he will count as if he had found it:
if not, he hath deprived him of his money,
and he hath gotten him an enemy without cause:
he payeth him with cursings and railings:
and for honour he will pay him disgrace.

7 Many therefore have refused to lend for other men's ill dealing,
fearing to be defrauded.

8 Yet have thou patience with a man in poor estate,
and delay not to show him mercy.

9 Help the poor for the commandment's sake,
and turn him not away because of his poverty.

10 Lose thy money for thy brother and thy friend,
and let it not rust under a stone to be lost.

11 Lay up thy treasure according to the commandments of the most
High,

and it shall bring thee more profit than gold.

¹² Shut up alms in thy storehouses:
and it shall deliver thee from all affliction.

¹³ It shall fight for thee against thy enemies
better than a mighty shield and strong spear.

¹⁴ An honest man is surety for his neighbour:
but he that is impudent will forsake him.

¹⁵ Forget not the friendship of thy surety,
for he hath given his life for thee.

¹⁶ A sinner will overthrow the good estate of his surety:

¹⁷ and he that is of an unthankful mind will leave him in danger
that delivered him.

¹⁸ Suretyship hath undone many of good estate,
and shaken them as a wave of the sea:
mighty men hath it driven from their houses,
so that they wandered among strange nations.

¹⁹ A wicked man transgressing the commandments of the Lord
shall fall into suretyship:
and he that undertaketh and followeth other men's business for
gain
shall fall into suits.

²⁰ Help thy neighbour according to thy power,
and beware that thou thyself fall not into the same.

²¹ The chief thing for life is water, and bread,
and clothing, and a house to cover shame.

²² Better is the life of a poor man in a mean cottage,
than delicate fare in another man's house.

²³ Be it little or much, hold thee contented,
that thou hear not the reproach of thy house.

²⁴ For it is a miserable life to go from house to house:
for where thou art a stranger, thou darest not open thy mouth.

²⁵ Thou shalt entertain, and feast, and have no thanks:
moreover, thou shalt hear bitter words:

²⁶ 'Come, thou stranger, and furnish a table,
and feed me of that thou hast ready.

²⁷ Give place, thou stranger, to an honourable man,
my brother cometh to be lodged, and I have need of my house.'

²⁸ These things are grievous to a man of understanding:
the upbraiding of houseroom, and reproaching of the lender.

30

He that loveth his son causeth him oft to feel the rod,
that he may have joy of him in the end.

² He that chastiseth his son shall have joy in him,
and shall rejoice of him among his acquaintance.

³ He that teacheth his son grieveth the enemy:
and before his friends he shall rejoice of him.

⁴ Though his father die, yet he is as though he were not dead:
  for he hath left one behind him that is like himself.
⁵ While he lived, he saw and rejoiced in him:
  and when he died, he was not sorrowful.
⁶ He left behind him an avenger against his enemies,
  and one that shall requite kindness to his friends.
⁷ He that maketh too much of his son shall bind up his wounds,
  and his bowels will be troubled at every cry.
⁸ A horse not broken becometh headstrong:
  and a child left to himself will be wilful.
⁹ Cocker thy child, and he shall make thee afraid:
  play with him, and he will bring thee to heaviness.
¹⁰ Laugh not with him, lest thou have sorrow with him,
  and lest thou gnash thy teeth in the end.
¹¹ Give him no liberty in his youth,
  and wink not at his follies.
¹² Bow down his neck while he is young,
  and beat him on the sides while he is a child,
  lest he wax stubborn, and be disobedient unto thee,
  and so bring sorrow to thy heart.
¹³ Chastise thy son, and hold him to labour,
  lest his lewd behaviour be an offence unto thee.

¹⁴ Better is the poor, being sound and strong of constitution,
  than a rich man that is afflicted in his body.
¹⁵ Health and good state of body are above all gold,
  and a strong body above infinite wealth.
¹⁶ There is no riches above a sound body,
  and no joy above the joy of the heart.
¹⁷ Death is better than a bitter life or continual sickness.
¹⁸ Delicates poured upon a mouth shut up
  are as messes of meat set upon a grave.
¹⁹ What good doeth the offering unto an idol?
  for neither can it eat nor smell:
  so is he that is persecuted of the Lord.
²⁰ He seeth with his eyes and groaneth,
  as a eunuch that embraceth a virgin and sigheth.

²¹ Give not over thy mind to heaviness,
  and afflict not thyself in thy own counsel.
²² The gladness of the heart is the life of man,
  and the joyfulness of a man prolongeth his days.
²³ Love thy own soul, and comfort thy heart,
  remove sorrow far from thee: for sorrow hath killed many,
  and there is no profit therein.
²⁴ Envy and wrath shorten the life,
  and carefulness bringeth age before the time.
²⁵ A cheerful and good heart will have a care of his meat and diet.

31

¹ Watching for riches consumeth the flesh,
and the care thereof driveth away sleep.

² Watching care will not let a man slumber,
as a sore disease breaketh sleep.

³ The rich hath great labour in gathering riches together,
and when he resteth, he is filled with his delicates.

⁴ The poor laboureth in his poor estate,
and when he leaveth off, he is still needy.

⁵ He that loveth gold shall not be justified,
and he that followeth corruption shall have enough thereof.

⁶ Gold hath been the ruin of many,
and their destruction was present.

⁷ It is a stumbling-block unto them that sacrifice unto it,
and every fool shall be taken therewith.

⁸ Blessed is the rich that is found without blemish,
and hath not gone after gold:

⁹ who is he? and we will call him blessed:
for wonderful things hath he done among his people.

¹⁰ Who hath been tried thereby, and found perfect?
then let him glory.
Who might offend, and hath not offended?
or done evil, and hath not done it?

¹¹ His goods shall be established,
and the congregation shall declare his alms.

¹² If thou sit at a bountiful table, be not greedy upon it,
and say not, 'There is much meat on it'.

¹³ Remember that a wicked eye is an evil thing:
and what is created more wicked than an eye?
therefore it weepeth upon every occasion.

¹⁴ Stretch not thy hand whithersoever it looketh,
and thrust it not with him into the dish.

¹⁵ Judge of thy neighbour by thyself:
and be discreet in every point.

¹⁶ Eat as it becometh a man those things which are set before
thee:
and devour not, lest thou be hated.

¹⁷ Leave off first for manners' sake,
and be not unsatiable, lest thou offend.

¹⁸ When thou sittest among many,
reach not thy hand out first of all.

¹⁹ A very little is sufficient for a man well nurtured,
and he fetcheth not his wind short upon his bed.

²⁰ Sound sleep cometh of moderate eating:
he riseth early, and his wits are with him:
but the pain of watching, and choler, and pangs of the belly
are with an unsatiable man.

²¹ And if thou hast been forced to eat,
  arise, go forth, vomit, and thou shalt have rest.

²² My son, hear me, and despise me not,
  and at the last thou shalt find as I told thee:
  in all thy works be quick,
  so shall there no sickness come unto thee.
²³ Whoso is liberal of his meat, men shall speak well of him,
  and the report of his good housekeeping will be believed.
²⁴ But against him that is a niggard of his meat the whole city shall
    murmur;
  and the testimonies of his niggardness shall not be doubted of.

²⁵ Show not thy valiantness in wine,
  for wine hath destroyed many.
²⁶ The furnace proveth the edge by dipping:
  so doth wine the hearts of the proud by drunkenness.
²⁷ Wine is as good as life to a man if it be drunk moderately:
  what life is then to a man that is without wine?
  for it was made to make men glad.
²⁸ Wine measurably drunk and in season
  bringeth gladness of the heart, and cheerfulness of the mind:
²⁹ but wine drunken with excess maketh bitterness of the mind,
  with brawling and quarrelling.
³⁰ Drunkenness increaseth the rage of a fool till he offend:
  it diminisheth strength, and maketh wounds.
³¹ Rebuke not thy neighbour at the wine,
  and despise him not in his mirth:
  give him no despiteful words,
  and press not upon him with urging him to drink.

32 If thou be made the master of the feast,
  lift not thyself up, but be among them as one of the rest;
  take diligent care for them, and so sit down.
² And when thou hast done all thy office, take thy place,
  that thou mayest be merry with them,
  and receive a crown for thy well ordering of the feast.

³ Speak, thou that art the elder, for it becometh thee,
  but with sound judgement, and hinder not music.
⁴ Pour not out words where there is a musician,
  and show not forth wisdom out of time.
⁵ A concert of music in a banquet of wine
  is as a signet of carbuncle set in gold.
⁶ As a signet of an emerald set in a work of gold,
  so is the melody of music with pleasant wine.

⁷ Speak, young man, if there be need of thee:
  and yet scarcely when thou art twice asked.
⁸ Let thy speech be short, comprehending much in few words;
  be as one that knoweth and yet holdeth his tongue.
⁹ If thou be among great men, make not thyself equal with them,
  and when ancient men are in place, use not many words.
¹⁰ Before the thunder goeth lightning:
  and before a shamefast man shall go favour.
¹¹ Rise up betimes, and be not the last:
  but get thee home without delay.
¹² There take thy pastime, and do what thou wilt:
  but sin not by proud speech.
¹³ And for these things bless him that made thee,
  and hath replenished thee with his good things.

¹⁴ Whoso feareth the Lord will receive his discipline,
  and they that seek him early shall find favour.
¹⁵ He that seeketh the law shall be filled therewith:
  but the hypocrite will be offended thereat.
¹⁶ They that fear the Lord shall find judgement,
  and shall kindle justice as a light.
¹⁷ A sinful man will not be reproved,
  but findeth an excuse according to his will.

¹⁸ A man of counsel will be considerate;
  but a strange and proud man is not daunted with fear,
  even when of himself he hath done without counsel.
¹⁹ Do nothing without advice,
  and when thou hast once done, repent not.
²⁰ Go not in a way wherein thou mayest fall,
  and stumble not among the stones.
²¹ Be not confident in a plain way.
²² And beware of thy own children.
²³ In every good work trust thy own soul:
  for this is the keeping of the commandments.
²⁴ He that believeth in the Lord taketh heed to the commandment:
  and he that trusteth in him shall fare never the worse.

33 There shall no evil happen unto him that feareth the Lord,
  but in temptation even again he will deliver him.
² A wise man hateth not the law,
  but he that is a hypocrite therein is as a ship in a storm.
³ A man of understanding trusteth in the law,
  and the law is faithful unto him, as an oracle.

⁴ Prepare what to say, and so thou shalt be heard:
  and bind up instruction, and then make answer.
⁵ The heart of the foolish is like a cartwheel:

and his thoughts are like a rolling axletree.

6 A stallion horse is as a mocking friend,
he neigheth under every one that sitteth upon him.

7 Why doth one day excel another,
when as all the light of every day in the year is of the sun?

8 By the knowledge of the Lord they were distinguished:
and he altered seasons and feasts.

9 Some of them hath he made high days, and hallowed them,
and some of them hath he made ordinary days.

10 And all men are from the ground,
and Adam was created of earth.

11 In much knowledge the Lord hath divided them,
and made their ways diverse.

12 Some of them hath he blessed and exalted,
and some of them hath he sanctified, and set near himself:
but some of them hath he cursed and brought low,
and turned out of their places.

13 As the clay is in the potter's hand, to fashion it at his pleasure:
so man is in the hand of him that made him,
to render to them as liketh him best.

14 Good is set against evil, and life against death:
so is the godly against the sinner, and the sinner against the
godly.

15 So look upon all the works of the most High,
and there are two and two, one against another.

16 I awoke up last of all,
as one that gathereth after the grapegatherers:
by the blessing of the Lord I profited,
and filled my wine-press like a gatherer of grapes.

17 Consider that I laboured not for myself only,
but for all them that seek learning.

18 Hear me, O ye great men of the people,
and hearken with your ears, ye rulers of the congregation.

19 Give not thy son and wife, thy brother and friend,
power over thee while thou livest,
and give not thy goods to another,
lest it repent thee, and thou entreat for the same again.

20 As long as thou livest and hast breath in thee,
give not thyself over to any.

21 For better it is that thy children should seek to thee,
than that thou shouldst stand to their courtesy.

22 In all thy works keep to thyself the pre-eminence,
leave not a stain in thy honour.

23 At the time when thou shalt end thy days, and finish thy life,
distribute thy inheritance.

²⁴ Fodder, a wand, and burdens are for the ass:
and bread, correction, and work for a servant.
²⁵ If thou set thy servant to labour, thou shalt find rest:
but if thou let him go idle, he shall seek liberty.
²⁶ A yoke and a collar do bow the neck:
so are tortures and torments for an evil servant.
²⁷ Send him to labour, that he be not idle:
for idleness teacheth much evil.
²⁸ Set him to work, as is fit for him:
if he be not obedient, put on more heavy fetters.
²⁹ But be not excessive toward any,
and without discretion do nothing.
³⁰ If thou have a servant, let him be unto thee as thyself,
because thou hast bought him with a price.
³¹ If thou have a servant, entreat him as a brother:
for thou hast need of him, as of thy own soul:
if thou entreat him evil, and he run from thee,
which way wilt thou go to seek him?

34 The hopes of a man void of understanding are vain and false:
and dreams lift up fools.
² Whoso regardeth dreams is like him that catcheth at a shadow,
and followeth after the wind.
³ The vision of dreams is the resemblance of one thing to another,
even as the likeness of a face to a face.
⁴ Of an unclean thing what can be cleansed?
and from that thing which is false what truth can come?
⁵ Divinations, and soothsayings, and dreams are vain:
and the heart fancieth as a woman's heart in travail.
⁶ If they be not sent from the most High in thy visitation,
set not thy heart upon them.
⁷ For dreams have deceived many,
and they have failed that put their trust in them.

⁸ The law shall be found perfect without lies:
and wisdom is perfection to a faithful mouth.
⁹ A man that hath travelled knoweth many things:
and he that hath much experience will declare wisdom.
¹⁰ He that hath no experience knoweth little:
but he that hath travelled is full of prudence.
¹¹ When I travelled, I saw many things:
and I understand more than I can express.
¹² I was ofttimes in danger of death,
yet I was delivered because of these things.

¹³ The spirit of those that fear the Lord shall live,
for their hope is in him that saveth them.
¹⁴ Whoso feareth the Lord shall not fear nor be afraid,

for he is his hope.

¹⁵ Blessed is the soul of him that feareth the Lord:
to whom doth he look? and who is his strength?

¹⁶ For the eyes of the Lord are upon them that love him,
he is their mighty protection and strong stay,
a defence from heat, and a cover from the sun at noon,
a preservation from stumbling, and a help from falling.

¹⁷ He raiseth up the soul, and lighteneth the eyes:
he giveth health, life, and blessing.

¹⁸ He that sacrificeth of a thing wrongfully gotten, his offering is
ridiculous,
and the gifts of unjust men are not accepted.

¹⁹ The most High is not pleased with the offerings of the wicked,
neither is he pacified for sin by the multitude of sacrifices.

²⁰ Whoso bringeth an offering of the goods of the poor
doeth as one that killeth the son before his father's eyes.

²¹ The bread of the needy is their life:
he that defraudeth him thereof is a man of blood.

²² He that taketh away his neighbour's living slayeth him:
and he that defraudeth the labourer of his hire is a
bloodshedder.

²³ When one buildeth, and another pulleth down,
what profit have they then but labour?

²⁴ When one prayeth, and another curseth,
whose voice will the Lord hear?

²⁵ He that washeth himself after the touching of a dead body,
if he touch it again, what availeth his washing?

²⁶ So is it with a man that fasteth for his sins,
and goeth again, and doeth the same:
who will hear his prayer?
or what doth his humbling profit him?

35 He that keepeth the law bringeth offerings enough:
he that taketh heed to the commandment offereth a peace
offering.

² He that requiteth a good turn offereth fine flour:
and he that giveth alms sacrificeth praise.

³ To depart from wickedness is a thing pleasing to the Lord:
and to forsake unrighteousness is a propitiation.

⁴ Thou shalt not appear empty before the Lord:

⁵ for all these things are to be done because of the commandment.

⁶ The offering of the righteous maketh the altar fat,
and the sweet savour thereof is before the most High.

⁷ The sacrifice of a just man is acceptable,
and the memorial thereof shall never be forgotten.

⁸ Give the Lord his honour with a good eye,

and diminish not the first-fruits of thy hands.
⁹ In all thy gifts show a cheerful countenance,
and dedicate thy tithes with gladness.
¹⁰ Give unto the most High according as he hath enriched thee,
and as thou hast gotten, give with a cheerful eye.
¹¹ For the Lord recompenseth,
and will give thee seven times as much.

¹² Do not think to corrupt with gifts,
for such he will not receive:
and trust not to unrighteous sacrifices,
for the Lord is judge, and with him is no respect of persons.
¹³ He will not accept any person against a poor man,
but will hear the prayer of the oppressed.
¹⁴ He will not despise the supplication of the fatherless:
nor the widow when she poureth out her complaint.
¹⁵ Do not the tears run down the widow's cheeks?
and is not her cry against him that causeth them to fall?
¹⁶ He that serveth the Lord shall be accepted with favour,
and his prayer shall reach unto the clouds.
¹⁷ The prayer of the humble pierceth the clouds:
and till it come nigh, he will not be comforted;
and will not depart, till the most High shall behold to judge
righteously,
and execute judgement.
¹⁸ For the Lord will not be slack,
neither will the Mighty be patient towards them,
till he hath smitten in sunder the loins of the unmerciful,
and repaid vengeance to the heathen:
till he have taken away the multitude of the proud,
and broken the sceptre of the unrighteous:
¹⁹ till he have rendered to every man according to his deeds,
and to the works of men according to their devices;
till he have judged the cause of his people,
and made them to rejoice in his mercy.
²⁰ Mercy is seasonable in the time of affliction,
as clouds of rain in the time of drought.

36 Have mercy upon us, O Lord God of all, and behold us:
²and send thy fear upon all the nations that seek not after thee.
³ Lift up thy hand against the strange nations,
and let them see thy power.
⁴ As thou wast sanctified in us before them:
so be thou magnified among them before us.
⁵ And let them know thee, as we have known thee,
that there is no God but only thou, O God.
⁶ Show new signs, and make other strange wonders:
glorify thy hand and thy right arm,

that they may set forth thy wondrous works.
7 Raise up indignation, and pour out wrath:
  take away the adversary, and destroy the enemy.
8 Make the time short, remember the covenant,
  and let them declare thy wonderful works.
9 Let him that escapeth be consumed by the rage of the fire,
  and let them perish that oppress the people.
10 Smite in sunder the heads of the rulers of the heathen,
  that say, 'There is no other but we'.

11 Gather all the tribes of Jacob together,
  and inherit thou them, as from the beginning.
12 O Lord, have mercy upon the people that is called by thy name,
  and upon Israel, whom thou hast named thy firstborn.
13 O be merciful unto Jerusalem, thy holy city,
  the place of thy rest.
14 Fill Sion with thy unspeakable oracles,
  and thy people with thy glory.
15 Give testimony unto those that thou hast possessed from the
    beginning,
  and raise up prophets that have been in thy name.
16 Reward them that wait for thee,
  and let thy prophets be found faithful.
17 O Lord, hear the prayer of thy servants,
  according to the blessing of Aaron over thy people,
  that all they which dwell upon the earth may know
  that thou art the Lord, the eternal God.

18 The belly devoureth all meats,
  yet is one meat better than another.
19 As the palate tasteth divers kinds of venison:
  so doth a heart of understanding false speeches.
20 A froward heart causeth heaviness:
  but a man of experience will recompense him.

21 A woman will receive every man,
  yet is one daughter better than another.
22 The beauty of a woman cheereth the countenance,
  and a man loveth nothing better.
23 If there be kindness, meekness, and comfort in her tongue,
  then is not her husband like other men.
24 He that getteth a wife beginneth a possession,
  a help like unto himself, and a pillar of rest.
25 Where no hedge is, there the possession is spoiled:
  and he that hath no wife will wander up and down mourning.
26 Who will trust a thief well appointed, that skippeth from city to
    city?

so who will believe a man that hath no house,
and lodgeth wheresoever the night taketh him?

37 Every friend saith, 'I am his friend also':
but there is a friend, which is only a friend in name.
² Is it not a grief unto death,
when a companion and friend is turned to an enemy?
³ O wicked imagination,
whence camest thou in to cover the earth with deceit?
⁴ There is a companion, which rejoiceth in the prosperity of a
friend:
but in the time of trouble will be against him.
⁵ There is a companion, which helpeth his friend for the belly,
and taketh up the buckler against the enemy.
⁶ Forget not thy friend in thy mind,
and be not unmindful of him in thy riches.

⁷ Every counsellor extolleth counsel;
but there is some that counselleth for himself.
⁸ Beware of a counsellor, and know before what need he hath;
for he will counsel for himself lest he cast the lot upon thee,
⁹ and say unto thee, 'Thy way is good':
and afterward he stand on the other side, to see what shall befall
thee.
¹⁰ Consult not with one that suspecteth thee:
and hide thy counsel from such as envy thee.
¹¹ Neither consult with a woman touching her of whom she is
jealous;
neither with a coward in matters of war;
nor with a merchant concerning exchange;
nor with a buyer of selling;
nor with an envious man of thankfulness;
nor with an unmerciful man touching kindness;
nor with the slothful for any work;
nor with a hireling for a year of finishing work;
nor with an idle servant of much business:
hearken not unto these in any matter of counsel.
¹² But be continually with a godly man,
whom thou knowest to keep the commandments of the Lord,
whose mind is according to thy mind,
and will sorrow with thee, if thou shalt miscarry.
¹³ And let the counsel of thy own heart stand:
for there is no man more faithful unto thee than it.
¹⁴ For a man's mind is sometimes wont to tell him more than seven
watchmen,
that sit above in a high tower.
¹⁵ And above all this pray to the most High,
that he will direct thy way in truth.

¹⁶ Let reason go before every enterprise,
and counsel before every action.
¹⁷ The countenance is a sign of changing of the heart.
¹⁸ Four manner of things appear: good and evil, life and death:
but the tongue ruleth over them continually.
¹⁹ There is one that is wise and teacheth many,
and yet is unprofitable to himself.
²⁰ There is one that showeth wisdom in words, and is hated:
he shall be destitute of all food.
²¹ For grace is not given him from the Lord:
because he is deprived of all wisdom.
²² Another is wise to himself:
and the fruits of understanding are commendable in his mouth.
²³ A wise man instructeth his people,
and the fruits of his understanding fail not.
²⁴ A wise man shall be filled with blessing,
and all they that see him shall count him happy.
²⁵ The days of the life of man may be numbered:
but the days of Israel are innumerable.
²⁶ A wise man shall inherit glory among his people,
and his name shall be perpetual.

²⁷ My son, prove thy soul in thy life,
and see what is evil for it, and give not that unto it.
²⁸ For all things are not profitable for all men,
neither hath every soul pleasure in everything.
²⁹ Be not insatiable in any dainty thing,
nor too greedy upon meats:
³⁰ for excess of meats bringeth sickness,
and surfeiting will turn into choler.
³¹ By surfeiting have many perished,
but he that taketh heed prolongeth his life.

38 Honour a physician with the honour due unto him
for the uses which you may have of him:
for the Lord hath created him.
² For of the most High cometh healing,
and he shall receive honour of the king.
³ The skill of the physician shall lift up his head:
and in the sight of great men he shall be in admiration.
⁴ The Lord hath created medicines out of the earth;
and he that is wise will not abhor them.
⁵ Was not the water made sweet with wood,
that the virtue thereof might be known?
⁶ And he hath given men skill,
that he might be honoured in his marvellous works.
⁷ With such doth he heal men, and taketh away their pains.
⁸ Of such doth the apothecary make a confection;

and of his works there is no end;
and from him is peace over all the earth.

⁹ My son, in thy sickness be not negligent:
but pray unto the Lord, and he will make thee whole.
¹⁰ Leave off from sin, and order thy hands aright,
and cleanse thy heart from all wickedness.
¹¹ Give a sweet savour, and a memorial of fine flour:
and make a fat offering, as not being.
¹² Then give place to the physician, for the Lord hath created him:
let him not go from thee, for thou hast need of him.
¹³ There is a time when in their hands there is good success.
¹⁴ For they shall also pray unto the Lord,
that he would prosper that which they give for ease and remedy
to prolong life.
¹⁵ He that sinneth before his Maker, let him fall into the hand of
the physician.

¹⁶ My son, let tears fall down over the dead,
and begin to lament, as if thou hadst suffered great harm
thyself:
and then cover his body according to the custom,
and neglect not his burial.
¹⁷ Weep bitterly, and make great moan, and use lamentation, as he
is worthy,
and that a day or two, lest thou be evil spoken of:
and then comfort thyself for thy heaviness.
¹⁸ For of heaviness cometh death,
and the heaviness of the heart breaketh strength.
¹⁹ In affliction also sorrow remaineth:
and the life of the poor is the curse of the heart.
²⁰ Take no heaviness to heart:
drive it away, and remember the last end.
²¹ Forget it not, for there is no turning again:
thou shalt not do him good, but hurt thyself.
²² Remember my judgement: for thine also shall be so;
yesterday for me, and today for thee.
²³ When the dead is at rest, let his remembrance rest,
and be comforted for him, when his spirit is departed from him.

²⁴ The wisdom of a learned man cometh by opportunity of leisure:
and he that hath little business shall become wise.
²⁵ How can he get wisdom that holdeth the plough,
and that glorieth in the goad,
that driveth oxen, and is occupied in their labours,
and whose talk is of bullocks?
²⁶ He giveth his mind to make furrows:
and is diligent to give the kine fodder.

²⁷ So every carpenter and workmaster,
   that laboureth night and day:
   and they that cut and grave seals,
   and are diligent to make great variety,
   and give themselves to counterfeit imagery,
   and watch to finish a work:
²⁸ the smith also sitting by the anvil,
   and considering the iron work;
   the vapour of the fire wasteth his flesh,
   and he fighteth with the heat of the furnace:
   the noise of the hammer and the anvil is ever in his ears,
   and his eyes look still upon the pattern of the thing that he
      maketh;
   he setteth his mind to finish his work,
   and watcheth to polish it perfectly:
²⁹ so doth the potter sitting at his work,
   and turning the wheel about with his feet,
   who is always carefully set at his work,
   and maketh all his work by number;
³⁰ he fashioneth the clay with his arm,
   and boweth down his strength before his feet:
   he applieth himself to lead it over;
   and he is diligent to make clean the furnace.
³¹ All these trust to their hands:
   and every one is wise in his work.
³² Without these cannot a city be inhabited:
   and they shall not dwell where they will, nor go up and down.
³³ They shall not be sought for in public counsel,
   nor sit high in the congregation:
   they shall not sit on the judges' seat,
   nor understand the sentence of judgement:
   they cannot declare justice and judgement,
   and they shall not be found where parables are spoken.
³⁴ But they will maintain the state of the world,
   and all their desire is in the work of their craft.

39

But he that giveth his mind to the law of the most High,
and is occupied in the meditation thereof,
will seek out the wisdom of all the ancient,
and be occupied in prophecies.
² He will keep the sayings of the renowned men:
   and where subtle parables are, he will be there also.
³ He will seek out the secrets of grave sentences,
   and be conversant in dark parables.
⁴ He shall serve among great men, and appear before princes:
   he will travel through strange countries,
   for he hath tried the good and the evil among men.
⁵ He will give his heart to resort early to the Lord that made him,

and will pray before the most High,
and will open his mouth in prayer,
and make supplication for his sins.

⁶ When the great Lord will, he shall be filled with the spirit of
  understanding:
he shall pour out wise sentences,
and give thanks unto the Lord in his prayer.

⁷ He shall direct his counsel and knowledge,
and in his secrets shall he meditate.

⁸ He shall show forth that which he hath learned,
and shall glory in the law of the covenant of the Lord.

⁹ Many shall commend his understanding,
and so long as the world endureth, it shall not be blotted out;
his memorial shall not depart away,
and his name shall live from generation to generation.

¹⁰ Nations shall show forth his wisdom,
and the congregation shall declare his praise.

¹¹ If he die, he shall leave a greater name than a thousand:
and if he live, he shall increase it.

¹² Yet have I more to say, which I have thought upon,
for I am filled as the moon at the full.

¹³ Hearken unto me, ye holy children,
and bud forth as a rose growing by the brook of the field:

¹⁴ and give ye a sweet savour as frankincense,
and flourish as a lily,
send forth a smell, and sing a song of praise,
bless the Lord in all his works.

¹⁵ Magnify his name, and show forth his praise
with the songs of your lips, and with harps,
and in praising him you shall say after this manner:

¹⁶ 'All the works of the Lord are exceeding good,
and whatsoever he commandeth shall be accomplished in due
  season'.

¹⁷ And none may say, 'What is this? wherefore is that?'
for at time convenient they shall all be sought out:
at his commandment the waters stood as a heap,
and at the words of his mouth the receptacles of waters.

¹⁸ At his commandment is done whatsoever pleaseth him,
and none can hinder, when he will save.

¹⁹ The works of all flesh are before him,
and nothing can be hid from his eyes.

²⁰ He seeth from everlasting to everlasting,
and there is nothing wonderful before him.

²¹ A man need not to say, 'What is this? wherefore is that?'
for he hath made all things for their uses.

²² His blessing covered the dry land as a river,
and watered it as a flood.

²³ As he hath turned the waters into saltness:
so shall the heathen inherit his wrath.
²⁴ As his ways are plain unto the holy,
so are they stumbling-blocks unto the wicked.

²⁵ For the good are good things created from the beginning:
so evil things for sinners.
²⁶ The principal things for the whole use of man's life are
water, fire, iron, and salt,
flour of wheat, honey, milk, and the blood of the grape,
and oil, and clothing.
²⁷ All these things are for good to the godly:
so to the sinners they are turned into evil.

²⁸ There be spirits that are created for vengeance,
which in their fury lay on sore strokes;
in the time of destruction they pour out their force,
and appease the wrath of him that made them.
²⁹ Fire, and hail, and famine, and death:
all these were created for vengeance:
³⁰ teeth of wild beasts, and scorpions,
serpents, and the sword,
punishing the wicked to destruction.
³¹ They shall rejoice in his commandment,
and they shall be ready upon earth when need is;
and when their time is come, they shall not transgress his word.

³² Therefore from the beginning I was resolved,
and thought upon these things, and have left them in writing.
³³ All the works of the Lord are good:
and he will give every needful thing in due season.
³⁴ So that a man cannot say, 'This is worse than that':
for in time they shall all be well approved.
³⁵ And therefore praise ye the Lord with the whole heart and
mouth,
and bless the name of the Lord.

40 Great travail is created for every man,
and a heavy yoke is upon the sons of Adam,
from the day that they go out of their mother's womb,
till the day that they return to the mother of all things.
² Their imagination of things to come, and the day of death,
trouble their thoughts, and cause fear of heart:
³ from him that sitteth on a throne of glory,
unto him that is humbled in earth and ashes;
⁴ from him that weareth purple and a crown,
unto him that is clothed with a linen frock.
⁵ Wrath, and envy, trouble, and unquietness,

fear of death, and anger, and strife,
and in the time of rest upon his bed
his night sleep do change his knowledge.
⁶ A little or nothing is his rest, and afterward he is in his sleep,
as in a day of keeping watch, troubled in the vision of his heart,
as if he were escaped out of a battle.
⁷ When all is safe, he awaketh,
and marvelleth that the fear was nothing.

⁸ Such things happen unto all flesh, both man and beast,
and that is sevenfold more upon sinners.
⁹ Death, and bloodshed, strife, and sword,
calamities, famine, tribulation, and the scourge:
¹⁰ these things are created for the wicked,
and for their sakes came the flood.
¹¹ All things that are of the earth shall turn to the earth again:
and that which is of the waters doth return into the sea.

¹² All bribery and injustice shall be blotted out:
but true dealing shall endure for ever.
¹³ The goods of the unjust shall be dried up like a river,
and shall vanish with noise, like a great thunder in rain.
¹⁴ While he openeth his hand he shall rejoice:
so shall transgressors come to nought.
¹⁵ The children of the ungodly shall not bring forth many
branches:
but are as unclean roots upon a hard rock.
¹⁶ The weed growing upon every water and bank of a river
shall be pulled up before all grass.
¹⁷ Bountifulness is as a most fruitful garden,
and mercifulness endureth for ever.

¹⁸ To labour and to be content with that a man hath, is a sweet life:
but he that findeth a treasure is above them both.
¹⁹ Children and the building of a city continue a man's name:
but a blameless wife is counted above them both.
²⁰ Wine and music rejoice the heart:
but the love of wisdom is above them both.
²¹ The pipe and the psaltery make sweet melody:
but a pleasant tongue is above them both.
²² Thy eye desireth favour and beauty:
but more than both, corn while it is green.
²³ A friend and companion never meet amiss:
but above both is a wife with her husband.
²⁴ Brethren and help are against time of trouble:
but alms shall deliver more than them both.
²⁵ Gold and silver make the foot stand sure:
but counsel is esteemed above them both.

²⁶ Riches and strength lift up the heart:
  but the fear of the Lord is above them both:
  there is no want in the fear of the Lord,
  and it needeth not to seek help.
²⁷ The fear of the Lord is a fruitful garden,
  and covereth him above all glory.

²⁸ My son, lead not a beggar's life:
  for better it is to die than to beg.
²⁹ The life of him that dependeth on another man's table is not to
    be counted for a life:
  for he polluteth himself with other men's meat:
  but a wise man well nurtured will beware thereof.
³⁰ Begging is sweet in the mouth of the shameless:
  but in his belly there shall burn a fire.

41 O death, how bitter is the remembrance of thee
  to a man that liveth at rest in his possessions,
  unto the man that hath nothing to vex him,
  and that hath prosperity in all things:
  yea unto him that is yet able to receive meat!
² O death, acceptable is thy sentence unto the needy,
  and unto him whose strength faileth,
  that is now in the last age, and is vexed with all things,
  and to him that despaireth, and hath lost patience.
³ Fear not the sentence of death,
  remember them that have been before thee, and that come
    after,
  for this is the sentence of the Lord over all flesh.
⁴ And why art thou against the pleasure of the most High?
  there is no inquisition in the grave,
  whether thou have lived ten, or a hundred, or a thousand years.

⁵ The children of sinners are abominable children,
  and they that are conversant in the dwelling of the ungodly.
⁶ The inheritance of sinners' children shall perish,
  and their posterity shall have a perpetual reproach.
⁷ The children will complain of an ungodly father,
  because they shall be reproached for his sake.

⁸ Woe be unto you, ungodly men, which have forsaken the law of
    the most high God:
  for if you increase, it shall be to your destruction.
⁹ And if you be born, you shall be born to a curse:
  and if you die, a curse shall be your portion.
¹⁰ All that are of the earth shall turn to earth again:
  so the ungodly shall go from a curse to destruction.

¹¹ The mourning of men is about their bodies:
but an ill name of sinners shall be blotted out.
¹² Have regard to thy name:
for that shall continue with thee above a thousand great
treasures of gold.
¹³ A good life hath but few days:
but a good name endureth for ever.

¹⁴ My children, keep discipline in peace:
for wisdom that is hid, and a treasure that is not seen,
what profit is in them both?
¹⁵ A man that hideth his foolishness
is better than a man that hideth his wisdom.
¹⁶ Therefore be shamefast according to my word:
for it is not good to retain all shamefastness,
neither is it altogether approved in everything.
¹⁷ Be ashamed of whoredom before father and mother,
and of a lie before a prince and a mighty man;
¹⁸ of an offence before a judge and ruler,
of iniquity before a congregation and people,
of unjust dealing before thy partner and friend;
¹⁹ and of theft in regard of the place where thou sojournest,
and in regard of the truth of God and his covenant;
and to lean with thy elbow upon the meat;
and of scorning to give and take;
²⁰ and of silence before them that salute thee;
and to look upon a harlot;
²¹ and to turn away thy face from thy kinsman;
or to take away a portion or a gift;
or to gaze upon another man's wife;
²² or to be overbusy with his maid, and come not near her bed;
or of upbraiding speeches before friends;
and after thou hast given, upbraid not;
²³ or of iterating and speaking again that which thou hast heard;
and of revealing of secrets.
²⁴ So shalt thou be truly shamefast,
and find favour before all men.

42 Of these things be not thou ashamed,
and accept no person to sin thereby:
² of the law of the most High, and his covenant;
and of judgement to justify the ungodly;
³ of reckoning with thy partners and travellers;
or of the gift of the heritage of friends;
⁴ of exactness of balance and weights;
or of getting much or little;
⁵ and of merchants' indifferent selling;
of much correction of children;

and to make the side of an evil servant to bleed.
⁶ Sure keeping is good, where an evil wife is;
and shut up where many hands are.
⁷ Deliver all things in number and weight,
and put all in writing that thou givest out, or receivest in.
⁸ Be not ashamed to inform the unwise and foolish,
and the extreme aged that contendeth with those that are young:
thus shalt thou be truly learned,
and approved of all men living.

⁹ The father waketh for the daughter, when no man knoweth,
and the care for her taketh away sleep;
when she is young, lest she pass away the flower of her age;
and being married, lest she should be hated;
¹⁰ in her virginity, lest she should be defiled
and gotten with child in her father's house;
and having a husband, lest she should misbehave herself;
and when she is married, lest she should be barren.
¹¹ Keep a sure watch over a shameless daughter,
lest she make thee a laughing-stock to thy enemies,
and a byword in the city,
and a reproach among the people,
and make thee ashamed before the multitude.

¹² Behold not everybody's beauty,
and sit not in the midst of women.
¹³ For from garments cometh a moth,
and from women wickedness.
¹⁴ Better is the churlishness of a man than a courteous woman,
a woman, I say, which bringeth shame and reproach.

¹⁵ I will now remember the works of the Lord,
and declare the things that I have seen:
in the words of the Lord are his works.
¹⁶ The sun that giveth light looketh upon all things,
and the work thereof is full of the glory of the Lord.
¹⁷ The Lord hath not given power to the saints to declare all his
marvellous works,
which the Almighty Lord firmly settled,
that whatsoever is might be established for his glory.
¹⁸ He seeketh out the deep, and the heart,
and considereth their crafty devices:
for the Lord knoweth all that may be known,
and he beholdeth the signs of the world.
¹⁹ He declareth the things that are past, and for to come,
and revealeth the steps of hidden things.
²⁰ No thought escapeth him,
neither any word is hidden from him.

²¹ He hath garnished the excellent works of his wisdom,
and he is from everlasting to everlasting:
unto him may nothing be added, neither can he be diminished,
and he hath no need of any counsellor.
²² O how desirable are all his works:
and that a man may see even to a spark.
²³ All these things live and remain for ever for all uses,
and they are all obedient.
²⁴ All things are double one against another:
and he hath made nothing imperfect.
²⁵ One thing establisheth the good of another:
and who shall be filled with beholding his glory?

43 The pride of the height, the clear firmament,
the beauty of heaven, with his glorious show;
² the sun when it appeareth,
declaring at his rising a marvellous instrument,
the work of the most High.
³ At noon it parcheth the country,
and who can abide the burning heat thereof?
⁴ A man blowing a furnace is in works of heat,
but the sun burneth the mountains three times more;
breathing out fiery vapours, and sending forth bright beams,
it dimmeth the eyes.
⁵ Great is the Lord that made it,
and at his commandment it runneth hastily.

⁶ He made the moon also to serve in her season
for a declaration of times, and a sign of the world.
⁷ From the moon is the sign of feasts,
a light that decreaseth in her perfection.
⁸ The month is called after her name,
increasing wonderfully in her changing,
being an instrument of the armies above,
shining in the firmament of heaven,
⁹ the beauty of heaven, the glory of the stars,
an ornament giving light in the highest places of the Lord.
¹⁰ At the commandment of the Holy One
they will stand in their order,
and never faint in their watches.

¹¹ Look upon the rainbow, and praise him that made it;
very beautiful it is in the brightness thereof.
¹² It compasseth the heaven about with a glorious circle,
and the hands of the most High have bent it.

¹³ By his commandment he maketh the snow to fall apace,
and sendeth swiftly the lightnings of his judgement.

¹⁴ Through this the treasures are opened,
and clouds fly forth as fowls.
¹⁵ By his great power he maketh the clouds firm,
and the hailstones are broken small.
¹⁶ At his sight the mountains are shaken,
and at his will the south wind bloweth.
¹⁷ The noise of the thunder maketh the earth to tremble:
so doth the northern storm and the whirlwind:
as birds flying he scattereth the snow,
and the falling down thereof is as the lighting of grasshoppers:
¹⁸ the eye marvelleth at the beauty of the whiteness thereof,
and the heart is astonished at the raining of it.
¹⁹ The hoar frost also as salt he poureth on the earth,
and being congealed, it lieth on the top of sharp stakes.
²⁰ When the cold north wind bloweth, and the water is congealed
into ice,
it abideth upon every gathering together of water,
and clotheth the water as with a breastplate.
²¹ It devoureth the mountains, and burneth the wilderness,
and consumeth the grass as fire.
²² A present remedy of all is a mist coming speedily:
a dew coming after heat refresheth.

²³ By his counsel he appeaseth the deep,
and planteth islands therein.
²⁴ They that sail on the sea tell of the danger thereof,
and when we hear it with our ears, we marvel thereat.
²⁵ For therein be strange and wondrous works,
variety of all kinds of beasts and whales created.
²⁶ By him the end of them hath prosperous success,
and by his word all things consist.

²⁷ We may speak much, and yet come short;
wherefore in sum, he is all.
²⁸ How shall we be able to magnify him?
for he is great above all his works.
²⁹ The Lord is terrible and very great,
and marvellous is his power.
³⁰ When you glorify the Lord, exalt him as much as you can:
for even yet will he far exceed:
and when you exalt him, put forth all your strength,
and be not weary: for you can never go far enough.
³¹ Who hath seen him, that he might tell us?
and who can magnify him as he is?
³² There are yet hid greater things than these be,
for we have seen but a few of his works.
³³ For the Lord hath made all things,
and to the godly hath he given wisdom.

44 Let us now praise famous men,
and our fathers that begot us.

[2] The Lord hath wrought great glory by them
through his great power from the beginning.

[3] Such as did bear rule in their kingdoms,
men renowned for their power,
giving counsel by their understanding,
and declaring prophecies:

[4] leaders of the people by their counsels,
and by their knowledge of learning meet for the people,
wise and eloquent in their instructions:

[5] such as found out musical tunes,
and recited verses in writing:

[6] rich men furnished with ability,
living peaceably in their habitations:

[7] all these were honoured in their generations,
and were the glory of their times.

[8] There be of them, that have left a name behind them,
that their praises might be reported.

[9] And some there be, which have no memorial,
who are perished, as though they had never been,
and are become as though they had never been born,
and their children after them.

[10] But these were merciful men,
whose righteousness hath not been forgotten.

[11] With their seed shall continually remain a good inheritance,
and their children are within the covenant.

[12] Their seed stands fast,
and their children for their sakes.

[13] Their seed shall remain for ever,
and their glory shall not be blotted out.

[14] Their bodies are buried in peace,
but their name liveth for evermore.

[15] The people will tell of their wisdom,
and the congregation will show forth their praise.

[16] Enoch pleased the Lord, and was translated,
being an example of repentance to all generations.

[17] Noah was found perfect and righteous;
in the time of wrath he was taken in exchange for the world;
therefore was he left as a remnant unto the earth, when the
flood came.

[18] An everlasting covenant was made with him,
that all flesh should perish no more by the flood.

[19] Abraham was a great father of many people:
in glory was there none like unto him:

²⁰ who kept the law of the most High,
and was in covenant with him:
he established the covenant in his flesh,
and when he was proved, he was found faithful.
²¹ Therefore he assured him by an oath, that he would bless the
nations in his seed,
and that he would multiply him as the dust of the earth,
and exalt his seed as the stars,
and cause them to inherit from sea to sea,
and from the river unto the utmost part of the land.

²² With Isaac did he establish likewise for Abraham his father's sake
the blessing of all men, and the covenant,
²³ and made it rest upon the head of Jacob.
He acknowledged him in his blessing,
and gave him a heritage, and divided his portions;
among the twelve tribes did he part them.

45

And he brought out of him a merciful man,
which found favour in the sight of all flesh,
even Moses, beloved of God and men,
whose memorial is blessed.
² He made him like to the glorious saints, and magnified him,
so that his enemies stood in fear of him.
³ By his words he caused the wonders to cease,
and he made him glorious in the sight of kings,
and gave him a commandment for his people,
and showed him part of his glory.
⁴ He sanctified him in his faithfulness and meekness,
and chose him out of all men.
⁵ He made him to hear his voice,
and brought him into the dark cloud,
and gave him commandments before his face,
even the law of life and knowledge,
that he might teach Jacob his covenants,
and Israel his judgements.

⁶ He exalted Aaron, a holy man like unto him,
even his brother, of the tribe of Levi.
⁷ An everlasting covenant he made with him,
and gave him the priesthood among the people,
he beautified him with comely ornaments,
and clothed him with a robe of glory.
⁸ He put upon him perfect glory:
and strengthened him with rich garments,
with breeches, with a long robe, and the ephod.
⁹ And he compassed him with pomegranates,
and with many golden bells round about,

that as he went there might be a sound,
and a noise made that might be heard in the temple,
for a memorial to the children of his people;
¹⁰ with a holy garment, with gold, and blue silk,
and purple, the work of the embroiderer,
with a breastplate of judgement,
and with Urim and Thummim;
¹¹ with twisted scarlet, the work of the cunning workman,
with precious stones graven like seals, and set in gold,
the work of the jeweller,
with a writing engraved for a memorial,
after the number of the tribes of Israel.
¹² He set a crown of gold upon the mitre,
wherein was engraved holiness,
an ornament of honour, a costly work,
the desires of the eyes, goodly and beautiful.
¹³ Before him there were none such,
neither did ever any stranger put them on,
but only his children and his children's children perpetually.
¹⁴ Their sacrifices shall be wholly consumed
every day twice continually.

¹⁵ Moses consecrated him, and anointed him with holy oil:
this was appointed unto him by an everlasting covenant,
and to his seed so long as the heavens should remain,
that they should minister unto him, and execute the office of
    the priesthood,
and bless the people in his name.
¹⁶ He chose him out of all men living to offer sacrifices to the Lord,
incense, and a sweet savour, for a memorial,
to make reconciliation for his people.
¹⁷ He gave unto him his commandments,
and authority in the statutes of judgements,
that he should teach Jacob the testimonies,
and inform Israel in his laws.

¹⁸ Strangers conspired together against him,
and maligned him in the wilderness,
even the men that were of Dathan's and Abiron's side,
and the congregation of Core, with fury and wrath.
¹⁹ This the Lord saw, and it displeased him,
and in his wrathful indignation were they consumed:
he did wonders upon them,
to consume them with the fiery flame.
²⁰ But he made Aaron more honourable,
and gave him a heritage,
and divided unto him the first-fruits of the increase;
especially he prepared bread in abundance:

21 for they eat of the sacrifices of the Lord,
  which he gave unto him and his seed.
22 Howbeit in the land of the people he had no inheritance,
  neither had he any portion among the people:
  for the Lord himself is his portion and inheritance.

23 The third in glory is Phinees the son of Eleazar,
  because he had zeal in the fear of the Lord,
  and stood up with good courage of heart when the people were
    turned back,
  and made reconciliation for Israel.
24 Therefore was there a covenant of peace made with him,
  that he should be the chief of the sanctuary and of his people,
  and that he and his posterity should have the dignity of the
    priesthood for ever.

25 According to the covenant made with David son of Jesse, of the
    tribe of Juda,
  that the inheritance of the king should be to his posterity alone:
  so the inheritance of Aaron should also be unto his seed.
26 God give you wisdom in your heart to judge his people in
    righteousness,
  that their good things be not abolished,
  and that their glory may endure for ever.

46 Jesus the son of Nave was valiant in the wars,
  and was the successor of Moses in prophecies,
  who according to his name was made great for the saving of the
    elect of God,
  and taking vengeance of the enemies that rose up against them,
  that he might set Israel in their inheritance.
2 How great glory got he, when he did lift up his hands,
  and stretched out his sword against the cities!
3 Who before him so stood to it?
  for the Lord himself brought his enemies unto him.
4 Did not the sun go back by his means?
  and was not one day as long as two?
5 He called upon the most high Lord,
  when the enemies pressed upon him on every side,
  and the great Lord heard him.
6 And with hailstones of mighty power
  he made the battle to fall violently upon the nations,
  and in the descent of Beth-horon he destroyed them that
    resisted,
  that the nations might know all their strength,
  because he fought in the sight of the Lord,
  and he followed the Mighty One.

⁷ In the time of Moses also he did a work of mercy,
 he and Caleb the son of Jephunne,
 in that they withstood the congregation,
 and withheld the people from sin,
 and appeased the wicked murmuring.
⁸ And of six hundred thousand people on foot,
 they two were preserved to bring them into the heritage,
 even unto the land that floweth with milk and honey.
⁹ The Lord gave strength also unto Caleb,
 which remained with him unto his old age,
 so that he entered upon the high places of the land,
 and his seed obtained it for a heritage:
¹⁰ that all the children of Israel might see
 that it is good to follow the Lord.

¹¹ And concerning the judges, every one by name,
 whose heart went not a-whoring, nor departed from the Lord,
 let their memory be blessed.
¹² Let their bones flourish out of their place,
 and let the name of them that were honoured be continued
  upon their children.

¹³ Samuel the prophet of the Lord, beloved of his Lord,
 established a kingdom, and anointed princes over his people.
¹⁴ By the law of the Lord he judged the congregation,
 and the Lord had respect unto Jacob.
¹⁵ By his faithfulness he was found a true prophet,
 and by his word he was known to be faithful in vision.
¹⁶ He called upon the mighty Lord,
 when his enemies pressed upon him on every side,
 when he offered the sucking lamb.
¹⁷ And the Lord thundered from heaven,
 and with a great noise made his voice to be heard.
¹⁸ And he destroyed the rulers of the Tyrians,
 and all the princes of the Philistines.
¹⁹ And before his long sleep he made protestations
 in the sight of the Lord and his anointed,
 'I have not taken any man's goods, so much as a shoe':
 and no man did accuse him.
²⁰ And after his death he prophesied, and showed the king his end,
 and lifted up his voice from the earth in prophecy,
 to blot out the wickedness of the people.

47

And after him rose up Nathan to prophesy in the time of
 David.

² As is the fat taken away from the peace offering,
 so was David chosen out of the children of Israel.
³ He played with lions as with kids,

and with bears as with lambs.

⁴ Slew he not a giant, when he was yet but young?
and did he not take away reproach from the people,
when he lifted up his hand with the stone in the sling,
and beat down the boasting of Goliath?

⁵ For he called upon the most high Lord,
and he gave him strength in his right hand to slay that mighty
warrior,
and set up the horn of his people:

⁶ so the people honoured him with ten thousands,
and praised him in the blessings of the Lord,
in that he gave him a crown of glory.

⁷ For he destroyed the enemies on every side,
and brought to nought the Philistines his adversaries,
and broke their horn in sunder unto this day.

⁸ In all his works he praised the Holy One most high with words of
glory;
with his whole heart he sang songs,
and loved him that made him.

⁹ He set singers also before the altar,
that by their voices they might make sweet melody,
and daily sing praises in their songs.

¹⁰ He beautified their feasts,
and set in order the solemn times until the end,
that they might praise his holy name,
and that the temple might sound from morning.

¹¹ The Lord took away his sins, and exalted his horn for ever:
he gave him a covenant of kings,
and a throne of glory in Israel.

¹² After him rose up a wise son,
and for his sake he dwelt at large.

¹³ Solomon reigned in a peaceable time, and was honoured;
for God made all quiet round about him,
that he might build a house in his name,
and prepare his sanctuary for ever.

¹⁴ How wise wast thou in thy youth,
and as a flood filled with understanding.

¹⁵ Thy soul covered the whole earth,
and thou filledst it with dark parables.

¹⁶ Thy name went far unto the islands,
and for thy peace thou wast beloved.

¹⁷ The countries marvelled at thee for thy songs,
and proverbs, and parables, and interpretations.

¹⁸ By the name of the Lord God, which is called the Lord God of
Israel,
thou didst gather gold as tin,
and didst multiply silver as lead.

¹⁹ Thou didst bow thy loins unto women,
  and by thy body thou wast brought into subjection.
²⁰ Thou didst stain thy honour, and pollute thy seed,
  so that thou broughtest wrath upon thy children,
  and wast grieved for thy folly.
²¹ So the kingdom was divided,
  and out of Ephraim ruled a rebellious kingdom.
²² But the Lord will never leave off his mercy,
  neither shall any of his works perish,
  neither will he abolish the posterity of his elect,
  and the seed of him that loveth him he will not take away:
  wherefore he gave a remnant unto Jacob,
  and out of him a root unto David.

²³ Thus rested Solomon with his fathers,
  and of his seed he left behind him Roboam,
  even the foolishness of the people and one that had no
    understanding,
  who turned away the people through his counsel.
  There was also Jeroboam the son of Nabat, who caused Israel to sin,
  and showed Ephraim the way of sin:
²⁴ and their sins were multiplied exceedingly,
  that they were driven out of the land.
²⁵ For they sought out all wickedness,
  till the vengeance came upon them.

48

Then stood up Elias the prophet as fire,
  and his word burnt like a lamp.
² He brought a sore famine upon them,
  and by his zeal he diminished their number.
³ By the word of the Lord he shut up the heaven,
  and also three times brought down fire.
⁴ O Elias, how wast thou honoured in thy wondrous deeds!
  and who may glory like unto thee!
⁵ who didst raise up a dead man from death,
  and his soul from the place of the dead by the word of the most
    High:
⁶ who broughtest kings to destruction,
  and honourable men from their bed:
⁷ who heardest the rebuke of the Lord in Sinai,
  and in Horeb the judgement of vengeance:
⁸ who anointedst kings to take revenge,
  and prophets to succeed after him:
⁹ who wast taken up in a whirlwind of fire,
  and in a chariot of fiery horses:
¹⁰ who wast ordained for reproofs in their times,
  to pacify the wrath of the Lord's judgement before it broke forth
    into fury,

and to turn the heart of the father unto the son,
and to restore the tribes of Jacob.

¹¹ Blessed are they that saw thee, and slept in love,
for we shall surely live.
¹² Elias it was, who was covered with a whirlwind:
and Eliseus was filled with his spirit:
whilst he lived, he was not moved with the presence of any
prince,
neither could any bring him into subjection.
¹³ No word could overcome him,
and after his death his body prophesied.
¹⁴ He did wonders in his life,
and at his death were his works marvellous.

¹⁵ For all this the people repented not,
neither departed they from their sins,
till they were spoiled and carried out of their land,
and were scattered through all the earth:
yet there remained a small people,
and a ruler in the house of David:
¹⁶ of whom some did that which was pleasing to God,
and some multiplied sins.

¹⁷ Ezekias fortified his city,
and brought in water into the midst thereof:
he digged the hard rock with iron,
and made wells for waters.
¹⁸ In his time Sennacherib came up, and sent Rabsaces,
and lifted up his hand against Sion, and boasted proudly.
¹⁹ Then trembled their hearts and hands,
and they were in pain, as women in travail.
²⁰ But they called upon the Lord which is merciful,
and stretched out their hands towards him:
and immediately the Holy One heard them out of heaven,
and delivered them by the ministry of Esay.
²¹ He smote the host of the Assyrians,
and his angel destroyed them.
²² For Ezekias had done the thing that pleased the Lord,
and was strong in the ways of David his father,
as Esay the prophet, who was great and faithful in his vision, had
commanded him.
²³ In his time the sun went backward,
and he lengthened the king's life.
²⁴ He saw by an excellent spirit what should come to pass at the last,
and he comforted them that mourned in Sion.
²⁵ He showed what should come to pass for ever,
and secret things or ever they came.

49

The remembrance of Josias is like the composition of the
perfume that is made by the art of the apothecary:
it is sweet as honey in all mouths,
and as music at a banquet of wine.
² He behaved himself uprightly in the conversion of the people,
and took away the abominations of iniquity.
³ He directed his heart unto the Lord,
and in the time of the ungodly he established the worship of
God.

⁴ All, except David and Ezekias and Josias, were defective:
for they forsook the law of the most High,
even the kings of Juda failed.
⁵ Therefore he gave their power unto others,
and their glory to a strange nation.
⁶ They burnt the chosen city of the sanctuary,
and made the streets desolate
according to the prophecy of Jeremias.
⁷ For they entreated him evil, who nevertheless was a prophet,
sanctified in his mother's womb,
that he might root out and afflict and destroy,
and that he might build up also, and plant.

⁸ It was Ezekiel who saw the glorious vision,
which was shown him upon the chariot of the cherubims.
⁹ For he made mention of the enemies under the figure of the
rain,
and directed them that went right.

¹⁰ And of the twelve prophets let the memorial be blessed,
and let their bones flourish again out of their place:
for they comforted Jacob,
and delivered them by assured hope.

¹¹ How shall we magnify Zorobabel?
even he was as a signet on the right hand.
¹² So was Jesus the son of Josedec:
who in their time built the house and set up a holy temple to the
Lord,
which was prepared for everlasting glory.
¹³ And among the elect was Neemias whose renown is great,
who raised up for us the walls that were fallen,
and set up the gates and the bars,
and raised up our ruins again.

¹⁴ But upon the earth was no man created like Enoch,
for he was taken from the earth.
¹⁵ Neither was there a man born like unto Joseph,

a governor of his brethren, a stay of the people,
whose bones were regarded of the Lord.
¹⁶ Sem and Seth were in great honour among men,
and so was Adam above every living thing in the creation.

50

Simon the high priest, the son of Onias,
who in his life repaired the house again,
and in his days fortified the temple:
² and by him was built from the foundation the double height,
the high fortress of the wall about the temple.
³ In his days the cistern to receive water, being in compass as the
sea, was covered with plates of brass.
⁴ He took care of the temple that it should not fall,
and fortified the city against besieging.
⁵ How was he honoured in the midst of the people
in his coming out of the sanctuary!
⁶ He was as the morning star in the midst of a cloud,
and as the moon at the full:
⁷ as the sun shining upon the temple of the most High,
and as the rainbow giving light in the bright clouds:
⁸ and as the flower of roses in the spring of the year,
as lilies by the rivers of waters,
and as the branches of the frankincense tree in the time of
summer:
⁹ as fire and incense in the censer,
and as a vessel of beaten gold set with all manner of precious
stones:
¹⁰ and as a fair olive tree budding forth fruit,
and as a cypress tree which groweth up to the clouds.

¹¹ When he put on the robe of honour,
and was clothed with the perfection of glory,
when he went up to the holy altar,
he made the garment of holiness honourable.
¹² When he took the portions out of the priests' hands,
he himself stood by the hearth of the altar,
compassed with his brethren round about,
as a young cedar in Libanus;
and as palm trees compassed they him round about.
¹³ So were all the sons of Aaron in their glory,
and the oblations of the Lord in their hands,
before all the congregation of Israel.
¹⁴ And finishing the service at the altar,
that he might adorn the offering of the most high Almighty,
¹⁵ he stretched out his hand to the cup,
and poured of the blood of the grape,
he poured out at the foot of the altar
a sweet-smelling savour unto the most high King of all.

¹⁶ Then shouted the sons of Aaron,
    and sounded the silver trumpets,
    and made a great noise to be heard,
    for a remembrance before the most High.
¹⁷ Then all the people together hasted,
    and fell down to the earth upon their faces
    to worship their Lord God Almighty, the most High.
¹⁸ The singers also sang praises with their voices,
    with great variety of sounds was there made sweet melody.
¹⁹ And the people besought the Lord, the most High,
    by prayer before him that is merciful,
    till the solemnity of the Lord was ended,
    and they had finished his service.
²⁰ Then he went down,
    and lifted up his hands over the whole congregation of the
        children of Israel,
    to give the blessing of the Lord with his lips,
    and to rejoice in his name.
²¹ And they bowed themselves down to worship the second time,
    that they might receive a blessing from the most High.

²² Now therefore bless ye the God of all,
    which only doeth wondrous things everywhere,
    which exalteth our days from the womb,
    and dealeth with us according to his mercy.
²³ He grant us joyfulness of heart,
    and that peace may be in our days in Israel for ever:
²⁴ that he would confirm his mercy with us,
    and deliver us at his time.

²⁵ There be two manner of nations which my heart abhorreth,
    and the third is no nation:
²⁶ they that sit upon the mountain of Samaria,
    and they that dwell amongst the Philistines,
    and that foolish people that dwell in Sichem.

²⁷Jesus the son of Sirach of Jerusalem hath written in this book the instruction of understanding and knowledge, who out of his heart poured forth wisdom.

²⁸ Blessed is he that shall be exercised in these things;
    and he that layeth them up in his heart shall become wise.
²⁹ For if he do them, he shall be strong to all things:
    for the light of the Lord leadeth him,
    who giveth wisdom to the godly.
    Blessed be the Lord for ever. Amen, Amen.

51
A Prayer of Jesus the son of Sirach.

I will thank thee, O Lord and King,
and praise thee, O God my Saviour:
I do give praise unto thy name:
² for thou art my defender and helper,
and hast preserved my body from destruction,
and from the snare of the slanderous tongue,
and from the lips that forge lies,
and hast been my helper against my adversaries:
³ and hast delivered me,
according to the multitude of thy mercies and greatness of thy
    name,
from the teeth of them that were ready to devour me,
and out of the hands of such as sought after my life,
and from the manifold afflictions which I had:
⁴ from the choking of fire on every side,
and from the midst of the fire which I kindled not:
⁵ from the depth of the belly of hell,
from an unclean tongue, and from lying words.
⁶ By an accusation to the king from an unrighteous tongue
my soul drew near even unto death,
my life was near to the hell beneath:
⁷ they compassed me on every side,
and there was no man to help me:
I looked for the succour of men, but there was none:
⁸ then thought I upon thy mercy, O Lord,
and upon thy acts of old,
how thou deliverest such as wait for thee,
and savest them out of the hands of the enemies.
⁹ Then lifted I up my supplication from the earth,
and prayed for deliverance from death.
¹⁰ I called upon the Lord, the Father of my Lord,
that he would not leave me in the days of my trouble,
and in the time of the proud when there was no help.
¹¹ 'I will praise thy name continually,
and will sing praise with thanksgiving',
and so my prayer was heard:
¹² for thou savedst me from destruction,
and deliveredst me from the evil time:
therefore will I give thanks, and praise thee,
and bless thy name, O Lord.

¹³ When I was yet young, or ever I went abroad,
I desired wisdom openly in my prayer.
¹⁴ I prayed for her before the temple,
and will seek her out even to the end.

¹⁵ Even from the flower till the grape was ripe hath my heart
   delighted in her:
   my foot went the right way,
   from my youth up sought I after her.
¹⁶ I bowed down my ear a little, and received her,
   and got much learning.
¹⁷ I profited therein,
   therefore will I ascribe the glory unto him that giveth me
      wisdom:
¹⁸ for I purposed to do after her,
   and earnestly I followed that which is good;
   so shall I not be confounded.
¹⁹ My soul hath wrestled with her,
   and in my doings I was exact:
   I stretched forth my hands to the heaven above,
   and bewailed my ignorances of her.
²⁰ I directed my soul unto her,
   and I found her in pureness:
   I have had my heart joined with her from the beginning,
   therefore shall I not be forsaken.
²¹ My heart was troubled in seeking her:
   therefore have I gotten a good possession.
²² The Lord hath given me a tongue for my reward,
   and I will praise him therewith.

²³ Draw near unto me, you unlearned,
   and dwell in the house of learning.
²⁴ Wherefore are you slow,
   and what say you of these things,
   seeing your souls are very thirsty?
²⁵ I opened my mouth, and said,
   'Buy her for yourselves without money.
²⁶ Put your neck under the yoke,
   and let your soul receive instruction:
   she is hard at hand to find.'
²⁷ Behold with your eyes, how that I have had but little labour,
   and have gotten unto me much rest.
²⁸ Get learning with a great sum of money,
   and get much gold by her.
²⁹ Let your soul rejoice in his mercy,
   and be not ashamed of his praise.
³⁰ Work your work betimes,
   and in his time he will give you your reward.

BARUCH

1 And these are the words of the book, which Baruch the son of Nerias, the son of Maasias, the son of Sedecias, the son of Asadias, the son of Chelcias, wrote in Babylon, [2]in the fifth year, and in the seventh day of the month, what time as the Chaldeans took Jerusalem, and burnt it with fire.

[3]And Baruch did read the words of this book in the hearing of Jechonias the son of Joachim king of Juda, and in the ears of all the people that came to hear the book, [4]and in the hearing of the nobles, and of the kings' sons, and in the hearing of the elders, and of all the people from the lowest unto the highest, even of all them that dwelt at Babylon, by the river Sud. [5]Whereupon they wept, fasted, and prayed before the Lord. [6]They made also a collection of money according to every man's power. [7]And they sent it to Jerusalem unto Joachim the high priest, the son of Chelcias, son of Salom, and to the priests, and to all the people which were found with him at Jerusalem, [8]at the same time when he received the vessels of the house of the Lord that were carried out of the temple, to return them into the land of Juda, the tenth day of the month Sivan, namely, silver vessels, which Sedecias the son of Josias king of Juda had made, [9]after that Nabuchodonosor king of Babylon had carried away Jechonias, and the princes, and the captives, and the mighty men, and the people of the land from Jerusalem, and brought them unto Babylon.

[10]And they said, 'Behold, we have sent you money to buy you burnt offerings, and sin offerings, and incense, and prepare ye manna, and offer upon the altar of the Lord our God, [11]and pray for the life of Nabuchodonosor king of Babylon, and for the life of Balthasar his son, that their days may be upon earth as the days of heaven. [12]And the Lord will give us strength, and lighten our eyes, and we shall live under the shadow of Nabuchodonosor king of Babylon, and under the shadow of Balthasar his son, and we shall serve them many days, and find favour in their sight. [13]Pray for us also unto the Lord our God, for we have sinned against the Lord our God, and unto this day the fury of the Lord and his wrath is not turned from us.

[14]'And ye shall read this book which we have sent unto you, to make confession in the house of the Lord, upon the feasts and solemn days. [15]And ye shall say, "To the Lord our God belongeth righteousness, but unto us the confusion of faces, as it is come to pass this day unto them of Juda, and to the inhabitants of Jerusalem, [16]and to our kings, and to our princes, and to our priests, and to our prophets, and to our fathers. [17]For we have sinned before the Lord, [18]and disobeyed him, and have not hearkened unto the voice of the Lord our God, to walk in the commandments that he gave us openly: [19]since the day that the Lord brought our forefathers out of the land of Egypt, unto this present day, we have been disobedient unto the Lord our God, and we have been

negligent in not hearing his voice. ²⁰Wherefore the evils cleaved unto us, and the curse which the Lord appointed by Moses his servant at the time that he brought our fathers out of the land of Egypt, to give us a land that floweth with milk and honey, like as it is to see this day. ²¹Nevertheless we have not hearkened unto the voice of the Lord our God, according unto all the words of the prophets, whom he sent unto us: ²²but every man followed the imagination of his own wicked heart, to serve strange gods, and to do evil in the sight of the Lord our God.

2 ¹'Therefore the Lord hath made good his word, which he pronounced against us, and against our judges that judged Israel, and against our kings, and against our princes, and against the men of Israel and Juda, ²to bring upon us great plagues, such as never happened under the whole heaven, as it came to pass in Jerusalem, according to the things that were written in the law of Moses, ³that a man should eat the flesh of his own son, and the flesh of his own daughter. ⁴Moreover he hath delivered them to be in subjection to all the kingdoms that are round about us, to be as a reproach and desolation among all the people round about, where the Lord hath scattered them. ⁵Thus we were cast down, and not exalted, because we have sinned against the Lord our God, and have not been obedient unto his voice. ⁶To the Lord our God appertaineth righteousness: but unto us and to our fathers open shame, as appeareth this day. ⁷For all these plagues are come upon us, which the Lord hath pronounced against us. ⁸Yet have we not prayed before the Lord, that we might turn every one from the imaginations of his wicked heart. ⁹Wherefore the Lord watched over us for evil, and the Lord hath brought it upon us: for the Lord is righteous in all his works which he hath commanded us. ¹⁰Yet we have not hearkened unto his voice, to walk in the commandments of the Lord, that he hath set before us.

¹¹'"And now, O Lord God of Israel, that hast brought thy people out of the land of Egypt with a mighty hand, and high arm, and with signs and with wonders, and with great power, and hast gotten thyself a name, as appeareth this day: ¹²O Lord our God, we have sinned, we have done ungodly, we have dealt unrighteously in all thy ordinances. ¹³Let thy wrath turn from us: for we are but a few left among the heathen, where thou hast scattered us. ¹⁴Hear our prayers, O Lord, and our petitions, and deliver us for thy own sake, and give us favour in the sight of them which have led us away: ¹⁵that all the earth may know that thou art the Lord our God, because Israel and his posterity is called by thy name.

¹⁶'"O Lord, look down from thy holy house, and consider us: bow down thy ear, O Lord, to hear us. ¹⁷Open thy eyes, and behold: for the dead that are in the graves, whose souls are taken from their bodies, will give unto the Lord neither praise nor righteousness: ¹⁸but the soul that is greatly vexed, which goeth stooping and feeble, and the eyes that fail, and the hungry soul, will give thee praise and righteousness, O Lord.

¹⁹'"Therefore we do not make our humble supplication before thee,

O Lord our God, for the righteousness of our fathers, and of our kings. [20] For thou hast sent out thy wrath and indignation upon us, as thou hast spoken by thy servants the prophets, saying, [21] 'Thus saith the Lord, "Bow down your shoulders to serve the king of Babylon: so shall ye remain in the land that I gave unto your fathers. [22] But if ye will not hear the voice of the Lord, to serve the king of Babylon, [23] I will cause to cease out of the cities of Juda, and from without Jerusalem, the voice of mirth, and the voice of joy, the voice of the bridegroom, and the voice of the bride: and the whole land shall be desolate of inhabitants."' [24] But we would not hearken unto thy voice, to serve the king of Babylon: therefore hast thou made good the words that thou spokest by thy servants the prophets, namely, that the bones of our kings, and the bones of our fathers, should be taken out of their places. [25] And lo, they are cast out to the heat of the day, and to the frost of the night, and they died in great miseries by famine, by sword, and by pestilence. [26] And the house which is called by thy name hast thou laid waste, as it is to be seen this day, for the wickedness of the house of Israel and the house of Juda.

[27] "'O Lord our God, thou hast dealt with us after all thy goodness, and according to all that great mercy of thine, [28] as thou spokest by thy servant Moses in the day when thou didst command him to write thy law before the children of Israel, saying, [29] 'If ye will not hear my voice, surely this very great multitude shall be turned into a small number among the nations, where I will scatter them. [30] For I knew that they would not hear me, because it is a stiff-necked people: but in the land of their captivities they shall remember themselves, [31] and shall know that I am the Lord their God: for I will give them a heart, and ears to hear. [32] And they shall praise me in the land of their captivity, and think upon my name, [33] and return from their stiff neck, and from their wicked deeds: for they shall remember the way of their fathers, which sinned before the Lord. [34] And I will bring them again into the land which I promised with an oath unto their fathers, Abraham, Isaac, and Jacob, and they shall be lords of it: and I will increase them, and they shall not be diminished. [35] And I will make an everlasting covenant with them to be their God, and they shall be my people: and I will no more drive my people of Israel out of the land that I have given them.'

3 "'O Lord Almighty, God of Israel, the soul in anguish, the troubled spirit crieth unto thee. [2] Hear, O Lord, and have mercy: for thou art merciful, and have pity upon us, because we have sinned before thee. [3] For thou endurest for ever, and we perish utterly. [4] O Lord Almighty, thou God of Israel, hear now the prayers of the dead Israelites, and of their children, which have sinned before thee, and not hearkened unto the voice of thee their God: for the which cause these plagues cleave unto us. [5] Remember not the iniquities of our forefathers: but think upon thy power and thy name now at this time. [6] For thou art the Lord our God, and thee, O Lord, will we praise. [7] And for this cause thou hast put thy fear in our hearts, to the intent that we should call upon thy name, and praise thee in our captivity: for we have called to mind all

the iniquity of our forefathers, that sinned before thee. [8]Behold, we are yet this day in our captivity, where thou hast scattered us, for a reproach and a curse, and to be subject to payments, according to all the iniquities of our fathers, which departed from the Lord our God.'"

[9] Hear, Israel, the commandments of life:
  give ear to understand wisdom.
[10] How happeneth it, Israel, that thou art in thy enemies' land,
  that thou art waxed old in a strange country,
  that thou art defiled with the dead,
[11] that thou art counted with them that go down into the grave?
[12] Thou hast forsaken the fountain of wisdom.
[13] For if thou hadst walked in the way of God,
  thou shouldst have dwelt in peace for ever.
[14] Learn where is wisdom, where is strength, where is
    understanding,
  that thou mayest know also where is length of days, and life,
  where is the light of the eyes, and peace.
[15] Who hath found out her place?
  or who hath come into her treasures?
[16] Where are the princes of the heathen become,
  and such as ruled the beasts upon the earth;
[17] they that had their pastime with the fowls of the air,
  and they that hoarded up silver and gold wherein men trust,
  and made no end of their getting?
[18] For they that wrought in silver, and were so careful,
  and whose works are unsearchable,
[19] they are vanished and gone down to the grave,
  and others are come up in their steads.
[20] Young men have seen light, and dwelt upon the earth:
  but the way of knowledge have they not known,
[21] nor understood the paths thereof, nor laid hold of it:
  their children were far off from that way.
[22] It hath not been heard of in Canaan,
  neither hath it been seen in Theman.
[23] The Agarenes that seek wisdom upon earth,
  the merchants of Merran and of Theman,
  the authors of fables, and searchers out of understanding:
  none of these have known the way of wisdom,
  or remember her paths.

[24] O Israel, how great is the house of God!
  and how large is the place of his possession!
[25] great, and hath no end:
  high, and immeasurable.

[26] There were the giants famous from the beginning,
  that were of so great stature, and so expert in war.

[27] Those did not the Lord choose,
neither gave he the way of knowledge unto them.
[28] But they were destroyed, because they had no wisdom,
and perished through their own foolishness.

[29] Who hath gone up into heaven, and taken her,
and brought her down from the clouds?
[30] Who hath gone over the sea, and found her,
and will bring her for pure gold?
[31] No man knoweth her way, nor thinketh of her path.
[32] But he that knoweth all things knoweth her,
and hath found her out with his understanding:
he that prepared the earth for evermore hath filled it with
fourfooted beasts:
[33] he that sendeth forth light, and it goeth,
calleth it again, and it obeyeth him with fear.
[34] The stars shone in their watches, and rejoiced:
when he calleth them, they say, 'Here we be',
and so with cheerfulness they showed light unto him that made
them.

[35] This is our God,
and there shall no other be accounted of in comparison of him.
[36] He hath found out all the way of knowledge,
and hath given it unto Jacob his servant,
and to Israel his beloved.
[37] Afterward did he show himself upon earth,
and conversed with men.

4 This is the book of the commandments of God,
and the law that endureth for ever:
all they that keep it shall come to life:
but such as leave it shall die.
[2] Turn thee, O Jacob, and take heed of it:
walk in the presence of the light thereof,
that thou mayest be illuminated.
[3] Give not thy honour to another,
nor the things that are profitable unto thee to a strange nation.
[4] O Israel, happy are we:
for things that are pleasing to God are made known unto us.

[5] Be of good cheer, my people, the memorial of Israel.
[6] Ye were sold to the nations, not for your destruction:
but because you moved God to wrath,
ye were delivered unto the enemies.
[7] For ye provoked him that made you
by sacrificing unto devils, and not to God.
[8] Ye have forgotten the everlasting God, that brought you up,

and ye have grieved Jerusalem that nursed you.

⁹ For when she saw the wrath of God coming upon you, she said,
'Hearken, O ye that dwell about Sion:
God hath brought upon me great mourning;

¹⁰ for I saw the captivity of my sons and daughters,
which the Everlasting brought upon them.

¹¹ With joy did I nourish them:
but sent them away with weeping and mourning.

¹² Let no man rejoice over me a widow and forsaken of many,
who for the sins of my children am left desolate:
because they departed from the law of God.

¹³ They knew not his statutes,
nor walked in the ways of his commandments,
nor trod in the paths of discipline in his righteousness.

¹⁴ 'Let them that dwell about Sion come,
and remember ye the captivity of my sons and daughters,
which the Everlasting hath brought upon them.

¹⁵ For he hath brought a nation upon them from far:
a shameless nation, and of a strange language,
who neither reverenced old man, nor pitied child.

¹⁶ These have carried away the dear beloved children of the widow,
and left her that was alone desolate without daughters.

¹⁷ But what can I help you?

¹⁸ For he that brought these plagues upon you
will deliver you from the hands of your enemies.

¹⁹ Go your way, O my children, go your way:
for I am left desolate.

²⁰ I have put off the clothing of peace,
and put upon me the sackcloth of my prayer.
I will cry unto the Everlasting in my days.

²¹ 'Be of good cheer, O my children, cry unto the Lord:
and he shall deliver you from the power and hand of the
enemies.

²² For my hope is in the Everlasting, that he will save you,
and joy is come unto me from the Holy One,
because of the mercy which shall soon come unto you
from the Everlasting our Saviour.

²³ For I sent you out with mourning and weeping:
but God will give you to me again with joy and gladness for ever.

²⁴ Like as now the neighbours of Sion have seen your captivity:
so shall they see shortly your salvation from our God,
which shall come upon you with great glory,
and brightness of the Everlasting.

²⁵ My children, suffer patiently the wrath that is come upon you
from God:
for thy enemy hath persecuted thee:

but shortly thou shalt see his destruction,
and shalt tread upon his neck.

²⁶ My delicate ones have gone rough ways,
and were taken away as a flock caught of the enemies.

²⁷ 'Be of good comfort, O my children, and cry unto God:
for you shall be remembered of him that brought these things
upon you.

²⁸ For as it was your mind to go astray from God:
so, being returned, seek him ten times more.

²⁹ For he that hath brought these plagues upon you
shall bring you everlasting joy again with your salvation.'

³⁰ Take a good heart, O Jerusalem:
for he that gave thee that name will comfort thee.

³¹ Miserable are they that afflicted thee, and rejoiced at thy fall.

³² Miserable are the cities which thy children served:
miserable is she that received thy sons.

³³ For as she rejoiced at thy ruin, and was glad of thy fall:
so shall she be grieved for her own desolation.

³⁴ For I will take away the rejoicing of her great multitude,
and her pride shall be turned into mourning.

³⁵ For fire shall come upon her from the Everlasting, long to
endure:
and she shall be inhabited of devils for a great time.

³⁶ O Jerusalem, look about thee toward the east,
and behold the joy that cometh unto thee from God.

³⁷ Lo, thy sons come, whom thou sentest away:
they come gathered together from the east to the west
by the word of the Holy One, rejoicing in the glory of God.

5 Put off, O Jerusalem, the garment of thy mourning and affliction,
and put on the comeliness of the glory that cometh from God for
ever.

² Cast about thee a double garment of the righteousness which
cometh from God,
and set a diadem on thy head of the glory of the Everlasting.

³ For God will show thy brightness unto every country under
heaven.

⁴ For thy name shall be called of God for ever,
'The peace of righteousness, and the glory of God's worship'.

⁵ Arise, O Jerusalem, and stand on high, and look about toward
the east,
and behold thy children gathered from the west unto the east by
the word of the Holy One,
rejoicing in the remembrance of God.

⁶ For they departed from thee on foot,

and were led away of their enemies:
but God bringeth them unto thee exalted with glory,
as children of the kingdom.
[7] For God hath appointed that every high hill,
and banks of long continuance should be cast down,
and valleys filled up, to make even the ground,
that Israel may go safely in the glory of God.
[8] Moreover even the woods and every sweet-smelling tree
shall overshadow Israel by the commandment of God.
[9] For God shall lead Israel with joy, in the light of his glory,
with the mercy and righteousness that cometh from him.

THE EPISTLE OF JEREMY

6 A copy of an epistle which Jeremy sent unto them which were to be led captives into Babylon by the king of the Babylonians, to certify them, as it was commanded him of God.

[2]Because of the sins which ye have committed before God, ye shall be led away captives unto Babylon by Nabuchodonosor king of the Babylonians. [3]So when ye be come unto Babylon, ye shall remain there many years, and for a long season, namely, seven generations: and after that I will bring you away peaceably from thence.

[4]Now shall ye see in Babylon gods of silver, and of gold, and of wood, borne upon shoulders, which cause the nations to fear. [5]Beware therefore that ye in no wise be like to strangers, neither be ye afraid of them, when ye see the multitude before them and behind them, worshipping them. [6]But say ye in your hearts, 'O Lord, we must worship thee'. [7]For my angel is with you, and I myself caring for your souls.

[8]As for their tongue, it is polished by the workman, and they themselves are gilded and laid over with silver, yet are they but false and cannot speak. [9]And taking gold, as it were for a virgin that loves to go gay, they make crowns for the heads of their gods. [10]Sometimes also the priests convey from their gods gold and silver, and bestow it upon themselves. [11]Yea, they will give thereof to the common harlots, and deck them as men with garments, being gods of silver, and gods of gold, and wood. [12]Yet cannot these gods save themselves from rust and moths, though they be covered with purple raiment. [13]They wipe their faces because of the dust of the temple, when there is much upon them. [14]And he that cannot put to death one that offendeth him holdeth a sceptre as though he were a judge of the country. [15]He hath also in his right hand a dagger and an axe: but cannot deliver himself from war and thieves. [16]Whereby they are known not to be gods: therefore fear them not.

[17]For like as a vessel that a man useth is nothing worth when it is broken; even so it is with their gods: when they be set up in the temple, their eyes be full of dust through the feet of them that come in. [18]And as the doors are made sure on every side

upon him that offendeth the king, as being committed to suffer death: even so the priests make fast their temples with doors, with locks and bars, lest their gods be spoiled with robbers. [19]They light them candles, yea, more than for themselves, whereof they cannot see one. [20]They are as one of the beams of the temple, yet they say their hearts are gnawed upon by things creeping out of the earth; and when they eat them and their clothes, they feel it not. [21]Their faces are blacked through the smoke that comes out of the temple. [22]Upon their bodies and heads sit bats, swallows, and birds, and the cats also. [23]By this you may know that they are no gods: therefore fear them not.

[24]Notwithstanding the gold that is about them to make them beautiful, except they wipe off the rust they will not shine: for neither when they were molten did they feel it. [25]The things wherein there is no breath are bought for a most high price. [26]They are borne upon shoulders, having no feet, whereby they declare unto men that they be nothing worth. [27]They also that serve them are ashamed: for if they fall to the ground at any time, they cannot rise up again of themselves: neither if one set them upright can they move of themselves: neither, if they be bowed down, can they make themselves straight: but they set gifts before them as unto dead men.

[28]As for the things that are sacrificed unto them, their priests sell and abuse: in like manner their wives lay up part thereof in salt: but unto the poor and impotent they give nothing of it. [29]Menstruous women and women in childbed eat their sacrifices: by these things ye may know that they are no gods: fear them not.

[30]For how can they be called gods? because women set meat before the gods of silver, gold, and wood. [31]And the priests sit in their temples, having their clothes rent, and their heads and beards shaven, and nothing upon their heads. [32]They roar and cry before their gods, as men do at the feast when one is dead. [33]The priests also take off their garments, and clothe their wives and children. [34]Whether it be evil that one doeth unto them, or good, they are not able to recompense it: they can neither set up a king, nor put him down. [35]In like manner, they can neither give riches nor money: though a man make a vow unto them, and keep it not, they will not require it. [36]They can save no man from death, neither deliver the weak from the mighty. [37]They cannot restore a blind man to his sight, nor help any man in his distress. [38]They can show no mercy to the widow, nor do good to the fatherless. [39]Their gods of wood, and which are overlaid with gold and silver, are like the stones that be hewn out of the mountain: they that worship them shall be confounded.

[40]How should a man then think and say that they are gods, when even the Chaldeans themselves dishonour them. [41]Who if they shall see one dumb that cannot speak, they bring him, and entreat Bel that he may speak, as though he were able to understand. [42]Yet they cannot understand this themselves, and leave

them: for they have no knowledge. ⁴³The women also with cords about them, sitting in the ways, burn bran for perfume: but if any of them, drawn by some that passeth by, lie with him, she reproacheth her fellow that she was not thought as worthy as herself, nor her cord broken. ⁴⁴Whatsoever is done among them is false: how may it then be thought or said that they are gods?

⁴⁵They are made of carpenters and goldsmiths: they can be nothing else than the workman will have them to be. ⁴⁶And they themselves that made them can never continue long; how should then the things that are made of them be gods? ⁴⁷For they left lies and reproaches to them that come after. ⁴⁸For when there cometh any war or plague upon them, the priests consult with themselves, where they may be hidden with them. ⁴⁹How then cannot men perceive that they be no gods, which can neither save themselves from war nor from plague? ⁵⁰For seeing they be but of wood, and overlaid with silver and gold, it shall be known hereafter that they are false. ⁵¹And it shall manifestly appear to all nations and kings that they are no gods, but the works of men's hands, and that there is no work of God in them. ⁵²Who then may not know that they are no gods?

⁵³For neither can they set up a king in the land, nor give rain unto men. ⁵⁴Neither can they judge their own cause, nor redress a wrong, being unable: for they are as crows between heaven and earth. ⁵⁵Whereupon when fire falleth upon the house of gods of wood, or laid over with gold or silver, their priests will fly away, and escape: but they themselves shall be burnt asunder like beams. ⁵⁶Moreover they cannot withstand any king or enemies: how can it then be thought or said that they be gods?

⁵⁷Neither are those gods of wood, and laid over with silver or gold, able to escape either from thieves or robbers. ⁵⁸Whose gold, and silver, and garments wherewith they are clothed, they that are strong do take, and go away withal: neither are they able to help themselves. ⁵⁹Therefore it is better to be a king that showeth his power, or else a profitable vessel in a house, which the owner shall have use of, than such false gods; or to be a door in a house to keep such things safe as be therein, than such false gods; or a pillar of wood in a palace, than such false gods.

⁶⁰For sun, moon, and stars, being bright, and sent to do their offices, are obedient. ⁶¹In like manner the lightning when it breaketh forth is easy to be seen, and after the same manner the wind bloweth in every country. ⁶²And when God commandeth the clouds to go over the whole world, they do as they are bidden. ⁶³And the fire sent from above to consume hills and woods doeth as it is commanded: but these are like unto them neither in show nor power. ⁶⁴Wherefore it is neither to be supposed nor said that they are gods, seeing they are able neither to judge causes, nor to do good unto men.

⁶⁵Knowing therefore that they are no gods, fear them not.

[66]For they can neither curse nor bless kings: [67]neither can they show signs in the heavens among the heathen, nor shine as the sun, nor give light as the moon. [68]The beasts are better than they: for they can get under a covert, and help themselves.

[69]It is then by no means manifest unto us that they are gods: therefore fear them not. [70]For as a scarecrow in a garden of cucumbers keepeth nothing: so are their gods of wood, and laid over with silver and gold. [71]And likewise their gods of wood, and laid over with silver and gold, are like to a whitethorn in an orchard that every bird sitteth upon: as also to a dead body, that is cast into the dark. [72]And you shall know them to be no gods by the bright purple that rotteth upon them: and they themselves afterward shall be eaten, and shall be a reproach in the country.

[73]Better therefore is the just man that hath no idols: for he shall be far from reproach.

THE SONG OF THE
THREE HOLY CHILDREN

which followeth in the third chapter of DANIEL
after this place, 'fell down bound into the midst
of the burning fiery furnace' (verse 23).
That which followeth is not in the Hebrew,
to wit, 'And they walked' unto these words,
'Then Nebuchadnezzar'—(verse 24).

And they walked in the midst of the fire, praising God, and blessing the Lord. ²Then Azarias stood up and prayed on this manner; and opening his mouth in the midst of the fire, said, ³'Blessed art thou, O Lord God of our fathers: thy name is worthy to be praised and glorified for evermore. ⁴For thou art righteous in all the things that thou hast done to us: yea, true are all thy works, thy ways are right, and all thy judgements truth. ⁵In all the things that thou hast brought upon us, and upon the holy city of our fathers, even Jerusalem, thou hast executed true judgement: for according to truth and judgement didst thou bring all these things upon us because of our sins. ⁶For we have sinned and committed iniquity, departing from thee. ⁷In all things have we trespassed, and not obeyed thy commandments, nor kept them, neither done as thou hast commanded us, that it might go well with us. ⁸Wherefore all that thou hast brought upon us, and everything that thou hast done to us, thou hast done in true judgement. ⁹And thou didst deliver us into the hands of lawless enemies, most hateful forsakers of God, and to an unjust king, and the most wicked in all the world. ¹⁰And now we cannot open our mouths, we are become a shame and reproach to thy servants, and to them that worship thee.

¹¹'Yet deliver us not up wholly, for thy name's sake, neither disannul thou thy covenant: ¹²and cause not thy mercy to depart from us, for thy beloved Abraham's sake, for thy servant Isaac's sake, and for thy holy Israel's sake; ¹³to whom thou hast spoken and promised, that thou wouldst multiply their seed as the stars of heaven, and as the sand that lieth upon the sea-shore. ¹⁴For we, O Lord, are become less than any nation, and be kept under this day in all the world because of our sins. ¹⁵Neither is there at this time prince, or prophet, or leader, or burnt offering, or sacrifice, or oblation, or incense, or place to sacrifice before thee, and to find mercy. ¹⁶Nevertheless in a contrite heart and a humble spirit let us be accepted. ¹⁷Like as in the burnt offering of rams and bullocks, and like as in ten thousands of fat lambs: so let our sacrifice be in thy sight this day, and grant that we may wholly go after thee: for they shall not be confounded that put their trust in thee. ¹⁸And now we follow thee with all our heart, we fear thee, and seek thy face. ¹⁹Put us not to shame: but deal with us after thy loving-kindness, and according to

the multitude of thy mercies. [20]Deliver us also according to thy marvellous works, and give glory to thy name, O Lord: and let all them that do thy servants hurt be ashamed; [21]and let them be confounded in all their power and might, and let their strength be broken; [22]and let them know that thou art Lord, the only God, and glorious over the whole world.'

[23]And the king's servants that put them in, ceased not to make the oven hot with rosin, pitch, tow, and small wood; [24]so that the flame streamed forth above the furnace forty and nine cubits. [25]And it passed through, and burnt those Chaldeans it found about the furnace. [26]But the angel of the Lord came down into the oven together with Azarias and his fellows, and smote the flame of the fire out of the oven: [27]and made the midst of the furnace as it had been a moist whistling wind, so that the fire touched them not at all, neither hurt nor troubled them.

[28]Then the three, as out of one mouth, praised, glorified, and blessed God in the furnace, saying,

[29] 'Blessed art thou, O Lord God of our fathers:
and to be praised and exalted above all for ever.
[30] And blessed is thy glorious and holy name:
and to be praised and exalted above all for ever.
[31] Blessed art thou in the temple of thy holy glory:
and to be praised and glorified above all for ever.
[32] Blessed art thou that beholdest the depths, and sittest upon the
cherubims:
and to be praised and exalted above all for ever.
[33] Blessed art thou on the glorious throne of thy kingdom:
and to be praised and glorified above all for ever.
[34] Blessed art thou in the firmament of heaven:
and above all to be praised and glorified for ever.

[35] 'O all ye works of the Lord, bless ye the Lord:
praise and exalt him above all for ever.
[36] O ye heavens, bless ye the Lord:
praise and exalt him above all for ever.
[37] O ye angels of the Lord, bless ye the Lord:
praise and exalt him above all for ever.
[38] O all ye waters that be above the heaven, bless ye the Lord:
praise and exalt him above all for ever.
[39] O all ye powers of the Lord, bless ye the Lord:
praise and exalt him above all for ever.
[40] O ye sun and moon, bless ye the Lord:
praise and exalt him above all for ever.
[41] O ye stars of heaven, bless ye the Lord:
praise and exalt him above all for ever.
[42] O every shower and dew, bless ye the Lord:
praise and exalt him above all for ever.
[43] O all ye winds, bless ye the Lord:

praise and exalt him above all for ever.
44 O ye fire and heat, bless ye the Lord:
    praise and exalt him above all for ever.
45 O ye winter and summer, bless ye the Lord:
    praise and exalt him above all for ever.
46 O ye dews and storms of snow, bless ye the Lord:
    praise and exalt him above all for ever.
47 O ye nights and days, bless ye the Lord:
    praise and exalt him above all for ever.
48 O ye light and darkness, bless ye the Lord:
    praise and exalt him above all for ever.
49 O ye ice and cold, bless ye the Lord:
    praise and exalt him above all for ever.
50 O ye frost and snow, bless ye the Lord:
    praise and exalt him above all for ever.
51 O ye lightnings and clouds, bless ye the Lord:
    praise and exalt him above all for ever.
52 O let the earth bless the Lord:
    praise and exalt him above all for ever.
53 O ye mountains and little hills, bless ye the Lord:
    praise and exalt him above all for ever.
54 O all ye things that grow on the earth, bless ye the Lord:
    praise and exalt him above all for ever.
55 O ye fountains, bless ye the Lord:
    praise and exalt him above all for ever.
56 O ye seas and rivers, bless ye the Lord:
    praise and exalt him above all for ever.
57 O ye whales, and all that move in the waters, bless ye the
    Lord:
    praise and exalt him above all for ever.
58 O all ye fowls of the air, bless ye the Lord:
    praise and exalt him above all for ever.
59 O all ye beasts and cattle, bless ye the Lord:
    praise and exalt him above all for ever.

60 'O ye children of men, bless ye the Lord:
    praise and exalt him above all for ever.
61 O Israel, bless ye the Lord:
    praise and exalt him above all for ever.
62 O ye priests of the Lord, bless ye the Lord:
    praise and exalt him above all for ever.
63 O ye servants of the Lord, bless ye the Lord:
    praise and exalt him above all for ever.
64 O ye spirits and souls of the righteous, bless ye the Lord:
    praise and exalt him above all for ever.
65 O ye holy and humble men of heart, bless ye the Lord:
    praise and exalt him above all for ever.

⁶⁶ 'O Ananias, Azarias, and Misael, bless ye the Lord:
 praise and exalt him above all for ever:
  for he hath delivered us from hell, and saved us from the hand of
   death,
  and delivered us out of the midst of the furnace and burning
   flame:
  even out of the midst of the fire hath he delivered us.

⁶⁷ 'O give thanks unto the Lord, because he is gracious:
 for his mercy endureth for ever:
⁶⁸ O all ye that worship the Lord, bless the God of gods,
 praise him, and give him thanks:
  for his mercy endureth for ever.'

THE HISTORY OF
SUSANNA

set apart from the beginning of DANIEL, because it is not in Hebrew, as neither the narration of BEL AND THE DRAGON.

There dwelt a man in Babylon, called Joacim. ²And he took a wife, whose name was Susanna, the daughter of Chelcias, a very fair woman, and one that feared the Lord. ³Her parents also were righteous, and taught their daughter according to the law of Moses. ⁴Now Joacim was a great rich man, and had a fair garden joining unto his house, and to him resorted the Jews: because he was more honourable than all others.

⁵The same year were appointed two of the ancients of the people to be judges, such as the Lord spoke of, that wickedness came from Babylon from ancient judges, who seemed to govern the people. ⁶These kept much at Joacim's house: and all that had any suits in law came unto them.

⁷Now when the people departed away at noon, Susanna went into her husband's garden to walk. ⁸And the two elders saw her going in every day, and walking: so that their lust was inflamed toward her. ⁹And they perverted their own mind, and turned away their eyes, that they might not look unto heaven, nor remember just judgements. ¹⁰And albeit they both were wounded with her love, yet durst not one show another his grief. ¹¹For they were ashamed to declare their lust, that they desired to have to do with her. ¹²Yet they watched diligently from day to day to see her.

¹³And the one said to the other, 'Let us now go home: for it is dinner time'. ¹⁴So when they were gone out, they parted the one from the other, and turning back again they came to the same place; and after that they had asked one another the cause, they acknowledged their lust: then appointed they a time both together, when they might find her alone. ¹⁵And it fell out, as they watched a fit time, she went in as before with two maids only, and she was desirous to wash herself in the garden: for it was hot. ¹⁶And there was nobody there save the two elders, that had hid themselves, and watched her. ¹⁷Then she said to her maids, 'Bring me oil and washing balls, and shut the garden doors, that I may wash me'. ¹⁸And they did as she bade them, and shut the garden doors, and went out themselves at privy doors to fetch the things that she had commanded them: but they saw not the elders, because they were hid.

¹⁹Now when the maids were gone forth, the two elders rose up, and ran unto her, saying, ²⁰'Behold, the garden doors are shut, that no man can see us, and we are in love with thee; therefore consent unto us, and lie with us. ²¹If thou wilt not, we will bear witness against thee, that a young man was with thee: and therefore thou didst send away thy

maids from thee.' ²²Then Susanna sighed, and said, 'I am straited on every side: for if I do this thing, it is death unto me: and if I do it not, I cannot escape your hands. ²³It is better for me to fall into your hands, and not do it, than to sin in the sight of the Lord.' ²⁴With that Susanna cried with a loud voice: and the two elders cried out against her. ²⁵Then ran the one, and opened the garden door. ²⁶So when the servants of the house heard the cry in the garden, they rushed in at a privy door, to see what was done unto her. ²⁷But when the elders had declared their matter, the servants were greatly ashamed: for there was never such a report made of Susanna.

²⁸And it came to pass the next day, when the people were assembled to her husband Joacim, the two elders came also full of mischievous imagination against Susanna to put her to death, ²⁹and said before the people, 'Send for Susanna, the daughter of Chelcias, Joacim's wife'. And so they sent. ³⁰So she came with her father and mother, her children and all her kindred. ³¹Now Susanna was a very delicate woman, and beauteous to behold. ³²And these wicked men commanded to uncover her face (for she was covered), that they might be filled with her beauty. ³³Therefore her friends and all that saw her wept.

³⁴Then the two elders stood up in the midst of the people, and laid their hands upon her head. ³⁵And she weeping looked up towards heaven: for her heart trusted in the Lord. ³⁶And the elders said, 'As we walked in the garden alone, this woman came in with two maids, and shut the garden doors, and sent the maids away. ³⁷Then a young man, who there was hid, came unto her, and lay with her. ³⁸Then we that stood in a corner of the garden, seeing this wickedness, ran unto them. ³⁹And when we saw them together, the man we could not hold: for he was stronger than we, and opened the door, and leapt out. ⁴⁰But having taken this woman, we asked who the young man was, but she would not tell us: these things do we testify.'

⁴¹Then the assembly believed them, as those that were the elders and judges of the people: so they condemned her to death. ⁴²Then Susanna cried out with a loud voice and said, 'O everlasting God, that knowest the secrets, and knowest all things before they be: ⁴³thou knowest that they have borne false witness against me, and behold, I must die: whereas I never did such things as these men have maliciously invented against me'.

⁴⁴And the Lord heard her voice. ⁴⁵Therefore when she was led to be put to death, the Lord raised up the holy spirit of a young youth, whose name was Daniel, ⁴⁶who cried with a loud voice, 'I am clear from the blood of this woman'. ⁴⁷Then all the people turned them towards him, and said, 'What mean these words that thou hast spoken?' ⁴⁸So he standing in the midst of them, said, 'Are ye such fools, ye sons of Israel, that without examination or knowledge of the truth ye have condemned a daughter of Israel? ⁴⁹Return again to the place of judgement: for they have borne false witness against her.'

⁵⁰Wherefore all the people turned again in haste, and the elders said unto him, 'Come sit down among us, and show it us, seeing God hath

given thee the honour of an elder'. [51]Then said Daniel unto them, 'Put these two aside one far from another, and I will examine them'. [52]So when they were put asunder one from another, he called one of them, and said unto him, 'O thou that art waxed old in wickedness, now thy sins which thou hast committed aforetime are come to light. [53]For thou hast pronounced false judgement, and hast condemned the innocent, and hast let the guilty go free, albeit the Lord saith, "The innocent and righteous shalt thou not slay". [54]Now then, if thou hast seen her, tell me, under what tree sawest thou them companying together?' Who answered, 'Under a mastic tree'. [55]And Daniel said, 'Very well: thou hast lied against thy own head: for even now the angel of God hath received the sentence of God to cut thee in two'.

[56]So he put him aside, and commanded to bring the other, and said unto him, 'O thou seed of Canaan, and not of Juda, beauty hath deceived thee, and lust hath perverted thy heart. [57]Thus have ye dealt with the daughters of Israel, and they for fear companied with you: but the daughter of Juda would not abide your wickedness. [58]Now therefore tell me, under what tree didst thou take them companying together?' Who answered, 'Under a holm tree'. [59]Then said Daniel unto him, 'Well: thou hast also lied against thy own head: for the angel of God waiteth with the sword to cut thee in two, that he may destroy you'.

[60]With that all the assembly cried out with a loud voice, and praised God, who saveth them that trust in him. [61]And they arose against the two elders (for Daniel had convicted them of false witness by their own mouth), [62]and according to the law of Moses they did unto them in such sort as they maliciously intended to do to their neighbour: and they put them to death. Thus the innocent blood was saved the same day. [63]Therefore Chelcias and his wife praised God for their daughter Susanna, with Joacim her husband, and all the kindred, because there was no dishonesty found in her.

[64]From that day forth was Daniel had in great reputation in the sight of the people.

THE HISTORY OF THE DESTRUCTION
OF
BEL AND THE DRAGON,
cut off from the end of DANIEL.

Ａnd king Astyages was gathered to his fathers, and Cyrus of Persia received his kingdom. ²And Daniel conversed with the king, and was honoured above all his friends.

³Now the Babylonians had an idol called Bel, and there were spent upon him every day twelve great measures of fine flour, and forty sheep, and six vessels of wine. ⁴And the king worshipped it, and went daily to adore it: but Daniel worshipped his own God. And the king said unto him, 'Why dost not thou worship Bel?' ⁵Who answered and said, 'Because I may not worship idols made with hands, but the living God, who hath created the heaven and the earth, and hath sovereignty over all flesh'. ⁶Then said the king unto him, 'Thinkest thou not that Bel is a living god? seest thou not how much he eateth and drinketh every day?' ⁷Then Daniel smiled, and said, 'O king, be not deceived: for this is but clay within, and brass without, and did never eat or drink anything'.

⁸So the king was wroth, and called for his priests, and said unto them, 'If ye tell me not who this is that devoureth these expenses, ye shall die. ⁹But if ye can certify me that Bel devoureth them, then Daniel shall die: for he hath spoken blasphemy against Bel.' And Daniel said unto the king, 'Let it be according to thy word'. ¹⁰(Now the priests of Bel were threescore and ten, besides their wives and children.) And the king went with Daniel into the temple of Bel. ¹¹So Bel's priests said, 'Lo, we go out: but thou, O king, set on the meat, and make ready the wine, and shut the door fast, and seal it with thy own signet: ¹²and tomorrow when thou comest in, if thou findest not that Bel hath eaten up all, we will suffer death; or else Daniel, that speaketh falsely against us'. ¹³And they little regarded it: for under the table they had made a privy entrance, whereby they entered in continually, and consumed those things.

¹⁴So when they were gone forth, the king set meats before Bel. Now Daniel had commanded his servants to bring ashes, and those they strewed throughout all the temple in the presence of the king alone: then went they out, and shut the door, and sealed it with the king's signet, and so departed. ¹⁵Now in the night came the priests with their wives and children (as they were wont to do), and did eat and drink up all. ¹⁶In the morning betime the king arose, and Daniel with him. ¹⁷And the king said, 'Daniel, are the seals whole?' And he said, 'Yea, O king, they be whole'. ¹⁸And as soon as he had opened the door, the king looked upon the table, and cried with a loud voice, 'Great art thou, O Bel, and with thee is no deceit at all'. ¹⁹Then laughed Daniel, and held

the king that he should not go in, and said, 'Behold now the pavement, and mark well whose footsteps are these'. [20]And the king said, 'I see the footsteps of men, women, and children'. And then the king was angry, [21]and took the priests with their wives and children, who showed him the privy doors, where they came in, and consumed such things as were upon the table. [22]Therefore the king slew them, and delivered Bel into Daniel's power, who destroyed him and his temple.

[23]And in that same place there was a great dragon, which they of Babylon worshipped. [24]And the king said unto Daniel, 'Wilt thou also say that this is of brass? lo, he liveth, he eateth and drinketh; thou canst not say that he is no living god: therefore worship him'. [25]Then said Daniel unto the king, 'I will worship the Lord my God: for he is the living God. [26]But give me leave, O king, and I shall slay this dragon without sword or staff.' The king said, 'I give thee leave'. [27]Then Daniel took pitch, fat, and hair, and did seethe them together, and made lumps thereof: this he put in the dragon's mouth, and so the dragon burst in sunder: and Daniel said, 'Lo, these are the gods you worship'.

[28]When they of Babylon heard that, they took great indignation, and conspired against the king, saying, 'The king is become a Jew, and he hath destroyed Bel, he hath slain the dragon, and put the priests to death'. [29]So they came to the king, and said, 'Deliver us Daniel, or else we will destroy thee and thy house'. [30]Now when the king saw that they pressed him sore, being constrained, he delivered Daniel unto them: [31]who cast him into the lions' den: where he was six days. [32]And in the den there were seven lions, and they had given them every day two carcases, and two sheep: which then were not given to them, to the intent they might devour Daniel.

[33]Now there was in Jewry a prophet called Habacuc, who had made pottage, and had broken bread in a bowl, and was going into the field, for to bring it to the reapers. [34]But the angel of the Lord said unto Habacuc, 'Go, carry the dinner that thou hast into Babylon unto Daniel, who is in the lions' den'. [35]And Habacuc said, 'Lord, I never saw Babylon: neither do I know where the den is'. [36]Then the angel of the Lord took him by the crown, and bore him by the hair of his head, and through the vehemence of his spirit set him in Babylon over the den. [37]And Habacuc cried, saying, 'O Daniel, Daniel, take the dinner which God hath sent thee'. [38]And Daniel said, 'Thou hast remembered me, O God: neither hast thou forsaken them that seek thee and love thee'. [39]So Daniel arose, and did eat: and the angel of the Lord set Habacuc in his own place again immediately.

[40]Upon the seventh day the king went to bewail Daniel: and when he came to the den, he looked in, and behold, Daniel was sitting. [41]Then cried the king with a loud voice, saying, 'Great art thou, O Lord God of Daniel, and there is no other besides thee'. [42]And he drew him out, and cast those that were the cause of his destruction into the den: and they were devoured in a moment before his face.

THE
PRAYER OF MANASSES
KING OF JUDA
WHEN HE WAS HELD CAPTIVE
IN BABYLON

O LORD, Almighty God of our fathers, Abraham, Isaac, and Jacob, and of their righteous seed; who hast made heaven and earth, with all the ornament thereof; who hast bound the sea by the word of thy commandment; who hast shut up the deep, and sealed it by thy terrible and glorious name; whom all men fear, and tremble before thy power: for the majesty of thy glory cannot be borne, and thy angry threatening towards sinners is importable: but thy merciful promise is immeasurable and unsearchable; for thou art the most high Lord, of great compassion, long-suffering, very merciful, and repentest of the evils of men. Thou, O Lord, according to thy great goodness hast promised repentance and forgiveness to them that have sinned against thee: and of thy infinite mercies hast appointed repentance unto sinners, that they may be saved.

Thou therefore, O Lord, that art the God of the just, hast not appointed repentance to the just, as to Abraham, and Isaac, and Jacob, which have not sinned against thee; but thou hast appointed repentance unto me that am a sinner: for I have sinned above the number of the sands of the sea. My transgressions, O Lord, are multiplied: my transgressions are multiplied, and I am not worthy to behold and see the height of heaven for the multitude of my iniquity. I am bowed down with many iron bands, that I cannot lift up my head, neither have any release: for I have provoked thy wrath, and done evil before thee: I did not thy will, neither kept I thy commandments: I have set up abominations, and have multiplied offences.

Now therefore I bow the knee of my heart, beseeching thee of grace. I have sinned, O Lord, I have sinned, and I acknowledge my iniquities, wherefore, I humbly beseech thee, forgive me, O Lord, forgive me, and destroy me not with my iniquities. Be not angry with me for ever, by reserving evil for me, neither condemn me into the lower parts of the earth. For thou art the God, even the God of them that repent: and in me thou wilt show all thy goodness: for thou wilt save me that am unworthy, according to thy great mercy. Therefore I will praise thee for ever all the days of my life: for all the powers of the heavens do praise thee, and thine is the glory for ever and ever. Amen.

THE FIRST BOOK OF THE
MACCABEES

1 And it happened, after that Alexander son of Philip, the Macedonian, who came out of the land of Chettiim, had smitten Darius king of the Persians and Medes, that he reigned in his stead, the first over Greece, ²and made many wars, and won many strongholds, and slew the kings of the earth, ³and went through to the ends of the earth, and took spoils of many nations, insomuch that the earth was quiet before him; whereupon he was exalted, and his heart was lifted up. ⁴And he gathered a mighty strong host, and ruled over countries, and nations, and kings, who became tributaries unto him.

⁵And after these things he fell sick, and perceived that he should die. ⁶Wherefore he called his servants, such as were honourable, and had been brought up with him from his youth, and parted his kingdom among them, while he was yet alive. ⁷So Alexander reigned twelve years, and then died. ⁸And his servants bore rule every one in his place. ⁹And after his death they all put crowns upon themselves; so did their sons after them many years: and evils were multiplied in the earth. ¹⁰And there came out of them a wicked root, Antiochus surnamed Epiphanes, son of Antiochus the king, who had been a hostage at Rome, and he reigned in the hundred and thirty and seventh year of the kingdom of the Greeks.

¹¹In those days went there out of Israel wicked men, who persuaded many, saying, 'Let us go and make a covenant with the heathen that are round about us: for since we departed from them we have had much sorrow'. ¹²So this device pleased them well. ¹³Then certain of the people were so forward herein, that they went to the king, who gave them licence to do after the ordinances of the heathen. ¹⁴Whereupon they built a place of exercise at Jerusalem according to the customs of the heathen, ¹⁵and made themselves uncircumcised, and forsook the holy covenant, and joined themselves to the heathen, and were sold to do mischief.

¹⁶Now when the kingdom was established before Antiochus, he thought to reign over Egypt, that he might have the dominion of two realms. ¹⁷Wherefore he entered into Egypt with a great multitude, with chariots, and elephants, and horsemen, and a great navy, ¹⁸and made war against Ptolemee king of Egypt: but Ptolemee was afraid of him, and fled; and many were wounded to death. ¹⁹Thus they got the strong cities in the land of Egypt, and he took the spoils thereof.

²⁰And after that Antiochus had smitten Egypt, he returned again in the hundred forty and three year, and went up against Israel and Jerusalem with a great multitude, ²¹and entered proudly into the sanctuary, and took away the golden altar, and the candlestick of light, and all the vessels thereof, ²²and the table of the showbread, and the pouring vessels, and the vials, and the censers of gold, and the veil, and the

crowns, and the golden ornaments that were before the temple, all which he pulled off. ²³He took also the silver and the gold, and the precious vessels: also he took the hidden treasures which he found. ²⁴And when he had taken all away, he went into his own land, having made a great massacre, and spoken very proudly.

²⁵Therefore there was great mourning in Israel, in every place where they were; ²⁶so that the princes and elders mourned, the virgins and young men were made feeble, and the beauty of women was changed. ²⁷Every bridegroom took up lamentation, and she that sat in the marriage-chamber was in heaviness. ²⁸The land also was moved for the inhabitants thereof, and all the house of Jacob was covered with confusion.

²⁹And after two years fully expired the king sent his chief collector of tribute unto the cities of Juda, who came unto Jerusalem with a great multitude, ³⁰and spoke peaceable words unto them, but all was deceit: for when they had given him credence, he fell suddenly upon the city, and smote it very sore, and destroyed much people of Israel. ³¹And when he had taken the spoils of the city, he set it on fire, and pulled down the houses and walls thereof on every side. ³²But the women and children took they captive, and possessed the cattle.

³³Then built they the city of David with a great and strong wall, and with mighty towers, and made it a stronghold for them. ³⁴And they put therein a sinful nation, wicked men, and fortified themselves therein. ³⁵They stored it also with armour and victuals, and when they had gathered together the spoils of Jerusalem, they laid them up there, and so they became a sore snare: ³⁶for it was a place to lie in wait against the sanctuary, and an evil adversary to Israel. ³⁷Thus they shed innocent blood on every side of the sanctuary, and defiled it: ³⁸insomuch that the inhabitants of Jerusalem fled because of them: whereupon the city was made a habitation of strangers, and became strange to those that were born in her, and her own children left her. ³⁹Her sanctuary was laid waste like a wilderness, her feasts were turned into mourning, her sabbaths into reproach, her honour into contempt. ⁴⁰As had been her glory, so was her dishonour increased, and her excellence was turned into mourning.

⁴¹Moreover king Antiochus wrote to his whole kingdom, that all should be one people, ⁴²and every one should leave his laws: so all the heathen agreed according to the commandment of the king. ⁴³Yea, many also of the Israelites consented to his religion, and sacrificed unto idols, and profaned the sabbath. ⁴⁴For the king had sent letters by messengers unto Jerusalem and the cities of Juda, that they should follow the strange laws of the land, ⁴⁵and forbid burnt offerings, and sacrifice, and drink offerings in the temple; and that they should profane the sabbaths and festival days: ⁴⁶and pollute the sanctuary and holy people: ⁴⁷set up altars, and groves, and chapels of idols, and sacrifice swine's flesh, and unclean beasts: ⁴⁸that they should also leave their children uncircumcised, and make their souls abominable with all manner of uncleanness and profanation: ⁴⁹to the end they might forget

the law, and change all the ordinances. ⁵⁰And whosoever would not do according to the commandment of the king, he said he should die.

⁵¹In the selfsame manner wrote he to his whole kingdom, and appointed overseers over all the people, commanding the cities of Juda to sacrifice, city by city. ⁵²Then many of the people were gathered unto them, to wit, every one that forsook the law; and so they committed evils in the land: ⁵³and drove the Israelites into secret places, even wheresoever they could fly for succour.

⁵⁴Now the fifteenth day of the month Casleu, in the hundred forty and fifth year, they set up the abomination of desolation upon the altar, and built idol altars throughout the cities of Juda on every side; ⁵⁵and burnt incense at the doors of their houses, and in the streets. ⁵⁶And when they had rent in pieces the books of the law which they found, they burnt them with fire. ⁵⁷And wheresoever was found with any the book of the testament, or if any consented to the law, the king's commandment was, that they should put him to death. ⁵⁸Thus did they by their authority unto the Israelites every month, to as many as were found in the cities.

⁵⁹Now the five and twentieth day of the month they did sacrifice upon the idol altar, which was upon the altar of God. ⁶⁰At which time according to the commandment they put to death certain women that had caused their children to be circumcised. ⁶¹And they hanged the infants about their necks, and rifled their houses, and slew them that had circumcised them. ⁶²Howbeit many in Israel were fully resolved and confirmed in themselves not to eat any unclean thing. ⁶³Wherefore they chose rather to die, that they might not be defiled with meats, and that they might not profane the holy covenant: so then they died. ⁶⁴And there was very great wrath upon Israel.

2 In those days arose Mattathias the son of John, the son of Simeon, a priest of the sons of Joarib, from Jerusalem, and dwelt in Modin. ²And he had five sons, Joannan, called Caddis: ³Simon, called Thassi: ⁴Judas, who was called Maccabeus: ⁵Eleazar, called Avaran, and Jonathan, whose surname was Apphus.

⁶And when he saw the blasphemies that were committed in Juda and Jerusalem, ⁷he said, 'Woe is me, wherefore was I born to see this misery of my people, and of the holy city, and to dwell there, when it was delivered into the hand of the enemy, and the sanctuary into the hand of strangers? ⁸Her temple is become as a man without glory. ⁹Her glorious vessels are carried away into captivity, her infants are slain in the streets, her young men with the sword of the enemy. ¹⁰What nation hath not had a part in her kingdom, and gotten of her spoils? ¹¹All her ornaments are taken away; of a free woman she is become a bondslave. ¹²And behold, our sanctuary, even our beauty and our glory, is laid waste, and the Gentiles have profaned it. ¹³To what end therefore shall we live any longer?' ¹⁴Then Mattathias and his sons rent their clothes, and put on sackcloth, and mourned very sore.

¹⁵In the mean while the king's officers, such as compelled the people to revolt, came into the city Modin to make them sacrifice. ¹⁶And when

many of Israel came unto them, Mattathias also and his sons came together. [17]Then answered the king's officers, and said to Mattathias on this wise, 'Thou art a ruler, and an honourable and great man in this city, and strengthened with sons and brethren: [18]now therefore come thou first, and fulfil the king's commandment, like as all the heathen have done, yea, and the men of Juda also, and such as remain at Jerusalem: so shalt thou and thy house be in the number of the king's friends, and thou and thy children shall be honoured with silver and gold, and many rewards.'

[19]Then Mattathias answered and spoke with a loud voice, 'Though all the nations that are under the king's dominion obey him, and fall away every one from the religion of their fathers, and give consent to his commandments: [20]yet will I and my sons and my brethren walk in the covenant of our fathers. [21]God forbid that we should forsake the law and the ordinances. [22]We will not hearken to the king's words, to go from our religion, either on the right hand, or the left.'

[23]Now when he had left speaking these words, there came one of the Jews in the sight of all to sacrifice on the altar which was at Modin, according to the king's commandment. [24]Which thing when Mattathias saw, he was inflamed with zeal, and his reins trembled, neither could he forbear to show his anger according to judgement: wherefore he ran, and slew him upon the altar. [25]Also the king's commissioner who compelled men to sacrifice, he killed at that time, and the altar he pulled down. [26]Thus dealt he zealously for the law of God, like as Phinees did unto Zambri the son of Salom. [27]And Mattathias cried throughout the city with a loud voice, saying, 'Whosoever is zealous of the law, and maintaineth the covenant, let him follow me'. [28]So he and his sons fled into the mountains, and left all that ever they had in the city.

[29]Then many that sought after justice and judgement went down into the wilderness, to dwell there: [30]both they, and their children, and their wives, and their cattle, because afflictions increased sore upon them. [31]Now when it was told the king's servants, and the host that was at Jerusalem, in the city of David, that certain men, who had broken the king's commandment, were gone down into the secret places in the wilderness, [32]they pursued after them a great number, and having overtaken them, they camped against them, and made war against them on the sabbath day. [33]And they said unto them, 'Let that which you have done hitherto suffice: come forth, and do according to the commandment of the king, and you shall live'. [34]But they said, 'We will not come forth, neither will we do the king's commandment to profane the sabbath day'. [35]So then they gave them the battle with all speed. [36]Howbeit they answered them not, neither cast they a stone at them, nor stopped the places where they lay hid, [37]but said, 'Let us die all in our innocence: heaven and earth shall testify for us, that you put us to death wrongfully'. [38]So they rose up against them in battle on the sabbath, and they slew them, with their wives and children, and their cattle, to the number of a thousand people.

³⁹Now when Mattathias and his friends understood hereof, they mourned for them right sore. ⁴⁰And one of them said to another, 'If we all do as our brethren have done, and fight not for our lives and laws against the heathen, they will now quickly root us out of the earth'. ⁴¹At that time therefore they decreed, saying, 'Whosoever shall come to make battle with us on the sabbath day, we will fight against him, neither will we die all, as our brethren that were murdered in the secret places'.

⁴²Then came there unto him a company of Asideans, who were mighty men of Israel, even all such as were voluntarily devoted unto the law. ⁴³Also all they that fled for persecution joined themselves unto them, and were a stay unto them. ⁴⁴So they joined their forces, and smote sinful men in their anger, and wicked men in their wrath: but the rest fled to the heathen for succour.

⁴⁵Then Mattathias and his friends went round about, and pulled down the altars. ⁴⁶And what children soever they found within the coast of Israel uncircumcised, those they circumcised valiantly. ⁴⁷They pursued also after the proud men, and the work prospered in their hand. ⁴⁸So they recovered the law out of the hand of the Gentiles, and out of the hand of kings, neither suffered they the sinner to triumph.

⁴⁹Now when the time drew near that Mattathias should die, he said unto his sons, 'Now hath pride and rebuke gotten strength, and the time of destruction, and the wrath of indignation: ⁵⁰now therefore, my sons, be ye zealous for the law, and give your lives for the covenant of your fathers. ⁵¹Call to remembrance what acts our fathers did in their time; so shall ye receive great honour and an everlasting name. ⁵²Was not Abraham found faithful in temptation, and it was imputed unto him for righteousness? ⁵³Joseph in the time of his distress kept the commandment, and was made lord of Egypt. ⁵⁴Phinees our father in being zealous and fervent obtained the covenant of an everlasting priesthood. ⁵⁵Jesus for fulfilling the word was made a judge in Israel. ⁵⁶Caleb for bearing witness before the congregation received the heritage of the land. ⁵⁷David for being merciful possessed the throne of an everlasting kingdom. ⁵⁸Elias for being zealous and fervent for the law was taken up into heaven. ⁵⁹Ananias, Azarias, and Misael, by believing were saved out of the flame. ⁶⁰Daniel for his innocence was delivered from the mouth of lions. ⁶¹And thus consider ye throughout all ages, that none that put their trust in him shall be overcome. ⁶²Fear not then the words of a sinful man: for his glory shall be dung and worms. ⁶³Today he shall be lifted up, and tomorrow he shall not be found, because he is returned into his dust, and his thought is come to nothing. ⁶⁴Wherefore you my sons be valiant, and show yourselves men in the behalf of the law, for by it shall you obtain glory.

⁶⁵'And behold, I know that your brother Simon is a man of counsel, give ear unto him always: he shall be a father unto you. ⁶⁶As for Judas Maccabeus, he hath been mighty and strong, even from his youth up: let him be your captain, and fight the battle of the people. ⁶⁷Take also unto you all those that observe the law, and avenge ye the wrong of

your people. ⁶⁸Recompense fully the heathen, and take heed to the commandments of the law.'

⁶⁹So he blessed them, and was gathered to his fathers. ⁷⁰And he died in the hundred forty and sixth year, and his sons buried him in the sepulchre of his fathers at Modin, and all Israel made great lamentation for him.

3 Then his son Judas, called Maccabeus, rose up in his stead. ²And all his brethren helped him, and so did all they that held with his father, and they fought with cheerfulness the battle of Israel. ³So he got his people great honour, and put on a breastplate as a giant, and girt his warlike harness about him, and he made battles, protecting the host with his sword. ⁴In his acts he was like a lion, and like a lion's whelp roaring for his prey. ⁵For he pursued the wicked, and sought them out, and burnt up those that vexed his people. ⁶Wherefore the wicked shrunk for fear of him, and all the workers of iniquity were troubled, because salvation prospered in his hand. ⁷He grieved also many kings, and made Jacob glad with his acts, and his memorial is blessed for ever. ⁸Moreover he went through the cities of Juda, destroying the ungodly out of them, and turning away wrath from Israel: ⁹so that he was renowned unto the utmost part of the earth, and he received unto him such as were ready to perish.

¹⁰Then Apollonius gathered the Gentiles together, and a great host out of Samaria to fight against Israel. ¹¹Which thing when Judas perceived, he went forth to meet him, and so he smote him, and slew him: many also fell down slain, but the rest fled. ¹²Wherefore Judas took their spoils, and Apollonius' sword also, and therewith he fought all his life long.

¹³Now when Seron, a prince of the army of Syria, heard say that Judas had gathered unto him a multitude and company of the faithful to go out with him to war, ¹⁴he said, 'I will get me a name and honour in the kingdom, for I will go fight with Judas and them that are with him, who despise the king's commandment'. ¹⁵So he made him ready to go up, and there went with him a mighty host of the ungodly to help him, and to be avenged of the children of Israel.

¹⁶And when he came near to the going up of Bethoron, Judas went forth to meet him with a small company: ¹⁷who, when they saw the host coming to meet them, said unto Judas, 'How shall we be able, being so few, to fight against so great a multitude and so strong, seeing we are ready to faint with fasting all this day?' ¹⁸Unto whom Judas answered, 'It is no hard matter for many to be shut up in the hands of a few; and with the God of heaven it is all one, to deliver with a great multitude, or a small company: ¹⁹for the victory of battle standeth not in the multitude of a host, but strength cometh from heaven. ²⁰They come against us in much pride and iniquity to destroy us, and our wives and children, and to spoil us: ²¹but we fight for our lives and our laws. ²²Wherefore the Lord himself will overthrow them before our face: and as for you, be ye not afraid of them.'

²³Now as soon as he had left off speaking, he leapt suddenly upon

them, and so Seron and his host was overthrown before him. ²⁴And they pursued them from the going down of Bethoron unto the plain, where were slain about eight hundred men of them; and the residue fled into the land of the Philistines.

²⁵Then began the fear of Judas and his brethren, and an exceeding great dread to fall upon the nations round about them: ²⁶insomuch as his fame came unto the king, and all nations talked of the battles of Judas. ²⁷Now when king Antiochus heard these things, he was full of indignation: wherefore he sent and gathered together all the forces of his realm, even a very strong army. ²⁸He opened also his treasure, and gave his soldiers pay for a year, commanding them to be ready whensoever he should need them. ²⁹Nevertheless, when he saw that the money of his treasures failed, and that the tributes in the country were small, because of the dissension and plague which he had brought upon the land in taking away the laws which had been of old time, ³⁰he feared that he should not be able to bear the charges any longer, nor to have such gifts to give so liberally as he did before: for he had abounded above the kings that were before him.

³¹Wherefore, being greatly perplexed in his mind, he determined to go into Persia, there to take the tributes of the countries, and to gather much money. ³²So he left Lysias, a nobleman, and one of the blood royal, to oversee the affairs of the king from the river Euphrates unto the borders of Egypt: ³³and to bring up his son Antiochus, until he came again. ³⁴Moreover he delivered unto him the half of his forces, and the elephants, and gave him charge of all things that he would have done, as also concerning them that dwelt in Juda and Jerusalem: ³⁵to wit, that he should send an army against them, to destroy and root out the strength of Israel, and the remnant of Jerusalem, and to take away their memorial from that place: ³⁶and that he should place strangers in all their quarters, and divide their land by lot. ³⁷So the king took the half of the forces that remained, and departed from Antioch, his royal city, the hundred forty and seventh year, and having passed the river Euphrates, he went through the high countries.

³⁸Then Lysias chose Ptolemee the son of Dorymenes, and Nicanor, and Gorgias, mighty men of the king's friends: ³⁹and with them he sent forty thousand footmen, and seven thousand horsemen to go into the land of Juda, and to destroy it, as the king commanded. ⁴⁰So they went forth with all their power, and came and pitched by Emmaus in the plain country. ⁴¹And the merchants of the country, hearing the fame of them, took silver and gold very much, with servants, and came into the camp to buy the children of Israel for slaves: a power also of Syria and of the land of the Philistines joined themselves unto them.

⁴²Now when Judas and his brethren saw that miseries were multiplied, and that the forces did encamp themselves in their borders (for they knew how the king had given commandment to destroy the people, and utterly abolish them), ⁴³they said one to another, 'Let us restore the decayed estate of our people, and let us fight for our people and the sanctuary'. ⁴⁴Then was the congregation gathered together, that they

might be ready for battle, and that they might pray, and ask mercy and compassion.

⁴⁵Now Jerusalem lay void as a wilderness, there was none of her children that went in or out: the sanctuary also was trodden down, and aliens kept the stronghold: the heathen had their habitation in that place; and joy was taken from Jacob, and the pipe with the harp ceased. ⁴⁶Wherefore the Israelites assembled themselves together, and came to Maspha, over against Jerusalem; for in Maspha was the place where they prayed aforetime in Israel. ⁴⁷Then they fasted that day, and put on sackcloth, and cast ashes upon their heads, and rent their clothes, ⁴⁸and laid open the book of the law, wherein the heathen had sought to paint the likeness of their images. ⁴⁹They brought also the priests' garments, and the first-fruits, and the tithes, and the Nazarites they stirred up, who had accomplished their days.

⁵⁰Then cried they with a loud voice toward heaven, saying, 'What shall we do with these, and whither shall we carry them away? ⁵¹for thy sanctuary is trodden down and profaned, and thy priests are in heaviness, and brought low. ⁵²And lo, the heathen are assembled together against us to destroy us: what things they imagine against us, thou knowest. ⁵³How shall we be able to stand against them, except thou, O God, be our help?' ⁵⁴Then sounded they with trumpets, and cried with a loud voice.

⁵⁵And after this Judas ordained captains over the people, even captains over thousands, and over hundreds, and over fifties, and over tens. ⁵⁶But as for such as were building houses, or had betrothed wives, or were planting vineyards, or were fearful, those he commanded that they should return, every man to his own house, according to the law. ⁵⁷So the camp removed, and pitched upon the south side of Emmaus. ⁵⁸And Judas said, 'Arm yourselves, and be valiant men, and see that ye be in readiness against the morning, that ye may fight with these nations, that are assembled together against us to destroy us and our sanctuary: ⁵⁹for it is better for us to die in battle, than to behold the calamities of our people and our sanctuary. ⁶⁰Nevertheless, as the will of God is in heaven, so let him do.'

4 Then took Gorgias five thousand footmen, and a thousand of the best horsemen, and removed out of the camp by night: ²to the end he might rush in upon the camp of the Jews, and smite them suddenly. And the men of the fortress were his guides. ³Now when Judas heard thereof, he himself removed, and the valiant men with him, that he might smite the king's army which was at Emmaus, ⁴while as yet the forces were dispersed from the camp. ⁵In the mean season came Gorgias by night into the camp of Judas: and when he found no man there, he sought them in the mountains: for said he, 'These fellows flee from us'.

⁶But as soon as it was day, Judas showed himself in the plain with three thousand men, who nevertheless had neither armour nor swords to their minds. ⁷And they saw the camp of the heathen, that it was strong and well harnessed, and compassed round about with horse-

men; and these were expert of war. ⁸Then said Judas to the men that were with him, 'Fear ye not their multitude, neither be ye afraid of their assault. ⁹Remember how our fathers were delivered in the Red Sea, when Pharaoh pursued them with an army. ¹⁰Now therefore let us cry unto heaven, if peradventure the Lord will have mercy upon us, and remember the covenant of our fathers, and destroy this host before our face this day: ¹¹that so all the heathen may know that there is one who delivereth and saveth Israel.'

¹²Then the strangers lifted up their eyes, and saw them coming over against them. ¹³Wherefore they went out of the camp to battle; but they that were with Judas sounded their trumpets. ¹⁴So they joined battle, and the heathen being discomfited fled into the plain. ¹⁵Howbeit all the hindmost of them were slain with the sword: for they pursued them unto Gazera, and unto the plains of Idumea, and Azotus, and Jamnia, so that there were slain of them upon a three thousand men.

¹⁶This done, Judas returned again with his host from pursuing them, ¹⁷and said to the people, 'Be not greedy of the spoils, inasmuch as there is a battle before us, ¹⁸and Gorgias and his host are here by us in the mountain, but stand ye now against your enemies, and overcome them, and after this you may boldly take the spoils'.

¹⁹As Judas was yet speaking these words, there appeared a part of them looking out of the mountain: ²⁰who when they perceived that the Jews had put their host to flight, and were burning the tents (for the smoke that was seen declared what was done): ²¹when therefore they perceived these things, they were sore afraid, and seeing also the host of Judas in the plain ready to fight, ²²they fled every one into the land of strangers.

²³Then Judas returned to spoil the tents, where they got much gold, and silver, and blue silk, and purple of the sea, and great riches. ²⁴After this they went home, and sung a song of thanksgiving, and praised the Lord in heaven: because it is good, because his mercy endureth for ever. ²⁵Thus Israel had a great deliverance that day.

²⁶Now all the strangers that had escaped came and told Lysias what had happened: ²⁷who, when he heard thereof, was confounded and discouraged because neither such things as he would were done unto Israel, nor such things as the king commanded him were come to pass.

²⁸The next year therefore following, Lysias gathered together threescore thousand choice men of foot, and five thousand horsemen, that he might subdue them. ²⁹So they came into Idumea, and pitched their tents at Bethsura, and Judas met them with ten thousand men. ³⁰And when he saw that mighty army, he prayed and said, 'Blessed art thou, O Saviour of Israel, who didst quell the violence of the mighty man by the hand of thy servant David, and gavest the host of strangers into the hands of Jonathan the son of Saul, and his armour-bearer. ³¹Shut up this army in the hand of thy people Israel, and let them be confounded in their power and horsemen. ³²Make them to be of no courage, and cause the boldness of their strength to fall away, and let them quake at their destruction. ³³Cast them down with the sword of them that love

thee, and let all those that know thy name praise thee with thanksgiving.'

[34] So they joined battle; and there were slain of the host of Lysias about five thousand men, even before them were they slain. [35] Now when Lysias saw his army put to flight, and the manliness of Judas's soldiers, and how they were ready either to live or die valiantly, he went into Antiochia, and gathered together a company of strangers, and having made his army greater than it was, he purposed to come again into Judea.

[36] Then said Judas and his brethren, 'Behold, our enemies are discomfited: let us go up to cleanse and dedicate the sanctuary'. [37] Upon this all the host assembled themselves together, and went up into mount Sion. [38] And when they saw the sanctuary desolate, and the altar profaned, and the gates burnt up, and shrubs growing in the courts as in a forest, or in one of the mountains, yea, and the priests' chambers pulled down, [39] they rent their clothes, and made great lamentation, and cast ashes upon their heads, [40] and fell down flat to the ground upon their faces, and blew an alarm with the trumpets, and cried towards heaven.

[41] Then Judas appointed certain men to fight against those that were in the fortress, until he had cleansed the sanctuary. [42] So he chose priests of blameless conversation, such as had pleasure in the law: [43] who cleansed the sanctuary, and bore out the defiled stones into an unclean place. [44] And when as they consulted what to do with the altar of burnt offerings, which was profaned, [45] they thought it best to pull it down, lest it should be a reproach to them, because the heathen had defiled it: wherefore they pulled it down, [46] and laid up the stones in the mountain of the temple in a convenient place, until there should come a prophet to show what should be done with them. [47] Then they took whole stones according to the law, and built a new altar according to the former: [48] and made up the sanctuary, and the things that were within the temple, and hallowed the courts. [49] They made also new holy vessels, and into the temple they brought the candlestick, and the altar of burnt offerings, and of incense, and the table. [50] And upon the altar they burnt incense, and the lamps that were upon the candlestick they lighted, that they might give light in the temple. [51] Furthermore they set the loaves upon the table, and spread out the veils, and finished all the works which they had begun to make.

[52] Now on the five and twentieth day of the ninth month, which is called the month Casleu, in the hundred forty and eighth year, they rose up betimes in the morning, [53] and offered sacrifice according to the law upon the new altar of burnt offerings, which they had made. [54] Look, at what time and what day the heathen had profaned it, even in that was it dedicated with songs, and citherns, and harps, and cymbals. [55] Then all the people fell upon their faces, worshipping and praising the God of heaven, who had given them good success.

[56] And so they kept the dedication of the altar eight days, and offered burnt offerings with gladness, and sacrificed the sacrifice of deliverance and praise. [57] They decked also the forefront of the temple with

crowns of gold, and with shields; and the gates and the chambers they renewed, and hanged doors upon them. ⁵⁸Thus was there very great gladness among the people, for that the reproach of the heathen was put away. ⁵⁹Moreover Judas and his brethren with the whole congregation of Israel ordained that the days of the dedication of the altar should be kept in their season from year to year by the space of eight days, from the five and twentieth day of the month Casleu, with mirth and gladness.

⁶⁰At that time also they built up the mount Sion with high walls and strong towers round about, lest the Gentiles should come and tread it down, as they had done before. ⁶¹And they set there a garrison to keep it, and fortified Bethsura to preserve it; that the people might have a defence against Idumea.

5 Now when the nations round about heard that the altar was built, and the sanctuary renewed as before, it displeased them very much. ²Wherefore they thought to destroy the generation of Jacob that was among them, and thereupon they began to slay and destroy the people. ³Then Judas fought against the children of Esau in Idumea at Arabattine, because they besieged Israel: and he gave them a great overthrow, and abated their courage, and took their spoils. ⁴Also he remembered the injury of the children of Bean, who had been a snare and an offence unto the people, in that they lay in wait for them in the ways. ⁵He shut them up therefore in the towers, and encamped against them, and destroyed them utterly, and burnt the towers of that place with fire, and all that were therein. ⁶Afterward he passed over to the children of Ammon, where he found a mighty power, and much people, with Timotheus their captain. ⁷So he fought many battles with them, till at length they were discomfited before him; and he smote them. ⁸And when he had taken Jazar, with the towns belonging thereto, he returned into Judea.

⁹Then the heathen that were at Galaad assembled themselves together against the Israelites that were in their quarters, to destroy them; but they fled to the fortress of Dathema, ¹⁰and sent letters unto Judas and his brethren,

The heathen that are round about us are assembled together against us to destroy us: ¹¹and they are preparing to come and take the fortress whereunto we are fled, Timotheus being captain of their host. ¹²Come now therefore, and deliver us from their hands, for many of us are slain. ¹³Yea, all our brethren that were in the places of Tobie are put to death: their wives and their children also they have carried away captives, and borne away their stuff, and they have destroyed there about a thousand men.

¹⁴While these letters were yet reading, behold, there came other messengers from Galilee with their clothes rent, who reported on this wise, ¹⁵and said, 'They of Ptolemais, and of Tyrus, and Sidon, and all Galilee of the Gentiles, are assembled together against us to consume us'.

¹⁶Now when Judas and the people heard these words, there assembled

a great congregation together, to consult what they should do for their brethren, that were in trouble, and assaulted of them. ¹⁷Then said Judas unto Simon his brother, 'Choose thee out men, and go and deliver thy brethren that are in Galilee, for I and Jonathan my brother will go into the country of Galaad'. ¹⁸So he left Joseph the son of Zacharias, and Azarias, captains of the people, with the remnant of the host in Judea to keep it, ¹⁹unto whom he gave commandment, saying, 'Take ye the charge of this people, and see that you make not war against the heathen until the time that we come again'. ²⁰Now unto Simon were given three thousand men to go into Galilee, and unto Judas eight thousand men for the country of Galaad.

²¹Then went Simon into Galilee, where he fought many battles with the heathen, so that the heathen were discomfited by him. ²²And he pursued them unto the gate of Ptolemais; and there were slain of the heathen about three thousand men, whose spoils he took. ²³And those that were in Galilee, and in Arbattis, with their wives and their children, and all that they had, took he away with him, and brought them into Judea, with great joy.

²⁴Judas Maccabeus also and his brother Jonathan went over Jordan, and travelled three days' journey in the wilderness, ²⁵where they met with the Nabathites, who came unto them in peaceable manner, and told them everything that had happened to their brethren in the land of Galaad: ²⁶and how that many of them were shut up in Bosora, and Bosor, in Alema, Casphor, Maked, and Carnaim (all these cities are strong and great), ²⁷and that they were shut up in the rest of the cities of the country of Galaad, and that against tomorrow they had appointed to bring their host against the forts, and to take them, and to destroy them all in one day.

²⁸Hereupon Judas and his host turned suddenly by the way of the wilderness unto Bosora; and when he had won the city, he slew all the males with the edge of the sword, and took all their spoils, and burnt the city with fire. ²⁹From whence he removed by night, and went till he came to the fortress. ³⁰And betimes in the morning they looked up, and behold, there was an innumerable people bearing ladders and other engines of war, to take the fortress: for they assaulted them. ³¹When Judas therefore saw that the battle was begun, and that the cry of the city went up to heaven, with trumpets, and a great sound, ³²he said unto his host, 'Fight this day for your brethren'. ³³So he went forth behind them in three companies, who sounded their trumpets, and cried with prayer. ³⁴Then the host of Timotheus, knowing that it was Maccabeus, fled from him: wherefore he smote them with a great slaughter: so that there were killed of them that day about eight thousand men.

³⁵This done, Judas turned aside to Maspha, and after he had assaulted it, he took it, and slew all the males therein, and received the spoils thereof, and burnt it with fire. ³⁶From thence went he, and took Casphon, Maged, Bosor, and the other cities of the country of Galaad.

³⁷After these things gathered Timotheus another host, and encamped

against Raphon beyond the brook. [38] So Judas sent men to espy the host, who brought him word, saying, 'All the heathen that be round about us are assembled unto them, even a very great host. [39] He hath also hired the Arabians to help them, and they have pitched their tents beyond the brook, ready to come and fight against thee.' Upon this Judas went to meet them.

[40] Then Timotheus said unto the captains of his host, 'When Judas and his host come near the brook, if he pass over first unto us, we shall not be able to withstand him, for he will mightily prevail against us. [41] But if he be afraid, and camp beyond the river, we shall go over unto him, and prevail against him.' [42] Now when Judas came near the brook, he caused the scribes of the people to remain by the brook: unto whom he gave commandment, saying, 'Suffer no man to remain in the camp, but let all come to the battle'. [43] So he went first over unto them, and all the people after him: then all the heathen, being discomfited before him, cast away their weapons, and fled unto the temple that was at Carnaim. [44] But they took the city, and burnt the temple with all that were therein. Thus was Carnaim subdued, neither could they stand any longer before Judas.

[45] Then Judas gathered together all the Israelites that were in the country of Galaad, from the least unto the greatest, even their wives, and their children, and their stuff, a very great host, to the end they might come into the land of Judea. [46] Now when they came unto Ephron (this was a great city in the way as they should go, very well fortified), they could not turn from it, either on the right hand or the left, but must needs pass through the midst of it. [47] Then they of the city shut them out, and stopped up the gates with stones. [48] Whereupon Judas sent unto them in peaceable manner, saying, 'Let us pass through your land to go into our own country, and none shall do you any hurt, we will only pass through on foot': howbeit they would not open unto him. [49] Wherefore Judas commanded a proclamation to be made throughout the host, that every man should pitch his tent in the place where he was. [50] So the soldiers pitched, and assaulted the city all that day and all that night, till at the length the city was delivered into his hands: [51] who then slew all the males with the edge of the sword, and rased the city, and took the spoils thereof, and passed through the city over them that were slain. [52] After this went they over Jordan into the great plain before Bethsan. [53] And Judas gathered together those that came behind, and exhorted the people all the way through, till they came into the land of Judea. [54] So they went up to mount Sion with joy and gladness, where they offered burnt offerings, because not one of them were slain until they had returned in peace.

[55] Now what time as Judas and Jonathan were in the land of Galaad, and Simon his brother in Galilee before Ptolemais, [56] Joseph the son of Zacharias, and Azarias, captains of the garrisons, heard of the valiant acts and warlike deeds which they had done. [57] Wherefore they said, 'Let us also get us a name, and go fight against the heathen that are round about us'. [58] So when they had given charge unto the garrison that was

with them, they went towards Jamnia. ⁵⁹Then came Gorgias and his men out of the city to fight against them. ⁶⁰And so it was, that Joseph and Azarias were put to flight, and pursued unto the borders of Judea: and there were slain that day of the people of Israel about two thousand men. ⁶¹Thus was there a great overthrow among the children of Israel, because they were not obedient unto Judas and his brethren, but thought to do some valiant act. ⁶²Moreover these men came not of the seed of those, by whose hand deliverance was given unto Israel.

⁶³Howbeit the man Judas and his brethren were greatly renowned in the sight of all Israel, and of all the heathen, wheresoever their name was heard of, ⁶⁴insomuch as the people assembled unto them with joyful acclamations.

⁶⁵Afterward went Judas forth with his brethren, and fought against the children of Esau in the land toward the south, where he smote Hebron, and the towns thereof, and pulled down the fortress of it, and burnt the towers thereof round about. ⁶⁶From thence he removed to go into the land of the Philistines, and passed through Samaria.

⁶⁷At that time certain priests, desirous to show their valour, were slain in battle, for that they went out to fight unadvisedly. ⁶⁸So Judas turned to Azotus in the land of the Philistines, and when he had pulled down their altars, and burnt their carved images with fire, and spoiled their cities, he returned into the land of Judea.

6 About that time king Antiochus travelling through the high countries, heard say that Elymais in the country of Persia was a city greatly renowned for riches, silver, and gold, ²and that there was in it a very rich temple, wherein were coverings of gold, and breastplates, and shields which Alexander, son of Philip, the Macedonian king, who reigned first among the Grecians, had left there. ³Wherefore he came and sought to take the city, and to spoil it, but he was not able, because they of the city having had warning thereof, ⁴rose up against him in battle: so he fled, and departed thence with great heaviness, and returned to Babylon.

⁵Moreover there came one who brought in tidings into Persia that the armies which went against the land of Judea, were put to flight: ⁶and that Lysias, who went forth first with a great power, was driven away of the Jews, and that they were made strong by the armour, and power, and store of spoils, which they had gotten of the armies, whom they had destroyed: ⁷also that they had pulled down the abomination, which he had set up upon the altar in Jerusalem, and that they had compassed about the sanctuary with high walls as before, and his city Bethsura. ⁸Now when the king heard these words, he was astonished and sore moved: whereupon he laid him down upon his bed, and fell sick for grief, because it had not befallen him as he looked for. ⁹And there he continued many days: for his grief was ever more and more, and he made account that he should die. ¹⁰Wherefore he called for all his friends, and said unto them, 'The sleep is gone from my eyes, and my heart faileth for very care. ¹¹And I thought with myself, into what tribulation am I come, and how great a flood of misery is it wherein

now I am! for I was bountiful and beloved in my power. [12]But now I remember the evils that I did at Jerusalem, and that I took all the vessels of gold and silver that were therein, and sent to destroy the inhabitants of Judea without a cause. [13]I perceive therefore that for this cause these troubles are come upon me, and behold, I perish through great grief in a strange land.'

[14]Then called he for Philip, one of his friends, whom he made ruler over all his realm, [15]and gave him the crown, and his robe, and his signet, to the end he should bring up his son Antiochus, and nourish him up for the kingdom. [16]So king Antiochus died there in the hundred forty and ninth year. [17]Now when Lysias knew that the king was dead, he set up Antiochus his son (whom he had brought up, being young) to reign in his stead, and his name he called Eupator.

[18]About this time they that were in the tower shut up the Israelites round about the sanctuary, and sought always their hurt, and the strengthening of the heathen. [19]Wherefore Judas, purposing to destroy them, called all the people together to besiege them. [20]So they came together, and besieged them in the hundred and fiftieth year, and he made mounts for shot against them, and other engines.

[21]Howbeit certain of them that were besieged got forth, unto whom some ungodly men of Israel joined themselves. [22]And they went unto the king, and said, 'How long will it be ere thou execute judgement, and avenge our brethren? [23]We have been willing to serve thy father, and to do as he would have us, and to obey his commandments. [24]For which cause they of our nation besiege the tower, and are alienated from us: moreover as many of us as they could light on they slew, and spoiled our inheritance. [25]Neither have they stretched out their hand against us only, but also against all their borders. [26]And behold, this day are they besieging the tower at Jerusalem, to take it: the sanctuary also and Bethsura have they fortified. [27]Wherefore if thou dost not prevent them quickly, they will do greater things than these, neither shalt thou be able to rule them.'

[28]Now when the king heard this, he was angry, and gathered together all his friends, and the captains of his army, and those that had charge of the horse. [29]There came also unto him from other kingdoms, and from isles of the sea bands of hired soldiers. [30]So that the number of his army was a hundred thousand footmen, and twenty thousand horsemen, and two and thirty elephants exercised in battle. [31]These went through Idumea, and pitched against Bethsura, which they assaulted many days, making engines of war: but they of Bethsura came out, and burnt them with fire, and fought valiantly.

[32]Upon this Judas removed from the tower, and pitched in Bathzacharias, over against the king's camp. [33]Then the king rising very early marched fiercely with his host toward Bathzacharias, where his armies made them ready to battle, and sounded the trumpets. [34]And to the end they might provoke the elephants to fight, they showed them the blood of grapes and mulberries. [35]Moreover they divided the beasts among the armies, and for every elephant they appointed a thousand

men, armed with coats of mail, and with helmets of brass on their heads; and besides this, for every beast were ordained five hundred horsemen of the best. ³⁶These were ready at every occasion: whereso-ever the beast was, and whithersoever the beast went, they went also, neither departed they from him. ³⁷And upon the beasts were there strong towers of wood, which covered every one of them, and were girt fast unto them with devices: there were also upon every one two and thirty strong men, that fought upon them, besides the Indian that ruled him. ³⁸As for the remnant of the horsemen, they set them on this side and that side at the two parts of the host, giving them signs what to do, and being harnessed all over amidst the ranks. ³⁹Now when the sun shone upon the shields of gold and brass, the mountains glistered therewith, and shone like lamps of fire. ⁴⁰So part of the king's army being spread upon the high mountains, and part on the valleys below, they marched on safely and in order. ⁴¹Wherefore all that heard the noise of their multitude, and the marching of the company, and the rattling of the harness, were moved: for the army was very great and mighty. ⁴²Then Judas and his host drew near, and entered into battle, and there were slain of the king's army six hundred men.

⁴³Eleazar also, surnamed Savaran, perceiving that one of the beasts, armed with royal harness, was higher than all the rest, and supposing that the king was upon him, ⁴⁴put himself in jeopardy, to the end he might deliver his people, and get him a perpetual name: ⁴⁵wherefore he ran upon him courageously through the midst of the battle, slaying on the right hand and on the left, so that they were divided from him on both sides. ⁴⁶Which done, he crept under the elephant, and thrust him under, and slew him: whereupon the elephant fell down upon him, and there he died. ⁴⁷Howbeit the rest of the Jews seeing the strength of the king, and the violence of his forces, turned away from them.

⁴⁸Then the king's army went up to Jerusalem to meet them, and the king pitched his tents against Judea, and against mount Sion. ⁴⁹But with them that were in Bethsura he made peace: for they came out of the city, because they had no victuals there to endure the siege, it being a year of rest to the land. ⁵⁰So the king took Bethsura, and set a garrison there to keep it.

⁵¹As for the sanctuary, he besieged it many days: and set there artillery with engines and instruments to cast fire and stones, and pieces to cast darts and slings. ⁵²Whereupon they also made engines against their engines, and held them battle a long season. ⁵³Yet at the last, their vessels being without victuals (for that it was the seventh year, and they in Judea, that were delivered from the Gentiles, had eaten up the residue of the store), ⁵⁴there were but a few left in the sanctuary, because the famine did so prevail against them, that they were fain to disperse themselves, every man to his own place.

⁵⁵At that time Lysias heard say, that Philip (whom Antiochus the king whilst he lived had appointed to bring up his son Antiochus, that he might be king) ⁵⁶was returned out of Persia and Media, and the king's host also that went with him, and that he sought to take unto him the

ruling of the affairs. ⁵⁷Wherefore he went in all haste, and said to the king and the captains of the host and the company, 'We decay daily, and our victuals are but small, and the place we lay siege unto is strong, and the affairs of the kingdom lie upon us. ⁵⁸Now therefore let us be friends with these men, and make peace with them, and with all their nation; ⁵⁹and covenant with them, that they shall live after their laws, as they did before: for they are therefore displeased, and have done all these things, because we abolished their laws.'

⁶⁰So the king and the princes were content: wherefore he sent unto them to make peace; and they accepted thereof. ⁶¹Also the king and the princes made an oath unto them: whereupon they went out of the stronghold. ⁶²Then the king entered into mount Sion, but when he saw the strength of the place, he broke his oath that he had made, and gave commandment to pull down the wall round about. ⁶³Afterward departed he in all haste, and returned unto Antiochia, where he found Philip to be master of the city: so he fought against him, and took the city by force.

7 In the hundred and one and fiftieth year Demetrius the son of Seleucus departed from Rome, and came up with a few men unto a city of the sea coast, and reigned there. ²And as he entered into the palace of his ancestors, so it was, that his forces had taken Antiochus and Lysias, to bring them unto him. ³Wherefore when he knew it, he said, 'Let me not see their faces'. ⁴So his host slew them.

Now when Demetrius was set upon the throne of his kingdom, ⁵there came unto him all the wicked and ungodly men of Israel, having Alcimus (who was desirous to be high priest) for their captain. ⁶And they accused the people to the king, saying, 'Judas and his brethren have slain all thy friends, and driven us out of our own land. ⁷Now therefore send some man whom thou trustest, and let him go and see what havoc he hath made amongst us, and in the king's land, and let him punish them with all them that aid them.' ⁸Then the king chose Bacchides, a friend of the king, who ruled beyond the flood, and was a great man in the kingdom, and faithful to the king. ⁹And him he sent with that wicked Alcimus, whom he made high priest, and commanded that he should take vengeance of the children of Israel. ¹⁰So they departed, and came with a great power into the land of Judea, where they sent messengers to Judas and his brethren with peaceable words deceitfully. ¹¹But they gave no heed to their words, for they saw that they were come with a great power.

¹²Then did there assemble unto Alcimus and Bacchides a company of scribes, to require justice. ¹³Now the Asideans were the first among the children of Israel that sought peace of them: ¹⁴for said they, 'One that is a priest of the seed of Aaron is come with this army, and he will do us no wrong'. ¹⁵So he spoke unto them peaceably, and swore unto them, saying, 'We will procure the harm neither of you nor your friends'. ¹⁶Whereupon they believed him: howbeit he took of them threescore men, and slew them in one day, according to the words which he wrote, ¹⁷'The flesh of thy saints have they cast out, and their blood have they

shed round about Jerusalem, and there was none to bury them'. [18]Wherefore the fear and dread of them fell upon all the people, who said, 'There is neither truth nor righteousness in them; for they have broken the covenant and oath that they made'.

[19]After this removed Bacchides from Jerusalem, and pitched his tents in Bezeth, where he sent and took many of the men that had forsaken him, and certain of the people also, and when he had slain them, he cast them into the great pit. [20]Then committed he the country to Alcimus, and left with him a power to aid him: so Bacchides went to the king.

[21]But Alcimus contended for the high priesthood. [22]And unto him resorted all such as troubled the people, who, after they had gotten the land of Juda into their power, did much hurt in Israel. [23]Now when Judas saw all the mischief that Alcimus and his company had done among the Israelites, even above the heathen, [24]he went out into all the coast of Judea round about, and took vengeance of them that had revolted from him, so that they durst no more go forth into the country. [25]On the other side, when Alcimus saw that Judas and his company had gotten the upper hand, and knew that he was not able to abide their force, he went again to the king, and said all the worst of them that he could.

[26]Then the king sent Nicanor, one of his honourable princes, a man that bore deadly hate unto Israel, with commandment to destroy the people. [27]So Nicanor came to Jerusalem with a great force: and sent unto Judas and his brethren deceitfully with friendly words, saying, [28]'Let there be no battle between me and you; I will come with a few men, that I may see you in peace'. [29]He came therefore to Judas, and they saluted one another peaceably. Howbeit the enemies were prepared to take away Judas by violence. [30]Which thing after it was known to Judas, to wit, that he came unto him with deceit, he was sore afraid of him, and would see his face no more. [31]Nicanor also, when he saw that his counsel was discovered, went out to fight against Judas beside Capharsalama: [32]where there were slain of Nicanor's side about five thousand men, and the rest fled into the city of David.

[33]After this went Nicanor up to mount Sion, and there came out of the sanctuary certain of the priests and certain of the elders of the people to salute him peaceably, and to show him the burnt sacrifice that was offered for the king. [34]But he mocked them, and laughed at them, and abused them shamefully, and spoke proudly, [35]and swore in his wrath, saying, 'Unless Judas and his host be now delivered into my hands, if ever I come again in safety, I will burn up this house': and with that he went out in a great rage. [36]Then the priests entered in, and stood before the altar and the temple, weeping, and saying, [37]'Thou, O Lord, didst choose this house to be called by thy name, and to be a house of prayer and petition for thy people. [38]Be avenged of this man and his host, and let them fall by the sword: remember their blasphemies, and suffer them not to continue any longer.'

[32]So Nicanor went out of Jerusalem, and pitched his tents in Bethoron,

where a host out of Syria met him. ⁴⁰But Judas pitched in Adasa with three thousand men, and there he prayed, saying, ⁴¹'O Lord, when they that were sent from the king of the Assyrians blasphemed, thy angel went out, and smote a hundred fourscore and five thousand of them. ⁴²Even so destroy thou this host before us this day, that the rest may know that he hath spoken blasphemously against thy sanctuary, and judge thou him according to his wickedness.'

⁴³So the thirteenth day of the month Adar the hosts joined battle: but Nicanor's host was discomfited, and he himself was first slain in the battle. ⁴⁴Now when Nicanor's host saw that he was slain, they cast away their weapons, and fled. ⁴⁵Then they pursued after them a day's journey from Adasa unto Gazera, sounding an alarm after them with their trumpets. ⁴⁶Whereupon they came forth out of all the towns of Judea round about, and closed them in, so that they, turning back upon them that pursued them, were all slain with the sword, and not one of them was left. ⁴⁷Afterwards they took the spoils, and the prey, and smote off Nicanor's head, and his right hand, which he stretched out so proudly, and brought them away, and hanged them up towards Jerusalem. ⁴⁸For this cause the people rejoiced greatly, and they kept that day a day of great gladness. ⁴⁹Moreover they ordained to keep yearly this day, being the thirteenth of Adar. ⁵⁰Thus the land of Juda was in rest a little while.

8 Now Judas had heard of the fame of the Romans, that they were mighty and valiant men, and such as would lovingly accept all that joined themselves unto them, and make a league of amity with all that came unto them, ²and that they were men of great valour. It was told him also of their wars and noble acts which they had done amongst the Galatians, and how they had conquered them, and brought them under tribute; ³and what they had done in the country of Spain, for the winning of the mines of the silver and gold which is there; ⁴And that by their policy and patience they had conquered all that place, though it were very far from them; and the kings also that came against them from the uttermost part of the earth, till they had discomfited them, and given them a great overthrow, so that the rest did give them tribute every year: ⁵besides this, how they had discomfited in battle Philip, and Perseus king of the Citims, with others that lifted up themselves against them, and had overcome them: ⁶how also Antiochus the great king of Asia that came against them in battle, having a hundred and twenty elephants, with horsemen, and chariots, and a very great army, was discomfited by them; ⁷and how they took him alive, and covenanted that he and such as reigned after him should pay a great tribute, and give hostages, and that which was agreed upon, ⁸and the country of India, and Media, and Lydia, and of the goodliest countries, which they took of him, and gave to king Eumenes: ⁹moreover how the Grecians had determined to come and destroy them; ¹⁰and that they, having knowledge thereof, sent against them a certain captain, and fighting with them slew many of them, and carried away captives their wives and their children, and spoiled them, and took possession of their lands, and pulled down their strongholds, and brought them to be their servants unto this day. ¹¹It was told him besides how they destroyed and brought under their dominion all other kingdoms and isles that at any time resisted them. ¹²But with their friends and such as relied upon them they kept amity: and that they had conquered kingdoms both far and nigh, insomuch as all that heard of their name were afraid of them: ¹³also that whom they would help to a kingdom, those reign, and whom again they would, they displace: finally, that they were greatly exalted. ¹⁴Yet for all this none of them wore a crown, or was clothed in purple, to be magnified thereby. ¹⁵Moreover how they had made for themselves a senate house, wherein three hundred and twenty men sat in council daily, consulting always for the people, to the end they might be well ordered: ¹⁶and that they committed their government to one man every year, who ruled over all their country, and that all were obedient to that one, and that there was neither envy nor emulation amongst them.

¹⁷In consideration of these things, Judas chose Eupolemus the son of John, the son of Accos, and Jason the son of Eleazar, and sent them to Rome, to make a league of amity and confederacy with them, ¹⁸and to entreat them that they would take the yoke from them; for they saw that the kingdom of the Grecians did oppress Israel with servitude. ¹⁹They went therefore to Rome, which was a very great journey, and came into the senate, where they spoke and said, ²⁰'Judas Maccabeus with his brethren, and the people of the Jews, have sent us unto you, to make a confederacy and peace with you, and that we might be registered your confederates and friends'. ²¹So that matter pleased the Romans well.

²²And this is the copy of the epistle which the senate wrote back again in tablets of brass, and sent to Jerusalem, that there they might have by them a memorial of peace and confederacy:

²³Good success be to the Romans, and to the people of the Jews, by sea and by land for ever: the sword also and enemy be far from them. ²⁴If there come first any war upon the Romans or any of their confederates throughout all their dominion, ²⁵the people of the Jews shall help them, as the time shall be appointed, with all their heart. ²⁶Neither shall they give anything unto them that make war upon them, or aid them with victuals, weapons, money, or ships, as it hath seemed good unto the Romans, but they shall keep their covenant without taking anything therefore. ²⁷In the same manner also, if war come first upon the nation of the Jews, the Romans shall help them with all their heart, according as the time shall be appointed them. ²⁸Neither shall victuals be given to them that take part against them, or weapons, or money, or ships, as it hath seemed good to the Romans; but they shall keep their covenants, and that without deceit.

²⁹According to these articles did the Romans make a covenant with the people of the Jews.

³⁰Howbeit, if hereafter the one party or the other shall think

meet to add or diminish anything, they may do it at their pleasures, and whatsoever they shall add or take away shall be ratified. ³¹And as touching the evils that Demetrius doeth to the Jews, we have written unto him, saying, 'Wherefore hast thou made thy yoke heavy upon our friends and confederates the Jews? ³²If therefore they complain any more against thee, we will do them justice, and fight with thee by sea and by land.'

9 Furthermore, when Demetrius heard that Nicanor and his host were slain in battle, he sent Bacchides and Alcimus into the land of Judea the second time, and with them the chief strength of his host: ²who went forth by the way that leadeth to Galgala, and pitched their tents before Masaloth, which is in Arbela, and after they had won it, they slew much people.

³Also the first month of the hundred fifty and second year they encamped before Jerusalem. ⁴From whence they removed, and went to Berea, with twenty thousand footmen and two thousand horsemen. ⁵Now Judas had pitched his tents at Eleasa, and three thousand chosen men with him: ⁶who seeing the multitude of the other army to be so great were sore afraid, whereupon many conveyed themselves out of the host, insomuch as there abode of them no more but eight hundred men. ⁷When Judas therefore saw that his host slipped away, and that the battle pressed upon him, he was sore troubled in mind, and much distressed, for that he had no time to gather them together. ⁸Nevertheless unto them that remained he said, 'Let us arise and go up against our enemies, if peradventure we may be able to fight with them'. ⁹But they dehorted him, saying, 'We shall never be able: let us now rather save our lives, and hereafter we will return with our brethren, and fight against them: for we are but few'. ¹⁰Then Judas said, 'God forbid that I should do this thing, and flee away from them: if our time be come, let us die manfully for our brethren, and let us not stain our honour'.

¹¹With that the host of Bacchides removed out of their tents, and stood over against them, their horsemen being divided into two troops, and their slingers and archers going before the host, and they that marched in the foreward were all mighty men. ¹²As for Bacchides, he was in the right wing: so the host drew near on the two parts, and sounded their trumpets. ¹³They also of Judas's side, even they sounded their trumpets also, so that the earth shook at the noise of the armies, and the battle continued from morning till night.

¹⁴Now when Judas perceived that Bacchides and the strength of his army were on the right side, he took with him all the hardy men, ¹⁵who discomfited the right wing, and pursued them unto the mount Azotus. ¹⁶But when they of the left wing saw that they of the right wing were discomfited, they followed upon Judas and those that were with him hard at the heels from behind: ¹⁷whereupon there was a sore battle, insomuch as many were slain on both parts. ¹⁸Judas also was killed, and the remnant fled.

¹⁹Then Jonathan and Simon took Judas their brother, and buried

him in the sepulchre of his fathers in Modin. ²⁰Moreover they bewailed him, and all Israel made great lamentation for him, and mourned many days, saying, ²¹'How is the valiant man fallen, that delivered Israel!'

²²As for the other things concerning Judas and his wars, and the noble acts which he did, and his greatness, they are not written: for they were very many.

²³Now after the death of Judas the wicked began to put forth their heads in all the coasts of Israel, and there arose up all such as wrought iniquity. ²⁴In those days also was there a very great famine, by reason whereof the country revolted, and went with them. ²⁵Then Bacchides chose the wicked men, and made them lords of the country. ²⁶And they made inquiry and search for Judas's friends, and brought them unto Bacchides, who took vengeance of them, and used them despitefully. ²⁷So was there a great affliction in Israel, the like whereof was not since the time that a prophet was not seen amongst them. ²⁸For this cause all Judas's friends came together, and said unto Jonathan, ²⁹'Since thy brother Judas died, we have no man like him to go forth against our enemies, and Bacchides, and against them of our nation that are adversaries to us. ³⁰Now therefore we have chosen thee this day to be our prince and captain in his stead, that thou mayest fight our battles.' ³¹Upon this Jonathan took the governance upon him at that time, and rose up instead of his brother Judas.

³²But when Bacchides got knowledge thereof, he sought for to slay him. ³³Then Jonathan, and Simon his brother, and all that were with him, perceiving that, fled into the wilderness of Thecoe, and pitched their tents by the water of the pool Asphar. ³⁴Which when Bacchides understood, he came near to Jordan with all his host upon the sabbath day. ³⁵Now Jonathan had sent his brother John, a captain of the people, to pray his friends the Nabathites that they might leave with them their carriage, which was much. ³⁶But the children of Jambri came out of Medaba, and took John, and all that he had, and went their way with it.

³⁷After this came word to Jonathan and Simon his brother that the children of Jambri made a great marriage, and were bringing the bride from Nadabatha with a great train, as being the daughter of one of the great princes of Canaan. ³⁸Therefore they remembered John their brother, and went up, and hid themselves under the covert of the mountain: ³⁹where they lifted up their eyes, and looked, and behold, there was much ado and great carriage: and the bridegroom came forth, and his friends and brethren, to meet them with drums, and instruments of music, and many weapons. ⁴⁰Then Jonathan and they that were with him rose up against them from the place where they lay in ambush, and made a slaughter of them in such sort, as many fell down dead, and the remnant fled into the mountain, and they took all their spoils. ⁴¹Thus was the marriage turned into mourning, and the noise of their melody into lamentation. ⁴²So when they had avenged fully the blood of their brother, they turned again to the marsh of Jordan.

⁴³Now when Bacchides heard hereof, he came on the sabbath day unto the banks of Jordan with a great power. ⁴⁴Then Jonathan said to his company, 'Let us go up now and fight for our lives, for it standeth not with us today, as in time past: ⁴⁵for behold, the battle is before us and behind us, and the water of Jordan on this side and that side, the marsh likewise and wood, neither is there place for us to turn aside. ⁴⁶Wherefore cry ye now unto heaven, that ye may be delivered from the hand of your enemies.' ⁴⁷With that they joined battle, and Jonathan stretched forth his hand to smite Bacchides, but he turned back from him. ⁴⁸Then Jonathan and they that were with him leapt into Jordan, and swam over unto the farther bank: howbeit the others passed not over Jordan unto them. ⁴⁹So there were slain of Bacchides' side that day about a thousand men.

⁵⁰Afterward returned Bacchides to Jerusalem, and repaired the strong cities in Judea: the fort in Jericho, and Emmaus, and Bethoron, and Bethel, and Thamnatha, Pharathoni, and Taphon, these did he strengthen with high walls, with gates, and with bars. ⁵¹And in them he set a garrison, that they might work malice upon Israel. ⁵²He fortified also the city Bethsura, and Gazara, and the tower, and put forces in them, and provision of victuals. ⁵³Besides, he took the chief men's sons in the country for hostages, and put them into the tower at Jerusalem to be kept.

⁵⁴Moreover in the hundred fifty and third year, in the second month, Alcimus commanded that the wall of the inner court of the sanctuary should be pulled down; he pulled down also the works of the prophets. ⁵⁵And as he began to pull down, even at that time was Alcimus plagued, and his enterprises hindered: for his mouth was stopped, and he was taken with a palsy, so that he could no more speak anything, nor give order concerning his house. ⁵⁶So Alcimus died at that time with great torment. ⁵⁷Now when Bacchides saw that Alcimus was dead, he returned to the king: whereupon the land of Judea was in rest two years.

⁵⁸Then all the ungodly men held a council, saying, 'Behold, Jonathan and his company are at ease, and dwell without care: now therefore we will bring Bacchides hither, who shall take them all in one night.' ⁵⁹So they went and consulted with him. ⁶⁰Then removed he, and came with a great host, and sent letters privily to his adherents in Judea, that they should take Jonathan and those that were with him: howbeit they could not, because their counsel was known unto them. ⁶¹Wherefore they took of the men of the country that were authors of that mischief, about fifty persons, and slew them. ⁶²Afterward Jonathan, and Simon, and they that were with him, got them away to Bethbasi, which is in the wilderness, and they repaired the decays thereof, and made it strong. ⁶³Which thing when Bacchides knew, he gathered together all his host, and sent word to them that were of Judea. ⁶⁴Then went he and laid siege against Bethbasi; and they fought against it a long season, and made engines of war. ⁶⁵But Jonathan left his brother Simon in the city, and went forth himself into the country, and with a certain num-

ber went he forth. ⁶⁶And he smote Odonarkes and his brethren, and the children of Phasiron in their tent. ⁶⁷And when he began to smite them, and came up with his forces, Simon and his company went out of the city, and burnt up the engines of war, ⁶⁸and fought against Bacchides, who was discomfited by them, and they afflicted him sore: for his counsel and travail was in vain. ⁶⁹Wherefore he was very wroth at the wicked men that gave him counsel to come into the country, insomuch as he slew many of them, and purposed to return into his own country. ⁷⁰Whereof when Jonathan had knowledge, he sent ambassadors unto him, to the end he should make peace with him, and deliver them the prisoners. ⁷¹Which thing he accepted, and did according to his demands, and swore unto him that he would never do him harm all the days of his life. ⁷²When therefore he had restored unto him the prisoners that he had taken aforetime out of the land of Judea, he returned and went his way into his own land, neither came he any more into their borders. ⁷³Thus the sword ceased from Israel: but Jonathan dwelt at Machmas, and began to govern the people, and he destroyed the ungodly men out of Israel.

10 In the hundred and sixtieth year Alexander, the son of Antiochus surnamed Epiphanes, went up and took Ptolemais: for the people had received him, by means whereof he reigned there. ²Now when king Demetrius heard thereof, he gathered together an exceeding great host, and went forth against him to fight. ³Moreover Demetrius sent letters unto Jonathan with loving words, so as he magnified him. ⁴'For,' said he, 'Let us first make peace with him, before he join with Alexander against us. ⁵Else he will remember all the evils that we have done against him, and against his brethren and his people.' ⁶Wherefore he gave him authority to gather together a host, and to provide weapons, that he might aid him in battle: he commanded also that the hostages that were in the tower should be delivered him. ⁷Then came Jonathan to Jerusalem, and read the letters in the audience of all the people, and of them that were in the tower: ⁸who were sore afraid when they heard that the king had given him authority to gather together a host. ⁹Whereupon they of the tower delivered their hostages unto Jonathan, and he delivered them unto their parents.

¹⁰This done, Jonathan settled himself in Jerusalem, and began to build and repair the city. ¹¹And he commanded the workmen to build the walls and the mount Sion round about with square stones for fortification; and they did so. ¹²Then the strangers, that were in the fortresses which Bacchides had built, fled away: ¹³insomuch as every man left his place, and went into his own country. ¹⁴Only at Bethsura certain of those that had forsaken the law and the commandments remained still: for it was their place of refuge.

¹⁵Now when king Alexander had heard what promises Demetrius had sent unto Jonathan: when also it was told him of the battles and noble acts which he and his brethren had done, and of the pains that they had endured, ¹⁶he said, 'Shall we find such another man? Now therefore we will make him our friend and confederate.' ¹⁷Upon this

he wrote a letter, and sent it unto him, according to these words, saying,

¹⁸King Alexander to his brother Jonathan sendeth greeting: ¹⁹we have heard of thee, that thou art a man of great power, and meet to be our friend. ²⁰Wherefore now this day we ordain thee to be the high priest of thy nation, and to be called the king's friend (and therewithal he sent him a purple robe and a crown of gold), and require thee to take our part, and keep friendship with us.

²¹So in the seventh month of the hundred and sixtieth year, at the feast of the tabernacles, Jonathan put on the holy robe, and gathered together forces, and provided much armour. ²²Whereof when Demetrius heard, he was very sorry, and said, ²³'What have we done that Alexander hath prevented us, in making amity with the Jews to strengthen himself? ²⁴I also will write unto them words of encouragement, and promise them dignities and gifts, that I may have their aid.' ²⁵He sent unto them therefore to this effect:

King Demetrius unto the people of the Jews sendeth greeting: ²⁶whereas you have kept covenants with us, and continued in our friendship, not joining yourselves with our enemies, we have heard hereof, and are glad. ²⁷Wherefore now continue ye still to be faithful unto us, and we will well recompense you for the things you do in our behalf, ²⁸and will grant you many immunities, and give you rewards.

²⁹And now I do free you, and for your sake I release all the Jews from tributes, and from the customs of salt, and from crown-taxes, ³⁰and from that which appertaineth unto me to receive for the third part of the seed, and the half of the fruit of the trees, I release it from this day forth, so that they shall not be taken of the land of Judea, nor of the three governments which are added thereunto out of the country of Samaria and Galilee, from this day forth for evermore. ³¹Let Jerusalem also be holy and free, with the borders thereof, both from tenths and tributes. ³²And as for the tower which is at Jerusalem, I yield up my authority over it, and give it to the high priest, that he may set in it such men as he shall choose to keep it. ³³Moreover I freely set at liberty every one of the Jews that were carried captives out of the land of Judea into any part of my kingdom, and I will that all my officers remit the tributes even of their cattle. ³⁴Furthermore I will that all the feasts, and sabbaths, and new moons, and solemn days, and the three days before the feast, and the three days after the feast, shall be all days of immunity and freedom for all the Jews in my realm. ³⁵Also no man shall have authority to meddle with them, or to molest any of them in any matter.

³⁶I will further, that there be enrolled amongst the king's forces about thirty thousand men of the Jews, unto whom pay shall be given, as belongeth to all the king's forces. ³⁷And of

them some shall be placed in the king's strongholds, of whom also some shall be set over the affairs of the kingdom, which are of trust: and I will that their overseers and governors be of themselves, and that they live after their own laws, even as the king hath commanded in the land of Judea.

³⁸And concerning the three governments that are added to Judea from the country of Samaria, let them be joined with Judea, that they may be reckoned to be under one, nor bound to obey other authority than the high priest's.

³⁹As for Ptolemais, and the land pertaining thereto, I give it as a free gift to the sanctuary at Jerusalem for the necessary expenses of the sanctuary. ⁴⁰Moreover I give every year fifteen thousand shekels of silver out of the king's accounts from the places appertaining. ⁴¹And all the overplus, which the officers paid not in as in former time, from henceforth shall be given towards the works of the temple. ⁴²And besides this, the five thousand shekels of silver, which they took from the uses of the temple out of the accounts year by year, even those things shall be released, because they appertain to the priests that minister. ⁴³And whosoever they be that flee unto the temple at Jerusalem, or be within the liberties thereof, being indebted unto the king, or for any other matter, let them be at liberty, and all that they have in my realm. ⁴⁴For the building also and repairing of the works of the sanctuary expenses shall be given of the king's accounts. ⁴⁵Yea, and for the building of the walls of Jerusalem, and the fortifying thereof round about, expenses shall be given out of the king's accounts, as also for building of the walls in Judea.

⁴⁶Now when Jonathan and the people heard these words, they gave no credit unto them, nor received them, because they remembered the great evil that he had done in Israel; for he had afflicted them very sore. ⁴⁷But with Alexander they were well pleased, because he was the first that entreated of true peace with them, and they were confederate with him always.

⁴⁸Then gathered king Alexander great forces, and camped over against Demetrius. ⁴⁹And after the two kings had joined battle, Demetrius' host fled: but Alexander followed after him, and prevailed against them. ⁵⁰And he continued the battle very sore until the sun went down: and that day was Demetrius slain.

⁵¹Afterward Alexander sent ambassadors to Ptolemee king of Egypt with a message to this effect: ⁵²'Forsomuch as I am come again to my realm, and am set in the throne of my progenitors, and have gotten the dominion, and overthrown Demetrius, and recovered our country ⁵³(for after I had joined battle with him, both he and his host was discomfited by us, so that we sit in the throne of his kingdom), ⁵⁴now therefore let us make a league of amity together, and give me now thy daughter to wife: and I will be thy son-in-law, and will give both thee and her gifts according to thy dignity.' ⁵⁵Then Ptolemee the king gave

answer, saying, 'Happy be the day wherein thou didst return into the land of thy fathers, and sattest in the throne of their kingdom. ⁵⁶And now will I do to thee, as thou hast written: meet me therefore at Ptolemais, that we may see one another, for I will marry my daughter to thee according to thy desire.'

⁵⁷So Ptolemee went out of Egypt with his daughter Cleopatra, and they came unto Ptolemais in the hundred threescore and second year: ⁵⁸where king Alexander meeting him, gave unto him his daughter Cleopatra, and celebrated her marriage at Ptolemais with great glory, as the manner of kings is.

⁵⁹Now king Alexander had written unto Jonathan, that he should come and meet him: ⁶⁰who thereupon went honourably to Ptolemais, where he met the two kings, and gave them and their friends silver and gold, and many presents, and found favour in their sight.

⁶¹At that time certain pestilent fellows of Israel, men of a wicked life, assembled themselves against him, to accuse him: but the king would not hear them. ⁶²Yea more than that, the king commanded to take off his garments, and clothe him in purple: and they did so. ⁶³Also he made him sit by himself, and said unto his princes, 'Go with him into the midst of the city, and make proclamation, that no man complain against him of any matter, and that no man trouble him for any manner of cause'. ⁶⁴Now when his accusers saw that he was honoured according to the proclamation, and clothed in purple, they fled all away.

⁶⁵So the king honoured him, and wrote him amongst his chief friends, and made him a duke, and partaker of his dominion. ⁶⁶Afterward Jonathan returned to Jerusalem with peace and gladness.

⁶⁷Furthermore in the hundred threescore and fifth year came Demetrius son of Demetrius out of Crete into the land of his fathers: ⁶⁸whereof when king Alexander heard tell, he was right sorry, and returned into Antioch. ⁶⁹Then Demetrius made Apollonius the governor of Coelosyria his general, who gathered together a great host, and camped in Jamnia, and sent unto Jonathan the high priest, saying, ⁷⁰'Thou alone liftest up thyself against us, and I am laughed to scorn for thy sake, and reproached: and why dost thou vaunt thy power against us in the mountains? ⁷¹Now therefore, if thou trustest in thy own strength, come down to us into the plain field, and there let us try the matter together: for with me is the power of the cities. ⁷²Ask and learn who I am, and the rest that take our part, and they shall tell thee that thy foot is not able to stand before our face; for thy fathers have been twice put to flight in their own land. ⁷³Wherefore now thou shalt not be able to abide the horsemen and so great a power in the plain, where is neither stone nor flint, nor place to flee unto.'

⁷⁴So when Jonathan heard these words of Apollonius, he was moved in his mind, and choosing ten thousand men, he went out of Jerusalem, where Simon his brother met him for to help him. ⁷⁵And he pitched his tents against Joppe: but they of Joppe shut him out of the city, because Apollonius had a garrison there. ⁷⁶Then Jonathan laid siege unto it:

whereupon they of the city let him in for fear: and so Jonathan won Joppe. [77]Whereof when Apollonius heard, he took three thousand horsemen, with a great host of footmen, and went to Azotus as one that journeyed, and therewithal drew him forth into the plain, because he had a great number of horsemen, in whom he put his trust. [78]Then Jonathan followed after him to Azotus, where the armies joined battle. [79]Now Apollonius had left a thousand horsemen in ambush. [80]And Jonathan knew that there was an ambushment behind him; for they had compassed in his host, and cast darts at the people, from morning till evening. [81]But the people stood still, as Jonathan had commanded them: and so the enemies' horses were tired. [82]Then brought Simon forth his host, and set them against the footmen (for the horsemen were spent), who were discomfited by him, and fled. [83]The horsemen also, being scattered in the field, fled to Azotus, and went into Bethdagon, their idol's temple, for safety. [84]But Jonathan set fire on Azotus, and the cities round about it, and took their spoils; and the temple of Dagon, with them that were fled into it, he burnt with fire. [85]Thus there were burnt and slain with the sword well nigh eight thousand men. [86]And from thence Jonathan removed his host, and camped against Ascalon, where the men of the city came forth, and met him with great pomp. [87]After this returned Jonathan and his host unto Jerusalem, having many spoils.

[88]Now when king Alexander heard these things, he honoured Jonathan yet more, [89]and sent him a buckle of gold, as the use is to be given to such as are of the kings' blood: he gave him also Accaron with the borders thereof in possession.

11 And the king of Egypt gathered together a great host, like the sand that lieth upon the sea-shore, and many ships, and went about through deceit to get Alexander's kingdom, and join it to his own. [2]Whereupon he took his journey into Syria in peaceable manner, so as they of the cities opened unto him, and met him: for king Alexander had commanded them so to do, because he was his father in law. [3]Now as Ptolemee entered into the cities, he set in every one of them a garrison of soldiers to keep it. [4]And when he came near to Azotus, they showed him the temple of Dagon that was burnt, and Azotus and the suburbs thereof that were destroyed, and the bodies that were cast abroad, and them that he had burnt in the battle, for they had made heaps of them by the way where he should pass. [5]Also they told the king whatsoever Jonathan had done, to the intent he might blame him: but the king held his peace. [6]Then Jonathan met the king with great pomp at Joppe, where they saluted one another, and lodged. [7]Afterward Jonathan, when he had gone with the king to the river called Eleutherus, returned again to Jerusalem.

[8]King Ptolemee therefore, having gotten the dominion of the cities by the sea unto Seleucia upon the sea coast, imagined wicked counsels against Alexander. [9]Whereupon he sent ambassadors unto king Demetrius, saying, 'Come, let us make a league betwixt us, and I will give thee my daughter whom Alexander hath, and thou shalt reign in

thy father's kingdom: ¹⁰for I repent that I gave my daughter unto him, for he sought to slay me'. ¹¹Thus did he slander him, because he was desirous of his kingdom. ¹²Wherefore he took his daughter from him, and gave her to Demetrius, and forsook Alexander, so that their hatred was openly known.

¹³Then Ptolemee entered into Antioch, where he set two crowns upon his head, the crown of Asia, and of Egypt. ¹⁴In the mean season was king Alexander in Cilicia, because those that dwelt in those parts had revolted from him. ¹⁵But when Alexander heard of this, he came to war against him: whereupon king Ptolemee brought forth his host, and met him with a mighty power, and put him to flight. ¹⁶So Alexander fled into Arabia, there to be defended; but king Ptolemee was exalted: ¹⁷for Zabdiel the Arabian took off Alexander's head, and sent it unto Ptolemee. ¹⁸King Ptolemee also died the third day after, and they that were in the strongholds were slain one of another. ¹⁹By this means Demetrius reigned in the hundred threescore and seventh year.

²⁰At the same time Jonathan gathered together them that were in Judea, to take the tower that was in Jerusalem: and he made many engines of war against it. ²¹Then certain ungodly persons who hated their own people, went unto the king, and told him that Jonathan besieged the tower. ²²Whereof when he heard, he was angry, and immediately removing, he came to Ptolemais, and wrote unto Jonathan, that he should not lay siege to the tower, but come and speak with him at Ptolemais in great haste. ²³Nevertheless Jonathan, when he heard this, commanded to besiege it still: and he chose certain of the elders of Israel and the priests, and put himself in peril; ²⁴and took silver and gold, and raiment, and divers presents besides, and went to Ptolemais unto the king, where he found favour in his sight. ²⁵And though certain ungodly men of the people had made complaints against him, ²⁶yet the king entreated him as his predecessors had done before, and promoted him in the sight of all his friends, ²⁷and confirmed him in the high priesthood, and in all the honours that he had before, and gave him pre-eminence among his chief friends.

²⁸Then Jonathan desired the king, that he would make Judea free from tribute, as also the three governments, with the country of Samaria; and he promised him three hundred talents. ²⁹So the king consented, and wrote letters unto Jonathan of all these things after this manner:

³⁰King Demetrius unto his brother Jonathan, and unto the nation of the Jews, sendeth greeting. ³¹We send you here a copy of the letter which we did write unto our cousin Lasthenes concerning you, that you might see it. ³²'King Demetrius unto his father Lasthenes sendeth greeting: ³³we are determined to do good to the people of the Jews, who are our friends, and keep covenants with us, because of their good will towards us. ³⁴Wherefore we have ratified unto them the borders of Judea, with the three governments of Apherema and Lydda and

Ramathem, that are added unto Judea from the country of Samaria, and all things appertaining unto them, for all such as do sacrifice in Jerusalem, instead of the payments which the king received of them yearly aforetime out of the fruits of the earth and of trees. ³⁵And as for other things that belong unto us, of the tithes and customs pertaining unto us, as also the salt pits, and the crown-taxes, which are due unto us, we discharge them of them all for their relief. ³⁶And nothing hereof shall be revoked from this time forth for ever. ³⁷Now therefore see that thou make a copy of these things, and let it be delivered unto Jonathan, and set upon the holy mount in a conspicuous place.

³⁸After this, when king Demetrius saw that the land was quiet before him, and that no resistance was made against him, he sent away all his forces, every one to his own place, except certain bands of strangers, whom he had gathered from the isles of the heathen: wherefore all the forces of his fathers hated him. ³⁹Moreover there was one Tryphon, that had been of Alexander's part afore, who, seeing that all the host murmured against Demetrius, went to Simalcue the Arabian, that brought up Antiochus the young son of Alexander, ⁴⁰and lay sore upon him to deliver him this young Antiochus, that he might reign in his father's stead: he told him therefore all that Demetrius had done, and how his men of war were at enmity with him, and there he remained a long season.

⁴¹In the mean time Jonathan sent unto king Demetrius, that he would cast those of the tower out of Jerusalem, and those also in the fortresses: for they fought against Israel. ⁴²So Demetrius sent unto Jonathan, saying, 'I will not only do this for thee and thy people, but I will greatly honour thee and thy nation, if opportunity serve. ⁴³Now therefore thou shalt do well if thou send me men to help me; for all my forces are gone from me.' ⁴⁴Upon this Jonathan sent him three thousand strong men unto Antioch: and when they came to the king, the king was very glad of their coming. ⁴⁵Howbeit they that were of the city gathered themselves together into the midst of the city, to the number of a hundred and twenty thousand men, and would have slain the king. ⁴⁶Wherefore the king fled into the court, but they of the city kept the passages of the city, and began to fight. ⁴⁷Then the king called to the Jews for help, who came unto him all at once, and dispersing themselves through the city, slew that day in the city to the number of a hundred thousand. ⁴⁸Also they set fire on the city, and got many spoils that day, and delivered the king.

⁴⁹So when they of the city saw that the Jews had got the city as they would, their courage was abated: wherefore they made supplication to the king, and cried, saying, ⁵⁰'Grant us peace, and let the Jews cease from assaulting us and the city'. ⁵¹With that they cast away their weapons, and made peace; and the Jews were honoured in the sight of the king, and in the sight of all that were in his realm; and they returned to Jerusalem, having great spoils. ⁵²So king Demetrius sat on the throne of his kingdom, and the land was quiet before him.

⁵³Nevertheless he dissembled in all that ever he spoke, and estranged himself from Jonathan, neither rewarded he him according to the benefits which he had received of him, but troubled him very sore.

⁵⁴After this returned Tryphon, and with him the young child Antiochus, who reigned, and was crowned. ⁵⁵Then there gathered unto him all the men of war whom Demetrius had put away, and they fought against Demetrius, who turned his back and fled. ⁵⁶Moreover Tryphon took the elephants, and won Antioch.

⁵⁷At that time young Antiochus wrote unto Jonathan, saying, 'I confirm thee in the high priesthood, and appoint thee ruler over the four governments, and to be one of the king's friends'. ⁵⁸Upon this he sent him golden vessels to be served in, and gave him leave to drink in gold, and to be clothed in purple, and to wear a golden buckle. ⁵⁹His brother Simon also he made captain from the place called the Ladder of Tyrus unto the borders of Egypt.

⁶⁰Then Jonathan went forth, and passed through the cities beyond the water, and all the forces of Syria gathered themselves unto him for to help him: and when he came to Ascalon, they of the city met him honourably. ⁶¹From whence he went to Gaza, but they of Gaza shut him out; wherefore he laid siege unto it, and burnt the suburbs thereof with fire, and spoiled them. ⁶²Afterward, when they of Gaza made supplication unto Jonathan, he made peace with them, and took the sons of the chief men for hostages, and sent them to Jerusalem, and passed through the country unto Damascus.

⁶³Now when Jonathan heard that Demetrius' princes were come to Cades, which is in Galilee, with a great power, purposing to remove him out of the country, ⁶⁴he went to meet them, and left Simon his brother in the country. ⁶⁵Then Simon encamped against Bethsura, and fought against it a long season, and shut it up: ⁶⁶but they desired to have peace with him, which he granted them, and then put them out from thence, and took the city, and set a garrison in it.

⁶⁷As for Jonathan and his host, they pitched at the water of Gennesar, from whence betimes in the morning they got them to the plain of Nasor. ⁶⁸And behold, the host of strangers met them in the plain, who, having laid men in ambush for him in the mountains, came themselves over against him. ⁶⁹So when they that lay in ambush rose out of their places, and joined battle, all that were of Jonathan's side fled; ⁷⁰insomuch as there was not one of them left, except Mattathias the son of Absalom, and Judas the son of Calphi, the captains of the host. ⁷¹Then Jonathan rent his clothes, and cast earth upon his head, and prayed. ⁷²Afterwards turning again to battle, he put them to flight, and so they ran away. ⁷³Now when his own men that were fled saw this, they turned again unto him, and with him pursued them to Cades, even unto their own tents, and there they camped. ⁷⁴So there were slain of the heathen that day about three thousand men: but Jonathan returned to Jerusalem.

12 Now when Jonathan saw that the time served him, he chose certain men, and sent them to Rome, for to confirm and renew the

friendship that they had with them. [2]He sent letters also to the Lacedemonians, and to other places, for the same purpose. [3]So they went unto Rome, and entered into the senate, and said, 'Jonathan the high priest, and the people of the Jews sent us unto you, to the end you should renew the friendship, which you had with them, and league, as in former time'. [4]Upon this the Romans gave them letters unto the governors of every place, that they should bring them into the land of Judea peaceably.

[5]And this is the copy of the letters which Jonathan wrote to the Lacedemonians:

[6]Jonathan the high priest, and the elders of the nation, and the priests, and the other people of the Jews, unto the Lacedemonians their brethren send greeting. [7]There were letters sent in times past unto Onias the high priest from Darius, who reigned then among you, to signify that you are our brethren, as the copy here underwritten doth specify. [8]At which time Onias entreated the ambassador that was sent honourably, and received the letters, wherein declaration was made of the league and friendship. [9]Therefore we also, albeit we need none of these things, for that we have the holy books of scripture in our hands to comfort us, [10]have nevertheless attempted to send unto you for the renewing of brotherhood and friendship, lest we should become strangers unto you altogether: for there is a long time passed since you sent unto us. [11]We therefore at all times without ceasing, both in our feasts, and other convenient days, do remember you in the sacrifices which we offer, and in our prayers, as reason is, and as it becometh us to think upon our brethren: [12]and we are right glad of your honour.

[13]As for ourselves, we have had great troubles and wars on every side, forsomuch as the kings that are round about us have fought against us. [14]Howbeit we would not be troublesome unto you, nor to others of our confederates and friends in these wars: [15]for we have help from heaven that succoureth us, so as we are delivered from our enemies, and our enemies are brought under foot. [16]For this cause we chose Numenius the son of Antiochus, and Antipater the son of Jason, and sent them unto the Romans, to renew the amity that we had with them, and the former league. [17]We commanded them also to go unto you, and to salute you, and to deliver you our letters concerning the renewing of our brotherhood. [18]Wherefore now ye shall do well to give us an answer thereto.

[19]And this is the copy of the letters which Oniares sent:

[20]Areus king of the Lacedemonians to Onias the high priest, greeting. [21]It is found in writing, that the Lacedemonians and Jews are brethren, and that they are of the stock of Abraham: [22]now therefore, since this is come to our knowledge, you shall do well to write unto us of your prosperity. [23]We do write back

again to you, that your cattle and goods are ours, and ours are yours. We do command therefore our ambassadors to make report unto you on this wise. [24]Now when Jonathan heard that Demetrius' princes were come to fight against him with a greater host than afore, [25]he removed from Jerusalem, and met them in the land of Amathis: for he gave them no respite to enter his country. [26]He sent spies also unto their tents, who came again, and told him that they were appointed to come upon them in the night season. [27]Wherefore so soon as the sun was down, Jonathan commanded his men to watch, and to be in arms, that all the night long they might be ready to fight: also he sent forth sentinels round about the host. [28]But when the adversaries heard that Jonathan and his men were ready for battle, they feared, and trembled in their hearts, and they kindled fires in their camp. [29]Howbeit Jonathan and his company knew it not till the morning: for they saw the lights burning. [30]Then Jonathan pursued after them, but overtook them not: for they were gone over the river Eleutherus. [31]Wherefore Jonathan turned to the Arabians, who were called Zabadeans, and smote them, and took their spoils. [32]And removing thence, he came to Damascus, and so passed through all the country.

[33]Simon also went forth, and passed through the country unto Ascalon, and the holds there adjoining, from whence he turned aside to Joppe, and won it. [34]For he had heard that they would deliver the hold unto them that took Demetrius' part; wherefore he set a garrison there to keep it.

[35]After this came Jonathan home again, and calling the elders of the people together, he consulted with them about building strongholds in Judea, [36]and making the walls of Jerusalem higher, and raising a great mount between the tower and the city, for to separate it from the city, that so it might be alone, that men might neither sell nor buy in it. [37]Upon this they came together to build up the city, forasmuch as part of the wall toward the brook on the east side was fallen down, and they repaired that which was called Caphenatha. [38]Simon also set up Adida in Sephela, and made it strong with gates and bars.

[39]Now Tryphon went about to get the kingdom of Asia, and to kill Antiochus the king, that he might set the crown upon his own head. [40]Howbeit he was afraid that Jonathan would not suffer him, and that he would fight against him; wherefore he sought a way how to take Jonathan, that he might kill him. So he removed, and came to Bethsan. [41]Then Jonathan went out to meet him with forty thousand men chosen for the battle, and came to Bethsan. [42]Now when Tryphon saw that Jonathan came with so great a force, he durst not stretch his hand against him, [43]but received him honourably, and commended him unto all his friends, and gave him gifts, and commanded his men of war to be as obedient unto him, as to himself. [44]Unto Jonathan also he said, 'Why hast thou put all this people to so great trouble, seeing there is no war betwixt us? [45]Therefore send them now home again, and choose a few men to wait on thee, and come thou with me to Ptolemais, for I will

give it thee, and the rest of the strongholds and forces, and all that have any charge: as for me, I will return and depart: for this is the cause of my coming.' ⁴⁶So Jonathan believing him did as he bade him, and sent away his host, who went into the land of Judea. ⁴⁷And with himself he retained but three thousand men, of whom he sent two thousand into Galilee, and one thousand went with him. ⁴⁸Now as soon as Jonathan entered into Ptolemais, they of Ptolemais shut the gates, and took him, and all them that came with him they slew with the sword.

⁴⁹Then sent Tryphon a host of footmen and horsemen into Galilee, and into the great plain, to destroy all Jonathan's company. ⁵⁰But when they knew that Jonathan and they that were with him were taken and slain, they encouraged one another, and went close together, prepared to fight. ⁵¹They therefore that followed upon them, perceiving that they were ready to fight for their lives, turned back again. ⁵²Whereupon they all came into the land of Judea peaceably, and there they bewailed Jonathan, and them that were with him, and they were sore afraid; wherefore all Israel made great lamentation. ⁵³Then all the heathen that were round about them sought to destroy them. 'For,' said they, 'they have no captain, nor any to help them: now therefore let us make war upon them, and take away their memorial from amongst men.'

13 Now when Simon heard that Tryphon had gathered together a great host to invade the land of Judea, and destroy it, ²and saw that the people was in great trembling and fear, he went up to Jerusalem, and gathered the people together, ³and gave them exhortation, saying, 'Ye yourselves know what great things I, and my brethren, and my father's house, have done for the laws and the sanctuary, the battles also and troubles which we have seen, ⁴by reason whereof all my brethren are slain for Israel's sake, and I am left alone. ⁵Now therefore be it far from me, that I should spare my own life in any time of trouble: for I am no better than my brethren. ⁶Doubtless I will avenge my nation, and the sanctuary, and our wives, and our children: for all the heathen are gathered to destroy us of very malice.'

⁷Now as soon as the people heard these words, their spirit revived. ⁸And they answered with a loud voice, saying, 'Thou shalt be our leader in stead of Judas and Jonathan thy brother. ⁹Fight thou our battles, and whatsoever thou commandest us, that will we do.'

¹⁰So then he gathered together all the men of war, and made haste to finish the walls of Jerusalem, and he fortified it round about. ¹¹Also he sent Jonathan the son of Absalom, and with him a great power, to Joppe: who casting out them that were therein remained there in it.

¹²So Tryphon removed from Ptolemais with a great power to invade the land of Judea, and Jonathan was with him in ward. ¹³But Simon pitched his tents at Adida, over against the plain. ¹⁴Now when Tryphon knew that Simon was risen up in stead of his brother Jonathan, and meant to join battle with him, he sent messengers unto him, saying,

¹⁵Whereas we have Jonathan thy brother in hold, it is for money that he is owing unto the king's treasure, concerning the business that was committed unto him. ¹⁶Wherefore now send a

hundred talents of silver, and two of his sons for hostages, that when he is at liberty he may not revolt from us, and we will let him go. [17]Hereupon Simon, albeit he perceived that they spoke deceitfully unto him, yet sent he the money and the children, lest peradventure he should procure to himself great hatred of the people: [18]who might have said, 'Because I sent him not the money and the children, therefore is Jonathan dead'. [19]So he sent them the children and the hundred talents: howbeit Tryphon dissembled, neither would he let Jonathan go.

[20]And after this came Tryphon to invade the land, and destroy it, going round about by the way that leadeth unto Adora: but Simon and his host marched against him in every place wheresoever he went. [21]Now they that were in the tower sent messengers unto Tryphon, to the end that he should hasten his coming unto them by the wilderness, and send them victuals. [22]Wherefore Tryphon made ready all his horsemen to come that night: but there fell a very great snow, by reason whereof he came not. So he departed, and came into the country of Galaad. [23]And when he came near to Bascama, he slew Jonathan, who was buried there. [24]Afterward Tryphon returned and went into his own land.

[25]Then sent Simon, and took the bones of Jonathan his brother, and buried them in Modin, the city of his fathers. [26]And all Israel made great lamentation for him, and bewailed him many days. [27]Simon also built a monument upon the sepulchre of his father and his brethren, and raised it aloft to the sight, with hewn stone behind and before. [28]Moreover he set up seven pyramids one against another, for his father, and his mother, and his four brethren. [29]And in these he made cunning devices, about the which he set great pillars, and upon the pillars he made all their armour for a perpetual memory, and by the armour ships carved, that they might be seen of all that sail on the sea. [30]This is the sepulchre which he made at Modin, and it standeth yet unto this day.

[31]Now Tryphon dealt deceitfully with the young king Antiochus, and slew him. [32]And he reigned in his stead, and crowned himself king of Asia, and brought a great calamity upon the land.

[33]Then Simon built up the strongholds in Judea, and fenced them about with high towers, and great walls, and gates, and bars, and laid up victuals therein. [34]Moreover Simon chose men, and sent to king Demetrius, to the end he should give the land an immunity, because all that Tryphon did was to spoil. [35]Unto whom king Demetrius answered and wrote after this manner:

[36]King Demetrius unto Simon the high priest, and friend of kings, as also unto the elders and nation of the Jews, sendeth greeting. [37]The golden crown, and the scarlet robe which ye sent unto us, we have received, and we are ready to make a steadfast peace with you, yea, and to write unto our officers to confirm the immunities which we have granted. [38]And whatsoever covenants we have made with you shall stand, and the strongholds which ye have built shall be your own. [39]As for any

oversight or fault committed unto this day, we forgive it, and the crown-tax also which ye owe us: and if there were any other tribute paid in Jerusalem, it shall no more be paid. ⁴⁰And look who are meet among you to be in our court, let them be enrolled, and let there be peace betwixt us.

⁴¹Thus the yoke of the heathen was taken away from Israel in the hundred and seventieth year. ⁴²Then the people of Israel began to write in their instruments and contracts, 'In the first year of Simon the high priest, the governor and leader of the Jews'.

⁴³In those days Simon camped against Gaza, and besieged it round about; he made also an engine of war, and set it by the city, and battered a certain tower, and took it. ⁴⁴And they that were in the engine leapt into the city, whereupon there was a great uproar in the city: ⁴⁵insomuch as the people of the city rent their clothes, and climbed upon the walls with their wives and children, and cried with a loud voice, beseeching Simon to grant them peace. ⁴⁶And they said, 'Deal not with us according to our wickedness, but according to thy mercy'. ⁴⁷So Simon was appeased towards them, and fought no more against them, but put them out of the city, and cleansed the houses wherein the idols were, and so entered into it with songs and thanksgiving. ⁴⁸Yea, he put all uncleanness out of it, and placed such men there as would keep the law, and made it stronger than it was before, and built therein a dwelling-place for himself.

⁴⁹They also of the tower in Jerusalem were kept so strait, that they could neither come forth, nor go into the country, nor buy, nor sell: wherefore they were in great distress for want of victuals, and a great number of them perished through famine. ⁵⁰Then cried they to Simon, beseeching him to be at one with them: which thing he granted them; and when he had put them out from thence, he cleansed the tower from pollutions: ⁵¹and entered into it the three and twentieth day of the second month, in the hundred seventy and first year, with thanksgiving, and branches of palm trees, and with harps, and cymbals, and with viols, and hymns, and songs: because there was destroyed a great enemy out of Israel. ⁵²He ordained also that that day should be kept every year with gladness. Moreover the hill of the temple that was by the tower he made stronger than it was, and there he dwelt himself with his company. ⁵³And when Simon saw that John his son was a valiant man, he made him captain of all the hosts; and dwelt in Gazara.

14 Now in the hundred threescore and twelfth year king Demetrius gathered his forces together, and went into Media, to get him help to fight against Tryphon. ²But when Arsaces, the king of Persia and Media, heard that Demetrius was entered within his borders, he sent one of his princes to take him alive: ³who went and smote the host of Demetrius, and took him, and brought him to Arsaces, by whom he was put in ward.

⁴As for the land of Judea, that was quiet all the days of Simon: for he sought the good of his nation in such wise, as that evermore his author-

ity and honour pleased them well. ⁵And as he was honourable in all his acts, so in this, that he took Joppe for a haven, and made an entrance to the isles of the sea, ⁶and enlarged the bounds of his nation, and recovered the country, ⁷and gathered together a great number of captives, and had the dominion of Gazara, and Bethsura, and the tower, out of the which he took all uncleanness, neither was there any that resisted him.

⁸Then did they till their ground in peace, and the earth gave her increase, and the trees of the field their fruit. ⁹The ancient men sat all in the streets, communing together of good things, and the young men put on glorious and warlike apparel. ¹⁰He provided victuals for the cities, and set in them all manner of munition, so that his honourable name was renowned unto the end of the world. ¹¹He made peace in the land, and Israel rejoiced with great joy: ¹²for every man sat under his vine and his fig tree, and there was none to fray them: ¹³neither was there any left in the land to fight against them: yea, the kings themselves were overthrown in those days. ¹⁴Moreover he strengthened all those of his people that were brought low: the law he searched out; and every contemner of the law and wicked person he took away. ¹⁵He beautified the sanctuary, and multiplied the vessels of the temple.

¹⁶Now when it was heard at Rome, and as far as Sparta, that Jonathan was dead, they were very sorry. ¹⁷But as soon as they heard that his brother Simon was made high priest in his stead, and ruled the country, and the cities therein, ¹⁸they wrote unto him in tablets of brass, to renew the friendship and league which they had made with Judas and Jonathan his brethren: ¹⁹which writings were read before the congregation at Jerusalem. ²⁰And this is the copy of the letters that the Lacedemonians sent:

The rulers of the Lacedemonians, with the city, unto Simon the high priest, and the elders and priests, and residue of the people of the Jews, our brethren, send greeting. ²¹The ambassadors that were sent unto our people certified us of your glory and honour: wherefore we were glad of their coming, ²²and did register the things that they spoke in the council of the people in this manner: 'Numenius son of Antiochus, and Antipater son of Jason, the Jews' ambassadors, came unto us to renew the friendship they had with us. ²³And it pleased the people to entertain the men honourably, and to put the copy of their ambassage in public records, to the end the people of the Lacedemonians might have a memorial thereof: furthermore we have written a copy thereof unto Simon the high priest.'

²⁴After this Simon sent Numenius to Rome with a great shield of gold of a thousand pound weight, to confirm the league with them.

²⁵Whereof when the people heard, they said, 'What thanks shall we give to Simon and his sons? ²⁶for he and his brethren and the house of his father have established Israel, and chased away in fight their enemies from them, and confirmed their liberty'. ²⁷So then they wrote it in tablets of brass, which they set upon pillars in mount Sion: and this is the copy of the writing:

The eighteenth day of the month Elul, in the hundred three-score and twelfth year, being the third year of Simon the high priest, ²⁸at Saramel in the great congregation of the priests and people, and rulers of the nation, and elders of the country, were these things notified unto us. ²⁹Forsomuch as oftentimes there have been wars in the country, wherein for the maintenance of their sanctuary, and the law, Simon the son of Mattathias, of the posterity of Jarib, together with his brethren, put themselves in jeopardy, and resisting the enemies of their nation did their nation great honour. ³⁰(For after that Jonathan, having gathered his nation together, and been their high priest, was added to his people, ³¹their enemies purposed to invade their country, that they might destroy it, and lay hands on the sanctuary. ³²At which time Simon rose up, and fought for his nation, and spent much of his own substance, and armed the valiant men of his nation, and gave them wages, ³³and fortified the cities of Judea, together with Bethsura, that lieth upon the borders of Judea, where the armour of the enemies had been before; but he set a garrison of Jews there. ³⁴Moreover he fortified Joppe, which lieth upon the sea, and Gazara, that bordereth upon Azotus, where the enemies had dwelt before: but he placed Jews there, and furnished them with all things convenient for the reparation thereof.)

³⁵The people therefore seeing the acts of Simon, and unto what glory he thought to bring his nation, made him their governor and chief priest, because he had done all these things, and for the justice and faith which he kept to his nation, and for that he sought by all means to exalt his people. ³⁶For in his time things prospered in his hands, so that the heathen were taken out of their country, and they also that were in the city of David in Jerusalem, who had made themselves a tower, out of which they issued, and polluted all about the sanctuary, and did much hurt in the holy place. ³⁷But he placed Jews therein, and fortified it for the safety of the country and the city, and raised up the walls of Jerusalem. ³⁸King Demetrius also confirmed him in the high priesthood according to those things, ³⁹and made him one of his friends, and honoured him with great honour. ⁴⁰For he had heard say, that the Romans had called the Jews their friends and confederates and brethren, and that they had entertained the ambassadors of Simon honourably; ⁴¹also that the Jews and priests were well pleased that Simon should be their governor and high priest for ever until there should arise a faithful prophet; ⁴²moreover that he should be their captain, and should take charge of the sanctuary, to set them over their works, and over the country, and over the armour, and over the fortresses, that, I say, he should take charge of the sanctuary; ⁴³besides this, that he should be obeyed of every man, and that all the writings in the country should be

made in his name, and that he should be clothed in purple, and wear gold: ⁴⁴also that it should be lawful for none of the people or priests to break any of these things, or to gainsay his words, or to gather an assembly in the country without him, or to be clothed in purple, or wear a buckle of gold: ⁴⁵and whosoever should do otherwise, or break any of these things, he should be punished.

⁴⁶Thus it liked all the people to deal with Simon, and to do as hath been said. ⁴⁷Then Simon accepted hereof, and was well pleased to be high priest, and captain and governor of the Jews and priests, and to defend them all.

⁴⁸So they commanded that this writing should be put in tablets of brass, and that they should be set up within the compass of the sanctuary in a conspicuous place; ⁴⁹also that the copies thereof should be laid up in the treasury, to the end that Simon and his sons might have them.

15 Moreover Antiochus son of Demetrius the king sent letters from the isles of the sea unto Simon the priest and prince of the Jews, and to all the people; ²the contents whereof were these:

King Antiochus to Simon the high priest and prince of his nation, and to the people of the Jews, greeting: ³forasmuch as certain pestilent men have usurped the kingdom of our fathers, and my purpose is to challenge it again, that I may restore it to the old estate, and to that end have gathered a multitude of foreign soldiers together, and prepared ships of war, ⁴my meaning also being to go through the country, that I may be avenged of them that have destroyed it, and made many cities in the kingdom desolate: ⁵now therefore I confirm unto thee all the oblations which the kings before me granted thee, and whatsoever gifts besides they granted. ⁶I give thee leave also to coin money for thy country with thy own stamp. ⁷And as concerning Jerusalem and the sanctuary, let them be free, and all the armour that thou hast made, and fortresses that thou hast built, and keepest in thy hands, let them remain unto thee. ⁸And if anything be, or shall be, owing to the king, let it be forgiven thee from this time forth for evermore. ⁹Furthermore, when we have obtained our kingdom, we will honour thee, and thy nation, and thy temple with great honour, so that your honour shall be known throughout the world.

¹⁰In the hundred threescore and fourteenth year went Antiochus into the land of his fathers, at which time all the forces came together unto him, so that few were left with Tryphon. ¹¹Wherefore being pursued by king Antiochus, he fled unto Dora, which lieth by the seaside: ¹²for he saw that troubles came upon him all at once, and that his forces had forsaken him. ¹³Then camped Antiochus against Dora, having with him a hundred and twenty thousand men of war, and eight thousand horsemen. ¹⁴And when he had compassed the city round about, and joined ships close to the town on the seaside, he vexed the city by land and by sea, neither suffered he any to go out or in.

¹⁵In the mean season came Numenius and his company from Rome, having letters to the kings and countries, wherein were written these things: ¹⁶Lucius, consul of the Romans, unto king Ptolemee, greeting. ¹⁷The Jews' ambassadors, our friends and confederates, came unto us to renew the old friendship and league, being sent from Simon the high priest, and from the people of the Jews: ¹⁸and they brought a shield of gold of a thousand pound. ¹⁹We thought it good therefore to write unto the kings and countries, that they should do them no harm, nor fight against them, their cities, or countries, nor yet aid their enemies against them. ²⁰It seemed also good to us to receive the shield of them. ²¹If therefore there be any pestilent fellows, that have fled from their country unto you, deliver them unto Simon the high priest, that he may punish them according to their own law.

²²The same thing wrote he likewise unto Demetrius the king, and Attalus, to Ariarathes, and Arsaces, ²³and to all the countries, and to Sampsames, and the Lacedemonians, and to Delus, and Myndus, and Sicyon, and Caria, and Samos, and Pamphylia, and Lycia, and Halicarnassus, and Rhodus, and Phaselis, and Cos, and Side, and Aradus, and Gortyna, and Cnidus, and Cyprus, and Cyrene. ²⁴And the copy hereof they wrote to Simon the high priest.

²⁵So Antiochus the king camped against Dora the second day, assaulting it continually, and making engines, by which means he shut up Tryphon, that he could neither go out nor in. ²⁶At that time Simon sent him two thousand chosen men to aid him: silver also, and gold, and much armour. ²⁷Nevertheless he would not receive them, but broke all the covenants which he had made with him afore, and became strange unto him. ²⁸Furthermore he sent unto him Athenobius, one of his friends, to commune with him, and say, 'You withhold Joppe and Gazara, with the tower that is in Jerusalem, which are cities of my realm. ²⁹The borders thereof ye have wasted and done great hurt in the land, and got the dominion of many places within my kingdom. ³⁰Now therefore deliver the cities which ye have taken, and the tributes of the places, whereof ye have gotten dominion without the borders of Judea: ³¹or else give me for them five hundred talents of silver; and for the harm that you have done, and the tributes of the cities, other five hundred talents: if not, we will come and fight against you.'

³²So Athenobius the king's friend came to Jerusalem: and when he saw the glory of Simon, and the cupboard of gold and silver plate, and his great attendance, he was astonished, and told him the king's message. ³³Then answered Simon, and said unto him, 'We have neither taken other men's land, nor held that which appertaineth to others, but the inheritance of our fathers, which our enemies had wrongfully in possession a certain time. ³⁴Wherefore we, having opportunity, hold the inheritance of our fathers. ³⁵And whereas thou demandest Joppe and Gazara, albeit they did great harm unto the people in our country, yet will we give a hundred talents for them.' Hereunto Athenobius

answered him not a word, ³⁶but returned in a rage to the king, and made report unto him of these speeches, and of the glory of Simon, and of all that he had seen: whereupon the king was exceeding wroth.

³⁷In the mean time fled Tryphon by ship unto Orthosias. ³⁸Then the king made Cendebeus captain of the sea coast, and gave him a host of footmen and horsemen, ³⁹and commanded him to remove his host toward Judea: also he commanded him to build up Cedron, and to fortify the gates, and to war against the people; but as for the king himself, he pursued Tryphon. ⁴⁰So Cendebeus came to Jamnia, and began to provoke the people, and to invade Judea, and to take the people prisoners, and slay them. ⁴¹And when he had built up Cedron, he set horsemen there, and a host of footmen, to the end that issuing out they might make outroads upon the ways of Judea, as the king had commanded him.

16 Then came up John from Gazara, and told Simon his father what Cendebeus had done. ²Wherefore Simon called his two eldest sons, Judas and John, and said unto them, 'I and my brethren, and my father's house have ever from our youth unto this day fought against the enemies of Israel, and things have prospered so well in our hands, that we have delivered Israel oftentimes. ³But now I am old, and ye, by God's mercy, are of a sufficient age: be ye in stead of me and my brother, and go and fight for our nation, and the help from heaven be with you.'

⁴So he chose out of the country twenty thousand men of war with horsemen, who went out against Cendebeus, and rested that night at Modin. ⁵And when as they rose in the morning, and went into the plain, behold, a mighty great host both of footmen and horsemen came against them: howbeit there was a water brook betwixt them. ⁶So he and his people pitched over against them: and when he saw that the people were afraid to go over the water brook, he went first over himself, and then the men seeing him passed through after him. ⁷That done, he divided his men, and set the horsemen in the midst of the footmen: for the enemies' horsemen were very many. ⁸Then sounded they with the holy trumpets: whereupon Cendebeus and his host were put to flight, so that many of them were slain, and the remnant got them to the stronghold. ⁹At that time was Judas John's brother wounded: but John still followed after them, until he came to Cedron, which Cendebeus had built. ¹⁰So they fled even unto the towers in the fields of Azotus: wherefore he burnt it with fire: so that there were slain of them about two thousand men. Afterward he returned into the land of Judea in peace.

¹¹Moreover in the plain of Jericho was Ptolemee the son of Abubus made captain, and he had abundance of silver and gold: ¹²for he was the high priest's son-in-law. ¹³Wherefore his heart being lifted up, he thought to get the country to himself, and thereupon consulted deceitfully against Simon and his sons to destroy them. ¹⁴Now Simon was visiting the cities that were in the country, and taking care for the good ordering of them; at which time he came down himself to Jericho with

his sons, Mattathias and Judas, in the hundred threescore and seventeenth year, in the eleventh month, called Sabat: [15]where the son of Abubus receiving them deceitfully into a little hold called Docus, which he had built, made them a great banquet: howbeit he had hid men there. [16]So when Simon and his sons had drunk largely, Ptolemee and his men rose up, and took their weapons, and came upon Simon into the banqueting place, and slew him, and his two sons, and certain of his servants. [17]In which doing he committed a great treachery, and recompensed evil for good.

[18]Then Ptolemee wrote these things, and sent to the king, that he should send him a host to aid him, and he would deliver him the country and cities. [19]He sent others also to Gazara to kill John: and unto the tribunes he sent letters to come unto him, that he might give them silver, and gold, and rewards. [20]And others he sent to take Jerusalem, and the mountain of the temple. [21]Now one had run afore to Gazara, and told John that his father and brethren were slain, and, quoth he, 'Ptolemee hath sent to slay thee also'. [22]Hereof when he heard, he was sore astonished: so he laid hands on them that were come to destroy him, and slew them, for he knew that they sought to make him away.

[23]As concerning the rest of the acts of John, and his wars, and worthy deeds which he did, and the building of the walls which he made, and his doings, [24]behold, these are written in the chronicles of his priesthood, from the time he was made high priest after his father.

THE SECOND BOOK
OF THE
MACCABEES

1 The brethren the Jews that be at Jerusalem and in the land of Judea, wish unto the brethren, the Jews that are throughout Egypt, health and peace. ²God be gracious unto you, and remember his covenant that he made with Abraham, Isaac, and Jacob, his faithful servants; ³and give you all a heart to serve him, and to do his will, with a good courage and a willing mind; ⁴and open your hearts in his law and commandments, and send you peace, ⁵and hear your prayers, and be at one with you, and never forsake you in time of trouble. ⁶And now we be here praying for you. ⁷What time as Demetrius reigned, in the hundred threescore and ninth year, we the Jews wrote unto you in the extremity of trouble that came upon us in those years, from the time that Jason and his company revolted from the holy land and kingdom, ⁸and burnt the porch, and shed innocent blood. Then we prayed unto the Lord, and were heard: we offered also sacrifices and fine flour, and lighted the lamps, and set forth the loaves. ⁹And now see that ye keep the feast of tabernacles in the month Casleu.

¹⁰In the hundred fourscore and eighth year, the people that were at Jerusalem and in Judea, and the council, and Judas, sent greeting and health unto Aristobulus, king Ptolemee's master, who was of the stock of the anointed priests, and to the Jews that were in Egypt:

¹¹Insomuch as God hath delivered us from great perils, we thank him highly, as having been in battle against a king. ¹²For he cast them out that fought within the holy city. ¹³For when the leader was come into Persia, and the army with him that seemed invincible, they were slain in the temple of Nanea by the deceit of Nanea's priests. ¹⁴For Antiochus, as though he would marry her, came into the place, and his friends that were with him, to receive money in name of a dowry. ¹⁵Which when the priests of Nanea had set forth, and he was entered with a small company into the compass of the temple, they shut the temple as soon as Antiochus was come in: ¹⁶and opening a privy door of the roof, they threw stones like thunderbolts, and struck down the captain, hewed them in pieces, smote off their heads, and cast them to those that were without. ¹⁷Blessed be our God in all things, who hath delivered up the ungodly.

¹⁸Therefore whereas we are now purposed to keep the purification of the temple upon the five and twentieth day of the month Casleu, we thought it necessary to certify you thereof, that ye also might keep it, as the feast of the tabernacles, and of

the fire, which was given us when Neemias offered sacrifice, after that he had built the temple and the altar. ¹⁹For when our fathers were led into Persia, the priests that were then devout took the fire of the altar privily, and hid it in a hollow place of a pit without water, where they kept it sure, so that the place was unknown to all men. ²⁰Now after many years, when it pleased God, Neemias, being sent from the king of Persia, did send of the posterity of those priests that had hid it to the fire: but when they told us they found no fire, but thick water, ²¹then commanded he them to draw it up, and to bring it: and when the sacrifices were laid on, Neemias commanded the priests to sprinkle the wood and the things laid thereupon with the water, ²²When this was done, and the time came that the sun shone which afore was hid in the cloud, there was a great fire kindled, so that every man marvelled.

²³And the priests made a prayer whilst the sacrifice was consuming, I say, both the priests, and all the rest, Jonathan beginning, and the rest answering thereunto, as Neemias did. ²⁴And the prayer was after this manner, 'O Lord, Lord God, Creator of all things, who art fearful and strong, and righteous, and merciful, and the only and gracious King, ²⁵the only giver of all things, the only just, almighty, and everlasting, thou that deliverest Israel from all trouble, and didst choose the fathers, and sanctify them: ²⁶receive the sacrifice for thy whole people Israel, and preserve thy own portion, and sanctify it. ²⁷Gather those together that are scattered from us, deliver them that serve among the heathen, look upon them that are despised and abhorred, and let the heathen know that thou art our God. ²⁸Punish them that oppress us, and with pride do us wrong. ²⁹Plant thy people again in thy holy place as Moses hath spoken.' ³⁰And the priests sang psalms of thanksgiving.

³¹Now when the sacrifice was consumed, Neemias commanded the water that was left to be poured on the great stones. ³²When this was done, there was kindled a flame: but it was consumed by the light that shone from the altar. ³³So when this matter was known, it was told the king of Persia, that in the place, where the priests that were led away had hid the fire, there appeared water, and that Neemias had purified the sacrifices therewith. ³⁴Then the king, enclosing the place, made it holy after he had tried the matter. ³⁵And the king took many gifts, and bestowed thereof on those whom he would gratify. ³⁶And Neemias called this thing Naphthar, which is as much to say as, a cleansing: but many men call it Nephi.

2 It is also found in the records, that Jeremy the prophet commanded them that were carried away to take of the fire, as it hath been signified, ²and how that the prophet, having given them the law, charged them not to forget the commandments of the Lord, and that they should not err in their minds, when

they see images of silver and gold, with their ornaments. ³And with other such speeches exhorted he them, that the law should not depart from their hearts.

⁴It was also contained in the same writing, that the prophet, being warned of God, commanded the tabernacle and the ark to go with him, as he went forth into the mountain, where Moses climbed up, and saw the heritage of God. ⁵And when Jeremy came thither, he found a hollow cave, wherein he laid the tabernacle, and the ark, and the altar of incense, and so stopped the door. ⁶And some of those that followed him came to mark the way, but they could not find it. ⁷Which when Jeremy perceived, he blamed them, saying, 'As for that place, it shall be unknown until the time that God gather his people again together, and receive them unto mercy. ⁸Then shall the Lord show them these things, and the glory of the Lord shall appear, and the cloud also as it was shown under Moses, and as when Solomon desired that the place might be honourably sanctified.'

⁹It was also declared that he being wise offered the sacrifice of dedication, and of the finishing of the temple. ¹⁰And as when Moses prayed unto the Lord, the fire came down from heaven, and consumed the sacrifices: even so prayed Solomon also, and the fire came down from heaven, and consumed the burnt offerings. ¹¹And Moses said, 'Because the sin offering was not to be eaten, it was consumed'. ¹²So Solomon kept those eight days.

¹³The same things also were reported in the writings and commentaries of Neemias, and how he founding a library gathered together the acts of the kings, and the prophets, and of David, and the epistles of the kings concerning the holy gifts. ¹⁴In like manner also Judas gathered together all those things that were lost by reason of the war we had, and they remain with us. ¹⁵Wherefore if ye have need thereof, send some to fetch them unto you.

¹⁶Whereas we then are about to celebrate the purification, we have written unto you, and ye shall do well, if ye keep the same days. ¹⁷We hope also that the God that delivered all his people, and gave them all a heritage, and the kingdom, and the priesthood, and the sanctuary, ¹⁸as he promised in the law, will shortly have mercy upon us, and gather us together out of every land under heaven into the holy place: for he hath delivered us out of great troubles, and hath purified the place.

¹⁹Now as concerning Judas Maccabeus, and his brethren, and the purification of the great temple, and the dedication of the altar, ²⁰and the wars against Antiochus Epiphanes, and Eupator his son, ²¹and the manifest signs that came from heaven unto those that behaved themselves manfully to their honour for Judaism: so that, being but a few, they overcame the whole country, and chased barbarous multitudes, ²²and recovered again the temple renowned all the world over, and

freed the city, and upheld the laws which were going down, the Lord being gracious unto them with all favour: ²³all these things, I say, being declared by Jason of Cyrene in five books, we will essay to abridge in one volume. ²⁴For considering the infinite number, and the difficulty which they find that desire to look into the narrations of the story, for the variety of the matter, ²⁵we have been careful, that they that will read may have delight, and that they that are desirous to commit to memory might have ease, and that all into whose hands it comes might have profit.

²⁶Therefore to us, that have taken upon us this painful labour of abridging, it was not easy, but a matter of sweat and watching; ²⁷even as it is no ease unto him that prepareth a banquet, and seeketh the benefit of others: yet for the pleasuring of many we will undertake gladly this great pains: ²⁸leaving to the author the exact handling of every particular, and labouring to follow the rules of an abridgement. ²⁹For as the master-builder of a new house must care for the whole building; but he that undertaketh to set it out, and paint it, must seek out fit things for the adorning thereof: even so I think it is with us. ³⁰To stand upon every point, and go over things at large, and to be curious in particulars, belongeth to the first author of the story. ³¹But to use brevity, and avoid much labouring of the work, is to be granted to him that will make an abridgement. ³²Here then will we begin the story: only adding thus much to that which hath been said, that it is a foolish thing to make a long prologue, and to be short in the story itself.

3 Now when the holy city was inhabited with all peace, and the laws were kept very well, because of the godliness of Onias the high priest, and his hatred of wickedness, ²it came to pass that even the kings themselves did honour the place, and magnify the temple with their best gifts; ³insomuch that Seleucus king of Asia of his own revenues bore all the costs belonging to the service of the sacrifices.

⁴But one Simon of the tribe of Benjamin, who was made governor of the temple, fell out with the high priest about disorder in the city. ⁵And when he could not overcome Onias, he got him to Apollonius the son of Thraseas, who then was governor of Coelosyria and Phenice, ⁶and told him that the treasury in Jerusalem was full of infinite sums of money, so that the multitude of their riches which did not pertain to the account of the sacrifices, was innumerable, and that it was possible to bring all into the king's hand. ⁷Now when Apollonius came to the king, and had shown him of the money whereof he was told, the king chose out Heliodorus his treasurer, and sent him with a commandment to bring him the foresaid money.

⁸So forthwith Heliodorus took his journey under a colour of visiting the cities of Coelosyria and Phenice, but indeed to fulfil the king's purpose. ⁹And when he was come to Jerusalem, and had been courteously received of the high priest of the city, he told him what intelligence was given of the money, and declared wherefore he came, and asked if these things were so indeed. ¹⁰Then the high priest told him that there was such money laid up for the relief of widows and fatherless chil-

dren, [11]and that some of it belonged to Hircanus son of Tobias, a man of great dignity, and not as that wicked Simon had misinformed: the sum whereof in all was four hundred talents of silver, and two hundred of gold, [12]and that it was altogether impossible that such wrong should be done unto them, that had committed it to the holiness of the place, and to the majesty and inviolable sanctity of the temple, honoured over all the world. [13]But Heliodorus, because of the king's commandment given him, said, 'That in any wise it must be brought into the king's treasury'.

[14]So at the day which he appointed he entered in to order this matter, wherefore there was no small agony throughout the whole city. [15]But the priests, prostrating themselves before the altar in their priests' vestments, called unto heaven upon him that made a law concerning things given to be kept, that they should safely be preserved for such as had committed them to be kept. [16]Then whoso had looked the high priest in the face, it would have wounded his heart: for his countenance and the changing of his colour declared the inward agony of his mind. [17]For the man was so compassed with fear and horror of the body, that it was manifest to them that looked upon him, what sorrow he had now in his heart. [18]Others ran flocking out of their houses to the general supplication, because the place was like to come into contempt. [19]And the women, girt with sackcloth under their breasts, abounded in the streets, and the virgins that were kept in ran, some to the gates, and some to the walls, and others looked out of the windows: [20]and all, holding their hands towards heaven, made supplication. [21]Then it would have pitied a man to see the falling down of the multitude of all sorts, and the fear of the high priest, being in such an agony.

[22]They then called upon the Almighty Lord to keep the things committed of trust safe and sure for those that had committed them. [23]Nevertheless Heliodorus executed that which was decreed. [24]Now as he was there present himself with his guard about the treasury, the Lord of spirits, and the Prince of all power, caused a great apparition, so that all that presumed to come in with him were astonished at the power of God, and fainted, and were sore afraid. [25]For there appeared unto them a horse with a terrible rider upon him, and adorned with a very fair covering, and he ran fiercely, and smote at Heliodorus with his forefeet, and it seemed that he that sat upon the horse had complete harness of gold. [26]Moreover two other young men appeared before him, notable in strength, excellent in beauty, and comely in apparel, who stood by him on either side, and scourged him continually, and gave him many sore stripes. [27]And Heliodorus fell suddenly unto the ground, and was compassed with great darkness: but they that were with him took him up, and put him into a litter. [28]Thus him that lately came with a great train and with all his guard into the said treasury, they carried out, being unable to help himself with his weapons: and manifestly they acknowledged the power of God. [29]For he by the hand of God was cast down, and lay speechless without all hope of life. [30]But they praised the Lord that had miraculously honoured his own place: for the tem-

ple, which a little afore was full of fear and trouble, when the Almighty Lord appeared, was filled with joy and gladness. [31]Then straightways certain of Heliodorus' friends prayed Onias that he would call upon the most High to grant him his life, who lay ready to give up the ghost. [32]So the high priest, suspecting lest the king should misconceive that some treachery had been done to Heliodorus by the Jews, offered a sacrifice for the health of the man. [33]Now as the high priest was making an atonement, the same young men in the same clothing appeared and stood beside Heliodorus, saying, 'Give Onias the high priest great thanks, insomuch as for his sake the Lord hath granted thee life. [34]And seeing that thou hast been scourged from heaven, declare unto all men the mighty power of God.' And when they had spoken these words, they appeared no more.

[35]So Heliodorus, after he had offered sacrifice unto the Lord, and made great vows unto him that had saved his life, and saluted Onias, returned with his host to the king. [36]Then testified he to all men the works of the great God, which he had seen with his eyes.

[37]And when the king asked Heliodorus, who might be a fit man to be sent yet once again to Jerusalem, he said, [38]'If thou hast any enemy or traitor, send him thither, and thou shalt receive him well scourged, if he escape with his life: for in that place, no doubt, there is an especial power of God. [39]For he that dwelleth in heaven hath his eye on that place, and defendeth it, and he beateth and destroyeth them that come to hurt it.'

[40]And the things concerning Heliodorus, and the keeping of the treasury, fell out on this sort.

4 This Simon now, of whom we spoke afore, having been a bewrayer of the money, and of his country, slandered Onias, as if he had terrified Heliodorus, and been the worker of these evils. [2]Thus was he bold to call him a traitor, that had deserved well of the city, and tendered his own nation, and was so zealous of the laws. [3]But when their hatred went so far, that by one of Simon's faction murders were committed, [4]Onias seeing the danger of this contention, and that Apollonius, as being the governor of Coelosyria and Phenice, did rage, and increase Simon's malice, [5]he went to the king, not to be an accuser of his countrymen, but seeking the good of all, both public and private: [6]for he saw that it was impossible that the state should continue quiet, and Simon leave his folly, unless the king did look thereunto.

[7]But after the death of Seleucus, when Antiochus, called Epiphanes, took the kingdom, Jason the brother of Onias laboured underhand to be high priest, [8]promising unto the king by intercession three hundred and threescore talents of silver, and of another revenue eighty talents: [9]besides this, he promised to assign a hundred and fifty more, if he might have licence to set him up a place for exercise, and for the training up of youth in the fashions of the heathen, and to write them of Jerusalem by the name of Antiochians. [10]Which when the king had granted, and he had gotten into his hand the rule, he forthwith brought his own nation to the Greekish fashion. [11]And the royal privi-

leges granted of special favour to the Jews by the means of John the father of Eupolemus, who went ambassador to Rome for amity and aid, he took away, and putting down the governments which were according to the law, he brought up new customs against the law. ¹²For he built gladly a place of exercise under the tower itself, and brought the chief young men under his subjection, and made them wear a hat. ¹³Now such was the height of Greek fashions, and increase of heathenish manners, through the exceeding profaneness of Jason, that ungodly wretch, and no high priest: ¹⁴that the priests had no courage to serve any more at the altar, but despising the temple, and neglecting the sacrifices, hastened to be partakers of the unlawful allowance in the place of exercise, after the game of discus called them forth; ¹⁵not setting by the honours of their fathers, but liking the glory of the Grecians best of all. ¹⁶By reason whereof sore calamity came upon them: for they had them to be their enemies and avengers, whose custom they followed so earnestly, and unto whom they desired to be like in all things. ¹⁷For it is not a light thing to do wickedly against the laws of God: but the time following shall declare these things.

¹⁸Now when the game that was used every fifth year was kept at Tyrus, the king being present, ¹⁹this ungracious Jason sent special messengers from Jerusalem, who were Antiochians, to carry three hundred drachms of silver to the sacrifice of Hercules, which even the bearers thereof thought fit not to bestow upon the sacrifice, because it was not convenient, but to be reserved for other charges. ²⁰This money then, in regard of the sender, was appointed to Hercules' sacrifice, but because of the bearers thereof, it was employed to the making of galleys.

²¹Now when Apollonius the son of Menestheus was sent unto Egypt for the coronation of king Ptolemee Philometor, Antiochus, understanding him not to be well-affected to his affairs, provided for his own safety: whereupon he came to Joppe, and from thence to Jerusalem: ²²where he was honourably received of Jason, and of the city, and was brought in with torchlight, and with great shoutings: and so afterward went with his host unto Phenice.

²³Three years afterward Jason sent Menelaus, the foresaid Simon's brother, to bear the money unto the king, and to put him in mind of certain necessary matters. ²⁴But he being brought to the presence of the king, when he had magnified him for the glorious appearance of his power, got the priesthood to himself, offering more than Jason by three hundred talents of silver. ²⁵So he came with the king's mandate, bringing nothing worthy the high priesthood, but having the fury of a cruel tyrant, and the rage of a savage beast. ²⁶Then Jason, who had undermined his own brother, being undermined by another, was compelled to flee into the country of the Ammonites. ²⁷So Menelaus got the principality: but as for the money that he had promised unto the king, he took no good order for it, albeit Sostratus the ruler of the castle required it: ²⁸for unto him appertained the gathering of the customs. Wherefore they were both called before the king. ²⁹Now Menelaus left

his brother Lysimachus in his stead in the priesthood, and Sostratus left Crates, who was governor of the Cyprians.

³⁰While those things were in doing, they of Tarsus and Mallos made insurrection, because they were given to the king's concubine, called Antiochis. ³¹Then came the king in all haste to appease matters, leaving Andronicus, a man in authority, for his deputy. ³²Now Menelaus, supposing that he had gotten a convenient time, stole certain vessels of gold out of the temple, and gave some of them to Andronicus, and some he sold into Tyrus and the cities round about. ³³Which when Onias knew of a surety, he reproved him, and withdrew himself into a sanctuary at Daphne, that lieth by Antiochia. ³⁴Wherefore Menelaus, taking Andronicus apart, prayed him to get Onias into his hands; who being persuaded thereunto, and coming to Onias in deceit, gave him his right hand with oaths; and though he were suspected by him, yet persuaded he him to come forth of the sanctuary: whom forthwith he shut up without regard of justice.

³⁵For the which cause not only the Jews, but many also of other nations, took great indignation, and were much grieved for the unjust murder of the man. ³⁶And when the king was come again from the places about Cilicia, the Jews that were in the city, and certain of the Greeks that abhorred the fact also, complained because Onias was slain without cause. ³⁷Therefore Antiochus was heartily sorry, and moved to pity, and wept, because of the sober and modest behaviour of him that was dead. ³⁸And being kindled with anger, forthwith he took away Andronicus' purple, and rent off his clothes, and leading him through the whole city unto that very place, where he had committed impiety against Onias, there slew he the cursed murderer. Thus the Lord rewarded him his punishment, as he had deserved.

³⁹Now when many sacrileges had been committed in the city by Lysimachus with the consent of Menelaus, and the bruit thereof was spread abroad, the multitude gathered themselves together against Lysimachus, many vessels of gold being already carried away. ⁴⁰Whereupon the common people rising, and being filled with rage, Lysimachus armed about three thousand men, and began first to offer violence; one Auranus being the leader, a man far gone in years, and no less in folly. ⁴¹They then seeing the attempt of Lysimachus, some of them caught stones, some clubs, others taking handfuls of dust, that was next at hand, cast them all together upon Lysimachus, and those that set upon them. ⁴²Thus many of them they wounded, and some they struck to the ground, and all of them they forced to flee: but as for the church-robber himself, him they killed beside the treasury.

⁴³Of these matters therefore there was an accusation laid against Menelaus. ⁴⁴Now when the king came to Tyrus, three men that were sent from the senate pleaded the cause before him: ⁴⁵but Menelaus, being now convicted, promised Ptolemee the son of Dorymenes to give him much money, if he would pacify the king towards him. ⁴⁶Whereupon Ptolemee taking the king aside into a certain gallery, as it were to take the air, brought him to be of another mind: ⁴⁷insomuch

that he discharged Menelaus from the accusations, who notwithstanding was cause of all the mischief: and those poor men, who, if they had told their cause, yea, before the Scythians, should have been judged innocent, them he condemned to death. [48]Thus they that followed the matter for the city, and for the people, and for the holy vessels, did soon suffer unjust punishment. [49]Wherefore even they of Tyrus, moved with hatred of that wicked deed, caused them to be honourably buried. [50]And so through the covetousness of them that were in power Menelaus remained still in authority, increasing in malice, and being a great traitor to the citizens.

5 About the same time Antiochus prepared his second voyage into Egypt: [2]and then it happened, that through all the city, for the space almost of forty days, there were seen horsemen running in the air, in cloth of gold, and armed with lances, like a band of soldiers, [3]and troops of horsemen in array, encountering, and running one against another with shaking of shields, and multitude of pikes, and drawing of swords, and casting of darts, and glittering of golden ornaments, and harness of all sorts. [4]Wherefore every man prayed that that apparition might turn to good.

[5]Now when there was gone forth a false rumour, as though Antiochus had been dead, Jason took at the least a thousand men, and suddenly made an assault upon the city; and they that were upon the walls being put back, and the city at length taken, Menelaus fled into the castle: [6]but Jason slew his own citizens without mercy, not considering that to get the day of them of his own nation would be a most unhappy day for him; but thinking they had been his enemies, and not his countrymen, whom he conquered. [7]Howbeit, for all this he obtained not the principality, but at the last received shame for the reward of his treason, and fled again into the country of the Ammonites. [8]In the end therefore he had an unhappy return, being accused before Aretas the king of the Arabians, fleeing from city to city, pursued of all men, hated as a forsaker of the laws, and being had in abomination as an open enemy of his country and countrymen, he was cast out into Egypt. [9]Thus he that had driven many out of their country perished in a strange land, retiring to the Lacedemonians, and thinking there to find succour by reason of his kindred. [10]And he that had cast out many unburied had none to mourn for him, nor any solemn funerals at all, nor sepulchre with his fathers.

[11]Now when this that was done came to the king's ear, he thought that Judea had revolted: whereupon removing out of Egypt in a furious mind, he took the city by force of arms, [12]and commanded his men of war not to spare such as they met, and to slay such as went up upon the houses. [13]Thus there was killing of young and old, making away of men, women, and children, slaying of virgins and infants. [14]And there were destroyed within the space of three whole days fourscore thousand, whereof forty thousand were slain in the conflict; and no fewer sold than slain.

[15]Yet was he not content with this, but presumed to go into the most

holy temple of all the world; Menelaus, that traitor to the laws, and to his own country, being his guide: ¹⁶and taking the holy vessels with polluted hands, and with profane hands pulling down the things that were dedicated by other kings to the augmentation and glory and honour of the place, he gave them away. ¹⁷And so haughty was Antiochus in mind, that he considered not that the Lord was angry for a while for the sins of them that dwelt in the city, and therefore his eye was not upon the place. ¹⁸For had they not been formerly wrapped in many sins, this man, as soon as he had come, had forthwith been scourged, and put back from his presumption, as Heliodorus was, whom Seleucus the king sent to view the treasury. ¹⁹Nevertheless God did not choose the people for the place's sake, but the place for the people's sake. ²⁰And therefore the place itself, that was partaker with them of the adversities that happened to the nation, did afterward communicate in the benefits sent from the Lord: and as it was forsaken in the wrath of the Almighty, so again, the great Lord being reconciled, it was set up with all glory.

²¹So when Antiochus had carried out of the temple a thousand and eight hundred talents, he departed in all haste unto Antiochia, weening in his pride to make the land navigable, and the sea passable by foot: such was the haughtiness of his mind. ²²And he left governors to vex the nation: at Jerusalem Philip, for his country a Phrygian, and for manners more barbarous than he that set him there; ²³and at Garizim, Andronicus; and besides, Menelaus, who worse than all the rest bore a heavy hand over the citizens, having a malicious mind against his countrymen the Jews. ²⁴He sent also that detestable ringleader Apollonius with an army of two and twenty thousand, commanding him to slay all those that were in their best age, and to sell the women and the younger sort: ²⁵who coming to Jerusalem, and pretending peace, did forbear till the holy day of the sabbath, when taking the Jews keeping holy day, he commanded his men to arm themselves. ²⁶And so he slew all them that were gone to the celebrating of the sabbath, and running through the city with weapons slew great multitudes.

²⁷But Judas Maccabeus with nine others, or thereabout, withdrew himself into the wilderness, and lived in the mountains after the manner of beasts, with his company, who fed on herbs continually, lest they should be partakers of the pollution.

6 Not long after this the king sent an old man of Athens to compel the Jews to depart from the laws of their fathers, and not to live after the laws of God: ²and to pollute also the temple in Jerusalem, and to call it the temple of Jupiter Olympius; and that in Garizim, of Jupiter the defender of strangers, as they did desire that dwelt in the place. ³The coming in of this mischief was sore and grievous to the people: ⁴for the temple was filled with riot and revelling by the Gentiles, who dallied with harlots, and had to do with women within the circuit of the holy places, and besides that, brought in things that were not lawful. ⁵The altar also was filled with profane things, which the law forbiddeth. ⁶Neither was it lawful for a man to keep sabbath days or ancient feasts, or to profess himself at all to be a Jew. ⁷And in the day of the king's birth every month they were brought by bitter constraint to eat of the sacrifices; and when the feast of Bacchus was kept, the Jews were compelled to go in procession to Bacchus, carrying ivy. ⁸Moreover there went out a decree to the neighbour cities of the heathen, by the suggestion of Ptolemee, against the Jews, that they should observe the same fashions, and be partakers of their sacrifices: ⁹and whoso would not conform themselves to the manners of the Gentiles should be put to death.

Then might a man have seen the present misery. ¹⁰For there were two women brought, who had circumcised their children; whom when they had openly led round about the city, the babes hanging at their breasts, they cast them down headlong from the wall. ¹¹And others that had run together into caves near by, to keep the sabbath day secretly, being discovered to Philip, were all burnt together, because they made a conscience to help themselves for the honour of the most sacred day.

¹²Now I beseech those that read this book, that they be not discouraged for these calamities, but that they judge those punishments not to be for destruction, but for a chastening of our nation. ¹³For it is a token of his great goodness, when wicked-doers are not suffered any long time, but forthwith punished. ¹⁴For not as with other nations whom the Lord patiently forbeareth to punish, till they be come to the fulness of their sins, so dealeth he with us, ¹⁵lest that being come to the height of sin, afterwards he should take vengeance of us. ¹⁶And therefore he never withdraweth his mercy from us: and though he punish with adversity, yet doth he never forsake his people. ¹⁷But let this that we have spoken be for a warning unto us. And now will we come to the declaring of the matter in few words.

¹⁸Eleazar, one of the principal scribes, an aged man, and of a well-favoured countenance, was constrained to open his mouth, and to eat swine's flesh. ¹⁹But he, choosing rather to die gloriously, than to live stained with such an abomination, spit it forth, and came of his own accord to the torment, ²⁰as it behoved them to come, that are resolute to stand out against such things, as are not lawful for love of life to be tasted. ²¹But they that had the charge of that wicked feast, for the old acquaintance they had with the man, taking him aside, besought him to bring flesh of his own provision, such as was lawful for him to use, and make as if he did eat of the flesh taken from the sacrifice commanded by the king, ²²that in so doing he might be delivered from death, and for the old friendship with them find favour. ²³But he began to consider discreetly, and as became his age, and the excellence of his ancient years, and the honour of his grey head, whereunto he was come, and his most honest education from a child, or rather the holy law made and given by God: therefore he answered accordingly, and willed them straightways to send him to the grave. ²⁴'For it becometh not our age,' said he, 'in any wise to dissemble, whereby many young persons might think that Eleazar, being fourscore years old and ten, were now gone to a strange religion, ²⁵and so they through my

hypocrisy, and desire to live a little time and a moment longer, should be deceived by me, and I get a stain to my old age, and make it abominable. ²⁶For though for the present time I should be delivered from the punishment of men: yet should I not escape the hand of the Almighty, neither alive, nor dead. ²⁷Wherefore now manfully changing this life, I will show myself such a one as my age requireth, ²⁸and leave a notable example to such as be young to die willingly and courageously for the honourable and holy laws.'

And when he had said these words, immediately he went to the torment: ²⁹they that led him changing the good will they bore him a little before into hatred, because the foresaid speeches proceeded, as they thought, from a desperate mind. ³⁰But when he was ready to die with stripes, he groaned, and said, 'It is manifest unto the Lord, that hath the holy knowledge, that whereas I might have been delivered from death, I now endure sore pains in body by being beaten: but in soul am well content to suffer these things, because I fear him'. ³¹And thus this man died, leaving his death for an example of a noble courage, and a memorial of virtue, not only unto young men, but unto all his nation.

7 It came to pass also, that seven brethren with their mother were taken, and compelled by the king against the law to taste swine's flesh, and were tormented with scourges and whips. ²But one of them that spoke first said thus, 'What wouldst thou ask or learn of us? we are ready to die, rather than to transgress the laws of our fathers'. ³Then the king, being in a rage, commanded pans and cauldrons to be made hot: ⁴which forthwith being heated, he commanded to cut out the tongue of him that spoke first, and to cut off the utmost parts of his body, the rest of his brethren and his mother looking on. ⁵Now when he was thus maimed in all his members, he commanded him being yet alive to be brought to the fire, and to be fried in the pan: and as the vapour of the pan was for a good space dispersed, they exhorted one another with the mother to die manfully, saying thus, ⁶'The Lord God looketh upon us, and in truth hath comfort in us, as Moses in his song, which witnessed to their faces, declared, saying, "And he shall be comforted in his servants"'.

⁷So when the first was dead after this manner, they brought the second to make him a mocking-stock: and when they had pulled off the skin of his head with the hair, they asked him, 'Wilt thou eat, before thou be punished throughout every member of thy body?' ⁸But he answered in his own language, and said, 'No'. Wherefore he also received the next torment in order, as the former did. ⁹And when he was at the last gasp, he said, 'Thou like a fury takest us out of this present life, but the King of the world shall raise us up, who have died for his laws, unto everlasting life'.

¹⁰After him was the third made a mocking-stock: and when he was required, he put out his tongue, and that right soon, holding forth his hands manfully, ¹¹and said courageously, 'These I had from heaven, and for his laws I despise them, and from him I hope to receive them again'.

¹²Insomuch that the king, and they that were with him, marvelled at the young man's courage, for that he nothing regarded the pains.

¹³Now when this man was dead also, they tormented and mangled the fourth in like manner. ¹⁴So when he was ready to die he said thus, 'It is good, being put to death by men, to look for hope from God to be raised up again by him: as for thee, thou shalt have no resurrection to life'.

¹⁵Afterward they brought the fifth also, and mangled him. ¹⁶Then looked he unto the king, and said, 'Thou hast power over men, thou art corruptible, thou doest what thou wilt; yet think not that our nation is forsaken of God. ¹⁷But abide a while, and behold his great power, how he will torment thee and thy seed.'

¹⁸After him also they brought the sixth, who being ready to die said, 'Be not deceived without cause: for we suffer these things for ourselves, having sinned against our God: therefore marvellous things are done unto us. ¹⁹But think not thou, that takest in hand to strive against God, that thou shalt escape unpunished.'

²⁰But the mother was marvellous above all, and worthy of honourable memory: for when she saw her seven sons slain within the space of one day, she bore it with a good courage, because of the hope that she had in the Lord. ²¹Yea, she exhorted every one of them in her own language, filled with courageous spirits; and stirring up her womanish thoughts with a manly stomach, she said unto them, ²²'I cannot tell how you came into my womb: for I neither gave you breath nor life, neither was it I that formed the members of every one of you. ²³But doubtless the Creator of the world, who formed the generation of man, and found out the beginning of all things, will also of his own mercy give you breath and life again, as you now regard not your own selves for his laws' sake.'

²⁴Now Antiochus, thinking himself despised, and suspecting it to be a reproachful speech, whilst the youngest was yet alive, did not only exhort him by words, but also assured him with oaths, that he would make him both a rich and a happy man, if he would turn from the laws of his fathers, and that also he would take him for his friend, and trust him with affairs. ²⁵But when the young man would in no case hearken unto him, the king called his mother, and exhorted her that she would counsel the young man to save his life. ²⁶And when he had exhorted her with many words, she promised him that she would counsel her son. ²⁷But she bowing herself towards him, laughing the cruel tyrant to scorn, spoke in her country language on this manner, 'O my son, have pity upon me that bore thee nine months in my womb, and gave thee suck three years, and nourished thee, and brought thee up unto this age, and endured the troubles of education. ²⁸I beseech thee, my son, look upon the heaven and the earth, and all that is therein, and consider that God made them of things that were not, and so was mankind made likewise. ²⁹Fear not this tormentor, but, being worthy of thy brethren, take thy death, that I may receive thee again in mercy with thy brethren.'

³⁰Whilst she was yet speaking these words, the young man said,

'Whom wait ye for? I will not obey the king's commandment: but I will obey the commandment of the law that was given unto our fathers by Moses. ³¹And thou, that hast been the author of all mischief against the Hebrews, shalt not escape the hands of God. ³²For we suffer because of our sins. ³³And though the living Lord be angry with us a little while for our chastening and correction, yet shall he be at one again with his servants. ³⁴But thou, O godless man, and of all others most wicked, be not lifted up without a cause, nor puffed up with uncertain hopes, lifting up thy hand against the servants of God: ³⁵for thou hast not yet escaped the judgement of Almighty God, who seeth all things. ³⁶For our brethren, who now have suffered a short pain, are dead under God's covenant of everlasting life: but thou, through the judgement of God, shalt receive just punishment for thy pride. ³⁷But I, as my brethren, offer up my body and life for the laws of our fathers, beseeching God that he would speedily be merciful unto our nation; and that thou by torments and plagues mayest confess, that he alone is God; ³⁸and that in me and my brethren the wrath of the Almighty, which is justly brought upon all our nation, may cease.'

³⁹Then the king, being in a rage, handled him worse than all the rest, and took it grievously that he was mocked. ⁴⁰So this man died undefiled, and put his whole trust in the Lord.

⁴¹Last of all after the sons the mother died.

⁴²Let this be enough now to have spoken concerning the idolatrous feasts, and the extreme tortures.

8 Then Judas Maccabeus, and they that were with him, went privily into the towns, and called their kinsfolks together, and took unto them all such as continued in the Jews' religion, and assembled about six thousand men. ²And they called upon the Lord, that he would look upon the people that was trodden down of all, and also pity the temple profaned of ungodly men, ³and that he would have compassion upon the city, sore defaced, and ready to be made even with the ground, and hear the blood that cried unto him, ⁴and remember the wicked slaughter of harmless infants, and the blasphemies committed against his name, and that he would show his hatred against the wicked.

⁵Now when Maccabeus had his company about him, he could not be withstood by the heathen: for the wrath of the Lord was turned into mercy. ⁶Therefore he came at unawares, and burnt up towns and cities, and got into his hands the most commodious places, and overcame and put to flight no small number of his enemies. ⁷But specially took he advantage of the night for such privy attempts, insomuch that the bruit of his manliness was spread everywhere.

⁸So when Philip saw that this man increased by little and little, and that things prospered with him still more and more, he wrote unto Ptolemeus, the governor of Coelosyria and Phenice, to yield more aid to the king's affairs. ⁹Then forthwith choosing Nicanor the son of Patroclus, one of his special friends, he sent him with no fewer than twenty thousand of all nations under him, to root out the whole generation of the Jews; and with him he joined also Gorgias a captain, who

in matters of war had great experience. [10]So Nicanor undertook to make so much money of the captive Jews, as should defray the tribute of two thousand talents, which the king was to pay to the Romans. [11]Wherefore immediately he sent to the cities upon the sea coast, proclaiming a sale of the captive Jews, and promising that they should have fourscore and ten bodies for one talent, not expecting the vengeance that was to follow upon him from the Almighty God.

[12]Now when word was brought unto Judas of Nicanor's coming, and he had imparted unto those that were with him that the army was at hand, [13]they that were fearful, and distrusted the justice of God, fled, and conveyed themselves away. [14]Others sold all that they had left, and withal besought the Lord to deliver them, being sold by the wicked Nicanor before they met together: [15]and if not for their own sakes, yet for the covenants he had made with their fathers, and for his holy and glorious name's sake, by which they were called.

[16]So Maccabeus called his men together unto the number of six thousand, and exhorted them not to be stricken with terror of the enemy, nor to fear the great multitude of the heathen, who came wrongfully against them, but to fight manfully, [17]and to set before their eyes the injury that they had unjustly done to the holy place, and the cruel handling of the city, whereof they made a mockery, and also the taking away of the government of their forefathers: [18]'For they,' said he, 'trust in their weapons and boldness, but our confidence is in the Almighty God, who at a beck can cast down both them that come against us, and also all the world.' [19]Moreover he recounted unto them what helps their forefathers had found, and how they were delivered, when under Sennacherib a hundred fourscore and five thousand perished. [20]And he told them of the battle that they had in Babylon with the Galatians, how they came but eight thousand in all to the business, with four thousand Macedonians, and that the Macedonians being perplexed, the eight thousand destroyed a hundred and twenty thousand because of the help that they had from heaven, and so received a great booty.

[21]Thus when he had made them bold with these words, and ready to die for the laws and the country, he divided his army into four parts: [22]and joined with himself his own brethren, leaders of each band, to wit, Simon, and Joseph, and Jonathan, giving each one fifteen hundred men. [23]Also he appointed Eleazar to read the holy book: and when he had given them this watchword, 'The help of God'; himself leading the first band, he joined battle with Nicanor. [24]And by the help of the Almighty they slew above nine thousand of their enemies, and wounded and maimed the most part of Nicanor's host, and so put all to flight: [25]and took their money that came to buy them, and pursued them far: but lacking time they returned: [26]for it was the day before the sabbath, and therefore they would no longer pursue them. [27]So when they had gathered their armour together, and spoiled their enemies, they occupied themselves about the sabbath, yielding exceeding praise and thanks to the Lord, who had preserved them unto that day, which was the beginning of mercy distilling upon them. [28]And after the sab-

bath, when they had given part of the spoils to the maimed, and the widows, and orphans, the residue they divided among themselves and their servants. ²⁹When this was done, and they had made a common supplication, they besought the merciful Lord to be reconciled with his servants for ever.

³⁰Moreover of those that were with Timotheus and Bacchides, who fought against them, they slew above twenty thousand, and very easily got high and strong holds, and divided amongst themselves many spoils more, and made the maimed, orphans, widows, yea, and the aged also, equal in spoils with themselves. ³¹And when they had gathered their armour together, they laid them up all carefully in convenient places, and the remnant of the spoils they brought to Jerusalem. ³²They slew also Philarches, that wicked person, who was with Timotheus, and had annoyed the Jews many ways. ³³Furthermore at such time as they kept the feast for the victory in their country, they burnt Callisthenes, that had set fire upon the holy gates, who was fled into a little house, and so he received a reward meet for his wickedness.

³⁴As for that most ungracious Nicanor, who had brought a thousand merchants to buy the Jews, ³⁵he was through the help of the Lord brought down by them, of whom he made least account; and putting off his glorious apparel, and discharging his company, he came like a fugitive servant through the midland unto Antioch, having very great dishonour, for that his host was destroyed. ³⁶Thus he, that took upon him to make good to the Romans their tribute by means of the captives in Jerusalem, told abroad, that the Jews had God to fight for them, and therefore they could not be hurt, because they followed the laws that he gave them.

9 About that time came Antiochus with dishonour out of the country of Persia. ²For he had entered the city called Persepolis, and went about to rob the temple, and to hold the city; whereupon the multitude running to defend themselves with their weapons put them to flight; and so it happened, that Antiochus being put to flight of the inhabitants returned with shame. ³Now when he came to Ecbatana, news was brought him what had happened unto Nicanor and Timotheus. ⁴Then swelling with anger, he thought to avenge upon the Jews the disgrace done unto him by those that made him fly. Therefore commanded he his chariot-man to drive without ceasing, and to dispatch the journey, the judgement of God now following him. For he had spoken proudly in this sort, that he would come to Jerusalem, and make it a common burying-place of the Jews.

⁵But the Lord Almighty, the God of Israel, smote him with an incurable and invisible plague: for as soon as he had spoken these words, a pain of the bowels that was remediless came upon him, and sore torments of the inner parts; ⁶and that most justly: for he had tormented other men's bowels with many and strange torments. ⁷Howbeit he nothing at all ceased from his bragging, but still was filled with pride, breathing out fire in his rage against the Jews, and commanding to haste the journey: but it came to pass that he fell down from his char-

iot, carried violently, so that having a sore fall, all the members of his body were much pained. ⁸And thus he that a little afore thought he might command the waves of the sea (so proud was he beyond the condition of man), and weigh the high mountains in a balance, was now cast on the ground, and carried in a horse-litter, showing forth unto all the manifest power of God. ⁹So that the worms rose up out of the body of this wicked man, and whilst he lived in sorrow and pain, his flesh fell away, and the filthiness of his smell was noisome to all his army. ¹⁰And the man that thought a little afore he could reach to the stars of heaven, no man could endure to carry for his intolerable stink.

¹¹Here therefore, being plagued, he began to leave off his great pride, and to come to the knowledge of himself by the scourge of God, his pain increasing every moment. ¹²And when he himself could not abide his own smell, he said these words, 'It is meet to be subject unto God, and that a man that is mortal should not proudly think of himself, as if he were God'. ¹³This wicked person vowed also unto the Lord, who now no more would have mercy upon him, saying thus, ¹⁴that the holy city (to the which he was going in haste, to lay it even with the ground, and to make it a common burying-place), he would set at liberty: ¹⁵and as touching the Jews, whom he had judged not worthy so much as to be buried, but to be cast out with their children to be devoured of the fowls and wild beasts, he would make them all equals to the citizens of Athens, ¹⁶and the holy temple, which before he had spoiled, he would garnish with goodly gifts, and restore all the holy vessels with many more, and out of his own revenue defray the charges belonging to the sacrifices: ¹⁷yea, and that also he would become a Jew himself, and go through all the world that was inhabited, and declare the power of God.

¹⁸But for all this his pains would not cease: for the just judgement of God was come upon him: therefore despairing of his health, he wrote unto the Jews the letter underwritten, containing the form of a supplication, after this manner:

¹⁹Antiochus, king and governor, to the good Jews his citizens, wisheth much joy, health, and prosperity. ²⁰If ye and your children fare well, and your affairs be to your contentment, I give very great thanks to God, having my hope in heaven. ²¹As for me, I was weak, or else I would have remembered kindly your honour and good will. Returning out of Persia, and being taken with a grievous disease, I thought it necessary to care for the common safety of all: ²²not distrusting my health, but having great hope to escape this sickness. ²³But considering that even my father, at what time he led an army into the high countries, appointed a successor, ²⁴to the end that if anything fell out contrary to expectation, or if any tidings were brought that were grievous, they of the land, knowing to whom the state was left, might not be troubled. ²⁵Again, considering how that the princes that are borderers and neighbours unto my kingdom wait for opportunities, and expect what shall be the event, I

have appointed my son Antiochus king, whom I often committed and commended unto many of you, when I went up into the high provinces, to whom I have written as followeth. ²⁶Therefore I pray and request you to remember the benefits that I have done unto you generally, and in special, and that every man will be still faithful to me and my son. ²⁷For I am persuaded that he understanding my mind will favourably and graciously yield to your desires.

²⁸Thus the murderer and blasphemer having suffered most grievously, as he entreated other men, so died he a miserable death in a strange country in the mountains. ²⁹And Philip, that was brought up with him, carried away his body, who also fearing the son of Antiochus went into Egypt to Ptolemee Philometor.

10 Now Maccabeus and his company, the Lord guiding them, recovered the temple and the city. ²But the altars which the heathen had built in the open street, and also the chapels they pulled down. ³And having cleansed the temple they made another altar, and striking stones they took fire out of them, and offered a sacrifice after two years, and set forth incense, and lights, and showbread. ⁴When that was done, they fell flat down, and besought the Lord that they might come no more into such troubles: but if they sinned any more against him, that he himself would chasten them with mercy, and that they might not be delivered unto the blasphemous and barbarous nations. ⁵Now upon the same day that the strangers profaned the temple, on the very same day it was cleansed again, even the five and twentieth day of the same month, which is Casleu. ⁶And they kept eight days with gladness, as in the feast of the tabernacles, remembering that not long afore they had held the feast of the tabernacles, when as they wandered in the mountains and dens like beasts. ⁷Therefore they bore branches, and fair boughs, and palms also, and sang psalms unto him that had given them good success in cleansing his place. ⁸They ordained also by a common statute and decree, that every year those days should be kept of the whole nation of the Jews.

⁹And this was the end of Antiochus, called Epiphanes. ¹⁰Now will we declare the acts of Antiochus Eupator, who was the son of this wicked man, gathering briefly the calamities of the wars. ¹¹So when he was come to the crown, he set one Lysias over the affairs of his realm, and appointed him chief governor of Coelosyria and Phenice. ¹²For Ptolemee, that was called Macron, choosing rather to do justice unto the Jews for the wrong that had been done unto them, endeavoured to continue peace with them. ¹³Whereupon being accused of the king's friends before Eupator, and called traitor at every word, because he had left Cyprus, that Philometor had committed unto him, and departed to Antiochus Epiphanes, and seeing that he was in no honourable place, he was so discouraged, that he poisoned himself and died.

¹⁴But when Gorgias was governor of the holds, he hired soldiers, and nourished war continually with the Jews: ¹⁵and therewithal the Idumeans, having gotten into their hands the most commodious holds,

kept the Jews occupied, and receiving those that were banished from Jerusalem, they went about to nourish war. [16]Then they that were with Maccabeus made supplication, and besought God that he would be their helper; and so they ran with violence upon the strongholds of the Idumeans, [17]and assaulting them strongly, they won the holds, and kept off all that fought upon the wall, and slew all that fell into their hands, and killed no fewer than twenty thousand. [18]And because certain, who were no less than nine thousand, were fled together into two very strong castles, having all manner of things convenient to sustain the siege, [19]Maccabeus left Simon and Joseph, and Zaccheus also, and them that were with him, who were enough to besiege them, and departed himself unto those places which more needed his help.

[20]Now they that were with Simon, being led with covetousness, were persuaded for money (through certain of those that were in the castle), and took seventy thousand drachms, and let some of them escape. [21]But when it was told Maccabeus what was done, he called the governors of the people together, and accused those men, that they had sold their brethren for money, and set their enemies free to fight against them. [22]So he slew those that were found traitors, and immediately took the two castles. [23]And having good success with his weapons in all things he took in hand, he slew in the two holds more than twenty thousand.

[24]Now Timotheus, whom the Jews had overcome before, when he had gathered a great multitude of foreign forces, and horses out of Asia not a few, came as though he would take Jewry by force of arms. [25]But when he drew near, they that were with Maccabeus turned themselves to pray unto God, and sprinkled earth upon their heads, and girded their loins with sackcloth, [26]and fell down at the foot of the altar, and besought him to be merciful to them, and to be an enemy to their enemies, and an adversary to their adversaries, as the law declareth. [27]So after the prayer they took their weapons, and went on farther from the city: and when they drew near to their enemies, they kept by themselves. [28]Now the sun being newly risen, they joined both together; the one part having together with their virtue their refuge also unto the Lord for a pledge of their success and victory: the other side making their rage leader of their battle. [29]But when the battle waxed strong, there appeared unto the enemies from heaven five comely men upon horses, with bridles of gold, and two of them led the Jews, [30]and took Maccabeus betwixt them, and covered him on every side with their weapons, and kept him safe, but shot arrows and lightnings against the enemies: so that being confounded with blindness, and full of trouble, they were killed. [31]And there were slain of footmen twenty thousand and five hundred, and six hundred horsemen.

[32]As for Timotheus himself, he fled into a very strong hold, called Gazara, where Chereas was governor. [33]But they that were with Maccabeus laid siege against the fortress courageously four days. [34]And they that were within, trusting to the strength of the place, blasphemed exceedingly, and uttered wicked words. [35]Nevertheless upon the fifth day early twenty young men of Maccabeus' company,

inflamed with anger because of the blasphemies, assaulted the wall manly, and with a fierce courage killed all that they met withal. ³⁶Others likewise ascending after them, whilst they were busied with them that were within, burnt the towers, and kindling fires burnt the blasphemers alive, and others broke open the gates, and, having received in the rest of the army, took the city, ³⁷and killed Timotheus that was hid in a certain pit, and Chereas his brother, with Apollophanes. ³⁸When this was done, they praised the Lord with psalms and thanksgiving, who had done so great things for Israel, and given them the victory.

11 Not long after this, Lysias the king's protector and cousin, who also managed the affairs, took sore displeasure for the things that were done. ²And when he had gathered about fourscore thousand with all the horsemen, he came against the Jews, thinking to make the city a habitation of the Gentiles, ³and to make a gain of the temple, as of the other chapels of the heathen, and to set the high priesthood to sale every year: ⁴not at all considering the power of God, but puffed up with his ten thousand footmen, and his thousand horsemen, and his fourscore elephants. ⁵So he came to Judea, and drew near to Bethsura, which was a strong town, but distant from Jerusalem about five furlongs, and he laid sore siege unto it.

⁶Now when they that were with Maccabeus heard that he besieged the holds, they and all the people with lamentation and tears besought the Lord that he would send a good angel to deliver Israel. ⁷Then Maccabeus himself first of all took weapons, exhorting the others that they would jeopard themselves together with him to help their brethren: so they went forth together with a willing mind. ⁸And as they were at Jerusalem, there appeared before them on horseback one in white clothing, shaking his armour of gold. ⁹Then they praised the merciful God all together, and took heart, insomuch that they were ready not only to fight with men, but with most cruel beasts, and to pierce through walls of iron. ¹⁰Thus they marched forward in their armour, having a helper from heaven: for the Lord was merciful unto them. ¹¹And giving a charge upon their enemies like lions, they slew eleven thousand footmen, and sixteen hundred horsemen, and put all the others to flight. ¹²Many of them also being wounded escaped naked, and Lysias himself fled away shamefully, and so escaped.

¹³Who, as he was a man of understanding, casting with himself what loss he had had, and considering that the Hebrews could not be overcome, because the Almighty God helped them, he sent unto them, ¹⁴and persuaded them to agree to all reasonable conditions, and promised that he would persuade the king that he must needs be a friend unto them. ¹⁵Then Maccabeus consented to all that Lysias desired, being careful of the common good; and whatsoever Maccabeus wrote unto Lysias concerning the Jews, the king granted it.

¹⁶For there were letters written unto the Jews from Lysias to this effect:
Lysias unto the people of the Jews sendeth greeting. ¹⁷John and Absalom, who were sent from you, delivered me the petition

subscribed, and made request for the performance of the contents thereof. [18]Therefore what things soever were meet to be reported to the king, I have declared them, and he hath granted as much as might be. [19]If then you will keep yourselves loyal to the state, hereafter also will I endeavour to be a means of your good. [20]But of the particulars I have given order both to these, and the others that came from me, to commune with you. [21]Fare ye well. The hundred and eight and fortieth year, the four and twentieth day of the month Dioscorinthius.

[22]Now the king's letter contained these words:

King Antiochus unto his brother Lysias sendeth greeting. [23]Since our father is translated unto the gods, our will is, that they that are in our realm live quietly, that every one may attend upon his own affairs. [24]We understand also that the Jews would not consent to our father for to be brought unto the custom of the Gentiles, but had rather keep their own manner of living: for the which cause they require of us, that we should suffer them to live after their own laws. [25]Wherefore our mind is, that this nation shall be in rest, and we have determined to restore them their temple, that they may live according to the customs of their forefathers. [26]Thou shalt do well therefore to send unto them, and grant them peace, that when they are certified of our mind, they may be of good comfort, and ever go cheerfully about their own affairs.

[27]And the letter of the king unto the nation of the Jews was after this manner:

King Antiochus sendeth greeting unto the council, and the rest of the Jews. [28]If ye fare well, we have our desire: we are also in good health. [29]Menelaus declared unto us, that your desire was to return home, and to follow your own business: [30]wherefore they that will depart shall have safe conduct till the thirtieth day of Xanthicus with security. [31]And the Jews shall use their own kind of meats and laws, as before, and none of them any manner of ways shall be molested for things ignorantly done. [32]I have sent also Menelaus, that he may comfort you. [33]Fare ye well. In the hundred forty and eighth year, and the fifteenth day of the month Xanthicus.

[34]The Romans also sent unto them a letter containing these words:

Quintus Memmius and Titus Manlius, ambassadors of the Romans, send greeting unto the people of the Jews. [35]Whatsoever Lysias the king's cousin hath granted, therewith we also are well pleased. [36]But touching such things as he judged to be referred to the king: after you have advised thereof, send one forthwith, that we may declare as it is convenient for you: for we are now going to Antioch. [37]Therefore send some with speed, that we may know what is your mind. [38]Farewell. This hundred and eight and fortieth year, the fifteenth day of the month Xanthicus.

12 When these covenants were made, Lysias went unto the king, and the Jews were about their husbandry. ²But of the governors of several places, Timotheus, and Apollonius the son of Genneus, also Hieronymus, and Demophon, and besides them Nicanor the governor of Cyprus would not suffer them to be quiet, and live in peace.

³The men of Joppe also did such an ungodly deed: they prayed the Jews that dwelt among them to go with their wives and children into the boats which they had prepared, as though they had meant them no hurt. ⁴Who accepted of it according to the common decree of the city, as being desirous to live in peace, and suspecting nothing: but when they were gone forth into the deep, they drowned no less than two hundred of them. ⁵When Judas heard of this cruelty done unto his countrymen, he commanded those that were with him to make them ready. ⁶And calling upon God the righteous Judge, he came against those murderers of his brethren, and burnt the haven by night, and set the boats on fire, and those that fled thither he slew. ⁷And when the town was shut up, he went backward, as if he would return to root out all them of the city of Joppe. ⁸But when he heard that the Jamnites were minded to do in like manner unto the Jews that dwelt among them, ⁹he came upon the Jamnites also by night, and set fire on the haven and the navy, so that the light of the fire was seen at Jerusalem two hundred and forty furlongs off.

¹⁰Now when they were gone from thence nine furlongs in their journey toward Timotheus, no fewer than five thousand men on foot and five hundred horsemen of the Arabians set upon him. ¹¹Whereupon there was a very sore battle; but Judas's side by the help of God got the victory, so that the Nomades of Arabia, being overcome, besought Judas for peace, promising both to give him cattle, and to pleasure him otherwise. ¹²Then Judas, thinking indeed that they would be profitable in many things, granted them peace: whereupon they shook hands, and so they departed to their tents.

¹³He went also about to make a bridge to a certain strong city, which was fenced about with walls, and inhabited by people of divers countries, and the name of it was Caspis. ¹⁴But they that were within it put such trust in the strength of the walls and provision of victuals, that they behaved themselves rudely towards them that were with Judas, railing and blaspheming, and uttering such words as were not to be spoken. ¹⁵Wherefore Judas with his company, calling upon the great Lord of the world (who without any rams or engines of war did cast down Jericho in the time of Joshua), gave a fierce assault against the walls, ¹⁶and took the city by the will of God, and made unspeakable slaughters, insomuch that a lake two furlongs broad near adjoining thereunto, being filled full, was seen running with blood.

¹⁷Then departed they from thence seven hundred and fifty furlongs, and came to Characa unto the Jews that are called Tubieni. ¹⁸But as for Timotheus, they found him not in the places, for before he had dispatched anything, he departed from thence, having left a very strong garrison in a certain hold. ¹⁹Howbeit Dositheus and Sosipater, who

were of Maccabeus' captains, went forth, and slew those that Timotheus had left in the fortress, above ten thousand men. [20]And Maccabeus ranged his army by bands, and set them over the bands, and went against Timotheus, who had about him a hundred and twenty thousand men of foot, and two thousand and five hundred horsemen. [21]Now when Timotheus had knowledge of Judas's coming, he sent the women and children and the other baggage unto a fortress called Carnion: for the town was hard to besiege, and uneasy to come unto, by reason of the straitness of all the places. [22]But when Judas's first band came in sight, the enemies, being smitten with fear and terror through the appearing of him that seeth all things, fled amain, one running this way, another that way, so as that they were often hurt of their own men, and wounded with the points of their own swords. [23]Judas also was very earnest in pursuing them, killing those wicked wretches, of whom he slew about thirty thousand men. [24]Moreover Timotheus himself fell into the hands of Dositheus and Sosipater, whom he besought with much craft to let him go with his life, because he had many of the Jews' parents, and the brethren of some of them, who, if they put him to death, should not be regarded. [25]So when he had assured them with many words that he would restore them without hurt, according to the agreement, they let him go for the saving of their brethren.

[26]Then Maccabeus marched forth to Carnion, and to the temple of Atargatis, and there he slew five and twenty thousand persons. [27]And after he had put to flight and destroyed them, Judas removed the host towards Ephron, a strong city, wherein Lysias abode, and a great multitude of divers nations, and the strong young men kept the walls, and defended them mightily: wherein also was great provision of engines and darts. [28]But when Judas and his company had called upon Almighty God, who with his power breaketh the strength of his enemies, they won the city, and slew twenty and five thousand of them that were within. [29]From thence they departed to Scythopolis, which lieth six hundred furlongs from Jerusalem. [30]But when the Jews that dwelt there had testified that the Scythopolitans dealt lovingly with them, and entreated them kindly in the time of their adversity: [31]they gave them thanks, desiring them to be friendly still unto them: and so they came to Jerusalem, the feast of the weeks approaching.

[32]And after the feast called Pentecost, they went forth against Gorgias the governor of Idumea, [33]who came out with three thousand men of foot and four hundred horsemen. [34]And it happened that in their fighting together a few of the Jews were slain. [35]At which time Dositheus, one of Bacenor's company, who was on horseback, and a strong man, was still upon Gorgias, and taking hold of his coat drew him by force; and when he would have taken that cursed man alive, a horseman of Thracia coming upon him smote off his shoulder, so that Gorgias fled unto Marisa. [36]Now when they that were with Gorgias had fought long, and were weary, Judas called upon the Lord, that he would show himself to be their helper and leader of the battle. [37]And with that he began in his

own language, and sang psalms with a loud voice, and rushing unawares upon Gorgias' men, he put them to flight. ³⁸So Judas gathered his host, and came into the city of Odollam. And when the seventh day came, they purified themselves, as the custom was, and kept the sabbath in the same place. ³⁹And upon the day following, as the use had been, Judas and his company came to take up the bodies of them that were slain, and to bury them with their kinsmen in their fathers' graves. ⁴⁰Now under the coats of every one that was slain they found things consecrated to the idols of the Jamnites, which is forbidden the Jews by the law. Then every man saw that this was the cause wherefore they were slain. ⁴¹All men therefore praising the Lord, the righteous Judge, who had opened the things that were hid, ⁴²betook themselves unto prayer, and besought him that the sin committed might wholly be put out of remembrance. Besides, that noble Judas exhorted the people to keep themselves from sin, forasmuch as they saw before their eyes the things that came to pass for the sin of those that were slain. ⁴³And when he had made a gathering throughout the company to the sum of two thousand drachms of silver, he sent it to Jerusalem to offer a sin offering, doing therein very well and honestly, in that he was mindful of the resurrection: ⁴⁴for if he had not hoped that they that were slain should have risen again, it had been superfluous and vain to pray for the dead. ⁴⁵And also in that he perceived that there was great favour laid up for those that died godly, it was a holy and good thought. Whereupon he made a reconciliation for the dead, that they might be delivered from sin.

13 In the hundred forty and ninth year it was told Judas that Antiochus Eupator was coming with a great power into Judea, ²and with him Lysias his protector, and ruler of his affairs, having either of them a Grecian power of footmen, a hundred and ten thousand, and horsemen five thousand and three hundred, and elephants two and twenty, and three hundred chariots armed with hooks. ³Menelaus also joined himself with them, and with great dissimulation encouraged Antiochus, not for the safeguard of the country, but because he thought to have been made governor. ⁴But the King of kings moved Antiochus' mind against this wicked wretch, and Lysias informed the king that this man was the cause of all mischief, so that the king commanded to bring him unto Berea, and to put him to death, as the manner is in that place. ⁵Now there was in that place a tower of fifty cubits high, full of ashes, and it had a round instrument which on every side hanged down into the ashes. ⁶And whosoever was condemned of sacrilege, or had committed any other grievous crime, there did all men thrust him unto death. ⁷Such a death it happened that wicked man to die, not having so much as burial in the earth; and that most justly: ⁸for inasmuch as he had committed many sins about the altar, whose fire and ashes were holy, he received his death in ashes.

⁹Now the king came with a barbarous and haughty mind to do far worse to the Jews than had been done in his father's time. ¹⁰Which things when Judas perceived, he commanded the multitude to call

upon the Lord night and day, that if ever at any other time, he would now also help them, being at the point to be put from their law, from their country, and from the holy temple: [11] and that he would not suffer the people, that had even now been but a little refreshed, to be in subjection to the blasphemous nations. [12] So when they had all done this together, and besought the merciful Lord with weeping and fasting, and lying flat upon the ground three days long, Judas, having exhorted them, commanded they should be in a readiness.

[13] And Judas, being apart with the elders, determined, before the king's host should enter into Judea and get the city, to go forth and try the matter in fight by the help of the Lord. [14] So when he had committed all to the Creator of the world, and exhorted his soldiers to fight manfully, even unto death, for the laws, the temple, the city, the country, and the commonwealth, he camped by Modin. [15] And having given the watchword to them that were about him, 'Victory is of God'; with the most valiant and choice young men he went in into the king's tent by night, and slew in the camp about four thousand men, and the chiefest of the elephants, with all that were upon him. [16] And at last they filled the camp with fear and tumult, and departed with good success. [17] This was done in the break of the day, because the protection of the Lord did help him.

[18] Now when the king had taken a taste of the manliness of the Jews, he went about to take the holds by policy, [19] and marched towards Bethsura, which was a strong hold of the Jews: but he was put to flight, failed, and lost of his men: [20] for Judas had conveyed unto them that were in it such things as were necessary. [21] But Rhodocus, who was in the Jews' host, disclosed the secrets to the enemies; therefore he was sought out, and when they had gotten him, they put him in prison. [22] The king treated with them in Bethsura the second time, gave his hand, took theirs, departed, fought with Judas, was overcome; [23] heard that Philip, who was left over the affairs in Antioch, was desperately bent, confounded, entreated the Jews, submitted himself, and swore to all equal conditions, agreed with them, and offered sacrifice, honoured the temple, and dealt kindly with the place, [24] and accepted well of Maccabeus, made him principal governor from Ptolemais unto the Gerrhenians; [25] came to Ptolemais: the people there were grieved for the covenants; for they stormed, because they would make their covenants void. [26] Lysias went up to the judgement seat, said as much as could be in defence of the cause, persuaded, pacified, made them well-affected, returned to Antioch. Thus it went touching the king's coming and departing.

14 After three years was Judas informed that Demetrius the son of Seleucus, having entered by the haven of Tripolis with a great power and navy, [2] had taken the country, and killed Antiochus, and Lysias his protector.

[3] Now one Alcimus, who had been high priest, and had defiled himself wilfully in the times of their mingling with the Gentiles, seeing that by no means he could save himself, nor have any more access to the holy

altar, ⁴came to king Demetrius in the hundred and one and fiftieth year, presenting unto him a crown of gold, and a palm, and also of the boughs which were used solemnly in the temple: and so that day he held his peace. ⁵Howbeit, having gotten opportunity to further his foolish enterprise, and being called into counsel by Demetrius, and asked how the Jews stood affected, and what they intended, he answered thereunto: ⁶'Those of the Jews that be called Asideans, whose captain is Judas Maccabeus, nourish war, and are seditious, and will not let the realm be in peace. ⁷Therefore I, being deprived of my ancestors' honour, I mean the high priesthood, am now come hither: ⁸first verily, for the unfeigned care I have of things pertaining to the king, and secondly, even for that I intend the good of my own countrymen: for all our nation is in no small misery through the unadvised dealing of them aforesaid. ⁹Wherefore, O king, seeing thou knowest all these things, be careful for the country, and our nation, which is pressed on every side, according to the clemency that thou readily showest unto all. ¹⁰For as long as Judas liveth, it is not possible that the state should be quiet.'

¹¹This was no sooner spoken of him, but others of the king's friends, being maliciously set against Judas, did more incense Demetrius. ¹²And forthwith calling Nicanor, who had been master of the elephants, and making him governor over Judea, he sent him forth, ¹³commanding him to slay Judas, and to scatter them that were with him, and to make Alcimus high priest of the great temple. ¹⁴Then the heathen, that had fled out of Judea from Judas, came to Nicanor by flocks, thinking the harm and calamities of the Jews to be their welfare.

¹⁵Now when the Jews heard of Nicanor's coming, and that the heathen were up against them, they cast earth upon their heads, and made supplication to him that had established his people for ever, and who always helpeth his portion with manifestation of his presence. ¹⁶So at the commandment of the captain they removed straightways from thence, and came near unto them at the town of Dessau. ¹⁷Now Simon, Judas's brother, had joined battle with Nicanor, but was somewhat discomfited through the sudden silence of his enemies. ¹⁸Nevertheless Nicanor, hearing of the manliness of them that were with Judas, and the courageousness that they had to fight for their country, durst not try the matter by the sword. ¹⁹Wherefore he sent Posidonius, and Theodotus, and Mattathias to make peace.

²⁰So when they had taken long advisement thereupon, and the captain had made the multitude acquainted therewith, and it appeared that they were all of one mind, they consented to the covenants, ²¹and appointed a day to meet in together by themselves: and when the day came, and stools were set for either of them, ²²Judas placed armed men ready in convenient places, lest some treachery should be suddenly practised by the enemies: so they made a peaceable conference.

²³Now Nicanor abode in Jerusalem, and did no hurt, but sent away the people that came flocking unto him. ²⁴And he would not willingly have Judas out of his sight: for he loved the man from his heart. ²⁵He prayed

him also to take a wife, and to beget children: so he married, was quiet, and took part of this life.

²⁶But Alcimus, perceiving the love that was betwixt them, and considering the covenants that were made, came to Demetrius, and told him that Nicanor was not well-affected towards the state, for that he had ordained Judas, a traitor to his realm, to be the king's successor. ²⁷Then the king being in a rage, and provoked with the accusations of the most wicked man, wrote to Nicanor, signifying that he was much displeased with the covenants, and commanding him that he should send Maccabeus prisoner in all haste unto Antioch. ²⁸When this came to Nicanor's hearing, he was much confounded in himself, and took it grievously that he should make void the articles which were agreed upon, the man being in no fault. ²⁹But because there was no dealing against the king, he watched his time to accomplish this thing by policy. ³⁰Notwithstanding, when Maccabeus saw that Nicanor began to be churlish unto him, and that he entreated him more roughly than he was wont, perceiving that such sour behaviour came not of good, he gathered together not a few of his men, and withdrew himself from Nicanor.

³¹But the other, knowing that he was notably prevented by Judas's policy, came into the great and holy temple, and commanded the priests that were offering their usual sacrifices, to deliver him the man. ³²And when they swore that they could not tell where the man was whom he sought, ³³he stretched out his right hand toward the temple, and made an oath in this manner: 'If you will not deliver me Judas as a prisoner, I will lay this temple of God even with the ground, and I will break down the altar, and erect a notable temple unto Bacchus'. ³⁴After these words he departed. Then the priests lifted up their hands towards heaven, and besought him that was ever a defender of their nation, saying in this manner: ³⁵'Thou, O Lord of all things, who hast need of nothing, wast pleased that the temple of thy habitation should be among us. ³⁶Therefore now, O holy Lord of all holiness, keep this house ever undefiled, which lately was cleansed, and stop every unrighteous mouth.'

³⁷Now was there accused unto Nicanor one Razis, one of the elders of Jerusalem, a lover of his countrymen, and a man of very good report, who for his kindness was called a father of the Jews. ³⁸For in the former times, when they mingled not themselves with the Gentiles, he had been accused of Judaism, and did boldly jeopard his body and life with all vehemence for the religion of the Jews. ³⁹So Nicanor, willing to declare the hate that he bore unto the Jews, sent above five hundred men of war to take him: ⁴⁰for he thought by taking him to do the Jews much hurt. ⁴¹Now when the multitude would have taken the tower, and violently broken into the outer door, and bade that fire should be brought to burn it, he being ready to be taken on every side fell upon his sword, ⁴²choosing rather to die manfully, than to come into the hands of the wicked, to be abused otherwise than beseemed his noble birth. ⁴³But missing his stroke through haste, the multitude also rushing within the doors, he ran boldly up to the wall, and cast himself

down manfully among the thickest of them. ⁴⁴But they quickly giving back, and a space being made, he fell down into the midst of the void place. ⁴⁵Nevertheless, while there was yet breath within him, being inflamed with anger, he rose up; and though his blood gushed out like spouts of water, and his wounds were grievous, yet he ran through the midst of the throng; and standing upon a steep rock, ⁴⁶when as his blood was now quite gone, he plucked out his bowels, and taking them in both his hands, he cast them upon the throng, and calling upon the Lord of life and spirit to restore him those again, he thus died.

15 But Nicanor, hearing that Judas and his company were in the strong places about Samaria, resolved without any danger to set upon them on the sabbath day. ²Nevertheless the Jews that were compelled to go with him said, 'O destroy not so cruelly and barbarously, but give honour to that day, which he, that seeth all things, hath honoured with holiness above other days'. ³Then this most ungracious wretch demanded, if there were a Mighty One in heaven that had commanded the sabbath day to be kept. ⁴And when they said, 'There is in heaven a living Lord, and mighty, who commanded the seventh day to be kept', ⁵then said the other, 'And I also am mighty upon earth, and I command to take arms, and to do the king's business'. Yet he obtained not to have his wicked will done.

⁶So Nicanor in exceeding pride and haughtiness determined to set up a public monument of his victory over Judas and them that were with him. ⁷But Maccabeus had ever sure confidence that the Lord would help him: ⁸wherefore he exhorted his people not to fear the coming of the heathen against them, but to remember the help which in former times they had received from heaven, and now to expect the victory and aid, which should come unto them from the Almighty. ⁹And so comforting them out of the law and the prophets, and withal putting them in mind of the battles that they won afore, he made them more cheerful. ¹⁰And when he had stirred up their minds, he gave them their charge, showing them therewithal the falsehood of the heathen, and the breach of oaths. ¹¹Thus he armed every one of them not so much with defence of shields and spears, as with comfortable and good words: and besides that, he told them a dream worthy to be believed, as if it had been so indeed, which did not a little rejoice them.

¹²And this was his vision: that Onias, who had been high priest, a virtuous and a good man, reverend in conversation, gentle in condition, well spoken also, and exercised from a child in all points of virtue, holding up his hands prayed for the whole body of the Jews. ¹³This done, in like manner there appeared a man with grey hairs, and exceeding glorious, who was of a wonderful and excellent majesty. ¹⁴Then Onias answered, saying, 'This is a lover of the brethren, who prayeth much for the people, and for the holy city, to wit, Jeremias the prophet of God'. ¹⁵Whereupon Jeremias holding forth his right hand gave to Judas a sword of gold, and in giving it spoke thus, ¹⁶'Take this holy sword, a gift from God, with the which thou shalt wound the adversaries'.

¹⁷Thus being well comforted by the words of Judas, which were very good, and able to stir them up to valour, and to encourage the hearts of the young men, they determined not to pitch camp, but courageously to set upon them, and manfully to try the matter by conflict, because the city and the sanctuary and the temple were in danger. ¹⁸For the care that they took for their wives, and their children, their brethren, and kinsfolks, was in least account with them: but the greatest and principal fear was for the holy temple. ¹⁹Also they that were in the city took not the least care, being troubled for the conflict abroad.

²⁰And now, when as all looked what should be the trial, and the enemies were already come near, and the army was set in array, and the beasts conveniently placed, and the horsemen set in wings, ²¹Maccabeus seeing the coming of the multitude, and the divers preparations of armour, and the fierceness of the beasts, stretched out his hands towards heaven, and called upon the Lord that worketh wonders, knowing that victory cometh not by arms, but even as it seemeth good to him, he giveth it to such as are worthy: ²²therefore in his prayer he said after this manner: 'O Lord, thou didst send thy angel in the time of Ezekias king of Judea, and didst slay in the host of Sennacherib a hundred fourscore and five thousand. ²³Wherefore now also, O Lord of heaven, send a good angel before us for a fear and dread unto them. ²⁴And through the might of thy arm let those be stricken with terror, that come against thy holy people to blaspheme.' And he ended thus.

²⁵Then Nicanor and they that were with him came forward with trumpets and songs. ²⁶But Judas and his company encountered the enemies with invocation and prayer. ²⁷So that fighting with their hands, and praying unto God with their hearts, they slew no less than thirty and five thousand men: for through the appearance of God they were greatly cheered.

²⁸Now when the battle was done, returning again with joy, they knew that Nicanor lay dead in his harness. ²⁹Then they made a great shout and a noise, praising the Almighty in their own language. ³⁰And Judas, who was ever the chief defender of the citizens both in body and mind, and who continued his love towards his countrymen all his life, commanded to strike off Nicanor's head, and his hand with his shoulder, and bring them to Jerusalem.

³¹So when he was there, and had called them of his nation together, and set the priests before the altar, he sent for them that were of the tower, ³²and showed them vile Nicanor's head, and the hand of that blasphemer, which with proud brags he had stretched out against the holy temple of the Almighty. ³³And when he had cut out the tongue of that ungodly Nicanor, he commanded that they should give it by pieces unto the fowls, and hang up the reward of his madness before the temple. ³⁴So every man praised towards the heaven the glorious Lord, saying, 'Blessed be he that hath kept his own place undefiled.' ³⁵He hanged also Nicanor's head upon the tower, an evident and manifest sign unto all of the help of the Lord. ³⁶And they ordained all with a common

decree in no case to let that day pass without solemnity, but to celebrate the thirteenth day of the twelfth month, which in the Syrian tongue is called Adar, the day before Mardocheus' day. [37]Thus went it with Nicanor: and from that time forth the Hebrews had the city in their power.

And here will I make an end. [38]And if I have done well, and as is fitting the story, it is that which I desired: but if slenderly and meanly, it is that which I could attain unto. [39]For as it is hurtful to drink wine or water alone; and as wine mingled with water is pleasant, and delighteth the taste: even so speech finely framed delighteth the ears of them that read the story. And here shall be an end.

THE END OF APOCRYPHA

THE NEW TESTAMENT

THE GOSPEL ACCORDING TO
SAINT MATTHEW

1 The book of the generation of Jesus Christ, the son of David, the son of Abraham. ²Abraham begot Isaac, and Isaac begot Jacob, and Jacob begot Judas and his brethren. ³And Judas begot Phares and Zara of Thamar, and Phares begot Esrom, and Esrom begot Aram. ⁴And Aram begot Aminadab, and Aminadab begot Naasson, and Naasson begot Salmon. ⁵And Salmon begot Booz of Rachab, and Booz begot Obed of Ruth, and Obed begot Jesse. ⁶And Jesse begot David the king, and David the king begot Solomon of her that had been the wife of Urias. ⁷And Solomon begot Roboam, and Roboam begot Abia, and Abia begot Asa. ⁸And Asa begot Josaphat, and Josaphat begot Joram, and Joram begot Ozias. ⁹And Ozias begot Joatham, and Joatham begot Achaz, and Achaz begot Ezekias. ¹⁰And Ezekias begot Manasses, and Manasses begot Amon, and Amon begot Josias. ¹¹And Josias begot Jechonias and his brethren, about the time they were carried away to Babylon. ¹²And after they were brought to Babylon, Jechonias begot Salathiel, and Salathiel begot Zorobabel. ¹³And Zorobabel begot Abiud, and Abiud begot Eliakim, and Eliakim begot Azor. ¹⁴And Azor begot Sadoc, and Sadoc begot Achim, and Achim begot Eliud. ¹⁵And Eliud begot Eleazar, and Eleazar begot Matthan, and Matthan begot Jacob. ¹⁶And Jacob begot Joseph the husband of Mary, of whom was born Jesus, who is called Christ.

¹⁷So all the generations from Abraham to David are fourteen generations: and from David until the carrying away into Babylon are fourteen generations: and from the carrying away into Babylon unto Christ are fourteen generations.

¹⁸Now the birth of Jesus Christ was on this wise: when as his mother Mary was espoused to Joseph, before they came together, she was found with child of the Holy Ghost. ¹⁹Then Joseph her husband, being a just man, and not willing to make her a public example, was minded to put her away privily. ²⁰But while he thought on these things, behold, the angel of the Lord appeared unto him in a dream, saying, 'Joseph, thou son of David, fear not to take unto thee Mary thy wife: for that which is conceived in her is of the Holy Ghost. ²¹And she shall bring forth a son, and thou shalt call his name Jesus: for he shall save his people from their sins.' ²²Now all this was done, that it might be fulfilled which was spoken of the Lord by the prophet, saying, ²³'Behold, a virgin shall be with child, and shall bring forth a son, and they shall call his name Emmanuel', which being interpreted is, God with us. ²⁴Then Joseph being raised from sleep did as the angel of the Lord had bidden him, and took unto him his wife: ²⁵and knew her not till she had brought forth her firstborn son: and he called his name Jesus.

2 Now when Jesus was born in Bethlehem of Judea in the days of Herod the king, behold, there came wise men from the east to Jerusalem, ²saying, 'Where is he that is born King of the Jews? for we have seen his star in the east, and are come to worship him'. ³When Herod the king had heard these things, he was troubled, and all Jerusalem with him. ⁴And when he had gathered all the chief priests and scribes of the people together, he demanded of them where Christ should be born. ⁵And they said unto him, 'In Bethlehem of Judea: for thus it is written by the prophet, ⁶"And thou Bethlehem, in the land of Juda, art not the least among the princes of Juda: for out of thee shall come a Governor, that shall rule my people Israel"'.

⁷Then Herod, when he had privily called the wise men, inquired of them diligently what time the star appeared. ⁸And he sent them to Bethlehem, and said, 'Go and search diligently for the young child, and when ye have found him, bring me word again, that I may come and worship him also'.

⁹When they had heard the king, they departed; and lo, the star, which they saw in the east, went before them, till it came and stood over where the young child was. ¹⁰When they saw the star, they rejoiced with exceeding great joy. ¹¹And when they were come into the house, they saw the young child with Mary his mother, and fell down, and worshipped him: and when they had opened their treasures, they presented unto him gifts, gold, and frankincense, and myrrh. ¹²And being warned of God in a dream that they should not return to Herod, they departed into their own country another way.

¹³And when they were departed, behold, the angel of the Lord appeareth to Joseph in a dream, saying, 'Arise, and take the young child and his mother, and flee into Egypt, and be thou there until I bring thee word: for Herod will seek the young child to destroy him'. ¹⁴When he arose, he took the young child and his mother by night, and departed into Egypt: ¹⁵and was there until the death of Herod: that it might be fulfilled which was spoken of the Lord by the prophet, saying, 'Out of Egypt have I called my son'.

¹⁶Then Herod, when he saw that he was mocked of the wise men, was exceeding wroth, and sent forth, and slew all the children that were in Bethlehem, and in all the coasts thereof, from two years old and under, according to the time which he had diligently inquired of the wise men. ¹⁷Then was fulfilled that which was spoken by Jeremy the prophet, saying, ¹⁸'In Rama was there a voice heard, lamentation, and weeping, and great mourning, Rachel weeping for her children, and would not be comforted, because they are not'.

¹⁹But when Herod was dead, behold, an angel of the Lord appeareth in a dream to Joseph in Egypt, ²⁰saying, 'Arise, and take the young child and his mother, and go into the land of Israel: for they are dead which sought the young child's life'. ²¹And he arose, and took the young child and his mother, and came into the land of Israel. ²²But when he heard that Archelaus did reign in Judea in the room of his father Herod, he was afraid to go thither: notwithstanding, being warned of God in a dream, he turned aside into the parts of Galilee: ²³and he came and dwelt in a city called Nazareth: that it might be fulfilled which was spoken by the prophets, 'He shall be called a Nazarene'.

3 In those days came John the Baptist, preaching in the wilderness of Judea, ²and saying, 'Repent ye: for the kingdom of heaven is at hand'. ³For this is he that was spoken of by the prophet Esaias, saying, 'The voice of one crying in the wilderness, "Prepare ye the way of the Lord, make his paths straight"'. ⁴And the same John had his raiment of camel's hair, and a leathern girdle about his loins, and his meat was locusts and wild honey. ⁵Then went out to him Jerusalem, and all Judea, and all the region round about Jordan, ⁶and were baptized of him in Jordan, confessing their sins.

⁷But when he saw many of the Pharisees and Sadducees come to his baptism, he said unto them, 'O generation of vipers, who hath warned you to flee from the wrath to come? ⁸Bring forth therefore fruits meet for repentance. ⁹And think not to say within yourselves, "We have Abraham to our father": for I say unto you, that God is able of these stones to raise up children unto Abraham. ¹⁰And now also the axe is laid unto the root of the trees: therefore every tree which bringeth not forth good fruit is hewn down, and cast into the fire. ¹¹I indeed baptize you with water unto repentance: but he that cometh after me is mightier than I, whose shoes I am not worthy to bear: he shall baptize you with the Holy Ghost, and with fire: ¹²whose fan is in his hand, and he will thoroughly purge his floor, and gather his wheat into the garner: but will burn up the chaff with unquenchable fire.'

¹³Then cometh Jesus from Galilee to Jordan unto John, to be baptized of him. ¹⁴But John forbad him, saying, 'I have need to be baptized of thee, and comest thou to me?' ¹⁵And Jesus answering said unto him, 'Suffer it to be so now: for thus it becometh us to fulfil all righteousness'. Then he suffered him. ¹⁶And Jesus, when he was baptized, went up straightway out of the water: and lo, the heavens were opened unto him, and he saw the Spirit of God descending like a dove, and lighting upon him: ¹⁷and lo, a voice from heaven, saying, 'This is my beloved Son, in whom I am well pleased'.

4 Then was Jesus led up of the Spirit into the wilderness to be tempted of the devil. ²And when he had fasted forty days and forty nights, he was afterward a-hungered. ³And when the tempter came to him, he said, 'If thou be the Son of God, command that these stones be made bread'. ⁴But he answered and said, 'It is written, "Man shall not live by bread alone, but by every word that proceedeth out of the mouth of God"'.

⁵Then the devil taketh him up into the holy city, and setteth him on a pinnacle of the temple, ⁶and saith unto him, 'If thou be the Son of God, cast thyself down: for it is written, "He shall give his angels charge concerning thee, and in their hands they shall bear thee up, lest at any time thou dash thy foot against a stone"'. ⁷Jesus said unto him, 'It is written again, "Thou shalt not tempt the Lord thy God"'.

⁸Again, the devil taketh him up into an exceeding high mountain, and showeth him all the kingdoms of the world, and the glory of them: ⁹and saith unto him, 'All these things will I give thee, if thou wilt fall down and worship me'. ¹⁰Then saith Jesus unto him, 'Get thee hence,

Satan: for it is written, "Thou shalt worship the Lord thy God, and him only shalt thou serve"'. ¹¹Then the devil leaveth him, and behold, angels came and ministered unto him.

¹²Now when Jesus had heard that John was cast into prison, he departed into Galilee. ¹³And leaving Nazareth, he came and dwelt in Capernaum, which is upon the sea-coast, in the borders of Zabulon and Nephthalim: ¹⁴that it might be fulfilled which was spoken by Esaias the prophet, saying, ¹⁵'The land of Zabulon, and the land of Nephthalim, by the way of the sea, beyond Jordan, Galilee of the Gentiles: ¹⁶the people which sat in darkness saw great light: and to them which sat in the region and shadow of death light is sprung up'.

¹⁷From that time Jesus began to preach, and to say, 'Repent: for the kingdom of heaven is at hand'.

¹⁸And Jesus, walking by the sea of Galilee, saw two brethren, Simon called Peter, and Andrew his brother, casting a net into the sea: for they were fishers. ¹⁹And he saith unto them, 'Follow me, and I will make you fishers of men'. ²⁰And they straightway left their nets, and followed him. ²¹And going on from thence, he saw other two brethren, James the son of Zebedee, and John his brother, in a ship with Zebedee their father, mending their nets: and he called them. ²²And they immediately left the ship and their father, and followed him.

²³And Jesus went about all Galilee, teaching in their synagogues, and preaching the gospel of the kingdom, and healing all manner of sickness and all manner of disease among the people. ²⁴And his fame went throughout all Syria: and they brought unto him all sick people that were taken with divers diseases and torments, and those which were possessed with devils, and those which were lunatic, and those that had the palsy, and he healed them. ²⁵And there followed him great multitudes of people from Galilee, and from Decapolis, and from Jerusalem, and from Judea, and from beyond Jordan.

5 And seeing the multitudes, he went up into a mountain: and when he was set, his disciples came unto him. ²And he opened his mouth, and taught them, saying, ³'Blessed are the poor in spirit: for theirs is the kingdom of heaven. ⁴Blessed are they that mourn: for they shall be comforted. ⁵Blessed are the meek: for they shall inherit the earth. ⁶Blessed are they which do hunger and thirst after righteousness: for they shall be filled. ⁷Blessed are the merciful: for they shall obtain mercy. ⁸Blessed are the pure in heart: for they shall see God. ⁹Blessed are the peacemakers: for they shall be called the children of God. ¹⁰Blessed are they which are persecuted for righteousness' sake: for theirs is the kingdom of heaven. ¹¹Blessed are ye, when men shall revile you, and persecute you, and shall say all manner of evil against you falsely, for my sake. ¹²Rejoice, and be exceeding glad: for great is your reward in heaven: for so persecuted they the prophets which were before you.

¹³'Ye are the salt of the earth: but if the salt have lost his savour, wherewith shall it be salted? It is thenceforth good for nothing, but to be cast out, and to be trodden under foot of men. ¹⁴Ye are the light of the world. A city that is set on a hill cannot be hid. ¹⁵Neither do men

light a candle, and put it under a bushel, but on a candlestick, and it giveth light unto all that are in the house. [16]Let your light so shine before men, that they may see your good works, and glorify your Father which is in heaven.

[17]'Think not that I am come to destroy the law, or the prophets. I am not come to destroy, but to fulfil. [18]For verily I say unto you, till heaven and earth pass, one jot or one tittle shall in no wise pass from the law, till all be fulfilled. [19]Whosoever therefore shall break one of these least commandments, and shall teach men so, he shall be called the least in the kingdom of heaven: but whosoever shall do and teach them, the same shall be called great in the kingdom of heaven. [20]For I say unto you, that except your righteousness shall exceed the righteousness of the scribes and Pharisees, ye shall in no case enter into the kingdom of heaven.

[21]'Ye have heard that it was said by them of old time, "Thou shalt not kill"; and "Whosoever shall kill shall be in danger of the judgement": [22]but I say unto you, that whosoever is angry with his brother without a cause shall be in danger of the judgement: and whosoever shall say to his brother, "Raca", shall be in danger of the council: but whosoever shall say, "Thou fool", shall be in danger of hell fire. [23]Therefore if thou bring thy gift to the altar, and there rememberest that thy brother hath aught against thee: [24]leave there thy gift before the altar, and go thy way; first be reconciled to thy brother, and then come and offer thy gift. [25]Agree with thy adversary quickly, whilst thou art in the way with him: lest at any time the adversary deliver thee to the judge, and the judge deliver thee to the officer, and thou be cast into prison. [26]Verily I say unto thee, thou shalt by no means come out thence, till thou hast paid the uttermost farthing.

[27]'Ye have heard that it was said by them of old time, "Thou shalt not commit adultery": [28]but I say unto you, that whosoever looketh on a woman to lust after her hath committed adultery with her already in his heart. [29]And if thy right eye offend thee, pluck it out, and cast it from thee. For it is profitable for thee that one of thy members should perish, and not that thy whole body should be cast into hell. [30]And if thy right hand offend thee, cut it off, and cast it from thee. For it is profitable for thee that one of thy members should perish, and not that thy whole body should be cast into hell. [31]It hath been said, "Whosoever shall put away his wife, let him give her a writing of divorcement": [32]but I say unto you, that whosoever shall put away his wife, saving for the cause of fornication, causeth her to commit adultery: and whosoever shall marry her that is divorced committeth adultery.

[33]'Again, ye have heard that it hath been said by them of old time, "Thou shalt not forswear thyself, but shalt perform unto the Lord thy oaths": [34]but I say unto you, swear not at all, neither by heaven, for it is God's throne: [35]nor by the earth, for it is his footstool: neither by Jerusalem, for it is the city of the great King. [36]Neither shalt thou swear by thy head, because thou canst not make one hair white or black. [37]But let your communication be, "Yea, yea"; "Nay, nay": for whatsoever is more than these cometh of evil.

³⁸'Ye have heard that it hath been said, "An eye for an eye, and a tooth for a tooth": ³⁹but I say unto you, that ye resist not evil: but whosoever shall smite thee on thy right cheek, turn to him the other also. ⁴⁰And if any man will sue thee at the law, and take away thy coat, let him have thy cloak also. ⁴¹And whosoever shall compel thee to go a mile, go with him twain. ⁴²Give to him that asketh thee: and from him that would borrow of thee turn not thou away.

⁴³'Ye have heard that it hath been said, "Thou shalt love thy neighbour, and hate thy enemy". ⁴⁴But I say unto you, love your enemies, bless them that curse you, do good to them that hate you, and pray for them which despitefully use you, and persecute you: ⁴⁵that ye may be the children of your Father which is in heaven: for he maketh his sun to rise on the evil and on the good, and sendeth rain on the just and on the unjust. ⁴⁶For if ye love them which love you, what reward have ye? Do not even the publicans the same? ⁴⁷And if ye salute your brethren only, what do you more than others? Do not even the publicans so? ⁴⁸Be ye therefore perfect, even as your Father which is in heaven is perfect.

6 ¹'Take heed that ye do not your alms before men, to be seen of them: otherwise ye have no reward of your Father which is in heaven. ²Therefore when thou doest thy alms, do not sound a trumpet before thee, as the hypocrites do in the synagogues and in the streets, that they may have glory of men. Verily I say unto you, they have their reward. ³But when thou doest alms, let not thy left hand know what thy right doeth: ⁴that thy alms may be in secret: and thy Father which seeth in secret himself shall reward thee openly.

⁵'And when thou prayest, thou shalt not be as the hypocrites are: for they love to pray standing in the synagogues and in the corners of the streets, that they may be seen of men. Verily I say unto you, they have their reward. ⁶But thou, when thou prayest, enter into thy closet, and when thou hast shut thy door, pray to thy Father which is in secret; and thy Father which seeth in secret shall reward thee openly. ⁷But when ye pray, use not vain repetitions, as the heathen do. For they think that they shall be heard for their much speaking. ⁸Be not ye therefore like unto them: for your Father knoweth what things ye have need of, before ye ask him.

⁹'After this manner therefore pray ye: "Our Father which art in heaven, hallowed be thy name. ¹⁰Thy kingdom come. Thy will be done in earth, as it is in heaven. ¹¹Give us this day our daily bread. ¹²And forgive us our debts, as we forgive our debtors. ¹³And lead us not into temptation, but deliver us from evil: for thine is the kingdom, and the power, and the glory, for ever. Amen." ¹⁴For if ye forgive men their trespasses, your heavenly Father will also forgive you: ¹⁵but if ye forgive not men their trespasses, neither will your Father forgive your trespasses.

¹⁶'Moreover when ye fast, be not as the hypocrites, of a sad countenance: for they disfigure their faces, that they may appear unto men to fast. Verily I say unto you, they have their reward. ¹⁷But thou, when thou fastest, anoint thy head, and wash thy face: ¹⁸that thou appear not

unto men to fast, but unto thy Father which is in secret: and thy Father, which seeth in secret, shall reward thee openly.

¹⁹'Lay not up for yourselves treasures upon earth, where moth and rust doth corrupt, and where thieves break through and steal. ²⁰But lay up for yourselves treasures in heaven, where neither moth nor rust doth corrupt, and where thieves do not break through nor steal. ²¹For where your treasure is, there will your heart be also. ²²The light of the body is the eye: if therefore thy eye be single, thy whole body shall be full of light. ²³But if thy eye be evil, thy whole body shall be full of darkness. If therefore the light that is in thee be darkness, how great is that darkness?

²⁴'No man can serve two masters: for either he will hate the one, and love the other; or else he will hold to the one, and despise the other. Ye cannot serve God and mammon. ²⁵Therefore I say unto you, take no thought for your life, what ye shall eat, or what ye shall drink, nor yet for your body, what ye shall put on. Is not the life more than meat, and the body than raiment? ²⁶Behold the fowls of the air: for they sow not, neither do they reap, nor gather into barns, yet your heavenly Father feedeth them. Are ye not much better than they? ²⁷Which of you by taking thought can add one cubit unto his stature? ²⁸And why take ye thought for raiment? Consider the lilies of the field, how they grow: they toil not, neither do they spin. ²⁹And yet I say unto you, that even Solomon in all his glory was not arrayed like one of these. ³⁰Wherefore, if God so clothe the grass of the field, which today is, and tomorrow is cast into the oven, shall he not much more clothe you, O ye of little faith? ³¹Therefore take no thought, saying, "What shall we eat?" or, "What shall we drink?" or, "Wherewithal shall we be clothed?" ³²(for after all these things do the Gentiles seek): for your heavenly Father knoweth that ye have need of all these things. ³³But seek ye first the kingdom of God, and his righteousness, and all these things shall be added unto you. ³⁴Take therefore no thought for the morrow: for the morrow shall take thought for the things of itself. Sufficient unto the day is the evil thereof.

7 'Judge not, that ye be not judged. ²For with what judgement ye judge, ye shall be judged: and with what measure ye mete, it shall be measured to you again. ³And why beholdest thou the mote that is in thy brother's eye, but considerest not the beam that is in thy own eye? ⁴Or how wilt thou say to thy brother, "Let me pull out the mote out of thy eye", and behold, a beam is in thy own eye? ⁵Thou hypocrite, first cast out the beam out of thy own eye: and then shalt thou see clearly to cast out the mote out of thy brother's eye.

⁶'Give not that which is holy unto the dogs, neither cast ye your pearls before swine, lest they trample them under their feet, and turn again and rend you.

⁷'Ask, and it shall be given you: seek, and ye shall find: knock, and it shall be opened unto you. ⁸For every one that asketh receiveth: and he that seeketh findeth: and to him that knocketh it shall be opened. ⁹Or what man is there of you, whom if his son ask bread, will he give him a

stone? [10]Or if he ask a fish, will he give him a serpent? [11]If ye then, being evil, know how to give good gifts unto your children, how much more shall your Father which is in heaven give good things to them that ask him? [12]Therefore all things whatsoever ye would that men should do to you, do ye even so to them: for this is the law and the prophets.

[13]'Enter ye in at the strait gate, for wide is the gate, and broad is the way that leadeth to destruction, and many there be which go in thereat: [14]because strait is the gate, and narrow is the way, which leadeth unto life, and few there be that find it.

[15]'Beware of false prophets, which come to you in sheep's clothing, but inwardly they are ravening wolves. [16]Ye shall know them by their fruits. Do men gather grapes of thorns, or figs of thistles? [17]Even so every good tree bringeth forth good fruit: but a corrupt tree bringeth forth evil fruit. [18]A good tree cannot bring forth evil fruit, neither can a corrupt tree bring forth good fruit. [19]Every tree that bringeth not forth good fruit is hewn down, and cast into the fire. [20]Wherefore by their fruits ye shall know them.

[21]'Not every one that saith unto me, "Lord, Lord", shall enter into the kingdom of heaven: but he that doeth the will of my Father which is in heaven. [22]Many will say to me in that day, "Lord, Lord, have we not prophesied in thy name? and in thy name have cast out devils? and in thy name done many wonderful works?" [23]And then will I profess unto them, "I never knew you: depart from me, ye that work iniquity".

[24]'Therefore whosoever heareth these sayings of mine, and doeth them, I will liken him unto a wise man, which built his house upon a rock: [25]and the rain descended, and the floods came, and the winds blew, and beat upon that house: and it fell not, for it was founded upon a rock. [26]And every one that heareth these sayings of mine, and doeth them not, shall be likened unto a foolish man, which built his house upon the sand: [27]and the rain descended, and the floods came, and the winds blew, and beat upon that house, and it fell, and great was the fall of it.'

[28]And it came to pass, when Jesus had ended these sayings, the people were astonished at his doctrine: [29]for he taught them as one having authority, and not as the scribes.

8 When he was come down from the mountain, great multitudes followed him. [2]And behold, there came a leper and worshipped him, saying, 'Lord, if thou wilt, thou canst make me clean'. [3]And Jesus put forth his hand, and touched him, saying, 'I will, be thou clean'. And immediately his leprosy was cleansed. [4]And Jesus saith unto him, 'See thou tell no man; but go thy way, show thyself to the priest, and offer the gift that Moses commanded, for a testimony unto them'.

[5]And when Jesus was entered into Capernaum, there came unto him a centurion, beseeching him, [6]and saying, 'Lord, my servant lieth at home sick of the palsy, grievously tormented'. [7]And Jesus saith unto him, 'I will come and heal him'. [8]The centurion answered and said, 'Lord, I am not worthy that thou shouldst come under my roof: but speak the word only, and my servant shall be healed. [9]For I am a man

under authority, having soldiers under me: and I say to this man, "Go", and he goeth; and to another, "Come", and he cometh; and to my servant, "Do this", and he doeth it.' [10]When Jesus heard it, he marvelled, and said to them that followed, 'Verily I say unto you, I have not found so great faith, no, not in Israel. [11]And I say unto you, that many shall come from the east and west, and shall sit down with Abraham, and Isaac, and Jacob, in the kingdom of heaven. [12]But the children of the kingdom shall be cast out into outer darkness: there shall be weeping and gnashing of teeth.' [13]And Jesus said unto the centurion, 'Go thy way, and as thou hast believed, so be it done unto thee'. And his servant was healed in the selfsame hour.

[14]And when Jesus was come into Peter's house, he saw his wife's mother laid, and sick of a fever. [15]And he touched her hand, and the fever left her: and she arose, and ministered unto them.

[16]When the even was come, they brought unto him many that were possessed with devils: and he cast out the spirits with his word, and healed all that were sick, [17]that it might be fulfilled which was spoken by Esaias the prophet, saying, 'Himself took our infirmities, and bore our sicknesses'.

[18]Now when Jesus saw great multitudes about him, he gave commandment to depart unto the other side. [19]And a certain scribe came, and said unto him, 'Master, I will follow thee whithersoever thou goest'. [20]And Jesus saith unto him, 'The foxes have holes, and the birds of the air have nests: but the Son of man hath not where to lay his head'. [21]And another of his disciples said unto him, 'Lord, suffer me first to go and bury my father'. [22]But Jesus said unto him, 'Follow me, and let the dead bury their dead'.

[23]And when he was entered into a ship, his disciples followed him. [24]And behold, there arose a great tempest in the sea, insomuch that the ship was covered with the waves: but he was asleep. [25]And his disciples came to him, and awoke him, saying, 'Lord, save us: we perish'. [26]And he saith unto them, 'Why are ye fearful, O ye of little faith?' Then he arose, and rebuked the winds and the sea, and there was a great calm. [27]But the men marvelled, saying, 'What manner of man is this, that even the winds and the sea obey him!'

[28]And when he was come to the other side into the country of the Gergesenes, there met him two possessed with devils, coming out of the tombs, exceeding fierce, so that no man might pass by that way. [29]And behold, they cried out, saying, 'What have we to do with thee, Jesus, thou Son of God? Art thou come hither to torment us before the time?' [30]And there was a good way off from them a herd of many swine feeding. [31]So the devils besought him, saying, 'If thou cast us out, suffer us to go away into the herd of swine'. [32]And he said unto them, 'Go'. And when they were come out, they went into the herd of swine: and behold, the whole herd of swine ran violently down a steep place into the sea, and perished in the waters. [33]And they that kept them fled, and went their ways into the city, and told everything, and what was befallen to the possessed of the devils. [34]And behold, the whole city

came out to meet Jesus: and when they saw him, they besought him that he would depart out of their coasts.

9 And he entered into a ship, and passed over, and came into his own city. ²And behold, they brought to him a man sick of the palsy, lying on a bed: and Jesus seeing their faith, said unto the sick of the palsy, 'Son, be of good cheer, thy sins be forgiven thee'. ³And behold, certain of the scribes said within themselves, 'This man blasphemeth'. ⁴And Jesus knowing their thoughts said, 'Wherefore think ye evil in your hearts? ⁵For whether is easier to say, "Thy sins be forgiven thee": or to say, "Arise, and walk"? ⁶But that ye may know that the Son of man hath power on earth to forgive sins' (then saith he to the sick of the palsy), 'Arise, take up thy bed, and go unto thy house.' ⁷And he arose, and departed to his house. ⁸But when the multitudes saw it, they marvelled, and glorified God, which had given such power unto men.

⁹And as Jesus passed forth from thence, he saw a man named Matthew, sitting at the receipt of custom: and he saith unto him, 'Follow me'. And he arose, and followed him.

¹⁰And it came to pass, as Jesus sat at meat in the house, behold, many publicans and sinners came and sat down with him and his disciples. ¹¹And when the Pharisees saw it, they said unto his disciples, 'Why eateth your master with publicans and sinners?' ¹²But when Jesus heard that, he said unto them, 'They that be whole need not a physician, but they that are sick. ¹³But go ye and learn what that meaneth, "I will have mercy, and not sacrifice": for I am not come to call the righteous, but sinners to repentance.'

¹⁴Then came to him the disciples of John, saying, 'Why do we and the Pharisees fast oft, but thy disciples fast not?' ¹⁵And Jesus said unto them, 'Can the children of the bride-chamber mourn, as long as the bridegroom is with them? But the days will come, when the bridegroom shall be taken from them, and then shall they fast. ¹⁶No man putteth a piece of new cloth unto an old garment: for that which is put in to fill it up taketh from the garment, and the rent is made worse. ¹⁷Neither do men put new wine into old bottles: else the bottles break, and the wine runneth out, and the bottles perish: but they put new wine into new bottles, and both are preserved.'

¹⁸While he spoke these things unto them, behold, there came a certain ruler, and worshipped him, saying, 'My daughter is even now dead: but come and lay thy hand upon her, and she shall live'. ¹⁹And Jesus arose, and followed him, and so did his disciples.

²⁰And behold, a woman, which was diseased with an issue of blood twelve years, came behind him, and touched the hem of his garment. ²¹For she said within herself, 'If I may but touch his garment, I shall be whole'. ²²But Jesus turned him about, and when he saw her, he said, 'Daughter, be of good comfort, thy faith hath made thee whole'. And the woman was made whole from that hour.

²³And when Jesus came into the ruler's house, and saw the minstrels and the people making a noise, ²⁴he said unto them, 'Give place, for the maid is not dead, but sleepeth'. And they laughed him to scorn. ²⁵But

when the people were put forth, he went in, and took her by the hand: and the maid arose. ²⁶And the fame hereof went abroad into all that land.

²⁷And when Jesus departed thence, two blind men followed him, crying, and saying, 'Thou Son of David, have mercy on us'. ²⁸And when he was come into the house, the blind men came to him: and Jesus saith unto them, 'Believe ye that I am able to do this?' They said unto him, 'Yea, Lord'. ²⁹Then touched he their eyes, saying, 'According to your faith, be it unto you'. ³⁰And their eyes were opened: and Jesus straitly charged them, saying, 'See that no man know it'. ³¹But they, when they were departed, spread abroad his fame in all that country.

³²As they went out, behold, they brought to him a dumb man possessed with a devil. ³³And when the devil was cast out, the dumb spoke: and the multitudes marvelled, saying, 'It was never so seen in Israel'. ³⁴But the Pharisees said, 'He casteth out the devils through the prince of the devils'.

³⁵And Jesus went about all the cities and villages, teaching in their synagogues, and preaching the gospel of the kingdom, and healing every sickness and every disease among the people. ³⁶But when he saw the multitudes, he was moved with compassion on them, because they fainted, and were scattered abroad, as sheep having no shepherd. ³⁷Then saith he unto his disciples, 'The harvest truly is plenteous, but the labourers are few. ³⁸Pray ye therefore the Lord of the harvest, that he will send forth labourers into his harvest.'

10 And when he had called unto him his twelve disciples, he gave them power against unclean spirits, to cast them out, and to heal all manner of sickness and all manner of disease. ²Now the names of the twelve apostles are these: the first, Simon, who is called Peter, and Andrew his brother; James the son of Zebedee, and John his brother; ³Philip, and Bartholomew; Thomas, and Matthew the publican; James the son of Alphaeus, and Lebbaeus, whose surname was Thaddaeus; ⁴Simon the Canaanite, and Judas Iscariot, who also betrayed him.

⁵These twelve Jesus sent forth, and commanded them, saying, 'Go not into the way of the Gentiles, and into any city of the Samaritans enter ye not: ⁶but go rather to the lost sheep of the house of Israel. ⁷And as ye go, preach, saying, "The kingdom of heaven is at hand". ⁸Heal the sick, cleanse the lepers, raise the dead, cast out devils: freely ye have received, freely give. ⁹Provide neither gold, nor silver, nor brass in your purses, ¹⁰nor scrip for your journey, neither two coats, neither shoes, nor yet staves: for the workman is worthy of his meat. ¹¹And into whatsoever city or town ye shall enter, inquire who in it is worthy, and there abide till ye go thence. ¹²And when ye come into a house, salute it. ¹³And if the house be worthy, let your peace come upon it: but if it be not worthy, let your peace return to you. ¹⁴And whosoever shall not receive you, nor hear your words, when ye depart out of that house or city, shake off the dust of your feet. ¹⁵Verily I say unto you, it shall be more tolerable for the land of Sodom and Gomorrha in the day of judgement, than for that city.

¹⁶'Behold, I send you forth as sheep in the midst of wolves: be ye therefore wise as serpents, and harmless as doves. ¹⁷But beware of men: for they will deliver you up to the councils, and they will scourge you in their synagogues, ¹⁸and ye shall be brought before governors and kings for my sake, for a testimony against them and the Gentiles. ¹⁹But when they deliver you up, take no thought how or what ye shall speak, for it shall be given you in that same hour what ye shall speak. ²⁰For it is not ye that speak, but the Spirit of your Father which speaketh in you. ²¹And the brother shall deliver up the brother to death, and the father the child: and the children shall rise up against their parents, and cause them to be put to death. ²²And ye shall be hated of all men for my name's sake: but he that endureth to the end shall be saved. ²³But when they persecute you in this city, flee ye into another: for verily I say unto you, ye shall not have gone over the cities of Israel, till the Son of man be come. ²⁴The disciple is not above his master, nor the servant above his lord. ²⁵It is enough for the disciple that he be as his master, and the servant as his lord. If they have called the master of the house Beelzebub, how much more shall they call them of his household? ²⁶Fear them not therefore: for there is nothing covered, that shall not be revealed; and hid, that shall not be known. ²⁷What I tell you in darkness, that speak ye in light: and what ye hear in the ear, that preach ye upon the house-tops. ²⁸And fear not them which kill the body, but are not able to kill the soul: but rather fear him which is able to destroy both soul and body in hell.

²⁹'Are not two sparrows sold for a farthing? And one of them shall not fall on the ground without your Father. ³⁰But the very hairs of your head are all numbered. ³¹Fear ye not therefore, ye are of more value than many sparrows.

³²'Whosoever therefore shall confess me before men, him will I confess also before my Father which is in heaven. ³³But whosoever shall deny me before men, him will I also deny before my Father which is in heaven.

³⁴'Think not that I am come to send peace on earth: I came not to send peace, but a sword. ³⁵For I am come to set a man at variance against his father, and the daughter against her mother, and the daughter-in-law against her mother-in-law ³⁶And a man's foes shall be they of his own household. ³⁷He that loveth father or mother more than me is not worthy of me: and he that loveth son or daughter more than me is not worthy of me. ³⁸And he that taketh not his cross, and followeth after me, is not worthy of me. ³⁹He that findeth his life shall lose it: and he that loseth his life for my sake shall find it.

⁴⁰'He that receiveth you receiveth me, and he that receiveth me receiveth him that sent me. ⁴¹He that receiveth a prophet in the name of a prophet shall receive a prophet's reward: and he that receiveth a righteous man in the name of a righteous man shall receive a righteous man's reward. ⁴²And whosoever shall give to drink unto one of these little ones a cup of cold water only in the name of a disciple, verily I say unto you, he shall in no wise lose his reward.'

11 And it came to pass, when Jesus had made an end of command-ing his twelve disciples, he departed thence to teach and to preach in their cities. ²Now when John had heard in the prison the works of Christ, he sent two of his disciples, ³and said unto him, 'Art thou he that should come, or do we look for another?' ⁴Jesus answered and said unto them, 'Go and show John again those things which ye do hear and see: ⁵the blind receive their sight, and the lame walk, the lep-ers are cleansed, and the deaf hear, the dead are raised up, and the poor have the gospel preached to them. ⁶And blessed is he, whosoever shall not be offended in me.'

⁷And as they departed, Jesus began to say unto the multitudes con-cerning John, 'What went ye out into the wilderness to see? A reed shaken with the wind? ⁸But what went ye out for to see? A man clothed in soft raiment? Behold, they that wear soft clothing are in kings' houses. ⁹But what went ye out for to see? A prophet? yea, I say unto you, and more than a prophet. ¹⁰For this is he, of whom it is written, "Behold, I send my messenger before thy face, which shall prepare thy way before thee". ¹¹Verily I say unto you, among them that are born of women there hath not risen a greater than John the Baptist: notwith-standing he that is least in the kingdom of heaven is greater than he. ¹²And from the days of John the Baptist until now the kingdom of heaven suffereth violence, and the violent take it by force. ¹³For all the prophets and the law prophesied until John. ¹⁴And if ye will receive it, this is Elias, which was for to come. ¹⁵He that hath ears to hear, let him hear.

¹⁶'But whereunto shall I liken this generation? It is like unto children sitting in the markets, and calling unto their fellows, ¹⁷and saying, "We have piped unto you, and ye have not danced: we have mourned unto you, and ye have not lamented". ¹⁸For John came neither eating nor drinking, and they say, "He hath a devil". ¹⁹The Son of man came eating and drinking, and they say, "Behold a man gluttonous, and a wine-bib-ber, a friend of publicans and sinners". But wisdom is justified of her children.'

²⁰Then began he to upbraid the cities wherein most of his mighty works were done, because they repented not. ²¹'Woe unto thee, Chorazin, woe unto thee, Bethsaida: for if the mighty works, which were done in you, had been done in Tyre and Sidon, they would have repented long ago in sackcloth and ashes. ²²But I say unto you, it shall be more tolerable for Tyre and Sidon at the day of judgement, than for you. ²³And thou Capernaum, which art exalted unto heaven, shalt be brought down to hell: for if the mighty works which have been done in thee, had been done in Sodom, it would have remained until this day. ²⁴But I say unto you, that it shall be more tolerable for the land of Sodom in the day of judgement, than for thee.'

²⁵At that time Jesus answered and said, 'I thank thee, O Father, Lord of heaven and earth, because thou hast hid these things from the wise and prudent, and hast revealed them unto babes. ²⁶Even so, Father, for so it seemed good in thy sight. ²⁷All things are delivered unto me of my

Father: and no man knoweth the Son, but the Father: neither knoweth any man the Father, save the Son, and he to whomsoever the Son will reveal him.

²⁸ 'Come unto me, all ye that labour and are heavy laden, and I will give you rest. ²⁹Take my yoke upon you, and learn of me, for I am meek and lowly in heart: and ye shall find rest unto your souls. ³⁰For my yoke is easy, and my burden is light.'

12 At that time Jesus went on the sabbath day through the corn; and his disciples were a-hungered, and began to pluck the ears of corn, and to eat. ²But when the Pharisees saw it, they said unto him, 'Behold, thy disciples do that which is not lawful to do upon the sabbath day'. ³But he said unto them, 'Have ye not read what David did, when he was a-hungered, and they that were with him, ⁴how he entered into the house of God, and did eat the showbread, which was not lawful for him to eat, neither for them which were with him, but only for the priests? ⁵Or have ye not read in the law, how that on the sabbath days the priests in the temple profane the sabbath, and are blameless? ⁶But I say unto you, that in this place is one greater than the temple. ⁷But if ye had known what this meaneth, "I will have mercy, and not sacrifice", ye would not have condemned the guiltless. ⁸For the Son of man is Lord even of the sabbath day.'

⁹And when he was departed thence, he went into their synagogue. ¹⁰And behold, there was a man which had his hand withered. And they asked him, saying, 'Is it lawful to heal on the sabbath days?' that they might accuse him. ¹¹And he said unto them, 'What man shall there be among you, that shall have one sheep, and if it fall into a pit on the sabbath day, will he not lay hold on it, and lift it out? ¹²How much then is a man better than a sheep? Wherefore it is lawful to do well on the sabbath days.' ¹³Then saith he to the man, 'Stretch forth thy hand'. And he stretched it forth, and it was restored whole, like as the other.

¹⁴Then the Pharisees went out, and held a council against him, how they might destroy him. ¹⁵But when Jesus knew it, he withdrew himself from thence: and great multitudes followed him, and he healed them all, ¹⁶and charged them that they should not make him known: ¹⁷that it might be fulfilled which was spoken by Esaias the prophet, saying, ¹⁸'Behold my servant, whom I have chosen, my beloved, in whom my soul is well pleased: I will put my spirit upon him, and he shall show judgement to the Gentiles. ¹⁹He shall not strive, nor cry, neither shall any man hear his voice in the streets. ²⁰A bruised reed shall he not break, and smoking flax shall he not quench, till he send forth judgement unto victory. ²¹And in his name shall the Gentiles trust.'

²²Then was brought unto him one possessed with a devil, blind, and dumb: and he healed him, insomuch that the blind and dumb both spoke and saw. ²³And all the people were amazed, and said, 'Is this the son of David?' ²⁴But when the Pharisees heard it, they said, 'This fellow doth not cast out devils, but by Beelzebub the prince of the devils'. ²⁵And Jesus knew their thoughts, and said unto them, 'Every kingdom

divided against itself is brought to desolation: and every city or house divided against itself shall not stand. ²⁶And if Satan cast out Satan, he is divided against himself; how shall then his kingdom stand? ²⁷And if I by Beelzebub cast out devils, by whom do your children cast them out? Therefore they shall be your judges. ²⁸But if I cast out devils by the Spirit of God, then the kingdom of God is come unto you. ²⁹Or else how can one enter into a strong man's house, and spoil his goods, except he first bind the strong man? and then he will spoil his house. ³⁰He that is not with me is against me: and he that gathereth not with me scattereth abroad.

³¹'Wherefore I say unto you, all manner of sin and blasphemy shall be forgiven unto men: but the blasphemy against the Holy Ghost shall not be forgiven unto men. ³²And whosoever speaketh a word against the Son of man, it shall be forgiven him: but whosoever speaketh against the Holy Ghost, it shall not be forgiven him, neither in this world, neither in the world to come. ³³Either make the tree good, and his fruit good: or else make the tree corrupt, and his fruit corrupt: for the tree is known by his fruit. ³⁴O generation of vipers, how can ye, being evil, speak good things? For out of the abundance of the heart the mouth speaketh. ³⁵A good man out of the good treasure of the heart bringeth forth good things: and an evil man out of the evil treasure bringeth forth evil things. ³⁶But I say unto you, that every idle word that men shall speak, they shall give account thereof in the day of judgement. ³⁷For by thy words thou shalt be justified, and by thy words thou shalt be condemned.'

³⁸Then certain of the scribes and of the Pharisees answered, saying, 'Master, we would see a sign from thee'. ³⁹But he answered and said unto them, 'An evil and adulterous generation seeketh after a sign, and there shall no sign be given to it, but the sign of the prophet Jonas. ⁴⁰For as Jonas was three days and three nights in the whale's belly: so shall the Son of man be three days and three nights in the heart of the earth. ⁴¹The men of Nineveh shall rise in judgement with this generation, and shall condemn it, because they repented at the preaching of Jonas; and behold, a greater than Jonas is here. ⁴²The queen of the south shall rise up in the judgement with this generation, and shall condemn it: for she came from the uttermost parts of the earth to hear the wisdom of Solomon; and behold, a greater than Solomon is here.

⁴³'When the unclean spirit is gone out of a man, he walketh through dry places, seeking rest, and findeth none. ⁴⁴Then he saith, "I will return into my house from whence I came out"; and when he is come, he findeth it empty, swept, and garnished. ⁴⁵Then goeth he, and taketh with himself seven other spirits more wicked than himself, and they enter in and dwell there: and the last state of that man is worse than the first. Even so shall it be also unto this wicked generation.'

⁴⁶While he yet talked to the people, behold, his mother and his brethren stood without, desiring to speak with him. ⁴⁷Then one said unto him, 'Behold, thy mother and thy brethren stand without, desiring to speak with thee'. ⁴⁸But he answered and said unto him that told

him, 'Who is my mother? And who are my brethren?' ⁴⁹And he stretched forth his hand toward his disciples, and said, 'Behold, my mother and my brethren. ⁵⁰For whosoever shall do the will of my Father which is in heaven, the same is my brother, and sister, and mother.'

13 The same day went Jesus out of the house, and sat by the seaside. ²And great multitudes were gathered together unto him, so that he went into a ship, and sat, and the whole multitude stood on the shore. ³And he spoke many things unto them in parables, saying, 'Behold, a sower went forth to sow. ⁴And when he sowed, some seeds fell by the wayside, and the fowls came and devoured them up. ⁵Some fell upon stony places, where they had not much earth: and forthwith they sprang up, because they had no deepness of earth. ⁶And when the sun was up, they were scorched: and because they had not root, they withered away. ⁷And some fell among thorns: and the thorns sprung up, and choked them. ⁸But others fell into good ground, and brought forth fruit, some a hundredfold, some sixtyfold, some thirtyfold. ⁹Who hath ears to hear, let him hear.'

¹⁰And the disciples came, and said unto him, 'Why speakest thou unto them in parables?' ¹¹He answered and said unto them, 'Because it is given unto you to know the mysteries of the kingdom of heaven, but to them it is not given. ¹²For whosoever hath, to him shall be given, and he shall have more abundance: but whosoever hath not, from him shall be taken away even that he hath. ¹³Therefore speak I to them in parables: because they seeing see not: and hearing they hear not, neither do they understand. ¹⁴And in them is fulfilled the prophecy of Esaias, which saith, "By hearing ye shall hear, and shall not understand: and seeing ye shall see, and shall not perceive. ¹⁵For this people's heart is waxed gross, and their ears are dull of hearing, and their eyes they have closed, lest at any time they should see with their eyes, and hear with their ears, and should understand with their heart, and should be converted, and I should heal them." ¹⁶But blessed are your eyes, for they see: and your ears, for they hear. ¹⁷For verily I say unto you, that many prophets and righteous men have desired to see those things which ye see, and have not seen them: and to hear those things which ye hear, and have not heard them.

¹⁸'Hear ye therefore the parable of the sower. ¹⁹When anyone heareth the word of the kingdom, and understandeth it not, then cometh the wicked one, and catcheth away that which was sown in his heart: this is he which received seed by the wayside. ²⁰But he that received the seed into stony places, the same is he that heareth the word, and anon with joy receiveth it: ²¹yet hath he not root in himself, but dureth for a while: for when tribulation or persecution ariseth because of the word, by and by he is offended. ²²He also that received seed among the thorns is he that heareth the word, and the care of this world, and the deceitfulness of riches choke the word, and he becometh unfruitful. ²³But he that received seed into the good ground is he that heareth the word, and understandeth it, which also beareth fruit, and bringeth forth, some a hundredfold, some sixty, some thirty.'

²⁴Another parable put he forth unto them, saying, 'The kingdom of heaven is likened unto a man which sowed good seed in his field: ²⁵but while men slept, his enemy came and sowed tares among the wheat, and went his way. ²⁶But when the blade was sprung up, and brought forth fruit, then appeared the tares also. ²⁷So the servants of the house-holder came and said unto him, "Sir, didst not thou sow good seed in thy field? from whence then hath it tares?" ²⁸He said unto them, "An enemy hath done this". The servants said unto him, "Wilt thou then that we go and gather them up?" ²⁹But he said, "Nay: lest while ye gather up the tares, ye root up also the wheat with them. ³⁰Let both grow together until the harvest: and in the time of harvest I will say to the reapers, 'Gather ye together first the tares, and bind them in bundles to burn them: but gather the wheat into my barn'."'

³¹Another parable put he forth unto them, saying, 'The kingdom of heaven is like to a grain of mustard seed, which a man took, and sowed in his field: ³²which indeed is the least of all seeds: but when it is grown, it is the greatest among herbs, and becometh a tree: so that the birds of the air come and lodge in the branches thereof'.

³³Another parable spoke he unto them, 'The kingdom of heaven is like unto leaven, which a woman took, and hid in three measures of meal, till the whole was leavened'.

³⁴All these things spoke Jesus unto the multitude in parables, and without a parable spoke he not unto them: ³⁵that it might be fulfilled which was spoken by the prophet, saying, 'I will open my mouth in parables, I will utter things which have been kept secret from the foundation of the world'.

³⁶Then Jesus sent the multitude away, and went into the house: and his disciples came unto him, saying, 'Declare unto us the parable of the tares of the field'. ³⁷He answered and said unto them, 'He that soweth the good seed is the Son of man. ³⁸The field is the world. The good seed are the children of the kingdom: but the tares are the children of the wicked one. ³⁹The enemy that sowed them is the devil. The harvest is the end of the world. And the reapers are the angels. ⁴⁰As therefore the tares are gathered and burnt in the fire: so shall it be in the end of this world. ⁴¹The Son of man shall send forth his angels, and they shall gather out of his kingdom all things that offend, and them which do iniquity: ⁴²and shall cast them into a furnace of fire: there shall be wailing and gnashing of teeth. ⁴³Then shall the righteous shine forth as the sun in the kingdom of their Father. Who hath ears to hear, let him hear.

⁴⁴'Again, the kingdom of heaven is like unto treasure hid in a field: the which when a man hath found, he hideth, and for joy thereof goeth and selleth all that he hath, and buyeth that field.

⁴⁵'Again, the kingdom of heaven is like unto a merchantman, seeking goodly pearls: ⁴⁶who, when he had found one pearl of great price, went and sold all that he had, and bought it.

⁴⁷'Again, the kingdom of heaven is like unto a net, that was cast into the sea, and gathered of every kind, ⁴⁸which, when it was full, they

drew to shore, and sat down, and gathered the good into vessels, but cast the bad away. ⁴⁹So shall it be at the end of the world: the angels shall come forth, and sever the wicked from among the just, ⁵⁰and shall cast them into the furnace of fire: there shall be wailing and gnashing of teeth.'

⁵¹Jesus saith unto them, 'Have ye understood all these things?' They say unto him, 'Yea, Lord'. ⁵²Then said he unto them, 'Therefore every scribe which is instructed unto the kingdom of heaven is like unto a man that is a householder, which bringeth forth out of his treasure things new and old'.

⁵³And it came to pass that when Jesus had finished these parables, he departed thence. ⁵⁴And when he was come into his own country, he taught them in their synagogue, insomuch that they were astonished, and said, 'Whence hath this man this wisdom, and these mighty works? ⁵⁵Is not this the carpenter's son? Is not his mother called Mary? and his brethren, James, and Joses, and Simon, and Judas? ⁵⁶And his sisters, are they not all with us? Whence then hath this man all these things?' ⁵⁷And they were offended in him. But Jesus said unto them, 'A prophet is not without honour, save in his own country, and in his own house'. ⁵⁸And he did not many mighty works there because of their unbelief.

14 At that time Herod the tetrarch heard of the fame of Jesus, ²and said unto his servants, 'This is John the Baptist, he is risen from the dead, and therefore mighty works do show forth themselves in him'.

³For Herod had laid hold on John, and bound him, and put him in prison for Herodias' sake, his brother Philip's wife. ⁴For John said unto him, 'It is not lawful for thee to have her'. ⁵And when he would have put him to death, he feared the multitude, because they counted him as a prophet. ⁶But when Herod's birthday was kept, the daughter of Herodias danced before them, and pleased Herod. ⁷Whereupon he promised with an oath to give her whatsoever she would ask. ⁸And she, being before instructed of her mother, said, 'Give me here John Baptist's head in a charger'. ⁹And the king was sorry: nevertheless for the oaths' sake, and them which sat with him at meat, he commanded it to be given her: ¹⁰and he sent, and beheaded John in the prison. ¹¹And his head was brought in a charger, and given to the damsel: and she brought it to her mother. ¹²And his disciples came, and took up the body, and buried it, and went and told Jesus.

¹³When Jesus heard of it, he departed thence by ship into a desert place apart: and when the people had heard thereof, they followed him on foot out of the cities. ¹⁴And Jesus went forth, and saw a great multitude, and was moved with compassion toward them, and he healed their sick.

¹⁵And when it was evening, his disciples came to him, saying, 'This is a desert place, and the time is now past; send the multitude away, that they may go into the villages, and buy themselves victuals'. ¹⁶But Jesus said unto them, 'They need not depart; give ye them to eat'. ¹⁷And they

say unto him, 'We have here but five loaves, and two fishes'. [18]He said, 'Bring them hither to me'. [19]And he commanded the multitude to sit down on the grass, and took the five loaves, and the two fishes, and looking up to heaven, he blessed, and broke, and gave the loaves to his disciples, and the disciples to the multitude. [20]And they did all eat, and were filled: and they took up of the fragments that remained twelve baskets full. [21]And they that had eaten were about five thousand men, besides women and children.

[22]And straightway Jesus constrained his disciples to get into a ship, and to go before him unto the other side, while he sent the multitudes away. [23]And when he had sent the multitudes away, he went up into a mountain apart to pray: and when the evening was come, he was there alone. [24]But the ship was now in the midst of the sea, tossed with waves: for the wind was contrary. [25]And in the fourth watch of the night Jesus went unto them, walking on the sea. [26]And when the disciples saw him walking on the sea, they were troubled, saying, 'It is a spirit': and they cried out for fear. [27]But straightway Jesus spoke unto them, saying, 'Be of good cheer: it is I, be not afraid'. [28]And Peter answered him and said, 'Lord, if it be thou, bid me come unto thee on the water'. [29]And he said, 'Come'. And when Peter was come down out of the ship, he walked on the water, to go to Jesus. [30]But when he saw the wind boisterous, he was afraid: and beginning to sink, he cried, saying, 'Lord, save me'. [31]And immediately Jesus stretched forth his hand, and caught him, and said unto him, 'O thou of little faith, wherefore didst thou doubt?' [32]And when they were come into the ship, the wind ceased. [33]Then they that were in the ship came and worshipped him, saying, 'Of a truth thou art the Son of God'.

[34]And when they were gone over, they came into the land of Gennesaret. [35]And when the men of that place had knowledge of him, they sent out into all that country round about, and brought unto him all that were diseased, [36]and besought him that they might only touch the hem of his garment: and as many as touched were made perfectly whole.

15 Then came to Jesus scribes and Pharisees, which were of Jerusalem, saying, [2]'Why do thy disciples transgress the tradition of the elders? for they wash not their hands when they eat bread'. [3]But he answered and said unto them, 'Why do you also transgress the commandment of God by your tradition? [4]For God commanded, saying, "Honour thy father and mother": and, "He that curseth father or mother, let him die the death". [5]But ye say, "Whosoever shall say to his father or his mother, 'It is a gift, by whatsoever thou mightest be profited by me', [6]and honour not his father or his mother, he shall be free". Thus have ye made the commandment of God of no effect by your tradition. [7]Ye hypocrites, well did Esaias prophesy of you, saying, [8]"This people draweth nigh unto me with their mouth, and honoureth me with their lips: but their heart is far from me. [9]But in vain they do worship me, teaching for doctrines the commandments of men."'

[10]And he called the multitude, and said unto them, 'Hear, and under-

stand. ¹¹Not that which goeth into the mouth defileth a man: but that which cometh out of the mouth, this defileth a man.'

¹²Then came his disciples, and said unto him, 'Knowest thou that the Pharisees were offended, after they heard this saying?' ¹³But he answered and said, 'Every plant which my heavenly Father hath not planted, shall be rooted up. ¹⁴Let them alone: they be blind leaders of the blind. And if the blind lead the blind, both shall fall into the ditch.'

¹⁵Then answered Peter and said unto him, 'Declare unto us this parable'. ¹⁶And Jesus said, 'Are ye also yet without understanding? ¹⁷Do not ye yet understand, that whatsoever entereth in at the mouth goeth into the belly, and is cast out into the draught? ¹⁸But those things which proceed out of the mouth come forth from the heart, and they defile the man. ¹⁹For out of the heart proceed evil thoughts, murders, adulteries, fornications, thefts, false witness, blasphemies. ²⁰These are the things which defile a man: but to eat with unwashed hands defileth not a man.'

²¹Then Jesus went thence, and departed into the coasts of Tyre and Sidon. ²²And behold, a woman of Canaan came out of the same coasts, and cried unto him, saying, 'Have mercy on me, O Lord, thou son of David, my daughter is grievously vexed with a devil'. ²³But he answered her not a word. And his disciples came and besought him, saying, 'Send her away, for she crieth after us'. ²⁴But he answered and said, 'I am not sent but unto the lost sheep of the house of Israel'. ²⁵Then came she and worshipped him, saying, 'Lord, help me'. ²⁶But he answered and said, 'It is not meet to take the children's bread, and to cast it to dogs'. ²⁷And she said, 'Truth, Lord: yet the dogs eat of the crumbs which fall from their masters' table'. ²⁸Then Jesus answered and said unto her, 'O woman, great is thy faith: be it unto thee even as thou wilt'. And her daughter was made whole from that very hour.

²⁹And Jesus departed from thence, and came nigh unto the sea of Galilee, and went up into a mountain, and sat down there. ³⁰And great multitudes came unto him, having with them those that were lame, blind, dumb, maimed, and many others, and cast them down at Jesus' feet; and he healed them: ³¹insomuch that the multitude wondered, when they saw the dumb to speak, the maimed to be whole, the lame to walk, and the blind to see: and they glorified the God of Israel.

³²Then Jesus called his disciples unto him, and said, 'I have compassion on the multitude, because they continue with me now three days, and have nothing to eat: and I will not send them away fasting, lest they faint in the way'. ³³And his disciples say unto him, 'Whence should we have so much bread in the wilderness, as to fill so great a multitude?' ³⁴And Jesus saith unto them, 'How many loaves have ye?' And they said, 'Seven, and a few little fishes'. ³⁵And he commanded the multitude to sit down on the ground. ³⁶And he took the seven loaves and the fishes, and gave thanks, and broke them, and gave to his disciples, and the disciples to the multitude. ³⁷And they did all eat, and were filled: and they took up of the broken meat that was left seven baskets full. ³⁸And they that did eat were four thousand men, besides women

and children. ³⁹And he sent away the multitude, and took ship, and came into the coasts of Magdala.

16 The Pharisees also with the Sadducees came, and tempting, desired him that he would show them a sign from heaven. ²He answered and said unto them, 'When it is evening, ye say, "It will be fair weather: for the sky is red". ³And in the morning, "It will be foul weather today: for the sky is red and louring". O ye hypocrites, ye can discern the face of the sky, but can ye not discern the signs of the times? ⁴A wicked and adulterous generation seeketh after a sign, and there shall no sign be given unto it, but the sign of the prophet Jonas.' And he left them, and departed.

⁵And when his disciples were come to the other side, they had forgotten to take bread. ⁶Then Jesus said unto them, 'Take heed and beware of the leaven of the Pharisees and of the Sadducees'. ⁷And they reasoned among themselves, saying, 'It is because we have taken no bread'. ⁸Which when Jesus perceived, he said unto them, 'O ye of little faith, why reason ye among yourselves, because ye have brought no bread? ⁹Do ye yet not understand, neither remember the five loaves of the five thousand, and how many baskets ye took up? ¹⁰neither the seven loaves of the four thousand, and how many baskets ye took up? ¹¹How is it that ye do not understand that I spoke it not to you concerning bread, that ye should beware of the leaven of the Pharisees and of the Sadducees?' ¹²Then understood they how that he bade them not beware of the leaven of bread, but of the doctrine of the Pharisees and of the Sadducees.

¹³When Jesus came into the coasts of Caesarea Philippi, he asked his disciples, saying, 'Whom do men say that I, the Son of man, am?' ¹⁴And they said, 'Some say that thou art John the Baptist, some, Elias, and others, Jeremias, or one of the prophets'. ¹⁵He saith unto them, 'But whom say ye that I am?' ¹⁶And Simon Peter answered and said, 'Thou art Christ, the Son of the living God'. ¹⁷And Jesus answered and said unto him, 'Blessed art thou, Simon Bar-jona: for flesh and blood hath not revealed it unto thee, but my Father which is in heaven. ¹⁸And I say also unto thee, that thou art Peter, and upon this rock I will build my church: and the gates of hell shall not prevail against it. ¹⁹And I will give unto thee the keys of the kingdom of heaven: and whatsoever thou shalt bind on earth shall be bound in heaven: whatsoever thou shalt loose on earth shall be loosed in heaven.' ²⁰Then charged he his disciples that they should tell no man that he was Jesus the Christ.

²¹From that time forth began Jesus to show unto his disciples, how that he must go unto Jerusalem, and suffer many things of the elders and chief priests and scribes, and be killed, and be raised again the third day. ²²Then Peter took him, and began to rebuke him, saying, 'Be it far from thee, Lord: this shall not be unto thee'. ²³But he turned, and said unto Peter, 'Get thee behind me, Satan, thou art an offence unto me: for thou savourest not the things that be of God, but those that be of men'.

²⁴Then said Jesus unto his disciples, 'If any man will come after me, let

him deny himself, and take up his cross, and follow me. ²⁵For whosoever will save his life shall lose it: and whosoever will lose his life for my sake shall find it. ²⁶For what is a man profited, if he shall gain the whole world, and lose his own soul? Or what shall a man give in exchange for his soul? ²⁷For the Son of man shall come in the glory of his Father with his angels: and then he shall reward every man according to his works. ²⁸Verily I say unto you, there be some standing here, which shall not taste of death, till they see the Son of man coming in his kingdom.'

17 And after six days Jesus taketh Peter, James, and John his brother, and bringeth them up into a high mountain apart, ²and was transfigured before them, and his face did shine as the sun, and his raiment was white as the light. ³And behold, there appeared unto them Moses and Elias talking with him. ⁴Then answered Peter, and said unto Jesus, 'Lord, it is good for us to be here: if thou wilt, let us make here three tabernacles: one for thee, and one for Moses, and one for Elias'. ⁵While he yet spoke, behold, a bright cloud overshadowed them: and behold, a voice out of the cloud, which said, 'This is my beloved Son, in whom I am well pleased: hear ye him'. ⁶And when the disciples heard it, they fell on their face, and were sore afraid. ⁷And Jesus came and touched them, and said, 'Arise, and be not afraid'. ⁸And when they had lifted up their eyes, they saw no man, save Jesus only.

⁹And as they came down from the mountain, Jesus charged them, saying, 'Tell the vision to no man, until the Son of man be risen again from the dead'. ¹⁰And his disciples asked him, saying, 'Why then say the scribes that Elias must first come?' ¹¹And Jesus answered and said unto them, 'Elias truly shall first come, and restore all things. ¹²But I say unto you, that Elias is come already, and they knew him not, but have done unto him whatsoever they listed. Likewise shall also the Son of man suffer of them.' ¹³Then the disciples understood that he spoke unto them of John the Baptist.

¹⁴And when they were come to the multitude, there came to him a certain man, kneeling down to him, and saying, ¹⁵'Lord, have mercy on my son, for he is lunatic, and sore vexed: for ofttimes he falleth into the fire, and oft into the water. ¹⁶And I brought him to thy disciples, and they could not cure him.' ¹⁷Then Jesus answered and said, 'O faithless and perverse generation, how long shall I be with you? how long shall I suffer you? bring him hither to me'. ¹⁸And Jesus rebuked the devil, and he departed out of him: and the child was cured from that very hour. ¹⁹Then came the disciples to Jesus apart, and said, 'Why could not we cast him out?' ²⁰And Jesus said unto them, 'Because of your unbelief: for verily I say unto you, if ye have faith as a grain of mustard seed, ye shall say unto this mountain, "Remove hence to yonder place": and it shall remove; and nothing shall be impossible unto you. ²¹Howbeit this kind goeth not out but by prayer and fasting.'

²²And while they abode in Galilee, Jesus said unto them, 'The Son of man shall be betrayed into the hands of men: ²³and they shall kill him, and the third day he shall be raised again'. And they were exceeding sorry.

²⁴And when they were come to Capernaum, they that received tribute money came to Peter, and said, 'Doth not your master pay tribute?' ²⁵He saith, 'Yes'. And when he was come into the house, Jesus prevented him, saying, 'What thinkest thou, Simon? of whom do the kings of the earth take custom or tribute? of their own children, or of strangers?' ²⁶Peter saith unto him, 'Of strangers'. Jesus saith unto him, 'Then are the children free. ²⁷Notwithstanding, lest we should offend them, go thou to the sea, and cast a hook, and take up the fish that first cometh up: and when thou hast opened his mouth, thou shalt find a piece of money: that take, and give unto them for me and thee.'

18 At the same time came the disciples unto Jesus, saying, 'Who is the greatest in the kingdom of heaven?' ²And Jesus called a little child unto him, and set him in the midst of them, ³and said, 'Verily I say unto you, except ye be converted, and become as little children, ye shall not enter into the kingdom of heaven. ⁴Whosoever therefore shall humble himself as this little child, the same is greatest in the kingdom of heaven. ⁵And whoso shall receive one such little child in my name receiveth me. ⁶But whoso shall offend one of these little ones which believe in me, it were better for him that a millstone were hanged about his neck, and that he were drowned in the depth of the sea.

⁷'Woe unto the world because of offences: for it must needs be that offences come: but woe to that man by whom the offence cometh. ⁸Wherefore if thy hand or thy foot offend thee, cut them off, and cast them from thee: it is better for thee to enter into life halt or maimed, rather than having two hands or two feet to be cast into everlasting fire. ⁹And if thy eye offend thee, pluck it out, and cast it from thee: it is better for thee to enter into life with one eye, rather than having two eyes to be cast into hell fire. ¹⁰Take heed that ye despise not one of these little ones: for I say unto you, that in heaven their angels do always behold the face of my Father which is in heaven. ¹¹For the Son of man is come to save that which was lost. ¹²How think ye? if a man have a hundred sheep, and one of them be gone astray, doth he not leave the ninety and nine, and goeth into the mountains, and seeketh that which is gone astray? ¹³And if so be that he find it, verily I say unto you, he rejoiceth more of that sheep, than of the ninety and nine which went not astray. ¹⁴Even so it is not the will of your Father which is in heaven, that one of these little ones should perish.

¹⁵'Moreover if thy brother shall trespass against thee, go and tell him his fault between thee and him alone: if he shall hear thee, thou hast gained thy brother. ¹⁶But if he will not hear thee, then take with thee one or two more, that in the mouth of two or three witnesses every word may be established. ¹⁷And if he shall neglect to hear them, tell it unto the church: but if he neglect to hear the church, let him be unto thee as a heathen man and a publican. ¹⁸Verily I say unto you, whatsoever ye shall bind on earth shall be bound in heaven: and whatsoever ye shall loose on earth shall be loosed in heaven. ¹⁹Again I say unto you, that if two of you shall agree on earth as touching anything that they shall ask, it shall be done for them of my Father which is in heaven.

²⁰For where two or three are gathered together in my name, there am I in the midst of them.'

²¹Then came Peter to him, and said, 'Lord, how oft shall my brother sin against me, and I forgive him? till seven times?' ²²Jesus saith unto him, 'I say not unto thee, until seven times: but, until seventy times seven. ²³Therefore is the kingdom of heaven likened unto a certain king, which would take account of his servants. ²⁴And when he had begun to reckon, one was brought unto him, which owed him ten thousand talents. ²⁵But forasmuch as he had not to pay, his lord commanded him to be sold, and his wife, and children, and all that he had, and payment to be made. ²⁶The servant therefore fell down, and worshipped him, saying, "Lord, have patience with me, and I will pay thee all". ²⁷Then the lord of that servant was moved with compassion, and loosed him, and forgave him the debt. ²⁸But the same servant went out, and found one of his fellow-servants, which owed him a hundred pence: and he laid hands on him, and took him by the throat, saying, "Pay me that thou owest". ²⁹And his fellow-servant fell down at his feet, and besought him, saying, "Have patience with me, and I will pay thee all". ³⁰And he would not: but went and cast him into prison, till he should pay the debt. ³¹So when his fellow-servants saw what was done, they were very sorry, and came and told unto their lord all that was done. ³²Then his lord, after that he had called him, said unto him, "O thou wicked servant, I forgave thee all that debt, because thou desiredst me: ³³shouldst not thou also have had compassion on thy fellow-servant, even as I had pity on thee? " ³⁴And his lord was wroth, and delivered him to the tormentors, till he should pay all that was due unto him. ³⁵So likewise shall my heavenly Father do also unto you, if ye from your hearts forgive not every one his brother their trespasses.'

19 And it came to pass that when Jesus had finished these sayings, he departed from Galilee, and came into the coasts of Judea beyond Jordan: ²and great multitudes followed him, and he healed them there.

³The Pharisees also came unto him, tempting him, and saying unto him, 'Is it lawful for a man to put away his wife for every cause?' ⁴And he answered and said unto them, 'Have ye not read, that he which made them at the beginning made them male and female, ⁵and said, "For this cause shall a man leave father and mother, and shall cleave to his wife: and they twain shall be one flesh?" ⁶Wherefore they are no more twain, but one flesh. What therefore God hath joined together, let not man put asunder.' ⁷They say unto him, 'Why did Moses then command to give a writing of divorcement, and to put her away?' ⁸He saith unto them, 'Moses, because of the hardness of your hearts, suffered you to put away your wives: but from the beginning it was not so. ⁹And I say unto you, whosoever shall put away his wife, except it be for fornication, and shall marry another, committeth adultery: and whoso marrieth her which is put away doth commit adultery.'

¹⁰His disciples say unto him, 'If the case of the man be so with his wife, it is not good to marry'. ¹¹But he said unto them, 'All men cannot

receive this saying, save they to whom it is given. ¹²For there are some eunuchs, which were so born from their mother's womb: and there are some eunuchs, which were made eunuchs of men: and there be eunuchs, which have made themselves eunuchs for the kingdom of heaven's sake. He that is able to receive it, let him receive it.'

¹³Then were there brought unto him little children, that he should put his hands on them, and pray: and the disciples rebuked them. ¹⁴But Jesus said, 'Suffer little children, and forbid them not to come unto me: for of such is the kingdom of heaven'. ¹⁵And he laid his hands on them, and departed thence.

¹⁶And behold, one came and said unto him, 'Good Master, what good thing shall I do, that I may have eternal life?' ¹⁷And he said unto him, 'Why callest thou me good? there is none good but one, that is, God: but if thou wilt enter into life, keep the commandments'. ¹⁸He saith unto him, 'Which?' Jesus said, 'Thou shalt do no murder, thou shalt not commit adultery, thou shalt not steal, thou shalt not bear false witness, ¹⁹honour thy father and thy mother: and, thou shalt love thy neighbour as thyself'. ²⁰The young man saith unto him, 'All these things have I kept from my youth up: what lack I yet?' ²¹Jesus said unto him, 'If thou wilt be perfect, go and sell that thou hast, and give to the poor, and thou shalt have treasure in heaven: and come and follow me'. ²²But when the young man heard that saying, he went away sorrowful: for he had great possessions.

²³Then said Jesus unto his disciples, 'Verily I say unto you, that a rich man shall hardly enter into the kingdom of heaven. ²⁴And again I say unto you, it is easier for a camel to go through the eye of a needle, than for a rich man to enter into the kingdom of God.' ²⁵When his disciples heard it, they were exceedingly amazed, saying, 'Who then can be saved?' ²⁶But Jesus beheld them, and said unto them, 'With men this is impossible; but with God all things are possible'.

²⁷Then answered Peter and said unto him, 'Behold, we have forsaken all, and followed thee; what shall we have therefore?' ²⁸And Jesus said unto them, 'Verily I say unto you, that ye which have followed me, in the regeneration when the Son of man shall sit in the throne of his glory, ye also shall sit upon twelve thrones, judging the twelve tribes of Israel. ²⁹And every one that hath forsaken houses, or brethren, or sisters, or father, or mother, or wife, or children, or lands, for my name's sake, shall receive a hundredfold, and shall inherit everlasting life. ³⁰But many that are first shall be last, and the last shall be first.

20 'For the kingdom of heaven is like unto a man that is a householder, which went out early in the morning to hire labourers into his vineyard. ²And when he had agreed with the labourers for a penny a day, he sent them into his vineyard. ³And he went out about the third hour, and saw others standing idle in the market-place, ⁴and said unto them, "Go ye also into the vineyard, and whatsoever is right I will give you". And they went their way. ⁵Again he went out about the sixth and ninth hour, and did likewise. ⁶And about the eleventh hour he went out, and found others standing idle, and saith unto them,

"Why stand ye here all the day idle?" ⁷They say unto him, "Because no man hath hired us". He saith unto them, "Go ye also into the vineyard: and whatsoever is right, that shall ye receive". ⁸So when even was come, the lord of the vineyard saith unto his steward, "Call the labourers, and give them their hire, beginning from the last unto the first". ⁹And when they came that were hired about the eleventh hour, they received every man a penny. ¹⁰But when the first came, they supposed that they should have received more, and they likewise received every man a penny. ¹¹And when they had received it, they murmured against the goodman of the house, ¹²saying, "These last have wrought but one hour, and thou hast made them equal unto us, which have borne the burden and heat of the day". ¹³But he answered one of them, and said, "Friend, I do thee no wrong: didst not thou agree with me for a penny? ¹⁴Take that thine is, and go thy way: I will give unto this last, even as unto thee. ¹⁵Is it not lawful for me to do what I will with my own? Is thy eye evil, because I am good?" ¹⁶So the last shall be first, and the first last: for many be called, but few chosen.'

¹⁷And Jesus going up to Jerusalem took the twelve disciples apart in the way, and said unto them, ¹⁸'Behold, we go up to Jerusalem, and the Son of man shall be betrayed unto the chief priests and unto the scribes, and they shall condemn him to death, ¹⁹and shall deliver him to the Gentiles to mock, and to scourge, and to crucify him: and the third day he shall rise again'.

²⁰Then came to him the mother of Zebedee's children with her sons, worshipping him, and desiring a certain thing of him. ²¹And he said unto her, 'What wilt thou?' She saith unto him, 'Grant that these my two sons may sit, the one on thy right hand, and the other on the left, in thy kingdom'. ²²But Jesus answered and said, 'Ye know not what ye ask. Are ye able to drink of the cup that I shall drink of, and to be baptized with the baptism that I am baptized with?' They say unto him, 'We are able'. ²³And he saith unto them, 'Ye shall drink indeed of my cup, and be baptized with the baptism that I am baptized with: but to sit on my right hand, and on my left, is not mine to give, but it shall be given to them for whom it is prepared of my Father'.

²⁴And when the ten heard it, they were moved with indignation against the two brethren. ²⁵But Jesus called them unto him, and said, 'Ye know that the princes of the Gentiles exercise dominion over them, and they that are great exercise authority upon them. ²⁶But it shall not be so among you: but whosoever will be great among you, let him be your minister. ²⁷And whosoever will be chief among you, let him be your servant: ²⁸even as the Son of man came not to be ministered unto, but to minister, and to give his life a ransom for many.'

²⁹And as they departed from Jericho, a great multitude followed him. ³⁰And behold, two blind men sitting by the wayside, when they heard that Jesus passed by, cried out, saying, 'Have mercy on us, O Lord, thou son of David'. ³¹And the multitude rebuked them, because they should hold their peace: but they cried the more, saying, 'Have mercy on us, O Lord, thou Son of David'. ³²And Jesus stood still, and called them, and

said, 'What will ye that I shall do unto you?' [33]They say unto him, 'Lord, that our eyes may be opened'. [34]So Jesus had compassion on them, and touched their eyes: and immediately their eyes received sight, and they followed him.

21 And when they drew nigh unto Jerusalem, and were come to Bethphage, unto the mount of Olives, then sent Jesus two disciples, [2]saying unto them, 'Go into the village over against you, and straightway ye shall find an ass tied, and a colt with her: loose them, and bring them unto me. [3]And if any man say aught unto you, ye shall say, "The Lord hath need of them", and straightway he will send them.' [4]All this was done, that it might be fulfilled which was spoken by the prophet, saying, [5]"Tell ye the daughter of Sion, "Behold, thy King cometh unto thee, meek, and sitting upon an ass, and a colt the foal of an ass"".

[6]And the disciples went, and did as Jesus commanded them, [7]and brought the ass, and the colt, and put on them their clothes, and they set him thereon. [8]And a very great multitude spread their garments in the way; others cut down branches from the trees, and strewed them in the way. [9]And the multitudes that went before, and that followed, cried, saying, 'Hosanna to the son of David: blessed is he that cometh in the name of the Lord, Hosanna in the highest'. [10]And when he was come into Jerusalem, all the city was moved, saying, 'Who is this?' [11]And the multitude said, 'This is Jesus the prophet of Nazareth of Galilee'.

[12]And Jesus went into the temple of God, and cast out all them that sold and bought in the temple, and overthrew the tables of the money-changers, and the seats of them that sold doves, [13]and said unto them, 'It is written, "My house shall be called the house of prayer", but ye have made it a den of thieves'.

[14]And the blind and the lame came to him in the temple, and he healed them. [15]And when the chief priests and scribes saw the wonderful things that he did, and the children crying in the temple, and saying, 'Hosanna to the son of David', they were sore displeased, [16]and said unto him, 'Hearest thou what these say?' And Jesus saith unto them, 'Yea, have ye never read, "Out of the mouth of babes and sucklings thou hast perfected praise"?' [17]And he left them, and went out of the city into Bethany, and he lodged there.

[18]Now in the morning as he returned into the city, he hungered. [19]And when he saw a fig tree in the way, he came to it, and found nothing thereon, but leaves only, and said unto it, 'Let no fruit grow on thee henceforward for ever'. And presently the fig tree withered away. [20]And when the disciples saw it, they marvelled, saying, 'How soon is the fig tree withered away?' [21]Jesus answered and said unto them, 'Verily I say unto you, if ye have faith, and doubt not, ye shall not only do this which is done to the fig tree, but also if ye shall say unto this mountain, "Be thou removed, and be thou cast into the sea", it shall be done. [22]And all things whatsoever ye shall ask in prayer, believing, ye shall receive.'

[23]And when he was come into the temple, the chief priests and the elders of the people came unto him as he was teaching, and said, 'By what

authority doest thou these things? and who gave thee this authority?' [24]And Jesus answered and said unto them, 'I also will ask you one thing, which if ye tell me, I in like wise will tell you by what authority I do these things. [25]The baptism of John, whence was it? from heaven, or of men?' And they reasoned with themselves, saying, 'If we shall say, "From heaven", he will say unto us, "Why did ye not then believe him?" [26]But if we shall say, "Of men", we fear the people, for all hold John as a prophet.' [27]And they answered Jesus, and said, 'We cannot tell'. And he said unto them, 'Neither tell I you by what authority I do these things.

[28]'But what think you? A certain man had two sons, and he came to the first, and said, "Son, go work today in my vineyard". [29]He answered and said, "I will not": but afterward he repented, and went. [30]And he came to the second, and said likewise. And he answered and said, "I go, sir", and went not. [31]Whether of them twain did the will of his father?' They say unto him, 'The first'. Jesus saith unto them, 'Verily I say unto you, that the publicans and the harlots go into the kingdom of God before you. [32]For John came unto you in the way of righteousness, and ye believed him not: but the publicans and the harlots believed him. And ye, when ye had seen it, repented not afterward, that ye might believe him.

[33]'Hear another parable. There was a certain householder, which planted a vineyard, and hedged it round about, and dug a wine-press in it, and built a tower, and let it out to husbandmen, and went into a far country. [34]And when the time of the fruit drew near, he sent his servants to the husbandmen, that they might receive the fruits of it. [35]And the husbandmen took his servants, and beat one, and killed another, and stoned another. [36]Again, he sent other servants more than the first, and they did unto them likewise. [37]But last of all he sent unto them his son, saying, "They will reverence my son". [38]But when the husbandmen saw the son, they said among themselves, "This is the heir, come, let us kill him, and let us seize on his inheritance". [39]And they caught him, and cast him out of the vineyard, and slew him. [40]When the lord therefore of the vineyard cometh, what will he do unto those husbandmen?' [41]They say unto him, 'He will miserably destroy those wicked men, and will let out his vineyard unto other husbandmen, which shall render him the fruits in their seasons'. [42]Jesus saith unto them, 'Did ye never read in the scriptures, "The stone which the builders rejected, the same is become the head of the corner: this is the Lord's doing, and it is marvellous in our eyes"? [43]Therefore say I unto you, the kingdom of God shall be taken from you, and given to a nation bringing forth the fruits thereof. [44]And whosoever shall fall on this stone shall be broken: but on whomsoever it shall fall, it will grind him to powder.' [45]And when the chief priests and Pharisees had heard his parables, they perceived that he spoke of them. [46]But when they sought to lay hands on him, they feared the multitude, because they took him for a prophet.

22 And Jesus answered and spoke unto them again by parables, and said, [2]'The kingdom of heaven is like unto a certain king, which made a marriage for his son, ³and sent forth his servants to call them that were bidden to the wedding, and they would not come. ⁴Again, he sent forth other servants, saying, "Tell them which are bidden, 'Behold, I have prepared my dinner: my oxen and my fatlings are killed, and all things are ready: come unto the marriage'". ⁵But they made light of it, and went their ways, one to his farm, another to his merchandise: ⁶and the remnant took his servants, and entreated them spitefully, and slew them. ⁷But when the king heard thereof, he was wroth, and he sent forth his armies, and destroyed those murderers, and burnt up their city. ⁸Then saith he to his servants, "The wedding is ready, but they which were bidden were not worthy. ⁹Go ye therefore into the highways, and as many as ye shall find, bid to the marriage." ¹⁰So those servants went out into the highways, and gathered together all as many as they found, both bad and good, and the wedding was furnished with guests. ¹¹And when the king came in to see the guests, he saw there a man which had not on a wedding garment, ¹²and he saith unto him, "Friend, how camest thou in hither not having a wedding garment?" And he was speechless. ¹³Then said the king to the servants, "Bind him hand and foot, and take him away, and cast him into outer darkness; there shall be weeping and gnashing of teeth". ¹⁴For many are called, but few are chosen.'

¹⁵Then went the Pharisees, and took counsel how they might entangle him in his talk. ¹⁶And they sent out unto him their disciples with the Herodians, saying, 'Master, we know that thou art true, and teachest the way of God in truth, neither carest thou for any man: for thou regardest not the person of men. ¹⁷Tell us therefore, what thinkest thou? Is it lawful to give tribute unto Caesar, or not?' ¹⁸But Jesus perceived their wickedness, and said, 'Why tempt ye me, ye hypocrites? ¹⁹Show me the tribute money.' And they brought unto him a penny. ²⁰And he saith unto them, 'Whose is this image and superscription?' ²¹They say unto him, 'Caesar's'. Then saith he unto them, 'Render therefore unto Caesar the things which are Caesar's: and unto God the things that are God's'. ²²When they had heard these words, they marvelled, and left him, and went their way.

²³The same day came to him the Sadducees, which say that there is no resurrection, and asked him, ²⁴saying, 'Master, Moses said, "If a man die, having no children, his brother shall marry his wife, and raise up seed unto his brother". ²⁵Now there were with us seven brethren: and the first, when he had married a wife, deceased, and, having no issue, left his wife unto his brother. ²⁶Likewise the second also, and the third, unto the seventh. ²⁷And last of all the woman died also. ²⁸Therefore in the resurrection whose wife shall she be of the seven? for they all had her.' ²⁹Jesus answered and said unto them, 'Ye do err, not knowing the scriptures, nor the power of God. ³⁰For in the resurrection they neither marry, nor are given in marriage, but are as the angels of God in heaven. ³¹But as touching the resurrection of the dead, have ye not read that which was spoken unto you by God, saying, ³²"I am the God of Abraham, and the God of Isaac, and the God of Jacob"? God is not the

God of the dead, but of the living.' ³³And when the multitude heard this, they were astonished at his doctrine.

³⁴But when the Pharisees had heard that he had put the Sadducees to silence, they were gathered together. ³⁵Then one of them, which was a lawyer, asked him a question, tempting him, and saying, ³⁶'Master, which is the great commandment in the law?' ³⁷Jesus said unto him, 'Thou shalt love the Lord thy God with all thy heart, and with all thy soul, and with all thy mind. ³⁸This is the first and great commandment. ³⁹And the second is like unto it, thou shalt love thy neighbour as thyself. ⁴⁰On these two commandments hang all the law and the prophets.'

⁴¹While the Pharisees were gathered together, Jesus asked them, ⁴²saying, 'What think ye of Christ? whose son is he?' They say unto him, 'The son of David'. ⁴³He saith unto them, 'How then doth David in spirit call him Lord, saying, ⁴⁴"The Lord said unto my Lord, 'Sit thou on my right hand, till I make thy enemies thy footstool'"? ⁴⁵If David then call him Lord, how is he his son?' ⁴⁶And no man was able to answer him a word, neither durst any man from that day forth ask him any more questions.

23 Then spoke Jesus to the multitude, and to his disciples, ²saying, 'The scribes and the Pharisees sit in Moses' seat: ³all therefore whatsoever they bid you observe, that observe and do, but do not ye after their works: for they say, and do not. ⁴For they bind heavy burdens and grievous to be borne, and lay them on men's shoulders, but they themselves will not move them with one of their fingers. ⁵But all their works they do for to be seen of men: they make broad their phylacteries, and enlarge the borders of their garments, ⁶and love the uppermost rooms at feasts, and the chief seats in the synagogues, ⁷and greetings in the markets, and to be called of men, "Rabbi, Rabbi". ⁸But be not ye called Rabbi: for one is your Master, even Christ, and all ye are brethren. ⁹And call no man your father upon the earth: for one is your Father, which is in heaven. ¹⁰Neither be ye called masters: for one is your Master, even Christ. ¹¹But he that is greatest among you shall be your servant. ¹²And whosoever shall exalt himself shall be abased: and he that shall humble himself shall be exalted.

¹³'But woe unto you, scribes and Pharisees, hypocrites: for ye shut up the kingdom of heaven against men: for ye neither go in yourselves, neither suffer ye them that are entering to go in. ¹⁴Woe unto you, scribes and Pharisees, hypocrites: for ye devour widows' houses, and for a pretence make long prayer: therefore ye shall receive the greater damnation. ¹⁵Woe unto you, scribes and Pharisees, hypocrites: for ye compass sea and land to make one proselyte, and when he is made, ye make him twofold more the child of hell than yourselves.

¹⁶'Woe unto you, ye blind guides, which say, "Whosoever shall swear by the temple, it is nothing; but whosoever shall swear by the gold of the temple, he is a debtor". ¹⁷Ye fools and blind: for whether is greater, the gold, or the temple that sanctifieth the gold? ¹⁸And, "Whosoever shall swear by the altar, it is nothing: but whosoever sweareth by the gift that is upon it, he is guilty". ¹⁹Ye fools and blind: for whether is greater, the gift, or the altar that sanctifieth the gift? ²⁰Whoso there-

fore shall swear by the altar, sweareth by it, and by all things thereon. [21]And whoso shall swear by the temple, sweareth by it, and by him that dwelleth therein. [22]And he that shall swear by heaven, sweareth by the throne of God, and by him that sitteth thereon.

[23]'Woe unto you, scribes and Pharisees, hypocrites: for ye pay tithe of mint and anise and cummin, and have omitted the weightier matters of the law, judgement, mercy, and faith: these ought ye to have done, and not to leave the others undone. [24]Ye blind guides, which strain at a gnat, and swallow a camel. [25]Woe unto you, scribes and Pharisees, hypocrites: for ye make clean the outside of the cup and of the platter, but within they are full of extortion and excess. [26]Thou blind Pharisee, cleanse first that which is within the cup and platter, that the outside of them may be clean also. [27]Woe unto you, scribes and Pharisees, hypocrites: for ye are like unto whited sepulchres, which indeed appear beautiful outward, but are within full of dead men's bones, and of all uncleanness. [28]Even so ye also outwardly appear righteous unto men, but within ye are full of hypocrisy and iniquity.

[29]'Woe unto you, scribes and Pharisees, hypocrites, because ye build the tombs of the prophets, and garnish the sepulchres of the righteous, [30]and say, "If we had been in the days of our fathers, we would not have been partakers with them in the blood of the prophets". [31]Wherefore ye be witnesses unto yourselves, that ye are the children of them which killed the prophets. [32]Fill ye up then the measure of your fathers. [33]Ye serpents, ye generation of vipers, how can ye escape the damnation of hell?

[34]'Wherefore behold, I send unto you prophets, and wise men, and scribes, and some of them ye shall kill and crucify, and some of them shall ye scourge in your synagogues, and persecute them from city to city: [35]that upon you may come all the righteous blood shed upon the earth, from the blood of righteous Abel unto the blood of Zacharias son of Barachias, whom ye slew between the temple and the altar. [36]Verily I say unto you, all these things shall come upon this generation. [37]O Jerusalem, Jerusalem, thou that killest the prophets, and stonest them which are sent unto thee, how often would I have gathered thy children together, even as a hen gathereth her chickens under her wings, and ye would not! [38]Behold, your house is left unto you desolate. [39]For I say unto you, ye shall not see me henceforth, till ye shall say, "Blessed is he that cometh in the name of the Lord".'

24 And Jesus went out, and departed from the temple: and his disciples came to him for to show him the buildings of the temple. [2]And Jesus said unto them, 'See ye not all these things? Verily I say unto you, there shall not be left here one stone upon another, that shall not be thrown down.'

[3]And as he sat upon the mount of Olives, the disciples came unto him privately, saying, 'Tell us, when shall these things be? and what shall be the sign of thy coming, and of the end of the world?' [4]And Jesus answered and said unto them, 'Take heed that no man deceive you. [5]For many shall come in my name, saying, "I am Christ": and shall deceive

many. ⁶And ye shall hear of wars and rumours of wars: see that ye be not troubled: for all these things must come to pass, but the end is not yet. ⁷For nation shall rise against nation, and kingdom against kingdom, and there shall be famines, and pestilences, and earthquakes, in divers places. ⁸All these are the beginning of sorrows.

⁹'Then shall they deliver you up to be afflicted, and shall kill you: and ye shall be hated of all nations for my name's sake. ¹⁰And then shall many be offended, and shall betray one another, and shall hate one another. ¹¹And many false prophets shall rise, and shall deceive many. ¹²And because iniquity shall abound, the love of many shall wax cold. ¹³But he that shall endure unto the end, the same shall be saved. ¹⁴And this gospel of the kingdom shall be preached in all the world for a witness unto all nations, and then shall the end come.

¹⁵'When ye therefore shall see the abomination of desolation, spoken of by Daniel the prophet, stand in the holy place (whoso readeth, let him understand), ¹⁶then let them which be in Judea flee into the mountains. ¹⁷Let him which is on the house-top not come down to take anything out of his house: ¹⁸neither let him which is in the field return back to take his clothes. ¹⁹And woe unto them that are with child, and to them that give suck in those days. ²⁰But pray ye that your flight be not in the winter, neither on the sabbath day: ²¹for then shall be great tribulation, such as was not since the beginning of the world to this time, no, nor ever shall be. ²²And except those days should be shortened, there should no flesh be saved: but for the elect's sake those days shall be shortened.

²³Then if any man shall say unto you, "Lo, here is Christ, or there": believe it not. ²⁴For there shall arise false Christs, and false prophets, and shall show great signs and wonders: insomuch that, if it were possible, they shall deceive the very elect. ²⁵Behold, I have told you before. ²⁶Wherefore if they shall say unto you, "Behold, he is in the desert", go not forth: "Behold, he is in the secret chambers", believe it not. ²⁷For as the lightning cometh out of the east, and shineth even unto the west: so shall also the coming of the Son of man be. ²⁸For wheresoever the carcase is, there will the eagles be gathered together.

²⁹'Immediately after the tribulation of those days shall the sun be darkened, and the moon shall not give her light, and the stars shall fall from heaven, and the powers of the heavens shall be shaken. ³⁰And then shall appear the sign of the Son of man in heaven: and then shall all the tribes of the earth mourn, and they shall see the Son of man coming in the clouds of heaven with power and great glory. ³¹And he shall send his angels with a great sound of a trumpet, and they shall gather together his elect from the four winds, from one end of heaven to the other.

³²'Now learn a parable of the fig tree: when his branch is yet tender, and putteth forth leaves, ye know that summer is nigh: ³³so likewise ye, when ye shall see all these things, know that it is near, even at the doors. ³⁴Verily I say unto you, this generation shall not pass, till all these things be fulfilled. ³⁵Heaven and earth shall pass away, but my words shall not pass away.

[36] 'But of that day and hour knoweth no man, no, not the angels of heaven, but my Father only. [37] But as the days of Noe were, so shall also the coming of the Son of man be. [38] For as in the days that were before the flood, they were eating and drinking, marrying and giving in marriage, until the day that Noe entered into the ark, [39] and knew not until the flood came, and took them all away: so shall also the coming of the Son of man be. [40] Then shall two be in the field: the one shall be taken, and the other left. [41] Two women shall be grinding at the mill: the one shall be taken, and the other left. [42] Watch therefore, for ye know not what hour your Lord doth come.

[43] 'But know this, that if the goodman of the house had known in what watch the thief would come, he would have watched, and would not have suffered his house to be broken up. [44] Therefore be ye also ready: for in such an hour as you think not the Son of man cometh. [45] Who then is a faithful and wise servant, whom his lord hath made ruler over his household, to give them meat in due season? [46] Blessed is that servant, whom his lord when he cometh shall find so doing. [47] Verily I say unto you, that he shall make him ruler over all his goods. [48] But and if that evil servant shall say in his heart, "My lord delayeth his coming", [49] and shall begin to smite his fellow-servants, and to eat and drink with the drunken: [50] the lord of that servant shall come in a day when he looketh not for him, and in an hour that he is not aware of, [51] and shall cut him asunder, and appoint him his portion with the hypocrites: there shall be weeping and gnashing of teeth.

25 'Then shall the kingdom of heaven be likened unto ten virgins, which took their lamps, and went forth to meet the bridegroom. [2] And five of them were wise, and five were foolish. [3] They that were foolish took their lamps, and took no oil with them: [4] but the wise took oil in their vessels with their lamps. [5] While the bridegroom tarried, they all slumbered and slept. [6] And at midnight there was a cry made, "Behold, the bridegroom cometh, go ye out to meet him". [7] Then all those virgins arose, and trimmed their lamps. [8] And the foolish said unto the wise, "Give us of your oil, for our lamps are gone out". [9] But the wise answered, saying, "Not so, lest there be not enough for us and you, but go ye rather to them that sell, and buy for yourselves". [10] And while they went to buy, the bridegroom came, and they that were ready went in with him to the marriage, and the door was shut. [11] Afterward came also the other virgins, saying, "Lord, Lord, open to us". [12] But he answered and said, "Verily I say unto you, I know you not". [13] Watch therefore, for ye know neither the day nor the hour wherein the Son of man cometh.

[14] 'For the kingdom of heaven is as a man travelling into a far country, who called his own servants, and delivered unto them his goods. [15] And unto one he gave five talents, to another two, and to another one, to every man according to his several ability, and straightway took his journey. [16] Then he that had received the five talents went and traded with the same, and made them other five talents. [17] And likewise he that had received two, he also gained other two. [18] But he that had received

one went and dug in the earth, and hid his lord's money. [19]After a long time the lord of those servants cometh, and reckoneth with them. [20]And so he that had received five talents came and brought other five talents, saying, "Lord, thou deliveredst unto me five talents: behold, I have gained besides them five talents more". [21]His lord said unto him, "Well done, thou good and faithful servant, thou hast been faithful over a few things, I will make thee ruler over many things: enter thou into the joy of thy lord". [22]He also that had received two talents came and said, "Lord, thou deliveredst unto me two talents: behold, I have gained two other talents besides them". [23]His lord said unto him, "Well done, good and faithful servant, thou hast been faithful over a few things, I will make thee ruler over many things: enter thou into the joy of thy lord". [24]Then he which had received the one talent came and said, "Lord, I knew thee that thou art a hard man, reaping where thou hast not sown, and gathering where thou hast not strewn: [25]and I was afraid, and went and hid thy talent in the earth: lo, there thou hast that is thine". [26]His lord answered and said unto him, "Thou wicked and slothful servant, thou knewest that I reap where I sowed not, and gather where I have not strewn: [27]thou oughtest therefore to have put my money to the exchangers, and then at my coming I should have received my own with usury. [28]Take therefore the talent from him, and give it unto him which hath ten talents. [29]For unto every one that hath shall be given, and he shall have abundance: but from him that hath not shall be taken away even that which he hath. [30]And cast ye the unprofitable servant into outer darkness: there shall be weeping and gnashing of teeth."

[31]'When the Son of man shall come in his glory, and all the holy angels with him, then shall he sit upon the throne of his glory: [32]and before him shall be gathered all nations, and he shall separate them one from another, as a shepherd divideth his sheep from the goats. [33]And he shall set the sheep on his right hand, but the goats on the left. [34]Then shall the King say unto them on his right hand, "Come, ye blessed of my Father, inherit the kingdom prepared for you from the foundation of the world. [35]For I was a-hungered, and ye gave me meat: I was thirsty, and ye gave me drink: I was a stranger, and ye took me in: [36]naked, and ye clothed me: I was sick, and ye visited me: I was in prison, and ye came unto me." [37]Then shall the righteous answer him, saying, "Lord, when saw we thee a-hungered, and fed thee? or thirsty, and gave thee drink? [38]When saw we thee a stranger, and took thee in? or naked, and clothed thee? [39]Or when saw we thee sick, or in prison, and came unto thee?" [40]And the King shall answer and say unto them, "Verily I say unto you, inasmuch as ye have done it unto one of the least of these my brethren, ye have done it unto me". [41]Then shall he say also unto them on the left hand, "Depart from me, ye cursed, into everlasting fire, prepared for the devil and his angels. [42]For I was a-hungered, and ye gave me no meat: I was thirsty, and ye gave me no drink: [43]I was a stranger, and ye took me not in: naked, and ye clothed me not: sick, and in prison, and ye visited me not." [44]Then shall they also answer

him, saying, "Lord, when saw we thee a-hungered, or athirst, or a stranger, or naked, or sick, or in prison, and did not minister unto thee?" ⁴⁵Then shall he answer them, saying, "Verily I say unto you, inasmuch as ye did it not to one of the least of these, ye did it not to me". ⁴⁶And these shall go away into everlasting punishment: but the righteous into life eternal.'

26 And it came to pass, when Jesus had finished all these sayings, he said unto his disciples, ²'Ye know that after two days is the feast of the passover, and the Son of man is betrayed to be crucified'. ³Then assembled together the chief priests, and the scribes, and the elders of the people, unto the palace of the high priest, who was called Caiaphas, ⁴and consulted that they might take Jesus by subtlety, and kill him. ⁵But they said, 'Not on the feast day, lest there be an uproar among the people'.

⁶Now when Jesus was in Bethany, in the house of Simon the leper, ⁷there came unto him a woman having an alabaster box of very precious ointment, and poured it on his head, as he sat at meat. ⁸But when his disciples saw it, they had indignation, saying, 'To what purpose is this waste? ⁹For this ointment might have been sold for much, and given to the poor.' ¹⁰When Jesus understood it, he said unto them, 'Why trouble ye the woman? for she hath wrought a good work upon me. ¹¹For ye have the poor always with you, but me ye have not always. ¹²For in that she hath poured this ointment on my body, she did it for my burial. ¹³Verily I say unto you, wheresoever this gospel shall be preached in the whole world, there shall also this, that this woman hath done, be told for a memorial of her.'

¹⁴Then one of the twelve, called Judas Iscariot, went unto the chief priests, ¹⁵and said unto them, 'What will ye give me, and I will deliver him unto you?' And they covenanted with him for thirty pieces of silver. ¹⁶And from that time he sought opportunity to betray him.

¹⁷Now the first day of the feast of unleavened bread, the disciples came to Jesus, saying unto him, 'Where wilt thou that we prepare for thee to eat the passover?' ¹⁸And he said, 'Go into the city to such a man, and say unto him, "The Master saith, 'My time is at hand, I will keep the passover at thy house with my disciples'"'. ¹⁹And the disciples did as Jesus had appointed them, and they made ready the passover.

²⁰Now when the even was come, he sat down with the twelve. ²¹And as they did eat, he said, 'Verily I say unto you, that one of you shall betray me'. ²²And they were exceeding sorrowful, and began every one of them to say unto him, 'Lord, is it I?' ²³And he answered and said, 'He that dippeth his hand with me in the dish, the same shall betray me. ²⁴The Son of man goeth as it is written of him: but woe unto that man by whom the Son of man is betrayed: it had been good for that man if he had not been born.' ²⁵Then Judas, which betrayed him, answered and said, 'Master, is it I?' He said unto him, 'Thou hast said'.

²⁶And as they were eating, Jesus took bread, and blessed it, and broke it, and gave it to the disciples, and said, 'Take, eat, this is my body'. ²⁷And he took the cup, and gave thanks, and gave it to them, saying,

'Drink ye all of it: [28]for this is my blood of the new testament, which is shed for many for the remission of sins. [29]But I say unto you, I will not drink henceforth of this fruit of the vine, until that day when I drink it new with you in my Father's kingdom.'

[30]And when they had sung a hymn, they went out into the mount of Olives. [31]Then saith Jesus unto them, 'All ye shall be offended because of me this night, for it is written, "I will smite the shepherd, and the sheep of the flock shall be scattered abroad". [32]But after I am risen again, I will go before you into Galilee.' [33]Peter answered and said unto him, 'Though all men shall be offended because of thee, yet will I never be offended'. [34]Jesus said unto him, 'Verily I say unto thee, that this night, before the cock crow, thou shalt deny me thrice'. [35]Peter said unto him, 'Though I should die with thee, yet will I not deny thee'. Likewise also said all the disciples.

[36]Then cometh Jesus with them unto a place called Gethsemane, and saith unto the disciples, 'Sit ye here, while I go and pray yonder'. [37]And he took with him Peter, and the two sons of Zebedee, and began to be sorrowful and very heavy. [38]Then saith he unto them, 'My soul is exceeding sorrowful, even unto death: tarry ye here, and watch with me'. [39]And he went a little farther, and fell on his face, and prayed, saying, 'O my Father, if it be possible, let this cup pass from me: nevertheless not as I will, but as thou wilt'.

[40]And he cometh unto the disciples, and findeth them asleep, and saith unto Peter, 'What, could ye not watch with me one hour? [41]Watch and pray, that ye enter not into temptation: the spirit indeed is willing, but the flesh is weak.'

[42]He went away again the second time, and prayed, saying, 'O my Father, if this cup may not pass away from me, except I drink it, thy will be done'. [43]And he came and found them asleep again: for their eyes were heavy. [44]And he left them, and went away again, and prayed the third time, saying the same words.

[45]Then cometh he to his disciples, and saith unto them, 'Sleep on now, and take your rest: behold, the hour is at hand, and the Son of man is betrayed into the hands of sinners. [46]Rise, let us be going: behold, he is at hand that doth betray me.'

[47]And while he yet spoke, lo, Judas, one of the twelve, came, and with him a great multitude with swords and staves, from the chief priests and elders of the people. [48]Now he that betrayed him gave them a sign, saying, 'Whomsoever I shall kiss, that same is he, hold him fast'. [49]And forthwith he came to Jesus, and said, 'Hail, master', and kissed him. [50]And Jesus said unto him, 'Friend, wherefore art thou come?' Then came they, and laid hands on Jesus, and took him.

[51]And behold, one of them which were with Jesus stretched out his hand, and drew his sword, and struck a servant of the high priest, and smote off his ear. [52]Then said Jesus unto him, 'Put up again thy sword into his place: for all they that take the sword shall perish with the sword. [53]Thinkest thou that I cannot now pray to my Father, and he shall presently give me more than twelve legions of

angels? ⁵⁴But how then shall the scriptures be fulfilled, that thus it must be?'

⁵⁵In that same hour said Jesus to the multitudes, 'Are ye come out as against a thief with swords and staves for to take me? I sat daily with you teaching in the temple, and ye laid no hold on me. ⁵⁶But all this was done, that the scriptures of the prophets might be fulfilled.' Then all the disciples forsook him, and fled.

⁵⁷And they that had laid hold on Jesus led him away to Caiaphas the high priest, where the scribes and the elders were assembled. ⁵⁸But Peter followed him afar off unto the high priest's palace, and went in, and sat with the servants to see the end. ⁵⁹Now the chief priests, and elders, and all the council, sought false witness against Jesus, to put him to death, ⁶⁰but found none: yea, though many false witnesses came, yet found they none. At the last came two false witnesses, ⁶¹and said, 'This fellow said, I am able to destroy the temple of God, and to build it in three days'. ⁶²And the high priest arose, and said unto him, 'Answerest thou nothing? what is it which these witness against thee?' ⁶³But Jesus held his peace. And the high priest answered and said unto him, 'I adjure thee by the living God, that thou tell us whether thou be the Christ, the Son of God'. ⁶⁴Jesus saith unto him, 'Thou hast said: nevertheless I say unto you, hereafter shall ye see the Son of man sitting on the right hand of power, and coming in the clouds of heaven'. ⁶⁵Then the high priest rent his clothes, saying, 'He hath spoken blasphemy: what further need have we of witnesses? Behold, now ye have heard his blasphemy. ⁶⁶What think ye?' They answered and said, 'He is guilty of death'.

⁶⁷Then did they spit in his face, and buffeted him, and others smote him with the palms of their hands, ⁶⁸saying, 'Prophesy unto us, thou Christ, who is he that smote thee?'

⁶⁹Now Peter sat without in the palace: and a damsel came unto him, saying, 'Thou also wast with Jesus of Galilee'. ⁷⁰But he denied before them all, saying, 'I know not what thou sayest'. ⁷¹And when he was gone out into the porch, another maid saw him, and said unto them that were there, 'This fellow was also with Jesus of Nazareth'. ⁷²And again he denied with an oath, 'I do not know the man'. ⁷³And after a while came unto him they that stood by, and said to Peter, 'Surely thou also art one of them, for thy speech bewrayeth thee'. ⁷⁴Then began he to curse and to swear, saying, 'I know not the man'. And immediately the cock crew. ⁷⁵And Peter remembered the words of Jesus, which said unto him, 'Before the cock crow, thou shalt deny me thrice'. And he went out, and wept bitterly.

27 When the morning was come, all the chief priests and elders of the people took counsel against Jesus to put him to death. ²And when they had bound him, they led him away, and delivered him to Pontius Pilate the governor.

³Then Judas, which had betrayed him, when he saw that he was condemned, repented himself, and brought again the thirty pieces of silver to the chief priests and elders, ⁴saying, 'I have sinned in that I have betrayed the innocent blood'. And they said, 'What is that to us? see

thou to that'. [5]And he cast down the pieces of silver in the temple, and departed, and went and hanged himself. [6]And the chief priests took the silver pieces, and said, 'It is not lawful for to put them into the treasury, because it is the price of blood'. [7]And they took counsel, and bought with them the potter's field, to bury strangers in. [8]Wherefore that field was called, the Field of Blood, unto this day. [9]Then was fulfilled that which was spoken by Jeremy the prophet, saying, 'And they took the thirty pieces of silver, the price of him that was valued, whom they of the children of Israel did value: [10]and gave them for the potter's field, as the Lord appointed me'.

[11]And Jesus stood before the governor, and the governor asked him, saying, 'Art thou the King of the Jews?' And Jesus said unto him, 'Thou sayest'. [12]And when he was accused of the chief priests and elders, he answered nothing. [13]Then said Pilate unto him, 'Hearest thou not how many things they witness against thee?' [14]And he answered him to never a word: insomuch that the governor marvelled greatly.

[15]Now at that feast the governor was wont to release unto the people a prisoner, whom they would. [16]And they had then a notable prisoner, called Barabbas. [17]Therefore when they were gathered together, Pilate said unto them, 'Whom will ye that I release unto you? Barabbas, or Jesus which is called Christ?' [18]For he knew that for envy they had delivered him.

[19]When he was set down on the judgement seat, his wife sent unto him, saying, 'Have thou nothing to do with that just man: for I have suffered many things this day in a dream because of him'. [20]But the chief priests and elders persuaded the multitude that they should ask Barabbas, and destroy Jesus. [21]The governor answered and said unto them, 'Whether of the twain will ye that I release unto you?' They said, 'Barabbas'. [22]Pilate said unto them, 'What shall I do then with Jesus which is called Christ?' They all say unto him, 'Let him be crucified'. [23]And the governor said, 'Why, what evil hath he done?' But they cried out the more, saying, 'Let him be crucified'.

[24]When Pilate saw that he could prevail nothing, but that rather a tumult was made, he took water, and washed his hands before the multitude, saying, 'I am innocent of the blood of this just person: see ye to it'. [25]Then answered all the people, and said, 'His blood be on us, and on our children'. [26]Then released he Barabbas unto them: and when he had scourged Jesus, he delivered him to be crucified.

[27]Then the soldiers of the governor took Jesus into the common hall, and gathered unto him the whole band of soldiers. [28]And they stripped him, and put on him a scarlet robe. [29]And when they had plaited a crown of thorns, they put it upon his head, and a reed in his right hand: and they bowed the knee before him, and mocked him, saying, 'Hail, King of the Jews'. [30]And they spat upon him, and took the reed, and smote him on the head. [31]And after that they had mocked him, they took the robe off from him, and put his own raiment on him, and led him away to crucify him. [32]And as they came out, they found a man of Cyrene, Simon by name: him they compelled to bear his cross.

³³And when they were come unto a place called Golgotha, that is to say, a place of a skull, ³⁴they gave him vinegar to drink mingled with gall: and when he had tasted thereof, he would not drink. ³⁵And they crucified him, and parted his garments, casting lots: that it might be fulfilled which was spoken by the prophet, 'They parted my garments among them, and upon my vesture did they cast lots'. ³⁶And sitting down they watched him there; ³⁷and set up over his head his accusation written, 'THIS IS JESUS THE KING OF THE JEWS'. ³⁸Then were there two thieves crucified with him, one on the right hand, and another on the left.

³⁹And they that passed by reviled him, wagging their heads, ⁴⁰and saying, 'Thou that destroyest the temple, and buildest it in three days, save thyself. If thou be the Son of God, come down from the cross.' ⁴¹Likewise also the chief priests mocking him, with the scribes and elders, said, ⁴²'He saved others, himself he cannot save. If he be the King of Israel, let him now come down from the cross, and we will believe him. ⁴³He trusted in God, let him deliver him now if he will have him: for he said, "I am the Son of God".' ⁴⁴The thieves also, which were crucified with him, cast the same in his teeth.

⁴⁵Now from the sixth hour there was darkness over all the land unto the ninth hour. ⁴⁶And about the ninth hour Jesus cried with a loud voice, saying, 'Eli, Eli, lama sabachthani?' that is to say, 'My God, my God, why hast thou forsaken me?' ⁴⁷Some of them that stood there, when they heard that, said, 'This man calleth for Elias'. ⁴⁸And straightway one of them ran, and took a sponge, and filled it with vinegar, and put it on a reed, and gave him to drink. ⁴⁹The rest said, 'Let be, let us see whether Elias will come to save him'.

⁵⁰Jesus, when he had cried again with a loud voice, yielded up the ghost. ⁵¹And behold, the veil of the temple was rent in twain from the top to the bottom, and the earth did quake, and the rocks rent. ⁵²And the graves were opened, and many bodies of saints which slept arose, ⁵³and came out of the graves after his resurrection, and went into the holy city, and appeared unto many. ⁵⁴Now when the centurion, and they that were with him, watching Jesus, saw the earthquake, and those things that were done, they feared greatly, saying, 'Truly this was the Son of God'.

⁵⁵And many women were there beholding afar off, which followed Jesus from Galilee, ministering unto him: ⁵⁶among which was Mary Magdalene, and Mary the mother of James and Joses, and the mother of Zebedee's children.

⁵⁷When the even was come, there came a rich man of Arimathaea, named Joseph, who also himself was Jesus' disciple: ⁵⁸he went to Pilate, and begged the body of Jesus. Then Pilate commanded the body to be delivered. ⁵⁹And when Joseph had taken the body, he wrapped it in a clean linen cloth, ⁶⁰and laid it in his own new tomb, which he had hewn out in the rock: and he rolled a great stone to the door of the sepulchre, and departed. ⁶¹And there was Mary Magdalene, and the other Mary, sitting over against the sepulchre.

⁶²Now the next day, that followed the day of the preparation, the chief priests and Pharisees came together unto Pilate, ⁶³saying, 'Sir, we remember that that deceiver said, while he was yet alive, "After three days I will rise again". ⁶⁴Command therefore that the sepulchre be made sure until the third day, lest his disciples come by night, and steal him away, and say unto the people, "He is risen from the dead": so the last error shall be worse than the first.' ⁶⁵Pilate said unto them, 'Ye have a watch, go your way, make it as sure as you can'. ⁶⁶So they went, and made the sepulchre sure, sealing the stone, and setting a watch.

28 In the end of the sabbath, as it began to dawn towards the first day of the week, came Mary Magdalene and the other Mary to see the sepulchre. ²And behold, there was a great earthquake: for the angel of the Lord descended from heaven, and came and rolled back the stone from the door, and sat upon it. ³His countenance was like lightning, and his raiment white as snow. ⁴And for fear of him the keepers did shake, and became as dead men. ⁵And the angel answered and said unto the women, 'Fear not ye: for I know that ye seek Jesus, which was crucified. ⁶He is not here: for he is risen, as he said: come, see the place where the Lord lay. ⁷And go quickly, and tell his disciples that he is risen from the dead. And behold, he goeth before you into Galilee, there shall ye see him: lo, I have told you.' ⁸And they departed quickly from the sepulchre with fear and great joy, and did run to bring his disciples word.

⁹And as they went to tell his disciples, behold, Jesus met them, saying, 'All hail'. And they came and held him by the feet, and worshipped him. ¹⁰Then said Jesus unto them, 'Be not afraid: go tell my brethren that they go into Galilee, and there shall they see me'.

¹¹Now when they were going, behold, some of the watch came into the city, and showed unto the chief priests all the things that were done. ¹²And when they were assembled with the elders, and had taken counsel, they gave large money unto the soldiers, ¹³saying, 'Say ye, "His disciples came by night, and stole him away while we slept". ¹⁴And if this come to the governor's ears, we will persuade him, and secure you.' ¹⁵So they took the money, and did as they were taught. And this saying is commonly reported among the Jews until this day.

¹⁶Then the eleven disciples went away into Galilee, into a mountain where Jesus had appointed them. ¹⁷And when they saw him, they worshipped him: but some doubted. ¹⁸And Jesus came and spoke unto them, saying, 'All power is given unto me in heaven and in earth. ¹⁹Go ye therefore, and teach all nations, baptizing them in the name of the Father, and of the Son, and of the Holy Ghost: ²⁰teaching them to observe all things whatsoever I have commanded you: and lo, I am with you always, even unto the end of the world.' Amen.

[handwritten: worked w/Paul and Peter]

THE GOSPEL ACCORDING TO
SAINT MARK

[handwritten: only Mark's opinion]

1 The beginning of the gospel of Jesus Christ, the Son of God, ²as it is written in the prophets, 'Behold, I send my messenger before thy face, which shall prepare thy way before thee'. ³'The voice of one crying in the wilderness, "Prepare ye the way of the Lord, make his paths straight".'

[handwritten: Jesus]

⁴John did baptize in the wilderness, and preach the baptism of repentance for the remission of sins. ⁵And there went out unto him all the land of Judea, and they of Jerusalem, and were all baptized of him in the river of Jordan, confessing their sins. ⁶And John was clothed with camel's hair, and with a girdle of a skin about his loins: and he did eat locusts and wild honey, ⁷and preached, saying, 'There cometh one mightier than I after me, the latchet of whose shoes I am not worthy to stoop down and unloose. ⁸I indeed have baptized you with water: but he shall baptize you with the Holy Ghost.'

⁹And it came to pass in those days that Jesus came from Nazareth of Galilee, and was baptized of John in Jordan. ¹⁰And straightway coming up out of the water, he saw the heavens opened, and the Spirit like a dove descending upon him. ¹¹And there came a voice from heaven, saying, 'Thou art my beloved Son, in whom I am well pleased'.

[handwritten: JESUS]

¹²And immediately the Spirit driveth him into the wilderness. ¹³And he was there in the wilderness forty days, tempted of Satan, and was with the wild beasts, and the angels ministered unto him.

¹⁴Now after that John was put in prison, Jesus came into Galilee, preaching the gospel of the kingdom of God, ¹⁵and saying, 'The time is fulfilled, and the kingdom of God is at hand: repent ye, and believe the gospel'. ¹⁶Now as he walked by the sea of Galilee, he saw Simon and Andrew his brother casting a net into the sea: for they were fishers. ¹⁷And Jesus said unto them, 'Come ye after me, and I will make you to become fishers of men'. ¹⁸And straightway they forsook their nets, and followed him. ¹⁹And when he had gone a little farther thence, he saw James the son of Zebedee, and John his brother, who also were in the ship mending their nets. ²⁰And straightway he called them: and they left their father Zebedee in the ship with the hired servants, and went after him.

²¹And they went into Capernaum, and straightway on the sabbath day he entered into the synagogue, and taught. ²²And they were astonished at his doctrine: for he taught them as one that had authority, and not as the scribes. ²³And there was in their synagogue a man with an unclean spirit, and he cried out, ²⁴saying, 'Let us alone, what have we to do with thee, thou Jesus of Nazareth? Art thou come to destroy us? I know thee who thou art, the Holy One of God.' ²⁵And Jesus rebuked him, saying, 'Hold thy peace, and come out of him'. ²⁶And when the unclean spirit had torn him, and cried with a loud voice, he came out

of him. [27]And they were all amazed, insomuch that they questioned among themselves, saying, 'What thing is this? What new doctrine is this? For with authority commandeth he even the unclean spirits, and they do obey him.' [28]And immediately his fame spread abroad throughout all the region round about Galilee.

[29]And forthwith, when they were come out of the synagogue, they entered into the house of Simon and Andrew, with James and John. [30]But Simon's wife's mother lay sick of a fever, and anon they tell him of her. [31]And he came and took her by the hand, and lifted her up, and immediately the fever left her, and she ministered unto them.

[32]And at even, when the sun did set, they brought unto him all that were diseased, and them that were possessed with devils. [33]And all the city was gathered together at the door. [34]And he healed many that were sick of divers diseases, and cast out many devils, and suffered not the devils to speak, because they knew him.

[35]And in the morning, rising up a great while before day, he went out, and departed into a solitary place, and there prayed. [36]And Simon and they that were with him followed after him. [37]And when they had found him, they said unto him, 'All men seek for thee'. [38]And he said unto them, 'Let us go into the next towns, that I may preach there also: for therefore came I forth'. [39]And he preached in their synagogues throughout all Galilee, and cast out devils.

[40]And there came a leper to him, beseeching him, and kneeling down to him, and saying unto him, 'If thou wilt, thou canst make me clean'. [41]And Jesus, moved with compassion, put forth his hand, and touched him, and saith unto him, 'I will, be thou clean'. [42]And as soon as he had spoken, immediately the leprosy departed from him, and he was cleansed. [43]And he straitly charged him, and forthwith sent him away, [44]and saith unto him, 'See thou say nothing to any man: but go thy way, show thyself to the priest, and offer for thy cleansing those things which Moses commanded, for a testimony unto them'. [45]But he went out, and began to publish it much, and to blaze abroad the matter, insomuch that Jesus could no more openly enter into the city, but was without in desert places: and they came to him from every quarter.

2 And again he entered into Capernaum after some days, and it was noised that he was in the house. [2]And straightway many were gathered together, insomuch that there was no room to receive them, no, not so much as about the door: and he preached the word unto them. [3]And they come unto him, bringing one sick of the palsy, which was borne of four. [4]And when they could not come nigh unto him for press, they uncovered the roof where he was: and when they had broken it up, they let down the bed wherein the sick of the palsy lay. [5]When Jesus saw their faith, he said unto the sick of the palsy, 'Son, thy sins be forgiven thee'. [6]But there were certain of the scribes sitting there, and reasoning in their hearts, [7]'Why doth this man thus speak blasphemies? Who can forgive sins but God only?' [8]And immediately when Jesus perceived in his spirit that they so reasoned within themselves, he said unto them, 'Why reason ye these things in your hearts? [9]Whether is it

easier to say to the sick of the palsy, "Thy sins be forgiven thee": or to say, "Arise, and take up thy bed, and walk"? ¹⁰But that ye may know that the Son of man hath power on earth to forgive sins' (he saith to the sick of the palsy), ¹¹'I say unto thee, arise, and take up thy bed, and go thy way into thy house.' ¹²And immediately he arose, took up the bed, and went forth before them all, insomuch that they were all amazed, and glorified God, saying, 'We never saw it on this fashion'.

¹³And he went forth again by the seaside, and all the multitude resorted unto him, and he taught them. ¹⁴And as he passed by, he saw Levi the son of Alpheus sitting at the receipt of custom, and said unto him, 'Follow me'. And he arose and followed him. ¹⁵And it came to pass that as Jesus sat at meat in his house, many publicans and sinners sat also together with Jesus and his disciples: for there were many, and they followed him. ¹⁶And when the scribes and Pharisees saw him eat with publicans and sinners, they said unto his disciples, 'How is it that he eateth and drinketh with publicans and sinners?' ¹⁷When Jesus heard it, he saith unto them, 'They that are whole have no need of the physician, but they that are sick: I came not to call the righteous, but sinners to repentance'.

¹⁸And the disciples of John and of the Pharisees used to fast: and they come and say unto him, 'Why do the disciples of John and of the Pharisees fast, but thy disciples fast not?' ¹⁹And Jesus said unto them, 'Can the children of the bride-chamber fast, while the bridegroom is with them? As long as they have the bridegroom with them, they cannot fast. ²⁰But the days will come, when the bridegroom shall be taken away from them, and then shall they fast in those days. ²¹No man also seweth a piece of new cloth on an old garment: else the new piece that filled it up taketh away from the old, and the rent is made worse. ²²And no man putteth new wine into old bottles, else the new wine doth burst the bottles, and the wine is spilt, and the bottles will be marred: but new wine must be put into new bottles.'

²³And it came to pass that he went through the corn fields on the sabbath day, and his disciples began, as they went, to pluck the ears of corn. ²⁴And the Pharisees said unto him, 'Behold, why do they on the sabbath day that which is not lawful?' ²⁵And he said unto them, 'Have ye never read what David did, when he had need, and was a-hungered, he, and they that were with him? ²⁶how he went into the house of God in the days of Abiathar the high priest, and did eat the showbread, which is not lawful to eat but for the priests, and gave also to them which were with him?' ²⁷And he said unto them, 'The sabbath was made for man, and not man for the sabbath: ²⁸therefore the Son of man is Lord also of the sabbath'.

3 And he entered again into the synagogue, and there was a man there which had a withered hand. ²And they watched him, whether he would heal him on the sabbath days, that they might accuse him. ³And he saith unto the man which had the withered hand, 'Stand forth'. ⁴And he saith unto them, 'Is it lawful to do good on the sabbath day, or to do evil? to save life, or to kill?' But they held their peace. ⁵And

when he had looked round about on them with anger, being grieved for the hardness of their hearts, he saith unto the man, 'Stretch forth thy hand'. And he stretched it out: and his hand was restored whole as the other. [6]And the Pharisees went forth, and straightway took counsel with the Herodians against him, how they might destroy him.

[7]But Jesus withdrew himself with his disciples to the sea: and a great multitude from Galilee followed him, and from Judea, [8]and from Jerusalem, and from Idumea, and from beyond Jordan, and they about Tyre and Sidon, a great multitude, when they had heard what great things he did, came unto him. [9]And he spoke to his disciples, that a small ship should wait on him because of the multitude, lest they should throng him. [10]For he had healed many, insomuch that they pressed upon him for to touch him, as many as had plagues. [11]And unclean spirits, when they saw him, fell down before him, and cried, saying, 'Thou art the Son of God'. [12]And he straitly charged them that they should not make him known.

[13]And he goeth up into a mountain, and calleth unto him whom he would: and they came unto him. [14]And he ordained twelve, that they should be with him, and that he might send them forth to preach, [15]and to have power to heal sicknesses, and to cast out devils. [16]And Simon he surnamed Peter. [17]And James the son of Zebedee, and John the brother of James (and he surnamed them Boanerges, which is, the sons of thunder). [18]And Andrew, and Philip, and Bartholomew, and Matthew, and Thomas, and James the son of Alphaeus, and Thaddaeus, and Simon the Canaanite, [19]and Judas Iscariot, which also betrayed him: and they went into a house.

[20]And the multitude cometh together again, so that they could not so much as eat bread. [21]And when his friends heard of it, they went out to lay hold on him, for they said, 'He is beside himself'. [22]And the scribes which came down from Jerusalem said, 'He hath Beelzebub, and by the prince of the devils casteth he out devils'. [23]And he called them unto him, and said unto them in parables, 'How can Satan cast out Satan? [24]And if a kingdom be divided against itself, that kingdom cannot stand. [25]And if a house be divided against itself, that house cannot stand. [26]And if Satan rise up against himself, and be divided, he cannot stand, but hath an end. [27]No man can enter into a strong man's house, and spoil his goods, except he will first bind the strong man, and then he will spoil his house. [28]Verily I say unto you, all sins shall be forgiven unto the sons of men, and blasphemies wherewith soever they shall blaspheme: [29]but he that shall blaspheme against the Holy Ghost hath never forgiveness, but is in danger of eternal damnation.' [30]Because they said, 'He hath an unclean spirit'.

[31]There came then his brethren and his mother, and, standing without, sent unto him, calling him. [32]And the multitude sat about him, and they said unto him, 'Behold, thy mother and thy brethren without seek for thee'. [33]And he answered them, saying, 'Who is my mother, or my brethren?' [34]And he looked round about on them which sat about him, and said, 'Behold my mother and my brethren. [35]For whosoever

shall do the will of God, the same is my brother, and my sister, and mother.'

4 And he began again to teach by the seaside: and there was gathered unto him a great multitude, so that he entered into a ship, and sat in the sea: and the whole multitude was by the sea on the land. ²And he taught them many things by parables, and said unto them in his doctrine, ³'Hearken, behold, there went out a sower to sow: ⁴and it came to pass, as he sowed, some fell by the wayside, and the fowls of the air came and devoured it up. ⁵And some fell on stony ground, where it had not much earth: and immediately it sprang up, because it had no depth of earth. ⁶But when the sun was up, it was scorched, and because it had no root, it withered away. ⁷And some fell among thorns, and the thorns grew up, and choked it, and it yielded no fruit. ⁸And other fell on good ground, and did yield fruit that sprang up and increased, and brought forth, some thirty, and some sixty, and some a hundred.' ⁹And he said unto them, 'He that hath ears to hear, let him hear'. ¹⁰And when he was alone, they that were about him with the twelve asked of him the parable. ¹¹And he said unto them, 'Unto you it is given to know the mystery of the kingdom of God: but unto them that are without, all these things are done in parables: ¹²that seeing they may see, and not perceive, and hearing they may hear, and not understand, lest at any time they should be converted, and their sins should be forgiven them'. ¹³And he said unto them, 'Know ye not this parable? And how then will you know all parables? ¹⁴The sower soweth the word. ¹⁵And these are they by the wayside, where the word is sown, but when they have heard, Satan cometh immediately, and taketh away the word that was sown in their hearts. ¹⁶And these are they likewise which are sown on stony ground, who, when they have heard the word, immediately receive it with gladness: ¹⁷and have no root in themselves, and so endure but for a time: afterward, when affliction or persecution ariseth for the word's sake, immediately they are offended. ¹⁸And these are they which are sown among thorns: such as hear the word, ¹⁹and the cares of this world, and the deceitfulness of riches, and the lusts of other things entering in, choke the word, and it becometh unfruitful. ²⁰And these are they which are sown on good ground, such as hear the word, and receive it, and bring forth fruit, some thirtyfold, some sixty, and some a hundred.'

²¹And he said unto them, 'Is a candle brought to be put under a bushel, or under a bed? and not to be set on a candlestick? ²²For there is nothing hid, which shall not be manifested: neither was anything kept secret, but that it should come abroad. ²³If any man have ears to hear, let him hear.'

²⁴And he said unto them, 'Take heed what you hear: with what measure ye mete, it shall be measured to you: and unto you that hear shall more be given. ²⁵For he that hath, to him shall be given: and he that hath not, from him shall be taken even that which he hath.'

²⁶And he said, 'So is the kingdom of God, as if a man should cast seed into the ground, ²⁷and should sleep, and rise night and day, and the

seed should spring and grow up, he knoweth not how. ²⁸For the earth bringeth forth fruit of herself, first the blade, then the ear, after that the full corn in the ear. ²⁹But when the fruit is brought forth, immediately he putteth in the sickle, because the harvest is come.'

³⁰And he said, 'Whereunto shall we liken the kingdom of God? Or with what comparison shall we compare it? ³¹It is like a grain of mustard seed, which, when it is sown in the earth, is less than all the seeds that be in the earth. ³²But when it is sown, it groweth up, and becometh greater than all herbs, and shooteth out great branches, so that the fowls of the air may lodge under the shadow of it.' ³³And with many such parables spoke he the word unto them, as they were able to hear it. ³⁴But without a parable spoke he not unto them, and when they were alone, he expounded all things to his disciples.

³⁵And the same day, when the even was come, he saith unto them, 'Let us pass over unto the other side'. ³⁶And when they had sent away the multitude, they took him even as he was in the ship. And there were also with him other little ships. ³⁷And there arose a great storm of wind, and the waves beat into the ship, so that it was now full. ³⁸And he was in the hinder part of the ship, asleep on a pillow: and they awake him, and say unto him, 'Master, carest thou not that we perish?' ³⁹And he arose, and rebuked the wind, and said unto the sea, 'Peace, be still'. And the wind ceased, and there was a great calm. ⁴⁰And he said unto them, 'Why are ye so fearful? How is it that you have no faith?' ⁴¹And they feared exceedingly, and said one to another, 'What manner of man is this, that even the wind and the sea obey him?'

5 And they came over unto the other side of the sea, into the country of the Gadarenes. ²And when he was come out of the ship, immediately there met him out of the tombs a man with an unclean spirit, ³who had his dwelling among the tombs, and no man could bind him, no, not with chains: ⁴because that he had been often bound with fetters and chains, and the chains had been plucked asunder by him, and the fetters broken in pieces: neither could any man tame him. ⁵And always, night and day, he was in the mountains, and in the tombs, crying, and cutting himself with stones. ⁶But when he saw Jesus afar off, he came and worshipped him, ⁷and cried with a loud voice, and said, 'What have I to do with thee, Jesus, thou Son of the most high God? I adjure thee by God, that thou torment me not.' ⁸For he said unto him, 'Come out of the man, thou unclean spirit'. ⁹And he asked him, 'What is thy name?' And he answered, saying, 'My name is Legion: for we are many'. ¹⁰And he besought him much that he would not send them away out of the country. ¹¹Now there was there nigh unto the mountains a great herd of swine feeding. ¹²And all the devils besought him, saying, 'Send us into the swine, that we may enter into them'. ¹³And forthwith Jesus gave them leave. And the unclean spirits went out, and entered into the swine, and the herd ran violently down a steep place into the sea (they were about two thousand), and were choked in the sea. ¹⁴And they that fed the swine fled, and told it in the city, and in the country. And they went out to see what it was that was done. ¹⁵And they come to

Jesus, and see him that was possessed with the devil, and had the legion, sitting, and clothed, and in his right mind: and they were afraid. ¹⁶And they that saw it told them how it befell to him that was possessed with the devil, and also concerning the swine. ¹⁷And they began to pray him to depart out of their coasts. ¹⁸And when he was come into the ship, he that had been possessed with the devil prayed him that he might be with him. ¹⁹Howbeit Jesus suffered him not, but saith unto him, 'Go home to thy friends, and tell them how great things the Lord hath done for thee, and hath had compassion on thee'. ²⁰And he departed, and began to publish in Decapolis how great things Jesus had done for him: and all men did marvel.

²¹And when Jesus was passed over again by ship unto the other side, much people gathered unto him, and he was nigh unto the sea. ²²And behold, there cometh one of the rulers of the synagogue, Jairus by name, and when he saw him, he fell at his feet, ²³and besought him greatly, saying, 'My little daughter lieth at the point of death, I pray thee, come and lay thy hands on her, that she may be healed, and she shall live'. ²⁴And Jesus went with him, and much people followed him, and thronged him.

²⁵And a certain woman, which had an issue of blood twelve years, ²⁶and had suffered many things of many physicians, and had spent all that she had, and was nothing bettered, but rather grew worse, ²⁷when she had heard of Jesus, came in the press behind, and touched his garment. ²⁸For she said, 'If I may touch but his clothes, I shall be whole'. ²⁹And straightway the fountain of her blood was dried up: and she felt in her body that she was healed of that plague. ³⁰And Jesus, immediately knowing in himself that virtue had gone out of him, turned him about in the press, and said, 'Who touched my clothes?' ³¹And his disciples said unto him, 'Thou seest the multitude thronging thee, and sayest thou, "Who touched me?"' ³²And he looked round about to see her that had done this thing. ³³But the woman fearing and trembling, knowing what was done in her, came and fell down before him, and told him all the truth. ³⁴And he said unto her, 'Daughter, thy faith hath made thee whole, go in peace, and be whole of thy plague'.

³⁵While he yet spoke, there came from the ruler of the synagogue's house certain which said, 'Thy daughter is dead, why troublest thou the Master any further?' ³⁶As soon as Jesus heard the word that was spoken, he saith unto the ruler of the synagogue, 'Be not afraid, only believe'. ³⁷And he suffered no man to follow him, save Peter, and James, and John the brother of James. ³⁸And he cometh to the house of the ruler of the synagogue, and seeth the tumult, and them that wept and wailed greatly. ³⁹And when he was come in, he saith unto them, 'Why make ye this ado, and weep? the damsel is not dead, but sleepeth'. ⁴⁰And they laughed him to scorn. But when he had put them all out, he taketh the father and the mother of the damsel, and them that were with him, and entereth in where the damsel was lying. ⁴¹And he took the damsel by the hand, and said unto her, 'Talitha cumi', which is, being interpreted, 'Damsel, I say unto thee, arise'. ⁴²And straightway

the damsel arose, and walked, for she was of the age of twelve years: and they were astonished with a great astonishment. ⁴³And he charged them straitly that no man should know it: and commanded that something should be given her to eat.

6 And he went out from thence, and came into his own country, and his disciples follow him. ²And when the sabbath day was come, he began to teach in the synagogue: and many hearing him were astonished, saying, 'From whence hath this man these things? And what wisdom is this which is given unto him, that even such mighty works are wrought by his hands? ³Is not this the carpenter, the son of Mary, the brother of James, and Joses, and of Juda, and Simon? And are not his sisters here with us?' And they were offended at him. ⁴But Jesus said unto them, 'A prophet is not without honour, but in his own country, and among his own kin, and in his own house'. ⁵And he could there do no mighty work, save that he laid his hands upon a few sick folk, and healed them. ⁶And he marvelled because of their unbelief. And he went round about the villages, teaching.

⁷And he calleth unto him the twelve, and began to send them forth by two and two, and gave them power over unclean spirits, ⁸and commanded them that they should take nothing for their journey, save a staff only: no scrip, no bread, no money in their purse: ⁹but be shod with sandals: and not put on two coats. ¹⁰And he said unto them, 'In what place soever ye enter into a house, there abide till ye depart from that place. ¹¹And whosoever shall not receive you, nor hear you, when ye depart thence, shake off the dust under your feet for a testimony against them. Verily I say unto you, it shall be more tolerable for Sodom and Gomorrha in the day of judgement, than for that city.' ¹²And they went out, and preached that men should repent. ¹³And they cast out many devils, and anointed with oil many that were sick, and healed them.

¹⁴And king Herod heard of him (for his name was spread abroad), and he said that John the Baptist was risen from the dead, and therefore mighty works do show forth themselves in him. ¹⁵Others said, 'That it is Elias'. And others said, 'That it is a prophet, or as one of the prophets'. ¹⁶But when Herod heard thereof, he said, 'It is John, whom I beheaded, he is risen from the dead'.

¹⁷For Herod himself had sent forth and laid hold upon John, and bound him in prison for Herodias' sake, his brother Philip's wife, for he had married her. ¹⁸For John had said unto Herod, 'It is not lawful for thee to have thy brother's wife'. ¹⁹Therefore Herodias had a quarrel against him, and would have killed him, but she could not. ²⁰For Herod feared John, knowing that he was a just man and a holy, and observed him: and when he heard him, he did many things, and heard him gladly. ²¹And when a convenient day was come, that Herod on his birthday made a supper to his lords, high captains, and chief estates of Galilee: ²²and when the daughter of the said Herodias came in, and danced, and pleased Herod, and them that sat with him, the king said unto the damsel, 'Ask of me whatsoever thou wilt, and I will give it

thee'. ²³And he swore unto her, 'Whatsoever thou shalt ask of me, I will give it thee, unto the half of my kingdom'. ²⁴And she went forth, and said unto her mother, 'What shall I ask?' And she said, 'The head of John the Baptist'. ²⁵And she came in straightway with haste unto the king, and asked, saying, 'I will that thou give me by and by in a charger the head of John the Baptist'. ²⁶And the king was exceeding sorry, yet for his oaths' sake, and for their sakes which sat with him, he would not reject her. ²⁷And immediately the king sent an executioner, and commanded his head to be brought: and he went and beheaded him in the prison, ²⁸and brought his head in a charger, and gave it to the damsel, and the damsel gave it to her mother. ²⁹And when his disciples heard of it, they came and took up his corpse, and laid it in a tomb.

³⁰And the apostles gathered themselves together unto Jesus, and told him all things, both what they had done, and what they had taught. ³¹And he said unto them, 'Come ye yourselves apart into a desert place, and rest a while'. For there were many coming and going, and they had no leisure so much as to eat. ³²And they departed into a desert place by ship privately. ³³And the people saw them departing, and many knew him, and ran afoot thither out of all cities, and outwent them, and came together unto him. ³⁴And Jesus, when he came out, saw much people, and was moved with compassion toward them, because they were as sheep not having a shepherd: and he began to teach them many things. ³⁵And when the day was now far spent, his disciples came unto him, and said, 'This is a desert place, and now the time is far passed. ³⁶Send them away, that they may go into the country round about, and into the villages, and buy themselves bread: for they have nothing to eat.' ³⁷He answered and said unto them, 'Give ye them to eat'. And they say unto him, 'Shall we go and buy two hundred pennyworth of bread, and give them to eat?' ³⁸He saith unto them, 'How many loaves have ye? go and see'. And when they knew, they say, 'Five, and two fishes'. ³⁹And he commanded them to make all sit down by companies upon the green grass. ⁴⁰And they sat down in ranks, by hundreds, and by fifties. ⁴¹And when he had taken the five loaves and the two fishes, he looked up to heaven, and blessed, and broke the loaves, and gave them to his disciples to set before them; and the two fishes divided he among them all. ⁴²And they did all eat, and were filled. ⁴³And they took up twelve baskets full of the fragments, and of the fishes. ⁴⁴And they that did eat of the loaves were about five thousand men.

⁴⁵And straightway he constrained his disciples to get into the ship, and to go to the other side before unto Bethsaida, while he sent away the people. ⁴⁶And when he had sent them away, he departed into a mountain to pray. ⁴⁷And when even was come, the ship was in the midst of the sea, and he alone on the land. ⁴⁸And he saw them toiling in rowing (for the wind was contrary unto them): and about the fourth watch of the night he cometh unto them, walking upon the sea, and would have passed by them. ⁴⁹But when they saw him walking upon the sea, they supposed it had been a spirit, and cried out: ⁵⁰for they all saw him, and were troubled. And immediately he talked with them, and saith unto

them, 'Be of good cheer, it is I, be not afraid'. [51]And he went up unto them into the ship, and the wind ceased: and they were sore amazed in themselves beyond measure, and wondered. [52]For they considered not the miracle of the loaves, for their heart was hardened.

[53]And when they had passed over, they came into the land of Gennesaret, and drew to the shore. [54]And when they were come out of the ship, straightway they knew him, [55]and ran through that whole region round about, and began to carry about in beds those that were sick, where they heard he was. [56]And whithersoever he entered, into villages, or cities, or country, they laid the sick in the streets, and besought him that they might touch if it were but the border of his garment: and as many as touched him were made whole.

7 Then came together unto him the Pharisees, and certain of the scribes, which came from Jerusalem. [2]And when they saw some of his disciples eat bread with defiled, that is to say, with unwashed, hands, they found fault. [3]For the Pharisees, and all the Jews, except they wash their hands oft, eat not, holding the tradition of the elders. [4]And when they come from the market, except they wash, they eat not. And many other things there be, which they have received to hold, as the washing of cups, and pots, brazen vessels, and of tables. [5]Then the Pharisees and scribes asked him, 'Why walk not thy disciples according to the tradition of the elders, but eat bread with unwashed hands?' [6]He answered and said unto them, 'Well hath Esaias prophesied of you hypocrites, as it is written, "This people honoureth me with their lips, but their heart is far from me. [7]Howbeit in vain do they worship me, teaching for doctrines the commandments of men." [8]For laying aside the commandment of God, ye hold the tradition of men, as the washing of pots and cups: and many other such like things ye do.'

[9]And he said unto them, 'Full well ye reject the commandment of God, that ye may keep your own tradition. [10]For Moses said, "Honour thy father and thy mother": and, "Whoso curseth father or mother, let him die the death". [11]But ye say, "If a man shall say to his father or mother, 'It is Corban'", that is to say, a gift, by whatsoever thou mightest be profited by me: he shall be free. [12]And ye suffer him no more to do aught for his father or his mother: [13]making the word of God of no effect through your tradition, which ye have delivered: and many such like things do ye.'

[14]And when he had called all the people unto him, he said unto them, 'Hearken unto me every one of you, and understand. [15]There is nothing from without a man, that entering into him can defile him: but the things which come out of him, those are they that defile the man. [16]If any man have ears to hear, let him hear.' [17]And when he was entered into the house from the people, his disciples asked him concerning the parable. [18]And he saith unto them, 'Are ye so without understanding also? Do ye not perceive, that whatsoever thing from without entereth into the man, it cannot defile him, [19]because it entereth not into his heart, but into the belly, and goeth out into the draught, purging all meats?' [20]And he said, 'That which cometh out of the man, that defileth

the man. [21]For from within, out of the heart of men, proceed evil thoughts, adulteries, fornications, murders, [22]thefts, covetousness, wickedness, deceit, lasciviousness, an evil eye, blasphemy, pride, foolishness: [23]all these evil things come from within, and defile the man.'

[24]And from thence he arose, and went into the borders of Tyre and Sidon, and entered into a house, and would have no man know it, but he could not be hid. [25]For a certain woman, whose young daughter had an unclean spirit, heard of him, and came and fell at his feet. [26]The woman was a Greek, a Syrophenician by nation: and she besought him that he would cast forth the devil out of her daughter. [27]But Jesus said unto her, 'Let the children first be filled: for it is not meet to take the children's bread, and to cast it unto the dogs'. [28]And she answered and said unto him, 'Yes, Lord, yet the dogs under the table eat of the children's crumbs'. [29]And he said unto her, 'For this saying go thy way, the devil is gone out of thy daughter'. [30]And when she was come to her house, she found the devil gone out, and her daughter laid upon the bed.

[31]And again, departing from the coasts of Tyre and Sidon, he came unto the sea of Galilee, through the midst of the coasts of Decapolis. [32]And they bring unto him one that was deaf, and had an impediment in his speech: and they beseech him to put his hand upon him. [33]And he took him aside from the multitude, and put his fingers into his ears, and he spat, and touched his tongue, [34]and looking up to heaven, he sighed, and saith unto him, 'Ephphatha', that is, 'Be opened'. [35]And straightway his ears were opened, and the string of his tongue was loosed, and he spoke plain. [36]And he charged them that they should tell no man: but the more he charged them, so much the more a great deal they published it; [37]and were beyond measure astonished, saying, 'He hath done all things well: he maketh both the deaf to hear, and the dumb to speak'.

8 In those days the multitude being very great, and having nothing to eat, Jesus called his disciples unto him, and saith unto them, [2]'I have compassion on the multitude, because they have now been with me three days, and have nothing to eat: [3]and if I send them away fasting to their own houses, they will faint by the way: for divers of them came from far'. [4]And his disciples answered him, 'From whence can a man satisfy these men with bread here in the wilderness?' [5]And he asked them, 'How many loaves have ye?' And they said, 'Seven'. [6]And he commanded the people to sit down on the ground: and he took the seven loaves, and gave thanks, and broke, and gave to his disciples to set before them: and they did set them before the people. [7]And they had a few small fishes: and he blessed, and commanded to set them also before them. [8]So they did eat, and were filled: and they took up of the broken meat that was left seven baskets. [9]And they that had eaten were about four thousand, and he sent them away.

[10]And straightway he entered into a ship with his disciples, and came into the parts of Dalmanutha. [11]And the Pharisees came forth, and began to question with him, seeking of him a sign from heaven, tempt-

ing him. [12]And he sighed deeply in his spirit, and saith, 'Why doth this generation seek after a sign? Verily I say unto you, there shall no sign be given unto this generation.' [13]And he left them, and entering into the ship again departed to the other side.

[14]Now the disciples had forgotten to take bread, neither had they in the ship with them more than one loaf. [15]And he charged them, saying, 'Take heed, beware of the leaven of the Pharisees, and of the leaven of Herod'. [16]And they reasoned among themselves, saying, 'It is because we have no bread'. [17]And when Jesus knew it, he saith unto them, 'Why reason ye, because ye have no bread? Perceive ye not yet, neither understand? Have ye your heart yet hardened? [18]Having eyes, see ye not? and having ears, hear ye not? And do ye not remember? [19]When I broke the five loaves among five thousand, how many baskets full of fragments took ye up?' They say unto him, 'Twelve'. [20]'And when the seven among four thousand, how many baskets full of fragments took ye up?' And they said, 'Seven'. [21]And he said unto them, 'How is it that ye do not understand?'

[22]And he cometh to Bethsaida, and they bring a blind man unto him, and besought him to touch him. [23]And he took the blind man by the hand, and led him out of the town, and when he had spat on his eyes, and put his hands upon him, he asked him if he saw aught. [24]And he looked up, and said, 'I see men as trees, walking'. [25]After that he put his hands again upon his eyes, and made him look up: and he was restored, and saw every man clearly. [26]And he sent him away to his house, saying, 'Neither go into the town, nor tell it to any in the town'.

[27]And Jesus went out, and his disciples, into the towns of Caesarea Philippi: and by the way he asked his disciples, saying unto them, 'Whom do men say that I am?' [28]And they answered, 'John the Baptist: but some say, Elias: and others, one of the prophets'. [29]And he saith unto them, 'But whom say ye that I am?' And Peter answereth and saith unto him, 'Thou art the Christ'. [30]And he charged them that they should tell no man of him. [31]And he began to teach them, that the Son of man must suffer many things, and be rejected of the elders, and of the chief priests, and scribes, and be killed, and after three days rise again. [32]And he spoke that saying openly. And Peter took him, and began to rebuke him. [33]But when he had turned about and looked on his disciples, he rebuked Peter, saying, 'Get thee behind me, Satan: for thou savourest not the things that be of God, but the things that be of men'.

[34]And when he had called the people unto him with his disciples also, he said unto them, 'Whosoever will come after me, let him deny himself, and take up his cross, and follow me. [35]For whosoever will save his life shall lose it, but whosoever shall lose his life for my sake and the gospel's, the same shall save it. [36]For what shall it profit a man, if he shall gain the whole world, and lose his own soul? [37]Or what shall a man give in exchange for his soul? [38]Whosoever therefore shall be ashamed of me and of my words in this adulterous and sinful generation, of him also shall the Son of man be ashamed, when he cometh in the glory of his Father with the holy angels.'

9 And he said unto them, 'Verily I say unto you, that there be some of them that stand here, which shall not taste of death, till they have seen the kingdom of God come with power'.

²And after six days Jesus taketh with him Peter, and James, and John, and leadeth them up into a high mountain apart by themselves: and he was transfigured before them. ³And his raiment became shining, exceeding white as snow: so as no fuller on earth can white them. ⁴And there appeared unto them Elias with Moses: and they were talking with Jesus. ⁵And Peter answered and said to Jesus, 'Master, it is good for us to be here, and let us make three tabernacles; one for thee, and one for Moses, and one for Elias'. ⁶For he wist not what to say, for they were sore afraid. ⁷And there was a cloud that overshadowed them: and a voice came out of the cloud, saying, 'This is my beloved Son: hear him'. ⁸And suddenly, when they had looked round about, they saw no man any more, save Jesus only with themselves.

⁹And as they came down from the mountain, he charged them that they should tell no man what things they had seen, till the Son of man were risen from the dead. ¹⁰And they kept that saying with themselves, questioning one with another what the rising from the dead should mean. ¹¹And they asked him, saying, 'Why say the scribes that Elias must first come?' ¹²And he answered and told them, 'Elias verily cometh first, and restoreth all things; and how it is written of the Son of man, that he must suffer many things, and be set at nought. ¹³But I say unto you, that Elias is indeed come, and they have done unto him whatsoever they listed, as it is written of him.'

¹⁴And when he came to his disciples, he saw a great multitude about them, and the scribes questioning with them. ¹⁵And straightway all the people, when they beheld him, were greatly amazed, and running to him saluted him. ¹⁶And he asked the scribes, 'What question ye with them?' ¹⁷And one of the multitude answered and said, 'Master, I have brought unto thee my son, which hath a dumb spirit: ¹⁸and wheresoever he taketh him, he teareth him, and he foameth, and gnasheth with his teeth, and pineth away: and I spoke to thy disciples that they should cast him out, and they could not'. ¹⁹He answereth him, and saith, 'O faithless generation, how long shall I be with you? how long shall I suffer you? Bring him unto me.' ²⁰And they brought him unto him: and when he saw him, straightway the spirit tore him, and he fell on the ground, and wallowed foaming. ²¹And he asked his father, 'How long is it ago since this came unto him?' And he said, 'Of a child'. ²²And ofttimes it hath cast him into the fire, and into the waters, to destroy him: but if thou canst do anything, have compassion on us, and help us. ²³Jesus said unto him, 'If thou canst believe, all things are possible to him that believeth'. ²⁴And straightway the father of the child cried out, and said with tears, 'Lord, I believe, help thou my unbelief'. ²⁵When Jesus saw that the people came running together, he rebuked the foul spirit, saying unto him, 'Thou dumb and deaf spirit, I charge thee, come out of him, and enter no more into him'. ²⁶And the spirit cried, and rent him sore, and came out of him, and he was as one dead,

insomuch that many said, 'He is dead'. ²⁷But Jesus took him by the hand, and lifted him up, and he arose. ²⁸And when he was come into the house, his disciples asked him privately, 'Why could not we cast him out?' ²⁹And he said unto them, 'This kind can come forth by nothing, but by prayer and fasting'.

³⁰And they departed thence, and passed through Galilee, and he would not that any man should know it. ³¹For he taught his disciples, and said unto them, 'The Son of man is delivered into the hands of men, and they shall kill him, and after that he is killed, he shall rise the third day'. ³²But they understood not that saying, and were afraid to ask him.

³³And he came to Capernaum; and being in the house he asked them, 'What was it that ye disputed among yourselves by the way?' ³⁴But they held their peace: for by the way they had disputed among themselves, who should be the greatest. ³⁵And he sat down, and called the twelve, and saith unto them, 'If any man desire to be first, the same shall be last of all, and servant of all'. ³⁶And he took a child, and set him in the midst of them: and when he had taken him in his arms, he said unto them, ³⁷'Whosoever shall receive one of such children in my name, receiveth me: and whosoever shall receive me, receiveth not me, but him that sent me'.

³⁸And John answered him, saying, 'Master, we saw one casting out devils in thy name, and he followeth not us, and we forbad him, because he followeth not us'. ³⁹But Jesus said, 'Forbid him not, for there is no man which shall do a miracle in my name, that can lightly speak evil of me. ⁴⁰For he that is not against us is on our part. ⁴¹For whosoever shall give you a cup of water to drink in my name, because ye belong to Christ, verily I say unto you, he shall not lose his reward. ⁴²And whosoever shall offend one of these little ones that believe in me, it is better for him that a millstone were hanged about his neck, and he were cast into the sea. ⁴³And if thy hand offend thee, cut it off: it is better for thee to enter into life maimed, than having two hands to go into hell, into the fire that never shall be quenched: ⁴⁴where their worm dieth not, and the fire is not quenched. ⁴⁵And if thy foot offend thee, cut if off: it is better for thee to enter halt into life, than having two feet to be cast into hell, into the fire that never shall be quenched: ⁴⁶where their worm dieth not, and the fire is not quenched. ⁴⁷And if thy eye offend thee, pluck it out: it is better for thee to enter into the kingdom of God with one eye, than having two eyes to be cast into hell fire: ⁴⁸where their worm dieth not, and the fire is not quenched. ⁴⁹For every one shall be salted with fire, and every sacrifice shall be salted with salt. ⁵⁰Salt is good: but if the salt have lost his saltness, wherewith will you season it? Have salt in yourselves, and have peace one with another.'

10 And he arose from thence, and cometh into the coasts of Judea by the farther side of Jordan: and the people resort unto him again, and as he was wont, he taught them again.

²And the Pharisees came to him, and asked him, 'Is it lawful for a man to put away his wife?' tempting him. ³And he answered and said unto

them, 'What did Moses command you?' ⁴And they said, 'Moses suffered to write a bill of divorcement, and to put her away'. ⁵And Jesus answered and said unto them, 'For the hardness of your heart he wrote you this precept. ⁶But from the beginning of the creation God made them male and female. ⁷For this cause shall a man leave his father and mother, and cleave to his wife, ⁸and they twain shall be one flesh: so then they are no more twain, but one flesh. ⁹What therefore God hath joined together, let not man put asunder.' ¹⁰And in the house his disciples asked him again of the same matter. ¹¹And he saith unto them, 'Whosoever shall put away his wife, and marry another, committeth adultery against her. ¹²And if a woman shall put away her husband, and be married to another, she committeth adultery.'

¹³And they brought young children to him, that he should touch them, and his disciples rebuked those that brought them. ¹⁴But when Jesus saw it, he was much displeased, and said unto them, 'Suffer the little children to come unto me, and forbid them not: for of such is the kingdom of God. ¹⁵Verily I say unto you, whosoever shall not receive the kingdom of God as a little child, he shall not enter therein.' ¹⁶And he took them up in his arms, put his hands upon them, and blessed them.

¹⁷And when he was gone forth into the way, there came one running, and kneeled to him, and asked him, 'Good Master, what shall I do that I may inherit eternal life?' ¹⁸And Jesus said unto him, 'Why callest thou me good? There is no man good but one, that is, God. ¹⁹Thou knowest the commandments, do not commit adultery, do not kill, do not steal, do not bear false witness, defraud not, honour thy father and mother.' ²⁰And he answered and said unto him, 'Master, all these have I observed from my youth'. ²¹Then Jesus beholding him loved him, and said unto him, 'One thing thou lackest: go thy way, sell whatsoever thou hast, and give to the poor, and thou shalt have treasure in heaven, and come, take up the cross, and follow me'. ²²And he was sad at that saying, and went away grieved: for he had great possessions.

²³And Jesus looked round about, and saith unto his disciples, 'How hardly shall they that have riches enter into the kingdom of God?' ²⁴And the disciples were astonished at his words. But Jesus answereth again, and saith unto them, 'Children, how hard is it for them that trust in riches to enter into the kingdom of God? ²⁵It is easier for a camel to go through the eye of a needle, than for a rich man to enter into the kingdom of God.' ²⁶And they were astonished out of measure, saying among themselves, 'Who then can be saved?' ²⁷And Jesus looking upon them saith, 'With men it is impossible, but not with God: for with God all things are possible'.

²⁸Then Peter began to say unto him, 'Lo, we have left all, and have followed thee'. ²⁹And Jesus answered and said, 'Verily I say unto you, there is no man that hath left house, or brethren, or sisters, or father, or mother, or wife, or children, or lands, for my sake, and the gospel's, ³⁰but he shall receive a hundredfold now in this time, houses, and brethren, and sisters, and mothers, and children, and lands, with per-

secutions; and in the world to come eternal life. ³¹But many that are first shall be last: and the last first.'

³²And they were in the way going up to Jerusalem: and Jesus went before them, and they were amazed, and as they followed, they were afraid. And he took again the twelve, and began to tell them what things should happen unto him, ³³saying, 'Behold, we go up to Jerusalem, and the Son of man shall be delivered unto the chief priests, and unto the scribes: and they shall condemn him to death, and shall deliver him to the Gentiles. ³⁴And they shall mock him, and shall scourge him, and shall spit upon him, and shall kill him, and the third day he shall rise again.'

³⁵And James and John, the sons of Zebedee, come unto him, saying, 'Master, we would that thou shouldst do for us whatsoever we shall desire'. ³⁶And he said unto them, 'What would ye that I should do for you?' ³⁷They said unto him, 'Grant unto us that we may sit, one on thy right hand, and the other on thy left hand, in thy glory'. ³⁸But Jesus said unto them, 'Ye know not what ye ask: can ye drink of the cup that I drink of? and be baptized with the baptism that I am baptized with?' ³⁹And they said unto him, 'We can'. And Jesus said unto them, 'Ye shall indeed drink of the cup that I drink of: and with the baptism that I am baptized withal shall ye be baptized: ⁴⁰but to sit on my right hand and on my left hand is not mine to give, but it shall be given to them for whom it is prepared'.

⁴¹And when the ten heard it, they began to be much displeased with James and John. ⁴²But Jesus called them to him, and saith unto them, 'Ye know that they which are accounted to rule over the Gentiles exercise lordship over them: and their great ones exercise authority upon them. ⁴³But so shall it not be among you: but whosoever will be great among you, shall be your minister: ⁴⁴and whosoever of you will be the chiefest, shall be servant of all. ⁴⁵For even the Son of man came not to be ministered unto, but to minister, and to give his life a ransom for many.'

⁴⁶And they came to Jericho: and as he went out of Jericho with his disciples and a great number of people, blind Bartimaeus, the son of Timaeus, sat by the highway side begging. ⁴⁷And when he heard that it was Jesus of Nazareth, he began to cry out, and say, 'Jesus, thou son of David, have mercy on me'. ⁴⁸And many charged him that he should hold his peace: but he cried the more a great deal, 'Thou son of David, have mercy on me'. ⁴⁹And Jesus stood still, and commanded him to be called: and they call the blind man, saying unto him, 'Be of good comfort, rise, he calleth thee'. ⁵⁰And he, casting away his garment, rose, and came to Jesus. ⁵¹And Jesus answered and said unto him, 'What wilt thou that I should do unto thee?' The blind man said unto him, 'Lord, that I might receive my sight'. ⁵²And Jesus said unto him, 'Go thy way, thy faith hath made thee whole'. And immediately he received his sight, and followed Jesus in the way.

11 And when they came nigh to Jerusalem, unto Bethphage and Bethany, at the mount of Olives, he sendeth forth two of his disciples, ²and saith unto them, 'Go your way into the village over against you: and as soon as ye be entered into it, ye shall find a colt tied, whereon never man sat, loose him, and bring him. ³And if any man say unto you, "Why do ye this?" say ye that the Lord hath need of him: and straightway he will send him hither.' ⁴And they went their way, and found the colt tied by the door without in a place where two ways met: and they loose him. ⁵And certain of them that stood there said unto them, 'What do ye, loosing the colt?' ⁶And they said unto them even as Jesus had commanded: and they let them go. ⁷And they brought the colt to Jesus, and cast their garments on him, and he sat upon him. ⁸And many spread their garments in the way: and others cut down branches of the trees, and strewed them in the way. ⁹And they that went before, and they that followed, cried, saying, 'Hosanna, blessed is he that cometh in the name of the Lord. ¹⁰Blessed be the kingdom of our father David, that cometh in the name of the Lord, Hosanna in the highest.' ¹¹And Jesus entered into Jerusalem, and into the temple, and when he had looked round about upon all things, and now the eventide was come, he went out unto Bethany with the twelve.

¹²And on the morrow, when they were come from Bethany, he was hungry. ¹³And seeing a fig tree afar off having leaves, he came, if haply he might find anything thereon, and when he came to it, he found nothing but leaves: for the time of figs was not yet. ¹⁴And Jesus answered and said unto it, 'No man eat fruit of thee hereafter for ever'. And his disciples heard it.

¹⁵And they come to Jerusalem, and Jesus went into the temple, and began to cast out them that sold and bought in the temple, and overthrew the tables of the money-changers, and the seats of them that sold doves, ¹⁶and would not suffer that any man should carry any vessel through the temple. ¹⁷And he taught, saying unto them, 'Is it not written, "My house shall be called of all nations the house of prayer"? but ye have made it a den of thieves'. ¹⁸And the scribes and chief priests heard it, and sought how they might destroy him: for they feared him, because all the people was astonished at his doctrine. ¹⁹And when even was come, he went out of the city.

²⁰And in the morning, as they passed by, they saw the fig tree dried up from the roots. ²¹And Peter calling to remembrance saith unto him, 'Master, behold, the fig tree which thou cursedst is withered away'. ²²And Jesus answering saith unto them, 'Have faith in God. ²³For verily I say unto you, that whosoever shall say unto this mountain, "Be thou removed, and be thou cast into the sea", and shall not doubt in his heart, but shall believe that those things which he saith shall come to pass: he shall have whatsoever he saith. ²⁴Therefore I say unto you, what things soever ye desire, when ye pray, believe that ye receive them, and ye shall have them. ²⁵And when ye stand praying, forgive, if ye have aught against any: that your Father also which is in heaven may forgive you your trespasses. ²⁶But if you do not forgive, neither will your Father which is in heaven forgive your trespasses.'

²⁷And they come again to Jerusalem, and as he was walking in the temple, there come to him the chief priests, and the scribes, and the

elders, ²⁸ and say unto him, 'By what authority doest thou these things? and who gave thee this authority to do these things?' ²⁹And Jesus answered and said unto them, 'I will also ask of you one question, and answer me, and I will tell you by what authority I do these things. ³⁰The baptism of John, was it from heaven, or of men? Answer me.' ³¹And they reasoned with themselves, saying, 'If we shall say, "From heaven", he will say, "Why then did ye not believe him?" ³²But if we shall say, "Of men"', they feared the people: for all men counted John, that he was a prophet indeed. ³³And they answered and said unto Jesus, 'We cannot tell'. And Jesus answering saith unto them, 'Neither do I tell you by what authority I do these things'.

12

And he began to speak unto them by parables. 'A certain man planted a vineyard, and set a hedge about it, and dug a place for the wine-vat, and built a tower, and let it out to husbandmen, and went into a far country. ²And at the season he sent to the husbandmen a servant, that he might receive from the husbandmen of the fruit of the vineyard. ³And they caught him, and beat him, and sent him away empty. ⁴And again he sent unto them another servant; and at him they cast stones, and wounded him in the head, and sent him away shamefully handled. ⁵And again he sent another, and him they killed: and many others, beating some, and killing some. ⁶Having yet therefore one son, his well-beloved, he sent him also last unto them, saying, "They will reverence my son". ⁷But those husbandmen said amongst themselves, "This is the heir, come, let us kill him, and the inheritance shall be ours". ⁸And they took him, and killed him, and cast him out of the vineyard. ⁹What shall therefore the lord of the vineyard do? He will come and destroy the husbandmen, and will give the vineyard unto others. ¹⁰And have ye not read this scripture? "The stone which the builders rejected is become the head of the corner: ¹¹this was the Lord's doing, and it is marvellous in our eyes". ¹²And they sought to lay hold on him, but feared the people: for they knew that he had spoken the parable against them: and they left him, and went their way.

¹³And they send unto him certain of the Pharisees and of the Herodians, to catch him in his words. ¹⁴And when they were come, they say unto him, 'Master, we know that thou art true, and carest for no man: for thou regardest not the person of men, but teachest the way of God in truth. Is it lawful to give tribute to Caesar, or not? ¹⁵Shall we give, or shall we not give?' But he, knowing their hypocrisy, said unto them, 'Why tempt ye me? Bring me a penny, that I may see it.' ¹⁶And they brought it. And he saith unto them, 'Whose is this image and superscription?' And they said unto him, 'Caesar's'. ¹⁷And Jesus answering said unto them, 'Render to Caesar the things that are Caesar's, and to God the things that are God's'. And they marvelled at him.

¹⁸Then come unto him the Sadducees, which say there is no resurrection, and they asked him, saying, ¹⁹'Master, Moses wrote unto us, "If a man's brother die, and leave his wife behind him, and leave no children, that his brother should take his wife, and raise up seed unto his brother". ²⁰Now there were seven brethren: and the first took a

wife, and dying left no seed. ²¹And the second took her, and died, neither left he any seed, and the third likewise. ²²And the seven had her, and left no seed: last of all the woman died also. ²³In the resurrection therefore, when they shall rise, whose wife shall she be of them? for the seven had her to wife.' ²⁴And Jesus answering said unto them, 'Do ye not therefore err, because ye know not the scriptures, neither the power of God? ²⁵For when they shall rise from the dead, they neither marry, nor are given in marriage: but are as the angels which are in heaven. ²⁶And as touching the dead, that they rise: have ye not read in the book of Moses, how in the bush God spoke unto him, saying, "I am the God of Abraham, and the God of Isaac, and the God of Jacob"? ²⁷He is not the God of the dead, but the God of the living: ye therefore do greatly err.'

²⁸And one of the scribes came, and having heard them reasoning together, and perceiving that he had answered them well, asked him, 'Which is the first commandment of all?' ²⁹And Jesus answered him, 'The first of all the commandments is, "Hear, O Israel, the Lord our God is one Lord: ³⁰and thou shalt love the Lord thy God with all thy heart, and with all thy soul, and with all thy mind, and with all thy strength": this is the first commandment. ³¹And the second is like, namely this, "Thou shalt love thy neighbour as thyself". There is no other commandment greater than these.' ³²And the scribe said unto him, 'Well, Master, thou hast said the truth: for there is one God, and there is no other but he. ³³And to love him with all the heart, and with all the understanding, and with all the soul, and with all the strength, and to love his neighbour as himself, is more than all whole burnt offerings and sacrifices.' ³⁴And when Jesus saw that he answered discreetly, he said unto him, 'Thou art not far from the kingdom of God'. And no man after that durst ask him any question.

³⁵And Jesus answered and said, while he taught in the temple, 'How say the scribes that Christ is the son of David? ³⁶For David himself said by the Holy Ghost, "The Lord said to my Lord, 'Sit thou on my right hand, till I make thy enemies thy footstool'". ³⁷David therefore himself calleth him Lord, and whence is he then his son?' And the common people heard him gladly.

³⁸And he said unto them in his doctrine, 'Beware of the scribes, which love to go in long clothing, and love salutations in the market-places, ³⁹and the chief seats in the synagogues, and the uppermost rooms at feasts: ⁴⁰which devour widows' houses, and for a pretence make long prayers: these shall receive greater damnation'.

⁴¹And Jesus sat over against the treasury, and beheld how the people cast money into the treasury: and many that were rich cast in much. ⁴²And there came a certain poor widow, and she threw in two mites, which make a farthing. ⁴³And he called unto him his disciples, and saith unto them, 'Verily I say unto you, that this poor widow hath cast more in, than all they which have cast into the treasury. ⁴⁴For all they did cast in of their abundance; but she of her want did cast in all that she had, even all her living.'

13 And as he went out of the temple, one of his disciples saith unto him, 'Master, see what manner of stones and what buildings are here'. ²And Jesus answering said unto him, 'Seest thou these great buildings? there shall not be left one stone upon another, that shall not be thrown down'. ³And as he sat upon the mount of Olives over against the temple, Peter and James and John and Andrew asked him privately, ⁴'Tell us, when shall these things be? And what shall be the sign when all these things shall be fulfilled?' ⁵And Jesus answering them began to say, 'Take heed lest any man deceive you. ⁶For many shall come in my name, saying, "I am Christ": and shall deceive many. ⁷And when ye shall hear of wars and rumours of wars, be ye not troubled: for such things must needs be, but the end shall not be yet. ⁸For nation shall rise against nation, and kingdom against kingdom: and there shall be earthquakes in divers places, and there shall be famines and troubles: these are the beginnings of sorrows.

⁹'But take heed to yourselves: for they shall deliver you up to councils, and in the synagogues ye shall be beaten, and ye shall be brought before rulers and kings for my sake, for a testimony against them. ¹⁰And the gospel must first be published among all nations. ¹¹But when they shall lead you, and deliver you up, take no thought beforehand what ye shall speak, neither do ye premeditate: but whatsoever shall be given you in that hour, that speak ye: for it is not ye that speak, but the Holy Ghost. ¹²Now the brother shall betray the brother to death, and the father the son: and children shall rise up against their parents, and shall cause them to be put to death. ¹³And ye shall be hated of all men for my name's sake: but he that shall endure unto the end, the same shall be saved.

¹⁴'But when ye shall see the abomination of desolation, spoken of by Daniel the prophet, standing where it ought not (let him that readeth understand), then let them that be in Judea flee to the mountains: ¹⁵and let him that is on the house-top not go down into the house, neither enter therein, to take anything out of his house. ¹⁶And let him that is in the field not turn back again for to take up his garment. ¹⁷But woe to them that are with child, and to them that give suck in those days. ¹⁸And pray ye that your flight be not in the winter. ¹⁹For in those days shall be affliction, such as was not from the beginning of the creation which God created unto this time, neither shall be. ²⁰And except that the Lord had shortened those days, no flesh should be saved: but for the elect's sake, whom he hath chosen, he hath shortened the days. ²¹And then if any man shall say to you, "Lo, here is Christ", or, "Lo, he is there": believe him not. ²²For false Christs and false prophets shall rise, and shall show signs and wonders, to seduce, if it were possible, even the elect. ²³But take ye heed: behold, I have foretold you all things.

²⁴'But in those days, after that tribulation, the sun shall be darkened, and the moon shall not give her light. ²⁵And the stars of heaven shall fall, and the powers that are in heaven shall be shaken. ²⁶And then shall they see the Son of man coming in the clouds with great power and glory. ²⁷And then shall he send his angels, and shall gather together his

elect from the four winds, from the uttermost part of the earth to the uttermost part of heaven.

²⁸'Now learn a parable of the fig tree. When her branch is yet tender, and putteth forth leaves, ye know that summer is near: ²⁹so ye in like manner, when ye shall see these things come to pass, know that it is nigh, even at the doors. ³⁰Verily I say unto you, that this generation shall not pass, till all these things be done. ³¹Heaven and earth shall pass away: but my words shall not pass away.

³²'But of that day and that hour knoweth no man, no, not the angels which are in heaven, neither the Son, but the Father. ³³Take ye heed, watch and pray: for ye know not when the time is. ³⁴For the Son of man is as a man taking a far journey, who left his house, and gave authority to his servants, and to every man his work, and commanded the porter to watch. ³⁵Watch ye therefore: for ye know not when the master of the house cometh, at even, or at midnight, or at the cock-crowing, or in the morning: ³⁶lest coming suddenly he find you sleeping. ³⁷And what I say unto you I say unto all, watch.'

14 After two days was the feast of the passover, and of unleavened bread: and the chief priests and the scribes sought how they might take him by craft, and put him to death. ²But they said, 'Not on the feast day, lest there be an uproar of the people'.

³And being in Bethany in the house of Simon the leper, as he sat at meat, there came a woman having an alabaster box of ointment of spikenard very precious, and she broke the box, and poured it on his head. ⁴And there were some that had indignation within themselves, and said, 'Why was this waste of the ointment made? ⁵For it might have been sold for more than three hundred pence, and have been given to the poor.' And they murmured against her. ⁶And Jesus said, 'Let her alone, why trouble you her? She hath wrought a good work on me. ⁷For ye have the poor with you always, and whensoever ye will ye may do them good: but me ye have not always. ⁸She hath done what she could: she is come aforehand to anoint my body to the burying. ⁹Verily I say unto you, wheresoever this gospel shall be preached throughout the whole world, this also that she hath done shall be spoken of for a memorial of her.'

¹⁰And Judas Iscariot, one of the twelve, went unto the chief priests, to betray him unto them. ¹¹And when they heard it, they were glad, and promised to give him money. And he sought how he might conveniently betray him.

¹²And the first day of unleavened bread, when they killed the passover, his disciples said unto him, 'Where wilt thou that we go and prepare that thou mayest eat the passover?' ¹³And he sendeth forth two of his disciples, and saith unto them, 'Go ye into the city, and there shall meet you a man bearing a pitcher of water: follow him. ¹⁴And wheresoever he shall go in, say ye to the goodman of the house, "The Master saith, 'Where is the guest-chamber, where I shall eat the passover with my disciples?'" ¹⁵And he will show you a large upper room furnished and prepared: there make ready for us.' ¹⁶And his disciples went forth,

and came into the city, and found as he had said unto them: and they made ready the passover.

¹⁷And in the evening he cometh with the twelve. ¹⁸And as they sat and did eat, Jesus said, 'Verily I say unto you, one of you which eateth with me shall betray me'. ¹⁹And they began to be sorrowful, and to say unto him one by one, 'Is it I?' And another said, 'Is it I?' ²⁰And he answered and said unto them, 'It is one of the twelve, that dippeth with me in the dish. ²¹The Son of man indeed goeth, as it is written of him: but woe to that man by whom the Son of man is betrayed: good were it for that man if he had never been born.'

²²And as they did eat, Jesus took bread, and blessed, and broke it, and gave to them, and said, 'Take, eat: this is my body'. ²³And he took the cup, and when he had given thanks, he gave it to them: and they all drank of it. ²⁴And he said unto them, 'This is my blood of the new testament, which is shed for many. ²⁵Verily I say unto you, I will drink no more of the fruit of the vine, until that day that I drink it new in the kingdom of God.'

²⁶And when they had sung a hymn, they went out into the mount of Olives. ²⁷And Jesus saith unto them, 'All ye shall be offended because of me this night: for it is written, "I will smite the shepherd, and the sheep shall be scattered". ²⁸But after that I am risen, I will go before you into Galilee.' ²⁹But Peter said unto him, 'Although all shall be offended, yet will not I'. ³⁰And Jesus saith unto him, 'Verily I say unto thee, that this day, even in this night, before the cock crow twice, thou shalt deny me thrice'. ³¹But he spoke the more vehemently, 'If I should die with thee, I will not deny thee in any wise'. Likewise also said they all.

³²And they came to a place which was named Gethsemane: and he saith to his disciples, 'Sit ye here, while I shall pray'. ³³And he taketh with him Peter and James and John, and began to be sore amazed, and to be very heavy, ³⁴and saith unto them, 'My soul is exceeding sorrowful unto death: tarry ye here, and watch'. ³⁵And he went forward a little, and fell on the ground, and prayed that, if it were possible, the hour might pass from him. ³⁶And he said, 'Abba, Father, all things are possible unto thee, take away this cup from me: nevertheless not that I will, but what thou wilt'.

³⁷And he cometh, and findeth them sleeping, and saith unto Peter, 'Simon, sleepest thou? Couldst not thou watch one hour? ³⁸Watch ye and pray, lest ye enter into temptation: the spirit truly is ready, but the flesh is weak.'

³⁹And again he went away, and prayed, and spoke the same words. ⁴⁰And when he returned, he found them asleep again (for their eyes were heavy), neither wist they what to answer him. ⁴¹And he cometh the third time, and saith unto them, 'Sleep on now, and take your rest: it is enough, the hour is come, behold, the Son of man is betrayed into the hands of sinners. ⁴²Rise up, let us go, lo, he that betrayeth me is at hand.'

⁴³And immediately, while he yet spoke, cometh Judas, one of the twelve, and with him a great multitude with swords and staves, from

the chief priests and the scribes and the elders. ⁴⁴And he that betrayed him had given them a token, saying, 'Whomsoever I shall kiss, that same is he; take him, and lead him away safely'. ⁴⁵And as soon as he was come, he goeth straightway to him, and saith, 'Master, master', and kissed him.

⁴⁶And they laid their hands on him, and took him. ⁴⁷And one of them that stood by drew a sword, and smote a servant of the high priest, and cut off his ear. ⁴⁸And Jesus answered and said unto them, 'Are ye come out, as against a thief, with swords and with staves to take me? ⁴⁹I was daily with you in the temple teaching, and ye took me not; but the scriptures must be fulfilled.' ⁵⁰And they all forsook him, and fled. ⁵¹And there followed him a certain young man, having a linen cloth cast about his naked body, and the young men laid hold on him: ⁵²and he left the linen cloth, and fled from them naked.

⁵³And they led Jesus away to the high priest, and with him were assembled all the chief priests and the elders and the scribes. ⁵⁴And Peter followed him afar off, even into the palace of the high priest: and he sat with the servants, and warmed himself at the fire.

⁵⁵And the chief priests and all the council sought for witness against Jesus to put him to death, and found none. ⁵⁶For many bore false witness against him, but their witness agreed not together. ⁵⁷And there arose certain, and bore false witness against him, saying, ⁵⁸'We heard him say, I will destroy this temple that is made with hands, and within three days I will build another made without hands'. ⁵⁹But neither so did their witness agree together.

⁶⁰And the high priest stood up in the midst, and asked Jesus, saying, 'Answerest thou nothing? What is it which these witness against thee?' ⁶¹But he held his peace, and answered nothing. Again the high priest asked him, and said unto him, 'Art thou the Christ, the Son of the Blessed?' ⁶²And Jesus said, 'I am: and ye shall see the Son of man sitting on the right hand of power, and coming in the clouds of heaven'. ⁶³Then the high priest rent his clothes, and saith, 'What need we any further witnesses? ⁶⁴Ye have heard the blasphemy: what think ye?' And they all condemned him to be guilty of death. ⁶⁵And some began to spit on him, and to cover his face, and to buffet him, and to say unto him, 'Prophesy': and the servants did strike him with the palms of their hands.

⁶⁶And as Peter was beneath in the palace, there cometh one of the maids of the high priest. ⁶⁷And when she saw Peter warming himself, she looked upon him, and said, 'And thou also wast with Jesus of Nazareth'. ⁶⁸But he denied, saying, 'I know not, neither understand I what thou sayest'. And he went out into the porch, and the cock crew. ⁶⁹And a maid saw him again, and began to say to them that stood by, 'This is one of them'. ⁷⁰And he denied it again. And a little after, they that stood by said again to Peter, 'Surely thou art one of them: for thou art a Galilean, and thy speech agreeth thereto'. ⁷¹But he began to curse and to swear, saying, 'I know not this man of whom ye speak'. ⁷²And the second time the cock crew. And Peter called to mind the word that

Jesus said unto him, 'Before the cock crow twice, thou shalt deny me thrice'. And when he thought thereon, he wept.

15 And straightway in the morning the chief priests held a consultation with the elders and scribes and the whole council, and bound Jesus, and carried him away, and delivered him to Pilate. ²And Pilate asked him, 'Art thou the King of the Jews?' And he answering said unto him, 'Thou sayest it'. ³And the chief priests accused him of many things: but he answered nothing. ⁴And Pilate asked him again, saying, 'Answerest thou nothing? behold how many things they witness against thee'. ⁵But Jesus yet answered nothing, so that Pilate marvelled.

⁶Now at that feast he released unto them one prisoner, whomsoever they desired. ⁷And there was one named Barabbas, which lay bound with them that had made insurrection with him, who had committed murder in the insurrection. ⁸And the multitude crying aloud began to desire him to do as he had ever done unto them. ⁹But Pilate answered them, saying, 'Will ye that I release unto you the King of the Jews?' ¹⁰For he knew that the chief priests had delivered him for envy. ¹¹But the chief priests moved the people, that he should rather release Barabbas unto them. ¹²And Pilate answered and said again unto them, 'What will ye then that I shall do unto him whom ye call the King of the Jews?' ¹³And they cried out again, 'Crucify him'. ¹⁴Then Pilate said unto them, 'Why, what evil hath he done?' And they cried out the more exceedingly, 'Crucify him'. ¹⁵And so Pilate, willing to content the people, released Barabbas unto them, and delivered Jesus, when he had scourged him, to be crucified.

¹⁶And the soldiers led him away into the hall, called Praetorium, and they call together the whole band. ¹⁷And they clothed him with purple, and plaited a crown of thorns, and put it about his head, ¹⁸and began to salute him, 'Hail, King of the Jews'. ¹⁹And they smote him on the head with a reed, and did spit upon him, and bowing their knees worshipped him. ²⁰And when they had mocked him, they took off the purple from him, and put his own clothes on him, and led him out to crucify him. ²¹And they compel one Simon a Cyrenian, who passed by, coming out of the country, the father of Alexander and Rufus, to bear his cross.

²²And they bring him unto the place Golgotha, which is, being interpreted, the place of a skull. ²³And they gave him to drink wine mingled with myrrh: but he received it not. ²⁴And when they had crucified him, they parted his garments, casting lots upon them, what every man should take. ²⁵And it was the third hour, and they crucified him. ²⁶And the superscription of his accusation was written over, 'THE KING OF THE JEWS'. ²⁷And with him they crucify two thieves, the one on his right hand, and the other on his left. ²⁸And the scripture was fulfilled, which saith, 'And he was numbered with the transgressors'.

²⁹And they that passed by railed on him, wagging their heads, and saying, 'Ah, thou that destroyest the temple, and buildest it in three days, ³⁰save thyself, and come down from the cross'. ³¹Likewise also the chief priests mocking said among themselves with the scribes, 'He saved others, himself he cannot save. ³²Let Christ the King of Israel descend now

from the cross, that we may see and believe.' And they that were crucified with him reviled him.

[33]And when the sixth hour was come, there was darkness over the
whole land until the ninth hour. [34]And at the ninth hour Jesus cried
with a loud voice, saying, 'Eloi, Eloi, lama sabachthani?' which is, being
interpreted, 'My God, my God, why hast thou forsaken me?' [35]And some
of them that stood by, when they heard it, said, 'Behold, he calleth
Elias'. [36]And one ran and filled a sponge full of vinegar, and put it on a
reed, and gave him to drink, saying, 'Let alone, let us see whether Elias
will come to take him down'. [37]And Jesus cried with a loud voice, and
gave up the ghost. [38]And the veil of the temple was rent in twain from
the top to the bottom. [39]And when the centurion, which stood over
against him, saw that he so cried out, and gave up the ghost, he said,
'Truly this man was the Son of God'.

[40]There were also women looking on afar off, among whom was Mary
Magdalene, and Mary the mother of James the less and of Joses, and
Salome: [41]who also, when he was in Galilee, followed him, and minis-
tered unto him, and many other women which came up with him unto
Jerusalem.

[42]And now when the even was come, because it was the preparation,
that is, the day before the sabbath, [43]Joseph of Arimathaea, an honourable counsellor, which also waited for the kingdom of God, came,
and went in boldly unto Pilate, and craved the body of Jesus. [44]And
Pilate marvelled if he were already dead, and calling unto him the centurion, he asked him whether he had been any while dead. [45]And when
he knew it of the centurion, he gave the body to Joseph. [46]And he
bought fine linen, and took him down, and wrapped him in the linen,
and laid him in a sepulchre which was hewn out of a rock, and rolled a
stone unto the door of the sepulchre. [47]And Mary Magdalene and Mary
the mother of Joses beheld where he was laid.

16 And when the sabbath was past, Mary Magdalene, and Mary the
mother of James, and Salome, had bought sweet spices, that
they might come and anoint him. [2]And very early in the morning the
first day of the week, they came unto the sepulchre at the rising of the
sun. [3]And they said among themselves, 'Who shall roll us away the
stone from the door of the sepulchre?' [4]And when they looked, they saw
that the stone was rolled away: for it was very great. [5]And entering into
the sepulchre, they saw a young man sitting on the right side, clothed
in a long white garment, and they were affrighted. [6]And he saith unto
them, 'Be not affrighted; ye seek Jesus of Nazareth, which was crucified: he is risen, he is not here: behold the place where they laid him.
[7]But go your way, tell his disciples and Peter that he goeth before you
into Galilee: there shall ye see him, as he said unto you.' [8]And they went
out quickly, and fled from the sepulchre, for they trembled and were
amazed, neither said they any thing to any man, for they were afraid.

[9]Now when Jesus was risen early the first day of the week, he appeared
first to Mary Magdalene, out of whom he had cast seven devils. [10]And
she went and told them that had been with him, as they mourned and

wept. [11]And they, when they had heard that he was alive, and had been seen of her, believed not.

[12]After that he appeared in another form unto two of them, as they walked, and went into the country. [13]And they went and told it unto the residue, neither believed they them.

[14]Afterward he appeared unto the eleven as they sat at meat, and upbraided them with their unbelief and hardness of heart, because they believed not them which had seen him after he was risen. [15]And he said unto them, 'Go ye into all the world, and preach the gospel to every creature. [16]He that believeth and is baptized shall be saved, but he that believeth not shall be damned. [17]And these signs shall follow them that believe, in my name shall they cast out devils, they shall speak with new tongues, [18]they shall take up serpents, and if they drink any deadly thing, it shall not hurt them, they shall lay hands on the sick, and they shall recover.'

[19]So then after the Lord had spoken unto them, he was received up into heaven, and sat on the right hand of God. [20]And they went forth, and preached everywhere, the Lord working with them, and confirming the word with signs following. Amen.

THE GOSPEL ACCORDING TO
SAINT LUKE

1 Forasmuch as many have taken in hand to set forth in order a declaration of those things which are most surely believed among us, [2]even as they delivered them unto us, which from the beginning were eyewitnesses, and ministers of the word: [3]it seemed good to me also, having had perfect understanding of things from the very first, to write unto thee in order, most excellent Theophilus, [4]that thou mightest know the certainty of those things wherein thou hast been instructed.

[5]There was in the days of Herod, the king of Judea, a certain priest named Zacharias, of the course of Abia, and his wife was of the daughters of Aaron, and her name was Elizabeth. [6]And they were both righteous before God, walking in all the commandments and ordinances of the Lord blameless. [7]And they had no child, because that Elizabeth was barren, and they both were now well stricken in years. [8]And it came to pass that while he executed the priest's office before God in the order of his course, [9]according to the custom of the priest's office, his lot was to burn incense when he went into the temple of the Lord. [10]And the whole multitude of the people were praying without at the time of incense. [11]And there appeared unto him an angel of the Lord standing on the right side of the altar of incense. [12]And when Zacharias saw him, he was troubled, and fear fell upon him. [13]But the angel said unto him, 'Fear not, Zacharias, for thy prayer is heard, and thy wife Elizabeth shall bear thee a son, and thou shalt call his name John. [14]And thou shalt have joy and gladness, and many shall rejoice at his birth: [15]for he shall be great in the sight of the Lord, and shall drink neither wine nor strong drink, and he shall be filled with the Holy Ghost, even from his mother's womb. [16]And many of the children of Israel shall he turn to the Lord their God. [17]And he shall go before him in the spirit and power of Elias, to turn the hearts of the fathers to the children, and the disobedient to the wisdom of the just, to make ready a people prepared for the Lord.'

[18]And Zacharias said unto the angel, 'Whereby shall I know this? For I am an old man, and my wife well stricken in years.' [19]And the angel answering said unto him, 'I am Gabriel that stand in the presence of God, and am sent to speak unto thee, and to show thee these glad tidings. [20]And behold, thou shalt be dumb, and not able to speak, until the day that these things shall be performed, because thou believest not my words, which shall be fulfilled in their season.'

[21]And the people waited for Zacharias, and marvelled that he tarried so long in the temple. [22]And when he came out, he could not speak unto them: and they perceived that he had seen a vision in the temple: for he beckoned unto them, and remained speechless. [23]And it came to pass that as soon as the days of his ministration were accomplished, he departed to his own house.

²⁴And after those days his wife Elizabeth conceived, and hid herself five months, saying, ²⁵'Thus hath the Lord dealt with me in the days wherein he looked on me, to take away my reproach among men'.

²⁶And in the sixth month the angel Gabriel was sent from God unto a city of Galilee, named Nazareth, ²⁷to a virgin espoused to a man whose name was Joseph, of the house of David, and the virgin's name was Mary. ²⁸And the angel came in unto her, and said, 'Hail, thou that art highly favoured, the Lord is with thee: blessed art thou among women'. ²⁹And when she saw him, she was troubled at his saying, and cast in her mind what manner of salutation this should be. ³⁰And the angel said unto her, 'Fear not, Mary, for thou hast found favour with God. ³¹And behold, thou shalt conceive in thy womb, and bring forth a son, and shalt call his name Jesus. ³²He shall be great, and shall be called the Son of the Highest, and the Lord God shall give unto him the throne of his father David. ³³And he shall reign over the house of Jacob for ever, and of his kingdom there shall be no end.'

³⁴Then said Mary unto the angel, 'How shall this be, seeing I know not a man?' ³⁵And the angel answered and said unto her, 'The Holy Ghost shall come upon thee, and the power of the Highest shall overshadow thee. Therefore also that holy thing which shall be born of thee shall be called the Son of God. ³⁶And behold, thy cousin Elizabeth, she hath also conceived a son in her old age, and this is the sixth month with her, who was called barren. ³⁷For with God nothing shall be impossible.' ³⁸And Mary said, 'Behold the handmaid of the Lord, be it unto me according to thy word'. And the angel departed from her.

³⁹And Mary arose in those days, and went into the hill-country with haste, into a city of Juda, ⁴⁰and entered into the house of Zacharias, and saluted Elizabeth. ⁴¹And it came to pass that when Elizabeth heard the salutation of Mary, the babe leapt in her womb, and Elizabeth was filled with the Holy Ghost. ⁴²And she spoke out with a loud voice, and said, 'Blessed art thou among women, and blessed is the fruit of thy womb. ⁴³And whence is this to me, that the mother of my Lord should come to me? ⁴⁴For lo, as soon as the voice of thy salutation sounded in my ears, the babe leapt in my womb for joy. ⁴⁵And blessed is she that believed, for there shall be a performance of those things which were told her from the Lord.'

⁴⁶And Mary said,

'My soul doth magnify the Lord,
⁴⁷ and my spirit hath rejoiced in God my Saviour.
⁴⁸ For he hath regarded the low estate of his handmaiden:
  for behold, from henceforth all generations shall call me blessed.
⁴⁹ For he that is mighty hath done to me great things,
  and holy is his name.
⁵⁰ And his mercy is on them that fear him
  from generation to generation.
⁵¹ He hath shown strength with his arm,
  he hath scattered the proud in the imagination of their hearts.

⁵² He hath put down the mighty from their seats,
and exalted them of low degree.
⁵³ He hath filled the hungry with good things,
and the rich he hath sent empty away.
⁵⁴ He hath helped his servant Israel,
in remembrance of his mercy,
⁵⁵ as he spoke to our fathers,
to Abraham, and to his seed for ever.'

⁵⁶And Mary abode with her about three months, and returned to her own house.

⁵⁷Now Elizabeth's full time came that she should be delivered, and she brought forth a son. ⁵⁸And her neighbours and her cousins heard how the Lord had shown great mercy upon her, and they rejoiced with her. ⁵⁹And it came to pass that on the eighth day they came to circumcise the child, and they called him Zacharias, after the name of his father. ⁶⁰And his mother answered and said, 'Not so, but he shall be called John'. ⁶¹And they said unto her, 'There is none of thy kindred that is called by this name'. ⁶²And they made signs to his father, how he would have him called. ⁶³And he asked for a writing-tablet, and wrote, saying, 'His name is John'. And they marvelled all. ⁶⁴And his mouth was opened immediately, and his tongue loosed, and he spoke, and praised God.

⁶⁵And fear came on all that dwelt round about them, and all these sayings were noised abroad throughout all the hill-country of Judea. ⁶⁶And all they that heard them laid them up in their hearts, saying, 'What manner of child shall this be?' And the hand of the Lord was with him.

⁶⁷And his father Zacharias was filled with the Holy Ghost, and prophesied, saying,

⁶⁸ 'Blessed be the Lord God of Israel,
for he hath visited and redeemed his people,
⁶⁹ and hath raised up a horn of salvation for us
in the house of his servant David,
⁷⁰ as he spoke by the mouth of his holy prophets,
which have been since the world began:
⁷¹ that we should be saved from our enemies,
and from the hand of all that hate us,
⁷² to perform the mercy promised to our fathers,
and to remember his holy covenant,
⁷³ the oath which he swore to our father Abraham,
⁷⁴ that he would grant unto us,
that we being delivered out of the hands of our enemies
might serve him without fear,
⁷⁵ in holiness and righteousness before him,
all the days of our life.

⁷⁶ 'And then thou, child, shalt be called the Prophet of the Highest:
for thou shalt go before the face of the Lord to prepare his ways,

⁷⁷ to give knowledge of salvation unto his people
by the remission of their sins,
⁷⁸ through the tender mercy of our God,
whereby the day-spring from on high hath visited us,
⁷⁹ to give light to them that sit in darkness and in the shadow of
death,
to guide our feet into the way of peace.'

⁸⁰And the child grew, and waxed strong in spirit, and was in the deserts till the day of his showing unto Israel.

2 And it came to pass in those days that there went out a decree from Caesar Augustus, that all the world should be taxed. ²(And this taxing was first made when Cyrenius was governor of Syria.) ³And all went to be taxed, every one into his own city. ⁴And Joseph also went up from Galilee, out of the city of Nazareth, into Judea, unto the city of David, which is called Bethlehem (because he was of the house and lineage of David), ⁵to be taxed with Mary his espoused wife, being great with child.

⁶And so it was, that, while they were there, the days were accomplished that she should be delivered. ⁷And she brought forth her first-born son, and wrapped him in swaddling-clothes, and laid him in a manger, because there was no room for them in the inn.

⁸And there were in the same country shepherds abiding in the field, keeping watch over their flock by night. ⁹And lo, the angel of the Lord came upon them, and the glory of the Lord shone round about them, and they were sore afraid. ¹⁰And the angel said unto them, 'Fear not: for behold, I bring you good tidings of great joy, which shall be to all people. ¹¹For unto you is born this day in the city of David a Saviour, which is Christ the Lord. ¹²And this shall be a sign unto you; ye shall find the babe wrapped in swaddling-clothes, lying in a manger.' ¹³And suddenly there was with the angel a multitude of the heavenly host praising God, and saying, ¹⁴'Glory to God in the highest, and on earth peace, good will towards men'.

¹⁵And it came to pass, as the angels were gone away from them into heaven, the shepherds said one to another, 'Let us now go even unto Bethlehem, and see this thing which is come to pass, which the Lord hath made known unto us'. ¹⁶And they came with haste, and found Mary, and Joseph, and the babe lying in a manger. ¹⁷And when they had seen it, they made known abroad the saying which was told them concerning this child. ¹⁸And all they that heard it wondered at those things which were told them by the shepherds. ¹⁹But Mary kept all these things, and pondered them in her heart. ²⁰And the shepherds returned, glorifying and praising God for all the things that they had heard and seen, as it was told unto them.

²¹And when eight days were accomplished for the circumcising of the child, his name was called Jesus, which was so named of the angel before he was conceived in the womb.

²²And when the days of her purification according to the law of

Moses were accomplished, they brought him to Jerusalem, to present him to the Lord [23](as it is written in the law of the Lord, 'Every male that openeth the womb shall be called holy to the Lord'), [24]and to offer a sacrifice according to that which is said in the law of the Lord, 'A pair of turtle doves, or two young pigeons'. [25]And behold, there was a man in Jerusalem, whose name was Simeon, and the same man was just and devout, waiting for the consolation of Israel: and the Holy Ghost was upon him. [26]And it was revealed unto him by the Holy Ghost, that he should not see death, before he had seen the Lord's Christ. [27]And he came by the Spirit into the temple: and when the parents brought in the child Jesus, to do for him after the custom of the law, [28]then took he him up in his arms, and blessed God, and said,

[29] 'Lord, now lettest thou thy servant depart in peace,
    according to thy word.
[30] For my eyes have seen thy salvation,
[31] which thou hast prepared before the face of all people;
[32] a light to lighten the Gentiles,
    and the glory of thy people Israel.'

[33]And Joseph and his mother marvelled at those things which were spoken of him. [34]And Simeon blessed them, and said unto Mary his mother, 'Behold, this child is set for the fall and rising again of many in Israel: and for a sign which shall be spoken against [35](yea, a sword shall pierce through thy own soul also), that the thoughts of many hearts may be revealed'.

[36]And there was one Anna, a prophetess, the daughter of Phanuel, of the tribe of Aser; she was of a great age, and had lived with a husband seven years from her virginity. [37]And she was a widow of about fourscore and four years, which departed not from the temple, but served God with fastings and prayers night and day. [38]And she coming in that instant gave thanks likewise unto the Lord, and spoke of him to all them that looked for redemption in Jerusalem. [39]And when they had performed all things according to the law of the Lord, they returned into Galilee, to their own city Nazareth. [40]And the child grew, and waxed strong in spirit, filled with wisdom, and the grace of God was upon him.

[41]Now his parents went to Jerusalem every year at the feast of the passover. [42]And when he was twelve years old, they went up to Jerusalem after the custom of the feast. [43]And when they had fulfilled the days, as they returned, the child Jesus tarried behind in Jerusalem, and Joseph and his mother knew not of it. [44]But they, supposing him to have been in the company, went a day's journey, and they sought him among their kinsfolk and acquaintance. [45]And when they found him not, they turned back again to Jerusalem, seeking him. [46]And it came to pass that after three days they found him in the temple, sitting in the midst of the doctors, both hearing them, and asking them questions. [47]And all that heard him were astonished at his understanding and

answers. ⁴⁸And when they saw him, they were amazed: and his mother said unto him, 'Son, why hast thou thus dealt with us? Behold, thy father and I have sought thee sorrowing.' ⁴⁹And he said unto them, 'How is it that ye sought me? Wist ye not that I must be about my Father's business?' ⁵⁰And they understood not the saying which he spoke unto them. ⁵¹And he went down with them, and came to Nazareth, and was subject unto them: but his mother kept all these sayings in her heart. ⁵²And Jesus increased in wisdom and stature, and in favour with God and man.

3 Now in the fifteenth year of the reign of Tiberius Caesar, Pontius Pilate being governor of Judea, and Herod being tetrarch of Galilee, and his brother Philip tetrarch of Ituraea and of the region of Trachonitis, and Lysanias the tetrarch of Abilene, ²Annas and Caiaphas being the high priests, the word of God came unto John the son of Zacharias in the wilderness. ³And he came into all the country about Jordan, preaching the baptism of repentance for the remission of sins, ⁴as it is written in the book of the words of Esaias the prophet, saying, 'The voice of one crying in the wilderness, "Prepare ye the way of the Lord, make his paths straight. ⁵Every valley shall be filled, and every mountain and hill shall be brought low, and the crooked shall be made straight, and the rough ways shall be made smooth. ⁶And all flesh shall see the salvation of God."'

⁷Then said he to the multitude that came forth to be baptized of him, 'O generation of vipers, who hath warned you to flee from the wrath to come? ⁸Bring forth therefore fruits worthy of repentance, and begin not to say within yourselves, "We have Abraham to our father": for I say unto you, that God is able of these stones to raise up children unto Abraham. ⁹And now also the axe is laid unto the root of the trees: every tree therefore which bringeth not forth good fruit is hewn down, and cast into the fire.'

¹⁰And the people asked him, saying, 'What shall we do then?' ¹¹He answereth and saith unto them, 'He that hath two coats, let him impart to him that hath none, and he that hath meat, let him do likewise'. ¹²Then came also publicans to be baptized, and said unto him, 'Master, what shall we do?' ¹³And he said unto them, 'Exact no more than that which is appointed you'. ¹⁴And the soldiers likewise demanded of him, saying, 'And what shall we do?' And he said unto them, 'Do violence to no man, neither accuse any falsely, and be content with your wages'.

¹⁵And as the people were in expectation, and all men mused in their hearts of John, whether he were the Christ, or not: ¹⁶John answered, saying unto them all, 'I indeed baptize you with water, but one mightier than I cometh, the latchet of whose shoes I am not worthy to unloose: he shall baptize you with the Holy Ghost and with fire: ¹⁷whose fan is in his hand, and he will thoroughly purge his floor, and will gather the wheat into his garner, but the chaff he will burn with fire unquenchable'.

¹⁸And many other things in his exhortation preached he unto the

people. ¹⁹But Herod the tetrarch, being reproved by him for Herodias his brother Philip's wife, and for all the evils which Herod had done, ²⁰added yet this above all, that he shut up John in prison.

²¹Now when all the people were baptized, it came to pass that Jesus also being baptized, and praying, the heaven was opened, ²²and the Holy Ghost descended in a bodily shape like a dove upon him, and a voice came from heaven, which said, 'Thou art my beloved Son, in thee I am well pleased'.

²³And Jesus himself began to be about thirty years of age, being (as was supposed) the son of Joseph, which was the son of Heli, ²⁴which was the son of Matthat, which was the son of Levi, which was the son of Melchi, which was the son of Janna, which was the son of Joseph, ²⁵which was the son of Mattathias, which was the son of Amos, which was the son of Naum, which was the son of Esli, which was the son of Nagge, ²⁶which was the son of Maath, which was the son of Mattathias, which was the son of Semei, which was the son of Joseph, which was the son of Juda ²⁷which was the son of Joanna, which was the son of Rhesa, which was the son of Zorobabel, which was the son of Salathiel, which was the son of Neri, ²⁸which was the son of Melchi, which was the son of Addi, which was the son of Cosam, which was the son of Elmodam, which was the son of Er, ²⁹which was the son of Jose, which was the son of Eliezer, which was the son of Jorim, which was the son of Matthat, which was the son of Levi, ³⁰which was the son of Simeon, which was the son of Juda, which was the son of Joseph, which was the son of Jonan, which was the son of Eliakim, ³¹which was the son of Melea, which was the son of Menan, which was the son of Mattatha, which was the son of Nathan, which was the son of David, ³²which was the son of Jesse, which was the son of Obed, which was the son of Booz, which was the son of Salmon, which was the son of Naasson, ³³which was the son of Aminadab, which was the son of Aram, which was the son of Esrom, which was the son of Phares, which was the son of Juda, ³⁴which was the son of Jacob, which was the son of Isaac, which was the son of Abraham, which was the son of Thara, which was the son of Nachor, ³⁵which was the son of Saruch, which was the son of Ragau, which was the son of Phalec, which was the son of Heber, which was the son of Sala, ³⁶which was the son of Cainan, which was the son of Arphaxad, which was the son of Sem, which was the son of Noe, which was the son of Lamech, ³⁷which was the son of Mathusala, which was the son of Enoch, which was the son of Jared, which was the son of Maleleel, which was the son of Cainan, ³⁸which was the son of Enos, which was the son of Seth, which was the son of Adam, which was the son of God.

4 And Jesus being full of the Holy Ghost returned from Jordan, and was led by the Spirit into the wilderness, ²being forty days tempted of the devil. And in those days he did eat nothing: and when they were ended, he afterward hungered. ³And the devil said unto him, 'If thou be the Son of God, command this stone that it be made bread'. ⁴And Jesus answered him, saying, 'It is written, that man shall not live by bread alone, but by every word of God'.

⁵And the devil, taking him up into a high mountain, showed unto him all the kingdoms of the world in a moment of time. ⁶And the devil said unto him, 'All this power will I give thee, and the glory of them; for that is delivered unto me; and to whomsoever I will I give it. ⁷If thou therefore wilt worship me, all shall be thine.' ⁸And Jesus answered and said unto him, 'Get thee behind me, Satan: for it is written, "Thou shalt worship the Lord thy God, and him only shalt thou serve"'.

⁹And he brought him to Jerusalem, and set him on a pinnacle of the temple, and said unto him, 'If thou be the Son of God, cast thyself down from hence. ¹⁰For it is written, "He shall give his angels charge over thee, to keep thee. ¹¹And in their hands they shall bear thee up, lest at any time thou dash thy foot against a stone."' ¹²And Jesus answering said unto him, 'It is said, "Thou shalt not tempt the Lord thy God"'. ¹³And when the devil had ended all the temptation, he departed from him for a season.

¹⁴And Jesus returned in the power of the Spirit into Galilee, and there went out a fame of him through all the region round about. ¹⁵And he taught in their synagogues, being glorified of all.

¹⁶And he came to Nazareth, where he had been brought up, and, as his custom was, he went into the synagogue on the sabbath day, and stood up for to read. ¹⁷And there was delivered unto him the book of the prophet Esaias. And when he had opened the book, he found the place where it was written, ¹⁸'The Spirit of the Lord is upon me, because he hath anointed me to preach the gospel to the poor, he hath sent me to heal the broken-hearted, to preach deliverance to the captives, and recovering of sight to the blind, to set at liberty them that are bruised, ¹⁹to preach the acceptable year of the Lord'. ²⁰And he closed the book, and he gave it again to the minister, and sat down. And the eyes of all them that were in the synagogue were fastened on him.

²¹And he began to say unto them, 'This day is this scripture fulfilled in your ears'. ²²And all bore him witness, and wondered at the gracious words which proceeded out of his mouth. And they said, 'Is not this Joseph's son?' ²³And he said unto them, 'Ye will surely say unto me this proverb, "Physician, heal thyself": whatsoever we have heard done in Capernaum, do also here in thy country'. ²⁴And he said, 'Verily I say unto you, no prophet is accepted in his own country. ²⁵But I tell you of a truth, many widows were in Israel in the days of Elias, when the heaven was shut up three years and six months, when great famine was throughout all the land: ²⁶but unto none of them was Elias sent, save unto Sarepta, a city of Sidon, unto a woman that was a widow. ²⁷And many lepers were in Israel in the time of Eliseus the prophet: and none of them was cleansed, saving Naaman the Syrian.'

²⁸And all they in the synagogue, when they heard these things, were filled with wrath, ²⁹and rose up, and thrust him out of the city, and led him unto the brow of the hill whereon their city was built, that they might cast him down headlong. ³⁰But he passing through the midst of them went his way, ³¹and came down to Capernaum, a city of Galilee, and taught them on the sabbath days. ³²And they were astonished at his doctrine: for his word was with power.

³³And in the synagogue there was a man, which had a spirit of an unclean devil, and cried out with a loud voice, ³⁴saying, 'Let us alone, what have we to do with thee, thou Jesus of Nazareth? art thou come to destroy us? I know thee who thou art, the Holy One of God'. ³⁵And Jesus rebuked him, saying, 'Hold thy peace, and come out of him'. And when the devil had thrown him in the midst, he came out of him, and hurt him not. ³⁶And they were all amazed, and spoke among themselves, saying, 'What a word is this? for with authority and power he commandeth the unclean spirits, and they come out'. ³⁷And the fame of him went out into every place of the country round about.

³⁸And he arose out of the synagogue, and entered into Simon's house: and Simon's wife's mother was taken with a great fever, and they besought him for her. ³⁹And he stood over her, and rebuked the fever, and it left her. And immediately she arose and ministered unto them.

⁴⁰Now when the sun was setting, all they that had any sick with divers diseases brought them unto him: and he laid his hands on every one of them, and healed them. ⁴¹And devils also came out of many, crying out, and saying, 'Thou art Christ the Son of God'. And he rebuking them, suffered them not to speak: for they knew that he was Christ.

⁴²And when it was day, he departed and went into a desert place: and the people sought him, and came unto him, and stayed him, that he should not depart from them. ⁴³And he said unto them, 'I must preach the kingdom of God to other cities also: for therefore am I sent'. ⁴⁴And he preached in the synagogues of Galilee.

5 And it came to pass that as the people pressed upon him to hear the word of God, he stood by the lake of Gennesaret, ²and saw two ships standing by the lake: but the fishermen were gone out of them, and were washing their nets. ³And he entered into one of the ships, which was Simon's, and prayed him that he would thrust out a little from the land: and he sat down, and taught the people out of the ship. ⁴Now when he had left speaking, he said unto Simon, 'Launch out into the deep, and let down your nets for a draught'. ⁵And Simon answering said unto him, 'Master, we have toiled all the night, and have taken nothing: nevertheless at thy word I will let down the net'. ⁶And when they had this done, they enclosed a great multitude of fishes, and their net broke: ⁷and they beckoned unto their partners, which were in the other ship, that they should come and help them. And they came, and filled both the ships, so that they began to sink. ⁸When Simon Peter saw it, he fell down at Jesus' knees, saying, 'Depart from me, for I am a sinful man, O Lord'. ⁹For he was astonished, and all that were with him, at the draught of the fishes which they had taken. ¹⁰And so was also James, and John, the sons of Zebedee, which were partners with Simon. And Jesus said unto Simon, 'Fear not, from henceforth thou shalt catch men'. ¹¹And when they had brought their ships to land, they forsook all, and followed him.

¹²And it came to pass, when he was in a certain city, behold a man full of leprosy: who seeing Jesus, fell on his face, and besought him, saying,

'Lord, if thou wilt, thou canst make me clean'. ¹³And he put forth his hand, and touched him, saying, 'I will: be thou clean'. And immediately the leprosy departed from him. ¹⁴And he charged him to tell no man: but 'Go, and show thyself to the priest, and offer for thy cleansing, according as Moses commanded, for a testimony unto them'. ¹⁵But so much the more went there a fame abroad of him, and great multitudes came together to hear, and to be healed by him of their infirmities. ¹⁶And he withdrew himself into the wilderness, and prayed.

¹⁷And it came to pass on a certain day, as he was teaching, that there were Pharisees and doctors of the law sitting by, which were come out of every town of Galilee, and Judea, and Jerusalem: and the power of the Lord was present to heal them. ¹⁸And behold, men brought in a bed a man which was taken with a palsy: and they sought means to bring him in, and to lay him before him. ¹⁹And when they could not find by what way they might bring him in because of the multitude, they went upon the house-top, and let him down through the tiling with his couch into the midst before Jesus. ²⁰And when he saw their faith, he said unto him, 'Man, thy sins are forgiven thee'.

²¹And the scribes and the Pharisees began to reason, saying, 'Who is this which speaketh blasphemies? Who can forgive sins, but God alone?' ²²But when Jesus perceived their thoughts, he answering said unto them, 'What reason ye in your hearts? ²³Whether is easier to say, "Thy sins be forgiven thee": or to say, "Rise up and walk?" ²⁴But that ye may know that the Son of man hath power upon earth to forgive sins' (he said unto the sick of the palsy), 'I say unto thee, arise, and take up thy couch, and go into thy house.' ²⁵And immediately he rose up before them, and took up that whereon he lay, and departed to his own house, glorifying God. ²⁶And they were all amazed, and they glorified God, and were filled with fear, saying, 'We have seen strange things today'.

²⁷And after these things he went forth, and saw a publican, named Levi, sitting at the receipt of custom: and he said unto him, 'Follow me'. ²⁸And he left all, rose up, and followed him. ²⁹And Levi made him a great feast in his own house: and there was a great company of publicans and of others that sat down with them. ³⁰But their scribes and Pharisees murmured against his disciples, saying, 'Why do ye eat and drink with publicans and sinners?' ³¹And Jesus answering said unto them, 'They that are whole need not a physician: but they that are sick. ³²I came not to call the righteous, but sinners to repentance.'

³³And they said unto him, 'Why do the disciples of John fast often, and make prayers, and likewise the disciples of the Pharisees: but thine eat and drink?' ³⁴And he said unto them, 'Can ye make the children of the bride-chamber fast, while the bridegroom is with them? ³⁵But the days will come, when the bridegroom shall be taken away from them, and then shall they fast in those days.'

³⁶And he spoke also a parable unto them, 'No man putteth a piece of a new garment upon an old: if otherwise, then both the new maketh a rent, and the piece that was taken out of the new agreeth not with the

old. [37]And no man putteth new wine into old bottles: else the new wine will burst the bottles, and be spilt, and the bottles shall perish. [38]But new wine must be put into new bottles, and both are preserved. [39]No man also having drunk old wine straightway desireth new: for he saith, "The old is better".'

6 And it came to pass on the second sabbath after the first, that he went through the corn fields: and his disciples plucked the ears of corn, and did eat, rubbing them in their hands. [2]And certain of the Pharisees said unto them, 'Why do ye that which is not lawful to do on the sabbath days?' [3]And Jesus answering them said, 'Have ye not read so much as this, what David did, when himself was a-hungered, and they which were with him: [4]how he went into the house of God, and did take and eat the showbread, and gave also to them that were with him, which it is not lawful to eat but for the priests alone?' [5]And he said unto them, that 'The Son of man is Lord also of the sabbath'.

[6]And it came to pass also on another sabbath, that he entered into the synagogue and taught: and there was a man whose right hand was withered. [7]And the scribes and Pharisees watched him, whether he would heal on the sabbath day: that they might find an accusation against him. [8]But he knew their thoughts, and said to the man which had the withered hand, 'Rise up, and stand forth in the midst'. And he arose and stood forth. [9]Then said Jesus unto them, 'I will ask you one thing, is it lawful on the sabbath days to do good, or to do evil? to save life, or to destroy it?' [10]And looking round about upon them all, he said unto the man, 'Stretch forth thy hand'. And he did so: and his hand was restored whole as the other. [11]And they were filled with madness, and communed one with another what they might do to Jesus.

[12]And it came to pass in those days, that he went out into a mountain to pray, and continued all night in prayer to God. [13]And when it was day, he called unto him his disciples: and of them he chose twelve; whom also he named apostles: [14]Simon (whom he also named Peter), and Andrew his brother, James and John, Philip and Bartholomew, [15]Matthew and Thomas, James the son of Alphaeus, and Simon called Zelotes, [16]and Judas the brother of James, and Judas Iscariot, which also was the traitor.

[17]And he came down with them, and stood in the plain, and the company of his disciples, and a great multitude of people out of all Judea and Jerusalem, and from the sea-coast of Tyre and Sidon, which came to hear him, and to be healed of their diseases, [18]and they that were vexed with unclean spirits: and they were healed. [19]And the whole multitude sought to touch him: for there went virtue out of him, and healed them all.

[20]And he lifted up his eyes on his disciples, and said, 'Blessed be ye poor: for yours is the kingdom of God. [21]Blessed are ye that hunger now: for ye shall be filled. Blessed are ye that weep now: for ye shall laugh. [22]Blessed are ye, when men shall hate you, and when they shall separate you from their company, and shall reproach you, and cast out your name as evil, for the Son of man's sake. [23]Rejoice ye in that day, and leap

for joy: for behold, your reward is great in heaven: for in the like manner did their fathers unto the prophets.

²⁴'But woe unto you that are rich: for ye have received your consolation. ²⁵Woe unto you that are full: for ye shall hunger. Woe unto you that laugh now: for ye shall mourn and weep. ²⁶Woe unto you, when all men shall speak well of you: for so did their fathers to the false prophets.

²⁷'But I say unto you which hear, love your enemies, do good to them which hate you, ²⁸bless them that curse you, and pray for them which despitefully use you. ²⁹And unto him that smiteth thee on the one cheek, offer also the other: and him that taketh away thy cloak, forbid not to take thy coat also. ³⁰Give to every man that asketh of thee, and of him that taketh away thy goods, ask them not again. ³¹And as ye would that men should do to you, do ye also to them likewise. ³²For if ye love them which love you, what thanks have ye? for sinners also love those that love them. ³³And if ye do good to them which do good to you, what thanks have ye? for sinners also do even the same. ³⁴And if ye lend to them of whom ye hope to receive, what thanks have ye? for sinners also lend to sinners, to receive as much again. ³⁵But love ye your enemies, and do good, and lend, hoping for nothing again: and your reward shall be great, and ye shall be the children of the Highest: for he is kind unto the unthankful and to the evil. ³⁶Be ye therefore merciful, as your Father also is merciful. ³⁷Judge not, and ye shall not be judged: condemn not, and ye shall not be condemned: forgive, and ye shall be forgiven. ³⁸Give, and it shall be given unto you, good measure, pressed down, and shaken together, and running over, shall men give into your bosom: for with the same measure that ye mete withal it shall be measured to you again.'

³⁹And he spoke a parable unto them, 'Can the blind lead the blind? Shall they not both fall into the ditch? ⁴⁰The disciple is not above his master: but every one that is perfect shall be as his master. ⁴¹And why beholdest thou the mote that is in thy brother's eye, but perceivest not the beam that is in thy own eye? ⁴²Either how canst thou say to thy brother, "Brother, let me pull out the mote that is in thy eye", when thou thyself beholdest not the beam that is in thy own eye? Thou hypocrite, cast out first the beam out of thy own eye, and then shalt thou see clearly to pull out the mote that is in thy brother's eye.

⁴³'For a good tree bringeth not forth corrupt fruit: neither doth a corrupt tree bring forth good fruit. ⁴⁴For every tree is known by his own fruit: for of thorns men do not gather figs, nor of a bramble bush gather they grapes. ⁴⁵A good man out of the good treasure of his heart bringeth forth that which is good: and an evil man out of the evil treasure of his heart bringeth forth that which is evil: for of the abundance of the heart his mouth speaketh.

⁴⁶'And why call ye me, "Lord, Lord", and do not the things which I say? ⁴⁷Whosoever cometh to me, and heareth my sayings, and doeth them, I will show you to whom he is like. ⁴⁸He is like a man which built a house, and dug deep, and laid the foundation on a rock. And when

the flood arose, the stream beat vehemently upon that house, and could not shake it: for it was founded upon a rock. ⁴⁹But he that heareth, and doeth not, is like a man that without a foundation built a house upon the earth: against which the stream did beat vehemently, and immediately it fell, and the ruin of that house was great.'

7 Now when he had ended all his sayings in the audience of the people, he entered into Capernaum. ²And a certain centurion's servant, who was dear unto him, was sick, and ready to die. ³And when he heard of Jesus, he sent unto him the elders of the Jews, beseeching him that he would come and heal his servant. ⁴And when they came to Jesus, they besought him instantly, saying, that he was worthy for whom he should do this. ⁵'For he loveth our nation, and he hath built us a synagogue'. ⁶Then Jesus went with them. And when he was now not far from the house, the centurion sent friends to him, saying unto him, 'Lord, trouble not thyself: for I am not worthy that thou shouldst enter under my roof. ⁷Wherefore neither thought I myself worthy to come unto thee: but say in a word, and my servant shall be healed. ⁸For I also am a man set under authority, having under me soldiers, and I say unto one, "Go", and he goeth: and to another, "Come", and he cometh: and to my servant, "Do this", and he doeth it.' ⁹When Jesus heard these things, he marvelled at him, and turned him about, and said unto the people that followed him, 'I say unto you, I have not found so great faith, no, not in Israel'. ¹⁰And they that were sent, returning to the house, found the servant whole that had been sick.

¹¹And it came to pass the day after, that he went into a city called Nain: and many of his disciples went with him, and much people. ¹²Now when he came nigh to the gate of the city, behold, there was a dead man carried out, the only son of his mother, and she was a widow: and much people of the city was with her. ¹³And when the Lord saw her, he had compassion on her, and said unto her, 'Weep not'. ¹⁴And he came and touched the bier (and they that bore him stood still). And he said, 'Young man, I say unto thee, arise'. ¹⁵And he that was dead sat up, and began to speak. And he delivered him to his mother. ¹⁶And there came a fear on all, and they glorified God, saying, that a great prophet is risen up among us, and, that God hath visited his people. ¹⁷And this rumour of him went forth throughout all Judea, and throughout all the region round about.

¹⁸And the disciples of John showed him of all these things. ¹⁹And John calling unto him two of his disciples, sent them to Jesus, saying, 'Art thou he that should come, or look we for another?' ²⁰When the men were come unto him, they said, 'John Baptist hath sent us unto thee, saying, "Art thou he that should come, or look we for another?"' ²¹And in that same hour he cured many of their infirmities and plagues, and of evil spirits, and unto many that were blind he gave sight. ²²Then Jesus answering said unto them, 'Go your way, and tell John what things ye have seen and heard, how that the blind see, the lame walk, the lepers are cleansed, the deaf hear, the dead are raised, to the poor the gospel is preached. ²³And blessed is he, whosoever shall not be offended in me.'

²⁴And when the messengers of John were departed, he began to speak unto the people concerning John, 'What went ye out into the wilderness for to see? A reed shaken with the wind? ²⁵But what went ye out for to see? A man clothed in soft raiment? Behold, they which are gorgeously apparelled, and live delicately, are in kings' courts. ²⁶But what went ye out for to see? A prophet? Yea, I say unto you, and much more than a prophet. ²⁷This is he, of whom it is written, "Behold, I send my messenger before thy face, which shall prepare thy way before thee". ²⁸For I say unto you, among those that are born of women there is not a greater prophet than John the Baptist: but he that is least in the kingdom of God is greater than he.' ²⁹And all the people that heard him, and the publicans, justified God, being baptized with the baptism of John. ³⁰But the Pharisees and lawyers rejected the counsel of God against themselves, being not baptized of him.

³¹And the Lord said, 'Whereunto then shall I liken the men of this generation? and to what are they like? ³²They are like unto children sitting in the market-place, and calling one to another, and saying, "We have piped unto you, and ye have not danced: we have mourned to you, and ye have not wept". ³³For John the Baptist came neither eating bread nor drinking wine, and ye say, "He hath a devil". ³⁴The Son of man is come eating and drinking, and ye say, "Behold a gluttonous man, and a wine-bibber, a friend of publicans and sinners". ³⁵But wisdom is justified of all her children.'

³⁶And one of the Pharisees desired him that he would eat with him. And he went into the Pharisee's house, and sat down to meat. ³⁷And behold, a woman in the city, which was a sinner, when she knew that Jesus sat at meat in the Pharisee's house, brought an alabaster box of ointment, ³⁸and stood at his feet behind him weeping, and began to wash his feet with tears, and did wipe them with the hairs of her head, and kissed his feet, and anointed them with the ointment. ³⁹Now when the Pharisee which had bidden him saw it, he spoke within himself, saying, 'This man, if he were a prophet, would have known who and what manner of woman this is that toucheth him: for she is a sinner'. ⁴⁰And Jesus answering said unto him, 'Simon, I have somewhat to say unto thee'. And he saith, 'Master, say on'. ⁴¹'There was a certain creditor which had two debtors: the one owed five hundred pence, and the other fifty. ⁴²And when they had nothing to pay, he frankly forgave them both. Tell me therefore, which of them will love him most?' ⁴³Simon answered and said, 'I suppose that he, to whom he forgave most'. And he said unto him, 'Thou hast rightly judged'. ⁴⁴And he turned to the woman, and said unto Simon, 'Seest thou this woman? I entered into thy house, thou gavest me no water for my feet: but she hath washed my feet with tears, and wiped them with the hairs of her head. ⁴⁵Thou gavest me no kiss: but this woman since the time I came in hath not ceased to kiss my feet. ⁴⁶My head with oil thou didst not anoint: but this woman hath anointed my feet with ointment. ⁴⁷Wherefore I say unto thee, her sins, which are many, are forgiven, for she loved much: but to whom little is forgiven, the same loveth little.'

⁴⁸And he said unto her, 'Thy sins are forgiven'. ⁴⁹And they that sat at meat with him began to say within themselves, 'Who is this that forgiveth sins also?' ⁵⁰And he said to the woman, 'Thy faith hath saved thee, go in peace'.

8 And it came to pass afterward, that he went throughout every city and village, preaching and showing the glad tidings of the kingdom of God: and the twelve were with him, ²and certain women, which had been healed of evil spirits and infirmities, Mary called Magdalene, out of whom went seven devils, ³and Joanna the wife of Chuza, Herod's steward, and Susanna, and many others, which ministered unto him of their substance.

⁴And when much people were gathered together, and were come to him out of every city, he spoke by a parable: ⁵'A sower went out to sow his seed: and as he sowed, some fell by the wayside, and it was trodden down, and the fowls of the air devoured it. ⁶And some fell upon a rock, and as soon as it was sprung up, it withered away, because it lacked moisture. ⁷And some fell among thorns, and the thorns sprang up with it, and choked it. ⁸And other fell on good ground, and sprang up, and bore fruit a hundredfold.' And when he said these things, he cried, 'He that hath ears to hear, let him hear'. ⁹And his disciples asked him, saying, 'What might this parable be?' ¹⁰And he said, 'Unto you it is given to know the mysteries of the kingdom of God: but to others in parables, that seeing they might not see, and hearing they might not understand. ¹¹Now the parable is this: the seed is the word of God. ¹²Those by the wayside are they that hear: then cometh the devil, and taketh away the word out of their hearts, lest they should believe and be saved. ¹³They on the rock are they, which, when they hear, receive the word with joy: and these have no root, which for a while believe, and in time of temptation fall away. ¹⁴And that which fell among thorns are they, which, when they have heard, go forth, and are choked with cares and riches and pleasures of this life, and bring no fruit to perfection. ¹⁵But that on the good ground are they, which in an honest and good heart, having heard the word, keep it, and bring forth fruit with patience.

¹⁶'No man, when he hath lighted a candle, covereth it with a vessel, or putteth it under a bed: but setteth it on a candlestick, that they which enter in may see the light. ¹⁷For nothing is secret, that shall not be made manifest: neither anything hid, that shall not be known and come abroad. ¹⁸Take heed therefore how ye hear: for whosoever hath, to him shall be given; and whosoever hath not, from him shall be taken even that which he seemeth to have.'

¹⁹Then came to him his mother and his brethren, and could not come at him for the press. ²⁰And it was told him by certain which said, 'Thy mother and thy brethren stand without, desiring to see thee'. ²¹And he answered and said unto them, 'My mother and my brethren are these which hear the word of God, and do it'.

²²Now it came to pass on a certain day, that he went into a ship with his disciples: and he said unto them, 'Let us go over unto the other side of the lake', and they launched forth. ²³But as they sailed he fell asleep,

and there came down a storm of wind on the lake, and they were filled with water, and were in jeopardy. ²⁴And they came to him, and awoke him, saying, 'Master, master, we perish'. Then he arose, and rebuked the wind and the raging of the water: and they ceased, and there was a calm. ²⁵And he said unto them, 'Where is your faith?' And they being afraid wondered, saying one to another, 'What manner of man is this! For he commandeth even the winds and water, and they obey him.'

²⁶And they arrived at the country of the Gadarenes, which is over against Galilee. ²⁷And when he went forth to land, there met him out of the city a certain man, which had devils long time, and wore no clothes, neither abode in any house, but in the tombs. ²⁸When he saw Jesus, he cried out, and fell down before him, and with a loud voice said, 'What have I to do with thee, Jesus, thou Son of God most high? I beseech thee, torment me not.' ²⁹(For he had commanded the unclean spirit to come out of the man. For oftentimes it had caught him, and he was kept bound with chains and in fetters: and he broke the bands, and was driven of the devil into the wilderness.) ³⁰And Jesus asked him, saying, 'What is thy name?' And he said, 'Legion': because many devils were entered into him. ³¹And they besought him that he would not command them to go out into the deep. ³²And there was there a herd of many swine feeding on the mountain: and they besought him that he would suffer them to enter into them: and he suffered them. ³³Then went the devils out of the man, and entered into the swine: and the herd ran violently down a steep place into the lake, and were choked. ³⁴When they that fed them saw what was done, they fled, and went and told it in the city and in the country. ³⁵Then they went out to see what was done, and came to Jesus, and found the man, out of whom the devils were departed, sitting at the feet of Jesus, clothed, and in his right mind: and they were afraid. ³⁶They also which saw it told them by what means he that was possessed of the devils was healed.

³⁷Then the whole multitude of the country of the Gadarenes round about besought him to depart from them, for they were taken with great fear: and he went up into the ship, and returned back again. ³⁸Now the man out of whom the devils were departed besought him that he might be with him: but Jesus sent him away, saying, ³⁹'Return to thy own house, and show how great things God hath done unto thee'. And he went his way, and published throughout the whole city how great things Jesus had done unto him.

⁴⁰And it came to pass that when Jesus was returned, the people gladly received him: for they were all waiting for him. ⁴¹And behold, there came a man named Jairus, and he was a ruler of the synagogue: and he fell down at Jesus' feet, and besought him that he would come into his house: ⁴²for he had one only daughter, about twelve years of age, and she lay a-dying.

But as he went the people thronged him. ⁴³And a woman having an issue of blood twelve years, which had spent all her living upon physicians, neither could be healed of any, ⁴⁴came behind him, and touched the border of his garment: and immediately her issue of blood stanched. ⁴⁵And Jesus said, 'Who touched me?' When all denied, Peter and they that were with him said, 'Master, the multitude throng thee and press thee, and sayest thou, "Who touched me?"' ⁴⁶And Jesus said, 'Somebody hath touched me: for I perceive that virtue is gone out of me'. ⁴⁷And when the woman saw that she was not hid, she came trembling, and falling down before him, she declared unto him before all the people for what cause she had touched him, and how she was healed immediately. ⁴⁸And he said unto her, 'Daughter, be of good comfort, thy faith hath made thee whole, go in peace'.

⁴⁹While he yet spoke, there cometh one from the ruler of the synagogue's house, saying to him, 'Thy daughter is dead, trouble not the Master'. ⁵⁰But when Jesus heard it, he answered him, saying, 'Fear not, believe only, and she shall be made whole'. ⁵¹And when he came into the house, he suffered no man to go in, save Peter, and James, and John, and the father and the mother of the maiden. ⁵²And all wept, and bewailed her: but he said, 'Weep not, she is not dead, but sleepeth'. ⁵³And they laughed him to scorn, knowing that she was dead. ⁵⁴And he put them all out, and took her by the hand, and called, saying, 'Maid, arise'. ⁵⁵And her spirit came again, and she arose straightway: and he commanded to give her meat. ⁵⁶And her parents were astonished: but he charged them that they should tell no man what was done.

9 Then he called his twelve disciples together, and gave them power and authority over all devils, and to cure diseases. ²And he sent them to preach the kingdom of God, and to heal the sick. ³And he said unto them, 'Take nothing for your journey, neither staves, nor scrip, neither bread, neither money, neither have two coats apiece. ⁴And whatsoever house ye enter into, there abide, and thence depart. ⁵And whosoever will not receive you, when ye go out of that city, shake off the very dust from your feet for a testimony against them.' ⁶And they departed, and went through the towns, preaching the gospel, and healing everywhere.

⁷Now Herod the tetrarch heard of all that was done by him: and he was perplexed, because that it was said of some, that John was risen from the dead; ⁸and of some, that Elias had appeared; and of others, that one of the old prophets was risen again. ⁹And Herod said, 'John have I beheaded: but who is this, of whom I hear such things?' And he desired to see him.

¹⁰And the apostles, when they were returned, told him all that they had done. And he took them, and went aside privately into a desert place belonging to the city called Bethsaida. ¹¹And the people, when they knew it, followed him, and he received them, and spoke unto them of the kingdom of God, and healed them that had need of healing. ¹²And when the day began to wear away, then came the twelve, and said unto him, 'Send the multitude away, that they may go into the towns and country round about, and lodge, and get victuals: for we are here in a desert place'. ¹³But he said unto them, 'Give ye them to eat'. And they said, 'We have no more but five loaves and two fishes, except we should go and buy meat for all this people'. ¹⁴For they were about

five thousand men. And he said to his disciples, 'Make them sit down by fifties in a company'. ¹⁵And they did so, and made them all sit down. ¹⁶Then he took the five loaves and the two fishes, and looking up to heaven, he blessed them, and broke, and gave to the disciples to set before the multitude. ¹⁷And they did eat, and were all filled. And there was taken up of fragments that remained to them twelve baskets.

¹⁸And it came to pass, as he was alone praying, his disciples were with him: and he asked them, saying, 'Whom say the people that I am?' ¹⁹They answering said, 'John the Baptist; but some say, Elias; and others say, that one of the old prophets is risen again'. ²⁰He said unto them, 'But whom say ye that I am?' Peter answering said, 'The Christ of God'. ²¹And he straitly charged them, and commanded them to tell no man that thing, ²²saying, 'The Son of man must suffer many things, and be rejected of the elders and chief priests and scribes, and be slain, and be raised the third day'.

²³And he said to them all, 'If any man will come after me, let him deny himself, and take up his cross daily, and follow me. ²⁴For whosoever will save his life shall lose it: but whosoever will lose his life for my sake, the same shall save it. ²⁵For what is a man advantaged, if he gain the whole world, and lose himself, or be cast away? ²⁶For whosoever shall be ashamed of me and of my words, of him shall the Son of man be ashamed, when he shall come in his own glory, and in his Father's, and of the holy angels. ²⁷But I tell you of a truth, there be some standing here, which shall not taste of death, till they see the kingdom of God.'

²⁸And it came to pass about an eight days after these sayings, he took Peter and John and James, and went up into a mountain to pray. ²⁹And as he prayed, the fashion of his countenance was altered, and his raiment was white and glistering. ³⁰And behold, there talked with him two men, which were Moses and Elias, ³¹who appeared in glory, and spoke of his decease which he should accomplish at Jerusalem. ³²But Peter and they that were with him were heavy with sleep: and when they were awake, they saw his glory, and the two men that stood with him. ³³And it came to pass, as they departed from him, Peter said unto Jesus, 'Master, it is good for us to be here, and let us make three tabernacles, one for thee, and one for Moses, and one for Elias': not knowing what he said. ³⁴While he thus spoke, there came a cloud, and overshadowed them, and they feared as they entered into the cloud. ³⁵And there came a voice out of the cloud, saying, 'This is my beloved Son, hear him'. ³⁶And when the voice was past, Jesus was found alone. And they kept it close, and told no man in those days any of those things which they had seen.

³⁷And it came to pass that on the next day, when they were come down from the hill, much people met him. ³⁸And behold, a man of the company cried out, saying, 'Master, I beseech thee, look upon my son, for he is my only child. ³⁹And lo, a spirit taketh him, and he suddenly crieth out, and it teareth him that he foameth again, and bruising him, hardly departeth from him. ⁴⁰And I besought thy disciples to cast him out, and they could not.' ⁴¹And Jesus answering said, 'O faithless and

perverse generation, how long shall I be with you, and suffer you? Bring thy son hither.' [42]And as he was yet a-coming, the devil threw him down, and tore him: and Jesus rebuked the unclean spirit, and healed the child, and delivered him again to his father.

[43]And they were all amazed at the mighty power of God. But while they wondered every one at all things which Jesus did, he said unto his disciples, [44]'Let these sayings sink down into your ears: for the Son of man shall be delivered into the hands of men'. [45]But they understood not this saying, and it was hid from them, that they perceived it not: and they feared to ask him of that saying.

[46]Then there arose a reasoning among them, which of them should be greatest. [47]And Jesus, perceiving the thought of their heart, took a child, and set him by him, [48]and said unto them, 'Whosoever shall receive this child in my name receiveth me: and whosoever shall receive me receiveth him that sent me: for he that is least among you all, the same shall be great'.

[49]And John answered and said, 'Master, we saw one casting out devils in thy name, and we forbad him, because he followeth not with us'. [50]And Jesus said unto him, 'Forbid him not: for he that is not against us is for us'.

[51]And it came to pass, when the time was come that he should be received up, he steadfastly set his face to go to Jerusalem, [52]and sent messengers before his face: and they went, and entered into a village of the Samaritans, to make ready for him. [53]And they did not receive him, because his face was as though he would go to Jerusalem. [54]And when his disciples James and John saw this, they said, 'Lord, wilt thou that we command fire to come down from heaven, and consume them, even as Elias did?' [55]But he turned, and rebuked them, and said, 'Ye know not what manner of spirit ye are of. [56]For the Son of man is not come to destroy men's lives, but to save them.' And they went to another village.

[57]And it came to pass that as they went in the way, a certain man said unto him, 'Lord, I will follow thee whithersoever thou goest'. [58]And Jesus said unto him, 'Foxes have holes, and birds of the air have nests, but the Son of man hath not where to lay his head'. [59]And he said unto another, 'Follow me'. But he said, 'Lord, suffer me first to go and bury my father'. [60]Jesus said unto him, 'Let the dead bury their dead: but go thou and preach the kingdom of God'. [61]And another also said, 'Lord, I will follow thee: but let me first go bid them farewell, which are at home at my house'. [62]And Jesus said unto him, 'No man, having put his hand to the plough, and looking back, is fit for the kingdom of God'.

10
After these things the Lord appointed other seventy also, and sent them two and two before his face into every city and place, whither he himself would come. [2]Therefore said he unto them, 'The harvest truly is great, but the labourers are few: pray ye therefore Lord of the harvest, that he would send forth labourers into his harvest. [3]Go your ways: behold, I send you forth as lambs among wolves. [4]Carry neither purse, nor scrip, nor shoes, and salute no man by the way. [5]And into whatsoever house ye enter, first say, "Peace be to this house". [6]And

if the son of peace be there, your peace shall rest upon it: if not, it shall turn to you again. [7]And in the same house remain, eating and drinking such things as they give: for the labourer is worthy of his hire. Go not from house to house. [8]And into whatsoever city ye enter, and they receive you, eat such things as are set before you: [9]and heal the sick that are therein, and say unto them, "The kingdom of God is come nigh unto you". [10]But into whatsoever city ye enter, and they receive you not, go your ways out into the streets of the same, and say, [11]"Even the very dust of your city, which cleaveth on us, we do wipe off against you: notwithstanding be ye sure of this, that the kingdom of God is come nigh unto you". [12]But I say unto you, that it shall be more tolerable in that day for Sodom, than for that city.

[13]'Woe unto thee, Chorazin, woe unto thee, Bethsaida: for if the mighty works had been done in Tyre and Sidon, which have been done in you, they had a great while ago repented, sitting in sackcloth and ashes. [14]But it shall be more tolerable for Tyre and Sidon at the judgement, than for you. [15]And thou, Capernaum, which art exalted to heaven, shalt be thrust down to hell. [16]He that heareth you heareth me: and he that despiseth you despiseth me: and he that despiseth me despiseth him that sent me.'

[17]And the seventy returned again with joy, saying, 'Lord, even the devils are subject unto us through thy name'. [18]And he said unto them, 'I beheld Satan as lightning fall from heaven. [19]Behold, I give unto you power to tread on serpents and scorpions, and over all the power of the enemy: and nothing shall by any means hurt you. [20]Notwithstanding in this rejoice not, that the spirits are subject unto you: but rather rejoice, because your names are written in heaven.'

[21]In that hour Jesus rejoiced in spirit, and said, 'I thank thee, O Father, Lord of heaven and earth, that thou hast hid these things from the wise and prudent, and hast revealed them unto babes: even so, Father, for so it seemed good in thy sight. [22]All things are delivered to me of my Father: and no man knoweth who the Son is, but the Father: and who the Father is, but the Son, and he to whom the Son will reveal him.'

[23]And he turned him unto his disciples, and said privately, 'Blessed are the eyes which see the things that ye see. [24]For I tell you, that many prophets and kings have desired to see those things which ye see, and have not seen them: and to hear those things which ye hear, and have not heard them.'

[25]And behold, a certain lawyer stood up, and tempted him, saying, 'Master, what shall I do to inherit eternal life?' [26]He said unto him, 'What is written in the law? how readest thou?' [27]And he answering said, 'Thou shalt love the Lord thy God with all thy heart, and with all thy soul, and with all thy strength, and with all thy mind, and thy neighbour as thyself'. [28]And he said unto him, 'Thou hast answered right: this do, and thou shalt live.'

[29]But he, willing to justify himself, said unto Jesus, 'And who is my neighbour?' [30]And Jesus answering said, 'A certain man went down from Jerusalem to Jericho, and fell among thieves, which stripped him

of his raiment, and wounded him, and departed, leaving him half dead. [31]And by chance there came down a certain priest that way, and when he saw him, he passed by on the other side. [32]And likewise a Levite, when he was at the place, came and looked on him, and passed by on the other side. [33]But a certain Samaritan, as he journeyed, came where he was: and when he saw him, he had compassion on him, [34]and went to him, and bound up his wounds, pouring in oil and wine, and set him on his own beast, and brought him to an inn, and took care of him. [35]And on the morrow when he departed, he took out two pence, and gave them to the host, and said unto him, "Take care of him, and whatsoever thou spendest more, when I come again, I will repay thee". [36]Which now of these three, thinkest thou, was neighbour unto him that fell among the thieves?' [37]And he said, 'He that showed mercy on him'. Then said Jesus unto him, 'Go, and do thou likewise'.

[38]Now it came to pass, as they went, that he entered into a certain village: and a certain woman named Martha received him into her house. [39]And she had a sister called Mary, which also sat at Jesus' feet, and heard his word. [40]But Martha was cumbered about much serving, and came to him, and said, 'Lord, dost thou not care that my sister hath left me to serve alone? Bid her therefore that she help me.' [41]And Jesus answered and said unto her, 'Martha, Martha, thou art careful and troubled about many things: [42]but one thing is needful, and Mary hath chosen that good part, which shall not be taken away from her'.

11 And it came to pass that as he was praying in a certain place, when he ceased, one of his disciples said unto him, 'Lord, teach us to pray, as John also taught his disciples'. [2]And he said unto them, 'When ye pray, say, "Our Father which art in heaven, hallowed be thy name. Thy kingdom come. Thy will be done, as in heaven, so in earth. [3]Give us day by day our daily bread. [4]And forgive us our sins: for we also forgive every one that is indebted to us. And lead us not into temptation, but deliver us from evil."'

[5]And he said unto them, 'Which of you shall have a friend, and shall go unto him at midnight, and say unto him, "Friend, lend me three loaves. [6]For a friend of mine in his journey is come to me, and I have nothing to set before him"? [7]and he from within shall answer and say, "Trouble me not, the door is now shut, and my children are with me in bed: I cannot rise and give thee". [8]I say unto you, though he will not rise and give him, because he is his friend, yet because of his importunity he will rise and give him as many as he needeth. [9]And I say unto you, ask, and it shall be given you: seek, and ye shall find: knock, and it shall be opened unto you. [10]For every one that asketh receiveth: and he that seeketh findeth: and to him that knocketh it shall be opened. [11]If a son shall ask bread of any of you that is a father, will he give him a stone? Or if he ask a fish, will he for a fish give him a serpent? [12]Or if he shall ask an egg, will he offer him a scorpion? [13]If ye then, being evil, know how to give good gifts unto your children: how much more shall your heavenly Father give the Holy Spirit to them that ask him?'

[14]And he was casting out a devil, and it was dumb. And it came to

pass, when the devil was gone out, the dumb spoke: and the people wondered. [15]But some of them said, 'He casteth out devils through Beelzebub the chief of the devils'. [16]And others, tempting him, sought of him a sign from heaven. [17]But he, knowing their thoughts, said unto them, 'Every kingdom divided against itself is brought to desolation: and a house divided against a house falleth. [18]If Satan also be divided against himself, how shall his kingdom stand? Because ye say that I cast out devils through Beelzebub. [19]And if I by Beelzebub cast out devils, by whom do your sons cast them out? therefore shall they be your judges. [20]But if I with the finger of God cast out devils, no doubt the kingdom of God is come upon you. [21]When a strong man armed keepeth his palace, his goods are in peace: [22]but when a stronger than he shall come upon him, and overcome him, he taketh from him all his armour wherein he trusted, and divideth his spoils. [23]He that is not with me is against me: and he that gathereth not with me scattereth. [24]When the unclean spirit is gone out of a man, he walketh through dry places, seeking rest: and finding none, he saith, "I will return unto my house whence I came out". [25]And when he cometh, he findeth it swept and garnished. [26]Then goeth he, and taketh to him seven other spirits more wicked than himself, and they enter in, and dwell there: and the last state of that man is worse than the first.'

[27]And it came to pass, as he spoke these things, a certain woman of the company lifted up her voice, and said unto him, 'Blessed is the womb that bore thee, and the paps which thou hast sucked'. [28]But he said, 'Yea rather, blessed are they that hear the word of God, and keep it'.

[29]And when the people were gathered thick together, he began to say, 'This is an evil generation: they seek a sign, and there shall no sign be given it, but the sign of Jonas the prophet. [30]For as Jonas was a sign unto the Ninevites, so shall also the Son of man be to this generation. [31]The queen of the south shall rise up in the judgement with the men of this generation, and condemn them: for she came from the utmost parts of the earth to hear the wisdom of Solomon: and behold, a greater than Solomon is here. [32]The men of Nineveh shall rise up in the judgement with this generation, and shall condemn it: for they repented at the preaching of Jonas, and behold, a greater than Jonas is here.

[33]'No man, when he hath lighted a candle, putteth it in a secret place, neither under a bushel, but on a candlestick, that they which come in may see the light. [34]The light of the body is the eye: therefore when thy eye is single, thy whole body also is full of light: but when thy eye is evil, thy body also is full of darkness. [35]Take heed therefore that the light which is in thee be not darkness. [36]If thy whole body therefore be full of light, having no part dark, the whole shall be full of light, as when the bright shining of a candle doth give thee light.'

[37]And as he spoke, a certain Pharisee besought him to dine with him: and he went in, and sat down to meat. [38]And when the Pharisee saw it, he marvelled that he had not first washed before dinner. [39]And the Lord said unto him, 'Now do ye Pharisees make clean the outside of the cup and the platter: but your inward part is full of ravening and wicked-

ness. ⁴⁰Ye fools, did not he that made that which is without make that which is within also? ⁴¹But rather give alms of such things as you have: and behold, all things are clean unto you. ⁴²But woe unto you, Pharisees: for ye tithe mint and rue and all manner of herbs, and pass over judgement and the love of God: these ought ye to have done, and not to leave the other undone. ⁴³Woe unto you, Pharisees: for ye love the uppermost seats in the synagogues, and greetings in the markets. ⁴⁴Woe unto you, scribes and Pharisees, hypocrites: for ye are as graves which appear not, and the men that walk over them are not aware of them.'

⁴⁵Then answered one of the lawyers, and said unto him, 'Master, thus saying thou reproachest us also'. ⁴⁶And he said, 'Woe unto you also, ye lawyers: for ye load men with burdens grievous to be borne, and ye yourselves touch not the burdens with one of your fingers. ⁴⁷Woe unto you: for ye build the sepulchres of the prophets, and your fathers killed them. ⁴⁸Truly ye bear witness that ye allow the deeds of your fathers: for they indeed killed them, and ye build their sepulchres. ⁴⁹Therefore also said the wisdom of God, "I will send them prophets and apostles, and some of them they shall slay and persecute": ⁵⁰that the blood of all the prophets, which was shed from the foundation of the world, may be required of this generation, ⁵¹from the blood of Abel unto the blood of Zacharias, which perished between the altar and the temple: verily I say unto you, it shall be required of this generation. ⁵²Woe unto you, lawyers: for ye have taken away the key of knowledge: ye entered not in yourselves, and them that were entering in ye hindered.'

⁵³And as he said these things unto them, the scribes and the Pharisees began to urge him vehemently, and to provoke him to speak of many things: ⁵⁴laying wait for him, and seeking to catch something out of his mouth, that they might accuse him.

12 In the mean time, when there were gathered together an innumerable multitude of people, insomuch that they trod one upon another, he began to say unto his disciples first of all, 'Beware ye of the leaven of the Pharisees, which is hypocrisy. ²For there is nothing covered, that shall not be revealed, neither hid, that shall not be known. ³Therefore whatsoever ye have spoken in darkness shall be heard in the light: and that which ye have spoken in the ear in closets shall be proclaimed upon the house-tops. ⁴And I say unto you my friends, be not afraid of them that kill the body, and after that have no more that they can do. ⁵But I will forewarn you whom you shall fear: fear him, which after he hath killed hath power to cast into hell; yea, I say unto you, fear him. ⁶Are not five sparrows sold for two farthings, and not one of them is forgotten before God? ⁷But even the very hairs of your head are all numbered: fear not therefore, ye are of more value than many sparrows. ⁸Also I say unto you, whosoever shall confess me before men, him shall the Son of man also confess before the angels of God. ⁹But he that denieth me before men shall be denied before the angels of God. ¹⁰And whosoever shall speak a word against the Son of man, it shall be forgiven him: but unto him that blasphemeth against the Holy Ghost it shall not be forgiven. [11]And when they bring you unto the synagogues, and unto magistrates, and powers, take ye no thought how or what thing ye shall answer, or what ye shall say: [12]for the Holy Ghost shall teach you in the same hour what ye ought to say.'

[13]And one of the company said unto him, 'Master, speak to my brother, that he divide the inheritance with me'. [14]And he said unto him, 'Man, who made me a judge or a divider over you?' [15]And he said unto them, 'Take heed, and beware of covetousness: for a man's life consisteth not in the abundance of the things which he possesseth'. [16]And he spoke a parable unto them, saying, 'The ground of a certain rich man brought forth plentifully. [17]And he thought within himself, saying, "What shall I do, because I have no room where to bestow my fruits?" [18]And he said, "This will I do, I will pull down my barns, and build greater, and there will I bestow all my fruits and my goods. [19]And I will say to my soul, 'Soul, thou hast much goods laid up for many years, take thy ease, eat, drink, and be merry'." [20]But God said unto him, "Thou fool, this night thy soul shall be required of thee: then whose shall those things be, which thou hast provided?" [21]So is he that layeth up treasure for himself, and is not rich towards God.'

[22]And he said unto his disciples, 'Therefore I say unto you, take no thought for your life, what ye shall eat, neither for the body, what ye shall put on. [23]The life is more than meat, and the body is more than raiment. [24]Consider the ravens, for they neither sow nor reap, which neither have storehouse nor barn, and God feedeth them: how much more are ye better than the fowls? [25]And which of you with taking thought can add to his stature one cubit? [26]If ye then be not able to do that thing which is least, why take ye thought for the rest? [27]Consider the lilies how they grow, they toil not; they spin not: and yet I say unto you, that Solomon in all his glory was not arrayed like one of these. [28]If then God so clothe the grass, which is today in the field, and tomorrow is cast into the oven: how much more will he clothe you, O ye of little faith? [29]And seek not ye what ye shall eat, or what ye shall drink, neither be ye of doubtful mind. [30]For all these things do the nations of the world seek after: and your Father knoweth that ye have need of these things. [31]But rather seek ye the kingdom of God, and all these things shall be added unto you. [32]Fear not, little flock, for it is your Father's good pleasure to give you the kingdom. [33]Sell that ye have, and give alms: provide yourselves bags which wax not old, a treasure in the heavens that faileth not, where no thief approacheth, neither moth corrupteth. [34]For where your treasure is, there will your heart be also. [35]Let your loins be girded about, and your lights burning, [36]and ye yourselves like unto men that wait for their lord, when he will return from the wedding, that when he cometh and knocketh, they may open unto him immediately. [37]Blessed are those servants, whom the lord when he cometh shall find watching: verily I say unto you, that he shall gird himself, and make them to sit down to meat, and will come forth and serve them. [38]And if he shall come in the second watch, or come in the third watch, and find them so, blessed are those servants. [39]And this

know, that if the goodman of the house had known what hour the thief would come, he would have watched, and not have suffered his house to be broken through. [40]Be ye therefore ready also: for the Son of man cometh at an hour when ye think not.'

[41]Then Peter said unto him, 'Lord, speakest thou this parable unto us, or even to all?' [42]And the Lord said, 'Who then is that faithful and wise steward, whom his lord shall make ruler over his household, to give them their portion of meat in due season? [43]Blessed is that servant, whom his lord when he cometh shall find so doing. [44]Of a truth I say unto you, that he will make him ruler over all that he hath. [45]But and if that servant say in his heart, "My lord delayeth his coming"; and shall begin to beat the menservants and maidens, and to eat and drink, and to be drunken: [46]the lord of that servant will come in a day when he looketh not for him, and at an hour when he is not aware, and will cut him in sunder, and will appoint him his portion with the unbelievers. [47]And that servant, which knew his lord's will, and prepared not himself, neither did according to his will, shall be beaten with many stripes. [48]But he that knew not, and did commit things worthy of stripes, shall be beaten with few stripes. For unto whomsoever much is given, of him shall be much required: and to whom men have committed much, of him they will ask the more.

[49]'I am come to send fire on the earth, and what will I, if it be already kindled? [50]But I have a baptism to be baptized with, and how am I straitened till it be accomplished? [51]Suppose ye that I am come to give peace on earth? I tell you, nay, but rather division. [52]For from henceforth there shall be five in one house divided, three against two, and two against three. [53]The father shall be divided against the son, and the son against the father: the mother against the daughter, and the daughter against the mother: the mother-in-law against her daughter-in-law, and the daughter-in-law against her mother-in-law.'

[54]And he said also to the people, 'When ye see a cloud rise out of the west, straightway ye say, "There cometh a shower", and so it is. [55]And when ye see the south wind blow, ye say, "There will be heat", and it cometh to pass. [56]Ye hypocrites, ye can discern the face of the sky and of the earth: but how is it that ye do not discern this time?

[57]'Yea, and why even of yourselves judge ye not what is right? [58]When thou goest with thy adversary to the magistrate, as thou art in the way, give diligence that thou mayest be delivered from him, lest he hale thee to the judge, and the judge deliver thee to the officer, and the officer cast thee into prison. [59]I tell thee, thou shalt not depart thence, till thou hast paid the very last mite.'

13 There were present at that season some that told him of the Galileans, whose blood Pilate had mingled with their sacrifices. [2]And Jesus answering said unto them, 'Suppose ye that these Galileans were sinners above all the Galileans, because they suffered such things? [3]I tell you, nay: but, except ye repent, ye shall all likewise perish. [4]Or those eighteen, upon whom the tower in Siloam fell, and slew them, think ye that they were sinners above all men that dwelt in

Jerusalem? ⁵I tell you, nay: but, except ye repent, ye shall all likewise perish.'

⁶He spoke also this parable: 'A certain man had a fig tree planted in his vineyard, and he came and sought fruit thereon, and found none. ⁷Then said he unto the dresser of his vineyard, "Behold, these three years I come seeking fruit on this fig tree, and find none: cut it down, why cumbereth it the ground?" ⁸And he answering said unto him, "Lord, let it alone this year also, till I shall dig about it, and dung it: ⁹and if it bear fruit, well: and if not, then after that thou shalt cut it down".'

¹⁰And he was teaching in one of the synagogues on the sabbath. ¹¹And behold, there was a woman which had a spirit of infirmity eighteen years, and was bowed together, and could in no wise lift up herself. ¹²And when Jesus saw her, he called her to him, and said unto her, 'Woman, thou art loosed from thy infirmity'. ¹³And he laid his hands on her, and immediately she was made straight, and glorified God. ¹⁴And the ruler of the synagogue answered with indignation, because that Jesus had healed on the sabbath day, and said unto the people, 'There are six days in which men ought to work: in them therefore come and be healed, and not on the sabbath day'. ¹⁵The Lord then answered him, and said, 'Thou hypocrite, doth not each one of you on the sabbath loose his ox or his ass from the stall, and lead him away to watering? ¹⁶And ought not this woman, being a daughter of Abraham, whom Satan hath bound, lo, these eighteen years, be loosed from this bond on the sabbath day?' ¹⁷And when he had said these things, all his adversaries were ashamed: and all the people rejoiced for all the glorious things that were done by him.

¹⁸Then said he, 'Unto what is the kingdom of God like? and whereunto shall I resemble it? ¹⁹It is like a grain of mustard seed, which a man took, and cast into his garden, and it grew, and waxed a great tree: and the fowls of the air lodged in the branches of it.' ²⁰And again he said, 'Whereunto shall I liken the kingdom of God? ²¹It is like leaven, which a woman took and hid in three measures of meal, till the whole was leavened.'

²²And he went through the cities and villages, teaching, and journeying towards Jerusalem. ²³Then said one unto him, 'Lord, are there few that be saved?' And he said unto them, ²⁴'Strive to enter in at the strait gate: for many, I say unto you, will seek to enter in, and shall not be able. ²⁵When once the master of the house is risen up, and hath shut to the door, and ye begin to stand without, and to knock at the door, saying, "Lord, Lord, open unto us", and he shall answer and say unto you, "I know you not whence you are": ²⁶then shall ye begin to say, "We have eaten and drunk in thy presence, and thou hast taught in our streets". ²⁷But he shall say, "I tell you, I know you not whence you are; depart from me, all ye workers of iniquity". ²⁸There shall be weeping and gnashing of teeth, when ye shall see Abraham, and Isaac, and Jacob, and all the prophets in the kingdom of God, and you yourselves thrust out. ²⁹And they shall come from the east, and from the west, and

from the north, and from the south, and shall sit down in the kingdom of God. ³⁰And behold, there are last which shall be first, and there are first which shall be last.'

³¹The same day there came certain of the Pharisees, saying unto him, 'Get thee out, and depart hence: for Herod will kill thee'. ³²And he said unto them, 'Go ye, and tell that fox, "Behold, I cast out devils, and I do cures today and tomorrow, and the third day I shall be perfected". ³³Nevertheless I must walk today, and tomorrow, and the day following: for it cannot be that a prophet perish out of Jerusalem. ³⁴O Jerusalem, Jerusalem, which killest the prophets, and stonest them that are sent unto thee; how often would I have gathered thy children together, as a hen doth gather her brood under her wings, and ye would not! ³⁵Behold, your house is left unto you desolate. And verily I say unto you, ye shall not see me, until the time come when ye shall say, "Blessed is he that cometh in the name of the Lord".'

14 And it came to pass, as he went into the house of one of the chief Pharisees to eat bread on the sabbath day, that they watched him. ²And behold, there was a certain man before him which had the dropsy. ³And Jesus answering spoke unto the lawyers and Pharisees, saying, 'Is it lawful to heal on the sabbath day?' ⁴And they held their peace. And he took him, and healed him, and let him go, ⁵and answered them, saying, 'Which of you shall have an ass or an ox fallen into a pit, and will not straightway pull him out on the sabbath day?' ⁶And they could not answer him again to these things.

⁷And he put forth a parable to those which were bidden, when he marked how they chose out the chief rooms, saying unto them, ⁸'When thou art bidden of any man to a wedding, sit not down in the highest room: lest a more honourable man than thou be bidden of him, ⁹and he that bade thee and him come and say to thee, "Give this man place": and thou begin with shame to take the lowest room. ¹⁰But when thou art bidden, go and sit down in the lowest room, that when he that bade thee cometh, he may say unto thee, "Friend, go up higher": then shalt thou have worship in the presence of them that sit at meat with thee. ¹¹For whosoever exalteth himself shall be abased: and he that humbleth himself shall be exalted.'

¹²Then said he also to him that bade him, 'When thou makest a dinner or a supper, call not thy friends, nor thy brethren, neither thy kinsmen, nor thy rich neighbours, lest they also bid thee again, and a recompense be made thee. ¹³But when thou makest a feast, call the poor, the maimed, the lame, the blind, ¹⁴and thou shalt be blessed, for they cannot recompense thee: for thou shalt be recompensed at the resurrection of the just.'

¹⁵And when one of them that sat at meat with him heard these things, he said unto him, 'Blessed is he that shall eat bread in the kingdom of God'. ¹⁶Then said he unto him, 'A certain man made a great supper, and bade many: ¹⁷and sent his servant at supper time to say to them that were bidden, "Come, for all things are now ready". ¹⁸And they all with one consent began to make excuse. The first said unto him, "I have

bought a piece of ground, and I must needs go and see it: I pray thee have me excused". ¹⁹And another said, "I have bought five yoke of oxen, and I go to prove them: I pray thee have me excused". ²⁰And another said, "I have married a wife: and therefore I cannot come". ²¹So that servant came, and showed his lord these things. Then the master of the house being angry said to his servant, "Go out quickly into the streets and lanes of the city, and bring in hither the poor, and the maimed, and the halt, and the blind". ²²And the servant said, "Lord, it is done as thou hast commanded, and yet there is room". ²³And the lord said unto the servant, "Go out into the highways and hedges, and compel them to come in, that my house may be filled. ²⁴For I say unto you, that none of those men which were bidden shall taste of my supper."'

²⁵And there went great multitudes with him: and he turned, and said unto them, ²⁶'If any man come to me, and hate not his father, and mother, and wife, and children, and brethren, and sisters, yea, and his own life also, he cannot be my disciple. ²⁷And whosoever doth not bear his cross, and come after me, cannot be my disciple. ²⁸For which of you, intending to build a tower, sitteth not down first, and counteth the cost, whether he have sufficient to finish it? ²⁹lest haply, after he hath laid the foundation, and is not able to finish it, all that behold it begin to mock him, ³⁰saying, "This man began to build, and was not able to finish". ³¹Or what king, going to make war against another king, sitteth not down first, and consulteth whether he be able with ten thousand to meet him that cometh against him with twenty thousand? ³²Or else, while the other is yet a great way off, he sendeth an ambassage, and desireth conditions of peace. ³³So likewise, whosoever he be of you that forsaketh not all that he hath, he cannot be my disciple.

³⁴'Salt is good: but if the salt have lost his savour, wherewith shall it be seasoned? ³⁵It is neither fit for the land, nor yet for the dunghill: but men cast it out. He that hath ears to hear, let him hear.'

15 Then drew near unto him all the publicans and sinners for to hear him. ²And the Pharisees and scribes murmured, saying, 'This man receiveth sinners, and eateth with them'.

³And he spoke this parable unto them, saying, ⁴'What man of you, having a hundred sheep, if he lose one of them, doth not leave the ninety and nine in the wilderness, and go after that which is lost, until he find it? ⁵And when he hath found it, he layeth it on his shoulders, rejoicing. ⁶And when he cometh home, he calleth together his friends and neighbours, saying unto them, "Rejoice with me, for I have found my sheep which was lost". ⁷I say unto you, that likewise joy shall be in heaven over one sinner that repenteth, more than over ninety and nine just persons, which need no repentance.

⁸'Either what woman having ten pieces of silver, if she lose one piece, doth not light a candle, and sweep the house, and seek diligently till she find it? ⁹And when she hath found it, she calleth her friends and her neighbours together, saying, "Rejoice with me, for I have found the piece which I had lost". ¹⁰Likewise, I say unto you, there is joy in the presence of the angels of God over one sinner that repenteth.'

[11]And he said, 'A certain man had two sons: [12]and the younger of them said to his father, "Father, give me the portion of goods that falleth to me". And he divided unto them his living. [13]And not many days after the younger son gathered all together, and took his journey into a far country, and there wasted his substance with riotous living. [14]And when he had spent all, there arose a mighty famine in that land, and he began to be in want. [15]And he went and joined himself to a citizen of that country, and he sent him into his fields to feed swine. [16]And he would fain have filled his belly with the husks that the swine did eat: and no man gave unto him. [17]And when he came to himself, he said, "How many hired servants of my father have bread enough and to spare, and I perish with hunger! [18]I will arise and go to my father, and will say unto him, 'Father, I have sinned against heaven, and before thee, [19]and am no more worthy to be called thy son: make me as one of thy hired servants'." [20]And he arose, and came to his father. But when he was yet a great way off, his father saw him, and had compassion, and ran, and fell on his neck, and kissed him. [21]And the son said unto him, "Father, I have sinned against heaven, and in thy sight, and am no more worthy to be called thy son". [22]But the father said to his servants, "Bring forth the best robe, and put it on him, and put a ring on his hand, and shoes on his feet. [23]And bring hither the fatted calf, and kill it, and let us eat, and be merry. [24]For this my son was dead, and is alive again; he was lost, and is found." And they began to be merry.

[25]'Now his elder son was in the field, and as he came and drew nigh to the house, he heard music and dancing. [26]And he called one of the servants, and asked what these things meant. [27]And he said unto him, "Thy brother is come, and thy father hath killed the fatted calf, because he hath received him safe and sound". [28]And he was angry, and would not go in: therefore came his father out, and entreated him. [29]And he answering said to his father, "Lo, these many years do I serve thee, neither transgressed I at any time thy commandment, and yet thou never gavest me a kid, that I might make merry with my friends: [30]but as soon as this thy son was come, which hath devoured thy living with harlots, thou hast killed for him the fatted calf". [31]And he said unto him, "Son, thou art ever with me, and all that I have is thine. [32]It was meet that we should make merry, and be glad: for this thy brother was dead, and is alive again: and was lost, and is found."'

16 And he said also unto his disciples, 'There was a certain rich man, which had a steward, and the same was accused unto him that he had wasted his goods. [2]And he called him, and said unto him, "How is it that I hear this of thee? Give an account of thy stewardship: for thou mayest be no longer steward." [3]Then the steward said within himself, "What shall I do? for my lord taketh away from me the stewardship: I cannot dig, to beg I am ashamed. [4]I am resolved what to do, that, when I am put out of the stewardship, they may receive me into their houses." [5]So he called every one of his lord's debtors unto him, and said unto the first, "How much owest thou unto my lord?" [6]And he said, "A hundred measures of oil". And he said unto him, "Take thy bill,

and sit down quickly, and write fifty". [7]Then said he to another, "And how much owest thou?" And he said, "A hundred measures of wheat". And he said unto him, "Take thy bill, and write fourscore". [8]And the lord commended the unjust steward, because he had done wisely: for the children of this world are in their generation wiser than the children of light. [9]And I say unto you, make to yourselves friends of the mammon of unrighteousness, that when ye fail, they may receive you into everlasting habitations. [10]He that is faithful in that which is least is faithful also in much: and he that is unjust in the least is unjust also in much. [11]If therefore ye have not been faithful in the unrighteous mammon, who will commit to your trust the true riches? [12]And if ye have not been faithful in that which is another man's, who shall give you that which is your own? [13]No servant can serve two masters, for either he will hate the one, and love the other: or else he will hold to the one, and despise the other. Ye cannot serve God and mammon.'

[14]And the Pharisees also, who were covetous, heard all these things: and they derided him. [15]And he said unto them, 'Ye are they which justify yourselves before men, but God knoweth your hearts: for that which is highly esteemed amongst men is abomination in the sight of God. [16]The law and the prophets were until John: since that time the kingdom of God is preached, and every man presseth into it. [17]And it is easier for heaven and earth to pass, than one tittle of the law to fail. [18]Whosoever putteth away his wife, and marrieth another, committeth adultery: and whosoever marrieth her that is put away from her husband committeth adultery.

[19]'There was a certain rich man, which was clothed in purple and fine linen, and fared sumptuously every day. [20]And there was a certain beggar named Lazarus, which was laid at his gate, full of sores, [21]and desiring to be fed with the crumbs which fell from the rich man's table: moreover the dogs came and licked his sores. [22]And it came to pass that the beggar died, and was carried by the angels into Abraham's bosom: the rich man also died, and was buried. [23]And in hell he lifted up his eyes, being in torments, and seeth Abraham afar off, and Lazarus in his bosom: [24]and he cried and said, "Father Abraham, have mercy on me, and send Lazarus, that he may dip the tip of his finger in water, and cool my tongue, for I am tormented in this flame". [25]But Abraham said, "Son, remember that thou in thy lifetime receivedst thy good things, and likewise Lazarus evil things, but now he is comforted, and thou art tormented. [26]And besides all this, between us and you there is a great gulf fixed, so that they which would pass from hence to you cannot, neither can they pass to us, that would come from thence." [27]Then he said, "I pray thee therefore, father, that thou wouldst send him to my father's house: [28]for I have five brethren, that he may testify unto them, lest they also come into this place of torment". [29]Abraham saith unto him, "They have Moses and the prophets, let them hear them". [30]And he said, "Nay, father Abraham: but if one went unto them from the dead, they will repent". [31]And he said unto him, "If they hear not Moses and the prophets, neither will they be persuaded, though one rose from the dead".'

17 Then said he unto the disciples, 'It is impossible but that offences will come, but woe unto him, through whom they come. ²It were better for him that a millstone were hanged about his neck, and he cast into the sea, than that he should offend one of these little ones. ³Take heed to yourselves: if thy brother trespass against thee, rebuke him, and if he repent, forgive him. ⁴And if he trespass against thee seven times in a day, and seven times in a day turn again to thee, saying, "I repent", thou shalt forgive him.'

⁵And the apostles said unto the Lord, 'Increase our faith'. ⁶And the Lord said, 'If ye had faith as a grain of mustard seed, ye might say unto this sycamine tree, "Be thou plucked up by the root, and be thou planted in the sea", and it should obey you. ⁷But which of you, having a servant ploughing or feeding cattle, will say unto him by and by, when he is come from the field, "Go and sit down to meat?" ⁸And will not rather say unto him, "Make ready wherewith I may sup, and gird thyself, and serve me, till I have eaten and drunken: and afterward thou shalt eat and drink?" ⁹Doth he thank that servant because he did the things that were commanded him? I trow not. ¹⁰So likewise ye, when ye shall have done all those things which are commanded you, say, "We are unprofitable servants: we have done that which was our duty to do".'

¹¹And it came to pass, as he went to Jerusalem, that he passed through the midst of Samaria and Galilee. ¹²And as he entered into a certain village, there met him ten men that were lepers, which stood afar off. ¹³And they lifted up their voices, and said, 'Jesus, Master, have mercy on us'. ¹⁴And when he saw them, he said unto them, 'Go show yourselves unto the priests'. And it came to pass that as they went, they were cleansed. ¹⁵And one of them, when he saw that he was healed, turned back, and with a loud voice glorified God, ¹⁶and fell down on his face at his feet, giving him thanks: and he was a Samaritan. ¹⁷And Jesus answering said, 'Were there not ten cleansed? but where are the nine? ¹⁸There are not found that returned to give glory to God, save this stranger.' ¹⁹And he said unto him, 'Arise, go thy way, thy faith hath made thee whole'.

²⁰And when he was demanded of the Pharisees, when the kingdom of God should come, he answered them and said, 'The kingdom of God cometh not with observation. ²¹Neither shall they say, "Lo here", or, "Lo there": for behold, the kingdom of God is within you.'

²²And he said unto the disciples, 'The days will come, when ye shall desire to see one of the days of the Son of man, and ye shall not see it. ²³And they shall say to you, "See here", or, "See there": go not after them, nor follow them. ²⁴For as the lightning that lighteneth out of the one part under heaven, shineth unto the other part under heaven: so shall also the Son of man be in his day. ²⁵But first must he suffer many things, and be rejected of this generation.

²⁶'And as it was in the days of Noe, so shall it be also in the days of the Son of man. ²⁷They did eat, they drank, they married wives, they were given in marriage, until the day that Noe entered into the ark, and the

flood came, and destroyed them all. [28]Likewise also as it was in the days of Lot, they did eat, they drank, they bought, they sold, they planted, they built: [29]but the same day that Lot went out of Sodom, it rained fire and brimstone from heaven, and destroyed them all: [30]even thus shall it be in the day when the Son of man is revealed. [31]In that day he which shall be upon the house-top, and his stuff in the house, let him not come down to take it away: and he that is in the field, let him likewise not return back. [32]Remember Lot's wife. [33]Whosoever shall seek to save his life shall lose it, and whosoever shall lose his life shall preserve it. [34]I tell you, in that night there shall be two men in one bed; the one shall be taken, the other shall be left. [35]Two women shall be grinding together; the one shall be taken, and the other left. [36]Two men shall be in the field; the one shall be taken, and the other left.' [37]And they answered and said unto him, 'Where, Lord?' And he said unto them, 'Wheresoever the body is, thither will the eagles be gathered together'.

18 And he spoke a parable unto them to this end, that men ought always to pray, and not to faint, [2]saying, 'There was in a city a judge, which feared not God, neither regarded man. [3]And there was a widow in that city, and she came unto him, saying, "Avenge me of my adversary". [4]And he would not for a while. But afterward he said within himself, "Though I fear not God, nor regard man, [5]yet because this widow troubleth me, I will avenge her, lest by her continual coming she weary me".' [6]And the Lord said, 'Hear what the unjust judge saith. [7]And shall not God avenge his own elect, which cry day and night unto him, though he bear long with them? [8]I tell you that he will avenge them speedily. Nevertheless when the Son of man cometh, shall he find faith on the earth?'

[9]And he spoke this parable unto certain which trusted in themselves that they were righteous, and despised others: [10]Two men went up into the temple to pray, the one a Pharisee, and the other a publican. [11]The Pharisee stood and prayed thus with himself, "God, I thank thee, that I am not as other men are, extortioners, unjust, adulterers, or even as this publican. [12]I fast twice in the week, I give tithes of all that I possess." [13]And the publican, standing afar off, would not lift up so much as his eyes unto heaven, but smote upon his breast, saying, "God be merciful to me a sinner". [14]I tell you, this man went down to his house justified rather than the other: for every one that exalteth himself shall be abased: and he that humbleth himself shall be exalted.'

[15]And they brought unto him also infants, that he would touch them: but when his disciples saw it, they rebuked them. [16]But Jesus called them unto him, and said, 'Suffer little children to come unto me, and forbid them not: for of such is the kingdom of God. [17]Verily I say unto you, whosoever shall not receive the kingdom of God as a little child shall in no wise enter therein.'

[18]And a certain ruler asked him, saying, 'Good Master, what shall I do to inherit eternal life?' [19]And Jesus said unto him, 'Why callest thou me good? None is good, save one, that is, God. [20]Thou knowest the commandments, do not commit adultery, do not kill, do not steal, do not

bear false witness, honour thy father and thy mother.' ²¹And he said, 'All these have I kept from my youth up'. ²²Now when Jesus heard these things, he said unto him, 'Yet lackest thou one thing: sell all that thou hast, and distribute unto the poor, and thou shalt have treasure in heaven, and come, follow me'. ²³And when he heard this, he was very sorrowful, for he was very rich. ²⁴And when Jesus saw that he was very sorrowful, he said, 'How hardly shall they that have riches enter into the kingdom of God? ²⁵For it is easier for a camel to go through a needle's eye, than for a rich man to enter into the kingdom of God.' ²⁶And they that heard it said, 'Who then can be saved?' ²⁷And he said, 'The things which are impossible with men are possible with God'. ²⁸Then Peter said, 'Lo, we have left all, and followed thee'. ²⁹And he said unto them, 'Verily I say unto you, there is no man that hath left house, or parents, or brethren, or wife, or children, for the kingdom of God's sake, ³⁰who shall not receive manifold more in this present time, and in the world to come life everlasting'.

³¹Then he took unto him the twelve, and said unto them, 'Behold, we go up to Jerusalem, and all things that are written by the prophets concerning the Son of man shall be accomplished. ³²For he shall be delivered unto the Gentiles, and shall be mocked, and spitefully entreated, and spat on: ³³and they shall scourge him, and put him to death, and the third day he shall rise again.' ³⁴And they understood none of these things: and this saying was hid from them, neither knew they the things which were spoken.

³⁵And it came to pass that as he was come nigh unto Jericho, a certain blind man sat by the wayside begging, ³⁶and hearing the multitude pass by, he asked what it meant. ³⁷And they told him that Jesus of Nazareth passeth by. ³⁸And he cried, saying, 'Jesus, thou Son of David, have mercy on me'. ³⁹And they which went before rebuked him, that he should hold his peace: but he cried so much the more, 'Thou Son of David, have mercy on me'. ⁴⁰And Jesus stood, and commanded him to be brought unto him: and when he was come near, he asked him, ⁴¹saying, 'What wilt thou that I shall do unto thee?' And he said, 'Lord, that I may receive my sight'. ⁴²And Jesus said unto him, 'Receive thy sight, thy faith hath saved thee'. ⁴³And immediately he received his sight, and followed him, glorifying God: and all the people, when they saw it, gave praise unto God.

19 And Jesus entered and passed through Jericho. ²And behold, there was a man named Zacchaeus, which was the chief among the publicans, and he was rich. ³And he sought to see Jesus who he was, and could not for the press, because he was little of stature. ⁴And he ran before, and climbed up into a sycamore tree to see him, for he was to pass that way. ⁵And when Jesus came to the place, he looked up, and saw him, and said unto him, 'Zacchaeus, make haste, and come down, for today I must abide at thy house'. ⁶And he made haste, and came down, and received him joyfully. ⁷And when they saw it, they all murmured, saying, that he was gone to be guest with a man that is a sinner. ⁸And Zacchaeus stood, and said unto the Lord, 'Behold, Lord, the half of my goods I give to the poor, and if I have taken anything from any man by false accusation, I restore him fourfold'. ⁹And Jesus said unto him, 'This day is salvation come to this house, forasmuch as he also is the son of Abraham. ¹⁰For the Son of man is come to seek and to save that which was lost.'

¹¹And as they heard these things, he added and spoke a parable, because he was nigh to Jerusalem, and because they thought that the kingdom of God should immediately appear. ¹²He said therefore, 'A certain nobleman went into a far country to receive for himself a kingdom, and to return. ¹³And he called his ten servants, and delivered them ten pounds, and said unto them, "Occupy till I come". ¹⁴But his citizens hated him, and sent a message after him, saying, "We will not have this man to reign over us". ¹⁵And it came to pass that when he was returned, having received the kingdom, then he commanded these servants to be called unto him, to whom he had given the money, that he might know how much every man had gained by trading. ¹⁶Then came the first, saying, "Lord, thy pound hath gained ten pounds". ¹⁷And he said unto him, "Well, thou good servant: because thou hast been faithful in a very little, have thou authority over ten cities". ¹⁸And the second came, saying, "Lord, thy pound hath gained five pounds". ¹⁹And he said likewise to him, "Be thou also over five cities". ²⁰And another came, saying, "Lord, behold, here is thy pound, which I have kept laid up in a napkin: ²¹for I feared thee, because thou art an austere man: thou takest up that thou layedst not down, and reapest that thou didst not sow". ²²And he saith unto him, "Out of thy own mouth will I judge thee, thou wicked servant. Thou knewest that I was an austere man, taking up that I laid not down, and reaping that I did not sow. ²³Wherefore then gavest not thou my money into the bank, that at my coming I might have required my own with usury?" ²⁴And he said unto them that stood by, "Take from him the pound, and give it to him that hath ten pounds". ²⁵And they said unto him, "Lord, he hath ten pounds". ²⁶"For I say unto you, that unto every one which hath shall be given, and from him that hath not, even that he hath shall be taken away from him. ²⁷But those my enemies, which would not that I should reign over them, bring hither, and slay them before me."'

²⁸And when he had thus spoken, he went before, ascending up to Jerusalem. ²⁹And it came to pass, when he was come nigh to Bethphage and Bethany, at the mount called the mount of Olives, he sent two of his disciples, ³⁰saying, 'Go ye into the village over against you, in the which at your entering ye shall find a colt tied, whereon yet never man sat: loose him, and bring him hither. ³¹And if any man ask you, "Why do ye loose him?" thus shall ye say unto him, "Because the Lord hath need of him".' ³²And they that were sent went their way, and found even as he had said unto them. ³³And as they were loosing the colt, the owners thereof said unto them, 'Why loose ye the colt?' ³⁴And they said, 'The Lord hath need of him'. ³⁵And they brought him to Jesus: and they cast their garments upon the colt, and they set Jesus thereon. ³⁶And as he went, they spread their clothes in the way. ³⁷And when he was come

nigh, even now at the descent of the mount of Olives, the whole multitude of the disciples began to rejoice and praise God with a loud voice for all the mighty works that they had seen, [38]saying, 'Blessed be the King that cometh in the name of the Lord, peace in heaven, and glory in the highest'. [39]And some of the Pharisees from among the multitude said unto him, 'Master, rebuke thy disciples'. [40]And he answered and said unto them, 'I tell you that, if these should hold their peace, the stones would immediately cry out'.

[41]And when he was come near, he beheld the city, and wept over it, [42]saying, 'If thou hadst known, even thou, at least in this thy day, the things which belong unto thy peace! but now they are hid from thy eyes. [43]For the days shall come upon thee, that thy enemies shall cast a trench about thee, and compass thee round, and keep thee in on every side, [44]and shall lay thee even with the ground, and thy children within thee: and they shall not leave in thee one stone upon another, because thou knewest not the time of thy visitation.'

[45]And he went into the temple, and began to cast out them that sold therein, and them that bought, [46]saying unto them, 'It is written, "My house is the house of prayer": but ye have made it a den of thieves'.

[47]And he taught daily in the temple. But the chief priests and the scribes and the chief of the people sought to destroy him, [48]and could not find what they might do: for all the people were very attentive to hear him.

20 And it came to pass that on one of those days, as he taught the people in the temple, and preached the gospel, the chief priests and the scribes came upon him with the elders, [2]and spoke unto him, saying, 'Tell us, by what authority doest thou these things? or who is he that gave thee this authority?' [3]And he answered and said unto them, 'I will also ask you one thing, and answer me. [4]The baptism of John, was it from heaven, or of men?' [5]And they reasoned with themselves, saying, 'If we shall say, "From heaven", he will say, "Why then believed ye him not?" [6]But and if we say, "Of men", all the people will stone us: for they be persuaded that John was a prophet.' [7]And they answered, that they could not tell whence it was. [8]And Jesus said unto them, 'Neither tell I you by what authority I do these things'.

[9]Then began he to speak to the people this parable: 'A certain man planted a vineyard, and let it forth to husbandmen, and went into a far country for a long time. [10]And at the season he sent a servant to the husbandmen, that they should give him of the fruit of the vineyard, but the husbandmen beat him, and sent him away empty. [11]And again he sent another servant, and they beat him also, and entreated him shamefully, and sent him away empty. [12]And again he sent the third, and they wounded him also, and cast him out. [13]Then said the lord of the vineyard, "What shall I do? I will send my beloved son: it may be they will reverence him when they see him." [14]But when the husbandmen saw him, they reasoned among themselves, saying, "This is the heir, come, let us kill him, that the inheritance may be ours". [15]So they cast him out of the vineyard, and killed him. What therefore shall the

lord of the vineyard do unto them? ¹⁶He shall come and destroy these husbandmen, and shall give the vineyard to others.' And when they heard it, they said, 'God forbid'. ¹⁷And he beheld them, and said, 'What is this then that is written, "The stone which the builders rejected, the same is become the head of the corner"? ¹⁸Whosoever shall fall upon that stone shall be broken: but on whomsoever it shall fall, it will grind him to powder.'

¹⁹And the chief priests and the scribes the same hour sought to lay hands on him, and they feared the people: for they perceived that he had spoken this parable against them. ²⁰And they watched him, and sent forth spies, which should feign themselves just men, that they might take hold of his words, that so they might deliver him unto the power and authority of the governor. ²¹And they asked him, saying, 'Master, we know that thou sayest and teachest rightly, neither acceptest thou the person of any, but teachest the way of God truly. ²²Is it lawful for us to give tribute unto Caesar, or no?' ²³But he perceived their craftiness, and said unto them, 'Why tempt ye me? ²⁴Show me a penny. Whose image and superscription hath it?' They answered and said, 'Caesar's'. ²⁵And he said unto them, 'Render therefore unto Caesar the things which be Caesar's, and unto God the things which be God's'. ²⁶And they could not take hold of his words before the people, and they marvelled at his answer, and held their peace.

²⁷Then came to him certain of the Sadducees, which deny that there is any resurrection, and they asked him, ²⁸saying, 'Master, Moses wrote unto us, "If any man's brother die, having a wife, and he die without children, that his brother should take his wife, and raise up seed unto his brother". ²⁹There were therefore seven brethren, and the first took a wife, and died without children. ³⁰And the second took her to wife, and he died childless. ³¹And the third took her, and in like manner the seven also. And they left no children, and died. ³²Last of all the woman died also. ³³Therefore in the resurrection whose wife of them is she? for seven had her to wife.' ³⁴And Jesus answering said unto them, 'The children of this world marry, and are given in marriage: ³⁵but they which shall be accounted worthy to obtain that world, and the resurrection from the dead, neither marry, nor are given in marriage. ³⁶Neither can they die any more: for they are equal unto the angels, and are the children of God, being the children of the resurrection. ³⁷Now that the dead are raised, even Moses showed at the bush, when he calleth the Lord the God of Abraham, and the God of Isaac, and the God of Jacob. ³⁸For he is not a God of the dead, but of the living: for all live unto him.'

³⁹Then certain of the scribes answering said, 'Master, thou hast well said'. ⁴⁰And after that they durst not ask him any question at all. ⁴¹And he said unto them, 'How say they that Christ is David's son? ⁴²And David himself saith in the book of Psalms, "The Lord said unto my Lord, 'Sit thou on my right hand, ⁴³till I make thy enemies thy footstool'". ⁴⁴David therefore calleth him Lord, how is he then his son?'

⁴⁵Then in the audience of all the people he said unto his disciples, ⁴⁶'Beware of the scribes, which desire to walk in long robes, and love

greetings in the markets, and the highest seats in the synagogues, and the chief rooms at feasts: ⁴⁷which devour widows' houses, and for a show make long prayers: the same shall receive greater damnation'.

21 And he looked up, and saw the rich men casting their gifts into the treasury. ²And he saw also a certain poor widow casting in thither two mites. ³And he said, 'Of a truth I say unto you, that this poor widow hath cast in more than they all. ⁴For all these have of their abundance cast in unto the offerings of God, but she of her penury hath cast in all the living that she had.'

⁵And as some spoke of the temple, how it was adorned with goodly stones and gifts, he said, ⁶'As for these things which ye behold, the days will come, in the which there shall not be left one stone upon another, that shall not be thrown down'. ⁷And they asked him, saying, 'Master, but when shall these things be? and what sign will there be when these things shall come to pass?' ⁸And he said, 'Take heed that ye be not deceived: for many shall come in my name, saying, "I am Christ", and the time draweth near: go ye not therefore after them. ⁹But when ye shall hear of wars and commotions, be not terrified: for these things must first come to pass, but the end is not by and by.'

¹⁰Then said he unto them, 'Nation shall rise against nation, and kingdom against kingdom: ¹¹and great earthquakes shall be in divers places, and famines, and pestilences: and fearful sights and great signs shall there be from heaven. ¹²But before all these, they shall lay their hands on you, and persecute you, delivering you up to the synagogues, and into prisons, being brought before kings and rulers for my name's sake. ¹³And it shall turn to you for a testimony. ¹⁴Settle it therefore in your hearts, not to meditate before what ye shall answer. ¹⁵For I will give you a mouth and wisdom, which all your adversaries shall not be able to gainsay nor resist. ¹⁶And ye shall be betrayed both by parents, and brethren, and kinsfolks, and friends, and some of you shall they cause to be put to death. ¹⁷And ye shall be hated of all men for my name's sake. ¹⁸But there shall not a hair of your head perish. ¹⁹In your patience possess ye your souls.

²⁰'And when ye shall see Jerusalem compassed with armies, then know that the desolation thereof is nigh. ²¹Then let them which are in Judea flee to the mountains, and let them which are in the midst of it depart out, and let not them that are in the countries enter thereinto. ²²For these be the days of vengeance, that all things which are written may be fulfilled. ²³But woe unto them that are with child, and to them that give suck, in those days, for there shall be great distress in the land, and wrath upon this people. ²⁴And they shall fall by the edge of the sword, and shall be led away captive into all nations, and Jerusalem shall be trodden down of the Gentiles, until the times of the Gentiles be fulfilled. ²⁵And there shall be signs in the sun, and in the moon, and in the stars, and upon the earth distress of nations, with perplexity, the sea and the waves roaring, ²⁶men's hearts failing them for fear, and for looking after those things which are coming on the earth: for the powers of heaven shall be shaken. ²⁷And then shall they see the Son of man

coming in a cloud with power and great glory. ²⁸And when these things begin to come to pass, then look up, and lift up your heads, for your redemption draweth nigh.'

²⁹And he spoke to them a parable, 'Behold the fig tree, and all the trees, ³⁰when they now shoot forth, ye see and know of your own selves that summer is now nigh at hand. ³¹So likewise ye, when ye see these things come to pass, know ye that the kingdom of God is nigh at hand. ³²Verily I say unto you, this generation shall not pass away, till all be fulfilled. ³³Heaven and earth shall pass away, but my words shall not pass away.

³⁴'And take heed to yourselves, lest at any time your hearts be overcharged with surfeiting, and drunkenness, and cares of this life, and so that day come upon you unawares. ³⁵For as a snare shall it come on all them that dwell on the face of the whole earth. ³⁶Watch ye therefore, and pray always, that ye may be accounted worthy to escape all these things that shall come to pass, and to stand before the Son of man.'

³⁷And in the day time he was teaching in the temple, and at night he went out, and abode in the mount that is called the mount of Olives. ³⁸And all the people came early in the morning to him in the temple, for to hear him.

22 Now the feast of unleavened bread drew nigh, which is called the Passover. ²And the chief priests and scribes sought how they might kill him; for they feared the people.

³Then entered Satan into Judas surnamed Iscariot, being of the number of the twelve. ⁴And he went his way, and communed with the chief priests and captains, how he might betray him unto them. ⁵And they were glad, and covenanted to give him money. ⁶And he promised, and sought opportunity to betray him unto them in the absence of the multitude.

⁷Then came the day of unleavened bread, when the passover must be killed. ⁸And he sent Peter and John, saying, 'Go and prepare us the passover, that we may eat'. ⁹And they said unto him, 'Where wilt thou that we prepare?' ¹⁰And he said unto them, 'Behold, when ye are entered into the city, there shall a man meet you, bearing a pitcher of water, follow him into the house where he entereth in. ¹¹And ye shall say unto the goodman of the house, "The Master saith unto thee, 'Where is the guest-chamber, where I shall eat the passover with my disciples?'" ¹²And he shall show you a large upper room furnished: there make ready.' ¹³And they went, and found as he had said unto them, and they made ready the passover.

¹⁴And when the hour was come, he sat down, and the twelve apostles with him. ¹⁵And he said unto them, 'With desire I have desired to eat this passover with you before I suffer. ¹⁶For I say unto you, I will not any more eat thereof, until it be fulfilled in the kingdom of God.' ¹⁷And he took the cup, and gave thanks, and said, 'Take this, and divide it among yourselves. ¹⁸For I say unto you, I will not drink of the fruit of the vine, until the kingdom of God shall come.'

¹⁹And he took bread, and gave thanks, and broke it, and gave unto

them, saying, 'This is my body which is given for you, this do in remembrance of me'. [20]Likewise also the cup after supper, saying, 'This cup is the new testament in my blood, which is shed for you.

[21]'But behold, the hand of him that betrayeth me is with me on the table. [22]And truly the Son of man goeth, as it was determined, but woe unto that man by whom he is betrayed.' [23]And they began to inquire among themselves, which of them it was that should do this thing.

[24]And there was also a strife among them, which of them should be accounted the greatest. [25]And he said unto them, 'The kings of the Gentiles exercise lordship over them, and they that exercise authority upon them are called benefactors. [26]But ye shall not be so: but he that is greatest among you, let him be as the younger, and he that is chief, as he that doth serve. [27]For whether is greater, he that sitteth at meat, or he that serveth? Is not he that sitteth at meat? But I am among you as he that serveth. [28]Ye are they which have continued with me in my temptations. [29]And I appoint unto you a kingdom, as my Father hath appointed unto me, [30]that ye may eat and drink at my table in my kingdom, and sit on thrones judging the twelve tribes of Israel.'

[31]And the Lord said, 'Simon, Simon, behold, Satan hath desired to have you, that he may sift you as wheat: [32]but I have prayed for thee, that thy faith fail not: and when thou art converted, strengthen thy brethren'. [33]And he said unto him, 'Lord, I am ready to go with thee, both into prison, and to death'. [34]And he said, 'I tell thee, Peter, the cock shall not crow this day, before that thou shalt thrice deny that thou knowest me'.

[35]And he said unto them, 'When I sent you without purse, and scrip, and shoes, lacked ye anything?' And they said, 'Nothing'. [36]Then said he unto them, 'But now, he that hath a purse, let him take it, and likewise his scrip: and he that hath no sword, let him sell his garment, and buy one. [37]For I say unto you, that this that is written must yet be accomplished in me, "And he was reckoned among the transgressors": for the things concerning me have an end.' [38]And they said, 'Lord, behold, here are two swords'. And he said unto them, 'It is enough'.

[39]And he came out, and went, as he was wont, to the mount of Olives, and his disciples also followed him. [40]And when he was at the place, he said unto them, 'Pray that ye enter not into temptation'. [41]And he was withdrawn from them about a stone's cast, and kneeled down, and prayed, [42]saying, 'Father, if thou be willing, remove this cup from me: nevertheless not my will, but thine, be done'. [43]And there appeared an angel unto him from heaven, strengthening him. [44]And being in an agony he prayed more earnestly, and his sweat was as it were great drops of blood falling down to the ground. [45]And when he rose up from prayer, and was come to his disciples, he found them sleeping for sorrow, [46]and said unto them, 'Why sleep ye? Rise and pray, lest ye enter into temptation.'

[47]And while he yet spoke, behold, a multitude, and he that was called Judas, one of the twelve, went before them, and drew near unto Jesus to kiss him. [48]But Jesus said unto him, 'Judas, betrayest thou the Son of

man with a kiss?' ⁴⁹When they which were about him saw what would follow, they said unto him, 'Lord, shall we smite with the sword?' ⁵⁰And one of them smote the servant of the high priest, and cut off his right ear. ⁵¹And Jesus answered and said, 'Suffer ye thus far'. And he touched his ear, and healed him. ⁵²Then Jesus said unto the chief priests, and captains of the temple, and the elders, which were come to him, 'Be ye come out as against a thief, with swords and staves? ⁵³When I was daily with you in the temple, ye stretched forth no hands against me: but this is your hour, and the power of darkness.'

⁵⁴Then took they him, and led him, and brought him into the high priest's house. And Peter followed afar off. ⁵⁵And when they had kindled a fire in the midst of the hall, and were set down together, Peter sat down among them. ⁵⁶But a certain maid beheld him as he sat by the fire, and earnestly looked upon him, and said, 'This man was also with him'. ⁵⁷And he denied him, saying, 'Woman, I know him not'. ⁵⁸And after a little while another saw him, and said, 'Thou art also of them'. And Peter said, 'Man, I am not'. ⁵⁹And about the space of one hour after another confidently affirmed, saying, 'Of a truth this fellow also was with him: for he is a Galilean'. ⁶⁰And Peter said, 'Man, I know not what thou sayest'. And immediately, while he yet spoke, the cock crew. ⁶¹And the Lord turned, and looked upon Peter. And Peter remembered the word of the Lord, how he had said unto him, 'Before the cock crow, thou shalt deny me thrice'. ⁶²And Peter went out, and wept bitterly.

⁶³And the men that held Jesus mocked him, and smote him. ⁶⁴And when they had blindfolded him, they struck him on the face, and asked him, saying, 'Prophesy, who is it that smote thee?' ⁶⁵And many other things blasphemously spoke they against him.

⁶⁶And as soon as it was day, the elders of the people and the chief priests and the scribes came together, and led him into their council, saying, ⁶⁷'Art thou the Christ? Tell us.' And he said unto them, 'If I tell you, you will not believe. ⁶⁸And if I also ask you, you will not answer me, nor let me go. ⁶⁹Hereafter shall the Son of man sit on the right hand of the power of God.' ⁷⁰Then said they all, 'Art thou then the Son of God?' And he said unto them, 'Ye say that I am'. ⁷¹And they said, 'What need we any further witness? For we ourselves have heard of his own mouth.'

23

And the whole multitude of them arose, and led him unto Pilate. ²And they began to accuse him, saying, 'We found this fellow perverting the nation, and forbidding to give tribute to Caesar, saying that he himself is Christ a King'. ³And Pilate asked him, saying, 'Art thou the King of the Jews?' And he answered him and said, 'Thou sayest it'. ⁴Then said Pilate to the chief priests and to the people, 'I find no fault in this man'. ⁵And they were the more fierce, saying, 'He stirreth up the people, teaching throughout all Jewry, beginning from Galilee to this place'. ⁶When Pilate heard of Galilee, he asked whether the man were a Galilean. ⁷And as soon as he knew that he belonged unto Herod's jurisdiction, he sent him to Herod, who himself also was at Jerusalem at that time.

⁸And when Herod saw Jesus, he was exceeding glad, for he was

desirous to see him of a long season, because he had heard many things of him, and he hoped to have seen some miracle done by him. ⁹Then he questioned with him in many words, but he answered him nothing. ¹⁰And the chief priests and scribes stood and vehemently accused him. ¹¹And Herod with his men of war set him at nought, and mocked him, and arrayed him in a gorgeous robe, and sent him again to Pilate.

¹²And the same day Pilate and Herod were made friends together: for before they were at enmity between themselves.

¹³And Pilate, when he had called together the chief priests and the rulers and the people, ¹⁴said unto them, 'Ye have brought this man unto me, as one that perverteth the people, and behold, I, having examined him before you, have found no fault in this man touching those things whereof ye accuse him. ¹⁵No, nor yet Herod: for I sent you to him, and lo, nothing worthy of death is done unto him. ¹⁶I will therefore chastise him, and release him.' ¹⁷For of necessity he must release one unto them at the feast. ¹⁸And they cried out all at once, saying, 'Away with this man, and release unto us Barabbas' ¹⁹(who for a certain sedition made in the city, and for murder, was cast in prison). ²⁰Pilate therefore, willing to release Jesus, spoke again to them. ²¹But they cried, saying, 'Crucify him, crucify him'. ²²And he said unto them the third time, 'Why, what evil hath he done? I have found no cause of death in him, I will therefore chastise him, and let him go.' ²³And they were instant with loud voices, requiring that he might be crucified. And the voices of them and of the chief priests prevailed. ²⁴And Pilate gave sentence that it should be as they required. ²⁵And he released unto them him that for sedition and murder was cast into prison, whom they had desired, but he delivered Jesus to their will. ²⁶And as they led him away, they laid hold upon one Simon, a Cyrenian, coming out of the country, and on him they laid the cross, that he might bear it after Jesus.

²⁷And there followed him a great company of people, and of women, which also bewailed and lamented him. ²⁸But Jesus turning unto them said, 'Daughters of Jerusalem, weep not for me, but weep for yourselves, and for your children. ²⁹For behold, the days are coming, in the which they shall say, "Blessed are the barren, and the wombs that never bore, and the paps which never gave suck". ³⁰Then shall they begin to say to the mountains, "Fall on us", and to the hills, "Cover us". ³¹For if they do these things in a green tree, what shall be done in the dry?'

³²And there were also two others, malefactors, led with him to be put to death. ³³And when they were come to the place, which is called Calvary, there they crucified him, and the malefactors, one on the right hand, and the other on the left.

³⁴Then said Jesus, 'Father, forgive them, for they know not what they do'. And they parted his raiment, and cast lots. ³⁵And the people stood beholding. And the rulers also with them derided him, saying, 'He saved others, let him save himself, if he be Christ, the chosen of God'. ³⁶And the soldiers also mocked him, coming to him, and offering him vinegar, ³⁷and saying, 'If thou be the king of the Jews, save thyself'.

³⁸And a superscription also was written over him in letters of Greek, and Latin, and Hebrew, 'THIS IS THE KING OF THE JEWS'.

³⁹And one of the malefactors which were hanged railed on him, saying, 'If thou be Christ, save thyself and us'. ⁴⁰But the other answering rebuked him, saying, 'Dost not thou fear God, seeing thou art in the same condemnation? ⁴¹And we indeed justly; for we receive the due reward of our deeds, but this man hath done nothing amiss.' ⁴²And he said unto Jesus, 'Lord, remember me when thou comest into thy kingdom'. ⁴³And Jesus said unto him, 'Verily I say unto thee, today shalt thou be with me in paradise'.

⁴⁴And it was about the sixth hour, and there was a darkness over all the earth until the ninth hour. ⁴⁵And the sun was darkened, and the veil of the temple was rent in the midst. ⁴⁶And when Jesus had cried with a loud voice, he said, 'Father, into thy hands I commend my spirit': and having said thus, he gave up the ghost. ⁴⁷Now when the centurion saw what was done, he glorified God, saying, 'Certainly this was a righteous man'. ⁴⁸And all the people that came together to that sight, beholding the things which were done, smote their breasts, and returned. ⁴⁹And all his acquaintance, and the women that followed him from Galilee, stood afar off, beholding these things.

⁵⁰And behold, there was a man named Joseph, a counsellor, and he was a good man, and a just ⁵¹(the same had not consented to the counsel and deed of them); he was of Arimathaea, a city of the Jews: who also himself waited for the kingdom of God. ⁵²This man went unto Pilate, and begged the body of Jesus. ⁵³And he took it down, and wrapped it in linen, and laid it in a sepulchre that was hewn in stone, wherein never man before was laid. ⁵⁴And that day was the preparation, and the sabbath drew on. ⁵⁵And the women also, which came with him from Galilee, followed after, and beheld the sepulchre, and how his body was laid. ⁵⁶And they returned, and prepared spices and ointments, and rested the sabbath day according to the commandment.

24 Now upon the first day of the week, very early in the morning, they came unto the sepulchre, bringing the spices which they had prepared, and certain others with them. ²And they found the stone rolled away from the sepulchre. ³And they entered in, and found not the body of the Lord Jesus. ⁴And it came to pass, as they were much perplexed thereabout, behold, two men stood by them in shining garments. ⁵And as they were afraid, and bowed down their faces to the earth, they said unto them, 'Why seek ye the living among the dead? ⁶He is not here, but is risen: remember how he spoke unto you when he was yet in Galilee, ⁷saying, "The Son of man must be delivered into the hands of sinful men, and be crucified, and the third day rise again".' ⁸And they remembered his words, ⁹and returned from the sepulchre, and told all these things unto the eleven, and to all the rest. ¹⁰It was Mary Magdalene, and Joanna, and Mary the mother of James, and other women that were with them, which told these things unto the apostles. ¹¹And their words seemed to them as idle tales, and they believed them not. ¹²Then arose Peter, and ran unto the sepulchre, and stooping down, he beheld the linen clothes laid by themselves, and departed, wondering in himself at that which was come to pass.

¹³And behold, two of them went that same day to a village called Emmaus, which was from Jerusalem about threescore furlongs. ¹⁴And they talked together of all these things which had happened. ¹⁵And it came to pass that while they communed together and reasoned, Jesus himself drew near, and went with them. ¹⁶But their eyes were held that they should not know him. ¹⁷And he said unto them, 'What manner of communications are these that ye have one to another, as ye walk, and are sad?' ¹⁸And the one of them, whose name was Cleopas, answering said unto him, 'Art thou only a stranger in Jerusalem, and hast not known the things which are come to pass there in these days?' ¹⁹And he said unto them, 'What things?' And they said unto him, 'Concerning Jesus of Nazareth, which was a prophet mighty in deed and word before God and all the people. ²⁰And how the chief priests and our rulers delivered him to be condemned to death, and have crucified him. ²¹But we trusted that it had been he which should have redeemed Israel: and besides all this, today is the third day since these things were done. ²²Yea, and certain women also of our company made us astonished, which were early at the sepulchre: ²³and when they found not his body, they came, saying, that they had also seen a vision of angels, which said that he was alive. ²⁴And certain of them which were with us went to the sepulchre, and found it even so as the women had said: but him they saw not.' ²⁵Then he said unto them, 'O fools, and slow of heart to believe all that the prophets have spoken: ²⁶ought not Christ to have suffered these things, and to enter into his glory?' ²⁷And beginning at Moses and all the prophets, he expounded unto them in all the scriptures the things concerning himself.

²⁸And they drew nigh unto the village, whither they went, and he made as though he would have gone farther. ²⁹But they constrained him, saying, 'Abide with us: for it is towards evening, and the day is far spent'. And he went in to tarry with them. ³⁰And it came to pass, as he sat at meat with them, he took bread, and blessed it, and broke, and gave to them. ³¹And their eyes were opened, and they knew him, and he vanished out of their sight. ³²And they said one to another, 'Did not our heart burn within us, while he talked with us by the way, and while he opened to us the scriptures?' ³³And they rose up the same hour, and returned to Jerusalem, and found the eleven gathered together, and them that were with them, ³⁴saying, 'The Lord is risen indeed, and hath appeared to Simon'. ³⁵And they told what things were done in the way, and how he was known of them in breaking of bread.

³⁶And as they thus spoke, Jesus himself stood in the midst of them, and saith unto them, 'Peace be unto you'. ³⁷But they were terrified and affrighted, and supposed that they had seen a spirit. ³⁸And he said unto them, 'Why are ye troubled? and why do thoughts arise in your hearts? ³⁹Behold my hands and my feet, that it is I myself: handle me, and see, for a spirit hath not flesh and bones, as ye see me have.' ⁴⁰And when he had thus spoken, he showed them his hands and his feet. ⁴¹And while

they yet believed not for joy, and wondered, he said unto them, 'Have ye here any meat?' [42]And they gave him a piece of a broiled fish, and of a honeycomb. [43]And he took it, and did eat before them. [44]And he said unto them, 'These are the words which I spoke unto you, while I was yet with you, that all things must be fulfilled, which were written in the law of Moses, and in the prophets, and in the psalms, concerning me'. [45]Then opened he their understanding, that they might understand the scriptures, [46]and said unto them, 'Thus it is written, and thus it behoved Christ to suffer, and to rise from the dead the third day: [47]and that repentance and remission of sins should be preached in his name among all nations, beginning at Jerusalem. [48]And ye are witnesses of these things. [49]And behold, I send the promise of my Father upon you: but tarry ye in the city of Jerusalem, until ye be endued with power from on high.'

[50]And he led them out as far as to Bethany, and he lifted up his hands, and blessed them. [51]And it came to pass, while he blessed them, he was parted from them, and carried up into heaven. [52]And they worshipped him, and returned to Jerusalem with great joy: [53]and were continually in the temple, praising and blessing God. Amen.

THE GOSPEL ACCORDING TO
SAINT JOHN

1 In the beginning was the Word, and the Word was with God, and the Word was God. ²The same was in the beginning with God. ³All things were made by him, and without him was not anything made that was made. ⁴In him was life, and the life was the light of men. ⁵And the light shineth in darkness, and the darkness comprehended it not.

⁶There was a man sent from God, whose name was John. ⁷The same came for a witness, to bear witness of the light, that all men through him might believe. ⁸He was not that light, but was sent to bear witness of that light. ⁹That was the true light, which lighteth every man that cometh into the world. ¹⁰He was in the world, and the world was made by him, and the world knew him not. ¹¹He came unto his own, and his own received him not. ¹²But as many as received him, to them gave he power to become the sons of God, even to them that believe on his name: ¹³which were born, not of blood, nor of the will of the flesh, nor of the will of man, but of God. ¹⁴And the Word was made flesh, and dwelt among us (and we beheld his glory, the glory as of the only begotten of the Father), full of grace and truth.

¹⁵John bore witness of him, and cried, saying, 'This was he of whom I spoke, "He that cometh after me is preferred before me", for he was before me'. ¹⁶And of his fulness have all we received, and grace for grace. ¹⁷For the law was given by Moses, but grace and truth came by Jesus Christ. ¹⁸No man hath seen God at any time: the only begotten Son, which is in the bosom of the Father, he hath declared him.

¹⁹And this is the record of John, when the Jews sent priests and Levites from Jerusalem to ask him, 'Who art thou?' ²⁰And he confessed, and denied not: but confessed, 'I am not the Christ'. ²¹And they asked him, 'What then? Art thou Elias?' And he saith, 'I am not'. 'Art thou that prophet?' And he answered, 'No'. ²²Then said they unto him, 'Who art thou? that we may give an answer to them that sent us. What sayest thou of thyself?' ²³He said, 'I am the voice of one crying in the wilderness, "Make straight the way of the Lord", as said the prophet Esaias'.

²⁴And they which were sent were of the Pharisees. ²⁵And they asked him, and said unto him, 'Why baptizest thou then, if thou be not that Christ, nor Elias, neither that prophet?' ²⁶John answered them, saying, 'I baptize with water, but there standeth one among you, whom ye know not; ²⁷he it is, who coming after me is preferred before me, whose shoe's latchet I am not worthy to unloose'. ²⁸These things were done in Bethabara beyond Jordan, where John was baptizing.

²⁹The next day John seeth Jesus coming unto him, and saith, 'Behold the Lamb of God, which taketh away the sin of the world. ³⁰This is he of whom I said, "After me cometh a man which is preferred before me": for he was before me. ³¹And I knew him not: but that he should be made

manifest to Israel, therefore am I come baptizing with water.' ³²And John bore record, saying, 'I saw the Spirit descending from heaven like a dove, and it abode upon him. ³³And I knew him not: but he that sent me to baptize with water, the same said unto me, "Upon whom thou shalt see the Spirit descending, and remaining on him, the same is he which baptizeth with the Holy Ghost". ³⁴And I saw, and bore record that this is the Son of God.'

³⁵Again the next day after, John stood, and two of his disciples. ³⁶And looking upon Jesus as he walked, he saith, 'Behold the Lamb of God'. ³⁷And the two disciples heard him speak, and they followed Jesus. ³⁸Then Jesus turned, and saw them following, and saith unto them, 'What seek ye?' They said unto him, 'Rabbi' (which is to say, being interpreted, Master), 'where dwellest thou?' ³⁹He saith unto them, 'Come and see'. They came and saw where he dwelt, and abode with him that day: for it was about the tenth hour. ⁴⁰One of the two which heard John speak, and followed him, was Andrew, Simon Peter's brother. ⁴¹He first findeth his own brother Simon, and saith unto him, 'We have found the Messiah', which is, being interpreted, the Christ. ⁴²And he brought him to Jesus. And when Jesus beheld him, he said, 'Thou art Simon the son of Jona: thou shalt be called Cephas', which is by interpretation, a stone.

⁴³The day following Jesus would go forth into Galilee, and findeth Philip, and saith unto him, 'Follow me'. ⁴⁴Now Philip was of Bethsaida, the city of Andrew and Peter. ⁴⁵Philip findeth Nathanael, and saith unto him, 'We have found him, of whom Moses in the law, and the prophets, did write, Jesus of Nazareth, the son of Joseph'. ⁴⁶And Nathanael said unto him, 'Can there any good thing come out of Nazareth?' Philip saith unto him, 'Come and see'. ⁴⁷Jesus saw Nathanael coming to him, and saith of him, 'Behold an Israelite indeed, in whom is no guile'. ⁴⁸Nathanael saith unto him, 'Whence knowest thou me?' Jesus answered and said unto him, 'Before that Philip called thee, when thou wast under the fig tree, I saw thee'. ⁴⁹Nathanael answered and saith unto him, 'Rabbi, thou art the Son of God, thou art the King of Israel'. ⁵⁰Jesus answered and said unto him, 'Because I said unto thee, I saw thee under the fig tree, believest thou? thou shalt see greater things than these'. ⁵¹And he saith unto him, 'Verily, verily, I say unto you, hereafter ye shall see heaven open, and the angels of God ascending and descending upon the Son of man'.

2 And the third day there was a marriage in Cana of Galilee, and the mother of Jesus was there. ²And both Jesus was called, and his disciples, to the marriage. ³And when they wanted wine, the mother of Jesus saith unto him, 'They have no wine'. ⁴Jesus saith unto her, 'Woman, what have I to do with thee? my hour is not yet come'. ⁵His mother saith unto the servants, 'Whatsoever he saith unto you, do it'. ⁶And there were set there six water-pots of stone, after the manner of the purifying of the Jews, containing two or three firkins apiece. ⁷Jesus saith unto them, 'Fill the water-pots with water'. And they filled them up to the brim. ⁸And he saith unto them, 'Draw out now, and bear unto

the governor of the feast'. And they bore it. ⁹When the ruler of the feast had tasted the water that was made wine, and knew not whence it was (but the servants which drew the water knew), the governor of the feast called the bridegroom, ¹⁰and saith unto him, 'Every man at the beginning doth set forth good wine, and when men have well drunk, then that which is worse: but thou hast kept the good wine until now'. ¹¹This beginning of miracles did Jesus in Cana of Galilee, and manifested forth his glory; and his disciples believed on him.

¹²After this he went down to Capernaum, he, and his mother, and his brethren, and his disciples, and they continued there not many days. ¹³And the Jews' passover was at hand, and Jesus went up to Jerusalem, ¹⁴and found in the temple those that sold oxen and sheep and doves, and the changers of money sitting. ¹⁵And when he had made a scourge of small cords, he drove them all out of the temple, and the sheep, and the oxen, and poured out the changers' money, and overthrew the tables, ¹⁶and said unto them that sold doves, 'Take these things hence, make not my Father's house a house of merchandise'. ¹⁷And his disciples remembered that it was written, 'The zeal of thy house hath eaten me up'. ¹⁸Then answered the Jews and said unto him, 'What sign showest thou unto us, seeing that thou doest these things?' ¹⁹Jesus answered and said unto them, 'Destroy this temple, and in three days I will raise it up'. ²⁰Then said the Jews, 'Forty and six years was this temple in building, and wilt thou rear it up in three days?' ²¹But he spoke of the temple of his body. ²²When therefore he was risen from the dead, his disciples remembered that he had said this unto them: and they believed the scripture, and the word which Jesus had said.

²³Now when he was in Jerusalem at the passover, in the feast day, many believed in his name, when they saw the miracles which he did. ²⁴But Jesus did not commit himself unto them, because he knew all men, ²⁵and needed not that any should testify of man: for he knew what was in man.

3 There was a man of the Pharisees, named Nicodemus, a ruler of the Jews: ²the same came to Jesus by night, and said unto him, 'Rabbi, we know that thou art a teacher come from God: for no man can do these miracles that thou doest, except God be with him'. ³Jesus answered and said unto him, 'Verily, verily, I say unto thee, except a man be born again, he cannot see the kingdom of God'. ⁴Nicodemus saith unto him, 'How can a man be born when he is old? can he enter the second time into his mother's womb, and be born?' ⁵Jesus answered, 'Verily, verily, I say unto thee, except a man be born of water and of the Spirit, he cannot enter into the kingdom of God. ⁶That which is born of the flesh is flesh, and that which is born of the Spirit is spirit. ⁷Marvel not that I said unto thee, "Ye must be born again". ⁸The wind bloweth where it listeth, and thou hearest the sound thereof, but canst not tell whence it cometh, and whither it goeth: so is every one that is born of the Spirit.'

⁹Nicodemus answered and said unto him, 'How can these things be?' ¹⁰Jesus answered and said unto him, 'Art thou a master of Israel, and

knowest not these things? [11]Verily, verily, I say unto thee, we speak that we do know, and testify that we have seen; and ye receive not our witness. [12]If I have told you earthly things, and ye believe not, how shall ye believe, if I tell you of heavenly things? [13]And no man hath ascended up to heaven, but he that came down from heaven, even the Son of man which is in heaven. [14]And as Moses lifted up the serpent in the wilderness, even so must the Son of man be lifted up: [15]that whosoever believeth in him should not perish, but have eternal life. [16]For God so loved the world, that he gave his only begotten Son, that whosoever believeth in him should not perish, but have everlasting life. [17]For God sent not his Son into the world to condemn the world: but that the world through him might be saved. [18]He that believeth on him is not condemned: but he that believeth not is condemned already, because he hath not believed in the name of the only begotten Son of God. [19]And this is the condemnation, that light is come into the world, and men loved darkness rather than light, because their deeds were evil. [20]For every one that doeth evil hateth the light, neither cometh to the light, lest his deeds should be reproved. [21]But he that doeth truth cometh to the light, that his deeds may be made manifest, that they are wrought in God.'

[22]After these things came Jesus and his disciples into the land of Judea, and there he tarried with them, and baptized. [23]And John also was baptizing in Aenon near to Salim, because there was much water there: and they came, and were baptized. [24]For John was not yet cast into prison.

[25]Then there arose a question between some of John's disciples and the Jews about purifying. [26]And they came unto John, and said unto him, 'Rabbi, he that was with thee beyond Jordan, to whom thou borest witness, behold, the same baptizeth, and all men come to him'. [27]John answered and said, 'A man can receive nothing, except it be given him from heaven. [28]Ye yourselves bear me witness, that I said, "I am not the Christ, but that I am sent before him". [29]He that hath the bride is the bridegroom: but the friend of the bridegroom, which standeth and heareth him, rejoiceth greatly because of the bridegroom's voice: this my joy therefore is fulfilled. [30]He must increase, but I must decrease.

[31]'He that cometh from above is above all: he that is of the earth is earthly, and speaketh of the earth: he that cometh from heaven is above all: [32]and what he hath seen and heard, that he testifieth, and no man receiveth his testimony: [33]he that hath received his testimony hath set to his seal that God is true. [34]For he whom God hath sent speaketh the words of God: for God giveth not the Spirit by measure unto him. [35]The Father loveth the Son, and hath given all things into his hand. [36]He that believeth on the Son hath everlasting life: and he that believeth not the Son shall not see life: but the wrath of God abideth on him.'

4 When therefore the Lord knew how the Pharisees had heard that Jesus made and baptized more disciples than John [2](though Jesus himself baptized not, but his disciples), [3]he left Judea, and departed

again into Galilee. ⁴And he must needs go through Samaria. ⁵Then cometh he to a city of Samaria, which is called Sychar, near to the parcel of ground that Jacob gave to his son Joseph. ⁶Now Jacob's well was there. Jesus therefore, being wearied with his journey, sat thus on the well: and it was about the sixth hour. ⁷There cometh a woman of Samaria to draw water: Jesus saith unto her, 'Give me to drink'. ⁸For his disciples were gone away unto the city to buy meat. ⁹Then saith the woman of Samaria unto him, 'How is it that thou, being a Jew, askest drink of me, which am a woman of Samaria?' For the Jews have no dealings with the Samaritans. ¹⁰Jesus answered and said unto her, 'If thou knewest the gift of God, and who it is that saith to thee, "Give me to drink"; thou wouldst have asked of him, and he would have given thee living water'. ¹¹The woman saith unto him, 'Sir, thou hast nothing to draw with, and the well is deep: from whence then hast thou that living water? ¹²Art thou greater than our father Jacob, which gave us the well, and drank thereof himself, and his children, and his cattle?' ¹³Jesus answered and said unto her, 'Whosoever drinketh of this water shall thirst again: ¹⁴but whosoever drinketh of the water that I shall give him shall never thirst: but the water that I shall give him shall be in him a well of water springing up into everlasting life'. ¹⁵The woman saith unto him, 'Sir, give me this water, that I thirst not, neither come hither to draw'. ¹⁶Jesus saith unto her, 'Go, call thy husband, and come hither'. ¹⁷The woman answered and said, 'I have no husband'. Jesus said unto her, 'Thou hast well said, "I have no husband": ¹⁸for thou hast had five husbands, and he whom thou now hast is not thy husband: in that saidst thou truly'. ¹⁹The woman saith unto him, 'Sir, I perceive that thou art a prophet. ²⁰Our fathers worshipped in this mountain, and ye say, that in Jerusalem is the place where men ought to worship.' ²¹Jesus saith unto her, 'Woman, believe me, the hour cometh, when ye shall neither in this mountain, nor yet at Jerusalem, worship the Father. ²²Ye worship ye know not what: we know what we worship: for salvation is of the Jews. ²³But the hour cometh, and now is, when the true worshippers shall worship the Father in spirit and in truth: for the Father seeketh such to worship him. ²⁴God is a Spirit, and they that worship him must worship him in spirit and in truth.' ²⁵The woman saith unto him, 'I know that Messiah cometh, which is called Christ: when he is come, he will tell us all things'. ²⁶Jesus saith unto her, 'I that speak unto thee am he'.

²⁷And upon this came his disciples, and marvelled that he talked with the woman: yet no man said, 'What seekest thou?' or, 'Why talkest thou with her?' ²⁸The woman then left her water-pot, and went her way into the city, and saith to the men, ²⁹'Come, see a man, which told me all things that ever I did: is not this the Christ?' ³⁰Then they went out of the city, and came unto him.

³¹In the mean while his disciples prayed him, saying, 'Master, eat'. ³²But he said unto them, 'I have meat to eat that ye know not of'. ³³Therefore said the disciples one to another, 'Hath any man brought him aught to eat?' ³⁴Jesus saith unto them, 'My meat is to do the will of

him that sent me, and to finish his work. ³⁵Say not ye, "There are yet four months, and then cometh harvest"? Behold, I say unto you, lift up your eyes, and look on the fields: for they are white already to harvest. ³⁶And he that reapeth receiveth wages, and gathereth fruit unto life eternal: that both he that soweth and he that reapeth may rejoice together. ³⁷And herein is that saying true, "One soweth, and another reapeth". ³⁸I sent you to reap that whereon ye bestowed no labour: other men laboured, and ye are entered into their labours.'

³⁹And many of the Samaritans of that city believed on him for the saying of the woman, which testified, 'He told me all that ever I did'. ⁴⁰So when the Samaritans were come unto him, they besought him that he would tarry with them, and he abode there two days. ⁴¹And many more believed because of his own word: ⁴²and said unto the woman, 'Now we believe, not because of thy saying, for we have heard him ourselves, and know that this is indeed the Christ, the Saviour of the world'.

⁴³Now after two days he departed thence, and went into Galilee. ⁴⁴For Jesus himself testified, that a prophet hath no honour in his own country. ⁴⁵Then when he was come into Galilee, the Galileans received him, having seen all the things that he did at Jerusalem at the feast: for they also went unto the feast. ⁴⁶So Jesus came again into Cana of Galilee, where he made the water wine. And there was a certain nobleman, whose son was sick at Capernaum. ⁴⁷When he heard that Jesus was come out of Judea into Galilee, he went unto him, and besought him that he would come down, and heal his son: for he was at the point of death. ⁴⁸Then said Jesus unto him, 'Except ye see signs and wonders, ye will not believe'. ⁴⁹The nobleman saith unto him, 'Sir, come down ere my child die'. ⁵⁰Jesus saith unto him, 'Go thy way, thy son liveth'. And the man believed the word that Jesus had spoken unto him, and he went his way. ⁵¹And as he was now going down, his servants met him, and told him, saying, 'Thy son liveth'. ⁵²Then inquired he of them the hour when he began to amend: and they said unto him, 'Yesterday at the seventh hour the fever left him'. ⁵³So the father knew that it was at the same hour, in the which Jesus said unto him, 'Thy son liveth', and himself believed, and his whole house. ⁵⁴This is again the second miracle that Jesus did, when he was come out of Judea into Galilee.

5 After this there was a feast of the Jews, and Jesus went up to Jerusalem. ²Now there is at Jerusalem by the sheep market a pool, which is called in the Hebrew tongue Bethesda, having five porches. ³In these lay a great multitude of impotent folk, of blind, halt, withered, waiting for the moving of the water. ⁴For an angel went down at a certain season into the pool, and troubled the water: whosoever then first after the troubling of the water stepped in was made whole of whatsoever disease he had. ⁵And a certain man was there, which had an infirmity thirty and eight years. ⁶When Jesus saw him lie, and knew that he had been now a long time in that case, he saith unto him, 'Wilt thou be made whole?' ⁷The impotent man answered him, 'Sir, I have no man, when the water is troubled, to put me into the pool: but while I am coming, another steppeth down before me'. ⁸Jesus saith unto him,

'Rise, take up thy bed, and walk'. ⁹And immediately the man was made whole, and took up his bed, and walked: and on the same day was the sabbath.

¹⁰The Jews therefore said unto him that was cured, 'It is the sabbath day, it is not lawful for thee to carry thy bed'. ¹¹He answered them, 'He that made me whole, the same said unto me, "Take up thy bed, and walk"'. ¹²Then asked they him, 'What man is that which said unto thee, "Take up thy bed, and walk"?' ¹³And he that was healed wist not who it was: for Jesus had conveyed himself away, a multitude being in that place. ¹⁴Afterward Jesus findeth him in the temple, and said unto him, 'Behold, thou art made whole: sin no more, lest a worse thing come unto thee'. ¹⁵The man departed, and told the Jews that it was Jesus, which had made him whole.

¹⁶And therefore did the Jews persecute Jesus, and sought to slay him, because he had done these things on the sabbath day. ¹⁷But Jesus answered them, 'My Father worketh hitherto, and I work'. ¹⁸Therefore the Jews sought the more to kill him, not only because he had broken the sabbath, but said also that God was his Father, making himself equal with God. ¹⁹Then answered Jesus and said unto them, 'Verily, verily, I say unto you, the Son can do nothing of himself, but what he seeth the Father do: for what things soever he doeth, these also doeth the Son likewise. ²⁰For the Father loveth the Son, and showeth him all things that himself doeth: and he will show him greater works than these, that ye may marvel. ²¹For as the Father raiseth up the dead, and quickeneth them: even so the Son quickeneth whom he will. ²²For the Father judgeth no man, but hath committed all judgement unto the Son: ²³that all men should honour the Son, even as they honour the Father. He that honoureth not the Son honoureth not the Father which hath sent him. ²⁴Verily, verily, I say unto you, he that heareth my word, and believeth on him that sent me, hath everlasting life, and shall not come into condemnation: but is passed from death unto life. ²⁵Verily, verily, I say unto you, the hour is coming, and now is, when the dead shall hear the voice of the Son of God: and they that hear shall live. ²⁶For as the Father hath life in himself: so hath he given to the Son to have life in himself: ²⁷and hath given him authority to execute judgement also, because he is the Son of man. ²⁸Marvel not at this: for the hour is coming, in the which all that are in the graves shall hear his voice, ²⁹and shall come forth, they that have done good, unto the resurrection of life, and they that have done evil, unto the resurrection of damnation. ³⁰I can of my own self do nothing: as I hear, I judge: and my judgement is just, because I seek not my own will, but the will of the Father which hath sent me.

³¹'If I bear witness of myself, my witness is not true. ³²There is another that beareth witness of me, and I know that the witness which he witnesseth of me is true. ³³Ye sent unto John, and he bore witness unto the truth. ³⁴But I receive not testimony from man: but these things I say, that ye might be saved. ³⁵He was a burning and a shining light: and ye were willing for a season to rejoice in his light. ³⁶But I have greater wit-

ness than that of John: for the works which the Father hath given me to finish, the same works that I do, bear witness of me, that the Father hath sent me. ³⁷And the Father himself, which hath sent me, hath borne witness of me. Ye have neither heard his voice at any time, nor seen his shape. ³⁸And ye have not his word abiding in you: for whom he hath sent, him ye believe not. ³⁹Search the scriptures, for in them ye think ye have eternal life, and they are they which testify of me. ⁴⁰And ye will not come to me, that ye might have life. ⁴¹I receive not honour from men. ⁴²But I know you, that ye have not the love of God in you. ⁴³I am come in my Father's name, and ye receive me not: if another shall come in his own name, him ye will receive. ⁴⁴How can ye believe, which receive honour one of another, and seek not the honour that cometh from God only? ⁴⁵Do not think that I will accuse you to the Father: there is one that accuseth you, even Moses, in whom ye trust. ⁴⁶For had ye believed Moses, ye would have believed me: for he wrote of me. ⁴⁷But if ye believe not his writings, how shall ye believe my words?'

6 After these things Jesus went over the sea of Galilee, which is the sea of Tiberias. ²And a great multitude followed him, because they saw his miracles which he did on them that were diseased. ³And Jesus went up into a mountain, and there he sat with his disciples. ⁴And the passover, a feast of the Jews, was nigh. ⁵When Jesus then lifted up his eyes, and saw a great company come unto him, he saith unto Philip, 'Whence shall we buy bread, that these may eat?' ⁶And this he said to prove him: for he himself knew what he would do. ⁷Philip answered him, 'Two hundred pennyworth of bread is not sufficient for them, that every one of them may take a little'. ⁸One of his disciples, Andrew, Simon Peter's brother, saith unto him, ⁹'There is a lad here, which hath five barley loaves, and two small fishes: but what are they among so many?' ¹⁰And Jesus said, 'Make the men sit down'. Now there was much grass in the place. So the men sat down, in number about five thousand. ¹¹And Jesus took the loaves, and when he had given thanks, he distributed to the disciples, and the disciples to them that were set down, and likewise of the fishes as much as they would. ¹²When they were filled, he said unto his disciples, 'Gather up the fragments that remain, that nothing be lost'. ¹³Therefore they gathered them together, and filled twelve baskets with the fragments of the five barley loaves, which remained over and above unto them that had eaten.

¹⁴Then those men, when they had seen the miracle that Jesus did, said, 'This is of a truth that prophet that should come into the world'. ¹⁵When Jesus therefore perceived that they would come and take him by force, to make him a king, he departed again into a mountain himself alone.

¹⁶And when even was now come, his disciples went down unto the sea, ¹⁷and entered into a ship, and went over the sea towards Capernaum. And it was now dark, and Jesus was not come to them. ¹⁸And the sea arose by reason of a great wind that blew. ¹⁹So when they had rowed about five and twenty or thirty furlongs, they see Jesus walking on the sea, and drawing nigh unto the ship: and they were afraid.

²⁰But he saith unto them, 'It is I, be not afraid'. ²¹Then they willingly received him into the ship, and immediately the ship was at the land whither they went.

²²The day following, when the people which stood on the other side of the sea saw that there was no other boat there, save that one whereinto his disciples were entered, and that Jesus went not with his disciples into the boat, but that his disciples were gone away alone ²³(howbeit there came other boats from Tiberias nigh unto the place where they did eat bread, after that the Lord had given thanks): ²⁴when the people therefore saw that Jesus was not there, neither his disciples, they also took shipping, and came to Capernaum, seeking for Jesus. ²⁵And when they had found him on the other side of the sea, they said unto him, 'Rabbi, when camest thou hither?' ²⁶Jesus answered them and said, 'Verily, verily, I say unto you, ye seek me, not because ye saw the miracles, but because ye did eat of the loaves, and were filled. ²⁷Labour not for the meat which perisheth, but for that meat which endureth unto everlasting life, which the Son of man shall give unto you: for him hath God the Father sealed.' ²⁸Then said they unto him, 'What shall we do, that we might work the works of God?' ²⁹Jesus answered and said unto them, 'This is the work of God, that ye believe on him whom he hath sent'. ³⁰They said therefore unto him, 'What sign showest thou then, that we may see, and believe thee? What dost thou work? ³¹Our fathers did eat manna in the desert, as it is written, "He gave them bread from heaven to eat".' ³²Then Jesus said unto them, 'Verily, verily, I say unto you, Moses gave you not that bread from heaven, but my Father giveth you the true bread from heaven. ³³For the bread of God is he which cometh down from heaven, and giveth life unto the world.' ³⁴Then said they unto him, 'Lord, evermore give us this bread'. ³⁵And Jesus said unto them, 'I am the bread of life: he that cometh to me shall never hunger: and he that believeth on me shall never thirst. ³⁶But I said unto you, that ye also have seen me, and believe not. ³⁷All that the Father giveth me shall come to me; and him that cometh to me I will in no wise cast out. ³⁸For I came down from heaven, not to do my own will, but the will of him that sent me. ³⁹And this is the Father's will which hath sent me, that of all which he hath given me I should lose nothing, but should raise it up again at the last day. ⁴⁰And this is the will of him that sent me, that every one which seeth the Son, and believeth on him, may have everlasting life: and I will raise him up at the last day.'

⁴¹The Jews then murmured at him, because he said, 'I am the bread which came down from heaven'. ⁴²And they said, 'Is not this Jesus, the son of Joseph, whose father and mother we know? How is it then that he saith, "I came down from heaven"?' ⁴³Jesus therefore answered and said unto them, 'Murmur not among yourselves. ⁴⁴No man can come to me, except the Father which hath sent me draw him: and I will raise him up at the last day. ⁴⁵It is written in the prophets, "And they shall be all taught of God". Every man therefore that hath heard, and hath learned of the Father, cometh unto me, ⁴⁶not that any man hath seen the Father, save he which is of God, he hath seen the Father. ⁴⁷Verily,

verily, I say unto you, he that believeth on me hath everlasting life. ⁴⁸I am that bread of life. ⁴⁹Your fathers did eat manna in the wilderness, and are dead. ⁵⁰This is the bread which cometh down from heaven, that a man may eat thereof, and not die. ⁵¹I am the living bread which came down from heaven. If any man eat of this bread, he shall live for ever: and the bread that I will give is my flesh, which I will give for the life of the world.'

⁵²The Jews therefore strove amongst themselves, saying, 'How can this man give us his flesh to eat?' ⁵³Then Jesus said unto them, 'Verily, verily, I say unto you, except ye eat the flesh of the Son of man, and drink his blood, ye have no life in you. ⁵⁴Whoso eateth my flesh, and drinketh my blood, hath eternal life, and I will raise him up at the last day. ⁵⁵For my flesh is meat indeed, and my blood is drink indeed. ⁵⁶He that eateth my flesh, and drinketh my blood, dwelleth in me, and I in him. ⁵⁷As the living Father hath sent me, and I live by the Father: so he that eateth me, even he shall live by me. ⁵⁸This is that bread which came down from heaven: not as your fathers did eat manna, and are dead: he that eateth of this bread shall live for ever.'

⁵⁹These things said he in the synagogue, as he taught in Capernaum. ⁶⁰Many therefore of his disciples, when they had heard this, said, 'This is a hard saying, who can hear it?' ⁶¹When Jesus knew in himself that his disciples murmured at it, he said unto them, 'Doth this offend you? ⁶²What and if ye shall see the Son of man ascend up where he was before? ⁶³It is the spirit that quickeneth, the flesh profiteth nothing: the words that I speak unto you, they are spirit, and they are life. ⁶⁴But there are some of you that believe not.' For Jesus knew from the beginning who they were that believed not, and who should betray him. ⁶⁵And he said, 'Therefore said I unto you, that no man can come unto me, except it were given unto him of my Father'.

⁶⁶From that time many of his disciples went back, and walked no more with him. ⁶⁷Then said Jesus unto the twelve, 'Will ye also go away?' ⁶⁸Then Simon Peter answered him, 'Lord, to whom shall we go? Thou hast the words of eternal life. ⁶⁹And we believe and are sure that thou art that Christ, the Son of the living God.' ⁷⁰Jesus answered them, 'Have not I chosen you twelve, and one of you is a devil?' ⁷¹He spoke of Judas Iscariot the son of Simon: for he it was that should betray him, being one of the twelve.

7 After these things Jesus walked in Galilee: for he would not walk in Jewry, because the Jews sought to kill him. ²Now the Jews' feast of tabernacles was at hand. ³His brethren therefore said unto him, 'Depart hence, and go into Judea, that thy disciples also may see the works that thou doest. ⁴For there is no man that doeth anything in secret, and he himself seeketh to be known openly: if thou do these things, show thyself to the world.' ⁵For neither did his brethren believe in him. ⁶Then Jesus said unto them, 'My time is not yet come: but your time is always ready. ⁷The world cannot hate you, but me it hateth, because I testify of it, that the works thereof are evil. ⁸Go ye up unto this feast: I go not up yet unto this feast, for my time is not yet full

come.' ⁹When he had said these words unto them, he abode still in Galilee.

¹⁰But when his brethren were gone up, then went he also up unto the feast, not openly, but as it were in secret. ¹¹Then the Jews sought him at the feast, and said, 'Where is he?' ¹²And there was much murmuring among the people concerning him: for some said, 'He is a good man': others said, 'Nay, but he deceiveth the people'. ¹³Howbeit no man spoke openly of him for fear of the Jews.

¹⁴Now about the midst of the feast Jesus went up into the temple, and taught. ¹⁵And the Jews marvelled, saying, 'How knoweth this man letters, having never learned?' ¹⁶Jesus answered them, 'My doctrine is not mine, but his that sent me. ¹⁷If any man will do his will, he shall know of the doctrine, whether it be of God, or whether I speak of myself. ¹⁸He that speaketh of himself seeketh his own glory: but he that seeketh his glory that sent him, the same is true, and no unrighteousness is in him.

¹⁹'Did not Moses give you the law, and yet none of you keepeth the law? Why go ye about to kill me?' ²⁰The people answered and said, 'Thou hast a devil: who goeth about to kill thee?' ²¹Jesus answered and said unto them, 'I have done one work, and ye all marvel. ²²Moses therefore gave unto you circumcision (not because it is of Moses, but of the fathers), and ye on the sabbath day circumcise a man. ²³If a man on the sabbath day receive circumcision, that the law of Moses should not be broken; are ye angry at me, because I have made a man every whit whole on the sabbath day? ²⁴Judge not according to the appearance, but judge righteous judgement.'

²⁵Then said some of them of Jerusalem, 'Is not this he, whom they seek to kill? ²⁶But lo, he speaketh boldly, and they say nothing unto him. Do the rulers know indeed that this is the very Christ? ²⁷Howbeit we know this man whence he is: but when Christ cometh, no man knoweth whence he is.' ²⁸Then cried Jesus in the temple as he taught, saying, 'Ye both know me, and ye know whence I am: and I am not come of myself, but he that sent me is true, whom ye know not. ²⁹But I know him, for I am from him, and he hath sent me.' ³⁰Then they sought to take him: but no man laid hands on him, because his hour was not yet come. ³¹And many of the people believed on him, and said, 'When Christ cometh, will he do more miracles than these which this man hath done?'

³²The Pharisees heard that the people murmured such things concerning him: and the Pharisees and the chief priests sent officers to take him. ³³Then said Jesus unto them, 'Yet a little while am I with you, and then I go unto him that sent me. ³⁴Ye shall seek me, and shall not find me: and where I am, thither ye cannot come.' ³⁵Then said the Jews among themselves, 'Whither will he go, that we shall not find him? will he go unto the dispersed among the Gentiles, and teach the Gentiles? ³⁶What manner of saying is this that he said, "Ye shall seek me, and shall not find me? and where I am, thither ye cannot come?"'

³⁷In the last day, that great day of the feast, Jesus stood and cried, say-

ing, 'If any man thirst, let him come unto me, and drink. ³⁸He that believeth on me, as the scripture hath said, out of his belly shall flow rivers of living water.' ³⁹(But this spoke he of the Spirit, which they that believe on him should receive. For the Holy Ghost was not yet given, because that Jesus was not yet glorified.)

⁴⁰Many of the people therefore, when they heard this saying, said, 'Of a truth this is the Prophet'. ⁴¹Others said, 'This is the Christ'. But some said, 'Shall Christ come out of Galilee? ⁴²Hath not the scripture said, that Christ cometh of the seed of David, and out of the town of Bethlehem, where David was?' ⁴³So there was a division among the people because of him. ⁴⁴And some of them would have taken him, but no man laid hands on him.

⁴⁵Then came the officers to the chief priests and Pharisees, and they said unto them, 'Why have ye not brought him?' ⁴⁶The officers answered, 'Never man spoke like this man'. ⁴⁷Then answered them the Pharisees, 'Are ye also deceived? ⁴⁸Have any of the rulers or of the Pharisees believed on him? ⁴⁹But this people who knoweth not the law are cursed.' ⁵⁰Nicodemus saith unto them (he that came to Jesus by night, being one of them), ⁵¹'Doth our law judge any man, before it hear him, and know what he doeth?' ⁵²They answered and said unto him, 'Art thou also of Galilee? Search, and look: for out of Galilee ariseth no prophet.' ⁵³And every man went unto his own house.

8 Jesus went unto the mount of Olives. ²And early in the morning he came again into the temple, and all the people came unto him, and he sat down, and taught them. ³And the scribes and Pharisees brought unto him a woman taken in adultery; and when they had set her in the midst, ⁴they say unto him, 'Master, this woman was taken in adultery, in the very act. ⁵Now Moses in the law commanded us, that such should be stoned: but what sayest thou?' ⁶This they said, tempting him, that they might have to accuse him. But Jesus stooped down, and with his finger wrote on the ground, as though he heard them not. ⁷So when they continued asking him, he lifted up himself, and said unto them, 'He that is without sin among you, let him first cast a stone at her'. ⁸And again he stooped down, and wrote on the ground. ⁹And they which heard it, being convicted by their own conscience, went out one by one, beginning at the eldest, even unto the last: and Jesus was left alone, and the woman standing in the midst. ¹⁰When Jesus had lifted up himself, and saw none but the woman, he said unto her, 'Woman, where are those thy accusers? Hath no man condemned thee?' ¹¹She said, 'No man, Lord'. And Jesus said unto her, 'Neither do I condemn thee: go, and sin no more'.

¹²Then spoke Jesus again unto them, saying, 'I am the light of the world: he that followeth me shall not walk in darkness, but shall have the light of life'. ¹³The Pharisees therefore said unto him, 'Thou bearest record of thyself, thy record is not true'. ¹⁴Jesus answered and said unto them, 'Though I bear record of myself, yet my record is true: for I know whence I came, and whither I go: but ye cannot tell whence I come, and whither I go. ¹⁵Ye judge after the flesh, I judge no man. ¹⁶And yet if I

judge, my judgement is true: for I am not alone, but I and the Father that sent me. [17]It is also written in your law, that the testimony of two men is true. [18]I am one that bear witness of myself, and the Father that sent me beareth witness of me.' [19]Then said they unto him, 'Where is thy Father?' Jesus answered, 'Ye neither know me, nor my Father: if ye had known me, ye should have known my Father also'. [20]These words spoke Jesus in the treasury, as he taught in the temple: and no man laid hands on him; for his hour was not yet come.

[21]Then said Jesus again unto them, 'I go my way, and ye shall seek me, and shall die in your sins: whither I go, ye cannot come'. [22]Then said the Jews, 'Will he kill himself? because he saith, "Whither I go, ye cannot come"'. [23]And he said unto them, 'Ye are from beneath, I am from above: ye are of this world, I am not of this world. [24]I said therefore unto you, that ye shall die in your sins: for if ye believe not that I am he, ye shall die in your sins.' [25]Then said they unto him, 'Who art thou?' And Jesus saith unto them, 'Even the same that I said unto you from the beginning. [26]I have many things to say and to judge of you: but he that sent me is true, and I speak to the world those things which I have heard of him.' [27]They understood not that he spoke to them of the Father. [28]Then said Jesus unto them, 'When ye have lifted up the Son of man, then shall ye know that I am he, and that I do nothing of myself: but as my Father hath taught me, I speak these things. [29]And he that sent me is with me: the Father hath not left me alone: for I do always those things that please him.' [30]As he spoke these words, many believed on him.

[31]Then said Jesus to those Jews which believed on him, 'If ye continue in my word, then are ye my disciples indeed. [32]And ye shall know the truth, and the truth shall make you free.' [33]They answered him, 'We be Abraham's seed, and were never in bondage to any man: how sayest thou, "Ye shall be made free"?' [34]Jesus answered them, 'Verily, verily, I say unto you, whosoever committeth sin is the servant of sin. [35]And the servant abideth not in the house for ever: but the Son abideth ever. [36]If the Son therefore shall make you free, ye shall be free indeed. [37]I know that ye are Abraham's seed, but ye seek to kill me, because my word hath no place in you. [38]I speak that which I have seen with my Father: and ye do that which ye have seen with your father.' [39]They answered and said unto him, 'Abraham is our father'. Jesus saith unto them, 'If ye were Abraham's children, ye would do the works of Abraham. [40]But now ye seek to kill me, a man that hath told you the truth, which I have heard of God: this did not Abraham. [41]Ye do the deeds of your father.'

Then said they to him, 'We be not born of fornication, we have one Father, even God'. [42]Jesus said unto them, 'If God were your Father, ye would love me, for I proceeded forth and came from God: neither came I of myself, but he sent me. [43]Why do ye not understand my speech? even because ye cannot hear my word. [44]Ye are of your father the devil, and the lusts of your father ye will do: he was a murderer from the beginning, and abode not in the truth, because there is no truth in him. When he speaketh a lie, he speaketh of his own: for he is a liar, and the father of it. ⁴⁵And because I tell you the truth, ye believe me not. ⁴⁶Which of you convinceth me of sin? And if I say the truth, why do ye not believe me? ⁴⁷He that is of God heareth God's words: ye therefore hear them not, because ye are not of God.'

⁴⁸Then answered the Jews, and said unto him, 'Say we not well that thou art a Samaritan, and hast a devil?' ⁴⁹Jesus answered, 'I have not a devil: but I honour my Father, and ye do dishonour me. ⁵⁰And I seek not my own glory: there is one that seeketh and judgeth. ⁵¹Verily, verily, I say unto you, if a man keep my saying, he shall never see death.'

⁵²Then said the Jews unto him, 'Now we know that thou hast a devil. Abraham is dead, and the prophets: and thou sayest, "If a man keep my saying, he shall never taste of death". ⁵³Art thou greater than our father Abraham, which is dead? and the prophets are dead: whom makest thou thyself?' ⁵⁴Jesus answered, 'If I honour myself, my honour is nothing: it is my Father that honoureth me, of whom ye say, that he is your God: ⁵⁵yet ye have not known him, but I know him: and if I should say, "I know him not", I shall be a liar like unto you: but I know him, and keep his saying. ⁵⁶Your father Abraham rejoiced to see my day: and he saw it, and was glad.' ⁵⁷Then said the Jews unto him, 'Thou art not yet fifty years old, and hast thou seen Abraham?' ⁵⁸Jesus said unto them, 'Verily, verily, I say unto you, before Abraham was, I am'.

⁵⁹Then took they up stones to cast at him: but Jesus hid himself, and went out of the temple, going through the midst of them, and so passed by. ¹And as Jesus passed by, he saw a man which was blind from his birth. ²And his disciples asked him, saying, 'Master, who did sin, this man, or his parents, that he was born blind?' ³Jesus answered, 'Neither hath this man sinned, nor his parents: but that the works of God should be made manifest in him. ⁴I must work the works of him that sent me, while it is day: the night cometh, when no man can work. ⁵As long as I am in the world, I am the light of the world.' ⁶When he had thus spoken, he spat on the ground, and made clay of the spittle, and he anointed the eyes of the blind man with the clay, ⁷and said unto him, 'Go, wash in the pool of Siloam' (which is by interpretation, Sent). He went his way therefore, and washed, and came seeing.

⁸The neighbours therefore, and they which before had seen him that he was blind, said, 'Is not this he that sat and begged?' ⁹Some said, 'This is he': others said, 'He is like him': but he said, 'I am he'. ¹⁰Therefore said they unto him, 'How were thy eyes opened?' ¹¹He answered and said, 'A man that is called Jesus made clay, and anointed my eyes, and said unto me, "Go to the pool of Siloam, and wash": and I went and washed, and I received sight'. ¹²Then said they unto him, 'Where is he?' He said, 'I know not'.

¹³They brought to the Pharisees him that aforetime was blind. ¹⁴And it was the sabbath day when Jesus made the clay, and opened his eyes. ¹⁵Then again the Pharisees also asked him how he had received his sight. He said unto them, 'He put clay upon my eyes, and I washed, and do see'. ¹⁶Therefore said some of the Pharisees, 'This man is not of God,

because he keepeth not the sabbath day'. Others said, 'How can a man that is a sinner do such miracles?' And there was a division among them. ¹⁷They say unto the blind man again, 'What sayest thou of him, that he hath opened thy eyes?' He said, 'He is a prophet'.

¹⁸But the Jews did not believe concerning him, that he had been blind, and received his sight, until they called the parents of him that had received his sight. ¹⁹And they asked them, saying, 'Is this your son, who ye say was born blind? how then doth he now see?' ²⁰His parents answered them and said, 'We know that this is our son, and that he was born blind: ²¹but by what means he now seeth, we know not, or who hath opened his eyes, we know not: he is of age, ask him: he shall speak for himself'. ²²These words spoke his parents, because they feared the Jews: for the Jews had agreed already, that if any man did confess that he was Christ, he should be put out of the synagogue. ²³Therefore said his parents, 'He is of age, ask him'.

²⁴Then again called they the man that was blind, and said unto him, 'Give God the praise, we know that this man is a sinner'. ²⁵He answered and said, 'Whether he be a sinner or no, I know not: one thing I know, that whereas I was blind, now I see'. ²⁶Then said they to him again, 'What did he to thee? How opened he thy eyes?' ²⁷He answered them, 'I have told you already, and ye did not hear: wherefore would you hear it again? Will ye also be his disciples?' ²⁸Then they reviled him, and said, 'Thou art his disciple, but we are Moses' disciples. ²⁹We know that God spoke unto Moses: as for this fellow, we know not from whence he is.' ³⁰The man answered and said unto them, 'Why herein is a marvellous thing, that ye know not from whence he is, and yet he hath opened my eyes. ³¹Now we know that God heareth not sinners: but if any man be a worshipper of God, and doeth his will, him he heareth. ³²Since the world began was it not heard that any man opened the eyes of one that was born blind. ³³If this man were not of God, he could do nothing.' ³⁴They answered and said unto him, 'Thou wast altogether born in sins, and dost thou teach us?' And they cast him out.

³⁵Jesus heard that they had cast him out; and when he had found him, he said unto him, 'Dost thou believe on the Son of God?' ³⁶He answered and said, 'Who is he, Lord, that I might believe on him?' ³⁷And Jesus said unto him, 'Thou hast both seen him, and it is he that talketh with thee'. ³⁸And he said, 'Lord, I believe'. And he worshipped him.

³⁹And Jesus said, 'For judgement I am come into this world, that they which see not might see, and that they which see might be made blind'. ⁴⁰And some of the Pharisees which were with him heard these words, and said unto him, 'Are we blind also?' ⁴¹Jesus said unto them, 'If ye were blind, ye should have no sin: but now ye say, "We see", therefore your sin remaineth.

10 'Verily, verily, I say unto you, he that entereth not by the door into the sheepfold, but climbeth up some other way, the same is a thief and a robber. ²But he that entereth in by the door is the shepherd of the sheep. ³To him the porter openeth, and the sheep hear his voice, and he calleth his own sheep by name, and leadeth them out.

⁴'And when he putteth forth his own sheep, he goeth before them, and the sheep follow him: for they know his voice. ⁵And a stranger will they not follow, but will flee from him, for they know not the voice of strangers.'

⁶This parable spoke Jesus unto them: but they understood not what things they were which he spoke unto them. ⁷Then said Jesus unto them again, 'Verily, verily, I say unto you, I am the door of the sheep. ⁸All that ever came before me are thieves and robbers: but the sheep did not hear them. ⁹I am the door: by me if any man enter in, he shall be saved, and shall go in and out, and find pasture. ¹⁰The thief cometh not, but for to steal, and to kill, and to destroy: I am come that they might have life, and that they might have it more abundantly. ¹¹I am the good shepherd: the good shepherd giveth his life for the sheep. ¹²But he that is a hireling, and not the shepherd, whose own the sheep are not, seeth the wolf coming, and leaveth the sheep, and fleeth: and the wolf catcheth them, and scattereth the sheep. ¹³The hireling fleeth, because he is a hireling, and careth not for the sheep. ¹⁴I am the good shepherd, and know my sheep, and am known of mine. ¹⁵As the Father knoweth me, even so know I the Father: and I lay down my life for the sheep. ¹⁶And other sheep I have, which are not of this fold: them also I must bring, and they shall hear my voice; and there shall be one fold, and one shepherd. ¹⁷Therefore doth my Father love me, because I lay down my life, that I might take it again. ¹⁸No man taketh it from me, but I lay it down of myself. I have power to lay it down, and I have power to take it again. This commandment have I received of my Father.'

¹⁹There was a division therefore again among the Jews for these sayings. ²⁰And many of them said, 'He hath a devil, and is mad, why hear ye him?' ²¹Others said, 'These are not the words of him that hath a devil. Can a devil open the eyes of the blind?'

²²And it was at Jerusalem the feast of the dedication, and it was winter. ²³And Jesus walked in the temple in Solomon's porch. ²⁴Then came the Jews round about him, and said unto him, 'How long dost thou make us to doubt? If thou be the Christ, tell us plainly.' ²⁵Jesus answered them, 'I told you, and ye believed not: the works that I do in my Father's name, they bear witness of me. ²⁶But ye believe not, because ye are not of my sheep, as I said unto you. ²⁷My sheep hear my voice, and I know them, and they follow me. ²⁸And I give unto them eternal life, and they shall never perish, neither shall any man pluck them out of my hand. ²⁹My Father, which gave them me, is greater than all: and no man is able to pluck them out of my Father's hand. ³⁰I and my Father are one.'

³¹Then the Jews took up stones again to stone him. ³²Jesus answered them, 'Many good works have I shown you from my Father; for which of those works do ye stone me?' ³³The Jews answered him, saying, 'For a good work we stone thee not, but for blasphemy; and because that thou, being a man, makest thyself God'. ³⁴Jesus answered them, 'Is it not written in your law, "I said, 'Ye are gods'"? ³⁵If he called them gods, unto whom the word of God came, and the scripture cannot be broken:

³⁶say ye of him, whom the Father hath sanctified, and sent into the world, "Thou blasphemest"; because I said, "I am the Son of God"? ³⁷If I do not the works of my Father, believe me not. ³⁸But if I do, though ye believe not me, believe the works: that ye may know, and believe, that the Father is in me, and I in him.'

³⁹Therefore they sought again to take him: but he escaped out of their hand, ⁴⁰and went away again beyond Jordan into the place where John at first baptized: and there he abode. ⁴¹And many resorted unto him, and said, 'John did no miracle: but all things that John spoke of this man were true'. ⁴²And many believed on him there.

11 Now a certain man was sick, named Lazarus, of Bethany, the town of Mary and her sister Martha. ²(It was that Mary which anointed the Lord with ointment, and wiped his feet with her hair, whose brother Lazarus was sick.) ³Therefore his sister sent unto him, saying, 'Lord, behold, he whom thou lovest is sick'. ⁴When Jesus heard that, he said, 'This sickness is not unto death, but for the glory of God, that the Son of God might be glorified thereby'. ⁵Now Jesus loved Martha, and her sister, and Lazarus. ⁶When he had heard therefore that he was sick, he abode two days still in the same place where he was.

⁷Then after that saith he to his disciples, 'Let us go into Judea again'. ⁸His disciples say unto him, 'Master, the Jews of late sought to stone thee, and goest thou thither again?' ⁹Jesus answered, 'Are there not twelve hours in the day? If any man walk in the day, he stumbleth not, because he seeth the light of this world. ¹⁰But if a man walk in the night, he stumbleth, because there is no light in him.' ¹¹These things said he, and after that he saith unto them, 'Our friend Lazarus sleepeth, but I go, that I may awake him out of sleep'. ¹²Then said his disciples, 'Lord, if he sleep, he shall do well'. ¹³Howbeit Jesus spoke of his death: but they thought that he had spoken of taking of rest in sleep. ¹⁴Then said Jesus unto them plainly, 'Lazarus is dead. ¹⁵And I am glad for your sakes that I was not there, to the intent ye may believe: nevertheless let us go unto him.' ¹⁶Then said Thomas, which is called Didymus, unto his fellow-disciples, 'Let us also go, that we may die with him'.

¹⁷Then when Jesus came, he found that he had lain in the grave four days already. ¹⁸Now Bethany was nigh unto Jerusalem, about fifteen furlongs off: ¹⁹and many of the Jews came to Martha and Mary, to comfort them concerning their brother. ²⁰Then Martha, as soon as she heard that Jesus was coming, went and met him: but Mary sat still in the house. ²¹Then said Martha unto Jesus, 'Lord, if thou hadst been here, my brother had not died. ²²But I know, that even now, whatsoever thou wilt ask of God, God will give it thee.' ²³Jesus saith unto her, 'Thy brother shall rise again'. ²⁴Martha saith unto him, 'I know that he shall rise again in the resurrection at the last day'. ²⁵Jesus said unto her, 'I am the resurrection, and the life: he that believeth in me, though he were dead, yet shall he live. ²⁶And whosoever liveth and believeth in me shall never die. Believest thou this?' ²⁷She saith unto him, 'Yea, Lord, I believe that thou art the Christ, the Son of God, which should come into the world'.

²⁸And when she had so said, she went her way, and called Mary her sister secretly, saying, 'The Master is come, and calleth for thee'. ²⁹As soon as she heard that, she arose quickly, and came unto him. ³⁰Now Jesus was not yet come into the town, but was in that place where Martha met him. ³¹The Jews then which were with her in the house, and comforted her, when they saw Mary, that she rose up hastily and went out, followed her, saying, 'She goeth unto the grave to weep there'.

³²Then when Mary was come where Jesus was, and saw him, she fell down at his feet, saying unto him, 'Lord, if thou hadst been here, my brother had not died'. ³³When Jesus therefore saw her weeping, and the Jews also weeping which came with her, he groaned in the spirit, and was troubled, ³⁴and said, 'Where have ye laid him?' They say unto him, 'Lord, come and see'. ³⁵Jesus wept. ³⁶Then said the Jews, 'Behold how he loved him'. ³⁷And some of them said, 'Could not this man, which opened the eyes of the blind, have caused that even this man should not have died?'

³⁸Jesus therefore again groaning in himself, cometh to the grave. It was a cave, and a stone lay upon it. ³⁹Jesus said, 'Take ye away the stone'. Martha, the sister of him that was dead, saith unto him, 'Lord, by this time he stinketh: for he hath been dead four days'. ⁴⁰Jesus saith unto her, 'Said I not unto thee, that if thou wouldst believe, thou shouldst see the glory of God?' ⁴¹Then they took away the stone from the place where the dead was laid. And Jesus lifted up his eyes, and said, 'Father, I thank thee that thou hast heard me. ⁴²And I knew that thou hearest me always: but because of the people which stand by I said it, that they may believe that thou hast sent me.' ⁴³And when he thus had spoken, he cried with a loud voice, 'Lazarus, come forth'. ⁴⁴And he that was dead came forth, bound hand and foot with grave-clothes: and his face was bound about with a napkin. Jesus saith unto them, 'Loose him, and let him go'.

⁴⁵Then many of the Jews which came to Mary, and had seen the things which Jesus did, believed on him. ⁴⁶But some of them went their ways to the Pharisees, and told them what things Jesus had done.

⁴⁷Then gathered the chief priests and the Pharisees a council, and said, 'What do we? for this man doeth many miracles. ⁴⁸If we let him thus alone, all men will believe on him, and the Romans shall come and take away both our place and nation.' ⁴⁹And one of them, named Caiaphas, being the high priest that same year, said unto them, 'Ye know nothing at all, ⁵⁰nor consider that it is expedient for us, that one man should die for the people, and that the whole nation perish not'. ⁵¹And this spoke he not of himself: but being high priest that year, he prophesied that Jesus should die for that nation: ⁵²and not for that nation only, but that also he should gather together in one the children of God that were scattered abroad. ⁵³Then from that day forth they took counsel together for to put him to death. ⁵⁴Jesus therefore walked no more openly among the Jews: but went thence unto a country near to the wilderness, into a city called Ephraim, and there continued with his disciples.

⁵⁵And the Jews' passover was nigh at hand: and many went out of the country up to Jerusalem before the passover, to purify themselves. ⁵⁶Then sought they for Jesus, and spoke among themselves, as they stood in the temple, 'What think ye, that he will not come to the feast?' ⁵⁷Now both the chief priests and the Pharisees had given a commandment, that, if any man knew where he were, he should show it, that they might take him.

12 Then Jesus six days before the passover came to Bethany, where Lazarus was which had been dead, whom he raised from the dead. ²There they made him a supper, and Martha served: but Lazarus was one of them that sat at the table with him. ³Then took Mary a pound of ointment of spikenard, very costly, and anointed the feet of Jesus, and wiped his feet with her hair: and the house was filled with the odour of the ointment. ⁴Then saith one of his disciples, Judas Iscariot, Simon's son, which should betray him, ⁵'Why was not this ointment sold for three hundred pence, and given to the poor?' ⁶This he said, not that he cared for the poor: but because he was a thief, and had the bag, and bore what was put therein. ⁷Then said Jesus, 'Let her alone: against the day of my burying hath she kept this. ⁸For the poor always ye have with you: but me ye have not always.'

⁹Much people of the Jews therefore knew that he was there: and they came not for Jesus' sake only, but that they might see Lazarus also, whom he had raised from the dead. ¹⁰But the chief priests consulted that they might put Lazarus also to death, ¹¹because that by reason of him many of the Jews went away, and believed on Jesus.

¹²On the next day much people that were come to the feast, when they heard that Jesus was coming to Jerusalem, ¹³took branches of palm trees, and went forth to meet him, and cried, 'Hosanna: blessed is the King of Israel that cometh in the name of the Lord'. ¹⁴And Jesus, when he had found a young ass, sat thereon, as it is written, ¹⁵'Fear not, daughter of Sion, behold, thy King cometh, sitting on an ass's colt'. ¹⁶These things understood not his disciples at the first: but when Jesus was glorified, then remembered they that these things were written of him, and that they had done these things unto him.

¹⁷The people therefore that was with him when he called Lazarus out of his grave, and raised him from the dead, bore record. ¹⁸For this cause the people also met him, for that they heard that he had done this miracle. ¹⁹The Pharisees therefore said among themselves, 'Perceive ye how ye prevail nothing? Behold, the world is gone after him.'

²⁰And there were certain Greeks among them that came up to worship at the feast: ²¹the same came therefore to Philip, which was of Bethsaida of Galilee, and desired him, saying, 'Sir, we would see Jesus'. ²²Philip cometh and telleth Andrew: and again Andrew and Philip told Jesus.

²³And Jesus answered them, saying, 'The hour is come, that the Son of man should be glorified. ²⁴Verily, verily, I say unto you, except a corn of wheat fall into the ground and die, it abideth alone: but if it die, it bringeth forth much fruit. ²⁵He that loveth his life shall lose it: and he

that hateth his life in this world shall keep it unto life eternal. ²⁶If any man serve me, let him follow me, and where I am, there shall also my servant be: if any man serve me, him will my Father honour.

²⁷'Now is my soul troubled, and what shall I say? "Father, save me from this hour", but for this cause came I unto this hour. ²⁸Father, glorify thy name.' Then came there a voice from heaven, saying, 'I have both glorified it, and will glorify it again'. ²⁹The people therefore, that stood by, and heard it, said that it thundered: others said, 'An angel spoke to him'. ³⁰Jesus answered and said, 'This voice came not because of me, but for your sakes. ³¹Now is the judgement of this world: now shall the prince of this world be cast out. ³²And I, if I be lifted up from the earth, will draw all men unto me.' ³³This he said, signifying what death he should die.

³⁴The people answered him, 'We have heard out of the law that Christ abideth for ever: and how sayest thou, "The Son of man must be lifted up"? Who is this Son of man?' ³⁵Then Jesus said unto them, 'Yet a little while is the light with you. Walk while ye have the light, lest darkness come upon you: for he that walketh in darkness knoweth not whither he goeth. ³⁶While ye have light, believe in the light, that ye may be the children of light.' These things spoke Jesus, and departed, and did hide himself from them.

³⁷But though he had done so many miracles before them, yet they believed not on him: ³⁸that the saying of Esaias the prophet might be fulfilled, which he spoke, 'Lord, who hath believed our report? and to whom hath the arm of the Lord been revealed?' ³⁹Therefore they could not believe, because that Esaias said again, ⁴⁰'He hath blinded their eyes, and hardened their heart, that they should not see with their eyes, nor understand with their heart, and be converted, and I should heal them'. ⁴¹These things said Esaias, when he saw his glory, and spoke of him.

⁴²Nevertheless among the chief rulers also many believed on him; but because of the Pharisees they did not confess him, lest they should be put out of the synagogue: ⁴³for they loved the praise of men more than the praise of God.

⁴⁴Jesus cried and said, 'He that believeth on me, believeth not on me, but on him that sent me. ⁴⁵And he that seeth me seeth him that sent me. ⁴⁶I am come a light into the world, that whosoever believeth on me should not abide in darkness. ⁴⁷And if any man hear my words, and believe not, I judge him not: for I came not to judge the world, but to save the world. ⁴⁸He that rejecteth me, and receiveth not my words, hath one that judgeth him: the word that I have spoken, the same shall judge him in the last day. ⁴⁹For I have not spoken of myself; but the Father which sent me, he gave me a commandment, what I should say, and what I should speak. ⁵⁰And I know that his commandment is life everlasting: whatsoever I speak therefore, even as the Father said unto me, so I speak.'

13 Now before the feast of the passover, when Jesus knew that his hour was come that he should depart out of this world unto the

Father, having loved his own which were in the world, he loved them unto the end. ²And supper being ended, the devil having now put into the heart of Judas Iscariot, Simon's son, to betray him; ³Jesus knowing that the Father had given all things into his hands, and that he was come from God, and went to God: ⁴he riseth from supper, and laid aside his garments, and took a towel, and girded himself. ⁵After that he poureth water into a basin, and began to wash the disciples' feet, and to wipe them with the towel wherewith he was girded. ⁶Then cometh he to Simon Peter: and Peter saith unto him, 'Lord, dost thou wash my feet?' ⁷Jesus answered and said unto him, 'What I do thou knowest not now: but thou shalt know hereafter'. ⁸Peter saith unto him, 'Thou shalt never wash my feet'. Jesus answered him, 'If I wash thee not, thou hast no part with me'. ⁹Simon Peter saith unto him, 'Lord, not my feet only, but also my hands and my head'. ¹⁰Jesus saith to him, 'He that is washed needeth not save to wash his feet, but is clean every whit: and ye are clean, but not all'. ¹¹For he knew who should betray him; therefore said he, 'Ye are not all clean'.

¹²So after he had washed their feet, and had taken his garments, and was set down again, he said unto them, 'Know ye what I have done to you? ¹³Ye call me Master and Lord, and ye say well: for so I am. ¹⁴If I then, your Lord and Master, have washed your feet, ye also ought to wash one another's feet. ¹⁵For I have given you an example, that ye should do as I have done to you. ¹⁶Verily, verily, I say unto you, the servant is not greater than his lord, neither he that is sent greater than he that sent him. ¹⁷If ye know these things, happy are ye if ye do them.

¹⁸'I speak not of you all: I know whom I have chosen: but that the scripture may be fulfilled, "He that eateth bread with me hath lifted up his heel against me". ¹⁹Now I tell you before it come, that when it is come to pass, ye may believe that I am he. ²⁰Verily, verily, I say unto you, he that receiveth whomsoever I send receiveth me: and he that receiveth me receiveth him that sent me.'

²¹When Jesus had thus said, he was troubled in spirit, and testified, and said, 'Verily, verily, I say unto you, that one of you shall betray me'. ²²Then the disciples looked one on another, doubting of whom he spoke. ²³Now there was leaning on Jesus' bosom one of his disciples, whom Jesus loved. ²⁴Simon Peter therefore beckoned to him, that he should ask who it should be of whom he spoke. ²⁵He then lying on Jesus' breast saith unto him, 'Lord, who is it?' ²⁶Jesus answered, 'He it is, to whom I shall give a sop, when I have dipped it'. And when he had dipped the sop, he gave it to Judas Iscariot, the son of Simon. ²⁷And after the sop Satan entered into him. Then said Jesus unto him, 'That thou doest, do quickly'. ²⁸Now no man at the table knew for what intent he spoke this unto him. ²⁹For some of them thought, because Judas had the bag, that Jesus had said unto him, 'Buy those things that we have need of against the feast': or, that he should give something to the poor. ³⁰He then having received the sop went immediately out: and it was night.

³¹Therefore, when he was gone out, Jesus said, 'Now is the Son of

man glorified, and God is glorified in him. [32]If God be glorified in him, God shall also glorify him in himself, and shall straightway glorify him. [33]Little children, yet a little while I am with you. Ye shall seek me, and as I said unto the Jews, "Whither I go, ye cannot come": so now I say to you. [34]A new commandment I give unto you, that ye love one another, as I have loved you, that ye also love one another. [35]By this shall all men know that ye are my disciples, if ye have love one to another.'

[36]Simon Peter said unto him, 'Lord, whither goest thou?' Jesus answered him, 'Whither I go, thou canst not follow me now: but thou shalt follow me afterwards'. [37]Peter said unto him, 'Lord, why cannot I follow thee now? I will lay down my life for thy sake.' [38]Jesus answered him, 'Wilt thou lay down thy life for my sake? Verily, verily, I say unto thee, the cock shall not crow, till thou hast denied me thrice.

14 'Let not your heart be troubled: ye believe in God, believe also in me. [2]In my Father's house are many mansions: if it were not so, I would have told you: I go to prepare a place for you. [3]And if I go and prepare a place for you, I will come again, and receive you unto myself, that where I am, there ye may be also. [4]And whither I go ye know, and the way ye know.'

[5]Thomas saith unto him, 'Lord, we know not whither thou goest: and how can we know the way?' [6]Jesus saith unto him, 'I am the way, the truth, and the life: no man cometh unto the Father, but by me. [7]If ye had known me, ye should have known my Father also: and from henceforth ye know him, and have seen him.'

[8]Philip saith unto him, 'Lord, show us the Father, and it sufficeth us'. [9]Jesus saith unto him, 'Have I been so long time with you, and yet hast thou not known me, Philip? he that hath seen me hath seen the Father, and how sayest thou then, "Show us the Father"? [10]Believest thou not that I am in the Father, and the Father in me? The words that I speak unto you I speak not of myself: but the Father that dwelleth in me, he doeth the works. [11]Believe me that I am in the Father, and the Father in me: or else believe me for the very works' sake. [12]Verily, verily, I say unto you, he that believeth on me, the works that I do shall he do also, and greater works than these shall he do, because I go unto my Father. [13]And whatsoever ye shall ask in my name, that will I do, that the Father may be glorified in the Son. [14]If ye shall ask anything in my name, I will do it.

[15]'If ye love me, keep my commandments. [16]And I will pray the Father, and he shall give you another Comforter, that he may abide with you for ever, [17]even the Spirit of truth, whom the world cannot receive, because it seeth him not, neither knoweth him: but ye know him, for he dwelleth with you, and shall be in you. [18]I will not leave you comfortless: I will come to you. [19]Yet a little while, and the world seeth me no more: but ye see me: because I live, ye shall live also. [20]At that day ye shall know that I am in my Father, and you in me, and I in you. [21]He that hath my commandments, and keepeth them, he it is that loveth me: and he that loveth me shall be loved of my Father, and I will love him, and will manifest myself to him.'

[22]Judas saith unto him, not Iscariot, 'Lord, how is it that thou wilt

manifest thyself unto us, and not unto the world?' ²³Jesus answered and said unto him, 'If a man love me, he will keep my words: and my Father will love him, and we will come unto him, and make our abode with him. ²⁴He that loveth me not keepeth not my sayings, and the word which you hear is not mine, but the Father's which sent me. ²⁵These things have I spoken unto you, being yet present with you. ²⁶But the Comforter, which is the Holy Ghost, whom the Father will send in my name, he shall teach you all things, and bring all things to your remembrance, whatsoever I have said unto you.

²⁷'Peace I leave with you, my peace I give unto you: not as the world giveth, give I unto you. Let not your heart be troubled, neither let it be afraid. ²⁸Ye have heard how I said unto you, "I go away, and come again unto you". If ye loved me, ye would rejoice, because I said, "I go unto the Father": for my Father is greater than I. ²⁹And now I have told you before it come to pass, that when it is come to pass, ye might believe. ³⁰Hereafter I will not talk much with you: for the prince of this world cometh, and hath nothing in me. ³¹But that the world may know that I love the Father: and as the Father gave me commandment, even so I do. Arise, let us go hence.

15 'I am the true vine, and my Father is the husbandman. ²Every branch in me that beareth not fruit he taketh away: and every branch that beareth fruit, he purgeth it, that it may bring forth more fruit. ³Now ye are clean through the word which I have spoken unto you. ⁴Abide in me, and I in you. As the branch cannot bear fruit of itself, except it abide in the vine: no more can ye, except ye abide in me. ⁵I am the vine, ye are the branches: he that abideth in me, and I in him, the same bringeth forth much fruit: for without me ye can do nothing. ⁶If a man abide not in me, he is cast forth as a branch, and is withered; and men gather them, and cast them into the fire, and they are burnt. ⁷If ye abide in me, and my words abide in you, ye shall ask what ye will, and it shall be done unto you. ⁸Herein is my Father glorified, that ye bear much fruit; so shall ye be my disciples. ⁹As the Father hath loved me, so have I loved you: continue ye in my love. ¹⁰If ye keep my commandments, ye shall abide in my love, even as I have kept my Father's commandments, and abide in his love. ¹¹These things have I spoken unto you, that my joy might remain in you, and that your joy might be full. ¹²This is my commandment, that ye love one another, as I have loved you. ¹³Greater love hath no man than this, that a man lay down his life for his friends. ¹⁴Ye are my friends, if ye do whatsoever I command you. ¹⁵Henceforth I call you not servants, for the servant knoweth not what his lord doeth, but I have called you friends: for all things that I have heard of my Father I have made known unto you. ¹⁶Ye have not chosen me, but I have chosen you, and ordained you, that you should go and bring forth fruit, and that your fruit should remain: that whatsoever ye shall ask of the Father in my name, he may give it you. ¹⁷These things I command you, that ye love one another.

¹⁸'If the world hate you, ye know that it hated me before it hated you. ¹⁹If ye were of the world, the world would love his own: but because ye

are not of the world, but I have chosen you out of the world, therefore the world hateth you. ²⁰Remember the word that I said unto you, "The servant is not greater than the lord". If they have persecuted me, they will also persecute you; if they have kept my saying, they will keep yours also. ²¹But all these things will they do unto you for my name's sake, because they know not him that sent me. ²²If I had not come and spoken unto them, they had not had sin: but now they have no cloak for their sin. ²³He that hateth me hateth my Father also. ²⁴If I had not done among them the works which no other man did, they had not had sin: but now have they both seen and hated both me and my Father. ²⁵But this cometh to pass, that the word might be fulfilled that is written in their law, "They hated me without a cause". ²⁶But when the Comforter is come, whom I will send unto you from the Father, even the Spirit of truth, which proceedeth from the Father, he shall testify of me. ²⁷And ye also shall bear witness, because ye have been with me from the beginning.

16 'These things have I spoken unto you, that ye should not be offended. ²They shall put you out of the synagogues: yea, the time cometh, that whosoever killeth you will think that he doeth God service. ³And these things will they do unto you, because they have not known the Father, nor me. ⁴But these things have I told you, that when the time shall come, ye may remember that I told you of them. And these things I said not unto you at the beginning, because I was with you. ⁵But now I go my way to him that sent me, and none of you asketh me, "Whither goest thou?" ⁶But because I have said these things unto you, sorrow hath filled your heart. ⁷Nevertheless I tell you the truth, it is expedient for you that I go away: for if I go not away, the Comforter will not come unto you: but if I depart, I will send him unto you. ⁸And when he is come, he will reprove the world of sin, and of righteousness, and of judgement: ⁹of sin, because they believe not on me; ¹⁰of righteousness, because I go to my Father, and ye see me no more; ¹¹of judgement, because the prince of this world is judged.

¹²'I have yet many things to say unto you, but ye cannot bear them now. ¹³Howbeit when he, the Spirit of truth, is come, he will guide you into all truth: for he shall not speak of himself: but whatsoever he shall hear, that shall he speak, and he will show you things to come. ¹⁴He shall glorify me, for he shall receive of mine, and shall show it unto you. ¹⁵All things that the Father hath are mine: therefore said I that he shall take of mine, and shall show it unto you. ¹⁶A little while, and ye shall not see me: and again, a little while, and ye shall see me, because I go to the Father.'

¹⁷Then said some of his disciples among themselves, 'What is this that he saith unto us, "A little while, and ye shall not see me: and again, a little while, and ye shall see me": and, "Because I go to the Father"?' ¹⁸They said therefore, 'What is this that he saith, "A little while"? we cannot tell what he saith.'

¹⁹Now Jesus knew that they were desirous to ask him, and said unto them, 'Do ye inquire among yourselves of that I said, "A little while,

and ye shall not see me: and again, a little while, and ye shall see me"? ²⁰Verily, verily, I say unto you, that ye shall weep and lament, but the world shall rejoice: and ye shall be sorrowful, but your sorrow shall be turned into joy. ²¹A woman when she is in travail hath sorrow, because her hour is come: but as soon as she is delivered of the child, she remembereth no more the anguish, for joy that a man is born into the world. ²²And ye now therefore have sorrow: but I will see you again, and your heart shall rejoice, and your joy no man taketh from you. ²³And in that day ye shall ask me nothing. Verily, verily, I say unto you, whatsoever ye shall ask the Father in my name, he will give it you. ²⁴Hitherto have ye asked nothing in my name: ask, and ye shall receive, that your joy may be full.

²⁵'These things have I spoken unto you in proverbs: the time cometh, when I shall no more speak unto you in proverbs, but I shall show you plainly of the Father. ²⁶At that day ye shall ask in my name: and I say not unto you that I will pray the Father for you: ²⁷for the Father himself loveth you, because ye have loved me, and have believed that I came out from God. ²⁸I came forth from the Father, and am come into the world: again, I leave the world, and go to the Father.'

²⁹His disciples said unto him, 'Lo, now speakest thou plainly, and speakest no proverb. ³⁰Now are we sure that thou knowest all things, and needest not that any man should ask thee: by this we believe that thou camest forth from God.' ³¹Jesus answered them, 'Do ye now believe? ³²Behold, the hour cometh, yea, is now come, that ye shall be scattered, every man to his own, and shall leave me alone: and yet I am not alone, because the Father is with me. ³³These things I have spoken unto you, that in me ye might have peace. In the world ye shall have tribulation: but be of good cheer; I have overcome the world.'

17 These words spoke Jesus, and lifted up his eyes to heaven, and said, 'Father, the hour is come, glorify thy Son, that thy Son also may glorify thee: ²as thou hast given him power over all flesh, that he should give eternal life to as many as thou hast given him. ³And this is life eternal, that they might know thee the only true God, and Jesus Christ, whom thou hast sent. ⁴I have glorified thee on the earth: I have finished the work which thou gavest me to do. ⁵And now, O Father, glorify thou me with thy own self with the glory which I had with thee before the world was.

⁶'I have manifested thy name unto the men which thou gavest me out of the world: thine they were, and thou gavest them me; and they have kept thy word. ⁷Now they have known that all things whatsoever thou hast given me are of thee. ⁸For I have given unto them the words which thou gavest me, and they have received them, and have known surely that I came out from thee, and they have believed that thou didst send me. ⁹I pray for them, I pray not for the world: but for them which thou hast given me, for they are thine. ¹⁰And all mine are thine, and thine are mine: and I am glorified in them.

¹¹'And now I am no more in the world, but these are in the world, and I come to thee. Holy Father, keep through thy own name those

whom thou hast given me, that they may be one, as we are. ¹²While I was with them in the world, I kept them in thy name: those that thou gavest me I have kept, and none of them is lost, but the son of perdition: that the scripture might be fulfilled.

¹³'And now come I to thee, and these things I speak in the world, that they might have my joy fulfilled in themselves. ¹⁴I have given them thy word, and the world hath hated them, because they are not of the world, even as I am not of the world. ¹⁵I pray not that thou shouldst take them out of the world, but that thou shouldst keep them from the evil. ¹⁶They are not of the world, even as I am not of the world. ¹⁷Sanctify them through thy truth: thy word is truth. ¹⁸As thou hast sent me into the world, even so have I also sent them into the world. ¹⁹And for their sakes I sanctify myself, that they also might be sanctified through the truth.

²⁰'Neither pray I for these alone, but for them also which shall believe on me through their word: ²¹that they all may be one: as thou, Father, art in me, and I in thee, that they also may be one in us: that the world may believe that thou hast sent me. ²²And the glory which thou gavest me I have given them: that they may be one, even as we are one: ²³I in them, and thou in me, that they may be made perfect in one, and that the world may know that thou hast sent me, and hast loved them, as thou hast loved me.

²⁴'Father, I will that they also, whom thou hast given me, be with me where I am, that they may behold my glory, which thou hast given me: for thou lovedst me before the foundation of the world. ²⁵O righteous Father, the world hath not known thee, but I have known thee, and these have known that thou hast sent me. ²⁶And I have declared unto them thy name, and will declare it: that the love wherewith thou hast loved me may be in them, and I in them.'

18 When Jesus had spoken these words, he went forth with his disciples over the brook Cedron, where was a garden, into the which he entered, and his disciples. ²And Judas also, which betrayed him, knew the place: for Jesus ofttimes resorted thither with his disciples. ³Judas then, having received a band of men and officers from the chief priests and Pharisees, cometh thither with lanterns and torches and weapons. ⁴Jesus therefore, knowing all things that should come upon him, went forth, and said unto them, 'Whom seek ye?' ⁵They answered him, 'Jesus of Nazareth'. Jesus saith unto them, 'I am he'. And Judas also, which betrayed him, stood with them. ⁶As soon then as he had said unto them, 'I am he', they went backward, and fell to the ground. ⁷Then asked he them again, 'Whom seek ye?' And they said, 'Jesus of Nazareth'. ⁸Jesus answered, 'I have told you that I am he: if therefore ye seek me, let these go their way': ⁹that the saying might be fulfilled, which he spoke, 'Of them which thou gavest me have I lost none'. ¹⁰Then Simon Peter having a sword drew it, and smote the high priest's servant, and cut off his right ear. The servant's name was Malchus. ¹¹Then said Jesus unto Peter, 'Put up thy sword into the sheath: the cup which my Father hath given me, shall I not drink it?'

¹²Then the band and the captain and officers of the Jews took Jesus, and bound him, ¹³and led him away to Annas first; for he was father-in-law to Caiaphas, which was the high priest that same year. ¹⁴Now Caiaphas was he which gave counsel to the Jews, that it was expedient that one man should die for the people.

¹⁵And Simon Peter followed Jesus, and so did another disciple: that disciple was known unto the high priest, and went in with Jesus into the palace of the high priest. ¹⁶But Peter stood at the door without. Then went out that other disciple, which was known unto the high priest, and spoke unto her that kept the door, and brought in Peter. ¹⁷Then saith the damsel that kept the door unto Peter, 'Art not thou also one of this man's disciples?' He saith, 'I am not'. ¹⁸And the servants and officers stood there, who had made a fire of coals (for it was cold), and they warmed themselves: and Peter stood with them, and warmed himself.

¹⁹The high priest then asked Jesus of his disciples, and of his doctrine. ²⁰Jesus answered him, 'I spoke openly to the world, I ever taught in the synagogue, and in the temple, whither the Jews always resort, and in secret have I said nothing: ²¹why askest thou me? Ask them which heard me, what I have said unto them: behold, they know what I said.' ²²And when he had thus spoken, one of the officers which stood by struck Jesus with the palm of his hand, saying, 'Answerest thou the high priest so?' ²³Jesus answered him, 'If I have spoken evil, bear witness of the evil: but if well, why smitest thou me?' ²⁴Now Annas had sent him bound unto Caiaphas the high priest.

²⁵And Simon Peter stood and warmed himself. They said therefore unto him, 'Art not thou also one of his disciples?' He denied it, and said, 'I am not'. ²⁶One of the servants of the high priest, being his kinsman whose ear Peter cut off, saith, 'Did not I see thee in the garden with him?' ²⁷Peter then denied again, and immediately the cock crew.

²⁸Then led they Jesus from Caiaphas unto the hall of judgement: and it was early; and they themselves went not into the judgement hall, lest they should be defiled: but that they might eat the passover. ²⁹Pilate then went out unto them, and said, 'What accusation bring you against this man?' ³⁰They answered and said unto him, 'If he were not a malefactor, we would not have delivered him up unto thee'. ³¹Then said Pilate unto them, 'Take ye him, and judge him according to your law'. The Jews therefore said unto him, 'It is not lawful for us to put any man to death': ³²that the saying of Jesus might be fulfilled, which he spoke, signifying what death he should die.

³³Then Pilate entered into the judgement hall again, and called Jesus, and said unto him, 'Art thou the King of the Jews?' ³⁴Jesus answered him, 'Sayest thou this thing of thyself, or did others tell it thee of me?' ³⁵Pilate answered, 'Am I a Jew? Thy own nation and the chief priests have delivered thee unto me: what hast thou done?' ³⁶Jesus answered, 'My kingdom is not of this world: if my kingdom were of this world, then would my servants fight, that I should not be delivered to the Jews: but now is my kingdom not from hence'. ³⁷Pilate therefore said unto him, 'Art thou a king then?' Jesus answered, 'Thou sayest that I am

a king. To this end was I born, and for this cause came I into the world, that I should bear witness unto the truth: every one that is of the truth heareth my voice.' [38]Pilate saith unto him, 'What is truth?'

And when he had said this, he went out again unto the Jews, and saith unto them, 'I find in him no fault at all. [39]But ye have a custom, that I should release unto you one at the passover: will ye therefore that I release unto you the King of the Jews?' [40]Then cried they all again, saying, 'Not this man, but Barabbas'. Now Barabbas was a robber.

19 Then Pilate therefore took Jesus, and scourged him. [2]And the soldiers plaited a crown of thorns, and put it on his head, and they put on him a purple robe, [3]and said, 'Hail, King of the Jews': and they smote him with their hands.

[4]Pilate therefore went forth again, and saith unto them, 'Behold, I bring him forth to you, that ye may know that I find no fault in him'. [5]Then came Jesus forth, wearing the crown of thorns, and the purple robe. And Pilate saith unto them, 'Behold the man'. [6]When the chief priests therefore and officers saw him, they cried out, saying, 'Crucify him, crucify him'. Pilate saith unto them, 'Take ye him, and crucify him: for I find no fault in him'. [7]The Jews answered him, 'We have a law, and by our law he ought to die, because he made himself the Son of God'.

[8]When Pilate therefore heard that saying, he was the more afraid, [9]and went again into the judgement hall, and saith unto Jesus, 'Whence art thou?' But Jesus gave him no answer. [10]Then saith Pilate unto him, 'Speakest thou not unto me? Knowest thou not that I have power to crucify thee, and have power to release thee?' [11]Jesus answered, 'Thou couldst have no power at all against me, except it were given thee from above: therefore he that delivered me unto thee hath the greater sin'.

[12]And from thenceforth Pilate sought to release him: but the Jews cried out, saying, 'If thou let this man go, thou art not Caesar's friend: whosoever maketh himself a king speaketh against Caesar'.

[13]When Pilate therefore heard that saying, he brought Jesus forth, and sat down in the judgement seat in a place that is called the Pavement, but in the Hebrew, Gabbatha. [14]And it was the preparation of the passover, and about the sixth hour: and he saith unto the Jews, 'Behold your King'. [15]But they cried out, 'Away with him, away with him, crucify him'. Pilate saith unto them, 'Shall I crucify your King?' The chief priests answered, 'We have no king but Caesar'. [16]Then delivered he him therefore unto them to be crucified.

And they took Jesus, and led him away. [17]And he bearing his cross went forth into a place called the place of a skull, which is called in the Hebrew, Golgotha: [18]where they crucified him, and two others with him, on either side one, and Jesus in the midst.

[19]And Pilate wrote a title, and put it on the cross. And the writing was, 'JESUS OF NAZARETH, THE KING OF THE JEWS'. [20]This title then read many of the Jews: for the place where Jesus was crucified was nigh to the city, and it was written in Hebrew, and Greek, and Latin.

²¹Then said the chief priests of the Jews to Pilate, 'Write not, "The King of the Jews": but that he said, "I am King of the Jews"'. ²²Pilate answered, 'What I have written I have written'.

²³Then the soldiers, when they had crucified Jesus, took his garments, and made four parts, to every soldier a part; and also his coat: now the coat was without seam, woven from the top throughout. ²⁴They said therefore among themselves, 'Let us not rend it, but cast lots for it, whose it shall be': that the scripture might be fulfilled, which saith, 'They parted my raiment among them, and for my vesture they did cast lots'. These things therefore the soldiers did.

²⁵Now there stood by the cross of Jesus his mother, and his mother's sister, Mary the wife of Cleophas, and Mary Magdalene. ²⁶When Jesus therefore saw his mother, and the disciple standing by, whom he loved, he saith unto his mother, 'Woman, behold thy son'. ²⁷Then saith he to the disciple, 'Behold thy mother'. And from that hour that disciple took her unto his own home.

²⁸After this, Jesus knowing that all things were now accomplished, that the scripture might be fulfilled, saith, 'I thirst'. ²⁹Now there was set a vessel full of vinegar: and they filled a sponge with vinegar, and put it upon hyssop, and put it to his mouth. ³⁰When Jesus therefore had received the vinegar, he said, 'It is finished', and he bowed his head, and gave up the ghost.

³¹The Jews therefore, because it was the preparation, that the bodies should not remain upon the cross on the sabbath day (for that sabbath day was a high day), besought Pilate that their legs might be broken, and that they might be taken away. ³²Then came the soldiers, and broke the legs of the first, and of the other which was crucified with him. ³³But when they came to Jesus, and saw that he was dead already, they broke not his legs. ³⁴But one of the soldiers with a spear pierced his side, and forthwith came there out blood and water. ³⁵And he that saw it bore record, and his record is true, and he knoweth that he saith true, that ye might believe. ³⁶For these things were done, that the scripture should be fulfilled, 'A bone of him shall not be broken'. ³⁷And again another scripture saith, 'They shall look on him whom they pierced'.

³⁸And after this Joseph of Arimathaea, being a disciple of Jesus, but secretly for fear of the Jews, besought Pilate that he might take away the body of Jesus, and Pilate gave him leave: he came therefore, and took the body of Jesus. ³⁹And there came also Nicodemus, which at the first came to Jesus by night, and brought a mixture of myrrh and aloes, about a hundred pound weight. ⁴⁰Then took they the body of Jesus, and wound it in linen clothes with the spices, as the manner of the Jews is to bury. ⁴¹Now in the place where he was crucified there was a garden, and in the garden a new sepulchre, wherein was never man yet laid. ⁴²There laid they Jesus therefore because of the Jews' preparation day, for the sepulchre was nigh at hand.

20 The first day of the week cometh Mary Magdalene early, when it was yet dark, unto the sepulchre, and seeth the stone taken away from the sepulchre. ²Then she runneth, and cometh to Simon Peter, and to the other disciple, whom Jesus loved, and saith unto them, 'They have taken away the Lord out of the sepulchre, and we know not where they have laid him'. ³Peter therefore went forth, and that other disciple, and came to the sepulchre. ⁴So they ran both together, and the other disciple did outrun Peter, and came first to the sepulchre. ⁵And he stooping down, and looking in, saw the linen clothes lying; yet went he not in. ⁶Then cometh Simon Peter following him, and went into the sepulchre, and seeth the linen clothes lie, ⁷and the napkin, that was about his head, not lying with the linen clothes, but wrapped together in a place by itself. ⁸Then went in also that other disciple, which came first to the sepulchre, and he saw, and believed. ⁹For as yet they knew not the scripture, that he must rise again from the dead.

¹⁰Then the disciples went away again unto their own home. ¹¹But Mary stood without at the sepulchre weeping: and as she wept, she stooped down, and looked into the sepulchre, ¹²and seeth two angels in white sitting, the one at the head, and the other at the feet, where the body of Jesus had lain. ¹³And they say unto her, 'Woman, why weepest thou?' She saith unto them, 'Because they have taken away my Lord, and I know not where they have laid him'.

¹⁴And when she had thus said, she turned herself back, and saw Jesus standing, and knew not that it was Jesus. ¹⁵Jesus saith unto her, 'Woman, why weepest thou? whom seekest thou?' She, supposing him to be the gardener, saith unto him, 'Sir, if thou have borne him hence, tell me where thou hast laid him, and I will take him away'. ¹⁶Jesus saith unto her, 'Mary'. She turned herself, and saith unto him, 'Rabboni', which is to say, 'Master'. ¹⁷Jesus saith unto her, 'Touch me not: for I am not yet ascended to my Father: but go to my brethren, and say unto them, I ascend unto my Father, and your Father, and to my God, and your God'. ¹⁸Mary Magdalene came and told the disciples that she had seen the Lord, and that he had spoken these things unto her.

¹⁹Then the same day at evening, being the first day of the week, when the doors were shut where the disciples were assembled for fear of the Jews, came Jesus and stood in the midst, and saith unto them, 'Peace be unto you'. ²⁰And when he had so said, he showed unto them his hands and his side. Then were the disciples glad, when they saw the Lord. ²¹Then said Jesus to them again, 'Peace be unto you: as my Father hath sent me, even so send I you'. ²²And when he had said this, he breathed on them, and saith unto them, 'Receive ye the Holy Ghost. ²³Whose soever sins ye remit, they are remitted unto them, and whose soever sins ye retain, they are retained.'

²⁴But Thomas, one of the twelve, called Didymus, was not with them when Jesus came. ²⁵The other disciples therefore said unto him, 'We have seen the Lord'. But he said unto them, 'Except I shall see in his hands the print of the nails, and put my finger into the print of the nails, and thrust my hand into his side, I will not believe'.

²⁶And after eight days again his disciples were within, and Thomas

with them: then came Jesus, the doors being shut, and stood in the midst, and said, 'Peace be unto you'. ²⁷Then saith he to Thomas, 'Reach hither thy finger, and behold my hands, and reach hither thy hand, and thrust it into my side, and be not faithless, but believing'. ²⁸And Thomas answered and said unto him, 'My Lord and my God'. ²⁹Jesus saith unto him, 'Thomas, because thou hast seen me, thou hast believed: blessed are they that have not seen, and yet have believed'.

³⁰And many other signs truly did Jesus in the presence of his disciples, which are not written in this book: ³¹but these are written, that ye might believe that Jesus is the Christ, the Son of God, and that believing ye might have life through his name.

21 After these things Jesus showed himself again to the disciples at the sea of Tiberias, and on this wise showed he himself. ²There were together Simon Peter, and Thomas called Didymus, and Nathanael of Cana in Galilee, and the sons of Zebedee, and two others of his disciples. ³Simon Peter saith unto them, 'I go a-fishing'. They say unto him, 'We also go with thee'. They went forth, and entered into a ship immediately, and that night they caught nothing.

⁴But when the morning was now come, Jesus stood on the shore: but the disciples knew not that it was Jesus. ⁵Then Jesus saith unto them, 'Children, have ye any meat?' They answered him, 'No'. ⁶And he said unto them, 'Cast the net on the right side of the ship, and ye shall find'. They cast therefore, and now they were not able to draw it for the multitude of fishes. ⁷Therefore that disciple whom Jesus loved saith unto Peter, 'It is the Lord'. Now when Simon Peter heard that it was the Lord, he girt his fisher's coat unto him (for he was naked), and did cast himself into the sea. ⁸And the other disciples came in a little ship (for they were not far from land, but as it were two hundred cubits), dragging the net with fishes. ⁹As soon then as they were come to land, they saw a fire of coals there, and fish laid thereon, and bread. ¹⁰Jesus saith unto them, 'Bring of the fish which ye have now caught'. ¹¹Simon Peter went up, and drew the net to land full of great fishes, a hundred and fifty and three: and for all there were so many, yet was not the net broken. ¹²Jesus saith unto them, 'Come and dine'. And none of the disciples durst ask him, 'Who art thou?' knowing that it was the Lord. ¹³Jesus then cometh, and taketh bread, and giveth them, and fish likewise. ¹⁴This is now the third time that Jesus showed himself to his disciples, after that he was risen from the dead.

¹⁵So when they had dined, Jesus saith to Simon Peter, 'Simon, son of Jonas, lovest thou me more than these?' He saith unto him, 'Yea, Lord, thou knowest that I love thee'. He saith unto him, 'Feed my lambs'. ¹⁶He saith to him again the second time, 'Simon, son of Jonas, lovest thou me?' He saith unto him, 'Yea, Lord, thou knowest that I love thee'. He saith unto him, 'Feed my sheep'. ¹⁷He said unto him the third time, 'Simon, son of Jonas, lovest thou me?' Peter was grieved because he said unto him the third time, 'Lovest thou me?' And he said unto him, 'Lord, thou knowest all things, thou knowest that I love thee'. Jesus saith unto him, 'Feed my sheep. ¹⁸Verily, verily, I say unto thee, when thou wast

young, thou girdedst thyself, and walkedst whither thou wouldst: but when thou shalt be old, thou shalt stretch forth thy hands, and another shall gird thee, and carry thee whither thou wouldst not.' ¹⁹This spoke he, signifying by what death he should glorify God. And when he had spoken this, he saith unto him, 'Follow me'.

²⁰Then Peter, turning about, seeth the disciple whom Jesus loved following, which also leaned on his breast at supper, and said, 'Lord, which is he that betrayeth thee?' ²¹Peter seeing him saith to Jesus, 'Lord, and what shall this man do?' ²²Jesus saith unto him, 'If I will that he tarry till I come, what is that to thee? Follow thou me.' ²³Then went this saying abroad among the brethren, that that disciple should not die: yet Jesus said not unto him, 'He shall not die': but, 'If I will that he tarry till I come, what is that to thee?'

²⁴This is the disciple which testifieth of these things, and wrote these things, and we know that his testimony is true.

²⁵And there are also many other things which Jesus did, the which, if they should be written every one, I suppose that even the world itself could not contain the books that should be written. Amen.

THE
ACTS OF THE APOSTLES

1 The former treatise have I made, O Theophilus, of all that Jesus began both to do and teach, [2]until the day in which he was taken up, after that he through the Holy Ghost had given commandments unto the apostles whom he had chosen: [3]to whom also he showed himself alive after his passion by many infallible proofs, being seen of them forty days, and speaking of the things pertaining to the kingdom of God: [4]and, being assembled together with them, commanded them that they should not depart from Jerusalem, but wait for the promise of the Father, 'which,' saith he, 'ye have heard of me. [5]For John truly baptized with water, but ye shall be baptized with the Holy Ghost not many days hence.'

[6]When they therefore were come together, they asked of him, saying, 'Lord, wilt thou at this time restore again the kingdom to Israel?' [7]And he said unto them, 'It is not for you to know the times or the seasons, which the Father hath put in his own power. [8]But ye shall receive power, after that the Holy Ghost is come upon you, and ye shall be witnesses unto me both in Jerusalem, and in all Judea, and in Samaria, and unto the uttermost part of the earth.'

[9]And when he had spoken these things, while they beheld, he was taken up, and a cloud received him out of their sight. [10]And while they looked steadfastly toward heaven as he went up, behold, two men stood by them in white apparel, [11]which also said, 'Ye men of Galilee, why stand ye gazing up into heaven? This same Jesus, which is taken up from you into heaven, shall so come in like manner as ye have seen him go into heaven.'

[12]Then returned they unto Jerusalem from the mount called Olivet, which is from Jerusalem a sabbath day's journey. [13]And when they were come in, they went up into an upper room, where abode both Peter, and James, and John, and Andrew, Philip, and Thomas, Bartholomew, and Matthew, James the son of Alphaeus, and Simon Zelotes, and Judas the brother of James. [14]These all continued with one accord in prayer and supplication, with the women, and Mary the mother of Jesus, and with his brethren.

[15]And in those days Peter stood up in the midst of the disciples, and said (the number of names together were about a hundred and twenty), [16]'Men and brethren, this scripture must needs have been fulfilled, which the Holy Ghost by the mouth of David spoke before concerning Judas, which was guide to them that took Jesus. [17]For he was numbered with us, and had obtained part of this ministry.' [18]Now this man purchased a field with the reward of iniquity, and falling headlong, he burst asunder in the midst, and all his bowels gushed out. [19]And it was known unto all the dwellers at Jerusalem, insomuch as that field is called in their proper tongue, Aceldama, that is to say, the Field of

Blood. ²⁰'For it is written in the book of Psalms, "Let his habitation be desolate, and let no man dwell therein": and "His bishopric let another take". ²¹Wherefore of these men which have companied with us all the time that the Lord Jesus went in and out among us, ²²beginning from the baptism of John, unto that same day that he was taken up from us, must one be ordained to be a witness with us of his resurrection.'

²³And they appointed two, Joseph called Barsabas, who was surnamed Justus, and Matthias. ²⁴And they prayed, and said, 'Thou, Lord, which knowest the hearts of all men, show whether of these two thou hast chosen, ²⁵that he may take part of this ministry and apostleship, from which Judas by transgression fell, that he might go to his own place'. ²⁶And they gave forth their lots, and the lot fell upon Matthias, and he was numbered with the eleven apostles.

2 And when the day of Pentecost was fully come, they were all with one accord in one place. ²And suddenly there came a sound from heaven as of a rushing mighty wind, and it filled all the house where they were sitting. ³And there appeared unto them cloven tongues like as of fire, and it sat upon each of them. ⁴And they were all filled with the Holy Ghost, and began to speak with other tongues, as the Spirit gave them utterance.

⁵And there were dwelling at Jerusalem Jews, devout men, out of every nation under heaven. ⁶Now when this was noised abroad, the multitude came together, and were confounded, because that every man heard them speak in his own language. ⁷And they were all amazed and marvelled, saying one to another, 'Behold, are not all these which speak Galileans? ⁸And how hear we every man in our own tongue, wherein we were born? ⁹Parthians, and Medes, and Elamites, and the dwellers in Mesopotamia, and in Judea, and Cappadocia, in Pontus, and Asia, ¹⁰Phrygia, and Pamphylia, in Egypt, and in the parts of Libya about Cyrene, and strangers of Rome, Jews and proselytes, ¹¹Cretes and Arabians, we do hear them speak in our tongues the wonderful works of God.' ¹²And they were all amazed, and were in doubt, saying one to another, 'What meaneth this?' ¹³Others mocking said, 'These men are full of new wine'.

¹⁴But Peter, standing up with the eleven, lifted up his voice, and said unto them, 'Ye men of Judea, and all ye that dwell at Jerusalem, be this known unto you, and hearken to my words: ¹⁵for these are not drunken, as ye suppose, seeing it is but the third hour of the day. ¹⁶But this is that which was spoken by the prophet Joel, ¹⁷"'And it shall come to pass in the last days,' saith God, 'I will pour out of my Spirit upon all flesh: and your sons and your daughters shall prophesy, and your young men shall see visions, and your old men shall dream dreams: ¹⁸and on my servants and on my handmaidens I will pour out in those days of my Spirit, and they shall prophesy: ¹⁹and I will show wonders in heaven above, and signs in the earth beneath: blood, and fire, and vapour of smoke. ²⁰The sun shall be turned into darkness, and the moon into blood, before that great and notable day of the Lord come. ²¹And it shall come to pass that whosoever shall call on the name of the Lord shall be saved.'"

[22]'Ye men of Israel, hear these words, Jesus of Nazareth, a man approved of God among you by miracles, wonders and signs, which God did by him in the midst of you, as ye yourselves also know: [23]him, being delivered by the determinate counsel and foreknowledge of God, ye have taken, and by wicked hands have crucified and slain: [24]whom God hath raised up, having loosed the pains of death: because it was not possible that he should be held of it. [25]For David speaketh concerning him, "I foresaw the Lord always before my face, for he is on my right hand, that I should not be moved. [26]Therefore did my heart rejoice, and my tongue was glad: moreover also my flesh shall rest in hope, [27]because thou wilt not leave my soul in hell, neither wilt thou suffer thy Holy One to see corruption. [28]Thou hast made known to me the ways of life, thou shalt make me full of joy with thy countenance."

[29]'Men and brethren, let me freely speak unto you of the patriarch David, that he is both dead and buried, and his sepulchre is with us unto this day. [30]Therefore being a prophet, and knowing that God had sworn with an oath to him, that of the fruit of his loins, according to the flesh, he would raise up Christ to sit on his throne: [31]he seeing this before, spoke of the resurrection of Christ, that his soul was not left in hell, neither his flesh did see corruption. [32]This Jesus hath God raised up, whereof we all are witnesses. [33]Therefore being by the right hand of God exalted, and having received of the Father the promise of the Holy Ghost, he hath shed forth this, which ye now see and hear. [34]For David is not ascended into the heavens, but he saith himself, "The Lord said unto my Lord, 'Sit thou on my right hand, [35]until I make thy foes thy footstool'". [36]Therefore let all the house of Israel know assuredly, that God hath made that same Jesus, whom ye have crucified, both Lord and Christ.'

[37]Now when they heard this, they were pricked in their heart, and said unto Peter and to the rest of the apostles, 'Men and brethren, what shall we do?' [38]Then Peter said unto them, 'Repent, and be baptized every one of you in the name of Jesus Christ for the remission of sins, and ye shall receive the gift of the Holy Ghost. [39]For the promise is unto you, and to your children, and to all that are afar off, even as many as the Lord our God shall call.' [40]And with many other words did he testify and exhort, saying, 'Save yourselves from this untoward generation'.

[41]Then they that gladly received his word were baptized: and the same day there were added unto them about three thousand souls. [42]And they continued steadfastly in the apostles' doctrine and fellowship, and in breaking of bread, and in prayers. [43]And fear came upon every soul: and many wonders and signs were done by the apostles.

[44]And all that believed were together, and had all things common, [45]and sold their possessions and goods, and parted them to all men, as every man had need. [46]And they, continuing daily with one accord in the temple, and breaking bread from house to house, did eat their meat with gladness and singleness of heart, [47]praising God, and having favour with all the people. And the Lord added to the church daily such as should be saved.

3 Now Peter and John went up together into the temple at the hour of prayer, being the ninth hour. [2]And a certain man lame from his mother's womb was carried, whom they laid daily at the gate of the temple which is called Beautiful, to ask alms of them that entered into the temple; [3]who seeing Peter and John about to go into the temple asked an alms. [4]And Peter, fastening his eyes upon him with John, said, 'Look on us'. [5]And he gave heed unto them, expecting to receive something of them. [6]Then Peter said, 'Silver and gold have I none, but such as I have give I thee: in the name of Jesus Christ of Nazareth rise up and walk'. [7]And he took him by the right hand, and lifted him up: and immediately his feet and ankle-bones received strength. [8]And he leaping up stood, and walked, and entered with them into the temple, walking, and leaping, and praising God. [9]And all the people saw him walking and praising God. [10]And they knew that it was he which sat for alms at the Beautiful gate of the temple: and they were filled with wonder and amazement at that which had happened unto him.

[11]And as the lame man which was healed held Peter and John, all the people ran together unto them in the porch that is called Solomon's, greatly wondering. [12]And when Peter saw it, he answered unto the people, 'Ye men of Israel, why marvel ye at this? or why look ye so earnestly on us, as though by our own power or holiness we had made this man to walk? [13]The God of Abraham, and of Isaac, and of Jacob, the God of our fathers, hath glorified his Son Jesus, whom ye delivered up, and denied him in the presence of Pilate, when he was determined to let him go. [14]But ye denied the Holy One and the Just, and desired a murderer to be granted unto you, [15]and killed the Prince of life, whom God hath raised from the dead, whereof we are witnesses. [16]And his name through faith in his name hath made this man strong, whom ye see and know: yea, the faith which is by him hath given him this perfect soundness in the presence of you all. [17]And now, brethren, I wot that through ignorance ye did it, as did also your rulers. [18]But those things, which God before had shown by the mouth of all his prophets, that Christ should suffer, he hath so fulfilled.

[19]'Repent ye therefore, and be converted, that your sins may be blotted out, when the times of refreshing shall come from the presence of the Lord. [20]And he shall send Jesus Christ, which before was preached unto you: [21]whom the heaven must receive until the times of restitution of all things, which God hath spoken by the mouth of all his holy prophets since the world began. [22]For Moses truly said unto the fathers, "A prophet shall the Lord your God raise up unto you of your brethren, like unto me; him shall ye hear in all things whatsoever he shall say unto you. [23]And it shall come to pass that every soul which will not hear that prophet, shall be destroyed from among the people." [24]Yea, and all the prophets from Samuel and those that follow after, as many as have spoken, have likewise foretold of these days. [25]Ye are the children of the prophets, and of the covenant which God made with our fathers, saying unto Abraham, "And in thy seed shall all the kindreds of the earth be blessed". [26]Unto you first God, having raised up his Son

Jesus, sent him to bless you, in turning away every one of you from his iniquities.'

4 And as they spoke unto the people, the priests, and the captain of the temple, and the Sadducees came upon them, ²being grieved that they taught the people, and preached through Jesus the resurrection from the dead. ³And they laid hands on them, and put them in hold unto the next day: for it was now eventide. ⁴Howbeit many of them which heard the word believed, and the number of the men was about five thousand.

⁵And it came to pass on the morrow, that their rulers, and elders, and scribes, ⁶and Annas the high priest, and Caiaphas, and John, and Alexander, and as many as were of the kindred of the high priest, were gathered together at Jerusalem. ⁷And when they had set them in the midst, they asked, 'By what power, or by what name have ye done this?' ⁸Then Peter, filled with the Holy Ghost, said unto them, 'Ye rulers of the people, and elders of Israel, ⁹if we this day be examined of the good deed done to the impotent man, by what means he is made whole, ¹⁰be it known unto you all, and to all the people of Israel, that by the name of Jesus Christ of Nazareth, whom ye crucified, whom God raised from the dead, even by him doth this man stand here before you whole. ¹¹This is the stone which was set at nought of you builders, which is become the head of the corner. ¹²Neither is there salvation in any other: for there is no other name under heaven given among men, whereby we must be saved.'

¹³Now when they saw the boldness of Peter and John, and perceived that they were unlearned and ignorant men, they marvelled, and they took knowledge of them, that they had been with Jesus. ¹⁴And beholding the man which was healed standing with them, they could say nothing against it. ¹⁵But when they had commanded them to go aside out of the council, they conferred among themselves, ¹⁶saying, 'What shall we do to these men? for that indeed a notable miracle hath been done by them is manifest to all them that dwell in Jerusalem, and we cannot deny it. ¹⁷But that it spread no further among the people, let us straitly threaten them, that they speak henceforth to no man in this name.' ¹⁸And they called them, and commanded them not to speak at all nor teach in the name of Jesus. ¹⁹But Peter and John answered and said unto them, 'Whether it be right in the sight of God to hearken unto you more than unto God, judge ye. ²⁰For we cannot but speak the things which we have seen and heard.' ²¹So when they had further threatened them, they let them go, finding nothing how they might punish them, because of the people: for all men glorified God for that which was done. ²²For the man was above forty years old, on whom this miracle of healing was shown.

²³And being let go, they went to their own company, and reported all that the chief priests and elders had said unto them. ²⁴And when they heard that, they lifted up their voice to God with one accord, and said, 'Lord, thou art God, which hast made heaven, and earth, and the sea, and all that in them is, ²⁵who by the mouth of thy servant David hast

said, "Why did the heathen rage, and the people imagine vain things? [26]The kings of the earth stood up, and the rulers were gathered together against the Lord, and against his Christ." [27]For of a truth against thy holy child Jesus, whom thou hast anointed, both Herod, and Pontius Pilate, with the Gentiles, and the people of Israel, were gathered together, [28]for to do whatsoever thy hand and thy counsel determined before to be done. [29]And now, Lord, behold their threatenings: and grant unto thy servants, that with all boldness they may speak thy word, [30]by stretching forth thy hand to heal: and that signs and wonders may be done by the name of thy holy child Jesus.'

[31]And when they had prayed, the place was shaken where they were assembled together, and they were all filled with the Holy Ghost, and they spoke the word of God with boldness.

[32]And the multitude of them that believed were of one heart and of one soul: neither said any of them that aught of the things which he possessed was his own, but they had all things common. [33]And with great power gave the apostles witness of the resurrection of the Lord Jesus, and great grace was upon them all. [34]Neither was there any among them that lacked: for as many as were possessors of lands or houses sold them, and brought the prices of the things that were sold, [35]and laid them down at the apostles' feet: and distribution was made unto every man according as he had need. [36]And Joses, who by the apostles was surnamed Barnabas (which is, being interpreted, the son of consolation), a Levite, and of the country of Cyprus, [37]having land, sold it, and brought the money, and laid it at the apostles' feet.

5 But a certain man named Ananias, with Sapphira his wife, sold a possession, [2]and kept back part of the price, his wife also being privy to it, and brought a certain part, and laid it at the apostles' feet. [3]But Peter said, 'Ananias, why hath Satan filled thy heart to lie to the Holy Ghost, and to keep back part of the price of the land? [4]Whilst it remained, was it not thy own? and after it was sold, was it not in thy own power? why hast thou conceived this thing in thy heart? thou hast not lied unto men, but unto God.' [5]And Ananias hearing these words fell down, and gave up the ghost: and great fear came on all them that heard these things. [6]And the young men arose, wound him up, and carried him out, and buried him.

[7]And it was about the space of three hours after, when his wife, not knowing what was done, came in. [8]And Peter answered unto her, 'Tell me whether ye sold the land for so much?' And she said, 'Yea, for so much'. [9]Then Peter said unto her, 'How is it that ye have agreed together to tempt the Spirit of the Lord? behold, the feet of them which have buried thy husband are at the door, and shall carry thee out.' [10]Then fell she down straightway at his feet, and yielded up the ghost: and the young men came in, and found her dead, and, carrying her forth, buried her by her husband. [11]And great fear came upon all the church, and upon as many as heard these things.

[12]And by the hands of the apostles were many signs and wonders wrought among the people (and they were all with one accord in

Solomon's porch. ¹³And of the rest durst no man join himself to them: but the people magnified them. ¹⁴And believers were the more added to the Lord, multitudes both of men and women), ¹⁵insomuch that they brought forth the sick into the streets, and laid them on beds and couches, that at the least the shadow of Peter passing by might over-shadow some of them. ¹⁶There came also a multitude out of the cities round about unto Jerusalem, bringing sick folks, and them which were vexed with unclean spirits: and they were healed every one.

¹⁷Then the high priest rose up, and all they that were with him (which is the sect of the Sadducees), and were filled with indignation, ¹⁸and laid their hands on the apostles, and put them in the common prison. ¹⁹But the angel of the Lord by night opened the prison doors, and brought them forth, and said, ²⁰'Go, stand and speak in the temple to the people all the words of this life.' ²¹And when they heard that, they entered into the temple early in the morning, and taught.

But the high priest came, and they that were with him, and called the council together, and all the senate of the children of Israel, and sent to the prison to have them brought. ²²But when the officers came, and found them not in the prison, they returned, and told, ²³saying, 'The prison truly found we shut with all safety, and the keepers standing without before the doors, but when we had opened, we found no man within'. ²⁴Now when the high priest and the captain of the temple and the chief priests heard these things, they doubted of them whereunto this would grow. ²⁵Then came one and told them, saying, 'Behold, the men whom ye put in prison are standing in the temple, and teaching the people'. ²⁶Then went the captain with the officers, and brought them without violence: for they feared the people, lest they should have been stoned.

²⁷And when they had brought them, they set them before the coun-cil, and the high priest asked them, ²⁸saying, 'Did not we straitly com-mand you that you should not teach in this name? And behold, ye have filled Jerusalem with your doctrine, and intend to bring this man's blood upon us.'

²⁹Then Peter and the other apostles answered and said, 'We ought to obey God rather than men. ³⁰The God of our fathers raised up Jesus, whom ye slew and hanged on a tree. ³¹Him hath God exalted with his right hand to be a Prince and a Saviour, for to give repentance to Israel, and forgiveness of sins. ³²And we are his witnesses of these things, and so is also the Holy Ghost, whom God hath given to them that obey him.' ³³When they heard that, they were cut to the heart, and took counsel to slay them. ³⁴Then stood there up one in the council, a Pharisee, named Gamaliel, a doctor of law, had in reputation among all the peo-ple, and commanded to put the apostles forth a little space, ³⁵and said unto them, 'Ye men of Israel, take heed to yourselves what ye intend to do as touching these men. ³⁶For before these days rose up Theudas, boasting himself to be somebody, to whom a number of men, about four hundred, joined themselves: who was slain, and all, as many as obeyed him, were scattered, and brought to nought. ³⁷After this man

rose up Judas of Galilee in the days of the taxing, and drew away much people after him: he also perished, and all, even as many as obeyed him, were dispersed. [38]And now I say unto you, refrain from these men, and let them alone: for if this counsel or this work be of men, it will come to nought. [39]But if it be of God, ye cannot overthrow it, lest haply ye be found even to fight against God.' [40]And to him they agreed: and when they had called the apostles, and beaten them, they commanded that they should not speak in the name of Jesus, and let them go.

[41]And they departed from the presence of the council, rejoicing that they were counted worthy to suffer shame for his name. [42]And daily in the temple, and in every house, they ceased not to teach and preach Jesus Christ.

6 And in those days, when the number of the disciples was multiplied, there arose a murmuring of the Grecians against the Hebrews, because their widows were neglected in the daily ministration. [2]Then the twelve called the multitude of the disciples unto them, and said, 'It is not reason that we should leave the word of God, and serve tables. [3]Wherefore, brethren, look ye out among you seven men of honest report, full of the Holy Ghost and wisdom, whom we may appoint over this business. [4]But we will give ourselves continually to prayer, and to the ministry of the word.' [5]And the saying pleased the whole multitude: and they chose Stephen, a man full of faith and of the Holy Ghost, and Philip, and Prochorus, and Nicanor, and Timon, and Parmenas, and Nicolas a proselyte of Antioch: [6]whom they set before the apostles: and when they had prayed, they laid their hands on them. [7]And the word of God increased, and the number of the disciples multiplied in Jerusalem greatly, and a great company of the priests were obedient to the faith.

[8]And Stephen, full of faith and power, did great wonders and miracles among the people. [9]Then there arose certain of the synagogue, which is called the synagogue of the Libertines, and Cyrenians, and Alexandrians, and of them of Cilicia and of Asia, disputing with Stephen. [10]And they were not able to resist the wisdom and the spirit by which he spoke. [11]Then they suborned men, which said, 'We have heard him speak blasphemous words against Moses, and against God'. [12]And they stirred up the people, and the elders, and the scribes, and came upon him, and caught him, and brought him to the council, [13]and set up false witnesses, which said, 'This man ceaseth not to speak blasphemous words against this holy place, and the law. [14]For we have heard him say, that this Jesus of Nazareth shall destroy this place, and shall change the customs which Moses delivered us.' [15]And all that sat in the council, looking steadfastly on him, saw his face as it had been the face of an angel.

7 Then said the high priest, 'Are these things so?' [2]And he said, 'Men, brethren, and fathers, hearken: the God of glory appeared unto our father Abraham, when he was in Mesopotamia, before he dwelt in Charran, [3]and said unto him, "Get thee out of thy country, and from thy kindred, and come into the land which I shall show thee". [4]Then

came he out of the land of the Chaldeans, and dwelt in Charran: and from thence, when his father was dead, he removed him into this land, wherein ye now dwell. ⁵And he gave him no inheritance in it, no, not so much as to set his foot on: yet he promised that he would give it to him for a possession, and to his seed after him, when as yet he had no child. ⁶And God spoke on this wise, that his seed should sojourn in a strange land, and that they should bring them into bondage, and entreat them evil four hundred years. ⁷"And the nation to whom they shall be in bondage will I judge," said God: "and after that shall they come forth, and serve me in this place." ⁸And he gave him the covenant of circumcision: and so Abraham begot Isaac, and circumcised him the eighth day: and Isaac begot Jacob, and Jacob begot the twelve patriarchs.

⁹'And the patriarchs, moved with envy, sold Joseph into Egypt: but God was with him, ¹⁰and delivered him out of all his afflictions, and gave him favour and wisdom in the sight of Pharaoh king of Egypt: and he made him governor over Egypt and all his house. ¹¹Now there came a dearth over all the land of Egypt and Canaan, and great affliction, and our fathers found no sustenance. ¹²But when Jacob heard that there was corn in Egypt, he sent out our fathers first. ¹³And at the second time Joseph was made known to his brethren, and Joseph's kindred was made known unto Pharaoh. ¹⁴Then sent Joseph, and called his father Jacob to him, and all his kindred, threescore and fifteen souls. ¹⁵So Jacob went down into Egypt, and died, he, and our fathers, ¹⁶and were carried over into Sychem, and laid in the sepulchre that Abraham bought for a sum of money of the sons of Emmor the father of Sychem.

¹⁷'But when the time of the promise drew nigh, which God had sworn to Abraham, the people grew and multiplied in Egypt, ¹⁸till another king arose, which knew not Joseph. ¹⁹The same dealt subtly with our kindred, and evil entreated our fathers, so that they cast out their young children, to the end they might not live. ²⁰In which time Moses was born, and was exceeding fair, and nourished up in his father's house three months: ²¹and when he was cast out, Pharaoh's daughter took him up, and nourished him for her own son. ²²And Moses was learned in all the wisdom of the Egyptians, and was mighty in words and in deeds.

²³'And when he was full forty years old, it came into his heart to visit his brethren the children of Israel. ²⁴And seeing one of them suffer wrong, he defended him, and avenged him that was oppressed, and smote the Egyptian: ²⁵for he supposed his brethren would have understood how that God by his hand would deliver them, but they understood not. ²⁶And the next day he showed himself unto them as they strove, and would have set them at one again, saying, "Sirs, ye are brethren, why do ye wrong one to another?" ²⁷But he that did his neighbour wrong thrust him away, saying, "Who made thee a ruler and a judge over us? ²⁸Wilt thou kill me, as thou didst the Egyptian yesterday?" ²⁹Then fled Moses at this saying, and was a stranger in the land of Madian, where he begot two sons.

³⁰'And when forty years were expired, there appeared to him in the

wilderness of mount Sinai an angel of the Lord in a flame of fire in a bush. ³¹When Moses saw it, he wondered at the sight: and as he drew near to behold it, the voice of the Lord came unto him, ³²saying, "I am the God of thy fathers, the God of Abraham, and the God of Isaac, and the God of Jacob". Then Moses trembled, and durst not behold. ³³Then said the Lord to him, "Put off thy shoes from thy feet: for the place where thou standest is holy ground. ³⁴I have seen, I have seen the afflic-tion of my people which is in Egypt, and I have heard their groaning, and am come down to deliver them. And now come, I will send thee into Egypt." ³⁵This Moses whom they refused, saying, "Who made thee a ruler and a judge?" the same did God send to be a ruler and a deliverer by the hands of the angel which appeared to him in the bush. ³⁶He brought them out, after that he had shown wonders and signs in the land of Egypt, and in the Red Sea, and in the wilderness forty years.

³⁷'This is that Moses, which said unto the children of Israel, "A prophet shall the Lord your God raise up unto you of your brethren, like unto me: him shall ye hear". ³⁸This is he that was in the church in the wilderness with the angel which spoke to him in the mount Sinai, and with our fathers: who received the lively oracles to give unto us: ³⁹to whom our fathers would not obey, but thrust him from them, and in their hearts turned back again into Egypt, ⁴⁰saying unto Aaron, "Make us gods to go before us. For as for this Moses, which brought us out of the land of Egypt, we wot not what is become of him." ⁴¹And they made a calf in those days, and offered sacrifice unto the idol, and rejoiced in the works of their own hands. ⁴²Then God turned, and gave them up to worship the host of heaven, as it is written in the book of the prophets, "O ye house of Israel, have ye offered to me slain beasts and sacrifices by the space of forty years in the wilderness? ⁴³Yea, ye took up the tabernacle of Moloch, and the star of your god Remphan, figures which ye made to worship them: and I will carry you away beyond Babylon."

⁴⁴'Our fathers had the tabernacle of witness in the wilderness, as he had appointed, speaking unto Moses, that he should make it according to the fashion that he had seen. ⁴⁵Which also our fathers that came after brought in with Jesus into the possession of the Gentiles, whom God drove out before the face of our fathers, unto the days of David, ⁴⁶who found favour before God, and desired to find a tabernacle for the God of Jacob. ⁴⁷But Solomon built him a house. ⁴⁸Howbeit the most High dwelleth not in temples made with hands, as saith the prophet, ⁴⁹"'Heaven is my throne, and earth is my footstool: what house will ye build me?' saith the Lord: 'or what is the place of my rest? ⁵⁰Hath not my hand made all these things?'"

⁵¹'Ye stiff-necked and uncircumcised in heart and ears, ye do always resist the Holy Ghost: as your fathers did, so do ye. ⁵²Which of the prophets have not your fathers persecuted? And they have slain them which showed before of the coming of the Just One, of whom ye have been now the betrayers and murderers: ⁵³who have received the law by the disposition of angels, and have not kept it.'

⁵⁴When they heard these things, they were cut to the heart, and they gnashed on him with their teeth. ⁵⁵But he, being full of the Holy Ghost, looked up steadfastly into heaven, and saw the glory of God, and Jesus standing on the right hand of God, ⁵⁶and said, 'Behold, I see the heavens opened, and the Son of man standing on the right hand of God'. ⁵⁷Then they cried out with a loud voice, and stopped their ears, and ran upon him with one accord, ⁵⁸and cast him out of the city, and stoned him: and the witnesses laid down their clothes at a young man's feet, whose name was Saul. ⁵⁹And they stoned Stephen, calling upon God, and saying, 'Lord Jesus, receive my spirit'. ⁶⁰And he kneeled down, and cried with a loud voice, 'Lord, lay not this sin to their charge'. And when he had said this, he fell asleep.

8 And Saul was consenting unto his death. And at that time there was a great persecution against the church which was at Jerusalem, and they were all scattered abroad throughout the regions of Judea and Samaria, except the apostles. ²And devout men carried Stephen to his burial, and made great lamentation over him. ³As for Saul, he made havoc of the church, entering into every house, and haling men and women, committed them to prison. ⁴Therefore they that were scattered abroad went everywhere preaching the word.

⁵Then Philip went down to the city of Samaria, and preached Christ unto them. ⁶And the people with one accord gave heed unto those things which Philip spoke, hearing and seeing the miracles which he did. ⁷For unclean spirits, crying with loud voice, came out of many that were possessed with them: and many taken with palsies, and that were lame, were healed. ⁸And there was great joy in that city. ⁹But there was a certain man, called Simon, which beforetime in the same city used sorcery, and bewitched the people of Samaria, giving out that himself was some great one: ¹⁰to whom they all gave heed, from the least to the greatest, saying, 'This man is the great power of God'. ¹¹And to him they had regard, because that of long time he had bewitched them with sorceries. ¹²But when they believed Philip preaching the things concerning the kingdom of God, and the name of Jesus Christ, they were baptized, both men and women. ¹³Then Simon himself believed also: and when he was baptized, he continued with Philip, and wondered, beholding the miracles and signs which were done.

¹⁴Now when the apostles which were at Jerusalem heard that Samaria had received the word of God, they sent unto them Peter and John: ¹⁵who, when they were come down, prayed for them, that they might receive the Holy Ghost ¹⁶(for as yet he was fallen upon none of them: only they were baptized in the name of the Lord Jesus). ¹⁷Then laid they their hands on them, and they received the Holy Ghost.

¹⁸And when Simon saw that through laying on of the apostles' hands the Holy Ghost was given, he offered them money, ¹⁹saying, 'Give me also this power, that on whomsoever I lay hands, he may receive the Holy Ghost'. ²⁰But Peter said unto him, 'Thy money perish with thee, because thou hast thought that the gift of God may be purchased with money. ²¹Thou hast neither part nor lot in this matter, for thy heart is

not right in the sight of God. ²²Repent therefore of this thy wickedness, and pray God, if perhaps the thought of thy heart may be forgiven thee. ²³For I perceive that thou art in the gall of bitterness, and in the bond of iniquity.' ²⁴Then answered Simon, and said, 'Pray ye to the Lord for me, that none of these things which ye have spoken come upon me'.

²⁵And they, when they had testified and preached the word of the Lord, returned to Jerusalem, and preached the gospel in many villages of the Samaritans.

²⁶And the angel of the Lord spoke unto Philip, saying, 'Arise, and go toward the south unto the way that goeth down from Jerusalem unto Gaza, which is desert'. ²⁷And he arose and went: and behold, a man of Ethiopia, a eunuch of great authority under Candace queen of the Ethiopians, who had the charge of all her treasure, and had come to Jerusalem for to worship, ²⁸was returning, and sitting in his chariot, read Esaias the prophet. ²⁹Then the Spirit said unto Philip, 'Go near, and join thyself to this chariot'. ³⁰And Philip ran thither to him, and heard him read the prophet Esaias, and said, 'Understandest thou what thou readest?' ³¹And he said, 'How can I, except some man should guide me?' And he desired Philip that he would come up and sit with him.

³²The place of the scripture which he read was this, 'He was led as a sheep to the slaughter, and like a lamb dumb before the shearer, so opened he not his mouth: ³³in his humiliation his judgement was taken away: and who shall declare his generation? for his life is taken from the earth'. ³⁴And the eunuch answered Philip, and said, 'I pray thee, of whom speaketh the prophet this? of himself, or of some other man?' ³⁵Then Philip opened his mouth, and began at the same scripture, and preached unto him Jesus. ³⁶And as they went on their way, they came unto a certain water: and the eunuch said, 'See, here is water, what doth hinder me to be baptized?' ³⁷And Philip said, 'If thou believest with all thy heart, thou mayest'. And he answered and said, 'I believe that Jesus Christ is the Son of God'. ³⁸And he commanded the chariot to stand still: and they went down both into the water, both Philip and the eunuch, and he baptized him. ³⁹And when they were come up out of the water, the Spirit of the Lord caught away Philip, that the eunuch saw him no more: and he went on his way rejoicing. ⁴⁰But Philip was found at Azotus: and passing through he preached in all the cities, till he came to Caesarea.

9 And Saul, yet breathing out threatenings and slaughter against the disciples of the Lord, went unto the high priest, ²and desired of him letters to Damascus to the synagogues, that if he found any of this way, whether they were men or women, he might bring them bound unto Jerusalem. ³And as he journeyed, he came near Damascus, and suddenly there shone round about him a light from heaven. ⁴And he fell to the earth, and heard a voice saying unto him, 'Saul, Saul, why persecutest thou me?' ⁵And he said, 'Who art thou, Lord?' And the Lord said, 'I am Jesus whom thou persecutest: it is hard for thee to kick against the pricks'. ⁶And he trembling and astonished said, 'Lord, what wilt thou have me to do?' And the Lord said unto him, 'Arise, and go into the city, and it shall be told thee what thou must do'. ⁷And the men which journeyed with him stood speechless, hearing a voice, but seeing no man. ⁸And Saul arose from the earth, and when his eyes were opened, he saw no man: but they led him by the hand, and brought him into Damascus. ⁹And he was three days without sight, and neither did eat nor drink.

¹⁰And there was a certain disciple at Damascus, named Ananias, and to him said the Lord in a vision, 'Ananias'. And he said, 'Behold, I am here, Lord'. ¹¹And the Lord said unto him, 'Arise, and go into the street which is called Straight, and inquire in the house of Judas for one called Saul, of Tarsus: for behold, he prayeth, ¹²and hath seen in a vision a man named Ananias coming in, and putting his hand on him, that he might receive his sight'. ¹³Then Ananias answered, 'Lord, I have heard by many of this man, how much evil he hath done to thy saints at Jerusalem: ¹⁴and here he hath authority from the chief priests to bind all that call on thy name'. ¹⁵But the Lord said unto him, 'Go thy way: for he is a chosen vessel unto me, to bear my name before the Gentiles, and kings, and the children of Israel. ¹⁶For I will show him how great things he must suffer for my name's sake.'

¹⁷And Ananias went his way, and entered into the house, and putting his hands on him said, 'Brother Saul, the Lord, even Jesus, that appeared unto thee in the way as thou camest, hath sent me, that thou mightest receive thy sight, and be filled with the Holy Ghost'. ¹⁸And immediately there fell from his eyes as it had been scales, and he received sight forthwith, and arose, and was baptized. ¹⁹And when he had received meat, he was strengthened. Then was Saul certain days with the disciples which were at Damascus.

²⁰And straightway he preached Christ in the synagogues, that he is the Son of God. ²¹But all that heard him were amazed, and said, 'Is not this he that destroyed them which called on this name in Jerusalem, and came hither for that intent, that he might bring them bound unto the chief priests?' ²²But Saul increased the more in strength, and confounded the Jews which dwelt at Damascus, proving that this is very Christ.

²³And after that many days were fulfilled, the Jews took counsel to kill him. ²⁴But their laying await was known of Saul. And they watched the gates day and night to kill him. ²⁵Then the disciples took him by night, and let him down by the wall in a basket. ²⁶And when Saul was come to Jerusalem, he essayed to join himself to the disciples, but they were all afraid of him, and believed not that he was a disciple. ²⁷But Barnabas took him, and brought him to the apostles, and declared unto them how he had seen the Lord in the way, and that he had spoken to him, and how he had preached boldly at Damascus in the name of Jesus. ²⁸And he was with them coming in and going out at Jerusalem. ²⁹And he spoke boldly in the name of the Lord Jesus, and disputed against the Grecians: but they went about to slay him. ³⁰Which when the brethren knew, they brought him down to Caesarea, and sent him forth to Tarsus. ³¹Then had the churches rest throughout all Judea and

Galilee and Samaria, and were edified; and walking in the fear of the Lord, and in the comfort of the Holy Ghost, were multiplied.

[32]And it came to pass, as Peter passed throughout all quarters, he came down also to the saints which dwelt at Lydda. [33]And there he found a certain man named Aeneas, which had kept his bed eight years, and was sick of the palsy. [34]And Peter said unto him, 'Aeneas, Jesus Christ maketh thee whole: arise, and make thy bed'. And he arose immediately. [35]And all that dwelt at Lydda and Saron saw him, and turned to the Lord.

[36]Now there was at Joppa a certain disciple named Tabitha, which by interpretation is called Dorcas: this woman was full of good works and alms-deeds which she did. [37]And it came to pass in those days, that she was sick, and died: whom when they had washed, they laid her in an upper chamber. [38]And forasmuch as Lydda was nigh to Joppa, and the disciples had heard that Peter was there, they sent unto him two men, desiring him that he would not delay to come to them. [39]Then Peter arose and went with them. When he was come, they brought him into the upper chamber: and all the widows stood by him weeping, and showing the coats and garments which Dorcas made, while she was with them. [40]But Peter put them all forth, and kneeled down, and prayed; and turning him to the body said, 'Tabitha, arise'. And she opened her eyes, and when she saw Peter, she sat up. [41]And he gave her his hand, and lifted her up, and when he had called the saints and widows, presented her alive. [42]And it was known throughout all Joppa, and many believed in the Lord. [43]And it came to pass that he tarried many days in Joppa with one Simon a tanner.

10 There was a certain man in Caesarea called Cornelius, a centurion of the band called the Italian band, [2]a devout man, and one that feared God with all his house, which gave much alms to the people, and prayed to God always. [3]He saw in a vision evidently, about the ninth hour of the day, an angel of God coming in to him, and saying unto him, 'Cornelius'. [4]And when he looked on him, he was afraid, and said, 'What is it, Lord?' And he said unto him, 'Thy prayers and thy alms are come up for a memorial before God. [5]And now send men to Joppa, and call for one Simon, whose surname is Peter. [6]He lodgeth with one Simon a tanner, whose house is by the seaside: he shall tell thee what thou oughtest to do.' [7]And when the angel which spoke unto Cornelius was departed, he called two of his household servants, and a devout soldier of them that waited on him continually. [8]And when he had declared all these things unto them, he sent them to Joppa.

[9]On the morrow, as they went on their journey, and drew nigh unto the city, Peter went up upon the house to pray about the sixth hour. [10]And he became very hungry, and would have eaten: but while they made ready, he fell into a trance, [11]and saw heaven opened, and a certain vessel descending unto him, as it had been a great sheet knit at the four corners, and let down to the earth: [12]wherein were all manner of four-footed beasts of the earth, and wild beasts, and creeping things, and fowls of the air. [13]And there came a voice to him, 'Rise, Peter: kill,

and eat'. [14]But Peter said, 'Not so, Lord; for I have never eaten anything that is common or unclean'. [15]And the voice spoke unto him again the second time, 'What God hath cleansed, that call not thou common'. [16]This was done thrice: and the vessel was received up again into heaven.

[17]Now while Peter doubted in himself what this vision which he had seen should mean, behold, the men which were sent from Cornelius had made inquiry for Simon's house, and stood before the gate, [18]and called, and asked whether Simon, which was surnamed Peter, were lodged there. [19]While Peter thought on the vision, the Spirit said unto him, 'Behold, three men seek thee. [20]Arise therefore, and get thee down, and go with them, doubting nothing: for I have sent them.' [21]Then Peter went down to the men which were sent unto him from Cornelius, and said, 'Behold, I am he whom ye seek: what is the cause wherefore ye are come?' [22]And they said, 'Cornelius the centurion, a just man, and one that feareth God, and of good report among all the nation of the Jews, was warned from God by a holy angel to send for thee into his house, and to hear words of thee'. [23]Then called he them in, and lodged them.

And on the morrow Peter went away with them, and certain brethren from Joppa accompanied him. [24]And the morrow after they entered into Caesarea. And Cornelius waited for them, and had called together his kinsmen and near friends. [25]And as Peter was coming in, Cornelius met him, and fell down at his feet, and worshipped him. [26]But Peter took him up, saying, 'Stand up, I myself also am a man'. [27]And as he talked with him, he went in, and found many that were come together. [28]And he said unto them, 'Ye know how that it is an unlawful thing for a man that is a Jew to keep company, or come unto one of another nation: but God hath shown me that I should not call any man common or unclean. [29]Therefore came I unto you without gainsaying, as soon as I was sent for. I ask therefore for what intent ye have sent for me?' [30]And Cornelius said, 'Four days ago I was fasting until this hour, and at the ninth hour I prayed in my house, and behold, a man stood before me in bright clothing, [31]and said, "Cornelius, thy prayer is heard, and thy alms are had in remembrance in the sight of God. [32]Send therefore to Joppa, and call hither Simon, whose surname is Peter; he is lodged in the house of one Simon a tanner by the seaside, who, when he cometh, shall speak unto thee." [33]Immediately therefore I sent to thee, and thou hast well done that thou art come. Now therefore are we all here present before God, to hear all things that are commanded thee of God.'

[34]Then Peter opened his mouth, and said, 'Of a truth I perceive that God is no respecter of persons: [35]but in every nation he that feareth him, and worketh righteousness, is accepted with him. [36]The word which God sent unto the children of Israel, preaching peace by Jesus Christ (he is Lord of all): [37]that word, I say, you know, which was published throughout all Judea, and began from Galilee, after the baptism which John preached: [38]how God anointed Jesus of Nazareth with the

Holy Ghost and with power, who went about doing good, and healing all that were oppressed of the devil: for God was with him. ³⁹And we are witnesses of all things which he did both in the land of the Jews, and in Jerusalem; whom they slew and hanged on a tree: ⁴⁰him God raised up the third day, and showed him openly, ⁴¹not to all the people, but unto witnesses chosen before of God, even to us, who did eat and drink with him after he rose from the dead. ⁴²And he commanded us to preach unto the people, and to testify that it is he which was ordained of God to be the Judge of quick and dead. ⁴³To him give all the prophets witness, that through his name whosoever believeth in him shall receive remission of sins.'

⁴⁴While Peter yet spoke these words, the Holy Ghost fell on all them which heard the word. ⁴⁵And they of the circumcision which believed were astonished, as many as came with Peter, because that on the Gentiles also was poured out the gift of the Holy Ghost. ⁴⁶For they heard them speak with tongues, and magnify God. Then answered Peter, ⁴⁷'Can any man forbid water, that these should not be baptized, which have received the Holy Ghost as well as we?' ⁴⁸And he commanded them to be baptized in the name of the Lord. Then prayed they him to tarry certain days.

11 And the apostles and brethren that were in Judea heard that the Gentiles had also received the word of God. ²And when Peter was come up to Jerusalem, they that were of the circumcision contended with him, ³saying, 'Thou wentest in to men uncircumcised, and didst eat with them'. ⁴But Peter rehearsed the matter from the beginning, and expounded it by order unto them, saying, ⁵'I was in the city of Joppa praying, and in a trance I saw a vision, a certain vessel descend, as it had been a great sheet, let down from heaven by four corners, and it came even to me. ⁶Upon the which when I had fastened my eyes, I considered, and saw four-footed beasts of the earth, and wild beasts, and creeping things, and fowls of the air. ⁷And I heard a voice saying unto me, "Arise, Peter, slay and eat". ⁸But I said, "Not so, Lord: for nothing common or unclean hath at any time entered into my mouth". ⁹But the voice answered me again from heaven, "What God hath cleansed, that call not thou common". ¹⁰And this was done three times: and all were drawn up again into heaven. ¹¹And behold, immediately there were three men already come unto the house where I was, sent from Caesarea unto me. ¹²And the Spirit bade me go with them, nothing doubting. Moreover these six brethren accompanied me, and we entered into the man's house: ¹³and he showed us how he had seen an angel in his house, which stood and said unto him, "Send men to Joppa, and call for Simon, whose surname is Peter: ¹⁴who shall tell thee words, whereby thou and all thy house shall be saved". ¹⁵And as I began to speak, the Holy Ghost fell on them, as on us at the beginning. ¹⁶Then remembered I the word of the Lord, how that he said, "John indeed baptized with water: but ye shall be baptized with the Holy Ghost". ¹⁷Forasmuch then as God gave them the like gift as he did unto us, who believed on the Lord Jesus Christ: what was I, that I could withstand God?'

¹⁸When they heard these things, they held their peace, and glorified God, saying, 'Then hath God also to the Gentiles granted repentance unto life'.

¹⁹Now they which were scattered abroad upon the persecution that arose about Stephen travelled as far as Phenice, and Cyprus, and Antioch, preaching the word to none but unto the Jews only. ²⁰And some of them were men of Cyprus and Cyrene, which, when they were come to Antioch, spoke unto the Grecians, preaching the Lord Jesus. ²¹And the hand of the Lord was with them: and a great number believed, and turned unto the Lord.

²²Then tidings of these things came unto the ears of the church which was in Jerusalem: and they sent forth Barnabas, that he should go as far as Antioch. ²³Who, when he came, and had seen the grace of God, was glad, and exhorted them all, that with purpose of heart they would cleave unto the Lord. ²⁴For he was a good man, and full of the Holy Ghost and of faith: and much people was added unto the Lord.

²⁵Then departed Barnabas to Tarsus, for to seek Saul. ²⁶And when he had found him, he brought him unto Antioch. And it came to pass that a whole year they assembled themselves with the church, and taught much people. And the disciples were called Christians first in Antioch.

²⁷And in these days came prophets from Jerusalem unto Antioch. ²⁸And there stood up one of them named Agabus, and signified by the Spirit that there should be great dearth throughout all the world: which came to pass in the days of Claudius Caesar. ²⁹Then the disciples, every man according to his ability, determined to send relief unto the brethren which dwelt in Judea: ³⁰which also they did, and sent it to the elders by the hands of Barnabas and Saul.

12 Now about that time Herod the king stretched forth his hands to vex certain of the church. ²And he killed James the brother of John with the sword. ³And because he saw it pleased the Jews, he proceeded further to take Peter also. (Then were the days of unleavened bread.) ⁴And when he had apprehended him, he put him in prison, and delivered him to four quaternions of soldiers to keep him, intending after Easter to bring him forth to the people. ⁵Peter therefore was kept in prison, but prayer was made without ceasing of the church unto God for him.

⁶And when Herod would have brought him forth, the same night Peter was sleeping between two soldiers, bound with two chains, and the keepers before the door kept the prison. ⁷And behold, the angel of the Lord came upon him, and a light shone in the prison: and he smote Peter on the side, and raised him up, saying, 'Arise up quickly'. And his chains fell off from his hands. ⁸And the angel said unto him, 'Gird thyself, and bind on thy sandals'. And so he did. And he saith unto him, 'Cast thy garment about thee, and follow me'. ⁹And he went out, and followed him, and wist not that it was true which was done by the angel: but thought he saw a vision. ¹⁰When they were past the first and the second ward, they came unto the iron gate that leadeth unto the city, which opened to them of his own accord: and they went out, and

passed on through one street, and forthwith the angel departed from him. ¹¹And when Peter was come to himself, he said, 'Now I know of a surety, that the Lord hath sent his angel, and hath delivered me out of the hand of Herod, and from all the expectation of the people of the Jews'.

¹²And when he had considered the thing, he came to the house of Mary the mother of John, whose surname was Mark, where many were gathered together praying. ¹³And as Peter knocked at the door of the gate, a damsel came to hearken, named Rhoda. ¹⁴And when she knew Peter's voice, she opened not the gate for gladness, but ran in, and told how Peter stood before the gate. ¹⁵And they said unto her, 'Thou art mad'. But she constantly affirmed that it was even so. Then said they, 'It is his angel'. ¹⁶But Peter continued knocking: and when they had opened the door, and saw him, they were astonished. ¹⁷But he, beckoning unto them with the hand to hold their peace, declared unto them how the Lord had brought him out of the prison: and he said, 'Go show these things unto James, and to the brethren'. And he departed, and went into another place.

¹⁸Now as soon as it was day, there was no small stir among the soldiers, what was become of Peter. ¹⁹And when Herod had sought for him, and found him not, he examined the keepers, and commanded that they should be put to death. And he went down from Judea to Caesarea, and there abode.

²⁰And Herod was highly displeased with them of Tyre and Sidon: but they came with one accord to him, and having made Blastus the king's chamberlain their friend, desired peace, because their country was nourished by the king's country. ²¹And upon a set day Herod, arrayed in royal apparel, sat upon his throne, and made an oration unto them. ²²And the people gave a shout, saying, 'It is the voice of a god, and not of a man'. ²³And immediately the angel of the Lord smote him, because he gave not God the glory, and he was eaten of worms, and gave up the ghost.

²⁴But the word of God grew and multiplied. ²⁵And Barnabas and Saul returned from Jerusalem, when they had fulfilled their ministry, and took with them John, whose surname was Mark.

13

Now there were in the church that was at Antioch certain prophets and teachers: as Barnabas, and Simeon that was called Niger, and Lucius of Cyrene, and Manaen, which had been brought up with Herod the tetrarch, and Saul. ²As they ministered to the Lord, and fasted, the Holy Ghost said, 'Separate me Barnabas and Saul for the work whereunto I have called them'. ³And when they had fasted and prayed, and laid their hands on them, they sent them away.

⁴So they, being sent forth by the Holy Ghost, departed unto Seleucia, and from thence they sailed to Cyprus. ⁵And when they were at Salamis, they preached the word of God in the synagogues of the Jews: and they had also John to their minister. ⁶And when they had gone through the isle unto Paphos, they found a certain sorcerer, a false prophet, a Jew, whose name was Bar-jesus: ⁷which was with the deputy of the country, Sergius Paulus, a prudent man: who called for Barnabas

and Saul, and desired to hear the word of God. [8]But Elymas the sorcerer (for so is his name by interpretation) withstood them, seeking to turn away the deputy from the faith. [9]Then Saul (who also is called Paul), filled with the Holy Ghost, set his eyes on him, [10]and said, 'O full of all subtlety and all mischief, thou child of the devil, thou enemy of all righteousness, wilt thou not cease to pervert the right ways of the Lord? [11]And now, behold, the hand of the Lord is upon thee, and thou shalt be blind, not seeing the sun for a season.' And immediately there fell on him a mist and a darkness, and he went about seeking some to lead him by the hand. [12]Then the deputy, when he saw what was done, believed, being astonished at the doctrine of the Lord.

[13]Now when Paul and his company loosed from Paphos, they came to Perga in Pamphylia: and John departing from them returned to Jerusalem. [14]But when they departed from Perga, they came to Antioch in Pisidia, and went into the synagogue on the sabbath day, and sat down. [15]And after the reading of the law and the prophets, the rulers of the synagogue sent unto them, saying, 'Ye men and brethren, if ye have any word of exhortation for the people, say on'. [16]Then Paul stood up, and beckoning with his hand said, 'Men of Israel, and ye that fear God, give audience. [17]The God of this people of Israel chose our fathers, and exalted the people when they dwelt as strangers in the land of Egypt, and with a high arm brought he them out of it. [18]And about the time of forty years suffered he their manners in the wilderness. [19]And when he had destroyed seven nations in the land of Canaan, he divided their land to them by lot. [20]And after that he gave unto them judges about the space of four hundred and fifty years, until Samuel the prophet. [21]And afterward they desired a king, and God gave unto them Saul the son of Cis, a man of the tribe of Benjamin, by the space of forty years. [22]And when he had removed him, he raised up unto them David to be their king, to whom also he gave testimony, and said, "I have found David the son of Jesse, a man after my own heart, which shall fulfil all my will". [23]Of this man's seed hath God according to his promise raised unto Israel a Saviour, Jesus: [24]when John had first preached before his coming the baptism of repentance to all the people of Israel. [25]And as John fulfilled his course, he said, "Whom think ye that I am? I am not he. But behold, there cometh one after me, whose shoes of his feet I am not worthy to loose."

[26]'Men and brethren, children of the stock of Abraham, and whosoever among you feareth God, to you is the word of this salvation sent. [27]For they that dwell at Jerusalem, and their rulers, because they knew him not, nor yet the voices of the prophets which are read every sabbath day, they have fulfilled them in condemning him. [28]And though they found no cause of death in him, yet desired they Pilate that he should be slain. [29]And when they had fulfilled all that was written of him, they took him down from the tree, and laid him in a sepulchre. [30]But God raised him from the dead: [31]and he was seen many days of them which came up with him from Galilee to Jerusalem, who are his witnesses unto the people.

[32]'And we declare unto you glad tidings, how that the promise which was made unto the fathers, [33]God hath fulfilled the same unto us their children, in that he hath raised up Jesus again, as it is also written in the second psalm, "Thou art my Son, this day have I begotten thee". [34]And as concerning that he raised him up from the dead, now no more to return to corruption, he said on this wise, "I will give you the sure mercies of David". [35]Wherefore he saith also in another psalm, "Thou shalt not suffer thy Holy One to see corruption". [36]For David, after he had served his own generation by the will of God, fell on sleep, and was laid unto his fathers, and saw corruption: [37]but he, whom God raised again, saw no corruption.

[38]'Be it known unto you therefore, men and brethren, that through this man is preached unto you the forgiveness of sins: [39]and by him all that believe are justified from all things, from which ye could not be justified by the law of Moses. [40]Beware therefore, lest that come upon you, which is spoken of in the prophets, [41]"Behold, ye despisers, and wonder, and perish: for I work a work in your days, a work which you shall in no wise believe, though a man declare it unto you".'

[42]And when the Jews were gone out of the synagogue, the Gentiles besought that these words might be preached to them the next sabbath. [43]Now when the congregation was broken up, many of the Jews and religious proselytes followed Paul and Barnabas, who speaking to them, persuaded them to continue in the grace of God.

[44]And the next sabbath day came almost the whole city together to hear the word of God. [45]But when the Jews saw the multitudes, they were filled with envy, and spoke against those things which were spoken by Paul, contradicting and blaspheming. [46]Then Paul and Barnabas waxed bold, and said, 'It was necessary that the word of God should first have been spoken to you: but seeing ye put it from you, and judge yourselves unworthy of everlasting life, lo, we turn to the Gentiles. [47]For so hath the Lord commanded us, saying, "I have set thee to be a light of the Gentiles, that thou shouldst be for salvation unto the ends of the earth".' [48]And when the Gentiles heard this, they were glad, and glorified the word of the Lord: and as many as were ordained to eternal life believed. [49]And the word of the Lord was published throughout all the region.

[50]But the Jews stirred up the devout and honourable women, and the chief men of the city, and raised persecution against Paul and Barnabas, and expelled them out of their coasts. [51]But they shook off the dust of their feet against them, and came unto Iconium. [52]And the disciples were filled with joy, and with the Holy Ghost.

14 And it came to pass in Iconium, that they went both together into the synagogue of the Jews, and so spoke, that a great multitude both of the Jews and also of the Greeks believed. [2]But the unbelieving Jews stirred up the Gentiles, and made their minds evil-affected against the brethren. [3]Long time therefore abode they speaking boldly in the Lord, which gave testimony unto the word of his grace, and granted signs and wonders to be done by their hands. [4]But the multitude of the city was divided: and part held with the Jews, and part with the apostles. [5]And when there was an assault made both of the Gentiles, and also of the Jews with their rulers, to use them despitefully, and to stone them, [6]they were aware of it, and fled unto Lystra and Derbe, cities of Lycaonia, and unto the region that lieth round about. [7]And there they preached the gospel.

[8]And there sat a certain man at Lystra, impotent in his feet, being a cripple from his mother's womb, who never had walked. [9]The same heard Paul speak: who steadfastly beholding him, and perceiving that he had faith to be healed, [10]said with a loud voice, 'Stand upright on thy feet'. And he leapt and walked. [11]And when the people saw what Paul had done, they lifted up their voices, saying in the speech of Lycaonia, 'The gods are come down to us in the likeness of men'. [12]And they called Barnabas Jupiter, and Paul Mercurius, because he was the chief speaker. [13]Then the priest of Jupiter, which was before their city, brought oxen and garlands unto the gates, and would have done sacrifice with the people. [14]Which when the apostles, Barnabas and Paul, heard of, they rent their clothes, and ran in among the people, crying out, [15]and saying, 'Sirs, why do ye these things? We also are men of like passions with you, and preach unto you that ye should turn from these vanities unto the living God, which made heaven, and earth, and the sea, and all things that are therein: [16]who in times past suffered all nations to walk in their own ways. [17]Nevertheless he left not himself without witness, in that he did good, and gave us rain from heaven, and fruitful seasons, filling our hearts with food and gladness.' [18]And with these sayings scarce restrained they the people, that they had not done sacrifice unto them.

[19]And there came thither certain Jews from Antioch and Iconium, who persuaded the people, and, having stoned Paul, drew him out of the city, supposing he had been dead. [20]Howbeit, as the disciples stood round about him, he rose up, and came into the city, and the next day he departed with Barnabas to Derbe. [21]And when they had preached the gospel to that city, and had taught many, they returned again to Lystra, and to Iconium, and Antioch, [22]confirming the souls of the disciples, and exhorting them to continue in the faith, and that we must through much tribulation enter into the kingdom of God. [23]And when they had ordained them elders in every church, and had prayed with fasting, they commended them to the Lord, on whom they believed.

[24]And after they had passed throughout Pisidia, they came to Pamphylia. [25]And when they had preached the word in Perga, they went down into Attalia, [26]and thence sailed to Antioch, from whence they had been recommended to the grace of God for the work which they fulfilled. [27]And when they were come, and had gathered the church together, they rehearsed all that God had done with them, and how he had opened the door of faith unto the Gentiles. [28]And there they abode long time with the disciples.

15 And certain men which came down from Judea taught the brethren, and said, 'Except ye be circumcised after the manner of Moses, ye cannot be saved'. [2]When therefore Paul and Barnabas had no small dissension and disputation with them, they determined that Paul and Barnabas, and certain other of them, should go up to Jerusalem unto the apostles and elders about this question. [3]And being brought on their way by the church, they passed through Phenice and Samaria, declaring the conversion of the Gentiles: and they caused great joy unto all the brethren. [4]And when they were come to Jerusalem, they were received of the church, and of the apostles and elders, and they declared all things that God had done with them. [5]But there rose up certain of the sect of the Pharisees which believed, saying, that it was needful to circumcise them, and to command them to keep the law of Moses.

[6]And the apostles and elders came together for to consider of this matter. [7]And when there had been much disputing, Peter rose up, and said unto them, 'Men and brethren, ye know how that a good while ago God made choice among us, that the Gentiles by my mouth should hear the word of the gospel, and believe. [8]And God, which knoweth the hearts, bore them witness, giving them the Holy Ghost, even as he did unto us, [9]and put no difference between us and them, purifying their hearts by faith. [10]Now therefore why tempt ye God, to put a yoke upon the neck of the disciples, which neither our fathers nor we were able to bear? [11]But we believe that through the grace of the Lord Jesus Christ we shall be saved, even as they.'

[12]Then all the multitude kept silence, and gave audience to Barnabas and Paul, declaring what miracles and wonders God had wrought among the Gentiles by them.

[13]And after they had held their peace, James answered, saying, 'Men and brethren, hearken unto me. [14]Simeon hath declared how God at the first did visit the Gentiles, to take out of them a people for his name. [15]And to this agree the words of the prophets, as it is written, [16]"'After this I will return, and will build again the tabernacle of David, which is fallen down: and I will build again the ruins thereof, and I will set it up: [17]that the residue of men might seek after the Lord, and all the Gentiles, upon whom my name is called,' saith the Lord, who doeth all these things". [18]Known unto God are all his works from the beginning of the world. [19]Wherefore my sentence is, that we trouble not them, which from among the Gentiles are turned to God: [20]but that we write unto them, that they abstain from pollutions of idols, and from fornication, and from things strangled, and from blood. [21]For Moses of old time hath in every city them that preach him, being read in the synagogues every sabbath day.'

[22]Then pleased it the apostles and elders, with the whole church, to send chosen men of their own company to Antioch with Paul and Barnabas: namely, Judas surnamed Barsabas, and Silas, chief men among the brethren: [23]and they wrote letters by them after this manner,

The apostles and elders and brethren send greeting unto the brethren which are of the Gentiles in Antioch, and Syria, and

Cilicia. ²⁴Forasmuch as we have heard, that certain which went out from us have troubled you with words, subverting your souls, saying, 'Ye must be circumcised, and keep the law', to whom we gave no such commandment: ²⁵it seemed good unto us, being assembled with one accord, to send chosen men unto you with our beloved Barnabas and Paul, ²⁶men that have hazarded their lives for the name of our Lord Jesus Christ. ²⁷We have sent therefore Judas and Silas, who shall also tell you the same things by mouth. ²⁸For it seemed good to the Holy Ghost, and to us, to lay upon you no greater burden than these necessary things; ²⁹that ye abstain from meats offered to idols, and from blood, and from things strangled, and from fornication: from which if ye keep yourselves, ye shall do well. Fare ye well.

³⁰So when they were dismissed, they came to Antioch: and when they had gathered the multitude together, they delivered the epistle: ³¹which when they had read, they rejoiced for the consolation. ³²And Judas and Silas, being prophets also themselves, exhorted the brethren with many words, and confirmed them. ³³And after they had tarried there a space, they were let go in peace from the brethren unto the apostles. ³⁴Notwithstanding it pleased Silas to abide there still. ³⁵Paul also and Barnabas continued in Antioch, teaching and preaching the word of the Lord, with many others also.

³⁶And some days after Paul said unto Barnabas, 'Let us go again and visit our brethren in every city where we have preached the word of the Lord, and see how they do'. ³⁷And Barnabas determined to take with them John, whose surname was Mark. ³⁸But Paul thought not good to take him with them; who departed from them from Pamphylia, and went not with them to the work. ³⁹And the contention was so sharp between them, that they departed asunder one from the other: and so Barnabas took Mark, and sailed unto Cyprus. ⁴⁰And Paul chose Silas, and departed, being recommended by the brethren unto the grace of God. ⁴¹And he went through Syria and Cilicia, confirming the churches.

16 Then came he to Derbe and Lystra: and behold, a certain disciple was there, named Timothy, the son of a certain woman, which was a Jewess, and believed: but his father was a Greek: ²which was well reported of by the brethren that were at Lystra and Iconium. ³Him would Paul have to go forth with him, and took and circumcised him because of the Jews which were in those quarters: for they knew all that his father was a Greek. ⁴And as they went through the cities, they delivered them the decrees for to keep, that were ordained of the apostles and elders which were at Jerusalem. ⁵And so were the churches established in the faith, and increased in number daily.

⁶Now when they had gone throughout Phrygia and the region of Galatia, and were forbidden of the Holy Ghost to preach the word in Asia, ⁷after they were come to Mysia, they essayed to go into Bithynia: but the Spirit suffered them not. ⁸And they passing by Mysia, came down to Troas. ⁹And a vision appeared to Paul in the night: there stood a man of Macedonia, and prayed him, saying, 'Come over into

Macedonia, and help us'. [10]And after he had seen the vision, immediately we endeavoured to go into Macedonia, assuredly gathering that the Lord had called us for to preach the gospel unto them. [11]Therefore loosing from Troas, we came with a straight course to Samothracia, and the next day to Neapolis: [12]and from thence to Philippi, which is the chief city of that part of Macedonia, and a colony: and we were in that city abiding certain days.

[13]And on the sabbath we went out of the city by a river side, where prayer was wont to be made, and we sat down, and spoke unto the women which resorted thither. [14]And a certain woman named Lydia, a seller of purple, of the city of Thyatira, which worshipped God, heard us: whose heart the Lord opened, that she attended unto the things which were spoken of Paul. [15]And when she was baptized, and her household, she besought us, saying, 'If ye have judged me to be faithful to the Lord, come into my house, and abide there'. And she constrained us.

[16]And it came to pass, as we went to prayer, a certain damsel possessed with a spirit of divination met us, which brought her masters much gain by soothsaying. [17]The same followed Paul and us, and cried, saying, 'These men are the servants of the most high God, which show unto us the way of salvation'. [18]And this did she many days. But Paul, being grieved, turned and said to the spirit, 'I command thee in the name of Jesus Christ to come out of her'. And he came out the same hour.

[19]And when her masters saw that the hope of their gains was gone, they caught Paul and Silas, and drew them into the market-place unto the rulers, [20]and brought them to the magistrates, saying, 'These men, being Jews, do exceedingly trouble our city, [21]and teach customs which are not lawful for us to receive, neither to observe, being Romans'. [22]And the multitude rose up together against them, and the magistrates rent off their clothes, and commanded to beat them. [23]And when they had laid many stripes upon them, they cast them into prison, charging the jailor to keep them safely: [24]who, having received such a charge, thrust them into the inner prison, and made their feet fast in the stocks.

[25]And at midnight Paul and Silas prayed, and sang praises unto God: and the prisoners heard them. [26]And suddenly there was a great earthquake, so that the foundations of the prison were shaken: and immediately all the doors were opened, and everyone's bands were loosed. [27]And the keeper of the prison awaking out of his sleep, and seeing the prison doors open, he drew out his sword, and would have killed himself, supposing that the prisoners had been fled. [28]But Paul cried with a loud voice, saying, 'Do thyself no harm, for we are all here'. [29]Then he called for a light, and sprang in, and came trembling, and fell down before Paul and Silas, [30]and brought them out, and said, 'Sirs, what must I do to be saved?' [31]And they said, 'Believe on the Lord Jesus Christ, and thou shalt be saved, and thy house'. [32]And they spoke unto him the word of the Lord, and to all that were in his house. [33]And he took them the same hour of the night, and washed their stripes, and was baptized, he and all his, straightway. [34]And when he had brought them into

his house, he set meat before them, and rejoiced, believing in God with all his house.

³⁵And when it was day, the magistrates sent the sergeants, saying, 'Let those men go'. ³⁶And the keeper of the prison told this saying to Paul, 'The magistrates have sent to let you go: now therefore depart, and go in peace'. ³⁷But Paul said unto them, 'They have beaten us openly uncondemned, being Romans, and have cast us into prison, and now do they thrust us out privily? Nay verily; but let them come themselves and fetch us out.' ³⁸And the sergeants told these words unto the magistrates: and they feared, when they heard that they were Romans. ³⁹And they came and besought them, and brought them out, and desired them to depart out of the city. ⁴⁰And they went out of the prison, and entered into the house of Lydia, and when they had seen the brethren, they comforted them, and departed.

17 Now when they had passed through Amphipolis and Apollonia, they came to Thessalonica, where was a synagogue of the Jews. ²And Paul, as his manner was, went in unto them, and three sabbath days reasoned with them out of the scriptures, ³opening and alleging, that Christ must needs have suffered, and risen again from the dead: and that 'This Jesus, whom I preach unto you, is Christ'. ⁴And some of them believed, and consorted with Paul and Silas: and of the devout Greeks a great multitude, and of the chief women not a few.

⁵But the Jews which believed not, moved with envy, took unto them certain lewd fellows of the baser sort, and gathered a company, and set all the city on an uproar, and assaulted the house of Jason, and sought to bring them out to the people. ⁶And when they found them not, they drew Jason and certain brethren unto the rulers of the city, crying, 'These that have turned the world upside down are come hither also, ⁷whom Jason hath received: and these all do contrary to the decrees of Caesar, saying that there is another king, one Jesus'. ⁸And they troubled the people and the rulers of the city, when they heard these things. ⁹And when they had taken security of Jason, and of the others, they let them go.

¹⁰And the brethren immediately sent away Paul and Silas by night unto Berea: who coming thither went into the synagogue of the Jews. ¹¹These were more noble than those in Thessalonica, in that they received the word with all readiness of mind, and searched the scriptures daily, whether those things were so. ¹²Therefore many of them believed: also of honourable women which were Greeks, and of men, not a few. ¹³But when the Jews of Thessalonica had knowledge that the word of God was preached of Paul at Berea, they came thither also, and stirred up the people. ¹⁴And then immediately the brethren sent away Paul to go as it were to the sea: but Silas and Timothy abode there still. ¹⁵And they that conducted Paul brought him unto Athens: and receiving a commandment unto Silas and Timothy for to come to him with all speed, they departed.

¹⁶Now while Paul waited for them at Athens, his spirit was stirred in him, when he saw the city wholly given to idolatry. ¹⁷Therefore dis-

puted he in the synagogue with the Jews, and with the devout persons, and in the market daily with them that met with him. [18]Then certain philosophers of the Epicureans, and of the Stoics, encountered him. And some said, 'What will this babbler say?' other some, 'He seemeth to be a setter-forth of strange gods': because he preached unto them Jesus, and the resurrection. [19]And they took him, and brought him unto Areopagus, saying, 'May we know what this new doctrine, whereof thou speakest, is? [20]For thou bringest certain strange things to our ears: we would know therefore what these things mean.' [21](For all the Athenians and strangers which were there spent their time in nothing else, but either to tell, or to hear some new thing.)

[22]Then Paul stood in the midst of Mars' hill, and said, 'Ye men of Athens, I perceive that in all things ye are too superstitious. [23]For as I passed by, and beheld your devotions, I found an altar with this inscription, "TO THE UNKNOWN GOD". Whom therefore ye ignorantly worship, him declare I unto you. [24]God that made the world and all things therein, seeing that he is Lord of heaven and earth, dwelleth not in temples made with hands: [25]neither is worshipped with men's hands, as though he needed anything, seeing he giveth to all life, and breath, and all things, [26]and hath made of one blood all nations of men for to dwell on all the face of the earth, and hath determined the times before appointed, and the bounds of their habitation: [27]that they should seek the Lord, if haply they might feel after him, and find him, though he be not far from every one of us. [28]For in him we live, and move, and have our being, as certain also of your own poets have said, "For we are also his offspring". [29]Forasmuch then as we are the offspring of God, we ought not to think that the Godhead is like unto gold, or silver, or stone, graven by art and man's device. [30]And the times of this ignorance God winked at, but now commandeth all men everywhere to repent: [31]because he hath appointed a day, in the which he will judge the world in righteousness by that man whom he hath ordained, whereof he hath given assurance unto all men, in that he hath raised him from the dead.'

[32]And when they heard of the resurrection of the dead, some mocked: and others said, 'We will hear thee again of this matter'. [33]So Paul departed from among them. [34]Howbeit certain men cleaved unto him, and believed: among the which was Dionysius the Areopagite, and a woman named Damaris, and others with them.

18 After these things Paul departed from Athens, and came to Corinth, [2]and found a certain Jew named Aquila, born in Pontus, lately come from Italy, with his wife Priscilla (because that Claudius had commanded all Jews to depart from Rome), and came unto them. [3]And because he was of the same craft, he abode with them, and wrought: for by their occupation they were tent-makers. [4]And he reasoned in the synagogue every sabbath, and persuaded the Jews and the Greeks.

[5]And when Silas and Timothy were come from Macedonia, Paul was pressed in spirit, and testified to the Jews that Jesus was Christ. [6]And when they opposed themselves, and blasphemed, he shook his rai-

ment, and said unto them, 'Your blood be upon your own heads, I am clean: from henceforth I will go unto the Gentiles'.

[7]And he departed thence, and entered into a certain man's house, named Justus, one that worshipped God, whose house joined hard to the synagogue. [8]And Crispus, the chief ruler of the synagogue, believed on the Lord with all his house: and many of the Corinthians hearing believed, and were baptized. [9]Then spoke the Lord to Paul in the night by a vision, 'Be not afraid, but speak, and hold not thy peace: [10]for I am with thee, and no man shall set on thee to hurt thee: for I have much people in this city'. [11]And he continued there a year and six months, teaching the word of God among them.

[12]And when Gallio was the deputy of Achaia, the Jews made insurrection with one accord against Paul, and brought him to the judgement seat, [13]saying, 'This fellow persuadeth men to worship God contrary to the law'. [14]And when Paul was now about to open his mouth, Gallio said unto the Jews, 'If it were a matter of wrong or wicked lewdness, O ye Jews, reason would that I should bear with you. [15]But if it be a question of words and names, and of your law, look ye to it: for I will be no judge of such matters.' [16]And he drove them from the judgement seat. [17]Then all the Greeks took Sosthenes, the chief ruler of the synagogue, and beat him before the judgement seat. And Gallio cared for none of those things.

[18]And Paul after this tarried there yet a good while, and then took his leave of the brethren, and sailed thence into Syria, and with him Priscilla and Aquila: having shorn his head in Cenchrea: for he had a vow. [19]And he came to Ephesus, and left them there: but he himself entered into the synagogue, and reasoned with the Jews. [20]When they desired him to tarry longer time with them, he consented not: [21]but bade them farewell, saying, 'I must by all means keep this feast that cometh in Jerusalem; but I will return again unto you, if God will'. And he sailed from Ephesus. [22]And when he had landed at Caesarea, and gone up, and saluted the church, he went down to Antioch. [23]And after he had spent some time there, he departed, and went over all the country of Galatia and Phrygia in order, strengthening all the disciples.

[24]And a certain Jew named Apollos, born at Alexandria, an eloquent man, and mighty in the scriptures, came to Ephesus. [25]This man was instructed in the way of the Lord, and being fervent in the spirit, he spoke and taught diligently the things of the Lord, knowing only the baptism of John. [26]And he began to speak boldly in the synagogue: whom when Aquila and Priscilla had heard, they took him unto them, and expounded unto him the way of God more perfectly. [27]And when he was disposed to pass into Achaia, the brethren wrote, exhorting the disciples to receive him: who, when he was come, helped them much which had believed through grace: [28]for he mightily convinced the Jews, and that publicly, showing by the scriptures that Jesus was Christ.

19
And it came to pass that while Apollos was at Corinth, Paul having passed through the upper coasts, came to Ephesus, and finding certain disciples, [2]he said unto them, 'Have ye received the Holy

Ghost since ye believed?' And they said unto him, 'We have not so much as heard whether there be any Holy Ghost'. ³And he said unto them, 'Unto what then were ye baptized?' And they said, 'Unto John's baptism'. ⁴Then said Paul, 'John verily baptized with the baptism of repentance, saying unto the people, that they should believe on him which should come after him, that is, on Christ Jesus'. ⁵When they heard this, they were baptized in the name of the Lord Jesus. ⁶And when Paul had laid his hands upon them, the Holy Ghost came on them, and they spoke with tongues, and prophesied. ⁷And all the men were about twelve.

⁸And he went into the synagogue, and spoke boldly for the space of three months, disputing and persuading the things concerning the kingdom of God. ⁹But when divers were hardened, and believed not, but spoke evil of that way before the multitude, he departed from them, and separated the disciples, disputing daily in the school of one Tyrannus. ¹⁰And this continued by the space of two years, so that all they which dwelt in Asia heard the word of the Lord Jesus, both Jews and Greeks. ¹¹And God wrought special miracles by the hands of Paul: ¹²so that from his body were brought unto the sick handkerchiefs or aprons, and the diseases departed from them, and the evil spirits went out of them.

¹³Then certain of the vagabond Jews, exorcists, took upon them to call over them which had evil spirits the name of the Lord Jesus, saying, 'We adjure you by Jesus whom Paul preacheth'. ¹⁴And there were seven sons of one Sceva, a Jew, and chief of the priests, which did so. ¹⁵And the evil spirit answered and said, 'Jesus I know, and Paul I know, but who are ye?' ¹⁶And the man in whom the evil spirit was, leapt on them, and overcame them, and prevailed against them, so that they fled out of that house naked and wounded. ¹⁷And this was known to all the Jews and Greeks also dwelling at Ephesus, and fear fell on them all, and the name of the Lord Jesus was magnified. ¹⁸And many that believed came, and confessed, and showed their deeds. ¹⁹Many also of them which used curious arts brought their books together, and burnt them before all men: and they counted the price of them, and found it fifty thousand pieces of silver. ²⁰So mightily grew the word of God and prevailed.

²¹After these things were ended, Paul purposed in the spirit, when he had passed through Macedonia and Achaia, to go to Jerusalem, saying, 'After I have been there, I must also see Rome'. ²²So he sent into Macedonia two of them that ministered unto him, Timothy and Erastus, but he himself stayed in Asia for a season.

²³And the same time there arose no small stir about that way. ²⁴For a certain man named Demetrius, a silversmith, which made silver shrines for Diana, brought no small gain unto the craftsmen: ²⁵whom he called together with the workmen of like occupation, and said, 'Sirs, ye know that by this craft we have our wealth. ²⁶Moreover ye see and hear, that not alone at Ephesus, but almost throughout all Asia, this Paul hath persuaded and turned away much people, saying that they be no gods, which are made with hands. ²⁷So that not only this our craft

is in danger to be set at nought: but also that the temple of the great goddess Diana should be despised, and her magnificence should be destroyed, whom all Asia and the world worshippeth.' [28]And when they heard these sayings, they were full of wrath, and cried out, saying, 'Great is Diana of the Ephesians'. [29]And the whole city was filled with confusion: and having caught Gaius and Aristarchus, men of Macedonia, Paul's companions in travel, they rushed with one accord into the theatre. [30]And when Paul would have entered in unto the people, the disciples suffered him not. [31]And certain of the chief of Asia, which were his friends, sent unto him, desiring him that he would not adventure himself into the theatre. [32]Some therefore cried one thing, and some another: for the assembly was confused, and the more part knew not wherefore they were come together. [33]And they drew Alexander out of the multitude, the Jews putting him forward. And Alexander beckoned with the hand, and would have made his defence unto the people. [34]But when they knew that he was a Jew, all with one voice about the space of two hours cried out, 'Great is Diana of the Ephesians'.

[35]And when the town-clerk had appeased the people, he said, 'Ye men of Ephesus, what man is there that knoweth not how that the city of the Ephesians is a worshipper of the great goddess Diana, and of the image which fell down from Jupiter? [36]Seeing then that these things cannot be spoken against, ye ought to be quiet, and to do nothing rashly. [37]For ye have brought hither these men, which are neither robbers of churches, nor yet blasphemers of your goddess. [38]Wherefore if Demetrius, and the craftsmen which are with him, have a matter against any man, the law is open, and there are deputies: let them implead one another. [39]But if ye inquire anything concerning other matters, it shall be determined in a lawful assembly. [40]For we are in danger to be called in question for this day's uproar, there being no cause whereby we may give an account of this concourse.' [41]And when he had thus spoken, he dismissed the assembly.

20 And after the uproar was ceased, Paul called unto him the disciples, and embraced them, and departed for to go into Macedonia. [2]And when he had gone over those parts, and had given them much exhortation, he came into Greece, [3]and there abode three months. And when the Jews laid wait for him, as he was about to sail into Syria, he purposed to return through Macedonia. [4]And there accompanied him into Asia Sopater of Berea; and of the Thessalonians, Aristarchus and Secundus; and Gaius of Derbe, and Timothy; and of Asia, Tychicus and Trophimus. [5]These going before tarried for us at Troas. [6]And we sailed away from Philippi after the days of unleavened bread, and came unto them to Troas in five days, where we abode seven days.

[7]And upon the first day of the week, when the disciples came together to break bread, Paul preached unto them, ready to depart on the morrow, and continued his speech until midnight. [8]And there were many lights in the upper chamber, where they were gathered together.

⁹And there sat in a window a certain young man named Eutychus, being fallen into a deep sleep: and as Paul was long preaching, he sank down with sleep, and fell down from the third loft, and was taken up dead. ¹⁰And Paul went down, and fell on him, and embracing him said, 'Trouble not yourselves, for his life is in him'. ¹¹When he therefore was come up again, and had broken bread, and eaten, and talked a long while, even till break of day, so he departed. ¹²And they brought the young man alive, and were not a little comforted.

¹³And we went before to ship, and sailed unto Assos, there intending to take in Paul: for so had he appointed, minding himself to go afoot. ¹⁴And when he met with us at Assos, we took him in, and came to Mitylene. ¹⁵And we sailed thence, and came the next day over against Chios, and the next day we arrived at Samos, and tarried at Trogyllium: and the next day we came to Miletus. ¹⁶For Paul had determined to sail by Ephesus, because he would not spend the time in Asia: for he hasted, if it were possible for him, to be at Jerusalem the day of Pentecost.

¹⁷And from Miletus he sent to Ephesus, and called the elders of the church. ¹⁸And when they were come to him, he said unto them, 'Ye know, from the first day that I came into Asia, after what manner I have been with you at all seasons, ¹⁹serving the Lord with all humility of mind, and with many tears, and temptations, which befell me by the lying in wait of the Jews: ²⁰and how I kept back nothing that was profitable unto you, but have shown you, and have taught you publicly, and from house to house, ²¹testifying both to the Jews, and also to the Greeks, repentance toward God, and faith toward our Lord Jesus Christ. ²²And now behold, I go bound in the spirit unto Jerusalem, not knowing the things that shall befall me there: ²³save that the Holy Ghost witnesseth in every city, saying that bonds and afflictions abide me. ²⁴But none of these things move me, neither count I my life dear unto myself, so that I might finish my course with joy, and the ministry, which I have received of the Lord Jesus, to testify the gospel of the grace of God. ²⁵And now behold, I know that ye all, among whom I have gone preaching the kingdom of God, shall see my face no more. ²⁶Wherefore I take you to record this day, that I am pure from the blood of all men. ²⁷For I have not shunned to declare unto you all the counsel of God.

²⁸'Take heed therefore unto yourselves, and to all the flock, over the which the Holy Ghost hath made you overseers, to feed the church of God, which he hath purchased with his own blood. ²⁹For I know this, that after my departing shall grievous wolves enter in among you, not sparing the flock. ³⁰Also of your own selves shall men arise, speaking perverse things, to draw away disciples after them. ³¹Therefore watch, and remember that by the space of three years I ceased not to warn every one night and day with tears.

³²'And now, brethren, I commend you to God, and to the word of his grace, which is able to build you up, and to give you an inheritance among all them which are sanctified. ³³I have coveted no man's silver, or gold, or apparel. ³⁴Yea, you yourselves know, that these hands have ministered unto my necessities, and to them that were with me. ³⁵I

have shown you all things, how that so labouring ye ought to support the weak, and to remember the words of the Lord Jesus, how he said, "It is more blessed to give than to receive".'

³⁶And when he had thus spoken, he kneeled down, and prayed with them all. ³⁷And they all wept sore, and fell on Paul's neck, and kissed him, ³⁸sorrowing most of all for the words which he spoke, that they should see his face no more. And they accompanied him unto the ship.

21 And it came to pass that after we were gotten from them, and had launched, we came with a straight course unto Cos, and the day following unto Rhodes, and from thence unto Patara. ²And finding a ship sailing over unto Phenice, we went aboard, and set forth. ³Now when we had discovered Cyprus, we left it on the left hand, and sailed into Syria, and landed at Tyre: for there the ship was to unlade her burden. ⁴And finding disciples, we tarried there seven days: who said to Paul through the Spirit, that he should not go up to Jerusalem. ⁵And when we had accomplished those days, we departed and went our way, and they all brought us on our way, with wives and children, till we were out of the city: and we kneeled down on the shore, and prayed. ⁶And when we had taken our leave one of another, we took ship, and they returned home again.

⁷And when we had finished our course from Tyre, we came to Ptolemais, and saluted the brethren, and abode with them one day. ⁸And the next day we that were of Paul's company departed, and came unto Caesarea, and we entered into the house of Philip the evangelist, which was one of the seven, and abode with him. ⁹And the same man had four daughters, virgins, which did prophesy. ¹⁰And as we tarried there many days, there came down from Judea a certain prophet, named Agabus. ¹¹And when he was come unto us, he took Paul's girdle, and bound his own hands and feet, and said, 'Thus saith the Holy Ghost, "So shall the Jews at Jerusalem bind the man that owneth this girdle, and shall deliver him into the hands of the Gentiles"'. ¹²And when we heard these things, both we, and they of that place, besought him not to go up to Jerusalem. ¹³Then Paul answered, 'What mean ye to weep and to break my heart? for I am ready not to be bound only, but also to die at Jerusalem for the name of the Lord Jesus'. ¹⁴And when he would not be persuaded, we ceased, saying, 'The will of the Lord be done'.

¹⁵And after those days we took up our carriages, and went up to Jerusalem. ¹⁶There went with us also certain of the disciples of Caesarea, and brought with them one Mnason of Cyprus, an old disciple, with whom we should lodge. ¹⁷And when we were come to Jerusalem, the brethren received us gladly.

¹⁸And the day following Paul went in with us unto James, and all the elders were present. ¹⁹And when he had saluted them, he declared particularly what things God had wrought among the Gentiles by his ministry. ²⁰And when they heard it, they glorified the Lord, and said unto him, 'Thou seest, brother, how many thousands of Jews there are which believe, and they are all zealous of the law. ²¹And they are informed of

thee, that thou teachest all the Jews which are among the Gentiles to forsake Moses, saying that they ought not to circumcise their children, neither to walk after the customs. ²²What is it therefore? the multitude must needs come together: for they will hear that thou art come. ²³Do therefore this that we say to thee: we have four men which have a vow on them; ²⁴them take, and purify thyself with them, and be at charges with them, that they may shave their heads: and all may know that those things whereof they were informed concerning thee, are nothing, but that thou thyself also walkest orderly, and keepest the law. ²⁵As touching the Gentiles which believe, we have written and concluded that they observe no such thing, save only that they keep themselves from things offered to idols, and from blood, and from strangled, and from fornication.' ²⁶Then Paul took the men, and the next day purifying himself with them entered into the temple, to signify the accomplishment of the days of purification, until that an offering should be offered for every one of them.

²⁷And when the seven days were almost ended, the Jews which were of Asia, when they saw him in the temple, stirred up all the people, and laid hands on him, ²⁸crying out, 'Men of Israel, help: this is the man that teacheth all men everywhere against the people, and the law, and this place: and further brought Greeks also into the temple, and hath polluted this holy place'. ²⁹(For they had seen before with him in the city Trophimus an Ephesian, whom they supposed that Paul had brought into the temple.) ³⁰And all the city was moved, and the people ran together: and they took Paul, and drew him out of the temple: and forthwith the doors were shut. ³¹And as they went about to kill him, tidings came unto the chief captain of the band, that all Jerusalem was in an uproar. ³²Who immediately took soldiers and centurions, and ran down unto them: and when they saw the chief captain and the soldiers, they left beating of Paul. ³³Then the chief captain came near, and took him, and commanded him to be bound with two chains, and demanded who he was, and what he had done. ³⁴And some cried one thing, some another, among the multitude: and when he could not know the certainty for the tumult, he commanded him to be carried into the castle. ³⁵And when he came upon the stairs, so it was, that he was borne of the soldiers for the violence of the people. ³⁶For the multitude of the people followed after, crying, 'Away with him'.

³⁷And as Paul was to be led into the castle, he said unto the chief captain, 'May I speak unto thee?' Who said, 'Canst thou speak Greek? ³⁸Art not thou that Egyptian, which before these days madest an uproar, and leddest out into the wilderness four thousand men that were murderers?' ³⁹But Paul said, 'I am a man which am a Jew of Tarsus, a city in Cilicia, a citizen of no mean city: and, I beseech thee, suffer me to speak unto the people'. ⁴⁰And when he had given him licence, Paul stood on the stairs, and beckoned with the hand unto the people.

And when there was made a great silence, he spoke unto them in the Hebrew tongue, saying, ¹'Men, brethren, and fathers, hear ye my defence which I make now unto you'. ²(And when they heard

22

that he spoke in the Hebrew tongue to them, they kept the more silence: and he saith), ³'I am verily a man which am a Jew, born in Tarsus, a city in Cilicia, yet brought up in this city at the feet of Gamaliel, and taught according to the perfect manner of the law of the fathers, and was zealous towards God, as ye all are this day. ⁴And I persecuted this way unto the death, binding and delivering into prisons both men and women. ⁵As also the high priest doth bear me witness, and all the estate of the elders: from whom also I received letters unto the brethren, and went to Damascus, to bring them which were there bound unto Jerusalem, for to be punished. ⁶And it came to pass that as I made my journey, and was come nigh unto Damascus about noon, suddenly there shone from heaven a great light round about me. ⁷And I fell unto the ground, and heard a voice saying unto me, "Saul, Saul, why persecutest thou me?" ⁸And I answered, "Who art thou, Lord?" And he said unto me, "I am Jesus of Nazareth, whom thou persecutest". ⁹And they that were with me saw indeed the light, and were afraid; but they heard not the voice of him that spoke to me. ¹⁰And I said, "What shall I do, Lord?" And the Lord said unto me, "Arise, and go into Damascus, and there it shall be told thee of all things which are appointed for thee to do". ¹¹And when I could not see for the glory of that light, being led by the hand of them that were with me, I came into Damascus.

¹²'And one Ananias, a devout man according to the law, having a good report of all the Jews which dwelt there, ¹³came unto me, and stood, and said unto me, "Brother Saul, receive thy sight". And the same hour I looked up upon him. ¹⁴And he said, "The God of our fathers hath chosen thee, that thou shouldst know his will, and see that Just One, and shouldst hear the voice of his mouth. ¹⁵For thou shalt be his witness unto all men of what thou hast seen and heard. ¹⁶And now why tarriest thou? Arise, and be baptized, and wash away thy sins, calling on the name of the Lord."

¹⁷'And it came to pass that when I was come again to Jerusalem, even while I prayed in the temple, I was in a trance, ¹⁸and saw him saying unto me, "Make haste, and get thee quickly out of Jerusalem: for they will not receive thy testimony concerning me". ¹⁹And I said, "Lord, they know that I imprisoned and beat in every synagogue them that believed on thee. ²⁰And when the blood of thy martyr Stephen was shed, I also was standing by, and consenting unto his death, and kept the raiment of them that slew him." ²¹And he said unto me, "Depart: for I will send thee far hence unto the Gentiles".'

²²And they gave him audience unto this word, and then lifted up their voices, and said, 'Away with such a fellow from the earth: for it is not fit that he should live'. ²³And as they cried out, and cast off their clothes, and threw dust into the air, ²⁴the chief captain commanded him to be brought into the castle, and bade that he should be examined by scourging: that he might know wherefore they cried so against him. ²⁵And as they bound him with thongs, Paul said unto the centurion that stood by, 'Is it lawful for you to scourge a man that is a Roman, and

uncondemned?' ²⁶When the centurion heard that, he went and told the chief captain, saying, 'Take heed what thou doest, for this man is a Roman'. ²⁷Then the chief captain came, and said unto him, 'Tell me, art thou a Roman?' He said, 'Yea'. ²⁸And the chief captain answered, 'With a great sum obtained I this freedom'. And Paul said, 'But I was free-born'. ²⁹Then straightway they departed from him which should have examined him: and the chief captain also was afraid, after he knew that he was a Roman, and because he had bound him.

³⁰On the morrow, because he would have known the certainty wherefore he was accused of the Jews, he loosed him from his bands, and commanded the chief priests and all their council to appear, and brought Paul down, and set him before them.

23 And Paul, earnestly beholding the council, said, 'Men and brethren, I have lived in all good conscience before God until this day'. ²And the high priest Ananias commanded them that stood by him to smite him on the mouth. ³Then said Paul unto him, 'God shall smite thee, thou whited wall: for sittest thou to judge me after the law, and commandest me to be smitten contrary to the law?' ⁴And they that stood by said, 'Revilest thou God's high priest?' ⁵Then said Paul, 'I wist not, brethren, that he was the high priest: for it is written, "Thou shalt not speak evil of the ruler of thy people"'.

⁶But when Paul perceived that the one part were Sadducees, and the other Pharisees, he cried out in the council, 'Men and brethren, I am a Pharisee, the son of a Pharisee: of the hope and resurrection of the dead I am called in question'. ⁷And when he had so said, there arose a dissension between the Pharisees and the Sadducees: and the multitude was divided. ⁸For the Sadducees say that there is no resurrection, neither angel, nor spirit: but the Pharisees confess both. ⁹And there arose a great cry: and the scribes that were of the Pharisees' part arose, and strove, saying, 'We find no evil in this man: but if a spirit or an angel hath spoken to him, let us not fight against God'. ¹⁰And when there arose a great dissension, the chief captain, fearing lest Paul should have been pulled in pieces of them, commanded the soldiers to go down, and to take him by force from among them, and to bring him into the castle.

¹¹And the night following the Lord stood by him, and said, 'Be of good cheer, Paul: for as thou hast testified of me in Jerusalem, so must thou bear witness also at Rome'.

¹²And when it was day, certain of the Jews banded together, and bound themselves under a curse, saying that they would neither eat nor drink till they had killed Paul. ¹³And they were more than forty which had made this conspiracy. ¹⁴And they came to the chief priests and elders, and said, 'We have bound ourselves under a great curse, that we will eat nothing until we have slain Paul. ¹⁵Now therefore ye with the council signify to the chief captain that he bring him down unto you tomorrow, as though ye would inquire something more perfectly concerning him: and we, or ever he come near, are ready to kill him.'

¹⁶And when Paul's sister's son heard of their lying in wait, he went

and entered into the castle, and told Paul. ¹⁷Then Paul called one of the centurions unto him, and said, 'Bring this young man unto the chief captain: for he hath a certain thing to tell him'. ¹⁸So he took him, and brought him to the chief captain, and said, 'Paul the prisoner called me unto him, and prayed me to bring this young man unto thee, who hath something to say unto thee'. ¹⁹Then the chief captain took him by the hand, and went with him aside privately, and asked him, 'What is that thou hast to tell me?' ²⁰And he said, 'The Jews have agreed to desire thee that thou wouldst bring down Paul tomorrow into the council, as though they would inquire somewhat of him more perfectly. ²¹But do not thou yield unto them: for there lie in wait for him of them more than forty men, which have bound themselves with an oath, that they will neither eat nor drink till they have killed him: and now are they ready, looking for a promise from thee.' ²²So the chief captain then let the young man depart, and charged him, 'See thou tell no man that thou hast shown these things to me'. ²³And he called unto him two centurions, saying, 'Make ready two hundred soldiers to go to Caesarea, and horsemen threescore and ten, and spearmen two hundred, at the third hour of the night. ²⁴And provide them beasts, that they may set Paul on, and bring him safe unto Felix the governor.'

²⁵And he wrote a letter after this manner:

²⁶Claudius Lysias unto the most excellent governor Felix sendeth greeting. ²⁷This man was taken of the Jews, and should have been killed of them: then came I with an army, and rescued him, having understood that he was a Roman. ²⁸And when I would have known the cause wherefore they accused him, I brought him forth into their council: ²⁹whom I perceived to be accused of questions of their law, but to have nothing laid to his charge worthy of death or of bonds. ³⁰And when it was told me how that the Jews laid wait for the man, I sent straightway to thee, and gave commandment to his accusers also to say before thee what they had against him. Farewell.

³¹Then the soldiers, as it was commanded them, took Paul, and brought him by night to Antipatris. ³²On the morrow they left the horsemen to go with him, and returned to the castle: ³³who, when they came to Caesarea, and delivered the epistle to the governor, presented Paul also before him. ³⁴And when the governor had read the letter, he asked of what province he was. And when he understood that he was of Cilicia, ³⁵'I will hear thee,' said he, 'when thy accusers are also come'. And he commanded him to be kept in Herod's judgement hall.

24 And after five days Ananias the high priest descended with the elders, and with a certain orator named Tertullus, who informed the governor against Paul. ²And when he was called forth, Tertullus began to accuse him, saying, 'Seeing that by thee we enjoy great quietness, and that very worthy deeds are done unto this nation by thy providence, ³we accept it always, and in all places, most noble Felix, with all thankfulness. ⁴Notwithstanding, that I be not further tedious unto thee, I pray thee that thou wouldst hear us of thy

ACTS 25

clemency a few words. ⁵For we have found this man a pestilent fellow, and a mover of sedition among all the Jews throughout the world, and a ringleader of the sect of the Nazarenes: ⁶who also hath gone about to profane the temple: whom we took, and would have judged according to our law. ⁷But the chief captain Lysias came upon us, and with great violence took him away out of our hands, ⁸commanding his accusers to come unto thee: by examining of whom thyself mayest take knowledge of all these things, whereof we accuse him.' ⁹And the Jews also assented, saying that these things were so.

¹⁰Then Paul, after that the governor had beckoned unto him to speak, answered, 'Forasmuch as I know that thou hast been of many years a judge unto this nation, I do the more cheerfully answer for myself: ¹¹because that thou mayest understand, that there are yet but twelve days since I went up to Jerusalem for to worship. ¹²And they neither found me in the temple disputing with any man, neither raising up the people, neither in the synagogues, nor in the city: ¹³neither can they prove the things whereof they now accuse me. ¹⁴But this I confess unto thee, that after the way which they call heresy, so worship I the God of my fathers, believing all things which are written in the law and the prophets, ¹⁵and have hope towards God, which they themselves also allow, that there shall be a resurrection of the dead, both of the just and unjust. ¹⁶And herein do I exercise myself to have always a conscience void of offence toward God, and toward men.

¹⁷'Now after many years I came to bring alms to my nation, and offerings. ¹⁸Whereupon certain Jews from Asia found me purified in the temple, neither with multitude, nor with tumult: ¹⁹who ought to have been here before thee, and object, if they had aught against me. ²⁰Or else let these same here say, if they have found any evil-doing in me, while I stood before the council, ²¹except it be for this one voice, that I cried standing among them, "Touching the resurrection of the dead I am called in question by you this day".'

²²And when Felix heard these things, having more perfect knowledge of that way, he deferred them, and said, 'When Lysias the chief captain shall come down, I will know the uttermost of your matter'. ²³And he commanded a centurion to keep Paul, and to let him have liberty, and that he should forbid none of his acquaintance to minister or come unto him.

²⁴And after certain days, when Felix came with his wife Drusilla, which was a Jew, he sent for Paul, and heard him concerning the faith in Christ. ²⁵And as he reasoned of righteousness, temperance, and judgement to come, Felix trembled, and answered, 'Go thy way for this time; when I have a convenient season, I will call for thee'. ²⁶He hoped also that money should have been given him of Paul, that he might loose him: wherefore he sent for him the oftener, and communed with him. ²⁷But after two years Porcius Festus came into Felix' room: and Felix, willing to show the Jews a pleasure, left Paul bound.

25 Now when Festus was come into the province, after three days he ascended from Caesarea to Jerusalem. ²Then the high priest

and the chief of the Jews informed him against Paul, and besought him, ³and desired favour against him, that he would send for him to Jerusalem, laying wait in the way to kill him. ⁴But Festus answered, that Paul should be kept at Caesarea, and that he himself would depart shortly thither. ⁵'Let them therefore,' said he, 'which among you are able, go down with me, and accuse this man, if there be any wickedness in him.'

⁶And when he had tarried among them more than ten days, he went down unto Caesarea, and the next day sitting in the judgement seat commanded Paul to be brought. ⁷And when he was come, the Jews which came down from Jerusalem stood round about, and laid many and grievous complaints against Paul, which they could not prove, ⁸while he answered for himself, 'Neither against the law of the Jews, neither against the temple, nor yet against Caesar, have I offended anything at all'. ⁹But Festus, willing to do the Jews a pleasure, answered Paul, and said, 'Wilt thou go up to Jerusalem, and there be judged of these things before me?' ¹⁰Then said Paul, 'I stand at Caesar's judgement seat, where I ought to be judged; to the Jews have I done no wrong, as thou very well knowest. ¹¹For if I be an offender, or have committed anything worthy of death, I refuse not to die: but if there be none of these things whereof these accuse me, no man may deliver me unto them. I appeal unto Caesar.' ¹²Then Festus, when he had conferred with the council, answered, 'Hast thou appealed unto Caesar? unto Caesar shalt thou go'.

¹³And after certain days king Agrippa and Bernice came unto Caesarea to salute Festus. ¹⁴And when they had been there many days, Festus declared Paul's cause unto the king, saying, 'There is a certain man left in bonds by Felix: ¹⁵about whom, when I was at Jerusalem, the chief priests and the elders of the Jews informed me, desiring to have judgement against him. ¹⁶To whom I answered, "It is not the manner of the Romans to deliver any man to die, before that he which is accused have the accusers face to face, and have licence to answer for himself concerning the crime laid against him". ¹⁷Therefore, when they were come hither, without any delay on the morrow I sat on the judgement seat, and commanded the man to be brought forth. ¹⁸Against whom when the accusers stood up, they brought no accusation of such things as I supposed: ¹⁹but had certain questions against him of their own superstition, and of one Jesus, which was dead, whom Paul affirmed to be alive. ²⁰And because I doubted of such manner of questions, I asked him whether he would go to Jerusalem, and there be judged of these matters. ²¹But when Paul had appealed to be reserved unto the hearing of Augustus, I commanded him to be kept till I might send him to Caesar.' ²²Then Agrippa said unto Festus, 'I would also hear the man myself'. 'Tomorrow,' said he, 'thou shalt hear him.'

²³And on the morrow, when Agrippa was come, and Bernice, with great pomp, and was entered into the place of hearing, with the chief captains, and principal men of the city, at Festus' commandment Paul was brought forth. ²⁴And Festus said, 'King Agrippa, and all men which

are here present with us, ye see this man, about whom all the multitude of the Jews have dealt with me, both at Jerusalem, and also here, crying that he ought not to live any longer. ²⁵But when I found that he had committed nothing worthy of death, and that he himself hath appealed to Augustus, I have determined to send him. ²⁶Of whom I have no certain thing to write unto my lord. Wherefore I have brought him forth before you, and specially before thee, O king Agrippa, that, after examination had, I might have somewhat to write. ²⁷For it seemeth to me unreasonable to send a prisoner, and not withal to signify the crimes laid against him.'

26 Then Agrippa said unto Paul, 'Thou art permitted to speak for thyself'. Then Paul stretched forth the hand, and answered for himself, ²'I think myself happy, king Agrippa, because I shall answer for myself this day before thee touching all the things whereof I am accused of the Jews: ³especially because I know thee to be expert in all customs and questions which are among the Jews: wherefore I beseech thee to hear me patiently.

⁴'My manner of life from my youth, which was at the first among my own nation at Jerusalem, know all the Jews, ⁵which knew me from the beginning, if they would testify, that after the most straitest sect of our religion I lived a Pharisee. ⁶And now I stand and am judged for the hope of the promise made of God unto our fathers: ⁷unto which promise our twelve tribes, instantly serving God day and night, hope to come: for which hope's sake, king Agrippa, I am accused of the Jews. ⁸Why should it be thought a thing incredible with you, that God should raise the dead? ⁹I verily thought with myself, that I ought to do many things contrary to the name of Jesus of Nazareth. ¹⁰Which thing I also did in Jerusalem, and many of the saints did I shut up in prison, having received authority from the chief priests; and when they were put to death, I gave my voice against them. ¹¹And I punished them oft in every synagogue, and compelled them to blaspheme, and being exceedingly mad against them, I persecuted them even unto strange cities.

¹²'Whereupon as I went to Damascus with authority and commission from the chief priests, ¹³at midday, O king, I saw in the way a light from heaven, above the brightness of the sun, shining round about me and them which journeyed with me. ¹⁴And when we were all fallen to the earth, I heard a voice speaking unto me, and saying in the Hebrew tongue, "Saul, Saul, why persecutest thou me? It is hard for thee to kick against the pricks." ¹⁵And I said, "Who art thou, Lord?" And he said, "I am Jesus whom thou persecutest. ¹⁶But rise, and stand upon thy feet, for I have appeared unto thee for this purpose, to make thee a minister and a witness both of these things which thou hast seen, and of those things in the which I will appear unto thee, ¹⁷delivering thee from the people, and from the Gentiles, unto whom now I send thee, ¹⁸to open their eyes, and to turn them from darkness to light, and from the power of Satan unto God, that they may receive forgiveness of sins, and inheritance among them which are sanctified by faith that is in me."

¹⁹'Whereupon, O king Agrippa, I was not disobedient unto the heav-

enly vision: ²⁰but showed first unto them of Damascus, and at Jerusalem, and throughout all the coasts of Judea, and then to the Gentiles, that they should repent and turn to God, and do works meet for repentance. ²¹For these causes the Jews caught me in the temple, and went about to kill me. ²²Having therefore obtained help of God, I continue unto this day, witnessing both to small and great, saying no other things than those which the prophets and Moses did say should come: ²³that Christ should suffer, and that he should be the first that should rise from the dead, and should show light unto the people, and to the Gentiles.'

²⁴And as he thus spoke for himself, Festus said with a loud voice, 'Paul, thou art beside thyself, much learning doth make thee mad'. ²⁵But he said, 'I am not mad, most noble Festus, but speak forth the words of truth and soberness. ²⁶For the king knoweth of these things, before whom also I speak freely: for I am persuaded that none of these things are hidden from him, for this thing was not done in a corner. ²⁷King Agrippa, believest thou the prophets? I know that thou believest.' ²⁸Then Agrippa said unto Paul, 'Almost thou persuadest me to be a Christian'. ²⁹And Paul said, 'I would to God, that not only thou, but also all that hear me this day, were both almost, and altogether such as I am, except these bonds'.

³⁰And when he had thus spoken, the king rose up, and the governor, and Bernice, and they that sat with them. ³¹And when they were gone aside, they talked between themselves, saying, 'This man doeth nothing worthy of death or of bonds'. ³²Then said Agrippa unto Festus, 'This man might have been set at liberty, if he had not appealed unto Caesar'.

27 And when it was determined that we should sail into Italy, they delivered Paul and certain other prisoners unto one named Julius, a centurion of Augustus' band. ²And entering into a ship of Adramyttium, we launched, meaning to sail by the coasts of Asia, one Aristarchus, a Macedonian of Thessalonica, being with us. ³And the next day we touched at Sidon: and Julius courteously entreated Paul, and gave him liberty to go unto his friends to refresh himself. ⁴And when we had launched from thence, we sailed under Cyprus, because the winds were contrary. ⁵And when we had sailed over the sea of Cilicia and Pamphylia, we came to Myra, a city of Lycia. ⁶And there the centurion found a ship of Alexandria sailing into Italy, and he put us therein. ⁷And when we had sailed slowly many days, and scarce were come over against Cnidus, the wind not suffering us, we sailed under Crete, over against Salmone, ⁸and hardly passing it, came unto a place which is called the Fair Havens, nigh whereunto was the city of Lasea.

⁹Now when much time was spent, and when sailing was now dangerous, because the fast was now already past, Paul admonished them, ¹⁰and said unto them, 'Sirs, I perceive that this voyage will be with hurt and much damage, not only of the lading and ship, but also of our lives'. ¹¹Nevertheless the centurion believed the master and the owner of the ship, more than those things which were spoken by Paul. ¹²And

because the haven was not commodious to winter in, the more part advised to depart thence also, if by any means they might attain to Phenice, and there to winter; which is a haven of Crete, and lieth toward the south-west and north-west. ¹³And when the south wind blew softly, supposing that they had obtained their purpose, loosing thence, they sailed close by Crete. ¹⁴But not long after there arose against it a tempestuous wind, called Euroclydon. ¹⁵And when the ship was caught, and could not bear up into the wind, we let her drive. ¹⁶And running under a certain island which is called Clauda, we had much work to come by the boat: ¹⁷which when they had taken up, they used helps, undergirding the ship; and, fearing lest they should fall into the quicksands, struck sail, and so were driven. ¹⁸And we being exceedingly tossed with a tempest, the next day they lightened the ship: ¹⁹and the third day we cast out with our own hands the tackling of the ship. ²⁰And when neither sun nor stars in many days appeared, and no small tempest lay on us, all hope that we should be saved was then taken away.

²¹But after long abstinence, Paul stood forth in the midst of them, and said, 'Sirs, ye should have hearkened unto me, and not have loosed from Crete, and to have gained this harm and loss. ²²And now I exhort you to be of good cheer: for there shall be no loss of any man's life among you, but of the ship. ²³For there stood by me this night the angel of God, whose I am, and whom I serve, ²⁴saying, "Fear not, Paul, thou must be brought before Caesar: and lo, God hath given thee all them that sail with thee". ²⁵Wherefore, sirs, be of good cheer: for I believe God, that it shall be even as it was told me. ²⁶Howbeit we must be cast upon a certain island.'

²⁷But when the fourteenth night was come, as we were driven up and down in Adria, about midnight the shipmen deemed that they drew near to some country: ²⁸and sounded, and found it twenty fathoms: and when they had gone a little farther, they sounded again, and found it fifteen fathoms. ²⁹Then fearing lest we should have fallen upon rocks, they cast four anchors out of the stern, and wished for the day. ³⁰And as the shipmen were about to flee out of the ship, when they had let down the boat into the sea, under colour as though they would have cast anchors out of the foreship, ³¹Paul said to the centurion and to the soldiers, 'Except these abide in the ship, ye cannot be saved'. ³²Then the soldiers cut off the ropes of the boat, and let her fall off.

³³And while the day was coming on, Paul besought them all to take meat, saying, 'This day is the fourteenth day that ye have tarried and continued fasting, having taken nothing. ³⁴Wherefore I pray you to take some meat, for this is for your health: for there shall not a hair fall from the head of any of you.' ³⁵And when he had thus spoken, he took bread, and gave thanks to God in presence of them all, and when he had broken it, he began to eat. ³⁶Then were they all of good cheer, and they also took some meat. ³⁷And we were in all in the ship two hundred threescore and sixteen souls. ³⁸And when they had eaten enough, they lightened the ship, and cast out the wheat into the sea.

³⁹And when it was day, they knew not the land: but they discovered a

certain creek with a shore, into the which they were minded, if it were possible, to thrust in the ship. ⁴⁰And when they had taken up the anchors, they committed themselves unto the sea, and loosed the rudder bands, and hoisted up the mainsail to the wind, and made toward shore. ⁴¹And falling into a place where two seas met, they ran the ship aground, and the forepart stuck fast, and remained immovable, but the hinder part was broken with the violence of the waves. ⁴²And the soldiers' counsel was to kill the prisoners, lest any of them should swim out, and escape. ⁴³But the centurion, willing to save Paul, kept them from their purpose, and commanded that they which could swim should cast themselves first into the sea, and get to land: ⁴⁴and the rest, some on boards, and some on broken pieces of the ship. And so it came to pass that they escaped all safe to land.

28 And when they were escaped, then they knew that the island was called Melita. ²And the barbarous people showed us no little kindness: for they kindled a fire, and received us every one, because of the present rain, and because of the cold. ³And when Paul had gathered a bundle of sticks, and laid them on the fire, there came a viper out of the heat, and fastened on his hand. ⁴And when the barbarians saw the venomous beast hang on his hand, they said among themselves, 'No doubt this man is a murderer, whom, though he hath escaped the sea, yet vengeance suffereth not to live'. ⁵And he shook off the beast into the fire, and felt no harm. ⁶Howbeit they looked when he should have swollen, or fallen down dead suddenly: but after they had looked a great while, and saw no harm come to him, they changed their minds, and said that he was a god.

⁷In the same quarters were possessions of the chief man of the island, whose name was Publius, who received us, and lodged us three days courteously. ⁸And it came to pass that the father of Publius lay sick of a fever and of a bloody flux, to whom Paul entered in, and prayed, and laid his hands on him, and healed him. ⁹So when this was done, others also, which had diseases in the island, came, and were healed: ¹⁰who also honoured us with many honours; and when we departed, they loaded us with such things as were necessary.

¹¹And after three months we departed in a ship of Alexandria, which had wintered in the isle, whose sign was Castor and Pollux. ¹²And landing at Syracuse, we tarried there three days. ¹³And from thence we fetched a compass, and came to Rhegium, and after one day the south wind blew, and we came the next day to Puteoli: ¹⁴where we found brethren, and were desired to tarry with them seven days: and so we went toward Rome. ¹⁵And from thence, when the brethren heard of us, they came to meet us as far as Appii Forum, and the Three Taverns: whom when Paul saw, he thanked God, and took courage.

¹⁶And when we came to Rome, the centurion delivered the prisoners to the captain of the guard: but Paul was suffered to dwell by himself with a soldier that kept him. ¹⁷And it came to pass that after three days Paul called the chief of the Jews together. And when they were come together, he said unto them, 'Men and brethren, though I have com-

mitted nothing against the people, or customs of our fathers, yet was I delivered prisoner from Jerusalem into the hands of the Romans. [18]Who, when they had examined me, would have let me go, because there was no cause of death in me. [19]But when the Jews spoke against it, I was constrained to appeal unto Caesar, not that I had aught to accuse my nation of. [20]For this cause therefore have I called for you, to see you, and to speak with you: because that for the hope of Israel I am bound with this chain.' [21]And they said unto him, 'We neither received letters out of Judea concerning thee, neither any of the brethren that came showed or spoke any harm of thee. [22]But we desire to hear of thee what thou thinkest: for as concerning this sect, we know that everywhere it is spoken against.'

[23]And when they had appointed him a day, there came many to him into his lodging, to whom he expounded and testified the kingdom of God, persuading them concerning Jesus, both out of the law of Moses, and out of the prophets, from morning till evening. [24]And some believed the things which were spoken, and some believed not. [25]And when they agreed not among themselves, they departed, after that Paul had spoken one word, 'Well spoke the Holy Ghost by Esaias the prophet unto our fathers, [26]saying, "Go unto this people, and say, 'Hearing ye shall hear, and shall not understand, and seeing ye shall see, and not perceive'. [27]For the heart of this people is waxed gross, and their ears are dull of hearing, and their eyes have they closed, lest they should see with their eyes, and hear with their ears, and understand with their heart, and should be converted, and I should heal them." [28]Be it known therefore unto you, that the salvation of God is sent unto the Gentiles, and that they will hear it.' [29]And when he had said these words, the Jews departed, and had great reasoning among themselves.

[30]And Paul dwelt two whole years in his own hired house, and received all that came in unto him, [31]preaching the kingdom of God, and teaching those things which concern the Lord Jesus Christ, with all confidence, no man forbidding him.

THE
EPISTLE OF PAUL THE APOSTLE
TO THE
ROMANS

1 Paul, a servant of Jesus Christ, called to be an apostle, separated unto the gospel of God ²(which he had promised afore by his prophets in the holy scriptures), ³concerning his Son Jesus Christ our Lord, which was made of the seed of David according to the flesh, ⁴ and declared to be the Son of God with power, according to the spirit of holiness, by the resurrection from the dead: ⁵by whom we have received grace and apostleship, for obedience to the faith among all nations, for his name, ⁶among whom are ye also the called of Jesus Christ: ⁷to all that be in Rome, beloved of God, called to be saints: grace to you and peace from God our Father, and the Lord Jesus Christ.

⁸First, I thank my God through Jesus Christ for you all, that your faith is spoken of throughout the whole world. ⁹For God is my witness, whom I serve with my spirit in the gospel of his Son, that without ceasing I make mention of you always in my prayers, ¹⁰making request, if by any means now at length I might have a prosperous journey by the will of God to come unto you. ¹¹For I long to see you, that I may impart unto you some spiritual gift, to the end you may be established, ¹²that is, that I may be comforted together with you by the mutual faith both of you and me. ¹³Now I would not have you ignorant, brethren, that oftentimes I purposed to come unto you (but was let hitherto), that I might have some fruit among you also, even as among other Gentiles. ¹⁴I am debtor both to the Greeks, and to the Barbarians, both to the wise, and to the unwise. ¹⁵So, as much as in me is, I am ready to preach the gospel to you that are at Rome also. ¹⁶For I am not ashamed of the gospel of Christ: for it is the power of God unto salvation to every one that believeth, to the Jew first, and also to the Greek. ¹⁷For therein is the righteousness of God revealed from faith to faith: as it is written, 'The just shall live by faith'.

¹⁸For the wrath of God is revealed from heaven against all ungodliness and unrighteousness of men, who hold the truth in unrighteousness; ¹⁹because that which may be known of God is manifest in them, for God hath shown it unto them. ²⁰For the invisible things of him from the creation of the world are clearly seen, being understood by the things that are made, even his eternal power and Godhead, so that they are without excuse: ²¹because that, when they knew God, they glorified him not as God, neither were thankful, but became vain in their imaginations, and their foolish heart was darkened. ²²Professing themselves to be wise, they became fools, ²³and changed the glory of the incorruptible God into an image made like to corruptible man, and to birds, and four-footed beasts, and creeping things. ²⁴Wherefore God also gave them up

to uncleanness through the lusts of their own hearts, to dishonour their own bodies between themselves: ²⁵who changed the truth of God into a lie, and worshipped and served the creature more than the Creator, who is blessed for ever. Amen.

²⁶For this cause God gave them up unto vile affections: for even their women did change the natural use into that which is against nature: ²⁷and likewise also the men, leaving the natural use of the woman, burnt in their lust one towards another, men with men working that which is unseemly, and receiving in themselves that recompense of their error which was meet. ²⁸And even as they did not like to retain God in their knowledge, God gave them over to a reprobate mind, to do those things which are not convenient: ²⁹being filled with all unrighteousness, fornication, wickedness, covetousness, maliciousness, full of envy, murder, debate, deceit, malignity, whisperers, ³⁰backbiters, haters of God, despiteful, proud, boasters, inventors of evil things, disobedient to parents, ³¹without understanding, covenant-breakers, without natural affection, implacable, unmerciful; ³²who knowing the judgement of God, that they which commit such things are worthy of death, not only do the same, but have pleasure in them that do them.

2 Therefore thou art inexcusable, O man, whosoever thou art that judgest: for wherein thou judgest another, thou condemnest thyself, for thou that judgest doest the same things. ²But we are sure that the judgement of God is according to truth against them which commit such things. ³And thinkest thou this, O man, that judgest them which do such things, and doest the same, that thou shalt escape the judgement of God? ⁴Or despisest thou the riches of his goodness and forbearance and long-suffering, not knowing that the goodness of God leadeth thee to repentance? ⁵but after thy hardness and impenitent heart treasurest up unto thyself wrath against the day of wrath and revelation of the righteous judgement of God: ⁶who will render to every man according to his deeds: ⁷to them who by patient continuance in well-doing seek for glory and honour and immortality, eternal life: ⁸but unto them that are contentious, and do not obey the truth, but obey unrighteousness, indignation and wrath, ⁹tribulation and anguish, upon every soul of man that doeth evil, of the Jew first, and also of the Gentile; ¹⁰but glory, honour, and peace, to every man that worketh good, to the Jew first, and also to the Gentile. ¹¹For there is no respect of persons with God.

¹²For as many as have sinned without law shall also perish without law: and as many as have sinned in the law shall be judged by the law ¹³(for not the hearers of the law are just before God, but the doers of the law shall be justified; ¹⁴for when the Gentiles, which have not the law, do by nature the things contained in the law, these, having not the law, are a law unto themselves, ¹⁵which show the work of the law written in their hearts, their conscience also bearing witness, and their thoughts the mean while accusing or else excusing one another): ¹⁶in the day when God shall judge the secrets of men by Jesus Christ according to my gospel.

[17]Behold, thou art called a Jew, and restest in the law, and makest thy boast of God, [18]and knowest his will, and approvest the things that are more excellent, being instructed out of the law, [19]and art confident that thou thyself art a guide of the blind, a light of them which are in darkness, [20]an instructor of the foolish, a teacher of babes, which hast the form of knowledge and of the truth in the law. [21]Thou therefore which teachest another, teachest thou not thyself? thou that preachest a man should not steal, dost thou steal? [22]Thou that sayest a man should not commit adultery, dost thou commit adultery? thou that abhorrest idols, dost thou commit sacrilege? [23]thou that makest thy boast of the law, through breaking the law dishonourest thou God? [24]For the name of God is blasphemed among the Gentiles through you, as it is written. [25]For circumcision verily profiteth, if thou keep the law: but if thou be a breaker of the law, thy circumcision is made uncircumcision. [26]Therefore if the uncircumcision keep the righteousness of the law, shall not his uncircumcision be counted for circumcision? [27]And shall not uncircumcision which is by nature, if it fulfil the law, judge thee, who by the letter and circumcision dost transgress the law? [28]For he is not a Jew, which is one outwardly, neither is that circumcision, which is outward in the flesh: [29]but he is a Jew, which is one inwardly, and circumcision is that of the heart, in the spirit, and not in the letter, whose praise is not of men, but of God.

3 What advantage then hath the Jew? or what profit is there of circumcision? [2]Much every way: chiefly, because that unto them were committed the oracles of God. [3]For what if some did not believe? shall their unbelief make the faith of God without effect? [4]God forbid: yea, let God be true, but every man a liar; as it is written, 'That thou mightest be justified in thy sayings, and mightest overcome when thou art judged'. [5]But if our unrighteousness commend the righteousness of God, what shall we say? Is God unrighteous who taketh vengeance (I speak as a man)? [6]God forbid: for then how shall God judge the world? [7]For if the truth of God hath more abounded through my lie unto his glory; why yet am I also judged as a sinner? [8]And not rather (as we be slanderously reported, and as some affirm that we say), 'Let us do evil that good may come'? whose damnation is just.

[9]What then? are we better than they? No, in no wise: for we have before proved both Jews and Gentiles, that they are all under sin, [10]as it is written, 'There is none righteous, no, not one: [11]there is none that understandeth, there is none that seeketh after God. [12]They are all gone out of the way, they are together become unprofitable, there is none that doeth good, no, not one. [13]Their throat is an open sepulchre, with their tongues they have used deceit, the poison of asps is under their lips: [14]whose mouth is full of cursing and bitterness: [15]their feet are swift to shed blood. [16]Destruction and misery are in their ways: [17]and the way of peace have they not known. [18]There is no fear of God before their eyes.' [19]Now we know that what things soever the law saith, it saith to them who are under the law: that every mouth may be stopped, and all the world may become guilty before God. [20]Therefore by the

deeds of the law there shall no flesh be justified in his sight: for by the law is the knowledge of sin.

²¹But now the righteousness of God without the law is manifested, being witnessed by the law and the prophets; ²²even the righteousness of God which is by faith of Jesus Christ unto all and upon all them that believe: for there is no difference: ²³for all have sinned, and come short of the glory of God, ²⁴being justified freely by his grace through the redemption that is in Jesus Christ: ²⁵whom God hath set forth to be a propitiation through faith in his blood, to declare his righteousness for the remission of sins that are past, through the forbearance of God; ²⁶to declare, I say, at this time his righteousness: that he might be just, and the justifier of him which believeth in Jesus.

²⁷Where is boasting then? It is excluded. By what law? of works? Nay: but by the law of faith. ²⁸Therefore we conclude that a man is justified by faith without the deeds of the law. ²⁹Is he the God of the Jews only? is he not also of the Gentiles? Yes, of the Gentiles also: ³⁰seeing it is one God, which shall justify the circumcision by faith, and uncircumcision through faith. ³¹Do we then make void the law through faith? God forbid: yea, we establish the law.

4 What shall we say then that Abraham our father, as pertaining to the flesh, hath found? ²For if Abraham were justified by works, he hath whereof to glory, but not before God. ³For what saith the scripture? 'Abraham believed God, and it was counted unto him for righteousness'. ⁴Now to him that worketh is the reward not reckoned of grace, but of debt. ⁵But to him that worketh not, but believeth on him that justifieth the ungodly, his faith is counted for righteousness. ⁶Even as David also describeth the blessedness of the man, unto whom God imputeth righteousness without works, ⁷saying, 'Blessed are they whose iniquities are forgiven, and whose sins are covered. ⁸Blessed is the man to whom the Lord will not impute sin.' ⁹Cometh this blessedness then upon the circumcision only, or upon the uncircumcision also? for we say that faith was reckoned to Abraham for righteousness. ¹⁰How was it then reckoned? When he was in circumcision, or in uncircumcision? not in circumcision, but in uncircumcision. ¹¹And he received the sign of circumcision, a seal of the righteousness of the faith which he had yet being uncircumcised: that he might be the father of all them that believe, though they be not circumcised, that righteousness might be imputed unto them also: ¹²and the father of circumcision to them who are not of the circumcision only, but also walk in the steps of that faith of our father Abraham, which he had being yet uncircumcised. ¹³For the promise that he should be the heir of the world, was not to Abraham, or to his seed, through the law, but through the righteousness of faith. ¹⁴For if they which are of the law be heirs, faith is made void, and the promise made of no effect: ¹⁵because the law worketh wrath: for where no law is, there is no transgression. ¹⁶Therefore it is of faith, that it might be by grace; to the end the promise might be sure to all the seed not to that only which is of the law, but to that also which is of the faith of Abraham, who is the father of us all

[17](as it is written, 'I have made thee a father of many nations'), before him whom he believed, even God, who quickeneth the dead, and calleth those things which be not as though they were, [18]who against hope believed in hope, that he might become the father of many nations, according to that which was spoken, 'So shall thy seed be'. [19]And being not weak in faith, he considered not his own body now dead, when he was about a hundred years old, neither yet the deadness of Sara's womb. [20]He staggered not at the promise of God through unbelief but was strong in faith, giving glory to God: [21]and being fully persuaded that, what he had promised, he was able also to perform. [22]And therefore it was imputed to him for righteousness. [23]Now it was not written for his sake alone, that it was imputed to him: [24]but for us also, to whom it shall be imputed, if we believe on him that raised up Jesus our Lord from the dead, [25]who was delivered for our offences, and was raised again for our justification.

5 Therefore being justified by faith, we have peace with God through our Lord Jesus Christ: [2]by whom also we have access by faith into this grace wherein we stand, and rejoice in hope of the glory of God. [3]And not only so, but we glory in tribulations also, knowing that tribulation worketh patience: [4]and patience, experience: and experience, hope: [5]and hope maketh not ashamed, because the love of God is shed abroad in our hearts by the Holy Ghost which is given unto us.

[6]For when we were yet without strength, in due time Christ died for the ungodly. [7]For scarcely for a righteous man will one die: yet peradventure for a good man some would even dare to die. [8]But God commendeth his love towards us, in that, while we were yet sinners, Christ died for us. [9]Much more then, being now justified by his blood, we shall be saved from wrath through him. [10]For if, when we were enemies, we were reconciled to God by the death of his Son, much more, being reconciled, we shall be saved by his life. [11]And not only so, but we also joy in God through our Lord Jesus Christ, by whom we have now received the atonement.

[12]Wherefore, as by one man sin entered into the world, and death by sin: and so death passed upon all men, for that all have sinned. [13]For until the law sin was in the world: but sin is not imputed when there is no law. [14]Nevertheless death reigned from Adam to Moses, even over them that had not sinned after the similitude of Adam's transgression, who is the figure of him that was to come. [15]But not as the offence, so also is the free gift. For if through the offence of one many be dead, much more the grace of God, and the gift by grace, which is by one man, Jesus Christ, hath abounded unto many. [16]And not as it was by one that sinned, so is the gift: for the judgement was by one to condemnation, but the free gift is of many offences unto justification. [17]For if by one man's offence death reigned by one, much more they which receive abundance of grace and of the gift of righteousness shall reign in life by one, Jesus Christ. [18]Therefore as by the offence of one judgement came upon all men to condemnation: even so by the righteousness of one the free gift came upon all men unto justification of life.

[19]For as by one man's disobedience many were made sinners, so by the obedience of one shall many be made righteous. [20]Moreover the law entered, that the offence might abound. But where sin abounded, grace did much more abound: [21]that as sin hath reigned unto death, even so might grace reign through righteousness unto eternal life by Jesus Christ our Lord.

6 What shall we say then? Shall we continue in sin, that grace may abound? [2]God forbid. How shall we, that are dead to sin, live any longer therein? [3]Know ye not, that so many of us as were baptized into Jesus Christ were baptized into his death? [4]Therefore we are buried with him by baptism into death, that like as Christ was raised up from the dead by the glory of the Father, even so we also should walk in newness of life. [5]For if we have been planted together in the likeness of his death, we shall be also in the likeness of his resurrection: [6]knowing this, that our old man is crucified with him, that the body of sin might be destroyed, that henceforth we should not serve sin. [7]For he that is dead is freed from sin. [8]Now if we be dead with Christ, we believe that we shall also live with him: [9]knowing that Christ being raised from the dead dieth no more, death hath no more dominion over him. [10]For in that he died, he died unto sin once: but in that he liveth, he liveth unto God. [11]Likewise reckon ye also yourselves to be dead indeed unto sin, but alive unto God through Jesus Christ our Lord.

[12]Let not sin reign therefore in your mortal body, that ye should obey it in the lusts thereof. [13]Neither yield ye your members as instruments of unrighteousness unto sin: but yield yourselves unto God, as those that are alive from the dead, and your members as instruments of righteousness unto God. [14]For sin shall not have dominion over you, for ye are not under the law, but under grace.

[15]What then? shall we sin, because we are not under the law, but under grace? God forbid. [16]Know ye not, that to whom ye yield yourselves servants to obey, his servants ye are to whom ye obey: whether of sin unto death, or of obedience unto righteousness? [17]But God be thanked, that ye were the servants of sin, but ye have obeyed from the heart that form of doctrine which was delivered you. [18]Being then made free from sin, ye became the servants of righteousness. [19]I speak after the manner of men because of the infirmity of your flesh: for as ye have yielded your members servants to uncleanness and to iniquity unto iniquity: even so now yield your members servants to righteousness unto holiness. [20]For when ye were the servants of sin, ye were free from righteousness. [21]What fruit had ye then in those things whereof ye are now ashamed? for the end of those things is death. [22]But now being made free from sin, and become servants to God, ye have your fruit unto holiness, and the end everlasting life. [23]For the wages of sin is death: but the gift of God is eternal life through Jesus Christ our Lord.

7 Know ye not, brethren (for I speak to them that know the law), how that the law hath dominion over a man as long as he liveth? [2]For the woman which hath a husband is bound by the law to her husband so long as he liveth: but if the husband be dead, she is loosed from the

law of the husband. ³So then if, while her husband liveth, she be married to another man, she shall be called an adulteress: but if her husband be dead, she is free from that law, so that she is no adulteress, though she be married to another man. ⁴Wherefore, my brethren, ye also are become dead to the law by the body of Christ, that ye should be married to another, even to him who is raised from the dead, that we should bring forth fruit unto God. ⁵For when we were in the flesh, the motions of sins, which were by the law, did work in our members to bring forth fruit unto death. ⁶But now we are delivered from the law, that being dead wherein we were held, that we should serve in newness of spirit, and not in the oldness of the letter.

⁷What shall we say then? Is the law sin? God forbid. Nay, I had not known sin, but by the law: for I had not known lust, except the law had said, 'Thou shalt not covet'. ⁸But sin, taking occasion by the commandment, wrought in me all manner of concupiscence. For without the law sin was dead. ⁹For I was alive without the law once, but when the commandment came, sin revived, and I died. ¹⁰And the commandment, which was ordained to life, I found to be unto death. ¹¹For sin, taking occasion by the commandment, deceived me, and by it slew me. ¹²Wherefore the law is holy, and the commandment holy, and just, and good.

¹³Was that then which is good made death unto me? God forbid. But sin, that it might appear sin, working death in me by that which is good: that sin by the commandment might become exceeding sinful. ¹⁴For we know that the law is spiritual: but I am carnal, sold under sin. ¹⁵For that which I do I allow not: for what I would, that do I not, but what I hate, that do I. ¹⁶If then I do that which I would not, I consent unto the law that it is good. ¹⁷Now then, it is no more I that do it, but sin that dwelleth in me. ¹⁸For I know that in me (that is, in my flesh) dwelleth no good thing. For to will is present with me: but how to perform that which is good I find not. ¹⁹For the good that I would I do not: but the evil which I would not, that I do. ²⁰Now if I do that I would not, it is no more I that do it, but sin that dwelleth in me.

²¹I find then a law, that, when I would do good, evil is present with me. ²²For I delight in the law of God after the inward man: ²³but I see another law in my members, warring against the law of my mind, and bringing me into captivity to the law of sin which is in my members. ²⁴O wretched man that I am: who shall deliver me from the body of this death? ²⁵I thank God through Jesus Christ our Lord. So then with the mind I myself serve the law of God; but with the flesh the law of sin.

8 There is therefore now no condemnation to them which are in Christ Jesus, who walk not after the flesh, but after the Spirit. ²For the law of the spirit of life in Christ Jesus hath made me free from the law of sin and death. ³For what the law could not do, in that it was weak through the flesh, God sending his own Son in the likeness of sinful flesh, and for sin, condemned sin in the flesh: ⁴that the righteousness of the law might be fulfilled in us, who walk not after the flesh, but after the Spirit.

[5]For they that are after the flesh do mind the things of the flesh: but they that are after the Spirit, the things of the Spirit. [6]For to be carnally minded is death: but to be spiritually minded is life and peace: [7]because the carnal mind is enmity against God: for it is not subject to the law of God, neither indeed can be. [8]So then they that are in the flesh cannot please God.

[9]But ye are not in the flesh, but in the Spirit, if so be that the Spirit of God dwell in you. Now if any man have not the Spirit of Christ, he is none of his. [10]And if Christ be in you, the body is dead because of sin: but the Spirit is life because of righteousness. [11]But if the Spirit of him that raised up Jesus from the dead dwell in you, he that raised up Christ from the dead shall also quicken your mortal bodies by his Spirit that dwelleth in you.

[12]Therefore, brethren, we are debtors, not to the flesh, to live after the flesh. [13]For if ye live after the flesh, ye shall die: but if ye through the Spirit do mortify the deeds of the body, ye shall live. [14]For as many as are led by the Spirit of God, they are the sons of God. [15]For ye have not received the spirit of bondage again to fear: but ye have received the Spirit of adoption, whereby we cry, 'Abba, Father'. [16]The Spirit itself beareth witness with our spirit, that we are the children of God: [17]and if children, then heirs, heirs of God, and joint-heirs with Christ: if so be that we suffer with him, that we may be also glorified together.

[18]For I reckon that the sufferings of this present time are not worthy to be compared with the glory which shall be revealed in us. [19]For the earnest expectation of the creature waiteth for the manifestation of the sons of God. [20]For the creature was made subject to vanity, not willingly, but by reason of him who hath subjected the same in hope, [21]because the creature itself also shall be delivered from the bondage of corruption into the glorious liberty of the children of God. [22]For we know that the whole creation groaneth and travaileth in pain together until now. [23]And not only they, but ourselves also, which have the firstfruits of the Spirit, even we ourselves groan within ourselves, waiting for the adoption, to wit, the redemption of our body. [24]For we are saved by hope: but hope that is seen is not hope: for what a man seeth, why doth he yet hope for? [25]But if we hope for that we see not, then do we with patience wait for it.

[26]Likewise the Spirit also helpeth our infirmities: for we know not what we should pray for as we ought: but the Spirit itself maketh intercession for us with groanings which cannot be uttered. [27]And he that searcheth the hearts knoweth what is the mind of the Spirit, because he maketh intercession for the saints according to the will of God. [28]And we know that all things work together for good to them that love God, to them who are the called according to his purpose. [29]For whom he did foreknow, he also did predestinate to be conformed to the image of his Son, that he might be the firstborn amongst many brethren. [30]Moreover whom he did predestinate, them he also called: and whom he called, them he also justified: and whom he justified, them he also glorified.

³¹What shall we then say to these things? If God be for us, who can be against us? ³²He that spared not his own Son, but delivered him up for us all, how shall he not with him also freely give us all things? ³³Who shall lay anything to the charge of God's elect? It is God that justifieth. ³⁴Who is he that condemneth? It is Christ that died, yea rather, that is risen again, who is even at the right hand of God, who also maketh intercession for us. ³⁵Who shall separate us from the love of Christ? shall tribulation, or distress, or persecution, or famine, or nakedness, or peril, or sword? ³⁶As it is written, 'For thy sake we are killed all the day long, we are accounted as sheep for the slaughter'. ³⁷Nay, in all these things we are more than conquerors through him that loved us. ³⁸For I am persuaded, that neither death, nor life, nor angels, nor principalities, nor powers, nor things present, nor things to come, ³⁹nor height, nor depth, nor any other creature, shall be able to separate us from the love of God, which is in Christ Jesus our Lord.

9 I say the truth in Christ, I lie not, my conscience also bearing me witness in the Holy Ghost, ²that I have great heaviness and continual sorrow in my heart. ³For I could wish that myself were accursed from Christ for my brethren, my kinsmen according to the flesh: ⁴who are Israelites: to whom pertaineth the adoption, and the glory, and the covenants, and the giving of the law, and the service of God, and the promises: ⁵whose are the fathers, and of whom as concerning the flesh Christ came, who is over all, God blessed for ever. Amen.

⁶Not as though the word of God hath taken no effect. For they are not all Israel, which are of Israel: ⁷neither, because they are the seed of Abraham, are they all children: but, 'In Isaac shall thy seed be called'. ⁸That is, they which are the children of the flesh, these are not the children of God: but the children of the promise are counted for the seed. ⁹For this is the word of promise, 'At this time will I come, and Sara shall have a son'. ¹⁰And not only this, but when Rebecca also had conceived by one, even by our father Isaac ¹¹(for the children being not yet born, neither having done any good or evil, that the purpose of God according to election might stand, not of works, but of him that calleth), ¹²it was said unto her, 'The elder shall serve the younger'. ¹³As it is written, 'Jacob have I loved, but Esau have I hated'.

¹⁴What shall we say then? Is there unrighteousness with God? God forbid. ¹⁵For he saith to Moses, 'I will have mercy on whom I will have mercy, and I will have compassion on whom I will have compassion'. ¹⁶So then it is not of him that willeth, nor of him that runneth, but of God that showeth mercy. ¹⁷For the scripture saith unto Pharaoh, 'Even for this same purpose have I raised thee up, that I might show my power in thee, and that my name might be declared throughout all the earth'. ¹⁸Therefore hath he mercy on whom he will have mercy, and whom he will he hardeneth.

¹⁹Thou wilt say then unto me, 'Why doth he yet find fault? For who hath resisted his will?' ²⁰Nay but, O man, who art thou that repliest against God? Shall the thing formed say to him that formed it, 'Why hast thou made me thus?' ²¹Hath not the potter power over the clay, of

the same lump to make one vessel unto honour, and another unto dis-honour? ²²What if God, willing to show his wrath, and to make his power known, endured with much long-suffering the vessels of wrath fitted to destruction: ²³and that he might make known the riches of his glory on the vessels of mercy, which he had afore prepared unto glory, ²⁴even us, whom he hath called, not of the Jews only, but also of the Gentiles? ²⁵As he saith also in Osee, 'I will call them my people, which were not my people: and her beloved, which was not beloved. ²⁶And it shall come to pass, that in the place where it was said unto them, "Ye are not my people", there shall they be called the chil-dren of the living God.' ²⁷Esaias also crieth concerning Israel, 'Though the number of the children of Israel be as the sand of the sea, a rem-nant shall be saved. ²⁸For he will finish the work, and cut it short in righteousness: because a short work will the Lord make upon the earth.' ²⁹And as Esaias said before, 'Except the Lord of Sabaoth had left us a seed, we had been as Sodoma, and been made like unto Gomorrha'.

³⁰What shall we say then? That the Gentiles, which followed not after righteousness, have attained to righteousness, even the righteous-ness which is of faith: ³¹but Israel, which followed after the law of right-eousness, hath not attained to the law of righteousness. ³²Wherefore? Because they sought it not by faith, but as it were by the works of the law: for they stumbled at that stumbling-stone, ³³as it is written, 'Behold, I lay in Sion a stumbling-stone and rock of offence: and whoso-ever believeth on him shall not be ashamed'.

10 Brethren, my heart's desire and prayer to God for Israel is, that they might be saved. ²For I bear them record that they have a zeal of God, but not according to knowledge. ³For they being ignorant of God's righteousness, and going about to establish their own right-eousness, have not submitted themselves unto the righteousness of God. ⁴For Christ is the end of the law for righteousness to every one that believeth. ⁵For Moses describeth the righteousness which is of the law, that the man which doeth those things shall live by them. ⁶But the righteousness which is of faith speaketh on this wise, 'Say not in thy heart, "Who shall ascend into heaven?"' That is to bring Christ down from above. ⁷'Or, "Who shall descend into the deep?"' That is to bring up Christ again from the dead. ⁸But what saith it? 'The word is nigh thee, even in thy mouth, and in thy heart': that is, the word of faith, which we preach, ⁹that if thou shalt confess with thy mouth the Lord Jesus, and shalt believe in thy heart that God hath raised him from the dead, thou shalt be saved. ¹⁰For with the heart man believeth unto righteousness, and with the mouth confession is made unto salva-tion. ¹¹For the scripture saith, 'Whosoever believeth on him shall not be ashamed'. ¹²For there is no difference between the Jew and the Greek: for the same Lord over all is rich unto all that call upon him. ¹³For whosoever shall call upon the name of the Lord shall be saved. ¹⁴How then shall they call on him in whom they have not believed? and how shall they believe in him of whom they have not heard? and how shall they hear without a preacher? ¹⁵and how shall they preach, except they be sent? As it is written, 'How beautiful are the feet of them that preach the gospel of peace, and bring glad tidings of good things!' ¹⁶But they have not all obeyed the gospel. For Esaias saith, 'Lord, who hath believed our report?' ¹⁷So then faith cometh by hearing, and hearing by the word of God. ¹⁸But I say, 'Have they not heard?' Yes verily, their sound went into all the earth, and their words unto the ends of the world. ¹⁹But I say, 'Did not Israel know?' First Moses saith, 'I will provoke you to jealousy by them that are no people, and by a foolish nation I will anger you'. ²⁰But Esaias is very bold, and saith, 'I was found of them that sought me not: I was made manifest unto them that asked not after me'. ²¹But to Israel he saith, 'All day long I have stretched forth my hands unto a disobedient and gainsaying people'.

11 I say then, 'Hath God cast away his people?' God forbid. For I also am an Israelite of the seed of Abraham, of the tribe of Benjamin. ²God hath not cast away his people which he foreknew. Wot ye not what the scripture saith of Elias? how he maketh intercession to God against Israel, saying, ³'Lord, they have killed thy prophets, and dug down thy altars, and I am left alone, and they seek my life'. ⁴But what saith the answer of God unto him? 'I have reserved to myself seven thousand men, who have not bowed the knee to the image of Baal'. ⁵Even so then at this present time also there is a remnant according to the election of grace. ⁶And if by grace, then is it no more of works: otherwise grace is no more grace. But if it be of works, then is it no more grace: otherwise work is no more work.

⁷What then? Israel hath not obtained that which he seeketh for, but the election hath obtained it, and the rest were blinded, ⁸according as it is written, 'God hath given them the spirit of slumber, eyes that they should not see, and ears that they should not hear unto this day'. ⁹And David saith, 'Let their table be made a snare, and a trap, and a stumbling-block, and a recompense unto them. ¹⁰Let their eyes be darkened, that they may not see, and bow down their back always.' ¹¹I say then, 'Have they stumbled that they should fall?' God forbid: but rather through their fall salvation is come unto the Gentiles, for to provoke them to jealousy. ¹²Now if the fall of them be the riches of the world, and the diminishing of them the riches of the Gentiles: how much more their fulness?

¹³For I speak to you Gentiles, inasmuch as I am the apostle of the Gentiles, I magnify my office: ¹⁴if by any means I may provoke to emulation them which are my flesh, and might save some of them. ¹⁵For if the casting away of them be the reconciling of the world, what shall the receiving of them be, but life from the dead? ¹⁶For if the first-fruit be holy, the lump is also holy: and if the root be holy, so are the branches. ¹⁷And if some of the branches be broken off, and thou, being a wild olive tree, wert grafted in amongst them, and with them partakest of the root and fatness of the olive tree: ¹⁸boast not against the branches. But if thou boast, thou bearest not the root, but the root thee. ¹⁹Thou wilt say then, 'The branches were broken off, that I might be grafted in'. ²⁰Well: because of unbelief they were broken off, and

thou standest by faith. Be not high-minded, but fear. ²¹For if God spared not the natural branches, take heed lest he also spare not thee. ²²Behold therefore the goodness and severity of God: on them which fell, severity; but towards thee, goodness, if thou continue in his goodness: otherwise thou also shalt be cut off. ²³And they also, if they bide not still in unbelief, shall be grafted in: for God is able to graft them in again. ²⁴For if thou wert cut out of the olive tree which is wild by nature, and wert grafted contrary to nature into a good olive tree: how much more shall these, which be the natural branches, be grafted into their own olive tree?

²⁵For I would not, brethren, that ye should be ignorant of this mystery, (lest ye should be wise in your own conceits), that blindness in part is happened to Israel, until the fulness of the Gentiles be come in. ²⁶And so all Israel shall be saved: as it is written, 'There shall come out of Sion the Deliverer, and shall turn away ungodliness from Jacob. ²⁷For this is my covenant unto them, when I shall take away their sins.' ²⁸As concerning the gospel, they are enemies for your sake: but as touching the election, they are beloved for the fathers' sakes. ²⁹For the gifts and calling of God are without repentance. ³⁰For as ye in times past have not believed God, yet have now obtained mercy through their unbelief: ³¹even so have these also now not believed, that through your mercy they also may obtain mercy. ³²For God hath concluded them all in unbelief, that he might have mercy upon all.

³³O the depth of the riches both of the wisdom and knowledge of God! how unsearchable are his judgements, and his ways past finding out! ³⁴For who hath known the mind of the Lord? or who hath been his counsellor? ³⁵Or who hath first given to him, and it shall be recompensed unto him again? ³⁶For of him, and through him, and to him are all things: to whom be glory for ever. Amen.

12 I beseech you therefore, brethren, by the mercies of God, that ye present your bodies a living sacrifice, holy, acceptable unto God, which is your reasonable service. ²And be not conformed to this world: but be ye transformed by the renewing of your mind, that ye may prove what is that good, that acceptable, and perfect will of God. ³For I say, through the grace given unto me, to every man that is among you, not to think of himself more highly than he ought to think, but to think soberly, according as God hath dealt to every man the measure of faith. ⁴For as we have many members in one body, and all members have not the same office: ⁵so we, being many, are one body in Christ, and every one members one of another. ⁶Having then gifts differing according to the grace that is given to us, whether prophecy, let us prophesy according to the proportion of faith: ⁷or ministry, let us wait on our ministering: or he that teacheth, on teaching: ⁸or he that exhorteth, on exhortation: he that giveth, let him do it with simplicity: he that ruleth, with diligence: he that showeth mercy, with cheerfulness.

⁹Let love be without dissimulation. Abhor that which is evil, cleave to that which is good. ¹⁰Be kindly affectioned one to another with

brotherly love, in honour preferring one another; [11]not slothful in business; fervent in spirit, serving the Lord; [12]rejoicing in hope, patient in tribulation, continuing instant in prayer; [13]distributing to the necessity of saints; given to hospitality. [14]Bless them which persecute you, bless, and curse not. [15]Rejoice with them that do rejoice, and weep with them that weep. [16]Be of the same mind one towards another. Mind not high things, but condescend to men of low estate. Be not wise in your own conceits. [17]Recompense to no man evil for evil. Provide things honest in the sight of all men. [18]If it be possible, as much as lieth in you, live peaceably with all men. [19]Dearly beloved, avenge not yourselves, but rather give place unto wrath: for it is written, '"Vengeance is mine, I will repay," saith the Lord'. [20]Therefore if thy enemy hunger, feed him, if he thirst, give him drink. For in so doing thou shalt heap coals of fire on his head. [21]Be not overcome of evil, but overcome evil with good.

13 Let every soul be subject unto the higher powers: for there is no power but of God. The powers that be are ordained of God. [2]Whosoever therefore resisteth the power, resisteth the ordinance of God: and they that resist shall receive to themselves damnation. [3]For rulers are not a terror to good works, but to the evil. Wilt thou then not be afraid of the power? do that which is good, and thou shalt have praise of the same. [4]For he is the minister of God to thee for good: but if thou do that which is evil, be afraid: for he beareth not the sword in vain: for he is the minister of God, a revenger to execute wrath upon him that doeth evil. [5]Wherefore ye must needs be subject, not only for wrath, but also for conscience sake. [6]For for this cause pay you tribute also: for they are God's ministers, attending continually upon this very thing. [7]Render therefore to all their dues, tribute to whom tribute is due, custom to whom custom, fear to whom fear, honour to whom honour. [8]Owe no man anything, but to love one another: for he that loveth another hath fulfilled the law. [9]For this, 'Thou shalt not commit adultery, thou shalt not kill, thou shalt not steal, thou shalt not bear false witness, thou shalt not covet': and if there be any other commandment, it is briefly comprehended in this saying, namely, 'Thou shalt love thy neighbour as thyself'. [10]Love worketh no ill to his neighbour: therefore love is the fulfilling of the law.

[11]And that, knowing the time, that now it is high time to awake out of sleep: for now is our salvation nearer than when we believed. [12]The night is far spent, the day is at hand: let us therefore cast off the works of darkness, and let us put on the armour of light. [13]Let us walk honestly, as in the day, not in rioting and drunkenness, not in chambering and wantonness, not in strife and envying. [14]But put ye on the Lord Jesus Christ, and make not provision for the flesh, to fulfil the lusts thereof.

14 Him that is weak in the faith receive you, but not to doubtful disputations. [2]For one believeth that he may eat all things: another, who is weak, eateth herbs. [3]Let not him that eateth despise him that eateth not: and let not him which eateth not: judge him that eateth: for God hath received him. [4]Who art thou that judgest another man's servant? to his own master he standeth or falleth. Yea, he shall be held up: for God is able to make him stand. ⁵One man esteemeth one day above another: another esteemeth every day alike. Let every man be fully persuaded in his own mind. ⁶He that regardeth a day, regardeth it unto the Lord; and he that regardeth not the day, to the Lord he doth not regard it. He that eateth, eateth to the Lord, for he giveth God thanks: and he that eateth not, to the Lord he eateth not, and giveth God thanks. ⁷For none of us liveth to himself, and no man dieth to himself. ⁸For whether we live, we live unto the Lord; and whether we die, we die unto the Lord: whether we live therefore, or die, we are the Lord's. ⁹For to this end Christ both died, and rose, and revived, that he might be Lord both of the dead and living. ¹⁰But why dost thou judge thy brother? or why dost thou set at nought thy brother? we shall all stand before the judgement seat of Christ. ¹¹For it is written, '"As I live," saith the Lord, "every knee shall bow to me, and every tongue shall confess to God"'. ¹²So then every one of us shall give account of himself to God.

¹³Let us not therefore judge one another any more: but judge this rather, that no man put a stumbling-block or an occasion to fall in his brother's way. ¹⁴I know, and am persuaded by the Lord Jesus, that there is nothing unclean of itself: but to him that esteemeth anything to be unclean, to him it is unclean. ¹⁵But if thy brother be grieved with thy meat, now walkest thou not charitably. Destroy not him with thy meat, for whom Christ died. ¹⁶Let not then your good be evil spoken of. ¹⁷For the kingdom of God is not meat and drink; but righteousness, and peace, and joy in the Holy Ghost. ¹⁸For he that in these things serveth Christ is acceptable to God, and approved of men.

¹⁹Let us therefore follow after the things which make for peace, and things wherewith one may edify another. ²⁰For meat destroy not the work of God. All things indeed are pure; but it is evil for that man who eateth with offence. ²¹It is good neither to eat flesh, nor to drink wine, nor anything whereby thy brother stumbleth, or is offended, or is made weak. ²²Hast thou faith? have it to thyself before God. Happy is he that condemneth not himself in that thing which he alloweth. ²³And he that doubteth is damned if he eat, because he eateth not of faith: for whatsoever is not of faith is sin.

15 We then that are strong ought to bear the infirmities of the weak, and not to please ourselves. ²Let every one of us please his neighbour for his good to edification. ³For even Christ pleased not himself, but, as it is written, 'The reproaches of them that reproached thee fell on me'. ⁴For whatsoever things were written aforetime were written for our learning, that we through patience and comfort of the scriptures might have hope. ⁵Now the God of patience and consolation grant you to be like-minded one towards another according to Christ Jesus: ⁶that ye may with one mind and one mouth glorify God, even the Father of our Lord Jesus Christ. ⁷Wherefore receive ye one another, as Christ also received us to the glory of God.

⁸Now I say that Jesus Christ was a minister of the circumcision for the truth of God, to confirm the promises made unto the fathers: ⁹and

that the Gentiles might glorify God for his mercy, as it is written, 'For this cause I will confess to thee among the Gentiles, and sing unto thy name'. ¹⁰And again he saith, 'Rejoice, ye Gentiles, with his people'. ¹¹And again, 'Praise the Lord, all ye Gentiles, and laud him, all ye people'. ¹²And again, Esaias saith, 'There shall be a root of Jesse, and he that shall rise to reign over the Gentiles, in him shall the Gentiles trust'. ¹³Now the God of hope fill you with all joy and peace in believing, that ye may abound in hope, through the power of the Holy Ghost.

¹⁴And I myself also am persuaded of you, my brethren, that ye also are full of goodness, filled with all knowledge, able also to admonish one another. ¹⁵Nevertheless, brethren, I have written the more boldly unto you in some sort, as putting you in mind, because of the grace that is given to me of God, ¹⁶that I should be the minister of Jesus Christ to the Gentiles, ministering the gospel of God, that the offering up of the Gentiles might be acceptable, being sanctified by the Holy Ghost. ¹⁷I have therefore whereof I may glory through Jesus Christ in those things which pertain to God. ¹⁸For I will not dare to speak of any of those things which Christ hath not wrought by me, to make the Gentiles obedient, by word and deed, ¹⁹through mighty signs and wonders, by the power of the Spirit of God, so that from Jerusalem, and round about unto Illyricum, I have fully preached the gospel of Christ. ²⁰Yea, so have I striven to preach the gospel, not where Christ was named, lest I should build upon another man's foundation: ²¹but as it is written, 'To whom he was not spoken of, they shall see: and they that have not heard shall understand'.

²²For which cause also I have been much hindered from coming to you. ²³But now having no more place in these parts, and having a great desire these many years to come unto you: ²⁴whensoever I take my journey into Spain, I will come to you: for I trust to see you in my journey, and to be brought on my way thitherward by you, if first I be somewhat filled with your company. ²⁵But now I go unto Jerusalem to minister unto the saints. ²⁶For it hath pleased them of Macedonia and Achaia to make a certain contribution for the poor saints which are at Jerusalem. ²⁷It hath pleased them verily, and their debtors they are. For if the Gentiles have been made partakers of their spiritual things, their duty is also to minister unto them in carnal things. ²⁸When therefore I have performed this, and have sealed to them this fruit, I will come by you into Spain. ²⁹And I am sure that when I come unto you, I shall come in the fulness of the blessing of the gospel of Christ.

³⁰Now I beseech you, brethren, for the Lord Jesus Christ's sake, and for the love of the Spirit, that ye strive together with me in your prayers to God for me, ³¹that I may be delivered from them that do not believe in Judea; and that my service which I have for Jerusalem may be accepted of the saints: ³²that I may come unto you with joy by the will of God, and may with you be refreshed. ³³Now the God of peace be with you all. Amen.

16 I commend unto you Phebe our sister, which is a servant of the church which is at Cenchrea: ²that ye receive her in the Lord, as becometh saints, and that ye assist her in whatsoever business she hath need of you: for she hath been a succourer of many, and of myself also. ³Greet Priscilla and Aquila my helpers in Christ Jesus: ⁴who have for my life laid down their own necks: unto whom not only I give thanks, but also all the churches of the Gentiles. ⁵Likewise greet the church that is in their house. Salute my well-beloved Epaenetus, who is the first-fruits of Achaia unto Christ. ⁶Greet Mary, who bestowed much labour on us. ⁷Salute Andronicus and Junia, my kinsmen, and my fellow-prisoners, who are of note among the apostles, who also were in Christ before me. ⁸Greet Amplias my beloved in the Lord. ⁹Salute Urbane, our helper in Christ, and Stachys my beloved. ¹⁰Salute Apelles approved in Christ. Salute them which are of Aristobulus' household. ¹¹Salute Herodion my kinsman. Greet them that be of the household of Narcissus, which are in the Lord. ¹²Salute Tryphena and Tryphosa, who labour in the Lord. Salute the beloved Persis, which laboured much in the Lord. ¹³Salute Rufus chosen in the Lord, and his mother and mine. ¹⁴Salute Asyncritus, Phlegon, Hermas, Patrobas, Hermes, and the brethren which are with them. ¹⁵Salute Philologus, and Julia, Nereus, and his sister, and Olympas, and all the saints which are with them. ¹⁶Salute one another with a holy kiss. The churches of Christ salute you.

¹⁷Now I beseech you, brethren, mark them which cause divisions and offences contrary to the doctrine which ye have learned, and avoid them. ¹⁸For they that are such serve not our Lord Jesus Christ, but their own belly, and by good words and fair speeches deceive the hearts of the simple. ¹⁹For your obedience is come abroad unto all men. I am glad therefore on your behalf: but yet I would have you wise unto that which is good, and simple concerning evil. ²⁰And the God of peace shall bruise Satan under your feet shortly. The grace of our Lord Jesus Christ be with you. Amen.

²¹Timothy my work-fellow, and Lucius, and Jason, and Sosipater, my kinsmen, salute you. ²²I Tertius, who wrote this epistle, salute you in the Lord. ²³Gaius my host, and of the whole church, saluteth you. Erastus the chamberlain of the city saluteth you, and Quartus a brother. ²⁴The grace of our Lord Jesus Christ be with you all. Amen.

²⁵Now to him that is of power to establish you according to my gospel, and the preaching of Jesus Christ, according to the revelation of the mystery, which was kept secret since the world began, ²⁶but now is made manifest, and by the scriptures of the prophets, according to the commandment of the everlasting God, made known to all nations for the obedience of faith: ²⁷to God only wise, be glory through Jesus Christ for ever. Amen.

Written to the Romans from Corinthus and sent by Phebe servant of the Church at Cenchrea.

THE FIRST EPISTLE
OF PAUL THE APOSTLE TO THE
CORINTHIANS

1 Paul, called to be an apostle of Jesus Christ through the will of God, and Sosthenes our brother, ²unto the church of God which is at Corinth, to them that are sanctified in Christ Jesus, called to be saints, with all that in every place call upon the name of Jesus Christ our Lord, both theirs and ours. ³Grace be unto you, and peace, from God our Father, and from the Lord Jesus Christ.

⁴I thank my God always on your behalf, for the grace of God which is given you by Jesus Christ, ⁵that in everything ye are enriched by him, in all utterance, and in all knowledge: ⁶even as the testimony of Christ was confirmed in you: ⁷so that ye come behind in no gift; waiting for the coming of our Lord Jesus Christ,⁸who shall also confirm you unto the end, that ye may be blameless in the day of our Lord Jesus Christ.⁹God is faithful by whom ye were called unto the fellowship of his Son Jesus Christ our Lord.

¹⁰Now I beseech you, brethren, by the name of our Lord Jesus Christ, that ye all speak the same thing, and that there be no divisions among you: but that ye be perfectly joined together in the same mind and in the same judgement. ¹¹For it hath been declared unto me of you, my brethren, by them which are of the house of Chloe, that there are contentions among you. ¹²Now this I say, that every one of you saith, 'I am of Paul', and 'I of Apollos', and 'I of Cephas', and 'I of Christ'. ¹³Is Christ divided? was Paul crucified for you? or were ye baptized in the name of Paul? ¹⁴I thank God that I baptized none of you, but Crispus and Gaius: ¹⁵lest any should say that I had baptized in my own name. ¹⁶And I baptized also the household of Stephanas: besides, I know not whether I baptized any others. ¹⁷For Christ sent me not to baptize, but to preach the gospel: not with wisdom of words, lest the cross of Christ should be made of no effect.

¹⁸For the preaching of the cross is to them that perish foolishness: but unto us which are saved, it is the power of God. ¹⁹For it is written, 'I will destroy the wisdom of the wise, and will bring to nothing the understanding of the prudent'. ²⁰Where is the wise? where is the scribe? where is the disputer of this world? Hath not God made foolish the wisdom of this world? ²¹For after that in the wisdom of God the world by wisdom knew not God, it pleased God by the foolishness of preaching to save them that believe. ²²For the Jews require a sign, and the Greeks seek after wisdom: ²³but we preach Christ crucified, unto the Jews a stumbling-block, and unto the Greeks foolishness: ²⁴but unto them which are called, both Jews and Greeks, Christ the power of God, and the wisdom of God. ²⁵Because the foolishness of God is wiser than men: and the weakness of God is stronger than men. ²⁶For ye see your

calling, brethren, how that not many wise men after the flesh, not many mighty, not many noble, are called. [27]But God hath chosen the foolish things of the world to confound the wise: and God hath chosen the weak things of the world to confound the things which are mighty. [28]And base things of the world, and things which are despised, hath God chosen, yea, and things which are not, to bring to nought things that are, [29]that no flesh should glory in his presence. [30]But of him are ye in Christ Jesus, who of God is made unto us wisdom, and righteousness, and sanctification, and redemption: [31]that, according as it is written, 'He that glorieth, let him glory in the Lord'.

2 And I, brethren, when I came to you, came not with excellence of speech or of wisdom, declaring unto you the testimony of God. [2]For I determined not to know anything among you, save Jesus Christ, and him crucified. [3]And I was with you in weakness, and in fear, and in much trembling. [4]And my speech and my preaching was not with enticing words of man's wisdom, but in demonstration of the Spirit and of power: [5]that your faith should not stand in the wisdom of men, but in the power of God.

[6]Howbeit we speak wisdom among them that are perfect: yet not the wisdom of this world, nor of the princes of this world, that come to nought: [7]but we speak the wisdom of God in a mystery, even the hidden wisdom, which God ordained before the world unto our glory: [8]which none of the princes of this world knew: for had they known it, they would not have crucified the Lord of glory. [9]But as it is written, 'Eye hath not seen, nor ear heard, neither have entered into the heart of man, the things which God hath prepared for them that love him'. [10]But God hath revealed them unto us by his Spirit: for the Spirit searcheth all things, yea, the deep things of God. [11]For what man knoweth the things of a man, save the spirit of man which is in him? Even so the things of God knoweth no man, but the Spirit of God. [12]Now we have received, not the spirit of the world, but the Spirit which is of God, that we might know the things that are freely given to us of God. [13]Which things also we speak, not in the words which man's wisdom teacheth, but which the Holy Ghost teacheth, comparing spiritual things with spiritual. [14]But the natural man receiveth not the things of the Spirit of God, for they are foolishness unto him: neither can he know them, because they are spiritually discerned. [15]But he that is spiritual judgeth all things, yet he himself is judged of no man. [16]For who hath known the mind of the Lord, that he may instruct him? But we have the mind of Christ.

3 And I, brethren, could not speak unto you as unto spiritual, but as unto carnal, even as unto babes in Christ. [2]I have fed you with milk, and not with meat: for hitherto ye were not able to bear it, neither yet now are ye able. [3]For ye are yet carnal: for whereas there is among you envying, and strife, and divisions, are ye not carnal, and walk as men? [4]For while one saith, 'I am of Paul', and another, 'I am of Apollos', are ye not carnal? [5]Who then is Paul, and who is Apollos, but ministers by whom ye believed, even as the Lord gave to every man? [6]I have planted,

Apollos watered: but God gave the increase. ⁷So then neither is he that planteth anything, neither he that watereth: but God that giveth the increase. ⁸Now he that planteth and he that watereth are one: and every man shall receive his own reward according to his own labour. ⁹For we are labourers together with God, ye are God's husbandry, ye are God's building.

¹⁰According to the grace of God which is given unto me, as a wise master-builder, I have laid the foundation, and another buildeth thereon. But let every man take heed how he buildeth thereupon. ¹¹For other foundation can no man lay than that is laid, which is Jesus Christ. ¹²Now if any man build upon this foundation gold, silver, precious stones, wood, hay, stubble: ¹³every man's work shall be made manifest. For the day shall declare it, because it shall be revealed by fire, and the fire shall try every man's work of what sort it is. ¹⁴If any man's work abide which he hath built thereupon, he shall receive a reward. ¹⁵If any man's work shall be burnt, he shall suffer loss: but he himself shall be saved: yet so as by fire. ¹⁶Know ye not that ye are the temple of God, and that the Spirit of God dwelleth in you? ¹⁷If any man defile the temple of God, him shall God destroy: for the temple of God is holy, which temple ye are.

¹⁸Let no man deceive himself. If any man among you seemeth to be wise in this world, let him become a fool, that he may be wise. ¹⁹For the wisdom of this world is foolishness with God: for it is written, 'He taketh the wise in their own craftiness'. ²⁰And again, 'The Lord knoweth the thoughts of the wise, that they are vain'. ²¹Therefore let no man glory in men, for all things are yours. ²²Whether Paul, or Apollos, or Cephas, or the world, or life, or death, or things present, or things to come, all are yours. ²³And ye are Christ's; and Christ is God's.

4 Let a man so account of us, as of the ministers of Christ, and stewards of the mysteries of God. ²Moreover it is required in stewards, that a man be found faithful. ³But with me it is a very small thing that I should be judged of you, or of man's judgement: yea, I judge not my own self. ⁴For I know nothing by myself, yet am I not hereby justified: but he that judgeth me is the Lord. ⁵Therefore judge nothing before the time, until the Lord come, who both will bring to light the hidden things of darkness, and will make manifest the counsels of the hearts: and then shall every man have praise of God.

⁶And these things, brethren, I have in a figure transferred to myself and to Apollos for your sakes: that ye might learn in us not to think of men above that which is written, that no one of you be puffed up for one against another. ⁷For who maketh thee to differ from another? And what hast thou that thou didst not receive? Now if thou didst receive it, why dost thou glory, as if thou hadst not received it? ⁸Now ye are full, now ye are rich, ye have reigned as kings without us, and I would to God ye did reign, that we also might reign with you. ⁹For I think that God hath set forth us the apostles last, as it were approved to death. For we are made a spectacle unto the world, and to angels, and to men. ¹⁰We are fools for Christ's sake, but ye are wise in Christ. We are weak,

but ye are strong: ye are honourable, but we are despised. ¹¹Even unto this present hour we both hunger, and thirst, and are naked, and are buffeted, and have no certain dwelling-place, ¹²and labour, working with our own hands: being reviled, we bless: being persecuted, we suffer it: ¹³being defamed, we entreat: we are made as the filth of the world, and are the offscouring of all things unto this day.

¹⁴I write not these things to shame you, but as my beloved sons I warn you. ¹⁵For though you have ten thousand instructors in Christ, yet have ye not many fathers: for in Christ Jesus I have begotten you through the gospel. ¹⁶Wherefore I beseech you, be ye followers of me. ¹⁷For this cause have I sent unto you Timothy, who is my beloved son, and faithful in the Lord, who shall bring you into remembrance of my ways which be in Christ, as I teach everywhere in every church. ¹⁸Now some are puffed up, as though I would not come to you. ¹⁹But I will come to you shortly, if the Lord will, and will know, not the speech of them which are puffed up, but the power. ²⁰For the kingdom of God is not in word, but in power. ²¹What will ye? Shall I come unto you with a rod, or in love, and in the spirit of meekness?

5 It is reported commonly that there is fornication among you, and such fornication as is not so much as named amongst the Gentiles, that one should have his father's wife. ²And ye are puffed up, and have not rather mourned, that he that hath done this deed might be taken away from among you. ³For I verily, as absent in body, but present in spirit, have judged already, as though I were present, concerning him that hath so done this deed, ⁴in the name of our Lord Jesus Christ, when ye are gathered together, and my spirit, with the power of our Lord Jesus Christ, ⁵to deliver such a one unto Satan for the destruction of the flesh, that the spirit may be saved in the day of the Lord Jesus.

⁶Your glorying is not good: know ye not that a little leaven leaveneth the whole lump? ⁷Purge out therefore the old leaven, that ye may be a new lump, as ye are unleavened. For even Christ our passover is sacrificed for us. ⁸Therefore let us keep the feast, not with old leaven, neither with the leaven of malice and wickedness: but with the unleavened bread of sincerity and truth.

⁹I wrote unto you in an epistle not to company with fornicators: ¹⁰yet not altogether with the fornicators of this world, or with the covetous, or extortioners, or with idolaters; for then must ye needs go out of the world. ¹¹But now I have written unto you not to keep company, if any man that is called a brother be a fornicator, or covetous, or an idolater, or a railer, or a drunkard, or an extortioner: with such a one, no, not to eat. ¹²For what have I to do to judge them also that are without? do not ye judge them that are within? ¹³But them that are without, God judgeth. Therefore put away from among yourselves that wicked person.

6 Dare any of you, having a matter against another, go to law before the unjust, and not before the saints? ²Do ye not know that the saints shall judge the world? And if the world shall be judged by you, are ye unworthy to judge the smallest matters? ³Know ye not that we shall judge angels? How much more things that pertain to this life?

[4]If then ye have judgements of things pertaining to this life, set them to judge who are least esteemed in the church. [5]I speak to your shame. Is it so, that there is not a wise man amongst you? no, not one that shall be able to judge between his brethren? [6]But brother goeth to law with brother, and that before the unbelievers. [7]Now therefore there is utterly a fault among you, because ye go to law one with another. Why do ye not rather take wrong? Why do ye not rather suffer yourselves to be defrauded? [8]Nay, you do wrong, and defraud, and that your brethren. [9]Know ye not that the unrighteous shall not inherit the kingdom of God? Be not deceived: neither fornicators, nor idolaters, nor adulterers, nor effeminate, nor abusers of themselves with mankind, [10]nor thieves, nor covetous, nor drunkards, nor revilers, nor extortioners, shall inherit the kingdom of God. [11]And such were some of you: but ye are washed, but ye are sanctified, but ye are justified in the name of the Lord Jesus, and by the Spirit of our God.

[12]All things are lawful unto me, but all things are not expedient: all things are lawful for me, but I will not be brought under the power of any. [13]Meats for the belly, and the belly for meats: but God shall destroy both it and them. Now the body is not for fornication, but for the Lord: and the Lord for the body. [14]And God hath both raised up the Lord, and will also raise up us by his own power. [15]Know ye not that your bodies are the members of Christ? Shall I then take the members of Christ, and make them the members of a harlot? God forbid. [16]What? know ye not that he which is joined to a harlot is one body? 'For two,' saith he, 'shall be one flesh.' [17]But he that is joined unto the Lord is one spirit. [18]Flee fornication: every sin that a man doeth is without the body: but he that committeth fornication sinneth against his own body. [19]What? know ye not that your body is the temple of the Holy Ghost which is in you, which ye have of God, and ye are not your own? [20]For ye are bought with a price: therefore glorify God in your body, and in your spirit, which are God's.

7 Now concerning the things whereof ye wrote unto me: 'It is good for a man not to touch a woman'. [2]Nevertheless, to avoid fornication, let every man have his own wife, and let every woman have her own husband. [3]Let the husband render unto the wife due benevolence: and likewise also the wife unto the husband. [4]The wife hath not power of her own body, but the husband: and likewise also the husband hath not power of his own body, but the wife. [5]Defraud you not one the other, except it be with consent for a time, that ye may give yourselves to fasting and prayer, and come together again, that Satan tempt you not for your incontinence. [6]But I speak this by permission, and not of commandment. [7]For I would that all men were even as I myself: but every man hath his proper gift of God, one after this manner, and another after that.

[8]I say therefore to the unmarried and widows, it is good for them if they abide even as I. [9]But if they cannot contain, let them marry: for it is better to marry than to burn.

[10]And unto the married I command, yet not I, but the Lord, let not

the wife depart from her husband: ¹¹but and if she depart, let her remain unmarried, or be reconciled to her husband: and let not the husband put away his wife.

¹²But to the rest speak I, not the Lord: if any brother hath a wife that believeth not, and she be pleased to dwell with him, let him not put her away. ¹³And the woman which hath an husband that believeth not, and if he be pleased to dwell with her, let her not leave him. ¹⁴For the unbelieving husband is sanctified by the wife, and the unbelieving wife is sanctified by the husband; else were your children unclean, but now are they holy. ¹⁵But if the unbelieving depart, let him depart. A brother or a sister is not under bondage in such cases: but God hath called us to peace. ¹⁶For what knowest thou, O wife, whether thou shalt save thy husband? or how knowest thou, O man, whether thou shalt save thy wife?

¹⁷But as God hath distributed to every man, as the Lord hath called every one, so let him walk. And so ordain I in all churches. ¹⁸Is any man called being circumcised? let him not become uncircumcised. Is any called in uncircumcision? let him not be circumcised. ¹⁹Circumcision is nothing, and uncircumcision is nothing, but the keeping of the commandments of God. ²⁰Let every man abide in the same calling wherein he was called. ²¹Art thou called being a servant? care not for it: but if thou mayest be made free, use it rather. ²²For he that is called in the Lord, being a servant, is the Lord's freeman: likewise also he that is called, being free, is Christ's servant. ²³Ye are bought with a price, be not ye the servants of men. ²⁴Brethren, let every man, wherein he is called, therein abide with God.

²⁵Now concerning virgins I have no commandment of the Lord: yet I give my judgement as one that hath obtained mercy of the Lord to be faithful. ²⁶I suppose therefore that this is good for the present distress, I say, that it is good for a man so to be. ²⁷Art thou bound unto a wife? seek not to be loosed. Art thou loosed from a wife? seek not a wife. ²⁸But and if thou marry, thou hast not sinned, and if a virgin marry, she hath not sinned. Nevertheless such shall have trouble in the flesh: but I spare you.

²⁹But this I say, brethren, the time is short. It remaineth, that both they that have wives be as though they had none: ³⁰and they that weep, as though they wept not: and they that rejoice, as though they rejoiced not: and they that buy, as though they possessed not: ³¹and they that use this world, as not abusing it: for the fashion of this world passeth away.

³²But I would have you without carefulness. He that is unmarried careth for the things that belong to the Lord, how he may please the Lord: ³³but he that is married careth for the things that are of the world, how he may please his wife. ³⁴There is difference also between a wife and a virgin: the unmarried woman careth for the things of the Lord, that she may be holy both in body and in spirit: but she that is married careth for the things of the world, how she may please her husband. ³⁵And this I speak for your own profit, not that I may cast a snare

upon you, but for that which is comely, and that you may attend upon the Lord without distraction. ³⁶But if any man think that he behaveth himself uncomely toward his virgin, if she pass the flower of her age, and need so require, let him do what he will, he sinneth not: let them marry. ³⁷Nevertheless he that standeth steadfast in his heart, having no necessity, but hath power over his own will, and hath so decreed in his heart that he will keep his virgin, doeth well. ³⁸So then he that giveth her in marriage doeth well: but he that giveth her not in marriage doeth better. ³⁹The wife is bound by the law as long as her husband liveth: but if her husband be dead, she is at liberty to be married to whom she will, only in the Lord. ⁴⁰But she is happier if she so abide, after my judgement: and I think also that I have the Spirit of God.

8 Now as touching things offered unto idols, we know that we all have knowledge. Knowledge puffeth up: but charity edifieth. ²And if any man think that he knoweth anything, he knoweth nothing yet as he ought to know. ³But if any man love God, the same is known of him. ⁴As concerning therefore the eating of those things that are offered in sacrifice unto idols, we know that an idol is nothing in the world, and that there is no other God but one. ⁵For though there be that are called gods, whether in heaven or in earth (as there be gods many, and lords many), ⁶but to us there is but one God, the Father, of whom are all things, and we in him, and one Lord Jesus Christ, by whom are all things, and we by him.

⁷Howbeit there is not in every man that knowledge: for some with conscience of the idol unto this hour eat it as a thing offered unto an idol, and their conscience being weak is defiled. ⁸But meat commendeth us not to God: for neither, if we eat, are we the better: neither, if we eat not, are we the worse. ⁹But take heed lest by any means this liberty of yours become a stumbling-block to them that are weak. ¹⁰For if any man see thee which hast knowledge sit at meat in the idol's temple, shall not the conscience of him which is weak be emboldened to eat those things which are offered to idols? ¹¹And through thy knowledge shall the weak brother perish, for whom Christ died? ¹²But when ye sin so against the brethren, and wound their weak conscience, ye sin against Christ. ¹³Wherefore, if meat make my brother to offend, I will eat no flesh while the world standeth, lest I make my brother to offend.

9 Am I not an apostle? am I not free? have I not seen Jesus Christ our Lord? Are not you my work in the Lord? ²If I be not an apostle unto others, yet doubtless I am to you: for the seal of my apostleship are ye in the Lord.

³My answer to them that do examine me is this, ⁴have we not power to eat and to drink? ⁵have we not power to lead about a sister, a wife, as well as other apostles, and as the brethren of the Lord, and Cephas? ⁶Or I only and Barnabas, have not we power to forbear working? ⁷Who goeth a warfare any time at his own charges? who planteth a vineyard, and eateth not of the fruit thereof? or who feedeth a flock, and eateth not of the milk of the flock? ⁸Say I these things as a man? or saith not the law the same also? ⁹For it is written in the law of Moses, 'Thou shalt

not muzzle the mouth of the ox that treadeth out the corn'. Doth God take care for oxen? [10]Or saith he it altogether for our sakes? For our sakes, no doubt, this is written: that he that plougheth should plough in hope: and that he that thresheth in hope should be partaker of his hope. [11]If we have sown unto you spiritual things, is it a great thing if we shall reap your carnal things? [12]If others be partakers of this power over you, are not we rather? Nevertheless we have not used this power: but suffer all things, lest we should hinder the gospel of Christ. [13]Do ye not know that they which minister about holy things live of the things of the temple? and they which wait at the altar are partakers with the altar? [14]Even so hath the Lord ordained that they which preach the gospel should live of the gospel. [15]But I have used none of these things. Neither have I written these things, that it should be so done unto me: for it were better for me to die, than that any man should make my glorying void. [16]For though I preach the gospel, I have nothing to glory of: for necessity is laid upon me, yea, woe is unto me, if I preach not the gospel. [17]For if I do this thing willingly, I have a reward: but if against my will, a dispensation of the gospel is committed unto me.

[18]What is my reward then? Verily that, when I preach the gospel, I may make the gospel of Christ without charge, that I abuse not my power in the gospel. [19]For though I be free from all men, yet have I made myself servant unto all, that I might gain the more. [20]And unto the Jews I became as a Jew, that I might gain the Jews: to them that are under the law, as under the law, that I might gain them that are under the law: [21]to them that are without law, as without law (being not without law to God, but under the law to Christ), that I might gain them that are without law. [22]To the weak became I as weak, that I might gain the weak: I am made all things to all men, that I might by all means save some. [23]And this I do for the gospel's sake, that I might be partaker thereof with you.

[24]Know ye not that they which run in a race run all, but one receiveth the prize? So run, that ye may obtain. [25]And every man that striveth for the mastery is temperate in all things. Now they do it to obtain a corruptible crown, but we an incorruptible. [26]I therefore so run, not as uncertainly: so fight I, not as one that beateth the air: [27]but I keep under my body, and bring it into subjection: lest that by any means, when I have preached to others, I myself should be a castaway.

10 Moreover, brethren, I would not that ye should be ignorant, how that all our fathers were under the cloud, and all passed through the sea: [2]and were all baptized unto Moses in the cloud and in the sea; [3]and did all eat the same spiritual meat: [4]and did all drink the same spiritual drink: for they drank of that spiritual Rock that followed them: and that Rock was Christ. [5]But with many of them God was not well pleased: for they were overthrown in the wilderness.

[6]Now these things were our examples, to the intent we should not lust after evil things, as they also lusted. [7]Neither be ye idolaters, as were some of them, as it is written, 'The people sat down to eat and drink, and rose up to play'. [8]Neither let us commit fornication, as some

of them committed, and fell in one day three and twenty thousand. ⁹Neither let us tempt Christ, as some of them also tempted, and were destroyed of serpents. ¹⁰Neither murmur ye, as some of them also murmured, and were destroyed of the destroyer.

¹¹Now all these things happened unto them for examples: and they are written for our admonition, upon whom the ends of the world are come. ¹²Wherefore let him that thinketh he standeth take heed lest he fall. ¹³There hath no temptation taken you but such as is common to man: but God is faithful, who will not suffer you to be tempted above that you are able: but will with the temptation also make a way to escape, that ye may be able to bear it.

¹⁴Wherefore, my dearly beloved, flee from idolatry. ¹⁵I speak as to wise men: judge ye what I say. ¹⁶The cup of blessing which we bless, is it not the communion of the blood of Christ? The bread which we break, is it not the communion of the body of Christ? ¹⁷For we being many are one bread, and one body: for we are all partakers of that one bread.

¹⁸Behold Israel after the flesh: are not they which eat of the sacrifices partakers of the altar? ¹⁹What say I then? that the idol is anything, or that which is offered in sacrifice to idols is anything? ²⁰But I say, that the things which the Gentiles sacrifice, they sacrifice to devils, and not to God: and I would not that ye should have fellowship with devils. ²¹Ye cannot drink the cup of the Lord, and the cup of devils: ye cannot be partakers of the Lord's table, and of the table of devils. ²²Do we provoke the Lord to jealousy? are we stronger than he?

²³All things are lawful for me, but all things are not expedient: all things are lawful for me, but all things edify not. ²⁴Let no man seek his own, but every man another's wealth.

²⁵Whatsoever is sold in the shambles, that eat, asking no question for conscience sake. ²⁶For the earth is the Lord's, and the fulness thereof.

²⁷If any of them that believe not bid you to a feast, and ye be disposed to go, whatsoever is set before you, eat, asking no question for conscience sake. ²⁸But if any man say unto you, 'This is offered in sacrifice unto idols', eat not for his sake that showed it, and for conscience sake. The earth is the Lord's, and the fulness thereof. ²⁹Conscience, I say, not thy own, but of the other: for why is my liberty judged of another man's conscience? ³⁰For if I by grace be a partaker, why am I evil spoken of for that for which I give thanks? ³¹Whether therefore ye eat or drink, or whatsoever ye do, do all to the glory of God. ³²Give no offence, neither to the Jews, nor to the Gentiles, nor to the church of God: ³³even as I please all men in all things, not seeking my own profit, but the profit of many, that they may be saved.

11 Be ye followers of me, even as I also am of Christ. ²Now I praise you, brethren, that you remember me in all things, and keep the ordinances, as I delivered them to you. ³But I would have you know, that the head of every man is Christ: and the head of the woman is the man, and the head of Christ is God. ⁴Every man praying or prophesying, having his head covered, dishonoureth his head. ⁵But every woman that prayeth or prophesieth with her head uncovered dishonoureth her head: for that is even all one as if she were shaven. ⁶For if the woman be not covered, let her also be shorn: but if it be a shame for a woman to be shorn or shaven, let her be covered. ⁷For a man indeed ought not to cover his head, forasmuch as he is the image and glory of God: but the woman is the glory of the man. ⁸For the man is not of the woman: but the woman of the man. ⁹Neither was the man created for the woman: but the woman for the man. ¹⁰For this cause ought the woman to have power on her head because of the angels. ¹¹Nevertheless neither is the man without the woman, neither the woman without the man, in the Lord. ¹²For as the woman is of the man, even so is the man also by the woman; but all things of God.

¹³Judge in yourselves, is it comely that a woman pray unto God uncovered? ¹⁴Doth not even nature itself teach you, that, if a man have long hair, it is a shame unto him? ¹⁵But if a woman have long hair, it is a glory to her: for her hair is given her for a covering. ¹⁶But if any man seem to be contentious, we have no such custom, neither the churches of God.

¹⁷Now in this that I declare unto you I praise you not, that you come together not for the better, but for the worse. ¹⁸For first of all, when ye come together in the church, I hear that there be divisions among you, and I partly believe it. ¹⁹For there must be also heresies among you, that they which are approved may be made manifest among you. ²⁰When ye come together therefore into one place, this is not to eat the Lord's supper. ²¹For in eating every one taketh before other his own supper: and one is hungry, and another is drunken. ²²What? have ye not houses to eat and to drink in? Or despise ye the church of God, and shame them that have not? What shall I say to you? shall I praise you in this? I praise you not. ²³For I have received of the Lord that which also I delivered unto you, that the Lord Jesus the same night in which he was betrayed took bread: ²⁴and when he had given thanks, he broke it, and said, 'Take, eat, this is my body, which is broken for you: this do in remembrance of me'. ²⁵After the same manner also he took the cup, when he had supped, saying, 'This cup is the new testament in my blood: this do ye, as oft as ye drink it, in remembrance of me'. ²⁶For as often as ye eat this bread, and drink this cup, ye do show the Lord's death till he come. ²⁷Wherefore whosoever shall eat this bread, and drink this cup of the Lord unworthily, shall be guilty of the body and blood of the Lord. ²⁸But let a man examine himself, and so let him eat of that bread, and drink of that cup. ²⁹For he that eateth and drinketh unworthily, eateth and drinketh damnation to himself, not discerning the Lord's body. ³⁰For this cause many are weak and sickly among you, and many sleep. ³¹For if we would judge ourselves, we should not be judged. ³²But when we are judged, we are chastened of the Lord, that we should not be condemned with the world. ³³Wherefore, my brethren, when ye come together to eat, tarry one for another. ³⁴And if any man hunger, let him eat at home, that ye come not together unto condemnation. And the rest will I set in order when I come.

12 Now concerning spiritual gifts, brethren, I would not have you ignorant. ²Ye know that ye were Gentiles, carried away unto these dumb idols, even as ye were led. ³Wherefore I give you to understand, that no man speaking by the Spirit of God calleth Jesus accursed: and that no man can say that Jesus is the Lord, but by the Holy Ghost.

⁴Now there are diversities of gifts, but the same Spirit. ⁵And there are differences of administrations, but the same Lord. ⁶And there are diversities of operations, but it is the same God which worketh all in all. ⁷But the manifestation of the Spirit is given to every man to profit withal. ⁸For to one is given by the Spirit the word of wisdom, to another the word of knowledge by the same Spirit: ⁹to another faith by the same Spirit: to another the gifts of healing by the same Spirit: ¹⁰to another the working of miracles, to another prophecy, to another discerning of spirits, to another divers kinds of tongues, to another the interpretation of tongues: ¹¹but all these worketh that one and the selfsame Spirit, dividing to every man severally as he will.

¹²For as the body is one, and hath many members, and all the members of that one body, being many, are one body: so also is Christ. ¹³For by one Spirit are we all baptized into one body, whether we be Jews or Gentiles, whether we be bond or free: and have been all made to drink into one Spirit. ¹⁴For the body is not one member, but many. ¹⁵If the foot shall say, 'Because I am not the hand, I am not of the body': is it therefore not of the body? ¹⁶And if the ear shall say, 'Because I am not the eye, I am not of the body': is it therefore not of the body? ¹⁷If the whole body were an eye, where were the hearing? If the whole were hearing, where were the smelling? ¹⁸But now hath God set the members every one of them in the body, as it hath pleased him. ¹⁹And if they were all one member, where were the body? ²⁰But now are they many members, yet but one body. ²¹And the eye cannot say unto the hand, 'I have no need of thee': nor again the head to the feet, 'I have no need of you'. ²²Nay, much more those members of the body, which seem to be more feeble, are necessary. ²³And those members of the body, which we think to be less honourable, upon these we bestow more abundant honour, and our uncomely parts have more abundant comeliness. ²⁴For our comely parts have no need: but God hath tempered the body together, having given more abundant honour to that part which lacked: ²⁵that there should be no schism in the body, but that the members should have the same care one for another. ²⁶And whether one member suffer, all the members suffer with it: or one member be honoured, all the members rejoice with it.

²⁷Now ye are the body of Christ, and members in particular. ²⁸And God hath set some in the church, first apostles, secondarily prophets, thirdly teachers, after that miracles, then gifts of healings, helps in governments, diversities of tongues. ²⁹Are all apostles? are all prophets? are all teachers? are all workers of miracles? ³⁰have all the gifts of healing? do all speak with tongues? do all interpret? ³¹But covet earnestly the best gifts: and yet show I unto you a more excellent way.

13 Though I speak with the tongues of men and of angels, and have not charity, I am become as sounding brass, or a tinkling cymbal. ²And though I have the gift of prophecy, and understand all mysteries, and all knowledge: and though I have all faith, so that I could remove mountains, and have no charity, I am nothing. ³And though I bestow all my goods to feed the poor, and though I give my body to be burnt, and have not charity, it profiteth me nothing.

⁴Charity suffereth long, and is kind: charity envieth not: charity vaunteth not itself, is not puffed up, ⁵doth not behave itself unseemly, seeketh not her own, is not easily provoked, thinketh no evil, ⁶rejoiceth not in iniquity, but rejoiceth in the truth: ⁷beareth all things, believeth all things, hopeth all things, endureth all things.

⁸Charity never faileth: but whether there be prophecies, they shall fail; whether there be tongues, they shall cease; whether there be knowledge, it shall vanish away. ⁹For we know in part, and we prophesy in part. ¹⁰But when that which is perfect is come, then that which is in part shall be done away.

¹¹When I was a child, I spoke as a child, I understood as a child, I thought as a child: but when I became a man, I put away childish things. ¹²For now we see through a glass, darkly: but then face to face: now I know in part; but then shall I know even as also I am known. ¹³And now abideth faith, hope, charity, these three, but the greatest of these is charity.

14 Follow after charity, and desire spiritual gifts, but rather that ye may prophesy. ²For he that speaketh in an unknown tongue speaketh not unto men, but unto God: for no man understandeth him: howbeit in the spirit he speaketh mysteries. ³But he that prophesieth speaketh unto men to edification, and exhortation, and comfort. ⁴He that speaketh in an unknown tongue edifieth himself: but he that prophesieth edifieth the church. ⁵I would that ye all spoke with tongues, but rather that ye prophesied: for greater is he that prophesieth than he that speaketh with tongues, except he interpret, that the church may receive edifying. ⁶Now, brethren, if I come unto you speaking with tongues, what shall I profit you, except I shall speak to you either by revelation, or by knowledge, or by prophesying, or by doctrine? ⁷And even things without life giving sound, whether pipe or harp, except they give a distinction in the sounds, how shall it be known what is piped or harped? ⁸For if the trumpet give an uncertain sound, who shall prepare himself to the battle? ⁹So likewise you, except ye utter by the tongue words easy to be understood, how shall it be known what is spoken? for ye shall speak into the air. ¹⁰There are, it may be, so many kinds of voices in the world, and none of them is without signification. ¹¹Therefore if I know not the meaning of the voice, I shall be unto him that speaketh a barbarian, and he that speaketh shall be a barbarian unto me. ¹²Even so ye, forasmuch as ye are zealous of spiritual gifts, seek that ye may excel to the edifying of the church. ¹³Wherefore let him that speaketh in an unknown tongue pray that he may interpret. ¹⁴For if I pray in an unknown tongue, my spirit prayeth, but my understanding is unfruitful. ¹⁵What is it then? I will pray with the spirit, and will pray with the understanding also: I will sing with the spirit, and I will sing with the understanding also. ¹⁶Else when thou shalt bless with the spirit, how shall he that occupieth the room of the unlearned say 'Amen' at thy giving of thanks, seeing he understandeth not what thou sayest? ¹⁷For thou verily givest thanks well, but the other is not edified.

¹⁸I thank my God, I speak with tongues more than you all. ¹⁹Yet in the church I had rather speak five words with my understanding, that by my voice I might teach others also, than ten thousand words in an unknown tongue.

²⁰Brethren, be not children in understanding: howbeit in malice be ye children, but in understanding be men. ²¹In the law it is written, '"With men of other tongues and other lips will I speak unto this people: and yet for all that will they not hear me," saith the Lord'. ²²Wherefore tongues are for a sign, not to them that believe, but to them that believe not: but prophesying serveth not for them that believe not, but for them which believe. ²³If therefore the whole church be come together into some place, and all speak with tongues, and there come in those that are unlearned, or unbelievers, will they not say that ye are mad? ²⁴But if all prophesy, and there come in one that believeth not, or one unlearned, he is convinced of all, he is judged of all. ²⁵And thus are the secrets of his heart made manifest, and so falling down on his face he will worship God, and report that God is in you of a truth.

²⁶How is it then, brethren? when ye come together, every one of you hath a psalm, hath a doctrine, hath a tongue, hath a revelation, hath an interpretation: let all things be done unto edifying. ²⁷If any man speak in an unknown tongue, let it be by two, or at the most by three, and that by course, and let one interpret. ²⁸But if there be no interpreter, let him keep silence in the church, and let him speak to himself, and to God. ²⁹Let the prophets speak two or three, and let the others judge. ³⁰If anything be revealed to another that sitteth by, let the first hold his peace. ³¹For ye may all prophesy one by one, that all may learn, and all may be comforted. ³²And the spirits of the prophets are subject to the prophets. ³³For God is not the author of confusion, but of peace, as in all churches of the saints.

³⁴Let your women keep silence in the churches, for it is not permitted unto them to speak; but they are commanded to be under obedience: as also saith the law. ³⁵And if they will learn anything, let them ask their husbands at home: for it is a shame for women to speak in the church.

³⁶What? came the word of God out from you? or came it unto you only? ³⁷If any man think himself to be a prophet, or spiritual, let him acknowledge that the things that I write unto you are the commandments of the Lord. ³⁸But if any man be ignorant, let him be ignorant. ³⁹Wherefore, brethren, covet to prophesy, and forbid not to speak with tongues. ⁴⁰Let all things be done decently and in order.

15 Moreover, brethren, I declare unto you the gospel which I preached unto you, which also you have received, and wherein ye stand; ²by which also ye are saved, if ye keep in memory what I preached unto you, unless ye have believed in vain. ³For I delivered unto you first of all that which I also received, how that Christ died for our sins according to the scriptures: ⁴and that he was buried, and that he rose again the third day according to the scriptures. ⁵And that he was seen of Cephas, then of the twelve. ⁶After that, he was seen of above five hundred brethren at once: of whom the greater part remain unto this present, but some are fallen asleep. ⁷After that, he was seen of James, then of all the apostles. ⁸And last of all he was seen of me also, as of one born out of due time. ⁹For I am the least of the apostles, that am not meet to be called an apostle, because I persecuted the church of God. ¹⁰But by the grace of God I am what I am: and his grace which was bestowed upon me was not in vain: but I laboured more abundantly than they all, yet not I, but the grace of God which was with me. ¹¹Therefore whether it were I or they, so we preach, and so ye believed.

¹²Now if Christ be preached that he rose from the dead, how say some among you that there is no resurrection of the dead? ¹³But if there be no resurrection of the dead, then is Christ not risen. ¹⁴And if Christ be not risen, then is our preaching vain, and your faith is also vain. ¹⁵Yea, and we are found false witnesses of God, because we have testified of God that he raised up Christ: whom he raised not up, if so be that the dead rise not. ¹⁶For if the dead rise not, then is not Christ raised. ¹⁷And if Christ be not raised, your faith is vain, ye are yet in your sins. ¹⁸Then they also which are fallen asleep in Christ are perished. ¹⁹If in this life only we have hope in Christ, we are of all men most miserable. ²⁰But now is Christ risen from the dead, and become the first-fruits of them that slept. ²¹For since by man came death, by man came also the resurrection of the dead. ²²For as in Adam all die, even so in Christ shall all be made alive. ²³But every man in his own order: Christ the first-fruits, afterward they that are Christ's at his coming.

²⁴Then cometh the end, when he shall have delivered up the kingdom to God, even the Father, when he shall have put down all rule and all authority and power. ²⁵For he must reign, till he hath put all enemies under his feet. ²⁶The last enemy that shall be destroyed is death. ²⁷For he hath put all things under his feet; but when he saith all things are put under him, it is manifest that he is excepted, which did put all things under him. ²⁸And when all things shall be subdued unto him, then shall the Son also himself be subject unto him that put all things under him, that God may be all in all. ²⁹Else what shall they do which are baptized for the dead, if the dead rise not at all? why are they then baptized for the dead? ³⁰And why stand we in jeopardy every hour? ³¹I protest by your rejoicing which I have in Christ Jesus our Lord, I die daily. ³²If after the manner of men I have fought with beasts at Ephesus, what advantageth it me, if the dead rise not? let us eat and drink, for tomorrow we die.

³³Be not deceived: evil communications corrupt good manners. ³⁴Awake to righteousness, and sin not: for some have not the knowledge of God: I speak this to your shame.

³⁵But some man will say, 'How are the dead raised up? and with what

body do they come?' ³⁶Thou fool, that which thou sowest is not quickened, except it die. ³⁷And that which thou sowest, thou sowest not that body that shall be, but bare grain, it may chance of wheat, or of some other grain: ³⁸but God giveth it a body as it hath pleased him, and to every seed his own body. ³⁹All flesh is not the same flesh, but there is one kind of flesh of men, another flesh of beasts, another of fishes, and another of birds. ⁴⁰There are also celestial bodies, and bodies terrestrial: but the glory of the celestial is one, and the glory of the terrestrial is another. ⁴¹There is one glory of the sun, another of the moon, and another glory of the stars: for one star differeth from another star in glory. ⁴²So also is the resurrection of the dead. It is sown in corruption, it is raised in incorruption. ⁴³It is sown in dishonour, it is raised in glory: it is sown in weakness, it is raised in power: ⁴⁴it is sown a natural body, it is raised a spiritual body.

There is a natural body, and there is a spiritual body. ⁴⁵And so it is written, 'The first man Adam was made a living soul', the last Adam was made a quickening spirit. ⁴⁶Howbeit that was not first which is spiritual: but that which is natural, and afterward that which is spiritual. ⁴⁷The first man is of the earth, earthy: the second man is the Lord from heaven. ⁴⁸As is the earthy, such are they that are earthy, and as is the heavenly, such are they also that are heavenly. ⁴⁹And as we have borne the image of the earthy, we shall also bear the image of the heavenly.

⁵⁰Now this I say, brethren, that flesh and blood cannot inherit the kingdom of God: neither doth corruption inherit incorruption. ⁵¹Behold, I show you a mystery: we shall not all sleep, but we shall all be changed, ⁵²in a moment, in the twinkling of an eye, at the last trump: for the trumpet shall sound, and the dead shall be raised incorruptible, and we shall be changed. ⁵³For this corruptible must put on incorruption, and this mortal must put on immortality. ⁵⁴So when this corruptible shall have put on incorruption, and this mortal shall have put on immortality, then shall be brought to pass the saying that is written, 'Death is swallowed up in victory'. ⁵⁵O death, where is thy sting? O grave, where is thy victory? ⁵⁶The sting of death is sin, and the strength of sin is the law. ⁵⁷But thanks be to God, which giveth us the victory through our Lord Jesus Christ. ⁵⁸Therefore, my beloved brethren, be ye steadfast, immovable, always abounding in the work of the Lord, forasmuch as you know that your labour is not in vain in the Lord.

16 Now concerning the collection for the saints, as I have given order to the churches of Galatia, even so do ye. ²Upon the first day of the week let every one of you lay by him in store, as God hath prospered him, that there be no gatherings when I come. ³And when I come, whomsoever you shall approve by your letters, them will I send to bring your liberality unto Jerusalem. ⁴And if it be meet that I go also, they shall go with me.

⁵Now I will come unto you, when I shall pass through Macedonia: for I do pass through Macedonia. ⁶And it may be that I will abide, yea, and winter with you, that ye may bring me on my journey whithersoever

I go. ⁷For I will not see you now by the way, but I trust to tarry a while with you, if the Lord permit. ⁸But I will tarry at Ephesus until Pentecost. ⁹For a great door and effectual is opened unto me, and there are many adversaries.

¹⁰Now if Timothy come, see that he may be with you without fear: for he worketh the work of the Lord, as I also do. ¹¹Let no man therefore despise him: but conduct him forth in peace, that he may come unto me: for I look for him with the brethren. ¹²As touching our brother Apollos, I greatly desired him to come unto you with the brethren, but his will was not at all to come at this time: but he will come when he shall have convenient time.

¹³Watch ye, stand fast in the faith, quit you like men, be strong. ¹⁴Let all your things be done with charity.

¹⁵I beseech you, brethren (ye know the house of Stephanas, that it is the first-fruits of Achaia, and that they have addicted themselves to the ministry of the saints), ¹⁶that ye submit yourselves unto such, and to every one that helpeth with us, and laboureth. ¹⁷I am glad of the coming of Stephanas and Fortunatus and Achaicus: for that which was lacking on your part they have supplied. ¹⁸For they have refreshed my spirit and yours: therefore acknowledge ye them that are such.

¹⁹The churches of Asia salute you. Aquila and Priscilla salute you much in the Lord, with the church that is in their house. ²⁰All the brethren greet you. Greet ye one another with a holy kiss.

²¹The salutation of me Paul with my own hand.

²²If any man love not the Lord Jesus Christ, let him be anathema, Maran-atha.

²³The grace of our Lord Jesus Christ be with you.

²⁴My love be with you all in Christ Jesus. Amen.

The first epistle to the Corinthians was written from Philippi by Stephanas, and Fortunatus, and Achaicus, and Timothy.

THE SECOND EPISTLE
OF PAUL THE APOSTLE TO THE
CORINTHIANS

1 Paul, an apostle of Jesus Christ by the will of God, and Timothy our brother, unto the church of God which is at Corinth, with all the saints which are in all Achaia: ²grace be to you and peace from God our Father, and from the Lord Jesus Christ.

³Blessed be God, even the Father of our Lord Jesus Christ, the Father of mercies, and the God of all comfort, ⁴who comforteth us in all our tribulation, that we may be able to comfort them which are in any trouble, by the comfort wherewith we ourselves are comforted of God. ⁵For as the sufferings of Christ abound in us, so our consolation also aboundeth by Christ. ⁶And whether we be afflicted, it is for your consolation and salvation, which is effectual in the enduring of the same sufferings which we also suffer: or whether we be comforted, it is for your consolation and salvation. ⁷And our hope of you is steadfast, knowing, that as you are partakers of the sufferings, so shall ye be also of the consolation. ⁸For we would not, brethren, have you ignorant of our trouble which came to us in Asia, that we were pressed out of measure, above strength, insomuch that we despaired even of life. ⁹But we had the sentence of death in ourselves, that we should not trust in ourselves, but in God which raiseth the dead: ¹⁰who delivered us from so great a death, and doth deliver: in whom we trust that he will yet deliver us: ¹¹you also helping together by prayer for us, that for the gift bestowed upon us by the means of many persons thanks may be given by many on our behalf.

¹²For our rejoicing is this, the testimony of our conscience, that in simplicity and godly sincerity, not with fleshly wisdom, but by the grace of God, we have had our conversation in the world, and more abundantly to you-wards. ¹³For we write no other things unto you, than what you read or acknowledge, and I trust you shall acknowledge even to the end; ¹⁴as also you have acknowledged us in part, that we are your rejoicing, even as ye also are ours in the day of the Lord Jesus.

¹⁵And in this confidence I was minded to come unto you before, that you might have a second benefit: ¹⁶and to pass by you into Macedonia, and to come again out of Macedonia unto you, and of you to be brought on my way toward Judea. ¹⁷When I therefore was thus minded, did I use lightness? or the things that I purpose, do I purpose according to the flesh, that with me there should be yea yea, and nay nay? ¹⁸But as God is true, our word toward you was not yea and nay. ¹⁹For the Son of God, Jesus Christ, who was preached among you by us, even by me and Silvanus and Timothy, was not yea and nay, but in him was yea. ²⁰For all the promises of God in him are yea, and in him 'Amen', unto the glory of God by us. ²¹Now he which establisheth us with you in Christ, and

hath anointed us, is God, [22]who hath also sealed us, and given the earnest of the Spirit in our hearts.

[23]Moreover I call God for a record upon my soul, that to spare you I came not as yet unto Corinth. [24]Not for that we have dominion over your faith, but are helpers of your joy: for by faith ye stand.

2 But I determined this with myself, that I would not come again to you in heaviness. [2]For if I make you sorry, who is he then that maketh me glad, but the same which is made sorry by me? [3]And I wrote this same unto you, lest, when I came, I should have sorrow from them of whom I ought to rejoice, having confidence in you all, that my joy is the joy of you all. [4]For out of much affliction and anguish of heart I wrote unto you with many tears, not that you should be grieved, but that ye might know the love which I have more abundantly unto you.

[5]But if any have caused grief, he hath not grieved me, but in part: that I may not overcharge you all. [6]Sufficient to such a man is this punishment, which was inflicted of many. [7]So that contrariwise ye ought rather to forgive him, and comfort him, lest perhaps such a one should be swallowed up with overmuch sorrow. [8]Wherefore I beseech you that you would confirm your love towards him. [9]For to this end also did I write, that I might know the proof of you, whether ye be obedient in all things. [10]To whom ye forgive anything, I forgive also: for if I forgave anything, to whom I forgave it, for your sakes forgave I it in the person of Christ, [11]lest Satan should get an advantage of us: for we are not ignorant of his devices.

[12]Furthermore, when I came to Troas to preach Christ's gospel, and a door was opened unto me of the Lord, [13]I had no rest in my spirit, because I found not Titus my brother, but taking my leave of them, I went from thence into Macedonia. [14]Now thanks be unto God, which always causeth us to triumph in Christ, and maketh manifest the savour of his knowledge by us in every place. [15]For we are unto God a sweet savour of Christ, in them that are saved, and in them that perish. [16]To the one we are the savour of death unto death; and to the other the savour of life unto life: and who is sufficient for these things? [17]For we are not as many, which corrupt the word of God: but as of sincerity, but as of God, in the sight of God speak we in Christ.

3 Do we begin again to commend ourselves? or need we, as some others, epistles of commendation to you, or letters of commendation from you? [2]Ye are our epistle written in our hearts, known and read of all men: [3]forasmuch as ye are manifestly declared to be the epistle of Christ ministered by us, written not with ink, but with the Spirit of the living God, not in tablets of stone, but in fleshy tablets of the heart. [4]And such trust have we through Christ to God-ward: [5]not that we are sufficient of ourselves to think anything as of ourselves: but our sufficiency is of God: [6]who also hath made us able ministers of the new testament, not of the letter, but of the spirit: for the letter killeth, but the spirit giveth life. [7]But if the ministration of death, written and engraved in stones, was glorious, so that the children of Israel could not steadfastly behold the face of Moses for the glory of his counte-

nance, which glory was to be done away: ⁸how shall not the ministration of the spirit be rather glorious? ⁹For if the ministration of condemnation be glory, much more doth the ministration of righteousness exceed in glory. ¹⁰For even that which was made glorious had no glory in this respect, by reason of the glory that excelleth. ¹¹For if that which is done away was glorious, much more that which remaineth is glorious.

¹²Seeing then that we have such hope, we use great plainness of speech: ¹³and not as Moses, which put a veil over his face, that the children of Israel could not steadfastly look to the end of that which is abolished; ¹⁴but their minds were blinded: for until this day remaineth the same veil untaken away in the reading of the old testament: which veil is done away in Christ. ¹⁵But even unto this day, when Moses is read, the veil is upon their heart. ¹⁶Nevertheless when it shall turn to the Lord, the veil shall be taken away. ¹⁷Now the Lord is that Spirit, and where the Spirit of the Lord is, there is liberty. ¹⁸But we all, with open face beholding as in a glass the glory of the Lord, are changed into the same image from glory to glory, even as by the Spirit of the Lord.

4 Therefore seeing we have this ministry, as we have received mercy, we faint not: ²but have renounced the hidden things of dishonesty, not walking in craftiness, nor handling the word of God deceitfully, but by manifestation of the truth commending ourselves to every man's conscience in the sight of God. ³But if our gospel be hid, it is hid to them that are lost: ⁴in whom the god of this world hath blinded the minds of them which believe not, lest the light of the glorious gospel of Christ, who is the image of God, should shine unto them. ⁵For we preach not ourselves, but Christ Jesus the Lord, and ourselves your servants for Jesus' sake. ⁶For God, who commanded the light to shine out of darkness, hath shone in our hearts, to give the light of the knowledge of the glory of God in the face of Jesus Christ.

⁷But we have this treasure in earthen vessels, that the excellence of the power may be of God, and not of us. ⁸We are troubled on every side, yet not distressed; we are perplexed, but not in despair, ⁹persecuted, but not forsaken; cast down, but not destroyed; ¹⁰always bearing about in the body the dying of the Lord Jesus, that the life also of Jesus might be made manifest in our body. ¹¹For we which live are always delivered unto death for Jesus' sake, that the life also of Jesus might be made manifest in our mortal flesh. ¹²So then death worketh in us, but life in you. ¹³We having the same spirit of faith, according as it is written, 'I believed, and therefore have I spoken': we also believe, and therefore speak; ¹⁴knowing that he which raised up the Lord Jesus shall raise up us also by Jesus, and shall present us with you. ¹⁵For all things are for your sakes, that the abundant grace might through the thanksgiving of many redound to the glory of God. ¹⁶For which cause we faint not, but though our outward man perish, yet the inward man is renewed day by day. ¹⁷For our light affliction, which is but for a moment, worketh for us a far more exceeding and eternal weight of glory, ¹⁸while we look not at the things which are seen, but at the things which are not

seen: for the things which are seen are temporal, but the things which are not seen are eternal.

5 For we know that if our earthly house of this tabernacle were dissolved, we have a building of God, a house not made with hand, eternal in the heavens. ²For in this we groan, earnestly desiring to be clothed upon with our house which is from heaven: ³if so be that being clothed we shall not be found naked. ⁴For we that are in this tabernacle do groan, being burdened, not for that we would be unclothed, but clothed upon, that mortality might be swallowed up of life. ⁵Now he that hath wrought us for the selfsame thing is God, who also hath given unto us the earnest of the Spirit. ⁶Therefore we are always confident, knowing that, whilst we are at home in the body, we are absent from the Lord ⁷(for we walk by faith, not by sight). ⁸We are confident, I say, and willing rather to be absent from the body, and to be present with the Lord. ⁹Wherefore we labour, that, whether present or absent, we may be accepted of him. ¹⁰For we must all appear before the judgement seat of Christ, that every one may receive the things done in his body, according to that he hath done, whether it be good or bad.

¹¹Knowing therefore the terror of the Lord, we persuade men; but we are made manifest unto God, and I trust also are made manifest in your consciences. ¹²For we commend not ourselves again unto you, but give you occasion to glory on our behalf, that you may have somewhat to answer them which glory in appearance, and not in heart. ¹³For whether we be beside ourselves, it is to God: or whether we be sober, it is for your cause. ¹⁴For the love of Christ constraineth us, because we thus judge, that if one died for all, then were all dead: ¹⁵and that he died for all, that they which live should not henceforth live unto themselves, but unto him which died for them, and rose again. ¹⁶Wherefore henceforth know we no man after the flesh: yea, though we have known Christ after the flesh, yet now henceforth know we him no more. ¹⁷Therefore if any man be in Christ, he is a new creature: old things are passed away, behold, all things are become new. ¹⁸And all things are of God, who hath reconciled us to himself by Jesus Christ, and hath given to us the ministry of reconciliation, ¹⁹to wit, that God was in Christ, reconciling the world unto himself, not imputing their trespasses unto them, and hath committed unto us the word of reconciliation. ²⁰Now then we are ambassadors for Christ, as though God did beseech you by us; we pray you in Christ's stead, be ye reconciled to God. ²¹For he hath made him to be sin for us, who knew no sin, that we might be made the righteousness of God in him.

6 We then, as workers together with him, beseech you also that ye receive not the grace of God in vain ²(for he saith, 'I have heard thee in a time accepted, and in the day of salvation have I succoured thee': behold, now is the accepted time, behold, now is the day of salvation), ³giving no offence in anything, that the ministry be not blamed: ⁴but in all things approving ourselves as the ministers of God, in much patience, in afflictions, in necessities, in distresses, ⁵in stripes, in imprisonments, in tumults, in labours, in watchings, in fastings; ⁶by pureness, by knowledge, by long-suffering, by kindness, by the Holy Ghost, by love unfeigned, [7]by the word of truth, by the power of God, by the armour of righteousness on the right hand and on the left, [8]by honour and dishonour, by evil report and good report, as deceivers, and yet true: [9]as unknown, and yet well known: as dying, and behold, we live: as chastened, and not killed: [10]as sorrowful, yet always rejoicing: as poor, yet making many rich, as having nothing, and yet possessing all things.

[11]O ye Corinthians, our mouth is open unto you, our heart is enlarged. [12]Ye are not straitened in us, but ye are straitened in your own bowels. [13]Now for a recompense in the same (I speak as unto my children), be ye also enlarged.

[14]Be ye not unequally yoked together with unbelievers: for what fellowship hath righteousness with unrighteousness? and what communion hath light with darkness? [15]and what concord hath Christ with Belial? or what part hath he that believeth with an infidel? [16]and what agreement hath the temple of God with idols? for ye are the temple of the living God; as God hath said, 'I will dwell in them, and walk in them, and I will be their God, and they shall be my people'. [17]Wherefore 'Come out from among them, and be ye separate,' saith the Lord, 'and touch not the unclean thing, and I will receive you, [18]and will be a Father unto you, and ye shall be my sons and daughters,' saith the Lord Almighty.

7 Having therefore these promises, dearly beloved, let us cleanse ourselves from all filthiness of the flesh and spirit, perfecting holiness in the fear of God.

[2]Receive us; we have wronged no man, we have corrupted no man, we have defrauded no man. [3]I speak not this to condemn you: for I have said before, that you are in our hearts to die and live with you. [4]Great is my boldness of speech toward you, great is my glorying of you: I am filled with comfort, I am exceeding joyful in all our tribulation.

[5]For when we were come into Macedonia, our flesh had no rest, but we were troubled on every side; without were fightings, within were fears. [6]Nevertheless God, that comforteth those that are cast down, comforted us by the coming of Titus; [7]and not by his coming only, but by the consolation wherewith he was comforted in you, when he told us your earnest desire, your mourning, your fervent mind toward me, so that I rejoiced the more. [8]For though I made you sorry with a letter, I do not repent, though I did repent: for I perceive that the same epistle hath made you sorry, though it were but for a season. [9]Now I rejoice, not that ye were made sorry, but that ye sorrowed to repentance: for ye were made sorry after a godly manner, that ye might receive damage by us in nothing. [10]For godly sorrow worketh repentance to salvation not to be repented of, but the sorrow of the world worketh death. [11]For behold this selfsame thing that ye sorrowed after a godly sort, what carefulness it wrought in you, yea, what clearing of yourselves, yea, what indignation, yea, what fear, yea, what vehement desire, yea, what zeal, yea, what revenge! In all things ye have approved yourselves to be

clear in this matter. ¹²Wherefore, though I wrote unto you, I did it not for his cause that had done the wrong, nor for his cause that suffered wrong, but that our care for you in the sight of God might appear unto you. ¹³Therefore we were comforted in your comfort, yea, and exceedingly the more joyed we for the joy of Titus, because his spirit was refreshed by you all. ¹⁴For if I have boasted anything to him of you, I am not ashamed; but as we spoke all things to you in truth, even so our boasting, which I made before Titus, is found a truth. ¹⁵And his inward affection is more abundant toward you, whilst he remembereth the obedience of you all, how with fear and trembling you received him. ¹⁶I rejoice therefore that I have confidence in you in all things.

8 Moreover, brethren, we do you to wit of the grace of God bestowed on the churches of Macedonia, ²how that in a great trial of affliction the abundance of their joy and their deep poverty abounded unto the riches of their liberality. ³For to their power, I bear record, yea, and beyond their power they were willing of themselves: ⁴praying us with much entreaty that we would receive the gift, and take upon us the fellowship of the ministering to the saints. ⁵And this they did, not as we hoped, but first gave their own selves to the Lord, and unto us by the will of God. ⁶Insomuch that we desired Titus, that as he had begun, so he would also finish in you the same grace also. ⁷Therefore, as ye abound in everything, in faith, and utterance, and knowledge, and in all diligence, and in your love to us, see that ye abound in this grace also. ⁸I speak not by commandment, but by occasion of the forwardness of others, and to prove the sincerity of your love. ⁹For ye know the grace of our Lord Jesus Christ, that, though he was rich, yet for your sakes he became poor, that ye through his poverty might be rich.

¹⁰And herein I give my advice, for this is expedient for you, who have begun before, not only to do, but also to be forward a year ago. ¹¹Now therefore perform the doing of it, that as there was a readiness to will, so there may be a performance also out of that which you have. ¹²For if there be first a willing mind, it is accepted according to that a man hath, and not according to that he hath not. ¹³For I mean not that other men be eased, and you burdened: ¹⁴but by an equality, that now at this time your abundance may be a supply for their want, that their abundance also may be a supply for your want, that there may be equality: ¹⁵as it is written, 'He that had gathered much had nothing over, and he that had gathered little had no lack'.

¹⁶But thanks be to God, which put the same earnest care into the heart of Titus for you. ¹⁷For indeed he accepted the exhortation, but being more forward, of his own accord he went unto you. ¹⁸And we have sent with him the brother, whose praise is in the gospel throughout all the churches; ¹⁹and not that only, but who was also chosen of the churches to travel with us with this grace, which is administered by us to the glory of the same Lord, and declaration of your ready mind: ²⁰avoiding this, that no man should blame us in this abundance which is administered by us: ²¹providing for honest things, not only in the sight of the Lord, but in the sight of men. ²²And we have sent with them our

brother, whom we have oftentimes proved diligent in many things, but now much more diligent, upon the great confidence which I have in you. [23]Whether any do inquire of Titus, he is my partner and fellow-helper concerning you: or our brethren be inquired of, they are the messengers of the churches, and the glory of Christ. [24]Wherefore show ye to them, and before the churches, the proof of your love, and of our boasting on your behalf.

9 For as touching the ministering to the saints, it is superfluous for me to write to you: [2]for I know the forwardness of your mind, for which I boast of you to them of Macedonia, that Achaia was ready a year ago, and your zeal hath provoked very many. [3]Yet have I sent the brethren, lest our boasting of you should be in vain in this behalf, that, as I said, ye may be ready: [4]lest haply if they of Macedonia come with me, and find you unprepared, we (that we say not, you) should be ashamed in this same confident boasting. [5]Therefore I thought it necessary to exhort the brethren, that they would go before unto you, and make up beforehand your bounty, whereof ye had notice before, that the same might be ready, as a matter of bounty, not of covetousness.

[6]But this I say, he which soweth sparingly shall reap sparingly: and he which soweth bountifully shall reap bountifully. [7]Every man according as he purposeth in his heart, so let him give; not grudgingly, or of necessity: for God loveth a cheerful giver. [8]And God is able to make all grace abound towards you, that ye, always having all sufficiency in all things, may abound to every good work [9](as it is written, 'He hath dispersed abroad: he hath given to the poor: his righteousness remaineth for ever'. [10]Now he that ministereth seed to the sower both minister bread for your food, and multiply your seed sown, and increase the fruits of your righteousness), [11]being enriched in everything to all bountifulness, which causeth through us thanksgiving to God. [12]For the administration of this service not only supplieth the want of the saints, but is abundant also by many thanksgivings unto God, [13]whilst by the experiment of this ministration they glorify God for your professed subjection unto the gospel of Christ, and for your liberal distribution unto them, and unto all men: [14]and by their prayer for you, which long after you for the exceeding grace of God in you. [15]Thanks be unto God for his unspeakable gift.

10 Now I Paul myself beseech you, by the meekness and gentleness of Christ, who in presence am base among you, but being absent am bold toward you: [2]but I beseech you, that I may not be bold when I am present with that confidence wherewith I think to be bold against some, which think of us as if we walked according to the flesh. [3]For though we walk in the flesh, we do not war after the flesh [4](for the weapons of our warfare are not carnal, but mighty through God to the pulling down of strongholds): [5]casting down imaginations, and every high thing that exalteth itself against the knowledge of God, and bringing into captivity every thought to the obedience of Christ: [6]and having in a readiness to revenge all disobedience, when your obedience is fulfilled.

⁷Do ye look on things after the outward appearance? If any man trust to himself that he is Christ's, let him of himself think this again, that, as he is Christ's, even so are we Christ's. ⁸For though I should boast somewhat more of our authority, which the Lord hath given us for edification, and not for your destruction, I should not be ashamed: ⁹that I may not seem as if I would terrify you by letters. ¹⁰'For his letters,' say they, 'are weighty and powerful, but his bodily presence is weak, and his speech contemptible.' ¹¹Let such a one think this, that such as we are in word by letters when we are absent, such will we be also in deed when we are present.

¹²For we dare not make ourselves of the number, or compare ourselves with some that commend themselves: but they measuring themselves by themselves, and comparing themselves amongst themselves, are not wise. ¹³But we will not boast of things without our measure, but according to the measure of the rule which God hath distributed to us, a measure to reach even unto you. ¹⁴For we stretch not ourselves beyond our measure, as though we reached not unto you, for we are come as far as to you also in preaching the gospel of Christ: ¹⁵not boasting of things without our measure, that is, of other men's labours, but having hope, when your faith is increased, that we shall be enlarged by you according to our rule abundantly, ¹⁶to preach the gospel in the regions beyond you, and not to boast in another man's line of things made ready to our hand. ¹⁷But he that glorieth, let him glory in the Lord. ¹⁸For not he that commendeth himself is approved, but whom the Lord commendeth.

11 Would to God you could bear with me a little in my folly, and indeed bear with me. ²For I am jealous over you with godly jealousy, for I have espoused you to one husband, that I may present you as a chaste virgin to Christ. ³But I fear, lest by any means, as the serpent beguiled Eve through his subtlety, so your minds should be corrupted from the simplicity that is in Christ. ⁴For if he that cometh preacheth another Jesus whom we have not preached, or if ye receive another spirit, which ye have not received, or another gospel, which ye have not accepted, ye might well bear with him. ⁵For I suppose I was not a whit behind the very chiefest apostles. ⁶But though I be rude in speech, yet not in knowledge; but we have been thoroughly made manifest among you in all things.

⁷Have I committed an offence in abasing myself that you might be exalted, because I have preached to you the gospel of God freely? ⁸I robbed other churches, taking wages of them, to do you service. ⁹And when I was present with you, and wanted, I was chargeable to no man: for that which was lacking to me the brethren which came from Macedonia supplied, and in all things I have kept myself from being burdensome unto you, and so will I keep myself. ¹⁰As the truth of Christ is in me, no man shall stop me of this boasting in the regions of Achaia. ¹¹Wherefore? because I love you not? God knoweth. ¹²But what I do, that I will do, that I may cut off occasion from them which desire occasion, that wherein they glory, they may be found even as we. ¹³For such are

false apostles, deceitful workers, transforming themselves into the apostles of Christ. ¹⁴And no marvel, for Satan himself is transformed into an angel of light. ¹⁵Therefore it is no great thing if his ministers also be transformed as the ministers of righteousness, whose end shall be according to their works.

¹⁶I say again, let no man think me a fool; if otherwise, yet as a fool receive me, that I may boast myself a little. ¹⁷That which I speak, I speak it not after the Lord, but as it were foolishly, in this confidence of boasting. ¹⁸Seeing that many glory after the flesh, I will glory also. ¹⁹For ye suffer fools gladly, seeing ye yourselves are wise. ²⁰For ye suffer if a man bring you into bondage, if a man devour you, if a man take of you, if a man exalt himself, if a man smite you on the face. ²¹I speak as concerning reproach, as though we had been weak.

Howbeit whereinsoever any is bold (I speak foolishly), I am bold also. ²²Are they Hebrews? so am I. Are they Israelites? so am I. Are they the seed of Abraham? so am I. ²³Are they ministers of Christ (I speak as a fool)? I am more: in labours more abundant, in stripes above measure, in prisons more frequent, in deaths oft. ²⁴Of the Jews five times received I forty stripes save one. ²⁵Thrice was I beaten with rods, once was I stoned, thrice I suffered shipwreck, a night and a day I have been in the deep; ²⁶in journeying often, in perils of waters, in perils of robbers, in perils by my own countrymen, in perils by the heathen, in perils in the city, in perils in the wilderness, in perils in the sea, in perils among false brethren, ²⁷in weariness and painfulness, in watchings often, in hunger and thirst, in fastings often, in cold and nakedness.

²⁸Besides those things that are without, that which cometh upon me daily, the care of all the churches. ²⁹Who is weak, and I am not weak? who is offended, and I burn not? ³⁰If I must needs glory, I will glory of the things which concern my infirmities. ³¹The God and Father of our Lord Jesus Christ, which is blessed for evermore, knoweth that I lie not. ³²In Damascus the governor under Aretas the king kept the city of the Damascenes with a garrison, desirous to apprehend me: ³³and through a window in a basket was I let down by the wall, and escaped his hands.

12 It is not expedient for me doubtless to glory. I will come to visions and revelations of the Lord. ²I knew a man in Christ above fourteen years ago, whether in the body, I cannot tell, or whether out of the body, I cannot tell, God knoweth: such a one, caught up to the third heaven. ³And I knew such a man (whether in the body, or out of the body, I cannot tell, God knoweth), ⁴how that he was caught up into paradise, and heard unspeakable words, which it is not lawful for a man to utter. ⁵Of such a one will I glory: yet of myself I will not glory, but in my infirmities. ⁶For though I would desire to glory, I shall not be a fool: for I will say the truth. But now I forbear, lest any man should think of me above that which he seeth me to be, or that he heareth of me. ⁷And lest I should be exalted above measure through the abundance of the revelations, there was given to me a thorn in the flesh, the messenger of Satan to buffet me, lest I should be exalted above measure. ⁸For this thing I besought the Lord thrice, that it might depart from me. ⁹And he said unto me, 'My grace is sufficient for thee: for my strength is made perfect in weakness'. Most gladly therefore will I rather glory in my infirmities, that the power of Christ may rest upon me. ¹⁰Therefore I take pleasure in infirmities, in reproaches, in necessities, in persecutions, in distresses for Christ's sake: for when I am weak, then am I strong. ¹¹I am become a fool in glorying, ye have compelled me. For I ought to have been commended of you: for in nothing am I behind the very chiefest apostles, though I be nothing. ¹²Truly the signs of an apostle were wrought among you in all patience, in signs, and wonders, and mighty deeds. ¹³For what is it wherein ye were inferior to other churches, except it be that I myself was not burdensome to you? forgive me this wrong.

¹⁴Behold, the third time I am ready to come to you, and I will not be burdensome to you; for I seek not yours, but you: for the children ought not to lay up for the parents, but the parents for the children. ¹⁵And I will very gladly spend and be spent for you, though the more abundantly I love you, the less I be loved. ¹⁶But be it so: I did not burden you: nevertheless, being crafty, I caught you with guile. ¹⁷Did I make a gain of you by any of them whom I sent unto you? ¹⁸I desired Titus, and with him I sent a brother. Did Titus make a gain of you? Walked we not in the same spirit? walked we not in the same steps?

¹⁹Again, think you that we excuse ourselves unto you? we speak before God in Christ: but we do all things, dearly beloved, for your edifying. ²⁰For I fear lest, when I come, I shall not find you such as I would, and that I shall be found unto you such as ye would not, lest there be debates, envyings, wraths, strifes, backbitings, whisperings, swellings, tumults, ²¹and lest, when I come again, my God will humble me among you, and that I shall bewail many which have sinned already, and have not repented of the uncleanness and fornication and lasciviousness which they have committed.

13 This is the third time I am coming to you. In the mouth of two or three witnesses shall every word be established. ²I told you before, and foretell you, as if I were present, the second time, and being absent now I write to them which heretofore have sinned, and to all others, that, if I come again, I will not spare: ³since ye seek a proof of Christ speaking in me, which to you-ward is not weak, but is mighty in you. ⁴For though he was crucified through weakness, yet he liveth by the power of God: for we also are weak in him, but we shall live with him by the power of God toward you.

⁵Examine yourselves, whether ye be in the faith: prove your own selves. Know ye not your own selves, how that Jesus Christ is in you, except ye be reprobates? ⁶But I trust that ye shall know that we are not reprobates. ⁷Now I pray to God that ye do no evil, not that we should appear approved, but that ye should do that which is honest, though we be as reprobates. ⁸For we can do nothing against the truth, but for the truth. ⁹For we are glad, when we are weak, and ye are strong: and this also we wish, even your perfection. ¹⁰Therefore I write these things being absent, lest being present I should use sharpness, according to

the power which the Lord hath given me to edification, and not to destruction. [11]Finally, brethren, farewell. Be perfect, be of good comfort, be of one mind, live in peace, and the God of love and peace shall be with you. [12]Greet one another with a holy kiss. [13]All the saints salute you.

[14]The grace of the Lord Jesus Christ, and the love of God, and the communion of the Holy Ghost, be with you all. Amen.

The second epistle to the Corinthians was written from Philippi, a city of Macedonia, by Titus and Luke.

THE
EPISTLE OF PAUL THE APOSTLE
TO THE
GALATIANS

1 Paul, an apostle, not of men, neither by man, but by Jesus Christ, and God the Father, who raised him from the dead, ²and all the brethren which are with me, unto the churches of Galatia: ³grace be to you and peace from God the Father, and from our Lord Jesus Christ, ⁴who gave himself for our sins, that he might deliver us from this present evil world, according to the will of God and our Father, ⁵to whom be glory for ever and ever. Amen.

⁶I marvel that you are so soon removed from him that called you into the grace of Christ, unto another gospel: ⁷which is not another; but there be some that trouble you, and would pervert the gospel of Christ. ⁸But though we, or an angel from heaven, preach any other gospel unto you than that which we have preached unto you, let him be accursed. ⁹As we said before, so say I now again, if any man preach any other gospel unto you than that ye have received, let him be accursed. ¹⁰For do I now persuade men, or God? or do I seek to please men? For if I yet pleased men, I should not be the servant of Christ.

¹¹But I certify you, brethren, that the gospel which was preached of me is not after man. ¹²For I neither received it of man, neither was I taught it, but by the revelation of Jesus Christ. ¹³For ye have heard of my conversation in time past in the Jews' religion, how that beyond measure I persecuted the church of God, and wasted it: ¹⁴and profited in the Jews' religion above many my equals in my own nation, being more exceedingly zealous of the traditions of my fathers. ¹⁵But when it pleased God, who separated me from my mother's womb, and called me by his grace, ¹⁶to reveal his Son in me, that I might preach him among the heathen, immediately I conferred not with flesh and blood: ¹⁷neither went I up to Jerusalem to them which were apostles before me, but I went into Arabia, and returned again unto Damascus. ¹⁸Then after three years I went up to Jerusalem to see Peter, and abode with him fifteen days. ¹⁹But others of the apostles saw I none, save James the Lord's brother. ²⁰Now the things which I write unto you, behold, before God, I lie not. ²¹Afterwards I came into the regions of Syria and Cilicia, ²²and was unknown by face unto the churches of Judea which were in Christ: ²³but they had heard only, that he which persecuted us in times past now preacheth the faith which once he destroyed. ²⁴And they glorified God in me.

2 Then fourteen years after I went up again to Jerusalem with Barnabas, and took Titus with me also. ²And I went up by revelation, and communicated unto them that gospel which I preach among the Gentiles, but privately to them which were of reputation, lest by any means I should run, or had run, in vain. ³But neither Titus, who was with me, being a Greek, was compelled to be circumcised: ⁴and that because of false brethren unawares brought in, who came in privily to spy out our liberty which we have in Christ Jesus, that they might bring us into bondage: ⁵to whom we gave place by subjection, no, not for an hour, that the truth of the gospel might continue with you. ⁶But of these who seemed to be somewhat (whatsoever they were, it maketh no matter to me: God accepteth no man's person), for they who seemed to be somewhat in conference added nothing to me: ⁷but contrariwise, when they saw that the gospel of the uncircumcision was committed unto me, as the gospel of the circumcision was unto Peter ⁸(for he that wrought effectually in Peter to the apostleship of the circumcision, the same was mighty in me towards the Gentiles): ⁹and when James, Cephas, and John, who seemed to be pillars, perceived the grace that was given unto me, they gave to me and Barnabas the right hands of fellowship, that we should go unto the heathen, and they unto the circumcision. ¹⁰Only they would that we should remember the poor, the same which I also was forward to do.

¹¹But when Peter was come to Antioch, I withstood him to the face, because he was to be blamed. ¹²For before that certain came from James, he did eat with the Gentiles: but when they were come, he withdrew and separated himself, fearing them which were of the circumcision. ¹³And the other Jews dissembled likewise with him, insomuch that Barnabas also was carried away with their dissimulation. ¹⁴But when I saw that they walked not uprightly according to the truth of the gospel, I said unto Peter before them all, 'If thou, being a Jew, livest after the manner of Gentiles, and not as do the Jews, why compellest thou the Gentiles to live as do the Jews?'

¹⁵We who are Jews by nature, and not sinners of the Gentiles, ¹⁶knowing that a man is not justified by the works of the law, but by the faith of Jesus Christ, even we have believed in Jesus Christ, that we might be justified by the faith of Christ, and not by the works of the law: for by the works of the law shall no flesh be justified. ¹⁷But if, while we seek to be justified by Christ, we ourselves also are found sinners, is therefore Christ the minister of sin? God forbid. ¹⁸For if I build again the things which I destroyed, I make myself a transgressor. ¹⁹For I through the law am dead to the law, that I might live unto God. ²⁰I am crucified with Christ. Nevertheless I live, yet not I, but Christ liveth in me, and the life which I now live in the flesh I live by the faith of the Son of God, who loved me, and gave himself for me. ²¹I do not frustrate the grace of God: for if righteousness come by the law, then Christ is dead in vain.

3 O foolish Galatians, who hath bewitched you, that you should not obey the truth, before whose eyes Jesus Christ hath been evidently set forth, crucified among you? ²This only would I learn of you, received ye the Spirit by the works of the law, or by the hearing of faith? ³Are ye so foolish? having begun in the Spirit, are ye now made perfect by the flesh? ⁴Have ye suffered so many things in vain? if it be yet in vain. ⁵He therefore that ministereth to you the Spirit, and worketh

miracles among you, doeth he it by the works of the law, or by the hearing of faith? [6]Even as Abraham believed God, and it was accounted to him for righteousness. [7]Know ye therefore that they which are of faith, the same are the children of Abraham. [8]And the scripture, foreseeing that God would justify the heathen through faith, preached before the gospel unto Abraham, saying, 'In thee shall all nations be blessed'. [9]So then they which be of faith are blessed with faithful Abraham. [10]For as many as are of the works of the law are under the curse: for it is written, 'Cursed is every one that continueth not in all things which are written in the book of the law to do them'. [11]But that no man is justified by the law in the sight of God, it is evident: for, 'The just shall live by faith'. [12]And the law is not of faith: but, 'The man that doeth them shall live in them'. [13]Christ hath redeemed us from the curse of the law, being made a curse for us: for it is written, 'Cursed is every one that hangeth on tree': [14]that the blessing of Abraham might come on the Gentiles through Jesus Christ: that we might receive the promise of the Spirit through faith.

[15]Brethren, I speak after the manner of men; though it be but a man's covenant, yet if it be confirmed, no man disannulleth, or addeth thereto. [16]Now to Abraham and his seed were the promises made. He saith not, 'And to seeds', as of many, but as of one, 'And to thy seed', which is Christ. [17]And this I say, that the covenant, that was confirmed before of God in Christ, the law, which was four hundred and thirty years after, cannot disannul, that it should make the promise of no effect. [18]For if the inheritance be of the law, it is no more of promise: but God gave it to Abraham by promise.

[19]Wherefore then serveth the law? It was added because of transgressions, till the seed should come to whom the promise was made, and it was ordained by angels in the hand of a mediator. [20]Now a mediator is not a mediator of one, but God is one.

[21]Is the law then against the promises of God? God forbid: for if there had been a law given which could have given life, verily righteousness should have been by the law. [22]But the scripture hath concluded all under sin, that the promise by faith of Jesus Christ might be given to them that believe.

[23]But before faith came, we were kept under the law, shut up unto the faith which should afterwards be revealed. [24]Wherefore the law was our schoolmaster to bring us unto Christ, that we might be justified by faith. [25]But after that faith is come, we are no longer under a schoolmaster. [26]For ye are all the children of God by faith in Christ Jesus. [27]For as many of you as have been baptized into Christ have put on Christ. [28]There is neither Jew nor Greek, there is neither bond nor free, there is neither male nor female: for ye are all one in Christ Jesus. [29]And if ye be Christ's, then are ye Abraham's seed, and heirs according to the promise.

4 Now I say, that the heir, as long as he is a child, differeth nothing from a servant, though he be lord of all, [2]but is under tutors and governors until the time appointed of the father. [3]Even so we, when we

were children, were in bondage under the elements of the world: ⁴but when the fulness of the time was come, God sent forth his Son, made of a woman, made under the law, ⁵to redeem them that were under the law, that we might receive the adoption of sons. ⁶And because ye are sons, God hath sent forth the Spirit of his Son into your hearts, crying, 'Abba, Father'. ⁷Wherefore thou art no more a servant, but a son; and if a son, then an heir of God through Christ.

⁸Howbeit then, when ye knew not God, ye did service unto them which by nature are no gods. ⁹But now, after that ye have known God, or rather are known of God, how turn ye again to the weak and beggarly elements, whereunto ye desire again to be in bondage? ¹⁰Ye observe days, and months, and times, and years. ¹¹I am afraid of you, lest I have bestowed upon you labour in vain.

¹²Brethren, I beseech you, be as I am; for I am as ye are: ye have not injured me at all. ¹³Ye know how through infirmity of the flesh I preached the gospel unto you at the first. ¹⁴And my temptation which was in my flesh ye despised not, nor rejected, but received me as an angel of God, even as Christ Jesus. ¹⁵Where is then the blessedness you spoke of? for I bear you record, that, if it had been possible, ye would have plucked out your own eyes, and have given them to me. ¹⁶Am I therefore become your enemy, because I tell you the truth? ¹⁷They zealously affect you, but not well: yea, they would exclude you, that you might affect them. ¹⁸But it is good to be zealously affected always in a good thing, and not only when I am present with you. ¹⁹My little children, of whom I travail in birth again until Christ be formed in you, ²⁰I desire to be present with you now, and to change my voice, for I stand in doubt of you.

²¹Tell me, ye that desire to be under the law, do ye not hear the law? ²²For it is written, that Abraham had two sons, the one by a bondmaid, the other by a freewoman. ²³But he who was of the bondwoman was born after the flesh: but he of the freewoman was by promise. ²⁴Which things are an allegory: for these are the two covenants; the one from the mount Sinai, which gendereth to bondage, which is Agar. ²⁵For this Agar is mount Sinai in Arabia, and answereth to Jerusalem which now is, and is in bondage with her children. ²⁶But Jerusalem which is above is free, which is the mother of us all. ²⁷For it is written, 'Rejoice, thou barren that bearest not, break forth and cry, thou that travailest not: for the desolate hath many more children than she which hath a husband'. ²⁸Now we, brethren, as Isaac was, are the children of promise. ²⁹But as then he that was born after the flesh persecuted him that was born after the Spirit, even so it is now. ³⁰Nevertheless what saith the scripture? 'Cast out the bondwoman and her son: for the son of the bondwoman shall not be heir with the son of the freewoman'. ³¹So then, brethren, we are not children of the bondwoman, but of the free.

5 Stand fast therefore in the liberty wherewith Christ hath made us free, and be not entangled again with the yoke of bondage. ²Behold, I Paul say unto you, that if ye be circumcised, Christ shall profit you nothing. ³For I testify again to every man that is circumcised, that he is

a debtor to do the whole law. ⁴Christ is become of no effect unto you, whosoever of you are justified by the law: ye are fallen from grace. ⁵For we through the Spirit wait for the hope of righteousness by faith. ⁶For in Jesus Christ neither circumcision availeth anything, nor uncircumcision, but faith which worketh by love. ⁷Ye did run well; who did hinder you that ye should not obey the truth? ⁸This persuasion cometh not of him that calleth you. ⁹A little leaven leaveneth the whole lump. ¹⁰I have confidence in you through the Lord, that you will be no otherwise minded; but he that troubleth you shall bear his judgement, whosoever he be. ¹¹And I, brethren, if I yet preach circumcision, why do I yet suffer persecution? then is the offence of the cross ceased. ¹²I would they were even cut off which trouble you.

¹³For, brethren, ye have been called unto liberty, only use not liberty for an occasion to the flesh, but by love serve one another. ¹⁴For all the law is fulfilled in one word, even in this: 'Thou shalt love thy neighbour as thyself'. ¹⁵But if ye bite and devour one another, take heed ye be not consumed one of another. ¹⁶This I say then, walk in the Spirit, and ye shall not fulfil the lust of the flesh. ¹⁷For the flesh lusteth against the Spirit, and the Spirit against the flesh: and these are contrary the one to the other: so that ye cannot do the things that ye would. ¹⁸But if ye be led of the Spirit, ye are not under the law.

¹⁹Now the works of the flesh are manifest, which are these, adultery, fornication, uncleanness, lasciviousness, ²⁰idolatry, witchcraft, hatred, variance, emulations, wrath, strife, seditions, heresies, ²¹envyings, murders, drunkenness, revellings, and such like: of the which I tell you before, as I have also told you in time past, that they which do such things shall not inherit the kingdom of God. ²²But the fruit of the Spirit is love, joy, peace, long-suffering, gentleness, goodness, faith, ²³meekness, temperance: against such there is no law. ²⁴And they that are Christ's have crucified the flesh with the affections and lusts. ²⁵If we live in the Spirit, let us also walk in the Spirit. ²⁶Let us not be desirous of vain glory, provoking one another, envying one another.

6 Brethren, if a man be overtaken in a fault, ye which are spiritual, restore such a one in the spirit of meekness, considering thyself, lest thou also be tempted. ²Bear ye one another's burdens, and so fulfil the law of Christ. ³For if a man think himself to be something, when he is nothing, he deceiveth himself. ⁴But let every man prove his own work, and then shall he have rejoicing in himself alone, and not in another. ⁵For every man shall bear his own burden. ⁶Let him that is taught in the word communicate unto him that teacheth in all good things. ⁷Be not deceived, God is not mocked: for whatsoever a man soweth, that shall he also reap. ⁸For he that soweth to his flesh shall of the flesh reap corruption: but he that soweth to the Spirit shall of the Spirit reap life everlasting. ⁹And let us not be weary in well-doing: for in due season we shall reap, if we faint not. ¹⁰As we have therefore opportunity, let us do good unto all men, especially unto them who are of the household of faith.

¹¹Ye see how large a letter I have written unto you with my own hand.

¹²As many as desire to make a fair show in the flesh, they constrain you to be circumcised: only lest they should suffer persecution for the cross of Christ. ¹³For neither they themselves who are circumcised keep the law, but desire to have you circumcised, that they may glory in your flesh. ¹⁴But God forbid that I should glory, save in the cross of our Lord Jesus Christ, by whom the world is crucified unto me, and I unto the world. ¹⁵For in Christ Jesus neither circumcision availeth anything, nor uncircumcision, but a new creature. ¹⁶And as many as walk according to this rule, peace be on them, and mercy, and upon the Israel of God.

¹⁷From henceforth let no man trouble me, for I bear in my body the marks of the Lord Jesus.

¹⁸Brethren, the grace of our Lord Jesus Christ be with your spirit. Amen.

Unto the Galatians written from Rome.

THE
EPISTLE OF PAUL THE APOSTLE
TO THE
EPHESIANS

1 Paul, an apostle of Jesus Christ by the will of God, to the saints which are at Ephesus, and to the faithful in Christ Jesus. [2]Grace be to you, and peace, from God our Father, and from the Lord Jesus Christ.

[3]Blessed be the God and Father of our Lord Jesus Christ, who hath blessed us with all spiritual blessings in heavenly places in Christ: [4]according as he hath chosen us in him before the foundation of the world, that we should be holy and without blame before him in love: [5]having predestinated us unto the adoption of children by Jesus Christ to himself, according to the good pleasure of his will, [6]to the praise of the glory of his grace, wherein he hath made us accepted in the beloved: [7]in whom we have redemption through his blood, the forgiveness of sins, according to the riches of his grace, [8]wherein he hath abounded toward us in all wisdom and prudence: [9]having made known unto us the mystery of his will, according to his good pleasure which he had purposed in himself, [10]that in the dispensation of the fulness of times he might gather together in one all things in Christ, both which are in heaven, and which are on earth, even in him: [11]in whom also we have obtained an inheritance, being predestinated according to the purpose of him who worketh all things after the counsel of his own will: [12]that we should be to the praise of his glory, who first trusted in Christ. [13]In whom ye also trusted, after that ye heard the word of truth, the gospel of your salvation: in whom also after that ye believed, ye were sealed with that holy Spirit of promise, [14]which is the earnest of our inheritance until the redemption of the purchased possession, unto the praise of his glory.

[15]Wherefore I also, after I heard of your faith in the Lord Jesus, and love unto all the saints, [16]cease not to give thanks for you, making mention of you in my prayers, [17]that the God of our Lord Jesus Christ, the Father of glory, may give unto you the spirit of wisdom and revelation in the knowledge of him: [18]the eyes of your understanding being enlightened: that ye may know what is the hope of his calling, and what the riches of the glory of his inheritance in the saints, [19]and what is the exceeding greatness of his power to us-ward who believe, according to the working of his mighty power, [20]which he wrought in Christ, when he raised him from the dead, and set him at his own right hand in the heavenly places, [21]far above all principality, and power, and might, and dominion, and every name that is named, not only in this world, but also in that which is to come: [22]and hath put all things under his feet, and gave him to be the head over all things to the church, [23]which is his body, the fulness of him that filleth all in all.

2 And you hath he quickened, who were dead in trespasses and sins, [2]wherein in time past ye walked according to the course of this world, according to the prince of the power of the air, the spirit that now worketh in the children of disobedience, [3]among whom also we all had our conversation in times past in the lusts of our flesh, fulfilling the desires of the flesh and of the mind, and were by nature the children of wrath, even as others. [4]But God, who is rich in mercy, for his great love wherewith he loved us, [5]even when we were dead in sins, hath quickened us together with Christ (by grace ye are saved), [6]and hath raised us up together, and made us sit together in heavenly places in Christ Jesus: [7]that in the ages to come he might show the exceeding riches of his grace in his kindness towards us through Christ Jesus. [8]For by grace are ye saved through faith, and that not of yourselves: it is the gift of God: [9]not of works, lest any man should boast. [10]For we are his workmanship, created in Christ Jesus unto good works, which God hath before ordained that we should walk in them.

[11]Wherefore remember, that ye being in time past Gentiles in the flesh, who are called Uncircumcision by that which is called the Circumcision in the flesh made by hands, [12]that at that time ye were without Christ, being aliens from the commonwealth of Israel, and strangers from the covenants of promise, having no hope, and without God in the world: [13]but now in Christ Jesus ye who sometime were far off are made nigh by the blood of Christ. [14]For he is our peace, who hath made both one, and hath broken down the middle wall of partition between us: [15]having abolished in his flesh the enmity, even the law of commandments contained in ordinances, for to make in himself of twain one new man, so making peace; [16]and that he might reconcile both unto God in one body by the cross, having slain the enmity thereby, [17]and came and preached peace to you which were afar off, and to them that were nigh. [18]For through him we both have access by one Spirit unto the Father.

[19]Now therefore ye are no more strangers and foreigners, but fellow-citizens with the saints, and of the household of God, [20]and are built upon the foundation of the apostles and prophets, Jesus Christ himself being the chief corner-stone, [21]in whom all the building fitly framed together groweth unto a holy temple in the Lord: [22]in whom you also are built together for a habitation of God through the Spirit.

3 For this cause I Paul, the prisoner of Jesus Christ for you Gentiles, [2]if ye have heard of the dispensation of the grace of God which is given me to you-ward: [3]how that by revelation he made known unto me the mystery (as I wrote afore in few words, [4]whereby, when ye read, ye may understand my knowledge in the mystery of Christ) [5]which in other ages was not made known unto the sons of men, as it is now revealed unto his holy apostles and prophets by the Spirit, [6]that the Gentiles should be fellow-heirs, and of the same body, and partakers of his promise in Christ by the gospel: [7]whereof I was made a minister, according to the gift of the grace of God given unto me by the effectual working of his power. [8]Unto me, who am less than the least of all saints,

is this grace given, that I should preach among the Gentiles the unsearchable riches of Christ, [9] and to make all men see what is the fellowship of the mystery, which from the beginning of the world hath been hid in God, who created all things by Jesus Christ: [10] to the intent that now unto the principalities and powers in heavenly places might be known by the church the manifold wisdom of God, [11] according to the eternal purpose which he purposed in Christ Jesus our Lord: [12] in whom we have boldness and access with confidence by the faith of him. [13] Wherefore I desire that ye faint not at my tribulations for you, which is your glory.

[14] For this cause I bow my knees unto the Father of our Lord Jesus Christ, [15] of whom the whole family in heaven and earth is named, [16] that he would grant you, according to the riches of his glory, to be strengthened with might by his Spirit in the inner man, [17] that Christ may dwell in your hearts by faith, that ye, being rooted and grounded in love, [18] may be able to comprehend with all saints what is the breadth, and length, and depth, and height: [19] and to know the love of Christ, which passeth knowledge, that ye might be filled with all the fulness of God.

[20] Now unto him that is able to do exceeding abundantly above all that we ask or think, according to the power that worketh in us, [21] unto him be glory in the church by Christ Jesus throughout all ages, world without end. Amen.

4 I therefore, the prisoner of the Lord, beseech you that ye walk worthy of the vocation wherewith ye are called, [2] with all lowliness and meekness, with long-suffering, forbearing one another in love; [3] endeavouring to keep the unity of the Spirit in the bond of peace. [4] There is one body, and one Spirit, even as ye are called in one hope of your calling; [5] one Lord, one faith, one baptism, [6] one God and Father of all, who is above all, and through all, and in you all. [7] But unto every one of us is given grace according to the measure of the gift of Christ. [8] Wherefore he saith, 'When he ascended up on high, he led captivity captive, and gave gifts unto men'. [9] (Now that he ascended, what is it but that he also descended first into the lower parts of the earth? [10] He that descended is the same also that ascended up far above all heavens, that he might fill all things.) [11] And he gave some, apostles; and some, prophets; and some, evangelists; and some, pastors and teachers: [12] for the perfecting of the saints, for the work of the ministry, for the edifying of the body of Christ: [13] till we all come in the unity of the faith, and of the knowledge of the Son of God, unto a perfect man, unto the measure of the stature of the fulness of Christ: [14] that we henceforth be no more children, tossed to and fro, and carried about with every wind of doctrine, by the sleight of men, and cunning craftiness, whereby they lie in wait to deceive: [15] but speaking the truth in love, may grow up into him in all things, which is the head, even Christ: [16] from whom the whole body fitly joined together and compacted by that which every joint supplieth, according to the effectual working in the measure of every part, maketh increase of the body unto the edifying of itself in love.

¹⁷This I say therefore, and testify in the Lord, that ye henceforth walk not as other Gentiles walk, in the vanity of their mind, ¹⁸having the understanding darkened, being alienated from the life of God through the ignorance that is in them, because of the blindness of their heart: ¹⁹who being past feeling have given themselves over unto lasciviousness, to work all uncleanness with greediness. ²⁰But ye have not so learned Christ: ²¹if so be that ye have heard him, and have been taught by him, as the truth is in Jesus, ²²that ye put off concerning the former conversation the old man, which is corrupt according to the deceitful lusts: ²³and be renewed in the spirit of your mind: ²⁴and that ye put on that new man, which after God is created in righteousness and true holiness.

²⁵Wherefore putting away lying, speak every man truth with his neighbour: for we are members one of another. ²⁶Be ye angry, and sin not, let not the sun go down upon your wrath: ²⁷neither give place to the devil. ²⁸Let him that stole steal no more: but rather let him labour, working with his hands the thing which is good, that he may have to give to him that needeth. ²⁹Let no corrupt communication proceed out of your mouth, but that which is good to the use of edifying, that it may minister grace unto the hearers. ³⁰And grieve not the holy Spirit of God, whereby ye are sealed unto the day of redemption. ³¹Let all bitterness, and wrath, and anger, and clamour, and evil speaking, be put away from you, with all malice, ³²and be ye kind one to another, tenderhearted, forgiving one another, even as God for Christ's sake hath forgiven you.

5 Be ye therefore followers of God, as dear children; ²and walk in love, as Christ also hath loved us, and hath given himself for us, an offering and a sacrifice to God for a sweet-smelling savour. ³But fornication, and all uncleanness, or covetousness, let it not be once named amongst you, as becometh saints: ⁴neither filthiness, nor foolish talking, nor jesting, which are not convenient: but rather giving of thanks. ⁵For this ye know, that no whoremonger, nor unclean person, nor covetous man, who is an idolater, hath any inheritance in the kingdom of Christ and of God. ⁶Let no man deceive you with vain words: for because of these things cometh the wrath of God upon the children of disobedience. ⁷Be not ye therefore partakers with them. ⁸For ye were sometime darkness, but now are ye light in the Lord: walk as children of light ⁹(for the fruit of the Spirit is in all goodness and righteousness and truth), ¹⁰proving what is acceptable unto the Lord. ¹¹And have no fellowship with the unfruitful works of darkness, but rather reprove them. ¹²For it is a shame even to speak of those things which are done of them in secret. ¹³But all things that are reproved are made manifest by the light: for whatsoever doth make manifest is light. ¹⁴Wherefore he saith, 'Awake thou that sleepest, and arise from the dead, and Christ shall give thee light'. ¹⁵See then that ye walk circumspectly, not as fools, but as wise, ¹⁶redeeming the time, because the days are evil. ¹⁷Wherefore be ye not unwise, but understanding what the will of the Lord is. ¹⁸And be not drunk with wine, wherein is excess: but be filled with the Spirit:

¹⁹speaking to yourselves in psalms and hymns and spiritual songs, singing and making melody in your heart to the Lord, ²⁰giving thanks always for all things unto God and the Father in the name of our Lord Jesus Christ, ²¹submitting yourselves one to another in the fear of God.

²²Wives, submit yourselves unto your own husbands, as unto the Lord. ²³For the husband is the head of the wife, even as Christ is the head of the church: and he is the saviour of the body. ²⁴Therefore as the church is subject unto Christ, so let the wives be to their own husbands in everything. ²⁵Husbands, love your wives, even as Christ also loved the church, and gave himself for it: ²⁶that he might sanctify and cleanse it with the washing of water by the word, ²⁷that he might present it to himself a glorious church, not having spot, or wrinkle, or any such thing: but that it should be holy and without blemish. ²⁸So ought men to love their wives as their own bodies. He that loveth his wife loveth himself. ²⁹For no man ever yet hated his own flesh: but nourisheth and cherisheth it, even as the Lord the church: ³⁰for we are members of his body, of his flesh, and of his bones. ³¹'For this cause shall a man leave his father and mother, and shall be joined unto his wife, and they two shall be one flesh.' ³²This is a great mystery: but I speak concerning Christ and the church. ³³Nevertheless let every one of you in particular so love his wife even as himself, and the wife see that she reverence her husband.

6 Children, obey your parents in the Lord: for this is right. ²Honour thy father and mother (which is the first commandment with promise), ³that it may be well with thee, and thou mayest live long on the earth. ⁴And, ye fathers, provoke not your children to wrath: but bring them up in the nurture and admonition of the Lord.

⁵Servants, be obedient to them that are your masters according to the flesh, with fear and trembling, in singleness of your heart, as unto Christ: ⁶not with eye-service, as men-pleasers, but as the servants of Christ, doing the will of God from the heart: ⁷with good will doing service, as to the Lord, and not to men, ⁸knowing that whatsoever good thing any man doeth, the same shall he receive of the Lord, whether he be bond or free. ⁹And, ye masters, do the same things unto them, forbearing threatening: knowing that your Master also is in heaven, neither is there respect of persons with him.

¹⁰Finally, my brethren, be strong in the Lord, and in the power of his might. ¹¹Put on the whole armour of God, that ye may be able to stand against the wiles of the devil. ¹²For we wrestle not against flesh and blood, but against principalities, against powers, against the rulers of the darkness of this world, against spiritual wickedness in high places. ¹³Wherefore take unto you the whole armour of God, that ye may be able to withstand in the evil day, and having done all, to stand. ¹⁴Stand therefore, having your loins girt about with truth, and having on the breastplate of righteousness: ¹⁵and your feet shod with the preparation of the gospel of peace; ¹⁶above all, taking the shield of faith, wherewith ye shall be able to quench all the fiery darts of the wicked. ¹⁷And take the helmet of salvation, and the sword of the Spirit, which is the word

of God: [18]praying always with all prayer and supplication in the Spirit, and watching thereunto with all perseverance and supplication for all saints, [19]and for me, that utterance may be given unto me, that I may open my mouth boldly, to make known the mystery of the gospel: [20]for which I am an ambassador in bonds, that therein I may speak boldly, as I ought to speak.

[21]But that ye also may know my affairs, and how I do, Tychicus, a beloved brother and faithful minister in the Lord, shall make known to you all things: [22]whom I have sent unto you for the same purpose, that ye might know our affairs, and that he might comfort your hearts.

[23]Peace be to the brethren, and love, with faith from God the Father and the Lord Jesus Christ. [24]Grace be with all them that love our Lord Jesus Christ in sincerity.

Written from Rome unto the Ephesians by Tychicus.

THE
EPISTLE OF PAUL THE APOSTLE
TO THE
PHILIPPIANS

1 Paul and Timothy, the servants of Jesus Christ, to all the saints in Christ Jesus which are at Philippi, with the bishops and deacons: ²grace be unto you, and peace, from God our Father, and from the Lord Jesus Christ.

³I thank my God upon every remembrance of you, ⁴always in every prayer of mine for you all making request with joy ⁵for your fellowship in the gospel from the first day until now; ⁶being confident of this very thing, that he which hath begun a good work in you will perform it until the day of Jesus Christ: ⁷even as it is meet for me to think this of you all, because I have you in my heart, inasmuch as both in my bonds, and in the defence and confirmation of the gospel, ye all are partakers of my grace. ⁸For God is my record, how greatly I long after you all in the bowels of Jesus Christ. ⁹And this I pray, that your love may abound yet more and more in knowledge and in all judgement; ¹⁰that ye may approve things that are excellent, that ye may be sincere and without offence till the day of Christ; ¹¹being filled with the fruits of righteousness, which are by Jesus Christ, unto the glory and praise of God.

¹²But I would ye should understand, brethren, that the things which happened unto me have fallen out rather unto the furtherance of the gospel; ¹³so that my bonds in Christ are manifest in all the palace, and in all other places. ¹⁴And many of the brethren in the Lord, waxing confident by my bonds, are much more bold to speak the word without fear. ¹⁵Some indeed preach Christ even of envy and strife, and some also of good will: ¹⁶the one preach Christ of contention, not sincerely, supposing to add affliction to my bonds: ¹⁷but the others of love, knowing that I am set for the defence of the gospel. ¹⁸What then? Notwithstanding, every way, whether in pretence, or in truth: Christ is preached, and I therein do rejoice, yea, and will rejoice. ¹⁹For I know that this shall turn to my salvation through your prayer, and the supply of the Spirit of Jesus Christ, ²⁰according to my earnest expectation and my hope, that in nothing I shall be ashamed: but that with all boldness, as always, so now also Christ shall be magnified in my body, whether it be by life, or by death. ²¹For to me to live is Christ, and to die is gain. ²²But if I live in the flesh, this is the fruit of my labour: yet what I shall choose I wot not. ²³For I am in a strait betwixt two, having a desire to depart, and to be with Christ, which is far better: ²⁴nevertheless to abide in the flesh is more needful for you. ²⁵And having this confidence, I know that I shall abide and continue with you all for your furtherance and joy of faith; ²⁶that your rejoicing may be more abundant in Jesus Christ for me by my coming to you again.

²⁷Only let your conversation be as it becometh the gospel of Christ, that whether I come and see you, or else be absent, I may hear of your affairs, that ye stand fast in one spirit, with one mind striving together for the faith of the gospel, ²⁸and in nothing terrified by your adversaries, which is to them an evident token of perdition, but to you of salvation, and that of God. ²⁹For unto you it is given in the behalf of Christ, not only to believe on him, but also to suffer for his sake, ³⁰having the same conflict which ye saw in me, and now hear to be in me.

2 If there be therefore any consolation in Christ, if any comfort of love, if any fellowship of the Spirit, if any bowels and mercies, ²fulfil ye my joy, that ye be like-minded, having the same love, being of one accord, of one mind. ³Let nothing be done through strife or vainglory, but in lowliness of mind let each esteem others better than themselves. ⁴Look not every man on his own things, but every man also on the things of others. ⁵Let this mind be in you, which was also in Christ Jesus: ⁶who, being in the form of God, thought it not robbery to be equal with God: ⁷but made himself of no reputation, and took upon him the form of a servant, and was made in the likeness of men: ⁸and being found in fashion as a man, he humbled himself, and became obedient unto death, even the death of the cross. ⁹Wherefore God also hath highly exalted him, and given him a name which is above every name: ¹⁰that at the name of Jesus every knee should bow, of things in heaven, and things in earth, and things under the earth: ¹¹and that every tongue should confess that Jesus Christ is Lord, to the glory of God the Father.

¹²Wherefore, my beloved, as ye have always obeyed, not as in my presence only, but now much more in my absence, work out your own salvation with fear and trembling. ¹³For it is God which worketh in you both to will and to do of his good pleasure. ¹⁴Do all things without murmurings and disputings: ¹⁵that ye may be blameless and harmless, the sons of God, without rebuke, in the midst of a crooked and perverse nation, among whom ye shine as lights in the world: ¹⁶holding forth the word of life, that I may rejoice in the day of Christ, that I have not run in vain, neither laboured in vain. ¹⁷Yea, and if I be offered upon the sacrifice and service of your faith, I joy, and rejoice with you all. ¹⁸For the same cause also do ye joy, and rejoice with me.

¹⁹But I trust in the Lord Jesus to send Timothy shortly unto you, that I also may be of good comfort, when I know your state. ²⁰For I have no man like-minded, who will naturally care for your state. ²¹For all seek their own, not the things which are Jesus Christ's. ²²But ye know the proof of him, that, as a son with the father, he hath served with me in the gospel. ²³Him therefore I hope to send presently, so soon as I shall see how it will go with me. ²⁴But I trust in the Lord that I also myself shall come shortly. ²⁵Yet I supposed it necessary to send to you Epaphroditus, my brother, and companion in labour, and fellow-soldier, but your messenger, and he that ministered to my wants. ²⁶For he longed after you all, and was full of heaviness, because that ye had heard that he had been sick. ²⁷For indeed he was sick nigh unto death,

but God had mercy on him: and not on him only, but on me also, lest I should have sorrow upon sorrow. ²⁸I sent him therefore the more carefully, that, when ye see him again, ye may rejoice, and that I may be the less sorrowful. ²⁹Receive him therefore in the Lord with all gladness, and hold such in reputation: ³⁰because for the work of Christ he was nigh unto death, not regarding his life, to supply your lack of service toward me.

3 Finally, my brethren, rejoice in the Lord. To write the same things to you, to me indeed is not grievous, but for you it is safe. ²Beware of dogs, beware of evil workers, beware of the concision. ³For we are the circumcision, which worship God in the spirit, and rejoice in Christ Jesus, and have no confidence in the flesh. ⁴Though I might also have confidence in the flesh. If any other man thinketh that he hath whereof he might trust in the flesh, I more: ⁵circumcised the eighth day, of the stock of Israel, of the tribe of Benjamin, a Hebrew of the Hebrews; as touching the law, a Pharisee: ⁶concerning zeal, persecuting the church: touching the righteousness which is in the law, blameless. ⁷But what things were gain to me, those I counted loss for Christ. ⁸Yea doubtless, and I count all things but loss for the excellence of the knowledge of Christ Jesus my Lord: for whom I have suffered the loss of all things, and do count them but dung, that I may win Christ, ⁹and be found in him, not having my own righteousness, which is of the law, but that which is through the faith of Christ, the righteousness which is of God by faith: ¹⁰that I may know him, and the power of his resurrection, and the fellowship of his sufferings, being made conformable unto his death, ¹¹if by any means I might attain unto the resurrection of the dead. ¹²Not as though I had already attained, either were already perfect: but I follow after, if that I may apprehend that for which also I am apprehended of Christ Jesus. ¹³Brethren, I count not myself to have apprehended: but this one thing I do, forgetting those things which are behind, and reaching forth unto those things which are before, ¹⁴I press toward the mark for the prize of the high calling of God in Christ Jesus. ¹⁵Let us therefore, as many as be perfect, be thus minded: and if in anything ye be otherwise minded, God shall reveal even this unto you. ¹⁶Nevertheless, whereto we have already attained, let us walk by the same rule, let us mind the same thing.

¹⁷Brethren, be followers together of me, and mark them which walk so as ye have us for an example. ¹⁸(For many walk, of whom I have told you often, and now tell you even weeping, that they are the enemies of the cross of Christ: ¹⁹whose end is destruction, whose God is their belly, and whose glory is in their shame, who mind earthly things.) ²⁰For our conversation is in heaven, from whence also we look for the Saviour, the Lord Jesus Christ: ²¹who shall change our vile body, that it may be fashioned like unto his glorious body, according to the working whereby he is able even to subdue all things unto himself.

4 Therefore, my brethren dearly beloved and longed for, my joy and crown, so stand fast in the Lord, my dearly beloved. ²I beseech Euodias, and beseech Syntyche, that they be of the same mind in the

Lord. ³And I entreat thee also, true yoke-fellow, help those women which laboured with me in the gospel, with Clement also, and with others my fellow-labourers, whose names are in the book of life.

⁴Rejoice in the Lord always: and again I say, rejoice. ⁵Let your moderation be known unto all men. The Lord is at hand. ⁶Be careful for nothing: but in everything by prayer and supplication with thanksgiving let your request be made known unto God. ⁷And the peace of God, which passeth all understanding, shall keep your hearts and minds through Christ Jesus. ⁸Finally, brethren, whatsoever things are true, whatsoever things are honest, whatsoever things are just, whatsoever things are pure, whatsoever things are lovely, whatsoever things are of good report: if there be any virtue, and if there be any praise, think on these things. ⁹Those things, which ye have both learned, and received, and heard, and seen in me, do: and the God of peace shall be with you.

¹⁰But I rejoiced in the Lord greatly, that now at the last your care of me hath flourished again, wherein ye were also careful, but ye lacked opportunity. ¹¹Not that I speak in respect of want: for I have learned, in whatsoever state I am, therewith to be content. ¹²I know both how to be abased, and I know how to abound: everywhere and in all things I am instructed both to be full and to be hungry, both to abound and to suffer need. ¹³I can do all things through Christ which strengtheneth me. ¹⁴Notwithstanding ye have well done, that ye did communicate with my affliction.

¹⁵Now ye Philippians know also, that in the beginning of the gospel, when I departed from Macedonia, no church communicated with me as concerning giving and receiving, but ye only. ¹⁶For even in Thessalonica ye sent once and again unto my necessity. ¹⁷Not because I desire a gift: but I desire fruit that may abound to your account. ¹⁸But I have all, and abound. I am full, having received of Epaphroditus the things which were sent from you, an odour of a sweet smell, a sacrifice acceptable, well-pleasing to God. ¹⁹But my God shall supply all your need according to his riches in glory by Christ Jesus. ²⁰Now unto God and our Father be glory for ever and ever. Amen.

²¹Salute every saint in Christ Jesus. The brethren which are with me greet you. ²²All the saints salute you, chiefly they that are of Caesar's household.

²³The grace of our Lord Jesus Christ be with you all. Amen.

It was written to the Philippians from Rome by Epaphroditus.

THE
EPISTLE OF PAUL THE APOSTLE
TO THE
COLOSSIANS

1 Paul, an apostle of Jesus Christ by the will of God, and Timothy our brother, [2] to the saints and faithful brethren in Christ which are at Colosse: grace be unto you, and peace, from God our Father and the Lord Jesus Christ.

[3] We give thanks to God and the Father of our Lord Jesus Christ, praying always for you, [4] since we heard of your faith in Christ Jesus, and of the love which ye have to all the saints, [5] for the hope which is laid up for you in heaven, whereof ye heard before in the word of the truth of the gospel, [6] which is come unto you, as it is in all the world, and bringeth forth fruit, as it doth also in you, since the day ye heard of it, and knew the grace of God in truth: [7] as ye also learned of Epaphras our dear fellow-servant, who is for you a faithful minister of Christ: [8] who also declared unto us your love in the Spirit.

[9] For this cause we also, since the day we heard it, do not cease to pray for you, and to desire that ye might be filled with the knowledge of his will in all wisdom and spiritual understanding: [10] that ye might walk worthy of the Lord unto all pleasing, being fruitful in every good work, and increasing in the knowledge of God: [11] strengthened with all might, according to his glorious power, unto all patience and long-suffering with joyfulness: [12] giving thanks unto the Father, which hath made us meet to be partakers of the inheritance of the saints in light: [13] who hath delivered us from the power of darkness, and hath translated us into the kingdom of his dear Son, [14] in whom we have redemption through his blood, even the forgiveness of sins: [15] who is the image of the invisible God, the firstborn of every creature. [16] For by him were all things created that are in heaven, and that are in earth, visible and invisible, whether they be thrones, or dominions, or principalities, or powers: all things were created by him, and for him. [17] And he is before all things, and by him all things consist. [18] And he is the head of the body, the church: who is the beginning, the firstborn from the dead, that in all things he might have the pre-eminence. [19] For it pleased the Father that in him should all fulness dwell, [20] and, having made peace through the blood of his cross, by him to reconcile all things unto himself; by him, I say, whether they be things in earth, or things in heaven.

[21] And you, that were sometime alienated and enemies in your mind by wicked works, yet now hath he reconciled [22] in the body of his flesh through death, to present you holy and unblameable and unreproveable in his sight, [23] if ye continue in the faith grounded and settled, and be not moved away from the hope of the gospel, which ye have heard, and which was preached to every creature which is under heaven,

whereof I Paul am made a minister; ²⁴who now rejoice in my sufferings for you, and fill up that which is behind of the afflictions of Christ in my flesh for his body's sake, which is the church, ²⁵whereof I am made a minister, according to the dispensation of God which is given to me for you, to fulfil the word of God: ²⁶even the mystery which hath been hid from ages and from generations, but now is made manifest to his saints, ²⁷to whom God would make known what is the riches of the glory of this mystery among the Gentiles, which is Christ in you, the hope of glory: ²⁸whom we preach, warning every man, and teaching every man in all wisdom, that we may present every man perfect in Christ Jesus: ²⁹whereunto I also labour, striving according to his working, which worketh in me mightily.

2 For I would that ye knew what great conflict I have for you, and for them at Laodicea, and for as many as have not seen my face in the flesh: ²that their hearts might be comforted, being knit together in love, and unto all riches of the full assurance of understanding, to the acknowledgement of the mystery of God, and of the Father, and of Christ, ³in whom are hid all the treasures of wisdom and knowledge. ⁴And this I say, lest any man should beguile you with enticing words. ⁵For though I be absent in the flesh, yet am I with you in the spirit, joying and beholding your order, and the steadfastness of your faith in Christ.

⁶As ye have therefore received Christ Jesus the Lord, so walk ye in him: ⁷rooted and built up in him, and established in the faith, as ye have been taught, abounding therein with thanksgiving. ⁸Beware lest any man spoil you through philosophy and vain deceit, after the tradition of men, after the rudiments of the world, and not after Christ. ⁹For in him dwelleth all the fulness of the Godhead bodily. ¹⁰And ye are complete in him, which is the head of all principality and power: ¹¹in whom also ye are circumcised with the circumcision made without hands, in putting off the body of the sins of the flesh by the circumcision of Christ: ¹²buried with him in baptism, wherein also you are risen with him through the faith of the operation of God, who hath raised him from the dead. ¹³And you, being dead in your sins and the uncircumcision of your flesh, hath he quickened together with him, having forgiven you all trespasses, ¹⁴blotting out the handwriting of ordinances that was against us, which was contrary to us, and took it out of the way, nailing it to his cross: ¹⁵and having spoiled principalities and powers, he made a show of them openly, triumphing over them in it.

¹⁶Let no man therefore judge you in meat, or in drink, or in respect of a holy day, or of the new moon, or of the sabbath days: ¹⁷which are a shadow of things to come, but the body is of Christ. ¹⁸Let no man beguile you of your reward in a voluntary humility and worshipping of angels, intruding into those things which he hath not seen, vainly puffed up by his fleshly mind, ¹⁹and not holding the head, from which all the body by joints and bands having nourishment ministered, and knit together, increaseth with the increase of God. ²⁰Wherefore if ye be dead with Christ from the rudiments of the world, why, as though liv-

ing in the world, are ye subject to ordinances ²¹(touch not, taste not, handle not: ²²which all are to perish with the using), after the commandments and doctrines of men? ²³which things have indeed a show of wisdom in will-worship, and humility, and neglecting of the body, not in any honour to the satisfying of the flesh.

3 If ye then be risen with Christ, seek those things which are above, where Christ sitteth on the right hand of God. ²Set your affection on things above, not on things on the earth. ³For ye are dead, and your life is hid with Christ in God. ⁴When Christ, who is our life, shall appear, then shall ye also appear with him in glory.

⁵Mortify therefore your members which are upon the earth: fornication, uncleanness, inordinate affection, evil concupiscence, and covetousness, which is idolatry: ⁶for which things' sake the wrath of God cometh on the children of disobedience, ⁷in the which ye also walked sometime, when ye lived in them. ⁸But now you also put off all these, anger, wrath, malice, blasphemy, filthy communication out of your mouth. ⁹Lie not one to another, seeing that ye have put off the old man with his deeds: ¹⁰and have put on the new man, which is renewed in knowledge after the image of him that created him, ¹¹where there is neither Greek nor Jew, circumcision nor uncircumcision, Barbarian, Scythian, bond nor free: but Christ is all, and in all.

¹²Put on therefore, as the elect of God, holy and beloved, bowels of mercies, kindness, humbleness of mind, meekness, long-suffering, ¹³forbearing one another, and forgiving one another, if any man have a quarrel against any: even as Christ forgave you, so also do ye. ¹⁴And above all these things put on charity, which is the bond of perfectness. ¹⁵And let the peace of God rule in your hearts, to the which also ye are called in one body: and be ye thankful. ¹⁶Let the word of Christ dwell in you richly in all wisdom, teaching and admonishing one another in psalms and hymns and spiritual songs, singing with grace in your hearts to the Lord. ¹⁷And whatsoever ye do in word or deed, do all in the name of the Lord Jesus, giving thanks to God and the Father by him.

¹⁸Wives, submit yourselves unto your own husbands, as it is fit in the Lord. ¹⁹Husbands, love your wives, and be not bitter against them. ²⁰Children, obey your parents in all things, for this is well-pleasing unto the Lord. ²¹Fathers, provoke not your children to anger, lest they be discouraged. ²²Servants, obey in all things your masters according to the flesh: not with eye-service, as men-pleasers, but in singleness of heart, fearing God: ²³and whatsoever ye do, do it heartily, as to the Lord, and not unto men: ²⁴knowing that of the Lord ye shall receive the reward of the inheritance: for ye serve the Lord Christ. ²⁵But he that doeth wrong shall receive for the wrong which he hath done: and there is no respect

4 of persons. ¹Masters, give unto your servants that which is just and equal, knowing that ye also have a Master in heaven.

²Continue in prayer, and watch in the same with thanksgiving: ³withal praying also for us, that God would open unto us a door of utterance, to speak the mystery of Christ, for which I am also in bonds: ⁴that I may make it manifest, as I ought to speak. ⁵Walk in wisdom

toward them that are without, redeeming the time. ⁶Let your speech be always with grace, seasoned with salt, that you may know how ye ought to answer every man.

⁷All my state shall Tychicus declare unto you, who is a beloved brother, and a faithful minister and fellow-servant in the Lord: ⁸whom I have sent unto you for the same purpose, that he might know your estate, and comfort your hearts; ⁹with Onesimus, a faithful and beloved brother, who is one of you. They shall make known unto you all things which are done here.

¹⁰Aristarchus my fellow-prisoner saluteth you, and Marcus, sister's son to Barnabas (touching whom ye received commandments: if he come unto you, receive him), ¹¹and Jesus, which is called Justus, who are of the circumcision. These only are my fellow-workers unto the kingdom of God, which have been a comfort unto me. ¹²Epaphras, who is one of you, a servant of Christ, saluteth you, always labouring fervently for you in prayers, that ye may stand perfect and complete in all the will of God. ¹³For I bear him record, that he hath a great zeal for you, and them that are in Laodicea, and them in Hierapolis. ¹⁴Luke, the beloved physician, and Demas, greet you. ¹⁵Salute the brethren which are in Laodicea, and Nymphas, and the church which is in his house. ¹⁶And when this epistle is read amongst you, cause that it be read also in the church of the Laodiceans: and that ye likewise read the epistle from Laodicea.

¹⁷And say to Archippus, 'Take heed to the ministry which thou hast received in the Lord, that thou fulfil it'.

¹⁸The salutation by the hand of me Paul. Remember my bonds. Grace be with you. Amen.

Written from Rome to the Colossians by Tychicus and Onesimus.

THE FIRST EPISTLE
OF PAUL THE APOSTLE
TO THE
THESSALONIANS

1 Paul, and Silvanus, and Timothy, unto the church of the Thessalonians which is in God the Father and in the Lord Jesus Christ: grace be unto you, and peace, from God our Father, and the Lord Jesus Christ.

²We give thanks to God always for you all, making mention of you in our prayers, ³remembering without ceasing your work of faith, and labour of love, and patience of hope in our Lord Jesus Christ, in the sight of God and our Father: ⁴knowing, brethren beloved, your election of God. ⁵For our gospel came not unto you in word only, but also in power, and in the Holy Ghost, and in much assurance; as ye know what manner of men we were among you for your sake. ⁶And ye became followers of us, and of the Lord, having received the word in much affliction, with joy of the Holy Ghost: ⁷so that ye were examples to all that believe in Macedonia and Achaia. ⁸For from you sounded out the word of the Lord not only in Macedonia and Achaia, but also in every place your faith to God-ward is spread abroad, so that we need not to speak anything. ⁹For they themselves show of us what manner of entering in we had unto you, and how ye turned to God from idols to serve the living and true God, ¹⁰and to wait for his Son from heaven, whom he raised from the dead, even Jesus, which delivered us from the wrath to come.

2 For yourselves, brethren, know our entrance in unto you, that it was not in vain: ²but even after that we had suffered before, and were shamefully entreated, as ye know, at Philippi, we were bold in our God to speak unto you the gospel of God with much contention. ³For our exhortation was not of deceit, nor of uncleanness, nor in guile: ⁴but as we were allowed of God to be put in trust with the gospel, even so we speak, not as pleasing men, but God, which trieth our hearts. ⁵For neither at any time used we flattering words, as ye know, nor a cloak of covetousness, God is witness: ⁶nor of men sought we glory, neither of you, nor yet of others, when we might have been burdensome, as the apostles of Christ. ⁷But we were gentle among you, even as a nurse cherisheth her children: ⁸so being affectionately desirous of you, we were willing to have imparted unto you, not the gospel of God only, but also our own souls, because ye were dear unto us. ⁹For ye remember, brethren, our labour and travail: for labouring night and day, because we would not be chargeable unto any of you, we preached unto you the gospel of God. ¹⁰Ye are witnesses, and God also, how holily and justly and unblameably we behaved ourselves among you that believe: ¹¹as you know how we exhorted and comforted and charged every one of

you, as a father doth his children, [12]that ye would walk worthy of God, who hath called you unto his kingdom and glory.

[13]For this cause also thank we God without ceasing, because, when ye received the word of God which ye heard of us, ye received it not as the word of men, but, as it is in truth, the word of God, which effectually worketh also in you that believe. [14]For ye, brethren, became followers of the churches of God which in Judea are in Christ Jesus: for ye also have suffered like things of your own countrymen, even as they have of the Jews: [15]who both killed the Lord Jesus, and their own prophets, and have persecuted us: and they please not God, and are contrary to all men: [16]forbidding us to speak to the Gentiles that they might be saved, to fill up their sins always: for the wrath is come upon them to the uttermost.

[17]But we, brethren, being taken from you for a short time in presence, not in heart, endeavoured the more abundantly to see your face with great desire. [18]Wherefore we would have come unto you, even I Paul, once and again: but Satan hindered us. [19]For what is our hope, or joy, or crown of rejoicing? Are not even ye in the presence of our Lord Jesus Christ at his coming? [20]For ye are our glory and joy.

3 Wherefore when we could no longer forbear, we thought it good to be left at Athens alone: [2]and sent Timothy, our brother, and minister of God, and our fellow-labourer in the gospel of Christ, to establish you, and to comfort you concerning your faith: [3]that no man should be moved by these afflictions: for yourselves know that we are appointed thereunto. [4]For verily, when we were with you, we told you before that we should suffer tribulation, even as it came to pass, and ye know. [5]For this cause, when I could no longer forbear, I sent to know your faith, lest by some means the tempter have tempted you, and our labour be in vain.

[6]But now when Timothy came from you unto us, and brought us good tidings of your faith and charity, and that ye have good remembrance of us always, desiring greatly to see us, as we also to see you: [7]therefore, brethren, we were comforted over you in all our affliction and distress by your faith: [8]for now we live, if ye stand fast in the Lord. [9]For what thanks can we render to God again for you, for all the joy wherewith we joy for your sakes before our God, [10]night and day praying exceedingly that we might see your face, and might perfect that which is lacking in your faith?

[11]Now God himself and our Father, and our Lord Jesus Christ, direct our way unto you. [12]And the Lord make you to increase and abound in love one towards another, and towards all men, even as we do towards you: [13]to the end he may establish your hearts unblameable in holiness before God, even our Father, at the coming of our Lord Jesus Christ with all his saints.

4 Furthermore then we beseech you, brethren, and exhort you by the Lord Jesus, that as ye have received of us how ye ought to walk and to please God, so ye would abound more and more. [2]For ye know what commandments we gave you by the Lord Jesus. [3]For this is the will of

God, even your sanctification, that ye should abstain from fornication: [4]that every one of you should know how to possess his vessel in sanctification and honour: [5]not in the lust of concupiscence, even as the Gentiles which know not God: [6]that no man go beyond and defraud his brother in any matter, because that the Lord is the avenger of all such; as we also have forewarned you and testified: [7]for God hath not called us unto uncleanness, but unto holiness. [8]He therefore that despiseth, despiseth not man, but God, who hath also given unto us his holy Spirit.

[9]But as touching brotherly love ye need not that I write unto you: for ye yourselves are taught of God to love one another. [10]And indeed ye do it towards all the brethren which are in all Macedonia: but we beseech you, brethren, that ye increase more and more: [11]and that ye study to be quiet, and to do your own business, and to work with your own hands, as we commanded you: [12]that ye may walk honestly toward them that are without, and that ye may have lack of nothing.

[13]But I would not have you to be ignorant, brethren, concerning them which are asleep, that ye sorrow not, even as others which have no hope. [14]For if we believe that Jesus died and rose again, even so them also which sleep in Jesus will God bring with him. [15]For this we say unto you by the word of the Lord, that we which are alive and remain unto the coming of the Lord shall not prevent them which are asleep. [16]For the Lord himself shall descend from heaven with a shout, with the voice of the archangel, and with the trump of God: and the dead in Christ shall rise first. [17]Then we which are alive and remain shall be caught up together with them in the clouds, to meet the Lord in the air: and so shall we ever be with the Lord. [18]Wherefore comfort one another with these words.

5 But of the times and the seasons, brethren, ye have no need that I write unto you. [2]For yourselves know perfectly that the day of the Lord so cometh as a thief in the night. [3]For when they shall say, 'Peace and safety': then sudden destruction cometh upon them, as travail upon a woman with child, and they shall not escape. [4]But ye, brethren, are not in darkness, that that day should overtake you as a thief. [5]Ye are all the children of light, and the children of the day: we are not of the night, nor of darkness. [6]Therefore let us not sleep, as do others: but let us watch and be sober. [7]For they that sleep sleep in the night, and they that be drunken are drunken in the night. [8]But let us, who are of the day, be sober, putting on the breastplate of faith and love, and for a helmet, the hope of salvation. [9]For God hath not appointed us to wrath, but to obtain salvation by our Lord Jesus Christ, [10]who died for us, that, whether we wake or sleep, we should live together with him. [11]Wherefore comfort yourselves together, and edify one another, even as also ye do.

[12]And we beseech you, brethren, to know them which labour among you, and are over you in the Lord, and admonish you: [13]and to esteem them very highly in love for their work's sake, and be at peace among yourselves. [14]Now we exhort you, brethren, warn them that are unruly,

comfort the feeble-minded, support the weak, be patient toward all men. ¹⁵See that none render evil for evil unto any man: but ever follow that which is good, both among yourselves, and to all men.

¹⁶Rejoice evermore: ¹⁷pray without ceasing: ¹⁸in everything give thanks: for this is the will of God in Christ Jesus concerning you. ¹⁹Quench not the Spirit: ²⁰despise not prophesyings: ²¹prove all things; hold fast that which is good. ²²Abstain from all appearance of evil.

²³And the very God of peace sanctify you wholly: and I pray God your whole spirit and soul and body be preserved blameless unto the coming of our Lord Jesus Christ. ²⁴Faithful is he that calleth you, who also will do it.

²⁵Brethren, pray for us. ²⁶Greet all the brethren with a holy kiss.

²⁷I charge you by the Lord that this epistle be read unto all the holy brethren.

²⁸The grace of our Lord Jesus Christ be with you. Amen.

The first epistle unto the Thessalonians was written from Athens.

THE SECOND EPISTLE OF PAUL THE APOSTLE TO THE
THESSALONIANS

1 Paul, and Silvanus, and Timothy, unto the church of the Thessalonians in God our Father and the Lord Jesus Christ: ²grace unto you, and peace, from God our Father and the Lord Jesus Christ.

³We are bound to thank God always for you, brethren, as it is meet, because that your faith groweth exceedingly, and the charity of every one of you all towards each other aboundeth: ⁴so that we ourselves glory in you in the churches of God for your patience and faith in all your persecutions and tribulations that ye endure: ⁵which is a manifest token of the righteous judgement of God, that ye may be counted worthy of the kingdom of God, for which ye also suffer; ⁶seeing it is a righteous thing with God to recompense tribulation to them that trouble you: ⁷and to you who are troubled rest with us, when the Lord Jesus shall be revealed from heaven with his mighty angels, ⁸in flaming fire taking vengeance on them that know not God, and that obey not the gospel of our Lord Jesus Christ: ⁹who shall be punished with everlasting destruction from the presence of the Lord, and from the glory of his power: ¹⁰when he shall come to be glorified in his saints, and to be admired in all them that believe (because our testimony among you was believed) in that day. ¹¹Wherefore also we pray always for you, that our God would count you worthy of this calling, and fulfil all the good pleasure of his goodness, and the work of faith with power: ¹²that the name of our Lord Jesus Christ may be glorified in you, and ye in him, according to the grace of our God and the Lord Jesus Christ.

2 Now we beseech you, brethren, by the coming of our Lord Jesus Christ, and by our gathering together unto him, ²that ye be not soon shaken in mind, or be troubled, neither by spirit, nor by word, nor by letter as from us, as that the day of Christ is at hand. ³Let no man deceive you by any means, for that day shall not come, except there come a falling away first, and that man of sin be revealed, the son of perdition, ⁴who opposeth and exalteth himself above all that is called God, or that is worshipped: so that he as God sitteth in the temple of God, showing himself that he is God. ⁵Remember ye not, that, when I was yet with you, I told you these things? ⁶And now ye know what withholdeth that he might be revealed in his time. ⁷For the mystery of iniquity doth already work: only he who now letteth will let, until he be taken out of the way. ⁸And then shall that wicked be revealed, whom the Lord shall consume with the spirit of his mouth, and shall destroy with the brightness of his coming: ⁹even him, whose coming is after the working of Satan with all power and signs and lying wonders, ¹⁰and with all deceivableness of unrighteousness in them that perish: because they received not the love of the truth, that they might be saved. ¹¹And for this cause God shall send them strong delusion, that they should believe a lie: [12] that they all might be damned who believed not the truth, but had pleasure in unrighteousness.

[13] But we are bound to give thanks always to God for you, brethren beloved of the Lord, because God hath from the beginning chosen you to salvation through sanctification of the Spirit and belief of the truth, [14] whereunto he called you by our gospel, to the obtaining of the glory of the Lord Jesus Christ. [15] Therefore, brethren, stand fast, and hold the traditions which ye have been taught, whether by word, or our epistle. [16] Now our Lord Jesus Christ himself, and God, even our Father, which hath loved us, and hath given us everlasting consolation and good hope through grace, [17] comfort your hearts, and establish you in every good word and work.

3 Finally, brethren, pray for us, that the word of the Lord may have free course, and be glorified, even as it is with you: [2] and that we may be delivered from unreasonable and wicked men: for all men have not faith. [3] But the Lord is faithful, who shall establish you, and keep you from evil. [4] And we have confidence in the Lord touching you, that ye both do and will do the things which we command you. [5] And the Lord direct your hearts into the love of God, and into the patient waiting for Christ.

[6] Now we command you, brethren, in the name of our Lord Jesus Christ, that ye withdraw yourselves from every brother that walketh disorderly, and not after the tradition which he received of us. [7] For yourselves know how ye ought to follow us: for we behaved not ourselves disorderly among you, [8] neither did we eat any man's bread for nought: but wrought with labour and travail night and day, that we might not be chargeable to any of you: [9] not because we have not power, but to make ourselves an example unto you to follow us. [10] For even when we were with you, this we commanded you, that if any would not work, neither should he eat. [11] For we hear that there are some which walk among you disorderly, working not at all, but are busybodies. [12] Now them that are such we command and exhort by our Lord Jesus Christ, that with quietness they work, and eat their own bread.

[13] But ye, brethren, be not weary in well-doing. [14] And if any man obey not our word by this epistle, note that man, and have no company with him, that he may be ashamed. [15] Yet count him not as an enemy, but admonish him as a brother.

[16] Now the Lord of peace himself give you peace always by all means. The Lord be with you all.

[17] The salutation of Paul with my own hand, which is the token in every epistle: so I write.

[18] The grace of our Lord Jesus Christ be with you all. Amen.

The second epistle to the Thessalonians was written from Athens.

THE FIRST EPISTLE
OF PAUL THE APOSTLE TO
TIMOTHY

1 Paul, an apostle of Jesus Christ by the commandment of God our Saviour, and Lord Jesus Christ, which is our hope, [2] unto Timothy, my own son in the faith: grace, mercy, and peace, from God our Father and Jesus Christ our Lord.

[3] As I besought thee to abide still at Ephesus, when I went into Macedonia, that thou mightest charge some that they teach no other doctrine, [4] neither give heed to fables and endless genealogies, which minister questions, rather than edifying which is in faith: so do. [5] Now the end of the commandment is charity out of a pure heart, and of a good conscience, and of faith unfeigned: [6] from which some having swerved have turned aside unto vain jangling, [7] desiring to be teachers of the law, understanding neither what they say, nor whereof they affirm. [8] But we know that the law is good, if a man use it lawfully; [9] knowing this, that the law is not made for a righteous man, but for the lawless and disobedient, for the ungodly and for sinners, for unholy and profane, for murderers of fathers and murderers of mothers, for man-slayers, [10] for whoremongers, for them that defile themselves with mankind, for men-stealers, for liars, for perjured persons, and if there be any other thing that is contrary to sound doctrine, [11] according to the glorious gospel of the blessed God, which was committed to my trust.

[12] And I thank Christ Jesus our Lord, who hath enabled me, for that he counted me faithful, putting me into the ministry, [13] who was before a blasphemer, and a persecutor, and injurious. But I obtained mercy, because I did it ignorantly in unbelief. [14] And the grace of our Lord was exceeding abundant with faith and love which is in Christ Jesus. [15] This is a faithful saying, and worthy of all acceptation, that Christ Jesus came into the world to save sinners, of whom I am chief. [16] Howbeit for this cause I obtained mercy, that in me first Jesus Christ might show forth all long-suffering, for a pattern to them which should hereafter believe on him to life everlasting. [17] Now unto the King eternal, immortal, invisible, the only wise God, be honour and glory for ever and ever. Amen.

[18] This charge I commit unto thee, son Timothy, according to the prophecies which went before on thee, that thou by them mightest war a good warfare, [19] holding faith, and a good conscience; which some having put away concerning faith have made shipwreck: [20] of whom is Hymeneus and Alexander, whom I have delivered unto Satan, that they may learn not to blaspheme.

2 I exhort therefore, that, first of all, supplications, prayers, intercessions, and giving of thanks, be made for all men: [2] for kings, and for all that are in authority, that we may lead a quiet and peaceable life in all godliness and honesty. [3] For this is good and acceptable in the sight

of God our Saviour, ⁴who will have all men to be saved, and to come unto the knowledge of the truth. ⁵For there is one God, and one mediator between God and men, the man Christ Jesus, ⁶who gave himself a ransom for all, to be testified in due time. ⁷Whereunto I am ordained a preacher, and an apostle (I speak the truth in Christ, and lie not), a teacher of the Gentiles in faith and verity.

⁸I will therefore that men pray everywhere, lifting up holy hands, without wrath and doubting. ⁹In like manner also, that women adorn themselves in modest apparel, with shamefastness and sobriety, not with braided hair, or gold, or pearls, or costly array, ¹⁰but (which becometh women professing godliness) with good works. ¹¹Let the woman learn in silence with all subjection. ¹²But I suffer not a woman to teach, nor to usurp authority over the man, but to be in silence. ¹³For Adam was first formed, then Eve. ¹⁴And Adam was not deceived, but the woman being deceived was in the transgression. ¹⁵Notwithstanding she shall be saved in child-bearing, if they continue in faith and charity and holiness with sobriety.

3 This is a true saying, 'If a man desire the office of a bishop, he desireth a good work'. ²A bishop then must be blameless, the husband of one wife, vigilant, sober, of good behaviour, given to hospitality, apt to teach, ³not given to wine, no striker, not greedy of filthy lucre, but patient, not a brawler, not covetous; ⁴one that ruleth well his own house, having his children in subjection with all gravity ⁵(for if a man know not how to rule his own house, how shall he take care of the church of God?); ⁶not a novice, lest being lifted up with pride he fall into the condemnation of the devil. ⁷Moreover he must have a good report of them which are without, lest he fall into reproach and the snare of the devil.

⁸Likewise must the deacons be grave, not double-tongued, not given to much wine, not greedy of filthy lucre, ⁹holding the mystery of the faith in a pure conscience. ¹⁰And let these also first be proved; then let them use the office of a deacon, being found blameless. ¹¹Even so must their wives be grave, not slanderers, sober, faithful in all things. ¹²Let the deacons be the husbands of one wife, ruling their children and their own houses well. ¹³For they that have used the office of a deacon well purchase to themselves a good degree, and great boldness in the faith which is in Christ Jesus.

¹⁴These things write I unto thee, hoping to come unto thee shortly: ¹⁵but if I tarry long, that thou mayest know how thou oughtest to behave thyself in the house of God, which is the church of the living God, the pillar and ground of the truth. ¹⁶And without controversy, great is the mystery of godliness: God was manifest in the flesh, justified in the Spirit, seen of angels, preached unto the Gentiles, believed on in the world, received up into glory.

4 Now the Spirit speaketh expressly, that in the latter times some shall depart from the faith, giving heed to seducing spirits, and doctrines of devils: ²speaking lies in hypocrisy, having their conscience seared with a hot iron, ³forbidding to marry, and commanding to

abstain from meats, which God hath created to be received with thanksgiving of them which believe and know the truth. ⁴For every creature of God is good, and nothing to be refused, if it be received with thanksgiving: ⁵for it is sanctified by the word of God and prayer.

⁶If thou put the brethren in remembrance of these things, thou shalt be a good minister of Jesus Christ, nourished up in the words of faith and of good doctrine, whereunto thou hast attained. ⁷But refuse profane and old wives' fables, and exercise thyself rather unto godliness. ⁸For bodily exercise profiteth little, but godliness is profitable unto all things, having promise of the life that now is, and of that which is to come. ⁹This is a faithful saying and worthy of all acceptation. ¹⁰For therefore we both labour and suffer reproach, because we trust in the living God, who is the Saviour of all men, specially of those that believe.

¹¹These things command and teach. ¹²Let no man despise thy youth, but be thou an example of the believers, in word, in conversation, in charity, in spirit, in faith, in purity. ¹³Till I come, give attendance to reading, to exhortation, to doctrine. ¹⁴Neglect not the gift that is in thee, which was given thee by prophecy, with the laying on of the hands of the presbytery. ¹⁵Meditate upon these things, give thyself wholly to them, that thy profiting may appear to all. ¹⁶Take heed unto thyself, and unto the doctrine: continue in them: for in doing this thou shalt both save thyself, and them that hear thee.

5 Rebuke not an elder, but entreat him as a father, and the younger men as brethren: ²the elder women as mothers, the younger as sisters, with all purity. ³Honour widows that are widows indeed. ⁴But if any widow have children or nephews, let them learn first to show piety at home, and to requite their parents: for that is good and acceptable before God. ⁵Now she that is a widow indeed, and desolate, trusteth in God, and continueth in supplications and prayers night and day. ⁶But she that liveth in pleasure is dead while she liveth. ⁷And these things give in charge, that they may be blameless. ⁸But if any provide not for his own, and specially for those of his own house, he hath denied the faith, and is worse than an infidel. ⁹Let not a widow be taken into the number under threescore years old, having been the wife of one man, ¹⁰well reported of for good works, if she have brought up children, if she have lodged strangers, if she have washed the saints' feet, if she have relieved the afflicted, if she have diligently followed every good work. ¹¹But the younger widows refuse: for when they have begun to wax wanton against Christ, they will marry, ¹²having damnation, because they have cast off their first faith. ¹³And withal they learn to be idle, wandering about from house to house; and not only idle, but tattlers also and busybodies, speaking things which they ought not. ¹⁴I will therefore that the younger women marry, bear children, guide the house, give no occasion to the adversary to speak reproachfully. ¹⁵For some are already turned aside after Satan. ¹⁶If any man or woman that believeth have widows, let them relieve them, and let not the church be charged, that it may relieve them that are widows indeed.

¹⁷Let the elders that rule well be counted worthy of double honour,

especially they who labour in the word and doctrine. [18]For the scripture saith, 'Thou shalt not muzzle the ox that treadeth out the corn': and, 'The labourer is worthy of his reward'. [19]Against an elder receive not an accusation, but before two or three witnesses. [20]Them that sin rebuke before all, that others also may fear. [21]I charge thee before God, and the Lord Jesus Christ, and the elect angels, that thou observe these things without preferring one before another, doing nothing by partiality. [22]Lay hands suddenly on no man, neither be partaker of other men's sins. Keep thyself pure.

[23]Drink no longer water, but use a little wine for thy stomach's sake and thy often infirmities. [24]Some men's sins are open beforehand, going before to judgement: and some men they follow after. [25]Likewise also the good works of some are manifest beforehand, and they that are otherwise cannot be hid.

6 Let as many servants as are under the yoke count their own masters worthy of all honour, that the name of God and his doctrine be not blasphemed. [2]And they that have believing masters, let them not despise them, because they are brethren: but rather do them service, because they are faithful and beloved, partakers of the benefit. These things teach and exhort.

[3]If any man teach otherwise, and consent not to wholesome words, even the words of our Lord Jesus Christ, and to the doctrine which is according to godliness: [4]he is proud, knowing nothing, but doting about questions and strifes of words, whereof cometh envy, strife, railings, evil surmisings, [5]perverse disputings of men of corrupt minds, and destitute of the truth, supposing that gain is godliness: from such withdraw thyself. [6]But godliness with contentment is great gain. [7]For we brought nothing into this world, and it is certain we can carry nothing out. [8]And having food and raiment let us be therewith content. [9]But they that will be rich fall into temptation and a snare, and into many foolish and hurtful lusts, which drown men in destruction and perdition. [10]For the love of money is the root of all evil, which while some coveted after, they have erred from the faith, and pierced themselves through with many sorrows.

[11]But thou, O man of God, fly these things; and follow after righteousness, godliness, faith, love, patience, meekness. [12]Fight the good fight of faith, lay hold on eternal life, whereunto thou art also called, and hast professed a good profession before many witnesses. [13]I give thee charge in the sight of God, who quickeneth all things, and before Christ Jesus, who before Pontius Pilate witnessed a good confession, [14]that thou keep this commandment without spot, unrebukeable, until the appearing of our Lord Jesus Christ: [15]which in his times he shall show, who is the blessed and only Potentate, the King of kings, and Lord of lords: [16]who only hath immortality, dwelling in the light which no man can approach unto, whom no man hath seen, nor can see: to whom be honour and power everlasting. Amen.

[17]Charge them that are rich in this world, that they be not highminded, nor trust in uncertain riches, but in the living God, who

giveth us richly all things to enjoy, [18] that they do good, that they be rich in good works, ready to distribute, willing to communicate, [19] laying up in store for themselves a good foundation against the time to come, that they may lay hold on eternal life.

[20] O Timothy, keep that which is committed to thy trust, avoiding profane and vain babblings, and oppositions of science falsely so called: [21] which some professing have erred concerning the faith.

Grace be with thee. Amen.

The first to Timothy was written from Laodicea, which is the chiefest city of Phrygia Pacatiana.

THE SECOND EPISTLE
OF PAUL THE APOSTLE TO
TIMOTHY

1 Paul, an apostle of Jesus Christ by the will of God, according to the promise of life which is in Christ Jesus, ²to Timothy, my dearly beloved son: grace, mercy, and peace, from God the Father and Christ Jesus our Lord.

³I thank God, whom I serve from my forefathers with pure conscience, that without ceasing I have remembrance of thee in my prayers night and day, ⁴greatly desiring to see thee, being mindful of thy tears, that I may be filled with joy, ⁵when I call to remembrance the unfeigned faith that is in thee, which dwelt first in thy grandmother Lois, and thy mother Eunice: and I am persuaded that in thee also. ⁶Wherefore I put thee in remembrance that thou stir up the gift of God, which is in thee by the putting on of my hands. ⁷For God hath not given us the spirit of fear, but of power, of love, and of a sound mind. ⁸Be not thou therefore ashamed of the testimony of our Lord, nor of me his prisoner, but be thou partaker of the afflictions of the gospel according to the power of God, ⁹who hath saved us, and called us with a holy calling, not according to our works, but according to his own purpose and grace, which was given us in Christ Jesus before the world began, ¹⁰but is now made manifest by the appearing of our Saviour Jesus Christ, who hath abolished death, and hath brought life and immortality to light through the gospel: ¹¹whereunto I am appointed a preacher, and an apostle, and a teacher of the Gentiles. ¹²For the which cause I also suffer these things; nevertheless I am not ashamed: for I know whom I have believed, and I am persuaded that he is able to keep that which I have committed unto him against that day. ¹³Hold fast the form of sound words, which thou hast heard of me, in faith and love which is in Christ Jesus. ¹⁴That good thing which was committed unto thee keep by the Holy Ghost which dwelleth in us.

¹⁵This thou knowest, that all they which are in Asia be turned away from me, of whom are Phygellus and Hermogenes. ¹⁶The Lord give mercy unto the house of Onesiphorus, for he oft refreshed me, and was not ashamed of my chain: ¹⁷but, when he was in Rome, he sought me out very diligently, and found me. ¹⁸The Lord grant unto him that he may find mercy of the Lord in that day: and in how many things he ministered unto me at Ephesus, thou knowest very well.

2 Thou therefore, my son, be strong in the grace that is in Christ Jesus. ²And the things that thou hast heard of me among many witnesses, the same commit thou to faithful men, who shall be able to teach others also. ³Thou therefore endure hardness, as a good soldier of Jesus Christ. ⁴No man that warreth entangleth himself with the affairs of this life, that he may please him who hath chosen him to be a soldier. [5]And if a man also strive for masteries, yet is he not crowned, except he strive lawfully. [6]The husbandman that laboureth must be first partaker of the fruits. [7]Consider what I say, and the Lord give thee understanding in all things.

[8]Remember that Jesus Christ of the seed of David was raised from the dead according to my gospel: [9]wherein I suffer trouble, as an evil doer, even unto bonds: but the word of God is not bound. [10]Therefore I endure all things for the elect's sakes, that they may also obtain the salvation which is in Christ Jesus with eternal glory.

[11]It is a faithful saying: 'For if we be dead with him, we shall also live with him: [12]if we suffer, we shall also reign with him: if we deny him, he also will deny us: [13]if we believe not, yet he abideth faithful: he cannot deny himself'.

[14]Of these things put them in remembrance, charging them before the Lord that they strive not about words to no profit, but to the subverting of the hearers. [15]Study to show thyself approved unto God, a workman that needeth not to be ashamed, rightly dividing the word of truth. [16]But shun profane and vain babblings, for they will increase unto more ungodliness. [17]And their word will eat as doth a canker: of whom is Hymeneus and Philetus; [18]who concerning the truth have erred, saying that the resurrection is past already, and overthrow the faith of some. [19]Nevertheless the foundation of God standeth sure, having the seal, 'The Lord knoweth them that are his'. And, 'Let every one that nameth the name of Christ depart from iniquity'. [20]But in a great house there are not only vessels of gold and of silver, but also of wood and of earth: and some to honour, and some to dishonour. [21]If a man therefore purge himself from these, he shall be a vessel unto honour, sanctified, and meet for the master's use, and prepared unto every good work.

[22]Fly also youthful lusts: but follow righteousness, faith, charity, peace, with them that call on the Lord out of a pure heart. [23]But foolish and unlearned questions avoid, knowing that they do gender strifes. [24]And the servant of the Lord must not strive: but be gentle unto all men, apt to teach, patient, [25]in meekness instructing those that oppose themselves, if God peradventure will give them repentance to the acknowledging of the truth; [26]and that they may recover themselves out of the snare of the devil, who are taken captive by him at his will.

3 This know also, that in the last days perilous times shall come. [2]For men shall be lovers of their own selves, covetous, boasters, proud, blasphemers, disobedient to parents, unthankful, unholy, [3]without natural affection, truce-breakers, false accusers, incontinent, fierce, despisers of those that are good, [4]traitors, heady, high-minded, lovers of pleasures more than lovers of God, [5]having a form of godliness, but denying the power thereof: from such turn away. [6]For of this sort are they which creep into houses, and lead captive silly women laden with sins, led away with divers lusts, [7]ever learning, and never able to come to the knowledge of the truth. [8]Now as Jannes and Jambres withstood Moses, so do these also resist the truth: men of corrupt minds, reprobate

concerning the faith. [9]But they shall proceed no further: for their folly shall be manifest unto all men, as theirs also was.

[10]But thou hast fully known my doctrine, manner of life, purpose, faith, long-suffering, charity, patience, [11]persecutions, afflictions, which came unto me at Antioch, at Iconium, at Lystra, what persecutions I endured: but out of them all the Lord delivered me. [12]Yea, and all that will live godly in Christ Jesus shall suffer persecution. [13]But evil men and seducers shall wax worse and worse, deceiving, and being deceived. [14]But continue thou in the things which thou hast learned and hast been assured of, knowing of whom thou hast learned them; [15]and that from a child thou hast known the holy scriptures, which are able to make thee wise unto salvation through faith which is in Christ Jesus. [16]All scripture is given by inspiration of God, and is profitable for doctrine, for reproof, for correction, for instruction in righteousness, [17]that the man of God may be perfect, thoroughly furnished unto all good works.

4 I charge thee therefore before God, and the Lord Jesus Christ, who shall judge the quick and the dead at his appearing and his kingdom: [2]preach the word, be instant in season, out of season, reprove, rebuke, exhort with all long-suffering and doctrine. [3]For the time will come when they will not endure sound doctrine, but after their own lusts shall they heap to themselves teachers, having itching ears: [4]and they shall turn away their ears from the truth, and shall be turned unto fables. [5]But watch thou in all things, endure afflictions, do the work of an evangelist, make full proof of thy ministry.

[6]For I am now ready to be offered, and the time of my departure is at hand. [7]I have fought a good fight, I have finished my course, I have kept the faith. [8]Henceforth there is laid up for me a crown of righteousness, which the Lord, the righteous judge, shall give me at that day: and not to me only, but unto them also that love his appearing.

[9]Do thy diligence to come shortly unto me: [10]for Demas hath forsaken me, having loved this present world, and is departed unto Thessalonica; Crescens to Galatia, Titus unto Dalmatia. [11]Only Luke is with me. Take Mark, and bring him with thee: for he is profitable to me for the ministry. [12]And Tychicus have I sent to Ephesus. [13]The cloak that I left at Troas with Carpus, when thou comest, bring with thee, and the books, but especially the parchments.

[14]Alexander the coppersmith did me much evil: the Lord reward him according to his works: [15]of whom be thou wary also, for he hath greatly withstood our words. [16]At my first answer no man stood with me, but all men forsook me: I pray God that it may not be laid to their charge. [17]Notwithstanding the Lord stood with me, and strengthened me, that by me the preaching might be fully known, and that all the Gentiles might hear: and I was delivered out of the mouth of the lion. [18]And the Lord shall deliver me from every evil work, and will preserve me unto his heavenly kingdom; to whom be glory for ever and ever. Amen.

[19]Salute Prisca and Aquila, and the household of Onesiphorus.

²⁰Erastus abode at Corinth: but Trophimus have I left at Miletum sick. ²¹Do thy diligence to come before winter.

Eubulus greeteth thee, and Pudens, and Linus, and Claudia, and all the brethren.

²²The Lord Jesus Christ be with thy spirit. Grace be with you. Amen.

The second epistle unto Timothy, ordained the first bishop of the church of the Ephesians, was written from Rome, when Paul was brought before Nero the second time.

THE EPISTLE OF PAUL TO
TITUS

1 Paul, a servant of God, and an apostle of Jesus Christ, according to the faith of God's elect, and the acknowledging of the truth which is after godliness, ²in hope of eternal life, which God, that cannot lie, promised before the world began: ³but hath in due times manifested his word through preaching, which is committed unto me according to the commandment of God our Saviour: ⁴to Titus, my own son after the common faith: grace, mercy, and peace from God the Father and the Lord Jesus Christ our Saviour.

⁵For this cause left I thee in Crete, that thou shouldst set in order the things that are wanting, and ordain elders in every city, as I had appointed thee: ⁶if any be blameless, the husband of one wife, having faithful children not accused of riot or unruly. ⁷For a bishop must be blameless, as the steward of God: not self-willed, not soon angry, not given to wine, no striker, not given to filthy lucre, ⁸but a lover of hospitality, a lover of good men, sober, just, holy, temperate, ⁹holding fast the faithful word as he hath been taught, that he may be able by sound doctrine both to exhort and to convince the gainsayers.

¹⁰For there are many unruly and vain talkers and deceivers, specially they of the circumcision: ¹¹whose mouths must be stopped, who subvert whole houses, teaching things which they ought not, for filthy lucre's sake. ¹²One of themselves, even a prophet of their own, said, 'The Cretians are always liars, evil beasts, slow bellies'. ¹³This witness is true: wherefore rebuke them sharply, that they may be sound in the faith; ¹⁴not giving heed to Jewish fables, and commandments of men that turn from the truth. ¹⁵Unto the pure all things are pure, but unto them that are defiled and unbelieving is nothing pure: but even their mind and conscience is defiled. ¹⁶They profess that they know God; but in works they deny him, being abominable, and disobedient, and unto every good work reprobate.

2 But speak thou the things which become sound doctrine: ²that the aged men be sober, grave, temperate, sound in faith, in charity, in patience. ³The aged women likewise, that they be in behaviour as becometh holiness, not false accusers, not given to much wine, teachers of good things, ⁴that they may teach the young women to be sober, to love their husbands, to love their children, ⁵to be discreet, chaste, keepers at home, good, obedient to their own husbands, that the word of God be not blasphemed. ⁶Young men likewise exhort to be sober-minded. ⁷In all things showing thyself a pattern of good works: in doctrine showing incorruptness, gravity, sincerity, ⁸sound speech that cannot be condemned, that he that is of the contrary part may be ashamed, having no evil thing to say of you. ⁹Exhort servants to be obedient unto their own masters, and to please them well in all things, not answering again: ¹⁰not purloining, but showing all good fidelity, that they may adorn the doctrine of God our Saviour in all things.

[11] For the grace of God that bringeth salvation hath appeared to all men, [12] teaching us that, denying ungodliness and worldly lusts, we should live soberly, righteously, and godly, in this present world, [13] looking for that blessed hope, and the glorious appearing of the great God and our Saviour Jesus Christ, [14] who gave himself for us, that he might redeem us from all iniquity, and purify unto himself a peculiar people, zealous of good works. [15] These things speak, and exhort, and rebuke with all authority. Let no man despise thee.

3 Put them in mind to be subject to principalities and powers, to obey magistrates, to be ready to every good work, [2] to speak evil of no man, to be no brawlers, but gentle, showing all meekness unto all men. [3] For we ourselves also were sometime foolish, disobedient, deceived, serving divers lusts and pleasures, living in malice and envy, hateful, and hating one another. [4] But after that the kindness and love of God our Saviour toward man appeared, [5] not by works of righteousness which we have done, but according to his mercy he saved us, by the washing of regeneration, and renewing of the Holy Ghost, [6] which he shed on us abundantly through Jesus Christ our Saviour: [7] that being justified by his grace, we should be made heirs according to the hope of eternal life. [8] This is a faithful saying, and these things I will that thou affirm constantly, that they which have believed in God might be careful to maintain good works. These things are good and profitable unto men. [9] But avoid foolish questions, and genealogies, and contentions, and strivings about the law; for they are unprofitable and vain. [10] A man that is a heretic, after the first and second admonition, reject; [11] knowing that he that is such is subverted, and sinneth, being condemned of himself.

[12] When I shall send Artemas unto thee, or Tychicus, be diligent to come unto me to Nicopolis: for I have determined there to winter. [13] Bring Zenas the lawyer and Apollos on their journey diligently, that nothing be wanting unto them. [14] And let ours also learn to maintain good works for necessary uses, that they be not unfruitful.

[15] All that are with me salute thee. Greet them that love us in the faith.

Grace be with you all. Amen.

It was written to Titus, ordained the first bishop of the church of the Cretians, from Nicopolis of Macedonia.

THE EPISTLE OF PAUL TO
PHILEMON

Paul, a prisoner of Jesus Christ, and Timothy our brother, unto Philemon our dearly beloved, and fellow-labourer, ²and to our beloved Apphia, and Archippus our fellow-soldier, and to the church in thy house: ³grace to you, and peace, from God our Father and the Lord Jesus Christ.

⁴I thank my God, making mention of thee always in my prayers, ⁵hearing of thy love and faith, which thou hast toward the Lord Jesus, and toward all saints: ⁶that the communication of thy faith may become effectual by the acknowledging of every good thing which is in you in Christ Jesus. ⁷For we have great joy and consolation in thy love, because the bowels of the saints are refreshed by thee, brother.

⁸Wherefore, though I might be much bold in Christ to enjoin thee that which is convenient, ⁹yet for love's sake I rather beseech thee, being such a one as Paul the aged, and now also a prisoner of Jesus Christ. ¹⁰I beseech thee for my son Onesimus, whom I have begotten in my bonds, ¹¹which in time past was to thee unprofitable, but now profitable to thee and to me: ¹²whom I have sent again: thou therefore receive him, that is, my own bowels: ¹³whom I would have retained with me, that in thy stead he might have ministered unto me in the bonds of the gospel: ¹⁴but without thy mind would I do nothing, that thy benefit should not be as it were of necessity, but willingly. ¹⁵For perhaps he therefore departed for a season, that thou shouldst receive him for ever: ¹⁶not now as a servant, but above a servant, a brother beloved, specially to me, but how much more unto thee, both in the flesh, and in the Lord?

¹⁷If thou count me therefore a partner, receive him as myself. ¹⁸If he hath wronged thee, or oweth thee aught, put that on my account. ¹⁹I Paul have written it with my own hand, I will repay it: albeit I do not say to thee how thou owest unto me even thy own self besides. ²⁰Yea, brother, let me have joy of thee in the Lord: refresh my bowels in the Lord. ²¹Having confidence in thy obedience I wrote unto thee, knowing that thou wilt also do more than I say. ²²But withal prepare me also a lodging: for I trust that through your prayers I shall be given unto you.

²³There salute thee Epaphras, my fellow-prisoner in Christ Jesus: ²⁴Marcus, Aristarchus, Demas, Luke, my fellow-labourers.

²⁵The grace of our Lord Jesus Christ be with your spirit. Amen.

Written from Rome to Philemon, by Onesimus a servant.

THE
EPISTLE OF PAUL THE APOSTLE
TO THE
HEBREWS

1 God, who at sundry times and in divers manners spoke in time past unto the fathers by the prophets, ²hath in these last days spoken unto us by his Son, whom he hath appointed heir of all things, by whom also he made the worlds, ³who being the brightness of his glory, and the express image of his person, and upholding all things by the word of his power, when he had by himself purged our sins, sat down on the right hand of the Majesty on high, ⁴being made so much better than the angels, as he hath by inheritance obtained a more excellent name than they. ⁵For unto which of the angels said he at any time, 'Thou art my Son, this day have I begotten thee'? And again, 'I will be to him a Father, and he shall be to me a Son'? ⁶And again, when he bringeth in the first-begotten into the world, he saith, 'And let all the angels of God worship him'. ⁷And of the angels he saith, 'Who maketh his angels spirits, and his ministers a flame of fire'. ⁸But unto the Son he saith, 'Thy throne, O God, is for ever and ever: a sceptre of righteousness is the sceptre of thy kingdom. ⁹Thou hast loved righteousness, and hated iniquity, therefore God, even thy God, hath anointed thee with the oil of gladness above thy fellows.' ¹⁰And, 'Thou, Lord, in the beginning hast laid the foundation of the earth: and the heavens are the works of thy hands. ¹¹They shall perish, but thou remainest: and they all shall wax old as doth a garment. ¹²And as a vesture shalt thou fold them up, and they shall be changed, but thou art the same, and thy years shall not fail.' ¹³But to which of the angels said he at any time, 'Sit on my right hand, until I make thy enemies thy footstool'? ¹⁴Are they not all ministering spirits, sent forth to minister for them who shall be heirs of salvation?

2 Therefore we ought to give the more earnest heed to the things which we have heard, lest at any time we should let them slip. ²For if the word spoken by angels was steadfast, and every transgression and disobedience received a just recompense of reward: ³how shall we escape, if we neglect so great salvation, which at the first began to be spoken by the Lord, and was confirmed unto us by them that heard him, ⁴God also bearing them witness, both with signs and wonders, and with divers miracles, and gifts of the Holy Ghost, according to his own will?

⁵For unto the angels hath he not put in subjection the world to come, whereof we speak. ⁶But one in a certain place testified, saying, 'What is man, that thou art mindful of him? or the son of man, that thou visitest him? ⁷Thou madest him a little lower than the angels, thou crownedst him with glory and honour, and didst set him over the

works of thy hands. ⁸Thou hast put all things in subjection under his feet.' For in that he put all in subjection under him, he left nothing that is not put under him. But now we see not yet all things put under him. ⁹But we see Jesus, who was made a little lower than the angels for the suffering of death, crowned with glory and honour, that he by the grace of God should taste death for every man.

¹⁰For it became him, for whom are all things, and by whom are all things, in bringing many sons unto glory, to make the captain of their salvation perfect through sufferings. ¹¹For both he that sanctifieth and they who are sanctified are all of one: for which cause he is not ashamed to call them brethren, ¹²saying, 'I will declare thy name unto my brethren, in the midst of the church will I sing praise unto thee'. ¹³And again, 'I will put my trust in him'. And again, 'Behold I and the children which God hath given me'. ¹⁴Forasmuch then as the children are partakers of flesh and blood, he also himself likewise took part of the same, that through death he might destroy him that had the power of death, that is, the devil: ¹⁵and deliver them who through fear of death were all their lifetime subject to bondage. ¹⁶For verily he took not on him the nature of angels: but he took on him the seed of Abraham. ¹⁷Wherefore in all things it behoved him to be made like unto his brethren, that he might be a merciful and faithful high priest in things pertaining to God, to make reconciliation for the sins of the people. ¹⁸For in that he himself hath suffered being tempted, he is able to succour them that are tempted.

3 Wherefore, holy brethren, partakers of the heavenly calling, consider the Apostle and High Priest of our profession, Christ Jesus, ²who was faithful to him that appointed him, as also Moses was faithful in all his house. ³For this man was counted worthy of more glory than Moses, inasmuch as he who hath built the house hath more honour than the house. ⁴For every house is built by some man, but he that built all things is God. ⁵And Moses verily was faithful in all his house, as a servant, for a testimony of those things which were to be spoken after; ⁶but Christ as a son over his own house, whose house are we, if we hold fast the confidence and the rejoicing of the hope firm unto the end.

⁷Wherefore as the Holy Ghost saith, 'Today if ye will hear his voice, ⁸harden not your hearts, as in the provocation, in the day of temptation in the wilderness: ⁹when your fathers tempted me, proved me, and saw my works forty years. ¹⁰Wherefore I was grieved with that generation, and said, "They do always err in their hearts, and they have not known my ways". ¹¹So I swore in my wrath, "They shall not enter into my rest".' ¹²Take heed, brethren, lest there be in any of you an evil heart of unbelief, in departing from the living God. ¹³But exhort one another daily, while it is called today, lest any of you be hardened through the deceitfulness of sin. ¹⁴For we are made partakers of Christ, if we hold the beginning of our confidence steadfast unto the end; ¹⁵whilst it is said, 'Today if ye will hear his voice, harden not your hearts, as in the provocation'. ¹⁶For some, when they had heard, did provoke: howbeit

not all that came out of Egypt by Moses. [17]But with whom was he grieved forty years? was it not with them that had sinned, whose carcases fell in the wilderness? [18]And to whom swore he that they should not enter into his rest, but to them that believed not? [19]So we see that they could not enter in because of unbelief.

4 Let us therefore fear, lest, a promise being left us of entering into his rest, any of you should seem to come short of it. [2]For unto us was the gospel preached, as well as unto them: but the word preached did not profit them, not being mixed with faith in them that heard it. [3]For we which have believed do enter into rest, as he said, 'As I have sworn in my wrath, if they shall enter into my rest', although the works were finished from the foundation of the world. [4]For he spoke in a certain place of the seventh day on this wise, 'And God did rest the seventh day from all his works'. [5]And in this place again, 'If they shall enter into my rest'. [6]Seeing therefore it remaineth that some must enter therein, and they to whom it was first preached entered not in because of unbelief: [7]again, he limiteth a certain day, saying in David, 'Today', after so long a time; as it is said, 'Today if ye will hear his voice, harden not your hearts'. [8]For if Jesus had given them rest, then would he not afterward have spoken of another day. [9]There remaineth therefore a rest to the people of God. [10]For he that is entered into his rest, he also hath ceased from his own works, as God did from his. [11]Let us labour therefore to enter into that rest, lest any man fall after the same example of unbelief.

[12]For the word of God is quick, and powerful, and sharper than any two-edged sword, piercing even to the dividing asunder of soul and spirit, and of the joints and marrow, and is a discerner of the thoughts and intents of the heart. [13]Neither is there any creature that is not manifest in his sight: but all things are naked and opened unto the eyes of him with whom we have to do. [14]Seeing then that we have a great high priest, that is passed into the heavens, Jesus the Son of God, let us hold fast our profession. [15]For we have not a high priest which cannot be touched with the feeling of our infirmities: but was in all points tempted like as we are, yet without sin. [16]Let us therefore come boldly unto the throne of grace, that we may obtain mercy, and find grace to help in time of need.

5 For every high priest taken from among men is ordained for men in things pertaining to God, that he may offer both gifts and sacrifices for sins: [2]who can have compassion on the ignorant, and on them that are out of the way, for that he himself also is compassed with infirmity. [3]And by reason hereof he ought, as for the people, so also for himself, to offer for sins. [4]And no man taketh this honour unto himself, but he that is called of God, as was Aaron. [5]So also Christ glorified not himself to be made a high priest: but he that said unto him, 'Thou art my Son, today have I begotten thee'. [6]As he saith also in another place, 'Thou art a priest for ever after the order of Melchisedec'. [7]Who in the days of his flesh, when he had offered up prayers and supplications with strong crying and tears unto him that was able to save him from death, and

was heard in that he feared. [8]Though he were a Son, yet learned he obedience by the things which he suffered: [9]and being made perfect, he became the author of eternal salvation unto all them that obey him, [10]called of God a high priest after the order of Melchisedec.

[11]Of whom we have many things to say, and hard to be uttered, seeing ye are dull of hearing. [12]For when for the time ye ought to be teachers, ye have need that one teach you again which be the first principles of the oracles of God, and are become such as have need of milk, and not of strong meat. [13]For every one that useth milk is unskilful in the word of righteousness: for he is a babe. [14]But strong meat belongeth to them that are of full age, even those who by reason of use have their senses exercised to discern both good and evil.

6 Therefore leaving the principles of the doctrine of Christ, let us go on unto perfection, not laying again the foundation of repentance from dead works, and of faith towards God, [2]of the doctrine of baptisms, and of laying on of hands, and of resurrection of the dead, and of eternal judgement. [3]And this will we do, if God permit. [4]For it is impossible for those who were once enlightened, and have tasted of the heavenly gift, and were made partakers of the Holy Ghost, [5]and have tasted the good word of God, and the powers of the world to come, [6]if they shall fall away, to renew them again unto repentance: seeing they crucify to themselves the Son of God afresh, and put him to an open shame. [7]For the earth which drinketh in the rain that cometh oft upon it, and bringeth forth herbs meet for them by whom it is dressed, receiveth blessing from God: [8]but that which beareth thorns and briers is rejected, and is nigh unto cursing, whose end is to be burnt.

[9]But, beloved, we are persuaded better things of you, and things that accompany salvation, though we thus speak. [10]For God is not unrighteous to forget your work and labour of love, which ye have shown toward his name, in that ye have ministered to the saints, and do minister. [11]And we desire that every one of you do show the same diligence to the full assurance of hope unto the end: [12]that ye be not slothful, but followers of them who through faith and patience inherit the promises.

[13]For when God made promise to Abraham, because he could swear by no greater, he swore by himself, [14]saying, 'Surely blessing I will bless thee, and multiplying I will multiply thee'. [15]And so, after he had patiently endured, he obtained the promise. [16]For men verily swear by the greater, and an oath for confirmation is to them an end of all strife. [17]Wherein God, willing more abundantly to show unto the heirs of promise the immutability of his counsel, confirmed it by an oath: [18]that by two immutable things, in which it was impossible for God to lie, we might have a strong consolation, who have fled for refuge to lay hold upon the hope set before us: [19]which hope we have as an anchor of the soul, both sure and steadfast, and which entereth into that within the veil, [20]whither the forerunner is for us entered, even Jesus, made a high priest for ever after the order of Melchisedec.

7 For this Melchisedec, king of Salem, priest of the most high God, who met Abraham returning from the slaughter of the kings, and

blessed him: [2]to whom also Abraham gave a tenth part of all: first being by interpretation king of righteousness, and after that also king of Salem, which is, king of peace; [3]without father, without mother, without descent, having neither beginning of days, nor end of life: but made like unto the Son of God, abideth a priest continually.

[4]Now consider how great this man was, unto whom even the patriarch Abraham gave the tenth of the spoils. [5]And verily they that are of the sons of Levi, who receive the office of the priesthood, have a commandment to take tithes of the people according to the law, that is, of their brethren, though they come out of the loins of Abraham: [6]but he whose descent is not counted from them received tithes of Abraham, and blessed him that had the promises. [7]And without all contradiction the less is blessed of the better. [8]And here men that die receive tithes: but there he receiveth them, of whom it is witnessed that he liveth. [9]And as I may so say, Levi also, who receiveth tithes, paid tithes in Abraham. [10]For he was yet in the loins of his father, when Melchisedec met him.

[11]If therefore perfection were by the Levitical priesthood (for under it the people received the law), what further need was there that another priest should rise after the order of Melchisedec, and not be called after the order of Aaron? [12]For the priesthood being changed, there is made of necessity a change also of the law. [13]For he of whom these things are spoken pertaineth to another tribe, of which no man gave attendance at the altar. [14]For it is evident that our Lord sprang out of Juda, of which tribe Moses spoke nothing concerning priesthood.

[15]And it is yet far more evident: for that after the similitude of Melchisedec there ariseth another priest, [16]who is made, not after the law of a carnal commandment, but after the power of an endless life. [17]For he testifieth, 'Thou art a priest for ever after the order of Melchisedec'. [18]For there is verily a disannulling of the commandment going before for the weakness and unprofitableness thereof. [19]For the law made nothing perfect, but the bringing in of a better hope did: by the which we draw nigh unto God.

[20]And inasmuch as not without an oath he was made priest [21](for those priests were made without an oath: but this with an oath by him that said unto him, 'The Lord swore and will not repent, "Thou art a priest for ever after the order of Melchisedec"'), [22]by so much was Jesus made a surety of a better testament. [23]And they truly were many priests, because they were not suffered to continue by reason of death. [24]But this man, because he continueth ever, hath an unchangeable priesthood. [25]Wherefore he is able also to save them to the uttermost that come unto God by him, seeing he ever liveth to make intercession for them.

[26]For such a high priest became us, who is holy, harmless, undefiled, separate from sinners, and made higher than the heavens; [27]who needeth not daily, as those high priests, to offer up sacrifice, first for his own sins, and then for the people's: for this he did once, when he offered up himself. [28]For the law maketh men high priests which have

infirmity, but the word of the oath, which was since the law, maketh the Son, who is consecrated for evermore.

8 Now of the things which we have spoken this is the sum: we have such a high priest, who is set on the right hand of the throne of the Majesty in the heavens: ²a minister of the sanctuary, and of the true tabernacle, which the Lord pitched, and not man. ³For every high priest is ordained to offer gifts and sacrifices: wherefore it is of necessity that this man have somewhat also to offer. ⁴For if he were on earth, he should not be a priest, seeing that there are priests that offer gifts according to the law: ⁵who serve unto the example and shadow of heavenly things, as Moses was admonished of God when he was about to make the tabernacle. For, 'See,' saith he, 'that thou make all things according to the pattern shown to thee in the mount'. ⁶But now hath he obtained a more excellent ministry, by how much also he is the mediator of a better covenant, which was established upon better promises.

⁷For if that first covenant had been faultless, then should no place have been sought for the second. ⁸For finding fault with them, he saith, '"Behold, the days come," saith the Lord, "when I will make a new covenant with the house of Israel and the house of Juda: ⁹not according to the covenant that I made with their fathers in the day when I took them by the hand to lead them out of the land of Egypt, because they continued not in my covenant, and I regarded them not," saith the Lord. ¹⁰"For this is the covenant that I will make with the house of Israel after those days," saith the Lord: "I will put my laws into their mind, and write them in their hearts: and I will be to them a God, and they shall be to me a people. ¹¹And they shall not teach every man his neighbour, and every man his brother, saying, "Know the Lord": for all shall know me, from the least to the greatest. ¹²For I will be merciful to their unrighteousness, and their sins and their iniquities will I remember no more."' ¹³In that he saith, 'A new covenant', he hath made the first old. Now that which decayeth and waxeth old is ready to vanish away.

9 Then verily the first covenant had also ordinances of divine service, and a worldly sanctuary. ²For there was a tabernacle made, the first, wherein was the candlestick, and the table, and the showbread, which is called the sanctuary. ³And after the second veil, the tabernacle which is called the Holiest of all: ⁴which had the golden censer, and the ark of the covenant overlaid round about with gold, wherein was the golden pot that had manna, and Aaron's rod that budded, and the tablets of the covenant; ⁵and over it the cherubims of glory shadowing the mercy-seat; of which we cannot now speak particularly.

⁶Now when these things were thus ordained, the priests went always into the first tabernacle, accomplishing the service of God. ⁷But into the second went the high priest alone once every year, not without blood, which he offered for himself, and for the errors of the people: ⁸the Holy Ghost this signifying, that the way into the holiest of all was not yet made manifest, while as the first tabernacle was yet standing: ⁹which was a figure for the time then present, in which were offered

both gifts and sacrifices, that could not make him that did the service perfect, as pertaining to the conscience, [10]which stood only in meats and drinks, and divers washings, and carnal ordinances, imposed on them until the time of reformation.

[11]But Christ being come a high priest of good things to come, by a greater and more perfect tabernacle, not made with hands, that is to say, not of this building: [12]neither by the blood of goats and calves, but by his own blood he entered in once into the holy place, having obtained eternal redemption for us. [13]For if the blood of bulls and of goats, and the ashes of a heifer sprinkling the unclean, sanctifieth to the purifying of the flesh: [14]how much more shall the blood of Christ, who through the eternal Spirit offered himself without spot to God, purge your conscience from dead works to serve the living God?

[15]And for this cause he is the mediator of the new testament, that by means of death, for the redemption of the transgressions that were under the first testament, they which are called might receive the promise of eternal inheritance. [16]For where a testament is, there must also of necessity be the death of the testator. [17]For a testament is of force after men are dead: otherwise it is of no strength at all whilst the testator liveth. [18]Whereupon neither the first testament was dedicated without blood. [19]For when Moses had spoken every precept to all the people according to the law, he took the blood of calves and of goats, with water, and scarlet wool, and hyssop, and sprinkled both the book, and all the people, [20]saying, 'This is the blood of the testament which God hath enjoined unto you'. [21]Moreover he sprinkled with blood both the tabernacle, and all the vessels of the ministry. [22]And almost all things are by the law purged with blood: and without shedding of blood is no remission.

[23]It was therefore necessary that the patterns of things in the heavens should be purified with these, but the heavenly things themselves with better sacrifices than these. [24]For Christ is not entered into the holy places made with hands, which are the figures of the true, but into heaven itself, now to appear in the presence of God for us: [25]nor yet that he should offer himself often, as the high priest entereth into the holy place every year with blood of others: [26]for then must he often have suffered since the foundation of the world: but now once in the end of the world hath he appeared to put away sin by the sacrifice of himself. [27]And as it is appointed unto men once to die, but after this the judgement: [28]so Christ was once offered to bear the sins of many, and unto them that look for him shall he appear the second time without sin unto salvation.

10 For the law having a shadow of good things to come, and not the very image of the things, can never with those sacrifices which they offered year by year continually make the comers thereunto perfect. [2]For then would they not have ceased to be offered, because that the worshippers once purged should have had no more conscience of sins? [3]But in those sacrifices there is a remembrance again made of sins every year. [4]For it is not possible that the blood of bulls and of goats should take away sins.

⁵Wherefore when he cometh into the world, he saith, 'Sacrifice and offering thou wouldst not, but a body hast thou prepared me: ⁶in burnt offerings and sacrifices for sin thou hast had no pleasure. ⁷Then said I, "Lo, I come (in the volume of the book it is written of me) to do thy will, O God".' ⁸Above when he said, 'Sacrifice and offering and burnt offerings and offering for sin thou wouldst not, neither hadst pleasure therein, which are offered by the law': ⁹then said he, 'Lo, I come to do thy will, O God'. He taketh away the first, that he may establish the second. ¹⁰By the which will we are sanctified through the offering of the body of Jesus Christ once for all.

¹¹And every priest standeth daily ministering and offering oftentimes the same sacrifices, which can never take away sins: ¹²but this man, after he had offered one sacrifice for sins for ever, sat down on the right hand of God, ¹³from henceforth expecting till his enemies be made his footstool. ¹⁴For by one offering he hath perfected for ever them that are sanctified. ¹⁵Whereof the Holy Ghost also is a witness to us: for after that he had said before, ¹⁶'"This is the covenant that I will make with them after those days," saith the Lord, "I will put my laws into their hearts, and in their minds will I write them: ¹⁷and their sins and iniquities will I remember no more"'. ¹⁸Now where remission of these is, there is no more offering for sin.

¹⁹Having therefore, brethren, boldness to enter into the holiest by the blood of Jesus, ²⁰by a new and living way, which he hath consecrated for us, through the veil, that is to say, his flesh: ²¹and having a high priest over the house of God: ²²let us draw near with a true heart in full assurance of faith, having our hearts sprinkled from an evil conscience, and our bodies washed with pure water. ²³Let us hold fast the profession of our faith without wavering (for he is faithful that promised), ²⁴and let us consider one another to provoke unto love and to good works: ²⁵not forsaking the assembling of ourselves together, as the manner of some is: but exhorting one another, and so much the more, as ye see the day approaching.

²⁶For if we sin wilfully after that we have received the knowledge of the truth, there remaineth no more sacrifice for sins, ²⁷but a certain fearful looking for of judgement and fiery indignation, which shall devour the adversaries. ²⁸He that despised Moses' law died without mercy under two or three witnesses. ²⁹Of how much sorer punishment, suppose ye, shall he be thought worthy, who hath trodden under foot the Son of God, and hath counted the blood of the covenant, wherewith he was sanctified, an unholy thing, and hath done despite unto the Spirit of grace? ³⁰For we know him that hath said, '"Vengeance belongeth unto me, I will recompense," saith the Lord'. And again, 'The Lord shall judge his people'. ³¹It is a fearful thing to fall into the hands of the living God.

³²But call to remembrance the former days, in which, after ye were illuminated, ye endured a great fight of afflictions: ³³partly whilst ye were made a gazing-stock both by reproaches and afflictions, and partly whilst ye became companions of them that were so used. ³⁴For ye

had compassion of me in my bonds, and took joyfully the spoiling of your goods, knowing in yourselves that ye have in heaven a better and an enduring substance. ³⁵Cast not away therefore your confidence, which hath great recompense of reward. ³⁶For ye have need of patience, that, after ye have done the will of God, ye might receive the promise. ³⁷'For yet a little while, and he that shall come will come, and will not tarry. ³⁸Now the just shall live by faith: but if any man draw back, my soul shall have no pleasure in him.' ³⁹But we are not of them who draw back unto perdition: but of them that believe to the saving of the soul.

11 Now faith is the substance of things hoped for, the evidence of things not seen. ²For by it the elders obtained a good report. ³Through faith we understand that the worlds were framed by the word of God, so that things which are seen were not made of things which do appear. ⁴By faith Abel offered unto God a more excellent sacrifice than Cain, by which he obtained witness that he was righteous, God testifying of his gifts: and by it he being dead yet speaketh. ⁵By faith Enoch was translated that he should not see death, and was not found, because God had translated him: for before his translation he had this testimony, that he pleased God. ⁶But without faith it is impossible to please him: for he that cometh to God must believe that he is, and that he is a rewarder of them that diligently seek him. ⁷By faith Noah, being warned of God of things not seen as yet, moved with fear, prepared an ark to the saving of his house, by the which he condemned the world, and became heir of the righteousness which is by faith. ⁸By faith Abraham, when he was called to go out into a place which he should after receive for an inheritance, obeyed, and he went out, not knowing whither he went. ⁹By faith he sojourned in the land of promise, as in a strange country, dwelling in tabernacles with Isaac and Jacob, the heirs with him of the same promise: ¹⁰for he looked for a city which hath foundations, whose builder and maker is God. ¹¹Through faith also Sara herself received strength to conceive seed, and was delivered of a child when she was past age, because she judged him faithful who had promised. ¹²Therefore sprang there even of one, and him as good as dead, so many as the stars of the sky in multitude, and as the sand which is by the sea-shore innumerable.

¹³These all died in faith, not having received the promises, but having seen them afar off, and were persuaded of them, and embraced them, and confessed that they were strangers and pilgrims on the earth. ¹⁴For they that say such things declare plainly that they seek a country. ¹⁵And truly, if they had been mindful of that country from whence they came out, they might have had opportunity to have returned. ¹⁶But now they desire a better country, that is, a heavenly: wherefore God is not ashamed to be called their God: for he hath prepared for them a city.

¹⁷By faith Abraham, when he was tried, offered up Isaac: and he that had received the promises offered up his only begotten son, ¹⁸of whom it was said, that 'In Isaac shall thy seed be called': ¹⁹accounting that God was able to raise him up, even from the dead: from whence also he received him in a figure. ²⁰By faith Isaac blessed Jacob and Esau con-

cerning things to come. ²¹By faith Jacob, when he was a-dying, blessed both the sons of Joseph, and worshipped, leaning upon the top of his staff. ²²By faith Joseph, when he died, made mention of the departing of the children of Israel: and gave commandment concerning his bones. ²³By faith Moses, when he was born, was hid three months of his parents, because they saw he was a proper child, and they were not afraid of the king's commandment. ²⁴By faith Moses, when he was come to years, refused to be called the son of Pharaoh's daughter, ²⁵choosing rather to suffer affliction with the people of God, than to enjoy the pleasures of sin for a season: ²⁶esteeming the reproach of Christ greater riches than the treasures in Egypt: for he had respect unto the recompense of the reward. ²⁷By faith he forsook Egypt, not fearing the wrath of the king: for he endured, as seeing him who is invisible. ²⁸Through faith he kept the passover, and the sprinkling of blood, lest he that destroyed the firstborn should touch them. ²⁹By faith they passed through the Red Sea as by dry land: which the Egyptians essaying to do were drowned. ³⁰By faith the walls of Jericho fell down, after they were compassed about seven days. ³¹By faith the harlot Rahab perished not with them that believed not, when she had received the spies with peace.

³²And what shall I more say? for the time would fail me to tell of Gideon, and of Barak, and of Samson, and of Jephthah, of David also, and Samuel, and of the prophets: ³³who through faith subdued kingdoms, wrought righteousness, obtained promises, stopped the mouths of lions, ³⁴quenched the violence of fire, escaped the edge of the sword, out of weakness were made strong, waxed valiant in fight, turned to flight the armies of the aliens. ³⁵Women received their dead raised to life again: and others were tortured, not accepting deliverance, that they might obtain a better resurrection. ³⁶And others had trial of cruel mockings and scourgings, yea, moreover of bonds and imprisonment. ³⁷They were stoned, they were sawn asunder, were tempted, were slain with the sword: they wandered about in sheepskins and goatskins, being destitute, afflicted, tormented ³⁸(of whom the world was not worthy): they wandered in deserts, and in mountains, and in dens and caves of the earth. ³⁹And these all, having obtained a good report through faith, received not the promise: ⁴⁰God having provided some better thing for us, that they without us should not be made perfect.

12 Wherefore seeing we also are compassed about with so great a cloud of witnesses, let us lay aside every weight, and the sin which doth so easily beset us, and let us run with patience the race that is set before us, ²looking unto Jesus the author and finisher of our faith, who for the joy that was set before him endured the cross, despising the shame, and is set down at the right hand of the throne of God. ³For consider him that endured such contradiction of sinners against himself, lest ye be wearied and faint in your minds. ⁴Ye have not yet resisted unto blood, striving against sin. ⁵And ye have forgotten the exhortation which speaketh unto you as unto children, 'My son, despise not thou the chastening of the Lord, nor faint when thou art

rebuked of him. ⁶For whom the Lord loveth he chasteneth, and scourgeth every son whom he receiveth.' ⁷If ye endure chastening, God dealeth with you as with sons: for what son is he whom the father chasteneth not? ⁸But if ye be without chastisement, whereof all are partakers, then are ye bastards, and not sons. ⁹Furthermore we have had fathers of our flesh which corrected us, and we gave them reverence: shall we not much rather be in subjection unto the Father of spirits, and live? ¹⁰For they verily for a few days chastened us after their own pleasure, but he for our profit, that we might be partakers of his holiness. ¹¹Now no chastening for the present seemeth to be joyous, but grievous: nevertheless afterward it yieldeth the peaceable fruit of righteousness unto them which are exercised thereby. ¹²Wherefore lift up the hands which hang down, and the feeble knees; ¹³and make straight paths for your feet, lest that which is lame be turned out of the way, but let it rather be healed. ¹⁴Follow peace with all men, and holiness, without which no man shall see the Lord: ¹⁵looking diligently lest any man fail of the grace of God, lest any root of bitterness springing up trouble you, and thereby many be defiled: ¹⁶lest there be any fornicator, or profane person, as Esau, who for one morsel of meat sold his birthright. ¹⁷For ye know how that afterward, when he would have inherited the blessing, he was rejected: for he found no place of repentance, though he sought it carefully with tears.

¹⁸For ye are not come unto the mount that might be touched, and that burnt with fire, nor unto blackness, and darkness, and tempest, ¹⁹and the sound of a trumpet, and the voice of words, which voice they that heard entreated that the word should not be spoken to them any more. ²⁰For they could not endure that which was commanded, 'And if so much as a beast touch the mountain, it shall be stoned, or thrust through with a dart'. ²¹And so terrible was the sight, that Moses said, 'I exceedingly fear and quake'. ²²But ye are come unto mount Sion, and unto the city of the living God, the heavenly Jerusalem, and to an innumerable company of angels: ²³to the general assembly and church of the firstborn, which are written in heaven, and to God the Judge of all, and to the spirits of just men made perfect: ²⁴and to Jesus the mediator of the new covenant, and to the blood of sprinkling, that speaketh better things than that of Abel. ²⁵See that ye refuse not him that speaketh: for if they escaped not who refused him that spoke on earth, much more shall not we escape, if we turn away from him that speaketh from heaven: ²⁶whose voice then shook the earth, but now he hath promised, saying, 'Yet once more I shake not the earth only, but also heaven'. ²⁷And this word, 'Yet once more', signifieth the removing of those things that are shaken, as of things that are made, that those things which cannot be shaken may remain. ²⁸Wherefore we receiving a kingdom which cannot be moved, let us have grace, whereby we may serve God acceptably with reverence and godly fear: ²⁹for our God is a consuming fire.

13 Let brotherly love continue. ²Be not forgetful to entertain strangers, for thereby some have entertained angels unawares.

³Remember them that are in bonds, as bound with them, and them which suffer adversity, as being yourselves also in the body. ⁴Marriage is honourable in all, and the bed undefiled: but whoremongers and adulterers God will judge. ⁵Let your conversation be without covetousness: and be content with such things as ye have. For he hath said, 'I will never leave thee, nor forsake thee'. ⁶So that we may boldly say, 'The Lord is my helper, and I will not fear what man shall do unto me'. ⁷Remember them which have the rule over you, who have spoken unto you the word of God: whose faith follow, considering the end of their conversation. ⁸Jesus Christ the same yesterday, and today, and for ever. ⁹Be not carried about with diverse and strange doctrines. For it is a good thing that the heart be established with grace, not with meats, which have not profited them that have been occupied therein.

¹⁰We have an altar, whereof they have no right to eat which serve the tabernacle. ¹¹For the bodies of those beasts, whose blood is brought into the sanctuary by the high priest for sin, are burnt without the camp. ¹²Wherefore Jesus also, that he might sanctify the people with his own blood, suffered without the gate. ¹³Let us go forth therefore unto him without the camp, bearing his reproach. ¹⁴For here have we no continuing city, but we seek one to come. ¹⁵By him therefore let us offer the sacrifice of praise to God continually, that is, the fruit of our lips giving thanks to his name. ¹⁶But to do good and to communicate forget not, for with such sacrifices God is well pleased. ¹⁷Obey them that have the rule over you, and submit yourselves: for they watch for your souls, as they that must give account, that they may do it with joy, and not with grief: for that is unprofitable for you.

¹⁸Pray for us: for we trust we have a good conscience in all things, willing to live honestly. ¹⁹But I beseech you the rather to do this, that I may be restored to you the sooner.

²⁰Now the God of peace, that brought again from the dead our Lord Jesus, that great shepherd of the sheep, through the blood of the everlasting covenant, ²¹make you perfect in every good work to do his will, working in you that which is well-pleasing in his sight, through Jesus Christ, to whom be glory for ever and ever. Amen.

²²And I beseech you, brethren, suffer the word of exhortation, for I have written a letter unto you in few words. ²³Know ye that our brother Timothy is set at liberty, with whom, if he come shortly, I will see you. ²⁴Salute all them that have the rule over you, and all the saints. They of Italy salute you.

²⁵Grace be with you all. Amen.

Written to the Hebrews from Italy by Timothy.

THE GENERAL EPISTLE OF
JAMES

1 James, a servant of God and of the Lord Jesus Christ, to the twelve tribes which are scattered abroad, greeting.

²My brethren, count it all joy when ye fall into divers temptations, ³knowing this, that the trying of your faith worketh patience. ⁴But let patience have her perfect work, that ye may be perfect and entire, wanting nothing. ⁵If any of you lack wisdom, let him ask of God, that giveth to all men liberally, and upbraideth not: and it shall be given him. ⁶But let him ask in faith, nothing wavering: for he that wavereth is like a wave of the sea driven with the wind and tossed. ⁷For let not that man think that he shall receive anything of the Lord. ⁸A double-minded man is unstable in all his ways. ⁹Let the brother of low degree rejoice in that he is exalted: ¹⁰but the rich, in that he is made low: because as the flower of the grass he shall pass away. ¹¹For the sun is no sooner risen with a burning heat, but it withereth the grass, and the flower thereof falleth, and the grace of the fashion of it perisheth: so also shall the rich man fade away in his ways.

¹²Blessed is the man that endureth temptation: for when he is tried, he shall receive the crown of life, which the Lord hath promised to them that love him. ¹³Let no man say when he is tempted, 'I am tempted of God': for God cannot be tempted with evil, neither tempteth he any man. ¹⁴But every man is tempted, when he is drawn away of his own lust, and enticed. ¹⁵Then when lust hath conceived, it bringeth forth sin: and sin, when it is finished, bringeth forth death. ¹⁶Do not err, my beloved brethren. ¹⁷Every good gift and every perfect gift is from above, and cometh down from the Father of lights, with whom is no variableness, neither shadow of turning. ¹⁸Of his own will begot he us with the word of truth, that we should be a kind of first-fruits of his creatures.

¹⁹Wherefore, my beloved brethren, let every man be swift to hear, slow to speak, slow to wrath. ²⁰For the wrath of man worketh not the righteousness of God. ²¹Wherefore lay apart all filthiness and superfluity of naughtiness, and receive with meekness the engrafted word, which is able to save your souls. ²²But be ye doers of the word, and not hearers only, deceiving your own selves. ²³For if any be a hearer of the word, and not a doer, he is like unto a man beholding his natural face in a glass: ²⁴for he beholdeth himself, and goeth his way, and straightway forgetteth what manner of man he was. ²⁵But whoso looketh into the perfect law of liberty, and continueth therein, he being not a forgetful hearer, but a doer of the work, this man shall be blessed in his deed. ²⁶If any man among you seem to be religious, and bridleth not his tongue, but deceiveth his own heart, this man's religion is vain. ²⁷Pure religion and undefiled before God and the Father is this, to visit the fatherless and widows in their affliction, and to keep himself unspotted from the world.

2 My brethren, have not the faith of our Lord Jesus Christ, the Lord of glory, with respect of persons. ²For if there come unto your assembly a man with a gold ring, in goodly apparel, and there come in also a poor man in vile raiment: ³and ye have respect to him that weareth the gay clothing, and say unto him, 'Sit thou here in a good place': and say to the poor, 'Stand thou there, or sit here under my footstool': ⁴are ye not then partial in yourselves, and are become judges of evil thoughts? ⁵Hearken, my beloved brethren, hath not God chosen the poor of this world, rich in faith, and heirs of the kingdom which he hath promised to them that love him? ⁶But ye have despised the poor. Do not rich men oppress you, and draw you before the judgement seats? ⁷Do not they blaspheme that worthy name by the which ye are called? ⁸If ye fulfil the royal law according to the scripture, 'Thou shalt love thy neighbour as thyself', ye do well. ⁹But if ye have respect to persons, ye commit sin, and are convinced of the law as transgressors. ¹⁰For whosoever shall keep the whole law, and yet offend in one point, he is guilty of all. ¹¹For he that said, 'Do not commit adultery', said also, 'Do not kill'. Now if thou commit no adultery, yet if thou kill, thou art become a transgressor of the law. ¹²So speak ye, and so do, as they that shall be judged by the law of liberty. ¹³For he shall have judgement without mercy, that hath shown no mercy, and mercy rejoiceth against judgement.

¹⁴What doth it profit, my brethren, though a man say he hath faith, and have not works? can faith save him? ¹⁵If a brother or sister be naked, and destitute of daily food, ¹⁶and one of you say unto them, 'Depart in peace, be you warmed and filled': notwithstanding ye give them not those things which are needful to the body: what doth it profit? ¹⁷Even so faith, if it hath not works, is dead, being alone. ¹⁸Yea, a man may say, 'Thou hast faith, and I have works': show me thy faith without thy works, and I will show thee my faith by my works. ¹⁹Thou believest that there is one God, thou doest well: the devils also believe, and tremble. ²⁰But wilt thou know, O vain man, that faith without works is dead? ²¹Was not Abraham our father justified by works, when he had offered Isaac his son upon the altar? ²²Seest thou how faith wrought with his works, and by works was faith made perfect? ²³And the scripture was fulfilled which saith, 'Abraham believed God, and it was imputed unto him for righteousness: and he was called the friend of God'. ²⁴Ye see then how that by works a man is justified, and not by faith only. ²⁵Likewise also was not Rahab the harlot justified by works, when she had received the messengers, and had sent them out another way? ²⁶For as the body without the spirit is dead, so faith without works is dead also.

3 My brethren, be not many masters, knowing that we shall receive the greater condemnation. ²For in many things we offend all. If any man offend not in word, the same is a perfect man, and able also to bridle the whole body. ³Behold, we put bits in the horses' mouths, that they may obey us, and we turn about their whole body. ⁴Behold also the ships, which though they be so great, and are driven of fierce winds, yet are they turned about with a very small helm, whithersoever the

governor listeth. ⁵Even so the tongue is a little member, and boasteth great things: behold, how great a matter a little fire kindleth. ⁶And the tongue is a fire, a world of iniquity: so is the tongue amongst our members, that it defileth the whole body, and setteth on fire the course of nature, and it is set on fire of hell. ⁷For every kind of beasts, and of birds, and of serpents, and of things in the sea, is tamed, and hath been tamed of mankind: ⁸but the tongue can no man tame; it is an unruly evil, full of deadly poison. ⁹Therewith bless we God, even the Father: and therewith curse we men, which are made after the similitude of God. ¹⁰Out of the same mouth proceedeth blessing and cursing: my brethren, these things ought not so to be. ¹¹Doth a fountain send forth at the same place sweet water and bitter? ¹²Can the fig tree, my brethren, bear olive berries? either a vine, figs? so can no fountain both yield salt water and fresh.

¹³Who is a wise man and endued with knowledge amongst you? let him show out of a good conversation his works with meekness of wisdom. ¹⁴But if ye have bitter envying and strife in your hearts, glory not, and lie not against the truth. ¹⁵This wisdom descendeth not from above, but is earthly, sensual, devilish. ¹⁶For where envying and strife is, there is confusion and every evil work. ¹⁷But the wisdom that is from above is first pure, then peaceable, gentle, and easy to be entreated, full of mercy and good fruits, without partiality, and without hypocrisy. ¹⁸And the fruit of righteousness is sown in peace of them that make peace.

4 From whence come wars and fightings among you? come they not hence, even of your lusts that war in your members? ²Ye lust, and have not: ye kill, and desire to have, and cannot obtain: ye fight and war, yet ye have not, because ye ask not. ³Ye ask, and receive not, because ye ask amiss, that ye may consume it upon your lusts. ⁴Ye adulterers and adulteresses, know ye not that the friendship of the world is enmity with God? whosoever therefore will be a friend of the world is the enemy of God. ⁵Do ye think that the scripture saith in vain, 'The spirit that dwelleth in us lusteth to envy'? ⁶But he giveth more grace, wherefore he saith, 'God resisteth the proud, but giveth grace unto the humble'. ⁷Submit yourselves therefore to God: resist the devil, and he will flee from you. ⁸Draw nigh to God, and he will draw nigh to you: cleanse your hands, ye sinners, and purify your hearts, ye doubleminded. ⁹Be afflicted, and mourn, and weep: let your laughter be turned to mourning, and your joy to heaviness. ¹⁰Humble yourselves in the sight of the Lord, and he shall lift you up.

¹¹Speak not evil one of another, brethren: he that speaketh evil of his brother, and judgeth his brother, speaketh evil of the law, and judgeth the law: but if thou judge the law, thou art not a doer of the law, but a judge. ¹²There is one lawgiver, who is able to save and to destroy: who art thou that judgest another?

¹³Go to now, ye that say, 'Today or tomorrow we will go into such a city, and continue there a year, and buy and sell, and get gain': ¹⁴whereas ye know not what shall be on the morrow. For what is your

life? It is even a vapour that appeareth for a little time, and then vanisheth away. [15]For that ye ought to say, 'If the Lord will, we shall live, and do this, or that'. [16]But now ye rejoice in your boastings: all such rejoicing is evil. [17]Therefore to him that knoweth to do good, and doeth it not, to him it is sin.

5 Go to now, ye rich men, weep and howl for your miseries that shall come upon you. [2]Your riches are corrupted, and your garments moth-eaten. [3]Your gold and silver is cankered, and the rust of them shall be a witness against you, and shall eat your flesh as it were fire: ye have heaped treasure together for the last days. [4]Behold, the hire of the labourers which have reaped down your fields, which is of you kept back by fraud, crieth: and the cries of them which have reaped are entered into the ears of the Lord of Sabaoth. [5]Ye have lived in pleasure on the earth, and been wanton: ye have nourished your hearts, as in a day of slaughter. [6]Ye have condemned and killed the just, and he doth not resist you.

[7]Be patient therefore, brethren, unto the coming of the Lord. Behold, the husbandman waiteth for the precious fruit of the earth, and hath long patience for it, until he receive the early and latter rain. [8]Be ye also patient; establish your hearts: for the coming of the Lord draweth nigh. [9]Grudge not one against another, brethren, lest ye be condemned: behold, the judge standeth before the door. [10]Take, my brethren, the prophets, who have spoken in the name of the Lord, for an example of suffering affliction, and of patience. [11]Behold, we count them happy which endure. Ye have heard of the patience of Job, and have seen the end of the Lord: that the Lord is very pitiful, and of tender mercy.

[12]But above all things, my brethren, swear not, neither by heaven, neither by the earth, neither by any other oath: but let your yea be yea, and your nay, nay: lest ye fall into condemnation.

[13]Is any among you afflicted? let him pray. Is any merry? let him sing psalms. [14]Is any sick among you? let him call for the elders of the church, and let them pray over him, anointing him with oil in the name of the Lord: [15]and the prayer of faith shall save the sick, and the Lord shall raise him up: and if he hath committed sins, they shall be forgiven him. [16]Confess your faults one to another, and pray one for another, that ye may be healed: the effectual fervent prayer of a righteous man availeth much. [17]Elias was a man subject to like passions as we are, and he prayed earnestly that it might not rain: and it rained not on the earth by the space of three years and six months. [18]And he prayed again, and the heaven gave rain, and the earth brought forth her fruit.

[19]Brethren, if any of you do err from the truth, and one convert him, [20]let him know, that he which converteth the sinner from the error of his way shall save a soul from death, and shall hide a multitude of sins.

THE
FIRST EPISTLE GENERAL OF
PETER

1 Peter, an apostle of Jesus Christ, to the strangers scattered throughout Pontus, Galatia, Cappadocia, Asia, and Bithynia, ²elect according to the foreknowledge of God the Father, through sanctification of the Spirit, unto obedience and sprinkling of the blood of Jesus Christ: grace unto you and peace be multiplied. ³Blessed be the God and Father of our Lord Jesus Christ, which according to his abundant mercy hath begotten us again unto a lively hope by the resurrection of Jesus Christ from the dead, ⁴to an inheritance incorruptible, and undefiled, and that fadeth not away, reserved in heaven for you, ⁵who are kept by the power of God through faith unto salvation ready to be revealed in the last time. ⁶Wherein ye greatly rejoice, though now for a season, if need be, ye are in heaviness through manifold temptations: ⁷that the trial of your faith, being much more precious than of gold that perisheth, though it be tried with fire, might be found unto praise and honour and glory at the appearing of Jesus Christ: ⁸whom having not seen, ye love; in whom, though now ye see him not, yet believing, ye rejoice with joy unspeakable and full of glory, ⁹receiving the end of your faith, even the salvation of your souls: ¹⁰of which salvation the prophets have inquired and searched diligently, who prophesied of the grace that should come unto you, ¹¹searching what, or what manner of time the Spirit of Christ which was in them did signify, when it testified beforehand the sufferings of Christ, and the glory that should follow. ¹²Unto whom it was revealed, that not unto themselves, but unto us they did minister the things which are now reported unto you by them that have preached the gospel unto you with the Holy Ghost sent down from heaven, which things the angels desire to look into.

¹³Wherefore gird up the loins of your mind, be sober, and hope to the end for the grace that is to be brought unto you at the revelation of Jesus Christ: ¹⁴as obedient children, not fashioning yourselves according to the former lusts in your ignorance: ¹⁵but as he which hath called you is holy, so be ye holy in all manner of conversation; ¹⁶because it is written, 'Be ye holy; for I am holy'. ¹⁷And if ye call on the Father, who without respect of persons judgeth according to every man's work, pass the time of your sojourning here in fear: ¹⁸forasmuch as ye know that ye were not redeemed with corruptible things, as silver and gold, from your vain conversation received by tradition from your fathers; ¹⁹but with the precious blood of Christ, as of a lamb without blemish and without spot, ²⁰who verily was foreordained before the foundation of the world, but was manifest in these last times for you, ²¹who by him do believe in God, that raised him up from the dead, and gave him glory, that your faith and hope might be in God. ²²Seeing ye have purified your souls in obeying the truth through the Spirit unto unfeigned love

of the brethren, see that ye love one another with a pure heart fervently, ²³being born again, not of corruptible seed, but of incorruptible, by the word of God, which liveth and abideth for ever. ²⁴For 'All flesh is as grass, and all the glory of man as the flower of grass. The grass withereth, and the flower thereof falleth away: ²⁵but the word of the Lord endureth for ever.' And this is the word which by the gospel is preached unto you.

2 Wherefore laying aside all malice, and all guile, and hypocrisies, and envies, and evil speakings, ²as newborn babes, desire the sincere milk of the word, that ye may grow thereby, ³if so be ye have tasted that the Lord is gracious. ⁴To whom coming, as unto a living stone, disallowed indeed of men, but chosen of God, and precious, ⁵ye also, as lively stones, are built up a spiritual house, a holy priesthood, to offer up spiritual sacrifice, acceptable to God by Jesus Christ. ⁶Wherefore it is contained in the scripture, 'Behold, I lay in Sion a chief corner-stone, elect, precious, and he that believeth on him shall not be confounded'. ⁷Unto you therefore which believe he is precious: but unto them which be disobedient, 'The stone which the builders disallowed, the same is made the head of the corner', ⁸and 'A stone of stumbling, and a rock of offence', even to them which stumble at the word, being disobedient, whereunto also they were appointed. ⁹But ye are a chosen generation, a royal priesthood, a holy nation, a peculiar people, that ye should show forth the praises of him who hath called you out of darkness into his marvellous light: ¹⁰which in time past were not a people, but are now the people of God: which had not obtained mercy, but now have obtained mercy.

¹¹Dearly beloved, I beseech you as strangers and pilgrims, abstain from fleshly lusts, which war against the soul, ¹²having your conversation honest among the Gentiles, that, whereas they speak against you as evil-doers, they may by your good works, which they shall behold, glorify God in the day of visitation.

¹³Submit yourselves to every ordinance of man for the Lord's sake, whether it be to the king, as supreme, ¹⁴or unto governors, as unto them that are sent by him for the punishment of evil-doers, and for the praise of them that do well. ¹⁵For so is the will of God, that with well-doing ye may put to silence the ignorance of foolish men: ¹⁶as free, and not using your liberty for a cloak of maliciousness, but as the servants of God. ¹⁷Honour all men. Love the brotherhood. Fear God. Honour the king.

¹⁸Servants, be subject to your masters with all fear, not only to the good and gentle, but also to the froward. ¹⁹For this is thanksworthy, if a man for conscience toward God endure grief, suffering wrongfully. ²⁰For what glory is it, if, when ye be buffeted for your faults, ye shall take it patiently? but if, when ye do well, and suffer for it, ye take it patiently, this is acceptable with God. ²¹For even hereunto were ye called: because Christ also suffered for us, leaving us an example, that ye should follow his steps: ²²who did no sin, neither was guile found in his mouth: ²³who, when he was reviled, reviled not again; when he suf-

fered, he threatened not, but committed himself to him that judgeth righteously: ²⁴who his own self bore our sins in his own body on the tree, that we, being dead to sins, should live unto righteousness, by whose stripes ye were healed. ²⁵For ye were as sheep going astray, but are now returned unto the Shepherd and Bishop of your souls.

3 Likewise, ye wives, be in subjection to your own husbands, that, if any obey not the word, they also may without the word be won by the conversation of the wives: ²while they behold your chaste conversation coupled with fear. ³Whose adorning let it not be that outward adorning of plaiting the hair, and of wearing of gold, or of putting on of apparel; ⁴but let it be the hidden man of the heart, in that which is not corruptible, even the ornament of a meek and quiet spirit, which is in the sight of God of great price. ⁵For after this manner in the old time the holy women also, who trusted in God, adorned themselves, being in subjection unto their own husbands: ⁶even as Sara obeyed Abraham, calling him lord, whose daughters ye are as long as ye do well, and are not afraid with any amazement. ⁷Likewise, ye husbands, dwell with them according to knowledge, giving honour unto the wife, as unto the weaker vessel, and as being heirs together of the grace of life, that your prayers be not hindered.

⁸Finally, be ye all of one mind, having compassion one of another, love as brethren, be pitiful, be courteous, ⁹not rendering evil for evil, or railing for railing: but contrariwise blessing, knowing that ye are thereunto called, that ye should inherit a blessing. ¹⁰For 'He that will love life, and see good days, let him refrain his tongue from evil, and his lips that they speak no guile: ¹¹let him eschew evil, and do good, let him seek peace, and ensue it. ¹²For the eyes of the Lord are over the righteous, and his ears are open unto their prayers: but the face of the Lord is against them that do evil.'

¹³And who is he that will harm you, if ye be followers of that which is good? ¹⁴But and if ye suffer for righteousness' sake, happy are ye, and be not afraid of their terror, neither be troubled: ¹⁵but sanctify the Lord God in your hearts, and be ready always to give an answer to every man that asketh you a reason of the hope that is in you with meekness and fear: ¹⁶having a good conscience, that, whereas they speak evil of you, as of evil-doers, they may be ashamed that falsely accuse your good conversation in Christ. ¹⁷For it is better, if the will of God be so, that ye suffer for well-doing, than for evil-doing. ¹⁸For Christ also hath once suffered for sins, the just for the unjust, that he might bring us to God, being put to death in the flesh, but quickened by the Spirit: ¹⁹by which also he went and preached unto the spirits in prison, ²⁰which sometime were disobedient, when once the long-suffering of God waited in the days of Noah, while the ark was a-preparing, wherein few, that is, eight souls were saved by water. ²¹The like figure whereunto, even baptism, doth also now save us (not the putting away of the filth of the flesh, but the answer of a good conscience toward God), by the resurrection of Jesus Christ: ²²who is gone into heaven, and is on the right hand of God, angels and authorities and powers being made subject unto him.

4 Forasmuch then as Christ hath suffered for us in the flesh, arm yourselves likewise with the same mind: for he that hath suffered in the flesh hath ceased from sin: ²that he no longer should live the rest of his time in the flesh to the lusts of men, but to the will of God. ³For the time past of our life may suffice us to have wrought the will of the Gentiles, when we walked in lasciviousness, lusts, excess of wine, revellings, banquetings, and abominable idolatries: ⁴wherein they think it strange that you run not with them to the same excess of riot, speaking evil of you: ⁵who shall give account to him that is ready to judge the quick and the dead. ⁶For for this cause was the gospel preached also to them that are dead, that they might be judged according to men in the flesh, but live according to God in the spirit.

⁷But the end of all things is at hand: be ye therefore sober, and watch unto prayer. ⁸And above all things have fervent charity among yourselves: for charity shall cover the multitude of sins. ⁹Use hospitality one to another without grudging. ¹⁰As every man hath received the gift, even so minister the same one to another, as good stewards of the manifold grace of God. ¹¹If any man speak, let him speak as the oracles of God: if any man minister, let him do it as of the ability which God giveth, that God in all things may be glorified through Jesus Christ, to whom be praise and dominion for ever and ever. Amen.

¹²Beloved, think it not strange concerning the fiery trial which is to try you, as though some strange thing happened unto you: ¹³but rejoice, inasmuch as ye are partakers of Christ's sufferings; that, when his glory shall be revealed, ye may be glad also with exceeding joy. ¹⁴If ye be reproached for the name of Christ, happy are ye, for the spirit of glory and of God resteth upon you: on their part he is evil spoken of, but on your part he is glorified. ¹⁵But let none of you suffer as a murderer, or as a thief, or as an evil-doer, or as a busybody in other men's matters. ¹⁶Yet if any man suffer as a Christian, let him not be ashamed, but let him glorify God on this behalf. ¹⁷For the time is come that judgement must begin at the house of God: and if it first begin at us, what shall the end be of them that obey not the gospel of God? ¹⁸And if the righteous scarcely be saved, where shall the ungodly and the sinner appear? ¹⁹Wherefore let them that suffer according to the will of God commit the keeping of their souls to him in well-doing, as unto a faithful Creator.

5 I exhort, who am also an elder, and a witness of the sufferings of Christ, and also a partaker of the glory that shall be revealed: ²feed the flock of God which is among you, taking the oversight thereof, not by constraint, but willingly: not for filthy lucre, but of a ready mind: ³neither as being lords over God's heritage, but being examples to the flock. ⁴And when the chief Shepherd shall appear, ye shall receive a crown of glory that fadeth not away.

⁵Likewise, ye younger, submit yourselves unto the elder: yea, all of you be subject one to another, and be clothed with humility: for God resisteth the proud, and giveth grace to the humble. ⁶Humble yourselves therefore under the mighty hand of God, that he may exalt

you in due time, ⁷casting all your care upon him, for he careth for you.

⁸Be sober, be vigilant: because your adversary the devil, as a roaring lion, walketh about, seeking whom he may devour: ⁹whom resist steadfast in the faith, knowing that the same afflictions are accomplished in your brethren that are in the world. ¹⁰But the God of all grace, who hath called us into his eternal glory by Christ Jesus, after that ye have suffered a while, make you perfect, establish, strengthen, settle you. ¹¹To him be glory and dominion for ever and ever. Amen.

¹²By Silvanus, a faithful brother unto you, as I suppose, I have written briefly, exhorting, and testifying that this is the true grace of God wherein ye stand.

¹³The church that is at Babylon, elected together with you, saluteth you, and so doth Marcus my son.

¹⁴Greet ye one another with a kiss of charity.

Peace be with you all that are in Christ Jesus. Amen.

THE
SECOND EPISTLE GENERAL OF
PETER

1 Simon Peter, a servant and an apostle of Jesus Christ, to them that have obtained like precious faith with us through the righteousness of God and our Saviour Jesus Christ. [2]Grace and peace be multiplied unto you through the knowledge of God, and of Jesus our Lord, [3]according as his divine power hath given unto us all things that pertain unto life and godliness, through the knowledge of him that hath called us to glory and virtue: [4]whereby are given unto us exceeding great and precious promises, that by these you might be partakers of the divine nature, having escaped the corruption that is in the world through lust.

[5]And besides this, giving all diligence, add to your faith virtue; and to virtue knowledge; [6]and to knowledge temperance; and to temperance patience; and to patience godliness; [7]and to godliness brotherly kindness; and to brotherly kindness charity. [8]For if these things be in you, and abound, they make you that ye shall neither be barren nor unfruitful in the knowledge of our Lord Jesus Christ. [9]But he that lacketh these things is blind, and cannot see far off, and hath forgotten that he was purged from his old sins. [10]Wherefore the rather, brethren, give diligence to make your calling and election sure: for if ye do these things, ye shall never fall: [11]for so an entrance shall be ministered unto you abundantly into the everlasting kingdom of our Lord and Saviour Jesus Christ.

[12]Wherefore I will not be negligent to put you always in remembrance of these things, though ye know them, and be established in the present truth. [13]Yea, I think it meet, as long as I am in this tabernacle, to stir you up by putting you in remembrance: [14]knowing that shortly I must put off this my tabernacle, even as our Lord Jesus Christ hath shown me. [15]Moreover I will endeavour that you may be able after my decease to have these things always in remembrance. [16]For we have not followed cunningly devised fables, when we made known unto you the power and coming of our Lord Jesus Christ, but were eyewitnesses of his majesty. [17]For he received from God the Father honour and glory, when there came such a voice to him from the excellent glory, 'This is my beloved Son, in whom I am well pleased'. [18]And this voice which came from heaven we heard, when we were with him in the holy mount. [19]We have also a more sure word of prophecy, whereunto ye do well that ye take heed, as unto a light that shineth in a dark place, until the day dawn, and the day star arise in your hearts: [20]knowing this first, that no prophecy of the scripture is of any private interpretation: [21]for the prophecy came not in old time by the will of man: but holy men of God spoke as they were moved by the Holy Ghost.

2 But there were false prophets also among the people, even as there shall be false teachers among you, who privily shall bring in damnable heresies, even denying the Lord that bought them, and bring upon themselves swift destruction. ²And many shall follow their pernicious ways, by reason of whom the way of truth shall be evil spoken of. ³And through covetousness shall they with feigned words make merchandise of you, whose judgement now of a long time lingereth not, and their damnation slumbereth not. ⁴For if God spared not the angels that sinned, but cast them down to hell, and delivered them into chains of darkness, to be reserved unto judgement; ⁵and spared not the old world, but saved Noah the eighth person, a preacher of righteousness, bringing in the flood upon the world of the ungodly; ⁶and turning the cities of Sodom and Gomorrha into ashes condemned them with an overthrow, making them an example unto those that after should live ungodly; ⁷and delivered just Lot, vexed with the filthy conversation of the wicked ⁸(for that righteous man dwelling among them, in seeing and hearing, vexed his righteous soul from day to day with their unlawful deeds): ⁹the Lord knoweth how to deliver the godly out of temptations, and to reserve the unjust unto the day of judgement to be punished: ¹⁰but chiefly them that walk after the flesh in the lust of uncleanness, and despise government. Presumptuous are they, self-willed: they are not afraid to speak evil of dignities. ¹¹Whereas angels, which are greater in power and might, bring not railing accusation against them before the Lord. ¹²But these, as natural brute beasts, made to be taken and destroyed, speak evil of the things that they understand not, and shall utterly perish in their own corruption, ¹³and shall receive the reward of unrighteousness, as they that count it pleasure to riot in the day time: spots they are and blemishes, sporting themselves with their own deceivings while they feast with you: ¹⁴having eyes full of adultery, and that cannot cease from sin, beguiling unstable souls: a heart they have exercised with covetous practices: cursed children: ¹⁵which have forsaken the right way, and are gone astray, following the way of Balaam the son of Bosor, who loved the wages of unrighteousness, ¹⁶but was rebuked for his iniquity: the dumb ass speaking with man's voice forbad the madness of the prophet.

¹⁷These are wells without water, clouds that are carried with a tempest, to whom the mist of darkness is reserved for ever. ¹⁸For when they speak great swelling words of vanity, they allure through the lusts of the flesh, through much wantonness, those that were clean escaped from them who live in error. ¹⁹While they promise them liberty, they themselves are the servants of corruption: for of whom a man is overcome, of the same is he brought in bondage. ²⁰For if after they have escaped the pollutions of the world through the knowledge of the Lord and Saviour Jesus Christ, they are again entangled therein, and overcome, the latter end is worse with them than the beginning. ²¹For it had been better for them not to have known the way of righteousness, than, after they have known it, to turn from the holy commandment delivered unto them. ²²But it is happened unto them according to the true proverb, 'The dog is turned to his own vomit again, and the sow that was washed to her wallowing in the mire'.

3 This second epistle, beloved, I now write unto you, in both which I stir up your pure minds by way of remembrance: ²that ye may be mindful of the words which were spoken before by the holy prophets, and of the commandment of us the apostles of the Lord and Saviour: ³knowing this first, that there shall come in the last days scoffers, walking after their own lusts, ⁴and saying, 'Where is the promise of his coming? for since the fathers fell asleep, all things continue as they were from the beginning of the creation'. ⁵For this they willingly are ignorant of, that by the word of God the heavens were of old, and the earth standing out of the water and in the water, ⁶whereby the world that then was, being overflowed with water, perished. ⁷But the heavens and the earth, which are now, by the same word are kept in store, reserved unto fire against the day of judgement and perdition of ungodly men.

⁸But, beloved, be not ignorant of this one thing, that one day is with the Lord as a thousand years, and a thousand years as one day. ⁹The Lord is not slack concerning his promise, as some men count slackness, but is long-suffering to us-ward, not willing that any should perish, but that all should come to repentance. ¹⁰But the day of the Lord will come as a thief in the night, in the which the heavens shall pass away with a great noise, and the elements shall melt with fervent heat, the earth also and the works that are therein shall be burnt up.

¹¹Seeing then that all these things shall be dissolved, what manner of persons ought ye to be in all holy conversation and godliness, ¹²looking for and hasting unto the coming of the day of God, wherein the heavens being on fire shall be dissolved, and the elements shall melt with fervent heat? ¹³Nevertheless we, according to his promise, look for new heavens and a new earth, wherein dwelleth righteousness.

¹⁴Wherefore, beloved, seeing that ye look for such things, be diligent that ye may be found of him in peace, without spot, and blameless. ¹⁵And account that the long-suffering of our Lord is salvation, even as our beloved brother Paul also according to the wisdom given unto him hath written unto you; ¹⁶as also in all his epistles, speaking in them of these things, in which are some things hard to be understood, which they that are unlearned and unstable wrest, as they do also the other scriptures, unto their own destruction. ¹⁷Ye therefore, beloved, seeing ye know these things before, beware lest ye also, being led away with the error of the wicked, fall from your own steadfastness. ¹⁸But grow in grace, and in the knowledge of our Lord and Saviour Jesus Christ. To him be glory both now and for ever. Amen.

THE FIRST EPISTLE GENERAL OF
JOHN

1 That which was from the beginning, which we have heard, which we have seen with our eyes, which we have looked upon, and our hands have handled, of the Word of life ²(for the life was manifested, and we have seen it, and bear witness, and show unto you that eternal life, which was with the Father, and was manifested unto us); ³that which we have seen and heard declare we unto you, that ye also may have fellowship with us; and truly our fellowship is with the Father, and with his Son Jesus Christ. ⁴And these things write we unto you, that your joy may be full.

⁵This then is the message which we have heard of him, and declare unto you, that God is light, and in him is no darkness at all. ⁶If we say that we have fellowship with him, and walk in darkness, we lie, and do not the truth. ⁷But if we walk in the light, as he is in the light, we have fellowship one with another, and the blood of Jesus Christ his Son cleanseth us from all sin. ⁸If we say that we have no sin, we deceive ourselves, and the truth is not in us. ⁹If we confess our sins, he is faithful and just to forgive us our sins, and to cleanse us from all unrighteousness. ¹⁰If we say that we have not sinned, we make him a liar, and his word is not in us.

2 My little children, these things write I unto you, that ye sin not. And if any man sin, we have an advocate with the Father, Jesus Christ the righteous: ²and he is the propitiation for our sins: and not for ours only, but also for the sins of the whole world. ³And hereby we do know that we know him, if we keep his commandments. ⁴He that saith, 'I know him', and keepeth not his commandments, is a liar, and the truth is not in him. ⁵But whoso keepeth his word, in him verily is the love of God perfected: hereby know we that we are in him. ⁶He that saith he abideth in him ought himself also so to walk, even as he walked.

⁷Brethren, I write no new commandment unto you, but an old commandment which ye had from the beginning. The old commandment is the word which ye have heard from the beginning. ⁸Again, a new commandment I write unto you, which thing is true in him and in you: because the darkness is past, and the true light now shineth. ⁹He that saith he is in the light, and hateth his brother, is in darkness even until now. ¹⁰He that loveth his brother abideth in the light, and there is no occasion of stumbling in him. ¹¹But he that hateth his brother is in darkness, and walketh in darkness, and knoweth not whither he goeth, because that darkness hath blinded his eyes.

¹²I write unto you, little children, because your sins are forgiven you for his name's sake. ¹³I write unto you, fathers, because ye have known him that is from the beginning. I write unto you, young men, because you have overcome the wicked one. I write unto you, little children,

because ye have known the Father. ¹⁴I have written unto you, fathers, because ye have known him that is from the beginning. I have written unto you, young men, because ye are strong, and the word of God abideth in you, and ye have overcome the wicked one.

¹⁵Love not the world, neither the things that are in the world. If any man love the world, the love of the Father is not in him. ¹⁶For all that is in the world, the lust of the flesh, the lust of the eyes, and the pride of life, is not of the Father, but is of the world. ¹⁷And the world passeth away, and the lust thereof: but he that doeth the will of God abideth for ever.

¹⁸Little children, it is the last time: and as ye have heard that antichrist shall come, even now are there many antichrists, whereby we know that it is the last time. ¹⁹They went out from us, but they were not of us: for if they had been of us, they would no doubt have continued with us: but they went out that they might be made manifest that they were not all of us. ²⁰But ye have an unction from the Holy One, and ye know all things. ²¹I have not written unto you because ye know not the truth, but because ye know it, and that no lie is of the truth.

²²Who is a liar but he that denieth that Jesus is the Christ? He is antichrist, that denieth the Father and the Son. ²³Whosoever denieth the Son, the same hath not the Father: but he that acknowledgeth the Son hath the Father also. ²⁴Let that therefore abide in you, which ye have heard from the beginning: if that which ye have heard from the beginning shall remain in you, ye also shall continue in the Son, and in the Father. ²⁵And this is the promise that he hath promised us, even eternal life.

²⁶These things have I written unto you concerning them that seduce you. ²⁷But the anointing which ye have received of him abideth in you, and ye need not that any man teach you: but as the same anointing teacheth you of all things, and is truth, and is no lie, and even as it hath taught you, ye shall abide in him. ²⁸And now, little children, abide in him, that when he shall appear, we may have confidence, and not be ashamed before him at his coming. ²⁹If ye know that he is righteous, ye know that every one which doeth righteousness is born of him.

3 Behold, what manner of love the Father hath bestowed upon us, that we should be called the sons of God: therefore the world knoweth us not, because it knew him not. ²Beloved, now are we the sons of God, and it doth not yet appear what we shall be: but we know that when he shall appear, we shall be like him: for we shall see him as he is. ³And every man that hath this hope in him purifieth himself, even as he is pure.

⁴Whosoever committeth sin transgresseth also the law: for sin is the transgression of the law. ⁵And ye know that he was manifested to take away our sins, and in him is no sin. ⁶Whosoever abideth in him sinneth not: whosoever sinneth hath not seen him, neither known him. ⁷Little children, let no man deceive you: he that doeth righteousness is righteous, even as he is righteous. ⁸He that committeth sin is of the devil, for the devil sinneth from the beginning: for this purpose the Son of God

was manifested, that he might destroy the works of the devil. ⁹Whosoever is born of God doth not commit sin: for his seed remaineth in him, and he cannot sin, because he is born of God. ¹⁰In this the children of God are manifest, and the children of the devil: whosoever doeth not righteousness is not of God, neither he that loveth not his brother.

¹¹For this is the message that ye heard from the beginning, that we should love one another. ¹²Not as Cain, who was of that wicked one, and slew his brother. And wherefore slew he him? Because his own works were evil, and his brother's righteous. ¹³Marvel not, my brethren, if the world hate you. ¹⁴We know that we have passed from death unto life, because we love the brethren: he that loveth not his brother abideth in death. ¹⁵Whosoever hateth his brother is a murderer, and ye know that no murderer hath eternal life abiding in him. ¹⁶Hereby perceive we the love of God, because he laid down his life for us, and we ought to lay down our lives for the brethren. ¹⁷But whoso hath this world's good, and seeth his brother hath need, and shutteth up his bowels of compassion from him, how dwelleth the love of God in him?

¹⁸My little children, let us not love in word, neither in tongue, but in deed and in truth. ¹⁹And hereby we know that we are of the truth, and shall assure our hearts before him. ²⁰For if our heart condemn us, God is greater than our heart, and knoweth all things. ²¹Beloved, if our heart condemn us not, then have we confidence towards God. ²²And whatsoever we ask, we receive of him, because we keep his commandments, and do those things that are pleasing in his sight. ²³And this is his commandment, that we should believe on the name of his Son Jesus Christ, and love one another, as he gave us commandment. ²⁴And he that keepeth his commandments dwelleth in him, and he in him: and hereby we know that he abideth in us, by the Spirit which he hath given us.

4 Beloved, believe not every spirit, but try the spirits whether they are of God: because many false prophets are gone out into the world. ²Hereby know ye the Spirit of God: every spirit that confesseth that Jesus Christ is come in the flesh is of God. ³And every spirit that confesseth not that Jesus Christ is come in the flesh is not of God: and this is that spirit of antichrist, whereof you have heard that it should come, and even now already is it in the world. ⁴Ye are of God, little children, and have overcome them: because greater is he that is in you, than he that is in the world. ⁵They are of the world: therefore speak they of the world, and the world heareth them. ⁶We are of God: he that knoweth God heareth us; he that is not of God heareth not us. Hereby know we the spirit of truth, and the spirit of error.

⁷Beloved, let us love one another; for love is of God: and every one that loveth is born of God, and knoweth God. ⁸He that loveth not knoweth not God: for God is love. ⁹In this was manifested the love of God towards us, because that God sent his only begotten Son into the world, that we might live through him. ¹⁰Herein is love, not that we loved God, but that he loved us, and sent his Son to be the propitiation for our sins.

[11]Beloved, if God so loved us, we ought also to love one another. [12]No man hath seen God at any time. If we love one another, God dwelleth in us, and his love is perfected in us. [13]Hereby know we that we dwell in him, and he in us, because he hath given us of his Spirit. [14]And we have seen and do testify that the Father sent the Son to be the Saviour of the world. [15]Whosoever shall confess that Jesus is the Son of God, God dwelleth in him, and he in God. [16]And we have known and believed the love that God hath to us. God is love, and he that dwelleth in love dwelleth in God, and God in him. [17]Herein is our love made perfect, that we may have boldness in the day of judgement, because as he is, so are we in this world. [18]There is no fear in love, but perfect love casteth out fear: because fear hath torment. He that feareth is not made perfect in love. [19]We love him, because he first loved us. [20]If a man say, 'I love God', and hateth his brother, he is a liar: for he that loveth not his brother whom he hath seen, how can he love God whom he hath not seen? [21]And this commandment have we from him, that he who loveth God love his brother also.

5 Whosoever believeth that Jesus is the Christ is born of God: and every one that loveth him that begot loveth him also that is begotten of him. [2]By this we know that we love the children of God, when we love God, and keep his commandments. [3]For this is the love of God, that we keep his commandments, and his commandments are not grievous. [4]For whatsoever is born of God overcometh the world, and this is the victory that overcometh the world, even our faith. [5]Who is he that overcometh the world, but he that believeth that Jesus is the Son of God? [6]This is he that came by water and blood, even Jesus Christ; not by water only, but by water and blood. And it is the Spirit that beareth witness, because the Spirit is truth. [7]For there are three that bear record in heaven, the Father, the Word, and the Holy Ghost: and these three are one. [8]And there are three that bear witness in earth, the Spirit, and the water, and the blood: and these three agree in one. [9]If we receive the witness of men, the witness of God is greater: for this is the witness of God which he hath testified of his Son. [10]He that believeth on the Son of God hath the witness in himself: he that believeth not God hath made him a liar, because he believeth not the record that God gave of his Son. [11]And this is the record, that God hath given to us eternal life, and this life is in his Son. [12]He that hath the Son hath life; and he that hath not the Son hath not life.

[13]These things have I written unto you that believe on the name of the Son of God, that ye may know that ye have eternal life, and that ye may believe on the name of the Son of God. [14]And this is the confidence that we have in him, that, if we ask anything according to his will, he heareth us. [15]And if we know that he hear us, whatsoever we ask, we know that we have the petitions that we desired of him.

[16]If any man see his brother sin a sin which is not unto death, he shall ask, and he shall give him life for them that sin not unto death. There is a sin unto death: I do not say that he shall pray for it. [17]All unrighteousness is sin, and there is a sin not unto death. [18]We know

that whosoever is born of God sinneth not: but he that is begotten of God keepeth himself, and that wicked one toucheth him not. ¹⁹And we know that we are of God, and the whole world lieth in wickedness. ²⁰And we know that the Son of God is come, and hath given us an understanding, that we may know him that is true, and we are in him that is true, even in his Son Jesus Christ. This is the true God, and eternal life. ²¹Little children, keep yourselves from idols. Amen.

THE SECOND EPISTLE OF
JOHN

The elder unto the elect lady and her children, whom I love in the truth: and not I only, but also all they that have known the truth: ²for the truth's sake, which dwelleth in us, and shall be with us for ever. ³Grace be with you, mercy, and peace, from God the Father, and from the Lord Jesus Christ, the Son of the Father, in truth and love.

⁴I rejoiced greatly that I found of thy children walking in truth, as we have received a commandment from the Father. ⁵And now I beseech thee, lady, not as though I wrote a new commandment unto thee, but that which we had from the beginning, that we love one another. ⁶And this is love, that we walk after his commandments. This is the commandment, that, as ye have heard from the beginning, ye should walk in it. ⁷For many deceivers are entered into the world, who confess not that Jesus Christ is come in the flesh. This is a deceiver and an antichrist. ⁸Look to yourselves, that we lose not those things which we have wrought, but that we receive a full reward. ⁹Whosoever transgresseth, and abideth not in the doctrine of Christ, hath not God. He that abideth in the doctrine of Christ, he hath both the Father and the Son. ¹⁰If there come any unto you, and bring not this doctrine, receive him not into your house, neither bid him God speed: ¹¹for he that biddeth him God speed is partaker of his evil deeds.

¹²Having many things to write unto you, I would not write with paper and ink, but I trust to come unto you, and speak face to face, that our joy may be full.

¹³The children of thy elect sister greet thee. Amen.

THE THIRD EPISTLE OF
JOHN

The elder unto the well-beloved Gaius, whom I love in the truth. [2]Beloved, I wish above all things that thou mayest prosper and be in health, even as thy soul prospereth. [3]For I rejoiced greatly, when the brethren came and testified of the truth that is in thee, even as thou walkest in the truth. [4]I have no greater joy than to hear that my children walk in truth. [5]Beloved, thou doest faithfully whatsoever thou doest to the brethren, and to strangers: [6]which have born witness of thy charity before the church: whom if thou bring forward on their journey after a godly sort, thou shalt do well: [7]because that for his name's sake they went forth, taking nothing of the Gentiles. [8]We therefore ought to receive such, that we might be fellow-helpers to the truth.

[9]I wrote unto the church, but Diotrephes, who loveth to have the preeminence among them, receiveth us not. [10]Wherefore, if I come, I will remember his deeds which he doeth, prating against us with malicious words: and not content therewith, neither doth he himself receive the brethren, and forbiddeth them that would, and casteth them out of the church.

[11]Beloved, follow not that which is evil, but that which is good. He that doeth good is of God: but he that doeth evil hath not seen God. [12]Demetrius hath good report of all men, and of the truth itself: yea, and we also bear record, and ye know that our record is true.

[13]I had many things to write, but I will not with ink and pen write unto thee. [14]But I trust I shall shortly see thee, and we shall speak face to face.

Peace be to thee. Our friends salute thee. Greet the friends by name.

THE GENERAL EPISTLE OF
JUDE

Jude, the servant of Jesus Christ, and brother of James, to them that
are sanctified by God the Father, and preserved in Jesus Christ, and
called: ²mercy unto you, and peace, and love, be multiplied.

³Beloved, when I gave all diligence to write unto you of the common
salvation, it was needful for me to write unto you, and exhort you that
ye should earnestly contend for the faith which was once delivered
unto the saints. ⁴For there are certain men crept in unawares, who
were before of old ordained to this condemnation, ungodly men, turning the grace of our God into lasciviousness, and denying the only Lord
God, and our Lord Jesus Christ.

⁵I will therefore put you in remembrance, though ye once knew this,
how that the Lord, having saved the people out of the land of Egypt,
afterward destroyed them that believed not. ⁶And the angels which
kept not their first estate, but left their own habitation, he hath
reserved in everlasting chains under darkness unto the judgement of
the great day. ⁷Even as Sodom and Gomorrha, and the cities about
them, in like manner giving themselves over to fornication, and going
after strange flesh, are set forth for an example, suffering the
vengeance of eternal fire. ⁸Likewise also these filthy dreamers defile
the flesh, despise dominion, and speak evil of dignities. ⁹Yet Michael
the archangel, when contending with the devil he disputed about the
body of Moses, durst not bring against him a railing accusation, but
said, 'The Lord rebuke thee'.

¹⁰But these speak evil of those things which they know not: but what
they know naturally, as brute beasts, in those things they corrupt
themselves. ¹¹Woe unto them, for they have gone in the way of Cain,
and ran greedily after the error of Balaam for reward, and perished in
the gainsaying of Core. ¹²These are spots in your feasts of charity, when
they feast with you, feeding themselves without fear: clouds they are
without water, carried about of winds, trees whose fruit withereth,
without fruit, twice dead, plucked up by the roots; ¹³raging waves of
the sea, foaming out their own shame, wandering stars, to whom is
reserved the blackness of darkness for ever.

¹⁴And Enoch also, the seventh from Adam, prophesied of these, saying, 'Behold, the Lord cometh with ten thousands of his saints, ¹⁵to execute judgement upon all, and to convince all that are ungodly among
them of all their ungodly deeds which they have ungodly committed,
and of all their hard speeches which ungodly sinners have spoken
against him.' ¹⁶These are murmurers, complainers, walking after their
own lusts, and their mouth speaketh great swelling words, having
men's persons in admiration because of advantage.

¹⁷But, beloved, remember ye the words which were spoken before of
the apostles of our Lord Jesus Christ: ¹⁸how that they told you there

should be mockers in the last time, who should walk after their own ungodly lusts. [19]These be they who separate themselves, sensual, having not the Spirit. [20]But ye, beloved, building up yourselves on your most holy faith, praying in the Holy Ghost, [21]keep yourselves in the love of God, looking for the mercy of our Lord Jesus Christ unto eternal life. [22]And of some have compassion, making a difference: [23]and others save with fear, pulling them out of the fire: hating even the garment spotted by the flesh.

[24]Now unto him that is able to keep you from falling, and to present you faultless before the presence of his glory with exceeding joy, [25]to the only wise God our Saviour, be glory and majesty, dominion and power, now and ever. Amen.

THE REVELATION

OF SAINT JOHN THE DIVINE

1 The Revelation of Jesus Christ, which God gave unto him, to show unto his servants things which must shortly come to pass; and he sent and signified it by his angel unto his servant John, ²who bore record of the word of God, and of the testimony of Jesus Christ, and of all things that he saw. ³Blessed is he that readeth, and they that hear the words of this prophecy, and keep those things which are written therein: for the time is at hand.

⁴John to the seven churches in Asia: grace be unto you, and peace, from him which is, and which was, and which is to come, and from the seven Spirits which are before his throne: ⁵and from Jesus Christ, who is the faithful witness, and the first-begotten of the dead, and the prince of the kings of the earth. Unto him that loved us, and washed us from our sins in his own blood, ⁶and hath made us kings and priests unto God and his Father: to him be glory and dominion for ever and ever. Amen.

⁷Behold, he cometh with clouds, and every eye shall see him, and they also which pierced him: and all kindreds of the earth shall wail because of him: even so. Amen.

⁸'I am Alpha and Omega, the beginning and the ending,' saith the Lord, 'which is, and which was, and which is to come, the Almighty.'

⁹I John, who also am your brother, and companion in tribulation, and in the kingdom and patience of Jesus Christ, was in the isle that is called Patmos, for the word of God, and for the testimony of Jesus Christ. ¹⁰I was in the Spirit on the Lord's day, and heard behind me a great voice, as of a trumpet, ¹¹saying, 'I am Alpha and Omega, the first and the last: and what thou seest, write in a book, and send it unto the seven churches which are in Asia, unto Ephesus, and unto Smyrna, and unto Pergamos, and unto Thyatira, and unto Sardis, and Philadelphia, and unto Laodicea'. ¹²And I turned to see the voice that spoke with me. And being turned, I saw seven golden candlesticks, ¹³and in the midst of the seven candlesticks one like unto the Son of man, clothed with a garment down to the foot, and girt about the paps with a golden girdle. ¹⁴His head and his hairs were white like wool, as white as snow, and his eyes were as a flame of fire, ¹⁵and his feet like unto fine brass, as if they burnt in a furnace: and his voice as the sound of many waters. ¹⁶And he had in his right hand seven stars: and out of his mouth went a sharp two-edged sword: and his countenance was as the sun shineth in his strength. ¹⁷And when I saw him, I fell at his feet as dead: and he laid his right hand upon me, saying unto me, 'Fear not, I am the first and the last. ¹⁸I am he that liveth, and was dead: and behold, I am alive for evermore, Amen, and have the keys of hell and of death. ¹⁹Write the things which thou hast seen, and the things which are, and the things which shall be hereafter, ²⁰the mystery of the seven stars which thou sawest in

my right hand, and the seven golden candlesticks. The seven stars are the angels of the seven churches: and the seven candlesticks which thou sawest are the seven churches.

2 'Unto the angel of the church of Ephesus write, "These things saith he that holdeth the seven stars in his right hand, who walketh in the midst of the seven golden candlesticks: ²'I know thy works, and thy labour, and thy patience, and how thou canst not bear them which are evil, and thou hast tried them which say they are apostles, and are not, and hast found them liars: ³and hast borne, and hast patience, and for my name's sake hast laboured, and hast not fainted. ⁴Nevertheless I have somewhat against thee, because thou hast left thy first love. ⁵Remember therefore from whence thou art fallen, and repent, and do the first works, or else I will come unto thee quickly, and will remove thy candlestick out of his place, except thou repent. ⁶But this thou hast, that thou hatest the deeds of the Nicolaitans, which I also hate. ⁷He that hath an ear, let him hear what the Spirit saith unto the churches: to him that overcometh will I give to eat of the tree of life, which is in the midst of the paradise of God.'"

⁸'And unto the angel of the church in Smyrna write, "These things saith the first and the last, which was dead, and is alive: ⁹'I know thy works, and tribulation, and poverty, but thou art rich, and I know the blasphemy of them which say they are Jews, and are not, but are the synagogue of Satan. ¹⁰Fear none of those things which thou shalt suffer: behold, the devil shall cast some of you into prison, that ye may be tried, and ye shall have tribulation ten days: be thou faithful unto death, and I will give thee a crown of life. ¹¹He that hath an ear, let him hear what the Spirit saith unto the churches. He that overcometh shall not be hurt of the second death.'"

¹²'And to the angel of the church in Pergamos write, "These things saith he which hath the sharp sword with two edges: ¹³'I know thy works, and where thou dwellest, even where Satan's seat is, and thou holdest fast my name, and hast not denied my faith, even in those days wherein Antipas was my faithful martyr, who was slain among you, where Satan dwelleth. ¹⁴But I have a few things against thee, because thou hast there them that hold the doctrine of Balaam, who taught Balak to cast a stumbling-block before the children of Israel, to eat things sacrificed unto idols, and to commit fornication. ¹⁵So hast thou also them that hold the doctrine of the Nicolaitans, which thing I hate. ¹⁶Repent, or else I will come unto thee quickly, and will fight against them with the sword of my mouth. ¹⁷He that hath an ear, let him hear what the Spirit saith unto the churches. To him that overcometh will I give to eat of the hidden manna, and will give him a white stone, and in the stone a new name written, which no man knoweth saving he that receiveth it.'"

¹⁸'And unto the angel of the church in Thyatira write, "These things saith the Son of God, who hath his eyes like unto a flame of fire, and his feet are like fine brass: ¹⁹'I know thy works, and charity, and service, and faith, and thy patience, and thy works, and the last to be more than

the first. ²⁰Notwithstanding I have a few things against thee, because thou sufferest that woman Jezebel, which calleth herself a prophetess, to teach and to seduce my servants to commit fornication, and to eat things sacrificed unto idols. ²¹And I gave her space to repent of her fornication, and she repented not. ²²Behold, I will cast her into a bed, and them that commit adultery with her into great tribulation, except they repent of their deeds. ²³And I will kill her children with death, and all the churches shall know that I am he which searcheth the reins and hearts: and I will give unto every one of you according to your works. ²⁴But unto you I say, and unto the rest in Thyatira, as many as have not this doctrine, and which have not known the depths of Satan, as they speak, I will put upon you no other burden: ²⁵but that which ye have already hold fast till I come. ²⁶And he that overcometh, and keepeth my works unto the end, to him will I give power over the nations ²⁷(and he shall rule them with a rod of iron: as the vessels of a potter shall they be broken to shivers): even as I received of my Father. ²⁸And I will give him the morning star. ²⁹He that hath an ear, let him hear what the Spirit saith unto the churches.'"

3 'And unto the angel of the church in Sardis write, "These things saith he that hath the seven Spirits of God, and the seven stars: 'I know thy works, that thou hast a name that thou livest, and art dead. ²Be watchful, and strengthen the things which remain, that are ready to die: for I have not found thy works perfect before God. ³Remember therefore how thou hast received and heard, and hold fast, and repent. If therefore thou shalt not watch, I will come on thee as a thief, and thou shalt not know what hour I will come upon thee. ⁴Thou hast a few names even in Sardis which have not defiled their garments, and they shall walk with me in white: for they are worthy. ⁵He that overcometh, the same shall be clothed in white raiment, and I will not blot out his name out of the book of life, but I will confess his name before my Father, and before his angels. ⁶He that hath an ear, let him hear what the Spirit saith unto the churches.'"

⁷'And to the angel of the church in Philadelphia write, "These things saith he that is holy, he that is true, he that hath the key of David, he that openeth, and no man shutteth, and shutteth, and no man openeth: ⁸'I know thy works: behold, I have set before thee an open door, and no man can shut it: for thou hast a little strength, and hast kept my word, and hast not denied my name. ⁹Behold, I will make them of the synagogue of Satan, which say they are Jews, and are not, but do lie: behold, I will make them to come and worship before thy feet, and to know that I have loved thee. ¹⁰Because thou hast kept the word of my patience, I also will keep thee from the hour of temptation, which shall come upon all the world, to try them that dwell upon the earth. ¹¹Behold, I come quickly, hold that fast which thou hast, that no man take thy crown. ¹²Him that overcometh will I make a pillar in the temple of my God, and he shall go no more out: and I will write upon him the name of my God, and the name of the city of my God, which is new Jerusalem, which cometh down out of heaven from my God: and I will

write upon him my new name. [13]He that hath an ear, let him hear what the Spirit saith unto the churches.'"

[14]'And unto the angel of the church of the Laodiceans write, "These things saith the Amen, the faithful and true witness, the beginning of the creation of God: [15]'I know thy works, that thou art neither cold nor hot: I would thou wert cold or hot. [16]So then because thou art luke-warm, and neither cold nor hot, I will spew thee out of my mouth: [17]because thou sayest, "I am rich, and increased with goods, and have need of nothing": and knowest not that thou art wretched, and miser-able, and poor, and blind, and naked. [18]I counsel thee to buy of me gold tried in the fire, that thou mayest be rich, and white raiment, that thou mayest be clothed, and that the shame of thy nakedness do not appear, and anoint thy eyes with eyesalve, that thou mayest see. [19]As many as I love, I rebuke and chasten: be zealous therefore, and repent. [20]Behold, I stand at the door, and knock: if any man hear my voice, and open the door, I will come in to him, and will sup with him, and he with me. [21]To him that overcometh will I grant to sit with me in my throne, even as I also overcame, and am set down with my Father in his throne. [22]He that hath an ear, let him hear what the Spirit saith unto the churches.'"'

4 After this I looked, and behold, a door was opened in heaven: and the first voice which I heard was as it were of a trumpet talking with me, which said, 'Come up hither, and I will show thee things which must be hereafter.' [2]And immediately I was in the spirit: and behold, a throne was set in heaven, and one sat on the throne. [3]And he that sat was to look upon like a jasper and a sardine stone: and there was a rainbow round about the throne, in sight like unto an emerald. [4]And round about the throne were four and twenty seats, and upon the seats I saw four and twenty elders sitting, clothed in white raiment, and they had on their heads crowns of gold. [5]And out of the throne pro-ceeded lightnings and thunderings and voices: and there were seven lamps of fire burning before the throne, which are the seven Spirits of God. [6]And before the throne there was a sea of glass like unto crystal: and in the midst of the throne, and round about the throne, were four beasts full of eyes before and behind. [7]And the first beast was like a lion, and the second beast like a calf, and the third beast had a face as a man, and the fourth beast was like a flying eagle. [8]And the four beasts had each of them six wings about him, and they were full of eyes within: and they rest not day and night, saying, 'Holy, holy, holy, Lord God Almighty, which was, and is, and is to come'. [9]And when those beasts give glory and honour and thanks to him that sat on the throne, who liveth for ever and ever, [10]the four and twenty elders fall down before him that sat on the throne, and worship him that liveth for ever and ever, and cast their crowns before the throne, saying, [11]'Thou art wor-thy, O Lord, to receive glory and honour and power: for thou hast cre-ated all things, and for thy pleasure they are and were created'.

5 And I saw in the right hand of him that sat on the throne a book written within and on the backside, sealed with seven seals. [2]And I saw a strong angel proclaiming with a loud voice, 'Who is worthy to

open the book, and to loose the seals thereof?' ³And no man in heaven, nor in earth, neither under the earth, was able to open the book, neither to look thereon. ⁴And I wept much, because no man was found worthy to open and to read the book, neither to look thereon.

⁵And one of the elders saith unto me, 'Weep not: behold, the Lion of the tribe of Juda, the root of David, hath prevailed to open the book, and to loose the seven seals thereof'. ⁶And I beheld, and lo, in the midst of the throne and of the four beasts, and in the midst of the elders, stood a Lamb as it had been slain, having seven horns and seven eyes, which are the seven Spirits of God sent forth into all the earth. ⁷And he came and took the book out of the right hand of him that sat upon the throne. ⁸And when he had taken the book, the four beasts and four and twenty elders fell down before the Lamb, having every one of them harps, and golden vials full of odours, which are the prayers of saints. ⁹And they sung a new song, saying, 'Thou art worthy to take the book, and to open the seals thereof: for thou wast slain, and hast redeemed us to God by thy blood out of every kindred, and tongue, and people, and nation: ¹⁰and hast made us unto our God kings and priests, and we shall reign on the earth'.

¹¹And I beheld, and I heard the voice of many angels round about the throne and the beasts and the elders, and the number of them was ten thousand times ten thousand, and thousands of thousands, ¹²saying with a loud voice, 'Worthy is the Lamb that was slain to receive power, and riches, and wisdom, and strength, and honour, and glory, and blessing'. ¹³And every creature which is in heaven, and on the earth, and under the earth, and such as are in the sea, and all that are in them, heard I saying, 'Blessing, honour, glory, and power, be unto him that sitteth upon the throne, and unto the Lamb for ever and ever'. ¹⁴And the four beasts said, 'Amen'. And the four and twenty elders fell down and worshipped him that liveth for ever and ever.

6 And I saw when the Lamb opened one of the seals, and I heard, as it were the noise of thunder, one of the four beasts saying, 'Come and see'. ²And I saw, and behold, a white horse: and he that sat on him had a bow, and a crown was given unto him, and he went forth conquering, and to conquer.

³And when he had opened the second seal, I heard the second beast say, 'Come and see'. ⁴And there went out another horse that was red: and power was given to him that sat thereon to take peace from the earth, and that they should kill one another: and there was given unto him a great sword.

⁵And when he had opened the third seal, I heard the third beast say, 'Come and see'. And I beheld, and lo, a black horse: and he that sat on him had a pair of balances in his hand. ⁶And I heard a voice in the midst of the four beasts say, 'A measure of wheat for a penny, and three measures of barley for a penny, and see thou hurt not the oil and the wine'.

⁷And when he had opened the fourth seal, I heard the voice of the fourth beast say, 'Come and see'. ⁸And I looked, and behold, a pale horse, and his name that sat on him was Death, and hell followed with

him: and power was given unto them over the fourth part of the earth, to kill with sword, and with hunger, and with death, and with the beasts of the earth.

[9]And when he had opened the fifth seal, I saw under the altar the souls of them that were slain for the word of God, and for the testimony which they held. [10]And they cried with a loud voice, saying, 'How long, O Lord, holy and true, dost thou not judge and avenge our blood on them that dwell on the earth?' [11]And white robes were given unto every one of them, and it was said unto them, that they should rest yet for a little season, until their fellow-servants also and their brethren, that should be killed as they were, should be fulfilled.

[12]And I beheld when he had opened the sixth seal, and lo, there was a great earthquake, and the sun became black as sackcloth of hair, and the moon became as blood. [13]And the stars of heaven fell unto the earth, even as a fig tree casteth her untimely figs when she is shaken of a mighty wind. [14]And the heaven departed as a scroll when it is rolled together, and every mountain and island were moved out of their places. [15]And the kings of the earth, and the great men, and the rich men, and the chief captains, and the mighty men, and every bondman, and every freeman, hid themselves in the dens and in the rocks of the mountains, [16]and said to the mountains and rocks, 'Fall on us, and hide us from the face of him that sitteth on the throne, and from the wrath of the Lamb: [17]for the great day of his wrath is come, and who shall be able to stand?'

7 And after these things I saw four angels standing on the four corners of the earth, holding the four winds of the earth, that the wind should not blow on the earth, nor on the sea, nor on any tree. [2]And I saw another angel ascending from the east, having the seal of the living God: and he cried with a loud voice to the four angels to whom it was given to hurt the earth and the sea, [3]saying, 'Hurt not the earth, neither the sea, nor the trees, till we have sealed the servants of our God in their foreheads'. [4]And I heard the number of them which were sealed: and there were sealed a hundred and forty and four thousand of all the tribes of the children of Israel. [5]Of the tribe of Juda were sealed twelve thousand. Of the tribe of Reuben were sealed twelve thousand. Of the tribe of Gad were sealed twelve thousand. [6]Of the tribe of Aser were sealed twelve thousand. Of the tribe of Nephthalim were sealed twelve thousand. Of the tribe of Manasses were sealed twelve thousand. [7]Of the tribe of Simeon were sealed twelve thousand. Of the tribe of Levi were sealed twelve thousand. Of the tribe of Isachar were sealed twelve thousand. [8]Of the tribe of Zabulon were sealed twelve thousand. Of the tribe of Joseph were sealed twelve thousand. Of the tribe of Benjamin were sealed twelve thousand.

[9]After this I beheld, and lo, a great multitude, which no man could number, of all nations, and kindreds, and people, and tongues, stood before the throne, and before the Lamb, clothed with white robes, and palms in their hands: [10]and cried with a loud voice, saying, 'Salvation to our God which sitteth upon the throne, and unto the Lamb'. [11]And all

the angels stood round about the throne, and about the elders and the four beasts, and fell before the throne on their faces, and worshipped God, [12]saying, 'Amen: blessing, and glory, and wisdom, and thanksgiving, and honour, and power, and might be unto our God for ever and ever. Amen.'

[13]And one of the elders answered, saying unto me, 'What are these which are arrayed in white robes? and whence came they?' [14]And I said unto him, 'Sir, thou knowest'. And he said to me, 'These are they which came out of great tribulation, and have washed their robes, and made them white in the blood of the Lamb. [15]Therefore are they before the throne of God, and serve him day and night in his temple: and he that sitteth on the throne shall dwell among them. [16]They shall hunger no more, neither thirst any more, neither shall the sun light on them, nor any heat. [17]For the Lamb which is in the midst of the throne shall feed them, and shall lead them unto living fountains of waters: and God shall wipe away all tears from their eyes.'

8 And when he had opened the seventh seal, there was silence in heaven about the space of half an hour.

[2]And I saw the seven angels which stood before God, and to them were given seven trumpets. [3]And another angel came and stood at the altar, having a golden censer, and there was given unto him much incense, that he should offer it with the prayers of all saints upon the golden altar which was before the throne. [4]And the smoke of the incense, which came with the prayers of the saints, ascended up before God out of the angel's hand. [5]And the angel took the censer, and filled it with fire of the altar, and cast it into the earth: and there were voices, and thunderings, and lightnings, and an earthquake: [6]and the seven angels which had the seven trumpets prepared themselves to sound.

[7]The first angel sounded, and there followed hail and fire mingled with blood, and they were cast upon the earth, and the third part of trees was burnt up, and all green grass was burnt up.

[8]And the second angel sounded, and as it were a great mountain burning with fire was cast into the sea, and the third part of the sea became blood. [9]And the third part of the creatures which were in the sea, and had life, died, and the third part of the ships were destroyed.

[10]And the third angel sounded, and there fell a great star from heaven, burning as it were a lamp, and it fell upon the third part of the rivers, and upon the fountains of waters: [11]and the name of the star is called Wormwood: and the third part of the waters became wormwood, and many men died of the waters, because they were made bitter.

[12]And the fourth angel sounded, and the third part of the sun was smitten, and the third part of the moon, and the third part of the stars, so as the third part of them was darkened: and the day shone not for a third part of it, and the night likewise. [13]And I beheld, and heard an angel flying through the midst of heaven, saying with a loud voice, 'Woe, woe, woe, to the inhabiters of the earth, by reason of the other voices of the trumpet of the three angels, which are yet to sound'.

9 And the fifth angel sounded, and I saw a star fall from heaven unto the earth: and to him was given the key of the bottomless pit. ²And he opened the bottomless pit, and there arose a smoke out of the pit, as the smoke of a great furnace, and the sun and the air were darkened by reason of the smoke of the pit. ³And there came out of the smoke locusts upon the earth, and unto them was given power, as the scorpions of the earth have power. ⁴And it was commanded them that they should not hurt the grass of the earth, neither any green thing, neither any tree: but only those men which have not the seal of God in their foreheads. ⁵And to them it was given that they should not kill them, but that they should be tormented five months, and their torment was as the torment of a scorpion, when he striketh a man. ⁶And in those days shall men seek death, and shall not find it, and shall desire to die, and death shall flee from them. ⁷And the shapes of the locusts were like unto horses prepared unto battle, and on their heads were as it were crowns like gold, and their faces were as the faces of men. ⁸And they had hair as the hair of women, and their teeth were as the teeth of lions. ⁹And they had breastplates, as it were breastplates of iron, and the sound of their wings was as the sound of chariots of many horses running to battle. ¹⁰And they had tails like unto scorpions, and there were stings in their tails: and their power was to hurt men five months. ¹¹And they had a king over them, which is the angel of the bottomless pit, whose name in the Hebrew tongue is Abaddon, but in the Greek tongue hath his name Apollyon. ¹²One woe is past, and behold, there come two woes more hereafter.

¹³And the sixth angel sounded, and I heard a voice from the four horns of the golden altar which is before God, ¹⁴saying to the sixth angel which had the trumpet, 'Loose the four angels which are bound in the great river Euphrates'. ¹⁵And the four angels were loosed, which were prepared for an hour, and a day, and a month, and a year, for to slay the third part of men. ¹⁶And the number of the army of the horsemen were two hundred thousand thousand: and I heard the number of them. ¹⁷And thus I saw the horses in the vision, and them that sat on them, having breastplates of fire, and of jacinth, and brimstone: and the heads of the horses were as the heads of lions, and out of their mouths issued fire and smoke and brimstone. ¹⁸By these three was the third part of men killed, by the fire, and by the smoke, and by the brimstone, which issued out of their mouths. ¹⁹For their power is in their mouth, and in their tails: for their tails were like unto serpents, and had heads, and with them they do hurt. ²⁰And the rest of the men which were not killed by these plagues yet repented not of the works of their hands, that they should not worship devils, and idols of gold, and silver, and brass, and stone, and of wood, which neither can see, nor hear, nor walk: ²¹neither repented they of their murders, nor of their sorceries, nor of their fornication, nor of their thefts.

10 And I saw another mighty angel come down from heaven, clothed with a cloud, and a rainbow was upon his head, and his face was as it were the sun, and his feet as pillars of fire. ²And he had in

his hand a little book open: and he set his right foot upon the sea, and his left foot on the earth, ³and cried with a loud voice, as when a lion roareth: and when he had cried, seven thunders uttered their voices. ⁴And when the seven thunders had uttered their voices, I was about to write: and I heard a voice from heaven saying unto me, 'Seal up those things which the seven thunders uttered, and write them not'. ⁵And the angel which I saw stand upon the sea and upon the earth lifted up his hand to heaven, ⁶and swore by him that liveth for ever and ever, who created heaven, and the things that therein are, and the earth, and the things that therein are, and the sea, and the things which are therein, that there should be time no longer. ⁷But in the days of the voice of the seventh angel, when he shall begin to sound, the mystery of God should be finished, as he hath declared to his servants the prophets.

⁸And the voice which I heard from heaven spoke unto me again, and said, 'Go and take the little book which is open in the hand of the angel which standeth upon the sea and upon the earth'. ⁹And I went unto the angel, and said unto him, 'Give me the little book'. And he said unto me, 'Take it, and eat it up, and it shall make thy belly bitter, but it shall be in thy mouth sweet as honey'. ¹⁰And I took the little book out of the angel's hand, and ate it up, and it was in my mouth sweet as honey: and as soon as I had eaten it, my belly was bitter. ¹¹And he said unto me, 'Thou must prophesy again before many peoples, and nations, and tongues, and kings'.

11 And there was given me a reed like unto a rod: and the angel stood, saying, 'Rise, and measure the temple of God, and the altar, and them that worship therein. ²But the court which is without the temple leave out, and measure it not: for it is given unto the Gentiles, and the holy city shall they tread under foot forty and two months. ³And I will give power unto my two witnesses, and they shall prophesy a thousand two hundred and threescore days, clothed in sackcloth.'

⁴These are the two olive trees, and the two candlesticks standing before the God of the earth. ⁵And if any man will hurt them, fire proceedeth out of their mouth, and devoureth their enemies: and if any man will hurt them, he must in this manner be killed. ⁶These have power to shut heaven, that it rain not in the days of their prophecy: and have power over waters to turn them to blood, and to smite the earth with all plagues, as often as they will. ⁷And when they shall have finished their testimony, the beast that ascendeth out of the bottomless pit shall make war against them, and shall overcome them, and kill them. ⁸And their dead bodies shall lie in the street of the great city, which spiritually is called Sodom and Egypt, where also our Lord was crucified. ⁹And they of the people and kindreds and tongues and nations shall see their dead bodies three days and a half, and shall not suffer their dead bodies to be put in graves. ¹⁰And they that dwell upon the earth shall rejoice over them, and make merry, and shall send gifts one to another, because these two prophets tormented them that dwelt

on the earth. ¹¹And after three days and a half the Spirit of life from God entered into them: and they stood upon their feet, and great fear fell upon them which saw them. ¹²And they heard a great voice from heaven saying unto them, 'Come up hither'. And they ascended up to heaven in a cloud, and their enemies beheld them. ¹³And the same hour was there a great earthquake, and the tenth part of the city fell, and in the earthquake were slain of men seven thousand: and the remnant were affrighted, and gave glory to the God of heaven. ¹⁴The second woe is past, and behold, the third woe cometh quickly.

¹⁵And the seventh angel sounded, and there were great voices in heaven, saying, 'The kingdoms of this world are become the kingdoms of our Lord, and of his Christ, and he shall reign for ever and ever'. ¹⁶And the four and twenty elders, which sat before God on their seats, fell upon their faces, and worshipped God, ¹⁷saying, 'We give thee thanks, O Lord God Almighty, which art, and wast, and art to come; because thou hast taken to thee thy great power, and hast reigned. ¹⁸And the nations were angry, and thy wrath is come, and the time of the dead, that they should be judged, and that thou shouldst give reward unto thy servants the prophets, and to the saints, and them that fear thy name, small and great, and shouldst destroy them which destroy the earth.' ¹⁹And the temple of God was opened in heaven, and there was seen in his temple the ark of his testament, and there were lightnings, and voices, and thunderings, and an earthquake, and great hail.

12 And there appeared a great wonder in heaven, a woman clothed with the sun, and the moon under her feet, and upon her head a crown of twelve stars: ²and she being with child cried, travailing in birth, and pained to be delivered. ³And there appeared another wonder in heaven, and behold, a great red dragon, having seven heads and ten horns, and seven crowns upon his heads. ⁴And his tail drew the third part of the stars of heaven, and did cast them to the earth: and the dragon stood before the woman which was ready to be delivered, for to devour her child as soon as it was born. ⁵And she brought forth a man-child, who was to rule all nations with a rod of iron: and her child was caught up unto God, and to his throne. ⁶And the woman fled into the wilderness, where she hath a place prepared of God, that they should feed her there a thousand two hundred and threescore days.

⁷And there was war in heaven: Michael and his angels fought against the dragon, and the dragon fought and his angels, ⁸and prevailed not, neither was their place found any more in heaven. ⁹And the great dragon was cast out, that old serpent, called the Devil, and Satan, which deceiveth the whole world: he was cast out into the earth, and his angels were cast out with him. ¹⁰And I heard a loud voice saying in heaven, 'Now is come salvation, and strength, and the kingdom of our God, and the power of his Christ: for the accuser of our brethren is cast down, which accused them before our God day and night. ¹¹And they overcame him by the blood of the Lamb, and by the word of their testimony, and they loved not their lives unto the death. ¹²Therefore rejoice,

ye heavens, and ye that dwell in them. Woe to the inhabiters of the earth and of the sea: for the devil is come down unto you, having great wrath, because he knoweth that he hath but a short time.'

¹³And when the dragon saw that he was cast unto the earth, he persecuted the woman which brought forth the man-child. ¹⁴And to the woman were given two wings of a great eagle, that she might fly into the wilderness, into her place, where she is nourished for a time, and times, and half a time, from the face of the serpent. ¹⁵And the serpent cast out of his mouth water as a flood after the woman, that he might cause her to be carried away of the flood. ¹⁶And the earth helped the woman, and the earth opened her mouth, and swallowed up the flood which the dragon cast out of his mouth. ¹⁷And the dragon was wroth with the woman, and went to make war with the remnant of her seed, which keep the commandments of God, and have the testimony of Jesus Christ.

13 And I stood upon the sand of the sea, and saw a beast rise up out of the sea, having seven heads and ten horns, and upon his horns ten crowns, and upon his heads the name of blasphemy. ²And the beast which I saw was like unto a leopard, and his feet were as the feet of a bear, and his mouth as the mouth of a lion: and the dragon gave him his power, and his seat, and great authority. ³And I saw one of his heads as it were wounded to death, and his deadly wound was healed: and all the world wondered after the beast. ⁴And they worshipped the dragon which gave power unto the beast, and they worshipped the beast, saying, 'Who is like unto the beast? Who is able to make war with him?'

⁵And there was given unto him a mouth speaking great things and blasphemies, and power was given unto him to continue forty and two months. ⁶And he opened his mouth in blasphemy against God, to blaspheme his name, and his tabernacle, and them that dwell in heaven. ⁷And it was given unto him to make war with the saints, and to overcome them: and power was given him over all kindreds, and tongues, and nations. ⁸And all that dwell upon the earth shall worship him, whose names are not written in the book of life of the Lamb slain from the foundation of the world.

⁹If any man have an ear, let him hear. ¹⁰He that leadeth into captivity shall go into captivity: he that killeth with the sword must be killed with the sword. Here is the patience and the faith of the saints.

¹¹And I beheld another beast coming up out of the earth, and he had two horns like a lamb, and he spoke as a dragon. ¹²And he exerciseth all the power of the first beast before him, and causeth the earth and them which dwell therein to worship the first beast, whose deadly wound was healed. ¹³And he doeth great wonders, so that he maketh fire come down from heaven on the earth in the sight of men, ¹⁴and deceiveth them that dwell on the earth by the means of those miracles which he had power to do in the sight of the beast, saying to them that dwell on the earth, that they should make an image to the beast, which had the wound by a sword, and did live. ¹⁵And he had power to give life

unto the image of the beast, that the image of the beast should both speak, and cause that as many as would not worship the image of the beast should be killed. [16]And he causeth all, both small and great, rich and poor, free and bond, to receive a mark in their right hand, or in their foreheads: [17]and that no man might buy or sell, save he that had the mark, or the name of the beast, or the number of his name. [18]Here is wisdom. Let him that hath understanding count the number of the beast: for it is the number of a man, and his number is six hundred threescore and six.

14 And I looked, and lo, a Lamb stood on the mount Sion, and with him a hundred forty and four thousand, having his Father's name written in their foreheads. [2]And I heard a voice from heaven, as the voice of many waters, and as the voice of a great thunder: and I heard the voice of harpers harping with their harps. [3]And they sung as it were a new song before the throne, and before the four beasts, and the elders, and no man could learn that song but the hundred and forty and four thousand, which were redeemed from the earth. [4]These are they which were not defiled with women: for they are virgins. These are they which follow the Lamb whithersoever he goeth. These were redeemed from among men, being the first-fruits unto God and to the Lamb. [5]And in their mouth was found no guile: for they are without fault before the throne of God.

[6]And I saw another angel fly in the midst of heaven, having the ever-lasting gospel, to preach unto them that dwell on the earth, and to every nation, and kindred, and tongue, and people, [7]saying with a loud voice, 'Fear God, and give glory to him, for the hour of his judgement is come: and worship him that made heaven, and earth, and the sea, and the fountains of waters'.

[8]And there followed another angel, saying, 'Babylon is fallen, is fallen, that great city, because she made all nations drink of the wine of the wrath of her fornication'.

[9]And the third angel followed them, saying with a loud voice, 'If any man worship the beast and his image, and receive his mark in his fore-head, or in his hand, [10]the same shall drink of the wine of the wrath of God, which is poured out without mixture into the cup of his indigna-tion, and he shall be tormented with fire and brimstone in the pres-ence of the holy angels, and in the presence of the Lamb: [11]and the smoke of their torment ascendeth up for ever and ever. And they have no rest day nor night, who worship the beast and his image, and whoso-ever receiveth the mark of his name.' [12]Here is the patience of the saints: here are they that keep the commandments of God, and the faith of Jesus.

[13]And I heard a voice from heaven saying unto me, 'Write, "Blessed are the dead which die in the Lord from henceforth": "Yea," saith the Spirit, "that they may rest from their labours, and their works do fol-low them"'.

[14]And I looked, and behold, a white cloud, and upon the cloud one sat like unto the Son of man, having on his head a golden crown, and in his

hand a sharp sickle. ¹⁵And another angel came out of the temple, crying with a loud voice to him that sat on the cloud, 'Thrust in thy sickle, and reap, for the time is come for thee to reap, for the harvest of the earth is ripe'. ¹⁶And he that sat on the cloud thrust in his sickle on the earth, and the earth was reaped.

¹⁷And another angel came out of the temple which is in heaven, he also having a sharp sickle. ¹⁸And another angel came out from the altar, which had power over fire, and cried with a loud cry to him that had the sharp sickle, saying, 'Thrust in thy sharp sickle, and gather the clusters of the vine of the earth, for her grapes are fully ripe'. ¹⁹And the angel thrust in his sickle into the earth, and gathered the vine of the earth, and cast it into the great wine-press of the wrath of God. ²⁰And the wine-press was trodden without the city, and blood came out of the wine-press, even unto the horse bridles, by the space of a thousand and six hundred furlongs.

15 And I saw another sign in heaven, great and marvellous, seven angels having the seven last plagues, for in them is filled up the wrath of God. ²And I saw as it were a sea of glass mingled with fire, and them that had gotten the victory over the beast, and over his image, and over his mark, and over the number of his name, stand on the sea of glass, having the harps of God. ³And they sing the song of Moses the servant of God, and the song of the Lamb, saying, 'Great and marvellous are thy works, Lord God Almighty, just and true are thy ways, thou King of saints. ⁴Who shall not fear thee, O Lord, and glorify thy name? for thou only art holy: for all nations shall come and worship before thee, for thy judgements are made manifest.'

⁵And after that I looked, and behold, the temple of the tabernacle of the testimony in heaven was opened: ⁶and the seven angels came out of the temple, having the seven plagues, clothed in pure and white linen, and having their breasts girded with golden girdles. ⁷And one of the four beasts gave unto the seven angels seven golden vials full of the wrath of God, who liveth for ever and ever. ⁸And the temple was filled with smoke from the glory of God, and from his power, and no man was able to enter into the temple, till the seven plagues of the seven angels were fulfilled.

16 And I heard a great voice out of the temple saying to the seven angels, 'Go your ways, and pour out the vials of the wrath of God upon the earth'. ²And the first went, and poured out his vial upon the earth, and there fell a noisome and grievous sore upon the men which had the mark of the beast, and upon them which worshipped his image.

³And the second angel poured out his vial upon the sea, and it became as the blood of a dead man: and every living soul died in the sea.

⁴And the third angel poured out his vial upon the rivers and fountains of waters, and they became blood. ⁵And I heard the angel of the waters say, 'Thou art righteous, O Lord, which art, and wast, and shalt be, because thou hast judged thus. ⁶For they have shed the blood of saints and prophets, and thou hast given them blood to drink: for they

are worthy.' ⁷And I heard another out of the altar say, 'Even so, Lord God Almighty, true and righteous are thy judgements'.

⁸And the fourth angel poured out his vial upon the sun, and power was given unto him to scorch men with fire. ⁹And men were scorched with great heat, and blasphemed the name of God, which hath power over these plagues: and they repented not, to give him glory.

¹⁰And the fifth angel poured out his vial upon the seat of the beast, and his kingdom was full of darkness, and they gnawed their tongues for pain, ¹¹and blasphemed the God of heaven because of their pains and their sores, and repented not of their deeds.

¹²And the sixth angel poured out his vial upon the great river Euphrates, and the water thereof was dried up, that the way of the kings of the east might be prepared. ¹³And I saw three unclean spirits like frogs come out of the mouth of the dragon, and out of the mouth of the beast, and out of the mouth of the false prophet. ¹⁴For they are the spirits of devils, working miracles, which go forth unto the kings of the earth and of the whole world, to gather them to the battle of that great day of God Almighty. ¹⁵'Behold, I come as a thief. Blessed is he that watcheth, and keepeth his garments, lest he walk naked, and they see his shame.' ¹⁶And he gathered them together into a place called in the Hebrew tongue Armageddon.

¹⁷And the seventh angel poured out his vial into the air, and there came a great voice out of the temple of heaven, from the throne, saying, 'It is done'. ¹⁸And there were voices, and thunders, and lightnings: and there was a great earthquake, such as was not since men were upon the earth, so mighty an earthquake, and so great. ¹⁹And the great city was divided into three parts, and the cities of the nations fell: and great Babylon came in remembrance before God, to give unto her the cup of the wine of the fierceness of his wrath. ²⁰And every island fled away, and the mountains were not found. ²¹And there fell upon men a great hail out of heaven, every stone about the weight of a talent, and men blasphemed God because of the plague of the hail: for the plague thereof was exceeding great.

17 And there came one of the seven angels which had the seven vials, and talked with me, saying unto me, 'Come hither, I will show unto thee the judgement of the great whore that sitteth upon many waters: ²with whom the kings of the earth have committed fornication, and the inhabiters of the earth have been made drunk with the wine of her fornication'. ³So he carried me away in the spirit into the wilderness: and I saw a woman sit upon a scarlet-coloured beast, full of names of blasphemy, having seven heads and ten horns. ⁴And the woman was arrayed in purple and scarlet colour, and decked with gold and precious stone and pearls, having a golden cup in her hand full of abominations and filthiness of her fornication. ⁵And upon her forehead was a name written, 'MYSTERY, BABYLON THE GREAT, THE MOTHER OF HARLOTS AND ABOMINATIONS OF THE EARTH'. ⁶And I saw the woman drunken with the blood of the saints, and with the blood of the martyrs of Jesus: and when I saw her, I wondered with great admiration.

⁷And the angel said unto me, 'Wherefore didst thou marvel? I will tell thee the mystery of the woman, and of the beast that carrieth her, which hath the seven heads and ten horns. ⁸The beast that thou sawest was, and is not, and shall ascend out of the bottomless pit, and go into perdition: and they that dwell on the earth shall wonder (whose names were not written in the book of life from the foundation of the world), when they behold the beast that was, and is not, and yet is. ⁹And here is the mind which hath wisdom. The seven heads are seven mountains, on which the woman sitteth. ¹⁰And there are seven kings: five are fallen, and one is, and the other is not yet come: and when he cometh, he must continue a short space. ¹¹And the beast that was, and is not, even he is the eighth, and is of the seven, and goeth into perdition. ¹²And the ten horns which thou sawest are ten kings, which have received no kingdom as yet: but receive power as kings one hour with the beast. ¹³These have one mind, and shall give their power and strength unto the beast. ¹⁴These shall make war with the Lamb, and the Lamb shall overcome them: for he is Lord of lords, and King of kings, and they that are with him are called, and chosen, and faithful.'

¹⁵And he saith unto me, 'The waters which thou sawest, where the whore sitteth, are peoples, and multitudes, and nations, and tongues. ¹⁶And the ten horns which thou sawest upon the beast, these shall hate the whore, and shall make her desolate and naked, and shall eat her flesh, and burn her with fire. ¹⁷For God hath put in their hearts to fulfil his will, and to agree, and give their kingdom unto the beast, until the words of God shall be fulfilled. ¹⁸And the woman which thou sawest is that great city which reigneth over the kings of the earth.'

18 And after these things I saw another angel come down from heaven, having great power, and the earth was lightened with his glory. ²And he cried mightily with a strong voice, saying, 'Babylon the great is fallen, is fallen, and is become the habitation of devils, and the hold of every foul spirit, and a cage of every unclean and hateful bird. ³For all nations have drunk of the wine of the wrath of her fornication, and the kings of the earth have committed fornication with her, and the merchants of the earth are waxed rich through the abundance of her delicacies.'

⁴And I heard another voice from heaven, saying, 'Come out of her, my people, that ye be not partakers of her sins, and that ye receive not of her plagues. ⁵For her sins have reached unto heaven, and God hath remembered her iniquities. ⁶Reward her even as she rewarded you, and double unto her double according to her works: in the cup which she hath filled, fill to her double. ⁷How much she hath glorified herself, and lived deliciously, so much torment and sorrow give her: for she saith in her heart, "I sit a queen, and am no widow, and shall see no sorrow". ⁸Therefore shall her plagues come in one day, death, and mourning, and famine, and she shall be utterly burnt with fire, for strong is the Lord God who judgeth her.

⁹'And the kings of the earth, who have committed fornication and lived deliciously with her, shall bewail her, and lament for her, when

they shall see the smoke of her burning, [10]standing afar off for the fear of her torment, saying, "Alas, alas, that great city Babylon, that mighty city: for in one hour is thy judgement come". [11]And the merchants of the earth shall weep and mourn over her, for no man buyeth their merchandise any more: [12]the merchandise of gold, and silver, and precious stones, and of pearls, and fine linen, and purple, and silk, and scarlet, and all thyine wood, and all manner vessels of ivory, and all manner vessels of most precious wood, and of brass, and iron, and marble, [13]and cinnamon, and odours, and ointments, and frankincense, and wine, and oil, and fine flour, and wheat, and beasts, and sheep, and horses, and chariots, and slaves, and souls of men. [14]And the fruits that thy soul lusted after are departed from thee, and all things which were dainty and goodly are departed from thee, and thou shalt find them no more at all. [15]The merchants of these things, which were made rich by her, shall stand afar off for the fear of her torment, weeping and wailing, [16]and saying, "Alas, alas, that great city, that was clothed in fine linen, and purple, and scarlet, and decked with gold, and precious stones, and pearls: [17]for in one hour so great riches is come to nought". And every shipmaster, and all the company in ships, and sailors, and as many as trade by sea, stood afar off, [18]and cried when they saw the smoke of her burning, saying, "What city is like unto this great city!" [19]And they cast dust on their heads, and cried, weeping and wailing, saying, "Alas, alas, that great city, wherein were made rich all that had ships in the sea by reason of her costliness, for in one hour is she made desolate". [20]Rejoice over her, thou heaven, and ye holy apostles and prophets, for God hath avenged you on her.'

[21]And a mighty angel took up a stone like a great millstone, and cast it into the sea, saying, 'Thus with violence shall that great city Babylon be thrown down, and shall be found no more at all. [22]And the voice of harpers, and musicians, and of pipers, and trumpeters, shall be heard no more at all in thee: and no craftsman, of whatsoever craft he be, shall be found any more in thee: and the sound of a millstone shall be heard no more at all in thee: [23]and the light of a candle shall shine no more at all in thee: and the voice of the bridegroom and of the bride shall be heard no more at all in thee: for thy merchants were the great men of the earth: for by thy sorceries were all nations deceived. [24]And in her was found the blood of prophets, and of saints, and of all that were slain upon the earth.'

19 And after these things I heard a great voice of much people in heaven, saying, 'Alleluia: salvation, and glory, and honour, and power unto the Lord our God: [2]for true and righteous are his judgements, for he hath judged the great whore which did corrupt the earth with her fornication, and hath avenged the blood of his servants at her hand'. [3]And again they said, 'Alleluia': and her smoke rose up for ever and ever. [4]And the four and twenty elders and the four beasts fell down and worshipped God that sat on the throne, saying, 'Amen, Alleluia'.

[5]And a voice came out of the throne, saying, 'Praise our God, all ye his servants, and ye that fear him, both small and great'. [6]And I heard

as it were the voice of a great multitude, and as the voice of many waters, and as the voice of mighty thunderings, saying, 'Alleluia: for the Lord God omnipotent reigneth. ⁷Let us be glad and rejoice, and give honour to him: for the marriage of the Lamb is come, and his wife hath made herself ready. ⁸And to her was granted that she should be arrayed in fine linen, clean and white: for the fine linen is the righteousness of saints.'

⁹And he saith unto me, 'Write, "Blessed are they which are called unto the marriage supper of the Lamb"'. And he saith unto me, 'These are the true sayings of God'. ¹⁰And I fell at his feet to worship him. And he said unto me, 'See thou do it not: I am thy fellow-servant, and of thy brethren that have the testimony of Jesus: worship God: for the testimony of Jesus is the spirit of prophecy'.

¹¹And I saw heaven opened, and behold, a white horse, and he that sat upon him was called Faithful and True, and in righteousness he doth judge and make war. ¹²His eyes were as a flame of fire, and on his head were many crowns, and he had a name written, that no man knew, but he himself. ¹³And he was clothed with a vesture dipped in blood, and his name is called The Word of God. ¹⁴And the armies which were in heaven followed him upon white horses, clothed in fine linen, white and clean. ¹⁵And out of his mouth goeth a sharp sword, that with it he should smite the nations: and he shall rule them with a rod of iron: and he treadeth the wine-press of the fierceness and wrath of Almighty God. ¹⁶And he hath on his vesture and on his thigh a name written, 'KING OF KINGS, AND LORD OF LORDS'.

¹⁷And I saw an angel standing in the sun, and he cried with a loud voice, saying to all the fowls that fly in the midst of heaven, 'Come and gather yourselves together unto the supper of the great God: ¹⁸that ye may eat the flesh of kings, and the flesh of captains, and the flesh of mighty men, and the flesh of horses, and of them that sit on them, and the flesh of all men, both free and bond, both small and great'. ¹⁹And I saw the beast, and the kings of the earth, and their armies, gathered together to make war against him that sat on the horse, and against his army. ²⁰And the beast was taken, and with him the false prophet that wrought miracles before him, with which he deceived them that had received the mark of the beast, and them that worshipped his image. These both were cast alive into a lake of fire burning with brimstone. ²¹And the remnant were slain with the sword of him that sat upon the horse, which sword proceeded out of his mouth: and all the fowls were filled with their flesh.

20 And I saw an angel come down from heaven, having the key of the bottomless pit and a great chain in his hand. ²And he laid hold on the dragon, that old serpent, which is the Devil, and Satan, and bound him a thousand years, ³and cast him into the bottomless pit, and shut him up, and set a seal upon him, that he should deceive the nations no more, till the thousand years should be fulfilled: and after that he must be loosed a little season.

⁴And I saw thrones, and they sat upon them, and judgement was

given unto them: and I saw the souls of them that were beheaded for the witness of Jesus, and for the word of God, and which had not worshipped the beast, neither his image, neither had received his mark upon their foreheads, or in their hands, and they lived and reigned with Christ a thousand years. ⁵But the rest of the dead lived not again until the thousand years were finished. This is the first resurrection. ⁶Blessed and holy is he that hath part in the first resurrection: on such the second death hath no power, but they shall be priests of God and of Christ, and shall reign with him a thousand years.

⁷And when the thousand years are expired, Satan shall be loosed out of his prison, ⁸and shall go out to deceive the nations which are in the four quarters of the earth, Gog and Magog, to gather them together to battle: the number of whom is as the sand of the sea. ⁹And they went up on the breadth of the earth, and compassed the camp of the saints about, and the beloved city: and fire came down from God out of heaven, and devoured them. ¹⁰And the devil that deceived them was cast into the lake of fire and brimstone, where the beast and the false prophet are, and shall be tormented day and night for ever and ever.

¹¹And I saw a great white throne, and him that sat on it, from whose face the earth and the heaven fled away, and there was found no place for them. ¹²And I saw the dead, small and great, stand before God: and the books were opened: and another book was opened, which is the book of life: and the dead were judged out of those things which were written in the books, according to their works. ¹³And the sea gave up the dead which were in it: and death and hell delivered up the dead which were in them: and they were judged every man according to their works. ¹⁴And death and hell were cast into the lake of fire. This is the second death. ¹⁵And whosoever was not found written in the book of life was cast into the lake of fire.

21 And I saw a new heaven and a new earth: for the first heaven and the first earth were passed away, and there was no more sea. ²And I John saw the holy city, new Jerusalem, coming down from God out of heaven, prepared as a bride adorned for her husband. ³And I heard a great voice out of heaven saying, 'Behold, the tabernacle of God is with men, and he will dwell with them, and they shall be his people, and God himself shall be with them, and be their God. ⁴And God shall wipe away all tears from their eyes: and there shall be no more death, neither sorrow, nor crying, neither shall there be any more pain: for the former things are passed away.'

⁵And he that sat upon the throne said, 'Behold, I make all things new'. And he said unto me, 'Write: for these words are true and faithful'. ⁶And he said unto me, 'It is done: I am Alpha and Omega, the beginning and the end. I will give unto him that is athirst of the fountain of the water of life freely. ⁷He that overcometh shall inherit all things, and I will be his God, and he shall be my son. ⁸But the fearful, and unbelieving, and the abominable, and murderers, and whoremongers, and sorcerers, and idolaters, and all liars, shall have their part in the lake which burneth with fire and brimstone: which is the second death.'

⁹And there came unto me one of the seven angels which had the seven vials full of the seven last plagues, and talked with me, saying, 'Come hither, I will show thee the bride, the Lamb's wife'. ¹⁰And he carried me away in the spirit to a great and high mountain, and showed me that great city, the holy Jerusalem, descending out of heaven from God, ¹¹having the glory of God: and her light was like unto a stone most precious, even like a jasper stone, clear as crystal; ¹²and had a wall great and high, and had twelve gates, and at the gates twelve angels, and names written thereon, which are the names of the twelve tribes of the children of Israel: ¹³on the east three gates, on the north three gates, on the south three gates, and on the west three gates. ¹⁴And the wall of the city had twelve foundations, and in them the names of the twelve apostles of the Lamb.

¹⁵And he that talked with me had a golden reed to measure the city, and the gates thereof, and the wall thereof. ¹⁶And the city lieth foursquare, and the length is as large as the breadth: and he measured the city with the reed, twelve thousand furlongs: the length and the breadth and the height of it are equal. ¹⁷And he measured the wall thereof, a hundred and forty and four cubits, according to the measure of a man, that is, of the angel. ¹⁸And the building of the wall of it was of jasper, and the city was pure gold, like unto clear glass. ¹⁹And the foundations of the wall of the city were garnished with all manner of precious stones. The first foundation was jasper, the second sapphire, the third a chalcedony, the fourth an emerald, ²⁰the fifth sardonyx, the sixth sardius, the seventh chrysolite, the eighth beryl, the ninth a topaz, the tenth a chrysoprasus, the eleventh a jacinth, the twelfth an amethyst. ²¹And the twelve gates were twelve pearls, every several gate was of one pearl, and the street of the city was pure gold, as it were transparent glass.

²²And I saw no temple therein: for the Lord God Almighty and the Lamb are the temple of it. ²³And the city had no need of the sun, neither of the moon, to shine in it: for the glory of God did lighten it, and the Lamb is the light thereof. ²⁴And the nations of them which are saved shall walk in the light of it: and the kings of the earth do bring their glory and honour into it. ²⁵And the gates of it shall not be shut at all by day: for there shall be no night there. ²⁶And they shall bring the glory and honour of the nations into it. ²⁷And there shall in no wise enter into it anything that defileth, neither whatsoever worketh abomination, or maketh a lie: but they which are written in the Lamb's book of life.

22 And he showed me a pure river of water of life, clear as crystal, proceeding out of the throne of God and of the Lamb. ²In the midst of the street of it, and of either side of the river, was there the tree of life, which bore twelve manner of fruits, and yielded her fruit every month: and the leaves of the tree were for the healing of the nations. ³And there shall be no more curse: but the throne of God and of the Lamb shall be in it; and his servants shall serve him. ⁴And they shall see his face, and his name shall be in their foreheads. ⁵And there

shall be no night there, and they need no candle, neither light of the sun, for the Lord God giveth them light: and they shall reign for ever and ever.

⁶And he said unto me, 'These sayings are faithful and true. And the Lord God of the holy prophets sent his angel to show unto his servants the things which must shortly be done.'

⁷'Behold, I come quickly: blessed is he that keepeth the sayings of the prophecy of this book.'

⁸And I John saw these things, and heard them. And when I had heard and seen, I fell down to worship before the feet of the angel which showed me these things. ⁹Then saith he unto me, 'See thou do it not: for I am thy fellow-servant, and of thy brethren the prophets, and of them which keep the sayings of this book: worship God'. ¹⁰And he saith unto me, 'Seal not the sayings of the prophecy of this book: for the time is at hand. ¹¹He that is unjust, let him be unjust still: and he which is filthy, let him be filthy still: and he that is righteous, let him be righteous still: and he that is holy, let him be holy still.'

¹²'And behold, I come quickly, and my reward is with me, to give every man according as his work shall be. ¹³I am Alpha and Omega, the beginning and the end, the first and the last. ¹⁴Blessed are they that do his commandments, that they may have right to the tree of life, and may enter in through the gates into the city. ¹⁵For without are dogs, and sorcerers, and whoremongers, and murderers, and idolaters, and whosoever loveth and maketh a lie.

¹⁶'I Jesus have sent my angel to testify unto you these things in the churches. I am the root and the offspring of David, and the bright and morning star.'

¹⁷And the Spirit and the bride say, 'Come'. And let him that heareth say, 'Come'. And let him that is athirst come. And whosoever will, let him take the water of life freely. ¹⁸For I testify unto every man that heareth the words of the prophecy of this book, if any man shall add unto these things, God shall add unto him the plagues that are written in this book. ¹⁹And if any man shall take away from the words of the book of this prophecy, God shall take away his part out of the book of life, and out of the holy city, and from the things which are written in this book.

²⁰He which testifieth these things saith, 'Surely I come quickly'. Amen. Even so, come, Lord Jesus.

²¹The grace of our Lord Jesus Christ be with you all. Amen.

THE END

NOTES

Each note begins with some basic information about the name of the book, its contents, the period covered where the book is historical, its author(s) and date of composition. Some of the information is traditional rather than historically certain, and sometimes authorship and date are unknown. A necessarily brief introduction follows, highlighting key aspects of the book. There are also general introductions to the Pentateuch, biblical poetry (p. 1883), the prophetic books (p. 1890), the Apocrypha, the New Testament, the Gospels and the Epistles (p. 1914).

ABBREVIATIONS

BOOKS OF THE BIBLE

Chr.	Chronicles
Col.	Colossians
Cor.	Corinthians
Deut.	Deuteronomy
Exod.	Exodus
Gen.	Genesis
Isa.	Isaiah
Macc.	Maccabees
Matt.	Matthew
Neh.	Nehemiah
Num.	Numbers
Rom.	Romans
Sam.	Samuel
Thess.	Thessalonians
Tim.	Timothy

OTHERS

BCE	Before Common Era
CE	Common Era
KJB	King James Bible
NT	New Testament
OT	Old Testament

THE OLD TESTAMENT

THE PENTATEUCH

The first five books of the OT, Genesis to Deuteronomy, are the heart of the Jewish Bible, and the Hebrew name for them, the Torah, captures one part of their significance: the law. Telling of the establishment of the nation of Israel from Adam, the first man, through to the escape from enslavement in Egypt and the wanderings in the desert before the arrival in the promised land of milk and honey, they also tell of the establishment of the Jewish law, so giving two of the three essential elements of the Jewish heritage. The third, overriding element is the relationship with God, expressed through various covenants. The first is a promise of God's care for all life, symbolised in the rainbow after the flood. The next begins to shape Jewish history: it is God's promise of a special relationship with Abram (Abraham) and his multitudinous descendants, and of a land for them to live in (Gen. 12:1–2). This becomes a covenant with obligations, most notably when the Ten Commandments are given.

There is a law, both simple, as in the commandments, and extensive, as in Leviticus and Deuteronomy, but always demanding. Much of the later narrative of the history of the children of Israel is dominated by alternating periods of failure to keep the law and of repentance.

The traditional ascription of the Pentateuch to Moses originated perhaps as early as the fourth century BCE, and was generally accepted in NT times. However, like the majority of the OT books, it is a composite structure. Oral and written tellings and retellings over centuries were compiled and revised by redactors (editors in modern terms). Original sources and events exist in layers which can sometimes only be guessed at. The final versions often reflect the views of the editors, but these men had a strong sense of the increasing, if not final, sacredness of the texts they worked on, so they were reluctant to lose material, and often did not fully harmonise their sources with each other or with their own views.

The Pentateuch has four major sources, partly identified by the name they use for God, either 'Elohim' (in the KJB, 'God', as in Gen. 1), or the tetragrammaton, the four Hebrew letters YHWH, 'Yahweh' (in the KJB, 'the LORD' or 'GOD', as in Gen. 2); such identification becomes difficult after Exod. 3:14, when God reveals his name to Moses. These sources are known as E, the Elohistic source; J, the Yahwistic source; P, the priestly source; and D, the Deuteronomic source. J is probably the oldest, approximately tenth century BCE, and comes from the southern kingdom (Judah); it is particularly notable for its storytelling qualities. E is a little later, from a priestly source in the northern kingdom (Israel); it is less lively and more didactic in its storytelling. P is the work of priests in Jerusalem, perhaps during the reign of Hezekiah (c. 715–687 BCE), or the time of the Babylonian exile (586–538 BCE), or even later; it is most concerned with ritual, and genealogical and chronological information. All three are found in Genesis and continue into the later books. D comes from a priestly source probably working in the reign of Josiah (d. 609 BCE), and perhaps with a continuation after the exile to Babylon; its contribution begins in Deuteronomy, and is especially notable for the theological shaping it gives to the narrative through the end of 2 Kings. A redactor (possibly Ezra working about 458 BCE) is thought to have combined these four main sources, and may be responsible for Deuteronomistic elements in the first four books.

Genesis ('origin' or 'creation'; Hebrew: Bereshith, 'in the beginning').* The creation of the world and of Adam and Eve; their Fall; Noah and the flood; stories of the patriarchs, notably Abraham, Isaac, Jacob and Joseph.

Period: traditionally 4004–1635 BCE (Archbishop James Ussher made the calculations that produced these dates, which are found in many editions of the KJB from 1701 onwards). Authorship: J, E, P and Redactor.

One must either believe or suspend disbelief to appreciate Genesis, one of the most revered and loved books of the OT. In the opening words, 'In the beginning God created the heaven and the earth', God simply is: a supreme power and also a character in a narrative. Like a master to a servant he can give orders, and they are instantly obeyed, but the orders are of such magnitude that he is at once like a character and infinitely beyond: 'God said, "Let there be light": and there was light' (1:3). Such simple writing both invokes the reader's idea of God (belief), and creates him (suspending disbelief). The way God is presented and understood develops. He is a physical presence to Adam and then Eve, instructing, warning and caring for them, as he will, on a larger scale and with gradual loss of a sense of his actual physical presence, instruct, warn, care for and punish the Jewish people throughout the OT. Though the focus in Genesis moves to individuals, acting either in keeping with or against their sense of God, the reader should stay alert to God throughout. He is a reality to them – and to their successors throughout the Bible – and he is a reality throughout the writing.

The same expressive power of action that creates God's power is also characteristic of the early narratives. They may be legendary but they are written with a sense of certainty that works equally on faith and imagination. After Jacob, loving Rachel the younger daughter of his uncle Laban, has been told he must serve seven years for her, we read, 'And Jacob served seven years for Rachel: and they seemed unto him but a few days, for the love he had to her' (29:20). The plain statement of fact invites reflection: for a moment Jacob is one of the world's great lovers. Some of the power, too, lies in the particular words used in the KJB (taken straight from William Tyndale's translation and closely following the Hebrew). The rhythmic monosyllables, finishing in a cadence that makes 'love' the most emphatic word, speak aloud.

The human characters in these stories are not just revered ancestors and heroes, but, like Adam and Eve, they are sinners: in their actions their faults are as clear as their virtues. This quality makes Genesis a book at least as human as it is divine. Jacob is not only a romantic hero but a swindler of his own brother whose talents as a schemer also allow him to get the better of his uncle Laban. Abraham, so faithful that he is willing to sacrifice his son Isaac at God's behest, also puts his wife Sarah at risk for his own safety. Stories of faith and heroism sit alongside stories of downright treachery, as in the terrible vengeance Jacob's sons Simeon and Levi wreak on the family of Shechem (34); in this story it is Shechem, the defiler of Dinah, who emerges as the honourable character.

The multiple sources of the stories lead to peculiar effects. Events sometimes seem to happen more than once, or the same event may happen in different ways. On the sixth day of creation God first creates the living creatures, then creates both man and woman 'in his own image' (1:27). He also 'formed man of the dust of the ground' (2:7; 'Adam' means both man and ground), then creates living creatures (2:19). Adam has time to name them all before God

---

* The Hebrew names for the first five books come from their opening words.

makes a woman from his rib (2:21–3). Before the flood animals go into the ark two by two, but also in sevens. In the first example two different creation stories are being told in succession: from P and from J. In the second, details from two different versions of the Noah story are combined. Whether or not we can reconcile these differences, it is important to note that the Redactor let them stand: it was all truth, all equally a part of the heritage. Our belief that truth is a singular thing sometimes does not fit with reading the Bible.

The exquisite miniatures of the first thirty-six chapters are followed by the extended narrative of Joseph and his brothers. The storytelling is thorough and often moving. There are vivid details, speeches, conversations and even racy action when Potiphar's wife tries to seduce Joseph. What is missing is explicit reflection on the story, yet it is unnecessary. The faith expressed especially by Joseph that the action fulfils God's plan allows the action, good and bad, to be presented nakedly, yet still to be expressive of man's faith in and his relation to God, and of God's hand guiding his chosen people.

At the end of the book the twelve tribes of Israel – named after eleven of the sons of Jacob, with two half-tribes named after Joseph's sons – are established and dominant in Egypt.

Exodus ('departure'; Hebrew: Shemoth, 'names', or Eleh Shemoth, 'these are the names'). The Israelites' servitude in Egypt, Moses' attempts to secure release from Pharaoh, the plagues, escape through the Red Sea and origin of the Passover, and the arrival at Sinai; the giving of the law and the making of the Tabernacle.
Period: traditionally 1571 (birth of Moses) to 1491 BCE; now thought to have been thirteenth century. Authorship: J, E, P and Redactor.

Whereas Genesis begins with God but is primarily about the human characters, Exodus begins with Moses but is primarily about God. It is hard to realise that the all-powerful creator shown in the first chapter of Genesis, the single God of Judaism, Christianity and Islam, was one god among many. Exodus is about God's establishment of his supremacy and what this means for his true followers, at this stage the ever-backsliding children of Israel. For them it means everything.

Four hundred years after Joseph, a pharaoh in fear of their power sets out to quash the Israelites in his kingdom, even decreeing that all male children shall be killed at birth. Enslavement in a state bent on exterminating them is a situation that will resonate through Jewish history, and the subsequent pattern of divinely directed escape through the sea to a promised land extends the resonance to, for instance, the Puritans settling in the promised land of America.

Through his servant Moses, the central human figure of this and the following three books, God demands liberation for his people, and demonstrates his power in ten plagues and finally the miraculous parting of the Red Sea. At first the plagues seem to follow conjuring contests between Moses and his brother Aaron, a priest, and their equivalents on the Egyptian side. While the Egyptians can duplicate some of the feats, only Moses, informed by God, knows what plague will come and how to avoid it and then to rid it from the land. The Israelites avoid the horrifying final plague, when all the firstborn of Egypt are killed, by marking their houses with lambs' blood. Seeing this, God passes over them. This, together with the consequent escape from Egypt, is commemorated as one of the major festivals of the Jewish year, Passover.

After each plague God hardened Pharaoh's heart. What might seem deliberate prolongation of agony is in fact essential demonstration of God's power, not only to the Egyptians but to the Israelites, for God raised up Pharaoh 'to show in thee my power' (9:16). All will 'know that there is none like unto the LORD our God' (8:10). After the repeated lessons of the plagues, the final destruction of the Egyptian army in the sea shows God getting himself 'honour upon Pharaoh' (14:17). In celebration, the children of Israel sing, 'Who is like unto thee, O LORD, amongst the gods?' (15:11).

In spite of this celebratory psalm, the recalcitrance of the children of Israel is almost as important as the power of God; as he observes, 'it is a stiff-necked people' (32:9). One might say that they are like Pharaoh, but while his was a heart purposefully hardened by God, in the wilderness God and Moses have to deal with basic human weakness. Again the lesson of God's power is enforced. He has chosen these people and made a covenant with them that is both merciful and demanding. It is now enshrined in the law, and they must, repeatedly through the generations, learn to obey.

The latter part of Exodus is principally concerned with this law. Its centre-piece is a theological and moral code, the Ten Commandments, that begins with the lesson of Exodus: 'I am the LORD thy God, which have brought thee out of the land of Egypt, out of the house of bondage. Thou shalt have no other gods before me' (20:2–3). Given amidst 'the thunderings, and the lightnings, and the noise of the trumpet, and the mountain smoking' (20:18), it is part of the new sense of God as an immense supernatural force. While he may speak to Moses 'face to face, as a man speaketh unto his friend' (33:11), for the people he is this fearsome power: directly encountered, this power is death. Reverence, which includes the taboo on speaking the holy name, is enforced. Moses comforts the people, 'for God is come to prove you, and that his fear may be before your faces, that ye sin not' (20:20).

Even so, the people continue most humanly recalcitrant. Starving in the desert before the giving of the manna and quails, they wish they had 'died by the hand of the LORD in the land of Egypt, when we sat by the flesh-pots, and when we did eat bread to the full' (16:3; 'flesh-pots' hold meat; 'meat' in the KJB means food of any sort). More culpably, while Moses is receiving the law for forty days on the holy mountain, Sinai or Horeb, they disobey the first two commandments, getting Aaron to make them 'gods which shall go before us' (32:1), the golden calf. What follows is gruesome, more horrifying than the flood, perhaps even than the killing of the firstborn, because the slaughter is so intimate: every Levite (priest) has to kill his brother, companion or neighbour, and does so. '[A]bout three thousand men' die (32:28). Such are the wages of sin.

Leviticus (Hebrew: Vayikra, 'and he called'). Laws for the Levites, including the Holiness Code.
Authorship: P and Redactor. The Holiness Code may be older than the rest of P.

Jewish children often start Bible study with Leviticus, traditionally because of what it teaches of purity, but more practically because it contains most of the laws that they will follow throughout their lives, especially those concerning food, sex, marriage, justice and religious observance. It is the most Jewish book of the Jewish Bible.

Much of it is alien to non-Jews, and some, such as the extensive laws of sacrifice, alien also to modern Judaism. From Exodus 25 through Leviticus and continuing on to Numbers 10, these comprise a law book for the library shelves: one might dust it off only when needed for reference. Yet its importance for Jewish children, its enormous presence in rabbinic learning and, above all, its importance for conduct throughout the OT and into the NT, make it a necessary book to have some sense of.

Leviticus, the book for the sons of Levi, the priests, presents itself as 'the statutes and judgements and laws, which the LORD made between him and the children of Israel in mount Sinai by the hand of Moses' (26:46). Throughout God speaks to Moses, dictating laws for the children of Israel and, where priestly practice is concerned, the sons of Aaron, the first high priest. The story is told of 'the son of an Israelitish woman' and an Egyptian who 'blasphemed the name of the LORD, and cursed' (24:10–11), and Moses consults God who delivers a judgement: the congregation are to stone him. This becomes the specific punishment for blasphemy. What is so striking is that this is the only instance in Leviticus of the law arising from a particular case (the only other story, that of Aaron's sons Nadab and Abihu offering 'strange fire before the LORD, which he commanded them not' (10:1), is exemplary in the way the stories of Exodus are, in showing the consequence of disobedience). Otherwise, the law is detailed and final. As such it is the work of P, attributing developed practice to the time of its beginnings.

Chapter 19 is summarised simply in the first edition of the KJB as 'a repetition of sundry laws', yet it stands out. The first nineteen verses constitute a more general moral code than the rest of the book. They restate some of the Ten Commandments, and include the second of the two laws that Jesus singled out when asked 'Which is the first commandment of all?' (Mark 12:28): 'thou shalt love thy neighbour as thyself' (19:18). There is also the charitable command that 'thou shalt not wholly reap the corners of thy field, neither shalt thou gather the gleanings of thy harvest . . . thou shalt leave them for the poor and stranger' (19:9–10). Boaz's obedience to this is a key point in Ruth – just one of many examples one might take of levitical law as basic to understanding later events.

Numbers (Hebrew: Bemidbar, 'in the wilderness'). Moses and the Israelites in the wilderness to the time of Joshua's appointment as Moses' successor, with many laws and two census records, whence 'Numbers'.
Period: traditionally 1490–1451 BCE. Authorship: J and E (particularly in chapters 11–25), P and Redactor.

Numbers gives episodes from the forty years of wandering in the wilderness after the escape from Egypt as the children of Israel develop as a fighting force and come close to the promised land. It has a direct narrative continuity from Exodus 20, and the story runs through into Joshua.

The first nine chapters, besides recounting the census, continue the legislative mode of Leviticus, detailing among other things priestly duties and the form of the Passover. Chapter 6 is especially notable for the blessing, 'The LORD bless thee, and keep thee: the LORD make his face shine upon thee, and be gracious unto thee: the LORD lift up his countenance upon thee, and give thee peace' (6:24–6). These simple words, familiar to church-goers, not only bless but create a feeling of peace. They have been found inscribed on a silver scroll or amulet probably from the sixth century BCE, perhaps the oldest extant inscription of a biblical text.

The most striking story concerns Balaam. Though he is not an Israelite, in his direct knowledge of God, his fidelity and his fearless obedience, he has the qualities of a prophet. The miraculous tale of Balaam's ass interrupts the narrative: in it a she-donkey can see more than the non-Israelite prophet and can even rebuke him with a memorable statement of her faithfulness and service. Two ideas of Balaam stand in contradiction. He is both a faithful prophet who knows God, and a false prophet whose blessings and curses are for sale. He is remembered in both ways later in the Bible.

For the rest of the story he is, crucially, the faithful prophet, memorably and repeatedly blessing Israel and cursing its enemies. Among his prophecies is this:

> Surely there is no enchantment against Jacob,
> neither is there any divination against Israel:
> according to this time it shall be said of Jacob and of Israel,
> 'What hath God wrought!'   (23:23)

The last words, taken directly from Tyndale but impossible to keep for modern English translations, resonate far beyond their context and show the KJB's enduring ability to give expression appropriate for the moment: on 24 May 1844, at the suggestion of a young girl, Samuel Morse used 'What hath God wrought' as the words for the first message ever telegraphed.

Deuteronomy ('second law'; Hebrew: Devarim, 'words'). Laws and exhortations framed as Moses' seven final addresses; death of Moses.
Period: traditionally 1451 BCE. Authorship: D.

The title comes from the Greek Septuagint by way of the Roman Catholic Vulgate translation of 17:18. The KJB translates the Hebrew more correctly as 'a copy of this law', but 'second law' is apt. This fifth book of Moses rehearses and elaborates much of the law that has gone before, but in a more readable form than Leviticus.

Deuteronomy is both the end of the Pentateuch and the beginning of the next series of books (through to 2 Kings) that all (except Ruth) seem to come from a single authorial tradition and together make up the Deuteronomic history. This history all but finishes with the religious reforms of the reign of Josiah, during which the book of the law, probably Deuteronomy in some form, was found (2 Kings 22).

With the children of Israel about to enter the promised land, and knowing that his death is close, Moses speaks to his followers, gathered as the only chosen nation. The heart of the speech, resonating across the centuries, is God's past and present covenantal love for this people, his mercy to those that love him and obey his commandments, and his vengeance on those who do not (7:1–11).

A key part is the Shema (6:4–9), so-called from its first word in Hebrew, 'Hear'. The Christian reader will recognise that it contains what Jesus called the first of the commandments (Matt. 22:38, etc.). For Jews it is the central religious statement, to be recited at morning and evening prayers, before sleep and before death. It begins: 'Hear, O Israel: the LORD our God is one LORD. And thou shalt love the LORD thy God with all thy heart, and with all thy soul, and with all thy might'. Part of what makes this so resonant is that it has mixed the starkness of the first commandment, 'Thou shalt have no other gods before me' (Exod. 20:3, Deut. 5:7), with the human element of strenuous love: there is a care for what is in the soul.

Though, as in the order to exterminate seven nations (7.2), there is a harshness that one wishes belonged only to primitive tribal societies, the positive human element and the caring, merciful picture of God combine with the personal address to give Deuteronomy its readability. Laws with a complex human wisdom jostle with 'eye for eye, tooth for tooth' (19:21; another of the Bible's famous phrases). For instance, the newly-wed man 'shall be free at home one year, and shall cheer up his wife which he hath taken' (24:5). The God of battles is also the God of a compassionate society.

Such laws and emphasis are part of how the second law has developed from that given at Sinai/Horeb. As one would expect from different human authors writing long after the events, there are inconsistencies among the continuities between Deuteronomy and the preceding books. They reflect not just different authorship but also a maturing sense of God, man and society.

The people, however, remain the same. Moses knows that they 'have been rebellious against the LORD from the day that I knew you' (9:24), and God prophesies that, after Moses' death, 'this people will rise up . . . and will forsake me, and break my covenant' (31:16). Nevertheless, Moses' final words are a blessing, 'Happy art thou, O Israel: who is like unto thee, O people! saved by the LORD' (33:29).

Joshua to 2 Kings, excluding Ruth, constitute the Former Prophets (Nevi'im Rishonim) in the Jewish Bible.

Joshua. The Israelites from the death of Moses to the death of Joshua, including the conquest of the promised land and its division among the twelve tribes. Period: traditionally 1451–1427 BCE. Authorship: D.

Chapters 1–12 mix stories of the conquest with a bare itemising of victories. The most famous is the conquest of Jericho, climaxing with the ritual marching around the walls for seven days, and their wonderful collapse.

Before this battle there is a story of real human interest that is somewhat puzzling in its significance. Two unnamed men are sent to spy out the land, and they come into the house of the harlot Rahab. She hides them, tells them of the terror among the inhabitants and then saves them. In part she is like Balaam, a foreigner who recognises that 'the LORD your God, he is God in heaven above, and in earth beneath' (2:11), and so an enlightened figure deserving of respect. Yet she may also be acting out of well-founded fear, and she is a prostitute, not a celebrated seer. Other non-Israelites such as the people of Nineveh in Jonah or the exemplary Ruth showed themselves faithful to the God of Israel, but in the NT Rahab is the only non-Israelite singled out along with famous Israelite ancestors (Hebrews 11:31 and James 2:25).

The conquest of the promised land is presented as the fulfilment of all God's promises to the Israelites, with all their enemies conquered, but close reading suggests something more partial. For example, the children of Judah fail to conquer the Jebusites in Jerusalem, so 'the Jebusites dwell with the children of Judah at Jerusalem unto this day' (15:63), and the same thing happens with the Canaanites in Gezer (16:10). Moreover, as God tells the aged Joshua, 'there remaineth yet very much land to be possessed' (13:1), and a catalogue of this follows (much of Joshua is material that would now be found in a land records office). Joshua's death-bed speech recognises this and presciently warns of the dangers facing the Israelites 'if ye do in any wise go back, and cleave unto the remnant of these nations' (23:12). Theological and nationalistic idealisation of this period rubs awkwardly against some of the memories of the time.

Judges. The Israelites from the death of Joshua to just before the beginning of the monarchy as they struggle to establish themselves in the promised land and endure uneven fortunes under a succession of tribal leaders called judges; includes the stories of Deborah, Gideon, Jephthah and Samson.
Period: traditionally 1425–1120 BCE. Authorship: D.

The largely unedifying saga of this period is presented with a nakedness made possible by a combination of reverence for traditional stories and an unfailing belief that the disasters come from failure to respect the covenant, and the triumphs from periodic returns to faith in God. These stories retain an often horrifying hold over the imagination. All but one of Gideon's seventy sons are slaughtered by Abimelech, his son by a concubine from Shechem. Jephthah's daughter is sacrificed because of his vow to God to sacrifice 'whatsoever cometh forth of the doors of my house to meet me' (11:31) if the promise of victory is fulfilled. The Levite's concubine is gang-raped to death by the Benjamites, and this almost leads to the extermination of that tribe. Most famously, there is the marauding violence of the most foolish womaniser in the Bible, Samson. Though the totals must be taken loosely, the body-count in Judges is 270,774, plus the unnumbered victims. This includes 45,100 Benjamites, for the fighting is between the tribes as well as with the other nations of Canaan.

Sometimes the narratives are full of powerful detail, sometimes bare facts are just as powerful. Samson, in quest of the Philistine woman who will be his first wife, finds himself confronted with a young lion roaring against him, 'And the Spirit of the LORD came mightily upon him, and he rent him as he would have rent a kid, and he had nothing in his hand' (14:6). The simile is remarkable: it takes a strong man to rend a kid bare-handed, yet this is easy for a Samson. Not long after the wedding comes one of the powerful bare facts. Samson returns to his father's house, and we read, 'But Samson's wife was given to his companion, whom he had used as his friend' (14:20). The last words, redolent of treachery, bring the reader to a stop, outraged on Samson's behalf.

Then comes Samson and Delilah. One moment we are told that he loves her, the next that the Philistines offer her a fabulous sum to entice from him the secret of his strength. After lying three times, he tells her that he has been a Nazirite from the womb, a man who never cut his hair in sign of his dedication to God: if it is cut, God departs from him. So Delilah, now rich with the Philistines' money, 'made him sleep upon her knees; and she called for a man, and she caused him to shave off the seven locks of his head' (16:19). No more words are needed to create a complete picture, and the story moves quickly to its melodramatic conclusion as he pulls the house down: 'the dead which he slew at his death were more than they which he slew in his life' (16:30).

Besides relishing such stories, it is important to keep the generalised historical and theological picture in mind. The partial conquest of the promised land noted but not stressed in Joshua is basic. The new generations of 'the children of Israel did evil in the sight of the LORD, and served Baalim' (2:11). They adopted local religious practices and mixed with the other inhabitants of the land, sometimes being beaten into submission, sometimes, led by the judges, gaining ascendancy, typically for forty years. The phrase, 'did evil in the sight of the LORD', always with the meaning of following false gods.

1878

first part of the book, and later becomes a refrain in the books of Kings. It is part of the Deuteronomistic view that lends a moral and religious shape to the stories.

Ruth. The Moabite Ruth, her mother-in-law, and how she came to marry Boaz. Period: traditionally 1322–1312 BCE. Authorship: unknown.

The subject matter of this perfect short story of honour – quietly called kindness – and fidelity could not be in sharper contrast with Judges. Ruth is from a tribe the children of Israel were at war with in Judges and which was forbidden to 'enter into the congregation of the LORD' (Deut. 23:3; see also 7:3–4), yet conditions now are different. Her beautifully balanced expression of loyalty to her Bethlehemite mother-in-law, Naomi, sets the tone for what follows: 'whither thou goest, I will go; and where thou lodgest, I will lodge: thy people shall be my people, and thy God my God' (1:16). The vow is fulfilled and reciprocated in a context where so much could go wrong. There are young men who might fall upon her (KJB's alternative translation of 'meet thee' (2:22)), there is no onus on Naomi's relative Boaz to treat her kindly, and there is a nearer relative to claim whatever is Naomi's, including Ruth. Key points in the action depend on characters inferring the true significance of each other's actions. Ruth, at Naomi's suggestion, does something that in any other context would make this a ribald tale like Chaucer's Reeve's, but she, Naomi and Boaz have read each other correctly, and the reader has read them in the same way.

  The story begins 'in the days when the judges ruled', and finishes with a genealogical epilogue that links the characters back to Gen. 38:29, and forward to David. Though it is not part of the Deuteronomic history, this amply justifies its placement in the Christian OT as a link between the patriarchs and the kings. In the Jewish Scriptures it follows the Song of Solomon, a good context for a spiritualised tale of faith and kindness that is finally a love story.

1, 2 Samuel (Hebrew: Shemuel, one book, but 1, 2 Kings in Greek and Latin Bibles). The prophet Samuel and the establishment of the monarchy; Saul's reign and death; David's reign, including the unification of the northern and southern kingdoms.
Period: traditionally 1171–1017 BCE. Authorship: D.

Samuel (1 and 2) is one of the most obviously composite books, with material from different sources put together apparently without concern for consistency. The overriding aim of D seems to have been the preservation, rather than the harmonisation, of stories. Because David especially was a figure of legendary proportions, an unusually large number of stories about him survived, and it is impossible either to reconstruct sources with any certainty or to disentangle history from legend. What is important is the hold that these stories have had on the beliefs and imaginations of Jews and Christians.

  The composite nature is most obvious in the repeated stories such as the death of Saul. Defeated by the Philistines, he unsuccessfully begs his armour-bearer to finish him off, then falls on his own sword (1 Sam. 31). But, in the next chapter (2 Sam. 1), a tattered Amalekite survivor comes to David and reports that, at Saul's earnest entreaty, 'slay me: for anguish is come upon me, because my life is yet whole in me' (1:9), he killed him. The narrator offers no comment on the apparent contradictions. The second version leads to characteristic actions by David. First he turns the tables on the Amalekite, who is executed for slaying the Lord's anointed, then he makes his magnificent lament for Saul and Jonathan. In such ways the books of Samuel resemble an anthology of Saul and David stories presented as a single narrative by a light editorial hand.

Besides the stories of Samuel's ascendancy to authority and leadership, the first part of 1 Samuel is dominated by the story of the Ark of the Covenant, the sacred chest that symbolised the presence of God. It brings destruction, military defeat and plague wherever it goes, even death to 50,070 of the Israelites of Beth-shemesh, who looked into it to see that nothing had been removed. The fearful power of God is paramount: 'Who is able to stand before this holy LORD God?' (6:20).

While 'there was sore war against the Philistines all the days of Saul' (14:52), and this continues into the reign of David, the stories of these two kings are largely personal and usually highly dramatic – so much so that D. H. Lawrence in his play *David* (1926) was able to transcribe substantial portions of the text such as chapter 15 and have it work as drama. Saul is a tragic figure, especially if one takes a sympathetic view of the two failures that lead to the loss of God's and Samuel's favour. He becomes a depressive, dangerous man, liable to hurl the javelin that is constantly at his side at any man, but liable also to sincere repentance, according to which spirit enters him: 'the Spirit of the LORD departed from Saul, and an evil spirit from the LORD troubled him' (16:14).

David is the dominant human figure of the OT. As their greatest king, his significance for the Jews is second only to that of Moses, and he is also the chief poet of the OT, while as legendary hero, as chief ancestor of Jesus and as poet, he is also of huge significance for Christians. He receives from God a promise similar to that given to Abraham: 'thy house and thy kingdom shall be established for ever before thee' (2 Sam. 7:16). The rest of the prophecy is about his son Solomon but also can be read as referring to Jesus, who is repeatedly called the son of David in the NT: 'I will establish the throne of his kingdom for ever. I will be his father, and he shall be my son' (7:13–14).

In choosing the youngest of Jesse's children, David, as Saul's successor, God tells the surprised Samuel, 'the LORD seeth not as man seeth; for man looketh on the outward appearance, but the LORD looketh on the heart' (1 Sam. 16:7). This is the clue to David. '[A] man after [God's] own heart' (13:14), David constantly shows a greatness of heart. No more than a shepherd boy and a 'stripling' (17:56), he conquers Goliath in the name of God. He constantly surprises with a kind of divine wisdom, as when he ceases to fast after his baby son's death, declaring, 'wherefore should I fast? Can I bring him back again? I shall go to him, but he shall not return to me' (2 Sam. 12:23). Jesus is the only other person in the Bible who constantly astonishes those around him with his actions and words. And the greatness of heart is never more powerful than when he is moved to poetic expression as in his lament for Saul and Jonathan (1:19–27), or his cry after rebellious Absalom: 'O my son Absalom, my son, my son Absalom: would God I had died for thee, O Absalom, my son, my son' (18:33).

Yet David is also a man with blatant faults. For much of his early career he is a rebel chief, even duplicitously siding with the Philistines. His greatest crime, seducing Bathsheba and sending her honourable husband Uriah the Hittite to certain death in battle, is worthy of the basest warlord. The rebellions of David's sons and the battle for succession that make up much of the last part of 2 Samuel are God's punishment on David for doing evil in his sight.

1, 2 Kings (Hebrew: Melakim, one book, but 3, 4 Kings in Greek and Latin Bibles). The monarchy from greatness under Solomon through the division into two kingdoms to the fall of Israel, and then the further history of the kingdom of Judah to the fall of Jerusalem and exile; includes the building of the Temple and stories of Elijah and Elisha.
Period: *c.* 962–586 BCE. Authorship: D.

The Temple at Jerusalem, the centre of Jewish worship, was built at the height of the monarchy under Solomon (*c.* 962–922 BCE). But then, because 'his heart was not perfect with the LORD his God, as was the heart of David his father' (1 Kings 11:4), God took the largest part of the kingdom away from his successors. Ten tribes formed the northern kingdom, called Israel, and Judah and Benjamin made up the southern kingdom, called Judah, with Jerusalem as its capital. Under nineteen or twenty kings of Israel and twenty kings and one queen of Judah, they fought each other – and sometimes made alliances against common enemies. All the kings of Israel 'did evil in the sight of the LORD', in other words, pursued various forms of idolatry in addition to miscellaneous wickedness, but eight of the kings of Judah 'did that which was right in the sight of the LORD'. Israel fell to Assyria in 722 BCE, and Judah to Babylon in 597, with Jerusalem and the Temple being finally destroyed in 587/6.

Some of the events can be dated accurately from Assyrian and Babylonian sources, but Kings itself is not principally a history, as the doing evil or doing right distinction suggests. Historical material, including some from several named but lost sources (acts of Solomon, chronicles of the kings of Judah and of Israel, etc.), is used within a strongly theological framework. D sees Judah as the true, Davidic kingdom, and so finds no good in the religious practices of Israel. He assesses the kings of Judah as he had previously done the judges by criteria taken from Deuteronomy.

Mixed in with the moralised saga are some famous stories such as the judgement of Solomon on the two mothers both claiming the same child and the miraculous doings of the prophets Elijah and Elisha, which constitute a largely separate strand.

1, 2 Chronicles (Hebrew: Divrei Hayamim, 'acts of the days', one book, but in Greek and Latin Bibles two books, Paraleipomena, 'things omitted', so called because they were considered a supplement to the historical books; the modern name comes from Jerome's phrase, 'chronicon totius divinae historiae', 'chronicle of the entire divine history'). Genealogies from Adam; death of Saul; David and preparations for building the Temple; Solomon and the building of the Temple; kings of Judah.
Period: 4004 (traditionally) to 538 BCE. Authorship: traditionally ascribed to Ezra but much debated; the Chronicler (or his school), possibly a Jerusalem Levite connected with the Second Temple in the latter part of the fourth century, using various sources, including earlier books of the Bible and lost works.

This relatively late work opens with nine chapters made up of names of people and occasional snippets of biographical information and speech. These people relate especially to the tribe of Judah and to the service of the Temple, and are part of the special focus of Chronicles on the heritage of the Jews as the true religious people. This is a significant change from the focus on Israel as a nation developing and finally losing both kingdoms. It reflects the later worldly situation of the Jews both as a subject people with no realistic political aspirations in the land they had once thought of as their own, and as a substantially scattered people.

The narrative part begins with the death of Saul, a preface to the reign of David and also the first example of the retribution that falls on a king. Rather than narrating Saul's life, the Chronicler characteristically assumes familiarity with the full story and is concerned to put a theological understanding on it.

While some of Samuel's stories of David as a successful warrior-king are repeated, the Chronicler's emphasis is on David as the king who restored the Ark to Jerusalem and made all the preparations for the building of the Temple and, especially, for serving it. The account of Solomon concentrates on the building of the Temple, culminating in a magnificent feast at which the Ark is brought into it. He delivers a speech of consecration, and elaborate sacrifices are offered. Finally, God appears to Solomon by night, confirming that the Temple is his chosen place and that there he will hear all that come to him in faith, but he warns that if the people are unfaithful he will cast the Temple out of his sight and 'make it to be a proverb and a byword among all nations'. To the question, 'Why hath the LORD done thus unto this land, and unto this house?', the answer will be, 'Because they forsook the LORD God of their fathers' (2 Chr. 7:20–22). Prospectively, this explains as retribution the destruction of the Temple and all the other calamities that had come on the people by the time of the Chronicler, but it also has a strong sense that a penitential return to true faith will be rewarded.

The seventeen chapters on the kings of Judah sometimes give a significantly different version from that found in Kings. Manasseh, for instance, was presented as so supremely wicked that he provoked God to the later destruction of Jerusalem, but in Chronicles he repents and prays successfully to God; he then evicts the strange gods and altars from the Temple, repairs the altar, makes peace and thanks offerings, 'and commanded Judah to serve the LORD God of Israel' (33:16). The emphasis on the efficacy of repentance and the repairing of the Temple is characteristic of Chronicles, and a strong lesson for the people.

The kings who do most to bring the people back to God and to restore the Temple are Hezekiah and Josiah. Chronicles all but finishes with the destruction of the Temple and the Babylonian exile, but the last two verses bring a note of hope and challenge, as the Persian king Cyrus proclaims that God 'hath charged me to build him a house in Jerusalem ... Who is there among you of all his people? The Lord his God be with him, and let him go up' (36:23).

From Chronicles the order and grouping of the Jewish Bible and the Christian OT vary considerably. Chronicles is placed at the end of the final section of the Jewish Bible, the Writings (Kethuvim). The Jewish order of the Writings is usually as follows: Psalms, Proverbs, Job, Song of Solomon, Ruth, Lamentations, Ecclesiastes, Esther, Daniel, Ezra and Nehemiah, Chronicles.

Ezra and **Nehemiah** (treated as a single book until divided by Origen, third century CE; different version given as 1 and 2 Esdras in the Apocrypha). The work and reforms of Ezra and Nehemiah following the Babylonian exile; expeditions to Jerusalem to rebuild the Temple and the city wall; the reading of the law and the renewal of the covenant. Two sections of Ezra (4:8–6:18 and 7:12–26) are in Aramaic (called Chaldee in the KJB).

Period: 538–444 BCE. Authorship: either as for Chronicles or independent compiler(s).

The Bible gives no straightforward account of the fifty years of exile in Babylon, but from that time emerged a new religious sense in which Ezra, like a second Moses, is the central figure. The Persian empire had taken over from the Babylonian, and with it came policies sympathetic to local religions and to repatriation. For the Jews, Cyrus' proclamation of 538 BCE, given at the end of Chronicles and repeated at Ezra 1:2–4 and 6:3–5, seemed divinely inspired (see Isa. 44:28–45:13), and mandated what became the Jerusalem Temple-centred restoration of Jewish religion. Nevertheless, while remnants from the old kingdom of Judah returned to Jerusalem, many stayed in exile. Judaism thus became both diasporic and centralised. Moreover, the people of the old Israelite kingdom had become absorbed into Samaria, and gradually developed different traditions, notably that the Pentateuch alone constituted their scriptures.

Ezra and Nehemiah present historical puzzles. They seem to assume more prior knowledge than is in the Bible, and they appear to have both men in Jerusalem at the same time, yet with little knowledge of each other. They give glimpses of nearly a century of history particularly through authentic documents and, uniquely in the OT, Ezra's and Nehemiah's personal memoirs.

The heart of Ezra is the rebuilding of the Temple and the restoration of a strict, separatist religious life. This follows returns to Jerusalem under Sheshbazzar and then Zerubbabel, and opposition from the local peoples. The list of returnees in chapter 2 concentrates on the leaders of Temple worship, who must be genealogically pure, sons of Judah and Benjamin from the exile. This is the first sign of the exclusiveness that will lead to Ezra's terrible rejection (so against the spirit of the books of Ruth and Jonah) of foreign wives and children.

Nehemiah the Tirshatha (Persian: governor) is of lesser importance than Ezra the priest, but, from the moment he hears of the destruction of Jerusalem and so appears sad and sorrowful before the Persian king Artaxerxes to his final prayer, 'Remember me, O my God, for good' (Neh. 13:31), he is more engaging. He recounts his expedition to Jerusalem, his secret survey of the walls, and how he managed their reconstruction despite the hostility of the surrounding people. The crucial part of the book is not the re-establishment of Jerusalem but Ezra's reading of the book of the law to the people and the consequent renewal of the covenant. In this the strongly legalistic and exclusive Judaism of the Second Temple is established. What was once a great kingdom has become a small but phenomenally influential theocracy.

Ezra 7:21 is a minor curiosity in the KJB, the only verse to have all the letters of the alphabet in it (I was printed J in early editions).

THE REST OF THE OLD TESTAMENT

Nehemiah is the last of the historical books in the OT. The books that follow either belong to or are set before the return to Jerusalem and represent various other kinds of Jewish writing: Esther to the Song of Solomon includes major poetic works in Job, Psalms and the Song of Solomon; reflective and moral works, Job again, Proverbs and Ecclesiastes; and a story, Esther. The OT finishes with the prophetic books (see p. 1890), while some later Jewish history is recounted in parts of the Apocrypha (see p. 1900).

Esther. An attempt to remove the Jews from the Persian empire is victoriously turned against the Jews' enemies by Esther and Mordecai; origin of the feast of Purim.

Authorship: unknown; date unknown.

Esther is a very unusual book to find in a collection of great religious writings, because it is a secular and – despite its historical setting in the reign of Ahasuerus (probably Xerxes, 486–465 BCE) – fictional tale of court intrigue and even farcical mistakes that never once mentions God. It begins with events similar to those at the end of Shakespeare's *The Taming of the Shrew* (1590–91): at a feast, Queen Vashti refuses to obey a command from King Ahasuerus and, rather than being tamed, is disposed of lest 'all women ... despise their husbands' (1:17). Even more than the omnipotent debauchee, Ahasuerus, the narrator forgets about her, and the Jewish Esther, a paragon of beauty and either obedience or the most deferential disobedience, becomes queen. She thus is in position to turn the genocidal schemes of the chief minister, Haman, on his own head. So the closely plotted tale becomes redolent of a recurrent situation in Jewish history, but with a happy outcome.

At the end Esther institutes Purim, named after the lot, or Pur, that Haman casts against the Jews. This major annual Jewish feast is still riotously celebrated. Esther is read aloud, with audience participation appropriate to a Victorian melodrama: whenever Haman's name occurs, whistles and catcalls, rattles and hooters drown it out. This unbridled spirit fits the story.

Esther might have been a different kind of narrative, much more like some of the stories in the historical books, and it was later expanded to take this kind of form. The additional passages found in the Greek version were placed by Jerome in the Vulgate following the Hebrew narrative; and the KJB gives them in the Apocrypha as The Rest of Esther. The story is framed by Mordecai's prophetic dream, giving a sense of divine purpose in the events. Two proclamations such as are found in Ezra and Nehemiah are added, as are prayers and some more details of the action, some of them, like Esther's fainting, quite dramatic. The Jewish text is almost bereft of characterisation and does not explain some key actions. In the Greek text, Esther and Mordecai (Mardocheus) become strictly religious characters. For instance, Mordecai's reason for offending Haman is now clear, that he would 'not prefer the glory of man above the glory of God' (Rest of Esther 13:14).

Confusingly, The Rest of Esther is numbered as a continuation of Esther. It begins with the end of the story (10:4–13), then goes to the beginning and gives parts to be inserted into the Hebrew version.

BIBLICAL POETRY

From Job to the end of the OT the Hebrew is mostly poetry. Though it was believed to be metrical, nobody could scan it satisfactorily. In the 1740s Robert Lowth changed perceptions by arguing that Hebrew poetry's only obvious formal quality was parallelism:

> The poetical conformation of the sentences ... consists chiefly in a certain equality, resemblance, or parallelism between the members of each period; so that in two lines ... things for the most part shall answer to things, and words to words, as if fitted to each other by a kind of rule or measure. This parallelism has much variety and many gradations; it

is sometimes more accurate and manifest, sometimes more vague and obscure.

(*Lectures on the Sacred Poetry of the Hebrews*, trans. George Gregory, 2 vols. (1787), vol. 2, p. 34)

Moreover, since this was a structure not of sound but of words or things, he argued 'that a poem translated literally from the Hebrew into the prose of any other language, whilst the same forms of the sentences remain, will still retain, even as far as relates to versification, much of its native dignity, and a faint appearance of versification' (ibid., vol. 1, p. 71).

The KJB is just such a prose translation. It was never intended to have English poetic form, yet it does preserve some sense of the poetic quality of the Hebrew. At its simplest, parallelism works like this:

'"Shall mortal man be more just than God?
shall a man be more pure than his maker? . . ."'   (Job 4:17)

The two questions are identical in structure and meaning: 'man' parallels 'mortal man', pure/just and maker/God. There is a rhythm of sense, and we have no difficulty in reading the translation as poetry. Here is the opening of Psalm 114:

When Israel went out of Egypt,
the house of Jacob from a people of strange language:
Judah was his sanctuary,
and Israel his dominion.

Again the parallelism is straightforward, Israel/Jacob, sanctuary/dominion, and so on. But immediately one notices there is flexibility: verbs are not necessarily repeated, a description of a quality of the Egyptians can parallel the name of a country. Moreover, it raises a question as to the effect. Is it simply repetitive, or is there a development? Does 'a people of strange language' enhance one's sense of 'Egypt'? Does one think of the two kingdoms in lines 3 and 4 and so see a contrast between the sanctuary, the Temple in Jerusalem, and the dominion over the northern kingdom? This latter reading is perfectly possible, but the nature of parallelism is that identity predominates over difference, for if the former is downplayed too much, misreading can result. When Job cries,

'Let the day perish wherein I was born,
and the night in which it was said,
"There is a man-child conceived".'   (3:3)

he is not giving two curses – on the day of his birth and on the night of his conception – but one: the night is part of his day of birth, the day on which the midwife said, 'It's a boy'. Similarly, in Zechariah's picture of Zion's king coming 'riding upon an ass,/and upon a colt the foal of an ass' (9:9), it is a single animal; implicit between the lines are the words 'that is to say'. Matthew misunderstood this verse, and believing Jesus to have fulfilled this prophecy, describes him impossibly as riding into Jerusalem on an ass and a colt (21:7). So, returning to Psalm 114, we should take Israel/Jacob and sanctuary/dominion as identical; any appreciation of possible differences is secondary.

Parallelism may sometimes look like tediousness, but so often it has a quality of rhythmic reflection and intensity that is part of the power of the poetry. Two poems identical in meaning could be picked out of Psalm 114 by taking alternate lines, but the sense of God's presence in the history of Israel would be – not destroyed, but – diminished.

Lowth noted that parallelism is sometimes hardly at all visible. We should not worry if the only thing that makes the words seem like poetry is their layout on the page, and that the poetry sometimes shades into prose. Parallelism also offers a further insight into the Hebrew sense of verbal truth: at the local level it shows what has been evident elsewhere: an appreciation of repetition with difference, as in Genesis and Samuel.

Things may indeed be said more than twice. Hebrew poetry depends on an accumulation of statements of a single idea, followed by statements of another idea without any obvious transition. Often the poetry seems to be dancing on one spot, and then, without having visibly made the move, to be dancing on another. It is more an art of accumulation than integration, with the reader often needing to supply the links. Psalm 127, for instance, has two verses about the futility of labour that has not God in it, followed by three about the blessings of children: the reader has to see God the giver of blessings as the uniting thread among the accumulated statements made vivid by their images.

Job. Poetic debate about innocent suffering and divine justice between the afflicted Job and four comforters, concluding with the voice of God and the restoration of Job's prosperity.
Authorship: unknown; the narrative framework may be pre-exilic, the body of the book post-exilic, fifth or fourth century BCE.

In the prose tale that frames the poetic debate, God gives Satan (or, as in the KJB margin, 'the adversary') permission to test his perfect servant, Job, a man rich in both family and material possessions. Is Job rich because he is virtuous or virtuous because he is rich? Is true faith only possible when it is easy? Will it disappear in adversity? Are the rich rich because they are good, and the poor blighted because they are bad? Afflicted by Satan, Job shows his proverbial patience (see James 5:11), neither sinning nor charging God foolishly (Job 1:22), but the nature of the book changes when the poetic debate begins and Eliphaz, Bildad and Zophar, followed by the youngster Elihu, come to comfort Job. All is generalised as Job is no longer patient but the patient, the sufferer, expressing all mankind's anguish and incomprehension that God should deal out such undeserved affliction. He curses the day he was born, thinks of the peace he would have known if he had died at birth and asks why life is given. The language is contorted with suffering, as shown by a comparison of 3:3ff., with the blander version of the same sentiments in Jeremiah 20:14–18.

The predominant elements in Job's later speeches are incomprehension as to why he is afflicted and his desire to defend himself to God against whatever charges have been brought against him. He is conscious of his own integrity and his perfect devotion to God: 'Though [God] slay me, yet will I trust in him: but I will maintain my own ways before him' (13:15).

Within these speeches come some of the KJB's (and the Prayer Book's) best-known words, for instance the passage beginning 'For I know that my redeemer liveth, and that he shall stand at the latter day upon the earth' (19:25), which presents what is at this point in the Christian OT a startlingly new conception of God; or this description of life:

> 'Man that is born of a woman is of few days,
> and full of trouble.
> He cometh forth like a flower, and is cut down:
> he fleeth also as a shadow, and continueth not.'   (14:1–2)

The mixture here of generalised reflection on life and similes and examples from the natural world makes up the whole book's characteristic mode of expression.

Job is by no means always easy to read. It is set up to be a theological argument yet is weak as such. Job clings to his integrity, the three comforters (who are uncharacterised and indistinguishable) argue that he has sinned. Elihu berates the comforters for failing to convince (convict or confute) Job, but then repeats their positions; finally God speaks, but has nothing new to argue: like the comforters, but more magnificently, he describes his creation, the natural world, again showing that his wisdom and power are beyond what man can understand. Because the voice is God's, Job accepts this, but the argument is not advanced. In short, the power of the book lies in its expression, not its theological points, and the reader may find it most effective to read it out of sequence, taking Job's speeches first, then those of the three comforters, and finally God's.

Also making Job difficult to read is the state of the Hebrew text. It may well be the product of several reworkings and a greater degree of textual corruption than was evident in the historical books, and it has a large number of unique words whose meaning is uncertain. Later translations sometimes offer quite different interpretations and deal with the apparent incoherence by rearranging the text and changing the attribution of some of the speeches. Chapter 25, for instance, might be a speech of Job's, not Bildad's, and vice versa for most of chapter 26.

Psalms (Hebrew: Tehilim, 'praises', 'hymns'). 150 songs sometimes divided into five books to reflect the Pentateuch (the divisions are marked by doxologies, or blessing formulas, at the ends of Psalms 41, 72, 89 and 106); numbering varies (the Greek text gives Psalm 9 as a continuation of 8, and divides Psalm 147); verse numbering also varies because some versions count the superscriptions as verses.
Authorship: unknown, traditionally ascribed to David; perhaps compiled between sixth and second centuries BCE.

This is the one book for which the KJB is not always the best-known text. Anglicans typically refer to the Prayer Book Psalter, which is, with slight variations, Miles Coverdale's version from the Great Bible (1539–40). Metrical versions were also extremely popular. From OT times the Psalms have been a central part of Jewish and then Christian worship, and a private source of comfort and inspiration. This has more to do with what they say than with their strength as poetry, for all that there are some outstanding achievements such as Psalm 23. They express fear, hope, faith and praise in ways that are accessible to every reader, hearer or singer. From ancient times people have found in them expression for their own situation, often in moments of extremity. Perhaps the most striking instance is Jesus on the cross crying, 'My God, my God, why hast thou forsaken me?' (Matt. 27:46, Mark 15:34, quoting Psalm 22:1).

This accessibility comes in part from their general escape from individuality – an aspect masked by contextualising headings, particularly among the psalms ascribed to David (these ascriptions are late additions to the text). Not one of them is strictly personal in the way that the apocryphal Psalm 151 is; it begins:

> I was smaller than my brothers, and younger than the sons of
>   my father.
> He made me shepherd of his flock, and a ruler over his kids.
>   (Geza Vermes (ed.), *The Complete Dead Sea Scrolls in English*, rev. edn
>   (Penguin Classics, 2004), p. 308)

Psalm 54, for instance, is headed, 'A psalm of David, when the Ziphims came and said to Saul, "Doth not David hide himself with us?"' Looking up 1 Sam. 23:19, we can see how the psalm could fit but it has no specific reference to the events there. Rather than the Ziphims, strangers and oppressors are the danger, making the psalm a prayer to God from anyone beset by enemies. As Job became everybody in his suffering, so the Psalmist becomes everybody in his prayer for help and his declaration of faith.

Characteristic themes run through the collection: affliction, penitence and faith; thanksgiving; praise and celebration of God as creator and saviour of both his chosen people and the individual. It is a narrow range inevitably leading to a degree of sameness. Sometimes there is repetition (14 and 53, 40:13–17 and 70), probably reflecting the compilers' use of various earlier collections whose exact contents are unknown. As a whole the final collection was used principally for liturgical purposes in Second Temple times.

The meaning of the recurrent 'Selah' (e.g. 3:8) is unknown. It may be some sort of musical instruction, as are some of the other Hebrew terms preserved in the KJB. It gives marginal interpretations for several, notably Maschil, 'giving instruction' (32:0) and Michtam, 'A golden psalm' (16:0). Some may be names of tunes.

Psalms 117 and 119 are the shortest and longest in the Bible. The latter consists of twenty-two sections, each one having lines beginning with one letter of the Hebrew alphabet, whence the marking of each section in the KJB with the name of the letter. One curiosity of the KJB has to do with the notion that, because its language is so good, Shakespeare, aged about 46, must have had a hand in it: his 'signature' can be found in Psalm 46 by counting 46 words from the beginning, then backwards 46 words from the end (omitting 'Selah').

Proverbs (Hebrew: Mishlei, 'proverbs', 'parables', 'passages of wisdom'). Several collections of wisdom writings.
Authorship: ascribed to Solomon, who probably wrote and collected part of the book; gathered together from various sources of uncertain age, possibly in the middle or late fourth century BCE.

> The wisest man that ever man begot
>   In heav'nly Proverbs shows what's good, what's not.

So summarised in children's Thumb Bibles (miniature books containing couplet summaries of the Bible), Proverbs is one of the lesser books, not living up to the description of Solomon's wisdom in 1 Kings 4:29–34. It is a collection of collections of wisdom writings for ordinary men (not women: it has much in it to rouse the ire of feminists).

The first section, chapters 1–9, begins with a description of the purpose of Solomon's proverbs, 'to know wisdom and instruction, to perceive the words of understanding, to receive the instruction of wisdom, justice, and judgement, and equity, to give subtlety to the simple, to the young man knowledge and discretion' (1:2–4). Immediately the wide sense of 'Mishlei' is evident as passages of advice follow, partly in the voice of a father, partly in the voice of wisdom. God sits in the background, for 'The fear of the LORD is the beginning of knowledge' (1:7), but the advice is predominantly moral, extolling the virtues of wisdom and exhorting the son to avoid the snares of wicked men and strange women. This is a section that one can read as a whole.

The second section, 10–22:16, is a miscellaneous collection of 'proverbs of Solomon' (10:1) united by their form: they are poetic couplets wherein the second half typically is the opposite of the first: their essence is simple moral contrast, as in 'A soft answer turneth away wrath: but grievous words stir up anger' (15:1). The stark antithetical parallelisms are the essence of their memorability. Here one might pick and choose from sentences to savour individually.

The remaining sections are variations on the modes found in the first two. The third, 22:17–24:22, is based on the *Instruction of Amen-em-ope*, an Egyptian collection of advice dating from about 1000 BCE, and is completed with two paragraphs of wisdom from another source. The last substantial section, chapters 25–9, proverbs of Solomon copied by the men of Hezekiah, is more like the second section, but less uniform in pattern and notable for its greater use of imagery, particularly similes. These are more like 'dark sayings' (1:6) on which one must meditate. Here Proverbs is at its most inventive and satisfying, teaching truth by suggestion. 'Where no wood is, there the fire goeth out: so where there is no tale-bearer, the strife ceaseth' (26:20) has more to say about muckrakers and the wisdom of silence than the earlier, 'A tale-bearer revealeth secrets: but he that is of a faithful spirit concealeth the matter' (11:13).

The final two pieces, chapters 30 and 31, come from otherwise unknown figures. Agur's stylised reflections have a real power in their images: to think of an adulteress as being as incomprehensible, even marvellous, as 'an eagle in the air' or 'a serpent upon a rock' (30:19), makes the final picture of her a little triumph of vividness:

> Such is the way of an adulterous woman:
> she eateth, and wipeth her mouth,
> and saith, 'I have done no wickedness'.   (30:20)

There she is, in all her insouciance. Such, though, is not the last word. In this heavily masculine book, it is given to a woman and to the praise of a virtuous woman.

Ecclesiastes ('preacher'; Hebrew: Koheleth, 'preacher', 'assembler', 'public speaker'). Reflections on the futility or vanity of human life.
Authorship: traditionally ascribed to Solomon; unknown, probably third century BCE, with a later addition.

Portraying himself as one who has had all opportunities, wealth, power and wisdom, the Preacher reflects on life, knowing that death comes equally to all people, creatures and things. In this long view, 'all is vanity' (1:2), windy, empty, worthless, senseless. '[T]he day of death' may be better 'than the day of one's birth' (7:1), yet this is not truly a book of despair. Doing may be pointless, yet the book is full of doing. The Preacher has thrown himself with energy into all things, giving his heart to know wisdom, throwing himself into mirth, pleasure and laughter, doing great works. The result may be vanity, he may hate life and 'all my labour which I had taken under the sun' (2:18), yet there is still the very energy with which he creates his vision: there is the power of the expression, there is still a great book of wisdom created. The negative vision wrestles with the energy of the book. It is as if the reader is invited to take 'vanity of vanities, all is vanity' ironically, as truth but not the whole truth. The epilogue puts the point: 'The words of the wise are as goads, and as nails fastened by the masters of assemblies' (12:11). This is a book of goads.

One of the most famous passages begins, 'To everything there is a season, and a time to every purpose under the heaven' (3:1). This, like various other parts of Ecclesiastes, gives a different vision, for the time of lamenting the vanity of life is only one time. God 'hath made everything beautiful in his time', and 'there is nothing better, than that a man should rejoice in his own works' (3:11, 22). Though 'childhood and youth are vanity', the Preacher counsels wholehearted enjoyment of them: 'Rejoice, O young man, in thy youth, and let thy heart cheer thee in the days of thy youth' (11:10, 9). Such sentiments may also be goads, inviting further reflection. Ecclesiastes is both outspoken and enigmatic. Part of its wisdom is to know that no wisdom is final.

The Song of Solomon (Hebrew: Shir Hashirim, 'song of songs'). Love poetry. Authorship: ascribed to Solomon; unknown, possibly fourth or third century BCE.

A man and a woman proclaim their love for each other in a series of speeches that make up a single poem, yet which might be a collection of fragments. There is no obvious story but, in a dream-like way, a series of situations are suggested as the voices seem to drift in and out of each other. Sometimes one person is speaking, sometimes several, as if a chorus echoes the solo voice. Sometimes the direct address to the beloved is varied with personal statements and declarations about the beloved to listeners such as the 'daughters of Jerusalem' (1:5, etc.), sometimes parts are repeated. The reader should be both confused and enchanted.

The enchantment lies in the unabashed absoluteness of the love and the quite extraordinary extent of the descriptions. From the opening two lines, both the frankness and the perfection are evident. We cannot tell if they have different speakers – one addresses the audience, one either the man or the woman – but this kind of escape from precision is also part of the enchantment. The Song never becomes tied to the absolutely personal and particular. Just as Job and the Psalmist are everyman, so these two beloveds are every ideal beloved.

What seems to be the first speech of the man moves from 'thou fairest among women' to comparisons that bring out this perfection. She is like 'a company of horses in Pharaoh's chariots' (1:8–9). It is a comparison of quality: she is as fine as the finest things he can imagine. Many of the images work this way. These two verses are characteristic:

Thy two breasts are like two young roes that are twins.
Thy neck is as a tower of ivory . . .
thy nose is as the tower of Lebanon which looketh toward
Damascus. (7:3–4)

We are accustomed to similes that suggest appearance, but the implicit words here are 'as beautiful as'. Her breasts do not look like fawns, her neck is not towering nor is her nose. Instead, by way of the slight physical connection, there is the overwhelming sense of beauty, and with it, of tenderness and love.

One might wonder what songs of human love, with no mention of God or religion or the nation in them, are doing in the Bible. The relationship between God and his people is frequently imaged in terms of the marriage relationship. More often than not the people are the unfaithful lover, 'for the land hath committed great whoredom, departing from the LORD' (Hosea 1:2), but, addressing Zion, Isaiah shows how the Song can work as an ideal religious vision: 'and as the bridegroom rejoiceth over the bride, so shall thy God rejoice over thee' (62:5). In Judaism the man is God, the beautiful woman Israel; in Christianity, Christ and the Church. The KJB's chapter summary for chapter 1 reads: '1 The Church's love unto Christ. 5 She confesseth her deformity, 7 and prayeth to be directed to his flock. 8 Christ directeth her to the shepherds' tents. 9 And showing his love to her, 11 giveth her gracious promises. 12 The Church and Christ congratulate one another.'

THE PROPHETIC BOOKS

In Genesis, Abraham passed off his wife Sarah as his sister, so Abimelech king of Gerar took her. In a dream God told Abimelech the truth, and added: 'Now therefore restore the man his wife: for he is a prophet, and he shall pray for thee, and thou shalt live' (20:7). This is the Bible's first use of 'prophet', indicating a man with a special relationship to God and with special power. After the crossing of the Red Sea, 'Miriam the prophetess . . . took a timbrel in her hand, and all the women went out after her with timbrels and with dances' (Exod. 15:20): a musician and a poet, she is the first prophetess. Moses, unable 'to bear all this people alone' (Num. 11:14), is relieved by the appointment of seventy elders, who also receive his God-given spirit, and 'when the spirit rested upon them, they prophesied' (11:25). Perhaps they spoke in tongues; more likely, inspired, they ruled the people with the word of God. God promises to raise up a prophet as successor of Moses, and to 'put my words in his mouth, and he shall speak unto them all that I shall command him' (Deut. 18:18). He adds that true prophets can be distinguished from false according to whether what they say comes to pass. Prophets are not only God's mouthpieces, they foretell the future.

Such examples begin to suggest the range of biblical ideas of prophets and prophecy, yet they do not explain the sometimes magnificent efflorescence of prophecy in the last part of the OT – nor its immense importance. The prime characteristic of a prophet is that he or she knows God and can speak on God's behalf. In this sense Moses is the chief prophet, for 'there arose not a prophet since in Israel like unto Moses, whom the LORD knew face to face' (Deut. 34:10). As well as this difference of degree, there is a difference in kind between Moses and the authors of the prophetic books. Whereas Moses is the lawgiver, they are the interpreters of the ways of God to man: from an intense and often stern religious viewpoint, their predominant role is as social and religious critics. They are intensely involved with the present in the light of the covenant and of the nation's history. As the religious conscience of Judah and Israel, they created essential parts of the OT religious vision. Their critical role also involves the future as they look forward either to consequences or to consolation. On the one hand, the nation or the individual has not kept faith with God, so punishment is foretold; on the other, God is merciful and forgiving, so a new Zion or Jerusalem, a new heaven and a new earth, and a Messiah can be foretold; projecting both punishment and salvation, even the end of the world can be foretold. Forgiveness, redemption and the Messiah: without these ideas there could have been no NT.

Isaiah to Malachi, excluding Lamentations and Daniel, constitute the Latter Prophets (Nevi'im Aharonim) in the Jewish Bible. Almost all of them overlap in time of writing with the later historical books (2 Kings to Nehemiah), and it is often valuable to look back at those books for historical background. One event, the exile, is pivotal. Seven prophets come before it, perhaps in this chronological order: Amos, Hosea, first Isaiah (i.e. Isaiah 1–39), Micah, Habakkuk, Zephaniah and Nahum. For them the collective and individual failures of the people, and an emphasis on punishment to come, predominate; this punishment could include the whole nation. From the time of the exile come Jeremiah, Obadiah, Isaiah 40–55, Ezekiel and, possibly later, Isaiah 56–66. In the face of disaster and actual destruction of the nation, for them lamentation, the promise of forgiveness and the vision of a Messiah become important. Haggai, Zechariah 1–8, Malachi, Joel and Zechariah 9–14 are short post-exilic books that address the new situation with some hope and more warning.

The last twelve books of the OT make up the Twelve Minor Prophets in the Hebrew text, a convenient grouping because, by reason of their brevity, they can be copied on a single scroll. A manuscript, dating from around 150 BCE, is among the Dead Sea Scrolls, and, slightly earlier, Ecclesiasticus mentions them as a group and summarises the positive aspect of their message: 'the twelve prophets . . . comforted Jacob, and delivered them by assured hope' (49:10).

Daniel and Jonah stand apart. Though set in Babylon, Daniel is a very late work that casts as prophecy events that have already happened and led to its writing. Jonah, the date of which is unknown, is a narrative about a prophet rather than a prophetic book.

As the chronological sequence above suggests, the order of the prophetic books in the Bible is somewhat arbitrary. Beyond a sense of the primacy of Isaiah as a prophetic book, and the value of finishing with the last chapter of Malachi, there is nothing useful in their order. The prophets as a whole are a great, disordered collection of collections of prophetic writings.

Isaiah ('the Lord has saved'*). Collections of visionary songs, often with a contemporary political content.
Authorship: Isaiah, late eighth century BCE (1–39); unknown writers in the tradition or school of Isaiah, probably in the later years of the exile, 549–538 BCE (40–55), and slightly later (56–66).

Isaiah includes some of the OT's most famous, influential and inspiring writing. '[B]ehold, a virgin shall conceive, and bear a son, and shall call his name

* Most biblical names have a meaning, though they are not always readily translated. Where the names of the prophets are significant, sometimes significant enough to suggest pen-names, possible translations are given.

Immanuel' and 'For unto us a child is born, unto us a son is given' (7:14, 9:6) are but two of its Messianic prophecies that have shaped Christian theology, and which annually ring in the ears of worshippers, and of listeners to Handel's *Messiah* (1742). The resounding declarations of a single, holy, merciful, saving God to whom the whole world can come are no less important: 'Look unto me, and be ye saved, all the ends of the earth: for I am God, and there is none else' (45:22). In such passages is born the idea of a religion that is not solely Jewish. Unsurprisingly, Isaiah is, after the Psalms, the OT book most quoted in the NT.

The visions, theology and language work together. Particularly in the second half of the book the parallelistic writing, full of exhortatory exclamations and questions, is of exceptional power. Some passages have been singled out as supreme examples of, as George Saintsbury put it, 'the best words of the best time in English, in the best order, on the best subjects' (*A History of English Prose Rhythm* (1912), p. 157). Following Saintsbury, Rudyard Kipling imagined Shakespeare as giving the final turn to the language in chapter 60 (' "Proofs of Holy Writ" ' (1934)). This is pre-eminently a book to be heard.

Isaiah is a collection of writings from an uncertain number of authors making up an anthology of pieces that have a general thematic and stylistic unity. Where one piece ends and another begins is often uncertain, and some from one time are mixed in with others from another. Isaiah is commonly divided into two parts, 1–39 and 40–66 (Deutero-Isaiah); 56–66 is sometimes regarded as a further division (Trito-Isaiah); within these broad outlines there are further divisions. Nevertheless, the reader may find it helpful to think of chapters 1–39 as a miscellaneous collection generally associated with Isaiah, who lived through the time of King Hezekiah (with some historical material, 36–9; similar to 2 Kings), and chapters 40–66 as a more homogeneous collection from the time of the Babylonian exile, changing tone slightly at chapter 56. Save for headings such as 'The burden of Babylon, which Isaiah the son of Amoz did see' (13:1), the text gives no clues as to where pieces begin. There is therefore more than the usual amount of guesswork in the way the text is divided into paragraphs. The same is true of speech marks because of the frequent fluidity of speech between indirect and direct, and between first or second and third person.

The KJB glosses some of the significant names as follows: Shear-jashub, 'the remnant shall return' (7:3); Maher-shalal-hash-baz, 'in making speed to the spoil he hasteneth the prey' (8:1); Hephzi-bah, 'my delight is in her', and Beulah, 'married' (62:4).

Jeremiah ('the Lord will rise'). Collection of prophetic and personal writings with historical material about the times and life of Jeremiah.
Period: 627–586 BCE. Authorship: Jeremiah with Baruch as amanuensis; possible other sources, and a later editing of Deuteronomic character.

Jeremiah lived through some of the darkest OT times. His forty-year prophetic vocation began with Judah subject to Assyria, included the possibility of an alliance with Egypt which he opposed, saw the destruction of the Temple, and finished with the conquest of Jerusalem by Nebuchadrezzar and the beginning of the Babylonian exile. Jeremiah gave a theological vision to these disastrous times. They were God's punishment for Judah's and Israel's infidelity, 'according to the fruit of your doings' (21:14). Babylon would be God's final instrument of deserved destruction, but a remnant of true believers would be left; Israel and Judah would be rebuilt. In a crucial passage for the NT, God will make a new covenant with them, not one of external law, but internal: 'I will put my law in their inward parts, and write it in their hearts' (31:33). So, though Jeremiah, 'full of the fury of the LORD' (6:11) and with a heart 'broken because of the prophets' (23:9), is far more a prophet of doom than Isaiah, important parts of his vision are consoling. His final note is extended, stirring and characteristic: Babylon, anticipating Revelation, will suffer a more final destruction than Judah and Israel at God's hands.

The book itself is a hotchpotch of sometimes repeated poetic and prose pieces given in no particular order. How it reached this form is unknown, but the Septuagint text is shorter and sometimes follows a different order: the poems denouncing various nations which here make up the final chapters (save for 52, which is a narrative appendix), there follow the beginning of 25:13. Such differences bespeak bittiness and editorial manipulation.

These characteristics do not make Jeremiah such a challenging book to read as Isaiah. He is a lesser poet and prophet, and the anguished essence of his vision, together with the moments of promise, is relatively straightforward, but his personal presence and story give the book some of its special appeal.

Lamentations (Hebrew: Ekhah, 'alas', from the opening word). Five laments for the destruction of Jerusalem.
Authorship: traditionally Jeremiah, as in full title in KJB; unknown, *c.* 586 BCE.

In various voices, including that of Jerusalem, generally pictured as a once-beautiful woman, the destruction of the city in 586 BCE is described and lamented. Moving images of horror accumulate, yet, as in Jeremiah, God's justice is accepted: 'The LORD is righteous, for I have rebelled against his commandment' (1:18). There is also belief and hope in God's mercies in the middle lament and at the end of the fourth. But destruction and weeping dominate, from the opening exclamation, 'How doth the city sit solitary that was full of people! how is she become as a widow!', to the closing gesture of hope that is overwhelmed by final despair.

Though the context is clear, as with so much biblical poetry the writing is sufficiently general and powerful to have become the timeless expression of lament in disaster, especially within Judaism, but also in Christian liturgies for Good Friday.

In the Hebrew there is a formal structure, invisible in translation, that may suggest the completeness of the laments. The first four are alphabetic acrostics (as Psalm 119); the fifth perhaps reflects this pattern by having twenty-two lines, the same as the number of letters in the Hebrew alphabet.

Ezekiel ('God strengthens'). Collection of Ezekiel's prophecies during the Babylonian exile, condemning first Jerusalem, then other countries, and finishing with the redemption of the Jewish people and the reconstructed Temple.
Authorship: Ezekiel; 595–571 BCE.

Condemnation and extravagant visions make up much of this largely chronological and largely prose work. The first half is dominated by vilification of 'the bloody city', Jerusalem, as Ezekiel pictures her as a harlot and shows 'all her abominations' (22:2). This is Jeremiah's vision with a greater intensity of loathing, as God, in keeping with Ezekiel's bitterness and heated spirit (3:14), speaks 'in the fire of my jealousy' (36:5). Chapter 16 is representative, even down to the unconvincing promise of forgiveness in verses 41–2, and the final paragraph, which does promise 'an everlasting covenant', but only when God is 'pacified' (16:60, 63). Ezekiel's God is a jealous God writ large.

From the beginning, highly-wrought supernatural visions feature. On a specific day when he 'was among the [Babylonian] captives by the river of Chebar . . . the heavens were opened, and I saw visions of God' (1:1). The detail is bizarre, but the overall effect unmistakable. The heavens and God are as unearthly as possible, but obviously fearful and magnificent, with fire and brightness predominant. Out of it all God speaks with celestial power, sending his spirit into Ezekiel. The tone and parameters for the book are set.

The best-known vision comes at 37:1–14, when Ezekiel is divinely transported to a valley of dry bones, prophesies as he is commanded, and the bones are restored to life. 'Doth he not speak parables?' (20:49), his contemporaries say of him. Here the parable, or metaphor, is that the bones are Israel: God will open their graves, put his spirit in them, and they will live, back in their own land. It is a passage that lends itself to developing ideas of resurrection, but its power comes from the stark realisation of the image.

The new life under a renewed covenant is quite different from that envisaged in Isaiah. It is exclusively Jewish, led by a Zadokite priesthood (Ezekiel was a priest of the line of Zadok, Solomon's chief priest), with ritual observance of Levitical laws in a rebuilt Temple at its centre. This is the burden of the last chapters as, in another transported vision, Ezekiel describes, in detail which recalls the instructions for the tabernacle in Exodus, the architecture of the new Temple.

Daniel ('judge of God'). Daniel (and three companions), captive in Babylon, gains favour with Nebuchadnezzar as an interpreter of dreams, including Belshazzar's feast and the episode in the lions' den; Daniel's own political and apocalyptic visions. 2:4–7:28 is in Aramaic (Chaldee).
Authorship: unknown; 167–164 BCE.

Over 400 years after the destruction of the Temple by the Babylonians, Antiochus IV Epiphanes was the latest foreign oppressor. Wanting to Hellenise his lands, he banned all Jewish religious practices, burnt the Scriptures and made their possession a capital offence. With troops stationed in the Temple, he had an altar to Zeus erected. The Maccabean revolt (related in the books of Maccabees) was one consequence; another was the book of Daniel, the latest of the OT books (this is probably why it is placed among the Writings rather than the Prophets in the Hebrew canon). Though set in Babylon, it speaks to these second-century BCE events.

Chapters 1–6 relate events in Daniel's life that establish him as a latter-day Joseph, gaining eminence in a foreign court through his 'understanding in all visions and dreams' (1:17). He and his companions are also pre-eminent examples of faith in the face of oppression. Together with the additions found in the Apocrypha (The Song of the Three Holy Children, Susanna, and Bel and the Dragon), this gives the Daniel who is a favourite in story and proverb. With God's aid, he can tell Nebuchadnezzar what he dreamt and what it signified, and Belshazzar the meaning of the writing on the wall that precedes his murder (the cliché, 'the writing on the wall', comes from this story but is not in the text (5:5); it appears as a header in some editions of the KJB). Daniel can survive being cast into the den of lions for his faith, just as his companions survived being cast into the 'burning fiery furnace' (3:6): these were stories to inspire in the face of Antiochus' pollution of the Temple (11:31; cf. 1 Macc. 1:54).

Chapters 7–12 are made up of Daniel's 'night visions' (7:7). Showing literary affinity with Ezekiel, they are an allegory of the changing shapes of power within which Jerusalem was a pawn. Israel's sinfulness is acknowledged, God's help prayed for and the passing of the abomination of desolation foreseen. Some of them have taken on a deeper significance; for example, 7:9–14 develops the vision of God as 'the Ancient of days' on a throne that 'was like the fiery flame', ministered to by 'thousand thousands', setting judgement in books that are to be opened. Then comes 'one like the Son of man' (verse 13) who is given an 'everlasting dominion'. The Aramaic phrase translated as 'the Son of man' lacks the definite article and may mean 'a human being' (Jewish Publication Society Tanakh translation). KJB's capital for 'Son' reflects the Christian interpretation of this passage and follows Jesus' own characteristic use of the phrase for himself (e.g. Matt. 8:20). The passage links with the vision of the Messiah coming sixty-nine weeks after the restoration of Jerusalem (Daniel 9:25).

Hosea ('deliverer'). Hosea's difficult marriage as an emblem of Israel's infidelity; denunciations of Israel and promises of redemption (the Hebrew text of this part is poor and the meaning often uncertain).
Authorship: Hosea; 785–725 BCE; some redaction.

Hosea lived in the latter days of the northern kingdom, Israel, which he frequently calls Ephraim, perhaps reflecting its collapse into a single tribal area. The almost irredeemable crime which preoccupies his writing and life is Baal worship, and the central image is adultery, 'for the spirit of whoredoms hath caused [my people] to err, and they have gone a-whoring from under their God' (4:12). This now-familiar marriage imagery for God and his people is especially apt here because of the fertility cult's sexual licence.

The opening three chapters take this imagery to an extreme. Hosea is commanded by God to enact the relationship by taking 'unto thee a wife of whoredoms and children of whoredoms' (1:2). Their children, Lo-ruhamah and Lo-ammi, 'not having obtained mercy' and 'not my people' (KJB margin), are named for God's judgement on Israel: 'I will no more have mercy upon the house of Israel . . . for ye are not my people, and I will not be your God' (1:6, 9). Yet the judgement contains a flat contradiction: Judah and Israel will be united and great (1:11), and Hosea's children will be called 'having obtained mercy' and 'my people' (KJB margin). Nowhere is the dual aspect of judgement and forgiveness so starkly presented. It is the heart of Hosea's vision.

The poems in Chapters 4–14 have a beauty to them somewhat similar to that of the Song of Solomon. God's voice dominates, but there are other voices, and the accumulating images of denunciation gradually turn into images of love, for God's 'heart is turned within me, my repentings are kindled together. I will not execute the fierceness of my anger' (11:8–9). At last the loving mode and imagery of the Song of Solomon take over, made the more moving by the extent of the forgiveness needed (14:5–6).

Joel ('the Lord is God'). Plague of locusts and the approaching day of the Lord; visions of judgement and salvation.
Authorship: Joel; perhaps c. 400 BCE.

The nation is depicted as a land blasted by a plague of locusts and by drought, then as invaded by an army of phenomenal power. The locusts are like 'a nation . . . come up upon my land, strong, and without number' (1:6); the army has the same effect: 'the land is as the garden of Eden before them, and behind them a desolate wilderness' (2:3). Whether both are literal or figurative invasions, or whether one is an image for the other, is not clear, but it is all 'a destruction from the Almighty' (1:15). Calls to repentance lead to a vision of exclusive restoration; the other nations will be left desolate, but Jerusalem, freed of foreigners, will be God's city for ever.

Joel makes significant use of phrases from other prophets, so 3:10 echoes Isa. 2:4 and Micah 4:3; 3:16 and 18 echo Amos 1:2 and 9:13; these latter links may be the reason a late book is placed among the earlier prophets. Joel also offers a vision of the people receiving the prophetic spirit (2:28–32) that Peter understood as prophesying Pentecost (Acts 2:16–21).

Amos ('burdensome'). Visions of a corrupt society and its demise, finishing with a promise of restoration.

Authorship: Amos; c. 760 BCE; some redaction.

The first of the writing prophets, Amos lived in prosperous times: Assyria was not yet a swarm on the horizon, and religion seemed quite efficacious. But social injustice was rife, and religion, though it paid lip-service to God, was thoroughly contaminated by the abuses his near-contemporary Hosea had inveighed against. Almost, 'It was the best of times, it was the worst of times', to use the opening words of *A Tale of Two Cities* (1859), another description of a period in prophetic terms. Amos saw all the corruption and, with special attention to the injustices, depicted it in ways not too different from those Dickens used.

The book opens with six powerful, patterned oracles of damnation from God against the transgressions of Damascus, Gaza, etc., and appropriate punishment is promised. The turn comes with the seventh and eighth oracles. Using the identical pattern, Judah and Israel are damned. 'You are as bad as those you scorn,' the pattern says. The description of Israel's transgressions shows Amos at his most distinctive: crimes of social injustice, made the more callous by the pettiness of the profit, are heaped up in one of the most structured pieces of writing in the OT, at once poetry and rhetoric.

In the final poem Amos is shown 'a basket of summer fruit' (8:1), an emblem of the land that God will destroy. Images of sins, still recognisable in many a modern nation, are multiplied, then with equal vividness images of God's inescapability. But at last restoration is promised: implicitly the 'basket of summer fruit' will be restored free from corruption.

Obadiah ('God's servant'). Destruction of Edom and a prophecy against nations.

Authorship: Obadiah; sometime after the destruction of Jerusalem, 586 BCE.

Edom, descended from Esau, should have been a brotherly kingdom in relation to the descendants of Jacob, but had been persistently hostile, and participated in the destruction of Jerusalem (verses 10–11). Obadiah prophesies that its deeds will redound on its own head, but the house of Jacob will be saved and holy, and will devour Edom. The same fate awaits all the heathen.

This is the shortest book in the OT.

Jonah ('dove'). Jonah's unwillingness to go and preach to Nineveh; his eventual obedience after maritime misadventures leads to Nineveh's repentance. Authorship: unknown; date unknown.

Rather than a book of prophecy, this is a book *about* prophecy, its effects, and Jewish exclusiveness set against God's inclusiveness. Using the name of a prophet mentioned once earlier (2 Kings 14:25), an unknown author has created a satiric parable quite remarkable for the quality of its storytelling. This prophet will not do as God tells him because he knows that if he cries against Nineveh, the great capital of the Assyrians, it will repent and be saved, for God is 'a gracious God, and merciful' (4:2, looking back to Exod. 34:6). Very literally fearing God, Jonah forgets the wisdom of Amos – 'Though they dig into hell, thence shall my hand take them' (9:2) – and attempts to flee 'from the presence of the LORD' (1:3). Jonah is indeed cast into hell, three days in the belly of a great fish, then fantastically belched up again. The command is given again, and with a bad grace Jonah delivers the OT's most perfunctory oracle: 'Yet forty days, and Nineveh shall be overthrown' (3:4). Never was so little prophecy so effective. Like the ship's crew in chapter 1, the Ninevites appear much more genuinely God-fearing than the bilious prophet: total repentance follows, and God forgives Nineveh. Jonah would rather be dead than have had this happen, and God asks Jonah whether he himself should have pity on Nineveh. It is a powerful rhetorical question: What is the nature of God's mercy? Can anyone who truly repents partake of it? Does Jonah, as a dove-like Israel (e.g. Psalm 74:19), learn a lesson directed to all Israel?

Jesus saw Jonah's three days in the whale's belly as a sign that 'the Son of man [shall] be three days and three nights in the heart of the earth', and the repentance of the Ninevites as a condemnation of the chosen people for their failure to listen to him (Matt. 12:39–41, Luke 11:29–32).

Micah (form of Micaiah, 'who is like the Lord?'). Prophecies of the destruction of Israel and Judah, with promises of future regeneration of the people and the coming of a Messiah.
Authorship: Micah; late eighth century BCE, with later revisions and additions.

Like Amos, Micah was a villager with a strong sense of the social injustices of his time. His vision of these is, for the most part, less vividly presented, but it can reach to horrifying hyperbole: the leaders of Israel are men

> 'who also eat the flesh of my people,
> and flay their skin from off them;
> and they break their bones, and chop them in pieces,
> as for the pot, and as flesh within the cauldron'. (3:3)

Destruction will be the inevitable result, but Micah, like Isaiah, has a vision of Jerusalem as the future leader among nations, and God as judge 'among many people' and rebuker of 'strong nations afar off' (4:3). Mixed in with this largely nationalistic vision is an ethical vision that summarises an important part of the prophetic message (6:8).

The text as it has come down to us is muddled and hard to follow closely, especially with the switches between different times that appear to reflect a multiple authorship, but the drift is clear, and some of the writing sharp enough to make Micah more than just a repetition of other prophets.

Nahum ('comfort'). Prophecies of the fall of Nineveh.
Authorship: Nahum; perhaps late seventh century BCE.

Nineveh, chief city of one of the most bloodthirsty invaders, Assyria, fell in 612 BCE, never to rise again, and this could give some comfort in the face of any oppressor. Nahum begins with a vivid passage on the terrible power of vengeance that God, though he 'is slow to anger' (1:3), reserves for his enemies. '[H]e will make an utter end: affliction shall not rise up the second time' (1:9). An exultant vision of Nineveh's destruction makes up the rest of the book.

Habakkuk ('embrace'). Dialogue with God about his slowness to punish and save; vision of God coming to deliver.
Authorship: Habakkuk; perhaps 609–598 BCE.

'O LORD, how long shall I cry, and thou wilt not hear!' (1:2) cries Habakkuk, as if beginning a psalm or echoing Job. It is a fundamental question. Why are violence and injustice abroad, and God appears to be doing nothing? God answers with a description of the Chaldeans (Babylonians) that he will raise up as invaders. The vivid writing continues through a series of woes and culminates in a prayer or psalm giving an extended description of God himself coming upon the earth. Poet and prophet Habakkuk concludes with a simple declaration of faith, made stirring with one last characteristic image:

> The LORD God is my strength,
> and he will make my feet like hinds' feet,
> and he will make me to walk upon my high places. (3:19)

This is blithe walking.

Among the Dead Sea Scrolls is a commentary on the first two chapters that identifies the Chaldeans as the Kittim, either the Greeks or the Romans. Habakkuk's vision fits to the recurring situation of oppression: man, in his impatience, can see neither God's purpose in it nor God bringing it to an end, yet in faith there is hope.

Zephaniah ('the Lord protects'). Approaching day of judgement, with hopes and encouragement.
Authorship: Zephaniah; late seventh century BCE.

The voice of God alternates with another voice as Zephaniah gives a stark outline of destruction and redemption. Initially, though he does not make the comparison, we are back with the situation that produced the flood in Genesis. Seeing the wickedness of man, God vows total destruction: 'The great day of the LORD is near' (1:14); it will be 'a day of wrath' (1:15), 'dies irae'. Images of desolation are heaped up, mixed with calls to repentance (2:3). The final promise is of salvation for a remnant of Israel, and of Jerusalem saved, joyful and praising God, while her enemies are destroyed. This is not quite the renewed covenant signalled by the rainbow, but an essential consolation to a people on the brink of annihilation.

Haggai ('festive'). Four addresses on the building of the Second Temple delivered by Haggai.
Authorship: Haggai; August–December 520 BCE.

Haggai elaborates Ezra's note that 'the elders of the Jews built, and they prospered through the prophesying of Haggai the prophet and Zechariah the son of Iddo' (Ezra 6:14). The prophet reports God's impatience with the stalled work at a time when the people are more concerned with the grandeur of their own houses, and adds three more divine communications as the work at last progresses, including a promise that the Second Temple will be greater than the first.

Zechariah ('the Lord remembers'). Eight visions, some connected with the building of the Second Temple; miscellaneous prophecies.
Authorship: chapters 1–8 Zechariah; 520–518 BCE; 9–14 may be late fourth century BCE. Matt. 27:9 attributes 11:12–13 to Jeremiah.

Though contemporary with Haggai and concerned with the rebuilding of the Temple and other issues of the time, Zechariah is a very different book in which the strange, symbolic, artful visionary mode, seen in parts of Ezekiel and Daniel, mixes with condemnations, promises and exhortations. The promises are notable for their inclusive vision of Jerusalem and the Temple restored, and 'many people and strong nations', even the enemies of Jerusalem, coming to worship there (8:22).

A strong Messianic vision is probably Zechariah's most important contribution to the prophetic books. The prophecy of the coming of Jerusalem's king helped make the gospel story (9:9; see p. 1884), and 11:12 looks forward to Judas' thirty pieces of silver (Matt. 27:9).

Malachi ('my messenger', or 'an angel of the Lord', 2 Esdras 1:40). The sins of post-exilic Israel and the promise of a messenger preparing the way before the day of the Lord.
Authorship: Malachi; sometime before 460 BCE.

The form of Malachi is unusual, a dialogue between God and his people as he reproves them and shows the fatuousness of their excuses for their corruptions. Bluntly, God declares that he has no pleasure in the people's polluted offerings but his 'name shall be great among the Gentiles' (1:11). The need for the reforms of Ezra and Nehemiah is clear, and forgiveness is still possible. Very simply, God tells the people, 'Return unto me, and I will return unto you' (3:7). The idea of the messenger, Elijah, preparing the way for judgement dominates the last two chapters.

The final three verses speak for much of the OT. The people are to remember 'the statutes and judgements' of the Mosaic law (4:4), and, through the action of a prophet, will have their hearts turned 'lest I come and smite the earth with a curse' (4:6). The law followed by the prophets may lead the people to salvation, but the threat of punishment is ever present.

NOTES

THE APOCRYPHA

None of the OT writings – except, obliquely, Daniel – deals with a time later than Ezra and Nehemiah's reforms following the return from exile, so the historical gap between the two Testaments is substantial, roughly 450 years. Israel went from being a small part of the Persian empire through domination by the Greeks (331 BCE onwards), and then, after Alexander the Great's death (323), the Syrian Seleucid empire. Following Antiochus' pollution of the Temple in 167 (see note to Daniel), there was a period of nationalistic revolt under the Maccabees that finally removed the Seleucids from Judah in 142. From 63 through the time of the NT, Rome was the dominant power. The Jewish religious and political leader was now the High Priest, and the Synagogue the place of worship; there were two important parties, the devoutly legalistic Pharisees who, in keeping with Christian attitudes, believed in the resurrection of the dead and the existence of angels and spirits, and the priestly Sadducees who did not (Acts 23:8). There was now general if not final agreement within Israel on the canon of Scripture, the Hebrew books represented in the Protestant OT.

The books collected in the Apocrypha do much to fill the historical gap and also to show the theological and intellectual developments that occurred between the Testaments. Though we now know of Hebrew versions of some of them, their origins lie principally in the Jewish communities living outside Israel, most notably the large Greek-speaking community at Alexandria. Its Scriptures were now in Greek, the Septuagint, and were more extensive: they included additions to OT books, alternative versions of Ezra and Nehemiah, and substantial and valuable works of wisdom, fiction and history.

Early Christianity, quickly spreading through the civilised world, became predominantly Greek-speaking, so knew and used the Septuagint. When St Jerome created the Vulgate OT he worked from the Hebrew, but, well aware of the differences between the Hebrew and the Greek versions, he placed the Greek books separately, misleadingly calling them 'apocrypha' or 'things hidden away'. Nevertheless, the Catholic Church (and similarly the Eastern Orthodox Church, which continued to use the Septuagint) kept a larger OT with most of these Greek books, following Nehemiah with Tobit, Judith, Esther (with the additions, often printed in italics) and 1 and 2 Maccabees (sometimes given at the end of the OT); the Wisdom of Solomon and Ecclesiasticus come after the Song of Solomon, and Baruch after Lamentations. It thought of them as deutero-canonical, that is, belonging to a second tier of the canon. Protestant Churches followed Jerome in giving these books as the Apocrypha. The Anglican Thirty-Nine Articles of 1571 states that 'the Church doth read [them] for example of life and instruction of manners; but yet doth it not apply them to establish any doctrine'. The Puritan Westminster Confession of Faith of 1646 takes a more hostile position that has been particularly influential in the United States: 'the books commonly called Apocrypha, not being of divine inspiration, are no part of the canon of Scripture; and therefore are of no authority in the Church of God, nor to be any otherwise approved, or made use of, than other human writings'. A Geneva Bible of 1640 seems to have been the first English Bible to omit the Apocrypha deliberately. When in 1827 the British and Foreign Bible Society decided to exclude it from all its innumerable editions, omission became the norm.

The Greek origin of both the Apocrypha and the NT affects the English of the KJB, especially in those books written with some sense of Greek forms and literary style. Most obviously, as also in the NT, names are based on their Greek form. 'LORD' is no longer used because that typographical form is reserved for the Hebrew holy name. Sentences tend to be longer and to make greater use of subordination; participial phrases such as those in 1 Esdras 1:2 become common. The vocabulary also becomes somewhat more Latinate.

1 Esdras ('Esdras' is the Greek form of 'Ezra'). Alternative version of 2 Chr. 35–6, Ezra and parts of Nehemiah; includes a wisdom competition.
Authorship: as for the above, by an unknown reviser. Included in the Vulgate and still accepted by some Orthodox churches, but not canonical for Roman Catholics.

In chapters 3–4, three of King Darius' bodyguards compete to see who can make the wisest sentence. The first claims that wine is the strongest thing in the world, the second that the king is and the third, Zorobabel (4:13; Zerubbabel in the OT, e.g. Ezra 2:2), that women are (an extraordinary assertion in so male-dominated a society). He wins by entertainingly showing how even the king is subject to his concubine, and then moves to a higher level of wisdom, declaring the superiority of truth. The resounding conclusion is 'Great is truth, and mighty above all things' (4:41, still known in its Latin form, 'magna est veritas et praevalet'). Having won the king's favour, Zorobabel asks for the fulfilment of his promise to rebuild Jerusalem and the Temple; this is granted, and the Ezra story, in which he is an important figure, resumes.

2 Esdras. Jewish-Christian prophetic introduction with NT echoes; the 'Ezra Apocalypse'.
Authorship: unknown; chapters 1–2, c. 150 CE; 3–14, c. 100 CE; 15–16, late third century CE. Not canonical for Roman Catholics but included in some editions of the Vulgate.

Jewish quasi-scriptural writing continued even beyond the writing of the NT, and the ending of 2 Esdras is the latest writing in the Bible (the connection with Ezra is in name only: the writers, as in Daniel, used a famous figure for their work). It is valuable as an example of the Jewish apocalyptic tradition that lies behind Revelation (others can be found in collections of OT Pseudepigrapha, that is, books with false titles). It is also notable for some echoes of the NT (Matt. 23:37 in 1:30, and Revelation 7:9 in 2:42), and the Christian additions, 'my son Jesus' and 'my son Christ' (7:28–9).

In the seven visions known as the 'Ezra Apocalypse', Esdras is guided to truth by the angel Uriel ('flame of God'). In the light of the sufferings of Jerusalem, Israel and righteous people in general, he is particularly concerned with God's justice and the day of judgement, which is not far off, for 'the times begin to wax old' (14:10).

Esdras' heartfelt grief for Jerusalem both allows him to see its glory and makes him highly blessed, so he is given 'visions of the high things, which the most High will do unto them that dwell upon earth in the last days' (10:59). One of these is a resumé of Roman history using the likeness of a twelve-winged, three-headed eagle that is explicitly connected with Daniel's vision (Daniel 7). Finally, he receives 'the wonderful visions of the night' (2 Esdras 14:42) which replace the law that has been burnt. At his dictation five men write 204 books in 40 days (14:44). Later translations give the number of books as 94, the 24 canonical books of the OT, plus 70 further only for 'such as be wise among the people' (14:46). This is a legendary expansion of Nehemiah 8.

A passage describing what happens in the seven days between death and the day of judgement was missing in the text the KJB translators worked from. Rediscovered in the nineteenth century, it follows 7:35 and can be found in some later English translations from the Revised Version (1895) onwards.

Tobit. The good Tobit and how his son Tobias, helped by the angel Raphael, came to marry Sara.
Authorship: unknown; c. 225–175 BCE.

This pleasing, popular story is, like Ruth, a romance full of honourable characters and homely narrative detail (with, unique in the Bible, a pet dog). It also has fairy-tale, miraculous elements: an angel and an evil spirit, a fish with healing properties, and wonderful cures. The picture of holy living, with its emphasis on faith, deeds and charity, is an important antidote to the visions of the wickedness of the people.

Revealing his true identity, Raphael ('God heals') says he is 'one of the seven holy angels, which present the prayers of the saints, and which go in and out before the glory of the Holy One' (12:15). Angels have been messengers and agents of God from Hagar's meeting with the angel (Gen. 16:7) onwards ('angel' is a Greek word interpreting a Hebrew word that means 'messenger'). Following the role of the spirit in Ezekiel, in Zechariah and 2 Esdras angels have become something more, wisdom figures. This reflects a changing understanding of God: where God could be met in person and spoke directly in earlier parts of the OT, he is now transcendent, so his word now typically comes through angels. Raphael shows further development in numbering the angels and ascribing to them an intercessory role. Moreover, he is an agent of good, in effect a guardian angel, something rather different from being an often-destructive agent of God. Set against him is the evil spirit Asmodeus, who had killed Sara's first seven husbands on their wedding night. Ideas of angels and demons as workers of good and evil take us into and beyond NT times.

The KJB translates from the shorter of the two Greek versions of Tobit; the longer version found in Codex Sinaiticus is generally thought to be better. Fragments of Aramaic and Hebrew versions are among the Dead Sea Scrolls, and it seems likely that Aramaic was the original language.

Judith. Unhistorical story of Judith saving a Jewish city from forces led by Holofernes, whom she entices and beheads.
Authorship: perhaps a Pharisee; probably late second century BCE.

This famous story is full of contrasts. We may see Judith as the saintly assassin, but the text has a heroic view of her. In the pantheon of Jewish heroes and heroines, she belongs with Ehud (Judges 3:15–30) and Jael (Judges 4:17–21, 5:24). As a female saviour of the nation she also belongs with Esther. The story's most important contrast is Nabuchodonosor (Nebuchadrezzar): he is a worldly parody of God. Swearing vengeance on 'all flesh, that did not obey the commandment of his mouth' (Judith 2:3), he sends his general, Holofernes, on a mission of conquest and extermination. Achior, the captain of the Ammonites, instructs Holofernes in Jewish history: if there is iniquity among them, Holofernes will win, but if there is not, God will fight for them and he will lose. Holofernes' scornful retort is 'who is God but Nabuchodonosor?' (6:2). Human power is set against divine, and Holofernes is defeated. Be faithful and fight, this is the inspiring message the book gives to Maccabean times. In non-historical terms, we are in the world of the wisdom competition in 1 Esdras. The idea that the king is mightiest is set against the idea that truth is mightiest of all. Truth prevails through those two other mighty things, wine and woman.

The Rest of Esther.
Authorship: unknown; perhaps *c*. 114 BCE.

See note on Esther.

The Wisdom of Solomon. Graeco-Judaic reflection on the righteous and the wicked, and the value of wisdom; review of Israel's early history and a diatribe against idolatry.
Authorship: probably an Alexandrian Jew; perhaps first half of first century BCE.

This and Ecclesiasticus are the wisdom books of the Apocrypha, making up a group with Job, Proverbs and Ecclesiastes. Though ascribed to Solomon and taking his persona in chapters 7–9, this is a late work that mixes Greek ideas with Jewish belief to create the Bible's most powerful expression of the idea of the 'loving spirit' (1:6) of wisdom. It leads well into John's Gospel and Paul's epistles. Rather as John links the Word and God (1:1), so an important group of words comes in the first paragraph: 'righteousness', 'the Lord', 'God', 'wisdom' and 'holy spirit of discipline'. God is highest, but praise of God, wisdom and the other qualities become one and the same thing. The writer, in one of his many fine phrases, puts the relationship this way: wisdom 'is the breath of the power of God' (Wisdom 7:25).

A central part of the author's idea of God and wisdom draws on Greek thought and is almost entirely new in Judaic writing. God 'created man to be immortal' (2:23), and 'to know [his] power is the root of immortality' (15:3). '[R]ighteousness is immortal' (1:15), and 'the righteous live for evermore' (5:15). 'Nevertheless through envy of the devil came death into the world: and they that do hold of his side do find it' (2:24). In keeping with these ideas, there are substantial sections contrasting the righteous with the unrighteous, and, similarly, the work of God, 'the first author of beauty' (13:3), with the writer's *bête noire*, idols ('the cause, and the end of all evil', 14:27). It is indicative of the power of this book that even the soliloquy of the unrighteous is a source of poetry: 'let us crown ourselves with rosebuds, before they be withered' (2:8) will become Robert Herrick's 'Gather ye Rose-buds while ye may' ('To the Virgins, to make much of Time' (1648)). Though there are some turgid and even incomprehensible parts, the power of belief, thought and language make the Wisdom of Solomon one of the outstanding books of the Apocrypha.

Ecclesiasticus, also known as **The Wisdom of Jesus the Son of Sirach**. Miscellaneous collection of instruction in religion, morality, manners, the way of the world; it includes the praise of famous men.
Authorship: Jesus Ben Sira, Jerusalem Jew; *c*. 180 BCE.

The two prologues give unusually detailed information about Jesus the son of Sirach, the nature of the book and how it was preserved. '[A] man of great diligence and wisdom', Jesus collected wise sayings and added some of his own, 'full of much understanding and wisdom' (first prologue). The collection was arranged by his son and translated from Hebrew into Greek by his grandson. Some of these sayings resonate with simple truth: 'A faithful friend is the medicine of life' (6:16), 'He that toucheth pitch shall be defiled therewith' (13:1), and 'The wisdom of a learned man cometh by opportunity of leisure' (38:24); this last is followed by a fine recognition of the need for manual labour, for not everyone has the leisure to pursue wisdom. Jesus' grandson describes the book's purpose: 'that those which are desirous to learn . . . might profit much more in living according to the law' (second prologue). Clearly directed at young men, it was widely used in the Church, whence its common name, Ecclesiasticus, 'Church book'.

Since Polonius borrowed from Ecclesiasticus, one might describe it in his words, as a 'few precepts in thy memory' (*Hamlet* (1600–1601) 1:3), save that 'few' does not fit this, the longest book of the Apocrypha. Too often pedestrian, Ecclesiasticus is Polonius without Shakespeare.

Baruch. Baruch's prayer read before the exiles in Babylon confessing sins and asking forgiveness; poems on wisdom, God and the law, and of comfort and promise; the Epistle of Jeremy, sermon against idol worship.
Authorship: ascribed to Baruch, secretary of Jeremiah; possibly three authors, second century BCE to 70 CE (if the destruction of Jerusalem is taken as a parallel for events of this time). The Epistle of Jeremy (chapter 6) is an independent work ascribed to Jeremiah; perhaps 300 BCE or later.

ADDITIONS TO DANIEL

The next three little books are found in the Greek but not the Hebrew-Aramaic text of Daniel. Unlike The Rest of Esther, they do not make up a single reshaping of the book. Rather, the Song brings in a prayer and a psalm which were probably in general circulation, while Susanna and Bel give three of a number of legends that accumulated round the figure of Daniel.

The Song of the Three Holy Children. A prayer and a psalm of praise.
Authorship: unknown; late second century or first century BCE.

The History of Susanna ('lily'). Susanna resists sexual advances by two elders, is accused by them but saved by Daniel.
Authorship: unknown; before 100 BCE.

The virtuous woman falsely accused by rejected predatory males is a familiar narrative situation. Here what is probably a folktale turns into a demonstration of young Daniel's legal talents as he cross-examines the elders and convicts them from their own testimony.

Bel and the Dragon. Two stories of idols exposed by Daniel; Daniel again in the lions' den.
Authorship: unknown; perhaps second century BCE.

The stories fit with the denunciations of idols and incidents such as the destruction of Dagon (1 Sam. 5). The destruction of the dragon (or snake) is slight and miraculous, but the exposure of Bel has special qualities as the first detective story. It uses forensic work worthy of Arthur Conan Doyle's Sherlock Holmes, who used the same ploy in 'The Golden Pince-Nez' (1904), also exposing a person in search of food.

The Prayer of Manasses. Penitent prayer of King Manasseh referred to in 2 Chr. 33:18–19.
Authorship: perhaps Jerusalem Jewish; before 70 CE. Not originally part of the Septuagint; not canonical for Roman Catholics.

1 Maccabees. The Maccabean (or Hasmonean) struggle to preserve Judaism and to free Judah from Syrian (Seleucid) oppression, from the accession of Antiochus IV Epiphanes to the death of Simon Maccabeus; origin of Hanukkah. Period: 175–135 BCE. Authorship: Palestinian Jewish; c. 100 BCE; Hebrew original lost.

This substantially authentic history tells of decades of war, alliances and treachery that not only played an important part in the preservation of Jewish, and therefore Christian, religion, but also continue to have political repercussions. The narrator's heroes are the Hasmonean family of Mattathias and his sons, Joannan, Simon, Eleazar, Jonathan and, above all, Judas, known as Maccabeus ('the hammerer'). Though they all are fanatical in their faith and believe that God fights with them, this is essentially a history of war for faith and nation rather than a narrative of God's power.

In the face of Antiochus Epiphanes' determination to eliminate all Jewish religious practices and to pillage the province (from another point of view, his 'effort to get rid of their primitive cult and hellenize them' (Tacitus, *The Histories* 5:8:3; trans. Kenneth Wellesley (Penguin Classics, 1972), p. 276), Mattathias began the revolt by killing an apostate Jew and the king's commissioner. After his death, Judas and his brothers 'fought with cheerfulness the battle of Israel' (3:2). Jerusalem, which 'lay void as a wilderness' (3:45), was gradually liberated, with the key moment being the rededication of the Temple in December 164 BCE (4:59), an event commemorated annually by the Jews at Hanukkah, 'the feast of the dedication' (John 10:22). At last 'the yoke of the heathen was taken away' (13:41) in 142 BCE.

The narrative shows both personal knowledge and documentary research, and gives a particularly interesting account of the Romans and a covenant that Judas made with them (8). There are some extraordinary events, such as the refusal of some of the early revolutionaries 'to profane the sabbath day' (2:34) by fighting on it (an easy massacre followed), and the death of Eleazar, crushed under an elephant which he has just killed (6:45–6).

2 Maccabees. The Maccabean wars to the victory of Judas Maccabeus. Period: 176–161 BCE. Authorship: perhaps Pharisaic; before 63 BCE.

2 Maccabees is a different account of the events covered in the first half of 1 Maccabees, ending with the equivalent of 1 Macc. 7:47, the death of Nicanor. Prefaced by two letters from Jerusalem to Egyptian Jews urging the observation of Hanukkah, it may be read as an inspirational account of the Maccabean history surrounding the feast. The real beginning comes at 2:19 where the author gives a self-conscious account of his work and its general purpose – delight, memorability, profit – that is unparalleled in the Bible. It is worthwhile pairing this with how he narrates the way Judas inspired his troops before the battle with Nicanor. With 'ever sure confidence that the Lord would help him . . . he exhorted his people not to fear the coming of the heathen against them, but to remember the help which in former times they had received from heaven . . . Thus he armed every one of them not so much with defence of shields and spears, as with comfortable and good words' (15:7–8, 11). Then Judas recounts a dream in which Jeremias appears and gives Judas a holy sword of gold, 'a gift from God, with the which thou shalt wound the adversaries' (15:16). His dream is described as 'worthy to be believed, as if it had been so indeed' (15:11): it is a truth-like, inspirational invention, testimony to the profitable power of words that the author himself aims at.

The watchword given by Judas to his soldiers, 'Victory is of God' (13:15), is the essence of how the history is told. Just as Judas tells of being given the sword of gold, so divine forces appear in the battles, as when 'there appeared unto the enemies from heaven five comely men upon horses' (10:29) leading the Jews and protecting Judas. Fitting with this intervention is the absolute faith of, for instance, the elderly scribe Eleazar, and of the mother and her seven sons: all go to moving deaths rather than eat swine's flesh. Anticipating the NT, a strong belief in God's judgement and mercy after death sustains them, and the narrator observes that Eleazar left 'his death for an example of a noble courage, and a memorial of virtue . . . unto all his nation' (6:31). So it is that the Apocrypha concludes with a powerful fictionalised history designed to inspire obedience to the law, belief in God's special protection and his mercy after death, and a picture of the Jewish people triumphant: 'from that time forth the Hebrews had the city in their power' (15:37).

THE NEW TESTAMENT

From 63 BCE Judah was a Roman province partly governed by the successors to the Hasmoneans, the Herodians, including Herod the Great, 47–4 BCE, in whose reign Jesus was born; Archelaus, 4 BCE–6 CE; and Antipas, ruler of Galilee, 4 BCE–69 CE, who had John the Baptist killed. Pontius Pilate was governor of Judea, 26–36 CE. The High Priesthood lost its political power to these rulers. The Jewish people were again subservient and subject to foreign taxation. Two parties, the Pharisees, associated with the scribes who were experts in the law, and the Sadducees, dominated Jewish religious life. The long-prophesied Messiah or anointed one (in Greek, the Christ) was still awaited, many hoping that he would be a Davidic king who would save the people from oppression as had the Maccabees.

Yet he came not from the dominant parties or the intellectual elite but from the common people, at once a carpenter's son from Nazareth and the son of

God. Nor did he come as a worldly but as an other-worldly king. The majority of the Jews did not recognise Jesus as the Messiah, but some, persuaded by his healing, miracles, wisdom, and, above all, his resurrection, became the first followers of a new religion built on Judaism. The NT is their book, mostly created in the second half of the first century CE as the first-hand memory of Jesus began to fade and the need to record what was known became inescapable, and as others, most notably Paul, wrote down their understanding of Jesus' significance.

Two aspects of Jesus dominate the NT: his teaching, and the recognition and significance he has as the resurrected son of God. The gospel story is shaped by the latter but dominated by the former. In the context of Jesus as Messiah, beginning with his Davidic genealogy, and finishing with the Crucifixion and Resurrection, the Gospels tell of his deeds and his teaching. Acts tells the stories of his disciples' and apostles' work, faith and trials in spreading the gospel. The rest of the NT consists of epistles and a prophetic-apocalyptic work, Revelation. The Epistles include the earliest NT writings as Paul, 'the minister of Jesus Christ to the Gentiles' (Rom. 15:16), and some of the other apostles write occasional letters to the expanding Christian community, preaching, encouraging and reprimanding.

The OT was essential to the early Christians, most of all for the way it spoke of the Messiah. It was also an immense source of debate, especially about its status as law. Jesus affirmed that he had not 'come to destroy the law, or the prophets . . . but to fulfil' them (Matt. 5:17). Yet the early Christians moved beyond the OT, whence the idea of a new covenant between God and man. Jesus speaks of 'the new testament' when he institutes Communion at the Last Supper (Mark 14:24, etc.). Paul sees the relationship between the two testaments or revelations (for 'testament' had yet to be used of the Jewish Scriptures, and the Christian writings were only then being created and would not be thought of as scripture for some time) in terms of the veil that Moses put on because of the brightness of his face after being with God (Exod. 34:30–34): God is veiled in the OT, but, through Jesus, the veil is removed, leaving Christians 'with open face beholding as in a glass the glory of the Lord' (2 Cor. 3:18).

GOSPELS (GREEK: EVANGELION, GOOD NEWS)

Mark is probably the earliest of the Gospels. Matthew and Luke draw on it substantially, and also on a lost collection of sayings. This commonality leads to Matthew, Mark and Luke being called the Synoptic Gospels. John, probably the latest of the four, stands somewhat apart in its theological emphasis, and also its style and structure. The literary relationships between the four have been much studied, and are still uncertain. More complex still – and not an entirely separate issue – is the question of the relationship between these narratives and the historical Jesus. The Gospels tell us much, but, as is natural with accounts written decades after the events by authors with differing skills, perceptions and audiences, they do not always agree. Moreover, there is much they do not tell us – 'there are also many other things which Jesus did' (John 21:25). They are not conventional history or biography, trying to tell everything we would want for a historical picture of the man. Only Matthew and Luke give Jesus' genealogy and the nativity stories; except for Luke's story of the twelve-year-old Jesus listening to and questioning the doctors in the Temple (2:41–52), there is nothing between his birth and his baptism at the hands of

John the Baptist, which marks the beginning of his ministry. Concentrating on what mattered, the ministry and the death and Resurrection, the Gospels probably began as aids to the memory for people who knew the elements of Jesus' teaching and divinity. This is explicit in Luke, who is writing in order that Theophilus might 'know the certainty of those things, wherein thou hast been instructed' (1:4). They continued as proclamation of the truth to men and women who had no connection to the historical Jesus, finishing with the most theologically-developed Gospel, John.

The most distinctive form of Jesus' teaching in the Synoptic Gospels, especially in Matthew and Luke, is the parable; as Mark comments, 'without a parable spoke he not unto them' (4:34). This is evidence of a most extraordinary teaching imagination, capable of putting often difficult ideas in thoroughly memorable form for everyone. The parables are either comparisons, usually ways of imaging the kingdom of heaven, or naturalistic stories that produce a vivid spiritual insight. Nevertheless, in Mark and Matthew the disciples typically find them obscure and have to have them explained. It is the accompanying explanation and our familiarity with them that makes them seem easy. 'Parable' is used for some thirty pieces of teaching in the Gospels, but by some counts there are more than double this number. Many are thoroughly easy to identify, but there are other sayings that might or might not be parables: what matters most is to realise that the kind of figurative imagination that produced the easily identifiable parables runs throughout Jesus' teaching. The whole of Matthew 7, for instance, is full of imagery that we might think of as incipient parables: the mote and the beam, pearls before swine, the strait gate, false prophets in sheep's clothing, and so on. As with, say, the prodigal son, the power of such images has made them proverbial.

Placed first, and sometimes thought to be the earliest of the Gospels, Matthew is the best known, and there is a sense in which general knowledge is best obtained from Matthew and supplemented by the remaining three. It has almost all the events from Palm Sunday to Easter Sunday, the most important week in the Christian calendar because its events affirm that the man who was crucified among thieves on Good Friday and then rose again from the dead, was indeed divine, the Christ. The triumphal entry into Jerusalem is followed by the cleansing of the Temple and the institution of Christianity's chief sacrament, the Eucharist (Holy Communion or Mass), at the Last Supper; there is the betrayal by Judas in the Garden of Gethsemane, Peter's triple denial that he knows Jesus, the trial before Pontius Pilate who washes his hands of 'the blood of this just person' (Matt. 27:24), the Crucifixion and the Resurrection. John adds some substantial passages of teaching, including the new commandment 'that ye love one another' (John 13:34), Pilate's resonant question, 'What is truth?' (18:38), and details such as the spear through Jesus' side at the Crucifixion (19:34). Luke and John give important stories that follow the Resurrection, including doubting Thomas (John), the road to Emmaus (Luke) and, most importantly, Jesus' ascension to heaven. Nevertheless, the reader interested in following the theological and literary development of the Gospels may find it valuable to read Mark first, and to come last to John's very different account.

Matthew. The gospel story, including genealogy, nativity and the Sermon on the Mount.
Authorship: probably a Jewish Christian in Antioch for a mixed Jewish-Gentile readership; 85–90.

The first and last parts of Matthew – nativity and baptism, last days in Jerusalem, death and Resurrection – are about Jesus the Saviour. The first revolves around the declaration by the voice from heaven at Jesus' baptism, 'This is my beloved Son, in whom I am well pleased' (3:17). It is the Synoptic Gospels' central assertion of divinity, coming both here and at the transfiguration (17:5). The genealogies establish that Jesus has the lineage the Messiah must have, from David and Abraham; the nativity stories establish his more-than-mortal nature, combining the miraculous with careful attention to the Messianic prophecies his birth and early life fulfil; the baptism story gives a double recognition of his divinity, by John the Baptist and the heavenly voice; finally, there is the supernatural set of temptations by the devil, underlining that Jesus is not a worldly leader, and inaugurating his teaching. There is a sense through all this of Matthew writing from his understanding of the prophets: they had prophesied the Messiah, Jesus had fulfilled their prophecies. It is a strong faith that shapes the story into this miraculous form, and that will go on giving a turn to some of the later events, such as the entry into Jerusalem on two asses (21:1–7), in literal fulfilment of the writer's misunderstanding of Zechariah 9:9 (see p. 1884).

The middle of Matthew (4:17–20:34) concentrates on Jesus as teacher and minister, with anticipation of his final days beginning to dominate the later chapters. The teaching begins with the calling of the disciples and a prophet-like cry, 'Repent: for the kingdom of heaven is at hand' (4:17). There follows the most famous extended teaching, the Sermon on the Mount (partly paralleled by Luke 6:20–49), perhaps a compilation of Jesus' teachings, true to the spirit of how he taught. In keeping with Christianity's origins among the people or 'babes' rather than 'the wise and prudent' (11:25), it begins with blessings for the poor and the oppressed, exhorting to joy, 'for great is your reward in heaven' (5:12). What follows is wise but hard, in its other-worldliness going far beyond its antecedents in the wisdom writings of the OT. Within it are some of Jesus' most famous sayings in their most familiar form, powerful thought expressed with appropriate power. Matthew's effectiveness is obvious if one compares his version of the Lord's Prayer (6:9–13) with Luke's (11:2–4), and his power and rhythm are obvious in sayings such as 'Consider the lilies of the field, how they grow: they toil not, neither do they spin' (6:28); compare Luke 12:27. The sermon's concluding image (7:24–7), comparing those who hear Jesus' words and follow them to those who hear but do not to the wise man who builds his house on rock and the foolish man who builds his house on sand, shows both the powerful imagination characteristic of much of Jesus' teaching and how individual Gospel-writers (and translators) can shape its expression. The differences from Luke 6:47–9 primarily reflect Matthew and Luke as writers: Matthew has the more poetic imagination. The result in the KJB's quite literal rendering of Matthew is a small masterpiece of the English language, the rhythm and structure of the writing creating the downfall of the house built on sand: 'and the rain descended, and the floods came, and the winds blew, and beat upon that house, and it fell, and great was the fall of it'.

Miracles, whether of healing or incidents like walking on water, show the divine power of Jesus. They beget faith, even, strikingly, among non-Jews. So Jesus reflects on the centurion whose servant he has cured, 'I have not found so great faith, no, not in Israel' (8:10). In Matthew this is the second healing, following a briefly mentioned healing of leprosy, whereas in Luke it comes in the middle of the healings (7:1–10), which perhaps shows Matthew emphasising that Jesus came to the Gentiles (non-Jews) as well as the Jews. The final declaration of faith in Matthew is worth noting: echoing Peter's affirmation, 'Thou art Christ, the Son of the living God' (16:16), it too comes from a centurion, 'Truly this was the Son of God' (27:54).

Mark. The gospel story from the baptism to the Resurrection.
Authorship: supposed to have been a follower of Peter, the John Mark mentioned at Acts 12:12, or the Marcus of 1 Peter 5:13 (they may be the same person), writing perhaps in Rome for Gentiles; 65–70.

Lacking much that is found in the other Gospels and supplying little that they do not have, crudely written and generally missing the famous phrasings of the others, Mark has been the least read of the Gospels. Yet Mark has two special claims to authenticity: the strong tradition that it derives from the apostle Peter and the probability that it is closest in time to Jesus. Moreover, there are places where it has been unreliably elaborated by Matthew and Luke, though this is not to say that they do not also have material that is more reliable than Mark. To take one example, the Lord's Prayer. Mark does not have it, but gives these comments on prayer by Jesus:

> [W]hat things soever ye desire, when ye pray, believe that ye receive them, and ye shall have them. And when ye stand praying, forgive, if ye have aught against any: that your Father also which is in heaven may forgive you your trespasses. But if you do not forgive, neither will your Father which is in heaven forgive your trespasses.   (11:24–6)

Though fitting with the Prayer, this lacks its compelling directness and simplicity. We might wonder if Luke invented the Prayer on the basis of this passage, and then suggest that Matthew developed it, but it is quite likely that Mark reflects something Jesus said, while the others give an actual form that he taught.

There are other aspects of weaker writing in Mark, such as the constant mixing of tenses, the abrupt opening and the even more abrupt ending (Mark proper finishes at 16:8; the brief account of Jesus' later appearances, instructions to the apostles and his ascension are a later addition). Yet such things are also strengths. Mark has an immediacy and urgency that are enhanced by the continual irruption of present tenses and the skeletal rush of the narrative. The constant use of 'And' to begin sentences and the frequent use of 'immediately', 'straightway', 'forthwith', 'as soon as' and 'anon', especially in the first chapter, enhance the effect. Jesus works with miraculous suddenness.

More than the other Gospels, Mark emphasises Jesus the healer. As the ministry begins he notes that Jesus taught with astonishing authority in the synagogue; then, rather than relating this 'doctrine' (1:22), he tells how Jesus cured the 'man with an unclean spirit' (1:23), an incident manifesting his 'new doctrine' (1:27). 'I know thee who thou art, the Holy One of God' (1:24), cries this spirit, giving testimony to Jesus' divinity that matches that of the voice from heaven at the baptism. The opposition between such possessing spirits of sickness and the divine spirit of Jesus is a key to Mark. Healing, preaching and forgiveness of sins become inseparable (see, e.g., 2:1–12, 6:2).

Luke. The gospel story, including the birth and preaching of John the Baptist, the nativity and Resurrection stories, concluding with the Ascension.

Authorship: traditionally but not certainly Luke 'the beloved physician' (Col. 4:14) who accompanied Paul on some of his journeys, writing outside Israel for Gentiles; *c.* 80–85.

Luke with Acts is a two-part work that takes the history of Jesus and early Christianity from its beginnings with the births of John and Jesus through to Paul's imprisonment in Rome. The short preface addressed to Theophilus ('lover of God', perhaps a real person, certainly a fitting name) calls it not a gospel but an orderly 'declaration of those things which are most surely believed among us' (1:1), based on eyewitness accounts. Though the content draws largely on Mark and the source shared with Matthew, there are unique parts, and the writing is distinctive. Mark's crude immediacy is replaced with a relatively educated and more detailed narrative that makes Luke read more like a biography.

Among Luke's best-known contributions to the gospel story are his nativity stories, and parables whose essence has become proverbial such as the good Samaritan (10:25–37) and the prodigal son. Whereas Matthew's account of the nativity is dominated by Messianic prophecies, Luke concentrates on the miraculous as testimony to Jesus' divinity. Yet this is pre-eminently the Gospel of historical and everyday detail: Luke is more a storyteller than the relatively poetic Matthew and the dramatic Mark. He begins by setting John the Baptist's parents in their time and place. The angel Gabriel appears to his father Zacharias in the midst of his daily activity, at once astonishing, as an angel should be, yet credible because of the sober context. With the passage of time carefully noted, Mary is introduced and a parallel annunciation follows. Luke emphasises Jesus' humble origins with famous lowly details: the swaddling clothes and the manger, and the visit not of wise men or kings but of shepherds. The narrative also grows through songs, now famous, expressing faith and blessing: Mary's song of praise, the Magnificat; Zacharias' Benedictus; and Simeon's Nunc Dimittis.

The parables in Mark and Matthew are usually followed by their interpretation and a sense that only the initiated can 'know the mystery of the kingdom of God' (Mark 4:11). Most of the distinctively Lucan parables illustrate a point already made, and they are told with a fullness of worldly detail. Having said that 'joy shall be in heaven over one sinner that repenteth, more than over ninety and nine just persons, which need no repentance' (15:7), Jesus first tells of the lost piece of silver, then his longest parable, the prodigal son (15:11–32). The heavenly point is made, but it is proverbial because it is so true to life, right down to details like 'the husks that the swine did eat' (15:16). The two brothers are instantly recognisable in their actions and their words, and the father, who might have been a King Lear, is an image of wisdom in his explanation of his actions to the disgruntled son.

Unique stories fully and knowingly told are Luke's greatest strength, but the limitations of his prosaic imagination and his language sometimes appear in comparison. Matthew's version of the parable of the talents is the more powerful because of the patterning created by there being only three servants; the giving to them of five, two and one talents; and the matching return generated by the first two servants. Luke's conclusion is sound (19:26), but Matthew's is resonantly balanced (25:29). The writers of the Gospels serve their story in different ways and with different strengths.

John. Extended account of Jesus' theological teaching, tied to selected gospel stories, including changing the water into wine and raising Lazarus from the dead, finishing with events following the Resurrection.

Authorship: uncertain, traditionally the disciple John; perhaps John the elder (or presbyter), author of the epistles of John, basing his work on the disciple John's memories (19:35, 21:24), and writing in Ephesus for a mixed early Christian community; 85–100.

The famous opening, 'In the beginning was the Word, and the Word was with God, and the Word was God' (a translation suggested by Thomas More), announces a very different Gospel. In keeping with these complex and mysterious words, John concentrates on Jesus' teaching about his relationship to God. This Gospel used to be thought of as a late expansion of some material from the Synoptics to create a uniquely Hellenised and enormously important theology that perhaps owes more to John than to Jesus, but archaeological discoveries have confirmed some of its circumstantial detail, and the Dead Sea Scrolls have shown that its mix of Jewish and Greek ideas antedates Jesus. It now appears rather more authentic and probably quite independent of the Synoptics. It adds to our knowledge of Jesus' story and is an invaluable re-creation of his theology.

Key elements of the theology are announced in the first chapter: Jesus is life and 'the light of men' (1:4), 'the Word . . . made flesh' (1:14), 'the only begotten Son' (1:18), 'the Lamb of God' (1:29), 'the Messiah', 'the Christ' (1:41), 'the Son of God' and 'the King of Israel' (1:49). Such declarations link and form the basis of the teaching; the events both express these ideas and lead to their development.

The greatest healing, the raising of Lazarus from the dead, is one such event. It comes between teaching whose central idea is, 'I am the good shepherd: the good shepherd giveth his life for the sheep' (10:11), and the Palm Sunday narrative that leads to Jesus indeed giving his life for the sheep. The context for the miracle of Lazarus is apt: John tells miracles less as a basis for belief (though he mentions several times that people believed because of miracles, 2:23, etc.) than as a source of understanding. The essential basis for belief is the words rather than the miracles. Jesus tells Martha, who knows that there will be 'resurrection at the last day', 'I am the resurrection, and the life: he that believeth in me, though he were dead, yet shall he live' (11:24, 25). In the emotional turmoil following Lazarus' death, during which, in the words of the famous shortest verse of the Bible, 'Jesus wept' (11:35), Jesus has the stone removed from the mouth of the cave in which Lazarus is buried, and calls him forth. 'And he that was dead came forth, bound hand and foot with grave-clothes' (11:44). Jesus' teaching is given living form, and his own resurrection is prefigured. This mixture of images, ideas, proclamation and deeds is characteristic of John.

The method continues into the Gospel's final story, the catching of the 153 fish (21:1–23). Reminiscent of Luke 5:1–11, in which Jesus tells Peter that 'henceforth thou shalt catch men', the event gives an image of the duty entrusted to the disciples. There were supposed to be 153 species of fish, so they are to go to all men, not just the Jews. In a symbolic reversal of Peter's threefold denial that he knows Jesus, the image changes to a more familiar one as Jesus three times asks Peter whether he loves him, and three times commands him, 'Feed my sheep'. Though generally thought to be a late addition, this chapter fits with the rest of John, and Jesus has passed on his mission.

The Synoptic Gospels all give the commandments to 'love the Lord thy God with all thy heart' and 'thy neighbour as thyself' (Mark 12:30–31, etc.), but John is pre-eminently the Gospel of love. 'God so loved the world, that he gave his only begotten Son' (3:16), and Jesus, 'having loved his own which were in the world . . . loved them unto the end' (13:1). He gives them 'A new commandment . . . that ye love one another' (13:34), and further memorable sayings such as 'Greater love hath no man than this, that a man lay down his life for his friends' (15:13). John's later statement, 'God is love' (1 John 4:8, 16), brings the development of such ideas from Isaiah onwards to a simple apotheosis.

Acts. The creation and expansion from Jerusalem to Rome of the early Church through the work of the apostles, especially Peter and Paul, from Jesus' promise of the Holy Ghost to Paul teaching in Rome.
Authorship: as for Luke, following the Gospel; c. 80–85.

This detailed and, in its latter parts, compelling account of the apostles' preaching and missionary work gives a unique insight into the Christians' early understanding of their faith ('Christians' is first used at Antioch (11:26), for what was hostilely called 'the sect of the Nazarenes' (24:5)). The teaching, theology and life of Jesus before the Resurrection find almost no place in Acts: the apostles and disciples preach Jesus as the risen Christ and giver of the Holy Ghost (the third part of the Christian Trinity: God the Father, God the Son and God the Holy Ghost). Typically 'showing by the scriptures', that is, 'out of the law of Moses, and out of the prophets' (28:23), 'that Jesus was Christ' (18:28), by miracles and, in Paul's case, personal testimony, they make their converts. So strong is the emphasis on the OT that Stephen, the first martyr, defends himself from the charge of blasphemy by summarising OT history without mentioning Jesus ('Jesus', 7:45, is Joshua), only the Holy Ghost. Philip finds the Ethiopian eunuch reading Isaiah 53:7–8 and tells him whom the prophet means by preaching Jesus from these verses (8:35). In response, the Ethiopian declares, 'I believe that Jesus Christ is the Son of God' (8:37), and is baptised. Such speeches and episodes are characteristic. Other men had been wise, had been great teachers, had had special understanding of God, but only Jesus was the Messiah and the Son of God. In the first thirty years after the Resurrection, the event that proved his divinity, this truth was paramount.

Dreams given by the Holy Spirit in chapters 10 and 11 are the turning-point in both Acts and the early history of the Church. Through them, Peter understands that 'God is no respecter of persons: but in every nation he that feareth him, and worketh righteousness, is accepted with him' (10:34–5). Jewish Christians protest, but the conclusion is clear: 'Then hath God also to the Gentiles granted repentance unto life' (11:18). Without such guidance from the Spirit, 'the sect of the Nazarenes' might have remained just that, a dissident body within Judaism.

Just before these dreams comes Acts' most famous incident, the visionary conversion of the Christians' main persecutor, Paul (previously called Saul), on the road to Damascus (9). It heralds the concentration of the latter part of the book on his extraordinary and tenacious – not to say adventurous – mission to the Gentiles.

THE EPISTLES

All but one of the remaining books of the NT are letters to the nascent churches or to individual Christians. Often written in response to particular situations, they mix everyday matters, greetings, requests and the like, with valuable information about the early church, castigation, exhortation and, most importantly, theology: they are a major source of Christian understanding and belief. They start with those thought to be by the single most important thinker of the early Church, Paul, arranged following the earliest collections in order of length. Not all are genuinely his (the ascriptions and superscriptions giving information about the writing of the letters are not found in the Greek). Next comes Hebrews, which was later ascribed to Paul, and letters attributed to other apostles, James, Peter, John and Jude. The later letters especially are dominated by the need to combat false teaching and belief. Seven epistles (James, 1–2 Peter, 1–3 John and Jude) are called the General or Catholic Epistles because they were intended for general circulation among churches.

Romans. The redemptive power or grace of God, and how it can be gained in the same way by both Jewish and Greek Christians.
Authorship: Paul, probably from Corinth; 58.

Romans is a thorough and profound argument about some of the most important theological issues, imparting, as Paul hopes to do in person when he comes to Rome, 'some spiritual gift, to the end you may be established' (1:11). Jew and Gentile alike are sinful, regardless of whether they have known the Jewish law, but both alike may be freed from sin, 'justified freely by [God's] grace through the redemption that is in Jesus Christ' (3:24). The cycle started by Adam is completed in Jesus: 'For as by one man's disobedience many were made sinners, so by the obedience of one shall many be made righteous' (5:19).

Paul teases out the identity and the difference between Jewish and Greek Christians. All are sons of Abraham, all can receive grace through faith in Jesus; as Paul finely puts it, 'there is no difference between the Jew and the Greek: for the same Lord over all is rich unto all that call upon him' (10:12; see also Galatians 3). Nevertheless, the Jews were called first. Unlike Jesus, Paul rarely uses extended images, but he brings these issues together in the olive tree representing the Jewish people growing into the Christian Church. Through lack of faith, branches are broken off; equally, the wild olive may be grafted on (11:13–24). The Greek Christians are not to be scorned because they did not have the law, and this leads him to a fine exhortation to tolerance in chapter 14.

Romans and Paul's 'weighty and powerful' (2 Cor. 10:10) epistles in general are not easy to read. The high road and the byways of thought and language need and reward reading and re-reading. Though never becoming as simply memorable as Jesus' oral teaching, Paul's writing does have striking phrases such as 'brotherly love' (12:10) and 'The powers that be' (13:1), whose familiarity is testimony to the closeness with which his epistles have been read and known.

1 Corinthians. Issues arising from problems in Corinth, including discussions of words versus spirit, prophecy and speaking in tongues, marriage and celibacy, the hierarchy of God, Jesus, men and women, charity, individuality, and the Resurrection.
Authorship: Paul from Ephesus; 54.

The notorious corruption and sexual immorality of the immense commercial seaport of Corinth had had its effect on the Christian community Paul founded there. 1 and 2 Corinthians respond to such problems and to the personal rivalries within the community and with Paul himself. A strong element of advice on particular issues and, especially in 2 Corinthians, self-defence and attack on enemies runs through them. These letters represent a more extensive correspondence, and the present text of 2 Corinthians may be a composite of two or more letters.

1 Corinthians is partly famous, partly infamous for its condemnation of what the KJB quaintly calls 'abusers of themselves with mankind' (6:9), its qualified advocacy of celibacy ('it is better to marry than to burn' (7:9)) and its subordination of women ('the head of the woman is the man' (11:3)), but its greatness lies in the ways it contrasts the worldly and the divine. Looking back on how he first came to the Corinthians, Paul declares that he has set aside the strength of the prized Greek art of rhetoric, 'enticing words of man's wisdom' (2:4), for the weakness of divine truth, knowing that 'the weakness of God is stronger than men' (1:25).

This opposition continues into the most famous NT passage outside the Gospels, the praise of charity in chapter 13. Usually read by itself as a passage of especial significance and, in the KJB, beauty, it takes on still more meaning as part of the whole argument, and in its immediate context. This is characteristic of Paul. It follows a striking passage in which he demolishes the idea that some gifts or abilities matter more than others – clearly some Corinthians were claiming superiority for their particular abilities. '[T]here are diversities of gifts,' Paul argues, 'but the same Spirit' (12:4). Using the classical analogy of society to the body, he argues the essentiality of all the members, even the weakest, for the less honourable parts have more abundant honour bestowed upon them (12:23). Acceptance of all who have received the Spirit in a single Church and the idea of one Spirit are key. The gifts include teaching, miracles, healing, speaking with tongues and interpreting. The transition to the passage about charity comes in the words, 'covet earnestly the best gifts: and yet show I unto you a more excellent way' (12:31).

Charity is another way of designating the Spirit. Without it, all the gifts are nothing because they are but worldly. Paul begins with the gift of rhetoric: 'Though I speak with the tongues of men and of angels, and have not charity, I am become as sounding brass, or a tinkling cymbal' (13:1). Without the Spirit, it is empty music, nothing, and 'nothing' resonates at the end of the next two sentences.

Though not drawn into a thoroughly logical whole, such a complex continuity of essential ideas so powerfully imagined and expressed is Paul at his best.

2 Corinthians. Paul's defence of himself and his ministry against accusations from some at Corinth; arrangements for a collection for the church in Jerusalem; and a final attack on his enemies.
Authorship: Paul from Macedonia; 56.

'O ye Corinthians,' cries Paul, 'our mouth is open unto you, our heart is enlarged' (6:11). The love, turmoil and confession he suggests here are characteristic of the first part of the book. What elevates this letter above the tantalisingly autobiographical is the spiritual light Paul brings to it. His faith allows him to place the trouble and despair 'even of life' (1:8) in the context of the fundamental contrast that runs through his writings, the deathly things of this world set against the living things of the Spirit. 2 Corinthians is full of telling contrasts between the 'earthen vessels' of men and the 'treasure' that is 'the light of the knowledge of the glory of God in the face of Jesus Christ' (4:6–7). See also note on 1 Corinthians.

Galatians. Attack on Judaising tendencies among the Galatians, and declaration of freedom in faith.
Authorship: Paul; place and date uncertain, Ephesus, *c.* 55, or Antioch, *c.* 48.

This polemical declaration of justification by faith and of Christian freedom has much in common with Romans, and has been a major influence on Christian thought. Paul argues vehemently that gentile Christians, people of the uncircumcision, should not subject themselves to the Jewish law, the law of circumcision. The Galatians had been idolaters before they knew God and now, in adopting Jewish practices, are returning to the same 'weak and beggarly elements' (4:8–10). Such an identification of idolatry and the Jewish law is daring and potentially highly offensive, but Paul is adamant in the theology that leads to it. The law is of this world and chains one to sin; the new revelation in Jesus is of the Spirit and liberates from sin. The Galatians, Christians, are children of the Spirit: 'if ye be led of the Spirit, ye are not under the law' (5:18).

As in 2 Corinthians, there is an important biographical section in the first two chapters, for again Paul must defend the Christ-given authenticity of the gospel he preaches. It may seem curious that he minimises his contact with the original apostles: three years after his conversion, he stayed with Peter for fifteen days, and saw none of the others except James. But his point is his full authority (evidently something his successors among the Galatians had denigrated): he 'neither received [the gospel] of man, neither was I taught it, but by the revelation of Jesus Christ' (1:12).

Ephesians. Essentials of the faith, and appropriate conduct therein.
Authorship: Paul (sometimes questioned; possibly pseudonymous, after Paul's death); place and date uncertain, from prison in Rome, *c.* 60, or in Caesarea, 57–9.

Ephesians is more likely to have been a circular letter than written specifically to a church Paul knew so intimately (see Acts 20:17–38). In effect it addresses all Gentile Christians, giving them 'the spirit of wisdom and revelation in the knowledge of [Christ]' (1:17). In the first part, through prose of considerable complexity, the writing moves from praising the glory of God's grace to description of the new life and union with God through Jesus: 'by grace are ye saved through faith, and that not of yourselves: it is the gift of God: not of works, lest any man should boast. For we are his workmanship, created in Christ Jesus unto good works' (2:8–10). Such subtlety of thought removes from people any sense of their own merit in being saved, yet keeps an absolute sense of the need for good works.

The second part, more simply written, starts from this idea: Paul (or the unknown man writing with his voice) begs his readers that 'ye walk worthy of the vocation wherewith ye are called' (4:1), and goes on to outline various aspects of this conduct, including the relationship between man and woman (see also Col. 3:18–4:1), and similar relationships between children and parents, and between servants and masters. The women are to be subject to their husbands as the Church is to Christ; equally, the husband is to love the wife as Christ does the Church. This is addressed more to the men than the women, enjoining them to true love.

Philippians. Letter of thanks and encouragement in the faith.
Authorship: Paul; from prison, probably in Rome, c. 61–2.

This most affectionate of Paul's letters was prompted by the latest of several gifts from one of the churches he had founded. Besides the thanks, prayers and love, the paragraph on rejoicing (4:4–9) is well worth noting. It includes words very familiar to church-goers: 'whatsoever things are true, whatsoever things are honest, whatsoever things are just, whatsoever things are pure, whatsoever things are lovely, whatsoever things are of good report: if there be any virtue, and if there be any praise, think on these things' (4:8).

Colossians. The pre-eminence of Christ; warning against heresy and immorality; and instruction in right living.
Authorship: Paul (sometimes questioned; possibly pseudonymous, after his death); from prison, probably in Rome, c. 61–2.

Writing to a predominantly Greek church he has never visited, Paul summarises the redemptive lordship of Christ and then warns against 'philosophy and vain deceit' (2:8), heretical tendencies appearing at Colossae that would adulterate pure Christianity. These appear to include ascetic practices such as dietary regulations, and mystical beliefs that seem to anticipate gnosticism, and worship of intermediary beings such as angels, something that is unnecessary because Christ has superseded them all.

1, 2 Thessalonians. The Thessalonian converts and how Paul preached to them, and the second coming; further teaching about the second coming and appropriate conduct in relation to it.
Authorship: Paul (authenticity of the second epistle sometimes questioned); from Corinth, 50 or 51, some months apart.

Unless the earlier dates for Galatians and James are right, these are the earliest NT writings. Their twofold interest is in the description Paul gives of the gentle way he converted the Thessalonians (1 Thess. 2:1–16), and in the teaching about the second coming (the parousia, the return of Christ to establish his kingdom on the earth) and the day of judgement. Then God will raise the dead ('the dead in Christ shall rise first' (4:16)), and the living will rise up to meet them. The suggestion that the second coming is imminent and that some of those presently alive will see it, together with the warning 'that the day of the Lord so cometh as a thief in the night' (5:2), seem to have led some of the Thessalonians to quit work and live idly. 2 Thessalonians addresses this, first developing the apocalyptic picture of the second coming (1:6–10), then seemingly pushing back its arrival until after the appearance of 'that man of sin . . . who opposeth and exalteth himself above all that is called God' (2:3–4), later called the antichrist (1 John 4:3). As for the layabouts, Paul is practical: no work, no food. Paul himself 'wrought with labour and travail night and day, that we might not be chargeable to any of you' (3:8), pursuing his trade as tent-maker (Acts 18:3): the Christian life is a working life.

1, 2 Timothy and Titus. Advice on church leadership.
Authorship: either by Paul late in his life, *c.* 65, with 2 Timothy the latest, traditionally shortly before his execution; or by a follower of Paul using some authentic material, *c.* 85; or by a pseudonymous writer, perhaps *c.* 100.

1 and 2 Timothy and Titus together are known as the Pastoral Epistles because of the insight they give into pastoral work as churches began to take institutional shape. Timothy, leader of the church at Ephesus, and Titus, leader at Crete, were trusted lieutenants of Paul, and these letters were written 'that thou mayest know how thou oughtest to behave thyself in . . . the church of the living God' (1 Tim. 3:15). The advice is often mundane, sometimes more like Ecclesiasticus than a Pauline epistle, as in 'Drink no longer water, but use a little wine for thy stomach's sake', and 'the love of money is the root of all evil' (5:23, 6:10), but there are also some important statements such as 'All scripture is given by inspiration of God, and is profitable for doctrine, for reproof, for correction, for instruction in righteousness, that the man of God may be perfect, thoroughly furnished unto all good works' (2 Tim. 3:16–17), and 'Unto the pure all things are pure, but unto them that are defiled and unbelieving is nothing pure' (Titus 1:15). If such things do indeed sound unlike Paul (the arguments about authorship are complex and not conclusive), they still have value, and it is difficult not to read 'I have fought a good fight, I have finished my course, I have kept the faith' (2 Tim. 4:7) as Paul's final words on himself.

Philemon. Note about a runaway slave, now a Christian.
Authorship: Paul; from prison in Rome, *c.* 62.

The Jewish-Christian Paul here begs his convert, the well-to-do Gentile, Philemon, to receive back his runaway slave, now also a convert of Paul's, as a brother. Without attacking slavery, Paul implies in this engaging note the embracing equality of the Church. In that common phrase of the KJB, the Church should have 'no respect of persons', that is, no regard to worldly status.

Hebrews. Teaching about the significance of Christ.
Authorship: unknown, often attributed to Paul; *c.* 60–95, perhaps no later than 70.

Hebrews is a sermon which finishes with some personal notes. It is best taken as addressed to teachers, ministers and growing churches which 'have need that one teach you again which be the first principles of the oracles of God' (5:12). It is an emphatic statement of 'Jesus Christ the same yesterday, and today, and for ever' (13:8). The idea that it is to the Hebrews, presumably Jewish Christians, comes from its uniquely intensive use of OT citations to build its arguments. First, through a concatenation of OT quotations, it shows Jesus' superiority to angels. Then, in the most substantial section, Psalm 110:4 ('Thou art a priest for ever after the order of Melchizedek') is used in an imaginative way characteristic of this letter to develop the idea of Jesus as the 'great high priest' (4:14). Melchizedek, that is, king of righteousness, is also king of Salem, that is, 'peace', and 'priest of the most high God' (Gen. 14:18): the titles fit Christ. Then the fact that almost nothing else is related of Melchizedek (something that might be said of innumerable OT figures) produces this: 'without father, without mother, without descent, having neither beginning of days, nor end of life: but made like unto the Son of God, [he] abideth a priest continually' (7:3). Such ingenuity of interpretation of so momentary and shadowy an OT figure is central to the teaching about Jesus as high priest, 'holy, harmless, undefiled, separate from sinners, and made higher than the heavens' (7:26). The Levitical priesthood has been superseded, and a new covenant established, with Christ as 'the mediator of the new testament, that by means of death, for the redemption of the transgressions that were under the first testament, they which are called might receive the promise of eternal inheritance' (9:15).

James. Practical reflections on Christian living.
Authorship: perhaps James the brother of Jesus, c. 45–8, or perhaps c. 60; perhaps pseudonymous, late first century.

James has had a mixed reception. It was late gaining acceptance into the canon of the Western Church, and was famously characterised by Martin Luther as an epistle of straw. It seems to come not from a hard-thinking mind but from a simple faith. Would not all the theologically astute writers of the Bible have protested at the assertion that 'Pure religion ... is this, to visit the fatherless and widows in their affliction' (1:27)? This is a practical version of the idea of loving one's neighbour as oneself, but it is neither all that religion is nor specific to Christianity. Yet the epistle's exhortations to living the effective good life, and reflections such as 'the effectual fervent prayer of a righteous man availeth much' (5:16), are an engaging reminder that 'faith without works is dead' (2:20): real faith necessarily leads to good works.

1 Peter. Encouragement to holy living.
Authorship: the disciple Simon Peter, c. 64; or possibly a pseudonymous later follower of Peter; from Rome (called Babylon, 5:13) to the Christians of Asia Minor (Turkey).

'Conversation' is a key word in 1 Peter; the translators use it in a now obsolete way to mean way of life, conduct, manners and, by extension in Peter's thought, good works: following Christ's holy example, 'be ye holy in all manner of conversation' (1:15). Peter joins this idea to suffering (possibly because the letter was written in a time of persecution), again urging his readers to follow Christ's example (2:21). He stresses that 'if ye suffer for righteousness' sake, happy are ye' (3:14; something quite different from suffering for one's own sins). The epistle in effect explains the idea of the meek inheriting the earth, for they will 'Honour all men' (2:17), regardless of their desert, and 'with well-doing . . . put to silence the ignorance of foolish men' (2:15). '[C]harity,' Peter declares, 'shall cover the multitude of sins' (4:8; cf. James 5:20).

2 Peter. False prophets and the last days.
Authorship: probably pseudonymous, c. 140, but datings vary widely; possibly Peter shortly before his death in 67 or 68.

Probably the latest of the NT writings (some parts of 2 Esdras are later), this brief letter is cast as an eve-of-death reminder of truths the writer's audience knows, but may be in danger of forgetting. It warns against false prophets, who appear to be multiplying and gathering followers, and explains why the day of judgement has not yet come. There is a notable description of Paul's epistles ('all', 3:16, may not mean all the epistles now taken to be Paul's).

1–3 John. Short letter and two notes warning against heresies and preaching love.
Authorship: perhaps the author of John's Gospel, John the elder (or presbyter); c. 100.

Addressing first little children, young men and fathers, then a sister church, called 'the elect lady and her children' (2 John 1), and Gaius, these were written to ensure 'that ye sin not' (1 John 2:1), and draw a series of contrasts between sin and truth. John affirms the central truths of John's Gospel, most memorably in the central statement of a chapter about love: 'God is love, and he that dwelleth in love dwelleth in God, and God in him' (4:16). A sense of the final days hangs over these letters as some schismatic heretical teachings are characterised as antichrist (a word only used here, e.g. 2:18), and refuted.

Jude. Urgent, vehement and vivid warning against 'ungodly men, turning the grace of our God into lasciviousness, and denying the only Lord God, and our Lord Jesus Christ' (verse 4).
Authorship: either Judas, brother of Jesus, or pseudonymous; date very uncertain.

Revelation. Vision of the last days.
Authorship: John of Patmos, sometimes identified with the apostle; c. 90–96.

This is a quite different book from anything else in the NT. Drawing on the prophetic and apocalyptic tradition seen in Ezekiel, Daniel and 2 Esdras, Revelation not only confuses but frightens and inspires as it moves to its climax with the marriage of the Lamb, that is, Jesus, with the shining new Jerusalem, the Church. The marriage is the centrepiece of John's vision of 'a new heaven and a new earth' (21:1) that will come when, after a millennium, this earth passes away. '[A] great voice out of heaven' affirms that the new Jerusalem is 'the tabernacle of God [that] is with men, and he will dwell with them, and they shall be his people, and God himself shall be with them, and be their God' (21:3).

The way to this gleaming ending is through a series of visions that starts with 'one like unto the Son of man' (1:13) standing in the midst of seven golden candlesticks holding seven stars. The candlesticks are the churches, the stars their angels (1:20) and the man Jesus, 'out of [whose] mouth went a sharp two-edged sword' (1:16); this last is not identified but suggests his role as judge. Though the method is quite different, this vision puts us in the world of the epistles, for Jesus commands John to write individually to each of the angels of the seven churches with a mixture of praise and warning against failings and heresies.

From chapter 4 the visions are of 'things which must be hereafter' (4:1). Much of it is deliberately mysterious, intended to impress more than en-lighten, and explanations are often omitted, for what is described is 'the mystery of God' (10:7). Sometimes initiation is needed for the reader, as, for instance, with the extensive use of numbers. Seven suggests completeness, so the seven churches are both particular churches and, by implication, all churches; twelve is the number of the tribes of Israel; and four has a sense of the completeness of the world. But some, such as the famous 666 for the 'beast' (13:18), are esoteric. The action is often powerfully metaphoric and works without explanation. Seven angels are given 'seven golden vials full of the wrath of God' (15:7). One by one they pour them out on the earth, the sea, the rivers and fountains, the sun, the seat of the beast, the Euphrates and the air. The end-days effects are horrifyingly vivid, as with the sea becoming 'as the blood of a dead man: and every living soul died in the sea' (16:3). The inscription on the forehead of the woman sitting 'upon a scarlet-coloured beast', 'MYSTERY, BABYLON THE GREAT, THE MOTHER OF HARLOTS AND ABOMINATIONS OF THE EARTH' (17:3, 5), says all that is needed. We could add that Babylon symbolises Rome, but this vision of 'the woman drunken with the blood of the saints, and with the blood of the martyrs of Jesus' (17:6), picking up the Bible's ubiquitous imagery of sexual infidelity, fully expresses the end-time persecuting and oppressing city, incarnation of all worldly evil.

The very end of the Bible echoes the beginning, suddenly giving a sense of completeness to this massive book and its vision of the cycle of human and divine history. John is shown 'a pure river of water of life, clear as crystal, proceeding out of the throne of God and of the Lamb' (22:1). By it the tree of life (but not the tree of the knowledge of good and evil (Gen. 2:9)) bears 'twelve manner of fruits ... and the leaves of the tree were for the healing of the nations' (22:2). The last words of Revelation contain an appeal and exhortation, 'the Spirit and the bride say, "Come". And let him that heareth say, "Come"' (22:17); a warning not to add to or subtract from the book (and, implicitly, from any part of the Bible); a promise of Jesus' imminent return, 'Surely I come quickly'; and a blessing: 'The grace of our Lord Jesus Christ be with you all. Amen' (22:20–21).

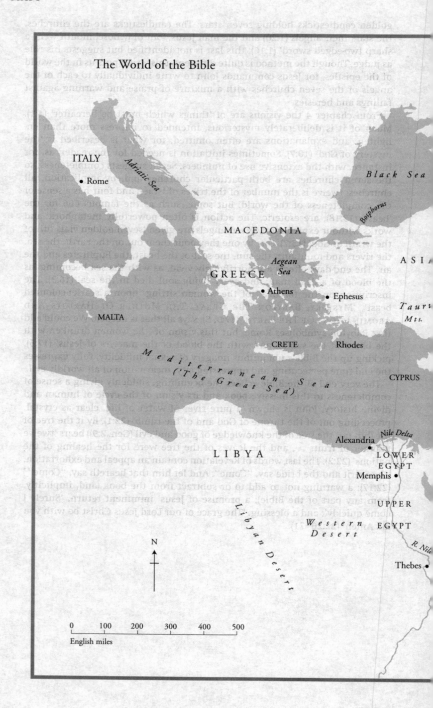

The World of the Bible

ITALY

• Rome

Adriatic Sea

Black Sea

Bosphorus

MACEDONIA

Aegean Sea

ASIA

GREECE

• Athens

• Ephesus

Taurus Mts.

MALTA

CRETE

Rhodes

Mediterranean Sea
('The Great Sea')

CYPRUS

Nile Delta

Alexandria •

LIBYA

LOWER EGYPT

Memphis •

UPPER EGYPT

Western Desert

Libyan Desert

R. Nile

Thebes •

N

0   100   200   300   400   500

English miles

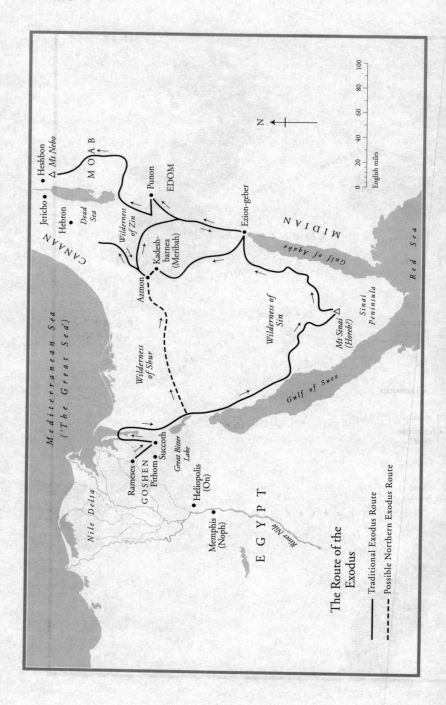

The Route of the
Exodus

—— Traditional Exodus Route

----- Possible Northern Exodus Route

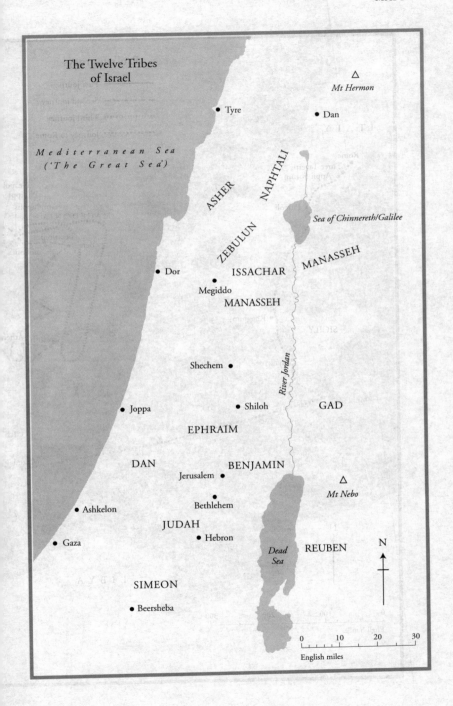

The Twelve Tribes
of Israel

*Mediterranean Sea
('The Great Sea')*

△
Mt Hermon

● Tyre

● Dan

ASHER

NAPHTALI

Sea of Chinnereth/Galilee

ZEBULUN

MANASSEH

● Dor

ISSACHAR

●
Megiddo

MANASSEH

Shechem ●

River Jordan

● Joppa

● Shiloh

GAD

EPHRAIM

DAN

BENJAMIN

Jerusalem ●

△
Mt Nebo

● Ashkelon

Bethlehem ●

JUDAH

● Gaza

● Hebron

*Dead
Sea*

REUBEN

N

SIMEON

● Beersheba

0   10   20   30

English miles

1925

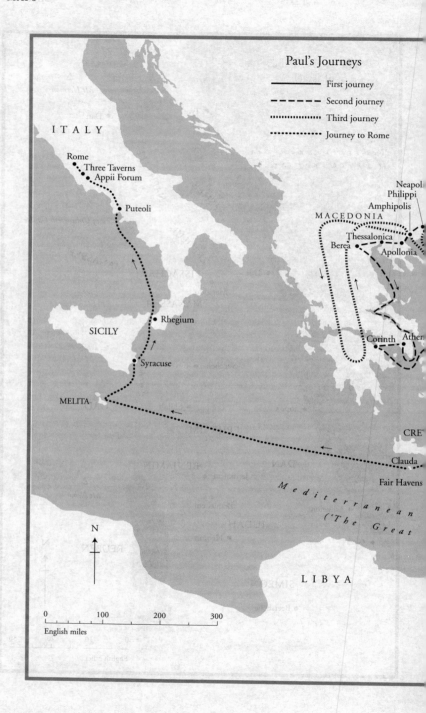

Paul's Journeys

First journey
Second journey
Third journey
Journey to Rome

ITALY

Rome
Three Taverns
Appii Forum

Puteoli

Neapol
Philippi
Amphipolis
MACEDONIA
Thessalonica
Berea
Apollonia

SICILY

Rhegium

Corinth   Athen

Syracuse

MELITA

CRE

Clauda

Fair Havens

Mediterranean
('*The Great*

N

LIBYA

0   100   200   300
English miles

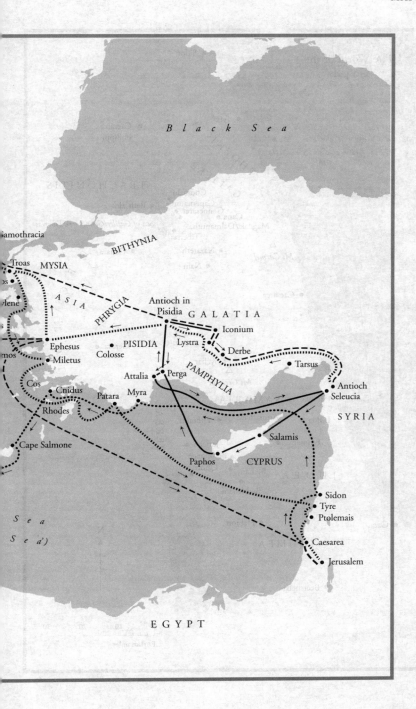

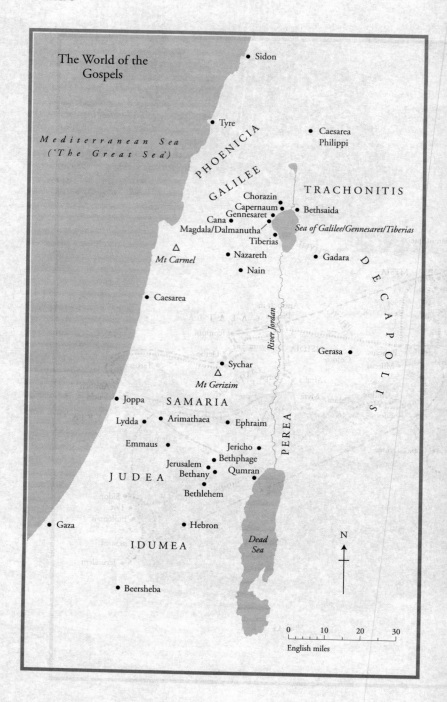

The World of the
Gospels

Sidon

Tyre

Mediterranean Sea
('The Great Sea')

PHOENICIA

Caesarea
Philippi

GALILEE

TRACHONITIS

Chorazin
Capernaum
Gennesaret
Cana
Magdala/Dalmanutha
Tiberias

Bethsaida

Sea of Galilee/Gennesaret/Tiberias

△
Mt Carmel

Nazareth
Nain

Gadara

D
E
C
A
P
O
L
I
S

Caesarea

River Jordan

Gerasa

Sychar
△
Mt Gerizim

Joppa

SAMARIA

Lydda
Arimathaea
Ephraim

PEREA

Emmaus

Jericho
Bethphage
Jerusalem
Bethany
Qumran

JUDEA

Bethlehem

Gaza
Hebron

Dead
Sea

IDUMEA

N

Beersheba

0   10   20   30

English miles

THE BOOKS OF THE BIBLE
IN ALPHABETICAL ORDER